Business Law

The Ethical, Global, and E-Commerce Environment

FOURTEENTH EDITION

14e

Business Law

The Ethical, Global, and E-Commerce Environment

FOURTEENTH EDITION
14e

Jane P. Mallor

A. James Barnes

Thomas Bowers

Arlen W. Langvardt

all of Indiana University

McGraw-Hill
Irwin

Boston   Burr Ridge, IL   Dubuque, IA   New York   San Francisco   St. Louis
Bangkok   Bogotá   Caracas   Kuala Lumpur   Lisbon   London   Madrid   Mexico City
Milan   Montreal   New Delhi   Santiago   Seoul   Singapore   Sydney   Taipei   Toronto

BUSINESS LAW: THE ETHICAL, GLOBAL, AND E-COMMERCE ENVIRONMENT
Published by McGraw-Hill/Irwin, a business unit of The McGraw-Hill Companies, Inc., 1221 Avenue of the Americas, New York, NY, 10020.
Copyright © 2010, 2007, 2004, 2001, 1998, 1995, 1992, 1989, 1986, 1982, 1978, 1974, 1970, 1966 by The McGraw-Hill Companies, Inc. All
rights reserved. No part of this publication may be reproduced or distributed in any form or by any means, or stored in a database or retrieval
system, without the prior written consent of The McGraw-Hill Companies, Inc., including, but not limited to, in any network or other electronic
storage or transmission, or broadcast for distance learning.

Some ancillaries, including electronic and print components, may not be available to customers outside the United States.

This book is printed on acid-free paper.

1 2 3 4 5 6 7 8 9 0 VNH/VNH 0 9

ISBN 978-0-07-337764-3
MHID 0-07-337764-3

Vice president and editor-in-chief: *Brent Gordon*
Publisher: *Paul Ducham*
Sponsoring editor: *Dana L. Woo*
Developmental editor: *Megan Richter*
Senior marketing manager: *Sarah Schuessler*
Project manager: *Dana M. Pauley*
Lead production supervisor: *Michael R. McCormick*
Designer: *Matt Diamond*
Lead media project manager: *Brian Nacik*
Typeface: *10/12 Times New Roman*
Compositor: *Macmillan Publishing Solutions*
Printer: *R. R. Donnelley*

Library of Congress Cataloging-in-Publication Data
Business law : the ethical, global, and e-commerce environment / Jane P. Mallor . . . [et al.].—14th ed.
    p. cm.
  Includes index.
  ISBN-13: 978-0-07-337764-3 (alk. paper)
  ISBN-10: 0-07-337764-3 (alk. paper)
  1. Commercial law—United States—Cases. 2. Business law—United States—Cases.
3. Business law—United States—Cases. 4. Commercial law—United States. 5. Business law—United States.
I. Mallor, Jane P.
KF888.B8 2010
346.7307—dc22   2008053699

www.mhhe.com

Jane P. Mallor has been a member of the Business Law faculty at Kelley School of Business, Indiana University, since 1976. She has a B.A. from Indiana University and a J.D. from Indiana University School of Law. She has been admitted to the Indiana Bar, the Bar of the Southern District of Indiana, and the Bar of the U.S. Supreme Court. She is a member of the Academy of Legal Studies in Business.

Professor Mallor has taught a range of courses, including an introductory legal environment course and a graduate-level legal concepts course, real estate law, university pedagogy courses for business doctoral students, and an online law and ethics graduate course. She is a member of Indiana University's Faculty Colloquium for Excellence in Teaching and was a Lilly Postdoctoral Teaching Fellow. She has won a number of teaching awards, including the Amoco Foundation Award for Distinguished Teaching, the Dow Technology Teaching Award, and the Innovative Teaching Award. Her research has focused primarily on punitive damages, product liability, and employment rights. Her work has been published in law reviews such as *Hastings Law Journal, North Carolina Law Review, American Business Law Journal,* and *Notre Dame Lawyer.*

A. James Barnes, J.D. Professor of Public and Environmental Affairs and Adjunct Professor of Law at Indiana University, Bloomington. He previously served as Dean of the School of Public and Environmental Affairs, and has taught business law at Indiana University and Georgetown University. His teaching interests include commercial law, environmental law, alternative dispute resolution, law and public policy, and ethics and the public official. He is the co-author of several leading books on business law.

From 1985 to 1988 Professor Barnes served as the deputy administrator of the U.S. Environmental Protection Agency. From 1983 to 1985 he was the EPA general counsel and in the early 1970s served as chief of staff to the first administrator of EPA. Professor Barnes also served as a trial attorney in the U.S. Department of Justice and as general counsel of the U.S. Department of Agriculture. For six years, from 1975 to 1981, he had a commercial and environmental law practice with the firm of Beveridge and Diamond in Washington, D.C.

Professor Barnes is a Fellow of the National Academy of Public Administration, the Chair of EPA's Environmental Finance Advisory Board, and a member of the U.S. Department of Energy's Environmental Management Advisory Board. From 1992 to 1998 he was a member of the Board of Directors of the Long Island Lighting Company (LILCO). He received his B.A. from Michigan State University and a Juris Doctor degree, *cum laude*, from Harvard Law School.

Thomas Bowers Thomas Bowers is the Argosy Gaming Faculty Fellow in the Kelley School of Business at Indiana University, Bloomington. Focusing primarily on the law of business organizations, securities regulation, professional responsibilities, and ethical and rational decision making, Dr. Bowers has taught three courses in the Kelley School's top-ranked Accounting Graduate Program. In 2005, he received the Kelley School's Innovative Teaching Award for his work with the GAP. In addition, his students and colleagues have honored him with 23 outstanding teaching awards. He joined the faculty at Indiana University in 1977 after obtaining a B.S. in finance *summa cum laude* from The Ohio State University and a J.D. from New York University. He is also Director of the Kelley MBA Sports & Entertainment Academy.

Arlen W. Langvardt Professor of Business Law, joined the faculty of Indiana University's Kelley School of Business in 1985. Professor Langvardt earned a B.A. (*summa cum laude*) form Hastings College and a J.D. (with distinction) from the University of Nebraska. From 1981 to 1985, he was a trial attorney with firms in Nebraska. He tried cases in a variety of legal areas, including tort, contract, constitutional, and miscellaneous commercial cases.

Professor Langvardt has received several teaching awards at the graduate and undergraduate levels. His graduate teaching assignments have included Legal Concepts and Trends Affecting Business, Managing Legal and Ethical Risk, Legal Issues in Marketing Management, and Legal Issues in the Arts. His undergraduate teaching assignments have included Legal Environment of Business, Legal Aspects of Marketing, Law and the Arts, and Personal Law. From 2000 through 2009, Professor served as chair of the Kelley School's Department of Business Law.

Professor Langvardt's wide-ranging research interests are reflected in his articles on such topics as intellectual property, commercial speech, medical malpractice, and other healthcare-related subjects. He has published numerous articles in journals such as the *Minnesota Law Review*, the *American Business Law Journal*, the *Journal of Marketing*, the *Trademark Reporter*, the *Journal of Law, Technology & Policy*, and the *University of Pennsylvania Journal of Business Law.* Professor Langvardt has won several research awards from professional associations, including the Holmes/Cardozo and Hoeber Awards from the Academy of Legal Studies in Business and the Ladas Memorial Award from the Brand Names Education Foundation.

Preface

This is the Fourteenth UCC Edition (and the twentieth overall edition) of a business law text that first appeared in 1935. Throughout its over 70 years of existence, this book has been a leader and an innovator in the fields of business law and the legal environment of business. One reason for the book's success is its clear and comprehensive treatment of the standard topics that form the traditional business law curriculum. Another reason is its responsiveness to changes in these traditional subjects and to new views about that curriculum. In 1976, this textbook was the first to inject regulatory materials into a business law textbook, defining the "legal environment" approach to business law. Over the years, this textbook has also pioneered by introducing materials on business ethics, corporate social responsibility, global legal issues, and e-commerce law. The Fourteenth Edition continues to emphasize change by integrating these four areas into its pedagogy.

Continuing Strengths

The Fourteenth UCC Edition continues the basic features that have made its predecessors successful. They include:

- *Comprehensive Coverage.* We believe that the text continues to excel both in the number of topics it addresses and the depth of coverage within each topic. This is true both of the basic business law subjects that form the core of the book and also of the regulatory and other subjects that are said to constitute the "legal environment" curriculum.
- *Style and Presentation.* This text is written in a style that is direct, lucid, and organized, yet also relatively relaxed and conversational. For this reason, we often have been able to cover certain topics by assigning them as reading without lecturing on them. As always, key points and terms are emphasized; examples, charts, figures, and concept summaries are used liberally; and elements of a claim and lists of defenses are stated in numbered paragraphs.
- *Case Selection.* We try very hard to find cases that clearly illustrate important points made in the text, that should interest students, and that are fun to teach. Except when older decisions are landmarks or continue to best illustrate particular concepts, we also try to select recent cases. Our collective in-class teaching experience with recent editions has helped us determine which of those cases best meet these criteria.
- *AACSB Curricular Standards.* The AACSB's curriculum standards say that both undergraduate and MBA curricula should include ethical and global issues; should address the influence of political, social, legal and regulatory, environmental, and technological issues on business; and should also address the impact of demographic diversity on organizations. In addition to its obvious emphasis on legal and regulatory issues, the book contains considerable material on business ethics, the legal environment for

international business, and environmental law, as well as Ethics in Action boxes. By putting legal changes in their social, political, and economic context, several text chapters enhance students' understanding of how political and social changes influence business and the law. For example, Chapter 4 discusses the ethical issues of recent years, and Chapter 43 addresses the credit crunch of 2008–2009 and options backdating. Chapter 51's discussion of employment discrimination law certainly speaks to the subject of workplace diversity. Finally, the Fourteenth UCC Edition examines many specific legal issues involving e-commerce and the Internet.

Features The Fourteenth Edition continues 10 features introduced by previous editions:

Opening Vignettes precede the chapter discussion in order to give students a context for the law they are about to study. Many opening vignettes raise issues that come from the corporate social responsibility crisis that students have read about the last few years. Others place students in the position of executives and entrepreneurs making management decisions and creating new business.

Ethics in Action boxes are interspersed where ethical issues arise, asking students to consider the ethics of actions and laws. The ethics boxes often ask students to apply their learning from Chapter 4, the chapter on ethical and rational decision making. The boxes also feature the most important corporate social responsibility legislation of the last 20 years, the Sarbanes–Oxley Act of 2002.

Cyberlaw in Action boxes discuss e-commerce and Internet law at the relevant points of the text.

The Global Business Environment boxes address the legal and business risks that arise in international business transactions, including being subject to the laws of other countries. By the integration of the global business environment boxes in each chapter, students are taught that global issues are an integral part of business decision making.

Log On boxes direct students to Internet sites where they can find additional legal and business materials that will aid their understanding of the law.

Online Research Boxes close each chapter by challenging students to use their Internet research skills to expand their understanding of the chapter.

Concept Reviews appear throughout the chapters. These Concept Reviews visually represent important concepts presented in the text to help summarize key ideas at a glance and simplify students' conceptualization of complicated issues.

Cases include the judicial opinions accompanying court decisions. These help to provide concrete examples of the rules stated in the text, and to provide a real-life application of the legal rule.

Problem Cases are included at the end of each chapter to provide review questions for students.

Key Terms are bolded throughout the text and defined in the Glossary at the end of the text for better comprehension of important terminology.

Important Changes in This Edition

In this edition, there are many new cases, the text has been thoroughly updated, and a good number of problem cases have been replaced with new ones. The cases continue to include both hypothetical cases as well as real-life cases so that we can target particular issues that deserve emphasis. The Fourteenth UCC Edition continues the development of components that were added to the text's previous edition. Examples of these components are as follows:

- Chapter 2 includes a discussion of the new federal rules governing discovery of electronically stored information.
- The **Sarbanes–Oxley Act of 2002** is covered thoroughly. This important legislation that intends to rein in corporate fraud is featured prominently in Chapters 4, 43, 45, and 46.
- Chapter 4, "Business Ethics, Corporate Social Responsibility, Corporate Governance, and Critical Thinking," contains a logical exposition of ethical thinking and sections with guidelines for making ethical decisions and resisting requests to act unethically.
- Chapter 8 includes, as new text cases, recent Supreme Court decisions on patent law. Chapter 8 also includes new material on the Trademark Dilution Revision Act of 2006.
- The contracts chapters integrate e-commerce issues at various points. Examples include treatments of the proposed Uniform Computer Information Transactions Act in Chapter 9, shrinkwrap and clickwrap contracts in Chapter 10, and digital or electronic signatures in Chapter 16.
- Chapter 20 includes a new section on the preemption and regulatory compliance defenses in product liability cases, and features the Supreme Court's recent *Riegel* decision in that section.
- Chapters 35 and 36 cover the new *Restatement (Third) of Agency*.
- Chapters 37 to 44 include business planning materials that help persons creating partnerships, LLPs, corporations, and other business forms. New materials give practical solutions that help business planners determine the compensation of partners in an LLP, ensure a return on investment for shareholders, anticipate management problems in partnerships and corporations, and provide for the repurchase of owners' interests in partnerships and corporations.
- Chapter 40 gives greater emphasis to the law affecting limited liability companies and covers the Revised Uniform Limited Liability Company Act.
- Recent Supreme Court cases, such as *Massachusetts v. EPA* (Chapter 52), have been integrated in this edition.
- Materials in Chapter 43 on complying with management duties give practical advice to boards of directors as well as consultants and investment bankers assisting corporate management. These materials help managers make prudent business decisions.
- Legal and ethical issues arising from the credit crunch of 2008–2009 and options backdating are addressed in Chapter 43. Included is a criminal options backdating case, *U.S. v. Jensen*.
- The latest case by Disney shareholders against former CEO Michael Eisner also is included in Chapter 43.
- Chapter 44 includes a new case, *Brodie v. Jordan*, in which the Supreme Court of Connecticut fashioned rights for a minority shareholder.
- The recent U.S. Supreme Court case, *Stoneridge Investment Partners, LLC v. Scientific-Atlanta, Inc.,* was added in Chapter 45. The case is the latest on the issue of aiding and abetting under Securities Exchange Act Rule 10b–5.
- The professional liability chapter, Chapter 46, was updated with three new text cases on issues ranging from liability for negligent misrepresentation to the definition of scienter under Rule 10b–5.
- Chapter 46 covers the liability of professionals in general, with emphasis on investment bankers, securities brokers, and securities analysts. The chapter is relevant not only to students studying accounting and auditing, but also to finance majors and MBA students who will work in the consulting and securities industries.
- Chapter 45 includes recent SEC changes that expand the communications permitted during registered offerings of securities.
- Chapter 48 contains new text material discussing recent amendments to the Consumer Product Safety Act.
- Chapter 49 includes, as a new text case, the recent *Leegin* decision, in which the Supreme Court held that vertical minimum price-fixing would be treated under the rule of reason rather than as a per se violation of the Sherman Act.

Acknowledgments

We would like to thank the many reviewers who have contributed their ideas and time to the development of this text. Our sincere appreciation to the following:

Kenneth Ackman, *Miami-Dade Community College, Kendall*
Miriam Albert, *Fordham University*
Joseph Allegretti, *Siena College*
Laura Barelman, *Wayne State University*
Laura Barnard, *Lakeland Community College*
Todd Barnet, *Pace University*
Lia Barone, *Norwalk Community College*
Karen Barr, *Pennsylvania State University*
Perry Binder, *Georgia State University*
Robert Bing, *William Paterson University*
William Bockanic, *John Carroll University*
Glenn Boggs, *Florida State University*
Joyce Boland-DeVito, *St. John's University*
Harvey Boller, *Loyola University*

Myra Bruegger, *Southeastern Community College*
Jeff Bruns, *Bacone College*
William Burke, *Trinity University*
Jeanne Calderon, *New York University*
Leandro Castillo, *Monterey Peninsula College*
Tom Cavenagh, *North Central College*
Wade Chumney, *Charleston Southern University*
Mark Conrad, *Fordham University*
Kathryn Coulter, *Mt. Mercy College*
Richard Custin, *Carthage College*
Barbara Danos, *Louisiana State University*
Larry Danks, *Camden Community College*
Diana Dawson, *Florida Atlantic University, Boca Raton*
Patrick Deane, *South Suburban College*
Alexander Devience, *DePaul University*
John Dowdy, *University of Texas, Arlington*
Paul Dwyer, *Siena College*
Craig Ehrlich, *Babson College*
Tony Enerva, *Lakeland Community College*
Pam Evers, *University of North Carolina–Wilmington*
Richard Finkley, *Governors State University*
Mahmoud Gaballa, *Mansfield University*
Sam Garber, *DePaul University*
Robert Garrett, *American River College*
Donna Gitter, *Fordham University*
Cheryl Gracie, *Washtennaw Community College*
Dale Grossman, *Cornell University, Ithaca*
Michelle Grunsted, *University of Oklahoma*
Jack Heinsius, *Yosemite Community College*
Patricia Hermann, *Coastal Bend College, Beeville*
Scott Hoover, *Lipscomb University*
Phillip Howard, *Ball State University*
Walt Janoski, *Luzerne County Community College*
Catherine Jones-Rokkers, *Grand Valley State University*
Steve Kaber, *Baldwin-Wallace College*
Warren Keck, *Thiel College*
Kevin Kern, *Rhodes College*
Edward Kissling, *Ocean County College*
Paul Klein, *Duquesne University*
Nancy Kubasek, *Bowling Green State University*
Elvin Lashbrooke, *Michigan State University, East Lansing*
Andrew Laviano, *University of Rhode Island, Kingston*
Daniel Levin, *Minnesota State University, Mankato*
Anne Levy, *Michigan State University, East Lansing*
Avi Liveson, *Hunter College*
Victor Lopez, *SUNY, Delhi*
James MacDonald, *Weber State University*
Julie Magid, *Indiana University–Purdue University Indianapolis*

Linda Marquis, *Northern Kentucky University*
Jim Marshall, *Michigan State University, East Lansing*
Brent McClintock, *Carthage College*
Brad McDonald, *Northern Illinois University*
Jane McNiven, *Ivy Tech State College*
Russell Meade, *Gardner-Webb University*
Ronald Meisberg, *University of Maryland, College Park*
Christine Mooney, *Queensborough Community College*
Georthia Moses, *Morris College*
Stephen Mumford, *Gwynedd Mercy College*
Marlene Murphy, *Governors State University*
Tonia Murphy, *University of Notre Dame*
Michael O'Hara, *University of Nebraska–Omaha*
Jim Owens, *California State University, Chico*
Sandra Perry, *Bradley University*
Ellen Pierce, *University of North Carolina*
Greg Rabb, *Jamestown Community College*
Roger Reinsch, *University of Wisconsin, La Crosse*
Daniel Reynolds, *Middle Tennessee State University*
Bob Richards, *Oklahoma State University*
Marvin Robertson, *Harding University*
Susan Samuelson, *Boston University*
Kurt Saunders, *California State University, Northridge*
David Scalise, *University of San Francisco*
Anne Schacherl, *Madison Area Technical College*
Robert Schupp, *University of North Florida*
Sean Scott, *St. Petersburg College*
Keith Shishido, *Santa Monica College*
Harold Silverman, *Bridgewater State College*
Jay Sklar, *Temple University*
Bradley Sleeper, *St. Cloud State University*
Michael Sommerville, *St. Mary's University*
John Sparks, *Grove City College*
John Thomas, *Northampton Community College*
David Trostel, *University of the Ozarks*
Donna Utley, *Okaloosa-Walton Community College*
Janet Velasquez, *Kansas City Community College*
Douglas Woods, *Wayne College*
Mary-Kathryn Zachary, *University of West Georgia*

We also acknowledge the assistance of Professors Sarah Jane Hughes and Dennis Long of the Indiana University Law School, graduate assistant Lauren Jeffries, and research assistant Laura Maul.

Jane P. Mallor
A. James Barnes
Thomas Bowers
Arlen W. Langvardt

A New Kind of Business Law

The 14th Edition of **Business Law** continues to focus on global, ethical, and e-commerce issues affecting legal aspects of business. The new edition contains a number of new features as well as an exciting new supplements package. Please take a few moments to page through some of the highlights of this new edition.

chapter 2

THE RESOLUTION OF PRIVATE DISPUTES

Victoria Wilson, a resident of Illinois, wishes to bring an invasion of privacy lawsuit against XYZ Co. because XYZ used a photograph of her, without her consent, in an advertisement for one of the company's products. Wilson will seek money damages of $150,000 from XYZ, whose principal offices are located in New Jersey. A New Jersey newspaper was the only print media outlet in which the advertisement was published. However, XYZ also placed the advertisement on the firm's Web site. This Web site may be viewed by anyone with Internet access, regardless of the viewer's geographic location.

Consider the following questions regarding Wilson's case as you read Chapter 2:

- Where, in a geographic sense, may Wilson properly file and pursue her lawsuit against XYZ?
- Must Wilson pursue her case in a state court, or does she have the option of litigating in federal court?
- Assuming that Wilson files her case in a state court, what strategic option may XYZ exercise if it acts promptly?
- Regardless of the court in which the case is litigated, what procedural steps will occur as the lawsuit proceeds from beginning to end?
- If Wilson requests copies of certain documents in XYZ's files, does XYZ have a legal obligation to provide the copies? What if Wilson requests copies of e-mails written by XYZ employees? Is XYZ legally required to provide the copies? What ethical obligations attend Wilson's making, and XYZ's responses to, such requests?

OPENING VIGNETTES

Each chapter begins with an opening vignette that presents students with a mix of real-life and hypothetical situations and discussion questions. These stories provide a motivational way to open the chapter and get students interested in the chapter content.

CHAPTER 43 UPDATED IN RESPONSE TO THE 2008 FINANCIAL CRISIS

Legal and ethical issues arising from the credit crunch of 2008–2009 and options backdating are addressed in Chapter 43. Included is a criminal options backdating case, *U.S. v. Jensen.*

United States v. Jensen   537 F. Supp. 2d 1069 (N.D. Cal. 2008)

On March 18, 2006, The Wall Street Journal published an article analyzing how some companies were granting stock options to their executives. According to the article, companies issued a suspiciously high number of options at times when the stock price hit a periodic low, followed by a sharp price increase. The odds of these well-timed grants occurring by chance alone were astronomical—less likely than winning the lottery. Eventually it was determined that such buy-low, sell-high returns simply could not be the product of chance. In testimony before Congress, Professor Erik Lie identified three potential strategies to account for these well-timed stock option grants. The first strategy included techniques called "spring-loading" and "bullet-dodging." The practice of "spring-loading" involved timing a stock option grant to precede an announcement of good news. The practice of "bullet-dodging" involved timing a stock option grant to follow an announcement of bad news. A second strategy included manipulating the flow of information—timing corporate announcements to match known future grant dates. A third strategy, backdating, involved cherry-picking past, and relatively low, stock prices to be the official grant date. Backdating occurs when the option's grant date is altered to an earlier date with a lower, more favorable price to the recipient.

A company grants stock options to its officers, directors, and employees at a certain "exercise price," giving the recipient the right to buy shares of the stock at that price, once the option vests. If the stock price rises after the date of the grant, the options have value. If the stock price falls after the date of the grant, the options have no value. Options with an exercise price equal to the stock's market price are called "at-the-money" options. Options with an exercise price lower than the stock's market price are called "in-the-money" options. By granting in-the-money, backdated options, a company effectively grants an employee an instant opportunity for profit.

Granting backdated options has important accounting consequences for the issuing company. For financial reporting purposes, companies granting in-the-money options have to recognize compensation expenses equal to the difference between the market price and the exercise price. APB 25 is the accounting rule that governed stock-based compensation through June 2005; it required companies to recognize this compensation expense for backdated options. For options granted at-the-money, a company did not have to recognize any compensation expenses under APB 25.

Backdating stock options by itself is not illegal. Purposefully backdated options that are properly accounted for and disclosed are legal. On the other hand, the backdating of options that is not disclosed or does not result in the recognition of a compensation expense is fraud.

A motive for fraudulent backdating may be to avoid recognizing a compensation expense, or a hit to the earnings, all the while awarding in-the-money options. To accomplish the fraud, those responsible assign an earlier date to the stock

CYBERLAW IN ACTION BOXES

In keeping with today's technological world, these boxes describe and discuss actual instances of how e-commerce and the Internet are affecting business law today.

CYBERLAW IN ACTION

Does the federal Computer Fraud and Abuse Act provide a basis for a lawsuit when the defendant allegedly misappropriated trade secret information from a database owned by the plaintiff? In *Garelli Wong & Associates, Inc. v. Nichols*, 2008 U.S. Dist. LEXIS 3288 (N.D. Ill. 2008), the court gave "no" as the answer.

Garelli Wong, a provider of accounting and financial personnel services, created a database containing confidential client tracking information. The firm took steps to maintain the confidentiality of the information and thereby obtain the competitive advantage that the information provided. The case arose when William Nichols, a former employee of Garelli Wong and a corporation that had later acquired the firm, allegedly used some of the confidential information in the database after he had taken a job with a competing firm. Nichols's supposed use of the information allegedly breached a contract he had entered into with Garelli Wong when he was employed there. Garelli Wong and the successor corporation sued Nichols in federal court, contending that his actions violated the Consumer

(ii) intentionally accesses a protected computer without authorization, and as a result of such conduct, recklessly causes damage; or

(iii) intentionally accesses a protected computer without authorization, and as a result of such conduct, causes damage . . . ; and

(5)(B)(i) by conduct described in clause (i), (ii), or (iii) of subparagraph (A), caused . . . loss to 1 or more persons during any 1-year period . . . aggregating at least $5,000 in value.

The court noted that in view of the above language, a plaintiff must properly plead both *damage* and *loss* in order to allege a civil CFAA violation. A definition section of the CFAA defines *damage* as "impairment to the integrity or availability of data, a program, a system, or information." Applying these definitions, the court agreed with Nichols that even if he used information in the database, he did not impair the integrity or availability of the information or the database. Accordingly, the court held that the CFAA does not extend to cases in which trade secret information is merely used—even if in violation of a contract or state trade secret law—because such conduct by itself does not constitute *damage* as that term is

Ethics in Action

Enron employee Sherron Watkins received considerable praise from the public, governmental officials, and media commentators when she went public in 2002 with her concerns about certain accounting and other business practices of her employer. These alleged practices caused Enron and high level executives of the firm to undergo considerable legal scrutiny in the civil and criminal arenas.

In deciding to become a whistle-blower, Sherron Watkins no doubt was motivated by what she regarded as a moral obligation. The decision she made was more highly publicized than most decisions of that nature, but was otherwise of a type that many employees have faced and will continue to face. You may be among those persons at some point in your career. Various questions, including the ones set forth below, may therefore be worth pondering. As you do so, you may find it

useful to consider the perspectives afforded by the ethical theories discussed in Chapter 4.

- When an employee learns of apparently unlawful behavior on the part of his or her employer, does the employee have an ethical duty to blow the whistle on the employer?
- Do any ethical duties or obligations of the employee come into conflict in such a situation? If so, what are they, and how does the employee balance them?
- What practical consequences may one face if he or she becomes a whistle-blower? What role, if any, should those potential consequences play in the ethical analysis?
- What other consequences are likely to occur if the whistle is blown? What is likely to happen if the whistle isn't blown? Should these likely consequences affect the ethical analysis? If so, how?

ETHICS IN ACTION BOXES

These boxes appear throughout the chapters and offer critical thinking questions and situations that relate to ethical/public policy concerns.

THE GLOBAL BUSINESS ENVIRONMENT BOXES

Since global issues affect people in many different aspects of business, this material now appears throughout the text instead of in a separate chapter on international issues. This feature brings to life global issues that are affecting business law.

The Global Business Environment

At varying times since the 1977 enactment of the Foreign Corrupt Practices Act, the United States has advocated the development of international agreements designed to combat bribery and similar forms of corruption on at least a regional, if not a global, scale. These efforts and those of other nations sharing similar views bore fruit during the past decade.

In 1996, the Organization of American States (OAS) adopted the Inter-American Convention Against Corruption (IACAC). When it ratified the IACAC in September 2000, the United States joined 20 other subscribing OAS nations. The IACAC prohibits the offering or giving of a bribe to a government official in order to influence the official's actions, the solicitation or receipt of such a bribe, and certain other forms of corruption on the part of government officials. It requires subscribing nations to make changes in their domestic laws, in order to make those laws consistent with the IACAC. The United States has taken the position that given the content of the Foreign Corrupt Practices Act and other U.S. statutes prohibiting the offering and solicitation of bribes as well as various other forms of corruption, its statutes already are consistent with the IACAC.

The Organization for Economic Cooperation and Development (OECD) is made up of 29 nations that are leading exporters. In 1997, the OECD adopted the Convention on

Combating Bribery of Officials in International Business Transactions. The OECD Convention, subscribed to by the United States, 28 other OECD member nations, and five non-member nations, prohibits the offering or giving of a bribe to a government official in order to obtain a business advantage from the official's action or inaction. It calls for subscribing nations to have domestic laws that contain such a prohibition. Unlike the IACAC, however, the OECD neither prohibits the government official's solicitation or receipt of a bribe nor contains provisions dealing with the other forms of official corruption contemplated by the IACAC.

In 1999, the Council of Europe adopted the Criminal Law Convention on Corruption, which calls upon European Union (EU) member nations to develop domestic laws prohibiting the same sorts of behaviors prohibited by the IACAC. Many European Union members have signed on to this convention, as have three nonmembers of the EU. One of those is the United States.

Because the IACAC, the OECD Convention, and the Criminal Law Convention are relatively recent developments, it is too early to determine whether they have been effective international instruments for combating bribery and similar forms of corruption. Much will depend upon whether the domestic laws contemplated by these conventions are enforced with consistency and regularity.

LOG ON

For a great deal of information about the U.S. Supreme Court and access to the Court's opinions in recent cases, see the Court's Web site at **http://www.supremecourtus.gov.**

LOG ON BOXES

These appear throughout the chapters and direct students, where appropriate, to relevant Web sites that will give them more information about each featured topic. Many of these are key legal sites that may be used repeatedly by business law students and business professionals alike.

CONCEPT REVIEW

The First Amendment

Type of Speech	Level of First Amendment Protection	Consequences When Government Regulates Content of Speech
Noncommercial	Full	Government action is constitutional only if action is necessary to fulfillment of compelling government purpose. Otherwise, government action violates First Amendment.
Commercial (*nonmisleading and about lawful activity*)	Intermediate	Government action is constitutional if government has substantial underlying interest, action directly advances that interest, and action is no more extensive than necessary to fulfillment of that interest (i.e., action is narrowly tailored).
Commercial (*misleading or about unlawful activity*)	None	Government action is constitutional.

CONCEPT REVIEWS

These boxes visually represent important concepts presented in the text to help summarize key ideas at a glance and simplify students' conceptualization of complicated issues.

ONLINE RESEARCH PROBLEMS

These end-of-chapter research problems drive students to the Internet and include discussion questions so they can be used in class or as homework.

Online Research

Josephson Institute Center for Business Ethics

Josephson Institute Center for Business Ethics is a leading source of materials for businesses and executives who want to act ethically.

- Locate the Josephson Web site.
- Find "The Seven-Step Path to Better Decisions" and the "Six Pillars of Character."
- List the "Obstacles to Ethical Decision Making: Rationalizations."

Bombliss v. Cornelsen   824 N.E.2d 1175 (Ill. App. 2005)

Ron and Catherine Bombliss were dog breeders who lived in Illinois. They bred Tibetan mastiffs, as did Oklahoma residents Anne and Jim Cornelsen. When Anne Cornelsen telephoned the Bomblisses and said she was ready to sell two litters of Tibetan mastiff puppies, Ron Bombliss expressed interest in purchasing two females of breeding quality.

A Tibetan mastiff named Mulan was the mother of one of the two litters of puppies the Cornelsens were offering for sale. Mulan was co-owned by Richard Eichhorn. Pursuant to an agreement containing a written guarantee that Mulan was free of genetic defects, Eichhorn provided Mulan to the Cornelsens for breeding purposes. The agreement between Eichhorn and the Cornelsens entitled Eichhorn to odd-numbered pups from Mulan's first two litters. However, in the event a genetic defect became apparent, Eichhorn would not receive any puppies. According to the complaint filed by the Bomblisses in the case described below, Anne Cornelsen was angry with Eichhorn because Mulan was infected with roundworms and ticks when Eichhorn delivered the dog to the Cornelsens. Anne allegedly told the Bomblisses that she wanted to prevent Eichhorn from getting any of Mulan's pups.

In January 2002, the Bomblisses traveled to Oklahoma to see the puppies. During their visit, they observed that Mulan and some of her pups appeared sick and worm-infested. They urged Anne to get the sick puppies to the veterinarian immediately. The Bomblisses selected one healthy female from each litter and paid the agreed price with the understanding that the Cornelsens would guarantee the puppies as breeding stock, free from genetic diseases or defects, for three years. According to the Bomblisses' complaint, Anne waited two weeks to take one of the sick pups to the veterinarian. It was then confirmed

CASES

The cases in each chapter help to provide concrete examples of the rules stated in the text. A list of cases appears at the front of the text.

PROBLEMS AND PROBLEM CASES

Problem cases appear at the end of each chapter for student review and discussion.

Problems and Problem Cases

1. Law enforcement officers arrived at a Minnesota residence in order to execute arrest warrants for Andrew Hyatt. During the officers' attempt to make the arrest, Hyatt yelled something such as "Go ahead, just shoot me, shoot me," and struck one of the officers. Another officer then called for assistance from City of Anoka, Minnesota, police officer Mark Yates, who was elsewhere in the residence with his leashed police dog, Chips. Yates entered the room where Hyatt was, saw the injured officer's bloodied face, and observed Hyatt standing behind his wife (Lena Hyatt). One of the officers acquired the impression that Lena may have been serving as a shield for her husband. When Andrew again yelled "Shoot me, shoot me" and ran toward the back of the room, Yates released Chips from the leash. Instead of pursuing Andrew, Chips apprehended Lena, taking her to the ground and performing a "bite and hold" on her leg and arm. Yates then pursued Andrew, who had fled through a window. When Yates later re-entered the room, he released Chips from Lena and instructed another officer to arrest her on suspicion of obstruction of legal process. Lena was taken by ambulance to a hospital and treated for lacerations on her elbow and knee. She later sued the City of Anoka, seeking compensation for medical expenses and pain and suffering. Her complaint alleged liability on the basis of Minnesota's dog bite statute, which read as follows:

   "If a dog, without provocation, attacks or injures any person who is acting peaceably in any place where the person may lawfully be, the owner of the dog is liable

YOU BE THE JUDGE

We have indicated where you can consider completing relevant You Be the Judge case segments.

INSTRUCTOR'S MANUAL

The Instructor's Manual, written by the authors, consists of objectives, suggestions for lecture preparation, recommended references, answers to problems and problem cases, and suggested answers to the Online Research Problems and Opening Vignettes. It also includes answers to the Student Study Guide questions and information/teaching notes for You Be the Judge case segments.

YOU BE THE JUDGE

You Be the Judge Online video segments include 18 hypothetical business law cases. All of the cases are based on real cases from our Business Law texts. Each case allows you to watch interviews of the plaintiff and defendant before the courtroom argument, see the courtroom proceedings, view relevant evidence, read other actual cases relating to the issues in the case, and then create your own ruling. After your verdict is generated, view what an actual judge ruled (unscripted) in the case and then get the chance to defend or change your ruling.

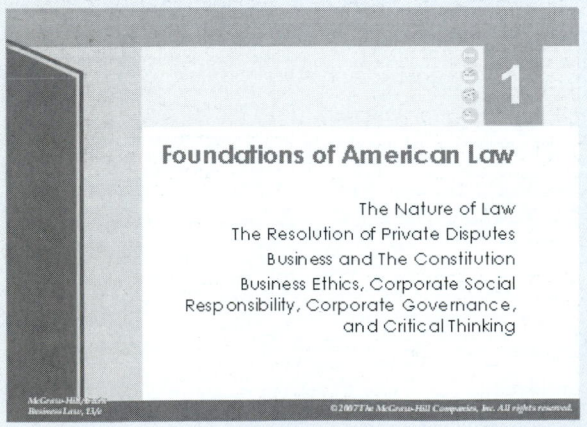

POWERPOINT® PRESENTATION ("BASIC" AND "DETAILED" VERSIONS)

The PowerPoint presentation is authored by Pamela S. Evers, Attorney and Associate Professor, University of North Carolina Wilmington. It has been significantly enhanced based on reviewer feedback to now include over 1,100 slides that provide lecture outline material, important concepts and figures in the text, photos for discussion, hyperlinks, and summaries of the cases in the book. Notes are also provided within the PowerPoint presentations for students and instructors to augment information and class discussion. Questions are included to use with the classroom performance system as well.

Supplements

TEST BANK

The Test Bank consists of true-false, multiple choice, and short essay questions in each chapter. Approximately 50 questions are included per chapter. Questions adapted from previous CPA exams are also included and highlighted to help Accounting students review for the exam.

STUDENT STUDY GUIDE

The Student Study Guide, has been revised and expanded for the 14th Edition by Evan Scheffel. The guide follows the text chapter by chapter, giving chapter outlines, lecture hints, and an outline of how each chapter topic fits into the larger Business Law course. Questions for review are also included to help students better retain concepts and put their learning into practice.

ONLINE LEARNING CENTER

www.mhhe.com/mallor14e The Online Learning Center (OLC) is a Web site that follows the text chapter by chapter. The 14th Edition OLC contains case updates, quizzes and review terms for students to study from, downloadable supplements for the instructors, links to professional resources for students and professors, and links to video clips to use for discussion.

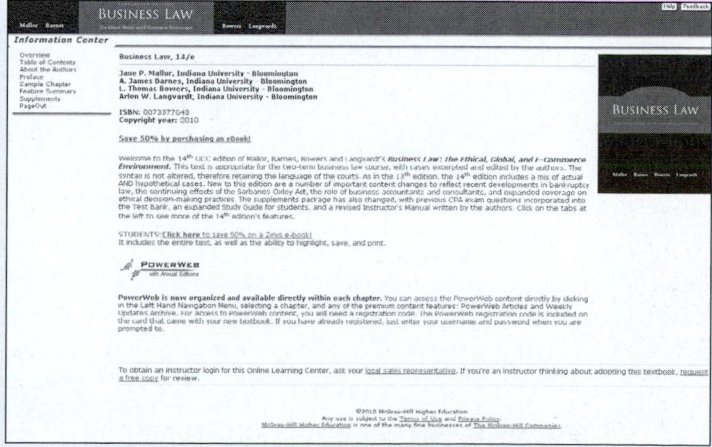

Brief Contents

▶ Part 1 Foundations of American Law

1 The Nature of Law 2
2 The Resolution of Private Disputes 29
3 Business and the Constitution 56
4 Business Ethics, Corporate Social Responsibility, Corporate Governance, and Critical Thinking 90

▶ Part 2 Crimes and Torts

5 Crimes 124
6 Intentional Torts 169
7 Negligence and Strict Liability 205
8 Intellectual Property and Unfair Competition 241

▶ Part 3 Contracts

9 Introduction to Contracts 290
10 The Agreement: Offer 307
11 The Agreement: Acceptance 325
12 Consideration 343
13 Reality of Consent 360
14 Capacity to Contract 378
15 Illegality 392
16 Writing 412
17 Rights of Third Parties 435
18 Performance and Remedies 453

▶ Part 4 Sales

19 Formation and Terms of Sales Contracts 480
20 Product Liability 504
21 Performance of Sales Contracts 546
22 Remedies for Breach of Sales Contracts 568

▶ Part 5 Property

23 Personal Property and Bailments 588
24 Real Property 613
25 Landlord and Tenant 645
26 Estates and Trusts 667
27 Insurance Law 687

▶ Part 6 Credit

28 Introduction to Credit and Secured Transactions 718
29 Security Interests in Personal Property 740
30 Bankruptcy 769

▶ Part 7 Commercial Paper

31 Negotiable Instruments 806

32 Negotiation and Holder in Due Course 822
33 Liability of Parties 846
34 Checks and Electronic Transfers 869

▶ Part 8 Agency Law

35 The Agency Relationship 896
36 Third-Party Relations of the Principal and the Agent 913

▶ Part 9 Partnerships

37 Introduction to Forms of Business and Formation of Partnerships 932
38 Operation of Partnerships and Related Forms 951
39 Partners' Dissociation and Partnerships' Dissolution and Winding Up 967
40 Limited Liability Companies, Limited Partnerships, and Limited Liability Limited Partnerships 985

▶ Part 10 Corporations

41 History and Nature of Corporations 1008
42 Organization and Financial Structure of Corporations 1027
43 Management of Corporations 1047
44 Shareholders' Rights and Liabilities 1084
45 Securities Regulation 1114
46 Legal and Professional Responsibilities of Auditors, Consultants, and Securities Professionals 1158

▶ Part 11 Regulation of Business

47 Administrative Agencies 1194
48 The Federal Trade Commission Act and Consumer Protection Laws 1225
49 Antitrust: The Sherman Act 1254
50 The Clayton Act, the Robinson–Patman Act, and Antitrust Exemptions and Immunities 1287
51 Employment Law 1315
52 Environmental Regulation 1345

▶ Appendix A

The Constitution of the United States of America A-1

▶ Appendix B

The Uniform Commercial Code, Articles 2, 2A, 3, 4, 7, and 9 B-1

Glossary G-1

Index I-1

Contents

Preface vi

Part 1   Foundations of American Law

1   The Nature of Law 2
Types and Classifications of Law 2
The Types of Law 2
Priority Rules 6
Classifications of Law 8
Jurisprudence 9
Legal Positivism 9
Natural Law 9
American Legal Realism 9
Sociological Jurisprudence 10
Other Schools of Jurisprudence 11
The Functions of Law 11
Legal Reasoning 11
Case Law Reasoning 12
Statutory Interpretation 15
Limits on the Power of Courts 23
APPENDIX: Reading and Briefing Cases 24

2   The Resolution of Private Disputes 29
State Courts and Their Jurisdiction 29
Courts of Limited Jurisdiction 29
Trial Courts 29
Appellate Courts 30
Jurisdiction and Venue 30
Federal Courts and Their Jurisdiction 34
Federal District Courts 34
Specialized Federal Courts 36
Federal Courts of Appeals 36
The U.S. Supreme Court 37
Civil Procedure 39
Service of the Summons 39
The Pleadings 39
Motion to Dismiss 40
Discovery 40
Summary Judgment 45
The Pretrial Conference 45
The Trial 45
Appeal 48
Enforcing a Judgment 48

Class Actions 48
Alternative Dispute Resolution 49
Common Forms of ADR 49
Other ADR Devices 53

3   Business and the Constitution 56
An Overview of the U.S. Constitution 56
The Evolution of the Constitution and the Role of the Supreme Court 57
The Coverage and Structure of This Chapter 58
State and Federal Power to Regulate 58
State Regulatory Power 58
Federal Regulatory Power 58
Independent Checks on the Federal Government and the States 63
Incorporation 63
Government Action 63
Means-Ends Tests 64
Business and the First Amendment 65
Due Process 71
Equal Protection 72
Independent Checks Applying Only to the States 80
The Contract Clause 80
Burden on, or Discrimination against, Interstate Commerce 81
Federal Preemption 84
The Takings Clause 84

4   Business Ethics, Corporate Social Responsibility, Corporate Governance, and Critical Thinking 90
Why Study Business Ethics? 91
The Corporate Social Responsibility Debate 91
Ethical Theories 93
Rights Theory 93
Justice Theory 95
Utilitarianism 96
Profit Maximization 97
Guidelines for Ethical Decision Making 105
What Facts Impact My Decision? 105
What Are the Alternatives? 106
Who Are the Stakeholders? 106
How Do the Alternatives Impact Society as a Whole? 106
How Do the Alternatives Impact My Firm? 107

How Do the Alternatives Impact Me, the Decision Maker? 107
What Are the Ethics of Each Alternative? 108
What Are the Practical Constraints of Each Alternative? 109
What Course of Action Should Be Taken and How Do We Implement It? 109
Knowing When to Use the Guidelines 110

Thinking Critically 110
Non Sequiturs 110
Appeals to Pity 111
False Analogies 111
Begging the Question 111
Argumentum ad Populum 111
Bandwagon Fallacy 112
Argumentum ad Baculum 112
Argumentum ad Hominem 112
Argument from Authority 113
False Cause 113
The Gambler's Fallacy 113
Reductio ad Absurdum 114
Appeals to Tradition 114
The Lure of the New 114
Sunk Cost Fallacy 114

Common Characteristics of Poor Decision Making 115
Failing to Remember Goals 115
Overconfidence 115
Complexity of the Issues 116

Resisting Requests to Act Unethically 116
Recognizing Unethical Requests and Bosses 116
Buying Time 117
Find a Mentor and a Peer Support Group 117
Find Win-Win Solutions 117
Work within the Firm to Stop the Unethical Act 118
Prepare to Lose Your Job 119

Leading Ethically 119
Be Ethical 119
Communicate the Firm's Core Ethical Values 119
Connect Ethical Behavior with the Firm's and Workers' Best Interests 119
Reinforce Ethical Behavior 119

Part 2 Crimes and Torts

5 Crimes 124
Role of the Criminal Law 125

Nature of Crimes 125
Purpose of the Criminal Sanction 126
Essentials of Crime 128

Criminal Procedure 137
Criminal Prosecutions: An Overview 137
Role of Constitutional Safeguards 138
The Fourth Amendment 139
The Fifth Amendment 148
The Sixth Amendment 153

White-Collar Crimes and the Dilemmas of Corporate Control 154
Introduction 154
Evolution of Corporate Criminal Liability 154
Corporate Criminal Liability Today 155
Individual Liability for Corporate Crime 156
New Directions 157

Important White-Collar Crimes 159
Regulatory Offenses 159
Fraudulent Acts 159
The Sarbanes–Oxley Act 159
Bribery and Giving of Illegal Gratuities 159
RICO 160

Computer Crime 163

6 Intentional Torts 169
Interference with Personal Rights 173
Battery 173
Assault 175
Intentional Infliction of Emotional Distress 176
False Imprisonment 177
Defamation 181
Invasion of Privacy 191
Misuse of Legal Proceedings 195
Deceit (Fraud) 195

Interference with Property Rights 196
Trespass to Land 196
Private Nuisance 196
Conversion 198

Other Examples of Intentional Tort Liability 198

7 Negligence and Strict Liability 205
Negligence 206
Duty and Breach of Duty 206
Causation of Injury 221
Res Ipsa Loquitur 231
Negligence Defenses 232

Strict Liability 234

Abnormally Dangerous Activities 234

Statutory Strict Liability 236

Tort Reform 236

8   Intellectual Property and Unfair
     Competition 241

Protection of Intellectual Property 242

Patents 242

Copyrights 251

Trademarks 263

Trade Secrets 273

Definition of a Trade Secret 273

Ownership and Transfer of Trade Secrets 274

Misappropriation of Trade Secrets 274

Commercial Torts 276

Injurious Falsehood 276

Interference with Contractual Relations 277

Interference with Prospective Advantage 278

Lanham Act Section 43(a) 280

Part 3   Contracts

9   Introduction to Contracts 290

The Nature of Contracts 290

The Functions of Contracts 290

The Evolution of Contract Law 291

The Methods of Contracting 291

Basic Elements of a Contract 291

Basic Contract Concepts and Types 294

Bilateral and Unilateral Contracts 294

Valid, Unenforceable, Voidable, and Void Contracts 295

Express and Implied Contracts 295

Executed and Executory Contracts 295

Sources of Law Governing Contracts 295

The Uniform Commercial Code: Origin and Purposes 295

Application of Article 2 296

Application of the Common Law of Contracts 296

Law Governing "Hybrid" Contracts 296

*Relationship of the UCC and the Common Law of
Contracts 298*

*Basic Differences in the Nature of Article 2 and the
Common Law of Contracts 298*

Influence of Restatement (Second) of Contracts 300

"Noncontract" Obligations 300

Quasi-Contract 300

Promissory Estoppel 302

10   The Agreement: Offer 307

Requirements for an Offer 307

Intent to Contract 307

Definiteness of Terms 309

Communication to Offeree 313

Special Offer Problem Areas 313

Advertisements 313

Rewards 314

Auctions 314

Bids 314

Which Terms Are Included in the Offer? 314

Termination of Offers 315

Terms of the Offer 315

Lapse of Time 316

Revocation 316

Rejection 317

Death or Insanity of Either Party 318

Destruction of Subject Matter 318

Intervening Illegality 318

11   The Agreement: Acceptance 325

What Is an Acceptance? 325

Intention to Accept 325

Intent and Acceptance on the Offeror's Terms 327

Communication of Acceptance 331

When Is Acceptance Communicated? 331

Acceptances by Instantaneous Forms of Communication 331

*Acceptances by Noninstantaneous Forms of
Communication 332*

Stipulated Means of Communication 334

Special Acceptance Problem Areas 334

Acceptance in Unilateral Contracts 334

Acceptance in Bilateral Contracts 334

Silence as Acceptance 335

Acceptance When a Writing Is Anticipated 337

Acceptance of Ambiguous Offers 337

Who Can Accept an Offer? 338

12   Consideration 343

Elements of Consideration 343

Legal Value 344

Bargained-For Exchange 344

**Exchanges That Fail to Meet Consideration
Requirements 346**

Illusory Promises 346

Preexisting Duties 348

Past Consideration 353

Exceptions to the Consideration Requirement 354
Promissory Estoppel 354
Promises to Pay Debts Barred by Statutes of Limitations 356
Promises to Pay Debts Barred by Bankruptcy Discharge 356
Charitable Subscriptions 356

13 Reality of Consent 360
Effect of Doctrines Discussed in This Chapter 360
Necessity for Prompt and Unequivocal Rescission 360
Misrepresentation and Fraud 361
Relationship between Misrepresentation and Fraud 361
Requirements for Rescission on the Ground of Misrepresentation 361
Mistake 365
Nature of Mistake 365
Requirements for Mutual Mistake 367
Requirements for Unilateral Mistake 369
Duress 370
Nature of Duress 370
Requirements for Duress 370
Economic Duress 371
Undue Influence 374
Nature of Undue Influence 374
Determining Undue Influence 374

14 Capacity to Contract 378
What Is Capacity? 378
Effect of Lack of Capacity 378
Capacity of Minors 379
Minors' Right to Disaffirm 379
Period of Minority 380
Emancipation 380
Time of Disaffirmance 381
Ratification 381
Duties upon Disaffirmance 381
Effect of Misrepresentation of Age 385
Capacity of Mentally Impaired Persons 385
Theory of Incapacity 385
Test for Mental Incapacity 385
The Effect of Incapacity Caused by Mental Impairment 386
Contracts of Intoxicated Persons 389
Intoxication and Capacity 389

15 Illegality 392
Meaning of Illegality 392
Determining Whether an Agreement Is Illegal 392
Agreements in Violation of Statute 394

Agreements Declared Illegal by Statute 394
Agreements That Violate the Public Policy of a Statute 395
Agreements That May Be in Violation of Public Policy Articulated by Courts 397
Agreements in Restraint of Competition 398
Exculpatory Clauses 400
Family Relationships and Public Policy 402
Unfairness in Agreements: Contracts of Adhesion and Unconscionable Contracts 403
Unconscionability 403
Contracts of Adhesion 406
Effect of Illegality 406
General Rule: No Remedy for Breach of Illegal Agreements 406
Exceptions 406

16 Writing 412
The Significance of Writing in Contract Law 412
Purposes of Writing 412
Writing and Contract Enforcement 412
Overview of the Statute of Frauds 413
History and Purposes 413
Effect of Violation of the Statute of Frauds 413
Contracts Covered by the Statute of Frauds 413
Collateral Contracts 414
Interest in Land 415
Contracts That Cannot Be Performed within One Year 416
Sale of Goods for $500 or More 418
Promise of Executor or Administrator to Pay a Decedent's Debt Personally 418
Contract in Which Marriage Is the Consideration 419
Meeting the Requirements of the Statute of Frauds 420
Nature of the Writing Required 420
UCC: Alternative Means of Satisfying the Statute of Frauds in Sale of Goods Contracts 421
Promissory Estoppel and the Statute of Frauds 425
The Parol Evidence Rule 425
Explanation of the Rule 425
Scope of the Parol Evidence Rule 426
Admissible Parol Evidence 426
Interpretation of Contracts 430

17 Rights of Third Parties 435
Assignment of Contracts 435
Nature of Assignment of Rights 435

Creating an Assignment 437
Assignability of Rights 437
Nature of Assignee's Rights 439
Subsequent Assignments 440
Successive Assignments 440
Assignor's Warranty Liability to Assignee 441

Delegation of Duties 441
Nature of Delegation 441
Delegable Duties 441
Language Creating a Delegation 442
Assumption of Duties by Delegatee 442
Discharge of Delegator by Novation 444

Third-Party Beneficiaries 446
Intended Beneficiaries versus Incidental Beneficiaries 446
Vesting of Beneficiary's Rights 448

18 **Performance and Remedies 453**

Conditions 453
Nature of Conditions 453
Types of Conditions 454
Creation of Express Conditions 456
Excuse of Conditions 457

Performance of Contracts 459
Level of Performance Expected of the Promisor 459
Good Faith Performance 460

Breach of Contract 460
Effect of Material Breach 461
Determining the Materiality of the Breach 461
Anticipatory Repudiation 464
Recovery by a Party Who Has Committed Material Breach 465

Excuses for Nonperformance 465
Impossibility 466
Commercial Impracticability 467

Other Grounds for Discharge 468
Discharge by Mutual Agreement 468
Discharge by Accord and Satisfaction 468
Discharge by Waiver 468
Discharge by Alteration 468
Discharge by Statute of Limitations 468
Discharge by Decree of Bankruptcy 469

Remedies for Breach of Contract 469
Types of Contract Remedies 469
Interests Protected by Contract Remedies 469
Legal Remedies (Damages) 469
Equitable Remedies 473
Restitution 474

Part 4 Sales

19 **Formation and Terms of Sales Contracts 480**

Sale of Goods 480

Leases 482

Merchants 483

Code Requirements 483

Terms of Sales Contracts 483
Gap Fillers 483
Price Terms 483
Quantity Terms 483
Output and Needs Contracts 483
Exclusive Dealing Contracts 487
Time for Performance 487
Delivery Terms 487

Title 487
Passage of Title 487
Importance of Title 488

Title and Third Parties 490
Obtaining Good Title 490
Transfers of Voidable Title 490
Buyers in the Ordinary Course of Business 492
Entrusting of Goods 492

Risk of Loss 493
Terms of the Agreement 493
Shipment Contracts 493
Destination Contracts 495
Goods in the Possession of Third Parties 496
Risk Generally 496
Effect of Breach on Risk of Loss 496
Insurable Interest 496

Sales on Trial 496
Sale on Approval 496
Sale or Return 497
Sale on Consignment 498

20 **Product Liability 504**

The Evolution of Product Liability Law 505
The 19th Century 505
The 20th and 21st Centuries 505
The Current Debate over Product Liability Law 506

Theories of Product Liability Recovery 506
Express Warranty 506
Implied Warranty of Merchantability 508
Implied Warranty of Fitness 512
Negligence 514

Strict Liability 517
The Restatement (Third) 520
Other Theories of Recovery 524

Time Limitations 526

Damages in Product Liability Cases 526

The No-Privity Defense 527

Tort Cases 527
Warranty Cases 527

Disclaimers and Remedy Limitations 532

Implied Warranty Disclaimers 532
Express Warranty Disclaimers 533
Disclaimers of Tort Liability 533
Limitation of Remedies 533

Defenses 533

The Traditional Defenses 534
Comparative Principles 534
Preemption and Regulatory Compliance? 535

21 Performance of Sales Contracts 546

General Rules 546

Good Faith 547
Course of Dealing 547
Usage of Trade 547
Modification 549
Waiver 549
Assignment 550

Delivery 550

Basic Obligation 550
Place of Delivery 550
Seller's Duty of Delivery 550

Inspection and Payment 550

Buyer's Right of Inspection 550
Payment 552

Acceptance, Revocation, and Rejection 553

Acceptance 553
Effect of Acceptance 554
Revocation of Acceptance 554
Buyer's Rights on Improper Delivery 556
Rejection 557
Right to Cure 559
Buyer's Duties after Rejection 559

Assurance, Repudiation, and Excuse 560

Assurance 560
Anticipatory Repudiation 563
Excuse 563

22 Remedies for Breach of Sales Contracts 568

Agreements as to Remedies 568

Statute of Limitations 571

Seller's Remedies 571

Remedies Available to an Injured Seller 571
Cancellation and Withholding of Delivery 571
Resale of Goods 572
Recovery of the Purchase Price 572
Damages for Rejection or Repudiation 572
Seller's Remedies Where Buyer Is Insolvent 575
Seller's Right to Stop Delivery 575
Liquidated Damages 576

Buyer's Remedies 576

Buyer's Remedies in General 576
Buyer's Right to Cover 577
Incidental Damages 578
Consequential Damages 578
Damages for Nondelivery 578
Damages for Defective Goods 581
Buyer's Right to Specific Performance 582
Buyer and Seller Agreements as to Remedies 582

Part 5 Property

23 Personal Property and Bailments 588

Nature of Property 588

Classifications of Property 589

Personal Property versus Real Property 589
Tangible versus Intangible Personal Property 589
Public and Private Property 589

Acquiring Ownership of Personal Property 589

Production or Purchase 589
Possession of Unowned Property 590
Rights of Finders of Lost, Mislaid, and Abandoned Property 590
Legal Responsibilities of Finders 593
Leasing 593
Gifts 593
Conditional Gifts 595
Uniform Transfers to Minors Act 597
Will or Inheritance 597
Confusion 597
Accession 597

Bailments 598

Nature of Bailments 598

Elements of a Bailment 598

Creation of a Bailment 598

Types of Bailments 599

Special Bailments 599

Duties of the Bailee 599

Duty of Bailee to Take Care of Property 599

Bailee's Duty to Return the Property 600

Bailee's Liability for Misdelivery 602

Limits on Liability 602

Right to Compensation 602

Bailor's Liability for Defects in the Bailed Property 602

Special Bailments 603

Common Carriers 603

Hotelkeepers 603

Safe-Deposit Boxes 605

Involuntary Bailments 605

Documents of Title 605

Warehouse Receipts 605

Bills of Lading 605

Duty of Care 607

Negotiation of Document of Title 608

Rights Acquired by Negotiation 608

Warranties of Tansferor of Document of Title 609

24 Real Property 613

Scope of Real Property 613

Fixtures 613

Rights and Interests in Real Property 617

Estates in Land 617

Co-ownership of Real Property 617

Interests in Real Property Owned by Others 619

Easements 619

Creation of Easements 619

Profits 620

Licenses 620

Restrictive Covenants 620

Acquisition of Real Property 623

Acquisition by Purchase 623

Acquisition by Gift 623

Acquisition by Will or Inheritance 623

Acquisition by Tax Sale 623

Acquisition by Adverse Possession 623

Transfer by Sale 625

Steps in a Sale 625

Contracting with a Real Estate Broker 625

Contract of Sale 626

Fair Housing Act 626

Deeds 627

Form and Execution of Deed 628

Recording Deeds 628

Methods of Assuring Title 628

Seller's Responsibilities regarding the Quality of Residential Property 629

Implied Warranty of Habitability 629

Duty to Disclose Hidden Defects 630

Other Property Condition–Related Obligations of Real Property Owners and Possessors 630

Expansion of Premises Liability 630

Americans with Disabilities Act 631

Land Use Control 632

Nuisance Law 632

Eminent Domain 633

Zoning and Subdivision Laws 636

Land Use Regulation and Taking 638

25 Landlord and Tenant 645

Leases and Tenancies 646

Nature of Leases 646

Types of Tenancies 646

Execution of a Lease 646

Rights, Duties, and Liabilities of the Landlord 647

Landlord's Rights 647

Landlord's Duties 648

Landlord's Responsibility for Condition of Leased Property 649

Landlord's Tort Liability 653

Rights, Duties, and Liabilities of the Tenant 659

Rights of the Tenant 659

Duty to Pay Rent 659

Duty Not to Commit Waste 659

Assignment and Subleasing 659

Tenant's Liability for Injuries to Third Persons 660

Termination of the Leasehold 660

Eviction 660

Agreement to Surrender 660

Abandonment 660

26 Estates and Trusts 667

The Law of Estates and Trusts 667

Estate Planning 667

Wills 667

Rights of Disposition by Will 667

Nature of a Will 668

Common Will Terminology 668

Testamentary Capacity 668

Execution of a Will 669

Incorporation by Reference 669

Informal Wills 669

Joint and Mutual Wills 670

Construction of Wills 670

Limitations on Disposition by Will 672

Revocation of Wills 673

Codicils 673

Advance Directives: Planning for Disability 673

Living Wills 673

Durable Power of Attorney 674

Durable Power of Attorney for Health Care 675

Federal Law and Advance Directives 675

Intestacy 675

Characteristics of Intestacy Statutes 675

Special Rules 677

Simultaneous Death 677

Administration of Estates 678

The Probate Estate 678

Determining the Existence of a Will 678

Selecting a Personal Representative 678

Responsibilities of the Personal Representative 678

Trusts 679

Nature of a Trust 679

Trust Terminology 679

Why People Create Trusts 679

Creation of Express Trusts 680

Charitable Trusts 680

Totten Trusts 680

Powers and Duties of the Trustee 680

Liability of Trustee 681

Spendthrift Trusts 681

Termination and Modification of a Trust 684

Implied and Constructive Trusts 684

27   **Insurance Law 687**

Nature and Benefits of Insurance Relationships 688

Insurance Policies as Contracts 688

Interested Parties 688

Offer, Acceptance, and Consideration 688

Effect of Insured's Misrepresentation 692

Legality 692

Form and Content of Insurance Contracts 692

Performance and Breach by Insurer 694

Property Insurance 694

The Insurable Interest Requirement 694

Covered and Excluded Perils 696

Nature and Extent of Insurer's Payment Obligation 699

Right of Subrogation 701

Duration and Cancellation of Policy 701

Liability Insurance 701

Types of Liability Insurance Policies 701

Liabilities Insured Against 702

Insurer's Obligations 705

Is There a Liability Insurance Crisis? 706

Bad Faith Breach of Insurance Contract 708

Part 6   Credit

28   **Introduction to Credit and Secured Transactions 718**

Credit 719

Unsecured Credit 719

Secured Credit 719

Development of Security 719

Security Interests in Personal Property 720

Security Interests in Real Property 720

Suretyship and Guaranty 720

Sureties and Guarantors 720

Creation of Principal and Surety Relation 721

Defenses of a Surety 721

Creditor's Duties to Surety 721

Subrogation, Reimbursement, and Contribution 723

Liens on Personal Property 724

Common Law Liens 724

Statutory Liens 724

Characteristics of Liens 724

Foreclosure of Lien 727

Security Interests in Real Property 727

Historical Development of Mortgages 728

Form, Execution, and Recording 728

Rights and Liabilities 729

Foreclosure 729

Right of Redemption 729

Recent Developments Concerning Foreclosures 730

Deed of Trust 732

Land Contracts 732

Mechanic's and Materialman's Liens 732

Rights of Subcontractors and Materialmen 732
Basis for Mechanic's or Materialman's Lien 733
Requirements for Obtaining Lien 734
Priorities and Foreclosure 734
Waiver of Lien 737

29 Security Interests in Personal Property 740
Article 9 740
Security Interests under the Code 741
Security Interests 741
Types of Collateral 741
Obtaining a Security Interest 742
Attachment of the Security Interest 742
Attachment 742
The Security Agreement 742
Future Advances 744
After-Acquired Property 744
Proceeds 744
Perfecting the Security Interest 744
Perfection 744
Perfection by Public Filing 744
Possession by Secured Party as Public Notice 745
Control 748
Perfection by Attachment/Automatic Perfection 748
Motor Vehicles 751
Fixtures 751
Priority Rules 752
Importance of Determining Priority 752
General Priority Rules 753
Purchase Money Security Interest in Inventory 753
Purchase Money Security Interest in Noninventory Collateral 756
Rationale for Protecting Purchase Money Security Interests 757
Buyers in the Ordinary Course of Business 758
Artisan's and Mechanic's Liens 758
Liens on Consumer Goods Perfected by Attachment/Automatic Perfection 758
Fixtures 758
Default and Foreclosure 761
Default 761
Right to Possession 761
Sale of the Collateral 761
Consumer Goods 761
Distribution of Proceeds 762
Liability of Creditor 763

30 Bankruptcy 769
The Bankruptcy Code 769
Bankruptcy Proceedings 770
Liquidations 770
Reorganizations 770
Family Farms 770
Consumer Debt Adjustments 770
The Bankruptcy Courts 770
Chapter 7: Liquidation Proceedings 771
Petitions 771
Involuntary Petitions 771
Automatic Stay Provisions 772
Order of Relief 772
Meeting of Creditors and Election of Trustee 772
Duties of the Trustee 773
The Bankruptcy Estate 773
Exemptions 773
Avoidance of Liens 776
Preferential Payments 777
Preferential Liens 777
Transactions in the Ordinary Course of Business 777
Fraudulent Transfers 778
Claims 781
Allowable Claims 781
Secured Claims 781
Priority Claims 781
Distribution of the Debtor's Estate 782
Discharge in Bankruptcy 782
Discharge 782
Objections to Discharge 782
Acts That Bar Discharge 784
Nondischargeable Debts 784
Reaffirmation Agreements 785
Dismissal for Substantial Abuse 786
Chapter 11: Reorganizations 790
Reorganization Proceeding 790
Use of Chapter 11 793
Collective Bargaining Agreements 794
Chapter 12: Family Farmers and Fishermen 794
Relief for Family Farmers and Fishermen 794
Chapter 13: Consumer Debt Adjustments 796
Relief for Individuals 796
Procedure 796
Discharge 798
Advantages of Chapter 13 800

Part 7   Commercial Paper

31   Negotiable Instruments 806
Nature of Negotiable Instruments 806
Uniform Commercial Code 807
Negotiable Instruments 807
Negotiability 807

Kinds of Negotiable Instruments 807
Promissory Notes 807
Certificates of Deposit 808
Drafts 808
Checks 808

Benefits of Negotiable Instruments 811
Rights of an Assignee of a Contract 811
Rights of a Holder of a Negotiable Instrument 811

Formal Requirements for Negotiability 811
Basic Requirements 811
Importance of Form 812

In Writing 812

Signed 812

Unconditional Promise or Order 813
Requirement of a Promise or Order 813
Promise or Order Must Be Unconditional 814

Fixed Amount of Money 815
Fixed Amount 815
Payable in Money 815

Payable on Demand or at a Definite Time 815
Payable on Demand 815
Payable at a Definite Time 815

Payable to Order or Bearer 816

Special Terms 818
Additional Terms 818
Ambiguous Terms 818

32   Negotiation and Holder in Due Course 822
Negotiation 822
Nature of Negotiation 822
Formal Requirements for Negotiation 823
Nature of Indorsement 823
Wrong or Misspelled Name 823
Checks Deposited without Indorsement 823
Transfer of Order Instrument 824

Indorsements 825
Effects of an Indorsement 825
Kinds of Indorsements 825

Rescission of Indorsement 828

Holder in Due Course 828
General Requirements 829
Holder 830
Value 831
Good Faith 831
Overdue or Dishonored 832
Notice of Unauthorized Signature or Alteration 832
Notice of Claims 832
Irregular and Incomplete Instruments 833
Shelter Rule 834

Rights of a Holder in Due Course 834
Claims and Defenses Generally 834
Importance of Being a Holder in Due Course 836
Real Defenses 836
Personal Defenses 837
Claims to the Instrument 838
Claims in Recoupment 839

Changes in the Holder in Due Course Rule for Consumer Credit Transactions 839
Consumer Disadvantages 839
State Consumer Protection Legislation 839
Federal Trade Commission Regulation 839

33   Liability of Parties 846
Liability in General 846
Contractual Liability 846
Primary and Secondary Liability 847
Obligation of a Maker 847
Obligation of a Drawee or an Acceptor 847
Obligation of a Drawer 849
Obligation of an Indorser 849
Obligation of an Accommodation Party 849
Signing an Instrument 850
Signature by an Authorized Agent 850
Unauthorized Signature 851

Contractual Liability in Operation 851
Presentment of a Note 852
Presentment of a Check or a Draft 852
Time of Presentment 853

Warranty Liability 854
Transfer Warranties 854
Presentment Warranties 856
Payment or Acceptance by Mistake 857
Operation of Warranties 857

Other Liability Rules 858

Negligence 858
Impostor Rule 859
Fictitious Payee Rule 859
Comparative Negligence Rule Concerning Impostors and
Fictitious Payees 860
Fraudulent Indorsements by Employees 860
Conversion 863

Discharge of Negotiable Instruments 863
Discharge of Liability 863
Discharge by Payment 864
Discharge by Cancellation 864
Altered Instruments; Discharge by Alteration 864
Discharge of Indorsers and Accommodation Parties 866

34 Checks and Electronic Transfers 869
The Drawer–Drawee Relationship 869
Bank's Duty to Pay 870
Bank's Right to Charge to Customer's Account 870
Stop-Payment Order 871
Bank's Liability for Payment after Stop-Payment Order 872
Certified Check 875
Cashier's Check 875
Death or Incompetence of Customer 876

Forged and Altered Checks 877
Bank's Right to Charge Account 877
Customer's Duty to Report Forgeries and Alterations 877

Check Collection and Funds Availability 880
Check Collection 880
Funds Availability 885
Check 21 886

Electronic Transfers 887
Electronic Funds Transfer Act 888
Wire Transfers 889

Part 8   Agency Law

35 The Agency Relationship 896
Creation of an Agency 897
Formation 897
Capacity 897
Nondelegable Obligations 897

Agency Concepts, Definitions, and Types 898
Authority 898
General and Special Agents 899
Gratuitous Agents 899

Subagents 899
Employees and Independent Contractors 899

Duties of Agent to Principal 901
Agent's Duty of Loyalty 902
Agent's Duty to Obey Instructions 903
Agent's Duty to Act with Care and Skill 903
Agent's Duty to Notify the Principal 904
Agent's Duties to Account 904

Duties of Principal to Agent 906
Duty to Compensate Agent 906
Duties of Reimbursement and Indemnity 907

Termination of an Agency 907
Termination by Act of the Parties 907
Termination by Operation of Law 907
Termination of Agency Powers Given as Security 908
Effect of Termination on Agent's Authority 909

36 Third-Party Relations of the Principal and
the Agent 913
Contract Liability of the Principal 914
Express Authority 914
Implied Authority 914
Apparent Authority 914
Agent's Notification and Knowledge 917
Ratification 917
Contracts Made by Subagents 919

Contract Liability of the Agent 919
The Nature of the Principal 919
Liability of Agent by Agreement 921
Implied Warranty of Authority 922

Tort Liability of the Principal 923
Respondeat Superior Liability 923
Direct Liability 924
Liability for Torts of Independent Contractors 926
Liability for Agent's Misrepresentations 926

Tort Liability of the Agent 927

Tort Suits against Principal and Agent 927

Part 9   Partnerships

37 Introduction to Forms of Business and
Formation of Partnerships 932
Choosing a Form of Business 932
Sole Proprietorship 932
Partnership 933

Limited Liability Partnership 933
Limited Partnership 934
Limited Liability Limited Partnership 934
Corporation 934
Professional Corporation 935
Limited Liability Company 935

Partnerships 938

Creation of Partnerships 938
RUPA Definition of Partnership 939
Creation of Joint Ventures 940
Creation of Mining Partnerships 942
Creation of Limited Liability Partnerships 942

Purported Partners 942
Purporting to Be a Partner 943
Reliance Resulting in a Transaction with the Partnership 943
Effect of Purported Partnership 943

Partnership Capital 945

Partnership Property 945
Examples 945

Partner's Partnership Interest 947
Partner's Transferable Interest 947
Effect of Partnership Agreement 948

38 **Operation of Partnerships and Related Forms 951**
Duties of Partners to the Partnership and Each Other 951
Having Interest Adverse to Partnership 952
Competing against the Partnership 952
Duty to Serve 952
Duty of Care 952
Duty to Act within Actual Authority 952
Duty to Account 952
Other Duties 953
Joint Ventures and Mining Partnerships 953

Compensation of Partners 953
Profits and Losses 953

Management Powers of Partners 956
Individual Authority of Partners 956
Special Transactions 957
Disagreement among Partners: Ordinary Course of Business 958
When Unanimous Partners' Agreement Required 958
Joint Ventures and Mining Partnerships 959
Effect of Partnership Agreement 959

Liability for Torts and Crimes 961
Torts 961
Tort Liability and Limited Liability Partnerships 962
Crimes 962

Lawsuits by and against Partnerships and Partners 962
Limited Liability Partnerships 963

39 **Partners' Dissociation and Partnerships' Dissolution and Winding Up 967**
Dissociation 967
Nonwrongful Dissociation 968
Wrongful Dissociation 968
Acts Not Causing Dissociation 969
Effect of Partnership Agreement 969

Dissolution and Winding Up the Partnership Business 969
Events Causing Dissolution and Winding Up 969
Joint Ventures and Mining Partnerships 972
Performing Winding Up 972
Partner's Authority during Winding Up 972
Distribution of Dissolved Partnership's Assets 974
Asset Distributions in a Limited Liability Partnership 975
Termination 975

When the Business Is Continued 975
Successor's Liability for Predecessor's Obligations 975
Dissociated Partner's Liability for Obligations Incurred While a Partner 976
Dissociated Partner's Liability for Obligations Incurred after Leaving the Partnership 976
Effect of LLP Status 977
Buyout of Dissociated Partners 978

Partners Joining an Existing Partnership 981
Liability of New Partners 981

40 **Limited Liability Companies, Limited Partnerships, and Limited Liability Limited Partnerships 985**
Limited Liability Companies 985
Tax Treatment of LLCs 986
Formation of LLCs 986
Members' Rights and Liabilities 986
Members' Dissociations and LLC Dissolution 990

Limited Partnerships and Limited Liability Limited Partnerships 993
The Uniform Limited Partnership Acts 993
Use of Limited Partnerships and LLLPs 993

Creation of Limited Partnerships and LLLPs 994
Creation of LLLPs 995
Defective Compliance with Limited Partnership Statute 995

Rights and Liabilities of Partners in Limited Partnerships or LLLPs 996
Rights and Liabilities Shared by General and Limited Partners 996
Other Rights of General Partners 997
Other Liabilities of General Partners 998
Other Rights of Limited Partners 998
Other Liabilities of Limited Partners 998
Partner Who Is Both a General Partner and a Limited Partner 998

Partners' Dissociations and Limited Partnership Dissolution 999
Partners' Dissociations 999
Limited Partnership Dissolutions 1000

Mergers and Conversions 1001

Part 10 Corporations

41 History and Nature of Corporations 1008
History of Corporations 1009
American Corporation Law 1009
Classifications of Corporations 1010
Regulation of For-Profit Corporations 1010
State Incorporation Statutes 1011
State Common Law of Corporations 1011
Regulation of Nonprofit Corporations 1011
Regulation of Foreign and Alien Corporations 1011
Due Process Clause 1012
Commerce Clause 1012
Subjecting Foreign Corporations to Suit 1012
Taxation 1014
Qualifying to Do Business 1014
Regulation of a Corporation's Internal Affairs 1017
Regulation of Foreign Nonprofit Corporations 1017
Piercing the Corporate Veil 1017
Nonprofit Corporations 1019

42 Organization and Financial Structure of Corporations 1027
Promoters and Preincorporation Transactions 1027
Corporation's Liability on Preincorporation Contracts 1027
Promoter's Liability on Preincorporation Contracts 1028

Obtaining a Binding Preincorporation Contract 1028
Preincorporation Share Subscriptions 1029
Relation of Promoter and Prospective Corporation 1029
Liability of Corporation to Promoter 1030

Incorporation 1030
Steps in Incorporation 1030
Close Corporation Elections 1032

Defective Attempts to Incorporate 1033
De Jure Corporation 1033
De Facto Corporation 1033
Corporation by Estoppel 1034
Liability for Defective Incorporation 1034
Modern Approaches to the Defective Incorporation Problem 1034

Incorporation of Nonprofit Corporations 1035
Liability for Preincorporation Transactions 1036

Financing For-Profit Corporations 1036
Equity Securities 1036
Authorized, Issued, and Outstanding Shares 1037
Options, Warrants, and Rights 1037
Debt Securities 1038

Consideration for Shares 1038
Quality of Consideration for Shares 1038
Quantity of Consideration for Shares 1038

Share Subscriptions 1040
Issuance of Shares 1040
Transfer of Shares 1040
Restrictions on Transferability of Shares 1041
Financing Nonprofit Corporations 1044

43 Management of Corporations 1047
Corporate Objectives 1047
Corporate Powers 1048
Purpose Clauses in Articles of Incorporation 1048
Powers of Nonprofit Corporations 1049
The Board of Directors 1049
Board Authority under Corporation Statutes 1049
Committees of the Board 1049
Powers, Rights, and Liabilities of Directors as Individuals 1050
Election of Directors 1050
Directors' Meetings 1053
Officers of the Corporation 1054
Managing Close Corporations 1055
Managing Nonprofit Corporations 1055

Directors' and Officers' Duties to the Corporation 1056

Acting within Authority 1056

Duty of Care 1056

Board Opposition to Acquisition of Control of a Corporation 1063

Duties of Loyalty 1067

Conflicting Interest Transactions 1067

Usurpation of a Corporate Opportunity 1069

Oppression of Minority Shareholders 1071

Trading on Inside Information 1072

Director's Right to Dissent 1073

Duties of Directors and Officers of Nonprofit Corporations 1073

Corporate and Management Liability for Torts and Crimes 1074

Liability of the Corporation 1074

Directors' and Officers' Liability for Torts and Crimes 1074

Insurance and Indemnification 1078

Mandatory Indemnification of Directors 1078

Permissible Indemnification of Directors 1078

Insurance 1079

Nonprofit Corporations 1079

44 Shareholders' Rights and Liabilities 1083

Shareholders' Meetings 1083

Notice of Meetings 1084

Conduct of Meetings 1084

Shareholder Action without a Meeting 1084

Shareholders' Election of Directors 1084

Straight Voting 1084

Cumulative Voting 1084

Classes of Shares 1085

Shareholder Control Devices 1085

Fundamental Corporate Changes 1088

Procedures Required 1089

Dissenters' Rights 1089

Shareholders' Inspection and Information Rights 1095

Preemptive Right 1095

Distributions to Shareholders 1096

Dividends 1096

Share Repurchases 1099

Ensuring a Shareholder's Return on Investment 1099

Shareholders' Lawsuits 1099

Shareholders' Individual Lawsuits 1099

Shareholder Class Action Suits 1099

Shareholders' Derivative Actions 1100

Defense of Corporation by Shareholder 1103

Shareholder Liability 1103

Shareholder Liability for Illegal Distributions 1103

Shareholder Liability for Corporate Debts 1103

Sale of a Control Block of Shares 1103

Shareholders as Fiduciaries 1104

Members' Rights and Duties in Nonprofit Corporations 1107

Members' Meeting and Voting Rights 1107

Member Inspection and Information Rights 1108

Distributions of Assets 1108

Resignation and Expulsion of Members 1108

Derivative Suits 1108

Dissolution and Termination of Corporations 1109

Winding Up and Termination 1110

Dissolution of Nonprofit Corporations 1110

45 Securities Regulation 1114

Purposes of Securities Regulation 1115

Securities and Exchange Commission 1115

SEC Actions 1115

What Is a Security? 1116

Securities Act of 1933 1119

Registration of Securities under the 1933 Act 1119

Mechanics of a Registered Offering 1119

Registration Statement and Prospectus 1120

Section 5: Timing, Manner, and Content of Offers and Sales 1120

Exemptions from the Registration Requirements of the 1933 Act 1124

Securities Exemptions 1124

Transaction Exemptions 1124

Intrastate Offering Exemption 1124

Private Offering Exemption 1124

Small Offering Exemptions 1126

Securities Offerings on the Internet 1127

Transaction Exemptions for Nonissuers 1127

Sale of Restricted Securities 1127

Consequence of Obtaining a Securities or Transaction Exemption 1128

Liability Provisions of the 1933 Act 1129

Liability for Defective Registration Statements 1130

Other Liability Provisions 1135

Criminal Liability 1135

Securities Exchange Act of 1934 1136

Registration of Securities under the 1934 Act 1136

Holdings and Trading by Insiders 1137

Proxy Solicitation Regulation 1138

Liability Provisions of the 1934 Act 1140

Liability for False Statements in Filed Documents 1140

Section 10(b) and Rule 10b–5 1140

Elements of a Rule 10b–5 Violation 1141

Regulation FD 1149

Criminal Liability 1151

Tender Offer Regulation 1151

Private Acquisition of Shares 1151

State Regulation of Tender Offers 1152

State Securities Law 1153

Registration of Securities 1153

46 Legal and Professional Responsibilities of Auditors, Consultants, and Securities Professionals 1158

General Standard of Performance 1159

Professionals' Liability to Clients 1160

Contractual Liability 1160

Tort Liability 1161

Breach of Trust 1165

Securities Law 1165

Professionals' Liability to Third Persons: Common Law 1165

Negligence and Negligent Misrepresentation 1166

Fraud 1170

Professionals' Liability to Third Parties: Securities Law 1171

Securities Act of 1933 1171

Securities Exchange Act of 1934 1173

State Securities Law 1176

Securities Analysts' Conflicts of Interest 1176

Limiting Professionals' Liability: Professional Corporations and Limited Liability Partnerships 1179

Qualified Opinions, Disclaimers of Opinion, Adverse Opinions, and Unaudited Statements 1180

Criminal, Injunctive, and Administrative Proceedings 1180

Criminal Liability under the Securities Laws 1180

Other Criminal Law Violations 1182

Injunctions 1183

Administrative Proceedings 1183

Securities Exchange Act Audit Requirements 1184

SOX Section 404 1184

Ownership of Working Papers 1185

Professional–Client Privilege 1185

Part 11   Regulation of Business

47 Administrative Agencies 1194

Origins of Administrative Agencies 1196

Agency Creation 1196

Enabling Legislation 1196

Administrative Agencies and the Constitution 1197

Agency Types and Organization 1201

Agency Types 1201

Agency Organization 1202

Agency Powers and Procedures 1202

Nature, Types, and Source of Powers 1202

Investigative Power 1202

Rulemaking Power 1205

Adjudicatory Power 1207

Controlling Administrative Agencies 1208

Presidential Controls 1208

Congressional Controls 1208

Judicial Review 1208

Information Controls 1216

Freedom of Information Act 1216

Privacy Act of 1974 1219

Government in the Sunshine Act 1219

Issues in Regulation 1219

"Old" Regulation versus "New" Regulation 1219

"Captive" Agencies and Agencies' "Shadows" 1219

Deregulation versus Reregulation 1219

Regulations That Preempt Private Lawsuits? 1220

48 The Federal Trade Commission Act and Consumer Protection Laws 1225

The Federal Trade Commission 1226

The FTC's Powers 1226

FTC Enforcement Procedures 1226

Anticompetitive Behavior 1227

Deception and Unfairness 1227

Deception 1227

Unfairness 1231

Remedies 1231

Consumer Protection Laws 1231
Telemarketing and Consumer Fraud and Abuse Prevention Act 1231
Do-Not-Call Registry 1232
Magnuson-Moss Warranty Act 1236
Truth in Lending Act 1237
Fair Credit Reporting Act 1238
FACT Act and the Identity Theft Problem 1242
Equal Credit Opportunity Act 1243
Fair Credit Billing Act 1243
Fair Debt Collection Practices Act 1244
Product Safety Regulation 1248

49 Antitrust: The Sherman Act 1254
The Antitrust Policy Debate 1255
Chicago School Theories 1255
Traditional Antitrust Theories 1255
Effect of Chicago School Notions 1256
Jurisdiction, Types of Cases, and Standing 1256
Jurisdiction 1256
Types of Cases and the Role of Pretrial Settlements 1256
Criminal Prosecutions 1256
Civil Litigation 1257
Standing 1257
Section 1—Restraints of Trade 1257
Concerted Action 1257
Per Se Analysis 1258
"Rule of Reason" Analysis 1258
Horizontal Price-Fixing 1259
Vertical Price-Fixing 1260
Horizontal Divisions of Markets 1267
Vertical Restraints on Distribution 1267
Group Boycotts and Concerted Refusals to Deal 1268
Tying Agreements 1268
Reciprocal Dealing Agreements 1272
Exclusive Dealing Agreements 1272
Joint Ventures by Competitors 1272
Section 2—Monopolization 1273
Monopolization 1273
Attempted Monopolization 1280
Conspiracy to Monopolize 1282

50 The Clayton Act, the Robinson–Patman Act, and Antitrust Exemptions and Immunities 1287
Clayton Act Section 3 1288

Tying Agreements 1288
Exclusive Dealing Agreements 1288
Clayton Act Section 7 1289
Introduction 1289
Relevant Market Determination 1289
Horizontal Mergers 1292
Vertical Mergers 1296
Conglomerate Mergers 1297
Clayton Act Section 8 1298
The Robinson–Patman Act 1299
Jurisdiction 1299
Section 2(a) 1299
Defenses to Section 2(a) Liability 1305
Indirect Price Discrimination 1306
Buyer Inducement of Discrimination 1306
Antitrust Exceptions and Exemptions 1306
Statutory Exemptions 1307
State Action Exemption 1307
The Noerr–Pennington Doctrine 1308
Patent Licensing 1311
Foreign Commerce 1311

51 Employment Law 1315
Legislation Protecting Employee Health, Safety, and Well-Being 1316
Workers' Compensation 1316
The Occupational Safety and Health Act 1319
The Family and Medical Leave Act 1319
Legislation Protecting Wages, Pensions, and Benefits 1320
Social Security 1320
Unemployment Compensation 1320
ERISA 1320
The Fair Labor Standards Act 1321
Collective Bargaining and Union Activity 1321
Equal Opportunity Legislation 1322
The Equal Pay Act 1322
Title VII 1323
Basic Features of Title VII 1323
Race or Color Discrimination 1327
National Origin Discrimination 1327
Religious Discrimination 1327
Sex Discrimination 1327
Section 1981 1330
The Age Discrimination in Employment Act 1330
The Americans with Disabilities Act 1331

Executive Order 11246 1333
State Antidiscrimination Laws 1333

Employee Privacy 1334
Polygraph Testing 1334
Drug and Alcohol Testing 1335
Employer Searches 1335
Records and References 1336
Employer Monitoring 1336

Job Security 1338
The Doctrine of Employment at Will 1338
The Common Law Exceptions 1338

52 Environmental Regulation 1345

Historical Perspective 1345
The Environmental Protection Agency 1346
The National Environmental Policy Act 1346

Air Pollution 1347
Background 1347
Clean Air Act 1347
Ambient Air Control Standards 1347
Acid Rain Controls 1347
Control of Toxic Air Pollutants 1347
New Source Controls 1348
Permits 1350
Enforcement 1351
Automobile Pollution 1351

Climate Change 1352

Water Pollution 1355
Background 1355
Early Federal Legislation 1355

Clean Water Act 1355
Discharge Permits 1355
Water Quality Standards 1356
Enforcement 1356
Wetlands 1358
Ocean Dumping 1359
Drinking Water 1360

Waste Disposal 1361
Background 1361
The Resource Conservation and Recovery Act 1361
Underground Storage Tanks 1361
State Responsibilities 1361
Enforcement 1361
Solid Waste 1364
Superfund 1364
Community Right to Know and Emergency Cleanup 1367

Appendix A   The Constitution of the United States of America A-1

Appendix B   The Uniform Commercial Code, Articles 2, 2A, 3, 4, 7, and 9 B-1

Glossary G-1
Index I-1

List of Cases

ABKCO Music Inc. v. Harrisongs Music, Ltd. 902

Adsit Co. v. Gustin 326

Allstate Indemnity Co. v. Ruiz 41

American Federal Bank, FSB v. Parker 865

Anza v. Ideal Steel Supply Corp. 161

Armstrong v. Rohm and Haas Company, Inc. 309

Armstrong Surgical Center, Inc. v. Armstrong County
Memorial Hospital 1308

Arnhold v. Ocean Atlantic Woodland Corp. 462

Arthur Andersen LLP v. United States 135, 1186

Atlantic Coast Airlines v. Cook 221

Auto-Owners Insurance Co. v. Harvey 702

Baker v. Burlington Coat Factory Warehouse 582

Baker v. International Record Syndicate, Inc. 569

Bank One, N.A. v. Streeter 854

Becknell v. Board of Education 1324

Bersani v. U.S. Environmental Protection Agency 1358

Black v. William Insulation Co. 225

Bombliss v. Cornelsen 31

Brehm v. Eisner 1058

Brodie v. Jordan 1105

Brooke Group Ltd. v. Brown & Williamson Tobacco Corp. 1300

Brooks v. Lewin Realty III, Inc. 650

Cabot Corporation v. AVX Corporation 372

Carey Station Village Homeowners Association,
Inc. v. Carey Station Village, Inc. 278

Carr v. CIGNA Securities, Inc. 1141

Carrow v. Arnold 427

C.B.C. Distribution & Marketing, Inc. v. Major League
Baseball Advanced Media, L.P 193

Christmas Lumber Co., Inc. v. Valiga 1034

Circuit City Stores, Inc. v. Mantor 404

Cisco v. King 1340

Coggins v. New England Patriots Football Club, Inc. . . . 1072

Coma Corporation v. Kansas Department of Labor 393

Commodity Futures Trading Commission v. Collins 1204

Corliss v. Wenner and Anderson 591

Coyle v. Schwartz 1043

Croskey v. BMW of North America, Inc. 515

Crowe v. CarMax Auto Superstores, Inc. 509

Currie v. Chevron U.S.A., Inc. 211

Darco Transportation v. Dulen 1318

Davenport v. Cotton Hope Plantation 233

Dealer Management Systems, Inc. v. Design
Automotive Group, Inc, ... 481

Delgado v. Trax Bar & Grill 215

DeNardo v. Bax 183

Denny's Marina, Inc. v. Renfro Productions, Inc. 1259

Department of the Interior v. Klamath Water Users
Protective Association 1217

Department of Revenue of Kentucky v. Davis 82

Detroit Institute of Arts v. Rose and Smith 600

Dirks v. SEC 1144

Dodge v. Ford Motor Co. 1097

Dodson v. Shrader 382

East Capitol View Community Development
Corporation v. Robinson 466

eBay, Inc. v. MercExchange, LLC 249

Eisenberg v. Advance Relocation & Storage, Inc. 900

Escott v. BarChris Construction Corp. 1131

Estate of McDaniel v. McDaniel 676

Estate of Nelson v. Rice 368

Estate of Shelly 670

Evory v. RJM Acquisitions Funding, L.L.C. 1244

Fair Housing Council of San Fernando Valley v.
Roommate.com, LLC 16

Family Video Movie Club v. Home Folks, Inc. 319

Federal Trade Commission v. Staples, Inc. 1293

Fehribach v. E&Y LLP 1162

Felley v. Singleton 507

Ferris, Baker Watts, Inc. v. Ernst & Young, LLP 1173

Finnin v. Bob Lindsay, Inc. 327

Firstar Bank, N.A. v. First Service Title Agency, Inc. 833

Fitl v. Strek 557

Fitzgerald v. Racing Association of Central Iowa 72

Franklin v. The Monadnock Company 1339

Furst v. Einstein Moomjy, Inc. 471

Galatia Community State Bank v. Kindy 818

Gardner v. Jefferys 621

General Credit Corp. v. New York Linen Co., Inc. 836

General Dynamics Land Systems, Inc. v. Cline 20

General Electric Capital Commercial Automotive Finance, Inc. v. Spartan Motors, Inc. 753

Giles v. First Virginia Credit Services, Inc. 763

Golden Years Nursing Home, Inc. v. Gabbard 830

Gonzales v. Raich 59

Gottlieb v. Tropicana Hotel and Casino 345

Grace Label, Inc. v. Kliff 547

Green Wood Industrial Company v. Forceman International Development Group, Inc. 579

Gribben v. Wal-Mart Stores, Inc. 3

Grimes v. Donald 1052

Guth v. Loft, Inc. 1069

Gyamfoah v. EG&G Dynatrend (now EG&G Technical Services) 607

Hagan v. Coca-Cola Bottling Co. 13

Harbor Park Market v. Gronda 457

Hargis v. Baize 218

Harrington v. MacNab 848

Hearst Corp. v. Skeen 188

Heye v. American Golf Corporation, Inc. 346

Hildreth v. Tidewater Equipment Co. 1019

Holt v. Home Depot, U.S.A., Inc. 303

Hudson v. Michigan 143

Hyundai Motor America, Inc. v. Goodin 528

Illinois Tool Works, Inc. v. Independent Ink, Inc. 1269

In re Borden 725

In re Burt 797

In re Corvette Collection of Boston, Inc. 499

In re Foreclosure Cases 730

In re Garrison-Ashburn, LC 991

In re Gerhardt 784

In re Interbank Funding Corp. v. Chadmoore Wireless Group Inc. 922

In re Kyllogen 774

In re Labrum & Doak, LLP 977

In re Made In Detroit, Inc. 791

In re Manhattan Investment Fund Ltd. 779

In re McAllister 756

In re Shirel 742

In re Siegenberg 786

Interbank of New York v. Fleet Bank 813

Internet Solutions Corp. v. Marshall 34

Jannusch v. Naffziger 311

Jet Wine & Spirits, Inc. v. Bacardi & Co., Ltd. 1013

Jewish Federation of Greater Des Moines v. Cedar Forrest Products Co. 574

Jones v. The Baran Company 423

Jordan v. Knafel 363

Kasky v. Nike, Inc. 68

Katris v. Carroll 988

Keeton v. Flying J, Inc. 1329

Kelo v. City of New London 634

Kenai Chrysler Center, Inc. v. Denison 386

KGM Harvesting Co. v. Fresh Network 577

Khan v. Parsons Global Services, Ltd. 176

Koch Materials Co. v. Shore Slurry Seal, Inc. 560

Kraft, Inc. v. Federal Trade Commission 1228

Kruser v. Bank of America NT & SA 888

KSR International Co. v. Teleflex, Inc. 244

Kulp v. Timmons 682

Kyllo v. United States 141

Lach v. Man O'War, LLC 1001

Lambert v. Barron 293

Leegin Creative Leather Products v. PSKS, Inc. 1263

Lehigh Presbytery v. Merchants Bancorp, Inc. 826

Lindh v. Surman 595

Lingle v. Chevron U.S.A., Inc. 639

Locke v. Ozark City Board of Education 447

Louis Vuitton Malletier, SA v. Haute Diggity Dog, LLC 269

Mainstream Marketing Services, Inc. v. Federal Trade Commission 1233

Mark v. FSC Securities Corp. 1125

Massachusetts v. Environmental Protection Agency 1209, 1353

Mathias v. Accor Economy Lodging, Inc. 171

Matthews v. Amberwood Associates Limited Partnership, Inc. 654

McCormick v. Brevig 946

McCune v. Myrtle Beach Indoor Shooting Range, Inc. . . . 401

McGurn v. Bell Microproducts, Inc. 335

MDM Group Associates, Inc. v. CX Reinsurance Company Ltd. 897

Meram v. MacDonald 308

Meskell v. Bertone 749

Metro-Goldwyn-Mayer Studios, Inc. v. Grokster, Ltd. . . . 255

Millan v. Dean Witter Reynolds, Inc. 925

Missouri v. Seibert 149

Montgomery Cellular Holding Co., Inc. v. Dobler 1090

Moren v. JAX Restaurant 963

Moser v. Moser 995

Moss v. Batesville Casket Co. 512

Music Acceptance Corp. v. Lofing 841

Mutual Savings Association v. Res/Com
Properties, L.L.C. 734

Nasc Services, Inc. v. Jervis 399

NBN Broadcasting, Inc. v. Sheridan Broadcasting
Networks, Inc. 959

New Jersey Economic Development Authority v.
Pavonia Restaurant, Inc. 722

Newton v. Standard Candy Co. 510

Noble Roman's, Inc. v. Pizza Boxes, Inc. 485

North Atlantic Instruments, Inc. v. Haber 275

Okosa v. Hall 332

Olbekson v. Huber 614

Olin Corporation v. Federal Trade Commission 1290

Opp v. Wheaton Van Lines, Inc. 916

Paciaroni v. Crane 973

Palese v. Delaware State Lottery Office 301

Palmer v. Claydon 944

Paramount Communications, Inc. v. Time, Inc. 1065

Parents Involved in Community Schools v. Seattle School
District No. 1 75

Pass v. Shelby Aviation 297

Pearson v. Shalala 1197

Pelican National Bank v. Provident Bank of Maryland . . . 817

Perfect 10, Inc. v. Amazon.com, Inc. 259

Pfaff v. Wells Electronics, Inc. 243

Phillips v. E.I. DuPont de Nemours & Co. (In re Hanford
Nuclear Reservation Litigation) 235

Pope v. Rostraver Shop and Save 178

PPG Industries Inc. v. JMB/Houston Center 437

Preston v. Ferrer 50

Raleigh v. Performance Plumbing and Heating, Inc. 207

Reynolds Health Care Services, Inc. v. HMNH, Inc. 1086

Riegel v. Medtronic, Inc. 536

Riggs v. Woman to Woman, P.C. 396

Rooney v. Tyson 1016

Rosenberg v. Son, Inc. 444

Ross v. May Company 349

Ryan v. Cerullo 1016

Safeco Insurance Co. of America v. Burr 1239

Sanders v. Madison Square Garden L.P. 905

Schaadt v. St. Jude Medical S.C., Inc. 417

Schlichting v. Cotter 624

Schwartz v. Family Dental Group, P.C. 970

SEC v. Edwards 1117

Seigel v. Merrill Lynch, Pierce, Fenner & Smith, Inc. 873

Shelter Mutual Insurance Co. v. Maples 698

Simo v. Mitsubishi Motors North America, Inc. 518

Skebba v. Kasch 354

Smith v. Carter & Burgess, Inc. 455

SmithStearn Yachts, Inc. v. Gyrographic
Communications, Inc. 1028

Southex Exhibitions, Inc. v. Rhode Island
Builders Association, Inc. 941

Spector v. Konover 955

Stahlecker v. Ford Motor Co. 228

Standard Bent Glass Corporation v. Glassrobots Oy 330

Star-Shadow Productions, Inc. v. Super 8 Sync Sound
System 570

State of Connecticut v. Cardwell 488

State Oil Co. v. Khan 1261

Stephens v. Pillen 196

Stoneridge Investment Partners, LLC v.
Scientific-Atlanta, Inc. 1146

Stoshak v. East Baton Rouge Parish School Board 174

Stroupes v. The Finish Line, Inc. 379

Sylva Shops Limited Partnership v. Hibbard 661

TBG Insurance Services Corp. v. Superior Court 1336

Tempur-Pedic International, Inc. v. Waste to Charity, Inc. . . 490

The Work Connection, Inc. v. Universal Forest
Products, Inc. 918

Time Warner Cable, Inc. v. DIRECTV, Inc. 280

Town of Freeport v. Ring 824

Treadwell v. J.D. Construction Co. 920

Trentadue v. Gorton 6

Trepanier v. Bankers Life & Casualty Co. 909

Tricontinental Industries, Ltd. v.
PricewaterhouseCoopers, LLP 1167

Union Planters Bank, N.A. v. Rogers 878

United States v. Dean 1361

United States v. Domenic Lombardi Realty 1365

United States v. Hall 139

United States v. Hopkins 1356

United States v. Jensen 1075

United States v. Microsoft Corp. 1275

United States v. Natelli 1181

United States v. Ohio Edison Company 1348

United States v. Santos 128

Valley Bank of Ronan v. Hughes 882

Victory Clothing Co., Inc. v. Wachovia Bank, N.A. 860

Vining v. Enterprise Financial Group, Inc. 709

Volvo Trucks North America, Inc. v. Reeder-Simco
GMC, Inc. 1302

Waddell v. L.V.R.V. Inc. 554

Warnick v. Warnick 979

Watts v. Simpson 443

Weil v. Murray 553

Whitman v. American Trucking Associations 1200

Windows, Inc. v. Jordan Panel Systems Corp. 494

Wintersport Ltd. v. Millionaire.com, Inc. 414

World Trade Center Properties, LLC v. Hartford Fire
Insurance Co. 689

Wright v. Brooke Group Limited 521

Yeadon Fabric Domes, Inc. v. Maine
Sports Complex, LLC 759

Young v. Weaver 384

Zapata Corp. v. Maldonado 1101

Part One

Foundations of American Law

chapter 1
The Nature of Law

chapter 2
The Resolution of Private Disputes

chapter 3
Business and the Constitution

chapter 4
Business Ethics, Corporate Social Responsibility, Corporate Governance, and Critical Thinking

chapter 1

THE NATURE OF LAW

Assume that you have taken on a management position at MKT Corp. If MKT is to make sound business decisions, you and your management colleagues must be aware of a broad array of legal considerations. These may range, to use a nonexhaustive list, from issues in contract, agency, and employment law to considerations suggested by tort, intellectual property, securities, and constitutional law. Sometimes legal principles may constrain MKT's business decisions; at other times, the law may prove a valuable ally of MKT in the successful operation of the firm's business.

Of course, you and other members of the MKT management group will rely on the advice of in-house counsel (an attorney who is an MKT employee) or of outside attorneys who are in private practice. The approach of simply "leaving the law to the lawyers," however, is likely to be counterproductive. It often will be up to nonlawyers such as you to identify a potential legal issue or pitfall about which MKT needs professional guidance. If you fail to spot the issue in a timely manner and legal problems are allowed to develop and fester, even the most skilled attorneys may have difficulty rescuing you and the firm from the resulting predicament. If, on the other hand, your failure to identify a legal consideration means that you do not seek advice in time to obtain an advantage that applicable law would have provided MKT, the corporation may lose out on a beneficial opportunity. Either way—that is, whether the relevant legal issue operates as a constraint or offers a potential advantage—you and the firm cannot afford to be unfamiliar with the legal environment in which MKT operates.

This may sound intimidating, but it need not be. The process of acquiring a working understanding of the legal environment of business begins simply enough with these basic questions:

- What major types of law apply to the business activities and help shape the business decisions of firms such as MKT?
- What ways of examining and evaluating law may serve as useful perspectives from which to view the legal environment in which MKT and other businesses operate?
- What role do courts play in making or interpreting law that applies to businesses such as MKT and to employees of those firms, and what methods of legal reasoning do courts utilize?
- What is the relationship between legal standards of behavior and notions of **ethical** conduct?

Types and Classifications of Law

The Types of Law

Constitutions Constitutions, which exist at the state and federal levels, have two general functions.[1] First, they set up the structure of government for the political unit they control (a state or the federal government). This involves creating the branches and subdivisions of the government and stating the powers given and denied to each. Through its **separation of powers,** the U.S. Constitution establishes the Congress and gives it power to legislate or *make* law in certain areas, provides for a chief executive (the president) whose function is to execute or *enforce* the laws, and helps create a federal judiciary to *interpret* the laws. The U.S. Constitution also structures the relationship between the federal government and the states. In the process, it

---

[1] Chapter 3 discusses constitutional law as it applies to government regulation of business.

respects the principle of **federalism** by recognizing the states' power to make law in certain areas.

The second function of constitutions is to prevent other units of government from taking certain actions or passing certain laws. Constitutions do so mainly by prohibiting government action that restricts certain individual rights. The Bill of Rights to the U.S. Constitution is an example.

Statutes Statutes are laws created by elected representatives in Congress or a state legislature. They are stated in an authoritative form in statute books or codes. As you will see, however, their interpretation and application are often difficult.

Throughout this text, you will encounter state statutes that were originally drafted as **uniform acts.** Uniform acts are model statutes drafted by private bodies of lawyers and/or scholars. They do not become law until a legislature enacts them. Their aim is to produce state-by-state uniformity on the subjects they address. Examples include the Uniform Commercial Code (which deals with a wide range of commercial law subjects), the Revised Uniform Partnership Act, and the Revised Model Business Corporation Act.

Common Law The **common law** (also called judge-made law or case law) is law made and applied by judges as they decide cases not governed by statutes or other types of law. Although common law exists only at the state level, both state courts and federal courts become involved in applying it. The common law originated in medieval England and developed from the decisions of judges in settling disputes. Over time, judges began to follow the decisions of other judges in similar cases, called **precedents.** This practice became formalized in the doctrine of *stare decisis* (let the decision stand). As you will see later in the chapter, *stare decisis* is not completely rigid in its requirement of adherence to precedent. It is flexible enough to allow the common law to evolve to meet changing social conditions. The common law rules in force today, therefore, often differ considerably from the common law rules of earlier times.

The common law came to America with the first English settlers, was applied by courts during the colonial period, and continued to be applied after the Revolution and the adoption of the Constitution. It still governs many cases today. For example, the rules of tort, contract, and agency discussed in this text are mainly common law rules. In some instances, states have codified (enacted into statute) some parts of the common law. States and the federal government also have passed statutes superseding the common law in certain situations. As discussed in Chapter 9, for example, the states have established special rules for contract cases involving the sale of goods by enacting Article 2 of the Uniform Commercial Code.

This text's torts, contracts, and agency chapters often refer to the *Restatement*—or *Restatement (Second)* or (*Third*)—rule on a particular subject. The *Restatements* are collections of common law (and occasionally statutory) rules covering various areas of the law. Because they are promulgated by the American Law Institute rather than by courts, the *Restatements* are not law and do not bind courts. However, state courts often find *Restatement* rules persuasive and adopt them as common law rules within their states. The *Restatement* rules usually are the rules followed by a majority of the states. Occasionally, however, the *Restatements* stimulate changes in the common law by suggesting new rules that the courts later decide to follow.

Because the judge-made rules of common law apply only when there is no applicable statute or other type of law, common law fills in gaps left by other legal rules if sound social and public policy reasons call for those gaps to be filled. Judges thus serve as policy makers in formulating the content of the common law. In the *Gribben* case, which follows shortly, the Supreme Court of Indiana surveys the relevant legal landscape and concludes that there was no need to develop a new common law rule to fill the supposed legal gap at issue in the case. A later section in the chapter will focus on the process of **case law reasoning,** in which courts engage when they make and apply common law rules.

Gribben v. Wal-Mart Stores, Inc.   824 N.E.2d 349 (Ind. Sup. Ct. 2005)

Chapters 6 and 7 of the text deal with torts, *a branch of the law focusing on behavior that violates recognized legal standards and causes harm to another person. When a tort allegedly occurs, the harmed party (the plaintiff) is entitled to take legal action against the party whose behavior caused the harm (the defendant). Various* intentional torts *are addressed in Chapter 6. Chapter 7 examines a different type of tort, known as* negligence. *You will see in Chapter 7 that key inquiries in negligence cases are whether the defendant failed to exercise reasonable care and, if so, whether the plaintiff experienced harm as a result. Most tort cases are governed by common law (i.e., judge-made law). As noted earlier in this chapter, common law is state law, but both state courts and federal courts become involved in applying it. (Chapter 2 will provide an overview of the state court and federal court systems.)*

This case arose when Patricia Gribben sustained injuries as the result of a fall at a store owned by Wal-Mart Stores, Inc. In an effort to recover monetary compensation for her injuries, Gribben filed a negligence lawsuit against Wal-Mart in a federal court, the United States District Court for the Southern District of Indiana. (Gribben could have sued Wal-Mart in state court, but exercised the option of bringing the case in federal court under a jurisdictional principle that will be explained in Chapter 2.) Later, Gribben sought to add to her case against Wal-Mart a claim for spoliation of evidence, because Wal-Mart had failed to preserve a surveillance videotape that, according to Gribben, would have helped support her negligence claim. The term "spoliation of evidence" is used to refer to situations in which evidence potentially relevant to a lawsuit is either destroyed or discarded. The federal magistrate to whom Gribben's case was assigned concluded that it was uncertain whether Indiana common law recognized a claim for spoliation of evidence. Therefore, the magistrate employed a procedure, allowed by Indiana law, under which the federal court certifies a question to the Supreme Court of Indiana (the highest court in the Indiana state court system) and asks that court for guidance on the question. The question certified by the federal court asked whether a spoliation of evidence claim is, or should be, allowed under Indiana common law. What follows is an edited version of the Supreme Court of Indiana's opinion regarding the certified question.

Dickson, Justice

The United States District Court for the Southern District of Indiana has certified . . . the following question of Indiana law: Does Indiana law recognize a claim for "first-party" spoliation of evidence; that is, if a [defendant] negligently or intentionally destroys or discards evidence that is relevant to a tort action [against the defendant], does the plaintiff in the tort action have an additional cognizable claim against the [defendant] for spoliation of evidence? In her certification order, [the federal magistrate] asserts that there is no controlling Indiana precedent and that courts in other [states] vary greatly [on this question]. The [certified] question is specifically limited to "first-party" spoliation, as distinguished from "third-party" spoliation. The former refers to spoliation of evidence by a party to the principal litigation, and the latter to spoliation by a nonparty.

The plaintiff [Gribben] asserts that Indiana should recognize an independent tort claim for intentional first-party spoliation of evidence. While the certified question includes both negligent and intentional destruction of evidence, the plaintiff here claims only intentional spoliation. She argues that spoliation and the underlying cause of action should be tried together and, if the jury finds intentional spoliation related to a relevant issue, the jury should be instructed to find for the plaintiff on that issue.

[Gribben] contends that a tort of intentional spoliation arises from standard Indiana jurisprudence regarding the existence of a duty of care, and that the tort is needed to discourage the growing occurrence of spoliation and its erosion of both the ability of courts to do justice and public confidence in legal processes. She argues that existing sanctions are insufficient deterrence to the practice of intentional destruction of evidence, and that any systemic burden upon courts and juries that might result from recognizing this new tort would be overwhelmingly outweighed by the importance of stopping cheating and assuring the availability of evidence to enable the fact finder to make a fair and informed decision.

The defendant [Wal-Mart] urges that Indiana's existing procedural and evidentiary safeguards are an adequate deterrent without adopting a new tort. It also contends that recognizing a new tort of spoliation would involve the speculative nature of harm and damages, significantly increase costs of litigation, cause jury confusion, result in duplicative and burdensome proceedings, be subject to abuse, and make collateral issues the focus of many disputes.

Already existing under Indiana law are important sanctions that not only provide remedy to persons aggrieved, but also deterrence to spoliation of evidence by litigants and their attorneys. It is well established in Indiana law that intentional first-party spoliation of evidence may be used to establish an inference that the spoliated evidence was unfavorable to the party responsible. *E.g., Cahoon v. Cummings*, 734 N.E.2d 535, 545 (Ind. Sup. Ct. 2000) (involving a jury instruction permitting the inference). Potent responses also exist under [an Indiana trial procedure rule] authorizing trial courts to respond to discovery violations with such sanctions "as are just," which may include, among others, ordering that designated facts be taken as established, prohibiting the introduction of evidence, dismissal of all or any part of an action, rendering a judgment by default against a disobedient party, and payment of reasonable expenses including attorney fees. We further note that [according to the Indiana Rules of Professional Conduct,] attorneys involved in destruction or concealment of evidence face penalties including disbarment. In addition, the destruction or concealment of evidence, or presentation of false testimony related thereto, may be criminally prosecuted [under Indiana's criminal statutes] as a felony for perjury or obstruction of justice.

Absent these sanctions, however, Indiana case law is inconsistent regarding whether one party to a civil action may obtain the relief sought therein solely based on the opposing party's intentional destruction of evidence. In 1941, this court expressed disfavor of such a claim, as did our Court of Appeals in 1991. [The Indiana Court of Appeals is a lower court in relation to the state's Supreme Court, so decisions of the Court of Appeals are not binding on the Supreme Court.] But two other cases from our Court of Appeals have [offered indications to the contrary, though in special circumstances not necessarily present here]. In light of Indiana's inconclusive case law, we agree with [the federal magistrate] that there is no controlling Indiana precedent as to the questions presented.

Courts uniformly condemn spoliation. [They regard it as improper, unjustifiable, and a threat to the judicial system's integrity.] Several [states], including West Virginia, Alaska, Montana, the District of Columbia, Illinois, New Mexico, and Ohio, recognize evidence spoliation as a cognizable tort. But several other [states] considering the issue, among them Florida, Mississippi, Arkansas, California, Iowa, Texas, Alabama, Georgia, Kansas, and Arizona, have rejected spoliation as an independent tort.

Notwithstanding the important considerations favoring the recognition of an independent tort of spoliation by parties to litigation, we are persuaded that these are minimized by existing remedies and outweighed by the attendant disadvantages [as noted by Wal-Mart]. We thus determine the common law of Indiana to be that, if an alleged tortfeasor negligently or intentionally destroys or discards evidence that is relevant to a tort action, the plaintiff in the tort action does not have an additional independent cognizable claim against the tortfeasor for spoliation of evidence under Indiana law. It may well be that the fairness and integrity of outcome and the deterrence of evidence destruction may require an additional tort remedy when evidence is destroyed or impaired by persons that are not parties to litigation and thus not subject to existing remedies and deterrence. But the certified question is directed only to first-party spoliation, and we therefore decline to address the issue with respect to third-party spoliation.

We answer the . . . certified question in the negative: Indiana law does not recognize a claim for "first-party" negligent or intentional spoliation of evidence.

Certified question answered; independent tort claim for first-party spoliation of evidence disallowed.

Equity The body of law called **equity** historically concerned itself with accomplishing "rough justice" when common law rules would produce unfair results. In medieval England, common law rules were technical and rigid and the remedies available in common law courts were too few. This meant that some deserving parties could not obtain adequate relief. As a result, separate equity courts began hearing cases that the common law courts could not resolve fairly. In these equity courts, procedures were flexible, and rigid rules of law were deemphasized in favor of general moral maxims.

Equity courts also provided several remedies not available in the common law courts (which generally awarded only money damages or the recovery of property). The most important of these *equitable remedies* was—and continues to be—the **injunction,** a court order forbidding a party to do some act or commanding him to perform some act. Others include the contract remedies of **specific performance** (whereby a party is ordered to perform according to the terms of her contract), **reformation** (in which the court rewrites the contract's terms to reflect the parties' real intentions), and **rescission** (a cancellation of a contract in which the parties are returned to their precontractual position).

As was the common law, equity principles were brought to the American colonies and continued to be used after the Revolution and the adoption of the Constitution. Over time, however, the once-sharp line between law and equity has become blurred. Nearly all states have abolished separate equity courts and have enabled courts to grant whatever relief is appropriate, whether it be the legal remedy of money damages or one of the equitable remedies discussed above. Equitable principles have been blended together with common law rules, and some traditional equity doctrines have been restated as common law or statutory rules. An example is the doctrine of unconscionability discussed in Chapter 15.

Administrative Regulations and Decisions As Chapter 47 reveals, the administrative agencies established by Congress and the state legislatures have acquired considerable power, importance, and influence over business. A major reason for the rise of administrative agencies was the collection of social and economic problems created by the industrialization of the United States that began late in the 19th century. Because legislatures generally lacked the time and expertise to deal with these problems on a continuing basis, the creation of specialized, expert agencies was almost inevitable.

Administrative agencies obtain the ability to make law through a *delegation* (or grant) of power from the legislature. Agencies normally are created by a statute that specifies the areas in which the agency can make law and the scope of its power in each area. Often, these statutory delegations are worded so broadly that the legislature has, in effect, merely pointed to a problem and given the agency wide-ranging powers to deal with it.

The two types of law made by administrative agencies are **administrative regulations** and **agency decisions.** As do statutes, administrative regulations appear in a precise form in one authoritative source. They differ from statutes, however, because the body enacting regulations is not an elected body. Many agencies have an internal courtlike structure that enables them to hear cases arising under the statutes and regulations they enforce. The resulting agency decisions are legally binding, though appeals to the judicial system are sometimes allowed.

Treaties According to the U.S. Constitution, **treaties** made by the president with foreign governments and approved by two-thirds of the U.S. Senate are "the supreme Law of the Land." As will be seen, treaties invalidate inconsistent state (and sometimes federal) laws.

Ordinances State governments have subordinate units that exercise certain functions. Some of these units, such as school districts, have limited powers. Others, such as counties, municipalities, and townships, exercise various governmental functions. The enactments of counties and municipalities are called **ordinances;** zoning ordinances are an example.

Executive Orders In theory, the president or a state's governor is a chief executive who enforces the laws but has no law-making powers. However, these officials sometimes have limited power to issue laws called **executive orders.** This power normally results from a legislative delegation.

Priority Rules
Because the different types of law conflict, rules for determining which type takes priority are necessary. Here, we briefly describe the most important such rules.

1. According to the principle of **federal supremacy,** the U.S. Constitution, federal laws enacted pursuant to it, and treaties are the supreme law of the land. This means that federal law defeats conflicting state law.

2. Constitutions defeat other types of law within their domain. Thus, a state constitution defeats all other state laws inconsistent with it. The U.S. Constitution, however, defeats inconsistent laws of whatever type.

3. When a treaty conflicts with a federal statute over a purely domestic matter, the measure that is later in time usually prevails.

4. Within either the state or the federal domain, statutes defeat conflicting laws that depend on a legislative delegation for their validity. For example, a state statute defeats an inconsistent state administrative regulation.

5. Statutes and any laws derived from them by delegation defeat inconsistent common law rules. Accordingly, either a statute or an administrative regulation defeats a conflicting common law rule. *Trentadue v. Gorton,* which follows, illustrates the application of this principle. In addition, the *Trentadue* court utilizes a statutory interpretation technique addressed later in this chapter.

Trentadue v. Gorton   738 N.W.2d 664 (Mich. Sup. Ct. 2007)

Margarette Eby resided in a Flint, Michigan, home that she had rented from Ruth Mott. In 1986, Eby was murdered at the residence. Eby's murder remained unsolved until 2002, when DNA evidence established that Jeffrey Gorton had committed the crime. At the time of the murder, Gorton was an employee of his parents' corporation, which serviced the sprinkler system on the grounds surrounding the residence where Eby lived. Gorton was convicted of murder and was sentenced to life imprisonment.

In August 2002, plaintiff Dayle Trentadue, Eby's daughter and the personal representative of her estate, filed a complaint against Gorton and various other defendants. The other defendants included Gorton's parents, their corporation, the personal representative of Mott's estate (Mott having died in 1999), the property management company that provided services to Mott, and two of Mott's employees. The claim against Gorton alleged battery resulting in death. Regarding the other defendants, the plaintiff alleged negligent hiring and monitoring of Gorton, negligence in allowing access to the area that led to Eby's residence, and negligence in failing to provide adequate security at the residence.

Each defendant except Gorton sought dismissal of the claims against them on the theory that the plaintiff's action was barred by Michigan's three-year statute of limitations for wrongful death actions. (Statutes of limitations require that a plaintiff who wishes to make a legal claim must file her lawsuit within a designated length of time after her claim accrues. Normally a claim accrues at the time the legal wrong was committed. The length of time set forth in statutes of limitation varies, depending upon the type of claim and the state whose law controls. If the plaintiff does not file her lawsuit within the time specified by the applicable statute of limitations, her claim cannot lawfully be pursued.) In particular, the defendants other than Gorton argued that Trentadue's case should be dismissed because her claim accrued when Eby was killed in 1986—meaning that the 2002 filing of the lawsuit occurred long after the three-year limitations period had expired. Trentadue asserted, on the other hand, that a common law rule known as the "discovery rule" should be applied so as to suspend the running of the limitations period until 2002, when she learned the identity of Eby's killer. Under the discovery rule argued for by Trentadue, the 2002 filing of the lawsuit would be seen as timely because the running of the limitations period would have been tolled—in other words, suspended—until the 2002 discovery that Gorton was the killer.

The trial court held that the common law discovery rule applied to the case and that, accordingly, Trentadue's lawsuit was filed in a timely manner. The Michigan Court of Appeals affirmed, concluding that the discovery rule coexists with the applicable statute of limitations and that because Trentadue could not have been aware of a possible cause of action against the defendants until the 2002 discovery that Gorton was Eby's killer, the statute of limitations did not bar Trentadue from proceeding with her case. The defendants other than Gorton appealed to the Supreme Court of Michigan.

Corrigan, Judge

This wrongful death case requires us to consider whether the common-law discovery rule, which allows tolling of the statutory period of limitations when a plaintiff could not have reasonably discovered the elements of a cause of action within the limitations period, can operate to toll the period of limitations, or whether Michigan Compiled Laws (MCL) 600.5827, which has no such provision, alone governs the time of accrual of the plaintiff's claims. The applicable statute of limitations in a wrongful death case is MCL 600.5805(10), which states: "The period of limitations is three years after the time of the death or injury for all other actions to recover damages for the death of a person, or for injury to a person or property." Thus, the period of limitations runs three years from "the death or injury."

Moreover, MCL 600.5827 defines the time of accrual for actions subject to the limitations period in MCL 600.5805(10). It provides: "Except as otherwise expressly provided, the period of limitations runs from the time the claim accrues. The claim accrues at the time provided in sections 5829 to 5838, and in cases not covered by these sections the claim accrues at the time the wrong upon which the claim is based was done regardless of the time when damage results." This is consistent with MCL 600.5805(10) because it indicates that the claim accrues "at the time the wrong upon which the claim is based was done."

[Other MCL sections provide] for tolling of the period of limitations in certain specified situations. These are actions alleging professional malpractice, actions alleging medical malpractice, actions brought against certain defendants alleging injuries from unsafe property, and actions alleging that a person who may be liable for the claim fraudulently concealed the existence of the claim or the identity of any person who is liable for the claim. Significantly, none of these tolling provisions covers this situation—tolling until the identity of the tortfeasor is discovered.

Trentadue contends, however, that, notwithstanding these statutes, when the claimant was unaware of any basis for an action, the harsh result of barring any lawsuit because the period of limitations has expired can be avoided by the operation of a court-created discovery rule, sometimes described as a common-law rule. Under a discovery-based analysis, a claim does not accrue until a plaintiff knows, or objectively should know, that he has a cause of action and can allege it in a proper complaint. Accordingly, Trentadue argues that her claims did not accrue until she discovered that Gorton was the killer because, before that time, she could not have known of and alleged each element of the claims. We reject this contention because the statutory scheme is exclusive and thus precludes this common law practice of tolling accrual based on discovery in cases where none of the statutory tolling provisions apply.

It is axiomatic that the Legislature has the authority to abrogate the common law. Further, if a statutory provision and the common law conflict, the common law must yield. Accordingly, this Court has observed: "In general, where comprehensive legislation prescribes in detail a course of conduct to pursue and the parties and things affected, and designates specific limitations and exceptions, the legislature will be found to have intended that the statute supersede and replace the common law dealing with the subject matter." [Case citation omitted.]

As we have explained, the relevant sections of the [Michigan statutes] comprehensively establish limitations periods, times of accrual, and tolling for civil cases. MCL 600.5827 explicitly states that a limitations period runs from the time a claim accrues "[e]xcept as otherwise expressly provided." Accordingly, the statutes designate specific limitations and exceptions for tolling based on discovery, as exemplified by [the sections dealing with malpractice claims and claims regarding unsafe property]. The [statutory] scheme also explicitly supersedes the common law, as can be seen in the area of medical malpractice, for instance, where this court's pre-statutory applications of the common-law discovery rule were superseded by MCL 600.5838a, in which the legislature codified the discovery rule for medical malpractice cases.

Finally, MCL 600.5855 is a good indication that the legislature intended the scheme to be comprehensive and exclusive. MCL 600.5855 provides for essentially unlimited tolling based on discovery when a claim is fraudulently concealed. If we may simply apply an extra-statutory discovery rule in any case not addressed by the statutory scheme, we will render § 5855 effectively meaningless. For, under a general extra-statutory discovery rule, a plaintiff could toll the limitations period simply by claiming that he reasonably had no knowledge of the tort or the identity of the tortfeasor. He would never need to establish that the claim or tortfeasor had been fraudulently concealed.

Since the legislature has exercised its power to establish tolling based on discovery under particular circumstances, but has not provided for a general discovery rule that tolls or delays the time of accrual if a plaintiff fails to discover the elements of a cause of action during the limitations period, no such tolling is allowed. Therefore, we conclude that courts may not employ an extra-statutory discovery rule to toll accrual in avoidance of the plain language of MCL 600.5827. Because the statutory scheme here is comprehensive, the legislature has undertaken the necessary task of balancing plaintiffs' and defendants' interests and has allowed for tolling only where it sees fit. This is a power the legislature has because such a statute of limitations bears a reasonable relationship to the permissible legislative objective of protecting defendants from stale or fraudulent claims. Accordingly, the lower courts erred when they applied an extra-statutory discovery rule to allow plaintiff to bring her claims 16 years after the death of her decedent. When the death occurred, the "wrong upon which the claim is based was done."

We hold that the plain language of MCL 600.5827 precludes the use of a broad common-law discovery rule to toll the accrual date of claims to which this statute applies. Here, the wrong was done when Eby was murdered in 1986. MCL 600.5827 was in effect at that time. Accordingly, plaintiff's claims accrued at the time of Eby's death. The legislature has evinced its intent that, despite this tragedy, the defendants [other than Gorton] may not face the threat of litigation 16 years later, merely because the plaintiff alleges she could not reasonably discover the facts underlying their potential negligence until 2002.

Judgment of Court of Appeals reversed and case remanded for further proceedings.

Classifications of Law

Classifications of Law   Three common classifications of law cut across the different types of law. These classifications involve distinctions between (1) criminal law and civil law; (2) substantive law and procedural law; and (3) public law and private law. One type of law might be classified in each of these ways. For example, a burglary statute would be criminal, substantive, and public; a rule of contract law would be civil, substantive, and private.

Criminal and Civil Law   **Criminal law** is the law under which the government prosecutes someone for committing a crime. It creates duties that are owed to the public as a whole. **Civil law** mainly concerns obligations that private parties owe to each other. It is the law applied when one private party sues another. The government, however, may also be a party to a civil case. For example, a city may sue, or be sued by, a construction contractor. Criminal penalties (e.g., imprisonment or fines) differ from civil remedies (e.g., money damages or equitable relief). Although most of the legal rules in this text are civil law rules, Chapter 5 deals specifically with the criminal law.

Even though the civil law and the criminal law are distinct bodies of law, the same behavior will sometimes violate both. For instance, if A commits an intentional act of physical violence on B, A may face both a criminal prosecution by the state and B's civil suit for damages.

Substantive Law and Procedural Law   **Substantive law** sets the rights and duties of people as they act in society. **Procedural law** controls the behavior of government bodies (mainly courts) as they establish and enforce rules of substantive law. A statute making murder a crime, for example, is a rule of substantive law. The rules describing the proper conduct of a trial, however, are procedural. This text focuses on substantive law. Chapters 2 and 5, however, examine some of the procedural rules governing civil and criminal cases.

Public and Private Law   **Public law** concerns the powers of government and the relations between government and private parties. Examples include constitutional law, administrative law, and criminal law. **Private law** establishes a framework of legal rules that enables parties to set the rights and duties they owe each other. Examples include the rules of contract, property, and agency.

Jurisprudence

The various types of law sometimes are called *positive law*. Positive law comprises the rules that have been laid down (or posited) by a recognized political authority. Knowing the types of positive law is essential to an understanding of the American legal system and the topics discussed in this text. Yet defining *law* by listing these different kinds of positive law is no more complete or accurate than defining "automobile" by describing all the vehicles going by that name. To define law properly, some say, we need a general description that captures its essence.

The field known as **jurisprudence** seeks to provide such a description. Over time, different schools of jurisprudence have emerged, each with its own distinctive view of law.

Legal Positivism   One feature common to all types of law is their enactment by a governmental authority such as a legislature or an administrative agency. This feature underlies the definition of law adopted by the school of jurisprudence known as **legal positivism.** Legal positivists define law as the *command of a recognized political authority*. As the British political philosopher Thomas Hobbes observed, "Law properly, is the word of him, that by right hath command over others."

The commands of recognized political authorities may be good, bad, or indifferent in moral terms. To legal positivists, such commands are valid law regardless of their "good" or "bad" content. In other words, positivists see legal validity and moral validity as entirely separate questions. Some (but not all) positivists say that every properly enacted positive law should be enforced and obeyed, whether just or unjust. Similarly, positivist judges usually try to enforce the law as written, excluding their own moral views from the process.

Natural Law   At first glance, legal positivism's "law is law, just or not" approach may seem to be perfect common sense. It presents a problem, however, for it could mean that *any* positive law—no matter how unjust—is valid law and should be enforced and obeyed so long as some recognized political authority enacted it. The school of jurisprudence known as **natural law** takes issue with legal positivism by rejecting the positivist separation of law and morality.

Natural law adherents usually contend that some higher law or set of universal moral rules binds all human beings in all times and places. The Roman statesman Marcus Cicero described natural law as "the highest reason, implanted in nature, which commands what ought to be done and forbids the opposite." Because this higher law determines what is ultimately good and ultimately bad, it serves as a criterion for evaluating positive law. To Saint Thomas Aquinas, for example, "every human law has just so much of the nature of law, as it is derived from the law of nature." To be genuine law, in other words, positive law must resemble the law of nature by being "good"—or at least by not being "bad."

Unjust positive laws, then, are not valid law under the natural law view. As Cicero put it: "What of the many deadly, the many pestilential statutes which are imposed on peoples? These no more deserve to be called laws than the rules a band of robbers might pass in their assembly." An "unjust" law's supposed invalidity does not translate into a natural law defense that is recognized in court, however.

Although a formal natural law defense is not recognized in court, judges may sometimes take natural law-oriented views into account when interpreting the law. As compared with positivist judges, judges influenced by natural law ideas may be more likely to read constitutional provisions broadly in order to strike down positive laws they regard as unjust. They also may be more likely to let morality influence their interpretation of the law. Of course, neither judges nor natural law thinkers always agree about what is moral and immoral—a major difficulty for the natural law position. This difficulty allows legal positivists to claim that only by keeping legal and moral questions separate can we obtain stability and predictability in the law.

American Legal Realism   To some, the debate between natural law and legal positivism may seem unreal. Not only is natural law unworkable, such people might say, but sometimes positive law does not mean much either. For example, juries sometimes pay little attention to the legal rules that are supposed to guide their decisions, and prosecutors have discretion concerning whether to enforce criminal statutes. In some legal proceedings, moreover, the background, biases, and values of the judge—and not the positive law—determine the result. An old joke reminds us that justice sometimes is what the judge ate for breakfast.

Remarks such as these typify the school of jurisprudence known as **American legal realism.** Legal realists regard the law-in-the-books as less important than the *law in action*—the conduct of those who enforce and interpret the positive law. American legal realism defines law as the *behavior of public officials (mainly judges) as they deal with matters before the legal system*. Because the actions of such decision makers—and not the rules in the books—really affect people's lives, the realists say, this behavior is what deserves to be called law.

It is doubtful whether the legal realists have ever developed a common position on the relation between law and morality or on the duty to obey positive law. They have been quick, however, to tell judges how to behave. Many realists feel that the modern judge should be a social engineer who weighs all relevant values and considers social science findings when deciding a case. Such a judge would make the positive law only one factor in her decision. Because judges inevitably base their decisions on personal considerations, the realists assert, they should at least do this honestly and intelligently. To promote this kind of decision making, the realists have sometimes favored fuzzy, discretionary rules that allow judges to decide each case according to its unique facts.

Sociological Jurisprudence
Sociological jurisprudence is a general label uniting several different approaches that examine law within its social context. The following quotation from Justice Oliver Wendell Holmes is consistent with such approaches:

> The life of the law has not been logic: it has been experience. The felt necessities of the time, the prevalent moral and political theories, intuitions of public policy, avowed or unconscious, even the prejudices which judges share with their fellow-men, have had a good deal more to do than the syllogism in determining the rules by which men should be governed. The law embodies the story of a nation's development through many centuries, and it cannot be dealt with as if it contained only the axioms and corollaries of a book of mathematics.[2]

Despite these approaches' common outlook, there is no distinctive sociological definition of law. If one were attempted, it might go as follows: *Law is a process of social ordering reflecting society's dominant interests and values*.

Different Sociological Approaches By examining examples of sociological legal thinking, we can add substance to the definition just offered. The "dominant interests" portion of the definition is exemplified by the writings of Roscoe Pound, an influential 20th-century American legal philosopher. Pound developed a detailed and changing catalog of the social interests that press on government and the legal system and thus shape positive law. An example of the definition's "dominant values" component is the *historical school* of jurisprudence identified with the 19th-century German legal philosopher Friedrich Karl von Savigny. Savigny saw law as an unplanned, almost unconscious, reflection of the collective spirit of a particular society. In his view, legal change could only be explained historically, as a slow response to social change.

By emphasizing the influence of dominant social interests and values, Pound and Savigny undermine the legal positivist view that law is nothing more than the command of some political authority. The early 20th-century Austrian legal philosopher Eugen Ehrlich went even further in rejecting positivism. He did so by identifying two different "processes of social ordering" contained within our definition of sociological jurisprudence. The first of these is positive law. The second is the "living law," informal social controls such as customs, family ties, and business practices. By regarding both as law, Ehrlich sought to demonstrate that positive law is only one element within a spectrum of social controls.

The Implications of Sociological Jurisprudence Because its definition of law includes social values, sociological jurisprudence seems to resemble natural law. Most sociological thinkers, however, are concerned only with the *fact* that moral values influence the law, and not with the goodness or badness of those values. Thus, it might seem that sociological jurisprudence gives no practical advice to those who must enforce and obey positive law.

Sociological jurisprudence has at least one practical implication, however: a tendency to urge that the law must change to meet changing social conditions and values. In other words, the law should keep up with the times. Some might stick to this view even when society's values are changing for the worse. To Holmes, for example, "[t]he first requirement of a sound body of law is, that it should correspond with the actual feelings and demands of the community, whether right or wrong."

---

[2]Holmes. *The Common Law* (1881).

Other Schools of Jurisprudence During approximately the past 30 years, legal scholars have fashioned additional ways of viewing law, explaining why legal rules are as they are, and exploring supposed needs for changes in legal doctrines. For example, the *law and economics* movement examines legal rules through the lens provided by economic theory and analysis. This movement's influence has extended beyond academic literature, with law and economics-oriented considerations, factors, and tests sometimes appearing in judicial opinions dealing with such matters as contract, tort, or antitrust law.

The *critical legal studies* (CLS) movement regards law as inevitably the product of political calculation (mostly of the right-wing variety) and long-standing class biases on the part of lawmakers, including judges. Articles published by CLS adherents provide controversial assessments and critiques of legal rules. Given the thrust of CLS and the view it takes of lawmakers, however, one would be hard-pressed to find CLS adherents in the legislature or the judiciary.

Other schools of jurisprudence that have acquired notoriety in recent years examine law and the legal system from the vantage points of particular groups of persons or sets of ideas. Examples include the feminist legal studies perspective and the gay legal studies movement.

The Functions of Law

In societies of the past, people often viewed law as unchanging rules that deserved obedience because they were part of the natural order of things. Most lawmakers today, however, treat law as a flexible tool or instrument for the accomplishment of chosen purposes. For example, the law of negotiable instruments discussed later in this text is designed to stimulate commercial activity by promoting the free movement of money substitutes such as promissory notes, checks, and drafts. Throughout the text, moreover, you see courts manipulating existing legal rules to achieve desired results. One strength of this *instrumentalist* attitude is its willingness to adapt the law to further the social good. A weakness, however, is the legal instability and uncertainty those adaptations often produce.

Just as individual legal rules advance specific purposes, law as a whole serves many general social functions. Among the most important of those functions are:

1. *Peacekeeping.* The criminal law rules discussed in Chapter 5 further this basic function of any legal system. Also, as Chapter 2 suggests, the resolution of private disputes serves as a major function of the civil law.

2. *Checking government power and promoting personal freedom.* Obvious examples are the constitutional restrictions examined in Chapter 3.

3. *Facilitating planning and the realization of reasonable expectations.* The rules of contract law discussed in Chapters 9–18 help fulfill this function of law.

4. *Promoting economic growth through free competition.* The antitrust laws discussed in Chapters 48–50 are among the many legal rules that help perform this function.

5. *Promoting social justice.* Throughout this century, government has intervened in private social and economic affairs to correct perceived injustices and give all citizens equal access to life's basic goods. Examples include the employer–employee regulations addressed in Chapter 51.

6. *Protecting the environment.* The most important federal environmental statutes are discussed in Chapter 52.

Obviously, the law's various functions can conflict. The familiar clash between economic growth and environmental protection is an example. Chapter 5's cases dealing with the constitutional aspects of criminal cases illustrate the equally familiar conflict between effective law enforcement and the preservation of personal rights. Only rarely does the law achieve one end without sacrificing others. In law, as in life, there generally is no such thing as a free lunch. Where the law's objectives conflict, lawmakers may try to strike the best possible balance among those goals. This suggests limits on the law's usefulness as a device for promoting particular social goals.

Legal Reasoning

This text seeks to describe important legal rules affecting business. As texts generally do, it states those rules in what lawyers call "black letter" form, using sentences saying that certain legal consequences will occur if certain events happen. Although it provides a clear statement of the law's commands, this black letter approach can be misleading. It suggests definiteness, certainty, permanence, and predictability—attributes the law frequently lacks. To illustrate, and to give you some idea how lawyers and judges think, we now discuss the two most important kinds of legal reasoning: **case law reasoning**

Ethics in Action

Some schools of jurisprudence discussed in this chapter—most notably *natural law* and the various approaches lumped under the *sociological jurisprudence* heading—concern themselves with the relationship between law and notions of morality. These schools of jurisprudence involve considerations related to key aspects of ethical theories that will be explored in Chapter 4, which addresses ethical issues arising in business contexts.

Natural law's focus on rights thought to be independent of positive law has parallels in ethical theories that are classified under the *rights theory* heading. In its concern over unjust laws, natural law finds common ground with the ethical theory known as *justice theory*. When subscribers to sociological jurisprudence focus on the many influences that shape law and the trade-offs involved in a dynamic legal system, they may explore considerations that relate not only to rights theory or justice theory but also to two other ethical theories, *utilitarianism* and *profit maximization*. As you study Chapter 4 and later chapters, keep the schools of jurisprudence in mind. Think of them as you consider the extent to which a behavior's probable legal treatment and the possible ethical assessments of it may correspond or, instead, diverge.

and **statutory interpretation**.[3] However, we first must examine legal reasoning in general.

Legal reasoning is basically deductive, or syllogistic. The legal rule is the major premise, the facts are the minor premise, and the result is the product of combining the two. Suppose a state statute says that a driver operating an automobile between 55 and 70 miles per hour must pay a $50 fine (the rule or major premise) and that Jim Smith drives his car at 65 miles per hour (the facts or minor premise). If Jim is arrested, and if the necessary facts can be proved, he will be required to pay the $50 fine. As you will now see, however, legal reasoning often is more difficult than this example would suggest.

Case Law Reasoning

In cases governed by the common law, courts find the appropriate legal rules in prior cases called *precedents*. The standard for choosing and applying prior cases to decide present cases is the doctrine of *stare decisis,* which states that like cases should be decided alike. That is, the present case should be decided in the same way as past cases presenting the same facts and the same legal issues. If no applicable precedent exists, the court is free to develop a new common law rule to govern the case, assuming the court believes that sound public policy reasons call for the development of a new rule. When an earlier case may seem similar enough to the present case to constitute a precedent but the court deciding the present case nevertheless identifies a meaningful difference between the cases, the court *distinguishes* the earlier decision.

Because every present case differs from the precedents in some respect, it is always possible to spot a factual distinction. For example, one could attempt to distinguish a prior case because both parties in that case had black hair, whereas one party in the present case has brown hair. Of course, such a distinction would be ridiculous, because the difference it identifies is insignificant in moral or social policy terms. A valid distinction involves a widely accepted ethical or policy reason for treating the present case differently from its predecessor. Because people disagree about moral ideas, public policies, and the degree to which they are accepted, and because all these factors change over time, judges may differ on the wisdom of distinguishing a prior case. This is a source of uncertainty in the common law, but it gives the common law the flexibility to adapt to changing social conditions.[4]

When a precedent has been properly distinguished, the common law rule it stated does not control the present case. The court deciding the present case may then fashion a new common law rule to govern the case. Consider, for instance, an example involving the employment-at-will rule, the prevailing common law rule regarding employees in the United States. Under this rule, an employee may be fired at any time—and without any reason, let alone a good one—unless a contract between the employer and the employee guaranteed a certain duration of employment or established that the employee could be fired only for certain recognized legal causes. Most employees are not parties to a contract containing such provisions. Therefore, they are employees-at-will. Assume that in a precedent case, an employee who had been doing good work challenged his firing, and that the court hearing the case ruled against him on the basis of the employment-at-will rule. Also assume that in a later case, a fired employee has challenged her dismissal. Although the fired employee would appear to be subject to the employment-at-will rule applied in the seemingly similar precedent case, the court deciding the later case

---

[3]The reasoning courts employ in constitutional cases resembles that used in common law cases, but often is somewhat looser. See Chapter 3.

[4]Also, though they exercise the power infrequently, courts sometimes completely *overrule* their own prior decisions.

nevertheless identifies an important difference: that in the later case, the employee was fired in retaliation for having reported to law enforcement authorities that her employer was engaging in seriously unlawful business-related conduct. A firing under such circumstances appears to offend public policy, notwithstanding the general acceptance of the employment-at-will rule. Having properly distinguished the precedent, the court deciding the later case would not be bound by the employment-at-will rule set forth in the precedent and would be free to develop a public policy–based exception under which the retaliatory firing would be deemed wrongful. (Chapter 51 will reveal that courts in a number of states have adopted such an exception to the employment-at-will rule.)

The *Hagan* case, which follows, provides a further illustration of the process of case law reasoning. In *Hagan,* the Florida Supreme Court scrutinizes various precedents as it attempts to determine whether Florida's courts should retain, modify, or abolish a common law rule under which a plaintiff in a negligence case could not recover damages for emotional harm unless she also sustained some sort of impact that produced physical injuries—that is, injuries to her body. (Negligence law is discussed in depth in Chapter 7.) Ultimately, the court determines that under circumstances of the sort presented in the case, damages for emotional distress should be recoverable even in the absence of a physical injury–producing impact.

Hagan v. Coca-Cola Bottling Co.   776 So. 2d 275 (Fla. Sup. Ct. 2000)

Linda Hagan and her sister Barbara Parker drank from a bottle of Coke which they both agreed tasted flat. Hagan then held the bottle up to a light and observed what she and Parker thought was a used condom with "oozy stringy stuff coming out of the top." Both women were distressed that they had consumed some foreign material, and Hagan immediately became nauseated. The bottle was later delivered to Coca-Cola for testing. Concerned about what they had drunk, the women went to a health care facility the next day and were given shots. The medical personnel at the facility told them they should be tested for HIV. Hagan and Parker were then tested and informed that the results were negative. Six months later, both women were again tested for HIV, and the results were again negative.

Hagan and Parker brought a negligence action against Coca-Cola. Coca-Cola's beverage analyst testified at trial that he had initially thought, as Hagan and Parker had, that the object in the bottle was a condom. However, upon closer examination, he concluded that the object was a mold, and that, to a "scientific certainty," the item floating in the Coke bottle was not a condom. At the conclusion of the trial, the jury returned a verdict in favor of the plaintiffs, awarding $75,000 each to Hagan and Parker. The trial court reduced the jury award to $25,000 each to Hagan and Parker. Both sides appealed to the Fifth District Court of Appeal.

The appellate court reversed the jury awards and concluded that under case law concerning the impact rule, Hagan and Parker had not established a claim because neither had suffered a physical injury. Under a special procedure allowed by Florida law, certain dissenting and concurring appellate court judges sent a certified question to the state Supreme Court asking whether the impact rule should be abolished or amended in Florida.

Anstead, Judge

We have for review a decision from the Fifth District Court of Appeal in which the court certified a question to be of great public importance: Should the impact rule be abolished or amended in Florida? Because we conclude that there was an impact here and the impact rule does not bar the claim, we rephrase the certified question [to ask whether] the impact rule preclude[s] a claim for damages for emotional distress caused by the consumption of a foreign substance in a beverage product where the plaintiff suffers no accompanying physical injuries[.]

Hagan and Parker (hereinafter "appellants") assert that a person should not be barred from recovering damages for emotional distress caused by the consumption of a beverage containing a foreign substance simply because she suffered distress but did not suffer any additional physical injury at the

time of consumption. Therefore, appellants contend that the "impact rule" should not operate to preclude relief under the circumstances of this case. We agree with appellants and hold that the impact rule does not apply to cases where a plaintiff suffers emotional distress as a direct result of the consumption of a contaminated beverage.

We begin by acknowledging that although many states have abolished the "impact rule," several states, including Florida, still adhere to the rule. This court, while acknowledging exceptions, has accepted the impact rule as a limitation on certain claims as a means for "assuring the validity of claims for emotional or psychic damages." *R. J. v. Humana of Florida, Inc.* (1995). Generally stated, the impact rule requires that before a plaintiff may recover damages for emotional distress, she must demonstrate that the emotional stress suffered flowed from injuries sustained in an impact. Notwithstanding our adherence to the rule, this Court has noted several instances where the impact rule should not preclude an otherwise viable claim.

For example, this Court modified the impact rule in bystander cases by excusing the lack of a physical impact. In such cases, recovery for emotional distress would be permitted where one person suffers "death or significant discernible physical injury when caused by psychological trauma resulting from a negligent injury imposed on a close family member within the sensory perception of the physically injured person." *Champion v. Gray* (1985). We also have held that the impact rule does not apply to claims for intentional infliction of emotional distress, wrongful birth, negligence claims involving stillbirth, and bad faith claims against an insurance carrier.

We believe that public policy dictates that a cause of action for emotional distress caused by the ingestion of a contaminated food or beverage should be recognized despite the lack of an accompanying physical injury. In *Doyle v. Pillsbury Co.* (1985), for example, this Court observed that the impact rule would not bar a cause of action for damages caused by the ingestion of a contaminated food or beverage. There, the plaintiffs, Mr. and Mrs. Doyle, opened a can of peas and observed an insect floating on top of the contents. Mrs. Doyle jumped back in alarm, fell over a chair and suffered physical injuries. The plaintiffs sued the Pillsbury Company, Green Giant Company, and Publix Supermarkets, alleging negligence, strict liability, and breach of warranty. The trial court granted summary judgment in favor of the defendants, finding that the impact rule barred the plaintiffs' cause of action, and the intermediate appellate court affirmed.

On review, this Court approved of the outcome but disapproved of the application of the impact rule. We initially recognized that ingestion of a food or drink product is a necessary prerequisite to a cause of action against restaurants, manufacturers, distributors and retailers of food. In doing so, we impliedly found that ingestion of a foreign food or substance constitutes an impact. [We wrote:]

> This ingestion requirement is grounded upon foreseeability rather than the impact rule. The public has become accustomed to believing in and relying on the fact that packaged foods are fit for consumption. A producer or retailer of food should foresee that a person may well become physically or mentally ill after consuming part of a food product and then discovering a deleterious foreign object, such as an insect or rodent, in presumably wholesome food or drink. The manufacturer or retailer must expect to bear the costs of the resulting injuries. The same foreseeability is lacking where a person simply observes the foreign object and suffers injury after the observation. The mere observance of unwholesome food cannot be equated to consuming a portion of the same. We should not impose virtually unlimited liability in such cases. When a claim is based on an inert foreign object

in a food product, we continue to require ingestion of a portion of the food before liability arises. Because Mrs. Doyle never ingested any portion of the canned peas, the trial court properly granted summary judgment against the Doyles.

Other jurisdictions have reached a similar conclusion, one, in fact, involving virtually the same facts presented here. In *Wallace v. Coca-Cola Bottling Plants, Inc.*, [Me. (1970)], the plaintiff drank from a Coke bottle which contained an unwrapped condom. The plaintiff became ill after he returned home and thought about his experience. The Maine Supreme Court held that where the plaintiff demonstrates a causal relationship between the negligent act and the reasonably foreseeable mental and emotional suffering by a reasonably foreseeable plaintiff, damages for emotional suffering are recoverable despite the lack of a "discernable trauma from external causes." The court found that such requirements had been met: "The foreign object was of such a loathsome nature it was reasonably foreseeable its presence would cause nausea and mental distress upon being discovered . . . The mental distress was manifested by the vomiting."

Several years later [in *Culbert v. Sampson Supermarkets Inc.*, 444 A.2d 433 [Me. (1982)], the Maine Supreme Court overruled *Wallace* to the extent that it had required a plaintiff to demonstrate actual physical manifestations of the mental injury. In overruling any physical injury requirement, the court noted that it could have permitted recovery in *Wallace* even under the impact rule because the condom had come in contact with the plaintiff. We find the reasoning of the Maine Supreme Court to be instructive, and consistent with our analysis in *Doyle,* to the extent it concludes that a plaintiff may recover for emotional injuries caused by the consumption of a contaminated food or beverage despite the lack of an additional physical injury.

As this Court [has] recognized [before], the impact rule does not apply where emotional damages are a "consequence of conduct that itself is a freestanding tort apart from any emotional injury." *Tanner v. Hartog,* (1997). [W]e hold that a plaintiff need not prove the existence of a physical injury in order to recover damages for emotional injuries caused by the consumption of a contaminated food or beverage. [T]hose who market foodstuffs should foresee and expect to bear responsibility for the emotional and physical harm caused by someone consuming a food product that is contaminated by a foreign substance. Further, since we have concluded that there was an impact in the case at hand by the ingestion of a contaminated substance, and the impact rule does not bar the action, we decline to rule on the broader question posed by the district court's certified question.

Intermediate appellate court decision reversed, and case remanded.

CYBERLAW IN ACTION

Section 230 of the Communications Decency Act (CDA), a federal statute, provides that "[n]o provider or user of an interactive computer service shall be treated as the publisher or speaker of any information provided by another information content provider." Although § 230 appears in a statute otherwise designed to protect minors against online exposure to indecent material, the broad language of § 230 has caused courts to apply it in contexts having nothing to do with indecent expression.

For instance, various courts have held that § 230 protects providers of an interactive computer service (ICS) against liability for defamation when a user of the service creates and posts false, reputation-harming statements about someone else. (ICS is defined in the statute as "any information service, system, or access software provider that provides or enables computer access by multiple users to a computer server.") With courts so holding, § 230 has the effect of superseding a common law rule of defamation that anyone treated as a publisher or speaker of defamatory material is liable to the same extent as the original speaker or writer of that material. Absent § 230, ICS providers could sometimes face defamation liability under the theory that they are publishers of statements made by someone else. (You will learn more about defamation in Chapter 6.) This application of § 230 illustrates two concepts noted earlier in the chapter: first, that federal law overrides state law when the two conflict; and second, that an applicable statute supersedes a common law rule.

Cases in other contexts have required courts to utilize statutory interpretation techniques discussed in this chapter as they determine whether § 230's shield against liability applies. For example, two recent cases presented the question whether § 230 protects Web site operators against liability for alleged Fair Housing Act (FHA) violations based on material that appears on their sites. The FHA states that it is unlawful to "make, print, or publish," or to "cause" the making, printing, or publishing, of notices, statements, or advertisements that "with respect to the sale or rental of a dwelling[,] . . . indicate[] any preference, limitation, or discrimination based on race, color, religion, sex, handicap, familial status, or national origin, or an intention to make any such preference, limitation, or discrimination." A civil rights organization sued Craigslist, Inc., which operates a well-known electronic forum for those who wish to buy, sell, or rent housing and miscellaneous goods and services. The plaintiff alleged that Craigslist users posted housing-related statements such as "No minorities" and "No children," and that those statements constituted FHA violations on the part of Craigslist.

In *Chicago Lawyers Committee for Civil Rights Under Law, Inc. v. Craigslist, Inc.*, 519 F.3d 666 (7th Cir. 2008), the U.S. Court of Appeals for the Seventh Circuit affirmed the district court's dismissal of the plaintiff's complaint. The Seventh Circuit held that a "natural reading" of § 230 of the CDA protected Craigslist against liability. The statements that allegedly violated the FHA were those of users of the electronic forum— meaning that Craigslist would be liable only if it were treated as a publisher or speaker of the users' statements. The plain language of § 230, however, prohibited classifying Craigslist, Inc., as a publisher or speaker of the content posted by the users. Neither did Craigslist "cause" users to make statements of the sort prohibited by the FHA. Using a commonsense interpretation of the word "cause," the court concluded that merely furnishing the electronic forum was not enough to implicate Craigslist in having "cause[d]" the users' statements. There were no facts indicating that Craigslist suggested or encouraged statements potentially running afoul of the FHA.

Less than a month after the decision just discussed, the U.S. Court of Appeals for the Ninth Circuit decided *Fair Housing Council of San Fernando Valley v. Roommate.com, LLC*, 2008 U.S. App. LEXIS 7066 (9th Cir. 2008). There, the court held that § 230 of the CDA did not protect Roommate.com against FHA liability for allegedly discriminatory housing-related statements posted by users of Roommate.com's electronic forum. An edited version of that decision appears nearby in the text. After reading it, compare it to the *Craigslist* decision summarized above. Given the different outcomes reached in the two cases, are the two decisions simply inconsistent, or can they be harmonized?

Statutory Interpretation Because statutes are written in one authoritative form, their interpretation might seem easier than case law reasoning. However, this is not so. The natural ambiguity of language serves as one reason courts face difficulties when interpreting statutes. The problems become especially difficult when statutory words are applied to situations the legislature did not foresee. In some instances, legislators may deliberately use ambiguous language when they are unwilling or unable to deal specifically with each situation the statute was enacted to regulate. When this happens, the legislature expects courts and/or administrative agencies to fill in the details on a case-by-case basis. Other reasons for deliberate ambiguity include the need for legislative compromise and legislators' desire to avoid taking controversial positions.

To deal with the problems just described, courts use various techniques of statutory interpretation. As you will see shortly, different techniques may dictate different results in a particular case. Sometimes judges employ the techniques in an instrumentalist or result-oriented fashion, emphasizing the technique that will produce the result they want and downplaying the others. It is therefore unclear which technique should control when different techniques yield different results. Judges have considerable latitude in this regard.

Plain Meaning Courts begin their interpretation of a statute with its actual language. If the statute's words have a clear, common, accepted meaning, courts often employ the *plain meaning rule*. This approach calls for the court to apply the statute according to the usual meaning of its words, without concerning itself with anything else.

Legislative History and Legislative Purpose Courts sometimes refuse to follow a statute's plain meaning when its legislative history suggests a different result. Almost all courts resort to legislative history when the statute's language is ambiguous. A statute's legislative history includes the following sources: reports of investigative committees or law revision commissions that led to the legislation; transcripts or summaries of hearings of legislative committees that originally considered the legislation; reports issued by such committees; records of legislative debates; reports of conference committees reconciling two houses' conflicting versions of the law; amendments or defeated amendments to the legislation; other bills not passed by the legislature but proposing similar legislation; and discrepancies between a bill passed by one house and the final version of the statute.

Sometimes a statute's legislative history provides no information or conflicting information about its meaning, scope, or purposes. Some sources prove to be more authoritative than others. The worth of debates, for instance, may depend on which legislator (e.g., the sponsor of the bill or an uninformed blowhard) is quoted. Some sources are useful only in particular situations; prior unpassed bills and amendments or defeated amendments are

examples. Consider, for instance, whether mopeds are covered by an air pollution statute applying to "automobiles, trucks, buses, and other motorized passenger or cargo vehicles." If the statute's original version included mopeds but this reference was removed by amendment, it is unlikely that the legislature wanted mopeds to be covered. The same might be true if six similar unpassed bills had included mopeds but the bill that was eventually passed did not, or if one house had passed a bill including mopeds but mopeds did not appear in the final version of the legislation.

Courts use legislative history in two overlapping but distinguishable ways. They may use it to determine what the legislature thought about the specific meaning of statutory language. They may also use it to determine the overall aim, end, or goal of the legislation. In this second case, they then ask whether a particular interpretation of the statute is consistent with this legislative purpose. To illustrate the difference between these two uses of legislative history, suppose that a court is considering whether our pollution statute's "other motorized passenger or cargo vehicles" language includes battery-powered vehicles. The court might scan the legislative history for specific references to battery-powered vehicles or other indications of what the legislature thought about their inclusion. However, the court might also use the same history to determine the overall aims of the statute, and then ask whether including battery-powered vehicles is consistent with those aims. Because the history probably would reveal that the statute's purpose was to reduce air pollution from internal combustion engines, the court might well conclude that battery-powered vehicles should not be covered.

Two statutory interpretation cases follow. In *Fair Housing Council v. Roommate.com,* the court carefully examines the relevant statutory language and considers the purposes underlying it. In *General Dynamics Land Systems, Inc. v. Cline,* the Supreme Court interprets a major employment discrimination statute by relying heavily on its legislative history and purpose.

Fair Housing Council of San Fernando Valley v. Roommate.com, LLC
2008 U.S. App. LEXIS 7066 (9th Cir. 2008)

Roommate.com, LLC ("Roommate") operated a Web site designed to match people renting out spare rooms with people looking for a place to live. At the time of the litigation referred to below, Roommate's Web site featured approximately 150,000 active listings and received roughly a million page views a day.

Before subscribers could search listings or post housing opportunities on Roommate's Web site, they had to create profiles. This process required subscribers to answer a series of questions. Besides requesting basic information such as name, location, and e-mail address, Roommate required each subscriber to disclose his or her sex and sexual orientation, and whether he or she would bring children to a household. Each subscriber was further required to describe his or her preferences in roommates with respect to the same three criteria: sex, sexual orientation, and whether children would be brought to the household. The Roommate site also encouraged subscribers to provide "Additional Comments" describing themselves and their desired roommate in an open-ended essay. After a new subscriber completed the application, Roommate would assemble his or her answers into a profile page. The profile page displayed the subscriber's pseudonym, description, and preferences, as divulged through answers to Roommate's questions.

Roommate's subscribers were able to choose between two levels of service. Those using the site's free service level could create their own personal profile page, search the profiles of others, and send personal e-mail messages. They could also receive periodic e-mails from Roommate, informing them of available housing opportunities matching their preferences. Subscribers who paid a monthly fee also gained the ability to read e-mails from other users, and to view other subscribers' "Additional Comments."

The Fair Housing Councils of the San Fernando Valley and San Diego ("Councils") sued Roommate in federal court, alleging that Roommate's activities violated the federal Fair Housing Act ("FHA"), 42 U.S.C. § 3601 et seq. The FHA prohibits, in the sale or rental of housing, discrimination on the basis of "race, color, religion, sex, familial status, or national origin." The FHA also includes a provision that makes it unlawful to

make, print, or publish, or cause to be made, printed, or published, any notice, statement, or advertisement, with respect to the sale or rental of a dwelling that indicates any preference, limitation, or discrimination based on race, color, religion, sex, handicap, familial status, or national origin, or an intention to make any such preference, limitation, or discrimination.

In their lawsuit, Councils claimed that Roommate was effectively a housing broker doing online what it could not lawfully do off-line. Roommate argued, however, that it was immune from liability under § 230 of the federal Communications Decency Act, which provides that "[n]o provider . . . of an interactive computer service shall be treated as the publisher or speaker of any information provided by another information content provider." The district court agreed, reasoning that imposition of liability on Roommate for a violation of the FHA would depend upon classifying Roommate as a publisher or speaker but that § 230 prohibited such an outcome. The district court therefore dismissed Councils' FHA claim without determining whether Roommate violated the FHA. Councils appealed to the U.S. Court of Appeals for the Ninth Circuit.

Kozinski, Chief Judge

We plumb the depths of the immunity provided by § 230 of the Communications Decency Act of 1996 ("CDA").

Section 230 of the CDA immunizes providers of interactive computer services against liability arising from content created by third parties: "No provider . . . of an interactive computer service shall be treated as the publisher or speaker of any information provided by another information content provider." This grant of immunity applies only if the interactive computer service provider is not also an "information content provider," which is defined as someone who is "responsible, in whole or in part, for the creation or development of" the offending content. Section 230 defines an "interactive computer service" as "any information service, system, or access software provider that provides or enables computer access by multiple users to a computer server." Today, the most common interactive computer services are websites. Councils do not dispute that Roommate's website is an interactive computer service.

A website operator can be both a service provider and a content provider. If it passively displays content that is created entirely by third parties, then it is only a service provider with respect to that content. But as to content that it creates itself, or is "responsible, in whole or in part" for creating or developing, the website is also a content provider. Thus, a website may be immune from liability for some of the content it displays to the public but be subject to liability for other content.

Section 230 was prompted by a state court case holding Prodigy responsible for a libelous message posted on one of its financial message boards. *See Stratton Oakmont v. Prodigy Servs. Co.,* 1995 N.Y. Misc. LEXIS (N.Y. Sup. Ct. 1995). The court there found that Prodigy had become a "publisher" under state law because it voluntarily deleted some messages from its message boards "on the basis of offensiveness and 'bad taste,'" and was therefore legally responsible for the content of defamatory messages that it failed to delete. Under the reasoning of *Stratton Oakmont,* online service providers that voluntarily filter some messages become liable for all messages transmitted, whereas providers that bury their heads in the sand and ignore problematic posts altogether escape liability. Prodigy claimed that the "sheer volume" of message board postings it received made manual review of every message impossible; thus, if it were forced to choose between taking responsibility for all messages and deleting no messages at all, it would have to choose the latter course.

In passing § 230, Congress sought to spare interactive computer services this grim choice by allowing them to perform some editing on user-generated content without thereby becoming liable for all defamatory or otherwise unlawful messages that they didn't edit or delete. In other words, [as the statute's legislative history indicates,] Congress sought to immunize the *removal* of user-generated content, not the *creation* of content.

With this backdrop in mind, we examine three specific functions performed by Roommate that are alleged to violate the FHA.

1. Councils first argue that the questions Roommate poses to prospective subscribers during the registration process violate the FHA. Councils allege that requiring subscribers to disclose their sex, family status and sexual orientation "indicates" an intent to discriminate against them, and thus runs afoul of the FHA. Roommate created the questions and choice of answers, and designed its website registration process around them. Therefore, Roommate is undoubtedly the "information content provider" as to the questions and can claim no immunity for posting them on its website, or for forcing subscribers to answer them as a condition of using its services.

Here, we must determine whether Roommate has immunity under the CDA because Councils have at least a plausible claim that Roommate violated the FHA by merely posing the questions. We need not decide whether any of Roommate's questions actually violate the FHA. [We leave that issue] for the district court on remand. Rather, we examine the scope of plaintiffs' substantive claims only insofar as necessary to determine whether § 230 immunity applies. However, we note that asking questions certainly *can* violate the FHA. For example, a real estate broker may not inquire as to the race of a prospective buyer, and an employer may not inquire as to the religion of a prospective employee. If such questions are unlawful when posed face-to-face or by telephone, they don't magically become lawful when asked electronically online. [Section 230 of the CDA] was not meant to create a lawless no-man's-land on the Internet.

Councils also claim that requiring subscribers to answer the questions as a condition of using Roommate's services unlawfully "cause[s]" subscribers to make a "statement . . . with respect to the sale or rental of a dwelling that indicates [a] preference, limitation, or discrimination," in violation of [the FHA]. The CDA does not grant immunity for inducing third parties to express illegal preferences. Roommate's own acts— posting the questionnaire and requiring answers to it—are entirely its doing and thus § 230 of the CDA does not apply to them. Roommate is entitled to no immunity [against this asserted basis of liability].

2. Councils also charge that Roommate's development and display of subscribers' discriminatory preferences is unlawful. Roommate publishes a "profile page" for each subscriber on its website. The page describes the client's personal information— such as his sex, sexual orientation and whether he has children— as well as the attributes of the housing situation he seeks.

The content of these pages is drawn directly from the registration process. For example, Roommate requires subscribers to specify, using a drop-down menu provided by Roommate, whether they are "Male" or "Female" and then displays that information on the profile page. Roommate also requires subscribers who are listing available housing to disclose whether there are currently "Straight male(s)," "Gay male(s)," "Straight female(s)" or "Lesbian(s)" living in the dwelling. Subscribers who are seeking housing must make a selection from a drop-down menu, again provided by Roommate, to indicate whether they are willing to live with "Straight or gay" males, only with "Straight" males, only with "Gay" males or with "No males." Similarly, Roommate requires subscribers listing housing to disclose whether there are "Children present" or "Children not present" and requires housing seekers to say "I will live with children" or "I will not live with children." Roommate then displays these answers, along with other information, on the subscriber's profile page. This information is obviously included to help subscribers decide which housing opportunities to pursue and which to bypass. In addition, Roommate itself uses this information to channel subscribers away from listings where the individual offering housing has expressed preferences that aren't compatible with the subscriber's answers.

[It is correct to conclude] that Roommate's subscribers are information content providers who create the profiles by picking among options and providing their own answers. But the fact that users are information content providers does not preclude Roommate from *also* being an information content provider by helping "develop" at least "in part" the information in the profiles. Here, the part of the profile that is alleged to offend the Fair Housing Act and state housing discrimination laws—the information about sex, family status and sexual orientation—is provided by subscribers in response to Roommate's questions, which they cannot refuse to answer if they want to use defendant's services. By requiring subscribers to provide the information as a condition of accessing its service, and by providing a limited set of pre-populated answers, Roommate becomes much more than a passive transmitter of information provided by others; it becomes the developer, at least in part, of that information. And § 230 provides immunity only if the interactive computer service does not "creat[e] or develop[ ]" the information "in whole or in part."

Roommate does much more than provide options [to subscribers as they provide information for their profiles]. To begin with, Roommate asks discriminatory questions. The FHA makes it unlawful to ask certain discriminatory questions for a very good reason: Unlawful questions solicit (a.k.a. "develop") unlawful answers. Not only does Roommate ask these questions, Roommate makes answering the discriminatory questions a condition of doing business. This is no different from a real estate broker in real life saying, "Tell me whether you're Jewish or you can find yourself another broker." When a business enterprise extracts such information from potential customers as a condition of accepting them as clients, it is no stretch to say that the enterprise is responsible, at least in part, for developing that information.

Similarly, Roommate is not entitled to CDA immunity for the operation of its search system, which filters listings, or of its email notification system, which directs emails to subscribers according to discriminatory criteria. Roommate designed its search system so it would steer users based on the preferences and personal characteristics that Roommate itself forces subscribers to disclose. If Roommate has no immunity for asking the discriminatory questions, as we concluded above, it can certainly have no immunity for using the answers to the unlawful questions to limit who has access to housing.

For example, a subscriber who self-identifies as a "Gay male" will not receive email notifications of new housing opportunities supplied by owners who limit the universe of acceptable tenants to "Straight male(s)," "Straight female(s)" and "Lesbian(s)." Similarly, subscribers with children will not be notified of new listings where the owner specifies "no children." Councils charge that limiting the information a subscriber can access based on that subscriber's protected status violates the FHA. It is, Councils allege, no different from a real estate broker saying to a client: "Sorry, sir, but I can't show you any listings on this block because you are [gay/female/black/a parent]." If such screening is prohibited when practiced in person or by telephone, we see no reason why Congress would have wanted to make it lawful to profit from it online.

Roommate's search function is similarly designed to steer users based on discriminatory criteria. Roommate's search engine thus differs materially from generic search engines such as Google, Yahoo! and MSN Live Search, in that Roommate designed its system to use allegedly unlawful criteria so as to limit the results of each search, and to force users to participate in its discriminatory process. In other words, Councils allege that Roommate's search is designed to make it more difficult or impossible for individuals with certain protected characteristics to find housing—something the law prohibits. By contrast, ordinary search engines do not use unlawful criteria to limit the scope of searches conducted on them, nor are they designed to achieve illegal ends—as Roommate's search function is alleged

to do here. Therefore, such search engines play no part in the "development" of any unlawful searches.

3. Councils finally argue that Roommate should be held liable for the discriminatory statements displayed in the "Additional Comments" section of profile pages. At the end of the registration process, on a separate page from the other registration steps, Roommate prompts subscribers to "tak[e] a moment to personalize your profile by writing a paragraph or two describing yourself and what you are looking for in a roommate." The subscriber is presented with a blank text box, in which he can type as much or as little about himself as he wishes. Such essays are visible only to paying subscribers.

Subscribers provide a variety of provocative, and often very revealing, answers. The contents range from subscribers who "[p]ref[er] white Male roommates" or require that "[t]he person applying for the room MUST be a BLACK GAY MALE" to those who are "NOT looking for black muslims." Some common themes are a desire to live without "drugs, kids or animals" or "smokers, kids or druggies," while a few subscribers express more particular preferences, such as preferring to live in a home free of "psychos or anyone on mental medication." Some subscribers are just looking for someone who will get along with their significant other or [will hold certain religious beliefs].

Roommate publishes these comments as written. It does not provide any specific guidance as to what the essay should contain, nor does it urge subscribers to input discriminatory preferences. Roommate is not responsible, in whole or in part, for the development of this content, which comes entirely from subscribers and is passively displayed by Roommate. Without reviewing every essay, Roommate would have no way to distinguish unlawful discriminatory preferences from perfectly legitimate statements. Nor can there be any doubt that this information was tendered to Roommate for publication online. This is precisely the kind of situation for which § 230 was designed to provide immunity.

We must keep firmly in mind that this is an immunity statute we are expounding, a provision enacted to protect websites against the evil of liability for failure to remove offensive content. Websites are complicated enterprises, and there will always be close cases where a clever lawyer could argue that *something* the website operator did encouraged the illegality. Such close cases, we believe, must be resolved in favor of immunity, lest we cut the heart out of § 230 by forcing websites to face death by ten thousand duck-bites, fighting off claims that they promoted or encouraged—or at least tacitly assented to—the illegality of third parties. Where it is very clear that the website directly participates in developing the alleged illegality—as it is clear here with respect to Roommate's questions, answers, and the resulting profile pages—immunity will be lost. But in cases of enhancement by implication or development by inference—such as with respect to the "Additional Comments" here—§ 230 must be interpreted to protect websites not merely from ultimate liability, but from having to fight costly and protracted legal battles.

[This decision's] message to website operators is clear: If you don't encourage illegal content, or design your website to require users to input illegal content, you will be immune. We believe that this distinction is consistent with the intent of Congress to preserve the free-flowing nature of Internet speech and commerce without unduly prejudicing the enforcement of other important state and federal laws. When Congress passed § 230 it didn't intend to prevent the enforcement of all laws online;

rather, it sought to encourage interactive computer services that provide users *neutral* tools to post content online to police that content without fear that through their [screening of offensive material], they would become liable for every single message posted by third parties on their website.

In light of our determination that the CDA does not provide immunity to Roommate for all of the content of its website and email newsletters, we remand for the district court to determine in the first instance whether the alleged actions for which Roommate is not immune violate the FHA.

District court's decision reversed in part and affirmed in part, and case remanded for further proceedings.

General Dynamics Land Systems, Inc. v. Cline   540 U.S. 581 (U.S. Sup. Ct. 2004)

Section 623 of the federal Age Discrimination in Employment Act (ADEA) makes it unlawful for an employer of at least 20 persons "to fail or refuse to hire or to discharge any individual or otherwise discriminate against any individual with respect to his compensation, terms, conditions, or privileges of employment, because of such individual's age." According to another ADEA section, the protection against discrimination afforded by § 623 applies only when the affected individual is at least 40 years of age.

A pre-1997 collective bargaining agreement between the United Auto Workers (UAW) and General Dynamics Land Systems, Inc., called for General Dynamics to furnish health benefits to retired employees who had worked for the company for a qualifying number of years. In 1997, however, the UAW and General Dynamics entered into a new collective bargaining agreement that eliminated the obligation of General Dynamics to provide health benefits to employees who retired after the effective date of the new agreement, except for then-current workers who were at least 50 years old at the time of the agreement. Employees in that 50-and-over category would still receive health benefits when they retired.

Dennis Cline was among the General Dynamics employees who were dissatisfied with the new collective bargaining agreement because they were under 50 years of age when the agreement was adopted, and thus would not receive health benefits when they retired. Although they were under 50 years old, Cline and the other employees who later became plaintiffs in the case described below were all at least 40 years of age. They therefore met the ADEA's minimum age threshold. In a proceeding before the Equal Employment Opportunity Commission (EEOC), Cline and the other plaintiffs asserted that the 1997 collective bargaining agreement violated the ADEA, because the plaintiffs were within the ADEA's protected class of persons (those at least 40 years of age) and because the agreement discriminated against them "with respect to . . . compensation, terms, conditions, or privileges of employment, because of [their] age" (quoting section 623 of the ADEA). The age discrimination alleged by the plaintiffs was that under the terms of the agreement, their under-50 age was the basis for denying them the more favorable treatment to be received by persons 50 years of age or older. Agreeing with this view of the case, the EEOC invited General Dynamics and the union to settle informally with Cline and the other plaintiffs (hereinafter referred to collectively as "Cline").

When no settlement occurred, Cline sued General Dynamics for a supposed violation of the ADEA. The federal district court dismissed the case. Cline appealed, and the U.S. Court of Appeals for the Sixth Circuit reversed. The Sixth Circuit reasoned that the prohibition of section 623, covering discrimination against "any individual . . . because of such individual's age," was so clear on its face that if Congress had meant to limit its coverage to protect only the older worker against the younger, it would have said so. The United States Supreme Court then granted General Dynamics' petition for writ of certiorari (i.e., the Supreme Court agreed to decide the case).

Souter, Justice

The Age Discrimination in Employment Act forbids discriminatory preference for the young over the old. The question in this case is whether it also prohibits favoring the old over the young.

The common ground in this case is the generalization that the ADEA's prohibition covers "discriminat[ion] . . . because of [an] individual's age," [if the discrimination] helps the younger by hurting the older. In the abstract, the phrase is open to an argument for a broader construction, since reference to "age" carries no express modifier and the word could be read to look two ways. This more expansive possible understanding does not, however, square with the natural reading of the whole provision prohibiting discrimination, and in fact Congress's interpretive clues speak almost unanimously to an understanding of discrimination as directed against workers who are older than the ones getting treated better.

Congress chose not to include age within discrimination forbidden by Title VII of the Civil Rights Act of 1964 [, which prohibits employment discrimination on the basis of race, color, sex, religion, or national origin]. Instead [Congress] called for a study of the issue by the Secretary of Labor, who concluded that age discrimination was a serious problem [centering around] disadvantage to older individuals from arbitrary and stereotypical employment distinctions (including then-common policies of age ceilings on hiring). . . . [T]he Secretary ultimately took the position that arbitrary discrimination against older workers was widespread and persistent enough to call for a federal legislative remedy. [The Secretary's report] was devoid of any indication that the Secretary had noticed unfair advantages accruing to older employees at the expense of their juniors.

[Congress then began considering legislation dealing with employment-related age discrimination.] Extensive House and Senate hearings ensued. The testimony at the hearings [focused] on unjustified assumptions about the effect of age on ability to work. [In addition, the hearings] specifically addressed higher pension and benefit costs as heavier drags on hiring workers the older they got. The record thus reflects the common facts that an individual's chances to find and keep a job get worse over time; as between any two people, the younger is in the stronger position, the older more apt to be tagged with demeaning stereotype. Not surprisingly, from the voluminous records of the hearings, we have found . . . nothing suggesting that any workers were registering complaints about discrimination in favor of their seniors.

Nor is there any such suggestion in the introductory provisions of the ADEA. [The congressional findings set forth in the introductory provisions] stress the impediments suffered by "older workers . . . in their efforts to retain . . . and especially to regain employment," the burdens of "arbitrary age limits regardless of potential for job performance," the costs of "otherwise desirable practices [that] may work to the disadvantage of older persons," and "the incidence of unemployment, especially long-term unemployment [, which] is, relative to the younger ages, high among older workers." The statutory objects [specified in the ADEA] were "to promote employment of older persons based on their ability rather than age; to prohibit arbitrary age discrimination in employment; [and] to help employers and workers find ways of meeting problems arising from the impact of age on employment." In sum, . . . all the findings and statements of objectives are either cast in terms of the effects of age as intensifying over time, or are couched in terms that refer to "older" workers, explicitly or implicitly relative to "younger" ones.

Such is the setting of the ADEA's core substantive provision, § 623, prohibiting employers and certain others from "discriminat[ion] . . . because of [an] individual's age," [assuming the individual is at least 40 years of age.] The prefatory provisions and their legislative history [of the ADEA] make a case that we think is beyond reasonable doubt, that the ADEA was concerned to protect a relatively old worker from discrimination that works to the advantage of the relatively young.

Nor is it remarkable that the record is devoid of any evidence that younger workers were suffering at the expense of their elders, let alone that a social problem required a federal statute to place a younger worker in parity with an older one. Common experience is to the contrary, and the testimony, reports, and congressional findings simply confirm that Congress used the phrase "discriminat[ion] . . . because of [an] individual's age" the same way that ordinary people in common usage might speak of age discrimination any day of the week. One commonplace conception of American society in recent decades is its character as a "youth culture," and in a world where younger is better, talk about discrimination because of age is naturally understood to refer to discrimination against the older.

This same, idiomatic sense of the statutory phrase is confirmed by the statute's restriction of the protected class to those 40 and above. If Congress had been worrying about protecting the younger against the older, it would not likely have ignored everyone under 40. The youthful deficiencies of inexperience and unsteadiness invite stereotypical and discriminatory thinking about those a lot younger than 40, and prejudice suffered by a 40-year-old is not typically owing to youth, as 40-year-olds sadly tend to find out. The enemy of 40 is 30, not 50. Thus, the 40-year threshold makes sense as identifying a class requiring protection against preference for their juniors, not as defining a class that might be threatened by favoritism toward seniors.

[Cline argues, however,] that the statute's meaning is plain when the word "age" receives its natural and ordinary meaning and the statute is read as a whole giving "age" the same meaning throughout. [Cline makes] the dictionary argument that "age" means the length of a person's life, with the phrase "because of such individual's age" stating a simple test of causation: "discriminat[ion] . . . because of [an] individual's age" is treatment that would not have occurred if the individual's span of years had been longer or shorter. The case for this reading calls attention to the other instances of "age" in the ADEA that are not limited to old age, such as [the section that] gives an employer a defense to charges of age discrimination when "age is a bona fide occupational qualification." Cline argues that if "age" meant old age, [the section just quoted] would then provide a defense (old age is a bona fide qualification) only for an employer's action that on our reading would never clash with the statute (because preferring the older is not forbidden).

The argument rests on two mistakes. First, it assumes that the word "age" has the same meaning wherever the ADEA uses it. But this is not so, and Cline simply misemploys the presumption that identical words used in different parts of the same act are intended to have the same meaning. The presumption of uniform usage relents when a word used has several commonly understood meanings among which a speaker can alternate in the course of an ordinary conversation, without being confused or getting confusing.

"Age" is that kind of word. [T]he word "age" standing alone can be readily understood either as pointing to any number of years lived, or as common shorthand for the longer span and concurrent aches that make youth look good. Which alternative was probably intended is a matter of context; we understand the different choices of meaning that lie behind a sentence [such as] "Age can be shown by a driver's license," and the statement, "Age has left him a shut-in." So it is easy to understand that Congress chose different meanings at different places in the ADEA, as the different settings readily show. Hence the second flaw in Cline's argument for uniform usage: it ignores the cardinal rule that statutory language must be read in context, [because] a phrase gathers meaning from the words around it. The point here is that we are not asking an abstract question about the meaning of "age"; we are seeking the meaning of the whole phrase "discriminate . . . because of such individual's age," where it occurs in the ADEA.

Here, regular interpretive method leaves no serious question. The word "age" takes on a definite meaning from being in the phrase "discriminat[ion] . . . because of such individual's age," occurring as that phrase does in a statute structured and manifestly intended to protect the older from arbitrary favor for the younger. We see the text, structure, purpose, and history of the ADEA . . . as showing that the statute does not mean to stop an employer from favoring an older employee over a younger one.

Judgment of Sixth Circuit Court of Appeals reversed in favor of General Dynamics.

General Public Purpose Occasionally, courts construe statutory language in the light of various *general public purposes*. These purposes are not the purposes underlying the statute in question; rather, they are widely accepted general notions of public policy. For example, the Supreme Court once used the general public policy against racial discrimination in education as an argument for denying tax-exempt status to a private university that discriminated on the basis of race.

Prior Interpretations Courts sometimes follow prior cases and administrative decisions interpreting a statute, regardless of the statute's plain meaning or legislative history. The main argument for following these prior interpretations is to promote stability and certainty by preventing each successive court that considers a statute from adopting its own interpretation. The courts' willingness to follow a prior interpretation depends on such factors as the number of past courts adopting the interpretation, the authoritativeness of those courts, and the number of years that the interpretation has been followed.

Maxims Maxims are general rules of thumb employed in statutory interpretation. There are many maxims, which courts tend to use or ignore at their discretion. One example of a maxim is the *ejusdem generis* rule, which says that when general words follow words of a specific, limited meaning, the general language should be limited to things of the same class as those specifically stated. Suppose that the pollution statute quoted earlier listed 12 types of gas-powered vehicles and ended with the words "and other motorized passenger or cargo vehicles." In that instance, *ejusdem generis* probably would dictate that battery-powered vehicles not be included.

Limits on the Power of Courts

By now, you may think that anything goes when courts decide common law cases or interpret statutes. Many factors, however, discourage courts from adopting a freewheeling approach. Their legal training and mental makeup cause judges to be likely to respect established precedents and the will of the legislature. Many courts issue written opinions, which expose judges to academic and professional criticism if the opinions are poorly reasoned. Lower court judges may be discouraged from innovation by the fear of being overruled by a higher court. Finally, political factors inhibit judges. For example, some judges are elected, and even judges with lifetime tenure can sometimes be removed.

An even more fundamental limit on the power of courts is that they cannot make or interpret law until parties present them with a case to decide. In addition, any such case must be a real dispute. That is, courts generally limit themselves to genuine, existing "cases or controversies" between real parties with tangible opposing interests in the lawsuit. Courts generally do not issue *advisory opinions* on abstract legal questions unrelated to a genuine dispute, and do not decide *feigned controversies* that parties concoct to seek answers to such questions. Courts may also refuse to decide cases that are insufficiently *ripe* to have matured into a genuine controversy, or that are *moot* because there no longer is a real dispute between the parties. Expressing similar ideas is the doctrine of **standing to sue,** which normally requires that the plaintiff have some direct, tangible, and substantial stake in the outcome of the litigation.

The Global Business Environment

Just as statutes may require judicial interpretation when a dispute arises, so may treaties. The techniques that courts use in interpreting treaties correspond closely to the statutory interpretation techniques discussed in this chapter. *Olympic Airways v. Husain,* 540 U.S. 644 (U.S. Sup. Ct. 2004), furnishes a useful example.

In *Olympic Airways,* the U.S. Supreme Court was faced with an interpretation question regarding a treaty, the Warsaw Convention, which deals with airlines' liability for passenger deaths or injuries on international flights. Numerous nations (including the United States) subscribe to the Warsaw Convention, a key provision of which provides that in regard to international flights, the airline "shall be liable for damages sustained in the event of the death or wounding of a passenger or any other bodily injury suffered by a passenger, if the accident which caused the damage so sustained took place on board the aircraft or in the course of any of the operations of embarking or disembarking." A separate provision imposes limits on the amount of money damages to which a liable airline may be subjected.

The *Olympic Airways* case centered around the death of Dr. Abid Hanson, a severe asthmatic, on an international flight operated by Olympic. Smoking was permitted on the flight. Hanson was given a seat in the nonsmoking section, but his seat was only three rows in front of the smoking section. Because Hanson was extremely sensitive to secondhand smoke, he and his wife, Rubina Husain, requested various times that he be allowed, for health reasons, to move to a seat farther away from the smoking section. Each time, the request was denied by an Olympic flight attendant. When smoke from the smoking section began to give Hanson difficulty, he used a new inhaler and walked toward the front of the plane to get some fresher air. Hanson went into respiratory distress, whereupon his wife and a doctor who was on board gave him shots of epinephrine from an emergency kit that Hanson carried. Although the doctor administered CPR and oxygen when Hanson collapsed, Hanson died. Husain, acting as personal representative of her late husband's estate, sued Olympic in federal court on the theory that the Warsaw Convention made Olympic liable for Hanson's death. The federal district court and the court of appeals ruled in favor of Husain.

In considering Olympic's appeal, the U.S. Supreme Court noted that the key issue was one of treaty interpretation: whether the flight attendant's refusals to reseat Hanson constituted an "accident which caused" the death of Hanson. Noting that the Warsaw Convention itself did not define "accident" and that different dictionary definitions of "accident" exist, the Court looked to a precedent case, *Air France v. Saks*, 470 U.S. 392 (U.S. Sup. Ct. 1985), for guidance. In the *Air France* case, the Court held that the term "accident" in the Warsaw Convention means "an unexpected or unusual event or happening that is external to the passenger." Applying that definition to the facts at hand, the Court concluded in *Olympic Airways* that the repeated refusals to reseat Hanson despite his health concerns amounted to unexpected and unusual behavior for a flight attendant. Although the refusals were not the sole reason why Hanson died (the smoke itself being a key factor), the refusals were nonetheless a significant link in the causation chain that led to Hanson's death. Given the definition of "accident" in the Court's earlier precedent, the phrasing, the Warsaw Convention, and the underlying public policies supporting it, the Court concluded that the refusals to reseat Hanson constituted an "accident" covered by the Warsaw Convention. Therefore, the Court affirmed the decision of the lower courts.

State and federal **declaratory judgment** statutes, however, allow parties to determine their rights and duties even though their controversy has not advanced to the point where harm has occurred and legal relief may be necessary. This enables them to determine their legal position without taking action that could expose them to liability. For example, if Darlene believes that something she plans to do would not violate Earl's copyright on a work of authorship but she recognizes that he may take a contrary view, she may seek a declaratory judgment on the question rather than risk Earl's lawsuit by proceeding to do what she had planned. Usually, a declaratory judgment is awarded only when the parties' dispute is sufficiently advanced to constitute a real case or controversy.

APPENDIX

Reading and Briefing Cases

Throughout this text, you will encounter cases—the judicial opinions accompanying court decisions. These cases are highly edited versions of their much longer originals. What follows are explanations and pointers to assist you in studying cases.

1. Each case has a *case name* that includes at least some of the parties to the case. Because the order of the parties may change when a case is appealed, do not assume that the first party listed is the plaintiff (the party suing) and the second the defendant (the party being sued). Also, because some cases have many plaintiffs and/or many defendants, the parties discussed in the court's opinion sometimes differ from those found in the case name.

2. Each case also has a *citation,* which includes the volume and page number of the legal reporter in which the full case appears, plus the year the case was decided. *General Dynamics v. Cline,* for instance, begins on page 581 of volume 540 of the United States Reports (the official reporter for U.S. Supreme Court decisions), and was decided in 2004. (Each of the many different legal reporters has its own abbreviation. The list is too long to include here.) In the parenthesis accompanying the date, we also give you some information about the court that decided the case. For example, "U.S. Sup. Ct." is the United States Supreme Court, "3d Cir." is the U.S. Court of Appeals for the Third Circuit, "S.D.N.Y." is the U.S. District Court for the Southern District of New York, "Minn. Sup. Ct."

is the Supreme Court of Minnesota, and "Mich. Ct. App." is the Michigan Court of Appeals (a Michigan intermediate appellate court). Chapter 2 describes the various kinds of courts.

3. At the beginning of each case, there is a *statement of facts* containing the most important facts that gave rise to the case.

4. Immediately after the statement of facts, we give you the case's *procedural history*. This history tells you what courts previously handled the case you are reading, and how they dealt with it.

5. Next comes your major concern: the *body of the court's opinion*. Here, the court determines the applicable law and applies it to the facts to reach a conclusion. The court's discussion of the relevant law may be elaborate; it may include prior cases, legislative history, applicable public policies, and more. The court's application of the law to the facts usually occurs after it has arrived at the applicable legal rule(s), but also may be intertwined with its legal discussion.

6. At the very end of the case, we complete the procedural history by stating the court's *decision*. For example, "Judgment reversed in favor of Smith" says that a lower court judgment against Smith was reversed on appeal. This means that Smith's appeal was successful and Smith wins.

7. The cases' main function is to provide concrete examples of rules stated in the text. (Frequently, the text tells you what point the case illustrates.) In studying law, it is easy to conclude that your task is finished once you have memorized a black letter rule. Real-life legal problems, however, seldom present themselves as abstract questions of law; instead, they are hidden in particular situations one encounters or particular actions one takes. Without some sense of a legal rule's real-life application, your knowledge of that rule is incomplete. The cases help provide this sense.

8. You may find it helpful to *brief* the cases. There is no one correct way to brief a case, but most good briefs contain the following elements: (1) a short statement of the relevant facts; (2) the case's prior history; (3) the question(s) or issue(s) the court had to decide; (4) the answer(s) to those question(s); (5) the reasoning the court used to justify its decision; and (6) the final result. Using "P" and "D" for the plaintiff and defendant, a brief of the *General Dynamics* case might look this way:

General Dynamics v. Cline

Facts Under a pre-1997 collective bargaining agreement between the United Auto Workers (UAW) and

General Dynamics, retired employees of General Dynamics received health benefits from the company if they had worked there a sufficiently long period of time. A 1997 agreement between the UAW and General Dynamics eliminated this company obligation as to employees who retired after the 1997 effective date of the agreement, except for workers who were already at least 50 years old when the agreement took effect. The latter workers would still receive health benefits when they retired. Because Cline, an employee of General Dynamics, was under 50 at the time of the 1997 agreement, he supposedly would not receive health benefits when he retired. However, Cline was at least 40 years of age—the minimum age necessary for a worker to be protected by the Age Discrimination in Employment Act (ADEA), which bars discrimination in a broad range of employment matters "because of [the] age" of the allegedly discriminated-against individual.

History   Cline (P) sued General Dynamics (D), alleging that the 1997 collective bargaining agreement violated the ADEA by discriminating against him "because of [his] age." P argued there was age discrimination because the fact that he was under 50 years old in 1997 meant that when he retired, he would not receive the health benefits that were still being guaranteed, upon retirement, to workers who were 50 or older in 1997. P lost in the federal district court, but the court of appeals reversed. D appealed to the U.S. Supreme Court.

Issue   Is the ADEA's ban on employment discrimination on the basis of "age" violated when the supposed discrimination works in favor of employees who are older and against employees who are younger but are at least 40 years old?

Holding   No, there is no ADEA violation in such a situation.

Reasoning   Even though the literal language of the relevant ADEA section's prohibition of employment discrimination "because of . . . age" could be read as allowing an ADEA claim even when an employer's age-based action favors older workers over younger workers, the statute should not be read that way. The social context in which the ADEA was enacted, the legislative history of the ADEA, and the congressional findings in the introductory sections of the ADEA all indicate that when the relevant ADEA section banned discrimination "because of . . . age," Congress was concerned about the persistent problem posed by employers who took age-based actions favoring younger workers over older workers. Nothing indicates that Congress was worried about employers' age-based actions that favored older employees, even when the disadvantaged younger employees were within the class of persons the ADEA normally protects (persons at least 40 years of age). In addition, a commonsense reading of the statutory context in which the "discrimination . . . because of such individual's age" language appeared bolsters the conclusion that Congress meant only to prohibit age-based employment discrimination that favored younger persons at the expense of older ones. Congress did not seek to stop employers from favoring older employees over younger workers.

Result   Court of appeals decision reversed. D wins.

Problems and Problem Cases

1. Law enforcement officers arrived at a Minnesota residence in order to execute arrest warrants for Andrew Hyatt. During the officers' attempt to make the arrest, Hyatt yelled something such as "Go ahead, just shoot me, shoot me," and struck one of the officers. Another officer then called for assistance from City of Anoka, Minnesota, police officer Mark Yates, who was elsewhere in the residence with his leashed police dog, Chips. Yates entered the room where Hyatt was, saw the injured officer's bloodied face, and observed Hyatt standing behind his wife (Lena Hyatt). One of the officers acquired the impression that Lena may have been serving as a shield for her husband. When Andrew again yelled "Shoot me, shoot me" and ran toward the back of the room, Yates released Chips from the leash. Instead of pursuing Andrew, Chips apprehended Lena, taking her to the ground and performing a "bite and hold" on her leg and arm. Yates then pursued Andrew, who had fled through a window. When Yates later re-entered the room, he released Chips from Lena and instructed another officer to arrest her on suspicion of obstruction of legal process. Lena was taken by ambulance to a hospital and treated for lacerations on her elbow and knee. She later sued the City of Anoka, seeking compensation for medical expenses and pain and suffering. Her complaint alleged liability on the basis of Minnesota's dog bite statute, which read as follows:

   "If a dog, without provocation, attacks or injures any person who is acting peaceably in any place where the person may lawfully be, the owner of the dog is liable in damages to the person so attacked or injured to the full amount of the injury sustained. The term "owner" includes any person harboring or keeping a dog but the owner shall be primarily liable. The term "dog" includes both male and female of the canine species."

In defense, the city argued that the dog bite statute does not apply to police dogs and municipalities that own them. Was the city correct?

2. As part of its collective bargaining agreement with the United Steelworkers of America, the Kaiser Aluminum and Chemical Company established an on-the-job craft training program at its Gramercy, Louisiana, plant. The selection of trainees for the program was generally based on seniority, but the selection guidelines included an affirmative action feature under which at least 50 percent of the new trainees had to be black until the percentage of black skilled craft workers in the plant approximated the percentage of blacks in the local labor force. The purposes of the affirmative action feature were to break down old patterns of racial segregation and hierarchy, and to open up employment opportunities for blacks in occupations that had traditionally been closed to them. Kaiser employee Brian Weber, who was white, applied for the program but was rejected. He would have qualified for the program had the affirmative action feature not existed. Weber sued Kaiser and the union in federal district court, arguing that the racial preference violated Title VII of the Civil Rights Act of 1964. Section 703(a) of the Act states: "It shall be an unlawful employment practice for an employer . . . to discriminate against any individual with respect to his compensation, terms, conditions, or privileges of employment, because of such individual's race, color, religion, sex, or national origin." Section 703(d) includes a similar provision specifically forbidding racial discrimination in admission to apprenticeship or other training programs. Weber won his case in the federal district court and in the federal court of appeals. Kaiser and the union appealed to the U.S. Supreme Court. Did the affirmative action feature of the training program violate Title VII's prohibition of employment discrimination on the basis of race?

3. The Freedom of Access to Clinic Entrances Act (FACE), a federal statute, provides for penalties against anyone who "by force or threat of force or by physical obstruction . . . intentionally injures, intimidates, or interferes . . . with any person . . . in order to intimidate such person . . . from obtaining or providing

reproductive health services." Two persons, Lynch and Moscinski, blocked access to a clinic that offered such services. The federal government sought an injunction barring Lynch and Moscinski from impeding access to, or coming within 15 feet of, the clinic. In defense, the defendants argued that FACE protects the taking of innocent human life, that FACE is therefore contrary to natural law, and that, accordingly, FACE should be declared null and void. A federal district court issued the injunction after finding that Lynch and Moscinski had violated FACE by making entrance to the clinic unreasonably difficult. On appeal, the defendants maintained that the district court erred in not recognizing their natural law argument as a defense. Were the defendants correct?

4. The Anti-Drug Abuse Act of 1988 provides that each "public housing agency shall utilize leases which . . . provide that any criminal activity that threatens the health, safety, or right to peaceful enjoyment of the premises by other tenants or any drug-related criminal activity on or off such premises, engaged in by a public housing tenant, any member of the tenant's household, or any guest or other person under the tenant's control, shall be cause for termination of tenancy." Department of Housing and Urban Development (HUD) regulations implementing the Act authorize local public housing authorities to evict tenants for drug-related activity of persons listed in the statute even if the tenants did not know of the activity. The Oakland Housing Authority (OHA) instituted eviction proceedings in state court against four tenants, alleging that they had violated a lease provision obligating tenants to "assure that . . . any member of the household, a guest, or another person under the tenant's control, shall not engage in . . . any drug-related criminal activity on or near the premises." Allegedly, the respective grandsons of tenants Lee and Hill were caught smoking marijuana in the apartment complex parking lot, and the daughter of tenant Rucker was found with cocaine and a crack cocaine pipe three blocks from Rucker's apartment. In addition, on three instances within a two-month period, 75-year-old tenant Walker's caregiver and two others were found with cocaine in Walker's apartment. Lee, Hill, and Rucker claimed to have been unaware of their grandsons' and daughter's illegal drug abuse, and Walker fired his caregiver upon receiving the eviction notice. In response to OHA's actions, the four tenants just mentioned filed suit in federal court,

arguing that the Anti-Drug Abuse Act should not be interpreted as authorizing the eviction of innocent tenants (i.e., tenants who did not know of the drug activity on or near the premises). Were the tenants correct?

5. The Federal Tort Claims Act (FTCA) waives the federal government's sovereign immunity concerning claims arising out of torts committed by federal employees. Therefore, the government generally can be sued for tort claims based on wrongful actions by federal employees. However, there are exceptions to this waiver of sovereign immunity. Where an exception applies, a tort claim cannot be brought against the government. One of the exceptions to the sovereign immunity waiver is set forth in FTCA § 2680(c). This exception is for "any claim arising in respect of the assessment or collection of any tax or customs duty, or the detention of any . . . property by any officer of customs or excise or any other law enforcement officer." When a prisoner was transferred from a federal prison in Georgia to another federal prison in Kentucky, he noticed that several items of religious and nostalgic significance were missing from his bags of personal property, which had been shipped to the new facility by the Federal Bureau of Prisons (FBOP). Alleging that FBOP officers had lost his property, petitioner filed suit under the FTCA. The district court dismissed the claim, concluding that it was barred by § 2680(c) and its broad reference to "any other law enforcement officer." The U.S. Court of Appeals for the Eleventh Circuit affirmed. In doing so, the Eleventh Circuit rejected the prisoner's argument that the statutory phrase "any officer of customs or excise or any other law enforcement officer" applies only to officers enforcing customs or excise laws and not to the FBOP officers (who obviously were not acting as enforcers of customs or excise laws). The prisoner appealed to the U.S. Supreme Court. In rejecting the prisoner's argument, did the Eleventh Circuit correctly interpret § 2680(c)?

6. As noted in the preceding problem case, the Federal Tort Claims Act (FTCA) waives the federal government's sovereign immunity concerning claims arising out of torts committed by federal employees. This waiver of sovereign immunity allows tort claims based on wrongful actions by federal employees, except when an exception to the waiver applies (in which event a tort claim cannot be brought or pursued against the government). One of the exceptions to the

sovereign immunity waiver is set forth in FTCA § 2680(b). This exception is for "loss, miscarriage, or negligent transmission of letters or postal matter." Barbara Dolan was injured when she tripped and fell over packages and letters that a U.S. Postal Service (USPS) mail carrier left on the porch of her home. Dolan sued the USPS under the FTCA on the theory that the USPS mail carrier had been negligent—in other words, had failed to use reasonable care—in leaving the items of mail on the porch. The USPS argued that the case should be dismissed because it fell within § 2680(b)'s reference to claims arising out of "negligent transmission of letters or postal matter." Agreeing with this argument, the district court dismissed the case. The U.S. Court of Appeals for the Third Circuit affirmed. Dolan appealed to the U.S. Supreme Court, arguing that the lower courts had erroneously interpreted § 2680(b). Were the lower courts correct in their interpretation of § 2680(b)? Was Dolan's claim barred by the "negligent transmission of letters or postal matter" language?

7. Many states and localities used to have so-called Sunday Closing laws—statutes or ordinances forbidding certain business from being conducted on Sunday. A few may still have such laws. Often, these laws have not been obeyed or enforced. What would an extreme legal positivist tend to think about the duty to enforce and obey such laws? What would a natural law exponent who strongly believes in economic freedom tend to think about this question? What about a natural law adherent who is a Christian religious traditionalist? What observation would almost any legal realist make about Sunday Closing laws? With these laws looked at from a sociological perspective, finally, what social factors help explain their original passage, their relative lack of enforcement today, and their continued presence on the books despite their lack of enforcement?

8. Assume that you are a trial court judge in Nebraska's state court system and that *Sigler v. Patrick* is one of the civil cases you must decide. Your research has revealed that the critical issue in *Sigler* is the same issue presented in *Churchich v. Duda,* a 1996 decision of the Supreme Court of Nebraska (the highest court in the Nebraska system). The *Churchich* decision established a new common law rule for Nebraska. Your research has also revealed that in 2007, the Nebraska legislature enacted a statute that states a rule different from the common law rule established

in *Churchich*. You believe, however, that the 2007 statute offers an unwise rule, and that the common law rule set forth in *Churchich* amounts to much better public policy. In deciding the *Sigler* case, are you free to apply the *Churchich* rule? Why or why not?

9. One wheel of a pre-1916 automobile manufactured by the Buick Motor Company was made of defective wood. Buick could have discovered the defect had it made a reasonable inspection after it purchased the wheel from another manufacturer. Buick sold the car to a retail dealer, who then sold it to MacPherson. While MacPherson was driving his new Buick, the defective wheel collapsed and he was thrown from the vehicle. Was Buick, which did not deal directly with MacPherson, liable for his injuries?

10. In 1997, the Drudge Report, a free Internet gossip page hosted by America Online (AOL), reported that Sidney Blumenthal, a Clinton Administration aide, had a "spousal abuse past that [had] been effectively covered up." Blumenthal and his wife then brought a defamation action against AOL and Matt Drudge, the operator of the Drudge Report. Although Drudge posted the content that appeared on the Drudge Report, AOL retained certain editorial rights in regard to the page. The Blumenthals took the position that the editorial rights retained by AOL made AOL a publisher of the Drudge Report's statements and, as such, a liable party in addition to Drudge under the common law of defamation. AOL argued, however, that § 230 of the federal Communications Decency Act protected it against liability. Section 230 states that "[n]o provider or user of an interactive computer service shall be treated as the publisher or speaker of any information provided by another information content provider." How did the court rule? Did AOL face potential liability under the common law of defamation, or did § 230 of the Communications Decency Act protect AOL against liability?

Online Research

Statutory Interpretation

Statutory interpretation was critical to the Supreme Court of Colorado's resolution of a 2007 case, *Pringle v. Valdez*. Using an online source or sources, locate the *Pringle* decision. Then do the following:

1. Read Justice Bender's majority opinion and prepare a case brief of the sort described in this chapter's appendix on "Reading and Briefing Cases."

2. Read the dissenting opinion authored by Justice Coats. Then prepare a one-page essay that (a) summarizes the principal arguments made in the dissenting opinion; (b) sets forth your view on which analysis—the majority opinion's or the dissenting opinion's—is better; and (c) provides the reasons for the view you have expressed in (b).

chapter 2

THE RESOLUTION OF
PRIVATE DISPUTES

Victoria Wilson, a resident of Illinois, wishes to bring an invasion of privacy lawsuit against XYZ Co. because XYZ used a photograph of her, without her consent, in an advertisement for one of the company's products. Wilson will seek money damages of $150,000 from XYZ, whose principal offices are located in New Jersey. A New Jersey newspaper was the only print media outlet in which the advertisement was published. However, XYZ also placed the advertisement on the firm's Web site. This Web site may be viewed by anyone with Internet access, regardless of the viewer's geographic location.

Consider the following questions regarding Wilson's case as you read Chapter 2:

- Where, in a geographic sense, may Wilson properly file and pursue her lawsuit against XYZ?
- Must Wilson pursue her case in a state court, or does she have the option of litigating in federal court?
- Assuming that Wilson files her case in a state court, what strategic option may XYZ exercise if it acts promptly?
- Regardless of the court in which the case is litigated, what procedural steps will occur as the lawsuit proceeds from beginning to end?
- If Wilson requests copies of certain documents in XYZ's files, does XYZ have a legal obligation to provide the copies? What if Wilson requests copies of e-mails written by XYZ employees? Is XYZ legally required to provide the copies? What ethical obligations attend Wilson's making, and XYZ's responses to, such requests?

BUSINESS LAW COURSES examine many substantive legal rules that tell us how to behave in business and in society. Examples include the principles of contract, tort, and agency law, as well as those of many other legal areas addressed later in this text. Most of these principles are applied by courts as they decide civil cases involving private parties. This chapter lays a foundation for the text's discussion of substantive legal rules by examining the court systems of the United States and by outlining how civil cases proceed from beginning to end. The chapter also explores related subjects, including *alternative dispute resolution,* a collection of processes for resolving private disputes outside the court systems.

State Courts and Their Jurisdiction

The United States has 52 court systems—a federal system plus a system for each state and the District of Columbia. This section describes the various types of state courts.

It also considers the important subject of *jurisdiction,* something a court must have if its decision in a case is to be binding on the parties.

Courts of Limited Jurisdiction Minor criminal cases and civil disputes involving small amounts of money or specialized matters frequently are decided in *courts of limited jurisdiction.* Examples include traffic courts, probate courts, and small claims courts. Such courts often handle a large number of cases. In some of these courts, procedures may be informal and parties often argue their own cases without representation by attorneys. Courts of limited jurisdiction often are not courts of record—meaning that they may not keep a transcript of the proceedings conducted. Appeals from their decisions therefore require a new trial (a trial *de novo*) in a trial court.

Trial Courts Courts of limited jurisdiction find the relevant facts, identify the appropriate rule(s) of law, and combine the facts and the law to reach a decision.

State trial courts do the same, but differ from inferior courts in two key ways. First, they are not governed by the subject-matter restrictions or the limits on civil damages or criminal penalties that govern courts of limited jurisdiction. Cases involving significant dollar amounts or major criminal penalties usually begin, therefore, at the trial court level. Second, trial courts are courts of record that keep detailed records of hearings, trials, and other proceedings. These records become important if a trial court decision is appealed. The trial court's fact-finding function may be handled by the judge or by a jury. Determination of the applicable law, however, is always the judge's responsibility. In cases pending in trial courts, the parties nearly always are represented by attorneys.

States usually have at least one trial court for each county. It may be called a circuit, superior, district, county, or common pleas court. Most state trial courts can hear a wide range of civil and criminal cases, with little or no subject-matter restriction. They may, however, have civil and criminal divisions. If no court of limited jurisdiction deals with these matters, state trial courts may also contain other divisions such as domestic relations courts or probate courts.

Appellate Courts
State appeals (or appellate) courts generally decide only legal questions. Instead of receiving new evidence or otherwise retrying the case, appellate courts review the record of the trial court proceedings. Although appellate courts correct legal errors made by the trial judge, they usually accept the trial court's findings of fact. Appellate courts also may hear appeals from state administrative agency decisions. Some states have only one appeals court (usually called the supreme court), but most also have an intermediate appellate court. The U.S. Supreme Court sometimes hears appeals from decisions of the state's highest court.

Jurisdiction and Venue
The party who sues in a civil case (the plaintiff) cannot sue the defendant (the party being sued) in whatever court the plaintiff happens to prefer. Instead, the chosen court—whether a state court or a federal court—must have **jurisdiction** over the case. Jurisdiction is a court's power to hear a case and to issue a decision binding on the parties. In order to render a binding decision in a civil case, a court must have not only subject-matter jurisdiction but also in personam jurisdiction or in rem jurisdiction. Even if a court has jurisdiction, applicable **venue** requirements must also be satisfied in order for the case to proceed in that court.

Subject-Matter Jurisdiction Subject-matter jurisdiction is a court's power to decide the *type* of dispute involved in the case. Criminal courts, for example, cannot hear civil matters. Similarly, a $500,000 claim for breach of contract cannot be pursued in a small claims court.

In Personam Jurisdiction Even a court with subject-matter jurisdiction cannot decide a civil case unless it also has either **in personam jurisdiction** or **in rem jurisdiction.** In personam jurisdiction is based on the residence, location, or activities of the defendant. A state court has in personam jurisdiction over defendants who are citizens or residents of the state (even if situated out-of-state), who are within the state's borders when process is served on them (even if nonresidents),[1] or who consent to the court's authority (for instance, by entering the state to defend against the plaintiff's claim).[2] The same principle governs federal courts' in personam jurisdiction over defendants.

In addition, most states have enacted "long-arm" statutes that give their courts in personam jurisdiction over certain out-of-state defendants. Under these statutes, nonresident individuals and businesses become subject to the jurisdiction of the state's courts by, for example, doing business within the state, contracting to supply goods or services within the state, or committing a tort (a civil wrong) within the state. Some long-arm statutes are phrased with even broader application in mind. Federal law, moreover, permits federal courts to rely on state long-arm statutes as a basis for obtaining in personam jurisdiction over nonresident defendants.

Even if a long-arm statute applies, however, a state or federal court's assertion of in personam jurisdiction over an out-of-state defendant is subject to federal due process standards. The *Bombliss* case, which follows shortly, addresses long-arm statute and due process issues arising in a context involving Internet communications. For further discussion of in personam jurisdiction issues, see the *Internet Solutions* case and the Global Business Environment box, both of which appear later in the chapter.

---

[1]Service of process is discussed later in the chapter.
[2]In many states, however, out-of-state defendants may make a *special appearance* to challenge the court's jurisdiction without consenting to the court's authority.

Bombliss v. Cornelsen   824 N.E.2d 1175 (Ill. App. 2005)

Ron and Catherine Bombliss were dog breeders who lived in Illinois. They bred Tibetan mastiffs, as did Oklahoma residents Anne and Jim Cornelsen. When Anne Cornelsen telephoned the Bomblisses and said she was ready to sell two litters of Tibetan mastiff puppies, Ron Bombliss expressed interest in purchasing two females of breeding quality.

A Tibetan mastiff named Mulan was the mother of one of the two litters of puppies the Cornelsens were offering for sale. Mulan was co-owned by Richard Eichhorn. Pursuant to an agreement containing a written guarantee that Mulan was free of genetic defects, Eichhorn provided Mulan to the Cornelsens for breeding purposes. The agreement between Eichhorn and the Cornelsens entitled Eichhorn to odd-numbered pups from Mulan's first two litters. However, in the event a genetic defect became apparent, Eichhorn would not receive any puppies. According to the complaint filed by the Bomblisses in the case described below, Anne Cornelsen was angry with Eichhorn because Mulan was infected with roundworms and ticks when Eichhorn delivered the dog to the Cornelsens. Anne allegedly told the Bomblisses that she wanted to prevent Eichhorn from getting any of Mulan's pups.

In January 2002, the Bomblisses traveled to Oklahoma to see the puppies. During their visit, they observed that Mulan and some of her pups appeared sick and worm-infested. They urged Anne to get the sick puppies to the veterinarian immediately. The Bomblisses selected one healthy female from each litter and paid the agreed price with the understanding that the Cornelsens would guarantee the puppies as breeding stock, free from genetic diseases or defects, for three years. According to the Bomblisses' complaint, Anne waited two weeks to take one of the sick pups to the veterinarian. It was then confirmed that the pup had pneumonia. Approximately one month later, Anne posted a message in a Tibetan mastiff chat room on the Internet. In the message, Anne sought advice as to why a three-month-old pup from Mulan's litter was critically ill, even though it had been wormed. She subsequently posted messages stating that she believed the puppy suffered from a genetic disease, and that all of the puppies from the same litter should be spayed or neutered rather than used for breeding. Nevertheless, in April 2002, Anne completed American Kennel Club (AKC) registration papers for Mohanna, one of the sick puppy's littermates that had been sold to plaintiffs in January. These papers, which Anne mailed to the Bomblisses' home in Illinois, stated that Mohanna was "for breeding."

After learning of Anne's chat room postings, the Bomblisses had blood tests done on Mohanna. The tests indicated that Mohanna had no genetic disorders. The Bomblisses later sued the Cornelsens in an Illinois court on various legal theories, including tortious interference with prospective business advantage. The various claims made by the plaintiffs centered around contentions that the defendants knowingly published false statements about Mohanna's genetic line in order to retaliate against Eichhorn, and that, as a consequence, the plaintiffs' negotiations with several potential puppy customers had fallen through. The plaintiffs also alleged that they were denied membership in Internet discussion groups, and that the defendants' comments harmed their reputations.

Because the defendants were residents of Oklahoma and because they believed that the Illinois long-arm statute did not apply, they asked the Illinois trial court to dismiss the complaint for lack of in personam jurisdiction. When the trial court granted the defendants' request, the plaintiffs appealed to the Illinois Court of Appeals.

McDade, Justice

The issue we are asked to determine is whether this state's long-arm statute permits Illinois courts to exercise personal jurisdiction over the Oklahoma defendants.

Specific jurisdiction refers to jurisdiction over a defendant in a suit arising out of or related to the defendant's contacts with the forum. Plaintiffs argue that specific in personam jurisdiction is established . . . because the Cornelsens intentionally directed tortious activities at the Illinois plaintiffs [and] because the assertion of jurisdiction comports with the due process clauses of the Illinois and United States Constitutions. Relevant to our inquiry are the following provisions of the Illinois long-arm statute:

(a) Any person, whether or not a citizen or resident of this State, who in person or through an agent does any

of the acts hereinafter enumerated, thereby submits such person, and, if an individual, his or her personal representative, to the jurisdiction of the courts of this State as to any cause of action arising from the doing of any of such acts:

* * * *

(2) The commission of a tortious act within this State;

* * * *

(c) A court may also exercise jurisdiction on any other basis now or hereafter permitted by the Illinois Constitution and the Constitution of the United States.

Subsection (c) [of the long-arm statute] has been interpreted to mean that if contacts between the defendant and Illinois are sufficient to satisfy due process under the state and federal constitutions, no further inquiry is necessary to satisfy the statute. Accordingly, if the constitutional guarantees of due process are satisfied in this case, we need not determine whether plaintiffs have established jurisdiction under the alternative "tortious act" provision.

The assertion of specific in personam jurisdiction satisfies federal due process guarantees so long as the defendant has sufficient "minimum contacts" with the forum state, such that maintaining an action there comports with "traditional notions of fair play and substantial justice." *International Shoe Co. v. Washington,* 326 U.S. 310 (1945). "Minimum contacts" must involve acts by which the defendant purposefully avails himself of the privilege of conducting activities within the forum state, thereby invoking the benefits and protection of its laws. *Hanson v. Denckla,* 357 U.S. 235 (1958). The defendant's conduct with respect to the forum state must be such that he would reasonably anticipate being haled into that state's court. *World-Wide Volkswagen Corp. v. Woodson,* 444 U.S. 286 (1980). The factors a court must consider include (1) whether the defendant has sufficient minimum contacts with the forum state, (2) whether the cause of action arises out of these contacts, and (3) whether it is reasonable to require the defendant to litigate in the forum state. *Burger King Corp. v. Rudzewicz,* 471 U.S. 462 (1985). We analyze each factor in turn.

When the parties have a contractual relationship, minimum contacts may be shown by the parties' negotiations preceding their agreement, the course of dealing between the parties, the terms of the agreement and foreseeable future consequences arising out of the agreement. Where the defendant is shown to have deliberately engaged in significant activities within the forum state or created ongoing obligations with a resident of the forum state, the defendant has accepted the privilege of doing business with the forum state, and it is not unreasonable to require him to litigate there.

In this case, plaintiffs allege that defendants telephoned plaintiffs at their residence in Illinois and initiated negotiations for the sale of pick-of-the-litter "breeding quality" puppies. After plaintiffs [visited Oklahoma, purchased Mohanna and another puppy, and] returned to Illinois, defendants forwarded AKC registration papers through the United States postal service to plaintiffs' Illinois residence. [The mailed papers] documented Mohanna's lineage and [stated] that she was sold "for breeding purposes." If the only contacts defendants had with Illinois consisted of a single telephone call and one mailing in connection with their sale of the two pups to plaintiffs, we might agree with the trial court that plaintiffs failed to establish sufficient minimum contacts to satisfy due process. But, plaintiffs insist, there was more.

Plaintiffs allege, and defendants agree, that defendants maintain an interactive commercial website advertising their pups and encouraging visitors to communicate with them about potential purchases of puppies via a direct link to defendants' e-mail address. Moreover, plaintiffs allege, defendants' publication of untrue statements about Mohanna's lineage in Tibetan mastiff chat rooms constitutes activity in Illinois. According to plaintiffs, defendants' statements targeted Mohanna and her littermates and falsely indicated that no genetically sound puppies would result from breeding Mohanna.

The type of Internet activity that is sufficient to establish personal jurisdiction remains an emerging area of jurisprudence. For ease of analysis, a "sliding scale" approach has been adopted. *Zippo Manufacturing Co. v. Zippo Dot Com, Inc.,* 952 F. Supp. 1119 (W.D. Pa. 1997). At one end, jurisdiction may be asserted if the [nonresident] defendant transacts business in [the forum state] via an interactive website where contracts are completed online and the defendant derives profits directly from web-related activity. At the opposite end of the scale, jurisdiction does not attach where the nonresident maintains a passive website that merely provides information about the defendant's products. Between these types of websites lies a third category that is interactive, in that it allows customers [in whatever states they are located] to communicate regarding the defendant's services or products. This third category may or may not be sufficient to assert in personam jurisdiction, depending on the level of interactivity and the commercial nature of the information exchanged.

It is clear to us that defendants' website falls within the third category. If defendants' commercial website inviting prospective puppy purchasers to communicate with them by e-mail were the full extent of their Internet activity, we would not find sufficient purposeful contacts with Illinois to assert long-arm jurisdiction. However, the pleadings at issue establish that defendants' activity in the Tibetan mastiff chat rooms also concerned the dog breeding business and should be considered, especially since defendants' messages in the chat rooms pertained to the lineage of plaintiffs' AKC-registered, "breeding quality" pup in Illinois. In our opinion, the totality of defendants' activities in Illinois, including (1) the contract negotiations and follow-up AKC registration of Mohanna, (2) maintenance of a commercial interactive website, and (3) use of Tibetan mastiff chat rooms to reach potential customers of Tibetan mastiff breeders, including plaintiffs, were of sufficient quantity and quality to constitute minimum contacts in Illinois under federal due process analysis.

Next, we must consider whether plaintiffs' cause of action arose out of defendants' contacts with Illinois. This question is easily resolved in plaintiffs' favor. Plaintiffs' primary complaint is of tortious interference with prospective business advantage. According to the complaint, defendants' initial contact was by telephone, offering to sell "pick-of-the-litter" female pups to plaintiffs. They followed up on the agreement with a contact by mail, forwarding AKC registration papers to plaintiffs' home showing that Mohanna was "for breeding." They subsequently published allegedly false information about Mohanna's lineage in Internet chat rooms targeting Tibetan mastiff owners and breeders, again reaching into Illinois and adversely affecting plaintiffs' Illinois dog-breeding operation. Accordingly, it is clear that defendants' contacts with Illinois gave rise to plaintiffs' cause of action.

Next, we consider whether it is reasonable to require defendants to litigate in Illinois. Again, several factors guide this inquiry: (1) the burden on the defendant of defending the action in the forum state; (2) the forum state's interest in adjudicating the dispute; (3) the plaintiff's interest in obtaining effective relief; (4) the interstate judicial system's interest in obtaining the most efficient resolution of the action; and (5) the shared - interests of the several states in advancing fundamental social policies. *World-Wide Volkswagen* [cited earlier]. If the plaintiff has established that the defendant purposely directed his activities at the forum state, it is the defendant's burden to show that litigating the dispute in that state would be unreasonable. *Burger King* [cited earlier].

Here, plaintiffs have shown that defendants purposely directed their activities at Illinois by initiating negotiations with regard to the sale of two pups. Defendants also purposely posted messages in Internet chat rooms impugning the genetic integrity of Mohanna and her littermates. Even if, as plaintiffs allege, defendants' primary purpose was to cover up a breach of their contractual obligation with Eichhorn in California, they

reasonably should have anticipated that messages to other Tibetan mastiff breeders and owners would cause economic damage to plaintiffs' Illinois dog-breeding enterprise. Under the circumstances, it was defendants' burden to show that litigating the cause in Illinois would be unreasonable. This, they have not done.

First, defendants have not shown that it would be unduly burdensome for them to defend this action in Illinois. It would appear that most of the documentary evidence and some of the witnesses are situated in Illinois. The inconvenience to defendants of litigating here is no more burdensome to them than the inconvenience of litigating in Oklahoma would be to plaintiffs. Turning to the second factor, Illinois has a strong interest in providing its residents with a convenient forum. Third, any damages sustained by plaintiffs would have affected their interests in Illinois. And, finally, defendants have advanced no compelling argument for finding that litigating the cause in Oklahoma would serve the interstate judicial system, or that the shared interests of both states in advancing fundamental social policies would be better served by litigating in Oklahoma.

In sum, we [conclude] that the Illinois court's assertion of in personam jurisdiction over the Cornelsens does not offend federal due process concerns. For [essentially] the same reasons that in personam jurisdiction does not offend the federal constitution's due process protections, we also . . . conclude that the assertion of in personam jurisdiction comports with this state's due process guaranty.

Trial court's dismissal for lack of in personam jurisdiction reversed, and case remanded for further proceedings.

In Rem Jurisdiction

In rem jurisdiction is based on the presence of *property* within the state. It empowers state courts to determine rights in that property even if the persons whose rights are affected are outside the state's in personam jurisdiction. For example, a state court's decision regarding title to land within the state is said to bind the world.[3]

---

[3]Another form of jurisdiction, *quasi in rem jurisdiction* or *attachment jurisdiction,* also is based on the presence of property within the state. Unlike cases based on in rem jurisdiction, cases based on quasi in rem jurisdiction do not necessarily determine rights in the property itself. Instead, the property is regarded as an extension of the out-of-state defendant—an extension that sometimes enables the court to decide claims unrelated to the property. For example, a plaintiff might attach the defendant's bank account in the state where the bank is located, sue the defendant on a tort or contract claim unrelated to the bank account, and recover the amount of the judgment from the account if the suit is successful.

Venue

Even if a court has jurisdiction, it may be unable to decide the case because **venue** requirements have not been met. Venue questions arise only after jurisdiction is established or assumed. In general, a court has venue if it is a territorially fair and convenient forum in which to hear the case. Venue requirements applicable to state courts typically are set by state statutes, which normally determine the county in which a case must be brought. For instance, the statute might say that a case concerning land must be filed in the county where the land is located, and that other suits must be brought in the county where the defendant resides or is doing business. If justice so requires, the defendant may be able to obtain a *change of venue.* This can occur when, for example, a fair trial would be impossible within a particular county.

Role of Forum Selection Clauses

Contracts sometimes contain a clause reciting that disputes between the parties regarding matters connected with the contract must be litigated in the courts of a particular state. Such a provision is known as a **forum selection clause.** Depending on its wording, a forum selection clause may have the effect of addressing both jurisdiction and venue issues. Although forum selection clauses may appear in agreements whose terms have been hammered out by the parties after extensive negotiation, they fairly often are found in form agreements whose terms were not the product of actual discussion or give-and-take. For example, an Internet access provider (IAP) may include a forum selection clause in a so-called "clickwrap" document that sets forth the terms of its Internet-related services— terms to which the IAP's subscribers are deemed to have agreed by virtue of utilizing the IAP's services. Forum selection clauses, whether expressly bargained for or included in a clickwrap agreement, are generally enforced by courts unless they are shown to be unreasonable in a given set of circumstances. Assume, for instance, that the IAP's terms of services document calls for the courts of Virginia to have "exclusive jurisdiction" over its subscribers' disputes with the company, but that a subscriber sues the IAP in a Pennsylvania court. Unless the subscriber performs the difficult task of demonstrating that application of the clickwrap agreement's forum selection clause would be unreasonable, the Pennsylvania court will be likely to dismiss the case and to hold that if the subscriber wishes to litigate the claim, he or she must sue in an appropriate Virginia court.

Federal Courts and Their Jurisdiction

Federal District Courts
In the federal system, lawsuits usually begin in the federal district courts. As do state trial courts, the federal district courts determine both the facts and the law. The fact-finding function may be entrusted to either the judge or a jury, but determining the applicable law is the judge's responsibility. Each state is designated as a separate district for purposes of the federal court system. Each district has at least one district court, and each district court has at least one judge.

District Court Jurisdiction   There are various bases of federal district court civil jurisdiction. The two most important are **diversity jurisdiction** and **federal question jurisdiction.** One traditional justification for diversity jurisdiction is that it may help protect out-of-state defendants from potentially biased state courts. *Diversity jurisdiction* exists when (1) the case is between citizens of different states, and (2) the amount in controversy exceeds $75,000. For an example, see the *Internet Solutions* case, which follows shortly. Diversity jurisdiction also exists in certain cases between citizens of a state and citizens or governments of foreign nations, if the amount in controversy exceeds $75,000. Under diversity jurisdiction, a corporation normally is a citizen of both the state where it has been incorporated and the state where it has its principal place of business.

Federal question jurisdiction exists when the case arises under the Constitution, laws, or treaties of the United States. The "arises under" requirement normally is met when a right created by federal law is a basic part of the plaintiff's case. There is no amount-in-controversy requirement for federal question jurisdiction.

Diversity jurisdiction and federal question jurisdiction are forms of subject-matter jurisdiction. Even if one of the two forms exists, a federal district court must also have in personam jurisdiction in order to render a decision that is binding on the parties. As noted earlier in the chapter, the analysis of in personam jurisdiction issues in the federal court system is essentially the same as in the state court systems. Further limiting the plaintiff's choice of federal district courts are the federal system's complex venue requirements, which are beyond the scope of this text.

The *Internet Solutions* case, which follows, illustrates the application of diversity jurisdiction and in personam jurisdiction principles in the federal court system.

| **Internet Solutions Corp. v. Marshall** | 2008 U.S. Dist. LEXIS 28261 (M.D. Fla. 2008) |

Internet Solutions Corp. (ISC), a Nevada corporation, has its principal place of business in Orlando, Florida. ISC, which operates various employment recruiting and Internet advertising Web sites, sued Tabatha Marshall, a resident of the State of Washington, in the U.S. District Court for the Middle District of Florida. In its lawsuit, ISC alleged that on her Web site, Marshall made false and defamatory statements asserting that ISC engaged in ongoing criminal activity, scams, and phishing. According to ISC, these statements caused injury to ISC's business in Florida. Marshall filed a motion to dismiss the case because, in her view, neither subject matter nor in personam jurisdiction existed.

Conway, District Judge

[Marshall's motion to dismiss presents the question] whether the district court has subject matter jurisdiction in the case at bar [and the question] whether the district court can exercise in personam jurisdiction over the nonresident defendant pursuant to [Florida law] and the Due Process Clause of the U.S. Constitution.

Pursuant to 28 U.S.C. § 1332, subject matter jurisdiction is proper in federal court when there is a matter in controversy between citizens of different states and . . . "the matter in controversy exceeds the sum or value of $75,000." [The damages sought by ISC make this a] case involv[ing] a controversy that exceeds the sum or value of $75,000. ISC is a Nevada corporation, which has its principal place of business in Orlando, Florida. Marshall is a private individual who resides in the State of Washington. Therefore, pursuant to 28 U.S.C. § 1332, this court has subject matter jurisdiction based on diversity of citizenship.

[The court now turns to the in personam jurisdiction question.] A district court's determination of in personam jurisdiction over a nonresident defendant generally entails a two-part inquiry. First, the court must determine whether the exercise of jurisdiction is appropriate under [the state's] long-arm statute. Second, the court must determine whether there are sufficient minimum contacts with the forum state to satisfy the Due Process Clause of the U.S. Constitution and traditional notions of fair play and substantial justice. See *International Shoe Co. v. Washington,* 326 U.S. 310 (1945). [Both parts of the] two-part inquiry must be satisfied before the court can properly exercise in personam jurisdiction over a nonresident defendant.

[Florida's long-arm statute and precedent cases indicate that in personam jurisdiction] may be found in certain instances where an out-of-state defendant commits a tort that produces an injury in Florida. ISC bears the burden of establishing a prima facie case of in personam jurisdiction through the long-arm statute. ISC contends that Marshall committed tortious conduct through her website, which caused injury to ISC's business in Florida. Specifically, ISC alleges that Marshall made false and defamatory statements on her website which harmed ISC's reputation in the community, deterred third persons from associating with ISC, and [adversely affected] ISC's business revenues.

Marshall has not adequately rebutted ISC's allegation of long-arm jurisdiction based on the claim that the tort was committed in Florida and that injury resulted in Florida. [An affidavit submitted by Marshall] explains the lack of minimum contacts that Marshall has with Florida, asserts that Marshall has never done business in Florida, denies directing any communications into Florida, and denies committing any tort in Florida. The affidavit does not discuss the issue of an injury resulting to ISC's business in Florida. It does not adequately refute that a tort was committed in Florida. [In] simply conclud[ing] that Marshall did not commit any tort in the State of Florida[,] Marshall's affidavit is insufficient to shift to ISC the burden of producing evidence supporting jurisdiction.

Therefore, the court finds that ISC has satisfied its [first] burden and assumes that there is jurisdiction under Florida's long-arm statute for the purposes of deciding the instant motion. However, the in personam jurisdiction inquiry does not end here. The court must now assess whether ISC has established the existence of sufficient minimum contacts and whether Due Process is otherwise satisfied.

[D]ue process requires that in order to subject a defendant to a judgment in personam [in a state in which she does not reside, she must] have certain minimum contacts with [the forum state, so that] the maintenance of the suit does not offend traditional notions of fair play and substantial justice. See *International Shoe.* The plaintiff bears the burden of establishing . . . that the constitutional requirement of minimum contacts has been satisfied.

[In *Posner v. Essex Ins. Co.,* 178 F.3d 1209 (11th Cir. 1999), the U.S. Court of Appeals for the Eleventh Circuit] adopted a three-part test to determine whether the minimum contacts requirement has been satisfied. First, "the contacts must be related to the plaintiff's cause of action." Second, "the contacts must involve some act by which the defendant purposefully avails itself of the privilege of conducting activities within the forum." Third, "the defendant's contacts with the forum must be such that the defendant should reasonably anticipate being haled into court there."

ISC contends that Marshall committed tortious acts by posting defamatory comments on her website and targeting individuals in Florida. ISC further alleges that Marshall's conduct resulted in contact or communications "into" Florida. However, "the minimum contacts must be 'purposeful' contacts." [Case citation omitted.] In *Calder v. Jones,* the United States Supreme Court found that an alleged single tortious act by a National Enquirer editor and reporter in Florida was sufficient to satisfy minimum contacts with the forum state of California. *Calder v. Jones,* 465 US 783, 789–790, 104 S. Ct. 1482, 79 L. Ed. 2d 804 (1984). The two National Enquirer employees were Florida residents who were sued in California for libel. The court reasoned that the writers purposefully availed themselves by specifically targeting a California audience, making large distributions into California, and publishing articles about a California resident. The court further explained that the alleged tortious conduct was purposeful and calculated to cause injury in California, and therefore the editors must have reasonably anticipated being haled into a California court.

Unlike *Calder,* in the case at bar there is no evidence that Marshall specifically targeted Florida residents. Marshall's website was not only made available to Florida residents, but the website was equally accessible to persons in all states. Under the *Calder* analysis, even if Marshall's alleged tortious conduct occurred or resulted in injury in Florida, the single tortious act would not be sufficient to satisfy minimum contacts absent a showing of purposeful availment. According to Marshall's affidavit, her contacts with Florida were nearly nonexistent. Marshall [states] that she does not own or lease property in the state of Florida, does not operate a business of any kind, and has only visited Florida on one occasion (which had no connection to her website). ISC has not provided evidence to the contrary. Besides, the website postings do not establish any Florida-specific postings or conduct by Marshall, [who] denies directing any communications into Florida.

In addition, the postings do not specifically mention Florida or its residents nor do they amount to purposeful availment. "The requirement for purposeful minimum contacts helps [to] ensure that non-residents have fair warning that a particular activity may subject them to litigation within the forum." [Case citation omitted.] Marshall's conduct is distinguishable from the purposeful contacts made in the *Calder* case. Marshall has not made Florida-specific contacts. The mere fact that Marshall's website was accessible to residents everywhere and a resident of Florida responded does not amount to purposeful availment.

ISC contends that Marshall should have known that her conduct would subject her to litigation in the court's jurisdiction. The fact that Marshall posted comments on her website which were accessible to residents everywhere does not indicate that Marshall could reasonably anticipate being haled into a Florida court. Based on the information presented, there is nothing to support [a conclusion] that Marshall should reasonably anticipate being called before a Florida court to answer for her alleged conduct.

Marshall's affidavit rebuts ISC's claim that there is jurisdiction under the minimum contacts requirement. [The] affidavit . . . was sufficient to shift the burden back to ISC[, which] did not refute or provide supporting evidence that there were minimum contacts. [Because] ISC has failed to meet its burden of establishing sufficient minimum contacts, . . . the court determines that exercising in personam jurisdiction over Marshall would not comport with the requirements of Due Process or the traditional notions of fair play and substantial justice. [Therefore,] in personam jurisdiction over the nonresident defendant in this court would be improper.

Defendant's motion granted and case dismissed.

Concurrent Jurisdiction and Removal The federal district courts have *exclusive jurisdiction* over some matters. Patent cases, for example, must be litigated in the federal system. Often, however, federal district courts have *concurrent jurisdiction* with state courts—meaning that both state and federal courts have jurisdiction over the case. For example, a plaintiff might assert state court in personam jurisdiction over an out-of-state defendant or might sue in a federal district court under that court's diversity jurisdiction. A state court, moreover, may sometimes decide cases involving federal questions. Where concurrent jurisdiction exists and the plaintiff opts for a state court, the defendant has the option to *remove* the case to an appropriate federal district court, assuming the defendant acts promptly.

Specialized Federal Courts The federal court system also includes certain specialized federal courts, including the Court of Federal Claims (which hears claims against the United States), the Court of International Trade (which is concerned with tariff, customs, import, and other trade matters), the Bankruptcy Courts (which operate as adjuncts of the district courts), and the Tax Court (which reviews certain IRS determinations). Usually, the decisions of these courts can be appealed to a federal court of appeals.

Federal Courts of Appeals The U.S. courts of appeals do not engage in fact-finding. Instead, they review only the legal conclusions reached by lower federal courts. As Figure 1 shows, there are 13 circuit courts of appeals: 11 numbered circuits covering several states each; a District of Columbia circuit; and a separate federal circuit.

Except for the Court of Appeals for the Federal Circuit, the most important function of the U.S. courts of appeals is to hear appeals from decisions of the federal district courts. Appeals from a district court ordinarily proceed to the court of appeals for that district court's region. Appeals from the District Court for the Southern District of New York, for example, go to the Second Circuit Court of Appeals. The courts of appeals also hear

Figure 1   The Thirteen Federal Judicial Circuits

First Circuit (*Boston, Mass.*) Maine, Massachusetts, New Hampshire, Puerto Rico, Rhode Island	**Second Circuit** (*New York, N.Y*.) Connecticut, New York, Vermont	**Third Circuit** (*Philadelphia, Pa.*) Delaware, New Jersey, Pennsylvania, Virgin Islands	**Fourth Circuit** (*Richmond, Va.*) Maryland, North Carolina, South Carolina, Virginia, West Virginia
Fifth Circuit (*New Orleans, La.*) Louisiana, Mississippi, Texas	**Sixth Circuit** (*Cincinnati, Ohio*) Kentucky, Michigan, Ohio, Tennessee	**Seventh Circuit** (*Chicago, Ill.*) Illinois, Indiana, Wisconsin	**Eighth Circuit** (*St. Louis, Mo.*) Arkansas, Iowa, Minnesota, Missouri, Nebraska, North Dakota, South Dakota
Ninth Circuit (*San Francisco, Calif.*) Alaska, Arizona, California, Guam, Hawaii, Idaho, Montana, Nevada, Northern Mariana Islands, Oregon, Washington	**Tenth Circuit** (*Denver, Colo.*) Colorado, Kansas, New Mexico, Oklahoma, Utah, Wyoming	**Eleventh Circuit** (*Atlanta, Ga.*) Alabama, Florida, Georgia	**District of Columbia Circuit** (*Washington, D.C.*)

Federal Circuit (*Washington, D.C.*)

appeals from the Tax Court, from many administrative agency decisions, and from some Bankruptcy Court decisions. The Court of Appeals for the Federal Circuit hears a wide variety of specialized appeals, including some patent and trademark matters, Court of Federal Claims decisions, and decisions by the Court of International Trade.

The U.S. Supreme Court

The United States Supreme Court, the highest court in the land, is mainly an appellate court. It therefore considers only questions of law when it decides appeals from the federal courts of appeals and the highest state courts.[4] Today, most appealable decisions from these courts fall within the Supreme Court's *certiorari* jurisdiction, under which the Court has discretion whether to hear the appeal. The Court hears only a small percentage of the many appeals it is asked to decide under its certiorari jurisdiction.

Nearly all appeals from the federal courts of appeals are within the Court's certiorari jurisdiction. Appeals from the highest state courts are within the certiorari jurisdiction when (1) the validity of any treaty or federal statute has been questioned; (2) any state statute is challenged as repugnant to federal law; or (3) any title, right, privilege, or immunity is claimed under federal law. The Supreme Court usually defers to the states' highest courts on questions of state law and does not hear appeals from those courts if the case involves only such questions.

In certain rare situations, the U.S. Supreme Court has **original jurisdiction,** which means that it acts as a trial court. The Supreme Court has *original and exclusive* jurisdiction over all controversies between two or more states. It has *original,* but not exclusive, jurisdiction over cases involving foreign ambassadors, ministers, and like parties, controversies between the United States and a state, and cases in which a state proceeds against citizens of another state or against aliens.

---

[4]In special situations that do not often arise, the Supreme Court will hear appeals directly from the federal district courts.

The in personam jurisdiction issues addressed earlier in the chapter also arise when a resident of the United States initiates legal action in the United States against a defendant from another country. *Benton v. Cameco Corp.,* 375 F.3d 1070 (10th Cir. 2004), furnishes a useful example.

A Colorado resident, Oren Benton, and a Canadian firm, Cameco Corp., entered into a Memorandum of Understanding (MOU) that called for Benton to purchase uranium from Cameco for purposes of resale. The MOU also set forth the key terms of a planned joint venture involving uranium trading activities. The transactions contemplated by the MOU did not take place, however, because Cameco's board of directors did not approve them. Benton later sued Cameco in federal district court in Colorado, asserting claims for breach of contract and tortious interference with existing and prospective business relationships. After determining that Cameco did not have sufficient contacts with Colorado to allow the court to exercise in personam jurisdiction over the Canadian firm, the district court granted Cameco's motion to dismiss. On appeal, the U.S. Court of Appeals for the Tenth Circuit concluded that Cameco did have the requisite minimum contacts with Colorado but that the district court's dismissal should be affirmed anyway, because "traditional notions of fair play and substantial justice" counseled against an exercise of in personam jurisdiction over Cameco.

The Tenth Circuit regarded the minimum contacts issue as a close call but based its conclusion that minimum contacts existed between Cameco and the state of Colorado on the basis of this combination of facts: the Canadian firm's supposed contract with a Colorado resident, Benton; the separate transactions that Cameco had engaged in with Benton during earlier years; the parties' contract negotiations, which, through the use of the telephone and mailed communications, had a connection with Colorado; the further connection with Colorado that would have resulted if contract performance had occurred; and the fact that Cameco sent representatives to Colorado to check on Benton's business. Because Benton's claim arose out of Cameco's contacts with Colorado, the facts just noted would have been sufficient to support in personam jurisdiction of the specific variety pursuant to Colorado's long-arm statute, if not for another critical requirement. (Specific jurisdiction is discussed more fully in the *Bombliss* case, which appears earlier in the chapter.) The other requirement was that an attempt to exert in personam jurisdiction over a nonresident defendant must be consistent with "traditional notions of fair play and substantial justice." *See International Shoe Co. v. Washington,* 326 U.S. 310 (U.S. Sup. Ct. 1945); *Asahi Metal Industry Co. v. Superior Court,* 480 U.S. 102 (U.S. Sup. Ct. 1987). In order to make the necessary determination regarding "fair play and substantial justice," the Tenth Circuit applied five factors drawn from precedent cases.

First, the court considered the burden on Cameco of having to litigate the case in what was, for the Canadian firm, a foreign forum. Important when a U.S. plaintiff files suit in the plaintiff's home state or federal district against a U.S. defendant from a different state, this factor assumes added significance when a defendant from another country is sued in the United States. In the latter situation, the court stressed, "'great care and reserve should be exercised' before [in personam] jurisdiction is exercised over the defendant" (quoting *Asahi*). The Tenth Circuit regarded the burden on Cameco as substantial, given that the firm's principal offices were in Saskatchewan, it had no offices, property, or employees in Colorado, and it was not licensed to do business there. If in personam jurisdiction were held to exist in this case, Cameco's officers and employees would not only have to travel to Colorado for trial but also litigate the case before judges who were unfamiliar with Canadian law (which the parties, in the MOU, had agreed would be controlling). The first factor, therefore, weighed against a conclusion that in personam jurisdiction should exist as to Cameco.

Second, the Tenth Circuit examined the forum state's interest in resolving the dispute. Although Colorado had an interest in providing a dispute-resolution forum for a Colorado resident (Benton), the parties' agreement that Canadian law would govern their dispute meant that the second factor did not substantially favor either party.

Third, the court considered whether the plaintiff could receive convenient and effective relief in a forum other than the U.S. court he chose. Because Canadian law governed the parties' dispute and because there was no showing that the inconvenience of traveling to Canada for trial would cause undue hardship to Benton, the Tenth Circuit concluded that the third factor favored Cameco and weighed against an exercise of in personam jurisdiction by the U.S. court.

Fourth, the court focused on whether Colorado was the most efficient place for the litigation to be conducted. The court observed that many of the witnesses in the dispute would be affiliated with Cameco and would thus be located in Canada, that the supposed wrong—the Cameco board's failure to approve the transactions contemplated by the MOU—occurred in Canada, and that Canadian law would govern the case. The Tenth Circuit therefore concluded that it would not be more efficient to litigate the case in Colorado than in Canada.

Fifth (and finally), the court considered whether an exercise of in personam jurisdiction would affect important Canadian policy interests. The Tenth Circuit noted that precedent cases required it to look carefully at whether allowing the case to proceed in the U.S. court would interfere with Canada's sovereignty. The court regarded an exertion of in personam jurisdiction over Cameco as likely to affect Canadian policy interests and interfere with Canada's sovereignty, mainly because Cameco was a Canadian firm and Canadian law was to govern the dispute. With most of the five "reasonableness factors" operating in Cameco's favor, the Tenth Circuit held that even though Cameco possessed minimum contacts with Colorado, "an exercise of in personam jurisdiction over Cameco would offend traditional notions of fair play and substantial justice."

Civil Procedure

Civil procedure is the set of legal rules establishing how a civil lawsuit proceeds from beginning to end.[5] Because civil procedure sometimes varies with the jurisdiction in question,[6] the following presentation summarizes the most widely accepted rules governing civil cases in state and federal courts. Knowledge of these basic procedural matters will be useful if you become involved in a civil lawsuit and will help you understand the cases in this text.

In any civil case, the *adversary system* is at work. Through their attorneys, the litigants take contrary positions before a judge and possibly a jury. To win a civil case, the plaintiff must prove each element of his, her, or its claim by a *preponderance of the evidence.*[7] This standard of proof requires the plaintiff to show that the greater weight of the evidence—by credibility, not quantity—supports the existence of each element. In other words, the plaintiff must convince the fact-finder that the existence of each factual element is more probable than its nonexistence. The attorney for each party presents his or her client's version of the facts, tries to convince the judge or jury that this version is true, and attempts to rebut conflicting factual allegations by the other party. Each attorney also seeks to persuade the court that his or her reading of the law is correct.

Service of the Summons
A **summons** notifies the defendant that he, she, or it is being sued. The summons typically names the plaintiff and states the time within which the defendant must enter an *appearance* in court (usually through an attorney). In most jurisdictions, it is accompanied by a copy of the plaintiff's complaint (which is described below).

The summons is usually served on the defendant by an appropriate public official after the plaintiff has filed her case. To ensure that the defendant is properly notified, statutes, court rules, and constitutional due process guarantees set standards for proper service of the summons. For example, personal delivery to the defendant almost always meets these standards. Many jurisdictions also permit the summons to be left at the defendant's home or place of business. Service to corporations often may be accomplished by delivery of the summons to the firm's managing agent. Many state long-arm statutes permit out-of-state defendants to be served by registered mail. Although inadequate service of process may sometimes defeat the plaintiff's claim, the defendant who participates in the case without making a prompt objection to the manner of service will be deemed to have waived the objection.

The Pleadings
The **pleadings** are the documents the parties file with the court when they first state their respective claims and defenses. They include the **complaint,** the **answer,** and, in some jurisdictions, the **reply.** Traditionally, the pleadings' main function was to define and limit the issues to be decided by the court. Only those issues raised in the pleadings were considered part of the case, amendments to the pleadings were seldom permitted, and litigants were firmly bound by allegations or admissions contained in the pleadings. Although many jurisdictions retain some of these rules, most have relaxed them significantly. The main reason is the modern view of the purpose of pleading rules: that their aim is less to define the issues for trial than to give the parties general notice of each other's claims and defenses.

The Complaint The complaint states the plaintiff's claim in separate, numbered paragraphs. It must allege sufficient facts to show that the plaintiff would be entitled to legal relief and to give the defendant reasonable notice of the nature of the plaintiff's claim. The complaint also must state the remedy requested.

The Answer Unless the defendant makes a successful motion to dismiss (described below), he must file an answer to the plaintiff's complaint within a designated time after service of the complaint. The amount of time is set by applicable law, with 30 to 45 days being typical. The answer responds to the complaint paragraph by paragraph, with an admission or denial of each of the plaintiff's allegations.

An answer may also include an **affirmative defense** to the claim asserted in the complaint. A successful affirmative defense enables the defendant to win the case even if all the allegations in the complaint are true and, by themselves, would have entitled the plaintiff to recover. For example, suppose that the plaintiff bases her lawsuit on a contract that she alleges the defendant has breached. The defendant's answer may admit or deny the existence of the contract or the assertion that the defendant breached it. In addition, the answer may make assertions that, if proven, would provide the defendant an affirmative defense on the basis of fraud committed by the plaintiff during the contract negotiation phase.

---

[5]Criminal procedure is discussed in Chapter 5.

[6]In the following discussion, the term *jurisdiction* refers to one of the 50 states, the District of Columbia, or the federal government.

[7]In a criminal case, however, the government must prove the elements of the alleged crime beyond a reasonable doubt. This standard of proof is discussed in Chapter 5.

Furthermore, the answer may contain a **counterclaim.**[8] A counterclaim is a *new* claim by the defendant arising from the matters stated in the complaint. Unlike an affirmative defense, it is not merely an attack on the plaintiff's claim, but is the defendant's attempt to obtain legal relief. In addition to using fraud as an affirmative defense to a plaintiff's contract claim, for example, a defendant might counterclaim for damages caused by that fraud.

The Reply   In some jurisdictions, the plaintiff is allowed or required to respond to an affirmative defense or a counterclaim by making a reply. The reply is the plaintiff's point-by-point response to the allegations in the answer or counterclaim. In jurisdictions that do not allow a reply to an answer, the defendant's new allegations are automatically denied. Usually, however, a plaintiff who wishes to contest a counterclaim must file a reply to it.

Motion to Dismiss   Sometimes it is evident from
the complaint or the pleadings that the plaintiff does not have a valid claim. In such a situation, it would be wasteful for the litigation to proceed further. The procedural device for ending the case at this early stage is commonly called the **motion to dismiss.** This motion often is made after the plaintiff has filed her complaint. A similar motion allowed by some jurisdictions, the **motion for judgment on the pleadings,** normally occurs after the pleadings have been completed. A successful motion to dismiss means that the defendant wins the case. If the motion fails, the case proceeds.

The motion to dismiss may be made on various grounds—for example, inadequate service of process or lack of jurisdiction. The most important type of motion to dismiss, however, is the motion to dismiss for failure to state a claim upon which relief can be granted, sometimes called the **demurrer.** This motion basically says "So what?" to the factual allegations in the complaint. It asserts that the plaintiff cannot recover even if all of his allegations are true because no rule of law entitles him to win on those facts. Suppose that Potter sues Davis on the theory that Davis's bad breath is a form of "olfactory pollution" entitling Potter to recover damages. Potter's

complaint describes Davis's breath and the distress it causes Potter in great detail. Even if all of Potter's factual allegations are true, Davis's motion to dismiss almost certainly will succeed. There is no rule of law allowing the "victim" of another person's bad breath to recover damages from that person.

Discovery   When a civil case begins, litigants do
not always possess all of the facts they need to prove their claims or establish their defenses. To help litigants obtain the facts and to narrow and clarify the issues for trial, the state and federal court systems permit each party to a civil case to exercise **discovery** rights. The discovery phase of a lawsuit normally begins when the pleadings have been completed. Each party is entitled to request information from the other party by utilizing the forms of discovery described in this section. Moreover, for civil cases pending in federal court, the Federal Rules of Civil Procedure require each party to provide the other party certain basic information at an early point in the case, even though the other party may not have made a formal discovery request.

Discovery is available for information that is not subject to a recognized legal privilege and is relevant to the case or likely to lead to other information that may be relevant. Information may be subject to discovery even if it would not ultimately be admissible at trial under the legal rules of evidence. The scope of permissible discovery is thus extremely broad. The broad scope of discovery stems from a policy decision to minimize the surprise element in litigation and to give each party the opportunity to become fully informed regarding facts known by the opposing party. Each party may then formulate trial strategies on the basis of that knowledge.

The *deposition* is one of the most frequently employed forms of discovery. In a deposition, one party's attorney conducts an oral examination of the other party or of a likely witness (usually one identified with the other party). The questions asked by the examining attorney and the answers given by the deponent—the person being examined—are taken down by a court reporter. The deponent is under oath, just as he or she would be if testifying at trial, even though the deposition occurs on a pretrial basis and is likely to take place at an attorney's office or at some location other than a courtroom. Some depositions are videotaped.

Interrogatories and *requests for admissions* are among the other commonly utilized forms of discovery. Interrogatories are written questions directed by the plaintiff to the defendant, or vice versa. The litigant on whom interrogatories are served must provide written

---

[8]In appropriate instances, a defendant also may file a *cross claim* against another defendant in the plaintiff's suit, or a *third-party complaint* against a party who was not named as a defendant in the plaintiff's complaint.

answers, under oath, within a time period prescribed by applicable law (30 days being typical). Requests for admissions are one party's written demand that the other party admit or deny, in writing, certain statements of supposed fact or of the application of law to fact, within a time period prescribed by law (30 days again being typical). The other party's failure to respond with an admission or denial during the legal time period is deemed an admission of the statements' truth or accuracy.

Requests for production of documents or other physical items (e.g., videotapes, photographs, and the like) are a discovery form employed by the parties in many civil cases. What about e-mail and other electronically stored information? For a discussion of the discoverability of such items, see the Cyberlaw in Action box that appears later in the chapter.

When the issues in a case make the opposing litigant's physical or mental condition relevant, a party may seek discovery in yet another way by filing a *motion for a court order requiring* that the opponent undergo *a physical or mental examination.* With the exception of the discovery form mentioned in the previous sentence, discovery generally takes place without a need for court orders or other judicial supervision. Courts become involved, however, if a party objects to a discovery request on the basis of privilege or other recognized legal ground, desires an order compelling a noncomplying litigant to respond to a discovery request, or seeks sanctions on a party who refused to comply with a legitimate discovery request or abusively invoked the discovery process. In the *Allstate* case, the court rejects Allstate's objections to the opposing parties' request for documents from the insurer's files.

Allstate Indemnity Co. v. Ruiz   2005 Fla. LEXIS 612 (Fla. Sup. Ct. 2005)

One month after securing insurance coverage from Allstate Indemnity Co. for their Chevrolet Blazer, Joaquin and Paulina Ruiz purchased an Oldsmobile Cutlass. They instructed Allstate agent Paul Cobb to add that vehicle to the policy. Cobb added the Cutlass to the policy but mistakenly deleted the Blazer. The Ruizes were not notified that the Blazer was no longer covered under their insurance policy.

Joaquin Ruiz was later involved in an accident while driving the Blazer. When the Ruizes submitted a claim for collision coverage, Allstate denied payment, asserting that the Blazer was not covered under the policy. The Ruizes filed suit, alleging that Cobb and Allstate had been negligent in deleting the Blazer from the insurance policy, and that Allstate had engaged in bad faith and unfair claim settlement practices in violation of a Florida statute. After the filing of the lawsuit, Allstate admitted its obligation to provide collision coverage. Even though the basic coverage issue was resolved, the bad faith claim remained pending.

In connection with the bad faith claim, the Ruizes sought discovery of certain documents, including Allstate's claim and investigative file and materials, Allstate internal manuals, and Cobb's file regarding the bad faith claim. Allstate refused to supply the requested documents, so the Ruizes asked the trial court to compel production of them. After reviewing the documents sought by the Ruizes, the trial judge ordered that the documents be provided to them because the documents contained relevant information regarding Allstate's handling of the underlying insurance claim. The judge also determined that the requested documents did not constitute work product or attorney-client communications and thus were not exempt from disclosure during the discovery process. (Because communications between an attorney and his or her client are privileged, they are not subject to discovery. Work product is a term used to describe documents and materials prepared by an attorney and his or her client in anticipation of litigation. In general, work product is not subject to discovery.)

Allstate appealed to Florida's intermediate court of appeals, arguing that the dispute over the Ruizes' insurance coverage was immediately apparent when Allstate refused to make payment, that litigation was anticipated at all pertinent times, and that all of the material sought by the Ruizes was nondiscoverable work product. The appellate court concluded that several requested items were not protected work product and therefore were properly discoverable, including Cobb's statement of January 7, 1997; computer diaries and entries from the date Joaquin Ruiz reported the accident on December 28, 1996, through January 10, 1997; and a January 7, 1997, memorandum from an Allstate insurance adjustor to her boss. However, the appellate court determined that the balance of the documents sought by the Ruizes were prepared by Allstate in anticipation of litigation and were thus nondiscoverable work product. Both parties were dissatisfied with the appellate court's decision, the Ruizes because some of what they sought was held nondiscoverable and Allstate because some of what it sought to withhold was held discoverable. The Supreme Court of Florida granted Allstate's request for review.

Lewis, Justice

The instant action causes us to review and revisit previous decisions regarding discovery issues that arise in bad faith insurance litigation. Section 624.155 of the Florida Statutes was designed and intended to provide a civil remedy for any person damaged by an insurer's conduct, including "not attempting in good faith to settle claims when, under all the circumstances, it could and should have done so, had it acted fairly and honestly toward its insured and with due regard for her or his interests." Fla. Stat. § 624.155(1)(b)(1). As implied by the statute, bad faith actions do not exist in a vacuum. A necessary prerequisite for any bad faith action is an underlying claim for coverage or benefits or an action for damages which the insured alleges was handled in bad faith by the insurer.

It is precisely this two-tiered nature of bad faith actions that engenders the discovery battles so often waged in bad faith litigation, and is at the heart of the matter now before the Court. Allstate asserts that work product protection should extend to and envelop the entire claim file and all files, whatever the name, in the underlying coverage or damage matter or dispute, including an extension into any bad faith litigation which may flow from the processing or litigating of the underlying claim. The insureds and injured third parties, on the other hand, often and logically seek disclosure of actual events in the claim processing as reflected in the studies, notes, memoranda, and other documentation comprising the claim file type material because such information is certainly material and relevant, if not crucial, to any intelligent and just resolution of the bad faith litigation. They assert that this is precisely the evidence upon which a "bad faith" determination is made. As the insureds succinctly posit, how is one to ever determine whether an insurance company has processed, analyzed, or litigated a claim in a fair, forthright, and good faith manner if access is totally denied to the underlying file materials that reflect how the matter was processed and contain the direct evidence of whether the claim was processed in "good" or "bad" faith? In other words, it is asserted that the claim litigation file material constitutes the best and only evidence of an insurer's conduct.

To resolve this bad faith discovery dispute, we must first review the nature of bad faith actions and case law pertaining to discovery. There are two distinct but very similar types of bad faith actions that may be initiated against an insurer: first-party and third-party. Third-party bad faith actions have a long and established pedigree, having been recognized at common law in this state since 1938. Third-party bad faith actions arose in response to the argument that there was a practice in the insurance industry of rejecting without sufficient investigation or consideration claims presented by third parties against an insured, thereby exposing the insured individual to judgments exceeding the coverage limits of the policy while the insurer

remained protected by a policy limit. With no actionable remedy, insureds in this state and elsewhere were left personally responsible for the excess judgment amount. This concern gave life to the concept that insurance companies had an obligation of good faith and fair dealing. Florida courts recognized common law third-party bad faith actions in part because the insurers had the power and authority to litigate or settle any claim, and thus owed the insured a corresponding duty of good faith and fair dealing in handling these third-party claims.

Traditionally and historically, the courts in this state did not, however, recognize a corresponding common law first-party action that would protect insured individuals and enable them to seek redress of harm against their insurers for the wrongful processing or denial of their own first-party claims or failure to deal fairly in claims processing. This void existed notwithstanding that insurers had the same incentive to deny an insured's first-party claim as may have existed with regard to the refusal to settle a claim presented by a third party against an insured. In both contexts, the insurer's ultimate responsibility could not exceed the policy limits in the absence of a viable bad faith cause of action.

However, with the enactment of § 624.155 in 1982, . . . the Florida Legislature resolved this inequity and recognized the power disparity as it created a statutory first-party bad faith cause of action for first-party insureds, thereby eliminating the disparity in the treatment of insureds aggrieved by an act of bad faith on the part of their insurers regardless of the nature of the type of claim presented. [T]his statutory remedy essentially extended the duty of an insurer to act in good faith and deal fairly in those instances where an insured seeks first-party coverage or benefits under a policy of insurance. It was pursuant to this provision that the Ruizes filed the statutory first-party bad faith action at issue in the instant proceeding.

Even though the enactment of § 624.155 ushered out the distinction between first- and third-party statutory claims for the purposes of initiating bad faith actions, some court decisions have continued to draw inappropriate distinctions in defining the parameters of discovery in those bad faith actions. In the context of both statutory and common law third-party bad faith actions for failure to settle a claim, discovery of the insurer's underlying claim file type material is permitted over the objections of work product protection.

By contrast, the rule permitting discovery of materials contained in claim type files in third-party bad faith actions has not been consistently applied in first-party bad faith actions. It appears that this inconsistency has resulted from and been engendered by a misdescription of the nature of the parties' relationship in first-party actions as being totally adversarial, an outdated pre-statutory analysis, as opposed to applying the responsibilities that have traditionally flowed in the third-party context, which are now codified for first-party actions. The Legislature has mandated that insurance companies act in good faith and deal fairly with insureds regardless of the nature of the claim presented, whether it be a first-party claim or one arising from a claim against an insured by a third party.

[A]ny distinction between first- and third-party bad faith actions with regard to discovery purposes is unjustified and without support under § 624.155 and creates an overly formalistic distinction between substantively identical claims. [S]ection 624.155 very clearly provides first-party claimants, upon compliance with statutory requirements, the identical opportunity to pursue bad faith claims against insurers as has been the situation in connection with third-party claims for decades at common law. The Legislature has clearly chosen to impose on insurance companies a duty to use good faith and fair dealing in processing and litigating the claims of their own insureds as insurers have had in dealing with third-party claims. Thus, there is no basis to apply different discovery rules to the substantively identical causes of action.

[T]o continue to recognize any such distinction and restriction would not only hamper but would impair the viability of first-party bad faith actions in a manner that would thwart the legislative intent in creating the right of action in the first instance. Just as we have concluded in the context of third-party actions, we conclude that the claim file type material presents virtually the only source of direct evidence with regard to the essential issue of the insurance company's handling of the insured's claim. Given the Legislature's recognition of the need to require that insurance companies deal fairly and act in good faith and the decision to provide insureds the right to institute first-party bad faith actions against their insurers, there is simply no logical or legally tenable basis upon which to deny access to the very information that is necessary to advance such action but also necessary to fairly evaluate the allegations of bad faith—information to which they would have unfettered access in the third-party bad faith context. We therefore hold, as does the substantial weight of authority elsewhere on the question, that the claim file is and was properly held producible in this first-party case.

[W]e determine that the [court of appeals] was correct in affirming the trial court's decision to compel the production of [the documents the trial court ordered to be produced]. We have reservations, however, with regard to the balance of the [appellate] court's determination, which reversed the trial court's decision to compel the production of other [requested documents]. Our review of the record reveals that [the other requested] documents included handwritten notes evaluating coverage issues, internal letters and memoranda drafted in September of 1997 regarding coverage issues, and other items that do appear to be relevant, discoverable, [and] not entitled to protection, and [that appear] to pertain to Allstate's conduct with regard to the coverage dispute. While we remand . . . for a careful review of each document requested in light of this holding, such documentation would appear to be freely discoverable in the bad faith action. In accordance with our decision today, work product protection that may otherwise be afforded to documents prepared in anticipation of litigation of the underlying coverage dispute does not automatically operate to protect such documents from discovery in the ensuing, or accompanying, bad faith action.

Court of appeals decision denying production of certain requested documents reversed, and case remanded for further proceedings.

Documents and similar items obtained through the discovery process may be used at trial if they fall within the legal rules governing admissible evidence. The same is true of discovery material such as answers to interrogatories and responses to requests for admissions. If a party or other witness who testifies at trial offers testimony that differs from her statements during a deposition, the deposition may be used to impeach her—that is, to cast doubt on her trial testimony. A litigant may offer as evidence the deposition of a witness who died prior to trial or meets the legal standard of unavailability to testify in person. In addition, selected parts or all of the deposition of the opposing party or of certain persons affiliated with the opposing party may be used as evidence at trial, regardless of whether such a deponent is available to testify "live."

Participation in the discovery process may require significant expenditures of time and effort, not only by the attorneys but also by the parties and their employees. Parties who see themselves as too busy to comply with discovery requests may need to think seriously about whether they should remain a party to pending litigation. The discovery process may also trigger significant ethical issues, such as those associated with uses of discovery requests simply to harass or cause expense to the other party, or the issues faced by one who does not wish to hand over legitimately sought material that may prove to be damaging to him or to his employer.

CYBERLAW IN ACTION

In recent years, the widespread uses of e-mail and information presented and stored in electronic form have raised questions about whether, in civil litigation, an opposing party's e-mails and electronic information are discoverable to the same extent as conventional written or printed documents. With the Federal Rules of Civil Procedure and comparable discovery rules applicable to state courts having been devised prior to the explosion in e-mail use and online activities, the rules' references to "documents" no doubt contemplated traditional on-paper items. Courts, however, frequently interpreted "documents" broadly, so as to include e-mails and certain electronic communications within the scope of what was discoverable.

Even so, greater clarity on the discoverability issue seemed warranted—especially as to electronic material that might be less readily classifiable than e-mails as "documents." Various states responded by updating their discovery rules to include electronic communications within the list of discoverable items. So did the Federal Judicial Conference. In Federal Rules of Civil Procedure amendments proposed by the Judicial Conference and ratified by Congress in 2006, "electronically stored information" became a separate category of discoverable material. The *electronically stored information (ESI)* category is broad enough to include e-mails and similar communications as well as electronic business records, Web pages, dynamic databases, and a host of other material existing in electronic form. So-called "E-Discovery" has become a standard feature of civil litigation because of the obvious value of having access to the opposing party's e-mails and other electronic communications.

Discovery regarding ESI occurs in largely the same manner as discovery regarding conventional documents. The party seeking discovery of ESI serves a specific request for production on the other. The served party must provide the requested ESI if it is relevant, is not protected by a legal privilege (e.g., the attorney-client privilege), and is reasonably accessible. Court involvement becomes necessary only if the party from whom discovery is sought fails to comply or raises an objection on lack of relevance, privilege, or burdensomeness grounds. The Federal Rules allow the party seeking discovery of ESI to request not only copies of the requested material but also, where appropriate, the ability to test or sample the ESI. The party seeking discovery of ESI may also specify the form in which the requested copies should appear (e.g., hard copies, electronic files, searchable CD, direct access to database, etc.). The party from whom discovery is sought may object to the specified form, in which event the court may have to resolve the dispute. If the party requesting discovery does not specify a form, the other party must provide the requested electronic material in a form that is reasonably usable.

The Federal Rules provide that if the requested electronic material is "not reasonably accessible because of undue burden or cost," the party from whom discovery is sought need not provide the material. When an objection along those lines is filed, the court decides whether the objection is valid in light of the particular facts and circumstances. For instance, if requested e-mails now appear only on backup tapes and searching those tapes would require the expenditures of significant time, money, and effort, are the requested e-mails "not reasonably accessible because of undue burden or costs"? Perhaps, but perhaps not. The court will rule, based on the relevant situation. The court may deny the discovery request, uphold the discovery request, or condition the upholding of the discovery request on the requesting party's covering part or all of the costs incurred by the other party in retrieving the requested ESI and making it available. When a party fails or refuses to comply with a legitimate discovery request and the party seeking discovery of ESI has to secure a court order compelling the release of the requested material, the court may order the noncompliant party to pay the attorney's fees incurred by the requesting party in seeking the court order. If a recalcitrant party does not abide by a court order compelling discovery, the court may assess attorney's fees against that party and/or impose evidentiary or procedural sanctions such as barring that party from using certain evidence or from raising certain claims or defenses at trial.

The above discussion suggests that discovery requests regarding ESI may be extensive and broad-ranging, with logistical issues often attending those requests. In recognition of these realities, the Federal Rules seek to head off the sorts of disputes outlined in the previous paragraph by requiring the parties to civil litigation to meet, at least through their attorneys, soon after the case is filed. The meeting's goal is development of a discovery plan that outlines the parties' intentions regarding discovery of ESI and sets forth an agreement on such matters as the form in which the requested ESI will be provided. If the parties cannot agree on certain issues concerning discovery of ESI, the court will have to become involved to resolve the disputes.

The discoverability of electronically stored information makes it incumbent upon businesses to retain and preserve such material not only when litigation to which the material may be related has already been instituted, but also when potential litigation might reasonably be anticipated. Failure to preserve the electronic communications could give rise to allegations of evidence spoliation and, potentially, sanctions imposed by a court. (For further discussion of legal and ethical issues concerning spoliation, see the *Gribben* case in Chapter 1 and this chapter's Ethics in Action box.)

Finally, given the now-standard requests of plaintiffs and defendants that the opposing party provide access to relevant e-mails, one should not forget this important piece of advice: Do not say anything in an e-mail that you would not say in a formal written memo or in a conversation with someone. There is a too-frequent tendency to think that because e-mails tend to be informal in nature, one is somehow free to say things in an e-mail that he or she would not say in another setting. Many individuals and companies have learned the hard way that comments made in their e-mails or those of their employees proved to be damning evidence against them in litigation and thus helped the opposing parties to win the cases.

Summary Judgment

Summary judgment is a device for disposing of relatively clear cases without a trial. It differs from a demurrer because it involves factual determinations. To prevail, the party moving for a summary judgment must show that (1) there is no genuine issue of material (legally significant) fact, and (2) she is entitled to judgment as a matter of law. A moving party satisfies the first element of the test by using the pleadings, relevant discovery information, and affidavits (signed and sworn statements regarding matters of fact) to show that there is no real question about any significant fact. She satisfies the second element by showing that, given the established facts, the applicable law clearly mandates that she win.

Either or both parties may move for a summary judgment. If the court rules in favor of either party, that party wins the case. (The losing party may appeal, however.) If the parties' summary judgment motions are denied, the case proceeds to trial. The judge may also grant a partial summary judgment, which settles some issues in the case but leaves others to be decided at trial.

The Pretrial Conference

Depending on the jurisdiction, a **pretrial conference** is either mandatory or held at the discretion of the trial judge. At this conference, the judge meets informally with the attorneys for both litigants. He or she may try to get the attorneys to stipulate, or agree to, the resolution of certain issues in order to simplify the trial. The judge may also urge them to convince their clients to settle the case by coming to an agreement that eliminates the need for a trial. If the case is not settled, the judge enters a pretrial order that includes the attorneys' stipulations and any other agreements. Ordinarily, this order binds the parties for the remainder of the case.

The Trial

Once the case has been through discovery and has survived any pretrial motions, it is set for trial. The trial may be before a judge alone (i.e., a bench trial), in which case the judge makes findings of fact and reaches conclusions of law before issuing the court's judgment. If the right to a jury trial exists and either party demands one, the jury finds the facts. The judge, however, continues to determine legal questions.[9] During a pretrial jury screening process known as *voir dire,* biased potential jurors may be removed for cause. In addition, the attorney for each party is allowed a limited number of *peremptory challenges,* which allow him to remove potential jurors without having to show bias or other cause.

Trial Procedure   At either a bench trial or a jury trial, the attorneys for each party make opening statements that outline what they expect to prove. The plaintiff's attorney then presents her client's case-in-chief by calling witnesses and introducing documentary evidence (relevant documents and written records, e-mails, videotapes, and other evidence having a physical form). The plaintiff's attorney asks questions of her client's witnesses in a process known as direct examination. If the plaintiff is an individual person rather than a corporation, he is very likely to testify. The plaintiff's attorney may choose to call the defendant to testify. In this respect, civil cases differ from criminal cases, in which the Fifth Amendment's privilege against self-incrimination bars the government from compelling the defendant to testify. After the plaintiff's attorney completes direct examination of a witness, the defendant's lawyer cross-examines the witness. This may be followed by redirect examination by the plaintiff's attorney and recross examination by the defendant's lawyer.

Once the plaintiff's attorney has completed the presentation of her client's case, defense counsel presents his client's case-in-chief by offering documentary evidence

---

[9]The rules governing availability of a jury trial are largely beyond the scope of this text. The U.S. Constitution guarantees a jury trial in federal court cases "at common law" whose amount exceeds $20. Most states have similar constitutional provisions, often with a higher dollar amount. Also, Congress and the state legislatures have chosen to allow jury trials in various other cases.

Ethics in Action

The broad scope of discovery rights in a civil case will often entitle a party to seek and obtain copies of e-mails, records, memos, and other documents and electronically stored information from the opposing party's files. In many cases, some of the most favorable evidence for the plaintiff will have come from the defendant's files, and vice versa. If your firm is, or is likely to be, a party to civil litigation and you know that the firm's files contain materials that may be damaging to the firm in the litigation, you may be faced with the temptation to alter or destroy the potentially damaging items. This temptation poses serious ethical dilemmas. Is it morally defensible to change the content of records or documents on an after-the-fact basis, in order to lessen the adverse effect on your firm in pending or probable litigation? Is document destruction or e-mail deletion ethically justifiable when you seek to protect your firm's interests in a lawsuit?

If the ethical concerns are not sufficient by themselves to make you leery of involvement in document alteration or destruction, consider the potential legal consequences for yourself and your firm. The much-publicized collapse of the Enron Corporation in 2001 led to considerable scrutiny of the actions of the Arthur Andersen firm, which had provided auditing and consulting services to Enron. An Andersen partner, David Duncan, pleaded guilty to a criminal obstruction of justice charge that accused him of having destroyed, or having instructed Andersen employees to destroy, certain Enron-related records in order to thwart a Securities and Exchange Commission (SEC) investigation of Andersen. The U.S. Justice Department also launched an obstruction of justice prosecution against Andersen on the theory that the firm altered or destroyed records pertaining to Enron in order to impede the SEC investigation. In 2002, a jury found Andersen guilty of obstruction of justice. Although the Andersen conviction was overturned by the U.S. Supreme Court in 2005 because the trial judge's instructions to the jury on relevant principles of law had been impermissibly vague regarding the critical issue of criminal intent, a devastating effect on the firm had already taken place.

Of course, not all instances of document alteration or destruction will lead to criminal prosecution for obstruction of justice. Other consequences of a noncriminal but clearly severe nature may result, however, from document destruction that interferes with legitimate discovery requests in a civil case. In such instances, courts have broad discretionary authority to impose appropriate sanctions on the document-destroying party. These sanctions may include such remedies as court orders prohibiting the document-destroyer from raising certain claims or defenses in the lawsuit, instructions to the jury regarding the wrongful destruction of the documents, and court orders that the document-destroyer pay certain attorney's fees to the opposing party. The *Gribben* case, which appears in Chapter 1, discusses some of the consequences just mentioned—consequences that the *Gribben* court regarded as severe enough to make a separate tort claim for spoliation of evidence unnecessary.

What about the temptation to simply refuse to cooperate regarding an opposing party's lawful request for discovery regarding material in one's possession? Although a refusal to cooperate seems less blameworthy than destruction or alteration of documents, extreme instances of recalcitrance during the discovery process may cause a party to experience adverse consequences similar to those imposed on parties who destroy or alter documents. Recent litigation between Ronald Perelman and the Morgan Stanley firm provides an illustration. Perelman had sued Morgan Stanley on the theory that the investment bank participated with Sunbeam Corp. in a fraudulent scheme that supposedly induced him to sell Sunbeam his stake in another firm in return for Sunbeam shares whose value plummeted when Sunbeam collapsed. During the discovery phase of the case, Perelman had sought certain potentially relevant e-mails from Morgan Stanley's files. Morgan Stanley repeatedly failed and refused to provide this discoverable material, and in the process ignored court orders to provide the e-mails.

Eventually, a fed-up trial judge decided to impose sanctions for Morgan Stanley's wrongful conduct during the discovery process. The judge ordered that Perelman's contentions would be presumed to be correct and that the burden of proof would be shifted to Morgan Stanley, so that Morgan Stanley would have to disprove Perelman's allegations. In addition, the trial judge prohibited Morgan Stanley from contesting certain allegations made by Perelman. The jury later returned a verdict in favor of Perelman and against Morgan Stanley for $604 million in compensatory damages and $850 million in punitive damages. The court orders sanctioning Morgan Stanley for its discovery misconduct undoubtedly played a key role in Perelman's victory, effectively turning a case that was not a sure-fire winner for Perelman into just that. The case illustrates that a party to litigation may be playing with fire if he, she, or it insists on refusing to comply with legitimate discovery requests.

and the testimony of witnesses. The same process of direct, cross-, redirect, and recross-examination is followed, except that the examination roles of the respective lawyers are reversed. After the plaintiff and defendant have presented their cases-in-chief, each party is allowed to present evidence rebutting the showing made by the other party. Throughout each side's presentations of evidence, the opposing attorney may object, on specified legal grounds, to certain questions asked of witnesses or to certain evidence that has been offered for admission. The trial judge utilizes the legal rules of evidence to determine whether to sustain the objection (meaning that the objected-to question cannot be answered by the witness or that the offered evidence will be disallowed) or, instead, overrule it (meaning that the question may be answered or that the offered evidence will be allowed).

After all of the evidence has been presented by the parties, each party's attorney makes a closing argument summarizing his or her client's position. In bench trials, the judge then usually takes the case under advisement rather than issuing a decision immediately. The judge later makes findings of fact and reaches conclusions of law, renders judgment, and, if the plaintiff is the winning party, states the relief to which the plaintiff is entitled.

Jury Trials At the close of a jury trial, the judge ordinarily submits the case to the jury after issuing **instructions** that set forth the legal rules applicable to the case. The jury then deliberates, makes the necessary determinations of the facts, applies the applicable legal rules to the facts, and arrives at a **verdict** on which the court's judgment will be based.

The verdict form used the majority of the time is the *general verdict,* which requires only that the jury declare which party wins and, if the plaintiff wins, the money damages awarded. The jury neither states its findings of fact nor explains its application of the law to the facts. Although the nature of the general verdict may permit a jury, if it is so inclined, to render a decision that is based on bias, sympathy, or some basis other than the probable facts and the law, one's belief regarding the extent to which juries engage in so-called "jury nullification" of the facts and law is likely to be heavily influenced by one's attitude toward the jury system. Most proponents of the jury system may be inclined to believe that "renegade" juries, though regrettable, are an aberration, and that the vast majority of juries make a good-faith effort to decide cases on the basis of the facts and controlling legal principles. Some jury system proponents, however, take a different view, asserting that juries *should* engage in jury nullification when they believe it is necessary to accomplish "rough justice." Those who take a dim view of the jury system perceive it as fundamentally flawed and as offering juries too much opportunity to make decisions that stray from a reasonable view of the evidence and the law. Critics of the jury system have little hope of abolishing it, however. Doing so would require amendments to the U.S. Constitution and many state constitutions, as well as the repeal of numerous federal and state statutes.

Another verdict form known as the *special verdict* may serve to minimize concerns that some observers have about jury decisions. When a special verdict is employed, the jury makes specific, written findings of fact in response to questions posed by the trial judge. The judge then applies the law to those findings. Whether a special verdict is utilized is a matter largely within the discretion of the trial judge. The special verdict is not as frequently employed, however, as the general verdict.

Directed Verdict Although the general verdict gives the jury considerable power, the American legal system also has devices for limiting that power. One device, the **directed verdict,** takes the case away from the jury and provides a judgment to one party before the jury gets a chance to decide the case. The motion for a directed verdict may be made by either party; it usually occurs after the other (nonmoving) party has presented her evidence. The moving party asserts that the evidence, even when viewed favorably to the other party, leads to only one result and need not be considered by the jury. Courts differ on the test governing a motion for a directed verdict. Some deny the motion if there is *any* evidence favoring the nonmoving party, whereas others deny the motion only if there is *substantial* evidence favoring the nonmoving party. More often than not, trial judges deny motions for a directed verdict.

Judgment Notwithstanding the Verdict On occasion, one party wins a judgment even after the jury has reached a verdict against that party. The device for doing so is the **judgment notwithstanding the verdict** (also known as the judgment *non obstante veredicto* or judgment n.o.v.). Some jurisdictions provide that a motion for judgment n.o.v. cannot be made unless the moving party previously moved for a directed verdict. In any event, the standard used to decide the motion for judgment n.o.v. usually is the same standard used to decide the motion for a directed verdict.

Motion for a New Trial In a wide range of situations that vary among jurisdictions, the losing party can successfully move for a new trial. Acceptable reasons for granting a new trial include legal errors by the judge during the trial, jury or attorney misconduct, the discovery of new evidence, or an award of excessive damages to the plaintiff. Most motions for a new trial are unsuccessful, however.

Appeal

A final judgment generally prevents the parties from relitigating the same claim. One or more parties still may appeal the trial court's decision, however. Normally, appellate courts consider only alleged errors of law made by the trial court. The matters ordinarily considered "legal" and thus appealable include the trial judge's decisions on motions to dismiss, for summary judgment, for directed verdict or judgment notwithstanding the verdict, and for a new trial. Other matters typically considered appealable include trial court rulings on service of process and admission of evidence at trial, as well as the court's legal conclusions in a nonjury trial, instructions to the jury in a jury case, and decision regarding damages or other relief. Appellate courts may *affirm* the trial court's decision, *reverse* it, or affirm parts of the decision and reverse other parts. One of three things ordinarily results from an appellate court's disposition of an appeal: (1) the plaintiff wins the case; (2) the defendant wins the case; or (3) the case is *remanded* (returned) to the trial court for further proceedings if the trial court's decision is reversed in whole or in part. For example, if the plaintiff appeals a trial court decision granting the defendant's motion to dismiss and the appellate courts affirm that decision, the plaintiff loses. On the other hand, if an appellate court reverses a trial court judgment in the plaintiff's favor, the defendant could win outright, or the case might be returned to the trial court for further proceedings consistent with the appellate decision.

Enforcing a Judgment

In this text, you may occasionally see cases in which someone was not sued even though he probably would have been liable to the plaintiff, who sued another party instead. One explanation is that the first party was "judgment-proof"—so lacking in assets as to make a civil lawsuit for damages a waste of time and money. The defendant's financial condition also affects a winning plaintiff's ability to collect whatever damages she has been awarded.

When the defendant fails to pay as required after losing a civil case, the winning plaintiff must enforce the judgment. Ordinarily, the plaintiff will obtain a *writ of execution* enabling the sheriff to seize designated property of the defendant and sell it at a judicial sale to help satisfy the judgment. A judgment winner may also use a procedure known as *garnishment* to seize property, money, and wages that belong to the defendant but are in the hands of a third party such as a bank or employer. Legal limits exist, however, concerning the portion of wages that may be garnished. If the property needed to satisfy the judgment is located in another state, the plaintiff must use that state's execution or garnishment procedures. Under the U.S. Constitution, the second state must give "full faith and credit" to the judgment of the state in which the plaintiff originally sued. Finally, when the court has awarded an equitable remedy such as an injunction, the defendant may be found in contempt of court and subjected to a fine or a jail term if he fails to obey the court's order.

Class Actions

So far, our civil procedure discussion has proceeded as if the plaintiff and the defendant were single parties. Various plaintiffs and defendants, however, may be parties to one lawsuit. In addition, each jurisdiction has procedural rules stating when other parties can be *joined* to a suit that begins without them.

One special type of multiparty case, the **class action,** allows one or more persons to sue on behalf of themselves and all others who have suffered similar harm from substantially the same wrong. Class action suits by consumers, environmentalists, and other groups now are reasonably common events. The usual justifications for the class action are that (1) it allows legal wrongs causing losses to a large number of widely dispersed parties to be fully compensated, and (2) it promotes economy of judicial effort by combining many similar claims into one suit.

The requirements for a class action vary among jurisdictions. The issues addressed by state and federal class action rules include the following: whether there are questions of law and fact common to all members of the alleged class; whether the class is small enough to allow all of its members to join the case as parties rather than use a class action; and whether the plaintiff(s) and their attorney(s) can adequately represent the class without conflicts of interest or other forms of unfairness. To protect the individual class members' right to be heard, some jurisdictions have required that unnamed or absent class members be given notice of the case if this is reasonably possible. The damages awarded in a successful class action usually are apportioned among the entire class. Establishing the total recovery and distributing it to the class, however, pose problems when the class is large, the class members' injuries are indefinite, or some members cannot be identified.

In 2005, Congress moved to restrict the filing of class actions in state courts by enacting a statute giving the federal district courts original jurisdiction over class actions in which the amount in controversy exceeds $5 million and any member of the plaintiff class resides in a state different from the state of any defendant.

Proponents of the measure describe it as being designed to curtail "forum shopping" by multistate plaintiffs for "friendly" state courts that might be especially likely to favor the claims of the plaintiffs. Critics assert that the 2005 enactment is too protective of corporate defendants and likely to curtail the bringing of legitimate civil rights, consumer-protection, and environmental-harm claims. As this book went to press, it remained too early to sort out the full effects of the 2005 class action legislation.

Alternative Dispute Resolution

Lawsuits are not the only devices for resolving civil disputes. Nor are they always the best means of doing so. Settling private disputes through the courts can be a cumbersome, lengthy, and expensive process for litigants. With the advent of a litigious society and the increasing caseloads it has produced, handling disputes in this fashion also imposes ever-greater social costs. For these reasons and others, various forms of **alternative dispute resolution (ADR)** have assumed increasing importance in recent years. Proponents of ADR cite many considerations in its favor. These include ADR's (1) quicker resolution of disputes; (2) lower costs in time, money, and aggravation for the parties; (3) lessening of the strain on an overloaded court system; (4) use of decision makers with specialized expertise; and (5) potential for compromise decisions that promote and reflect consensus between the parties. Those who are skeptical of ADR worry about its potential for sloppy or biased decisions. They also worry that it may sometimes mean second-class justice for ordinary people who deal with powerful economic interests. Sometimes, for example, agreements to submit disputes to alternative dispute resolution are buried in complex standard-form contracts drafted by a party with superior size, knowledge, and business sophistication and are unknowingly agreed to by less knowledgeable parties. Such clauses, critics charge, may compel ADR proceedings before decision makers who are biased in favor of the stronger party.

Common Forms of ADR

Settlement The settlement of a civil lawsuit is not everyone's idea of an alternative dispute resolution mechanism. It is an important means, however, of avoiding protracted litigation—one that often is a sensible compromise for the parties. Most cases settle at some stage in the proceedings described previously. The usual settlement agreement is a contract whereby the defendant agrees to pay the plaintiff a sum of money, in exchange for the plaintiff's promise to release the defendant from liability for the plaintiff's claims. Such agreements must satisfy the requirements of contract law discussed later in this text. In some cases, moreover, the court must approve the settlement in order for it to be enforceable. Examples include class actions and litigation involving minors.

Arbitration Arbitration is the submission of a dispute to a neutral, nonjudicial third party (the *arbitrator*) who issues a binding decision resolving the dispute. Arbitration usually results from the parties' agreement. That agreement normally is made before the dispute arises (most often through an *arbitration clause* in a contract). As noted in the *Preston* case, which follows shortly, the Federal Arbitration Act requires judicial enforcement of a wide range of agreements to arbitrate claims. This means that if a contract contains a clause requiring arbitration of certain claims but one of the parties attempts to litigate such a claim in court, the court is very likely to dismiss the case and compel arbitration of the dispute.

Arbitration may also be compelled by other statutes. One example is the *compulsory arbitration* many states require as part of the collective bargaining process for certain public employees. Finally, parties who have not agreed in advance to submit future disputes to arbitration may agree upon arbitration after the dispute arises.

Arbitration usually is less formal than regular court proceedings. The arbitrator may or may not be an attorney. Often, she is a professional with expertise in the subject matter of the dispute. Although arbitration hearings often resemble civil trials, the applicable procedures, the rules for admission of evidence, and the record-keeping requirements typically are not as rigorous as those governing courts. Arbitrators sometimes have freedom to ignore rules of substantive law that would bind a court.

The arbitrator's decision, called an *award,* is filed with a court, which will enforce it if necessary. The losing party may object to the arbitrator's award, but judicial review of arbitration proceedings is limited. According to the Federal Arbitration Act (FAA), grounds for overturning an arbitration award include (1) a party's use of fraud, (2) the arbitrator's partiality or corruption, and (3) other misconduct by the arbitrator.

In *Hall Street Associates v. Mattel. Inc.,* 128 S. Ct. 1396 (2008), the U.S. Supreme Court noted that the exclusive grounds for having an arbitration award vacated are the ones listed in the FAA. The Court then held that parties to an arbitration agreement cannot add to the statutory list of grounds for overturning an arbitration award by contractually calling for judicial review that would allow an arbitration award to be vacated because of ordinary legal errors on the part of the arbitrator. Thus, even if a party believes that the arbitrator's decision resulted from an erroneous application of the law, the arbitration award will stand.

Preston v. Ferrer, which follows, discusses the purposes of the FAA. The Supreme Court goes on to hold that when parties have agreed to arbitrate disputes, the FAA controls and the dispute must therefore be submitted to arbitration even if otherwise applicable state law appears to give initial decision-making authority to a court or an administrative agency.

Preston v. Ferrer   128 S. Ct. 978 (U.S. Sup. Ct. 2008)

Alex Ferrer, a former judge who appears as "Judge Alex" on a Fox television network program, entered into a contract with Arnold Preston, a California attorney who renders services to persons in the entertainment industry. Seeking fees allegedly due under the contract, Preston invoked the clause setting forth the parties' agreement to arbitrate "any dispute . . . relating to the terms of [the contract] or the breach, validity, or legality thereof . . . in accordance with the rules [of the American Arbitration Association]." Preston's demand for arbitration was countered shortly thereafter by Ferrer's petition to the California Labor Commissioner. In that petition, Ferrer contended that the contract was unenforceable under the California Talent Agencies Act (CTAA). Ferrer asserted that Preston acted as a talent agent without the license required by the CTAA, and that Preston's unlicensed status rendered the entire contract void.

The Labor Commissioner's hearing officer determined that Ferrer had stated a plausible basis for invoking the Labor Commissioner's authority. The hearing officer denied Ferrer's motion to stay the arbitration, however, on the ground that the Labor Commissioner lacked the specific power to order such relief. Ferrer then filed suit in a California Superior Court, seeking a declaration that the controversy between the parties "arising from the [c]ontract, including in particular the issue of the validity of the [c]ontract, is not subject to arbitration." Ferrer sought an injunction restraining Preston from proceeding before the arbitrator. Preston responded by moving to compel arbitration. The Superior Court denied Preston's motion to compel arbitration and enjoined Preston from proceeding before the arbitrator "unless and until the Labor Commissioner determines that . . . she is without jurisdiction over the disputes between Preston and Ferrer."

Preston appealed to the California Court of Appeal, which affirmed the lower court's decision. The California Supreme Court denied Preston's petition for review. The U.S. Supreme Court, however, granted Preston's petition for a writ of certiorari and thereby agreed to decide the issue presented by Preston's appeal: whether the Federal Arbitration Act overrides a state law vesting initial adjudicatory authority in an administrative agency.

Ginsburg, Justice

As this Court recognized in *Southland Corp. v. Keating,* 465 U.S. 1 (1984), the Federal Arbitration Act (FAA) establishes a national policy favoring arbitration when the parties contract for that mode of dispute resolution. The FAA . . . supplies not simply a procedural framework applicable in federal courts; it also calls for the application, in state as well as federal courts, of federal substantive law regarding arbitration. More recently, in *Buckeye Check Cashing, Inc. v. Cardegna,* 546 U.S. 440 (2006), the Court clarified that when parties agree to arbitrate all disputes arising under their contract, questions concerning the validity of the entire contract are to be resolved by the arbitrator in the first instance, not by a federal or state court.

The instant petition presents the following question: Does the FAA override not only state statutes that refer certain state-law controversies initially to a judicial forum, but also state statutes that refer certain disputes initially to an administrative agency? We hold today that when parties agree to arbitrate all questions arising under a contract, state laws lodging primary jurisdiction in another forum, whether judicial or administrative, are superseded by the FAA.

An easily stated question underlies this controversy. Ferrer claims that Preston was a talent agent who operated without a license in violation of the CTAA. Accordingly, he urges, the contract between the parties . . . is void and Preston is entitled to no compensation for any services he rendered. Preston, on the other hand, maintains that he acted as a personal manager, not as a talent agent, hence his contract with Ferrer is not governed by the CTAA and is both lawful and fully binding on the parties.

Because the contract between Ferrer and Preston provides that "any dispute . . . relating to the . . . validity, or legality" of the agreement "shall be submitted to arbitration," Preston urges that Ferrer must litigate his CTAA defense in the arbitral forum. Ferrer insists, however, that the "personal manager" or "talent agent" inquiry falls, under California law, within the exclusive original jurisdiction of the Labor Commissioner, and that the FAA does not displace the Commissioner's primary jurisdiction. The dispositive issue, then, contrary to Ferrer's suggestion, is not whether the FAA preempts the CTAA wholesale. The FAA plainly has no such destructive aim or effect. Instead, the question is simply who decides whether Preston acted as personal manager or as talent agent.

Section 2 of the FAA states: "A written provision in any . . . contract evidencing a transaction involving commerce to settle by arbitration a controversy thereafter arising out of such contract or transaction . . . shall be valid, irrevocable, and enforceable, save upon such grounds as exist at law or in equity for the revocation of any contract." Section 2 "declare[s] a national policy favoring arbitration" of claims that parties contract to settle in that manner. *Southland Corp.,* 465 U.S. at 10. That national policy, we held in *Southland,* "appli[es] in state as well as federal courts" and "foreclose[s] state legislative attempts to undercut the enforceability of arbitration agreements." *Id.* at 16. The FAA's displacement of conflicting state law is now well-established and has been repeatedly reaffirmed. [Case citations omitted.]

A recurring question under § 2 is who should decide whether "grounds . . . exist at law or in equity" to invalidate an arbitration agreement. In *Prima Paint Corp. v. Flood & Conklin Mfg. Co.,* 388 U.S. 395 (1967), we held that attacks on the validity of an entire contract, as distinct from attacks aimed at the arbitration clause, are within the arbitrator's ken. The litigation in *Prima Paint* originated in federal court, but the same rule, we held in *Buckeye,* applies in state court. The plaintiffs in *Buckeye* alleged that the contracts they signed, which contained arbitration clauses, were illegal under state law and void *ab initio.* Relying on *Southland,* we held that the plaintiffs' challenge was within the province of the arbitrator to decide.

Buckeye largely, if not entirely, resolves the dispute before us. The contract between Preston and Ferrer clearly "evidenc[ed] a transaction involving commerce" [quoting FAA § 2], and Ferrer has never disputed that the written arbitration provision in the contract falls within the purview of § 2. Moreover, Ferrer sought invalidation of the contract as a whole. In the proceedings below, he made no discrete challenge to the validity of the arbitration clause. Ferrer thus urged the Labor Commissioner and California courts to override the contract's arbitration clause on a ground that *Buckeye* requires the arbitrator to decide in the first instance.

Ferrer attempts to distinguish *Buckeye* by arguing that the CTAA merely requires exhaustion of administrative remedies before the parties proceed to arbitration. We reject that argument.

The CTAA regulates talent agents and talent agency agreements. "Talent agency" is defined, with exceptions not relevant here, as "a person or corporation who engages in the occupation of procuring, offering, promising, or attempting to procure employment or engagements for an artist or artists." The definition "does not cover other services for which artists often contract, such as personal and career management (i.e., advice, direction, coordination, and oversight with respect to an artist's career or personal or financial affairs)." [Case citation omitted.] The CTAA requires talent agents to procure a license from the Labor Commissioner. "In furtherance of the [CTAA's] protective aims, an unlicensed person's contract with an artist to provide the services of a talent agency is illegal and void." [Case citation omitted.]

The CTAA states [that] "[i]n cases of controversy arising under this chapter, the parties involved shall refer the matters in dispute to the Labor Commissioner, who shall hear and determine the same, subject to an appeal within 10 days after determination, to the superior court where the same shall be heard de novo." . . . Procedural prescriptions of the CTAA thus conflict with the FAA's dispute resolution regime [by granting] the Labor Commissioner exclusive jurisdiction to decide an issue that the parties agreed to arbitrate. . . . Ferrer contends that the CTAA is nevertheless compatible with the FAA because [the CTAA] merely postpones arbitration until after the Labor Commissioner has exercised her primary jurisdiction. The party that loses before the Labor Commissioner may file for *de novo* review in [a California Superior Court]. At that point, Ferrer asserts, either party could move to compel arbitration under [California law] and thereby obtain an arbitrator's determination prior to judicial review.

Ferrer's . . . argument—that [the CTAA] merely postpones arbitration—[does not] withstand examination. [The CTAA] provides for *de novo* review in [California] Superior Court, not elsewhere. From Superior Court an appeal lies in the Court of Appeal. Thereafter, the losing party may seek review in the California Supreme Court. Arbitration, if it ever occurred following the Labor Commissioner's decision, would likely be long delayed, in contravention of Congress' intent "to move the parties to an arbitrable dispute out of court and into arbitration as quickly and easily as possible." [Case citation omitted.] If Ferrer prevailed in the California courts, moreover, he would no doubt argue that judicial findings of fact and conclusions of law, made after a full and fair *de novo* hearing in court, are binding on the parties and preclude the arbitrator from making any contrary rulings.

A prime objective of an agreement to arbitrate is to achieve "streamlined proceedings and expeditious results." [Case citation omitted.] That objective would be frustrated even if Preston could compel arbitration in lieu of *de novo* Superior Court review. Requiring initial reference of the parties' dispute to the Labor Commissioner would, at the least, hinder speedy resolution of the controversy.

Ferrer asks us to overlook the apparent conflict between the arbitration clause and [the CTAA] because proceedings before the Labor Commissioner are administrative rather than judicial. Allowing parties to proceed directly to arbitration, Ferrer contends, would undermine the Labor Commissioner's ability to stay informed of potentially illegal activity, and would deprive artists protected by the TAA of the Labor Commissioner's expertise. In *Gilmer v. Interstate/Johnson Lane Corp.*, 500 U.S. 20 (1991), we considered and rejected a similar argument, namely, that arbitration of age discrimination claims would undermine the role of the Equal Employment Opportunity Commission (EEOC) in enforcing federal law. The "mere involvement of an administrative agency in the enforcement of a statute," we held, does not limit private parties' obligation to comply with their arbitration agreements.

Ferrer points to our holding in *EEOC v. Waffle House, Inc.*, 534 U.S. 279 (2002), that an arbitration agreement signed by an employee who becomes a discrimination complainant does not bar the EEOC from filing an enforcement suit in its own name. He further emphasizes our observation in *Gilmer* that individuals who agreed to arbitrate their discrimination claims would "still be free to file a charge with the EEOC." Consistent with these decisions, Ferrer argues, the arbitration clause in his contract with Preston leaves undisturbed the Labor Commissioner's independent authority to enforce the CTAA. And so it

may. Enforcement of the parties' arbitration agreement in this case does not displace any independent authority the Labor Commissioner may have to investigate and rectify violations of the CTAA. But in [the CTAA] proceedings [Ferrer desires], the Labor Commissioner [would] function[] not as an advocate advancing a cause before a tribunal authorized to find the facts and apply the law; instead, the Commissioner [would] serve[] as impartial arbiter. That role is just what the FAA-governed agreement between Ferrer and Preston reserves for the arbitrator. In contrast, in *Waffle House* and in the *Gilmer* aside [that] Ferrer quotes, the Court addressed the role of an agency, not as adjudicator but as prosecutor, pursuing an enforcement action in its own name or reviewing a discrimination charge to determine whether to initiate judicial proceedings.

Finally, it bears repeating that Preston's petition presents precisely and only a question concerning the forum in which the parties' dispute will be heard. "By agreeing to arbitrate a statutory claim, a party does not forgo the substantive rights afforded by the statute; it only submits to their resolution in an arbitral . . . forum." [Case citation omitted.] So here, Ferrer relinquishes no substantive rights the CTAA or other California law may accord him. But under the contract he signed, he cannot escape resolution of those rights in an arbitral forum.

In sum, we disapprove the distinction between judicial and administrative proceedings drawn by Ferrer and adopted by the [California Court of Appeal in ruling in favor of Ferrer]. When parties agree to arbitrate all questions arising under a contract, the FAA supersedes state laws lodging primary jurisdiction in another forum, whether judicial or administrative.

Decision of California Court of Appeal reversed, and case remanded for further proceedings.

Court-Annexed Arbitration In this form of ADR, certain civil lawsuits are diverted into arbitration. One example might be cases in which less than a specified dollar amount is at issue. Most often, court-annexed arbitration is mandatory and is ordered by the judge, but some jurisdictions merely offer litigants the option of arbitration. The losing party in a court-annexed arbitration still has the right to a regular trial.

Mediation In mediation, a neutral third party called a *mediator* helps the parties reach a cooperative resolution of their dispute by facilitating communication between them, clarifying their areas of agreement and disagreement, helping them to see each other's viewpoints, and suggesting settlement options. Mediators, unlike arbitrators,

cannot make decisions that bind the parties. Instead, a successful mediation process results in a *mediation agreement*. Such agreements normally are enforced under regular contract law principles.

Mediation is used in a wide range of situations, including labor, commercial, family, and environmental disputes. It may occur by agreement of the parties after a dispute has arisen. It also may result from a previous contractual agreement by the parties. Increasingly, court-annexed mediation is either compelled or made available by courts in certain cases.

Summary Jury Trial Sometimes settlement of civil litigation is impeded because the litigants have vastly different perceptions about the merits of their cases. In such cases, the summary jury trial may give the parties a needed dose of reality. The summary jury trial is an abbreviated, non-public mock jury trial that does not bind the parties. If the parties do not settle after completion of the summary jury trial, they still are entitled to a regular court trial. There is some disagreement over whether courts can compel the parties to take part in a summary jury trial.

Minitrial   A minitrial is an informal, abbreviated private "trial" whose aim is to promote settlement of disputes. Normally, it arises out of a private agreement that also describes the procedures to be followed. In the typical minitrial, counsel for the parties present their cases to a panel composed of senior management from each side. Sometimes a neutral advisor such as an attorney or a retired judge presides. This advisor may also offer an opinion about the case's likely outcome in court. After the presentations, the managers attempt to negotiate a settlement.

Other ADR Devices   Other ADR devices include (1) *med/arb* (a hybrid of mediation and arbitration in which a third party first acts as a mediator, and then as an arbitrator); (2) the use of *magistrates* and *special masters* to perform various tasks during complex litigation in the federal courts; (3) *early neutral evaluation (ENE)* (a court-annexed procedure involving early, objective evaluation of the case by a neutral private attorney with experience in its subject matter); (4) *private judging* (in which litigants hire a private referee to issue a decision that may be binding but that usually does not preclude recourse to the courts); and (5) *private panels* instituted by an industry or an organization to handle claims of certain kinds (e.g., the Better Business Bureau). In addition, some formal legal processes are sometimes called ADR devices. Examples include small claims courts and the administrative procedures used to handle claims for veterans' benefits or Social Security benefits.

Problems and Problem Cases

1. Peters sues Davis. At trial, Peters's lawyer attempts to introduce certain evidence to help make his case. Davis's attorney objects, and the trial judge refuses to allow the evidence. Peters eventually loses the case at the trial court level. On appeal, his attorney argues that the trial judge's decision not to admit the evidence was erroneous. Davis's attorney argues that the appellate court cannot consider this question, because appellate courts review only errors of *law* (not fact) at the trial court level. Is Davis's attorney correct? Why or why not?

2. Eric Baker, who had agreed in his employment application to resolve any employment-related dispute through arbitration, was fired after suffering a seizure on the job. Baker did not initiate arbitration proceedings. Instead, he filed a charge of discrimination with the Equal Employment Opportunity Commission (EEOC). Alleging that Baker's employer violated the Americans with Disabilities Act (ADA), the EEOC filed an enforcement action against the employer in federal court. The EEOC sought an injunction and punitive damages against the employer, and backpay, reinstatement, and compensatory damages for Baker. The Federal Arbitration Act (FAA) does not allow Baker to step outside the bounds of his agreement by bringing a judicial action against Waffle House. Does it prohibit the EEOC from bringing such an action, demanding victim-specific relief for Baker?

3. Alabama resident Lynda Butler sued Beer Across America, an Illinois firm, for having sold her minor son 12 bottles of beer. The son ordered the beer from the defendant's Web site while his parents were on vacation. Butler based her lawsuit on an Alabama statute and filed it in an Alabama state court. Exercising an option described in Chapter 2, the defendant removed the case to a federal court, the U.S. District Court for the Northern District of Alabama. Alabama's long-arm statute, rather than being restricted to certain listed behaviors on the part of nonresident defendants, contained an authorization for courts in the state and federal district of Alabama to exert in personam jurisdiction over nonresident defendants in any case in which the exertion of such jurisdiction would be consistent with the U.S. Constitution's due process guarantee. Beer Across America filed a motion asking the federal court to dismiss the case for lack of in personam jurisdiction. The facts showed that Beer Across America owned no property in Alabama, had no offices or sales personnel located there, and did not advertise there. Beer Across America's $24.95 sale to Butler's son was the only sale made by the firm to him, and the firm had not directly solicited him as a customer. Sales to Alabama residents represented a very small percentage of Beer Across America's

revenue. Beer Across America's Web site allowed the ordering of products but was not highly interactive in nature. In view of the facts and the relevant legal principles, how did the court rule on Beer Across America's motion to dismiss?

4. Sandra Wheeler and Darrin Green were involved in litigation in which Wheeler was not represented by an attorney. Green's attorney served 64 requests for admission on Wheeler. For the most part, the requests for admission set forth substantive legal allegations that Green needed to prove in order to win the case, as opposed to being requests that sought admissions regarding purely factual matters. Wheeler provided responses to the requests but did so two days after the responses were due under applicable law of the state of Texas. Because the responses he received from Wheeler were not timely and because he took the position that the requests for admission were to be deemed admitted, Green's attorney filed a motion for summary judgment against Wheeler. The trial court granted summary judgment in favor of Green. Wheeler retained an attorney and appealed to the intermediate court of appeals, which affirmed the trial court's decision. Wheeler then appealed to the Supreme Court of Texas, arguing that even though her responses to the requests for admission were submitted after the due date, the requests should not have been deemed admitted, and the lower courts should not have granted summary judgment in favor of Green. Was Wheeler correct?

5. Adams, a worker at a Circuit City retail electronics store in California, signed an employment application that included an agreement to resolve all future employment disputes exclusively by binding arbitration. Later, Adams filed a state-law-based employment discrimination suit against Circuit City in a California state court. Circuit City then filed suit in a federal district court, asking the court to enjoin the state court action and compel arbitration under the Federal Arbitration Act (FAA). The coverage provision of the FAA states that "[a] written provision in . . . a contract evidencing a transaction involving commerce to settle by arbitration a controversy thereafter arising out of such contract . . . shall be valid, irrevocable, and enforceable. . . ." However, another section of the FAA excludes from the FAA's coverage "contracts of employment of seamen, railroad employees, or any other class or workers engaged in foreign or interstate commerce." Concluding that the FAA applied

to the Adams–Circuit City contract, the federal district court issued an order compelling arbitration of the dispute. Adams appealed, and the U.S. Court of Appeals for the Ninth Circuit reversed. The Ninth Circuit reasoned that in view of the above-quoted exclusion, the FAA does not apply to contracts of employment. Circuit City appealed to the U.S. Supreme Court, which agreed to decide the case. Was the Ninth Circuit correct? Are all contracts of employment excluded from the FAA's coverage?

6. Jerrie Gray worked at a Tyson Foods plant where she was exposed to comments, gestures, and physical contact that, she alleged, constituted sexual harassment. Tyson disputed the allegation, arguing that the behavior was not unwelcome, that the complained-about conduct was not based on sex, that the conduct did not affect a term, condition, or privilege of employment, and that proper remedial action was taken in response to any complaint by Gray of sexual harassment. During the trial in federal court, a witness for Gray repeatedly volunteered inadmissible testimony that the judge had to tell the jury to disregard. At one point, upon an objection from the defendant's counsel, the witness asked, "May I say something here?" The judge told her she could not. Finally, after the jury left the courtroom, the witness had an angry outburst that continued into the hallway, in view of some of the jurors.

   The jury awarded Gray $185,000 in compensatory and $800,000 in punitive damages. Tyson believed that it should not have been liable, that the awards of damages were excessive and unsupported by evidence, and that the inadmissible evidence and improper conduct had tainted the proceedings. What courses of action may Tyson pursue?

7. Preston is the plaintiff in a civil lawsuit against Dalton. During the discovery phase of the case, Dalton's attorney took Preston's deposition. The trial of the case is in process. Dalton's attorney has offered Preston's deposition as evidence. Preston's attorney has objected, arguing that Preston is neither dead nor unavailable to testify in person, and that the deposition therefore should not be allowed admitted into evidence. Is Preston's attorney correct?

8. Abbott Laboratories manufactured and sold the Life Care PCA, a pump that delivers medication into a person intravenously at specific time intervals. Beverly Lewis sued Abbott in a Mississippi state court, alleging that a defective Life Care PCA had

injured her by delivering an excessive quantity of morphine. Abbott served Lewis with a request for admission calling for her to admit that her damages did not exceed $75,000. Lewis did not answer the request for admission. Abbott removed the case to the U.S. District Court for the Southern District of Mississippi, predicating the court's subject-matter jurisdiction on diversity of citizenship and an amount in controversy exceeding $75,000. Contending that her silence had amounted to an admission that her damages were less than $75,000, Lewis filed a motion asking that the federal court remand the case to the state court. Did the federal court have subject-matter jurisdiction? How did the federal court rule on Lewis's motion to send the case back to the state court?

9. The state of New Jersey says it is sovereign over certain landfilled portions of Ellis Island. The state of New York disagrees, asserting that it is sovereign over the whole of the island. New Jersey brings an action in the U.S. District Court for the Southern District of New York. Should the court hear the case?

10. New Jersey residents Richard Goldhaber and his daughter, Danna, joined an Internet newsgroup that provided information about cruises and cruise ships. California resident Charles Kohlenberg was a member of the same group. According to the Goldhabers, Kohlenberg began posting on this newsgroup certain messages that alleged the Goldhabers had engaged in unlawful and immoral acts. These allegations were false, the Goldhabers maintained. They filed a defamation lawsuit against Kohlenberg in a New Jersey court. Kohlenberg sought to have the case dismissed, contending that the court lacked in personam jurisdiction over him. Did the New Jersey court have in personam jurisdiction over Kohlenberg?

Online Research

The American Arbitration Association

The American Arbitration Association (AAA) furnishes dispute resolution services in cases that fall within a wide variety of legal categories identified on the AAA's official Web site. Locate and review the organization's Web site. Then prepare a list of the legal categories of cases concerning which the AAA provides dispute resolution services.

chapter 3

BUSINESS AND THE CONSTITUTION

A federal statute and related regulations prohibited producers of beer from listing, on a product label, the alcohol content of the beer in the container on which the label appeared. The regulation existed because the U.S. government believed that if alcohol content could be disclosed on labels, certain producers of beer might begin marketing their brand as having a higher alcohol content than competing beers. The government was concerned that "strength wars" among producers could then develop, that consumers would seek out beers with higher alcohol content, and that adverse public health consequences would follow. Because it wished to include alcohol content information on container labels for its beers, Coors Brewing Co. filed suit against the United States government and asked the court to rule that the statute and regulations violated Coors's constitutional right to freedom of speech.

Consider the following questions as you read Chapter 3:

- On which provision in the U.S. Constitution was Coors relying in its challenge of the statute and regulations?
- Does a corporation such as Coors possess the same constitutional right to freedom of speech possessed by an individual human being, or does the government have greater latitude to restrict the content of a corporation's speech?
- The alcohol content disclosures that Coors wished to make with regard to its product would be classified as *commercial speech.* Does commercial speech receive the same degree of constitutional protection that political or other noncommercial speech receives?
- Which party—Coors or the federal government—won the case, and why?
- Do producers and other sellers of alcoholic beverages have, in connection with the sale of their products, special ethical obligations that sellers of other products might not have? If so, what are those obligations and why do they exist?

CONSTITUTIONS SERVE TWO general functions. First, they set up the structure of government, allocating power among its various branches and subdivisions. Second, they prevent government from taking certain actions—especially actions that restrict individual or, as suggested by the Coors scenario with which this chapter opened, corporate rights. This chapter examines the U.S. Constitution's performance of these functions and considers how that performance affects government regulation of business.

An Overview of the U.S. Constitution

The U.S. Constitution exhibits the principle of **separation of powers** by giving distinct powers to Congress, the president, and the federal courts. Article I of the Constitution establishes a Congress composed of a Senate and a House of Representatives, gives it sole power to legislate at the federal level, and sets out rules for the enactment of legislation. Article I, section 8 also defines when Congress can make law by stating its *legislative powers*. Three of those powers—the commerce, tax, and spending powers—are discussed later in the chapter.

Article II gives the president the *executive power*—the power to execute or enforce the laws passed by Congress. Section 2 of that article lists other presidential powers, including the powers to command the nation's armed forces and to make treaties. Article III gives the *judicial power* of the United States to the Supreme Court and the other federal courts later established by Congress. Article III also determines the types of cases the federal courts may decide.

Besides creating a separation of powers, Articles I, II, and III set up a system of **checks and balances** among Congress, the president, and the courts. For example, Article I gives the president the power to veto legislation passed by Congress, but allows Congress to override such a veto by a two-thirds vote of each House. Article I and Article II provide that the president, the vice president, and other federal officials may be impeached and removed from office by a two-thirds vote of the Senate. Article II states that treaties made by the president must be approved by a two-thirds vote of the Senate. Article III gives Congress some control over the Supreme Court's appellate jurisdiction.

The Constitution recognizes the principle of **federalism** in the way it structures power relations between the federal government and the states. After Article I lists the powers Congress holds, a later section in Article I lists certain powers that Congress cannot exercise. The Tenth Amendment provides that those powers the Constitution neither gives to the federal government nor denies to the states are reserved to the states or the people.

Article VI, however, makes the Constitution, laws, and treaties of the United States supreme over state law. As will be seen, this principle of **federal supremacy** may cause federal statutes to *preempt* inconsistent state laws. The Constitution also puts limits on the states' lawmaking powers. One example is Article I's command that states shall not pass laws impairing the obligation of contracts.

Article V sets forth the procedures for amending the Constitution. The Constitution has been amended 27 times. The first 10 of these amendments comprise the Bill of Rights. Although the rights guaranteed in the first 10 amendments once restricted only federal government action, most of them now limit state government action as well. As you will learn, this results from their *incorporation* within the Due Process Clause of the Fourteenth Amendment.

The Evolution of the Constitution and the Role of the Supreme Court

According to the legal realists discussed in Chapter 1, written "book law" is less important than what public decision makers *actually do*. Using this approach, we discover a Constitution that differs from the written Constitution just described. The actual powers of today's presidency, for instance, exceed anything one would expect from reading Article II. As you will see, moreover, some constitutional provisions have acquired a meaning different from their meaning when first enacted. American constitutional law is much more evolving than static.

Many of these changes result from the way one public decision maker—the nine-member U.S. Supreme Court—has interpreted the Constitution over time. Formal constitutional change can be accomplished only through the amendment process. Because this process is difficult to employ, however, amendments to the Constitution have been relatively infrequent. As a practical matter, the Supreme Court has become the Constitution's main "amender" through its many interpretations of constitutional provisions. Various factors help explain the Supreme Court's ability and willingness to play this role. Because of their vagueness, some key constitutional provisions invite diverse interpretations; "due process of law" and "equal protection of the laws" are examples. In addition, the history surrounding the enactment of constitutional provisions sometimes is sketchy, confused, or contradictory. Probably more important, however, is the perceived need to adapt the Constitution to changing social conditions. As the old saying goes, Supreme Court decisions tend to "follow the election returns." (Regardless of where one finds himself or herself on the political spectrum, the old saying has taken on a new twist after *Bush v. Gore,* the historic 2000 decision referred to later in this chapter.)

Under the power of **judicial review,** courts can declare the actions of other government bodies unconstitutional. How courts exercise this power depends on how they choose to read the Constitution. This means that courts—especially the Supreme Court—have political power. Indeed, the Supreme Court's justices are, to a considerable extent, public policy makers. Their beliefs are important in the determination of how America is governed. This is why the justices' nomination and confirmation often involve so much political controversy.

Yet even though the Constitution frequently is what the courts say it is, judicial power to shape the Constitution has limits. Certain limits spring from the Constitution's language, which sometimes is quite clear. Others result from the judges' adherence to the *stare decisis* doctrine discussed in Chapter 1. Perhaps the most significant limits on judges' power, however, stem from the tension between modern judicial review and democracy. Legislators are chosen by the people, whereas judges—especially appellate level judges—often are appointed, not elected. Today, judges exercise political power by declaring the actions of legislatures unconstitutional under standards largely of the judiciary's own devising. This sometimes leads to charges that courts are undemocratic, elitist institutions. Such charges put political constraints on judges because courts depend on the other branches of government—and ultimately on public belief in judges' fidelity to the rule of law—to make their decisions effective. Judges, therefore, may be reluctant to declare statutes unconstitutional because they are wary of power struggles with a more representative body such as Congress.

LOG ON

For a great deal of information about the U.S. Supreme Court and access to the Court's opinions in recent cases, see the Court's Web site at **http://www.supremecourtus.gov.**

The Coverage and Structure of This Chapter

This chapter examines certain constitutional provisions that are important to business; it does not discuss constitutional law in its entirety. These provisions help define federal and state power to regulate the economy. The U.S. Constitution limits government regulatory power in two general ways. First, it restricts *federal* legislative authority by listing the powers Congress can exercise. These are known as the **enumerated powers.** Federal legislation cannot be constitutional if it is not based on a power specifically stated in the Constitution. Second, the U.S. Constitution limits both *state and federal* power by placing certain **independent checks** in the path of each. In effect, the independent checks establish that even if Congress has an enumerated power to legislate on a particular matter or a state constitution authorizes a state to take certain actions, there still are certain protected spheres into which neither the federal government nor the state government may reach.

Accordingly, a federal law must meet two general tests in order to be constitutional: (1) it must be based on an enumerated power of Congress, and (2) it must not collide with any of the independent checks. For example, Congress has the power to regulate commerce among the states. This power might seem to allow Congress to pass legislation forbidding women from crossing state lines to buy or sell goods. Yet such a law, though arguably based on an enumerated power, surely would be unconstitutional because it conflicts with an independent check—the equal protection guarantee discussed later in the chapter. Today, the independent checks are the main limitations on congressional power. The most important reason for the decline of the enumerated powers limitation is the perceived need for active federal regulation of economic and social life. Recently, however, the enumerated powers limitation has begun to assume somewhat more importance, as will be seen.

After discussion of the most important state and federal powers to regulate economic matters, the chapter explores certain independent checks that apply to the federal government and the states. The chapter then examines some independent checks that affect the states alone. It concludes by discussing a provision—the Takings Clause of the Fifth Amendment—that both recognizes a governmental power and limits its exercise.

State and Federal Power to Regulate

State Regulatory Power
Although state constitutions may do so, the U.S. Constitution does not list the powers state legislatures can exercise. The U.S. Constitution does place certain independent checks in the path of state lawmaking, however. It also declares that certain powers (e.g., creating currency and taxing imports) can be exercised only by Congress. In many other areas, though, Congress and the state legislatures have *concurrent powers*. Both can make law within those areas unless Congress preempts state regulation under the supremacy clause. A very important state legislative power that operates concurrently with many congressional powers is the **police power,** a broad state power to regulate for the public health, safety, morals, and welfare.

Federal Regulatory Power
Article I, section 8 of the U.S. Constitution specifies a number of ways in which Congress may legislate concerning business and commercial matters. For example, it empowers Congress to coin and borrow money, regulate commerce

with foreign nations, establish uniform laws regarding bankruptcies, create post offices, and enact copyright and patent laws. The most important congressional powers contained in Article I, section 8, however, are the powers to regulate commerce among the states, to lay and collect taxes, and to spend for the general welfare. Because they now are read so broadly, these three powers are the main constitutional bases for the extensive federal social and economic regulation that exists today.

The Commerce Power   Article I, section 8 states that "The Congress shall have Power . . . To regulate Commerce . . . among the several States." The original reason for giving Congress this power to regulate *interstate commerce* was to nationalize economic matters by blocking the protectionist state restrictions on interstate trade that were common after the Revolution. As discussed later in the chapter, the Commerce Clause serves as an independent check on state regulation that unduly restricts interstate commerce. Our present concern, however, is the Commerce Clause's role as a source of congressional regulatory power.

The literal language of the Commerce Clause simply gives Congress power to regulate commerce that occurs among the states. Today, however, the clause is regarded as an all-purpose federal police power enabling Congress to regulate many activities within a state's borders (*intrastate matters*). How has this transformation occurred?

The most important step in the transformation was the Supreme Court's conclusion that the power to regulate *interstate* commerce includes the power to regulate *intrastate* activities that affect interstate commerce. For example, in a 1914 decision, the Supreme Court upheld the Interstate Commerce Commission's regulation of railroad rates within Texas (an intrastate matter outside the language of the Commerce Clause) because those rates affected rail traffic between Texas and Louisiana (an interstate matter within the clause's language). This "affecting commerce" doctrine eventually was used to justify federal police power measures with significant intrastate reach. For instance, the Supreme Court upheld the application of the 1964 Civil Rights Act's "public accommodations" section to a family-owned restaurant in Birmingham, Alabama. It did so because the restaurant's racial discrimination affected interstate commerce by reducing the restaurant's business and limiting its purchases of out-of-state meat, and by restricting the ability of blacks to travel among the states.

As the above example suggests, Congress may Constitutionally regulate many predominantly intrastate activities. Yet two Supreme Court decisions during roughly the past 15 years offered indications that the commerce power is not as broad as many had come to believe. Harmonizing those two decisions with the earlier "affecting commerce" decisions was the Court's task in a 2005 case, *Gonzales v. Raich,* which follows.

Gonzales v. Raich   545 U.S. 1 (U.S. Sup. Ct. 2005)

Although marijuana possession and sale are outlawed by state and federal statutes, a 1996 California law, the Compassionate Use Act, made California the first of approximately 10 states to authorize limited use of the drug for medicinal purposes. The Compassionate Use Act created an exemption from criminal prosecution for patients and primary caregivers who possess or cultivate marijuana for medicinal purposes with a physician's approval.

California residents Angel Raich and Diane Monson suffered from a variety of serious medical conditions. After prescribing numerous conventional medicines, physicians had concluded that marijuana was the only effective treatment for Raich and Monson. Both women had been using marijuana as a medication pursuant to their doctors' recommendations, and both relied heavily on marijuana so that they could function on a daily basis without extreme pain. Monson cultivated her own marijuana. Two caregivers provided Raich with locally grown marijuana at no charge.

In 2002, county deputy sheriffs and agents from the federal Drug Enforcement Administration (DEA) came to Monson's home. Although the deputies concluded that Monson's use of marijuana was lawful under California law, the federal agents seized and destroyed all six of her cannabis plants. Raich and Monson thereafter initiated legal action against the Attorney General of the United States and the head of the DEA in an effort to obtain an injunction barring the enforcement of the federal Controlled Substances Act (CSA), to the extent that it prevented them from possessing, obtaining, or manufacturing cannabis for their personal medical use in accordance with California law. The CSA classifies marijuana as a controlled substance and criminalizes its possession and sale. In their complaint, Raich and Monson claimed that enforcing the CSA against them would violate the U.S. Constitution's Commerce Clause and the Due Process Clause of the Fifth Amendment. The federal district court denied the request for a preliminary injunction. The U.S. Court of Appeals for the Ninth Circuit, however, agreed with the Commerce Clause argument made by Raich and Monson. The Court of Appeals therefore directed the lower court to issue a preliminary injunction prohibiting enforcement of the CSA against Raich and Monson (often referred to below as "respondents"). The U.S. Supreme Court granted the federal government's petition for a writ of certiorari.

Stevens, Justice

Article I, section 8 of the Constitution [empowers Congress] "to make all Laws which shall be necessary and proper for carrying into Execution" [the federal] authority to "regulate Commerce with foreign Nations, and among the several States." The question presented in this case is whether the power vested in Congress by [the Commerce Clause] includes the power to prohibit the local cultivation and use of marijuana in compliance with California law. [This] case is made difficult by respondents' strong arguments that they will suffer irreparable harm because, despite a congressional finding to the contrary, marijuana does have valid therapeutic purposes. The [issue] before us, however, is not whether it is wise to enforce the statute in these circumstances; rather, it is whether Congress' power to regulate interstate markets for medicinal substances encompasses the portions of those markets that are supplied with drugs produced and consumed locally.

[Enacted in 1970 as part of a broader legislative package known as the Comprehensive Drug Abuse Prevention and Control Act], the CSA repealed most of the earlier [federal] drug laws in favor of a comprehensive regime to combat the international and interstate traffic in illicit drugs. The main objectives of the CSA [center around monitoring] legitimate and illegitimate traffic in controlled substances. Congress devised a closed regulatory system making it unlawful to manufacture, distribute, dispense, or possess any controlled substance except in a manner authorized by the CSA, [which] categorizes all controlled substances into five schedules. The drugs are grouped together based on their accepted medical uses, the potential for abuse, and their psychological and physical effects on the body. Each schedule is associated with a distinct set of controls regarding the manufacture, distribution, and use of the substances listed therein.

Congress classified marijuana [in] Schedule I [of the CSA]. Schedule I drugs are categorized as such because of their high potential for abuse, lack of any accepted medical use, and absence of any accepted safety for use in medically supervised treatment. These three factors, in varying gradations, are also used to categorize drugs in the other four schedules. [As Congress acknowledged in the CSA, many drugs listed on the other schedules do have accepted medical uses.] By classifying marijuana as a Schedule I drug, [Congress made] the manufacture, distribution, or possession of marijuana . . . a criminal offense.

Respondents . . . do not dispute that passage of the CSA, as part of the Comprehensive Drug Abuse Prevention and Control Act, was well within Congress' commerce power. Rather, respondents' challenge is actually quite limited; they argue that the CSA's categorical prohibition of the manufacture and possession of marijuana as applied to the intrastate manufacture and possession of marijuana for medical purposes pursuant to California law exceeds Congress' authority under the Commerce Clause.

[This Court's Commerce Clause cases] have identified three general categories of regulation in which Congress is authorized to engage under its commerce power. First, Congress can regulate the channels of interstate commerce. Second, Congress has authority to regulate and protect the instrumentalities of interstate commerce, and persons or things in interstate commerce. Third, Congress has the power to regulate activities that substantially affect interstate commerce. Only the third category is implicated in the case at hand.

Our case law firmly establishes Congress' power to regulate purely local activities that are part of an economic "class of activities" [having] a substantial effect on interstate commerce. See, e.g., *Wickard v. Filburn*, 317 U.S. 111 (1942). As we stated in *Wickard*, "even if appellee's activity be local and though it may not be regarded as commerce, it may still, whatever its nature, be reached by Congress if it exerts a substantial economic effect on interstate commerce." In *Wickard*, we upheld the application of regulations promulgated under the Agricultural Adjustment Act of 1938, which were designed to control the volume of wheat moving in interstate and foreign commerce in order to avoid surpluses and consequent abnormally low prices. The regulations established an allotment of 11.1 acres for Filburn's 1941 wheat crop, but he sowed 23 acres, intending to use the excess by consuming it on his own farm. Filburn argued that even though Congress [had the] power to regulate the production of goods for commerce, that power did not authorize "federal regulation [of] production not intended in any part for commerce but wholly for consumption on the farm." Justice Jackson's opinion for a unanimous Court rejected this submission. He wrote:

> The effect of the statute before us is to restrict the amount which may be produced for market and the extent as well to which one may forestall resort to the market by producing to meet his own needs. That appellee's own contribution to the demand for wheat may be trivial by itself is not enough to remove him from the scope of federal regulation where, as here, his contribution, taken together with that of many others similarly situated, is far from trivial.

Wickard thus establishes that Congress can regulate purely intrastate activity that is not itself "commercial," in that it is not produced for sale, if it concludes that failure to regulate that class of activity would undercut the regulation of the interstate market in that commodity.

The similarities between this case and *Wickard* are striking. Like the farmer in *Wickard,* respondents are cultivating, for home consumption, a fungible commodity for which there is an established, albeit illegal, interstate market. Just as the Agricultural Adjustment Act was designed "to control the volume [of wheat] moving in interstate and foreign commerce in order to avoid surpluses" and consequently control the market price, a primary purpose of the CSA is to control the supply and demand of controlled substances in both lawful and unlawful drug markets. In *Wickard,* we had no difficulty concluding that Congress had a rational basis for believing that . . . leaving home-consumed wheat outside the regulatory scheme would have a substantial influence on price and market conditions. Here too, Congress had a rational basis for concluding that leaving home-consumed marijuana outside federal control would similarly affect price and market conditions.

More concretely, one concern prompting inclusion of wheat grown for home consumption in the 1938 Act was that rising market prices could draw such wheat into the interstate market, resulting in lower market prices. The parallel concern making it appropriate to include marijuana grown for home consumption in the CSA is the likelihood that the high demand in the interstate market will draw such marijuana into that market. While the diversion of homegrown wheat tended to frustrate the federal interest in stabilizing prices by regulating the volume of commercial transactions in the interstate market, the diversion of homegrown marijuana tends to frustrate the federal interest in eliminating commercial transactions in the interstate market in their entirety. In both cases, the regulation is squarely within Congress' commerce power because production of the commodity meant for home consumption, be it wheat or marijuana, has a substantial effect on supply and demand in the national market for that commodity.

To support their [argument that applying the CSA to them would violate the Commerce Clause], respondents rely heavily on two of our more recent Commerce Clause cases, *United States v. Lopez,* 514 U.S. 549 (1995), and *United States v. Morrison,* 529 U.S. 598 (2000). [However, respondents] overlook the larger context of modern-era Commerce Clause jurisprudence preserved by those cases. [T]he statutory challenges in *Lopez* and *Morrison* were markedly different from the [statutory] challenge in the case at hand. Here, respondents ask us to excise individual applications of a concededly valid statutory scheme. In contrast, in both *Lopez* and *Morrison,* the parties asserted that a particular statute or provision fell outside Congress' commerce power in its entirety. This distinction is pivotal, for we have often reiterated that "where the class of activities is

regulated and that class is within the reach of federal power, the courts have no power 'to excise, as trivial, individual instances' of the class." [Citations of authority omitted.]

At issue in *Lopez* was the validity of the Gun-Free School Zones Act of 1990, which was a brief, single-subject statute making it a [federal] crime for an individual to possess a gun in a school zone. The Act did not regulate any economic activity and did not contain any requirement that the possession of a gun have any connection to past interstate activity or a predictable impact on future commercial activity. Distinguishing our earlier cases holding that comprehensive regulatory statutes may be validly applied to local conduct that does not, when viewed in isolation, have a significant impact on interstate commerce, we held the statute invalid. We explained:

[The Gun-Free School Zones Act] is a criminal statute that by its terms has nothing to do with 'commerce' or any sort of economic enterprise, however broadly one might define those terms. [The statute] is not an essential part of a larger regulation of economic activity, in which the regulatory scheme could be undercut unless the intrastate activity were regulated. It cannot, therefore, be sustained under our cases upholding regulations of activities that arise out of or are connected with a commercial transaction, which viewed in the aggregate, substantially affects interstate commerce.

The statutory scheme that the government is defending in this litigation is at the opposite end of the regulatory spectrum. [The CSA is] a lengthy and detailed statute creating a comprehensive framework for regulating the production, distribution, and possession of five classes of controlled substances. [The CSA's classification of marijuana], unlike the discrete prohibition established by the Gun-Free School Zones Act of 1990, was merely one of many "essential parts of a larger regulation of economic activity, in which the regulatory scheme could be undercut unless the intrastate activity were regulated." [Citation omitted.] Our opinion in *Lopez* casts no doubt on the validity of such a program.

Nor does this Court's holding in *Morrison.* The Violence Against Women Act of 1994 created a federal civil remedy for the victims of gender-motivated crimes of violence. The remedy . . . generally depended on proof of the violation of a state law. Despite congressional findings that such crimes had an adverse impact on interstate commerce, we held the statute unconstitutional because, like the statute in *Lopez,* it did not regulate economic activity.

Unlike those at issue in *Lopez* and *Morrison,* the activities regulated by the CSA are quintessentially economic. The CSA is a statute that regulates the production, distribution, and consumption of commodities for which there is an established, and lucrative, interstate market. Prohibiting the intrastate possession or manufacture of an article of commerce is a rational (and commonly utilized) means of regulating commerce in that product. Because the CSA is a statute that directly regulates economic, commercial activity, our opinion in *Morrison* casts no doubt on its constitutionality.

The Court of Appeals was able to conclude otherwise only by isolating a "separate and distinct" class of activities that it held to be beyond the reach of federal power, defined as "the intrastate, noncommercial cultivation, possession and use of marijuana for personal medical purposes on the advice of a physician and in accordance with state law." The court characterized this class as "different in kind from drug trafficking." The differences between the members of a class so defined and the principal traffickers in Schedule I substances might be sufficient to justify a policy decision exempting the narrower class from the coverage of the CSA. The question, however, is whether Congress' contrary policy judgment, i.e., its decision to include this narrower "class of activities" within the larger regulatory scheme, was constitutionally deficient. We have no difficulty concluding that Congress acted rationally in determining that none of the characteristics making up the purported class . . . compelled an exemption from the CSA.

We acknowledge that evidence proffered by respondents in this case regarding the effective medical uses for marijuana, if found credible after trial, would cast serious doubt on the accuracy of the [congressional] findings that require marijuana to be listed in Schedule I. But the possibility that the drug may be reclassified in the future has no relevance to the question whether Congress now has the power to regulate its production and distribution. One need not have a degree in economics to understand why a nationwide exemption for the vast quantity of marijuana . . . locally cultivated for personal use (which presumably would include use by friends, neighbors, and family members) may have a substantial impact on the interstate market for this extraordinarily popular substance. The congressional judgment that an exemption for such a significant segment of the total market would undermine the orderly enforcement of the entire regulatory scheme is entitled to a strong presumption of validity.

[T]hat the California exemptions will have a significant impact on both the supply and demand sides of the market for marijuana is . . . readily apparent. [Although] most prescriptions for legal drugs . . . limit the dosage and duration of the usage, under California law the doctor's permission to recommend marijuana use is open-ended. The [Compassionate Use Act's authorization for the doctor] to grant permission whenever the doctor determines that a patient is afflicted with "any other illness for which marijuana provides relief" is broad enough to allow even the most scrupulous doctor to conclude that some recreational uses would be therapeutic. And our cases have taught us that there are some unscrupulous physicians who overprescribe when it is sufficiently profitable to do so.

The exemption for cultivation by patients and caregivers can only increase the supply of marijuana in the California market. The likelihood that all such production will promptly terminate when patients recover or will precisely match the patients' medical needs during their convalescence seems remote, whereas the danger that excesses will satisfy some of the admittedly enormous demand for recreational use seems obvious. Moreover, that the national and international narcotics trade has thrived in the face of vigorous criminal enforcement efforts suggests that no small number of unscrupulous people will make use of the California exemptions to serve their commercial ends whenever it is feasible to do so.

[T]he case for the exemption comes down to the claim that a locally cultivated product that is used domestically rather than sold on the open market is not subject to federal regulation. Given the findings in the CSA and the undisputed magnitude of the commercial market for marijuana, our decisions in *Wickard v. Filburn* and the later [cases] endorsing its reasoning foreclose that claim.

Respondents also raise a substantive due process claim and seek to avail themselves of [a] medical necessity defense. These theories of relief were set forth in their complaint but were not reached by the Court of Appeals. We therefore do not address the question whether judicial relief is available to respondents on these alternative bases. We do note, however, the presence of another avenue of relief: [the CSA-authorized procedures that can lead to] reclassification of Schedule I drugs. But perhaps even more important than these legal avenues is the democratic process, in which the voices of voters allied with these respondents may one day be heard in the halls of Congress. Under the present state of the law, however, the judgment of the Court of Appeals [cannot stand].

Court of Appeals decision vacated; case remanded for further proceedings.

The Taxing Power   Article I, section 8 of the Constitution states that "The Congress shall have Power To lay and collect Taxes, Duties, Imposts and Excises." The main purpose of this *taxing power* is to provide a means of raising revenue for the federal government. The taxing power, however, may also serve as a regulatory device. Because the power to tax is the power to destroy, Congress may choose, for instance, to regulate a disfavored activity by imposing a heavy tax on it. Although some past regulatory taxes were struck down, today the reach of the taxing power is seen as very broad. Sometimes it is said that a regulatory tax is constitutional if its purpose could be furthered by another power belonging to Congress. The broad scope of the commerce power may therefore mean that the taxing power has few limits.

The Spending Power If taxing power regulation uses a federal club, congressional *spending power* regulation employs a federal carrot. Article I, section 8 also gives Congress a broad ability to spend for the general welfare. By basing the receipt of federal money on the performance of certain conditions, Congress can use the spending power to advance specific regulatory ends. Conditional federal grants to the states, for instance, are common today.

Over the past several decades, congressional spending power regulation routinely has been upheld. There are limits, however, on its use. First, an exercise of the spending power must serve *general* public purposes rather than particular interests. Second, when Congress conditions the receipt of federal money on certain conditions, it must do so clearly. Third, the condition must be reasonably related to the purpose underlying the federal expenditure. This means, for instance, that Congress probably could not condition a state's receipt of federal highway money on the state's adoption of a one-house legislature.

Independent Checks on the Federal Government and the States

Even if a regulation is within Congress's enumerated powers or a state's police power, it still is unconstitutional if it collides with one of the Constitution's *independent checks*. This section discusses three checks that limit both federal and state regulation of the economy: freedom of speech; due process; and equal protection. Before discussing these guarantees, however, we must consider three foundational matters.

Incorporation The Fifth Amendment prevents the federal government from depriving "any person of life, liberty, or property, without due process of law." The Fourteenth Amendment creates the same prohibition with regard to the states. The literal language of the First Amendment, however, restricts only federal government action. Moreover, the Fourteenth Amendment says that no *state* shall "deny to any person . . . the equal protection of the laws."

Thus, although the due process guarantees clearly apply to both the federal government and the states, the First Amendment seems to apply only to the federal government and the Equal Protection Clause only to the states. The First Amendment's free speech guarantee, however, has been included within the "liberty" protected by Fourteenth Amendment due process as a result of Supreme Court decisions. The free speech guarantee, therefore, restricts state governments as well as the federal government. This is an example of the process of *incorporation,* by which almost all Bill of Rights provisions now apply to the states. The Fourteenth Amendment's equal protection guarantee, on the other hand, has been made applicable to federal government action through incorporation of it within the Fifth Amendment's Due Process Clause.

Government Action People often talk as if the Constitution protects them against anyone who might threaten their rights. However, most of the Constitution's individual rights provisions block only the actions of *government* bodies, federal, state, and local.[1] Private behavior that denies individual rights, while perhaps forbidden by statute, is very seldom a constitutional matter. This **government action** or **state action** requirement forces courts to distinguish between governmental behavior and private behavior. Judicial approaches to this problem have varied over time.

Before World War II, only formal arms of government such as legislatures, administrative agencies, municipalities, courts, prosecutors, and state universities were deemed state actors. After the war, however, the scope of government action increased considerably, with various sorts of traditionally private behavior being subjected to individual rights limitations. The Supreme Court, in *Marsh v. Alabama* (1946), treated a privately owned company town's restriction of free expression as government action under the *public function* theory because the town was nearly identical to a regular municipality in most respects. In *Shelley v. Kraemer* (1948), the Court held that when state courts enforced certain white homeowners' private agreements not to sell their homes to blacks, there was state action that violated the Equal Protection Clause. Later, in *Burton v. Wilmington Parking Authority* (1961), the Court concluded that racial discrimination by a privately owned restaurant located in a state-owned and state-operated parking garage was unconstitutional state

---

[1]However, the Thirteenth Amendment, which bans slavery and involuntary servitude throughout the United States, does not have a state action requirement. Some state constitutions, moreover, have individual rights provisions that lack a state action requirement.

action, in part because the garage and the restaurant were intertwined in a mutually beneficial "symbiotic" relationship. Among the other factors leading courts to find state action during the 1960s and 1970s were extensive government regulation of private activity and government financial aid to a private actor.

The Court, however, severely restricted the reach of state action during the 1970s and 1980s. Since then, private behavior generally has not been held to constitute state action unless a regular unit of government is directly *responsible* for the challenged private behavior because it has coerced or encouraged such behavior. The public function doctrine, moreover, has been limited to situations in which a private entity exercises powers that have *traditionally* been *exclusively* reserved to the state; private police protection is a possible example. In addition, government regulation and government funding have become somewhat less important factors in state action determinations. Despite all these changes, however, state action doctrine has not returned to its narrow pre–World War II definition. Some uncertainty remains in this area, as brief discussion of two cases will demonstrate.

Consider, first, the Supreme Court's decision in *Rendell-Baker v. Cohn* (1982). There, the Court rejected various constitutional challenges to the firing of teachers and counselors at a private school for maladjusted high school students because no state action was present. Although the school was extensively regulated by the state, that did not matter because no state regulation compelled or even influenced the challenged firings. The school depended heavily on state funding, but that fact was not sufficient for state action either. The Court found the public function doctrine inapplicable because the education of maladjusted high school students, though public in nature, is not *exclusively* a state function.

In a 2001 decision, however, a six-justice majority of the Supreme Court concluded that the Tennessee Secondary School Athletic Association (TSSAA) was a state actor for purposes of the Constitution's Fourteenth Amendment when it enforced an association rule against a member school. The TSSAA, a privately organized, not-for-profit entity, regulated interscholastic sports competition among public and private high schools in Tennessee. Although no school was required to join the TSSAA, nearly all public schools and many private schools had done so. All members of the association's governing bodies were school officials, most of whom were from public schools. Public school systems provided considerable financial support for the TSSAA, which worked closely with the state board of education, a governmental body. For many years, the TSSAA was designated in a state

board of education rule as the regulator of athletics in the state's public schools. Stressing the "pervasive entwinement of public institutions and public officials in [the TSSAA's] composition and workings" and the lack of any "substantial reason to claim unfairness in applying constitutional standards to it," the Supreme Court held in *Brentwood Academy v. Tennessee Secondary School Athletic Association* that the TSSAA was a government actor. *Brentwood Academy*'s "entwinement" rationale appears to provide an additional way in which state action can be found, though the Court emphasized that each decision on the state action issue is highly fact-specific.

Means-Ends Tests

Throughout this chapter, you will see tests of constitutionality that may seem strange at first glance. One example is the test for determining whether laws that discriminate on the basis of sex violate equal protection. This test says that to be constitutional, such laws must be substantially related to the achievement of an important government purpose. The Equal Protection Clause does not contain such language. It simply says that "No State shall . . . deny to any person . . . the equal protection of the laws." What is going on here?

The sex discrimination test just stated is a **means-ends test** developed by the Supreme Court. Such tests are judicially created because no constitutional right is absolute, and because judges therefore must weigh individual rights against the social purposes served by laws that restrict those rights. In other words, means-ends tests determine how courts strike the balance between individual rights and the social needs that may justify their suppression. The "ends" component of a means-ends test specifies how *significant* a social purpose must be in order to justify the restriction of a right. The "means" component states how *effectively* the challenged law must promote that purpose in order to be constitutional. In the sex discrimination test, for example, the challenged law must serve an "important" government purpose (the significance of the end) and must be "substantially" related to the achievement of that purpose (the effectiveness of the means).

Some constitutional rights are deemed more important than others. Accordingly, courts use tougher tests of constitutionality in certain cases and more lenient tests in other situations. Sometimes these tests are lengthy and complicated. Throughout the chapter, therefore, we will simplify by referring to three general kinds of means-ends tests:

1. *The rational basis test.* This is a very relaxed test of constitutionality that challenged laws usually pass with ease. A typical formulation of the rational basis

test might say that government action need only have a *reasonable* relation to the achievement of a *legitimate* government purpose to be constitutional.

2. *Intermediate scrutiny.* This comes in many forms; the sex discrimination test discussed above is an example.

3. *Full strict scrutiny.* Here, the court might say that the challenged law must be *necessary* to the fulfillment of a *compelling* government purpose. Government action that is subjected to this rigorous test of constitutionality is usually struck down.

Business and the First Amendment

The First Amendment provides that "Congress shall make no law . . . abridging the freedom of speech." Despite its absolute language ("*no* law"), the First Amendment does not prohibit every law that restricts speech. As Justice Oliver Wendell Holmes famously remarked, the First Amendment does not protect someone who falsely shouts "Fire!" in a crowded theater. Although the First Amendment's free speech guarantee is not absolute, government action restricting the content of speech usually receives very strict judicial scrutiny. One justification for this high level of protection is the "marketplace" rationale, under which the free competition of ideas is seen as the surest means of attaining truth. The marketplace of ideas operates most effectively, according to this rationale, when restrictions on speech are kept to a minimum and all viewpoints can be considered.

During recent decades, the First Amendment has been applied to a wide variety of government restrictions on the expression of individuals and organizations, including corporations. This chapter does not attempt a comprehensive discussion of the many applications of the freedom of speech guarantee. Instead, it explores basic First Amendment concepts before turning to an examination of the free speech rights of corporations.

Political and Other Noncommercial Speech Political speech—expression that deals in some fashion with government, government issues or policies, public officials, or political candidates—is often described as being at the "core" of the First Amendment. Various Supreme Court decisions have held, however, that the freedom of speech guarantee applies not only to political speech but also to noncommercial expression that does not have a political content or flavor. According to these decisions, the First Amendment protects speech of a literary or artistic nature, speech dealing with scientific, economic, educational, and ethical issues, and expression on many other matters of public interest or concern. Government attempts to

restrict the content of political or other noncommercial speech normally receive full strict scrutiny when challenged in court. Unless the government is able to meet the exceedingly difficult burden of proving that the speech restriction is *necessary* to the fulfillment of a *compelling government purpose,* a First Amendment violation will be found. Because government restrictions on political or other noncommercial speech trigger the full strict scrutiny test, such speech is referred to as carrying "full" First Amendment protection.

Do *corporations,* however, have the same First Amendment rights that individual human beings possess? The Supreme Court has consistently provided a "yes" answer to this question. Therefore, if a corporation engages in political or other noncommercial expression, it is entitled to full First Amendment protection, just as an individual would be if he or she engaged in such speech. This does not mean, however, that all speech of a corporation is fully protected. Some corporate speech is classified as **commercial speech,** a category of expression to be examined shortly. As will be seen, commercial speech receives First Amendment protection but not the full variety extended to political or noncommercial speech. The mere fact, however, that a profit motive underlies speech does not make the speech commercial in nature. Books, movies, television programs, musical works, works of visual art, and newspaper, magazine, and journal articles are normally classified as noncommercial speech—and are thus fully protected—despite the typical existence of an underlying profit motive. Their informational, educational, artistic, or entertainment components are thought to outweigh, for First Amendment purposes, the profit motive.

Commercial Speech The exact boundaries of the commercial speech category are not certain, though the Supreme Court has usually defined commercial speech as speech that proposes a commercial transaction. As a result, most cases on the subject involve advertisements for the sale of products or services or for the promotion of a business. In 1942, the Supreme Court held that commercial speech fell outside the First Amendment's protective umbrella. The Court reversed its position, however, during the 1970s. It reasoned that informed consumer choice would be furthered by the removal of barriers to the flow of commercial information in which consumers would find an interest. Since the mid-1970s, commercial speech has received an intermediate level of First Amendment protection if it deals with a lawful activity and is nonmisleading. Commercial speech receives no protection, however, if it misleads or seeks to promote

CYBERLAW IN ACTION

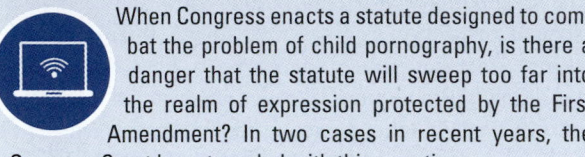

When Congress enacts a statute designed to combat the problem of child pornography, is there a danger that the statute will sweep too far into the realm of expression protected by the First Amendment? In two cases in recent years, the Supreme Court has struggled with this question.

Child pornography—sexually explicit visual depictions of actual minors—has long been held to fall outside the First Amendment's protective umbrella. Therefore, the Supreme Court has held that criminal prosecutions for purveying or possessing child pornography do not violate the First Amendment. In *Ashcroft v. Free Speech Coalition*, 535 U.S. 234 (2002), the Court was faced with determining the constitutionality of a statute in which Congress banned the possession and distribution of material meant to create the impression of minors engaging in sexually explicit conduct even if the persons actually depicted were adults. The Court struck down this statute because it would reach beyond actual child pornography and would ban expression protected by the First Amendment—in particular, nonobscene depictions of nudity or sexual content involving adults. (Although obscene expression receives no First Amendment protection, most descriptions or depictions of nudity or other sexual content involving adults are seen as having literary, artistic, political, or scientific value and thus are not obscene under the controlling test established by the Supreme Court.)

After the *Free Speech Coalition* decision, Congress again tackled the child pornography problem in a 2003 statute, the Protect Act (Prosecutorial Remedies and Other Tools to End the Exploitation of Children Act). The Protect Act made it a crime to knowingly promote, distribute, or solicit, by means of a computer or by any other means, "material or purported material in a manner that reflects the belief, or that is intended to cause another to believe, that the material or purported material is or contains . . . a visual depiction of an actual minor engaging in sexually explicit conduct." Rejecting the argument that this statute was effectively the same as the one struck down in *Free Speech Coalition*, the Supreme Court held in *United States v. Williams*, 2008 U.S. LEXIS 4314 (2008), that the

Protect Act did not violate the First Amendment. In his opinion for a seven-justice majority, Justice Scalia noted that the Protect Act's focus on pandering or soliciting distinguished it from the earlier statute. He also observed that "[t]he emergence of new technology and the repeated retransmission of picture files over the Internet could make it nearly impossible to prove that a particular image was produced using real children" even though evidence seemed to indicate that child pornography-type images being circulated over the Internet generally did involve actual children. Thus, the Court saw the Protect Act as a reasonable response to the child pornography problem.

In upholding the Protect Act, the Court sustained the defendant's conviction of pandering in violation of the statute. The defendant had represented in an Internet chat room to an undercover federal agent that he could provide certain pictures amounting to child pornography, when in reality he did not have the particular pictures he purported to have. When the government obtained a warrant to search the defendant's computer, however, federal agents found other images of actual child pornography—images whose possession by the defendant caused him to be convicted of a separate charge of possession of child pornography. Therefore, the defendant was convicted of the possession charge concerning the images he actually had on his computer in addition to being convicted of pandering—in violation of the Protect Act—regarding the images he purported to have but did not actually have.

Addressing the concern that the Protect Act might ensnare the grandparent who offers to provide a "cute" picture of her grandchild in the bathtub or the advertiser of R-rated movies that contain scenes suggesting sexual activity, the *Williams* majority opinion stressed the need to read the Protect Act narrowly. Justice Scalia reasoned that a strict reading of the statute and its "knowingly" requirement—coupled with the likely good faith of mainstream movie makers and the public's expectation that movies containing sex scenes are not usually made with minor actors—should not leave the grandparent or the movie advertiser at any serious risk of a Protect Act conviction.

---

an illegal activity. As a result, there is no First Amendment obstacle to federal or state regulation of deceptive commercial advertising. (Political or other noncommercial speech, on the other hand, generally receives—with very few exceptions—full First Amendment protection even if it misleads or deals with unlawful matters.)

Because nonmisleading commercial speech about a lawful activity receives intermediate protection, the government has greater ability to regulate such speech without

violating the First Amendment than when the government seeks to regulate fully protected political or other noncommercial speech. Nearly three decades ago, the Supreme Court developed a still-controlling test that amounts to intermediate scrutiny. Under this test, a government restriction on protected commercial speech does not violate the First Amendment if the government proves each of these elements: that a *substantial government interest* underlies the restriction; that the restriction

The First Amendment

Type of Speech	Level of First Amendment Protection	Consequences When Government Regulates Content of Speech
Noncommercial	Full	Government action is constitutional only if action is necessary to fulfillment of compelling government purpose. Otherwise, government action violates First Amendment.
Commercial (*nonmisleading and about lawful activity*)	Intermediate	Government action is constitutional if government has substantial underlying interest, action directly advances that interest, and action is no more extensive than necessary to fulfillment of that interest (i.e., action is narrowly tailored).
Commercial (*misleading or about unlawful activity*)	None	Government action is constitutional.

directly advances the underlying interest; and that the restriction is *no more extensive than necessary* to further the interest (i.e., that the restriction is narrowly tailored). It usually is not difficult for the government to prove that a substantial interest supports the commercial speech restriction. Almost any asserted interest connected with the promotion of public health, safety, or welfare will suffice. The government is likely to encounter more difficulty, however, in proving that the restriction at issue directly advances the underlying interest without being more extensive than necessary—the elements that address the "fit" between the restriction and the underlying interest. If the government fails to prove any element of the test, the restriction violates the First Amendment.

Although the same test has been used in evaluating commercial speech restrictions for nearly three decades, the Supreme Court has varied the intensity with which it has applied the test. From the mid-1980s until 1995, the Court sometimes applied the test loosely and in a manner favorable to the government. The Court has applied the test—especially the "fit" elements—more strictly since 1995, however. For instance, in *Coors v. Rubin* (1995), the Court struck down federal restrictions that kept beer producers from listing the alcohol content of their beer on product labels. (The *Coors* case was the subject of the introductory problem with which this chapter began.) In *44 Liquormart v. Rhode Island* (1996), the Court held that Rhode Island's prohibition on price disclosures in alcoholic beverage advertisements violated the First Amendment. A 1999 decision, *Greater New Orleans Broadcasting Association v. United States,* established

that a federal law barring broadcast advertisements for a variety of gambling activities could not constitutionally be applied to radio and television stations located in the same state as the gambling casino whose lawful activities were being advertised. In each of the cases just noted, the Court emphasized that the government's restrictions on commercial speech suffered from "fit" problems—usually because the restrictions prohibited more speech than would have been necessary if the government had adopted available alternative measures that would have furthered the underlying public health, safety, or welfare interest just as well, if not better.

Two key conclusions may be drawn from the Court's recent commercial speech decisions: (1) the government has found it more difficult to justify restrictions on commercial speech; and (2) the gap between the intermediate protection for commercial speech and the full protection for political and other noncommercial speech has effectively become smaller than it was approximately 20 years ago. Although the Court has hinted in recent cases that it might consider formal changes in commercial speech doctrine (so as to enhance First Amendment protection for commercial speech), it had not made formal doctrinal changes as of the time this book went to press in 2008.

In the following case, *Kasky v. Nike, Inc.,* the Supreme Court of California addresses a classification question: whether Nike engaged in fully protected noncommercial speech or, instead, commercial speech, when it made allegedly misleading statements in the course of a public relations campaign designed to refute claims about its overseas labor practices.

Kasky v. Nike, Inc.   45 P.3d 243 (Cal. Sup. Ct. 2002)

Nike, Inc. mounted a public relations campaign in order to refute news media allegations that its labor practices overseas were unfair and unlawful. This campaign involved the use of press releases, letters to newspapers, a letter to university presidents and athletic directors, and full-page advertisements in leading newspapers. Relying on California statutes designed to curb false and misleading advertising and other forms of unfair competition, California resident Mark Kasky filed suit in a California court on behalf of the general public of the state. Kasky contended that Nike had made false statements in its campaign and that the court should therefore grant the legal relief contemplated by the California statutes. Nike demurred on the ground, among others, that the First Amendment barred Kasky's action. The court, holding Nike's campaign to be fully protected under the First Amendment as noncommercial speech, sustained Nike's demurrer and dismissed Kasky's complaint. Kasky appealed, and the California Court of Appeal affirmed. The Supreme Court of California granted Kasky's petition for review.

Kennard, Justice

The U.S. Supreme Court has not adopted an all-purpose test to distinguish commercial from noncommercial speech under the First Amendment, nor do we propose to do so here. A close reading of the high court's commercial speech decisions suggests, however, that it is possible to formulate a limited-purpose test. We conclude, therefore, that *when a court must decide whether particular speech may be subjected to laws aimed at preventing false advertising or other forms of commercial deception,* categorizing a particular statement as commercial or noncommercial speech requires consideration of three elements: the speaker, the intended audience, and the content of the message.

In typical commercial speech cases, the *speaker* is likely to be someone engaged in commerce—that is, generally, the production, distribution, or sale of goods or services—or someone acting on behalf of a person so engaged. [T]he *intended audience* is likely to be actual or potential buyers or customers of the speaker's goods or services, or persons acting for actual or potential buyers or customers, or persons (such as reporters or reviewers) likely to repeat the message to or otherwise influence actual or potential buyers or customers. Considering the identity of both the speaker and the target audience is consistent with, and implicit in, the U.S. Supreme Court's commercial speech decisions. The Court has frequently spoken of commercial speech as speech proposing a commercial transaction, thus implying that commercial speech typically is communication between persons who engage in such transactions.

In addition, the factual content of the message should be commercial in character. In the context of regulation of false or misleading advertising, this typically means that the speech consists of representations of fact about the business operations, products, or services of the speaker (or the individual or company that the speaker represents), made for the purpose of promoting sales of, or other commercial transactions in, the speaker's products or services. This is consistent with . . . the Supreme Court's commercial speech decisions[, including *Bolger v. Youngs Drug Products Corp.,* 463 U.S. 60 (1983), in which the Court identified "product references" as a usual characteristic of commercial speech]. By "product references," we do not understand the Court to mean only statements about the price, qualities, or availability of individual items offered for sale. Rather, we understand "product references" to include also, for example, statements about the manner in which the products are manufactured, distributed, or sold, about repair or warranty services that the seller provides to purchasers of the product, or about the identity or qualifications of persons who manufacture, distribute, sell, service, or endorse the product. Similarly, references to services would include not only statements about the price, availability, and quality of the services themselves, but also, for example, statements about the education, experience, and qualifications of the persons providing or endorsing the services. This broad definition of "product references" is necessary, we think, to adequately categorize statements made in the context of a modern, sophisticated public relations campaign intended to increase sales and profits by enhancing the image of a product or of its manufacturer or seller.

Our understanding of the content element of commercial speech is also consistent with the reasons that the Court has given for denying First Amendment protection to false or misleading commercial speech. The Court stated[, in *Virginia State Board of Pharmacy v. Virginia Citizens Consumer Council, Inc.,* 425 U.S. 748 (1976),] that false or misleading commercial speech may be prohibited because the truth of commercial speech is "more easily verifiable by its disseminator" and because commercial speech, being motivated by the desire for economic profit, is less likely than noncommercial speech to be chilled by proper regulation.

Apart from this consideration of the identities of the speaker and the audience, and the contents of the speech, we find nothing in the U. S. Supreme Court's commercial speech decisions that is essential to a determination that particular speech is commercial in character. Although in *Bolger* the Court noted that the [commercial] speech at issue there was in a traditional advertising format, the court cautioned that it was not holding that this factor would always be necessary to the characterization of speech as commercial. Advertising format is by no means essential to characterization as commercial speech.

Here, the first element—a commercial speaker—is satisfied because the speakers—Nike and its officers and directors—are engaged in commerce. The second element—an intended commercial audience—is also satisfied. Nike's letters to university presidents and directors of athletic departments were addressed directly to actual and potential purchasers of Nike's products, because college and university athletic departments are major purchasers of athletic shoes and apparel. [Kasky] has alleged that Nike's press releases and letters to newspaper editors, although addressed to the public generally, were also intended to reach and influence actual and potential purchasers of Nike's products. Specifically, plaintiff has alleged that Nike made these statements about its labor policies and practices "to maintain and/or increase its sales and profits." To support this allegation, [he] has included as an exhibit a letter to a newspaper editor, written by Nike's director of communications, referring to Nike's labor policies practices and stating that "consumers are savvy and want to know they support companies with good products and practices" and that "during the shopping season, we encourage shoppers to remember that Nike is the industry's leader in improving factory conditions."

The third element—representations of fact of a commercial nature—is also present. In describing its own labor policies, and the practices and working conditions in factories where its products are made, Nike was making factual representations about its own business operations. In speaking to consumers about working conditions and labor practices in the factories where its products are made, Nike addressed matters within its own knowledge. The wages paid to the factories' employees, the hours they work, the way they are treated, and whether the environmental conditions under which they work violate local health and safety laws, are all matters likely to be within the personal knowledge of Nike executives, employees, or subcontractors. Thus, Nike was in a position to readily verify the truth of any factual assertions it made on these topics.

In speaking to consumers about working conditions in the factories where its products are made, Nike engaged in speech that is particularly hardy or durable. Because Nike's purpose in making these statements, at least as alleged in [Kasky's] complaint, was to maintain its sales and profits, regulation aimed at preventing false and actually or inherently misleading speech is unlikely to deter Nike from speaking truthfully or at all about the conditions in its factories. To the extent that application of these laws may make Nike more cautious, and cause it to make greater efforts to verify the truth of its statements, these laws will serve the purpose of commercial speech protection by[, as

noted in *Virginia Board of Pharmacy,*] "insuring that the stream of commercial information flows cleanly as well as freely."

Because Nike was acting as a commercial speaker, because its intended audience was primarily the buyers of its products, and because the statements consisted of factual representations about its own business operations, we conclude that the statements were commercial speech for purposes of applying state laws designed to prevent false advertising and other forms of commercial deception. Nike argues[, however,] that its allegedly false and misleading statements were not commercial speech because they were part of "an international media debate on issues of intense public interest." This argument falsely assumes that speech cannot properly be categorized as commercial speech if it relates to a matter of significant public interest or controversy. As the U.S. Supreme Court has [made clear], commercial speech commonly concerns matters of intense public and private interest. The individual consumer's interest in the price, availability, and characteristics of products and services "may be as keen, if not keener by far, than his interest in the day's most urgent political debate" (quoting *Virginia Board of Pharmacy*).

Nike's speech is not removed from the category of commercial speech because it is intermingled with noncommercial speech. To the extent Nike's press releases and letters discuss policy questions such as the degree to which domestic companies should be responsible for working conditions in factories located in other countries, or what standards domestic companies ought to observe in such factories, or the merits and effects of economic "globalization" generally, Nike's statements are noncommercial speech. Any content-based regulation of these noncommercial messages would be subject to the strict scrutiny test for fully protected speech. But Nike may not "immunize false or misleading product information from government regulation simply by including references to public issues" (quoting *Bolger*). Here, the alleged false and misleading statements all relate to the commercial portions of the speech in question—the description of actual conditions and practices in factories that produce Nike's products—and thus the proposed regulations reach only that commercial portion.

We also reject Nike's argument that regulating its speech to suppress false and misleading statements is impermissible because it would restrict or disfavor expression of one point of view (Nike's) and not the other point of view (that of the critics of Nike's labor practices). The argument is misdirected because the regulations in question do not suppress points of view but instead suppress false and misleading statements of fact. Moreover, differential treatment of speech about products and services based on the identity of the speaker is inherent in the commercial speech doctrine as articulated by the U.S. Supreme Court. A noncommercial speaker's statements criticizing a product are generally noncommercial speech, for which damages may be awarded only upon proof of both falsehood and actual malice. A commercial speaker's statements in praise or support of the same product, by comparison, are commercial speech that may be prohibited entirely to the extent the statements are either false or actually or inherently misleading.

We conclude, accordingly, that the trial court and the Court of Appeal erred in characterizing as noncommercial speech Nike's allegedly false and misleading statements about labor practices and working conditions in factories where Nike products are made. In concluding . . . that Nike's speech at issue here is commercial speech, we do not decide whether that speech was, as plaintiff has alleged, false or misleading. [That issue, as well as others, should be addressed on remand.]

Court of Appeal decision reversed and case remanded.

Figure 1   *A Note on Government Speech*

"Beef. It's What's for Dinner." This familiar tagline has been featured in numerous television commercials during recent years. Given the pro-beef messages being communicated, one might logically assume that a private association of beef marketers chose to pay for these commercials and selected the particular content included in them. Such an assumption would be inaccurate, however, because the beef advertisements referred to here were government-initiated and government-approved. The U.S. government has implemented various industry-specific regulatory regimes that require advertisements for a particular type of product—for example, beef, mushrooms, cotton, potatoes, watermelons, blueberries, pork, and eggs—and levy monetary assessments on producers or marketers of such products as a means of paying for the advertisements.

If producers or marketers of the regulated products disagree with the advertisements' content but are still compelled by federal law to help pay for the advertisements, are those parties' First Amendment rights violated? That was the issue presented in *Johanns v. Livestock Marketing Association,* 544 U.S. 550 (2005), in which the U.S. Supreme Court considered numerous livestock marketers' First Amendment challenge to the government's beef advertising program. The familiar "Beef. It's What's for Dinner" commercials were part of that program. In the Beef Promotion and Research Act of 1985 (Beef Act), Congress established a federal policy of promoting the marketing and consumption of beef. The Beef Act called for the Secretary of Agriculture (Secretary) to issue an order setting up an advisory board and operating committee charged with, among other things, designing a beef advertising program that would be subject to the Secretary's approval. To fund the advertisements, the Beef Act directed the Secretary to impose a $1-per-head assessment on all sales or importations of cattle and a similar assessment on imported beef products. Although the members of the advisory board and operating committee were private parties rather than government officials, the Secretary possessed and exercised final approval rights over the content of the advertisements.

The beef marketers who challenged the advertising program objected to its generic pro-beef message, which they saw as impeding their individual efforts to advertise their particular beef (e.g., grain-fed, certified Angus, or Hereford) as superior to other beef. They based their challenge on two lines of cases: the *compelled speech* decisions, which found First Amendment problems with governmental attempts to require persons to communicate messages with which they disagreed; and the *compelled subsidy* decisions, which established that the First Amendment is implicated when the government requires one party to subsidize (in a financial sense) the speech of another party even though the subsidizing party disagrees with the speech. A federal district court and court of appeals both ruled in favor of the beef marketers, holding largely on the basis of the compelled subsidy line of cases that the beef advertising program violated the First Amendment.

In *Johanns v. Livestock Marketing Association,* however, the Supreme Court reversed the lower courts' decisions. The Supreme Court stressed that the compelled speech and compelled subsidy cases apply only when the mandated message, or the speech being subsidized, is private in nature, as opposed to that of the government. The Court held that when *government speech* is involved, there is no First Amendment barrier to the government's requirement that individuals or corporations contribute financially—whether through general tax revenues or targeted assessments—to the communication of that speech. According to the Court, the advertising program at issue in *Livestock Marketing* was government speech because Congress set up the legal parameters of the beef promotions initiative, required the Secretary to take certain actions to launch and maintain it, and gave the Secretary final authority to approve the content of the advertisements. Despite the presence of private parties on the advisory board and the operating committee, the legal structure just noted made the message of the beef advertisements "from beginning to end the message established by the federal government."

The Court further noted that the pervasive nature of the statutory and administrative regime made the beef advertisements government speech even though the advertisements' reference to sponsorship by "America's Beef Producers" did not send a clear government speech signal to readers and viewers. The Court conceded that the beef promotions program upheld in *Livestock Marketing* was exceedingly similar to the federal government's mushroom promotions program, which the Court had struck down as a violation of the First Amendment only four years earlier. In that earlier case, however, the government speech issue had not been before the Court. Because the government speech issue was properly presented in *Livestock Marketing,* the Court reasoned that it was not bound by the earlier decision and was free to sustain the beef promotions program on the government speech ground.

Although the specifics of each regulatory initiative requiring subsidization of advertisements for a type of product must be examined in order to make a clear determination of whether the advertising at issue is government speech, the analysis in *Livestock Marketing* appears to give the government considerable latitude to implement such programs without violating the First Amendment rights of product producers and marketers who are unhappy with the advertising they must subsidize.

Due Process

Due Process The Fifth and Fourteenth Amendments require that the federal government and the states observe **due process** when they deprive a person of life, liberty, or property. Due process has both *procedural* and *substantive* meanings.

Procedural Due Process The traditional conception of due process, called **procedural due process,** establishes the *procedures* that government must follow when it takes life, liberty, or property. Although the requirements of procedural due process vary from situation to situation, their core idea is that one is entitled to adequate *notice* of the government action to be taken against him and to some sort of *fair trial or hearing* before that action can occur.

For purposes of procedural due process claims, *liberty* includes a very broad and poorly defined range of freedoms. It even includes certain interests in personal reputation. For example, the firing of a government employee may require some kind of due process hearing if it is publicized, the fired employee's reputation is sufficiently damaged, and her future employment opportunities are restricted. The Supreme Court has said that procedural due process *property* is not created by the Constitution but by existing rules and understandings that stem from an independent source such as state law. These rules and understandings must give a person a *legitimate claim of entitlement* to a benefit, not merely some need, desire, or expectation for it. This definition includes almost all of the usual forms of property, as well as utility service, disability benefits, welfare benefits, and a driver's license. It also includes the job rights of tenured public employees who can be discharged only for cause, but not the rights of untenured or probationary employees.

Substantive Due Process Procedural due process does not challenge rules of *substantive law*—the rules that set standards of behavior for organized social life. For example, imagine that State X makes adultery a crime and allows people to be convicted of adultery without a trial. Arguments that adultery should not be a crime go to the substance of the statute, whereas objections to the lack of a trial are procedural in nature.

Sometimes, the due process clauses have been used to attack the substance of government action. For our purposes, the most important example of this **substantive due process** occurred early in the 20th century, when courts struck down various kinds of social legislation as denying due process. They did so mainly by reading freedom of contract and other economic rights into the liberty and property protected by the Fifth and Fourteenth Amendments, and then interpreting "due process of law" to require that laws denying such rights be subjected to means-ends scrutiny. The best-known example is the Supreme Court's 1905 decision in *Lochner v. New York,* which struck down a state law setting maximum hours of work for bakery employees because the statute limited freedom of contract and did not directly advance the legitimate state goal of promoting worker health.

Since 1937, however, this "economic" form of substantive due process has been largely abandoned by the Supreme Court and has not amounted to a significant check on government regulation of economic matters. Substantive due process attacks on such regulations now trigger only a lenient type of rational basis review and thus have had little chance of success. During the 1970s and 1980s, however, substantive due process became increasingly important as a device for protecting *noneconomic* rights. The most important example is the constitutional right of privacy, which consists of several rights that the Supreme Court regards as fundamental and as entitled to significant constitutional protection. The Court has declared that these include the rights to marry, have children and direct their education and upbringing, enjoy marital privacy, use contraception, and elect to have an abortion. Laws restricting these rights must be narrowly tailored to meet a compelling government purpose in order to avoid being declared unconstitutional.

Equal Protection
The Fourteenth Amendment's Equal Protection Clause says that "[n]o State shall . . . deny to any person . . . the equal protection of the laws." Because the equal protection guarantee has been incorporated within Fifth Amendment due process, it also restricts the federal government. As currently interpreted, the equal protection guarantee potentially applies to all situations in which government *classifies* or *distinguishes* people. The law inevitably makes distinctions among people, benefiting or burdening some groups but not others. Equal protection doctrine, as developed by the Supreme Court, sets the standards such distinctions must meet in order to be constitutional.

The Basic Test   The basic equal protection standard is the *rational basis* test described earlier. This is the standard usually applied to social and economic regulations that are challenged as denying equal protection. As the following case illustrates, this lenient test usually does not impede state and federal regulation of social and economic matters.

Fitzgerald v. Racing Association of Central Iowa
539 U.S. 103 (U.S. Sup. Ct. 2003)

Before 1989, Iowa permitted only one form of gambling: parimutuel betting at racetracks. A 1989 Iowa statute authorized other forms of gambling, including slot machines on riverboats. The 1989 law established that adjusted revenues from riverboat slot machine gambling would be taxed at graduated rates, with a top rate of 20 percent. In 1994, Iowa enacted a law that authorized racetracks to operate slot machines. That law also imposed a graduated tax upon racetrack slot machine adjusted revenues, with a top rate that started at 20 percent and would automatically rise over time to 36 percent. The 1994 enactment left in place the 20 percent tax rate on riverboat slot machine adjusted revenues.

Contending that the 1994 legislation's 20 percent versus 36 percent tax rate difference violated the federal Constitution's Equal Protection Clause, a group of racetracks and an association of dog owners brought suit against the State of Iowa (through its state treasurer, Michael Fitzgerald). A state district court upheld the statute, but the Iowa Supreme Court reversed. The U.S. Supreme Court granted Iowa's petition for a writ of certiorari.

Breyer, Justice

We here consider whether a difference in state tax rates violates the Fourteenth Amendment's mandate that "no State shall . . . deny to any person . . . the equal protection of the laws." The law in question does not distinguish on the basis of, for example, race or gender. It does not distinguish between in-state and out-of-state businesses. Neither does it favor a State's long-time residents at the expense of residents who have more recently arrived from other States. Rather, the law distinguishes for tax purposes among revenues obtained within the State of Iowa by two enterprises, each of which does business in the State. Where that is so, the law is subject to rational-basis review:

> The Equal Protection Clause is satisfied so long as there is a plausible policy reason for the classification, the legislative facts on which the classification is apparently based rationally may have been considered to be true by the governmental decisionmaker, and the relationship of the classification to its goal is not so attenuated as to render the distinction arbitrary or irrational.

[Case citation omitted.] [We have also held that] rational-basis review "is especially deferential in the context of classifications made by complex tax laws." [Case citation omitted.]

The Iowa Supreme Court found that the 20 percent/36 percent tax rate differential failed to meet this standard because, in its view, that difference frustrated what it saw as the law's basic objective, namely, rescuing the racetracks from economic distress. And no rational person, it believed, could claim the contrary. The Iowa Supreme Court could not deny, however, that the Iowa law, like most laws, might predominately serve one general objective, say, helping the racetracks, while containing subsidiary provisions that seek to achieve other desirable (perhaps even contrary) ends as well, thereby producing a law that balances objectives but still serves the general objective when seen as a whole. After all, if *every* subsidiary provision in a law designed to help racetracks had to help those racetracks and nothing more, then (since any tax rate hurts the racetracks when compared with a lower rate) there could be no taxation of the racetracks at all.

Neither could the Iowa Supreme Court deny that the 1994 legislation, *seen as a whole,* can rationally be understood to do what that court says it seeks to do, namely, advance the racetracks' economic interests. Its grant to the racetracks of authority to operate slot machines should help the racetracks economically to some degree—even if its simultaneous imposition of a tax on slot machine adjusted revenue means that the law provides less help than respondents might like. At least a rational legislator might so believe. And the Constitution grants legislators, not courts, broad authority (within the bounds of rationality) to decide whom they wish to help with their tax laws and how much help those laws ought to provide. "The 'task of classifying persons for . . . benefits . . . inevitably requires that some persons who have an almost equally strong claim to favored treatment be placed on different sides of the line,' and the fact the line might have been drawn differently at some points is a matter for legislative, rather than judicial, consideration." [Case citation omitted.]

Once one realizes that not every provision in a law must share a single objective, one has no difficulty finding the necessary rational support for the 20 percent/36 percent differential here at issue. That difference, harmful to the racetracks, is helpful to the riverboats, which, as [those challenging the 1994 statute]

concede, were also facing financial peril. These two characterizations are but opposite sides of the same coin. Each reflects a rational way for a legislator to view the matter. And aside from simply aiding the financial position of the riverboats, the legislators may have wanted to encourage the economic development of river communities or to promote riverboat history, say, by providing incentives for riverboats to remain in the State, rather than relocate to other States. Alternatively, they may have wanted to protect the reliance interests of riverboat operators, whose adjusted slot machine revenue had previously been taxed at the 20 percent rate. All these objectives are rational ones, which lower riverboat tax rates could further and which suffice to uphold the different tax rates.

We conclude that there is "a plausible policy reason for the classification," that the legislature "rationally may have . . . considered . . . true" the related justifying "legislative facts," and that the "relationship of the classification to its goal is not so attenuated as to render the distinction arbitrary or irrational." [Case citation omitted.] Consequently the State's differential tax rate does not violate the Federal Equal Protection Clause.

Iowa Supreme Court decision reversed, and case remanded for further proceedings.

Stricter Scrutiny The rational basis test is the basic equal protection standard. Some classifications, however, receive tougher means-ends scrutiny. According to Supreme Court precedent, laws that discriminate regarding **fundamental rights** or **suspect classes** must undergo more rigorous review.

Although the list of rights regarded as "fundamental" for equal protection purposes is not completely clear, it includes certain criminal procedure protections as well as the rights to vote and engage in interstate travel. Laws creating unequal enjoyment of these rights receive full strict scrutiny. In 1969, for instance, the Supreme Court struck down the District of Columbia's one-year residency requirement for receiving welfare benefits because that requirement unequally and impermissibly restricted the right of interstate travel.

An equal protection claim involving the fundamental right to vote was addressed in high-profile fashion by the Supreme Court in *Bush v. Gore,* 531 U.S. 98 (2000). A five-justice majority in the historic and controversial decision terminated an ongoing vote recount in Florida because, in the majority's view, Florida law's "intent of the voter" test was not a sufficiently clear standard for determining whether a ballot not counted in the initial machine count should be counted as valid during the

manual recount. The majority was concerned that in the absence of a more specific standard, vote counters taking part in the recount might apply inconsistent standards in determining what the voter supposedly intended, and might thereby value some votes over others. The termination of the Florida recount meant that then-Governor Bush won the state of Florida, giving him enough Electoral College votes to win the presidency despite the fact that candidate Gore tallied more popular votes nationally. The four dissenters in *Bush v. Gore* faulted the majority for focusing on the supposed equal protection violation it identified, when, in the dissenters' view, the Court ignored a potentially bigger equal protection problem created by termination of the recount: the prospect that large numbers of ballots not counted during the machine count would never be counted, even though they may have been valid votes under Florida's "intent of the voter" test.

In *Crawford v. Marion County Election Board,* 128 S. Ct. 1610 (2008), the Supreme Court again addressed the fundamental right to vote. This time, the Court was faced with determining whether an Indiana law violated the Equal Protection Clause by requiring that voters produce a government-issued photo ID as a precondition to being allowed to vote. Those who raised the equal protection challenge to the requirement asserted that its burdens would fall disproportionately on low-income and elderly voters, who would be less likely than other persons to have a driver's license or other photo ID and would not be able to exercise the right to vote if they lacked the necessary photo ID. The Court upheld the Indiana law, ruling that it did not violate the Equal Protection Clause. The six justices in the majority split into two three-justice camps on the details of the appropriate supporting reasoning. They agreed, however, that even though voter fraud at the polls had not been a demonstrated problem in Indiana, the photo ID requirement was a generally applicable and not excessively burdensome way of furthering the state's purposes of preventing voter fraud and preserving voter confidence in the integrity of elections.

Certain "suspect" bases of classification also trigger more rigorous equal protection review. As of 2008, the **suspect classes** and the level of scrutiny they attract are as follows:

1. *Race and national origin.* Classifications disadvantaging racial or national minorities receive the most rigorous kind of strict scrutiny and are almost never constitutional. Still, the Supreme Court has sometimes upheld government-required affirmative action plans and what critics have called reverse racial discrimination—government action that benefits racial minorities and allegedly disadvantages whites. In 1989, however, a majority of the Court concluded that state action of this kind should receive the same full strict scrutiny as discrimination *against* racial or national minorities. Reversing a 1990 ruling, a 1995 Supreme Court decision held that this is true of federal government action as well as state action. These developments have curtailed certain government-created affirmative action programs but have not eliminated them.

In the companion cases of *Gratz v. Bollinger,* 539 U.S. 244 (2003), and *Grutter v. Bollinger,* 539 U.S. 306 (2003), the Supreme Court considered whether the University of Michigan violated the Equal Protection Clause by taking minority students' race into account in its undergraduate and law school admissions policies. The Court recognized in the two cases that seeking student diversity in a higher education context is a compelling government interest. However, in *Gratz,* a five-justice majority of the Court held that the university's undergraduate admissions policy violated the Equal Protection Clause because the policy's consideration of minority applicants' race became effectively the automatic determining factor in admission decisions regarding minority applicants. In *Grutter,* on the other hand, a different five-justice majority held that the university's law school admissions policy did not violate the Equal Protection Clause. The *Grutter* majority reasoned that the law school's policy, in considering minority applicants' race, did so as part of individualized consideration of applicants and of various types of diversity, not simply race. Thus, the law school's policy did not make race *the* determining factor in the impermissible way that the undergraduate policy did.

After the decisions in *Gratz* and *Grutter,* two new justices—Chief Justice Roberts and Justice Alito—joined the Court as replacements for Chief Justice Rehnquist (who died) and Justice O'Connor (who retired). In a much-anticipated decision, *Parents Involved in Community Schools v. Seattle School District No. 1,* 127 S. Ct. 2738 (2007), the Court held that public school districts in Washington and Kentucky violated the Equal Protection Clause in the ways that they considered race when assigning students to schools. There was a five-justice majority for this holding, but Justice Kennedy's crucial fifth vote came in a concurring

Ethics in Action

As discussion in this chapter reveals, Supreme Court precedent establishes that when government action discriminates on the basis of race or sex, the action will receive heightened scrutiny from the Court in an equal protection case. Sexual orientation, however, has not been treated by the Supreme Court as a classification basis that justifies heightened scrutiny. This means that the lenient rational basis review will be employed by a court deciding an equal protection case in which the government is alleged to have discriminated on the basis of sexual orientation. In a *legal* sense, then, the government has more latitude to regulate in ways that draw lines on the basis of persons' sexual preference than in ways that classify on the basis of persons' race or gender. Now view this set of issues from an *ethical* perspective. Should the government be any more free to take actions that discriminate against homosexuals—or, for that matter, against heterosexuals—than it is to take actions that discriminate on the basis of race or sex? As you consider this question, you may wish to examine Chapter 4's discussion of ethical theories and ethical decision making.

opinion that rejected much of the reasoning in the plurality opinion authored by Chief Justice Roberts (and joined by Justices Scalia, Thomas, and Alito). Justice Breyer authored a lengthy dissent in which he spoke for himself and Justices Stevens, Souter, and Ginsburg. In order to provide a sense of the Court's divisions on the questions before it, the edited version of *Parents Involved in Community Schools* (which follows shortly), includes portions of the Chief Justice's plurality opinion, the Kennedy concurrence in the judgment, and the Breyer dissent. (Students may want to look back at Chapter 1's discussion of legal reasoning before reading the case.)

2. *Alienage.* Classifications based on one's status as an alien also receive strict scrutiny of some kind, but this standard almost certainly is not as tough as the full strict scrutiny normally used in race discrimination cases. Under the "political function" exception, moreover, laws restricting aliens from employment in positions that are intimately related to democratic self-government only receive *rational basis* review. This exception has been read broadly to allow the upholding of laws that exclude aliens from being state troopers, public school teachers, and probation officers.

3. *Sex.* Although the Supreme Court has been hesitant to make a formal declaration that sex is a suspect class, for well more than 30 years laws discriminating on the basis of gender have been subjected to a fairly rigorous form of *intermediate scrutiny.* As the Court said in 1996, such laws require an "exceedingly persuasive" justification. The usual test is that government action discriminating on the basis of sex must be *substantially* related to the furtherance of an *important* government purpose. Under this test, measures discriminating against women have almost always been struck down. The Supreme Court has said that laws disadvantaging men receive the same scrutiny as those disadvantaging women, but this has not prevented the Court from upholding men-only draft registration and a law making statutory rape a crime for men alone.

4. *Illegitimacy.* Classifications based on one's illegitimate birth receive a form of *intermediate scrutiny* that probably is less strict than the scrutiny given gender-based classifications. Under this vague standard, the Court has struck down state laws discriminating against illegitimates in areas such as recovery for wrongful death, workers' compensation benefits, Social Security payments, inheritance, and child support.

Parents Involved in Community Schools v. Seattle School District No. 1
127 S. Ct. 2738 (U.S. Sup. Ct. 2007)

School districts in Seattle, Washington, and Jefferson County, Kentucky, voluntarily adopted student assignment plans that relied on race to determine which schools certain children may attend. The Seattle district, which had neither created segregated schools nor been subject to court-ordered desegregation, generally allowed students to choose what high school they wished to attend. However, the district classified students as white or nonwhite and used the racial classifications as a "tiebreaker" to allocate available slots in particular high schools and thereby seek to achieve racially diverse schools despite the existence of housing patterns that would have produced little racial diversity at schools in certain areas of the city. The Jefferson County district was subject to a federal court's desegregation decree from 1975 until 2000, when the court dissolved the decree after finding that the district had eliminated the vestiges of prior segregation to the greatest extent feasible. In 2001, the district adopted a plan that classified students as black or "other" in order to make certain elementary school assignments and to rule on transfer requests. By doing so, the district sought to achieve racial diversity in schools that otherwise would have reflected less racial diversity in light of traditional housing patterns.

An organization of Seattle parents and the mother of a Jefferson County student, whose children were or could be assigned under the plans described above, filed separate suits contending that allocating children to different public schools based solely on their race violated the Fourteenth Amendment's Equal Protection Clause. In the Seattle case, the district court granted the school district summary judgment, finding that its plan survived strict scrutiny because it was narrowly tailored to serve a compelling government interest in achieving a racially diverse educational environment. The U. S. Court of Appeals for the Ninth Circuit affirmed. In the Jefferson County case, the district court found that the school district had asserted a compelling interest in maintaining racially diverse schools, and that its plan was narrowly tailored to serve that interest. The U.S. Court of Appeals for the Sixth Circuit affirmed. The U.S. Supreme Court consolidated the cases for decision and granted the respective school districts' petitions for a writ of certiorari.

Roberts, Chief Justice

Both cases present the same underlying legal question— whether a public school that had not operated legally segregated schools or has been found to be unitary may choose to classify students by race and rely upon that classification in making school assignments.

It is well-established that when the government distributes burdens or benefits on the basis of individual racial classifications, that action is reviewed under strict scrutiny. [*E.g.,*] *Grutter v. Bollinger,* 539 U.S. 306 (2003). As the Court recently reaffirmed, "racial classifications are simply too pernicious to permit any but the most exact connection between justification and classification." *Gratz v. Bollinger,* 539 U.S. 244, 270 (2003). In order to satisfy this searching standard of review, the school districts must demonstrate that the use of individual racial classifications in the assignment plans here under review is narrowly tailored to achieve a compelling government interest.

Without attempting to set forth all the interests a school district might assert, it suffices to note that our prior cases, in evaluating the use of racial classifications in the school context, have recognized two interests that qualify as compelling. The first is the compelling interest of remedying the effects of past intentional discrimination. Yet the Seattle public schools have not shown that they were ever segregated by law, and were not subject to court-ordered desegregation decrees. The Jefferson County public schools were previously segregated by law and were subject to a desegregation decree entered in 1975. In 2000, the District Court that entered that decree dissolved it, finding that Jefferson County had eliminated the vestiges associated with the former policy of segregation and its pernicious effects, and thus had achieved unitary status. Jefferson County accordingly does not rely upon an interest in remedying the effects of past intentional discrimination in defending its present use of race in assigning students.

The second government interest we have recognized as compelling for purposes of strict scrutiny is the interest in diversity in higher education upheld in *Grutter.* The specific interest found compelling in *Grutter* was student body diversity "in the context of higher education." The diversity interest was not focused on race alone but encompassed "all factors that may contribute to student body diversity." We described the various types of diversity that the law school sought[, noting that the law school's policy] "makes clear there are many possible bases for diversity admissions, and provides examples of admittees who have lived or traveled widely abroad, are fluent in several languages, have overcome personal adversity and family hardship, have exceptional records of extensive community service, and have had successful careers in other fields."

The entire gist of the analysis in *Grutter* was that the admissions program at issue there focused on each applicant as an individual, and not simply as a member of a particular racial group. The classification of applicants by race upheld in *Grutter* was only as part of a "highly individualized, holistic review." The point of the narrow tailoring analysis in which the *Grutter* Court engaged was to ensure that the use of racial classifications was indeed part of a broader assessment of diversity, and not simply an effort to achieve racial balance, which the Court explained would be "patently unconstitutional."

In the present cases, by contrast, race is not considered as part of a broader effort to achieve "exposure to widely diverse people, cultures, ideas, and viewpoints." Race, for some students, is determinative standing alone. The districts argue that other factors, such as student preferences, affect assignment decisions under their plans, but under each plan when race comes into play, it is decisive by itself. It is not simply one factor weighed with others in reaching a decision, as in *Grutter;* it is the factor. Like the University of Michigan undergraduate plan struck down in *Gratz,* the plans here do not provide for a meaningful individualized review of applicants but instead rely on racial classifications in a nonindividualized, mechanical way.

In upholding the admissions plan in *Grutter,* . . . this Court relied upon considerations unique to institutions of higher education, noting that in light of "the expansive freedoms of speech and thought associated with the university environment, universities occupy a special niche in our constitutional tradition." The Court in *Grutter* expressly articulated key limitations on its holding—defining a specific type of broad-based diversity and noting the unique context of higher education—but these limitations were largely disregarded by the lower courts in extending *Grutter* to uphold race-based assignments in elementary and secondary schools. The present cases are not governed by *Grutter*.

Perhaps recognizing that reliance on *Grutter* cannot sustain their plans, both school districts assert additional interests, distinct from the interest upheld in *Grutter,* to justify their race-based assignments. Seattle contends that its use of race helps to reduce racial concentration in schools and to ensure that racially concentrated housing patterns do not prevent nonwhite students from having access to the most desirable schools. Jefferson County has articulated a similar goal, phrasing its interest in terms of educating its students in a racially integrated environment. Each school district argues that educational and broader socialization benefits flow from a racially diverse learning environment, and each contends that because the diversity they seek is racial diversity—not the broader diversity at issue in *Grutter*—it makes sense to promote that interest directly by relying on race alone.

The parties dispute whether racial diversity in schools in fact has a marked impact on test scores and other objective yardsticks or achieves intangible socialization benefits. The debate is not one we need to resolve, however, because it is clear that the racial classifications employed by the districts are not narrowly tailored to the goal of achieving the educational and social benefits asserted to flow from racial diversity. In design and operation, the plans are directed only to racial balance, pure and simple, an objective this Court has repeatedly condemned as illegitimate.

The plans are tied to each district's specific racial demographics, rather than to any pedagogic concept of the level of diversity needed to obtain the asserted educational benefits. In Seattle, the district seeks white enrollment of between 31 and 51 percent (within 10 percent of the district white average of 41 percent), and nonwhite enrollment of between 49 and 69 percent (within 10 percent of the district minority average of 59 percent). In Jefferson County, by contrast, the district seeks black enrollment of no less than 15 or more than 50 percent, a range designed to be equally above and below black student enrollment systemwide. In Seattle, then, the benefits of racial diversity require enrollment of at least 31 percent white students; in Jefferson County, at least 50 percent. There must be at least 15 percent nonwhite students under Jefferson County's plan; in Seattle, more than three times that figure. This comparison makes clear that the racial demographics in each district—whatever they happen to be—drive the required "diversity" numbers. The plans here are not tailored to achieving a degree of diversity necessary to realize the asserted educational benefits; instead the plans are tailored [to a goal of attaining a level of diversity within the schools that approximates the district's overall demographics]. The districts offer no evidence that the level of racial diversity necessary to achieve the asserted educational benefits happens to coincide with the racial demographics of the respective school districts.

In Grutter, the number of minority students the school sought to admit was an undefined "meaningful number" necessary to achieve a genuinely diverse student body. Although the matter was the subject of disagreement on the Court, the majority concluded that the law school did not count back from its applicant pool to arrive at the "meaningful number" it regarded as necessary to diversify its student body. Here the racial balance the districts seek is a defined range set solely by reference to the demographics of the respective school districts.

This working backward to achieve a particular type of racial balance, rather than working forward from some demonstration of the level of diversity that provides the purported benefits, is a fatal flaw under our existing precedent. We have many times

over reaffirmed that "racial balance is not to be achieved for its own sake." [Case citation omitted.] Grutter itself reiterated that "outright racial balancing" is "patently unconstitutional."

Accepting racial balancing as a compelling state interest would justify the imposition of racial proportionality throughout American society, contrary to our repeated recognition that "at the heart of the Constitution's guarantee of equal protection lies the simple command that the Government must treat citizens as individuals, not as simply components of a racial, religious, sexual or national class." [Case citation omitted.] Racial balancing is not transformed from "patently unconstitutional" to a compelling state interest simply by relabeling it "racial diversity." While the school districts use various verbal formulations to describe the interest they seek to promote—racial diversity, avoidance of racial isolation, racial integration—they offer no definition of the interest that suggests it differs from racial balance.

The districts have also failed to show that they considered methods other than explicit racial classifications to achieve their stated goals. Narrow tailoring requires "serious, good faith consideration of workable race-neutral alternatives," [case citation omitted,] and yet in Seattle several alternative assignment plans—many of which would not have used express racial classifications—were rejected with little or no consideration. Jefferson County has failed to present any evidence that it considered alternatives.

In Brown v. Board of Education, 347 U.S. 483 (1954), we held that segregation deprived black children of equal educational opportunities regardless of whether school facilities and other tangible factors were equal, because government classification and separation on grounds of race themselves denoted inferiority. It was not the inequality of the facilities but the fact of legally separating children on the basis of race on which the Court relied to find a constitutional violation in 1954. The parties . . . debate which side is more faithful to the heritage of Brown, but the position of the plaintiffs in Brown was spelled out in their brief and could not have been clearer: "The Fourteenth Amendment prevents states from according differential treatment to American children on the basis of their color or race." What do the racial classifications at issue here do, if not accord differential treatment on the basis of race? As counsel who appeared before this Court for the plaintiffs in Brown put it: "We have one fundamental contention which we will seek to develop in the course of this argument, and that contention is that no State has any authority under the equal-protection clause of the Fourteenth Amendment to use race as a factor in affording educational opportunities among its citizens." There is no ambiguity in that statement. And it was that position that prevailed in this Court. What do the racial classifications do in these cases, if not determine admission to a public school on a racial basis?

Before *Brown,* schoolchildren were told where they could and could not go to school based on the color of their skin. The school districts in these cases have not carried the heavy burden of demonstrating that we should allow this once again—even for very different reasons. For schools that never segregated on the basis of race, such as Seattle, or that have removed the vestiges of past segregation, such as Jefferson County, the way "to achieve a system of determining admission to the public schools on a nonracial basis" [quoting *Brown*] is to stop assigning students on a racial basis. The way to stop discrimination on the basis of race is to stop discriminating on the basis of race.

Decisions of Sixth and Ninth Circuit Courts of Appeal reversed, and cases remanded for further proceedings.

Kennedy, Justice, concurring in part and concurring in the judgment

In my view the state-mandated racial classifications at issue . . . are unconstitutional as the cases now come to us. I agree with The Chief Justice that [the Seattle and Jefferson County plans violate the Equal Protection Clause]. My views[, however,] do not allow me to join the balance of the [plurality] opinion by The Chief Justice. The plurality [opinion] does not acknowledge that the school districts have identified a compelling interest here. For this reason, among others, I [join only portions of the plurality opinion]. Diversity, depending on its meaning and definition, is a compelling educational goal a school district may pursue.

[P]arts of the opinion by The Chief Justice imply an all-too-unyielding insistence that race cannot be a factor in instances when, in my view, it may be taken into account. The plurality opinion is too dismissive of the legitimate interest government has in ensuring all people have equal opportunity regardless of their race. The plurality's postulate that "the way to stop discrimination on the basis of race is to stop discriminating on the basis of race" is not sufficient to decide these cases. Fifty years of experience since *Brown v. Board of Education* should teach us that the problem before us defies so easy a solution. School districts can seek to reach *Brown*'s objective of equal educational opportunity. The plurality opinion is at least open to the interpretation that the Constitution requires school districts to ignore the problem of de facto resegregation in schooling. I cannot endorse that conclusion. To the extent the plurality opinion suggests the Constitution mandates that state and local school authorities must accept the status quo of racial isolation in schools, it is, in my view, profoundly mistaken.

In the administration of public schools by the state and local authorities it is permissible to consider the racial makeup of schools and to adopt general policies to encourage a diverse student body, one aspect of which is its racial composition. If school authorities are concerned that the student-body compositions of certain schools interfere with the objective of offering an equal educational opportunity to all of their students, they are free to devise race-conscious measures to address the problem in a general way and without treating each student in different fashion solely on the basis of a systematic, individual typing by race. School boards may pursue the goal of bringing together students of diverse backgrounds and races through other means, including strategic site selection of new schools; drawing attendance zones with general recognition of the demographics of neighborhoods; allocating resources for special programs; recruiting students and faculty in a targeted fashion; and tracking enrollments, performance, and other statistics by race. These mechanisms are race-conscious but do not lead to different treatment based on a classification that tells each student he or she is to be defined by race, so [none of them should be found unconstitutional].

This Nation has a moral and ethical obligation to fulfill its historic commitment to creating an integrated society that ensures equal opportunity for all of its children. A compelling interest exists in avoiding racial isolation, an interest that a school district, in its discretion and expertise, may choose to pursue. Likewise, a district may consider it a compelling interest to achieve a diverse student population. Race may be one component of that diversity, but other demographic factors, plus special talents and needs, should also be considered. What the government is not permitted to do, absent a showing of necessity not made here, is to classify every student [solely] on the basis of race and to assign each of them to schools based on that classification.

The decision today should not prevent school districts from continuing the important work of bringing together students of different racial, ethnic, and economic backgrounds. Due to a variety of factors—some influenced by government, some not—neighborhoods in our communities do not reflect the diversity of our Nation as a whole. Those entrusted with directing our public schools can bring to bear the creativity of experts, parents, administrators, and other concerned citizens to find a way to achieve the compelling interests they face without resorting to widespread governmental allocation of benefits and burdens on the basis of racial classifications.

Breyer, Justice, dissenting

The school board plans before us resemble many others adopted in the last 50 years by primary and secondary schools throughout the Nation. All of those plans represent local efforts to bring about the kind of racially integrated education that *Brown v. Board of Education* long ago promised—efforts that this Court has repeatedly required, permitted, and encouraged local authorities to undertake. This Court has recognized that the public interests at stake in such cases are "compelling." We have approved of "narrowly tailored" plans that are no less race-conscious than the plans before us. And we have understood that the Constitution permits local communities to adopt desegregation plans even where it does not require them to do so.

The plurality pays inadequate attention to this law, to past opinions' rationales, their language, and the contexts in which they arise. As a result, it reverses course and reaches the wrong conclusion. In doing so, it distorts precedent, it misapplies the relevant constitutional principles, it announces legal rules that will obstruct efforts by state and local governments to deal effectively with the growing resegregation of public schools, it threatens to substitute for present calm a disruptive round of race-related litigation, and it undermines *Brown*'s promise of integrated primary and secondary education that local communities have sought to make a reality. This cannot be justified in the name of the Equal Protection Clause.

There is reason to believe that those who drafted [the Equal Protection Clause] would have understood the legal and practical difference between the use of race-conscious criteria . . . to keep the races apart, and the use of race-conscious criteria . . . to bring the races together. Although the Constitution almost always forbids the former, it is significantly more lenient in respect to the latter. Until today, this Court understood the Constitution as affording the people, acting through their elected representatives, freedom to select the use of "race-conscious" criteria from among their available options [in an effort to promote integration]. Yesterday, the citizens of this Nation could look for guidance to this Court's unanimous pronouncements concerning desegregation. Today, they cannot. Yesterday, school boards had available to them a full range of means to combat segregated schools. Today, they do not.

The Court's decision undermines other basic institutional principles as well. What has happened to *stare decisis?* The history of the plans before us, their educational importance, their highly limited use of race—all these and more—make clear that the compelling interest here is stronger than in *Grutter*. The plans here are more narrowly tailored than the law school admissions program there at issue. Hence, applying *Grutter*'s strict test, their lawfulness follows *a fortiori*.

And what of the long history and moral vision that the Fourteenth Amendment itself embodies? The plurality cites in support those who argued in *Brown* against segregation. But segregation policies did not simply tell schoolchildren "where they could and could not go to school based on the color of their skin" [quoting the plurality opinion]; they perpetuated a caste system rooted in the institutions of slavery and 80 years of legalized subordination. The lesson of history is not that efforts to continue racial segregation are constitutionally indistinguishable from efforts to achieve racial integration. Indeed, it is a cruel distortion of history to compare Topeka, Kansas, in the 1950s [the setting in *Brown*] to Louisville and Seattle in the modern day—to equate the plight of Linda Brown (who was ordered to attend a Jim Crow school [in 1950s Topeka]) to the circumstances of Joshua McDonald (whose request to transfer to a [Jefferson County] school closer to home was initially declined).

Finally, what of the hope and promise of *Brown?* It was not long ago that people of different races drank from separate fountains, rode on separate buses, and studied in separate schools. In this Court's finest hour, *Brown v. Board of Education* challenged this history and helped to change it. For *Brown* held out a promise . . . of true racial equality—not as a matter of fine words on paper, but as a matter of everyday life in the Nation's cities and schools. [*Brown*'s promise] was about the nature of a democracy that must work for all Americans. It sought one law, one Nation, one people, not simply as a matter of legal principle but in terms of how we actually live.

Not everyone welcomed this Court's decision in *Brown*. Three years after that decision was handed down, the Governor of Arkansas ordered state militia to block the doors of a white schoolhouse so that black children could not enter. The President of the United States dispatched the 101st Airborne Division to Little Rock, Arkansas, and federal troops were needed to enforce a desegregation decree. Today, 50 years later, attitudes toward race in this Nation have changed dramatically. Many parents, white and black alike, want their children to attend schools with children of different races. Indeed, the very school districts that once spurned integration now strive for it. The long history of their efforts reveals the complexities and difficulties they have faced. And in light of those challenges, they have asked us not to take from their hands the instruments they have used to rid their schools of racial segregation, instruments that they believe are needed to overcome the problems of cities divided by race and poverty. The plurality would decline their modest request.

The plurality is wrong to do so. The last half-century has witnessed great strides toward racial equality, but we have not yet realized the promise of *Brown*. To invalidate the plans under review is to threaten the promise of *Brown*. The plurality's position, I fear, would break that promise. This is a decision that the Court and the Nation will come to regret.

Equal Protection and Levels of Scrutiny

Type of Government Action	Controlling Test	Operation and Effect of Test
Government action that discriminates but neither affects exercise of fundamental right nor discriminates against suspect class (e.g., most social and economic regulation)	Rational basis	Lenient test—government action is constitutional if rationally related to legitimate government purpose.
Government action that discriminates concerning ability to exercise fundamental right	Full strict scrutiny	Very rigorous test—government action is unconstitutional unless necessary to fulfillment of compelling government purpose.
Government action that discriminates on basis of race or national origin	Full strict scrutiny	Very rigorous test—government action is unconstitutional unless necessary to fulfillment of compelling government purpose.
Government action that discriminates on basis of alienage	Less than full strict scrutiny as general rule; rational basis when public function exception applies	Rigorous test—though softer application of full strict scrutiny requirements. When public function exception applies, test is lenient.
Government action that discriminates on basis of sex (gender)	Intermediate scrutiny	Moderately rigorous test—government action is unconstitutional unless substantially related to fulfillment of important government purpose.
Government action that discriminates on basis of illegitimacy	Intermediate scrutiny, but to lesser degree than in gender discrimination cases	Moderately rigorous test—though softer application of intermediate scrutiny requirements.

Independent Checks Applying Only to the States

The Contract Clause

Article I, section 10 of the Constitution states: "No State shall . . . pass any . . . Law impairing the Obligation of Contracts." Known as the *Contract Clause,* this provision deals with state laws that change the parties' performance obligations under an *existing* contract *after* that contract has been made.[2] The original purpose of the Contract Clause was to strike down the many debtor relief statutes passed by the states after the Revolution. These statutes impaired the obligations of existing private contracts by relieving debtors of what they owed to creditors. In two early 19th-century cases, however, the Contract Clause also was held to protect the obligations of *governmental* contracts, charters, and grants.

The Contract Clause probably was the most important constitutional check on state regulation of the economy for much of the 19th century. Beginning in the latter part of that century, the clause gradually became subordinate to legislation based on the states' police powers. By the mid-20th century, most observers treated the clause as being of historical interest only. In 1977, however, the Supreme Court gave the Contract Clause new life by announcing a fairly strict constitutional test governing situations in which a state impairs *its own* contracts, charters, and grants. Such impairments, the Court said, must be "reasonable and necessary to serve an important public purpose."

---

[2]Under the Fifth Amendment's Due Process Cause, standards similar to those described in this section apply to the federal government.

During recent decades, the Court has continued its deference toward state regulations that impair the obligations of *private* contracts. Consider, for instance, *Exxon Corp. v. Eagerton* (1983). For years, Exxon had paid a severance tax under Alabama law on oil and gas it drilled within the state. As the tax increased, appropriate provisions in Exxon's contracts with the purchasers of its oil and gas allowed Exxon to pass on the amounts of the increases to the purchasers. Alabama, however, enacted a law that not only increased the severance tax but also forbade producers of oil and gas from passing on the increase to purchasers. Exxon filed suit, seeking a declaration that the law's pass-on prohibition was unconstitutional under the Contract Clause. Affirming Alabama's highest court, the U.S. Supreme Court observed that the Contract Clause allows the states to adopt broad regulatory measures without having to be concerned that private contracts will be affected. The pass-on prohibition was designed to advance a broad public interest in protecting consumers against excessive prices and was applicable to all oil and gas producers regardless of whether they were then parties to contracts containing pass-on provisions. Therefore, the Court reasoned, the Alabama statute did not violate the Contract Clause.

Burden on, or Discrimination against, Interstate Commerce

In addition to empowering Congress to regulate interstate commerce, the Commerce Clause limits the states' ability to *burden* or discriminate against such commerce. This limitation is not expressly stated in the Constitution. Instead, it arises by implication from the Commerce Clause and reflects that clause's original purpose of blocking state protectionism and ensuring free interstate trade. (Because this limitation arises by implication, it is often referred to as the "dormant" Commerce Clause—a term used by the Supreme Court in the *Davis* case, which follows shortly.) The burden-on-commerce limitation and the nondiscrimination principle operate independently of congressional legislation under the commerce power or other federal powers. If appropriate federal regulation is present, the preemption questions discussed in the next section may also arise.

Many different state laws can raise burden-on-commerce problems. For example, state regulation of transportation (e.g., limits on train or truck lengths) has been a prolific source of litigation. The same is true of state restrictions on the importation of goods or resources, such as laws forbidding the sale of out-of-state food products unless they meet certain standards. Such restrictions sometimes benefit local economic interests and reflect their political influence. Burden-on-commerce issues also arise if states try to aid their own residents by blocking the export of scarce or valuable products, thus denying out-of-state buyers access to those products.

In part because of the variety of state regulations it has had to consider, the Supreme Court has not adhered to one consistent test for determining when such regulations impermissibly burden interstate commerce. In a 1994 case, the Court said that if a state law *discriminates* against interstate commerce, the strictest scrutiny will be applied in the determination of the law's constitutionality. Discrimination is *express* when state laws treat local and interstate commerce unequally on their face.

State laws might also discriminate even though on their face, they seem neutral regarding interstate commerce. This occurs when their *effect* is to burden or hinder such commerce. In one case, for example, the Supreme Court considered a North Carolina statute that required all closed containers of apples sold within the state to bear only the applicable U.S. grade or standard. The State of Washington, the nation's largest apple producer, had its own inspection and grading system for Washington apples. This system generally was regarded as superior to the federal system. The Court struck down the North Carolina statute because it benefited local apple producers by forcing Washington sellers to regrade apples sold in North Carolina (thus raising their costs of doing business) and by undermining the competitive advantage provided by Washington's superior grading system.

On the other hand, state laws that regulate evenhandedly and have only incidental effects on interstate commerce are constitutional if they serve legitimate state interests and their local benefits exceed the burden they place on interstate commerce. There is no sharp line between such regulations and those that are almost always unconstitutional under the tests discussed above. In a 1981 Supreme Court case, a state truck-length limitation that differed from the limitations imposed by neighboring states failed to satisfy the tests for constitutionality. The Court concluded that the measure did not further the state's legitimate interest in highway safety because the trucks banned by the state generally were as safe as those it allowed. In addition, whatever marginal safety advantage the law provided was outweighed by the numerous problems it posed for interstate trucking companies.

Laws may also unconstitutionally burden interstate commerce when they *directly regulate* that commerce. This can occur, for example, when state price regulations require firms to post the prices at which they will sell within the state and to promise that they will not sell below those prices in other states. Because they affect prices in other states, such regulations directly regulate interstate commerce and usually are unconstitutional.

Department of Revenue of Kentucky v. Davis, which follows, addresses a number of the principles discussed in the foregoing section. The Supreme Court goes on in *Davis* to explain an important analytical wrinkle: the greater latitude given, in dormant Commerce Clause cases, to states that have acted as market *participants* rather than merely as market *regulators*.

Department of Revenue of Kentucky v. Davis
2008 U.S. LEXIS 4312 (U.S. Sup. Ct. 2008)

As most other states do, the Commonwealth of Kentucky taxes its residents' income. Kentucky law establishes that income subject to taxation includes "interest income derived from obligations of sister states and political subdivisions thereof," but not interest income from obligations of Kentucky. Interest on bonds issued by Kentucky and its political subdivisions is thus exempt from Kentucky income tax, whereas interest on municipal bonds of other states and their subdivisions is taxable. The tax exemption for Kentucky bonds helps make those bonds attractive to in-state purchasers even if they carry somewhat lower rates of interest than other states' bonds or those issued by private companies. Most other states have differential tax schemes that resemble Kentucky's.

George and Catherine Davis are Kentucky residents who paid state income tax on interest from out-of-state municipal bonds, and then sued the Department of Revenue of Kentucky (hereinafter, Kentucky) in state court in an effort to obtain a refund. The Davises claimed that Kentucky's differential taxation of municipal bond interest impermissibly discriminates against interstate commerce in violation of the U.S. Constitution's Commerce Clause. The trial court ruled in favor of Kentucky, but the Court of Appeals of Kentucky reversed. In doing so, the appellate court rejected the reasoning of an Ohio decision upholding a similar tax scheme that had been challenged under the Commerce Clause. The Supreme Court of Kentucky denied review. However, the U.S. Supreme Court granted Kentucky's petition for a writ of certiorari because of the conflict between the Kentucky and Ohio courts on an important question of constitutional law, and because the result reached by the Kentucky court cast constitutional doubt on a tax regime adopted by a majority of the states.

Souter, Justice

For the better part of two centuries States and their political subdivisions have issued bonds for public purposes, and for nearly half that time some States have exempted interest on their own bonds from their state income taxes, which are imposed on bond interest from other States. The question here is whether Kentucky's version of this differential tax scheme offends the Commerce Clause.

The significance of the scheme is immense. Between 1996 and 2002, Kentucky and its subdivisions issued $7.7 billion in long-term bonds to pay for spending on transportation, public safety, education, utilities, and environmental protection, among other things. Across the Nation during the same period, States issued over $750 billion in long-term bonds, with nearly a third of the money going to education, followed by transportation (13%) and utilities (11%). Municipal bonds currently finance roughly two-thirds of capital expenditures by state and local governments.

Funding the work of government this way follows a tradition going back as far as the 17th century. Municipal bonds first appeared in the United States in the early 19th century. The municipal bond market had swelled by the mid-1840s.

Bonds funded some of the great public works of the day, including New York City's first water system. At the turn of the 20th century, the total state and municipal debt was closing in on $2 billion, and by the turn of the millennium, over $1.5 trillion in municipal bonds were outstanding.

Differential tax schemes [such as] Kentucky's have a long pedigree, too. State income taxation became widespread in the early 20th century, and along with the new tax regimes came exemptions and deductions to induce all sorts of economic behavior. Today, 41 States have [differential tax laws similar to] the one before us.

The Commerce Clause empowers Congress "[t]o regulate Commerce . . . among the several States," and although its terms do not expressly restrain "the several States" in any way, we have sensed a negative implication in the provision since the early days. The modern law of what has come to be called the dormant Commerce Clause is driven by concern about "economic protectionism—that is, regulatory measures designed to benefit in-state economic interests by burdening out-of-state competitors." [Case citation omitted.] The point is to "effectuat[e] the Framers' purpose to prevent a State from retreating into [the] economic isolation" [case citation omitted] "that had plagued relations among the Colonies and later among the States under the Articles of Confederation." [Case citation omitted.] The law has had to respect a cross purpose as well, for the Framers' distrust of economic Balkanization was limited by their federalism favoring a degree of local autonomy.

Under the resulting protocol for dormant Commerce Clause analysis, we ask whether a challenged law discriminates against interstate commerce. See *Oregon Waste Systems, Inc. v. Department of Environmental Quality of Ore.,* 511 U.S. 93, 99, 114 S. Ct. 1345, 128 L. Ed. 2d 13 (1994). [We noted in *Oregon Waste Systems* that] a discriminatory law is "virtually *per se* invalid," and will survive only if it "advances a legitimate local purpose that cannot be adequately served by reasonable nondiscriminatory alternatives." Absent discrimination for the forbidden purpose, however, the law "will be upheld unless the burden imposed on [interstate] commerce is clearly excessive in relation to the putative local benefits." [Case citation omitted.]

Some cases run a different course, however, and an exception covers States that go beyond regulation and themselves "participat[e] in the market" so as to "exercis[e] the right to favor [their] own citizens over others." *Hughes v. Alexandria Scrap Corp.,* 426 U.S. 794 (1976). This "market-participant" exception reflects a "basic distinction . . . between States as market participants and States as market regulators," [t]here [being] no indication of a constitutional plan to limit the ability of the States themselves to operate freely in the free market." [Case citation omitted.] Thus, in *Alexandria Scrap,* we found that a state law authorizing state payments to processors of automobile hulks validly burdened out-of-state processors with more onerous documentation requirements than their in-state counterparts. Likewise, [later decisions] accepted South Dakota's policy of giving in-state customers first dibs on cement produced by a state-owned plant, and [upheld] a Boston executive order requiring half the workers on city-financed construction projects to be city residents.

Our most recent look at the reach of the dormant Commerce Clause came just last Term, in a case decided independently of the market participation precedents. *United Haulers,* [cited earlier,] upheld a "flow control" ordinance requiring trash haulers to deliver solid waste to a processing plant owned and operated by a public authority in New York State. We found "[c]ompelling reasons" for "treating [the ordinance] differently from laws favoring particular private businesses over their competitors." [As noted in *United Haulers,*] state and local governments that provide public goods and services on their own, unlike private businesses, are "vested with the responsibility of protecting the health, safety, and welfare of [their] citizens," and laws favoring such States and their subdivisions may "be directed toward any number of legitimate goals unrelated to protectionism." That was true in *United Haulers,* where the ordinance

addressed waste disposal, "both typically and traditionally a local government function." And if more had been needed to show that New York's object was consequently different from forbidden protectionism, we pointed out that "the most palpable harm imposed by the ordinances—more expensive trash removal—[was] likely to fall upon the very people who voted for the laws," rather than out-of-state interests. Being concerned that a "contrary approach . . . would lead to unprecedented and unbounded interference by the courts with state and local government," we held that the ordinance did "not discriminate against interstate commerce for purposes of the dormant Commerce Clause."

It follows *a fortiori* from *United Haulers* that Kentucky must prevail. In *United Haulers,* we explained that a government function is not susceptible to standard dormant Commerce Clause scrutiny owing to its likely motivation by legitimate objectives distinct from the simple economic protectionism the Clause abhors. This logic applies with even greater force to laws favoring a State's municipal bonds, given that the issuance of debt securities to pay for public projects is a quintessentially public function, with the venerable history we have already sketched. By issuing bonds, state and local governments spread the costs of public projects over time, much as one might buy a house with a loan subject to monthly payments. Bonds place the cost of a project on the citizens who benefit from it over the years, and they allow for public work beyond what current revenues could support. Bond proceeds are thus the way to shoulder the cardinal civic responsibilities listed in *United Haulers:* protecting the health, safety, and welfare of citizens. It should go without saying that the apprehension in *United Haulers* about "unprecedented . . . interference" with a traditional government function is just as warranted here, where the Davises would have us invalidate a century-old taxing practice presently employed by 41 States and affirmatively supported by all of them [in an amicus curiae ("friend of the court") brief submitted to the Court].

Thus, *United Haulers* provides a firm basis for reversal. Just like the ordinances upheld there, Kentucky's tax exemption . . . does "not 'discriminate against interstate commerce' for purposes of the dormant Commerce Clause."

[Our dissenting colleagues] rightly praise the virtues of the free market, and [warn] that our decision to uphold Kentucky's tax scheme will result in untoward consequences for that market. But the warning is alarmism; going back to 1919 the state regimes of differential bond taxation have been elements of the national commerce without wilting the Commerce Clause. The threat would come, instead, from the dissent[ers'] approach, which to a certainty would upset the market in bonds and the settled expectations of their issuers based on the experience of nearly a century.

We have been here before. Our predecessors on this Court responded to an earlier invitation to the adventurism of overturning a traditional local taxing practice. Justice Holmes answered that "the mode of taxation is of long standing, and upon questions of constitutional law the long settled habits of the community play a part. . . . [T]he fact that the system has been in force for a very long time is of itself a strong reason . . . for leaving any improvement that may be desired to the legislature." *Paddell v. City of New York,* 211 U.S. 446, 448, 29 S. Ct. 139, 53 L. Ed. 275 (1908).

Decision of Court of Appeals of Kentucky reversed, and case remanded for further proceedings.

Federal Preemption   The constitutional principle of **federal supremacy** dictates that when state law conflicts with valid federal law, the federal law is supreme. In such a situation, the state law is said to be *preempted* by the federal regulation. The central question in most federal preemption cases is the intent of Congress. Thus, such cases often present complex questions of statutory interpretation.

Federal preemption of state law generally occurs for one or more of four reasons:

1. *There is a literal conflict between the state and federal measures, so that it is impossible to follow both simultaneously.*

2. *The federal law specifically states that it will preempt state regulation in certain areas.* Similar statements may also appear in the federal statute's legislative history. Courts sometimes find such statements persuasive even when they appear only in the legislative history and not in the statute itself.

3. *The federal regulation is pervasive.* If Congress has "occupied the field" by regulating a subject in great breadth and/or in considerable detail, such action by Congress may suggest an intent to displace state regulation of the subject. This may be especially likely where Congress has given an administrative agency broad regulatory power in a particular area.

4. *The state regulation is an obstacle to fulfilling the purposes of the federal law.* Here, the party challenging the state law's constitutionality typically claims that the state law interferes with the purposes she attributes to the federal measure (purposes usually found in its legislative history).

The Takings Clause

The Fifth Amendment states that "private property [shall not] be taken for public use, without just compensation." Because this **Takings Clause** has been incorporated within Fourteenth Amendment due process, it applies to the states. Traditionally, it has come into play when the government formally condemns land through its power of **eminent domain**,[3] but it has many other applications as well.

The Takings Clause both recognizes government's power to take private property and limits the exercise of that power. It does so by requiring that when *property* is subjected to a governmental *taking,* the taking must be for a *public use* and the property owner must receive *just compensation.* We now consider these four aspects of the Takings Clause in turn.

1. *Property.* The Takings Clause protects other property interests besides land and interests in land. Although its full scope is unclear, the clause has been held to cover takings of personal property, liens, trade secrets, and contract rights.

2. *Taking.* Because of the range of property interests it may cover, the Takings Clause potentially has a broad scope. Another reason for the clause's wide possible application is the range of government activities that may be considered takings. Of course, the government's use of formal condemnation procedures to acquire private property is a taking. There also may be a taking when the government physically invades private property or allows someone else to do so.

It has long been recognized, moreover, that overly extensive land use regulation may so diminish the value of property or the owner's enjoyment of it as to constitute a taking. Among the factors courts consider in such "regulatory taking" cases are the degree to which government deprives the owner of free possession, use, and disposition of his property; the overall economic impact of the regulation on the owner; and how much the regulation interferes with the owner's reasonable investment-backed expectations regarding the future use of the property. In *Lucas v. South*

---

[3]Eminent domain and the Takings Clause's application to land use problems are discussed in Chapter 24.

Carolina Coastal Council (1992), the Supreme Court held that there is an automatic taking when the government denies the owner *all* economically beneficial uses of the land. When this is not the case, courts tend to apply some form of means-ends scrutiny in determining whether land use regulation has gone too far and thus amounts to a regulatory taking.

3. *Public use.* Once a taking of property has occurred, it is unconstitutional unless it is for a public use. The public use element took center stage in a widely

publicized 2005 Supreme Court decision, *Kelo v. City of New London.* For discussion of *Kelo,* see Figure 2.

4. *Just compensation.* Even if a taking of property is for a public use, it still is unconstitutional if the property owner does not receive just compensation. Although the standards for determining just compensation vary with the circumstances, the basic test is the fair market value of the property (or of the lost property right) at the time of the taking.

Figure 2   *Economic Development as Public Use?*

Does the government's taking of private property for the purpose of economic development satisfy the *public use* requirement set forth in the Fifth Amendment's Takings Clause? In *Kelo v. City of New London,* 545 U.S. 469 (2005), the U.S. Supreme Court answered "yes."

New London, Connecticut, experienced economic decline for a considerable number of years. The city therefore made economic revitalization efforts, which included a plan to acquire 115 parcels of real estate in a 90-acre area and create, in collaboration with private developers, a multifaceted zone that would combine commercial, residential, and recreational elements. The planned development was designed to increase tax revenue, create jobs, and otherwise capitalize on the economic opportunities that city officials expected would flow from a major pharmaceutical company's already-announced plan to construct a large facility near the area the city wished to develop.

The city was able to negotiate the purchase of most parcels of property in the 90-acre area, but some property owners refused to sell. The latter group included homeowners Susette Kelo and Wilhelmina Dery. Kelo had lived in her home for several years, had made substantial improvements to it, and especially enjoyed the water view it afforded. Dery, who was born in 1918, had lived her entire life in the home the city sought to acquire. Both homes were well maintained. After the city decided to use its eminent domain power to acquire the properties of those owners who refused to sell, Kelo, Dery, and the other nonselling owners filed suit in state court. They contended that the city's plan to take their property for the purpose of economic development did not involve a public use and thus would violate the Fifth Amendment's Takings Clause. The dispute made its way through the Connecticut courts and then to the U.S. Supreme Court, where a five-justice majority ruled in favor of the city.

Writing for the majority in *Kelo v. City of New London,* Justice Stevens noted that earlier decisions had identified three types of eminent domain settings in which the government's acquisition of private property satisfied the constitutional

public use element: first, when the government planned to develop a government-owned facility (e.g., a military base); second, when the government planned to construct, or allow others to construct, improvements to which the public would have broad access (e.g., highways or railroads); and third, when the government sought to further some meaningful public purpose. Justice Stevens observed that precedents had recognized the *public purpose* type of public use even if the government would not ultimately retain legal title to the acquired property (unlike the military base example) and the acquired property would not be fully opened up for public access (unlike the highway and railroad examples). The Court acknowledged that the public use requirement clearly would not be satisfied if the government took private party A's property simply to give it to private party B. However, the Court stressed, the prospect that private parties might ultimately own or control property the government had acquired through eminent domain would not make the taking unconstitutional if an overriding public purpose prompted the government's use of eminent domain. Similarly, even if certain private parties (e.g., the pharmaceutical company and private developers in the *Kelo* facts) would stand to benefit from the government's exercise of eminent domain, such a fact would not make the taking unconstitutional if a public purpose supported the taking.

The *Kelo* majority stressed the particular relevance of two earlier Supreme Court decisions, *Berman v. Parker,* 348 U.S. 26 (1954), and *Hawaii Housing Authority v. Midkiff,* 467 U.S. 299 (1984). In *Berman,* the Court sustained Washington, D.C.'s use of eminent domain to take property that included businesses and "blighted" dwellings in order to construct a low-income housing project and new streets, schools, and public facilities. In *Midkiff,* the Court upheld Hawaii's use of eminent domain to effectuate a legislative determination that Hawaii's long-standing land oligopoly, under which property ownership was highly concentrated among a small number of property owners, had to be broken up for social and economic reasons. The *Kelo* majority concluded that significant public purposes were present in both *Berman* and *Midkiff* and that those decisions led logically to the conclusion that economic development was a public purpose weighty enough to constitute public use for purposes of the Takings Clause. Therefore, the Court upheld the city's exercise of eminent domain in *Kelo*.

In his majority opinion, Justice Stevens was careful to point out that because the constitutional question was whether a public use existed, it was not the Court's job to determine the wisdom of the government's attempt to exercise eminent domain. Neither should the Court allow its decision to be guided by the undoubted hardship that eminent domain places on unwilling property owners who must yield their homes to the state (albeit in return for "just compensation"). Justice Stevens emphasized that if state legislatures believed an economic development purpose such as the one the City of New London had in mind should not be used to support an exercise of eminent domain, the legislatures were free to specify, in their state statutes, that eminent domain could not be employed for an economic development purpose. The Court's determination of what is a public use for purposes of the Takings Clause sets a protective floor for property owners, with states being free to give greater protection against takings by the government.

The four dissenting justices in *Kelo* issued sharply worded opinions expressing their disagreement with the majority's characterization of *Berman* and *Midkiff* as having led logically to the conclusion that economic development was a public use. In emotional terms, the dissenters accused the majority of having effectively erased the public use requirement from the Takings Clause. The *Kelo* decision drew considerable media attention, perhaps more because of what appeared to be considerable hardship to property owners such as Kelo and Dery than because of new legal ground—if any—broken in the decision. For many observers, the case's compelling facts led to a perception that the city had engaged in overreaching. The Court's decision in *Kelo* meant that in a legal sense, there was no overreaching on the part of the city. Was there, however, overreaching in an *ethical* sense? How would *utilitarians* answer that question? What about *rights theorists?* (As you consider the questions, you may wish to consult Chapter 4.)

Problems and Problem Cases

1. In 1967, Gary Jones purchased a house on North Bryan Street in Little Rock, Arkansas. He and his wife lived in the house until they separated in 1993. Jones then moved into an apartment in Little Rock, and his wife continued to live in the house. Jones paid his mortgage each month for 30 years. The mortgage company paid the property taxes on the house. After Jones paid off his mortgage in 1997, the property taxes went unpaid. In April 2000, the Arkansas Commissioner of State Lands (Commissioner) attempted to notify Jones of his tax delinquency and his right to redeem the property by paying the past-due taxes. The Commissioner sought to provide this notice by mailing a certified letter to Jones at the North Bryan Street address. Arkansas law approved the use of such a method of providing notice. The packet of information sent by the Commissioner stated that unless Jones redeemed the property, it would be subject to public sale two years later. No one was at home to sign for the letter. No one appeared at the post office to retrieve the letter within the next 15 days. The post office then returned the unopened packet to the Commissioner with an "unclaimed" designation on it. In the spring of 2002, a few weeks before the public sale scheduled for Jones's house, the Commissioner published a notice of public sale in a local newspaper. No bids were submitted, meaning that under Arkansas law, the state could negotiate a private sale of the property.

Several months later, Linda Flowers submitted a purchase offer. The Commissioner then mailed another certified letter to Jones at the North Bryan Street address, attempting to notify him that his house would be sold to Flowers if he did not pay his delinquent taxes. As with the first letter, the second letter was returned to the Commissioner with an "unclaimed" designation. Flowers purchased the house. Immediately after the expiration of the 30-day period in which Arkansas law would have allowed Jones to make a post-sale redemption of the property by paying the past-due taxes, Flowers had an eviction notice delivered to the North Bryan Street property. The notice was served on Jones's daughter, who contacted Jones and notified him of the tax sale. Jones then filed a lawsuit in Arkansas state court against the Commissioner and Flowers. In his lawsuit, Jones contended that the Commissioner's failure to provide notice of the tax sale and of Jones's right to redeem resulted in the taking of his property without due process. The trial court ruled in favor of the Commissioner and Flowers, and the Arkansas Supreme Court affirmed. The U.S. Supreme Court agreed to decide the case and its central question of whether Jones was afforded due process. How did the U.S. Supreme Court rule?

2. The Food and Drug Administration Modernization Act of 1997 (FDAMA) exempted "compounded drugs" from the rigorous Food and Drug Administration approval process that new drugs must ordinarily undergo. Compounded drugs are "cocktails" whose ingredients are combined, mixed, or altered by pharmacists or doctors to accommodate patients with individualized needs. Congress exempted compounded drugs from the usual drug approval process because the high costs of going through the process would likely make compounded drug production financially unfeasible for many pharmacists, given the special-order nature of such medications. Providers of compounded drugs, however, were exempted from the approval process only if they adhered to certain conditions set by the FDAMA. These conditions required, among other things, that the providers not advertise or promote the compounding of any particular drug, class of drug, or type of drug. Congress adopted the advertising restriction because it believed that the inability to advertise the compounding of drugs would keep the amounts of compounded drugs produced from becoming large enough to compromise the integrity of the approval process that new drugs generally must complete. A group of pharmacies specializing in compounded drugs filed suit against the U.S. Secretary of Health and Human Services and the commissioner of the FDA, alleging that the FDAMA's advertising restrictions violated First Amendment free speech rights. What type of speech did the FDAMA restrict, and what level of First Amendment protection attaches to such speech? Were the pharmacists entitled to win their case?

3. A federal statute, 8 U.S.C. § 1409, sets requirements for acquisition of U.S. citizenship by a child born outside the United States to unwed parents, only one of whom is a U.S. citizen. If the mother is the U.S. citizen, the child acquires citizenship at birth. Section 1409(a) states that when the father is the citizen parent, the child acquires citizenship only if, before the child reaches the age of 18, the child is legitimized under the law of the child's residence or domicile, the father acknowledges paternity in writing under oath, or paternity is established by a competent court. Tuan Anh Nguyen was born in Vietnam to a Vietnamese mother and a U.S. citizen father, Joseph Boulais. At six years of age, Nguyen came to the United States, where he became a lawful permanent resident and was raised by his father. When Nguyen was 22, he pleaded guilty in a Texas court to two counts of sexual assault. The U.S. Immigration and Naturalization Service initiated deportation proceedings against Nguyen, and an immigration judge found him deportable. While Nguyen's appeal to the U.S. Board of Immigration Appeals was pending, Boulais obtained from a state court an order of parentage that was based on DNA testing. The board dismissed Nguyen's appeal, denying his citizenship claim on the ground that he had not established compliance with § 1409(a). Nguyen and Boulais appealed to the U.S. Court of Appeals for the Fifth Circuit, which rejected their contention that § 1409 discriminated on the basis of gender and thus violated the Constitution's equal protection guarantee. Was the Fifth Circuit's decision correct?

4. A Dallas, Texas, city ordinance restricted admission to so-called "Class E" dance halls to persons between the ages of 14 and 18. The ordinance did not impose similar age limitations on most other establishments where teenagers might congregate—for example, skating rinks. Charles Stanglin, who in one building operated both a Class E dance hall and a roller-skating rink, filed suit in a Texas trial court in an effort to obtain an injunction against enforcement of the ordinance. He argued that the ordinance violated the U.S. Constitution's Equal Protection Clause. The trial court rejected Stanglin's argument, but a Texas appellate court struck down the age restriction. The U.S. Supreme Court agreed to decide the case. Did the age restriction in the Dallas ordinance violate the Equal Protection Clause?

5. A Stratton, Ohio, ordinance prohibited "canvassers" from "going in and upon" private residential property to promote a "cause" without first obtaining a permit from the office of the mayor. The ordinance sought to prevent fraud and crime and to protect residents' privacy. Permits were free of charge, and were routinely issued after an applicant had filled out a "Solicitor's Registration Form." After receiving a permit, a solicitor was authorized to go upon the premises she had listed on the registration form. At a resident's or a policeman's request, the solicitor was required to display the permit. If a resident had filled out a "No Solicitation Registration Form" from the mayor's office and posted a "no solicitation" sign on

his property, not even solicitors with permits were allowed to enter the premises unless the resident had listed them as exceptions on the "No Solicitation Registration Form."

The Watchtower Bible and Tract Society of New York, a society and congregation of Jehovah's Witnesses that distributed and published religious materials, did not apply for a permit. Watchtower claimed that God orders Jehovah's Witnesses to preach the gospel, and that applying for a permit would insult God by subordinating the scripture to local code. Watchtower therefore brought an action in federal court seeking to have the village of Stratton enjoined from enforcing the solicitation ordinance. Watchtower contended that the ordinance violated First Amendment rights to free speech, free press, and the free exercise of religion. Was Watchtower's allegation correct?

6. On August 26, while employed as a policeman at a state university, Richard Homar was arrested by the state police and charged with a drug felony. University officials then suspended Homar without pay. Although the criminal charges were dismissed on September 1, Homar's suspension remained in effect. On September 18, he finally was provided the opportunity to tell his side of the story to university officials. Subsequently, he was demoted to groundskeeper. He then filed suit under a federal civil rights statue, claiming that university officials' failure to provide him with notice and a hearing before suspension without pay had violated due process. Was Homar correct?

7. In the Violence Against Women Act, Congress provided a federal civil remedy for victims of gender-motivated violence. A female student who had attended a Virginia university brought a claim under the Violence Against Women Act against two male students who allegedly had sexually assaulted her and caused her to experience severe emotional distress. The defendants challenged the Violence Against Women Act on constitutional grounds, arguing that the statute did not fall within the power granted to Congress by the U.S. Constitution's Commerce Clause. Were the defendants correct in this argument?

8. The Minnesota legislature passed a statute banning the sale of milk in plastic nonrefillable, nonreusable containers. However, it allowed sales of milk in other nonrefillable, nonreusable containers such as paperboard cartons. One of the justifications for this ban on plastic jugs was that it would ease the state's solid waste disposal problems because plastic jugs occupy more space in landfills than other nonreturnable milk

containers. A group of dairy businesses challenged the statute, arguing that its distinction between plastic containers and other containers was unconstitutional under the Equal Protection Clause. What means-ends test or level of scrutiny applies in this case? Under that test, is easing the state's solid waste disposal problems a sufficiently important *end*? Under that test, is there a sufficiently close "fit" between the classification and that end to make the statutory *means* constitutional? In answering the last question, assume for the sake of argument that there were better ways of alleviating the solid waste disposal problem than banning plastic jugs while allowing paperboard cartons.

9. Oklahoma statutes set the age for drinking 3.2 beer at 21 for men and 18 for women. The asserted purpose behind the statutes (and the sex-based classification that they established) was traffic safety. The statutes were challenged as a denial of equal protection by male residents of Oklahoma. What level of scrutiny would this measure receive if *women* had been denied the right to drink 3.2 beer until they were 21 but men had been allowed to consume it at age 18? Should this standard change because the measure discriminates against *men?* Is the male challenge to the statute likely to be successful?

10. While it was preparing a comprehensive land use plan in the area, the Tahoe Regional Planning Agency (TRPA) imposed two moratoria on development of property in the Lake Tahoe Basin. The moratoria together lasted 32 months. A group of property developers affected by the moratoria filed suit in federal court alleging that the moratoria constituted an unconstitutional taking without just compensation. Were the developers correct?

11. During the 14 years it was in effect until its repeal in 1933, the 18th Amendment to the U.S. Constitution called for Prohibition, a nationwide outlawing of alcoholic beverage production and distribution. The repeal of Prohibition was accomplished by § 1 of the 21st Amendment. In its § 2, however, the 21st Amendment preserved an ability on the part of the individual states to regulate alcohol distribution by providing that "[t]he transportation or importation into any State, Territory, or possession of the United States for delivery or use therein of intoxicating liquors, in violation of the laws thereof, is hereby prohibited." As did the laws of many states, Michigan law on alcoholic beverage distribution set up a three-tiered system under which, as a general rule, alcoholic

beverage producers could sell only to licensed in-state wholesalers. Wholesalers were allowed to sell only to licensed in-state retailers, which then could sell to consumers. Michigan law, however, included an exception to the three-tier system for the approximately 40 wineries located in that state. The in-state wineries were eligible for licenses that allowed direct shipment to in-state consumers. Out-of-state wineries could apply for an "outside seller of wine" license, but such a license allowed those wineries to sell only to in-state wholesalers and not directly to consumers. New York law channeled alcohol sales through a similar three-tiered system, subject to exceptions for in-state wineries. These exceptions allowed in-state wineries to make direct sales to New York consumers on terms not available to out-of-state wineries. Out-of-state wineries were allowed to ship directly to New York consumers only if they became licensed New York wineries—a process that required the establishment of a branch factory, office, or storeroom within New York.

In separate cases filed in federal district courts in Michigan and New York, residents of Michigan and New York who wished to receive direct shipments of wine from out-of-state wineries sued appropriate state officials. The plaintiffs in each case contended that the direct-shipment laws of the relevant state (Michigan or New York) discriminated against interstate commerce in violation of the U.S. Constitution's Commerce Clause. In each case, the defendants argued that the ban on direct shipment from out-of-state wineries was a valid exercise of the relevant state's power under § 2 of the 21st Amendment. Because the cases led to inconsistent decisions of federal courts of appeal on the questions presented, the U.S. Supreme Court granted certiorari in both cases and consolidated them for decision. Did the Michigan and New York direct-shipment laws violate the Commerce Clause? Were the states' bans on direct shipment from out-of-state wineries valid exercises of the states' power under § 2 of the 21st Amendment?

12. In the Motor Carrier Act of 1980, Congress deregulated trucking by eliminating federal regulations that had previously applied to the trucking industry. Fourteen years later, Congress sought to preempt trucking regulation at the state level by enacting a law providing that "a State . . . may not enact or enforce a law . . . related to a price, route, or service of any motor carrier . . . with respect to the transportation of property." After the enactment of the 1994 federal statute just quoted, the State of Maine enacted a statute titled "An Act To Regulate the Delivery and Sales of Tobacco Products and To Prevent the Sale of Tobacco Products to Minors." One section of the Maine statute forbade anyone other than a Maine-licensed tobacco retailer to accept an order for delivery of tobacco. The statute went on to state that when a licensed retailer accepted an order and shipped tobacco, the retailer had to "utilize a delivery service" that provided a special kind of recipient-verification service. The statute required the delivery service to make certain that (1) the person who bought the tobacco was the person to whom the package was addressed; (2) the person to whom the package was addressed was of legal age to purchase tobacco; (3) the person to whom the package was addressed had himself or herself signed for the package; and (4) the person to whom the package was addressed, if under the age of 27, had produced a valid government-issued photo identification with proof of age. Violations of the statute were punishable by civil penalties of a monetary nature. Another section of the Maine statute forbade any person "knowingly" to "transport" a "tobacco product" to "a person" in Maine unless either the sender or the receiver had a Maine license. It further stated that a "person is deemed to know that a package contains a tobacco product" (1) if the package was marked as containing tobacco and displayed the name and license number of a Maine-licensed tobacco retailer, or (2) if the person received the package from someone whose name appears on a list of unlicensed tobacco retailers that Maine's Attorney General made available to various package-delivery companies. Violations again were made punishable by civil penalties of a monetary nature. Various trucking associations sued in federal court, claiming that the 1994 federal statute quoted earlier preempted the Maine statute. Were the trucking associations correct in this claim?

Online Research

The First Amendment

Using an online legal research tool, locate the U.S. Supreme Court's 2006 decision in *Garcetti v. Ceballos*. Read the opinion of Justice Kennedy, who wrote for a five-justice majority. Then prepare a one-page summary of why the majority rejected the First Amendment claim made by Ceballos.

BUSINESS ETHICS, CORPORATE SOCIAL RESPONSIBILITY, CORPORATE GOVERNANCE, AND CRITICAL THINKING

You are a senior associate consultant at Accent Pointe Consulting LLP, a consulting firm. The engagement partner has asked you to prepare an engagement plan and budget, which you dutifully complete on time. This is the first time you have prepared an engagement plan and budget. You make sure that your plan and budget are in line with your knowledge of what can and must be done to meet the client's needs. The proposed fee is $100,000. When you present the budget to the engagement partner, she goes ballistic. "What's this $100,000? This is Accent Pointe Consulting. This is the big time. What kind of consultant are you?"

"A good one," you reply. "I've created a reasonable plan, and for what we are doing for the client, that is a high-end fee."

The partner, however, does not buy your arguments. "You make this contract $200,000," she orders you, "and find a way in your engagement plan to back up that price."

- What action will you take?
- What process and guidelines will you use to determine what is the right thing to do in this context?
- If you decide that $100,000 is the correct contract price, how do you resist the partner's request to make you bill the client for $200,000?
- Will you take a different action if you know that a year from now the firm's partners will vote on whether you should be made a partner, and you believe the engagement partner's recommendation will be critical to your becoming a partner?
- Will you take a different action if you are the engagement partner and have been ordered to bill the client $200,000 by a managing partner? Note that as a partner, your share of firm profits is determined by the number of "units" you have, which is largely a function of the amount the firm bills clients for whom you are the engagement partner.
- What action will you take if you discover that the managing partner's request to bill more is a relatively isolated incident in a firm that generally bills clients accurately? You don't know the managing partner's motivation for asking you to overbill the client.
- What action will you take if you discover that the firm has a culture that encourages overbilling clients? The overbilling culture evolved within the last decade from a desire of managing partners to enjoy a financial status more nearly equal to the corporate executives of their clients, many of whom receive annual compensation in the millions of dollars.

Why Study Business Ethics?

Enron. WorldCom. Tyco. Adelphia. Global Crossing. ImClone. These business names from the front pages of the last decade conjure images of unethical and socially irresponsible behavior by business executives. The United States Congress, employees, investors, and other critics of the power held and abused by some corporations and their management have demanded that corporate wrongdoers be punished and that future wrongdoers be deterred. Consequently shareholders, creditors, and state and federal attorneys general have brought several civil and criminal actions against wrongdoing corporations and their executives. Congress has also got in on the action, passing the Sarbanes–Oxley Act, which increased penalties for corporate wrongdoers and established rules designed to deter and prevent future wrongdoing. The purpose of the statute is to encourage and enable corporate executives to be ethical and socially responsible.

But statutes and civil and criminal actions can go only so far in directing business managers down an ethical path. And while avoiding liability by complying with the law is one reason to be ethical and socially responsible, there are noble and economic reasons that encourage current and future business executives to study business ethics.

Although it is tempting to paint all businesses and all managers with the same brush that colors unethical and irresponsible corporations and executives, in reality corporate executives are little different from you, your friends, and your acquaintances. All of us from time to time fail to do the right thing, and we know that people have varying levels of commitment to acting ethically. The difference between most of us and corporate executives is that they are in positions of power that allow them to do greater damage to others when they act unethically or socially irresponsibly. They also act under the microscope of public scrutiny.

It is also tempting to say that current business managers are less ethical than managers historically. But as former Federal Reserve Chairman Alan Greenspan said, "It is not that humans have become any more greedy than in generations past. It is that the avenues to express greed have grown enormously."

This brings us to the first and most important reason why we need to study business ethics: to make better decisions for ourselves, the businesses we work for, and the society we live in. As you read this chapter, you will study not only the different theories that attempt to define ethical conduct, but more importantly you will learn to use a framework or strategy for making decisions. This framework will increase the likelihood you have considered all the facts affecting your decision. By learning a methodology for ethical decision making and studying common thinking errors, you will improve your ability to make ethical decisions.

Another reason we study ethics is to understand ourselves and others better. While studying the various ethical theories, you will see concepts that reflect your own thinking and the thinking of others. This chapter, by exploring ethical theories systematically and pointing out the strengths and weaknesses of each ethical theory, should help you understand better why you think the way you do and why others think the way they do. By studying ethical theories, learning a process for ethical decision making, and understanding common reasoning fallacies, you should also be better able to decide how you should think and whether you should be persuaded by the arguments of others. Along the way, by better understanding where others are coming from and avoiding fallacious reasoning, you should become a more persuasive speaker and writer.

There are also cynical reasons for executives to study business ethics. By learning how to act ethically and in fact doing so, businesses forestall public criticism, reduce lawsuits against them, prevent Congress from passing onerous legislation, and make higher profits. For many corporate actors, however, these are not reasons to act ethically, but instead the natural consequences of so acting.

While we are studying business ethics, we will also examine the role of the law in defining ethical conduct. Some argue that it is sufficient for corporations and executives to comply with the requirements of the law; commonly, critics of the corporation point out that since laws cannot and do not encompass all expressions of ethical behavior, compliance with the law is necessary but not sufficient to ensure ethical conduct. This introduces us to one of the major issues in the corporate social responsibility debate.

The Corporate Social Responsibility Debate

Although interest in business ethics education has increased greatly in the last few decades, that interest is only the latest stage in a long struggle to control corporate misbehavior. Ever since large corporations emerged in the late 19th century, such firms have been heroes to some and villains to others. Large corporations perform essential national and global economic functions, including raw material extraction, energy production, transportation, and communication, as well as providing consumer goods and entertainment to millions of people.

Critics, however, claim that corporations in their pursuit of profits ruin the environment, mistreat employees, sell shoddy and dangerous products, produce immoral television shows and motion pictures, and corrupt the political process. Critics claim that even when corporations provide vital and important services, business is not nearly as accountable to the public as are organs of government. For example, the public has little to say about the election of corporate directors or the appointment of corporate officers. This lack of accountability is aggravated by the large amount of power that big corporations wield in America and much of the rest of the world.

These criticisms and perceptions have led to calls for changes in how corporations and their executives make decisions. The main device for checking corporate misdeeds has been the law. The perceived need to check abuses of business power was a force behind the New Deal laws of the 1930s and extensive federal regulations enacted in the 1960s and 1970s. Some critics, however, believe that legal regulation, while an important element of any corporate control scheme, is insufficient by itself. They argue that businesses should adhere to a standard of ethical or socially responsible behavior that is higher than the law.

One such standard is the stakeholder theory of corporate social responsibility. It holds that rather than merely striving to maximize profits for its shareholders, a corporation should balance the interests of shareholders against the interests of other corporate stakeholders, such as employees, suppliers, customers, and the community. To promote such behavior, some corporate critics have proposed changes that increase the influence of the various stakeholders in the internal governance of a corporation. We will study many of these proposals later in the chapter in the subsection on profit maximization. You will also learn later that an ethical decision-making process requires a business executive to anticipate the effects of a corporate decision on the various corporate stakeholders.

Despite concerns about abuses of power, big business has contributed greatly to the unprecedented abundance in America and elsewhere. Partly for this reason and partly because many businesses attempt to be ethical actors, critics have not totally dominated the debate about control of the modern corporation. Defenders of businesses argue that in a society founded on capitalism, profit maximization should be the main goal of businesses: the only ethical norms firms must follow are those embodied

Ethics in Action

American physicist, mathematician, and futurist Freeman Dyson gave insight into why we humans may have difficulty determining which ethical viewpoint to embrace. His insights also help explain why different people have different ethical leanings.

The destiny of our species is shaped by the imperatives of survival on six distinct time scales. To survive means to compete successfully on all six time scales. But the unit of survival is different for each of the six time scales. On a time scale of years, the unit is the individual. On a time scale of decades, the unit is the family. On a time scale of centuries, the unit is the tribe or nation. On a time scale of millennia, the unit is the culture. On a time scale of tens of millennia, the unit is the species. On a time scale of eons, the unit is the whole web of life on our planet. That is why conflicting loyalties are deep in our nature. In order to survive, we need to be loyal to ourselves, to our families, to our tribes, to our culture, to our species, to our planet. If our psychological impulses are complicated, it is because they were shaped by complicated and conflicting demands.[1]

Dyson goes on to write, "Nature gave us greed, a robust desire to maximize our personal winnings. Without greed we would not have survived at the individual level." Yet he points out that Nature also gave us the connections and tools to survive at the family level (Dyson calls this tool love of family), the tribal level (love of friends), the cultural level (love of conversation), the species level (love of people in general), and the planetary level (love of nature).

If Dyson is correct, why are humans sometimes vastly different from each other in some of their ethical values? Why do some of us argue, for example, that universal health care is a right for each citizen, while others believe health care coverage should be an individual decision? The answer lies in the degree to which each of us embraces, innately or rationally, Dyson's six units of survival and the extent to which each of us possesses the connections and tools to survive on each of those levels.

[1]Freeman Dyson, *From Eros to Gaia,* (London: Penguin Books, 1993), pp. 341–42.

in the law or those impacting profits. In short, they argue that businesses that maximize profits within the limits of the law are acting ethically. Otherwise, the marketplace would discipline them for acting unethically by reducing their profits.

Former Fed Chairman Alan Greenspan wrote in 1963 that moral values are the power behind capitalism. He wrote, "Capitalism is based on self-interest and self-esteem; it holds integrity and trustworthiness as cardinal virtues and makes them pay off in the marketplace, thus demanding that men survive by means of virtue, not of vices." Note that companies that are successful decade after decade, like Procter & Gamble and Johnson & Johnson, adhere to society's core values.

We will cover other arguments supporting and criticizing profit maximization later in the chapter, where we will consider fully proposals to improve corporate governance and accountability. For now, however, having set the stage for the debate about business ethics and corporate social responsibility, we want to study the definitions of ethical behavior.

Ethical Theories

For centuries, religious and secular scholars have explored the meaning of human existence and attempted to define a "good life." In this section, we will define and examine some of the most important theories of ethical conduct.

As we cover these theories, much of what you read will be familiar to you. The names may be new, but almost certainly you have previously heard speeches and read writings of politicians, religious leaders, and commentators that incorporate the values in these theories. You will discover that your own thinking is consistent with one or more of the theories. You can also recognize the thinking of friends and antagonists in these theories.

None of these theories is necessarily invalid, and many people believe strongly in any one of them. Whether you believe your theory to be right and the others to be wrong, it is unlikely that others will accept what you see as the error of their ways and agree with all your values. Instead, it is important for you to recognize that people's ethical values can be as diverse as human culture. Therefore, no amount of argumentation appealing to theories you accept is likely to influence someone who subscribes to a different ethical viewpoint.

This means that if you want to be understood by and to influence someone who has a different ethical underpinning than you do, you must first determine his ethical viewpoint and then speak in an ethical language that will be understood and accepted by him. Otherwise, you and

your opponent are like the talking heads on nighttime cable TV news shows, whose debates often are reduced to shouting matches void of any attempt to understand the other side.

LOG ON

Go to
www.iep.utm.edu

The Internet Encyclopedia of Philosophy gives you background on all the world's great philosophers from Abelard to Zizek. You can also study the development of philosophy from ancient times to the present. Many of the world's great philosophers addressed the question of ethical or moral conduct.

The four ethical theories we will study are rights theory, justice theory, utilitarianism, and profit maximization. Some of these theories focus on results of our decisions or actions: do our decisions or actions produce the right results? Theories that focus on the consequences of a decision are **teleological** ethical theories. For example, a teleological theory may justify a manufacturing company laying off 5,000 employees, because the effect is to keep the price of manufactured goods low and to increase profits for the company's shareholders.

Other theories focus on the decision or action itself, irrespective of what results it produces. Theories that focus on decisions or actions alone are **deontological** ethical theories. For example, a deontological theory may find unacceptable that any competent employee loses his job, even if the layoff's effect is to reduce prices to consumers and increase profits.

First, we will cover rights theory, which is a deontological theory. Next will be justice theory, which has concepts common to rights theory, but a focus primarily on outcomes. Our study of ethical theories will conclude with two additional teleological theories, utilitarianism and profit maximization.

Rights Theory   Rights theory encompasses a variety of ethical philosophies holding that certain human rights are fundamental and must be respected by other humans. The focus is on each individual member of society and her rights. As an actor, each of us faces a moral compulsion not to harm the fundamental rights of others.

Kantianism   Few rights theorists are strict deontologists, and one of the few is 18th-century philosopher Immanuel Kant. Kant viewed humans as moral actors that are free to make choices. He believed humans are able to judge the morality of any action by applying his famous **categorical imperative.** One formulation of the categorical imperative is, "Act only on that maxim whereby at the same time you can will that it shall become a universal law." This means that we judge an action by applying it universally.

Suppose you want to borrow money even though you know that you will never repay it. To justify this action using the categorical imperative, you state the following maxim or rule: "When I want money, I will borrow money and promise to repay it, even though I know I won't repay." According to Kant, you would not want this maxim to become a universal law, because no one would believe in promises to repay debts and you would not be able to borrow money when you want. Thus, your maxim or rule fails to satisfy the categorical imperative. You are compelled, therefore, not to promise falsely that you will repay a loan.

Kant had a second formulation of the categorical imperative: "Always act to treat humanity, whether in yourself or in others, as an end in itself, never merely as a means." That is, we may not use or manipulate others to achieve our own happiness. In Kant's eyes, if you falsely promise a lender to repay a loan, you are using that person because she would not agree to the loan if she knew all the facts.

Modern Rights Theories Strict deontological ethical theories like Kant's face an obvious problem: the duties are absolute. We can never lie and never kill, even though most of us find lying and killing acceptable in some contexts, such as in self-defense. Responding to these difficulties, some modern philosophers have proposed mixed deontological theories. There are many theories here, but one popular theory requires us to abide by a moral rule unless a more important rule conflicts with it. In other words, our moral compulsion is not to compromise a person's right unless a greater right takes priority over it.

For example, members of society have the right not to be lied to. Therefore, in most contexts you are morally compelled not to tell a falsehood. That is an important right, because it is critical to a society that we be able to rely on someone's word. If, however, you could save someone's life by telling a falsehood, such as telling a lie to a criminal about where a witness who will testify against him can be found, you probably will be required to save that person's life by lying about his whereabouts.

The Global Business Environment

The Golden Rule in the World's Religions and Cultures

Immanuel Kant's categorical imperative, which is one formulation of rights theory, has its foundations in the Golden Rule. Note that the Golden Rule exists in all cultures and in all countries of the world. Here is a sampling.

> BUDDHISM: Hurt not others in ways that you would find hurtful.

> CHRISTIANITY: Do to others as you would have others do to you.

> CONFUCIANISM: Do not to others what you would not like yourself.

> GRECIAN: Do not that to a neighbor which you shall take ill from him.

> HINDUISM: This is the sum of duty: do nothing to others which if done to you would cause you pain.

> HUMANISM: Individual and social problems can only be resolved by means of human reason, intelligent effort, and critical thinking joined with compassion and a spirit of empathy for all living beings.

> ISLAM: No one of you is a believer until he desires for his brother that which he desires for himself.

> JAINISM: In happiness and suffering, in joy and grief, we should regard all creatures as we regard our own self.

> JUDAISM: Whatever is hateful to you, do not to another.

> NATIVE AMERICAN SPIRITUALITY: Respect for all life is the foundation.

> PERSIAN: Do as you would be done by.

> ROMAN: Treat your inferiors as you would be treated by your superiors.

> SHINTOISM: The heart of the person before you is a mirror. See there your own form.

> SIKHISM: As you deem yourself, so deem others.

> TAOISM: Regard your neighbor's gain as your own gain, and your neighbor's loss as your own loss.

> YORUBAN: One going to take a pointed stick to pinch a baby bird should first try it on himself to feel how it hurts.

> ZOROASTRIANISM: That nature alone is good which refrains from doing to another whatsoever is not good for itself.

In this context, the witness's right to live is a more important right than the criminal's right to hear the truth. In effect, one right "trumps" the other right.

What are these fundamental rights? How do we rank them in importance? Seventeenth-century philosopher John Locke argued for fundamental rights that we see embodied in the constitutions of modern democratic states: the protection of life, liberty, and property. Libertarians and others include the important rights of freedom of contract and freedom of expression. Modern liberals, like Bertolt Brecht, argued that all humans have basic rights to employment, food, housing, and education. Since the 1990s, the right to health care has become part of the liberal rights agenda.

Strengths of Rights Theory The major strength of rights theory is that it protects fundamental rights, unless some greater right takes precedence. This means that members of modern democratic societies have extensive liberties and rights that they need not fear will be taken away by their government or other members of society.

Criticisms of Rights Theory Most of the criticisms of rights theory deal with the near absolute yet relative value of the rights protected, making it difficult to articulate and administer a comprehensive rights theory. First, it is difficult to achieve agreement about which rights are protected. Rights fundamental to modern countries like the United States (such as many women's rights) are unknown or severely restricted in countries like Pakistan or Saudi Arabia. Even within one country, citizens disagree on the existence and ranking of rights. For example, some Americans argue that the right to health care is an important need that should be met by government or a person's employer. Other Americans believe funding universal health care would interfere with the libertarian right to limited government intervention in our lives.

In addition, rights theory does not concern itself with the costs or benefits of requiring respect for another's right. For example, rights theory probably justifies the protection of a neo-Nazi's right to spout hateful speech, even though the costs of such speech, including damage to relations between ethnic groups, may far outweigh any benefits the speaker, listeners, and society receives from the speech.

Moreover, rights theory promotes moral fanaticism and creates a sense of entitlement reducing innovation, entrepreneurship, and production. If, for example, I am entitled to a job, a place to live, food, and health care regardless of how hard I work, how motivated am I to work to earn those things?

Justice Theory   In 1971, John Rawls published his book *A Theory of Justice,* the philosophical underpinning for the bureaucratic welfare state. Rawls reasoned that it was right for governments to redistribute wealth in order to help the poor and disadvantaged. He argued for a just distribution of society's resources by which a society's benefits and burdens are allocated fairly among its members.

Rawls expressed this philosophy in his **Greatest Equal Liberty Principle:** each person has an equal right to basic rights and liberties. He qualified or limited this principle with the **Difference Principle:** social inequalities are acceptable only if they cannot be eliminated without making the worst-off class even worse off. The basic structure is perfectly just, he wrote, when the prospects of the least fortunate are as great as they can be.

Rawls's justice theory has application in the business context. Justice theory requires decision makers to be guided by fairness and impartiality. It holds that businesses should focus on outcomes: are people getting what they deserve? It would mean, for example, that a business deciding in which of two communities to build a new manufacturing plant should consider which community has the greater need for economic development.

Chief among Rawls's critics was his Harvard colleague Robert Nozick. Nozick argued that the rights of the individual are primary and that nothing more was justified than a minimal government that protected against violence and theft and ensured the enforcement of contracts. Nozick espoused a libertarian view that unequal distribution of wealth is moral if there is equal opportunity. Applied to the business context, Nozick's formulation of justice would permit a business to choose between two manufacturing plant sites after giving each community the opportunity to make its best bid for the plant. Instead of picking the community most in need, the business may pick the one offering the best deal.

Strengths of Justice Theory The strength of Rawls's justice theory lies in its basic premise, the protection of those who are least advantaged in society. Its motives are consistent with the religious and secular philosophies that urge humans to help those in need. Many religions and cultures hold basic to their faith the assistance of those who are less fortunate.

Criticisms of Justice Theory Rawls's justice theory shares some of the criticisms of rights theory. It treats equality as an absolute, without examining the costs of producing equality, including reduced incentives for innovation, entrepreneurship, and production. Moreover, any attempt to rearrange social benefits requires an accurate measurement of current wealth. For example, if a business is unable to measure accurately which employees are in greater need of benefits due to their wealth level, application of justice theory may make the business a Robin Hood in reverse: taking from the poor to give to the rich.

Utilitarianism

Utilitarianism requires a decision maker to maximize utility for society as a whole. Maximizing utility means achieving the highest level of satisfactions over dissatisfactions. This means that a person must consider the benefits and costs of her actions to everyone in society.

A utilitarian will act only if the benefits of the action to society outweigh the societal costs of the action. Note that the focus is on society as a whole. This means a decision maker may be required to do something that harms her if society as a whole is benefited by her action.

A teleological theory, utilitarianism judges our actions as good or bad depending on their consequences. This is sometimes expressed as "the ends justify the means."

Utilitarianism is most identified with 19th-century philosophers Jeremy Bentham and John Stuart Mill. Bentham argued that maximizing utility meant achieving the greatest overall balance of pleasure over pain. A critic of utilitarianism, Thomas Carlyle, called utilitarianism "pig philosophy," because it appeared to base the goal of ethics on the swinish pleasures of the multitude.

Mill thought Bentham's approach too narrow and broadened the definition of utility to include satisfactions such as health, knowledge, friendship, and aesthetic delights. Responding to Carlyle's criticisms, Mill also wrote that some satisfactions count more than others. For example, the pleasure of seeing wild animals free in the world may be a greater satisfaction morally than shooting them and seeing them stuffed in one's den.

How does utilitarianism work in practice? It requires that you consider not just the impact of decisions on yourself, your family, and your friends, but also the impact on everyone in society. Before deciding whether to ride a bicycle to school or work rather than to drive a car, a utilitarian would consider the wear and tear on her clothes, the time saved or lost by riding a bike, the displeasure of riding in bad weather, her improved physical condition, her feeling of satisfaction for not using fossil fuels, the cost of buying more food to fuel her body for the bike trips, the dangers of riding near automobile traffic, and a host of other factors that affect her satisfaction and dissatisfaction.

But her utilitarian analysis doesn't stop there. She has to consider her decision's effect on the rest of society. Will she interfere with automobile traffic flow and decrease the driving pleasure of automobile drivers? Will commuters be encouraged to ride as she does and benefit from doing so? Will her lower use of gasoline for her car reduce demand and consumption of fossil fuels, saving money for car drivers and reducing pollution? Will her and other bike riders' increased food consumption drive up food prices and make it less affordable for poor families? This only scratches the surface of her utilitarian analysis.

The process we used above, so-called **act utilitarianism,** judges each act separately, assessing a single act's benefits and costs to society's members. Obviously, a person cannot make an act utilitarian analysis for every decision. It would take too much time.

Utilitarianism recognizes that human limitation. **Rule utilitarianism** judges actions by a rule that over the long run maximizes benefits over costs. For example, you may find that taking a shower every morning before school or work maximizes society's satisfactions, as a rule. Most days, people around you will be benefited by not having to smell noisome odors, and your personal and professional prospects will improve by practicing good hygiene. Therefore, you are likely to be a rule utilitarian and shower each morning, even though some days you may not contact other people.

Many of the habits we have are the result of rule utilitarian analysis. Likewise, many business practices, such as a retailer's regular starting and closing times, also are based in rule utilitarianism.

Strengths of Utilitarianism

What are the strengths of utilitarianism as a guide for ethical conduct? It is easy to articulate the standard of conduct: you merely need to do what is best for society as a whole. It also coincides with values of most modern countries like the United States: it is capitalist in nature by focusing on total social satisfactions, benefits, welfare, and wealth, not on the allocations of pleasures and pains, satisfactions and dissatisfactions, and wealth.

Criticisms of Utilitarianism

Those strengths also expose some of the criticisms of utilitarianism as an ethical construct. It is difficult to measure one's own pleasures and pains and satisfactions and dissatisfactions, let alone those of all of society's members. In addition, those benefits and costs almost certainly are unequally distributed across society's members. It can foster a tyranny of the majority that may result in morally monstrous behavior, such as a decision by a 100,000-person community to use a lake as a dump for human waste because only one person otherwise uses or draws drinking water from the lake.

That example exhibits how utilitarianism differs from rights theory. While rights theory may protect a person's right to clean drinking water regardless of its cost, utilitarianism considers the benefits and costs of that right as only one factor in the total mix of society's benefits and costs. In some cases, the cost of interfering with someone's right may outweigh the benefits to society, resulting in the same decision that rights theory produces. But where rights theory is essentially a one-factor analysis, utilitarianism requires a consideration of that factor and a host of others as well.

A final criticism of utilitarianism is that it is not constrained by law. Certainly, the law is a factor in utilitarian analysis. Utilitarian analysis must consider, for example, the dissatisfactions fostered by not complying with the law and by creating an environment of lawlessness in a society. Yet the law is only one factor in utilitarian analysis. The pains caused by violating the law may be offset by benefits the violation produces. Most people, however, are rule utilitarian when it comes to law, deciding that obeying the law in the long run maximizes social utility.

Profit Maximization

Profit maximization as an ethical theory requires a decision maker to maximize a business's long-run profits within the limits of the law. It is based in the *laissez faire* theory of capitalism first expressed by Adam Smith in the 18th century and more recently promoted by economists such as Milton Friedman and Thomas Sowell. Laissez faire economists argue total social welfare is optimized if humans are permitted to work toward their own selfish goals. The role of governments and law is solely to ensure the workings of a free market by not interfering with economic liberty, eliminating collusion among competitors, and promoting accurate information in the marketplace.

By focusing on results—maximizing total social welfare—profit maximization is a teleological ethical theory. It is closely related to utilitarianism, but it differs fundamentally in how ethical decisions are made. While utilitarianism maximizes social utility by focusing the actor on everyone's satisfactions and dissatisfactions, profit maximization optimizes total social utility by narrowing the actor's focus, requiring the decision maker to make a decision that merely maximizes profits for himself or his organization.

Strengths of Profit Maximization How can we define ethical behavior as acting in one's selfish interest? As

you probably already learned in a microeconomics course, this apparent contradiction is explained by the consequences of all of us being profit maximizers. By working in our own interests, we compete for society's scarce resources (iron ore, labor, and land, to name a few), which are allocated to those people and businesses that can use them most productively. By allocating society's resources to their most efficient uses, as determined by a free market, we maximize total social utility or benefits. Society as a whole is bettered if all of us compete freely for its resources by trying to increase our personal or business profits. If we fail to maximize profits, some of society's resources will be allocated to less productive uses that reduce society's total welfare.

In addition, profit maximization results in ethical conduct because it requires society's members to act within the constraints of the law. A profit maximizer, therefore, acts ethically by complying with society's mores as expressed in its laws.

Moreover, each decision maker and business is disciplined by the marketplace. Consequently, profit maximization analysis probably requires a decision maker to consider the rights protected by rights theory and justice theory. Ignoring important rights of employees, customers, suppliers, communities, and other stakeholders may negatively impact a corporation's profits. A business that engages in behavior that is judged unethical by consumers and other members of society is subject to boycotts, adverse publicity, demands for more restrictive laws, and other reactions that damage its image, decrease its revenue, and increase its costs.

Consider for example, the reduced sales of Martha Stewart branded goods at Kmart after Ms. Stewart was accused of trading ImClone stock while possessing inside information. Consider also the fewer number of college graduates willing to work for Waste Management, Inc., in the wake of adverse publicity and indictments against its executives for misstating its financial results. Note also the higher cost of capital for firms like Dell as investors bid down the stock price of companies accused of accounting irregularities and other wrongdoing.

All these reactions to perceived unethical conduct impact the business's profitability in the short and long run, motivating that business to make decisions that comply with ethical views that transcend legal requirements.

Criticisms of Profit Maximization The strengths of profit maximization as a model for ethical behavior also suggest criticisms and weaknesses of the theory. Striking at the heart of the theory is the criticism that corporate managers are subject to human failings that make it impossible for them to maximize corporate profits. The failure to discover and process all relevant information and varying levels of aversion to risk can result in one manager making a different decision than another manager. Group decision making in the business context introduces other dynamics that interfere with rational decision making. Social psychologists have found that groups often accept a higher level of risk than they would as individuals. There is also the tendency of a group to internalize the group's values and suppress critical thought.

Furthermore, even if profit maximization results in an efficient allocation of society's resources and maximization of total social welfare, it does not concern itself with how wealth is allocated within society. In America, more than 50 percent of all wealth is held by 10 percent of the population. To some people, that wealth disparity is unacceptable. To *laissez faire* economists, wealth disparity is a necessary component of a free market that rewards hard work, acquired skills, innovation, and risk taking. Yet critics of profit maximization respond that market imperfections and a person's position in life at birth interfere with his ability to compete.

Critics charge that the ability of laws and market forces to control corporate behavior is limited, because it requires lawmakers, consumers, employees, and other constituents to detect unethical corporate acts and take appropriate steps. Even if consumers notice irresponsible behavior and inform a corporation, a bureaucratic corporate structure may interfere with the information being received by the proper person inside the corporation. If instead consumers are silent and refuse to buy corporate products because of perceived unethical acts, corporate management may notice a decrease in sales, yet attribute it to something other than the corporation's unethical behavior.

Critics also argue that equating ethical behavior with legal compliance is a tautology in countries like the United States where businesses distort the lawmaking process by lobbying legislators and making political contributions. It cannot be ethical, they argue, for businesses to comply with laws reflecting the interests of businesses.

Profit maximization proponents respond that many laws restraining businesses are passed despite businesses lobbying against those laws. The Sarbanes–Oxley Act, which increases penalties for wrongdoing executives, requires CEOs to certify financial statements, and imposes internal governance rules on public companies, is such an example. So are laws restricting drug companies from selling a drug unless it is approved by the Food and Drug Administration and requiring environmental impact studies before a business may construct a new manufacturing plant. Moreover, businesses are nothing other than a collection of individual stakeholders, which includes employees, shareholders, and their communities. When they lobby, they lobby in the best interests of all these stakeholders.

Critics respond that ethics transcends law, requiring in some situations that businesses adhere to a higher standard than required by law. We understand this in our personal lives. For example, despite the absence of law dictating for the most part how we treat friends, we know that ethical behavior requires us to be loyal to friends and to spend time with them when they need our help. In the business context, a firm may be permitted to release employees for nearly any reason, except the few legally banned bases of discrimination (such as race, age, and gender), yet some critics will argue businesses should not terminate an employee for other reasons currently not banned by most laws (such as sexual orientation or appearance). Moreover, these critics further argue that businesses—due to their influential role in a modern society—should be leaders in setting a standard for ethical conduct.

Profit maximizers respond that such an ethical standard is difficult to define and hampers efficient decision making. Moreover, they argue that experience shows the law has been a particularly relevant definition of ethical conduct. Consider that all the recent corporate scandals would have been prevented had the executives merely complied with the law. For example, Enron executives illegally kept some liabilities off the firm's financial statements. Tyco and Adelphia executives illegally looted corporate assets. Had these executives simply complied with the law and maximized their firms' long-run profits, none of the recent ethical debacles would have occurred.

Critics of profit maximization respond that the recent corporate crises at companies like Enron and WorldCom prove that flaws in corporate governance encourage executives to act unethically. These examples, critics say, show that many executives do not maximize profits for their firms. Instead, they maximize their own profits at the expense of the firm and its shareholders. They claim that stock options and other incentives intended to align the interests of executives with those of shareholders promote decisions that raise short-term profits to the long-run detriment of the firms. They point out that many CEOs and other top executives negotiate compensation plans that do not require them to stay with the firm long term and which allow them to benefit enormously from short-term profits. Executive greed, encouraged by these perverse executive compensation plans, also encourage CEOs and other executives to violate the law.

Defenders of business, profit maximization, and capitalist economics point out that it is nearly impossible to stop someone who is bent on fraud. A dishonest executive will lie to shareholders, creditors, board members, and the public and also treat the law as optional. Yet enlightened proponents of the modern corporation accept that there are problems with corporate management culture that require changes. They know that an unconstrained CEO, ethically uneducated executives, perverse compensation incentives, and inadequate supervision of executives by the firm's CEOs, board of directors, and shareholders present golden opportunities to the unscrupulous person and make unwitting accomplices of the ignorant and the powerless.

Improving Corporate Governance and Corporate Social Responsibility

Even if we cannot stop all fraudulent executives, we can modify the corporate governance model to educate, motivate, and supervise executives and thereby improve corporate social responsibility. Corporate critics have proposed a wide variety of cures, all of which have been implemented to some degree and with varying degrees of success.

Ethics Codes Many large corporations and several industries have adopted codes of ethics or codes of conduct to guide executives and other employees. The Sarbanes–Oxley Act requires a public company to disclose whether it has adopted a code of ethics for senior financial officers, and to disclose any change in the code or waiver of the code's application.

There are two popular views of such codes. One sees the codes as genuine efforts to foster ethical behavior within a firm or an industry. The other view regards them as thinly disguised attempts to make the firm function better, to mislead the public into believing the firm behaves ethically, to prevent the passage of legislation that would impose stricter constraints on business, or to limit competition under the veil of ethical standards. Even where the first view is correct, ethical codes fail to address concretely all possible forms of corporate misbehavior. Instead, they often emphasize either the behavior required for the firm's effective internal function, such as not accepting gifts from customers, or the relations between competitors within a particular industry, such as prohibitions on some types of advertising.

Better corporate ethics codes make clear that the corporation expects employees not to violate the law in a mistaken belief that loyalty to the corporation or corporate profitability requires it. Such codes work best, however, when a corporation also gives its employees an outlet for dealing with a superior's request to do an unethical act. That outlet may be the corporate legal department or corporate ethics office. One example is Google's Code of Ethics, which appears on the next page.

Ethical Instruction Some corporations require their employees to enroll in classes that teach ethical decision making. The idea is that a manager trained in ethical conduct will recognize unethical actions before they are taken and deter herself and the corporation from the unethical acts.

While promising in theory, in practice many managers are resistant to ethical training that requires them to examine their principles. They are reluctant to set aside a set of long-held principles with which they are comfortable. Therefore, there are some doubts whether managers are receptive to ethical instruction. Even if the training is accepted, will managers retain the ethical lessons of their training and use it, or will time and other job-related pressures force a manager to think only of completing the job at hand?

Moreover, what ethical values should be taught? Is it enough to teach only one, a few, or all the theories of ethical conduct? Corporations mostly support profit maximization, because it maximizes shareholder value. But should a corporation also teach rights theory and expect its employees to follow it? Or should rights theory be treated as only a component of profit maximization?

Most major corporations today express their dedication to ethical decision making by having an ethics officer who is not only responsible for ethical instruction, but also in charge of ethical supervision. The ethics officer may attempt to instill ethical decision making as a component of daily corporate life by sensitizing employees to the perils of ignoring ethical issues. The ethics officer may also be a mentor or sounding board for all employees who face ethical issues.

Whether an ethics officer is effective, however, is determined by the level of commitment top executives make to ethical behavior and the position and power granted to the ethics officer. For example, will top executives and the board of directors allow an ethics officer to nix an important deal on ethical grounds or will they replace the ethics officer with another executive whose ethical views permit the deal? Therefore, probably more important than an ethics officer is a CEO with the character to do the right thing.

Greater Shareholder Role in Corporations Since shareholders are the ultimate stakeholders in a corporation in a capitalist economy, some corporate critics argue that businesses should be more attuned to shareholders' ethical values and that shareholder control of the board of directors and executives should be increased. This

Ethics in Action

Google Code of Conduct

Internet giant Google Inc. is one of many international corporations to adopt an ethics code. Here are excerpts from Google's Code of Ethics for its employees and board of directors. For a look at Google's complete Code of Ethics, go to http://investor.google.com/conduct.html.

Preface "Don't be evil." Googlers generally apply those words to how we serve our users. But "Don't be evil" is much more than that. Yes, it's about providing our users unbiased access to information, focusing on their needs and giving them the best products and services that we can. But it's also about doing the right thing more generally—following the law, acting honorably and treating each other with respect.

The Google Code of Conduct is one of the ways we put "Don't be evil" into practice. It's built around the recognition that everything we do in connection with our work at Google will be, and should be, measured against the highest possible standards of ethical business conduct. We hire great people who work hard to build great products, and it's essential that we build an environment of trust—among ourselves and with our users. That trust and mutual respect underlie our success, and we need to earn it every day.

So, please do read the Code, and follow it, always bearing in mind that each of us has a personal responsibility to incorporate, and to encourage other Googlers to incorporate, the principles of the Code into our work.

I. Serve Our Users Our users value Google not only because we deliver great products and services, but [also] because we hold ourselves to a higher standard in how we treat users and operate more generally. Keeping the following principles in mind will help us to maintain that high standard:

a. Integrity
Our reputation as a company that our users can trust is our most valuable asset, and it is up to all of us to make sure that we continually earn that trust. All of our communications and other interactions with our users should increase their trust in us.

c. Privacy
As we develop great products that serve our users' needs, always remember that we are asking users to trust us with their personal information. Preserving that trust requires that each of us respect and protect the privacy of that information. Our security procedures strictly limit access to and use of users' personal information. Know your responsibilities under these procedures, and access data only as authorized by them, our Privacy Policy, and applicable local data protection laws.

II. Respect Each Other We are committed to a supportive work environment, where employees have the opportunity to reach their fullest potential. Each Googler is expected to do his or her utmost to create a respectful workplace culture that is free of harassment, intimidation, bias and unlawful discrimination of any kind.

III. Avoid Conflicts of Interest In working at Google, we have an obligation to always do what's best for the company and our users. When you are in a position to influence a decision or situation that may result in personal benefit for you or your friends or family at the expense of Google or our users, you may be subject to a conflict of interest. All of us should avoid circumstances that present even the appearance of such a conflict.

When faced with a potential conflict of interest, ask yourself:

- Would this relationship or situation embarrass me or Google if it showed up on the front page of a newspaper or the top of a blog?
- Am I reluctant to disclose the relationship or situation to my manager, Legal, or Ethics & Compliance?
- If I wanted to, could I exploit the potential relationship or situation in a way that benefited me, my friends or family or an associated business, at the expense of Google?

If the answer to any of these questions is "yes," the relationship or situation is likely to create a conflict of interest, and you should avoid it.

VI. Ensure Financial Integrity and Responsibility Financial integrity and fiscal responsibility are core aspects of corporate professionalism. This is more than accurate reporting of our financials, though that's certainly important. The money we spend on behalf of Google is not ours; it's the company's and, ultimately, our shareholders'. Each person at Google—not just those in Finance—has a role in making sure that money is appropriately spent, our financial records are complete and accurate and internal controls are honored.

VII. Obey the Law Google takes its responsibilities to comply with laws and regulations very seriously and each of us is expected to comply with applicable legal requirements and prohibitions. While it's impossible for anyone to know all aspects of every applicable law, you should understand the major laws and regulations that apply to your work. Take advantage of Legal and Ethics & Compliance to assist you here.

VIII. Conclusion Google aspires to be a different kind of company. It's impossible to spell out every possible ethical scenario we might face. Instead, we rely on one another's good judgment to uphold a high standard of integrity for ourselves and our company. We expect all Googlers to be guided by both the letter and the spirit of this Code. Sometimes, identifying the right thing to do isn't an easy call. If you aren't sure, don't be afraid to ask questions of your manager, Legal, or Ethics & Compliance.

And remember . . . don't be evil, and if you see something that you think isn't right—speak up!

decentralization of ethical decision making, the theory goes, should result in corporate decisions that better reflect shareholders' ethical values.

Yet this decentralization of power flies in the face of the rationale for the modern corporation, which in part is designed to centralize management in the board of directors and top officers and to free shareholders from the burden of managing their investments in the corporation. Significant efficiencies are lost if corporate executives are required to divine and apply shareholders' ethical values before making a decision.

In addition, divining the shareholders' ethical viewpoint may be difficult. While nearly all shareholders are mostly profit driven, a small minority of shareholders have other agendas, such as protecting the environment or workers' rights, regardless of the cost to the corporation. It is often not possible to please all shareholders.

Nonetheless, increasing shareholder democracy by enhancing the shareholders' role in the nomination and election of board members is essential to uniting the interests of shareholders and management. So is facilitating the ability of shareholders to bring proposals for ethical policy to a vote of shareholders. In the last several years, for public companies at least, the Securities and Exchange Commission has taken several steps to increase shareholder democracy. These steps, which are covered fully in Chapter 45, are having their intended effect. For example, shareholders of EMC Corporation approved a proposal recommending that the company's board comprise a majority of independent directors. Mentor Graphics Corporation shareholders voted in a resolution that any significant stock option plan be shareholder-approved. Moreover, the New York Stock Exchange and NASDAQ require companies listed on those exchanges to submit for shareholder approval certain actions, such as approval of stock option plans.

Consider All Stakeholders' Interests Utilitarianism analysis clearly requires an executive to consider a decision's impact on all stakeholders. How else can one determine all the benefits and costs of the decision? Likewise, modern rights theory also dictates considering all stakeholders' rights, including not compromising an important right unless trumped by another. Kant's categorical imperative also mandates a concern for others by requiring one to act as one would require others to act.

Critics of corporations and modern proponents of profit maximization argue that more responsible and ethical decisions are made when corporate managers consider the interests of all stakeholders, including not only shareholders, but also employees, customers, suppliers, the community, and others impacted by a decision. For profit

maximizers, the wisdom of considering all stakeholders is apparent, because ignoring the interests of any stakeholder may negatively affect profits. For example, a decision may impact a firm's ability to attract high quality employees, antagonize consumers, alienate suppliers, and motivate the public to lobby lawmakers to pass laws that increase a firm's cost of doing business. This wisdom is reflected in the Guidelines for Ethical Decision Making, which you will learn in the next section.

Nonetheless, there are challenges when a corporate manager considers the interests of all stakeholders. Beyond the enormity of identifying all stakeholders, stakeholders' interests may conflict, requiring a compromise that harms some stakeholders and benefits others. In addition, the impact on each stakeholder group may be difficult to assess accurately.

For example, if a manager is considering whether to terminate the 500 least productive employees during an economic downturn, the manager will note that shareholders will benefit from lower labor costs and consumers may find lower prices for goods, but the manager also knows that the terminated employees, their families, and their communities will likely suffer from the loss of income. Yet if the employees terminated are near retirement and have sizable retirement savings or if the termination motivates employees to return to college and seek better jobs, the impact on them, their families, and their communities may be minimal or even positive. On the other hand, if the manager makes the decision to retain the employees, shareholder wealth may decrease and economic inefficiency may result, which harms all society.

Independent Boards of Directors In some of the instances in which corporate executives have acted unethically and violated the law, the board of directors was little more than a rubber stamp or a sounding board for the CEO and other top executives. The CEO handpicked a board that largely allowed the CEO to run the corporation with little board supervision.

CEO domination of the board is a reality in most large corporations, because the market for CEO talent has skewed the system in favor of CEOs. Few CEOs are willing to accept positions in which the board exercises real control. Often, therefore, a CEO determines which board members serve on the independent board nominating committee and selects who is nominated by the committee. Owing their positions to the CEO and earning handsome fees sometimes exceeding $100,000, many directors are indisposed to oppose the CEO's plans.

For more than three decades, corporate critics have demanded that corporate boards be made more nearly independent of the CEO. The corporate ethical crisis of recent years has increased those calls for independence. The New York Stock Exchange and NASDAQ require companies with securities listed on the exchanges to have a majority of directors independent of the company and top management. Their rules also require independent management compensation, board nomination, and audit committees. The Sarbanes–Oxley Act requires public companies to have board audit committees comprising only independent directors.

One criticism of director independence rules is the belief that no director can remain independent after joining the board, because every director receives compensation from the corporation. There is a concern that an independent director, whose compensation is high, will side with management to ensure his continuing nomination, election, and receipt of high fees.

More extreme proposals of corporate critics include recommendations that all corporate stakeholders, such as labor, government, environmentalists, and communities, have representation on the board or that special directors or committees be given responsibility over special areas, such as consumer protection and workers' rights. Other critics argue for contested elections for each board vacancy. Few corporations have adopted these recommendations.

While honestly motivated, these laws and recommendations often fail to produce greater corporate social responsibility because they ignore the main reason for management's domination of the board: the limited time, information, and resources that directors have. One solution is to give outside directors a full-time staff with power to acquire information within the corporation. This solution, while providing a check on management, also may produce inefficiency by creating another layer of management in the firm.

In addition, some of the recommendations complicate management by making the board less cohesive. Conflicts between stakeholder representatives or between inside and outside directors may be difficult to resolve. For example, the board could be divided by disputes between shareholders who want more dividends, consumers who want lower prices, and employees who want higher wages.

Changing the Internal Management Structure Some corporate critics argue that the historic shift of corporate powers away from a public corporation's board and shareholders to its managers is irreversible. They recommend, therefore, that the best way to produce responsible corporate behavior is to change the corporation's management structure.

The main proponent of this view, Christopher Stone, recommended the creation of offices dedicated to areas such as environmental affairs and workers' rights, higher educational requirements for officers in positions like occupational safety, and procedures to ensure that important information inside and outside the corporation is directed to the proper person within the corporation. He also recommended that corporations study certain important issues and create reports of the study before making decisions.

These requirements aim to change the process by which corporations make decisions. The objective is to improve decision making by raising the competency of decision makers, increasing the amount of relevant information they hold, and enhancing the methodology by which decisions are made.

More information held by more competent managers using better tools should produce better decisions. Two of the later sections in this chapter in part reflect these recommendations. The Guidelines for Ethical Decision Making require a decision maker to study a decision carefully before making a decision. This includes acquiring all relevant facts, assessing a decision's impact on each stakeholder, and considering the ethics of one's decision from each ethical perspective. In addition, the Critical Thinking section below will help you understand when fallacious thinking interferes with a manager's ability to make good decisions.

Eliminating Perverse Incentives and Supervising Management Even if a corporation modifies its internal management structure by improving the decision-making process, there are no guarantees more responsible decisions will result. To the extent unethical corporate behavior results from faulty perception and inadequate facts, a better decision-making process helps. But if a decision maker is motivated solely to increase short-term profits, irresponsible decisions may follow. When one examines closely recent corporate debacles three things are clear: the corporate wrongdoers acted in their selfish interests; the corporate reward system encouraged them to act selfishly, illegally, and unethically; the wrongdoers acted without effective supervision. These facts suggest other changes that should be made in the internal management structure.

During the high flying stock market of the 1990s, stock options were the compensation package preferred by high level corporate executives. Shareholders and boards of directors were more than willing to accommodate them. On one level, stock options seem to align the interests of executives with those of the corporation and its shareholders. Issued at an exercise price usually far below the current market price of the stock, stock options have no value until the corporation's stock price exceeds the exercise price of the stock options. Thus, executives are motivated to increase the corporation's profits, which should result in an increase in the stock's market price. In the 1990s stock market, in which some stock prices were doubling yearly, the exercise price of executives' stock options was quickly dwarfed by the market price. Executives exercised the stock options, buying and then selling stock, and in the process generating profits for a single executive in the tens and hundreds of millions of dollars. Shareholders also benefited from the dramatic increase in the value of their stock.

So what is the problem with stock options? As executives accepted more of their compensation in the form of stock options and became addicted to the lifestyle financed by them, some executives felt pressure to keep profits soaring to ever higher levels. In companies like Enron and WorldCom, which had flawed business models and suspect accounting practices, some executives were encouraged to create business deals that had little if any economic justification and could be accounted for in ways that kept profits growing. In what were essentially pyramid schemes, once the faulty economics of the deals were understood by prospective partners, no new deals were possible and the schemes crashed like houses of cards. But until the schemes were discovered, many executives, including some who were part of the fraudulent schemes, pocketed tens and hundreds of millions of dollars in stock option profits.

The Sarbanes–Oxley Act attempts to recover fraudulently obtained stock option profits by requiring the CEO and CFO to reimburse the company when the corporation is required to restate its financial statements filed with the SEC. The CEO and CFO must disgorge any bonus or stock compensation that was received within 12 months after a false financial report was filed with the SEC.

It is easy to see how fraudulent actions subvert the objective of stock options to motivate executives to act in the best interests of shareholders. Adolph Berle, however, has argued for more than 40 years that stock options are flawed compensation devices that allow executives to profit when stock market prices rise in general, even when executives have no positive effect on profitability. He proposed that the best way to compensate executives is to allow them to trade on inside information they possess about a corporation's prospects, information they possess because they helped produce those prospects. His proposal, however, is not likely ever to be legal compensation because insider trading creates the appearance that the securities markets are rigged.

Even with incentives in place to encourage executives to inflate profits artificially, it is unlikely that the recent fraudulent schemes at Enron, WorldCom, and other companies would have occurred had there been better scrutiny of upper management and its actions by the CEO and the board of directors. At Enron, executives were given great freedom to create partnerships that allowed Enron to keep liabilities off the balance sheet yet generate income that arguably could be recognized in the current period. It is not surprising that this freedom from scrutiny when combined with financial incentives to create the partnerships resulted in executives creating partnerships that had little economic value to Enron.

Better supervision of management is mostly the responsibility of the CEO, but the board of directors bears this duty also. We addressed earlier proposals to create boards of directors that are more nearly independent of the CEO and, therefore, better able to supervise the CEO and other top managers. Primarily, however, better supervision is a matter of attitude, or a willingness to devote time and effort to discover the actions of those under your charge and to challenge them to justify their actions. It is not unlike the responsibility a parent owes to a teenage child to scrutinize her actions and her friends to make sure that she is acting consistent with the values of the family. So too, boards must make the effort to scrutinize their CEOs and hire CEOs who are able and willing to scrutinize the work of the managers below them.

Yet directors must also be educated and experienced. Poor supervision of management has also been shown to be partly due to some directors' ignorance of business disciplines like finance and accounting. Unless board members are able to understand accounting numbers and other information that suggests management wrongdoing, board scrutiny of management is a process with no substance.

The Law   The law has been a main means of controlling corporate misdeeds. Lawmakers usually assume that corporations and executives are rational actors that can be deterred from unethical and socially irresponsible behavior by the threats law presents. Those threats are fines and civil damages, such as those imposed and increased by the Sarbanes–Oxley Act. For deterrence to work, however, corporate decision makers must know when the law's penalties will be imposed, fear those penalties, and act rationally to avoid them.

To some extent, the law's ability to control executive misbehavior is limited. As we discussed earlier in this chapter, corporate lobbying may result in laws reflecting the views of corporations, not society as a whole. Some

The Global Business Environment

Foreign Businesses Face Tougher Laws in U.S. than at Home

Although American executives accused of defrauding shareholders are prosecuted or hauled before congressional hearings, wrongdoing managers in the rest of the world often escape the grasp of their countries' regulators. In most of Asia, Europe, and Latin America, regulations and enforcement are weak. Some legal systems are poorly equipped to handle executive misconduct. The Japanese Securities and Exchange Surveillance Commission brought only 108 enforcement actions in 2007 compared to 655 brought by the United States Securities and Exchange Commission.

Taiwan's Securities and Futures Commission has no power to conduct its own investigations, and local prosecutors who do have that power have little expertise in market and accounting fraud. Germany has been labeled the Wild West, with numerous scandals in newly public companies, yet few actions against the perpetrators. The German Association for Shareholder Protection, a shareholder rights group, regularly brings abuse allegations to state prosecutors, yet the cases are often too complicated for untrained prosecutors to handle. Fewer than 5 percent are investigated. In Italy, false accounting was decriminalized in 2001, making it merely a misdemeanor.

Yet if those executives manage foreign businesses that register their securities on a stock exchange in the United States, such as the New York Stock Exchange, the Sarbanes–Oxley Act (SOX) requires them to comply with some of the Act's toughest provisions. More than 1,300 foreign corporations, such as Sony, Nokia, and Daimler, and their executives are affected by the Act's provisions that ban loans to officers, require independent audit committees, and impose personal liability on officers for errors in the corporate books. The additional paperwork caused Sony to delay an earnings release in 2007.

Foreign governments and businesses have lobbied to be granted exemptions from the Sarbanes–Oxley Act. The European Union wrote to U.S. legislators that the Act gives the SEC unjustified authority over foreign auditing firms that could chill trans-Atlantic trade. The president of the Japanese Institute of Certified Public Accountants argued that the Act places U.S. law above Japanese securities and CPA law, violates international treaties, and infringes Japanese sovereignty.

For a year or so, the European Union considered enacting a law similar to SOX. That threat, however, appears to have passed.

corporate executives may not know the law exists. Others may view the penalties merely as a cost of doing business. Some may think the risk of detection is so low that the corporation can avoid detection. Other executives believe they are above the law, that it does not apply to them out of arrogance or a belief that they know better than lawmakers. Some rationalize their violation of the law on the grounds that "everybody does it."

Nonetheless, for all its flaws, the law is an important means by which society controls business misconduct. Of all the devices for corporate control we have considered, only market forces and the law impose direct penalties for corporate misbehavior. Although legal rules have no special claim to moral correctness, at least they are knowable. Laws also are the result of an open political process in which competing arguments are made and evaluated. This cannot be said about the intuitions of a corporate ethics officer, edicts from public interest groups, or the theories of economists or philosophers, except to the extent they are reflected in law. Moreover, in mature political systems like the United States, respect for and adherence to law is a well-entrenched value.

Where markets fail to promote socially responsible conduct, the law can do the job. For example, the antitrust laws discussed in Chapter 49, while still controversial,

have eliminated the worst anticompetitive business practices. The federal securities laws examined in Chapters 45 and 46 arguably restored investor confidence in the securities markets after the stock market crash of 1929. Although environmentalists often demand more regulation, the environmental laws treated in Chapter 52 have improved the quality of water and reduced our exposure to toxic substances. Employment regulations discussed in Chapter 51—especially those banning employment discrimination—have forced significant changes in the American workplace. Thus, the law has an accomplished record as a corporate control device.

Indeed, sometimes the law does the job too well, often imposing a maze of regulations that deter socially valuable profit seeking without producing comparable benefits. Former Fed chairman Greenspan once wrote, "Government regulation is not an alternative means of protecting the consumer. It does not build quality into goods, or accuracy into information. Its sole 'contribution' is to substitute force and fear for incentive as the 'protector' of the consumer."

The hope was that the Sarbanes–Oxley Act would restore investor confidence in audited financial statements and corporate governance. A 2007 survey by Financial Executives International found that 69 percent of financial executives agreed that compliance with SOX section 404 resulted in more investor confidence in their companies' financial reports. Fifty percent agreed that financial reports were more accurate. Those results came despite the high cost of complying with the Act: an average of $1.7 million for 168 companies with market capitalization above $75 million. For larger companies, like General Electric, the cost is even higher. In each of 2004 and 2005, GE spent more than $30 million to comply with section 404, which requires verification of adequate internal controls.

Guidelines for Ethical Decision Making

Now that you understand the basics of ethical theories and the issues in the corporate governance debate, how do you use this information to make decisions for your business that are ethical and socially responsible? That is, what process will ensure that you have considered all the ethical ramifications and arrived at a decision that is good for your business, good for your community, good for society as a whole, and good for you.

Figure 1 lists nine factors in the Guidelines for Ethical Decision Making. Let's consider each Guideline and explain how each helps you make better decisions.

What Facts Impact My Decision?
This is such an obvious component of any good decision that it hardly seems necessary to mention. Yet it is common that people make only a feeble attempt to acquire *all* the facts necessary to a good decision.

Many people enter a decision-making process biased in favor of a particular option. As a result, they look only for facts that support that option. You have seen this done many times by your friends and opponents, and since you are an honest person, you have seen yourself do this as well from time to time. In addition, demands on our time, fatigue, laziness, ignorance of where to look for facts, and aversion to inconvenience someone who has information contribute to a reluctance or inability to dig deep for relevant facts.

Since good decisions cannot be made in a partial vacuum of information, it is important to recognize when you need to acquire more facts. That is primarily the function of your other classes, which may teach you how to make stock market investment decisions, how to audit a company's financial records, and how to do marketing research.

For our purposes, let's consider this example. Suppose we work for a television manufacturing company that has a factory in Sacramento, California. Our company has placed you in charge of investigating the firm's decision whether to move the factory to Juarez, Mexico. What facts are needed to make this decision, and where do you find those facts?

Among the facts you need are: What are the firm's labor costs in Sacramento and what will those costs be in Juarez? How much will labor costs increase in subsequent years? What is the likelihood of good labor relations in each location? What is and will be the productivity level of employees in each city? What are and will be the transportation costs of moving the firm's inventory to market? What impact will the move have on employees, their families, the communities, the schools, and other stakeholders in each community? Will Sacramento employees find other jobs in Sacramento or elsewhere? How much will we have to pay in severance pay?

Figure 1   *Guidelines for Ethical Decision Making*

1. What **FACTS** impact my decision?

2. What are the **ALTERNATIVES?**

3. Who are the **STAKEHOLDERS?**

4. How do the alternatives impact **SOCIETY AS A WHOLE?**

5. How do the alternatives impact **MY BUSINESS FIRM?**

6. How do the alternatives impact **ME, THE DECISION MAKER?**

7. What are the **ETHICS** of each alternative?

8. What are the **PRACTICAL CONSTRAINTS** of each alternative?

9. What **COURSE OF ACTION** should be taken and how do we **IMPLEMENT** it?

How will our customers and suppliers be impacted by our decision? If we move to Juarez, will our customers boycott our products even if our televisions are better and cheaper than before? If we move, will our suppliers' costs increase or decrease? How will our profitability be affected? How will shareholders view the decision? Who are our shareholders? Do we have a lot of Mexican shareholders, or do Americans dominate our shareholder list? What tax concessions and other benefits will the City of Sacramento give our firm if we promise to stay in Sacramento? What will Ciudad Juarez and the government of Mexico give us if we move to Juarez? How will our decision impact U.S.–Mexican economic and political relations?

This looks like a lot of facts, but we have only scratched the surface. You can probably come up with another 100 facts that should be researched. To give you another example of how thorough managers must be to make prudent decisions, consider that the organizers for the 2000 Summer Olympics in Sydney, Australia, created 800 different terrorist scenarios before developing an antiterrorism plan.

You can see that to some extent we are discussing other factors in the Guidelines as we garner facts. The factors do overlap to some degree. Note also that some of the facts you want to find are not facts at all, but estimates, such as cost and sales projections. We'll discuss in the Eighth Guideline the practical problems with the facts we find.

What Are the Alternatives?

A decision maker must be thorough in listing the alternative courses of actions. For many of us, the temptation is to conclude that there are only two options: to do something or not to do something. Let's take our decision whether to move our factory to Juarez, Mexico. You might think that the only choices are to stay in Sacramento or to move to Juarez. Yet there are several combinations that fall in between those extremes.

For example, we could consider maintaining the factory in Sacramento temporarily, opening a smaller factory in Juarez, and gradually moving production to Mexico as employees in Sacramento retire. Another alternative is to offer jobs in the Juarez factory to all Sacramento employees who want to move. If per-unit labor costs in Sacramento are our concern, we could ask employees in Sacramento to accept lower wages and fringe benefits or to increase their productivity.

There are many other alternatives that you can imagine. It is important to consider all reasonable alternatives. If you do not, you increase the risk that the best course of action was not chosen only because it was not considered.

Who Are the Stakeholders?

In modern societies, where diversity is valued as an independent virtue, considering the impacts of your decision on the full range of society's stakeholders has taken on great significance in prudent and ethical decision making. While a public corporation with thousands of shareholders obviously owes a duty to its shareholders to maximize shareholder wealth, corporate managers must also consider the interests of other important stakeholders, including employees, suppliers, customers, and the communities in which they live. Stakeholders also include society as a whole, which can be defined as narrowly as your country or more expansively as an economic union of countries, such as the European Union of 27 countries, or even the world as a whole.

Not to be omitted from stakeholders is you, the decision maker who is also impacted by your decisions for your firm. The legitimacy of considering your own selfish interests will be considered fully in the Sixth Guideline.

Listing all the stakeholders is not a goal by itself, but helps the decision maker apply more completely other factors in the Ethical Guidelines. Knowing whom your decision affects will help you find the facts you need. It also helps you evaluate the alternatives using the next three Guidelines: how the alternatives we have proposed impact society as whole, your firm, and the decision maker.

How Do the Alternatives Impact Society as a Whole?

We covered some aspects of this Guideline above when we made an effort to discover all the facts that impact our decision. We can do a better job discovering the facts if we try to determine how our decision impacts society as a whole.

For example, if the alternative we evaluate is keeping the factory in Sacramento after getting property tax and road building concessions from the City of Sacramento, how is society as a whole impacted? What effect will tax concessions have on the quality of Sacramento schools (most schools are funded with property taxes)? Will lower taxes cause the Sacramento infrastructure (roads and governmental services) to decline to the detriment of the ordinary citizen? Will the economic benefits to workers in Sacramento offset the harm to the economy and workers in Juarez?

Will our firm's receiving preferential concessions from the Sacramento government undermine the ordinary citizen's faith in our political and economic institutions? Will we contribute to the feelings of some citizens that government grants privileges only to the powerful? Will our staying in Sacramento foster further economic growth in Sacramento? Will staying in Sacramento allow our suppliers to stay in business and continue to hire employees who will buy goods from groceries and malls in Sacramento?

What impact will our decision have on efforts to create a global economy in which labor and goods can freely travel between countries? Will our decision increase international tension between the United States and Mexico?

Note that the impact of our decision on society as a whole fits neatly with one of the ethical theories we discussed earlier: utilitarianism. Yet profit maximization, rights theory, and justice theory also require a consideration of societal impacts.

How Do the Alternatives Impact My Firm?

The most obvious impact any alternative has on your firm is its effect on the firm's bottom line: what are the firm's profits. Yet that answer requires explaining, because what you really want to know is what smaller things leading to profitability are impacted by an alternative.

For example, if our decision is to keep the factory in Sacramento open temporarily and gradually move the plant to Juarez as retirements occur, what will happen to employee moral and productivity in Sacramento? Will our suppliers in Sacramento abandon us to serve more permanent clients instead? Will consumers in Sacramento and the rest of California boycott our televisions? Will they be able to convince other American laborers to boycott our TVs? Will a boycott generate adverse publicity and media coverage that will damage our brand name? Will investors view our firm as a riskier business, raising our cost of capital?

Again, you can see some redundancy here as we work through the guidelines, but that redundancy is all right, for it ensures that we are examining all factors important to our decision.

How Do the Alternatives Impact Me, the Decision Maker?

At first look, considering how a decision you make for your firm impacts *you* hardly seems to be a component of ethical and responsible decision making. The term "selfish" probably comes to mind.

Many of the corporate ethical debacles of the last few years comprised unethical and imprudent decisions that probably were motivated by the decision makers' selfish interests. Mortgage brokers' desires to earn large fees encouraged them to falsify borrowers' financial status and to make imprudent loans to high-risk clients. Several of Enron's off-balance-sheet partnerships, while apparently helping Enron's financial position, lined the pockets of conflicted Enron executives holding stock options and receiving management fees from the partnerships.

Despite these examples, merely because a decision benefits you, the decision maker, does not always mean it is imprudent or unethical. Even decisions by some Enron executives in the late 1990s, while motivated in part by the desire to increase the value of the executives' stock options, could have been prudent and ethical if the off-balance-sheet partnerships had real economic value to Enron (as they did when Enron first created off-balance-sheet partnerships in the 1980s) and accounting for them complied with the law.

At least two reasons explain why you can and should consider your own interest yet act ethically for your firm. First, as the decision maker, you are impacted by the decision. Whether deservedly or not, the decision maker is often credited or blamed for the success or failure of the course of action chosen. You may also be a stakeholder in other ways. For example, if you are an executive in the factory in Sacramento, you and your family may be required to move to Juarez (or El Paso, Texas, which borders Juarez) if the factory relocates. It is valid to consider a decision's impact on you and your family, although it should not be given undue weight.

A second, and more important, reason to consider your own interest is that your decision may be better for your firm and other stakeholders if you also consider your selfish interest. For example, suppose when you were charged to lead the inquiry into the firm's decision whether to move to Juarez, it was made clear that the CEO preferred to close the Sacramento factory and move operations to Juarez.

Suppose also that you would be required to move to Juarez. Your spouse has a well-paying job in Sacramento, and your teenage children are in a good school system and have very supportive friends. You have a strong relationship with your parents and siblings, who also live within 50 miles of your family in Sacramento. You believe that you and your family could find new friends and good schools in El Paso or Juarez, and the move would enhance your position in the firm and increase your chances of a promotion. Nonetheless, overall you and your spouse have determined that staying in the Sacramento area is best for your family. So you are considering quitting your job with the firm and finding another job in the Sacramento area rather than make an attempt to oppose the CEO's preference.

If you quit your job, even in protest, you will have no role in the decision and your resignation will likely have no impact on the firm's Sacramento–Juarez decision.

Had you stayed with the firm, you could have led a diligent inquiry into all the facts that may have concluded that the prudent and ethical decision for the firm was to stay in Sacramento. Without your input and guidance, the firm may make a less prudent and ethical decision.

You can think of other examples where acting selfishly also results in better decisions. Suppose a top-level accounting executive, to whom you are directly responsible, has violated accounting standards and the law by pressuring the firm's auditors to book as income in the current year a contract that will not be performed for two years. You could quit your job and blow the whistle, but you may be viewed as a disgruntled employee and your story given no credibility. You could confront the executive, but you may lose your job or at least jeopardize your chances for a promotion while tipping off the executive, who will cover her tracks. As an alternative, the more effective solution may be to consider how you can keep your job and prospects for promotion while achieving your objective to blow the whistle on the executive. One alternative may be to go through appropriate channels in the firm, such as discussing the matter with the firm's audit committee or legal counsel.

Finding a way to keep your job will allow you to make an ethical decision that benefits your firm, whereas your quitting may leave the decision to someone else who would not act as prudently. The bottom line is this: while sometimes ethical conduct requires acting unselfishly, in other contexts consideration of your self-interest is not only consistent with ethical conduct, but also necessary to produce a moral result.

What Are the Ethics of Each Alternative?

Because our goal is to make a decision that is not only prudent for the firm but also ethical, we must consider the ethics of each alternative, not from one but a variety of ethical viewpoints. Our stakeholders' values comprise many ethical theories; ignoring any one theory will likely cause an incomplete consideration of the issues and may result in unforeseen consequences.

What Would a Utilitarian Do? A utilitarian would choose the alternative that promises the highest net welfare to society as a whole. If we define our society as the United States, moving to Juarez may nonetheless produce the highest net benefit, because the benefits to American citizens from a lower cost of televisions and to American shareholders from higher profits may more than offset the harm to our employees and other citizens of Sacramento. Another benefit of the move may be the reduced cost of the American government dealing with illegal immigration as Mexican workers decide to work at our plant in Juarez. Another cost may be the increased labor cost for a Texas business that would have hired Mexican workers had we not hired them.

If we define society as all countries in the North American Free Trade Agreement (NAFTA was signed by the United States, Mexico, and Canada), the benefit to workers in Juarez may completely offset the harm to workers in Sacramento. For example, the benefit to Juarez workers may be greater than the harm to Sacramento employees if many Juarez employees would otherwise be underemployed and Sacramento employees can find other work or are protected by a severance package or retirement plan.

As we discussed above in the discussion of ethical theories, finding and weighing all the benefits and costs of an alternative are difficult tasks. Even if we reject this theory as the final determinant, it is a good exercise for ensuring that we maximize the number of facts we consider when making a decision.

What Would a Profit Maximizer Do? A profit maximizer will choose the alternative that produces the most long-run profits for the company, within the limits of the law. This may mean, for example, that the firm should keep the factory in Sacramento if that will produce the most profits for the next 10 to 15 years.

This does not mean that the firm may ignore the impact of the decision on Juarez's community and workers. It may be that moving to Juarez will create a more affluent population in Juarez and consequently increase the firm's television sales in Juarez. But that impact is judged not by whether society as a whole is bettered (as with utilitarian analysis) or whether Juarez workers are more deserving of jobs (as with justice theory analysis), but is solely judged by how it impacts the firm's bottom line.

Nonetheless, profit maximization compels a decision maker to consider stakeholders other than the corporation and its shareholders. A decision to move to Juarez may mobilize American consumers to boycott our TVs, for example, or cause a public relations backlash if our Juarez employees receive wages far below our Sacramento workers. These and other impacts on corporate stakeholders may negatively impact the firm's profits.

Although projecting profits is not a precise science, tools you learned in finance classes should enhance your ability to select an alternative that maximizes your firm's profits within the limits of the law.

What Would a Rights Theorist Do? A follower of modern rights theory will determine whether anyone's rights are negatively affected by an alternative. If several rights are affected, the rights theorist will determine which right is more important or trumps the other rights, and choose the alternative that respects the most important right.

For example, if the alternative is to move to Juarez, the Sacramento employees, among others, are negatively affected. Yet if we do not move, potential employees in Juarez are harmed. Are these equal rights, a mere wash, or is it more important to retain a job one already has than to be deprived of a job one has never had?

Are other rights at work here, and how are they ranked? Is it more important to maintain manufacturing production in the firm's home country for national security and trade balance reasons than to provide cheaper televisions for the firm's customers? Does the right of all citizens to live in a global economy that spreads wealth worldwide and promotes international harmony trump all other rights?

While apparently difficult to identify and rank valid rights, this theory has value even to a utilitarian and a profit maximizer. By examining rights that are espoused by various stakeholders, we are more likely to consider all the costs and benefits of our decision and know which rights can adversely affect the firm's profitability if we fail to take them into account.

What Would a Justice Theorist Do?   A justice theorist would choose the alternative that allocates society's benefits and burden most fairly. This requires the decision maker to consider whether everyone is getting what he deserves. If we follow the preaching of John Rawls, the firm should move to Juarez if the workers there are less advantaged than those in Sacramento, who may be protected by savings, severance packages, and retirement plans.

If we follow Nozick's libertarian approach, it is sufficient that the firm gives Sacramento workers an opportunity to compete for the plant by matching the offer the firm has received from Juarez workers. Under this analysis, if Sacramento workers fail to match the Juarez workers' offer of lower wages, for example, it would be fair to move the factory to Juarez, even if Sacramento workers are denied their right to jobs.

Even if the firm has difficulty determining who most deserves jobs with our firm, justice theory, like rights theory, helps the firm identify constituents who suffer from our decision and who can create problems impacting the firm's profitability if the firm ignores their claims.

What Are the Practical Constraints of Each Alternative?

As we evaluate alternatives, it is important to consider each alternative's practical problems before we implement it. For example, is it feasible for us to implement an alternative? Do we have the necessary money, labor, and other resources?

Suppose one alternative is to maintain our manufacturing plant in Sacramento as we open a new plant in Juarez, gradually shutting down the Sacramento plant as employees retire and quit. That alternative sounds like an ethical way to protect the jobs of all existing and prospective employees, but what are the costs of having two plants? Will the expense make that alternative infeasible? Will the additional expense make it difficult for the firm to compete with other TV manufacturers? Is it practicable to have a plant in Sacramento operating with only five employees who are 40 years old and will not retire for 15 years?

It is also necessary to consider potential problems with the facts that have led us to each alternative. Did we find all the facts relevant to our decision? How certain are we of some facts? For example, are we confident about our projections of labor and transportation costs if we move to Juarez? Are we sure that sales of our products will drop insubstantially due to consumer boycotts?

What Course of Action Should Be Taken and How Do We Implement It?

Ultimately, we have to stop our analysis and make a decision by choosing one alternative. Yet even then our planning is not over.

We must determine how to put the alternative into action. How do we implement it? Who announces the decision? Who is told of the decision and when? Do some people, like our employee's labor union, receive advance notice of our plans and have an opportunity to negotiate a better deal for our Sacramento employees? When do we tell shareholders, government officials, lenders, suppliers, investments analysts, and the media and in what order? Do we antagonize a friend or an enemy and risk killing a deal if we inform someone too soon or too late?

Finally, we have to prepare for the worst-case scenario. What do we do if, despite careful investigation, analysis, and planning, our course of action fails? Do we have backup plans? Have we anticipated all the possible ways our plan may fail and readied responses to those failures?

In 1985, the Coca-Cola Company decided to change the flavor of Coke in response to Coke's shrinking share of the cola market. Despite careful market research, Coca-Cola failed to anticipate Coke drinkers' negative response to the new Coke formula and was caught without a response to the outcry. Within three months, Coca-Cola realized it had to revive the old Coke formula under the brand name Coca-Cola Classic. In the meantime, Coke lost significant market share to rival Pepsi. Today, one would expect Coke executives introducing a reformulated drink to predict more consumers' reactions to the drink and to prepare a response to each reaction.

Knowing When to Use the Guidelines

You can probably see that following these factors will result in better decisions in a variety of contexts, including some that appear to have no ethical concerns. For example, in the next few years, most of you will consider what major course of study to select at college or what job to take with which firm in which industry. This framework can help you make a better analysis that should result in a better decision.

The Guidelines can be used also to decide mundane matters in your personal life, such as whether to eat a high-fat hamburger or a healthful salad for lunch, whether to spend the next hour exercising at the gym or visiting a friend in the hospital, and whether or not to brush your teeth every day after lunch. But for most of us, using the Guidelines every day for every decision would occupy so much of our time that little could be accomplished, what is sometimes called "paralysis by analysis."

Practicality, therefore, requires us to use the Guidelines only for important decisions and those that create a potential for ethical problems. We can identify decisions requiring application of the Guidelines if we carefully reflect from time to time about what we have done and are doing. This requires us to examine our past, current, and future actions.

It may not surprise you how seldom people, including business executives, carefully preview and review their actions. The pressures and pace of daily living give us little time to examine our lives critically. Most people are reluctant to look at themselves in the mirror and ask themselves whether they are doing the right thing for themselves, their families, their businesses, and their communities. Few know or follow the words of Socrates, "The unexamined life is not worth living."

Ask yourself whether you believe that mortgage brokers used anything like the Guidelines for Ethical Decision Making before signing low-income borrowers to loans exceeding $500,000. Did executives at bankrupt energy trader Enron consider any ethical issues before creating off-balance-sheet partnerships with no economic value to Enron? Do you think the employees at accounting firm Arthur Andersen carefully examined their decision to accept Enron's accounting for off-balance-sheet partnerships?

Merely by examining our past and prospective actions, we can better know when to apply the Guidelines.

In the last section of this chapter, Resisting Requests to Act Unethically, you will learn additional tools to help you identify when to apply the Guidelines.

LOG ON

Go to
www.scu.edu/ethics
This Web site maintained by the Markkula Center for Applied Ethics at the University of Santa Clara has links to business ethics resources and guides for ethical/moral decision making.

Thinking Critically

Part of ethical decision making is being able to think critically, that is, to evaluate arguments logically, honestly, and without bias in favor of your own arguments and against those of others.

Even if someone uses the Guidelines for Ethical Decision Making, there is a risk that they have been misapplied if a person makes errors of logic or uses fallacious arguments. In this section, we want to help you identify when your arguments and thinking may be flawed and how to correct them. Equally important, we want to help you identify flaws in others' thinking. The purpose is to help you think critically and not to accept at face value everything you read or hear and to be careful before you commit your arguments to paper or voice them.

This chapter's short coverage of critical thinking covers only a few of the errors of logic and argument that are covered in a college course or book devoted to the subject. Here are 15 common fallacies.

Non Sequiturs A *non sequitur* is a conclusion that does not follow from the facts or premises one sets out. The speaker is missing the point or coming to an irrelevant conclusion. For example, suppose a consumer uses a corporation's product and becomes ill. The consumer argues that because the corporation has lots of money, the corporation should pay for his medical expenses. Clearly, the consumer is missing the point. The issue is whether the corporation's product *caused* his injuries, not whether money should be transferred from a wealthy corporation to a poor consumer.

You see this also used when employees attempt to justify stealing pens, staplers, and paper from their employers. The typical *non sequitur* goes like this: "I don't get paid enough, so I'll take a few supplies. My employer won't even miss them."

Business executives fall prey to this fallacy also. Our firm may consider which employees to let go during a downturn. Company policy may call for retaining the best employees in each department, yet instead we release those employees making the highest salary in each position in order to save more money. Our decision does not match the standards the company set for downsizing decisions and is a *non sequitur,* unless we admit that we have changed company policy.

Appeals to Pity
A common fallacy seen in the American press is the appeal to pity or compassion. This argument generates support for a proposition by focusing on a victim's predicament. It usually is also a *non sequitur.* Examples are news stories about elderly, retired people who find it hard to afford expensive, life-prolonging drugs. None of these stories point out that many of these people squandered their incomes when working rather than saving for retirement.

Appeals to pity are effective because humans are compassionate. We have to be careful, however, not to be distracted from the real issues at hand. For example, in the trial against accused 9/11 co-conspirator Zacarias Moussaoui, federal prosecutors wanted to introduce testimony by the families of the victims. While what the families of 9/11 suffered is terrible, the victims' families hold no evidence of Moussaoui's role in 9/11. Instead, their testimonies are appeals to pity likely to distract the jury from its main task of determining whether Moussaoui was a part of the 9/11 conspiracy.

You see many appeals to pity used against corporations. Here is a typical argument: a corporation has a chemical plant near a neighborhood; children are getting sick and dying in the neighborhood; someone should pay for this suffering; the corporation should pay. You can also see that this reasoning is a *non sequitur.* Better reasoning requires one to determine not whether two events are coincidental or correlated, but whether one (the chemical plant) caused the other (the children's illnesses).

False Analogies
An analogy essentially argues that since something is like something else in one or more ways, it is also like it in another respect. Arguers often use analogies to make a point vividly, and therefore analogies have strong appeal. Nonetheless, while some analogies are apt, we should make sure that the two situations are sufficiently similar to make the analogy valid.

Suppose an executive argues that our bank should not make loans to lower-income borrowers because the bank will suffer huge losses like Countrywide Financial. This analogy may be invalid because we may do a better job

verifying a borrower's income and ability to repay a loan than did Countrywide.

Analogies can also be used to generate support for a proposal, such as arguing that since Six Sigma worked for General Electric, it will work for our firm also. It is probable that factors other than Six Sigma contributed to GE's success during the Jack Welch era, factors our firm may or may not share with GE.

Nonetheless, analogies can identify potential opportunities, which we should evaluate prudently to determine whether the analogy is valid. Analogies can also suggest potential problems that require us to examine a decision more carefully before committing to it.

Begging the Question
An arguer begs the question when she takes for granted or assumes the thing that she is setting out to prove. For example, you might say that we should tell the truth because lying is wrong. That is **circular reasoning** and makes no sense, because telling the truth and not lying are the same things. Another example is arguing that democracy is the best form of government because the majority is always right.

Examples of begging the question are difficult to identify sometimes because they are hidden in the language of the speaker. It is best identified by looking for arguments that merely restate what the speaker or questioner has already stated, but in different words. For an example in the business context, consider this interchange between you and someone working under you.

You: Can I trust these numbers you gave to me?

Co-worker: Yes, you can trust them.

You: Why can I trust them?

Co-worker: Because I'm an honest person.

The co-worker used circular reasoning, since whether the numbers can be trusted is determined by whether he is honest, yet he provided no proof of his honesty or trustworthiness.

Argumentum ad Populum
Argumentum ad populum means argument to the people. It is an emotional appeal to popular beliefs, values, or wants. The fallacy is that merely because many or all people believe something does not mean it is true. It is common for newspapers to poll its readers about current issues, such as support for a presidential decision. For example, a newspaper poll may show that 60 percent of Americans support the president. The people may be right, but it is also possible that the president's supporters are wrong: they may be uninformed or base their support of the president on invalid reasoning.

Arguments to the people are commonly used by corporations in advertisements, such as beer company ads showing friends having a good time while drinking beer. The point of such ads is that if you want to have a good time with friends, you should drink beer. While some beer drinkers do have fun with friends, you probably can also point to other people who drink beer alone.

Bandwagon Fallacy

The bandwagon fallacy is similar to *argumentum ad populum*. A bandwagon argument states that we should or should not do something merely because one or more other people or firms do or do not do it. *Sports Illustrated* quoted baseball player Ken Caminiti's justification for using steroids: "At first I felt like a cheater. But I looked around, and everyone was doing it." Some people justify cheating on their taxes for the same reason.

This reasoning can be fallacious because probably not everyone is doing it, and even if many or all people do something, it is not necessarily right. For example, while some baseball players do use steroids, there are serious negative side effects including impotency and acute psychosis, which make its use risky. Cheating on taxes may be common, but it is still illegal and can result in the cheater's imprisonment.

Bandwagon thinking played a large part in the credit crunch of 2008, as many loan buyers like Bear Stearns bought high-risk loans only because their competitors were buying the loans, thereby encouraging lenders to continue to make high-risk loans.

Argumentum ad Baculum

Argumentum ad baculum means argument to club. The arguer uses threats or fear to bolster his position. This is a common argument in business and family settings. For example, when a parent asks a child to take out the garbage, the child may ask, "Why?" Some parents respond, "Because if you don't, you'll spend the rest of the afternoon in your room." Such an argument is a *non sequitur* as well.

In the business context, bosses explicitly and implicitly use the club, often generating support for their ideas from subordinates who fear they will not be promoted unless they support the boss's plans. An executive who values input from subordinates will ensure that they do not perceive that the executive is wielding a club over them.

Enron's CFO Andrew Fastow used this argument against investment firm Goldman Sachs when it balked at lending money to Enron. He told Goldman that he would not do anything with a presentation Goldman had prepared unless it made the loan.

By threatening to boycott a company's products, consumers and other interest groups use this argument against corporations perceived to act unethically. It is one reason that profit maximization requires decision makers to consider a decision's impact on all stakeholders.

Argumentum ad Hominem

Argumentum ad hominem means "argument against the man." This tactic attacks the speaker, not his reasoning. For example, a Republican senator criticizes a Democratic senator who supports the withdrawal of American troops from a war zone by saying, "You can't trust him. He never served in the armed forces." Such an argument attacks the Democratic senator's character, not the validity of his reasons for withdrawing troops.

When a CEO proposes a new compensation plan for corporate executives, an opponent may argue, "Of course he wants the new plan. He'll make a lot of money from it." Again, this argument doesn't address whether the plan is a good one or not; it only attacks the CEO's motives. While the obvious conflict of interest the CEO has may cause us to doubt the sincerity of the reasons he presents for the plan (such as to attract and retain better management talent), merely pointing out this conflict does not rebut his reasons.

One form of *ad hominem* argument is attacking a speaker's consistency, such as, "Last year you argued for something different." Another common form is appealing to personal circumstances. One woman may say to another, "As a woman, how can you be against corporate policies that set aside executive positions for women?" By personalizing the argument, the speaker is trying to distract the listener from the real issue. A proper response to the personal attack may be, "As a women and a human, I believe in equal opportunity for all people. I see no need for any woman or myself to have special privileges to compete with men. I can compete on my own. By having quotas, the corporation cheapens my accomplishments by suggesting that I need the quota. Why do you, as a woman, think you need a quota?"

Guilt by association is the last *ad hominem* argument we will consider. This argument attacks the speaker by linking her to someone unpopular. For example, if you make the libertarian argument that government should not restrict or tax the consumption of marijuana, someone may attack you by saying, "Mass murderer Charles Manson also believed that." Your attacker suggests that by believing as you do, you are as evil as Charles Manson. Some corporate critics use guilt by association to paint all executives as unethical people motivated to cheat their corporations. For example, if a CEO asks for stock options as part of her compensation package, someone may say, "Enron's executives wanted stock options also." The implication is that the CEO should not be trusted because some Enron executives who were corrupt also wanted stock options.

No *ad hominem* argument is necessarily fallacious, because a person's character, motives, consistency, personal characteristics, and associations may suggest further scrutiny of a speaker's arguments is necessary. However, merely attacking the speaker does not expose flaws in her arguments.

Argument from Authority

Arguments from authority rely on the quality of an expert or person in a position of authority, not the quality of the expert's or authority's argument. For example, if someone says, "The president says we need to stop drug trafficking in the United States, and that is good enough for me," he has argued from authority. He and the president may have good reasons to stop drug trafficking, but we cannot know that from his statement.

Another example is "Studies show that humans need to drink 10 glasses of water a day." What studies? What were their methodologies? Did the sample sizes permit valid conclusions? A form of argument to authority is **argument to reverence or respect,** such as "Who are you to disagree with the CEO's decision to terminate 5,000 employees?" The arguer is trying to get you to abandon your arguments, not because they are invalid, but because they conflict with the views of an authority. Your response to this question should not attack the CEO (to call the CEO an idiot would be *ad hominem* and also damage your prospects in the firm), but state the reasons you believe the company would be better off not terminating 5,000 employees.

It is natural to rely on authorities who have expertise in the area on which they speak. But should we give credibility to authorities speaking on matters outside the scope of their competency? For example, does the fact that Julia Roberts is an Academy Award–winning actress have any relevance when she is testifying before Congress about Rett Syndrome, a neurological disorder that leaves infants unable to communicate and control body functions? Is she any more credible as a Rett Syndrome authority because she narrated a film on the Discovery Health Channel about children afflicted with the disease?

This chapter includes several examples of arguments from authority when we cite Kant, Bentham, and others who have formulated ethical theories. What makes their theories valid, however, is not whether they are recognized as experts, but whether their reasoning is sound.

False Cause

This fallacy results from observing two events and concluding that there is a causal link between them when there is no such link. Often we commit this fallacy because we do not attempt to find all the evidence proving or disproving the causal connection. For example, if as a store manager you change the opening hour for your store to 6 AM from 8 AM, records for the first month of operation under the new hours may show an increase in revenue. While you may be tempted to infer that the revenue increase is due to the earlier opening hour, you should not make that conclusion until at the very least you examine store receipts showing the amount of revenue generated between 6 AM and 8 AM. The increase in revenue could have resulted from improved general economic conditions unconnected to the new hours: people just had more money to spend.

The fallacy of false cause is important to businesses, which need to make valid connections between events in order to judge the effectiveness of decisions. Whether, for example, new products and an improved customer relations program increases revenues and profits should be subjected to rigorous testing, not some superficial causal analysis. Measurement tools you learn in other business classes help you eliminate false causes.

The Gambler's Fallacy

This fallacy results from the mistaken belief that independent prior outcomes affect future outcomes. Consider this example. Suppose you flip a coin five times and each time it comes up heads. What is the probability that the next coin flip will be heads? If you did not answer 50 percent, you committed the gambler's fallacy. Each coin flip is an independent event, so no number of consecutive flips producing heads will reduce the likelihood that the next flip will also be heads. That individual probability is true even though the probability of flipping six consecutive heads is 0.5 to the sixth power, or only 1.5625 percent.

What is the relevance of the gambler's fallacy to business? We believe and are taught that business managers and professionals with higher skills and better decision-making methods are more likely to be successful than those with lesser skills and worse methods. Yet we have not discussed the importance of luck or circumstance to success. When a corporation has five years of profits rising by 30 percent, is it due to good management or because of expanding consumer demand or any number of other reasons? If a mutual fund has seven years of annual returns of at least 15 percent, is the fund's manager an investment genius or is she lucky? If it is just luck, one should not expect the luck to continue. The point is that you should not be seduced by a firm's, manager's, or even your own string of successes and immediately jump to the conclusion that the successes were the result of managerial excellence. Instead, you should use measurement tools taught in your finance, marketing, and other courses to determine the real reasons for success.

Reductio ad Absurdum

Reductio ad absurdum carries an argument to its logical end, without considering whether it is an inevitable or probable result. This is often called the **slippery slope fallacy.**

For example, if I want to convince someone not to eat fast food, I might argue, "Eating fast food will cause you to put on weight. Putting on weight will make you overweight. Soon you will weigh 400 pounds and die of heart disease. Therefore, eating fast food leads to death. Don't eat fast food." In other words, if you started eating fast food, you are on a slippery slope and will not be able to stop until you die. Although you can see that this argument makes some sense, it is absurd for most people who eat fast food.

Scientist Carl Sagan noted that the slippery slope argument is used by both sides of the abortion debate. One side says, "If we allow abortion in the first weeks of pregnancy, it will be impossible to prevent the killing of a full-term infant." The other replies, "If the state prohibits abortion even in the ninth month, it will soon be telling us what to do with our bodies around the time of conception."

Business executives face this argument frequently. Human resource managers use it to justify not making exceptions to rules, such as saying, "If we allow you time off to go to your aunt's funeral, we have to let anyone off anytime they want." Well, no, that was not what you were asking for. Executives who reason this way often are looking for administratively simple rules that do not require them to make distinctions. That is, they do not want to think hard or critically.

Pushing an argument to its limits is a useful exercise in critical thinking, often helping us to discover whether a claim has validity. The fallacy is carrying the argument to its extreme without recognizing and admitting that there are many steps along the way that are more likely consequences.

Appeals to Tradition

Appeals to tradition infer that because something has been done a certain way in the past, it should be done the same way in the future. You probably have heard people say, "I don't know why we do it, but we've always done it that way, and it's always worked, so we'll continue to do it that way." Although there is some validity to continuing to do what has stood the test of time, the reasons a business strategy has succeeded in the past may be independent of the strategy itself. The gambler's fallacy would suggest that perhaps we have just been lucky in the past. Also, changed circumstances may justify departing from previous ways of doing business.

The Lure of the New

The opposite of appeals to tradition is the lure of the new, the idea that we should do or buy something merely because it is "just released" or "improved." You see this common theme in advertising that promotes "new and improved" Tide or Windows 2009. Experience tells us that sometimes new products are better. But we can also recount examples of new car models with defects and new software with bugs that were fixed in a later version.

The lure of the new is also a common theme in management theories, as some managers have raced to embrace one new craze after another, depending on which is the hottest fad, be it Strategic Planning, Total Quality Management, Reengineering the Corporation, or Customer Relationship Management. The point here is the same. Avoid being dazzled by claims of newness. Evaluations of ideas should be based on substance.

Sunk Cost Fallacy

The sunk cost fallacy is an attempt to recover invested time, money, and other resources, by spending still more time, money, or other resources. It is sometimes expressed as "throwing good money after bad." Stock market investors do this often. They invest $30,000 in the latest tech stock. When the investment declines to $2,000, rather than evaluate whether it is better to withdraw that $2,000 and invest it elsewhere, an investor who falls for the sunk cost fallacy might say, "I can't stop investing now, otherwise what I've invested so far will be lost." While the latter part of the statement is true, the fallacy is in the first part. Of the money already invested, $28,000 is lost whether or not the investor continues to invest. If the tech stock is not a good investment *at this time,* the rational decision is to withdraw the remaining $2,000 and not invest more money.

There are other statements that indicate business executives may fall victim to the sunk cost fallacy: "It's too late for us to change plans now." Or "If we could go back to square one, then we could make a different decision." The best way to spend the firm's remaining labor and money may be to continue a project. But that decision should be unaffected by a consideration of the labor and money already expended. The proper question is this: What project will give the firm the best return on its investment of money and other resources *from this point forward.* To continue to invest in a hopeless project is irrational, and may be a pathetic attempt to delay having to face the consequences of a poor decision.

A decision maker acts irrationally when he attempts to save face by throwing good money after bad. If you want a real-world example of ego falling prey to the sunk cost fallacy, consider that President Lyndon Johnson committed American soldiers to the Vietnam Conflict after he had determined that America and South Vietnam could never defeat the Viet Cong. By falling for the sunk cost fallacy, the United States lost billions of dollars and tens of thousands of soldiers in the pursuit of a hopeless cause.

LOG ON

Go to
www.fallacyfiles.org
Maintained by Gary Curtis, *The Fallacy Files* cover more than 150 fallacies with links to explanations and valuable resources.
Go to
www.austhink.org/critical
Tim van Gelder's *Critical Thinking on the Web* lists some of the best Web sites with information about reasoning and critical thinking.

Common Characteristics of Poor Decision Making

Most business managers during the course of their formal education in school or informal education on the job have learned most of the techniques we have discussed in this chapter for making ethical and well-reasoned decisions. Yet business managers continue to make unethical and poor decisions, most often in disregard of the very principles that they otherwise view as essential to good decision making. Each of us can also point to examples when we have failed to analyze a situation properly before making a decision, even though at the time we possessed the ability to make better decisions.

Why do we and other well-intentioned people make bad decisions? What is it that interferes with our ability to use all the decision-making tools at our disposal, resulting sometimes in unethical and even catastrophic decisions? What causes a basically honest accountant to agree to cook the books for his corporation? What causes a drug company to continue to market a drug when internal tests and user experience show a high incidence of harmful side effects? What causes a corporation to continue to operate a chemical plant when its safety systems have been shut down? While business scholars and other writers have suggested several attributes that commonly interfere with good decision making, we believe they can be distilled into three essential traits that are useful to you, a decision maker who has already learned the Guidelines for Ethical Decision Making and the most common critical thinking errors.

Failing to Remember Goals

Friedrich Nietzsche wrote, "Man's most enduring stupidity is forgetting what he is trying to do." If, for example, our company's goal as a retailer is to garner a 30 percent market share in the retail market in five years, you may think that would translate into being dominant in each segment of our business, from housewares to video games. But should our retailer strive to dominate a market segment that is declining, such as portable cassette players, when the consumer market has clearly moved to iPods and other similar digital recorders? If we focus on the wrong goal—dominating the cassette player market, which may not exist in five years—we have failed to remember our goal of acquiring a 30 percent overall market share.

In another example, suppose we are a luxury home-builder with two goals that go hand-in-hand: producing high quality housing and maintaining an annual 15 percent return on equity. The first goal supports the second goal: by having a reputation for producing high quality housing, we can charge more for our houses. Suppose, however, one of our project managers is under pressure to bring her development in line with cost projections. She decides, therefore, to use lower quality, lower cost materials. The consequence is we meet our profit target in the short run, but in the long run when the shoddy materials are detected and our reputation is sullied, both of our goals of building high quality housing and achieving a 15 percent return on equity will be compromised. Again, we have failed to remember the most important goal, maintaining high quality, which allowed us to achieve our ROE goal.

Overconfidence

While confidence is a personal trait essential to success, overconfidence or overoptimism is one of the most common reasons for bad decisions. We all have heard ourselves and others say, "Don't worry. Everything will work out OK." That statement is likely a consequence of overconfidence, not careful analysis that is necessary to make sure everything will work out as we hope.

There are several corollaries or other ways to express this overoptimism. Sometimes businesses executives will do something that they know to be wrong with the belief that it is only a small or temporary wrong that will be fixed next year. They may rationalize that no one will notice the wrongdoing and that only big companies and big executives get caught, not small companies and little managers like them.

Many of the accounting scandals of the last ten years started small, rationalized as temporary attempts to cook the books that would be corrected in the following years when business turned around. As we now know, finance managers and accountants who thought things would turn around were being overconfident about the economy and their companies.

Another aspect of overconfidence is confirmation bias; that is, we must be doing things the right way because all has gone well in the past. Or at least we have not been caught doing something wrong in the past, so we will not be caught in the future. In part this reveals a thinking error we have studied, appeal to tradition. In the home-builder example above, the project manager's cutting quality in years past may not have been detected by home-owners who knew nothing about construction quality. And none of the project manager's workers may have told top management about the project manager's actions. That past, however, does not guarantee the future. New homeowners may be more knowledgeable, and future workers may inform management of the project manager's quality-cutting actions.

Another consequence of overoptimism is believing that complex problems have simple solutions. That leads to the next common trait of bad decision making.

Complexity of the Issues

Closely aligned to and aggravated by overconfidence is the failure of decision makers to understand the complexity of an issue. A manager may perceive that the facts are simpler than reality and, therefore, not see that there is little margin for error. Consequently, the executive has not considered the full range of possible solutions and has failed to find the one solution that best matches the facts.

Restated, the decision maker has not done all the investigation and thinking required by the Guidelines for Ethical Decision Making and, therefore, has not discovered all the facts and considered all the reasonable courses of action necessary to making a prudent decision.

The impediments to knowing all the facts, understanding the complexity of a problem, and doing the hard work to create and evaluate all possible solutions to a problem are known to all of us. Fatigue, laziness, overconfidence, and forgetting goals play roles in promoting ignorance of critical facts. We may also want to be team players, by following the lead of a colleague or the order of a boss. These human tendencies deter us from making the effort to find the facts and to consider all options.

Resisting Requests to Act Unethically

Even if we follow the Guidelines for Ethical Decision Making and avoid the pitfalls of fallacious reasoning, not everyone is a CEO or his own boss and able to make decisions that everyone else follows. Sure, if you control a firm, you will do the right thing. But the reality is that for most people in the business world, other people make many decisions that you are asked to carry out. What do you do when asked to do something unethical? How can you resist a boss's request to act unethically? What could employees at WorldCom have done when its CFO instructed them to falsify the firm's books, or mortgage brokers when their bosses asked them to falsify borrowers' incomes?

Recognizing Unethical Requests and Bosses

A person must recognize whether he has been asked to do something unethical. While this sounds simple considering we have spent most of this chapter helping you make just that kind of decision, there are structural problems that interfere with your ability to perform an ethical analysis when a boss or colleague asks you to do something. Many of us are inclined to be team players and "do as we are told" by a superior. Therefore, it is important to recognize any tendency to accept appeals to authority and to resist the temptation to follow orders blindly. We do not want to be like the Enron accounting employee who returned to his alma mater and was asked by a student, "What do you do at Enron?" When considering that question, a question he never posed to himself, he realized that his only job was to remove liabilities from Enron's balance sheet.

For most bosses' orders, such an analysis will be unnecessary. Most of the time, a boss is herself ethical and will not ask us to do something wrong. But there are exceptions that require us to be on the lookout. Moreover, some bosses have questionable integrity, and they are more likely to give us unethical orders. Therefore, it will be helpful if we can identify bosses who have shaky ethics, for whom we should put up our ethical antennae when they come to us with a task.

Business ethicists have attempted to identify executives with questionable integrity by their actions. Ethical bosses have the ability to "tell it like it is" while those with less integrity say one thing and do another. Ethical bosses have the ability to acknowledge that they have failed, whereas those with low integrity often insist on being right all the time. Ethical bosses try to build a consensus before making an important decision; unethical bosses may generate support for their decisions with intimidation through anger and threats. Ethical bosses can think about the needs of others beside themselves. Bosses with low integrity who misuse their workers by asking them to act unethically often mistreat other people also, like secretaries and waiters.

If we pay attention to these details, we will be better able to consider the "source" when we are asked to do something by a boss and, therefore, more sensitive to the need to scrutinize the ethics of a boss's request.

Buying Time

If we think a requested action is or might be unethical, what is done next? How can we refuse to do something a boss has ordered us to do? One key is to buy some time before you have to execute the boss's order. Buying time allows you to find more facts, to understand an act's impact on the firm's stakeholders, and to evaluate the ethics of the action. It also lets you find other alternatives that achieve the boss's objectives without compromising your values. Delay also gives you time to speak with the firm's ethics officer and other confidants.

How do you buy time? If the request is in an e-mail, you might delay responding to it. Or you could answer that you have received the e-mail and will give your attention to it when you finish with the task you are working on. Similar tactics can be used with phone calls and other direct orders. Even a few hours can help your decision. Depending on the order and your ability to stack delay on top of delay, you may be able to give yourself days or weeks to find a solution to your dilemma.

The most important reason for buying time is it allows you to seek advice and assistance from other people, especially those in the firm. That brings us to the next tactic for dealing with unethical requests.

Find a Mentor and a Peer Support Group

Having a support system is one of the most important keys to survival in any organization, and it is best to put a system in place when you start working at the firm. Your support system can improve and help defend your decisions. It can also give you access to executives who hold the power to overrule your boss. Your support system should include a mentor and a network of other employees with circumstances similar to your own.

A mentor who is well established, well respected, and highly placed in the firm will help you negotiate the pitfalls that destroy employees who are ignorant of a firm's culture. A mentor can be a sounding board for your decisions; he can provide information on those who can be expected to help you and those who could hurt you; he can advise you of the procedures you should follow to avoid antagonizing potential allies. A mentor can also defend you and provide protection when you oppose a boss's decision. Many firms have a mentorship program, but if not or if your assigned mentor is deficient, you should find an appropriate mentor soon after you join the firm. Be sure to keep him updated regularly on what you are doing. By letting a mentor know that you care to keep him informed, he becomes invested in you and your career.

You should also build a community of your peers by creating a network of other workers who share your values and interests. You may want to find others who joined the firm at about the same time you did, who are about the same age, who share your passion for the firm's products and services, and who have strong ethical values. To cement the relationship, your peer support group should meet regularly, such as twice a week at work during 15-minute coffee breaks. This group can give you advice, help with difficult decisions, and unite to back up your ethical decisions.

Find Win-Win Solutions

As we learned from the Guidelines for Ethical Decision Making, many times there are more than the two options of doing and not doing something. There are a number of choices in between those extremes, and the best solution may be one unconnected to them. For example, suppose your boss has ordered you to fire someone who works under you. The worker's productivity may be lagging, and perhaps he has made a few costly mistakes. Yet you think it would be wrong to fire the worker at this time. What do you do?

Find a win-win solution, that is, a compromise that works for you and your boss. First, discover your boss's wants. Probably you will find that your boss wants an employee who makes no or few mistakes and has a certain level of productivity. Next determine what is needed for the affected employee to reach that level. If you find the employee is having emotional problems that interfere with his work, are they temporary or can we help him handle them? Can we make him more productive by giving him more training? Is the employee unmotivated or is he unaware that he lags behind other workers? Should we give him a warning and place him on probationary status for a month, releasing him if there is no satisfactory improvement? These alternatives may address your boss's concerns about the employee without compromising your ethical values.

Resisting Requests to Do Unethical Acts

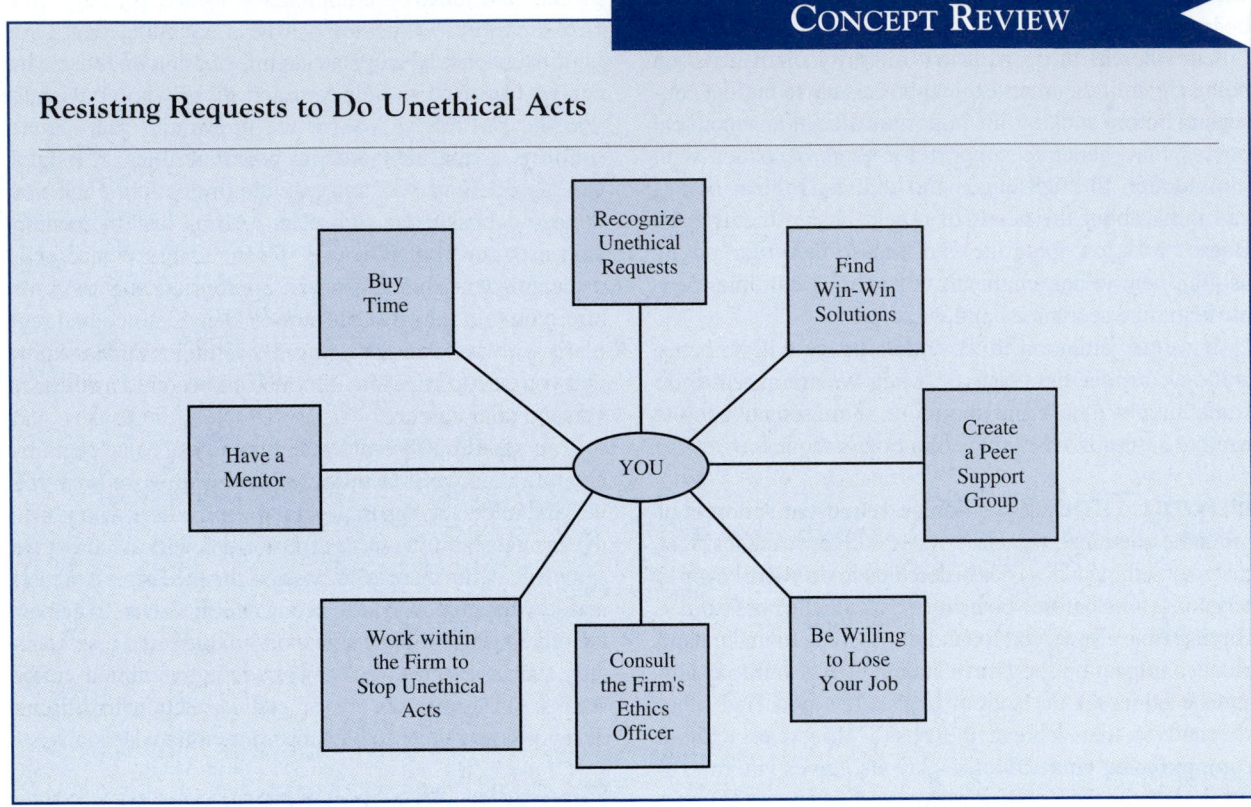

In other contexts, you may need to approach your boss directly and show that her order is not right for the firm. Using the Guidelines for Ethical Decision Making and valid arguments, you may be able to persuade your boss to accept your perspective and avoid an otherwise unethical decision. Finding a win-win solution is possible only when there is room for compromise. The Ethical Guidelines and logical arguments are effective when your boss respects reason and wants to act ethically. However, when you face an intractable executive demanding you do something illegal, a different response is needed.

Work within the Firm to Stop the Unethical Act Suppose you receive an order from an executive you know or suspect to be corrupt. For example, a CFO is motivated to increase the price of the firm's stock in order to make her stock options more valuable. She orders you to book in the current year revenue that in fact will not be received for at least two years, if ever. Booking that revenue would be fraudulent, unethical, and illegal. You are convinced the CFO knows of the illegality and will find someone else to book the

revenue if you refuse. You probably will lose your job if you do not cooperate. What do you do?

This is when your mentor, peer support group, and corporate ethics officer can help you. Your mentor may have access to the CEO or audit committee, who if honest, should back you and fire the CFO. Your peer support group might have similar access. The corporate ethics officer, especially if she is a lawyer in the firm's legal department, can also provide her backing and that of the legal department.

There is one large caveat, however. While the situation just described should and probably will result in your support system rallying to your support, in other situations that are ethically ambiguous, you, your mentor, and your support group may find that fighting a battle against a top corporate executive ineffectively expends your and your colleagues' political capital. In other words, you need to pick your battles carefully lest you and your colleagues at the firm be labeled whiners and troublemakers who unnecessarily seek intervention from higher level corporate executives. This is why we have listed this alternative near the end of our discussion. In most situations, it is better to rely on your colleagues as advisors and to execute win-win solutions in cooperation with your boss.

But if neither compromise nor other intrafirm tactics protect you from unethical requests, you are left with a final tactic.

Prepare to Lose Your Job
This is the last tactic, because by quitting or losing your job you are deprived of your ability to help the firm make ethical decisions. Only as an employee can you craft win-win solutions or work within the firm to do the right thing.

But if a firm's executives and its internal governance are so corrupted that neither compromise nor reason can steer the firm away from an unethical and illegal course, you must be willing to walk away from your job or be fired for standing up for your values. Do not want your job and the status it brings so much that you are willing to compromise more important values. It is tough losing a job when one has obligations to family, banks, and other creditors as well as aspirations for a better life. But if you prepare yourself financially from day one, putting away money for an ethical rainy day, you will protect more important values.

Leading Ethically

Some day, perhaps today, you will be in charge of other people in your business organization. You may be managing a four-person team, you may be a vice president of marketing in charge of a department, or you may eventually be a CEO directing an entire company. You give the people under your charge tasks to complete, supervise their work, help them complete the tasks, and provide motivation and feedback to ensure that the current job will be done well and that future work will be done better. So how do you also ensure that all those people under your charge act ethically? This is the daily challenge of ethical business leaders, who must not only act ethically themselves, but also promote ethical behavior of their workers.

Be Ethical
No one can lead ethically who does not attempt and mostly succeed in behaving ethically in her business and personal life. Few underlings respect an unethical leader, and many will be tempted to rationalize their own unethical conduct when they see their leaders acting unethically. They fall prey to the bandwagon fallacy, arguing for example that since the CFO is doing something wrong, so may they. For the same reason, ethical behavior by good managers encourages ethical behavior by underlings, who often view their bosses as role

models and guides for advancing in the corporation. If they see an ethical boss moving up in the business, they will believe that the system is fair and that they, too, by acting ethically, can advance at the firm.

Communicate the Firm's Core Ethical Values
For CEOs, creating, communicating, and emphasizing the firm's core values are essential to creating an ethical environment that rubs off on all employees. For other managers, recommunicating and reemphasizing the firm's value are also important.

All public companies today have ethics codes, as do many smaller companies. Yet the CEO who leads ethically must continually emphasize in written messages and speeches the importance and necessity that everyone comply with the code. Other top level managers, such as the vice president of finance, should ensure that their staffs understand the ethics code's application to their corporate tasks and make ethical reviews part of the staffs' annual evaluations. A lower level manager who supervises a small staff for a single project should also do her part to encourage compliance with the ethics code by pointing out how the code relates to the project assignment and including ethics in the project team's progress reports.

Connect Ethical Behavior with the Firm's and Workers' Best Interests
It is one thing to educate your staff about ethical behavior and another to obtain compliance. One good way to increase compliance with the firm's core ethical values is to convince the staff that their best interests—and the firm's—are met by acting ethically. Management should help employees understand that the firm's profitability and the employee's advancement in the firm are optimized by each employee taking responsibility for acting ethically. Staff must understand that adverse publicity caused by unethical conduct harms a firm's ability to promote itself and its products and services. The ethical manager also clearly establishes ethical behavior as a prerequisite for salary increases and promotions, or at least that unethical behavior is a disqualifier.

Reinforce Ethical Behavior
When a manager knows a staff member has acted ethically in a situation in which employees in less ethical firms would be tempted to act unethically, the manager should congratulate and find other ways to reinforce the staff member's behavior. For example, if a staff member reports that a supplier has attempted to bribe him in order to do business with the firm, the ethical manager will praise the staff member and may include a letter commending him in his employment file.

In addition, management should set up a mechanism for its employees to report instances of unethical behavior by the staff. While some employees will view whistle blowing as an act of disloyalty, management should recharacterize whistle blowing as necessary to the protection of the firm's decision-making processes and reputation. Undetected ethical decisions often lead to poor decisions and harm corporate profits. While management does not want witch hunts, good managers must garner evidence of alleged unethical behavior so they may investigate and stop conduct that is harmful to the firm.

A necessary corollary is not reinforcing unethical behavior, including behavior that may lead to an unethical act or foster an environment that appears tolerant of ethical missteps. As with childrearing, and so too with manag-ing a staff, it is usually not acceptable to ignore bad behavior. The ethical leader must reprimand staff for unethical actions and must not tolerate statements that suggest the firm should engage in unethical conduct. For example, if during discussions about how to increase revenue for a product line, one staff member suggests obtaining competitors' agreements to fix prices, a manager running the meeting should make clear that the firm will not engage in that or any other conduct that is illegal. To let the price-fixing comment pass without comment may send the message that the manager and the firm condone illegal or unethical acts.

Collectively, these reinforcing mechanisms should create a culture in which ethical practices define the firm and its employees rather than being imposed on them.

Problems and Problem Cases

1. You are a middle manager with responsibility over a staff of 16 workers. One of your workers is six months pregnant. Over the last month, she has missed work an average of two days a week and seems to be frequently distracted at work. You are concerned about her welfare and about her work performance, but are unsure what to do. What do the Guidelines for Ethical Decision Making suggest you do first?

2. You are an outside director of Hook, Inc., a manufacturer of surgical instruments. Hook has 19,000 employees worldwide, including 6,000 mostly manufacturing workers in China, 5,000 mostly manufacturing workers in Mexico, and 3,500 manufacturing and 1,500 executive employees in Springfield, Illinois, where it maintains its corporate headquarters. The CEO has proposed to Hook's board of directors that Hook close its manufacturing facility in Springfield and replace it with a larger facility in Honduras. Using the Guidelines for Ethical Decision Making, what do you want to know before you decide whether you will support the decision of the CEO?

3. You are a director of SeaGold Canning Company. SeaGold's business is canning tuna and salmon for sale to consumers. Its annual revenue is $575,000,000, 75 percent from tuna sales. SeaGold buys tuna from independent fishermen whose fishing methods do not always permit them to determine whether they are catching tuna or dolphins. The result is that many dolphins are killed. The Society to Protect All Sea Mammals (SPASM) has discovered that fishermen selling to SeaGold have been killing dolphins and has asked SeaGold to demand that the fishermen not kill dolphins and to refuse to buy tuna from fishermen who kill dolphins. If SeaGold does not comply with SPASM's request, SPASM will call a press conference to urge consumers to stop buying SeaGold tuna and salmon.

For fishermen to change their fishing methods would result in SeaGold paying an additional $20,000,000 each year for tuna. If SeaGold passes the cost on to consumers, the price of tuna will increase to $2.05 per can from the present $1.95 per can. Since SeaGold tuna now sells for the same price as other tuna brands, SeaGold expects its sales to fall by 10 percent if it increases the price of its tuna. What would a rights theorist do? What would you do as a SeaGold director?

4. You own a consulting firm with 32 employees and annual billings of $29,000,000. One of your clients, whom you bill an average of $1,200,000 annually, has asked you to hire her grandson. You know that the grandson has been recently graduated from a top-20 business school. He is 31 years old, has a solid academic record, and possesses the personal and professional skills to be successful as a consultant. You also know, however, that he is a recovering cocaine addict, having struggled with the addiction for five years prior to his attending business school.

Your firm has a strict no-drugs policy, which you usually interpret to exclude those who previously abused drugs. Using justice theory, justify a decision to exempt the grandson from your firm's no-drugs policy. Could you make the same decision as a profit maximizer?

5. Marigold Dairy Corporation sells milk products, including powdered milk formula for infants. Marigold hopes to increase sales of its powdered milk formula in Liberia and other African nations where mothers are often malnourished due to drought and civil war. Marigold's marketing department has created a marketing plan to convince mothers and expectant mothers not to breastfeed their babies and instead to use Marigold formula. Doctors generally favor breastfeeding as beneficial to mothers (it helps the uterus return to normal size), to babies (it is nutritious and strengthens the bonds between the infant and the mother), and to families (it is inexpensive). Marigold's marketing plan stresses the good nutrition of its formula and the convenience to parents of using it, including not having to breastfeed.

You are the Senior Vice President of Marketing for Marigold. Do you approve this marketing plan? What would a rights theorist do? What would a utilitarian do? What would a profit maximizer do?

6. During World War II, the insecticide DDT was used successfully to halt a typhus epidemic spread by lice and to control mosquitoes and flies. After World War II, it was used extensively to control agricultural and household pests. Today, DDT may not be used legally in the United States and most other countries. Although DDT has a rather low immediate toxicity to humans and other vertebrates, it becomes concentrated in fatty tissues of the body. In addition, it degrades slowly, remaining toxic in the soil for years after its application. But there has never been any credible evidence that this residue has caused any harm. Even so, DDT has been blamed for the near extinction of bald eagles, whose population has increased greatly since DDT was banned, although evidence tends to point to oil, lead, mercury, stress from noise, and other factors as the likely causes.

In 2007, over 3,600 people in the United States were infected by and 124 people killed after contracting West Nile virus, which is carried to humans by mosquitoes. CDC director Julie Gerberding called West Nile virus an "emerging, infectious disease epidemic" that could be spread all the way to the Pacific Coast by birds and mosquitoes. Pesticides such as malathion, resmethrin, and sumithrin can be effective in killing mosquitoes but are significantly limited because they do not stay in the environment after spraying. In Mozambique, indoor spraying of DDT has caused malaria rates to drop 88 percent among children.

As an executive for Eartho Chemical Company, you have been asked by Eartho's CEO to study whether Eartho should resume the manufacture of DDT. What would a utilitarian decide? What would a profit maximizer do?

7. You are assigned by your employer, Jay-Mart Corporation, an international discount retailer, to supervise the construction of ten new retail superstores in Shanghai, China. All construction is being done by a Chinese-owned contractor in compliance with Jay-Mart's construction standards. After an earthquake in China kills over 70,000 people, China's legislature passes a statute requiring new buildings to have a greater ability to withstand a large earthquake. The Chinese contractor has approached you and suggested that the new Chinese construction standards are unnecessarily high, that Jay-Mart's construction standards are sufficient to protect against any earthquake likely to occur, and that the cost of complying with the new Chinese construction standards will increase construction costs 20 percent.

What do you do if you believe that ethical behavior requires you to maximize Jay-Mart's profits?

8. You are the CFO of Ridgeway Bank, which makes loans to consumers and businesses totaling $870 million annually. Ridgeway Bank receives promissory notes from its borrowers, which notes the bank typically sells in bulk to investment banks, hedge funds, and other institutional investors within days after making the loans to its borrowers. By doing so, Ridgeway Bank is able to turn over its assets many times and optimize its profits. Finding buyers for the notes, however, can be challenging and depends in large part on the quality of the promissory notes, especially the collateral backing the notes and the borrowers' abilities to pay the notes. You are considering expanding Ridgeway's loan business by making loans to riskier borrowers. Before doing so, you want commitments from institutional investors that they will be willing to buy the risky notes. Because other banks made a large number of bad loans in 2005 and 2006 on which borrowers defaulted, Ridgeway has

found it especially difficult to sell higher-risk notes, as institutional investors have greatly restricted their buying of risky notes. You know that if you can convince one institutional investor to purchase some of the risky notes, you can tell other institutional investors that they are missing an opportunity that one of their competitors is taking. Do you think it is ethical to use that tactic to convince institutional investors to buy the notes? What fallacy are you expecting the institutional investors to make when they agree to do what their competitors do?

9. In 2007, NFL Commissioner Roger Goodell determined that the New England Patriots and its head coach, Bill Belichick, had violated NFL rules by videotaping opposing teams' sideline signals during games. Goodell docked the Patriots a 2008 first-round draft pick, and he fined Belichick $500,000 and the team $250,000. In 2008, Goodell interviewed the Patriots' employee who had done the videotaping and concluded that the employee's information was consistent with the behavior for which the Patriots and Belichick had been disciplined in 2007. Therefore, Goodell termed the matter over and said it was not necessary to discipline further the Patriots or Belichick. Immediately thereafter, Arlen Specter, a U.S. senator from Pennsylvania, called the NFL investigation "neither objective nor adequate." Specter stated, "If the commissioner doesn't move for an independent investigation, . . . depending on the public reaction, I may ask the Senate Judiciary Committee to hold hearings on the NFL antitrust exemption." Specter further stated that Goodell has made "ridiculous" assertions that wouldn't fly "in kindergarten." The senator said Goodell was caught in an "apparent conflict of interest" because the NFL doesn't want the public to lose confidence in the league's integrity. Terming the videotaping of opposing teams' signals a form of cheating equivalent to steroid use, Specter called for an independent investigation similar to the 2007 Mitchell Report on performance enhancing drugs in baseball.

Can you identify the fallacies in Senator Specter's arguments?

10. For the last five years, you have been a corporate accountant for Farrless Company, a public company that has seen explosive growth though acquisitions of smaller competitors in its industry, retail pharmacy.

Farrless's CFO tells you that Farrless's per store revenue for the fiscal quarter, as yet not publicly disclosed, has dropped by 15 percent. As a result, Farrless has had insufficient cash flow to pay some suppliers, many of whom are refusing to ship additional inventory to Farrless until it pays its outstanding debt to them. The CFO tells you he believes that the revenue drop, while temporary, will continue for the rest of the fiscal year. Next year, he says, per store revenue will be 20 percent more than last year's historic high. Consequently, to avoid a temporary drop in the market price of Farrless's stock, which will reduce the value of the CFO's stock options and make it more expensive for Farrless to raise capital, the CFO wants you to create false accounting entries that will smooth Farrless's revenues.

Can you identify the common characteristics of poor decision making that the CFO is exhibiting? Draft a plan that will help you resist the CFO's request for you to make false accounting entries. What should you have done during the five years you have been working for Farrless to help you now resist the CFO's request?

11. You have been a marketing manager at Pramat-Glomer Company for 10 years. Last week, you were promoted to the position of Assistant Vice President of Marketing. Overseeing a staff of 50 marketing professionals, you report directly to the Executive Vice President of Marketing. Draft a plan that will help ensure that every member of your staff acts ethically in compliance with Pramat-Glover's code of ethics.

Online Research

Josephson Institute Center for Business Ethics

Josephson Institute Center for Business Ethics is a leading source of materials for businesses and executives who want to act ethically.

- Locate the Josephson Web site.
- Find "The Seven-Step Path to Better Decisions" and the "Six Pillars of Character."
- List the "Obstacles to Ethical Decision Making: Rationalizations."

Part Two

Crimes and Torts

chapter 5
Crimes

chapter 6
Intentional Torts

chapter 7
Negligence and Strict Liability

chapter 8
Intellectual Property and
Unfair Competition

CRIMES

Nicolai Caymen worked as a desk clerk at a hotel in Ketchikan, Alaska. After a woman called a Ketchikan business supply store and complained that the store had charged her credit card for a laptop computer she did not purchase, the store discovered that Caymen had used a credit card in placing a telephone order for the laptop and that when he picked up the computer, the store clerk had not asked for identification. Store personnel then contacted the Ketchikan police department to report the incident and to pass along information, acquired from other stores, indicating that Caymen may have attempted similar credit card trickery elsewhere.

In order to look for the laptop and other evidence of credit card fraud, the police obtained a search warrant for the house where Caymen rented a room. Caymen, who was present while his room was searched, denied the allegation that he had used someone else's credit card to acquire the laptop. Instead, he stated that he had bought it with his own credit card. During the search, the police found the laptop and a tower computer. It was later determined that Caymen had rented the tower computer from a store but had never made any of the required payments. In Caymen's wallet, which the police examined in connection with the search of his room, the officers found receipts containing the names and credit card information of guests who had stayed at the hotel where Caymen was employed.

The police seized the laptop, took it to the police station, and contacted the store where Caymen had acquired it to ask whether officers could examine the laptop's hard drive before they returned the computer to the store. The store's owner consented to this request. In examining the laptop's hard drive for evidence of credit card fraud, the police found evidence indicating Caymen's probable commission of federal crimes unrelated to credit card fraud. The police then temporarily suspended their search of the hard drive and obtained another search warrant, because they had probable cause to believe that Caymen had committed federal offenses. Under that search warrant, officers checked the hard drives and storage media from the laptop and tower computers and found further evidence pertaining to the federal crimes.

Caymen was prosecuted in state court for credit card fraud and was indicted in federal court for the separate federal offenses. In the federal proceeding, he asked the court to suppress (i.e., rule inadmissible) the evidence obtained by the police in their examinations of the hard drives of the laptop and tower computers. Caymen based his suppression request on this multipart theory: that the police had no valid warrant for their initial look at the laptop's hard drive; that in the absence of a valid warrant, his consent (rather than the store owner's) was needed to justify a search of the laptop's hard drive; that the evidence obtained during the initial examination of the laptop's hard drive was the result of an unconstitutional search and was therefore inadmissible; and that the evidence obtained in the later examinations of the hard drives of the laptop and tower computers amounted to inadmissible "fruit of the poisonous tree."

As you read Chapter 5, consider these questions:

- On what constitutional provision was Caymen basing his challenge to the validity of the searches conducted by the police?
- Must law enforcement officers always have a warrant before they conduct a search, or are warrantless searches sometimes permissible? If warrantless searches are sometimes permissible, when?

- What is the usual remedy when law enforcement officers conduct an unconstitutional search?
- Did Caymen succeed with his challenge to the validity of the searches conducted by the police? Why or why not?
- What if a guilty person goes free as a result of a court's ruling that he was subjected to an unconstitutional search by law enforcement officers? From an ethical perspective, how would *utilitarians* view that outcome? What about *rights theorists?*

THE LIST FEATURES FAMILIAR corporate names: Enron, Arthur Andersen, WorldCom, Adelphia, ImClone, Global Crossing, and Tyco. Individuals such as Bernard Ebbers, John and Timothy Rigas, and Dennis Kozlowski also make the list. These names sometimes dominated the business headlines during recent years, but not for reasons any corporation or executive would find desirable. Instead, they acquired the notoriety associated with widely publicized financial scandals, related civil litigation, and criminal prosecutions that were actually pursued by the government, seriously contemplated by prosecutors, or argued for by the public and political figures of varying stripes.

For instance, former WorldCom CEO Ebbers was sentenced to 25 years in prison for his role in an $11 billion accounting and securities fraud. The Rigases were sentenced to substantial prison terms because of their involvement in bank and securities fraud while serving as high level executives at Adelphia. Kozlowski, convicted of financial wrongdoing in connection with his former position as Tyco's CEO, also faced incarceration.

In an earlier edition of this text, the first paragraph of Chapter 5 noted the importance of studying criminal law as part of a business manager's education but conceded that "[w]hen one lists legal topics relevant to business, criminal law comes to mind less readily than contracts, torts, agency, corporations, and various other subjects dealt with in this text." That statement, of course, was written approximately 10 years ago. Given the media, public, and governmental attention devoted to recent corporate scandals, it might be argued that criminal law now comes to mind *more* readily than certain other subjects on the list of legal topics relevant to business. At the very least, recent events involving high-profile firms and executives have demonstrated that business managers create considerable risk for themselves and their firms if they ignore the criminal law or lack a working understanding of it.

Role of the Criminal Law

This century has witnessed society's increasing tendency to use the criminal law as a major device for controlling corporate behavior. Many regulatory statutes establish criminal and civil penalties for statutory violations. The criminal penalties often apply to individual employees as well as to their employers.

Advocates of using the criminal law in this way typically argue that doing so achieves a deterrence level superior to that produced by damage awards and other civil remedies. Corporations may be inclined to treat damage awards as simply a business cost and to violate regulatory provisions when doing so makes economic sense. Criminal prosecutions, however, threaten corporations with the reputation-harming effect of a criminal conviction. In some cases, the criminal law allows society to penalize employees who would not be directly affected by a civil judgment against their employer. Moreover, by alerting private parties to a violation that could also give rise to a civil lawsuit for damages, criminal prosecutions may increase the likelihood that a corporation will bear the full costs of its actions.

Our examination of the criminal law's role in today's business environment begins with consideration of the nature and essential components of the criminal law. The chapter then explores various problems encountered in applying the criminal law to the corporate setting.

Nature of Crimes
Crimes are *public wrongs*—acts prohibited by the state or federal government. Criminal prosecutions are initiated by a prosecutor (an elected or appointed government employee) in the name of the state or the United States, whichever is appropriate. Persons convicted of crimes bear the stigma of a criminal conviction and face the punitive force of the criminal sanction.

Our legal system also contemplates noncriminal consequences for violations of legal duties. The next two chapters deal with *torts,* private wrongs for which the wrongdoer must pay money damages to compensate the harmed victim. In some tort cases, the court may also assess punitive damages in order to punish the wrongdoer. Only the criminal sanction, however, combines the threat to life or liberty with the stigma of conviction.

Crimes are typically classified as felonies or misdemeanors. A **felony** is a serious crime such as murder, sexual assault, arson, drug-dealing, or a theft or fraud offense of sufficient magnitude. Most felonies involve significant moral culpability on the offender's part. Felonies are punishable by lengthy confinement of the convicted offender to a penitentiary, as well as by a fine. A person convicted of a felony may experience other adverse consequences, such as disenfranchisement (loss of voting rights) and disqualification from the practice of certain professions (e.g., law or medicine). A **misdemeanor** is a lesser offense such as disorderly conduct or battery resulting in minor physical harm to the victim. Misdemeanor offenses usually involve less—sometimes much less—moral culpability than felony offenses. As such, misdemeanors are punishable by lesser fines and/or limited confinement in jail. Depending on their seriousness and potential for harm to the public, traffic violations are classified either as misdemeanors or as less serious **infractions.** Really only quasi-criminal, infractions usually are punishable by fines but not by confinement in jail.

Purpose of the Criminal Sanction

Disagreements about when the criminal sanction should be employed sometimes stem from a dispute over its purpose. Persons accepting the *utilitarian* view believe that prevention of socially undesirable behavior is the only proper purpose of criminal penalties. This prevention goal includes three major components: deterrence, rehabilitation, and incapacitation.

Deterrence theorists maintain that the threat or imposition of punishment deters the commission of crimes in two ways. The first, *special deterrence,* occurs when punishment of an offender deters him from committing further crimes. The second, *general deterrence,* results when punishment of a wrongdoer deters other persons from committing similar offenses. Factors influencing the probable effectiveness of deterrence include the respective likelihoods that the crime will be detected, that detection will be followed by prosecution, and that prosecution will result in a conviction. The severity of the probable punishment also serves as a key factor.

A fundamental problem attending deterrence theories is that we cannot be certain whether deterrence works, because we cannot determine reliably what the crime rate would be in the absence of punishment. Similarly, high levels of crime and recidivism (repeat offenses by previously punished offenders) may indicate only that sufficiently severe and certain criminal sanctions have not been employed, not that criminal sanctions in general cannot effectively deter. Deterrence theory's other major problem is its assumption that potential offenders are rational beings who consciously weigh the threat of punishment against the benefits derived from an offense. The threat of punishment, however, may not deter the commission of criminal offenses produced by irrational or unconscious drives.

Rehabilitation of convicted offenders—changing their attitudes or values so that they are not inclined to commit future offenses—serves as another way to prevent undesirable behavior. Critics of rehabilitation commonly point to high rates of recidivism as evidence of the general failure of rehabilitation efforts to date. Even if rehabilitation efforts fail, however, *incapacitation* of convicted offenders contributes to the goal of prevention. While incarcerated, offenders have much less ability to commit other crimes.

Prevention is not the only asserted goal of the criminal sanction. Some persons see *retribution*—the infliction of deserved suffering on violators of society's most fundamental rules—as the central focus of criminal punishment. Under this theory, punishment satisfies community and individual desires for revenge and reinforces important social values.

As a general rule, state laws on criminal punishments seek to further the deterrence, rehabilitation, and incapacitation purposes just discussed. State statutes usually set forth ranges of sentences (e.g., minimum and maximum amounts of fines and imprisonment) for each crime established by law. The court sets the convicted offender's sentence within the appropriate range unless the court places the defendant on probation.

Probation is effectively a conditional sentence that suspends the usual imprisonment and/or fine if the offender "toes the line" and meets other judicially imposed conditions for the period specified by the court. It is sometimes granted to first-time offenders and other convicted defendants deemed suitable candidates by the court. In deciding whether to order probation or an appropriate sentence within the statutory range, the court normally places considerable reliance on information contained in a presentence investigation conducted by the state probation office.

Figure 1 explains how federal law approaches the proper determination of a convicted offender's punishment.

Figure 1   The Federal Sentencing Guidelines and the Booker Decision

The federal approach to sentencing closely resembled the typical state approach discussed in the text until the Federal Sentencing Guidelines took effect in the mid-1980s. The significantly different sentencing model contemplated by the Sentencing Guidelines was largely upended, however, by the U.S. Supreme Court's decision in *United States v. Booker,* 543 U.S. 220 (2005), and decisions that followed it. To understand *Booker,* one must first know how the Sentencing Guidelines operated for the approximately 20 years preceding the Supreme Court's decision.

In the Sentencing Reform Act of 1984, Congress created the U.S. Sentencing Commission and authorized it to develop the Sentencing Guidelines. Congress took this action to reduce judicial discretion in sentencing and to minimize disparities among sentences imposed on defendants who committed the same offenses. Although pre–Sentencing Guidelines statutes setting forth sentencing ranges for particular crimes generally remained on the books, the Sentencing Guidelines developed by the Sentencing Commission assumed a legally controlling status under provisions of the Sentencing Reform Act. The Guidelines contain a table with more than 40 levels of seriousness of offense. Where an offender's crime and corresponding sentence range are listed on the table depends on the offender's prior criminal history and on various factors associated with the offense. The Sentencing Reform Act established that federal courts were bound by the table and usually were required to sentence convicted defendants in accordance with the range set in the table for the crime at issue. However, if the court found the existence of certain additional circumstances to be present (such as a leadership role in a crime committed by more than one person or similar facts seeming to enhance the defendant's level of culpability), the Guidelines required the court to sentence the defendant to a harsher penalty than would otherwise have been the maximum under the Guidelines.

Many federal judges voiced displeasure with the Guidelines because their mandatory nature deprived judges of the sentencing discretion they believed they needed in order to do justice in individual cases. In another key effect, the Guidelines led to the imposition of more severe sentences than had previously been imposed. Although the prospect of probation for certain offenses was not eliminated, the Guidelines led to an increased use of incarceration of individuals convicted of serious crimes. (A special subset of rules known as the Corporate Sentencing Guidelines, discussed later in the chapter, pertains to the sentencing of organizations convicted of federal crimes.)

In recent years, questions began to arise concerning the constitutionality of the Sentencing Guidelines. The questions focused on the cases in which the Guidelines effectively required—if the requisite additional circumstances were present—a sentence going beyond what would otherwise have been the maximum called for by the Guidelines. These cases were troublesome because nearly always the additional circumstances triggering the enhanced sentence were identified by the trial judge on the basis of evidence submitted to him or her at a posttrial sentencing hearing. The jury, on the other hand, would have heard and seen only the evidence produced at the trial—evidence that went toward guilt and presumably the standard range of punishment, but not toward an enhanced punishment harsher than the usual maximum. All of this was problematic, critics contended, in view of criminal defendants' Sixth Amendment right to a jury trial.

United States v. Booker provided the Supreme Court an opportunity to address the concerns raised by critics of the Guidelines. A jury had convicted Booker of the offense of possessing, with intent to distribute, at least 50 grams of crack cocaine. The evidence the jury heard at trial was to the effect that Booker possessed approximately 90 grams of crack. The Sentencing Guidelines called for a sentence of 20 to 22 years in prison for possessing at least 50 grams. However, evidence presented to the judge at the posttrial sentencing hearing indicated that Booker possessed some 650 grams. Possession of a much larger amount of crack than the amount for which he was convicted was a special circumstance that, under the Guidelines, necessitated a harsher sentence. Upon finding by a preponderance of the evidence that Booker possessed 650 grams (rather than the smaller quantity about which the jury heard evidence), the judge was required by the Guidelines to sentence Booker to at least 30 years in prison—even though the evidence presented to the jury would have justified a lesser sentence of 20 to 22 years. The judge imposed a 30-year sentence on Booker, who contended on appeal that the enhanced sentence required by the Guidelines violated his Sixth Amendment jury trial right.

In the 2005 *Booker* decision, the Supreme Court held that in view of the Sixth Amendment, any facts calling for the imposition of a sentence harsher than the usual maximum must be facts found by a jury rather than merely a judge (unless a jury has been validly waived by the defendant). The Federal Sentencing Guidelines and the statute contemplating their creation were thus unconstitutional insofar as they mandated a sentence going beyond the usual maximum if a judge's factual findings supporting such a sentence were made on the basis of evidence that the jury had not heard and seen. To remedy the constitutional defect, the Court determined it was necessary to excise certain Sentencing Reform Act sections that made the Sentencing Guidelines mandatory. The elimination of those statutory sections caused the Sentencing Guidelines to become *advisory* to judges as they make sentencing decisions. Judges must still consider what the Guidelines call for in regard to sentencing, but they are not required to impose the particular sentences specified in the Guidelines. The Court also stated in *Booker* that when a judge's sentencing decision is challenged on appeal, the governing standard will be one of reasonableness.

After *Booker*, lower courts were faced with determining what the "reasonableness" standard of review meant, as well as how far trial courts' discretion regarding the Guidelines really extended. In *Rita v. United States*, 127 S. Ct. 2456 (2007), the Supreme Court held that it was permissible for courts of appeal to adopt and apply a presumption of reasonableness if the sentence imposed by the trial court fell within the range set by the Guidelines. *Gall v. United States*, 128 S. Ct. 586 (2007), made clear, however, that the converse was not true. The Court held there that courts of appeal cannot apply a presumption of unreasonableness to a sentence that departed from the range set by the Guidelines. Instead, according

to *Gall*, consideration of the Guidelines is only "the starting point and the initial benchmark" for the trial judge as he or she makes an "individualized assessment" based on the facts and circumstances. Appellate courts are to give "due deference" to the trial judge's sentencing determinations, regardless of whether the sentence fell within or outside the Guidelines' range. In *Kimbrough v. United States*, 128 S. Ct. 558 (2007), a companion case to *Gall*, the Court underscored this standard of review and expressed disapproval of appellate court micromanagement of trial judges' sentencing decisions. The Court also suggested in *Kimbrough* that considerable deference to the trial judge's sentencing determinations remains appropriate even if it appears that the sentence departed from the Guidelines because of the judge's philosophical disagreement with the Guidelines.

Booker and its progeny—especially *Gall* and *Kimbrough*—have restored to trial judges most of the sentencing latitude they had prior to the Guidelines. This latitude is subject to two constraints: first, the sentence must be consistent with relevant *statutes* (as opposed to the now-advisory Guidelines); and second, the sentence must be based upon facts found by the jury (or by the judge, if a jury was waived).

Essentials of Crime
To convict a defendant of a crime, the government ordinarily must (1) demonstrate that his alleged acts violated a criminal statute; (2) prove beyond a reasonable doubt that he committed those acts; and (3) prove that he had the capacity to form a criminal intent. Crimes are *statutory* offenses. A given behavior is not a crime unless Congress or a state legislature has criminalized it.[1] As illustrated by the *Santos* case, which follows, courts normally interpret criminal statutes narrowly.

---

[1]Infractions of a minor criminal or quasi-criminal nature (such as traffic offenses) are often established by city or county ordinances but will not be considered here. For discussion of ordinances as a type of law, see Chapter 1.

United States v. Santos	2008 U.S. LEXIS 4699 (U.S. Sup. Ct. 2008)

From the 1970s until 1994, Efrain Santos operated an illegal lottery in Indiana. He employed a number of helpers to run the lottery. At bars and restaurants, Santos's runners gathered bets from gamblers, kept a portion of the bets as their commissions, and delivered the rest to Santos's collectors. Collectors, one of whom was Benedicto Diaz, then delivered the money to Santos, who used some of it to pay the salaries of collectors (including Diaz) and to pay the lottery winners.

These payments to runners, collectors, and winners formed the basis of a 10-count indictment filed against Santos and Diaz in the United States District Court for the Northern District of Indiana. A jury found Santos guilty of one count of conspiracy to run an illegal gambling business, one count of running an illegal gambling business, one count of conspiracy to launder money, and two counts of money laundering. Diaz pleaded guilty to conspiracy to launder money. The relevant provision of the money-laundering statute, 18 U.S.C. § 1956(a)(1), reads as follows:

Whoever, knowing that the property involved in a financial transaction represents the proceeds of some form of unlawful activity, conducts or attempts to conduct such a financial transaction which in fact involves the proceeds of specified unlawful activity . . . with the intent to promote the carrying on of specified unlawful activity . . . shall be sentenced to a fine of not more than $ 500,000 or twice the value of the property involved in the transaction, whichever is greater, or imprisonment for not more than twenty years, or both.

After the district court sentenced Santos and Diaz to prison, the U.S. Court of Appeals for the Seventh Circuit affirmed the convictions and sentences in a 2000 decision. Santos and Diaz later attacked the validity of the convictions and sentences by seeking a writ of habeas corpus. In the habeas corpus proceeding, the district court rejected all of their claims except for one, a challenge to their money-laundering convictions. The district court took note of a 2002 decision in which the Seventh Circuit held that the money-laundering statute's prohibition of transactions involving criminal "proceeds" applies only to transactions involving criminal profits, not criminal receipts. Applying that holding to the cases of Santos and Diaz, the district court found no evidence that the transactions on which the money-laundering convictions were based (Santos's payments to runners, winners, and collectors and Diaz's receipt of payment for his collection services) involved profits, as opposed to receipts, of the illegal lottery. Accordingly, the district court vacated the money-laundering convictions. The Seventh Circuit affirmed. The U.S. Supreme Court granted the government's petition for a writ of certiorari.

Scalia, Justice

We consider whether the term "proceeds" in the federal money-laundering statute means "receipts" or "profits."

The statute prohibits a number of activities involving criminal "proceeds." Most relevant to this case is 18 U.S.C. § 1956(a)(1), which criminalizes transactions to promote criminal activity. [The statute is quoted above.] This provision uses the term "proceeds" in describing two elements of the offense: the government must prove that a charged transaction "in fact involve[d] the proceeds of specified unlawful activity" (the proceeds element), and it also must prove that a defendant knew "that the property involved in" the charged transaction "represent[ed] the proceeds of some form of unlawful activity" (the knowledge element).

The money-laundering statute does not define "proceeds." When a term is undefined, we give it its ordinary meaning. "Proceeds" can mean either "receipts" or "profits." Both meanings . . . have long been accepted in ordinary usage[, as dictionaries indicate]. "Proceeds," moreover, has not acquired a common meaning in the provisions of the Federal Criminal Code. Most leave the term undefined. Recognizing the word's inherent ambiguity, Congress has defined "proceeds" in various criminal provisions, but sometimes has defined it to mean "receipts" and sometimes "profits."

Since context gives meaning, we cannot say the money-laundering statute is truly ambiguous until we consider "proceeds" not in isolation but as it is used in the money-laundering statute. The word appears repeatedly throughout the statute, but all of those appearances leave the ambiguity intact. Section 1956(a)(1) itself, for instance, makes sense under either [the "receipts" definition or the "profits" definition]. The same is true of all the other provisions of this legislation in which the term "proceeds" is used.

Under either of the word's ordinary definitions, all provisions of the federal money-laundering statute are coherent; no provisions are redundant; and the statute is not rendered utterly absurd. From the face of the statute, there is no more reason to think that "proceeds" means "receipts" than there is to think that "proceeds" means "profits." Under a long line of our decisions, the tie must go to the defendant. The rule of lenity requires ambiguous criminal laws to be interpreted in favor of the defendants subjected to them. [Case citations omitted.] This venerable rule not only vindicates the fundamental principle that no citizen should be held accountable for a violation of a statute whose commands are uncertain, or subjected to punishment that is not clearly prescribed. It also places the weight of inertia upon the party that can best induce Congress to speak more clearly and keeps courts from making criminal law in Congress's stead. Because the "profits" definition of "proceeds" is always more defendant-friendly than the "receipts" definition, the rule of lenity dictates that it should be adopted.

[The government asserts that] if we do not read "proceeds" to mean "receipts," we will disserve the purpose of the federal money-laundering statute, which is, the government says, to penalize criminals who conceal or promote their illegal activities. [According to] the government's [brief,] "[t]he gross receipts of a crime accurately reflect the scale of the criminal activity, because the illegal activity generated all of the funds."

When interpreting a criminal statute, we do not play the part of a mind-reader. In our seminal rule-of-lenity decision, Chief Justice Marshall rejected the impulse to speculate regarding a dubious congressional intent. "[P]robability is not a guide which a court, in construing a penal statute, can safely take." [Case citation omitted.] And Justice Frankfurter, writing for the Court in another case, said the following: "When Congress leaves to the Judiciary the task of imputing to Congress an undeclared will, the ambiguity should be resolved in favor of lenity." [Case citation omitted.]

The statutory purpose advanced by the government to construe "proceeds" is a textbook example of begging the question. To be sure, if "proceeds" meant "receipts," one could say that the statute was aimed at the dangers of concealment and promotion. But whether "proceeds" means "receipts" is the very issue in the case. If "proceeds" means "profits," one could say that the statute is aimed at the distinctive danger that arises from leaving in criminal hands the yield of a crime. A rational Congress could surely have decided that the risk of leveraging one criminal activity into the next poses a greater threat to society than the mere payment of crime-related expenses and justifies the money-laundering statute's harsh penalties.

If we accepted the government's invitation to speculate about congressional purpose, we would also have to confront and explain the strange consequence of the "receipts" interpretation, which [Santos and Diaz] have described [in their brief] as a "merger problem." If "proceeds" meant "receipts," nearly every violation of the illegal-lottery statute would also be a violation of the money-laundering statute, because paying a winning bettor is a transaction involving receipts that the defendant intends to promote the carrying on of the lottery. Since few lotteries, if any, will not pay their winners, the statute criminalizing illegal lotteries would "merge" with the money-laundering statute. Congress evidently decided that lottery operators ordinarily deserve up to five years of imprisonment, [as specified in the lottery statute], but as a result of merger they would face an additional 20 years [under the money-laundering statute]. Prosecutors, of course, would acquire the discretion to charge the lesser lottery offense, the greater money-laundering offense, or both—which would predictably be used to induce a plea bargain to the lesser charge.

The merger problem is not limited to lottery operators. For a host of predicate crimes, merger would depend on the manner and timing of payment for the expenses associated with the commission of the crime. Few crimes are entirely free of cost, and costs are not always paid in advance. Anyone who pays for the costs of a crime with its proceeds—for example, the felon who uses the stolen money to pay for the rented getaway car—would violate the money-laundering statute. And any wealth-acquiring crime with multiple participants would become money-laundering when the initial recipient of the wealth gives his confederates their shares.

The government suggests no explanation for why Congress would have wanted a transaction that is a normal part of a crime it had duly considered and appropriately punished elsewhere in the Criminal Code to radically increase the sentence for that crime. Interpreting "proceeds" to mean "profits" eliminates the merger problem. Transactions that normally occur during the course of running a lottery are not identifiable uses of profits and thus do not violate the money-laundering statute. More generally, a criminal who enters into a transaction paying the expenses of his illegal activity cannot possibly violate the money-laundering statute, because by definition profits consist of what remains after expenses are paid. Defraying an activity's costs with its receipts simply will not be covered.

The government also argues for the "receipts" interpretation because—quite frankly—it is easier to prosecute. Proving the proceeds and knowledge elements of the federal money-laundering offense under the "profits" interpretation will unquestionably require proof that is more difficult to obtain. Essentially, the government asks us to resolve the statutory ambiguity in light of Congress's presumptive intent to facilitate money-laundering prosecutions. That position turns the rule of lenity upside-down. We interpret ambiguous criminal statutes in favor of defendants, not prosecutors.

The money-laundering charges brought against Santos were based on his payments to the lottery winners and his employees, and the money-laundering charge brought against Diaz was based on his receipt of payments as an employee. Neither type of transaction can fairly be characterized as involving the lottery's profits. We accordingly affirm the [lower court decisions to vacate the money-laundering convictions.]

Seventh Circuit Court of Appeals decision affirmed; money-laundering convictions vacated.

Stevens, Justice, concurring in the judgment

When Congress fails to define potentially ambiguous statutory terms, it effectively delegates to federal judges the task of filling gaps in a statute. Congress has included definitions of the term "proceeds" in some criminal statutes, but it has not done so in the money-laundering statute at issue in this case. That statute is somewhat unique because it applies to the proceeds of a varied and lengthy list of specified unlawful activities, [including, among others,] controlled substance violations, murder, bribery, smuggling, various forms of fraud, concealment of assets, various environmental offenses, and health care offenses).

Although it did not do so, it seems clear that Congress could have provided that the term "proceeds" shall have one meaning when referring to some specified unlawful activities and a different meaning when referring to others. We have previously recognized that the same word can have different meanings in the same statute. If Congress could have expressly defined the term "proceeds" differently when applied to different specified unlawful activities, it seems to me that judges filling the gap in a statute with such a variety of applications may also do so, as long as they are conscientiously endeavoring to carry out the intent of Congress.

The consequences of applying a "gross receipts" definition of "proceeds" to the gambling operation conducted by respondents are so perverse that I cannot believe they were contemplated by Congress. The revenue generated by a gambling business that is used to pay the essential expenses of operating that business is not "proceeds" within the meaning of the money-laundering statute. As the plurality notes, there is "no explanation for why Congress would have wanted a transaction that is a normal part of a crime it had duly considered and appropriately punished elsewhere in the Criminal Code, to radically increase the sentence for that crime." This conclusion dovetails with what common sense and the rule of lenity would require.

Faced with both a lack of legislative history speaking to the definition of "proceeds" when operating a gambling business is the "specified unlawful activity" and my conviction that Congress could not have intended the perverse result that would obtain in this case under [the "gross receipts" interpretation], the rule of lenity may weigh in the determination. And in that respect the plurality's opinion is surely persuasive. Accordingly, I concur in the judgment.

Constitutional Limitations on Power to Criminalize Behavior

The U.S. Constitution prohibits *ex post facto* criminal laws. This means that a defendant's act must have been prohibited by statute at the time she committed it and that the penalty imposed must be the one provided for at the time of her offense.

The Constitution places other limits on legislative power to criminalize behavior. If behavior is constitutionally protected, it cannot be deemed criminal. For example, the **right of privacy** held implicit in the Constitution caused the Supreme Court, in *Griswold v. Connecticut* (1965), to strike down state statutes that prohibited the use of contraceptive devices and the counseling or assisting of others in the use of such devices. This decision provided the constitutional basis for the Court's historic *Roe v. Wade* (1973) decision, which limited the states' power to criminalize abortions.

By prohibiting laws that unreasonably restrict **freedom of speech,** the First Amendment plays a major role in limiting governmental power to enact and enforce criminal laws. As explained in Chapter 3, the First Amendment protects a broad range of noncommercial speech, including expression of a political, literary, or artistic nature as well as speech that deals with economic, scientific, or ethical issues or with other matters of public interest or concern. The First Amendment protection for noncommercial speech is so substantial that it is called "full" protection.

Commercial speech, on the other hand, receives a less substantial First Amendment shield known as "intermediate" protection. Does a speaker or writer with a profit motive (e.g., the author who hopes to make money on her book) therefore receive only intermediate First Amendment protection? No, as a general rule, because the mere presence of a profit motive does not keep expression from being fully protected noncommercial speech. Moreover, the commercial speech designation is usually reserved for what the Supreme Court has termed "speech that does no more than propose a commercial transaction." The best example of commercial speech is an advertisement for a product, service, or business.

Despite receiving less-than-full protection, commercial speech is far from a First Amendment outcast. Recent Supreme Court decisions, as noted in Chapter 3, have effectively raised commercial speech's intermediate protection to a level near that of full protection. Therefore, regardless of whether it is full or intermediate in strength, the First Amendment protection extended to expression means that governmental attempts to hold persons criminally liable for the content of their written or spoken statements are often unconstitutional.

Some speech falls outside the First Amendment umbrella, however. In a long line of cases, the Supreme Court has established that *obscene* expression receives no First Amendment protection. Purveyors of obscene books, movies, and other similar works may therefore be criminally convicted of violating an obscenity statute even though it is the works' content (i.e., the speech) that furnishes the basis for the conviction. Expression is obscene only if the government proves each element of the controlling obscenity test, which the Supreme Court established in *Miller v. California* (1973):

> (a) [That] the average person, applying contemporary community standards, would find that the work, taken as a whole, appeals to the prurient interest; (b) [that] the work depicts or describes, in a patently offensive way, [explicit] sexual conduct specifically defined by the applicable state law; and (c) [that] the work, taken as a whole, lacks serious literary, artistic, political, or scientific value.

If any of the three elements is not proven, the work is not obscene; instead, it is entitled to First Amendment protection.

The *Miller* test's final element is the one most likely to derail the government's obscenity case against a defendant. Books, movies, and other materials that contain explicit sexual content are not obscene if they have serious literary, artistic, political, or scientific value—and they generally do. In view of the *Miller* test's final element, moreover, certain publications that might fairly be regarded as "pornographic" are likely to escape being classified as obscene.

Although nonobscene expression carries First Amendment protection, Supreme Court decisions have allowed the government limited latitude to regulate *indecent* speech in order to protect minors from being exposed to such material. Indecent expression contains considerable sexual content but stops short of being obscene, often because of the presence of serious literary, artistic, political, or scientific value (for adults, at least). Assume that a state statute requires magazines available for sale at a store to be located behind a store counter rather than on an unattended display rack, if the magazines feature nudity and sexual content and the store is open to minors. This statute primarily restricts indecent expression because most magazines contemplated by the law are unlikely to be obscene. If the statute is challenged on First Amendment grounds and the court concludes that it is narrowly tailored to further the protection-of-minors purpose, it will survive First Amendment scrutiny. A law that restricts too much expression suitable for adults, however, will violate the First Amendment even if the government's aim was to safeguard minors.

Recent years have witnessed decisions in which the Supreme Court determined the First Amendment fate of statutes designed to protect minors against online exposure to material that is indecent though not obscene. (If the material were obscene, there would be no First Amendment obstacle to banning such material and imposing criminal consequences on those involved in the distribution of it.) In *Reno v. American Civil Liberties Union,* 521 U.S. 844 (1997), the Court struck down most of the Communications Decency Act of 1996 (CDA), which sought to ban Internet distribution of indecent material in a manner that would make the material accessible by minors. The Court reasoned that notwithstanding the statute's protection-of-minors purpose, the sweeping nature of the ban on indecent material extended too far into the realm of expression that adults were entitled to receive. In *Ashcroft v. American Civil Liberties Union,* 542 U.S. 665 (2004), the Court considered the constitutionality of the Child Online Protection Act (COPA), the next congressional attempt to restrict minors' exposure to indecent material in online contexts. According to the Court, the same problem that plagued the CDA—restricting too much expression that adults were entitled to communicate and receive—doomed the COPA to a determination of unconstitutionality.

As noted above, much of the material often referred to as pornography would not be considered obscene under the *Miller* test and thus would normally carry First Amendment protection. Safeguarding-of-minors concerns have proven critical, however, to the very different legal treatment extended to child pornography—

sexually explicit visual depictions of actual minors (as opposed to similar depictions of adults). Because of the obvious dangers and harms that child pornography poses for minors, child pornography has long been held to fall outside the First Amendment's protective umbrella. Therefore, the Supreme Court has held that there is no First Amendment bar to criminal prosecutions for purveying or possessing child pornography. In *Ashcroft v. Free Speech Coalition,* 535 U.S. 234 (2002), the Court decided a constitutional challenge to a statute in which Congress attempted to expand the treatment of child pornography by banning the possession and distribution of material meant to create the impression of minors engaging in sexually explicit conduct, even if the persons actually depicted were adults. The Court struck down this statute because it would reach beyond actual child pornography and would ban expression protected by the First Amendment.

After *Free Speech Coalition* was decided, Congress again took on the child pornography problem in a 2003 enactment, the Protect Act (Prosecutorial Remedies and Other Tools to End the Exploitation of Children Act). This statute criminalized the knowing promotion, distribution, or solicitation, by means of a computer or by any other means, of "material or purported material in a manner that reflects the belief, or that is intended to cause another to believe, that the material or purported material is or contains . . . a visual depiction of an actual minor engaging in sexually explicit conduct." Turning aside the argument that the statute was effectively the same as the law struck down in *Free Speech Coalition,* the Supreme Court held in *United States v. Williams,* 2008 U.S. LEXIS 4314 (2008), that the Protect Act did not violate the First Amendment. Justice Scalia's opinion for a seven-justice majority stressed that the Protect Act's focus on pandering or soliciting distinguished it from the earlier statute. The majority opinion also included considerable interpretive language meant to narrow the application of the statute and minimize potential First Amendment concerns. For a more complete discussion of the Court's reasoning in *Williams,* see the Cyberlaw in Action box in Chapter 3.

In addition to limiting the sorts of behavior that may be made criminal, the Constitution limits the manner in which behavior may be criminalized. The **Due Process** Clauses of the Fifth and Fourteenth Amendments (discussed in Chapter 3) require that criminal statutes define the prohibited behavior precisely enough to enable law enforcement officers and ordinary members of the public to understand which behavior violates the law. Statutes that fail to provide such fair notice may be challenged as unconstitutionally vague. The Fourteenth Amendment's

Equal Protection Clause (also discussed in Chapter 3) prohibits criminal statutes that discriminatorily treat certain persons of the same class or arbitrarily discriminate among different classes of persons. Legislatures usually are extended considerable latitude in making statutory classifications if the classifications have a rational basis. "Suspect" classifications, such as those based on race, are subjected to much closer judicial scrutiny, however.

Finally, the Constitution limits the type of punishment imposed on convicted offenders. The Eighth Amendment forbids **cruel and unusual punishments.** This prohibition furnishes, for example, the constitutional basis for judicial decisions establishing limits on imposition of the death penalty. Although various Supreme Court cases indicate that the Eighth Amendment may bar a sentence whose harshness is disproportionate to the seriousness of the defendant's offense, the Court has signaled that any Eighth Amendment concerns along these lines are unlikely to be triggered unless the sentence–crime disproportionality is exceedingly gross.

CYBERLAW IN ACTION

As noted in the text, criminal statutes that do not provide reasonable notice of prohibited behavior may be struck down as unconstitutionally vague. *United States v. Twombly,* 475 F. Supp. 2d 1019 (S.D. Cal. 2007), involved an unsuccessful attempt by criminal defendants to win a void-for-vagueness challenge.

The statute at issue in *Twombly,* 18 U.S.C. § 1037, prohibits a variety of misleading electronic mail-related actions in commercial settings. These include instances in which a person who, with knowledge of doing so, "materially falsifies header information in multiple commercial electronic mail messages and intentionally initiates the transmission of such messages," § 1037(a)(3), or "registers, using information that materially falsifies the identity of the actual registrant, for five or more electronic mail accounts or online user accounts or two or more domain names, and intentionally initiates the transmission of multiple commercial electronic mail messages from any combination of such accounts or domain names." § 1037 (a)(4). Violators of these prohibitions may be punished by fines or imprisonment, or both.

In *Twombly*, a criminal indictment charged that Michael Twombly and Joshua Eveloff violated §§ 1037(a)(3) and (a)(4). The government claimed that Twombly leased dedicated servers using an alias, including one server from Biznesshosting, Inc., and that shortly after it provided logon credentials to Twombly, Biznesshosting began receiving complaints regarding spam electronic mail messages originating from its network. These spam messages allegedly numbered approximately 1 million, followed several days later by another 1.5 million. The spam messages contained computer software advertising and directed recipients to the Web site of a company with a Canadian address. The government maintained that this Web site was falsely registered under the name of a nonexistent business, and that the messages' routing information and "From" lines had been falsified. As a result, the government contended, recipients, Internet service providers, and law enforcement agencies were prevented from identifying, locating, or responding to the senders. When Biznesshosting investigated the complaints, it traced the spam to the server leased by Twombly. A search conducted by the FBI allegedly uncovered roughly 20 dedicated servers leased by Twombly using false credentials. According to the government, Twombly leased the servers for an unnamed person—later determined to be defendant Eveloff—and received payment from that person for each set of logon credentials provided. Under the government's theory of the case, both Twombly and Eveloff caused the spam messages to be sent.

Twombly and Eveloff moved for dismissal of the indictment on the ground that §§ 1037(a)(3) and (a)(4) were unconstitutionally vague. Before examining the statutory language at issue, the court outlined basic principles governing void-for-vagueness challenges to criminal statutes. The court noted that in order to avoid being so vague as to violate the Constitution's Due Process Clause, a criminal statute must give persons of ordinary intelligence fair warning of the conduct being criminalized. Quoting the U.S. Supreme Court's decision in *Colten v. Kentucky*, 407 U.S. 104 (1972), the court emphasized that "'[t]he root of the vagueness doctrine is a rough idea of fairness'" and that "'[i]t is not a principle designed to convert into a constitutional dilemma the practical difficulties in drawing criminal statutes both general enough to take into account a variety of human conduct and sufficiently specific to provide fair warning that certain kinds of conduct are prohibited.'" In addition, the court observed that "the degree of vagueness that the Constitution tolerates depends in part on the nature of the enactment," that "[e]conomic regulation of businesses is subject to less strict requirements," and that a statute "threaten[ing] to inhibit the exercise of constitutionally protected rights may . . . require a stricter vagueness test."

Turning to the statutory language under which the defendants had been charged, the *Twombly* court observed that the meaning of §§ 1037(a)(3) and (a)(4) could be discerned more clearly by reviewing a later subsection, § 1037(d)(2). In § 1037(d)(2), Congress stated that

[f]or purposes of [§§ 1037(a)(3) and (a)(4),] header information or registration information is materially falsified if it is altered or concealed in a manner that would impair the ability of a recipient

of the message, an Internet access service processing the message on behalf of a recipient, a person alleging a violation of this section, or a law enforcement agency to identify, locate, or respond to a person who initiated the electronic mail message or to investigate the alleged violation.

Twombly and Eveloff contended that the meanings of "impair" and "materially," as explained in § 1037(d)(2), were no less vague than §§ 1037(a)(3) and (a)(4), the provisions § 1037(d)(2) purported to clarify. The defendants argued that a header does not necessarily identify the sender, and that a layperson has little or no ability to trace a sender's location based on the address. The court acknowledged that e-mail addresses do not necessarily identify the sender by name, but countered by stressing that even if an e-mail address does not necessarily identify the sender, "it does tell a recipient where to send replies to the sender, much in the same way a return address on an envelope [operates]." Thus, the court concluded that "[a] material falsification of header or registration information can violate [the statute] by hindering a recipient's ability to respond to the sender of an e-mail," as set forth in § 1037(d)(2).

Continuing its analysis, the court stated that even if identifying senders by header information may be difficult for many laypeople, the defendants erred in basing their argument "solely on the ability of an individual recipient to identify the sender of spam e-mails." The court stressed that §§ 1037(a)(3) and (a)(4), as augmented by § 1037(d)(2), "are expressly also designed to protect the ability of internet access services and government agencies to investigate spam." In "fail[ing] to show that falsified header or registration information would not impair the ability of either of these to investigate the source of spam or identify senders," the defendants fell short in their challenge to the statute. With the relevant statutory sections having survived the defendants' vagueness challenge, the court denied the defendants' motion to dismiss the indictment.

Proof beyond a Reasonable Doubt The serious matters at stake in a criminal case—the life and liberty of the accused—justify our legal system's placement of significant limits on the government's power to convict a person of a crime. A fundamental safeguard is the *presumption of innocence;* defendants in criminal cases are presumed innocent until proven guilty. The Due Process Clauses require the government to overcome this presumption by proving beyond a reasonable doubt every element of the offense charged against the defendant.[2] Requiring the government to meet this stern burden of proof minimizes the risk of erroneous criminal convictions.

Defendant's Criminal Intent and Capacity Most serious crimes require *mens rea,* or criminal intent, as an element. The level of fault required for a criminal violation depends on the wording of the relevant statute. Many criminal statutes require proof of intentional wrongdoing. Others impose liability for reckless conduct or, in rare instances, mere negligence. In the criminal context, recklessness generally means that the accused consciously disregarded a substantial risk that the harm prohibited by the statute would result from her actions. Negligence means that the accused failed to perceive a substantial risk of harm that a reasonable person would have perceived. As a general rule, negligent behavior is left to the civil justice system rather than being criminalized. In the *Arthur Andersen* case, which follows shortly, the Supreme Court issues a reminder regarding the importance of the element of criminal intent.

Criminal intent may be inferred from an accused's behavior, because a person is normally held to have intended the natural and probable consequences of her acts. The intent requirement furthers the criminal law's general goal of punishing conscious wrongdoers. Accordingly, proof that the defendant had the capacity to form the required intent is a traditional prerequisite of criminal responsibility. The criminal law recognizes three general types of incapacity: *intoxication, infancy,* and *insanity.*

Although it is not a complete defense to criminal liability, voluntary intoxication may sometimes diminish the degree of a defendant's responsibility. For example, many first-degree murder statutes require proof of *premeditation,* a conscious decision to kill. One who kills while highly intoxicated may be incapable of premeditation—meaning that he would not be guilty of first-degree murder. He may be convicted, however, of another homicide offense that does not require proof of premeditation.

The criminal law historically presumed that children younger than 14 years of age ("infants," for legal purposes) could not form a criminal intent. Today, most states treat juvenile offenders below a certain statutory age—usually 16 or 17—differently from adult offenders, with special juvenile court systems and separate detention facilities. Current juvenile law emphasizes

---

[2]The beyond-a-reasonable-doubt standard required of the government in criminal cases contemplates a stronger and more convincing showing than that required of plaintiffs in civil cases. As explained in Chapter 2, plaintiffs in civil cases need only prove the elements of their claims by a preponderance of the evidence.

rehabilitation rather than capacity issues. Repeat offenders or offenders charged with very serious offenses, however, may sometimes be treated as adults.

An accused's insanity at the time the charged act was committed may constitute a complete defense. This possible effect of insanity has generated public dissatisfaction. The controlling legal test for whether a defendant was insane varies among court systems. The details of the possible tests are beyond the scope of this text. Suffice it to say that as applied by courts, the tests make it a rare case in which the defendant succeeds with an insanity defense.

Arthur Andersen LLP v. United States   544 U.S. 696 (U.S. Sup. Ct. 2005)

In a 1990s move accompanied by aggressive accounting practices, Enron Corporation rapidly expanded beyond its original business of operating natural gas pipelines and became an energy conglomerate. The public accounting firm Arthur Andersen LLP (Andersen) audited Enron's publicly filed financial statements and provided internal audit and consulting services to the corporation. David Duncan headed Andersen's engagement team for Enron.

Enron's financial performance began to suffer in 2000 and worsened during 2001. On August 14, 2001, Enron CEO Jeffrey Skilling unexpectedly resigned. The corporation's former CEO, Kenneth Lay, then reassumed the CEO position. Within days after Skilling's resignation, Sherron Watkins, a senior accountant at Enron, warned Lay that Enron could "implode in a wave of accounting scandals." Watkins also mentioned the looming problems to Duncan and Michael Odom, an Andersen partner who had supervisory responsibility over Duncan. A key concern was Enron's use of "Raptors," which were special purpose entities engaging in "off-balance-sheet" activities. Andersen's engagement team had allowed Enron to "aggregate" the Raptors for accounting purposes so that they reflected a positive return. This was, in the words of an expert who testified in the case described below, a "black-and-white" violation of Generally Accepted Accounting Principles.

An August 28, 2001, Wall Street Journal *article suggested improprieties at Enron. That same day, the Securities and Exchange Commission (SEC) opened an informal investigation. By early September, Andersen had formed an Enron "crisis-response" team, which included Nancy Temple, an in-house attorney for Andersen. On October 8, Andersen retained outside counsel to represent it in any litigation that might arise from the Enron matter. The next day, Temple discussed Enron with other in-house attorneys. Her notes from that meeting stated that "some SEC investigation" is "highly probable."*

On October 10, Odom spoke at a meeting attended by 89 Andersen employees, including 10 from the Enron engagement team. Odom urged everyone to comply with Andersen's document retention policy. He added: "If [documents are] destroyed in the course of [the] normal policy and litigation is filed the next day, that's great. . . . We've followed our own policy, and whatever there was that might have been of interest to somebody is gone and irretrievable." Andersen's policy on documents called for a single central engagement file, which "should contain only that information which is relevant to supporting our work." The policy stated that "in cases of threatened litigation, . . . no related information will be destroyed." In addition, the policy provided that if Andersen was "advised of litigation or subpoenas regarding a particular engagement, the related information should not be destroyed. See Policy Statement No. 780—Notification of Litigation." Statement No. 780 set forth notification procedures for instances when "professional practice litigation against [Andersen] or any of its personnel has been commenced, has been threatened or is judged likely to occur, or when governmental or professional investigations that may involve [Andersen] or any of its personnel have been commenced or are judged likely."

On October 12, Temple entered the Enron matter into her computer, designating the "Type of Potential Claim" as "Professional Practice—Government/Regulatory Investigation." Temple also e-mailed Odom, suggesting that he "remind the engagement team" of the documents policy. In an October 16 announcement, Enron released its third quarter results and disclosed a $1.01 billion charge to earnings. The following day, the SEC notified Enron by letter that it had opened an investigation in August. The letter also contained the SEC's request for certain information and documents. On October 19, Enron forwarded a copy of the letter to Andersen.

The Enron crisis-response team held an October 20 conference call, during which Temple instructed everyone to "make sure to follow the [documents] policy." On October 23, Enron CEO Lay declined to answer questions during a call with analysts because of "potential lawsuits, as well as the SEC inquiry." After the call, Duncan met with other Andersen partners on the Enron engagement team and told them that they should ensure team members were complying with the documents policy. During a later meeting for all team members, Duncan distributed the policy and told everyone to comply. These meetings, and other smaller ones, were followed by substantial destruction of paper and electronic documents.

On October 26, an Andersen senior partner circulated, by e-mail, a New York Times *article discussing the SEC's response to Enron. His e-mail commented that "the problems are just beginning and we will be in the cross hairs. The marketplace is going to keep the pressure on this and is going to force the SEC to be tough." On October 30, the SEC opened a formal investigation and sent Enron a letter that requested accounting documents.*

Throughout this time period, the document destruction continued, despite reservations on the part of some Andersen managers. For example, on October 26, an Andersen partner saw Duncan shredding documents and told him that "this wouldn't be the best time in the world for you guys to be shredding a bunch of stuff." On October 31, a forensics investigator for Andersen met with Duncan. During the meeting, Duncan picked up a document with the words "smoking gun" written on it and began to destroy it, adding that "we don't need this." The forensics investigator cautioned Duncan on the need to maintain documents and later informed Temple that Duncan needed advice regarding the documents policy.

On November 8, Enron announced that it would issue a comprehensive restatement of its earnings and assets. Also on November 8, the SEC served Enron and Andersen with subpoenas for records. The next day, Duncan's secretary sent an e-mail that stated: "Per Dave—No more shredding. . . . We have been officially served for our documents." Enron filed for bankruptcy less than a month later. Andersen fired Duncan, who later pleaded guilty to a criminal charge of witness tampering.

In March 2002, Andersen was indicted in federal court in Texas on one count of violating 18 U.S.C. §§ 1512(b)(2)(A) and (B), which, under the version then in effect, made it a crime if one "knowingly uses intimidation or physical force, threatens, or corruptly persuades another person . . . with intent to . . . cause" that person to "withhold" documents from, or "alter" documents for use in, an "official proceeding." The indictment alleged that, between October 10 and November 9, 2001, Andersen "did knowingly, intentionally and corruptly persuade" its employees to destroy documents so that the documents would not be available for use in "official proceedings, namely regulatory and criminal proceedings and investigations." A jury trial followed, with the jury returning a verdict of guilty. The U.S. Court of Appeals for the Fifth Circuit affirmed, holding that the trial judge's instructions to the jury on controlling principles of law properly conveyed the meaning of "corruptly persuades" for purposes of the relevant federal statute. The U.S. Supreme Court granted Andersen's petition for certiorari.

Rehnquist, Chief Justice

As Enron Corporation's financial difficulties became public in 2001, petitioner Andersen [directed] its employees to destroy documents pursuant to its document retention policy. A jury found that this action made petitioner guilty of violating 18 U.S.C. §§ 1512(b)(2)(A) and (B). The Court of Appeals for the Fifth Circuit affirmed. We hold[, however,] that the jury instructions [given by the trial judge] failed to convey properly the elements of a "corrupt persuasion" conviction under § 1512(b).

Title 18 of the United States Code provides criminal sanctions for those who obstruct justice. Sections 1512(b)(2)(A) and (B), part of the witness tampering provisions, provide in relevant part:

Whoever knowingly uses intimidation or physical force, threatens, or corruptly persuades another person, or attempts to do so, or engages in misleading conduct toward another person, with intent to . . . cause or induce any person to . . . withhold testimony, or withhold a record, document, or other object, from an official proceeding [or] alter, destroy, mutilate, or conceal an object with intent to impair the object's integrity or availability for use in an official proceeding . . . shall be fined under this title or imprisoned not more than ten years, or both.

In this case, our attention is focused on what it means to "knowingly . . . corruptly persuade" another person "with intent to . . . cause" that person to "withhold" documents from, or "alter" documents for use in, an "official proceeding."

"We have traditionally exercised restraint in assessing the reach of a federal criminal statute, both out of deference to the prerogatives of Congress and out of concern that 'a fair warning should be given to the world in language that the common world will understand, of what the law intends to do if a certain line is passed.'" [Citations of quoted cases omitted.] Such restraint is particularly appropriate here, where the act underlying the conviction—"persuasion"—is by itself innocuous. Indeed, "persuading" a person "with intent to . . . cause" that person to "withhold" testimony or documents from a government proceeding or government official is not inherently malign. Consider, for instance, a mother who suggests to her son that he invoke his [constitutional] right against compelled self-incrimination, or a wife who persuades her husband not to disclose marital confidences.

Nor is it necessarily corrupt for an attorney to "persuade" a client "with intent to . . . cause" that client to "withhold" documents from the government. In *Upjohn Co. v. United States,* 449 U.S. 383 (1981), for example, we held that Upjohn was justified in withholding documents that were covered by the attorney-client privilege from the Internal Revenue Service (IRS). No one would suggest that an attorney who "persuaded" Upjohn to take that step acted wrongfully, even though he surely intended that his client keep those documents out of the IRS' hands.

Document retention policies, which are created in part to keep certain information from getting into the hands of others, including the government, are common in business. It is, of course, not wrongful for a manager to instruct his employees to comply with a valid document retention policy under ordinary circumstances.

Acknowledging this point, the parties have largely focused their attention on the word "corruptly" as the key to what may or may not lawfully be done in the situation presented here. Section 1512(b) punishes not just "corruptly persuading" another, but "*knowingly . . . corruptly persuading*" another. (Emphasis added.) The government suggests that "knowingly" does not modify "corruptly persuades," but that is not how the statute most naturally reads. It provides the *mens rea*—"knowingly"— and then a list of acts—"uses intimidation or physical force, threatens, or corruptly persuades." [In earlier decisions, we] have recognized with regard to similar statutory language that the *mens rea* at least applies to the acts that immediately follow, if not to *other* elements down the statutory chain. The government suggests [in its brief] that it is "questionable whether Congress would employ such an inelegant formulation as 'knowingly . . . corruptly persuades.'" Long experience has not taught us to share the government's doubts on this score, and we must simply interpret the statute as written.

The parties have not pointed us to another interpretation of "knowingly . . . corruptly" to guide us here. In any event, the natural meaning of these terms provides a clear answer. "Knowledge" and "knowingly" are normally associated with awareness, understanding, or consciousness. See *Black's Law Dictionary* 888 (8th ed. 2004) (hereinafter *Black's*) [and other dictionaries]. "Corrupt" and "corruptly" are normally associated with wrongful, immoral, depraved, or evil. See *Black's* 371 [and other dictionaries]. Joining these meanings together here makes sense both linguistically and in the statutory scheme. Only persons conscious of wrongdoing can be said to "knowingly . . . corruptly persuade."

The outer limits of this element need not be explored here because the jury instructions at issue simply failed to convey the requisite consciousness of wrongdoing. Indeed, it is striking how little culpability the instructions required. For example, the jury was told [in the trial judge's instructions] that "even if [petitioner] honestly and sincerely believed that its conduct was lawful, you may find [petitioner] guilty." The instructions also diluted the meaning of "corruptly" so that it covered innocent conduct.

The parties vigorously disputed how the jury would be instructed on "corruptly." The district court based its instruction on the definition of that term found in the Fifth Circuit Pattern Jury Instruction for [18 U.S.C.] § 1503. This pattern instruction defined "corruptly" as "knowingly and dishonestly, with the specific intent to subvert or undermine the integrity" of a proceeding. The government, however, insisted on excluding "dishonestly" and adding the term "impede" to the phrase "subvert or undermine." The district court agreed over [Andersen's] objections, and the jury was told to convict if it found petitioner intended to "subvert, undermine, or impede" governmental factfinding by suggesting to its employees that they enforce the document retention policy.

These changes were significant. No longer was any type of "dishonesty" necessary to a finding of guilt, and it was enough for [Andersen] to have simply "impeded" the government's factfinding ability. As the government conceded at oral argument, "impede" has broader connotations than "subvert" or even "undermine," and many of these connotations do not incorporate any "corruptness" at all. [A commonly used] dictionary defines "impede" as "to interfere with or get in the way of the progress of" or "hold up" or "detract from." By definition, anyone who innocently persuades another to withhold information from the government "gets in the way of the progress of" the government. With regard to such innocent conduct, the "corruptly" instructions did no limiting work whatsoever.

[In view of the flawed jury instructions, Andersen's conviction cannot stand.]

Court of Appeals decision upholding Andersen's conviction reversed; case remanded for further proceedings.

Criminal Procedure
Criminal Prosecutions: An Overview

Persons arrested for allegedly committing a crime are taken to the police station and booked. *Booking* is an administrative procedure for recording the suspect's arrest. In some states, temporary release on bail may be available at this stage. After booking, the police file an arrest report with the prosecutor, who decides whether to charge the suspect with an offense. If she decides to prosecute, the prosecutor prepares a complaint identifying the accused and detailing the charges. Most states require that arrested suspects be taken promptly before a magistrate or other judicial officer (such as a justice of the peace or judge whose court is of limited jurisdiction) for an *initial appearance*. During this appearance, the magistrate informs the accused of the charges and outlines the accused's constitutional rights. In misdemeanor cases in which the accused pleads guilty, the sentence may be (but need not be) imposed without a later hearing. If the accused pleads not guilty to a misdemeanor charge, the case is set for trial. In felony cases, as well as misdemeanor cases in which the accused pleads not guilty, the magistrate sets the amount of bail.

In many states, defendants in felony cases are protected against unjustified prosecutions by an additional procedural step, the *preliminary hearing*. The prosecutor must introduce enough evidence at this hearing to persuade a magistrate that there is *probable cause* to believe the accused committed a felony.[3] If persuaded that probable cause exists, the magistrate binds over the defendant for trial in the appropriate court.

After a bindover, the formal charge against the defendant is filed with the trial court. The formal charge consists of either an *information* filed by the prosecutor or an *indictment* returned by a grand jury. Roughly half of the states require that a grand jury approve the decision to prosecute a person for a felony. Grand juries are bodies of citizens selected in the same manner as the members of a trial (petit) jury; often, they are chosen through random drawings from a list of registered voters. Indictment of an accused prior to a preliminary hearing normally eliminates the need for a preliminary hearing because the indictment serves essentially the same function as a magistrate's probable cause determination.

The remainder of the states allow felony defendants to be charged by either indictment or information, at the prosecutor's discretion. An *information* is a formal charge signed by the prosecutor outlining the facts supporting the charges against the defendant. In states allowing felony prosecution by information, prosecutors elect the information method in the vast majority of felony cases. Misdemeanor cases are prosecuted by information in nearly all states.[4]

---

[3]The state need not satisfy the beyond a reasonable doubt standard of proof at the preliminary hearing stage. The prosecutor sufficiently establishes probable cause by causing the magistrate to believe it is more likely than not that the defendant committed the felony alleged.

[4]For federal crimes, a prosecutor in the relevant U.S. Attorney's office files an information to institute the case if the offense involved carries a penalty of not more than one year of imprisonment. Federal prosecutions for more serious crimes with potentially more severe penalties are commenced by means of a grand jury indictment.

Once an information or indictment has been filed with a trial court, an *arraignment* occurs. The defendant is brought before the court, informed of the charges, and asked to enter a plea. The defendant may plead guilty, not guilty, or nolo contendere. Although technically not an admission of guilt, nolo contendere pleas indicate that the defendant does not contest the charges. This decision by the defendant will lead to a finding of guilt. Unlike evidence of a guilty plea, however, evidence of a defendant's nolo plea is inadmissible in later civil cases against that defendant based on the same conduct amounting to the criminal violation. Individuals and corporate defendants therefore may find nolo pleas attractive when their chances of mounting a successful defense to the criminal prosecution are poor and the prospect of later civil suits is likely.

At or shortly after the arraignment, the defendant who pleads not guilty chooses the type of trial that will take place. Persons accused of serious crimes for which incarceration for more than six months is possible have a constitutional right to be tried by a jury of their peers. The accused, however, may waive this right and opt for a bench trial (i.e., before a judge only).

Role of Constitutional Safeguards

The preceding pages referred to various procedural devices designed to protect persons accused of crime. The Bill of Rights, the first 10 amendments to the U.S. Constitution, sets forth other rights of criminal defendants. These rights guard against unjustified or erroneous criminal convictions and serve as reminders of government's proper role in the administration of justice in a democratic society. Justice Oliver Wendell Holmes aptly addressed this latter point when he said, "I think it less evil that some criminals should escape than that the government should play an ignoble part."

Although the literal language of the Bill of Rights refers only to federal government actions, the U.S. Supreme Court has applied the most important Bill of Rights guarantees to state government actions by "selectively incorporating" those guarantees into the Fourteenth Amendment's due process protection. Once a particular safeguard has been found to be "implicit in the concept of ordered liberty" or "fundamental to the American scheme of justice," it has been applied equally in state and federal criminal trials. This has occurred with the constitutional protections examined earlier in this chapter as well as with the Fourth, Fifth, and Sixth Amendment guarantees discussed in the following pages.

The Fourth Amendment

The Fourth Amendment protects persons against arbitrary and unreasonable governmental violations of their privacy rights. It states:

> The right of the people to be secure in their persons, houses, papers, and effects, against unreasonable searches and seizures, shall not be violated, and no Warrants shall issue, but upon probable cause, supported by Oath or affirmation, and particularly describing the place to be searched, and the persons or things to be seized.

Reasonable Expectation of Privacy

The Fourth Amendment's language and judicial interpretations of it reflect the difficulties inherent in balancing citizens' legitimate expectations of privacy and government's legitimate interest in securing evidence of wrongdoing. Citizens are not protected against all searches and seizures—only against unreasonable ones. Because the Fourth Amendment safeguards reasonable privacy expectations, the Supreme Court has extended the amendment's protection to such places or items as private dwellings and immediately surrounding areas (often called the *curtilage*), telephone booths, sealed containers, and first-class mail. The Court has denied protection to places, items, or matters as to which it found no reasonable expectations of privacy, such as open fields, personal bank records, and voluntary conversations between criminal defendants and government informants. In *United States v. Hall,* which follows, the court considered whether a corporation and one of its executives possessed a reasonable expectation of privacy in the contents of garbage bags that had been placed in a dumpster on the corporation's property.

United States v. Hall   47 F.3d 1091 (11th Cir. 1995)

William T. Parks, a special agent of the U.S. Customs Service, was investigating allegations that Bet-Air, Inc. (a Miami-based seller of spare aviation parts and supplies) had supplied restricted military parts to Iran. Parks entered Bet-Air's property and removed, from a garbage dumpster, a bag of shredded documents. The dumpster was located near the Bet-Air offices in a parking area reserved for the firm's employees. To reach the dumpster, Parks had to travel 40 yards on a private paved road. No signs indicated that the road was private. In later judicial proceedings, Parks testified that at the time he traveled on the road, he did not know he was on Bet-Air's property.

When reconstructed, some of the previously shredded documents contained information seemingly relevant to the investigation. Parks used the shredded documents and the information they revealed as the basis for obtaining a warrant to search the Bet-Air premises. In executing the search warrant, Parks and other law enforcement officers seized numerous documents and Bet-Air records.

A federal grand jury later indicted Bet-Air's chairman, Terrence Hall, and other defendants on various counts related to the alleged supplying of restricted military parts to Iran. Contending that the Fourth Amendment had been violated, Hall filed a motion asking the court to suppress (i.e., exclude) all evidence derived from the warrantless search of the dumpster and all evidence seized during the search of the Bet-Air premises (the search pursuant to the warrant). The federal district court denied Hall's motion. Following a jury trial, Hall was convicted on all counts and sentenced to prison. Hall appealed to the 11th Circuit Court of Appeals.

Hatchett, Circuit Judge

In *California v. Greenwood* (1988), the Supreme Court held that a warrantless search and seizure of garbage left in a plastic bag on the curb in front of, but outside the curtilage of, a private house did not violate the Fourth Amendment. The Court held that such a search would only violate the Fourth Amendment if the persons discarding the garbage manifested a subjective expectation of privacy in their garbage that society accepts as objectively reasonable. The Court concluded that Greenwood had exposed his garbage to the public sufficiently to render his subjective expectation of privacy objectively unreasonable.

Hall points to the fact that Parks obtained documents that were shredded, then placed inside a green garbage bag, which was in turn placed inside a garbage dumpster. We believe that the manner in which Bet-Air disposed of its garbage serves only to demonstrate that Bet-Air manifested a subjective expectation of privacy in its discarded garbage. Whether Parks's actions were proscribed by the Fourth Amendment, however, turns on whether society is prepared to accept Bet-Air's subjective expectation of privacy as objectively reasonable.

It is well established that the Fourth Amendment protections apply [not only to residential property but also] to commercial premises. The Supreme Court's treatment of the expectation of privacy that the owner of commercial property enjoys in such property has differed significantly from the protection accorded an individual's home, [however]. Such distinctions are inevitable given the fundamental difference in the nature and uses of a residence as opposed to commercial property. These distinctions are drawn into sharp focus when, as in this case, the government intrudes into the area immediately surrounding the structure. In order for persons to preserve Fourth Amendment protection in the area immediately surrounding the residence, they must not conduct an activity or leave an object in the plain view of those outside the area. The occupant of a commercial building, in contrast, must take the additional precaution of affirmatively barring the public from the area. The Supreme Court has consistently held that the government is required to obtain a search warrant only when it wishes to search those areas of commercial property from which the public has been excluded.

Relying on the fact that the dumpster was within the "commercial curtilage" of Bet-Air's property and that it could only be accessed by traveling 40 yards on a private road, Hall asserts that the company's subjective expectation of privacy was objectively reasonable. Hall's heavy emphasis on Parks's trespass onto Bet-Air's private property is misplaced. The law of trespass forbids intrusions onto land that the Fourth Amendment would not proscribe. We note that although the road leading to Bet-Air's dumpster was private, the magistrate judge found that no "objective signs of restricted access such as signs, barricades, and the like" were present. Moreover, the magistrate judge also found that at the time Parks traveled the road, he believed it was a public road. [Bet-Air's] failure to exclude the public takes on increased significance when the asserted expectation of privacy is in discarded garbage. A commercial proprietor incurs a diminished expectation of privacy when garbage is placed in a dumpster which is located in a parking lot that the business shares with other businesses, and no steps are taken to limit the public's access to the dumpster. It is common knowledge that commercial dumpsters have long been a source of fruitful exploration for scavengers.

The Supreme Court used the concept of curtilage in *Hester v. United States* (1924) to distinguish between the area outside a person's house which the Fourth Amendment protects, and the open fields, which are afforded no Fourth Amendment protection. The Supreme Court has not squarely addressed the applicability of the common law concept of curtilage to commercial property. Given the Court's view of the relationship between the Fourth Amendment and commercial premises, however, we have little doubt that were the Court to embrace the so-called "business curtilage" concept, it would, at a minimum, require that the commercial proprietor take affirmative steps to exclude the public. In light of Bet-Air's failure to exclude the public from the area immediately surrounding its offices, we refuse to apply the so-called "business curtilage" concept in this case.

[W]e do not believe that Parks infringed upon any societal values the Fourth Amendment protects when he searched Bet-Air's garbage. Bet-Air did not take sufficient steps to restrict the public's access to its discarded garbage; therefore, its subjective expectation of privacy is not one that society is prepared to accept as objectively reasonable.

District court's denial of Hall's suppression motion affirmed.

Even when plainly protected areas or items are involved, not every governmental action is deemed sufficiently intrusive to constitute a search or seizure for Fourth Amendment purposes. Thus, for example, the Supreme Court held, in *United States v. Place* (1983), that exposing an airline traveler's luggage to a narcotics detection dog in a public place was not a search, considering the minimally intrusive nature of the intrusion and the narrow scope of information it revealed. Relying on *Place*, the Supreme Court concluded in *Illinois v. Caballes* (2005) that no search occurred when law enforcement officers used a drug-sniffing dog on the exterior of a car whose driver had been stopped for speeding. If a law enforcement officer stops an automobile, examines its interior, and sorts through items located there, a search has occurred. Because the driver of the stopped car has been seized for Fourth Amendment purposes, she has legal standing to challenge the validity of the search. What about a passenger in the stopped vehicle? In *Brendlin v. California*, 127 S. Ct. 2400 (2007), the Supreme Court held that the passenger has also been seized for Fourth Amendment purposes and therefore has standing to challenge the search on Fourth Amendment grounds. As will be seen shortly, however, the search—whether challenged by the driver or by the passenger—may not violate the Fourth Amendment if the law enforcement officer had sufficient justification to stop the vehicle.

Did a search occur when law enforcement officers, operating from a public street, aimed a thermal imaging device at a private home? The Supreme Court addressed that question in the *Kyllo* case, which follows.

Kyllo v. United States   533 U.S. 27 (U.S. Sup Ct. 2001)

Suspicious that marijuana was being grown in Danny Lee Kyllo's home, federal agents used a thermal imaging device to scan his triplex to determine whether the amount of heat emanating from it was consistent with the amount emanated from high-intensity lamps typically used for indoor marijuana growth. The scan showed that Kyllo's roof and a side wall were relatively hot compared to the rest of his home and substantially warmer than the neighboring units. Based in part on the thermal imaging results, a federal magistrate judge issued a warrant to search Kyllo's home, where the agents found marijuana growing. After Kyllo was indicted on a federal drug charge, he unsuccessfully moved to suppress the evidence seized from his home and then entered a conditional guilty plea. The Ninth Circuit Court of Appeals ultimately affirmed, upholding the warrant and holding that the evidence was admissible. Kyllo appealed, and the U.S. Supreme Court granted certiorari.

Scalia, Justice

The Fourth Amendment provides that "the right of the people to be secure in their persons, houses, papers, and effects, against unreasonable searches and seizures, shall not be violated." "At the very core" of the Fourth Amendment "stands the right of a man to retreat into his own home and there be free from unreasonable governmental intrusion." *Silverman v. United States,* 507 U.S. 990 (1961). With few exceptions, the question whether a warrantless search of a home is reasonable and hence constitutional must be answered no.

On the other hand, the antecedent question of whether or not a Fourth Amendment "search" has occurred is not so simple under our precedent. The lawfulness of warrantless visual surveillance [has long been accepted]. As we observed in *California v. Ciraolo,* 476 U.S. 207, 213 (1986), "the Fourth Amendment protection of the home has never been extended to require law enforcement officers to shield their eyes when passing by a home on public thoroughfares."

One might think that examining the portion of a house that is in plain public view [amounts to] a "search," [though] not an "unreasonable" one under the Fourth Amendment. But in fact we have held that visual observation is no "search" at all—perhaps in order to preserve somewhat more intact our doctrine that warrantless searches are presumptively unconstitutional. In assessing when a search is not a search, we have applied somewhat in reverse the principle first enunciated in *Katz v. United States,* 389 U.S. 347 (1967). *Katz* involved eavesdropping by means of an electronic listening device placed on the outside of a telephone booth—a location not within the catalog ("persons, houses, papers, and effects") that the Fourth Amendment protects against unreasonable searches. We held that the Fourth Amendment nonetheless protected Katz from the warrantless eavesdropping because he justifiably relied upon the privacy of the telephone booth. As Justice Harlan's oft-quoted concurrence described it, a Fourth Amendment search occurs when the government violates a subjective expectation of privacy that society recognizes as reasonable. We have subsequently applied this principle to hold that a Fourth Amendment

search does *not* occur—even when the explicitly protected location of a *house* is concerned—unless "the individual manifested a subjective expectation of privacy in the object of the challenged search," and "society [is] willing to recognize that expectation as reasonable." *Ciraolo,* 476 U.S. at 211. We have applied this test in holding that it is not a search for the police to use a pen register at the phone company to determine what numbers were dialed in a private home, and we have applied the test on two different occasions in holding that aerial surveillance of private homes and surrounding areas does not constitute a search.

The present case involves officers on a public street engaged in more than naked-eye surveillance of a home. We have previously reserved judgment as to how much technological enhancement of ordinary perception from such a vantage point, if any, is too much. While we upheld enhanced aerial photography of an industrial complex in *Dow Chemical Co. v. United States,* 476 U.S. 227 (1986), we noted that we found it "important that this is *not* an area immediately adjacent to a private home, where privacy expectations are most heightened." *Id.* at 237, n. 4. It would be foolish to contend that the degree of privacy secured to citizens by the Fourth Amendment has been entirely unaffected by the advance of technology. The question we confront today is what limits there are upon this power of technology to shrink the realm of guaranteed privacy.

The *Katz* test—whether the individual has an expectation of privacy that society is prepared to recognize as reasonable—has often been criticized as circular, and hence subjective and unpredictable. While it may be difficult to refine *Katz* when the search of areas such as telephone booths, automobiles, or even the curtilage and uncovered portions of residences are at issue, in the case of the search of the interior of homes—the prototypical and hence most commonly litigated area of protected privacy—there is a ready criterion, with roots deep in the common law, of the [minimum] expectation of privacy that *exists,* and that is acknowledged to be *reasonable.* To withdraw protection of this minimum expectation would be to permit police technology to erode the privacy guaranteed by the Fourth Amendment. We think that obtaining by sense-enhancing technology any information regarding the interior of the home that could not otherwise have been obtained without physical "intrusion into a constitutionally protected area," *Silverman,* 507 U.S. at 512, constitutes a search—at least where (as here) the technology in question is not in general public use. This assures preservation of that degree of privacy against government that existed when the Fourth Amendment was adopted. On the basis of this criterion, the information obtained by the thermal imager in this case was the product of a search.

The Government maintains, however, that the thermal imaging must be upheld because it detected "only heat radiating from the external surface of the house." [However,] just as a thermal imager captures only heat emanating from a house, so also a powerful directional microphone picks up only sound emanating from a house and a satellite capable of scanning from many miles away would pick up only visible light emanating from a house. We rejected such a mechanical interpretation of the Fourth Amendment in *Katz,* where the eavesdropping device picked up only sound waves that reached the exterior of the phone booth. Reversing that approach would leave the homeowner at the mercy of advancing technology—including imaging technology that could discern all human activity in the home. While the technology used in the present case was relatively crude, the rule we adopt must take account of more sophisticated systems that are already in use or in development.

The Government also contends that the thermal imaging was constitutional because it did not "detect private activities occurring in private areas." It points out that in *Dow Chemical* we observed that the enhanced aerial photography did not reveal any "intimate details." *Dow Chemical,* however, involved enhanced aerial photography of an industrial complex, which does not share the Fourth Amendment sanctity of the home. The Fourth Amendment's protection of the home has never been tied to measurement of the quality or quantity of information obtained. In *Silverman,* for example, we made clear that any physical invasion of the structure of the home, "by even a fraction of an inch," was too much, and there is certainly no exception to the warrant requirement for the officer who barely cracks open the front door and sees nothing but the nonintimate rug on the vestibule floor. In the home, our cases show, *all* details are intimate details, because the entire area is held safe from prying government eyes.

Limiting the prohibition of thermal imaging to "intimate details" would not only be wrong in principle; it would be impractical in application, failing to provide "a workable accommodation between the needs of law enforcement and the interests protected by the Fourth Amendment," *Oliver v. United States,* 466 U.S. 170, 181 (1984). To begin with, there is no necessary connection between the sophistication of the surveillance equipment and the "intimacy" of the details that it observes—which means that one cannot say (and the police cannot be assured) that use of the relatively crude equipment at issue here will always be lawful. The Agema Thermovision 210 might disclose, for example, at what hour each night the lady of the house takes her daily sauna and bath—a detail that many would consider "intimate"; and a much more sophisticated system might detect nothing more intimate than the fact that someone left a closet light on. We could not, in other words, develop a rule approving only that through-the-wall surveillance which identifies objects no smaller than 36 by 36 inches, but would have to develop a jurisprudence specifying which home activities are "intimate" and which are not. And even when (if ever) that jurisprudence were fully developed, no police officer would be able to know *in advance* whether his through-the-wall surveillance picks up "intimate" details—and thus would be unable to know in advance whether it is constitutional.

We have said that the Fourth Amendment draws "a firm line at the entrance to the house." *Payton v. New York,* 445 U.S. 573, 590 (1980). That line, we think, must be not only firm but also bright—which requires clear specification of those methods of surveillance that require a warrant. While it is certainly possible to conclude from the videotape of the thermal imaging that occurred in this case that no "significant" compromise of the homeowner's privacy has occurred, we must take the long view, from the original meaning of the Fourth Amendment forward. "The Fourth Amendment is to be construed in the light of what was deemed an unreasonable search and seizure when it was adopted, and in a manner which will conserve public interests as well as the interests and rights of individual citizens." *Carroll v. United States,* 267 U.S. 132, 149 (1925).

Where, as here, the Government uses a device that is not in general public use, to explore details of the home that would previously have been unknowable without physical intrusion, the surveillance is a "search" and is presumptively unreasonable without a warrant. Since we hold the Thermovision imaging to have been an unlawful search, it will remain for the District Court to determine whether, without the evidence it provided, the search warrant issued in this case was supported by probable cause.

Judgment of Ninth Circuit Court of Appeals reversed and case remanded for further proceedings.

Warrant Requirement and Exceptions In its treatment of the Fourth Amendment's warrant clause, the Supreme Court has engaged in similar balancing of individual and governmental interests. The warrant requirement further protects privacy interests by mandating that a judge or magistrate authorize and define the scope of intrusive governmental action. As a general rule, the Court has held that searches carried out without a proper warrant are unreasonable.

Nevertheless, the Court has devised a lengthy list of exceptions to this general rule. Warrantless searches of the arrestee himself, of items of property in his possession, and of the area within his immediate control have long been upheld, assuming the arrest was supported by probable cause. In *Virginia v. Moore,* 128 S. Ct. 1598 (2008), the Court reiterated this exception to the warrant requirement and held that the exception applies even when the arrest violates a procedure set by otherwise applicable state law, as long as there was probable cause for the arrest. The Court has also upheld warrantless searches of premises police enter in hot pursuit of an armed suspect, and of motor vehicles (and containers located therein) when the vehicle has been stopped by law enforcement officers for sufficient reason. The mobile nature of motor vehicles furnishes the justification for this exception to the warrant requirement. Warrantless seizures of contraband items in the plain view of officers acting lawfully have likewise been upheld. The same is true of customs searches, stop-and-frisk searches for weapons, and administrative inspections of closely regulated businesses, despite the absence of a warrant in each of these instances.

Finally, consensual searches without warrants do not violate the Fourth Amendment. For instance, if a homeowner consents to a search of her home, the search is considered to be reasonable. If there are co-occupants of a residence and any co-occupant gives law enforcement officers consent to search the property, the consent of that co-occupant will normally insulate the search against a Fourth Amendment challenge brought by a nonpresent and nonconsenting occupant. However, as the Supreme Court recognized in *Georgia v. Randolph,* 547 U.S. 103 (2006), the consent to search given by one co-occupant of a residence does not protect the search against a Fourth Amendment challenge by another co-occupant who was present at the time of the search and objected to its occurrence.

Exclusionary Rule The exclusionary rule serves as the basic remedial device in cases of Fourth Amendment violations. Under this judicially crafted rule, evidence seized in illegal searches cannot be used in a subsequent trial against an accused whose constitutional rights were violated.[5] In addition, if information obtained in an illegal search leads to the later discovery of further evidence, that further evidence is considered "fruit of the poisonous tree" and is therefore excluded from use at trial under the rule established in *Wong Sun v. United States* (1963). Because the exclusionary rule may result in suppression of convincing evidence of crime, it has generated controversy. The rule's supporters regard it as necessary to deter police from violating citizens' constitutional rights. The rule's opponents assert that it has no deterrent effect on police who believed they were acting lawfully. A loudly voiced complaint in some quarters has been that "because of a policeman's error, a criminal goes free."

During roughly the past 25 years, the Court has responded to such criticism by rendering decisions that restrict the operation of the exclusionary rule. For example, the Court has held that illegally obtained evidence may be introduced at trial if the prosecution convinces the trial judge that the evidence would inevitably have been obtained anyway by lawful means. The Court has also created a "good faith" exception to the exclusionary rule. This exception allows the use of evidence seized by police officers who acted pursuant to a search warrant later held invalid if the officers reasonably believed that the warrant was valid. Although the Court has not extended the good faith exception to the warrantless search setting, it has expanded the exception's scope to include searches made in reliance on a statute that is later declared invalid.

Hudson v. Michigan, which follows, illustrates recent years' narrowing in the application of the exclusionary rule.

---

[5]The Supreme Court initially authorized application of the exclusionary rule in federal criminal cases only. In *Mapp v. Ohio* (1961), the Court made the exclusionary rule applicable to state criminal cases as well.

Hudson v. Michigan   547 U.S. 586 (U.S. Sup. Ct. 2006)

Police obtained a warrant authorizing a search for drugs and firearms at the home of Booker Hudson. When the officers arrived to execute the warrant, they announced their presence but waited only a short time—perhaps three to five seconds— before turning the knob of the unlocked front door and entering Hudson's home. Once inside the home, the officers discovered large quantities of drugs. They also found a loaded gun lodged between the cushion and armrest of the chair in which Hudson was sitting. Hudson was charged under Michigan law with unlawful drug and firearm possession.

Arguing that the officers' premature entry into his home violated the "knock-and-announce" rule and therefore his Fourth Amendment rights, Hudson moved for suppression of the drugs and the gun. (In other words, Hudson's motion sought a court order that the drugs and the gun discovered by the officers not be allowed as evidence at trial.) The Michigan trial court granted his motion, but the Michigan Court of Appeals reversed the suppression order. After the Michigan Supreme Court denied leave to appeal, Hudson was convicted of drug possession. He renewed his Fourth Amendment claim on appeal, but the Court of Appeals rejected it and affirmed the conviction. After the Michigan Supreme Court again declined review, the U.S. Supreme Court granted Hudson's petition for a writ of certiorari.

Scalia, Justice

We [must] decide whether violation of the "knock-and-announce" rule requires the suppression of all evidence found in the search.

The common-law principle that law enforcement officers must announce their presence and provide residents an opportunity to open the door is an ancient one. See *Wilson v. Arkansas,* 514 U.S. 927 (1995). Since 1917, . . . this traditional protection has been part of federal statutory law. In *Wilson,* we were asked whether the rule was also a command of the Fourth Amendment. Tracing its origins in our English legal heritage, we concluded that it was.

When the knock-and-announce rule does apply, it is not easy to determine precisely what officers must do. How many seconds' wait are too few? Our "reasonable wait time" standard, see *United States v. Banks,* 540 U.S. 31 (2003), is necessarily vague. *Banks* (a drug case, like this one) held that the proper measure was not how long it would take the resident to reach the door, but how long it would take to dispose of the suspected drugs—but that such a time (15 to 20 seconds in that case) would necessarily be extended when, for instance, the suspected contraband was not easily concealed. If our *ex post* evaluation is subject to such calculations, it is unsurprising that, *ex ante,* police officers about to encounter someone who may try to harm them will be uncertain how long to wait.

Happily, these issues do not confront us here. From the trial level onward, Michigan has conceded that the entry was a knock-and-announce violation. The issue here is remedy. *Wilson* specifically declined to decide whether the exclusionary rule is appropriate for violation of the knock-and-announce requirement. That question is squarely before us now.

In *Weeks v. United States,* 232 U.S. 383 (1914), we adopted the federal exclusionary rule for evidence that was unlawfully seized from a home without a warrant in violation of the Fourth Amendment. We began applying the same rule to the States, through the Fourteenth Amendment, in *Mapp v. Ohio,* 367 U.S. 643 (1961).

Suppression of evidence, however, has always been our last resort, not our first impulse. The exclusionary rule generates "substantial social costs," which sometimes include setting the guilty free and the dangerous at large. We have therefore been "cautio[us] against expanding" it. [Case citations omitted.] We have rejected indiscriminate application of the rule, and have held it to be applicable only "where its remedial objectives are thought most efficaciously served"—that is, "where its deterrence benefits outweigh its 'substantial social costs.'" [Case citations omitted.]

We did not always speak so guardedly. Expansive dicta in *Mapp,* for example, suggested wide scope for the exclusionary rule. ("[A]ll evidence obtained by searches and seizures in violation of the Constitution is, by that same authority, inadmissible in a state court.") But we have long since rejected that [sweeping] approach. [More recently, we have noted that] "whether the exclusionary sanction is appropriately imposed in a particular case, . . . is 'an issue separate from the question whether the Fourth Amendment rights of the party seeking to invoke the rule were violated by police conduct.'" [Case citations omitted.]

[C]ases excluding the fruits of unlawful warrantless searches say nothing about the appropriateness of exclusion to vindicate the interests protected by the knock-and-announce requirement. Until a valid warrant has issued, citizens are entitled to shield "their persons, houses, papers, and effects," U.S. Const., Amdt. 4, from the government's scrutiny. Exclusion of the evidence obtained by a warrantless search vindicates that entitlement. The interests protected by the knock-and-announce requirement are quite different—and do not include the shielding of potential evidence from the government's eyes.

One of those interests is the protection of human life and limb, because an unannounced entry may provoke violence in supposed self-defense by the surprised resident. Another interest is the protection of property. The knock-and-announce rule gives individuals "the opportunity to comply with the law and to avoid the destruction of property occasioned by a forcible entry." [Case citation omitted.] And thirdly, the knock-and-announce rule protects those elements of privacy and dignity that can be destroyed by a sudden entrance. [It] assures the opportunity to collect oneself before answering the door.

What the knock-and-announce rule has never protected, however, is one's interest in preventing the government from seeing or taking evidence described in a warrant. Since the interests that were violated in this case have nothing to do with the seizure of the evidence, the exclusionary rule is inapplicable.

[T]he exclusionary rule has never been applied except "where its deterrence benefits outweigh its 'substantial social costs.'" [Case citations omitted.] The costs here are considerable. In addition to the grave adverse consequence that exclusion of relevant incriminating evidence always entails (viz., the risk of releasing dangerous criminals into society), imposing that massive remedy for a knock-and-announce violation would generate a constant flood of alleged failures to observe the rule, and claims that any asserted justification for a no-knock entry had inadequate support. The cost of entering this lottery would be small, but the jackpot enormous: suppression of all evidence, amounting in many cases to a get-out-of-jail-free card. Courts would experience as never before the reality that "[t]he exclusionary rule frequently requires extensive litigation to determine whether particular evidence must be excluded." [Case citation omitted.] Unlike the warrant or *Miranda* requirements, compliance with which is readily determined . . . , what constituted a reasonable wait time in a particular case [or whether there were suitable justifications for a failure to knock and announce], is difficult for the trial court to determine and even more difficult for an appellate court to review.

Next to these substantial social costs we must consider the deterrence benefits, existence of which is a necessary condition for exclusion. [T]he value of deterrence depends upon the strength of the incentive to commit the forbidden act. Viewed from this perspective, deterrence of knock-and-announce violations is not worth a lot. Violation of the warrant requirement sometimes produces incriminating evidence that could not otherwise be obtained. But ignoring knock-and-announce can realistically be expected to achieve absolutely nothing except the prevention of destruction of evidence and the avoidance of life-threatening resistance by occupants of the premises— dangers which, if there is even "reasonable suspicion" of their existence, suspend the knock-and-announce requirement anyway. Massive deterrence is hardly required.

It seems to us not even true, as Hudson contends, that without suppression there will be no deterrence of knock-and-announce violations at all. Assuming [for the sake of argument] that civil suit [against the police officers] is not an effective deterrent, one can think of many forms of police misconduct that are similarly "undeterred." When, for example, a confessed suspect in the killing of a police officer, arrested (along with incriminating evidence) in a lawful warranted search, is subjected to physical abuse at the station house, would it seriously be suggested that the evidence must be excluded, since that is the only "effective deterrent"? And what, other than civil suit, is the effective deterrent of police violation of an already-confessed suspect's Sixth Amendment rights by denying him prompt access to counsel? Many would regard these violated rights as more significant than the right not to be intruded upon in one's nightclothes—and yet nothing but "ineffective" civil suit is available as a deterrent.

We cannot assume that exclusion in this context is necessary deterrence simply because we found that it was necessary deterrence in different contexts and long ago. That would be forcing the public today to pay for the sins and inadequacies of a legal regime that existed almost half a century ago.

[Hudson's attorney asserted at oral argument that] "it would be very hard to find a lawyer to take a [civil rights case against police officers who violated the knock-and-announce rule]" but 42 U.S.C. § 1988(b) answers this objection. Since some civil-rights violations would yield damages too small to justify the expense of litigation, Congress has authorized attorney's fees for civil-rights plaintiffs. This remedy was unavailable in the heydays of our exclusionary-rule jurisprudence, because it is tied to the availability of a cause of action. For years after *Mapp,* "very few lawyers would even consider representation of persons who had civil rights claims against the police," but now "much has changed. Citizens and lawyers are much more willing to seek relief in the courts for police misconduct." [Citation of authority omitted.] The number of public-interest law firms and lawyers who specialize in civil-rights grievances has greatly expanded.

Hudson points out that few published decisions to date announce huge awards for knock-and-announce violations. [However, it] is clear, at least, that the lower courts are allowing colorable knock-and-announce suits [for damages and potentially large attorney's fees] to go forward. As far as we know, civil liability is an effective deterrent here.

Another development over the past half-century that deters civil-rights violations is the increasing professionalism of police forces, including a new emphasis on internal police discipline. [W]e now have increasing evidence that police forces across the United States take the constitutional rights of citizens seriously. Numerous sources are now available to teach officers and their supervisors what is required of them under this Court's cases, how to respect constitutional guarantees in various situations, and how to craft an effective regime for internal discipline. Failure to teach and enforce constitutional requirements exposes municipalities to financial liability. Moreover, modern police forces are staffed with professionals; it is not credible to assert that internal discipline, which can limit successful careers, will not have a deterrent effect. There is also evidence that the increasing use of various forms of citizen review can enhance police accountability.

In sum, the social costs of applying the exclusionary rule to knock-and-announce violations are considerable; the incentive to such violations is minimal to begin with, and the extant deterrences against them are substantial—incomparably greater than the factors deterring warrantless entries when *Mapp* was decided. Resort to the massive remedy of suppressing evidence of guilt is unjustified.

Judgment of Michigan Court of Appeals affirmed.

Kennedy, Justice, concurring in part and concurring in the judgment

Two points should be underscored with respect to today's decision. First, the knock-and-announce requirement protects rights and expectations linked to ancient principles in our constitutional order. The Court's decision should not be interpreted as suggesting that violations of the requirement are trivial or beyond the law's concern. Second, the continued operation of the exclusionary rule, as settled and defined by our precedents, is not in doubt. Today's decision determines only that in the specific context of the knock-and-announce requirement, a violation is not sufficiently related to the later discovery of evidence to justify suppression.

Breyer, Justice, with whom Justices Stevens, Souter, and Ginsburg join, dissenting

In *Wilson v. Arkansas,* a unanimous Court held that the Fourth Amendment normally requires law enforcement officers to knock and announce their presence before entering a dwelling. Today's opinion holds that evidence seized from a home following a violation of this requirement need not be suppressed. As a result, the Court destroys the strongest legal incentive to comply with the Constitution's knock-and-announce requirement. And the Court does so without significant support in precedent. At least I can find no such support in the many Fourth Amendment cases the Court has decided in the near century since it first set forth the exclusionary principle.

Today's opinion is thus doubly troubling. It represents a significant departure from the Court's precedents. And it weakens, perhaps destroys, much of the practical value of the Constitution's knock-and-announce protection.

The Global Business Environment

If an arrestee who is a foreign national makes incriminating statements to law enforcement authorities without having been informed of his right under an international agreement to have his detention reported to his country's consulate, does the exclusionary rule apply? The U.S. Supreme Court confronted that question in *Sanchez-Llamas v. Oregon,* 548 U.S. 331 (2006).

The relevant international agreement in *Sanchez-Llamas* was the Vienna Convention on Consular Relations, which was drafted in 1963 with the purpose, as set forth in its preamble, of "contribut[ing] to the development of friendly relations among nations, irrespective of their differing constitutional and social systems." Approximately 170 countries have subscribed to the Vienna Convention. The United States became a party to it in 1969. Article 36 of the Vienna Convention provides that "if he so requests, the competent authorities of the receiving State shall, without delay, inform the consular post of the sending State if, within its consular district, a national of that State is arrested or committed to prison or to custody pending trial or is detained in any other manner." Thus, when a national of one country is detained by authorities in another, the authorities must notify the consular officers of the detainee's home country if the detainee so requests. Article 36 further provides that "[t]he said authorities shall inform the [detainee] without delay of his rights under this sub-paragraph." The Convention also states that the rights provided by Article 36 "shall be exercised in conformity with the laws and regulations of the receiving State, subject to the proviso, however, that the said laws and regulations must enable full effect to be given to the purposes for which the rights accorded under this Article are intended."

Moises Sanchez-Llamas, a Mexican national, was arrested in Oregon in 1999 for alleged involvement in an exchange of gunfire in which a police officer was wounded. Following the arrest, police officers gave Sanchez-Llamas the *Miranda* warnings in both English and Spanish. However, the officers did not inform Sanchez-Llamas that he could ask to have the Mexican Consulate notified of his detention. Article 36 of the Vienna Convention was thus violated. During the interrogation that followed the issuance of the *Miranda* warnings, Sanchez-Llamas made incriminating statements that led to attempted murder charges, as well as various other charges, against him. After he made the incriminating statements and the formal charges were filed, Sanchez-Llamas learned of his Article 36 rights. He then moved for suppression of his incriminating statements (i.e., for an order that those statements be excluded from evidence at the trial) because of the Article 36 violation. The Oregon trial court denied the suppression motion. Sanchez-Llamas was convicted and sentenced to prison. After the appellate courts in Oregon affirmed, the U.S. Supreme Court agreed to decide the case.

Assuming that—but without deciding whether—individuals have a right to invoke Article 36 in a judicial proceeding (as opposed to nations enforcing the Convention through political or other appropriate channels), the Supreme Court held in *Sanchez-Llamas* that the exclusionary rule was not a proper remedy for an Article 36 violation. The Court noted that the Vienna Convention itself said nothing about the exclusionary rule as a remedy. Instead, through the statement that Article 36 rights are to be "exercised in conformity with the laws and regulations of the receiving State," the Convention left the implementation of Article 36 to domestic law. The Court stated that it "would be startling" if the Convention were interpreted as requiring suppression of evidence as a remedy for an Article 36 violation, because "[t]he exclusionary rule as we know it is an entirely American legal creation." The Court stressed that there was "no reason to suppose that Sanchez-Llamas would be afforded the relief he seeks here in any of the other 169 countries party to the Vienna Convention." (Presumably, then, a U.S. national should not assume that the exclusionary rule will apply to his case if he is arrested in another Vienna Convention nation and makes incriminating statements to law enforcement officers without having been informed of his Article 36 rights.)

The Court emphasized that "[b]ecause the [exclusionary] rule's social costs are considerable, suppression is warranted only where the rule's "'remedial objectives are thought most efficaciously served.'" [Case citations omitted.] The Court emphasized that "[w]e have applied the exclusionary rule primarily to deter constitutional violations"—normally those involving unreasonable searches in violation of the Fourth Amendment or incriminating statements of accused persons whose Fifth Amendment rights had been violated because their confessions were not voluntary or because they had not been given the *Miranda* warnings. No such problems attended the incriminating statements made by Sanchez-Llamas. From the Court's perspective, "[t]he violation of the right to consular notification . . . is at best remotely connected to the gathering of evidence," and "there is likely to be little connection between an Article 36 violation and evidence or statements obtained by police." The Court reasoned that even if law enforcement officers fail to provide detained foreign nationals notice of their Article 36 rights, the same general interests served by Article 36 would be safeguarded by other protections available to persons in the situation in which Sanchez-Llamas found himself. The Court stressed that "[a] foreign national detained on suspicion of crime, like anyone else in our country, enjoys under our system the protections of the Due Process Clause[,] . . . is entitled to an attorney, and is protected against compelled self-incrimination."

Finally, the Court stated that Vienna Convention rights could be vindicated in ways other than suppression of evidence. The Court observed that a defendant could make an Article 36 argument "as part of a broader challenge to the voluntariness of his statements to police," and that if a defendant alludes to a supposed Article 36 violation at trial, "a court can make appropriate accommodations to ensure that the defendant secures, to the extent possible, the benefits of consular assistance." Having concluded that the exclusionary rule was not an appropriate remedy for the Article 36 violation at issue, the Court upheld the conviction of Sanchez-Llamas.

The USA PATRIOT Act Approximately six weeks after the September 11, 2001, terrorist attacks on the United States, Congress enacted the Uniting and Strengthening America by Providing Appropriate Tools Required to Intercept and Obstruct Terrorism Act. This statute, commonly known as the USA PATRIOT Act or as simply the Patriot Act, contains numerous and broad-ranging provisions designed to protect the public against international and domestic terrorism.

Included in the Patriot Act are measures allowing the federal government significantly expanded ability, in terrorism-related investigations, to conduct searches of property, monitor Internet activities, and track electronic communications. Most, though not all, actions of that nature require a warrant from a special court known as the Foreign Intelligence Surveillance Court. The statute contemplates, however, that such warrants may be issued upon less of a showing by the government than would ordinarily be required, and may be more sweeping than usual in terms of geographic application. Moreover, warrants issued by the special court for the search of property can be of the so-called "sneak and peek" variety, under which the FBI need not produce the warrant for the property owner or possessor to see and need not notify an absent property owner or possessor that the search took place (unlike the rules typically applicable to execution of "regular" warrants).

The Patriot Act also calls for banks to report seemingly suspicious monetary deposits, as well as any deposits exceeding $10,000, not only to the Treasury Department (as required by prior law) but also to the Central Intelligence Agency and other federal intelligence agencies. In addition, the statute enables federal law enforcement authorities to seek a Surveillance Court warrant for the obtaining of individuals' credit, medical, and student records, regardless of state or federal privacy laws that would otherwise have applied.

Commentators critical of the Patriot Act have argued that despite the importance of safeguarding the public against acts of terrorism, the statute tips the balance too heavily in favor of law enforcement. They have characterized the statute's definition of "domestic terrorism" as so broad that various suspected activities not normally regarded as terrorism (or as harboring or aiding terrorists) could be considered as such for purposes of the federal government's expanded investigatory tools. If that happens, the critics contend, Fourth Amendment and other constitutional rights may easily be subverted. Others with reservations about the statute maintain that its allowance of expanded monitoring of Internet activities and electronic communications and its provisions for retrieval of library records and other records normally protected by privacy laws could give the government ready access to communications and private information of many wholly innocent persons. Two federal district courts gave added voice to such concerns with 2007 decisions holding portions of the Patriot Act unconstitutional. As of the time this book went to press in 2008, appeals were pending in those cases.

In apparent recognition of the extraordinary action it was taking in a time of national crisis, Congress included provisions stating that unless renewed, portions of the statute would expire at the end of 2005. Congress also included provisions requiring the attorney general to report to Congress on the use of the enhanced investigatory powers. Congress later renewed the bulk of the Patriot Act—meaning that it will remain in force for the foreseeable future unless those who have raised civil liberties concerns about it can succeed in cutting back its scope and application.

The expanded investigatory tools provided by the Patriot Act have existed alongside those provided by an older statute, the Foreign Intelligence Surveillance Act (FISA), which was enacted long before the September 11, 2001, attacks and has been amended various times both before and since. Under FISA, monitoring of a suspected terrorist's electronic communications generally required that an individualized warrant be obtained from the previously mentioned Foreign Intelligence Surveillance Court (FISA Court), which operates in secret and whose decisions, unlike those of other courts, are not published. Applications for warrants from the FISA Court have historically been approved a very high percentage of the time.

In December 2005, it was revealed that the Bush Administration had implemented a program of monitoring telephone calls of suspected terrorists when one party to the conversation was located outside the United States. This monitoring had occurred without an attempt by the government to obtain warrants from the FISA Court. Critics of this action by the government complained that

it violated not only FISA but also the Fourth Amendment. The Bush Administration took the position, however, that the monitoring program was within the inherent powers of the executive branch. Disputes over the validity of the monitoring program led to discussions over possible amendments to strengthen or loosen FISA's requirements. These discussions resulted in a temporary amendment under which the FISA Court could issue blanket warrants for electronic monitoring of groups of terrorism suspects for set periods of time (as opposed to the previous sole option of individualized warrants). With such loosening of what it saw as FISA's constraints, the Bush Administration shut down its warrantless monitoring program and resumed going to the FISA Court for warrants. As this book went to press in 2008, Congress had just enacted a further amendment to FISA. This amendment expanded the government's ability to monitor the phone calls of suspected terrorists, established FISA's requirement of warrants from the FISA Court as the exclusive way of exercising this surveillance power, and provided immunity from legal liability for telephone companies that had assisted the Bush Administration in the phone call monitoring activities for which FISA Court warrants had not been obtained.

The Fifth Amendment
The Fifth and Fourteenth Amendments' Due Process Clauses guarantee basic procedural and substantive fairness to criminal defendants. The Due Process Clauses are discussed earlier in this chapter and in Chapter 3.

Privilege against Self-Incrimination In another significant provision, the Fifth Amendment protects against *compelled testimonial self-incrimination* by establishing that "[n]o person . . . shall be compelled in any criminal case to be a witness against himself." This provision prevents the government from coercing a defendant into making incriminating statements and thereby assisting in his own prosecution.

In *Miranda v. Arizona* (1966), the Supreme Court established procedural requirements—the now-familiar *Miranda* warnings—to safeguard this Fifth Amendment right and other constitutional guarantees. The Court did so by requiring police to inform criminal suspects, before commencing custodial interrogation of them, that they have the right to remain silent, that any statements they make may be used as evidence against them, and that they have the right to the presence and assistance of a retained or court-appointed attorney (with court appointment occurring when suspects lack the financial ability to retain counsel).[6] Incriminating statements that an in-custody suspect makes without first having been given the *Miranda* warnings are inadmissible at trial. If the suspect invokes her right to silence, custodial interrogation must cease. If, on the other hand, the suspect knowingly and voluntarily waives her right to silence after having been given the *Miranda* warnings, her statements will be admissible.

The right to silence is limited, however, in various ways. For example, the traditional view that the Fifth Amendment applies only to *testimonial* admissions serves as the basis for allowing the police to compel an accused to furnish nontestimonial evidence such as fingerprints, samples of body fluids, and hair. Supreme Court decisions have recognized further limitations on the right to silence. For instance, the right has been held to include a corresponding implicit prohibition of prosecutorial comments at trial about the accused's failure to speak in his own defense. Although Supreme Court decisions still support this prohibition in general, the Court has sometimes allowed prosecutors to use the defendant's pretrial silence to impeach his trial testimony. For example, the Court has held that the Fifth Amendment is not violated by prosecutorial use of a defendant's silence (either prearrest or postarrest, but in advance of any *Miranda* warnings) to discredit his trial testimony that he killed the victim in self-defense.

Further inclination to narrow *Miranda*'s applicability and effect has sometimes been displayed by the Supreme Court during roughly the past 30 years. In one case, for example, the Court upheld a suspect's waiver of his *Miranda* rights and approved the use of his confession at trial, despite the police's failure to notify the suspect that an attorney retained for him by a family member was seeking to contact him. Another decision established that an undercover police officer posing as a fellow inmate need not give a jailed suspect the *Miranda* warnings before asking questions that could lead to incriminating admissions.

Although the *Miranda* warnings have been a required feature of law enforcement practice since the Supreme Court handed down its landmark decision more than four decades ago, a surprising 1999 decision of the U.S. Court of Appeals for the Fourth Circuit labeled the *Miranda* warnings as merely judicially created rules of procedure that were neither grounded in, nor required by, the Constitution. The Fourth Circuit's holding that the *Miranda* warnings were not of constitutional dimension led it to conclude that the warnings' required status could be eliminated by appropriate legislation, and that Congress, in a largely ignored 1968 statute, indeed had legislatively overruled *Miranda*. In *Dickerson v. United States* (2000), however, the Supreme Court overturned the Fourth Circuit's decision and classified the *Miranda* warnings as a constitutional rule, which Congress could not legislatively overrule.

An interrogation tactic designed to subvert the purpose of the *Miranda* warnings drew the disapproval of the Supreme Court in *Missouri v. Seibert,* which follows.

---

[6] The portions of the *Miranda* warnings dealing with the right to an attorney further Sixth Amendment interests. The Sixth Amendment is discussed later in this chapter.

Missouri v. Seibert   542 U.S. 600 (U.S. Sup. Ct. 2004)

Patrice Seibert's 12-year-old son, Jonathan, had cerebral palsy. When Jonathan died in his sleep, Seibert feared charges of neglect because there were bedsores on his body. In Seibert's presence, two of her teenage sons and two of their friends devised a plan to conceal the facts surrounding Jonathan's death by incinerating his body in the course of burning the family's mobile home. Under the plan, the fire would be set while Donald Rector, a mentally ill teenager who lived with the family, was asleep in the mobile home. The presence of Rector's body would negate any appearance that Jonathan had been unattended. Seibert's son Darian and a friend set the fire as planned, and Rector died.

Five days later, Rolla, Missouri, police officers awakened Seibert at 3 AM at a hospital where Darian was being treated for burns. An officer arrested Seibert but, in accordance with instructions from Officer Richard Hanrahan, refrained from giving Miranda warnings at the time of the arrest. After Seibert had been taken to the police station and left alone in an interview room for 15 to 20 minutes, Hanrahan questioned her without Miranda warnings for 30 to 40 minutes, squeezing her arm and repeating, "Donald was also to die in his sleep." When Seibert finally admitted she knew Donald was meant to die in the fire, she was given a 20-minute coffee and cigarette break. Hanrahan then turned on a tape recorder, gave Seibert the Miranda warnings, and obtained a signed waiver of rights from her. He resumed the questioning with "OK, [Pa]trice, we've been talking for a little while about what happened on Wednesday the twelfth, haven't we?" Hanrahan then confronted

Seibert with her prewarning statements about the plan to set the fire and the understanding that Donald Rector would be left sleeping in the mobile home. Specifically, Hanrahan referred to Seibert's prewarning statements by asking, in regard to Rector, "[D]idn't you tell me he was supposed to die in his sleep?" and "So he was supposed to die in his sleep?" Seibert answered "Yes" to the second of these postwarning questions.

After being charged with first-degree murder for her role in Rector's death, Seibert sought to have her prewarning and postwarning statements suppressed (i.e., excluded from evidence) as the remedy for what she alleged were Fifth Amendment, Fourteenth Amendment, and Miranda *violations. At the hearing on Seibert's motion to suppress, Hanrahan testified that he made a "conscious decision" to withhold* Miranda *warnings and to resort to an interrogation technique he had been taught: question first, then give the warnings, and then repeat the question "until I get the answer that she's already provided once." Hanrahan acknowledged that Seibert's ultimate statement was "largely a repeat of information . . . obtained" prior to the giving of the* Miranda *warnings.*

The trial court suppressed the prewarning statement but allowed, as evidence at Seibert's trial, the responses given after the Miranda *recitation. After a jury convicted Seibert of second-degree murder, the Missouri Court of Appeals affirmed the conviction. However, the Supreme Court of Missouri reversed, holding that "the second statement, clearly the product of the invalid first statement, should have been suppressed." The U.S. Supreme Court granted the state of Missouri's petition for certiorari.*

Souter, Justice

This case tests a police protocol for custodial interrogation that calls for giving no warnings of the rights to silence and counsel until interrogation has produced a confession. Although such a statement is generally inadmissible [i.e., cannot be used as evidence], since taken in violation of *Miranda v. Arizona,* 384 U.S. 436 (1966), the interrogating officer follows it with *Miranda* warnings and then leads the suspect to cover the same ground a second time. The question here is the admissibility of the repeated statement.

[Because the Fifth and Fourteenth Amendments to the Constitution afford defendants protection against compelled self-incrimination in federal and state criminal cases, a defendant's confession is not admissible evidence unless it was voluntarily given. Until the mid-1960s, courts determined whether a confession was voluntary by applying a totality-of-the-circumstances test that called for the court to examine all of the facts surrounding the interrogation and the confession in the particular case at issue.] In *Miranda,* we explained that the "voluntariness doctrine . . . encompasses all interrogation practices which are likely to exert such pressure upon an individual as to disable him from making a free and rational choice." We [also] appreciated the difficulty of judicial enquiry *post hoc* into the circumstances of a police interrogation. [In] *Dickerson v. United States,* 530 U.S. 428 (2000), [we noted *Miranda*'s recognition] that "the coercion inherent in custodial interrogation blurs the line between voluntary and involuntary statements, and thus heightens the risk" that the privilege against self-incrimination will not be observed. Hence our concern that the traditional totality-of-the-circumstances test posed an "unacceptably great" risk that involuntary custodial confessions would escape detection.

Accordingly, to reduce the risk of a coerced confession and to implement the [constitutional privilege against] self-incrimination . . . , this Court in *Miranda* concluded that "the accused must be adequately and effectively apprised of his rights and the exercise of those rights must be fully honored." *Miranda* conditioned the admissibility at trial of any custodial confession on warning a suspect of his rights: failure to give the prescribed warnings and obtain a waiver of rights before custodial questioning generally requires exclusion of any statements obtained. Conversely, giving the warnings and getting a waiver has generally produced a virtual ticket of admissibility.

There are those, of course, who preferred the old way of doing things: giving no warnings and litigating the voluntariness of any statement in nearly every instance. In the aftermath of *Miranda,* Congress even passed a statute seeking to restore that old regime, although the [statute] lay dormant for years until finally invoked and challenged [on constitutional grounds]. [In] *Dickerson v. United States*[, we] reaffirmed *Miranda* and held that its constitutional character prevailed against the statute.

The technique of interrogating in successive unwarned and warned phases raises a new challenge to *Miranda.* Although we have no statistics on the frequency of this practice, it is not confined to Rolla, Missouri. An officer of that police department testified that the strategy of withholding *Miranda* warnings until after interrogating and drawing out a confession was promoted not only by his own department, but by a national police training organization and other departments in which he had worked. [T]he Police Law Institute, for example, instructs [in one of its manuals] that officers may "conduct a two-stage interrogation" [and that] "during the pre-*Miranda* interrogation, usually after arrestees have confessed, officers may then read the *Miranda* warnings and ask for a waiver. If the arrestees waive their *Miranda* rights, officers will be able to repeat any *subsequent* incriminating statements later in court." The upshot of all this advice is a question-first practice of some popularity, as one can see from the reported cases describing its use, sometimes in obedience to departmental policy. [Citations of representative cases omitted.]

When a confession so obtained is offered and challenged, attention must be paid to the conflicting objects of *Miranda* and question-first. *Miranda* addressed "interrogation practices . . . likely . . . to disable [an individual] from making a free and rational choice" about speaking, and held that a suspect must be "adequately and effectively" advised of the choice the Constitution guarantees. The object of question-first is to render *Miranda* warnings ineffective by waiting for a particularly opportune time to give them, after the suspect has already confessed.

[I]t would be absurd to think that mere recitation of the [*Miranda*] litany suffices to satisfy *Miranda* in every conceivable circumstance. The threshold issue when interrogators question first and warn later is . . . whether it would be reasonable to find that in these circumstances the warnings could function "effectively" as *Miranda* requires. Could the warnings effectively advise the suspect that he had a real choice about giving an admissible statement at that juncture? Could they reasonably convey that he could choose to stop talking even if he had talked earlier? For unless the warnings could place a suspect who has just been interrogated in a position to make such an informed choice, there is no practical justification for accepting the formal warnings as compliance with *Miranda,* or for treating the second stage of interrogation as distinct from the first, unwarned and inadmissible segment.

There is no doubt about the answer that proponents of question-first give to this question about the effectiveness of warnings given only after successful interrogation, and we think their answer is correct. By any objective measure, applied to circumstances exemplified here, it is likely that if the interrogators employ the technique of withholding warnings until after interrogation succeeds in eliciting a confession, the warnings will be ineffective in preparing the suspect for successive interrogation, close in time and similar in content. After all, the reason that question-first is catching on is as obvious as its manifest purpose, which is to get a confession the suspect would not make if he understood his rights at the outset; the sensible underlying assumption is that with one confession in hand before the warnings, the interrogator can count on getting its duplicate, with trifling additional trouble. Upon hearing warnings only in the aftermath of interrogation and just after making a confession, a suspect would hardly think he had a genuine right to remain silent, let alone persist in so believing once the police began to lead him over the same ground again.

Thus, when *Miranda* warnings are inserted in the midst of coordinated and continuing interrogation, they are likely to mislead and "depriv[e] a defendant of knowledge essential to his ability to understand the nature of his rights and the consequences of abandoning them." [Citation omitted.] By the same token, it would ordinarily be unrealistic to treat two spates of integrated and proximately conducted questioning as independent interrogations subject to independent evaluation simply because *Miranda* warnings formally punctuate them in the middle.

Missouri argues that a confession repeated at the end of an interrogation sequence envisioned in a question-first strategy is admissible on the authority of *Oregon v. Elstad,* 470 U.S. 298 (1985), but the argument disfigures that case. In *Elstad,* the police went to the young suspect's house to take him into custody on a charge of burglary. Before the arrest, one officer spoke with the suspect's mother, while the other one joined the suspect in a "brief stop in the living room," where the officer said he "felt" the young man was involved in a burglary. The suspect acknowledged he had been at the scene. This Court noted that the pause in the living room "was not to interrogate the suspect but to notify his mother of the reason for his arrest," and described the incident as having "none of the earmarks of coercion." The Court, indeed, took care to mention that the officer's initial failure to warn was an "oversight" that "may have been the result of confusion as to whether the brief exchange qualified as 'custodial interrogation' or . . . may simply have reflected . . . reluctance to initiate an alarming police procedure before [an officer] had spoken with respondent's mother." At the outset of a later and systematic station house interrogation going well beyond the scope of the laconic prior admission, the suspect was given *Miranda* warnings and made a full confession.

In holding the second statement admissible and voluntary, *Elstad* rejected the "cat out of the bag" theory that any short, earlier admission, obtained in arguably innocent neglect of *Miranda,* determined the character of the later, warned confession. [O]n the facts of that case, the Court thought any causal connection between the first and second responses to the police was "speculative and attenuated." Although the *Elstad* Court expressed no explicit conclusion about either officer's state of mind, it is fair to read *Elstad* as treating the living room conversation as a good-faith *Miranda* mistake, not only open to correction by careful warnings before systematic questioning in that particular case, but posing no threat to warn-first practice generally.

The contrast between *Elstad* and this case reveals a series of relevant facts that bear on whether *Miranda* warnings delivered midstream could be effective enough to accomplish their object: the completeness and detail of the questions and answers in the first round of interrogation, the overlapping content of the two statements, the timing and setting of the first and the second, the continuity of police personnel, and the degree to which the interrogator's questions treated the second round as continuous with the first. In *Elstad,* it was not unreasonable to see the occasion for questioning at the station house as presenting a markedly different experience from the short conversation at home; since a reasonable person in the suspect's shoes could have seen the station house questioning as a new and distinct experience, the *Miranda* warnings could have made sense as presenting a genuine choice whether to follow up on the earlier admission.

At the opposite extreme are the facts here, which by any objective measure reveal a police strategy adapted to undermine the *Miranda* warnings. (Because the intent of the officer will rarely be as candidly admitted as it was here . . . , [our] focus is on facts apart from intent that show the question-first tactic at work.) The unwarned interrogation was conducted in the station house, and the questioning was systematic, exhaustive, and managed with psychological skill. When the police were finished there was little, if anything, of incriminating potential left unsaid. The warned phase of questioning proceeded after a pause of only 15 to 20 minutes, in the same place as the unwarned segment. When the same officer who had conducted the first phase recited the *Miranda* warnings, he said nothing to counter the probable misimpression that the advice that anything Seibert said could be used against her also applied to the details of the inculpatory statement previously elicited. In particular, the police did not advise that her prior statement could not be used. The impression that the further questioning was a mere continuation of the earlier questions and responses was fostered by references back to the confession already given. It would have been reasonable to regard the two sessions as parts of a continuum, in which it would have been unnatural to refuse to repeat at the second stage what had been said before. These circumstances must be seen as challenging the comprehensibility and efficacy of the *Miranda* warnings to the point that a reasonable person in the suspect's shoes would not have understood them to convey a message that she retained a choice about continuing to talk.

Strategists dedicated to draining the substance out of *Miranda* cannot accomplish by training instructions what *Dickerson* held Congress could not do by statute. Because the question-first tactic effectively threatens to thwart *Miranda*'s purpose of reducing the risk that a coerced confession would be admitted, and because the facts here do not reasonably support a conclusion that the warnings given could have served their purpose, Seibert's postwarning statements are inadmissible.

Supreme Court of Missouri's decision affirmed.

Note: The opinion of Justice Souter was a plurality opinion in regard to *reasoning* because Justice Souter spoke for four justices (himself and Justices Stevens, Ginsburg, and Breyer). In his concurrence in the judgment, Justice Kennedy provided a fifth vote—and hence a majority—on the case's *outcome:* that Seibert's post-*Miranda* warnings statement could not be used as evidence. Justice Kennedy condemned what he saw as a clear attempt to "circumvent" *Miranda.* He also expressed agreement with much of what the plurality opinion stated. Justice Kennedy did not join that opinion, however, because he would have adopted a different controlling test. Instead of the plurality's test of whether the midinterrogation giving of the *Miranda* warnings could reasonably be seen as effective to accomplish the purposes of those warnings, Justice Kennedy would have held that if law enforcement officers deliberately employed the two-step interrogation technique of the sort used in *Seibert,* the defendant's post-*Miranda* warnings statement would be inadmissible unless the interrogating officers implemented adequate "curative measures." Justice Kennedy noted that such measures could include the use of a significant time delay or change in location between the prewarning and postwarning phases of the interrogation, or the making of a specific statement, along with the *Miranda* warnings, that the defendant's earlier (i.e., prewarning) statement probably could not be used against him.

Production of Records The preceding discussion of the privilege against self-incrimination applies to criminal defendants in general. The Fifth Amendment's scope, however, has long been of particular concern to businesspersons charged with crimes. Documentary evidence often is quite important to the government's case in white-collar crime prosecutions. To what extent does the Fifth Amendment protect business records? More than a century ago, the Supreme Court held, in *Boyd v. United States* (1886), that the Fifth Amendment protects individuals against compelled production of their private papers.

In more recent years, however, the Court has drastically limited the scope of the protection contemplated by *Boyd.* The Court has held various times that the private papers privilege is personal and thus cannot be asserted by a corporation, partnership, or other "collective entity." Because such entities have no Fifth Amendment rights, the Court has held that when an organization's individual officer or agent has custody of organization records, the officer or agent cannot assert any personal privilege to prevent their disclosure. This rule holds even if the contents of the records incriminate her personally. Finally, various decisions allow the government to require business proprietors to keep certain records relevant to transactions that are appropriate subjects for government regulation. These "required records" are not entitled to private papers protection. They may be subpoenaed and used against the record keeper in prosecutions for regulatory violations.

The Court's business records decisions during the past three decades cast further doubt on the future of the private papers doctrine. Instead of focusing on whether subpoenaed records are private in nature, the Court now considers whether the *act of producing* the records would be sufficiently testimonial to trigger the privilege against self-incrimination. In *Fisher v. United States* (1976), the Court held that an individual subpoenaed to produce personal documents may assert his Fifth Amendment privilege only if the act of producing the documents would involve incriminating testimonial admissions. This is likely when the individual producing the records is in effect certifying the records' authenticity or admitting the existence of records previously unknown to the government (demonstrating that he had access to the records and, therefore, possible knowledge of any incriminating contents).

In *United States v. Doe* (1984), the Court extended the act-of-production privilege to a sole proprietor whose proprietorship records were subpoenaed. The Court, however, held that normal business records were not themselves protected by the Fifth Amendment because they were voluntarily prepared and thus not the product of compulsion. In view of *Doe's* emphasis on the testimonial and potentially incriminating nature of the act of producing business records, some observers thought that officers of collective entities under government investigation might be able to assert their personal privileges against self-incrimination as a way to avoid producing incriminating business records.

Braswell v. United States (1988) dashed such hopes, however, as the Court refused to extend its *Doe* holding to cover a corporation's sole shareholder who acted in his capacity as custodian of corporate records. The Court held that Braswell (the sole shareholder), having chosen to operate his business under the corporate form, was bound by the rule that corporations and similar entities have no Fifth Amendment privilege. Because Braswell acted in a representative capacity in producing the requested records, the government could not make evidentiary use of his act of production. The government, however, was free to use the contents of the records against Braswell and the corporation.

Double Jeopardy   Another important Fifth Amendment provision is the Double Jeopardy Clause. This provision protects defendants from multiple criminal prosecutions for the same offense. It prevents a second criminal prosecution for the same offense after the defendant has been acquitted or convicted of that offense. Moreover, it bars the imposition of multiple punishments for the same offense.

The Double Jeopardy Clause does not, however, preclude the possibility that a single criminal act may lead to more than one criminal prosecution. One criminal act may produce several statutory violations, all of which may give rise to prosecution. For example, a defendant who commits rape may also be prosecuted for battery, assault with a deadly weapon, and kidnapping if the facts of the case indicate that the relevant statutes were violated. In addition, the Supreme Court has long used a "same elements" test to determine what constitutes the same offense. This means that a single criminal act with multiple victims (e.g., a restaurant robbery in which several patrons are robbed) could result in several prosecutions because the identity of each victim would be an additional fact or element of proof in each case.

In addition, the Double Jeopardy Clause does not protect against multiple prosecutions by different sovereigns. A conviction or acquittal in a state prosecution does not prevent a subsequent federal prosecution for a federal offense arising out of the same event, or vice versa. Finally, the Double Jeopardy Clause does not bar a private plaintiff from pursuing a *civil* case (normally for one or more of the intentional torts discussed in Chapter 6) against a defendant who was criminally prosecuted by the government for the same alleged conduct. The headline-dominating criminal and civil cases against O. J. Simpson furnish perhaps the best-known example of this principle.

The Sixth Amendment   The Sixth Amendment applies to criminal cases in various ways. It entitles criminal defendants to a speedy trial by an impartial jury and guarantees them the right to confront and cross-examine the witnesses against them. The Sixth Amendment also gives the accused in a criminal case the right "to have the assistance of counsel" in her defense. This provision has been interpreted to mean not only that the accused may employ her own attorney but also that an indigent criminal defendant is entitled to court-appointed counsel. Included in the previously discussed *Miranda* warnings is a requirement that the police inform the accused of his right to counsel before custodial interrogation begins. *Edwards v. Arizona* (1981) established that once the accused has requested the assistance of counsel, he may not as a general rule be interrogated further until counsel is made available to him. The Supreme Court later held that the *Edwards* rule against further questioning is triggered only by an *unambiguous* request for counsel.[7] In *McNeil v. Wisconsin* (1991), the Court provided further latitude for law enforcement officers by holding that if a defendant has made an in-court request for an attorney's assistance regarding a crime with which he has been formally charged, that request does not preclude police interrogation of him—in the absence of counsel—regarding another unrelated crime.

Finally, an accused is entitled to *effective* assistance of counsel. This means that the accused is entitled to representation at a point in the proceedings when an attorney may effectively assist him, and to reasonably competent representation by that attorney. Inadequate assistance of counsel is a proper basis for setting aside a conviction and ordering a new trial, but the standard applied to these cases makes ineffective assistance of counsel claims difficult ones for convicted defendants to invoke successfully.

White-Collar Crimes and the Dilemmas of Corporate Control

Introduction *White-collar crime* is the term used to describe a wide variety of nonviolent criminal offenses committed by businesspersons and business organizations. This term includes offenses committed by employees against their employers, as well as corporate officers' offenses that harm the corporation and its shareholders. It also includes criminal offenses committed by corporate employers and employees against society. Each year, corporate crime costs consumers billions of dollars. It takes various forms, from consumer fraud, securities fraud, mail or wire fraud, and tax evasion to price-fixing, environmental pollution, and other regulatory violations. Corporate crime presents our legal system with various problems that we have failed to resolve satisfactorily.

Corporations form the backbone of the most successful economic system in history. They dominate the international economic scene and provide us with substantial benefits in the forms of efficiently produced goods and services. Yet these same corporations may pollute the environment, swindle their customers, mislead investors, produce dangerously defective products, and conspire with others to injure or destroy competition. How are we to achieve effective control over these large organizations so important to our existence? Increasingly, we have come to rely on the criminal law as a major corporate control instrument. The criminal law, however, was developed with individual wrongdoers in mind. Corporate crime is *organizational* in nature. Any given corporate action may be the product of the combined actions of many individuals acting within the corporate hierarchy. It may be that no individual had sufficient knowledge to possess the *mens rea* necessary for criminal responsibility under usual criminal law principles. Moreover, criminally penalizing corporations raises special problems in view of the obvious inability to apply standard sanctions such as imprisonment to legal entities.

Evolution of Corporate Criminal Liability The law initially rejected the notion that corporations could be criminally responsible for their employees' actions. Early corporations, small in size and number, had little impact on public life. Their small size made it relatively easy to pinpoint individual wrongdoers within the corporation.

As corporations grew in size and power, however, the social need to control their activities grew accordingly. Legislatures enacted statutes creating regulatory offenses that did not require proof of *mens rea*. By 1900, American courts had begun to impose criminal liability on corporations for general criminal offenses that required proof of *mens rea*. This expansion of corporate criminal liability involved imputing the criminal intent of employees to the corporation in a fashion similar to the imposition of tort liability on corporations under the *respondeat superior* doctrine.[8]

Corporations now may face criminal liability for almost any offense if the statute in question indicates a legislative intent to hold corporations responsible. This legislative intent requirement is sometimes problematic. Many state criminal statutes may contain language suggesting an intent to hold only humans liable. For example, manslaughter statutes often define the offense as "the killing of one human being by the act of another." When statutes are framed, however, in more

---

[7]In *Davis v. United States* (1994), the court concluded that "Maybe I should talk to a lawyer" was too ambiguous to trigger the *Edwards* rule.

[8]Chapter 36 discusses *respondeat superior* in detail.

Ethics in Action

The highly publicized financial scandals involving Enron, WorldCom, and other firms mentioned near the beginning of this chapter involved conduct that in some instances was alleged to be criminal. Regardless of whether criminal violations occurred, the alleged conduct was widely perceived to be questionable on ethical grounds and motivated by a desire for short-term gains notwithstanding the costs to others. Consider the broad-ranging and sometimes devastating effects of the perceived ethical lapses and the related legal proceedings (civil and/or criminal) faced by the firms and certain executives. These effects included:

• The crippling or near-crippling blow to the viability of the firms involved.

• The collapse in value of the firms' stock and the resulting loss to disillusioned and angry shareholders who felt they had been hoodwinked.

• The harm to the professional and personal reputations of the individuals involved in the business decisions that triggered legal scrutiny and raised serious ethical concerns.

• The job losses experienced by large numbers of employees who had nothing whatsoever to do with the questionable actions that effectively brought down the firm or made massive layoffs necessary.

• The effects on the families of those who lost their jobs.

• The lack of confidence on the part of would-be investors in the profit figures and projections put forth every day by corporations—including those that have done nothing irregular.

• The ripple effects of the above on the economy generally.

---

general terms—such as by referring to "persons"—courts are generally willing to apply them to corporate defendants.

Corporate Criminal Liability Today

Under the modern rule, a corporation may be held liable for criminal offenses committed by employees who *acted within the scope of their employment and for the benefit of the corporation.* A major corporate criminal liability issue centers around the classes of corporate employees whose intent can be imputed to the corporation. Some commentators argue that a corporation should be criminally responsible only for offenses committed by high corporate officials or those linked to them by authorization or acquiescence. (Nearly all, if not all, courts impose criminal liability on a corporation under such circumstances.) This argument reflects fairness notions, for if any group of corporate employees can fairly be said to constitute a corporation's mind, that group is its top officers and directors.

The problem with imposing corporate liability only on the basis of top corporate officers' actions or knowledge is that such a policy often insulates the corporation from liability. Many corporate offenses may be directly traceable only to middle managers or more subordinate employees. It may be impossible to demonstrate that any higher level corporate official had sufficient knowledge to constitute *mens rea.* Recognizing this problem, the federal courts have adopted a general rule that a corporation may be criminally liable for the actions of any of its agents, regardless of whether any link between the agents and higher level corporate officials can be demonstrated.

Problems with Punishing Corporations Despite the legal theories that justify corporate criminal liability, the punishment of corporations remains problematic. Does a criminal conviction stigmatize a corporation in the same way it stigmatizes an individual? Perhaps the only stigma resulting from a corporate criminal conviction is felt by the firm's employees, many of whom are entirely innocent of wrongdoing. Is it just to punish the innocent in an attempt to punish the guilty?

Consider, for instance, the effects that innocent employees of the Arthur Andersen firm experienced as a result of Andersen's obstruction of justice conviction in 2002. Although the conviction was overturned by the Supreme Court in 2005 because of faulty jury instructions (see the decision that appears earlier in the chapter), the Andersen firm had already been knocked out of existence. Many partners of the firm acquired positions elsewhere, but nonpartner employees of the firm no doubt experienced hardship despite having had nothing to do with any alleged wrongdoing. Concern about preservation of the firm and minimizing hardship for employees appeared to motivate another leading accounting firm, KPMG, to take the unusual step of acknowledging possibly criminal behavior before being formally charged in connection with certain questionable tax shelters designed by the firm. By acknowledging wrongdoing, it was thought, the firm might be able to head off criminal prosecution and remain viable as a firm.

What about the cash fine, the primary punishment imposed on convicted corporations? Most critics of corporate control strategies maintain that fines imposed on convicted firms tend to be too small to provide effective deterrence. These critics urge the use of fines keyed in some fashion to the corporate defendant's wealth. Larger fines may lead to undesirable results, however, if the corporate defendant ultimately passes along the fines to its customers (through higher prices), shareholders (through lower dividends or no dividends), or employees (through lower wages). Moreover, fines large enough to threaten corporate solvency may harm employees and those economically dependent on the corporation's financial well-being. Most of those persons, however, neither had the power to prevent the violation nor derived any benefit from it. Moreover, the managers responsible for a violation may avoid the imposition of direct burdens on them when the fine is assessed against the corporation.

Still other deficiencies make fines less-than-adequate corporate control devices. Fine strategies assume that all corporations are rationally acting profit-maximizers. Fines of sufficient size, it is argued, will erode the profit drive underlying most corporate violations. Numerous studies of actual corporate behavior, however, suggest that many corporations are neither profit-maximizers nor rational actors. Mature firms with well-established market shares may embrace goals other than profit maximization, such as technological prominence, increased market share, or higher employee salaries. In addition, the interests of managers who make corporate decisions and establish corporate policies may not coincide with the long-range economic interests of their corporate employers. The prospect that their employer could have to pay a substantial fine at some future point may not trouble top managers, who tend to have relatively short terms in office and are often compensated in part by large bonuses keyed to year-end profitability.

Individual Liability for Corporate Crime

Individuals who commit crimes while acting in corporate capacities have always been subjected to personal criminal liability. Most European nations reject corporate criminal liability and rely exclusively on individual criminal responsibility. In view of the problems associated with imposing criminal liability on corporations, individual liability may seem a more attractive control device. Besides being more consistent with traditional criminal law notions about the personal nature of guilt, individual liability may provide better deterrence than corporate liability if it enables society to use the criminal punishment threat against those who make important corporate decisions. The prospect of personal liability may cause individuals to resist corporate pressures to violate the law. If guilty individuals are identified and punished, the criminal law's purposes may be achieved without harm to innocent employees, shareholders, and consumers.

Problems with Individual Liability   Attractive as it may sound, individual liability also poses significant problems when applied to corporate acts. Identifying responsible individuals within the corporate hierarchy becomes difficult—and frequently impossible—if we follow traditional notions and require proof of criminal intent. Business decisions leading to corporate wrongs often result from the collective actions of numerous corporate employees, none of whom had complete knowledge or specific criminal intent. Other corporate crimes are structural in the sense that they result from internal bureaucratic failures rather than the conscious actions of any individual or group.

Proving culpability on the part of high level executives may be particularly difficult. Bad news sometimes does not reach them; other times, they consciously avoid knowledge that would lead to criminal responsibility. It therefore may be possible to demonstrate culpability only on the part of middle level managers. Juries may be unwilling to convict such individuals, however, if they seem to be scapegoats for their unindicted superiors.

The difficulties in imposing criminal penalties on individual employees have led to the creation of regulatory offenses that impose strict or vicarious liability on corporate officers. Strict liability offenses dispense with the requirement of proof of criminal intent but ordinarily require proof that the defendant committed some wrongful act. Vicarious liability offenses impose criminal liability on a defendant for the acts of third parties (normally, employees under the defendant's personal supervision), but may require proof of some form of *mens rea,* such as the defendant's negligent or reckless failure to supervise. Statutes often combine these two approaches by making corporate executives liable for the acts or omissions of corporate employees without requiring proof of criminal intent on the part of the employees. *United States v. Park,* discussed in Figure 2, is a famous example of such a prosecution.

Critics of strict liability offenses often argue that *mens rea* is a basic principle in our legal system and that it is unjust to stigmatize with a criminal conviction persons who are not morally culpable. In addition, critics doubt that strict liability statutes produce the deterrence sought by their proponents. Such statutes may reduce the

Figure 2   A *Note on* United States v. Park, *421 U.S. 658 (U.S. Sup. Ct. 1975)*

Facts and Procedural History

John R. Park was CEO of Acme Markets, Inc., a national retail food chain with approximately 36,000 employees, 874 retail outlets, and 16 warehouses. Acme and Park were charged with five counts of violating the federal Food, Drug, and Cosmetic Act (the Act) by storing food shipped in interstate commerce in warehouses where it was exposed to rodent contamination. The violations were detected during Food and Drug Administration (FDA) inspections of Acme's Baltimore warehouse. Inspectors saw evidence of rodent infestation and unsanitary conditions, such as mouse droppings on the floor of the hanging meat room and alongside bales of lime Jell-O, and a hole chewed by a rodent in a bale of Jell-O. The FDA notified Park by letter of these findings.

Upon checking with Acme's vice president for legal affairs, Park learned that the Baltimore division vice president "was investigating the situation immediately and would be taking corrective action." An FDA inspection three months after the first one disclosed continued rodent contamination at the Baltimore warehouse despite improved sanitation there. The criminal charges were then filed against Acme and Park. Acme pleaded guilty; Park refused to do so. Park was convicted on each count, but the court of appeals overturned the conviction.

The Supreme Court's Decision

The Supreme Court, however, reversed. In sustaining Park's conviction, the Court noted that in view of the substantial public interest in purity of food, the Act did not require awareness of wrongdoing as an element of criminal conduct. This did not mean, however, that a person "remotely entangled in the proscribed shipment" was at risk of being criminally convicted. Instead, the defendant must be shown to have had "a responsible share" in the violation, such as by failing to exercise authority and supervisory responsibility. The Court emphasized that the Act imposes on supervisory personnel the "highest standard of foresight and vigilance." This includes a duty to seek out and remedy violations when they occur, and a duty to implement measures to prevent violations from occurring.

Although one who was "powerless" to prevent or correct the violation cannot be held criminally responsible under the Act, the Court emphasized that Park was hardly powerless. He had the authority and responsibility to prevent or correct the prohibited condition. The evidence showed that prior to the Baltimore warehouse inspections giving rise to the criminal charges, Park was advised by the FDA of unsanitary conditions in another Acme warehouse. According to the Court, Park thus acquired notice—prior to the time that the Baltimore warehouse violations were discovered—that he could not rely on his previously employed system of delegation to subordinates to prevent or correct unsanitary conditions at company warehouses. Despite evidence indicating Park's prior awareness of this system's deficiencies well before the Baltimore violations were discovered, Park had not instituted any new procedures designed to prevent violations of the Act. The Court therefore concluded that his conviction should stand.

---

moral impact of the criminal sanction if they apply it to relatively trivial offenses. Moreover, they may not result in enough convictions or sufficiently severe penalties to produce deterrence because juries and judges are unwilling to convict or punish defendants who may not be morally culpable. Although statutes creating strict liability offenses are generally held constitutional, they are disfavored by courts. Most courts require a clear indication of a legislative intent to dispense with the *mens rea* element.

Strict liability offenses are also criticized on the ground that even if responsible individuals within the corporation are convicted and punished appropriately, individual liability unaccompanied by corporate liability is unlikely to achieve effective corporate control. If immune from criminal liability, corporations could benefit financially from employees' violations of the law.

Individual liability, unlike a corporate fine, does not force a corporation to give up the profits flowing from a violation. Thus, the corporation would have no incentive to avoid future violations. Incarcerated offenders would merely be replaced by others who might eventually yield to the pressures that produced the violations in the first place. Corporate liability, however, may sometimes encourage corporate efforts to prevent future violations. When an offense has occurred but no identifiable individual is sufficiently culpable to justify an individual prosecution of him or her, corporate liability is uniquely appropriate.

New Directions

The preceding discussion suggests that future efforts at corporate control are likely to include both corporate and individual criminal liability. It also suggests, however, that new approaches are

Ethics in Action

Enron employee Sherron Watkins received considerable praise from the public, governmental officials, and media commentators when she went public in 2002 with her concerns about certain accounting and other business practices of her employer. These alleged practices caused Enron and high level executives of the firm to undergo considerable legal scrutiny in the civil and criminal arenas.

In deciding to become a whistle-blower, Sherron Watkins no doubt was motivated by what she regarded as a moral obligation. The decision she made was more highly publicized than most decisions of that nature, but was otherwise of a type that many employees have faced and will continue to face. You may be among those persons at some point in your career. Various questions, including the ones set forth below, may therefore be worth pondering. As you do so, you may find it useful to consider the perspectives afforded by the ethical theories discussed in Chapter 4.

- When an employee learns of apparently unlawful behavior on the part of his or her employer, does the employee have an ethical duty to blow the whistle on the employer?
- Do any ethical duties or obligations of the employee come into conflict in such a situation? If so, what are they, and how does the employee balance them?
- What practical consequences may one face if he or she becomes a whistle-blower? What role, if any, should those potential consequences play in the ethical analysis?
- What other consequences are likely to occur if the whistle is blown? What is likely to happen if the whistle isn't blown? Should these likely consequences affect the ethical analysis? If so, how?

necessary if society is to gain more effective control over corporate activities.

Various novel criminal penalties have been suggested in the individual liability setting. For example, white-collar offenders could be sentenced to render public service in addition to, or in lieu of, being incarcerated or fined. Some have even suggested the licensing of managers, with license suspensions as a penalty for offenders. The common thread in these and other similar approaches is an attempt to create penalties that are meaningful yet not so severe that judges and juries are unwilling to impose them.

A promising suggestion regarding corporate liability involves imaginative judicial use of corporate probation for convicted corporate offenders. For example, courts could require convicted corporations to do self-studies identifying the source of a violation and proposing appropriate steps to prevent future violations. If bureaucratic failures caused the violation, the court could order a limited restructuring of the corporation's internal decision-making processes as a condition of obtaining probation or avoiding a penalty. Possible orders might include requiring the collection and monitoring of the data necessary to discover or prevent future violations and mandating the creation of new executive positions to monitor such data. Restructuring would minimize the previously discussed harm to innocent persons that often accompanies corporate financial penalties. In addition, restructuring could be a more effective way to achieve corporate rehabilitation than relying exclusively on a

corporation's desire to avoid future fines as an incentive to police itself.

The Federal Sentencing Guidelines, discussed earlier in this chapter in Figure 1, contain good reasons for corporations to institute measures to prevent regulatory violations. This is true even though, as Figure 1 indicates, the Supreme Court's 2005 decision in *Booker* made the Guidelines advisory rather than mandatory. Under the subset of rules known as the Corporate Sentencing Guidelines, organizations convicted of violating federal law may face greatly increased penalties for certain offenses, with some crimes carrying fines as high as $290 million. The penalty that may be imposed on an organization depends on its "culpability score," which increases (thus calling for a more severe penalty) if, for example, high level corporate officers were involved in the offense or the organization had a history of such offenses. Even apart from the potentially severe penalties, however, the Corporate Sentencing Guidelines provide an incentive for corporations to adopt compliance programs designed "to prevent and detect violations of the law." The presence of an effective compliance program may reduce the corporation's culpability score for sentencing purposes. Prior to the time the Corporate Sentencing Guidelines were developed, courts generally concluded that the existence of a compliance program should not operate as a mitigating factor in the sentencing of a convicted organization.

In recent years, the Justice Department has made increased use of deferred prosecution agreements (DPAs), under which corporations avoid formal criminal charges and trials in return for their agreement to pay monetary penalties and submit to outside monitoring of their activities. Proponents of DPAs see them as a way to encourage more responsible behavior from corporations without the "hammer" of the criminal sanction. Critics, however, see the increased use of DPAs as sending a signal to corporations that they may engage in wrongful activities but still have available, in a figurative sense, a "get-out-of-jail-almost-free" card.

Important White-Collar Crimes

Regulatory Offenses Numerous state and federal regulatory statutes on a wide range of subjects prescribe criminal as well as civil liability for violations. The Food, Drug, and Cosmetic Act, at issue in the case discussed in Figure 2, is an example of such a statute. Other major federal regulatory offenses are discussed in later chapters. These include violations of the Sherman Antitrust Act, the Securities Act of 1933, the Securities Exchange Act of 1934, and certain environmental laws.

Fraudulent Acts Many business crimes involve some fraudulent conduct. In most states, it is a crime to obtain money or property by fraudulent pretenses, issue fraudulent checks, make false credit statements, or give short weights or measures. Certain forms of fraud in bankruptcy proceedings, such as false claims by creditors or fraudulent concealment or transfer of a debtor's assets, are federal criminal offenses. The same is true of securities fraud. In addition, federal mail fraud and wire fraud statutes make criminal the use of the mail, telephone, or telegrams to accomplish a fraudulent scheme. (See, for instance, the case asked about in the Online Research section at the end of this chapter.) Another federal law makes it a crime to travel or otherwise use facilities in interstate commerce in order to commit criminal acts.

The Sarbanes–Oxley Act In response to a series of highly publicized financial scandals and accounting controversies involving Enron, Arthur Andersen, Global Crossing, WorldCom, and other firms, Congress enacted the Sarbanes–Oxley Act of 2002. The Sarbanes–Oxley Act created the Public Company Accounting Oversight Board and charged it with regulatory responsibilities concerning public accounting firms' audits of corporations. The statute also established various requirements designed to ensure auditor independence; bring about higher levels of accuracy in corporate reporting of financial information; and promote responsible conduct on the part of corporate officers and directors, auditors, and securities analysts.

Additional portions of the broad-ranging Sarbanes–Oxley Act were given separate and more informative titles such as the Corporate and Criminal Fraud Accountability Act and the White-Collar Crime Penalty Enhancement Act. In those other portions of the statute, Congress:

- Established substantial fines and/or a maximum of 20 years of imprisonment as punishment for the knowing alteration or destruction of documents or records with the intent to impede a government investigation or proceeding.
- Made it a crime for an accountant to destroy corporate audit records prior to the appropriate time set forth in the statute and in regulations to be promulgated by the Securities and Exchange Commission.
- Classified debts resulting from civil judgments for securities fraud as nondischargeable in bankruptcy.
- Lengthened the statute of limitations period within which certain securities fraud cases may be filed.
- Provided legal protections for corporate employees who act as whistle-blowers regarding instances of fraud on the part of their employers.
- Established substantial fines and/or imprisonment of up to 25 years as the punishment for certain securities fraud offenses.
- Increased the maximum term of imprisonment for mail fraud and wire fraud to 20 years.
- Made attempts and conspiracies to commit such offenses subject to the same penalties established for the offenses themselves.
- Enhanced the penalties for certain violations of the Securities Exchange Act of 1934 by providing for a maximum fine of $5 million or a maximum 20-year prison term for individual violators, and a maximum fine of $25 million for corporate violators.
- Instructed the U.S. Sentencing Commission to review the Federal Sentencing Guidelines' treatment of obstruction of justice offenses, white-collar crimes, and securities fraud offenses, in order to ensure that deterrence and punishment purposes were being adequately served.

Bribery and Giving of Illegal Gratuities

State and federal law has long made it a crime to offer public officials gifts, favors, or anything of value to influence official decisions for private benefit. In 1977, Congress enacted the Foreign Corrupt Practices Act (FCPA), which criminalized the offering or giving of anything of value to officials of *foreign* governments in an attempt to influence their official actions. Individuals who violate the FCPA's bribery prohibition may be fined up to $100,000 and/or imprisoned for a maximum of five years. Corporate violators of the FCPA may be fined as much as $2 million. Chapter 45 discusses the FCPA in more depth. As explained in the nearby Global Business Environment box, the 1990s marked the emergence of international agreements as additional devices for addressing the problem of bribery of government officials.

Most states in the United States also have commercial bribery statutes. These laws prohibit offering or providing kickbacks and similar payoffs to private parties in order to secure some commercial advantage.

RICO
When Congress passed the Racketeer Influenced and Corrupt Organizations Act (RICO) as part of the Organized Crime Control Act of 1970, lawmakers were primarily concerned about organized crime's increasing entry into legitimate business enterprises. RICO's broad language, however, allows the statute to be applied in a wide variety of cases having nothing to do with organized crime. As a result, RICO has become one of the most controversial pieces of legislation affecting business. Supporters of RICO argue that it is an effective and much-needed tool for attacking unethical business practices. Its critics, however, see RICO as an overbroad statute that needlessly taints business reputations. Critics also argue that RICO has operated unduly to favor plaintiffs in civil litigation rather than serving as an aid to law enforcement.

Criminal RICO Under RICO, it is a federal crime for any person to (1) use income derived from a "pattern of racketeering activity" to acquire an interest in, establish, or operate an enterprise; (2) acquire or maintain an interest in an enterprise through a pattern of racketeering activity; (3) conduct or participate in, through a pattern of racketeering activity, the affairs of an enterprise by which he is employed or with which he is affiliated; or (4) conspire to do any of the preceding acts.

RICO is a compound statute because it requires proof of "predicate" criminal offenses that constitute the necessary pattern of racketeering activity. *Racketeering*

The Global Business Environment

At varying times since the 1977 enactment of the Foreign Corrupt Practices Act, the United States has advocated the development of international agreements designed to combat bribery and similar forms of corruption on at least a regional, if not a global, scale. These efforts and those of other nations sharing similar views bore fruit during the past decade.

In 1996, the Organization of American States (OAS) adopted the Inter-American Convention Against Corruption (IACAC). When it ratified the IACAC in September 2000, the United States joined 20 other subscribing OAS nations. The IACAC prohibits the offering or giving of a bribe to a government official in order to influence the official's actions, the solicitation or receipt of such a bribe, and certain other forms of corruption on the part of government officials. It requires subscribing nations to make changes in their domestic laws, in order to make those laws consistent with the IACAC. The United States has taken the position that given the content of the Foreign Corrupt Practices Act and other U.S. statutes prohibiting the offering and solicitation of bribes as well as various other forms of corruption, its statutes already are consistent with the IACAC.

The Organization for Economic Cooperation and Development (OECD) is made up of 29 nations that are leading exporters. In 1997, the OECD adopted the Convention on Combating Bribery of Officials in International Business Transactions. The OECD Convention, subscribed to by the United States, 28 other OECD member nations, and five nonmember nations, prohibits the offering or giving of a bribe to a government official in order to obtain a business advantage from the official's action or inaction. It calls for subscribing nations to have domestic laws that contain such a prohibition. Unlike the IACAC, however, the OECD neither prohibits the government official's solicitation or receipt of a bribe nor contains provisions dealing with the other forms of official corruption contemplated by the IACAC.

In 1999, the Council of Europe adopted the Criminal Law Convention on Corruption, which calls upon European Union (EU) member nations to develop domestic laws prohibiting the same sorts of behaviors prohibited by the IACAC. Many European Union members have signed on to this convention, as have three nonmembers of the EU. One of those is the United States.

Because the IACAC, the OECD Convention, and the Criminal Law Convention are relatively recent developments, it is too early to determine whether they have been effective international instruments for combating bribery and similar forms of corruption. Much will depend upon whether the domestic laws contemplated by these conventions are enforced with consistency and regularity.

activity includes the commission of any of more than 30 state or federal criminal offenses. Although most offenses that qualify (e.g., arson, gambling, extortion) have no relation to normal business transactions, such offenses as mail and wire fraud, securities fraud, and bribery are also included. Thus, many forms of business fraud may be alleged to be a racketeering activity. To show a *pattern* of such activity, the prosecution must first prove the defendant's commission of at least two acts of racketeering activity within a 10-year period. The pattern requirement also calls for proof that these acts are related and amount to, or pose the threat of, continuing racketeering activity. Most courts have interpreted the statutory term *enterprise* broadly, so that it includes partnerships and unincorporated associations as well as corporations.

Individuals found guilty of RICO violations are subject to substantial fines and imprisonment for up to 20 years. In addition, RICO violators risk the forfeiture of any interest gained in any enterprise as a result of a violation, as well as forfeiture of property derived from the prohibited racketeering activity. To prevent defendants from hiding assets that may be forfeitable upon conviction, federal prosecutors may seek pretrial orders freezing a defendant's assets. Some RICO critics argue that the harm such a freeze may work on a defendant's ability to conduct business, coupled with the threat of forfeiture of most or all of the business upon conviction, has led some defendants to make plea bargains rather than risk all by fighting prosecutions they believe to be unjustified.

Civil RICO   Under RICO, the government may also seek various civil penalties for violations. These include divestiture of a defendant's interest in an enterprise, dissolution or reorganization of the enterprise, and injunctions against future racketeering activities.

RICO's most controversial sections, however, allow private individuals to recover treble damages (three times their actual loss) and attorney's fees for injuries caused by a statutory violation. To qualify for recovery under RICO, a plaintiff must prove that the defendant violated RICO's provisions (as explained above) and that the plaintiff was "injured in his business or property by reason of" the RICO violation. In the *Anza* case, which appears shortly, the Supreme Court emphasizes the direct causation link that must exist between the RICO violation and the harm experienced by the plaintiff.

Aided by the Supreme Court's refusal, in *Sedima, S.P.R.L. v. Imrex Co.* (1985), to give a narrowing construction to the broadly phrased RICO, private plaintiffs have brought a large number of civil RICO cases in recent years. In *Sedima,* the Court rejected, as an erroneous statutory interpretation, some lower federal courts' approach of requiring civil RICO plaintiffs to prove that the defendant had actually been criminally convicted of a predicate offense. The Court also rejected the argument that civil RICO plaintiffs should be expected to prove a "distinct racketeering injury" as a precondition of recovery. The Court acknowledged lower courts' concern about RICO's breadth and noted the fact that most civil RICO cases are filed against legitimate businesses rather than against "the archetypal, intimidating mobster." Nevertheless, the Court observed that "[t]his defect—if defect it is—is inherent in the statute as written, and its correction must lie with Congress."

Various RICO reform proposals have been unsuccessfully introduced in Congress. A 1995 reform measure that did become law, however, established that a civil RICO case cannot be based on conduct that would have been actionable as securities fraud unless the conduct amounting to securities fraud had resulted in a criminal conviction.

Anza v. Ideal Steel Supply Corp.   547 U.S. 451 (U.S. Sup. Ct. 2006)

Ideal Steel Supply Corporation sold steel mill products along with related supplies and services. National Steel Supply, Inc., owned by Joseph and Vincent Anza, was Ideal's principal competitor. Both Ideal and National had stores in New York City. Ideal sued the Anzas and National (often referred to below as "the petitioners") in federal district court in New York. Ideal based its claim on the Racketeer Influenced and Corrupt Organizations Act (RICO), 18 U.S.C. §§ 1961–1968. In § 1962, RICO prohibits certain conduct involving a "pattern of racketeering activity." RICO's § 1964(c) recognizes a private right of action in favor of "[a]ny person injured in his business or property by reason of a violation" of the statute's substantive restrictions.

In its complaint, Ideal alleged that National had adopted a practice of failing to charge the requisite New York sales tax to cash-paying customers. This practice supposedly allowed National to reduce its prices without affecting its profit margin. Ideal asserted that the petitioners submitted fraudulent tax returns to the New York State Department of Taxation and Finance in an effort to conceal their conduct. According to Ideal's complaint, the petitioners' submission of the fraudulent tax returns constituted various acts of mail fraud (when they sent the returns by mail) and wire fraud (when they sent the returns electronically). Mail fraud and wire fraud are forms of "racketeering activity," according to RICO's § 1961. Ideal contended that the petitioners' conduct amounted to a "pattern of racketeering activity" because the fraudulent returns were submitted on an ongoing and regular basis. In particular, Ideal claimed that the petitioners violated RICO's § 1962(c), which makes it unlawful for "any person employed by or associated with any enterprise engaged in, or the activities of which affect, interstate or foreign commerce, to conduct or participate, directly or indirectly, in the conduct of such enterprise's affairs through a pattern of racketeering activity or collection of unlawful debt." The complaint asserted that the allegedly unlawful racketeering scheme gave National a competitive advantage over Ideal in terms of sales and market share, and that Ideal had therefore been injured "by reason of" the scheme for purposes of § 1964(c)'s private right of action.

Ruling that Ideal's complaint failed to state a claim upon which relief could be granted, the district court granted the petitioners' motion to dismiss the case. The U.S. Court of Appeals for the Second Circuit reversed, concluding that Ideal had adequately pleaded a causation link between the alleged pattern of racketeering activity and the harm experienced by Ideal. The U.S. Supreme Court granted certiorari at the petitioners' request.

Kennedy, Justice

RICO prohibits certain conduct involving a "pattern of racketeering activity." One of RICO's enforcement mechanisms is a private right of action, available to "[a]ny person injured in his business or property by reason of a violation" of the Act's substantive restrictions. § 1964(c). In *Holmes v. Securities Investor Protection Corp.*, 503 U.S. 258 (1992), this Court held that a plaintiff may sue under § 1964(c) only if the alleged RICO violation was the proximate cause of the plaintiff's injury. The instant case requires us to apply the principles discussed in *Holmes* to a dispute between two competing businesses.

Our analysis begins—and, as will become evident, largely ends—with *Holmes*. That case arose from a complaint filed by the Securities Investor Protection Corporation (SIPC), a private corporation with a duty to reimburse the customers of registered broker-dealers who became unable to meet their financial obligations. SIPC claimed that Robert Holmes conspired with others to manipulate stock prices. When the market detected the fraud, the share prices plummeted, and the "decline caused [two] broker-dealers' financial difficulties resulting in their eventual liquidation and SIPC's advance of nearly $13 million to cover their customers' claims." SIPC sued on several theories, including that Holmes participated in the conduct of an enterprise's affairs through a pattern of racketeering activity in violation of § 1962(c) and conspired to do so in violation of § 1962(d).

The Court held that SIPC could not maintain its RICO claims against Holmes for his alleged role in the scheme. The decision relied on a careful interpretation of § 1964(c), which provides a civil cause of action to persons injured "by reason of" a defendant's RICO violation. The Court recognized that the phrase "by reason of" could be read broadly to require merely that the claimed violation was a "but for" cause of the plaintiff's injury. It rejected this reading, however, noting the

"unlikelihood that Congress meant to allow all factually injured plaintiffs to recover." Proper interpretation of § 1964(c) required consideration of the statutory history, which [caused the *Holmes* Court to conclude that § 1964(c)'s "by reason of" language called for private plaintiffs to prove that the defendants' violations directly caused the plaintiffs' harm and thus were the "proximate cause" thereof].

The *Holmes* Court turned to the common-law foundations of the proximate-cause requirement, and specifically the "demand for some direct relation between the injury asserted and the injurious conduct alleged." It concluded that [SIPC's] RICO claims could not satisfy this requirement of directness. The deficiency, the Court explained, was that "the link is too remote between the stock manipulation alleged and the customers' harm, being purely contingent on the harm suffered by the broker-dealers."

Applying the principles of *Holmes* to the present case, we conclude Ideal cannot maintain its claim based on § 1962(c). [That section], as noted above, forbids conducting or participating in the conduct of an enterprise's affairs through a pattern of racketeering activity. The Court has indicated that the compensable injury flowing from a violation of that provision "necessarily is the harm caused by predicate acts sufficiently related to constitute a pattern, for the essence of the violation is the commission of those acts in connection with the conduct of an enterprise." [Case citation omitted.]

Ideal's theory is that Joseph and Vincent Anza harmed it by defrauding the New York tax authority and using the proceeds from the fraud to offer lower prices designed to attract more customers. The RICO violation alleged by Ideal is that the Anzas conducted National's affairs through a pattern of mail fraud and wire fraud. The direct victim of this conduct was the State of New York, not Ideal. It was the State that was being defrauded and the state that lost tax revenue as a result.

To be sure, Ideal asserts it suffered its own harms when the Anzas failed to charge customers for the applicable sales tax. The cause of Ideal's asserted harms, however, is a set of actions (offering lower prices) entirely distinct from the alleged RICO violation (defrauding the state). The attenuation between the plaintiff's harms and the claimed RICO violation arises from a different source in this case than in *Holmes,* where the alleged violations were linked to the asserted harms only through the broker-dealers' inability to meet their financial obligations. Nevertheless, the absence of proximate causation is equally clear in both cases.

This conclusion is confirmed by considering the directness requirement's underlying premises. One motivating principle is the difficulty that can arise when a court attempts to ascertain the damages caused by some remote action. [As noted in *Holmes,*] "the less direct an injury is, the more difficult it becomes to ascertain the amount of a plaintiff's damages attributable to the violation, as distinct from other, independent, factors." The instant case is illustrative. The injury Ideal alleges is its own loss of sales resulting from National's decreased prices for cash-paying customers. National, however, could have lowered its prices for any number of reasons unconnected to the asserted pattern of fraud. It may have received a cash inflow from some other source or concluded that the additional sales would justify a smaller profit margin. Its lowering of prices in no sense required it to defraud the state tax authority. Likewise, the fact that a company commits tax fraud does not mean the company will lower its prices; the additional cash could go anywhere from asset acquisition to research and development to dividend payouts.

There is . . . a second discontinuity between the RICO violation and the asserted injury. Ideal's lost sales could have resulted from factors other than petitioners' alleged acts of fraud. Businesses lose and gain customers for many reasons, and it would require a complex assessment to establish what portion of Ideal's lost sales were the product of National's decreased prices.

The attenuated connection between Ideal's injury and the Anzas' injurious conduct thus implicates fundamental concerns expressed in *Holmes*. [A further problem] is the speculative nature of the proceedings that would follow if Ideal were permitted to maintain its claim. A court considering the claim would need to begin by calculating the portion of National's price drop attributable to the alleged pattern of racketeering activity. It next would have to calculate the portion of Ideal's lost sales attributable to the relevant part of the price drop. The element of proximate causation recognized in *Holmes* is meant to prevent these types of intricate, uncertain inquiries from overrunning RICO litigation.

The requirement of a direct causal connection is especially warranted where the immediate victims of an alleged RICO violation can be expected to vindicate the laws by pursuing their own claims. [As stated in *Holmes,*] "directly injured victims can generally be counted on to vindicate the law as private attorneys general, without any of the problems attendant upon suits by plaintiffs injured more remotely." [Here,] Ideal accuses the Anzas of defrauding the State of New York out of a substantial amount of money. If the allegations are true, the state can be expected to pursue appropriate remedies. The adjudication of the state's claims, moreover, would be relatively straightforward; while it may be difficult to determine facts such as the number of sales Ideal lost due to National's tax practices, it is considerably easier to make the initial calculation of how much tax revenue the Anzas withheld from the state. There is no need to broaden the universe of actionable harms to permit RICO suits by parties who have been injured only indirectly.

The Court of Appeals [reasoned] that because the Anzas allegedly sought to gain a competitive advantage over Ideal, it is immaterial whether they took an indirect route to accomplish their goal. This rationale does not accord with *Holmes*. A RICO plaintiff cannot circumvent the proximate-cause requirement simply by claiming that the defendant's aim was to increase market share at a competitor's expense. When a court evaluates a RICO claim for proximate causation, the central question it must ask is whether the alleged violation led directly to the plaintiff's injuries. In the instant case, the answer is no.

Second Circuit's judgment reversed and case remanded for further proceedings.

Computer Crime

As computers have come to play an increasingly important role in our society, new opportunities for crime have arisen. In some instances, computers may be used to accomplish crimes such as theft, embezzlement, espionage, and fraud. In others, computers or the information stored there may be targets of crimes such as unauthorized access, vandalism, tampering, or theft of services. The law's response to computer crimes has evolved with this new technology. For example, computer hacking—once viewed by some as a mischievous but clever activity—can now lead to significant prison sentences and fines.

CYBERLAW IN ACTION

Does the federal Computer Fraud and Abuse Act provide a basis for a lawsuit when the defendant allegedly misappropriated trade secret information from a database owned by the plaintiff? In *Garelli Wong & Associates, Inc. v. Nichols*, 2008 U.S. Dist. LEXIS 3288 (N.D. Ill. 2008), the court gave "no" as the answer.

Garelli Wong, a provider of accounting and financial personnel services, created a database containing confidential client tracking information. The firm took steps to maintain the confidentiality of the information and thereby obtain the competitive advantage that the information provided. The case arose when William Nichols, a former employee of Garelli Wong and a corporation that had later acquired the firm, allegedly used some of the confidential information in the database after he had taken a job with a competing firm. Nichols's supposed use of the information allegedly breached a contract he had entered into with Garelli Wong when he was employed there. Garelli Wong and the successor corporation sued Nichols in federal court, contending that his actions violated the Consumer Fraud and Abuse Act (CFAA), 18 U.S.C. § 1030 *et seq.*, and constituted breach of contract in violation of state common law. Nichols moved to dismiss the plaintiffs' CFAA claim because of a supposed failure to state a claim upon which relief could be granted.

Section 1030(a)(5) of the CFAA calls for liability to be imposed on one who:

(5)(A)(i) knowingly causes the transmission of . . . information . . . and as a result of such conduct, intentionally causes damage without authorization, to a protected computer;

(ii) intentionally accesses a protected computer without authorization, and as a result of such conduct, recklessly causes damage; or

(iii) intentionally accesses a protected computer without authorization, and as a result of such conduct, causes damage . . . ; and

(5)(B)(i) by conduct described in clause (i), (ii), or (iii) of subparagraph (A), caused . . . loss to 1 or more persons during any 1-year period . . . aggregating at least $5,000 in value.

The court noted that in view of the above language, a plaintiff must properly plead both *damage* and *loss* in order to allege a civil CFAA violation. A definition section of the CFAA defines *damage* as "impairment to the integrity or availability of data, a program, a system, or information." Applying these definitions, the court agreed with Nichols that even if he used information in the database, he did not impair the integrity or availability of the information or the database. Accordingly, the court held that the CFAA does not extend to cases in which trade secret information is merely used—even if in violation of a contract or state trade secret law—because such conduct by itself does not constitute *damage* as that term is defined in the CFAA. Because the plaintiffs could not properly allege damage, their CFAA claim was subject to dismissal regardless of whether they had properly pleaded loss.

With the CFAA claim having been dismissed, the court agreed with Nichols that the basis for federal court jurisdiction was gone and that the plaintiff's state law–based claim for breach of contract should also be dismissed. The plaintiffs' recourse, then, would be to refile the breach of contract claim in a state court, perhaps along with a misappropriation of trade secret claim under state law. (For more information on misappropriation of trade secret claims, see Chapter 8.)

The technical nature of computer crime complicates its detection and prosecution. Traditional criminal statutes have often proven inadequate because they tend not to address explicitly the types of crime associated with the use of computers. Assume, for example, that a general statute on theft defines the offense in terms of stealing "property," and that the defendant is charged with violating the statute by taking and using computer data without authorization. The court could decide to dismiss this case if categorizing data stored in a computer as "property" strikes the court as a strained interpretation of the statute. Although some courts have interpreted existing criminal laws narrowly so as to exclude instances of computer abuse, other courts have construed them more broadly. In light of the uncertainties attending statutory

interpretation, legislatures on the state and federal levels have become increasingly aware of the need to revise their criminal codes to be certain that they explicitly cover computer crime.

Almost all states have now enacted criminal statutes specifically outlawing certain abuses of computers. Common provisions prohibit such acts as obtaining access to a computer system without authorization, tampering with files or causing damage to a system (e.g., by spreading a virus or deleting files), invading the privacy of others, using a computer to commit fraud or theft, and trafficking in passwords or access codes.

On the federal level, computer crime has been prosecuted with some success under existing federal statutes, primarily those forbidding mail fraud, wire fraud, transportation of stolen property, and thefts of property. As has been true at the state level, successful prosecution of these cases often depends on broad interpretation of the statutory prerequisites. Another federal law deals more directly with improper uses of computers. Among the crimes covered by this federal statute are intentionally gaining unauthorized access to a computer used by or for the U.S. government, trafficking in passwords and other access devices, and using a computer to obtain government information that is protected from disclosure. It is also a crime to gain unauthorized access to the computer system of a private financial institution that has a connection with the federal government (such as federal insurance for the deposits in the financial institution). In addition, the statute criminalizes the transmission of codes, commands, or information if the transmission was intended to damage such an institution's computers, computer system, data, or programs.

The federal Computer Fraud and Abuse Act (CFAA) allows the imposition of criminal and civil liability on one who "knowingly, and with intent to defraud, accesses a protected computer without authorization, or exceeds authorized access, and by means of such conduct furthers the intended fraud and obtains anything of value." In addition, the CFAA provides that criminal and civil liability may attach to one who transmits a program, information, code, or command knowingly, intentionally, and without authorization, if the act results in damage to a computer system used by the government or a financial institution or otherwise in interstate commerce. For a case applying the CFAA, see the nearby Cyberlaw in Action box.

Problems and Problem Cases

1. Ahmad Ressam attempted to enter the United States by car ferry at Port Angeles, Washington. Hidden in his rental car's trunk were explosives that he intended to detonate at the Los Angeles International Airport. After the ferry docked, a customs official questioned Ressam. On the customs declaration form the official instructed Ressam to complete, Ressam identified himself on the form by a false name and falsely referred to himself as a Canadian citizen even though he was Algerian. Ressam was then directed to a secondary inspection station, where another official performed a search of his car. This search uncovered explosives and related items in the car's spare tire well. Ressam was later convicted of a number of crimes, including the felony of making a false statement to a United States customs official, in violation of 18 U.S.C. § 1001, and the offense of carrying an explosive "during the commission of" the just-noted felony, in violation of 18 U.S.C. § 844(h)(2). The latter offense was "Count 9" in the indictment against Ressam. The U.S. Court of Appeals for the Ninth Circuit set aside Ressam's conviction on Count 9 because it interpreted the word "during," as used in § 844(h)(2), as including an implicit requirement that the explosive be carried *in relation to* the underlying felony. The Ninth Circuit concluded that because Ressam's carrying of explosives did not relate to the underlying felony of making a false statement to a customs official, the conviction on Count 9 could not stand. Did the Ninth Circuit correctly interpret the "during the commission of" language in the statute on which Count 9 was based?

2. An informant told the Eagan, Minnesota, police that while walking past the window of a ground-floor apartment, he had observed people putting a white powder into bags. Officer Thielen went to the apartment building to investigate. He looked in the window through a gap in the closed blind and observed the bagging operation for several minutes. When two men left the building in a previously identified Cadillac, other police officers stopped the car. While one of the car's doors was open, the officers observed a black zippered pouch and a handgun on the floor of the vehicle. The officers arrested the car's occupants, Carter and Johns. A later search of the vehicle resulted in the discovery of pagers, a scale, and 47 grams of cocaine in plastic baggies. After seizing the car, the officers returned to the apartment and arrested its occupant, Thompson. A search of the apartment (conducted on the basis of a warrant) revealed cocaine residue on the kitchen table and plastic baggies similar to those found in the Cadillac. Officer Thielen identified Carter, Johns, and Thompson as the persons he had observed taking part in the bagging operation. It was later learned that Thompson was the apartment's lessee and that Carter and Johns, both of whom lived in Chicago, had come to the apartment for the sole purpose of packaging the cocaine. Carter and Johns had never been to the apartment before and were in the apartment for approximately two and one-half hours

at the general time the bagging operation was conducted. In return for the use of the apartment, Carter and Johns had given some of the cocaine to Thompson. Carter and Johns were charged with controlled substance–related crimes. Prior to trial, they moved to suppress all evidence obtained from the apartment and the Cadillac. They contended that Officer Thielen's observation of them through the apartment window was an unreasonable search in violation of the Fourth Amendment and that all evidence obtained as a result was inadmissible. Were Carter and Johns entitled to claim the protection of the Fourth Amendment?

3. A federal grand jury was investigating "John Doe," president and sole shareholder of "XYZ" corporation, concerning possible violations of federal securities and money-laundering statutes. During the investigation, the government learned that XYZ had paid the bills for various telephone lines, including those used in Doe's homes and car. Grand jury subpoenas calling for the production of documents were then served on the custodian of XYZ's corporate records, on Doe, and on the law firm Paul, Weiss, Rifkind, Wharton & Garrison (Paul–Weiss), which represented Doe. These subpoenas sought production of telephone bills, records, and statements of account regarding certain telephone numbers, including those used by Doe. The District Court determined after an evidentiary hearing that the documents sought were XYZ's, and not Doe's.

   Paul–Weiss, which had received copies of these documents from its client, refused to produce them, arguing that it was exempted from doing so by Doe's privilege against self-incrimination. Was Paul–Weiss correct in its assertion?

4. Dow Chemical Company operated a 2,000-acre chemical manufacturing facility at Midland, Michigan. The facility consisted of numerous covered buildings, with manufacturing equipment and piping conduits between various buildings plainly visible from the air. Dow maintained elaborate security around the perimeter of the complex to bar ground-level public views of these areas. It also investigated any low level flights by aircraft over the facility. Dow did not, however, attempt to conceal all manufacturing equipment within the complex from aerial views because the cost would have been prohibitive. With Dow's consent, enforcement officials of the Environmental Protection Agency (EPA) made an on-site inspection of two power plants in this complex. When Dow denied EPA's request for another inspection, EPA did not seek an administrative search warrant. Instead, EPA employed a commercial aerial photographer, who used a standard floor-mounted, precision aerial mapping camera to take photographs of the facility from altitudes of 12,000, 3,000, and 1,200 feet. At all times, the aircraft was lawfully within navigable airspace. EPA did not inform Dow of this aerial photography. Was EPA's taking of aerial photographs of the Dow complex a search prohibited by the Fourth Amendment?

5. Sun-Diamond Growers of California was a trade association engaged in marketing and lobbying activities on behalf of its member cooperatives, which were owned by 5,000 producers of raisins, figs, walnuts, prunes, and hazelnuts. A federal grand jury indicted Sun-Diamond for an alleged violation of the illegal gratuity statute, 18 U.S.C. § 201(1)(A), which criminalizes a private party's giving of "anything of value" to a public official "for or because of any official act performed or to be performed" by the public official. According to the indictment, Sun-Diamond violated the statute by giving then-Secretary of Agriculture Michael Espy gratuities valued at approximately $5,900 (tickets to the U.S. Open Tennis Tournament, luggage, meals, a framed print, and a crystal bowl). The indictment alluded to two Department of Agriculture–related matters in which Sun-Diamond had an interest in favorable treatment at the time Sun-Diamond gave the gifts to Secretary Espy. Nevertheless, the indictment did not allege a specific connection between either of the two matters and Sun-Diamond's conferral of the gifts. A federal district court jury found Sun-Diamond guilty. Holding that the district judge erred in instructing the jury that "it is sufficient if Sun-Diamond provided Espy with unauthorized compensation simply because he held public office," the U.S. Court of Appeals for the District of Columbia Circuit reversed and remanded. The U.S. Supreme Court granted certiorari. How did the Supreme Court rule?

6. Border Patrol Agent Cesar Cantu boarded a bus in Texas to check the immigration status of its passengers. As he walked off the bus, he squeezed the soft luggage that passengers had placed in the storage racks above their seats. After squeezing a green canvas bag belonging to Steven DeWayne Bond, Cantu concluded that it contained a "brick-like" object. Bond allowed Cantu to open the bag. Upon doing so, Cantu found a "brick" of methamphetamine, which had been wrapped in duct tape and then

rolled in a pair of pants. Did Cantu's physical manipulation of Bond's luggage constitute an "unreasonable search and seizure" for purposes of the Fourth Amendment?

7. Cedric Kushner Promotions Ltd. (Kushner), a corporate promoter of boxing matches, sued Don King, the president and sole shareholder of a rival corporation, alleging that King had conducted his corporation's affairs in violation of § 1962(c) of the Racketeer Influenced and Corrupt Organizations Act. A federal district court dismissed the complaint. In affirming, the U.S. Court of Appeals for the Second Circuit expressed its view that § 1962(c) applies only where a plaintiff shows the existence of two separate entities, a "person" and a distinct "enterprise," whose affairs that "person" improperly conducts. It was undisputed that King was an employee of his corporation and was acting within the scope of his authority. Under the Second Circuit's analysis, King was part of the corporation rather than a "person" distinct from the "enterprise." In cases presenting similar facts, other federal courts of appeal had concluded that the sole shareholder of a corporation was a "person" distinct from the corporate "enterprise." Kushner appealed the Second Circuit's decision, and the U.S. Supreme Court granted certiorari. Which interpretation of § 1962(c) did the Supreme Court adopt—the Second Circuit's or the one followed by other federal courts of appeal?

8. Muniz was arrested on a charge of driving under the influence of alcohol. He was taken to a booking center, where he was asked several questions by a police officer without first being given the *Miranda* warnings. Videotape (which included an audio portion) was used to record the questions and Muniz's answers. The officer asked Muniz his name, address, height, weight, eye color, date of birth, and current age. Muniz stumbled over answers to two of these questions. The officer then asked Muniz the date of his sixth birthday, but Muniz did not give the correct date. At a later point, Muniz was read the *Miranda* warnings for the first time. He was later convicted of the charged offense, with the trial court denying his motion to exclude the videotape (both video and audio portions) from evidence. Assume that the video portion of the tape violated neither the Fifth Amendment nor *Miranda*. Should all or any part of the audio portion of the tape (which contained Muniz's stumbling responses to two questions plus his incorrect answer to the sixth birthday date question) have been

excluded as a violation of either the Fifth Amendment or *Miranda?*

9. Explorica, Inc., was founded to compete with EF Cultural Travel, which dominated the market in global tours for high school students. Setting Explorica's tour prices lower than EF's became an important Explorica objective. EF's tour prices were accessible through the firm's Web site, where the user who desired information would enter various price-determining factors, such as desired date of departure and destination. The Web site would translate the user's preferences to a special code, decipherable only by the site's servers and human operators, and would submit the code to the server. The server would determine travel options and prices suited to the user's specifications, and then send them to the user's computer. In view of the large number of possible factor combinations that a user might submit to EF, Explorica realized that manually obtaining price information on every tour that EF could offer would be nearly impossible. Explorica therefore wrote a "scraper" program, using code information provided by Explorica Vice President Phil Gormley, a former employee of EF. The scraper automatically submitted codes representing all possible factor combinations to EF's server and then recorded the results in a spreadsheet. Explorica's use of the scraper resulted in a compilation of 60,000 lines—the rough equivalent of eight telephone books—of data. Explorica used this information to undercut EF's prices. When EF learned of Explorica's actions, EF sued Explorica, alleging civil violations of the Computer Fraud and Abuse Act (CFAA). Section 1030(a)(4) of the CFAA is violated when a person "knowingly, and with intent to defraud, accesses a protected computer without authorization, or exceeds authorized access, and by means of such conduct furthers the intended fraud and obtains anything of value." EF sought a preliminary injunction that would bar further use of the scraper and would require the return of all materials generated by the scraper. Was EF entitled to the preliminary injunction?

10. Notra Trulock served as Director of the Office of Intelligence of the U.S. Department of Energy (DOE) from 1994 to 1998. During those years, Trulock claimed to have uncovered evidence that Chinese spies had infiltrated U.S. weapons facilities and that the White House, the Federal Bureau of Investigation (FBI), and the Central Intelligence Agency (CIA) had ignored his warnings about the espionage.

Trulock testified before congressional committees on this subject and, after he no longer worked for the DOE, published a related article that criticized the White House, the FBI, and the CIA. Trulock contended that he did not reveal any classified information in the article. Linda Conrad, a DOE employee, owned a townhouse at which she and Trulock lived. After Trulock had left the DOE, Conrad's DOE supervisor told her that FBI agents wanted to talk with her about Trulock, that the FBI had a warrant to search her townhouse, and that if she did not cooperate, FBI agents would break down the townhouse's door while the press observed. Conrad submitted to a three-hour interview by FBI agents, who asked about Trulock's personal records and computer files. Conrad told the agents that she and Trulock shared a computer, which was located at the townhouse. She also said that she and Trulock maintained separate password-protected files on the computer's hard drive, and that neither knew the other's password. At the end of the interview, Conrad signed a form whose terms revealed her supposed consent to a search of the townhouse. The agents said nothing to Conrad about whether they had, or did not have, a search warrant. In fact, they did not have one.

The agents searched the townhouse pursuant to Conrad's supposed consent and without seeking Trulock's permission. During the search, the agents found the computer Conrad had mentioned. Aided by an FBI computer specialist, an agent examined the computer's files, including Trulock's password-protected files. In a civil action in which they alleged that the FBI had acted unconstitutionally, Conrad and Trulock contended that their Fourth Amendment rights had been violated. Was Conrad's supposed consent to the search of the townhouse valid and hence sufficient to defeat *her* claim of a Fourth Amendment violation? If Conrad legitimately consented to the search, was her consent binding on *Trulock* with regard to the FBI agents' (a) search of the townhouse itself, (b) examination of computer files to which both Conrad and Trulock had access, and (c) examination of Trulock's password-protected computer files?

11. A grand jury indicted Automated Medical Laboratories, Inc. (AML), Richmond Plasma Corporation (RPC) (a wholly owned AML subsidiary), and three former RPC managers for engaging in a conspiracy that included falsification of logbooks and records required to be maintained by businesses producing blood plasma. The falsification was designed to conceal from the Food and Drug Administration (FDA) various violations of federal regulations governing the plasmapheresis process and facilities. The evidence introduced at trial indicated that the managers and several other members of the team charged with ensuring compliance with FDA regulations had actively participated in record falsification. AML was convicted and appealed on the ground that there was no evidence that any officer or director of AML knowingly or willfully participated in or authorized the unlawful practices at RPC. Was AML's conviction in the absence of such proof proper?

12. While under arrest for an unrelated offense, Raymond Levi Cobb confessed to a home burglary, but denied knowledge relating to the disappearance of a woman and child from the home. Cobb was indicted on a charge of burglary, and an attorney was appointed to represent him. Later, while Cobb was out on bond, Cobb's father informed police that Cobb had confessed to him that he (Cobb) had murdered the woman and child. Police then took Cobb into custody. Cobb waived his *Miranda* rights, confessed to the murders, and led officers to the place where the bodies were buried. He appealed his consequent conviction and death sentence, arguing that because police had not secured the permission of his attorney from the burglary case before conducting the interrogation regarding the murders, his confession should have been suppressed. Was he correct?

Online Research

Wire Fraud

According to the federal wire fraud statute, it is a criminal offense to use interstate wires to carry out "any scheme or artifice to defraud, or for obtaining money or property by means of false or fraudulent pretenses." Can a plot to deprive the Canadian government of tax revenue violate this statute if the plot is hatched in the United States through the use of telephones? The U.S. Supreme Court answered this question in a 2005 decision. Use an online source to locate this decision. After reading the case, prepare a case brief of the sort described in the Appendix to Chapter 1.

chapter 6

INTENTIONAL TORTS

"The Mating Habits of the Suburban High School Teenager" served as the headline for a *Boston* magazine article that addressed sexuality and promiscuity among teenagers in the Boston area. An accompanying subheading, which appeared in lettering smaller than that used for the headline, read this way: "They hook up online. They hook up in real life. With prom season looming, meet your kids—they might know more about sex than you do."

According to the article, sexual experimentation had become increasingly common among high school students in recent years, with today's teenagers being both "sexually advanced" and "sexually daring." The author wrote that it had become common for "single boys and girls with nothing to do [to] go in a group to a friend's house . . . drink or smoke pot, then pair off and engage in no-strings hookups." Concerning the supposed prevalence of sexual promiscuity, the author quoted a teenager as saying that "everybody's having casual sex and pretty much everybody's doing it with multiple partners." Throughout the article, the author included excerpts from her interviews with Boston-area students about their sexual experiences and views on sexuality.

A large photograph accompanied the beginning portion of the article. The photograph, which took up a full page plus part of a facing page, showed five formally attired students standing near an exit door at a high school prom. Three students were smoking cigarettes, and a fourth was drinking from a plastic cup. The fifth student, Stacey Stanton, was looking in the direction of the camera with an apparently friendly expression. Her face and a portion of her body were readily visible. She wore a formal dress and was neither smoking nor drinking. Beneath the headlines and the article's opening text, and on the same page as the large photograph, there appeared the following caption and disclaimer: *"The photos on these pages are from an award-winning five-year project on teen sexuality by photojournalist Dan Habib. The individuals pictured are unrelated to the people or events described in this story. The names of the teenagers interviewed for the story have been changed."* Of the type sizes used on the page, the one used for the caption and disclaimer was the smallest. Other pictures that did not depict Stanton accompanied later portions of the article.

Stanton, who was not named in the article, neither consented to the use of the large photograph nor participated in Habib's supposed "project on teen sexuality." She filed suit against Metro Corporation, the publisher of *Boston* magazine. According to Stanton's complaint, the juxtaposition of the large photograph and the article created the false impression that she was a person engaged in the activities described in the article. Therefore, Stanton contended that she had been the victim of defamation. She also regarded the caption's reference to "project on teen sexuality" as having created the false and defamatory impression that she had participated in the project. Moreover, Stanton contended that the publication of the large photograph amounted to an invasion of her privacy.

The federal district court, however, ruled that Stanton had stated neither a valid defamation claim nor a valid invasion of privacy claim. Therefore, the court granted Metro's motion to dismiss Stanton's complaint. Stanton then appealed.

As you read Chapter 6, decide whether you agree with the district court's ruling on the defamation and invasion of privacy claims, and identify the reasons why or why not. Then make a prediction about how the appellate court ruled. Regardless of your conclusion on whether Stanton alleged valid defamation and invasion of privacy claims, think about this question: Did *Boston* magazine personnel act *ethically* in connection with the use of the large photograph, the caption, and the disclaimer? Be prepared to justify your position.

A **TORT** IS A *civil wrong* that is not a breach of a contract. Tort cases and treatises identify different types of wrongfulness, culpability, or fault and define them in varying ways. In this chapter and in Chapter 7, we will refer to the four types of wrongfulness defined below.

1. *Intent.* We define intent as the desire to cause certain consequences or the substantial certainty that those consequences will result from one's behavior. For example, if D pulls the trigger of a loaded handgun while aiming it at P for the purpose of killing him or with a substantial certainty that P would be killed, D intended to kill P. This chapter discusses several *intentional torts,* most of which require, as the name of this category of torts suggests, intent on the part of the defendant.

2. *Recklessness.* The form of intent involving substantial certainty blends by degrees into a different kind of fault: recklessness (sometimes called "willful and wanton conduct"). We define recklessness as a conscious indifference to a known and substantial risk of harm created by one's behavior. Suppose that simply because he likes the muzzle flash and the sound, D fires his handgun at random in a crowded subway station. One of D's shots injures P. D acted recklessly if he had no desire to hit P or anyone else and was not substantially certain that anyone would be hit, but nonetheless knew that this could easily result from his behavior. When legal responsibility is assigned in the civil context, recklessness is often treated as a near equivalent of intentional wrongdoing. Recklessness is considered a more severe degree of fault than the next type to be discussed: negligence.

3. *Negligence.* We define negligence as a failure to use reasonable care, with harm to another party occurring as a result. Negligent conduct falls below the level necessary to protect others against unreasonable risks of harm. Assume that without checking, D pulls the trigger on what he incorrectly and unreasonably thinks is an unloaded handgun. If the gun goes off and wounds P, D has negligently harmed P. Chapter 7 discusses negligence law in detail.

4. *Strict liability.* Strict liability is liability without fault or more precisely, liability irrespective of fault. In a strict liability case, the plaintiff need not prove intent, recklessness, negligence, or any other kind of wrongfulness on the defendant's part. However, strict liability is not automatic liability. A plaintiff must prove certain things in any strict liability case, but fault is not one of them. Chapter 7 discusses various types of strict liability, some of which are examined more fully in other chapters.

Tort law contemplates civil liability for those who commit torts. This distinguishes it from the criminal law, which also involves wrongful behavior. As you saw in Chapter 1, a civil case is normally a suit between private parties. In criminal cases, a prosecutor represents the government in confronting the defendant. The standard of proof that the plaintiff must satisfy in a tort case is the *preponderance of the evidence* standard, not the more stringent beyond-a-reasonable-doubt standard applied in criminal cases. This means that the greater weight of the evidence introduced at the trial must support the plaintiff's position on every element of the tort case. Finally, the remedy allowed in civil cases (most often, damages) differs from the punishment imposed in criminal cases (e.g., imprisonment or a fine). Of course, the same behavior may sometimes give rise to both civil and criminal liability. For example, one who commits a sexual assault is criminally liable and will also be liable for some or all of the torts of assault, battery, false imprisonment, and intentional infliction of emotional distress.

A plaintiff who wins a tort case usually recovers **compensatory damages** for the harm she suffered as a result of the defendant's wrongful act. Depending on the facts of the case, these damages may be for direct and immediate harms such as physical injuries, medical expenses, and lost wages and benefits, or for seemingly less tangible harms such as loss of privacy, injury to reputation, and emotional distress. If the defendant's behavior was particularly bad, injured victims may also be able to recover **punitive damages.** Punitive damages are not intended to compensate tort victims for their losses.

Instead, they are designed to punish flagrant wrongdoers and to deter them, as well as others, from engaging in similar conduct in the future. Punitive damages are reserved for the worst kinds of wrongdoing and thus are not routinely assessed against the losing defendant in a tort case. Certainly, however, some behaviors amounting to recklessness or giving rise to intentional tort liability are regarded as reprehensible enough to justify an assessment of punitive damages.

The *Mathias* case, which follows, reviews the types of fault discussed above and explains the role that punitive damages may play in certain cases.

Mathias v. Accor Economy Lodging, Inc.   347 F.3d 672 (7th Cir. 2003)

Burl and Desire Mathias were bitten by bedbugs when they stayed at a Motel 6 in downtown Chicago. They filed suit against the corporation that owns and operates the Motel 6 chain. Alleging that the defendant's personnel refused to act in response to the complaints of various guests and otherwise knowingly disregarded clear evidence of a bedbug infestation problem, the plaintiffs sought both compensatory and punitive damages on the theory that the defendant had engaged in "willful and wanton conduct." A federal court jury returned a verdict in favor of the Mathiases, awarding them compensatory damages for their injuries and assessing a punitive damages award against the defendant. On appeal to the U.S. Court of Appeals for the Seventh Circuit, the defendant argued that any fault on its part did not amount to willful and wanton conduct and that the award of punitive damages was therefore unwarranted. Further facts pertinent to the case are discussed in the edited version of the Seventh Circuit's opinion, which appears below.

Posner, Circuit Judge

[B]edbugs . . . are making a comeback in the U.S. as a consequence of more conservative use of pesticides. The plaintiffs claim that in allowing guests to be attacked by bedbugs in a motel that charges upwards of $100 a day for a room and would not like to be mistaken for a flophouse, the defendant was guilty of "willful and wanton conduct" and thus [should be] liable for punitive as well as compensatory damages. The jury agreed and awarded each plaintiff $186,000 in punitive damages, though only $5,000 in compensatory damages.

The defendant argues that at worst it is guilty of simple negligence, and if this is right the plaintiffs were not entitled . . . to any award of punitive damages. [The defendant] also complains that the [punitive damages] award was excessive. . . . The first complaint has no possible merit, as the evidence of . . . recklessness, in the strong sense of an unjustifiable failure to avoid a *known* risk, was amply shown. In 1998, EcoLab, the extermination service that the motel used, discovered bedbugs in several rooms in the motel and recommended that it be hired to spray every room, for which it would charge the motel only $500; the motel refused. The next year, bedbugs were again discovered in a room but EcoLab was asked to spray just that room. The motel tried to negotiate "a building sweep [by EcoLab] free of charge," but, not surprisingly, the negotiation failed. By the spring of 2000, the motel's manager "started noticing that there were refunds being given by my desk clerks and reports coming back from the guests that there were ticks in the rooms and bugs in the rooms that were biting." She looked in some of the rooms and discovered bedbugs. The defendant asks us to disregard her testimony as that of a disgruntled ex-employee,

but of course her credibility was for the jury, not the defendant, to determine.

Further incidents of guests being bitten by insects and demanding and receiving refunds led the manager to recommend to her superior in the company that the motel be closed while every room was sprayed, but this was refused. This superior, a district manager, was a management-level employee of the defendant, and his knowledge of the risk and failure to take effective steps either to eliminate it or to warn the motel's guests are imputed to his employer for purposes of determining whether the employer should be liable for punitive damages. The employer's liability for compensatory damages is of course automatic on the basis of the principle of *respondeat superior,* since the district manager was acting within the scope of his employment. [Under the *respondeat superior* principle, employers are liable for torts committed by employees if those torts occurred within the scope of employment.]

The infestation continued and began to reach farcical proportions, as when a guest, after complaining of having been bitten repeatedly by insects while asleep in his room in the hotel, was moved to another room only to discover insects there; and within 18 minutes of being moved to a third room he discovered insects in that room as well and had to be moved still again. (Odd that at that point he didn't flee the motel.) By July, the motel's management was acknowledging to EcoLab that there was a "major problem with bedbugs" and that all that was being done about it was "chasing them from room to room." Desk clerks were instructed to call the "bedbugs" "ticks," apparently on the theory that customers would be less alarmed, though in fact ticks are more dangerous than bedbugs because they spread Lyme Disease and Rocky Mountain Spotted Fever. Rooms that the motel had placed on "Do not rent, bugs in room" status nevertheless were rented.

It was in November that the plaintiffs checked into the motel. They were given Room 504, even though the motel had classified the room as "DO NOT RENT UNTIL TREATED," and it had not been treated. Indeed, that night 190 of the hotel's 191 rooms were occupied, even though a number of them had been placed on the same don't-rent status as Room 504.

Although bedbug bites are not as serious as the bites of some other insects, they are painful and unsightly. Motel 6 could not have rented any rooms at the prices it charged had it informed guests that the risk of being bitten by bedbugs was appreciable. Its failure either to warn guests or to take effective measures to eliminate the bedbugs amounted to fraud and probably to [the intentional tort of] battery as well. [See, for example,] the famous case of *Garratt v. Dailey*, 279 P.2d 1091 (Wash. Sup. Ct. 1955), [in which the court] held that the defendant would be guilty of battery if he knew with substantial certainty that when he moved a chair the plaintiff would try to sit down where the chair had been and would land on the floor instead. There was, in short, sufficient evidence of "willful and wanton conduct" [that is, of recklessness as opposed to mere negligence] to permit an award of punitive damages in this case.

But in what amount? In arguing that $20,000 was the maximum amount of punitive damages that a jury could constitutionally have awarded each plaintiff, the defendant points to the U.S. Supreme Court's recent statement that "few awards [of punitive damages] exceeding a single-digit ratio between punitive and compensatory damages, to a significant degree, will satisfy due process." *State Farm Mutual Automobile Insurance Co. v. Campbell,* 538 U.S. 408 (2003). The Court went on to suggest that "four times the amount of compensatory damages might be close to the line of constitutional impropriety." Hence the defendant's proposed ceiling in this case of $20,000, four times the compensatory damages awarded to each plaintiff. The ratio of punitive to compensatory damages determined by the jury was, in contrast, 37.2 to 1.

The Supreme Court did not, however, lay down a 4-to-1 or single-digit-ratio rule—it said merely that "there is a presumption against an award that has a 145-to-1 ratio"—and it would be unreasonable to do so. We must consider why punitive damages are awarded and why the Court has decided that due process requires that such awards be limited. The second question is easier to answer than the first. The term "punitive damages" implies punishment, and a standard principle of penal theory is that "the punishment should fit the crime" in the sense of being proportional to the wrongfulness of the defendant's action, though the principle is modified when the probability of

detection is very low (a familiar example is the heavy fines for littering) or the crime is potentially lucrative (as in the case of trafficking in illegal drugs).

Another penal precept is that a defendant should have reasonable notice of the sanction for unlawful acts, so that he can make a rational determination of how to act; and so there have to be reasonably clear standards for determining the amount of punitive damages for particular wrongs. [A] third precept, the core of the Aristotelian notion of corrective justice, and more broadly of the principle of the rule of law, is that sanctions should be based on the wrong done rather than on the status of the defendant; a person is punished for what he does, not for who he is, even if the who is a huge corporation.

What follows from these principles, however, is that punitive damages should be admeasured by standards or rules rather than in a completely ad hoc manner, and this does not tell us what the maximum ratio of punitive to compensatory damages should be in a particular case. To determine that, we have to consider why punitive damages are awarded in the first place.

England's common law courts first confirmed their authority to award punitive damages in the eighteenth century, at a time when the institutional structure of criminal law enforcement was primitive and it made sense to leave certain minor crimes to be dealt with by the civil law. And still today one function of punitive-damages awards is to relieve the pressures on an overloaded system of criminal justice by providing a civil alternative to criminal prosecution of minor crimes. An example is deliberately spitting in a person's face, a criminal assault but because minor readily deterrable by the levying of what amounts to a civil fine through a suit for damages for the tort of battery. Compensatory damages [unaccompanied by punitive damages] would not do the trick in such a case, . . . for three reasons: because [compensatory damages] are difficult to determine in the case of acts that inflict largely [dignity-related] harms; because in the spitting case [compensatory damages] would be too slight to give the victim an incentive to sue, and he might decide instead to respond with violence—and an age-old purpose of the law of torts is to provide a substitute for violent retaliation against wrongful injury; and because to limit the plaintiff to compensatory damages would enable the defendant to commit the offensive act with impunity provided that he was willing to pay.

When punitive damages are sought for billion-dollar oil spills and other huge economic injuries, the considerations that we have just canvassed fade. As the Court emphasized in *Campbell,* the fact that the plaintiffs in that case had been awarded very substantial compensatory damages—$1 million for a dispute over insurance coverage—greatly reduced the need for giving them a huge award of punitive damages ($145 million) as well in order to provide an effective remedy. Our case is closer to the spitting case. The defendant's behavior was outrageous but the compensable harm done was slight and at the same time difficult to quantify because a large element of it was emotional. And the defendant may well have profited from its misconduct because by concealing the infestation it was able to keep renting rooms. Refunds were frequent but may have cost less than the cost of closing the hotel for a thorough fumigation. The hotel's attempt to pass off the bedbugs as ticks, which some guests might ignorantly have thought less unhealthful, may have postponed the instituting of litigation to rectify the hotel's misconduct. The award of punitive damages in this case thus serves the additional purpose of limiting the defendant's ability to profit from its fraud by escaping detection and (private) prosecution. If a tortfeasor is "caught" only half the time he commits torts, then when he is caught he should be punished twice as heavily in order to make up for the times he gets away.

Finally, if the total stakes in the case were capped at $50,000 (2 × [$5,000 + $20,000]), the plaintiffs might well have had difficulty financing this lawsuit. It is here that the defendant's aggregate net worth of $1.6 billion becomes relevant. A defendant's wealth is not a sufficient basis for awarding punitive damages. *BMW of North America, Inc. v. Gore,* 517 U.S. 559 (1996). That would be discriminatory and would violate the rule of law, as we explained earlier, by making punishment depend on status rather than conduct. Where wealth in the sense of resources enters is in enabling the defendant to mount an extremely aggressive defense against suits such as this and by doing so to make litigating against it very costly, which in turn may make it difficult for the plaintiffs to find a lawyer willing to handle their case, involving as it does only modest stakes, for the usual 33–40 percent contingent fee. In other words, the defendant is investing in developing a reputation intended to deter plaintiffs. It is difficult otherwise to explain the great stubbornness with which it has defended this case, making a host of frivolous evidentiary arguments despite the very modest stakes even when the punitive damages awarded by the jury are included.

All things considered, we cannot say that the award of punitive damages was excessive, albeit the precise number chosen by the jury was arbitrary. It is probably not a coincidence that $5,000 + $186,000 = $191,000/191 = $1,000: that is, $1,000 per room in the hotel. But as there are no [rigid] punitive-damages guidelines, . . . it is inevitable that the specific amount of punitive damages awarded . . . will be arbitrary. (Which is perhaps why the plaintiffs' lawyer did not suggest a number to the jury.) The judicial function is to police a range, not a point.

But it would have been helpful had the parties presented evidence concerning the regulatory or criminal penalties to which the defendant exposed itself by deliberately exposing its customers to a substantial risk of being bitten by bedbugs. That is an inquiry recommended by the Supreme Court [in *Campbell*]. [However,] we do not think its omission invalidates the award. We can take judicial notice that deliberate exposure of hotel guests to the health risks created by insect infestations [potentially] exposes the hotel's owner to [criminal fines] under Illinois and Chicago law that in the aggregate are comparable in severity to that of the punitive damage award in this case. [W]hat is much more important, a Chicago hotel that permits unsanitary conditions to exist is subject to revocation of its license, without which it cannot operate. [Citation of city ordinance omitted.] We are sure that the defendant would prefer to pay the punitive damages assessed in this case than to lose its license.

District court's judgment in favor of plaintiffs affirmed.

Interference with Personal Rights

This chapter examines two categories of intentional torts: (1) those involving interference with personal rights, and (2) those involving interference with property rights. A third category, business or competitive torts, will be discussed in Chapter 8.

Battery   **Battery** is the intentional and harmful or offensive touching of another without his consent. Contact is *harmful* if it produces bodily injury. However, battery also includes nonharmful contact that is *offensive—* calculated to offend a reasonable sense of personal dignity. The *intent* required for battery is either (1) the intent to cause harmful or offensive contact or (2) the intent to cause apprehension that such contact is imminent. Assume, for instance, that in order to scare Pine, Delano threatens to "shoot" Pine with a gun that Delano mistakenly believes is unloaded. If Delano ends up shooting Pine even though that had not been his specific intent, Delano is liable for battery. For battery to occur, moreover, the person who suffers the harmful or offensive contact need not be the person the wrongdoer intended to injure. Under a concept known as *transferred intent,* a defendant who intends to injure one person but actually injures another is liable to the person injured, despite

the absence of any specific desire to injure him. So, if Dudley throws a rock at Thomas and hits Pike instead, Dudley is liable to Pike for battery. The *Stoshak* case, which follows shortly, provides a further example of the transferred intent principle's operation.

As the previous examples suggest, the *touching* necessary for battery does not require direct contact between the defendant's body and the plaintiff's body. Dudley is therefore liable if he successfully lays a trap for Pike or poisons him. There is also a touching if the defendant causes contact with anything attached to the plaintiff's body. If the other elements of a battery are present, Dudley is thus liable to Pike if he shoots off Pike's hat. Finally, the plaintiff need not be aware of the battery at the time it occurs. This means that Dudley is liable if he sneaks up behind Pike and knocks Pike unconscious, without Pike's ever knowing what hit him.

There is no liability for battery, however, if the plaintiff *consented* to the touching. As a general rule, consent must be freely and intelligently given to be a defense to battery. Consent also may be inferred from a person's voluntary participation in an activity, but it is ordinarily limited to contacts that are a normal consequence of the activity. A professional boxer injured by his opponent's punches to the head, therefore, would not win a battery lawsuit against the opponent. However, a professional boxer whose ear is partially bitten off by his opponent should have a valid battery claim against the ear-biter. In addition, the law infers consent to many touchings that are customary or reasonably necessary in normal social life. Thus, Preston could not recover for battery if Dean tapped him on the shoulder to ask directions or brushed against him on a crowded street. Of course, many such contacts are neither harmful nor offensive anyway.

Stoshak v. East Baton Rouge Parish School Board
959 So.2d 996 (La. App. 2007)

The statutes of Louisiana establish two different injury leave pay provisions for public school teachers who sustain injuries on the job, depending on the cause of the injury. A statute commonly referred to as the physical contact pay *provision states that if a public school teacher "is injured or disabled as a result of physical contact with a student while providing physical assistance to a student to prevent danger or risk of injury to the student," the teacher is entitled to "receive sick leave for a period up to one calendar year without reduction in pay . . . while injured or disabled as a result of rendering such assistance." A separate statute, commonly referred to as the* assault or battery pay *provision, states that if a public school teacher "is injured or disabled while acting in his official capacity as a result of assault or battery by any student or person[, the teacher] shall receive sick leave without reduction in pay . . . while disabled as a result of such assault or battery."*

John Stoshak, a teacher at a Baton Rouge, Louisiana, public high school, was injured when he attempted to break up a fistfight between two of his male students. During the fight, a punch thrown by one of the students struck Stoshak in the back of the head, causing him to fall to the ground and lose consciousness. Although neither student admitted to hitting Stoshak, one acknowledged that when Stoshak tried to break up the fight, the two students continued fighting. Stoshak later stated that he did not believe either of the boys had punched him deliberately; rather, he was struck when he sought to separate the boys who, in Stoshak's words, were "tear[ing] each other up."

Stoshak's employer, the East Baton Rouge Parish School Board (Board), placed Stoshak on leave without reduction in pay for a period of one year following the incident, in accordance with the physical contact pay *statute quoted above. When it became clear that the Board would not pay benefits for more than a year after the incident, Stoshak sued the Board in a Lousiana court. Stoshak contended that he was injured as a result of an "assault or battery by any student or person," that he continued to suffer a resulting disability, and that in accordance with the* assault or battery pay *statute, he was entitled to leave without reduction in pay for the disability's full duration. Stoshak and the Board filed opposing motions for summary judgment. The trial court granted the Board's motion, concluding that Stoshak's injuries fell under the* physical contact pay *statute. The court therefore dismissed Stoshak's claim for continued benefits. Stoshak appealed to the Court of Appeals of Louisiana.*

McClendon, Judge

The parties' motions for summary judgment required a determination of whether Stoshak's injures fell under the *assault or battery pay* provision, which would entitle Stoshak to leave without reduction in pay for the duration of his disability, or the *physical contact pay* provision, pursuant to which Mr. Stoshak's entitlement to leave without reduction in pay would cease one year after the incident causing his injury. Appellate courts review summary judgments [by asking] the same questions as does the trial court in determining whether summary judgment is appropriate: whether there is any genuine issue of material fact, and whether the mover is entitled to summary judgment as a matter of law.

In this case, the material facts are undisputed. Stoshak attested that he was hit in the head by a punch that was delivered by one of two students engaged in a fistfight. The Board did not introduce any evidence to controvert Stoshak's version of the incident. Moreover, while there is no evidence to suggest that the student intended to punch Stoshak, it is undisputed that the student who struck Stoshak intended to strike the other student and was physically attempting to injure the other student.

Stoshak contends the student who hit him committed an assault or battery as those terms are defined under Louisiana's criminal and civil law, entitling him to benefits under the *assault or battery pay* provision. The Board submits that the *assault or battery pay* provision applies only when a teacher is the direct, targeted victim of an assault or battery by a student or other person, while the *physical contact pay* provision applies in all other circumstances where there is a mere physical contact with a student resulting in injury to the teacher. The Board contends that the *physical contact pay* provision applies in this case because it is undisputed that the student intended to cause harmful physical contact to the other student, but not to Stoshak.

We disagree with the Board's narrow interpretation of [the *assault or battery pay* statute]. It is well-settled that the starting point for the interpretation of any statute is the language of the statute itself. When a law is clear and unambiguous and its application does not lead to absurd consequences, the law is applied as written, and no further interpretation may be made in search of legislative intent. It is presumed that in enacting a law, the legislature was aware of existing statutes, rules of construction, and judicial decisions interpreting those statutes.

The term "assault" is defined in the criminal law [of Louisiana] as "an attempt to commit a battery, or the intentional placing of another in reasonable apprehension of receiving a battery." [Statutory citation omitted.] The term "battery" is defined in the criminal law as the "intentional use of force or violence upon the person of another." [Statutory citation omitted.] Under the tort law, a battery has been defined as a "harmful or offensive contact with a person, resulting from an act intended to cause the plaintiff to suffer such a contact." [Case citation omitted.]

In defining what type of conduct constitutes a battery, our courts have employed the doctrine of transferred intent. Under this theory, if a person intended to inflict serious bodily injury while trying to hit another person, but missed and accidentally hit someone else instead, such intent is transferred to the actual victim. We must presume that in enacting [the *assault or battery pay* provision], the legislature was cognizant of the fact that our courts have interpreted the term "battery" to encompass an unintentional injury of one person if the person inflicting the injury specifically intended to injure someone else. The legislature authorized . . . benefits [that could extend beyond one year] to a teacher injured as a result of "assault or battery by any student or person." There is no language in this provision requiring that the teacher be the intended victim of an assault or battery, and we decline to read such a requirement into the statute.

Accordingly, we construe the benefits provided for in the *assault or battery pay* provision to apply whenever the teacher is the victim of a battery at the hands of a student. The benefits provided for under the *physical contact pay* provision apply to injuries a teacher sustains when coming to the aid of a student [if the injuries] result from physical contacts that do not rise to the level of an assault or battery. See, e.g., *Garnier v. Orleans Parish School Board,* 829 So.2d 433 (La. App. 2001) (holding that the *physical contact pay* provision applied to injuries sustained by a teacher who fell to the ground when a student she was attempting to restrain from harming another student jerked away from her).

Applying this construction of the statute, we hold that as a matter of law, Stoshak is entitled to benefits under the *assault or battery pay* [statute]. [T]he student who hit Stoshak committed a battery because he intended the physical act of throwing the punch, and he intended to injure another person by throwing the punch. Under the doctrine of transferred intent, the student who hit Stoshak while attempting to hit the other student is deemed to have had the requisite intent to commit a battery on Stoshak. Therefore, because Stoshak's injuries resulted from a battery by a student, the Board was obligated to provide him with leave without reduction in pay for the duration of his disability.

Trial court's grant of summary judgment in favor of the Board reversed; summary judgment entered in favor of Stoshak.

Assault   **Assault** occurs when there is an intentional attempt or offer to cause a harmful or offensive contact with another person, if that attempt or offer causes a reasonable apprehension of imminent battery in the other person's mind. The necessary *intent* is the same as the intent required for battery. In an assault case, however, it is irrelevant whether the threatened contact actually occurs. Instead, the key thing is the plaintiff's *apprehension* of a harmful or offensive contact. Apprehension need not involve fear; it might be described as a mental state consistent with this thought: "I'm just about to be hit."

The plaintiff's apprehension must pertain to an anticipated battery that would be *imminent or immediate*. Threats of some future battery, therefore, do not create liability for assault. In addition, the plaintiff must experience apprehension *at the time the threatened battery occurs*. For instance, if Dinwiddie fires a rifle at Porter from a great distance and misses him, and only later does Porter learn of the attempt on his life, Dinwiddie is not liable to Porter for assault. The plaintiff's apprehension must also be *reasonable*. As a result, threatening words normally are not an assault unless they are accompanied by acts or circumstances indicating the defendant's intent to carry out the threat.

Intentional Infliction of Emotional Distress

For many years, courts refused to allow recovery for purely emotional injuries unless the defendant had committed some recognized tort. Victims of such torts as assault, battery, and false imprisonment could recover for the emotional injuries resulting from these torts, but courts would not recognize an independent tort of infliction of emotional distress. The reasons for this judicial reluctance included a fear of spurious or trivial claims, concerns about proving purely emotional harms, and uncertainty about the proper boundaries of an independent tort. However, increased confidence in our knowledge about emotional injuries and a greater willingness to compensate such harms have helped to overcome these judicial impediments. Most courts today allow recovery for severe emotional distress, under appropriate circumstances, regardless of whether the elements of any other tort are proven.

The courts are not, however, in complete agreement on the elements of this relatively new tort. All courts do require that a wrongdoer's conduct be *outrageous* before liability for emotional distress arises. The *Restatement (Second) of Torts* speaks of conduct "so outrageous in character, and so extreme in degree, as to go beyond all possible bounds of decency, and to be regarded as atrocious, and utterly intolerable in a civilized community." This means that many instances of boorish, insensitive behavior are not "bad enough" to give rise to liability for this tort. Courts also agree in requiring *severe* emotional distress. The *Restatement (Second)* sets forth another clear majority rule: that the defendant must *intentionally* or *recklessly* inflict the distress in order to be liable. A few courts, however, still fear fictitious claims and require proof of some bodily harm resulting from the victim's emotional distress.

In addition, some courts say that the plaintiff's distress must be distress that a reasonable person of ordinary sensibilities would suffer. The focus on whether the severely distressed person had ordinary sensibilities is sometimes minimized, however, when the defendant behaves outrageously by abusing a position or relation that gives him authority over another. Examples include employers, police officers, landlords, and school authorities.

The courts also differ in the extent to which they allow recovery for emotional distress suffered as a result of witnessing outrageous conduct directed at persons other than the plaintiff. The *Restatement (Second)* suggests that, at minimum, plaintiffs should be allowed to recover for severe emotional distress resulting from witnessing outrageous behavior toward a member of their immediate family.

The *Khan* case, which follows, addresses the elements of intentional infliction of emotional distress.

Khan v. Parsons Global Services, Ltd.   521 F.3d 421 (D.C. Cir. 2008)

Azhar Ali Khan, an employee of Parsons Global Services, Ltd., was working for Parsons in the Phillipines. On one of his days off, when Parsons' offices were closed, Khan was kidnapped. He was later tortured. According to allegations made by Mr. Khan and his wife, Asma Azhar Khan, in the complaint referred to below, Parsons delayed paying the ransom that was demanded until after Mr. Khan's kidnappers carried out their threat to cut off part of his ear.

The Khans filed suit against Parsons in an effort to obtain damages for the physical and emotional harms they experienced as a result of the kidnapping incident and Parsons' response to it. In a portion of the complaint not addressed here, Mr. Khan sought damages from Parsons on a negligence theory. In another portion of the complaint, Mrs. Khan brought an intentional infliction of emotional distress claim against Parsons. Ruling that Mrs. Khan had failed to state a lawful cause of action, the federal district court dismissed Mrs. Khan's claim. Mrs. Khan then appealed to the U.S. Court of Appeals for the D.C. Circuit.

Rogers, Circuit Judge

[Mrs. Khan's intentional infliction of emotional distress claim focuses on] Parsons' alleged mishandling of ransom demands by Mr. Khan's kidnappers.

Under District of Columbia law, a claim of intentional infliction of emotional distress requires a showing of "(1) extreme and outrageous conduct on the part of the defendant which (2) intentionally or recklessly (3) causes the plaintiff severe emotional distress." [Case citation omitted.] Whether conduct is "extreme and outrageous" depends on "applicable contemporary community standards of offensiveness and decency, and the specific context in which the conduct took place." [Case citation omitted.] More specifically, the conduct must constitute, as Parsons notes [in its brief], behavior that is "atrocious and utterly intolerable." Although this standard is demanding, the allegations in the Khans' complaint are sufficient to state a claim.

[In its written opinion,] the district court reasoned that Parsons had not engaged in "extreme or outrageous" conduct and that "there is no evidence that this situation was caused either directly or indirectly by [Parsons]." As to the former, the Khans alleged, among other things, that Parsons had disregarded Mr. Khan's safety in favor of minimizing future corporate kidnappings, thereby provoking Mr. Khan's kidnappers to torture him, to cut off a piece of his ear, and to send a videotape of the event to Parsons, causing the Khans severe mental distress. Mrs. Khan certainly can allege facts, consistent with the complaint, that are "so outrageous in character, and so extreme in degree, as to go beyond all possible bounds of decency." [Case citation omitted.] For example, Parsons' alleged successful efforts to prevent Mrs. Khan from privately paying the ransom, despite threats of torture and mutilation, may have exposed her to the guilt of knowing that she could have prevented Mr. Khan's suffering and disfigurement if she had been able to convince Parsons to provide the ransom details that Parsons withheld from her. In the context of Mr. Khan's employment by Parsons, this could certainly be considered "atrocious" conduct. The complaint also alleges that Parsons' actions were intentional and that Mrs. Khan suffered severe emotional distress.

We hold that the Khans' allegations are sufficient to meet the criteria for intentional infliction of emotional distress [and that the district therefore court erred in dismissing Mrs. Khan's claim].

District court's dismissal of intentional infliction of emotional distress claim reversed, and case remanded for further proceedings.

Most intentional infliction of emotional distress cases are based on allegedly outrageous *conduct*. What about allegedly outrageous *speech*? May it be the basis of a valid emotional distress claim? The potential First Amendment implications of allowing emotional distress liability to be based on speech—particularly when the plaintiff is a famous person who was the target or subject of the defendant's statements—occupied the attention of the U.S. Supreme Court in *Hustler Magazine, Inc. v. Falwell* (1986). On First Amendment grounds, the Court unanimously struck down a damages award received in the lower courts by the Rev. Jerry Falwell as a result of offensive statements about him in an adult magazine. In doing so, the Court severely restricted the ability of *public figures* to win speech-related intentional infliction of emotional distress cases by requiring that such plaintiffs prove the same stern First Amendment–based requirements imposed on public figure plaintiffs in defamation cases. (A later section in this chapter includes extensive discussion of defamation law, including the First Amendment–based requirements that public figures must satisfy when they sue for defamation.)

The Court had no occasion to rule in *Falwell* on whether the First Amendment would restrict the ability of a private figure (i.e., a person who is not well known and thus is not a public figure) to base an emotional distress claim on a defendant's allegedly outrageous speech. Presumably, however, the First Amendment would have less of a role to play in such a case than in the public figure's case. Of course, when a defendant's *conduct*—as opposed to speech—is what the plaintiff complains about in an emotional distress case, the First Amendment does not even potentially furnish the defendant any protection against liability.

False Imprisonment
False imprisonment is the intentional *confinement* of another person for an *appreciable time* (a few minutes is enough) *without his consent.* The confinement element essentially involves the defendant's keeping the plaintiff within a circle that the defendant has created. It may result from physical barriers to the plaintiff's freedom of movement, such as locking a person in a room with no other doors or windows, or from the use or threat of physical force against the plaintiff.

Confinement also may result from the unfounded assertion of legal authority to detain the plaintiff, or from the detention of the plaintiff's property (e.g., a purse containing a large sum of money). Likewise, a threat to harm another, such as the plaintiff's spouse or child, can also cause confinement if it prevents the plaintiff from moving.

The confinement must be *complete*. Partial confinement of another by blocking her path or by depriving her of one means of escape where several exist, such as locking one door of a building having several unlocked doors, is not false imprisonment. The fact that a means of escape exists, however, does not relieve the defendant of liability if the plaintiff cannot reasonably be expected to know of its existence. The same is true if using the escape route would present some unreasonable risk of harm to the plaintiff or would involve some affront to the plaintiff's sense of personal dignity.

Although there is some disagreement on the subject, courts usually hold that the plaintiff must have *knowledge* of his confinement in order for liability for false imprisonment to arise. In addition, there is no liability if the plaintiff has *consented* to his confinement. Such consent, however, must be freely given; consent in the face of an implied or actual threat of force or an assertion of legal authority is not freely given.

Today, many false imprisonment cases involve a store's detention of persons suspected of shoplifting. In an attempt to accommodate the legitimate interests of store owners, most states have passed statutes giving them a *conditional privilege* to stop suspected shoplifters. To obtain this defense, the owner usually must act with reasonable cause and in a reasonable manner, and must detain the suspect for no longer than a reasonable length of time. These privilege statutes typically extend to other intentional torts besides false imprisonment.

The *Pope* case, which follows, examines the elements of false imprisonment and considers the role a privilege statute may play.

Pope v. Rostraver Shop and Save   2008 U.S. Dist. LEXIS 31690 (W.D. Pa. 2008)

Nicky Pope filed a false imprisonment lawsuit against the Rostraver Shop 'n Save store (Shop 'n Save) and its manager, Howard Russell, on the basis of the incident described below. In addition, Pope named Rostraver Township, the township's police department, and one of its police officers, George Milkent, as defendants. Pope claimed that those three defendants were liable for assault, battery, and false imprisonment, along with violations of federal civil rights laws. Pope, Russell, and Milkent all gave deposition testimony in the case.

The lawsuit-triggering incident began when Pope entered the Shop 'n Save store, stopped at the bakery counter, and purchased a cup of coffee and a piece of cake to eat while in the store. She then browsed through the store, walking through every aisle. Upon notification by another employee that Pope was walking back and forth without much in her shopping cart, Russell began watching her. Russell observed that she was wearing a long-sleeved, unbuttoned flannel shirt over a T-shirt. He testified in his deposition that he saw Pope's hand going "underneath and back into the . . . flannel shirt," followed by a "movement made down, possibly into the pants." Thereafter, her "arm came back out." Russell further observed what appeared to be a "protrusion . . . from the left area of [Pope's] back, at about the belt area." Finally, Russell testified that because of Pope's shirt as well as her movement and "the way she was positioned at the cart," he could not see whether Pope had actually concealed any item.

After Pope proceeded to the checkout stand and paid for her items, Russell stopped her in the store's vestibule area and asked to see her receipt. Russell verified that Pope's bakery receipt and store receipt matched her purchased items. He then asked Pope to lift up her outer shirt so that he could see whether she had concealed any items. Pope refused. As Pope acknowledged in her deposition, Russell did not touch her and did not create any physical barrier to prevent her from exiting the store. During their in-store exchange, however, Pope became upset at being accused of shoplifting. Pope told Russell that she believed she was being stopped because she was black and that she intended to sue. Russell informed Pope that he was calling the police and that she should not leave the premises. According to her deposition testimony, Pope believed that because the police had been called, she was not free to leave. During the five to ten minutes it took for the police to arrive, Pope neither asked to leave the store premises nor made any attempt to leave. She also stated in her deposition that she decided to wait for the police.

Officer Milkent was dispatched to Shop 'n Save in response to Russell's call. Upon his arrival, Milkent observed Russell waiting for him outside the store and Pope waiting alone in the vestibule area. Russell informed Milkent of what he had observed. Pope exited the store and approached Milkent, who, according to his deposition testimony, told Pope that she could leave any time she wished and that she was not under arrest. When Milkent asked Pope whether she had any items under her shirt, she responded "no." Milkent then asked Pope to lift up her outer shirt, and Pope complied. Milkent testified that based upon his observations, he could not be sure whether Pope had a concealed item. When asked at his deposition why he did not arrest Pope, Milkent responded that he did not feel comfortable escalating the situation. Pope alleged that after she lifted her shirt, Milkent proceeded to poke her pants area two or three times. Milkent denied having done so. Pope testified that after the alleged poking occurred, she was told she could leave. The exchange with Milkent took approximately 10 minutes. Pope, who was never charged with shoplifting, testified in her deposition that since the incident, she had suffered from panic attacks and lack of sleep.

A Pennsylvania statute, the Retail Theft Act, provides as follows:

> A peace officer, merchant or merchant's employee or an agent under contract with a merchant, who has probable cause to believe that retail theft has occurred or is occurring on or about a store or other retail mercantile establishment and who has probable cause to believe that a specific person has committed or is committing the retail theft may detain the suspect in a reasonable manner for a reasonable time on or off the premises for all or any of the following purposes: to require the suspect to identify himself, to verify such identification, to determine whether such suspect has in his possession unpurchased merchandise taken from the mercantile establishment and, if so, to recover such merchandise, to inform a peace officer, or to institute criminal proceedings against the suspect. Such detention shall not impose civil or criminal liability upon the peace officer, merchant, employee, or agent so detaining.

Following the completion of discovery in the case, Pope filed a motion for summary judgment. All defendants also moved for summary judgment. The U.S. District Court for the Western District of Pennsylvania considered all of the summary judgment motions together.

Fischer, District Judge

Summary judgment under Federal Rule of Civil Procedure 56(c) is appropriate "if the pleadings, the discovery and disclosure materials on file, and any affidavits show that there is no genuine issue as to any material fact and that the movant is entitled to judgment as a matter of law." The Court will first address the . . . claim of false imprisonment against [Shop 'n Save and Russell, referred to here as] the Shop 'n Save Defendants.

In a claim for false imprisonment, the plaintiff seeks to protect his or her interest in the freedom from restraint of movement. Under the law of Pennsylvania, a plaintiff bears the burden of proving (1) that the defendant acted intentionally to confine the plaintiff within boundaries fixed by the defendant; (2) that the act of the defendant either directly or indirectly resulted in said confinement of the plaintiff; and (3) that the plaintiff is either conscious of said confinement or is harmed by it. Caswell v. BJ's Wholesale Co., 5 F.Supp.2d 312, 319 (E.D. Pa. 1998).

In order for there to be a false imprisonment, the confinement must be complete. [Caswell indicates that] "[i]f a known, safe means of escape, involving only a slight inconvenience exists, there is no false imprisonment." The confinement can be effectuated either through physical means and barriers or through threats or coercion. [As noted in Caswell,] "[t]he fact that a plaintiff merely believes she is not free to leave is not enough to support a claim of false imprisonment. A plaintiff must make some attempt to determine whether her belief that her freedom of movement has been curtailed has basis." [Such

an] attempt could be made if the plaintiff [requests to leave but the request is denied].

The Shop 'n Save Defendants cite Caswell as an example of an unreasonable belief of confinement. [They argue] that Pope's belief of confinement is equally unreasonable. Caswell involved a plaintiff claiming to have been confined in a back room of the store when the store managers sought to question the plaintiff about incriminating photographs that the plaintiff had developed at the store [(photographs evidencing possible child abuse)]. The managers informed the plaintiff that they were calling the police. The plaintiff spoke to the managers for approximately 10 minutes [before leaving] the room to move her car from a no-parking zone. At no time during this incident did the managers touch the plaintiff or make any threats toward her. Based upon these facts, the court held that no reasonable jury could find that the managers falsely imprisoned the plaintiff [and] that the calling of the police and the standing in the doorway [were] not enough to create an issue of confinement for the jury. [T]he court [also] held [that] there could not be any confinement when the plaintiff was able to and did walk out of the room to her car unimpeded by the managers.

In contrast, Pope cites Pinkett v. Super Fresh Food Markets, Inc., 1988 U.S. Dist. LEXIS 2553 (E.D. Pa.1988). [There,] the plaintiff was in line at a grocery store when an employee came up from behind her, grabbed [her] arm, demanded that he [be allowed to] look in her purse, and accused her of shoplifting. The plaintiff told the employee that she was not going to let him search her purse. The employee responded . . . that she [would not be allowed to] leave the store unless he was able to check her bag. [After] the employee's repeated insistence that "you are not going to leave the store until I search your bag," the plaintiff summoned a store security guard and opened her purse for him. The security guard indicated that there were no stolen goods in her purse. The plaintiff was then able to finish checking out and [leave] the store unimpeded. The whole incident took approximately 10 minutes. The court held that the jury's verdict in favor of the plaintiff that there was a false imprisonment was not unreasonable given the repeated threats of the store employee. [The court noted that] "[w]hile there was no confinement in the literal sense of physical barriers, the repeated threats of the store employee that 'you are not going to leave the store until I search your bag' could reasonably be construed as constituting confinement by submission to duress or coercion." Further, when combined with the store employee grabbing the plaintiff's arm, the Court concluded that sufficient evidence existed to support the jury's verdict.

Using *Caswell* and *Pinkett* as guideposts for what is a reasonable or unreasonable belief of confinement, respectively, the Court finds that the facts of this case are more closely aligned with *Caswell* and that Pope's belief that she was imprisoned is not well-founded. It is undisputed by the parties that at no time did Russell touch Pope or any of her property. Hence, it is only what Russell allegedly said to Pope that could possibly constitute a threat to coerce her into being confined within the Shop 'n Save. Pope's deposition indicates that Russell informed her that he was going to call the police and that she [could] not leave. However, her deposition further indicates that she never tested whether she could leave or made a request to leave. In addition, Milkent stated at his deposition that Pope wasn't being detained when he arrived at the scene.

The Court recognizes that while the facts of this case have some similarity to *Pinkett*, the differences are material and determine a different outcome. The store employee in *Pinkett* grabbed the plaintiff's arm and repeatedly demanded that the plaintiff show the employee what was inside her purse. Here, Pope does not claim that Russell asked to search her repeatedly. In *Pinkett*, the store employee informed the plaintiff that she was not going to leave the store until he searched her purse. Such a statement made in conjunction with the grabbing of the plaintiff's arm allowed for a reasonable inference that the store employee was making a threat of physical force. Here, Pope was never touched by Russell and she stated it was her choice to wait and to talk to the police. As a result, Russell's actions never resulted in Pope being confined.

Pope argues that Russell confined her by asserting legal authority when he stated that he intended to call the police. [However], Russell's statement does not constitute an assertion of legal authority merely because he told her that he intended to call the police. In *Caswell,* the plaintiff was not confined when the store managers told her that the police were being called and that the store managers had seen what they thought was evidence of a crime. Although the context of *Caswell* is different, the result is the same.

The Shop 'n Save defendants argue that even if there was a confinement of Pope, it was not a complete confinement because there was a means of escape that Pope did not use. Pope admitted that she never asked [whether] she could leave, nor did she make any attempts to leave. When Russell told Pope that he was calling the police and not to leave, she was in the front vestibule area and had an open means of escape, i.e., the doors to exit the store. Because Pope never tested whether her confinement was complete, Pope is only left with her belief that her confinement was complete and, as previously stated, a belief of confinement is not sufficient to prove a claim of false imprisonment. Moreover, Pope chose to wait, thus making her belief that she was confined all the more unreasonable.

In addition, [although the issue was] not raised in the Shop 'n Save defendants' motion for summary judgment, this Court finds that the Pennsylvania Retail Theft Immunity Act would apply to [Russell's] actions. Russell's observations of Pope provided him with probable cause to reasonably detain Pope for a reasonable time. Hence, Russell [and Shop 'n Save are] entitled to immunity from liability [on] Plaintiff's false imprisonment claim [even if there had otherwise been a confinement for purposes of potential false imprisonment liability].

As a result, because Russell's conduct did not constitute a confinement and Pope never tested the reasonableness of her belief of confinement, Pope's claim for false imprisonment fails. [Alternatively], . . . Russell [and Shop 'n Save are] entitled to immunity under the Pennsylvania Retail Theft Immunity Act [even if the elements of false imprisonment had been present]. Accordingly, the Shop 'n Save defendants' motion for summary judgment will be granted.

[*Note:* In a portion of the opinion not included here, the court granted the motions for summary judgment filed by Milkent, the police department, and the township (the Rostraver defendants). The court concluded that based on what Russell had told him and based on his own observations, Milkent had probable cause to detain Pope briefly before releasing her. Therefore, the Pennsylvania Retail Theft Immunity Act protected the Rostraver defendants against liability for false imprisonment. Although the court indicated that the elements of assault and battery probably were not present anyway, the Retail Theft Immunity Act would provide an alternative ground for insulating the Rostraver defendants against any liability in connection with those supposed causes of action. Finally, the court saw no basis on which the Rostraver defendants could be held liable under federal civil rights laws.]

Defendants' motions for summary judgment granted.

Defamation   The tort of defamation protects the individual's interest in his reputation. Defamation is ordinarily defined as the (1) unprivileged (2) publication of (3) false and defamatory (4) statements concerning another. Before examining each of these elements, we must consider the distinction between two forms of defamation: **libel** and **slander.**

The Libel–Slander Distinction   Libel refers to written or printed defamation or to other defamation having a more or less permanent physical form, such as a defamatory picture, sign, or statue. Slander refers to all other defamatory statements—mainly oral defamation. Today, however, the great majority of courts treat defamatory statements in radio and television broadcasts as libel. The same is true of defamatory statements made on the Internet.

Why does the libel–slander distinction matter? Because of libel's more permanent nature and the seriousness we usually attach to the written word, the common law has traditionally allowed plaintiffs to recover for libel without proof of **special damages** (actual reputational injury and other actual harm). **Presumed damages** have long been allowed by the common law in libel cases. Described by the U.S. Supreme Court as an "oddity of tort law," presumed damages "compensate" for reputational harm that is presumed to have occurred but does not have to be proven by the plaintiff.

Slander, on the other hand, is generally not actionable without proof of special damages, unless the nature of the slanderous statement is so serious that it can be classified as *slander per se.* In cases of slander per se, presumed damages are allowed by the common law. Slander per se ordinarily includes false statements that the plaintiff (1) has committed a crime involving moral turpitude or potential imprisonment, (2) has a loathsome disease, (3) is professionally incompetent or guilty of professional misconduct, or (4) is guilty of serious sexual misconduct.

False and Defamatory Statement   Included among the elements of defamation are the separate requirements that the defendant's statement be both *false* and *defamatory.* Truth is a complete defense in a defamation case. A defamatory statement is one that is likely to harm the reputation of another by injuring his community's estimation of him or by deterring others from associating or dealing with him.

"Of and Concerning" the Plaintiff   Because the defamation cause of action serves to protect reputation, an essential element of the tort is that the alleged defamatory statement must be "of and concerning" the plaintiff. That is, the statement must be about—and thus bear upon the reputation of—the party who brought the case. This requirement presents problems whose many complexities are beyond the scope of this text. The rules sketched below, therefore, are sometimes subject to exceptions not explained here.

What about allegedly *fictional accounts* whose characters resemble real people? Most courts say that fictional accounts may be defamatory if a reasonable reader would identify the plaintiff as the subject of the story. Similarly, *humorous or satirical accounts* ordinarily are not defamation unless a reasonable reader would believe that they purport to describe real events.

Statements of pure *opinion* do not amount to defamation because they are not statements of "fact" concerning the plaintiff. However, statements that mix elements of opinion with elements of supposed "fact" may be actionable. *Mann v. Abel,* 885 N.E.2d 884 (N.Y App. 2008), furnishes a recent example of a fact-versus-opinion determination. The plaintiff, Mann, was the attorney for the Town of Rye. He based his defamation case on statements that appeared in "The Town Crier" column, a feature in a newspaper that served the Rye area. The writer of the column referred to Mann as a "political hatchet man" and as "one of the biggest powers behind the throne" in local government. The writer also asserted that "Mann pulls the strings" and raised the question whether Mann was "leading the Town of Rye to destruction." Although Mann won his case in the lower courts, the New York Court of Appeals reversed and ordered that his complaint be dismissed. The Court of Appeals held that considering the tone of the statements, the column's content as a whole, and the fact that the column was accompanied by an editor's note indicating that the column set forth the views of the writer, the statements complained about by Mann were nonactionable opinion rather than false statements of supposed fact.

Do defamatory statements concerning particular *groups* of people also defame the individuals who belong to those groups? Generally, an individual member of a defamed group cannot recover for damage to her own reputation unless the group is so small that the statement can reasonably be understood as referring to individual group members.

Finally, courts have placed some limits on the persons or entities that can suffer injury to reputation. No liability attaches, for example, to defamatory statements concerning the dead. Corporations and other business entities have reputational interests and can recover for defamatory statements that harm them in their business or deter others from dealing with them. Statements about a corporation's officers, employees, or shareholders normally are not defamatory regarding the corporation, however, unless the statements also reflect on the manner in which the corporation conducts its business.[1]

Publication Liability for defamation requires **publication** of the defamatory statement. As a general rule, no widespread communication of a defamatory statement is necessary for publication. The defendant's communication of the defamatory statement to one person other than the person defamed ordinarily suffices.

So long as no one else receives or overhears it, however, an insulting message communicated directly from the defendant to the plaintiff is not actionable. The long-standing rule is that publication does not take place when *the plaintiff herself* communicates the offensive statement to another. In recent years, some courts have made an exception to this rule in cases where a discharged employee is forced to tell a potential future employer about false and defamatory statements made to her by her prior employer.

Some courts still follow the older rule that intracorporate statements (statements by one corporate officer or employee to another officer of the same corporation) do not involve publication. Most courts, however, follow the modern trend and hold that there is publication in such situations.

The general rule is that one who repeats a false and defamatory statement is liable for defamation. This is true even if he identifies the source of the statement or expresses his disagreement with it.

A party other than the person who initially made a defamatory statement may be liable along with the original speaker or writer if that other party served as a *publisher* of the defamatory falsehood, but not if the other party was a mere *distributor.* According to defamation law's traditional publisher vs. distributor distinction, a company that publishes a book or a newspaper may be held liable for defamation on the basis of statements that appear in the book or in the newspaper's articles. The rationale is that the publishing company possessed considerable editorial control over the content of the book or the articles, and would have had the ability to remove the defamatory falsehoods. (The writer of the statements, of course, would be liable as well.) Libraries and bookstores,

however, are mere distributors because they lack the editorial control that publishers have. Therefore, libraries and bookstores are not liable for defamation even if defamatory falsehoods appear in books they lend to users or sell to customers.

What about Internet service providers and Web site operators? Can they be held liable as publishers of statements posted online by other parties? The answer might initially seem to be "yes" in instances where the service provider or Web site operator reserved some measure of editorial control, but the actual answer is "no." Section 230 of the federal Communications Decency Act establishes a national rule that "no provider or user of an interactive computer service shall be treated as the publisher or speaker of any information provided by another information content provider." This section has been applied by courts in a significant number of defamation cases and in various other types of cases in which liability for someone else's online statements is at issue. (For further discussion of § 230, refer back to the Cyberlaw in Action box in Chapter 1.)

Defenses and Privileges Even though defamation is called an intentional tort, the common law contemplated a form of strict liability for defamation. Defenses are available, however, in certain defamation cases. Of course, the truth of the defamatory statement is a complete defense to liability. Defamatory statements may be *privileged* as well. Privileges to defamation liability recognize that in some circumstances, other social interests are more important than an individual's right to reputation. Privileges can be *absolute* or *conditional.*

An **absolute privilege** shields the author of a defamatory statement regardless of her knowledge, motive, or intent. When such a privilege applies, it operates as a complete defense to defamation liability. Absolutely privileged statements include those made by participants in judicial proceedings, by legislators or witnesses in the course of legislative proceedings, by certain executive officials in the course of their duties, and by one spouse to the other in private. In each case, the theory underlying the privilege is that complete freedom of expression is essential to the proper functioning of the relevant activity, and that potential liability for defamation would inhibit free expression.

Conditional (or qualified) privileges give the defendant a defense unless the privilege is *abused.* What constitutes abuse varies with the privilege in question. In general, conditional privileges are abused when the statement is made with knowledge of its falsity or with reckless disregard for the truth, when the statement does not

---

[1]As Chapter 8 reveals, statements concerning the quality of a corporation's products or the quality of its title to land or other property may be the basis of an injurious falsehood claim.

advance the purposes supporting the privilege, or when it is unnecessarily made to inappropriate people.

There are various conditional privileges. One important conditional privilege involves *statements made to protect or further the legitimate interests of another.* One of the most common business-related examples is the employment reference. Suppose that Parker's former employer, Dorfman, has good reason to believe— and does in fact believe—that Parker embezzled money from Dorfman's business while Parker was a Dorfman employee. Trumbull, who is deciding whether to hire Parker, contacts Dorfman to ask about Parker's work record and performance as an employee. During the conversation, Dorfman tells Trumbull that he believes Parker committed embezzlement while working for him. On these facts, Dorfman will be protected by a conditional privilege against defamation liability to Parker because Dorfman's statement was designed to further Trumbull's legitimate interest in making an

intelligent hiring decision. Dorfman's good faith and reasonably based belief in the truth of his statement about Parker is critical to his ability to rely on the conditional privilege. If Dorfman had known his statement was false or had made it with reckless disregard for the truth, Dorfman would have abused the conditional privilege and would have lost its protection against liability.

A second important type of conditional privilege concerns *statements made to promote a common interest.* Intracorporate communications are one example. Such communications normally would abuse the privilege, however, if they are also communicated to the public at large. Finally, the privilege called *fair comment* protects fair and accurate media reports of defamatory matter that appears in proceedings of official government action or originates from public meetings.

DeNardo v. Box, which follows, addresses conditional privilege issues.

DeNardo v. Bax   147 P.3d 672 (Alaska Sup. Ct. 2006)

Daniel DeNardo and Joy Bax had been co-workers at Alaska Newspapers, Inc. (ANI). After DeNardo no longer worked for ANI, he filed a defamation lawsuit against Bax because she had told other employees of the company she was "worried" that DeNardo was "stalking" her. DeNardo contended that he had not stalked Bax and that her statements were therefore false. Bax moved for summary judgment, arguing that her statements were not false because they were based on her own observations and subjective concern that DeNardo was following and possibly stalking her. She also asserted that her conversations with co-workers were conditionally privileged because co-workers share a common interest in workplace safety. DeNardo countered by arguing that Bax had abused any conditional privilege to which she might otherwise have been entitled.

An Alaska trial court granted Bax's summary judgment motion, concluding that Bax's statements to co-workers were conditionally privileged and that DeNardo had not produced evidence demonstrating abuse of the privilege. DeNardo appealed to the Alaska Supreme Court.

Fabe, Justice

We review a grant of summary judgment de novo, affirming if the record contains no genuine issue of material fact and the moving party is entitled to judgment as a matter of law. When considering a motion for summary judgment, all reasonable inferences of fact from the proffered evidence must be drawn against the moving party and in favor of the non-moving party.

Whether a statement is defamatory and whether a statement is afforded privilege are questions of law. If the relevant facts of the case are disputed, a jury must determine [whether] a conditional privilege has been abused. When considering legal issues of first impression, such as whether a previously unrecognized privilege applies, we will adopt the rule of law that is most persuasive in light of precedent, reason, and policy.

In order for a defamation claim to succeed [under Alaska law], a plaintiff must establish: (1) a false and defamatory statement; (2) an unprivileged publication to a third party; (3) fault amounting at least to negligence; and (4) the existence of either "per se" actionability or special harm. The superior court determined that DeNardo failed to establish the second element, an unprivileged communication, and granted summary judgment in favor of Bax. The superior court reasoned that the statements Bax made to coworkers that she felt she was being stalked were conditionally privileged as statements of concern about personal safety in the workplace.

DeNardo does not challenge the superior court's determination that Bax's statements were privileged. Rather, he raises a claim that he was entitled to a jury trial on whether Bax abused the conditional privilege. But because we have never directly addressed the question whether a conditional privilege exists with respect to statements among coworkers about personal safety in the workplace, we first recognize that such a privilege applies.

In the past, "we have recognized a conditional privilege based on a joint business interest or an employer/employee relationship when a statement is made 'for the protection of a lawful business, professional, property or other pecuniary interest.'" [Case citation omitted.] And in [another case] we found that "speech on matters of public safety is privileged." While communications among coworkers concerning personal safety in the workplace do not fall squarely within the ambit of either of these recognized privileges, our previous acknowledgment of the importance of protecting speech regarding business interests and public health and safety lends support to recognition of a privilege in this case.

We will acknowledge a conditional privilege when a person "having a common interest in a particular subject matter believes that there is information that another sharing the common interest is entitled to know." [Case citation omitted.] According to the *Restatement (Second) of Torts,* "[a]n occasion makes a publication conditionally privileged if the circumstances induce a correct or reasonable belief that (a) there is information that affects a sufficiently important interest of the publisher, and (b) the recipient's knowledge of the defamatory matter will be of service in the lawful protection of the interest." Where, as here, a worker reveals to coworkers that she is concerned that another coworker might be stalking her, a sufficiently important interest to the statement's publisher, her personal safety, is at stake. Furthermore, by alerting coworkers to her fears, Bax protected her interest in personal safety by attuning coworkers to the possibility that she was the victim of dangerous behavior. Recognition of a privilege under these circumstances is necessary in order to facilitate an environment in which employees feel safe while performing their duties.

At the summary judgment stage, it was Bax's initial burden to establish that she was entitled to prevail as a matter of law, by demonstrating that a conditional privilege applies and that she did not abuse the applicable conditional privilege. In the trial court, Bax satisfied this initial burden [by] present[ing] evidence that she did not abuse the privilege. [In particular, she pointed to an affidavit she submitted in a separate wrongful termination case that DeNardo filed against his former employer. That affidavit stated:] "When we [Bax and DeNardo] worked together at ANI, there were several occasions when Mr. DeNardo followed me in his vehicle. I was worried that he was 'stalking' me." Bax's affidavit shows that [the very similar stalking-related statements she made to coworkers—the statements giving rise to DeNardo's defamation case against her—] were not made [with knowledge that] they were false [or] with reckless disregard for the truth.

Once Bax established a prima facie case that a conditional privilege applied and that she did not abuse the privilege, the burden shifted to DeNardo to show that the privilege had been abused. We have established that a conditional privilege may be abused:

(1) when there is malice—the publisher had knowledge or reckless disregard as to the falsity of the defamatory matter;
(2) because the defamatory matter is published for some purpose other than that for which the particular privilege is given;
(3) because the publication is made to some person not reasonably believed to be necessary for the accomplishment of the purpose of the particular privilege; or
(4) because the publication includes defamatory matter not reasonably believed to be necessary to accomplish the purpose for which the occasion is privileged.

Before the superior court, DeNardo contended that Bax abused the conditional privilege because she acted with [actual] malice: knowledge or reckless disregard as to the falsity of her statements. Because the actual malice test for determining abuse of a conditional privilege is subjective, at the summary judgment stage the court must determine "whether there is a genuine issue of material fact on whether [the defendant] entertained serious doubts as to the truth of the statements." We note that the false and defamatory comment that Bax allegedly made was that Bax was worried that DeNardo was stalking her and not that he was in fact stalking her. On summary judgment, DeNardo therefore has the burden of raising a material issue of fact on the question whether Bax entertained serious doubts about the truth of her statement that she was subjectively worried DeNardo was stalking her.

In support of DeNardo's claim that Bax's statement was made with [actual] malice, DeNardo essentially makes [these] arguments: (1) since Bax did not publish her statement of concern widely enough, she was not actually worried that DeNardo was stalking her; [and] (2) Bax had a motive to lie because she and DeNardo had a workplace rivalry. Even drawing all reasonable inferences in favor of DeNardo as the non-moving party, these allegations fail to raise a genuine issue of material fact on the question whether Bax entertained serious doubts as to the truth of her statement that she subjectively believed DeNardo was stalking her.

On the issue of the narrow scope of publication, DeNardo noted in his opposition to Bax's summary judgment motion that Bax only spoke to her "sales manager . . . and [two] coworkers. . . . Bax never told her husband, children, family, neighbors, [corporate] management, . . . or any governmental authority about plaintiff's stalking!" DeNardo does not meet his burden by pointing to the limited scope of Bax's publication. As DeNardo concedes, Bax expressed her concerns solely to her coworkers—those who knew DeNardo and were in the best position to observe the interaction between Bax and DeNardo in the workplace on a daily basis. It would not be reasonable to infer that Bax had serious doubts that her statements were true simply because she only discussed her concerns with those most familiar with her situation and those best able to assist her if DeNardo, [then] a coworker, turned out to in fact be stalking her.

Moreover, excessive publication to persons not reasonably believed to be necessary for the accomplishment of the purpose of the privilege would constitute abuse of the privilege. That Bax limited the publication of her statement to two coworkers and her supervisor—those most suited to respond if Bax's subjective fear that DeNardo was stalking her proved true—supports the conclusion that her statement was well within the bounds of the common interest privilege in workplace safety, and not that Bax doubted the truth of her statements.

DeNardo points to evidence that Bax had a motive to defame him because she coveted his customer lists and commissions and because there was ill will between DeNardo and Bax when they were coworkers at ANI. But evidence of ill will alone is not sufficient to establish abuse of the privilege. In most jurisdictions, evidence that a defendant disliked a plaintiff

is insufficient to establish abuse of the privilege. "If the defendant's statements were made to further the interest protected by the privilege, it matters not that defendant also despised plaintiff." [Case citation omitted.] Here DeNardo alleges that Bax harbored ill will toward him because she competed with him for customers and commissions when they were employees at ANI and [for other reasons]. But evidence that Bax might have disliked DeNardo does not cast doubt upon her statement that she feared DeNardo was stalking her.

Bax's publication was made for the purpose of protecting the interest in question, workplace safety, and therefore the fact that the publication might have been "inspired in part by resentment or indignation [in regard to DeNardo] does not constitute an abuse of the privilege." [Case citation omitted.] While DeNardo arguably set forth sufficient evidence to establish that Bax disliked him, he set forth no evidence to establish that Bax entertained serious doubts as to the truth of the statements. Because DeNardo has failed to meet his burden, we affirm the superior court's decision.

Trial court's grant of summary judgment in favor of defendant affirmed.

CYBERLAW IN ACTION

The late Evel Knievel, a motorcycle daredevil, acquired considerable fame as a result of his widely publicized and dangerous stunts during a career that began in the mid-1960s. Knievel's exploits have been featured in several books and movies and in a Smithsonian Museum exhibit. Prior to his death in 2007, Knievel served as an advertising spokesman for various well-known corporations. He also devoted considerable time to the promotion of antidrug and motorcycle safety programs.

In 2001, ESPN held its Action Sports and Music Awards ceremony. Celebrities from the field of "extreme" sports attended, as did famous rap and heavy-metal musicians. Knievel, sometimes known as the "father of extreme sports," attended along with his wife, Krystal. In one of the many photographs ESPN arranged to have taken at the ceremony, Knievel was pictured with his right arm around his wife and his left arm around an unidentified woman. Knievel was wearing a motorcycle jacket and rose-tinted sunglasses.

The photograph of the Knievels and the unidentified woman was one of 17 photographs that ESPN published on the "Green Carpet Gallery" section of its "EXPN.com" Web site. That site featured information and photographs concerning motorcycle racing and various other "extreme" sports.

The Green Carpet Gallery section was devoted to pictures of celebrity attendees of the Action Sports and Music Awards ceremony. A viewer who clicked on the Green Carpet Gallery icon was first directed to a photograph of two men grasping hands, with an accompanying caption stating that "Colin McKay and Cary Hart share the love." By clicking on the "next" icon, the viewer could scroll through the remaining photographs and corresponding captions. A photograph of a woman in a black dress had this caption: "Tara Dakides lookin' sexy, even though we all know she is hardcore." Another photograph showed a sunglasses-wearing man, with a caption stating that "Ben Hinkley rocks the shades so the ladies can't see him scoping." The photograph of the Knievels was the tenth in the sequence and could not be viewed without first viewing the photographs that preceded it. Its caption read this way: "Evel Knievel proves that you're never too old to be a pimp."

Evel and Krystal Knievel sued ESPN for defamation, contending that the caption, as used in connection with the photograph, falsely charged them with "immoral and improper behavior" and otherwise harmed their reputations. In particular, they alleged that after the publication of the photograph and caption, several of the corporations for which Evel had done product endorsements no longer wanted him associated with their products.

ESPN moved to dismiss the Knievels' complaint for failure to state a claim on which relief could be granted. According to the defendant, defamation could not have occurred because reasonable persons would not have interpreted the caption as an allegation that Evel was a criminal "pimp" or that Krystal was a prostitute. The federal district court granted the motion to dismiss. The Knievels appealed to the U.S. Court of Appeals for the Ninth Circuit.

In *Knievel v. ESPN*, 393 F.3d 1068 (9th Cir. 2005), the Ninth Circuit affirmed the lower court's dismissal of the plaintiffs' complaint. The court began its analysis by noting that "[i]n enforcing laws that impose liability for mere speech, a right explicitly guaranteed to the people in the United States Constitution, states tread perilously close to the limits of their authority." The court stated that "to survive ESPN's motion to dismiss, the Knievels must not only establish that the photograph and caption about which they complain are 'reasonably capable of sustaining a defamatory meaning,' they must also show that they are not mere 'comment within the ambit of the First Amendment.'" [Citation of quoted case omitted.]

The Ninth Circuit noted that in determining whether a statement can reasonably be seen as communicating a defamatory message, courts must view the statement as an average reader would, and must consider the statement in the context in which it appeared rather than in isolation. Applying that standard, the court concluded that even though "the word 'pimp' may be reasonably capable of a defamatory meaning when read in isolation," the district court had been correct in determining that the term lost its defamatory meaning when it was used in the context of the defendant's Web site. The Ninth Circuit also emphasized that as interpreted in *Milkovich v. Lorain Journal Co.,* 497 U.S. 1 (U.S. Sup. Ct. 1990), and *Hustler Magazine v. Falwell,* 485 U.S. 46 (1988), the First Amendment bars holding a speaker or writer liable for statements that cannot reasonably be regarded as having stated actual facts about the plaintiff. Such a rule is necessary to provide "assurance that public debate will not suffer for lack of 'imaginative expression' or the 'rhetorical hyperbole' which has traditionally added much to the discourse of our Nation." *Milkovich* (quoting *Falwell*).

As part of its consideration of the context in which the statement about the Knievels appeared, the court took into account the general nature and tone of the EXPN.com main page. The Ninth Circuit observed that the main page was "lighthearted, jocular, and intended for a youthful audience." The court also noted that in directing the viewer to "'check

out what the rock stars and prom queens were wearing'" and in offering a "'behind the scenes look at all the cool kids, EXPN-style,'" the page employed various slang phrases that were not subject to literal interpretation and almost certainly would not be "uttered by anyone but a teenager or young adult." This caused the court to conclude that "[a] reasonable viewer exposed to the main page would expect to find precisely that type of youthful, non-literal language on the rest of the site."

Continuing its consideration of the relevant context, the court examined the Green Carpet Gallery photographs and captions that viewers of the Web site would have seen when viewing the Knievel photograph and caption. The court again found an "overwhelming presence of slang," noting captions using terms such as "hardcore," "scoping," "throwing down a pose," "put a few back," and "hottie of the year." These terms, the court observed, were not "intended to be interpreted literally, if indeed they have a literal meaning at all." Accordingly, the court believed that "any reasonable viewer would have interpreted the word 'pimp' in the same loose, figurative sense as well." Although the Ninth Circuit conceded that the traditional dictionary definition of "pimp" contemplates a man who is in charge of prostitutes, the court cited online dictionaries of slang terms as indicating that slang uses of "pimp" may be in the nature of a compliment to a man for being "cool" or for having mastered some subject matter. Alternatively, "pimp" may be meant as a way of commenting negatively on a man's appearance, behavior, or attitudes.

Importantly, however, the court emphasized that even if a viewer of the Green Carpet Gallery had interpreted "pimp" literally, he or she would have "interpreted the photograph and caption, in the context in which they were published, as an attempt at humor." A reader or viewer who recognizes that a statement is an attempt at humor presumably does not take the statement as one of actual fact. The Ninth Circuit stressed that the Green Carpet Gallery poked fun at celebrities pictured there, with captions such as "Shannon Dunn and Leslee Olson make it look easy to be cheesy" and "Todd Richards tells the camera man to step off his lady." The court reasoned that "[j]ust as no reasonable reader would interpret those captions as allegations of fact, no reasonable reader would interpret the photograph of the Knievels [and the accompanying caption] as a serious allegation of criminal wrongdoing." In view of the context created by the "satirical, risque, and sophomoric slang found on the rest of the site," the word "pimp" could not reasonably be seen as a defamatory statement of supposed fact.

Defamation and the Constitution Until less than 50 years ago, the First Amendment's guarantees of freedom of speech and press were not considered relevant to defamation cases. The common law's strict liability

approach meant that unless one of the privileges discussed earlier applied, a speaker or writer who made a false statement believing it to be true had no more protection against defamation liability than the deliberate liar had. In a series of cases dating back to 1964, however, the U.S. Supreme Court has concluded that the common law's approach may be too heavily weighted in favor of plaintiffs' reputational interests and not sufficiently protective of defendants' free speech and free press interests. The Court has recognized that when coupled with the potential availability of presumed damages, a strict liability regime could deter would-be speakers from contributing true statements to public debate out of fear of the costly liability that might result if the jury somehow concluded that the statements were false. Recognizing the need to guard against this "chilling effect" and the resulting restriction on the flow of information that is important to a free society, the Court determined in *New York Times Co. v. Sullivan* (1964) that the First Amendment has a role to play in certain defamation cases. The Court reasoned that judicial enforcement of the legal rules of defamation served as the government action necessary to trigger application of the First Amendment.

Public Official Plaintiff Cases In *New York Times,* the Court held that when a *public official* brings a defamation case, he or she must prove not only the usual elements of defamation but also a First Amendment–based fault requirement known as **actual malice.** The Court gave actual malice a special meaning: knowledge of falsity or reckless disregard for the truth. Thus, after *New York Times,* a defendant who makes a false and defamatory statement about a public official plaintiff will not be held liable unless the public official proves that the defendant made the statement either (1) knowing it was false, or (2) recklessly. Moreover, the Court held in *New York Times* that as a further First Amendment–based safeguard, the public official plaintiff must prove actual malice by *clear and convincing evidence*—a higher standard of proof than the preponderance of the evidence standard applicable to every other element of a defamation claim and to civil cases generally. The public official category includes many high level government officials, whether elected or appointed.

Public Figure Plaintiff Cases Three years after *New York Times,* the Supreme Court extended the proof-of-actual-malice requirement to defamation cases in which the plaintiff is a *public figure.* The Court also mandated that such a plaintiff prove actual malice by clear and convincing evidence. Individual persons or corporations are public figures if they either (1) are well known to large segments of society through their own voluntary efforts, or (2) have voluntarily placed themselves, in the words of the Supreme Court, at "the forefront of a particular public controversy." The first type of public figure,

sometimes given the "general-purpose" designation, includes well-known corporations, political candidates who are not already holders of public office, and ex-government officials. It also includes a diverse collection of celebrities, near celebrities, and well-known persons ranging from familiar actors, entertainers, and media figures to famous athletes or coaches and others with high public visibility in their chosen professions. The second type of public figure, sometimes assigned the "limited-purpose" label, is not well known by large segments of society but has chosen to take a prominent leadership role regarding a matter of public debate (e.g., the abortion rights controversy, the debate over whether certain drugs should be legalized, or disputes over the extent to which environmental regulations should restrict business activity). A general-purpose public figure must prove actual malice in any defamation case in which he, she, or it is the plaintiff. A limited-purpose public figure, on the other hand, must prove actual malice when the statement giving rise to the case relates in some sense to the public controversy as to which the plaintiff is a public figure.

The proof-of-actual-malice requirement poses a very substantial hurdle for public officials and public figures to clear. That is by design, according to the Supreme Court. Defendants have especially strong First Amendment interests in regard to statements about public officials and public figures, given the high level of public interest and concern that attaches almost automatically to matters involving such persons.

Knowledge of falsity—one of the two forms of actual malice—is difficult to prove. When the defendant who made a false statement can point to an arguably credible source on which he, she, or it relied as a supposed indicator of the statement's truth, the defendant presumably did not have knowledge of the statement's falsity. Neither did the defendant speak or write with the other form of actual malice—*reckless disregard for the truth*—in such an instance. According to the Supreme Court, reckless disregard has been demonstrated when the plaintiff proves either (1) that the defendant "in fact entertained serious doubts" about the statement's truth but made the statement anyway or (2) that the defendant consciously rejected overwhelming evidence of falsity and chose instead to rely on a much less significant bit of evidence that would have indicated truth only if the contrary evidence had not also been part of the picture. When the defendant relied on an arguably credible source that tended to indicate the statement was true, the defendant presumably did not entertain serious doubts and did not consciously reject overwhelming evidence of falsity. Such a defendant, therefore, did not display reckless disregard for the truth. If a reasonable person in the defendant's position would not have relied on a lone source despite its credibility and would have ascertained the statement's falsity through further investigation, the defendant who failed to investigate further has been negligent. Negligence, however, is not as severe a degree of fault as reckless disregard and does not constitute actual malice.

Most defamation cases brought by public official or public figure plaintiffs are won by the defendant—if not at trial, then on appeal. That is often the result because the plaintiff was unable to prove actual malice even though the statement was false and tended to harm reputation. Sometimes, however, the public official or public figure plaintiff accomplishes the daunting task of proving actual malice. When that occurs, the First Amendment does not bar such a plaintiff from winning the case and recovering compensatory damages (including those of the presumed variety) as well as punitive damages.

The *Hearst* case, which follows, focuses on the actual malice element that public official plaintiffs and public figure plaintiffs must prove.

Hearst Corp. v. Skeen   159 S.W.3d 633 (Tex. Sup. Ct. 2005)

The Hearst Corporation publishes the Houston Chronicle, *whose June 11, 2000, edition included an article headlined "Justice Under Fire." Written by Evan Moore, the article contained pointed criticisms of the Smith County, Texas, criminal justice system. Under the subheading "'Win at all costs' is Smith County's rule, critics claim," the lead article reported that Smith County "is noted for its own brand of justice," which is "driven by aggressive prosecutors who achieve some of the state's longest sentences." The article stated that "[c]ritics say Smith County's justice system is tainted and inequitable." It also declared that Smith County prosecutors "have been accused of serious infractions," including "suppressing evidence, encouraging perjury, and practicing selective prosecution."*

Claiming that the article contained defamatory falsehoods, three Smith County prosecutors named in the article, District Attorney Jack Skeen and Assistant District Attorneys David Dobbs and Alicia Cashell, filed a defamation lawsuit against Hearst and Moore. A Texas trial court denied the defendants' motion for summary judgment. The state's intermediate court of appeals affirmed. Hearst and Moore appealed to the Supreme Court of Texas.

Per Curiam

To recover for defamation, the public-figure plaintiffs must prove that Hearst and Moore published a false and defamatory statement with actual malice. Although the parties disputed whether the article was capable of a defamatory meaning before the court of appeals, the issue was not raised here. Moreover, we need not decide whether the article was actually false to resolve this appeal. The plaintiffs can prevail here only if there is some evidence that Hearst and Moore published the article with actual malice.

To establish actual malice, the plaintiffs must prove Hearst and Moore published the article with either knowledge of falsity or reckless disregard for the truth. Knowledge of falsity is a relatively clear standard, but reckless disregard is much less so. Reckless disregard is a subjective standard, requiring evidence that Hearst and Moore entertained serious doubts as to the truth of the article at the time it was published.

A libel defendant is entitled to summary judgment [if the defendant] can negate actual malice as a matter of law. Hearst and Moore supported their motion for summary judgment with numerous exhibits, including Moore's affidavit, which stated he believed the article was true and accurate based on his extensive research. [With the defendants seemingly having] negated actual malice, the burden shifted to the plaintiffs to raise a fact issue.

The plaintiffs contend that Moore knew the article was false because the ten cases discussed in the article were a relatively insignificant sample from which to conclude that the Smith County D.A.'s office routinely engaged in unethical practices to win convictions. At Moore's deposition, the plaintiffs' attorney pointed out that these ten cases amounted to only .04 percent of the total indictments handled during D.A. Skeen's service. Moore admitted that he had done no statistical analysis but had only focused on the problem cases he had discovered. The fact that Moore had not reviewed every indictment during D.A. Skeen's service or discussed a larger number of problem cases is not evidence that he knew the article contained false statements.

Arguing the article was published with reckless disregard for the truth, the plaintiffs claim Hearst and Moore purposefully avoided the truth, relied on dubious information from biased sources, deviated from professional standards of care, and were motivated to fabricate. "A failure to investigate fully is not evidence of actual malice; a purposeful avoidance of the truth is." *Bentley v. Bunton,* 94 S.W.3d 561 (Tex. Sup. Ct. 2002). We analyzed evidence of purposeful avoidance in *Bentley* when a talk show host was sued for libel after repeatedly accusing a judge of being corrupt. Although the host claimed that his accusations were based on his investigations, there was a "complete absence of any evidence that a single soul . . . ever concurred in [the host's] accusations of misconduct against [the judge]. All those who could have shown [the host] that his charges were wrong [were] deliberately ignored [by the host]." For example, the host made a false accusation that the judge had improperly delayed a criminal trial without even contacting any attorney involved in the case to inquire about the delay.

Similarly, in *Harte-Hanks Communications, Inc. v. Connaughton,* 491 U.S. 657 (U.S. Sup. Ct. 1989), a newspaper deliberately avoided verifying false allegations it printed about a judicial candidate. The candidate had persuaded a certain Stephens to give him a recorded statement concerning bribes that she had made to his opponent's employee. Stephens' sister, who was present for the recorded statement, told the newspaper that the candidate used "dirty tricks" to get Stephens' statement with the intent of blackmailing his incumbent opponent into resigning before the election. Before printing the sister's allegations, the newspaper failed to interview Stephens, the key witness, or listen to the tape provided of Stephens' recorded statement. By ignoring the two sources that could objectively verify the sister's allegations, the newspaper had purposefully avoided discovering facts that might show the falsity of the allegations.

In contrast, we held in *Huckabee v. Time Warner Entertainment Co.,* 19 S.W.3d 413 (Tex. Sup. Ct. 2000), that the purposeful avoidance theory did not apply because "no source could have easily proved or disproved the documentary's allegations." When a documentary criticized a judge's order granting an allegedly abusive father custody of a child, the judge sued, arguing the filmmakers had purposefully avoided discovering the truth. The filmmakers' extensive research, which involved interviewing several people on both sides of the story, including the judge, and reading transcripts of the case, precluded a finding of purposeful avoidance. "Although the filmmakers did not interview [the father or his lawyers], they were not required to continue their research until they could find one more person who agreed with [the judge's] order." [This statement indicates that] failure to track down every possible source is not purposeful avoidance.

Like the filmmakers' research in *Huckabee,* Moore's five months of research involved interviewing parties on both sides of the issue, including the plaintiffs, and reviewing the court records of the cases discussed in the article. Furthermore, no source existed that could have easily disproved the criticisms of the Smith County D.A.'s office included in the article. The evidence simply does not support a purposeful avoidance theory.

"An understandable misinterpretation of ambiguous facts does not show actual malice, but inherently improbable assertions and statements made on information that is obviously

dubious may show actual malice." [Quoting *Bentley.*] In the current case, Moore had many sources corroborating the criticisms of the Smith County D.A.'s office. Moore testified that he spoke to over twenty attorneys, who told him that the Smith County D.A.'s office: was too aggressive; was too closely aligned with law enforcement; was overly influenced by prominence of the victim or accused; [had obtained] sentences that were harsh or excessive as compared to other jurisdictions; and had suppressed evidence or encouraged false testimony to win convictions. Although most conditioned their responses on anonymity, several attorneys, including perhaps most significantly a former Smith County D.A., allowed their names to appear in the article. The criticisms were not inherently improbable because Moore had reviewed multiple statements in court-filed documents alleging prosecutorial misconduct. Such documents included: a Court of Criminal Appeals opinion stating an assistant D.A. attempted to interview a defendant without his attorney's knowledge; a writ of habeas corpus petition alleging the Smith County D.A.'s office suppressed exculpatory evidence . . . ; a deposition . . . of chief prosecutor Dobbs, in which he admitted confronting [a] malicious prosecution [case's plaintiff] in a bar and asking "how much money would it take to make [the case] go away"; and [another case's] motion for new trial [, which] included affidavits accusing the prosecutor, Cashell, of soliciting a key witness to perjure her testimony. Moore's article was based on many sources that corroborated the criticisms, which his research showed were not inherently improbable. Therefore, no fact issue exists as to whether Moore relied on obviously doubtful sources of information for his article.

[In an attempt to] establish motivation for recklessly disregarding the truth, the plaintiffs presented evidence that Hearst and Moore ignored the plaintiffs' letter questioning the truth of the article because they received the letter two days before the article's publication deadline. This, however, is no evidence of actual malice. First, Hearst and Moore incorporated a portion of the letter into the article in the form of a quote by the plaintiffs. Second, "the mere fact that a defamation defendant knows that a public figure has denied harmful allegations or offered an alternative explanation of events is not evidence that the defendant doubted the allegations." [Quoting *Huckabee.*] Third, without more, mere evidence that a newspaper was motivated to meet a publication deadline is no evidence of actual malice. *See Harte-Hanks.*

Viewing the evidence in its entirety, no fact issue is raised as to whether the article was published with actual malice. Accordingly, [we] reverse the court of appeals' judgment and render summary judgment in favor of Hearst and Moore.

Denial of defendants' summary judgment motion reversed; summary judgment entered in favor of defendants.

Private Figure Plaintiff Cases What about defamation cases brought by *private figures,* those corporations that are not public figures and those individual persons who are neither public figures nor public officials? In *Gertz v. Robert Welch, Inc.* (1974), the Supreme Court concluded that private figure plaintiffs should not be expected to prove actual malice in order to win defamation cases, despite defendants' meaningful free speech and press interests. The Court noted that such plaintiffs have neither sought, nor do they command, the higher level of attention desired and achieved by public officials and public figures. Requiring private figure plaintiffs to prove actual malice would tip the balance too heavily in favor of defendants' First Amendment interests and would do so at the expense of plaintiffs' reputational interests. The Court sought to balance the respective interests more suitably by developing, in *Gertz,* a two-rule approach under which the first rule focused on liability and the second focused on damages.

The first *Gertz* rule provided that in order to win a defamation case, the private figure plaintiff must prove some level of fault as set by state law, so long as that level of fault was at least negligence (in the sense discussed earlier). After *Gertz,* nearly every state chose negligence as the applicable fault requirement. The second *Gertz* rule addressed recoverable damages. It provided that if a private figure plaintiff proved only negligence on the defendant's part—the level of fault necessary to enable the plaintiff to win the case—the recoverable damages would be restricted to compensatory damages for proven reputational harm and other actual injury. Presumed damages and punitive damages would not be recoverable in such an instance. The second *Gertz* rule also spoke to the availability of presumed and punitive damages by providing that if the private figure plaintiff wanted to recover such damages (either instead of or in addition to damages for demonstrated harm), he, she, or it would need to prove actual malice by clear and convincing evidence.

In a 1985 decision, *Dun & Bradstreet, Inc. v. Greenmoss Builders, Inc.,* the Court injected a *public concern vs. private concern* distinction into at least the second, if not both, of the two *Gertz* rules. The Court held in *Dun & Bradstreet* that the second *Gertz* rule (the one requiring proof of actual malice as a condition of recovering presumed and punitive damages) applies only when the private figure plaintiff's case is based on a statement that addressed a matter of public concern. If the private figure plaintiff's case pertains to a statement that addressed a matter of only private concern, the second *Gertz* rule does not apply—meaning that presumed and punitive damages are recoverable instead of or in addition to

damages for proven actual injury, even though the plaintiff established nothing more than the negligence presumably necessary to win the case. "Presumably necessary" is an apt characterization because it is a matter of interpretation and debate whether, after *Dun & Bradstreet,* the basic fault requirement of negligence still applies to a private figure plaintiff case involving a statement on a matter of private concern.

Only the second *Gertz* rule was at issue in *Dun & Bradstreet,* which, according to the Court, was a private figure/private concern case. Negligence on the defendant's part was present in the facts and was not a contested issue when the case reached the Supreme Court. Even so, it is not unreasonable to assert that if the Court was injecting a public concern qualifier into the second *Gertz* rule, it logically would also have been contemplating a public concern qualifier for the first *Gertz* rule (the rule requiring proof of at least negligence to establish liability). Under this reading of *Dun & Bradstreet,* the common law's liability-without-fault approach would again govern defamation cases of the private figure/private concern variety. Those who read *Dun & Bradstreet* more narrowly, however, are inclined to restrict it to what the Supreme Court actually held (i.e., that a public concern element is part of the second *Gertz* rule) and to assume that the basic fault requirement of negligence continues to apply to *all* private figure plaintiff cases until the Supreme Court specifically holds to the contrary. The narrower reading of *Dun & Bradstreet* may have slightly more adherents among lower courts and legal commentators, but it is a close call.

As the above discussion indicates, public concern determinations have become important in private figure plaintiff cases. (Note that the Supreme Court has not made the public concern–private concern distinction a requirement for public officials' and public figures' defamation cases—probably because the public concern character of statements about such prominent persons is essentially a "given" that may safely be assumed.) What sorts of statements, then, deal with matters of public concern? The Supreme Court provided little guidance on this issue in *Dun & Bradstreet.* Lower court decisions, however, have consistently established that statements dealing with crime address matters of public concern. The same is true of a broad range of statements dealing with public health, safety, or welfare, or with comparably important matters that capture society's attention.

The Media–Nonmedia Issue (or Nonissue?) A final set of issues concerning defamation's First Amendment–based fault requirements is whether they apply only when the defendant is a member of the media (i.e., the press), or in all defamation cases regardless of the defendant's media or nonmedia status. In phrasing its holdings in certain defamation decisions, the Supreme Court has sometimes employed media-oriented language. That may have been done, however, because the cases involved media defendants. The Court contributed to confusion on this point in one decision with an inaccurate footnote asserting that the Court had never decided whether the First Amendment–based fault requirements apply in nonmedia defendant cases. Yet the Court clearly had made such a decision. The landmark *New York Times* case included media and nonmedia defendants. There, the Court held that the public official plaintiff needed to prove actual malice on the part of all of the defendants.

Although the Court has not officially addressed the media–nonmedia issue in recent decisions, some justices have unofficially "rejected" such a distinction by making comments along those lines in concurring and dissenting opinions. In view of those comments, the decision in *New York Times,* the equal billing the First Amendment gives to freedom of "speech" and freedom of the "press," and the disapproval of a media–nonmedia distinction by most lower courts and an overwhelming majority of legal commentators, it seems extremely likely that if the Supreme Court now faced the issue squarely, it would hold that the First Amendment–based fault requirements apply to all defamation cases without regard for whether the defendant is a member of the media.

Figure 1 summarizes the major First Amendment aspects of defamation law.

Invasion of Privacy

Invasion of Privacy In tort law, the term **invasion of privacy** refers to four distinct torts. Each involves a different sense of the term privacy.

Intrusion on Solitude or Seclusion Any intentional intrusion on the solitude or seclusion of another constitutes an invasion of privacy if that intrusion would be highly offensive to a reasonable individual. The intrusion in question may be physical, such as an illegal search of a person's home or body or the opening of his mail. It may also be a nonphysical intrusion such as tapping another's telephone, examining her bank account, or subjecting her to harassing telephone calls. However, the tort applies only where there is a reasonable expectation of privacy. As a general rule, therefore, there is no liability for examining public records concerning a person, or for observing or photographing him in a public place.

Public Disclosure of Private Facts Publicizing facts concerning someone's private life can be an invasion of privacy if the publicity would be highly offensive to a reasonable person. The idea is that the public has no legitimate right to know certain aspects of a person's private life. Thus, publicity concerning someone's failure to pay his debts, humiliating illnesses he has suffered, or information about his sex life constitutes an invasion of privacy. Truth is *not* a defense to this type of invasion of privacy because the essence of the tort is giving unjustified publicity to purely private matters. Here, in further contrast to defamation, publicity means a *widespread*

Figure 1	*Constitutional Aspects of Defamation—Fault Requirements and Rules on Damages***		
	Public Official Plaintiff or Public Figure Plaintiff	**Private Figure Plaintiff and Subject of Public Concern**	**Private Figure Plaintiff and Subject of Private Concern**
What Plaintiff Must Prove to Win Case	Actual malice, by clear and convincing evidence	Fault—at least negligence	Perhaps (probably?) fault—at least negligence
Damages Recoverable If Plaintiff Wins Case	Damages for proven actual injury and/or presumed damages, as well as punitive damages	Damages for proven actual injury, if plaintiff proves only negligence. For presumed and punitive damages, plaintiff must prove actual malice, by clear and convincing evidence.	Damages for proven actual injury and/or presumed damages, as well as punitive damages

*These requirements and rules apply at least in defamation cases against a media defendant. Although the Supreme Court has left some uncertainty on this point, the requirements and rules set forth here probably apply in all defamation cases, regardless of the defendant's media or nonmedia status.

Ethics in Action

In *Hernandez v. Hillsides, Inc.,* 48 Cal. Rptr. 3d 780 (2006), the California Court of Appeal considered an invasion of privacy case arising out of the defendants' installation of a video surveillance system in an office shared by the plaintiffs. The defendants were the director of a residential facility for abused children and the two companies that operated the facility. The two plaintiffs were employees at the facility. The defendant director had the video surveillance system installed in the plaintiffs' office without their knowledge because of reports from the defendants' computer technician that someone—evidently neither of the plaintiffs—had been accessing pornographic Web sites at night from one of the computers in the plaintiffs' office. After the plaintiffs discovered the surveillance system, they also learned that it had been allowed to run not only at night (when the unauthorized computer use had occurred) but also during the daytime. This meant that the plaintiffs' activities during working hours had been recorded. They sued on the theory that the installation and operation of the surveillance system constituted an unlawful intrusion on solitude.

Although a lower court granted summary judgment in favor of the defendants, the California Court of Appeal reversed, holding that the plaintiffs had a reasonable expectation of privacy in their office and that the defendants' actions would have been highly offensive to a reasonable person. As this book went to press in 2008, the defendants' appeal to the Supreme Court of California remained pending.

Regardless of the ultimate outcome in *Hernandez,* think about behaviors such as those giving rise to the case and consider relevant ethical questions that go beyond the pure legal issues facing the courts. Give some thought, for instance, to these questions:

- When employers seek to monitor employees' actions during working hours, are there ethical obligations that constrain—or should constrain—employers? If so, what are those obligations, and how are they satisfied? Does it matter whether the employers have reason to suspect wrongdoing on the part of employees?
- In the situation that led to the plaintiffs' lawsuit in *Hernandez,* did the defendants act ethically (a) in installing the surveillance system, (b) in allowing it to run during daytime hours as well as nighttime hours, and (c) in not informing the plaintiffs about the system? If the defendants had informed the plaintiffs of the plan to install the surveillance system but the plaintiffs objected, would it have been ethical for the defendants to proceed with the installation of the system anyway?
- If an employer owns the computers in employees' offices and the employer operates the network or system of which those machines are a part, is it ethical for the employer to engage in secret monitoring of employees' use of the computers?

Be prepared to discuss the above questions and the reasons for the conclusions you draw.

---

communication of private details. For example, publication on the Internet would suffice.

As does defamation, this form of invasion of privacy potentially conflicts with the First Amendment. Courts have attempted to resolve this conflict in two major ways. First, no liability ordinarily attaches to publicity concerning matters of public record or legitimate public interest. Second, public figures and public officials have no right of privacy concerning information that is reasonably related to their public lives.

False Light Publicity Publicity that places a person in a false light in the public eye can be an invasion of privacy if that false light would be highly offensive to a reasonable person. What is required is unreasonable and highly objectionable publicity attributing to a person characteristics that she does not possess or beliefs that she does not hold. Examples include signing a person's name to a public letter that violates her deeply held beliefs or attributing authorship of an inferior scholarly or artistic

work to her. As in defamation cases, truth is a defense to liability. It is not necessary, however, that a person be defamed by the false light in which he is placed. For instance, signing a pro-life person's name to a petition urging increased abortion rights would create liability for false light publicity but probably not for defamation.

In view of the overlap between false light publicity and defamation, and the obvious First Amendment issues at stake, defendants in false light cases enjoy constitutional protections matching those enjoyed by defamation defendants.

Commercial Appropriation of Name or Likeness
Liability for invasion of privacy can exist when, without that person's consent, the defendant commercially uses someone's name or likeness, normally to imply his endorsement of a product or service or a nonexistent connection with the defendant's business.

This form of invasion of privacy also draws on the personal property right connected with a person's identity and his exclusive right to control it. In recent decades, recognition of this property right has given rise to a separate legal doctrine known as the *right of publicity,* under which public figures, celebrities, and entertainers have a cause of action against defendants who, without consent, use the right holders' names, likenesses, or identities for commercial purposes. Protected attributes of a celebrity's identity may include such things as a distinctive singing voice. Use of a celebrity's name or a "soundalike" of her in an advertisement for a product would be a classic example of a commercial use, as would use of an entertainer's picture as a commercially sold poster. Not all uses are commercial in nature, however, even if there is an underlying profit motive at stake. For example, though the cases are not entirely consistent on this point, a television show or movie that uses a celebrity's name, likeness, or identity is likely to be classified as noncommercial and thus not a violation of the right of publicity. Some uses are close to the line and require courts to make difficult determinations regarding the use's commercial or noncommercial nature. Moreover, First Amendment issues sometimes arise in these cases, as indicated in the *C.B.C. Distribution* case, which follows shortly.

States that recognize the right of publicity usually consider it inheritable—meaning that it may survive the death of the celebrity who held the right during his or her lifetime. There is little agreement among the states, however, on how long the right persists after the celebrity's death.

C.B.C. Distribution & Marketing, Inc. v. Major League Baseball Advanced Media, L.P.   505 F.3d 818 (8th Cir. 2007)

C.B.C. Distribution & Marketing, Inc. (CBC), sells fantasy sports products via its Internet Web site, e-mail, mail, and the telephone. Its fantasy baseball products use the names of actual major league baseball players, as well as their performance and biographical data. Before the commencement of the major league baseball season each spring, participants form their fantasy baseball teams by "drafting" players from various major league baseball teams. Participants compete against other fantasy baseball "owners" who have also drafted their own teams. The success of a participant's team depends on the actual performance of the fantasy team's players on their respective actual teams during the course of the major league season. Participants in CBC's fantasy games pay fees to play and additional fees to trade players during the course of the season.

From 1995 through the end of 2004, CBC licensed its use of the names of and information about major league players from the Major League Baseball Players Association (Players Association) pursuant to agreements that it entered into with the association in 1995 and 2002. The 2002 agreement licensed to CBC "the names, nicknames, likenesses, signatures, pictures, playing records, and/or biographical data of each player" (the "Rights") to be used in association with CBC's fantasy baseball products.

In 2005, after the 2002 agreement expired, the Players Association licensed to Major League Baseball Advanced Media, L.P. (Advanced Media), the exclusive right to use baseball players' names and performance information "for exploitation via all interactive media." Advanced Media began providing fantasy baseball games on its Web site, MLB.com, the official Web site of major league baseball. It offered CBC, in exchange for a commission, a license to promote the MLB.com fantasy baseball games on CBC's Web site but did not offer CBC a license to continue to offer its own fantasy baseball products.

This conduct by Advanced Media prompted CBC to file a declaratory judgment action against Advanced Media. Alleging that it reasonably anticipated being sued by Advanced Media if it continued to operate its fantasy baseball games, CBC asked the federal district court to rule that CBC has the right to use, without license, the names of and information about major league baseball players in connection with its fantasy baseball products. Advanced Media counterclaimed, maintaining that CBC's fantasy baseball products violated rights of publicity belonging to major league baseball players and that the players, through their association, had licensed those rights to Advanced Media. The Players Association intervened in the case, joining in Advanced Media's claims. When the district court granted summary judgment in favor of CBC, Advanced Media and the Players Association appealed to the U.S. Court of Appeals for the Eighth Circuit.

Arnold, Circuit Judge

Because this appeal is from the district court's grant of summary judgment, our review is *de novo,* and we . . . view the evidence in the light most favorable to the nonmoving party. Summary judgment is appropriate only if there is no genuine issue as to any material fact and the moving party is entitled to judgment as a matter of law. We also review *de novo* the district court's interpretation of state law, including its interpretation of

Missouri law regarding the right of publicity. When state law is ambiguous, we must predict how the highest court of that state would resolve the issue.

An action based on the right of publicity is a state-law claim. In Missouri, "the elements of a right of publicity action include: (1) That defendant used plaintiff's name as a symbol of his identity (2) without consent (3) and with the intent to obtain a commercial advantage." *Doe v. TCI Cablevision,* 110 S.W.3d 363, 369 (Mo. 2003). The parties all agree that CBC's continued use of the players' names and playing information after the expiration of the 2002 agreement was without consent. The district court concluded, however, that the evidence was insufficient to make out the other two elements of the claim, and we address each of these in turn.

With respect to the symbol-of-identity element, the Missouri Supreme Court has observed that "'the name used by the defendant must be understood by the audience as referring to the plaintiff'" [and] that "[i]n resolving this issue, the fact-finder may consider evidence including 'the nature and extent of the identifying characteristics used by the defendant, the defendant's intent, the fame of the plaintiff, evidence of actual identification made by third persons, and surveys or other evidence indicating the perceptions of the audience.'" *Doe,* 110 S.W.3d at 370 (quoting *Restatement (Third) of Unfair Competition* § 46 cmt. d). Here, we entertain no doubt that the players' names that CBC used are understood by it and its fantasy baseball subscribers as referring to actual major league baseball players. CBC itself admits that. In responding to the appellants' argument that "this element is met by the mere confirmation that the name used, in fact, refers to the famous person asserting the violation," CBC stated in its brief that "if this is all the element requires, CBC agrees that it is met." We think that by reasoning that "identity," rather than "mere use of a name," "is a critical element of the right of publicity," the district court did not understand that when a name alone is sufficient to establish identity, the defendant's use of that name satisfies the plaintiff's burden to show that a name was used as a symbol of identity.

It is true that with respect to the "commercial advantage" element of a cause of action for violating publicity rights, CBC's use does not fit neatly into the more traditional categories of commercial advantage, namely, using individuals' names for advertising and merchandising purposes in a way that states or intimates that the individuals are endorsing a product. See *Restatement (Third) of Unfair Competition* § 47 cmt. a, b. But the *Restatement,* which the Missouri Supreme Court has recognized as authority in this kind of case, also says that a name is used for commercial advantage when it is used "in connection with services rendered by the user" and that the plaintiff need not show that "prospective purchasers are likely to believe" that he or she endorsed the product or service. We note, moreover,

that in Missouri, "the commercial advantage element of the right of publicity focuses on the defendant's intent or purpose to obtain a commercial benefit from use of the plaintiff's identity." *Doe,* 110 S.W.3d at 370–71. Because we think it is clear that CBC uses baseball players' identities in its fantasy baseball products for purposes of profit, we believe that their identities are being used for commercial advantage and that the players therefore offered sufficient evidence to make out a cause of action for violation of their rights of publicity under Missouri law.

CBC argues that the First Amendment nonetheless trumps the right-of-publicity action that Missouri law provides. Though this dispute is between private parties, the state action necessary for First Amendment protections exists because the right-of-publicity claim exists only insofar as the courts enforce state-created obligations.

The Supreme Court has directed that state-law rights of publicity must be balanced against First Amendment considerations. See *Zacchini v. Scripps-Howard Broadcasting Co.,* 433 U.S. 562 (1977). [H]ere we conclude that the former must give way to the latter. First, the information used in CBC's fantasy baseball games is all readily available in the public domain, and it would be strange law that a person would not have a First Amendment right to use information that is available to everyone. It is true that CBC's use of the information is meant to provide entertainment, but "[s]peech that entertains, like speech that informs, is protected by the First Amendment because '[t]he line between the informing and the entertaining is too elusive for the protection of that basic right.'" *Cardtoons, L.C. v. Major League Baseball Players Ass'n,* 95 F.3d 959, 969 (10th Cir. 1996) (quoting *Winters v. New York,* 333 U.S. 507, 510, 68 S. Ct. 665, 92 L. Ed. 840 (1948)).

We also find no merit in the argument that CBC's use of players' names and information in its fantasy baseball games is not speech at all. We have held that "the pictures, graphic design, concept art, sounds, music, stories, and narrative present in video games" is speech entitled to First Amendment protection. See *Interactive Digital Software Ass'n v. St. Louis County,* 329 F.3d 954, 957 (8th Cir. 2003). Similarly, here CBC uses the "names, nicknames, likenesses, signatures, pictures, playing records, and/or biographical data of each player" in an interactive form in connection with its fantasy baseball products. This use is no less expressive than the use that was at issue in *Interactive Digital.*

Courts have also recognized the public value of information about the game of baseball and its players, referring to baseball as "the national pastime." *Cardtoons,* 95 F.3d at 972. A California court, in a case where Major League Baseball was itself defending its use of players' names, likenesses, and information against the players' asserted rights of publicity, observed,

"Major league baseball is followed by millions of people across this country on a daily basis. . . . The public has an enduring fascination in the records set by former players and in memorable moments from previous games. . . . The records and statistics remain of interest to the public because they provide context that allows fans to better appreciate (or deprecate) today's performances." *Gionfriddo v. Major League Baseball,* 114 Cal. Rptr. 2d 307 (Cal. App. 2001). The Court in *Gionfriddo* concluded that the "recitation and discussion of factual data concerning the athletic performance of [players on Major League Baseball's Web site] command a substantial public interest, and, therefore, is a form of expression due substantial constitutional protection." We find these views persuasive.

In addition, the facts in this case barely, if at all, implicate the interests that states typically intend to vindicate by providing rights of publicity to individuals. Economic interests that states seek to promote include the right of an individual to reap the rewards of his or her endeavors and an individual's right to earn a living. Other motives for creating a publicity right are the desire to provide incentives to encourage a person's productive activities and to protect consumers from misleading advertising. See *Zacchini,* 433 U.S. at 573, 576; *Cardtoons,* 95 F.3d at 973. But major league baseball players are rewarded, and handsomely, too, for their participation in games and can earn additional large sums from endorsements and sponsorship arrangements. Nor is there any danger here that consumers will be misled, because the fantasy baseball games depend on the inclusion of all players and thus cannot create a false impression that some particular player with "star power" is endorsing CBC's products.

Then there are so-called nonmonetary interests that publicity rights are sometimes thought to advance. These include protecting natural rights, rewarding celebrity labors, and avoiding emotional harm. See *Cardtoons,* 95 F.3d at 973. We do not see that any of these interests are especially relevant here, where baseball players are rewarded separately for their labors, and where any emotional harm would most likely be caused by a player's actual performance, in which case media coverage would cause the same harm. We also note that some courts have indicated that the right of publicity is intended to promote only economic interests and that noneconomic interests are more directly served by so-called rights of privacy. For instance, although the court in *Cardtoons* conducted a separate discussion of noneconomic interests when weighing the countervailing rights, it ultimately concluded that the noneconomic justifications for the right of publicity were unpersuasive as compared with the interest in freedom of expression. "Publicity rights . . . are meant to protect against the loss of financial gain, not mental anguish." We see merit in th[e] approach [taken in *Cardtoons*].

[W]e hold that CBC's First Amendment rights in offering its fantasy baseball products supersede the players' rights of publicity.

District court's grant of summary judgment in favor of CBC affirmed.

Misuse of Legal Proceedings

Misuse of Legal Proceedings Three intentional torts protect people against the harm that can result from wrongfully instituted legal proceedings. **Malicious prosecution** affords a remedy for the wrongful institution of criminal proceedings. Recovery for malicious prosecution requires proof that (1) the defendant caused the criminal proceedings to be initiated against the plaintiff without probable cause to believe that an offense had been committed; (2) the defendant did so for an improper purpose; and (3) the criminal proceedings eventually were terminated in the plaintiff's favor. **Wrongful use of civil proceedings** is designed to protect people from wrongfully instituted civil suits. Its elements are very similar to those for malicious prosecution.

Abuse of process imposes liability on those who initiate legal proceedings, whether criminal or civil, for a primary purpose other than the one for which the proceedings were designed. Abuse of process cases often involve situations in which the legal proceedings compel the other person to take some action unrelated to the subject of the suit. For example, Rogers wishes to buy Herbert's property, but Herbert refuses to sell. To pressure him into selling, Rogers files a private nuisance suit against Herbert, contending that Herbert's activities on his land interfere with Rogers's use and enjoyment of his adjoining property. Rogers may be liable to Herbert for abuse of process even if Rogers had reason to file the case, and even if Rogers won the case.

Deceit (Fraud)

Deceit (Fraud) Deceit (or fraud) is the formal name for the tort claim that is available to victims of knowing misrepresentations. Liability for fraud usually requires proof of a false statement of material fact that was knowingly or recklessly made by the defendant with the intent to induce reliance by the plaintiff, along with actual, justifiable, and detrimental reliance on the plaintiff's past. Because most fraud actions arise in a contractual setting, and because a tort action is only one of the remedies available to a victim of fraud, a more complete discussion of this topic is deferred until Chapter 13.

Interference with Property Rights

Trespass to Land

Trespass to land may be defined as any unauthorized or unprivileged intentional intrusion upon another's real property. Such intrusions include (1) physically entering the plaintiff's land; (2) causing another to do so (e.g., by chasing someone onto the land); (3) remaining on the land after one's right to remain has ceased (e.g., staying past the term of a lease); (4) failing to remove from the land anything one has a duty to remove; (5) causing an object or other thing to enter the land (although some overlap with nuisance exists here); and (6) invading the airspace above the land or the subsurface beneath it (if property law and federal, state, and local regulations give the plaintiff rights to the airspace or subsurface and do not allow the defendant to intrude).

The intent required for trespass liability is simply the intent to be on the land or to cause it to be invaded. A person therefore may be liable for trespass even though the trespass resulted from his mistaken belief that his entry was legally justified. Where the trespass was specifically intended, no actual harm to the land is required for liability, but actual harm is required for reckless or negligent trespasses.

Private Nuisance

In general, a **private nuisance** involves some interference with the plaintiff's use and enjoyment of her land. Unlike trespass to land, nuisance usually does not involve any physical invasion of the plaintiff's property. Trespass usually requires an invasion of tangible matter, whereas nuisance involves other interferences. Examples of such other interferences include odors, noise, smoke, light, and vibration. For nuisance liability to exist, however, the interference must be *substantial* and *unreasonable*. The defendant, moreover, must intend the interference.

The *Stephens* case, which follows, illustrates nuisance principles and explores issues concerning recoverable damages.

Stephens v. Pillen	681 N.W.2d 59 (Neb. App. 2004)

In December 2000, a group of 18 plaintiffs sued James D. Pillen and various other defendants, seeking injunctive relief and damages on the theory that the defendants' hog confinement operation constituted a private nuisance. The plaintiffs alleged that the hog confinement operation, which was conducted at four facilities in two different Nebraska counties, had been a nuisance since 1997. In addition, the plaintiffs alleged that they had been deprived of the normal use and enjoyment of their property, and that the defendants had been notified of the plaintiffs' concerns but had failed to take corrective action.

At a 2002 bench trial in a state district court, Pillen testified about the relevant facilities, each of which was classified as a "5,000 sow unit." The first of the four facilities was put into operation in 1996. The most recent facility was added in 1999. Pillen testified that he knew in May 1997 of a complaint from Nebraska's Department of Environmental Quality (DEQ) concerning "the odor from [an] incinerator" constructed at one of the facilities. Pillen believed that the DEQ complaint resulted from a complaint made to the DEQ by one of the plaintiffs. In addition, Pillen testified that he had discussed an odor problem with some of the plaintiffs prior to the end of September 1997.

All 18 plaintiffs testified concerning how the hog confinement operations had affected their lives and the use and enjoyment of their property. The testimony generally concerned the impact of odors from the hog confinement operation. The plaintiffs described the odors from the defendants' facilities as "unbearable," as "overwhelmingly a suffocating stench," as a "musty hog [excrement] smell," as a "sewage odor," as a "gas[-like] smell," and as an odor that "chokes you." Various plaintiffs said the smell was so bad that they had to keep their houses closed up at all times. The odor problem prevented them from spending time in their yards or gardens, from hanging laundry on outdoor clotheslines, and from participating in outside activities with children or grandchildren. One plaintiff testified that she was a "prisoner" in her own home.

According to Pillen's testimony, the defendants had tried various procedures to diminish the odors emanating from the facilities and the waste lagoons located there. These measures included the use of food additives, waste additives, and lagoon treatments. Pillen further testified that he did not think the hog confinement operation had changed the plaintiffs' quality of life or would ever disrupt their daily activities to such an extent that the operation should be changed.

The trial court ruled in favor of the plaintiffs and held that the defendants' four-facility operation constituted an intentional nuisance. The court ordered the defendants to explore the utility of processes to mitigate the odors and to implement such processes. In addition, the court ordered that the defendants must, within 12 months, "abate the nuisance or cease operating" their hog confinement facilities. Although the court found that the plaintiffs had suffered at least "some damage" as a result of the nuisance, the court noted that "none of the plaintiffs [was] able to quantify any request for damages" and that the plaintiffs "had not adduced any evidence sufficient for the court to award them specific damages." As a result, the court awarded no monetary recovery to any of the plaintiffs. On appeal to the Nebraska Court of Appeals, the defendants challenged the trial court's conclusion that the hog confinement operation constituted a nuisance. The plaintiffs challenged the trial court's failure to award damages.

Irwin, Chief Judge

We first address . . . whether the district court was correct in finding that the plaintiffs proved that the hog confinement facilities constitute a nuisance. The defendants assert that the district court erred in this regard and should have sustained the defendants' motion to dismiss. We disagree because we conclude that the evidence supports a finding that the defendants have known since 1997 that the hog confinement facilities have invaded the plaintiffs' private use and enjoyment of their land.

The appellate courts of Nebraska have adopted the law of nuisance as articulated in the *Restatement (Second) of Torts* (1979). A private nuisance is a nontrespassory invasion of another's interest in the private use and enjoyment of his or her land. Section 822 of the *Restatement (Second)* provides that one is subject to liability for a private nuisance if, but only if, his or her conduct is a legal cause of an invasion of another's interest in the private use and enjoyment of land and the invasion is intentional and unreasonable.

An intentional invasion of another's interest in the private use and enjoyment of land exists when an actor purposefully causes the invasion, knows that the invasion is resulting from the actor's conduct, or knows that the invasion is substantially certain to result from the actor's conduct. To be "intentional," an invasion of another's interest in the use and enjoyment of land, or of the public right, need not be inspired by malice or ill will on the actor's part toward the other. An invasion so inspired is intentional, but so is an invasion that the actor knowingly causes in the pursuit of a laudable enterprise without any desire to cause harm. It is the knowledge that the actor has at the time he acts or fails to act that determines whether the invasion resulting from his conduct is intentional or unintentional.

In this case, our review of the record indicates that the defendants knew, at least as early as September 1997 and perhaps as early as May 1997, that the operation of these facilities was causing an interference with the plaintiffs' enjoyment of their land. Several of the plaintiffs testified that they complained to the defendants about the odor from the facilities. Pillen testified that he discussed the odor with some of the plaintiffs and wrote them a letter on the subject in September 1997. Pillen also testified that he had received complaints about [some of the] facilities in the past. Further, as discussed more fully below,

the evidence indicates that the interference with the plaintiffs' enjoyment of their land was substantial and unreasonable. [T]he record adequately supports the district court's finding that the plaintiffs proved that the defendants' operation of these facilities constituted a knowing and intentional nuisance. As such, the [defendants'] assertions . . . are meritless.

The issue raised [by the plaintiffs] is whether the record supported an award of monetary damages, i.e., whether the district court erred in finding that it did not. Our review of the record indicates that many of the plaintiffs did present sufficient evidence to entitle them to an award of monetary damages. Some plaintiffs did not present sufficient evidence, and still other plaintiffs presented evidence which would have supported an award of monetary damages but affirmatively testified that they did not want any monetary damages.

We find that 11 of the plaintiffs presented sufficient evidence to support an award of monetary damages. [List of the 11 plaintiffs' names omitted.] Each of these plaintiffs presented testimony that he or she has suffered significant discomfort, annoyance, and inconvenience in the use of his or her property.

Our review of the district court's order leads us to conclude that the district court mistakenly applied rules applicable to special damages to the plaintiffs' request for general damages. Although damages such as depreciation in market or rental value of property, medical expenses, and psychological expenses may be recoverable in a nuisance action, such damages would be special damages and would require specific proof to be awarded. General damages, however, do not require specific proof. General damages are such as the jury may give when the judge cannot point to any measure by which they are to be assessed except the opinion and judgment of a reasonable person. By definition, the very nature of general damages [means] that a court cannot point out any measure of damages for things such as discomfort, annoyance, or inconvenience. Nonetheless, such damages are recoverable in a nuisance action.

The 11 plaintiffs [referred to] above all presented sufficient testimony to establish significant damage to their way of life and their quality of life as a result of the nuisance in this case. They variously testified about significant interferences with their abilities to use and enjoy their homes and yards, including hanging laundry on the clothesline, spending time outside with children and grandchildren, opening their windows to enjoy fresh air, and generally enjoying time outside. They [also] testified that they are forced to make sure windows and doors to their homes are closed at all times so that the odor does not invade the inside of their homes. Some of them testified that they had air conditioning and used it to keep their homes cool when the windows were shut. Kathleen Stephens identified herself as a "prisoner" in her own home and testified that she could not even eat things grown in her own garden because they had been "out in that smell" and thus were unappetizing as a result of the hog confinement facilities. Earl Stephens testified that he and Kathleen Stephens were considering moving and leaving land that had been in his family for years. James McIntosh testified that as a result of the odors, his family no longer plans any outdoor activities. Wanda Loseke testified that she has to put Mentholatum in her nose to be able to tolerate sitting on her porch to read. The 11 plaintiffs listed above all presented . . . similar testimony [sufficient] to establish that they have suffered compensable general damages as a result of the nuisance.

Although many of the 11 plaintiffs [referred to] above testified that they could not put a specific monetary value on these damages, none of them testified that he or she actually did not want compensation for such damages. [We therefore] reverse the order of the district court denying monetary damages to these 11 plaintiffs and remand the matter to the district court with directions to award appropriate monetary damages to each of them, considering the extent of interference demonstrated by their testimony.

Note: In the remainder of its opinion, the Nebraska Court of Appeals concluded that two other plaintiffs had not presented sufficient evidence to support an award of damages because they testified only that they sometimes noticed a foul smell and not that there had been any significant effect on their lives or on their ability to use their property. The court also concluded that five other plaintiffs had presented evidence otherwise supportive of an award of general damages, but that those plaintiffs, when cross-examined, had specifically said they did not wish to recover damages. Therefore, the court ruled that the trial court had been correct in denying those plaintiffs an award of damages.

Trial court's nuisance determination and issuance of injunction affirmed; trial court's denial of damages to plaintiffs affirmed in part and reversed in part; case remanded for determination of damages to be awarded to qualifying plaintiffs.

Conversion

Conversion is the defendant's intentional exercise of dominion or control over the plaintiff's personal property without the plaintiff's consent. Usually, the personal property in question is the plaintiff's goods. This can happen through the defendant's (1) *acquisition* of the plaintiff's property (e.g., theft, fraud, and even the purchase of stolen property); (2) *removal* of the plaintiff's property (e.g., taking that property to the dump or moving the plaintiff's car); (3) *transfer* of the plaintiff's property (e.g., selling stolen goods or misdelivering property); (4) *withholding possession* of the plaintiff's property (e.g., refusing to return a car one was to repair); (5) *destruction or alteration* of the plaintiff's property; or (6) *using* the plaintiff's property (e.g., driving a car left by its owner for storage purposes only).

In each case, the necessary intent is merely the intent to exercise dominion or control over the property. It is therefore possible for the defendant to be liable if she buys or sells stolen property in good faith. However, conversion is limited to *serious* interferences with the plaintiff's property rights.

If there is a serious interference and conversion, the defendant is liable for the *full value* of the property. What happens when the interference is nonserious? Although it has largely been superseded by conversion and its elements are hazy, a tort called **trespass to personal property** may come into play here. Suppose that Richards goes to McCrory Motors and asks to test-drive a new Corvette. If Richards either wrecks the car, causing major damage, or drives it across the United States, he is probably liable for conversion and obligated to pay McCrory the reasonable value of the car. On the other hand, if Richards is merely involved in a fender-bender, or keeps the car for eight hours, he is probably only liable for trespass. Therefore, he is only obligated to pay damages to compensate McCrory for the loss in value of the car or for its loss of use of the car.

A very different attempted application of trespass principles was unsuccessful in the *Intel* case, which is discussed in the nearby Cyberlaw in Action box.

Other Examples of Intentional Tort Liability

Chapter 8 discusses three additional intentional torts that protect various economic interests and often involve unfair competition: *injurious falsehood* (a type of business "defamation"); *intentional interference with contractual relations;* and *interference with prospective advantage.* Chapter 51 examines an intentional tortlike recovery for wrongful discharge called the *public policy* exception to employment at will. In Chapter 27, the text discusses the recoveries some states allow for *bad faith breach of contract.*

CYBERLAW IN ACTION

If a person uses a corporation's e-mail system to distribute unsolicited e-mails to large numbers of the corporation's employees and does so without the consent of the corporation, has the distributor committed the tort of trespass to personal property? That was the issue addressed by the Supreme Court of California in a 2003 decision.

After being fired from his job at Intel, Kourosh Hamidi obtained the company's e-mail address list without breaching Intel's computer security system; instead, an anonymous source sent the list to Hamidi on a computer disk. Over a period of approximately two years, Hamidi sent six e-mails to each of at least 8,000, and perhaps as many as 35,000, Intel employees. Hamidi's e-mails discussed his grievances against Intel and criticized the company's employment practices. A number of Intel employees complained to their employer about having received Hamidi's e-mails. Hamidi offered, however, to remove from his distribution list the addresses of Intel employees who requested that their addresses be removed. When employees so requested, Hamidi followed through on his removal offer.

After Intel's attempts to block Hamidi's e-mails proved largely unsuccessful and Hamidi ignored Intel's demands that he cease sending messages to the firm's employees, Intel sued Hamidi. Intel alleged that it owned the e-mail system, that the system was intended primarily for business use by Intel employees, that the address list was confidential, and that Hamidi had continued his mass e-mailings despite demands from Intel that he stop. Contending that Hamidi's actions amounted to trespass to chattels (i.e., trespass to personal property), Intel asked the court for an injunction barring Hamidi from sending further e-mails to Intel employees at their Intel addresses. A California trial court later granted summary judgment in favor of Intel and issued the requested injunction.

Hamidi appealed to the California Court of Appeal, which affirmed the lower court's decision. The appellate court conceded that injunctive relief was appropriate in view of the disruption to Intel's business that resulted from Hamidi's intentional interference with the company's e-mail system. This interference, the court reasoned, brought the case within the ownership and possession-related interests protected by the legal theory of trespass to personal property. The appellate court regarded its application of that "somewhat arcane" theory to the modern e-mail context as an illustration of how "[t]he common law adapts to human endeavor."

Again Hamidi appealed, this time to the Supreme Court of California. In *Intel Corp. v. Hamidi,* 71 P.3d 296 (2003), the Supreme Court reversed the lower courts' decisions.

The court observed that Hamidi's e-mails neither physically damaged nor functionally disrupted Intel's computers and did not prevent Intel from using its computers. These key facts caused the court to regard trespass to personal property as an ill-fitting theory. The court held that the trespass theory

> does not encompass, and should not be extended to encompass, an electronic communication that neither damages the recipient computer system nor impairs its functioning. Such an electronic communication does not constitute an actionable trespass to personal property, i.e., the computer system, because it does not interfere with the possessor's use or possession of, or any other legally protected interest in, the personal property itself.

Although Intel argued that it had suffered harm in the form of lost productivity resulting from the fact that employees read and reacted to Hamidi's messages, the Supreme Court noted that any such harm did not help Intel establish the necessary elements of a trespass claim. Such supposed harm was "not an injury to the company's interest in its computers—which worked as intended and were unharmed by the communications—any more than the personal distress caused by reading an unpleasant letter would be an injury to the recipient's mailbox. . . ." Intel's real concern, the court concluded, pertained to the content of Hamidi's messages. The court was unwilling to allow the trespass to personal property theory, whether in traditional or modified form, to be employed as a means of squelching speech that Intel found objectionable. Although the court only briefly touched on the potential First Amendment implications of a contrary holding, the decision appeared to have been influenced by the free speech arguments of organizations that had filed *amicus curiae* (friend-of-the-court) briefs in the case.

In rejecting Intel's attempt to employ the trespass to personal property theory to the facts at hand, the Supreme Court emphasized that its holding would not prohibit Internet service providers (ISPs) from invoking trespass principles as a basis for legal relief against senders of "unsolicited commercial bulk e-mail, also known as 'spam.'" Citing cases in which spammers had been held liable to ISPs, the court noted that in those cases, the trespass to personal property theory was applicable because "the extraordinary quantity of [spam] impaired the [relevant] computer system's functioning." The supposed injury in *Intel v. Hamidi,* by contrast, took the form of "the disruption or distraction caused to recipients by the *contents* of the e-mail messages, an injury . . . not directly affecting the possession or value of personal property."

Problems and Problem Cases

1. Betty England worked at a Dairy Queen restaurant owned by S&M Foods in Tallulah, Louisiana. One day while she was at work, her manager, Larry Garley, became upset when several incorrectly prepared hamburgers were returned by a customer. Garley expressed his dissatisfaction by throwing a hamburger that hit England on the leg. Assume that while Garley was not trying to hit England with the hamburger, he was aware that she was substantially certain to be hit as a result of his action. Also, assume that England was not harmed by the hamburger. England sued Garley for battery. Did Garley have the necessary intent for battery liability? Does England's not suffering harm defeat her battery claim?

2. Martin Wishnatsky worked as a paralegal for attorney Peter Crary. While Crary was engaged in a conversation with North Dakota Assistant Attorney General David Huey in Crary's office, Wishnatsky attempted to enter the office. Huey then pushed the door closed in Wishnatsky's face, forcing him back into the hall. Wishnatsky, who suffered no physical injury as a result of Huey's action, sued Huey for battery. In an affidavit filed in opposition to Huey's motion for summary judgment, Wishnatsky stated that he was offended, shocked, and frightened as a result of Huey's action and the "You get out of here" statement Huey allegedly made to Wishnatsky as he (Huey) pushed the door closed. After the trial court granted Huey's motion for summary judgment, Wishnatsky appealed. Was Huey entitled to summary judgment?

3. Drs. Fuste and Vanden Hoek, the plaintiffs in the lawsuit referred to below, were employed as pediatricians by Riverside Healthcare Association, Inc. (RHA), for approximately five years until a dispute between the plaintiffs and RHA caused both physicians to terminate their employment with RHA. After opening a new medical practice, Drs. Fuste and Vanden Hoek filed a defamation lawsuit in a Virginia court against RHA, Riverside Hospital, Inc., and Riverside Physician Services, Inc. Also named as defendants were Peninsula Healthcare, Inc., and Healthkeepers, Inc. The plaintiffs based their defamation claim on false statements supposedly made about them after they left their employment with RHA. According to their complaint, the statements were made by employees of RHA and the other defendants. The statements, supposedly made to patients, agents of other hospitals, and credentialing officials at area hospitals, charged that Drs. Fuste and Vanden Hoek were "unprofessional" and "uncooperative," that they had "left suddenly" and "abandoned their patients," and that there were "concerns about their competence." In addition, the plaintiffs alleged in their complaint that a caller to Healthkeepers was told that Drs. Fuste and Vanden Hoek would "never be put back on the Healthkeepers list of providers because of the way they left Riverside." When parents and grandparents of the plaintiffs' former patients inquired about the plaintiffs' whereabouts, RHA employees said that Drs. Fuste and Vanden Hoek had "left suddenly," that they "were not able to work in the area," that "their whereabouts were unknown," and that callers "should find another pediatrician." Finally, the plaintiffs alleged in their complaint that an RHA employee contacted a person who was contemplating working for Drs. Fuste and Vanden Hoek and told her that the plaintiffs' new practice "would be immediately shut down the day it opened" and that if she took a job there, she "would never have a future job with Riverside."

   The defendants filed demurrers to the plaintiffs' complaint. A Virginia state court judge sustained the defendants' demurrers and dismissed the plaintiffs' complaint. In remarks from the bench, the judge observed that Drs. Fuste and Vanden Hoek had not stated a valid defamation claim because "the defamatory statements as alleged, on balance, appear to be opinions by and between people involved in the health care field." The plaintiffs appealed to the Supreme Court of Virginia. Did the trial judge rule correctly in sustaining the defendants' demurrers on the ground that the statements were nonactionable opinion?

4. While at a Dillard's department store that was located in a shopping mall, Lakesha Millbrook tried on a pair of jeans. She decided not to purchase that pair, but she eventually purchased a different pair and then proceeded to another area of the store to wait on a friend. Shortly thereafter, Millbrook and her companion exited Dillard's and entered the public area of the mall. A security officer wearing a police uniform (because he was an off-duty police officer retained by Dillard's) then approached Millbrook, grabbed

her shoulder, and stated that Millbrook needed to come back to Dillard's with him. The officer accompanied Millbrook to the store. The officer and a Dillard's employee then escorted Millbrook into a room. Millbrook's friend tried to join them, but the officer would not let him do so. Once they were in the room, the officer stated that Millbrook was responsible for a missing pair of jeans. Millbrook informed them that she had purchased a pair of jeans and offered her receipt as evidence. According to Millbrook, the officer, without looking at her receipt, searched her bag before he left the room. When the officer left the room, he stood outside the room in front of the door. The Dillard's employee remained inside the room with Millbrook. After roughly 20 minutes, the officer came back into the room and told Millbrook that she was free to leave. According to Millbrook, the incident caused her to start crying because she was hurt and embarrassed. Furthermore, she stated that she had done considerable crying at nights and had become fearful of being wrongly approached or accused. Millbrook missed no work as a result of the incident. Nor did she see any doctors, psychologists, therapists, or counselors as a result of the incident. Millbrook later sued Dillard's, bringing claims for assault, battery, and false imprisonment. Dillard's moved for summary judgment. How did the court rule in regard to each of Millbrook's claims?

5. Cindy Lourcey worked as a mail carrier for the United States Postal Service. While delivering mail by postal vehicle in Lebanon, Tennessee, Lourcey saw Charles Scarlett and his wife, Joanne Scarlett, in the middle of the street. Lourcey stopped her vehicle to provide assistance and spoke with Charles Scarlett, who said his wife was having a seizure. As Lourcey used her cell phone to call 911 to request help, Charles Scarlett pulled out a pistol and shot his wife in the head. He then turned and faced Lourcey, pointed the pistol at his head, and fatally shot himself.

Lourcey sued the estate of Charles Scarlett in a Tennessee court on the theory that Scarlett's conduct constituted intentional infliction of emotional distress. According to Lourcey's complaint, Scarlett's conduct caused Lourcey to experience post-traumatic stress disorder, depression, and emotional harm. Lourcey also alleged that the incident's lingering effects left her unable to return to work and caused her to experience lost earning capacity. Arguing that the allegations in Lourcey's complaint were insufficient to state a legal claim, Scarlett's estate moved for dismissal. Were Loucey's allegations sufficient to state a legal claim for intentional infliction of emotional distress?

6. Irma White, a churchgoing woman in her late forties, was employed at a Monsanto refinery. While working in the canning department, she and three other employees were told to transfer a corrosive and hazardous chemical from a larger container into smaller containers. After they asked for rubber gloves and goggles, a supervisor sent for the equipment. In the meantime, White began cleaning up the work area and one of the other employees went to another area to do some work. The other two employees sat around waiting for the safety equipment, contrary to a work rule requiring employees to busy themselves in such situations.

After learning that the group was idle, Gary McDermott, the canning department foreman, went to the work station. Once there, he launched into a profane one-minute tirade directed at White and the other two workers present, calling them "motherf—s," accusing them of sitting on their "f—g asses," and threatening to "show them to the gate." At this, White became upset and began to experience pain in her chest, pounding in her head, and difficulty in breathing. Her family physician met her at the hospital, where he admitted her, fearing that she was having a heart attack. She was later diagnosed as having had an acute anxiety reaction.

White later sued Monsanto for intentional infliction of emotional distress. Was her distress sufficiently severe for liability? Was McDermott's behavior sufficiently outrageous for liability?

7. Jonathan Harr's best-selling book, *A Civil Action,* is a dramatized account of real-life toxic tort litigation involving a tannery. The book discusses evidence that the protagonist, attorney Jan Schlictmann, regarded as implicating tannery owner John Riley in the deaths of several children. Riley brought a defamation action against Harr and the book's publisher because, in Riley's view, the book had depicted him as a liar, a perjurer, a "killer," and a bully. One passage cited by Riley described Schlictmann's reaction upon discovering a certain incriminating document:

> This document was thirty years old and it dealt only with tannery waste, which might or might not have

contained TCE [a potentially harmful chemical]. But even so, Schlichtmann thought it had great value. Riley had sworn at his deposition that he had never dumped anything on the fifteen acres. Riley had lied then, and Schlichtmann—who didn't need much convincing—believed that Riley was also lying about using TCE.

Another passage described Schlichtmann's efforts to build a case against the tannery:

> It seemed that everyone but Riley recognized the fifteen acres as a toxic waste dump. Riley must have known about the condition of the property. Perhaps, thought Schlichtmann, the tanner really had been running an unauthorized waste dump. Perhaps he had charged his neighbor, Whitney Barrel, a fee for the use of the land.

Did Riley have a meritorious defamation claim against Harr and the publishing company on the basis of the above statements?

8. Joseph Doescher, a hospital operating room perfusionist (the person who operates the heart/lung machine during open-heart surgeries) filed an assault lawsuit against Dr. Daniel Raess, a cardiovascular surgeon, following a verbal altercation that occurred near an Indiana hospital's open-heart surgery area. The case proceeded to trial. The evidence indicated that Raess was angry at Doescher over reports to the hospital administration about the defendant's treatment of other perfusionists. Doescher testified that Raess aggressively and rapidly advanced on Doescher with clenched fists, piercing eyes, a beet-red face, and popping veins, and that Raess was screaming and swearing at him. Doescher further testified that he (Doescher) backed up against a wall and put his hands up, believing that Raess was going to hit him, "[t]hat [Raess] was going to smack the s**t out of me or do something." Then, Raess suddenly stopped, turned, stormed past Doescher, and left the room, momentarily stopping to declare to Doescher that "you're finished, you're history." After the jury returned a verdict in favor of Doescher and awarded him damages, Raess appealed. Was there sufficient evidence to support the jury's conclusion that the elements of assault were present?

9. Wade Banks sued John Fritsch for false imprisonment, assault, and battery on the basis of an incident that occurred at a Kentucky high school. Prior to the incident, Banks had skipped out of or left agricultural wood construction class several times during the spring semester of his junior year at the school.

Banks testified at the trial that while he was walking to class, another student told him that the teacher, Fritsch, had a chain and was planning to chain Banks up to keep him from skipping class. When Banks entered the classroom, Fritsch had a large log chain over his shoulder and several key locks on his belt loop. Fritsch told Banks to put his leg up on a chair so that Fritch could fasten the chain to Banks's ankle. Banks refused, but Fritsch repeated the instruction and Banks then complied. The entire class followed as Fritsch led Banks outside to a tree in an area where the class was painting wood troughs. Fritch locked the chain to the tree and returned to the classroom. After several minutes of effort, Banks managed to free his ankle. When he attempted to leave the school premises, several classmates chased him down, tackled him, and carried him back to the tree. Fritsch returned and placed another chain around Banks's neck. Banks initially stood up and held up the chain to keep its weight off his neck. After 15 minutes, he tired of holding the chain, sat down, and began crying. When he told another student that the chain was bothering him, the student went to tell Fritsch. Fritsch came out and unfastened the neck chain, but tightened the ankle chain. Fritch began discussing Banks's grade in the class and told Banks that he could pass if he painted the three remaining wood troughs. Fritsch removed the ankle chain when Banks agreed to do that painting.

Banks testified at the trial that he was deeply upset about the chaining and thought about it often. He received unwelcome attention from other students and the media about the incident. As a result, he spent his senior year in Columbia, Missouri, where his father lived. Banks testified that the move was traumatic, that he found it difficult to fit in at his new school, that he saw a psychologist once to discuss the chaining incident, and that he continued to cry and have flashbacks from it. His family stated that he seemed emotionally withdrawn. At the close of all of the evidence, Fritsch moved for a directed verdict. The trial judge granted the motion, ruling as a matter of law in favor of Fritsch instead of submitting the case to the jury. Was the trial court correct in granting Fritsch a directed verdict?

10. Bruno and Norma Ahnert lived across the street and approximately 500 feet from the Getty Granite Company. Asserting that Getty's business produced excessive noise and dust, the Ahnerts sued Getty for nuisance and trespass to land. They alleged that the

noise disturbed their sleep and made conversation, television watching, and radio or stereo listening difficult. In addition, the Ahnerts alleged that the dust prevented them from opening their windows for ventilation and rendered their outdoor premises unfit for use and enjoyment. Getty asked the court to dismiss the Ahnerts' claims for failure to state claims upon which relief could be granted. Did the Ahnerts state a valid trespass claim? Did they state a valid nuisance claim?

11. At the time of the events described below, California's statute dealing with a deceased celebrity's right of publicity read as follows: "Any person who uses a deceased personality's name, voice, signature, photograph, and likeness, in any manner, on or in products, merchandise, or goods, or for purposes of advertising or selling, or soliciting purchases of products, merchandise, goods, or services, without prior consent from [the legal owner of the deceased personality's right of publicity] shall be liable" to the right of publicity owner. The statute also set forth exemptions from the consent requirement for uses in news, public affairs, or sports broadcasts; in plays, books, magazines, newspapers, musical compositions, or film, television, or radio programs; or in other works of political or news-related value. There was also an exemption for "single and original works of fine art."

   Comedy III Production, Inc., owns the rights of publicity of the deceased celebrities who, through their comedy act and films, had become familiar to the public as "The Three Stooges." Relying on the statute quoted above, Comedy III brought a right of publicity action against artist Gary Saderup and the corporation of which he was a principal. Without Comedy III's consent, the defendants (referred to here collectively as "Saderup") had produced and profited from the sale of lithographs and T-shirts bearing a depiction of The Three Stooges. The depiction had been reproduced from Saderup's charcoal drawing, which featured an accurate and easily recognizable image of the Stooges. The trial court awarded damages to Comedy III after concluding that Saderup had violated the right of publicity statute and that neither the exemptions set forth in statute nor the First Amendment furnished a defense. When the California Court of Appeals affirmed, Saderup appealed to the Supreme Court of California. Were the lower courts correct in ruling in favor of Comedy III?

12. James Albright began working as a bodyguard for Madonna in 1992. From that year until 1994, Albright was involved in a romantic relationship with the famous singer. Many details about this relationship, including its sexual aspects, appeared in a 2000 book about Madonna. The book, written by Andrew Morton, also contained a photograph of Madonna walking with a man. The photograph's caption identified the man as "Jimmy Albright" and stated that Albright had been Madonna's "secret lover and one-time bodyguard." The same picture later appeared in other books and magazines, with the man consistently being identified as Albright. However, the man pictured with Madonna was not Albright. Instead, the man was Jose Guitierez, another former employee of Madonna. Albright filed a defamation lawsuit against author Morton, the publisher of Morton's book, and the publishers of the books and magazines in which the photograph later appeared. According to Albright's complaint, Guitierez was a homosexual who "clearly represents his homosexual ideology in what many would refer to as sometimes graphic and offensive detail." Albright contended that the incorrect association of his name with what was actually a picture of Guitierez would convey the erroneous impression that he (Albright) was gay. Did Albright state a valid claim for defamation?

13. Five passengers were injured when two cars collided during the operation of the "Starchaser," an indoor steel roller coaster at the Kentucky Kingdom amusement park. The collision and resulting investigation attracted immediate and continuing news coverage from WHAS-TV (a television station) and other media outlets. Kentucky Kingdom Amusement Co. (KKAC), which owns and operates Kentucky Kingdom, filed a defamation lawsuit against WHAS on the basis of certain statements made during the WHAS reports. At the trial, KKAC introduced evidence indicating that the statements were false and harmful to the reputation of Kentucky Kingdom. The jury returned a verdict calling for a substantial amount of damages to be awarded to KKAC. Among the issues on appeal was whether KKAC had adequately proved the fault requirement necessitated by the First Amendment. Assuming that KKAC is a public figure, what First Amendment–based fault requirement did KKAC have to prove in order to win the case? What does that fault requirement contemplate, and how does it differ from the fault requirement that would have been applicable if KKAC had been a private figure?

14. R&J Associates leased certain commercial real estate from T&C Associates, Inc., for a one-year period beginning May 1. The lease required that T&C give R&J 10 days' notice before canceling the lease. R&J operated the leased premises as a bar that featured seminude dancers but discontinued the business during the following March when it lost a necessary dance permit. In late March and early April, T&C noticed that the bar was not open and learned that R&J had lost its permit. R&J was behind on its rent at this time. Utility companies were seeking to shut off service to the premises because R&J was also behind on its utility bills. When T&C informed R&J that its monthly rent would be higher if it renewed the lease, R&J said it had no interest in renewing. For the above reasons, T&C took possession of the premises in April. T&C, however, did not give R&J the 10 days' notice referred to in the lease. T&C leased the premises to a new tenant later that month. At approximately the same time, R&J demanded the return of certain personal property items it had left on the premises. T&C told R&J to contact the new tenant, adding that there should be no problem with the return of the items of personal property. R&J contacted the new tenant, who told R&J to submit a list of its personal property because other parties were also claiming rights to what had been left on the premises. R&J did not submit this list and did not contact T&C again about the personal property items. Later, R&J sued T&C for conversion of the personal property. Did R&J have a valid conversion claim?

Online Research

The *Stanton* Case

In this chapter's opening problem, you were asked to make a prediction about the ruling of a federal court of appeals in a case involving claims of defamation and invasion of privacy. Now, using an online source, locate the 2006 decision of the appellate court in that case, *Stanton v. Metro Corp.* Read the decision and see how its content matches up—or does not match up—with the prediction you made earlier. Then, prepare a brief memo that sets forth the appellate court's holdings and explains the court's supporting reasoning.

Consider completing the case "Defamation: Trashing the French Maid" from the You Be the Judge Web site element after you have read this chapter. Visit our Web site at **www.mhhe.com/mallor14e** for more information and activities regarding this case segment.

chapter 7

NEGLIGENCE AND STRICT LIABILITY

Tracey Bantz and Crystal Kiesau served as deputy sheriffs for the Buchanan County, Iowa, Sheriff's Department. In connection with her employment, Kiesau was involved with a K-9 training program for dogs. The Web site for the K-9 program included a photograph of a uniformed Kiesau standing with a police dog in front of a Sheriff's Department car. Bantz obtained the photograph from his home computer and digitally altered it so that Kiesau appeared to be exposing her breasts. During the next several months, Bantz showed and electronically mailed the altered photograph to numerous other persons. When she learned what Bantz had done, Kiesau sued him for defamation and invasion of privacy (legal theories about which you read in Chapter 6). A jury eventually returned a verdict in favor of Kiesau and against Bantz for compensatory and punitive damages totaling approximately $160,000.

In addition, Kiesau's lawsuit named Buchanan County and its sheriff, Leonard Davis, as defendants. Making claims based on a legal theory about which you will read in this chapter, Kiesau contended that Davis and the county should face liability for negligent supervision of Bantz and for negligent retention of him as an employee. Davis and the county moved for summary judgment and sought dismissal of the claims made against them.

Evidence produced by Kiesau in opposition of the summary judgment motion revealed that Davis, who was Bantz's father-in-law, had received numerous complaints about Bantz's attitude and work habits. These complaints were lodged during a four-year period preceding Bantz's alteration and distribution of the photograph of Kiesau. For instance, a sergeant complained about Bantz's refusal to respond to a dispatch call and sent Davis a memo saying that "I am getting tired of people complaining that nothing ever happens to Deputy Bantz when a complaint is written up." As part of a recommendation that Davis terminate Bantz as a canine handler, a Lieutenant Furness mentioned Bantz's supposed lack of honesty, integrity, and sound judgment; his inability to work without supervision; and his failures to cooperate with other members of the Sheriff's Department. Furness, who described Bantz as "a lawsuit waiting to happen even without a dog," later provided Davis a written complaint asserting that Bantz was the cause of turmoil and low morale in the department. In addition, the lieutenant informed Davis that Bantz was "arrogant in his knowledge that he can do anything and nothing will happen to him." Furness also expressed the supposed view of fellow deputies that Bantz's actions would eventually lead to a lawsuit. The evidence also included a statement by a Captain Hepke, who noted that the number of complaints lodged against Bantz was the most he had seen filed against a single deputy in his 22 years of law enforcement experience. Davis apparently took no action in response to these complaints about Bantz.

The trial court granted summary judgment to Davis and the county and dismissed Kiesau's negligence claims against those defendants. Therefore, only the claims against Bantz were considered by the jury. Kiesau appealed the trial court's decision regarding her negligence claims against Davis and the county. As you read Chapter 7, consider these questions:

• What legal elements would Kiesau have to prove in order to win her negligent supervision and negligent retention claims against Davis and the county?

- Did Davis and the county owe any legally cognizable duty to Kiesau in connection with the supervision of Bantz and the retention of him as an employee? Was it foreseeable to Davis and the county that unless supervised closely, Bantz could cause harm to a fellow employee such as Kiesau?
- Was the trial court correct in dismissing Kiesau's negligence claims against Davis and the county?
- If Davis and the county were to argue that they should not be held liable for a wrong committed by Bantz, what would be the appropriate response for Kiesau to make?
- When an employer decides to hire a particular employment applicant, does the employer owe any ethical obligations to persons other than the applicant? If so, what are they? If not, why not? Once a particular employee has been hired, does the employer owe others any ethical obligations in connection with the actions of that employee? If so, what are they? If not, why not?

THE INDUSTRIAL REVOLUTION THAT changed the face of 19th-century America created serious strains on tort law. Railroads, factories, machinery, and new technologies meant increased injuries to persons and harm to their property. These injuries did not fit within the intentional torts framework because most were unintended. In response, courts created the law of **negligence.**

Negligence law initially was not kind to injured plaintiffs. One reason was the fear that if infant industries were held responsible for all the harms they caused, the country's industrial development would be seriously restricted. As a viable industrial economy emerged in the 20th century, this concern began to fade. Also fading over the same period was the 19th-century belief that there should be no tort liability without genuine fault on the defendant's part. More and more, the injuries addressed by tort law have come to be seen as the inevitable consequences of life in a high-speed, technologically advanced society. Although modern negligence rules have not eliminated the fault feature, they sometimes seem consistent with a goal of imposing tort liability on the party better positioned to bear the financial costs of these consequences. That party often is the defendant. Negligence law has become more proplaintiff in recent decades, though statistics indicate that defendants tend to win negligence cases as often as plaintiffs do.

Because most tort cases that do not involve intentional torts are governed by the law of negligence, the bulk of this chapter will deal with negligence principles. In a narrow range of cases, however, courts dispense with the fault requirement of negligence and impose **strict liability** on defendants. Strict liability's more limited application will be addressed during the latter part of this chapter. The chapter will conclude with discussion of recent years' **tort reform** movement, whose primary aims are to reduce plaintiffs' ability to prevail in tort cases and limit the amounts of damages they may receive when they win such cases.

Negligence

The previous chapter characterized negligence as conduct that falls below the level reasonably necessary to protect others against significant risks of harm. The elements of a negligence claim are (1) that the defendant owed a **duty** of care to the plaintiff; (2) that the defendant committed a **breach** of this duty; and (3) that this breach was the **actual and proximate cause of injury** experienced by the plaintiff. In order to win a negligence case, the plaintiff must prove each of these elements, which will be examined in the following pages. Later in the chapter, **defenses** to negligence liability will be considered.

Duty and Breach of Duty

Duty of Reasonable Care Negligence law rests on the premise that members of society normally should behave in ways that avoid the creation of unreasonable risks of harm to others. As a general rule, therefore, negligence law contemplates that each person must act as a *reasonable person of ordinary prudence* would have acted under the same or similar circumstances. This standard for assessing conduct is often called either the "reasonable person" test or the "reasonable care" standard. In most cases, the duty to exercise reasonable care serves as the relevant duty for purposes of a negligence claim's first element. The second element—breach of duty—requires the plaintiff to establish that the defendant failed to act as a reasonable person would have acted. Negligence law's focus on reasonableness of behavior leads to a broad range of applications in everyday personal life (e.g., a person's negligent driving of a car) and in business and professional contexts (e.g., an employer's negligent hiring of a certain employee, or an accountant's, attorney's, or physician's negligent performance of professional obligations).

Was the Duty Owed? Of course, there could not have been a breach of duty if the defendant did not owe the plaintiff a duty in the first place. It therefore becomes important, before we look further at *how* the reasonable person test is applied, to consider the ways in which courts determine *whether* the defendant owed the plaintiff a duty of reasonable care.

Courts typically hold that the defendant owed the plaintiff a duty of reasonable care if the plaintiff was among those who would foreseeably be at risk of harm stemming from the defendant's activities or conduct, or if a special relationship logically calling for such a duty existed between the parties. Most courts today broadly define the group of foreseeable "victims" of a defendant's activities or conduct. As a result, a duty of reasonable care is held to run from the defendant to the plaintiff in a high percentage of negligence cases—meaning that the outcome of the case will hinge on whether the defendant breached the duty or on whether the requisite causation link between the defendant's breach and the plaintiff's injury is established.

The particular circumstances present in some cases, however, cause the court to conclude that the defendant did not owe the plaintiff a duty of reasonable care. When the court so holds, the plaintiff's negligence claim is dismissed for failure to prove the required initial element of such a claim. The *Raleigh* case, which follows, serves as an example.

Raleigh v. Performance Plumbing and Heating, Inc.
130 P.3d 1011 (Colo. Sup. Ct. 2006)

Performance Plumbing and Heating, Inc., was in the business of installing underground and in-house water and sewer plumbing at Denver-area construction sites. Unless assigned a company vehicle, employees of Performance Plumbing used their own vehicles to commute to and from work. Whether employees drove a company vehicle or their own vehicle, Performance Plumbing did not treat driving to work at the beginning of the day and back home at the end as part of the workday. Employees were neither compensated for such commute time nor reimbursed for commuting mileage.

Because Performance Plumbing employees were expected to drive for the company during the workday in order to transport job materials and company tools from the company's construction trailers to job sites (and vice versa), the employer required a valid driver's license as part of the employment application process. However, it relied on the applicant's truthfulness in stating whether he or she held a valid license. Performance Plumbing checked driver's licenses and driving records only as required by its insurance company when it assigned an employee a company vehicle to drive.

In 1996, Performance Plumbing hired Cory Weese as an apprentice plumber. Weese had completed a standard employment application that contained inquiries into the status of his driver's license and driving history. Weese stated in his application that he had a valid license and no moving violations. In reality, his license was then under suspension, though he was eligible for reinstatement of the license upon providing proof of insurance. Weese signed a standard release form, enabling Performance Plumbing to investigate the status of his driver's license, but in accordance with the company's practice, it conducted no further investigation because it was not assigning him a company vehicle to drive. If it had reviewed Weese's driving record, Performance Plumbing would have discovered two accident-related careless driving convictions during the early 1990s, along with other traffic violations during the same general time. At the time of one of the accidents giving rise to a careless driving citation, Weese was found to have been driving without insurance. Because of too many accumulated points resulting from his careless driving convictions and other violations, Weese's driver's license was suspended until August 1992. He drove without a valid license prior to reinstatement, causing reinstatement to be deferred for an additional year. Had it checked Weese's driving record, Performance Plumbing also would have discovered that in November 1995, Weese was convicted of another traffic violation and was again found to have been driving without insurance. His license was suspended as a result. When Performance Plumbing hired Weese in April 1996, he was eligible for license reinstatement upon providing proof of insurance coverage and paying a reinstatement fee, but he had not proceeded to obtain insurance and have his license reinstated.

In early 1997, Performance Plumbing equipped Weese's personal truck with a rack for transporting pipe from the company's construction trailers to work sites. The company paid Weese for travel time between the construction trailers and job sites because it was part of his workday, but it did not pay or reimburse Weese for the use of his vehicle. In September 1997, after Weese's workday had ended and he was driving home, his truck collided with two cars. The collision resulted solely from negligence on Weese's part. Carolyn Raleigh and her son, Kevin, sustained severe injuries in the accident. They sued Performance Plumbing on two legal theories: respondeat superior *(a doctrine under which an employer is held liable for the tort of an employee if the tort was committed within the scope of employment); and negligent hiring. (For a discussion of* respondeat superior, *see Chapter 36.) A Colorado jury ruled against the Raleighs on the* respondeat superior *claim because Weese was not acting within the scope of employment at the time of the accident. On the negligent hiring claim, however, the jury returned a verdict in favor of the Raleighs for a substantial amount of damages.*

Colorado's intermediate court of appeals upheld the decision against the Raleighs on the respondeat superior *claim. Concerning the negligent hiring claim, the appellate court concluded that Performance Plumbing was obligated to inquire into Weese's driving record as part of a duty of reasonable care to hire a safe driver who would not create an undue risk of harm to the public in performing his employment duties. The court of appeals also concluded that there was sufficient evidence for the jury to find a breach of the company's duty to the driving public. However, stressing what it regarded as the absence of the necessary element of causation, the appellate court invalidated the jury's negligent hiring award in light of the jury's determination that Weese was not acting within the scope of his employment when the accident occurred. The Raleighs appealed to the Supreme Court of Colorado. In a portion of the opinion not included here, the Supreme Court affirmed the lower courts' rulings on the* respondeat superior *claim. The edited portion included here focuses on the Raleighs' negligent hiring claim.*

Hobbs, Justice

To obtain submittal of a negligence claim to a jury, the plaintiff must establish a prima facie case demonstrating the following elements: (1) the existence of a legal duty to the plaintiff; (2) the defendant breached that duty; (3) the plaintiff was injured; and (4) the defendant's breach of duty caused the injury. Thus, the first question in any negligence case is whether the defendant owed a legal duty to protect the plaintiff from injury. Whether a specific defendant owes a duty to a specific plaintiff under the circumstances involved with a tort claim is a question of law.

Negligent hiring cases are complex because they involve the employer's responsibility for the dangerous propensities of the employee, which were known or should have been known by the employer at the time of hiring, gauged in relation to the duties of the job for which the employer hires the employee. The employee's later intentional or non-intentional tort is the predicate for the plaintiff's action against the employer, so proof in the case involves both the employer's and the employee's tortious conduct. The lesson to be learned from a successful negligent hiring suit is that the employer should not have hired the employee in light of that person's dangerous propensities or, having hired him or her, must exercise that degree of control over the employee necessary to avert that employee from injuring persons to whom the employer owed the duty of care when making the hiring decision. But "[a] negligence claim against an employer will fail if it is based on circumstances in which the employer owed no duty of care." [Supporting citation omitted.]

We conclude in the case before us that the court of appeals erred in its ruling that the causation element of the tort of negligent hiring came into play to bar the jury's award on the Raleighs' cause of action. The court of appeals utilized the jury's special verdict finding that Weese was not acting within the scope of his employment when he caused the accident. However, conduct of the employee outside of his or her employment can nonetheless be actionable as a breach of the employer's duty of care in a negligent hiring case, if the employer owed a duty of care to the plaintiff when making the hiring decision. Accordingly, we focus in this case on whether Performance Plumbing owed a duty of care to the Raleighs in the first instance.

In 1992, we joined the majority of states in formally recognizing the tort of negligent hiring. *Connes v. Molalla Transp. Sys., Inc.,* 831 P.2d 1316, 1321 (Colo. 1992). *Connes* focused on the duty element of the tort. We posited the scope of the employer's legal duty upon the employer's actual knowledge at the time of hiring or reason to believe that the person being hired, by reason of some attribute of character or prior conduct, would create an undue risk of harm in carrying out his or her employment responsibilities. We observed that foreseeability of harm to the plaintiff is a prime factor in the duty analysis. A court should also weigh other factors, including the social utility of the defendant's conduct, the magnitude of the burden of guarding against the harm caused to the plaintiff, the practical consequences of placing such a burden on the defendant, and any additional elements disclosed by the particular circumstances of the case. No one factor is controlling; the question whether a duty should be imposed in a particular case is essentially one of fairness under contemporary standards—whether reasonable persons would recognize a duty and agree that it exists.

The tort of negligent hiring is independent of a *respondeat superior* theory; under appropriate circumstances, [negligent hiring principles] may apply to impose liability even though the employee is acting outside the scope of the employment. *Connes,* 831 P.2d at 1320–21. In fact, the vast majority of negligent hiring cases involve intentional torts committed by an employee who is not acting within the scope of his or her employment. In *Connes,* although we recognized a duty upon the employer of a commercial truck driver to hire a safe driver, we declined to require the employer to check the employee's criminal record which, if checked, would have revealed a criminal record that included violent acts. In that case, the employee sexually assaulted a woman while he was on a cross-country commercial trip. We held that the driver's contact with the woman was incidental to his employment, and the employer had no duty to further inquire into the employee's denial of a criminal record in the course of the hiring process.

When the duties of the job will bring the employee into frequent contact with members of the public, or will involve close contact with particular individuals as a result of a special relationship between such persons and the employer, some courts have expanded the employer's duty and have required the employer to go beyond the job application and make an independent inquiry into the applicant's background. [However,] when the employment calls for incidental contact between the employee and other persons, there may be no reason for an employer to conduct any investigation of the applicant's background beyond obtaining past employment information and personal data during the application process.

The employer's duty to members of the public in both negligent hiring and negligent supervision cases stems from the principle that the employer receives benefits from having customers and business invitees and incurs responsibilities to them. The *Restatement (Second) of Agency* addresses the tort of negligent hiring as follows: "A person conducting an activity through servants or other agents is subject to liability for harm resulting from his conduct if he is negligent or reckless . . . in the employment of improper persons or instrumentalities in work involving risks of harm to others. *Restatement (Second) of Agency* § 213. The [official] comment to this [*Restatement* section] reveals that liability is predicated on the employer's reason to believe at the time of hiring that undue risk of harm would exist from employing that person. [According to the comment,] "[l]iability results under the rule stated in [§ 213], not because of the relation of the parties, but because the employer antecedently had reason to believe that an undue risk of harm would exist because of the employment."

The key word in this formulation, "antecedently," refers to the time of hiring. In explaining the nature of the employer's duty at the time of hiring, we have reiterated that the scope of the employer's duty in exercising reasonable care in a hiring decision depends on the employee's anticipated degree of contact with other persons in carrying out the job for which the employee was hired. The job for which the defendant was hired in *Connes* consisted primarily of commercial vehicle driving. We recognized that employers of commercial drivers have a duty to investigate an applicant's driving record, in addition to what he or she provides in response to application questions or an employment interview. But, we cautioned in *Connes* that the tort of negligent hiring does not function as an insurance policy for all persons injured by persons an employer hires. [*Connes* indicates that when] driving is involved in performance of the job responsibilities, the duty is "to use reasonable care in hiring a safe driver who would not create a danger to the public in carrying out the duties of the job."

The Raleighs claim that Performance Plumbing owed a duty of care to them because Weese possessed a dangerous propensity in that he was a dangerous driver; had Performance Plumbing conducted a further investigation into his driving record, it would have discovered that Weese's license was under suspension and he had a record of moving violations and automobile accidents, despite his false statements in answer to the employment application questions. They contend that Weese was expected to drive as part of his employment, and they put much emphasis on the benefit the employer obtained by outfitting his private vehicle with a pipe rack.

We agree with the Raleighs that Weese was expected to drive as part of his employment, but only as part of his work day from construction trailers to job sites and back from the job site to construction trailers. The job required employees to commute to and from work on their own time. In this regard, this company is no different from any of a large number of Colorado employers who expect their employees to get to work on their own time and in their own way, and do not assume liability as part of their hiring decision to act as a surety for automobile accidents their employees may cause when commuting to and from work.

Whether Performance Plumbing owed a duty of care to the Raleighs boils down to whether reasonable persons would recognize and agree that a duty exists. The scope of the employer's duty of care in making the hiring decision extends to persons the employer should have reasonably foreseen the employee—who possesses the dangerous propensity the employer knew of, or reasonably should have known of—would come into contact with through the employment. Thus, [especially in light of the accidents that a check of Weese's driving record would have revealed,] the case before us could have presented a jury question on the negligent hiring claim had the accident occurred when Weese was driving to a job site from a construction trailer or from a job site to a construction trailer as part of his work. But our research has not disclosed any case that extends employer negligent hiring liability to off-duty driving of the type citizens undertake normally to get to and from their jobs.

There is precedent that cautions courts against extending the tort of negligent hiring to off-duty commute accidents. Otherwise, any employer who fails to check the license status of employees, and who knows that it is necessary that employees drive to and from work, could be considered to have brought the employee into contact with the third person via the vehicular collision, and could face potential liability for negligent hiring and retention as to injuries occurring from such a collision. We . . . make the further observation that this is properly part of the scope-of-the-employer's-duty analysis—however it might also play into a causation analysis—because the duty of reasonable care in hiring the employee appropriately focuses on the job duties for which the employee is being hired in relation to persons the employer would reasonably foresee the employee coming into contact with through the employment.

We recognize that the Raleighs suffered serious injuries for which Weese bears responsibility. [He] caused the accident when he was commuting from his job on his way home from work. But, we conclude as a matter of law that the Raleighs are not among the members of the public to whom Performance Plumbing owed a legal duty. They did not come into contact with Weese through his employment. Accordingly, we affirm the judgment of the court of appeals dismissing the . . . negligent hiring claim against Performance Plumbing [, though we do so on a ground different from the one on which the court of appeals relied].

Judgment of court of appeals affirmed.

Was the Duty Breached? Assuming that the defendant owed the plaintiff a duty of reasonable care, whether the defendant satisfied or instead breached that duty depends upon the application of the reasonable person test. This test is *objective* in two senses. First, it compares the defendant's actions with those that a hypothetical person with ordinary prudence and sensibilities would have taken (or not taken) under the circumstances. Second, the test focuses on the defendant's behavior rather than on the defendant's *subjective* mental state. The reasonable person test has another noteworthy characteristic: flexibility. In contemplating that courts consider all of the relevant facts and circumstances, the test allows courts to tailor their decisions to the facts of the particular case being decided.

When applying this objective yet flexible standard to specific cases, courts consider and balance various factors. The most important such factor is the *reasonable foreseeability* of harm. This factor does double duty, helping to determine not only whether the defendant owed the plaintiff a duty (as noted above) but also what the defendant's duty of reasonable care entailed in the case at hand. Suppose that Donald falls asleep at the wheel and causes a car accident in which another motorist, Peter, is injured. Falling asleep at the wheel involves a foreseeable risk of harm to others, so a reasonable person would remain awake while driving. Because Donald's conduct fell short of this behavioral standard, he has breached a duty to Peter. However, this probably would not be true if Donald's loss of awareness resulted from a sudden, severe, and unforeseeable blackout. On the other hand, there probably would be a breach of duty if Donald was driving and had a blackout to which a doctor had warned him he was subject.

Negligence law does not require that we protect others against all foreseeable risks of harm. Instead, the risk created by the defendant's conduct need only be an *unreasonable* one. In determining the reasonableness of the risk, courts consider other factors besides the foreseeability of harm. One such factor is the *seriousness* or *magnitude* of the foreseeable harm. As the seriousness of the harm increases, so does the need to take action to avoid it. Another factor is the *social utility* of the defendant's conduct. The more valuable that conduct, the less likely that it will be regarded as a breach of duty. A further consideration is the *ease or difficulty of avoiding the risk.* Negligence law normally does not require that defendants make superhuman efforts to avoid harm to others.

To a limited extent, negligence law also considers the *personal characteristics* of the defendant. For example, children are generally required to act as would a reasonable person of similar age, intelligence, and experience. A physically disabled person must act as would a reasonable person with the same disability. Mental deficiencies, however, ordinarily do not relieve a person from the duty to conform to the usual reasonable person standard. The same is true of voluntary and negligent intoxication.

Finally, negligence law is sensitive to the *context* in which the defendant acted. For example, someone confronted with an emergency requiring rapid decisions and action need not employ the same level of caution and deliberation as someone in circumstances allowing for calm reflection and deliberate action.

The *Currie* case, which follows, focuses mainly on the duty and breach of duty elements of a negligence claim. It also furnishes an introduction to concepts dealt with more fully later in the chapter.

Currie v. Chevron U.S.A., Inc.   2008 U.S. App. LEXIS 4269 (11th Cir. 2008)

Acting in her own right and as personal representative of the estate of her deceased daughter (Nodiana Antoine), Tracye Currie sued Chevron U.S.A., Inc., and Chevron Stations, Inc. (collectively, "Chevron"), on the theory that Chevron negligently caused Antoine's death. The facts giving rise to the case are summarized here.

For approximately two years, Antoine and Anjail Muhammad had had a close personal relationship. The relationship between the two women was a stormy one, with Muhammad sometimes threatening to inflict physical harm on Antoine. On the morning of May 25, 2003, Muhammad and Antoine were in Muhammad's car, which Muhammad had parked in a restaurant parking lot in Marietta, Georgia. According to a statement Muhammad later made to the police, Muhammad and Antoine became involved in an argument, during which Antoine said that she wanted to end their relationship. Muhammad also said in her statement that Antoine left the car and started walking toward a Chevron gas station across the street to call her family. Muhammad followed her, and the women continued arguing as they walked across the street.

Pamela Robinson, a customer at the Chevron station, testified at the trial in Currie's case that when she pulled into the station, she saw Muhammad and Antoine approach the Chevron station. Muhammad was pulling on Antoine's neck or the collar of her clothing and essentially dragging Antoine. Robinson also stated that Muhammad appeared to tighten her grip on Antoine when Antoine tried to pull away. Robinson, who watched the two women move in the direction of gas pump number one, went inside the Chevron station when she realized that the pump she was seeking to use had to be activated by a Chevron cashier before it would work. Jyotika Shukla was the cashier at the Chevron station on that day. Robinson testified that she entered the station and "told [Shukla] immediately that there was something going on with the two young ladies out here and that she needed to contact the police immediately." Robinson explained that she then pointed out the two women to Shukla.

Shukla testified at the trial that she did not know there was anything wrong outside until Robinson came into the station and told her, though an earlier statement by Shukla to the police indicated that Shukla saw the women before Robinson came into the station. Regardless of when she first saw the women, Shukla said that she did see the two women "verbally fighting" and that one woman was holding the other by her shirt. Shukla did not call the police because, according to her testimony, she thought the two women were or would be leaving the Chevron property.

Evidence adduced at the trial indicated that when customers at the Chevron station sought to use a gas pump, they had to lift a lever on the pump. A beeping sound inside the station would then inform the cashier that a customer had lifted the lever on a pump. In order for the customer to receive gas through the pump, the cashier would then have to hit the "authorize pump" button. After the gas pump was authorized, the beeping sound would stop.

The evidence established that Shukla authorized gas pump number one by pushing the appropriate button inside the station. This authorization of the pump enabled Muhammad to use it, even though Muhammad did not have a car on the premises. Shukla testified at trial that she authorized pump number one before Robinson came into the station and before she (Shukla) saw the women fighting, but Shukla's deposition testimony and an earlier statement given to the police indicated that she could not remember whether she knew about or had seen the fighting before she authorized the pump.

Robinson's testimony suggested that Shukla authorized a pump after Robinson told Shukla about the two women fighting. Based on her prior experience of working at a gas station, Robinson recognized that a beeping sound informed the cashier that a gas pump needed to be activated. Robinson testified that she heard a beeping sound when she entered the Chevron station. She also testified that the beeping sound stopped "right after" she told Shukla to call the police. Robinson also stated that she did not ask Shukla to authorize her gas pump until after she talked to Shukla about the two women fighting outside and showed Shukla where they were standing—by gas pump number one. Moreover, there were no other customers waiting for other pumps to be authorized.

Shukla's testimony was inconsistent about whether she looked at gas pump number one before authorizing it. She first testified that she did not remember whether she had looked at pump number one before authorizing it, but later she said "[m]aybe yes." In her statement to the police, Muhammad said that Shukla looked at pump number one before authorizing it.

Muhammad stated that "[e]verybody was really helpful like the lady . . . in the store. . . . [S]he just turned the pump on." When a police detective asked, "Even though ya'll didn't have a car?" Muhammad responded, "Didn't even have a car right next to it, she just turned it on, she looked at us and just turned the pump on."

After Shukla authorized pump number one, Muhammad sprayed 65 cents worth of gasoline on Antoine. Robinson testified that she exited the station to return to her car to pump gas and immediately saw the two women "in the same position with [Muhammad] holding [Antoine]." Before Robinson got to her car, Muhammad asked Robinson whether she had a cigarette lighter. Robinson said she did not. She then watched the two women as they left the Chevron station, with Muhammad still pulling Antoine by her shirt.

According to Muhammad's statement to the police, she and Antoine left the Chevron station and went back to Muhammad's car. Muhammad then found a cigarette lighter in the car and used the lighter to set Antoine on fire. Antoine ran through the parking lot while on fire and tried to roll over in a grassy area in an effort to put out the flames. A passerby called 911, and Antoine was taken to the hospital. Several weeks later, Antoine died as a result of the burns she had suffered. Muhammad, who confessed to police that she set Antoine on fire, was later indicted on criminal charges of murder, aggravated battery, aggravated assault, and arson.

In Currie's wrongful death lawsuit against Chevron, Currie alleged that Shukla negligently authorized the gas pump used by Muhammad and that Antoine died as a result. Under the respondeat superior *principle discussed in Chapter 36 of this text, Chevron would be liable for any negligence on the part of its employee, Shukla, if that negligence occurred within the scope of Shukla's employment. A federal district court jury returned a $3,500,000 verdict in Currie's favor. The court issued a judgment against Chevron for $2,625,000, an amount that reflected a 25 percent reduction from $3,500,000 because of the jury's finding that Antoine's own negligence accounted for 25 percent of the reason why she was killed. (Later in this chapter, you will learn about the comparative negligence principle applied by the court in reducing the amount of damages awarded.) Chevron unsuccessfully moved for judgment as a matter of law or, in the alternative, a new trial. Chevron then appealed to the U.S. Court of Appeals for the Eleventh Circuit.*

Per Curiam

In this diversity case controlled by Georgia law, . . . Currie contended at trial that Chevron's Shukla negligently activated the gas pump for Muhammad only after: (1) Shukla saw Muhammad pulling Antoine around the Chevron station's property by her shirt and thought that something was wrong; (2) Shukla saw that Muhammad and Antoine did not have a vehicle; and (3) customer Pamela Robinson warned Shukla that there was a problem with the two women outside, asked Shukla to call the police, and showed Shukla where the two women were standing by gas pump number one. Currie claimed that, given this evidence, Shukla should have foreseen that Antoine would suffer some injury as a result of Shukla's activating the gas pump for Muhammad. On appeal, Chevron argues that . . . Muhammad's actions were not a reasonably foreseeable consequence of Shukla's negligence; [that] Antoine failed to exercise ordinary care to avoid the consequences of Shukla's negligence; [and that] Antoine's negligence was equal to or greater than Shukla's negligence.

A cause of action for negligence in Georgia must contain the following elements: (1) a legal duty to conform to a standard of conduct for the protection of others against unreasonable risks of harm; (2) a breach of this standard; (3) a legally attributable causal connection between the conduct and the resulting injury; and (4) some loss or damage resulting from the breach of the legal duty. In order to establish a breach of the

applicable standard of conduct, there must be evidence that the alleged negligent act (or omission) created a foreseeable, unreasonable risk of harm. "'That is, it must appear that the alleged negligent condition was such as to put an ordinarily prudent person on notice that some injury might result therefrom.'" [Case citations omitted.] As to foreseeability of injury, Georgia courts have stated that "'in order for a party to be held liable for negligence, it is not necessary that he should have been able to anticipate the particular consequences which ensued. It is sufficient if, in ordinary prudence, he might have foreseen that some injury would result from his act or omission, and that consequences of a generally injurious nature might result.'" [Case citations omitted.]

In Georgia, questions of negligence, proximate cause, and foreseeability are generally for the jury. [After reviewing the record in this case, we] conclude that reasonable minds could differ as to whether Shukla was aware at the moment she authorized gas pump number one that her action would create a foreseeable risk of injury to Antoine. There was evidence from which the jury could have inferred that Shukla was aware that Muhammad and Antoine were involved in a serious fight on the Chevron station's property. In her statement to police on the day of the incident, Shukla said that she saw the two women walking on the station's property, that Muhammad had "grabbed" and "pulled" Antoine by the front of her shirt, and that Shukla "thought something was wrong." Shukla also testified at trial that she saw the women fighting on the Chevron station's property. Robinson's testimony confirmed Shukla's observation that the fight was serious. Robinson testified that [Muhammad tightened her grip on Antoine] when Antoine try to pull away from her. Robinson [also testified] that Muhammad then pulled Antoine "down to the ground like an animal."

There also was evidence from which the jury could have found that Shukla was aware that Muhammad and Antoine were involved in a serious fight at the Chevron station *before* she activated gas pump number one for Muhammad. [Robinson's testimony so suggested. Moreover, Shukla's statement to the police and her testimony were subject to such an interpretation by the jury.] [In addition,] there was evidence from which the jury could have concluded that Shukla looked at Muhammad before authorizing gas pump number one. Muhammad told police on the day of the incident that ". . . she looked at us and just turned the pump on. . . . " Based on Muhammad's statement and Shukla's own testimony, the jury could have found that Shukla looked at gas pump number one before she authorized it, saw Muhammad (whom Shukla had seen fighting with Antoine on the station's property and had recognized did not have a car), and nevertheless authorized gas pump number one for Muhammad.

[Considering] the totality of this evidence . . . , the jury could have found that the beeping sound that Robinson heard inside the Chevron station was Muhammad seeking authorization of gas pump number one and that Shukla looked at Muhammad and authorized gas pump number one for her (thus stopping the beeping sound) *after* Shukla's conversation with Robinson. The jury also could have found that Shukla was aware at the time she authorized gas pump number one for Muhammad that: (1) Muhammad had been pulling Antoine around the Chevron station's property by her shirt as they were fighting; (2) the fight was sufficiently serious that Shukla herself thought something was wrong and that Robinson came into the station to warn Shukla that something was going on with the two women outside and to ask her to call the police; (3) Muhammad and Antoine were fighting by gas pump number one; and (4) Muhammad and Antoine did not have a car on the station's property. Thus, we conclude that there was, at the very least, a substantial conflict in the evidence such that reasonable and fair-minded jurors might reach different conclusions as to whether Shukla was aware before she authorized gas pump number one that her negligent action would create a foreseeable risk of injury to Antoine.

Chevron presented expert testimony from Rosemary Erickson, Ph.D., a forensic sociologist, that it was not reasonably foreseeable to Shukla that Muhammad would douse Antoine with gas and set her on fire. Dr. Erickson based her opinion on a review of the depositions, the police records, the

low crime rate in the area surrounding the Chevron station, the lack of previous violent crimes at this specific Chevron station, and the rarity of the particular crime that occurred here. In addition to Dr. Erickson's testimony, Shukla testified that she had never [witnessed] a crime or fire at the Chevron station before that day and never had to call the police. [The] former Chevron station manager testified that there had not been any criminal activity at the Chevron station in his eight to ten years working there before this incident.

However, in cross-examining Dr. Erickson, plaintiff's counsel asked, "You would agree with me . . . would you not, that if something is going on at a gas station and a clerk sees one person holding another at a gas pump and there's no car and no container, that it's foreseeable that the gas may be used inappropriately and harm can result. . . . " Dr. Erickson replied, "If all those factors were in evidence." Thus, even from Chevron's own witness, there was in effect testimony to support Currie's claim that Shukla should not have authorized the gas pump after Shukla saw Muhammad and Antoine fighting (or was told by Robinson they were fighting) and where Muhammad and Antoine had no car or gas container. [In addition, both the former station manager and Robinson[, who had worked at a gas station,] testified that they would not activate a gas pump if they saw people at the gas pump without a car or gas can.

In arguing that this incident was not foreseeable, Chevron cites Georgia premises liability cases providing that property owners have a duty to exercise ordinary care to protect invitees from foreseeable third-party criminal attacks where there are prior similar criminal acts occurring on the premises that put the property owner on notice of the dangerous condition. Chevron argues that the criminal attack by Muhammad on Antoine was not foreseeable because this particular Chevron station was in a low crime area and had not been the site of any criminal activity in previous years, much less violent crime.

First, while Currie raised a premises liability theory at trial, her primary theory of liability was that given the particularly serious events unfolding before Shukla and given Robinson's warning, Shukla then committed her own affirmative negligent act in activating gas pump number one for Muhammad, not that Chevron breached its duty to Antoine to keep its premises safe generally. Second, the lack of prior criminal activity at this Chevron station does not wholly foreclose the foreseeability issue. Even in cases grounded solely on a premises liability theory, Georgia courts have stated that "a showing of prior similar incidents on a proprietor's premises is not always required to establish that a danger was reasonably foreseeable. An absolute requirement of this nature would create the equivalent of a one free bite rule for premises liability, even if the proprietor otherwise knew that the danger existed." [Case citation omitted.]

This Court applied this same reasoning in a premises liability case to conclude that there was a jury question of whether hostilities throughout the evening of which bowling alley employees were, or should have been, aware were sufficient to make it reasonably foreseeable to them that a fight would erupt, even though there had been no similar prior altercations on the premises. [Case citation omitted.] Similarly, in this case, there was a sufficient conflict in the evidence for reasonable minds to differ as to whether the particular serious and exigent events unfolding right before Shukla at the Chevron station that morning, together along with Robinson's warning, should have put her on notice that activating the gas pump for Muhammad would pose an unreasonable risk of harm to Antoine, even though there was no history of prior similar incidents at this specific Chevron station.

Therefore, we cannot say that the district court erred in denying Chevron's motion for judgment as a matter of law or a new trial.

[*Note:* In a later portion of the opinion not included here, the Eleventh Circuit concluded that the district judge had correctly instructed the jury on issues related to Antoine's own failure to use reasonable care, that the jury's assignment of a 25 percent degree of responsibility to Antoine was supported by the evidence, and that the court had therefore properly reduced the award of damages by 25 percent.]

Judgment in favor of Currie affirmed.

Special Duties In some situations, courts have fashioned particular negligence duties to supplement the general reasonable person standard. When performing their professional duties, for example, professionals such as doctors, lawyers, and accountants generally must exercise the knowledge, skill, and care ordinarily possessed and employed by members of the profession.[1] Also, common carriers and (sometimes) innkeepers are held to an extremely high duty of care approaching strict liability when they are sued for damaging or losing their customers' property. Many courts say that they also must exercise great caution to protect their passengers and lodgers against personal injury—especially against the foreseeable wrongful acts of third persons. This is true even though the law has long refused to recognize any general duty to aid and protect others from third-party wrongdoing unless the defendant's actions foreseeably increased the risk of such wrongdoing. Some recent decisions have imposed a duty on landlords to protect their tenants against the foreseeable criminal acts of others.

Duties to Persons on Property Another important set of special duties runs from possessors of real estate (land and buildings) to those who enter that property. Negligence cases that address these duties are often called *premises liability* cases. Traditionally, the duty owed by the possessor has depended on the classification into which the entering party fits. The three classifications are:

1. *Invitees.* Invitees are of two general types, the first of which is the "business visitor" who is invited to enter the property for a purpose connected with the possessor's business. Examples include customers, patrons, and delivery persons. The second type of invitees consists of "public invitees" who are invited to enter property that is held open to the public. Examples include persons using government or municipal facilities such as parks, swimming pools, and public offices; attendees of free public lectures and church services; and people responding to advertisements that something will be given away. The entry, however, must be for the purpose for which the property is held open. Accordingly, some—though not all—courts would hold that a person who enters a public library merely to meet a friend is not an invitee.

A possessor of property must exercise reasonable care for the safety of his invitees. In particular, he must take appropriate steps to protect an invitee against dangerous on-premises conditions that he knows about, or reasonably should discover, and that the invitee is unlikely to discover.

2. *Licensees.* A licensee enters the property for her own purposes, not for a purpose connected with the possessor's business. She does, however, enter with the possessor's consent. In some states, social guests are licensees, though they are invitees in other states. Other examples of licensees are door-to-door salespeople, solicitors of money for charity, and sometimes persons taking a shortcut across the property. As these examples suggest, consent to enter the property is often implied. The possessor usually is obligated only to warn licensees of dangerous on-premises conditions that they are unlikely to discover.

3. *Trespassers.* A trespasser enters the land without its possessor's consent and without any other privilege. Traditionally, a possessor of land owed trespassers no duty

---

[1]Chapter 46 discusses professional liability in greater detail.

Ethics in Action

Suppose that during regular work hours, an employee of XYZ Co. commits a sexual assault or other violent attack upon a member of the public. The employee, of course, is liable for the intentional tort of battery (about which you learned in Chapter 6), as well as a criminal offense. Although the doctrine of *respondeat superior* makes employers liable for their employees' torts when those torts are committed within the scope of employment, XYZ is quite unlikely to face *respondeat superior* liability for its employee's flagrantly wrongful act because a sexual assault or violent attack, even if committed during regular work hours, presumably would be outside the scope of employment.

However, as the principles explained in this chapter suggest, XYZ could be liable for its *own* tort if XYZ was negligent in hiring, supervising, or retaining the employee who committed the attack. A determination of whether XYZ was negligent would depend upon all of the relevant facts and circumstances.

Regardless of whether XYZ would or would not face legal liability, the scenario described above suggests related ethical questions that may confront employers. Consider the following:

- Does an employer have an ethical obligation to take corrective or preventive action when the employer knows, or has reason to know, that the employee poses a danger to others?
- Does it matter whether the employer has irrefutable evidence that the employee poses a danger, or whether the employer has only a reasonable suspicion to that effect?
- If the employer has an ethical obligation to take corrective or preventive action, to whom does that obligation run and what should that obligation entail?
- Does the employer owe any ethical duty to the *employee* in such situations?

You may find it helpful to consider these questions through the frames of reference provided by the ethical theories discussed in Chapter 4 (e.g., utilitarianism, rights theories, and profit maximization). Then compare and contrast the results of the respective analyses.

---

to exercise reasonable care for their safety; instead, there was only a duty not to willfully and wantonly injure trespassers once their presence was known.

Recent years have seen some tendency to erode these traditional distinctions. Most notably, some courts no longer distinguish between licensees and invitees. These courts hold that the possessor owes a duty of reasonable care to persons regardless of whether they are licensees or invitees. Some courts have created additional duties that possessors owe to trespassers. For example, a higher level of care is often required as to trespassers who are known to regularly enter the land, and as to children known to be likely to trespass.

In the *Delgado* case, which follows, the court discusses and applies the duty of reasonable care owed to invitees.

Delgado v. Trax Bar & Grill   113 P.3d 1159 (Cal. Sup. Ct. 2005)

On weekend nights, the employees on duty at Trax Bar & Grill (a California establishment) typically included two persons referred to here as "security guards," "guards," or "bouncers." One bouncer would be stationed inside the bar. The second would be stationed in the bar's parking lot.

At the trial in the case described below, Trax's manager testified that the guards were large, strong men who had been instructed to (1) patrol the parking lot to ensure that persons did not congregate or consume intoxicating beverages there; (2) check identifications in order to keep out underage patrons; and (3) call 911, rather than physically intervening, in any altercation involving patrons. In response to a question about whether the bar "had any responsibility for the safety of [its] customers in the parking lot," the manager testified, "To a certain point, yeah, to see that they got to their car."

The manager testified that the local police had recommended the no-physical-intervention policy, but he acknowledged that Trax's bouncers sometimes ignored the no-physical-intervention policy and personally interceded in fights between patrons, and that when the bouncers did so, they were not disciplined for a violation of procedure. A former guard at Trax testified as an expert witness that the practice of guards at local bars generally, and his own practice at the Trax bar, was to treat the safety of patrons as a "top priority" and to actively and physically intervene in altercations rather than simply to telephone 911. He also testified that prior to terminating his employment at Trax, he advised the manager that security was inadequate on busy nights.

The incident that gave rise to the case described below occurred on a Saturday night. Michael Delgado and his wife arrived at Trax between 10:00 PM and 10:30 PM. The 6 foot 1 inch, 230-pound Delgado had consumed two beers earlier in the evening. After entering the bar, and over the course of the following 60 to 90 minutes, he consumed one more beer. During this time, bar patron Jacob Joseph and his three or four companions stared at Delgado on numerous occasions, and Delgado stared back at the group. There was no verbal or physical interaction between Delgado and Joseph or his companions during this exchange of stares.

Prior to midnight, Delgado had become uncomfortable as a result of the continued staring, so he and his wife, Linette, considered leaving the bar. According to the trial testimony of Trax's interior guard, Jason Nichols, Linette approached him and expressed concern that "there was going to be a fight." Nichols himself then observed what appeared to be hostile stares between Delgado and Joseph and his companions. Concluding that a fight was imminent, Nichols determined that he would ask the Delgados to leave the bar because it would be easier to get them to depart than to get Jacob's group to do so. Nichols made that request and the Delgados exited the bar. Nichols did not escort the Delgados to their car, which was parked in Trax's lot approximately 40 feet from the door to the bar. Trax's second bouncer, who earlier had been posted outside the bar, no longer was present outside.

As the Delgados walked through the parking lot toward their car, a group of 12 to 20 men stood in the parking lot. This circumstance was contrary to the bar's policy of dispersing such gatherings. Joseph and his companions followed the Delgados into the parking lot and then accosted Michael Delgado, beating him severely. Some of the other persons who had congregated in the parking lot soon joined in on the attack on Delgado. During or immediately after the attack, a Trax employee telephoned 911 to seek police assistance. The police arrested Joseph, who later was convicted of felony assault.

Delgado suffered a fractured skull and a subdural hematoma, was hospitalized for 16 days, and experienced adverse personality changes as well as chronic headaches. He sued Joseph and Trax, alleging that Joseph committed battery and that Trax was negligent. After Joseph filed for bankruptcy, Delgado ceased pursuing the claim against him. In proceeding with his negligence claim against Trax, Delgado relied on premises liability principles. A California state court jury returned a verdict in favor of Delgado for approximately $81,000 in damages. Trax appealed to the California Court of Appeal, which held that because there had been no evidence of prior parking lot incidents in which a Trax patron was attacked by a group of assailants (as opposed to fights of a more minor nature), foreseeability was lacking. Concluding that Trax therefore owed Delgado no obligation to furnish an outside security guard or to intervene to protect him, the Court of Appeal ruled that the jury's verdict for the plaintiff could not stand. Delgado appealed to the Supreme Court of California.

George, Chief Justice

Although "[a]s a general principle, a defendant owes a duty of care to all persons who are foreseeably endangered by his conduct," . . . it also is well established that, as a general matter, there is no duty to act to protect others from the conduct of third parties. [Case citation omitted.] But . . . courts have recognized exceptions to the general no-duty-to-protect rule, one of which—the "special relationship" doctrine—is dispositive in this case.

A defendant may owe an affirmative duty to protect another from the conduct of third parties if he or she has a "special relationship" with the other person. Courts have found such a special relationship in cases involving . . . business proprietors such as shopping centers, restaurants, and bars, and their tenants, patrons, or invitees. Accordingly, in *Ann M. v. Pacific Plaza Shopping Center,* 863 P.2d 207 (Cal. Sup. Ct. 1993), we recognized as "well established" the proposition that a proprietor's "general duty of maintenance, which is owed to tenants and patrons, . . . include[s] the duty to take reasonable steps to secure common areas against foreseeable criminal acts of third

parties that are likely to occur in the absence of such precautionary measures."

[The "reasonable steps" contemplated by the proposition just stated may or may not include an obligation to furnish security guards. As noted in *Ann M.,*] the scope of the duty is determined . . . by balancing the foreseeability of the harm against the burden of the duty to be imposed." [We also] stated in *Ann M.* that although

> there may be circumstances where the hiring of security guards will be required to satisfy a landowner's duty of care, such action will rarely, if ever, be found to be a minimal burden. The monetary cost of security guards is not insignificant. Moreover, the obligation to provide patrols adequate to deter criminal conduct is not well defined. . . . Finally, the social costs of imposing a duty on landowners to hire private police forces are also not insignificant. For these reasons, we conclude that a high degree of foreseeability is required in order to find that the scope of a landlord's duty of care includes the hiring of security guards. We further conclude that the requisite degree of foreseeability rarely, if ever, can be proven in the absence of prior similar incidents of violent

crime on the landowner's premises. To hold otherwise would be to impose an unfair burden upon landlords and, in effect, would force landlords to become the insurers of public safety, contrary to well-established policy in this state.

[However, we followed the above statement in *Ann M.* with a footnote observing that] evidence other than prior similar crimes occurring on the proprietor's premises might [sometimes] be adequate to establish foreseeability. We stated: "It is possible that some other circumstances such as immediate proximity to a substantially similar business establishment that has experienced violent crime on its premises could provide the requisite degree of foreseeability. Because . . . no such evidence [was presented], we need not further consider this possibility."

Even when [a proprietor] has no duty under *Ann M.* to hire a security guard or to undertake other similarly burdensome preventative measures, [the proprietor] still owes a duty of due care to a patron or invitee by virtue of the special relationship. [T]here are circumstances, apart from the failure to provide a security guard or undertake other similarly burdensome preventative measures, that may give rise to liability based upon the proprietor's special relationship. For example, . . . a restaurant or bar proprietor also has a duty to warn patrons of known dangers and, in circumstances in which a warning alone is insufficient, has a duty to take other reasonable and appropriate measures to protect patrons or invitees from imminent or ongoing criminal conduct. Such measures may include telephoning the police or 911 for assistance or protecting patrons or invitees from an imminent and known peril lurking in a parking lot by providing an escort . . . to a car in that parking lot. [Case citations omitted.]

Moreover, . . . California decisions long have recognized, under the special relationship doctrine, that a proprietor who serves intoxicating drinks to customers for consumption on the premises must "exercis[e] reasonable care to protect his patrons from injury at the hands of fellow guests." *Saatzer v. Smith,* 122 Cal. App. 3d 512 (1981). [As noted in *Saatzer,* such] a duty arises

when one or more of the following circumstances exists: (1) [the] tavern keeper allowed a person on the premises who has a known propensity for fighting; (2) the tavern keeper allowed a person to remain on the premises whose conduct had become obstreperous and aggressive to such a degree the tavern keeper knew or ought to have known he endangered others; (3) the tavern keeper had been warned of danger from an obstreperous patron and failed to take suitable measures for the protection of others; (4) the tavern keeper failed to stop a fight as soon as possible after it started; (5) the tavern keeper failed to provide a staff adequate to police the premises; and (6) the tavern keeper tolerated disorderly conditions.

[In the case at hand,] Trax asserts that a showing of heightened foreseeability as defined by *Ann M.* and its progeny *always* is required when a plaintiff seeks to impose special-relationship-based liability upon a proprietor [in regard to] the criminal conduct of a third party. [This assertion is] inconsistent with our decisions in *Ann M.* and its progeny.

[W]e observe that [when] the burden of preventing future harm caused by third party criminal conduct is great or onerous (as when a plaintiff . . . asserts the defendant had a legal duty to provide guards or undertake equally onerous measures, or as when a plaintiff . . . asserts the defendant had a legal duty to provide bright lighting, activate and monitor security cameras, provide periodic "walk-throughs" by existing personnel, or provide stronger fencing), heightened foreseeability . . . will be required. [When heightened foreseeability is required, it may be] shown by prior similar criminal incidents or other indications of a reasonably foreseeable risk of violent criminal assaults in [the relevant] location. By contrast, [when] harm can be prevented by simple means or by imposing merely minimal burdens, only "regular" reasonable foreseeability, as opposed to heightened foreseeability, is required.

[I]t is undisputed that Trax, a bar proprietor, stood in a special relationship with Delgado, its patron and invitee. [Hence, Trax] owed a duty to undertake "reasonable steps to secure common areas against foreseeable criminal acts of third parties that [were] likely to occur in the absence of such precautionary measures" [quoting *Ann M.*] and to take such appropriate action as is reasonable under the circumstances to protect patrons. To the extent Delgado's special-relationship-based claim rests upon an assertion that the defendant was legally required to provide a guard or guards or to undertake any similarly burdensome measures, we initially must consider whether the defendant was obligated to do so under *Ann M.* and [later decisions]. In this respect, of course, Delgado was required to demonstrate heightened foreseeability in the form of prior similar criminal incidents *or* other indications of a reasonably foreseeable risk of violent criminal assaults in the bar or its parking lot. [W]e reject the suggestion of the Court of Appeal that in order to establish heightened foreseeability under *Ann M.,* the plaintiff was required to produce evidence not only of prior similar criminal assaults, but of "a coordinated gang attack on an individual patron." Heightened foreseeability is satisfied by a showing of prior *similar* criminal incidents (or other indications of a reasonably foreseeable risk of violent criminal assaults in that location) and does not require a showing of prior *nearly identical* criminal incidents.

Although the record refers to a few prior altercations between patrons, we agree with the conclusion of the Court of Appeal that the plaintiff produced insufficient evidence of heightened foreseeability in the form of prior similar incidents or other indications of a reasonably foreseeable risk of a violent criminal assault . . . that would have imposed upon Trax an obligation to provide any guard, or additional guards, to protect against third party assaults. But the absence of heightened foreseeability in this case merely signifies that Trax owed no special-relationship-based duty to provide guards or undertake other similarly burdensome preventative measures; it does not signify that the defendant owed no *other* special-relationship-based duty to the plaintiff, such as a duty to respond to events unfolding in its presence by undertaking reasonable, relatively simple, and minimally burdensome measures. Indeed, the record clearly establishes the existence of such a minimally burdensome duty here.

[T]he record contains evidence that the defendant's employee, Nichols, was aware of facts that led him to conclude . . . that a fight was likely to occur between Joseph, his three or four companions, and the plaintiff, absent some intervention on Nichols's part. The record also establishes that Nichols formed the opinion that in order to avoid an altercation, it was necessary to separate Delgado from Joseph and his group by removing Delgado from the bar while simultaneously leaving Joseph and his group inside.

[U]nder the circumstances, it was foreseeable that an assault would occur absent separation of Joseph and his group from Delgado. [The other relevant facts] similarly support a determination that Trax had a special-relationship-based duty to respond to the unfolding events by taking reasonable, relatively simple, and minimally burdensome steps . . . to address the imminent danger that Nichols perceived, and . . . to accomplish the separation that he had determined was necessary.

Such minimally burdensome measures may have included, for example, Nichols attempting to maintain separation between the plaintiff and Joseph's group . . . by turning his attention to Joseph and his companions in order to dissuade them from following Delgado (who, at Nichols's direction, was departing from the bar). And, in the face of the continuing threat of a five-on-one altercation if Nichols were unable to dissuade Joseph and his companions from following Delgado outside, [Nichols or other Trax personnel] also might have confirmed that the outside guard was at his post in the parking lot and was available, as necessary, to help maintain the desired separation between the plaintiff and Joseph and his companions.

We stress that . . . Trax's duty was to *attempt* to dissuade Joseph and his group from following the plaintiff. [W]e do not suggest that the defendant had a duty to guarantee that separation, or . . . to prevent any resulting attack and injury to the plaintiff. The question whether the ultimate group attack upon Delgado in the parking lot would not have occurred had Nichols successfully dissuaded Joseph and his companions from following Delgado implicates the sufficiency of the evidence to support the jury's implied findings of breach of duty and causation—issues that are not relevant to, and do not influence, our analysis of whether the defendant owed a duty of care under the circumstances.

We conclude that the Court of Appeal erred in [holding that] the defendant owed no duty to the plaintiff. Instead, . . . because Trax had actual notice of an impending assault involving Joseph and Delgado, its special-relationship-based duty included an obligation to take reasonable, relatively simple, and minimally burdensome steps to attempt to avert that danger. Whether there was sufficient evidence to support the jury's determinations of breach of duty and causation are matters to be addressed by the Court of Appeal on remand.

Decision of Court of Appeal reversed; case remanded for further proceedings.

Negligence Per Se Courts sometimes use statutes, ordinances, and administrative regulations to determine how a reasonable person would behave. Under the doctrine of **negligence per se,** the defendant's violation of such laws may create a breach of duty and may allow the plaintiff to win the case if the plaintiff (1) was within the class of persons intended to be protected by the statute or other law, and (2) suffered harm of a sort that the statute or other law was intended to protect against. In the *Hargis* case, which follows, the court approves of the plaintiff's attempt to use the negligence per se principle against a defendant who violated a workplace safety regulation.

Hargis v. Baize   168 S.W.3d 36 (Ky. Sup. Ct. 2005)

Allen Baize owned a Kentucky lumberyard and sawmill known as Greenville Log and Lumber Co. Baize hired Darrell Hargis on an independent contractor basis to haul logs to and from Greenville and various other locations. For these services, Baize paid Hargis by the board-feet hauled. Hargis owned his own truck but hauled the logs on a semitrailer owned by Baize. Baize supposedly leased the trailer to Hargis and deducted the rentals from Hargis's weekly paycheck. During the last six months of his life, Hargis worked exclusively for Baize.

In November 1998, Baize dispatched Hargis to pick up a load of logs that Baize had purchased from Whitney & Whitney Lumber Co. Whitney's employees loaded the logs. Upon returning to Greenville, Hargis began releasing the binders on the logs in preparation for unloading by one of Baize's forklift drivers. Hargis did so in accordance with Baize's policy, which required all truck drivers to release the binders on their loads and then move at least two truck lengths in front of the truck in order to be in full view of the forklift operator while the logs were being unloaded. A Baize employee was standing by in his forklift waiting for Hargis to release the binders so that he could unload the logs. When Hargis released the binders, however, a large log rolled off the trailer, struck Hargis, and killed him.

Hargis's widow sued Baize in a Kentucky court. The plaintiff alleged that the fatal accident resulted from Baize's failure to comply with a certain Kentucky administrative regulation, which had been promulgated by the Kentucky Occupational Safety and Health Standards Board (KOSHSB) under authority granted by a state statute, the Kentucky Occupational Safety and Health Act [hereinafter "Kentucky OSHA"]. The KOSHSB regulation at issue in the case incorporated by reference the content of a federal administrative regulation dealing with the unloading of logs. That federal regulation, promulgated pursuant to the federal Occupational Safety and Health Act, provided in pertinent part that "[b]inders on logs shall not be released prior to securing with unloading ties or other unloading device."

Under the factual circumstances giving rise to the plaintiff's case, "securing" the logs with an "unloading device" meant using the forks of the forklift to stabilize the logs and keep them from rolling off the truck when the binders were released. Baize admitted that it was not his company's policy to comply with the above-quoted regulation. Baize's former safety officer testified in a deposition that an insurance representative had visited the Greenville site two weeks before Hargis was killed and had recommended implementation of the log-securing procedures required by the KOSHSB regulation. According to the safety officer, Baize's operations manager rejected the recommendation even though the operations manager himself had been injured recently in a similar accident. A state investigative report prepared after Hargis's death also recommended implementation of the securing procedure required by the KOSHSB regulation. When confronted with this recommendation, Baize's sales manager responded that the recommendation was "[n]ot implemented."

Following completion of discovery, the plaintiff moved for partial summary judgment on the issue of Baize's negligence. The plaintiff argued that the violation of the KOSHSB regulation was negligence per se and that the jury should be allowed to consider only issues of damages and contributory fault, if any, on the part of Hargis. Baize also moved for summary judgment, arguing that a violation of the KOSHSB regulation did not create a private right of action in favor of the plaintiff and that in any event, Baize's only duty to an independent contractor such as Hargis was to warn him of any hidden dangers on the premises. Agreeing with Baize, the trial court overruled the plaintiff's motion for partial summary judgment and granted summary judgment in favor of Baize. After the Kentucky Court of Appeals affirmed, the plaintiff appealed to the Supreme Court of Kentucky.

Cooper, Justice

[According to a Kentucky statute of general applicability,] "[a] person injured by the violation of any statute may recover from the offender such damages as he sustained by reason of the violation, although a penalty or forfeiture is imposed for such violation." [The Kentucky OSHA, under which the KOSHSB regulation at issue in this case was promulgated,] specifically provides that "each employer . . . shall comply with occupational safety and health standards promulgated [by the KOSHSB] under this chapter." Since those standards include the ones set forth in the KOSHSB regulation on unloading of logs,] the violation of [that] regulation would constitute a violation of the Kentucky OSHA, thus triggering the right of action created by [the above-quoted statute of general applicability].

Baize [relies] on *Carman v. Dunaway Timber Co., Inc.,* 949 S.W.2d 569 (Ky. Sup. Ct. 1997), [but that reliance] is misplaced. While the accident in *Carman* occurred under facts almost identical to those in this case, the [injured] plaintiff in *Carman* was not within the class of persons . . . intended to be protected [by the Kentucky OSHA and the KOSHSB regulation on log unloading]. Carman was a private businessman . . . who was on Dunaway's premises for the purpose of selling his own logs to Dunaway. [Because] Carman was "neither an independent contractor nor an employee" [of Dunaway, he was not among those persons that Kentucky's workplace safety statute and regulations were meant to protect. Therefore, Carman could not rely on the negligence per se principle even though the log-unloading requirement of the KOSHSB regulation had been violated].

[The plaintiff in the case at hand erroneously asserts that in *Carman,* we adopted the rule stated in] *Teal v. E.I. DuPont de Nemours & Co.,* 728 F.2d 799 (6th Cir. 1984), which extended [the federal] Occupational Safety and Health Act's coverage [beyond an employer's own employees] to employees of independent contractors who work at another employer's workplace. [W]e did not . . . adopt *Teal* [in *Carman*]; there was no need to do so because the holding in *Teal* did not apply to the facts in *Carman.* The holding in *Teal,* however, does apply to the facts of this case.

If this were a workers' compensation claim, it would be a close question whether Hargis was an employee or an independent contractor. In addition to the facts that Baize dispatched Hargis to pick up Baize's logs and transport them to Baize's place of business on a semi-trailer owned by Baize are the facts that Hargis had worked exclusively for Baize for six months immediately preceding the accident and [that Hargis,] though paid by the board-feet hauled, was paid on a weekly basis [instead of after] each individual trip. [These facts might seem to point toward a conclusion that Hargis was Baize's employee.] Nevertheless, the parties agree that Hargis was an independent contractor (for otherwise, the plaintiff's complaint would have been summarily dismissed as barred by . . . the "exclusive remedy" provision of [Kentucky's] Workers' Compensation Act).

Thus, we now reach the issue that we did not reach in *Carman,* i.e., whether the protections of the Kentucky OSHA [and the KOSHSB regulations promulgated thereunder] extend to workers on the job site other than direct employees of the owner or other person in control of the job site. We conclude, as did the Sixth Circuit in *Teal* [in regard to the similar federal statute], that the protections [of the Kentucky statute and regulations] extend to any employee, including an employee of an independent contractor, who is performing work at another employer's workplace. We adopt *Teal*'s analysis of the relevant [federal] provisions as our construction of the same provisions replicated in the Kentucky OSHA [and related regulations].

[The *Teal* court noted] that in the federal Occupational Safety and Health Act (OSHA), Congress imposed on employers a general duty "to protect its employees from hazards that are likely to cause death or serious bodily injury," [and] a specific duty . . . "to comply with the . . . regulations [promulgated under the federal statute]." [According to the *Teal* court's reading of the general duty clause in the statute,] "every employer owes [the general] duty regardless of whether it controls the workplace, whether it is responsible for the hazard, or whether it has the best opportunity to abate the hazard. In contrast, [in] the specific duty provision[, the] class of employers who owe a duty to comply with the OSHA regulations is defined with reference to control of the workplace and opportunity to comply with the OSHA regulations." [The content of OSHA's specific duty provision and the "broad remedial nature" of OSHA caused the court to conclude that]

Congress enacted [OSHA] for the special benefit of all employees, including the employees of an independent contractor, who perform work at another employer's workplace. . . . Consistent with the broad remedial nature of [OSHA], we interpret the scope of intended beneficiaries . . . in a broad fashion. In our view, once an employer is deemed responsible for complying with OSHA regulations, it is obligated to protect every employee who works at its workplace[, regardless of whether that person is the employer's own employee or the employee of an independent contractor].

[Because the Kentucky OSHA is so similar in content and purpose to the federal OSHA, and because the KOSHSB regulations are so similar to regulations promulgated under OSHA, the analysis employed in *Teal* applies to this case as well. Therefore, the KOSHSB regulation on log unloading applies to all employees working at an employer's workplace, regardless of whether those persons are employees of that employer or employees of an independent contractor.]

Baize asserts that even if [the *Teal* rule] would apply to Hargis if he [had been] an *employee* of an independent contractor, it does not apply to him because Hargis was, in fact, *the* independent contractor. As illustrated by the analysis in *Teal,* to draw such a distinction would be ludicrous. Except for providing his own truck, Hargis was performing the same work duties and was exposed to the same work hazards as Baize's own truck-driver employees. [I]f Hargis had incorporated himself and paid himself a salary, as do many independent truckers, he would have been an "employee of an independent contractor." He is no less entitled to the Kentucky OSHA's protections because, technically, he was self-employed.

[Therefore, the negligence per se principle applies and enables the plaintiff to satisfy the first two elements of negligence, duty and breach of duty. The applicability of negligence per se] does not necessarily create liability[, however.] [T]he violation [of the statute and administrative regulation] must have been a substantial factor in causing the result. Baize claims the accident occurred because of Hargis's own negligence in permitting his truck to be overloaded so as to increase the amount of board-feet hauled and, thus, his remuneration for the trip; and that such was the only substantial factor in causing his injuries. But even if Hargis's truck were overloaded, a jury could conclude that Baize's compliance with the applicable KOSHA regulations would have prevented Hargis's death and, conversely, that his failure, nay refusal, to comply with those regulations was a substantial factor in causing that death. "In many negligence per se cases, the statute or ordinance violated was intended to protect individuals from their own carelessness in certain dangerous situations." [Citation of authority omitted.] The issue of comparative fault in this case is one to be decided by a properly instructed jury.

Decision of Court of Appeals reversed; case remanded to trial court for entry of partial summary judgment in favor of plaintiff on issue of Baize's liability and for trial on remaining issues.

Causation of Injury

Proof that the defendant breached a duty does not guarantee that the plaintiff will win a negligence case. The plaintiff must also prove that the defendant's breach caused her to experience injury. We shall look briefly at the injury component of this *causation of injury* requirement before examining the necessary causation link in greater depth.

Types of Injury and Damages

Personal injury—also called "physical" or "bodily" injury—is harm to the plaintiff's body. It is the type of injury present in many negligence cases. Plaintiffs who experienced personal injury and have proven all elements of a negligence claim are entitled to recover compensatory damages. These damages may include not only amounts for losses such as medical expenses or lost wages but also sums for pain and suffering. Although the nature of the harm may make it difficult to assign a dollar value to pain and suffering, we ask judges and juries to determine the dollar value anyway. The rationale is that the plaintiff's pain and suffering is a distinct harm resulting from the defendant's failure to use reasonable care, and that merely totaling up the amounts of the plaintiff's medical bills and lost wages would not compensate the plaintiff for the full effects of the defendant's wrongful behavior.

Property damage—harm to the plaintiff's real estate or a personal property item such as a car—is another recognized type of injury for which compensatory damages are recoverable in negligence litigation. In other negligence cases, many of which arise in business or professional contexts, no personal injury or property damage is involved. Instead, the plaintiff's injury may take the form of *economic loss* such as out-of-pocket expenses, lost profits, or similar financial harms that resulted from the defendant's breach of duty but have no connection to personal injury or property damages. Compensatory damages are available, of course, for losses of this nature.

Whatever the type of injury experienced by the plaintiff, the usual rule is that only compensatory damages are recoverable in a negligence case. As noted in Chapter 6, punitive damages tend to be reserved for cases involving flagrant wrongdoing. Negligence amounts to wrongdoing, but not of the more reprehensible sort typically necessary to trigger an assessment of punitive damages.

What if the plaintiff's claimed injury is *emotional* in nature? As you learned in Chapter 6, the law has long been reluctant to afford recovery for purely emotional harms. Until fairly recently, most courts would not allow a plaintiff to recover for emotional injuries resulting from a defendant's negligence without some impact on or contact with the plaintiff's person. Many courts have now abandoned this "impact rule" and allow recovery for foreseeable emotional injuries standing alone. Many such courts, however, still require proof that physical injury or symptoms resulted from the plaintiff's emotional distress. Other courts have dispensed with the injury requirement where the plaintiff has suffered serious emotional distress as a foreseeable consequence of the defendant's negligent conduct.

Atlantic Coast Airlines v. Cook, which follows, addresses issues that arise in negligent infliction of emotional distress litigation.

Atlantic Coast Airlines v. Cook   857 N.E.2d 989 (Ind. Sup. Ct. 2006)

On February 8, 2002—five months after the September 11, 2001, hijackings of airplanes and less than two months after a passenger on a Paris to Miami flight attempted to detonate explosives hidden in his shoe—Bryan and Jennifer Cook took a flight from Indianapolis to New York City. Delta Airlines handled the ticketing and Atlantic Coast Airlines operated the flight. While passengers waited to board, a man later identified as French national Frederic Girard ran toward the gate and abruptly stopped. Mr. Cook observed that the unaccompanied Girard had two tickets in his possession and that airline security had detained him at the boarding gate before allowing him to board. Mr. Cook further noticed that Girard's face was red and that his eyes were bloodshot and glassy.

In boarding the 32-passenger capacity plane, Girard ran up the steps and jumped inside. Rather than proceeding to his assigned seat, he attempted to sit in a seat nearest the cockpit. However, the flight attendant instructed him to sit in the back row. After taking a seat there, Girard repeatedly pressed the attendant call button and light switch above his head. Prior to takeoff, Mr. Cook approached the flight attendant and expressed concern that Girard was a possible security threat. The attendant acknowledged as much and explained that he had directed Girard to sit in the rear of the plane so he could keep an eye on him.

During takeoff, Girard disregarded instructions to remain seated. He lit a cigarette, disregarding directives from the flight attendant that smoking onboard was prohibited. Despite this admonition, Girard was permitted to retain his lighter. Mr. Cook approached three male passengers and asked for their assistance in the event that Girard's behavior grew dangerous. Girard moved about the plane, sat in various empty seats, and finally walked up the aisle toward the cockpit. Mr. Cook blocked his path and instructed him to sit. Without any physical contact with Mr. Cook, Girard returned to his seat and lit another cigarette. The flight attendant again told him to extinguish the cigarette, and in response Girard stood and shouted, "Get back! Get back!" Mr. Cook and other passengers approached Girard and ordered him to sit down. Instead, Girard stomped his feet and shouted, mostly in French. The Cooks were able to discern the words "World Trade Center," "Americans," and "New York City." Eventually, a Delta employee convinced Girard to sit after speaking to him in French. The employee spent the remainder of the flight sitting across from Girard in the rear of the plane. The pilot diverted the flight to Cleveland, where police arrested Girard. The flight then continued to New York City.

Recalling the events of September 11th and reports of the shoe-bomber incident, the Cooks described their ordeal as one in which they "have never been so scared in their entire lives" (quoting a brief they filed in the litigation about to be described). They filed a small claims court action in Marion County, Indiana, naming Atlantic Coast as a defendant. The Cooks sought damages for negligent infliction of emotional distress. After the small claims court entered judgment against the Cooks, they appealed to the Marion County Superior Court, which denied Atlantic Coast's motion for summary judgment on the negligent infliction of emotional distress claim. Atlantic Coast appealed to the Indiana Court of Appeals. In upholding the Superior Court's denial of the summary judgment motion, the Court of Appeals rejected Atlantic Coast's argument that the Cooks' negligent infliction of emotional distress claim was precluded by Indiana's "modified impact" rule. Atlantic Coast appealed to the Supreme Court of Indiana.

Rucker, Justice

Claims for the negligent infliction of mental or emotional distress have long been the subject of scholarly debate. Creating rules, formulating tests, and applying them to address such claims have proven a challenge for most courts. The majority of jurisdictions employ some variation or combination of the following common law limiting tests for evaluating these claims: the "physical injury" rule, under which . . . the plaintiff's emotional distress must be accompanied by a physical injury or symptom; the "zone of danger" rule, under which recovery is limited to those plaintiffs who themselves were not physically injured but were placed in immediate risk of harm by a defendant's negligent conduct which injured another; and the "bystander" test, . . . which allows recovery to certain plaintiffs [who] witness the injury or death of a third party (typically a close relative of the bystander) that is caused by the defendant's negligence. [Case citations omitted.] The underlying policy reason binding together these judicially created approaches is that absent certain limitations, allowing recovery for emotional distress will open the floodgates to spurious claims.

Before 1991, Indiana followed the rule that damages for emotional distress were recoverable only when accompanied by and resulting from a physical injury. The underlying rationale for this rule was that "absent physical injury, mental anguish is speculative, subject to exaggeration, likely to lead to fictitious claims, and often so unforeseeable that there is no rational basis for awarding damages." [Case citation omitted.] But this court modified the rule in *Shuamber v. Henderson,* 579 N.E.2d 452, 456 (Ind. 1991). We held instead:

When . . . a plaintiff sustains a direct impact by the negligence of another and, by virtue of that direct involvement sustains an emotional trauma which is serious in nature and

of a kind and extent normally expected to occur in a reasonable person, . . . such a plaintiff is entitled to maintain an action to recover for that emotional trauma without regard to whether the emotional trauma arises out of or accompanies any physical injury to the plaintiff.

We further expounded upon the contours of what is now commonly referred to as the "modified impact rule" in two [1999] cases. In *Conder v. Wood,* 716 N.E.2d 432, 435 (Ind. 1999), we held [that]

"direct impact" is properly understood as the requisite measure of "direct involvement" in the incident giving rise to the emotional trauma. Viewed in this context, we find that it matters little how the physical impact occurs, so long as that impact arises from the plaintiff's direct involvement in the tortfeasor's negligent conduct.

[In *Conder,* we concluded] that a pedestrian suffered a direct impact by pounding upon the panels of a truck that was running over her co-worker. In *Ross v. Cheema,* 716 N.E.2d 435, 437 (Ind. 1999), we held [that]

[i]n causing the requisite physical injuries, the direct impact is properly understood as being physical in nature. Though removing the physical injury element, *Shuamber* in no way altered the impact element of the rule. For purposes of the modified rule, the direct impact sustained by the plaintiff must necessarily be a physical one.

[We held in *Ross* that the plaintiff did not sustain] the direct physical impact necessary to recover damages for negligent infliction of emotional distress [when she proved only that she heard] a loud pounding at her door.

As *Shuamber, Conder,* and *Ross* make clear, the modified impact rule maintains the requirement of a direct physical impact. The impact, however, does not need to cause physical injury to the plaintiff. Additionally, the emotional trauma suffered by the plaintiff does not need to result from a physical injury caused by the impact. But how do we assess whether the degree of impact is sufficient to satisfy the requirement of the rule? We have answered this question as follows:

> [W]hen the courts have been satisfied that the facts of a particular case are such that the alleged mental anguish was not likely speculative, exaggerated, fictitious, or unforeseeable, then the claimant has been allowed to proceed with an emotional distress claim for damages even though the physical impact was slight, or the evidence of physical impact seemed to have been rather tenuous.

Bader v. Johnson, 732 N.E.2d 1212, 1221 (Ind. 2000) (finding that mother's continued pregnancy and the physical transformation that her body underwent satisfied the direct impact requirement) (citing *Alexander v. Scheid,* 726 N.E.2d 272, 283–84 (Ind. 2000) (holding that patient suffering from the destruction of healthy lung tissue due to physician's failure to diagnose cancer was sufficient for negligent infliction of emotional distress); *Holloway v. Bob Evans Farms, Inc.,* 695 N.E.2d 991, 996 (Ind. Ct. App. 1998) (concluding that restaurant patron's ingestion of a portion of vegetables cooked with a worm was a direct physical impact under the modified impact rule); *Dollar Inn, Inc., v. Slone,* 695 N.E.2d 185, 189 (Ind. Ct. App. 1998) (finding that hotel guest stabbing herself in the thumb with a hypodermic needle concealed in a roll of toilet paper was sufficient for claim of emotional distress associated with guest's fear of contracting AIDS).

We acknowledge there have been calls to abandon the impact rule altogether. Among other things there are concerns that Indiana's impact rule, even as modified, may prohibit some litigants from recovering damages for bona fide emotional injury even though there has been no physical impact. These are respectable positions. It is our view[, however,] that the requirements under Indiana's rule are modest and that a less restrictive rule would raise the potential for a flood of trivial suits, pose the possibility of fraudulent claims that are difficult for judges and juries to detect, and result in unlimited and unpredictable liability. We therefore reaffirm that Indiana's impact rule continues to require a plaintiff to demonstrate a direct physical impact resulting from the negligence of another.

This Court [, however,] has carved out an exception to the physical impact requirement. [W]e recognized that there may be circumstances under which a "plaintiff does not sustain a direct impact" but is nonetheless "sufficiently directly involved in the incident giving rise to the emotional trauma that we are able to distinguish legitimate claims from the mere spurious." *Groves v. Taylor,* 729 N.E.2d 569, 572 (Ind. 2000). We thus adopted what is now commonly referred to as the bystander rule. [As noted in *Groves,*]

> where the direct impact test is not met, a bystander may nevertheless establish "direct involvement" by proving that the plaintiff actually witnessed or came on the scene soon after the death or severe injury of a loved one with a relationship to the plaintiff analogous to a spouse, parent, child, grandparent, grandchild, or sibling caused by the defendant's negligent or otherwise tortious conduct.

In sum, in order to recover damages for the negligent infliction [of] emotional distress, a plaintiff must satisfy either the modified impact rule or the bystander rule.

Turning to the case before us, the Cooks do not contend that the bystander rule applies to them. Rather, their claim rises or falls on whether they suffered a direct physical impact from the alleged negligence of Atlantic Coast. According to the Cooks, breathing the smoke from Girard's lit cigarette and experiencing the vibrations from Girard's stomping feet caused an actual physical impact. [In addition, the Cooks asserted in their brief that] "constructive impact occurred by virtue of the physical effects on the [Cooks'] vital body functions in increased breathing, sweating, pulse, heart rate, adrenaline, and acuteness of the senses." [N]either this Court nor the Court of Appeals has ever addressed or adopted a theory of "constructive impact" as part of Indiana's impact rule, and we decline to do so today.

In any event, citing this Court's opinion in *Alexander,* the Court of Appeals characterized what the Cooks contend amounts to constructive impact as "physical changes" that are "good enough" to satisfy the rule. In *Alexander,* the plaintiff sued her physician for failure to diagnose her lung cancer. Among other things she sought damages for emotional distress. Her healthcare providers argued that the plaintiff failed to satisfy the impact rule. We disagreed[, observing that] "allegedly as a result of the defendants' negligence, [the plaintiff] suffered the destruction of healthy lung tissue by a cancerous tumor. . . . This is good enough."

We decline to equate a physical change resulting from the destruction of healthy lung tissue with what can best be described[, in the Cooks' case,] as the human body's natural responses to fear and anxiety. Indeed, "increased breathing, sweating, pulse, heart rate, adrenaline, and acuteness of the senses" are more descriptive of stress-like symptoms experienced by many passengers during a normal airplane flight that is undergoing turbulence. They simply are not physical changes as anticipated by *Alexander.* Nor are they physical transformations [of the sort present in] *Bader* ([holding that the] plaintiff's "continued pregnancy and the physical transformation her body underwent as a result satisfy the direct impact requirement of our modified impact rule").

This leaves for our consideration whether smelling cigarette smoke and feeling floor vibrations satisfy the direct physical impact requirement of the rule. [A]t the very least, this stretches the outer limits of the impact requirement. But even assuming that in some theoretical sense these experiences may be characterized as physical impact, the impact was certainly very "slight" and "the evidence of physical impact seem[s] to have been rather tenuous" (quoting *Bader*). We thus explore whether the Cooks' alleged mental anguish is "not likely speculative, exaggerated, fictitious, or unforeseeable" (quoting *Bader*).

Mr. Cook acknowledges that neither he nor his spouse has sought medical or mental health treatment for emotional distress. In his deposition, Mr. Cook described his emotional state as being "shaken up . . . anxious, just upset" and [stated] that he remained so "until [he and his wife] got to New York and got on the ground." Mr. Cook also testified that he was "distraught" and "probably didn't sleep well for at least a week and a half." He further asserted "whenever I get on a flight, I'm concerned that something could happen."

In her deposition, Mrs. Cook, who was seven months pregnant at the time of the incident, [stated] that after arriving in New York, she "was just having lower abdominal pains. Could have been brought on by stress." Further, she reported that she started to feel better "[o]nce we got home and I got back into my normal routine." Mrs. Cook also testified that she and her husband have traveled by air probably four times since this incident. On those flights, Mrs. Cook [is] "always nervous." When asked about the harm she incurred from the flight of February 8, 2002, Mrs. Cook said, "I feared for my life. I thought I was going to die." But she stopped having those fears "[w]hen we landed." According to Mrs. Cook, "[i]t bothered me until we landed. It bothered me that it happened. It bothers me every time I get on a plane."

Apparently the alleged mental and emotional distress the Cooks experienced manifested itself in fear and anxiety at the time the events were unfolding. But this fear and anxiety were transitory, disappearing once the Cooks completed their flight. Since that time, in their own words, the Cooks have experienced feelings of being "bothered," "concerned," and "nervous." But these feelings about the world around us in general and air travel in particular is the plight of many citizens in this country, living as we do in a post-September 11 environment. As [the *Restatement (Second) of Torts* § 46 cmt. j (1965)] has explained:

[S]ome degree of transient and trivial emotional distress is a part of the price of living among people. The law intervenes only where the distress inflicted is so severe that no reasonable [person] could be expected to endure it. The intensity and the duration of the distress are factors to be considered in determining its severity.

We do not suggest that the Cooks' fear and anxiety during the flight were trivial. But there was simply nothing before the trial court, and by extension before this Court, suggesting that the Cooks' fear and anxiety were anything other than temporary. And it is pure speculation to assume that the Cooks' later feelings of being bothered, concerned, and nervous are causally related to the events aboard the flight. Because the physical impact in this case was slight to nonexistent, allowing an emotional distress claim to proceed based on the Cooks' lingering mental anguish would essentially abrogate the requirements of Indiana's modified impact rule. In essence we view the alleged mental anguish here as speculative. Accordingly, the [lower courts] erred in denying Atlantic Coast's motion for summary judgment on this issue.

Denial of Atlantic Coast's summary judgment motion reversed.

The Causation Link   Even if the defendant has breached a duty and the plaintiff has suffered actual injury, there is no liability for negligence without the necessary causation link between breach and injury. The causation question involves three issues: (1) Was the breach an *actual cause* of the injury? (2) Was the breach a *proximate cause* of the injury? and (3) What was the effect of any *intervening cause* arising after the breach and helping to cause the injury? Both actual and proximate cause are necessary for a negligence recovery. Special rules dealing with intervening causes sometimes apply, depending on the facts of the case.

Actual Cause   Suppose that Dullard drove his car at an excessive speed on a crowded street and was therefore unable to stop the car in time to avoid striking and injuring Pence, who had lawfully entered the crosswalk. Dullard's conduct, being inconsistent with the behavior of a reasonable driver, was a breach of duty that served as the actual cause of Pence's injuries. To determine the existence of actual cause, courts often employ a "but-for" test. This test provides that the defendant's conduct is the actual cause of the plaintiff's injury when the plaintiff would not have been hurt but for (i.e., if not for) the defendant's breach of duty. In the example employed above, Pence clearly would not have been injured if not for Dullard's duty-breaching conduct.

In some cases, however, a person's negligent conduct may combine with another person's negligent conduct to cause a plaintiff's injury. Suppose that fires negligently started by Dustin and Dibble combine to burn down Potter's house. If each fire would have destroyed Potter's house on its own, the but-for test could absolve both Dustin and Dibble. In such cases, courts apply a different test by asking whether each defendant's conduct was a *substantial factor* in bringing about the plaintiff's injury. Under this test, both Dustin and Dibble are likely to be liable for Potter's loss.

Proximate Cause   The plaintiff who proves actual cause has not yet established the causation link necessary to enable her to win the case. She must also establish the existence of proximate cause—a task that sometimes, though clearly not always, is more difficult than proving actual cause.

Questions of proximate cause assume the existence of actual cause. Proximate cause concerns arise because it may sometimes seem unfair to hold a defendant liable for all the injuries actually caused by his breach—no matter how remote, bizarre, or unforeseeable they are. Thus, courts typically say that a negligent defendant is liable only for the *proximate* results of his breach. Proximate cause, then, concerns the required degree of proximity or closeness between the defendant's breach and the injury it actually caused.

Courts have not reached complete agreement on the appropriate test for resolving the proximate cause question. In reality, the question is one of social policy. When deciding which test to adopt, courts must recognize that negligent defendants may be exposed to catastrophic liability by a lenient test for proximate cause, but that a restrictive test prevents some innocent victims from recovering damages for their losses. Courts have responded in various ways to this difficult question.

A significant number of courts have adopted a test under which a defendant who has breached a duty of care is liable only for the "natural and probable consequences" of his actions. In many negligence cases, the injuries actually caused by the defendant's breach would easily qualify as natural and probable consequences because they are the sorts of harms that are both likely and logical effects of such a breach. The Dullard–Pence scenario discussed earlier would be an example. It is to be expected that a pedestrian struck by a car would sustain personal injury.

In other negligence cases, however, either the fact that the plaintiff was injured or the nature of his harms may seem unusual or in some sense remote from the defendant's breach, despite the existence of an actual causation link. The presence or absence of proximate cause becomes a more seriously contested issue in a case of that nature. A great deal will depend upon how narrowly or broadly the court defines the scope of what is natural and probable.

Other courts have limited a breaching defendant's liability for unforeseeable harms by stating that he is liable only to plaintiffs who were within the "scope of the foreseeable risk." Although this test is often characterized as a proximate cause rule, it is actually a rule dealing with the *duty* element, because courts adopting this rule hold that a defendant owes no duty to those who are not foreseeable "victims" of his actions. The *Restatement (Second) of Torts* takes yet another approach to the proximate cause question. It suggests that a defendant's breach of duty is not the legal (i.e., proximate) cause of a plaintiff's injury if, looking back after the harm, it appears "highly extraordinary" to the court that the breach would have brought about the injury.

Further discussion of proximate cause issues can be found in the *Stahlecker* case, which appears in this chapter's later discussion of intervening causes. In *Black v. William Insulation Co.,* which follows, the court rests its decision on the duty element of a negligence claim but engages in considerable discussion of the proximate cause concept.

Black v. William Insulation Co.   141 P.3d 123 (Wyo. Sup. Ct. 2006)

William Insulation Co. (WIC) was a subcontractor on an expansion project at the Exxon/LaBarge Shute Creek Plant. The plant was located in a remote Wyoming area approximately 26 and 40 miles, respectively, from the nearest population centers, the towns of Green River and Kemmerer. Given the remoteness of the work site, WIC provided $30 per day in subsistence pay to each of its employees to defer part of the cost of a motel room or apartment in Green River or Kemmerer. WIC did not require its employees to spend the money on lodging. The employees were free to spend it—or not spend it—as they saw fit.

David Ibarra-Viernes, a WIC employee, was assigned by WIC to work on the above-described expansion project. Ibarra-Viernes received the $30 per day subsistence pay from WIC, but he elected to make the commute to the plant from his home in Evanston, Wyoming, which was 90 miles away. Ibarra-Viernes carpooled with a group of co-workers, who took turns driving.

Ibarra-Viernes's work schedule was Monday through Friday, 7:00 AM to 5:30 PM, with a half-hour lunch and no, or minimal, breaks. In addition to his employment with WIC, Ibarra-Viernes worked a second job at night, washing dishes at a restaurant.

Ibarra-Viernes completed his regular shift at the plant on Tuesday, January 20, 2004, and returned to Evanston at 8:30 PM. He then worked his second job before going to bed around 11:00 PM. Ibarra-Viernes rose at 4:00 AM on January 21 to get his vehicle and collect his co-workers for the daily commute to the plant, where he worked his normal shift. The car pool, with Ibarra-Viernes driving, left the plant around 6:00 PM. Shortly thereafter, Ibarra-Viernes fell asleep at the wheel. His vehicle crossed the centerline of the highway and collided head-on with a vehicle in which Richard Black was a passenger. Richard Black died in the accident. His widow, Peggy Ann Cook Black, acting in her own right and as personal representative of her late husband's estate, filed a negligence-based wrongful death action against WIC in a Wyoming state court.

In her lawsuit, Black claimed that WIC owed a duty of care to other travelers on the highway to prevent injury caused by employees who had become exhausted after being required to commute long distances and work long hours. She contended in her complaint that WIC breached its duty by "failing to take precautionary measures to prevent employees from becoming so exhausted that they pose a threat of harm to the traveling public and failing to provide alternative transportation to its exhausted employees or, in the alternative, failing to provide living quarters to its employees within a reasonable distance from the plant site." WIC moved for summary judgment. The district court granted WIC's motion, concluding that WIC did not owe a duty to the decedent. Black appealed to the Supreme Court of Wyoming.

Hill, Justice

Black sets out [this issue] on appeal: Did the trial court err in failing to recognize a duty of care from an employer to innocent third parties who are injured, or in this case, killed, by its employees who are exhausted due to the working conditions imposed by the employer and thus fall asleep at the wheel? WIC responds [by arguing that] Wyoming law does not, and should not, impose a legal duty of reasonable care on Wyoming employers to protect the motoring public from the negligence of their off-duty employees when those off-duty employees drive to and from their Wyoming worksites in their personal vehicles outside the scope of their employment.

[Prior Supreme Court of Wyoming decisions have] set out in detail the analytical framework for determining whether a duty exists. "Whether a legal duty exists is a question of a law, and absent a duty, there is no liability." [Case citation omitted.] " 'Duty' is not sacrosanct in itself, but is only an expression of the sum total of those considerations of policy which lead the law to say that the plaintiff is entitled to protection.' " *Andersen v. Two Dot Ranch, Inc.,* 49 P.3d 1011, 1024 (Wyo. 2002) (quoting *Gates v. Richardson,* 719 P.2d 193, 195 (Wyo. 1986)). A duty may arise by contract, statute, common law, "or when the relationship of the parties is such that the law imposes an obligation on the defendant to act reasonably for the protection of the plaintiff." [Case citation omitted.] The legal question to be answered by the court is

> whether, upon the facts in evidence, such a relation exists between the parties that the community will impose a legal obligation upon one for the benefit of the other—or, more simply, whether the interest of the plaintiff which has suffered invasion was entitled to legal protection at the hands of the defendant.

[Case citation omitted.]

In deciding whether to adopt a particular tort duty, a court's focus must be much broader than just the case at hand. The judge's function in a duty determination involves complex considerations of legal and social policies which will directly affect the essential determination of the limits to government protection. Consequently, "the imposition and scope of a legal duty is dependent not only on the factor of foreseeability but involves other considerations, including the magnitude of the risk involved in defendant's conduct, the burden of requiring defendant to guard against that risk, and the consequences of placing that burden upon the defendant." [Case citations omitted.] In *Gates,* we further detailed the factors to be considered:

> (1) the foreseeability of harm to the plaintiff, (2) the closeness of the connection between the defendant's conduct and the injury suffered, (3) the degree of certainty that the plaintiff suffered injury, (4) the moral blame attached to the defendant's conduct, (5) the policy of preventing future harm, (6) the extent of the burden upon the defendant, (7) the consequences to the community and the court system, and (8) the availability, cost and prevalence of insurance for the risk involved.

[Other supporting case citations omitted.]

Before we can proceed to our analysis, we must identify the nature of the duty that Black seeks to impose on WIC. Black insists that she is not seeking . . . to establish a broad duty of care for an employer to control an off-duty employee's conduct. Instead, she argues that an employer has an obligation to ensure that the conditions of employment do not cause an employee to become fatigued and, to the extent that they do, the employer has a duty to take reasonable actions to protect the traveling public from the foreseeable consequences of those employees traveling from their worksite. Essentially, the question of duty that we must determine in this case is whether WIC's actions and/or inactions prior to the accident created a foreseeable risk of harm that the employer had a duty to guard against. In other words: whether or not Ibarra-Viernes's fatigue arose out of, and in the course of, his employment.

We turn to the first *Gates* factor: *The foreseeability of harm to the plaintiff.* We recently stated that this factor is essentially a consideration of proximate cause. Proximate cause [exists when] "the accident or injury [is] the natural and probable consequence of the act of negligence." [Case citation omitted.] The ultimate test of proximate cause is foreseeability of injury. In order to qualify as a legal cause, the conduct must be a substantial factor in bringing about the plaintiff's injuries.

The question then is whether or not WIC's conduct was a substantial factor in bringing about the death of the decedent. Or more precisely, a showing of causation necessitates a showing that Ibarra-Viernes's work was a substantial contributing factor to his fatigue. This means that for an "employer to be liable for the actions of a fatigued employee on a theory of negligence, the fatigue must arise out of and in the course of employment . . . [because] . . . [t]o hold otherwise would charge an employer with knowledge of circumstances beyond his control." [Citation of quoted article omitted.] Naturally then, the scope of an employer's duty is "bound by activity that the employer can actually control within the employment relationship." [Article citation omitted.]

Black contends that the accident was a foreseeable consequence of WIC's conduct. Specifically, she claims that . . . WIC required its employees to work long hours and make long commutes. She argues that workers who were commuting and working twelve to fourteen hours a day would not have sufficient time in the day to take care of life activities and still get sufficient sleep. Given these conditions, Black contends that without employer supplied alternatives such as bus transport, it was foreseeable that sleep-deprived workers would likely fall asleep and cause injury to other travelers on the roads.

The most obvious factor within the employer's control that could cause fatigue in an employee is the number of hours the employee is required to work. On the day of the accident and those preceding it, Ibarra-Viernes worked his normal shift of ten hours. A ten-hour shift within a twenty-four-hour period is not, on its face, an objectively unreasonable period of work when compared with those situations where an employer was held liable for the damages caused by a fatigued employee driving home from work. Compare *Robertson v. LeMaster,* 301 S.E.2d 563, 568–69 (W.Va. 1983) (employee required to work 32 consecutive hours) and *Faverty v. McDonald's Restaurants of Oregon, Inc.,* 892 P.2d 703, 705 (Ore. App. 1995) (18-year-old employee worked 12½ hours in a 17-hour period). Crucially, in both of those cases, the employers had actual knowledge of their employee's fatigued state. There is no evidence that WIC had notice that Ibarra-Viernes was fatigued on the day of the accident.

Black seeks to expand Ibarra-Viernes's hours of work to include the time of his commute, claiming that WIC "required" him to make the lengthy drive to and from the plant [by not providing alternative transportation such as a bus]. First, Black cites no authority for the proposition that WIC was required to provide its employees with alternatives, such as busing, to commuting. Furthermore, WIC did, in fact, provide an alternative to long-distance commuting for its employees: WIC provided its employees, including Ibarra-Viernes, with a daily $30 subsistence payment to partially offset the cost of taking lodging closer to the worksite. Ibarra-Viernes, however, elected to pocket that money and commute every day from his home in Evanston. That was a voluntary choice made by Ibarra-Viernes.

In making her argument, Black fails to address a significant factor: Ibarra-Viernes's decision to work a second job. After returning to Evanston upon completion of his work day for WIC, Ibarra-Viernes would go to a second job at a restaurant. On the night before the accident, Ibarra-Viernes stated that he returned home about 8:30 PM and then went to work [at] his second job. Ibarra-Viernes said he got to bed around 11:00 PM that night. Certainly, the second job had an effect on Ibarra-Viernes's ability to get rest, if not actual sleep. Ibarra-Viernes admitted that he normally got only about five to six hours of sleep a night. Nevertheless, Black neglects to discuss the consequences of the second job in her brief. Her failure to do so seriously undermines her argument.

Ibarra-Viernes had 13½ hours between shifts during the work week. The burden was on him to manage his own time to ensure that he was capable of performing his job. Ibarra-Viernes elected to expend a significant portion of his time making a lengthy commute and working a second job. These were voluntary decisions made by Ibarra-Viernes for which he is responsible. Under these circumstances, it cannot be said that his employment was the substantial factor in contributing to Ibarra-Viernes's fatigue.

We conclude that decedent's injuries were not the "natural and probable consequence of" any acts of negligence by WIC in the course of Ibarra-Viernes's employment; rather, the decisions and conduct of Ibarra-Viernes were the substantial factor that brought about the injuries. Since the harm to Black's decedent was not a foreseeable consequence of WIC's actions (or inactions), we decline to impose a duty under the circumstances. Given this conclusion, the remaining *Gates* factors are not persuasive, and we decline to discuss them.

Under the circumstances of this case, the defendant employer did not owe a duty to the plaintiff's decedent.

Grant of summary judgment to WIC affirmed.

Later Acts, Forces, or Events   In some cases, an act, force, or event occurring *after* a defendant's breach of duty may play a significant role in bringing about or worsening the plaintiff's injury. For example, suppose that after Davis sets a fire, a high wind comes up and spreads the fire to Parker's home, or that after Davis negligently runs Parker down with his car, a thief steals Parker's wallet while he lies unconscious. If the later act, force, or event was *foreseeable,* it will not relieve the defendant of liability. So, if high winds are an occurrence that may reasonably be expected from time to time in the locality, Davis is liable for the damage to Parker's home even though his fire might not have spread that far under the wind conditions that existed when he started it. In the second example, Davis is liable not only for Parker's physical injuries but also for the theft of Parker's wallet if the theft was foreseeable, given the time and location of the accident. (The thief, of course, would also be liable for the theft.)

Intervening Causes   On the other hand, if the later act, force, or event that contributes to the plaintiff's injury was *unforeseeable,* most courts hold that it is an intervening cause, which absolves the defendant of liability for harms that resulted directly from the intervening cause. For example, Dalton negligently starts a fire that causes injury to several persons. The driver of an ambulance summoned to the scene has been drinking on duty and, as a result, loses control of his ambulance and runs up onto a sidewalk, injuring several pedestrians. Given the nature of the ambulance driver's position, his drinking while on duty is likely to make the ambulance crash an unforeseeable event and thus an intervening cause. Most courts, therefore, would not hold Dalton responsible for the pedestrians' injuries. The ambulance driver, of course, would be liable to those he injured.

An important exception to the liability-absolving effect of an intervening cause deals with unforeseeable later events that produce a foreseeable harm identical to the harm risked by the defendant's breach of duty. Why should the defendant escape liability on the basis that an easily foreseeable consequence of its conduct came about through unforeseeable means? For example, if the owners of a concert hall negligently fail to install the number of emergency exits required by law, the owners will not escape liability to those burned and trampled during a fire just because the fire was caused by an insane concertgoer who set himself ablaze.

As suggested by some of the examples used above, when a defendant's breach of duty is followed by a third party's criminal or other wrongful act, the later act may be either foreseeable or unforeseeable, depending on the facts and circumstances. This state of affairs reflects the prevailing modern approach, which differs sharply from the traditional view that third parties' criminal acts were unforeseeable as a matter of law and thus were always intervening causes serving to limit or eliminate the original defendant's negligence liability. Today, courts do not hesitate to classify a third party's criminal act as foreseeable if the time and place of its commission and other relevant facts point to such a conclusion.

Assume, for instance, that XYZ, Inc., owns an apartment complex at which break-ins and prior instances of criminal activity had occurred. XYZ nevertheless fails to adopt the security-related measures that a reasonable apartment complex owner would adopt. As a result, a criminal intruder easily enters the complex. He then physically attacks a tenant. Because the intruder's act is likely to be seen as foreseeable—and thus not an intervening cause—XYZ faces negligence liability to the tenant for the injuries that the intruder directly inflicted on the tenant. (The intruder, of course, would face both criminal and civil liability for battery, but if his financial assets are limited, the injured tenant may find collecting a damages award from him either difficult or impossible.) Note that for purposes of the tenant's negligence claim, XYZ's breach of duty was a substantial factor in bringing about the plaintiff's injuries because the lack of reasonable security measures allowed the intruder to gain easy access to the premises. XYZ's breach thus would be considered the *actual cause* of the tenant's injuries under the previously discussed substantial factor test. It would also be considered the proximate cause under the various tests described earlier.

The *Stahlecker* case, which follows, illustrates the operation of intervening cause principles.

Stahlecker v. Ford Motor Co.   667 N.W.2d 244 (Neb. Sup. Ct. 2003)

During the early morning hours of April 29, 2000, Amy Stahlecker was driving a 1997 Ford Explorer equipped with Firestone Wilderness AT radial tires in a remote area of Nebraska. One of the tires failed, rendering the vehicle inoperable. Richard Cook encountered Amy while she was stranded as a result of the tire failure. Cook abducted Amy, sexually assaulted her, and then murdered her.

Susan and Dale Stahlecker, acting on behalf of themselves and as personal representatives of their daughter's estate, brought a wrongful death action in a Nebraska court against Cook, the Ford Motor Co. (manufacturer of the Explorer), and Bridgestone/Firestone Inc. (manufacturer of the tire that failed). The Stahleckers sought to make out negligence claims against Ford and Firestone. The plaintiffs alleged that Ford and Firestone knew of prior problems with the model of tire that was on the Explorer driven by Amy; knew those problems posed a greater-than-normal danger of tire failure; continued using a problematic model of Firestone tire on Explorers despite knowledge that tire failure would create a special risk of rollover and vehicle inoperability; failed to warn consumers of these dangers; and continued to advertise their tires and vehicles as suitable for uses of the sort Amy made immediately prior to the tire failure, even though they knew that drivers could become stranded in the event of tire failure. There was no allegation that the tire failure directly caused Amy to sustain physical harm prior to the obvious harm inflicted by Cook.

A state district court sustained demurrers filed by Ford and Firestone and dismissed the case as to those parties. The court concluded that the Stahleckers had not stated a valid cause of action against Ford and Firestone because Cook's criminal acts constituted an intervening cause that would relieve Ford and Firestone of any liability they might otherwise have had. The Stahleckers successfully petitioned to bypass the Nebraska Court of Appeals and pursue their appeal in the Supreme Court of Nebraska.

Stephan, Judge

In order to withstand a demurrer, a plaintiff must plead . . . "a narrative of events, acts, and things done or omitted which show a legal liability of the defendant to the plaintiff." [Case citation omitted.] In determining whether a cause of action has been stated, a petition is to be construed liberally.

In order to prevail in a negligence action, a plaintiff must establish the defendant's duty to protect the plaintiff from injury, a failure to discharge that duty, and damages proximately caused by the failure to discharge that duty. The concept of "foreseeability" is a component of both duty and proximate cause, although its meaning is somewhat different in each context. We have noted this distinction in recent cases:

> Foreseeability as a determinant of a [defendant's] duty of care . . . is to be distinguished from foreseeability as a determinant of whether a breach of duty is a proximate cause of an ultimate injury. Foreseeability as it impacts duty determinations refers to the knowledge of the risk of injury to be apprehended. The risk reasonably to be perceived defines the duty to be obeyed; it is the risk reasonably within the range of apprehension, of injury to another person, that is taken into account in determining the existence of the duty to exercise care. . . . Foreseeability that affects proximate cause, on the other hand, relates to the question of whether the specific act or omission of the defendant was such that the ultimate injury to the plaintiff reasonably flowed from defendant's breach of duty. . . . Foreseeability in the proximate cause context relates to remoteness rather than the existence of a duty.

[Case citations omitted.]

[B]y alleging that Ford and Firestone failed to exercise reasonable care in designing and manufacturing their tires, and failed to warn users of potential tire defects, the Stahleckers have alleged the existence of a legal duty and a breach thereof by both Ford and Firestone. The remaining issue is whether the breach of this duty was the proximate cause of Amy's harm.

The proximate cause of an injury is "that cause which, in a natural and continuous sequence, without any efficient, intervening cause, produces the injury, and without which the injury would not have occurred." [Case citation omitted.] Stated another way, a plaintiff must meet [these] basic requirements in establishing [causation]: (1) [the actual cause requirement] that without the negligent action, the injury would not have occurred, commonly known as the " but-for" rule; [and] (2) [the proximate cause requirement] that the injury was a natural and probable result of the negligence. [In addition, there cannot have been] an efficient intervening cause.

As to the first requirement, a defendant's conduct is the cause of the event if "the event would not have occurred but for that conduct; conversely, the defendant's conduct is not a cause of the event if the event would have occurred without it." [Case citation omitted.] The petition alleges that Cook "found Amy alone and stranded as a direct result of the failure of the Firestone Wilderness AT Radial Tire and proceeded to abduct, terrorize, rape and murder Amy." Firestone concedes that under the factual allegations of the Stahleckers' petition—that "but for" the failure of its tire—Amy would not have been at the place where she was assaulted and murdered.

The [tests governing] proximate cause [and intervening cause] are somewhat interrelated. Was the criminal assault and murder the "natural and probable" result of the failure to warn of potential tire failure, or did the criminal acts constitute an effective intervening cause that would preclude any causal link between the failure to warn and the injuries and wrongful death for which damages are claimed in this action? An efficient intervening cause is a new, independent force intervening between the defendant's negligent act and the plaintiff's injury. This force may be the conduct of a third person who had full control of the situation, whose conduct the defendant could not anticipate or contemplate, and whose conduct resulted directly in the plaintiff's injury. An efficient intervening cause must break the causal connection between the original wrong and the injury.

In *Shelton v. Board of Regents,* 320 N.W.2d 748 (Neb. Sup. Ct. 1982), we considered whether criminal conduct constituted an intervening cause. *Shelton* involved wrongful death claims brought on behalf of persons who were poisoned by a former employee of the Eugene C. Eppley Institute for Research in Cancer and Allied Diseases (the Institute). In their actions against the Institute . . . , the plaintiffs alleged that [even though] the former employee had a prior criminal conviction involving an attempted homicide, the Institute hired him as a research technologist and gave him access to the poisonous substance which he subsequently used to commit the murders. The plaintiffs alleged that the Institute was negligent in hiring the employee, in allowing him to have access to the poisonous substance, and in failing to monitor its inventory of the substance. The plaintiffs further alleged that the Institute's negligence was the proximate cause of the injuries and deaths of the victims. The district court sustained a demurrer filed by the Institute and dismissed the actions. This court affirmed, holding . . . that the criminal acts of stealing the drug and administering it to the victims "were of such nature as to constitute an efficient intervening cause which destroys any claim that the alleged negligence of the [Institute] was the proximate cause of the appellants' injuries and damage." In reaching this conclusion, we relied upon *Restatement (Second) of Torts* § 448 (1965), which states the following rule:

> The act of a third person in committing an intentional tort or crime is a superseding cause of harm to another resulting therefrom, although the actor's negligent conduct created a situation which afforded an opportunity to the third person to commit such a tort or crime, unless the actor at the time of his negligent conduct realized or should have realized the likelihood that such a situation might be created, and that a third person might avail himself of the opportunity to commit such a tort or crime.

We held [in *Shelton*] that the employee's criminal acts were the cause of the injuries for which damages were claimed and that "nothing which the [plaintiffs] claim the . . . Institute failed to do was in any manner related to those acts, nor could they have been reasonably contemplated by the . . . Institute."

We have, however, determined in certain premises liability cases and in cases involving negligent custodial entrustment that the criminal act of a third person does not constitute an efficient intervening cause. For example, in [one such case], a patron of a bar was seriously injured by another patron in the parking lot after the two were instructed by the bartender to take their argument "outside." The injured patron sued the owner of the bar, alleging that the owner negligently failed to contact law enforcement, maintain proper security on the premises, and properly train his personnel. [R]evers[ing] a judgment on a jury verdict in favor of the owner, . . . [w]e reasoned that

> because the harm resulting from a fight is precisely the harm against which [the owner] is alleged to have had a duty to protect [the patron], the "intervention" of [the other patron] cannot be said to be an independent act that would break the causal connection between [the owner's] negligence and [the patron's] injuries.

[Case citation omitted.]

We employed similar reasoning in [two other cases that] involved negligent placement of juvenile wards of the state in foster homes without disclosure of their known histories of violent acts. In each of those cases, we held that criminal acts of foster children perpetrated upon members of the foster parents' households could not be asserted as intervening causes to defeat liability for the negligent placement. Similarly, we recently held that a psychiatric patient's criminal assault upon a nurse was not an intervening cause as to the negligence of a state agency which breached its duty to disclose the violent propensities of the patient at the time of his admission to the hospital where the assault occurred. These decisions were based upon the principle . . . that "once it is shown that a defendant had a duty to anticipate [a] criminal act and guard against it, the criminal act cannot supersede the defendant's liability." [Case citation omitted.]

This principle requires that we determine whether the duty owed to Amy by Ford and Firestone, as manufacturers and sellers of the allegedly defective tires, included a duty to anticipate and guard against criminal acts perpetrated against the users of such tires. [As illustrated by the previously discussed cases dealing with juvenile wards and psychiatric patients,] we have recognized a duty to anticipate and protect another against criminal acts where the party charged with the duty has some right of control over the perpetrator of such acts or the physical premises upon which the crime occurs. [We have] recognized a duty on the part of the owner of business premises to protect invitees from criminal assault where there had been documented criminal activity in the immediate vicinity of the premises. [In addition, we have] held that a university had a duty to protect a student from physical hazing conducted in a fraternity house where similar incidents were known to have occurred previously[, and] that a university "owes a landowner-invitee duty to its students to take reasonable steps to protect against foreseeable acts of violence on its campus and the harm that naturally flows therefrom." [Case citation omitted.] However, we have adopted *Restatement (Second) of Torts* § 315 (1965), which provides:

> There is no duty so to control the conduct of a third person as to prevent him from causing physical harm to another unless . . . a special relation exists between the actor and the third person which imposes a duty upon the actor to control the third person's conduct, or . . . a special relation exists between the actor and the other which gives to the other a right to protection.

We have found no authority recognizing a duty on the part of the manufacturer of a product to protect a consumer from criminal activity at the scene of a product failure where no physical harm is caused by the product itself.

The Stahleckers argue that a duty to anticipate criminal acts associated with product failure arises from their allegations that Ford and Firestone knew or should have known of "the potential for similar dangerous situations arising as a result of a breakdown of a Ford Explorer and/or its tires." They also allege that Ford and Firestone had or should have had "knowledge, to include statistical information, regarding the likelihood of criminal conduct and/or sexual assault against auto and tire industry consumers as a result of unexpected auto and/or tire failures in general." Assuming the truth of these allegations, the most that can be inferred is that Ford and Firestone had general knowledge that criminal assaults can occur at the scene of a vehicular product failure. However, it is generally known that violent crime can and does occur in a variety of settings, including the relative safety of a victim's home. The facts alleged do not present the type of knowledge concerning a specific individual's criminal propensity, or right of control over premises known to have been the scene of prior criminal activity, upon which we have recognized a tort duty to protect another from criminal acts.

The Stahleckers have not alleged, and could not allege, any special relationship between Ford and Firestone and the criminal actor (Cook) or the victim of his crime (Amy) that would extend their duty, as manufacturers and sellers of products, to protect a consumer from harm caused by a criminal act perpetrated at the scene of a product failure. In the absence of such a duty, [we must] conclude as a matter of law that the criminal assault constituted an efficient intervening cause which precludes a determination that negligence on the part of Ford and Firestone was the proximate cause of the harm [to Amy].

[Therefore,] the district court did not err in sustaining the demurrers of Ford and Firestone . . . and in dismissing the action as to them.

District court's decision affirmed.

Special Rules Whatever test for proximate cause a court adopts, most courts agree on certain basic causation rules. In case of a conflict, these rules supersede the proximate cause and intervening cause rules stated earlier. One such rule is that persons who are negligent "take their victims as they find them." This means that a negligent defendant is liable for the full extent of her victim's injuries if those injuries are aggravated by some preexisting physical susceptibility of the victim—even though this susceptibility could not have been foreseen. Similarly, negligent defendants normally are liable for diseases contracted by their victims while in a weakened state caused by their injuries. Negligent defendants typically are jointly liable—along with the attending physician—for negligent medical care that their victims receive for their injuries.

Res Ipsa Loquitur

In some cases, negligence may be difficult to prove because the defendant has superior knowledge of the circumstances surrounding the plaintiff's injury. It may not be in the defendant's best interests to disclose those circumstances if they point to liability on his part. The classic example is an 1863 case, *Byrne v. Boadle.* The plaintiff was a pedestrian who had been hit on the head by a barrel of flour that fell from a warehouse owned by the defendant. The plaintiff had no way of knowing what caused the barrel to fall; he merely knew he had been injured. The only people likely to have known the relevant facts were the owners of the warehouse and their employees, but they most likely were the ones responsible for the accident. After observing that "[a] barrel could not roll out of a warehouse without some negligence," the court required the defendant owner to show that he was not at fault.

Byrne v. Boadle eventually led to the doctrine of **res ipsa loquitur** ("the thing speaks for itself"). *Res ipsa* applies when (1) the defendant has exclusive control of the instrumentality of harm (and therefore probable knowledge of, and responsibility for, the cause of the harm); (2) the harm that occurred would not ordinarily occur in the absence of negligence; and (3) the plaintiff was in no way responsible for his own injury. Most courts hold that when these three elements are satisfied, a presumption of breach of duty and causation arises. The defendant then

CYBERLAW IN ACTION

A *Cyberlaw in Action* box in Chapter 1 addressed the effect of §230 of the federal Communications Decency Act (CDA) on certain defamation and injurious falsehood claims. As *Gentry v. eBay, Inc.,* 99 Cal. App. 4th 816 (2002) reveals, §230 may also apply to certain negligence claims.

Gentry was a case brought by buyers of sports memorabilia that bore autographs later determined not to be genuine. The plaintiffs contended that eBay, an online marketplace on which the items were sold, should bear legal responsibility on various legal grounds, including negligence. According to the plaintiffs, eBay had been negligent: (1) by maintaining an online forum that allowed any user, regardless of his or her purchase history, to give positive or negative feedback regarding dealers; and (2) by endorsing certain dealers on the basis of this feedback and the dealers' sales volume. The plaintiffs contended that these actions by eBay created a false sense of confidence in the collectibles' authenticity because most, if

not all, of the positive feedback about a dealer would be generated either by that dealer or by another cooperating dealer.

A California appellate court held in *Gentry* that §230 of the CDA provided eBay a meritorious defense against the plaintiffs' negligence claim. Section 230 states that "[n]o provider or user of an interactive computer service shall be treated as the publisher or speaker of any information provided by another information content provider." The court reasoned that eBay was a "provider . . . of an interactive computer service" and that the plaintiffs' negligence claim amounted, in substance, to an attempt to have eBay held liable for the effects of statements made by "another information content provider" or providers (i.e., those who, in the online forum, posted arguably misleading "feedback"). The court therefore regarded the plaintiffs' negligence claim as an effort to have eBay treated as the "publisher" of information provided by another party. Section 230, the court held, prohibited such treatment of eBay.

---

runs a significant risk of losing the case if he does not produce evidence to rebut this presumption.

Negligence Defenses
The common law traditionally recognized two defenses to negligence: **contributory negligence** and **assumption of risk.** In many states, however, these traditional defenses have been superseded by new defenses called **comparative negligence** and **comparative fault.**

Contributory Negligence Contributory negligence is the plaintiff's failure to exercise reasonable care for her own safety. Where it still applies, contributory negligence is a complete defense for the defendant if it was a substantial factor in producing the plaintiff's injury. So, if Preston steps into the path of Doyle's speeding car without first checking to see whether any cars are coming, Preston would be denied any recovery against Doyle, in view of the clear causal relationship between Preston's injury and his failure to exercise reasonable care for his own safety.

Comparative Negligence Traditionally, even a minor failure to exercise reasonable care for one's own safety—only a slight departure from the standard of reasonable self-protectiveness—gave the defendant a complete contributory negligence defense. This rule, which probably stemmed from the 19th-century desire to protect railroads

and infant manufacturing interests from negligence liability, came under increasing attack in the 20th century. The main reasons were the traditional rule's harsh impact on many plaintiffs. The rule frequently prevented slightly negligent plaintiffs from recovering any compensation for their losses, even though the defendants may have been much more at fault.

In response to such complaints, all but a few states have adopted **comparative negligence** systems either by statute or by judicial decision. The details of these systems vary, but the principle underlying them is essentially the same: courts seek to determine the relative negligence of the parties and award damages in proportion to the degrees of negligence determined. The formula is:

$$\text{Plaintiff's recovery} = \text{Defendant's percentage share of the negligence causing the injury} \times \text{Plaintiff's proven damages}$$

For example, assume that Dunne negligently injures Porter and that Porter suffers $100,000 in damages. A jury determines that Dunne was 80 percent at fault and Porter 20 percent at fault. Under comparative negligence, Porter would recover $80,000 from Dunne. What if Dunne's share of the negligence is determined to be 40 percent and Porter's 60 percent? Here, the results vary depending on whether the state in question has adopted a *pure* or a *mixed* comparative negligence system. Under a pure system, courts apply the preceding formula regardless of the plaintiff's and the defendant's percentage shares of the negligence. Porter therefore would recover $40,000 in a pure comparative negligence state. Under a mixed system, the formula operates only when the defendant's share of the negligence is greater than (or, in some states, greater than or equal to) 50 percent. If the plaintiff's share of the negligence exceeds 50 percent, mixed systems provide that the defendant has a complete defense against liability. In such states, therefore, Porter would lose the case.

The *Currie* case, which appears earlier in the chapter, furnishes a further example of how comparative negligence principles are applied.

Assumption of Risk   Assumption of risk is the plaintiff's *voluntary* consent to a *known* danger. Voluntariness means that the plaintiff accepted the risk of her own free will; knowledge means that the plaintiff was aware of the nature and extent of the risk. Often, the plaintiff's knowledge and voluntariness are inferred from the facts. This type of assumption of risk is sometimes called **implied** assumption of risk. For example, Pilson voluntarily goes for a ride in Dudley's car, even though Dudley has told Pilson that her car's brakes frequently fail. Pilson probably has assumed the risk of injury from the car's defective brakes.

A plaintiff can also **expressly** assume the risk of injury by entering into a contract that purports to relieve the defendant of a duty of care he would otherwise owe to the plaintiff. Such contract provisions are called *exculpatory clauses.* Chapter 15 discusses exculpatory clauses and the limitations that courts have imposed on their enforceability. The most important such limitations are that the plaintiff have knowledge of the exculpatory clause (which often boils down to a question of its conspicuousness), and that the plaintiff must accept it voluntarily (which does not happen when the defendant has greatly superior bargaining power).

What happens to assumption of risk in comparative negligence states? Some of these states maintain assumption of risk as a separate and complete defense. Many other states now incorporate implied assumption of risk within the state's comparative negligence scheme. In such states, comparative negligence basically becomes **comparative fault.** Although the terms comparative negligence and comparative fault often are used interchangeably, technically the former involves only negligence and the latter involves all kinds of fault. In a comparative fault state, therefore, the fact-finder determines the plaintiff's and the defendant's relative shares of the fault—including assumption of risk—that caused the plaintiff's injury.

In the *Davenport* case, which follows, the court made implied assumption of risk part of the state's mixed comparative negligence scheme (effectively making it comparative fault). Note, however, that this was not true for express assumption of risk.

Davenport v. Cotton Hope Plantation   508 S.E.2d 565 (S.C. Sup. Ct. 1998)

Alvin Davenport, who leased a condominium at the Cotton Hope Plantation on Hilton Head Island, South Carolina, complained to Cotton Hope that the floodlights at the bottom of the stairway to his unit were not working. Before Cotton Hope got around to fixing the floodlights, Davenport was injured when he tried to descend the stairway one night. Specifically, he fell after attempting to place his foot on what appeared to be a step but actually was a shadow caused by the inoperative floodlight.

Davenport sued Cotton Hope for negligence in a South Carolina trial court. The trial court directed a verdict against him because he had assumed the risk of his injury, and, in the alternative, because he was more than 50 percent at fault in causing the injury. After Davenport appealed, the intermediate appellate court reversed, holding that under South Carolina's comparative negligence system, assumption of risk no longer was an independent defense, that it instead was just a factor to be considered in determining the parties' relative fault, and that that issue should have gone to the jury. Cotton Hope appealed to the South Carolina Supreme Court.

Toal, Judge

A threshold question is whether assumption of risk survives as a complete bar to recovery under South Carolina's comparative negligence system. In 1991, we adopted a modified version of comparative negligence. Under this system, a plaintiff in a negligence action may recover damages if his or her negligence is not greater than that of the defendant. Not so clear was what would become of assumption of risk.

An overwhelming majority of jurisdictions that have adopted some form of comparative negligence have abolished assumption of risk as an absolute bar to recovery. In analyzing the continuing viability of assumption of risk in a comparative negligence system, many courts distinguish between express assumption of risk and implied assumption of risk. Express assumption of risk applies when the parties expressly agree in advance, either in writing or orally, that the plaintiff will relieve the defendant of his or her legal duty toward the plaintiff. Even in those comparative fault jurisdictions that have abrogated assumption of risk, the rule remains that express assumption of risk continues as an absolute defense in an action for negligence. The reason is that express assumption of risk sounds in contract, not tort, and is based upon an express manifestation of consent. Implied assumption of risk arises when the plaintiff implicitly, rather than expressly, assumes known risks.

It is contrary to the basic premise of our fault system to allow a defendant, who is at fault in causing an accident, to escape bearing any of its cost, while requiring a plaintiff, who is no more than equally at fault, to bear all of its costs. The defendant's fault is not diminished solely because the plaintiff knowingly assumes a risk. In our comparative fault system, it would be incongruous to absolve the defendant of all liability based only on whether the plaintiff assumed the risk of injury. Comparative negligence seeks to assess and compare the negligence of both the plaintiff and the defendant. This goal would clearly be thwarted by adhering to the common law defense of assumption of risk. Our conclusion that the absolute defense of assumption of risk is inconsistent with South Carolina's comparative negligence system is buttressed by our recent opinion in *Spahn v. Town of Port Royal* (1998), [where] we held that last clear chance had been subsumed by our adoption of comparative negligence. We therefore hold that a plaintiff is not barred from recovery by assumption of risk unless the degree of fault arising therefrom is greater than the negligence of the defendant.

Cotton Hope argues that we should affirm the trial court's ruling that, as a matter of law, Davenport was more than 50 percent negligent. The trial court based its ruling on the fact that Davenport knew of the danger weeks before his accident, and had a safe alternate route. However, there also was evidence suggesting that Cotton Hope was negligent in failing to properly maintain the lighting in the stairway. It could be reasonably concluded that Davenport's negligence in proceeding down the stairway did not exceed Cotton Hope's negligence. Thus, [that issue] is properly submitted for jury determination.

Court of Appeals decision returning the case to the trial court affirmed.

Strict Liability

Strict liability is liability without fault or, perhaps more precisely, irrespective of fault. This means that in strict liability cases, the defendant is liable even though he did not intend to cause the harm and did not bring it about through recklessness or negligence.

The imposition of strict liability is a social policy decision that the risk associated with an activity should be borne by those who pursue it, rather than by innocent persons who are exposed to that risk. Such liability is premised on the defendant's voluntary decision to engage in a particularly risky activity. When the defendant is a corporation that has engaged in such an activity, the assumption is that the firm can pass the costs of liability on to consumers in the form of higher prices for goods or services. Through strict liability, therefore, the economic costs created by certain harms are "socialized" by being transferred from the victims to defendants to society at large.

Strict liability, however, does not apply to the vast majority of activities. It therefore becomes important to consider which activities do trigger the liability-without-fault approach. The owners of trespassing livestock and the keepers of naturally dangerous wild animals were among the first classes of defendants on whom the courts imposed strict liability. Today, the two most important activities subject to judicially imposed strict liability are abnormally dangerous (or ultrahazardous) activities and the manufacture or sale of defective and unreasonably dangerous products. We discuss the latter in Chapter 20 and the former immediately below.

Abnormally Dangerous Activities
Abnormally dangerous (or ultrahazardous) activities are those necessarily involving a risk of harm that cannot be eliminated by the exercise of reasonable care. Among the activities treated as abnormally dangerous are blasting, crop dusting, stunt flying, and, in one case, the transportation of large quantities of gasoline by truck. (Most courts, however, would be unlikely to label the latter as abnormally dangerous.) Traditionally, contributory negligence has not been a defense in ultrahazardous activity cases, but assumption of risk has been a defense. The *Phillips* case, which follows, discusses the various factors that courts consider before deciding whether a particular activity should be classified as abnormally dangerous.

Phillips v. E.I. DuPont de Nemours & Co. (In re Hanford Nuclear Reservation Litigation)   521 F.3d 1028 (9th Cir. 2008)

During World War II, the U.S. government constructed the Hanford Nuclear Weapons Reservation in the state of Washington. The facility's mission was to produce plutonium for military purposes. Because it was not clear that the government possessed the expertise to operate Hanford, the government solicited E.I. DuPont de Nemours & Co. to run the facility. Despite initial reluctance, DuPont undertook operation of Hanford as a patriotic duty and neither sought nor earned a profit from its Hanford activities. Hanford ultimately helped make the atomic bomb that was dropped on Nagasaki, Japan, in World War II. (The bomb dropped on Hiroshima was uranium-based.) General Electric, Inc. (GE), took over operation of Hanford from DuPont in 1946 and continued in that role for a substantial number of years. As was the case with DuPont, GE neither sought nor earned a profit in regard to Hanford.

As part of the plutonium-production process, the Hanford facility emitted I-131, a fission byproduct known as radioiodine. I-131 was regarded in the 1940s and thereafter as having the potential to cause adverse health effects in humans. Although emissions of I-131 continued at Hanford for many years, a late-1980s study by the Centers for Disease Control and Prevention concluded that 88 percent of the I-131 emissions at Hanford occurred from 1944 to 1946. Emissions levels decreased significantly in later years after stronger restrictions on emissions were put in place. This study, which focused on potentially adverse health effects of the I-131 emissions, sparked a considerable amount of litigation. More than 2,000 persons sued DuPont, GE, and other defendants, contending that the I-131 emissions at Hanford caused them to experience thyroid disorders, thyroid cancer, and other forms of cancer.

Because the plaintiffs claimed to have been harmed by a nuclear incident (the I-131 emissions), the cases were filed under a federal statute, the Price-Anderson Act (PAA). That statute allows parties harmed in nuclear incidents to sue potentially liable private companies such as DuPont and GE, but calls for government indemnification for liable private companies in order to give them an incentive to take part in the nuclear industry. The PAA gives federal courts exclusive jurisdiction over claims arising from nuclear incidents, and allows such claims to be consolidated in a single federal court. However, according to the PAA, the substantive legal rules governing the case are the rules provided by state law.

The many Hanford-related lawsuits were consolidated in a single federal court. After litigation that extended for approximately 15 years, the parties agreed to a bellwether trial that was designed to produce a verdict highlighting the strengths and weaknesses of the parties' respective cases and increase the chances of a settlement to resolve the long-running litigation. The bellwether trial focused on six plaintiffs who were representative of the larger group of plaintiffs. The six bellwether plaintiffs claimed that they suffered thyroid cancer or other thyroid disorders as a result of the I-131 emissions at Hanford, and that the defendants should be held strictly liable under Washington law. With causation proving to be the key issue in the strict liability case, two of the bellwether plaintiffs ended up winning their claims and receiving a judgment for damages. DuPont, GE, and the other defendants appealed to the U.S. Court of Appeals for the Ninth Circuit.

Schroeder, Circuit Judge

A threshold issue [in this appeal] is whether the defendants may seek complete immunity under the common law government contractor defense, because they were operating Hanford at the request of the federal government. We hold that the defense is inapplicable as a matter of law, because Congress enacted the PAA before the courts recognized the government contractor defense, and the PAA provides a comprehensive liability scheme that precludes the defendants' reliance on such a defense.

In the alternative, the defendants argue that even if they are not immune, they are not strictly liable for any I-131 emissions. Specifically, the defendants contend that operating the Hanford facility does not constitute an "abnormally dangerous activity" under Washington law. We review *de novo* the question of whether an activity is abnormally dangerous.

Washington has adopted the *Restatement (Second) of Torts*, §§ 519 and 520, which outline the strict liability regime for abnormally dangerous activities. See *Klein v. Pyrodyne Corp.*, 810 P.2d 917 (Wash. 1991). Section 519 provides:

(1) One who carries on an abnormally dangerous activity is subject to liability for harm to the person, land, or chattels of another resulting from the activity, although he has exercised the utmost care to prevent such harm.

(2) Such strict liability is limited to the kind of harm, the risk of which makes the activity abnormally dangerous.

Section 520 lists the factors to be used when determining what constitutes an abnormally dangerous activity:

(a) Whether the activity involves a high degree of risk of some harm to the person, land or chattels of another;

(b) Whether the gravity of the harm which may result from it is likely to be great;

(c) Whether the risk cannot be eliminated by the exercise of reasonable care;

(d) Whether the activity is not a matter of common usage;

(e) Whether the activity is inappropriate to the place where it is carried on; and

(f) The value of the activity to the community.

A court does not have to weigh each of the elements listed in § 520 equally. One factor alone, however, is generally not sufficient to find an activity abnormally dangerous.

The defendants argue that at the time of the emissions in the 1940s, they did not know the risks that were attributable to radioiodine exposure, and therefore § 520's factors (a)–(c) cannot be weighed against them. Any possible injury from radiation, however, need not have been actually known by the defendants at the time of exposure in order to impose strict liability. Under Washington law, if the actual harm fell within a general field of danger which should have been anticipated, strict liability may be appropriate. Whether an injury should have been anticipated does not depend on whether the particular harm was actually expected to occur. It is sufficient that "the risk created [be] so unusual, either because of its magnitude or because of the circumstances surrounding it. . . ." [Case citation omitted.]

There is no question that the defendants should have anticipated some of the many risks associated with operating a nuclear facility, creating plutonium, and releasing I-131 into the atmosphere. It is exactly because of these risks, and the potential exposure to liability arising from them, that the government contracted with the defendants to limit liability in case of an accident. For these same reasons, . . . scientists [with whom the government contracted] recommended dosage limits.

We agree with the district court that the defendants' conduct at Hanford was an abnormally dangerous activity under the § 520 factors. There was a high degree of risk to people and property associated with the Hanford facility and the gravity of any harm was likely to be great. Regardless of the defendants' efforts to exercise reasonable care, some I-131 would be released, and developing plutonium is hardly an activity of common usage. While the value to the community at large, i.e., the nation, of developing an atomic bomb was perceived as high and there is pragmatically no very appropriate place to carry on such an activity, the § 520 factors on balance support holding that the defendants' activities were abnormally dangerous.

District court's judgment against defendants on strict liability claims affirmed.

Statutory Strict Liability Strict liability principles are also embodied in modern legislation. The most important examples are the workers' compensation acts passed by most states early in this century. Chapter 51 contains more detailed discussion of such statutes, which allow employees to recover statutorily limited amounts from their employers without any need to show fault on the employer's part and without any consideration of contributory fault on the employee's part. Employers participate in a compulsory liability insurance system and are expected to pass the costs of the system on to consumers, who then become the ultimate bearers of the human costs of industrial production. Other examples of statutory strict liability vary from state to state.

Tort Reform

The risk-spreading strategy of tort law has not been trouble-free. During roughly the past 25 years, there has been considerable talk about a supposed crisis in the liability insurance system. From time to time over that period, the insurance system has been marked by outright refusals of coverage, reductions in coverage, and escalating premiums when coverage remains available. To some, this intermittent liability insurance crisis is largely the fault of the insurance industry. Among other things, such observers argue that insurers have manufactured the crisis to obtain unjustified premium increases and to divert attention from insurer mismanagement of invested premium income.

To other observers, however, the reason for the crisis is an explosion in tort liability in recent years. Examples include the tendency toward somewhat greater imposition of strict liability, increases in the frequency and size of punitive damage awards, and similar increases in awards for noneconomic harms such as pain and suffering. The greater costs imposed on defendants, observers say, operate to increase the price and diminish the availability of liability insurance. In some cases, therefore, businesses may be required to self-insure or go without insurance coverage. In others, they may be able to obtain insurance—but only at a price that cannot be completely passed on to consumers. Where the costs can be fully passed on, the argument continues, they depress the economy by diminishing consumers' purchasing power or adding to inflation, or both. In addition, the argument concludes, the liability explosion impedes the development of new products and technologies that might result in huge awards for injured plaintiffs.

These beliefs have fueled a movement for tort reform. By the mid-1990s, most states had enacted some form of tort reform legislation. Such legislation typically follows one or both of two strategies: (1) limiting defendants' tort *liability* (plaintiffs' ability to obtain a judgment); and (2) limiting the *damages* plaintiffs can recover once they get a judgment. One example of the former is some states' legislation restricting the liability of social hosts or businesses for the damage caused by intoxicated people to whom they serve alcohol. The most common examples

of the latter are statutory caps or other limits on recoveries for punitive damages and noneconomic harm.

The battle for tort reform has not ended, however. Proponents continue to seek additional reform measures. Tort reform opponents who lost the fight in the legislature have sometimes continued it in the courts. They have done so primarily by challenging tort reform measures on state constitutional grounds. Such challenges have succeeded in some states but have been rebuffed in others.

In recent years, there have been calls in some quarters for Congress to enact caps on dollar amounts of damages for pain and suffering and similar noneconomic harm in certain negligence cases, most notably those involving alleged medical malpractice. As of the time this book went to press in 2008, no such federal measures had been enacted.

Problems and Problem Cases

1. Terry Williams sustained physical injuries in an accident involving a vehicle driven by Kellie Meagher. At the time of the accident, Meagher was allegedly using a cellular phone furnished by Cingular Wireless. Williams later sued Meagher and Cingular in an Indiana court. In the portion of the complaint pertaining to Cingular, Williams alleged that Cingular was negligent in furnishing a cellular phone to Meagher when it knew, or should have known, that the phone would be used while the user operated a motor vehicle. Cingular filed a motion to dismiss for failure to state a claim on which relief could be granted. After the trial court granted Cingular's motion, Williams appealed to the Indiana Court of Appeals. Was the trial court correct in granting Cingular's motion to dismiss?

2. A young man abducted R.M.V., age 10, from the sidewalk in front of her home and dragged her across the street to a vacant apartment at the Chalmette Apartments. He raped her, put her in the closet, told her not to leave, and disappeared. The apartment in question was described by the police officer called to the scene as "empty, filthy, dirty, and full of debris." Glass was broken from its windows and the front door was off its hinges. In the two years prior to the attack on R.M.V., Dallas police had investigated many serious crimes committed at the Chalmette Apartments complex. A Dallas City Ordinance established minimum standards for property owners, requiring them, among other things, to "keep the

doors and windows of a vacant structure or vacant portion of a structure securely closed to prevent unauthorized entry." Gaile Nixon, R.M.V.'s mother, filed a negligence suit against Chalmette's owner and Mr. Property Management Company, Inc., the manager of the complex. Were the defendants correct in arguing that they owed no duty to R.M.V.?

3. Ludmila Hresil and her niece were shopping at a Sears retail store. There were few shoppers in the store at the time. Hresil spent about 10 minutes in the store's women's department, where she observed no other shoppers. After Hresil's niece completed a purchase in another part of the store, the two women began to walk through the women's department. Hresil, who was pushing a shopping cart, suddenly lost her balance and struggled to avoid a fall. As she did so, her right leg struck the shopping cart and began to swell. Hresil observed a "gob" on the floor where she had slipped. Later, a Sears employee said that "it looked like someone spat on the floor, like it was phlegm." Under the reasonable person standard, did Sears breach a duty to Hresil by not cleaning up the gob? *Hint:* Assume that Hresil could prove that the gob was on the floor only for the 10 minutes she spent in the women's department.

4. Daniel Scully operated a travel agency from a storefront that he leased in a one-story commercial building owned by William Fitzgerald. Attached to the back portion of that structure was a two-story building, which Fitzgerald also owned. The two-story building contained two apartments, one on each floor.

The rear portion of the first-floor apartment was a storage area, over which a deck extended from the second-floor apartment. During a summer heat wave, a fire that started in the storage area spread and destroyed most of the apartment building. The attached commercial building was significantly damaged by smoke and by water that firefighters used to extinguish the blaze. Scully suffered a total loss of his office property and had to relocate his business. In the area where the fire started, Fitzgerald had stored mulch, construction debris, gasoline, a gas engine lawn mower, a gas engine snowblower, old papers and other refuse that had accumulated over time, and garbage that was both in and out of trash cans. Because the storage area was unenclosed, it was freely accessible. The tenants who lived in the second-floor apartment regularly smoked cigarettes on the deck above the storage areas and dropped cigarette butts in and near the storage area. Fire officials who investigated the blaze found cigarette butts in that general area.

Scully sued Fitzgerald for negligence, alleging that Fitzgerald had failed to use reasonable care to maintain the storage area and that this failure caused the fire. The local fire chief, who determined that the fire originated in the storage area, testified in his deposition that he could not pinpoint the fire's exact cause but that he was able to eliminate potential causes such as the building's air conditioning units, the lawn mower and snowblower, the electrical outlets and lights, and the mulch. The fire chief offered his "best guess" that the fire started accidentally when a lit cigarette or match ignited loose debris. An expert witness for the plaintiff provided a report concluding that the storage of construction materials, equipment containing gasoline, and various other combustibles in the open storage area created an "unreasonable risk of fire" that "could have been avoided or greatly reduced by properly securing the area and/or prohibiting smoking in the area." In the expert's opinion, the failure to take those remedial steps led to the fire.

Fitzgerald moved for summary judgment. A New Jersey court granted his motion after ruling that Scully had failed to produce evidence of a breach of duty on the defendant's part. The court rejected the testimony of the plaintiff's expert because he did not identify a standard of care by reference to a building or fire code. Did the trial court rule correctly in granting Fitzgerald's motion for summary judgment?

5. While Sandra and Michael Morris were shopping at a Sam's Club store, Michael was pushing a shopping cart and Sandra was walking generally alongside him. The Morrises were proceeding through the frozen foods section of the store when, after rounding a corner, Sandra slipped on a wet substance. Sandra then fell, hitting a small portable freezer known as a "spot box" and landing on her lower back and buttocks. She attempted to pull herself up using the cart that Michael was holding, but slipped halfway up and fell a second time. Once Sandra was finally standing up, she noticed that her clothes and shoes were soaked. She thought that the substance on which she slipped was water from the spot box freezer. The store manager arrived on the scene and ordered an employee to clean up the pool of liquid. The employee who did so noted that the pool was approximately ten inches in diameter and was located "right there under the drain of the freezer." According to the Morrises, the store manager told them he thought the liquid was water that had leaked from the spot box freezer. They also contended that the manager pointed out to them that the plug on the bottom of the spot box freezer was out. Sandra, who was treated at a hospital emergency room, experienced severe bruises and considerable pain, for which she was prescribed medication. In accordance with her physician's advice, she remained off her feet for a week. Sandra filed a negligence lawsuit against Wal-Mart Stores, Inc., the owner of the Sam's Club store. In particular, she attempted to rely on the *res ipsa loquitur* theory. At the close of her case-in-chief, however, the court granted judgment as a matter of law in favor of the defendant. The court did so because it did not think Sandra had proven what was necessary to enable her to rely on *res ipsa loquitur*. Was the court correct?

6. Pyrodyne Corp. was hired to display the fireworks as part of a July 4 celebration at the Western Washington State Fairgrounds. During the display, a five-inch mortar was knocked into a horizontal position. A rocket inside the mortar then ignited, flew 500 feet parallel to the earth, and exploded near the crowd of onlookers. Danny and Marion Klein were injured as a result of the explosion. They filed a strict liability lawsuit against Pyrodyne. Pyrodyne moved for summary judgment, arguing that the Kleins' case should be governed by negligence principles rather than strict liability. Was Pyrodyne correct in arguing that that this was not a case in which strict liability should apply?

7. Ricky East was employed by Interim Personnel of Central Virginia, Inc., a firm that provided temporary employees to business and other organizations. When East applied at Interim, he falsely stated that he possessed a valid driver's license. In reality, however, his license had been suspended because of two criminal convictions for driving under the influence of alcohol (DUI). He later left Interim's employ before applying to return to work there. Again he falsely stated that he possessed a valid driver's license, and he did not list his DUI convictions in response to an application question about whether he had been convicted of criminal offenses. Interim rehired East without asking to see his driver's license and without performing a criminal background check. Later, Interim assigned East to work for the Alumni Association of the University of Virginia in a part-time building assistant's position that required driving for short distances during his work hours. In recommending East to the Alumni Association, Interim represented that East had a good driving record, that he had not been involved in any traffic accidents, that he had never "shown up drunk on the job," and that he had not been the subject of complaints from other employers to whom he had been assigned. The Alumni Association accepted East without asking him whether he had a valid driver's license.

East worked for the Alumni Association for two months, during which he regularly drove an Alumni Association truck for short distances as part of his job duties. On Wednesday of Thanksgiving week, East was told to keep a key to the alumni building during the holiday weekend because his supervisor, who normally locked and unlocked the alumni building, would be out of town. East was instructed to lock the building on Wednesday and unlock it on Saturday. On Wednesday, East used the building key to help him gain access to a key to the Alumni Association truck he usually drove. Without permission, East drove the truck to Richmond, Virginia, and then back to his home in Charlottesville, Virginia, on Friday. During the day on Friday, he consumed excessive amounts of alcohol and became intoxicated. While intoxicated, he drove the Alumni Association truck and caused an accident in which Mildred Messer was injured. Messer sued East, but also named the Alumni Association and Interim Personnel as defendants on the theory that they were negligent in hiring East. A Virginia jury returned a verdict in favor of Messer and against all three defendants.

East did not appeal, but the Alumni Association and Interim did, arguing that they should not have been held liable for negligent hiring. Were they correct in making this argument?

8. While he was a freshman at Auburn University, Jason Jones became a pledge at the Kappa Alpha (KA) fraternity. Over the next year, KA brothers hazed Jones in various ways, including (1) making him jump into a ditch filled with urine, feces, dinner leftovers, and vomit; (2) paddling his buttocks; (3) pushing and kicking him; (4) making him run a gauntlet in which he was pushed, hit, and kicked; and (5) making him attend 2:00 AM hazing meetings. Jones continued to participate in these and other hazing activities until he was suspended from Auburn for poor academic performance. Even though he knew that 20 to 40 percent of his pledge class had withdrawn from the pledge program, Jones kept participating because he wanted to become a full member of KA. Jones later sued the local and national KA organizations for, among other things, negligent hazing in violation of a state criminal statute that outlawed hazing. The defendants moved for summary judgment on Jones's negligence per se claim. They contended that in view of the facts, Jones had assumed the risk of hazing. Were the defendants entitled to summary judgment?

9. On April 16, 1947, the SS *Grandchamp,* a cargo ship owned by the Republic of France and operated by the French Line, was loading a cargo of fertilizer grade ammonium nitrate (FGAN) at Texas City, Texas. A fire began on board the ship, apparently as a result of a longshoreman's having carelessly discarded a cigarette or match into one of the ship's holds. Despite attempts to put out the fire, it spread quickly. Approximately an hour after the fire was discovered, the *Grandchamp* exploded with tremendous force. Fire and burning debris spread throughout the waterfront, touching off further fires and explosions in other ships, refineries, gasoline storage tanks, and chemical plants. When the conflagration was over, 500 persons had been killed and more than 3,000 had been injured. The United States paid out considerable sums to victims of the disaster. The United States then sought to recoup these payments as damages in a negligence case against the Republic of France and the French Line. The evidence revealed that even though ammonium nitrate (which constituted approximately 95 percent of the FGAN) was known throughout the transportation industry as an

oxidizing agent and a fire hazard, no one in charge on the *Grandchamp* had made any attempt to prohibit smoking in the ship's holds. The defendants argued that they should not be held liable because FGAN was not known to be capable of *exploding* (as opposed to simply being a fire hazard) under circumstances such as those giving rise to the disaster. Did the defendants succeed with this argument?

10. A railroad car leased by American Cyanamid (American) and containing 20,000 gallons of acrylonitrile manufactured by American began leaking while the car was sitting just south of Chicago in the Blue Island yard of the Indiana Harbor Belt Railroad (Indiana). The car was awaiting switching to Conrail for delivery to its final destination. Indiana's employees stopped the leak but were uncertain about how much of the car's contents had escaped. Because acrylonitrile is flammable, highly toxic, and possibly carcinogenic, Illinois authorities ordered homes near the yard temporarily evacuated. Later, it was discovered that only about a quarter of the car's contents had leaked, but the Illinois Department of Environmental Protection, fearing that the soil and water had been contaminated, ordered Indiana to take decontamination measures costing $981,000. Indiana sued American on negligence and strict liability theories, seeking to recover its expenses. Evidence introduced at the trial included a list of 125 hazardous materials that are shipped in highest volume on the nation's railroads. Acrylonitrile was the 53rd most hazardous on the list. Was the trial court's entry of summary judgment for Indiana on the strict liability claim proper?

11. Universal Metrics, Inc. (UMI) sponsored an evening social gathering for its employees at a Wisconsin country club. UMI provided each attendee with two vouchers, each of which was redeemable for an alcoholic or a nonalcoholic beverage. Once the vouchers had been used, attendees could purchase additional beverages from a country club bartender. Michael Devine and John Kreuser were among the UMI employees in attendance. They drove separately to the event. At approximately 8:30 PM, Kreuser heard the bartender ask Devine whether he (Devine) had a ride home. Kreuser saw Devine make a motion with his head, suggesting that Kreuser would be responsible for driving Devine home. Kreuser then indicated to the bartender that he would give Devine a ride home. After this indication by Kreuser, the bartender served Devine more drinks. Between 9:00 and 9:15 PM, Devine approached Kreuser and asked Kreuser to buy him a drink because the bartender had cut him off. Kreuser declined. He neither talked to nor saw Devine again during the evening. Kreuser and his wife left the party at approximately 10:00 PM. As they were leaving, Kreuser decided not to give Devine a ride home. Kreuser, who had driven Devine home under similar circumstances on two other occasions, did not tell Devine or anyone else that he did not intend to drive Devine home this time.

At approximately 10:40 PM, Devine was driving his own vehicle when he crossed the center line of the highway and struck a vehicle driven by Kathy Stephenson. Both drivers died as a result of injuries they suffered in the collision. Test results showed that Devine's blood alcohol concentration was more than three times greater than the legal limit. Devine's estate, of course, was legally liable to Kathy Stephenson's estate. Ricky Stephenson, Kathy's surviving spouse and personal representative of her estate, believed that others should be held liable as well. He therefore filed a negligence lawsuit against UMI and Kreuser. Were UMI and Kreuser liable for negligence?

Online Research

Negligent Hiring

Using an online source, find *Schecter v. Merchants Home Delivery, Inc.*, a 2006 decision of the District of Columbia Court of Appeals. Negligent hiring was one of the claims raised by the plaintiff in *Schecter*. Read the court's decision, draft a written case brief (see the appendix at the end of Chapter 1), and prepare a one-page essay in which you compare *Schecter* with *Raleigh v. Performance Plumbing and Heating, Inc.*, a case that appears early in Chapter 7. In your essay, state whether you think the courts in *Schecter* and *Raleigh* took irreconcilable approaches to determining whether a duty of care existed, or whether the two decisions can be harmonized. Explain your reasoning.

chapter 8

INTELLECTUAL PROPERTY AND UNFAIR COMPETITION

asterCard International, Inc., issues credit cards through more than 23,000 banks and other financial institutions. Since 1997, MasterCard has aired television commercials that have come to be known as the "Priceless Advertisements." These advertisements include a sequence of names and pictures of goods and services purchased by persons using their credit cards. Voiceovers and visual displays convey to the viewer the prices of these items. Each Priceless Advertisement concludes with mention of a priceless intangible that cannot be purchased (e.g., "a day where all you have to do is breathe"). The reference to the priceless intangible is followed with this statement: "Priceless. There are some things money can't buy. For everything else there's MasterCard."

In August 2000, it came to MasterCard's attention that Ralph Nader's campaign committee was promoting Nader's presidential campaign through use of a television advertisement that bore similarities to MasterCard's commercials. Nader's political advertisement listed this series of items and their supposed prices:

> Grilled tenderloin for fund-raiser: $1,000 a plate.
> Campaign ads filled with half-truths: $10 million.
> Promises to special interest groups: over $100 billion.

The advertisement concluded with "[f]inding out the truth: priceless. There are some things that money can't buy." Besides being aired on television during a period of roughly two weeks in August 2000, the Nader advertisement appeared on the candidate's Web site during the remainder of the 2000 presidential campaign.

MasterCard complained to Nader's campaign organization about the Nader advertisement's similarity to the long-running MasterCard commercials, suggested in a letter that the Nader campaign develop a more "original" advertisement, and threatened litigation if use of the Nader advertisement continued. It soon became clear that there would be no agreement to resolve the dispute. Therefore, MasterCard filed suit against Nader and his campaign organization.

Consider this scenario and the following questions as you read Chapter 8:

- Which area of intellectual property law provides MasterCard the rights it sought to enforce against the defendants? Was this, for instance, a patent infringement case? Alternatively, was it a copyright infringement case? Or was it a trademark rights case? Could MasterCard have been relying on more than one of these areas of intellectual property law?
- What specific rights would MasterCard have been attempting to enforce in this litigation?
- What arguments would the defendants have made in an effort to avoid liability to MasterCard?
- What public policy issues are at stake in cases of this nature?
- How did this case turn out?
- What ethical questions are suggested by a person's use of someone else's intellectual property? What ethical issues attend intellectual property owners' attempts to enforce their supposed rights?

THIS CHAPTER DISCUSSES LEGAL rules that allow civil recoveries for abuses of free competition. These abuses are (1) infringement of intellectual property rights protected by patent, copyright, and trademark law; (2) misappropriation of trade secrets; (3) the intentional torts of injurious falsehood, interference with contractual relations, and interference with prospective advantage; and (4) the various forms of unfair competition addressed by § 43(a) of the Lanham Act. Indeed, the term *unfair competition* describes the entire chapter. In general, competition is deemed unfair when (1) it discourages creative endeavor by robbing creative people of the fruits of their innovations, or (2) it renders commercial life too uncivilized for the law to tolerate.

Protection of Intellectual Property

Patents Patent law is exclusively federal in nature. A patent may be viewed as an agreement between an inventor and the federal government. Under that agreement, the inventor obtains the exclusive right (for a limited time) to exclude others from making, using, or selling his invention, in return for making the invention public by giving the government certain information about it. The patent holder's (or **patentee's**) monopoly encourages the creation and disclosure of inventions by stopping third parties from appropriating them once they become public.

The above reference to "inventor" should be taken literally. U.S. law adheres to the "first-to-invent" rule—meaning that only the true inventor is eligible for a patent on an invention. The first-to-invent rule places U.S. law at odds with the patent laws in many other nations, where the party eligible for a patent on an invention is the one who was first to file a patent application with the relevant government office. If a U.S. patent is issued to someone who appeared to be the first to invent but actually was not, the true inventor may use the first-to-invent rule as a basis for seeking cancellation of the erroneously granted patent. There has periodically been legislative discussion about whether to amend the Patent Act to make the United States a first-to-file nation. However, as of the time this book went to press in 2008, no such legislation had advanced beyond preliminary stages.

What Is Patentable? An inventor may patent (1) a *process* (a mode of treatment of certain materials to produce a given result), (2) a *machine,* (3) a *manufacture* or product, (4) a *composition of matter* (a combination of elements with qualities not present in the elements taken individually, such as a new chemical compound), (5) an *improvement* of any of the above, (6) an *ornamental design* for a product, and (7) a *plant* produced by asexual reproduction. Certain business methods may also be patentable. As later discussion will reveal, the patentability of business methods has become a controversial matter. Naturally occurring things (e.g., a new wild plant) are not patentable. In addition, abstract ideas and scientific or mathematical concepts are not patentable, although their practical applications often are. In *Diamond v. Diehr* (1981), for instance, the Supreme Court held that a computer program may be patentable if it is part of a patentable process.[1]

Even though an invention fits within one of the above categories, it is not patentable if it lacks novelty, is obvious, or has no utility.[2] One aspect of the *novelty* requirement is the rule that no patent should be issued if *before the invention's creation,* it has been (1) known or used in the United States, (2) patented in the United States or a foreign country, or (3) described in a printed publication in the United States or a foreign country. Another aspect is the requirement that no patent should be issued if more than one year before the *patent application,* the invention was (1) patented in the United States or a foreign country, (2) described in a printed publication in the United States or a foreign country, or (3) in public use or on sale in the United States. The *Pfaff* case, the first of two Supreme Court decisions that follow shortly, deals with the rule just noted.

In addition, there can be no patent if the invention would have been *obvious* to a person having ordinary skill in the area. *KSR International Co. v. Teleflex, Inc.,* which appears immediately after the *Pfaff* decision, addresses the obviousness basis for denial of a patent application. A patentable invention must also have *utility,* or usefulness. Finally, there can be no patent if the applicant did not create the invention in question, or if she abandoned the invention. *Creation* problems frequently arise where several persons allegedly contributed to the invention. *Abandonment* may be by express statement, such as publicly devoting an invention to humanity, or by implication from conduct, such as delaying for an unreasonable length of time before making a patent application.

---

[1]As discussed later in this chapter, computer programs may obtain copyright and trade secret protection.

[2]Plant and design patents are subject to requirements that are slightly different from those stated here.

Obtaining a Patent The United States Patent and Trademark Office handles patent applications. The application must include a *specification* describing the invention with sufficient detail and clarity to enable a person skilled in the relevant field to make and use the invention. The application must also contain a *drawing* when this is necessary for understanding the subject matter to be patented. The Patent Office then determines whether the invention meets the various tests for patentability. If the application is rejected, the applicant may resubmit it. Once any of the applicant's claims have been rejected twice, the applicant may appeal to the Office's Board of Patent Appeals and Interferences. Subsequent appeals to the federal courts are also possible.

Pfaff v. Wells Electronics, Inc.   525 U.S. 55 (1998)

Wayne Pfaff began development work on a new computer chip socket in November 1980. He prepared detailed engineering drawings that described the design and dimensions of the socket and the materials to be used in making it. Pfaff sent the drawings to a manufacturer in February or March 1981. Prior to March 17, 1981, he showed a sketch of his concept to representatives of Texas Instruments. On April 8, 1981, the Texas Instruments representatives provided Pfaff a written confirmation of a previously placed oral purchase order for 30,100 of the new sockets. The total purchase price was $91,155. In accordance with his usual business practice, Pfaff did not make and test a prototype of the socket before offering to sell it.

The manufacturer to which Pfaff sent his drawings took a few months to develop the customized tooling necessary to produce the socket. The first actual sockets were not produced until the summer of 1981. Pfaff filled the Texas Instruments order in July 1981. Other orders followed, as the socket became a commercial success. On April 19, 1982, Pfaff applied for a patent on the socket. A patent was issued to him in January 1985. Pfaff later filed an infringement action against Wells Electronics, Inc., which produced a competing socket. Wells Electronics argued that Pfaff's patent was invalid under section 102(b) of the Patent Act of 1952, which states that a patent cannot be obtained for an invention if it has been "on sale" for more than a year before the filing of the patent application.

The federal district court rejected Wells Electronics' section 102(b) defense because Pfaff had filed the patent application less than a year after reducing the invention to practice (i.e., less than a year after the first actual sockets were produced and available for sale). The district court held Wells Electronics liable for infringement but the U.S. Court of Appeals for the Federal Circuit reversed. The Court of Appeals held that Pfaff's patent was invalid because the socket had been offered for sale on a commercial basis more than a year before the filing of the patent application. The U.S. Supreme Court granted certiorari.

Stevens, Justice

Section 102(b) of the Patent Act of 1952 provides that no person is entitled to patent an "invention" that has been "on sale" for more than one year before filing a patent application. We granted certiorari to determine whether the commercial marketing of a newly invented product may mark the beginning of the one-year period even though the invention has not yet been reduced to practice.

On April 19, 1982, Pfaff filed an application for a patent on the computer chip socket. Therefore, April 19, 1981 constitutes the critical date for purposes of the on-sale bar of section 102(b); if the one-year period began to run before that date, Pfaff lost his right to patent his invention.

The primary meaning of the word "invention" in the Patent Act unquestionably refers to the inventor's conception rather than to a physical embodiment of the idea. The statute does not contain any express requirement that an invention must be reduced to practice before it can be patented. Neither the statutory definition of the term nor the basic conditions for obtaining a patent make any mention of "reduction to practice."

It is well settled that an invention may be patented before it is reduced to practice. In 1888, this Court upheld a patent issued to Alexander Graham Bell even though he had filed his application before constructing a working telephone. [In upholding the issuance of the patent to Bell, the Court stated:]

The law does not require that a discoverer or inventor, in order to get a patent for a process, must have succeeded in bringing his art to the highest degree of perfection. It is enough if he describes his method with sufficient clearness and precision to enable those skilled in the matter to understand what the process is, and if he points out some practicable way of putting it into operation.

The Telephone Cases, 126 U.S. 1 (1888).

When we apply the reasoning of *The Telephone Cases* to the facts of the case before us today, it is evident that Pfaff could have obtained a patent on his novel socket when he accepted the purchase order from Texas Instruments for 30,100 units. At that time he provided the manufacturer with a description and drawings that had "sufficient clearness and precision to enable those skilled in the matter" to produce the device. The parties agree that the sockets manufactured to fill that order embody Pfaff's conception. We can find no basis in the text of section 102(b) or in the facts of this case for concluding that Pfaff's invention was not "on sale" within the meaning of the statute until after it has been reduced to practice.

When Pfaff accepted the purchase order for his new sockets prior to April 8, 1981, his invention was ready for patenting. The fact that the manufacturer was able to produce the socket using his detailed drawings and specifications demonstrates this fact. Furthermore, those sockets contained all the elements of the invention claimed in the patent. Therefore, Pfaff's patent is invalid because the invention had been on sale for more than one year in this country before he filed his patent application.

Judgment of Court of Appeals affirmed.

KSR International Co. v. Teleflex, Inc.   127 S. Ct. 1727 (U.S. Sup. Ct. 2007)

In car engines without computer-controlled throttles, the accelerator pedal interacts with the throttle via cable or other mechanical link. During the 1990s, it became common to install computers in cars to control engine operation. Computer-controlled throttles open and close valves in response to electronic signals rather than through force transferred from the accelerator pedal by a mechanical link. For a computer-controlled throttle to respond to a driver's operation of the car, the computer must know what is happening with the pedal. A cable or other mechanical link does not suffice for this purpose. At some point, an electronic sensor is necessary to translate the mechanical operation into digital data the computer can understand.

The traditional mechanical design of an accelerator pedal permitted the pedal to be pushed down or released, but its position in the footwell area of the car could not be adjusted by sliding the pedal forward or back. As a result, a driver who wished to be closer or farther from the pedal had to reposition himself in the driver's seat or move the seat in some way. In cars with deep footwells, those were imperfect solutions for drivers of smaller stature. Inventors therefore designed pedals that could be adjusted to change their location in the footwell. The Asano patent, granted in 1989, used a mechanical link and revealed a pedal support housing that kept one of the pedal's pivot points fixed even when the pedal location was adjusted relative to the driver.

Other patents granted during the 1990s contemplated the addition of electronic pedal sensors for computer-controlled throttles. These patents called for differing locations for the sensor but did not refer to mounting the sensor on a fixed pivot point. In a 1998 invention that resulted in the 2001 grant of a patent to him, Steven Engelgau developed an adjustable pedal involving use of an electronic sensor. Claim 4 of the Engelgau patent called for the sensor to be mounted on a fixed pivot point in the pedal assembly. Besides differing from the sensor locations contemplated in the earlier patents, the Engelgau patent's sensor location appeared likely to lessen problems that had been experienced when the previously patented technology was used.

Engelgau licensed his patent on an exclusive basis to Teleflex, Inc.—meaning that Teleflex effectively stepped into Engelgau's shoes in terms of ability to enforce rights under the patent. Teleflex soon learned that pursuant to a contract to supply adjustable pedal technology to General Motors for use in the company's vehicles, KSR International, Inc., planned to add an electronic sensor to the adjustable pedal technology reflected in a patent it (KSR) had obtained some years earlier. KSR ignored Teleflex's insistence that KSR's plan would infringe the Engelgau patent and that KSR should therefore enter into a licensing agreement with Teleflex. When KSR refused to obtain a license and proceeded with its plan, Teleflex sued KSR for patent infringement, arguing in particular that KSR's actions violated claim 4 of the Engelgau patent. In defense, KSR contended that the Engelgau patent was invalid on the ground of obviousness. A federal district court agreed that claim 4 of Engelgau's invention was obvious, in light of the prior art. Therefore, the district court granted summary judgment in favor of KSR and held the Engelgau patent invalid. However, the U.S. Court of Appeals for the Federal Circuit reversed, holding that the district court had not properly applied the "teaching, suggestion, or motivation" (TSM) test for obviousness. The U.S. Supreme Court granted KSR's petition for a writ of certiorari.

Kennedy, Justice

Section 103 [of the Patent Act, 35 U.S.C. § 103,] forbids issuance of a patent when "the differences between the subject matter sought to be patented and the prior art are such that the subject matter as a whole would have been obvious at the time the invention was made to a person having ordinary skill in the art to which said subject matter pertains." In *Graham v. John Deere Co.,* 383 U.S. 1, 17–18 (1966), the Court set out a framework for applying the statutory language of § 103. The analysis is objective:

> Under § 103, the scope and content of the prior art are to be determined; differences between the prior art and the claims at issue are to be ascertained; and the level of ordinary skill in the pertinent art resolved. Against this background the obviousness or nonobviousness of the subject matter is determined. Such secondary considerations as commercial success, long felt but unsolved needs, failure of others, etc., might be utilized to give light to the circumstances surrounding the origin of the subject matter sought to be patented.

Seeking to resolve the question of obviousness with more uniformity and consistency, the Court of Appeals for the Federal Circuit has employed an approach referred to by the parties as the "teaching, suggestion, or motivation" test (TSM test), under which a patent claim is only proved obvious if "some motivation or suggestion to combine the prior art teachings" can be found in the prior art, the nature of the problem, or the knowledge of a person having ordinary skill in the art. [Case citation omitted.] [T]he Court of Appeals . . . ruled that the District Court had not been strict enough in applying the [TSM] test, having failed to make "findings as to the specific understanding or principle within the knowledge of a skilled artisan that would have motivated one with no knowledge of the invention to attach an electronic control to the support bracket of the Asano assembly." The Court of Appeals held that . . . unless the "prior art references address[ed] the precise problem that the patentee was trying to solve," the problem would not motivate an inventor to look at those references.

Here, the Court of Appeals found, the Asano pedal was designed to solve the "constant ratio problem"—that is, to ensure that the force required to depress the pedal is the same no matter how the pedal is adjusted—whereas Engelgau sought to provide a simpler, smaller, cheaper adjustable electronic pedal. As for [the] Rixon [patent, one of the pre-Engelgau patents calling for use of an electronic sensor,] the court explained that [Rixon's adjustable] pedal suffered from the problem of wire chafing [and that the patent governing it] did not teach anything helpful to Engelgau's purpose. [Another pre-Engelgau patent dealing with the use of an electronic

sensor] did not relate to adjustable pedals and did not "necessarily go to the issue of motivation to attach the electronic control [in the manner called for in the Engelgau patent]." When the [earlier] patents were interpreted in this way, the Court of Appeals held, they would not have led a person of ordinary skill to put a sensor on the sort of pedal described in Asano. That it might have been obvious to try the combination of Asano and a sensor was likewise irrelevant, in the court's view, because "'obvious to try' has long been held not to constitute obviousness."

We [reject] the rigid approach of the Court of Appeals. Throughout this Court's engagement with the question of obviousness, [*Graham* and our other decisions] have set forth an expansive and flexible approach inconsistent with the way the Court of Appeals applied its TSM test here. [It is important to exercise] caution in granting [or upholding] a patent based on the combination of elements found in the prior art. For over a half century, the Court has held that a "patent for a combination which only unites old elements with no change in their respective functions . . . obviously withdraws what is already known into the field of its monopoly and diminishes the resources available to skillful men." [Case citation omitted.] This is a principal reason for declining to allow patents for what is obvious. The combination of familiar elements according to known methods is likely to be obvious when it does no more than yield predictable results.

[*Graham* and later decisions following the principles outlined there] are instructive when the question is whether a patent claiming the combination of elements of prior art is obvious. When a work is available in one field of endeavor, design incentives and other market forces can prompt variations of it, either in the same field or a different one. If a person of ordinary skill can implement a predictable variation, § 103 likely bars its patentability. For the same reason, if a technique has been used to improve one device, and a person of ordinary skill in the art would recognize that it would improve similar devices in the same way, using the technique is obvious unless its actual application is beyond his or her skill.

Following these principles may be more difficult in other cases than it is here because the claimed subject matter may involve more than the simple substitution of one known element for another or the mere application of a known technique to a piece of prior art ready for the improvement. Often, it will be necessary for a court to look to interrelated teachings of multiple patents; the effects of demands known to the design community or present in the marketplace; and the background knowledge possessed by a person having ordinary skill in the art, all in order to determine whether there was an apparent reason to combine the known elements in the fashion claimed by the patent at issue. As our precedents make clear, however, the analysis need not seek out precise teachings directed to the specific subject matter of the challenged claim, for a court can take account of the inferences and creative steps that a person of ordinary skill in the art would employ.

When it first established the requirement of demonstrating a teaching, suggestion, or motivation to combine known elements in order to show that the combination is obvious, the Court of Customs and Patent Appeals captured a helpful insight. As is clear from [previous] cases . . . , a patent composed of several elements is not proved obvious merely by demonstrating that each of its elements was, independently, known in the prior art. Although common sense directs one to look with care at a patent application that claims as innovation the combination of two known devices according to their established functions, it can be important to identify a reason that would have prompted a person of ordinary skill in the relevant field to combine the elements in the way the claimed new invention does. This is so because inventions in most, if not all, instances rely upon building blocks long since uncovered, and claimed discoveries almost of necessity will be combinations of what, in some sense, is already known.

Helpful insights, however, need not become rigid and mandatory formulas; and when it is so applied, the TSM test is incompatible with our precedents. The obviousness analysis cannot be confined by a formalistic conception of the words teaching, suggestion, and motivation, or by overemphasis on the importance of published articles and the explicit content of issued patents. In many fields it may be that there is little discussion of obvious techniques or combinations, and it often may be the case that market demand, rather than scientific literature, will drive design trends. Granting patent protection to advances that would occur in the ordinary course without real innovation retards progress and may, in the case of patents combining previously known elements, deprive prior inventions of their value or utility.

In determining whether the subject matter of a patent claim is obvious, neither the particular motivation nor the avowed purpose of the patentee controls. What matters is the objective reach of the claim. If the claim extends to what is obvious, it is invalid under § 103. One of the ways in which a patent's subject matter can be proved obvious is by noting that there existed at the time of invention a known problem for which there was an obvious solution encompassed by the patent's claims. The first error of the Court of Appeals in this case was to foreclose this reasoning by holding that courts and patent examiners should look only to the problem the patentee was trying to solve. The Court of Appeals failed to recognize that the problem motivating the patentee may be only one of many addressed by the patent's subject matter. The question is not whether the combination was obvious to the patentee but whether the combination was obvious to a person with ordinary skill in the art. Under the correct analysis, any need or problem known in the field of endeavor at the time of invention and addressed by the patent can provide a reason for combining the elements in the manner claimed.

The second error of the Court of Appeals lay in its assumption that a person of ordinary skill attempting to solve a problem will be led only to those elements of prior art designed to solve the same problem. The primary purpose of Asano was solving the constant ratio problem; so, the court concluded, an inventor considering how to put a sensor on an adjustable pedal would have no reason to consider putting it on the Asano pedal. Common sense teaches, however, that familiar items may have obvious uses beyond their primary purposes, and in many cases a person of ordinary skill will be able to fit the teachings of multiple patents together like pieces of a puzzle. Regardless of Asano's primary purpose, the design provided an obvious example of an adjustable pedal with a fixed pivot point. The idea that a designer hoping to make an adjustable electronic pedal would ignore Asano because Asano was designed to solve the constant ratio problem makes little sense. A person of ordinary skill is also a person of ordinary creativity, not an automaton.

The same constricted analysis led the Court of Appeals to conclude, in error, that a patent claim cannot be proved obvious merely by showing that the combination of elements was "obvious to try." When there is a design need or market pressure to solve a problem and there are a finite number of identified, predictable solutions, a person of ordinary skill has good reason to pursue the known options within his or her technical grasp. If this leads to the anticipated success, it is likely the product not of innovation but of ordinary skill and common sense. In that instance the fact that a combination was obvious to try might show that it was obvious under § 103.

When we apply the standards we have explained to the instant facts, claim 4 must be found obvious. [W]e see little difference between the teachings of Asano and [other earlier patents] and the adjustable electronic pedal disclosed in claim 4 of the Engelgau patent. The District Court was correct to conclude that, as of the time Engelgau designed the subject matter in claim 4, it was obvious to a person of ordinary skill to combine Asano with a pivot-mounted pedal position sensor. There then existed a marketplace that created a strong incentive to convert mechanical pedals to electronic pedals, and the prior art taught a number of methods for achieving this advance. The Court of Appeals considered the issue too narrowly by, in effect, asking whether a pedal designer writing on a blank slate would have chosen both Asano and a modular sensor similar to the ones used in [other previous patents]. The proper question to have asked was whether a pedal designer of ordinary skill, facing the wide range of needs created by developments in the field of endeavor, would have seen a benefit to upgrading Asano with a sensor.

In automotive design, as in many other fields, the interaction of multiple components means that changing one component often requires the others to be modified as well. Technological developments made it clear that engines using computer-controlled throttles would become standard. As a result, designers might have decided to design new pedals from scratch; but they also would have had reason to make pre-existing pedals work with the new engines. Indeed, upgrading its own pre-existing model led KSR to design the pedal now accused of infringing the Engelgau patent.

For a designer starting with Asano, the question was where to attach the sensor. The consequent legal question, then, is whether a pedal designer of ordinary skill starting with Asano would have found it obvious to put the sensor on a fixed pivot point. The prior art discussed above leads us to the conclusion that attaching the sensor where both KSR and Engelgau put it would have been obvious to a person of ordinary skill.

We build and create by bringing to the tangible and palpable reality around us new works based on instinct, simple logic, ordinary inferences, extraordinary ideas, and sometimes even genius. These advances, once part of our shared knowledge, define a new threshold from which innovation starts once more. And as progress beginning from higher levels of achievement is expected in the normal course, the results of ordinary innovation are not the subject of exclusive rights under the patent laws. Were it otherwise, patents might stifle, rather than promote, the progress of useful arts. See U.S. Const., Art. I, § 8, cl. 8. These premises led to [§ 103's] bar on patents claiming obvious subject matter. Application of the bar must not be confined within a test or formulation too constrained to serve its purpose.

KSR provided convincing evidence that mounting a modular sensor on a fixed pivot point of the Asano pedal was a design step well within the grasp of a person of ordinary skill in the relevant art. Its arguments, and the record, demonstrate that claim 4 of the Engelgau patent is obvious.

Court of Appeals judgment in favor of Teleflex reversed, and case remanded for further proceedings.

Ownership and Transfer of Patent Rights

Until a relatively recent change in federal law, a patent normally gave the patentee exclusive rights regarding the patented invention for 17 years from the date the patent was granted. In order to bring the United States into compliance with the General Agreement on Tariffs and Trade (an international agreement commonly known as GATT), Congress amended the patent law to provide that the patentee's exclusive rights to exclude others from making, using, or selling the patented invention generally exist until the expiration of 20 years from the date the patent application was filed. This duration rule applies to patents that result from applications filed on or after June 8, 1995. (A design patent, however, exists for 14 years from the date it was granted.) A 1999 enactment of Congress allowed for the possible extension of a patent's duration if the Patent Office delayed an unreasonably long time in acting on and approving the patentee's application.

The patentee may transfer ownership of the patent by making a written *assignment* of it to another party. Alternatively, the patentee may retain ownership and *license* others to exercise some or all of the patent rights. As the Supreme Court recently made clear in *Quanta Computer v. LG Electronics,* 2008 U.S. LEXIS 4701 (U.S. Sup. Ct. 2008), once the patent owner licenses another party to make, use, or sell an item embodying the patented invention, the sale of the item exhausts the patent owner's rights regarding that item. For instance, if A licenses B to produce and sell an item that requires use of A's patent, B's production and sale of the item entitles A, of course, to payment of the licensing fee called for by the agreement between A and B. However, A is not entitled to enforce its patent against C in the event that B sells the licensed item to C and C then makes some use of the item (and hence of A's patented invention). B's sale of the item to C—a sale contemplated by the license A granted B—exhausted A's patent rights in regard to the item purchased by C. International licensing and patent rights issues are discussed in a Global Business Environment box that appears later in the chapter.

Usually, the party who created the invention is the patent holder. What happens, however, when the creator of the invention is an employee and her employer seeks rights in the invention? If the invention was developed by an employee *hired to do inventive or creative work,* she must use the invention solely for the employer's benefit and must assign any patents she obtains to the employer. If the employee was hired for purposes *other than invention or creation,* however, she owns any patent she acquires. Finally, regardless of the purpose for which the employee was hired, the *shop right* doctrine gives the employer a nonexclusive, royalty-free *license* to use the employee's invention if it was created on company time and through the use of company facilities. Any patent the employee might retain is still effective against parties other than the employer.

Patent Infringement   Patent infringement occurs when a defendant, without authorization from the patentee, usurps the patentee's rights by making, using, or selling the patented invention. Because the Patent Act does not have an extraterritorial reach, the allegedly infringing activities must have occurred within the United States in order for a valid infringement claim to be triggered. The making of an item that would infringe a U.S. patent if the item were made within the United States will not constitute infringement if the item is made, for instance, in China. However, a provision of the Patent Act potentially allows infringement liability to be imposed on a party who ships components of the patented invention from the United States with the intended result that the components are assembled, in another country, to produce an item covered by the terms of the patent.

Infringement may be established under principles of *literal* infringement or under a judicially developed approach known as the *doctrine of equivalents.* Infringement is literal in nature when the subject matter made, used, or sold by the defendant clearly falls within the stated terms of the claims of invention set forth in the patentee's application. Under the doctrine of equivalents, a defendant may be held liable for infringement even though the subject matter he made, used, or sold contained elements that were not identical to those described in the patentee's claim of invention, if the elements of the defendant's subject matter nonetheless may be seen as equivalent to those of the patented invention. A traditional formulation of the test posed by the doctrine of equivalents is whether the alleged infringer's subject matter performs substantially the same function as the protected invention in substantially the same way, in order to obtain the same result.

During the 1990s, an alleged infringer sought to convince the Supreme Court to abolish the doctrine of equivalents on the ground that it effectively allows patentees to extend the scope of patent protection beyond the stated terms approved by the Patent Office when it issued the patent. In *Warner-Jenkinson Co. v. Hilton Davis Chemical Co.* (1997), however, the Court rejected this attack on the doctrine. The Court observed that in view of courts' long-standing use of the doctrine (use in which Congress seemingly acquiesced by not legislatively prohibiting it), arguments for abolishing the doctrine would be better addressed to Congress. The *Warner-Jenkinson* Court did acknowledge, however, that overly broad application of the doctrine of equivalents could lead to an unwarranted expansion of patent owners' rights. Therefore, the Court held that the doctrine of equivalents must be applied to the *individual elements* of the patentee's claims of invention rather than to the patentee's invention *as a whole.*

One who *actively induces* another's infringement of a patent is liable as an infringer if he knows and intends that the infringement occur. For example, if Ingram directly infringes Paxton's patent on a machine and Doyle knowingly sold Ingram an instruction manual for the machine, Doyle may be liable as an infringer. Finally, if one knowingly sells a direct patent infringer a component of a patented invention or something useful in employing a patented process, the seller may be liable for *contributory infringement.* The thing sold must be a material part of the invention and must not be a staple article of commerce with some other significant use. Suppose that Irving directly infringes Potter's patent for a certain electronic device by selling essentially identical electronic devices. If Davis sells Irving sophisticated circuitry with knowledge of Irving's infringement, Davis may be liable for contributory infringement, assuming that the circuitry is an important component of the electronic devices at issue and has no other significant uses.

The basic recovery for patent infringement is damages adequate to compensate for the infringement, plus court costs and interest. The damages cannot be less than a reasonable royalty for the use made of the invention by the infringer. The court may in its discretion award damages of up to three times those actually suffered. Injunctive relief is also available, and attorney's fees may be awarded in exceptional cases.

Because injunctions have so frequently been issued against defendants held liable for patent infringement, some courts had concluded that injunctions were effectively a mandatory remedy. In *eBay, Inc. v. MercExchange, LLC,* which follows shortly, the Supreme Court ruled that courts are not required to issue an injunction against a defendant who committed patent infringement, if damages would be an adequate remedy and the public interest would not be served by the granting of an injunction.

eBay, Inc. v. MercExchange, LLC   547 U.S. 388 (2006)

EBay, Inc., operates a popular Internet Web site that allows private sellers to list goods they wish to sell, either through an auction or at a fixed price. MercExchange, LLC, holds a number of patents, including a business method patent for an electronic market designed to facilitate the sale of goods between private individuals by establishing a central authority to promote trust among participants. MercExchange sought to license this patent to eBay, as it had previously done with other companies, but the parties failed to reach an agreement. Later, MercExchange sued eBay for patent infringement in a federal district court. A jury found that MercExchange's patent was valid, that eBay had infringed it, and that MercExchange was entitled to an award of damages.

Following the jury verdict, the district court denied MercExchange's motion for a permanent injunction to bar eBay from using MercExchange's patented method. The U.S. Court of Appeals for the Federal Circuit reversed the denial of the requested injunction. The U.S. Supreme Court granted eBay's petition for a writ of certiorari.

Thomas, Justice

[In reversing, the Court of Appeals applied] its "general rule that courts will issue permanent injunctions against patent infringement absent exceptional circumstances." We granted certiorari to determine the appropriateness of this general rule.

According to well-established principles of equity, a plaintiff seeking a permanent injunction must satisfy a four-factor test before a court may grant such relief. A plaintiff must demonstrate: (1) that it has suffered an irreparable injury; (2) that remedies available at law, such as monetary damages, are inadequate to compensate for that injury; (3) that, considering the balance of hardships between the plaintiff and defendant, a remedy in equity is warranted; and (4) that the public interest would not be disserved by a permanent injunction. The decision to grant or deny permanent injunctive relief is an act of equitable discretion by the district court, reviewable on appeal for abuse of discretion.

These familiar principles apply with equal force to disputes arising under the Patent Act. As this Court has long recognized, "a major departure from the long tradition of equity practice should not be lightly implied." [Case citation omitted.] Nothing in the Patent Act indicates that Congress intended such a departure. To the contrary, the Patent Act expressly provides that injunctions "may" issue "in accordance with the principles of equity." 35 U.S.C. § 283.

To be sure, the Patent Act also declares that "patents shall have the attributes of personal property," § 261, including "the right to exclude others from making, using, offering for sale, or selling the invention," § 154(a)(l). According to the Court of Appeals, this statutory right to exclude alone justifies its general rule in favor of permanent injunctive relief. But the creation of a right is distinct from the provision of remedies for violations of that right. Indeed, the Patent Act itself indicates that patents shall have the attributes of personal property "[s]ubject to the provisions of this title," 35 U.S.C. § 261, including, presumably, the provision that injunctive relief "may" issue only "in accordance with the principles of equity," § 283.

This approach is consistent with our treatment of injunctions under the Copyright Act. Like a patent owner, a copyright holder possesses "the right to exclude others from using his property." [Case citation omitted.] Like the Patent Act, the Copyright Act provides that courts "may" grant injunctive relief "on such terms as it may deem reasonable to prevent or restrain infringement of a copyright." 17 U.S.C. § 502(a). And as in our decision today, this Court has consistently rejected invitations to replace traditional equitable considerations with a rule that an injunction automatically follows a determination that a copyright has been infringed.

Neither the District Court nor the Court of Appeals below fairly applied these traditional equitable principles in deciding respondent's motion for a permanent injunction. Although the District Court recited the traditional four-factor test, it appeared to adopt certain expansive principles suggesting that injunctive relief could not issue in a broad swath of cases. Most notably, it concluded that a "plaintiff's willingness to license its patents" and "its lack of commercial activity in practicing the patents" would be sufficient to establish that the patent holder would not suffer irreparable harm if an injunction did not issue. But traditional equitable principles do not permit such broad classifications. For example, some patent holders, such as university researchers or self-made inventors, might reasonably prefer to license their patents, rather than undertake efforts to secure the financing necessary to bring their works to market themselves. Such patent holders may be able to satisfy the traditional four-factor test, and we see no basis for categorically denying them the opportunity to do so. To the extent that the District Court adopted such a categorical rule, then, its analysis cannot be squared with the principles of equity adopted by Congress.

In reversing the District Court, the Court of Appeals departed in the opposite direction from the four-factor test. The court articulated a "general rule," unique to patent disputes, "that a permanent injunction will issue once infringement and validity have been adjudged." The court further indicated that injunctions should be denied only in the "unusual" case, under "exceptional circumstances" and "'in rare instances . . . to protect the public interest.'" Just as the District Court erred in its categorical denial of injunctive relief, the Court of Appeals erred in its categorical grant of such relief.

Because we conclude that neither court below correctly applied the traditional four-factor framework that governs the award of injunctive relief, we vacate the judgment of the Court of Appeals, so that the District Court may apply that framework in the first instance. In doing so, we take no position on whether permanent injunctive relief should or should not issue in this particular case, or indeed in any number of other disputes arising under the Patent Act. We hold only that the decision whether to grant or deny injunctive relief rests within the equitable discretion of the district courts, and that such discretion must be exercised consistent with traditional principles of equity, in patent disputes no less than in other cases governed by such standards.

Court of Appeals judgment vacated and case remanded for further proceedings.

Roberts, Chief Justice, joined by Justices Scalia and Ginsburg, concurring

I agree with the Court's holding [and] I join the opinion of the Court. That opinion rightly rests on the proposition that "a major departure from the long tradition of equity practice should not be lightly implied." [Case citation omitted.]

From at least the early 19th century, courts have granted injunctive relief upon a finding of infringement in the vast majority of patent cases. This "long tradition of equity practice" . . . does not entitle a patentee to a permanent injunction or justify a general rule that such injunctions should issue. At the same time, there is a difference between exercising equitable discretion pursuant to the established four-factor test and writing on an entirely clean slate. When it comes to discerning and applying those standards, in this area as others, "a page of history is worth a volume of logic." [Case citation omitted.]

Kennedy, Justice, joined by Justices Stevens, Souter, and Breyer, concurring

The Court is correct . . . to hold that courts should apply the well-established, four-factor test—without resort to categorical rules—in deciding whether to grant injunctive relief in patent cases. The Chief Justice is also correct that history may be instructive in applying this test. The lesson of the historical practice, [however], is most helpful and instructive when the circumstances of a case bear substantial parallels to litigation the courts have confronted before.

In cases now arising trial courts should bear in mind that in many instances the nature of the patent being enforced and the economic function of the patent holder present considerations quite unlike earlier cases. An industry has developed in which firms use patents not as a basis for producing and selling goods but, instead, primarily for obtaining licensing fees. For these firms, an injunction, and the potentially serious sanctions arising from its violation, can be employed as a bargaining tool to charge exorbitant fees to companies that seek to buy licenses to practice the patent. When the patented invention is but a small component of the product the companies seek to produce and the threat of an injunction is employed simply for undue leverage in negotiations, legal damages may well be sufficient to compensate for the infringement and an injunction may not serve the public interest. In addition injunctive relief may have different consequences for the burgeoning number of patents over business methods, which were not of much economic and legal significance in earlier times. The potential vagueness and suspect validity of some of these patents may affect the calculus under the four-factor test.

The equitable discretion over injunctions, granted by the Patent Act, is well-suited to allow courts to adapt to the rapid technological and legal developments in the patent system. For these reasons it should be recognized that district courts must determine whether past practice fits the circumstances of the cases before them. With these observations, I join the opinion of the Court.

Defenses to Patent Infringement One defense to a patent infringement suit is that the subject matter of the alleged infringement is neither within the literal scope of the patent nor substantially equivalent to the patented invention. This defense centers around the assertion that the defendant "designed around" the patent.

The alleged infringer may also defend by attacking the validity of the patent. Usually, the patent invalidity defense rests on the argument that the invention was not sufficiently novel or was obvious, and thus did not merit a patent. Despite the fact that the patent was issued by the supposed experts at the U.S. Patent and Trademark

Office (PTO), courts have the ability to second-guess the PTO and order the cancellation of a patent on the ground of invalidity. Challenges to the validity of patents prove to be successful with reasonable frequency.

One may also challenge a patent's validity without first being sued for infringement by filing a declaratory judgment action that seeks a court ruling of invalidity. What if one who wants to challenge the validity of the patent is a party to a licensing agreement with the patent owner? A formerly applicable rule provided that the patent challenger could not raise the issue of patent invalidity without first breaching the licensing agreement by refusing to pay the licensing fees and thereby risking an infringement lawsuit. In *MedImmune v. Genentech,* 127 S. Ct. 764 (2007), however, the U.S. Supreme Court held that the licensee need not breach the licensing agreement as a precondition to taking legal action to challenge the patent's validity.

In appropriate cases, the defendant can assert that the patentee has committed *patent misuse.* This is behavior that unjustifiably exploits the patent monopoly. For example, the patentee may require the purchaser of a license on his patent to buy his unpatented goods, or may tie the obtaining of a license on one of his patented inventions to the purchase of a license on another. One who refuses the patentee's terms and later infringes the patent may attempt to escape liability by arguing that the patentee misused his monopoly position.

Current Issues As this book went to press in 2008, various patent law issues were acquiring public attention. Most of these issues had a common ring to them: the notion among critics that the patent rights pendulum may have swung too far in favor of patent owners. For instance, the issuance of business method patents—first held appropriate in a late 1990s decision of the U.S. Court of Appeals for the Federal Circuit—continued to be controversial. Critics assert that many of the patents issued for business methods should never have been granted because the methods were nonnovel, obvious retreads of old business practices with merely a modern, Internet-oriented gloss placed on them. Thus, the argument goes, parties who should have been free to use certain business methods have had to expend time and money challenging the patents' validity. Although the continued patentability (and perhaps special conditions of patentability) of business methods could become the subject of legislative treatment at some future point, Congress had not taken such action as of the time this book went to press.

In recent years, other critics of the patent regime have lamented the size of the awards of damages sometimes granted to patent owners when they win infringement cases. Still others have seen a problem with so-called "patent trolls"—parties that acquire patents from others, not for the purpose of producing the patented invention themselves but solely in order to exercise licensing leverage against users of the invention. Justice Kennedy's concurrence in *eBay v. MercExchange,* which appears above, suggests such a concern. Others, however, do not regard patent trolls as problematic. Legislative proposals regarding damages rules and trolling behavior have been floated but had not advanced beyond preliminary stages as of 2008.

Finally, those who regard patent law as having swung too far in favor of patent owners should take note of the Supreme Court's recent decisions in the *KSR v. Teleflex, eBay v. MercExchange, Quanta Computers v. LG Electronics,* and *MedImmune v. Genentech* cases (which either appear earlier as text cases or are discussed in earlier sections). In each of those cases, the Court's decision seems more aligned with the interests of users and of the public than with advancing or expanding the rights of patent owners.

LOG ON

United States government Web sites contain a wealth of information on patent, copyright, and trademark law and procedures. For information on patents and trademarks, visit the site of the U.S. Patent and Trademark Office, at **www.uspto.gov**. Information on copyrights may be found at **www.loc.gov/copyright,** the site of the U.S. Copyright Office.

Copyrights Copyright law gives certain exclusive rights to creators of *original works of authorship.* It prevents others from using their work, gives them an incentive to innovate, and thereby benefits society. Yet copyright law also tries to balance these purposes against the equally compelling public interest in the free movement of ideas, information, and commerce. It does so mainly by limiting the intellectual products it protects and by allowing the fair use defense described later.

Coverage The federal Copyright Act protects a wide range of works of authorship, including books, periodical articles, dramatic and musical compositions, works of art, motion pictures and other audiovisual works, sound recordings, lectures, computer programs, and architectural plans. To merit copyright protection, such works must be *fixed*—set out in a tangible medium of expression from which they can be perceived, reproduced, or communicated. They also must be *original* (the author's own work) and *creative* (reflecting exercise of the creator's judgment). Unlike the inventions protected by patent law, however, copyrightable works need not be novel.

Copyright protection does not extend to ideas, facts, procedures, processes, systems, methods of operation, concepts, principles, or discoveries. Instead, it protects the *ways in which they are expressed.* The story line of a play, for instance, is protected, but the ideas, themes, or messages underlying it are not. Although there is no copyright protection over facts, the expression in nonfiction works and compilations of fact is protected.

Computer programs involve their own special problems. It is fairly well settled that copyright law protects a program's *object code* (program instructions that are machine-readable but not intelligible to humans) and *source code* (instructions intelligible to humans). There is less agreement, however, about the copyrightability of a program's nonliteral elements such as its organization, its structure, and its presentation of information on the screen. Most courts that have considered the issue hold that nonliteral elements may sometimes be protected by copyright law, but courts differ about the extent of this protection.

Creation and Notice A copyright comes into existence upon the creation and fixing of a protected work. Although a copyright owner may register the copyright with the U.S. Copyright Office, registration is not necessary for the copyright to exist. However, registration normally is a procedural prerequisite to filing a suit for copyright infringement. Even though it is not required, copyright owners often provide *notice* of the copyright. Federal law authorizes a basic form of notice for use with most copyrighted works. A book, for example, might include the term *Copyright* (or the abbreviation *Copr.* or the symbol ©), the year of its first publication, and the name of the copyright owner in a location likely to give reasonable notice to readers.

Duration The U.S. Constitution's Copyright Clause (Article I, section 8) empowers Congress to "promote the progress of Science and useful arts" by enacting copyright and patent laws that "secur[e] for limited Times to Authors and Inventors the exclusive Right to their respective Writings and Discoveries." Thus, copyrights and patents cannot last forever. Even so, the history of copyright protection in the United States has featured various significant lengthenings of the "limited time" a copyright endures. When a copyright's duration ends, the underlying work enters the public domain and becomes available for any uses other parties wish to make of it. The former copyright owner, therefore, loses control over the work and forfeits what had been valuable legal rights.

With the enactment of the Sonny Bono Copyright Term Extension Act (hereinafter "CTEA") in 1998, Congress conferred a substantial benefit on copyright owners. The CTEA added 20 years to the duration of copyrights, not only for works created after the CTEA's enactment *but also for any preexisting work that was still under valid copyright protection* as of the CTEA's October 1998 effective date. Copyright owners—especially some high-profile corporations whose copyrights on older works would soon have expired if not for the enactment of the CTEA—mounted a significant lobbying effort in favor of the term extension provided by the CTEA.

The CTEA's effect cannot be understood without discussion of the copyright duration rules that existed immediately before the CTEA's enactment. One set of rules applied to works created in 1978 or thereafter; another set applied to pre-1978 works. The copyright on pre-1978 works was good for a term of 28 years from first publication of the work, plus a renewal term of 47 years. (The renewal term had been only 28 years until Congress changed the law roughly three decades ago and added 19 more years to the renewal term for any work then under valid copyright protection.) As a result, 75 years of protection was available for pre-1978 works.

For works created in 1978 or thereafter, Congress scrapped the initial-term-plus-renewal-term approach, opting instead for a normally applicable rule that the copyright lasts for the life of the author/creator plus 50 years. This basic duration rule did not apply, however, if the copyrighted work, though created in 1978 or thereafter, was a work-for-hire. (The two types of work-for-hire will be explained below.) In a work-for-hire situation, the copyright would exist for 75 years from first publication of the work or 100 years from creation of it, whichever came first.

The CTEA tacked on 20 years to the durations contemplated by the rules discussed in the preceding two paragraphs. A pre-1978 work that was still under valid copyright protection as of late 1998 (when the CTEA took effect) now has a total protection period of 95 years from first publication—a 28-year initial term plus a renewal term that has been lengthened from 47 to 67 years. The copyright on Disney's "Steamboat Willie" cartoon—best known for its introduction of the famous

Mickey Mouse character—serves as an example. The protection period for the Steamboat Willie copyright began to run in the late 1920s, when the cartoon was released and distributed (i.e., published, for purposes of copyright law). Given the rule that existed immediately before the CTEA's enactment (an initial term of 28 years plus a renewal term of 47 years), the Steamboat Willie copyright would have expired within the first few years of the current century. The CTEA, however, gave Disney an additional 20 years of rights over the Steamboat Willie cartoon before it would pass into the public domain.

With the enactment of the CTEA, the basic duration rule for works created in 1978 or thereafter is now life of the author/creator plus 70 years (up from 50). The duration rule for a work-for-hire is now 95 years from first publication (up from 75) or 120 years from creation (up from 100), whichever comes first.

Critics of the CTEA mounted a constitutional challenge to the statute in *Eldred v. Ashcroft,* a case that made its way to the Supreme Court. Those challenging the CTEA argued that the statute violated the purpose of the "limited times" provision in the Constitution's Copyright Clause by making copyright protection so lengthy in duration. They also contended that the Copyright Clause's language empowering Congress to enact copyright laws to "promote the progress of science and useful arts" served as an *incentive-to-create* limitation on the exercise of that power, and that the CTEA—at least insofar as it applied to works already created as of 1998—unconstitutionally violated the incentive-to-create limitation. In its 2003 decision in *Eldred,* the Supreme Court rejected the constitutional challenge to the CTEA. The Court concluded that the CTEA may have been an unwise enactment as a matter of public policy, but that it fell within the authority extended to Congress by the Copyright Clause.

Works-for-Hire   A work-for-hire exists when (1) an employee, in the course of her regular employment duties, prepares a copyrightable work; or (2) an individual or corporation and an independent contractor (i.e., nonemployee) enter into a written agreement under which the independent contractor is to prepare, for the retaining individual or corporation, one of several types of copyrightable works designated in the Copyright Act. In the first situation, the employer is legally classified as the work's author and copyright owner. In the second situation, the party who (or which) retained the independent contractor is considered the resulting work's author and copyright owner.

Ownership Rights   A copyright owner has exclusive rights to reproduce the copyrighted work, prepare derivative works based on it (e.g., a movie version of a novel), and distribute copies of the work by sale or otherwise. With certain copyrighted works, the copyright owner also obtains the exclusive right to perform the work or display it publicly. The *Perfect 10* case, which appears later in this chapter's section on fair use, contains discussion of the rights held by copyright owners.

Copyright ownership initially resides in the creator of the copyrighted work, but the copyright may be transferred to another party. Also, the owner may individually transfer any of her ownership rights, or a portion of each, without losing ownership of the remaining rights. Most transfers of copyright ownership require a writing signed by the owner or his agent. The owner may also retain ownership while licensing the copyrighted work or a portion of it.

Infringement   Those who violate any of the copyright owner's exclusive rights may be liable for copyright infringement. Infringement is fairly easily proven when direct evidence of significant copying exists; verbatim copying of protected material is an example. Usually, however, proof of infringement involves establishing that (1) the defendant had *access* to the copyrighted work; (2) the defendant engaged in enough *copying*—either deliberately or subconsciously—that the resemblance between the allegedly infringing work and the copyrighted work does not seem coincidental; and (3) there is *substantial similarity* between the two works.

Access may be proven circumstantially, such as by showing that the copyrighted work was widely circulated. The copying and substantial similarity elements, which closely relate to each other, necessarily involve discretionary case-by-case determinations. Of course, the copying and substantial similarity must exist with regard to the copyrighted work's protected expression. Copying of general ideas, facts, themes, and the like (i.e., copying of unprotected matter) is not infringement. The defendant's having paraphrased protected expression does not constitute a defense to what otherwise appears to be infringement. Neither does the defendant's having credited the copyrighted work as the source from which the defendant borrowed.

Recent years' explosion in Internet usage has led to difficult copyright questions. For instance, services such as Napster, Grokster, and StreamCast have allowed easy and free-of-charge access to musical recordings in digital files. Owners of copyrights on songs and recordings have

CYBERLAW IN ACTION

In the Digital Millennium Copyright Act of 1998 (DMCA), Congress addressed selected copyright issues as to which special rules seemed appropriate, in view of recent years' technological advances and explosion in Internet usage. One such issue was how narrowly or broadly to define the class of parties potentially liable for copyright infringement in an Internet context. If, without Osborne's consent, Jennings posts Osborne's copyrighted material in an online context made available by Devaney (an Internet service provider), is only Jennings liable to Osborne, or is Devaney also liable? In the DMCA, Congress enacted "safe harbor" provisions designed to protect many service providers such as Devaney from liability for the actions of direct infringers who posted or transmitted copyrighted material.

The DMCA also addressed the actions of persons who seek to circumvent technological measures (e.g., encryption, password-protection measures, and the like) that control access to or copying of a copyrighted work. With certain narrowly defined exceptions of very limited applicability, Congress outlawed both (1) the circumvention of such technological measures and (2) the activity of trafficking in programs or other devices meant to accomplish such circumvention.

In *Universal City Studios, Inc. v. Corley,* 273 F.3d 429 (2d Cir. 2001), the U.S. Court of Appeals for the Second Circuit rejected the arguments of an individual (Corley) who had been held liable to various movie studios for violating the antitrafficking provisions of the DMCA. Corley had written an article about the decryption program known as "DeCSS" and had posted the article on his Web site, along with a copy of the DeCSS program itself and links to other sites where DeCSS could be found. DeCSS had been developed by parties other than Corley as a means of decrypting the "CSS" encryption technology that movie studios place on copyrighted DVDs of their movies. If it is not circumvented, CSS prevents the copying of the movie that appears on the DVD. A federal district court, holding that Corley had violated the DMCA's antitrafficking provisions, issued an injunction barring Corley from posting DeCSS on his Web site and from posting links to other sites where DeCSS could be found.

On appeal, Corley argued that his publication of the DeCSS program's codes was speech protected by the First Amendment and that the application of the DMCA to him was thus unconstitutional. The Second Circuit concluded that Corley was to some extent engaged in speech but that his actions also had a substantial nonspeech component. In any event, the Second Circuit reasoned, the DMCA's antitrafficking provisions served a substantial government interest in protecting the rights of intellectual property owners and were content-neutral restrictions unrelated to the suppression of free expression. The court therefore held that the antitrafficking provisions did not violate the First Amendment.

Some critics of the DMCA's anticircumvention and antitrafficking provisions have asserted that those provisions may operate to restrict users' ability to make fair use of copyrighted materials. Evidently attempting to convert this policy-based objection about what Congress enacted into a constitutional objection on which the court might be more inclined to rule, Corley argued that the fair use doctrine was required by the First Amendment and that the DMCA, insofar as it limited users' ability to rely on the fair use doctrine, was unconstitutional. The Second Circuit called it "extravagant" to assert that the fair use doctrine was constitutionally required, for there was no substantial authority to support such a contention. Moreover, the court reasoned that even if Corley's contention were not otherwise questionable, "[f]air use has never been held to be a guarantee of access to copyrighted material in order to copy it by the fair user's preferred technique or in the format of the original."

---

expressed concern over these services and have resorted to litigation against such providers on the theory that they materially contributed to or induced copyright infringement by their users. In its 2005 *Grokster* decision, the Supreme Court focused on the inducement basis for imposing liability on services such as Grokster and StreamCast. That case follows shortly.

The basic recovery for copyright infringement is the owner's actual damages plus the attributable profits received by the infringer. In lieu of the basic remedy, however, the plaintiff may usually elect to receive *statutory*

damages. The statutory damages set by the trial judge or jury must fall within the range of $750 to $30,000 unless the infringement was willful, in which event the maximum rises to $150,000. These limits do not apply if the plaintiff elects the basic remedy, however. Injunctive relief and awards of costs and attorney's fees are possible in appropriate cases. Although it seldom does so, the federal government may pursue a criminal copyright infringement prosecution if the infringement was willful and for purposes of commercial advantage or private financial gain.

Metro-Goldwyn-Mayer Studios, Inc. v. Grokster, Ltd.
545 U.S. 913 (U.S. Sup. Ct. 2005)

Grokster, Ltd., and StreamCast Networks, Inc., defendants in the case described below, distributed free software products allowing computer users to share electronic files through peer-to-peer networks. The networks are called "peer-to-peer" because users' computers communicate directly with each other rather than through central servers. Because they need no central computer server to mediate the exchange of information or files among users, the high-bandwidth communications capacity for a server may be dispensed with, and the need for costly server storage space is eliminated. The lack of a need for a central server eliminates possible server glitches and resulting server downtime. Given these benefits in security, cost, and efficiency, peer-to-peer networks are employed to store and distribute electronic files by universities, government agencies, corporations, and libraries.

Other users of peer-to-peer networks include individual recipients of Grokster's and StreamCast's software. Although the networks these persons enjoy through using the software can be employed for the sharing of any type of digital file, evidence produced in the case described below indicated that most users employed the networks in order to share copyrighted music and video files without authorization. Numerous copyright owners—including motion picture studios, recording companies, songwriters, and music publishers, but referred to here as "MGM" for convenience—filed separate lawsuits against Grokster and StreamCast in an effort to have them held liable for their users' copyright infringements. The various cases were consolidated into one case in a federal district court.

Grokster's software employed the FastTrack technology. StreamCast distributed a similar product except that its software, called Morpheus, relied on the Gnutella technology. A user who downloaded and installed either software possessed the protocol to send requests for files directly to the computers of others using software compatible with FastTrack or Gnutella. If the requested file was found, the requesting user could download it directly from the computer where it was located. The copied file would be placed in a designated sharing folder on the requesting user's computer, where it was available for other users to download in turn, along with any other file in that folder. Grokster and StreamCast used no servers to intercept the content of the search requests or to mediate the file transfers conducted by users of the software.

Although Grokster and StreamCast therefore did not know when particular files were copied, searches using their software revealed what was available on the networks the software reached. A study by a statistician for MGM showed that nearly 90 percent of the files available for download on the FastTrack system were copyrighted works. Grokster and StreamCast disputed this figure and argued that free copying of copyrighted works is sometimes authorized by the copyright holders. The defendants also argued that potential noninfringing uses of their software were significant. Some musical performers, they noted, had gained new audiences by distributing their copyrighted works for free across peer-to-peer networks, and some distributors of public domain content (e.g., Shakespeare's plays) had used peer-to-peer networks to disseminate files. MGM provided evidence tending to indicate, however, that the vast majority of users' downloads were acts of infringement. With more than 100 million copies of the software in question having been downloaded, and billions of files being shared across the FastTrack and Gnutella networks each month, the number of instances of copyright infringement by users was potentially huge.

Grokster and StreamCast conceded that users employed their software primarily to download copyrighted files, even if the decentralized FastTrack and Gnutella networks failed to reveal which files were being copied. MGM produced evidence tending to indicate that from the time Grokster and StreamCast began to distribute their free software, each one voiced the objective that recipients use it to download copyrighted works. MGM presented further evidence suggesting that after a successful lawsuit by copyright owners effectively shut down the Napster file-sharing service, Grokster and StreamCast sought to promote their software as a device by which former Napster users could obtain ready access to desired files. Although Grokster and StreamCast distributed their software free of charge, they made money by selling advertising space and streaming the advertising to users of the software.

After discovery, all parties moved for summary judgment. The federal district court held that those who used the Grokster and StreamCast software to download copyrighted media files directly infringed MGM's copyrights. However, the court granted summary judgment in favor of Grokster and StreamCast. Distributing their software gave rise to no liability, in the court's view, because its use did not provide the distributors with actual knowledge of specific acts of infringement. The U.S. Court of Appeals for the Ninth affirmed, reading Sony Corp. of America v. Universal City Studios, Inc., *464 U.S. 417 (1984), as holding that distribution of a commercial product capable of substantial noninfringing uses could not give rise to contributory liability for infringement unless the distributor had actual knowledge of specific instances of infringement and failed to act on that knowledge. Because the defendants' software was capable of substantial noninfringing uses and because the decentralized architecture of their software meant that the defendants had no actual knowledge of specific instances of infringement, the Ninth Circuit concluded that the defendants could not be held liable on a contributory infringement basis. The Ninth Circuit also ruled that Grokster and StreamCast could not be liable under a theory of vicarious infringement because the defendants did not monitor or control the use of the software, had no ability to supervise its use, and had no independent duty to police infringement. The U.S. Supreme Court granted MGM's petition for a writ of certiorari.*

Souter, Justice

The question is under what circumstances the distributor of a product capable of both lawful and unlawful use is liable for acts of copyright infringement by third parties using the product.

MGM . . . fault[s] the Court of Appeals' holding for upsetting a sound balance between the respective values of supporting creative pursuits through copyright protection and promoting innovation in new communication technologies by limiting the incidence of liability for copyright infringement. The more artistic protection is favored, the more technological innovation may be discouraged; the administration of copyright law is an exercise in managing the trade-off.

The tension between the two values is the subject of this case, with its claim that digital distribution of copyrighted material threatens copyright holders as never before, because every copy is identical to the original, copying is easy, and many people (especially the young) use file-sharing software to download copyrighted works. [I]ndications are that the ease of copying songs or movies using software [such as] Grokster's and Napster's is fostering disdain for copyright protection. As the case has been presented to us, these fears are said to be offset by the different concern that imposing liability, not only on infringers but on distributors of software based on its potential for unlawful use, could limit further development of beneficial technologies.

The argument for imposing indirect liability in this case is, however, a powerful one, given the number of infringing downloads that occur every day using StreamCast's and Grokster's software. When a widely shared service or product is used to commit infringement, it may be impossible to enforce rights in the protected work effectively against all direct infringers, the only practical alternative being to go against the distributor of the copying device for secondary liability on a theory of contributory or vicarious infringement.

One infringes contributorily by intentionally inducing or encouraging direct infringement, and infringes vicariously by profiting from direct infringement while declining to exercise a right to stop or limit it. In the present case, MGM has argued [not only a contributory infringement theory but also] a vicarious liability theory. Because we resolve the case based on an inducement theory, there is no need to analyze separately MGM's vicarious liability theory.

Despite the currency of these principles of secondary liability, this Court has dealt with secondary copyright infringement in only one recent case. In *Sony Corp. v. Universal City Studios,* 464 U.S. 417 (1984), this Court addressed a claim that secondary liability for infringement can arise from the very distribution of a commercial product. There, the product, novel at the time, was what we know today as the videocassette recorder, or VCR. Copyright holders sued Sony, the manufacturer, claiming it was contributorily liable for infringement that occurred when VCR owners taped copyrighted programs because it supplied the means used to infringe, and it had constructive knowledge that infringement would occur. [T]he evidence showed that the principal use of the VCR was for "'time-shifting,'" or taping a program for later viewing at a more convenient time, which the Court found to be a fair, not an infringing, use. There was no evidence that Sony had expressed an object of bringing about taping in violation of copyright or had taken active steps to increase its profits from unlawful taping. Although Sony's advertisements urged consumers to buy the VCR to "'record favorite shows'" or "'build a library'" of recorded programs, neither of these uses was necessarily infringing.

On those facts, with no evidence of stated or indicated intent to promote infringing uses, the only conceivable basis for imposing liability was on a theory of contributory infringement arising from its sale of VCRs to consumers with knowledge that some would use them to infringe. But because the VCR was "capable of commercially significant noninfringing uses," we [borrowed an approach followed in patent law] and held the manufacturer could not be faulted solely on the basis of its distribution. [This approach was designed to leave] breathing room for innovation and a vigorous commerce.

The parties . . . think the key to resolving [this case] is the *Sony* rule and, in particular, what it means for a product to be "capable of commercially significant noninfringing uses." MGM advances the argument that granting summary judgment to Grokster and StreamCast . . . gave too much weight to the value of innovative technology, and too little to the copyrights infringed by users of their software, given that 90 percent of works available on one of the networks was shown to be copyrighted. Assuming the remaining 10 percent to be its noninfringing use,

MGM says this should not qualify as "substantial." Grokster and StreamCast reply by citing evidence that their software can be used to reproduce public domain works, and they point to copyright holders who actually encourage copying. Even if infringement is the principal practice with their software today, they argue, the noninfringing uses are significant and will grow.

We agree with MGM that the Court of Appeals misapplied *Sony,* which it read as limiting secondary liability quite beyond the circumstances to which the case applied. *Sony* barred secondary liability based on presuming or imputing intent to cause infringement solely from the design or distribution of a product capable of substantial lawful use, which the distributor knows is in fact used for infringement. The Ninth Circuit read *Sony*'s limitation to mean that whenever a product is capable of substantial lawful use, the producer can never be held contributorily liable for third parties' infringing use of it; it read the rule as being this broad, even when an actual purpose to cause infringing use is shown by evidence independent of design and distribution of the product, unless the distributors had "specific knowledge of infringement at a time at which they contributed to the infringement, and failed to act upon that information" [quoting the Ninth Circuit's opinion]. Because the Ninth Circuit found the StreamCast and Grokster software capable of substantial lawful use, it concluded on the basis of its reading of *Sony* that neither company could be held liable, since there was no showing that their software, being without any central server, afforded them knowledge of specific unlawful uses.

This view of *Sony,* however, was in error, converting the case from one about liability resting on imputed intent to one about liability on any theory. *Sony*'s rule limits imputing culpable intent as a matter of law from the characteristics or uses of a distributed product. But nothing in *Sony* requires courts to ignore evidence of intent if there is such evidence, and the case was never meant to foreclose rules of fault-based liability derived from the common law. Thus, where evidence goes beyond a product's characteristics or the knowledge that it may be put to infringing uses, and shows statements or actions directed to promoting infringement, *Sony*'s . . . rule will not preclude liability.

The classic case of direct evidence of unlawful purpose occurs when one induces commission of infringement by another, or entices or persuades another to infringe, as by advertising. Thus at common law [and later under the Patent Act,] a patent defendant who "not only expected but invoked [infringing use] by advertisement" was liable for infringement "on principles recognized in every part of the law." [Case citation omitted.]

For the same reasons that *Sony* [looked to] patent law as a model for its copyright safe-harbor rule [regarding the prospect of substantial noninfringing uses], the inducement rule, too, is a sensible one for copyright. We adopt it here, holding that one who distributes a device with the object of promoting its use to infringe copyright, as shown by clear expression or other affirmative steps taken to foster infringement, is liable for the resulting acts of infringement by third parties. We are, of course, mindful of the need to keep from trenching on regular commerce or discouraging the development of technologies with lawful and unlawful potential. Accordingly, just as *Sony* did not find intentional inducement despite the knowledge of the VCR manufacturer that its device could be used to infringe, mere knowledge of infringing potential or of actual infringing uses would not be enough here to subject a distributor to liability. Nor would ordinary acts incident to product distribution, such as offering customers technical support or product updates, support liability in themselves. The inducement rule, instead, premises liability on purposeful, culpable expression and conduct, and thus does nothing to compromise legitimate commerce or discourage innovation having a lawful promise.

The only apparent question about treating MGM's evidence as sufficient to withstand summary judgment under the theory of inducement goes to the need on MGM's part to adduce evidence that StreamCast and Grokster communicated an inducing message to their software users. The classic instance of inducement is by advertisement or solicitation that broadcasts a message designed to stimulate others to commit violations. MGM claims that such a message is shown here. It is undisputed that StreamCast beamed onto the computer screens of users of Napster-compatible programs ads urging the adoption of [Streamcast's] OpenNap program, which was designed, as its name implied, to [appeal to users] of Napster, then under attack in the courts for facilitating massive infringement. [See *A & M Records, Inc. v. Napster, Inc.,* 239 F.3d 1004 (9th Cir. 2001).] Those who accepted StreamCast's OpenNap program were offered software to perform the same services, which a factfinder could conclude would readily have been understood in the Napster market as the ability to download copyrighted music files.

Grokster distributed an electronic newsletter containing links to articles promoting its software's ability to access popular copyrighted music. And anyone whose Napster or free file-sharing searches turned up a link to Grokster would have understood Grokster to be offering the same file-sharing ability as Napster, and to the same people who probably used Napster for infringing downloads; that would also have been the understanding of anyone offered Grokster's suggestively named Swaptor software, its version of OpenNap.

In StreamCast's case, . . . the evidence just described was supplemented by other unequivocal indications of unlawful purpose in the internal communications and advertising designs aimed at Napster users. A kit developed by StreamCast to be delivered to advertisers, for example, contained press articles about StreamCast's potential to capture former Napster users, and it introduced itself to some potential advertisers as a company "which is similar to what Napster was." It broadcast banner advertisements to users of other Napster-compatible software, urging them to adopt its OpenNap. An internal e-mail from a company executive stated: "'We have put this network in place so that when Napster pulls the plug on their free service . . . or if the Court orders them shut down prior to that . . . we will be positioned to capture the flood of their 32 million users that will be actively looking for an alternative.'" Here, the summary judgment record is replete with other evidence that Grokster and StreamCast, unlike the manufacturer and distributor in *Sony,* acted with a purpose to cause copyright violations by use of software suitable for illegal use.

Three features of this evidence of intent are particularly notable. First, each company showed itself to be aiming to satisfy a known source of demand for copyright infringement, the market comprising former Napster users. Grokster and StreamCast's efforts to supply services to former Napster users, deprived of a mechanism to copy and distribute what were overwhelmingly infringing files, indicate a principal, if not exclusive, intent on the part of each to bring about infringement. Second, this evidence of unlawful objective is given added significance by MGM's showing that neither company attempted to develop filtering tools or other mechanisms to diminish the infringing activity using their software.

Third, there is a further complement to the direct evidence of unlawful objective. It is useful to recall that StreamCast and Grokster make money by selling advertising space, by directing ads to the screens of computers employing their software. As the number of users of each program increases, advertising opportunities become worth more. While there is doubtless some demand for free Shakespeare, the evidence shows that substantive volume is a function of free access to copyrighted work. Users seeking Top 40 songs, for example, or the latest release by Modest Mouse, are certain to be far more numerous than those seeking [free public domain works], and Grokster and StreamCast translated that demand into dollars. [T]he commercial sense of [the defendants'] enterprise turns on high-volume use, which the record shows is infringing [an extremely high percentage of the time]. The unlawful objective is unmistakable.

In addition to intent to bring about infringement and distribution of a device suitable for infringing use, the inducement theory of course requires evidence of actual infringement by recipients of the device, the software in this case. [In this case,] there is evidence of infringement on a gigantic scale, and there is no serious issue of the adequacy of MGM's showing on this point in order to survive the [defendants'] summary judgment requests.

In sum, this case is significantly different from *Sony,* and reliance on that case to rule in favor of StreamCast and Grokster was error. *Sony* dealt with a claim of liability based solely on distributing a product with alternative lawful and unlawful uses, with knowledge that some users would follow the unlawful course. The case struck a balance between the interests of protection and innovation by holding that the product's capability of substantial lawful employment should bar the imputation of fault and consequent secondary liability for the unlawful acts of others.

MGM's evidence in this case most obviously addresses a different basis of liability for distributing a product open to alternative uses. Here, evidence of the distributors' words and deeds going beyond distribution as such shows a purpose to cause and profit from third-party acts of copyright infringement.

Judgment of Court of Appeals vacated; case remanded for further proceedings.

Fair Use The Copyright Act states that uses for such purposes as criticism or comment, news reporting, teaching, scholarship, or research may be good candidates for the protection of the fair use defense against infringement liability. However, a court's fair use determination requires the weighing of factors whose application varies from case to case. These factors are (1) the purpose and character of the use, (2) the nature of the copyrighted work, (3) the amount and substantiality of the portion used in relation to the copyrighted work as a whole, and (4) the effect of the use on the potential markets for the copyrighted work or on its value. Even one of the supposedly good candidates may be held not to be fair use once all of the factors are weighed and balanced.

The *Perfect 10* case, which follows, illustrates the application of the fair use factors and other fair use principles. Although the use at issue in *Perfect 10* was not a parody, the court engages in some discussion of why parody is often a good candidate for fair use treatment. After you read *Perfect 10*'s discussion of the fair use factors in the context of a nonparody case, think about how the factors would probably be applied in a case involving a parody of a copyrighted work.

Perfect 10, Inc. v. Amazon.com, Inc.   508 F.3d 1146 (9th Cir. 2007)

Google Inc. operates a search engine that automatically accesses thousands of Web sites and indexes them within a database stored on Google's computers. When a user accesses the Google site and types in a search query, Google's software searches for sites responsive to the query. Google then sends relevant information to the user's computer, providing the search results in the form of text, images, or videos. The technology known as Google Image Search furnishes search results as a Web page of small images called "thumbnails," which are stored in Google's servers. The thumbnail images are reduced, lower-resolution versions of full-sized images stored on third-party computers.

When a user clicks on a thumbnail image, the user's browser program interprets HTML instructions on Google's Web page. These HTML instructions direct the browser to cause a rectangular window to appear on the user's computer screen. The browser fills the top section of the window with information from the Google Web page, including the thumbnail image and text. The HTML instructions also give the user's browser the address of the Web site publisher's computer, which stores the full-size version of the thumbnail. By following the HTML instructions, the user's browser connects to the Web site publisher's computer, downloads the full-size image, and makes the image appear at the bottom of the window on the user's screen. Google does not store the images that fill this lower part of the window and does not communicate the images to the user; Google simply provides HTML instructions directing a user's browser to access a third-party Web site. However, the top part of the window (containing the information from the Google Web page) appears to frame and comment on the bottom part of the window. Thus, the user's window appears to be filled with a single integrated presentation of the full-size image, but it is actually an image from a third-party site framed by information from Google's site. The process by which the Web page directs a user's browser to incorporate content from different computers into a single window is referred to as "in-line linking." The term "framing" refers to the process by which information from one computer appears to frame and annotate the in-line linked content from another computer.

Google generates revenue through a business program called "AdSense." Under this program, the owner of a Web site can register with Google to become an AdSense "partner." The Web site owner then places HTML instructions on its Web pages in order to signal Google's server to place relevant advertising on the Web pages. AdSense participants agree to share, with Google, the revenues that flow from such advertising.

As another revenue source, Google authorized Amazon.com to in-line link to Google's search results. Amazon.com gave its users the impression that it was providing search results, but Google actually did so. Amazon.com routed users' search queries to Google and automatically transmitted Google's responses to its users.

Perfect 10, Inc., which markets and sells copyrighted images of nude models, operates a subscription Web site. Subscribers pay a monthly fee to view Perfect 10 images in a password-protected "members' area" of the site. Google does not include the password-protected images from the members' area in Google's index or database. Perfect 10 has also licensed Fonestarz Media Limited to sell and distribute Perfect 10's reduced-size copyrighted images for download and use on cell phones.

Some Web site publishers republish Perfect 10's copyrighted images on the Internet without authorization. Google's search engine automatically indexes the Web pages containing these images and then provides thumbnail versions of images in response to user queries. When a user clicks on the thumbnail image, the user's browser accesses the third-party Web page and in-line links to the full-sized image stored on the third party's computer. This image appears, in its original context, on the lower portion of the window on the user's computer screen, framed by information from Google's Web page.

Perfect 10 sued Google, claiming that Google's thumbnail images and in-line linking to the full-size images infringed Perfect 10's copyrights on the images. Perfect 10 later filed a similar lawsuit against Amazon.com. In each case, Perfect 10 sought a preliminary injunction to prevent the defendants from continuing the actions that Perfect 10 regarded as infringing in nature. After consolidating the two cases, the federal district court denied the motion for a preliminary injunction against Amazon.com, but granted the motion for a preliminary injunction against Google in regard to its thumbnail images. In so ruling, the court held that the thumbnail images violated Perfect 10's right, as copyright owner, to display its copyrighted images, and that the thumbnail images did not amount to fair use. Concerning Google's in-line linking to the full-size images, the court held that Google's actions in that regard did not warrant preliminary injunctive relief because Google neither displayed nor distributed those images and thus did not violate rights belonging to Perfect 10. Both Google and Perfect 10 appealed to the U.S. Court of Appeals for the Ninth Circuit. The following edited version of the Ninth Circuit's opinion focuses on Perfect 10's claim against Google.

Ikuta, Circuit Judge

Preliminary injunctive relief is available to a party who demonstrates either: (1) a combination of probable success on the merits and the possibility of irreparable harm; or (2) that serious questions are raised and the balance of hardships tips in its favor. Perfect 10 claims that Google's search engine program directly infringes two exclusive rights granted to copyright holders: its display right and its distribution right. Even if [Perfect 10 establishes an apparent violation of either of these rights, Google] may avoid liability if it can establish that its use of the images is a "fair use" as set forth in [the Copyright Act].

Display Right

In considering whether Perfect 10 made a prima facie case of violation of its display right, the district court reasoned that a computer owner that stores an image as electronic information and [provides] that electronic information directly to the user is displaying the electronic information in violation of a copyright holder's exclusive display right. Conversely, the owner of a computer that does not store and serve the electronic information to a user is not displaying that information, even if such owner in-line links to or frames the electronic information. The district court referred to this test as the "server test." Applying the server test, the district court concluded that Perfect 10 was likely to succeed in its claim that Google's thumbnails constituted direct infringement but was unlikely to succeed in its claim that Google's in-line linking to full-size infringing images constituted a direct infringement. [T]his analysis comports with the language of the Copyright Act, we agree with the district court's resolution of both these issues.

Section 106(5) [of the Copyright Act] states that a copyright owner has the exclusive right "to display the copyrighted work publicly." The Copyright Act explains that "display" means "to show a copy of it, either directly or by means of a film, slide, television image, or any other device or process. . . ." 17 U.S.C. § 101. Section 101 defines "copies" as "material objects, other than phonorecords, in which a work is fixed by any method now known or later developed, and from which the work can be perceived, reproduced, or otherwise communicated, either directly or with the aid of a machine or device." Finally, [§ 101] provides that "[a] work is 'fixed' in a tangible medium of expression when its embodiment in a copy or phonorecord, by or under the authority of the author, is sufficiently permanent or stable to permit it to be perceived, reproduced, or otherwise communicated for a period of more than transitory duration."

We must now apply these definitions to the facts of this case. A photographic image is a work that is "fixed in a tangible medium of expression," for purposes of the Copyright Act, when embodied (i.e., stored) in a computer's server (or hard disk, or other storage device). The image stored in the computer is the "copy" of the work for purposes of copyright law. The computer owner shows a copy "by means of a . . . device or process" when the owner uses the computer to fill the computer screen with the photographic image stored on that computer, or by communicating the stored image electronically to another person's computer. In sum, based on the plain language of the statute, a person displays a photographic image by using a computer to fill a computer screen with a copy of the photographic image fixed in the computer's memory.

There is no dispute that Google's computers store thumbnail versions of Perfect 10's copyrighted images and communicate copies of those thumbnails to Google's users. Therefore, Perfect 10 has made a prima facie case that Google's communication of its stored thumbnail images directly infringes Perfect 10's display right.

Google does not, however, display a copy of full-size infringing photographic images for purposes of the Copyright Act when Google frames in-line linked images that appear on a user's computer screen. Because Google's computers do not store the photographic images, Google does not have a copy of the images for purposes of the Copyright Act. In other words, Google does not have any "material objects . . . in which a work is fixed . . . and from which the work can be perceived, reproduced, or otherwise communicated" and thus cannot communicate a copy. 17 U.S.C. § 101.

Instead of communicating a copy of the image, Google provides HTML instructions that direct a user's browser to a website publisher's computer, [which] stores the full-size photographic image. Providing these HTML instructions is not equivalent to showing a copy. First, the HTML instructions are lines of text, not a photographic image. Second, HTML instructions do not themselves cause infringing images to appear on the user's computer screen. The HTML merely gives the address of the image to the user's browser. The browser then interacts with the computer that stores the infringing image. [T]his interaction . . . causes an infringing image to appear on the user's computer screen [but does not amount to a display by Google of Perfect 10's copyrighted images].

Perfect 10 argues that Google displays a copy of the full-size images by framing the full-size images, which gives the impression that Google is showing the image within a single Google webpage. While in-line linking and framing may cause some computer users to believe they are viewing a single Google webpage, the Copyright Act, unlike [trademark law], does not protect a copyright holder against acts that cause consumer confusion. [For the reasons already noted, framing of the sort relevant to this case does not constitute a display by Google of Perfect 10's copyrighted images.]

Distribution Right

The district court also concluded that Perfect 10 would not likely prevail on its claim that Google directly infringed Perfect 10's right to distribute its full-size images. The district court reasoned that distribution requires an "actual dissemination" of a copy. Because Google did not communicate the full-size images to the user's computer, Google did not distribute these images.

Again, the district court's conclusion on this point is consistent with the language of the Copyright Act. Section 106(3) provides that the copyright owner has the exclusive right "to distribute copies or phonorecords of the copyrighted work to the public by sale or other transfer of ownership, or by rental, lease, or lending." As noted, "copies" means "material objects . . . in which a work is fixed." 17 U.S.C. § 101. The Supreme Court has indicated that in the electronic context, copies may be distributed electronically. *See N.Y. Times Co. v. Tasini,* 533 U.S. 483, 498 (2001). Google's search engine communicates HTML instructions that tell a user's browser where to find full-size images on a website publisher's computer, but Google does not itself distribute copies of the infringing photographs. It is the website publisher's computer that distributes copies of the images by transmitting the photographic image electronically to the user's computer. Accordingly, the district court correctly concluded that Perfect 10 does not have a likelihood of success in proving that Google violates Perfect 10's distribution rights with respect to full-size images.

Fair Use Defense

Because Perfect 10 has succeeded in showing it would prevail in its prima facie case that Google's thumbnail images infringe Perfect 10's display rights, the burden shifts to Google to show that it will likely succeed [with the defense] that its use of thumbnails is a fair use of the images. The fair use defense permits the use of copyrighted works without the copyright owner's consent under certain situations. The defense encourages and allows the development of new ideas that build on earlier ones, thus providing a necessary counterbalance to the copyright law's goal of protecting creators' work product.

[Congress provided for the fair use defense in 17 U.S.C. § 107, which states that] "the fair use of a copyrighted work, including such use by reproduction in copies or phonorecords or by any other means . . . , for purposes such as criticism, comment, news reporting, teaching (including multiple copies for classroom use), scholarship, or research, is not an infringement of copyright." We must be flexible in applying a fair use analysis; it "is not to be simplified with bright-line rules, for the statute . . . calls for case-by-case analysis" [in which four factors required by § 107 are weighed and balanced]. *Campbell v. Acuff-Rose Music, Inc.,* 510 U.S. 569, 577–78 (1994).

In applying the fair use analysis in this case, we are guided by *Kelly v. Arriba Soft Corp.,* 336 F.3d 811 (9th Cir. 2003), which considered substantially the same use of copyrighted photographic images as is at issue here. In *Kelly,* a photographer brought a direct infringement claim against Arriba, the operator of an Internet search engine. The search engine provided thumbnail versions of the photographer's images in response to search queries. We held that Arriba's use of thumbnail images was a fair use primarily based on the transformative nature of a search engine and its benefit to the public. We also concluded that Arriba's use of the thumbnail images did not harm the photographer's market for his image. [In comparing the case before us with *Kelly,* we use] the context of the four-factor fair use analysis [required by § 107].

The first factor requires a court to consider "the purpose and character of the use, including whether such use is of a commercial nature or is for nonprofit educational purposes." 17 U.S.C. § 107. The central purpose of this inquiry is to determine whether and to what extent the new work is "transformative." *Campbell,* 510 U.S. at 579. [According to *Campbell,* a new] work is "transformative" when [it] does not "merely supersede the objects of the original creation" but rather "adds something new, with a further purpose or different character, altering the first with new expression, meaning, or message." Conversely, if the new work "supersede[s] the use of the original," the use is likely not a fair use. *Harper & Row Publishers, Inc. v. Nation Enterprises,* 471 U.S. 539, 550–51 (1985) (publishing the "heart" of an unpublished work and thus supplanting the copyright holder's first publication right was not a fair use).

In *Kelly,* we concluded that Arriba's use of thumbnails was transformative because "Arriba's use of the images serve[d] a different function than Kelly's use—improving access to information on the Internet versus artistic expression." *Kelly,* 336 F.3d at 819. Although an image may have been created originally to serve an entertainment, aesthetic, or informative function, a search engine transforms the image into a pointer directing a user to a source of information. Just as a "parody has an obvious claim to transformative value" because "it can provide social benefit, by shedding light on an earlier work, and, in the process, creating a new one," *Campbell,* 510 U.S. at 579, a search engine provides social benefit by incorporating an original work into a new work, namely, an electronic reference tool. Indeed, a search engine may be more transformative than a parody because a search engine provides an entirely new use for the original work, while a parody typically has the same entertainment purpose as the original work. *See, e.g., id.* at 594–96 (holding that 2 Live Crew's parody of "Oh, Pretty Woman" using the words "hairy woman" or "bald headed woman" was a transformative work, and thus [a strong candidate for] fair use [treatment]); *Mattel, Inc. v. Walking Mountain Productions,* 353 F.3d 792, 796–98, 800–06 (9th Cir. 2003) (concluding that photos parodying Barbie by depicting "nude Barbie dolls juxtaposed with vintage kitchen appliances" was a fair use). In other words, a search engine puts images "in a different context" so that they are "transformed into a new creation." [Case citation omitted.]

The fact that Google incorporates the entire Perfect 10 image into the search engine results does not diminish the transformative nature of Google's use. As the district court correctly noted, we determined in *Kelly* that even making an exact copy of a work may be transformative so long as the copy serves a different function than the original work. Here, Google uses Perfect 10's images in a new context to serve a different purpose.

The district court nevertheless determined that Google's use of thumbnail images was less transformative than Arriba's use of thumbnails in *Kelly* because Google's use of thumbnails superseded Perfect 10's right to sell its reduced-size images for use on cell phones. The district court stated that "mobile users can download and save the thumbnails displayed by Google Image Search onto their phones," and concluded [that] "to the extent that users may choose to download free images to their phone rather than purchase [Perfect 10's] reduced-size images, Google's use supersedes [Perfect 10's]." Additionally, the district court determined that the commercial nature of Google's use weighed against its transformative nature. Although *Kelly* held that the commercial use of the photographer's images by Arriba's search engine was less exploitative than typical commercial use, and thus weighed only slightly against a finding of fair use, the district court here distinguished *Kelly* on the ground that some website owners in the AdSense program had infringing Perfect 10 images on their websites. The district court held that because Google's thumbnails "lead users to sites that directly benefit Google's bottom line," the AdSense program increased the commercial nature of Google's use of Perfect 10's images.

In conducting our case-specific analysis of fair use in light of the purposes of copyright, we must weigh Google's superseding and commercial uses of thumbnail images against Google's significant transformative use, as well as the extent to which Google's search engine promotes the purposes of copyright and serves the interests of the public. Although the district court acknowledged the "truism that search engines such as Google Image Search provide great value to the public," the district court did not expressly consider whether this value outweighed the significance of Google's superseding use or the commercial nature of Google's use. The Supreme Court,

however, has directed us to be mindful of the extent to which a use promotes the purposes of copyright and serves the interests of the public. *See Campbell,* 510 U.S. at 579.

We note that the superseding use in this case is not significant at present: the district court did not find that any downloads for mobile phone use had taken place. Moreover, while Google's use of thumbnails to direct users to AdSense partners containing infringing content adds a commercial dimension that did not exist in *Kelly,* the district court did not determine that this commercial element was significant. The district court stated that Google's AdSense programs as a whole contributed "$630 million, or 46% of total revenues" to Google's bottom line, but noted that this figure did not "break down the much smaller amount attributable to websites that contain infringing content."

We conclude that the significantly transformative nature of Google's search engine, particularly in light of its public benefit, outweighs Google's superseding and commercial uses of the thumbnails in this case. In reaching this conclusion, we note the importance of analyzing fair use flexibly in light of new circumstances. We are also mindful of the Supreme Court's direction that "the more transformative the new work, the less will be the significance of other factors, like commercialism, that may weigh against a finding of fair use." *Campbell,* 510 U.S. at 579.

Accordingly, we disagree with the district court's conclusion that because Google's use of the thumbnails could supersede Perfect 10's cell phone download use and because the use was more commercial than Arriba's, this fair use factor weighed "slightly" in favor of Perfect 10. Instead, we conclude that the transformative nature of Google's use is more significant than any incidental superseding use or the minor commercial aspects of Google's search engine and website. Therefore, this factor weighs heavily in favor of Google.

With respect to . . . "the nature of the copyrighted work," [the second factor required by § 107], our decision in *Kelly* is directly on point. There we held that the photographer's images were "creative in nature" and thus "closer to the core of intended copyright protection than are more fact-based works." However, because the photos appeared on the Internet before Arriba used thumbnail versions in its search engine results, this factor weighed only slightly in favor of the photographer.

Here, the district court found that Perfect 10's images were creative but also previously published. The right of first publication is "the author's right to control the first public appearance of his expression." *Harper & Row,* 471 U.S. at 564. Because this right encompasses [what *Harper &. Row* termed] "the choices of when, where, and in what form first to publish a work," an author exercises and exhausts [the first publication] right by publishing the work in any medium. Once Perfect 10 . . . exploited this commercially valuable right of first publication by putting its images on the Internet for paid subscribers, Perfect 10 [was] no longer entitled to the enhanced protection available for an unpublished work. Accordingly the district court did not err in holding that this factor weighed only slightly in favor of Perfect 10.

The third factor [set forth in § 107 requires consideration of] the amount and substantiality of the portion [of the copyrighted work] used, in relation to the work as a whole. [The key issue is whether the extent of the use was] "reasonable in relation to the purpose of the copying." *Campbell,* 510 U.S. at 586. In *Kelly,* we held Arriba's use of the entire photographic image was reasonable in light of the purpose of a search engine. Specifically, we noted, "[i]t was necessary for Arriba to copy the entire image to allow users to recognize the image and decide whether to pursue more information about the image or the originating [website]." Accordingly, we concluded that this factor did not weigh in favor of either party. Because the same analysis applies to Google's use of Perfect 10's image, the district court did not err in finding that this factor favored neither party.

The fourth factor is "the effect of the use upon the potential market for or value of the copyrighted work." 17 U.S.C. § 107. In *Kelly,* we concluded that Arriba's use of the thumbnail images did not harm the market for the photographer's full-size images. We reasoned that because thumbnails were not a substitute for the full-sized images, they did not harm the photographer's ability to sell or license his full-sized images. The district court here followed *Kelly's* reasoning, holding that Google's use of thumbnails did not hurt Perfect 10's market for full-size images. We agree.

Perfect 10 also has a market for reduced-size images, an issue not considered in *Kelly.* The district court held that "Google's use of thumbnails likely does harm the potential market for the downloading of [Perfect 10's] reduced-size images onto cell phones." The district court reasoned that persons who can obtain Perfect 10 images free of charge from Google are less likely to pay for a download, and [that] the availability of Google's thumbnail images would harm Perfect 10's market for cell phone downloads. As we discussed above, the district court did not make a finding that Google users have downloaded thumbnail images for cell phone use. This potential harm to Perfect 10's market remains hypothetical. We conclude that this factor favors neither party.

Having undertaken a case-specific analysis of all four factors, we now weigh these factors together. Google has put Perfect 10's thumbnail images (along with millions of other thumbnail images) to a use fundamentally different than the use intended by Perfect 10. In doing so, Google has provided a significant benefit to the public. Weighing this significant transformative use against the unproven use of Google's thumbnails for cell phone downloads, and considering the other fair use factors, all in light of the purpose of copyright, we conclude that Google's use of Perfect 10's thumbnails is a fair use. [Because the district court erred in concluding that Google is not likely to succeed with the fair use defense,] we vacate the preliminary injunction regarding Google's use of thumbnail images.

District court's preliminary injunction against Google vacated.

Note: In a portion of the opinion not included here, the Ninth Circuit affirmed the district court's holdings that Amazon.com had neither displayed nor distributed Perfect 10's copyrighted images and that, accordingly, a preliminary injunction against Amazon.com would be inappropriate. In another portion of the opinion not included here, the Ninth Circuit remanded the case to the district court for further consideration of Perfect 10's alternative claims that Google and Amazon.com contributed to other parties' acts of infringement or should be held vicariously liable for those acts. The Ninth Circuit determined that additional fact-finding and a more expansive inquiry on the part of the district court would be necessary in order for the contributory and vicarious infringement claims to be fairly evaluated.

Trademarks

Trademarks Trademarks help purchasers identify favored products and services. For this reason, they also give sellers and manufacturers an incentive to innovate and strive for quality. However, both these ends would be defeated if competitors were free to appropriate each other's trademarks. Thus, the federal Lanham Act protects trademark owners against certain uses of their marks by third parties.[3]

Protected Marks The Lanham Act recognizes four kinds of marks. It defines a **trademark** as any word, name, symbol, device, or combination thereof used by a manufacturer or seller to identify its products and distinguish them from the products of competitors. Although trademarks consisting of single words or names are most commonly encountered, federal trademark protection has sometimes been extended to colors, pictures, label and package designs, slogans, sounds, arrangements of numbers and/or letters (e.g., "7-Eleven"), and shapes of goods or their containers (e.g., Coca-Cola bottles).

---

[3]In addition, the owner of a trademark may enjoy legal protection under common law trademark doctrines and state trademark statutes.

Ethics in Action

Significant ethical issues may arise as part of the clash between intellectual property rights and the claims of those who wish to make use of the protected invention, work, or item. Consider, for instance, these copyright-related questions:

- Is it ethical to use a Grokster-like service to obtain free-of-charge access to copyrighted musical compositions and recordings? Does it make a difference if the user downloads music only for his or her own personal use, as opposed to sharing files with other users? Does it make a difference whether the record companies supposedly have—or have not—made significant profits already on their copyrighted recordings? Is it ethical for record companies to seek, from Internet access providers, the names of their customers who

have a significant history of using Grokster-like services? (In thinking about these questions, you may find it useful to review the ethical theories discussed in Chapter 4.)
- If one has a plausible claim to the protection of the fair use doctrine, is it ethical to use portions of another party's copyrighted work even though the copyright owner has refused to grant permission for the use?
- How would profit maximizers, utilitarians, and rights theorists, respectively, be likely to assess the lobbying efforts of copyright owners who desired the significant increase in copyright duration that Congress enacted in the Sonny Bono Copyright Term Extension Act of 1998? (Feel free to review Chapter 4's discussion of the theories referred to in this question.)

Service marks resemble trademarks but identify and distinguish services. **Certification marks** certify the origin, materials, quality, method of manufacture, and other aspects of goods and services. Here, the user of the mark and its owner are distinct parties. A retailer, for example, may sell products bearing the Good Housekeeping Seal of Approval. **Collective marks** are trademarks or service marks used by organizations to identify themselves as the source of goods or services. Trade union and trade association marks fall into this category. Although all four kinds of marks receive federal protection, this chapter focuses on trademarks and service marks, using the terms *mark* or *trademark* to refer to both.

Distinctiveness Because their purpose is to help consumers identify products and services, trademarks must be *distinctive* to merit maximum Lanham Act protection. Marks fall into five general categories of distinctiveness (or nondistinctiveness):

1. *Arbitrary or fanciful marks.* These marks are the most distinctive—and the most likely to be protected—because they do not describe the qualities of the product or service they identify. The "Exxon" trademark is an example.

2. *Suggestive marks.* These marks convey the nature of a product or service only through imagination, thought, and perception. They do not actually describe the underlying product or service. The "Dietene" trademark for a dietary food supplement is an example. Although not

as clearly distinctive as arbitrary or fanciful marks, suggestive marks are nonetheless classified as distinctive. Hence, they are good candidates for protection.

3. *Descriptive marks.* These marks directly describe the product or service they identify (e.g., "Realemon," for bottled lemon juice). Descriptive marks are not protected unless they acquire *secondary meaning*. This occurs when their identification with a particular source of goods or services has become firmly established in the minds of a substantial number of buyers. "Realemon," of course, now has secondary meaning. Among the factors considered in secondary-meaning determinations are the length of time the mark has been used, the volume of sales associated with that use, and the nature of the advertising employing the mark. When applied to a package delivery service, for instance, the term *overnight* is usually descriptive and thus not protectible. It may come to deserve trademark protection, however, through long use by a single firm that advertised it extensively and made many sales while doing so. As will be seen, the same approach is taken concerning deceptively misdescriptive and geographically descriptive marks.

4. *Marks that are not inherently distinctive.* Although these marks are not distinctive in the usual senses of arbitrary nature, fanciful quality, or suggestiveness, proof of secondary meaning effectively makes these marks distinctive. They are therefore protectible if secondary meaning exists. The Supreme Court has held that under appropriate circumstances, product color is a potentially protectible trademark of this type.

5. *Generic terms.* Generic terms (e.g., "diamond" or "truck") simply refer to the general class of which the particular product or service is one example. Because any seller has the right to call a product or service by its common name, generic terms are ineligible for trademark protection.

Federal Registration Once the seller of a product or service uses a mark in commerce or forms a bona fide intention to do so very soon, she may apply to register the mark with the U.S. Patent and Trademark Office. The office reviews applications for distinctiveness. Its decision to deny or grant the application may be contested by the applicant or by a party who feels that he would be injured by registration of the mark. Such challenges may eventually reach the federal courts.

Trademarks of sufficient distinctiveness are placed on the Principal Register of the Patent and Trademark Office. A mark's inclusion in the Principal Register (1) is prima facie evidence of the mark's ownership, validity, and registration (which is useful in trademark infringement suits); (2) gives nationwide constructive notice of the owner's claim of ownership (thus eliminating the need to show that the defendant in an infringement suit had notice of the mark); (3) entitles the mark owner to assistance from the Bureau of Customs in stopping the importation of certain goods that, without the consent of the mark owner, bear a likeness of the mark; and (4) means that the mark will be incontestable after five years of registered status (as described later).

Even though they are not distinctive, certain other marks may merit placement on the Principal Register if they have acquired secondary meaning. These include (1) marks that are *not inherently distinctive* (as discussed earlier); (2) *descriptive marks* (as discussed earlier); (3) *deceptively misdescriptive* marks (such as "Dura-Skin," for plastic gloves); (4) *geographically descriptive* marks (such as "Indiana-Made"); and (5) marks that are *primarily a surname* (because as a matter of general policy, persons who have a certain last name should be fairly free to use that name in connection with their businesses). Once a mark in one of these classifications achieves registered status, the mark's owner obtains the legal benefits described in the previous paragraph.

Regardless of their distinctiveness, however, some kinds of marks are denied placement on the Principal Register. These include marks that (1) consist of the flags or other insignia of governments; (2) consist of the name, portrait, or signature of a living person who has not given consent to the trademark use; (3) are immoral, deceptive, or scandalous; or (4) are likely to cause confusion because they resemble a mark previously registered or used in the United States.

Transfer of Rights Because of the purposes underlying trademark law, transferring trademark rights is more difficult than transferring copyright or patent interests. A trademark owner may license the use of the mark, but only if the owner reserves control over the nature and quality of the goods or services as to which the licensee will use the mark. An uncontrolled "naked license" would allow the sale of goods or services bearing the mark but lacking the qualities formerly associated with it, and could confuse purchasers. Trademark rights may also be assigned or sold, but only along with the sale of the goodwill of the business originally using the mark.

Losing Federal Trademark Protection Federal registration of a trademark lasts for 10 years, with renewals for additional 10-year periods possible. However, trademark protection may be lost before the period expires. The government must cancel a registration six years after its date unless the registrant files with the Patent and Trademark Office, within the fifth and sixth years following the registration date, an affidavit detailing that the mark is in use or explaining its nonuse.

Any person who believes that he has been or will be damaged by a mark's registration may petition the Patent and Trademark Office to cancel that registration. Normally, the petition must be filed within five years of the mark's registration, because the mark becomes *incontestable* regarding goods or services with which it has continuously been used for five consecutive years after the registration. A mark's incontestability means that the permissible grounds for canceling its registration are limited. Even an incontestable mark, however, may be canceled *at any time* if, among other things, it was obtained by fraud, has been abandoned, or has become the generic name for the goods or services it identifies. *Abandonment* may occur through an express statement or agreement to abandon, through the mark's losing its significance as an indication of origin, or through the owner's failure to use it. A mark acquires a *generic meaning* when it comes to refer to a class of

The Global Business Environment

Piracy and other unauthorized uses of American goods or technology protected by U.S. patent, copyright, and trademark law have become a major problem of American businesses. For example, foreign jeans manufacturers may without authorization place the Levi's label on their jeans, thereby damaging the business of Levi Strauss & Co. by depriving it of some of the jeans' market and damaging the value of the Levi trademark, especially if the imported jeans are of inferior quality. This is an example of **counterfeit goods**—goods that copy or otherwise purport to be those of the trademark owner whose mark has been unlawfully used on the nongenuine goods. Counterfeit goods may also unlawfully appropriate patented technology or copyrighted material. For example, a foreign musical recording company may pirate the latest Beck album and import thousands of copies of it into the United States without copyright permission.

American firms harmed by the importation of counterfeit goods may obtain injunctions and damages under the Tariff Act of 1930, the Lanham Act, the Copyright Act, and the patent statute. In addition, the Trademark Counterfeiting Act of 1984 establishes civil and criminal penalties for counterfeiting goods. It also allows an American firm to recover from a counterfeiter three times its damages or three times the counterfeiter's profits (whichever is greater).

Patent, copyright, and trademark piracy is increasing in many parts of the world, especially in developing nations. Some developing nations believe that technology should be transferred freely to foster their economic growth. Consequently, they either encourage piracy or choose not to oppose it.

Gray market goods are goods lawfully bearing trademarks or using patents and copyrighted material but entering the American market without authorization. For example, Parker Pen Co. may authorize a Japanese manufacturer to make and sell Parker pens only in Japan. When an American firm imports the Japanese-made Parker pens into the United States, the goods become gray market goods.

While importing gray market goods may violate the contract between the American firm and its foreign licensee, it is not clear in what contexts it violates U.S. importation, trademark, patent, or copyright law. Some courts find a Lanham Act or Tariff Act violation, but other courts do not. The Trademark Counterfeiting Act of 1984 specifically excludes gray market goods from its coverage. The Copyright Act deals with gray market goods in a provision barring the "[i]mportation into the United States, without the authority of the owner of the copyright . . . of copies or phonorecords of a work that has been acquired outside the United States." Whether the items may lawfully enter the United States depends, therefore, on whether the copyright owner has provided "authority" for this to occur.

products or services rather than a particular source's product or service. For example, this has happened to such once-protected marks as aspirin, escalator, and thermos.

Trademark Infringement A trademark is infringed when, without the owner's consent, another party uses a substantially similar mark in connection with the sale of goods or services and this use is likely to cause confusion concerning their source or concerning whether there is an endorsement relationship or other affiliation between the mark's owner and the other party. The *Louis Vuitton* case, which appears later in the chapter, deals with trademark infringement. It also discusses many of the factors courts consider when determining whether the use is likely to cause confusion. A trademark owner who wins an infringement suit may obtain an injunction against uses of the mark that are likely to cause confusion. In addition, the owner may obtain money damages for provable injury resulting from the infringement, and sometimes the attributable profits realized by the infringing defendant.

Trademark Dilution Although trademark infringement is the usual legal theory employed when a mark owner seeks legal relief against one who used the mark without the owner's consent, trademark dilution—a legal theory to be explained more fully below—sometimes serves as an alternative to the standard claim of infringement. Roughly half the states have had laws recognizing the dilution doctrine for many years. Because of the geographic limitations inherent in state laws and because not all states have dilution statutes, trademark owners had long advocated enactment of a federal law recognizing dilution as a trademark rights theory. Congress finally obliged with the Federal Trademark Dilution Act of 1996 (FTDA), which was placed in the Lanham Act as § 43(c). However, a 2003 Supreme Court decision interpreting the FTDA made the statute less useful to trademark owners than it initially appeared to be. The Court concluded that in view of the FTDA's wording, proof of a § 43(c) violation required a showing of actual dilution of the plaintiff's mark rather than the likelihood of dilution required by state dilution laws. For trademark owners, the proof-of-actual-dilution requirement enhanced the difficulty of winning dilution cases under the federal statute.

Congress responded to the 2003 Supreme Court decision by enacting the Trademark Dilution Revision Act of 2006 (TDRA), which amended § 43(c) to state explicitly that a showing of likelihood of dilution was sufficient. Under the TDRA, one who makes a commercial use of a "famous mark" without the mark owner's consent faces liability if the use is "likely to cause dilution by blurring or dilution by tarnishment of the famous mark." The TDRA thus makes clear that there are two types of dilution (to be explained below): "dilution by blurring" and "dilution by tarnishment." In so providing, the TDRA responded to an expression of skepticism in the same 2003 Supreme Court decision over whether the tarnishment variety of dilution was contemplated by the federal law. Proof of a likelihood of either type of dilution satisfies the TDRA, assuming that the famous mark and commercial use elements are also met. Likelihood of confusion—the critical element in a trademark infringement case—need not be proven in a dilution case. Proof of competition between the plaintiff and the defendant is likewise unnecessary in a dilution case, as is proof of actual economic injury resulting from the defendant's actions.

According to the TDRA, a mark is "famous" if it is "widely recognized by the general consuming public." The TDRA goes on to define "dilution by blurring" as an "association arising from the similarity between a mark or trade name and a famous mark that impairs the distinctiveness of the famous mark." Also recognized by the FTDA (the TDRA's predecessor) and the patchwork quilt of state dilution laws, this type of dilution takes place when the defendant's use of the plaintiff's mark causes, or is likely to cause, the public to cease associating the mark solely with the plaintiff and instead to associate it with both the plaintiff and the defendant. When this occurs or appears likely to occur, the mark's distinctiveness as a clear identifier of the plaintiff is in danger of being blurred or whittled away—in other words, diluted—even if the public recognizes that the plaintiff and defendant are not affiliated and that they provide very different products or services. Consider a classic example: the dilution claim won by Polaroid (the camera company) against a small heating and air conditioning business whose chosen name, Polaraid, presented the danger of blurring the source-identification image conjured up by the Polaroid name. Clearly, however, dilution by blurring does not occur in every instance in which the plaintiff's mark and the defendant's version are quite similar, as Mead Data Central found out when it unsuccessfully

sought to prove that its LEXIS mark (for legal research services) was diluted by Toyota's use of LEXUS (for a luxury car model and division). For further discussion of the dilution by blurring theory, its potential application in appropriate cases, and its differences from the trademark infringement theory, see the *Louis Vuitton* case, which follows shortly.

The TDRA defines "dilution by tarnishment," the other type of dilution it recognizes, as an "association arising from the similarity between a mark or trade name and a famous mark that harms the reputation of the famous mark." This form of tarnishment is also recognized in state dilution laws. Although courts do not agree completely on what is necessary for likely tarnishment of a mark, various courts have concluded that the defendant's use of the plaintiff's mark in an unwholesome context—normally one suggesting illicit sexual or drug-related associations—may dilute a mark by tarnishing its reputation. The *Louis Vuitton* case contains a brief discussion of dilution by tarnishment.

Presumably to guard against overuse of the dilution theory, the TDRA states that certain uses cannot constitute dilution by blurring or dilution by tarnishment. The TDRA lists noncommercial uses and uses amounting to "news reporting and news commentary" in the protected category. In addition, the TDRA's exclusions from dilution liability apply to "[a]ny fair use" of a famous mark to identify or describe that mark or its owner, as opposed to a defendant's use of a version of the plaintiff's mark "as a designation of source for the [defendant's] own goods or services." These fair uses may include a defendant's references to the plaintiff's mark in the context of comparative advertising of the parties' respective goods or services, as well as a defendant's references to the plaintiff's mark in the course of "identifying and parodying, criticizing, or commenting upon the famous mark owner or the goods or services of the mark owner." In the *Louis Vuitton* case, the court interprets this parodist-protection provision in the TDRA and engages in further analysis of the role that parody may play when defendants seek to avoid dilution liability.

When the mark owner makes out a TDRA-based dilution claim, the standard (and normally sole) remedy is an injunction against the defendant's continued use of the diluting version of the plaintiff's mark. The same is true of successful dilution cases brought under state laws. The TDRA allows the prospect of recovering damages and the defendant's attributable profits only if the evidence reveals that the defendant willfully sought to harm the mark's reputation or to trade on the recognition associated with the mark.

The Global Business Environment

An American firm may enter the world market by licensing its product or service to a foreign manufacturer. In exchange for granting a license to the foreign licensee, the American licensor will receive royalties from the sale of the licensed product or service. Usually, the licensed product or service or the name under which it is sold will be protected by American intellectual property law, such as patent, trade secret, copyright, or trademark law. Because American intellectual property law does not protect the property outside the boundaries of the United States, a licensor needs to take steps to ensure that its intellectual property will acquire protection in the foreign nation. Otherwise, the licensor risks that a competitor may appropriate the intellectual property without penalty.

The World Trade Organization has attempted to increase the protection of intellectual property through passage of the Agreement on Trade-Related Aspects of Intellectual Property Rights (**TRIPS**). Effective in 1995, TRIPS covers patents, trade secrets, copyrights, and trademarks. It sets out minimum standards of intellectual property protection to be provided by each member nation. Some signatory nations, such as the United States, provide greater protection of intellectual property.

Patents and Trade Secrets

A patent filing must be made in each nation in which protection is desired. It is not especially difficult for a firm to acquire parallel patents in each of the major countries maintaining a patent system, because many countries (including the United States) are parties to the Paris Convention for the Protection of Industrial Property. This convention recognizes the date of the first filing in any nation as the filing date for all, but only if subsequent filings are in fact made within a year of the first filing.

When technology is not patented, either because it is not patentable or because a firm makes a business decision not to patent it, a licensor may control its use abroad under **trade secret** law. For example, an American firm can license its manufacturing know-how to a foreign manufacturer for use in a defined territory in return for promises to pay royalties and to keep the trade secret confidential.

Copyright

An American firm may license a foreign manufacturer to produce literary, artistic, or musical materials for which the firm holds an American copyright. For example, a computer software development firm may grant a license to a foreign manufacturer of software, or the American owner of copyrights protecting cartoon characters from the television program *The Simpsons* may license a Chinese firm to manufacture Homer, Marge, and Bart dolls.

There is no international copyright that automatically protects a copyrighted work everywhere in the world. Instead, copyright protection for a work must be secured under the laws of the individual nations in which protection is sought. International agreements, however, may smooth the way to copyright acquisition in many countries. The most notable is the Berne Convention, to which the United States and approximately 150 other nations subscribe. The Berne Convention guarantees that a work eligible for copyright in any signatory nation will be eligible for protection in all signatory nations. Although the Berne Convention does not completely standardize the copyright laws of the member nations, it does require each country's copyright laws to contain certain minimum guarantees of rights.

Another key aspect of the Berne Convention is its principle of *national treatment,* under which each signatory nation agrees to treat copyright owners from other subscribing countries according to the same rules it applies to copyright owners who are its own residents or citizens. Other international agreements to which the United States is a party operate in generally similar fashion. These include the Universal Copyright Convention and the World Intellectual Property Organization Copyright Treaty.

Trademarks

The holder of an American trademark may license the use of its trademark in a foreign nation. For example, McDonald's may license a French firm to use the McDonald's name and golden arches at a restaurant on the Champs-Élysées, or the holder of the Calvin Klein trademark may license a South Korean firm to manufacture Calvin Klein jeans.

An American trademark's owner, when licensing its product or services abroad, runs the risk of experiencing unwanted and largely uncontrollable uses of its trademark in a foreign market unless it has acquired trademark rights in that nation.

Trademark registrations normally must be made in each nation in which protection is desired. Parallel trademark registrations, however, may be made in compliance with the Paris Convention for the Protection of Industrial Property. Under the Paris Convention, the date of the first filing in any nation is the filing date for all nations, if the subsequent filings are made within six months of the first filing.

The European Union allows a single filing to be effective in all EU nations. An agreement known as the Madrid Protocol also permits a firm to register a trademark in all its signatory nations simultaneously by filing an application for registration in any signatory nation and with the World Intellectual Property Organization (WIPO) in Geneva. The United States joined the Madrid Protocol in 2003.

Louis Vuitton Malletier, SA v. Haute Diggity Dog, LLC
507 F.3d 252 (4th Cir. 2007)

Louis Vuitton Malletier, SA (LVM) is a well-known manufacturer of luxury luggage, leather goods, handbags, and accessories, which it markets and sells worldwide. In connection with the sale of its products, LVM has used certain widely recognized trademarks for many years. LVM has registered trademarks for LOUIS VUITTON (in connection with luggage and ladies' handbags), for a stylized monogram of LV (in connection with traveling bags and other goods), and for designs that combine the LV mark with images of stars, flowers, and circles (in connection with traveling bags and other products).

LVM's luggage, handbags, and other items featuring these marks are expensive. For instance, LVM's handbags cost $1,000 or more at retail and LVM's travel bags sometimes fall in the $5,000 range. LVM sells its products in LVM stores and in its own in-store boutiques that are contained within department stores. Although better known for its handbags and luggage, LVM also markets a limited selection of luxury pet accessories—collars, leashes, and dog carriers—which bear the above-described designs. These items range in price from approximately $200 to $1,600. LVM does not make dog toys.

Haute Diggity Dog, LLC, a Nevada company, manufactures and sells nationally—primarily through pet stores—a line of pet chew toys and beds whose names parody elegant high-end brands of products such as perfume, cars, shoes, sparkling wine, and handbags. In addition to Chewy Vuiton (LOUIS VUITTON), these include Chewnel No. 5 (Chanel No. 5), Furcedes (Mercedes), Jimmy Chew (Jimmy Choo), Dog Perignonn (Dom Perignon), Sniffany & Co. (Tiffany & Co.), and Dogior (Dior). The chew toys and pet beds are plush, made of polyester, and have a shape and design that loosely imitate the signature product of the targeted brand. They are mostly distributed and sold through pet stores. The dog toys generally sell for less than $20. Larger versions of some of Haute Diggity Dog's plush dog beds sell for more than $100.

Haute Diggity Dog's Chewy Vuiton dog toys loosely resemble miniature handbags and undisputedly evoke LVM handbags of similar shape, design, and color. Instead of the LOUIS VUITTON mark, the dog toy uses "Chewy Vuiton"; in lieu of the LV mark, it uses "CV"; and the other symbols and colors employed are imitations, but not exact ones, of those used in LVM's designs.

In view of the above facts, LVM sued Haute Diggity Dog in a federal district court, alleging claims of trademark infringement, trademark dilution, trade dress infringement, and copyright infringement. The district court granted Haute Diggity Dog's motion for summary judgment on all of LVM's claims. LVM appealed to the U.S. Court of Appeals for the Fourth Circuit.

Niemeyer, Circuit Judge

Trademark Infringement Claim

LVM contends that Haute Diggity Dog's marketing and sale of its Chewy Vuiton dog toys infringe its trademarks because the advertising and sale of the Chewy Vuiton [items] is likely to cause confusion. Haute Diggity Dog contends that [no] reasonable factfinder [could] conclude that there is a likelihood of confusion, because it successfully markets its products as parodies of famous marks such as those of LVM.

To prove trademark infringement, LVM must show (1) that it owns a valid and protectable mark; (2) that Haute Diggity Dog uses [the same mark or a substantially similar version] of that mark in commerce and without LVM's consent; and (3) that Haute Diggity Dog's use is likely to cause confusion. The validity . . . of LVM's marks [is] not at issue in this case, nor is the fact that Haute Diggity Dog uses a colorable imitation of LVM's mark. To determine whether the Chewy Vuiton product line creates a likelihood of confusion, we have identified several nonexclusive factors to consider: (1) the strength or distinctiveness of the plaintiff's mark; (2) the similarity of the two marks; (3) the similarity of the goods or services the marks identify; (4) the similarity of the facilities the two parties use in their businesses; (5) the similarity of the advertising used by the two parties; (6) the defendant's intent; and (7) actual confusion. *See Pizzeria Uno Corp. v. Temple,* 747 F.2d 1522, 1527 (4th Cir. 1984). These *Pizzeria Uno* factors are not always weighted equally, and not all factors are relevant in every case.

Because Haute Diggity Dog's arguments with respect to the *Pizzeria Uno* factors depend to a great extent on whether its products and marks are successful parodies, we consider first whether Haute Diggity Dog's products, marks, and trade dress are indeed successful parodies of LVM's marks and trade dress. For trademark purposes, "[a] 'parody' is defined as a simple form of entertainment conveyed by juxtaposing the irreverent representation of the trademark with the idealized image created by the mark's owner." *People for the Ethical Treatment of Animals v. Doughney ("PETA"),* 263 F.3d 359, 366 (4th Cir. 2001). [According to *PETA,*] "[a] parody must convey two simultaneous—and contradictory—messages: that it is the original, but also that it is *not* the original and is instead a parody." Thus, "[a] parody relies upon a difference from the original mark, presumably a humorous difference, in order to produce its desired effect." *Jordache Enterprises, Inc. v. Hogg Wyld, Ltd.,* 828 F.2d 1482, 1486 (10th Cir. 1987) (finding the use of "Lardashe" jeans for larger women to be a successful and permissible parody of "Jordache" jeans).

[W]e agree with the district court that the Chewy Vuiton dog toys are successful parodies of LVM handbags and the LVM marks and trade dress used in connection with the marketing and sale of those handbags. The dog toy is shaped roughly like a handbag; its name Chewy Vuiton sounds like and rhymes with LOUIS VUITTON; its monogram CV mimics LVM's LV mark; the repetitious design clearly imitates the design on the LVM handbag; and the coloring is similar. In short, the dog toy is a small, plush imitation of an LVM handbag carried by women, which invokes the marks and design of the handbag, albeit irreverently and incompletely. No one can doubt that LVM handbags are the target of the imitation.

At the same time, no one can doubt also that the Chewy Vuiton dog toy is not the "idealized image" of the mark created by LVM. The differences are immediate, beginning with the fact that the Chewy Vuiton product is a dog toy, not [a] luxury handbag. The toys are inexpensive; the handbags are expensive and marketed to be expensive. And, of course, [because it is] a dog toy, one must buy it with pet supplies and cannot buy it at an exclusive LVM store or boutique within a department store. In short, the Chewy Vuiton dog toy undoubtedly and deliberately conjures up the famous LVM marks and trade dress, but at the same time, it communicates that it is not the LVM product.

Finally, the juxtaposition of the similar and dissimilar—the irreverent representation and the idealized image of an LVM handbag—immediately conveys a joking and amusing parody. The furry little Chewy Vuiton imitation, as something to be *chewed by a dog,* pokes fun at the elegance and expensiveness of an LVM handbag, which must *not* be chewed by a dog. The LVM handbag is provided for the most elegant and well-to-do celebrity, to proudly display to the public and the press, whereas the imitation Chewy Vuiton "handbag" is designed to mock the celebrity and be used by a dog. The dog toy irreverently presents haute couture as an object for casual canine destruction. The satire is unmistakable. This parody is enhanced by the fact that Chewy Vuiton dog toys are sold with similar parodies of other famous and expensive brands—"Chewnel No. 5" targeting "Chanel No. 5"; "Dog Perignonn" targeting "Dom Perignon"; and "Sniffany & Co. "targeting "Tiffany & Co."

Finding [as we do] that Haute Diggity Dog's parody is successful, however, does not end the inquiry into whether Haute Diggity Dog's Chewy Vuiton products create a likelihood of confusion. The finding of a successful parody only influences the way in which the *Pizzeria Uno* factors are applied.

As to the first *Pizzeria Uno* factor, the parties agree that LVM's marks are strong and widely recognized. LVM maintains that a strong, famous mark is entitled, as a matter of law, to broad protection. While it is true that finding a mark to be strong and famous usually favors the plaintiff in a trademark infringement case, the opposite may be true when a legitimate claim of parody is involved. It is a matter of common sense that the strength of a famous mark allows consumers immediately to perceive the target of the parody, while simultaneously allowing them to recognize the changes to the mark that make the parody funny or biting. [P]recisely because LOUIS VUITTON is so strong a mark and so well-recognized as a luxury handbag brand from LVM, consumers readily recognize that when they see a Chewy Vuiton pet toy, they see a parody. Thus, the strength of LVM's marks in this case does not help LVM establish a likelihood of confusion.

With respect to the second *Pizzeria Uno* factor, the similarities between the marks, the usage by Haute Diggity Dog again converts what might be a problem for Haute Diggity Dog into a disfavored conclusion for LVM. Haute Diggity Dog concedes that its marks are and were designed to be somewhat similar to LVM's marks. But that is the essence of a parody. . . . While a trademark parody necessarily copies enough of the original design to bring it to mind as a target, a successful parody also distinguishes itself and, because of the implicit message communicated by the parody, allows the consumer to appreciate it. [Here, the] differences are sufficiently obvious and the parody sufficiently blatant that a consumer encountering a Chewy Vuiton dog toy would not mistake its source or sponsorship on the basis of mark similarity.

Nor does LVM find support from the third *Pizzeria Uno* factor, the similarity of the products themselves. It is obvious that a Chewy Vuiton plush imitation handbag, which does not open and is manufactured as a dog toy, is not a LOUIS VUITTON handbag sold by LVM. Even LVM's most proximate products—dog collars, leashes, and pet carriers—are fashion accessories, not dog toys.

The fourth and fifth *Pizzeria Uno* factors [pertain] to the similarity of facilities and advertising channels. . . . LVM products are sold exclusively through its own stores or its own boutiques within department stores. It also sells its products on the Internet through an LVM-authorized website. In contrast, Chewy Vuiton products are sold primarily through traditional and Internet pet stores, although they might also be sold in some department stores. As a general matter, however, there is little overlap in the individual retail stores selling the brands. Likewise with respect to advertising, there is little or no overlap. LVM markets LOUIS VUITTON handbags through high-end fashion magazines, [whereas] Chewy Vuiton products are advertised primarily through pet-supply channels. The overlap in facilities and advertising demonstrated by the record is so minimal as to be practically nonexistent. The *de minimis* overlap lends insignificant support to LVM on this factor.

The sixth factor, relating to Haute Diggity Dog's intent, again is neutralized by the fact that Haute Diggity Dog markets a parody of LVM products. As other courts have recognized, "[a]n intent to parody is not an intent to confuse the public." *Jordache,* 828 F.2d at 1486. Despite Haute Diggity Dog's obvious intent to profit from its use of parodies, this action does not amount to a bad-faith intent to create consumer confusion. To the contrary, the intent is to do just the opposite—to evoke a humorous, satirical association that *distinguishes* the products. This factor does not favor LVM.

On the actual confusion factor, it is well established that no actual confusion is required to prove a case of trademark infringement, although the presence of actual confusion can be persuasive evidence relating to a likelihood of confusion. LVM conceded in the district court that there was no evidence of actual confusion. . . . We conclude that this factor favors Haute Diggity Dog.

Recognizing that Chewy Vuiton is an obvious parody and applying the *Pizzeria Uno* factors, we conclude that LVM has failed to demonstrate any likelihood of confusion. Accordingly, we [agree that the district court correctly ruled] in favor of Haute Diggity Dog on the issue of trademark infringement.

Trademark Dilution Claim

LVM also contends that Haute Diggity Dog's advertising, sale, and distribution of the Chewy Vuiton dog toys dilutes its . . . famous and distinctive [marks]. Claims for trademark dilution are authorized by the Trademark Dilution Revision Act of 2006 ("TDRA"), which provides in relevant part:

> Subject to the principles of equity, the owner of a *famous* mark . . . shall be entitled to an injunction against another person who . . . commences use of a mark or trade name in commerce that is likely to cause *dilution by blurring* or *dilution by tarnishment* of the famous mark, regardless of the presence or absence of actual or likely confusion, of competition, or of actual economic injury.

15 U.S.C. § 1125(c)(1) (emphasis added). A mark is "famous" when it is "widely recognized by the general consuming public of the United States as a designation of source of the goods or services of the mark's owner." § 1125(c)(2)(A). [T]he TDRA defines "dilution by blurring" as the "association arising from the similarity between a mark or trade name and a famous mark that impairs the distinctiveness of the famous mark." § 1125(c)(2)(B). It defines "dilution by tarnishment" as the "association arising from the similarity between a mark or trade name and a famous mark that harms the reputation of the famous mark." § 1125(c)(2)(C).

In the context of blurring, distinctiveness refers to the ability of the famous mark uniquely to identify a single source and thus maintain its selling power. In proving a dilution claim under the TDRA, the plaintiff need not show actual or likely confusion, the presence of competition, or actual economic injury. The TDRA creates three defenses based on the defendant's (1) "fair use" (with exceptions); (2) "news reporting and news commentary"; and (3) "noncommercial use." *Id.* § 1125(c)(3).

We address first LVM's claim for dilution by blurring. The first three elements of a trademark dilution claim are not at issue in this case. LVM owns famous marks that are distinctive; Haute Diggity Dog has commenced using Chewy Vuiton, CV, and designs and colors that are allegedly diluting LVM's marks; and the similarity between Haute Diggity Dog's marks and LVM's marks gives rise to an association between the marks, albeit a parody. The issue for resolution is whether the association between Haute Diggity Dog's marks and LVM's marks is likely to impair the distinctiveness of LVM's famous marks.

LVM suggests that any use by a third person of an imitation of its famous marks dilutes the famous marks as a matter of law. This contention misconstrues the TDRA. To determine whether a junior mark is likely to dilute a famous mark through blurring, the TDRA directs the court to consider all factors relevant to the issue, including six factors that are enumerated in the statute:

(i) The degree of similarity between the mark or trade name and the famous mark.

(ii) The degree of inherent or acquired distinctiveness of the famous mark.

(iii) The extent to which the owner of the famous mark is engaging in substantially exclusive use of the mark.

(iv) The degree of recognition of the famous mark.

(v) Whether the user of the mark or trade name intended to create an association with the famous mark.

(vi) Any actual association between the mark or trade name and the famous mark.

15 U.S.C. § 1125(c)(2)(B).

We begin by noting that parody is not automatically a complete *defense* to a claim of dilution by blurring where the defendant uses the parody as its own designation of source, i.e., *as a trademark*. Although the TDRA does provide that fair use is a complete defense and allows that a parody can be considered fair use, it does not extend the fair use defense to parodies used as a trademark. [The statute provides that uses] "not . . . actionable as dilution by blurring or dilution by tarnishment [include] [a]ny fair use . . . *other than as a designation of source for the person's own goods or services,* including use in connection with . . . *parodying.* . . ." 15 U.S.C. § 1125(c)(3)(A)(ii) (emphasis added). Under the statute's plain language, parodying a famous mark is protected by the fair use defense . . . if the parody is *not* "a designation of source for the person's own goods or services."

The TDRA, however, does not require a court to ignore the existence of a parody that is used as a trademark, and it does not preclude a court from considering parody as part of the circumstances to be considered for determining whether the plaintiff has made out a claim for dilution by blurring. Indeed, the statute permits a court to consider "all relevant factors," including the six factors supplied in § 1125(c)(2)(B).

Thus, it would appear that a defendant's use of a mark as a parody is relevant to the overall question of whether the defendant's use is likely to impair the famous mark's distinctiveness. Moreover, the fact that the defendant uses its marks as a parody is specifically relevant to several of the listed factors. For example, factor (v) (whether the defendant intended to create an association with the famous mark) and factor (vi) (whether there exists an actual association between the defendant's mark and the famous mark) directly invite inquiries into the defendant's intent in using the parody, the defendant's actual use of the parody, and the effect that its use has on the famous mark. While a parody intentionally creates an association with the famous mark in order to be a parody, it also intentionally communicates, if it is successful, that it is *not* the famous mark, but rather a satire of the famous mark. That the defendant is using its mark as a parody is therefore relevant in the consideration of these statutory factors.

Similarly, factors (i), (ii), and (iv)—the degree of similarity between the two marks, the degree of distinctiveness of the famous mark, and its recognizability—are directly implicated by consideration of the fact that the defendant's mark is a successful parody. Indeed, by making the famous mark an object of the parody, a successful parody might actually enhance the famous mark's distinctiveness by making it an icon. The brunt of the joke becomes yet more famous. In sum, while a defendant's use of a parody as a mark does not support a "fair use" defense, it may be considered in determining whether the plaintiff-owner of a famous mark has proved its claim that the defendant's use of a parody mark is likely to impair the distinctiveness of the famous mark.

[W]hen considering factors (ii), (iii), and (iv), it is readily apparent . . . that LVM's marks are distinctive, famous, and strong. While the establishment of these facts satisfies essential elements of LVM's dilution claim, the facts impose on LVM an increased burden to demonstrate that the distinctiveness of its famous marks is likely to be impaired by a successful parody. Even as Haute Diggity Dog's parody mimics the famous mark, it communicates simultaneously that it is not the famous mark, but is only satirizing it. And because the famous mark is particularly strong and distinctive, it becomes more likely that a parody will not impair the distinctiveness of the mark. In short, as Haute Diggity Dog's Chewy Vuiton marks are a successful parody, we conclude that they will not blur the distinctiveness of the famous mark as a unique identifier of its source.

It is important to note, however, that this might not be true if the parody is so similar to the famous mark that it likely could be construed as actual use of the famous mark itself. If Haute Diggity Dog used the actual marks of LVM (as a parody or otherwise), it could dilute LVM's marks by blurring, regardless of whether Haute Diggity Dog's use was confusingly similar, whether it was in competition with LVM, or whether LVM sustained actual injury. Thus, "the use of DUPONT shoes, BUICK aspirin, and KODAK pianos would be actionable" under the TDRA because the unauthorized use of the famous marks *themselves* on unrelated goods might diminish the capacity of these trademarks to distinctively identify a single source. [Citation of authority omitted.]

But in this case, Haute Diggity Dog mimicked the famous marks; it did not come so close to them as to destroy the success of its parody and, more importantly, to diminish the LVM marks' capacity to identify a single source. In a similar vein, when considering factors (v) and (vi), it becomes apparent that Haute Diggity Dog intentionally associated its marks, but only partially and certainly imperfectly, so as to convey the simultaneous message that it was not in fact a source of LVM products. [W]e readily [conclude] that LVM has failed to make out a case of trademark dilution by blurring.

LVM's claim for dilution by tarnishment does not require an extended discussion. To establish [this] claim . . . , LVM must show . . . that Haute Diggity Dog's use of the Chewy Vuiton mark on dog toys harms the reputation of [LVM's] marks. LVM argues that the possibility that a dog could choke on a Chewy Vuiton toy causes this harm. It relies only on speculation about whether a dog could choke on the chew toys and a logical concession that a $10 dog toy made in China was of "inferior quality" to the $1,190 Louis Vuitton handbag. There is no record support, however, [indicating] that any dog has choked on a pet chew toy such as a Chewy Vuiton toy. [Nor is] there any basis from which to conclude that a dog would likely choke on such a toy. We agree with the district court that LVM failed to demonstrate a claim for dilution by tarnishment.

Other Claims

LVM raises [other] claims premised on the same basic facts. [It] argues that the district court erred in failing to address LVM's trade dress claims. Although the district court did not explicitly discuss the trade dress issue, we find that this reflects economy rather than error. LVM's trade dress claims under § 43(a) of the Lanham Act, 15 U.S.C. § 1125(a)(l), and under Virginia common law are based on essentially the same facts as its trademark infringement claims. Haute Diggity Dog does not challenge LVM's claim that its trade dress is protectable. The only question before the court was whether confusion was likely. But the same *Pizzeria Uno* likelihood-of-confusion factors used for trademark infringement claims are applied to trade dress claims, and the two issues rise or fall together. Consequently, our conclusion affirming the district court that no confusion is likely to result with regard to LVM's trademarks is sufficient also to dispose of LVM's trade dress claims as well.

LVM [also] argues that the district court erred in finding that Haute Diggity Dog's use of "CV" and the background design was a fair use of [one of] LVM's copyrighted designs. Because LVM attempts to use a copyright claim to pursue what is at its core a trademark and trade dress infringement claim, application of the fair-use factors under the Copyright Act to these facts is awkward. Nonetheless, after examining the record, we agree with the district court that Haute Diggity Dog's use as a parody of certain altered elements of LVM's design does not support a claim for copyright infringement.

District court's grant of summary judgment in favor of Haute Diggity Dog affirmed.

Trade Secrets

The law provides two partially overlapping means of protecting creative inventions. Owners of such inventions may go public and obtain monopoly patent rights. As an alternative, they may sometimes keep the invention secret and rely on trade secrets law to protect it.

The policies underlying patent protection and trade secrets protection differ. The general aim of patent law is to encourage the creation and disclosure of inventions by granting the patentee a temporary monopoly in the patented invention in exchange for his making it public.

Trade secrets, however, are nonpublic by definition. Although protecting trade secrets may stimulate creative activity, it also keeps the information from becoming public knowledge. Thus, the main justification for trade secrets protection is simply to preserve certain standards of commercial morality.

Definition of a Trade Secret A trade secret can be defined as any secret formula, pattern, process, program, device, method, technique, or compilation of information used in the owner's business, if it gives its owner an advantage over competitors who do not know it

CYBERLAW IN ACTION

Trademark infringement principles sometimes govern conflicts between one party's claim of trademark rights and another's claim of rights over a World Wide Web domain name. Such disputes sometimes raise dilution issues as well.

In a 1999 enactment, Congress paid special attention to the trademark rights–domain name rights conflict by enacting the Anticybersquatting Consumer Protection Act (hereinafter "ACPA"). The ACPA authorizes a civil action in favor of a trademark owner against any person who, having a "bad faith intent to profit" from the owner's mark, registers, sells, purchases, licenses, or otherwise uses a domain name that is identical or confusingly similar to the owner's mark (or would dilute the mark, if it is famous). Among the factors listed in the ACPA as relevant to the existence of bad faith intent to profit are a defendant's intent to divert consumers from the mark owner's online location to a site that could harm the mark's goodwill, and a defendant's offer to sell the domain name to the mark owner without having used, or intended to use, the domain name in the offering of goods or services.

If the trademark owner wins a cybersquatting action, the court may order the forfeiture or cancellation of the domain name or may order that it be transferred to the mark owner. The successful trademark owner may also recover actual damages as well as the cybersquatter's attributable profits. Borrowing the statutory damages concept from the Copyright Act, the ACPA provides that in lieu of actual damages plus profits, the trademark owner may elect to recover statutory damages falling within a range of $1,000 to $100,000 per domain name, "as the court considers just."

Many cases in which a trademark owner complains about another party's registration of a domain name have been submitted to arbitration, rather than to a court, in recent years. When a party registers an Internet address with the Internet Corporation for Assigned Names and Numbers, the registrant must agree to submit to arbitration in the event that a trademark owner claims a right to the domain name. The World Intellectual Property Organization is a leading provider of arbitrators for this process.

or use it.[4] Examples include chemical formulas, computer software, manufacturing processes, designs for machines, and customer lists. To be protectible, a trade secret must usually have sufficient value or originality to provide an actual or potential competitive advantage. It need not possess the novelty required for patent protection, however.

The *North Atlantic Instruments* case, which follows shortly, considers factors courts may examine when determining whether a trade secret exists. As some of the factors suggest, a trade secret must actually be *secret.* A substantial measure of secrecy is necessary, but it need not be absolute. Thus, information that becomes public knowledge or becomes generally known in the industry cannot be a trade secret. Similarly, information that is reasonably discoverable by proper means may not be protected. "Proper means" include independent invention of the secret, observation of a publicly displayed product, the owner's advertising, published literature, product analysis, and reverse engineering (starting with a legitimately acquired product and working backward to discover how it was developed).

In addition, a firm claiming a trade secret must usually show that it took *reasonable measures to ensure secrecy.* Examples include advising employees about the secret's secrecy, limiting access to the secret on a need-to-know basis, requiring those given access to sign a nondisclosure agreement, disclosing the secret only on a confidential basis, and controlling access to an office or plant. Computer software licensing agreements commonly forbid the licensee to copy the program except for backup and archival purposes, require the licensee and its employees to sign confidentiality agreements, call for those employees to use the program only in the course of their jobs, and require the licensee to use the program only in a central processing unit. Because the owner must only make *reasonable* efforts to ensure secrecy, however, she need not adopt extreme measures to block every ingenious form of industrial espionage.

Ownership and Transfer of Trade Secrets

The owner of a trade secret is usually the person who developed it or the business under whose auspices it was generated. Establishing the ownership of a trade secret can pose problems, however, when an employee develops a secret in the course of her employment. In such cases, courts often find the *employer* to be the owner if (1) the employee was hired to do creative work related to the secret, (2) the employee agreed not to divulge or use trade secrets, or (3) other employees contributed to the development of the secret. Even when the employee owns the secret, the employer still may obtain a royalty-free license to use it through the shop right doctrine discussed in the section on patents.

The owner of a trade secret may transfer rights in the secret to third parties. This may occur by assignment (in which case the owner loses title) or by license (in which case the owner retains title but allows the transferee certain uses of the secret).

Misappropriation of Trade Secrets

Misappropriation of a trade secret can occur in various ways, most of which involve *disclosure* or *use* of the secret. For example, misappropriation liability occurs when the secret is disclosed or used by one who did one of the following:

1. Acquired it by *improper means.* Improper means include theft, trespass, wiretapping, spying, bugging, bribery, fraud, impersonation, and eavesdropping.

2. Acquired it from a party who *is known or should be known* to have obtained it by improper means. For example, a freelance industrial spy might obtain one firm's trade secrets by improper means and sell them to the firm's competitors. If those competitors know or have reason to know that the spy obtained the secrets by improper means, they are liable for misappropriation along with the spy.

3. *Breached a duty of confidentiality regarding the secret.* If an employer owns a trade secret, for example, an employee is generally bound not to use or disclose it during his employment or thereafter.[5] The *North Atlantic Instruments* case, which follows shortly, presents an application of this rule. The employee may, however, utilize general knowledge and skills acquired during her employment.

Remedies for misappropriation of a trade secret include damages, which may involve both the actual loss caused by the misappropriation and the defendant's unjust enrichment. In some states, punitive damages are awarded for willful and malicious misappropriations. Also, an injunction may be issued against actual or threatened misappropriations.

---

[4]This definition comes mainly from *Restatement (Third) of Unfair Competition* § 39 (1995), with some additions from *Uniform Trade Secrets Act* § 1(4) (1985). Many states have adopted the Uniform Trade Secrets Act (UTSA) in some form. The discussion in this chapter is a composite of the *Restatement*'s and the UTSA's rules.

[5]This is an application of the agent's duty of loyalty, which is discussed in Chapter 35.

North Atlantic Instruments, Inc. v. Haber   188 F.3d 38 (2d Cir. 1999)

North Atlantic Instruments, Inc., manufactured electronic equipment used on ships, tanks, and aircraft. In August 1994, North Atlantic acquired Transmagnetics, Inc. (TMI), which designed, manufactured, and sold customized electronic devices to a limited number of engineers in the aerospace and high-tech industries. At the time North Atlantic acquired TMI, Fred Haber was a one-third owner of TMI, as well as its president and head of sales. This position allowed Haber to develop extensive client contacts. North Atlantic conditioned its agreement to acquire TMI on Haber's continuing to work for North Atlantic in a role similar to the role he had played at TMI.

The specialized nature of TMI's business made the identity of the relatively small number of engineers who required its products especially crucial to its business success. Even in companies employing thousands of engineers, a very small number of those engineers—sometimes only two—might need the technology produced by TMI. The identity and needs of that small number of engineers (i.e., TMI's client contacts) would have been very difficult for any company to derive on its own. TMI's list of client contacts was among the intangible assets for which North Atlantic paid when it acquired TMI.

North Atlantic retained Haber as president of its new TMI division. An employment agreement between North Atlantic and Haber ran until July 31, 1997. Its terms obligated Haber not to disclose North Atlantic's customer lists, trade secrets, or other confidential information, either during his employment by North Atlantic or after that employment ceased. As president of the TMI division, Haber had access through desktop and laptop computers to information about North Atlantic's technology and customer bases, including lists of clients and information about their individual product needs and purchases. In July 1997, Haber left North Atlantic to join Apex Signal Corp., which manufactured products targeted toward the same niche market as North Atlantic's TMI division. According to North Atlantic, Apex began targeting North Atlantic's customer base, with Haber allegedly asking clients he had dealt with at North Atlantic and TMI to do business with Apex. North Atlantic also contended that Haber had taken its confidential client information with him when he joined Apex.

North Atlantic sued Haber and Apex for misappropriation of trade secrets and requested a preliminary injunction. The federal district court referred the injunction request to a magistrate, who conducted an extensive hearing and issued a report recommending issuance of the injunction. The district court adopted the magistrate's report and preliminarily enjoined Haber and Apex from using the individual client contacts Haber had developed at North Atlantic and TMI. Haber and Apex appealed.

Straub, Circuit Judge

To succeed on a claim for the misappropriation of trade secrets under New York law, a party must demonstrate: (1) that it possessed a trade secret, and (2) that the defendants used the trade secret in breach of an agreement, confidential relationship, or duty, or as a result of discovery by improper means.

A trade secret is any formula, pattern, device, or compilation of information which is used in one's business, and which gives the owner an opportunity to obtain an advantage over competitors who do not know or use it. [Precedent cases indicate that a] customer list developed by a business through substantial effort and kept in confidence may be treated as a trade secret and protected at the owner's instance against disclosure to a competitor, provided the information it contains is not otherwise readily ascertainable.

The Magistrate Judge concluded that the list of *companies* to which North Atlantic's TMI division sold was not a trade secret. By contrast, [he] determined that the *identities of individual contact people* with whom Haber dealt while at North Atlantic or TMI were protectable trade secrets. The Magistrate Judge . . . determin[ed] that information on specific contact people was

not readily available to others in the industry. That is, Haber generated the list of specific contact people—the people who required the customized technology produced by TMI and North Atlantic's TMI division—over the 50 years he had worked in the industry, more than half of which he spent at TMI. The Magistrate Judge relied . . . on the testimony of North Atlantic's chief executive, who described the needle-in-the-haystack character of the search for the handful of engineers in companies of 100,000 employees who might have a use for one of North Atlantic's customized products.

The Magistrate Judge [also] conclud[ed] that North Atlantic took numerous appropriate measures to prevent unauthorized disclosure of the information contained in its list of client contacts. [These measures included the use of nondisclosure provisions in employment agreements and other access restrictions.] The Magistrate Judge next assessed the value of the list of client contacts and the energy and effort necessary to create it. [H]e pointed to the testimony by North Atlantic's chief executive stating that "in the technology business, the most expensive thing to replicate is your relationships with your customers." [In addition,] the Magistrate Judge concluded that the client contact list assembled over Haber's years at TMI and North Atlantic's TMI division could probably be duplicated, but only with great difficulty.

We hold that the District Court did not err in adopting the Magistrate Judge's extensive and detailed factual determination that the identity of North Atlantic's client contacts was a protectable trade secret. Numerous cases applying New York law have held that where, as here, it would be difficult to duplicate a customer list because it reflected individual customer preferences, trade secret protection should apply.

We next consider whether the defendants' use of a trade secret—specifically the list of client contacts—was in breach of a duty. Both this Circuit and numerous New York courts have held that an agent has a duty not to use confidential knowledge acquired in his employment in competition with his principal. Such a duty exists as well after the employment is terminated as during its continuance . . . and is implied in every contract of employment. [Moreover, the employment agreement between North Atlantic and Haber] provided expressly that Haber had a comparable duty to maintain the confidentiality of TMI's and North Atlantic's trade secrets. In this way, [the employment agreement] makes explicit an employee's implied duties under New York law with respect to confidential information.

[A]t the hearing before the Magistrate Judge, North Atlantic produced a printout of confidential client information from North Atlantic's customer database, printed by Haber on September 5, 1997—over one month after he had left North Atlantic—and found in Apex's files. Haber clearly used the information on the day he printed the file. That day, he sent a fax to a contact listed on the form. Testimony at the hearing suggested that it would have been impossible for Haber to have generated th[e] information [in the file printed on September 5, 1997] unless he had taken files with him when he left North Atlantic.

Based on the facts in the record, it is clear that Haber violated the duties imposed both by the employment agreement and by New York's laws. [T]he District Court properly concluded that North Atlantic has demonstrated a likelihood of success on the merits of its misappropriation of trade secrets claim. Finally, [w]e have held [in a prior case] that the loss of trade secrets cannot be measured in money damages because a trade secret, once lost, is, of course, lost forever. We conclude that North Atlantic would be irreparably harmed in the absence of an injunction.

Decision of District Court affirmed.

Commercial Torts

In addition to the intentional torts discussed in Chapter 6, other intentional torts involve business or commercial competition. These torts may help promote innovation by protecting creative businesses against certain competitive abuses. Their main aim, however, is simply to uphold certain minimum standards of commercial morality.

Injurious Falsehood
Injurious falsehood also goes by names such as product disparagement, slander of title, and trade libel. This tort involves the publication of false statements that disparage another's business, property, or title to property, and thus harm her economic interests. One common kind of injurious falsehood involves false statements that disparage either a person's *property rights* in land, things, or intangibles, or their *quality.* The property rights in question include virtually all legally protected property interests that can be sold; examples include leases, mineral rights, trademarks, copyrights, and corporate stock. Injurious falsehood also includes false statements that harm another's economic interests even though they do not disparage property or

property rights as such. For example, the seller of a bodybuilding program was held to have stated a valid claim for injurious falsehood against a book publisher regarding a false statement that the plaintiff's program was isometric in nature. The harm to the plaintiff's economic interest in the sale of its bodybuilding program stemmed from the juxtaposition of the untrue statement about the program with a statement concerning supposed dangers of isometric exercise programs.

Elements and Damages   In injurious falsehood cases, the plaintiff must prove that the defendant made a false statement of the sort just described, and that the statement was communicated to a third party. The degree of fault required for liability is unclear. Sources often say that the standard is malice, but formulations of this differ. The *Restatement* requires either knowledge that the statement is false, or reckless disregard as to its truth or falsity. There is usually no liability for false statements that are made negligently and in good faith.

The plaintiff must also prove that the false statement played a substantial part in causing him to suffer *special damages.* These may include losses resulting from the diminished value of disparaged property; the expense of measures for counteracting the false statement (e.g., advertising or litigation expenses); losses resulting from the breach of an existing contract by a third party; and the loss of prospective business. In cases involving the loss of prospective business, the plaintiff is usually required to show that some specific person or persons refused to buy because of the disparagement. This rule is often relaxed, however, where these losses are difficult to prove.

The special damages that the plaintiff is required to prove are his usual—and typically his only—remedy in injurious falsehood cases. Damages for personal injury or emotional distress, for instance, are generally not recoverable. However, punitive damages and injunctive relief are sometimes obtainable.

Injurious Falsehood and Defamation   Injurious falsehood may or may not overlap with the tort of defamation discussed in Chapter 6. Statements impugning a businessperson's character or conduct are probably defamatory. If, on the other hand, the false statement is limited to the plaintiff's business, property, or economic interests, his normal claim is for injurious falsehood. Both claims are possible when the injurious falsehood implies something about the plaintiff's character and affects his overall reputation. An example is a defendant's false allegation that the plaintiff knowingly sells dangerous products to children. As in defamation cases, statements of pure opinion (as opposed to false statements of supposed fact) do not give rise to injurious falsehood liability.

Defamation law's absolute and conditional privileges generally apply in injurious falsehood cases.[6] Certain other privileges protect defendants who are sued for injurious falsehood. For example, a rival claimant may in good faith disparage another's property rights by asserting his own competing rights. Similarly, one may make a good faith allegation that a competitor is infringing one's patent, copyright, or trademark. Finally, a person may sometimes make unfavorable comparisons between her product and that of a competitor. This privilege is generally limited to sales talk asserting the superiority of one's own product and does not cover unfavorable statements about a competitor's product.

Interference with Contractual Relations   In a lawsuit for intentional interference with contractual relations, one party to a contract claims that the defendant's interference with the other party's performance

of the contract wrongly caused the plaintiff to lose the benefit of that performance. One can interfere with the performance of a contract by causing a party to repudiate it, or by wholly or partly preventing that party's performance. The means of interference can range from mere persuasion to threatened or actual violence. The agreement whose performance is impeded, however, must be an *existing* contract. This includes contracts that are voidable, unenforceable, or subject to contract defenses, but *not* void bargains, contracts that are illegal on public policy grounds, or contracts to marry. Finally, the defendant must have *intended* to cause the breach; there is usually no liability for negligent contract interferences.

Even if the plaintiff proves these threshold requirements, the defendant is liable only if his behavior was *improper.* Despite the flexible, case-by-case nature of such determinations, a few generalizations about improper interference are possible.

1. If the contract's performance was blocked by such clearly improper means as threats of physical violence, misrepresentations, defamatory statements, bribery, harassment, or bad faith civil or criminal actions, the defendant usually is liable. Liability is also likely where the interference was motivated *solely* by malice, spite, or a simple desire to meddle.

2. If his means and motives are legitimate, a defendant generally escapes liability when his contract interference is in the *public interest*—for example, when he informs an airport that an air traffic controller habitually uses hallucinogenic drugs. The same is true when the defendant acts to *protect a person for whose welfare she is responsible*—for example, when a mother induces a private school to discharge a diseased student who could infect her children.

3. A contract interference resulting from the defendant's good faith effort to protect her own *existing* legal or economic interests usually does not create liability so long as appropriate means are used. For example, a landowner can probably induce his tenant to breach a sublease to a party whose business detracts from the land's value. However, business parties generally cannot interfere with existing contract rights merely to further some *prospective* competitive advantage. For example, a seller cannot entice its competitors' customers to break existing contracts with those competitors.

The *Carey Station Village* case, which follows shortly, explores the issues surrounding a defendant's privilege to interfere with a contract in order to protect his own interests. In addition, *Carey Station Village* reveals that

---

[6]Chapter 6 discusses those privileges.

liability for interference with contractual relations will not attach to one who is not a "stranger" to the relationship at issue.

4. Finally, competitors are unlikely to incur liability where, as is still often true of employment contracts, the agreement interfered with is *terminable at will.* The reason is that in such cases, the plaintiff has only an expectancy that the contract will continue, and not a right to have it continued. Thus, a firm that hires away its competitors' at-will employees usually escapes liability.

The basic measure of damages for intentional interference with contractual relations is the value of the lost contract performance. Some courts also award compensatory damages reasonably linked to the interference (including emotional distress and damage to reputation). Sometimes the plaintiff may obtain an injunction prohibiting further interferences.

Interference with Prospective Advantage The rules and remedies for intentional interference with prospective advantage parallel those for interference with contractual relations. The main difference is that the former tort involves interferences with *prospective* relations rather than existing contracts. The protected future relations are mainly potential contractual relations of a business or commercial sort. Liability for interference with such relations requires intent; negligence does not suffice.

The "improper interference" factors weighed in interference-with-contract cases generally apply to interference with prospective advantage as well. One difference, however, is that interference with prospective advantage can be justified if (1) the plaintiff and the defendant are in competition for the prospective relation with which the defendant interferes; (2) the defendant's purpose is at least partly competitive; (3) the defendant does not use such improper means as physical threats, misrepresentations, and bad faith lawsuits; and (4) the defendant's behavior does not create an unlawful restraint of trade under the antitrust laws or other regulations. Thus, a competitor ordinarily can win customers by offering lower prices and attract suppliers by offering higher prices. Unless this is otherwise illegal, he can also refuse to deal with suppliers or buyers who also deal with his competitors.

Carey Station Village Homeowners Association, Inc. v. Carey Station Village, Inc.
602 S.E.2d 233 (Ga. App. 2004)

Carey Station Village, Inc., referred to below as "the developer," purchased real estate near a Georgia lake in 1987. The developer planned to create a large residential subdivision known as Carey Station Village. Although the developer continued to own a number of the lots in the subdivision, it relinquished control of the subdivision to Carey Station Village Homeowners Association, Inc., referred to below as "the association," in 1994. In 1999, the developer began to sell off some of the lots whose ownership it had retained. These lots had been improved with double-wide, modular homes. The developer provided owner financing for a number of the purchases. Within the first three months of advertising the lots for sale, the developer had sold over one-half of the lots. Later, however, the developer was required to foreclose on 16 of the 21 parcels of property it had sold.

The association brought suit against the developer in 2001 to recover dues and assessments it claimed were owed by the developer in regard to the developer's remaining lots. The developer and the association had been involved in an earlier lawsuit that resulted in a settlement in which the developer forgave a promissory note from the association, and in exchange, the association released the developer from any liability for association dues or assessments through the year 1999. The developer paid all dues and assessments owing in 2000, but did not make any payments during the subsequent years.

The developer filed a counterclaim asserting that the association committed the tort of interference with contractual relations. According to the developer, actions by the association caused a number of purchasers of the developer's lots to default on their promissory notes. In addition, the developer contended that the association's actions adversely affected the developer's ability to sell its remaining lots at market value. The developer sought to recover damages resulting from the foreclosures referred to above, as well as damages allegedly incurred when the developer's remaining 27 lots were sold at a price below market value.

The case was tried to a jury in a Georgia court. The trial judge denied the association's motion for a directed verdict on the developer's interference with contractual relations counterclaim. The jury found in favor of the association on its claim for unpaid dues and assessments and awarded it $40,527.09. The jury also found in favor of the developer on its counterclaim and awarded it $211,250. The trial judge entered a judgment in favor of the developer in the amount of $170,722.91, the net amount once the damages awarded to the association were offset against the greater amount of damages awarded to the developer. The trial judge denied the association's motions for new trial and judgment notwithstanding the verdict. The association appealed to the Georgia Court of Appeals.

Adams, Judge

The association asserts that the trial court erred in failing to grant [it a] directed verdict [and a judgment notwithstanding the verdict] on the developer's claim of tortious interference with contractual relations. The association contends that it is not liable because it acted with privilege and because it was not a stranger to the relationship between the developer and the purchasers. [This argument causes us to explore the elements of interference with contractual relations.]

To establish [its] claim of interference with a contract or business relations, [the developer] must prove:

(1) improper action or wrongful conduct by the [association] without privilege; (2) the [association] acted purposely and . . . with the intent to injure; (3) the [association] induced a breach of a contractual obligation or caused a . . . third party to discontinue or fail to enter into an anticipated . . . relationship with the [developer]; and (4) the [association's] tortious conduct proximately caused damage to the developer.

Culpepper v. Thompson, 562 S.E.2d 837 (Ga. App. 2002). "Privilege" in this context means "a legitimate or bona fide . . . interest of the defendant or a legitimate relationship of the defendant with the contract, which causes the defendant not to be considered a stranger, interloper, or meddler to the contract." [Case citation omitted.]

In *Culpepper,* . . . we held that the president of a county farm bureau could not be liable for tortious interference with the employment contract between Georgia Farm Bureau Mutual Insurance Company and one of its agents because the president had a legitimate interest in that contract, and thus acted with privilege in requesting the agent's transfer to another county. [We] reached this conclusion based upon the fact that the agent was required to maintain good relations with the local board of directors of the farm bureau, because the farm bureau had a vested business interest in the success of the insurance company from premiums generated in the county, and [because] the farm bureau's board also approved the placement of the agent within the county.

Here, the evidence at trial showed that each subdivision lot, including those owned by the developer, was subject to "An Amended and Restated Declaration of Protective Covenants" governing the subdivision. That document was signed by both the developer and the association. Under these protective covenants, the association was granted the power to enforce the covenants and collect dues and assessments. And the Georgia Property Owners' Association Act gives the covenants the force of law. Thus, each of the warranty deeds executed in connection with the developer's sale of its lots recites that the property is subject to these protective covenants. Accordingly, the association acted with privilege when it took action as outlined under the protective covenants, such as attempting to collect dues and assessments.

But even if the actions of the association exceeded this privilege, as the developer asserts, the interference [with contractual relations] claim fails because the association is not a stranger to the relationship between the developer and the purchasers. To be liable for interference with contractual or business relations, "one must be a stranger to both the contract and the business relationship giving rise to and underpinning the contract. In other words, . . . parties to a comprehensive interwoven set of contracts [cannot be held] liable for tortious interference with any of the contracts or business relationships." *Galardi v. Steele-Inman,* 597 S.E.2d 571 (Ga. App. 2004).

Under the circumstances here, we cannot say that the association was a stranger to the contracts or relationship between the developer and the purchasers of the developer's lots. Rather, they are all parties to a "comprehensive interwoven set of contracts." [We conclude] that the association cannot be liable for interference with the contracts or business relationship between the developer and the lot purchasers. [Therefore,] the trial court erred in denying the association's motion for judgment notwithstanding the verdict.

Trial court's decision reversed; judgment to be entered in favor of association on developer's counterclaim.

Lanham Act Section 43(a)

Section 43(a) of the Lanham Act basically creates a federal law of unfair competition. Section 43(a) is not a consumer remedy; it is normally available only to commercial parties, who usually are the defendant's competitors. The section creates civil liability for a wide range of false, misleading, confusing, or deceptive representations made in connection with goods or services. Section 43(a)'s many applications include:

1. *Tort claims for "palming off" or "passing off."* This tort involves false representations that are likely to induce third parties to believe that the defendant's goods or services are those of the plaintiff. Such representations include imitations of the plaintiff's trademarks, trade names, packages, labels, containers, employee uniforms, and place of business.

2. *Trade dress infringement claims.* These claims resemble passing-off claims. A product's trade dress is its overall appearance and sales image. Section 43(a) prohibits a party from passing off its goods or services as those of a competitor by employing a substantially similar trade dress that is likely to confuse consumers as to the source of its products or services. For example, a competitor that sells antifreeze in jugs that are similar in size, shape, and color to a well-known competitor's jugs may face section 43(a) liability.

3. *Claims for infringement of both registered and unregistered trademarks.*

4. *Commercial appropriation of name or likeness claims and right of publicity claims* (discussed in Chapter 6).

5. *False advertising claims.* This important application of section 43(a) includes ads that misrepresent the nature, qualities, or characteristics of either the *advertiser's* products and services or a *competitor's* products and services. Section 43(a) applies to ads that are likely to mislead buyers even if they are not clearly false on their face, and to ads with certain deceptive *omissions.* In the *Time Warner Cable* case, the court discusses the types of statements that may violate section 43(a) and those that may not.

Time Warner Cable, Inc. v. DIRECTV, Inc.   497 F.3d 144 (2d Cir. 2007)

Time Warner Cable, Inc. (TWC), and DIRECTV, Inc., are major players in the multichannel video service industry. TWC is the second-largest cable company in the United States. TWC and other cable providers are required by law to operate through franchises issued by local government entities. At the time of the litigation described below, TWC was the franchisee in the greater part of New York City. DIRECTV is one of the country's largest satellite service providers. Because DIRECTV broadcasts directly via satellite, it is not subject to the franchise limitations applicable to cable companies. Therefore, in the markets where TWC is the franchisee, DIRECTV and other satellite providers pose the greatest threat to its market share.

Both TWC and DIRECTV offer high-definition (HD) service on some of their respective channels. HD provides the home viewer with theater-like picture quality on a wider screen. The picture quality of HD is governed by standards recommended by an international nonprofit organization that develops voluntary standards for digital television. TWC and DIRECTV meet these standards in their HD programming. To view programming in HD format, customers of either provider must have an HD television set. Evidence adduced in the litigation described below established that the HD programming consumers could see on TWC and DIRECTV was equivalent in picture quality.

In 2006, DIRECTV launched a multimedia advertising campaign based on the "Source Matters" theme. The campaign was designed to educate consumers that to obtain HD-standard picture quality, it is not enough to buy an HD television set; consumers must also receive HD programming from the "source," that is, the television service provider. As part of this campaign, DIRECTV began running a television commercial featuring celebrity Jessica Simpson. In the commercial, Simpson, portraying her character of Daisy Duke from the movie The Dukes of Hazzard, *says to some of her customers at the local diner:*

Y'all ready to order? Hey, 253 straight days at the gym to get this body and you're not gonna watch me on DIRECTV HD? You're just not gonna get the best picture out of some fancy big screen TV without DIRECTV. It's broadcast in 1080i [a reference to a technical term dealing with HD resolution]. I totally don't know what that means, but I want it.

The commercial concluded with a narrator saying, "For an HD picture that can't be beat, get DIRECTV."

Another television commercial in the DIRECTV campaign featured actor William Shatner as Captain James T. Kirk, his character from the popular Star Trek *television show and film series. The following conversation takes place on the starship* Enterprise:

Mr. Chekov: Should we raise our shields, Captain?

Captain Kirk: At ease, Mr. Chekov. Again with the shields. I wish he'd just relax and enjoy the amazing picture clarity of the DIRECTV HD we just hooked up. With what Starfleet just ponied up for this big screen TV, settling for cable would be illogical.

The commercial ended with the announcer saying, "For an HD picture that can't be beat, get DIRECTV."

As a further part of its advertising campaign, DIRECTV placed banner advertisements on various Web sites. The banner ads opened by showing an image so blurry that it was impossible to discern what was being depicted. On top of this indistinct image was superimposed the slogan, "Source Matters." After about a second, a vertical line split the screen into two parts, one labeled "Other TV" and the other "DIRECTV." On the other TV side of the line, the picture was extremely distorted, as the opening image had been. In contrast, the picture on the DIRECTV side was exceptionally sharp and clear. The DIRECTV screen revealed that what viewers had been looking at was an image of New York Giants quarterback Eli Manning; in another ad, it was a picture of two women snorkeling in tropical waters. The ads then invited browsers to "[f]ind out why DIRECTV's picture beats cable" and to "[l]earn more" about a special offer by clicking on a link to the HDTV section of DIRECTV's Web site.

In addition to the banner ads, DIRECTV created an ad that it featured on its own Web site. The visual content of this was very similar to that of the banner ads. The "Other TV" part of the split screen was later identified in the ad as representing "basic cable." The very blurry picture on the "Other TV" side was accompanied by the following text: "If you're hooking up your high-definition TV to basic cable, you're not getting the best picture on every channel. For unparalleled clarity, you need DIRECTV HD."

Shortly after DIRECTV began running the above-described television commercials and Internet ads, TWC sued DIRECTV in the U.S. District Court for the Southern District of New York. TWC, which claimed that DIRECTV had engaged in false advertising in violation of § 43(a) of the Lanham Act, moved for a preliminary injunction against the commercials and ads. When the federal district court granted the preliminary injunction, DIRECTV appealed to the U.S. Court of Appeals for the Second Circuit.

Straub, Circuit Judge

A party seeking preliminary injunctive relief must establish: (1) either (a) a likelihood of success on the merits of its case or (b) sufficiently serious questions going to the merits to make them a fair ground for litigation and a balance of hardships tipping decidedly in its favor, *and* (2) a likelihood of irreparable harm if the requested relief is denied.

Section 43(a) of the Lanham Act provides, in pertinent part, that

[a]ny person who, on or in connection with any goods or services . . . uses in commerce . . . any . . . false or misleading description of fact, or false or misleading representation of fact, which—

. . . .

(B) in commercial advertising or promotion, misrepresents the nature, characteristics, qualities, or geographic origin of his or her or another person's goods, services, or commercial activities, shall be liable in a civil action by any person who believes that he or she is or is likely to be damaged by such act.

15 U.S.C. § 1125(a)(l). Two different theories of recovery are available to a plaintiff who brings a false advertising action under § 43(a). First, the plaintiff can demonstrate that the challenged advertisement is literally false, *i.e.*, false on its face. When an advertisement is shown to be literally or facially false, consumer deception is presumed and "the court may grant relief without reference to the advertisement's [actual] impact on the buying public." [Case citation omitted.] "This is because plaintiffs alleging a literal falsehood are claiming that a statement, on its face, conflicts with reality, a claim that is best supported by comparing the statement itself with the reality it purports to describe." [Case citation omitted.] Alternatively, a plaintiff can show that the advertisement, while not literally false, is nevertheless likely to mislead or confuse consumers. Therefore, whereas "plaintiffs seeking to establish a literal falsehood must generally show the substance of what is conveyed, . . . a district court *must* rely on extrinsic evidence [of consumer deception or confusion] to support a finding of an implicitly false message." [Case citation omitted.]

Here, TWC chose to pursue only the first path of literal falsity, and the District Court granted the preliminary injunction against the television commercials on that basis. In this appeal, DIRECTV does not dispute that it would be a misrepresentation to claim that the picture quality of DIRECTV HD is superior to that of cable HD. Rather, it argues that neither commercial explicitly makes such a claim, and therefore cannot be literally false.

DIRECTV's argument is easily dismissed with respect to the Simpson commercial. In the critical lines, Simpson tells audiences, "You're just not gonna get the best picture out of some fancy big screen TV without DIRECTV. It's broadcast in 1080i." These statements make the explicit assertion that it is impossible to obtain "the best picture"—*i.e.*, a "1080i"-resolution picture—from any source other than DIRECTV. This claim is flatly untrue; the uncontroverted factual record establishes that viewers can, in fact, get the same "best picture" by ordering HD programming from their cable service provider. We therefore affirm the District Court's determination that the Simpson commercial's contention "that a viewer cannot 'get the best picture' without DIRECTV is . . . likely to be proven literally false."

The issue of whether the Shatner commercial is likely to be proven literally false requires more analysis. When interpreting the controversial statement [that] "[w]ith what Starfleet just ponied up for this big screen TV, settling for cable would be illogical," the District Court looked not only at that particular text, but also at the surrounding context. In light of Shatner's opening comment extolling the "amazing picture quality of . . . DIRECTV HD" and the announcer's closing remark highlighting the unbeatable "HD picture" provided by DIRECTV, the District Court found that the line in the middle—"settling for cable would be illogical"—clearly referred to cable's HD picture quality. Since it would only be "illogical" to "settle" for cable's HD picture if it was materially inferior to DIRECTV's HD picture, the District Court concluded that TWC was likely to establish that the statement was literally false.

DIRECTV argues that the District Court's ruling was clearly erroneous because the actual statement at issue, "settling for cable would be illogical," does not explicitly compare the picture quality of DIRECTV HD with that of cable HD, and indeed, does not mention HD at all. In DIRECTV's view, the District Court based its determination of literal falsity not on the words actually used, but on what it subjectively perceived to be the general message conveyed by the commercial as a whole. DIRECTV contends that this was plainly improper.

TWC, on the other hand, maintains that the District Court properly took context into account in interpreting the commercial. TWC argues that . . . an advertisement can be literally false even though no [statements in it are] untrue, if the clear meaning of the statement, considered in context, is false. Given the commercial's repeated references to "HD picture," TWC

contends that the District Court correctly found that "settling for cable would be illogical" literally made the false claim that cable's HD picture quality is inferior to DIRECTV's.

[A review of relevant decisions causes] us to now formally adopt what is known in other [circuit courts of appeal] as the "false by necessary implication" doctrine. Under this doctrine, a district court evaluating whether an advertisement is literally false "must analyze the message conveyed in full context," *i.e.,* it "must consider the advertisement in its entirety and not . . . engage in disputatious dissection." [Case citations omitted.] If the words or images, considered in context, necessarily imply a false message, the advertisement is literally false and no extrinsic evidence of consumer confusion is required. However, . . . if the language or graphic is susceptible to more than one reasonable interpretation, the advertisement cannot be literally false. [In that event, there] may still be a basis for a claim that the advertisement is misleading, but to resolve such a claim, the district court must look to consumer data to determine what "the person to whom the advertisement is addressed find[s] to be the message." [Case citation omitted.]

Here, the District Court found that Shatner's assertion that "settling for cable would be illogical," considered in light of the advertisement as a whole, unambiguously made the false claim that cable's HD picture quality is inferior to that of DIRECTV's. We cannot say that this finding was clearly erroneous, especially given that in the immediately preceding line, Shatner praises the "amazing picture clarity of . . . DIRECTV HD." We accordingly affirm the District Court's conclusion that TWC established a likelihood of success on its claim that the Shatner commercial is literally false.

[We now consider DIRECTV's Internet ads.] We had made clear that a district court must examine not only the words, but also the "visual images . . . to assess whether [the advertisement] is literally false." [Citation omitted.] It is uncontroverted that the images used in the Internet ads to represent cable are inaccurate depictions of the picture quality provided by cable's digital or analog service.

DIRECTV does not contest this point. Rather, it asserts that the images are so grossly distorted and exaggerated that no reasonable buyer would take them to be accurate depictions of how a consumer's television picture would look when connected to cable. Consequently, DIRECTV argues, the images are obviously just puffery, which cannot form the basis of a Lanham Act violation.

This Court has had little occasion to explore the concept of puffery in the false advertising context. In . . . one case where we discussed the subject in some depth, we characterized puffery as "[s]ubjective claims about products, which cannot be proven either true or false." [Case citation omitted.] We also cited to the Third Circuit's description of puffery in *Castrol, Inc. v.*

Pennzoil Co., 987 F.2d 939, 945 (3d Cir. 1993): "Puffery is an exaggeration or overstatement expressed in broad, vague, and commendatory language." Such sales talk, "or puffing, as it is commonly called, is considered to be offered and understood as an expression of the seller's opinion only, which is to be discounted as such by the buyer. . . . The puffing rule amounts to a seller's privilege to lie his head off, so long as he says nothing specific." W. Page Keeton et al., *Prosser and Keeton on the Law of Torts* § 109, at 756–57 (5th ed. 1984).

[The above] definition of puffery does not translate well into the world of images. Unlike words, images cannot be vague or broad. To the contrary, visual depictions of a product are generally specific and measurable, and can therefore be proven either true or false. Yet, if a visual representation is so grossly exaggerated that no reasonable buyer would take it at face value, there is no danger of consumer deception and hence, no basis for a false advertising claim.

Other circuits have recognized that puffery can come in at least two different forms. The first form [is] "a general claim of superiority over comparable products that is so vague that it can be understood as nothing more than a mere expression of opinion." [Case citation omitted.] The second form of puffery . . . is "an exaggerated, blustering, and boasting statement upon which no reasonable buyer would be justified in relying." [Case citation omitted.] We believe that this second conception of puffery is a better fit where, as here, the "statement" at issue is expressed not in words, but through images.

The District Court determined that the Internet Advertisements did not satisfy this alternative definition of puffery because DIRECTV's own evidence showed that "many HDTV equipment purchasers are confused as to what image quality to expect when viewing non-HD broadcasts, as their prior experience with the equipment is often limited to viewing HD broadcasts or other digital images on floor model televisions at large retail chains." Given this confusion, the District Court reasoned

that "consumers unfamiliar with HD equipment could be led to believe that using an HD television set with [a] cable feed might result in the sort of distorted images showcased in DIRECTV's Internet Advertisements, especially since those advertisements make reference to 'basic cable.'" *Id.*

Our review of the record persuades us that the District Court clearly erred in rejecting DIRECTV's puffery defense. The "Other TV" images in the Internet Advertisements are . . . unwatchably blurry, distorted, and pixilated, and . . . nothing like the images a customer would ordinarily see using TWC's cable service. [T]he Internet ads' depictions of cable are not just inaccurate; they are not even remotely realistic. It is difficult to imagine that any consumer, whatever the level of sophistication, would actually be fooled by the Internet ads into thinking that cable's picture quality is so poor that the image is nearly entirely obscured. As DIRECTV states in its brief, "even a person not acquainted with cable would realize TWC could not realistically supply an unwatchably blurry image and survive in the marketplace." For these reasons, we conclude that the District Court exceeded its permissible discretion in preliminarily enjoining DIRECTV from disseminating the Internet ads.

A plaintiff seeking a preliminary injunction under the Lanham Act must persuade a court not only that it is likely to succeed on the merits, but also that it is likely to suffer irreparable harm in the absence of immediate relief. [Because the District Court properly concluded that the Simpson and Shatner commercials were literally false, it was also proper for the court, utilizing applicable precedent, to conclude that TWC would suffer irreparable harm because of its competitor's literally false commercials.]

District Court's grant of preliminary injunction regarding DIRECTV's television commercials affirmed; preliminary injunction regarding Internet ads vacated; case remanded for further proceedings.

Problems and Problem Cases

1. Huey J. Rivet patented an "amphibious marsh craft" for hauling loads and laying pipeline in swamps. Rivet's model could "walk" over stumps for extended periods while carrying heavy loads. Later, Robert Wilson, who had once worked for Rivet as a welder, began marketing a similar craft. The craft sold by Wilson differed from the craft described in the specification accompanying Rivet's patent application in

several respects. Overall, though, the Wilson boat performed much the same functions about as effectively as the Rivet craft, and used much the same engineering techniques and concepts to do so. Has Wilson infringed Rivet's patent?

2. Visual artist Jeff Koons created a painting called "Niagara." The painting consisted of fragmentary images collaged against the backdrop of a landscape. It depicted four pairs of women's feet and

lower legs dangling prominently over images of confections—a large chocolate fudge brownie topped with ice cream, a tray of donuts, and a tray of apple danish pastries—with a grassy field and Niagara Falls in the background. The images of the legs were placed side by side, each pair pointing vertically downward. Koons drew the images in "Niagara" from fashion magazines and advertisements. One of the pairs of legs in the painting was adapted from a copyrighted photograph taken by Andrea Blanch, an accomplished professional fashion and portrait photographer. The Blanch photograph used by Koons in "Niagara" was titled "Silk Sandals." It appeared in the August 2000 issue of *Allure* magazine. While working on "Niagara" and other paintings, Koons saw "Silk Sandals" in *Allure.* In an affidavit submitted in the litigation referred to below, Koons stated that "certain physical features of the legs [in the photograph] represented for me a particular type of woman frequently presented in advertising." He considered this typicality to further his purpose of commenting on the "commercial images . . . in our consumer culture." Koons scanned the image of "Silk Sandals" into his computer and incorporated a version of the scanned image into "Niagara." He omitted certain aspects of the scanned image from his painting and modified certain other aspects of the image, such as by making the woman's legs angle downward rather than upward (the opposite of how they had appeared in Blanch's photograph). Koons did not seek permission from Blanch before using her photograph. He later earned approximately $125,000 from financial exploitation of "Niagara." When Blanch sued Koons for copyright infringement, what defense would Koons have attempted to establish? Did Koons succeed with that defense?

3. Tom Forsythe, who does business as "Walking Mountain Productions," produces photographs that have social and political overtones. Among Forsythe's works is a 78-photograph series titled "Food Chain Barbie." These photographs depict Mattel, Inc.'s famous "Barbie" doll in absurd positions and settings, many of which have sexual overtones. In some of the titles of individual photographs, Forsythe uses the "Barbie" name. Although the photographs vary in content, Forsythe generally depicts Barbie dolls juxtaposed with vintage kitchen appliances. For example, "Malted Barbie" features a nude Barbie placed on a malt machine. "Fondue a la Barbie" depicts Barbie heads in a fondue pot. "Barbie Enchiladas" shows a lit oven and a pan containing four tortilla-wrapped, salsa-covered Barbies.

In a declaration accompanying his summary judgment motion in the litigation described below, Forsythe described his photographic series as an attempt to "critique the objectification of women associated with [Barbie], and [to] lambaste the conventional beauty myth and the societal acceptance of women as objects." He said he parodied Barbie because he regards Barbie as "the most enduring of those products that feed on the insecurities of our beauty and perfection-obsessed consumer culture." Forsythe also said he sought to communicate, through artistic expression, a serious message with an element of humor. Forsythe's market success was limited. He displayed his works at two art festivals and several exhibitions. He printed 2,000 promotional postcards depicting the "Barbie Enchiladas" photograph, but only 500 postcards were circulated. Forsythe also produced 1,000 business cards, which depicted "Champagne Barbie." His name and self-given title ("Artsurdist") appeared on the cards. In addition, Forsythe had a Web site on which he depicted low-resolution images of his photographs. The Web site was not configured for online purchasing. "Tom Forsythe's Artsurdist Statement," in which he described his intent to critique and ridicule Barbie, was featured on the Web site. Prior to the lawsuit described below, Forsythe received only four or five unsolicited calls inquiring about his work. The "Food Chain Barbie" series earned him gross income of $3,659—at least half of which stemmed from purchases by Mattel investigators. Mattel sued Forsythe in federal district court, contending that the "Food Chain Barbie" series violated Mattel's copyright and trademark rights in regard to the Barbie doll's appearance and name. The district court granted Forsythe's motion for summary judgment. In so ruling, the court held that Forsythe's use of Mattel's copyrighted work was fair use and thus not copyright infringement. In addition, the court rejected Mattel's trademark infringement and dilution claims. Mattel appealed to the U.S. Court of Appeals for the Ninth Circuit. Was the district court's decision correct? How did the Ninth Circuit rule?

4. Qualitex Co. produces pads that dry-cleaning firms use on their presses. Since the 1950s, Qualitex has colored its press pads a shade of green-gold. In 1989, Jabcobson Products Co. began producing

press pads for sale to dry-cleaning firms. Jacobson colored its pads a green-gold resembling the shade used by Qualitex. Later in 1989, the United States Patent & Trademark Office granted Qualitex a trademark registration for the green-gold color (as used on press pads). Qualitex then added a trademark infringement claim to an unfair competition lawsuit it had previously filed against Jacobson. Qualitex won the case, but the Ninth Circuit Court of Appeals set aside the judgment on the trademark infringement claim. In the Ninth Circuit's view, the Lanham Act did not allow any party to have color alone registered as a trademark. The Supreme Court granted certiorari. How did the Supreme Court rule on the question whether color is a registrable trademark?

5. Peter Deptula owns a federal trademark registration on "Surfvivor," an amalgamation of the words "surf" and "survivor." Deptula has used the Surfvivor mark for a significant number of years on his many Hawaiian beach–themed products, which include sunscreen, T-shirts, and surfboards. Deptula's mark consists of the term "Surfvivor" in block or cursive writing, often accompanied by a stylized graphic such as a sun or a surfer. Deptula has advertised his products on local television and radio shows, on his Web site, and at local trade shows. Surfvivor goods are primarily sold in Hawaii through a local university, a drugstore chain, military outlets, and Hawaiian branches of major retailers. Deptula would like to expand Surfvivor's out-of-state presence, but has not made firm plans to do so. Several years after Deptula coined the "Surfvivor" name, the CBS television network and a television programming organization known as Survivor Productions began broadcasting a reality television show called *Survivor*. The *Survivor* program deals with the experiences of competitors who seek to survive in extreme outdoor conditions. The show has been a viewer favorite. Survivor Productions created a special *Survivor* logo for advertising and marketing purposes. As with the Surfvivor mark, the *Survivor* mark is emblazoned on a wide range of consumer merchandise, including T-shirts, shorts, and hats. The *Survivor* mark consists of the word "Survivor" in block script. It is often accompanied by the words "outwit[,] outplay[, and] outlast," or is superimposed on a stylized graphic suggesting the location of a particular series. When *Survivor*'s producers began their use of the *Survivor* name and mark, they were aware of Deptula's Surfvivor mark.

After *Survivor* began airing on television, Deptula encountered a few persons who wondered whether his business was sponsored by the entities that produced and aired the television program. One retailer and one customer mistook *Survivor* sunscreen for Deptula's product, and one trade show attendee thought that Deptula's business was endorsed by *Survivor*'s producers. Survivor Productions and CBS never received any complaints from confused customers. A survey commissioned by Survivor Productions revealed that fewer than 2 percent of more than 400 sunscreen purchasers were confused by the two marks. None of Deptula's customers returned any Surfvivor goods because of a mistaken belief that the goods they purchased were produced or endorsed by the producers of *Survivor*. No merchant stopped doing business with Deptula on account of confusion between the product lines.

Deptula filed a trademark infringement lawsuit against Survivor Productions and CBS on the basis of the facts set forth above. The federal district court granted summary judgment in favor of the defendants. Did the court rule correctly?

6. E. I. du Pont de Nemours & Co. was building a plant to develop a highly secret unpatented process for producing methanol. During the construction, some of its trade secrets were exposed to view from the air because the plant in which they were contained did not yet have a roof. These secrets were photographed from an airplane by two photographers who were hired by persons unknown to take pictures of the new construction. Did this action amount to a misappropriation of Du Pont's trade secrets?

7. AT&T Corp. owns a patent on an apparatus for digitally encoding and compressing recorded speech. Microsoft Corp.'s Windows operating system includes software that will enable a computer to process speech in a manner covered by AT&T's patent. However, the patent would not be infringed unless and until Windows was installed on a computer and the computer would then be able to perform in the way contemplated by the patent. Microsoft sells Windows to computer manufacturers, some of which are foreign companies. The purchasing manufacturers install Windows on the computers they build and sell. To each of the foreign manufacturers, Microsoft sends a master version of Windows, either on a disk or in an encrypted electronic transmission.

The foreign manufacturers then use the master version of Windows to create copies of it. The copies of Windows—rather than the master version provided by Microsoft—are installed on the foreign manufacturers' computers, which are then sold to users outside the United States. In a U.S. district court, AT&T sued Microsoft for patent infringement on the basis of the above facts. Was Microsoft liable for patent infringement in regard to its dealings with the foreign manufacturers?

8. In February 1999, Bob D'Amato registered the domain name www.audisport.com. He posted content to his Web site in June 1999 and April 2000. Believing that employees of a dealership that sold Audi automobiles had given him verbal permission to use Audi trademarks on his Web site, D'Amato commissioned another party to create a logo that incorporated portions of an Audi trademark, the company's rings logo. He used the commissioned logo on his site and posted links to another party's site, www.audisportline.com, which sold Audi-related items. Other content posted on D'Amato's site used the Audi name and other Audi trademarks. The site also contained a statement that "[w]e are a cooperative with Audi of America, and will be providing the latest products for your [Audi automobiles]." Although he requested the dealership's written permission to use Audi trademarks, D'Amato never received the written permission. Audi's agreements with its dealerships forbade them from granting anyone permission to use Audi trademarks. D'Amato later ceased using the Audi trademarks on his Web site. He ended up earning no profits from the site. Even so, Audi sued him for trademark infringement and dilution when it learned of his activities. Was D'Amato liable for trademark infringement? Was he liable for trademark dilution?

9. David Hudesman leased commercial property housing the Red Dog Saloon to Don Harris, the saloon's owner and operator. The lease said that Harris could assign it to any subtenant or assignee who was financially responsible and would properly care for the premises. It also required that Hudesman consent to such an assignment, but added that this consent could not be withheld unreasonably. After Harris decided to relocate his business, he was contacted by Richard Stone, president of the RAN Corporation. Stone wanted to use the property for an artifacts gallery. Harris and Stone agreed that Harris would assign the lease for $15,000, conditional on Hudesman's approval.

About this time, a politically influential man named Jerry Reinwand contacted Hudesman about the property. In exchange for Reinwand's promise to help Hudesman secure government leases for a large building Hudesman owned, Hudesman promised Reinwand that if Harris relocated his business, Reinwand would be assigned the property. Then Hudesman told Harris that he would not consent to Harris's assignment of the lease to RAN, and that Harris would be "looking at litigation" if he tried to assign the lease to Stone. Therefore, Harris told Stone that the deal was off, returned his $15,000 deposit, and assigned the lease to Reinwand for $15,000.

RAN then sued in an effort to invalidate Reinwand's lease and enforce its assignment contract with Harris. After RAN settled with several defendants, its main remaining claims were interference with contractual relations and interference with prospective advantage claims against Hudesman. When both parties moved for summary judgment, the trial court held for Hudesman. RAN appealed. Was RAN entitled to win on appeal?

10. The Jefferson County, Colorado, School District decided to refinance part of its bonded indebtedness by issuing refunding bonds. The School District selected two firms other than Moody's Investor Services, Inc. (hereinafter, "Moody"), to rate the bonds, even though it had used Moody's services in the past. When the School District brought the bonds to market, they initially sold well. Less than two hours into the sales period, however, Moody published an article about the bonds on its "Rating News," an electronically distributed information service sent to subscribers and news services. Moody stated in the article that even though it had not been asked to rate the bonds, it intended to assign a rating after the sale. The article went on to discuss the bonds and the School District's financial condition, concluding that "the outlook on the district's general obligation debt is negative, reflecting the district's ongoing financial pressure due in part to the state's [Colorado's] past underfunding of the school finance act as well as legal uncertainties and financial constraints under Amendment I." Amendment I, a then-recent change in the Colorado Constitution, required voter approval of certain tax increases.

According to the School District, Moody's article adversely affected the sale of the bonds. Purchase orders ceased, several buyers canceled prior orders, and the School District found it necessary to reprice the bonds at a higher interest in order to sell them. As a result, the School District asserted, it suffered a net loss of more than $700,000. Contending the statement in Moody's article falsely indicated that the School District was not in a creditworthy financial condition, the School District sued Moody for injurious falsehood. The federal district court dismissed the School District's claim for failure to state a claim on which relief could be granted. The court based its ruling on a conclusion that Moody's statement, rather than being demonstrably false, was a protected statement of opinion. Was the district court's decision correct?

11. American Italian Pasta Co. (American) sells dried pasta under numerous brand names, as does its competitor, New World Pasta Co. (New World). From 1997 to 2000, American manufactured Mueller's brand (Mueller's) dried pasta for Best Foods. In 2000, American purchased Mueller's and took on all packaging, distributing, pricing, and marketing for the brand. Since purchasing Mueller's, American has placed the phrase "America's Favorite Pasta" on Mueller's packaging. On different packages used for the Mueller's brand, the phrases "Quality Since 1867," "Made from 100% Semolina," or "Made with Semolina" accompany the phrase "America's Favorite Pasta." The packaging also contains a paragraph in which the phrase "America's Favorite Pasta" appears. The paragraph (1) states that pasta lovers have enjoyed Mueller's pasta for 130 years; (2) claims that Mueller's "pasta cooks to perfect tenderness every time," because Mueller's uses "100% pure semolina milled from the highest quality durum wheat"; and (3) encourages consumers to "taste why Mueller's is America's favorite pasta."

New World sent American a demand letter calling for American to cease and desist using the phrase "America's Favorite Pasta." Consequently, American filed a declaratory judgment action in federal court and named New World as the defendant. American asked the court to declare that its use of the phrase "America's Favorite Pasta" did not constitute false or misleading advertising under § 43(a) of the Lanham Act. New World counterclaimed, asserting that American's use of "America's Favorite Pasta" violated § 43(a). New World argued that American's use

of the phrase was false or misleading advertising, because, according to a consumer survey commissioned by New World, the phrase conveyed either of two inaccurate impressions: that Mueller's is a national pasta brand; or that Mueller's is the nation's number one selling pasta. American and New World agreed that American's brands (including Mueller's) are regional in nature and that a pasta producer other than American and New World sells the most dried pasta in the United States.

American argued that the phrase "America's Favorite Pasta" did not violate § 43(a) because the phrase constituted nonactionable puffery. The federal district court agreed with this argument by American and rejected New World's contention that the phrase "America's Favorite Pasta" made a deceptive factual claim. Therefore, the court ruled in favor of American on its request for declaratory relief and against New World on its counterclaim. Was the district court's ruling correct? Was "America's Favorite Pasta" mere puffery or, instead, a false statement of supposed fact?

Online Research

The United States Copyright Office

Go to the United States Copyright Office Web site, at **www.loc.gov/copyright**. Then find the answers to these questions:

1. What is the fee for a basic registration of a claim to copyright?

2. Does the Copyright Office maintain a list of works that have fallen into the public domain (i.e., works whose copyright protection has expired)?

Consider completing these two case segments from the You Be the Judge Web site element after you have read this chapter:

"INTELLECTUAL PROPERTY: Click Here, Get Sued"
"INTELLECTUAL PROPERTY: The Yoga Posture Puzzle"

Visit our Web site at **www.mhhe.com/mallor14e** for more information and activities regarding these case segments.

Part Three

Contracts

chapter 9
Introduction to Contracts

chapter 10
The Agreement: Offer

chapter 11
The Agreement: Acceptance

chapter 12
Consideration

chapter 13
Reality of Consent

chapter 14
Capacity to Contract

chapter 15
Illegality

chapter 16
Writing

chapter 17
Rights of Third Parties

chapter 18
Performance and Remedies

chapter 9

INTRODUCTION TO CONTRACTS

The 2001 catalog that Gigantic State University Web site sent out to prospective students described a merit-based scholarship called the "Eagle Scholarship." The catalog stated that GSU offers the Eagle Scholarship to all incoming students who are in the top 10 percent of their high school classes and have SAT scores of 1250 or above. Paul, a prospective student, read the 2001 catalog that GSU had sent to him. Money was tight for Paul, so he paid particular attention to the part of the catalog that described financial aid. He read about the Eagle Scholarship and realized that he qualified for the scholarship. Paul picked GSU over other schools in large part because of the Eagle Scholarship. He applied to GSU and GSU admitted him. Before his freshman orientation, Paul called GSU and checked to be sure that he met the requirements of the Eagle Scholarship, and the GSU representative that he talked to informed him that he did. When Paul arrived at GSU for freshman orientation, however, he received a copy of the 2002 catalog and learned that the qualifications for the Eagle Scholarship had changed and that he no longer qualified.

- Was there a contract between GSU and Paul for the Eagle Scholarship?
- If so, what kind of contract was it?
- What body of legal rules would apply to the contract?
- If it wasn't a contract, is there any other basis for a legal obligation on the part of GSU?
- Would it be ethical for GSU not to honor its promise to Paul?

The Nature of Contracts

The law of contracts deals with the enforcement of promises. It is important to realize from the outset of your study of contracts that *not every promise is legally enforceable.* (If every promise were enforceable, this chapter could be one sentence long!) We have all made and broken promises without fear of being sued. If you promise to take a friend out to dinner and then fail to do so, you would be shocked to be sued for breach of contract. What separates such promises from legally enforceable contracts? The law of contracts sorts out what promises are enforceable, to what extent, and how they will be enforced.

The essence of a contract is that it is a *legally enforceable* promise or set of promises. In other words, when a set of promises has the status of *contract,* a person injured by a breach of that contract is entitled to call on the government (courts) to force the breaching party to honor the contract.

The Functions of Contracts

Contracts give us the ability to enter into agreements with others with confidence that we may call on the *law*—not merely the good faith of the other party—to make sure that those agreements will be honored. Within limitations that you will study later, *contracting lets us create a type of private law*—the terms of the agreements we make—that governs our relations with others.

Contracts facilitate the planning that is necessary in a modern, industrialized society. Who would invest in a business if she could not rely on the fact that the builders and suppliers of the facilities and equipment, the suppliers of the raw materials necessary to manufacture products, and the customers who agree to purchase those products would all honor their commitments? How could we make loans, sell goods on credit, or rent property unless loan agreements, conditional sales agreements, and leases were backed by the force of the law? Contract, then, is necessary to the world as we know it. Like that world, its particulars tend to change over time, while its general characteristics remain largely stable.

The Evolution of Contract Law

The idea of contract is ancient. Thousands of years ago, Egyptians and Mesopotamians recognized devices like contracts; by the 15th century, the common law courts of England had developed a variety of theories to justify enforcing certain promises. Contract law did not, however, assume major importance in our legal system until the 19th century, when the Industrial Revolution created the necessity for greater private planning and certainty in commercial transactions.

The central principle of contract law that emerged from this period was *freedom of contract.* Freedom of contract is the idea that contracts should be enforced because they are the products of the free wills of their creators, who should, within broad limits, be free to determine the extent of their obligations. The proper role of the courts in such a system of contract was to enforce these freely made bargains but otherwise to adopt a hands-off stance. The freedom to make good deals carried with it the risk of making bad deals. As long as a person voluntarily entered a contract, it would generally be enforced against him, even if the result was grossly unfair. And since equal bargaining power tended to be assumed, the courts were usually unwilling to hear defenses based on unequal bargaining power. This judicial posture allowed the courts to create a pure contract law consisting of precise, clear, and technical rules that were capable of general, almost mechanical, application. Such a law of contract met the needs of the marketplace by affording the predictable and consistent results necessary to facilitate private planning.

The emergence of large business organizations after the Civil War produced obvious disparities of bargaining power in many contract situations, however. These large organizations found it more efficient to standardize their numerous transactions by employing standard form contracts, which also could be used to exploit their greater bargaining power by dictating the terms of their agreements.

Contract law evolved to reflect these changes in social reality. During the 20th century, there was a dramatic increase in government regulation of private contractual relationships. Think of all the statutes governing the terms of what were once purely private contractual relationships. Legislatures commonly dictate many of the basic terms of insurance contracts. Employment contracts are governed by a host of laws concerning maximum hours worked, minimum wages paid, employer liability for on-the-job injuries, unemployment compensation, and retirement benefits. In some circumstances, product liability statutes impose liability on the manufacturers and sellers of products regardless of the terms of their sales contracts. The purpose of much of this regulation has been to protect persons who lack sufficient bargaining power to protect themselves.

Courts have been increasingly concerned with creating contract rules that produce fair results. The precise, technical rules that characterized traditional common law contract have given way to permit some broader, imprecise standards such as good faith, injustice, reasonableness, and unconscionability. Despite the increased attention to fairness in contract law, the agreement between the parties is still the heart of every contract.

The Methods of Contracting

Many students reading about contract law for the first time may have the idea that contracts must be in writing to be enforceable. Generally speaking, that is not true. There are some situations in which the law requires certain kinds of contracts to be evidenced by a writing to be enforced. The most common examples of those situations are covered in Chapter 16. Unless the law specifically requires a certain kind of contract to be in writing, an oral contract that can be proven is as legally enforceable as a written one.

Contracts can be and are made in many ways. When most of us imagine a contract, we envision two parties bargaining for a deal, then drafting a contract on paper and signing it or shaking hands. Some contracts are negotiated and formed in that way. Far more common today, both online and offline, is the use of **standardized form contracts.** Standardized form contracts are contracts that are preprinted by one party and presented to the other party for signing. In most situations, the party who drafts and presents the standardized contract is the party who has the most bargaining power and/or sophistication in the transaction. Frequently, the terms of standardized contracts are nonnegotiable. Such contracts have the advantage of providing an efficient method of standardizing common transactions. On the other hand, they present the dangers that the party who signs the contract will not know what he is agreeing to and that the party who drafts and presents the contract will take advantage of his bargaining power to include terms that are oppressive or abnormal in that kind of transaction.

Basic Elements of a Contract

Over the years, the law has developed a number of requirements that a set of promises must meet before they are treated as a contract. To qualify as a contract, a set of promises must be based on a voluntary agreement, which is made up of

Figure 1   *Getting to Contract*

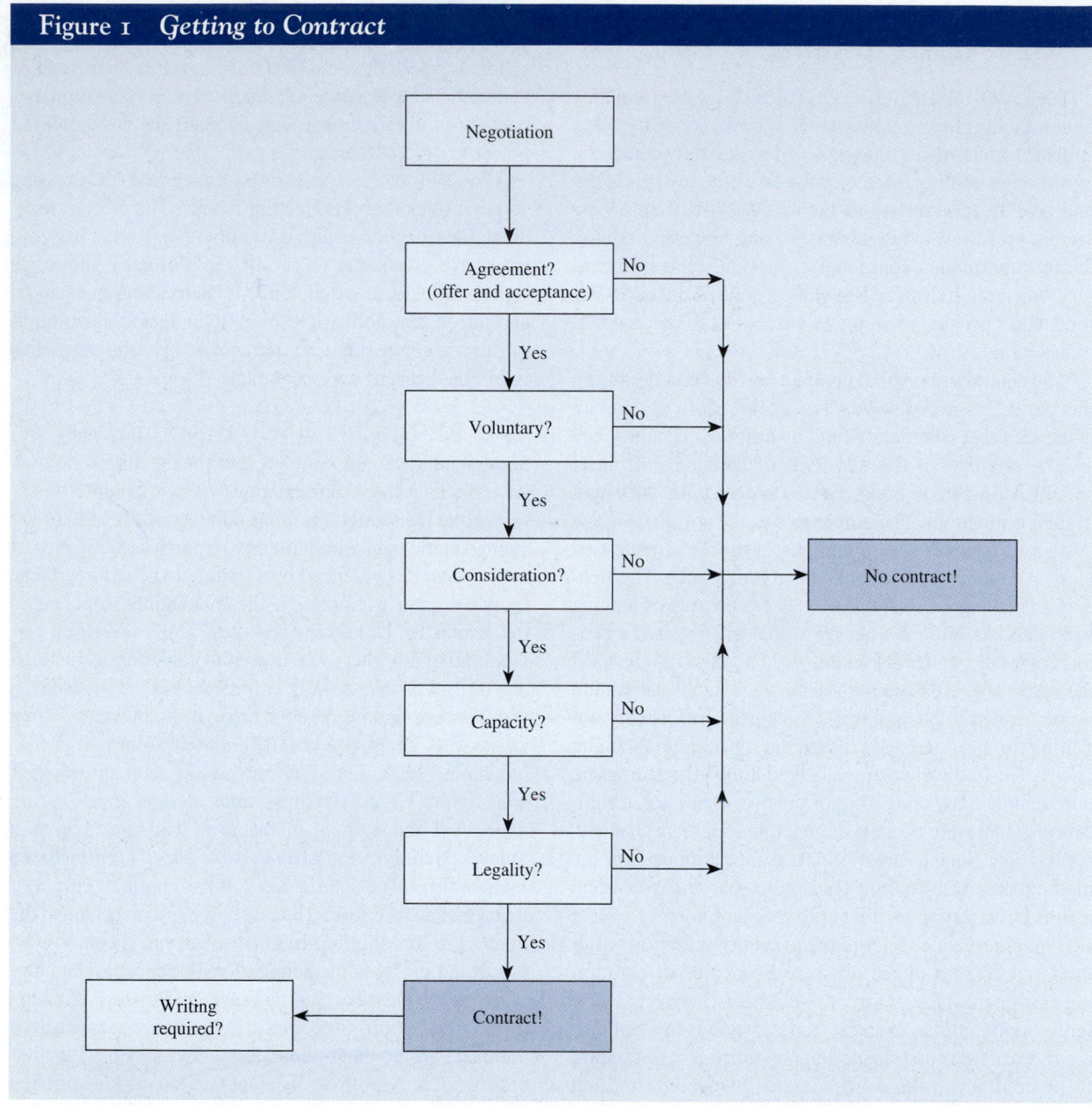

an **offer** and an **acceptance** of that offer. In addition, there usually must be **consideration** to support each party's promise. The contract must be between parties who have **capacity** to contract, and the objective and performance of the contract must be **legal.** (See Figure 1). Each of the elements of a contract will be discussed individually in subsequent chapters.

The elements of a contract can be found in all kinds of settings, from commercial dealings between strangers to agreements between family members. In determining whether a contract exists, courts scrutinize the parties' communications and conduct in light of the context in which the parties interacted. This process is illustrated by the following *Lambert v. Barron* case.

Lambert v. Barron   974 So.2d 198 (La. Ct. App. 2008)

Donald Lambert and Don Barron were friends. They had a long-standing professional relationship based on their public service together on the Louisiana State Board of Licensed Contractors from the 1980s. Lambert had been chairman of the state board, and had established his experience in resolving construction disputes. Barron is a commercial construction contractor doing business in Farmerville, Louisiana. In 1998, Barron's business began experiencing financial strain because five of his construction projects became mired in various difficulties. Barron and Lambert talked by phone during the summer of 1998 about Barron's personal problems and financial difficulties, and Lambert was concerned about his friend's depressed mental state.

On November 11, 1998, Lambert flew from New Orleans to Farmerville to meet with Barron. Prior to Lambert's flight, Barron's employee had faxed and overnighted copies of various construction contracts and correspondence relating to Barron's problematic construction projects for Lambert to review. Lambert contends that, while standing on the airport runway before he boarded the plane for his return trip home that day, he and Barron contracted for Lambert to provide consulting services for Barron. Lambert told Barron at that time that he customarily charged his clients $3,100 per month, and the minimum term for his services was one year. He also charged 10 percent of any amount recouped by his clients in settlement.

In late 2000, Lambert billed Barron for a $34,100 balance owed on the alleged oral contract. Lambert's letter dated October 30, 2000, requested payment and stated, "I have preformed (sic) my service for you and I must request that you pay me the balance due me of $34,100." Two weeks later, Barron wrote Lambert back:

I received your bill last week and was very shocked. I do not know where you are coming from, and what you have done to think you deserve any kind of pay. I sent the plane down for you to come up and look over some paper work and later we sent you some documents for you to take a look at. For your service for a full day and the one to three hours it may have taken, I was planning to pay you $2,000.00 and thought that would be around $150.00 an hour. My people knew you had been here so they paid the $3,100.00 invoice you sent. Then awhile later you called about money and I told you that we had paid you plenty and would not pay you any more. I remember you showing me a long list of people that paid you $3,100.00 a month. I did not tell you I wanted to be on that list. I have not called for any advice since then. All my calls have been to return your call.

Lambert filed suit against Barron for breach of contract. The trial court dismissed Lambert's suit, and Lambert appealed.

Caraway, Judge

This case involves the disputed formation of a contract for consulting services. A contract is an agreement by the parties whereby obligations are created. A contract is bilateral when the parties obligate themselves reciprocally, so that the obligation of each party is correlative to the obligation of the other. Unless the law prescribes a certain formality for the intended contract, offer and acceptance may be made orally, in writing, or by action or inaction that under the circumstances is clearly indicative of consent.

The trial court's ruling credited Barron's testimony that he never orally accepted Lambert's offer for consulting services under the proposed one-year arrangement with $3,100 per month payments. There was no writing reflecting the parties' consent. Nevertheless, the trial court's task was also to review Barron's alleged acceptance of the agreement from the implications of his actions or inaction. In this regard, Civil Code Article 1942 provides: "When, because of special

circumstances, the offeree's silence leads the offeror reasonably to believe that a contract has been formed, the offer is deemed accepted."

This case involves the special setting of parties with a prior friendship and the aid and advice freely given between friends that existed before Lambert first broached the subject of a consulting contract. In *Chaisson v. Chaisson,* this court found in a similar setting that an oral loan agreement had been reached between parents and their son. The son admittedly had understood his parents' intent for a loan for college expenses, but denied his acceptance of the loan agreement. Nevertheless, the son's actions in receiving the benefits of the loan proceeds in that setting and his subsequent partial payments on the loan were enough for this court to affirm the lower court's factual determination of a binding contract. A family setting or close friendship requires the finder-of-fact to determine the offeree's acceptance of an onerous contract and the offeror's reasonable belief that a contract has been formed, thus overcoming the competing implications of a benefit extended by one to a friend for a gratuitous reason without obtaining any advantage in return.

From our review of the testimony of the two men, we also conclude that there was no clear agreement given by Barron on November 11, 1998, as Lambert boarded the plane to return to New Orleans. Absent a direct oral or written acceptance by Barron, Lambert's proof of the contract rests on his receipt of certain documentation of Barron's troubled construction projects and invoices for consulting fees sent to Barron. The bulk of the documentation regarding Barron's five construction projects was forwarded to Lambert days before the Farmerville meeting. Lambert's review of the details of those construction contracts and Barron's problems with the projects would have been performed in preparation for the Farmerville meeting without any contract binding his friend. More importantly, Barron provided Lambert that documentation without any indication that his friend's review of the projects would require compensation.

After Lambert expressed at the Farmerville airport his offer and desire for a consulting contract, some further documentation was provided to him between April and August 1999. These were transmitted by fax to Lambert without any request

for specific services. The faxed documents primarily concerned correspondence from Barron's attorney to Barron reflecting the scheduling of mediation and arbitration hearings. Significantly, Barron's attorney never consulted Lambert, and Lambert never responded in writing to Barron regarding any substance concerning the status of the construction project disputes during that time. Moreover, Barron never used the principal subject matter of Lambert's expertise, arbitration, to resolve disputed construction project issues during the year following the alleged oral contract.

From our review of this evidence, we find that the trial court could determine that no tacit acceptance of Lambert's offer for services was made by Barron. Particularly lacking from the record is evidence of any substantive business benefit realized by Barron from his consultant friend. The trial court ultimately held that the parties' relationship was that of a "friend helping a friend," such that Lambert could not have reasonably believed that a contract had been formed.

For the reasons expressed above, the trial court's determination that no contract was formed between the parties is affirmed.

Affirmed in favor of Barron.

CYBERLAW IN ACTION

Standardized contracts are common online as well as in the physical world. You have probably entered into online standardized contracts when you downloaded software from the Internet, joined an online service, initialized an e-mail account, or purchased goods online. The terms of standardized contracts online are usually presented in a manner that requires the viewer to click on an icon indicating agreement before he can proceed in the program. Standardized online contracts presented in this way are often called **clickwrap**

contracts. If you have purchased mass-marketed software in a package, you have probably noticed that the program disk is packaged in a sealed package with a notice that states that your opening the package constitutes agreement with the terms of a proposed standardized license agreement. These are called **shrinkwrap contracts** or **shrinkwrap licenses,** a name that refers to the practice of packaging software in shrinkwrapped packaging. The enforceability of clickwraps and shrinkwraps, which has been a controversial topic, will be discussed in Chapters 10 and 11.

LOG ON

For a helpful overview of the law of contracts, see Findlaw for Small Business, *Contract Law: The Basics,* **http://smallbusiness.findlaw.com/business-forms-contracts/business-forms-contracts-overview.html.**

Basic Contract Concepts and Types

Bilateral and Unilateral Contracts

Contracts have traditionally been classified as **bilateral** or **unilateral,** depending on whether one or both of the parties have made a promise. In unilateral contracts, only one party makes a promise. For example, Perks Café issues "frequent buyer" cards to its customers, and stamps the cards each time a customer buys a cup of coffee. Perks promises to give any customer a free cup of coffee if the customer buys 10 cups of coffee and has his "frequent buyer" card stamped 10 times. In this case, Perks has made an offer for a unilateral contract, a contract that will be created with a customer only if and when the customer buys 10 cups of coffee and has his card stamped ten times. In a bilateral contract, by contrast, *both* parties exchange promises and the contract is formed as soon as the promises are exchanged. For example, if Perks Café promises to pay Willowtown Mall $1,000 a month if Willowtown Mall will promise to lease a kiosk in the mall to Perks for the holiday season, Perks has made an offer for a bilateral contract because it is offering a promise in exchange for a promise. If Willowtown Mall makes the requested promise, a bilateral contract is formed at that point—even before the parties begin performing any of the acts that they have promised to do.

Valid, Unenforceable, Voidable, and Void Contracts

A **valid contract** is one that meets all of the legal requirements for a binding contract. Valid contracts are, therefore, enforceable in court.

An **unenforceable contract** is one that meets the basic legal requirements for a contract but may not be enforceable because of some other legal rule. You'll learn about an example of this in Chapter 16, which discusses the statute of frauds, a rule that requires certain kinds of contracts to be evidenced by a writing. If a contract is one of those for which the statute of frauds requires a writing, but no writing is made, the contract is said to be unenforceable. Another example of an unenforceable contract is an otherwise valid contract whose enforcement is barred by the applicable contract statute of limitations.

Voidable contracts are those in which one or more of the parties have the legal right to cancel their obligations under the contract. For example, a contract that is induced by fraud or duress is voidable (cancelable) at the election of the injured party. Other situations in which contracts are voidable are discussed in Chapters 13 and 14. The important feature of a voidable contract is that the injured party has the *right* to cancel the contract *if he chooses*. That right belongs only to the injured party, and if he does not cancel the contract, it can be enforced by either party.

Void contracts are agreements that create no legal obligations and for which no remedy will be given. Contracts to commit crimes, such as "hit" contracts, are classic examples of void contracts. Illegal contracts such as these are discussed in Chapter 15.

Express and Implied Contracts

In an **express contract,** the parties have directly stated the terms of their contract orally or in writing at the time the contract was formed. However, the mutual agreement necessary to create a contract may also be demonstrated by the conduct of the parties. When the surrounding facts and circumstances indicate that an agreement has in fact been reached, an **implied contract** (also called a contract implied in fact) has been created. When you go to a doctor for treatment, for example, you do not ordinarily state the terms of your agreement in advance, although it is clear that you do, in fact, have an agreement. A court would infer a promise by your doctor to use reasonable care and skill in treating you and a return promise on your part to pay a reasonable fee for her services.

Executed and Executory Contracts

A contract is **executed** when all of the parties have fully performed their contractual duties, and it is **executory** until such duties have been fully performed.

Any contract may be described using one or more of the above terms. For example, Eurocars, Inc., orders five new Mercedes-Benz 500 SLs from Mercedes. Mercedes sends Eurocars its standard acknowledgment form accepting the order. The parties have a *valid, express, bilateral* contract that will be *executory* until Mercedes delivers the cars and Eurocars pays for them.

Sources of Law Governing Contracts

Two bodies of law—Article 2 of the Uniform Commercial Code and the common law of contracts—govern contracts today. The Uniform Commercial Code, or UCC, is statutory law in every state. The common law of contracts is court-made law that, like all court-made law, is in a constant state of evolution. Determining what body of law applies to a contract problem is a very important first step in analyzing that problem.

The Uniform Commercial Code: Origin and Purposes

The UCC was created by the American Law Institute and the National Conference of Commissioners on Uniform State Laws. All of the states have adopted it except Louisiana, which has adopted only part of the Code. The drafters of the Code had several purposes in mind, the most obvious of which was to establish a uniform set of rules to govern commercial

CYBERLAW IN ACTION

Currently, many courts are using the Uniform Commercial Code in cases involving disputes over software and other information contracts. However, the UCC was designed to deal with sales of goods and may not sufficiently address the concerns that parties have when making contracts to create or distribute information. During the 1990s, contract scholars, representatives of the affected information industries, consumer groups, and others worked as a drafting committee of the National Conference of Commissioners on Uniform State Laws to draft a uniform law that would be tailored to "information contracts." Internet access contracts and software licenses are two familiar examples of information contracts. Initially, this uniform statute was conceived of as a new article of the UCC. Later, however, attempts to fit the uniform law within the UCC were abandoned, and it was ultimately released as a proposed statute called the Uniform Computer Information Transactions Act, or UCITA. Several UCITA positions—notably those dealing with shrinkwrap and clickwrap licenses—have been quite controversial, and at the time of this writing, only two states have adopted UCITA in full as part of their state law.

---

transactions, which are often conducted across state lines.[1]

In addition to promoting uniformity, the drafters of the Code sought to create a body of rules that would realistically and fairly solve the common problems occurring in everyday commercial transactions. Finally, the drafters tried to formulate rules that would promote fair dealing and higher standards in the marketplace.

The UCC contains nine articles, most of which are discussed in detail in Parts 4, 6, and 7 of this book. The most important Code article for our present purposes is Article 2, which deals with the sale of goods.

The UCC has changed and is in the process of continuing to change in response to changes in technology and business transactions. In some instances, the creation of new bodies of uniform law have been necessary to govern transactions that are similar to but different in significant ways from the sale of goods. For example, as leasing became a more common way of executing and financing transactions in goods, a separate UCC article, Article 2A, was enacted to govern the *lease* of goods. In 2003, the private organizations that draft and revise the Uniform Commercial Code—the National Conference of Commissioners on Uniform State Laws and the American Law Institute—approved revisions of Article 2 of the UCC. These revisions will not become law unless and until they are adopted by legislatures. The revisions are meant to modernize the UCC to accommodate changes in business and technology, but they have been controversial. As this textbook is going to press, no states have adopted the new revisions.

Application of Article 2
Article 2 expressly applies only to *contracts for the sale of goods* [2-102] (the numbers in brackets refer to specific Code sections). The essence of the definition of goods in the UCC [1-105] is that *goods are tangible, movable, personal property.* So, contracts for the sale of such items as motor vehicles, books, appliances, and clothing are covered by Article 2.

Application of the Common Law of Contracts
Article 2 of the UCC applies to contracts for the sale of goods, but it does *not* apply to contracts for the sale of real estate or intangibles such as stocks and bonds, because those kinds of property do not constitute goods. Article 2 also does not apply to *service* contracts. Contracts for the sale of real estate, services, and intangibles are governed by the common law of contracts.

Law Governing "Hybrid" Contracts
Many contracts involve a hybrid of both goods and services. As the following *Pass* case discusses, the test that the courts most frequently use to determine whether Article 2 applies to such a contract is to ask which element, goods or services, *predominates* in the contract. Is the major purpose or thrust of the agreement the rendering of a service, or is it the sale of goods, with any services involved being merely incidental to that sale? This means that contracts calling for services that involve significant elements of personal skill or judgment in addition to goods probably are not governed by Article 2.

---

[1]Despite the Code's almost national adoption, however, complete uniformity has not been achieved. Many states have varied or amended the Code's language in specific instances, and some Code provisions were drafted in alternative ways, giving the states more than one version of particular Code provisions to choose from. Also, the various state courts have reached different conclusions about the meaning of particular Code sections.

Pass v. Shelby Aviation   2000 Tenn. App. LEXIS 247 (Ct. App. Tenn. 2000)

Max Pass owned and piloted a single engine Piper airplane. On April 15, 1994, Pass and his wife, Martha Pass, left Plant City, Florida, in the plane, bound for Clarksville, Tennessee. Somewhere over Alabama, the couple flew into turbulence. Pass lost control of the plane and it crashed to the ground in Alabama, killing the Passes. The administrators of the Passes' estates brought a lawsuit for breach of express and implied warranty under the UCC against Shelby Aviation, which is a fixed-base operator that services aircraft at an airport in Tennessee. Four and a half months prior to the Passes' fatal flight, Pass took his plane to Shelby Aviation for inspection and service. In servicing the plane, Shelby Aviation replaced both rear wing attach point brackets. The Passes' estates claimed that the rear wing attach point brackets sold and installed by Shelby Aviation were defective because they lacked the bolts necessary to secure them to the plane. Their complaint stated that Shelby Aviation employees failed to provide and install the bolts and that the missing bolts resulted in a failure of both wings of the plane to withstand the torque applied to an aircraft during turbulence, leading to Pass's loss of control of the plane and ultimately causing the crash.

Shelby Aviation filed a motion to dismiss, arguing that its contract with Pass had been primarily for the sale of services, rather than goods, and so the transaction was not covered by Article 2 of the Uniform Commercial Code. The trial court ruled against Shelby Aviation and Shelby Aviation appealed.

Lillard, Judge

Article 2 of the Uniform Commercial Code governs the sale of goods. Many contracts, however, like the one at bar, involve a mixture of both goods and services. The problem in such "mixed" transactions is to determine whether Article 2 governs the contract. Most jurisdictions follow one of two different approaches to address the problem. The first approach, sometimes called the "gravamen test," looks to that portion of the transaction upon which the complaint is based, to determine if it involved goods or services. The other approach, known as the "predominant factor" test, looks at the transaction as a whole to determine whether its predominant purpose was the sale of goods or the provision of a service. In *Hudson v. Town and Country True Value Hardware,* a mixed transaction involving a contract for the sale of both goods and real estate, Tennessee elected to follow the predominant factor approach, finding it "preferable to adopt a test that views the transaction as a whole."

Under the predominant factor test, the transaction between Shelby Aviation and Pass is examined to determine whether its predominant purpose was the sale of goods or the sale of services. If it was predominantly a contract for the sale of goods, it falls under the UCC and the warranty provisions of Article 2 apply. If it was predominantly a contract for service, it falls outside the UCC, and the warranty provisions of Article 2 are inapplicable. To determine whether the predominant purpose of a mixed transaction is the sale of goods or the provision of a service, we examine the language of the parties' contract, the nature of the business of the supplier of the goods and services, the reason the parties entered into the contract (i.e., what each bargained to receive), and the respective amounts charged under the contract for goods and for services.

In this case, Shelby Aviation argues that the predominant factor, thrust, and purpose of its transaction with Pass was the sale of services, with the sale of goods incidentally involved. Shelby Aviation notes the language in the invoice, which refers to the plane being brought in for "repair" and "100 hour inspection." Shelby Aviation also observes that the nature of its business is primarily service.

The Passes' estates argue that the predominant factor was the sale of goods. In analyzing the costs of the goods and services, the estates argue that the cost to install the parts should be included within the cost of the parts. If it is, the estates assert that 75 percent of the total amount charged by Shelby Aviation was for the sale of goods. The written document evidencing the transaction is the invoice prepared by Shelby Aviation. The invoice is preprinted with a handwritten description of repairs performed and parts used. In the top left hand corner, blocked off from the rest of the writing, is a preprinted paragraph that states that the owner is authorizing "the following repair work to be done along with the necessary material." On the top right hand side, under a heading entitled "Description," the box stating "annual 100 hour periodic inspection" is checked. On the left side of the invoice, beneath the authorization for repair, is a section entitled "Part number and description" with a handwritten list of the parts used and the amount charged for each. The right hand lower side of the page, under the heading "Service Description" lists the service performed and the amount charged. Finally, the bottom left corner of the page contains a block for "owner's signature" acknowledging "acceptance of repaired plane." As a whole, the invoice clearly emphasizes the repair and inspection aspect of the transaction, indicating that the predominant purpose was the sale of service, with the sale of goods incidental to that service.

We must also consider the nature of Shelby Aviation's business. The estates' complaint asserts that Shelby Aviation is "in the business of maintenance, service, storage, and upkeep of aircraft." Shelby Aviation's president stated in his affidavit that the parts sold to Pass in conjunction with the service performed on his airplane were ordered specifically for his airplane. In addition, the invoice indicates that one part installed by the defendant, the right engine mag, was supplied by Pass. Shelby Aviation argues that if it were primarily in the business of selling parts, rather than service, it would not have permitted a customer to supply his own part to be installed. Overall, the nature of Shelby Aviation's business appears to be service rather than the sale of parts.

It is also clear that Pass took the plane to Shelby Aviation primarily to have a service performed, i.e., the annual inspection. What the purchaser sought to procure when he entered into the contract is a strong indication of the predominant purpose of the contract. The "final product" Pass "bargained to receive" appears to be the annual inspection of his airplane.

The last factor to be considered is the respective amounts charged under the contract for goods and services. By adding the labor charge to install the parts sold to the cost of the parts themselves, the estates calculate that 75 percent of the amount Shelby Aviation charged is attributable to the sale of goods rather than service. The estates cite no case law in support of this method of calculation. Indeed, at least one case appears to indicate that the cost of labor for installing parts would *not* be included in the cost of the goods for purpose of ascertaining the purpose of the contract. If the cost of labor is not considered part of the cost of goods, the percentage of the invoice attributable to goods is 37 percent.

Regardless of how the percentage of the cost of goods is calculated, viewing the transaction as a whole, we must conclude that the predominant purpose of the transaction was the provision of a service rather than the sale of goods. The language of the invoice, the nature of the defendant's business, and the purpose for which Pass took his airplane to Shelby Aviation all indicate that service was the predominant factor in the transaction. Even where the cost of goods exceeds the cost of the services, the predominant purpose of the contract may still be deemed the provision of service where the other factors support such a finding. Therefore, we hold that the transaction between Shelby Aviation and Pass was predominantly a contract for service, with the sale of goods incidentally involved. As such, it is not subject to the warranty provisions of Article 2 of the UCC. Shelby Aviation is entitled to judgment as a matter of law on the UCC breach of warranty claims.

Reversed and remanded in favor of Shelby Aviation.

Relationship of the UCC and the Common Law of Contracts

Two important qualifications must be made concerning the application of Code contract principles. First, the Code does not change *all* of the traditional contract rules. Where no specific Code rule exists, traditional contract law rules apply to contracts for the sale of goods (see Figure 2). Second, and ultimately far more important, the courts have demonstrated a significant tendency to apply Code contract concepts by analogy to some contracts that are not technically covered by Article 2. For example, the Code concepts of good faith dealing and unconscionability have enjoyed wide application in cases that are technically outside the scope of Article 2. Thus, the Code is an important influence in shaping the evolution of contract law in general.

Basic Differences in the Nature of Article 2 and the Common Law of Contracts

Many of the provisions of Article 2 differ from traditional common law rules in a variety of important ways. The Code is more concerned with rewarding people's legitimate expectations than with technical rules, so it is generally more flexible than the common law of contracts. A court that applies the Code is more likely to find that the parties had a contract than is a court that applies the common law of contracts [2–204]. In some cases, the Code gives less weight to technical requirements such as consideration [2–205 and 2–209].

The drafters of the Code sought to create practical rules to deal with what people actually do in today's marketplace. We live in the day of the form contract, so some of the Code's rules try to deal fairly with that fact [2–205, 2–207, 2–209(2), and 2–302]. The words *reasonable, commercially reasonable,* and *seasonably* (within a reasonable time) are found throughout the Code. This reasonableness standard is different from the hypothetical reasonable person standard in tort law. A court that tries to decide what is reasonable under the Code is more likely to be concerned with what people really do in the marketplace than with what a nonexistent reasonable person would do.

The drafters of the Code wanted to promote fair dealing and higher standards in the marketplace, so they imposed a **duty of good faith** [1–203] in the performance

Figure 2   *When the Uniform Commercial Code Applies*

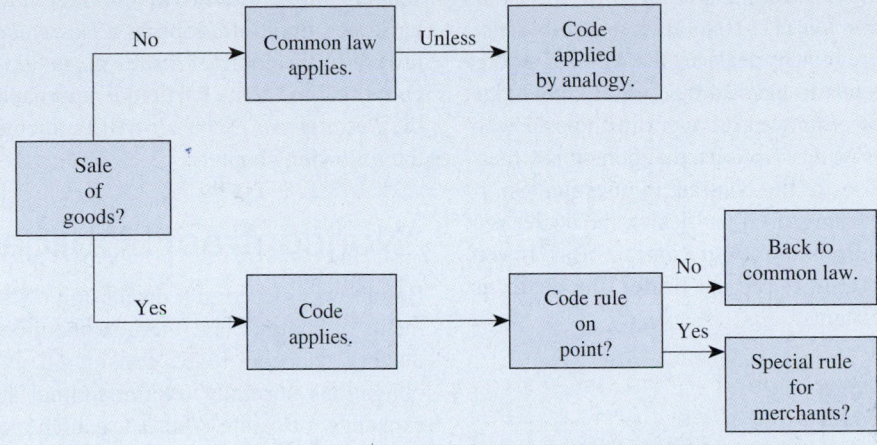

 ## The Global Business Environment

Dealing with Contract Disputes in International Transactions

The **United Nations Convention on Contracts for the International Sale of Goods,** or **CISG,** is an international body of contract rules that harmonizes contract principles from many legal systems. Seventy-one countries, including the United States and Canada, have adopted the CISG to date. The CISG is intended to provide a uniform code for international commercial contracts in much the same way as the UCC provides uniformity for transactions among contracting parties in different states in the United States. Like the UCC, though, the CISG does not have provisions to cover every contract problem that might occur. It applies only to sales of goods, not services, and only to commercial parties, not consumers. When there is a contract for the sale of goods between commercial parties whose relevant places of business are located in two different countries that have agreed to the CISG, the CISG applies by default unless the parties have opted out of the CISG in their contract. Since the CISG emphasizes freedom of contract, it does permit the parties to agree to exclude or vary any of the CISG rules or to opt out of the CISG completely by stating in their contract that some other body of law (such as the UCC) will apply to their contract.

Companies entering international transactions often protect themselves from disputes over what body of laws applies to their disputes by including a **choice of law clause** in their contracts. This is a provision that states the parties' agreement that a particular country or state's law will apply to their contract. (Of course, choice of law clauses are used extensively in domestic transactions as well.) In addition, it is very common for parties in international transactions to include an **arbitration clause** in their contracts, providing that future disputes between them will be resolved by arbitration.[2] Using arbitration gives the parties a relatively speedy and affordable dispute resolution process. An added benefit is that there are several international treaties that will enforce arbitration awards.

---

[2]Arbitration is discussed in more detail in Chapter 2.

---

and enforcement of every contract under the Code. Good faith means "honesty in fact," which is required of all parties to sales contracts [1–201(19)]. In addition, merchants are required to observe "reasonable commercial standards of fair dealing" [2–103(1)(b)]. The parties cannot alter this duty of good faith by agreement [1–102(3)]. Finally, the Code expressly recognizes the concept of an **unconscionable contract,** one that is grossly unfair or one-sided, and it gives the courts broad discretionary powers to deal fairly with such contracts [2–302].[3]

The Code also recognizes that buyers tend to place more reliance on professional sellers and that professionals are generally more knowledgeable and better able to protect themselves than nonprofessionals. So, the

---

[3]Chapter 15 discusses unconscionability in detail.

Code distinguishes between **merchants** and nonmerchants by holding merchants to a higher standard in some cases [2–201(2), 2–205, and 2–207(2)]. The Code defines the term *merchant* [2–104(1)] on a case-by-case basis. If a person regularly deals in the kind of goods being sold, or pretends to have some special knowledge about the goods, or employed an agent in the sale who fits either of these two descriptions, that person is a merchant for the purposes of the contract in question. So, if you buy a used car from a used-car dealer, the dealer is a merchant for the purposes of your contract. But, if you buy a refrigerator from a used-car dealer, the dealer is probably not a merchant.

LOG ON

For links to everything you might ever want to know about the CISG, visit Pace University School of Law Database on the CISG and International Commercial Law, **www.cisg.law.pace.edu/**.

Influence of *Restatement (Second) of Contracts* In 1932, the American Law Institute published the first *Restatement of Contracts,*[4] an attempt to codify and systematize the soundest principles of contract law gleaned from thousands of often conflicting judicial decisions. As the product of a private organization, the *Restatement* did not have the force of law, but as the considered judgment of some of the leading scholars of the legal profession, it was highly influential in shaping the evolution of contract law. The *Restatement (Second) of Contracts,* issued in 1979, is an attempt to reflect the significant changes that have occurred in contract law in the years following the birth of the first *Restatement*. The *Restatement (Second)* reflects the "shift from rules to standards" in modern contract law—the shift from precise, technical rules to broader, discretionary principles that produce just results.[5] In fact, many *Restatement (Second)* provisions are virtually identical to their Code analogues. For example, the *Restatement (Second)* has explicitly embraced the Code concepts of *good faith*[6] and *unconscionability.*[7]

---

[4]See Chapter 1 for a general discussion of the *Restatement* phenomenon.

[5]Speidel, "Restatement Second: Omitted Terms and Contract Method," 67 *Cornell L. Rev.* 785, 786 (1982).

[6]*Restatement (Second) of Contracts* § 205 (1981).

[7]*Restatement (Second) of Contracts* § 208 (1981).

The *Restatement (Second)* does *not* have the force of law. Nonetheless, it can be and has been influential in shaping the evolution of contract law because courts have the option of adopting a *Restatement (Second)* approach to the contract issues presented in the cases that come before them. Particular approaches suggested by the *Restatement (Second)* will be mentioned in some of the following chapters.

"Noncontract" Obligations

Before we proceed to a discussion of the individual elements of contract law, there is one more group of introductory concepts to be considered. Although contract obligations normally require mutual agreement and an exchange of value, there are some circumstances in which the law enforces an obligation to pay for certain losses or benefits even in the absence of mutual agreement and exchange of value. We will refer to these circumstances as "noncontract" obligations because they impose the duty on a person to pay for a loss or benefit yet they do not meet the criteria for formation of a contract. These noncontract doctrines give a person who cannot establish the existence of a contract a chance to obtain compensation.

Quasi-Contract Requiring all the elements of a binding contract before contractual obligation is imposed can cause injustice in some cases. One person may have provided goods or services to another person who benefited from them but has no contractual obligation to pay for them because no facts exist that would justify a court in implying a promise to pay for them. Such a situation can also arise in cases where the parties contemplated entering into a binding contract but some legal defense exists that prevents the enforcement of the agreement. Consider the following examples:

1. Jones paints Smith's house by mistake, thinking it belongs to Reed. Smith knows that Jones is painting his house but does not inform him of his error. There are no facts from which a court can infer that Jones and Smith have a contract because the parties have had no prior discussions or dealings.

2. Thomas Products fraudulently induces Perkins to buy a household products franchise by grossly misstating the average revenues of its franchisees. Perkins discovers the misrepresentation after he has resold some products that he has received but before he has paid Thomas for them. Perkins elects to rescind (cancel) the franchise contract on the basis of the fraud.

In the preceding examples, both Smith and Perkins have good defenses to contract liability; however, enabling Smith to get a free paint job and Perkins to avoid paying for the goods he resold would *unjustly enrich* them at the expense of Jones and Thomas. To deal with such cases and to prevent such unjust enrichment, the courts imply *as a matter of law* a promise by the benefited party to pay the *reasonable value* of the benefits he received. This idea is called **quasi-contract** (also called unjust enrichment or contract implied in law) because it represents an obligation imposed by law to avoid injustice, not a contractual obligation created by voluntary consent. Quasi-contract liability has been imposed in situations too numerous and varied to detail. In general, however, quasi-contract liability is imposed when one party *confers a benefit* on another who *knowingly accepts it* and *retains it* under circumstances that make it *unjust* to do so without paying for it. So, if Jones painted Smith's house while Smith was away on vacation, Smith would probably not be liable for the reasonable value of the paint job because he did *not* knowingly accept it and because he has no way to return it to Jones. As a general rule, however, quasi-contract is not available when a valid contract covering the disputed subject matter exists between the parties. The following *Palese* case provides another example of the application of the concept "unjust enrichment."

Palese v. Delaware State Lottery Office
2006 Del. Ch. LEXIS 126 (Del. Chancery 2006)

On March 21, 2003, Robert Palese bought five Delaware State Lottery tickets from a liquor store in Newark, Delaware. To select his number for the game, Palese used a "play slip" that contained five game panels. Each panel had a selection grid with numbers 1 through 38, and Palese chose six numbers from each of these grids by manually filling in the grids. After purchasing the tickets, Palese placed them in his pants pocket and returned home. Several days later, Palese learned that someone had won the March 21, 2003, lottery but that the winner had not yet come forward. He searched for his ticket to see if he had selected the winning numbers, but was unable to find it. Eventually, he remembered that he had done laundry the evening he purchased the ticket; thus he concluded that the ticket—which had been left in his pants pocket—had probably been destroyed in the wash. Although the lottery ticket was gone, Palese still possessed the play slip he used when he purchased the ticket. He checked the numbers on the play slip and discovered that the numbers he selected on the play slip's fifth game panel—9, 13, 19, 24, 27, and 35—were the winning numbers for the March 21, 2003, lottery.

Reasoning that the play slip would satisfy the Lottery office that he had selected the winning numbers, Palese wrote the Lottery Office and described his predicament. The Lottery Office advised him that he would need to wait one year "before the Lottery can even review your claim. If no other claims are made to this winning prize by March 21, 2004, the Lottery will then determine whether it has the legal authority under the Lottery laws and regulations to consider your letter claiming the winning prize." About eleven months later, Palese read in the newspaper that the unclaimed lottery jackpot had been transferred to the State's General Fund. Palese immediately contacted the Lottery Office. He was asked to provide further information about the ticket he purchased and how it had been destroyed. Palese complied and again explained that, although the ticket itself had been inadvertently destroyed in the laundry, he still had the play slip. The Lottery Office took the position that Palese needed to produce the actual winning ticket, and it denied his claim.

Palese brought suit against the Lottery Office and others, seeking to collect the lottery jackpot. The defendants moved to dismiss the claim on the ground that Palese failed to state a claim for which relief can be granted.

Noble, Vice Chancellor

The Delaware Constitution of 1897 contained a general prohibition against gambling. In 1973, [this provision] was amended to permit, among other exceptions, a state-operated Lottery. Within a few months, enabling legislation (the "Lottery Act") was passed which created the State Lottery Office and the position of Director of the State Lottery Office. The Lottery Act delegated to the Director the authority "to promulgate such rules and regulations governing the establishment and operation of the lottery." Pursuant to its mandate under the Lottery Act, the Lottery Office has promulgated rules and regulations that set forth the procedures for claiming prizes. These rules advance the Lottery Act's directive that payment of prizes be made to holders of winning tickets. As stated in Lottery Regulation 18, "[a]ll winning tickets will be validated. A winning ticket must not be counterfeit in whole or in part and *must be presented* by a person authorized to play the Lottery." Furthermore, Lottery Regulation 11.3 provides that the Lottery "shall not be responsible for lost, stolen, or mutilated tickets after sale of same to the public." Finally, under Lottery Regulation 19, "a lottery ticket which has been sold shall be owned by the *physical possessor* of said ticket." Thus, in accordance with the Lottery Regulations, the winning ticket must be presented in order to claim the prize.

By purchasing a lottery ticket, Palese entered into a contractual relationship with the Lottery Office, one evidenced, in the first instance, by the lottery ticket. The majority rule in American jurisprudence is that the relationship between a lottery ticket holder and the state lottery agency is primarily contractual in nature, and the purchase of a ticket in the proper manner constitutes acceptance of an offer, forming a binding contract. The text on the back of the lottery ticket placed Palese on notice that his rights as player of the lottery would be subject to the following terms:

> This ticket is a bearer instrument, therefore you should sign your ticket for safety. Valid only for date(s) shown. *Determination of winners and transactions are subject to Delaware State Lottery laws, rules, regulations and directives.* Void if mutilated, altered illegible or incomplete. Not responsible for torn or stolen tickets.

The ticket unequivocally stated that the right to payment is controlled by applicable laws and regulations (which, as discussed above, restrict payment of prizes to holders of winning tickets). Furthermore, the purchaser is advised to sign the back of the ticket because it is a "bearer instrument," meaning it is "payable to the person who holds it rather than to the order of a specific person." Just as the Court is bound to honor the plain language of the Lottery Act, it also must honor the express terms of the parties' agreement. Under the plain language of the parties' agreement, which Palese consented to when he purchased the ticket, payment of prize money is restricted to winning ticket holders.

Palese alleges that the State has been unjustly enriched by retaining a benefit to his detriment. He asks the Court to impose a quasi-contractual duty upon the defendants to pay the, allegedly, unjustly retained prize to him. Courts developed unjust enrichment, or quasi-contract, as a theory of recovery to remedy the absence of a formal contract. A party cannot seek recovery under an unjust enrichment theory if a contract is the measure of the plaintiff's right. Palese is precluded from prevailing on his claim for unjust enrichment because a binding contract exists between the parties that addresses the particular subject matter—the procedure for claiming the prize money. Because an enforceable contract exists between the parties and that contract requires presentment of the ticket, Palese's claim for unjust enrichment must be dismissed. Even if the express terms established under the contractual relationship between Palese and the Lottery Office were not dispositive, Palese would nonetheless be denied the equitable relief he seeks under the doctrine of unjust enrichment. The facts, as alleged by Palese, could support no such a finding here. Under Delaware law, only persons with a winning ticket are eligible to receive the prize money. The defendants denied Palese's claim based on their interpretation—which the Court accepts—that the Delaware lottery laws and regulations require presentation of the winning ticket. As a consequence, not only is his claim defeated by a controlling contract term, it also is deficient because the Defendants' conduct was not absent of justification; on the contrary, the defendants acted within the bounds of their prescribed legal authority and in conformity with the governing statute and regulations. Thus, Palese's claim under the doctrine of unjust enrichment must be dismissed.

Palese's complaint dismissed for failure to state a claim on which relief can be granted.

Promissory Estoppel

Promissory Estoppel Another very important idea that courts have developed to deal with the unfairness that would sometimes result from the strict application of traditional contract principles is the doctrine of **promissory estoppel.** In numerous situations one person may *rely* on a promise made by another even though the promise and surrounding circumstances are not sufficient to justify the conclusion that a contract has been created because one or more of the required elements is missing. To allow the person who made such a promise (the promisor) to argue that no contract was created would sometimes work an injustice on the person who relied on the promise (the promisee). For example, in

Ricketts v. Scothorn, a grandfather's promise to pay his granddaughter interest on a demand note he gave her so that she would not have to work was enforced against him after she had quit her job in reliance on his promise.[8] The Nebraska Supreme Court acknowledged that such promises were traditionally unenforceable because they were gratuitous and not supported by any consideration, but held that the granddaughter's reliance prevented her grandfather from raising his lack of consideration defense. In the early decades of this century, many courts began to extend similar protection to relying promisees.

---

[8]57 Neb. 51, 77 N.W. 365 (1898).

They said that persons who made promises that produced such reliance were *estopped,* or equitably prevented, from raising any defense they had to the enforcement of their promise. Out of such cases grew the doctrine of promissory estoppel. Section 90 of the *Restatement (Second) of Contracts* states:

A promise which the promisor should reasonably expect to induce action or forbearance on the part of the promisee or a third person and which does induce such action or forbearance is binding if injustice can be avoided only by enforcement of the promise. The remedy granted for breach may be limited as justice requires.

Thus, the elements of promissory estoppel are a *promise* that the *promisor should foresee is likely to induce reliance, reliance* on the promise by the promisee, and *injustice* as a result of that reliance. (See Figure 3.) The following *Holt* case provides an example of promissory estoppel.

When you consider these elements, it is obvious that promissory estoppel is fundamentally different from traditional contract principles. Contract is traditionally thought of as protecting *agreements* or bargains. Promissory

estoppel, on the other hand, protects *reliance.* Early promissory estoppel cases applied the doctrine only to gift promises like the one made by the grandfather in the previous example. As subsequent chapters demonstrate, however, promissory estoppel is now being used by the courts to prevent offerors from revoking their offers, to enforce indefinite promises, and to enforce oral promises that would ordinarily have to be in writing.

Figure 3 Contract and Noncontract Theories of Recovery

Theory	Key Concept	Remedy
Contract	Voluntary agreement	Enforce promise
Quasi-Contract	Unjust enrichment	Reasonable value of services
Promissory Estoppel	Foreseeable reliance	Enforce promise or recover reliance losses

Holt v. Home Depot, U.S.A., Inc.
2004 U.S. Dist. LEXIS 824 (U.S. Dist Ct. D. Conn. 2004)

Bruce Holt worked as a manager for Home Depot from January 1995 to July 1999. Throughout those years, Home Depot assured employees through statements in the employee handbook and other means of communication that if they took advantage of the company's open-door procedure to complain to management about their supervisors, they would not be penalized. In March 1999, Home Depot moved Holt and his family to Connecticut so he could manage a new distribution center in Bloomfield. Soon after he started there, he began to have difficulties and disagreements with his immediate supervisor, Ms. Gray. In June, he contacted a senior manager, Brian Bender, regarding his problems with her. On July 3, he called Home Depot's Impact Line to ask that forms be sent to him so he could make a formal complaint. On July 9, two senior Home Depot managers went to the Bloomfield center accompanied by Gray and terminated Holt's employment. Holt sued Home Depot, claiming promissory estoppel. The jury found in favor of Holt and awarded him $467,000 in compensatory damages. Home Depot moved for relief of several kinds, including judgment as a matter of law and a new trial.

Chatigny, District Judge

The jury was correctly charged that Holt could not prevail on this claim unless he proved the following: (1) Home Depot made a clear, definite promise that it would not retaliate against employees for using its internal complaint procedure; (2) Home Depot reasonably should have expected the plaintiff to rely on the promise; (3) he did reasonably rely on it; (4) his employment with Home Depot was terminated as a result; and (5) enforcement of the promise is necessary to prevent injustice.

Home Depot argues that it made no definite promise on which Holt could reasonably rely. While conceding that its

employee handbook contained an explicit promise that no employee would be penalized for using the open-door procedure, it contends that Holt could not reasonably rely on the promise because of disclaimers of contractual intent contained in the handbook and his employment application. I disagree. I think the jury could reasonably find that Home Depot's promise not to retaliate against employees for using the open-door procedure was so clear, emphatic, highly touted, and widely proclaimed that Holt could reasonably believe it was inviolable and thus not covered by general disclaimers in the handbook and application. Home Depot relies on cases in which similar disclaimers precluded claims of promissory estoppel, but those cases are factually distinguishable.

Home Depot next argues that the jury could not reasonably find that Holt proved reliance because there is no evidence he used the open-door procedure to complain about Gray. Here again, I disagree. The evidence is sufficient to support the jury's finding that he undertook to complain about Gray in reliance on the no-retaliation guarantee.

Home Depot next argues that the jury could not reasonably find that Holt's employment was terminated because of any complaint he made about Gray. It argues that the persons who terminated his employment did not know about his attempts to complain about her, and that he was terminated for incompetence, insubordination, and violating an ethics policy. It supports both arguments primarily with the testimony of the three people involved in the termination decision. The jury was entitled to reject their testimony as pretextual, particularly in light of the close temporal proximity between Holt's initial steps to complain to higher-ups about Gray and the termination of his employment, as well as the sequence of events immediately preceding the termination, which fit Holt's theory that he was the victim of a preemptive strike instigated by Gray.

Home Depot's motions denied in favor of Holt.

Ethics in Action

The idea that contracts should be enforced because they are voluntary agreements can obviously be justified on ethical grounds. But what about quasi-contracts and promissory estoppel? What ethical justifications can you give for departing from the notion of voluntary agreement in quasi-contract and promissory estoppel cases?

Problems and Problem Cases

1. The Joswicks bought a mobile home manufactured by Brigadier Homes of North Carolina, Inc., from Chesapeake Mobile Homes, Inc., in March 1988. In February 1995, they noticed for the first time that the roof was leaking due to the fact that the shingles at the eaves had been improperly installed and did not permit sufficient overhang to allow rain water to drip off the roof. That condition caused water to back up and rot facia boards and plywood, the repair of which would cost $4,275. The leak also damaged the interior of the mobile home. The defect was present when Chesapeake delivered the mobile home to the Joswicks in 1988, which was a breach of the warranty that the Joswicks had received from Brigadier. The Joswicks sued Chesapeake and Brigadier for breach of warranty. The defendants argued that the UCC statute of limitations applied to the case and that the Joswicks had waited too long to bring their case. Did the UCC apply to this case?

2. Clarence Jackson went to the Snack Plus convenience store in Hamden, Connecticut, and bought a Connecticut Lotto "Quick Pick" ticket for the drawing of October 13, 1995. On the back of the ticket are various provisions, including the admonition that "Prize must be claimed within one year from the drawing date. Determination of winners subject to DOSR rules and regulations." It also stated instructions for claiming the prize by presentment to any online agent or to "Lottery Claims" in Newington, Connecticut. The drawing was held on October 13, and the winning six-number combination was announced. One of the six-number combinations on Jackson's Lotto ticket matched the six-number combination drawn in the October 13 drawing, for a prize of $5.8 million dollars. Jackson only learned of the match 15 minutes before the one-year deadline that he had won. Instead of claiming his prize online, Jackson waited several more days until after the Columbus Day holiday to present it in person at the Lottery Claims Center because he was under the impression that it had to be presented there. The Connecticut Lottery Corporation (CLC) denied Jackson's claim because the one-year presentment period had elapsed. Does contract law give Jackson the right to claim the prize under these circumstances?

3. Mill Creek, a design fabrication firm, prepared and presented preliminary designs, sketches, and budgets

for a museum display of a London street scene to the Jackson Foundation, which operated a museum. Mill Creek's employee, Cooper, had put in approximately 156 hours working on the project on Mill Creek's behalf when the Jackson Foundation hired Cooper to take the project "in house." Jackson Foundation used some of Cooper's design to build a small portion of the London street scene and the display remained as part of Cooper's workload as an employee of Jackson Foundation. Mill Creek sought recovery from Jackson Foundation under a quasi-contract theory. Will it be successful?

4. In July 2006, Hernandez was employed by Nestlé as an industrial engineer. Hernandez learned of a job opening at UPS Supply Chain Solutions, Inc., and applied for it. He interviewed with UPS representatives and received a written job offer from UPS for a management trainee position in the El Paso, Texas, Industrial Engineering Department. He was assured by UPS supervisors that the job was his, so he accepted the UPS offer and quit his job with Nestlé. Hernandez terminated the lease on his apartment, discarded his furniture, and incurred moving and traveling expenses by relocating his family to El Paso. When he arrived at UPS, he was informed that his starting date would be delayed, but was assured once again that he would be employed by UPS. Hernandez worked at UPS for three days, from September 5 through September 7, 2006. Hernandez's work duties consisted of attending UPS orientation for approximately two days and working at home one day. After the second day of orientation, a UPS supervisor told Hernandez that he should go home because he was not an official employee. The next week, a UPS human resources representative informed Hernandez that UPS would not honor the job offer. In addition, Hernandez was not paid for the hours worked from September 5 to September 7, 2006. Hernandez sued UPS on the ground of promissory estoppel to recover his out-of-pocket expenses. Will he win?

5. Chow arranged through a travel agent to fly from Indianapolis to Singapore on June 27, 1986. Singapore Airlines gave him a round-trip ticket that included a TWA flight to Los Angeles. Shortly before the trip, Chow's flight was rerouted so that he had to fly to St. Louis first and then to San Francisco. During the St. Louis stopover, the flight developed engine trouble, causing a substantial delay. TWA personnel assured Chow that if he missed his connecting flight, TWA would arrange for him to take the next Singapore flight out of San Francisco. After the engine problem was fixed, TWA delayed the flight's departure an additional two hours to board additional passengers. Chow was again assured that if he missed his scheduled flight, TWA would make arrangements for him. Chow missed his Singapore flight by minutes, and was housed overnight at TWA's expense in San Francisco after once more being assured that TWA would make arrangements to get him on the next Singapore flight. When he called Singapore Airlines the next morning to see whether TWA had made him a reservation, Chow was told that no arrangements had been made. When he contacted TWA, he was told TWA would make the arrangements immediately. After waiting several hours, Chow learned TWA had still not made the arrangements and was told that TWA could no longer help him. Because Singapore Airlines no longer had economy class seats available, Chow had to buy a business class seat at an additional cost of $928. When he filed suit against TWA for that amount, TWA argued that the Conditions of Contract printed on Chow's ticket disclaimed any liability for failure to make connections. Did Chow have a valid claim against TWA?

6. Houston repeatedly promised his daughter, Allyson, that he would pay one-half of the costs of Allyson attending a private, historically African-American, college or university. Relying on this promise, Allyson applied to and was accepted into Clark Atlanta University. Houston reiterated this promise after Allyson's acceptance and specifically agreed to pay one-half of the costs of her tuition, room, board, books, and other expenses at Clark (less certain scholarship, work study, and grant monies). Allyson relied on this reiterated promise and, forgoing opportunities to apply to and enroll in other colleges or universities of significantly less cost, enrolled in Clark. Houston nevertheless refused to honor his commitment. Allyson sued her father alleging promissory estoppel. Does she have a good case for promissory estoppel?

7. Star Coach is in the business of converting sport utility vehicles and pickup trucks into custom vehicles. It performs the labor involved in installing parts supplied by other companies onto vehicles owned by dealers. Heart of Texas Dodge purchased a new

Dodge Durango from Chrysler Motors and entered into a contract with Star Coach for Star Coach to convert the Durango to a Shelby SP 360 custom performance vehicle and then return the converted vehicle to Heart of Texas Dodge. The manufacturer delivered the dealer's Durango to Star Coach and over a period of several months, Star Coach converted the vehicle using another company's parts. Several months later, Star Coach delivered the vehicle to Heart of Texas Dodge, which paid Star Coach the contract price of $15,768 without inspecting the vehicle. When Heart of Texas Dodge inspected the vehicle several days later, it found the workmanship faulty. Heart of Texas Dodge stopped payment on its check and Star Coach filed suit. An important issue in the case was whether the remedies of the UCC apply. Does the UCC apply to this case?

8. Emergency Physicians Integrated Care (EPIC) is a company that provides billing and collection services to various emergency physicians around Utah. EPIC provided medical services to county inmates incarcerated in Salt Lake County. The county denied any legal responsibility to pay the physicians for the services. Would EPIC have a valid claim against the county under quasi-contract?

9. Stephen Gall and his family became ill after drinking contaminated water supplied to their home by the McKeesport Municipal Water Authority. They filed suit against the utility, arguing, among other things, that the utility had breached the UCC implied warranty of merchantability when it sold them contaminated water. The utility moved to dismiss their complaint, arguing that since water was not "goods," the UCC did not apply. Should the Galls' complaint be dismissed?

10. In 1994, Schumacher and his wife and their two daughters moved to Finland, Minnesota, to operate a bar and restaurant called the Trestle Inn, which was owned by his parents. Schumacher claims that his parents induced him to leave his previous job and to make the move by orally agreeing to provide him a job managing the inn for life and to leave the business and a large parcel of land to him when his first parent died. Schumacher was given free reign in managing the inn and was allowed to retain all profits of the business but was not given any salary or wage. While he was operating the inn, Schumacher used his own funds to build a home for his family on his parents' land, install a well, buy equipment for the business, and develop various marketing tools for the business. In the fall of 1998, Schumacher suspected that his parents were about to sell the inn and the adjoining property. He brought suit for a restraining order to prevent them from doing so, claiming breach of contract and unjust enrichment, among other claims. In October 1998, the parents notified Schumacher that his employment at the inn and his right to possess the adjoining property were terminated. The parents moved for summary judgment. The trial court held that Schumacher's oral contract claim was invalid because the contract needed to be in writing under applicable Minnesota law. However, does Schumacher have a valid claim for unjust enrichment?

Online Research

Finding Sources of Contract Law

Find out which countries have signed the CISG (Contracts for International Sale of Goods). Create a hypothetical scenario in which the CISG would be applied to a contract. Use a CISG Web site such as Pace University School of Law's Database on the CISG and International Commercial Law, **www.cisg.law.pace.edu/** or simply do a key word search on your favorite search engine.

chapter 10

THE AGREEMENT: OFFER

J ackson read an ad in the newspaper that had been placed by the owner of a local dog track. The ad stated that the Pic-6 Jackpot for the last evening of the racing season would be $825,000. Jackson went to the track on that date, picked the winner in the six designated races, and won the jackpot. However, the owner of the track refused to pay Jackson more than $25,000, stating that it had intended the amount of the jackpot to be $25,000 and not $825,000. The reason the newspaper ad said "$825,000" was that a newspaper employee had misread the ad copy that the dog track owners had submitted to the newspaper, and had read the dollar sign in front of the 25,000 as an "8."

- Was the ad an offer?
- Does the actual intent of the dog track owner determine whether the offered jackpot was $25,000 or $825,000?
- Did the dog track owner have the right to terminate the offer?
- Is it ethically wrong for Jackson to take advantage of the dog track owner's mistake?

THE CONCEPT OF MUTUAL agreement lies at the heart of traditional contract law. Courts faced with deciding whether two or more persons entered into a contract look first for an *agreement* between the parties. Because the formation of an agreement is normally a two-step process by which one party makes a proposal and the other responds to the proposal, it is customary to analyze the agreement in two parts: *offer* and *acceptance.* This chapter, which concerns itself with the offer, and the next chapter, which covers acceptance, focus on the tools used by courts to determine whether the parties have reached the kind of agreement that becomes the foundation of a contract.

Requirements for an Offer

An **offer** is the critically important first step in the contract formation process. An offer says, in effect, "This is it—if you agree to these terms, we have a contract." The person who makes an offer (**the offeror**) gives the person to whom she makes the offer (**the offeree**) the power to bind her to a contract simply by accepting the offer.

Not every proposal qualifies as an offer. Some proposals are vague, for example, or made in jest, or thrown out merely as a way of opening negotiations. To distinguish an offer, courts look for three requirements. First, they look for some objective indication of a *present intent to contract* on the part of the offeror. Second, they look for specificity, or *definiteness,* in the terms of the alleged offer. Third, they look to see whether the alleged offer has been *communicated to the offeree.*

The preceding chapter discussed the fact that contracts for the sale of goods are governed by Article 2 of the UCC whereas contracts for services, real estate, and intangibles are generally governed by the common law of contracts. Common law and UCC standards for contract formation have a great deal in common, but they also differ somewhat. This chapter will point out those areas in which an offer for the sale of goods would be treated somewhat differently from an offer for services, real estate, and intangibles.

Intent to Contract For a proposal to be considered an offer, the offeror must indicate *present intent to contract.* Present intent means the intent to enter the contract upon acceptance. It signifies that the offeror is not joking, haggling, or equivocating. It makes sense that intent on the part of the offeror would be required for an offer—otherwise, an unwilling person might wrongly be bound to a contract. But what is meant by intent? Should courts look at what the offeror actually in his own mind (*subjectively*) intended? Or should intent be judged by the impression that he has given to the rest of the world through words, acts, and circumstances that *objectively* indicate that intent?

The Objective Standard of Intent Early American courts took a subjective approach to contract formation, asking whether there was truly a "meeting of the minds" between the parties. This subjective standard, however, created uncertainty in the enforcement of contracts because it left every contract vulnerable to disputes about actual intent. The desire to meet the needs of the marketplace by affording predictable and consistent results in contracts cases dictated a shift toward an *objective theory of contracts.* By the middle of the 19th century, the objective approach to contract formation, which judges agreement by looking at the parties' outward manifestations of intent, was firmly established in American law. Judge Learned Hand once described the effect of the objective contract theory as follows:

> A contract has, strictly speaking, nothing to do with the personal, or individual, intent of the parties. A contract is an obligation attached by the mere force of law to certain acts of the parties, usually words, which ordinarily accompany and represent a known intent. If however, it were proved by 20 bishops that either party when he used the words intended something else than the usual meaning which the law imposes on them, he would still be held, unless there were mutual mistake or something else of that sort.[1]

Following the objective theory of contracts, then, an offeror's intent will be judged by an objective standard—that is, what his words, acts, and the circumstances signify about his intent. If a reasonable person familiar with all the circumstances would be justified in believing that the offeror intended to contract, a court would find that the intent requirement of an offer was satisfied even if the offeror himself says that he did not intend to contract. The following *Meram v. MacDonald* case illustrates the objective standard of intent.

_____
[1]*Hotchkiss v. National City Bank,* 200 F. 287, 293 (S.D.N.Y. 1911).

Meram v. MacDonald　　2006 U.S. Dist. LEXIS 79069 (U.S. Dist. Ct. S.D. Cal.)

Allianz Sales invited Frank Meram to attend a presentation on September 29, 2005, to meet Robert MacDonald, who was promoting his new book, Cheat to Win. *MacDonald was a multimillionaire who had started as an insurance agent and built LifeUSA, a billion dollar company, which was owned by Allianz at the time of the presentation. Meram attended the presentation along with approximately 100 other financial representatives.*

At the beginning of the presentation, MacDonald announced that one of the attendees would leave that day with one million dollars. All that was required was to place a business card in the basket that was passed around, and to stay until the end of the presentation. At the end, MacDonald would select one card from the basket, and the person whose name was on the card would leave with a million dollars. Meram placed his business card in the basket and attended the presentation until the end. At the end of the presentation, MacDonald pulled Meram's business card out of the basket. He congratulated Meram and then explained how "this works." MacDonald said Meram would receive one dollar per year for a million years. He gave Meram $100 in cash for the first 100 years. According to MacDonald, all Meram had to do was attend a presentation once a year to claim the rest of the million dollars. MacDonald then laughed and thanked everyone for coming.

Meram filed an action for breach of contract against MacDonald and Allianz, seeking the remainder of the promised one million dollars. The defendants moved to dismiss Meram's case for failure to state a claim.

Lorenz, Judge

Defendants maintain no valid contract was created because MacDonald's statements at the seminar did not constitute a valid offer. To establish an offer, the defendant must communicate to the plaintiff that he is willing to enter into a contract with the plaintiff, the communication must contain specific terms, and, based on the communication, the plaintiff could have reasonably concluded that a contract with these terms would result if he accepted the offer. The issue is whether, under the circumstances, a reasonable person would conclude, from the words and conduct of each party, that there was an agreement. Defendants contend MacDonald's alleged offer was too good to be true, and Meram could not have reasonably concluded the offer was for a million dollars.

Meram alleges he concluded the offer was genuine, since he was aware that MacDonald was a multi-millionaire, that Allianz was a billion dollar company, and that each had the financial means to pay the promised sum. More significantly, MacDonald elaborated on the offer, and mentioned it at least twice. Based on these facts, Meram alleges he reasonably believed that defendants would pay the promised sum.

Reading the allegations in the light most favorable to the plaintiff, the allegations do not lead to an inescapable conclusion that the offer was a joke or that MacDonald meant anything other than what he said. Accordingly, the court cannot conclude that no reasonable person could conclude the offer was genuine. Meram therefore sufficiently alleged the offer and its terms.

Defendants next argue that there was no valid contract because the offer was too vague for failure to indentify who would receive the million dollars or the terms of payment. To form an enforceable contract, its terms must be clear enough that the parties could understand what each was required to do. By the alleged terms of the offer, the pool of potential winners was defined by the business cards placed in the basket. The winner's name was pulled out of the basket, and he or she would receive the prize so long as he or she also attended the presentation. Furthermore, MacDonald stated the winner would "walk out of here with a million dollars today." Accordingly, the alleged offer is sufficiently definite to support formation of a contract.

Motion to dismiss the action for breach of contract denied in favor of Meram.

Definiteness of Terms

Definiteness of Terms If Smith says to Ford, "I'd like to buy your house," and Ford responds, "You've got a deal," has a contract been formed? An obvious problem here is lack of specificity. A proposal that fails to state specifically what the offeror is willing to do and what he asks in return for his performance is unlikely to be considered an offer. One reason for the requirement of definiteness is that definiteness and specificity in an offer tend to indicate an intent to contract, whereas indefiniteness and lack of specificity tend to indicate that the parties are still negotiating and have not yet reached agreement. In the conversation between Smith and Ford, Smith's statement that he'd like to buy Ford's house is merely an invitation to offer or an invitation to negotiate. It indicates a willingness to contract in the future if the parties can reach agreement on mutually acceptable terms, but not a present intent to contract. If, however, Smith sends Ford a detailed and specific written document stating all of the material terms and conditions on which he is willing to buy the house and Ford writes back agreeing to Smith's terms, the parties' intent to contract would be objectively indicated and a contract probably would be created.

A second reason definiteness is important is that courts need to know the terms on which the parties agreed in order to determine if a breach of contract has occurred and calculate a remedy if it has. Keep in mind that the offer often contains all the terms of the parties' contract. This is so because all that an offeree is allowed to do in most cases is to accept or reject the terms of the offer. If an agreement is too indefinite, a court would not have a basis for giving a remedy if one of the parties alleged that the "contract" was breached. The following *Armstrong* case raises the issue of definiteness.

Armstrong v. Rohm and Haas Company, Inc.
349 F. Supp. 2d 71 (U.S. Dist. Ct. D. Mass. 2004)

Robert Armstrong and Marc Pottle worked for Morton International as ceramic grinders at its facility in Spencer, Massachusetts. In 1999, Rohm and Haas (RH) acquired Morton and announced that it would close the Spencer facility. RH gave Morton employees one month to decide whether to accept a severance package and quit their jobs. Employees who chose instead to transfer to the Woburn facility would receive an incentive payment larger than the payment offered as part of the severance package.

Armstrong and Pottle wanted to remain with the company, but Thomas Payne, the plant manager at the Spencer facility, suggested that they could make substantially more money if they resigned, accepted the severance package, and started their own company to handle RH's outsourced grinding work. At the time of Payne's statements, the grinding work was being out-sourced to a company called Chand Associates, and Payne indicated that the company wanted to end its dependence on Chand. Payne represented to Armstrong and Pottle that the company would give their new business "all the [outsourced grinding] work they could handle" and that the company "would like to" give the plaintiffs "all of its outsourced work in ceramic grinding, which had been in the neighborhood of $10,000 per month."

In reliance on Payne's representations, Armstrong and Pottle resigned from RH and accepted the severance package. After their resignations, Armstrong and Pottle invested in shop space and tools so that they could begin handling RH's outsourced work. During the first few months after the resignations of Armstrong and Pottle, RH gave them a small amount of work and assured them that it was all the work that was available because of a decrease in production. That trend continued into late 2001 when Pottle accepted a job with Chand due to the lack of work in his new business. When he began to work for Chand, he discovered that RH was still outsourcing large amounts of grinding work to Chand.

Armstrong and Pottle filed suit against RH on a number of grounds, including breach of contract. RH filed a motion to dismiss for failure to state a claim upon which relief can be granted.

Saylor, District Judge

In order to create an enforceable contract, "it is a necessary requirement that [the] agreement . . . be sufficiently definite to enable the courts to give it an exact meaning." *Williston on Contracts* § 4:18 (4th ed. 1990). While it is not required that parties specify *all* terms of an agreement, they must have progressed beyond the stage of imperfect negotiation. A lack of definiteness in an agreement might be based on a lack of specificity regarding the time of performance, price to be paid, work to be done, or property to be transferred. In determining whether such an agreement is nonetheless enforceable, courts should ask whether the parties intended to contract with one another and there is a reasonably certain basis for providing an appropriate remedy. That determination varies according to the facts of each case.

Here, defendant's alleged promise is too vague for this court to ascertain a reasonably certain basis for providing an appropriate remedy. As an initial matter, it is unclear what the volume of work was to be performed—that is, what the parties meant by the phrase "all the work" plaintiffs could "handle." How could this court determine what volume of work the two individual plaintiffs could handle? Was it the amount of work typically outsourced from the company to Chand? Was it the amount plaintiffs *wanted* to handle (i.e., did plaintiffs have the power to determine the volume)? Was it the amount that they *actually* could handle, in light of their apparent lack of experience in running a business? Was it an amount they *reasonably* should have been able to handle? What if the amount they could handle changed over time, as they gained experience? What if Morton's needs declined, increased, or fluctuated—how could the court take that into account? What was the nature and scope of the work? Was it all of the ceramic grinding work of the company? Only that work which had formerly gone to Chand?

Was it necessary to meet certain quality standards? Certain delivery times? Both? How could the court determine whether Armstrong and Pottle had performed their end of the bargain, that is, whether they had properly "handled" the work? What price would be paid for the work? Were there different prices for different types of work? When and how would Armstrong and Pottle be paid? What would be the duration of the contract? If it was terminable at will, how can plaintiffs make out a claim for breach? If it was not, what is its term?

Not all of these issues are insurmountable for Armstrong and Pottle, taken separately. The law provides a variety of mechanisms to fill in missing contractual details where appropriate to effectuate the intent of the parties to make a binding agreement. Taken together, however, the omissions are fatal. This court cannot supply the missing terms without writing a contract for the parties which they themselves did not make. RH's alleged promise is therefore unenforceable as a matter of law.

It should be obvious that there is not perfect congruence between the result that fairness might seem to dictate and the result dictated by law. The law strongly favors certainty and precision of contracts, even at the expense of occasional injustice, on the theory that a contrary rule would lead to even greater injustices. Thus, the law will refuse to enforce a simple and direct promise if it is unduly vague (e.g., "Don't worry, we'll take care of you") but insist on enforcing boilerplate contract language that neither party even read or understood. Of course, a person of principle and character would keep his word; but if his word is sufficiently imprecise, the law will not force him to do so. The alleged oral contract here is too imprecise to be enforceable as a matter of law. Armstrong and Pottle's claim for breach of oral contract will be dismissed for failure to state a claim.

Motion to dismiss granted in favor of RH.

Definiteness Standards under the Common Law

Classical contract law took the position that courts are contract enforcers, not contract makers. The prospect of enforcing an agreement in which the parties had omitted terms or left terms open for later agreement was unthinkable to courts that took a traditional, hands-off approach to contracts. Traditionally, contract law required a relatively high standard of definiteness for offers, requiring that all the essential terms of a proposed contract be stated in the offer. The traditional insistence on definiteness can serve useful ends. It can prevent a person from being held to an agreement when none was reached or from being bound by a contract term to which he never assented. Often, however, it can operate to frustrate the expectations of parties who intend to contract but, for whatever reason, fail to procure an agreement that specifies all the terms of the contract. The definiteness standard, like much of contract law, is constantly evolving. The trend of modern contract law is to tolerate a lower degree of specificity in agreements than classical contract law would have tolerated, although it is still unlikely that an agreement that leaves open important aspects of a transaction will be enforced.

Definiteness Standards under the UCC   The UCC, with its increased emphasis on furthering people's justifiable expectations and its encouragement of a hands-on approach by the courts, often creates contractual liability in situations where no contract would have resulted at common law. Perhaps no part of the Code better illustrates this basic difference between the UCC and classical common law than does the basic Code section on contract formation [2–204]. This section says that sales contracts under Article 2 can be created "in any manner sufficient to show agreement, including conduct which recognizes the existence of a contract" [2–204(1)]. So, if the parties are acting as though they have a contract by delivering or accepting goods or payment, for example, this may be enough to create a binding contract, even if it is impossible to point to a particular moment in time when the contract was created [2–204(2)]. The *Jannusch*

case, which follows, provides an example of these UCC standards.

An important difference between Code and classical common law standards for definiteness is that under the Code, the fact that the parties left open one or more terms of their agreement does not necessarily mean that their agreement is too indefinite to enforce. A sales contract is created if the court finds that the parties intended to make a contract and that their agreement is complete enough to allow the court to reach a fair settlement of their dispute ("a reasonably certain basis for giving an appropriate remedy" [2–204(3)]). If a term is left open in a contract that meets these two standards, that open term or "gap" can be "filled" by inserting a presumption found in the Code's "gap-filling" rules. The gap-filling rules allow courts to fill contract terms left open on matters of price [2–305], quantity [2–306], delivery [2–307, 2–308, and 2–309(1)], and time for payment [2–310] when such terms have been left open by the parties.[2] Of course, if a term was left out because the parties were *unable* to reach agreement about it, this would indicate that the intent to contract was absent and no contract would result, even under the Code's more liberal rules. *Intention is still at the heart of these modern contract rules;* the difference is that courts applying Code principles seek to further the parties' *underlying* intent to contract even though the parties have failed to express their intention about specific aspects of their agreement.

---

[2]Chapter 19 discusses these Code provisions in detail.

Jannusch v. Naffziger   883 N.E.2d 711 (Ill. Ct. App. 2008)

Gene Jannusch and his wife, Martha, operated Festival Foods, a business that served concessions at festivals and events throughout Illinois and Indiana from late April to late October each year. The assets of the business included a truck and servicing trailer and equipment such as refrigerators and freezers, roasters, chairs and tables, fountain service, and signs and lighting equipment. Lindsey Naffziger and her mother, Louann, were interested in purchasing the business. They met several times with the Jannuschs and observed the business in operation. According to Gene, he and Martha had entered into an oral agreement on August 13, 2005, to sell Festival Foods to the Naffzigers for $150,000. For the $150,000, the Naffzigers would receive the truck and trailer, all necessary equipment, and the opportunity to work at event locations secured by the Jannuschs. The Naffzigers paid $10,000 immediately, with the balance to be paid when they received their loan money from the bank. The Naffzigers took possession of Festival Foods the next day and operated Festival Foods for the remainder of the 2005 season. The insurance and titles to the truck and trailer remained in Gene's name because he had not yet received the purchase price from the Naffzigers.

Louann acknowledged testifying during a deposition that an oral agreement to purchase Festival Foods for $150,000 existed but later testified that she could not recall specifically making an oral agreement on any particular date. Lindsey testified that she and Louann met with the Jannuschs on August 13, 2005, and paid the $10,000 for the right to continue to *purchase the business because the Jannuschs had another interested buyer. The parties agreed that the Naffzigers would run Festival Foods as they pursued buying the business. According to Lindsey, Gene suggested the parties sign something and she replied that they were "in no position to sign anything" because they had not received any loan money from the bank and did not have an attorney. The following week, Lindsey consulted with an attorney about the legal aspects of buying and owning a business. She asked the attorney to prepare a contract for the purchase. Ultimately, the bank approved the Naffzigers for a loan. Lindsey took possession of Festival Foods, receiving the income from the business, purchasing inventory, replacing equipment, paying taxes on the business, and paying employees.*

The Naffzigers operated six events, three in Indiana and three in Illinois. Gene attended the first two festivals in Valparaiso and Auburn, Indiana, with the Naffzigers, who paid him $10 an hour plus lodging. The Jannuschs' minimal involvement with the operations after August 13 was in the nature of advisors to the Naffzigers, who were unfamiliar with this type of business. The income from Festival Foods was lower than the Naffzigers expected, and two days after the business season ended, they returned Festival Foods to the storage facility where Gene had stored it in the past. Gene had canceled his lease with the storage facility, however, telling the owner that he had sold his business. Someone at the storage facility called Gene and reported that Festival Foods had been returned. Gene then tried to sell Festival Foods, but was unsuccessful. The Jannuschs brought an action for breach of an oral contract against the Naffzigers. Following a bench trial, the trial court found in favor of the Naffzigers. The trial court then found that there was a contract formed but that the evidence was insufficient to establish that there was a meeting of the minds as to what that agreement was. The Jannuschs appealed.

Cook, Justice

The Naffzigers argue the UCC should not apply because this case involves the sale of a business rather than just the sale of goods. The "predominant purpose" test is used to determine whether a contract for both the sale of goods and the rendition of services falls within the scope of Article 2 of the UCC. A contract that is primarily for services, with the sale of goods being incidental, will not fall within the scope of Article 2 of the UCC. Certainly significant tangible assets were involved in this case. The evidence presented in this case was sufficient to support the conclusion that the proposed agreement was predominantly one for the sale of goods.

Under the UCC [section 2-204]:

(1) A contract for sale of goods may be made in any manner sufficient to show agreement, including conduct by both parties which recognizes the existence of such a contract.

(2) An agreement sufficient to constitute a contract for sale may be found even though the moment of its making is undetermined.

(3) Even though one or more terms are left open a contract for sale does not fail for indefiniteness if the parties have intended to make a contract and there is a reasonably certain basis for giving an appropriate remedy.

The Naffzigers argue that nothing was said in the contract about allocating a price for good will, a covenant not to compete, allocating a price for the equipment, how to release liens, what would happen if there was no loan approval, and other issues. They argue these are essential terms for the sale of a business and the Internal Revenue Service requires that parties allocate the sales price. "None of these items were even discussed much

less agreed to. There is not an enforceable agreement when there are so many essential terms missing."

A contract may be enforced even though some contract terms may be missing or left to be agreed upon, but if the essential terms are so uncertain that there is no basis for deciding whether the agreement has been kept or broken, there is no contract. The essential terms were agreed upon in this case. The purchase price was $150,000, and the items to be transferred were specified. No essential terms remained to be agreed upon; the only action remaining was the performance of the contract. The Naffzigers took possession of the items to be transferred and used them as their own. They paid $10,000 of the purchase price. The fact that the Naffzigers were disappointed in the income from the events they operated is not inconsistent with the existence of a contract.

The trial court noted that "the parties have very, very different views about what transpired in the course of the contract-formation discussions." It is not necessary that the parties share a subjective understanding as to the terms of the contract; the parties' conduct may indicate an agreement to the terms. The conduct in this case is clear. Parties discussing the sale of goods do not transfer those goods and allow them to be retained for a substantial period before reaching agreement. The Naffzigers replaced equipment, reported income, paid taxes, and paid Gene for his time and expenses, all of which is inconsistent with the idea that they were only "pursuing buying the business." An agreement to make an agreement is not an agreement, but there was clearly more than that here. The trial court believed it was significant that Lindsey told Gene that defendants were "in no position to sign anything" because they had not received any loan money from the bank and did not have any attorney. The fact that a formal written document is anticipated does not preclude enforcement of a specific preliminary promise. The Naffzigers' loan was eventually approved, they did consult with an attorney, and they remained in possession of and continued to operate Festival Foods. The parties' agreement could have been fleshed out with additional terms, but the essential terms were agreed upon. Louann admitted there was an agreement to purchase Festival Foods for $150,000 but could not recall specifically making an oral agreement on any particular date. "An agreement sufficient to constitute a contract for sale may be found even though the moment of its making is undetermined." 2-204(2). Returning the goods at the end of the season was not a rejection of the Jannuschs' offer to sell, it was a breach of contract.

We conclude there was an agreement to sell Festival Foods for the price of $150,000 and that the Naffzigers breached that agreement.

Reversed and remanded in favor of the Jannuschs.

The Global Business Environment

Under the CISG, a proposal will be considered an offer to contract if it is addressed to one or more specific persons, is sufficiently definite, and indicates the intent of the offeror to be bound in case of acceptance. Unlike the UCC, the CISG does not consider an offer to be sufficiently definite when the price term for goods is left open. The CISG states that the offer must indicate the goods and either expressly or impliedly make a provision for determining the quantity and price.

Communication to Offeree

When an offeror communicates the terms of an offer to an offeree, he objectively indicates an intent to be bound by those terms. The fact that an offer has *not* been communicated, on the other hand, may be evidence that the offeror has not yet decided to enter into a binding agreement. For example, assume that Stevens and Meyer have been negotiating over the sale of Meyer's restaurant. Stevens confides in his friend Reilly that he plans to offer Meyer $150,000 for the restaurant. Reilly goes to Meyer and tells Meyer that Stevens has decided to offer him $150,000 for the restaurant and has drawn up a written offer to that effect. After learning the details of the offer from Reilly, Meyer telephones Stevens and says, "I accept your offer." Is Stevens now contractually obligated to buy the restaurant? No. Since *Stevens* did not communicate the proposal to Meyer, there was no offer for Meyer to accept.

Special Offer Problem Areas

Advertisements   Generally speaking, advertisements for the sale of goods at specified prices are *not* considered to be offers. Rather, they are treated as being invitations to offer or negotiate. The same rule is generally applied to signs, handbills, catalogs, price lists, and price quotations. This rule is based on the presumed intent of the sellers involved. It is not reasonable to conclude that a seller who has a limited number of items to sell intends to give every person who sees her ad, sign, or catalog the power to bind her to contract. Thus, if Customer sees Retailer's advertisement of Whizbang XL laptop computers for $2,000 and goes to Retailer's store indicating his intent to buy the computer, Customer is making an offer, which Retailer is free to accept or reject. This is so because *Customer* is manifesting a present intent to contract on the definite terms of the ad.

In some cases, however, particular ads have been held to amount to offers. Such ads limit the power of acceptance to one offeree or a small number of offerees, are highly specific about the nature and number of items offered for sale and what is requested in return, and they leave nothing further to be negotiated. This specificity precludes the possibility that the offeror could become contractually bound to an infinite number of offerees. In addition, many of the ads treated as offers have required some special performance by would-be buyers or have in some other way clearly indicated that immediate action by the buyer creates a binding agreement.

For example, in one classic case,[3] a newspaper advertisement that stated, "Saturday 9 AM. . . . 1 Black Lapin Stole Beautiful, worth $139.50 . . . $1.00 First Come First Served" was held to be an offer. The ad was clear and specific about what was being offered and asked for in exchange—one had to be the first one to appear at the seller's place of business and pay $1.00—and there were no terms left open for further discussion or negotiation. Moreover, the "first come first served" language limits the number of people who would have the power of acceptance. The potential for unfairness to those who attempt to accept such ads and their fundamental difference from ordinary ads justify treating them as offers.

Rewards
Advertisements offering rewards for lost property, for information, or for the capture of criminals are generally treated as offers for unilateral contracts. To accept the offer and be entitled to the stated reward, offerees must perform the requested act—return the lost property, supply the requested information, or capture the wanted criminal. Some courts have held that only offerees who started performance with knowledge of the offer are entitled to the reward. Other courts, however, have indicated the only requirement is that the offeree know of the reward before completing performance. In reality, the result in most such cases probably reflects the court's perception of what is fairer given the facts involved in the particular case at hand.

Auctions
Sellers at auctions are generally treated as making an invitation to offer. Those who bid on offered goods are, therefore, treated as making offers that the owner of the goods may accept or reject. Acceptance occurs only when the auctioneer strikes the goods off to the highest bidder; the auctioneer may withdraw the goods at any time before acceptance. However, when an auction is advertised as being "without reserve," the seller is treated as having made an offer to sell the goods to the highest bidder and the goods cannot be withdrawn after a call for bids has been made unless no bids are made within a reasonable time.[4]

---

[3]*Lefkowitz v. Great Minneapolis Surplus Store,* 86 N.W.2d 689 (Sup. Ct. Minn. 1957).

[4]These rules and others concerned with the sale of goods by auction are contained in section 2–328 of the UCC.

Bids
The bidding process is a fertile source of contract disputes. Advertisements for bids are generally treated as invitations to offer. Those who submit bids are treated as offerors. According to general contract principles, bidders can withdraw their bids at any time prior to acceptance by the offeree inviting the bids and the offeree is free to accept or reject any bid. The previously announced terms of the bidding may alter these rules, however. For example, if the advertisement for bids unconditionally states that the contract will be awarded to the lowest responsible bidder, this will be treated as an offer that is accepted by the lowest bidder. Only proof by the offeror that the lowest bidder is not responsible can prevent the formation of a contract. Also, under some circumstances discussed later in this chapter, promissory estoppel may operate to prevent bidders from withdrawing their bids.

Bids for governmental contracts are generally covered by specific statutes rather than by general contract principles. Such statutes ordinarily establish the rules governing the bidding process, often require that the contract be awarded to the lowest bidder, and frequently establish special rules or penalties governing the withdrawal of bids.

Which Terms Are Included in the Offer?
After making a determination that an offer existed, a court must decide which terms were included in the offer so that it can determine the terms of the parties' contract. Put another way, which terms of the offer are binding on the offeree who accepts it? Should offerees, for example, be bound by fine-print clauses or by clauses on the back of the contract? Originally, the courts tended to hold that offerees were bound by all the terms of the offer on the theory that every person had a duty to protect himself by reading agreements carefully before signing them.

In today's world of lengthy, complex form contracts, however, people often sign agreements that they have not fully read or do not fully understand. Modern courts tend to recognize this fact by saying that offerees are bound only by terms of which they had actual or reasonable notice. If the offeree actually read the term in question, or if a reasonable person should have been aware of it, it will probably become part of the parties' contract. A fine-print provision on the back of a theater ticket would probably not be binding on a theater patron, however, because a reasonable person would not normally expect such a ticket to contain contractual terms. By contrast, the terms printed on a multipage airline ticket might well be considered binding on the purchaser if such documents would be expected to contain terms of the contract.

CYBERLAW IN ACTION

One controversy regarding the terms that are included in the offer has been raised by the standardized contracting techniques that almost always accompany the transfer of computer software. For example, Stacy goes to Gigantic State University Bookstore and purchases software in a package. When Stacy opens the package, she finds that the CD containing the program is sealed in an envelope and that it bears a label stating that by opening the envelope, Stacy is accepting the terms of a license agreement that is contained somewhere in the packaging. The label states that if Stacy does not want to accept the terms of the license, she can return the software. The license contains a variety of terms that generally protect the software manufacturer. This method of contracting is often called **shrinkwrap** contracting. Stacy rips open the envelope without reading the license agreement and installs the software. If a conflict arises later concerning one of the terms of the license agreement, should the law hold that the terms of the license agreement are contractually binding? A critic of shrinkwrap contracting would argue that

the terms should not be part of the contract because the contract was formed when Stacy purchased the program from Gigantic State University Bookstore and Stacy did not know of the license or its terms at that point. Also, consumers like Stacy may not understand that by opening the sealed package they are entering a contract, the terms of which they are unlikely to have read and may not understand.

The early cases dealing with shrinkwrap contracts generally decided against the enforceability of shrinkwraps. Since the late 1990s, however, judicial opinion has tended toward the enforcement of shrinkwraps, but opinion is still mixed.

Other forms of standardized contracting online are familiar to us: the **clickwrap** agreement, which requires us to read terms presented online and click buttons indicating our agreement, and the so-called **browsewrap** agreement, which presents purported contract terms and conditions but does not require the reader to click to indicate agreement. The enforcement of browsewrap agreements depends on whether the Web site viewer knew or had reason to know of the terms and conditions.

Ethics in Action

Jerry, who was in the process of opening a new small business in Connecticut, ordered an expensive new computer system from ABC Computing. As part of this transaction, ABC presented Jerry with a contract of sale. The contract was written on lightweight paper that was difficult to read. The signature line was on the bottom of the first page, but there were more contract terms on the reverse side of the page. On the reverse side, under the heading "Warranty Service" was a provision that disclaimed all implied warranties and

stated that any dispute that might arise between the parties would be resolved by arbitration in California (where ABC is headquartered). Jerry signed the contract without reading the reverse side. The computer system was defective and never worked correctly. Jerry wants to sue ABC Computing but cannot afford to go to California to do so. Is it ethical for businesses who deal with consumers and other less sophisticated parties to "hide" contract terms under misleading headings, in small print, deep in a Web site, or on the reverse side of the contract?

Termination of Offers

After a court has determined the existence and content of an offer, it must determine the duration of the offer. Was the offer still in existence when the offeree attempted to accept it? If not, no contract was created and the offeree is treated as having made an offer that the original offeror is free to accept or reject. This is so because, by attempting to accept an offer that has terminated, the offeree has indicated a present intent to contract on the terms of the original offer though he lacks the power to bind the offeror to a contract due to the original offer's termination.

Terms of the Offer The offeror is often said to be "the master of the offer." This means that offerors have the power to determine the terms and conditions under which they are bound to a contract. An offeror may include terms in the offer that limit its effective life. These may be specific terms, such as "you must accept by December 5, 2010," or "this offer is good for five days," or more general terms such as "for immediate acceptance," "prompt wire acceptance," or "by return mail." General time-limitation language in an offer can raise difficult problems of interpretation for courts trying to decide whether an offeree accepted before the offer terminated. Even more specific language, such as "this offer is good for five days," can cause problems if the offer does not specify whether the five-day period begins when the offer is sent or when the offeree receives it. Not all courts agree on such questions, so wise offerors should be as specific as possible in stating when their offers terminate.

Lapse of Time Offers that fail to provide a specific time for acceptance are valid for a reasonable time. What constitutes a reasonable time depends on the circumstances surrounding the offer. How long would a reasonable person in the offeree's position believe she had to accept the offer? Offers involving things subject to rapid fluctuations in value, such as stocks, bonds, or commodities futures, have a very brief duration. The same is true for offers involving goods that may spoil, such as produce.

The context of the parties' negotiations is another factor relevant to determining the duration of an offer. For example, most courts hold that when parties bargain face-to-face or over the telephone, the normal time for acceptance does not extend past the conclusion of their conversation unless the offeror indicates a contrary intention. Where negotiations are carried out by mail or telegram, the time for acceptance would ordinarily include at least the normal time for communicating the offer and a prompt response by the offeree. Finally, in cases where the parties have dealt with each other on a regular basis in the past, the timing of their prior transactions would be highly relevant in measuring the reasonable time for acceptance.

Revocation

General Rule: Offers Are Revocable As the masters of their offers, offerors can give offerees the power to bind them to contracts by making offers. They can also terminate that power by revoking their offers. The general common law rule on revocations is that offerors may revoke their offers at any time prior to acceptance, *even if they have promised to hold the offer open for a stated period of time.*

Exceptions to the General Rule In the following situations (summarized in Figure 1), however, offerors are *not* free to revoke their offers:

1. *Options.* An **option** is a separate contract in which an offeror agrees not to revoke her offer for a stated time in exchange for some valuable consideration. You can think of it as a contract in which an offeror sells her right to revoke her offer. For example, Jones, in

Figure 1	*When Offerors Cannot Revoke*
Options	Offeror has promised to hold offer open and has received consideration for that promise.
Firm Offers	Merchant offeror makes written offer to buy or sell goods, giving assurances that the offer will be held open.
Unilateral Contract Offers	Offeree has started to perform requested act before offeror revokes.
Promissory Estoppel	Offeree foreseeably and reasonably relies on offer being held open, and will suffer injustice if it is revoked.

exchange for $5,000, agrees to give Dewey Development Co. a six-month option to purchase her farm for $550,000. In this situation, Jones would not be free to revoke the offer during the six-month period of the option. The offeree, Dewey Development, has no obligation to accept Jones's offer. In effect, it has merely purchased the right to consider the offer for the stated time without fear that Jones will revoke it.

2. *Offers for unilateral contracts.* Suppose Franklin makes the following offer for a unilateral contract to Waters: "If you mow my lawn, I'll pay you $25." Given that an offeree in a unilateral contract must fully perform the requested act to accept the offer, can Franklin wait until Waters is almost finished mowing the lawn and then say "I revoke!"? Obviously, the application of the general rule that offerors can revoke at any time before acceptance creates the potential for injustice when applied to offers for unilateral contracts, because it would allow an offeror to revoke after the offeree has begun performance but before he has had a chance to complete it. To prevent injustice to offerees who rely on such offers by beginning performance, two basic approaches are available to modern courts.

Some courts have held that once the offeree has begun to perform, the offeror's power to revoke is suspended for the amount of time reasonably necessary for the offeree to complete performance. Another approach to the unilateral contract dilemma is to hold that a bilateral contract is created once the offeree begins performance.

3. *Promissory estoppel.* In some cases in which the offeree *relies* on the offer being kept open, the doctrine

of promissory estoppel can operate to prevent offerors from revoking their offers prior to acceptance. Section 87(2) of the *Restatement (Second)* says:

An offer which the offeror should reasonably expect to induce action or forbearance of a substantial character on the part of the offeree before acceptance and which does induce such action or forbearance is binding as an option contract to the extent necessary to avoid injustice.

Many of the cases in which promissory estoppel has been used successfully to prevent revocation of offers involve the bidding process. For example, Gigantic General Contractor seeks to get the general contract to build a new high school gymnasium for Shadyside School District. It receives bids from subcontractors. Liny Electric submits the lowest bid to perform the electrical work on the job, and Gigantic uses Liny's bid in preparing its bid for the general contract. Here, Liny has made an offer to Gigantic, but Gigantic cannot accept that offer until it knows whether it has gotten the general contract. The school district awards the general contract to Gigantic. Before Gigantic can accept Liny's offer, however, Liny attempts to revoke it. In this situation, a court could use the doctrine of promissory estoppel to hold that the offer could not be revoked.

4. *Firm offers for the sale of goods [Note: This applies to offers for the sale of goods ONLY!].* The Code makes a major change in the common law rules governing the revocability of offers by recognizing the concept of a **firm offer** [2–205]. Like an option, a firm offer is irrevocable for a period of time. In contrast to an option, however, a firm offer does not require consideration to be given in exchange for the offeror's promise to keep the offer open. Not all offers to buy or sell goods qualify as firm offers, however. To be a firm offer, an offer must:

- Be made by an offeror who is a *merchant.*
- Be contained in a signed writing.[5]
- Give assurances that the offer will be kept open.

An offer to buy or sell goods that fails to satisfy these three requirements is governed by the general common law rule and is revocable at any time prior to acceptance. If an offer *does* meet the requirements of a firm offer, however, it will be irrevocable for the time stated in the offer. If no specific time is stated in the offer, it will be irrevocable for a *reasonable* time. Regardless of the terms of the firm offer, the outer limit on a firm

offer's irrevocability is *three months.* For example, if Worldwide Widget makes an offer in a signed writing in which it proposes to sell a quantity of its XL Turbo Widget to Howell Hardware and gives assurances that the offer will be kept open for a year, the offer is a firm offer, but it can be revoked after three months if Howell Hardware has not yet accepted it.

In some cases, however, offerees are the true originators of an assurance term in an offer. When offerees have effective control of the terms of the offer by providing their customers with preprinted purchase order forms or order blanks, they may be tempted to take advantage of their merchant customers by placing an assurance term in their order forms. This would allow offerees to await market developments before deciding whether to fill the order, while their merchant customers, who may have signed the order without reading all of its terms, would be powerless to revoke. To prevent such unfairness, the Code requires that assurance terms on forms provided by offerees be separately signed by the offeror to effect a firm offer. For example, if Fashionable Mfg. Co. supplies its customer, Retailer, with preprinted order forms that contain a fine-print provision giving assurances that the customer's offer to purchase goods will be held open for one month, the purported promise to keep the offer open would not be enforceable unless Retailer separately signed that provision.

Time of Effectiveness of Revocations   The question of *when* a revocation is effective to terminate an offer is often a critical issue in the contract formation process. For example, Davis offers to landscape Winter's property for $1,500. Two days after making the offer, Davis changes his mind and mails Winter a letter revoking the offer. The next day, Winter, who has not received Davis's letter, telephones Davis and attempts to accept. Contract? Yes. The general rule on this point is that revocations are effective only when they are actually *received* by the offeree.

The only major exception to the general rule on effectiveness of revocations concerns offers to the general public. Because it would be impossible in most cases to reach every offeree with a revocation, it is generally held that a revocation made in the same manner as the offer is effective when published, without proof of communication to the offeree.

Rejection   An offeree may expressly reject an offer by indicating that he is unwilling to accept it. He may also impliedly reject it by making a counteroffer, an offer to contract on terms materially different from the terms

---

[5]Under the UCC [1–201(39)], the word *signed* includes any symbol that a person makes or adopts with the intent to authenticate a writing.

The Global Business Environment

Several of the kinds of factors that make offers irrevocable in the United States—such as consideration and, in the case of firm offers, writing—are not required to make offers irrevocable under the CISG. The CISG states that an offer cannot be revoked if it indicates that it is irrevocable or if it was reasonable for the offeree to rely on the offer as being irrevocable and the offeree has acted in reliance on the offer. However, even when an offer is irrevocable, the CISG allows it to be revoked if the revocation reaches the offeree before or at the same time as the offer.

of the offer. As a general rule, either form of rejection by the offeree terminates his power to accept the offer. This is so because an offeror who receives a rejection may rely on the offeree's expressed desire not to accept the offer by making another offer to a different offeree.

One exception to the general rule that rejections terminate offers concerns offers that are the subject of an option contract. Some courts hold that a rejection does not terminate an option contract and that the offeree who rejects still has the power to accept the offer later, so long as the acceptance is effective within the option period.

Time of Effectiveness of Rejections As a general rule, rejections, like revocations, are effective only when actually received by the offeror. Therefore, an offeree who has mailed a rejection could still change her mind and accept if she communicates the acceptance before the offeror receives the rejection.[6]

Death or Insanity of Either Party

The death or insanity of either party to an offer automatically terminates the offer without notice. A meeting of the minds is obviously impossible when one of the parties has died or become insane.[7]

Destruction of Subject Matter

If, prior to an acceptance of an offer, the subject matter of a proposed contract is destroyed without the knowledge or fault of either party, the offer is terminated.[8] So, if Marks offers to sell Wiggins his lakeside cottage and the cottage is destroyed by fire before Wiggins accepts, the offer was terminated on the destruction of the cottage. Subsequent acceptance by Wiggins would not create a contract. The following *Family Video Movie Club* case provides an illustration of lapse of time and destruction of the subject matter.

Intervening Illegality

An offer is terminated if the performance of the contract it proposes becomes illegal before the offer is accepted. So, if a computer manufacturer offered to sell sophisticated computer equipment to another country, but two days later, before the offer was accepted, Congress placed an embargo on all sales to this country, the offer was terminated by the embargo.[9]

---

[6]Chapter 11 discusses this subject in detail.

[7]Death or insanity of a party that occurs after a contract has been formed can excuse performance in contracts that call for personal services to be performed by the person who has died or become insane. This is discussed in Chapter 18.

[8]In some circumstances, destruction of subject matter can also serve as a legal excuse for a party's failure to perform his obligations under an existing contract. Chapter 18 discusses this subject.

[9]In some circumstances, intervening illegality can also serve as a legal excuse for a party's failure to perform his obligations under an existing contract. Chapter 18 discusses this subject.

Family Video Movie Club v. Home Folks, Inc.
827 N.E.2d 582 (Ind. Ct. App. 2005)

Home Folks, Inc., operated a restaurant on property that it leased from the owner, whose son, Tony Spachtholz, acted as her agent. Family Video Movie Club contacted Spachtholz in 2002 about buying the property for use as a video store. Home Folks' lease ran through 2005. The lease also contained a term that permitted either Home Folks or the landlord to cancel the lease if the property was destroyed.

In mid-2002, Family Video began negotiating with Home Folks about buying out the lease at the same time it was negotiating with Spachtholz about purchasing the property. Late in 2002, Home Folks and Family Video agreed on some terms regarding a buyout, including $35,000 that was to be paid to Home Folks. This was a partial oral agreement that was contingent and incomplete, and both parties knew that it was to be finalized in written form.

On November 25, 2002, Family Video sent a letter to Home Folks' operators, the Misners, outlining the proposed buyout. The letter said the following:

> As discussed, Family Video Movie Club, Inc. has entered into a Purchase Agreement to purchase said premises. We have the right to confirm our ability to replat the property, properly zone the property, and perform due diligence.
>
> Until a title has been delivered to us, and in the event we do not purchase said premises, you are obligated to fulfill the terms and conditions of your Lease Agreement with Anthony Spachtholtz [sic]. After closing, you will have ninety days (90) to vacate the premises. At such time that you vacate the premises and deliver possession to Family Video Movie Club, Inc., Family Video Movie Club, Inc. agrees to pay you the full sum of Thirty-five Thousand and 00/100 Dollars, ($35,000.00).

The letter contained a space for the Misners to sign, indicating "I agree with the above terms and conditions." On February 1, 2003, the building housing Home Folks burned to the ground as a result of arson. At this point, the Misners still had not signed the written offer that Family Video had sent to them.

Two days after the fire, the Misners signed the offer letter they had received from Family Video the previous November, indicating that they "agreed with" the terms and conditions of the buyout proposed by Family Video. They signed the offer letter on the advice of their attorney. The next day, February 4, 2003, Home Folks' attorney wrote to Family Video's representative, indicating "we are cancelling the lease, conditioned upon payment of the agreed upon amount." The day after that, February 5, 2003, the Misners wrote Spachtholz to state that Home Folks was canceling the lease.

Home Folks sought payment of the $35,000 from Family Video, but no payment occurred. Home Folks sued Family Video, alleging that a contract was formed and that Family Video should pay Home Folks the $35,000 contemplated by the contract. After a bench trial, the trial court concluded that a contract existed and ordered Family Video to pay Home Folks $35,000 in damages.

Vaidik, Judge

Unless an offer to form a contract specifically states how long it is open to acceptance, an offer is open only for a reasonable time. A reasonable time "is the time that a reasonable person in the exact position of the offeree would believe to be satisfactory to the offeror." 1 Joseph M. Perillo, *Corbin on Contracts* § 2.16, at 203–04 (rev. ed. 1995 & 2004 Supp.). How much time is reasonable for an offeree to accept an offer depends on the facts of each case. "The purpose of the offeror, to be attained by the making and performance of the contract, will affect the time allowed for acceptance, if it is or should be known to the offeree. In such case there is no power to accept after it is too late to attain that purpose." Id. at 211.

In this case, Family Video clearly bargained for Home Folks to abandon its interest in the leasehold well before Home Folks' lease would otherwise terminate. The fiery destruction of Home Folks' building made it impossible for Family Video to get what it had bargained for. The unexpected and premature destruction of a significant portion of the subject matter of the offer made it unreasonable to continue the time for Home Folks to accept the offer. Also, because Home Folks knew Family Video's purpose in the making and performance of the contract, Home Folks was on notice that it was no longer a reasonable time to accept the offer once the structure ceased to exist. Moreover, "the power of acceptance may be terminated by the death or destruction of a person or thing essential for performance . . ." *Restatement (Second) of Contracts* § 36, cmt. c. In this case, the destruction by fire of the structure subject to Home Folks' leasehold terminated Home Folks' time to accept Family Video's offer. The structure's existence was essential for performance of the contract, and Home Folks lost its capacity to accept the offer from Family Video when it was destroyed by fire.

This principle is illustrated by *White v. Arizona Property & Casualty Insurance Guaranty Fund* (Ariz. 1997), where an insurance company became insolvent after offering to settle a particular claim. As a result of the insolvency, the company was under court order not to dispose of any assets. The court held that the insolvency order terminated the offeree's power of acceptance because it imposed a legal impediment to the insurer's ability to pay the settlement. *White* is similar to this case, where an event occurred after the offer but before the acceptance that terminated the offeree's power of accept-

ance because something essential to the contract's performance was destroyed. This conclusion is buttressed by the well-established line of cases holding that the offeree's power of acceptance is terminated by the death of the offeror. Because the structure, an element essential to the achievement of the purpose of the contract, was destroyed before Home Folks accepted the offer, the power of acceptance was terminated and no contract was formed.

Judgment reversed in favor of Family Video.

Problems and Problem Cases

1. In 1989, the New Jersey Highway Authority increased its tolls from 25 cents to 35 cents. In connection with this increase, it authorized the sale of tokens for a discounted price—$10 for a roll of 40 tokens, a savings of $4 per roll for customers—for a limited time. The authority advertised this sale through several media, including signs on the parkway itself. Shortly after the discount sale began, complaints were made that the tokens were not available. The authority explained that the shortage probably resulted from an unanticipated demand for the tokens resulting from purchasers hoarding them. The authority then began limiting the sales to certain days of the week, but even with that limitation, the demand could not be satisfied. Schlictman, a motorist who used the toll roads, sued the authority for breach of contract after trying unsuccessfully, on five different occasions within the authorized sale dates and times, to buy the discounted tokens. What should the result be?

2. The Castagnas decided to sell their house. Through the Castagna's realtor, Baffone offered to purchase the house for $2.1 million. As a sign that he was serious, he provided a $50,000 deposit. The Castagnas rejected Baffone's offer, and, on August 19, 2004, they made a counteroffer, through the realtor, to sell the property to Baffone for $2.3 million. Baffone told the realtor that he would buy the house for $2.3 million, but only if the settlement date were December 31, 2004, and only if the Castagnas agreed to permit

Baffone to settle at any time up to that date. The realtor told the Castagnas about this latest counteroffer, but they never responded either affirmatively or negatively. Baffone later made yet another offer to buy the house, this time offering $2.5 million with no contingencies. The Castagnas never responded to this offer. Baffone later sued the Castagnas for breach of contract, claiming that he accepted the Castagnas' counteroffer to sell the property for $2.3 million. Is this a good argument?

3. Rodziewicz was driving a 1999 Volvo conventional tractor-trailer on I-90 in Lake County, Indiana, when he struck a concrete barrier. His truck was stuck on top of the barrier, and the state police contacted Waffco Heavy Duty Towing to help in the recovery. Before Waffco began working, Rodziewicz asked how much it would cost to tow the truck. He was told that the fee would be $275, and there was no discussion of labor or other costs. Rodziewicz instructed Waffco to take his truck to a Volvo dealership. After a few minutes of work, Waffco pulled Rodziewicz's truck off the barrier and towed the truck to its towing yard a few miles away. Subsequently, Waffco notified Rodziewicz that, in addition to the $275 towing fee, he would have to pay $4,070 in labor costs. Waffco calculated its labor charges as $.11 cents per pound. Waffco would not release the truck until payment was made, so Rodziewicz paid the total amount. Was Rodziewicz contractually obligated to pay Waffco the $4,070 labor fee?

4. Schiff, a self-styled tax rebel who had made a career out of his tax protest activities, appeared live on the February 7, 1983, CBS News *Nightwatch* program. During the course of the program, which had a viewer participant format, Schiff repeated his long-standing position that "there is nothing in the Internal Revenue Code which says anyone is legally required to pay the tax." Later in the program, Schiff stated: "If anybody calls this show and cites any section of this Code that says an individual is required to file a tax return, I will pay them $100,000." Newman, an attorney, did not see Schiff live on *Nightwatch,* but saw a two-minute taped segment of the original *Nightwatch* interview several hours later on the *CBS Morning News.* Certain that Schiff's statements were incorrect, Newman telephoned and wrote *CBS Morning News,* attempting to accept Schiff's offer by citing Internal Revenue Code provisions requiring individuals to pay federal income tax. CBS forwarded Newman's letter to Schiff, who refused to pay on the ground that Newman had not properly accepted his offer. Newman sued Schiff for breach of contract. Will Newman win?

5. Leonard saw a "Pepsi Stuff" commercial encouraging consumers to collect "Pepsi Points" from specially marked packages of Pepsi or Diet Pepsi and redeem these points for merchandise featuring the Pepsi logo. The commercial depicts a teenager preparing to leave for school, dressed in a shirt emblazoned with the Pepsi logo. The drumroll sounds as the subtitle "T-SHIRT 75 PEPSI POINTS" scrolled across the screen. The teenager strides down the hallway wearing a leather jacket, and the subtitle "LEATHER JACKET 1450 PEPSI POINTS" appears. The teenager opens the door of his house and puts on a pair of sunglasses. The drum roll then accompanies the subtitle "SHADES 175 PEPSI POINTS." A voiceover then intones, "Introducing the new Pepsi Stuff catalog." The scene then shifts to three young boys sitting in front of a high school building. The boy in the middle is intent on his Pepsi Stuff catalog, while the boys on either side are drinking Pepsi. The three boys gaze in awe at an object approaching overhead. The military music swelled, and the viewer senses the presence of a mighty plane as the extreme winds generated by its flight create a paper maelstrom in a classroom devoted to an otherwise dull physics lesson. Finally, a Harrier jet swings into view and lands by the side of the school building, next to a bicycle rack. Several students run for cover, and the velocity of the wind strips one faculty member down to his underwear. The voiceover announces, "Now the more Pepsi you drink, the more great stuff you're gonna get." The teenager opens the cockpit of the fighter and can be seen, holding a Pepsi. "Sure beats the bus," he says. The military drum roll swells a final time and the following words appear: "HARRIER FIGHTER 7,000,000 PEPSI POINTS." Inspired by the commercial, Leonard set out to get a Harrier jet. He consulted the Pepsi Stuff catalog, but it did not contain any entry or description of the Harrier jet. The amount of Pepsi Points necessary to get the listed merchandise ranged from 15 for a "jacket tattoo" to 3,300 for a mountain bike. The rear foldout pages of the catalog contained directions for redeeming Pepsi Points for merchandise. These directions note that merchandise may be ordered "only" with the original Order Form. The catalog notes that in the event that a consumer lacks enough Pepsi Points to obtain a desired item, additional Pepsi Points may be purchased for 10 cents each; however, at least 15 original Pepsi Points must accompany each order. Leonard initially set out to collect 7,000,000 Pepsi Points by consuming Pepsi products, but then switched to buying Pepsi Points. Leonard ultimately raised about $700,000. In March 1996, Leonard submitted an Order Form, fifteen original Pepsi Points, and a check for $700,008.50. At the bottom of the Order Form, Leonard wrote in "1 Harrier Jet" in the "Item" column and "7,000,000" in the "Total Points" column. In a letter accompanying his submission, he stated that the check was to purchase additional Pepsi Points for obtaining a new Harrier jet as advertised in the Pepsi Stuff commercial. Several months later, Pepsico's fulfillment house rejected Leonard's submission and returned the check, explaining that the item he requested was not part of the Pepsi Stuff collection, and only catalog merchandise could be redeemed under this program. It also stated, "The Harrier jet in the Pepsi commercial is fanciful and is simply included to create a humorous and entertaining ad." Leonard sued Pepsico for breach of contract. Will he win?

6. Pernal owned a parcel of real estate adjacent to property owned by St. Nicholas Greek Orthodox Church. Pernal sent a letter to the church indicating that he was offering it for sale for "$825,000 cash/mortgage,

'as is,' with no conditions, no contingencies related to zoning and 120 days post closing occupancy for the present tenants." This offer was dated June 3, 2003, and expressly provided that it would remain open for a two-week period. On the same day, Pernal also sent the same offer to sell the property on the same terms to another prospective purchaser, White Chapel Memorial Association Park Perpetual Care Trust. On June 4, the church sent a letter indicating that it accepted the terms of the offer that Pernal had set forth in his letter. However, the church's letter also referenced an attached purchase agreement. The purchase agreement agreed with Pernal's purchase price and the close occupancy period, but contrary to the offer, it contained additional terms. The church's president signed this attached purchase agreement, but defendant did not sign it. The offer by letter dated June 3, 2003, did not reference other potential purchasers. On June 10, White Chapel, by letter, offered to pay $900,000 cash for the property, with no conditions or contingencies related to zoning and 180 days post closing occupancy rent free. On that same date (June 10), Pernal sent a letter to both potential purchasers. This letter indicated that "amended offers" had been received. The letter further provided that the offer would remain open for two weeks' time as provided in the initial offering letter. On June 13, the church sent a letter to Pernal, stating that the offer had been accepted on June 4, and that an enforceable contract was formed. The church sued Pernal for breach of contract. Will it win?

7. Calvin and Audrey Bones are the trustees of the Calvin R. and Audrey J. Bones Family Trust. The trust owned a ranch in Nebraska that the trust decided to sell. On June 11, 1997, the Boneses listed the ranch for sale with Agri Affiliates, a real estate agent. According to the listing agreement between the Boneses and Agri, if the listing sold to the current tenants, Lydic Brothers, the agent would receive only a 1 percent commission. On the other hand, if the listing sold to anyone else, the agent would receive a 6 percent commission. On July 17, 1997, Dean Keller submitted to Agri a written offer to buy the ranch for $490,000. The offer also stated that it would be withdrawn if not accepted by July 21 at 5 PM. Paragraph 15 of the offer states in part that "upon execution by Seller, this agreement shall be-

come a binding contract." At 4:53 PM on July 21, the Boneses faxed a signed copy of the offer to Agri. In addition, at 5:12 PM on July 21, Loren Johnson, Agri's representative, telephoned Keller and left a voicemail message to inform him of the Boneses' acceptance. On July 22, 1997, Don Lydic, a representative of Lydic Brothers, informed the Boneses and the agent that Lydic Brothers would match Keller's offer for the ranch. The Boneses wanted to accept Don Lydic's offer and sell the ranch to Lydic Brothers. Later that same day, Agri asked Keller if he would be willing to release the Boneses from the agreement and "back out" of the deal. Keller refused and asserted that he wanted to go forward with the sale. The Boneses unequivocally informed Keller on December 5, 1997, that they would not sell the ranch to him. After the Boneses failed to close, Keller brought suit against the Boneses, seeking relief for breach of contract. The Boneses asserted that no contract existed (1) because their acceptance was not communicated to the buyer within the time specified in the offer and the attempted acceptance thus became a counteroffer and (2) because the buyer did not communicate to the sellers that he accepted their counteroffer. Are they correct?

8. Mariah Carey is a famous entertainer. Vian, who was Carey's stepfather before she achieved stardom, was in the business of designing, producing, and marketing gift and novelty items. Vian claimed that Carey agreed orally to give him a license to produce "Mariah dolls," which would be statuettes of the singer that would play her most popular songs. Vian asserted that this right was given in exchange for his financial and emotional support of Carey, including picking her up from late-night recording sessions, providing her with the use of a car, paying for dental care, allowing her to use his boat for business meetings and rehearsals, and giving her various items to help furnish her apartment. Vian based his claim of an oral contract on three conversations, twice in the family car and once on Vian's boat. Vian said to Carey, "Don't forget about the Mariah dolls," and "I get the Mariah dolls." According to Vian, on one occasion Carey responded, "Okay" and on other occasions, she merely smiled and nodded. Although Carey admits that Vian mentioned the dolls two or three times, she testified that

she thought it was a joke. Claiming that Carey breached the contract to license dolls in her likeness, Vian brought this action for breach of contract. Was a contract formed?

9. In July 1985, Congress passed the Statue of Liberty–Ellis Island Commemorative Coin Act. The Act instructed the Secretary of the Treasury to mint and sell a stated number of coins. In November and December 1985, the U.S. Mint mailed advertising materials about the coins to people whose names were included on a list of previous customers/coin collectors. These materials described the various coins the issuance of which was authorized by the Act, and encouraged potential purchasers to forward early payment for commemorative coins. Payment could be made either by check, money order, or credit card. The Mint had not previously dealt with credit card sales and the processing of credit card orders. Directly above the space provided on this form for the customer's signature on the order form was the following:

> VERY IMPORTANT—PLEASE READ: YES, Please accept my order for the U.S. Liberty Coins I have indicated. I understand that all sales are final and not subject to refund. Verification of my order will be made by the Department of the Treasury, U.S. Mint. . . . If my order is received by December 31, 1985, I will be entitled to purchase the coins at the Pre-Issue Discount price shown. I have read, understand and agree to the above. . . .
>
>   Please allow 6 to 8 weeks for delivery after issue date of January 1, 1986. The U.S. Mint reserves the right to limit quantities shipped, subject to availability. Mint may discontinue accepting orders should bullion prices increase significantly. Credit card orders will be billed upon receipt by the U.S. Mint.

In November 1985, Mrs. Mesaros sent an order to the Mint for certain Statue of Liberty coins. She provided information about her husband's credit card, reflecting that $1,675 should be charged to Mr. Mesaros's credit card account. Later in November, Mr. Mesaros sent additional orders for another 18 gold coins to the Mint. These orders were placed in the names of members of the Mesaros family, and were paid for with nine separate checks.

   Demand for the coins far exceeded the Mint's expectations, and there were not enough five-dollar gold coins to fill all the orders of those who had responded to the Mint's promotional materials. The last order for gold coins that was filled was accepted some time between December 31, 1985, and January 6, 1986. This exhausted the supply of the 500,000 gold coins that were authorized by the Act. These gold coins increased in value by approximately 200 percent within the first few months of 1986. In February 1986, the Mesaroses were informed by a form letter that the Mint "had tried but was unable" to process the Mesaroses' November credit card order. The Mesaroses did receive the 18 coins that had been paid for by checks. Investigation revealed that the Mesaroses' bank had given authorization to the Mellon Bank (responsible for processing credit card orders for the Mint) with respect to the coin order charged to Mr. Mesaros's account. However, the Mint and the Mellon Bank were swamped with a deluge of 756,000 orders, of which 186,000 were credit card orders. Cash orders were filled fairly promptly by the Mint, but credit card orders before being filled had to be sent by the Mint to the Mellon Bank in Pittsburgh for verification, investigation, and determination of validity, which was a slow process. Credit card orders, when approved by the Mellon Bank were certified as valid and returned to the Mint to be filled. Before all of the 186,000 credit card orders could be verified by the Mellon Bank and thereafter filled by the Mint, all of the gold coins had been sold by the Mint in filling cash orders, and no more coins were available. As a result, 13,000 credit card orders could not be filled, and were rejected by the Mint. The Mesaros order was in this rejected group. The Mesaroses brought suit against the government for breach of contract. They claimed that the Mint's promotional material and order form was an offer. Are they correct?

10. Jeff visited a car dealership and test-drove a used car. After discussing the price with the salesman, Jake, and learning that he could purchase the car for $500 less than the sticker price, Jeff asked Jake to hold the car for him until 8:00 that evening so that he could bring his wife back to see the car. Jake agreed, writing out a note promising not to sell the car before 8:00 PM. The note was written on dealership stationery, but Jake did not sign his name. The dealership broke its promise and sold the car to Jones

before 8:00 PM. Was it free to revoke its offer to Jeff? Jones, the new purchaser of the car (and a nonmerchant), later offered in a signed writing to sell the car to Jill and to hold the car for her until she returned with her husband. Could Jones revoke this offer?

Online Research

Finding Offers on the Internet

1. Browse various commercial Web sites, classified sections of online newspapers, and other online commercial solicitations. Select an example of an ad or solicitation that would be considered an invitation to negotiate rather than an offer and one that would constitute an offer. Explain why the examples you have chosen would or would not constitute offers under the standards discussed in this chapter.

2. Browse an online auction Web site such as eBay (**www.ebay.com**), and determine under what circumstances a seller's listing of items for auction on that site constitutes an offer. That is, does the bidder form a contract by submitting the highest bid, or can the seller legally refuse to sell the item to the highest bidder? Tip: Be sure to check out the site's User Agreement and its instructions for sellers.

chapter 11

THE AGREEMENT: ACCEPTANCE

O n April 1, 2006, Carlos received a letter from Clear Creek School Corporation (CCSC) offering him a job as a high school mathematics teacher for the academic year 2007–08, at a salary of $32,000. Carlos considered the offer for several days and then, on April 4, he sent CCSC a letter in which he stated that he accepted its offer. In this letter, Carlos also stated, "Is CCSC willing to pay me the $2,000 signing bonus that many of my classmates are getting from other school districts?" On April 5, before CCSC had received Carlos's letter, Carlos received a letter from CCSC's superintendent stating that CCSC had decided to hire someone else and was revoking its offer to him.

- Did Carlos accept CCSC's offer?
- If so, when was Carlos's acceptance effective?
- Did CCSC have the legal right to revoke its offer?
- Was it ethical for CCSC to revoke its offer?

THE PRECEDING CHAPTER DISCUSSED the circumstances under which a proposal will constitute the first stage of an agreement: the offer. This chapter focuses on the final stage of forming an agreement: the acceptance. The acceptance is vitally important because it is with the acceptance that the contract is formed. This chapter discusses the requirements for making a valid acceptance as well as the rules concerning the time at which a contract comes into being.

What Is an Acceptance?

An **acceptance** is "a manifestation of assent to the terms [of the offer] made by the offeree in the manner invited or required by the offer."[1] In determining if an offeree accepted an offer and created a contract, a court will look for evidence of three factors: (1) the offeree intended to

enter the contract, (2) the offeree accepted on the terms proposed by the offeror, and (3) the offeree communicated his acceptance to the offeror.

Intention to Accept

In determining whether an offeree accepted an offer, the court is looking for the same *present intent to contract* on the part of the offeree that it found on the part of the offeror. And, as is true of intent to make an offer, intent to accept is judged by an objective standard. The difference is that the offeree must objectively indicate a present intent to contract on the terms of the offer for a contract to result. As the master of the offer, the offeror may specify in detail what behavior is required of the offeree to bind him to a contract. If the offeror does so, the offeree must ordinarily comply with all the terms of the offer before a contract results.

The following *Adsit* case analyzes how these concepts about manifestion of assent apply in the context of *clickwrap* contracts presented online.

---

[1] *Restatement (Second) of Contracts* § 50(1)(1981).

Adsit Co. v. Gustin   874 N.E.2d 1018 (Ind. Ct. App. 2007)

Adsit is an Indiana-based retailer of new, used, and rebuilt parts and accessories for Mercedes-Benz automobiles. It does business over the phone and the Internet. Mary Gustin lives in Texas, and Julie Gustin, Mary's daughter-in-law, lives in Alabama. Julie's husband, Kevin, owned a classic 1967 Mercedes-Benz roadster. Mary wanted to buy leather seat covers and armrest covers for the car.

Prior to placing an online order on Adsit's Web site, a customer must click a button reading "I Accept," which is located at the bottom of a Web page describing the company policy. The policy stated that there would be absolutely no refunds or returns, that there was a warranty for 30 days on an exchange basis, and that all sales were final. The policy also included a forum selection clause:

AGREEMENT ON JURISDICTION TO DAMAGES:

[Adsit] and Customers agree that any suit, claim or legal proceedings of any nature between the parties must be filed and prosecuted in Delaware County, Indiana and shall be controlled by the laws of the State of Indiana then in effect. . . .

The page of Adsit's Web site regarding seat upholstery states that

[a]ll seat upholstery is manufactured using the original german leathers or mb tex vinyls to the original pattern for the correct look. Most original colors are available. If you have any questions about the color of your interior, please supply us with your vin# or send a sample of your old interior. All interior items are special order and nonreturnable so please order carefully.

On December 15, 2004, Mary placed an order on Adsit's Web site for two camel-colored leather seat covers and two camel-colored leather armrest covers. Mary also entered a vehicle identification number (VIN) on the Web site but wrote down an incorrect number. Consequently, when Adsit employees looked at the VIN, they dismissed it because it was not a VIN for a Mercedes-Benz vehicle. Originally, Mary placed the order on her credit card with instructions to ship the goods to Kevin and Julie. Two days later, an Adsit employee called Mary to inform her that because of a company policy, the credit card to which the order was billed needed to match the address to which it was shipped. Therefore, with Julie's permission, Mary provided Adsit with Julie's credit card number and information. Julie had no direct contact with Adsit. After verifying the order, Adsit placed an order for camel-colored leather seat and armrest covers from its supplier, German Auto Tops in North Hollywood, California. Because the factory was closed for the holidays, Julie and Kevin did not receive the goods until January 22, 2005. At that time, they discovered that the color of the seat covers did not match their vehicle's interior. Within six days of receiving the seat covers, Julie and Kevin returned them to the California address from which they were sent. They sent the seat covers via certified United States mail and received confirmation of delivery. They also reversed the charge on their credit card. A representative of Adsit testified that the company did not receive the goods.

On July 12, 2005, Adsit filed a breach of contract complaint against Julie, later adding Mary as a defendant. Following a bench trial, the trial court entered judgment for Adsit, but awarded a smaller amount of money than Adsit thought it was entitled to. Adsit and Mary and Julie appealed. Among the Gustins' arguments on appeal was that the Indiana court lacked jurisdiction over Mary and Julie, both of whom lived in other states.

Baker, Judge

As a threshold matter, we must consider whether the trial court properly exercised personal jurisdiction over the Gustins. Parties may consent by contract to the exercise of personal jurisdiction by courts that otherwise might not have such jurisdiction. Forum selection clauses—even those occurring in form contracts—are enforceable if they are reasonable and just under the circumstances and there is no evidence of fraud or overreaching. Additionally, the provision must have been freely negotiated. Thus, it is well settled that to determine the validity of a forum selection clause, we are to examine whether the clause is freely negotiated and just and reasonable under the circumstances.

Here, Adsit's policy contains a forum selection clause providing that "any suit, claim or legal proceedings of any nature between the parties must be filed and prosecuted in Delaware County Indiana and shall be controlled by the laws of the State of Indiana." To complete the transaction, Mary was required to click on a button reading "I Accept" that was placed at the bottom of the web-page containing the policy. This type of web-based contract is commonly referred to as a "clickwrap" agreement. A clickwrap agreement appears on an internet webpage and requires that a user consent to any terms and conditions by clicking on a dialog box on the screen in order to proceed with the internet transaction. Even though they are electronic, clickwrap agreements are considered to be writings because they are printable and storable. To determine whether a clickwrap agreement is enforceable, courts presented with the issue apply traditional principles of contract law and focus on whether the plaintiffs had reasonable notice of and manifested assent to the clickwrap agreement.

Here, the Adsit policy gave reasonable notice of its terms. To complete a transaction, a user must accept the policy, the text of which is immediately visible to the user. The user is required to take affirmative action by clicking on the "I Accept" button; if the user refuses to agree to the terms, she cannot engage in the transaction. The entire policy is essentially three short paragraphs—one-half of a page. Moreover, the paragraph that contains the forum selection clause begins with the following heading, which is bolded and in all capital letters: **"AGREEMENT ON JURISDICTION TO DAMAGES."**

Under these circumstances, we find that Mary had reasonable notice of and manifested assent to the clickwrap agreement containing the forum selection clause. We also find that she was capable of understanding its terms, consented to them, and could have rejected the agreement with impunity. Finally, we note that Mary was not deprived of her day in court, inasmuch as she and Julie retained counsel, requested and obtained permission to participate telephonically in hearings, and did, in fact, participate telephonically. Given these facts, we find that the forum selection clause contained in Adsit's clickwrap agreement was valid, enforceable, and binding on Mary.

Whether the forum selection clause also binds Julie is a closer call. Julie's only role in the transaction was to provide Mary with her credit card number after Adsit informed Mary that company policy required that a customer's shipping and billing addresses be the same. Mary then placed the order, using Julie's credit card number and address to complete the transaction. Thus, Julie did not personally accept Adsit's policy, including the forum selection clause. If Mary was acting as Julie's agent, however, then Julie is bound to the terms of the contract, including the forum selection clause. Although the record does not reveal the precise nature of the communication between Mary and Julie regarding the purchase from Adsit, it is undisputed that Julie did, in fact, provide Mary with her credit card number so that Mary could complete the purchase. We find that under these circumstances, Julie's conduct was sufficient to give Mary actual authority to engage in the transaction on her behalf. Consequently, Julie is likewise bound by Adsit's forum selection clause. In sum, we find that the trial court properly exercised personal jurisdiction over Mary and Julie.

Affirmed in favor of Adsit.

Intent and Acceptance on the Offeror's Terms

Common Law: Traditional "Mirror Image" Rule The traditional contract law rule is that an acceptance must be the *mirror image* of the offer. Attempts by offerees to change the terms of the offer or to add new terms to it are treated as counteroffers because they impliedly indicate an intent by the offeree to reject the offer instead of being bound by its terms. However, recent years have witnessed a judicial tendency to apply the mirror image rule in a more liberal fashion by holding that only *material* (important) variances between an offer and a purported acceptance result in an implied rejection of the offer.

Even under the mirror image rule, no rejection is implied if an offeree merely asks about the terms of the offer without indicating its rejection (an *inquiry regarding terms*), or accepts the offer's terms while complaining about them (a *grumbling acceptance*). Distinguishing among a counteroffer, an inquiry regarding terms, and a grumbling acceptance is often a difficult task. The fundamental issue, however, remains the same: Did the offeree objectively indicate a present intent to be bound by the terms of the offer? You will see an application of the traditional mirror image rule in the following *Finnin* case.

| Finnin v. Bob Lindsay, Inc. | 852 N.E.2d 446 (Ill. Ct. App. 2006) |

In March 2002, plaintiffs Michael Finnin, D. J. McPherson, and David Wright approached Bob Lindsay about selling his Honda-Toyota dealership. Negotiations continued over the next few months, and the agreement was drafted in writing. Both parties then made several suggestions, modifications, and counterproposals to the draft. On August 13, 2002, a few final changes to the agreement were discussed between the lawyers for both parties. On August 13 or 14, the legal assistant who worked for Lindsay's lawyer sent a letter to the plaintiffs' attorney enclosing a revised agreement for the sale of Lindsay's stock. This copy contained all of the corrections previously discussed and Lindsay signed it.

Upon receipt of the agreement, the plaintiffs' attorney noticed two errors that did not conform to the parties' intent. The parties had previously agreed that the plaintiffs would pay $1.1 million for the stock. The purchase price provision of the agreement stated the correct amount. However, Exhibit A to the agreement still stated that the purchase price was $700,000. Second, the agreement made reference to another agreement for the sale of goodwill between the parties that had since been incorporated into the agreement for the sale of stock. The plaintiffs' attorney contacted Lindsay's attorneys, and they discussed the errors. On August 19, 2002, Lindsay's attorney wrote to the plaintiffs' lawyer, suggesting that plaintiffs' lawyer send the draft back and he would send the plaintiffs a corrected version of the agreement. However, the plaintiffs' lawyer never returned the contract.

On the morning of August 22, Lindsay telephoned Finnin and informed him that he had received another offer from a third party. The plaintiffs' attorney recommended that the three partners sign the agreement and return it. Finnin called Lindsay and told him that the plaintiffs intended to go through with the deal. That same day, the plaintiffs' attorney made the previously discussed changes to the written agreement by striking out the incorrect purchase price and inserting the correct amount of money in Exhibit A and by removing all references to the "agreement for the sale of goodwill." The plaintiffs then initialed the corrections, signed the agreement, and returned the contract to Lindsay's attorney.

Lindsay refused to sell the dealership to the plaintiffs. They then filed a breach of contract complaint against Lindsay. The trial court granted summary judgment in favor of Lindsay. The plaintiffs appealed. They maintained that the modifications made after Lindsay signed the agreement were simply corrections to errors in the writing and did not change the terms agreed to by the parties; thus, a valid contract was formed.

Lytton, Justice

It is well settled that in order to constitute a contract by offer and acceptance, the acceptance must conform exactly to the offer. Under Illinois contract law, an acceptance requiring any modification or change in terms constitutes a rejection of the original offer and becomes a counteroffer that must be accepted by the original offeror before a valid contract is formed. Our supreme court [has] held that any changes to an offer, even minor changes, constitute a counteroffer rather than an acceptance.

Illinois' strict compliance rule of law was recently noted and applied by the Seventh Circuit in *Venture Associates Corp. v. Zenith Data Systems, Corp*. In that case, plaintiff and defendant were attempting to negotiate the sale of defendant's subsidiary company. The parties exchanged several drafts of a proposed agreement. After months of negotiations, the plaintiff returned a proposed purchase agreement "with minor, non-substantive changes on it in writing." The defendant seller eventually refused to proceed, and the sale was never completed. The plaintiff filed suit in federal court, alleging that the parties had entered into a binding agreement when it returned the agreement with only minor changes. The district court granted defendant's motion to dismiss. On appeal, the Seventh Circuit held that the plaintiff's conduct did not create a binding contract between the parties. The court concluded: "Because Illinois law demands that an acceptance comply strictly with the terms of the offer, [Plaintiff's] modifications of [defendant's] proposed agreement, however minor, precluded formation of a contract at that point. Indeed, [plaintiff's] changes created a counteroffer which [defendant] never accepted."

Here, plaintiffs argue that they made only non-substantive, typographical modifications to the proposed agreement for the sale of stock. We agree that plaintiffs' changes were minor and that they apparently conformed to the agreement of the parties. Nevertheless, Illinois case law clearly mandates that any modification, however slight, prevents the creation of a valid contract. Plaintiffs attempt to correct or modify the terms of the agreement formed a counteroffer that Lindsay refused to accept. We recognize that many courts in other jurisdictions disagree with our disposition. Other states have found that immaterial or minor differences or variances between the offer and acceptance do not prevent the formation of a contract. Those courts have concluded that a modification of an offer constitutes a counteroffer only if the modification is a material one. Although the material modification analysis may be more appropriately applied to the facts of this case, Illinois has yet to adopt that rule. Therefore, the trial court properly granted summary judgment in favor of Lindsay.

Affirmed in favor of Lindsay.

UCC Standard for Acceptance on the Offeror's Terms: The "Battle of the Forms" Strictly applying the mirror image rule to modern commercial transactions, most of which are carried out by using preprinted form contracts, would often result in frustrating the parties' true intent. Offerors use standard order forms prepared by their lawyers, and offerees use standard acceptance or acknowledgment forms drafted by their

Figure 1   The "Battle of the Forms"—A Section 2–207 Flowchart

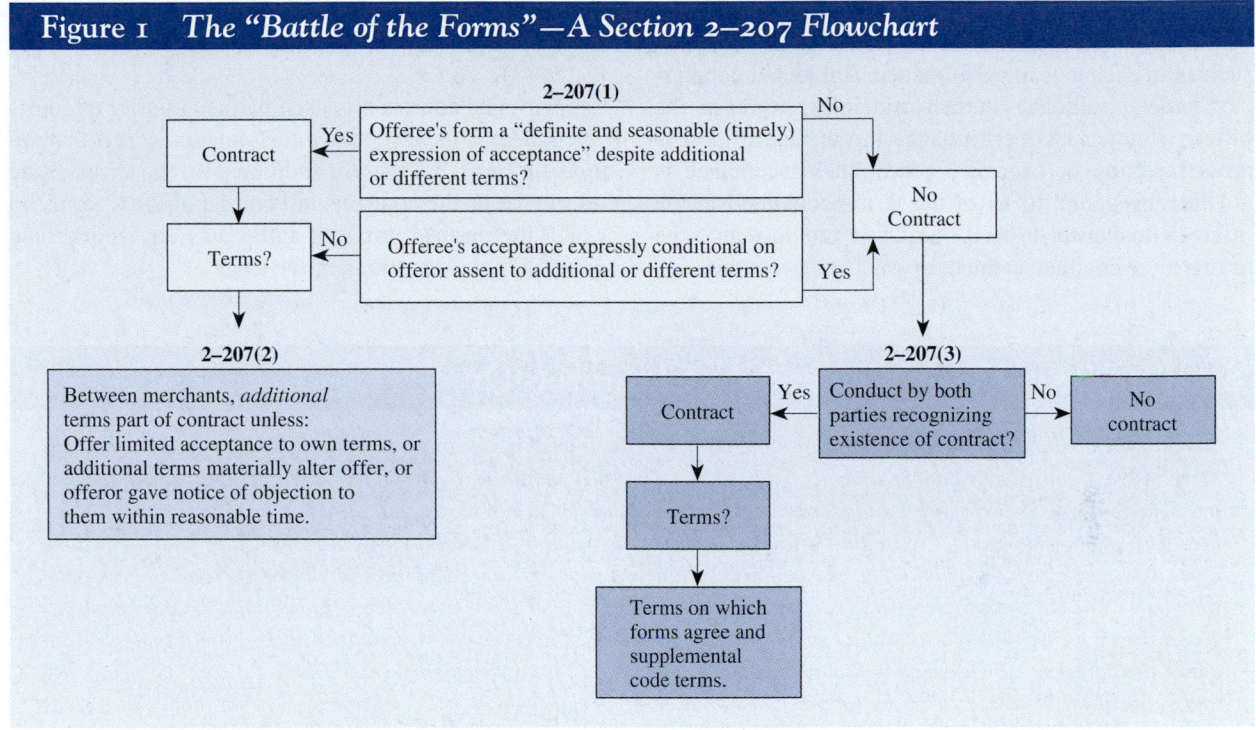

counter. The odds that these forms will agree in every detail are slight, as are the odds that the parties will read each other's forms in their entirety. Instead, the parties to such transactions are likely to read only crucial provisions concerning the goods ordered, the price, and the delivery date called for, and if these terms are agreeable, believe that they have a contract.

If a dispute arose before the parties started to perform, a court strictly applying the mirror image rule would hold that no contract resulted because the offer and acceptance forms did not match exactly. If a dispute arose after performance had commenced, the court would probably hold that the offeror had impliedly accepted the offeree's counteroffer and was bound by its terms.

Because neither of these results is very satisfactory, the Code, in a very controversial provision often called the "Battle of the Forms" section [2–207] (see Figure 1), has changed the mirror image rule for contracts involving the sale of goods. UCC section 2–207 allows the formation of a contract even when there is some variance between the terms of the offer and the terms of the acceptance. It also makes it possible, under *some* circumstances, for a term contained in the acceptance form to become part of the contract. The Code provides that a *definite and timely expression of acceptance* creates a contract, even if it includes terms that are *different from*

those stated in the offer or even if it states *additional terms* that the offer did not address [2–207(1)]. An attempted acceptance that *was expressly conditioned* on the offeror's agreement to the offeree's terms would *not* be a valid acceptance, however [2–207(1)]. You will see an example of the operation of 2–207 in the following *Standard Bent Glass* case.

What are the terms of a contract created by the exchange of standardized forms? The *additional* terms contained in the offeree's form are treated as "proposals for addition to the contract." If the parties are both *merchants,* the additional terms become part of the contract *unless:*

1. The offer *expressly limited acceptance* to its own terms.

2. The new terms would *materially alter* the offer, or

3. The offeror gives notice of objection to the new terms within a reasonable time after receiving the acceptance [2–207(2)].

When the offeree has made his acceptance expressly conditional on the offeror's agreement to the new terms or when the offeree's response to the offer is clearly not "an expression of acceptance" (e.g., an express rejection), no contract is created under section 2–207(1). A contract will only result in such cases if the parties engage in conduct that "recognizes the existence of a contract," such as an exchange of performance. Unlike her counterpart under traditional contract principles, however, the offeror who accepts performance in the face of an express rejection or expressly conditional acceptance is not thereby bound to all of the terms contained in the offeree's response. Instead, the Code provides that the terms of a contract created by such performance are those on which the parties' writings agree, supplemented by appropriate gap-filling provisions from the Code [2–207(3)].

That same approach is used by the majority of courts when there is an acceptance that contains terms that are *different* from (not merely additional to) the terms of the offer. That is, the contract will consist of those terms on which the parties' writings agree *plus* any appropriate gap-filling presumptions of the Code.

Standard Bent Glass Corporation v. Glassrobots Oy   333 F.3d 440 (3rd Cir. 2003)

Standard Bent Glass, a Pennsylvania corporation, wanted to buy a machine for its factory that would produce cut glass. In March 1998, it started negotiations with Glassrobots Oy, a Finnish corporation. By February 1999, negotiations had reached a critical juncture. On February 1, Standard Bent Glass faxed an offer to purchase a glass fabricating system from Glassrobots. The offer sheet began, "Please find below our terms and conditions related to ORDER #DKH2199," and defined the items to be purchased; the quantity; the price of $1.1 million; the payment terms; and installation specifics, instructions, and warranties. The letter concluded, "Please sign this ORDER and fax to us if it is agreeable." On February 2, Glassrobots responded with a cover letter, invoice, and standard sales agreement. The cover letter recited: "Attached you'll find our standard sales agreement. Please read it through and let me know if there is anything you want to change. If not, I'll send 2 originals, which will be signed." The contract included an arbitration clause and several references to arbitration. Glassrobots did not return, nor refer to, Standard Bent Glass's order.

Later that day, Standard Bent Glass faxed a return letter that began, "Please find our changes to the Sales Agreement," by which it meant Glassrobots's standard sales agreement. This letter apparently accepted Glassrobots's standard sales agreement as a template and requested five specific changes. The letter closed, "Please call me if the above is not agreeable. If it is we will start the wire today." On February 4, Standard Bent Glass wired the down payment to Glassrobots, and on February 8, the wire transfer cleared Glassrobots's bank account.

On February 5, Glassrobots sent Standard Bent Glass a revised sales agreement that incorporated almost all of the requested changes. Glassrobots's cover letter stated, "Attached you'll find the revised sales agreement. . . . Please return one signed to us; the other one is for your files." A provision of this agreement stated that "this Agreement shall come into force when signed by both parties." Standard Bent Glass never signed the agreement. On February 9, Standard Bent Glass sent another fax to Glassrobots in which it stated, "Just noticed on our sales agreement that the power is 440 ± 5. We must have 480 ± 5 on both pieces of equipment." There was no further written correspondence after February 9 and no contract was ever signed by both parties. Nevertheless, both parties continued to perform. Glassrobots installed the glass fabricating system and Standard Bent Glass made its final payment to Glassrobots.

Standard Bent Glass noticed defects in the equipment, and the parties disputed the cause of the defects. Standard Bent Glass sued Glassrobots. Glassrobots filed a motion to compel arbitration under an appendix to the standard sales agreement that Standard Bent Glass claims it never received. The trial court granted Glassrobots's motion and Standard Bent Glass appealed.

Scirica, Chief Judge

At issue is whether there was a valid agreement and whether that agreement contained a binding arbitration clause. Glassrobots's standard sales agreement contained a reference to binding arbitration. Because this dispute involves the sale of goods, the Uniform Commercial Code applies, specifically section 2–207.

Under UCC section 2–207(1), the offeree's expression of acceptance or transmission of a written confirmation generally results in the formation of a contract. This is true unless the offeree makes that expression or confirmation "expressly conditional" on the offeror's assent to the proposed additional or different terms. The flexibility permitted under section 2–207 allows parties to begin performance expediently rather than wait for all contract details to be resolved. This structure is well suited to the fast-paced environment of commercial dealings. Where parties perform but do not explicitly agree on a single uniform document, sections 2–207(2) and (3) govern proposed additional or different terms to the contract.

Here, Standard Bent Glass initiated written negotiations between the parties on February 1. This exchange represented an offer from Standard Bent Glass to purchase the glass fabricating machine from Glassrobots. The Standard Bent Glass offer contained a set of terms and conditions. On February 2, Glassrobots responded by enclosing its standard sales agreement, which contained a different set of terms and conditions. Later that day, Standard Bent Glass sent its own response, accepting the terms of the Glassrobots standard sales agreement and proposing five specific modifications. Referring to the Glassrobots agreement, the Standard Bent Glass letter began, "Please find our changes to the Sales Agreement."

This communication from Standard Bent Glass constituted either: (1) a definite and seasonable expression of acceptance under section 2–207(1); (2) a counteroffer; or (3) a rejection followed by conduct by both parties sufficient to recognize a valid contract under section 2–207(3). By using the Glassrobots standard sales agreement as a template and by authorizing a wire transfer of the down payment, Standard Bent Glass demonstrated its intent to perform under the essential terms of Glassrobots's standard sales agreement. Accordingly, its response was a definite and seasonable expression of acceptance of Glassrobots's offer. Noteworthy was Standard Bent Glass's own immediate performance on the February 2 agreement. On February 4, Standard Bent Glass initiated a wire transfer to Glassrobots for the down payment. The following day, Glassrobots adopted most, but not all, of the proposed modifications, and began to perform on the agreement. This was the last significant exchange of written documents between the parties. The parties continued to perform, with Glassrobots constructing and installing the desired equipment and Standard Bent Glass timely paying for it.

In sum, Standard Bent Glass's conduct constituted a definite and seasonable expression of acceptance that evinced the formation of a contract rather than a counteroffer or rejection. For these reasons, there was a valid contract on the Glassrobots terms of February 2 that incorporated any nonmaterial additions proposed by Standard Bent Glass.

Affirmed in favor of Glassrobots.

LOG ON

This helpful site leads a student through a §2–207 analysis: Professor Bell, *A Brief Working Guide to UCC §2–207*, **www.tomwbell.com/teaching/ UCC2-207.html.**

Communication of Acceptance

To accept an offer for a bilateral contract, the offeree must make the promise requested by the offer. In Chapter 10, you learned that an offeror must communicate the terms of his proposal to the offeree before an offer results. This is so because communication is a necessary component of the present intent to contract required for the creation of an offer. For similar reasons, it is generally held that an offeree must communicate his intent to be bound by the offer before a contract can be created. To accept an offer for a unilateral contract, however, the offeree must perform the requested act. The traditional contract law rule on this point assumes that the offeror will learn of the offeree's performance and holds that no further notice from the offeree is necessary to create a contract unless the offeror specifically requests notice.

Manner of Communication The offeror, as the master of the offer, has the power to specify the precise time, place, and manner in which acceptance must be communicated. This is called a *stipulation.* If the offeror stipulates a particular manner of acceptance, the offeree must respond in this way to form a valid acceptance. Suppose Prompt Printing makes an offer to Jackson and the offer states that Jackson must respond by certified mail. If Jackson deviates from the offer's instructions in any significant way, no contract results unless Prompt Printing indicates a willingness to be bound by the deviating acceptance. If, however, the offer merely *suggests* a method or place of communication or is *silent* on such matters, the offeree may accept within a *reasonable time* by *any reasonable means* of communication. So, if Prompt Printing's offer did not *require* any particular manner of accepting the offer, Jackson could accept the offer by any reasonable manner of communication within a reasonable time.

When Is Acceptance Communicated?

Acceptances by Instantaneous Forms of Communication

When the parties are dealing face-to-face, by telephone, or by other means of communication that are virtually instantaneous, there are few problems determining when the acceptance was communicated. As soon as the offeree says, "I accept," or words to that effect, a contract is created, assuming that the offer is still in existence.

Acceptances by Noninstantaneous Forms of Communication

Suppose the circumstances under which the offer was made reasonably led the offeree to believe that acceptance by some noninstantaneous form of communication is acceptable, and the offeree responds by using mail, telegraph, or some other means of communication that creates a time lag between the dispatching of the acceptance and its actual receipt by the offeror. The practical problems involving the timing of acceptance multiply in such transactions. The offeror may be attempting to revoke the offer while the offeree is attempting to accept it. An acceptance may get lost and never be received by the offeror. The time limit for accepting the offer may be rapidly approaching. Was the offer accepted before a revocation was received or before the offer expired? Does a lost acceptance create a contract when it is dispatched, or is it totally ineffective?

Under the so-called *mailbox rule,* properly addressed and dispatched acceptances can become effective when they are *dispatched,* even if they are lost and never received by the offeror. The mailbox rule, which is discussed further in the following *Okosa* case, protects the offeree's reasonable belief that a binding contract was created when the acceptance was dispatched. By the same token, it exposes the offeror to the risk of being bound by an acceptance that she has never received. The offeror, however, has the ability to minimize this risk by stipulating in her offer that she must actually receive the acceptance for it to be effective. Offerors who do this maximize the time that they have to revoke their offers

and ensure that they will never be bound by an acceptance that they have not received.

Operation of the Mailbox Rule: Common Law of Contracts As traditionally applied by the common law of contracts, the mailbox rule would make acceptances effective upon dispatch when the offeree used a manner of communication that was expressly or impliedly **authorized** (invited) by the offeror. Any manner of communication *suggested* by the offeror (e.g., "You may respond by mail") would be expressly authorized, resulting in an acceptance sent by the suggested means being effective on dispatch. Unless circumstances indicated to the contrary, a manner of communication *used by the offeror in making the offer* would be impliedly authorized (e.g., an offer sent by mail would impliedly authorize an acceptance by mail), as would a manner of communication common in the parties' trade or business (e.g., a trade usage in the parties' business that offers are made by mail and accepted by telegram would authorize an acceptance by telegram). Conversely, an improperly dispatched acceptance or one that was sent by some means of communication that was *nonauthorized* would be effective when *received,* assuming that the offer was still open at that time. This placed on the offeree the risk of the offer being revoked or the acceptance being lost. The following *Okosa* case illustrates the operation of the mailbox rule.

The mailbox rule is often applied more liberally by courts today. A modern version of the mailbox rule that is sanctioned by the *Restatement (Second)* holds that an offer that does not indicate otherwise is considered to invite acceptance by *any reasonable means* of communication, and a properly dispatched acceptance sent by a reasonable means of communication within a reasonable time is effective on dispatch.

Okosa v. Hall   718 A.2d 1223 (N.J. Super. Ct., App. Div. 1998)

Obianuju Okosa and her husband, Peter, were insured under an automobile policy with New Jersey Citizens United Reciprocal Exchange. The Okosas' policy required a quarterly premium payment to be made on February 28, 1994. At the close of business on February 28, 1994, the insurance carrier wrote a letter to the Okosas, which it posted on March 1, 1994. The letter advised the Okosas that they had failed to pay the $347.50 installment that was due and that their policy would be automatically canceled at 12:01 AM on March 16, 1994, unless payment was made by that date. The letter further advised the Okosas:

> If we receive payment on or before the cancellation date, we will continue your policy with no interruption in the protection it affords. If you've recently mailed your payment, please disregard this notice.

On March 15, 1994, while the policy was still in effect, the Okosas mailed, by certified mail, a check for the required payment. The very next day, Okosa was involved in an accident with Tawn D. Hall, who was uninsured. It is not known exactly when the Okosas' check was received, but the insurance carrier deposited and cashed the check on March 22, 1994. The Okosas sought Personal Injury Protection (PIP) benefits pursuant to their policy, but the insurance carrier rejected their claim on the ground that the policy had been canceled prior to the accident. The Okosas brought an action against Hall and the insurance carrier. The insurance carrier moved for and was granted summary judgment, and the Okosas' claim was dismissed. The Okosas appealed.

Kimmelman, J.A.D.

The Okosas contend that the so-called "Mailbox Rule" applies to the facts of this case and that the installment payment mailed on March 15, 1994, constituted a timely payment made prior to 12:01 AM on March 16, 1994. Generally speaking, the Mailbox Rule sanctions the formation or completion of a contractual undertaking upon the act of mailing where the use of the mail is authorized by the other party as the medium for response. The rule is succinctly set forth as follows:

> Where parties are at distance from one another, and an offer is sent by mail, it is universally held in this country that the reply accepting the offer may be sent through the same medium, and, if it is so sent, the contract will be complete when the acceptance is mailed, . . . and beyond the acceptor's control; the theory being that, when one makes an offer through the mail, he authorizes the acceptance to be made through the same medium, and constitutes that medium his agent to receive his acceptance; that the acceptance, when mailed, is then constructively communicated to the offeror.

Dickey v. Hurd.

There is no question in this case that the carrier addressed the Okosas by mail concerning their tardy payment. Its letter of February 28, 1994, posted March 1, 1994, invited the Okosas' response with payment by mail. In so responding, the Okosas did so by means of certified mail. The use of certified mail by the Okosas was perspicacious because it insured proof of mailing and its use avoided the thorny issue which would arise from a fraudulent response by them that post-dated the accident.

In *Rugala v. New Jersey Ins. Underwriting Ass'n,* we recognized the factual mechanics underlying in the Mailbox Rule without mentioning the rule itself. However, we rejected its applicability to the facts of that case. Plaintiffs in *Rugala* had sent their payment to renew an insurance policy by regular mail. Plaintiffs suffered a fire loss on the next day and the insurer did not receive plaintiffs' renewal check until the following day. It was held that the policy had expired at 12:01 AM on the previous day because the renewal payment had not been received prior to the expiration. The mailing of payment by regular mail was not deemed a renewal because the insured's contractual documents drew a distinction between certified mail and regular mail. The contract specifically provided that if regular mail was used instead of certified mail, the carrier would be bound only from the date on which the payment was actually received. The payment was received on the day after the fire loss occurred. In permitting the contractual distinction between regular and certified mail, we held that certified mailing was deemed sufficient because that method enabled the sender to obtain proof of the date of mailing and guarded against a fraudulent back-dated submission.

We have completely reviewed the record and are satisfied that by authorizing the use of mail as a means of paying premiums, the carrier constituted the postal authorities as its agent. Accordingly, the decision in this matter is controlled by the Mailbox Rule. As a consequence, the entry of summary judgment in favor of the carrier is reversed.

Reversed and remanded in favor of the Okosas.

Operation of the Mailbox Rule: UCC   The UCC, like the *Restatement (Second),* provides that an offer that does not specify a particular means of acceptance is considered to invite acceptance by *any reasonable means* of communication. It also provides that a properly dispatched acceptance sent by a reasonable means of communication within a reasonable time is effective on dispatch. What is reasonable depends on the circumstances in which the offer was made. These include the speed and reliability of the means used by the offeree, the nature of the transaction (e.g., does the agreement involve goods subject to rapid price fluctuations?), the existence of any trade

usage governing the transaction, and the existence of prior dealings between the parties (e.g., has the offeree previously used the mail to accept telegraphed offers from the offeror?). So, under proper circumstances, a mailed response to a telegraphed offer or a telegraphed response to a mailed offer might be considered reasonable and therefore effective on dispatch.

What if an offeree attempts to accept the offer by some means that is *unreasonable* under the circumstances or if the acceptance is not properly addressed or dispatched (e.g., misaddressed or accompanied by insufficient postage)? The UCC rejects the traditional rule

Figure 2   *Time of Acceptance*

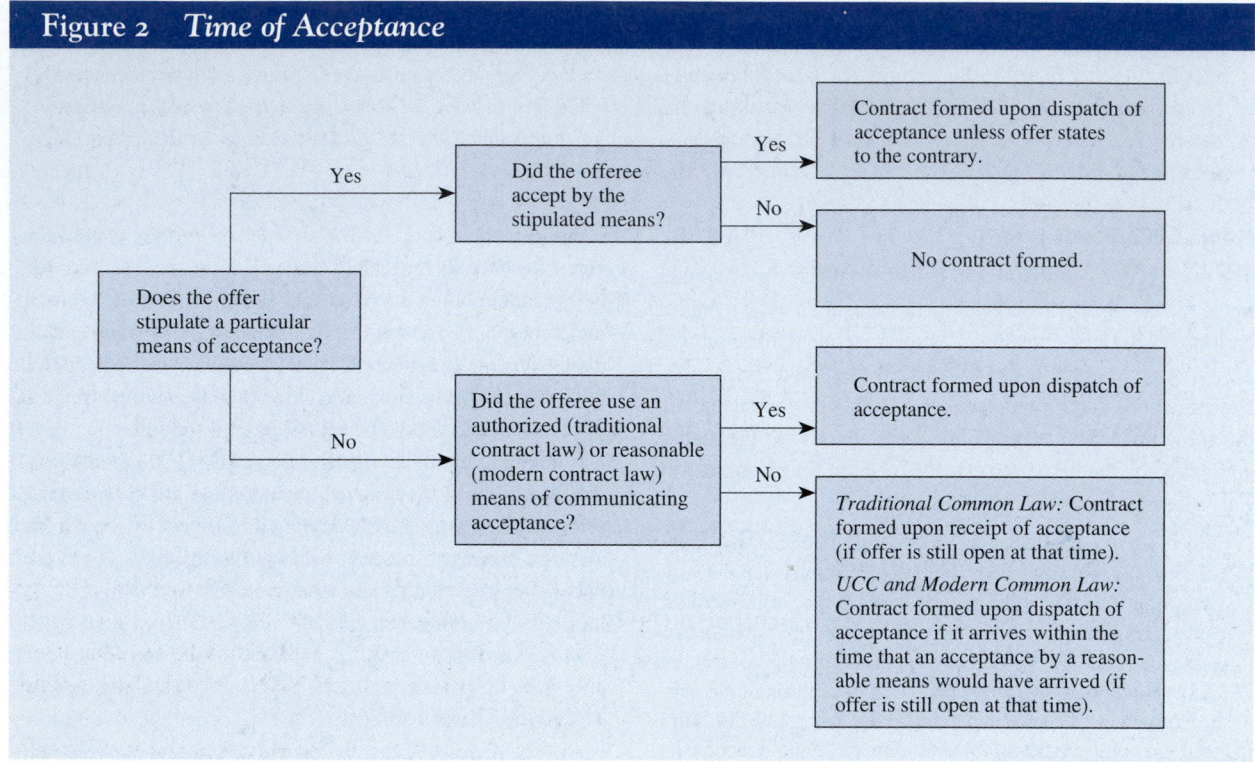

that such acceptances cannot be effective until received. It provides that an acceptance sent by an unreasonable means would be effective on dispatch *if* it is received within the time that an acceptance by a reasonable means would normally have arrived.

Stipulated Means of Communication

As we discussed earlier, an offer may stipulate the means of communication that the offeree must use to accept by saying, in effect: "You must accept by mail." An acceptance by the stipulated means of communication is effective on dispatch, just like an acceptance by any other reasonable or authorized means of communication (see Figure 2). The difference is that an acceptance by other than the stipulated means does not create a contract because it is an acceptance at variance with the terms of the offer.

LOG ON

For a thorough outline of the mailbox rule complete with some helpful diagrams and examples, see Tom W. Bell, *The Mailbox Rule and Related Rules*, **www.tomwbell.com/teaching/KMailbox.html.**

Special Acceptance Problem Areas

Acceptance in Unilateral Contracts

A unilateral contract involves the exchange of a promise for an act. To accept an offer to enter such a contract, the offeree must perform the requested act. As you learned in the last chapter, however, courts applying modern contract rules may prevent an offeror from revoking such an offer once the offeree has begun performance. This is achieved by holding either that a bilateral contract is created by the beginning of performance or that the offeror's power to revoke is suspended for the period of time reasonably necessary for the offeree to complete performance.

Acceptance in Bilateral Contracts

A bilateral contract involves the exchange of a promise for a promise. As a general rule, to accept an offer to enter such a contract, an offeree must *make the promise requested by the offer.* This may be done in a variety of ways. For example, Wallace sends Stevens a detailed offer for the purchase of Stevens's business. Within the time period prescribed by the offer, Stevens sends Wallace a letter that says, "I accept your offer." Stevens has *expressly* accepted

Wallace's offer, creating a contract on the terms of the offer. Acceptance, however, can be *implied* as well as expressed. Offerees who take action that objectively indicates agreement risk the formation of a contract. For example, offerees who act in a manner that is inconsistent with an offeror's ownership of offered property are commonly held to have accepted the offeror's terms. So, if Arnold, a farmer, leaves 10 bushels of corn with Porter, the owner of a grocery store, saying, "Look this corn over. If you want it, it's $5 a bushel," and Porter sells the corn, he has impliedly accepted Arnold's offer. But what if Porter just let the corn sit and, when Arnold returned a week later, Porter told Arnold that he did not want it? Could Porter's failure to act ever amount to an acceptance?

Silence as Acceptance
Since contract law generally requires some objective indication that an offeree intends to contract, the general rule is that an offeree's silence, without more, is *not* an acceptance. In addition, it is generally held that an offeror cannot impose on the offeree a duty to respond to the offer. So, even if Arnold made an offer to sell corn to Porter and said, "If I don't hear from you in three days, I'll assume you're buying the corn," Porter's silence would still not amount to acceptance.

On the other hand, the circumstances of a case sometimes impose a duty on the offeree to reject the offer affirmatively or be bound by its terms. These are cases in which the offeree's silence objectively indicates an intent to accept. Customary trade practice or prior dealings between the parties may indicate that silence signals acceptance. So, if Arnold and Porter had dealt with each other on numerous occasions and Porter had always promptly returned items that he did not want, Porter's silent retention of the goods for a week would probably constitute an acceptance. Likewise, an offeree's silence can also operate as an acceptance if the offeree has indicated that it will. For example, Porter (the *offeree*) tells Arnold, "If you don't hear from me in three days, I accept."

Finally, it is generally held that offerees who accept an offeror's performance knowing what the offeror expects in return for his performance have impliedly accepted the offeror's terms. So, if Apex Paving Corporation offers to do the paving work on a new subdivision being developed by Majestic Homes Corporation, and Majestic fails to respond to Apex's offer but allows Apex to do the work, most courts would hold that Majestic is bound by the terms of Apex's offer.

The application of this exception is analyzed in the context of an employment contract in the following case, *McGurn v. Bell Microproducts, Inc.*

McGurn v. Bell Microproducts, Inc.   284 F.3d 86 (1st Cir. 2002)

Donald Bell, President of Bell Microproducts, met with George McGurn and discussed with him the position of Vice President for the Eastern Region. At this meeting, McGurn said that if he came to work for Bell, he would require a written contract that included a termination clause stipulating that he would receive six months salary and half his commissions in the event that he was fired. After several discussions with a Bell official, Bell extended an offer of employment to McGurn, but this initial offer had no termination clause in it, and the parties held further discussions about a termination clause. During one of these conversations, McGurn said that he would consider a termination clause that was limited to the first 24 months of his employment, and according to McGurn, Bell said that this would be acceptable. Bell issued another offer containing a termination clause, but McGurn did not agree with its termination clause. Finally, Bell sent a third offer, dated July 3, 1997. This offer contained the following termination clause:

> The Company may terminate your employment without cause. In the event that this occurs within your first twelve months of employment, you will continue to receive your base salary for a period of six (6) months following your termination of employment, [and] you will receive an additional lump-sum amount equal to $40,000 or 50 percent of annual incentive.

The letter ended with the request that McGurn "sign an acknowledgment of this offer of employment and return to me for our files." The following appeared under the signature of Bell's Director of Human Resources:

> I acknowledge my acceptance of the offer as described above and my start date will be_____.
>
> Signed_____ Date_____

McGurn signed his name and entered "7–8–97" in the other two blank spaces. In addition, he crossed out the word twelve in the termination clause, inserted "twenty-four" directly above it, and initialed the change. The alteration was in the center of the second page of the two-page letter, five inches above McGurn's signatures. McGurn returned the letter and began work on July 8, 1997. McGurn did not tell anyone at Bell that he had modified the offer letter, and Bell officials denied having viewed the letter upon its return. Bell's Human Resources Department did receive the letter and kept it in its files.

In April 1998, McGurn's supervisor began to be dissatisfied with his performance, and on August 3, 1998, he fired McGurn. At some point after becoming dissatisfied with McGurn's performance but before firing him, McGurn's supervisor learned of McGurn's alteration of his offer letter. When he learned of his termination, approximately 13 months after McGurn began work at Bell, McGurn advised Bell officials that he believed his contract included a two-year termination clause. Bell refused to pay, and McGurn sued Bell for breach of contract. The district court granted summary judgment for McGurn and entered judgment for him in the amount of $120,000. Bell appealed.

Lipez, Circuit Judge

The parties agree that McGurn's alteration of Bell's offer letter constituted a rejection of that offer and created a counteroffer. What is in dispute is whether Bell accepted McGurn's counteroffer. As a general rule, silence in response to an offer to enter into a contract does not constitute an acceptance of the offer. There is, however, an exception to the rule against acceptance by silence where an offeree takes the benefit of offered services with reasonable opportunity to reject them and reason to know that they were offered with the expectation of compensation. *Restatement (Second) of Contracts* §69.

In *Gateway C. v. Charlotte Theatres, Inc.,* a case similar to this one, the defendant had sent the plaintiff two copies of a document which reduced to writing an oral agreement for the defendant to install air conditioning in the plaintiff's movie theater, with one copy to be countersigned and returned. The plaintiff signed, but also inserted a provision that the work would be performed by a certain date. The plaintiff returned the countersigned contract with a cover letter noting its understanding that the work would be performed by that date (although the letter made no reference to the alteration of the contract itself). We stated that "in the absence of actual knowledge [of the alteration of the contract], the test is whether there was reason for [the defendant] to suppose that such addition might have been made." We held that because of the cover letter flagging the issue, defendant's silence could constitute acceptance of plaintiff's counteroffer.

Importantly, we also noted in *Gateway* that "absent the [cover] letter, the case would seem more like" *Kidder v. Greenman.* In *Kidder,* a tenant had signed and returned a lease to her landlord with the understanding that the landlord would fill in certain blank spaces pursuant to an oral agreement. The landlord then completed the lease so as to include a term contrary to the oral understanding, signed it, and returned it to the tenant, who "did not look at the lease at the time she received it." The court declined to enforce the disputed term against the tenant on the ground that she had no reason to think that the [landlord] had not completed the lease in the authorized manner and, therefore, [had] no occasion to examine it, when it was returned to her, to see if he had done so.

We distill from the *Restatement* and the *Gateway* and *Kidder* precedents the legal rule in Massachusetts that silence in response to an offer may constitute an acceptance if an offeree who takes the benefit of offered services knew or had reason to know of the existence of the offer, and had a reasonable opportunity to reject it. We turn now to the application of that rule in this case.

The relevant question is why, as a matter of law, Bell should be expected to re-read an offer it had written and signed, upon its return with McGurn's countersignature. In response to that question the district court declared that "[a] presumably sophisticated employer who receives a signed letter of engagement from a prospective employee and fails to read the letter, particularly after weeks of negotiation, does so at its own peril." Although the logic of this generalization has some appeal, its generality is an insurmountable problem. Unless the record establishes that Bell knew or had reason to know that McGurn had modified what Bell had written—and the district court points to no facts in the record that would support such a conclusion—we cannot say that Bell's silence, as a matter of law, constituted an acceptance of McGurn's counteroffer.

We have stated that ordinarily the question of whether a contract has been made is for the jury, except where the words and actions that allegedly formed a contract are so clear themselves that reasonable people could not differ over their meaning. When, as is the case here, the facts support plausible but conflicting inferences on a pivotal issue in the case, the judge may not choose between those inferences at the summary judgment stage. In sum, we cannot say that the facts in the record compel a conclusion that Bell noticed or should have noticed McGurn's modification of Bell's offer letter, and that its silence, therefore, constituted acceptance of McGurn's offer. Instead, those issues must be resolved by the factfinder at trial.

Judgment vacated in favor of Bell and remanded for further proceedings consistent with this opinion.

Selya, Circuit Judge (dubitante)

There is no hint here of chicanery on McGurn's part, and I doubt that ignorance induced by a party's own negligence or lassitude is a basis for escaping from contractual obligations. To the contrary, the acceptance of offered services, under circumstances in which the beneficiary of those services ought to know that the provider expected to be compensated for them in a certain way, is the functional equivalent of express assent. I believe that a party should not be able to insulate itself from contract liability by professing that it neglected to read the very document essential for the formation of the contract, especially when that document has reposed in its own files at all relevant times. Were the law otherwise and the majority's view taken to its logical extreme, an offeree could completely redefine its own responsibilities by the simple expedient of claiming that it was not aware of what its own records plainly showed. Given this doubt, I respectfully decline to join the court's opinion.

Acceptance When a Writing Is Anticipated

Frequently, the parties to a contract intend to prepare a written draft of their agreement for both parties to sign. This is a good idea not only because the law requires written evidence of some contracts,[2] but also because it provides written evidence of the terms of the agreement if a dispute arises at a later date. If a dispute arises before such a writing has been prepared or signed, however, a question may arise concerning whether the signing of the agreement was a necessary condition to the creation of a contract. A party to the agreement who now wants out of the deal may argue that the parties did not intend to be bound until both parties signed the writing. A clear expression of such an intent by the parties during the negotiation process prevents the formation of a contract until both parties have signed. However, in the absence of such a clear expression of intent, the courts ask whether a reasonable person familiar with all the circumstances of the parties' negotiations would conclude that the parties intended to be bound only when a formal agreement was signed. If it appears that the parties had concluded their negotiations and reached agreement on all the essential aspects of the transaction, most courts would probably find a contract at the time agreement was reached, even though no formal agreement had been signed.

Acceptance of Ambiguous Offers

Although offerors have the power to specify the manner in which their offers can be accepted by requiring that the offeree make a return promise (a bilateral contract) or perform a specific act (a unilateral contract), often an offer is unclear about which form of acceptance is necessary to create a contract. In such a case, the offer may be accepted in any manner that is *reasonable* in light of the circumstances surrounding the offer. Thus, either a promise to perform or performance, if reasonable, creates a contract.

Acceptance by Shipment The Code specifically elaborates on the rule stated in the preceding section by stating that an order requesting prompt or current shipment of goods may be accepted either by a *prompt promise to ship* or by a *prompt or current shipment* of the goods [2–206(1)(b)]. So, if Ampex Corporation orders 500 IBM personal computers from Marks Office Supply, to be shipped immediately, Marks could accept either by promptly promising to ship the goods or by promptly shipping them. If Marks accepts by shipping, any subsequent attempt by Ampex to revoke the order will be ineffective.

---

[2]Chapter 16 discusses this subject in detail.

Ethics in Action

Marble Publications is a publisher of various magazines and newsletters. Samantha has a subscription to one of Marble's publications, *Parent's World*. In 2003, Marble sends Samantha a complimentary copy of another of its publications, *Gardens Unlimited*, along with a letter that states that Samantha will receive *Gardens Unlimited* free of charge for three months, but if she does not want to receive any further copies of *Gardens* *Unlimited*, she must contact Marble and cancel. The letter states that if Samantha fails to contact Marble, she will be subscribed for one year at a cost of $24.95. Samantha does not read the letter carefully and never contacts Marble. After three months, she receives a bill for $24.95. Is this an ethical way of marketing *Gardens Unlimited?* What ethical problems might arise if silence were generally considered to constitute acceptance?

The Global Business Environment

Under the CISG, as under U.S. law, statements or other conduct by the offeree that shows assent is an acceptance, and silence alone generally does not suffice as acceptance. And, as is true under U.S. law, a contract is concluded when an acceptance of an offer becomes effective. There are several notable differences between acceptance doctrines under U.S. law and the CISG, however. For one, the "battle of the forms," as it is formulated under the Uniform Commercial Code, does not exist under the CISG. Rather, under the CISG, a reply to an offer purports to be an acceptance but in fact contains new or different terms or limitations that are *material* is a rejection and *not* an acceptance. Examples of terms that would be considered material are terms relating to price, payment, quality, the extent of a party's liability, and settlement of disputes (such as arbitration clauses). However, a reply purporting to be an acceptance that contains *nonmaterial* new or different terms can be an acceptance. Another major difference between U.S. law and the CISG is that, unlike the U.S. "mailbox rule," the CISG generally holds acceptances to be effective when they are received.

What if Marks did not have 500 IBMs in stock and Marks knew that Ampex desperately needed the goods? Marks might be tempted to ship another brand of computers (that is, *nonconforming goods*—goods different from what the buyer ordered), hoping that Ampex would be forced by its circumstances to accept them because by the time they arrived it would be too late to get the correct goods elsewhere. Marks would argue that by shipping the wrong goods it had made a counteroffer because it had not performed the act requested by Ampex's order. If Ampex accepts the goods, Marks could argue that Ampex has impliedly accepted the counteroffer. If Ampex rejects the goods, Marks would arguably have no liability since it did not accept the order.

The Code prevents such a result by providing that prompt shipment of either conforming goods (what the order asked for) or nonconforming goods (something else) operates as an acceptance of the order [2–206(1)(b)]. This protects buyers such as Ampex because sellers who ship the wrong goods have simultaneously accepted their offers and breached the contract by sending the wrong merchandise.[3]

---

[3]Chapter 19 discusses the rights and responsibilities of the buyer and seller following the shipment of nonconforming goods.

But what if Marks is an honest seller merely trying to help out a customer that has placed a rush order? Must Marks expose itself to liability for breach of contract in the process? The Code prevents such a result by providing that no contract is created if the seller notifies the buyer within a reasonable time that the shipment of nonconforming goods is intended as an accommodation (an attempt to help the buyer) [2–206(1)(b)]. In this case, the shipment is merely a counteroffer that the buyer is free to accept or reject and the seller's notification gives the buyer the opportunity to seek the goods he needs elsewhere.

Who Can Accept an Offer?
As the masters of their offers, offerees have the right to determine who can bind them to a contract. So, the only person with the legal power to accept an offer and create a contract is the *original offeree*. An attempt to accept by anyone other than the offeree is treated as an offer, because the party attempting to accept is indicating a present intent to contract on the original offer's terms. For example, Price offers to sell his car to Waterhouse for $5,000. Anderson learns of the offer, calls Price, and attempts to accept. Anderson has made an offer that Price is free to accept or reject.

Problems and Problem Cases

1. In December 1999, Wilson applied for a Citibank credit card and signed an acceptance certificate in which she agreed to be bound by the terms and conditions of the credit card agreement. Citibank then issued a credit card to her, which Wilson began using. In July 2001, Citibank mailed Wilson her credit card statement, which informed her that it was modifying the terms of the original agreement. This revised agreement was enclosed with the credit card statement. After the July 2001 statement was made to her, Wilson continued using her credit card and

made monthly payments on her account balance. Wilson made her last payment to Citibank in March 2002 and failed to make payments thereafter. Citibank then filed suit against her to collect her overdue balance, which was $12,272.84. In this action, Citibank attempted to enforce the revised agreement rather than the original agreement. Wilson argued that she never accepted the revised agreement. Is this a good argument?

2. First Texas Savings Association promoted a "$5,000 Scoreboard Challenge" contest. Contestants who completed an entry form and deposited it with First Texas were eligible for a random drawing. The winner was to receive an $80 savings account with First Texas, plus four tickets to a Dallas Mavericks home basketball game chosen by First Texas. If the Mavericks held their opponent in the chosen game to 89 or fewer points, the winner was to receive an additional $5,000 money market certificate. In October 1982, Jergins deposited a completed entry form with First Texas. On November 1, 1982, First tried to amend the contest rules by posting notice at its branches that the Mavericks would have to hold their opponent to 85 or fewer points before the contest winner would receive the $5,000. In late December, Jergins was notified that she had won the $80 savings account and tickets to the January 22, 1983, game against the Utah Jazz. The notice contained the revised contest terms. The Mavericks held the Jazz to 88 points. Was Jergins entitled to the $5,000?

3. In 1997, Rubbermaid launched its "Tidal Wave Project" to introduce into the marketplace new and improved sponge mops named for a wave pattern that would be cut into the sponges. This included a "butterfly" mop that was assembled for Rubbermaid by an independent corporation, New Knight, and a roller mop that was produced "in house" by Rubbermaid. Target Stores had agreed to stock Tidal Wave sponge mop line at its stores nationwide. Rubbermaid contacted Reilly Foam to see if it could fulfill its needs. Reilly Foam was able to deliver the needed products in time, and Rubbermaid began talking with Reilly Foam about a longer-term relationship. Reilly Foam needed to retool its equipment and license technology to produce the "tidal wave" sponges, and Reilly Foam was concerned that its profits on the contract would permit it to recoup its costs. On March 26, 1999, Reilly Foam sent a letter to Rubbermaid. The letter stated that it related to the two laminates that Reilly Foam was currently working on, the roller mop and the butterfly mop, and three other products produced by New Knight. It referred to and attached a list of price quotations and quantities for these products, listing annual quantities for three products that were identified as "Other Affected Products": 340,000 for the brown sponge, 350,000 for the yellow ester with wave pattern sponge, and 300,000 for the yellow ester and white "scrubmate." The letter proposed that Rubbermaid commit to two million pieces of product under the subheading "Other Affected Products" over a period of two years and that the price include a surcharge of $.015 per part to amortize the cost of tooling for the wave pattern. It also proposed that Rubbermaid commit to buying all of its butterfly and roller mop laminates from Reilly Foam. On March 30, 1999, Tony Ferrante, a Rubbermaid product manager, responded by a letter that stated in part:

> This letter is to serve as Rubbermaid's commitment and authorization to procure tooling so that Reilly Foam will be in a position to make sponge products with Rubbermaid's patent pending Tidal Wave TM design. I understand that $.015 will be added to the cost of the sponge purchase price until we have made purchases of 2 million sponges, thereby covering the tooling cost of $30,000.
>
> Referencing the attached quotation, our commitment is as follows:
>
> 1. Any sponge mop product produced by New Knight, Inc. on behalf of Rubbermaid will source the sponge component from Reilly Foam. This includes the current product offering, as referenced in your quotation, as well as any future new products that New Knight will produce for us. . . .

Attached to this letter was Reilly Foam's price list, marked "Approved" and signed by Ferrante. After this exchange, Rubbermaid instructed New Knight to purchase sponges solely from Reilly Foam. Rubbermaid itself made purchases of sponges listed under the "other affected products" category. At the same time, Rubbermaid continued to purchase sponges from another supplier for use in the Tidal Wave line of mops. Moreover, Rubbermaid did not purchase 2 million sponges within the two-year window that Reilly Foam sought. Reilly Foam sued Rubbermaid for breach of contract. Will it be successful?

4. Ellefson and Mustaine are original members of the heavy metal rock band, Megadeth. The band was

initially formed in 1983, with Mustaine as the lead guitarist, lead vocalist, and lead songwriter, and Ellefson as the band's bassist. In 1990, they formed a formal corporation, Megadeth, Inc., with Mustaine receiving 80 percent of the stock and Ellefson 20 percent. Years later, Ellefson claimed that Mustaine, Megadeth, Inc., and others ("the Megadeth defendants") had defrauded him out of his share of the corporation's profits. Beginning in October 2003, Ellefson and the Megadeth defendants entered into negotiations to settle their disputes. On April 16, Ellefson's attorney, Abdo, received an initial draft of a proposed "Settlement and General Release," whereby Ellefson's interest in the corporation and various other licensing/recording agreements would be purchased. Negotiations over this proposed settlement continued uneventfully over the next four weeks as the attorneys incorporated various comments and changes. The pace of negotiations accelerated in May, however, because Mustaine imposed a deadline of five o'clock on Friday, May 14, 2004, for completion of the settlement. To that end, the parties' attorneys began working in earnest to put together a final draft of the agreement by the end of the week. On the morning of Thursday, May 13, Abdo received an e-mail reminding him "that Dave Mustaine has instructed us to pull the offer to Ellefson off the table and to terminate this deal as of 5 PM PST on Friday 5/14/04, if we do not have a signed agreement in hand." The following day, Friday, May 15, attorneys for both sides worked to finalize a draft of the agreement in time to meet the five o'clock deadline. After an exchange of e-mails between the attorneys, Abdo e-mailed Lurie, the Megadeth defendants' lawyer, that he was faxing his final comments, and that Lurie should "make the changes and we are done." At 4:45 PM PST, 15 minutes prior to expiration of the offer, Lurie sent Abdo a finalized copy of the agreement. In a covering document to the final agreement, Lurie stated that "attached is an execution copy of the above-referenced Settlement Agreement," reiterated the five o'clock deadline, and stated that defendants reserved "the right to make further changes pending our finalizing Exhibits A and B and the full execution of the agreement early next week." In the final e-mail of the day between the attorneys, sent on Friday, May 14, 2004, 5:16 PM, Abdo e-mailed Lurie and stated that "Dave Ellefson told me he signed and faxed the signature page to you. Thanks for the drafting work." Ellefson did sign and fax a completed

signature page shortly after receiving the final agreement at 4:45 PM on Friday, but there was no evidence that the fax was sent prior to the 5 PM deadline. On Thursday, May 20, 2004, four business days after Ellefson's signature fax was received, the Megadeth defendants' attorney, Lurie, sent all the parties fully executed copies of the agreement by regular mail. On May 24, four days after Lurie had mailed the agreement and 10 days after Ellefson had faxed the signed signature page, Lurie received an e-mail from Abdo stating that Ellefson "withdraws from these negotiations and withdraws all proposals." In response to this e-mail, Lurie stated, "we are not certain what you are talking about, but, as you know, there is a signed settlement agreement in place, which Dave [Ellefson] faxed to us more than a week ago." Finally, nine days later, on June 2, 2004, Abdo received the finalized agreement that Lurie had mailed on May 20, 2004. Ellefson filed suit against the Megadeth defendants. The Megadeth defendants moved to enforce the settlement agreement and dismiss Ellefson's action, arguing that any and all disputes between the parties were resolved by an agreement entitled "Settlement and General Release" and signed by all of the parties. Are they correct?

5. Netscape offered its SmartDownload software free of charge on its Web site. Visitors who wished to obtain SmartDownload from Netscape's Web site arrived at a page pertaining to the download of the software. On this page, there appeared a tinted box labeled "Download." By clicking on the box, a visitor initiated the download. The sole reference on this page to the License Agreement appeared in text that was visible only if a visitor scrolled down through the page to the next screen. If a visitor did so, he or she would see the following invitation to review the License Agreement: "Please review and agree to the terms of the Netscape SmartDownload software license agreement before downloading and using the software." Visitors were not required affirmatively to indicate their assent to the License Agreement by clicking on it, or even to view the License Agreement, before proceeding with a download of the software. But if a visitor chose to click on the underlined text in the invitation, a hypertext link would take the visitor to a Web page entitled "License & Support Agreements." The first paragraph on this page read in pertinent part: "The use of each Netscape software product is governed by a license

agreement. You must read and agree to the license agreement terms BEFORE acquiring a product. Please click on the appropriate link below to review the current license agreement for the product of interest to you before acquisition. For products available for download, you must read and agree to the license agreement terms BEFORE you install the software. If you do not agree to the license terms, do not download, install or use the software. . . ." A further click would be required before the visitor was brought to another Web page containing the full text of the License Agreement. Among the terms of the License Agreement was a term requiring that virtually all disputes be submitted to arbitration in Santa Clara County, California, with the losing party paying all costs of arbitration. Several people who downloaded SmartDownload filed suit against Netscape because of a privacy issue with the software. Netscape moved to compel arbitration, claiming that the arbitration clause in the License Agreement was valid and enforceable. Was Netscape correct?

6. Parker agreed to buy real estate that was jointly owned by Mr. and Mrs. Glosson. A written contract was prepared for the parties' signatures. One clause of the agreement stated: "This Agreement shall become an enforceable contract when a fully executed copy has been communicated to both parties." Although both Mr. and Mrs. Glosson were listed in the document as "Sellers," only Mr. Glosson signed the contract and Mrs. Glosson never signed it. The Glossons did not sell the property to Parker, and Parker sued them for breach of contract. Was there a valid contract to sell the property?

7. Cantu was hired as a special education teacher by the San Benito Consolidated Independent School District under a one-year contract for the 1990–91 school year. On August 18, 1990, shortly before the start of the school year, Cantu hand-delivered to her supervisor a letter of resignation, effective August 17, 1990. In this letter, Cantu requested that her final paycheck be forwarded to an address in McAllen, Texas, some 50 miles from the San Benito office where she tendered the resignation. The San Benito superintendent of schools, the only official authorized to accept resignations on behalf of the school district, received Cantu's resignation on Monday, August 20. The superintendent wrote a letter accepting Cantu's resignation the same day and deposited the letter, properly stamped and addressed, in the mail at approximately 5:15 PM that afternoon. At about 8:00 AM the next morning, August 21, Cantu hand-delivered to the superintendent's office a letter withdrawing her resignation. This letter contained a San Benito return address. In response, the superintendent hand-delivered that same day a copy of his letter mailed the previous day to inform Cantu that her resignation had been accepted and could not be withdrawn. The dispute was taken to the state commissioner of education, who concluded that the school district's refusal to honor Cantu's contract was lawful, because the school district's acceptance of Cantu's resignation was effective when mailed, which resulted in the formation of an agreement to rescind Cantu's employment contract. Cantu argued that the mailbox rule should not apply because her offer was made in person and the superintendent was not authorized to accept by using mail. Is this a good argument?

8. The Montgomerys owned a house that was listed for sale. English submitted an offer to pay the Montgomerys $272,000 for their home. English included in her offer a request to purchase several items of the Montgomerys' personal property and also indicated on the offer that an "As Is" rider was applicable to the transaction. After the Montgomerys received English's offer, they made several changes to the document, including (1) deleting certain items from the personal property section of the contract; (2) deleting a provision regarding latent defects; (3) deleting a provision regarding building inspections; and (4) adding a specific "As Is" rider. The Montgomerys signed their counteroffer and delivered it to English's real estate agent. The agent took the counteroffer to English later that same day. English initialed some, but not all, of the Montgomerys' suggested changes. Specifically, English did not initial the changes set forth by the Montgomerys in the personal property section of the document or explicitly confirm her acceptance of those terms by cover letter or otherwise. English's real estate agent thereafter faxed the document to the Montgomerys' attorney. Was an enforceable contract formed in this case?

9. In 1985, State Farm Mutual Insurance issued Casto an automobile insurance policy on her Jaguar. Casto also insured a second car, a Porsche, with State Farm. Some time in September or early October 1987, Casto received two renewal notices for her policy on

the Jaguar, indicating that the next premium was due on October 10, 1987. State Farm sent a notice of cancellation on October 15, indicating that the policy would be canceled on October 29. Casto denied having received this notice. On October 20, Casto placed two checks, one for the Jaguar and one for the Porsche, in two preaddressed envelopes that had been supplied by State Farm. She gave these envelopes to Donald Dick, who mailed them on the same day. The envelope containing the Porsche payment was timely delivered to State Farm, but State Farm never received the Jaguar payment, and that policy was canceled. Casto was involved in an accident on November 20 while driving the Jaguar. When she made a claim with State Farm, she learned that the policy had been canceled. After the accident, the envelope containing the Jaguar payment was returned to her stamped, "Returned for postage." The envelope did not bear any postage when returned to Casto. Casto brought a declaratory judgment action seeking a declaration that her insurance policy was in effect as of the date of the accident. Was it?

10. Paulaner is an importer of German beer, and Domanik Sales Company was one of Paulaner's distributors. The distributorship agreement provided that Paulaner could terminate the agreement if a default in payment by Domanik remained uncured five days after Domanik received a demand for payment. The contract also gave Paulaner the right to establish the terms of payment. Because of a previous default, Paulaner had placed Domanik on "COD status" and refused to afford it further credit. On March 10, 1998, Paulaner delivered a shipment of beer to Domanik. On March 18, 1998, Paulaner notified Domanik that the payment for the March 10 shipment was past due, that the amount due was $23,842.54, that payment was to be received no later than March 25, 1998, and that the agreement would

be terminated if payment was not received by that date. The invoice for the March 10 delivery was sent by fax to Domanik on March 18, arriving after receipt of the default notice. Domanik wrote a check for the full amount due on Friday, March 20, 1998, and placed the payment in the mail. The envelope was postmarked Monday, March 23, 1998. Payment was not received by Paulaner in its Colorado offices until March 26, 1998. The distributorship agreement was terminated by Paulaner that same day, since payment had not been received as required by the default notice. Domanik contends that placing the payment in the mail constituted payment under the mailbox rule. Is it correct?

chapter 12

CONSIDERATION

The Valley Area Anti-Smoking Foundation (VAAF) offered to pay any Valley Area resident $500 if he or she would refrain from smoking for one year. Chad, a Valley Area resident, decided to accept this offer. He quit smoking immediately and did not smoke for a whole year. When Chad contacted VAAF to inform it of his success and collect his $500, VAAF informed him that it was only able to pay $250 because so many Valley Area residents had taken advantage of its offer. Chad reluctantly agreed to accept $250 instead of $500.

- Was VAAF contractually obligated to pay Chad for refraining from smoking?
- Was there consideration to support its promise to pay $500?
- Are there other facts you need to know to make that determination?
- Is Chad entitled to receive the entire $500 or only $250?
- Was VAAF ethically required to pay the entire $500?

ONE OF THE THINGS that separates a contract from an unenforceable social promise is that a contract requires voluntary agreement by two or more parties. Not all agreements, however, are enforceable contracts. At a fairly early point in the development of classical contract law, the common law courts decided not to enforce gratuitous (free) promises. Instead, only promises supported by consideration were enforceable in a court of law. This was consistent with the notion that the purpose of contract law was to enforce freely made bargains. As one 19th-century work on contracts put it: "The common law . . . gives effect only to contracts that are founded on the mutual exigencies of men, and does not compel the performance of any merely gratuitous agreements."[1] The concept of consideration distinguishes agreements that the law will enforce from gratuitous promises, which are normally unenforceable. This chapter focuses on the concept of consideration.

Elements of Consideration

A common definition of **consideration** is *legal value, bargained for and given in exchange for an act or a promise.* Thus, a promise generally cannot be enforced against the person who made it (the *promisor*) unless the person to whom the promise was made (the *promisee*) has given up something of legal value in exchange for the promise. In effect, the requirement of consideration means that a promisee must pay the price that the promisor asked to gain the right to enforce the promisor's promise. So, if the promisor did not ask for anything in exchange for making her promise or if what the promisor asked for did not have legal value (e.g., because it was something to which she was already entitled), her promise is not enforceable against her because it is not supported by consideration.

Consider the early case of *Thorne v. Deas,* in which the part owner of a sailing ship named the *Sea Nymph* promised his co-owners that he would insure the ship for an upcoming voyage.[2] He failed to do so, and when the ship was lost at sea, the court found that he was not liable to his co-owners for breaching his promise to insure the ship. Why? Because his promise was purely gratuitous; he had neither asked for nor received anything in exchange for making it. Therefore, it was unenforceable because it was not supported by consideration.

This early example illustrates two important aspects of the consideration requirement. First, the requirement *tended to limit the scope of a promisor's liability for his*

---

[1] T. Metcalf, *Principles of the Law of Contracts* (1874), p. 161.

[2] Johns. 84 (N.Y. 1809).

promises by insulating him from liability for gratuitous promises and by protecting him against liability for reliance on such promises. Second, the mechanical application of the requirement *often produced unfair results.* This potential for unfairness has produced considerable dissatisfaction with the consideration concept. As the rest of this chapter indicates, the relative importance of consideration in modern contract law has been somewhat eroded by numerous exceptions to the consideration requirement and by judicial applications of consideration principles designed to produce fair results.

Legal Value Consideration can be an act in the case of a unilateral contract or a promise in the case of a bilateral contract. An act or a promise can have legal value in one of two ways. If, in exchange for the promisor's promise, the promisee does, or agrees to do, something he had no prior legal duty to do, that provides legal value. If, in exchange for the promisor's promise, the promisee refrains from doing, or agrees not to do, something she has a legal right to do, that also provides legal value. Note that this definition does not require that an act or a promise have monetary (economic) value to amount to consideration. Thus, in a famous 19th-century case, *Hamer v. Sidway,*[3] an uncle's promise to pay his nephew $5,000 if he refrained from using tobacco, drinking, swearing, and playing cards or billiards for money until his 21st birthday was held to be supported by consideration. Indeed, the nephew had refrained from doing any of these acts, even though he may have benefited from so refraining. He had a legal right to indulge in such activities, yet he had refrained from doing so at his uncle's request and in exchange for his uncle's promise. This was all that was required for consideration.

Adequacy of Consideration The point that the legal value requirement is not concerned with actual value is further borne out by the fact that the courts generally will not concern themselves with questions regarding the adequacy of the consideration that the promisee gave. This means that as long as the promisee's act or promise satisfies the legal value test, the courts do not ask whether that act or promise was worth what the promisor gave, or promised to give, in return for it. This rule on adequacy of consideration reflects the laissez-faire assumptions underlying classical contract law. Freedom of contract includes the freedom to make bad bargains as well as good ones, so promisors' promises are enforceable if they got

what they asked for in exchange for making their promises, even if what they asked for was not nearly so valuable in worldly terms as what they promised in return. Also, a court taking a hands-off stance concerning private contracts would be reluctant to step in and second-guess the parties by setting aside a transaction that both parties at one time considered satisfactory. Finally, the rule against considering the adequacy of consideration can promote certainty and predictability in commercial transactions by denying legal effect to what would otherwise be a possible basis for challenging the enforceability of a contract—the inequality of the exchange.

Several qualifications must be made concerning the general rule on adequacy of consideration. First, if the inadequacy of consideration is apparent on the face of the agreement, most courts conclude that the agreement was a disguised gift rather than an enforceable bargain. Thus, an agreement calling for an unequal exchange of money (e.g., $500 for $1,000) or identical goods (20 business law textbooks for 40 identical business law textbooks) and containing no other terms would probably be unenforceable. Gross inadequacy of consideration may also give rise to an inference of fraud, duress,[4] lack of capacity,[5] unconscionability,[6] or some other independent basis for setting aside a contract. However, inadequacy of consideration, standing alone, is never sufficient to prove lack of true consent or contractual capacity. Although gross inadequacy of consideration is not, by itself, ordinarily a sufficient reason to set aside a contract, the courts may refuse to grant specific performance or other equitable remedies to persons seeking to enforce unfair bargains.

Finally, some agreements recite "$1," or "$1 and other valuable consideration," or some other small amount as consideration for a promise. If no other consideration is actually exchanged, this is called *nominal consideration.* Often, such agreements are attempts to make gratuitous promises look like true bargains by reciting a nonexistent consideration. Most courts refuse to enforce such agreements unless they find that the stated consideration was truly bargained for.

Bargained-For Exchange Up to this point, we have focused on the legal value component of our consideration definition. But the fact that a promisee's act or promise provides legal value is not, in itself, a sufficient

---

[3]27 N.E. 256 (N.Y.Ct. App. 1891).

[4]Fraud and duress are discussed in Chapter 13.

[5]Lack of capacity is discussed in Chapter 14.

[6]Chapter 15 discusses unconscionability in detail.

basis for finding that it amounted to consideration. In addition, the promisee's act or promise must have been bargained for and given in exchange for the promisor's promise. In effect, it must be the price that the promisor asked for in exchange for making his promise. Over a hundred years ago, Oliver Wendell Holmes, one of our most renowned jurists, expressed this idea when he said,

"It is the essence of a consideration that, by the terms of the agreement, it is given and accepted as the motive or inducement of the promise."[7]

The following *Gottlieb* case illustrates the concept of bargained-for legal value.

[7]O. W. Holmes, *The Common Law* (1881), p. 239.

Gottlieb v. Tropicana Hotel and Casino
109 F. Supp. 2d 324 (U.S. Dist. Ct. E.D. Pa. 2000)

During the summer of 1999, Rena and Sheldon Gottlieb were vacationing in Atlantic City, New Jersey, and on July 24, they visited the Tropicana casino. Tropicana offers people membership in its "Diamond Club." To become a Diamond Club member, an individual must visit a promotional booth in the casino, obtain and fill out an application form, and show identification. There is no charge. The application form lists the person's name, address, telephone number, and e-mail address, and this information is entered into the casino's computer database. Each member receives a Diamond Club card that has a unique identification number. The member then presents or "swipes" the card in a machine each time he or she plays a game at the casino, and the casino obtains information about the member's gambling habits. The casino's marketing department then uses that information to tailor its promotions.

Rena Gottlieb was, and had been for a number of years, a member of the Diamond Club. When she entered the casino on July 24, she immediately went to the Fun House Million Dollar Wheel Promotion, which offers participants the chance to win a grand prize of $1 million. Diamond Club members were entitled to one free spin of the Million Dollar Wheel each day. She presented her Diamond Club card, a casino operator swiped it through the card reader, she pressed a button to activate the wheel, and the wheel began spinning. Gottlieb claims that the wheel landed on the $1 million grand prize, but when it did so, the casino attendant immediately swiped another card through the machine, reactivated the wheel, and the wheel landed on a prize of two show tickets. Tropicana denies that its attendant intervened and reactivated the wheel, and contends that the wheel simply landed on the lesser prize. Ms. Gottlieb sued Tropicana for breach of contract, among other theories, and Tropicana moved for summary judgment.

Bartle, III, Judge

According to Tropicana, participation in a promotion such as the Million Dollar Wheel cannot constitute consideration that would support the formation of an enforceable contract. We find the decision of the New Jersey Supreme Court in *Lucky Calendar Co. v. Cohen* to be on point. There, an advertising company brought a declaratory judgment action, seeking a determination that its promotional advertisement campaign for Acme Super Markets did not violate New Jersey's Lottery Act. The centerpiece of the campaign was a calendar that had Acme coupons bordering it, which was distributed by mass mailings. The calendar contained an explanation of the "Lucky Calendar Prize Contest." Entrants had the opportunity to win prizes in monthly drawings. All they had to do to enter was tear the entry form off the calendar, enter a name, address, and phone number, and have the form deposited in a box at any Acme store. There was no charge, and they were not required to be present for the drawing. The question in *Lucky Calendar* was whether there had been consideration for participation in the drawings.

The Supreme Court of New Jersey noted that, assuming consideration was required in order for something to qualify as an illegal lottery, it need only be the minimum consideration that is necessary to form a contract. It explained:

> The consideration in a lottery, as in any form of simple contract, need not be money or the promise of money. Nor need it be of intrinsic value; "a rose, a hawk or a peppercorn" will suffice, provided it is what is asked for by the promisor and is not illegal . . . Whether a "peppercorn" or the filling in and delivering of a coupon is sufficient consideration for a promise depends only on whether it was the requested detriment to the promisee induced by the promise.

The court determined that consideration was present "both in the form of a detriment or inconvenience to the promisee at the request of the promisor and of a benefit to the promisor. . . . Completing the coupon and arranging for the deposit of it in the box" at the store was the detriment to the promisee, and the "increase in volume of business" was the benefit to the promisor and its customer, the owner of the Acme stores. As the court pointed out, "The motives of the plaintiff and its customer [in offering the Lucky Calendar Prize Contest] . . . are in nowise altruistic."

In *Cobaugh v. Klick-Lewis, Inc.,* the Superior Court of Pennsylvania decided that there was adequate consideration to form a binding contract where a golfer, who was participating in a tournament, shot a hole-in-one after seeing a contest announcement offering a new car to anyone who could ace the particular hole. The court noted that the promisor benefited from the publicity of the promotional advertising, and the golfer performed an act that he was under no legal obligation to perform.

Ms. Gottlieb had to go to the casino to participate in the promotion. She had to wait in line to spin the wheel. By presenting her Diamond Club card to the casino attendant and allowing it to be swiped into the casino's machine, she was permitting the casino to gather information about her gambling habits. Additionally, by participating in the game, she was a part of the entertainment that casinos, by their very nature,

are designed to offer to all of those present. All of these detriments to Ms. Gottlieb were the requested detriments to the promisee induced by the promise of Tropicana to offer her a chance to win $1 million. Tropicana's motives in offering the promotion were "in nowise altruistic." It offered the promotion in order to generate patronage of and excitement within the casino. In short, Ms. Gottlieb provided adequate consideration to form a contract with Tropicana.

Tropicana further challenges Ms. Gottlieb's breach of contract claim on the grounds that it is clear as a matter of law that she did not win the $1 million prize. Tropicana points to computer records in support of its position that Ms. Gottlieb did not win the grand prize. Ms. Gottlieb relies in part on her own testimony and the testimony of her husband, who witnessed her spin of the promotional wheel. It is for the jury, and not for the court, to resolve this factual dispute.

Motion for summary judgment on the contract claim denied in favor of Ms. Gottlieb.

Exchanges That Fail to Meet Consideration Requirements

Illusory Promises For a promise to serve as consideration in a bilateral contract, the promisee must have promised to do, or to refrain from doing, something at the promisor's request. It seems obvious, therefore, that if the promisee's promise is illusory because it really does not bind the promisee to do or refrain from doing anything, such a promise could not serve as consideration. Such agreements are often said to lack the mutuality of

obligation required for an agreement to be enforceable. So, a promisee's promise to buy "all the sugar that I want" or to "paint your house if I feel like it" would not be sufficient consideration for a promisor's return promise to sell sugar or hire a painter. In neither case has the promisee given the promisor anything of legal value in exchange for the promisor's promise. The following *Heye* case provides an example of an illusory promise. Remember, though: So long as the promisee has given legal value, the agreement will be enforceable even though what the promisee gave is worth substantially less than what the promisor promised in return.

Heye v. American Golf Corporation, Inc.   80 P.3d 495 (N.M. Ct. App. 2003)

In March 1999, American Golf Corporation (AGC) hired Melissa Heye for a job in the pro shop at the Paradise Hills Golf Course, a club that it managed. On March 19, 1999, after Heye was hired but before she began working, AGC gave Heye a number of documents, including the Co-Worker Alliance Handbook.

On page 20 of the handbook was a reference to arbitration that essentially stated that binding arbitration would be the exclusive means of resolving all disputes about unlawful harassment, discrimination, wrongful discharge, and other causes of action and that the employee was agreeing to waive her right to pursue such claims in court. Page 23 of the handbook contained the following acknowledgment:

My signature below indicates that I have read this AGC Co-Worker Alliance agreement and handbook and promise and agree to abide by its terms and conditions.

I further understand that the Company reserves the right to amend, supplement, rescind or revise any policy, practice, or benefit described in this handbook—other than employment at-will provisions—as it deems appropriate.

I acknowledge that my employment is at-will, which means that either the Company or I have the absolute right to end the employment relationship at any time with or without notice or reason. I further understand that the president of American Golf Corporation is the only authorized representative of the Company who can modify this at-will employment relationship and the contents of this handbook, and that any such modifications must be made in writing.

I further acknowledge that I have read and agree to be bound by the arbitration policy set forth on page 20 of this handbook.

Heye signed the acknowledgment

Heye worked for AGC until January 2000. She later sued AGC on a variety of grounds, including sex discrimination and sexual harassment. AGC moved to compel arbitration under the acknowledgment form that Heye signed. The trial court initially granted this motion, but after Heye filed a motion for reconsideration, the trial court denied AGC's motion. AGC appealed.

Castillo, Judge

We interpret an arbitration agreement under the rules of state contract law. For a contract to be legally valid and enforceable, it must be factually supported by an offer, an acceptance, consideration, and mutual assent. AGC asserts that the arbitration agreement is supported by consideration in the form of AGC's agreement to arbitrate and in Heye's employment or continued employment. We first look to AGC's agreement to arbitrate.

A valid contract must possess mutuality of obligation. Mutuality means both sides must provide consideration. Consideration consists of a promise to do something that a party is under no legal obligation to do or to forbear from doing something he has a legal right to do. Furthermore, a promise must be binding. When a promise puts no constraints on what a party may do in the future—in other words, when a promise, in reality, promises nothing—it is illusory, and it is not consideration. AGC points to language on page 20 of the handbook, stating that arbitration is the "exclusive means of resolving any dispute(s)," and argues that this language does not allow AGC to modify or ignore the agreement to arbitrate. Heye counters that the language on page 20 conflicts with that of the acknowledgment form on page 23; the language on page 23 provides "that the Company reserves the right to amend, supplement, rescind or revise any policy, practice, or benefit described in this handbook—other than employment at-will provisions—as it deems appropriate." As a result, Heye contends, AGC is "free to amend, supplement, rescind or revise the policy regarding arbitration at its whim." Heye concludes that "at best, [AGC] is left with conflicting, and therefore ambiguous, terms regarding its ability to unilaterally change the contract."

We disagree with AGC that it was "equally obligated to . . . arbitrate all claims." To the contrary, the agreement provided in effect that only one thing would remain unchangeable, namely, Heye's at-will employment status. It expressly reserved for itself the "right to amend, supplement, rescind or revise any policy, practice, or benefit described in this handbook—other than employment at-will provisions—as it deems appropriate." The agreement, in essence, gives AGC unfettered discretion to terminate arbitration at any time, while binding Heye to arbitration. AGC remains free to selectively abide by its promise to arbitrate; the promise, therefore, is illusory. Thus, AGC's promise to arbitrate does not provide the consideration necessary to enforce the arbitration agreement.

Denial of motion to compel arbitration affirmed in favor of Heye.

Effect of Cancellation or Termination Clauses The fact that an agreement allows one or both of the parties to cancel or terminate their contractual obligations does not necessarily mean that the party (or parties) with the power to cancel has given an illusory promise. Such provisions are a common and necessary part of many business relationships. The central issue in such cases concerns whether a promise subject to cancellation or termination actually represents a binding obligation. A right to cancel or terminate at any time, for any reason, and without any notice would clearly render illusory any other promise by the party possessing such a right. However, limits on the circumstances under which cancellation may occur (such as a dealer's failure to live up to dealership obligations), or the time in which cancellation may occur (such as no cancellations for the first 90 days), or a requirement of advance notice of cancellation (such as a 30-day notice requirement) would all effectively remove a promise from the illusory category. This is so because in each case the party making such a promise has bound himself to do *something* in exchange for the other party's promise. A party's duty of good faith and fair dealing can also limit the right to terminate and prevent its promise from being considered illusory.

Effect of Output and Requirements Contracts Contracts in which one party to the agreement agrees to buy all of the other party's production of a particular commodity (*output* contracts) or to supply all of another party's needs for a particular commodity (*requirements* contracts) are common business transactions that serve legitimate business purposes. They can reduce a seller's selling costs and provide buyers with a secure source of supply. Prior to the enactment of the UCC, however, many common law courts used to refuse to enforce such agreements on the ground that their failure to specify the quantity of goods to be produced or purchased rendered them illusory. The courts also feared that a party to such an agreement might be tempted to exploit the other party. For example, subsequent market conditions could make it profitable for the seller in an output contract or the buyer in a requirements contract to demand that the other party buy or provide more of the particular commodity than the other party had actually intended to buy or sell. The Code legitimizes requirements and output contracts. It addresses the concern about the potential for exploitation by limiting a party's demands to those quantity needs that occur in *good faith* and are not unreasonably disproportionate to any quantity estimate contained in the contract, or to any normal prior output or requirements if no estimate is stated [2–306(1)]. Chapter 19, Formation and Terms of Sales Contracts, discusses this subject in greater detail.

Effect of Exclusive Dealing Contracts When a manufacturer of goods enters an agreement giving a distributor the exclusive right to sell the manufacturer's products in a particular territory, does such an agreement impose sufficient obligations on both parties to meet the legal value test? Put another way, does the distributor have any duty to sell the manufacturer's products and does the manufacturer have any duty to supply any particular number of products? Such agreements are commonly encountered in today's business world, and they can serve the legitimate interests of both parties. The Code recognizes this fact by providing that, unless the parties agree to the contrary, an exclusive dealing contract imposes a duty on the distributor to use her best efforts to sell the goods and imposes a reciprocal duty on the manufacturer to use his best efforts to supply the goods [2–306(2)].

Preexisting Duties The legal value component of our consideration definition requires that promisees do, or promise to do, something in exchange for a promisor's promise that they had no prior legal duty to do. Thus, as a general rule, performing or agreeing to perform a preexisting duty is not consideration. This seems fair because the promisor in such a case has effectively made a gratuitous promise, since she was already entitled to the promisee's performance.

Preexisting Public Duties Every member of society has a duty to obey the law and refrain from committing crimes or torts. Therefore, a promisee's promise not to commit such an act can never be consideration. So, Thomas's promise to pay Brown $100 a year in exchange for Brown's promise not to burn Thomas's barn would not be enforceable against Thomas. Since Brown has a preexisting duty not to burn Thomas's barn, his promise lacks legal value.

Similarly, public officials, by virtue of their offices, have a preexisting legal duty to perform their public responsibilities. For example, Smith, the owner of a liquor store, promises to pay Fawcett, a police officer whose beat includes Smith's store, $50 a week to keep an eye on the store while walking her beat. Smith's promise is unenforceable because Fawcett has agreed to do something that she already has a duty to do.

Preexisting Contractual Duties and Modifications of Contracts under the Common Law The most important preexisting duty cases are those involving preexisting *contractual* duties. These cases generally occur when the parties to an existing contract agree to *modify* that contract. The general common law rule on contract modifications holds that an agreement to modify an existing contract requires *some new consideration* to be binding.

For example, Turner enters into a contract with Acme Construction Company for the construction of a new office building for $350,000. When the construction is partially completed, Acme tells Turner that due to rising labor and materials costs it will stop construction unless Turner agrees to pay an extra $50,000. Turner, having already entered into contracts to lease office space in the new building, promises to pay the extra amount. When the construction is finished, Turner refuses to pay more than $350,000. Is Turner's promise to pay the extra $50,000 enforceable against him? No. All Acme has done in exchange for Turner's promise to pay more is build the building, something that Acme had a preexisting contractual duty to do. Therefore, Acme's performance is not consideration for Turner's promise to pay more.

Although the result in the preceding example seems fair (why should Turner have to pay $400,000 for something he had a right to receive for $350,000?) and is consistent with consideration theory, the application of the preexisting duty rule to contract modifications has generated a great deal of criticism. Plainly, the rule can protect a party to a contract such as Turner from being pressured into paying more because the other party to the contract is trying to take advantage of his situation by demanding an additional amount for performance. However, mechanical application of the rule could also produce unfair results when the parties have freely agreed to a fair modification of their contract. Some critics argue that the purpose of contract modification law should be to enforce freely made modifications of existing contracts and to deny enforcement to coerced modifications. Such critics commonly suggest that general principles such as good faith and unconscionability, rather than technical consideration rules, should be used to police contract modifications.

Other observers argue that most courts in fact apply the preexisting duty rule in a manner calculated to reach fair results, because several exceptions to the rule can be used to enforce a fair modification agreement. For example, any new consideration furnished by the promisee provides sufficient consideration to support a promise to modify an existing contract. So, if Acme had promised to finish construction a week before the completion date called for in the original contract, or had promised to make some change in the original contract specifications such as to install a better grade of carpet, Acme would have done something that it had no legal duty to do in exchange for Turner's new promise. Turner's promise to pay more would then be enforceable because it would be supported by new consideration.

Many courts also enforce an agreement to modify an existing contract if the modification resulted from *unforeseen circumstances* that a party could not reasonably be expected to have foreseen, and which made that party's performance far more difficult than the parties originally anticipated. For example, if Acme had requested the extra payment because abnormal subsurface rock formations made excavation on the construction site far more costly and time-consuming than could have been reasonably expected, many courts would enforce Turner's promise to pay more.

Courts can also enforce fair modification agreements by holding that the parties mutually agreed to terminate their original contract and then entered a new one. Because contracts are created by the will of the parties, they can be terminated in the same fashion. Each party agrees to release the other party from his contractual obligations in exchange for the other party's promise to do the same. Because such a mutual agreement terminates all duties owed under the original agreement, any subsequent agreement by the parties would not be subject to the preexisting duty rule. A court is likely to take this approach, however, only when it is convinced that the modification agreement was fair and free from coercion. The following *Ross* case illustrates the common law approach to modification of contracts.

Ross v. May Company 880 N.E.2d 210 (Ill. Ct. App. 2007)

Gary Ross was employed by May Company. When Ross went to work for May in 1968, he was given an employee handbook that described particular steps that had to be taken before an employee could be fired. In addition, a May manager told Ross that he would have a job as long as he wanted to work. Later on, however, in 1987 or 1989, May published a new handbook that contained disclaimers of any rights to continued employment that its employees might have.

After working for May for more than 40 years, Ross got in trouble for drawing stick figures depicting a female co-worker being electrocuted, boiled, guillotined, run over by a train, shot out of a cannon, tied to a rocket, and standing precariously under a 10,000-pound weight. The co-worker's son brought the pictures to the attention of May. May suspended Ross and told him to see a psychologist. Ross alleged that after two visits, the psychologist found he was not a threatening individual and determined that he required no treatment other than perhaps treatment for depression resulting from the suspension and possible job loss. Shortly thereafter, May fired Ross. Ross claimed he was terminated without cause and was not afforded procedures described in the 1968 handbook, such as an appeal or review of the decision. He sued May under a theory of breach of contract based upon the 1968 employee handbook. The trial court dismissed Ross's claim, and Ross appealed.

Hall, Justice

Under Illinois law, an employee hired without a fixed term is presumed to be an at-will employee whose employment may be terminated for any cause or reason, provided the employer does not violate clearly mandated public policy. Our supreme court crafted an exception to this rule where an employee handbook or other policy statement creates enforceable contractual rights if the traditional requirements for contract formation are present. Three requirements must be met for an employee handbook or policy statement to form an employee contract. First, the language of the policy statement must contain a promise clear enough that an employee would reasonably believe that an offer has been made. Second, the statement must be disseminated to the employee in such a manner that the employee is aware of its contents and reasonably believes it to be an offer. Third, the employee must accept the offer by commencing or continuing to work after learning of the policy statement. When these requirements are met, the employee's continued work constitutes consideration for the promises contained in the statement, and under traditional principles a valid contract is formed.

In this case, the trial court determined that promissory language set forth in the 1968 employee handbook defendant issued to Ross along with oral assurances of job security by May's agent created an employment contract between May and Ross, altering Ross's at-will status and binding May to certain procedures before it could terminate plaintiff's employment. However, the court went on to dismiss Ross's breach of contract claim, finding that disclaimers contained in revised employee handbooks issued to May served to invalidate his previously existing employment contract. May maintains that disclaimers set forth in employee handbooks issued to Ross in the late 1980s unilaterally modified May's employment contract, converting him to an at-will employee. May counters that the disclaimers did not modify his employment status because they were not supported by consideration.

The trial court determined that new benefits May offered to Ross and his coemployees in 1990 constituted consideration for the unilateral modification of Ross's employment contract. The new benefits consisted of paid personal days, short- and long-term disability, an insurance reimbursement plan, and a supplemental retirement savings plan. Ross accepted the new benefits and enrolled in the new long-term disability plan and in the enhanced supplemental retirement savings plan. Ross acknowledges that he experienced a benefit by receiving the enhanced pension and other new benefits. However, he maintains that the new benefits he received from May did not serve as consideration supporting the unilateral modification of his employment contract because they were offered to all eligible employees and

there was never any bargained-for exchange between him and May in which he agreed to modify or terminate his contract rights in exchange for the benefits. We agree.

Modification of a contract is a change in one or more respects that introduces new elements into the details of the contract and cancels others, but leaves the general purpose and effect undisturbed. No contract can be modified or amended in *ex parte* fashion by one of the contracting parties without the knowledge and consent of the remaining party to the agreement. A valid modification must satisfy all criteria essential for a valid contract, including offer, acceptance, and consideration.

The essential element of consideration is a bargained-for exchange of promises or performances that may consist of a promise, an act, a forbearance, or the creation, modification, or destruction of a legal relation. A bargained-for exchange exists if one party's promise induces the other party's promise or performance. A performance or return promise is bargained for if it is sought by the promisor in exchange for his promise and is given by the promisee in exchange for that promise. In the employer-employee context, consideration will be found when an employer and its employees make a bargained-for exchange to support the employees' relinquishment of the protections they were entitled to under the existing contract. Here, May does not contend that it bargained for Ross to modify his employment status and become an at-will employee. In this case, there was no bargained-for exchange, and no promises were made where Ross agreed to relinquish his contractual rights in exchange for the new benefits. The additional benefits, which were offered in 1990, were in no way related to, bargained for, or referenced to any preexisting contractual rights; the benefits were offered to all eligible employees whether or not they possessed contractual rights. May acted unilaterally, not in a bargained-for exchange, when it offered the additional benefits to its employees. No consideration flowed from May to Ross to compensate him for relinquishing the protections he enjoyed under the 1968 employee handbook. Under these circumstances, the additional benefits May offered Ross and his co-employees did not constitute consideration for the unilateral modification of Ross's employment contract.

In the typical bargain, the consideration and the promise "bear a reciprocal relation of motive or inducement: the consideration induces the making of the promise and the promise induces the furnishing of the consideration." *Restatement (Second) of Contracts* § 71, Comment *b*, at 173 (1981). Here, there was no reciprocal agreement or consideration. When May distributed the 1987/1989 revised handbooks containing the disclaimers allowing for the unilateral modification or termination of Ross's employment contract, it did not bargain with him or other pre-1987 employees who had contractual rights under the old employee handbooks, did not ask for or obtain their assent, and did not purport to provide any consideration other than their continued employment. However, our courts have determined that mere continued employment, standing alone, does not constitute consideration supporting the unilateral modification of an existing employment contract. In sum, the trial court erred in dismissing Ross's breach of contract claim.

Before leaving this issue, we note that May has expressed concern that adopting Ross's arguments would lead to a logistical nightmare for employers where they would be required to individually bargain with each employee anytime they wished to change policies or give better benefits. May's concerns are exaggerated. Our decision is not novel. It is well settled that a contract, once made, must be performed according to its terms and that any modification of those terms must be made by mutual assent and for consideration.

Reversed in favor of Ross.

Preexisting Duty and Contract Modification under the UCC

The drafters of the Code sought to avoid many of the problems caused by the consideration requirement by dispensing with it in two important situations: As discussed in Chapter 10, The Agreement: Offer, the Code does not require consideration for firm offers [2–205]. The Code also provides that an agreement to modify a contract for the sale of goods needs *no consideration* to be binding [2–209(1)]. For example, Electronics World orders 200 XYZ televisions at $150 per unit from XYZ Corp. Electronics World later seeks to cancel its order, but XYZ refuses to agree to cancellation. Instead, XYZ seeks to mollify a valued customer by offering to reduce the price to $100 per unit. Electronics World agrees, but when the televisions arrive, XYZ bills Electronics World for $150 per unit. Under classical contract principles, XYZ's promise to reduce the price of the goods would not be enforceable because Electronics World has furnished no new consideration in exchange for XYZ's promise. Under the Code, no new consideration is necessary and the agreement to modify the contract is enforceable.

Several things should be made clear about the operation of this Code rule. First, XYZ had no duty to agree to a modification and could have insisted on payment of $150 per unit. Second, modification agreements under the Code are still subject to scrutiny under the general Code principles of good faith and unconscionability, so unfair agreements or agreements that are the product of coercion are unlikely to be enforced. Finally, the Code contains two provisions to protect people from fictitious claims that an agreement has been modified. If the original agreement requires any modification to be in writing, an oral modification is unenforceable [2–209(2)]. Regardless of what the original agreement says, if the price of the goods in the modified contract is $500 or more, the modification is unenforceable unless the requirements of the Code's statute of frauds section [2–201] are satisfied [2–209(3)].[8]

Preexisting Duty and Agreements to Settle Debts

One special variant of the preexisting duty rule that causes considerable confusion occurs when a debtor offers to pay a creditor a sum less than the creditor is demanding in exchange for the creditor's promise to accept the part payment as full payment of the debt. If the creditor later sues for the balance of the debt, is the creditor's promise to take less enforceable? The answer depends on the nature of the debt and on the circumstances of the debtor's payment.

Liquidated Debts A **liquidated debt** is a debt that is both due and certain; that is, the parties have no good faith dispute about either the existence or the amount of

---

[8]Chapter 16 discusses § 2–201 of the Code in detail.

The Global Business Environment

Like the UCC, the CISG does not require new consideration to modify a contract. The CISG states that contracts can be modified by the "mere agreement" of the parties. Another similarity between the UCC and CISG is that under the CISG, a term in a written contract stating that modifications of that contract can only be made in writing will generally preclude oral modifications.

the original debt. If a debtor does nothing more than pay less than an amount he clearly owes, how could this be consideration for a creditor's promise to take less? Such a debtor has actually done less than he had a preexisting legal duty to do—namely, to pay the full amount of the debt. For this reason, the creditor's promise to discharge a liquidated debt for part payment of the debt at or after its due date is *unenforceable* for lack of consideration.

For example, Connor borrows $10,000 from Friendly Finance Company, payable in one year. On the day payment is due, Connor sends Friendly a check for $9,000 marked: "Payment in full for all claims Friendly Finance has against me." Friendly cashes Connor's check, thus impliedly promising to accept it as full payment by cashing it, and later sues Connor for $1,000. Friendly is entitled to the $1,000 because Connor has given no consideration to support Friendly's implied promise to accept $9,000 as full payment.

However, had Connor done something he had no preexisting duty to do in exchange for Friendly's promise to settle for part payment, he could enforce Friendly's promise and avoid paying the $1,000. For example, if Connor had paid early, before the loan contract called for payment, or in a different medium of exchange from that called for in the loan contract (such as $4,000 in cash and a car worth $5,000), he would have given consideration for Friendly's promise to accept early or different payment as full payment.

Unliquidated Debts   A good faith dispute about either the existence or the amount of a debt makes the debt an **unliquidated debt.** The settlement of an unliquidated debt is called an **accord and satisfaction.**[9] When an accord and satisfaction has occurred, the creditor cannot maintain an action to recover the remainder of the debt that he alleges is due. For example, Computer Corner, a retailer, orders 50 personal computers and associated software packages from Computech for $75,000. After receiving the goods, Computer Corner refuses to pay Computech the full $75,000, arguing that some of the computers were defective and that some of the software it received did not conform to its order. Computer Corner sends Computech a check for $60,000 marked: "Payment in full for all goods received from Computech." A creditor in Computech's position obviously faces a real dilemma. If Computech cashes Computer Corner's check, it will be held to have impliedly promised to accept $60,000 as full payment. Computech's promise to accept part payment as full payment would be enforceable because Computer

Corner has given consideration to support it: Computer Corner has given up its right to have a court determine the amount it owes Computech. This is something that Computer Corner had no duty to do; by giving up this right and the $60,000 in exchange for Computech's implied promise, the consideration requirement is satisfied. The result in this case is supported not only by consideration theory but also by a strong public policy in favor of encouraging parties to settle their disputes out of court. Who would bother to settle disputed claims out of court if settlement agreements were unenforceable?

Computech could refuse to accept Computer Corner's settlement offer and sue for the full $75,000, but doing so involves several risks. A court may decide that Computer Corner's arguments are valid and award Computech less than $60,000. Even if Computech is successful, it may take years to resolve the case in the courts through the expensive and time-consuming litigation process. In addition, there is always the chance that Computer Corner may file for bankruptcy before any judgment can be collected. Faced with such risks, Computech may feel that it has no practical alternative other than to cash Computer Corner's check.[10]

Composition Agreements   Composition agreements are agreements between a debtor and two or more creditors who agree to accept as full payment a stated percentage of their liquidated claims against the debtor at or after the date on which those claims are payable. Composition agreements are generally enforced by the courts despite the fact that enforcement appears to be contrary to the general rule on part payment of liquidated debts. Many courts have justified enforcing composition agreements on the ground that the creditors' mutual agreement to accept less than the amount due them provides the necessary consideration. The main reason why creditors agree to compositions is that they fear that their failure to do so may force the debtor into bankruptcy proceedings, in which case they might ultimately recover a smaller percentage of their claims than that agreed to in the composition.

Forbearance to Sue   An agreement by a promisee to refrain, or forbear, from pursuing a legal claim against a promisor can be valid consideration to support a return promise—usually to pay a sum of money—by a promisor. The promisee has agreed not to file suit, something that

---

[9]Accord and satisfaction is also discussed in Chapter 18.

[10]A provision of Article 3 of the Uniform Commercial Code, section 3–311, covers accord and satisfaction by use of an instrument such as a "full payment" check. With a few exceptions, the basic provisions of section 3–311 parallel the common law rules regarding accord and satisfaction that are described in this chapter and Chapter 18.

she has a legal right to do, in exchange for the promisor's promise. The courts do not wish to sanction extortion by allowing people to threaten to file spurious claims against others in the hope that those threatened will agree to some payment to avoid the expense or embarrassment associated with defending a lawsuit. On the other hand, we have a strong public policy favoring private settlement of disputes. Therefore, it is generally said that the promisee must have a good faith belief in the validity of his or her claim before forbearance amounts to consideration.

Past Consideration
Past consideration—despite its name—is not consideration at all. Past consideration is an act or other benefit given in the past that was *not* given in exchange for the promise in question. Because the past act was not given in exchange for the present promise, it cannot be consideration. Consider again the facts of the famous case of *Hamer v. Sidway,* discussed earlier in this chapter. There, an uncle's promise to pay his nephew $5,000 for refraining from smoking, drinking, swearing, and other delightful pastimes until his 21st birthday was supported by consideration because the nephew had given legal value by refraining from participating in the prohibited activities. However, what if the uncle had said to his nephew on the eve of his 21st birthday: "Your mother tells me you've been a good lad and abstained from tobacco, hard drink, foul language, and gambling. Such goodness should be rewarded. Tomorrow, I'll give you a check for $5,000." Should the uncle's promise be enforceable against him? Clearly not, because although his nephew's behavior still passes the legal value test, in this case it was not bargained for and given in exchange for the uncle's promise.

Ethics in Action

Rex Roofing contracted with the O'Neills to install a new roof on their house for $2,500. Rex began the work and soon realized that he had underbid the job. He informed the O'Neills that he would not do the job for $2,500 after all, but that he would complete the work for $3,200. The O'Neills promised to pay him $3,200. Assuming that there were no unforeseen conditions that affected the roof and no obvious mistakes in the bid calculations, was it ethical for Rex Roofing to refuse to do the job at the agreed-upon price? Since the O'Neills agreed to pay the higher price, are they ethically obligated to do so, even if the law does not require them to pay more than the originally agreed-upon price?

CONCEPT REVIEW

Consideration

Consideration*	Not Consideration
Doing something you had no preexisting duty to do	Doing something you had a preexisting duty to do
Promising to do something you had no preexisting duty to do	Promising to do something you had a preexisting duty to do
Paying part of a liquidated debt prior to the date the debt is due	Nominal consideration (unless actually bargained for)
Paying a liquidated debt in a different medium of exchange than originally agreed to	Paying part of a liquidated debt at or after the date the debt is due
Agreeing to settle an unliquidated debt	Making an illusory promise
Agreeing not to file suit when you have a good faith belief in your claim's validity	Past consideration
	Preexisting moral obligation

*Assuming bargained for.

Moral Obligation As a general rule, promises made to satisfy a preexisting moral obligation are unenforceable for lack of consideration. The fact that a promisor or some member of the promisor's family, for example, has received some benefit from the promisee in the past (e.g., food and lodging, or emergency care) would not constitute consideration for a promisor's promise to pay for that benefit, due to the absence of the bargain element. Some courts find this result distressing and enforce such promises despite the absence of consideration. In addition, a few states have passed statutes making promises to pay for past benefits enforceable if such a promise is contained in a writing that clearly expresses the promisor's intent to be bound.

Exceptions to the Consideration Requirement

The consideration requirement is a classic example of a traditional contract law rule. It is precise, abstract, and capable of almost mechanical application. It can also, in some instances, result in significant injustice. Modern courts and legislatures have responded to this potential for injustice by carving out numerous exceptions to the requirement of consideration. Some of these exceptions (for example, the Code firm offer and contract modification rules) have already been discussed in this and preceding chapters. In the remaining portion of this chapter, we focus on several other important exceptions to the consideration requirement.

Promissory Estoppel As discussed in Chapter 9, Introduction to Contracts, the doctrine of promissory estoppel first emerged from attempts by courts around the turn of this century to reach just results in donative (gift) promise cases. Classical contract consideration principles did not recognize a promisee's reliance

on a donative promise as a sufficient basis for enforcing the promise against the promisor. Instead, donative promises were unenforceable because they were not supported by consideration. In fact, the essence of a donative promise is that it does not seek or require any bargained-for exchange. Yet people continued to act in reliance on donative promises, often to their considerable disadvantage.

Refer to the facts of *Thorne v. Deas,* discussed earlier in this chapter. The co-owners of the *Sea Nymph* clearly relied on their fellow co-owner's promise to get insurance for the ship. Some courts in the early years of this century began to protect such relying promisees by *estopping* promisors from raising the defense that their promises were not supported by consideration. In a wide variety of cases involving gratuitous agency promises (as in *Thorne v. Deas*), promises of bonuses or pensions made to employees, and promises of gifts of land, courts began to use a promisee's detrimental (harmful) reliance on a donative promise as, in effect, a *substitute* for consideration.

In 1932, the first *Restatement of Contracts* legitimized these cases by expressly recognizing promissory estoppel in section 90. The elements of promissory estoppel were then essentially the same as they are today: a *promise* that the promisor should reasonably expect to induce reliance, *reliance* on the promise by the promisee, and *injustice* to the promisee as a result of that reliance. Promissory estoppel is now widely used as a consideration substitute, not only in donative promise cases but also in cases involving commercial promises contemplating a bargained-for exchange. The construction contract bid cases discussed in Chapter 10 are another example of this expansion of promissory estoppel's reach. In fact, promissory estoppel has expanded far beyond its initial role as a consideration substitute into other areas of contract law.

The following *Skebba* case applies promissory estoppel and discusses the remedies that might be given in cases of promissory estoppel.

Skebba v. Kasch   724 N.W.2d 408 (Wis. Ct. App. 2006)

Jeffrey Kasch, with his brother, owned M.W. Kasch Co. Kasch hired William Skebba as a sales representative. Kasch's father was the original owner of the business, and had hired Skebba's father. Skebba's father mentored Kasch. Over the years, Kasch promoted Skebba to account manager, then to customer service manager, field sales manager, vice president of sales, senior vice president of sales and purchasing, and finally to vice president of sales. When M.W. Kasch Co. experienced serious financial problems in 1993, another company solicited Skebba to leave Kasch and work for it. When Skebba told Kasch he was accepting the new opportunity, Kasch asked what it would take to get him to stay, and noted that Skebba's leaving at this time would be viewed very negatively within the industry. Shortly thereafter, Skebba told Kasch that he needed security for his retirement and family and would stay if Kasch agreed to pay Skebba $250,000 if one of these three conditions *occurred: (1) the company was sold; (2) Skebba was lawfully terminated; or (3) Skebba retired. Kasch agreed to this proposal and Kasch promised to have the agreement drawn up. Skebba turned down the job opportunity and stayed with Kasch from December 1993 (when this discussion occurred) through 1999 when the company assets were sold.*

Over the years, Skebba repeatedly asked Kasch for a written summary of this agreement; however, none was forthcoming. Eventually, Kasch sold the business. Kasch received $5.1 million dollars for his 51 percent share of the business when it was sold. Upon the sale of the business, Skebba asked Kasch for the $250,000 Kasch had previously promised to him, but Kasch refused, and denied ever having made such an agreement. Instead, Kasch gave Skebba a severance agreement that had been drafted by Kasch's lawyers in 1993. This agreement promised two years of salary continuation on the sale of the company, but only if Skebba was not hired by the successor company and the severance agreement required a set off against the salary continuation of any sums Skebba earned from any activity during the two years of the severance agreement. Skebba sued Kasch, alleging breach of contract and promissory estoppel.

The case went to trial. The jury found there was no contract, but that Kasch had made a promise upon which Skebba relied to his detriment, that the reliance was foreseeable, and that Skebba was damaged in the amount of $250,000. The trial court ruled against Skebba, however, on the ground that applicable case law did not allow the court to order Kasch to pay the sum that he had promised. Instead, it took the position that Skebba had not proved his damages because he had not proved how much he would have earned if he had taken the job that he turned down. Skebba appealed.

Kessler, Judge

The purpose of promissory estoppel is to enforce promises where the failure to do so is unjust. *Hoffman v. Red Owl Food Stores* was the first case in Wisconsin to adopt promissory estoppel. The facts in *Hoffman* present a long and complex history of Red Owl Food Stores inducing Mr. Hoffman to do a number of things (sell his bakery; sell his grocery store; move to another city to get larger grocery store management experience; commit to investing ever increasing sums of money in order to get a Red Owl store; buy a lot on which the store would be built, then sell the same lot; and other activities) in order to own a Red Owl grocery store to be built in the future. Mr. Hoffman did all of the things required, but finally balked at the last demand for increased capital. Although there was never a specific contract between Mr. Hoffman and Red Owl, yet Mr. Hoffman had obviously changed position in a number of ways in reliance on Red Owl's promise of a store, the court was faced with the need to provide a remedy to Mr. Hoffman and the impracticality of enforcing the promise of a store against Red Owl. In that context, the *Hoffman* court explained its adoption of a cause of action based on promissory estoppel. The conditions imposed are:

(1) Was the promise one which the promisor should reasonably expect to induce action or forbearance of a definite and substantial character on the part of the promisee?

(2) Did the promise induce such action or forbearance?

(3) Can injustice be avoided only by enforcement of the promise?

The *Hoffman* court explains that the first two of these requirements are facts to be found by a jury or other factfinder, while the third is a policy decision to be made by the court. In making this policy decision, a court must consider a number of factors in determining whether injustice can only be avoided by enforcement of the promise. A court, in fashioning a remedy, can consider any remedy which will prevent injustice.

In this case, Skebba performed—he remained at M.W. Kasch—in reliance on Kasch's promise to pay $250,000 to him if one of three conditions occurred. Kasch enjoyed the fruits of Skebba's reliance—he kept on a top salesperson to help the company through tough financial times and he avoided the damage that he believed Skebba's leaving could have had on M.W. Kasch's reputation in the industry. Accordingly, to prevent injustice, the remedy for Skebba to receive is Kasch's specific performance promised—payment of the $250,000. Otherwise Kasch will enjoy all of the benefits of induced reliance while Skebba will be deprived of that which he was promised, with no other available remedy to substitute fairly for the promised reward. Skebba did not spend money in reliance on the promise, so neither restitution nor cancellation of an obligation Skebba incurred would be relevant to these facts.

"The definite and substantial character of the action or forbearance in relation to the remedy sought" supports enforcing the promise. Skebba's forbearance of other employment for six years from the 1993 promise the jury found occurred was both definite and substantial. "The reasonableness of the action or forbearance" and "the extent to which the action or forbearance was foreseeable by the promisor" is supported by the undisputed fact that Kasch knew Skebba had another job opportunity in 1993, that Kasch believed Skebba's leaving would damage the company in the industry, and that Kasch wanted Skebba to stay. Kasch's promise achieved Kasch's objectives: Skebba stayed even though the company was in severe financial difficulties. In short, every factor this court requires to be considered supports enforcement of the promise through promissory estoppel.

Skebba's loss has nothing to do with what he might have earned on another job. Income from the rejected job was never a part of the calculus of the promise made and relied upon. Kasch never proposed to better the salary or bonus offered. Neither Kasch nor Skebba mention any discussion about a way for Kasch to retain Skebba other than the now disputed payment.

Hence, the damage calculation required by the trial court, which might be appropriate in other cases, has no reasonable application to the facts here. In this case, specific performance *is* the *necessary* enforcement mechanism to prevent injustice for Skebba's reliance on the promise the jury found Kasch had made to him.

Reversed and remanded in favor of Skebba.

Promises to Pay Debts Barred by Statutes of Limitations

Statutes of limitations set an express statutory time limit on a person's ability to pursue any legal claim. A creditor who fails to file suit to collect a debt within the time prescribed by the appropriate statute of limitations loses the right to collect it. Many states, however, enforce a new promise by a debtor to pay such a debt, even though technically such promises are not supported by consideration because the creditor has given nothing in exchange for the new promise. Most states afford debtors some protection in such cases, however, by requiring that the new promise be in writing to be enforceable.

Promises to Pay Debts Barred by Bankruptcy Discharge

Once a bankrupt debtor is granted a discharge,[11] creditors no longer have the legal right to collect discharged debts. Most states enforce a new promise by the debtor to pay (reaffirm) the debt regardless of whether the creditor has given any consideration to support it. To reduce creditor attempts to pressure debtors to reaffirm, the Bankruptcy Reform Act of 1978 made it much more difficult for debtors to reaffirm debts discharged in bankruptcy proceedings. The act requires that a reaffirmation promise be made prior to the date of the discharge and gives the debtor the right to revoke his promise within 30 days after it becomes enforceable. This act also requires the Bankruptcy Court to counsel individual (as opposed to corporate) debtors about the legal effects of reaffirmation and requires Bankruptcy Court approval of reaffirmations by individual debtors. In addition, a few states require reaffirmation promises to be in writing to be enforceable.

Charitable Subscriptions

Promises to make gifts for charitable or educational purposes are often enforced, despite the absence of consideration, when the institution or organization to which the promise was made has acted in reliance on the promised gift. This result is usually justified on the basis of either promissory estoppel or public policy.

---

[11]Chapter 30 discusses bankruptcy in detail.

Problems and Problem Cases

1. Calabro's parents were divorced, and she lived with her mother in Oklahoma while her father lived in Tennessee. Calabro had an excellent academic record in high school. During her senior year, her father offered to pay her expenses to attend a distinguished, private university if she received at least $10,000 in financial aid. At the time that Calabro was applying to colleges, she knew that she was eligible to attend the University of Oklahoma and receive a full scholarship, sufficient to pay tuition, room, board, books, and student activity fee. Knowing that her father would be willing to finance her college education at a private college if she received $10,000 in financial aid, Calabro applied to and was accepted at a number of private schools, including Vanderbilt University. In the fall of 1991, Calabro enrolled in Vanderbilt University with her father paying expenses that exceeded her scholarship. During the Christmas break of 1992, however, Calabro's father informed her that he was no longer willing to pay for her college expenses. At that time he had prepaid her tuition for the spring of 1993 at Vanderbilt. Calabro continued to attend Vanderbilt and completed her course by taking out student loans that became due upon her graduation. Calabro brought an action for promissory estoppel

against her father, but the trial court granted a summary judgment in favor of her father. Was this a correct decision by the court?

2. On February 1, 2004, Zhang entered into a contract with Sorichetti to buy Sorichetti's Las Vegas home for $532,500. The contract listed a March closing date and a few household furnishings as part of the sale. On February 3, Sorichetti told Zhang that he was terminating the sale "to stay in the house a little longer," and (incorrectly) that Nevada law allows the rescission of real property purchase agreements within three days of contracting. Sorichetti stated that he would sell the home, however, if Zhang paid more money. Zhang agreed. Another contract was drafted, reciting a new sales price, $578,000. This contract added to the included household furnishings drapes that were not listed in the February 1 agreement, and set an April, rather than March, closing date. Was this a valid modification of the contract?

3. On April 25, 2005, Poux hired Hernandez to sell organic produce for her sole proprietorship, Access Organics Sales. In July 2005, Hernandez was promoted to sales manager. On August 29, 2005, four months after his employment began, Hernandez signed a noncompete agreement and a nondisclosure agreement. The noncompete agreement provided in relevant part: "For good consideration and as an inducement for Access Organics (the Company) to employ Andy Hernandez, the undersigned Employee hereby agrees not to directly or indirectly compete with the business of the Company and it successors and assigns during the period of employment and for a period of two years following termination of employment. . . ." Shortly thereafter, Access Organics began experiencing financial difficulties and laid off Hernandez and several other employees. Hernandez voluntarily returned to the company on a part-time basis but resigned a short time later. Hernandez then entered into business with another former Access Organics employee. Full Circle Sales, Hernandez's new company, was located in the Kalispell area and dealt in both organic and conventional produce. Access Organics brought suit to enforce the noncompete and nondisclosure agreements signed by Hernandez. Was the noncompete and non-disclosure agreement a valid contract that was supported by consideration?

4. In April 1997, Buchholz entered into a written contract with Schneider's Milling to provide between 500 and 590 segregated early weaned (SEW) pigs every three weeks beginning October 15, 1997. The parties agreed to a price of $36.50 per pig. The contract was to continue for a period of 48 months. Because Buchholz was just starting a SEW pig program, the parties recognized that the number of pigs could vary in the first four months. Even after the first four months passed, however, Buchholz was unable to provide at least 500 pigs every three weeks. At the same time, the market price for pigs decreased significantly. In September 1998, a representative of Schneider's discussed reducing the price to $28 per pig. After some discussion, Buchholz proposed a price of $30 per pig. On October 8, 1998, the parties agreed to a price of $30 per pig and that Buchholz would produce at least 500 pigs every three weeks until April 1, 1999, or the contract would be terminated. Buchholz had two deliveries of over 500 pigs, but the other deliveries were less than 500 pigs. In February 1999, Schneider's terminated its agreement with Buchholz. Buchholz filed suit against Schneider's for breach of contract, claiming Schneider's had failed to pay the full contract price for the pigs, which was $36.50 per pig. Schneider's asserted that the contract had been modified in October 1998 to reduce the price to $30 per pig. Was this modification enforceable?

5. Approximately four years before his death, Dr. Martin Luther King, Jr., gave Boston University possession of some of his correspondence, manuscripts, and other papers. He did this pursuant to a letter, which read as follows:

On this 16th day of July, 1964, I name the Boston University Library the Repository of my correspondence, manuscripts, and other papers, along with a few of my awards and other material which may come to be of interest in historical and other research.

In accordance with this action I have authorized the removal of most of the above-mentioned papers and other objects to Boston University, including most correspondence through 1961, at once. It is my intention that after the end of each calendar year, similar files of materials for an additional year should be sent to Boston University.

All papers and other objects which thus pass into the custody of Boston University remain my legal property until otherwise indicated, according to the statements below. However, if, despite scrupulous care, any such materials are damaged or lost while in custody of Boston University, I absolve Boston University of responsibility to me for such damage or loss.

I intend each year to indicate a portion of the materials deposited with Boston University to become the absolute property of Boston University as an outright gift from me, until all shall have been thus given to the University. In the event of my death, all such materials deposited with the University shall become from that date the absolute property of Boston University.

Sincerely,
Martin Luther King, Jr.

Acting in her capacity as administrator of Dr. King's estate, his widow, Coretta Scott King, sued Boston University, alleging that the King Estate, not BU, owned the papers that had been housed in the BU Library's special collection since the 1964 delivery of them. BU contended that it owned them because Dr. King had made an enforceable charitable pledge to give them to BU. Was Dr. King's promise to give ownership of his papers to BU enforceable?

6. Smith hired Jones Construction to build a detached garage on her property according to certain specifications for $15,000. The contract called for Smith to pay Jones $5,000 "up front," to disburse an additional $7,000 at various stages of the construction, and to make a final payment of $3,000 at the completion of construction. Jones built the garage, but Smith complained that Jones's workmanship was substandard and that Jones had failed to build the garage to the specifications provided in the contract. Smith refused to make the final $3,000 payment. After Jones threatened to sue Smith for the $3,000, the parties came to an agreement that Smith would pay Jones $1,500 and Jones would accept the $1,500 as full payment of the contract. Smith paid Jones $1,500, making clear that it was for full payment of the contract, and Jones accepted the payment. However, Jones continued to try to collect the additional $1,500 provided for in the original contract, and when Smith refused to pay it, ultimately filed suit against Smith in small claims court. Is Smith legally obligated to pay the additional $1,500?

7. Ruth and Bryan Davis owned seven acres of land in Warren, Massachusetts. On August 19, 1997, Ruth and Bryan conveyed one and one-half acres of that parcel to Bryan's mother, Corinne, for "$1.00 in valuable consideration." Corinne built a house on the property and lived there for the next seven years. In the spring of 2004, Corinne decided to sell her house. She marketed her home herself, arranging five showings, negotiating a sales price,

and satisfactorily performing other tasks involved in selling the house and moving. Apparently prompted by Corinne's sales activity, Ruth drafted the following typewritten document:

As promised, I will give the amount of $40,000.00 to Ruth and Bryan Davis, for the value of the land at 1388 Brimfield Road.

Sincerely,
Corinne Davis.

Ruth and Bryan requested that Corinne sign it. On May 2, 2004, Bryan took the document to his mother's home and told her that if she signed it, it "might save his marriage." Corinne signed the document that day and Ruth and Bryan signed it sometime thereafter. When Corrine sold the home, she did not pay $40,000 of the sale proceeds to Bryan and Ruth. Ruth sued Corrine for breach of contract. Was there consideration to support Corrine's promise to pay part of the proceeds to Bryan and Ruth?

8. Brads became pastor of the First Baptist Church in January 1958. In June 1971, Brads had a heart attack. While he was recuperating, an officer of the church told Brads that the church had voted to pay his full salary for the remainder of his lifetime. That promise was unperformed because Brads later recovered and returned to work. In April 1980, Brads again had heart problems. On the advice of his doctor, Brads approached the deacons of the church about retirement. Brads proposed that his salary be reduced after retirement through a series of gradual step-downs to an amount approximately one-third the salary he was then receiving. Brads's proposal was accepted by the deacons. Under the terms of the agreement, the church placed Brads on disability retirement status, conferred an honorary title on him, gave him office space in the church, and allotted him retirement benefits according to the step-down schedule. Brads was required to aid, assist, and advise whomever the church called as a new pastor, to the extent Brads's health would allow. Brads and the church deacons jointly recommended to the congregation that it adopt the agreement, which the congregation did, unanimously. Brads then left his position as pastor and his benefits commenced. In 1985, the congregation was advised by a church officer that the benefits paid to Brads under the 1980 agreement should continue for Brads's lifetime. The congregation once again unanimously approved and reaffirmed the

agreement. Brads received his benefits from 1980 through early July 1990, when he was notified by church officials that he had been dismissed from the membership of the church and that no more payments would be made to him. Other benefits, such as free office space, were also discontinued. Brads sued the church, contending that it breached its contract. The church contended that there was no consideration to support its promise to pay retirement benefits to Brads for life. Is the church correct?

9. In October 2002, real estate developer Lotus Property entered into a contract with the Greers to purchase 148 acres of land. The contract contained a section entitled "Other Terms," which included the following statement: "Property shall be granted a zoning by the Henry County Board of Commissioners." Further, the contract was contingent upon Lotus obtaining sufficient financing and securing sewage easements to run sewage pipes to the property. The closing date under the contract was to be on or before January 10, 2003. In November 2002, the Greers sent a request to the Henry County Planning Commission asking it to rezone the property, and the Greers authorized an officer of Lotus to represent them at the commission's hearing. By early January 2003, however, the county had not approved the rezoning request. Further, Lotus had not yet secured financing for the project, obtained the sewage easements, or applied for any building permits. On January 9, 2003, the day before the sales contract expired, the parties signed an extension of the contract allowing Lotus to close on the property "on or before 30 days after rezoning has been approved" by the county. It is undisputed that Lotus did not pay any additional compensation to the Greers in exchange for the execution of the extension

agreement. It is also undisputed that Lotus was not ready and willing to close on the property on or before January 10, 2003, because the property had not been rezoned. Was this a valid modification of the contract?

10. Tinker Construction had a contract with Scroge to build a factory addition for Scroge by a particular date. The contract contained a penalty clause exacting daily penalties for late performance, and Tinker was working hard to complete the building on time. Because prompt completion of the addition was so important to Scroge, however, Scroge offered Tinker a bonus if it completed the factory addition on time. Scroge also learned that the supplier of parts for machinery that he had contracted for had called and said that it could not deliver the parts on Scroge's schedule for the price it had agreed to. Because there was no other supplier, Scroge promised to pay the requested higher price. The factory addition was completed on time and the parts arrived on time. Scroge then refused to pay both the bonus to Tinker and the higher price for the parts. Were these promises enforceable?

Online Research

Identifying Consideration on the Web

Browse various ads in online publications or commercial Web sites, and identify the consideration that the advertiser is proposing to give and the consideration that it requests in return.

chapter 13

REALITY OF CONSENT

In August of 2002, Duncan went to Smith Motors to look for a used car to buy. He test-drove a 1995 Corvette with an odometer reading of 52,000. Duncan assumed that the heater worked, but he did not turn it on to test it because it was so hot outside. The salesperson assured him that the car was in "mint condition." Duncan decided to buy the car. He later learned that the heater was broken, the radio would not work, the car would not start when the temperature dropped below 40 degrees, and that the car really had 152,000—not 52,000—miles on it.

- Can Duncan get out of this contract and get his money back?
- Did Smith Motors have a duty to disclose the defects in the car?
- Was the statement that the car was in "mint condition" a misrepresentation?
- Did Duncan have the obligation to investigate the car more thoroughly?
- What are the ethical concerns involved in this situation?

IN A COMPLEX ECONOMY that depends on planning for the future, it is crucial that the law can be counted on to enforce contracts. In some situations, however, there are compelling reasons for permitting people to escape or *avoid* their contracts. An agreement obtained by force, trickery, unfair persuasion, or error is not the product of mutual and voluntary consent. A person who has made an agreement under these circumstances will be able to avoid it because his consent was not *real.*

This chapter discusses five doctrines that permit people to avoid their contracts because of the absence of real consent: misrepresentation, fraud, mistake, duress, and undue influence. Doctrines that involve similar considerations will be discussed in Chapter 14, Capacity to Contract, and in Chapter 15, Illegality.

Effect of Doctrines Discussed in This Chapter

Contracts induced by misrepresentation, fraud, mistake, duress, or undue influence are generally considered to be **voidable.** This means that the person whose consent was not real has the power to **rescind** (cancel) the contract. A person who rescinds a contract is entitled to the return of anything he gave the other party. By the same token, he must offer to return anything he has received from the other party.

Necessity for Prompt and Unequivocal Rescission

Suppose Johnson, who recently bought a car from Sims Motors, learns that Sims Motors made fraudulent statements to her to induce her to buy the car. She believes the contract was induced by fraud and wants to rescind it. How does she act to protect her rights? To rescind a contract based on fraud or any of the other doctrines discussed in this chapter, she must act promptly and unequivocally. She must object promptly upon learning the facts that give her the right to rescind and must clearly express her intent to cancel the contract. She must also avoid any behavior that would suggest that she affirms or **ratifies** the contract. (Ratification of a voidable contract means that a person who had the right to rescind has elected not to do so. Ratification ends the right to rescind.) This means that she should avoid unreasonable delay in notifying the other party of her rescission, because unreasonable delay communicates that she has ratified the contract. She should also avoid any conduct that would send a "mixed message," such as continuing to accept benefits from the other party or behaving in any other way that is inconsistent with her expressed intent to rescind. You will see an example of ratification in the *Cabot Corporation v. AVX Corporation* case, which appears later in this chapter.

Misrepresentation and Fraud

Relationship between Misrepresentation and Fraud
A misrepresentation is an assertion that is not in accord with the truth. When a person enters a contract because of his justifiable reliance on a misrepresentation about some important fact, the contract is voidable.

It is not necessary that the misrepresentation be intentionally deceptive. Misrepresentations can be either "innocent" (not intentionally deceptive) or "fraudulent" (made with knowledge of falsity and intent to deceive). A contract may be voidable even if the person making the misrepresentation believes in good faith that what he says is true. Either innocent misrepresentation or fraud gives the complaining party the right to rescind a contract.

Fraud is the type of misrepresentation that is committed knowingly, with the intent to deceive. The legal term for this knowledge of falsity, which distinguishes fraud from innocent misrepresentation, is **scienter.** A person making a misrepresentation would be considered to do so "knowingly" if she knew that her statement was false, if she knew that she did not have a basis for making the statement, or even if she just made the statement without being confident that it was true. The intent to deceive can be inferred from the fact that the defendant knowingly made a misstatement of fact to a person who was likely to rely on it.

As is true for innocent misrepresentation, the contract remedy for fraudulent misrepresentation is rescission. The tort liability of a person who commits fraud is different from that of a person who commits innocent misrepresentation, however. A person who commits fraud may be liable for damages, possibly including punitive damages, for the tort of **deceit.**[1] As you will learn in following

sections, innocent misrepresentation and fraud share a common core of elements.

Election of Remedies In some states, a person injured by fraud cannot rescind the contract *and* sue for damages for deceit; he must elect (choose) between these remedies. In other states, however, an injured party may pursue both rescission and damage remedies and does not have to elect between them.[2]

Requirements for Rescission on the Ground of Misrepresentation
The fact that one of the parties has made an untrue assertion does not in itself make the contract voidable. Courts do not want to permit people who have exercised poor business judgment or poor common sense to avoid their contractual obligations, nor do they want to grant rescission of a contract when there have been only minor and unintentional misstatements of relatively unimportant details. A drastic remedy such as rescission should be used only when a person has been seriously misled about a fact important to the contract by someone he had the right to rely on. A person seeking to rescind a contract on the ground of innocent or fraudulent misrepresentation must be able to establish each of the following elements:

1. An untrue assertion of fact was made.
2. The fact asserted was material *or* the assertion was fraudulent.
3. The complaining party entered the contract because of his reliance on the assertion.
4. The reliance of the complaining party was reasonable.

In tort actions in which the plaintiff is seeking to recover damages for deceit, the plaintiff would have to establish a *fifth* element: injury. He would have to prove that he had suffered actual economic injury because of his reliance on the fraudulent assertion. In cases in which the injured person seeks only rescission of the contract, however, proof of economic injury usually is not required.

Untrue Assertion of Fact To have misrepresentation, one of the parties must have made an untrue assertion of fact or engaged in some conduct that is the equivalent of

---

[1]The tort of deceit is discussed in Chapter 6, Intentional Torts.

[2]Under every state's law, however, a person injured by fraud in a contract for the *sale of goods* can both rescind the contract and sue for damages. This is made clear by section 2–721 of the Uniform Commercial Code, which specifically states that no election of remedies is required in contracts for the sale of goods.

an untrue assertion of fact. The fact asserted must be a *past or existing fact,* as distinguished from an opinion or a promise or prediction about some future happening.

The **concealment** of a fact through some active conduct intended to prevent the other party from discovering the fact is considered to be the equivalent of an assertion. Like a false statement of fact, concealment can be the basis for a claim of misrepresentation or fraud. For example, if Summers is offering his house for sale and paints the ceilings to conceal the fact that the roof leaks, his active concealment constitutes an assertion of fact.

Nondisclosure can also be the equivalent of an assertion of fact. Nondisclosure differs from concealment in that concealment involves the active hiding of a fact, while nondisclosure is the failure to volunteer information. Disclosure of a fact—even a fact that will harm the speaker's bargaining position—is required in a number of situations, such as when the person has already offered *some* information but further information is needed to give the other party an accurate picture, or when there is a relationship of trust and confidence between the parties. In recent years, courts and legislatures have tended to impose a duty to disclose when a party has access to information that is not readily available to the other party. This is consistent with modern contract law's emphasis on influencing ethical standards of conduct and achieving fair results. Transactions involving the sale of real estate are among the most common situations in which this duty to disclose arises. Most states now hold that a seller who knows about a latent (hidden) defect that materially affects the value of the property he is selling has the obligation to speak up about this defect.

Materiality If the misrepresentation was innocent, the person seeking to rescind the contract must establish that the fact asserted was **material.** A fact will be considered to be material if it is likely to play a significant role in inducing a reasonable person to enter the contract or if the person asserting the fact knows that the other person is likely to rely on the fact. For example, Rogers, who is trying to sell his car to Ferguson and knows that Ferguson idolizes professional bowlers, tells Ferguson that a professional bowler once rode in the car. Relying on that representation, Ferguson buys the car. Although the fact Rogers asserted might not be important to most people, it would be material here because Rogers knew that his representation would be likely to induce Ferguson to enter the contract.

Even if the fact asserted was not material, the contract may be rescinded if the misrepresentation was *fraudulent*. The rationale for this rule is that a person who fraudulently misrepresents a fact, even one that is not material under the standards previously discussed, should not be able to profit from his intentionally deceptive conduct.

Actual Reliance Reliance means that a person pursues some course of action because of his faith in an assertion made to him. For misrepresentation to exist, there must have been a causal connection between the assertion and the complaining party's decision to enter the contract. If the complaining party knew that the assertion was false or was not aware that an assertion had been made, there has been no reliance.

Justifiable Reliance Courts also scrutinize the reasonableness of the behavior of the complaining party by requiring that his reliance be *justifiable*. A person does not act justifiably if he relies on an assertion that is obviously false or not to be taken seriously.

One problem involving the justifiable reliance element is determining the extent to which the relying party is responsible for investigating the accuracy of the statement on which he relies. Classical contract law held that a person who did not attempt to discover readily discoverable facts generally was not justified in relying on the other party's statements about them. For example, under traditional law, a person would not be entitled to rely on the other party's assertions about facts that are a matter of public record or that could be discovered through a reasonable inspection of available documents or records. The extent of the responsibility placed on a relying party to conduct an independent investigation has declined in modern contract law, however. Today, a court might be more likely to follow the approach of section 172 of the *Restatement,* which provides that a relying party's failure to discover facts before entering the contract does not make his reliance unjustifiable unless the degree of his fault was so extreme as to amount to a failure to act in good faith and in accordance with reasonable standards of fair dealing. Thus, today's courts tend to place a greater degree of accountability on the person who makes the assertion rather than the person who relies on the assertion.

You will see a discussion of the elements of misrepresentation (in this case, allegedly fraudulent misrepresentation) in the following *Jordan* case.

Jordan v. Knafel   378 Ill. App.3d 219 (Ill. Ct. App. 2007)

In the spring of 1989, Karla Knafel, a singer, was performing in a band at a hotel in Indianapolis, Indiana. The Chicago Bulls were also in town to play the Indiana Pacers. After her performance, Knafel was approached by a National Basketball Association referee, who eventually introduced her to Michael Jordan over the telephone. Although Knafel declined Jordan's invitations to meet during the spring and summer of 1989, she and Jordan continued long-distance telephone conversations during that time.

In December 1989, three months after Jordan had married his wife, Knafel traveled to Chicago to meet Jordan, where they had unprotected sex. Thereafter, in November 1990, Knafel stayed with Jordan in Phoenix, Arizona, where they again had unprotected sex. In early 1991, Knafel learned that she was pregnant. Knafel "was convinced that she was carrying Jordan's baby," but kept silent about the pregnancy for some time. The Bulls were on their way to their first NBA championship and Jordan was earning large sums of money in product endorsements. Knafel alleged that as a result, Jordan was "troubled" when she told him "she was pregnant with his child" in the spring of 1991. He was worried about destroying his public image, which he and his agent had carefully cultivated, and was concerned about the loss of future endorsements. Knafel further alleged that Jordan demanded that she abort the baby, but because of her personal beliefs, she refused.

According to Knafel, during several conversations about the impending birth of the baby, she and Jordan discussed possible resolutions of their dilemma. In the spring of 1991, Jordan offered, and urged Knafel to accept, his proposed settlement agreement to "resolve their problems." Jordan offered to pay her $5 million when he retired from professional basketball in return for her agreement not to file a paternity suit against him and for her agreement to keep their romantic involvement publicly confidential. Knafel accepted Jordan's offer. In consideration for his promise to pay her, she agreed to forbear filing a public paternity action against him and agreed to keep their romantic relationship confidential.

In July 1991, Knafel's child was born. Jordan paid certain hospital bills and medical costs and paid Knafel $250,000 for "her mental pain and anguish arising from her relationship with him." Knafel did not file a paternity suit against Jordan and she kept their relationship confidential. A month after Knafel's baby's birth, a physician collected blood samples from Jordan, Knafel, and the baby and concluded that the "test exclude[d] Mr. Jordan from being the father" of the baby.

In October 1993, Jordan announced his retirement from the Bulls, but in March 1995, he returned again to the NBA to play for the Bulls. Knafel had not contacted Jordan to demand her payment of the $5 million which he had allegedly promised her until the summer of 1998, amid public speculation that Jordan would soon retire again. In September 1998, Knafel approached Jordan while he was vacationing in Las Vegas. During their conversation, Knafel reminded Jordan of his obligation to pay her the money under their agreement. Knafel alleged that Jordan reaffirmed his agreement to pay her the $5 million. A few months later, Jordan again retired from professional basketball.

Two years later, after Jordan had failed to pay the $5 million under the alleged agreement, Knafel's counsel contacted Jordan's counsel to resolve their contract dispute. Jordan filed for a declaratory judgment alleging that Knafel was attempting to extort $5 million from him and that, even if an agreement was made, the agreement was unenforceable because of fraud and mutual mistake. Knafel filed a counterclaim for breach of contract and Jordan filed a motion to dismiss this claim. The trial court dismissed Jordan's complaint and also dismissed Knafel's counterclaim. Both parties appealed.

The Illinois Court of Appeals reversed and remanded the case to the trial court for further proceedings. On remand, Jordan filed an amended complaint and motion for summary judgment on Knafel's counterclaim. In support, he attached an affidavit of the doctor who had done the genetic testing on Knafel's baby. Knafel filed an affidavit stating that she had believed in good faith that she was pregnant with Jordan's child, that she had informed Jordan throughout their relationship that she was having sex with another man, and that she had never told Jordan that she was using birth control. She also included a signed and dated office note from her physician, Dr. Grisanti, that stated that the baby was conceived on November 19 or 20, 1990, which is the same time period that she was with Jordan in Phoenix. After a hearing, the trial court granted Jordan's motion for summary judgment. Knafel appealed.

Theis, Justice

We must now consider what impact the paternity evidence has on the enforceability of the alleged agreement. Knafel argues that Jordan's actual paternity is irrelevant to the enforceability of the alleged settlement agreement as long as she has alleged a good-faith belief at the time of contracting that she was pregnant with Jordan's child. Jordan maintains that, based upon the uncontroverted evidence that he is not the father of Knafel's child, her statement to him at the time of the alleged settlement that "she was pregnant with his child" is a fraudulent misrepresentation as a matter of law which makes the contract voidable, permitting rescission.

Fraud in the inducement of a contract is a defense that renders the contract voidable at the election of the injured party. In order for a representation to constitute fraud that would permit a court to set aside a contract, the party seeking such relief must establish that the representation was: (1) one of material fact; (2) made for the purpose of inducing the other party to act; (3) known to be false by the maker, or not actually believed by him on reasonable grounds to be true, but reasonably believed to be true by the other party; and (4) was relied upon by the other party to his detriment.

Knafel asserts that there is a genuine issue of fact as to whether her affirmative representation to Jordan that "she was pregnant with his child" was material to the alleged settlement agreement and induced Jordan to act. Specifically, she argues that Jordan's actual paternity (1) was not a subject of discussion when they reached their settlement agreement; (2) it was not a term or contingent condition of their settlement agreement; and (3) Jordan has never actually stated that it was material to the agreement. Additionally, she maintains that she is entitled to an inference that Jordan's only motive was to preserve his image and protect his lucrative endorsements. A misrepresentation is "material" if the party seeking rescission would have acted differently had he been aware of the fact or if it concerned the type of information upon which he would be expected to rely when making his decision to act. To be material, the representation need not have been the "paramount or decisive inducement, so long as it was a substantial factor." R. Lord, *Williston on Contracts* § 69:12.

Contrary to Knafel's assertions, her own allegations establish that paternity was material to the alleged settlement agreement and was made for the purposes of inducing Jordan to act. Knafel alleged that in the spring of 1991, when she told Jordan "she was pregnant with his child," Jordan "became worried" and they "discussed possible resolutions of their dilemma." When she refused to get an abortion, Jordan then "proposed a settlement agreement which would resolve their problems." In her verified statement, she asserted that it was not until "after [she] told Jordan of [her] pregnancy" that "Jordan said he was troubled at the prospect of destroying his public image" and he agreed to the alleged settlement. Thus, although a general fear of public exposure of their relationship may well have been a factor when Jordan proposed the alleged settlement, it was not Jordan's only inducement. Rather, by Knafel's own account, her statement to Jordan that he was the father of her child was indeed material and a substantial factor in inducing Jordan to act. To hold otherwise would render her agreement not to file a paternity claim to have been a mere pretense to extort money. If Jordan's paternity was immaterial to the parties' settlement agreement, then her claim that she had a good-faith basis for a paternity action against Jordan would be unfounded. Without a good-faith basis, they would have lacked the necessary consideration for their bargain. Since consideration is a material element of a contract, Jordan's paternity must have been material to a good-faith settlement of her paternity claim.

Next, we consider whether there is a genuine issue of fact as to whether Knafel's representation was known to be false or not reasonably believed by her to be true at the time of the alleged agreement. Jordan argues that because Knafel represented to him with certainty that "she was pregnant with his child," yet paternity testing ultimately revealed that someone else was the father, it necessarily follows that at the time she told Jordan he was the father, she must have lacked certainty about the paternity of the child. Therefore, Knafel's knowledge of her uncertainty regarding paternity satisfies the "knowledge" element of fraudulent misrepresentation. When a party claims to know a material fact with certainty, yet knows that she does not have that certainty, the assertion constitutes a fraudulent misrepresentation. As applied to this context, when a woman categorically represents to a man that he is the father of her child, it is implicit in her representation that during the period of conception she had only one sexual partner. If the man is actually not the father, that representation is categorically false, and constitutes a fraudulent misrepresentation.

Here, at the time of contract formation, Knafel represented with certainty that she knew Jordan was the father of her child. However, the paternity tests reveal that it was also the case that she was having sexual relations with someone other than Jordan around the time of conception. Therefore, the evidence presented establishes that she knew that she lacked the certainty about the paternity of the child or, at least, knew that she did not have the basis that she stated or implied for that categorical representation, thus making it fraudulent.

To rebut that finding, Knafel asserts that she believed she had certainty about the paternity of her child, and in support of that state of mind, she relies on Dr. Grisanti's office memo regarding the timing of conception. However, the memo is insufficient to defeat summary judgment. Knafel merely states that the doctor's information regarding the dates of conception coincided with the dates she was with Jordan in Phoenix. That assertion does not discount that she knew she was also with another partner around that same time period. Although one could contemplate a situation where a pregnant woman could be subjectively certain about paternity, Knafel has presented no such affirmative evidence to support an adequate basis for her certainty. Additionally, Knafel argues that she indeed disclosed to Jordan throughout their relationship that she was having sex with another man. Nevertheless, the question is not whether she told him about her relationships with other men at some previous time, but whether she failed to disclose material information in the process of contract formation that would render the contract voidable.

Here, at the time of negotiating the settlement, Knafel was not forthcoming that she had sex with another partner at the time of conception. Instead, she made an affirmative representation with certainty that she was pregnant with Jordan's child. Her failure to disclose the information when she alone had access to that information amounts to a failure to act in good faith and in accordance with reasonable standards of fair dealing.

Finally, with respect to the element of reliance, Knafel initially argues that Jordan's failure to state that he relied upon Knafel's representation precludes summary judgment. However, "[w]here representations have been made in regard to a material matter and action has been taken, in the absence of evidence showing the contrary, it will be presumed that the representations were relied on." R. Lord, *Williston on Contracts* § 69:32. Knafel argues that Jordan's statements to her in 1998, that he remembered their agreement and would still pay her, despite his knowledge that he was not the child's father, supports an inference that, at the time he entered into the contract, he never relied on her representation that he was the father of the child. However, as stated previously, if the alleged agreement had nothing to do with his paternity, then the agreement was merely an agreement to keep their romantic relationship confidential and could no longer be construed as a settlement of her paternity claim with a confidentiality provision. Accordingly, based upon Knafel's own allegations, Jordan must have relied on the representation or the alleged settlement agreement was otherwise untenable. Furthermore, Jordan had a right to rely upon the categorical representation by Knafel that he was the father because [i]t would make little sense to compel a putative father to conduct an independent investigation in the face of a clear and categorical representation of a mother (who is also his sexual partner) as to his parentage. Additionally, we find no merit to Knafel's contention that Jordan should not have relied on the representation. Accordingly, for all of the foregoing reasons, the alleged settlement agreement was premised on a fraudulent misrepresentation and, therefore, was voidable by Jordan.

Alternatively, we consider Jordan's defense of mutual mistake of fact. Mutual mistake of fact provides that if a mistake by both parties "as to a basic assumption on which the contract was made has a material effect on the agreed exchange of performances, the contract is voidable by the adversely affected party unless he bears the risk of the mistake." *Restatement (Second) of Contracts* section 152. Here, even if Knafel's representation was not fraudulent and was made in good faith, her representation regarding paternity was ultimately mistaken as Jordan was not the father of the child. As we have already held, the issue of paternity went to a basic assumption upon which the contract was made because it was the consideration for the alleged settlement of her paternity claim. Knafel's certainty regarding Jordan's paternity had a material effect on the agreed exchange of performances, and Jordan did not bear the risk of mistake as a matter of law as he was not obligated to infer that Knafel had another sexual partner at the time of conception in the face of Knafel's categorical representation that Jordan was the father. Accordingly, Jordan is entitled to rescission based upon a mutual mistake of fact regarding paternity and summary judgment was properly granted in his favor on that basis.

Affirmed in favor of Jordan.

LOG ON

A number of useful sites provide information about the nature of Internet fraud and how to reduce the chances of being victimized. Some even provide a method of reporting Internet fraud. Here are a few examples:
National Fraud Information Center,
www.fraud.org/,
U.S. Securities and Exchange Commission, Internet Fraud: How to Avoid Internet Investment Scams,
www.sec.gov/investor/pubs/cyberfraud.htm.
For a good resource on identity theft and identity fraud, see the U.S. Department of Justice's Web page on the topic at
www.usdoj.gov/criminal/fraud/websites/idtheft.html.

Mistake

Nature of Mistake Anyone who enters a contract does so on the basis of his understanding of the facts that are relevant to the contract. His decision about what he is willing to exchange with the other party is based on this understanding. If the parties are wrong about an important fact, the exchange that they make is likely to be quite different than what they contemplated when they entered the contract, and this difference is due to simple error rather than to any external events such as an increase in market price. For example, Fox contracts to sell to Ward a half-carat stone, which both believe to be a tourmaline, at a price of $65. If they are

---

Misrepresentation and Fraud

	Innocent Misrepresentation	Fraud
Remedy Elements	Rescission	Rescission *and/or* tort action for damages
	1. Untrue assertion of fact (or equivalent)	1. Untrue assertion of fact (or equivalent)
	2. Assertion relates to material fact	2. Assertion made with knowledge of falsity (scienter) and intent to deceive
	3. Actual reliance	3. Justifiable reliance
	4. Justifiable reliance	4. Economic loss (in a tort action for damages)

---

wrong and the stone is actually a diamond worth at least $2,500, Fox will have suffered an unexpected loss and Ward will have reaped an unexpected gain. The contract would not have been made at a price of $65 if the parties' belief about the nature of the stone had been in accord with the facts. In such cases, the person adversely affected by the mistake can avoid the contract under the doctrine of mistake. The purpose of the doctrine of mistake is to prevent unexpected and unbargained for losses that result when the parties are mistaken about a fact central to their contract.

What Is a Mistake? In ordinary conversation, we may use the term *mistake* to mean an error in judgment or an unfortunate act. In contract law, however, a mistake is a *belief* about a fact that is *not in accord with the truth*.[3] The mistake must relate to facts as they exist at the time the contract is created. An erroneous belief or prediction about facts that might occur in the future would not qualify as a mistake.

As in misrepresentation cases, the complaining party in a mistake case enters a contract because of a belief that is at variance with the actual facts. Mistake is unlike misrepresentation, however, in that the erroneous belief is not the result of the other party's untrue statements.

Mistakes of Law A number of the older mistake cases state that mistake about a principle of law will not justify rescission. The rationale for this view was

that everyone was presumed to know the law. More modern cases, however, have granted relief even when the mistake is an erroneous belief about some aspect of law.

Negligence and the Right to Avoid for Mistake Although courts sometimes state that relief will not be granted when a person's mistake was caused by his own negligence, they often have granted rescission even when the mistaken party was somewhat negligent. Section 157 of the *Restatement (Second) of Contracts* focuses on the *degree* of a party's negligence in making the mistake. It states that a person's fault in failing to know or discover facts before entering the contract will not bar relief unless his fault amounted to a failure to act in good faith.

Effect of Mistake The mere fact that the contracting parties have made a mistake is not, standing alone, a sufficient ground for avoidance of the contract. The right to avoid a contract because of mistake depends on several factors that are discussed in following sections. One important factor that affects the right to avoid is whether the mistake was made by just one of the parties (**unilateral mistake**) or by both parties (**mutual mistake**).

Mutual Mistakes in Drafting Writings Sometimes, mutual mistake takes the form of erroneous *expression* of an agreement, frequently caused by a clerical error in drafting or typing a contract, deed, or other document. In such cases, the remedy is *reformation* of the writing

---

[3]*Restatement (Second) of Contracts* § 151.

rather than avoidance of the contract. Reformation means modification of the written instrument to express the agreement that the parties made but failed to express correctly. Suppose Arnold agrees to sell Barber a vacant lot next to Arnold's home. The vacant lot is "Lot 3, block 1"; Arnold's home is on "Lot 2, block 1." The person typing the contract strikes the wrong key, and the contract reads, "Lot 2, block 1." Neither Arnold nor Barber notices this error when they read and sign the contract, yet clearly they did not intend to have Arnold sell the lot on which his house stands. In such a case, a court will reform the contract to conform to Arnold and Baker's true agreement.

Requirements for Mutual Mistake   A mutual mistake exists when both parties to the contract have erroneous assumptions about the same fact. When *both* parties are mistaken, the resulting contract can be avoided if the three following elements are present:

1. The mistake relates to a basic assumption on which the contract was made.
2. The mistake has a material effect on the agreed-upon exchange.
3. The party adversely affected by the mistake does not bear the risk of the mistake.[4]

Note that the *Jordan* case, which appeared earlier in this chapter in the discussion of misrepresentation, also applied the doctrine of mutual mistake.

Mistake about a Basic Assumption   Even if the mistake is mutual, the adversely affected party will not have the right to avoid the contract unless the mistake concerns a basic assumption on which the contract was based. Assumptions about the identity, existence, quality, or quantity of the subject matter of the contract are among the basic assumptions on which contracts typically are founded. It is not necessary that the parties be consciously aware of the assumption; an assumption may be so basic that they take it for granted. For example, if Peterson contracts to buy a house from Tharp, it is likely that both of them assume at the time of contracting that the house is in existence and that it is legally permissible for the house to be used as a residence.

An assumption would not be considered a basic assumption if it concerns a matter that bears an indirect or collateral relationship to the subject matter of the contract. For example, mistakes about matters such as a party's financial ability or market conditions usually would not give rise to avoidance of the contract.

Material Effect on Agreed-Upon Exchange   It is not enough for a person claiming mistake to show that the exchange is something different from what he expected. He must show that the imbalance caused by the mistake is so severe that it would be unfair for the law to require him to perform the contract. He will have a better chance of establishing this element if he can show not only that the contract is *less* desirable for him because of the mistake but also that the other party has received an unbargained-for advantage.

Party Harmed by Mistake Did Not Bear the Risk of Mistake   Even if the first two elements are present, the person who is harmed by the mistake cannot avoid the contract if he is considered to bear the risk of mistake.[5] Courts have the power to allocate the risk of a mistake to the adversely affected person whenever it is reasonable under the circumstances to do so.

One situation in which an adversely affected person would bear the risk of mistake is when he has expressly contracted to do so. For example, if Buyer contracted to accept property "as is," he may be considered to have accepted the risk that his assumption about the quality of the property may be erroneous.

The adversely affected party also bears the risk of mistake when he contracts with *conscious awareness* that he is ignorant or has limited information about a fact—in other words, he *knows that he does not know* the true state of affairs about a particular fact but he binds himself to perform anyway. Suppose someone gives you an old, locked safe. Without trying to open it, you sell it and "all of its contents" to one of your friends for $25. When your friend succeeds in opening the safe, he finds $10,000 in cash. In this case, you would not be able to rescind the contract because, in essence, you gambled on your limited knowledge . . . and lost. *Estate of Nelson v. Rice,* which follows, illustrates the effect of conscious awareness and contractual assignments of risk.

---

[4]*Restatement (Second) of Contracts* § 152.

[5]*Restatement (Second) of Contracts* § 154.

Estate of Nelson v. Rice   12 P.3d 238 (Ariz. Ct. App. 2000)

Martha Nelson died in 1996, and Kenneth Newman and Edward Franz were appointed co-personal representatives of her estate. Newman and Franz hired Judith McKenzie-Larson to appraise the estate's personal property in preparation for an estate sale. McKenzie-Larson told them that she did not appraise fine art, and that if she saw any, they would need to hire an additional appraiser. McKenzie-Larson did not report finding any fine art, and relying on her silence and her appraisal, Newman and Franz priced the personal property and held an estate sale.

Carl Rice responded to the newspaper advertisement for the sale and attended it. At the sale he bought two oil paintings, paying the asking price of $60 for the two paintings. Rice had bought and sold some art, but he was not an educated purchaser, had never made more than $55 on any single piece, and had bought many pieces that turned out to be frauds, forgeries, or the work of lesser artists. Rice assumed that the paintings were not originals, given their price and the fact that the estate was managed by professionals. At home, he compared the signatures on the paintings to those in a book of artists' signatures, noticing that they appeared to be similar to that of Martin Johnson Heade. As they had done in the past, Rice and his wife sent pictures of the paintings to Christie's in New York, hoping that they might be Heade's work. Christie's authenticated the paintings, Magnolia Blossoms on Blue Velvet *and* Cherokee Roses, *as paintings by Heade and offered to sell them on consignment. Christie's subsequently sold the paintings at auction for $1,072,000. After subtracting the buyer's premium and the commission, the Rices realized $911,780 from the sale.*

Newman and Franz learned about the sale in February 1997 and sued McKenzie-Larson on behalf of the estate, believing that she was responsible for the estate's loss. The following November, they settled the lawsuit because McKenzie-Larson had no assets. In January 1998, the estate sued the Rices, alleging that the sale contract should be rescinded or reformed because of mistake and unconscionability. The estate moved for summary judgment, arguing that the parties were not aware that the transaction had involved fine art, believing instead that the paintings were relatively valueless decorations. The Rices filed a cross-motion for summary judgment arguing that the estate bore the risk of the mistake. The trial court denied the estate's motion for summary judgment and granted the Rices' cross-motion. The estate's motion for a new trial was denied, and the estate appealed.

Espinosa, Chief Judge

A contract may be rescinded on the ground of mutual mistake as to a basic assumption on which both parties made the contract. Furthermore, the parties' mutual mistake must have had such a material effect on the agreed exchange of performances as to upset the very bases of the contract. However, the mistake must not be one on which the party seeking relief bears the risk under the rules stated in § 154(b) of the Restatement. In concluding that the estate was not entitled to rescind the sale, the trial court found that, although a mistake had existed as to the value of the paintings, the estate bore the risk of that mistake under § 154(b) of the Restatement. Section 154(b) states that a party bears the risk of mistake when he is aware, at the time the contract is made, that he has only limited knowledge with respect to the facts to which the mistake relates but treats his limited knowledge as sufficient. In explaining that provision, the Washington Supreme Court stated, "In such a situation there is no mistake. Instead, there is an awareness of uncertainty or conscious ignorance of the future."

The estate contends neither party bore the risk of mistake. Through its personal representatives, the estate hired two appraisers, McKenzie-Larson and an Indian art expert, to evaluate the estate's collection of Indian art and artifacts. McKenzie-Larson specifically told Newman that she did not appraise fine art. In his deposition, Newman testified that he had not been concerned that McKenzie-Larson had no expertise in fine art, believing the estate contained nothing of "significant value" except the house and the Indian art collection. Despite the knowledge that the estate contained framed art other than the Indian art, and that McKenzie-Larson was not qualified to appraise fine art, the personal representatives relied on her to notify them of any fine art or whether a fine arts appraiser was needed. Because McKenzie-Larson did not say they needed an additional appraiser, Newman and Franz did not hire anyone qualified to appraise fine art. By relying on the opinion of someone who was admittedly unqualified to appraise fine art to determine its existence, the personal representatives consciously ignored the possibility that the estate's assets might include fine art, thus assuming that risk. See *Klas v. Van Wagoner* (real estate buyers not entitled to rescind sale contract because they bore risk of mistake as to property's value; by hiring architects, decorators, and electricians to examine realty, but failing to have it appraised, purchasers executed sale contract knowing they had only limited knowledge with respect to the value of the home). Accordingly, the trial court correctly found that the estate bore the risk of mistake as to the paintings' value.

The estate asserts that the facts here are similar to those in *Renner [v. Kehl]*, in which real estate buyers sued to rescind a contract for acreage upon which they wished to commercially grow jojoba after discovering the water supply was inadequate for that purpose. The Supreme Court concluded that the buyers could rescind the contract based upon mutual mistake because both the buyers and the sellers had believed there was an adequate water supply, a basic assumption underlying formation of the contract. The parties' failure to thoroughly investigate the water supply did not preclude rescission when the risk of mistake was not allocated among the parties. The estate's reliance on *Renner* is unavailing because, as stated above, the estate bore the risk of mistake based on its own conscious ignorance.

Furthermore, under Restatement § 154(c), the court may allocate the risk of mistake to one party "on the ground that it is reasonable in the circumstances to do so." In making this determination, "the court will consider the purposes of the parties and will have recourse to its own general knowledge of human behavior in bargain transactions." Here, the estate had had ample opportunity to discover what it was selling and failed to do so; instead, it ignored the possibility that the paintings were valuable and attempted to take action only after learning of their worth as a result of the efforts of the Rices. Under these circumstances, the estate was a victim of its own folly and it was reasonable for the court to allocate to it the burden of its mistake.

Affirmed in favor of the Rices.

Requirements for Unilateral Mistake

A unilateral mistake exists when only one of the parties makes a mistake about a basic assumption on which he made the contract. For example, Plummer contracts to buy from Taylor 25 shares of Worthwright Enterprises, Inc., mistakenly believing that he is buying 25 shares of the much more valuable Worthwrite Industries. Taylor knows that the contract is for the sale of shares of Worthwright. Taylor (the "nonmistaken party") is correct in his belief about the identity of the stock he is selling; only Plummer (the "mistaken party") is mistaken in his assumption about the identity of the stock. Does Plummer's unilateral mistake give him the right to avoid the contract? Courts are more likely to allow avoidance of a contract when both parties are mistaken than when only one is mistaken. The rationale for this tendency is that in cases of unilateral mistake, at least one party's assumption about the facts was correct, and allowing avoidance disappoints the reasonable expectations of that nonmistaken party.

It is possible to avoid contracts for unilateral mistake, but to do so, proving the elements necessary for mutual mistake is just a starting point. *In addition to* proving the elements of mistake discussed earlier, a person trying to avoid on the ground of unilateral mistake must show *either* one of the following:

1. *The nonmistaken party caused or had reason to know of the mistake.* Courts permit avoidance in cases of unilateral mistake if the nonmistaken party caused the mistake, knew of the mistake, or even if the mistake was so obvious that the nonmistaken party had reason to realize that a mistake had been made.[6] For example, Ace Electrical Company makes an error when preparing a bid that it submits to Gorge General Contracting. If the mistake in Ace's bid was so obvious that Gorge knew about it when it accepted Ace's offer, Ace could avoid the contract even though Ace is the only party who was mistaken. The reasoning behind this rule is that the nonmistaken person could have prevented the loss by acting in good faith and informing the person in error that he had made a mistake. It also reflects the judgment that people should not take advantage of the mistakes of others. *Or*

2. *It would be unconscionable to enforce the contract.* A court could also permit avoidance because of unilateral mistake when the effect of the mistake was such that it would be unconscionable to enforce the contract. To show that it would be unconscionable to enforce the contract, the mistaken party would have to show that the consequences of the mistake were severe enough that it would be unreasonably harsh or oppressive to enforce the contract.[7] In the example above, Ace Electrical Company made an error when preparing a bid that it submits to Gorge General Contracting. Suppose that Gorge had no reason to realize that a mistake had been made, and accepted the bid. Ace might show that it would be unconscionable to enforce the contract by showing that not only will its profit margin not be what Ace contemplated when it made its offer, but also that it would suffer a grave loss by having to perform at the mistaken price.

---

[6]*Restatement (Second) of Contracts* § 153.

[7]The concept of unconscionability is developed more fully in Chapter 15.

Avoidance on the Ground of Mistake

	Mutual Mistake	Unilateral Mistake
Description	Both parties mistaken about same fact	Only one party mistaken about a fact
Needed for Avoidance of Contract	Elements of mistake: 1. Mistake about basic assumption on which contract was made 2. Material effect on agreed exchange 3. Person adversely affected by mistake does not bear the risk of the mistake	Same elements as mutual mistake *Plus* a. Nonmistaken party caused mistake or had reason to know of mistake *Or* b. Effect of mistake is to make it unconscionable to enforce contract

Duress

Nature of Duress
Duress is wrongful coercion that induces a person to enter or modify a contract. One kind of duress is physical compulsion to enter a contract. For example, Thorp overpowers Grimes, grasps his hand, and forces him to sign a contract. This kind of duress is rare, but when it occurs, a court would find that the contract was void. A far more common type of duress occurs when a person is induced to enter a contract by a *threat* of physical, emotional, or economic harm. In these cases, the contract is considered *voidable* at the option of the victimized person. This is the form of duress addressed in this chapter.

The elements of duress have undergone dramatic changes. Classical contract law took a very narrow view of the type of coercion that constituted duress, limiting duress to threats of imprisonment or serious physical harm. Today, however, courts take a much broader view of the types of coercion that will constitute duress. For example, modern courts recognize that threats to a person's economic interests can be duress.

Requirements for Duress
To rescind a contract because of duress, one must be able to establish both of the following elements:

1. The contract was induced by an improper threat.
2. The victim had no reasonable alternative but to enter the contract.

Improper Threat It would not be desirable for courts to hold that every kind of threat constituted duress. If they did, the enforceability of all contracts would be in question, because every contract negotiation involves at least the implied threat that a person will not enter into the transaction unless her demands are met. What degree of wrongfulness, then, is required for a threat to constitute duress? Traditionally, a person would have to threaten to do something she was not legally entitled to do—such as threaten to commit a crime or a tort—for that threat to be duress. Some courts still follow that rule. Other courts today follow the *Restatement* position that, to be duress, the threat need not be wrongful or illegal but must be *improper*—that is, improper to use as leverage to induce a contract.

Under some circumstances, threats to institute legal actions can be considered improper threats that will constitute duress. A threat to file either a civil or a criminal suit without a legal basis for doing so would clearly be improper. What of a threat to file a well-founded lawsuit or prosecution? Generally, if there is a good faith dispute over a matter, a person's threat to file a lawsuit to resolve that dispute is *not* considered to be improper. Otherwise, every person who settled a suit out of court could later claim duress. However, if the threat to sue is made in bad faith and for a purpose unrelated to the issues in the lawsuit, the threat can be considered improper. In one case, for example, duress was found when a husband who was in the process of divorcing his wife threatened to sue for custody of their children—something he had the right to

CYBERLAW IN ACTION

Pricing Glitches on the Web: Legal, Ethical, and Marketing Issues

The accidental advertisement of a mistaken price for a product or service occurs sometimes in bricks-and-mortar businesses. But when e-tailers make price glitches, the impact is likely to be far greater, because news of extremely low prices travels fast on the Web through various bargain hunter Web sites and online bulletin boards, and by the time the company learns of and repairs the error, it may have confirmed hundreds of orders for the product or service. Amazon.com, United Air Lines, and Staples.com are a few of the e-commerce leaders that have experienced pricing glitches. In one widely reported incident, for example, United Air Lines' Web site accidentally listed mistaken fares to Paris and various other cities—$24.98 for a flight from San Francisco to Paris—for five hours on one day, and in that time, more than 140 people had booked trips based on the mistaken fares.[8]

Legally, the doctrine of mistake presents at least a possible avenue for avoidance of contracts that are formed based on a mistaken price, but this would depend on factors such as the size and obviousness of the discrepancy between the mistaken price and the intended price. Of equal or greater concern to the e-tailer is likely to be the issue of how to maintain good customer relations. Should it sell the product at the advertised price and absorb the loss? Refuse to honor the mistaken deal and perhaps offer the customer something else of value to preserve goodwill? Some commercial Web sites have a provision in their "Terms and Conditions" link that notifies customers of the possibility of pricing mistakes and purports to protect the company in cases of price glitches.

Ethical issues are also present in these situations. Is it ethical for an e-tailer to refuse to honor a contract that is based on a mistaken price? Is it ethical for a customer to insist on a contract that is based on a mistaken price?

[8]Frank Hayes, *A Deal's a Deal: Should Pricing Glitches Be Honored? Computerworld* 2/26/01, www.itworld.com/Tech/2403/CWSTO58053.

do—unless the wife transferred to him stock that she owned in his company.[9]

Victim Had No Reasonable Alternative The person complaining of duress must be able to prove that the coercive nature of the improper threat was such that he had no reasonable alternative but to enter or modify the contract. Classical contract law applied an objective standard of coercion, which required that the degree of coercion exercised had to be sufficient to overcome the will of a person of ordinary courage. The more modern standard for coercion focuses on the alternatives open to the complaining party. For example, Barry, a traveling salesman, takes his car to Cheatum Motors for repair. Barry pays Cheatum the full amount previously agreed upon for the repair, but Cheatum refuses to return Barry's car to him unless Barry agrees to pay substantially more than the contract price for the repairs. Because of his urgent need for the return of his car, Barry agrees to do this. In this case, Barry technically had the alternative of filing a legal action to recover his car. However, this would not be a *reasonable alternative* for someone who needs the car urgently because of the time, expense, and uncertainty involved in pursuing a lawsuit. Thus, Barry

[9]*Link v. Link,* 179 S.E.2d 697 (1971).

could avoid his agreement to pay more money under a theory of duress.

Economic Duress   Today, the doctrine of duress is often applied in a business context. *Economic duress,* or *business compulsion,* are terms commonly used to describe situations in which one person induces the formation or modification of a contract by threatening another person's economic interests. A common coercive strategy is to threaten to breach the contract unless the other party agrees to modify its terms. For example, Moore, who has contracted to sell goods to Stephens, knows that Stephens needs timely delivery of the goods. Moore threatens to withhold delivery unless Stephens agrees to pay a higher price. Another common situation involving economic duress occurs when one of the parties offers a disproportionately small amount of money in settlement of a debt and refuses to pay more. Such a strategy can exert great economic pressure on a creditor who is in a desperate financial situation to accept the settlement because he cannot afford the time and expense of bringing a lawsuit.

When are negotiation tactics improper and coercive and when are they merely hard but permissible bargaining? The following *Cabot Corporation* case concerns that question.

Cabot Corporation v. AVX Corporation
863 N.E.2d 503 (Sup. Jud. Ct. Mass. 2007)

AVX Corporation manufactures capacitors for electronic products. Tantalum, an elemental metal as rare in nature as uranium, is used in the manufacture of AVX's products. Cabot Corporation is a major supplier of tantalum powder and wire and supplied AVX with tantalum products for many years.

The market for tantalum has been volatile. In the late 1990s, the tantalum market favored buyers and AVX purchased tantalum from Cabot at preferable prices without entering binding, long-term contracts. Each year, the parties signed "letters of intent," setting forth estimates of AVX's anticipated needs and agreed-on prices for each type of product. Cabot attempted to convince AVX to enter into long-term supply or "take or pay" contracts—contracts that set forth a mandatory amount of product to be purchased and require a buyer to pay for the product even if the buyer does not take it—but AVX resisted this alteration to their relationship.

By April 2000, Cabot was supplying about 20 percent of AVX's total tantalum requirements. Later in 2000, a worldwide shortage of tantalum developed and demand for electronic products using tantalum capacitors reached unprecedented levels. Orders from some of AVX's customers increased by more than 200 percent and AVX announced a dramatic increase in sales over prior years. Supplies of raw tantalum were severely limited. Cabot and other tantalum product manufacturers found it difficult to satisfy the rising demand for tantalum products, resulting in a steep rise in its price throughout the industry.

In August 2000, Cabot notified all of its customers that, in the future, it proposed to commit its limited production capacity to those customers who were prepared to enter into binding, long-term supply contracts. Between August and November 2000, Cabot and AVX negotiated the terms of a binding, long-term supply contract. Proposals and counterproposals were exchanged. Both parties were represented by highly competent legal counsel throughout the process. Cabot and AVX memorialized the terms of a basic agreement to a binding, five-year contract, under which AVX would purchase specified quantities of tantalum powder and wire at stated prices. In an e-mail sent to a Cabot executive regarding the agreed terms, the president and chief executive officer of AVX wrote, "I think we have a fair agreement for both parties . . . hope you agree." The prices agreed to were no higher than the then-current market prices for tantalum products. Cabot agreed to AVX's demand of "most favored customer" protection. AVX also obtained a right to purchase additional tantalum products in the event that Cabot was to expand its plant capacity. In addition, the parties agreed that the agreement would supersede all prior agreements (including the letters of intent) and released each other from all claims arising under any prior agreements. The supply contract was signed and effective as of January 1, 2001. During the first half of 2001, demand for tantalum products and capacitors remained high. AVX insisted that Cabot make deliveries of tantalum products in strict compliance with the terms of the supply contract. When Cabot fell behind on shipments because of production constraints, AVX pressed Cabot "to catch up on the contract." Throughout the supply contract's five-year term, both AVX and Cabot performed under its terms.

In July 2002, more than 20 months after the supply contract was negotiated, and more than 18 months after it was signed, AVX filed an action against Cabot in federal court. AVX alleged that the 2000 letters of intent were binding contracts and that the supply contract was void because it had been executed by AVX under economic duress. AVX asserted that in the negotiation of the supply contract, Cabot had pursued a strategy of starving it of product and threatening to breach the existing short-term agreement unless AVX agreed to its terms. This action was dismissed for lack of jurisdiction. Cabot then filed an action for a declaratory judgment, seeking a declaration that the supply contract was a valid and binding contract, and that the 2000 letters of intent were not binding contracts, and were, in any event, superseded by the supply contract. In its answer, AVX asserted economic duress with regard to the supply contract, and filed various counterclaims. Cabot filed a motion for partial summary judgment, which the trial court granted. AVX appealed.

Cordy, Judge

It is well established that a contract entered into under duress is voidable. Such duress need not be physical; it may be economic in nature. To show economic duress (1) a party must show that he has been the victim of a wrongful or unlawful act or threat, and (2) such act or threat must be one which deprives the victim of his unfettered will. To show duress, a victim "must go beyond the mere showing of a reluctance to accept [and] financial embarrassment" and show that acts of the other party produced these factors. S. 28 Williston, *Contracts,* at § 71:7. Thus, in order to substantiate the allegation of economic duress or business compulsion, there must be a showing of acts on the part of the defendant which produced [the financial embarrassment]. The assertion of duress must be proved by evidence that the duress resulted from defendant's wrongful and oppressive conduct and not by plaintiff's necessities.

AVX bears the burden of proving that the supply contract it entered into with Cabot was executed under economic duress. AVX and Cabot are sophisticated and substantial commercial parties. They were represented by highly competent counsel in their negotiations of a contract that was to govern their commercial relationship over the long term, and to settle their differences over the validity of prior agreements, purchase orders, and letters of intent. In these circumstances, we will strictly construe the requirements of economic duress against the party asserting it, so as not to undercut the well-established public policy favoring the private settlement of disputes.

There is no dispute that the strength of Cabot's bargaining position in negotiating the supply contract, as well as AVX's weakened position, were the result of a worldwide shortage of the rare tantalum product, at a time when AVX was facing a rapidly growing demand from its customers for the type of capacitors it manufactured. Cabot did not create the situation— it merely took advantage of it. The parties also acknowledge, as they must, that it is not infrequent that when two commercial parties enter into an agreement, one of them has a decided economic advantage over the other, and that the weaker party often must enter into the bargain because of his economic circumstances, a disparity in bargaining power to his disadvantage, or some combination of the two. Because an element of economic duress is thus present when many contracts are formed or releases given, the ability of a party to disown his obligations under a contract or release on that basis is reserved for extreme and extraordinary cases. Hard bargaining is not unlawful.

Absent any legally cognizable restraint, Cabot was free to drive whatever bargain the market would bear. AVX contends, however, that Cabot did not just engage in hard bargaining, it acted wrongfully in threatening to withhold tantalum deliveries to AVX in violation of the terms of the letters of intent, in order to coerce AVX into signing the supply contract. Of course, if the letters of intent were not binding contracts, it would not have been wrongful for Cabot to have declined to abide by them. Nor would it have been wrongful (in the sense of economic duress) if there was a good faith belief by Cabot that its position represented a plausible one under the letters of intent. The language in the letters of intent that "[i]t is AVX's intention to purchase the following materials" is not a binding commitment by AVX to make any purchases at all. There is no evidence in the record that Cabot threatened to withhold this product in the fall of 2000 in an attempt to coerce AVX into signing the supply contract.

In addition to establishing that Cabot acted wrongfully in order to coerce AVX into signing the supply contract, AVX must also prove that it had no feasible alternative in the face of this wrongful conduct but to enter into the supply contract. If AVX believed that Cabot was threatening to commit a breach of a binding contract by withholding a scarce product critical to its business in order to coerce a disproportionate bargain, AVX could have gone immediately to court and sought preliminary injunctive relief followed by declaratory relief on the merits of its claim. While recourse to courts of law may not be an adequate remedy if it is not quick enough to save the victim's business or property interests, that is not the case here. Such relief is ordinarily granted, if meritorious, within ten days of the filing of a complaint in State or Federal court. In contrast, the negotiations prompted by Cabot's threats took almost four months to complete.

Even if we were to conclude that material facts regarding the existence of economic duress remain in dispute, Cabot nonetheless would be entitled to summary judgment because AVX ratified the contract by its actions. A contract that is voidable for duress may be ratified and affirmed. A party must complain promptly of coercive acts that allegedly forced it into the contract or the defense of duress is waived, and the contract ratified. The requirement that the party claiming duress disclaim the contract or release about which he is complaining promptly or be held to have forfeited his right to do so protects the stability and reliability of such agreements by denying the weaker party the "heads I win, tails you lose" option of waiting to see how the arrangement works out and then deciding whether to seek to undo it. A party may ratify an agreement entered into under duress in a number of different ways: first, by intentionally accepting benefits under the contract; second, by remaining silent or acquiescing in the contract for a period of time after he has the opportunity to avoid it; and third, by recognizing its validity by acting upon it, performing under it, or by affirmatively acknowledging it.

The supply agreement was executed in January 2001, and the first time AVX asserted duress was in July 2002. This lengthy period of silence is powerful (if not conclusive) evidence of ratification. Ratification is further evidenced by AVX's performance under the contract. During 2001, while the market for electronic capacitors remained strong, AVX accepted the benefits afforded it under the terms of the supply contract, purchased Cabot's tantalum products necessary to its manufacture of capacitors, and demanded that Cabot deliver those products in the quantities and in the time frames specified therein. AVX cannot simply accept the terms of a supply contract favorable to it, obtain the supply it needs, and claim it did not intend to ratify the contract because some terms were unfavorable to it. Stated otherwise, it cannot wait to see how the arrangement works out and then decide whether to seek to undo it.

Judgment affirmed in favor of Cabot.

CONCEPT REVIEW

Wrongful Pressure in the Bargaining Process

	Duress	Undue Influence
Nature of Pressure	Coercion	Unfair persuasion of susceptible individual
Elements	1. Contract induced by improper threat 2. Threat leaves party no reasonable alternative but to enter or modify contract	1. Relationship of trust and confidence or dominance 2. Unfair persuasion

Undue Influence

Nature of Undue Influence
Undue influence is unfair persuasion. Like duress, undue influence involves wrongful pressure exerted on a person during the bargaining process. In undue influence, however, the pressure is exerted through *persuasion* rather than through coercion. The doctrine of undue influence was developed to give relief to persons who are unfairly persuaded to enter a contract while in a position of weakness that makes them particularly vulnerable to being preyed upon by those they trust or fear. A large proportion of undue influence cases arise after the death of the person who has been the subject of undue influence, when his relatives seek to set aside that person's contracts or wills.

Determining Undue Influence
All contracts are based on persuasion. There is no precise dividing line between permissible persuasion and impermissible persuasion. Nevertheless, several hallmarks of undue influence cases can be identified. Undue influence cases normally involve both of the following elements:

1. The relationship between the parties is either one of trust and confidence or one in which the person exercising the persuasion dominates the person being persuaded.

2. The persuasion is unfair.[10]

Relation between the Parties   Undue influence cases involve people who, though they have capacity to enter a contract, are in a position of particular vulnerability in relationship to the other party to the contract. This relationship can be one of trust and confidence, in which the person being influenced justifiably believes that the other party is looking out for his interests, or at least that he would not do anything contrary to his welfare. Examples of such relationships would include parent and child, husband and wife, or lawyer and client.

The relationship also can be one in which one of the parties holds dominant psychological power that is not derived from a confidential relationship. For example, Royce, an elderly man, is dependent on his housekeeper, Smith, to care for him. Smith persuades Royce to withdraw most of his life savings from the bank and make an interest-free loan to her. If the persuasion Smith used was unfair, the transaction could be voided because of undue influence.

Unfair Persuasion   The mere existence of a close or dependent relationship between the parties that results in economic advantage to one of them is not sufficient for undue influence. It must also appear that the weaker person entered the contract because he was subjected to unfair methods of persuasion. In determining this, a court will look at all of the surrounding facts and circumstances. Was the person isolated and rushed into the contract, or did he have access to outsiders for advice and time to consider his alternatives? Was the contract discussed and consummated in the usual time and place that would be expected for such a transaction, or was it discussed or consummated at an unusual time or in an unusual place? Was the contract a reasonably fair one that a person might have entered voluntarily, or was it so lopsided and unfair that one could infer that he probably would not have entered it unless he had been unduly influenced by the other party? The answers to these and similar questions help determine whether the line between permissible and impermissible persuasion has been crossed.

---

[10]*Restatement (Second) of Contracts* § 177.

Problems and Problem Cases

1. Mestrovic, the widow of an internationally known sculptor and artist, owned a large number of works of art created by her late husband. Mestrovic died, leaving a will in which she directed that all the works of art created by her husband were to be sold and the proceeds distributed to surviving members of the Mestrovic family. Mestrovic also owned real estate at the time of her death. 1st Source Bank, as the personal representative of the Mestrovic estate, entered into a contract to sell this real estate to the Wilkins. After taking possession of the property, the Wilkins complained to the bank that the property was left in a cluttered condition and would require substantial cleaning efforts. The trust officer of the bank offered the Wilkins two options: Either the bank would get a rubbish removal service to clean the property or the Wilkins could clean the property and keep any items of personal property they wanted. The Wilkins opted to clean the property themselves. At the time these arrangements were made, neither the bank nor the Wilkins suspected that any works of art remained on the property. During the cleanup efforts, the Wilkins found eight drawings apparently created by Mestrovic's husband. They also found a plaster sculpture of the figure of Christ with three small children. The Wilkins claimed ownership of these works of art by virtue of their agreement with the bank. The bank claimed that there was no agreement for the sale of the artwork and that there had been mutual mistake. Is the bank correct?

2. In 2001, Turner applied for a life insurance policy from Alfa Life Insurance through Eddins, an Alfa agent. Eddins read the questions to Turner, and he recorded her answers on the application. The application specifically provided: "IF ANY ANSWER TO THE FOLLOWING QUESTIONS IS 'YES,' THE PROPOSED INSURED IS NOT ELIGIBLE FOR COVERAGE." Question 12 following this statement was: "Have you ever been diagnosed with insulin-dependent diabetes?" Question 14 was: "In the past 24 months have you been diagnosed WITH or hospitalized for Congestive Heart Failure?" The application also contained the following:

AGREEMENT: The foregoing answers are complete and true to the best of my knowledge and belief.

I HAVE TRULY ANSWERED THE ABOVE QUESTIONS AND I HAVE READ OR HAD READ TO ME, THE COMPLETE APPLICATION. I REALIZE THAT MY FALSE STATEMENTS or MISREPRESENTATIONS OR CONCEALMENTS WHICH WOULD AFFECT THE ACCEPTANCE OF THE RISK ASSUMED MAY RESULT IN LOSS OF COVERAGE . . .

Turner signed the application completed by Eddins. This application indicated a negative response to questions 12 and 14. Alfa issued the policy, naming Turner's daughter, Lewis, as the owner and the beneficiary of the policy. In March 2002, Turner died. Shortly thereafter, Lewis submitted a Request for Insurance Benefits. In that request, Lewis indicated that the cause of Turner's death was congestive heart failure. Alfa began an investigation into Lewis's request for benefits and, as part of that investigation, obtained Turner's medical records from her physician. Upon reviewing those medical records, Alfa learned that Turner had been an insulin-dependent diabetic before the date on which Turner completed the application for life insurance. Turner's medical records also indicated that she had been diagnosed with congestive heart failure within the 24 months preceding her filing the application for life insurance with Alfa. Turner's primary treating physician listed on Alfa's Attending Physician Statement that the immediate cause of Turner's death was a pulmonary embolus, but congestive heart failure and diabetes were contributory causes of her death. Upon learning this information, Alfa sought to rescind the life insurance policy issued to Turner, arguing that the incorrect statements provided on the application regarding Turner's health were material to its acceptance of the risk and to the amount and cost of the policy coverage. Lewis argued that during the application process, Turner had told Eddins she was a diabetic and that she had previously been on insulin but that she "now took pills instead." Lewis and Phillips also attested that Eddins responded that the fact that Turner was diabetic could be a problem but that he would "put [the application] through." Lewis also claimed that neither Turner nor any of her family members had ever been told of her physician's diagnosis of congestive heart failure. Lewis asserted that Turner answered question 14 (regarding congestive heart failure) to the best of her ability and knowledge and that Turner could not provide information to Alfa that she did not have. Did Alfa have the right to rescind the insurance contract based on misrepresentation?

3. Rodi was recruited to the defendant law school, which had provisional accreditation, by statements indicating that accreditation would be forthcoming.

(However, the school's catalog, which was sent to Rodi, stated that it made no representations about accreditation.) After his first year, the school was still unaccredited and he considered transfer. Accreditation was essential for him to sit for the New Jersey bar. The acting dean of the school learned of Rodi's intentions and wrote him that there was "no cause for pessimism" about accreditation. In fact, however, the school had strayed farther away from accreditation standards. The school was not accredited by the time Rodi graduated, and he was unable to sit for the New Jersey bar. He sued the acting dean and the law school for fraud. Should his complaint be dismissed?

4. Odorizzi, an elementary school teacher, was arrested on criminal charges involving illegal sexual activity. After he was arrested, questioned by police, booked, and released on bail, and had gone 40 hours without sleep, he was visited in his home by the superintendent of the school district and the principal of his school. They told him that they were trying to help him and that they had his best interests at heart. They advised him to resign immediately, stating that there was no time to consult an attorney. They said that if he did not resign immediately, the district would dismiss him and publicize the proceedings, but that if he resigned at once, the incident would not be publicized and would not jeopardize his chances of securing employment as a teacher elsewhere. Odorizzi gave them a written letter of resignation, which they accepted. The criminal charges against Odorizzi were later dismissed, and he sought to resume his employment. When the school district refused to reinstate him, Odorizzi attempted to rescind his letter of resignation on several grounds, including undue influence. (He also alleged duress, but the facts of his case did not constitute duress under applicable state law.) Can Odorizzi avoid the contract on the ground of undue influence?

5. The Cherrys bought a home from the McCalls. After the Cherrys bought the home, they discovered a walled-in room in the basement. The room was filled with trash, including rusty plumbing fixtures, bathtubs, sinks, commodes, boards, pipes, rocks, and used building materials. The trash was damp and contaminated with mold. In the sales contract with the McCalls, the Cherrys contracted to accept the property "in its present condition," or "as is." The Cherrys claim that the walled-in room

constitutes a mutual mistake justifying rescission. Are they correct?

6. Boskett, a part-time coin dealer, paid $450 for a dime purportedly minted in 1916 at Denver and two additional coins of relatively small value. After carefully examining the dime, Beachcomber Coins, a retail coin dealer, bought the coin from Boskett for $500. Beachcomber then received an offer from a third party to purchase the dime for $700, subject to certification of its genuineness from the American Numismatic Society. That organization labeled the coin a counterfeit. Can Beachcomber rescind the contract with Boskett on the ground of mistake?

7. Retailer opened a baseball card store in vacant premises next to an existing store. The card shop was very busy on opening day, so Retailer got a clerk from the adjacent store to help out. The clerk knew nothing about baseball cards. A boy who had a large baseball card collection asked to see an Ernie Banks rookie card, which was in a plastic case with an adhesive dot attached that read "1200." The boy asked the salesclerk, "Is it really worth $12?" The salesclerk responded, "I guess so," or "I'm sure it is." The boy bought the card for $12. In fact, the true price intended by Retailer was $1,200. Can Retailer get the card back from the boy?

8. Keith contracted to build a house for Radford. Shortly before the closing, he met with Radford, accused her of fraud, and threatened to prevent the deal from closing. During the meeting, Keith's associate stood outside the door for two hours to prevent her from leaving. He gave her the choice of signing a Note and Deed of Trust promising to pay him more money or of going to court to settle the matter. Radford signed the agreement, but later sought to rescind it. Should she be able to rescind the agreement?

9. The Fritzes owned a home and five acres of land. They decided to move and rent the house, placing it with a rental agent to manage the property as a rental. The rental agent rented the house to a group of tenants who used the house for illegal drug activity. They used the rear deck and hot tub of the house as a methamphetamine lab and the basement as a marijuana growing operation. These activities were discovered by the local Narcotics Task Force, and two of the tenants were charged with manufacturing methamphetamine. The local newspaper published

an article in which it identified the property and the people involved in the illegal activity. The Fritzes learned from law enforcement that the task force had confiscated a marijuana growing operation and implements of a methamphetamine lab from their property. The tenants were evicted and the Fritzes subsequently decided to sell the property. In preparation for the sale, they cleaned the house, painted it, and changed the floor coverings. The Bloors moved to the area in 2004 and began looking for a home to purchase. When they were shown the Fritzes' property, they decided to make an offer to buy it. Mr. Fritz completed a seller's disclosure statement in which he represented that the property had never been used as an illegal drug manufacturing site. Although there was evidence that the real estate broker who represented both the Fritzes and the Bloors knew that the drug task force had discovered a marijuana growing operation and methamphetamine lab on the property, he did not disclose it to the Bloors. The Fritzes accepted the Bloors' offer, and the Bloors moved into the house in August 2004. In September, the Bloors' son heard from a member of the community that the property was known as a "drug house." The Bloors then began investigating and found an online version of the news article about the drug bust. Mrs. Bloor contacted the drug task force and learned that the task force had confiscated a methamphetamine lab at the property. In October, the County Health Department notified the Bloors that the property was contaminated by the methamphetamine manufacturing and was not fit for occupancy. Occupancy of buildings contaminated by methamphetamine manufacturing is dangerous to the health and safety of occupants. The Bloors were not even allowed to remove their personal property from the house because of the risk of cross-contamination. They left the house, leaving nearly all of their personal belongings in the house and garage. The health department posted an order prohibiting use of the property. The order stated that the Bloors were financially responsible for the cost of remediation, that a certified decontamination contractor would have to perform the remediation, and that use of the property was subject to criminal charges. The Bloors stayed with relatives until they could secure a place to live, eventually moving to another city. They had to repurchase clothing, bedding, furniture, and other necessities. They were unable to both support themselves and make their monthly mortgage payments. Do the Bloors have grounds for rescinding the purchase of the house?

10. Stambovky, a resident of New York City, contracted to buy a house in the Village of Nyack, New York, from Ackley. The house was widely reputed to be possessed by poltergeists, which Ackley and members of her family had reportedly seen and reported to both *Reader's Digest* and the local press. In 1989, the house was included in a five-home walking tour of Nyack and described in a newspaper article as a "riverfront Victorian (with ghost)." Ackley did not tell Stambovsky about the poltergeists before he bought the house. When Stambovsky learned of the house's reputation, however, he promptly sued for rescission. Will he be successful?

Online Research

Researching Internet Fraud

Using your favorite search engine, locate an article on Internet fraud. What is the number one form of Internet fraud in recent years?

Consider completing the case "FRAUD: Blind Dates Go Bust" from the You Be the Judge Web site element after you have read this chapter. Visit our Web site at **www.mhhe.com/mallor14e** for more information and activities regarding this case segment.

chapter 14

CAPACITY TO CONTRACT

In a state in which the age of majority for contracting purposes is 18, 17-year-old Daniel was married, employed, and living with his wife in their own apartment. Daniel and his wife went to Mattox Motors, a used car dealership, and purchased a used car for $500 cash. After driving the car for several months, Daniel was involved in a serious collision and damaged the car. He was one week over the age of 18 at this time. The next day, Daniel sent a letter to Mattox Motors stating that he was disaffirming the sales contract because he was underage at the time he entered the contract, and that he wanted his money back.

- Does Daniel have the right to get out of his contract?
- Does Mattox Motors have to give him his money back?
- Would it make a difference if Daniel had used the car to earn a living?
- If, instead of being a minor at the time the contract was made, Daniel had been mentally disabled or intoxicated, would he have the right to get out of the contract?
- Is it ethical for Daniel to disaffirm the contract after having wrecked the car?

ONE OF THE MAJOR justifications for enforcing a contract is that the parties voluntarily consented to be bound by it. It follows, then, that a person must have the *ability* to give consent before he can be legally bound to an agreement. For truly voluntary agreements to exist, this ability to give consent must involve more than the mere physical ability to say yes or shake hands or sign one's name. Rather, the person's maturity and mental ability must be such that it is fair to presume that he is capable of representing his own interests effectively. This concept is embodied in the legal term *capacity*.

What Is Capacity?

Capacity means the ability to incur legal obligations and acquire legal rights. Today, the primary classes of people who are considered to lack capacity are minors (who, in legal terms, are known as *infants*), persons suffering from mental illnesses or defects, and intoxicated persons.[1] Contract law gives them the right to *avoid* (escape) contracts that they enter during incapacity. This rule provides

a means of protecting people who, because of mental impairment, intoxication, or youth and inexperience, are disadvantaged in the normal give-and-take of the bargaining process.

Usually, lack of capacity to contract comes up in court in one of two ways. In some cases, it is asserted by a plaintiff as the basis of a lawsuit for the money or other benefits that he gave the other party under their contract. In others, it arises as a defense to the enforcement of a contract when the defendant is the party who lacked capacity. The responsibility for alleging and proving incapacity is placed on the person who bases his claim or defense on his lack of capacity.

Effect of Lack of Capacity Normally, a contract in which one or both parties lack capacity because of infancy, mental impairment, or intoxication is considered to be voidable. People whose capacity is impaired in any of these ways are able to enter a contract and enforce it if they wish, but they also have the right to avoid the contract. There are, however, some individuals whose capacity is so impaired that they do not have the ability to form even a voidable contract. A bargain is considered to be void if, at the time of formation of the bargain, a court had already **adjudicated** (adjudged or decreed) one or more of the parties to be mentally incompetent or one or

---

[1] In times past, married women, convicts, and aliens were also among the classes of persons who lacked capacity to contract. These limitations on capacity have been removed by statute and court rule, however.

more of the parties was so impaired that he could not even manifest assent (for example, he was comatose or unconscious).

Capacity of Minors

Minors' Right to Disaffirm
Courts have long recognized that minors are in a vulnerable position in their dealings with adults. Courts granted minors the right to avoid contracts as a means of protecting against their own improvidence and against overreaching by adults. The exercise of this right to avoid a contract is called **disaffirmance.** The right to disaffirm is personal to the minor. That is, only the minor or a legal representative

such as a guardian may disaffirm the contract. No formal act or written statement is required to make a valid disaffirmance. Any words or acts that effectively communicate the minor's desire to cancel the contract can constitute disaffirmance.

If, on the other hand, the minor wishes to enforce the contract instead of disaffirming it, the adult party must perform. You can see that the minor's right to disaffirm puts any adult contracting with a minor in an undesirable position: He is bound on the contract unless it is to the minor's advantage to disaffirm it. The right to disaffirm has the effect of discouraging adults from dealing with minors.

The following *Stroupes* case illustrates the application of the minor's right to disaffirm.

Stroupes v. The Finish Line, Inc.
2005 U.S. Dist. LEXIS 6975 (U.S. Dist. Ct. E.D. Tenn. 2005)

In the spring of 2003, Lindsey Stroupes was 16 years old and a sophomore in high school. While Lindsey was working at the Cookie Company, a store in Northgate Mall, Anthony Bradley, the manager of Finish Line's retail store in the mall, approached Lindsey and invited her to apply for a position at Finish Line. Lindsey accepted this invitation and applied for a position as a sales associate at Finish Line. Finish Line and Bradley hired Lindsey for this position. At some point, Lindsey signed an employment application. Part of this required that all claims against Finish Line be submitted to binding arbitration. Lindsey claims that Bradley sexually harassed her and committed assault, battery, and outrageous conduct. She and her parents (as her guardians) sued both Finish Line and Bradley. Both defendants moved to dismiss her suit and compel arbitration based on the arbitration clause in the employment application that Lindsey signed, which became part of her contract of employment.

R. Allan Edgar, Chief U.S. District Judge

In determining whether there is a valid arbitration agreement "courts . . . should apply ordinary state-law principles that govern formation of contracts." *First Options of Chicago, Inc. v. Kaplan* (1995). The general law in Tennessee regarding the validity of minor's contracts is clear: A minor's contracts, generally speaking, are voidable. The minor can repudiate such contracts or can elect to claim their advantage. Based on this infancy doctrine, the plaintiffs contend that, because Lindsey was sixteen years old when she began working for Finish Line, her Finish Line employment contract was voidable, and Lindsey effectively voided the contract by filing the instant action.

Essentially, the defendants urge this court to hold that the infancy doctrine does not apply to minor's employment contracts. To support the proposition that minors cannot void employment contracts, the defendants point to *Sheller v. Frank's Nursery & Crafts, Inc.* (N.D. Ill. 1997). In *Sheller* the district court considered whether minors pursuing sexual harassment claims against their employer must submit their claims to arbitration pursuant to an arbitration agreement in their employment contract. The minors argued that their employment contracts, including the

arbitration agreement, were voidable under Illinois' infancy doctrine. The district court rejected the minors' argument, finding that the employment contracts were not voidable under the infancy doctrine. As a basis for its holding, the court relied on three public policy rationales.

Because *Sheller* is an opinion of the Northern District of Illinois involving Illinois law, it is of limited precedential value here. Further, the court disagrees with the reasoning in that case. As its first support, *Sheller* relies on the policy rationale that the infancy doctrine "is to be used as a shield and not as a sword." However, this limitation is inapplicable to the instant situation. Lindsey is not using her minority as a sword to injure the defendants. Indeed, the only issue affected by Lindsey's use of the infancy doctrine is the appropriate forum to adjudicate her claims.

As a second basis for its holding, *Sheller* notes that the infancy "doctrine is to protect the inexperienced minor in their dealings with others." Applying this policy to the facts, *Sheller* reasoned that the plaintiffs' status as "minors was irrelevant to their signing of the employment application agreeing to arbitrate all claims against the company. Indeed, defendant required all of its employees, including adults, to sign the same agreement." Based in part on this reasoning, *Sheller* prohibited the minors from using the infancy doctrine to disaffirm their employment contracts. If *Sheller*'s reasoning in this regard were extended, it would eviscerate the infancy doctrine altogether. For example, under *Sheller*, any employment contract in which minors and adults alike must sign is not voidable by minors, because adults are bound by the same agreement. To extend the example to the consumer context, any contract for the purchase of an automobile signed by minors and adults alike is not voidable by minors, because adults are bound by the same agreement. If such were true, the infancy doctrine, permitting minors to disaffirm their contracts, would cease to exist.

As its final point, *Sheller* notes that "the minor is not entitled to retain an advantage from a transaction which he repudiates." Applying this policy to prohibit minors from disaffirming their employment contracts with the infancy doctrine, *Sheller* reasoned as follows:

> The fundamental reason Plaintiffs are able to bring this lawsuit is because they were employed by Defendant. Had they not been employed by Defendant, they would not be eligible to maintain the instant Title VII suit, obviously. Had they not signed the employment application which contained the arbitration clause, they would not have been hired by Defendant. Thus, if the Court were to allow the minor Plaintiffs to disaffirm the contract, Plaintiffs would be retaining the advantage of employment—

which entitled them to bring the instant Title VII suit—while repudiating their entire basis of, employment—the employment application.

Here *Sheller* seems to be saying that a minor cannot both disaffirm a contract and sue on the contract. That is not what is happening here. A minor suing an employer for sexual harassment is not suing on the contract. As *Sheller* recognizes, a minor suing an employer for sexual harassment could not maintain the suit but for the employment, which requires signing the employment contract. However, this fact does not morph a suit for sexual harassment against an employer into a suit on the employment contract. There are other cases which reach a different conclusion from that reached in *Sheller*. Most recently, in considering whether a minor must arbitrate his claims pursuant to an arbitration provision in the purchase contract, the Alabama Supreme Court recognized that infancy is a valid defense to the enforcement of a properly supported motion to compel arbitration. Facing a similar issue, a federal district court in North Carolina refused to require arbitration on the ground that plaintiff, as a minor, is not bound by the arbitration provision.

The court concludes that, under Tennessee law, a minor's employment contracts, including arbitration agreements, are voidable by the minor. The court finds that Lindsey's employment contract with Finish Line was voidable by Lindsey, and was voided by filing this action.

Motion denied in favor of Lindsey.

Exceptions to the Minor's Right to Disaffirm Not every contract involving a minor is voidable, however. State law often creates statutory exceptions to the minor's right to disaffirm. These statutes prevent minors from disaffirming such transactions as marriage, agreements to support their children, educational loans, life and medical insurance contracts, contracts for transportation by common carriers, and certain types of contracts approved by a court (such as contracts to employ a child actor).

LOG ON

Are you interested in the way in which concepts about capacity of minors are applied to professional child actors, athletes, and performers? In a number of states, special statutes have been enacted that create a procedure for judicial approval of such contracts. Check out this Web site for more information: Wallace Collins, *A Guide to Judicial Approval of Contracts for Services of Minors*, **http://wallacecollins.com/minors.html.**

LOG ON

If you'd like to learn about some of the special considerations that may apply when one of the parties to a lawsuit is a minor, see John J. Davis, *"Kid Law": Problems and Issues in Defending against the Minor Plaintiff*, **http://library.findlaw.com/1999/Nov/1/126318.html.**

Period of Minority At common law, the age of majority was 21. However, the ratification in 1971 of the Twenty-sixth Amendment to the Constitution giving 18-year-olds the right to vote stimulated a trend toward reducing the age of majority. The age of majority has been lowered by 49 states. In almost all of these states, the age of majority for contracting purposes is now 18.

Emancipation Emancipation is the termination of a parent's right to control a child and receive services and wages from him. There are no formal requirements for emancipation. It can occur by the parent's express or implied consent or by the occurrence of some events such as the marriage of the child. In most states, the mere fact that a minor is emancipated does *not* give him capacity to contract. A person younger than the legal age of majority is generally held to lack capacity to enter a contract, even if he is married and employed full time.

Time of Disaffirmance

Contracts entered during minority that affect title to *real estate* cannot be disaffirmed until majority. This rule is apparently based on the special importance of real estate and on the need to protect a minor from improvidently disaffirming a transaction (such as a mortgage or conveyance) involving real estate. All other contracts entered during minority may be disaffirmed as soon as the contract is formed. The minor's power to avoid his contracts does not end on the day he reaches the age of majority. It continues for a period of time after he reaches majority.

How long after reaching majority does a person retain the right to disaffirm the contracts he made while a minor? A few states have statutes that prescribe a definite time limit on the power of avoidance. In Oklahoma, for example, a person who wishes to disaffirm a contract must do so within one year after reaching majority.[2] In most states, however, there is no set limit on the time during which a person may disaffirm after reaching majority. In determining whether a person has the right to disaffirm, a major factor that courts consider is whether the adult has rendered performance under the contract or relied on the contract. If the adult has relied on the contract or has given something of value to the minor, the minor must disaffirm within a reasonable time after reaching majority. If he delays longer than a period of time that is considered to be reasonable under the circumstances, he will run the risk of *ratifying* (affirming) the contract. (The concept and consequences of ratification are discussed in the next section.) If the adult has neither performed nor relied on the contract, however, the former minor is likely to be accorded a longer period of time in which to disaffirm, sometimes even years after he has reached majority.

Ratification

Though a person has the right to disaffirm contracts made during minority, this right can be given up after the person reaches the age of majority. When a person who has reached majority indicates that he intends to be bound by a contract that he made while

still a minor, he surrenders his right to disaffirm. This act of affirming the contract and surrendering the right to avoid the contract is known as **ratification.** Ratification makes a contract valid from its inception. Because ratification represents the former minor's election to be bound by the contract, he cannot later disaffirm. Ratification can be done effectively only after the minor reaches majority. Otherwise, it would be as voidable as the initial contract.

There are no formal requirements for ratification. Any of the former minor's words or acts after reaching majority that indicate with reasonable clarity his intent to be bound by the contract are sufficient. Ratification can be *expressed* in an oral or written statement, or, as is more often the case, it can be *implied* by conduct on the part of the former minor. Naturally, ratification is clearest when the former minor has made some express statement of his intent to be bound. Predicting whether a court will determine that a contract has been ratified is a bit more difficult when the only evidence of the alleged ratification is the conduct of the minor. A former minor's acceptance or retention of benefits given by the other party for an unreasonable time after he has reached majority can constitute ratification. Also, a former minor's continued performance of his part of the contract after reaching majority has been held to imply his intent to ratify the contract.

Duties upon Disaffirmance

Duty to Return Consideration If neither party has performed his part of the contract, the parties' relationship will simply be canceled by the disaffirmance. Since neither party has given anything to the other party, no further adjustments are necessary. But what about the situation where, as is often the case, the minor has paid money to the adult and the adult has given property to the minor? Upon disaffirmance, each party has the duty to return to the other any consideration that the other has given. This means that the minor must return any consideration given to him by the adult that remains in his possession. However, if the minor is unable to return the consideration, most states will still permit him to disaffirm the contract.

The duty to return consideration also means that the minor has the right to recover any consideration he has given to the adult party. He even has the right to recover some property that has been transferred to third parties. One exception to the minor's right to recover property from third parties is found in section 2–403 of the Uniform Commercial Code, however. Under this section, a

---

[2]Okla. Stat. Ann. tit. 15 sec. 18 (1983).

minor cannot recover *goods* that have been transferred to a good faith purchaser. For example, Simpson, a minor, sells a 1980 Ford to Mort's Car Lot. Mort's then sells the car to Vane, a good faith purchaser. If Simpson disaffirmed the contract with Mort's, he would *not* have the right to recover the Ford from Vane.

Must the Disaffirming Minor Make Restitution? A Split of Authority

If the consideration given by the adult party has been lost, damaged, destroyed, or simply has depreciated in value, is the minor required to make restitution to the adult for the loss? The traditional rule is that the minor who cannot fully return the consideration that was given to her is *not* obligated to pay the adult for the benefits she has received or to compensate the adult for loss or depreciation of the consideration. Some states still follow this traditional rule. (As you will read in the next section, however, a minor's misrepresentation of age can, even in some of these states, make her responsible for reimbursing the other party upon disaffirmance.)

The rule that restitution is not required is designed to protect minors by discouraging adults from dealing with them. After all, if an adult knew that he might be able to demand the return of anything that he transferred to a minor, he would have little incentive to refrain from entering into contracts with minors.

The traditional rule, however, can work harsh results for innocent adults who have dealt fairly with minors. It strikes many people as unprincipled that a doctrine intended to protect against unfair exploitation of one class of people can be used to unfairly exploit another class of people. As courts sometimes say, the minor's right to disaffirm was designed to be used as a "shield rather than as a sword." For these reasons, a growing number of states have rejected the traditional rule. The courts and legislatures of these states have adopted rules that require minors who disaffirm their contracts and seek refunds of purchase price to reimburse adults for the use or depreciation of their property. The *Dodson* case follows this approach.

Dodson v. Shrader   824 S.W.2d 545 (Tenn. Sup. Ct. 1992)

Joseph Dodson, age 16, bought a 1984 Chevrolet truck from Burns and Mary Shrader, owners of Shrader's Auto Sales, for $4,900 cash. At the time, Burns Shrader, believing Dodson to be 18 or 19, did not ask Dodson's age and Dodson did not volunteer it. Dodson drove the truck for about eight months, when he learned from an auto mechanic that there was a burned valve in the engine. Dodson did not have the money for the repairs, so he continued to drive the truck without repair for another month until the engine "blew up" and stopped operating. He parked the car in the front yard of his parents' house. He then contacted the Shraders, rescinding the purchase of the truck and requesting a full refund. The Shraders refused to accept the truck or to give Dodson a refund. Dodson then filed an action seeking to rescind the contract and recover the amount paid for the truck. Before the court could hear the case, a hit-and-run driver struck Dodson's parked truck, damaging its left front fender. At the time of the circuit court trial, the truck was worth only $500. The Shraders argued that Dodson should be responsible for paying the difference between the present value of the truck and the $4,900 purchase price. The trial court found in Dodson's favor, ordering the Shraders to refund the $4,900 purchase price upon delivery of the truck. The Tennessee Court of Appeals affirmed this judgment, and the Shraders appealed.

O'Brien, Justice

The law on the subject of the protection of infants' rights has been slow to evolve. The underlying purpose of the "infancy doctrine" is to protect minors from their lack of judgment and from squandering their wealth through improvident contracts with crafty adults who would take advantage of them in the marketplace.

There is, however, a modern trend among the states, either by judicial action or by statute, in the approach to the problem of balancing the rights of minors against those of innocent merchants. As a result, two minority rules have developed which allow the other party to a contract with a minor to refund less than the full consideration paid in the event of rescission. The

first of these minority rules is called the "Benefit Rule." This rule holds that, upon rescission, recovery of the full purchase price is subject to a deduction for the minor's use of the merchandise. This rule recognizes that the traditional rule in regard to necessaries has been extended so far as to hold an infant bound by his contracts, where he failed to restore what he has received under them to the extent of the benefit actually derived by him from what he has received from the other party to the transaction. The other minority rule holds that the minor's recovery of the full purchase price is subject to a deduction for the minor's "use" of the consideration he or she received under the contract, or for the "depreciation" or "deterioration" of the consideration in his or her possession.

We are impressed by the statement made by the Court of Appeals of Ohio:

> At a time when we see young persons between 18 and 21 years of age demanding and assuming more responsibilities in their daily lives; when we see such persons charged with the responsibility for committing crimes; when we see such persons being sued in tort claims for acts of negligence; when we see such persons subject to military service; when we see such persons engaged in business and acting in almost all other respects as an adult, it seems timely to re-examine the case law pertaining to contractual rights and responsibilities of infants to see if the law as pronounced and applied by the courts should be redefined.

We state the rule to be followed hereafter, in reference to a contract of a minor, to be where the minor has not been overreached in any way, and there has been no undue influence, and the contract is a fair and reasonable one, and the minor has actually paid money on the purchase price, and taken and used the article purchased, that he ought not to be permitted to recover the amount actually paid, without allowing the vendor of the goods reasonable compensation for the use of, depreciation, and willful or negligent damage to the article purchased, while in his hands. If there has been any fraud or imposition on the part of the seller or if the contract is unfair, or any unfair advantage has been taken of the minor inducing him to make the purchase, then the rule does not apply. This rule will fully and fairly protect the minor against injustice or imposition, and at the same time it will be fair to a business person who has dealt with such minor in good faith.

This rule is best adapted to modern conditions under which minors are permitted to, and do in fact, transact a great deal of business for themselves, long before they have reached the age of legal majority. Many young people work and earn money and collect it and spend it oftentimes without any oversight or restriction. The law does not question their right to buy if they have the money to pay for their purchases. It seems intolerably burdensome on everyone concerned if merchants cannot deal with them safely, in a fair and reasonable way. Further, it does not appear consistent with practice of proper moral influence upon young people, tend to encourage honesty and integrity, or lead them to a good and useful business future if they are taught that they can make purchases with their own money, for their own benefit, and after paying for them, and using them until they are worn out and destroyed, go back and compel the vendor to return to them what they have paid upon the purchase price. Such a doctrine can only lead to the corruption of principles and encourage young people in habits of trickery and dishonesty.

Reversed and remanded in favor of the Shraders.

Minors' Obligation to Pay Reasonable Value of Necessaries

Though the law regarding minors' contracts is designed to discourage adults from dealing with (and possibly taking advantage of) minors, it would be undesirable for the law to discourage adults from selling minors the items that they need for basic survival. For this reason, disaffirming minors are required to pay the reasonable value of items that have been furnished to them that are classified as **necessaries.** A necessary is something that is essential for the minor's continued existence and general welfare that has not been provided by the minor's parents or guardian. Examples of necessaries include food, clothing, shelter, medical care, tools of the minor's trade, and basic educational or vocational training.

A minor's liability for necessaries supplied to him is **quasi contractual.** That is, the minor is liable for the *reasonable value* of the necessaries that she actually receives. She is not liable for the entire price agreed on if that price exceeds the actual value of the necessaries, and she is not liable for necessaries that she contracted for but did not receive. For example, Joy Jones, a minor, signs a one-year lease for an apartment in Mountain Park at a rent of $300 per month. After living in the apartment for three months, Joy breaks her lease and moves out. Because she is a minor, Joy has the right to disaffirm the lease. If shelter is a necessary in this case, however, she must pay the reasonable value of what she has actually received—three months' rent. If she can establish that the actual value of what she has received is less than $300 per month, she will be bound to pay only that lesser amount. Furthermore, she will not be obligated to pay for the remaining nine months' rent, because she has not received any benefits from the remainder of the lease.

Whether a given item is considered a necessary depends on the facts of a particular case. The minor's age, station in life, and personal circumstances are all relevant to this issue. An item sold to a minor is not considered a necessary if the minor's parent or guardian has already supplied him with similar items. For this reason, the range of items that will be considered necessaries is broader for married minors and other emancipated minors than it is for unemancipated minors.

The following *Young* case involves a situation in which the court is challenged to determine whether a minor has been provided with a necessary.

Young v. Weaver   883 So.2d 234 (Ala. Ct. Civ. App. 2003)

In the fall of 2001, Kim Young, who at the time was 18 years old and had been living with her parents all of her life, decided that she "wanted to move out and get away from [her] parents and be on [her] own." Young and a friend, Ashley Springer, also a minor at the time, signed a contract for the lease of an apartment with Phillip Weaver on September 20, 2001. No adult signed the lease as a guarantor. Young was employed on a full-time basis at a Lowe's hardware store at the time she entered into the lease agreement. Young paid a security deposit in the amount of $300; the rent for the apartment was $550 per month, and the lease was set to expire on July 31, 2002. Young and Springer moved into the apartment in late September and, together, paid rent at the agreed-upon rate for the portion of that month in which they lived in the apartment. Young and Springer continued to live in the apartment during October and most of November 2001. Young moved out near the end of November and returned to live with her parents. Young paid the full amount of her portion of the rent for October and November, but she stopped making any rent payments after she moved out of the apartment. Young had a dog that stayed in the apartment with the roommates, and the dog damaged part of the floor and the bathroom door in the apartment, causing $270 in damage. Young did not pay for this damage before vacating the apartment. Weaver managed to rent the apartment to someone else in June 2002. Weaver filed a claim against Young in Small Claims, seeking damages for the unpaid rent and the damage done by Young's dog to the apartment. The court ruled in favor of Weaver and awarded $1,370 in damages. Young appealed the decision to the Tuscaloosa Circuit Court, which tried the case and also entered a judgment in favor of Weaver and awarded him $1,095, the amount of Young's share of the unpaid rent for December 2001 and January and February 2002, as well as the $270 in damage caused by Young's dog. Young appealed.

Murdock, Judge

Young argues on appeal that the apartment was not a "necessity" and that, therefore, as a minor, she was not legally bound by the lease and owes Weaver nothing. Under Alabama law, one who is unmarried and has not reached the age of 19 years is deemed to be a minor. It is a well-established general rule at common-law, and recognized in this state, that a minor is not liable on any contract he makes and that he may disaffirm the same. Alabama law, like the law of most other states, provides that persons providing "necessaries" of life to minors may recover the reasonable value of such necessaries irrespective of the existence, or nonexistence, of a voidable contract respecting those necessaries.

Determining whether the subject of a contract is a necessity to a minor entails a two-step analysis. First, a court must determine whether the subject of the contract is generally considered a necessity. If the subject is so considered, then it is for the fact-finder to determine, on the particular facts and circumstances of the case, whether the subject of the contract is, in fact, a necessity to that minor. The first inquiry is a question of law; the second inquiry entails a factual determination.

There is little question that, in general, lodging is considered a necessity. Typical necessities include things for bodily need—food, support and maintenance, clothing, medicine and medical attention, and lodging. Thus, the question in this case is whether the trial court erred in concluding as a factual matter that the apartment leased by Young was a necessity for her. Young contends that the apartment was not a necessity to her because, she argues, her parents did not "kick" her out of their house and they kept her room waiting so that she could return

to their home at any time. Young's father testified that every time he talked to his daughter on the telephone while she lived in the apartment he asked her to move back in with them; he also testified that he was willing to take Young back at any time. In essence, because Young's parents were able and willing to house Young at the same time she contracted to lease the apartment, Young argues that in this case the particular lodging at issue was not a necessity.

Several authorities from other states support this position. *Webster Street Partnership, Ltd. v. Sheridan* (Neb. 1985), involved facts similar to those in this case. In *Sheridan,* two minor boys signed a lease with a real estate company for an apartment in mid-September 1982. The lease was to last through mid-August 1983. The boys paid the required rent for September and October, but in mid-November they found themselves financially unable to make that month's rental payment. Because they were unable to pay, the boys vacated the premises. The real estate company sued the boys to obtain damages for unpaid rent and expenses for November and December of the previous year. The boys denied any liability based on their status as minors. The Nebraska Supreme Court noted that "[j]ust what are necessaries, however, has no exact definition. The term is flexible and varies according to the facts of each individual case." The court then observed that the evidence showed that the two boys "were living away from home, apparently with the understanding that they could return home at any time," and that "[i]t would therefore appear that neither [minor] was in need of shelter but, rather, had chosen to voluntarily leave home, with the understanding that they could return whenever they desired." Based on this evidence, the Nebraska Supreme Court ruled that the apartment was not a necessity.

Likewise, in *Ballinger v. Craig* (Ohio Ct. App. 1933), the defendants were husband and wife and were minors at the time they purchased a house trailer. Both were employed. However, before they purchased the trailer, the defendants were living with the parents of the husband. The Ohio Court of Appeals ruled that under the facts presented the house trailer was not a necessity, reasoning that "to enable an infant to contract for articles as necessaries, he must have been in actual need of them, and obliged to procure them for himself. They are not necessaries as to him, however necessary they may be in their nature, if he was already supplied with sufficient articles of the kind, or if he had a parent or guardian who was able and willing to supply them."

As discussed above, Young's parents were willing and able to provide lodging for their daughter at the time she rented the apartment from Weaver. Given the authorities cited above and the particular facts of this case, we conclude that the trial court erred in its determination that the apartment in question was a necessity for Young. Therefore, as a minor, Young is not legally bound under the lease agreement. This result may seem unjust in some ways, but as the Supreme Court observed: "The law has fixed its policy with reference to the protection of infants with regard to their contracts, and those who deal with them, except when actually supplying them with necessaries, deal with them at their peril."

Reversed and remanded in favor of Young.

Effect of Misrepresentation of Age

It is not unheard of for a minor to occasionally pretend to be older than he is. The normal rules dealing with the minor's right to disaffirm and his duties upon disaffirmance can be affected by a minor's misrepresentation of his age.[3] Suppose, for example, that Jones, age 17, wants to lease a car from Acme Auto Rentals, but knows that Acme rents only to people who are at least 18. Jones induces Acme to lease a car to him by showing a false identification that represents his age to be 18. Acme relies on the misrepresentation. Jones wrecks the car, attempts to disaffirm the contract, and asks for the return of his money. What is the effect of Jones's misrepresentation? State law is not uniform on this point.

The traditional rule was that a minor's misrepresentation about his age did not affect his right to disaffirm and did not create any obligation to reimburse the adult for damages or pay for benefits received. The theory behind this rule is that one who lacks capacity cannot acquire it merely by claiming to be of legal age. As you can imagine, this traditional approach does not "sit well" with modern courts, at least in those cases in which the adult has dealt with the minor fairly and in good faith, because it creates severe hardship for innocent adults who have relied on minors' misrepresentations of age.

State law today is fairly evenly divided among those states that take the position that the minor who misrepresents his age will be *estopped* (prevented) from asserting his infancy as a defense and those that will allow a minor to disaffirm regardless of his misrepresentation of age. Among the states that allow disaffirmance despite the minor's misrepresentation, most hold the disaffirming minor responsible for the losses suffered by the adult, either by allowing the adult to counterclaim against the minor for the tort of deceit or by requiring the minor to reimburse the adult for use or depreciation of his property.

Capacity of Mentally Impaired Persons

Theory of Incapacity

Like minors, people who suffer from a mental illness or defect are at a disadvantage in their ability to protect their own interests in the bargaining process. Contract law makes their contracts either void or voidable to protect them from the results of their own impaired perceptions and judgment and from others who might take advantage of them.

Test for Mental Incapacity

Incapacity on grounds of mental illness or defect, which is often referred to in cases and texts as "insanity," encompasses a broad range of causes of impaired mental functioning, such as mental illness, brain damage, mental retardation, or senility. The mere fact that a person suffers from some mental illness or defect does not necessarily mean that he lacks capacity to contract, however. He could still have full capacity unless the defect or illness affects the particular transaction in question.

---

[3]You might want to refer back to Chapter 13 to review the elements of misrepresentation.

The usual test for mental incapacity is a *cognitive* one; that is, courts ask whether the person had sufficient mental capacity to understand the nature and effect of the contract. Some courts have criticized the traditional test as unscientific because it does not take into account the fact that a person suffering from a mental illness or defect might be unable to *control* his conduct. Section 15 of the *Restatement (Second) of Contracts* provides that a person's contracts are voidable if he is unable to *act* in a reasonable manner in relation to the transaction and the other party has reason to know of his condition. Where the other party has reason to know of the condition of the mentally impaired person, the *Restatement (Second)* standard would provide protection to people who understood the transaction but, because of some mental defect or illness, were unable to exercise appropriate judgment or to control their conduct effectively.

The Effect of Incapacity Caused by Mental Impairment

The contracts of people who are suffering from a mental defect at the time of contracting are usually considered to be *voidable*. In some situations, however, severe mental or physical impairment may prevent a person from even being able to manifest consent. In such a case, no contract could be formed.

As mentioned at the beginning of this chapter, contract law makes a distinction between a contract involving a person who has been *adjudicated* (judged by a court) incompetent at the time the contract was made and a contract involving a person who was suffering from some mental impairment at the time the contract was entered but whose incompetency was not established until *after* the contract was formed. If a person is under guardianship at the time the contract is formed—that is, if a court has found a person mentally incompetent after holding a hearing on his mental competency and has appointed a guardian for him—the contract is considered *void*. You will see an example of this in the following *Kenai Chrysler v. Denison* case. On the other hand, if *after* a contract has been formed, a court finds that the person who manifested consent lacked capacity on grounds of mental illness or defect, the contract is usually considered *voidable* at the election of the party who lacked capacity (or his guardian or personal representative).

The Right to Disaffirm

If a contract is found to be voidable on the ground of mental impairment, the person who lacked capacity at the time the contract was made has the right to disaffirm the contract. A person formerly incapacitated by mental impairment can ratify a contract if he regains his capacity. Thus, if he regains capacity, he must disaffirm the contract unequivocally within a reasonable time, or he will be deemed to have ratified it.

As is true of a disaffirming minor, a person disaffirming on the ground of mental impairment must return any consideration given by the other party that remains in his possession. A person under this type of mental incapacity is liable for the reasonable value of necessaries in the same manner as are minors. Must the incapacitated party reimburse the other party for loss, damage, or depreciation of nonnecessaries given to him? This is generally said to depend on whether the contract was basically fair and on whether the other party had reason to be aware of his impairment. If the contract is fair, bargained for in good faith, and the other party had no reasonable cause to know of the incapacity, the contract cannot be disaffirmed unless the other party is placed in *status quo* (the position she was in before the creation of the contract). However, if the other party had reason to know of the incapacity, the incapacitated party is allowed to disaffirm without placing the other party in status quo. This distinction discourages people from attempting to take advantage of mentally impaired people, but it spares those who are dealing in good faith and have no such intent.

Kenai Chrysler Center, Inc. v. Denison　　167 P.3d 1240 (Alaska Sup. Ct. 2007)

David Denison is a developmentally disabled young man who has been under the legal guardianship of his parents since 1999, when he turned 18. In October 2002, David was living in his own apartment, but his parents strictly controlled his finances. They visited him at least once each week to make sure he had a clean and safe place to live and was budgeting his food money properly. They also visited him socially several times every week and spoke with him nearly every day.

The Denisons first learned that David wanted to buy a car when David called his father, Michael, from Kenai Chrysler and asked him to cosign for a used car; David did not tell his father where he was when he called. Michael refused to cosign. The next day, David again tried to purchase a car from Kenai Chrysler. This time, he was trying to buy a new car, a Dodge

Neon, which he could finance without a cosigner. David called his mother, Dorothy, to ask for money for a down payment. Dorothy refused and told him not to buy a car. She assumed her word would be final because she did not realize that David could obtain any appreciable amount of money with his debit card. David used his debit card and bought the Neon. Kenai Chrysler charged a total price of $17,802, including taxes, fees, and extended service plan. Kenai Chrysler gave David credit for trading in his 1994 Pontiac Grand Am, and applied a $2,000 factory rebate to the down payment, which allowed David to buy the new Neon with only $500 in cash. Kenai Chrysler financed the remaining $12,851.77 at 11.99 percent APR for five years.

One or two days after David signed the contract, Dorothy came to Kenai Chrysler with David and informed the salesman who had sold the car to David and a Kenai Chrysler manager that David was under the legal guardianship of his parents and had no legal authority to enter into a contract to buy the Neon. Dorothy showed the manager David's guardianship papers and asked him to take back the car. The manager refused; according to Dorothy, he told her that Kenai Chrysler would not take back the car, and that the company sold cars to "a lot of people who aren't very smart." Dorothy insisted that the contract was void, but the Kenai Chrysler manager ignored her and handed the keys to David over Dorothy's objection. David drove off in the new car. Dorothy contacted Duane Bannock, the general manager of Kenai Chrysler, the next day; he told her that he had seen the guardianship papers, but he still thought that the contract was valid and that David was bound by it.

A couple of days after Kenai Chrysler gave David the keys, David damaged the Neon in a one-car accident. The Denisons then managed to get the car away from David and return it to Kenai Chrysler, but six days later, when David called Kenai Chrysler to ask for his Pontiac back, someone at the dealership told him that he could not have it but could pick up his new car any time. David got a ride to Kenai Chrysler and picked up the Neon. The next day the Denisons were able to convince David to return the car to Kenai Chrysler yet again, and this time he left the car there.

While they were trying to handle the immediate challenge of returning the Neon to Kenai Chrysler and preventing anyone there from giving it back to David, the Denisons also sought legal advice about the validity of the contract. They consulted the Alaska State Association for Guardianship and Advocacy and the Disability Law Center; advocates at both offices confirmed Dorothy's belief that the contract was void. Michael Denison also contacted the court-appointed investigator for David's guardianship case. The investigator contacted Kenai Chrysler's general manager, Bannock, and advised Bannock that the guardianship did indeed make the contract legally void; Bannock refused to listen to the advice. An advocate from the Disability Law Center contacted Robert Favretto, the owner of Kenai Chrysler, on the Denisons' behalf. Favretto would not listen to the advocate's advice. Despite these contacts, Kenai Chrysler sought no legal advice concerning the validity of the sales contract until November 15, a full month after the sale.

During this time, Kenai Chrysler continued in its active efforts to enforce the contract. The company promptly assigned David's loan to the General Motors Acceptance Corporation (GMAC) but never informed GMAC of David's incapacity. It also demanded storage fees from David for keeping the Neon on its lot. It sold David's Pontiac trade-in on the same day the Denisons brought the Neon back for the second time, even though the Denisons were still contesting the sale. GMAC eventually repossessed the Neon and sold it, resulting in a deficiency on the loan. After the Denisons' attorney informed GMAC of David's guardianship, GMAC agreed to treat the loan as uncollectible. Kenai Chrysler paid GMAC the deficiency without asking whether GMAC intended to collect the loan.

The Denisons sued the company, seeking a judgment declaring that the sales contract was void because of the guardianship and seeking additional relief. Kenai Chrysler counterclaimed for restitution, including reimbursement for paying the deficiency to GMAC. The Denisons moved for summary judgment on their claim for declaratory relief and the trial court granted it. Kenai Chrysler appealed.

Bryner, Chief Justice

The Denisons moved for summary judgment on their claim for a declaratory judgment that the contract between David and Kenai Chrysler was void and not merely voidable. On appeal, Kenai Chrysler contests the order granting summary judgment. Kenai Chrysler points out that Alaska has not expressly held that a valid guardianship order automatically voids an attempt by the ward to create a binding contract. In Kenai Chrysler's view, the party contracting with the ward should at least be entitled to restitution; and in any event, Kenai Chrysler maintains, factual issues existed here as to the validity of David's guardianship.

These arguments lack merit. Under the *Restatement (Second) of Contracts,* the existence of a valid legal guardianship precludes the formation of a valid contract with the guardianship's ward. In keeping with the *Restatement*'s view, we ruled in *Pappert v. Sargent* that a party who attempted to enter into a contract with a ward would be entitled to restitution only in the absence of actual or constructive knowledge of the ward's incompetence. Kenai Chrysler nevertheless cites *Pappert* as a case supporting its position that a genuine issue of material fact existed as to whether the dealership had notice of David's guardianship. But Kenai Chrysler misreads *Pappert*. The incompetent party in *Pappert* was not under a legal guardianship, and the circumstances of the disputed transaction in that case failed to create any reason to suspect incompetence. By contrast, in the present case, David Denison was a ward under a formal guardianship order that declared him incompetent to enter into a contract. And under the *Restatement (Second) of Contracts,* the guardianship order gave notice to the public of David's incapacity:

> The guardianship proceedings are treated as giving public notice of the ward's incapacity and establish his status with respect to transactions during guardianship even though the other party to a particular transaction may have no knowledge or reason to know of the guardianship: the guardian is not required to give personal notice to all persons who may deal with the ward. *Restatement (Second) of Contracts* § 13, cmt. a(1981).

Since Kenai Chrysler had constructive notice of David's incapacity, it was not entitled to restitution.

Kenai Chrysler's position also ignores Alaska's territorial case law. In *The Emporium v. Boyle,* the Alaska territorial court followed opinions from several states recognizing that an adjudication of insanity is notice to all the world of the fact that from that time on neither the lunatic nor his estate can be held upon any contract except those completed before that time. Applying this principle, the court in *The Emporium* held that a letter of credit authorizing another person to purchase goods on account was automatically revoked when the person who wrote the letter was declared incompetent. This conclusion was justified, the court explained, "because the world was charged with notice of the adjudication." Based on these authorities, we conclude that the superior court correctly interpreted and applied the law.

The *Restatement* makes it clear that a ward does not regain the ability to enter into a contract merely by having a "lucid interval"; instead, to establish restored ability to enter into a contract, the evidence must show that the guardianship was "terminated or abandoned." Although Kenai Chrysler argues here that evidence of the Denisons' neglect might have supported a finding of restored capacity, the *Restatement*'s standard requires more than a showing of mere neglect. The *Restatement* refers to the termination of a guardianship occurring by death or removal of the guardian, or by lapse where the "ward resumes full control of his property without interference over a substantial period of time."

To support its claim that the Denisons abandoned David as their ward, Kenai Chrysler alleges that the Denisons (1) failed to produce evidence that they had filed a visitor report as required by [Alaska law]; (2) allowed David to use his own bank account; (3) permitted David to work in a retail establishment where he used a cash register; (4) failed to prevent David from entering into the Dodge Neon transaction; (5) failed to inform Kenai Chrysler promptly of the guardianship's existence; (6) failed to prevent David from driving the Neon; and (7) failed to appoint a conservator for David when they encountered trouble controlling his purchases. But these circumstances fail to raise a genuine question of material fact on the issue of abandonment. The absence of a routine report hardly amounts to abandonment. Nor can abandonment be shown by evidence suggesting that the Denisons encouraged David to act independently. To the contrary, the terms of David's guardianship order instructed his guardians to encourage David to be as independent as possible while still protecting him. Allowing David a bank account and a job falls squarely within the scope of these instructions by encouraging David's development. Furthermore, the guardianship order did not oblige the Denisons to watch David's every movement in order to prevent him from trying to enter into contracts. Instead, as we have already observed, the guardianship order itself gave legal notice to all potential contracting parties to avoid entering into a bargain with David. Accordingly, neither the Denisons' failure to prevent the Kenai Chrysler contract nor their failure to give Kenai Chrysler advance warnings could reasonably be construed to imply abandonment of the guardianship.

We also note that Dorothy Denison unequivocally informed Kenai Chrysler of the guardianship within two days of the sale, when she tried to return the car. And in any event, the Denisons' inability to prevent David from driving the Neon after Kenai Chrysler refused to accept the car has no bearing on the guardianship's validity earlier, or when David actually signed the contract. Finally, the Denisons' supposed inability to control David's spending does not reasonably suggest an abandonment; the uncontradicted evidence of their ongoing efforts to control David's finances shows just the opposite. The Denisons are David's guardians, not his guarantors. We thus affirm the superior court's summary judgment order declaring the contract void as a matter of law.

Affirmed in favor of the Denisons.

Contracts of Intoxicated Persons

Intoxication and Capacity

Intoxication (either from alcohol or the use of drugs) can deprive a person of capacity to contract. The mere fact that a party to a contract had been drinking when the contract was formed would *not* normally affect his/her capacity to contract, however. Intoxication is a ground for lack of capacity only when it is so extreme that the person is unable to understand the nature of the business at hand. Section 16 of the *Restatement (Second) of Contracts* further provides that intoxication is a ground for lack of capacity only if *the other party has reason to know* that the affected person is so intoxicated that he/she cannot understand or act reasonably in relation to the transaction.

The rules governing the capacity of intoxicated persons are very similar to those applied to the capacity of people who are mentally impaired. The basic right to disaffirm contracts made during incapacity, the duties upon disaffirmance, and the possibility of ratification upon regaining capacity are the same for an intoxicated person as for a person under a mental impairment. In practice, however, courts traditionally have been less sympathetic with a person who was intoxicated at the time of contracting than with minors or those suffering from a mental impairment. It is rare for a person to actually escape his contractual obligations on the ground of intoxication. A person incapacitated by intoxication at the time of contracting might nevertheless be bound to his/her contract if he/she fails to disaffirm in a timely manner.

Problems and Problem Cases

1. Williams was 18 years old when she was admitted to Baptist Health Systems for treatment of serious health conditions. The age of majority for contracting in Williams's state was 19. Williams was hospitalized for two days, during which she had a variety of medical procedures and tests. At this time, Williams had been admitted to college and was awaiting enrollment, did not work, had no source of income, and was dependent on her mother to provide support. According to her, she believed that she was covered by her mother's health insurance, and that is what she told the hospital, but in fact, she was not covered. Williams's mother was listed in the hospital records as "guarantor." The hospital bill was $12,144. Williams's mother did not pay the bill. The hospital sued both Williams and her mother for the principal amount plus interest. Was Williams legally obligated to pay the bill, despite the fact that she was a minor when the contract was formed?

2. Robertson, while a minor, contracted to borrow money from his father for a college education. His father mortgaged his home and took out loans against his life insurance policies to get some of the money he lent to Robertson, who ultimately graduated from dental school. Two years after Robertson's graduation, his father asked him to begin paying back the amount of $30,000 at $400 per month. Robertson agreed to pay $24,000 at $100 per month. He did this for three years before stopping the payments. His father sued for the balance of the debt. Could Robertson disaffirm the contract?

3. Green, age 16, contracted to buy a Camaro from Star Chevrolet. Green lived about six miles from school and one mile from his job, and used the Camaro to go back and forth to school and work. When he did not have the car, he used a car pool to get to school and work. Several months later, the car became inoperable with a blown head gasket, and Green gave notice of disaffirmance to Star Chevrolet. Star Chevrolet refused to refund the purchase price, claiming, in part, that the car was a necessary. Was it?

4. In 1987, Hauer suffered a brain injury in a motorcycle accident. She was subsequently adjudicated to be incompetent, resulting in a guardian being appointed by the court. On September 20, 1988, Hauer's guardianship was terminated based upon a letter from her treating physician, who opined that Hauer had recovered to the point where she had ongoing memory, showed good judgment, was reasonable in her goals and plans, and could manage her own affairs. Her monthly income after the accident was $900, which consisted of Social Security disability and interest income from a mutual fund worth approximately $80,000. Around June of 1989, Hauer met Eilbes. Eilbes had been trying to raise sufficient funds for a new business venture. He had borrowed some money from Union State Bank but had been unable to borrow

as much as he needed and had defaulted on the loan. Hauer's daughter told Eilbes about the existence of Hauer's mutual fund. Eilbes subsequently discussed his business with Hauer on several occasions and Hauer expressed an interest in becoming an investor in the business. Because Hauer could only sell her stocks at certain times, Eilbes suggested that she take out a short-term loan using the stocks as collateral. Eilbes told Hauer that if she loaned him money, he would give her a job, pay her interest on the loan, and pay the loan when it came due. Hauer agreed. Eilbes then contacted Schroeder, assistant vice president of Union State Bank, and told Schroeder that Hauer wanted to invest in his business but that she needed short-term financing and could provide adequate collateral. Eilbes told Schroeder that he would use the money invested by Hauer in part to either bring the payments current on his defaulted loan or pay the loan off in full. Schroeder then called Hauer's stockbroker and financial consultant, Landolt, in an effort to verify the existence of Hauer's fund. Landolt told Schroeder that Hauer needed the interest income to live on and that he wished the bank would not use it as collateral for a loan. Schroeder also conceded that it was possible that Landolt told him that Hauer was suffering from brain damage, but did not specifically recall that part of their conversation. At some later date Eilbes met personally with Schroeder in order to further discuss the potential loan to Hauer, after which Schroeder indicated that the bank would be willing to loan Hauer $30,000. Schroeder gave Eilbes a loan application to give to Hauer to fill out. In October 1989, Hauer and Eilbes went to the Bank to meet with Schroeder and sign the necessary paperwork to borrow $30,000. Prior to this date, Schroeder had not spoken to or met with Hauer. During this meeting Schroeder explained the terms of the loan to Hauer: that she would sign a consumer single-payment note due in six months and give the bank a security interest in her mutual fund as collateral. Schroeder did not notice anything that would cause him to believe that Hauer did not understand the loan transaction. In April 1990, the date on which the loan matured, Hauer filed suit against the bank and Eilbes. Hauer's testimony indicated a complete lack of understanding of the nature and consequences of the transaction. Also, Hauer's psychological expert testified that when he treated her in 1987, Hauer was "very deficient in her cognitive abilities, her abilities to remember and to read, write and spell . . . she was very malleable,

gullible, people could convince her of almost anything." He further testified that because Hauer's condition had not changed in any significant way by 1990 when he next evaluated her, she was "incompetent and . . . unable to make reasoned decisions" on the date she made the loan. Was the loan contract voidable?

5. At a time when the age of majority in Ohio was 21, Lee, age 20, contracted to buy a 1964 Plymouth Fury for $1,552 from Haydocy Pontiac. Lee represented herself to be 21 when entering the contract. She paid for the car by trading in another car worth $150 and financing the balance. Immediately following delivery of the car to her, Lee permitted one John Roberts to take possession of it. Roberts delivered the car to someone else, and it was never recovered. Lee failed to make payments on the car, and Haydocy Pontiac sued her to recover the car or the amount due on the contract. Lee repudiated the contract on the ground that she was a minor at the time of purchase. Can Lee disaffirm the contract without reimbursing Haydocy Pontiac for the value of the car?

6. On or about December 8, 1989, Joseph Muller and Tina Muller, who are brother and sister, both signed a loan application with CES Credit Union. Tina was seeking the loan so that she could purchase Joseph's 1987 Buick Skylark. The loan application indicated that Joseph's birth date was February 10, 1972, and indicated that he had an automobile loan with BancOhio in the amount of $7,200 that would be paid off if the loan to Tina was approved. Once the loan application was approved, both Joseph and Tina Muller signed the loan contract. While Tina signed the contract on December 26, 1989, as the debtor, Joseph, on December 22, 1989, signed as a co-signor. At this time, Joseph was two months shy of his eighteenth birthday and the age of majority for contracting in his state was 18. The amount of the loan was $6,160.00. Joseph then transferred the Buick Skylark to his sister and his auto loan with BancOhio was paid off. Tina later defaulted on the loan, the Skylark was repossessed and sold at auction, leaving a balance of $4,915.73 owing to the credit union. In January 2003, the credit union sued Tina and Joseph seeking a judgment against them for the remaining principal and interest. Joseph defended on the ground that he was a minor when he signed the contact and that he therefore lacked capacity to contract. Is this a good argument?

7. In 1984, when Andrew Kavovit was 12 years of age, he and his parents entered into a contract with Scott Eden Management whereby Scott Eden became the exclusive personal manager to supervise and promote Andrew's career in the entertainment industry. This agreement ran from February 8, 1984, to February 8, 1986, with an extension for another three years to February 8, 1989. It provided that Scott Eden was entitled to a 15 percent commission on Andrew's gross compensation. It stated, "With respect to contracts entered into by [Andrew] . . . during the term of this agreement . . . [Scott Eden] shall be entitled to [its] commission from the residuals or royalties of such contracts, the full term of such contracts, including all extensions or renewals thereof, notwithstanding the earlier termination of this agreement." In 1986, Andrew signed an agency contract with the Andreadis Agency, a licensed agent selected by Scott Eden pursuant to industry requirements. This involved an additional 10 percent commission. Thereafter, Andrew signed several contracts for his services. The most important contract, from a financial and career point of view, secured a role for Andrew on *As the World Turns*, a long-running television soap opera. Income from this employment contract appears to have begun on December 28, 1987, and continued through December 28, 1990, with a strong possibility for renewal. One week before the contract with Scott Eden was to expire, Andrew's attorney notified Scott Eden that his "clients hereby disaffirm the contract on the grounds [sic] of infancy." Up until then, the Andreadis Agency had been forwarding Scott Eden its commissions, but by letter of February 4, 1989, Andrew's father advised Andreadis that Andrew's salary would go directly to Andrew and that he would send Andreadis its 10 percent. No further commissions were sent to Scott Eden. Was Scott Eden legally entitled to commissions for contracts entered into by Andrew during the term of his contract with Scott Eden?

8. In October 1995, Mitchell, a 17-year-old married minor, was injured in an auto accident while riding in a car owned by her father and driven by her husband. Subsequently, while Mitchell was still 17, she signed a release with State Farm Mutual Automobile Insurance Co. to settle her bodily injury claims for $2,500. No guardian or conservator was appointed at the time Mitchell signed this release. Mitchell then claimed that the release was voidable because she lacked capacity at the time she signed it. State Farm argued that the release was enforceable because she was married at the time she signed it. Will Mitchell be able to disaffirm the contract?

9. A boy bought an Ernie Banks rookie card for $12 from an inexperienced clerk in a baseball card store owned by Johnson. The card had been marked "1200," and Johnson, who had been away from the store at the time of the sale, had intended the card to be sold for $1,200, not $12. Can Johnson get the card back by asserting the boy's lack of capacity?

Online Research

Researching the Age of Majority

Using your favorite search engine and key word requests such as "age of majority AND states," determine what states have an age of majority older than 18.

chapter 15

ILLEGALITY

W ilson had been licensed to practice architecture in Hawaii, but his license lapsed in 1971 because he had failed to pay a required $15 renewal fee. A Hawaii statute provides that any person who practices architecture without having been registered and "without having a valid unexpired certificate of registration . . . shall be fined not more than $500 or imprisoned not more than one year, or both." In 1972, Wilson performed architectural and engineering services for Kealakekua Ranch, and billed the Ranch over $33,000 for the work.

- Is this a legal contract?
- Would it matter if Wilson had never met the licensing requirements to be licensed in Hawaii?
- Is Kealakekua Ranch required to pay Wilson anything for his work?
- Is it ethical for the Ranch to refuse to pay Wilson, even if he is unlicensed?

ALTHOUGH THE PUBLIC INTEREST normally favors the enforcement of contracts, there are times when the interests that usually favor the enforcement of an agreement are subordinated to conflicting social concerns. As you read in Chapter 13, Reality of Consent, and Chapter 14, Capacity to Contract, for example, people who did not truly consent to a contract or who lacked the capacity to contract have the power to cancel their contracts. In these situations, concerns about protecting disadvantaged persons and preserving the integrity of the bargaining process outweigh the usual public interest in enforcing private agreements. Similarly, when an agreement involves an act or promise that violates some legislative or court-made rule, the public interests threatened by the agreement outweigh the interests that favor its enforcement. Such an agreement will be denied enforcement on the ground of *illegality*, even if there is voluntary consent between two parties who have capacity to contract.

Meaning of Illegality

When a court says that an agreement is illegal, it does not necessarily mean that the agreement violates a criminal law, although an agreement to commit a crime is one type of illegal agreement. Rather, an agreement is illegal either because the legislature has declared that particular type of contract to be unenforceable or void or because the agreement violates a **public policy** that has been developed by courts or that has been manifested in constitutions, statutes, administrative regulations, or other sources of law.

The term *public policy* is impossible to define precisely. Generally, it is taken to mean a widely shared view about what ideas, interests, institutions, or freedoms promote public welfare. For example, in our society, there are strong public policies favoring the protection of human life and health, free competition, and private property. Judges' and legislators' perceptions of desirable public policy influence the decisions they make about the resolution of cases or the enactment of statutes. Public policy may be based on a prevailing moral code, on an economic philosophy, or on the need to protect a valued social institution such as the family or the judicial system. If the enforcement of an agreement would create a threat to a public policy, a court may determine that it is illegal.

Determining Whether an Agreement Is Illegal If a statute states that a particular type of agreement is unenforceable or void, courts will apply the statute and refuse to enforce the agreement. Relatively few such statutes exist, however. More frequently, a legislature will forbid certain conduct but will not address the enforceability of contracts that involve the forbidden

conduct. In such cases, courts must determine whether the importance of the public policy that underlies the statute in question and the degree of interference with that policy are sufficiently great to outweigh any interests that favor enforcement of the agreement.

In some cases, it is relatively easy to predict that an agreement will be held to be illegal. For example, an agreement to commit a serious crime is certain to be illegal. However, the many laws enacted by legislatures are of differing degrees of importance to the public welfare. The determination of **illegality** would not be so clear if the agreement violated a statute that was of relatively small importance to the public welfare. For example, in one Illinois case,[1] a seller of fertilizer failed to comply with an Illinois statute requiring that a descriptive statement accompany the delivery of the fertilizer. The sellers prepared the statements and offered them to the buyers but did not give them to the buyers at the time of delivery.

The court enforced the contract despite the sellers' technical violation of the law because the contract was not seriously injurious to public welfare. You will see that approach in the *Riggs* case later in this chapter.

Similarly, the public policies developed by courts are rarely absolute; they, too, depend on a balancing of several factors. In determining whether to hold an agreement illegal, a court will consider the importance of the public policy involved and the extent to which enforcement of the agreement would interfere with that policy. They will also consider the seriousness of any wrongdoing involved in the agreement and how directly that wrongdoing was connected with the agreement.

For purposes of our discussion, illegal agreements will be classified into three main categories: (1) agreements that violate statutes, (2) agreements that violate public policy developed by courts, and (3) unconscionable agreements and contracts of adhesion.

You will see the court grapple with conflicting public policies in deciding the following *Coma Corporation* case.

---

[1]*Amoco Oil Co. v. Toppert,* 56 Ill. App. 3d 1294 (Ill. Ct. App. 1978).

Coma Corporation v. Kansas Department of Labor
154 P.3d 1080 (Kan. Sup. Ct. 2007)

Cesar Martinez Corral was an undocumented worker who was not legally permitted to work in the United States. He was nevertheless employed by Coma Corporation, which did business as Burrito Express. Corral stated that Coma's manager, Luis Calderon, had agreed to pay him $6 per hour, with payment made weekly. Corral maintained that he worked 50 to 60 hours per week, 6 or 7 days per week, but that he was paid "$50 or $60 bucks a week."

Coma fired Corral, and Corral filed a claim with the Kansas Department of Labor for earned but unpaid wages under the Kansas Wage Payment Act. He was awarded a total of $7,657 against Coma and its president. Coma filed a petition for judicial review of final order. The district court held that the employment contract was illegal due to Corral's status as an undocumented worker and remanded to the Kansas Department of Labor for recalculation at the applicable minimum wage. The Kansas Department of Labor appealed.

Nuss, Judge

Coma argues that Corral's employment contract was illegal and unenforceable because he is an illegal alien. Intertwined with this argument is another: Coma claims that federal immigration law preempts the Kansas Wage Payment Act. Coma's purported trumping argument is based upon [The Immigration Reform and Control Act (IRCA)], which makes employment of unauthorized aliens illegal. Preemption, however is not presumed. It is well established that the states enjoy broad authority under their police powers to regulate employment relationships to protect workers within the state. Minimum and other wage laws and workmen's compensation law are only a few examples of the exercise of this broad authority. We conclude that under this case's facts, Coma has not overridden the presumption against federal preemption. Finally, we agree with the rationale set forth in *Flores v. Amigon,* where the court granted Fair Labor Standards Act protections to an undocumented worker and determined that payment of unpaid wages for work actually performed furthers the federal immigration policy:

> Indeed, it is arguable that enforcing the FLSA's provisions requiring employers to pay proper wages to undocumented aliens when the work had been performed actually furthers the goal of the IRCA, which requires the employer to discharge any worker upon discovery of the worker's undocumented alien status. If employers know that they will not only be subject to civil penalties when they hire illegal aliens, but they will also be required to pay them at the same rates as legal workers for work actually performed, there are

virtually no incentives left for an employer to hire an undocumented alien in the first instance. Whatever benefit an employer might have gained by paying less than the minimum wage is eliminated and the employer's incentive would be to investigate and obtain proper documentation from each of his workers.

Coma also asserts that Corral's employment contract is illegal under state law. Specifically, it argues that Kansas Department of Labor regulations require that a contract of employment contain lawful provisions in order to be enforceable. Coma reasons that because Corral does not have a legal right to be or to work in the United States, his contract violates IRCA and is unenforceable under Kansas Department of Labor regulations and state law.

Prior to IRCA's enactment, the Alaska Supreme Court confronted the issue of whether a contract of employment entered into by a Canadian alien was barred by illegality. *Gates v. Rivers Construction Co., Inc*. The court first discussed the nature of illegal contracts:

> Generally, a party to an illegal contract cannot recover damages for its breach. But as in the case of many such simplifications, the exceptions and qualifications to the general rule are numerous and complex. Thus, when a statute imposes sanctions but does not specifically declare a contract to be invalid, it is necessary to ascertain whether the legislature intended to make unenforceable contracts entered into in violation of the statute.

The *Gates* court then concluded that enforcement of the employment contract with the Canadian alien was not barred. It looked at the statutory language:

> [I]t is clear that the contract involved here should be enforced. First, it is apparent that the statute itself does not specifically declare the labor or service contracts of aliens seeking to enter the United States for the purpose of performing such labor or services to be void. The statute only specifies that aliens who enter this country for such purpose, without having received the necessary certification, "shall be ineligible to receive visas and shall be excluded from admission into the United States."

The court next advanced the concept of equity and fairness to the employee:

> Second, that the employer, who knowingly participated in an illegal transaction, should be permitted to profit thereby at the expense of the employee is a harsh and undesirable consequence of the doctrine that illegal contracts are not to be enforced. This result, so contrary to general considerations of equity and fairness, should be countenanced only when clearly demonstrated to have been intended by the legislature.

Finally, in a general foreshadowing of the benefit described in *Flores,* that is, of reducing employer incentives to violate the law, the *Gates* court stated:

> Third, since the purpose of this section would appear to be the safeguarding of American labor from unwanted competition, the appellant's contract should be enforced, because such an objective would not be furthered by permitting employers knowingly to employ excludable aliens and then, with impunity, to refuse to pay them for their services. *Indeed, to so hold could well have the opposite effect from the one intended, by encouraging employers to enter into the very type of contracts sought to be prevented.*

We agree with Kansas Department of Labor's position concerning the strong and longtime Kansas public policy of protecting wages and wage earners. As we stated in *Burriss v. Northern Assurance Co.,* "[t]hroughout the history of this state, the protection of wages and wage earners has been a principal objective of many of our laws in order that they and the families dependent upon them are not destitute." Accordingly, we conclude that to deny or to dilute an action for wages earned but not paid on the ground that such employment contracts are "illegal," would thus directly contravene the public policy of the State of Kansas. We hold for the above reasons that the district court erred in concluding that Corral's employment contract was illegal and therefore not enforceable.

Reversed in favor of Kansas Department of Labor.

Agreements in Violation of Statute

Agreements Declared Illegal by Statute

State legislatures occasionally enact statutes that declare certain types of agreements unenforceable, void, or voidable. In a case in which a legislature has specifically stated that a particular type of contract is void, a court need only interpret and apply the statute. These statutes differ from state to state. Some are relatively uncommon. For example, an Indiana statute declares surrogate birth contracts to be void.[2] Others, such as statutes setting limits on the amount of interest that can be charged for a

---

[2]Ind. Code 31-20-1-1 and 31-20-1-2.

loan or forbearance (usury statutes) and statutes prohibiting or regulating wagering or gambling are common.

Agreements That Violate the Public Policy of a Statute

As stated earlier, an agreement can be illegal even if no statute specifically states that that particular sort of agreement is illegal. Legislatures enact statutes in an effort to resolve some particular problem. If courts enforced agreements that involve the violation of a statute, they would frustrate the purpose for which the legislature passed the statute. They would also promote disobedience of the law and disrespect for the courts.

Agreements to Commit a Crime

For the reasons stated above, contracts that require the violation of a criminal statute are illegal. If Grimes promises to pay Judge John Doe a bribe of $5,000 to dismiss a criminal case against Grimes, for example, the agreement is illegal. Sometimes the very formation of a certain type of contract is a crime, even if the acts agreed on are never carried out. An example of this is an agreement to murder another person. Naturally, such agreements are considered illegal under contract law as well as under criminal law.

Agreements That Promote Violations of Statutes

Sometimes a contract of a type that is usually perfectly legal—say, a contract to sell goods—is deemed to be illegal under the circumstances of the case because it promotes or facilitates the violation of a statute. Suppose Davis sells Sims goods on credit. Sims uses the goods in some illegal manner and then refuses to pay Davis for the goods. Can Davis recover the price of the goods from Sims? The answer depends on whether Davis knew of the illegal purpose and whether he intended the sale to further that illegal purpose. Generally speaking, such agreements will be legal unless there is a direct connection between the illegal conduct and the agreement in the form of active, intentional participation in or facilitation of the illegal act. Knowledge of the other party's illegal purpose, standing alone, is generally not sufficient to render an agreement illegal. When a person is aware of the other's illegal purpose *and* actively helps to accomplish that purpose, an otherwise legal agreement—such as a sale of goods—might be labeled illegal.

Licensing Laws: Agreement to Perform an Act for Which a Party Is Not Properly Licensed

Congress and the state legislatures have enacted a variety of statutes that regulate professions and businesses. A common type of regulatory statute is one that requires a person to obtain a license, permit, or registration before engaging in a certain business or profession. For example, state statutes require lawyers, physicians, dentists, teachers, and other professionals to be licensed to practice their professions. In order to obtain the required license, they must meet specified requirements such as attaining a certain educational degree and passing an examination. Real estate brokers, stockbrokers, insurance agents, sellers of liquor and tobacco, pawnbrokers, electricians, barbers, and others too numerous to mention are also often required by state statute to meet licensing requirements to perform services or sell regulated commodities to members of the public.

What is the status of an agreement in which one of the parties agrees to perform an act regulated by state law for which she is not properly licensed? This will often be determined by looking at the purpose of the legislation that the unlicensed party has violated. If the statute is **regulatory**—that is, the purpose of the legislation is to protect the public against dishonest or incompetent practitioners—an agreement by an unlicensed person is generally held to be unenforceable. For example, if Spencer, a first-year law student, agrees to draft a will for Rowen for a fee of $150, Spencer could not enforce the agreement and collect a fee from Rowen for drafting the will because she is not licensed to practice law. This result makes sense, even though it imposes a hardship on Spencer. The public interest in ensuring that people on whose legal advice others rely have an appropriate educational background and proficiency in the subject matter outweighs any interest in seeing that Spencer receives what she bargained for.

On the other hand, where the licensing statute was intended primarily as a **revenue-raising** measure—that is, as a means of collecting money rather than as a means of protecting the public—an agreement to pay a person for performing an act for which she is not licensed will generally be enforced. For example, suppose that in the example used above, Spencer is a lawyer who is licensed to practice law in her state and who met all of her state's educational, testing, and character requirements but neglected to pay her annual registration fee. In this situation, there is no compelling public interest that would justify the harsh measure of refusing enforcement and possibly inflicting forfeiture on the unlicensed person.

Whether a statute is a regulatory statute or a revenue-raising statute depends on the intent of the legislature, which may not always be expressed clearly. Generally, statutes that require proof of character and skill and impose penalties for violation are considered to be regulatory in nature. Their requirements indicate that they were intended for the protection of the public. Those that impose a significant license fee and allow anyone who pays the fee to obtain a license are usually classified as revenue raising. The fact that no requirement other than the payment of the fee is imposed indicates that the purpose of the law is to raise money rather than to protect the public. Because such a statute is not designed for the protection of the public, a violation of the statute is not as threatening to the public interest as is a violation of a regulatory statute.

It would be misleading to imply that cases involving unlicensed parties always follow such a mechanical test. In some cases, courts may grant recovery to an unlicensed party even where a regulatory statute is violated. If the public policy promoted by the statute is relatively trivial in relation to the amount that would be forfeited by the unlicensed person and the unlicensed person is neither dishonest nor incompetent, a court may conclude that the statutory penalty for violation of the regulatory statute is sufficient to protect the public interest and that enforcement of the agreement is appropriate.

The following *Riggs* case illustrates how courts consider the degree of threat to the public interest when deciding whether to enforce a contract involving a violation of statute.

Riggs v. Woman to Woman, P.C.   812 N.E.2d 1027 (Ill. Ct. App. 2004)

In September 2000, Dr. Mary Riggs entered into a physician agreement with Woman to Woman Obstetrics and Gynecology, P.C., whereby she joined its medical practice. This agreement contained a covenant not to compete. At the time of the agreement, Woman to Woman assured Dr. Riggs in writing that the "Corporation [was] registered to practice medicine in the State of Illinois." Dr. Riggs started working for Woman to Woman in October 2000. Dr. Riggs resigned from Woman to Woman on December 20, 2002, after she discovered that Woman to Woman allegedly had engaged in a fraudulent accounting scheme designed to reduce her compensation and that Woman to Woman was not a licensed professional corporation.

On that same date, Dr. Riggs filed suit against Woman to Woman, based on various breaches and misrepresentations allegedly made by it. Dr. Riggs also sought a declaration that she was not required to abide by the terms, including the covenant not to compete, contained in her physician agreement. Dr. Riggs claimed that Woman to Woman's failure to register as a professional corporation with the Illinois Department of Professional Regulation (IDPR) under Illinois's Professional Service Corporation Act rendered the agreement void. Woman to Woman counterclaimed, seeking enforcement of Dr. Riggs's covenant not to compete.

The trial court granted Dr. Riggs's motion for summary judgment and dismissed Woman to Woman's counterclaim, finding that the professional registration act was intended to be regulatory for the protection of the public health and safety in the practice of medicine and that the physician agreement was void. However, finding that there was substantial ground for difference of opinion regarding its legal conclusion, the trial certified the following questions for review by the appellate court:

(1) Whether the Act's licensing requirements for medical corporations is intended to protect the public's health, safety, or welfare.

(2) Whether defendant's failure to comply with the Act's certificate of registration requirement rendered the employment agreement void.

Byrne, Judge

The facts pertaining to Woman to Woman's lack of a certificate of registration from the IDPR are undisputed. Woman to Woman was originally formed as a professional corporation in July 1999. At that time, Woman to Woman's legal counsel requested that the IDPR issue a certificate of registration for the corporation. Although Woman to Woman did not realize it at the time, the IDPR followed up on Woman to Woman's application by requesting that some minor, technical changes be made in the application. However, Woman to Woman never received the letter from the IDPR with respect to those defects because IDPR sent the letter to the wrong address. Around November 2002, the IDPR again sent a letter to Woman to Woman to the wrong address. This time, however, the letter was forwarded to Woman to Woman's office. In that notice, dated November 12, 2002, the IDPR explained that Woman to Woman's application for a certificate of registration had expired and, therefore, was denied. Woman to Woman later determined that its original application for registration was defective because the IDPR required that a suite number be added to the address and that the statement of purpose for the corporation be modified to remove the phrase "rendering the profession of obstetrics and gynecology." As soon as Woman to Woman discovered the circumstances relating to its original application, it promptly proceeded to file a new application and pay the necessary $50 fee for registering with the IDPR. Ultimately, a certificate of registration was issued to Woman to Woman by the IDPR, effective January 14, 2003, after the suit was filed. The IDPR has not fined Woman to Woman, conducted any investigation, or otherwise taken any action, except to issue the new certificate of registration to Woman to Woman as a result of the inadvertent expiration of Woman to Woman's initial application. At all times, every physician-employee of Woman to Woman has been duly licensed by the IDPR to practice medicine in the State of Illinois.

The first question we are called upon to answer is whether the Act's licensing requirements for medical corporations is intended to protect the public's health, safety, or welfare. We find nothing in any section of the Act that leads to this conclusion. It is clear that the function of the Act is primarily permissive, allowing professionals, who would otherwise not be entitled to enjoy the benefits of incorporating, to establish corporate entities for their professional practices. We find nothing in the Act that signifies that it was enacted for the protection of the public. Section 12 requires a corporation to pay an annual fee to renew its registration, but there are no civil or criminal penalties for noncompliance. The Act assigns only minor, administrative functions to the IDPR, whose tasks are more ministerial than regulatory. The only enforcement authority provided to the IDPR under the Act is the ability to suspend or revoke a certificate of registration or to collect an additional $100 fee when a registrant's certificate lapses and it continues to practice without a certificate. It is generally recognized that professional service corporation legislation, similar to the Act, arose "out of the desire of professional groups to realize the tax benefits open to employees under the qualified pension, profit-sharing, and annuity plan provisions of the Internal Revenue Code." J. Rydstrom, *Practice by Attorneys & Physicians as Corporate Entities or Associations Under Professional Service Corporation Statutes* (2003). In addition to providing certain tax breaks, incorporation under the Act reduces potential civil liability.

Clearly, the intent of the legislature here is not to advance the public welfare but to allow professionals to incorporate in order to enjoy certain tax benefits and to reduce their potential civil liability.

Furthermore, statutes that have been interpreted as necessary for the public safety are those that have been enacted to provide assurance of adequately trained professionals, such as those statutes requiring licenses for doctors or lawyers. Indeed, the Act does not include any of the indicia of such regulatory intent, including examinations for competency. Our supreme court in *People v. Brigham* (1992) determined that a lawyer's failure to pay his registration fee did not prevent him from providing competent legal advice. Similarly, we do not believe that a medical corporation's failure to pay its corporate registration fees would undermine the public's trust that its licensed doctors can practice medicine competently. Dr. Riggs appears to equate the lack of a certificate of registration under the Act to practice as a professional corporation with the lack of a license to practice medicine. Clearly, there is a difference. Those statutes requiring licenses to practice a profession are necessary for the public safety because they have been enacted to provide assurance of adequately trained professionals. A violation of the Act does not necessarily mean that the doctors lack the requisite medical skills to practice medicine. Accordingly, because we find nothing that signifies that the Act was enacted for the benefit of the health, safety, or welfare of the public, we answer the first question in the negative.

The second question we are called upon to answer is whether Woman to Woman's failure to comply with the Act's certificate of registration requirement rendered the employment agreement void. Dr. Riggs attempts to be excused from her contractual obligations due to Woman to Woman's failure to register as a corporation. Dr. Riggs, no doubt, enjoyed certain corporate benefits when she was employed by Woman to Woman. To excuse Dr. Riggs from her contractual obligations due to Woman to Woman's failure to register would be disproportionate to the wrong committed by Woman to Woman.

Certified questions answered in favor of Woman to Woman.

Agreements That May Be in Violation of Public Policy Articulated by Courts

Courts have broad discretion to articulate public policy and to decline to lend their powers of enforcement to an agreement that would contravene what they deem to be in the best interests of society. There is no simple rule for determining when a particular agreement is contrary to public policy. Public policy may change with the times; changing social and economic conditions may make behavior that was acceptable in an earlier time unacceptable today, or vice versa. The following are examples of agreements that are frequently considered vulnerable to attack on public policy grounds.

Agreements in Restraint of Competition

The policy against restrictions on competition is one of the oldest public policies declared by the common law. This same policy is also the basis of federal and state antitrust statutes. The policy against restraints on competition is based on the economic judgment that the public interest is best served by free competition. Nevertheless, courts have long recognized that some contractual restrictions on competition serve legitimate business interests and should be enforced. Therefore, agreements that limit competition are scrutinized very closely by the courts to determine whether the restraint imposed is in violation of public policy.

If the *sole* purpose of an agreement is to restrain competition, it violates public policy and is illegal. For example, if Martin and Bloom, who own competing businesses, enter an agreement whereby each agrees not to solicit or sell to the other's customers, such an agreement would be unenforceable. Where the restriction on competition was part of (*ancillary to*) an otherwise legal contract, the result may be different because the parties may have a legitimate interest to be protected by the restriction on competition.

For example, if Martin had *purchased* Bloom's business, the goodwill of the business was part of what she paid for. She has a legitimate interest in making sure that Bloom does not open a competing business soon after the sale and attract away the very customers whose goodwill she paid for. Or suppose that Martin hired Walker to work as a salesperson in her business. She wants to assure herself that she does not disclose trade secrets, confidential information, or lists of regular customers to Walker only to have Walker quit and enter a competing business.

To protect herself, the buyer or the employer in the above examples might bargain for a contractual clause that would provide that the seller or employee agrees not to engage in a particular competing activity in a specified *geographic area* for a specified *time* after the sale of the business or the termination of employment. This type of clause is called an **ancillary covenant not to compete,** or, as it is more commonly known, a **noncompetition clause** or **"noncompete."** Such clauses most frequently appear in *employment contracts, contracts for the sale of a business, partnership agreements,* and *small-business buy–sell agreements.* In an employment contract, the noncompetition clause might be the only part of the contract that the parties put in writing.

Enforceability of Noncompetition Clauses

Although noncompetition clauses restrict competition and thereby affect the public policy favoring free competition, courts enforce them if they meet the following three criteria.

1. *Clause must serve a legitimate business purpose.* This means that the person protected by the clause must have some justifiable interest—such as an interest in protecting goodwill or trade secrets—that is to be protected by the noncompetition clause. It also means that the clause must be *ancillary* to, or part of, an otherwise valid contract. For example, a noncompetition clause that is one term of an existing employment contract would be ancillary to that contract. By contrast, a promise not to compete would not be enforced if the employee made the promise *after* he had already resigned his job, because the promise not to compete was not ancillary to any existing contract.

2. *The restriction on competition must be reasonable in time, geographic area, and scope.* Another way of stating this is that the restrictions must not be any greater than necessary to protect a legitimate interest. It would be unreasonable for an employer or buyer of a business to restrain the other party from engaging in some activity that is not a competing activity or from doing business in a territory in which the employer or buyer does not do business, because this would not threaten his legitimate interests.

3. *The noncompetition clause should not impose an undue hardship.* A court will not enforce a noncompetition clause if its restraints are unduly burdensome either on the public or on the party whose ability to compete would be restrained. In one case, for example, the court refused to enforce a noncompetition clause against a gastroenterologist because of evidence that the restriction would have imposed a hardship on patients and other physicians requiring his services.[3] Noncompetition clauses in employment contracts that have the practical effect of preventing the restrained person from earning a livelihood are unlikely to be enforced as well. This is discussed further in the next section.

Noncompetition Clauses in Employment Contracts

In employment contracts, noncompetition clauses are one form of agreement that places restrictions on an employee's conduct after the employment is over. Other restrictions on employees' postemployment conduct can include **confidentiality** or **nondisclosure agreements,** which constrain the employee from divulging or using certain information gained during his employment, and **nonsolicitation agreements,** which forbid an employee from soliciting the employer's employees, clients, or

---

[3]*Iredell Digestive Disease Clinic, P.A. v. Petrozza,* 373 S.E.2d 449 (N.C. Ct. App. 1988).

customers. In many cases, employees sign all these forms of postemployment restrictions. In others, the postemployment restriction may reflect just one or two of these forms of restraints.

Restrictions on competition work a greater hardship on an employee than on a person who has sold a business. For this reason, courts tend to judge noncompetition clauses contained in employment contracts by a stricter standard than they judge similar clauses contained in contracts for the sale of a business. In some states, statutes limit or even prohibit noncompetition clauses in employment contracts. In others, there is a trend toward refusing enforcement of these clauses in employment contracts unless the employer can bring forth very good evidence that he has a protectible interest that compels enforcement of the clause. The employer can do this by showing that he has entrusted the employee with trade secrets or confidential information,

or that his goodwill with "near-permanent" customers is threatened. In the absence of this kind of proof, a court might conclude that the employer is just trying to avoid competition with a more efficient competitor and refuse enforcement because there is no legitimate business interest that requires protection.

Furthermore, many courts refuse to enforce noncompetition clauses if they restrict employees from engaging in a "common calling." A common calling is an occupation that does not require extensive or highly sophisticated training but instead involves relatively simple, repetitive tasks. Under this common calling restriction, various courts have refused to enforce noncompetition clauses against salespersons, a barber, and an auto trim repairperson.

In the following *Nasc Services* case, the court determines whether to enjoin employees from violating their noncompete agreement.

Nasc Services, Inc. v. Jervis
2008 U.S. Dist. LEXIS 40502 (U.S. Dist. Ct. D. N.J. 2008)

Gary Russell began running a soccer camp program in 1969 and, over the years, grew his business into a large organization, Nasc Services, which does business as MLS Camps. Nasc Services and Russell ("the plaintiffs") operate soccer camps and provide soccer instruction to youths throughout the United States. The New York–New Jersey area is one of their most active regions. In this area, plaintiffs provided soccer camp services to roughly 185 soccer clubs in the past year, accounting for approximately $1.5 million in annual revenue.

David Jervis, Adrian Moses, Steven Jones, Simon Barrow, Benjamin Moffett, and Simon Nee ("the defendants") are citizens of the United Kingdom and have played, taught, coached, and worked in the soccer industry most of their lives. The plaintiffs hired them to provide services for its soccer camps in the New York–New Jersey area. Each of the defendants entered into an employment contract with the plaintiffs. These employment contracts all included three relevant covenants: a covenant not to compete with the plaintiffs, a covenant not to solicit the plaintiffs' customers, and a covenant not to disclose the plaintiffs' confidential information.

The plaintiffs placed the defendants in positions in which they were responsible for developing and nurturing the plaintiffs' relationships with customers in the area. Some of the defendants were stationed in Red Bull New York, a soccer organization in Secaucus, New Jersey, to which the plaintiffs provided soccer camp services. Although defendants worked at the Red Bull facilities, they were the plaintiffs' employees. Between August and November of 2007, the defendants separated from the plaintiffs and assumed positions with the Red Bull, where they helped Red Bull launch soccer camps in the New York–New Jersey area in direct competition with their former employer. Though their specific reasons for leaving the plaintiffs differ, defendants all wished to distance themselves from Russell, MLS Camps' owner, because of alleged mistreatment, deception, bullying, and abuse.

Plaintiffs allege that, since defendants left their employment with plaintiffs, plaintiffs have experienced an immediate drop in customers in the New York–New Jersey area. They filed a motion for a preliminary injunction to prevent the defendants from violating the noncompetition, nonsolicitation, and nondisclosure clauses of their employment contracts.

Cavanaugh, U.S. District Judge

An employer's ongoing professional relationship with its clients is generally recognized as a legitimate business interest which may be protected through a restrictive covenant. Every employer has a patently legitimate interest in protecting his

trade secrets as well as his confidential business information and he has an equally legitimate interest in protecting his customer relationships. Plaintiffs argue that the covenants are reasonable both as to duration and geographic extent. Plaintiffs' soccer camp business is nationwide, with special concentration in the New York–New Jersey area. Furthermore, a two-year limitation is reasonable.

According to defendants, however, the noncompetition clauses appear to be unreasonable because they are unnecessary to protect plaintiffs' legitimate business interest. Defendants provide no unique services nor possess any extraordinary skills that could harm plaintiffs if they continue to work for the Red Bull or for any other employer in the soccer industry. Under Connecticut law, it would be an extraordinary stretch to extend mandatory injunctive relief under these circumstances. Plaintiffs nonetheless claim that the noncompetition clauses must be enforced because defendants possess allegedly confidential information concerning plaintiffs' methods of teaching soccer.

Plaintiffs have no legitimate protectable interest in preventing defendants from continuing to teach children how to play soccer. In the course of their work for MLS Camps, defendants were not exposed to information that represents a trade secret. Their jobs required them to coach, teach, organize, sell and manage youth soccer camps. There is nothing confidential about how to teach soccer. Moreover, the "secrets" of Russell's allegedly proprietary "Strengths-Based Coaching" program are readily available to anyone. For a nominal fee, anyone can sign-up *via* one of Russell's websites to purchase all of the materials necessary to master Russell's program. Russell's teaching methodology is nothing more than a collection of practices obtained from a variety of public sources. Likewise, plaintiffs' "client-list" constitutes nothing more than names of area soccer clubs who might be interested in youth programs, clinics or camps for children in their programs. It appears likely that plaintiffs' list could be easily replicated from the vast array of information available *via* the Internet. Furthermore, plaintiffs have not submitted evidence that defendants misappropriated confidential or proprietary information. Defendants claim that they have not divulged any information to Red Bull that they acquired from plaintiffs and that they have no intention in doing so. Likewise, defendants claim that none of Red Bull's employees have asked them to disclose any of plaintiffs' information.

There are strong public policy reasons for supporting noncompetition agreements. Such legally enforceable agreements make it possible for an employer to hire and train employees, to entrust them with responsibilities and to work with them in developing marketing strategies, secure in the knowledge that they will not, having gained these confidences, take them to a competitor's establishment and turn them against their former employer. Thus, judicial enforcement of noncompetition provisions of employment contracts serves the public interest by promoting stability and certainty in business and employment relationships.

In the current case, however, the balancing of the equities supports denial of plaintiffs' application for injunctive relief. If plaintiffs' application is granted, defendants will be forced to stop working for the Red Bull and be barred from working for any comparable business in any capacity in any part of the world. Five of the six defendants will also be forced to leave the United States because their visas depend upon their employment. This would create an oppressive and unfair scenario for defendants.

Motion for preliminary injunction denied in favor of the defendants.

The Effect of Overly Broad Noncompetition Clauses

The courts of different states treat unreasonably broad noncompetition clauses in different ways. Some courts will strike the entire restriction if they find it to be unreasonable and will refuse to grant the buyer or employer any protection. Others will refuse to enforce the restraint as written, but will adjust the clause and impose such restraints as would be reasonable. In case of breach of an enforceable noncompetition clause, the person benefited by the clause may seek damages or an injunction (a court order preventing the promisor from violating the covenant).

Exculpatory Clauses

An **exculpatory clause** (often called a "release" or "liability waiver") is a provision in a contract that purports to relieve one of the parties from tort liability. Exculpatory clauses are suspect on public policy grounds for two reasons. First, courts are concerned that a party who can contract away his liability for negligence will not have the incentive to use care to avoid hurting others. Second, courts are concerned that an agreement that accords one party such a powerful advantage might have been the result of the abuse of superior bargaining power rather than truly voluntary choice.

LOG ON

Want to know more about noncompetition agreements? Try this Web site: Business Owner's Toolkit, *Noncompete Agreements,* **www.toolkit.com/ small_business_guide/sbg.aspx?nid=P05_5750.**

Although exculpatory agreements are often said to be "disfavored" in the law, courts do not want to prevent parties who are dealing on a fair and voluntary basis from determining how the risks of their transaction shall be borne if their agreement does not threaten public health or safety.

Courts enforce exculpatory clauses in some cases and refuse to enforce them in others, depending on the circumstances of the case, the identity and relationship of the parties, and the language of the agreement. A few ground rules can be stated. First, an exculpatory clause cannot protect a party from liability for any wrongdoing greater than negligence. One that purports to relieve a person from liability for fraud or some other willful tort will be considered to be against public policy. In some states, in fact, exculpatory clauses have been invalidated on this ground because of broad language stating that one of the parties was relieved of "all liability." Second, exculpatory clauses will not be effective to exclude tort liability on the part of a party who owes a duty to the public (such as an airline) because this would present an obvious threat to the public health and safety.

A third possible limitation on the enforceability of exculpatory clauses arises from the increasing array of statutes and common law rules that impose certain obligations on one party to a contract for the benefit of the other party to the contract. Workers' compensation statutes and laws requiring landlords to maintain leased property in a habitable condition are examples of such

laws. Sometimes the person on whom such an obligation is placed will attempt to escape it by inserting an exculpatory or waiver provision in a contract. Such clauses are often—though not always—found to be against public policy because, if enforced, they would frustrate the very purpose of imposing the duty in question. For example, an employee's agreement to relieve her employer from workers' compensation liability is likely to be held illegal as a violation of public policy.

Even if a clause is not against public policy on any of the above three grounds, a court may still refuse to enforce it if a court finds that the clause was **unconscionable,** a **contract of adhesion,** or some other product of abuse of superior bargaining power. (Unconscionability and contracts of adhesion are discussed later in this chapter.) This determination depends on all of the facts of the case. Facts that tend to show that the exculpatory clause was not the product of *knowing* consent increase the likelihood that the clause will not be enforced. A clause that is written in clear language and conspicuous print is more likely to be enforced than one written in "legalese" and presented in fine print. Facts that tend to show that the exculpatory clause was the product of *voluntary* consent increase the likelihood of enforcement of the clause. For example, a clause contained in a contract for a frivolous or unnecessary activity is more likely to be enforced than is an exculpatory clause contained in a contract for a necessary activity such as medical care.

You will see an example of the analysis of an exculpatory clause in the following *McCune* case.

McCune v. Myrtle Beach Indoor Shooting Range, Inc.
612 S.E.2d 462 (S.C. Ct. App. 2005)

Christine McCune went to the Myrtle Beach Indoor Shooting Range to participate in a paintball game with her husband and friends. Before being allowed to participate, McCune signed and dated a waiver that purported to release the Range from liability for all known or unknown dangers for any reason with the exception of gross negligence on the part of the Range. The language of the release provided in part:

I, for myself and on behalf of my heirs HEREBY RELEASE AND HOLD HARMLESS THE AMERICAN PAINTBALL LEAGUE (APL), THE APL CERTIFIED MEMBER FIELD, the owners and lessors of premises used to conduct the paintball activities, their Officers, officials, agents, and/or employees, WITH RESPECT TO ANY AND ALL INJURY, DISABILITY, DEATH, or loss or damage to person or property, WHETHER CAUSED BY THE NEGLIGENCE OF THE RELEASEES OR OTHERWISE, except that which is the result of gross negligence and/or wanton misconduct.

I HAVE READ THIS RELEASE OF LIABILITY AND ASSUMPTION OF RISK AGREEMENT, FULLY UNDERSTANDING ITS TERMS, UNDERSTAND THAT I HAVE GIVEN UP SUBSTANTIAL RIGHTS BY SIGNING IT, AND SIGN IT FREELY AND VOLUNTARILY WITHOUT ANY INDUCEMENT.

During her paintball session, McCune used a mask provided by the Range. During her play, the mask was loose and ill fitting. She tried to have the mask tightened or replaced several times and an employee of the Range attempted to properly fit the mask for McCune. While playing in a match, McCune caught the mask on the branch of a tree. The tree was obscured from her field of vision by the top of the mask. The mask was raised off her face because it was loose, and provided no protection against an incoming paintball pellet. The pellet struck McCune in the eye, rendering her legally blind in the eye.

McCune brought a negligence suit against the Range. The Range filed a motion for summary judgment, alleging the waiver barred liability on its part. The court granted the Range's motion, and McCune appealed.

Beatty, Judge

McCune maintains the trial court erred in granting summary judgment to the Range on the basis of the exculpatory language in the release of liability signed by McCune. McCune asserts she did not anticipate the harm that was inflicted or the manner in which it occurred. Additionally, she contends the failure of the equipment was unexpected and she could not have voluntarily assumed such a risk. We disagree. Express assumption of risk is contrasted with implied assumption of risk, which arises when the plaintiff implicitly, rather than expressly, assumes known risks.

In the instant case, we are confronted with a defense based upon McCune's express assumption of the risk. She signed a release from liability prior to participating in the paintball match. The courts of South Carolina have analyzed express assumption of the risk cases in terms of exculpatory contracts. Exculpatory contracts, such as the one in this case, have previously been upheld by the courts of this state. However, notwithstanding the general acceptance of exculpatory contracts, since such provisions tend to induce a want of care, they are not favored by the law and will be strictly construed against the party relying thereon.

The release in the instant case explicitly and unambiguously limited the Range's liability. The agreement was voluntarily signed and specifically stated: (1) she assumed the risks, whether known or unknown; and (2) she released the Range from liability, even from injuries sustained because of the Range's own negligence. It is clear McCune voluntarily entered into the release in exchange for being allowed to participate in the paintball match. Additionally, she expressly assumed the risk for all known and unknown risks while participating and cannot now complain because she did not fully appreciate the exact risk she faced.

We find the release entered into by the parties does not contravene public policy. In *Huckaby v. Confederate Motor Speedway, Inc.,* the plaintiff signed a waiver similar to the one above, which was required before he could participate in a sanctioned automobile race. He maintained his injuries were caused by the speedway's faulty installation and maintenance of a guardrail. As was found in *Huckaby,* participation in a paintball match is voluntary. "If these agreements, voluntarily entered into, were not upheld, the effect would be to increase the liability of those organizing or sponsoring such events to such an extent that no one would be willing to undertake to sponsor a sporting event. Clearly, this would not be in the public interest."

Although our research reveals no South Carolina case that deals specifically with a release for paintball, other jurisdictions have found similarly worded releases to be unambiguous. Accordingly, we hold the trial court properly determined the release signed by McCune was sufficient to release the Range from all liability in this incident.

Affirmed in favor of the Range.

Family Relationships and Public Policy

In view of the central position of the family as a valued social institution, it is not surprising that an agreement that unreasonably tends to interfere with family relationships will be considered illegal. Examples of this type of contract include agreements whereby one of the parties agrees to divorce a spouse or agrees not to marry.

In recent years, courts have been presented with an increasing number of agreements between unmarried cohabitants that purport to agree upon the manner in which the parties' property will be shared or divided upon separation. It used to be widely held that contracts between unmarried cohabitants were against public policy because they were based on an immoral relationship.

As unmarried cohabitation has become more widespread, however, the law concerning the enforceability of agreements between unmarried couples has changed. For example, in the 1976 case of *Marvin v. Marvin,* the California Supreme Court held that an agreement between an unmarried couple to pool income and share property could be enforceable.[4] Today, most courts hold that agreements between unmarried couples are not against public policy unless they are explicitly based on illegal sexual relations as the consideration for the contract or unless one or more of the parties is married to someone else.

[4]134 Cal. Rptr. 815 (1976).

Unfairness in Agreements: Contracts of Adhesion and Unconscionable Contracts

Under classical contract law, courts were reluctant to inquire into the fairness of an agreement. Because the prevailing social attitudes and economic philosophy strongly favored freedom of contract, American courts took the position that so long as there had been no fraud, duress, misrepresentation, mistake, or undue influence in the bargaining process, unfairness in an agreement entered into by competent adults did not render it unenforceable.

As the changing nature of our society produced many contract situations in which the bargaining positions of the parties were grossly unequal, the classical contract assumption that each party was capable of protecting himself was no longer persuasive. The increasing use of standardized contracts (preprinted contracts) enabled parties with superior bargaining power and business sophistication to virtually dictate contract terms to weaker and less sophisticated parties.

Legislatures responded to this problem by enacting a variety of statutory measures to protect individuals against the abuse of superior bargaining power in specific situations. Examples of such legislation include minimum wage laws and rent control ordinances. Courts became more sensitive to the fact that superior bargaining power often led to **contracts of adhesion** (contracts in which a stronger party is able to determine the terms of a contract, leaving the weaker party no practical choice but to "adhere" to the terms). Some courts responded by borrowing a doctrine that had been developed and used for a long time in courts of equity,[5] the doctrine of **unconscionability.** Under this doctrine, courts would refuse to grant the equitable remedy of specific performance for breach of a contract if they found the contract to be oppressively unfair. Courts today can use the concepts of unconscionability or adhesion to analyze contracts that are alleged to be so unfair that they should not be enforced.

Unconscionability

Unconscionability One of the most far-reaching efforts to correct abuses of superior bargaining power was the enactment of section 2–302 of the Uniform Commercial Code, which gives courts the power to refuse to enforce all or part of a contract for the sale of goods or to modify such a contract if it is found to be

unconscionable. By virtue of its inclusion in Article 2 of the Uniform Commercial Code, the prohibition against unconscionable terms applies to every contract for the sale of goods. The concept of unconscionability is not confined to contracts for the sale of goods, however. Section 208 of the *Restatement (Second) of Contracts,* which closely resembles the unconscionability section of the UCC, provides that courts may decline to enforce unconscionable terms or contracts. The prohibition of unconscionability has been adopted as part of the public policy of many states by courts in cases that did not involve the sale of goods, such as banking transactions and contracts for the sale or rental of real estate. It is therefore fair to state that the concept of unconscionability has become part of the general body of contract law.

Consequences of Unconscionability The UCC and the *Restatement (Second) sections* on unconscionability give courts the power to manipulate a contract containing an unconscionable provision so as to reach a just result. If a court finds that a contract or a term in a contract is unconscionable, it can do one of three things: it can refuse to enforce the entire agreement; it can refuse to enforce the unconscionable provision but enforce the rest of the contract; or it can "limit the application of the unconscionable clause so as to avoid any unconscionable result." This last alternative has been taken by courts to mean that they can make adjustments in the terms of the contract.

Meaning of Unconscionability Neither the UCC nor the *Restatement (Second) of Contracts* attempts to define the term *unconscionability.* Though the concept is impossible to define with precision, unconscionability is generally taken to mean the *absence of meaningful choice* together with *terms unreasonably advantageous* to one of the parties.

The facts of each individual case are crucial to determining whether a contract term is unconscionable. Courts will scrutinize the process by which the contract was reached to see if the agreement was reached by fair methods and whether it can fairly be said to be the product of knowing and voluntary consent.

Procedural Unconscionability Courts and writers often refer to unfairness in the bargaining process as *procedural unconscionability.* Some facts that may point to procedural unconscionability include the use of fine print or inconspicuously placed terms, complex, legalistic language, and high-pressure sales tactics. One of the most significant facts pointing to procedural unconscionability is the lack of voluntariness as shown by a

---

[5]Chapter 1 discusses courts of equity.

marked imbalance in the parties' bargaining positions, particularly where the weaker party is unable to negotiate more favorable terms because of economic need, lack of time, or market factors. In fact, in most contracts that have been found to be unconscionable, there has been a serious inequality of bargaining power between the parties. It is important to note, however, that the mere existence of unequal bargaining power does not make a contract unconscionable. If it did, every consumer's contract with the telephone company or the electric company would be unenforceable. Rather, in an unconscionable contract, the party with the stronger bargaining power *exploits* that power by driving a bargain containing a term or terms that are so unfair that they "shock the conscience of the court."

Substantive Unconscionability In addition to looking at facts that might indicate procedural unconscionability, courts will scrutinize the contract terms themselves to determine whether they are oppressive, unreasonably one-sided, or unjustifiably harsh. This aspect of unconscionability is often referred to as *substantive unconscionability*. Examples include situations in which a party to the contract bears a disproportionate amount of the risk or other negative aspects of the transaction and situations in which a party is deprived of a remedy for the other party's breach. In some cases, unconscionability has been found in situations in which the contract provides for a price that is greatly in excess of the usual market price.

There is no mechanical test for determining whether a clause is unconscionable. Generally, in cases in which courts have found a contract term to be unconscionable, there are elements of *both* procedural and substantive unconscionability. Though courts have broad discretion to determine what contracts will be deemed to be unconscionable, it must be remembered that the doctrine of unconscionability is designed to prevent oppression and unfair surprise—not to relieve people of the effects of bad bargains.

The cases concerning unconscionability are quite diverse. Some courts have found unconscionability in contracts involving grossly unfair sales prices. Although the doctrine of unconscionability has been raised primarily by victimized consumers, there have been cases in which businesspeople in an inherently weak bargaining position have been successful in asserting unconscionability.

You will see an example of unconscionability analysis in the following *Circuit City* case.

Circuit City Stores, Inc. v. Mantor   335 F.3d 1101 (9th Cir. 2003)

Paul Mantor began working for Circuit City in August 1992. When Circuit City hired Mantor, it had no arbitration program. In 1995, Circuit City instituted an arbitration program called the "Associate Issue Resolution Program" (AIRP). Circuit City emphasized to managers the importance of full participation in the AIRP, claiming that the company had been losing money because of lawsuits filed by employees. Circuit City management stressed that employees had little choice in this matter. It suggested that employees should sign the agreement or prepare to be terminated. Although Circuit City circulated the forms regarding the AIRP in 1995, Mantor was able to avoid either signing up or openly refusing to participate in the AIRP for three years. In 1998, two Circuit City managers arranged a meeting with Mantor to discuss his participation in the AIRP. During this meeting, Mantor asked the two Circuit City managers what would happen should he decline to participate in the arbitration program. They responded to the effect that he would have no future with Circuit City. In February 1998, Mantor agreed to participate in the AIRP, acknowledging in writing his receipt of (1) an "Associate Issue Resolution Handbook," (2) the "Circuit City Dispute Resolution Rules and Procedures," and (3) a "Circuit City Arbitration Opt-Out Form."

In October 2000, Circuit City terminated Mantor's employment. A year later, Mantor brought a civil action in state court, alleging 12 causes of action. To preserve his right to arbitrate his claims in the event that a court determined that his claims were subject to arbitration, he also submitted an Arbitration Request Form to Circuit City's arbitration coordinator. Circuit City petitioned the district court to compel arbitration, and the district court granted Circuit City's motion to compel arbitration. Mantor appealed, arguing that the arbitration agreement was unenforceable because it was unconscionable.

Pregerson, Circuit Judge

In California, courts may refuse to enforce an arbitration agreement if it is unconscionable. Unconscionability exists when one party lacks meaningful choice in entering a contract or negotiating its terms and the terms are unreasonably favorable to the other party. Accordingly, a contract to arbitrate is unenforceable under the doctrine of unconscionability when there is both a procedural and substantive element of unconscionability. But procedural and substantive unconscionability need not be present in the same degree. The more substantively oppressive the contract term, the less evidence of procedural uncon-scionability is required to come to the conclusion that the term is unenforceable, and vice versa. To determine whether Circuit City's arbitration agreement with Mantor is procedu-rally unconscionable we must evaluate how the parties nego-tiated the contract and the circumstances of the parties at that time. One factor courts consider to determine whether a contract is procedurally unconscionable is whether the con-tract is oppressive. Courts have defined oppression as spring-ing from an inequality of bargaining power [that] results in no real negotiation and an absence of meaningful choice. Another factor courts look to is surprise, defined as the extent to which the supposedly agreed-upon terms of the bargain are hidden in the prolix printed form drafted by the party seeking to enforce the disputed terms.

Circuit City argues that because Mantor was given an op-portunity to "opt-out" of the arbitration agreement, the agree-ment was not oppressive—and therefore not procedurally un-conscionable. In support of its argument, Circuit City cites our decisions in *Circuit City Stores, Inc. v. Najd,* and *Circuit City Stores, Inc. v. Ahmed.* We do not agree that *Najd* and *Ahmed* guide our analysis here; in both *Najd* and *Ahmed,* the arbitra-tion agreement did not prove procedurally unconscionable specifically because both Najd and Ahmed had a *meaningful* opportunity to opt-out of the arbitration program. Mantor had no such *meaningful* opportunity. In 1995, Mantor was given an "opt-out" form by which he could elect not to participate in the arbitration program. But Circuit City management impliedly and expressly pressured Mantor not to opt-out, and even re-sorted to threatening his job outright should Mantor exercise his putative "right" to opt-out. The fact that Circuit City man-agement pressured and even threatened Mantor into assenting to the arbitration agreement demonstrates that he had no *meaningful* opportunity to opt-out of the program. When a party to a contract possesses far greater bargaining power than another party, or when the stronger party pressures, harasses, or compels another party into entering into a contract, oppression and, therefore, procedural unconscionability, are present. A meaningful opportunity to negotiate or reject the terms of a contract must mean something more than an empty choice. At a minimum, a party must have reasonable notice of his oppor-tunity to negotiate or reject the terms of a contract, *and* he must have an actual, meaningful, and reasonable choice to exercise that discretion. In light of Circuit City's insistence that Mantor sign the arbitration agreement—under pain of forfeiting his fu-ture with the company—the fact that in 1995 Mantor was pre-sented with an opt-out form does not save the agreement from being oppressive, for Mantor had no meaningful choice, nor any legitimate opportunity, to negotiate or reject the terms of the arbitration agreement. Accordingly, because Circuit City

presented the arbitration agreement to Mantor on an "adhere-or-reject" basis we conclude that the arbitration agreement was procedurally unconscionable.

We turn now to consider whether the arbitration agreement is substantively unconscionable. Substantive unconscionability concerns the terms of the agreement and whether those terms are so one-sided as to shock the conscience. To evaluate the substantive terms of a contract, a court must analyze the con-tract as of the time [it] was made. Many of the terms we have already held to be substantively unconscionable in earlier ver-sions of Circuit City's arbitration agreement remain in the 2001 version we review in this case. The substantively uncon-scionable provisions concerning the statute of limitations, class actions, cost-splitting, and Circuit City's unilateral power to modify or terminate the arbitration agreement remain in the version of the agreement we review in this case. For the reasons expressed in prior decisions, we again hold that these terms are substantively unconscionable.

Under its arbitration program, Circuit City requires an em-ployee to pay a seventy-five dollar filing fee to initiate an arbi-tration proceeding. In *Ingle v. Circuit City Stores, Inc.,* we crit-icized the filing fee rule in the 1998 version of the arbitration agreement because the employee is required to pay Circuit City for the privilege of bringing a complaint. This, we held, was not the *type* of expense that the employee would be required to bear in federal court. Thus, we concluded that it was improperly one-sided. We also observed that "Circuit City's arbitration agreement makes no provision for waiver of the filing fee (or other fees and costs of arbitration). In federal court, indigent plaintiffs may be exempt from having to pay court fees. In the 2001 version of the arbitration agreement we review here, Circuit City has revised the rule to allow for waiver of the fil-ing fee. But the fact that Circuit City vests in itself the sole dis-cretion to consider applications for waivers indicates that the process of filing could be halted unilaterally by Circuit City if an employee does not have the means to pay the seventy-five dollar filing fee. The fee waiver provision might not be one-sided if the discretion to waive the fee were assigned to a disin-terested party. However, because the fee waiver rule (1) pro-vides that an employee must pay an interested party for the privilege of bringing a complaint and (2) assigns Circuit City, an interested party, the responsibility for the decision whether to waive the filing fee, this rule is manifestly one-sided, and therefore, substantively unconscionable.

Under California law, a court has discretion whether to sever particular unconscionable terms or invalidate a contract entirely. To assess whether unconscionable terms can be sev-ered, a court considers whether the illegality is central or collat-eral to the purpose of the contract to determine whether an en-tire contract should be invalidated or whether only a particular term or set of terms should be severed. Under California contract law, a party may not fashion an adhesive arbitration agreement that significantly limits the other party's ability to substantiate his legal claims. The arbitration agreement between Circuit City and Mantor violates that rule: the arbitration agreement was procedurally unconscionable and numerous provisions in Circuit City's arbitration agreement operate to benefit itself at its employees' expense. Because any earnest attempt to ameliorate the unconscionable aspects of Circuit City's arbitration agreement would require this court to assume the role of contract author rather than interpreter, we hold that this agreement is unenforceable in its entirety.

Reversed and remanded in favor of Mantor.

Contracts of Adhesion

A contract of adhesion is a contract, usually on a standardized form, offered by a party who is in a superior bargaining position on a "take-it-or-leave-it" basis. The person presented with such a contract has no opportunity to negotiate the terms of the contract; they are imposed on him if he wants to receive the goods or services offered by the stronger party. In addition to not having a "say" about the terms of the contract, the person who signs a standardized contract of adhesion may not even know or understand the terms of the contract that he is signing. When these factors are present, the objective theory of contracts and the normal duty to read contracts before signing them may be modified. These factors may be viewed as a form of procedural unconscionability. A court may use the word *adhesion* to describe procedural unconscionability.

All of us have probably entered contracts of adhesion at one time or another. The mere fact that a contract is a contract of adhesion does not, in and of itself, mean that the contract is unenforceable. Courts will not refuse enforcement to such a contract unless the term complained of is either substantively unconscionable or is a term that the adhering party could not reasonably expect to be included in the form that he was signing.

Unenforceable contracts of adhesion can take different forms. The first is seen when the contract of adhesion contains a term that is harsh or oppressive. In this kind of case, the party offering the contract of adhesion has used his superior bargaining power to dictate unfair terms. The second situation in which contracts of adhesion are refused enforcement occurs when a contract of adhesion contains a term that, while it may not be harsh or oppressive, is a term that the adhering party could *not* be expected to have been aware that he was agreeing to. This type of case relates to the fundamental concept of agreement in an era in which lengthy, complex, standardized contracts are common. If a consumer presented with a contract of adhesion has no opportunity to negotiate terms and signs the contract without knowing or fully understanding what he is signing, is it fair to conclude that he has consented to the terms? It is reasonable to conclude that he has consented at least to the terms that he could have expected to be in the contract, but *not* to any terms that he could not have expected to be contained in the contract.

Effect of Illegality

General Rule: No Remedy for Breach of Illegal Agreements
As a general rule, courts will refuse to give any remedy for the breach of an illegal agreement. A court will refuse to enforce an illegal agreement and will also refuse to permit a party who has fully or partially performed her part of the agreement to recover what she has parted with. The reason for this rule is to serve the public interest, not to punish the parties.

In some cases, the public interest is best served by allowing some recovery to one or both of the parties. Such cases constitute exceptions to the "hands-off" rule. The following discussion concerns the most common situations in which courts will grant some remedy even though they find the agreement to be illegal.

Exceptions

Excusable Ignorance of Facts or Legislation Though it is often said that ignorance of the law is no excuse, courts will, under certain circumstances, permit a party to an illegal agreement who was excusably ignorant of facts or legislation that rendered the agreement illegal to recover damages for breach of the agreement. This exception is used where only *one* of the parties acted in ignorance of the illegality of the agreement and the other party was aware that the agreement was illegal. For this exception to apply, the facts or legislation of which the person

Ethics in Action

Murphy, a welfare recipient with four minor children, saw an advertisement in the local newspaper that had been placed by McNamara, a television and stereo dealer. It stated:

Why buy when you can rent? Color TV and stereos. *Rent to own!* Use our Rent-to-own plan and let TV Rentals deliver either of these models to your home. *We feature—*Never a repair bill—No deposit—No credit needed—No long term obligation—Weekly or monthly rates available—Order by phone—Call today—Watch color TV tonight.

As a result of the advertisement, Murphy leased a 25-inch Philco color console TV set from McNamara under the "Rent to Own" plan. The lease agreement provided that Murphy would pay a $20 delivery charge and 78 weekly payments of $16. At the end of the period, Murphy would own the set. The agreement also provided that the customer could return the set at any time and terminate the lease as long as all rental payments had been made up to the return date. Murphy entered the lease because she believed that she could acquire ownership of a TV set without first establishing credit as was stressed in McNamara's ads. At no time did McNamara inform Murphy that the terms of the lease required her to pay a total of $1,268 for the TV. The retail sales price for the same TV was $499. After making $436 in payments over a period of about six months, Murphy read a newspaper article criticizing the lease plan and realized the amount that the agreement required her to pay. She stopped making payments and McNamara sought to repossess the TV. Murphy argued that the agreement was unconscionable. Was it ethical to market the Rent to Own plan? Was McNamara ethically required to inform Murphy that the total price of the TV would be $1,268 under the Rent to Own plan?

claiming damages was ignorant must be of a relatively minor character—that is, it must not involve an immoral act or a serious threat to the public welfare. Finally, the person who is claiming damages cannot recover damages for anything that he does after learning of the illegality. For example, Warren enters a contract to perform in a play at Craig's theater. Warren does not know that Craig does not have the license to operate a theater as required by statute. Warren can recover the wages agreed on in the parties' contract for work that he performed before learning of the illegality.

When *both* of the parties are ignorant of facts or legislation of a relatively minor character, courts will not permit them to enforce the agreement and receive what they had bargained for, but they will permit the parties to recover what they have parted with.

Rights of Parties Not Equally in the Wrong

The courts will often permit a party who is not equally in the wrong (in technical legal terms, not in *pari delicto*) to recover what she has parted with under an illegal agreement. One of the most common situations in which this exception is used involves the rights of "protected parties"—people who were intended to be protected by a regulatory statute—who contract with parties who are not properly licensed under that statute. Most regulatory statutes are intended to protect the public. As a general rule if a person guilty of violating a regulatory statute enters into an agreement with another person for whose protection the statute was adopted, the agreement will be enforceable by the party whom the legislature intended to protect.

Another common situation in which courts will grant a remedy to a party who is not equally in the wrong is one in which the less guilty party has been induced to enter the agreement by misrepresentation, fraud, duress, or undue influence.

Rescission before Performance of Illegal Act

Obviously, public policy is best served by any rule that encourages people not to commit illegal acts. People who have fully or partially performed their part of an illegal contract have little incentive to raise the question of illegality if they know that they will be unable to recover what they have given because of the courts' hands-off approach to illegal agreements. To encourage people to cancel illegal contracts, courts will allow a person who rescinds such a contract before any illegal act has been performed to recover any consideration that he has given. For example, Dixon, the owner of a restaurant, pays O'Leary, an employee of a competitor's restaurant, $1,000 to obtain some of the competitor's recipes. If Dixon has second thoughts and tells O'Leary the deal is off before receiving any recipes, he can recover the $1,000 he paid O'Leary.

Divisible Contracts

If part of an agreement is legal and part is illegal, the courts will enforce the legal part so long as it is possible to separate the two parts. A contract is said to be *divisible*—that is, the legal part can be separated from the illegal part—if the contract consists of several promises or acts by one party, each of which corresponds with an act or a promise by the other party. In other words, there must be a separate consideration for each promise or act for a contract to be considered divisible.

Where no separate consideration is exchanged for the legal and illegal parts of an agreement, the agreement is said to be *indivisible*. As a general rule, an indivisible

---

Figure 1 *Effect of Illegality*

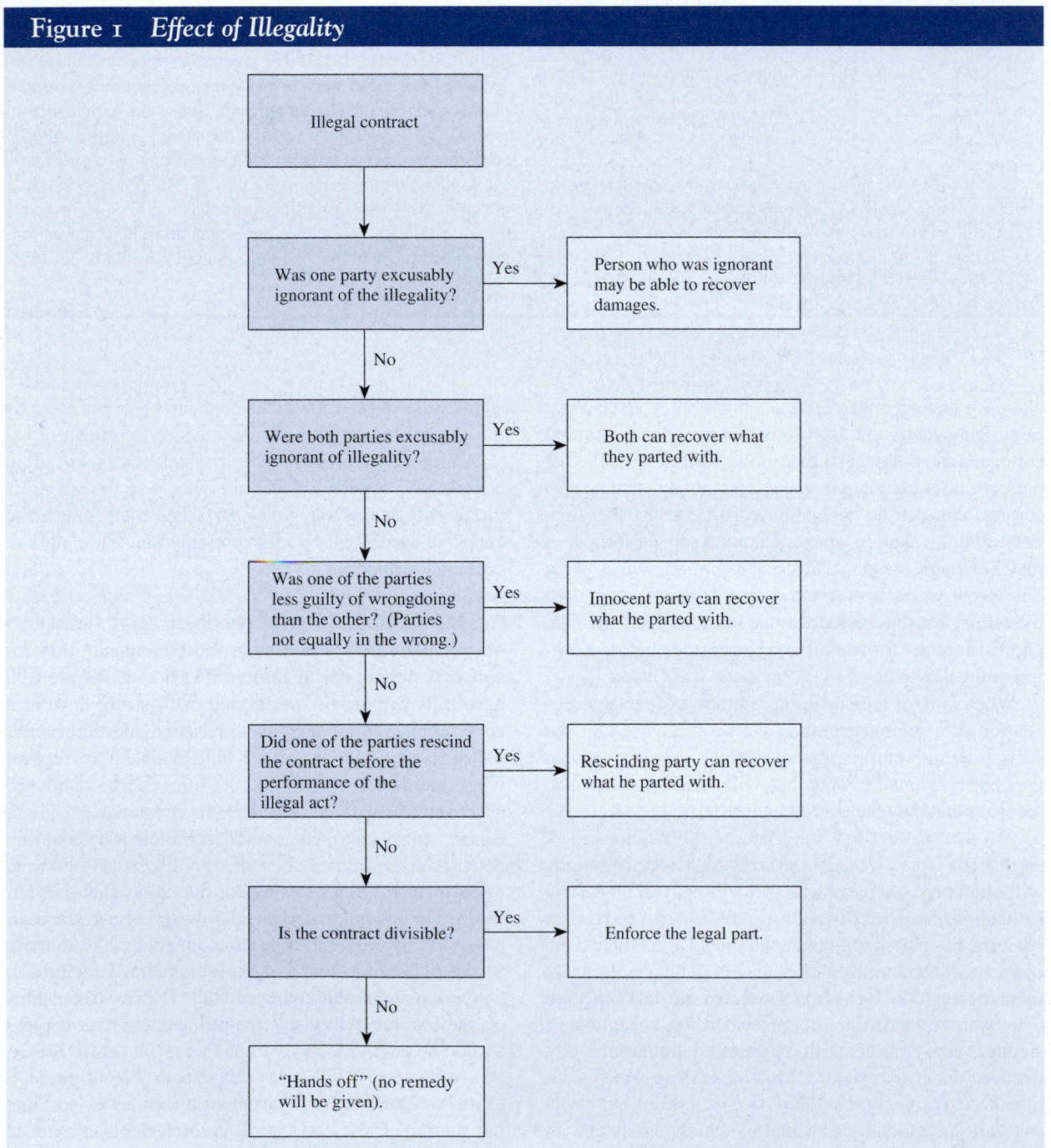

contract that contains an illegal part will be entirely un-enforceable unless it comes within one of the exceptions discussed above. However, if the major portion of a contract is legal but the contract contains an illegal provision that does not affect the primary, legal portion, courts will often enforce the legal part of the agreement and simply decline to enforce the illegal part. For example, suppose Alberts sells his barbershop to Bates. The contract of sale provides that Alberts will not engage in barbering anywhere in the world for the rest of his life. The major portion of the contract—the sale of the business—is perfectly legal. A provision of the contract—the ancillary covenant not to compete—is overly restrictive, and thus illegal. A court would enforce the sale of the business but modify or refuse to enforce the restraint provision. See Figure 1.

Problems and Problem Cases

1. Goldstein, an attorney, hired Patterson as a paralegal in her law firm. Goldstein orally agreed to pay Patterson an annual salary plus bonus wages calculated as 10 percent of Goldstein's attorney's fees from cases on which Patterson worked. At that time, Patterson did not know that the bonus arrangement violated the Florida Bar's Rules of Professional Conduct. When Goldstein failed to pay Patterson more than a portion of the bonus wages due under their agreement, Patterson pressed Goldstein for the unpaid bonuses. Goldstein promised that she would pay them, but stated that she could not put that promise into writing because of a problem with "the Bar." Goldstein thereafter refused to pay Patterson the remaining bonus wages due under their agreement. The employment relationship terminated, Patterson sued Goldstein for $87,300 in unpaid wages. Goldstein argued that the agreement was not enforceable against her because her own promise to pay Patterson the bonus wages was "unethical and thus void as against public policy." Will Goldstein's promise to give Patterson the bonus wages be enforced?

2. Broemmer, age 21, was unmarried and 16 or 17 weeks pregnant. She was a high school graduate earning less than $100 a week and had no medical benefits. Broemmer was in considerable turmoil and confusion. The father-to-be insisted that she have an abortion, but her parents advised against it. Broemmer went to Abortion Services with her mother and was escorted into an adjoining room and asked to complete three forms: a consent to treatment form, a questionnaire asking for a detailed medical history, and an agreement to arbitrate. The agreement to arbitrate stated that "any dispute arising between the Parties as a result of the fees and/or services: would be settled by binding arbitration" and that "any arbitrators appointed by the AAA [American Arbitration Association] shall be licensed medical doctors who specialize in obstetrics/gynecology." No one made any effort to explain this to Broemmer, and she was not provided with a copy of the agreement. She completed all three forms in less than five minutes. After Broemmer returned the forms to the front desk, she was taken into an examination room where preoperation procedures were performed. She was then instructed to return at 7:00 AM the next morning. She returned the following day and a physician performed the abortion. As a result of this procedure, Broemmer suffered a punctured uterus, which required medical treatment. Broemmer later filed a malpractice lawsuit against Abortion Services. Abortion Services moved to dismiss the suit on the ground that arbitration was required under the agreement. Should the arbitration clause be enforced in this situation?

3. Piatek had served a 10-year term in San Quentin State Prison for assault with a deadly weapon with great bodily injury. His criminal background prevented him from acquiring the license to sell insurance that was required by state law. Nevertheless, he sold insurance for American Income Life Insurance Company under several false names. He then sued American Income Life Insurance to recover commissions on the sales that he had made. Will he be successful?

4. Strickland attempted to bribe Judge Sylvania Woods to show leniency toward one of Strickland's friends who had a case pending before the judge. Judge Woods immediately reported this to the state's attorney and was asked to play along with Strickland until the actual payment of money occurred. Strickland gave $2,500 to the judge, who promptly turned it over to the state's attorney's office. Strickland was indicted for bribery, pled guilty, and was sentenced to a four-year prison term. Three months after the

criminal trial, Strickland filed a motion for the return of his $2,500. Will the court order the return of his money?

5. Steamatic of Kansas City, Inc., specialized in cleaning and restoring property damaged by fire, smoke, water, or other elements. It employed Rhea as a marketing representative. His duties included soliciting customers, preparing cost estimates, supervising restoration work, and conducting seminars. At the time of his employment, Rhea signed a noncompetition agreement prohibiting him from entering into a business in competition with Steamatic within six counties of the Kansas City area for a period of two years after the termination of his employment with Steamatic. Late in 1987, Rhea decided to leave Steamatic. In contemplation of the move, he secretly extracted the agreement restricting his postemployment activity from the company's files and destroyed it. Steamatic learned of this and discharged Rhea. Steamatic filed suit against Rhea to enforce the noncompetition agreement when it learned that he was entering a competing business. Will the noncompetition agreement be enforced?

6. Deno, Tisdale, Adams, Fairley, and Dickerson were all employees at the Waffle House restaurant in Grand Bay, Alabama. Seward was a regular customer at the restaurant. On several occasions, Seward would travel to Florida and buy lottery tickets. On his return, he would give the tickets to various friends and family members, including the employees of the Waffle House. A drawing for the Florida lottery was scheduled for Saturday night, March 6, 1999. Seward traveled to Florida in the week before that drawing and purchased several lottery tickets. He placed each individual ticket in a separate envelope and wrote the name of the intended recipient on the outside of the envelope. On the eve of the drawing, Seward presented three of the employees with an envelope containing a ticket, but none of them won. The day after the drawing, Seward gave Dickerson and another employee envelopes containing tickets. When Dickerson opened her envelope, she determined that the numbers of her ticket matched the winning numbers drawn in the lottery the night before. The ticket won a prize of approximately $5 million. Shortly afterward, Dickerson's four co-employees sued her, alleging that they and Dickerson had orally contracted with each other that if any one of them should win, the winner would share any lottery winnings with the other ticket recipients. An Alabama statute states that "all contracts founded in whole or in part on a gambling consideration are void." Must Dickerson share the lottery proceeds with her co-employees?

7. Kelly Services is a staffing services company that provides a range of employment staffing and consulting services. Greene, who was 24 years old, began working for Kelly Services six months after graduating from college. At the beginning of her employment, she signed an agreement that contained both noncompete and confidentiality clauses. The noncompete clause stated in part: "I will not compete against Kelly or associate myself with any Kelly competitor as an employee, owner, partner. . . . These same limitations apply for one year after I leave Kelly in any market area in which I worked or had responsibility during the past five years of my employment with Kelly."

She was a "staffing supervisor" for Kelly Services for more than two years. As a staffing supervisor, Greene serviced and maintained relationships with customers, developed new business, and recruited candidates throughout Cumberland and York Counties in Maine. About 75 percent of Greene's work at Kelly Services involved recruiting activities for Anthem Blue Cross/Blue Shield, Unum, and Citigroup Financial, including spending one full year on-site at Unum. Greene voluntarily resigned from Kelly Services in December 2007, at least in part because of repeated statements about possible layoffs made by a supervisor at Kelly Services. She began working for the Portland office of Maine Staffing Group as a "staffing specialist," where her duties were primarily clerical. The Portland office of Maine Staffing recruits blue-collar positions for the construction and trade industries and does not recruit for clients seeking to fill office or clerical positions. In her new job she did not seek new accounts or customers and did not solicit business involving white-collar personnel. She did not retain any Kelly Services documents and has not used any protected information from Kelly Services in her new job. Kelly Services filed a motion for a preliminary injunction against Greene for violating the noncompete that she signed. Is the noncompete clause likely to be enforced so as to prevent her from working at Maine Staffing?

8. Carlos Leon joined the Family Fitness Center, signing a contract called a "Club Membership Agreement (Retail Installment Contract)." The contract is

a legal-length, single sheet of paper covered with writing front and back. The front page was divided into two columns, with the right-hand column containing blanks for insertion of financial and "Federal Truth in Lending" data plus approximately 76 lines of text of varying sizes, some highlighted with bold print. The left-hand column contains approximately 90 lines of text undifferentiated in size, with no highlighting and no paragraph headings or any other indication of its contents. The back of the agreement contains approximately 90 lines of text. The exculpatory clause is located at the bottom of the left-hand column of the front page and states the following:

> Buyer is aware that participation in a sport or physical exercise may result in accidents or injury, and Buyer assumes the risk connected with the participation in a sport or exercise and represents that Member is in good health and suffers from no physical impairment which would limit their use of FFC's facilities. Buyer acknowledges that FFC has not and will not render any medical services including medical diagnosis of Member's physical condition. Buyer specifically agrees that FFC, its officers, employees and agents shall not be liable for any claim, demand, cause of action of any kind whatsoever for, or on account of death, personal injury, property damage or loss of any kind resulting from or related to Member's use of the facilities or participation in any sport, exercise or activity within or without the club premises, and Buyer agrees to hold FFC harmless from same.

Months later, Leon sustained head injuries when a sauna bench on which he was lying collapsed beneath him at Family Fitness. Leon filed an action against Family Fitness for personal injuries. Will the exculpatory agreement he signed be enforced?

9. A New York statute states that surrogate parenting agreements—agreements whereby insemination or impregnation is done specifically for the purpose of creating a child for adoption, and a surrogate mother agrees at the time of insemination or impregnation to surrender the child for adoption—are against public policy and void. Itskov alleges that Dr. Sultan had agreed to perform in vitro fertilization on a surrogate mother in order to create a child for Itskov to adopt. Later, she sued Dr. Sultan for breach of contract. Is the contract enforceable?

10. Gianni Sport was a New York manufacturer and distributor of women's clothing. Gantos was a clothing retailer headquartered in Grand Rapids, Michigan. In 1980, Gantos's sales total was 20 times greater than Gianni Sport's, and in this industry, buyers were "in the driver's seat." In June 1980, Gantos submitted to Gianni Sport a purchase order for women's holiday clothing to be delivered on October 10, 1980. The purchase order contained the following clause:

> Buyer reserves the right to terminate by notice to Seller all or any part of this Purchase Order with respect to Goods that have not actually been shipped by Seller or as to Goods which are not timely delivered for any reason whatsoever.

Gianni Sport made the goods in question especially for Gantos. This holiday order comprised 20 to 22 percent of Gianni Sport's business. In late September 1980, before the goods were shipped, Gantos canceled the order. Was the cancellation clause unconscionable?

Online Research

Examples of Noncompetes and Exculpatory Agreements

Using your favorite search engine, find an example of a noncompetition agreement and an example of a liability release (exculpatory agreement).

chapter 16

WRITING

Moore went to First National Bank and requested the president of the bank to allow his adult sons, Rocky and Mike, to open an account in the name of Texas Continental Express, Inc. Moore promised to bring his own business to the bank and orally agreed to make good any losses that the bank might incur from receiving dishonored checks from Texas Continental. The bank then furnished a regular checking account and bank draft services to Texas Continental. Several years later, Texas Continental wrote checks totaling $448,942.05 that were returned for insufficient funds. Texas Continental did not cover the checks and the bank turned to Moore for payment.

- Was Moore's **oral** promise to pay Texas Continental's dishonored checks enforceable?
- If not, what would have been required in the nature of a writing to make the promise enforceable?
- Suppose there had been a written agreement between Moore and the bank: Would the bank have been able to enforce an oral promise made by Moore that was **not** stated in the written contract?
- Would it be ethical of Moore *not* to pay the bank?

YOUR STUDY OF CONTRACT law so far has focused on the requirements for the formation of a valid contract. You should be aware, however, that even when all the elements of a valid contract exist, the enforceability of the contract and the nature of the parties' obligations can be greatly affected by the *form* in which the contract is set out and by the *language* that is used to express the agreement. This chapter discusses the ways in which the enforceability of a contract and the scope of contractual obligations can be affected by the manner in which people express their agreements.

The Significance of Writing in Contract Law

Purposes of Writing Despite what many people believe, there is no general requirement that contracts be in writing. In most situations, oral contracts are legally enforceable, assuming that they can be proven. Still, oral contracts are less desirable than written contracts in many ways. They are more easily misunderstood or forgotten than written contracts. They are also more subject to the danger that a person might fabricate terms or fraudulently claim to have made an oral contract when none exists.

Writing is important in contract law and practice for a number of reasons. When people memorialize their contracts in a writing, they are enhancing their chances of proving that an obligation was undertaken and making it harder for the other party to deny making the promise. A person's signature on a written contract allows a basis for the contract to be authenticated, or proved to be genuinely the contract of the signer. In addition, signing a writing also communicates to any of us entering the contract the seriousness of the occasion. Occasionally there are problems with proving the genuineness of the writing and often there are disagreements about the interpretation of language in a contract, but the written form is still very useful in increasing the chances that you will be able to depend on the enforcement of your contracts.

Writing and Contract Enforcement In contract law, there are certain situations in which a promise that is not in writing can be denied enforcement. In such situations, an otherwise valid contract can become unenforceable if it does not comply with the formalities required by state law. These situations are controlled by a type of statute called the Statute of Frauds.

Overview of the Statute of Frauds

History and Purposes
In 17th-century England, the dangers inherent in oral contracts were exacerbated by a legal rule that prohibited parties to a lawsuit from testifying in their own cases. Since the parties to an oral contract could not give testimony, the only way they could prove the existence of the contract was through the testimony of third parties. As you might expect, third parties were sometimes persuaded to offer false testimony about the existence of contracts. In an attempt to stop the widespread fraud and perjury that resulted, Parliament enacted the Statute of Frauds in 1677. It required written evidence before certain classes of contracts would be enforced. Although the possibility of fraud exists in every contract, the statute focused on contracts in which the potential for fraud was great or the consequences of fraud were especially serious. The legislatures of American states adopted very similar statutes, also known as statutes of frauds. These statutes, which require certain kinds of contracts to be evidenced by a signed writing, are exceptions to the general rule that oral contracts are enforceable.

Statutes of frauds have produced a great deal of litigation, due in part to the public's ignorance of their provisions. It is difficult to imagine an aspect of contract law that is more practical for businesspeople to know about than the circumstances under which an oral contract will not suffice.

Effect of Violation of the Statute of Frauds
The statute of frauds applies only to executory contracts. If an oral contract has been completely performed by both parties, the fact that it did not comply with the statute of frauds would not be a ground for rescission of the contract.

What happens if an executory contract is within the statute of frauds but has not been evidenced by the type of writing required by the statute? It is not treated as an illegal contract because the statute of frauds is more of a formal rule than a rule of substantive law. Rather, the contract that fails to comply with the statute of frauds is *unenforceable*. Although the contract will not be enforced, a person who has conferred some benefit on the other party pursuant to the contract can recover the reasonable value of his performance in an action based on *quasi-contract*.

Contracts Covered by the Statute of Frauds

A contract is said to be "within" (covered by) the statute of frauds if the statute requires that sort of contract to be evidenced by a writing. In almost all states, the following types of contracts are *within* the statute of frauds:

1. Collateral contracts in which a person promises to perform the obligation of another person.
2. Contracts for the sale of an interest in real estate.
3. Bilateral contracts that cannot be performed within a year from the date of their formation.
4. Contracts for the sale of goods for a price of $500 or more.
5. Contracts in which an executor or administrator promises to be personally liable for the debt of an estate.
6. Contracts in which marriage is the consideration.

Of this list, the first four sorts of contracts have the most significance today, and our discussion will focus primarily on them.

The statutes of frauds of the various states are not uniform. Some states require written evidence of other contracts in addition to those listed above. For example, a number of states require written evidence of contracts to pay a commission for the sale of real estate. Others require written evidence of ratifications of infants' promises or promises to pay debts that have been barred by the statute of limitations or discharged by bankruptcy.

The following discussion examines in greater detail the sorts of contracts that are within most states' statute of frauds.

The Global Business Environment

Under the CISG, there is no requirement that a contract be evidenced by a writing. A contract need not take any particular form, and can be proven by any means. The CISG does permit parties to a written contract to require that any modifications of the contract be in writing, however.

Collateral Contracts

A **collateral contract** is one in which one person (the *guarantor*) agrees to pay the debt or obligation that a second person (the *principal debtor*) owes to a third person (the *obligee*) if the principal debtor fails to perform. For example, Cohn, who wants to help Davis establish a business, promises First Bank that he will repay the loan that First Bank makes to Davis if Davis fails to pay it. Here, Cohn is the guarantor, Davis is the principal debtor, and First Bank is the obligee. Cohn's promise to First Bank must be in writing to be enforceable.

Figure 1 shows that a collateral contract involves at least three parties and at least two promises to perform (a promise by the principal debtor to pay the obligee and a promise by the guarantor to pay the obligee). In a collateral contract, the guarantor promises to pay *only if the principal debtor fails to do so*. The essence of the collateral contract is that the debt or obligation is owed primarily by the principal debtor and the guarantor's debt is *secondary*. Thus, not all three-party transactions are collateral contracts.

When a person undertakes an obligation that is *not* conditioned on the default of another person, and the debt is his own rather than that of another person, his obligation is said to be *original,* not collateral. For example, when Timmons calls Johnson Florist Company and says, "Send flowers to Elrod," Timmons is undertaking an obligation to pay *her own*—not someone else's—debt.

When a contract is determined to be collateral, however, it will be unenforceable unless it is evidenced by a writing. You will see an example of this principle in the *Wintersport* case which follows below.

Exception: Main Purpose or Leading Object Rule

There are some situations in which a contract that is technically collateral is treated like an original contract because the person promising to pay the debt of another

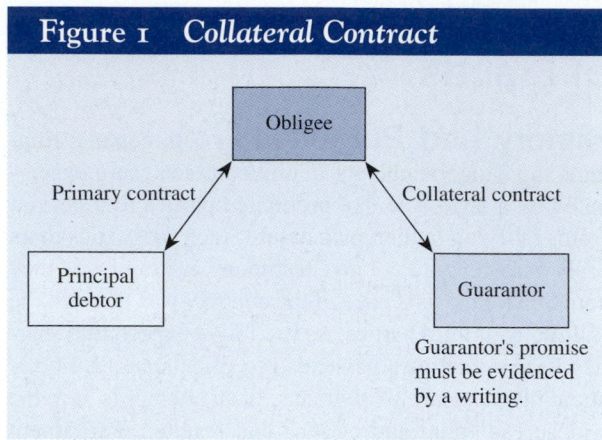

Figure 1   Collateral Contract

Obligee

Primary contract   Collateral contract

Principal debtor   Guarantor

Guarantor's promise must be evidenced by a writing.

does so for the primary purpose of securing some personal benefit. Under the **main purpose** or **leading object** rule, no writing is required where the guarantor makes a collateral promise for the main purpose of obtaining some personal economic advantage. When the consideration given in exchange for the collateral promise is something the guarantor seeks primarily for his own benefit rather than for the benefit of the primary debtor, the contract is outside the statute of frauds and does not have to be in writing. Suppose, for example, that Penn is a major creditor of Widgetmart, a retailer. To help keep Widgetmart afloat and increase the chances that Widgetmart will repay the debt it owes him, Penn orally promises Rex Industries, one of the Widgetmart's suppliers, that he will guarantee Widgetmart's payment for goods that Rex sells to Widgetmart. In this situation, Penn's oral agreement could be enforced under the main purpose rule if the court finds that Penn was acting for his own personal financial benefit.

In the following *Wintersport* case, the court considers whether the main purpose or leading object rule applies to a shareholder who guarantees a corporation's debt.

Wintersport Ltd. v. Millionaire.com, Inc.
2004 Wash. App. LEXIS 1071 (Ct. App. Wash. 2004) (unpublished opinion)

Wintersport Ltd. contacted Millionaire.com, Inc., to offer advertising, production, and printing services for Millionaire.com's magazine, Opulence. *Wintersport and Millionaire.com entered into a $170,000 contract for the printing of one monthly issue in October 2000. They performed that contract and entered negotiations to print the next month's issue. David Strong, senior vice president of Millionaire.com, and Ron Leiter, president of Wintersport, handled most of the negotiations and communications. Due to financial difficulties, Millionaire.com reduced the size of its order for the second issue and requested payment terms on the reduced price of $80,000. Concerned about Millionaire.com's creditworthiness, Leiter told Strong that Wintersport would only extend credit to Millionaire.com if Millionaire.com paid a $10,000 down payment and White personally guaranteed the balance due. During a phone call between their respective offices in Washington and South Carolina,*

Leiter requested and received White's oral agreement to the personal guaranty. Leiter then sent a confirming fax to White's office, and White express-mailed to Wintersport a $10,000 check drawn on Millionaire.com's account. When Millionaire.com failed to pay the amount due on the contract, Wintersport filed suit against White and others.

The trial court entered judgment in Wintersport's favor against Millionaire.com and White. White appealed, arguing that the action should have been dismissed because the statute of frauds prevented the enforcement of his oral guaranty.

Coleman, Judge

The statute of frauds provides that "every special promise to answer for the debt, default, or misdoings of another person" must be in writing. There is a distinction, however, between original promises, which do not fall within the statute, and collateral promises, which do. Wintersport argues that White's oral guaranty is outside the statute of frauds because White received a personal benefit from the guaranty due to his interest in continuing the business of Millionaire.com. White argues, however, that standing alone, ownership of stock is insufficient to support a finding that his promise was original. An original promise occurs when the promisor receives some consideration or direct benefit from the promise. If the leading object is to benefit the promisor, it does not matter if the effect of the promise is to pay the debt of another. A frequent scenario in which courts enforce oral original promises is when promisors agree to be billed directly for services provided to a third party. White contends that this case presents the classic example of an unenforceable promise in which a promisor agrees to pay the debts of another if that party fails to pay.

Smith v. Twohy held that in such circumstances a showing of direct benefit is necessary to take the promise out of the statute of frauds. *Twohy* further held that the benefits accruing as incidents of stock ownership are insufficient to show a direct benefit. The direct benefit inquiry here is the sole criteria for determining whether the promise was original or collateral. This case presents a situation where White promises to pay if Millionaire.com does not; but under *Twohy,* mere status as a shareholder is insufficient to take this kind of promise out of the statute of frauds. Wintersport has not shown that White's benefit amounted to anything more than an indirect incident of share ownership. Although White owned stock in Millionaire.com, there is not substantial evidence to support the trial court's findings that White received a personal benefit from Millionaire.com's successful completion of the printing contract with Wintersport.

At trial, Wintersport argued that Millionaire.com's future and White's job depended on the success of *Opulence* and that White received a substantial benefit to his company by entering into a guaranty. There is, however, no direct evidence of this. White describes Wintersport's claims as "speculative," and he is correct. The record is devoid of any evidence that could support these arguments. Since the burden was on Wintersport to prove the benefit White received and it failed to sustain its burden, we conclude that White's oral guaranty fell within the statute of frauds.

Reversed and dismissed in favor of White.

Interest in Land Any contract that creates or transfers an interest in land is within the statute of frauds. The inclusion of real estate contracts in the statute of frauds reflects the values of an earlier, agrarian society in which land was the primary basis of wealth. Our legal system historically has treated land as being more important than other forms of property. Courts have interpreted the land provision of the statute of frauds broadly to require written evidence of any transaction that will affect the ownership of an interest in land. Thus, a contract to sell or mortgage real estate must be evidenced by a writing, as must an option to purchase real estate or a contract to grant an easement or permit the mining and removal of minerals on land. A lease is also a transfer of an interest in land, but most states' statutes of frauds do not require leases to be in writing unless they are long-term leases, usually those for one year or more. On the other hand, a contract to erect a building or to insure a building would not be within the real estate provision of the statute of frauds because such contracts do not involve the transfer of interests in land.[1]

Exception: Full Performance by the Vendor An oral contract for the sale of land that has been completely performed by the vendor (seller) is "taken out of the statute of frauds"—that is, is enforceable without a writing. For example, Peterson and Lincoln enter into an oral contract for the sale of Peterson's farm at an agreed-on price and Peterson, the vendor, delivers a deed to the farm to

---

[1]Note, however, that a writing might be required under state insurance statutes.

Lincoln. In this situation, the vendor has completely performed and most states would treat the oral contract as being enforceable.

Exception: Part Performance (Action in Reliance) by the Vendee

When the vendee (purchaser of land) does an act in clear reliance on an oral contract for the sale of land, an equitable doctrine commonly known as the "part performance doctrine" permits the vendee to enforce the contract notwithstanding the fact that it was oral. The part performance doctrine is based on both evidentiary and reliance considerations. The doctrine recognizes that a person's conduct can "speak louder than words" and can indicate the existence of a contract almost as well as a writing can. The part performance doctrine is also based on the desire to avoid the injustice that would otherwise result if the contract were repudiated after the vendee's reliance.

Under section 129 of the *Restatement (Second) of Contracts,* a contract for the transfer of an interest in land can be enforced even without a writing if the person seeking enforcement:

1. Has *reasonably relied* on the contract and on the other party's assent.

2. Has changed his position to such an extent that *enforcement of the contract is the only way to prevent injustice.*

In other words, the vendee must have done some act in reliance on the contract and the nature of the act must be such that restitution (returning his money) would not be an adequate remedy. The part performance doctrine will not permit the vendee to collect damages for breach of contract, but it will permit him to obtain the equitable remedy of **specific performance,** a remedy whereby the court orders the breaching party to perform his contract.[2]

A vendee's reliance on an oral contract could be shown in many ways. Traditionally, many states have required that the vendee pay part or all of the purchase price and either make substantial improvements on the property or take possession of it. For example, Contreras and Miller orally enter into a contract for the sale of Contreras's land. If Miller pays Contreras a substantial part of the purchase price and either takes possession of the land or begins to make improvements on it, the contract would be enforceable without a writing under the part performance doctrine. These are not the only sorts of acts in reliance that would make an oral contract enforceable, however. Under the *Restatement (Second)* approach, if the promise to

transfer land is clearly proven or is admitted by the breaching party, it is not necessary that the act of reliance include making payment, taking possession, or making improvements.[3] It still is necessary, however, that the reliance be such that restitution would not be an adequate remedy. For this reason, a vendee's payment of the purchase price, standing alone, is usually *not* sufficient for the part performance doctrine.

Contracts That Cannot Be Performed within One Year

A bilateral, executory contract that cannot be performed within one year from the day on which it comes into existence is within the statute of frauds and must be evidenced by a writing. The apparent purpose of this provision is to guard against the risk of faulty or willfully inaccurate recollection of long-term contracts. Courts have tended to construe it very narrowly.

One aspect of this narrow construction is that most states hold that a contract that has been fully performed by *one* of the parties is "taken out of the statute of frauds" and is enforceable without a writing. For example, Nash enters into an oral contract to perform services for Thomas for 13 months. If Nash has already fully performed his part of the contract, Thomas will be required to pay him the contract price.

In addition, this provision of the statute has been held to apply only when the terms of the contract make it impossible for the contract to be completed within one year. You will see an example of this principle in the following *Schaadt v. St. Jude Medical S.C.* case. If the contract is for an indefinite period of time, it is not within the statute of frauds. This is true even if, in retrospect, the contract was not completed within a year. Thus, Weinberg's agreement to work for Wolf for an indefinite period of time would not have to be evidenced by a writing, even if Weinberg eventually works for Wolf for many years. The mere fact that performance is unlikely to be completed in one year does not bring the contract within the statute of frauds. In most states, a contract "for life" is not within the statute of frauds because it is possible—since death is an uncertain event—for the contract to be performed within a year. In a few states such as New York, contracts for life are within the statute of frauds.

Computing Time

In determining whether a contract is within the one-year provision, courts begin counting time on the day when the contract comes into existence. If, under the terms of the contract, it is possible to perform

---

[2]Specific performance is discussed in more detail in Chapter 18.

[3]*Restatement (Second) of Contracts* § 129, comment *d.*

it within one year from this date, the contract does not fall within the statute of frauds and does not have to be in writing. If, however, the terms of the contract make it impossible to complete performance of the contract (without breaching it) within one year from the date on which the contract came into existence, the contract falls within the statute and must meet its requirements to be enforceable. Thus, if Hammer Co. and McCrea agree on

August 1, 2009, that McCrea will work for Hammer Co. for one year, beginning October 1, 2009, the terms of the contract dictate that it is not possible to complete performance until October 1, 2010. Because that date is more than one year from the date on which the contract came into existence, the contract falls within the statute of frauds and must be evidenced by a writing to be enforceable.

Schaadt v. St. Jude Medical S.C., Inc.
2007 U.S. Dist. LEXIS 59586 (U.S. Dist. Ct. D. Minn. 2007)

St. Jude is a large medical device manufacturer. In July 2001, Schaadt began working as a product manager in St. Jude's Cardiac Rhythm Management Division. By all accounts, she performed well. Eventually, though, she became frustrated by sexual harassment and sexual discrimination within her division, so she applied for and obtained a position within another St. Jude division, the U.S. Sales Division (USD).

Schaadt began working in USD as a field marketing manager in May 2004. Shortly after she started her new position, USD asked her and all of the other field marketing managers to sign a written contract containing nonsolicitation and confidentiality provisions. In return for agreeing to these provisions, the field marketing managers—who would otherwise be employees at will—were given one-year terms of employment. The contract required St. Jude to employ Schaadt for a minimum of one year, and it prohibited Schaadt from soliciting St. Jude's employees for one year after the termination of her employment with St. Jude. USD gave the employment agreement to Schaadt and asked her to sign it. The parties dispute whether Schaadt signed it—she alleged that she did sign it—but there is no proof that any representative of St. Jude signed the contract.

Schaadt had conflicts with her supervisor in USD and began looking for another job. She told recruiters that she did not like her current position and wanted to pursue another opportunity. Before Schaadt could quit, though, she was fired. Schaadt sued St. Jude for breach of contract as well as other claims, and St. Jude moved for summary judgment of the breach of contract claim on the ground that it was barred by the statute of frauds.

Schlitz, U.S. District Judge

A contract falls within the statute of frauds unless the contract, by its terms, is capable of being fully performed within one year.

1. *Performance Within One Year*

Schaadt argues that the statute of frauds is inapplicable because her contract with St. Jude was capable of being fully performed within one year. According to Schaadt, she could have quit her job 30 seconds after she agreed to the contract. That would have triggered the running of the one-year nonsolicitation commitment, and she could have fulfilled that commitment within one year of the date that she entered the contract.

Schaadt's argument is unavailing. The test under the statute of frauds is whether the parties to a contract—all parties—can perform their obligations within one year. In any contract, something might arise within one year that excuses performance. That obviously cannot be enough to defeat application of the statute of frauds, or no contract would ever be covered by the statute. For purposes of the statute of frauds, the question is not whether something might arise within one year that would

excuse performance, but whether the parties can fully perform their obligations under the contract within one year if those obligations are not excused.

The St. Jude–Schaadt contract contains two commitments: a commitment by St. Jude to employ Schaadt for at least one year, and a commitment by Schaadt not to solicit St. Jude's employees for one year after leaving the employ of St. Jude. The parties could not fully perform all of their duties under the contract within one year. True, if Schaadt quit her job 30 seconds (or 30 days) after entering the contract, St. Jude would be excused from performing its obligation to employ Schaadt for a year. But St. Jude would not have performed its obligation. St. Jude needed one full year to perform its obligation under the employment provision, and Schaadt, of course, needed an additional year to perform her obligation under the nonsolicitation provision.

If the law were as Schaadt would have it, then no employment contract would ever fall within the statute of frauds because an employee can always quit (or become disabled or die) a few seconds after entering the contract. For example, an employee could allege that an employment contract for a term of five years was not within the statute of frauds because the employee could have quit the day after agreeing to the contract. Minnesota courts have consistently rejected such arguments. In sum, the St. Jude–Schaadt "agreement [was] . . . by its terms . . . not to be performed within one year from the making thereof." Minn. Stat. § 513.01. St. Jude, the party charged with breach, did not sign the contract, and therefore, under the Minnesota statute of frauds, the contract is unenforceable at St. Jude's option.

2. Necessity of a Signature

Schaadt argues that, despite the fact that St. Jude did not sign the contract, St. Jude drafted the agreement and that is sufficient to satisfy the statute of frauds. Schaadt relies most heavily on *Beach v. Anderson* (Minn. Ct. App. 1988). In *Beach,* the parties entered into an oral contract that included a six-year noncompete provision. The oral contract in *Beach* was transcribed by a court reporter. In addition, both parties in *Beach* explicitly assented to be bound by the contract, and their assent was transcribed by the court reporter. Disputes later arose between the parties, and one of the parties attempted to avoid the contract by arguing that it was subject to the statute of frauds (because of the six-year noncompete provision) and that the statute had not been satisfied because the contract had never been reduced to writing and signed. The Minnesota Court of Appeals agreed that

the contract was within the statute of frauds, but held that the statute's requirements were met because not merely the terms of the contract, but the parties' assent to those terms, had been transcribed. *Beach* is obviously distinguishable from the present case. Here, as was true in *Beach,* there is no real doubt about the terms of the contract. St. Jude asked Schaadt to sign the same form contract that it provided to many other employees. But here, as was not true in *Beach,* there is substantial doubt about whether both parties assented to the contract.

The court has a great deal of sympathy for Schaadt. When there is no real doubt about the terms of the proposed St. Jude–Schaadt contract—and no real doubt that St. Jude would have signed the contract if it had timely received a signed copy from Schaadt—it does seem that dismissing Schaadt's breach-of-contract claim exults form over substance. But the statute of frauds is, by its nature, a formalistic statute; it provides that, in some circumstances, form is just as important as substance. This is the decision of the Minnesota legislature, and this court is obligated to honor that decision. When the Minnesota statute of frauds clearly requires that the St. Jude–Schaadt contract be reduced to writing and signed by the party against whom enforcement is sought, the court will not expand *Beach* to eliminate the need for any objective evidence of assent.

Summary judgment granted in favor of St. Jude.

Sale of Goods for $500 or More
The original English Statute of Frauds required a writing for contracts for the sale of goods for a price of 10 pounds sterling or more. In the United States today, the writing requirement for the sale of goods is governed by section 2–201 of the Uniform Commercial Code. This section provides that contracts for the sale of goods for the price of $500 or more are not enforceable without a writing or other specified evidence that a contract was made. There are a number of alternative ways of satisfying the requirements of section 2–201. These will be explained later in this chapter.

Modifications of Existing Sales Contracts
Just as some contracts to extend the time for performance fall within the one-year provision of the statute of frauds, agreements to modify existing sales contracts can fall within the statute of frauds if the contract as modified is for a price of $500 or more.[4] UCC section 2–209(3) provides that the requirements of the statute of frauds

must be satisfied if the contract as modified is within its provisions. For example, if Carroll and Kestler enter into a contract for the sale of goods at a price of $490, the original contract does *not* fall within the statute of frauds. However, if they later modify the contract by increasing the contract price to $510, the modification falls within the statute of frauds and must meet its requirements to be enforceable.

Promise of Executor or Administrator to Pay a Decedent's Debt Personally
When a person dies, a personal representative is appointed to administer his estate. One of the important tasks of this personal representative, who is called an executor if the person dies leaving a will or an administrator if the person dies without a will, is to pay the debts owed by the decedent. No writing is required when an executor or administrator—acting in his representative capacity—promises to pay the decedent's debts from the funds of the decedent's estate. The statute of frauds requires a writing, however, if the executor, acting in her capacity as a private individual rather than in her representative capacity, promises to pay one of the decedent's

[4]Modifications of sales contracts are discussed in greater detail in Chapter 12.

CONCEPT REVIEW

Contracts within the Statute of Frauds

Provision	Description	Exceptions (Situations in Which Contract Does Not Require a Writing)
Marriage	Contracts, other than mutual promises to marry, where marriage is the consideration	—
Year	Bilateral contracts that, *by their terms,* cannot be performed within one year from the date on which the contract was formed	Full (complete) performance by one of the parties
Land	Contracts that create or transfer an ownership interest in real property	1. Full performance by vendor (vendor deeds property to vendees) or 2. "Part performance" doctrine: Vendee relies on oral contract—for example, by: a. Paying substantial part of purchase price, and b. Taking possession or making improvements
Executor's Promise	Executor promises to pay estate's debt out of his own funds	—
Sale of Goods at Price $500 or More (UCC § 2–201)	Contracts for the sale of goods for a contract price of $500 or more; also applies to modifications of contracts for goods where price as modified is $500 or more	See alternative ways of satisfying statute of frauds under UCC
Collateral Contracts Guaranty	Contracts where promisor promises to pay the debt of another if the primary debtor fails to pay	"Main purpose" or "leading object" exception: Guarantor makes promise primarily for her own economic benefit

debts out of her own (the executor's) funds. For example, Thomas, who has been appointed executor of his Uncle Max's estate, is presented with a bill for $10,500 for medical services rendered to Uncle Max during his last illness by the family doctor, Dr. Barnes. Feeling bad that there are not adequate funds in the estate to compensate Dr. Barnes for his services, Thomas promises to pay Dr. Barnes from his own funds. Thomas's promise would have to be evidenced by a writing to be enforceable.

Contract in Which Marriage Is the Consideration
The statute of frauds also requires a writing when marriage is the consideration to support a contract. The marriage provision has been interpreted to be inapplicable to agreements that involve only mutual

promises to marry. It can apply to any other contract in which one party's promise is given in exchange for marriage or the promise to marry on the part of the other party. This is true whether the promisor is one of the parties to the marriage or a third party. For example, if Hicks promises to deed his ranch to Everett in exchange for Everett's agreement to marry Hicks's son, Everett could not enforce Hicks's promise without written evidence of the promise.

Prenuptial (or antenuptial) agreements present a common contemporary application of the marriage provision of the statute of frauds. These are agreements between couples who contemplate marriage. They usually involve such matters as transfers of property, division of property upon divorce or death, and various lifestyle issues. Assuming that marriage or the promise to marry is the consideration supporting these agreements, they are within the statute of frauds and must be evidenced by a writing.[5]

Meeting the Requirements of the Statute of Frauds

Nature of the Writing Required
The statutes of frauds of the various states are not uniform in their formal requirements. However, most states require only a *memorandum* of the parties' agreement; they do not require that the entire contract be in writing. Essential terms of the contract must be stated in the writing. The memorandum must provide written evidence that a contract was made, but it need not have been created with the intent that the memorandum itself would be binding. In fact, in some cases, written offers that were accepted orally have been held sufficient to satisfy the writing requirement. Typical examples include letters, telegrams, receipts, or any other writing indicating that the parties had a contract. The memorandum need not be made at the same time the contract comes into being; in fact, the memorandum may be made at any time before suit is filed. If a memorandum of the parties' agreement is lost, its loss and its contents may be proven by oral testimony.

Contents of the Memorandum
Although there is a general trend away from requiring complete writings to satisfy the statute of frauds, an adequate memorandum must still contain several things. The essential terms of the contract generally must be indicated in the memorandum. States differ in their requirements concerning how specifically the terms must be stated, however. The identity of the parties must be indicated in some way, and the subject matter of the contract must be identified with reasonable certainty. This last requirement causes particular problems in contracts for the sale of land, since many statutes require a detailed description of the property to be sold.

Contents of Memorandum under the UCC
The standard for determining the sufficiency of the contents of a memorandum is more flexible in cases concerning contracts for the sale of goods. This looser standard is created by the language of UCC section 2–201, which states that the writing must be sufficient to indicate that a contract for sale has been made between the parties, but a writing can be sufficient even if it omits or incorrectly states a term agreed on. However, the memorandum is not enforceable for more than the quantity of goods stated in the memorandum. Thus, a writing that does not indicate the *quantity* of goods to be sold would not satisfy the Code's writing requirement.

Signature Requirement
The memorandum must be signed by the *party to be charged* or his authorized agent. (The party to be charged is the person using the statute of frauds as a defense—generally the defendant unless the statute of frauds is asserted as a defense to a counterclaim.) This means that it is not necessary for purposes of meeting the statute of frauds for both parties' signatures to appear on the document. It is, however, in the best interests of both parties for both signatures to appear on the writing; otherwise, the contract evidenced by the writing is enforceable only against the signing party. Unless the statute expressly provides that the memorandum or contract must be signed at the end, the signature may appear anyplace on the memorandum. Any writing, mark, initials, stamp, engraving, or other symbol placed or printed on a memorandum will suffice as a signature, as long as the party to be charged intended it to authenticate (indicate the genuineness of) the writing.

Memorandum Consisting of Several Writings
In many situations, the elements required for a memorandum are divided among several documents. For example, Wayman and Allen enter into a contract for the sale of real estate, intending to memorialize their agreement in a formal written document later. While final drafts of a written contract are being prepared, Wayman repudiates the contract. Allen has a copy of an unsigned preliminary draft of the contract that identifies the parties and contains all of the material terms of the parties' agreement, an unsigned note written by Wayman that contains the legal description of the property, and a letter signed by Wayman that refers to the contract and to

---

---

[5]Note, however, that "nonmarital" agreements between unmarried cohabitants who do not plan marriage are not within the marriage provision of the statute of frauds, even though the agreement may concern the same sorts of matters that are typically covered in a prenuptial agreement.

the other two documents. None of these documents, standing alone, would be sufficient to satisfy the statute of frauds. However, Allen can combine them to meet the requirements of the statute, provided that they all relate to the same agreement. This can be shown by physical attachment, as where the documents are stapled or bound together, or by references in the documents themselves that indicate that they all apply to the same transaction. In some cases, it has also been shown by the fact that the various documents were executed at the same time.

UCC: Alternative Means of Satisfying the Statute of Frauds in Sale of Goods Contracts

As you have learned, the basic requirement of the UCC statute of frauds [2–201] is that a contract for the sale of goods for the purchase price of $500 or more must be evidenced by a written memorandum that indicates the existence of the contract, states the quantity of goods to be sold, and is signed by the party to be charged. Recognizing that the underlying purpose of the statute of frauds is to provide more evidence of the existence of a contract than the mere oral testimony of one of the parties, however, the Code also permits the statute of frauds to be satisfied by any of four other types of evidence. These different methods of satisfying the UCC statute of frauds are depicted in Figure 2. Under the UCC, then, a contract for the sale of goods for a purchase price of $500 or more for which there is no written memorandum signed by the party to be charged can meet the requirements of the statute of frauds in any of the following ways:

1. *Confirmatory memorandum between merchants.* Suppose Gardner and Roth enter into a contract over the telephone for the sale of goods at a price of $5,000. Gardner then sends a memorandum to Roth confirming the deal they made orally. If Roth receives the memo and does not object to it, it would be fair to say that the parties' conduct provides some evidence that a contract exists. Under some circumstances, the UCC permits such confirmatory memoranda to satisfy the statute of frauds even though the writing is signed by the party who is seeking to enforce the contract rather than the party against whom enforcement is sought [2–201(2)]. This exception applies only when *both* of the parties to a contract are *merchants*. Furthermore, the memo must be sent within a reasonable time after the contract is made and must be sufficient to bind the person who sent it if enforcement were sought against him (that is, it must indicate that a contract was made, state a quantity, and be signed by the sender). If the party against whom enforcement is sought receives the memo, has reason to know its contents, and yet fails to give written notice of objection to the contents of the memo within 10 days after receiving it, the memo can be introduced to meet the requirements of the statute of frauds.

2. *Part payment or part delivery.* Suppose Rice and Cooper enter a contract for the sale of 1,000 units of goods at $1 each. After Rice has paid $600, Cooper refuses to deliver the goods and asserts the statute of frauds as a defense to enforcement of the contract. The Code permits part payment or part delivery to satisfy the statute of frauds, but only for the quantity of goods that have been delivered or paid for [2–201(3)(c)]. Thus, Cooper would be required to deliver only 600 units rather than the 1,000 units Rice alleges that he agreed to sell.

3. *Admission in pleadings or court.* Another situation in which the UCC statute of frauds can be satisfied without a writing occurs when the party being sued admits the existence of the oral contract in his trial testimony or in any document that he files with the court. For example, Nelson refuses to perform an oral contract he made with Smith for the sale of $2,000 worth of goods, and Smith sues him. If Nelson admits the existence of the oral contract in pleadings or in court proceedings, his admission is sufficient to meet the statute of frauds. This exception is justified by the strong evidence that such an admission provides. After all, what better evidence of a contract can there be than is provided when the party being sued admits under penalty of perjury that a contract exists? When such an admission is made, the statute of frauds is satisfied as to the quantity of goods admitted [2–201(3)(b)]. For example, if Nelson admits contracting only for $1,000 worth of goods, the contract is enforceable only to that extent. The following *Jones* case illustrates this method of satisfying the statute of frauds.

4. *Specially manufactured goods.* Finally, an oral contract within the UCC statute of frauds can be enforced without a writing in some situations involving the sale of specially manufactured goods. This exception to the writing requirement will apply only if the nature of the specially manufactured goods is such that they are not suitable for sale in the ordinary course of the seller's business. Completely executory oral contracts are not enforceable under this exception. The seller must have made a substantial beginning in manufacturing the goods for the buyer, or must have made commitments for their procurement, before receiving notice that the buyer was repudiating the sale [2–201(3)(a)]. For example, Bennett Co. has an oral

Figure 2   *Satisfying the Statute of Frauds through a Contract for the Sale of Goods with a Price of $500 or More*

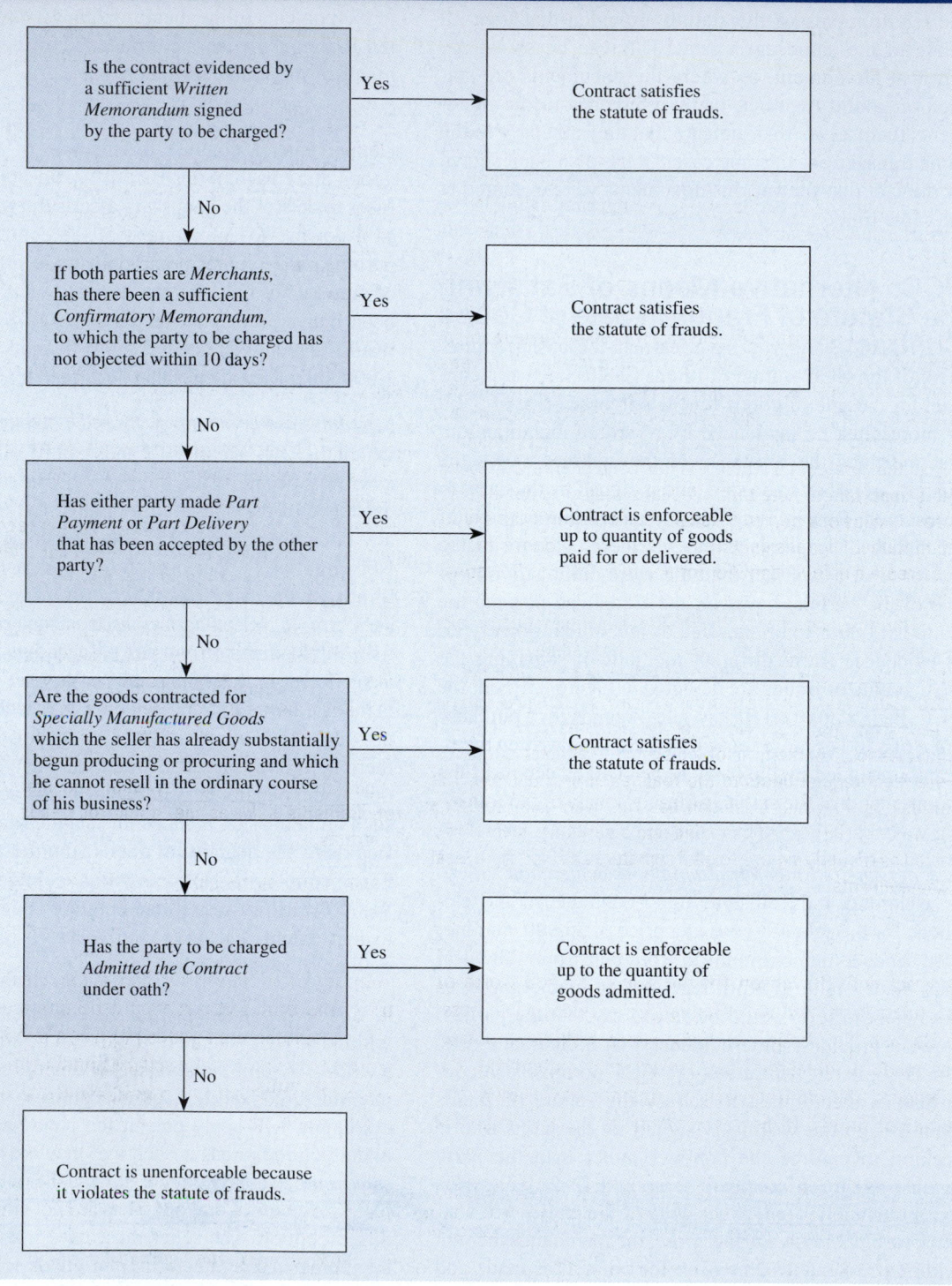

CYBERLAW IN ACTION

E-Signatures and the Statute of Frauds

The necessity of being able to prove the existence of a contract is as great online as it is in offline transactions. When we communicate or transact business online, we cannot depend on the traditional means of authenticating a contract—reading a person's distinctive signature, seeing the face, or hearing the voice of the other party, for example. Practical questions flow from this state of affairs, such as how can we be sure that a transmission arrives in the same condition as it left the sender, and that it has not been altered or forged? Technologies to increase security online have been developed and new ones are emerging all the time. One method of increasing security in electronic transmissions is the use of **digital signatures.** A digital signature is an electronic identifier that tells a person receiving the document whether it is genuinely from the sender and whether it has been altered in any way. It is important to note that a digital signature is not an electronic image of a person's signature or a person's name typed out. Rather, digital signatures employ encryption technology to create a unique identifier for a sender that can be verified by the receiver.

The absence of traditional authentication methods also raises legal questions as well, such as whether a contract formed electronically, such as over e-mail or on an e-tailer's Web site, satisfies the statute of frauds. Few courts have dealt with this issue. However, the vast majority of states have enacted some form of legislation to accommodate formal legal requirements to the realities of e-commerce. The trouble is that this legislation has not been uniform. Some states' legislation has been tied into a particular technology, such as recognizing only digital signatures as satisfying legal requirements.

The **Uniform Electronic Transactions Act** (UETA) takes a different approach. It is a proposed uniform state law that was designed to "remove barriers to electronic commerce by validating and effectuating electronic records and signatures."[6] It is not tied to any particular technology. The UETA states that an "electronic signature" (defined as an "electronic sound, symbol, or process attached to or logically associated with an electronic record and executed or adopted by a person with the intent to sign the electronic record") satisfies any law requiring a signature. Thus, digital signatures, which are one form of electronic signature, would satisfy the UETA, but so would a more commonplace symbol or event such as a typewritten name at the end of an e-mail or a click of a mouse. The UETA has been enacted in 47 states and the District of Columbia at the time of this writing.

Against the background of lack of uniformity in state law, the federal government enacted the **Electronic Signatures in Global and National Commerce Act** (E-Sign) in 2000. E-Sign provides that in transactions that are in or affecting interstate commerce, "a signature, contract, or other record relating to such transaction may not be denied legal effect, validity, or enforceability solely because it is in electronic form," nor can "a contract relating to such a transaction be denied legal effect, validity, or enforceability solely because an electronic signature or electronic record was used in its formation." Like UETA, E-Sign broadly interprets the concept of electronic signature—using, in fact, the same statutory definition of electronic signature as that which is used in UETA. E-Sign overrides any state law that is inconsistent with UETA, thus helping to harmonize U.S. law about the interaction of formal requirements such as the statute of frauds and electronic contracts.

---

[6]Uniform Electronic Transactions Act, Prefatory Note (1999).

contract with Stevenson for the sale of $2,500 worth of calendars imprinted with Bennett Co.'s name and address. If Bennett Co. repudiates the contract before Stevenson has made a substantial beginning in manufacturing the calendars, the contract will be unenforceable under the statute of frauds. If, however, Bennett Co. repudiated the contract after Stevenson had made a substantial beginning, the oral contract would be enforceable. The specially manufactured goods provision is based both on the evidentiary value of the seller's conduct and on the need to avoid the injustice that would otherwise result from the seller's reliance.

Jones v. The Baran Company   660 S.E.2d 420 (Ga. Ct. App. 2008)

In June 2003, Clifton Jones sought to buy a Mercedes-Benz McLaren SLR, an exotic race car that was hand built and manufactured in an extremely limited quantity. Jones planned to buy the vehicle and resell it for a profit. As such, he wanted to buy the vehicle at a price equal to the manufacturer's suggested retail price (MSRP), rather than at fair market value as independently determined by a dealership. Jones and his wife contacted a dealership, Mercedes-Benz of Buckhead.

The dealership had recently opened for business, operations were chaotic, and no one was able to quote a specific price for the vehicle. However, the salesperson told Jones that, in return for a $50,000 deposit, he would be entitled to purchase the vehicle at the MSRP once it was manufactured and delivered to the dealership. The salesperson further informed Jones that the dealership's general manager had approved the sale at MSRP. According to the salesperson, the MSRP would "probably [be] somewhere in the mid-[$400,000] range," but no actual price had been determined at that time. At the salesperson's request, Jones signed a preprinted form entitled "Additional Terms and Conditions of Order Agreement for a Mercedes-Benz SLR McLaren Coupe Vehicle." Jones subsequently sent his $50,000 deposit to the dealership, which retained the funds for over one-and-a-half years pending the manufacture and delivery of the vehicle.

The vehicle was delivered from the factory to the dealership in December 2004 with an MSRP established as $465,650. By that time, the original salesperson was no longer employed by the dealership, and her pending sales transactions had been taken over by another salesperson. The new salesperson had no knowledge of the prior price agreement reached with Jones and was instructed to quote Jones a final sales price of fair market value. As such, the new salesperson quoted Jones a final sales price of $800,000, the alleged fair market value of the vehicle. Jones disputed the quoted final sales price and refused to pay any amount above the MSRP. The dealership's counsel later wrote a letter to Jones offering a sales price of $700,000. Jones rejected the offer, and his deposit was returned to him by the dealership. The dealership later sold the vehicle to another customer for $505,000.

Jones filed suit for breach of contract seeking against the dealership, alleging that the dealership had entered into a contract to sell him the vehicle at a price equal to the MSRP. Jones moved for summary judgment and the trial court denied his motion. Jones appealed.

Newkirk, Judge

A contract for sale of goods may be made in any manner sufficient to show agreement, including conduct by both parties which recognizes the existence of such a contract. Furthermore, "[e]ven though one or more terms are left open a contract for sale does not fail for indefiniteness if the parties have intended to make a contract and there is a reasonably certain basis for giving an appropriate remedy." UCC § 2–204(3). Hence, if otherwise sufficient, the contract need not reflect an agreement on a specific price term.

Here, Jones presented testimony that there was an oral agreement under which the dealership was to sell Jones the vehicle at the MSRP in return for Jones making a $50,000 deposit and agreeing to purchase the vehicle once it was manufactured and delivered to the dealership, and that the terms of the oral agreement were supplemented by the "Additional Terms & Conditions of Order" form signed by Jones. Jones testified to this effect in his deposition, and the dealership's salesperson confirmed that she had promised Jones that he would be entitled to purchase the vehicle at the MSRP in return for his deposit and that the general manager had approved the agreement. The dealership failed to present any direct evidence that contradicted the positive testimony of Jones and its salesperson. We therefore conclude that the uncontroverted evidence shows that an oral contract had been formed for the sale of the vehicle, with the price term being the MSRP ultimately arrived at by the manufacturer.

Since evidence shows the existence of the oral agreement, the next issue is whether the agreement is enforceable. In this respect, the dealership argues that Jones's version of the contract is unenforceable because it violates the Statute of Frauds. It is true that:

> a contract for the sale of goods for the price of $500.00 or more is not enforceable by way of action or defense unless there is some writing sufficient to indicate that a contract for sale has been made between the parties and signed by the party against whom enforcement is sought or by his authorized agent or broker.

UCC § 2–201(1). Notwithstanding the writing and signature requirements of the Statute of Frauds, however, a contract for the sale of goods is still enforceable "[i]f the party against whom enforcement is sought admits in his pleading, testimony, or otherwise in court that a contract for sale was made." UCC § 2–201(3)(b).

It is sufficient that the party admit both that a contract was made and that the contract specified a quantity of goods. In the present case, the dealership's answer to the complaint admitted that the dealership had entered into a contract with Jones. The dealership did not otherwise dispute the existence of a contract, and in fact, retained Jones's deposit for the vehicle. Furthermore, the dealership's representative deposed under [Georgia law] testified that there was a contract between the parties. The dealership disagreed, however, as to the terms of the contract of sale. Under these circumstances, where the dealership admitted that a contract existed for the sale of a specific quantity of goods (namely, one vehicle) but on different terms and conditions than those alleged by Jones, the oral agreement between Jones and the dealership was enforceable under the exception to the Statute of Frauds set forth in UCC § 2–201(3)(b).

We conclude that the trial court erred in granting summary judgment to the dealership on the breach of contract claim. Furthermore, the trial court should have granted summary judgment to Jones on the issue of liability, since the dealership failed to present evidence sufficient to contradict the direct evidence brought forward by Jones as to the existence and terms of the contract between the parties.

Summary judgment reversed in favor of Jones.

Promissory Estoppel and the Statute of Frauds

The statute of frauds, which was created to prevent fraud and perjury, has often been criticized because it can create unjust results. One of the troubling features of the statute is that it can as easily be used to defeat a contract that was actually made as to defeat a fictitious agreement. As you have seen, courts and legislatures have created several exceptions to the statute of frauds that reduce the statute's potential for creating unfair results. In recent years, courts in some states have allowed the use of the doctrine of **promissory estoppel**[7] to enable some parties to recover under oral contracts that the statute of frauds would ordinarily render unenforceable.

Courts in these states hold that, when one of the parties would suffer serious losses because of her reliance on an oral contract, the other party is estopped from raising the statute of frauds as a defense. This position has been approved in the *Restatement (Second) of Contracts.* Section 139 of the *Restatement (Second)* provides that a promise that induces action or forbearance can be enforceable notwithstanding the statute of frauds if the reliance was foreseeable to the person making the promise and if injustice can be avoided only by enforcing the promise. The idea behind this section and the cases employing promissory estoppel is that the statute of frauds, which is designed to prevent injustice, should not be allowed to work an injustice. Section 139 and these cases also impliedly recognize the fact that the reliance required by promissory estoppel to some extent provides evidence of the existence of a contract between the parties, since it is unlikely that a person would materially rely on a nonexistent promise.

The use of promissory estoppel as a means of circumventing the statute of frauds is still controversial, however. Many courts fear that enforcing oral contracts on the basis of a party's reliance will essentially negate the statute. In cases involving the UCC statute of frauds, an additional source of concern involves the interpretation of section 2–201. Some courts have construed the provisions listing specific alternative methods of satisfying section 2–201's formal requirements to be *exclusive,* precluding the creation of any further exceptions by courts.

The Parol Evidence Rule

Explanation of the Rule

In many situations, contracting parties prefer to express their agreements in writing even when they are not required to do so by the statute of frauds. Written contracts rarely come into being without some prior discussions or negotiations between the parties, however. Various promises, proposals, or representations are usually made by one or both of the parties before the execution of a written contract. What happens when one of those prior promises, proposals, or representations is not included in the terms of the written contract? For example, suppose that Jackson wants to buy Stone's house. During the course of negotiations, Stone states that he will pay for any major repairs that the house needs for the first year that Jackson owns it. The written contract that the parties ultimately sign, however, does not say anything about Stone paying for repairs, and, in fact, states that Jackson will take the house "as is." The furnace breaks down three months after the sale, and Stone refuses to pay for its repair. What is the status of Stone's promise to pay for repairs? The basic problem is one of defining the boundaries of the parties' agreement. Are all the promises made in the process of negotiation part of the contract, or do the terms of the written document that the parties signed supersede any preliminary agreements?

The **parol evidence rule** provides the answer to this question. The term *parol evidence* means written or spoken statements that are *not contained in the written contract.* The parol evidence rule provides that, when parties enter a *written contract* that they intend as a complete **integration** (a complete and final statement of their agreement), a court will not permit the use of evidence of

---

[7]The doctrine of promissory estoppel is discussed in Chapters 9 and 12.

prior or *contemporaneous* statements to add to, alter, or contradict the terms of the written contract. This rule is based on the presumption that when people enter into a written contract, the best evidence of their agreement is the written contract itself. It also reflects the idea that later expressions of intent are presumed to prevail over earlier expressions of intent. In the hypothetical case involving Stone and Jackson, assuming that they intended the written contract to be the final integration of their agreement, Jackson would not be able to introduce evidence of Stone's promise to pay for repairs. The effect of excluding preliminary promises or statements from consideration is, of course, to confine the parties' contract to the terms of the written agreement. The lesson to be learned from this example is that people who put their agreements in writing should make sure that all the terms of their agreement are included in the writing. The *Carrow v. Arnold* case illustrates the application of the parol evidence rule.

Scope of the Parol Evidence Rule

The parol evidence rule is relevant only in cases in which the parties have expressed their agreement in a written contract. Thus, it would not apply to a case involving an oral contract or to a case in which writings existed that were not intended to embody the final statement of at least part of the parties' contract. The parol evidence rule has been made a part of the law of sales in the Uniform Commercial Code [2–202], so it is applicable to contracts for the sale of goods as well as to contracts governed by the common law of contracts. Furthermore, the rule excludes only evidence of statements made *prior to* or *during* the signing of the written contract. It does not apply to statements made after the signing of the contract. Thus, evidence of subsequent statements is freely admissible.

Admissible Parol Evidence

In some situations, evidence of statements made outside the written contract is admissible notwithstanding the parol evidence rule. Parol evidence is permitted in the situations discussed below either because the writing is not the best evidence of the contract or because the evidence is offered, not to contradict the terms of the writing, but to explain the writing or to challenge the underlying contractual obligation that the writing represents.

1. *Additional terms in partially integrated contracts.* In many instances, parties will desire to introduce evidence of statements or agreements that would supplement rather than contradict the written contract. Whether they can do this depends on whether the written contract is characterized as *completely integrated* or *partially integrated.* A completely integrated contract is one that the parties intend as a *complete and exclusive statement* of their entire agreement. A partially integrated contract is one that expresses the parties' final agreement as to some but not all of the terms of their contract. When a contract is only partially integrated, the parties are permitted to use parol evidence to prove the *additional* terms of their agreement. Such evidence cannot, however, be used to contradict the written terms of the contract. To determine whether a contract is completely or partially integrated, a court must determine the parties' intent. A court judges intent by looking at the language of the contract, the apparent completeness of the writing, and all the surrounding circumstances. It will also consider whether the contract contains a **merger clause** (also known as an **integration clause**). These clauses, which are very common in form contracts and commercial contracts, provide that the written contract is the complete integration of the parties' agreement. They are designed to prevent a party from giving testimony about prior statements or agreements and are generally effective in indicating that the writing was a complete integration. Even though a contract contains a merger clause, parol evidence could be admissible under one of the following exceptions.

2. *Explaining ambiguities.* Parol evidence can be offered to explain an ambiguity in the written contract. Suppose a written contract between Lowen and Matthews provides that Lowen will buy "Matthews's truck," but Matthews has two trucks. The parties could offer evidence of negotiations, statements, and other circumstances preceding the creation of the written contract to identify the truck to which the writing refers. Used in this way, parol evidence helps the court interpret the contract. It does not contradict the written contract.

3. *Circumstances invalidating contract.* Any circumstances that would be relevant to show that a contract is not valid can be proven by parol evidence. For example, evidence that Holden pointed a gun at Dickson and said, "Sign this contract, or I'll kill you," would be admissible to show that the contract was voidable because of duress. Likewise, parol evidence would be admissible to show that a contract was illegal or was induced by fraud, misrepresentation, undue influence, or mistake.

4. *Existence of condition.* It is also permissible to use parol evidence to show that a writing was executed with the understanding that it was *not to take effect until the*

CONCEPT REVIEW

Parol Evidence Rule

Parol Evidence Rule	Applies when:	Provides that:
	Parties create a writing intended as a final and complete integration of at least part of the parties' contract.	Evidence of statements of promises made before or during the creation of the writing cannot be used to supplement, change, or contradict the terms of the written contract.
But Parol Evidence *Can* Be Used to	1. Prove consistent, additional terms when the contract is *partially integrated*. 2. Explain an ambiguity in the written contract. 3. Prove that the contract is void, voidable, or unenforceable. 4. Prove that the contract was subject to a condition. 5. Prove that the parties subsequently modified the contract or made a new agreement.	

occurrence of a condition (a future, uncertain event that creates a duty to perform). Suppose Farnsworth signs a contract to purchase a car with the agreement that the contract is not to be effective unless and until Farnsworth gets a new job. If the written contract is silent about any conditions that must occur before it becomes effective, Farnsworth could introduce parol evidence to prove the existence of the condition. Such proof merely elaborates on, but does not contradict, the terms of the writing.

5. *Subsequent agreements.* As you read earlier, the parol evidence rule does not forbid parties to introduce proof of *subsequent agreements.* This is true even if the terms of the later agreement cancel, subtract from, or add to the obligations stated in the written contract. The idea here is that when a writing is followed by a later statement or agreement, the writing is no longer the best evidence of the agreement. You should be aware, however, that subsequent modifications of contracts may sometimes be unenforceable because of lack of consideration or failure to comply with the statute of frauds. In addition, contracts sometimes expressly provide that modifications must be written. In this situation, an oral modification would be unenforceable.

Carrow v. Arnold   2006 Del. Ch. LEXIS 191 (Del. Ct. Ch. 2006)

Lloyd Carrow owned a farm consisting of approximately 223 acres. Lloyd Arnold and Rodney Mitchell are partners in a real estate partnership. Al Moor, a long-time acquaintance of Carrow, had heard a rumor that Carrow wanted to sell his farm. He knew that Arnold and Mitchell were looking to buy real estate in the area, so he introduced them to Carrow. In mid-April 2003, Arnold, Mitchell, and Moor met with Carrow at his farm. At their first meeting, Carrow gave his visitors a tour of his farm but expressed reservations about selling it. Indeed, Arnold offered Carrow $1.2 million for the farm, but Carrow declined. During the meeting, Carrow showed Arnold a letter from the New Jersey Nature Conservancy offering to buy his farm for $1.5 million. During their discussions, Arnold told Carrow that if Carrow sold him the farm, he could continue to live on the farm and to till the land as long as Arnold owned it.

Approximately a week later, Arnold and Mitchell returned to the farm and negotiated with Carrow over the terms and conditions of a sale. During these negotiations, Carrow again expressed reservations about selling the farm because he did not want to leave it. Carrow testified that Arnold assured him that "Nothing would ever change for you, nothing. . . ." and that Carrow could "go right on farming this farm the rest of your life. . . ." Carrow claimed that Arnold assured him that he wanted to buy the land to use strictly as a hunting farm, and he understood this to mean that Arnold did not intend to develop the property or to transfer it any time in the near future. Carrow later testified that he would not have sold the farm without these representations.

Arnold admitted that during various stages of the negotiations he assured Carrow that Carrow could continue to live on and farm the land and that Arnold would never develop it. He also agreed that he told Carrow that he wanted the land for hunting purposes. According to Arnold, however, in making this and other assurances to Carrow, he always included the qualifier "as long as I own it." After some back and forth bargaining, Carrow agreed to sell the farm to Arnold for $1.4 million, not including the farm equipment.

Within a few days of their second meeting, Arnold returned to the farm and left a draft of a written contract with Carrow. Carrow put the contract on a shelf and did not discuss it with anyone for approximately one week. Although he saw provisions in the draft agreement that he did not like, he did not pay too much attention to it and did not "look at [the agreement] like I should have." Carrow did not seek the advice of an attorney, nor did he tell his adult children that he was selling the farm. He instead sought the assistance of his accountant. On April 28, 2003, Carrow and Arnold met in the accountant's office to discuss the proposed contract. Carrow expressed reservations about certain provisions in the contract, and the parties changed those provisions in response to Carrow's concerns. One section of the contract, for example, gave Carrow a life interest in the farmhouse and the approximately two acres around it. At least two provisions in the agreement were qualified by the statement "for as long as Purchaser shall own" the property or a similar language. At the conclusion of the meeting, the parties signed the Agreement and Arnold gave Carrow a $200,000 deposit. Within days of executing the Agreement, Arnold and Mitchell began to have the land surveyed for subdivision.

On May 16, Mitchell submitted plans to the Kent County Department of Planning Services to have the land approved for residential development. Arnold and Mitchell testified that they never had any intention to actually develop the land, but submitted the plans to the county because the land would be more valuable if approved for residential development. Consistent with this testimony, Arnold and Mitchell tried to enter into a transaction whereby they would sell the land for less than its appraised value to the Delaware Chapter of The Nature Conservancy, a nonprofit organization dedicated to preserving undeveloped land. Since part of the transaction would be considered a charitable contribution, the higher the appraised value of the land, the higher the tax deduction Arnold and Mitchell would receive. After learning that the Carrow farm was under a contract to be sold, the Conservancy had contacted Mitchell to see if it could purchase the farm. During the negotiations with the Conservancy, Arnold bargained for contractual provisions that would allow Carrow to remain on the farm and continue to till it for as long as he wanted. Eventually, the proposed transaction with the Conservancy fell apart, mostly because of tax difficulties.

By early May, Carrow was having reservations about selling his farm, so he called Arnold and told him that he wanted to return the deposit. Arnold replied that Carrow could not back out of the deal. Carrow says that he began to reconsider the agreement after he saw surveyors on various parts of the property. He asserted that he did not know that Arnold and Mitchell were professional real estate developers, and he thought he sold the farm for substantially less than its true value. Arnold, on the other hand, argued that Carrow simply had seller's remorse and wanted more money. Carrow filed suit to have the agreement rescinded, and Arnold later counterclaimed for enforcement of the contract.

Parsons, Vice Chancellor

Carrow alleges that the agreement was procured through fraud and misrepresentation. His allegation of fraud, however, consists entirely of the claim that Arnold made oral representations and promises before the execution of the written agreement and that such representations and promises have not been honored. Arnold contends that the agreement is an integrated agreement and the parol evidence rule bars consideration of earlier representations or promises that he allegedly made. These competing contentions raise several legal and factual issues.

The first issue that must be resolved, however, is whether the court is precluded from considering Arnold's oral representations because their consideration is barred by the parol evidence rule. I find that the parol evidence rule generally would bar admission of the oral representations, but the analysis cannot stop

there. Carrow argues that parol evidence is admissible under one or both of two exceptions to the rule: (1) for instances where the contract language is ambiguous; and (2) when the contract is the product of fraud or misrepresentation.

The Parol Evidence Rule

When a written contract is intended to be the final expression of the parties' agreement, the parol evidence rule bars the introduction of evidence of prior or contemporaneous oral understandings that vary the written terms of the agreement. The parol evidence rule prevents the use of extrinsic evidence of an oral agreement to vary a fully integrated agreement that the parties have reduced to writing. Where a written agreement is meant to be final and complete, it is a totally integrated contract. If a written agreement is final and incomplete, it is a partially integrated contract. The parol evidence rule prevents the consideration of oral evidence that would contradict either total or partial[ly] integrated agreements.

Thus, to apply the parol evidence rule, the court first must decide whether the parties' written contract was intended to be the final expression of their agreement, and second whether the alleged oral representations would contradict the written terms of the agreement.

1. Integration

When determining whether a written contract is the final expression of the parties' agreement, a court should consider the facts and circumstances surrounding the execution of the instrument. Some of the factors a court should consider are: the intent of the parties, where such intent is discernible; the language of the contract itself and whether it contains an integration clause; whether the instrument was carefully and formally drafted; the amount of time the parties had to consider the terms of the contract; whether the parties bargained over specific terms; and whether the contract addresses questions that naturally arise out of the subject matter.

The Agreement of Sale [in this case] is a final, integrated contract. The written contract does not contain an integration clause stating that it is intended to be the parties' final agreement. Such a clause would create a presumption of integration. The absence of an integration clause, however, does not necessarily mean that the parties did not intend the contract to be the final and complete expression of their agreement. Although lacking an integration clause, the Agreement of Sale is a formally drafted instrument. It is typewritten, and Carrow and Arnold had their signatures witnessed by a notary. Having the contract witnessed reflects a certain solemnity which shows that the parties acted deliberately and intended to be legally bound to the contract as written.

Furthermore, Carrow had approximately a week to study the proposed contract. Nothing prevented Carrow from reviewing the draft agreement with an attorney or discussing the sale with his family. Instead, Carrow chose to consult only his accountant about the agreement. At the meeting with Arnold in [the accountant's] office, Carrow and his accountant bargained over, and achieved concessions on, several specific terms in the final Agreement. If, as Carrow contends, the written contract was inconsistent with oral promises and representations Arnold had made earlier, Carrow had ample opportunity and motive to raise these issues with Arnold before signing the Agreement. He did not. In addition, the written Agreement addresses issues that normally arise in connection with the sale of land.

I find that the Agreement of Sale is a final, integrated contract. Because it is a final, integrated contract, the parol evidence rule bars the admission of oral promises and representations that are inconsistent with its written terms, unless an exception to the rule applies in this case.

2. Consistency

The Court further finds that the alleged oral representations Arnold made to Carrow during their negotiations, if admitted for purposes of construing their contract, would be inconsistent with the written terms of their final Agreement. Thus, in the absence of an exception such as ambiguity or fraud, the parol evidence rule precludes the admission of Carrow's evidence of alleged oral modifications.

3. Ambiguity

Carrow argues that the Agreement is ambiguous and that extrinsic evidence should be admitted to clarify the alleged ambiguity. To avoid repeating points made elsewhere in this opinion, I will not discuss each argument for ambiguity advanced by Carrow. The following is fairly representative. Carrow argues that the phrase "as long as Purchaser shall own it" is ambiguous as to the length of time that it represents. Carrow claims to have understood this phrase as implying that his rights to remain on the farm would last into the foreseeable future. I find the challenged language unambiguous. A contract is only ambiguous if its language is susceptible to two competing reasonable interpretations. I consider Carrow's interpretation unreasonable. Merely disliking the implications of a contractual provision does not render it ambiguous. The ordinary meaning of the phrase "as long as Purchaser shall own it" places no restriction on the length of time that ultimately may turn out to be.

4. The Fraud Exception to the Parol Evidence Rule

Carrow argues that parol evidence should be admitted because Arnold fraudulently induced Carrow to enter the Agreement. Courts have long recognized that where fraud or misrepresentation is alleged, evidence of oral promises or representations which are made prior to the written agreement will be admitted. To successfully allege fraudulent misrepresentation, a plaintiff must show that: (1) the defendant made a false representation, usually one of fact; (2) the defendant knew or believed that the representation was false, or made it with reckless indifference to the truth; (3) the defendant's false representation was intended to induce the plaintiff to act or refrain from acting; (4) the plaintiff's action or inaction was taken in justifiable reliance upon the representation; and (5) the plaintiff was damaged by such reliance.

Carrow alleges that Arnold committed fraud by making the following promises and representations: (1) that Carrow could remain on the land and continue to farm it; (2) that if Carrow sold his farm to Arnold, nothing would change for him; (3) that

Arnold intended to use the farm for agricultural and hunting purposes, which Carrow understood to mean that he did not intend to transfer the property for a long time; and (4) that Arnold would not develop or build on the land. Even assuming that Arnold promised each of these things, Carrow's arguments suffer from two serious flaws. First, these promises preceded the execution of the written contract and are not false statements of fact. Second, Carrow knew that there were provisions in the proposed Agreement that he did not like because they seemed inconsistent with the alleged oral promises. He had the opportunity to, and actually did, bargain for specific terms ameliorating some of those concerns, but not others. Thus, any reliance Carrow placed on the prior oral representations was unjustified.

Prior oral promises usually do not constitute "false representations of fact" that would satisfy the first element of fraudulent misrepresentation. A viable claim of fraud concerning a contract must allege misrepresentations of present facts (rather than merely of future intent) that were collateral to the contract and which induced the allegedly defrauded party to enter into the contract. All of the statements Carrow characterizes as fraudulent are either promises or statements of future intent. The problem with allowing a party to use promises and statements of intention to invoke the fraud exception to the parol evidence rule is that the very point of the rule is to exclude such things. Parties exchange various representations and supposed offers during negotiations, and reasonable misunderstandings can, and do, occur. By putting their understandings into a written contract, the parties highlight the points on which they have reached agreement and in some cases, the points on which they still diverge. The presumption embodied in the parol evidence rule is that the final written contract reflects the positions and compromises upon which the parties finally reached agreement. If the only showing required to invoke the fraud exception to the parol evidence rule were inconsistent prior oral statements, such oral statements would often (usually) be admitted, and the exception would swallow the rule.

The parties have entered a binding contract, represented by a written instrument, for the sale of Carrow's farm to Arnold. The parol evidence rule bars the admission of the oral statements and representations Carrow alleges Arnold made during the course of negotiations because those alleged representations are inconsistent with the express written terms of the Agreement.

Rescission denied and contract enforced in favor of Arnold.

Interpretation of Contracts

Once a court has decided what promises are included in a contract, it is faced with *interpreting* the contract to determine the *meaning* and *legal effect* of the terms used by the parties. Courts have adopted broad, basic standards of interpretation that guide them in the interpretation process.

The court will first attempt to determine the parties' *principal objective*. Every clause will then be determined in the light of this principal objective. Ordinary words will be given their usual meaning and technical words (such as those that have a special meaning in the parties' trade or business) will be given their technical meaning, unless a different meaning was clearly intended.

Guidelines grounded in common sense are also used to determine the relationship of the various terms of the contract. Specific terms that follow general terms are presumed to qualify those general terms. Suppose that a provision that states that the subject of the contract is "guaranteed for one year" is followed by a provision describing the "one-year guarantee against defects in workmanship." Here, it is fair to conclude that the more specific term qualifies the more general term and that the guarantee described in the contract is a guarantee of workmanship only, and not of parts and materials.

Sometimes, there is internal conflict in the terms of an agreement and courts must determine which term should prevail. When the parties use a form contract or some other type of contract that is partially printed and partially handwritten, the handwritten provisions will prevail. If the contract was drafted by one of the parties, any ambiguities will be resolved against the party who drafted the contract.

If both parties to the contract are members of a trade, profession, or community in which certain words are commonly given a particular meaning (this is called a *usage*), the courts will presume that the parties intended the meaning that the usage gives to the terms they use. For example, if the word *dozen* in the bakery business means 13 rather than 12, a contract between two bakers for the purchase of 10 dozen loaves of bread will be presumed to mean 130 loaves of bread rather than 120. Usages can also add provisions to the parties' agreement. If the court finds that a certain practice is a matter of

Ethics in Action

For those who draft and proffer standardized form contracts, the parol evidence rule can be a powerful ally because it has the effect of limiting the scope of an integrated, written contract to the terms of the writing. Although statements and promises made to a person before he signs a contract might be highly influential in persuading him to enter the contract, the parol evidence rule effectively prevents these precontract communications from being legally enforceable. Consider also that standardized form contracts are usually drafted for the benefit of and proffered by the more sophisticated and powerful party in a contract (e.g., the landlord rather than the tenant, the bank rather than the customer). Considering all of this, do you believe that the parol evidence rule promotes ethical behavior?

common usage in the parties' trade, it will assume that the parties intended to include that practice in their agreement. If contracting parties are members of the same trade, business, or community but do not intend to be bound by usage, they should specifically say so in their agreement.

Problems and Problem Cases

1. In August 2003, R.F. Cunningham & Co., a farms product dealer, and Driscoll, a farmer in Cayuga County, entered into an oral contract for the sale of 4,000 bushels of soybeans at a price of $5.50 per bushel, to be picked up after harvest time. Immediately afterward, Cunningham sent to Driscoll a "purchase confirmation," and Driscoll did not object to its contents. Later in October 2003, Driscoll's lawyer claimed that his client had no legal obligation to complete the contract and refused to sell his soybeans. As a result, Cunningham was forced to purchase replacement soybeans at the then-prevailing market price of $7.74 per bushel, and suffered a financial loss of $8,960.00, which was the difference between the contract price and Cunningham's costs to obtain the replacement soybeans. Cunningham sued Driscoll for breach of contract. Driscoll moved for summary judgment on the ground that the contract did not satisfy the statute of frauds. Will he win?

2. For several years, AutoZone sponsored events conducted by Professional Bull Riders (PBR). For the years 2001 and 2002, PBR prepared a written agreement to provide for AutoZone's sponsorship. Section I of that agreement states:

   The term of this agreement shall commence as of December 29, 2000, and end on December 31, 2002, unless terminated earlier in accordance with the provisions of this Agreement. Notwithstanding the preceding sentence, AutoZone may, at its option, elect to terminate this Agreement and its sponsorship of PBR and the Series effective as of the end of the Finals in 2001, by giving PBR written notice of termination by no later than August 15, 2001.

   AutoZone never signed this agreement. However PBR alleges that by its actions, AutoZone tacitly accepted its terms set forth in the proposed written agreement and that, as a result, the parties entered into an oral agreement on the terms set forth in writing. In January 2002, AutoZone notified PBR that AutoZone would not be sponsoring PBR events in 2002. However, despite this notice, PBR allegedly continued to use AutoZone's trademark and service mark in connection with its programs. PBR then sued AutoZone for breach of the oral sponsorship agreement. Was this agreement unenforceable because of the statute of frauds?

3. On two occasions in 1980, Hodge met with Tilley, president and chief operating officer of Evans Financial Corporation, to discuss Hodge's possible employment by Evans. Hodge was 54 years old at that time and was assistant counsel and assistant secretary of Mellon National Corporation and Mellon Bank of Pittsburgh. During these discussions, Tilley asked Hodge what his conditions were for accepting employment with Evans, and Hodge replied, "Number 1, the job must be permanent. Because of my age, I have a great fear about going back into the marketplace again. I want to be here until I retire." Tilley

allegedly responded, "I accept that condition." Regarding his retirement plans, Hodge later testified, "I really questioned whether I was going to go much beyond 65." Hodge later accepted Evans's offer of employment as vice president and general counsel. He moved from Pittsburgh to Washington, D.C., in September 1980 and worked for Evans from that time until he was fired by Tilley on May 7, 1981. Hodge brought a breach of contract suit against Evans. Evans argued that the oral contract was unenforceable because of the statute of frauds. Is this correct?

4. Green owns a lot (Lot S) in the Manomet section of Plymouth, Massachusetts. In July 1980, she advertised it for sale. On July 11 and 12, the Hickeys discussed with Green purchasing Lot S and orally agreed to a sale for $15,000. On July 12, Green accepted the Hickeys' check for $500. Hickey had left the payee line of the deposit check blank because of uncertainty whether Green or her brother was to receive the check. Hickey asked Green to fill in the appropriate name. Green, however, held the check, did not fill in the payee's name, and neither cashed nor endorsed it. Hickey told Green that his intention was to sell his home and build on the lot he was buying from Green. Relying on the arrangements with Green, the Hickeys advertised their house in newspapers for three days in July. They found a purchaser quickly. Within a short time, they contracted with a purchaser for the sale of their house and accepted the purchaser's deposit check. On the back of this check, above the Hickeys' signatures endorsing the check, was noted: "Deposit on purchase of property at Sachem Rd. and First St., Manomet, Ma. Sale price, $44,000." On July 24, Green told Hickey that she no longer intended to sell her property to him and instead had decided to sell it to someone else for $16,000. Hickey offered to pay Green $16,000 for the lot, but she refused this offer. The Hickeys then filed a complaint against Green seeking specific performance. Green asserted that relief was barred by the statute of frauds. Is this correct?

5. Iams is in the business of manufacturing and selling pet foods. For many years, Watkins was a nonexclusive distributor of Iams products in Michigan. In 1986 or 1987, Iams began to require Watkins (as well as its other distributors) to sign yearly written distributorship agreements. Until 1987, Watkins was the sole distributor of Iams products in Michigan, but in 1986, Wolverton, Inc., also began selling Iams products in the state. In 1989, Iams began offering its distributors a 2 percent discount on its products in return for a commitment from the distributors to sell Iams products exclusively. The discount was significant, given the low profit margins customary in the business. Watkins alleges that in 1990, Iams promised it that if it became an exclusive Iams distributor, Iams would grant it an exclusive sales territory in Michigan when Iams changed to a distribution system of exclusive territories. Watkins claims that it became an exclusive distributor in reliance on this promise. It entered into an exclusivity agreement in July 1990 and annually thereafter through 1993. The contract of January 31, 1993, between Iams and Watkins contains the following provisions:

> Notwithstanding the appointment herein the Company [Iams] reserves the right for itself to sell Products within the Territory. In addition, the Company may appoint any other distributor to sell Products within the Territory.

> This Agreement shall be effective on February 1, 1993, and shall automatically expire, without any further action by either party required, on January 31, 1994, unless earlier terminated as set forth in Section 4.2 or 4.3 or otherwise in accordance with the provisions of this Agreement. This Agreement may be renewed thereafter on terms mutually agreeable to the parties only in a writing signed by the parties hereto . . .

> With the exception of Schedule I, which may be unilaterally amended by the Company as provided in this Agreement . . . and except as otherwise provided in this Agreement, no change, modification or amendment of any provision of this Agreement will be binding unless made in writing and signed by the parties hereto.

> THIS AGREEMENT TOGETHER WITH THE COMPANY'S STANDARD TERMS AND CONDITIONS OF SALE REPRESENT THE ENTIRE AGREEMENT BETWEEN THE PARTIES AND SUPERSEDES ALL PRIOR, EXISTING, AND CONTEMPORANEOUS AGREEMENTS, WHETHER WRITTEN OR ORAL . . .

Instead of making Watkins its exclusive dealer, Iams notified Watkins in September 1993, that it would not renew its distributorship contract, and the contract expired, in accordance with its terms, on January 31, 1994. Iams subsequently entered into an exclusive distribution contract in Michigan with Wolverton.

Watkins brought suit against Iams on a number of grounds, including breach of contract, fraud, and promissory estoppel. Will Watkins win?

6. Southridge Presbyterian Church, owner of a residential home, placed it on the market for $134,500. Ayalla viewed the home and made a written offer to buy the home for $130,000. The written offer was made on a residential real estate sale contract form furnished by Southridge Presbyterian's real estate agent, Henderson. Ayalla gave Henderson a check for $1,000 as an earnest money deposit. Henderson orally notified Ayalla's mortgage broker that Southridge Presbyterian had accepted Ayalla's offer. The mortgage broker left a message with Ayalla's nephew about this acceptance. The following day, Henderson orally told Ayalla personally of Southridge Presbyterian's acceptance. They agreed to meet on May 1, 2005, to complete the paperwork, and Ayalla made plans to take that day off work. She also scheduled a home inspection to take place on May 2 or 3. Ayalla and her friends and family gathered together on May 1 to celebrate. Before her scheduled meeting with Henderson, however, Henderson called and told Ayalla that Southridge Presbyterian had accepted a higher offer of $142,500 from a third party. Was Southridge Presbyterian legally obligated to sell the home to Ayalla?

7. Dyer purchased a used Ford from Walt Bennett Ford for $5,895. She signed a written contract, which showed that no taxes were included in the sales price. Dyer contended, however, that the salesperson who negotiated the purchase with her told her both before and after her signing of the contract that the sales tax on the automobile had been paid. The contract Dyer signed contained the following language:

> The above comprises the entire agreement pertaining to this purchase and no other agreement of any kind, verbal understanding, representation, or promise whatsoever will be recognized.

It also stated:

> This contract constitutes the entire agreement between the parties and no modification hereof shall be valid in any event and Buyer expressly waives the right to rely thereon, unless made in writing, signed by Seller.

Later, when Dyer attempted to license the automobile, she discovered that the Arkansas sales tax had not been paid on it. She paid the sales tax and sued Bennett for breach of contract. What result?

8. In July 2004, the Harrises entered into a contract with the Hallbergs to purchase a home in Waccabuc, New York, for the sum of $1.9 million. Later, they had second thoughts about the purchase. In November 2004, the Harrises and Hallbergs signed an agreement which provided that, upon the forfeiture of the Harrises' down payment, "all contractual obligations" that the parties owed each other under the contract of sale would be terminated, and each party would "have no further obligation" toward the other. The release was consistent with the terms of the contract of sale, which had specified the Hallbergs' remedy in the event of a default by the Harrises. Both parties were represented by independent counsel during the transaction and Mr. Harris is a lawyer. Later, the Harrises alleged that, prior to signing the release, the parties entered into an oral agreement whereby the Hallbergs agreed that, if they could sell the property for more than the sum of $1.9 million, they would return all or part of the Harrises' down payment. The Harrises alleged that, although the Hallbergs had apparently sold the property for the sum of $2.4 million, they had refused to return any part of the down payment. Do the Harrises have the legal right to enforce the alleged oral agreement for the return of the down payment?

9. Roose hired the law firm of Gallagher, Langlas and Gallagher, P.C., to represent her in her divorce. Langlas, an attorney in the firm, signed an attorney fee contract and gave it to Roose to sign and return. He also requested a $2,000 retainer fee. Roose never signed or returned the contract, and did not pay the retainer fee in full. The firm represented Roose even though she did not sign the contract or pay the retainer fee in full. In April 1995, the Gallagher attorneys met with Roose and her father, Burco. The attorneys told Burco that the expense of his daughter's child custody trial would be approximately $1,000 per day. The firm would not guarantee Burco that the trial would last for only two or three days. The firm contends that during that meeting, Burco gave the firm a check for $1,000 to pay the outstanding balance on Roose's account and said he would pay for future services. Before the trial, an attorney with the firm contacted Burco and requested an additional retainer to secure fees to be incurred. Burco told her, "My word as a gentleman should be enough . . . I told Mr. Langlas I would pay and I will pay." Roose failed to pay her legal fees. In July 1995,

the attorneys sent Burco a letter requesting $5,000 for Roose's legal fees or the signing of a promissory note. At the end of July 1995, they sent Burco another letter asking him to sign a promissory note for $10,000. Neither Roose nor Burco paid the fees or signed the note. The firm represented Roose in the July 1995 trial. Burco took an active part in the trial by testifying and participating in conferences with counsel during recesses. After trial, Burco returned the second letter and promissory note with a notation stating that he was not responsible for his daughter's attorney fees. The firm sued Roose and Burco for the unpaid fees. Is Burco legally responsible for the fees?

10. Rosenfeld, an art dealer, claimed that Jean-Michel Basquiat, an acclaimed neoexpressionist artist, had agreed to sell to her three paintings entitled *Separation of the "K," Atlas,* and *Untitled Head.* She claimed that she went to Basquiat's apartment on October 25, 1982, and while she was there he agreed to sell her three paintings for $4,000 each, and that she picked out the three works. According to Rosenfeld, Basquiat asked for a cash deposit of 10 percent. She left his loft and later returned with $1,000 in cash, which she paid him. When she asked for a receipt, he insisted on drawing up a "contract," and got down on the floor and wrote it out in crayon on a large piece of paper, remarking that "some day this contract will be worth money." She identified a handwritten document listing the three paintings, bearing her signature and that of Basquiat, which stated: "$12,000—$1,000 DEPOSIT—OCT 25 82." Is this writing sufficient to satisfy the statute of frauds?

Online Research

Coverage of the Statute of Frauds

Using your favorite search engine, find a state statute of frauds. Study the list of contracts that must be evidenced by a writing under that statute, and note whether there are any classes of contracts listed in addition to the ones discussed in this chapter.

chapter 17

RIGHTS OF THIRD PARTIES

Peterson was employed by Post-Network as a newscaster-anchorman on station WTOP-TV Channel 9 under a three-year employment contract with two additional one-year terms at the option of Post-Network. During the first year of Peterson's employment, Post-Network sold its operation license to Evening News in a sale that provided for the assignment of all contracts, including Peterson's employment contract. Peterson continued working for the station for more than a year after the change of ownership, but then found a job at a competing station and resigned. Evening News sued Peterson for breach of the employment contract.

- Can a person who was not an original party to a contract sue to enforce it?
- Was the assignment of Peterson's employment contract a valid transfer, or does Peterson have a right not to have his employment transferred to another employer?
- Does Peterson have any right to enforce the contract between Post-Network and Evening News?
- Would it be ethical for Evening News to prevent Peterson from changing jobs and working for a competing station?

IN PRECEDING CHAPTERS, WE have emphasized the way in which an agreement between two or more people creates legal rights and duties *on the part of the contracting parties.* Since a contract is founded on the consent of the contracting parties, it might seem to follow that they are the only ones who have rights and duties under the contract. Although this is generally true, there are two situations in which people who were not parties to a contract have legally enforceable rights under it: when a contract has been *assigned* (transferred) to a third party and when a contract is *intended to benefit a third person* (a *third-party beneficiary*). This chapter discusses the circumstances in which third parties have rights under a contract.

Assignment of Contracts

Contracts give people both rights and duties. If Murphy buys Wagner's motorcycle and promises to pay him $1,000 for it, Wagner has the *right* to receive Murphy's promised performance (the payment of the $1,000) and Murphy has the *duty* to perform the promise by paying $1,000. In most situations, contract rights can be transferred to a third person and contract duties can be delegated to a third person. The transfer of a *right* under a contract is called an **assignment.** The appointment of another person to perform a *duty* under a contract is called a **delegation.**

Nature of Assignment of Rights A person who owes a duty to perform under a contract is called an **obligor.** The person to whom he owes the duty is called the **obligee.** For example, Samson borrows $500 from Jordan, promising to repay Jordan in six months. Samson, who owes the duty to pay the money, is the obligor, and Jordan, who has the right to receive the money, is the obligee. An assignment occurs when the obligee transfers his right to receive the obligor's performance to a third person. When there has been an assignment, the person making the assignment—the original obligee—is then called the **assignor.** The person to whom the right has been transferred is called the **assignee.** Figure 1 summarizes these key terms.

Suppose that Jordan, the obligee in the example above, assigns his right to receive Samson's payment to Kane. Here, Jordan is the assignor and Kane is the assignee. The relationship between the three parties is represented in Figure 2. Notice that the assignment is a separate transaction: It occurs after the formation of the original contract.

Figure 1   Assignment: Key Terms

Obligor	Obligee	Assignment	Assignor	Assignee
Person who owes the duty to perform	Person who has the right to receive obligor's performance	Transfer of the right to receive obligor's performance	Obligee who transfers the right to receive obligor's performance	Person to whom the right to receive obligor's performance is transferred

Figure 2   Assignment

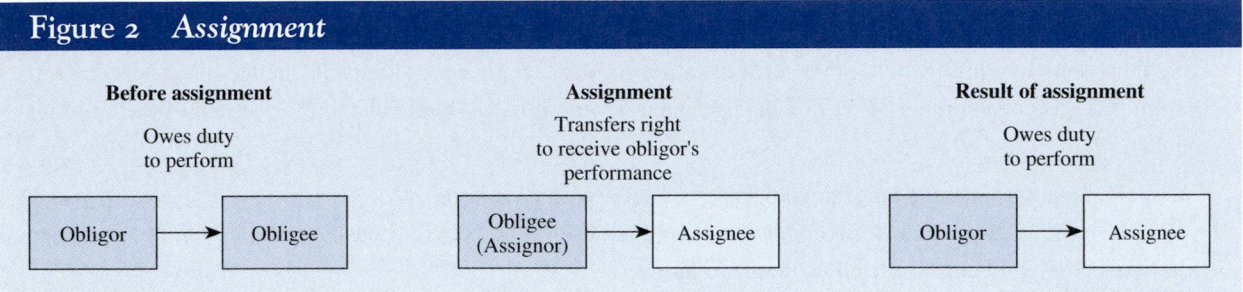

The effect of the assignment is to extinguish the assignor's right to receive performance and to transfer that right to the assignee. In the above example, Kane now owns the right to collect payment from Samson. If Samson fails to pay, Kane, as an assignee, now has the right to file suit against Samson to collect the debt.

People assign rights for a variety of reasons. A person might assign a right to a third party to satisfy a debt that he owes. For example, Jordan, the assignor in the above example, owes money to Kane, so he assigns to Kane the right to receive the $500 that Samson owes him. A person might also sell or pledge the rights owed to him to obtain financing. In the case of a business, the money owed to the business by customers and clients is called *accounts receivable.* A business's accounts receivable are an asset to the business that can be used to raise money in several ways. For example, the business may pledge its accounts receivable as collateral for a loan. Suppose Ace Tree Trimming Co. wants to borrow money from First Bank and gives First Bank a security interest (an interest in the debtor's property that secures the debtor's performance of an obligation) in its accounts receivable.[1] If Ace defaults in its payments to First Bank, First Bank will acquire Ace's rights to collect the accounts receivable. A person might also make an assignment of a contract right as a gift. For example, Lansing owes $2,000 to Father. Father assigns the right to receive Lansing's performance to Son as a graduation gift.

Evolution of the Law Regarding Assignments   Contract rights have not always been transferable. Early common law refused to permit assignment or delegation because debts were considered to be too personal to transfer. A debtor who failed to pay an honest debt was subject to severe penalties, including imprisonment, because such a failure to pay was viewed as the equivalent of theft. The identity of the creditor was of great importance to the debtor, since one creditor might be more lenient than another. Courts also feared that the assignment of debts would stir up unwanted litigation. In an economy that was primarily land-based, the extension of credit was of relatively small importance. As trade increased and became more complex, however, the practice of extending credit became more common. The needs of an increasingly commercial society demanded that people be able to trade freely in intangible assets such as debts. Consequently, the rules of law regarding the assignment of contracts gradually became more liberal. Today, public policy favors free assignability of contracts.

Sources of Assignment Law Today   Legal principles regarding assignment are found not only in the common law of contracts but also in Articles 2 and 9 of the

---

[1]Security interests in accounts and other property are discussed in Chapter 29.

Uniform Commercial Code. Section 2–210 of Article 2 contains principles applicable to assignments of rights under a contract for the sale of *goods*. Article 9 governs security interests in accounts and other contract rights as well as the outright sale of accounts. Article 9's treatment of assignments will be discussed in more detail in Chapter 29, Security Interests in Personal Property, but some provisions of Article 9 relating to assignments will be discussed in this chapter.

Creating an Assignment
An assignment can be made in any way that is sufficient to show the assignor's intent to assign. No formal language is required, and a writing is not necessary unless required by a provision of the statute of frauds or some other statute. Many states do have statutes requiring certain types of assignments to be evidenced by a writing, however. Additionally, an assignment for the purposes of security must meet Article 9's formal requirements for security interests.[2]

It is not necessary that the assignee give any consideration to the assignor in exchange for the assignment. Gratuitous assignments (those for which the assignee

gives no value) are generally revocable until such time as the obligor satisfies the obligation, however. They can be revoked by the assignor's death or incapacity or by notification of revocation given by the assignor to the assignee.

Assignability of Rights
Most, but not all, contract rights are assignable. Although the free assignability of contract rights performs a valuable function in our modern credit-based economy, assignment is undesirable if it would adversely affect some important public policy or if it would materially vary the bargained-for expectations of the parties. There are several basic limitations on the assignability of contract rights.

First, an assignment will not be effective if it is *contrary to public policy*. For example, most states have enacted statutes that prohibit or regulate a wage earner's assignment of future wages. These statutes are designed to protect people against unwisely impoverishing themselves by signing away their future incomes. State law may prohibit assignment of lottery prizes or certain kinds of lawsuits on grounds of public policy. You will see an example of an assignment that is invalid based on public policy in the following *PPG Industries* case.

---

[2]These requirements are discussed in Chapter 29.

PPG Industries, Inc. v. JMB/Houston Center
146 S.W.3d 79 (Tex. Sup. Ct. 2004)

One Houston Center, a 46-story skyscraper in downtown Houston, was completed in April 1978 and originally owned by Houston Center Corporation (HCC). The exterior included more than 12,000 Twindows, a dual-pane glass window unit manufactured and installed by PPG. Twindows were chosen for their insulating ability and color, which blended with other buildings in the Houston Center complex. By July 1982, a large number of the Twindows showed fogging and discoloration. At HCC's request, PPG manufactured and installed replacements for one-fourth of the building's windows pursuant to a contractual warranty. The replacement project took more than two years.

Several years later, HCC entered negotiations to sell One Houston Center to JMB. During its due diligence, JMB learned of the earlier window problems, and that to a limited extent they continued. When JMB inquired whether any warranties still applied, PPG replied that all had expired. JMB bought the building "as is" in December 1989 as part of a $375 million purchase. HCC assigned to JMB all warranties relating to the building, and JMB waived all Deceptive Trade Practices Act (DTPA)—a state statute that provides remedies for certain unfair trade practices—claims against HCC.

When extensive Twindows problems appeared in 1991, JMB sued PPG for violating the DTPA and breaching warranties issued to HCC. A jury found for JMB on all claims, assessing the cost to replace every Twindow in the building with comparable but nondefective window units at $4,745,037. The trial court trebled the award under the mandatory provisions of the 1973 DTPA, and after a bench trial awarded another $1,716,181 in attorney fees. The court of appeals affirmed the judgment. PPG appealed.

Brister, Judge

PPG first attacks the DTPA award, asserting that DTPA claims cannot be assigned. To determine whether DTPA claims are assignable, we look first to the words of the statute. The UCC

expressly provides that warranty claims are assignable, while the DTPA says nothing about assignment. In some cases of statutory silence, we have looked to the statute's purpose for guidance. Accordingly, we next look to the purposes of the

DTPA to determine whether assignment of claims is consistent with its goals. The DTPA's primary goal was to protect consumers by encouraging them to bring consumer complaints. While the DTPA allows the attorney general to bring consumer protection actions, one of the statute's primary purposes is to encourage consumers themselves to file their own complaints. One purpose of the DTPA's treble damages provisions is to encourage privately initiated consumer litigation, reducing the need for public enforcement. Making DTPA claims assignable would have just the opposite effect: instead of swindled consumers bringing their own DTPA claims, they will be brought by someone else.

The Legislature did not intend the DTPA for everybody. It limited DTPA complaints to "consumers," and excluded a number of parties and transactions from the DTPA, including claims by businesses with more than $25 million in assets, and certain claims in which consumers were represented by legal counsel. If DTPA claims can be assigned, a party excluded by the statute (such as JMB here) could nevertheless assert DTPA claims by stepping into the shoes of a qualifying assignor. This would frustrate the clear intent of the Legislature. Commercial trading in almost any kind of claim would likely encourage its proliferation, but raises a host of other concerns. First, the DTPA's treble-damage provisions were intended to motivate affected consumers; they may provide a different motivation for those who might traffic in such claims. It is one thing to place the power of treble damages in the hands of aggrieved parties or the attorney general; it is quite another to place it in the hands of those considering litigation for commercial profit.

Second, appraising the value of a chose in action is never easy, due to the absence of objective measures or markets. Consumers are likely to be at a severe negotiating disadvantage with the kinds of entrepreneurs willing to buy DTPA claims cheap and settle them dear. The result of making DTPA claims assignable is likely to be that some consumers will be deceived twice. Third, in many cases consumers may not even know they have DTPA claims when they sign a general assignment included in contractual boilerplate. If such assignments are valid, the claims meant to protect consumers will quite literally be gone before they know it. Every conceivable purpose of the statute is defeated if consumers may lose their claims by accident.

With respect to the assignment of claims, we have recognized the collapse of the common-law rule that generally prohibited such assignments. But the assignability of most claims does not mean all are assignable; exceptions may be required due to equity and public policy. Courts addressing assignability have often distinguished between claims that are property-based and remedial and claims that are personal and punitive,

holding that the former are assignable and the latter are not. The DTPA claims here clearly fall in the latter category. There must be a "personal" aspect in being "duped" that does not pass to subsequent buyers the way a warranty does. DTPA claims generally are also punitive rather than remedial. Frequently, the DTPA is pleaded not because it is the only remedy, but because it is the most favorable remedy. In this case, for example, the contract and warranty claims offered a remedy, but only the DTPA offered treble damages.

Finally, we must consider whether assignment of DTPA claims may increase or distort litigation. We have prohibited assignments that may skew the trial process, confuse or mislead the jury, promote collusion among nominal adversaries, or misdirect damages from more culpable to less culpable defendants. First, DTPA claims are unlike most contract-related claims in providing for mental anguish and punitive damages. Jurors are bound to experience some confusion in assessing mental anguish of a consumer, or punitive damages based on the situation and sensibilities of the parties, when the affected consumer is not a party. The Legislature intended DTPA lawsuits to be efficient and economical; assessing personal and punitive damages in these circumstances is likely to make that goal difficult.

But more important, there is a serious risk here of skewing the adversarial process. When A sells goods to B who sells them to C, if the goods prove defective and there were no dealings between A and C (as is often the case in the stream of commerce), C will naturally look to B for a breach-of-contract remedy. But if DTPA claims are assignable, B and C both have a strong incentive to direct the suit elsewhere for relief. If B settles with C for a small amount and assigns any DTPA claims it may have against A, C now has a case with potential punitive damages, and B has avoided potential liability. In this case JMB made no complaints against HCC, even though the window problems JMB discovered were very similar to the ones HCC encountered a few years before. Further, to avoid any discovery rule problems, HCC joined JMB in downplaying the earlier problems that must have seemed disastrous to HCC at the time. We cast no aspersions on the litigants here; we only note that assignability of DTPA claims may encourage some buyers to cooperate—if not collude—with a seller who may have been the one that actually misled them.

The DTPA is primarily concerned with people—both the deceivers and the deceived. This gives the entire act a personal aspect that cannot be squared with a rule that allows assignment of DTPA claims as if they were merely another piece of property.

Reversed in favor of PPG.

Second, an assignment will not be effective if it *adversely affects the obligor* in some significant way. An assignment is ineffective if it materially changes the obligor's duty or increases the burden or risk on the obligor. Naturally, any assignment will change an obligor's duty to some extent. The obligor will have to pay money or deliver goods or render some other performance to one party instead of to another. These changes are not considered to be sufficiently material to render an assignment ineffective. Thus, a right to receive money or goods or land is generally assignable. In addition, covenants not to compete are generally considered to be assignable to buyers of businesses. For example, Jefferson sells RX Drugstore to Waldman, including in the contract of sale a covenant whereby Jefferson promises not to operate a competing drugstore within a 30-mile radius of RX for 10 years after the sale. Waldman later sells RX to Tharp. Here, Tharp could enforce the covenant not to compete against Jefferson. The reason for permitting assignment of covenants not to compete is that the purpose of such covenants is to protect an asset of the business—goodwill—for which the buyer has paid.

An assignment could be ineffective because of its variation of the obligor's duty, however, if the contract right involved a *personal relationship* or an element of *personal skill, judgment,* or *character.* For this reason, contracts of employment in which an employee works under the direct and personal supervision of an employer cannot be assigned to a new employer. An employer could assign a contract of employment, however, if the assignee-employer could perform the contract without adversely affecting the interests of the employee, such as would be the case when an employment relationship does not involve personal supervision by an individual employer.

A purported assignment is ineffective if it significantly increases the burden of the obligor's performance. For example, if Walker contracts to sell Dwyer all of its requirements of wheat, a purported assignment of Dwyer's rights to a corporation that has much greater requirements of wheat would probably be ineffective because it would significantly increase the burden on Walker.

Contract Clauses Prohibiting Assignment A contract right may also be nonassignable because the original contract expressly forbids assignment. For example, leases often contain provisions forbidding assignment or requiring the tenant to obtain the landlord's permission for assignment.[3]

------

[3]The assignment of leases is discussed further in Chapter 25.

Antiassignment clauses in contracts are generally enforceable. Because of the strong public policy favoring assignability, however, such clauses are often interpreted narrowly. For example, a court might view an assignment made in violation of an antiassignment clause as a breach of contract for which damages may be recovered but not as an invalidation of the assignment. Another tactic is to interpret a contractual ban on assignment as prohibiting only the delegation of duties.

The UCC takes this latter position. Under section 2–210(2), general language prohibiting assignment of "the contract" or "all my rights under the contract" is interpreted as forbidding only the delegation of duties, unless the circumstances indicate to the contrary. Section 2–210 also states that a right to damages for breach of a whole sales contract or a right arising out of the assignor's performance of his entire obligation may be assigned even if a provision of the original sales contract prohibited assignment. In addition, UCC section 9–318(4) invalidates contract terms that prohibit (or require the debtor's consent to) an assignment of an account or creation of a security interest in a right to receive money that is now due or that will become due.

Nature of Assignee's Rights

When an assignment occurs, the assignee is said to "step into the shoes of his assignor." This means that the assignee acquires all of the rights that his assignor had under the contract. The assignee has the right to receive the obligor's performance, and if performance is not forthcoming, the assignee has the right to sue in his own name for breach of the obligation. By the same token, the assignee acquires no greater rights than those possessed by the assignor.

Because the assignee has no greater rights than did the assignor, the obligor may assert any defense or claim against the assignee that he could have asserted against the assignor, subject to certain time limitations discussed below. A contract that is void, voidable, or unenforceable as between the original parties does not become enforceable just because it has been assigned to a third party. For example, if Richards induces Dillman's consent to a contract by duress and subsequently assigns his rights under the contract to Keith, Dillman can assert the doctrine of duress against Keith as a ground for avoiding the contract.

Importance of Notifying the Obligor An assignee should promptly notify the obligor of the assignment. Although notification of the obligor is not necessary for the assignment to be valid, such notice is of great practical importance. One reason notice is important is that an obligor who does not have reason to know of the assignment could render performance to the assignor and claim that his obligation had been discharged by performance. An obligor who renders performance to the assignor without notice of the assignment has no further liability under the contract. For example, McKay borrows $500 from Goodheart, promising to repay the debt by June 1. Goodheart assigns the debt to Rogers, but no one informs McKay of the assignment, and McKay pays the $500 to Goodheart, the assignor. In this case, McKay is not liable for any further payment. But if Rogers had immediately notified McKay of the assignment and, after receiving notice, McKay had mistakenly paid the debt to Goodheart, McKay would still have the legal obligation to pay $500 to Rogers. Having been given adequate notice of the assignment, he may remain liable to the assignee even if he later renders performance to the assignor.

An assignor who accepts performance from the obligor after the assignment holds any benefits that he receives as a trustee for the assignee. If the assignor fails to pay those benefits to the assignee, however, an obligor who has been notified of the assignment and renders performance to the wrong person may have to pay the same debt twice.

An obligor who receives notice of an assignment from the assignee will want to assure himself that the assignment has in fact occurred. He may ask for written evidence of the assignment or contact the assignee and ask for verification of the assignment. Under UCC section 9–318(3), a notification of assignment is ineffective unless it reasonably identifies the rights assigned. If requested by the account debtor (an obligor who owes money for goods sold or leased or services rendered), the assignee must furnish reasonable proof that the assignment has been made, and, unless he does so, the account debtor may disregard the notice and pay the assignor.

Defenses against the Assignee An assignee's rights in an assignment are subject to the defenses that the obligor could have asserted against the assignor. Keep in mind that the assignee's rights are limited by the terms of the underlying contract between the assignor and the obligor. When defenses arise from the terms or performance of that contract, they can be asserted against the assignee even if they arise after the obligor receives notice of the assignment. For example, on June 1, Worldwide Widgets assigns to First Bank its rights under a contract with Widgetech, Inc. This contract obligates Worldwide Widgets to deliver a quantity of widgets to Widgetech by September 1, in return for

which Widgetech is obligated to pay a stated purchase price. First Bank gives prompt notice of the assignment to Widgetech. Worldwide Widget fails to deliver the widgets and Widgetech refuses to pay. If First Bank brought an action against Widgetech to recover the purchase price of the widgets, Widgetech could assert Worldwide Widget's breach as a defense, even though the breach occurred after Widgetech received notice of the assignment.[4]

In determining what other defenses can be asserted against the assignee, the time of notification plays an important role. After notification, as we discussed earlier, payment by the obligor to the assignor will not discharge the obligor.

Subsequent Assignments An assignee may "reassign" a right to a third party, who would be called a **subassignee.** The subassignee then acquires the rights held by the prior assignee. He should give the obligor prompt notice of the subsequent assignment, because he takes his interest subject to the same principles discussed above regarding the claims and defenses that can be asserted against him.

Successive Assignments Notice to the obligor may be important in one other situation. If an assignor assigns the same right to two assignees in succession, both of whom pay for the assignment, a question of priority results. An assignor who assigns the same right to different people will be held liable to the assignee who acquires no rights against the obligor, but which assignee is entitled to the obligor's performance? Which assignee will have recourse only against the assignor? There are several views on this point.

In states that follow the "American rule," the first assignee has the better right. This view is based on the rule of property law that a person cannot transfer greater rights in property than he owns. In states that follow the "English rule," however, the assignee who first gives notice of the assignment to the obligor, without knowledge of the other assignee's claim, has the better right. The *Restatement (Second) of Contracts* takes a third position. Section 342 of the *Restatement (Second)* provides that

---

[4]Similarly, if the assignor's rights were subject to discharge because of other factors such as the nonoccurrence of a condition, impossibility, impracticability, or public policy, this can be asserted as a defense against the assignee even if the event occurs after the obligor receives notice of assignment. See *Restatement (Second) of Contracts* § 336(3). The doctrines relating to discharge from performance are explained in Chapter 18.

the first assignee has priority unless the subsequent assignee gives value (pays for the assignment) and, without having reason to know of the other assignee's claim, does one of the following: obtains payment of the obligation, gets a judgment against the obligor, obtains a new contract with the obligor by novation, or possesses a writing of a type customarily accepted as a symbol or evidence of the right assigned (such as a passbook for a savings account).

Assignor's Warranty Liability to Assignee

Suppose that Ross, a 16-year-old boy, contracts to buy a used car for $2,000 from Donaldson. Ross pays Donaldson $500 as a down payment and agrees to pay the balance in equal monthly installments. Donaldson assigns his right to receive the balance of the purchase price to Beckman, who pays $1,000 in cash for the assignment. When Beckman later attempts to enforce the contract, however, Ross disaffirms the contract on grounds of lack of capacity. Thus, Beckman has paid $1,000 for a worthless claim. Does Beckman have any recourse against Donaldson? When an assignor is paid for making an assignment, the assignor is held to have made certain implied warranties about the claim assigned.

The assignor impliedly warrants that the claim assigned is valid. This means that the obligor has capacity to contract, the contract is not illegal, the contract is not voidable for any other reason known to the assignor (such as fraud or duress), and the contract has not been discharged prior to assignment. The assignor also warrants that he has good title to the rights assigned and that any written instrument representing the assigned claim is genuine. In addition, the assignor impliedly agrees that he will not do anything to impair the value of the assignment. These guarantees are imposed by law unless the assignment agreement clearly indicates to the contrary. One important aspect of the assigned right that the assignor does not impliedly warrant, however, is that the obligor is solvent.

Delegation of Duties

Nature of Delegation

A **delegation** of duties occurs when an obligor indicates his intent to appoint another person to perform his duties under a contract. For example, White owns a furniture store. He has numerous existing contracts to deliver furniture to customers, including a contract to deliver a sofa to Coombs. White is the *obligor* of the duty to deliver the sofa and Coombs is the *obligee*. White decides to sell his business to Rosen. As a part of the sale of the business, White assigns the rights in the existing contracts to Rosen and delegates to him the performance of those contracts, including the duty to deliver the sofa to Coombs. Here, White is the *delegator* and Rosen is the *delegatee*. White is appointing Rosen to carry out his duties to the obligee, Coombs. Figure 3 summarizes the key terms regarding delegation.

In contrast to an assignment of a right, which extinguishes the assignor's right and transfers it to the assignee, the delegation of a *duty* does *not* extinguish the duty owed by the delegator. The delegator remains liable to the obligee unless the obligee agrees to substitute the delegatee's promise for that of the delegator (this is called a *novation* and will be discussed in greater detail later in this chapter). This makes sense because, if it were possible for a person to escape his duties under a contract by merely delegating them to another, any party to a contract could avoid liability by delegating duties to an insolvent acquaintance. The significance of an effective delegation is that performance by the delegatee will discharge the delegator. In addition, if the duty is a delegable one, the obligee cannot insist on performance by the delegator; he must accept the performance of the delegatee. The relationship between the parties in a delegation is shown in Figure 4.

Delegable Duties

A duty that can be performed fully by a number of different persons is delegable. Not all duties are delegable, however. The grounds for

Figure 3 *Delegation: Key Terms*				
Obligor	Obligee	Delegation	Delegator	Delegatee
Person who owes the duty to perform	Person who has the right to receive obligor's performance	Appointment of another person to perform the obligor's duty to the obligee	Obligor who appoints another to perform his duty to obligee	Person who is appointed to perform the obligor's duty to the obligee

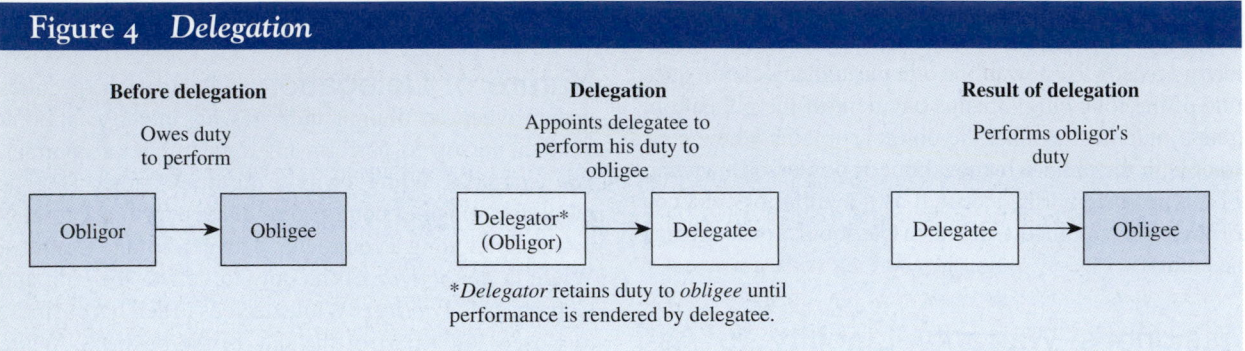

Figure 4   *Delegation*

Before delegation

Owes duty
to perform

Obligor → Obligee

Delegation

Appoints delegatee to
perform his duty to
obligee

Delegator*
(Obligor) → Delegatee

Delegator retains duty to *obligee* until
performance is rendered by delegatee.

Result of delegation

Performs obligor's
duty

Delegatee → Obligee

finding a duty to be nondelegable resemble closely the grounds for finding a right to be nonassignable. A duty is nondelegable if delegation would violate public policy or if the original contract between the parties forbids delegation. In addition, both section 2–210(1) of the UCC and section 318(2) of the *Restatement (Second) of Contracts* take the position that a party to a contract may delegate his duty to perform to another person unless the parties have agreed to the contrary or unless the other party has a *substantial interest* in having the original obligor perform the acts required by the contract. The key factor used in determining whether the obligee has such a substantial interest is the degree to which performance is dependent on the individual traits, skill, or judgment of the person who owes the duty to perform. For example, if Jansen hires Skelton, an artist, to paint her portrait, Skelton could not effectively delegate the duty to paint the portrait to another artist. Similarly, an employee could not normally delegate her duties under an employment contract to some third person, because employment contracts are made with the understanding that the person the employer hires will perform the work. The situation in which a person hires a general contractor to perform specific work is distinguishable, however. In that situation, the person hiring the general contractor would normally understand that at least part of the work would be delegated to subcontractors.

Language Creating a Delegation
No special, formal language is necessary to create an effective delegation of duties. In fact, since parties frequently confuse the terms *assignment* and *delegation,* one of the problems frequently presented to courts is determining whether the parties intended an assignment only or both an assignment and a delegation. Unless the agreement indicates a contrary intent, courts tend to interpret assignments as including a delegation of the assignor's

duties. Both the UCC 2–210(4) and section 328 of the *Restatement (Second) of Contracts* provide that, unless the language or the circumstances indicate to the contrary, general language of assignment such as language indicating an assignment of "the contract" or of "all my rights under the contract" is to be interpreted as creating *both* an assignment and a delegation.

Assumption of Duties by Delegatee
A delegation gives the delegatee the right to perform the duties of the delegator. The mere fact that duties have been delegated does not always place legal responsibility on the delegatee to perform. This is discussed in the following *Watts* case. The delegatee who fails to perform will not be liable to either the delegator or the obligee unless the delegatee has assumed the duty by expressly or impliedly undertaking the obligation to perform. However, both section 2–210(4) of the UCC and section 328 of the *Restatement (Second)* provide that an assignee's acceptance of an assignment is to be construed as a promise by him to perform the duties under the contract, unless the language of the assignment or the circumstances indicate to the contrary. Frequently, a term of the contract between the delegator and the delegatee provides that the delegatee assumes responsibility for performance. A common example of this is the assumption of an existing mortgage debt by a purchaser of real estate. Suppose Morgan buys a house from Friedman, agreeing to assume the outstanding mortgage on the property held by First Bank. By this assumption, Morgan undertakes personal liability to both Friedman and First Bank. If Morgan fails to make the mortgage payments, First Bank has a cause of action against Morgan personally. An assumption does *not* release the delegator from liability, however. Rather, it creates a situation in which both the delegator and the assuming delegatee owe duties to the obligee. If the assuming delegatee fails to pay,

the delegator can be held liable. Thus, in the example described above, if Morgan fails to make mortgage payments and First Bank is unable to collect the debt from Morgan, Friedman would have secondary liability. Friedman, of course, would have an action against Morgan for breach of their contract.

Watts v. Simpson   2007 Ky. App. LEXIS 247 (Ky. Ct. App. 2007)

On June 12, 2003, J. R. and Lillian Watts entered into a real estate contract with MW Development for the sale of a 40-acre tract of land. The contract provided that the closing would occur on or before July 31, 2003. MW Development paid the Wattses $212,000 as a down payment, which left $1,917,222 to be paid. According to the contract terms, if MW Development failed to close by the designated date for reasons not attributable to the fault of the Wattses, MW Development would pay 8 percent interest on the amount due to the Wattses until the date of closing.

Harry D. Simpson, Jr., was not a party to the real estate contract. However, Simpson loaned MW Development $212,000 for the down payment. To provide security for the repayment of the loan, Richard Taylor, as manager of MW Development, executed a promissory note to Simpson and an assignment pursuant to which MW Development assigned "all of its right, title and interest in and to" the real estate contract entered into with the Wattses. Because he was recuperating in Florida from an injury, Simpson did not see the note and assignment until June 22, 2003. Upon realizing that the promissory note did not become due until August 4, 2003, and that it further provided for a 10-day grace period before Simpson could pursue collection or exercise his rights under the terms of the assignment, he contacted an attorney requesting an agreement granting him the exclusive right to purchase the property if MW Development defaulted on the real estate contract and the promissory note.

After the agreement was drafted, Simpson met with the Wattses' son, Wayne Watts, and discussed the potential for the loss of the deposit money and the need for a 14-day period in which he could purchase the property after any default by MW Development. The precise content of their conversation differs. Simpson states that at no time was there any conversation or agreement that he would purchase the 40-acre tract while the Wattses recalled that Simpson affirmatively represented that if MW Development defaulted, he would purchase the property. As a result of their discussions, the Wattses and Simpson executed the prepared written agreement which states in part that:

> In consideration of the respective rights of the parties, IT IS HEREBY AGREED AS FOLLOWS: In the event M.W. defaults on the CONTRACT and defaults on the PROMISSORY NOTE, SIMPSON is hereby granted the exclusive right, for a period of fourteen (14) days after M.W. defaults on the CONTRACT, to purchase the property described in the CONTRACT for the sum of $2,129,222.00 in cash. Less the sum of $212,900.00, the amount paid to WATTS as a deposit, all according to the other terms and conditions of the CONTRACT.

A copy of the real estate sales contract, promissory note, and assignment were attached to the agreement and, by reference, incorporated into the agreement.

After MW Development failed to purchase the property, the Wattses sued MW Development, Richard Taylor, and Simpson for breach of contract. In January 2004, the court approved an agreed order which gave Simpson the right to purchase the property pursuant to the June 2003 real estate contract through and including February 25, 2004. The order further provided that if Simpson did not exercise his right to purchase, the Wattses could sell the property to a third party. After Simpson declined to exercise his right to purchase the property, the property was sold to a third party for $1,800,000. The trial court entered partial summary judgment in favor of the Wattses against MW Development in the amount of $91,605.78, which represented the interest accrued on the $1,917,222. It denied the Wattses' motions for summary judgment against Simpson. It also dismissed the complaint against Simpson. The Wattses appealed. They argued that because of the assignment contract entered into between Simpson and MW Development, Simpson is obligated to perform all of the obligations set forth in the real estate contract, including the purchase of the property.

Thompson, Judge

The question, therefore, is whether Simpson can be held responsible for damages, including the difference with the original sale price as stated in the real estate contract between the Wattses and MW Development and the interest due after default. Although the parties have failed to cite a Kentucky case specifically addressing the assignment of a real estate purchase contract, the law is well settled in other jurisdictions and is summarily recited in *Kneberg v. H.L. Green Co.,* wherein it stated:

> It is quite generally the law that a contract for the sale of land, which has been assigned by the purchaser, cannot be specifically enforced against the assignee, by reason of the assignment, unless the assignee has entered into a binding contract with the assignor or vendor to assume the assignor's obligations. It is also the rule, however, that if the assignee expressly assumes the burdens of the contract or if he accepts the benefits thereof and adopts the same by seeking performance of the contract or by any equivalent act, indicative of an intention upon his part to adopt and become bound, so that he may be held impliedly to have assumed the burdens thereof, specific performance will lie against him.

In this case, there is no language in the assignment contract between Simpson and the Wattses which can be reasonably construed to obligate him to purchase the property pursuant to the terms of the real estate contract between MW Development and the Wattses. The purpose of the assignment was to secure the $212,000 loan to MW Development. Thus, the assignment contract expressly states that: "As security for the above loan, First Party (MWD) hereby conditionally assigns unto the Second Party (Simpson), all of its right, title and interest in and to that certain real estate purchase agreement. . . ." It continues to state that the assignment "shall become effective and absolute upon any default by First Party in the payment of the aforesaid note according to its terms." The assignment, therefore, was not effective until MW Development defaulted on the promissory note, which was after the closing date stated in the real estate contract. The unambiguous language of the assignment contradicts the Wattses' argument that it operated as an assignment of MW Development's obligation to purchase the property. To construe the assignment contract to have also assigned MW Development's obligation to purchase the Wattses' property, would be contrary to the ordinary meaning of the language used and the intention of Simpson and MW Development. Thus, the Wattses cannot assert a claim against Simpson on the basis of the assignment contract entered into between Simpson and MW Development.

The Wattses contend that even if the assignment did not assign MW Development's obligation under the purchase contract, the July 31, 2003, agreement entered into between them and Simpson imposed the obligation on Simpson to purchase the property if MW Development defaulted. We find that the Wattses' reliance on the July 2003 agreement is misplaced. Like the assignment, the agreement unambiguously states that it is conditioned upon MW Development's default on the real estate contract. Notably absent from the agreement are any words which impose an obligation upon Simpson to purchase the property. Although during the 14 days after MW Development's default Simpson had the right to purchase the property, he did not have the obligation to do so.

Affirmed in favor of Simpson.

Discharge of Delegator by Novation

As you have seen, the mere delegation of duties—even when the delegatee assumes those duties—does not release the delegator from his legal obligation to the obligee. A delegator can, however, be discharged from performance by **novation.**

A novation is a particular type of substituted contract in which the obligee agrees to discharge the original obligor and to substitute a new obligor in his place. The effects of a novation are that the original obligor has no further obligation under the contract and the obligee has the right to look to the new obligor for fulfillment of the contract. A novation requires more than the obligee's consent to having the delegatee perform the duties. In the example used above, the mere fact that First Bank accepted mortgage payments from Morgan would not create a novation. Rather, there must be some evidence that the obligee agrees to discharge the old obligor and substitute a new obligor. As you will see in the following *Rosenberg* case, this can be inferred from language of a contract or such other factors as the obligee's conduct or the surrounding circumstances.

Rosenberg v. Son, Inc.	491 N.W.2d 71 (Sup. Ct. N.D. 1992)

In February 1980, Mary Pratt entered into a contract to buy a Dairy Queen restaurant located in Grand Forks's City Center Mall from Harold and Gladys Rosenberg. The terms of the contract for the franchise, inventory, and equipment were a purchase price totaling $62,000, a $10,000 down payment, and $52,000 due in quarterly payments at 10 percent interest over a 15-year period. The sales contract also contained a provision denying the buyer a right of prepayment for the first five years of the contract. In October 1982, Pratt assigned her rights and delegated her duties under this contract to Son, Inc. The *assignment between Pratt and Son contained a "Consent to Assignment" clause, which was signed by the Rosenbergs. It also contained a "save harmless" clause, in which Son promised to indemnify Pratt for any claims, demands, or actions that might result from Son's failure to perform the agreement. After this transaction, Pratt moved to Arizona and had no further knowledge of or involvement with the Dairy Queen business. Also following the assignment, the Dairy Queen was moved from the mall to a different location in Grand Forks.*

Son assigned the contract to Merit Corporation in June 1984. This assignment did not include a consent clause, but the Rosenbergs knew of the assignment and apparently acquiesced in it. They accepted a large prepayment from Merit, reducing the principal balance to $25,000. After the assignment, Merit pledged the inventory and equipment of the Dairy Queen as collateral for a loan from Valley Bank and Trust. Payments from Merit to the Rosenbergs continued until June 1988, at which time the payments ceased, leaving an unpaid principal balance of $17,326.24 plus interest. The Rosenbergs attempted collection of the balance from Merit, but Merit filed bankruptcy. The business assets pledged as collateral for the loan from Valley Bank and Trust were repossessed. The Rosenbergs brought this action for collection of the outstanding debt against Son and Pratt. The trial court granted summary judgment in favor of Son and Pratt and against the Rosenbergs, and the Rosenbergs appealed.

Erickstad, Chief Justice

It is a well-established principle in the law of contracts that a contracting party cannot escape its liability on the contract by merely assigning its duties and rights under the contract to a third party. This rule of law applies to all categories of contracts, including contracts for the sale of goods, which is present in the facts of this case.

Thus, when Pratt entered into the "assignment agreement" with Son, a simple assignment alone was insufficient to release her from any further liability on the contract. It is not, however, a legal impossibility for a contracting party to rid itself of an obligation under a contract. It may seek the approval of the other original party for release, and substitute a new party in its place. In such an instance, the transaction is no longer called an assignment; instead, it is called a novation. If a novation occurs in this manner, it must be clear from the terms of the agreement that a novation is intended by all parties involved. Both original parties to the contract must intend and mutually assent to the discharge of the obligor from any further liability on the original contract.

It is evident from the express language of the assignment agreement between Pratt and Son that only an assignment was intended, not a novation. The agreement made no mention of discharging Pratt from any further liability on the contract. To the contrary, the latter part of the agreement contained an indemnity clause holding Pratt harmless in the event of a breach by Son. Thus, it is apparent that Pratt contemplated being held ultimately responsible for performance of the obligation. Furthermore, the agreement was between Pratt and Son; they were the parties signing the agreement, not the Rosenbergs. An agreement between Pratt and Son cannot unilaterally affect the Rosenbergs' rights under the contract. The Rosenbergs did sign a consent to the assignment at the bottom of the agreement. However, by merely consenting to the assignment the Rosenbergs did not consent to a discharge of the principal obligor—Pratt. Nothing in the language of the consent clause supports such an allegation. A creditor is free to consent to an assignment without releasing the original obligor. Thus, the express language of the agreement and intent of the parties at the time the assignment was made did not contemplate a novation by releasing Pratt and substituting Son in her stead. The inquiry as to Pratt's liability does not end at this juncture. The trial court released Pratt from any liability on the contract due to the changes or alterations which took place following her assignment to Son. While it is true that Pratt cannot be forced to answer on the contract irrespective of events occurring subsequent to her assignment, it is also true that she cannot be exonerated for every type of alteration or change that may develop.

The trial court decided that any alteration in the underlying obligation resulted in a release of Pratt on the contract. It appears that not every type of alteration is sufficient to warrant discharge of the assignor. As suggested by Professor Corbin in the language highlighted above, the alteration must "prejudice the position of the assignor." 4 *Corbin on Contracts* section 866 at *459.*

If the changes in the obligation prejudicially affect the assignor, a new agreement has been formed between the assignee and the other original contracting party. More concisely, a novation has occurred and the assignor's original obligation has been discharged. Although we have previously determined that the terms of the assignment agreement between Pratt and Son did not contemplate a novation, there are additional methods of making a novation besides doing so in the express terms of an agreement. The question of whether or not there has been a novation is a question of fact. The trial court should not have granted summary judgment. There are questions of fact remaining as to the result of the changes in the contract. Thus, we reverse the summary judgment and remand for further proceedings.

Reversed and remanded in favor of the Rosenbergs.

Third-Party Beneficiaries

There are many situations in which the performance of a contract would constitute some benefit to a person who was not a party to the contract. Despite the fact that a nonparty may expect to derive advantage from the performance of a contract, the general rule is that no one but the parties to a contract or their assignees can enforce it. In some situations, however, parties contract for the purpose of benefiting some third person. In such cases, the benefit to the third person is an essential part of the contract, not just an incidental result of a contract that was really designed to benefit the parties. Where the parties to a contract *intended* to benefit a third party, courts will give effect to their intent and permit the third party to enforce the contract. Such third parties are called **third-party beneficiaries.** Figure 5 illustrates the relationship of third-party beneficiaries to the contracting parties.

Intended Beneficiaries versus Incidental Beneficiaries

For a third person (other than an assignee) to have the right to enforce a contract, she must be able to establish that the contract was made with the intent to benefit her. A few courts have required that both parties must have intended to benefit the third party. Most courts, however, have found it to be sufficient if the person to whom the promise to perform was made (the *promisee*) intended to benefit the third party. In ascertaining intent to benefit the third party, a court will look at the language used by the parties and all the surrounding circumstances. That point is made in the *Locke* case, which follows shortly. One factor that is frequently important in determining intent to benefit is whether the party making the promise to perform (the *promisor*) was to render performance directly to the third party. For example, if Allison contracts with Jones Florist to deliver flowers to Kirsch, the fact that performance was to be rendered to Kirsch would be good evidence that the parties intended to benefit Kirsch. This factor is not conclusive, however. There are some cases in which intent to benefit a third party has been found even though performance was to be rendered to the promisee rather than to the third party. Intended beneficiaries are often classified as either *creditor* or *donee beneficiaries*. These classifications are discussed in greater detail below.

A third party who is unable to establish that the contract was made with the intent to benefit her is called an *incidental beneficiary*. A third party is classified as an incidental beneficiary when the benefit derived by that third party was merely an unintended by-product of a contract that was created for the benefit of those who were parties to it. Incidental beneficiaries acquire no rights under a contract. For example, Hutton contracts with Long Construction Company to build a valuable structure on his land. The performance of the contract would constitute a benefit to Keller, Hutton's next-door neighbor, by increasing the value of Keller's land. The contract between Hutton and Long was made for the purpose of benefiting themselves, however. Any advantage derived by Keller is purely incidental to their primary purpose. Thus, Keller could not sue and recover damages if either Hutton or Long breaches the contract.

As a general rule, members of the public are held to be incidental beneficiaries of contracts entered into by

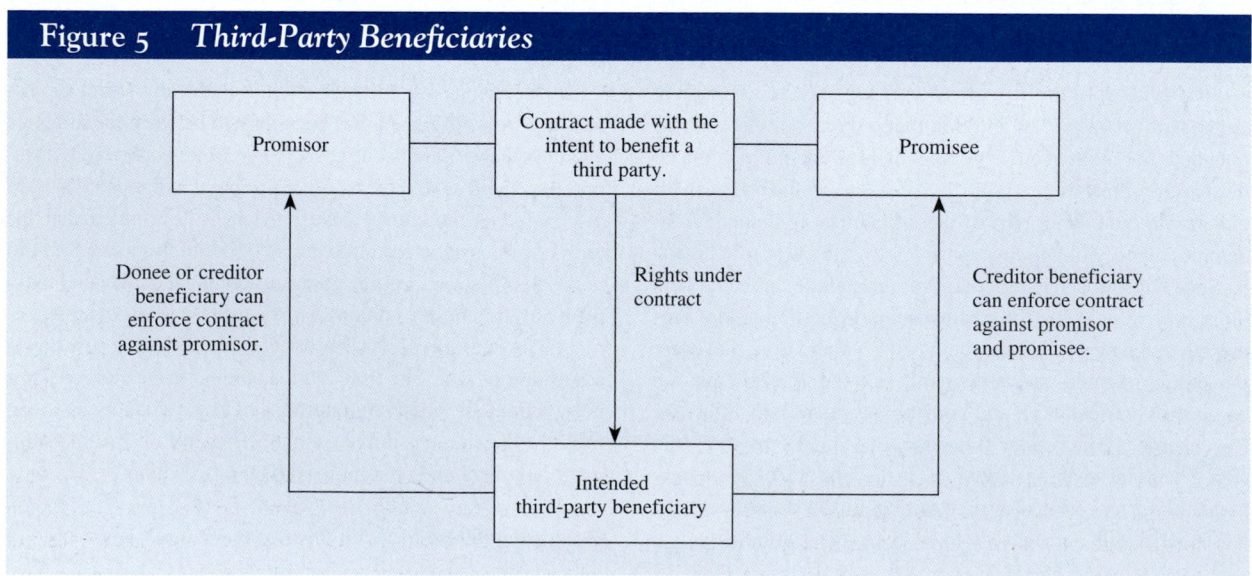

Figure 5   *Third-Party Beneficiaries*

their municipalities or other governmental units in the regular course of carrying on governmental functions. A member of the public cannot recover a judgment in a suit against a promisor of such a contract, even though all taxpayers will suffer some injury from nonperformance. A different result may be reached, however, if a party contracting with a governmental unit agrees to reimburse members of the public for damages or if the party undertakes to perform some duty for individual members of the public.

Creditor Beneficiaries If the promisor's performance is intended to satisfy a legal duty that the promisee owes to a third party, the third party is a **creditor beneficiary.** The creditor beneficiary has rights against both the promisee (because of the original obligation) and the promisor. For example, Smith buys a car on credit from Jones Auto Sales. Smith later sells the car to Carmichael, who agrees to pay the balance due on the car to Jones

Auto Sales. (Note that Smith is delegating his duty to pay to Carmichael, and Carmichael is assuming the personal obligation to do so.) In this case, Jones Auto Sales is a creditor beneficiary of the contract between Smith and Carmichael. It has rights against both Carmichael and Smith if Carmichael does not perform.

Donee Beneficiaries If the promisee's primary purpose in contracting is to make a gift of the agreed-on performance to a third party, that third party is classified as a *donee beneficiary.* If the contract is breached, the donee beneficiary will have a cause of action against the promisor, but not against the promisee (donor). For example, Miller contracts with Perpetual Life Insurance Company, agreeing to pay premiums in return for which Perpetual agrees to pay $100,000 to Miller's husband when Miller dies. Miller's husband is a donee beneficiary and can bring suit and recover judgment against Perpetual if Miller dies and Perpetual does not pay.

Locke v. Ozark City Board of Education   2005 Ala. LEXIS 55 (Ala. Sup. Ct. 2005)

Wesley Locke is a physical education teacher employed by the Dale County Department of Education. For a number of years, Locke also served as an umpire for high school baseball games. Locke was a member of the Southeast Alabama Umpires Association (SAUA), which provides officials to athletic events sponsored by the Alabama High School Athletic Association (AHSAA). On March 30, 1999, Locke was serving as the head umpire in a baseball game between Carroll High School and George W. Long High School. The game was being played at Carroll High School, and the principal and the athletic director of Carroll High School were in attendance; however, Carroll High School did not provide police protection or other security personnel for the game. After the baseball game, Mixon Cook, the parent of one of the baseball players for Carroll High School, attacked Locke, punching him three times in the face—in his right eye, on the right side of his face, and on the left side of his neck. As a result, Locke sustained physical injuries to his neck and face that caused him pain, discomfort, scarring, and blurred vision. Locke sued the Ozark City Board of Education, alleging breach of contract.

Locke specifically alleged that because Carroll High School, through the Board, is a member of the AHSAA, it is therefore required to follow the rules and regulations of the AHSAA. According to Locke, the AHSAA Directory provides that all school principals have the duty to "insure good game administration and supervision by providing for the following: . . . adequate police protection" at athletic events. Locke alleged that, by not fulfilling its duty under the Directory, the Board breached its contract with the ASHAA by failing to provide police protection at the baseball game, that he was an intended third-party beneficiary of the contract, and that he was injured as a result of the Board's breach of the contract. The trial court entered a summary judgment in favor of the Board, and Locke appealed.

See, Justice

Locke argues that he is an intended third-party beneficiary of a contract between the Board and the AHSAA. To recover under a third-party beneficiary theory, the complainant must show: 1) that the contracting parties intended, at the time the contract was created, to bestow a direct benefit upon a third party; 2) that the complainant was the intended beneficiary of the contract; and 3) that the contract was breached. Further, it has long been the rule in Alabama that one who seeks recovery as a third-party beneficiary of a contract must establish that the

contract was intended for his direct, as opposed to incidental, benefit. We look to the complaints and the surrounding circumstances of the parties to ascertain the existence of that direct benefit.

In *Zeigler v. Blount Bros. Construction Co.,* this court addressed what is necessary to establish status as a third-party beneficiary of a contract. In that case, a dam commissioned by a power company and built by a contractor collapsed. Zeigler, a customer of the electrical power company, sued the contractor that had built the dam, arguing that his status as a consumer of electrical power made him a third-party beneficiary of the contract between the electrical power company and the contractor. Specifically, Zeigler argued that because the contractor failed to construct the dam properly and the dam subsequently collapsed, he was being forced to pay higher bills for electricity than he would have had to pay had the dam been properly constructed. In determining whether Zeigler was a third-party beneficiary of the contract under the "surrounding circumstances" test, this court looked to whether the power company itself was directly benefited by the contract, or whether the benefit manifested itself mainly to third parties. This court noted that the contract itself did not mention third parties or any benefits third parties would reap from the construction of the dam. This court found that performance of the contracts would, and did, result in an enhancement of [the power company's] property holdings, to the direct benefit of the [power company] itself. This court further noted that there was no evidence indicating that the power company had considered the fees their customers would have to pay if the dam was built, and that there was no evidence indicating that a properly constructed dam would have necessarily resulted in lower electrical bills for the consumer. Therefore, this court held that because the contract directly benefited the power company and would not necessarily benefit the customer, Zeigler was an incidental, rather than an intended direct, beneficiary of the contract between the power company and the contractor.

On the other hand, in *H.R.H. Metals, Inc. v. Miller,* Vulcan Materials Company contracted with H.R.H Metals, Inc., to purchase and remove three buildings located on property belonging to Vulcan. H.R.H. signed a contract with Vulcan that provided, in pertinent part:

> [H.R.H.] covenants to follow Vulcan's safety rules and to maintain its own safety and health program for its employees, subcontractors, and agents sufficient to prevent injury or illness to such persons resulting from their presence on the Vulcan premises . . .

H.R.H. hired a subcontractor, Miller, to demolish and remove one of the buildings. While in the process of demolishing the building, Miller walked across a skylight and fell 20 feet, seriously injuring himself. Miller sued H.R.H., alleging, among other things, that H.R.H. had breached its contract with Vulcan to provide safety equipment to subcontractors, that he

was a third-party beneficiary of the contract between Vulcan and H.R.H., that H.R.H. had breached that contract, and that he had been injured by H.R.H.'s breach of the contract. This Court noted that in order for a person to be a third-party beneficiary of a contract, the contracting parties must have intended to bestow benefits on third parties. This Court held that to ascertain the intent of the parties, we must first look to the contract itself, because the intention of the parties is to be derived from the contract itself where the language is plain and unambiguous. This court held that the language reflects an intention on the part of the contracting parties to bestow a direct benefit on [the plaintiff].

In this case, the Board argues that Locke was not an intended beneficiary of the AHSAA contract. The contract between the Board and the AHSAA specifically provides that principals are to "provide good game administration and supervision by providing . . . adequate police protection." The contract before us between the Board and the AHSAA, like the one in *H.R.H.* and unlike the one in *Zeigler,* anticipates the existence of a third party. SAUA, which provided umpires, specifically Locke, for the game, provides officials only to athletic events that are sponsored by the AHSAA. The contract states that the purpose of "adequate police protection" is to "provide good game administration and supervision." Game administration and supervision necessarily involve umpires. The fact that the AHSAA and the Board intended for the police protection to directly benefit the umpires, who are involved in game administration and supervision, is evidenced by the letter from the AHSAA sanctioning Carroll High School for the incident involving Locke. Because this matter is before us on the appeal of a summary judgment, we need determine only whether Locke has presented substantial evidence creating a genuine issue of material fact as to whether he was an intended direct beneficiary of the contract. We hold, based on the plain language of the contract and on the surrounding circumstances, that the contract anticipates third-party umpires, that the contract was intended to directly benefit umpires like Locke, and that Locke has presented substantial evidence creating a genuine issue of fact as to whether he was an intended direct beneficiary of the contract between the Board and the AHSAA.

Reversed and remanded in favor of Locke.

Vesting of Beneficiary's Rights

Another possible threat to the interests of the third-party beneficiary is that the promisor and the promisee might modify or discharge their contract so as to extinguish or alter the beneficiary's rights. For example, Gates, who owes $500 to Sorenson, enters into a contract with Connor whereby Connor agrees to pay the $500 to Sorenson. What happens if, before Sorenson is paid, Connor pays the money to Gates and Gates accepts it or Connor and Gates otherwise modify the contract? Courts have held that there is

Ethics in Action

Westendorf bought her friend a Gateway computer, which, at her request, Gateway delivered directly to her friend. Several months later, the same friend purchased a Gateway computer, which he requested be delivered directly to Westendorf. Westendorf received and kept that computer. In the shipment, Gateway included its Standard Terms and Conditions Agreement, which contains an arbitration clause. Westendorf allegedly began experiencing numerous and serious difficulties when attempting to use the Gateway.net service. She brought a class action against Gateway. Westendorf argues that she is not bound by the arbitration clause because as a nonpurchasing user of the computer she never expressly agreed to arbitration. Is it ethical to obligate a donee beneficiary such as Westendorf to the arbitration clause that was part of the contract between the friend who gave her the computer and Gateway?

a point at which the rights of the beneficiary vest—that is, the beneficiary's rights cannot be lost by modification or discharge. A modification or discharge that occurs after the beneficiary's rights have vested cannot be asserted as a defense to a suit brought by the beneficiary. The exact time at which the beneficiary's rights vest differs from jurisdiction to jurisdiction. Some courts have held that vesting occurs when the contract is formed, while others hold that vesting does not occur until the beneficiary learns of the contract and consents to it or does some act in reliance on the promise.

The contracting parties' ability to vary the rights of the third-party beneficiary can also be affected by the terms of their agreement. A provision of the contract between the promisor and the promisee stating that the duty to the beneficiary cannot be modified would be effective to prevent modification. Likewise, a contract provision in which the parties specifically reserved the right to change beneficiaries or modify the duty to the beneficiary would be enforced. For example, provisions reserving the right to change beneficiaries are very common in insurance contracts.

Problems and Problem Cases

1. Schauer and Erstad went shopping for an engagement ring on August 15, 1999. After looking at diamonds in premier jewelry establishments such as Tiffany and Company and Cartier, they went to Mandarin Gem's store, where they found a ring that salesperson Joy said featured a 3.01 carat diamond with a clarity grading of "SI1." Erstad bought the ring the same day for $43,121.55. The following month, for insurance purposes, Mandarin Gem provided Erstad a written appraisal verifying the ring had certain characteristics, including an SI1 clarity rating and an average replacement value of $45,500. Lam, a graduate gemologist with the European Gemological Laboratory (EGL), signed the appraisal. The couple's subsequent short-term marriage was dissolved in a North Dakota judgment awarding each party "the exclusive right, title and possession of all personal property . . . which such party now owns, possesses, holds or hereafter acquires." Schauer's personal property included the engagement ring given to her by Erstad. On June 3, 2002, after the divorce, Schauer had the ring evaluated by the Gem Trade Laboratory, which gave the diamond a rating of "SI2" quality, an appraisal with which other unidentified jewelers, including one at Mandarin Gem's store agreed. Schauer alleged that the true clarity of the diamond and its actual worth, which is some $23,000 less than what Erstad paid for it. Schauer sued Mandarin Gems on several theories, alleging that she was a third-party beneficiary of Erstad's contract with Mandarin Gems. Is she correct?

2. Douglass was a highly trained servicer of hardness-testing machinery, who was employed by Page-Wilson. In August and April 1983, Douglass signed two employment agreements governing the terms and conditions of his employment with Page-Wilson. The first agreement prohibited Douglass, while he was working for Page-Wilson and for one year after the termination of his employment, from using, to Page-Wilson's detriment, any of its customer list or other intellectual property acquired from his job there. The

second agreement, which applied to the same time period, prohibited Douglass from accepting employment from or serving as a consultant to any business that was in competition with Page-Wilson. In April 1987, Canrad Corporation purchased all assets and contractual rights of Page-Wilson, including Douglass's two employment contracts. Special Products Manufacturing, a wholly owned subsidiary of Canrad, assumed plant operations. Douglas worked for Special Products until his resignation in February 1988. Shortly after that time, Special Products filed suit against Douglass, alleging that Douglass had affixed his name and home telephone number to the machines he serviced, so that the ensuing maintenance calls would reach him personally. It also alleged that, following his resignation, Douglass established a competing business and actively solicited Special Products' clientele. Douglass claims that Special Products did not have the right to enforce the agreements not to compete. Is Douglass correct?

3. Kethan's employment contract with his employer, MedEcon, included a noncompete. No clause in the contract directly addressed the issue of whether Kethan's contract could be assigned. Most of MedEcon's assets, including Kethan's employment contract, were acquired by the plaintiff, MHA. A short time after this acquisition, Kethan resigned and, in violation of the noncompete, went to work for a competitor. MHA brought suit seeking to enforce Kethan's noncompete with MedEcon. Was the noncompete assignable?

4. Perry sold its Auto Works Division to Northern Retail. Northern Retail's parent, Northern Pacific (later called NP Holding) agreed to assume Perry's debts and indemnify Perry for damages relating to Auto Works Division. After the contract was formed but before the closing, Northern Retail assigned the purchase contract to Auto Works, Inc. At the closing, Perry transferred the Auto Works Division to Auto Works, Inc. (not to Northern Retail), with the assumption instrument being executed by Auto Works, Inc., Later, Northern Retail sold Auto Works, Inc., to a third party, who put it into bankruptcy, thereby failing to pay rent due under leases that it had assumed from Perry. NP Holding dissolved. Northern Retail became CSKG (a subsidiary of CSK Auto), and then was dissolved, with a transfer of its assets to CSK Auto. Perry claimed that CSK and NP Holding were obligated to indemnify it for the leases. Perry argued that the sale of the Auto Works Division to Auto Works, Inc., did not release Northern Retail from its obligations and was not a novation. Was this a good argument?

5. Jones paid Sullivan, the chief of the Addison Police Department, $6,400 in exchange for Sullivan's cooperation in allowing Jones and others to bring marijuana by airplane into the Addison airport without police intervention. Instead of performing the requested service, Sullivan arrested Jones. The $6,400 was turned over to the district attorney's office and was introduced into evidence in the subsequent trial in which Jones was tried for and convicted of bribery. After his conviction, Jones assigned his alleged claim to the $6,400 to Melvyn Bruder. Based on the assignment, Bruder brought suit against the state of Texas to obtain possession of the money. Will he be successful?

6. GWI is a manufacturer of beauty supply products. Sullivan is a distributor of beauty supply products in New England and operates more than two dozen wholesale beauty supply stores in that region. In February 1998, the parties entered into a distribution agreement, pursuant to which GWI granted Sullivan the exclusive right to sell its products to professional stores in New Hampshire, Vermont, and Maine, and to sell its products to both professional stores and salons in Massachusetts. Among other things, the agreement provided that "[a]ll disputes and claims relating to or arising under or out of this Agreement shall be fully and finally settled by arbitration." This agreement expired in 2003, but the parties continued their relationship under the same terms and conditions as had governed the relationship during the duration of the contract. In 2006, another of GWI's regional distributors—Kaleidoscope/BOA, Inc.—assigned to Sullivan all of its "right, title, and interest under the Kaleidoscope Distribution Agreement [with GWI] dated August 16, 2004, save and except the right to distribute Graham Webb Classic line products to salons in the territory." GWI consented to this assignment. By acquiring an assignment of Kaleidoscope's rights under its distribution agreement with GWI, Sullivan obtained the exclusive right to distribute GWI products to professional salons in Maine, New Hampshire, and Vermont (previously, it had the exclusive right to distribute GWI products only to professional stores in those states). Like the original distribution agreement between GWI and Sullivan, both the distribution agreement between Kaleidoscope and GWI (the rights under which were assigned

to Sullivan) and the agreement evidencing that assignment contained arbitration provisions. Despite the fact that the Sullivan Distribution Agreement (SDA) had expired, the Assignment Agreement specifically referenced that document, describing the parties' respective rights and obligations and noting that the SDA will have to be amended to take into account Sullivan's newly expanded distribution rights. The parties' reference to the SDA in the Assignment Agreement provides strong evidence that, although the SDA agreement had expired, the parties were continuing their business relationship pursuant to its terms. A little more than a year later, GWI notified Sullivan of its intention to terminate its distribution relationship with Sullivan, effective April 1, 2007. In that letter, GWI specifically invoked the termination provisions contained in both the SDA and the Kaleidoscope Distribution Agreement. When Sullivan was unable to persuade GWI to change its mind, it sued GWI for breach of contract and other claims. Sullivan asserted that the arbitration provision in the Assignment Agreement was not relevant to this dispute and that it was not bound by the arbitration provisions in the Kaleidoscope Distribution Agreement. Is this a good argument?

7. Francis brought suit against Piper and his law firm, alleging Piper committed legal malpractice when he drafted a series of wills for Heine, Francis's brother. Heine, who had never married, had no children; Francis was his sole sibling and closest living relative. In 1987, after Heine suffered a stroke, the district court appointed a conservator for him. In 1990, Heine met Resick, a waitress at a deli he frequented. In December 1991, Resick referred Heine, who did not have a will, to Piper. Piper prepared three successive wills for Heine. The first left all of Heine's estate to a church. The second left $20,000 to Resick and the remainder of Heine's estate to a church. The third left all of Heine's estate to Resick. If Heine had not executed a will, Francis would have been Heine's sole heir under the intestacy laws. After Heine's death, Resick submitted the third will to probate. Francis challenged the will, and eventually reached a settlement with Resick that provided Resick would receive $80,000 and Francis the remainder of Heine's estate. Francis then brought this action against Piper, alleging Piper was negligent because Heine was under a conservatorship, lacked testamentary capacity, and was suffering from the effects of undue influence. Piper moved

for summary judgment, asserting Francis could not bring a legal malpractice action against him. Under applicable state law, an attorney is liable to a nonclient third party only if the client's sole purpose in retaining an attorney is to provide a benefit directly to the third party. Was Francis such an intended beneficiary?

8. The Sheriff of Polk County employed Prison Health Services (PHS) to provide total health care services for inmates and detainees housed in Polk County Jail and Jail Annex. In 1992, employees of the Sheriff's office booked Cherry into the jail to begin serving a 30-day sentence for driving under the influence of alcohol. At the time of his incarceration, Cherry informed the PHS medical staff that he consumed approximately a case of beer daily. Over the next two days, Cherry repeatedly requested medical attention for symptoms of alcohol withdrawal. Cherry's wife notified a Sheriff's office employee that her husband had a history of delirium tremens during alcohol withdrawal and that he was in immediate need of a doctor's attention. About two hours later, the inmates sharing Cherry's cell asked Sheriff's office to check on Cherry's condition. The employees found Cherry in his cell hallucinating and shaking violently. The employee notified PHS Nurse Gill, who examined Cherry and reported his symptoms to PHS Nurse Smith. Nurse Smith requested that Cherry be sent to the infirmary for observation. At the infirmary, a Sheriff's office employee shackled Cherry, who was still hallucinating, to his bed, with the knowledge and acquiescence of Nurse Smith. The next morning, while still suffering from hallucinations associated with delirium tremens, Cherry either walked or jumped off the end of his bed. Because the leg shackle did not allow his feet to advance beyond the top of the bed, Cherry landed head first on the concrete floor. Cherry died five days later as a result of his injuries. Cherry's estate filed suit against PHS, Nurse Smith, and the Sheriff's office for breach of contract, alleging that Cherry was a third-party beneficiary to the contract between the Sheriff and PHS. Will Cherry's estate prevail?

9. Lewis, a dairyman, was a member of the Mountain Empire Dairymen's Association (MEDA). MEDA was the exclusive agent for marketing Lewis's dairy products. Lewis borrowed $194,850 from Mid-States Sales and secured the loan with certain of his cattle and their products. Lewis assigned his right to receive some of the proceeds from the sale of his

milk each month to Mid-States, and notified MEDA of the assignment. After paying Mid-States for over a year under this agreement, MEDA received notice from Lewis that he was canceling his membership in MEDA. MEDA notified Mid-States and other assignees of Lewis that Lewis was canceling his membership, and asked them to sign a release of assignment. The other assignees signed the releases, but Mid-States did not. MEDA made the last payout on the milk it sold for Lewis directly to Lewis rather than to Mid-States. After Lewis filed for bankruptcy, Mid-States sued MEDA for the payment. Will it prevail?

Online Research

Assignment of Leases

Leases often contain clauses that specifically address the right to assign the lease. Using your favorite search engine and key words such as lease AND assignment, locate a lease that contains a provision addressing assignment. How would the concepts of this chapter apply if the lessor or the lessee of the lease you found assigns the lease?

PERFORMANCE AND REMEDIES

T he Warrens hired Denison, a building contractor, to build a house on their property for $73,400. Denison's construction deviated somewhat from the specifications for the project. These deviations were presumably unintentional, and the cost of repairing them was $1,941.50. The finished house had a market value somewhat higher than the market value would have been without the deviations. The Warrens refused to pay the $48,400 balance due under the contract, alleging that Denison had used poor workmanship in building the house and they were under no obligation to perform further duties under the contract.

- Do the Warrens have the right to withhold all further payment?
- What are the consequences of Denison's breach of contract?
- What are the appropriate remedies for Denison's breach of contract?
- Are the Warrens under an ethical duty to pay Denison?

CONTRACTS ARE GENERALLY FORMED before either of the parties renders any actual performance to the other. A person may be content to bargain for and receive the other person's promise at the formation stage of a contract because this permits him to plan for the future. Ultimately, however, all parties bargain for the *performance* of the promises that have been made to them.

In most contracts, each party carries out his promise and is *discharged* (released from all of his obligations under the contract) when his performance is complete. Sometimes, however, a party fails to perform or performs in an unsatisfactory manner. In such cases, courts are often called on to determine the respective rights and duties of the parties. This frequently involves deciding such questions as whether performance was due, whether the contract was breached, to what extent it was breached, and whether performance was excused. This task is made more difficult by the fact that contracts often fail to specify the consequences of nonperformance or defective performance. In deciding questions involving the performance of contracts and remedies for breach of contract, courts draw on a variety of legal principles that attempt to do justice, prevent forfeiture and unjust enrichment, and effectuate the parties' presumed intent.

This chapter presents an overview of the legal concepts that are used to resolve disputes arising in the performance stage of contracting. It describes how courts determine whether performance is due and what kind of performance is due, the consequences of contract breach, and the excuses for a party's failure to perform. It also includes a discussion of the remedies that are used when a court determines that a contract has been breached.

Conditions

Nature of Conditions
One issue that frequently arises in the performance stage of a contract is whether a party has the duty to perform. Some duties are *unconditional* or *absolute*—that is, the duty to perform does not depend on the occurrence of any further event other than the passage of time. For example, if Root promises to pay Downing $100, Root's duty is unconditional. When a party's duty is unconditional, he has the duty to perform unless his performance is excused. (The various excuses for nonperformance will be discussed later in this chapter.) When a duty is unconditional, the promisor's failure to perform constitutes a *breach of contract*.

In many situations, however, a promisor's duty to perform depends on the occurrence of some event that is called a **condition.** A condition is an uncertain, future event that affects a party's duty to perform. For example, if Melman contracts to buy Lance's house on condition that First Bank approve Melman's application for a mortgage loan by January 10, Melman's duty to buy Lance's

Figure 1   *Effect of Conditions*

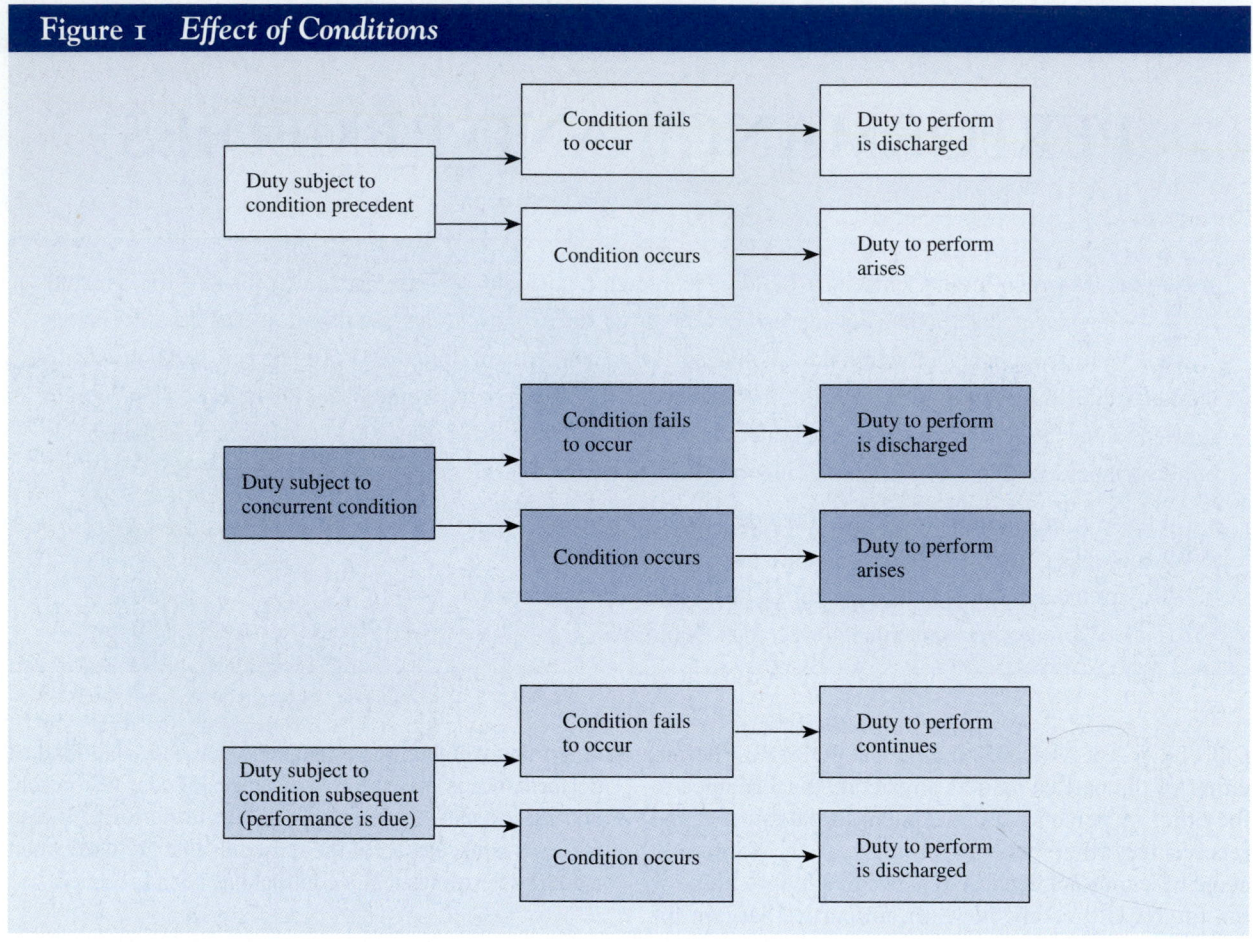

house is *conditioned* on the bank's approving his loan application by January 10. When a promisor's duty is conditional, his duty to perform is affected by the occurrence of the condition. In this case, if the condition does not occur, Melman has no duty to buy the house. His failure to buy it because of the nonoccurrence of the condition will *not* constitute a breach of contract. Rather, he is discharged from further obligation under the contract.

Almost any event can be a condition. Some conditions are beyond the control of either party, such as when Morehead promises to buy Pratt's business if the prime rate drops by a specified amount. Others are within the control of a party, such as when one party's performance of a duty under the contract is a condition of the other party's duty to perform.

Types of Conditions

There are two ways of classifying conditions. One way of classifying conditions focuses on the effect of the condition on the duty to perform. The other way focuses on the way in which the condition is created.

Classifications of Conditions Based on Their Effect on the Duty to Perform   As Figure 1 illustrates, conditions vary in their effects on the duty to perform.

1. *Condition precedent.* A condition precedent is a future, uncertain event that creates the duty to perform. If the condition does not occur, performance does not become due. If the condition does occur, the duty to perform arises. In the following *Smith* case, you will see an example of a condition precedent.

2. *Concurrent condition.* When the contract calls for the parties to perform at the same time, each person's performance is conditioned on the performance or tender of performance (offer of performance) by the other. Such conditions are called **concurrent conditions.** For example, if Martin promises to buy Johnson's car for $5,000, the parties' respective duties to perform are subject to a concurrent condition. Martin does not have the duty to perform unless Johnson tenders his performance, and vice versa.

3. *Condition subsequent.* A **condition subsequent** is a future, uncertain event that **discharges** the duty to perform. When a duty is subject to a condition subsequent, the duty to perform arises but is discharged if the future, uncertain event occurs. For example, Wilkinson and Jones agree that Wilkinson will begin paying Jones $2,000 per month, but that if XYZ Corporation dissolves, Wilkinson's obligation to pay will cease. In this case, Wilkinson's duty to pay is subject to being discharged by a condition subsequent. The major significance of the distinction between conditions precedent and conditions subsequent is that the plaintiff bears the burden of proving the occurrence of a condition precedent, while the defendant bears the burden of proving the occurrence of a condition subsequent.

Smith v. Carter & Burgess, Inc.   2005 Tex. App. LEXIS 1140 (Tex. Ct. App. 2005)

Chris Smith and 14 co-workers signed identical employment agreements with Carter & Burgess, Inc. (C&B). The employment agreements provided the employees could be terminated "for any reason, or no reason at all" after completion of an initial eight-week orientation period. The employment contracts also provided for an incentive payment under certain circumstances:

In the event Employee remains employed with Carter & Burgess for two years after the Effective Date of this Agreement, complies with the terms of this Agreement, and reaffirms the commitment to comply with the provisions of Paragraphs 3 and 4 of this Agreement [dealing with nondisclosure of information], Employee shall be eligible to receive deferred salary in the sum of $15,000. In the event Employee resigns before two years after the Effective Date of this Agreement or is terminated for Cause (as defined in paragraph 1), Employee is responsible for all costs for Employee to return to his/her home location and also forfeits the Incentive Payment.

Smith and the 14 co-workers were terminated after the orientation period but before the expiration of two years' employment when the project for which they were hired was canceled. C&B did not make any incentive payments. The employees sued for breach of contract and promissory estoppel, claiming they were entitled to the incentive payments because they had not resigned or been terminated for cause. The trial court granted a summary judgment in favor of C&B, and Smith and the other employees appealed.

Gardner, Judge

The first sentence of the contracts in this case provides that if an employee completes two years of service with the employer, the employee is eligible for an incentive bonus. The parties disagree as to the effect of the language in the second sentence of the contracts. Plaintiffs interpret the contracts to provide the incentive bonus even if the employees did not work for the employer for two years, so long as they were not terminated for cause or did not voluntarily cease working for C&B. Conversely, C&B contends that the contracts provide the bonus incentive if, and only if, plaintiffs worked for the employer for two years and also provide that even if the employee has served more than two years with the employer and is terminated for cause or quits, the employee must not only provide for his or her own transportation home, but also forfeit the incentive bonus.

We conclude that the only reasonable interpretation of the incentive payment contract provisions is that they required the plaintiffs to remain employed for two years before becoming eligible for the incentive bonus. Reading the contracts to allow the eligibility for an incentive bonus even if the plaintiffs did not remain an employee for two years would render the first sentence of the employment contracts meaningless.

We must next determine whether the two-year employment requirement is a condition precedent. To determine whether a condition precedent exists, the court will ascertain the intention of the parties, and that can be done only by looking at the entire contract. In order to make performance specifically conditional, a term such as "if," "provided that," "on condition that," or some similar language normally must be included. If no such language is used, the terms will be construed as a covenant in order to avoid forfeiture. While such language is not required, absence of such language is probative of the parties' intention that a promise be made, rather than a condition imposed. The contracts in this case use such words.

Thus, we conclude that the only reasonable interpretation of the contracts is that they contained a condition precedent requiring plaintiffs to complete two years of service before becoming eligible for the incentive bonus. The words "in the event that" evidence an intent to create a condition precedent. Furthermore, if a contract is to be interpreted as to give effect to all provisions of the contract, interpreting the employment contract to contain a promise to be made, rather than a condition precedent to performance, would render the first sentence of the contract meaningless. Therefore, a proper interpretation of the employment contracts would be to construe as a condition precedent the requirement that appellants complete two years of employment in order to be eligible for the incentive bonus.

Because we hold that the contract was unambiguous and contained a condition precedent requiring plaintiffs to be employed by C&B for two years before they would become eligible for an incentive payment, we affirm the trial court's summary judgment.

Affirmed in favor of C&B.

Classifications of Conditions Based on the Way in Which They Were Created

Another way of classifying conditions is to focus on the means by which the condition was created.

1. *Express condition.* An **express condition** is a condition that is specified in the language of the parties' contract. For example, if Grant promises to sell his regular season football tickets to Carson on condition that Indiana University wins the Rose Bowl, Indiana's winning the Rose Bowl is an express condition of Grant's duty to sell the tickets.

When the contract expressly provides that a party's duty is subject to a condition, courts take it very seriously. When a duty is subject to an express condition, that condition must be strictly complied with in order to give rise to the duty to perform.

2. *Implied-in-fact condition.* An **implied-in-fact condition** is one that is not specifically stated by the parties but is *implied* by the nature of the parties' promises. For example, if Summers promises to unload cargo from Knight's ship, the ship's arrival in port would be an implied-in-fact condition of Summer's duty to unload the cargo.

3. *Constructive condition.* **Constructive conditions** (also known as *implied-in-law conditions*) are conditions that are imposed by law rather than by the agreement of the parties. The law imposes constructive conditions to do justice between the parties. In contracts in which one of the parties is expected to perform before the other, the law normally infers that performance is a constructive condition of the other party's duty to perform. For example, if Thomas promises to build a house for King, and the parties' understanding is that King will pay Thomas an agreed-on price when the house is built, King's duty to pay is subject to the constructive condition that Thomas complete the house. Without such a constructive condition, a person who did not receive the performance promised him would still have to render his own performance.

Creation of Express Conditions

Although no particular language is required to create an express condition, the conditional nature of promises is usually indicated by such words as *provided that, subject to, on condition that, if, when, while, after,* and *as soon as.* The process of determining the meaning of conditions is not a mechanical one. Courts look at the parties' overall intent as indicated in language of the entire contract.

The following discussion explores two common types of express conditions.

Example of Express Condition: Satisfaction of Third Parties

It is common for building and construction contracts to provide that the property owner's duty to pay is conditioned on the builder's production of certificates to be issued by a specific architect or engineer. These certificates indicate the satisfaction of the architect or engineer with the builder's work. They are often issued at each stage of completion, after the architect or engineer has inspected the work done.

The standard usually used to determine whether the condition has occurred is a *good faith* standard. As a general rule, if the architect or engineer is acting honestly and has some good faith reason for withholding a certificate, the builder cannot recover payments due. In legal terms, the condition that will create the owner's duty to pay has not occurred.

If the builder can prove that the withholding of the certificate was fraudulent or done in bad faith (as a result of collusion with the owner, for example), the court may order that payment be made despite the absence of the certificate. In addition, production of the certificate may be excused by the death, insanity, or incapacitating illness of the named architect or engineer.

Example of Express Condition: Personal Satisfaction

Contracts sometimes provide that a promisee's duty to perform is conditioned on his personal satisfaction with the promisee's performance. For example, Moore commissions Allen to paint a portrait of Moore's wife, but the contract provides that Moore's duty to pay is conditioned on his personal satisfaction with the portrait.

In determining which standard of satisfaction to apply, courts distinguish between cases in which the performance bargained for involves personal taste and comfort and cases that involve mechanical fitness or suitability for a particular purpose. If personal taste and comfort are involved, as they would be in the hypothetical case described above, a promisor who is honestly dissatisfied with the promisee's performance has the right to reject the performance without being liable to the promisee. If, however, the performance involves mechanical fitness or suitability, the court will apply a reasonable person test. If the court finds that a reasonable person would be satisfied with the performance, the condition of personal satisfaction has been met and the promisor must accept the performance and pay the contract price.

Excuse of Conditions

In most situations involving conditional duties, the promisor does not have the duty to perform unless and until the condition occurs. There are, however, a variety of situations in which the occurrence of a condition will be excused. In such a case, the person whose duty is conditional will have to perform even though the condition has not occurred.

One ground for excusing a condition is that the occurrence of the condition has been *prevented* or *hindered* by the party who is benefited by the condition. For example, Connor hires Ingle to construct a garage on Connor's land, but when Ingle attempts to begin construction, Connor refuses to allow Ingle access to the land. In this case, Connor's duty to pay would normally be subject to a constructive condition that Ingle build the garage.

However, since Connor prevented the occurrence of the condition, the condition will be excused, and Ingle can sue Connor for damages for breach of contract even though the condition has not occurred. The following *Harbor Park Market* case considers whether a condition should be excused because of prevention.

Other grounds for excuse of a condition include **waiver** and **estoppel.** When a person whose duty is conditional voluntarily gives up his right to the occurrence of the condition (waiver), the condition will be excused. Suppose that Buchman contracts to sell his car to Fox on condition that Fox pay him $2,000 by June 14. Fox fails to pay on June 14, but, when he tenders payment on June 20, Buchman accepts and cashes the check without reservation. Buchman has thereby *waived* the condition of payment by June 14.

When a person whose duty is conditional leads the other party to rely on his noninsistence on the condition, the condition will be excused because of estoppel. For example, McDonald agrees to sell his business to Brown on condition that Brown provide a credit report and personal financial statement by July 17. On July 5, McDonald tells Brown that he can have until the end of the month to provide the necessary documents. Relying on McDonald's assurances, Brown does not provide the credit report and financial statement until July 29. In this case, McDonald would be *estopped* (precluded) from claiming that the condition did not occur.

A condition may also be excused when performance of the act that constitutes the condition becomes *impossible.* For example, if a building contract provides that the owner's duty to pay is conditioned on the production of a certificate from a named architect, the condition would be excused if the named architect died or became incapacitated before issuing the certificate.

Harbor Park Market v. Gronda   743 N.W.2d 585 (Mich. Ct. App. 2007)

William and Linda Gronda owned a party store and land along with fixtures, equipment, and a liquor license. On October 11, 2004, Harbor Park Market submitted a $55,000 offer to the Grondas for the purchase of their liquor license and fixtures. On October 14, 2004, the Grondas accepted Harbor Park Market's offer to buy the liquor license and fixtures, but their "acceptance" was expressly conditioned (and agreed to by Harbor Park Market) on their attorney's approval of the purchase agreement. The specific language within the agreement was: "This Purchase Agreement is subject to review & approval of attorney Lynn Stedman, on or before Oct. 22, 2004."

Before their attorney had an opportunity to review the purchase agreement, the Grondas conditionally accepted a second offer, this one from Carleton Enterprises, to purchase the real property, along with the business, liquor license, and fixtures, for $250,000. That acceptance, too, was expressly conditioned on the approval of the purchase agreement by the Grondas' attorney.

Lynn Stedman, the Grondas' attorney, reviewed the competing agreements together when he returned from a vacation. He approved the Carleton agreement. The Grondas thereafter refused to complete the sale to Harbor Park Market, and, instead, attempted to close their sale with Carleton. However, Harbor Park Market filed suit for breach of contract against the Grondas and Carleton and asked the court to require the Grondas to perform the contract.

After a one-day bench trial, the trial court concluded that, by soliciting and submitting a competing purchase agreement to Stedman for review, the Grondas placed an obstacle in the way of Stedman's approval of Harbor Park Market's agreement and hindered the fulfillment of the condition precedent. It found in favor of Harbor Park Market and ordered the Grondas to perform the contract. The Grondas appealed.

Murray, Judge

The dispositive issue on appeal is whether the Grondas interfered with, and therefore waived, the condition precedent by simultaneously submitting to Stedman a second conditional agreement. The goal of contract interpretation is to first determine, and then enforce, the intent of the parties based on the plain language of the agreement. If no reasonable person could dispute the meaning of ordinary and plain contract language, the Court must accept and enforce the language as written, unless the contract is contrary to law or public policy. Plain and unambiguous contract language cannot be rewritten by the Court "under the guise of interpretation," as the parties must live by the words of their agreement.

The parties agree that the attorney-approval clause was a condition precedent. A condition precedent, like the one at issue in this case, is a fact or event that the parties intend must take place before there is a right to performance. If the condition is not satisfied, there is no cause of action for a failure to perform the contract. However, the Grondas, as promisors, cannot avoid liability on the contract for the failure of a condition precedent where they caused the failure of the condition. As the Supreme Court has stated, when a contract contains a condition precedent, "there is an implied agreement that the promisor will place no obstacle in the way of the happening of such event. . . ." *Mehling v. Evening News Ass'n.* Where a party prevents the occurrence of a condition, the party, in effect, waives the performance of the condition. Hence, the performance of a condition precedent is discharged or excused, and the conditional promise made an absolute one.

Our case law generally reflects that a party must prevent the condition from occurring by either taking some affirmative action, or by refusing to take action required under the contract, before a court will find a waiver of a condition precedent. For example, in *Mehling,* the Court concluded that the plaintiffs waived the condition precedent that the parties agree on the appraiser's compensation before the property was appraised, because the plaintiffs refused to meet with the defendant and two other appraisers to discuss compensation.

Here, the language of the contract was clear and unambiguous. Quite simply, the agreement stated that the Grondas'

acceptance of Harbor Park Market's offer was subject to their attorney's review and approval of "this agreement." Thus, because there was no limitation on what aspects of the agreement were subject to Stedman's approval, Stedman was authorized to review and approve (or disapprove) any part of the contract, or the entire contract as a whole. Since the parties failed to include an express limitation in the language of the condition precedent that restricted Stedman's approval authority, we will not judicially impose one ourselves. Certainly, language limiting the scope of Stedman's approval could have been included by the parties, but it was not. Hence, because the contract language giving the Grondas' attorney complete discretion to approve or disapprove the agreement for whatever reason was clear and unambiguous, it has to be accepted and enforced as written.

Additionally, there was no finding by the trial court that the Grondas otherwise actively interfered with Stedman's approval, such as instructing the attorney to disapprove the agreement. The attorney-approval clause in Harbor Park Market's agreement required the Grondas to submit the purchase agreement to their lawyer for review. The Grondas submitted the agreement to Stedman in a timely manner, and the agreement required them to do no more. Nor did it prevent the Grondas from submitting other offers to Stedman before he decided whether to approve the Harbor Park Market offer. Thus, it cannot be disputed that the Grondas did not fail to perform as required under the contract. In similar situations, courts have routinely held that submitting a second, competing agreement for review when not precluded by the contract does not constitute a waiver of the condition precedent. Several of our sister states have provided some insightful cases on this precise point. In *Stevens v. Manchester,* the Ohio Court of Appeals held that a broad attorney-approval clause gave the attorneys the right to reject the contract for any reason, including a better competing offer.

In short, the evidence does not support the trial court's finding that the sellers or their attorneys acted in bad faith in disapproving Stevens's offer. The attorney-approval clause gave the sellers' attorneys the right to disapprove Stevens's offer for any reason. Stevens did not object to the language contained in the clause. The sellers' attorneys testified that they disapproved the contract based on potential tax problems for their clients associated with the purchase-price-allocation clause and the architect, inspection, and financing contingencies contained in Stevens's offer. Even assuming, as the trial court did, that the attorneys rejected Stevens's offer solely to accept the more favorable offer, such action does not constitute bad faith. As we have already made clear, the contract did not forbid the Grondas from considering other offers, and it did not require them to take their property off the market while the attorney was reviewing plaintiff's offer. Considering that the second purchase agreement was not legally impermissible where the first was only conditionally accepted, it was not a bad-faith act to accept it and submit it for review.

Reversed and remanded in favor of the Grondas.

Performance of Contracts

When a promisor has performed his duties under a contract, he is discharged. Because his performance constitutes the occurrence of a constructive condition, the other party's duty to perform is also triggered, and the person who has performed has the right to receive the other party's performance. In determining whether a promisor is discharged by performance and whether the constructive condition of his performance has been fulfilled, courts must consider the standard of performance expected of him.

Level of Performance Expected of the Promisor

In some situations, no deviation from the promisor's promised performance is tolerated; in others, less-than-perfect performance will be sufficient to discharge the promisor and give him the right to recover under the contract.

Strict Performance Standard A **strict performance** standard is a standard of performance that requires virtually perfect compliance with the contract terms. Remember that when a party's duty is subject to an express condition, that condition must be strictly and completely complied with in order to give rise to a duty of performance. Thus, when a promisor's performance is an express condition of the promisee's duty to perform, that performance must strictly and completely comply with the contract in order to give rise to the other promisee's duty to perform. For example, if McMillan agrees to pay Jester $500 for painting his house "on condition that" Jester finish the job no later than June 1, 2006, a standard of strict or complete performance would be applied to Jester's performance. If Jester does not finish the job by June 1, his breach will have several consequences: First, since the condition precedent to McMillan's duty to pay has not occurred, McMillan does not have a duty to pay the contract price. Second, since it is now too late for the condition to occur, McMillan is discharged. Third, McMillan can sue Jester for breach of contract. The law's commitment to freedom of contract justifies such results in cases in which the parties have expressly bargained for strict compliance with the terms of the contract.

The strict performance standard is also applied to contractual obligations that can be performed either exactly or to a high degree of perfection. Examples of this type of obligation include promises to pay money, deliver deeds, and, generally, promises to deliver goods. A promisor who performs such promises completely and in strict compliance with the contract is entitled to receive the entire contract price. The promisor whose performance deviates from perfection is not entitled to receive the other party's performance if he does not render perfect performance within an appropriate time. He may, however, be able to recover the value of any benefits that he has conferred on the other party under a theory of quasi-contract.

Substantial Performance Standard A **substantial performance** standard is a somewhat lower standard of performance that is applied to duties that are difficult to perform without some deviation from perfection *if* performance of those duties is *not* an express condition. A common example of this type of obligation is a promise to erect a building. Other examples include promises to construct roads, to cultivate crops, and to render some types of personal or professional services. Substantial performance is performance that falls short of complete performance in minor respects. It does not apply when a contracting party has been deprived of a material part of the consideration he bargained for. When a substantial performance standard is applied, the promisor who has substantially performed is discharged. His substantial performance triggers the other party's duty to pay the contract price less any damages resulting from the defects

Substantial Performance

Definition	Application	Effects	Limitation
Performance that falls short of complete performance in some minor respect but that does not deprive the other party of a material part of the consideration for which he bargained	Applies to performance that (1) is *not* an express condition of the other party's duty to perform and (2) is difficult to do perfectly	Triggers other party's duty to perform; requires other party to pay the contract price minus any damages caused by defects in performance	Breach cannot have been willful

in his performance. The obvious purpose behind the doctrine of substantial performance is to prevent forfeiture by a promisor who has given the injured party most of what he bargained for. Substantial performance is generally held to be inapplicable to a situation in which the breach of contract has been *willful,* however.

Good Faith Performance

One of the most significant trends in modern contract law is that courts and legislatures have created a duty to perform in good faith in an expanding range of contracts.[1] The Uniform Commercial Code specifically imposes a duty of good faith in every contract within the scope of any of the articles of the Code [1–203]. A growing number of courts have applied the duty to use good faith in transactions between lenders and their customers as well as insurance contracts, employment contracts, and contracts for the sale of real property.

This obligation to carry out a contract in good faith is usually called the **implied covenant of good faith and fair dealing.** It is a broad and flexible duty that is imposed by law rather than by the agreement of the parties. It is generally taken to mean that neither party to a contract will do anything to prevent the other from obtaining the benefits that he has the right to expect from the parties' agreement or their contractual relationship. The law's purpose in imposing such a term in contracts is to prevent abuses of power and encourage ethical behavior.

Breach of the implied covenant of good faith gives rise to a contract remedy. In some states, it can also constitute a tort, depending on the severity of the breach. A tort action for breach of the implied covenant of good faith is more likely to be recognized in situations in which a contract involves a special relationship of dependency and trust between the parties or where the public interest is adversely affected by a contracting party's practices. Numerous cases exist, for example, in which insurance companies' bad faith refusal to settle claims or perform duties to their insured and lenders' failure to exercise good faith in their dealings with their customers have led to large damage verdicts. Likewise, in states in which the implied duty of good faith has been held applicable to contracts of employment, employers who discharge employees in bad faith have been held liable for damages.[2]

Breach of Contract

When a person's performance is due, any failure to perform that is not excused is a breach of contract. Not all breaches of contract are of equal seriousness, however. Some are relatively minor deviations, whereas others are so extreme that they deprive the promisee of the essence of what he bargained for. The legal consequences of a given breach depend on the extent of the breach.

At a minimum, a party's breach of contract gives the nonbreaching party the right to sue and recover for any damages caused by that breach. When the breach is serious enough to be called a **material breach,** further legal consequences ensue.

---

[1]This trend is discussed in Chapter 9.

[2]This is discussed in Chapter 51.

Effect of Material Breach

A material breach occurs when the promisor's performance fails to reach the level of performance that the promisee is justified in expecting under the circumstances. In a situation in which the promisor's performance is judged by a substantial performance standard, saying that he failed to give substantial performance is the same thing as saying that he materially breached the contract.

The party who is injured by a material breach has the right to withhold his own performance. He is discharged from further obligations under the contract and may cancel it. He also has the right to sue for damages for total breach of contract.

Effect of Nonmaterial Breach

By contrast, when the breach is not serious enough to be material, the nonbreaching party may sue for only those damages caused by the particular breach. In addition, he does not have the right to cancel the contract, although a nonmaterial breach can give him the right to suspend his performance until the breach is remedied. Once the breach is remedied, however, the nonbreaching party must go ahead and render his performance, minus any damages caused by the breach.

Determining the Materiality of the Breach

The standard for determining materiality is a flexible one that takes into account the facts of each individual case. The key question is whether the breach deprives the injured party of the benefits that he reasonably expected. For example, Norman, who is running for mayor, orders campaign literature from Prompt Press, to be delivered in September. Prompt Press's failure to deliver the literature until after the election in November deprives Norman of the essence of what he bargained for and would be considered a material breach.

In determining materiality, courts take into account the extent to which the breaching party will suffer forfeiture if the breach is held to be material. They also consider the magnitude (amount) of the breach and the willfulness or good faith exercised by the breaching party. The timing of the breach can also be important. A breach that occurs early on in the parties' relationship is more likely to be viewed as material than is one that occurs after an extended period of performance. Courts also consider the extent to which the injured party can be adequately compensated by the payment of damages. The *Arnhold* case, which follows shortly, contains an analysis of whether a breach is material.

Time for Performance

A party's failure to perform on time is a breach of contract that may be serious enough to constitute a material breach, or it may be relatively trivial under the circumstances.

At the outset, it is necessary to determine when performance is due. Some contracts specifically state the time for performance, which makes it easy to determine the time for performance. In some contracts that do not specifically state the time for performance, such a time can be inferred from the circumstances surrounding the contract. In the Norman and Prompt Press campaign literature example, the circumstances surrounding the contract probably would have implied that the time for performance was some time before the election, even if the parties had not specified the time for performance. In still other contracts, no time for performance is either stated or implied. When no time for performance is stated or implied, performance must be completed within a "reasonable time," as judged by the circumstances of each case.

Consequences of Late Performance

After a court determines when performance was due, it must determine the consequences of late performance. In some contracts, the parties expressly state that "time is of the essence" or that timely performance is "vital." This means that each party's timely performance by a specific date is an express condition of the other party's duty to perform. Thus, in a contract that contains a time is of the essence provision, any delay by either party normally constitutes a material breach. Sometimes, courts will imply such a term even when the language of the contract does not state that time is of the essence. A court would be likely to do this if late performance is of little or no value to the promisee. For example, Schrader contracts with the local newspaper to run an advertisement for Christmas trees from December 15, 2000, to December 24, 2000, but the newspaper does not run the ad until December 26, 2000. In this case, the time for performance is an essential part of the contract and the newspaper has committed a material breach.

When a contract does not contain language indicating that time is of the essence and a court determines that the time for performance is not a particularly important part of the contract, the promisee must accept late performance rendered within a reasonable time after performance was due. The promisee is then entitled to deduct or set off from the contract price any losses caused by the delay. Late performance is not a material breach in such cases unless it is unreasonably late.

Arnhold v. Ocean Atlantic Woodland Corp.   284 F.3d 693 (7th Cir. 2002)

Edith Arnhold and John Argoudelis are lifelong farmers who own 280 acres of land near Plainfield, Illinois, a far south-western suburb of Chicago that is presently regarded as one of the fastest growing areas in the state. In exchange for $7.56 million payable over three years, Arnhold and Argoudelis agreed in August 1997 to sell their farm to Ocean Atlantic, a sophisticated development corporation that planned to transform the land into a residential subdivision with more than 700 homes. The parties scheduled the initial closing on November 15, 1997, and agreed to cooperate and ensure that all the conditions precedent to initial closing—such as the rezoning and annexation of the land by the Plainfield Village Board—would be met in a timely manner. Despite their best efforts, however, the parties realized that they were in no position to meet the November 15, 1997, deadline, for they had neither executed the necessary documents nor obtained the Board's approval of the annexation. At this juncture, Arnhold and Argoudelis granted Ocean Atlantic's request to extend the initial closing to January 15, 1999.

Throughout the spring and summer of 1998, Ocean Atlantic met with local planning officials to discuss their proposed development involving the sellers' land. However, by the fall, Ocean Atlantic still had not presented the Board with a petition for annexation of the property. Arnhold and Argoudelis accused Ocean Atlantic of dragging its feet. Ocean Atlantic repeatedly proposed to renegotiate the purchase price of the land as well. The parties negotiated and even litigated their respective rights. They then agreed to a second extension of the contract, which pushed back the initial date of closing to November 30, 1999. The sellers thereafter notified Ocean Atlantic on numerous occasions that they would consider the contract terminated if the closing failed to occur by that date.

As the November 30 deadline loomed, Ocean Atlantic sought to delay the initial closing for a third time. After more negotiation and litigation, Arnhold and Argoudelis and Ocean Atlantic signed the settlement agreement containing the time-essence clause that is the basis of this lawsuit. The new date was scheduled for January 25, 2001. Throughout the negotiations preceding the settlement agreement, the sellers insisted upon a rigid, absolute closing date. Ocean Atlantic had the right to schedule the closing on any of the 91 days between October 26, 2000, and January 25, 2001. Nevertheless, it exercised that right by informing the sellers that it had chosen to close January 24—a mere one day prior to the "drop-dead" date. On January 18, Ocean Atlantic sent the sellers a letter demanding that they move the closing to May 1 and pay an additional $680,000 in development fees. These fees had never been the subject of any prior negotiations nor were they embodied in any prior agreement between the parties. The sellers rejected Ocean Atlantic's demand and warned that "if the closing does not occur in accordance with the terms of the settlement agreement, your clients will have no rights whatsoever to the property after January 25, 2001, as clearly spelled out in that same agreement." At this point, Ocean Atlantic withdrew its proposals and thereafter assured the sellers that it would "fully participate in the scheduled closing [January 24], pursuant to the settlement agreement." However, when the sellers arrived for the closing on the morning of January 24, they executed each and every document and were ready to close that day, but the closing failed to occur on either January 24 (the date selected by Ocean Atlantic) or January 25 (the absolute, final drop-dead date in the Settlement Agreement) because Ocean Atlantic failed to tender the purchase price of $7.267 million for deposit into the sellers' escrow account. Arnhold and Argoudelis's attorneys notified Ocean Atlantic that the contract was terminated. After receiving this notice, Ocean Atlantic pleaded with Arnhold and Argoudelis to go forward with the sale, but they refused. Ocean Atlantic sued Arnhold and Argoudelis, seeking specific performance of the contract. Arnhold and Argoudelis asked the district court to rule that the contract was null and void. The district court decided in favor of Arnhold and Argoudelis, and Ocean Atlantic appealed.

Coffey, Circuit Judge

"What a diff'rence a day makes . . . twenty-four little hours."

The only issue before us is whether Ocean Atlantic materially breached the Settlement Agreement by failing to tender $7.267 million and close on the property by January 25, 2001.

A. The Two-Step Materiality Inquiry

Parties to a contract may make "time is of the essence" a provision of the contract, meaning that performance by one party at the time or within the time frame specified in the contract is essential to enable him to require counterperformance by the other party. Timely performance often is an absolute requirement even if the contract does not contain the talismanic phrase "time is of the essence"; it is well-settled that the intention of the parties as expressed by the agreement controls, and courts will give effect to this provision when no peculiar circumstances have intervened to prevent or excuse strict compliance. A party that fails to perform its contractual duties is liable for breach of contract, and a material breach of the terms of the contract will serve to excuse the other party from its duty of counterperformance.

The materiality inquiry focuses on two interrelated issues: (1) the intent of the parties with respect to the disputed provision; and (2) the equitable factors and circumstances surrounding the breach of the provision. When analyzing the materiality of a time-essence clause, the factfinder initially must ask whether performance by a particular date was truly of such significance that the contract would not have been made if the provision had not been included. A negative answer to this initial question means that the clause did not meet the materiality test and that the breach was minor, provided that the party has completed performance within a reasonable period of time. On the other hand, an affirmative answer to the first question does not end the materiality inquiry. Even where the parties clearly intended to regard a specific payment date as crucial, equity will refuse to enforce such a provision when to do so would be unconscionable or would give one party an unfair advantage over the other. As a result, even if the factfinder concludes that timely performance is an essential element of the contract, he or she must also decide whether to award damages and require counterperformance in spite of the breach.

The factfinder must take into account the totality of the circumstances and focus on the inherent justice of the matter. The focus should be on factors such as: whether the breach defeated the bargained-for objective of the parties, whether the nonbreaching party suffered disproportionate prejudice, and whether undue economic inefficiency and waste, or an unreasonable or unfair advantage, would inure to the nonbreaching party. We review the district court's analysis of these factors below.

1. Step one: Intent of the parties

Paragraph 15 of the settlement agreement states:

It is intended by Sellers and Purchasers that January 25, 2001 shall be the absolute final date for closing. . . . If closing has not occurred on or before January 25, 2001, for any reason other than Sellers' default. . . . Purchaser shall have no right to purchase or otherwise encumber the Property or Homestead parcel, the Contract shall be terminated, and Purchaser shall have no rights with respect to the Property or Homestead Parcel.

The magistrate judge found that this clause was "an essential (if not 'the' essential) term of the Settlement Agreement," and we agree. In the case before us, the district court considered the language of the settlement agreement, along with the substance of the parties' negotiations and their course of performance. All three categories of evidence support a finding of materiality. The explicit and unequivocal language of the contract is an unambiguous expression of intent, referring to January 25, 2001 as an "absolute, final date for closing" that "shall" be enforced without exception. The record reflects that the initial contract contemplated closing in November 1997, and nearly three years had passed without reaching that objective. Thus, by the time the most recent settlement agreement was drafted, the sellers testified that their heart was no longer in selling their property to Ocean Atlantic, and Ocean Atlantic's president similarly testified that he was "sick and tired" of dealing with the sellers.

We are convinced that the settlement agreement reflects a compromise. The sellers agreed to continue their relationship through January 25, 2001 and give Ocean Atlantic one last, final chance to comply with the language of the contract and purchase the farmland. In exchange, Ocean Atlantic agreed that absolutely no further delays would be tolerated. We agree that the clause was a material term of the contract.

2. Step two: Totality of the circumstances

Even when the parties agree to make timely performance an essential element of the contract, the factfinder must also consider whether the breach was material as to justify the other party's subsequent refusal to perform, based upon the totality of the circumstances.

b. The relevant factors

i. Bargained-for objective

When Ocean Atlantic failed to pay the sellers any money and failed to take title to the property by January 25, 2001, it deprived the sellers of the finality for which they had bargained. This breach went to the very heart and substance of the contract. It was material; indeed, it is difficult to imagine anything more material, given nearly three years of delays, three contract extensions, and two federal lawsuits involving the sale of this very property. The sellers displayed the patience of Job by waiting nearly 3½ years to accomplish the sale of farmland that was originally intended to be transferred within six months.

ii. Proportionality of prejudice

The proportionality-of-prejudice element of the materiality test requires the factfinder to compare the relative burdens that each side would suffer if the contract were terminated. In the case before us, the district court found that Ocean Atlantic spent $1.7 million in fees and expenses related to the annexation, rezoning, planning, preliminary engineering, and marketing of the property between 1997 and 2001. However, a reasonable factfinder, believing that promises conditioned upon timely performance should be kept when made, could have determined that the loss was not enough to warrant granting Ocean Atlantic's motion for specific performance.

iii. Unreasonable, unfair advantage

Two important factors to consider at this juncture are: (1) whether the breaching party used reasonable efforts to perform its contractual obligations; and (2) whether the parties contemplated that the breaching party would forfeit its contractual rights if it committed the type of breach that is at issue. Neither of these factors favors Ocean Atlantic. Although Ocean Atlantic blames its investment partner and its lender of choice for its failure to comply with the drop-dead clause, it appears to us that the problem more likely was caused by Ocean Atlantic waiting until the eleventh hour to execute and revise all the requisite documents. When parties wait until the last minute to comply with a deadline, they are playing with fire.

Conclusion

"Never put off until tomorrow what you can do today."

Although contract law allows parties to choose the reasonable extent of their duties and obligations towards one another, neither law nor equity guarantees that a party may specifically enforce a contract if it fails to perform its material obligations thereunder. A reasonable factfinder concluded that Ocean Atlantic treated the material, bargained-for deadlines in this agreement as if they were trivial details that could be flouted with impunity. As a result, Ocean Atlantic has lost any and all rights to purchase the sellers' farmland.

Affirmed in favor of Arnhold and Argoudelis.

CONCEPT REVIEW

Time for Performance

Contract Language	Time for Performance	Consequences of Late Performance
"Time is of the essence" or similar language	The time stated in the contract	Material breach
Specific time is stated in or implied by the contract and later performance would have little or no value	The time stated in or implied by the contract	Material breach
Specific time is stated in or implied by the contract, but the time for performance is a relatively unimportant part of the contract	The time stated in or implied by the contract	Not a material breach unless performance is unreasonably late
No time for performance is stated in or implied by the contract	Within a reasonable time	Not material breach unless performance is unreasonably late

---

Anticipatory Repudiation One type of breach of contract occurs when the promisor indicates before the time for his performance that he is unwilling or unable to carry out the contract. This is called **anticipatory repudiation** or **anticipatory breach.** Anticipatory breach generally constitutes a material breach of contract that discharges the promisee from all further obligation under the contract.

In determining what constitutes anticipatory repudiation, courts look for some unequivocal statement or voluntary act that clearly indicates that the promisor cannot or will not perform his duties under the contract. This may take the form of an express statement by the promisor. The promisor's intent not to perform could also be implied from actions of the promisor such as selling to a third party the property that the promisor was obligated to sell to the promisee. For example, if Ross, who is obligated to convey real estate to Davis, conveys the property to some third person instead, Ross has repudiated the contract.

When anticipatory repudiation occurs, the promisee is faced with several choices. For example, Marsh and Davis enter a contract in which Davis agrees to deliver a quantity of bricks to Marsh on September 1, 2007, and

Marsh agrees to pay Davis a sum of money in two installments. The agreement specifies that Marsh will pay 50 percent of the purchase price on July 15, 2007, and 50 percent of the purchase price within 30 days after delivery. On July 1, 2007, Davis writes Marsh and unequivocally states that he will not deliver the bricks. Must Marsh go ahead and send the payment that is due on July 15? Must he wait until September 1 to bring suit for total breach of contract? The answer to both questions is no.

When anticipatory repudiation occurs, the nonbreaching party is justified in withholding his own performance and suing for damages right away, without waiting for the time for performance to arrive.[3] If he can show that he was ready, willing, and able to perform his part of the contract, he can recover damages for total breach of the contract. The nonbreaching party is not obligated to do this, however. If he chooses, he may wait until the time for performance in case the other party changes his mind and decides to perform.

Recovery by a Party Who Has Committed Material Breach

A party who has materially breached the contract (that is, has not substantially performed) does not have the right to recover the contract price. If a promisor who has given some performance to the promisee cannot recover under the contract, however, the promisor will face forfeiture and the promisee will have obtained an unearned gain. There are two possible avenues for a party who has committed material breach to obtain some compensation for the performance he has conferred on the nonbreaching party.

1. *Quasi-contract.* A party who has materially breached a contract might recover the reasonable value of any benefits he has conferred on the promisee by bringing an action under quasi-contract.[4] This would enable him to obtain compensation for the value of any performance he has given that has benefited the nonbreaching party. Some courts take the position that a person in material breach should not be able to recover for benefits he has conferred, however.

2. *Partial performance of a divisible contract.* Some contracts are divisible; that is, each party's performance can be divided in two or more parts and each part is exchanged for some corresponding consideration from the other party. For example, if Johnson agrees to mow Peterson's lawn for $20 and clean Peterson's gutters for $50, the contract is divisible. When a promisor performs one part of the contract but materially breaches another part, he can recover at the contract price for the part that he did perform. For example, if Johnson breached his duty to clean the gutters but fully performed his obligation to mow the lawn, he could recover at the contract price for the lawn-mowing part of the contract.

Excuses for Nonperformance

Although nonperformance of a duty that has become due will ordinarily constitute a breach of contract, there are some situations in which nonperformance is excused because of factors that arise after the formation of the contract. When this occurs, the person whose performance is made impossible or impracticable by these

---

[3]Uniform Commercial Code rules regarding anticipatory repudiation in contracts for the sale of goods are discussed in Chapter 21.

[4]Quasi-contract is discussed in Chapter 9. It involves the use of the remedy of restitution, which is discussed later in this chapter.

Ethics in Action

Marsh, a contractor, enters into a contract with Needmore Tree Farm to build a structure on Needmore's property that Needmore plans to use as a sales office for selling Christmas trees to the public. The contract provides that Needmore will pay Marsh $110,000 for the structure, with 50 percent of the payment in advance and 50 percent upon completion. It also provides that Marsh will complete the construction and have the structure ready for occupation by December 1. With regard to this last provision, the contract states, "time is of the essence." The December 1 date is significant to Needmore because it wanted to be sure to have the sales office ready for Christmas season. On December 1, the construction has progressed substantially, but the structure is not going to be ready for occupation for several more weeks. Needmore fires Marsh and refuses to pay him the remaining 50 percent due under the contract. Assuming that Marsh has materially breached the contract, does Needmore have an ethical duty to pay Marsh for the benefit that Marsh has conferred on it?

factors is discharged from further obligation under the contract. The following discussion concerns the most common grounds for excuse of nonperformance.

Impossibility

Impossibility When performance of a contractual duty becomes impossible after the formation of the contract, the duty will be discharged on grounds of **impossibility.** This does not mean that a person can be discharged merely because he has contracted to do something that he is simply unable to do or that causes him hardship or difficulty. Impossibility in the legal sense of the word means "it cannot be done by anyone" rather than "I cannot do it." Thus, promisors who find that they have agreed to perform duties that are beyond their capabilities or that turn out to be unprofitable or burdensome are generally not excused from performance of their duties. This principle is illustrated in the following *East Capitol* case. Impossibility will provide an excuse for nonperformance, however, when some unexpected event arises after the formation of the contract and renders performance objectively impossible. The event that causes the impossibility need not have been entirely unforeseeable. Normally, however, the event will be one that the parties would not have reasonably thought of as a real possibility that would affect performance.

There are a variety of situations in which a person's duty to perform may be discharged on grounds of impossibility. The three most common situations involve illness or death of the promisor, supervening illegality, and destruction of the subject matter of the contract.

East Capitol View Community Development Corporation v. Robinson
941 A.2d 1036 (D.C. Ct. App. 2008)

East Capitol hired Denean Robinson in a written employment contract for a one-year term. Before the end of that term, however, East Capitol informed her that her employment would be terminated early for lack of funding. Although the employment contract stated that Robinson's "continued employment with [East Capitol] will be contingent on successfully achieving all performance goals and outcomes," there was no language stating that a lack of funding could excuse East Capitol from prematurely terminating Robinson's contract. Robinson filed suit against East Capitol for breach of contract. The trial judge declined to give the jury an instruction about the impossibility of performance defense. The jury returned a verdict in favor of Robinson, and East Capitol appealed.

Washington, Chief Judge

East Capitol contends that the trial court erred in failing to instruct the jury on the impossibility of performance defense. In essence, East Capitol argues that it was entitled to an impossibility of performance instruction "because the central issue in the case was whether East Capitol had an excuse for terminating the contract with Robinson because its [g]rant funding had been cancelled and it was no longer able to pay her salary." A jury instruction is not warranted without some evidence to support it. In order to receive an impossibility of performance instruction, East Capitol must demonstrate that there was evidence that could at least support such a defense.

A party's obligation to perform under a contract may be excused if performance is rendered impossible. To establish impossibility or commercial impracticability, a party must show (1) the unexpected occurrence of an intervening act; (2) the risk of the unexpected occurrence was not allocated by agreement or custom; and (3) the occurrence made performance impractical. The doctrine of impossibility relieves nonperformance only in extreme circumstances. Moreover, courts will generally only excuse nonperformance where performance is objectively impossible—that is, the contract is incapable of performance by anyone—rather than instances where the party subjectively claims the inability to perform. The *Restatement* recognizes the objective/subjective distinction, concluding that while a party's duty to perform is discharged if it is made objectively impracticable, "if the performance remains practicable and it is merely beyond the party's capacity to render it, he is ordinarily not discharged." *Restatement (Second) of Contracts* § 261 cmt. e (1981).

Under this analysis, a party's alleged financial inability to perform a contract that it voluntarily entered would rarely, if ever, excuse nonperformance; though a party may prove that it can no longer afford performance, it will be hard-pressed to prove that nonperformance exist[s] in the nature of the thing to be done. Although this court has not directly ruled on whether financial inability to meet a contractual obligation excuses nonperformance, most, if not all, other jurisdictions that have addressed this issue agree that it does not. Indeed, even insolvency is unlikely to excuse performance. Nor does the promisor's reliance on some third party for the ability to perform convert financial inability to perform into an objective impossibility.

"[T]he rationale is that a party generally assumes the risk of his own inability to perform his duty. Even if a party contracts to render a performance that depends on some act by a third party, he is not ordinarily discharged because of a failure by that party because this is also a risk that is commonly understood to be on the obligor." *Restatement (Second) of Contracts* § 261 cmt. e. For example, in *International Bhd. of Firemen & Oilers v. Board of Education,* the Pennsylvania Supreme Court rejected a school district's claimed inability to comply with a new bargaining agreement to pay increased salaries and benefits to its employees because the Philadelphia City Council failed to provide it with sufficient funding. Thus, the anticipation of funding from one source does not alter the party's duty to perform.

Of course, parties may contractually reallocate risk to the other party. However, in this case, there is no evidence that East Capitol assigned the risk of its financial instability to [Robinson]. Though East Capitol maintained that the revocation of funding deprived the corporation of sufficient assets to continue paying its employees, it failed to include such a possibility as a condition precedent in the employment agreement. Indeed, while East Capitol specifically included language warning Robinson that her continued employment was contingent upon successful performance, it failed to address funding in any way. The agreement does not mention the source of the salary, let alone warn Robinson that her continued employment was contingent upon continued grant funding. Robinson's employment contract was objectively capable of performance, and East Capitol did nothing to reallocate the risk of its own inability to pay. As East Capitol was not entitled to a defense of impossibility, the trial court's decision to withhold the impossibility defense jury instruction was not error.

Affirmed in favor of Robinson.

Illness or Death of Promisor Incapacitating illness or death of the promisor excuses nonperformance when the promisor has contracted to perform personal services. For example, if Pauling, a college professor who has a contract with State University to teach for an academic year, dies before the completion of the contract, her estate will not be liable for breach of contract. The promisor's death or illness does not, however, excuse the nonperformance of duties that can be delegated to another, such as the duty to deliver goods, pay money, or convey real estate. For example, if Odell had contracted to convey real estate to Ruskin and died before the closing date, Ruskin could enforce the contract against Odell's estate.

Supervening Illegality If a statute or governmental regulation enacted after the creation of a contract makes performance of a party's duties illegal, the promisor is excused from performing. Statutes or regulations that merely make performance more difficult or less profitable do not, however, excuse nonperformance.

Destruction of the Subject Matter of the Contract If something that is essential to the promisor's performance is destroyed after the formation of the contract through no fault of the promisor, the promisor is excused from performing. For example, Woolridge contracts to sell his car to Rivkin. If an explosion destroys the car after the contract has been formed but before Woolridge has made delivery, Woolridge's nonperformance will be excused.

The destruction of nonessential items that the promisor intended to use in performing does not excuse nonperformance if substitutes are available, even though securing them makes performance more difficult or less profitable. Suppose that Ace Construction Company had planned to use a particular piece of machinery in fulfilling a contract to build a building for Worldwide Widgets Company. If the piece of machinery is destroyed but substitutes are available, destruction of the machinery before the contract is performed would *not* give Ace an excuse for failing to perform.

Commercial Impracticability Section 2–615 of the Uniform Commercial Code has extended the scope of the common law doctrine of impossibility to cases in which unforeseen developments make performance by the promisor highly impracticable, unreasonably expensive, or of little value to the promisee. Rather than using a standard of impossibility, then, the Code uses the more relaxed standard of **impracticability.** Despite the less stringent standard applied, cases actually excusing nonperformance on grounds of impracticability are relatively rare. To be successful in claiming excuse based on impracticability, a promisor must be able to establish that the event that makes performance impracticable occurred without his fault and that the contract was made with the basic assumption that this event would not occur. This basically means that the event was beyond the scope of the risks that the parties contemplated at the time of contracting and that the promisor did not

expressly or impliedly assume the risk that the event would occur.

Case law and official comments to UCC section 2–615 indicate that neither increased cost nor collapse of a market for particular goods is sufficient to excuse nonperformance, because those are the types of business risks that every promisor assumes. However, drastic price increases or severe shortages of goods resulting from unforeseen circumstances such as wars and crop failures can give rise to impracticability.

If the event causing impracticability affects only a part of the seller's capacity to perform, the seller must allocate production and deliveries among customers in a "fair and reasonable" manner and must notify them of any delay or any limited allocation of the goods. You can read more about commercial impracticability in Chapter 21, Performance of Sales Contracts.

Other Grounds for Discharge

Earlier in this chapter, you learned about several situations in which a party's duty to perform could be discharged even though that party had not himself performed. These include the nonoccurrence of a condition precedent or concurrent condition, the occurrence of a condition subsequent, material breach by the other party, and excuse from performance by impossibility, impracticability, or frustration. The following discussion deals with additional ways in which a discharge can occur.

Discharge by Mutual Agreement
Just as contracts are created by mutual agreement, they can also be discharged by *mutual agreement.* An agreement to discharge a contract must be supported by consideration to be enforceable.

Discharge by Accord and Satisfaction
An **accord** is an agreement whereby a promisee who has an existing claim agrees with the promisor that he will accept some performance different from that which was originally agreed on. When the promisor performs the accord, that is called a **satisfaction.**[5] When an accord and satisfaction occurs, the parties are discharged. For example, Root contracts with May to build a garage on May's property for $30,000. After Root has performed his part of the bargain, the parties then agree that instead of paying money, May will transfer a one-year-old Porsche to Root instead. When this is done, both parties are discharged.

[5]Accord and satisfaction is also discussed in Chapter 12.

Discharge by Waiver
A party to a contract may voluntarily relinquish any right he has under a contract, including the right to receive return performance. Such a relinquishment of rights is known as a **waiver.** If one party tenders an incomplete or defective performance and the other party accepts that performance without objection, knowing that the defects will not be remedied, the party to whom performance was due will have discharged the other party from his duty of performance. For example, a real estate lease requires Long, the tenant, to pay a $5 late charge for late payments of rent. Long pays his rent late each month for five months, but the landlord accepts it without objection and without assessing the late charge. In this situation, the landlord has probably waived his right to collect the late charge.

To avoid waiving rights, a person who has received defective performance should give the other party prompt notice that she expects complete performance and will seek damages if the defects are not corrected.

Discharge by Alteration
If the contract is represented by a *written* instrument, and one of the parties intentionally makes a material alteration in the instrument without the other's consent, the alteration acts as a discharge of the other party. If the other party consents to the alteration or does not object to it when he learns of it, he is not discharged. Alteration by a third party without the knowledge or consent of the contracting parties does not affect the parties' rights.

Discharge by Statute of Limitations
Courts have long refused to grant a remedy to a person who delays bringing a lawsuit for an unreasonable time. All of the states have enacted statutes known as **statutes of limitation,** which specify the period of time in which a person can bring a lawsuit.

The time period for bringing a contract action varies from state to state, and many states prescribe time periods for cases concerning oral contracts that are different from those for cases concerning written contracts. Section 2–725 of the Uniform Commercial Code provides for a four-year statute of limitations for contracts involving the sale of goods.

The statutory period ordinarily begins to run from the date of the breach. It may be delayed if the party who has the right to sue is under some incapacity at that time (such as minority or insanity) or is beyond the jurisdiction of the state. A person who has breached a contractual duty is discharged from liability for breach if no lawsuit is brought before the statutory period elapses.

Discharge by Decree of Bankruptcy

The contractual obligations of a debtor are generally discharged by a decree of bankruptcy. Bankruptcy is discussed in Chapter 30.

Remedies for Breach of Contract

Our discussion of the performance stage of contracts so far has focused on the circumstances under which a party has the duty to perform or is excused from performing. In situations in which a person is injured by a breach of contract and is unable to obtain compensation by a settlement out of court, a further important issue remains: What remedy will a court fashion to compensate for breach of contract?

Contract law seeks to encourage people to rely on the promises made to them by others. Contract remedies focus on the economic loss caused by breach of contract, not on the moral obligation to perform a promise. The objective of granting a remedy in a case of breach of contract is simply to compensate the injured party.

Types of Contract Remedies

There are a variety of ways in which this can be done. The basic categories of contract remedies include:

1. Legal remedies (money damages).
2. Equitable remedies.
3. Restitution.

The usual remedy is an award of money damages that will compensate the injured party for his losses. This is called a **legal remedy** or **remedy at law**, because the imposition of money damages in our legal system originated in courts of law. Less frequently used but still important are **equitable remedies** such as specific performance. Equitable remedies are those remedies that had their origins in courts of equity rather than in courts of law.[6] Today, they are available at the discretion of the judge. A final possible remedy is **restitution**, which requires the defendant to pay the value of the benefits that the plaintiff has conferred on him.

Interests Protected by Contract Remedies

Remedies for breach of contract protect one or more of the following interests that a promisee may have:[7]

1. *Expectation interest.* A promisee's **expectation interest** is his interest in obtaining the objective or opportunity for gain that he bargained for and "expected." Courts attempt to protect this interest by formulating a remedy that will place the promisee in the position he would have been in if the contract had been performed as promised.

2. *Reliance interest.* A promisee's **reliance interest** is his interest in being compensated for losses that he has suffered by changing his position in reliance on the other party's promise. In some cases, such as when a promisee is unable to prove his expectation interest with reasonable certainty, the promisee may seek a remedy to compensate for the loss suffered as a result of relying on the promisor's promise rather than for the expectation of profit.

3. *Restitution interest.* A **restitution interest** is a party's interest in recovering the amount by which he has enriched or benefited the other. Both the reliance and restitution interests involve promisees who have changed their position. The difference between the two is that the reliance interest involves a loss to the promisee that does not benefit the promisor, whereas the restitution interest involves a loss to the promisee that does constitute an unjust enrichment to the promisor. A remedy based on restitution enables a party who has performed or partially performed her contract and has benefited the other party to obtain compensation for the value of the benefits that she has conferred.

Legal Remedies (Damages)

Limitations on Recovery of Damages in Contract Cases An injured party's ability to recover damages in a contract action is limited by three principles:

1. *A party can recover damages only for those losses that he can prove with reasonable certainty.* Losses that are purely speculative are not recoverable. Thus, if Jones

---

[6]The nature of equitable remedies is also discussed in Chapter 1.

[7]*Restatement (Second) of Contracts* § 344.

Publishing Company breaches a contract to publish Powell's memoirs, Powell may not be able to recover damages for lost royalties (her expectation interest), since she may be unable to establish, beyond speculation, how much money she would have earned in royalties if the book had been published. (Note, however, that Powell's reliance interest might be protected here; she could be allowed to recover provable losses incurred in reliance on the contract.)

2. *A breaching party is responsible for paying only those losses that were foreseeable to him at the time of contracting.* A loss is foreseeable if it would ordinarily be expected to result from a breach or if the breaching party had reason to know of particular circumstances that would make the loss likely. For example, if Prince Manufacturing Company renders late performance in a contract to deliver parts to Cheatum Motors without knowing that Cheatum is shut down waiting for the parts, Prince will not have to pay the business losses that result from Cheatum's having to close its operation.

3. *Plaintiffs injured by a breach of contract have the duty to mitigate (avoid or minimize) damages.* A party cannot recover for losses that he could have avoided without undue risk, burden, or humiliation. For example, an employee who has been wrongfully fired would be entitled to damages equal to his wages for the remainder of the employment period. The employee, however, has the duty to minimize the damages by making reasonable efforts to seek a similar job elsewhere.

Compensatory Damages Subject to the limitations discussed above, a person who has been injured by a breach of contract is entitled to recover **compensatory damages.** In calculating the compensatory remedy, a court will attempt to protect the expectation interest of the injured party by giving him the "benefit of his bargain" (placing him in the position he would have been in *had the contract been performed as promised*). To do this, the court must compensate the injured person for the provable losses he has suffered as well as for the provable gains that he has been prevented from realizing by the breach of contract. Normally, compensatory damages include one or more of three possible items: loss in value, any allowable consequential damages, and any allowable incidental damages.

1. *Loss in value.* The starting point in calculating compensatory damages is to determine the **loss in value** of the performance that the plaintiff had the right to expect. This is a way of measuring the expectation interest. The

calculation of the loss in value experienced by an injured party differs according to the sort of contract involved and the circumstances of the breach. In contracts involving nonperformance of the sale of real estate, for example, courts normally measure loss in value by the difference between the contract price and the market price of the property. Thus, if Willis repudiates a contract with Renfrew whereby Renfrew was to purchase land worth $20,000 from Willis for $10,000, Renfrew's loss in value was $10,000. Where a seller has failed to perform a contract for the sale of goods, courts may measure loss in value by the difference between the contract price and the price that the buyer had to pay to procure substitute goods.[8] In cases in which a party breaches by rendering defective performance—say, by breaching a warranty in the sale of goods—the loss in value would be measured by the difference between the value of the goods if they had been in the condition warranted by the seller and the value of the goods in their defective condition.[9] You will see an example of this concept in the *Furst* case later in this chapter.

2. *Consequential damages.* **Consequential damages** (also called **special damages**) compensate for losses that occur as a consequence of the breach of contract. Consequential losses occur because of some special or unusual circumstances of the particular contractual relationship of the parties. For example, Apex Trucking Company buys a computer system from ABC Computers. The system fails to operate properly, and Apex is forced to pay its employees to perform the tasks manually, spending $10,000 in overtime pay. In this situation, Apex might seek to recover the $10,000 in overtime pay in addition to the loss of value that it has experienced.

Lost profits flowing from a breach of contract can be recovered as consequential damages if they are foreseeable and can be proven with reasonable certainty. It is important to remember, however, that the recovery of consequential damages is subject to the limitations on damage recovery discussed earlier.

3. *Incidental damages.* **Incidental damages** compensate for reasonable costs that the injured party incurs after the breach in an effort to avoid further loss. For example, if Smith Construction Company breaches an employment contract with Brice, Brice could recover as incidental damages those reasonable expenses he must

---

[8]Remedies under Article 2 of the Uniform Commercial Code are discussed in detail in Chapter 22.

[9]See Chapter 20 for further discussion of the damages for breach of warranty in the sale of goods.

incur in attempting to procure substitute employment, such as long-distance telephone tolls or the cost of printing new résumés.

Alternative Measures of Damages

The foregoing discussion has focused on the most common formulation of damage remedies in contracts cases. The normal measure of compensatory damages is not appropriate in every case, however. When it is not appropriate, a court may use an alternative measure of damages. For example, where a party has suffered losses by performing or preparing to perform, he might seek damages based on his *reliance interest* instead of his expectation interest. In such a case, he would be compensated for the provable losses he suffered by relying on the other party's promise. This measure of damages is often used in cases in which a promise is enforceable under promissory estoppel.[10]

Nominal Damages

Nominal damages are very small damage awards that are given when a technical breach of contract has occurred without causing any actual or provable economic loss. The sums awarded as nominal damages typically vary from 2 cents to a dollar.

Liquidated Damages

The parties to a contract may expressly provide in their contract that a specific sum shall be recoverable if the contract is breached. Such provisions are called **liquidated damages** provisions. For example, Murchison rents space in a shopping mall in which she plans to operate a retail clothing store. She must make improvements in the space before opening the store, and it is very important to her to have the store opened for the Christmas shopping season. She hires Ace Construction Company to construct the improvements. The parties agree to include in the contract a liquidated damages provision stating that, if Ace is late in completing the construction, Murchison will be able to recover a specified sum for each day of delay. Such a provision is highly desirable from Murchison's point of view because, without a liquidated damages provision, she would have a difficult time in establishing the precise losses that would result from delay. Courts scrutinize these agreed-on damages carefully, however.

If the amount specified in a liquidated damages provision is reasonable and if the nature of the contract is such that actual damages would be difficult to determine, a court will enforce the provision. When liquidated damages provisions are enforced, the amount of damages agreed on will be the injured party's exclusive damage remedy. If the amount specified is unreasonably great in relation to the probable loss or injury, however, or if the amount of damages could be readily determined in the event of breach, the courts will then declare the provision to be a penalty and will refuse to enforce it.

---

[10]Promissory estoppel is discussed in Chapters 9 and 12.

| **Furst v. Einstein Moomjy, Inc.** | **860 A.2d 435 (N.J. Sup. Ct. 2004)** |

Einstein Moomjy, Inc. is a large retail distributor of carpets with stores located in Paramus, North Plainfield, Whippany, and Manhattan. In August 1999, at an annual clearance sale held by Einstein Moomjy, Henry Furst purchased five remnant carpets for his home for $10,139.68. One of these carpets was the "Mystery Ivory" carpet. Attached to the Mystery Ivory carpet at the time of its sale was a tag containing the following information:

The Back Yd.
Einstein Moomjy, The Carpet Department Store
REMNANT
REDUCED FOR CLEARANCE
SIZE: n1 11'4" in × 31'
REGULAR PRICE $5,775-
SALE PRICE
$1,499-
QUALITY: Mystery
COLOR: Ivory
Fibre: Wool
Sale
1,199

When the Mystery Ivory carpet was delivered to his home, Furst noticed that the carpet was damaged and smaller than the size indicated on the sales invoice. He complained about the condition and size of the carpet to Einstein Moomjy, who offered either a refund of the sale price of $1,199 or a similar carpet at an additional price. Einstein Moomjy claimed that the Mystery Ivory carpet was a high quality "Ireloom" white wool carpet that had been tagged mistakenly with the wrong sale price. Furst demanded that Einstein Moomjy comply with the warranty on the back of the sales invoice. The invoice promised that if the carpets purchased were not delivered by the scheduled delivery date, Furst had the choice of canceling the "order with a prompt full refund" or "accepting delivery at a specific later date." Furst insisted on delivery of an undamaged Ireloom carpet at the size he ordered and at the price he paid.

When Einstein Moomjy refused to replace the Ireloom carpet at that price, Furst filed a multicount lawsuit against Einstein Moomjy. The trial court entered summary judgment on liability in favor of Furst, finding that Einstein Moomjy had violated the Consumer Protection Act. Einstein Moomjy does not contest that ruling. The court also determined that Furst's "ascertainable loss" was the fair market or replacement value of the carpet, but it would not permit him to introduce evidence of the price tag to prove replacement value. The trial court determined that replacement value had to be proved through expert testimony and excluded the use of the unmarked-down regular price on the sales tag as evidence of the market value of the Ireloom carpet. The court also barred testimony from Furst's interior decorator regarding her investigation of market prices and testimony from defendant Moomjy regarding the market value of the Ireloom carpet. Because Furst could not prove replacement value, the court awarded him the purchase price. Under the Consumer Protection Act, an injured consumer's ascertainable losses are trebled, so the trial court awarded Furst the trebled purchase price of $1,199 and attorney fees, a remedy permitted by the act. Both parties appealed. The Appellate Division agreed that replacement value was the proper measure of ascertainable loss and the sales tag was sufficient evidence to create a triable issue of fact. Einstein Moomjy appealed.

Albin, Judge

Our analysis is informed by basic principles of contract law. In an ordinary breach-of-contract case, the function of damages is simply to make the injured party whole. Under the Uniform Commercial Code, the remedy for a buyer who has accepted defective goods is the difference between the "value of the goods accepted and the value they would have had if they had been as warranted." Similarly, in a breach-of-contract case, the innocent party must be given the "benefit of his bargain" and placed in "as good a position as he would have been in had the contract been performed." Indeed, under the *Restatement,* the innocent party has a right to damages "based on his expectation interest as measured by . . . the loss in the value to him" caused by the breaching party's nonperformance. *Restatement (Second) of Contracts* at § 347. If we apply those fundamental principles of contract law, we are led inexorably to the conclusion that replacement cost is the proper measure of damages sustained by the consumer in this case. In light of the Legislature's clear intent, it would be incongruous to provide consumers with a form of damages less than what is available in an ordinary breach-of-contract case. The "expectation interest" of the consumer who purchases merchandise at a discount is the benefit of the bargain. We conclude that a consumer who suffers an ascertainable loss is entitled to the benefit of the bargain in this case, the replacement value of the carpet trebled under the Act.

We next address whether Furst proffered sufficient evidence of the replacement value of the carpet to warrant a damages trial. The sales tag advertised a carpet "reduced for clearance" and contained the following information: the quality, color, and fiber of the carpet; its size; and its regular price ($5,775), its pre-marked-down price ($1,499), and its final marked-down price ($1,199). The description of the damaged carpet as Mystery Ivory Wool is relevant for the purpose of identifying the item for replacement value. The final marked-down price, the price paid for the carpet, is relevant as one possible measure of damages. We also find that the regular price on the sales sticker is evidence that tends to establish replacement value. In deciding that the regular price on the Ireloom carpet sales sticker is evidence of replacement value, we look to the reality of the marketplace and the role that advertising plays in inducing consumers to purchase products. The strong remedial policy undergirding the Consumer Fraud Act leads us to conclude that the regular price advertised on the sales sticker is a relevant benchmark from which to impute replacement value. Accordingly, there will be a rebuttable presumption that the regular price on the sales sticker is the replacement value of the carpet.

Reversed and remanded in favor of Furst.

Punitive Damages **Punitive damages** are damages awarded in addition to the compensatory remedy that are designed to punish a defendant for particularly reprehensible behavior and to deter the defendant and others from committing similar behavior in the future. The traditional rule is that punitive damages are not recoverable in contracts cases unless a specific statutory provision (such as some consumer protection statutes) allows them or the defendant has committed *fraud* or some other independent tort. A few states will permit the use of punitive damages in contracts cases in which the defendant's conduct, though not technically a tort, was malicious, oppressive, or tortious in nature.

Punitive damages have also been awarded in many of the cases involving breach of the implied covenant of good faith. In such cases, courts usually circumvent the traditional rule against awarding punitive damages in contracts cases by holding that breach of the duty of good faith is an independent tort. The availability of punitive damages in such cases operates to deter a contracting party from deliberately disregarding the other party's rights. Insurance companies have been the most frequent target for punitive damages awards in bad faith cases, but employers and banks have also been subjected to punitive damages verdicts.

Equitable Remedies
In exceptional cases in which money damages alone are not adequate to fully compensate for a party's injuries, a court may grant an **equitable remedy** either alone or in combination with a legal remedy. Equitable relief is subject to several limitations, however, and will be granted only when justice is served by doing so. The primary equitable remedies for breach of contract are specific performance and injunction.[11]

Specific Performance **Specific performance** is an equitable remedy whereby the court orders the breaching party to perform his contractual duties as promised. For example, if Barnes breached a contract to sell a tract of land to Metzger and a court granted specific performance of the contract, the court would require Barnes to deed the land to Metzger. (Metzger, of course, must pay the purchase price.) This remedy can be advantageous to the injured party because he is not faced with the complexities of proving damages, he does not have to worry

about whether he can actually collect the damages, and he gets exactly what he bargained for. However, the availability of this remedy is subject to the limitations discussed below.

The Availability of Specific Performance Specific performance, like other equitable remedies, is available only when the injured party has no adequate remedy at law—in other words, when money damages do not adequately compensate the injured party. This generally requires a showing that the subject of the contract is unique or at least that no substitutes are available. Even if this requirement is met, a court will withhold specific performance if the injured party has acted in bad faith, if he unreasonably delayed in asserting his rights, or if specific performance would require an excessive amount of supervision by the court.

Contracts for the sale of real estate are the most common subjects of specific performance decrees because every tract of real estate is considered to be unique. Specific performance is rarely granted for breach of a contract for the sale of goods because the injured party can usually procure substitute goods. However, there are situations involving sales of goods contracts in which specific performance is given. These cases involve goods that are unique or goods for which no substitute can be found. Examples include antiques, heirlooms, works of art, and objects of purely sentimental value.[12] Specific performance is not available for the breach of a promise to perform a personal service (such as a contract for employment, artistic performance, or consulting services). A decree requiring a person to specifically perform a personal-services contract would probably be ineffective in giving the injured party what he bargained for. It would also require a great deal of supervision by the court. In addition, an application of specific performance in such cases would amount to a form of involuntary servitude.

Injunction Injunction is an equitable remedy that is employed in many different contexts and is sometimes used as a remedy for breach of contract. An **injunction** is a court order requiring a person to do something (**mandatory injunction**) or ordering a person to refrain from doing something (**negative injunction**). Unlike legal remedies that apply only when the breach has already occurred, the equitable remedy of injunction can be invoked when a breach has merely been *threatened*.

---

[11]Another equitable remedy, *reformation,* allows a court to reform or "rewrite" a written contract when the parties have made an error in expressing their agreement. Reformation is discussed, along with the doctrine of mistake, in Chapter 13.

[12]Specific performance under § 2–716(1) of the UCC is discussed in Chapter 22.

Injunctions are available only when the breach or threatened breach is likely to cause *irreparable injury*.

In the contract context, specific performance is a form of mandatory injunction. Negative injunctions are appropriately used in several situations, such as contract cases in which a party whose duty under the contract is forbearance threatens to breach the contract. For example, Norris sells his restaurant in Gas City, Indiana, to Ford. A term of the contract of sale provides that Norris agrees not to own, operate, or be employed in any restaurant within 30 miles of Gas City for a period of two years after the sale.[13] If Norris threatens to open a new restaurant in Gas City several months after the sale is consummated, a court could *enjoin* Norris from opening the new restaurant.

Restitution
Restitution is a remedy that can be obtained either at law or in equity. Restitution applies when one party's performance or reliance has conferred a benefit on the other. A party's restitution interest is protected by compensating him for the value of benefits he has conferred on the other person.[14] This can be done through

---

[13]Ancillary covenants not to compete, or noncompetition agreements, are discussed in detail in Chapter 15.

[14]Quasi-contract is discussed in detail in Chapter 9.

specific restitution, in which the defendant is required to return the exact property conferred on him by the plaintiff, or **substitutionary restitution,** in which a court awards the plaintiff a sum of money that reflects the amount by which he benefited the defendant. In an action for damages based on quasi-contract, substitutionary restitution would be the remedy.

Restitution can be used in a number of circumstances. Sometimes, parties injured by breach of contract seek restitution as an alternative remedy instead of damages that focus on their expectation interest. In other situations, a *breaching party* who has partially performed seeks restitution for the value of benefits he conferred in excess of the losses he caused. In addition, restitution often applies in cases in which a person rescinds a contract on the grounds of lack of capacity, misrepresentation, fraud, duress, undue influence, or mistake. Upon rescission, each party who has been benefited by the other's performance must compensate the other for the value of the benefit conferred. Another application of restitution occurs when a party to a contract that violates the statute of frauds confers a benefit on the other party. For example, Boyer gives Blake a $10,000 down payment on an oral contract for the sale of a farm. Although the contract is unenforceable (that is, Boyer could not get compensation for his expectation interest), the court would give Boyer restitution of his down payment.

Problems and Problem Cases

1. Smith hired attorney Lewis to represent her as a plaintiff in a personal injury suit. They signed a contract of employment that provided that attorney fees would be paid based upon a "contingency fee of forty percent (40%) of final recovery whether by trial or by settlement. . . ." Lewis pursued the litigation on Smith's behalf for almost two years. Smith spoke little English, so Lewis communicated with her using interpreters. Lewis arranged for a settlement, and he claims that Lee, an interpreter for Smith, expressed Smith's authorization of the settlement. Later, however, another interpreter called to ask about the status of the case and indicated that Smith had not authorized the settlement. Lewis then rescinded the settlement and successfully prevented the other party from enforcing it. However, Smith fired Lewis and hired another attorney to pursue the case further. Lewis filed an attorney's lien and sued

Smith for $5,000, which represented 40 percent of the rejected $12,500 settlement that he negotiated, plus the $883.44 in expenses that he had paid. Does the contract of employment give Lewis the right to a 40 percent fee?

2. Optus hired Silvestri under a two-year employment contract that provided that Optus had the right to terminate him for failure to perform his duties to the satisfaction of the company. Silvestri had been hired to help resolve difficulties with technical support. The company continued to receive complaints from customers and resellers about technical support, however, and ultimately Optus fired Silvestri. Silvestri brought a breach of contract action, alleging that there was no objective reason for lack of satisfaction with his performance. Will Silvestri prevail?

3. Light contracted to build a house for the Mullers. After the job was completed, the Mullers refused to pay Light the balance they owed him under the

contract, claiming that he had done some of the work in an unworkmanlike manner. When Light sued for the money, the Mullers counterclaimed for $5,700 damages for delay under a liquidated damages clause in the contract. The clause provided that Light must pay $100 per day for every day of delay in completion of the construction. The evidence indicated that the rental value of the home was between $400 and $415 per month. Should the liquidated damages provision be enforced?

4. In 1992, White and J.M. Brown Amusement Co. entered into a contract giving Brown exclusive rights to place "certain coin-operated amusement machines" in 13 of White's stores, all in Oconee and Anderson counties in South Carolina. The contract was for a term of 15 years. Under the contract, White agreed "not to allow other machines on the premises without the express written consent of [Brown]." Brown placed the machines in White's stores as the contract provided. In 1993, the state legislature enacted a local option law as part of the Video Game Machines Act, permitting counties to hold an individual referendum to determine whether cash payouts for video gaming should remain legal. As a result of local referenda held in November 1994, 12 counties, including Oconee and Anderson, voted to ban cash payouts. The South Carolina Department of Revenue revoked the licenses required to operate the machines Brown had placed in White's stores, effective July 1, 1995, as required by the Act. Consequently, Brown removed the video poker machines from White's stores. Brown did not replace the machines with any other coin-operated amusement machines. In November 1996, the South Carolina Supreme Court struck down the local option law contained in the Act as unconstitutional. Given this Court's ruling, Brown planned to return the video poker machines to White's stores, but White informed Brown that the contract was no longer valid. White then filed suit seeking to have the contract declared void and unenforceable so that he would be free to sign a contract with another provider of legal video and amusement machines. Approximately one month after filing suit, White entered into an agreement with Hughes Entertainment, Inc. giving Hughes exclusive rights to place "all video game terminals and all coin operated music and amusement machines" in 12 of the same stores listed in the Brown contract. Was White's duty to perform the contract with Brown excused?

5. The Bassos contracted with Dierberg to purchase her property for $1,310,000. One term of the contract stated, "[t]he sale under this contract shall be closed . . . at the office of Community Title Company . . . on May 16, 1988 at 10:00 AM. . . . Time is of the essence of this contract." After forming the contract, the Bassos assigned their right to purchase Dierberg's property to Miceli and Slonim Development Corp. At 10:00 AM on May 16, 1988, Dierberg appeared at Community Title for closing. No representative of Miceli and Slonim was there, nor did anyone from Miceli and Slonim inform Dierberg that there would be any delay in the closing. At 10:20 AM, Dierberg declared the contract null and void because the closing did not take place as agreed, and she left the title company office shortly thereafter. Dierberg had intended to use the purchase money to close another contract to purchase real estate later in the day. At about 10:30 AM, a representative of Miceli and Slonim appeared at Community Title to begin the closing, but the representative did not have the funds for payment until 1:30 PM. Dierberg refused to return to the title company, stating that Miceli and Slonim had breached the contract by failing to tender payment on time. She had already made alternative arrangements to finance her purchase of other real estate to meet her obligation under that contract. Miceli and Slonim sued Dierberg, claiming that the contract did not require closing exactly at 10:00 AM, but rather some time on the day of May 16. Will they prevail?

6. Hart entered into a contract with Brad Smith Roofing on October 16, 2000, for the company to install gutters and replace, prime, and paint the facia board on two buildings he owned, for the price of $1,073. Hart then paid $300 as a deposit on the contract. Brad Smith Roofing never began performance, and, in April 2001, Hart wrote to the company requesting a schedule of completion and also informing it of his intention to seek another bid if it failed to respond. Having received no reply to this letter, Hart then obtained a bid for the gutter work from Broadview Roofing & Remodeling, Inc., for the price of $1,375. He again wrote to Brad Smith Roofing in June 2001, notifying it of his receipt of that bid and his intention to have Broadview perform the work unless Brad Smith Roofing started performance as contracted, as well as his intention to hold it liable for the differences in the contract prices. Subsequently, Broadview

did the gutter work for Hart in October 2001, for which Hart paid $1,375. Hart then sued Brad Smith Roofing, seeking damages in the amount of $602. After a hearing, a magistrate filed a report awarding Hart $300 for his deposit only, but denying recovery on the $302 damages claim. Was this a correct ruling?

7. Faulconer served as an employee of Wysong & Miles Company for approximately 30 years. In October 1981, Faulconer and Wysong & Miles entered into an agreement that provided for Faulconer to receive supplemental retirement and death benefits from Wysong & Miles in recognition of his years of faithful service, loyalty to the company (including a noncompete provision), and required physical check-ups. Faulconer retired from Wysong & Miles in 1987. Wysong & Miles was obligated to him in the sum of $2,620.80 per month under the agreement. It made all payments until the fall of 2000. At that point, Wysong & Miles suspended its payments to Faulconer. Faulconer filed suit against Wysong & Miles, claiming that it had missed eight payments, and owed him the principal sum of $20,966.40 plus interest. Wysong & Miles admitted that it had failed to make the payments, but it claimed that its duty to perform was discharged by impracticability. It stated that the precipitous decline in the metalworking machine manufacturing industry, for which Wysong was not in any way responsible, and the nonoccurrence of which was a basic assumption on which the agreement was made, made its performance impracticable. Will Wysong & Miles prevail on this argument?

8. In May 2001, Bush purchased an African safari package for herself and her fiancé. She paid a 20 percent deposit. The contract stated that in case of cancellation more than 60 days in advance of the tour, there would be a $50 per person penalty, and in case of cancellation 30–60 days in advance, the penalty would be 20 percent of the total retail tour rate. Sixty-four days before the tour was to begin, September 11 terror attacks on New York City occurred. As a result of the concern about terrorism surrounding that time, Bush and her fiancé decided to cancel the trip. They began to attempt to cancel on September 12, but phones were down and offices were closed, so Bush did not manage to convey her cancellation to ProTravel until September 27, which was within the 30–60 day period. ProTravel did

not manage to convey the cancellation to Micato, the tour operator, until October 4, also within the 30–60 days/20 percent penalty period. Because of this, the tour operator and travel agency kept the deposit. Bush claimed that impossibility because of frustration of the means of performance prevented her from canceling within the more-than-60-day period. ProTravel filed a motion for summary judgment. Should the court grant it?

9. Ross was recruited to play basketball at Creighton University. He came from an academically disadvantaged background, and at the time he enrolled, Ross was at an academic level far below that of the average Creighton student. Creighton realized Ross's academic limitations when it admitted him, and to induce him to attend and play basketball, assured him that he would receive sufficient tutoring so that he "would receive a meaningful education while at Creighton." Ross attended Creighton from 1978 to 1982. He maintained a D average and earned 96 of the 128 credits needed to graduate. On the advice of the athletics department, he took many of these credits in courses such as marksmanship and theory of basketball, which did not count toward a university degree. He also alleged that the university hired a secretary to read his assignments and prepare and type his papers. When he left Creighton, Ross had the overall language skills of a fourth grader and the reading skills of a seventh grader. He took remedial classes for a year at a preparatory school at Creighton's expense, attending classes with grade-school children, and then enrolled at Roosevelt University. He was forced to withdraw there for lack of funds. Ross sued Creighton for breach of contract, among other theories. Can Ross win this suit?

10. Dove had been employed by Rose Acre Farm, operated by Rust, its president and principal owner, in the summers and other times from 1972 to 1979. Rust had instituted and maintained extensive bonus programs. In June 1979, Rust called in Dove and other construction crew leaders and offered a bonus of $6,000 each if certain detailed construction work was completed in 12 weeks. In addition to completing the work, Dove would be required to work at least five full days a week for 12 weeks to qualify for the bonus. On the same day Dove's bonus agreement, by mutual consent, was amended to 10 weeks with a bonus of $5,000 to enable him to return to law school by September 1. To qualify for the bonus

he would have to work 10 weeks, five days a week, commencing at starting time and quitting only at quitting time. Dove was aware of the provisions concerning absenteeism and tardiness as they affected bonuses, and knew that if he missed any work, for any reason, including illness, he would forfeit the bonus. No exception had ever been made except as may have occurred by clerical error or inadvertence. In the tenth week, Dove came down with strep throat. On Thursday of that week he reported to work with a temperature of 104 degrees, and told Rust that he was unable to work. Rust told him, in effect, that if he went home, he would forfeit the bonus. Rust offered him the opportunity to stay there and lie on a couch, or make up his lost days on Saturday and/or Sunday. Rust told him he could sleep and still qualify for the bonus. Dove left to seek medical treatment and missed two days in the tenth week of the bonus program. Rust refused Dove the bonus based

solely upon his missing the two days of work. Was Rust within his legal rights to refuse to pay the bonus?

Online Research

Researching Remedies in Web Site Terms and Conditions

Many Web sites have pages called "Terms of Use" or "Terms & Conditions," and these pages often restrict the remedies that can be recovered in case of nonperformance or loss. Find a "Terms of Use" page and look for a provision that addresses remedies. What does the page you found have to say about remedies that will or will not be available in case of nonperformance?

Part Four

Sales

chapter 19
Formation and Terms
of Sales Contracts

chapter 20
Product Liability

chapter 21
Performance of Sales Contracts

chapter 22
Remedies for Breach
of Sales Contracts

chapter 19

FORMATION AND TERMS OF SALES CONTRACTS

P aul Reynolds used the Trek Web site to purchase a racing bike with a frame utilizing a newly developed high-strength but lightweight alloy. He selected the model he wanted and provided the company with the necessary information to place the $2,200 purchase price and $75.00 shipping costs on his Visa card. The bicycle was damaged during shipment when the box was punctured by a forklift truck that was loading other boxes onto the carrier's truck. Paul took the damaged bicycle to a local bicycle dealer to have it repaired. After the bicycle was repaired, but before Paul could pick it up, a clerk in the store, by mistake, sold the bicycle for $1,500 to Melissa Stevenson who bought it as a birthday gift for her boyfriend. This situation raises a number of legal issues that, among others, will be covered in this chapter, including:

- Can a legally enforceable contract for the sale of goods be formed electronically?
- Between Paul and Trek, who had the risk of loss or damage to the bicycle during the time it was under shipment to him?
- Would Paul be entitled to recover possession of the bicycle from Melissa and her boyfriend?
- Even if Melissa and her boyfriend are not legally required to return the bicycle to Paul, would returning it be the ethical thing to do?

IN PART 3, CONTRACTS, we introduced the common law rules that govern the creation and performance of contracts generally. Throughout much of history, special rules, known as the law merchant, were developed to control mercantile transactions in goods. Because transactions in goods commonly involve buyers and sellers located in different states—and even different countries—a common body of law to control these transactions can facilitate the smooth flow of commerce. To address this need, the Uniform Commercial Code (UCC or Code) was prepared to simplify and modernize the rules of law governing commercial transactions.

In 2003, the American Law Institute adopted a series of proposed amendments to Article 2 (Sales) of the UCC that are intended to further modernize and clarify some of its provisions. The amendments are not effective until they have been adopted by a state and incorporated into its version of Article 2. There is some controversy concerning the proposed amendments, and because at the time this book went to press they had not been adopted by any state, they are not incorporated in the discussion of Article 2 that follows.

This chapter reviews some Code rules that govern the formation of sales contracts previously discussed. It also covers some key terms in sales contracts, such as delivery terms, title, and risk of loss. Finally, it discusses the rules governing sales on trial, such as sales on approval and consignments.

Sale of Goods

The **sale of goods** is the transfer of ownership to tangible personal property in exchange for money, other goods, or the performance of services. The law of sales of goods is codified in Article 2 of the Uniform Commercial Code. While the law of sales is based on the fundamental principles of contract and personal property, it has been modified to accommodate current practices of merchants. In large measure, the Code discarded many technical requirements of earlier law that did not serve any useful purpose in the marketplace and replaced them with rules that are consistent with commercial expectations.

Article 2 of the Code applies only to *transactions in goods*. Thus, it does not cover contracts to provide

Figure 1   *Choice of Law*

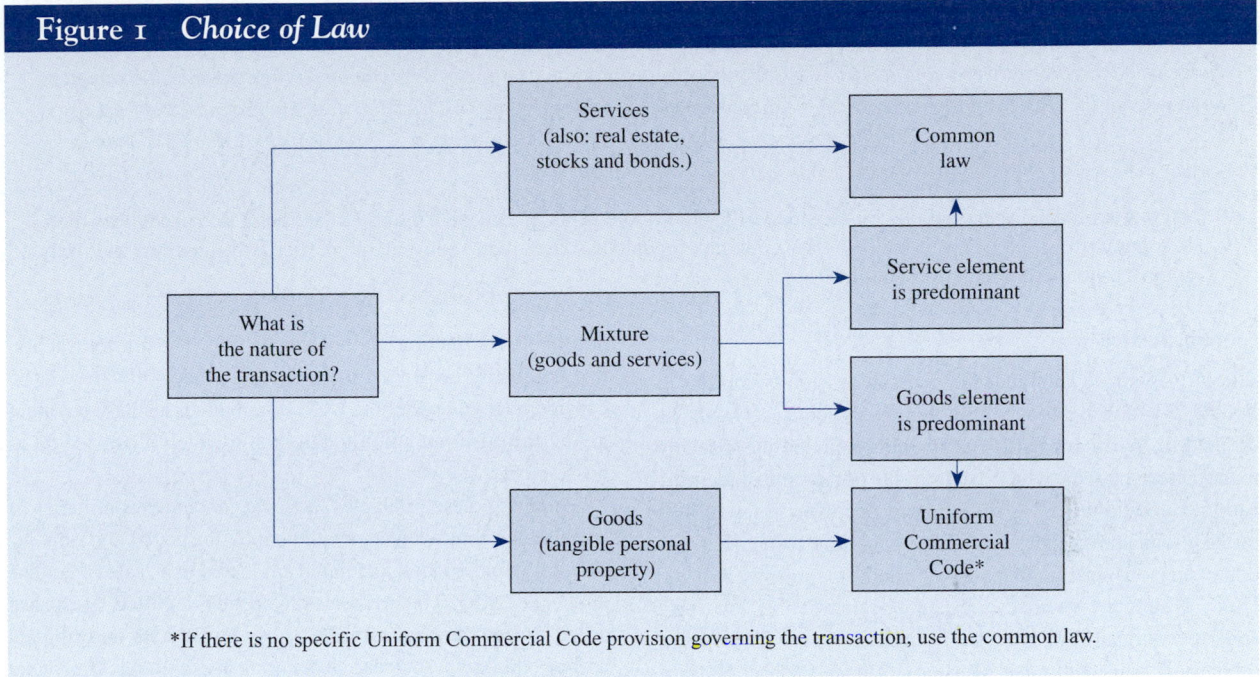

*If there is no specific Uniform Commercial Code provision governing the transaction, use the common law.

services or to sell real property. However, some courts have applied the principles set out in the Code to such transactions. When a contract appears to call for the furnishing of both goods and services, a question may arise as to whether the Code applies. For example, the operator of a hair salon may use a commercial solution intended to be used safely on humans that causes injury to a person's head. The injured person then might bring a lawsuit claiming that there was a breach of the Code's warranty of the suitability of the solution. In such cases, the courts commonly ask whether the sale of goods is the *predominant* part of the transaction or merely an *incidental* part; where the sale of goods predominates, courts normally apply Article 2. The *Dealer Management Systems* case, which follows, illustrates the type of analysis courts use to determine whether a particular contract should be governed by the Code.

Thus, the first question you should ask when faced with a contracts problem is: Is this a contract for the sale of goods? If it is not, then the principles of common law that were discussed in Part 3, Contracts, apply. If the contract is one for the sale of goods, then the Code applies. This analysis is illustrated in Figure 1.

Dealer Management Systems, Inc. v. Design Automotive Group, Inc.
822 N.E.2d 556 (App. Ct. Ill. 2005)

In 2000, Design Automotive Group, Inc., issued a purchase order to Dealer Management Systems, Inc. (DMS), for "computer programs and other services." In the purchase order, DMS agreed to provide Design Automotive with an "Accounting Information Management" system consisting of various separately priced software components. The price of the individual components totaled $24,000, but DMS agreed to provide them as a package for $20,000 plus an additional $795 for an item described a "RMCOBALRUNTIME SYSTEM FOR UNIX 16." The purchase order also contained the following language:

Software changes to AIM System to provide the same or better function as compared with current system. Develop a MRP subsystem to meet manufacturing needs. Also, includes data file conversion program from our current system and load programs in the AIM system. Also includes user training and support for 1 year.

@$15,000

Includes source code license for internal use only and not for resale to anyone or any company.

DMS brought suit against Design Automotive alleging that it had breached the contract for failing to pay the $20,000 purchase price for the software, and also seeking recovery in quantum meruit *for other computer programs that it claimed to have written for Design Automotive. Design Automotive moved to dismiss the contract claim on the grounds that because it had not signed the purchase order, the agreement was unenforceable under section 2–201(1) of the Uniform Commercial Code—Sales—the statute of frauds—which provides in pertinent part:*

A contract for the sale of goods for the price of $500 or more is not enforceable by way of action or defense unless there is some writing sufficient to indicate that a contract for sale has been made between the parties and signed by the party against whom enforcement is sought.

Callam, Justice

The UCC's statue of frauds for the sale of goods appears in Article 2, which applies to "transactions in goods." "Goods" is defined, in pertinent part, as "all things, including specially manufactured goods, which are movable at the time of identification to the contract." A sampling of decisions from various jurisdictions shows that courts have generally recognized that computer software qualifies as a "good" for purposes of the UCC. However, whether a particular transaction involving computer software constitutes a "transaction in goods" depends on various considerations. Most courts would probably agree that an ordinary sale of "off-the-rack" software is a transaction in goods. In contrast, a transaction predominantly involving the intellectual property rights to the software is outside the scope of Article 2.

Some courts have concluded that a contract to develop entirely new software is one for services rather than goods. On the other hand, a contract that calls for the modification or customization of existing software may still be a transaction in goods.

Contracts for the sale of software often also involve the provision of services. Where there is a mixed contract for goods and services, there is a "transaction in goods" only if the contract is predominantly for goods and incidentally for services. Article 2 applies to software transactions where the services provided are not substantially different from those generally accompanying package sales of computer systems consisting of hardware and software. Comparing the relative costs of materials and labor may be helpful in the analysis, but is not dispositive.

Finally, although the statute of frauds applies only to contracts for the "sale" of goods, the labels used by the parties to describe a transaction are not controlling. Thus, a transaction that nominally involves a mere license to use software will be considered a sale under the UCC if it involves a single payment giving the buyer an unlimited period in which it has a right to possession.

Applying these principles here, we conclude, as a matter of law, that the contract was predominantly for goods and only incidentally for services, and that it amounted to a "sale of goods" under the UCC. The written agreement is entitled "purchase order." It lists various software "subsystems" with descriptions corresponding to standard accounting tasks (e.g., "Accounts Receivable Subsys.," "Inventory Control Subsys."). There is nothing in the purchase order to suggest that these components were developed "from scratch." The subsystems are separately priced, but sold as a package for $20,000.

The price for services, in comparison, is only $15,000. Moreover, this amount includes customization of the software. Customization may be treated as the "manufacture" of the good from existing software rather than as a service. Thus, more than $20,000 of the contract price is for goods and less than $15,000 is for services. In addition, the services provided—installation, training, and support—are not substantially different from those generally accompanying package sales of computer systems consisting of hardware and software. The agreement is a sale subject to the statute of frauds because it provided for the transfer of the software for an unlimited time for a single payment. Accordingly, DMS has not shown the existence of a meritorious claim that could have withstood the UCC's statute of frauds.

Judgment affirmed for Design Automotive Group, Inc.

Leases

A lease of goods is a transfer of the right to possess and use goods belonging to another. Although the rights of one who leases goods (a lessee) do not constitute ownership of the goods, leasing is mentioned here because it is an important way of acquiring the use of many kinds of goods, from automobiles to farm equipment. In most states, Article 2 and Article 9 of the UCC are applied to such leases by analogy. However, rules contained in these articles sometimes are inadequate to resolve special problems presented by leasing. For this reason, a new article of the UCC dealing exclusively with leases of goods, Article 2A, was written in 1987 and has been adopted by 49 states and the District of Columbia. Because of space limitations, this textbook does not cover Article 2A in detail. However, the article itself is reprinted in its entirety in Appendix B.

Merchants

Many of the Code's provisions apply only to **merchants** or to transactions between merchants.[1] In addition, the Code sets a higher standard of conduct for merchants because persons who regularly deal in goods are expected to be familiar with the practices of that trade and with commercial law. Ordinary consumers and nonmerchants, on the other hand, frequently have little knowledge of or experience in these matters.

Code Requirements

The Code requires that parties to sales contracts act in good faith and in a commercially reasonable manner. Further, when a contract contains an unfair or unconscionable clause, or the contract as a whole is unconscionable, the courts have the right to refuse to enforce the unconscionable clause or contract [2–302].[2] The Code's treatment of unconscionability is discussed in detail in Chapter 15, Illegality.

A number of the Code provisions concerning the sale of goods were discussed in the chapters on contracts. The Concept Review (page 484) lists some of the important provisions discussed earlier, together with the chapters in the text where the discussion can be found.

Terms of Sales Contracts

Gap Fillers The Code recognizes the fact that parties to sales contracts frequently omit terms from their agreements or state terms in an indefinite or unclear manner. The Code deals with these situations by filling in the blanks with common trade practices, or by giving commonly used terms a specific meaning that is applied unless the parties' agreement clearly indicates a contrary intent.

Price Terms A fixed price is not essential to the creation of a binding sales contract. Of course, if price has been the subject of a dispute between the parties that has never been resolved, no contract is created because a "meeting of the minds" never occurred. However, if the parties omitted a price term or left the price to be determined at a future date or by some external means, the Code supplies a price term [2–305]. Under the common law, such contracts would have failed due to "indefiniteness." If a price term is simply omitted, or if the parties agreed that the price would be set by some external agency (like a particular market or trade journal) that fails to set the price, the Code says the price is a *reasonable price at the time for delivery* [2–305(1)]. If the agreement gives either party the power to fix the price, that party must do so in *good faith* [2–305(2)]. If the surrounding circumstances clearly indicate that the parties did not intend to be bound in the event a price was not determined in the agreed-upon manner, no contract results [2–305(4)].

Quantity Terms In some cases, the parties may state the quantity of goods covered by their sales contract in an indefinite way. Contracts that obligate a buyer to purchase a seller's *output* of a certain item or all of the buyer's *requirements* of a certain item are commonly encountered. These contracts caused frequent problems under the common law because of the indefiniteness of the parties' obligations. If the seller decided to double its output, did the buyer have to accept the entire amount? If the market price of the item soared much higher than the contract price, could the buyer double or triple its demands?

Output and Needs Contracts In an "output" contract, one party is bound to sell its entire output of particular goods and the other party is bound to buy that output. In a "needs" or "requirements" contract, the quantity of goods is based on the needs of the buyer. In determining the quantity of goods to be produced or taken pursuant to an output or needs contract, the rule of *good faith* applies. Thus, no quantity can be demanded or taken that is unreasonably disproportionate to any stated estimate in the contract or to "normal" prior output or requirements if no estimate is stated [2–306(2)].

For example, assume the Manhattan Ice Company enters into a five-year agreement with the Madison Square

---

[1]Under the Code, a "merchant" is defined as a "person who deals in goods of the kind or otherwise by his occupation holds himself out as having knowledge or skill peculiar to the practices or goods involved in the transaction or to whom such knowledge or skill may be attributed by his employment of an agent or broker or other intermediary who by his occupation holds himself out as having such knowledge or skill" [2–104(1)].

[2]The numbers in brackets refer to sections of the Uniform Commercial Code.

Formation of Contracts

Offer and Acceptance (Chapters 10 and 11)	1. A contract can be formed in any manner sufficient to show agreement, including conduct by both parties that recognizes the existence of a contract.
	2. The fact that the parties did not agree on all the terms of their contract does not prevent the formation of a contract.
	3. A firm written offer by a merchant that contains assurances it will be held open is irrevocable for a period of up to three months.
	4. Acceptance of an offer may be made by any reasonable manner and is effective on dispatch.
	5. A timely expression of acceptance creates a contract even if it contains terms different from the offer or states additional terms *unless* the attempted acceptance is expressly conditioned on the offer's agreement to the terms of the acceptance.
	6. An offer inviting a prompt shipment may be accepted either by a prompt promise to ship or a prompt shipment of the goods.
Consideration (Chapter 12)	1. Consideration is not required to make a firm offer in writing by a merchant irrevocable for a period of up to three months.
	2. Consideration is not required to support a modification of a contract for the sale of goods.
Statute of Frauds (Chapter 16)	1. Subject to several exceptions, all contracts for the sale of goods for $500 or more must be evidenced by a writing signed by the party against whom enforcement of the contract is sought. It is effective only as to the quantity of goods stated in the writing.
	2. A signed writing is not required if the party against whom enforcement is sought is a merchant, received a written memorandum from the other party, and did not object in writing within 10 days of his receipt of it.
	3. An exception to the statute of frauds is made for specially manufactured goods not suitable for sale to others on which the seller has made a substantial beginning in manufacturing or has entered into a binding contract to acquire.
	4. An exception to the statute of frauds is made for contracts that a party admits the existence of in court testimony or pleadings.
	5. If a party accepts goods or payment for goods, the statute of frauds is satisfied to the extent of the payment made or the goods accepted.
Unconscionability (Chapter 15)	If a court finds a contract for the sale of goods to be unconscionable, it can refuse to enforce it entirely, enforce it without any unconscionable clause, or enforce it in a way that avoids an unconscionable result.

CYBERLAW IN ACTION

Electronic Writings and the Statute of Frauds

The Electronic Signatures in Global and National Commerce Act (the "E-Sign" act) was enacted by Congress and became effective in the United States on October 1, 2000. The E-Sign law covers many everyday transactions including sales transactions even where the law of the state involved still has a version of Article 2 that requires a "signed writing" or another means of satisfying the Article 2 statute of frauds found in Section 2–201. Federal laws "preempt," that is, displace state laws if the two sets of laws are in conflict. If state law requires a signed writing or another indicator that the purported buyer and seller actually intended to form a contract, E-Sign allows the parties to use electronic authentications instead of signed writings. E-mail messages and online orders sent by the buyer would suffice. States that have adopted the Uniform Electronic Transactions Act (UETA) also allow online communications to satisfy the Section 2–201 statute of frauds requirement.

Garden Corporation to provide at a fixed, specified price all the ice required for the concession stands at Madison Square Garden. Manhattan Ice expands its capacity to make ice to fulfill the anticipated requirements and during the first two years of the contract delivers between 1.25 and 1.5 million pounds of ice to the Garden. If in the third year of the agreement, Madison Square Garden wants Manhattan Ice to deliver approximately twice that much ice so that it can be used at other arenas owned by the corporation, Manhattan Ice would not be obligated to provide the additional ice. Similarly, Madison Square Garden would not be able to reduce its request to 100,000 pounds of ice because it decides to make its own ice on the premises. In the latter case, it is obligated to continue to acquire all of its requirements for ice from Manhattan Ice.

In the *Noble Roman's* case that follows, the court looked to the contract and to the parties' course of performance to conclude that the contract was a "requirements" contract and not an order for a specified number of pizza boxes.

Noble Roman's, Inc. v. Pizza Boxes, Inc.
57 UCCRep.2d 901 (Ct. App. Indiana 2005)

Noble Roman's is a franchisor of pizza restaurants, but the company does not own or operate any restaurants. Noble Roman's franchisees order supplies approved by Noble Roman's. Pizza Boxes is a broker that acts as an intermediary for vendors who manufacture pizza boxes.

In 2002 William Gilbert, director of R&D and distribution for Noble Roman's, e-mailed Michael Rosenberg, vice president of Pizza Boxes, regarding Noble Roman's interest in "clamshell" boxes for use in a new "pizza-by-the-slice" program. Gilbert stated that the estimated usage at this stage is from 400,000 to a million units per year to start. After Noble Roman's approved the box design, the parties worked out the details for the purchase. Gilbert explained that the pizza-by-the-slice program was just getting started at one of its franchise locations, but he anticipated that other locations would implement the program over time. The two agreed that 2.5 million boxes would be needed annually; that Multifoods, Noble Roman's distributor, would submit orders for the boxes and pay the invoices; and that Multifoods would pick up the boxes after the orders were filled.

On November 1, 2002, Rosenberg sent Gilbert a confirming letter, which stated:

Dear Bill:

Please sign in the space below to confirm the following order:

Item: 18/6 Slice Box 220/case

Quantity: 2,500,000

Print: Two colors

Price: $101.45/M

FOB: Bakersfield or Stockton, Ca. (in trailer load quantity—approx. 230,000 per load)

To be picked up by Multifoods. PBI remits invoice Multifoods.

Extras for printing preps are included at $4,500 ($1.80/M) and amortized over the entire order. In the event that the total of 2.5 million boxes are not manufactured, Noble Roman's is responsible for any portion of the prep charge remaining.

Gilbert signed and dated the letter and returned it to Rosenberg. On its own initiative, Pizza Boxes, through its vendor, Dopaco, Inc., manufactured 519,200 boxes in anticipation of Multifoods' future orders. Multifoods submitted an initial purchase order to Pizza Boxes for six cases (12,000 boxes), and Multifoods paid Pizza Boxes for that order. However, after the initial order, Multifoods did not order any more boxes. When Rosenberg called Multifoods to inquire why it had not ordered more boxes, he was told that the franchisees were "not using this product."

Pizza Boxes then asked Noble Roman's to pay for approximately 500,000 boxes that Pizza Boxes had made but Multifoods had not ordered. Noble Roman's responded that it was a franchisor and not an operator of restaurants that specifies and arranges for the manufacture of products and supplies sold by its franchisees, and that Noble Roman's does not purchase any supplies or products. Once Noble Roman's includes products or supplies in its specifications, then any purchase order is signed by the distributor who buys all of the supplies and distributes them to the franchisees who sign purchase orders with the distributor.

Pizza Boxes then filed suit against Noble Roman's alleging breach of contract, seeking $54,901.44 for the unpaid inventory and tooling charges. The trial court entered summary judgment in favor of Pizza Boxes and Noble Roman's appealed.

Najam, Judge

Noble Roman's contends that the trial court erred when it entered summary judgment in favor of Pizza Boxes. In particular, Noble Roman's maintains that its only obligation under the November 1, 2002, letter was to pay the "printing prep" charges remaining in the event Pizza Boxes did not manufacture the 2.5 million boxes. We agree.

Initially, we note that Pizza Boxes' complaint suggests that the November 1, 2002, letter is a purchase order, that is, "[a] document authorizing a seller to deliver goods with payment to be made later." But the plain and ordinary meaning of the letter shows that it is a requirements contract. See UCC 2–306. The letter is not an order for 2.5 million boxes but, on its face, contemplates the possibility that not all 2.5 million boxes would be manufactured. Thus, it is not a purchase order. And, despite the inclusion in the letter of a specific estimate of quantity, it is clear that there was no meeting of the minds on how many boxes Pizza Boxes would ultimately produce under the requirements contract.

Noble Roman's contends, and we agree, that the letter is unambiguous and provides that it is only responsible for the unpaid "printing prep" charges "in the event that the toal of 2.5 million boxes are not manufactured." In interpreting an unambiguous contact, a court gives effect to the parties' intentions as expressed in the four corners of the instrument, and clear, plain and unambiguous terms are conclusive of that intent. Particular words and phrases cannot be read alone, and the parties' intentions must be determined by reading the contract as a whole.

The terms of the November 1 letter show that: (1) Multifoods would pick up the boxes; (2) Pizza Boxes would remit the invoices to Multifoods; and (3) Noble Roman's was responsible for "any portion of the [printing] prep charges remaining in the event that not all 2.5 boxes were manufactured." While the terms regarding quantity and price might, at first glance, suggest the letter is a purchase order from Noble Roman's for 2.5 million boxes, when the letter is read as a whole it shows that it is a requirements contract under which, Multifoods, not Noble Roman's, is the purchaser. In effect, Multifoods is a third-party beneficiary of the contract, in that Noble Roman's established the specifications for the manufacture, and negotiated the price of the boxes for the benefit of Multifoods.

In addition, the parties' course of performance shows that Pizza Boxes did not expect that Noble Roman's would be responsible for paying for the boxes. Indiana Code Section 2–208 provides in relevant part:

> Where the contract for sale involves repeated occasions for performance by either party with knowledge of the nature of the performance and opportunity for objection to it by the other, any course of performance accepted or acquiesced in without objection shall be relevant to determine the meaning of the agreement.

Indiana Code Section 2–202 provides in relevant part:

> Terms with respect to which the confirmatory memoranda of the parties agree or which are otherwise set forth in a writing intended by the parties as a final expression of their

agreement with respect to such terms as are included therein may not be contradicted by evidence of any prior agreement or a contemporaneous oral agreement but *may be explained or supplemented:*

(a) by course of dealing or usage of trade (1–205) or *by course of performance* (2–208).

Here, the requirements contract involved "repeated occasions for performance" in that not all 2.5 million boxes would be ordered, manufactured, and purchased at once.

Multifoods submitted a purchase order for sixty cases to Pizza Boxes; Pizza Boxes submitted an invoice to Multifoods; and Multifoods paid Pizza Boxes for the boxes. When Multifoods did not submit any subsequent orders, Rosenberg looked to Multifoods for an explanation and telephoned its buyer to ask why no other orders had been submitted. The conduct of Multifoods in submitting the order to Pizza Boxes and paying Pizza Boxes, and Pizza Boxes in submitting the invoice to Multifoods and contacting Multifoods to inquire about additional orders, establish a course of performance between them, consistent with the terms of the letter, all of which shows that Multifoods is the purchaser. Pizza Boxes did not suggest that the November 1, 2002, letter obligated Noble Roman's until it realized that Multifoods was not going to submit any additional purchase orders.

Noble Roman's did not order the boxes in dispute and is entitled to summary judgment on Pizza Boxes' breach of contract claim for the cost of the boxes as a matter of law. However, under the terms of contract, Noble Roman's is liable to Pizza Boxes for the portion of the prep charges still owed for the boxes that were not manufactured.

Judgment reversed in favor of Noble Roman's and remanded with instructions.

Exclusive Dealing Contracts

The Code takes a similar approach to *exclusive dealing contracts.* Under the common law, these contracts were sources of difficulty due to the indefinite nature of the parties' duties. Did the dealer have to make any effort to sell the manufacturer's products, and did the manufacturer have any duty to supply the dealer? The Code says that unless the parties agree to the contrary, sellers have an obligation to use their best efforts to supply the goods to the buyer and the buyers are obligated to use their best efforts to promote their sale [2–306(2)].

Time for Performance

If no time for performance is stated in the sales contract, a *reasonable time* for performance is implied. If a contract requires successive performances over an indefinite period of time, the contract is valid for a reasonable time; however, either party can terminate it at any time upon the giving of reasonable notice unless the parties have agreed otherwise as to termination [2–309]. For example, Farmer Jack agrees to sell his entire output of apples each fall to a cannery at the then-current market price. If the contract does not contain a provision spelling out how and when the contract can be terminated, Farmer Jack can terminate it if he gives the cannery a reasonable time to make arrangements to acquire apples from someone else.

Delivery Terms

Standardized shipping terms that through commercial practice have come to have a specific meaning are customarily used in sales contracts. The terms **FOB (free on board)** and **FAS (free alongside ship)** are basic delivery terms. If the delivery term of the contract is FOB or FAS the place at which the goods originate, the seller is obligated to deliver to the carrier goods that *conform to the contract* and *are properly prepared for shipment* to the buyer, and the seller must make a *reasonable contract for transportation of the goods* on behalf of the buyer. Under such delivery terms, the goods are at the risk of the buyer during transit and he must pay the shipping charges. If the term is *FOB destination,* the seller must deliver the goods to the designated destination and they are at the seller's risk and expense during transit. These terms will be discussed in more detail later in this chapter.

Title

Passage of Title

Title to goods cannot pass from the seller to the buyer until the goods are identified to the contract [2–401(1)]. For example, if Seller agrees to sell Buyer 50 chairs and Seller has 500 chairs in his warehouse, title to 50 chairs will not pass from Seller to Buyer until the 50 chairs that Buyer has purchased are selected and identified as the chairs sold to Buyer.

The parties may agree between themselves when title to the goods will pass from the seller to the buyer. If there is no agreement, then the general rule is that the *title to*

CYBERLAW IN ACTION

Buying Beer on the Internet

While his parents were away from home on vacation, Hunter Butler, a minor, used a credit card in his name to order 12 bottles of beer through Beer Across America's Internet site on the World Wide Web. When his mother, Lynda Butler, returned home she found several bottles from the shipment of beer remaining in the refrigerator. Lynda Butler then filed a civil lawsuit against Beer Across America seeking damages under Section 6–5–70 of the Alabama Civil Damages Act. The Civil Damages Act provides for a civil action by the parent or guardian of a minor against anyone who knowingly sells or furnishes liquor to the minor. A threshold issue in the lawsuit was whether the sale of the beer had taken place in Alabama so that a court in Alabama would have personal jurisdiction over Beer Across America.

Beer Across America was an Illinois corporation involved in the marketing and sale of alcoholic beverages and other merchandise. The beer was brought by carrier from Illinois to Alabama. The sales invoice and shipping documents provided that the sale was FOB the seller, with the carrier acting as the buyer's agent. Moreover, the invoice included a charge for sales tax but no charge for beer tax; Alabama law requires that sales tax be collected for out-of-state sale of goods which are then shipped to Alabama but requires beer tax be collected only on sales within Alabama.

The court held that the sale arranged over the Internet took place in Illinois. The court noted that under the versions of the Uniform Commercial Code in effect in both Illinois and Alabama, a sale consists in the passing of title from the seller to the buyer. Title to goods passes at the time and place of the shipment when the contract does not require the seller to make delivery at the destination. Accordingly, ownership to the beer passed to Hunter Butler upon tender of the beer to the carrier. The court then transferred the case to the U.S. District Court for the Northern District of Illinois. *Butler v. Beer Across America,* 40 UCC Rep.2d 1008 (U.S.D.C. N.D. Ala. 2000).

the goods passes to the buyer when the seller completes his obligations as to delivery of the goods:

1. If the contract requires the seller to "ship" the goods to the buyer, then title passes to the buyer when the seller delivers conforming goods to the carrier.

2. If the contract requires the seller to "deliver" the goods to the buyer, title does not pass to the buyer until the goods are delivered to the buyer and tendered to him.

3. If delivery is to be made without moving the goods, then title passes at the time and place of contracting. An exception is made if title to the goods is represented by a document of title such as a warehouse receipt; then, title passes when the document of title is delivered to the buyer.

4. If the buyer rejects goods tendered to him, title reverts to the seller [2–401(4)].

Importance of Title At common law, most of the problems relating to risks, insurable interests in goods, remedies, and similar rights and liabilities were determined on the basis of who was the technical title owner at the particular moment the right or liability arose. Under the Code, however, the rights of the seller and buyer and of third persons are determined irrespective of the technicality of who has the title, unless the provision of the Code expressly refers to title.

Determination of who has title to the goods is important in instances in which the rights of the seller's or the buyer's creditors in the goods are an issue. Another instance in which the identity of the title holder may be important is in determining whether the seller's insurance policy covers a particular loss.

The *Cardwell* case, which follows, illustrates the application of these rules.

State of Connecticut v. Cardwell   718 A.2d 954 (Conn. Sup. Ct. 1998)

The State of Connecticut brought suit against Roderick Cardwell, a resident of Connecticut and the owner of Ticketworld, contending that he was engaged in "ticket scalping" in violation of Connecticut law. A Connecticut statute makes it an unfair or deceptive trade practice to sell tickets to sporting and entertainment events to be held in Connecticut to purchasers located in Connecticut, for a price more than $3 in excess of the price, including tax, printed on the face of the ticket, or fixed for admission.

Cardwell was engaged in the business of selling tickets to entertainment and sporting events to be held in Connecticut. Ticketworld operated from two locations, one in Hartford and one in Springfield, Massachusetts. In order to obtain business, Ticketworld advertised in newspapers, including newspapers that circulate in Connecticut. The advertisements that appeared in Connecticut newspapers instructed prospective purchasers to telephone the Hartford office of Ticketworld for tickets to events that would take place outside of Connecticut, and to telephone the Springfield office for tickets to events that would be held in Connecticut. In the event that a prospective customer telephoned the Hartford office for tickets to a Connecticut event, the prospective customer was instructed to telephone the Springfield office in order to purchase those tickets.

On many occasions, Ticketworld sold tickets to Connecticut events from its Springfield office for which it charged a price that exceeded the fixed price of the ticket, tax included, by more than $3. The trial court found, specifically, that Ticketworld (1) had charged Mary Lou Lupovitch $125 per ticket for tickets to an event at the Connecticut Tennis Court in New Haven, although those tickets had a fixed price of $32.50 per ticket; and (2) had charged Cyrilla Bergeron $137 per ticket for tickets to an event in Hartford, although those tickets had a fixed price of $53.50 per ticket. The court determined that Ticketworld, in selling these tickets for a price in excess of the fixed price for admission, had violated section 53–289. Consequently, it issued a permanent injunction prohibiting Cardwell from engaging in any activity within the state in connection with selling, offering for sale, attempting to sell, mailing or otherwise delivering, or advertising or promoting the sale of any ticket to an event to be held in Connecticut sold for a price more than $3 in excess of the fixed price of the ticket, including tax.

Cardwell appealed, contending that since he sold tickets to events in Connecticut only through Ticketworld's office in Springfield, Massachusetts, the "sales" did not take place in Connecticut and thus did not violate Connecticut law.

Berdon, Associate Justice

In Connecticut, the sale of goods is governed by the Connecticut Uniform Commercial Code—Sales (code). Under the code, a "sale" is defined as "the passing of title from the seller to the buyer for a price. . . ." Section 2–106(1). The code further provides that "[u]nless otherwise explicitly agreed title passes to the buyer at the time and place at which the seller completes his performance with reference to the physical delivery of the goods, despite any reservation of a security interest and even though a document of title is to be delivered at a different time or place. . . ." Section 2–401(2). In addition, the code provides that "if the contract requires or authorizes the seller to send the goods to the buyer but does not require him to deliver them at destination, title passes to the buyer at the time and place of shipment. . . ." Section 2–401(2)(a).

The latter provision reflects the distinction made by the code between "shipment" and "destination" contracts. Under the code, when a carrier is used to transport the goods sold, shipment contracts and destination contracts are the only two types of sales contracts recognized. Section 2–401(2). Furthermore, under the code, "[t]he 'shipment' contract is regarded as the [general rule]." Under a shipment contract, the seller is either required or authorized to ship the goods to the buyer, but is not required to deliver them at a particular destination, and delivery to the carrier constitutes delivery to the buyer. Section 2–401(2)(a). Under a destination contract,

the seller is required to deliver the goods to the buyer at the named destination and delivery occurs upon tender of the goods at that destination. A strong presumption against the creation of destination contracts is contained in the code such that, in the absence of specific proof of agreement by the seller to deliver the goods to a particular destination and to bear the attendant risk of loss until such delivery, a sales contract that merely provides that the goods will be shipped to a certain location will be deemed to be a shipment contract.

In this case, the contracts made by Cardwell for the sale of tickets do not contain any explicit agreement by Cardwell to deliver the goods to a particular destination or to bear the attendant risk of loss until such time as the goods are delivered. Therefore, the contracts at issue in this case are properly classified as shipment contracts. Because delivery of the goods to the carrier constitutes delivery to the buyer under a shipment contract, section 2–401(2)(a), with respect to each sale of tickets made by Cardwell, delivery is made to the post office or other commercial carrier, and hence to the buyer, within Massachusetts. As a result, the "sale" of the tickets, as defined by the code, occurs in Massachusetts. Consequently, the trial court's determination that Cardwell sells tickets within Connecticut, and thereby violates the Connecticut statute, was incorrect.

Judgment reversed in favor of Cardwell.

Title and Third Parties

Obtaining Good Title

A fundamental rule of property law is that a buyer cannot receive better title to goods than the seller had. If Thief steals a digital camera from Adler and sells it to Brown, Brown does not get good title to the camera, because Thief had no title to it. Adler would have the right to recover the camera from Brown. Similarly, if Brown sold the camera to Carroll, Carroll could get no better title to it than Brown had. Adler would have the right to recover the camera from Carroll.

Under the Code, however, there are several exceptions to the general rule that a buyer cannot get better title to goods than his seller had. The most important exceptions include the following: (1) a person who has a voidable title to goods can pass good title to a bona fide purchaser for value; (2) a person who buys goods in the regular course of a retailer's business usually takes free of any interests in the goods that the retailer has given to others; and (3) a person who buys goods in the ordinary course of a dealer's business takes free of any claim of a person who entrusted those goods to the dealer.

Transfers of Voidable Title

A seller who has a **voidable title** has the power to pass good title to a *good faith purchaser for value* [2–403(1)]. A seller has a voidable title to goods if he has obtained his title through fraudulent representations. For example, a person would have a voidable title if he obtained goods by impersonating another person or by paying for them with a bad check or if he obtained goods without paying the agreed purchase price when it was agreed that the transaction was to be a cash sale. Under the Code, **good faith** means "honesty in fact in the conduct or transaction concerned" [1–201(19)] and a buyer has given **value** if he has given any consideration sufficient to support a simple contract [1–201(44)].

For example, Jones goes to the ABC Appliance Store, convinces the clerk that he is really Clark, who is a good customer of ABC, and leaves with a DVD player charged to Clark's account. If Jones sells the DVD player to Davis, who gives Jones value for it and has no knowledge of the fraud that Jones perpetrated on ABC, Davis gets good title to the DVD player. ABC cannot recover the DVD player from Davis; instead, it must look for Jones, the person who deceived it. In this situation, both ABC and Davis were innocent of wrongdoing, but the law considers Davis to be the more worthy of its protection because ABC was in a better position to have prevented the wrongdoing by Jones and because Davis bought the goods in good faith and for value.

The same result would be reached if Jones had given ABC a check that later bounced and then sold the DVD player to Davis, who was a good faith purchaser for value. Davis would have good title to the DVD player, and ABC would have to pursue its right against Jones on the bounced check.

These principles are illustrated in the *Tempur-Pedic* case that follows.

Tempur-Pedic International, Inc. v. Waste to Charity, Inc.
62 UCC Rep.2d 457 (U.S.D.C., W.D. Ark. 2007)

Tempur-Pedic (TP) manufactures, markets, and distributes mattresses, pillows, cushions, slippers, and similar products through a network of authorized and approved retail distributors. Each mattress model references the TEMPUR-PEDIC mark in its name.

Mattresses sold in the ordinary course of business by authorized TP distributors are enclosed in a hypoallergenic cover, sealed in a plastic bag, and packed in cardboard boxes labeled with TP's registered trademarks. Goods packaged for charitable donations are packaged differently. The mattresses do not include the hypoallergenic cover and are not boxed in the cardboard boxes. Instead, the mattresses are wrapped in clear plastic, stacked on wooden pallets, and then the entire load is wrapped in another layer of heavy-duty plastic. There were similar differences between the packing of pillows and slippers intended for retail distribution and those intended for donation.

In 2005, TP decided to make a donation of approximately $15 million in mattress, slipper, and pillow inventory to Gulf Coast residents victimized by Hurricane Katrina. The donations included approximately 7,800 mattresses to Waste to Charity (WCT), which was supposed to distribute those products to Hurricane Katrina victims. On November 14, 2005, TP entered into a charitable donation agreement with Jack Fitzgerald and his company, WCT, to distribute mattresses, slippers, and pillows. As a recipient of charitable produce donations, WCT agreed to the following restrictions:

1. All products donated by Tempur-Pedic are not to be resold, distributed for sale or otherwise sold for profit in any venue.

***

5. Should you wish to dispose of the Tempur-Pedic Products or any of them, you will notify us and give us an opportunity to retrieve them or designate their disposition, and you will comply with any reasonable request for their disposition.

TP made approximately 50 deliveries of donated goods to WTC. After these deliveries were made, TP learned that the donated products were not being provided to Hurricane Katrina victims but were instead being sold for profit in violation of the terms of the charitable donation agreement. Fitzgerald represented that all the property donated by TP had been distributed to three charitable organizations, Operation Compassion, Rhema International, and Hope Ministries.

An investigation by TP, a consultant it hired, and the FBI discovered the donated mattresses being offered for sale in a variety of ways: from trucks parked in shopping centers, from a warehouse where WTC had stored some of the donations, by a number of individuals affiliated in various ways with the warehouse, and on eBay. When an effort to sell a large quantity of TP mattresses from a warehouse in Booneville, Arkansas, was uncovered by the FBI and TP, the owner of a company known as CSS, Inc., stepped forward and claimed to be the legitimate owner of the mattresses. It maintained that they were used TP mattresses that had been returned to TP pursuant to its full refund within 30 days policy and that because the mattresses could not be sold by TP again as new, TP had sold them to Action Distributors, Inc. (ADI). CSS said it had purchased the mattresses from ADI, a company that it had been doing business with for several years.

TP brought an action for replevin, breach of contract, and fraud against WTC and CSS, and sought a temporary restraining order enjoining any sale or other disposition of the mattresses until the case could be decided by the court. The district court judge, relying on a report and recommendation from the magistrate judge, issued the preliminary injunction. A critical question for the magistrate judge was whether TP was likely to prevail on its claim against CSS.

Marschewski, Magistrate Judge

The crux of the parties' arguments can be simply summarized. TP maintains WTC misappropriated the donated property and that a purchaser from a thief acquires no title against the true owner. It therefore contends CSS acquired no title to the mattresses. Alternatively, if the court determines WTC did obtain "voidable title" to the donated property, TP argues CSS is not a good-faith purchaser for value based on the circumstances surrounding the alleged sale.

In contrast, CSS maintains the provisions of the Uniform Commercial Code apply to the transaction and WTC held "voidable title" and could therefore pass good title to good-faith purchasers for value without knowledge of WTC's alleged fraudulent conduct. CSS maintains that having purchased its mattresses from ADI it is such a good-faith purchaser for value without knowledge of WTC's fraudulent conduct. CSS contends TP cannot, therefore, show a likelihood of success on the merits and the motion for a preliminary injunction must be denied.

The Uniform Commercial Code applies to all "transactions in goods." [2–102] A purchase is defined to include "taking by sale . . . gift, or any other voluntary transaction creating an interest in property." [1–201(32)]

Section 2–403 recognizes a legal distinction between a sale of stolen goods and a sale of goods procured through fraud. Absent exigent circumstances, one who purchases from a thief acquires no title as against the true owner. However, under section 2–403, the result is different when property obtained by fraud is conveyed to a bona fide purchaser.

Section 2–403 in applicable part provides as follows:

(1) A purchaser of goods acquires all title which his transferor had or had power to transfer except that a purchaser of a limited interest acquires rights only to the extent of the interest purchased. A person with voidable title has power to transfer a good title to a good faith purchaser for value. When goods have been delivered under a transaction of purchase the purchaser has such power even though

    (a) the transferor was deceived as to the identity of the purchaser; or

    (b) the delivery was in exchange for a check which is later dishonored; or

    (c) it was agreed that the transaction was to be a "cash sale"; or

    (d) the delivery was procured through fraud punishable as larcenous under the criminal law.

The good-faith purchaser exception is designed to promote finality in commercial transactions and thus encourage purchases and to foster commerce. It does so by protecting the title of a purchaser who acquires property for valuable consideration and who, at the time of the purchase, is without notice that the seller lacks valid and transferable title to the property.

Here, TP voluntarily gave the property to WTC. There is no showing that WTC was just a sham operation. From the evidence before the court, the court believes that WTC lawfully came into possession of the property. Thus, it appears clear that WTC did acquire voidable title to the donated property.

After the donations were made, TP has presented evidence that at least a portion of the donated products were sold at various places around the country rather than put to their intended charitable use. WTC, although it claimed no knowledge of the sales, had sufficient control over the property, at least with respect to the Bowling Green warehouse, to represent that it had moved slippers from it after it was discovered they were being sold from that facility.

With respect to the mattresses purchased by CSS from ADI, the issue becomes whether CSS was a good-faith purchaser. "Good faith" is defined to mean "honesty in fact in the conduct or transaction concerned. [1–201(19)]. . . . I conclude TP has shown a probability that it will succeed on the merits of establishing that CSS was not a good-faith purchaser for value of the mattresses.

A number of factors lead the court to this conclusion. First, the price of the mattresses was substantially below market value. The average price per mattress paid by CSS was $125. TP's witness testified that the value of these mattresses would be substantially above that figure and that some of these mattresses could go from $600 and up. Even a witness for the defendants acknowledged that the range of TP mattresses, on the Web page, would go from $600 to $1,995. Second, the terms of the purported sale were suspicious: all tags had been removed; while the mattresses were confirmed to be TP mattresses they could not be sold as such; no sales could be made to TP dealers; and the representation was made that TP has confirmed the mattresses would not have tags on them.

Third, both the timing of the attempted sales, and the use of a building material supplier re some of the offered sales, lends support to the conclusion that CSS was not a good-faith purchaser for value. Fourth, the president of CSS acknowledged that he knew TP did not authorize the sale of used mattresses. Fifth, the corporate charter of ADI had been revoked both before and during the relevant period of time. It should be noted that Michael H. Lowe was listed as the Agent for the defunct ADI corporation in New Jersey. This is the same individual that was operating the fork lift at the Boonville warehouse. Sixth, the president of CSS had done a Web search of another representative of ADI and the search revealed very negative information.

Motion for preliminary injunction granted.

Buyers in the Ordinary Course of Business

A person who buys goods in the ordinary course of business from a person dealing in goods of that type takes free of any security interest in the goods given by his seller to another person [9–307(1)]. **A buyer in ordinary course** is a person who in good faith and without knowledge that the sale to him is in violation of the ownership rights of a third party buys goods in the ordinary course of business of a person selling goods of that kind, other than a pawnbroker [1–201(9)].

For example, Brown Buick may borrow money from Bank in order to finance its inventory of new Buicks; in turn, Bank may take a security interest in the inventory to secure repayment of the loan. If Carter buys a new Buick from Brown Buick, he gets good title to the Buick free and clear of the Bank's security interest if he is a buyer in the ordinary course of business and without knowledge that the sale is in violation of a security interest. The basic purpose of this exception is to protect those who innocently buy from merchants and thereby to promote confidence in such commercial transactions. The exception also reflects the fact that the bank is more interested in the proceeds from the sale than in the inventory. Security interests and the rights of buyers in the ordinary course of business are discussed in more detail in Chapter 29, Security Interests in Personal Property.

Entrusting of Goods

A third exception to the general rule is that if goods are entrusted to a merchant who deals in goods of that kind, the merchant has the power to transfer all rights of the entruster to a buyer in the ordinary course of business [2–403(2)]. In the scenario presented at the beginning of this chapter, Paul takes his damaged bicycle for repair to a shop that sells and repairs bicycles. By mistake, a clerk in the bicycle shop sells the bicycle to Melissa. The bicycle shop can pass good title to Melissa, a buyer in the ordinary course of business. In such a case, Paul would have to sue the bicycle shop for damages for conversion of the bicycle; he could not get it back from Melissa. The purpose behind this rule is to protect commerce by giving confidence to buyers that they will get good title to the goods they buy from merchants in the ordinary course of business. However, a merchant-seller cannot pass

CONCEPT REVIEW

Title and Third Parties

General Rule	A seller cannot pass better title to goods than he has.
Exceptions to General Rule	1. A person who has voidable title to goods can pass good title to a bona fide purchaser for value.
	2. A buyer in the ordinary course of a retailer's business usually takes free of any interests in the goods that the retailer has given to others.
	3. A person who buys goods in the ordinary course of a dealer's business takes free of any claims of a person who entrusted those goods to the dealer.

good title to stolen goods even if the buyer is a buyer in the ordinary course of business. This is because the original owner did nothing to facilitate the transfer.

Risk of Loss

The transportation of goods from sellers to buyers can be a risky business. The carrier of the goods may lose, damage, or destroy them; floods, hurricanes, and other natural catastrophes may take their toll; thieves may steal all or part of the goods. If neither party is at fault for the loss, who should bear the risk? If the buyer has the risk when the goods are damaged or lost, the buyer is liable for the contract price. If the seller has the risk, he is liable for damages unless substitute performance can be tendered.

The common law placed the risk on the party who had technical title at the time of the loss. The Code rejects this approach and provides specific rules governing risk of loss that are designed to provide certainty and to place the risk on the party best able to protect against loss and most likely to be insured against it. Risk of loss under the Code depends on the terms of the parties' agreement, on the moment the loss occurs, and on whether one of the parties was in breach of contract when the loss occurred.

Terms of the Agreement

The contracting parties, subject to the rule of good faith, may specify who has the risk of loss in their agreement [2–509(4)]. This they may do directly or by using certain commonly accepted shipping terms in their contract. In addition, the Code has certain general rules on risk of loss that amplify specific shipping terms and control risk of loss in cases where specific terms are not used [2–509].

Shipment Contracts

If the contract requires the seller to ship the goods by carrier but does not require their delivery to a specific destination, the risk passes to the buyer when the seller delivers the goods to the carrier [2–509(1)(a)]. Shipment contracts are considered to be the normal contract where the seller is required to send goods to the buyer but is not required to guarantee delivery at a particular location.

The following are commonly used shipping terms that create shipment contracts:

1. *FOB (free on board) point of origin.* This term calls for the seller to deliver the goods free of expense and at the seller's risk at the place designated. For example, a contract between a seller located in Chicago and a buyer in New York calls for delivery FOB Chicago. The seller must deliver the goods at his expense and at his risk to a carrier in the place designated in the contract, namely Chicago, and arrange for their carriage. Because the shipment term in this example is FOB Chicago, the seller bears the risk and expense of delivering the goods to the carrier, but the seller is not responsible for delivering the goods to a specific destination. If the term is "FOB vessel, car, or other vehicle," the seller must load the goods on board at his own risk and expense [2–319(1)].

2. *FAS (free alongside ship).* This term is commonly used in maritime contracts and is normally accompanied by the name of a specific vessel and port—for example, "FAS Calgary [the ship], Chicago Port Authority." The

Ethics in Action

Perils of Entrusting Goods

Suppose you are the owner of a small jewelry store that sells new and antique jewelry. A customer leaves a family heirloom—an elaborate diamond ring—with you for cleaning and resetting. By mistake, a clerk in your store sells it to another customer. What would you do? If you were the buyer of the ring and had given it to your fiancée as a gift and then were informed of the circumstances, what would you do?

---

seller must deliver the goods alongside the vessel *Calgary* at the Chicago Port Authority at his own risk and expense [2–319(2)].

3. *CIF (cost, insurance, and freight).* This term means that the price of the goods includes the cost of shipping and insuring them. The seller bears this expense and the risk of loading the goods [2–320].

4. *C & F.* This term is the same as CIF, except that the seller is not obligated to insure the goods [2–320].

The *Windows, Inc.* case, which follows, provides an example of the risk borne by a buyer in a shipment contract.

Windows, Inc. v. Jordan Panel Systems Corp.
38 UCC Rep.2d 267 (2nd Cir. 1999)

Windows, Inc., was a fabricator and seller of windows, based in South Dakota. Jordan Panel Systems, Inc., was a construction subcontractor, which contracted to install window wall panels at an air cargo facility at JFK International Airport in New York City. Jordan ordered custom-made windows from Windows. The purchase contract specified that the windows were to be shipped properly packaged for cross-country motor freight transit and "delivered to New York City."

Windows constructed the windows according to Jordan's specifications. It arranged to have them shipped to Jordan by a common carrier, Consolidated Freightways Corp., and delivered them to Consolidated intact and properly packaged. During the course of shipment, however, the goods sustained extensive damage. Much of the glass was broken and many of the window frames were gouged and twisted. Jordan's president signed a delivery receipt noting that approximately two-thirds of the shipment was damaged due to "load shift." Jordan, seeking to stay on its contractor's schedule, directed its employees to disassemble the window frames in an effort to salvage as much of the shipment as possible.

Jordan made a claim with Consolidated for damages it had sustained as a result of the casualty, including labor costs from its salvage efforts and other costs from Jordan's inability to perform its own contractual obligations on schedule. Jordan also ordered a new shipment from Windows, which was delivered without incident.

Jordan did not pay Windows for either the first shipment of damaged windows or the second, intact shipment. Windows filed suit to recover payment from Jordan for both shipments. Jordan counterclaimed, seeking incidental and consequential damages resulting from the damaged shipment. Windows then brought a third-party claim against Consolidated. Windows settled its claims against Consolidated, and Windows later withdrew its claims against Jordan.

The district court granted Windows' motion for summary judgment on Jordan's counterclaim against Windows for incidental and consequential damages. Jordan appealed.

Leval, Circuit Judge

Jordan seeks to recover incidental and consequential damages pursuant to UCC section 2–715. Under that provision, Jordan's entitlement to recover incidental and consequential damages depends on whether those damages "result[ed] from the seller's breach." A destination contract is covered by section 2–503(3); it arises where "the seller is *required to deliver* at a particular destination." Section 2–504 (emphasis added). Under a shipment contract, the seller must "put the goods in the possession of such a carrier and make such a contract for their transportation as may be reasonable having regard to the nature of the goods and other circumstances of the case." Section 2–504(a).

Where the terms of an agreement are ambiguous, there is a strong presumption under the UCC favoring shipment contracts. Unless the parties "expressly specify" that the contract requires the seller to deliver to a particular destination, the contract is generally construed as one for shipment.

Jordan's confirmation of its purchase order, by letter to Windows dated September 22, 1993, provided, "All windows to be shipped properly crated/packaged/boxed suitable for cross-country motor freight transit and delivered to New York City." We conclude that this was a shipment contract rather than a destination contract.

To overcome the presumption favoring shipment contracts, the parties must have explicitly agreed to impose on Windows the obligation to effect delivery at a particular destination. The language of this contract does not do so. Nor did Jordan use any commonly recognized industry term indicating that a seller is obligated to deliver the goods to the buyer's specified destination.

Given the strong presumption favoring shipment contracts and the absence of explicit terms satisfying both requirements for a destination contract, we conclude that the contract should be deemed a shipment contract.

Under the terms of its contract, Windows thus satisfied its obligations to Jordan when it put the goods, properly packaged, into the possession of the carrier for shipment. Upon Windows' proper delivery to the carrier, Jordan assumed the risk of loss, and cannot recover incidental or consequential damages from the seller caused by the carrier's negligence.

The allocation of risk is confirmed by the terms of UCC section 2–509(1)(a), entitled "Risk of Loss in the Absence of Breach." It provides that where the contract "does not require [the seller] to deliver [the goods] at a particular destination, the risk of loss passes to the buyer when the goods are duly delivered to the carrier." UCC section 2–509(1)(a). As noted earlier, Jordan does not contest the court's finding that Windows duly delivered conforming goods to the carrier. Accordingly, as Windows had already fulfilled its contractual obligations at the time the goods were damaged and Jordan had assumed the risk of loss, there was no "seller's breach" as is required for a buyer to claim incidental and consequential damages under section 2–715. Summary judgment for Windows was therefore proper.

We are mindful of Jordan's concern that it not be left "holding the bag" for the damages it sustained through no fault of its own. The fact that Jordan had assumed the risk of loss under section 2–509(1)(a) by the time the goods were damaged does not mean it is without a remedy. Under the 1906 Carmack Amendment to the Interstate Commerce Act, a buyer or seller has long been able to recover directly from an interstate common carrier in whose care their goods are damaged. Liability attaches unless the carrier can establish one of several affirmative defenses; for example, by showing that the damage was the fault of the shipper or caused by an Act of God.

Judgment affirmed in favor of Windows.

Destination Contracts If the contract requires the seller to deliver the goods to a specific destination, the seller bears the risk and expense of delivery to that destination [2–509(1)(b)]. The following are commonly used shipping terms that create destination contracts:

1. *FOB destination.* An FOB term coupled with the place of destination of the goods puts the expense and risk of delivering the goods to that destination on the seller [2–319(1)(b)]. For example, a contract between a seller in Chicago and a buyer in Phoenix might call for shipment FOB Phoenix. The seller must ship the goods to Phoenix at her own expense, and she also retains the risk of delivery of the goods to Phoenix.

2. *Ex-ship.* This term does not specify a particular ship, but it places the expense and risk on the seller until the goods are unloaded from whatever ship is used [2–322].

3. *No arrival, no sale.* This term places the expense and risk during shipment on the seller. If the goods fail to arrive through no fault of the seller, the seller has no further liability to the buyer [2–324].

For example, a Chicago-based seller contracts to sell a quantity of Weber grills to a buyer FOB Phoenix, the buyer's place of business. The grills are destroyed en route when the truck carrying the grills is involved in an accident. The risk of the loss of the grills is on the seller, and the buyer is not obligated to pay for them. The seller may have the right to recover from the trucking company, but between the seller and the buyer, the seller has the risk of loss. If the contract had called for delivery FOB the seller's manufacturing plant, then the risk of loss would have been on the buyer. The buyer would have had to pay for the grills and then pursue any claims that he had against the trucking company.

Goods in the Possession of Third Parties

If the goods are in the possession of a bailee and are to be delivered without being moved, the risk of loss passes to the buyer upon delivery to him of a negotiable document of title for the goods; if no negotiable document of title has been used, the risk of loss passes when the bailee indicates to the buyer that the buyer has the right to the possession of the goods [2–509(2)]. For example, if Farmer sells Miller a quantity of grain currently stored at Grain Elevator, the risk of loss of the grain will shift from Farmer to Miller (1) when a negotiable warehouse receipt for the grain is delivered to Miller or (2) when Grain Elevator notifies Miller that it is holding the grain for Miller.

Risk Generally

If the transaction does not fall within the situations discussed above, the risk of loss passes to the buyer upon *receipt* of the goods if the seller is a merchant; if the seller is not a merchant, then the risk of loss passes to the buyer upon the *tender of delivery* of the goods to the buyer [2–509(3)]. If Jones bought a television set from ABC Appliance on Monday, intending to pick it up on Thursday, and the set was stolen on Wednesday, the risk of loss remained with ABC. However, if Jones had purchased the set from his next-door neighbor and could have taken delivery of the set on Monday (i.e., delivery was tendered then), the risk of loss was Jones's.

Effect of Breach on Risk of Loss

When a seller tenders goods that do not conform to the contract and the buyer has the right to reject the goods, the risk of loss remains with the seller until any defect is cured or until the buyer accepts the goods [2–510(1)]. Where the buyer rightfully revokes his acceptance of goods, the risk of loss is with the seller to the extent that any loss is not covered by the buyer's insurance [2–510(2)]. This rule gives the seller the benefit of any insurance carried by the buyer.

For example, if Adler bought a new Buick from Brown Buick that he later returned to Brown because of serious defects in it and if through no fault of Adler the automobile was damaged while in his possession, then the risk of loss would be with Brown. However, if Adler had insurance on the automobile covering the damage to it and recovered from the insurance company, Adler would have to turn the insurance proceeds over to Brown or use them to fix the car before returning it to Brown.

When a buyer repudiates a contract for goods and those goods have already been set aside by the seller, the risk of loss stays with the buyer for a commercially reasonable time after the repudiation if the seller's insurance is not sufficient to cover any loss [2–510(3)].

Suppose Popcorn, Inc., contracts to buy Farmer's entire crop of popcorn. Farmer picks the popcorn, shells it, stores it in his barn, and informs Popcorn, Inc., that he is preparing to have the popcorn shipped to it. Popcorn, Inc., then tells Farmer that it does not intend to honor the contract because the market for popcorn has dropped and it can acquire the popcorn it desires at a lower price from someone else. Shortly thereafter, but before Farmer has an opportunity to find another buyer for the popcorn, there is a fire in his barn and the popcorn is ruined when it pops prematurely. If Farmer's insurance covers only part of the loss, Popcorn, Inc., must bear the rest of the loss.

Insurable Interest

The general practice of insuring risks is recognized and provided for under the Code. A buyer may protect his interest in goods that are the subject matter of a sales contract before he actually obtains title. The buyer obtains an insurable interest in existing goods when they are identified as the goods covered by the contract even though they are in fact nonconforming. The seller retains an insurable interest in goods so long as he has either title or a security interest in them [2–501(2)].

Sales on Trial

A common commercial practice is for a seller of goods to entrust possession of goods to a buyer to either give the buyer an opportunity to decide whether or not to buy them or to try to resell them to a third person. The entrusting may be known as a **sale on approval,** a **sale or return,** or a **consignment,** depending on the terms of the entrusting. Occasionally, the goods may be damaged, destroyed, or stolen, or the creditors of the buyer may try to claim them; on such occasions, the form of the entrusting will determine whether the buyer or the seller had the risk of loss and whether the buyer's creditors can successfully claim the goods.

Sale on Approval

In a sale on approval, the goods are delivered to the buyer with an understanding that he may use or test them for the purpose of determining whether he wishes to buy them [2–326(1)(a)]. In a sale on approval, neither the risk of loss nor title to the goods passes to the buyer until he accepts the goods. The buyer has the right to use the goods in any manner consistent with the purpose of the trial, but any unwarranted exercise of ownership over the goods is considered to be

Risk of Loss

The point at which the risk of loss or damage to goods identified to a contract passes to the buyer is as follows:

1. If there is an agreement between the parties, the risk of loss passes to the buyer at the time they have agreed to.

2. If the contract requires the seller to ship the goods by carrier but does not require that the seller guarantee their delivery to a specific destination (shipment contract), the risk of loss passes to the buyer when the seller has delivered the goods to the carrier and made an appropriate contract for their carriage.

3. If the contract requires the seller to guarantee delivery of the goods to a specific destination (destination contract), the risk of loss passes to the buyer when the seller delivers the goods to the designated destination.

4. If the goods are in the hands of a third person and the contract calls for delivery without moving the goods, the risk of loss passes to the buyer when the buyer has the power to take possession of the goods—for example, when he receives a document of title.

5. In any situation other than those noted above where the seller is a merchant, the risk of loss passes to the buyer on his receipt of the goods.

6. In any situation other than those noted above where the seller is not a merchant, the risk of loss passes to the buyer on the tender of delivery to the buyer by the seller.

7. When a seller tenders goods that the buyer lawfully could reject because they do not conform to the contract description, the risk of loss stays on the seller until the defect is cured or the buyer accepts them.

8. When a buyer rightfully revokes acceptance of goods, the risk of loss is on the seller from the beginning to the extent it is not covered by the buyer's insurance.

9. If a buyer repudiates a contract for identified, conforming goods before risk of loss has passed to the buyer, the buyer is liable for a commercially reasonable time for any loss or damage to the goods that is not covered by the seller's insurance.

an acceptance of the goods. Similarly, if the buyer fails to notify the seller of his election to return the goods, he is considered to have accepted them [2–327]. For example, if Dealer agrees to let Hughes take a new automobile home to drive for a day to see whether she wants to buy it and Hughes takes the car on a two-week vacation trip, Hughes will be considered to have accepted the automobile because she used it in a manner beyond that contemplated by the trial and as if she were its owner. If Hughes had driven the automobile for a day, decided not to buy it, and parked it in her driveway for two weeks without telling Dealer of her intention to return it, Hughes would also be deemed to have accepted the automobile.

Once the buyer has notified the seller of his election to return the goods, the return of the goods is at the seller's expense and risk. Because the title and risk of loss of goods delivered on a sale on approval remain with the seller, goods held on approval are not subject to the claims of the buyer's creditors until the buyer accepts them [2–326].

Sale or Return

In a sale or return, goods are delivered to a buyer for resale with the understanding that the buyer has the right to return them [2–326(1)(b)]. Under a sale or return, the title and risk of loss are with the buyer. While the goods are in the buyer's possession, they are subject to the claims of his creditors [2–326 and 2–327]. For example, if Publisher delivers some paperbacks to Bookstore on the understanding that Bookstore may return any of the paperbacks that remain unsold at the end of six months, the transaction is a sale or return. If Bookstore is destroyed by a fire, the risk of loss of the paperbacks was Bookstore's and it is responsible to Publisher for the purchase price. Similarly, if Bookstore becomes

The Global Business Environment

Risk of Loss in International Sales

Risk of loss is an important concept in the sale of goods—and takes on additional significance in international sales because of the substantial distances and multiple modes of transportation that may be involved. Between the time a contract is formed and the time the obligations of the parties are completed, the goods that are the subject of the contract may be lost, damaged, or stolen. Both the UCC and the Convention on Contracts for International Sale of Goods (CISG) explicitly address risk of loss in four different situations: (1) where goods are being held by the seller; (2) where goods are being held by a third person or bailee; (3) where goods are in transit; and (4) where goods are in the control of the buyer. Moreover, the CISG deals with risk of loss where goods have been sold or resold while in transit. Under both the UCC and the CISG, breach by a party may alter the basic rules regarding risk of loss.

Before discussing the CISG provisions, it is important to note that the definitions of some terms in the UCC differ from the meaning those terms may have in international trade. The International Chamber of Commerce has compiled a list of widely accepted international shipping terms in a document known as "INCOTERMS." The most recent version, INCOTERMS 2000, includes 13 different terms that are placed in four different categories, depending on the seller's responsibilities concerning the goods.

Under the first category (known as Group "E"), the seller's obligation is only to make the goods available to the buyer at the seller's place of business. This is referred to as an EXW, or EX Works, term. Risk passes from the seller to the buyer when the goods are placed at the buyer's disposal. Under the second category (known as Group "F"), the seller is required to deliver the goods to a carrier designated by the buyer. This category includes terms like "F.O.B." (Free on Board) and "F.A.S." (Free Along Side Ship). Passage of risk varies with the term.

Terms in the third category (Group "C") require the seller to contract for carriage of the goods but not to assume the risk of loss after shipment. Terms in the fourth category (Group "D") impose on the seller the costs and risks of bringing the goods to the country of destination. Under one such term, "D.A.F." (Delivered at Frontier), the seller must pay for the carriage of goods to some defined point after that where goods have been cleared for export in the country of origin but before the customs boundary of another identified, usually adjoining, country.

The CISG, like the UCC, provides a set of default rules governing risk of loss where the parties do not explicitly address risk of loss in their contract. However, it also permits parties to contract out of those rules. Parties to international agreements commonly utilize the INCOTERMS and incorporate them into contracts otherwise governed by the CISG. Thus, the INCOTERMS are used to define when risk of loss passes, and CISG, in turn, provides the legal consequences of the passage of the risk of loss in a particular case.

---

insolvent and is declared a bankrupt, the paperbacks will be considered part of the bankruptcy estate. If the buyer elects to return goods held on a sale or return basis, the return is at the buyer's risk and expense.

Sale on Consignment

Sometimes, goods are delivered to a merchant on consignment. If the merchant to whom goods are consigned maintains a place of business dealing in goods of that kind under a name other than that of the person consigning the goods, then the consignor must take certain steps to protect his interest in the goods or they will be subject to the claims of the merchant's creditors. The consignor must (1) make sure that a sign indicating the consignor's interest is prominently posted at the place of business, or (2) make sure that the merchant's creditors know that he is generally in the business of selling goods owned by others, or (3) comply with the filing provisions of Article 9 of the Code—Secured Transactions.

For example, Jones operates a retail music store under the name of City Music Store. Baldwin Piano Company delivers some pianos to Jones on consignment. If no notices are posted indicating Baldwin's interest in the pianos, if Jones is not generally known to be selling from a consigned inventory, and if Baldwin does not file its interest with the recording office pursuant to Article 9 of the Code, then the goods are subject to the claims of Jones's creditors. This is crucial to Baldwin because it may have intended to retain title. However, the Code treats a consignment to a person doing business under a name other than that of the consignor as a "sale or return" [2–326(3)]. If Jones did business as the Baldwin Piano Company, Baldwin's interest would be protected from the claims of Jones's creditors without the need for Baldwin to post a sign or to file under Article 9.

The risk taken by a consignor who does not take appropriate steps to protect his interest is illustrated in the following case, *In re Corvette Collection of Boston, Inc.*

In Re Corvette Collection of Boston, Inc.
294 B.R. 409 (U.S.B.C., S.D. Fla. 2003)

Corvette Collection of Boston, Inc., was a used Corvette dealership located in Pompano Beach, Florida. Corvette Collection owned some of its inventory and held the rest on consignment. In addition, the company also serviced Corvettes and sold Corvette parts. On November 20, 2001, Corvette Collection (the debtor) filed a voluntary Chapter 11 (reorganization) petition in bankruptcy. On January 22, 2002, the petition was converted to a case under Chapter 7 (liquidation).

On the date the petition in bankruptcy was filed, Corvette Collection had in its possession six Corvettes that had been consigned to it by The Corvette Experience, Inc. Three of the cars were assigned pursuant to written consignment agreements and three by oral consignment agreements. In each case, the cars were owned by individuals who held title to them, and the cars had been assigned to Corvette Experience. Corvette Experience had not filed a UCC financing statement or recorded a security agreement with the Florida Department of Motor Vehicles (see Chapter 29—Security Interests in Personal Property for a discussion of these concepts). Rather, Corvette Experience withheld the respective Corvette certificates of title prior to placing the vehicles on consignment with Corvette Collection. Pursuant to the consignment agreements, if Corvette Collection had sold the Corvettes at the minimum price permitted by the agreement, Corvette Experience would have been required to turn over the titles.

The Bankruptcy Trustee asserted that the six vehicles were consigned by Corvette Experience to Corvette Collection and that because Corvette Experience did not properly perfect its consignment interest by complying with the Florida UCC section 2–326, Corvette Collection held the consigned Corvettes "sale or return," thereby subjecting the vehicles to the claims of Corvette Collection's creditors. On the other hand, Corvette Experience contended that because the creditors of Corvette Collection were aware that it was substantially engaged in selling the consigned vehicles, the vehicles were held by Corvette Collection "sale on approval." As such, the Corvettes would not be subject to the claims of Corvette Collection's creditors.

Friedman, Bankruptcy Judge

Consignments are governed by UCC section 2–326(1). This provision recognizes two types of consignments. In a "sale on approval" transaction, the consignor delivers goods to the consignee primarily for use. Goods held on approval are not subject to the claims of the consignee's creditors until acceptance, and the consignor need not take any action to protect its interest in the goods. On the other hand, in a "sale or return" consignment, the consignor delivers goods to the consignee primarily for resale. Goods held "sale or return" are subject to the claims of the consignee's creditors. More importantly, pursuant to section 544(a) of the Bankruptcy Code, all goods held by the debtor sale or return become assets of the estate.

With regard to consigned goods, there is a presumption that goods are held by the debtor "sale or return"; therefore, the goods are subject to the claims of the debtor's creditors. However, the consignor may overcome this presumption by proving (1) he or she has complied with an applicable law providing for a consignor's interest or the like to be evidenced by a sign, or (2) he or she established that the person conducting the business is generally known by his or her creditors to be substantially engaged in selling the goods of others, or (3) he or she complied with the filing provisions of the chapter on secured transactions. In the instant case, it is undisputed that Corvette Experience had not complied with two of the exceptions since they neither recorded a UCC–1 financing statement nor placed

a sign above the Corvettes stating that they were held on consignment. Thus, the second issue before this Court is whether the debtor is a company that is generally known by its creditors to be substantially engaged in selling the goods of others.

Since there is a presumption that the debtor holds the Corvettes on a "sale or return" basis, the burden of proof is on Corvette Experience to prove by a preponderance of the evidence that the debtor was generally known by its creditors to be substantially engaged in the sale of goods of others. Corvette Experience must prove by a preponderance of the evidence (1) that the consignee is substantially engaged in selling the goods of others and (2) that the debtor is generally known by the creditors of the consignee that this is the case. Both prongs of this test must be satisfied in order for the consignor to overcome the presumption that the goods are held "sale or return."

As to the first prong, whether the debtor was substantially engaged in selling the goods of others, Corvette Experience presented no evidence regarding the debtor's inventory on the petition date. The parties stipulated that the debtor was a used Corvette dealership that also serviced Corvettes and sold Corvette parts. The parties also stipulated that the debtor owned some of its used Corvettes and consigned the rest. To meet their burden, Corvette Experience, experienced consignors, testified that most of the debtor's inventory was held on consignment and that everybody who wanted to sell a Corvette knew that the debtor primarily sold consigned vehicles. This testimony falls well short of Corvette Collection's burden of proving by a preponderance of the evidence that the consignee was substantially engaged in selling the goods of others.

With regard to the second prong, Corvette Experience, the defendants, also fell short of its burden. To satisfy the "generally known" prong of the test, the consignors must prove that a majority of the debtor-consignee's creditors were aware that the consignee was substantially engaged in selling the goods of others, that is, consignment sales. That majority is determined by the number of creditors, not by the amount of their claims.

According to the debtor's schedules, consignors constitute only a portion of the debtor's creditors. The debtor has a number of trade creditors such as utility companies and parts suppliers. The trustee presented the testimony of representatives of two trade creditors, Inter-Tel Technologies (a telephone leasing company) and Dixie Staffing (an employee staffing company), both of whom testified that they had no knowledge as to whether the debtor owned any inventory on consignment. Corvette Experience provided no evidence to establish that a traditional trade creditor would believe that the debtor was substantially engaged in the sale of goods of others. In fact, Mr. Finley testified that it would have been detrimental to the debtor had third parties known that the debtor was a consignment shop because potential purchasers would try to contact the Corvette owners directly to "cut out the middle-man" and obtain a better price. Furthermore, in order to satisfy their burden of proof, Corvette Experience testified that they believed Corvette Collection's creditors perceived the debtor to be a consignment shop. This testimony is insufficient to satisfy Corvette Experience's burden of proof. Testimony as to general knowledge in the industry is insufficient to prove knowledge by a majority of creditors.

This case is factually similar to *In re Valley Media, Inc., (Bankr. D. Del. 2002).* In *Valley Media,* some of the debtor's vendors had entered into consignment arrangements with the debtor prior to the debtor's filing for bankruptcy. The consigned inventory was commingled with all of the other inventory of the debtor at two warehouse locations. No signs were posted at the warehouses, and there were no signs or markings on the consigned inventory indicating that the inventory had been obtained on a consignment basis. When the debtor moved the bankruptcy court to sell all of its inventory, the consignment vendors objected arguing that they owned their consignment inventory by virtue of their consignment arrangements. The court observed that the consignors could have obtained a prior interest in their consigned goods if they had either (1) filed UCC–1 financing statements identifying their goods as required under UCC Article 9, or (2) proved that the consignee was generally known by its creditors to be substantially engaged in selling the goods of others.

In the instant case, like in *Valley Media,* Corvette Experience could have obtained a prior interest in their consigned goods if they had either filed UCC–1 financing statements identifying their goods as required under UCC Article 9, or proved that the debtor was generally known by its creditors to be substantially engaged in selling the goods of others. However, the instant Corvette Experience did neither. They did not file an appropriate UCC financing statement, and they did not prove by a preponderance of the evidence that the debtor was substantially engaged in selling the goods of others. Therefore, the debtor held the Corvettes on a "sale or return" basis at the time the debtor filed for bankruptcy. Accordingly, the Corvettes are subject to the claims of the debtor's creditors, and the trustee may, for the benefit of the estate, sell the Corvettes free and clear of Corvette Experience's (and its assignees') interests.

Judgment in favor of the Bankruptcy Trustee.

Problems and Problem Cases

1. Star Coach, L.L.C., is in the business of converting sport utility vehicles and pickup trucks into custom vehicles. Star Coach performs the labor involved in installing parts supplied by other companies onto vehicles owned by dealers. Heart of Texas Dodge purchased a new Dodge Durango from Chrysler Motors and entered into an agreement with Star coach whereby Star Coach would convert the Durango to a Shelby 360 custom performance vehicle and then return the converted vehicle to Heart of Texas Dodge. The manufacturer delivered the dealer's Durango to Star Coach and, over a period of several months, Star Coach converted the vehicle using parts supplied by another company, Performance West. Several months later, Star Coach delivered the vehicle to Heart of Texas Dodge, and Heart of Texas Dodge paid Star Coach the contract price of $15,768 without inspecting the vehicle. Two days later, Heart of Texas Dodge

inspected the vehicle and concluded that the workmanship was faulty. It stopped payment on the check and Star Coach filed suit against Heart of Texas Dodge. One of the issues in the litigation was whether the UCC applied to the contract in this case. Does the UCC apply to a contract for the conversion of a van that involves both goods and services?

2. Keith Russell, a boat dealer, contracted to sell a 19-foot Kinsvater boat to Robert Clouser for $8,500. The agreement stipulated that Clouser was to make a down payment of $1,700, with the balance due when he took possession of the boat. According to the contract, Russell was to retain possession of the boat in order to install a new engine and drive train. While the boat was still in Russell's possession, it was completely destroyed when it struck a seawall. Transamerica, Russell's insurance company, refused to honor Russell's claim for the damages to the boat.

   The insurance policy between Transamerica and Russell covered only watercraft under 26 feet in length that were not owned by Russell. Transamerica argued that the boat was not covered by the policy since Russell still owned it at the time of the accident. Did Russell have title to the boat at the time of the accident?

3. In December 1990, Arlene Bradley entered Alsafi Oriental Rugs and advised the owner that she was an interior decorator and that she was interested in selling some of his rugs to one of her customers. Alsafi did not know Bradley and had never done business with her. However, he allowed her to take three rugs out on consignment with the understanding that she would return them if her customer was not interested. In fact, however, Bradley was not obtaining the rugs for a "customer" but was instead working for another individual, Walid Salaam, a rug dealer.

   A friend of Bradley's had introduced her to Salaam earlier. Salaam had advised the two women that he was the owner of a recently closed oriental rug store that he was attempting to reopen. He offered to teach them how to become decorators and told them that when his store reopened, they could operate out of the store. Salaam advised them that until he got his store restocked, however, he wanted them to "check out" rugs on approval from other rug dealers in town. As they had no experience with oriental rugs, Salaam instructed them which rugs to look for. He then instructed them to go to rug dealers in Memphis and

advise them that they were interior decorators with customers that wanted to purchase oriental rugs.

After Bradley obtained possession of the three rugs from Alsafi, she turned them over to Salaam, who in turn took them to a pawnshop operated by the American Loan Company. There Salaam pawned the rugs, obtaining approximately $5,000 after filling out the required paperwork. Salaam failed to redeem the rugs. Following the default, the pawnshop gave the appropriate notice that it intended to dispose of them.

In April 1991 Alsafi learned that his rugs were at the pawnshop. After visiting the pawnshop and identifying the three rugs as his, he brought suit to recover possession of them.

Was Alsafi entitled to recover the rugs from the pawnshop?

4. On May 8, 2000, Paul Sutton delivered his 1995 Harley Davidson Model FLF motorcycle to Super Bikes to allow it to display the motorcycle for sale. Sutton retained the keys and the certificate of title to the motorcycle, but the keys were not necessary to drive it. The written consignment agreement provided that Sutton would receive $18,000 on the sale of the motorcycle and that Super Bikes would retain everything over that; there also was a pencil notation of "low dollars 17,000." On August 17, 2000, Mike Snider paid Super Bikes $17,500, the price it asked for the vehicle, and took possession of the motorcycle. He was aware that Super Bikes held it on consignment but was not aware of the consignor or of any of the terms of the consignment. Snider testified that Super Bikes said it would deliver the title to him as soon as his check cleared.

   Super Bikes never paid Sutton for the motorcycle. Sutton discovered that Snider had the motorcycle and sent letters to both Snider and to the owners of Super Bikes demanding either the return of possession of the motorcycle or the payment of $17,500. Sutton then brought a lawsuit against Snider seeking return of the motorcycle. Snider asserted that he had obtained good title to the motorcycle as a buyer in the ordinary course of business from a dealer in goods of that kind. Did Snider get good title to the motorcycle as a buyer in the ordinary course of business?

5. Legendary Homes, a home builder, purchased various appliances from Ron Mead T.V. & Appliance, a retail merchant selling home appliances. They were intended

to be installed in one of Legendary Homes' houses and were to be delivered on February 1. At 5 o'clock on that day, the appliances had not been delivered. Legendary Homes' employees closed the home and left. Sometime between 5 and 6:30, Ron Mead delivered the appliances. No one was at the home so the deliveryman put the appliances in the garage. During the night, someone stole the appliances. Legendary Homes denied it was responsible for the loss and refused to pay Ron Mead for the appliances. Ron Mead then brought suit for the purchase price. Did Legendary Homes have the risk of loss of the appliances?

6. The Cedar Rapids YMCA bought a large number of cases of candy from Seaway Candy under an agreement by which any unused portion could be returned. The YMCA was to sell the candy to raise money to send boys to camp. The campaign was less than successful, and 688 cases remained unsold. They were returned to Seaway Candy by truck. When delivered to the common carrier, the candy was in good condition; when it arrived at Seaway four days later, it had melted and was completely worthless. Seaway then brought suit against the YMCA to recover the purchase price of the candy spoiled in transit. Between Seaway and the YMCA, which had the risk of loss?

7. In June, Ramos entered into a contract to buy a motorcycle from Big Wheel Sports Center. He paid the purchase price of $893 and was given the papers necessary to register the cycle and get insurance on it. Ramos registered the cycle but had not attached the license plates to it. He left on vacation and told the salesperson for Big Wheel Sports Center that he would pick up the cycle on his return. While Ramos was on vacation, there was an electric power blackout in New York City and the cycle was stolen by looters. Ramos then sued Big Wheel Sports Center to get back his $893. Did Big Wheel Sports Center have the risk of loss of the motorcycle?

8. On December 14, 1998, Shepherd Machinery Co. sold five Caterpillar tractors to O.C.T. Equipment. At the time of the sale, the tractors were parked at the Keen Transport yard in Santa Paula, California, and were shown to Mike Clark, O.C.T.'s representative, on that date. The parties agreed, among other things, that all of the tractors would be painted yellow and that a winch would be installed on one of the tractors before delivery. An invoice was faxed to O.C.T. on December 22,

and it wired payment to Shepherd later that day. The tractors remained at Keen from the time Clark viewed them and agreed to purchase them. Shepherd sent instructions to Keen not to release any of the tractors to O.C.T.'s carrier until Keen had received a bill of lading for each tractor and a release from a Shepherd employee.

On December 23, Shepherd sent O.C.T. a fax indicating that the tractors would be ready for pickup on December 28. O.C.T. had asked that each of the tractors be checked for antifreeze levels because of a concern they would be going through high elevations en route to Oklahoma. The levels were checked and sent to O.C.T. The list showed that tractor JAK0012531 had no antifreeze level, and Keen was asked to recheck that tractor for antifreeze.

Keen contacted Shepherd on December 31 to advise it that on the prior evening, before the tractor had been picked up, a security guard at Keen had driven tractor JA0012531 at a point when it had no antifreeze/coolant in it and that the engine was burned up and ruined. Shepherd then reported the problem to O.C.T. and also took the position that O.C.T. owned the tractor and would have to work with Keen to resolve the damage. O.C.T. refused to take delivery of the damaged tractor, and after it and Shepherd were unable to agree on who had the risk of loss to the tractor, O.C.T. brought suit to recover from Shepherd the $43,000 it had paid Shepherd for the tractor. Had the risk of loss passed to O.C.T. at the time the tractor was damaged while in the hands of the bailee?

9. Edd and Diane Auclair maintained a place of business in Covington County, Alabama, where they operated a gun shop and convenience store named Heath Grocery and Final Chapter Firearms. In November 1989, Luke Jackson delivered about 70 firearms to the Auclairs to sell on consignment. The consignment agreement provided as follows: "I Edd Auclair have received a number of guns, of which a list will be attached and I will sign. As I sell a gun I will pay James E. 'Luke' Jackson or Betty King with them giving me a receipt for that particular gun. If something should happen to Luke Jackson the guns are to be returned to Betty King or at that time Betty King and Edd Auclair can enter into an agreement. If something should happen to Edd Auclair, Diane agrees to return all guns that have not been paid for to Luke Jackson or Betty King and pay for any that has [sic] been sold." The agreement was signed by Jackson, King, and the Auclairs.

On June 28, 1990, the Auclairs filed a petition in bankruptcy under Chapter 11 of the Bankruptcy Act. Shortly thereafter Jackson removed the firearms he had consigned from the Auclairs' store. The bankruptcy trustee representing the Auclairs' creditors claimed that the firearms were the property of the bankruptcy estate. Were the firearms that Jackson had delivered to the Auclairs pursuant to the consignment agreement subject to the claims of the Auclairs' creditors?

Online Research

Using the Internet to Buy a Computer

Assume you are considering the purchase of a new computer. Use the Internet to access the Web site of the manufacturer of the computer you are considering. Ascertain the following: (1) the purchase price of the model you prefer; (2) the cost of having the computer shipped to you; (3) the warranties, if any, that will be provided; and (4) whether you would be able to get a full refund if you do not find the computer acceptable after it is delivered to you.

chapter 20

PRODUCT LIABILITY

In recent years, newly developed prescription pain relievers known as COX-2 Inhibitors proved to be especially effective for arthritis sufferers and other persons who experienced chronic pain. Various pharmaceutical companies, including Merck & Co., produced such pain relievers. Merck's heavily advertised Vioxx brand became one of the most widely prescribed COX-2 Inhibitors and generated very large sales figures from 1999 to 2004. As 2004 wore on, however, news stories began to focus on a growing number of complaints that certain Vioxx users had experienced a heart attack or a stroke after using Vioxx over a prolonged period of time.

With the public reading and hearing about a possible—and previously undisclosed—relationship between long-term Vioxx use and greater risk of heart attack or stroke, there were calls in some quarters for the federal Food and Drug Administration (FDA) to order the removal of Vioxx from the market. Similar views were expressed regarding other firms' COX-2 Inhibitors. Merck decided, on its own, to cease Vioxx sales after a 2004 Merck study indicated a potential link between Vioxx use of at least 18 months and an increased heart attack or stroke risk. (The FDA later required the withdrawal from the market of Bextra, one of two COX-2 Inhibitors produced by Pfizer, Inc. Pfizer's Celebrex remained on the market but was subject to a requirement to warn users of a possible increase in their heart attack and stroke risks.)

By mid-2005, Merck faced approximately 4,000 pending or threatened lawsuits in which former Vioxx users or their estates contended that Vioxx use had caused the users to experience heart attacks or strokes. In these product liability cases, the plaintiffs typically alleged that Merck had known of such a link as far back as 1997 but had failed to inform physicians and their patients of the potential danger. The first of these cases to go to trial resulted in an August 2005 verdict in favor of the estate of Robert Ernst, a Vioxx user who experienced a heart arrhythmia that proved fatal. The verdict of approximately $250 million in damages—$25 million compensatory and $225 million punitive—shocked Merck, whose spokespersons asserted that the jury had erred in finding the existence of adequate proof of a specific causation link between Vioxx use and Ernst's heart condition. In addition, Merck protested that no study had linked Vioxx use with heart arrhythmia, as opposed to other cardiac problems. Despite its vow to appeal the verdict, and its later success in several of the Vioxx cases brought against it, Merck found itself having to decide whether to continue following its previously announced policy of aggressively defending against all Vioxx cases instead of attempting to settle them. In November 2007, Merck agreed to set up a fund of $4.85 billion to settle Vioxx-related claims against the company. Approximately 45,000 of 60,000 potentially eligible claimants had enrolled in the settlement plan as of March 2008.

As you read this chapter, think about the preceding paragraphs and consider the following questions:

- On what product liability theory or theories would the plaintiffs in the Vioxx cases have been relying?
- What legal elements must the plaintiffs prove in order to win the Vioxx cases?
- Are punitive damages routinely awarded, in addition to compensatory damages, in product liability cases? What would the plaintiff in the *Ernst* case have had to prove in order for punitive damages to have been assessed against Merck?

- If a manufacturer's product works well for most users but the manufacturer is aware that some users may experience harm as a result of using it, what would utilitarians and rights theorists say concerning whether the manufacturer has an ethical obligation to warn about the risk of harm or to suspend sales of the product? (You may wish to consult the discussion of ethical theories in Chapter 4 as you answer this question.)

SUPPOSE YOU HOLD AN executive position in a firm that makes products for sale to the public. One of your concerns would be the company's exposure to civil liability for defects in those products. In particular, you might worry about legal developments that make such liability more likely or more expensive. In other situations, however, such developments might appeal to you—especially if *you* are harmed by defective products you purchase as a consumer. You might also appreciate certain liability-imposing legal theories if your firm wants to sue a supplier that has sold it defective products.

Each of these situations involves the law of *product liability,* the body of legal rules governing civil lawsuits for losses and harms resulting from a defendant's furnishing of defective goods. After sketching product liability law's historical evolution, this chapter discusses the most important *theories of product liability* on which plaintiffs rely. The second part of the chapter considers certain legal problems that may be resolved differently under different theories of recovery.

The Evolution of Product Liability Law

The 19th Century   A century or so ago, the rules governing suits for defective goods were very much to manufacturers' and other sellers' advantage. This was the era of *caveat emptor* (let the buyer beware). In contract cases involving defective goods, there usually was no liability unless the seller had made an express promise to the buyer and the goods did not conform to that promise. In negligence cases, the "no liability without fault" principle was widely accepted, and plaintiffs often had difficulty proving negligence because the necessary evidence was under the defendant's control. In both contract and negligence cases, finally, the doctrine of "no liability outside privity of contract"—that is, no liability without a direct contractual relationship between plaintiff and defendant—often prevented plaintiffs from recovering against parties with whom they had not directly dealt.

The laissez-faire approach that influenced public policy and the law helped lead to such prodefendant rules. One illustration of that approach was the notion that manufacturers and other sellers should be contractually bound only when they deliberately assumed such liability by making a promise to someone with whom they dealt directly. Another factor limiting manufacturers' liability for defective products was the perceived importance of promoting industrialization by preventing potentially crippling damage recoveries against infant industries. Even though the 19th century's approach to product liability was prodefendant, some commentators maintain that most plaintiffs were not especially disadvantaged by the applicable legal rules. Goods tended to be simple, so buyers often could inspect them for defects. Before the emergence of large corporations late in the 19th century, moreover, sellers and buyers often were of relatively equal size, sophistication, and bargaining power. Thus, they could deal on a relatively equal footing.

The 20th and 21st Centuries   Today, laissez-faire values, while still influential, do not pack the weight they once did. With the development of a viable industrial economy, there has been less perceived need to protect manufacturers from liability for defective goods. The emergence of long chains of distribution has meant that consumers often do not deal directly with the parties responsible for defects in the products they buy. Because large corporations tend to dominate the economy, consumers are less able to bargain freely with the corporate sellers with which they deal. Finally, the growing complexity of goods has made buyers' inspections of the goods more difficult.

In response to these changes, product liability law has moved from its earlier *caveat emptor* emphasis to a stance of *caveat venditor* (let the seller beware). To protect consumers, modern courts and legislatures effectively intervene in private contracts for the sale of goods and sometimes impose liability regardless of fault. As a result, sellers and manufacturers face greater liability and higher damage assessments for defects in their products. Underlying the shift toward *caveat venditor* is the belief that sellers, manufacturers, and their insurers are better able to bear the economic costs associated with product defects, and that they usually can pass on these costs through higher prices. Thus, the economic risk associated with defective products has been effectively spread throughout society, or "socialized."

The Current Debate over Product Liability Law
Modern product liability law and its socialization-of-risk rationale have come under increasing attack over the past three decades. Such attacks often focus on the difficulty sellers and manufacturers encounter in obtaining product liability insurance and the increased costs of such insurance. Some observers blame insurance industry practices for these developments, whereas others trace them to the increased liability and greater damage recoveries just discussed. Whatever their origin, these problems have sometimes put sellers and manufacturers in a difficult spot. Businesses unwilling or unable to buy expensive product liability insurance run the risk of being crippled by large damage awards unless they self-insure, which can be an expensive option. Firms that purchase insurance, on the other hand, often must pay higher prices for it. In either case, the resulting costs may be difficult to pass on to consumers. Those costs may also deter the development and marketing of innovative new products.

For these reasons and others, recent years have witnessed many efforts to scale back the proplaintiff aspects of modern product liability law. This is one aspect of the tort reform movement discussed in Chapter 7. However, despite calls for federal reform bills, Congress had not made significant changes in product liability law as of the time this book went to press in 2008. As we note later in this chapter, however, some tort reform efforts have occurred in the states.

Theories of Product Liability Recovery

Some theories of product liability recovery are contractual and some are tort-based. The contract theories involve a product **warranty**—an express or implied promise about the nature of the product sold. In warranty cases, plaintiffs claim that the product failed to live up to the seller's promise. In tort cases, on the other hand, plaintiffs usually argue that the defendant was negligent or that strict liability should apply.

Express Warranty

Creation of an Express Warranty UCC section 2–313(1) states that an **express warranty** may be created in any of three ways.

1. *If an affirmation of fact or promise* regarding the goods becomes part of the basis of the bargain (a requirement to be discussed shortly), there is an express warranty that the goods will conform to the affirmation or promise. For instance, if a computer manufacturer's Web site says that a computer has a certain amount of memory, this statement may create an express warranty to that effect.

2. Any *description* of the goods that becomes part of the basis of the bargain creates an express warranty that the goods will conform to the description. Descriptions include (1) statements that goods are of a certain brand, type, or model (e.g., a Hewlett-Packard laser printer); (2) adjectives that characterize the product (e.g., shatterproof glass); and (3) drawings, blueprints, and technical specifications.

3. Assuming it becomes part of the basis of the bargain, a *sample* or *model* of goods to be sold creates an express warranty that the goods will conform to the sample or model. A sample is an object drawn from an actual collection of goods to be sold, whereas a model is a replica offered for the buyer's inspection when the goods themselves are unavailable.

The first two types of express warranties may often overlap; also, each may be either written or oral. "Magic" words such as *warrant* or *guarantee* are not necessary for creation of an express warranty.

Value, Opinion, and Sales Talk Statements of *value* ("This chair would bring you $2,000 at an auction") or *opinion* ("I think this chair might be an antique") do not create an express warranty. The same is true of statements that amount to *sales talk* or *puffery* ("This chair is a good buy"). No sharp line separates such statements from express warranties. In close cases, a statement is more likely to be an express warranty if it is specific rather than indefinite, if it is stated in the sales contract rather than elsewhere,[1] or if it is unequivocal rather than hedged or qualified. The relative knowledge possessed by the seller and the buyer also matters. For instance, a

---

[1]Parol evidence rule problems may arise in express warranty cases. For example, a seller who used a written contract may argue that the rule excludes an alleged oral warranty. On the parol evidence rule, see Chapter 16.

car salesperson's statement about a used car may be more likely to be an express warranty where the buyer knows little about cars than where the buyer is another car dealer. The *Felley* case, which follows shortly, discusses some of the express warranty issues addressed so far, as well as the important basis-of-the-bargain requirement to which we now turn.

The Basis-of-the-Bargain Requirement

Under pre-UCC law, there was no recovery for breach of an express warranty unless the buyer significantly relied on that warranty in making the purchase. The UCC, however, requires—though ambiguously—that the affirmation, promise, description, or sample or model have become *part of the basis of the bargain* in order for an express warranty to be created. Some courts read the Code's basis-of-the-bargain test as saying that significant reliance still is necessary. Others require only that the seller's warranty have been a *contributing factor* in the buyer's decision to purchase. Still others do not require any specific reliance on the buyer's part.

Advertisements

Statements made in advertisements, catalogs, or brochures may be express warranties. However, such sources often are filled with sales talk. Basis-of-the-bargain problems may arise if it is unclear whether or to what degree the statement induced the buyer to make the purchase. For example, suppose that the buyer read an advertisement containing a supposed express warranty one month before actually purchasing the product.

Multiple Express Warranties

What happens when a seller gives two or more express warranties and those warranties arguably conflict? UCC section 2–317 says that such warranties should be read as consistent with each other and as cumulative if this is reasonable. If not, the parties' intention controls. In determining that intention (1) exact or technical specifications defeat a sample, a model, or general descriptive language; and (2) a sample defeats general descriptive language.

As indicated by the *Felley* case, which follows, any seller—professional or not—may make an express warranty. When such a warranty has been breached (because the goods were not as warranted), the plaintiff who demonstrates resulting losses is entitled to compensatory damages.

Felley v. Singleton   705 N.E.2d 930 (Ill. App. 1999)

On June 8, 1997, Brian Felley went to the home of Thomas and Cheryl Singleton to look at a used car that the Singletons had offered for sale. The car, a 1991 Ford Taurus, had approximately 126,000 miles on it. Felley test-drove the car and discussed its condition with the Singletons. The Singletons told him that the car was in "good mechanical condition" and that they had experienced no brake problems. This was a primary consideration for Felley, who purchased the car from the Singletons for $5,800. Felley soon began experiencing problems with the car. On the second day after he bought it, he noticed a problem with the clutch. Over the next few days, the clutch problem worsened to the point where he was unable to shift the gears, no matter how far he pushed in the clutch pedal. He had to pay $942.76 for the removal and repair of the clutch. Within the first month that Felley owned the car, it developed serious brake problems, the repairs of which cost Felley more than $1,400.

Felley brought a small claims action against the Singletons, claiming that they had made and breached an express warranty to him. At trial, an expert witness testified that based on his examination of the car and discussion with Felley about the car and other factors, it was his opinion that the car's brake and clutch problems probably existed when Felley bought the car. The trial court ruled in Felley's favor and ordered the Singletons to pay him $2,343.03. The Singletons appealed.

Bowman, Presiding Justice

On appeal, the Singletons contend that the trial court erred when it determined that the statements they made to Felley regarding the condition of the car constituted an express warranty. The Singletons argue that their statements were nothing more than expressions of opinion in the nature of puffery that could not properly be deemed an express warranty.

Section 2–313 of the Uniform Commercial Code governs the formation of express warranties by affirmation in the context of a sale of goods such as a used car. Section 2–313 provides, in relevant part:

(1) Express warranties by the seller are created as follows:

(a) Any affirmation of fact or promise made by the seller to the buyer which relates to the goods and becomes part of the basis of the bargain creates an express warranty that the goods shall conform to the affirmation or promise.

(2) It is not necessary to the creation of an express warranty that the seller use formal words such as "warrant" or "guarantee" or that he have a specific intention to make a warranty, but an affirmation merely of the value of the goods or a statement purporting to be merely the seller's opinion or commendation of the goods does not create a warranty.

The Singletons point to subsection (2) of section 2–313 as support for their argument that their statements to Felley did not constitute an express warranty. The Singletons also cite the official comments to subsection (2), which state:

Concerning affirmations of value or a seller's opinion or commendation under subsection (2), the basic question remains the same: What statements of the seller have in the circumstances and in objective judgment become part of the basis of the bargain? As indicated above, all of the statements of the seller do so unless good reason is shown to the contrary. The provisions of subsection (2) are included, however, since common experience discloses that some statements or predictions cannot fairly be viewed as entering into the bargain.

In the Singletons' view, their statements to Felley cannot fairly be viewed as entering into the bargain. They assert that they are not automobile dealers or mechanics with specialized knowledge of the brake and clutch systems of the car and therefore their statements were merely expressions of a vendor's opinion that did not constitute an express warranty. Felley responds that the trial court correctly determined that the Singletons' statements were affirmations of fact that became a basis of the bargain and therefore constituted an express warranty. In support of his position, Felley cites *Weng v. Allison* (Ill. App. 1997).

Whether an express warranty exists is a factual issue to be determined by the trier of fact. Consequently, it is well settled that a reviewing court may not reverse a trial court judgment regarding the existence of an express or implied warranty merely because different conclusions might have been drawn. *Weng* involved the sale of a 10-year-old used car for $800. The car had 96,000 miles on it. When the buyers attempted to drive the car home, it failed to operate properly. An inspection at an automobile dealership revealed that the car was unsafe to drive and needed repairs costing about $1,500. The seller had told the

buyers that the car was "mechanically sound," "in good condition," "a reliable car," "a good car," and had "no problems." The trial court ruled that such representations could not become part of the basis of the bargain unless the buyer relied on them and that no one could reasonably rely on such statements with respect to such a car. In *Weng,* the appellate court disagreed and reversed the trial court. The appellate court determined that the representations made by the sellers were affirmations of fact that created an express warranty. The court stated that affirmations of fact made during a bargaining process regarding the sale of goods are presumed to be part of the basis of the bargain unless clear affirmative proof to the contrary is shown; that a showing of reliance on the affirmations by the buyer is not necessary for the creation of an express warranty; and that the seller has the burden to establish by clear affirmative proof that the affirmations did not become part of the basis of the bargain. The court also stated that the seller may be accountable for breach of warranty where affirmations are a basis of the bargain and the goods fail to conform to the affirmations.

We believe that the principles set out in *Weng* are correct. We agree with the *Weng* court that, in the context of a used car sale, representations by the seller such as the car is "in good mechanical condition" are presumed to be affirmations of fact that become part of the basis of the bargain. Because they are presumed to be part of the basis of the bargain, such representations constitute express warranties, regardless of the buyer's reliance on them, unless seller shows by clear affirmative proof that the representations did not become part of the basis of the bargain. In this case, it is undisputed that Felley asked the Singletons about the car's mechanical condition and the Singletons responded that the car was in good mechanical condition. Under the foregoing principles, the Singletons' representations are presumed to be affirmations of fact that became a part of the basis of the bargain. Nothing in the record indicates that the Singletons made a clear and affirmative showing that their representations did not become part of the basis of the bargain. The trial court, as the fact finder in this case, could have reasonably found that the Singletons asserted a fact of which Felley was ignorant when they told Felley that the car was in good mechanical condition.

Judgment in favor of Felley affirmed.

Implied Warranty of Merchantability

An **implied warranty** is a warranty created by operation of law rather than the seller's express statements. UCC section 2–314(1) creates the Code's **implied warranty of merchantability** with this language: "[A] warranty that the goods shall be merchantable is implied in a contract for their sale if the seller is a merchant with respect to goods of that kind." This is a clear example of the modern tendency of legislatures to intervene in private contracts to protect consumers.

In an implied warranty of merchantability case, the plaintiff argues that the seller breached the warranty by selling unmerchantable goods and that the plaintiff should therefore recover damages. Under section 2–314, such claims can succeed only where the seller is a *merchant with respect to goods of the kind sold.*[2] An accounting professor's sale of homemade preserves and a hardware store owner's sale of a used car, for example, do not trigger the implied warranty of merchantability.

UCC section 2–314(2) states that, to be merchantable, goods must at least (1) pass without objection in the trade; (2) be fit for the ordinary purposes for which such goods are used; (3) be of even kind, quality, and quantity within each unit (case, package, or carton); (4) be adequately contained, packaged, and labeled; (5) conform to any promises or statements of fact made on the container or label; and (6) in the case of fungible goods, be of fair average quality. The most important of these requirements is that the goods must be *fit for the ordinary purposes for which such goods are used.* (In the *Moss* case, which appears later in the chapter, the implied warranty of merchantability was made but was not breached, because the relevant goods were suitable for ordinary purposes.) As indicated by the *Crowe* case,

which follows below, the goods need not be perfect to be fit for their ordinary purposes. Rather, they need only meet the reasonable expectations of the average consumer.

This broad, flexible test of merchantability is almost inevitable given the wide range of products sold in the United States today and the varied defects they may present. Still, a few generalizations about merchantability determinations are possible. Goods that fail to function properly or that have harmful side effects normally are not merchantable. A computer that fails to work properly or that destroys the owner's programs, for example, is not fit for the ordinary purposes for which computers are used. In cases involving allergic reactions to drugs or other products, courts may find the defendant liable if it was reasonably foreseeable that an appreciable number of consumers would suffer the reaction. As revealed by *Newton v. Standard Candy Co.,* which appears immediately after the *Crowe* case, there is disagreement over the standard for food products that are alleged to be unmerchantable because they contain harmful objects or substances. Under the *foreign–natural* test, the defendant is liable if the object or substance is "foreign" to the product, but not liable if it is "natural" to the product. Increasingly, however, courts ask whether the food product met the consumer's reasonable expectations.

---

[2]The term *merchant* is defined in Chapter 9.

Crowe v. CarMax Auto Superstores, Inc.   612 S.E.2d 90 (Ga. App. 2005)

In October 2002, Tina and Thad Crowe purchased a 1999 Dodge Durango automobile from CarMax Auto Superstores, Inc. They received a 30-day/1,000-mile express warranty from CarMax. In addition, the Crowes purchased an 18-month/18,000-mile "Mechanical Repair Agreement" (MRA). The obligated party on this extended warranty was a corporation other than CarMax. Over the course of the next year, the Crowes brought the vehicle to CarMax and other repair facilities numerous times for a variety of repairs. Some of these repairs are discussed in the edited version of the court's opinion that appears below. All repairs within the original and extended warranty periods were done at little or no cost to the Crowes. However, the Crowes lost confidence in the vehicle because of the numerous times repairs had been necessary. In May 2003, the Crowes sued CarMax, contending that CarMax had breached the implied warranty of merchantability. After the trial court granted summary judgment in favor of CarMax, the Crowes appealed to the Georgia Court of Appeals.

Adams, Judge

We recently considered the implied warranty of merchantability [in] *Soto v. CarMax Auto Superstores,* 611 S.E.2d 108 (Ga. App. 2005):

Under [a Georgia statute], "a warranty that the goods shall be merchantable is implied in a contract for their sale if the seller is a merchant with respect to goods of that kind." This warranty protects consumers from defects or conditions existing at the time of sale. . . . [I]t is clear that "the implied warranties warrant against defects or conditions existing at

the time of sale, but [they] do not provide a warranty of continuing serviceability." [Case citation omitted.] It follows that proof that the [vehicle] was defective *when it was sold* is an essential element of [a] claim for breach of the implied warranty of merchantability.

The Crowes contend the trial court erred by finding that they did not meet their burden of showing that a jury question exists concerning whether the vehicle was defective at the time of sale. We find no error. Although the vehicle was first returned to CarMax just five days after it was sold [shortly before mid-October 2002], the record shows that those repairs were primarily to remedy cosmetic defects that CarMax agreed to fix at the time of sale. The Crowes returned the car again on October 22, after what they contend was 11 days of actual use. (The odometer reading on that date was 41,536. At the time of purchase it was 40,376, indicating the car had been driven over 1,100 miles.) The problems noted on that visit were that the vehicle was consuming massive amounts of oil, that the instrument panel lights were flickering, and that the four-wheel-drive illumination light was not working. Tina Crowe testified that the problems were fixed on that visit.

The vehicle was returned to CarMax on November 13, 2002, because the "check engine" light was on. The repair ticket indicated that "false codes" were detected and removed. However, the problem with the check engine light reappeared in January 2003, and the vehicle was returned to CarMax. At this time a broken ground wire was found. Tina Crowe testified the problem was fixed to her satisfaction, as was a problem with the rear windshield wiper, which was remedied by replacing the wiper motor.

On the January visit, it was also noted that the vehicle was jerking and the engine was revving up to 6,000 rpm when [the car was being driven]. Tina Crowe testified that the problem with the engine revving persisted for several months and that she returned the car for repairs several times before the control module was replaced and the problem fixed in April 2003. The record shows that during this same period the engine was running rough, but that problem was attributed to carbon build-up in the cylinders and was also remedied. Tina Crowe testified she did not take the vehicle back to CarMax after the MRA expired, but instead took it to another facility for repair when it began stalling out in June 2003. At that time, a fuel system tune-up was performed. [A] speed sensor was replaced in August, and a ball bearing was replaced on the front of the car in October 2003. At that time, the Crowes had owned the vehicle a little over a year, and the odometer reading was at 65,621 miles, indicating the car had been driven over 25,000 miles

during [the Crowe's ownership of the car]. Tina Crowe testified that at the time of her deposition in December 2003 there were no current problems with the car.

Based on this evidence, the trial court found that the Crowes failed to establish that the vehicle was defective when sold. We agree that this evidence does not present a jury question on this essential element of their claim. Although the vehicle was repaired on numerous occasions over the course of the first year of ownership, . . . for the most part these repairs were for different items or concerns on each occasion, and the problems were all remedied at the time the car was first brought in or on a subsequent visit. And although the Crowes argue strenuously that at least some evidence of a defect at the time of sale is shown by the fact that the car had to be returned for repairs after it was driven for just 11 days, the record shows that the primary complaint at that time was that the vehicle was consuming massive amounts of oil. [T]hat problem was remedied on that repair visit and did not recur. Moreover, although the vehicle had only been owned for a short period, it had already been driven in excess of 1,100 miles. The recurring problem with the engine revving was not detected until about three months later, and at that time the car had been driven almost 5,000 more miles. Although it took several attempts, that problem was also fixed. We note also that by the time the bearings had to be replaced in October 2003, the car had been driven over 25,000 miles since it was purchased about 13 months previously. Moreover, at the time of Tina Crowe's deposition in December 2003, there were no current problems with the car.

Under these facts, we agree that no defect has been shown to exist at the time of purchase. [T]o find otherwise would require the jury to rely on speculation or conjecture, improper bases for imposing liability. The trial court did not err in granting summary judgment [in favor of CarMax].

Trial court's grant of summary judgment to defendant affirmed.

Newton v. Standard Candy Co.   2008 U.S. Dist. LEXIS 21886 (D. Neb. 2008)

Standard Candy Co., a Tennessee firm, produces candy bars, including one known as the "Goo Goo Cluster." The Goo Goo Cluster candy bar contains peanuts provided to Standard Candy by an outside supplier. When Nebraska resident James Newton II purchased a Goo Goo Cluster and bit into it, he encountered what he claimed to be an undeveloped peanut. Newton maintained that biting the undeveloped peanut caused him to experience a damaged tooth as well as recurring jaw-locking and hearing loss problems. Relying on diversity of citizenship jurisdiction, Newton filed a breach of implied warranty of merchantability lawsuit against Standard Candy in the U.S. District Court for the District of Nebraska. Standard Candy moved for summary judgment in its favor.

Bataillon, Chief District Judge

On a motion for summary judgment, the question before the court is whether the record, when viewed in the light most favorable to the nonmoving party, shows that there is no genuine issue as to any material fact and that the moving party is entitled to judgment as a matter of law.

Standard Candy argues there are two potential theories of recovery for Newton: (1) the "foreign-natural" doctrine, and (2) the "reasonable expectation of the consumer" test. [Asserting] that there are no clear cases in Nebraska dealing with this issue, [Standard Candy] relies on cases from other [states in an effort] to show that no matter what doctrine Nebraska follows, Newton would not win [his breach of implied warranty of merchantability claim]. Standard Candy contends that Newton must produce an expert under either of these theories and has failed to do so. [Newton's witness list contains] two dental experts, but he has not listed any experts regarding an undeveloped peanut.

The "foreign-natural" doctrine provides there is no liability if the food product is natural to the ingredients, whereas liability exists [for resulting injuries] if the substance is foreign to the ingredients. *See, e.g., Mitchell v. T.G.I. Fridays,* 748 N.E.2d 89, 93 (Ohio App. 2000) (applying both tests, but concluding that a consumer who eats meat dishes knows there might be bones present under the foreign-natural doctrine). Standard Candy argues that if Nebraska follows this doctrine, it is clearly not liable. Newton's injuries were a result of a peanut, which is part of the ingredients found in a Goo Goo Cluster.

Likewise, under the "reasonable expectation of the consumer" doctrine, Standard Candy argues that Newton cannot assert liability. *Jackson v. Nestle-Beich, Inc.,* 589 N.E.2d 547, 548 (Ill. 1992). In the *Jackson* case, the court stated: "The reasonable expectation test provides that, regardless whether a substance in a food product is natural to an ingredient thereof, liability will lie for injuries caused by the substance where the consumer of the product would not reasonably have expected to find the substance in the product." Standard Candy argues that under this test, Newton would [have been] reasonably aware of peanuts in a Goo Goo Cluster candy bar. Further, Standard Candy contends that this is not a fact issue, but is a legal one. *See Mitchell* (clam shell piece in a clam strip was, as a matter of law, under either foreign-natural test or reasonable expectation test, reasonably expected to be there by the consumer); *Allen v. Grafton,* 164 N.E.2d 167, 174–75 (1960) (oyster shell in fried oysters did not create liability); *Koperwas v. Publix Supermarkets, Inc.,* 534 So.2d 872, 873 (Fla. App. 1988) (clam shell in clam chowder known to consumer and can be expected to reasonably guard against it); *Ex parte Morrison's Cafeteria of Montgomery, Inc.,* 431 So.2d 975, 979 (Ala. 1983) (bone in fish filet not [a basis for liability]).

In response to Standard Candy's motion for summary judgment, . . . Newton argues that [the supposed] undeveloped peanut [in the Goo Goo Cluster was] much like a rock. [Although Newton did not identify an expert witness who could testify on his behalf about undeveloped peanuts,] Newton took the deposition of Scott Sherry, [a Standard Candy employee on whom Standard Candy relies to make determinations concerning suitability of peanuts for use in Standard Candy products]. Sherry [testified] that when peanuts have skins on them, it [is] difficult to find peanuts that should not be used. He also [stated that he] knows there is a risk of an undeveloped peanut in [Standard Candy's products] . . . but that Standard Candy . . . does nothing to reinspect beyond what is done by [Standard Candy's peanuts supplier]. When he attempted to cut through one peanut in Newton's candy wrapper during the deposition, Sherry was unable to initially do so. He determined that [the peanut] looked more like a burnt peanut [than an undeveloped one]. [Sherry] agreed that this peanut was either undeveloped or overcooked, which made it rock-like. [He also conceded] in his deposition that Standard Candy knew as far back as 1997 that rock-like peanuts were [sometimes] included in the candy bars.

Newton also took the deposition of Zhaneta Shraybman, who has worked for Standard Candy since 2002 and deals with incoming claims [by consumers against the company]. She testified as to exhibits showing injuries as far back as 1991 where people damaged their teeth on hard or rock-like peanuts in the Goo Goo Clusters candy bar.

Newton argues that this court should adopt the reasonable expectation test, as even Standard Candy admits it is the more modern and accepted approach. Newton cites a series of cases in his brief indicating disfavor with the foreign-natural approach. Further, he argues that there is no need for an additional expert in this case. The two employees of Standard Candy [should] be sufficient, argues Newton, to make his case.

The court concludes that the motion for summary judgment must be denied. There are significant factual disputes that must be decided by the jury. The court also finds that Newton does not necessarily need an expert [on undeveloped peanuts] to prove his case. The testimony of Standard Candy's employees, Sherry and Shraybman, [is] sufficient to establish the existence of both burnt and undeveloped peanuts. Mr. Sherry will be able to testify as to his knowledge regarding undeveloped peanuts based on his work observations. In addition, he might very well qualify as an expert in this regard. Additionally, Ms. Shraybman . . . will be permitted to testify . . . based on [her] experience working for Standard Candy.

Standard Candy's motion for summary judgment denied; case to proceed to trial.

Implied Warranty of Fitness

UCC section 2–315's **implied warranty of fitness for a particular purpose** arises where (1) the seller has reason to know a particular purpose for which the buyer requires the goods; (2) the seller has reason to know that the buyer is relying on the seller's skill or judgment for the selection of suitable goods; and (3) the buyer actually relies on the seller's skill or judgment in purchasing the goods. If these tests are met, there is an implied warranty that the goods will be fit for the buyer's *particular* purpose. Any seller—merchant or nonmerchant—may make this implied warranty, the breach of which will give rise to liability for damages.

In many fitness warranty cases, buyers effectively put themselves in the seller's hands by making their needs known and by saying that they are relying on the seller to select goods that will satisfy those needs. This may happen, for example, when a seller sells a computer system specially manufactured or customized for a buyer's particular needs. Sellers also may be liable when the circumstances reasonably indicate that the buyer has a particular purpose and is relying on the seller to satisfy that purpose, even though the buyer fails to make either explicit. However, buyers may have trouble recovering if they are more expert than the seller, submit specifications for the goods they wish to buy, inspect the goods, actually select them, or insist on a particular brand.

As indicated in *Moss v. Batesville Casket Co.*, which follows shortly, the implied warranty of fitness differs from the implied warranty of merchantability. The tests for the creation of each warranty plainly are different. Under section 2–315, moreover, sellers warrant only that the goods are fit for the buyer's *particular* purposes, not the *ordinary* purposes for which such goods are used. If a 400-pound man asks a department store for a hammock that will support his weight but is sold a hammock that can support only average-sized people, there is a breach of the implied warranty of fitness but no breach of the implied warranty of merchantability. Depending on the facts of the case, therefore, one of the implied warranties may be breached but the other is satisfied, both implied warranties may be breached, or, as in *Moss*, neither ends up being breached.

Moss v. Batesville Casket Co.   935 So.2d 393 (Miss. Sup. Ct. 2006)

Nancy Moss Minton, a Mississippi resident, died on March 7, 1999. Her four adult children became the plaintiffs in the lawsuit described below and will be referred to as "the plaintiffs" during this summary of the facts giving rise to their case. The plaintiffs engaged Ott & Lee Funeral Home, a Mississippi firm, to handle the arrangements for their mother's burial. From the models on Ott & Lee's showroom floor, the plaintiffs selected a cherry wood casket manufactured by Batesville Casket Co. According to the deposition testimony later provided by each of the plaintiffs, aesthetic reasons played a key role in the choice of the cherry wood casket. The casket "looked like" their mother and "suited her" because all the furniture in her home was cherry wood. The plaintiffs contended that Ott & Lee told them the casket was "top of the line."

At the time the wooden casket was selected, Ott & Lee informed the plaintiffs that unlike a metal casket, a wooden casket could not be sealed. The plaintiffs testified in their depositions that Ott & Lee so informed them and that at Ott & Lee's suggestion, they chose to use a concrete vault with the wooden casket. According to the plaintiffs, Ott & Lee said the vault would keep the pressure of the dirt off the casket and would prevent water from reaching the casket. Ott & Lee made no representations to the plaintiffs about the ability of a wooden casket to preserve the remains contained inside it. The plaintiffs made no inquiry about whether the casket could or would preserve the remains.

The wooden casket chosen by the plaintiffs carried Batesville's written limited warranty, which specified that Batesville would replace the casket if, "at any time prior to the interment of this casket," defects in materials or workmanship were discovered. Thus, Batesville expressly warranted the casket until the time of Ms. Minton's burial, which took place on March 9, 1999. Later, believing that a medical malpractice claim may have existed against Ms. Minton's medical care providers, the plaintiffs had their mother's body exhumed for an autopsy on August 10, 2001. When the casket was exhumed, the plaintiffs observed visible cracks and separation in the casket. As the casket was removed, it began to dismantle. The body remained in the casket, and none of the plaintiffs saw the body.

After the exhumation, the plaintiffs filed suit against Ott & Lee and Batesville in a Mississippi court. The plaintiffs claimed that given the casket's cracked, separated, and partially dismantled condition, as revealed during the exhumation, the defendants had breached the implied warranties of merchantability and fitness for particular purpose. Ott & Lee and Batesville each moved for summary judgment. The plaintiffs presented affidavits from expert witnesses whose specialties were wood rot and adhesives, as opposed to caskets per se. These experts opined that the casket appeared as it did during the exhumation because of a probable failure of the adhesives used when it was manufactured. There was no evidence that Ms. Minton's body had not been properly preserved or that there was any damage to the body because of the cracks and separation in the casket. After the Mississippi circuit court granted the defendants' motions for summary judgment, the plaintiffs appealed to the Supreme Court of Mississippi.

Easley, Justice

The Mississippi Rules of Civil Procedure provide that summary judgment shall be granted by a court if there is no genuine issue as to any material fact and the moving party is entitled to a judgment as a matter of law. The moving party has the burden of demonstrating that there is no genuine issue of material fact in existence, while the non-moving party should be given the benefit of every reasonable doubt.

Implied Warranty of Fitness for Particular Purpose
Miss. Code Ann. § 75-2-315 establishes the foundation for the concept of an implied warranty for fitness for a particular purpose. The statute provides in pertinent part [that] "where the seller at the time of contracting has reason to know any particular purpose for which the goods are required and that the buyer is relying on the seller's skill or judgment to select or furnish suitable goods, there is an implied warranty that the goods shall be fit for such purpose." The warranty of fitness for a particular purpose does not arise unless there is reliance on the seller by the buyer, and the seller selects goods which are unfit for the particular purpose.

During discovery, depositions were taken from the plaintiffs. These depositions, which were provided to the trial court [in connection with] the motion for summary judgment, demonstrate that the plaintiffs purchased the wooden casket for its aesthetic value. [One plaintiff] testified:

> We spotted the cherry wood casket. [An Ott & Lee employee] walked us over there to it and we all decided, standing there—us four—that it looked like our mother. That's—I mean—she had everything in her house was cherry wood. I mean, it just looked like her. We asked . . . about the casket. I mean, I'm not stupid. I know a casket won't seal—a wood casket.

[Another plaintiff] testified: "We were looking at the different caskets, and when we saw the wood casket, we knew that we wanted this one for Mother because it looked just like her—a wood cherry casket. And we were just all . . . agreement with it." [A third plaintiff] testified that the reason he chose this casket was because his mother "just liked cherry wood furniture." He further stated [that] "[i]t just suited her."

In [its] conclusions of law, the trial court stated: "The court is convinced from the deposition testimony that the plaintiffs were well aware of the characteristic differences between a wooden casket as compared to a metal one, but that the former was selected because of their mother's love of cherry wood." The trial court found that "the fitness-purpose aspect was served during the time the decedent's body was placed in the casket and viewed by family members, loved ones, and friends at the funeral home."

Here, the evidence did not justify the submission of this case to a jury on the [implied] warranty of fitness for a particular purpose [claim]. Nothing in the record provides that the plaintiffs identified any particular purpose to the defendants when the casket was selected. Furthermore, assuming arguendo that the plaintiffs sought to preserve their mother's remains for some unspecified, indefinite period of time in the wooden casket, the record is completely devoid of any proof that the body had been damaged in any way by the alleged problems with the casket. As such, the burial had preserved the remains until the plaintiffs had their mother's remains unearthed and the autopsy performed. [T]he trial court did not err in granting summary judgment [in favor of the defendants on this implied warranty claim].

Implied Warranty of Merchantability Miss. Code Ann. § 75-2-314 establishes the statutory foundation for the concept of an implied warranty for merchantability. [The statute] provides in pertinent part: "[A] warranty that the goods shall be merchantable is implied in a contract for their sale if the seller is a merchant with respect to goods of that kind." [The statute also states that in order for goods to be merchantable, they must be] "fit for the ordinary purposes for which such goods are used."

The plaintiffs argue that, as reasonable consumers, they expected the casket to preserve the remains for an indefinite period of time. The defendants contend that even if the plaintiffs' theory that the ordinary purpose of the casket was to preserve the remains for an indefinite or some unknown period of time is accepted as true, there is no evidence in the record which indicates the remains were not in fact properly preserved for an indefinite or unknown period of time. When the remains were exhumed by the plaintiffs approximately two and one-half years after burial, the record reflects the remains were preserved. The plaintiffs present no claim that the remains had been damaged in any way by the cracks and separations. As such, the defendants assert the plaintiffs' alleged ordinary purpose of the casket was satisfied.

In *Craigmiles v. Giles,* 110 F. Supp. 2d 658, 662 (E.D. Tenn. 2000), the district court stated:

> A casket is nothing more than a container for human remains. Caskets are normally constructed of metal or wood, but can be made of other materials. Some have "protective seals," but those seals do not prevent air and bacteria from exiting. All caskets leak sooner or later, and all caskets, like their contents, eventually decompose.

Likewise, Batesville contends that the ordinary purpose of a wooden casket is to house the remains of the departed until interment. Batesville argues that the ordinary purpose includes uses which the manufacturer intended and those which are reasonably foreseeable. Accordingly, Batesville asserts that it would not be reasonably foreseeable that any customer would expect a wooden casket to preserve the remains for an indefinite period of time, as claimed by the plaintiffs.

[T]he record does not indicate that the plaintiffs ever stated a specified period of time that they, as reasonable customers, would have reasonably expected the wooden casket to last. The plaintiffs contend that they reasonably expected the casket to protect the remains for an indefinite period of time. *Indefinite* is defined as "without fixed boundaries or distinguishing characteristics; not definite, determinate, or precise." *Black's Law Dictionary* 393 (5th ed. 1983). [Under the circumstances, the] trial court [appropriately] found that the ordinary purpose for which the casket was designed ceased once the pallbearers bore the casket from the hearse to the grave site for burial. [In any event,] [a]s previously stated, the record also fails to demonstrate that the remains were damaged in any way from the alleged cracks and separation when the casket and body were exhumed.

Accordingly, [we reject] the plaintiffs' assignment of error [concerning the lower court's grant of summary judgment in favor of the defendants on the breach of implied warranty of merchantability claim].

Summary judgment in favor of defendants affirmed.

Negligence

Negligence Product liability lawsuits brought on the **negligence** theory discussed in Chapter 7 usually allege that the seller or manufacturer breached a duty to the plaintiff by failing to eliminate a reasonably foreseeable risk of harm associated with the product. Such cases typically involve one or more of the following claims: (1) negligent *manufacture* of the goods (including improper materials and packaging), (2) negligent *inspection,* (3) negligent failure to provide *adequate warnings,* and (4) negligent *design.*

Negligent Manufacture Negligence claims alleging the manufacturer's improper assembly, materials, or packaging often encounter obstacles because the evidence needed to prove a breach of duty is under the defendant's control. However, modern discovery rules and the doctrine of *res ipsa loquitur* may help plaintiffs establish a breach in such situations.[3]

Negligent Inspection Manufacturers have a duty to inspect their products for defects that create a reasonably foreseeable risk of harm, if such an inspection would be practicable and effective. As noted above, *res ipsa loquitur* and modern discovery rules may help plaintiffs prove their case against the manufacturer.

Most courts have held that middlemen such as retailers and wholesalers have a duty to inspect the goods they sell only when they have actual knowledge or reason to know of a defect. In addition, such parties generally have no duty to inspect if inspection would be unduly difficult, burdensome, or time-consuming. Unless the product defect is obvious, for example, middlemen usually are not liable for failing to inspect goods sold in the manufacturer's original packages or containers.

On the other hand, sellers that prepare, install, or repair the goods they sell ordinarily have a duty to inspect those goods. Examples include restaurants, automobile dealers, and installers of household products. In general, the scope of the inspection need only be consistent with the preparation, installation, or repair work performed. It is unlikely, therefore, that such sellers must unearth hidden or latent defects.

If there is a duty to inspect and the inspection reveals a defect, further duties may arise. For example, a manufacturer or other seller may be required not to sell the product in its defective state, or at least to give a suitable warning.

Negligent Failure to Warn Sellers and manufacturers often have a duty to give an appropriate warning when their products pose a reasonably foreseeable risk of harm. In determining whether there was a duty to warn and whether the defendant's warning was adequate, however, courts often consider other factors besides the reasonable

---

[3]Chapter 2 discusses discovery. Chapter 7 discusses *res ipsa loquitur.*

foreseeability of the risk. These include the *magnitude or severity* of the likely harm, the *ease or difficulty of providing an appropriate warning,* and the likely *effectiveness of a warning.* Many courts, moreover, hold there is no duty to warn if the risk is *open and obvious.*

Negligent Design   Manufacturers have a duty to design their products so as to avoid reasonably foreseeable risks of harm. As in failure-to-warn cases, however, design defect cases frequently involve other factors such as the *magnitude or severity* of the foreseeable harm. Three other factors are *industry practices* at the time the product was manufactured, the *state of the art* (the state of existing scientific and technical knowledge) at that time,

and the product's compliance or noncompliance with *government safety regulations.*

Sometimes courts employ *risk–benefit analysis* when weighing these factors. In such analyses, three other factors—the design's *social utility,* the *effectiveness of alternative designs,* and the *cost of safer designs*—may figure in the weighing process. Even when the balancing process indicates that the design was not defective, courts still may require a suitable warning.

The *Croskey* case, which follows, illustrates various issues that arise in negligent design cases involving motor vehicles, including the role that evidence of prior similar incidents may play. In addition, *Croskey* addresses negligent failure to warn issues.

Croskey v. BMW of North America, Inc.
2008 U.S. App. LEXIS 14544 (6th Cir. 2008)

William Croskey was seriously injured in July 2000 when his girlfriend's 1992 BMW automobile overheated and he opened the hood to add fluid. Because the plastic neck on the car's radiator failed, scalding radiator fluid spewed out and came in contact with Croskey, severely burning him. Relying on diversity of citizenship jurisdiction, Croskey filed suit in the U.S. District Court for the Eastern District of Michigan against the car's manufacturer, Bayerische Motoren Werk Aktiengesellschaft (BMW AG), and the North American distributor of BMW vehicles, BMW of North America, Inc. (BMW NA).

Croskey pleaded two alternative claims: (1) negligent design on the part of BMW AG; and (2) negligent failure to warn on the part of BMW AG and BMW NA. Deciding an evidentiary question prior to trial, the district court ruled that Croskey could use evidence of substantially similar incidents of plastic neck failure if those incidents came to the attention of the defendants and if the incidents occurred between 1991 and the date Croskey was injured. However, the court allowed this evidence to be used only in regard to the negligent failure to warn claim, and prohibited its use in regard to the negligent design claim. The court also ruled that concerning the negligent failure to warn claim, the defendants could introduce evidence of the number of BMWs sold with plastic-necked radiators between 1994 (when the defendants first learned of a neck failure) and the date of the Croskey incident. The purpose of such evidence was to show the likelihood—or lack of likelihood—of a neck failure.

The case proceeded to trial. Rejecting Croskey's negligent design and negligent failure to warn claims, the jury returned a verdict in favor of the defendants. Croskey appealed to the U.S. Court of Appeals for the Sixth Circuit.

Merritt, Circuit Judge

A negligence claim in a product liability action looks to the [defendant's] *conduct* and not the mere existence of a product's defect to determine whether the [defendant's] conduct was reasonable under the circumstances. [The plaintiff, Croskey,] claims that the defendants were negligent because they knew that the plastic used on the radiator "neck" could become brittle and break over time (the "defect"), exposing consumers to the possibility of severe burns if the consumer was standing near the car with the hood up when the neck failed and allowed hot liquid to escape from the radiator. The plaintiff also claims that [available] alternative designs . . . could have been used to minimize the type of radiator neck failure that led to the plaintiff's injuries.

[Croskey's other] negligence theory contends that even if the defendants did not know the product was defective when it left [their] possession, [they] became aware later of the defect and were under a duty to warn consumers. This . . . theory of negligence arises from the plaintiff's allegation that even if the radiator neck was not defective when it left the defendants' possession due to either a design defect or a manufacturing defect, over time the defendants became aware of the problem in older model cars and had a duty to warn customers about the problem in BMWs manufactured with this type of plastic radiator neck.

The primary issue in this appeal [centers around] the plaintiff's efforts to prove negligence under a theory of design defect. To prove a design defect under Michigan law, a plaintiff must show that the product was not reasonably safe for its foreseeable uses and that a risk-utility analysis favored a safer design. Under this approach, a plaintiff must show that (1) the product was not reasonably safe when it left the control of the manufacturer; and (2) a "feasible alternative production practice was available that would have prevented the harm without significantly impairing the usefulness or desirability of the product to users." [Citations of authority omitted.] Plaintiffs may use both direct and circumstantial evidence to prove a design defect claim.

A risk-utility balancing test invites the trier of fact to consider the alternatives and risks faced by the manufacturer in designing the product and to determine whether in light of certain factors "the manufacturer exercised reasonable care in making the design choices it made." [Case citation omitted.] Under Michigan's risk-utility test, a plaintiff must show:

(1) that the severity of the injury was foreseeable by the manufacturer;

(2) that the likelihood of the occurrence of the injury was foreseeable by the manufacturer at the time of distribution of the product;

(3) that there was a reasonable alternative design available;

(4) that the alternative available design was practicable;

(5) that the available and practicable reasonable alternative design would have reduced the foreseeable risk of harm posed by the defendant's product; and

(6) that the omission of the available and practicable reasonable alternative design rendered the defendant's product not reasonably safe.

The plaintiff may demonstrate a defendant's negligence under these factors through a "battle of the experts," with [each party] introducing expert testimony concerning the efficacy and practicability of using a certain design versus an alternative design. Or the plaintiff may demonstrate that the defendants knew or should have known about the risk of the radiator neck failures by introducing evidence of similar incidents involving the same neck piece.

The Michigan Supreme Court stated the general rule concerning the admissibility of other incidents in *Savage v. Peterson Dist. Co.,* 150 N.W.2d 804 (1967), [in which the court] rejected the defendant's argument that the trial court erred in admitting testimony of other consumers who experienced the same problems [complained about by the plaintiff]. [According to the *Savage* court, it] "was proper to show these circumstantial facts as some evidence from which the jury might conclude that there was a pattern of causally connected carelessness at [the defendant's] plant in manufacturing, for the market at the particular time, [the defendant's] various types of mink food [the allegedly defective product]."

A recent case in the Michigan Court of Appeals, decided after the district court's ruling in the trial below, relied upon the *Savage* case to allow the introduction of similar incidents to prove negligence in a design defect case. *City of Madison Heights v. Elgin Sweeper Co.,* 2007 Mich. App. LEXIS 1219 (Mich. App. 2007). In *City of Madison Heights,* the City purchased a 1998 Elgin GeoVac Street Sweeper. In 2003, a fire destroyed a number of vehicles owned by the [City's] Public Works Department. Experts testified that the most likely cause of the fire was the GeoVac's electrical system and that the fire originated in the GeoVac's auxiliary engine compartment. The City claimed that a design defect in the GeoVac caused the fire. Discovery revealed seven other incidents of GeoVacs involved in fires between 1998 and 2004, all involving GeoVacs produced in 1997 or 1998. The City sought to introduce evidence of other fires involving the Elgin GeoVac Street Sweeper, and it filed an interlocutory appeal after the trial court granted defendant's motion to exclude evidence of other fires involving Elgin GeoVac Street Sweepers. The Michigan Court of Appeals concluded that two of the incidents were "substantially similar" to the incident giving rise to the City's allegations and that the trial court should have found the incidents relevant.

Relying on *Savage* and *City of Madison Heights,* . . . we hold it was error for the district court to make a blanket exclusion of all "other incidents" evidence by plaintiff to prove a negligence claim involving a design defect. Prior accidents must be "substantially similar" to the one at issue before they will be admitted into evidence. Substantial similarity means that the accidents must have occurred under similar circumstances or share the same cause. The plaintiff has the burden of showing the substantial similarity between prior accidents and his own.

The plaintiff also claims that it was an abuse of discretion for the district court to allow testimony concerning the number of BMWs sold with the same type of radiator as the subject product between 1994 (the date that BMW received notice of the first breakage of a radiator neck) and the date of the plaintiff's accident. In the trial below, the plaintiff was allowed to introduce evidence of similar incidents between 1991 and July 2000 to prove defendants were negligent in their failure to warn. On retrial, the plaintiff will also be allowed to put on similar incidents evidence to prove his design defect claim. To rebut that evidence, the defendants should be allowed to put on evidence of the total number of cars sold during that same time with the same radiator neck piece to demonstrate the likelihood of failure of the radiator neck. Evidence of a small number of incidents versus the total number of similar model cars on the road has been permitted to refute evidence of prior accidents. A positive safety history may be admissible under certain conditions. *See McCormick On Evidence* § 200 (where a plaintiff has presented evidence of prior accidents to the jury, "it would seem perverse to tell a jury that one or two persons besides the plaintiff tripped on defendant's stairwell while withholding from them the further information that another thousand persons descended the same stairs without incident").

The plaintiff argues that any number that includes all cars—new and old—is misleading as it skews the numbers in such a way as to make the percentage of neck failures artificially small because new cars are counted equally with the older cars that are more prone to the problem. The district court properly ruled that the plaintiff would be able to cross-examine defendants on the statistics to help the jury understand that the plastic necks generally do not fail until after the cars have been on the road for a few years.

District court's decision reversed; case remanded for new trial on negligent design claim.

Strict Liability

Strict liability for certain defective products has been a feature of the legal landscape for roughly the past 45 years. The movement toward imposing strict liability received a critical boost when the American Law Institute promulgated section 402A of the *Restatement (Second) of Torts* in 1965. By now, the vast majority of the states have adopted some form of strict liability, either by statute or under the common law. The most important reason is the socialization-of-risk strategy discussed earlier. By not requiring plaintiffs to prove a breach of duty, strict liability makes it easier for them to recover; sellers then may pass on the costs of this liability through higher prices. Another justification for strict liability is that it stimulates manufacturers to design and build safer products.

Section 402A's Requirements

Because it is the most common version of strict liability in the products context, we limit our discussion of the subject to section 402A. It provides that a "seller . . . engaged in the business of selling" a product is liable for physical harm or property damage suffered by the ultimate user or consumer of that product, if the product was "in a defective condition unreasonably dangerous to the user or consumer or to his property." This rule applies even though "the seller has exercised all possible care in the preparation and sale of his product." Thus, section 402A states a strict liability rule, which does not require plaintiffs to prove a breach of duty.

Each element required by section 402A must be present in order for strict liability to be imposed.

1. The seller must be *engaged in the business of selling the product that harmed the plaintiff*. Thus, section 402A binds only parties who resemble UCC merchants because they regularly sell the product at issue. For example, the section does not apply to a plumber's or a clothing store's sale of a used car.

2. The product must be in a *defective condition* when sold, and also must be *unreasonably dangerous* because of that condition. The usual test of a product's defective condition is whether the product meets the reasonable expectations of the average consumer. An unreasonably dangerous product is one that is dangerous to an extent beyond the reasonable contemplation of the average consumer. For example, good whiskey is not unreasonably dangerous even though it can cause harm, but whiskey contaminated with a poisonous substance qualifies. Some courts balance the product's social utility against its danger when determining whether it is unreasonably dangerous.

Section 402A's requirement of unreasonable dangerousness means that strict liability applies to a smaller range of product defects than does the implied warranty of merchantability. A power mower that simply fails to operate is not unreasonably dangerous, although it would not be merchantable. Some courts, however, blur the requirements of defective condition and unreasonable dangerousness, and a few have done away with the latter requirement.

3. Finally, defendants may avoid section 402A liability where the product was *substantially modified* by the plaintiff or another party after the sale, and the modification contributed to the plaintiff's injury or other loss.

Applications of Section 402A

Design defect and failure-to-warn claims can be brought under section 402A. Even though section 402A is a strict liability provision, the factors considered in such cases resemble those taken into account in the negligence cases discussed in the previous section. (Sometimes plaintiffs bring alternative claims for strict liability and negligence in the same case.)

Because it applies to professional sellers, section 402A covers retailers and other middlemen who market goods containing defects that they did not create and may not have been able to discover. Even though such parties often escape negligence liability, courts have held them liable under section 402A's strict liability rule.

The Global Business Environment

By virtue of a 1985 European Union (EU) Council Directive premised on consumer protection grounds, *producers* of defective products face strict liability for the personal injuries and property damage those products cause. The 1985 Directive defined *product* as

all movables, with the exception of primary agricultural products and game, even though incorporated into another movable or into an immovable. "Primary agricultural products" means the products of the soil, of stock-farming and of fisheries, excluding products which have undergone initial processing. "Product" includes electricity.

A 1999 amendment, however, broadened the Directive's definition of *product* and coverage of the strict liability regime by eliminating the original version's exclusion of agricultural products. After the 1999 amendment, *product* includes "all movables even if incorporated into another movable or into an immovable." The 1999 amendment also retained the original version's inclusion of "electricity" within the definition of *product*.

The Directive states that a product is considered *defective* when it does not provide the safety which a person is entitled to expect, taking all circumstances into account, including: (a) the presentation of the product; (b) the use to which it could reasonably be expected that the product would be put; [and] (c) the time when the product was put into circulation.

Because the Directive contemplates strict liability, the harmed consumer need not show a failure to use reasonable care on the part of the producer. The typical tendency among the states of the United States is to require, in a strict liability case, proof that the product was both defective and unreasonably dangerous. The Directive, however, takes a different approach to strict liability. Although the consumer must demonstrate personal injury or property damage resulting from use of the product, the Directive's definition of *defective* does not contemplate a separate showing that the harm-causing product was defective to the point of being unreasonably dangerous. Only limited possible defenses against liability are provided for producers in the Directive.

Some states, however, have given middlemen protection against 402A liability or have required the manufacturer or other responsible party to indemnify them.

What about products, such as some medications, that have great social utility but pose serious and unavoidable risks? Imposing strict liability regarding such "unavoidably unsafe" products might deter manufacturers from developing and marketing them. When products of this kind cause harm and a lawsuit follows, many courts follow comment k to section 402A. Comment k says that unavoidably unsafe products are neither defective nor unreasonably dangerous if they are properly prepared and accompanied by proper directions and a proper warning. For this rule to apply, the product must be genuinely incapable of being made safer.

In the *Simo* case, which follows, the court examines the legal requirements that govern a strict liability case involving a claim of defective design of an SUV. The case also illustrates the role that expert testimony may play in product liability litigation.

Simo v. Mitsubishi Motors North America, Inc.
2007 U.S. App. LEXIS 19421 (4th Cir. 2007)

In the early morning hours of October 11, 2002, Chefik Simo was a passenger in a 2000 Mitsubishi P45 Montero Sport, a sport-utility vehicle (SUV), The vehicle was designed, manufactured, and sold by Mitsubishi Motors Corp. and Mitsubishi Motors North America, Inc. Simo suffered severe injuries when the Montero Sport rolled over on an interstate highway in South Carolina, after the driver suddenly steered left to avoid another vehicle and then attempted to correct his course by quickly turning back to the right. While the vehicle was on its side, it was struck by a Federal Express truck.

At the time of the accident, Simo was an 18-year-old freshman on the varsity soccer team at Furman University. In the litigation referred to below, Simo presented testimony that he was the top soccer recruit in the country the year he entered college and was among the best players on the United States' "Under-20" national team. Simo had intended to begin his professional career in Europe following the conclusion of the soccer season at Furman. Many European teams, including some at the top levels, had expressed interest in signing Simo when he became available.

Simo's injuries from the accident included a fractured shoulder blade, a fractured pelvis, a dislocated shoulder, a ruptured small intestine, a broken wrist, a knee dislocation in his left leg involving a complete separation of the thigh bone from the shin bone, and tears of three of the four major ligaments in the knee. He suffered irreparable nerve damage that resulted in a "drop foot." As a result of these injuries, Simo underwent a number of surgeries and incurred more than $277,000 in medical bills. He engaged in arduous rehabilitation efforts in an attempt to resume his soccer career. When he returned to the field, however, he ended up overcompensating for his injuries to his left side, leading to painful stress fractures that forced him to terminate his comeback.

Relying on diversity jurisdiction, Simo filed a strict liability lawsuit in the U.S. District Court for the District of South Carolina against Mitsubishi Motors and Mitsubishi Motors North America (collectively referred to here as "Mitsubishi"). Simo contended in his complaint that the Montero Sport was unreasonably dangerous because its center of gravity was too high, causing it to roll over in certain circumstances on flat, dry pavement (to roll over "untripped"). At the trial, Simo presented the expert testimony of David Bilek, a mechanical engineering specialist who had run stability tests and utilized data to evaluate vehicle dynamics for over 20 years in a litigation-consultant capacity. Bilek discussed stability tests he performed on the Montero Sport, a wider and lower prototype that he designed, and various SUVs comparable to the Montero Sport. Bilek explained that an unreasonably top-heavy vehicle (such as, in his view, the Montero Sport) could roll over untripped when the lateral forces on the vehicle reached a certain level. Had the Montero Sport been wider and a few inches shorter, Bilek asserted, the untripped rollover danger would not have been present. Bilek also opined that in light of information disseminated from other manufacturers, a reasonable manufacturer would have tested its vehicles to ensure that they would not roll over untripped. He stated his view that handling tests performed by Mitsubishi, in which the drivers did not expose the vehicles to forces strong enough to roll the vehicles over, were not sufficient.

Also providing testimony for Simo was engineer Michael Gilbert, who testified that the Montero Sport rolled over untripped under certain circumstances, whereas on-the-market SUVs with different designs did not. He further testified that designing an SUV so as to avoid untripped rollovers was not difficult, and offered the opinion that if the Montero Sport had been designed to have the stability of other SUVs, the accident in which Simo was injured would not have occurred.

Simo offered expert testimony regarding earnings that he lost as a result of the accident. Patrick McCabe, a former collegiate and professional soccer player and then-current soccer agent and talent scout, was his chief expert in that regard. McCabe testified concerning his familiarity with talent levels of soccer players, his experience in identifying players chosen for North American and European professional soccer teams, and his knowledge of players' market values in North America and Europe. McCabe offered the opinion that prior to his injuries, Simo was destined to become a top professional player, that he could have expected to play for 15 years in Europe, and that his career earnings would have fallen within the range of $3 million to $10 million.

Mitsubishi moved for a directed verdict at the close of all of the evidence, but the district court denied the motion and allowed Simo's strict liability claim to go to the jury. The jury returned a verdict in favor of Simo and awarded him $7 million in compensatory damages, an amount the district judge reduced to just over $6 million after giving Mitsubishi credit for amounts Simo received in settlement of claims against other parties. Mitsubishi appealed to the U.S. Court of Appeals for the Fourth Circuit.

Traxler, Circuit Judge

Mitsubishi first argues that Simo failed to establish the existence of an alternative feasible design that would have prevented or reduced Simo's injuries, and that the district court [therefore] erred in denying its motion for [a directed verdict]. We disagree.

Under South Carolina law, which the parties agree applies in this diversity suit, . . . a plaintiff must show [the following in order to win a strict liability claim]: (1) he was injured by the product; (2) the injury occurred because the product was in a defective condition, unreasonably dangerous to the user; and (3) the product at the time of the accident was in essentially the same condition as when it left the hands of the defendant. Prov-

ing the existence of an alternative feasible design is a crucial aspect of this required showing.

Simo presented expert testimony that designing an SUV that will not roll over untripped is not difficult so long as the issue is addressed early in the design process. *See Restatement (Third) of Torts: Product Liability* § 2 cmt. f (1998) (explaining that qualified expert testimony may establish that an alternative feasible design existed "if it reasonably supports the conclusion that [such a] design could have been practically adopted at the time of sale"). Indeed, Simo presented evidence that, at the time Mitsubishi sold the Montero Sport at issue here, several other SUVs already on the market had centers of gravity sufficiently low that the vehicles would not roll over untripped.

Thus, the district court correctly denied Mitsubishi's motion [insofar as it was premised on a supposed failure of Simo to identify a reasonable alternative design]. *See Restatement (Third)* § 2 cmt. f (noting that "other products already available on the market . . . may serve as reasonable alternatives to the product in question").

Mitsubishi also contends that the district court erred in admitting expert testimony from David Bilek. We disagree. The admissibility of expert testimony is governed by Federal Rule of Evidence 702, which provides:

> If scientific, technical, or other specialized knowledge will assist the trier of fact to understand the evidence or to determine a fact in issue, a witness qualified as an expert by knowledge, skill, experience, training, or education, may testify there to in the form of an opinion or otherwise, if (1) the testimony is based upon sufficient facts or data, (2) the testimony is the product of reliable principles and methods, and (3) the witness has applied the principles and methods reliably to the facts of the case.

Bilek was experienced in applying mechanical engineering principles. After obtaining his bachelor of science degree in mechanical engineering technology, Bilek received training in vehicle stability issues. In doing litigation consulting-type work, Bilek gained extensive experience and knowledge over twenty years concerning how to perform stability testing on vehicles. He has specialized knowledge concerning the tests that manufacturers employ and experience in evaluating the effectiveness of different design modifications in protecting against rollovers. Bilek also has reviewed many documents and reports prepared by vehicle engineers, the National Highway Traffic Safety Administration, and the Society of Automotive Engineers. All of this training qualified Bilek to testify, as he did, regarding the physics involved in rollovers, his testing of the various vehicles to determine whether they roll over untripped, and the state of knowledge of the risk of SUV rollovers.

Mitsubishi appears to argue, however, that Bilek was not qualified to offer expert testimony concerning whether his notion of designing the Montero Sport to be lower and wider could be feasibly implemented. Even assuming that Bilek was not qualified to offer testimony concerning the feasibility of his own design—the prototype—he did not purport to do so. As we have explained, there was no need for Bilek to theorize about whether Mitsubishi could design an SUV with utility equal to the Montero Sport that would not roll over untripped because Simo presented testimony that several such vehicles were already on the market.

Mitsubishi next maintains that the district court erred in admitting the expert testimony of Patrick McCabe. Mitsubishi argues that the testimony violated the standard of admissibility established in Federal Rule of Evidence 702. [Given McCabe's background and experience, we] conclude that the district court was within its discretion in admitting McCabe's testimony. While neither McCabe nor anyone else could predict with certainty what the future would have held for Simo, South Carolina damages law did not require such certainty. *See South Carolina Fin. Corp. of Anderson v. W. Side Fin. Co.,* 113 S.E.2d 329, 336 (S.C. 1960) ("The law does not require absolute certainty of data upon which lost profits are to be estimated, but all that is required is such reasonable certainty that damages may not be based wholly upon speculation and conjecture, and it is sufficient if there is a certain standard or fixed method by which profits sought to be recovered may be estimated and determined with a fair degree of accuracy"). McCabe explained that his [income] projections encompassed "a range of averages," rather than a precise prediction of Simo's future. And, it is noteworthy that even Mitsubishi's expert testified that he was sufficiently informed to offer a "probable career path" for Simo.

District court's judgment in favor of Simo affirmed.

The *Restatement (Third)*

In 1998, the American Law Institute published its *Restatement (Third) of Torts: Product Liability.* Although many courts now discuss the new *Restatement,* it has not supplanted negligence and section 402A in most states as we write in 2008. The *Restatement (Third),* however, may signal the likely evolution of product liability law in the coming years. As indicated by citations to it in the *Simo* case, which appeared earlier, the *Restatement (Third)* may be influential even when courts continue to adhere to the traditional product liability theories of negligence and strict liability.

Basic Provisions The *Restatement (Third)*'s basic product liability rule states: "One engaged in the business of selling or otherwise distributing products who sells or distributes a defective product is subject to liability for harm to persons or property caused by the defect." As does section 402A, this rule covers only those who are engaged in the business of selling the kind of product that injured the plaintiff. The rule also resembles 402A in covering not only manufacturers, but other sellers down the product's chain of distribution. Unlike 402A, however, the *Restatement (Third)* does not require that the product be unreasonably dangerous.

Specific Rules The *Restatement (Third)* states special rules governing the sale of product components, prescription drugs, medical devices, food products, and used goods. More importantly, it adds substance to the general rule just stated by describing three kinds of product defects.

1. *Manufacturing defects.* A manufacturing defect occurs when the product does not conform to its intended design at the time it leaves the manufacturer's hands. This includes products that are incorrectly assembled, physically flawed, or damaged.

2. *Inadequate instructions or warnings.* Although the *Restatement (Third)* applies strict liability to manufacturing defects, liability for inadequate instructions or warnings resembles negligence more than strict liability. (The *Restatement (Third)* rules regarding failures to warn do not use the term *negligence*, however.) This liability exists when reasonable instructions or warnings could have reduced the product's foreseeable risk of harm, but the seller did not provide such instructions or warnings and the product thus was not reasonably safe.

Manufacturers and sellers are liable only for failing to instruct or warn about *reasonably foreseeable* harms, and not about every conceivable risk their products might present. As with negligence and 402A, moreover, they need not warn about obvious and generally known risks. The other failure-to-warn factors discussed earlier probably apply under the new *Restatement* as well.

3. *Design defects.* Design defect liability under the *Restatement (Third)* is determined under principles resembling those of negligence (though the *Restatement (Third)* rule for such cases again avoids using the term *negligence*). A product is defective in design when its foreseeable risks of harm could have been reduced or avoided by a reasonable alternative design, and the omission of that design rendered the product not reasonably safe. The plaintiff must prove that a reasonable alternative design was possible at the time of the sale.

In the *Wright* case, which follows, the Iowa Supreme Court announces that in design defect cases, Iowa will follow the *Restatement (Third)*'s rule rather than the previously applied rules of strict liability and negligence.

Wright v. Brooke Group Limited   652 N.W. 2d 159 (Iowa Sup. Ct. 2002)

Robert and DeAnn Wright sued various cigarette manufacturers in federal district court in an effort to obtain damages for harms allegedly resulting from Robert's cigarette smoking. The plaintiffs made various claims, including negligence, strict liability, breach of implied warranty, breach of express warranty, fraudulent misrepresentation and nondisclosure, and civil conspiracy. The defendants' motion to dismiss was largely overruled by the federal court. Thereafter, the defendants asked the federal court to certify questions of law to the Iowa Supreme Court, in accordance with Iowa Code § 684A.1.

Concluding that the case presented potentially determinative state law questions as to which there was either no controlling precedent or ambiguous precedent, the federal court certified various questions to the Iowa Supreme Court. Two of the certified questions dealt with strict liability. They read as follows: "In a design defect products liability case, what test applies under Iowa law to determine whether cigarettes are unreasonably dangerous? What requirements must be met under the applicable test?"

The Iowa Supreme Court issued an opinion answering the various questions certified by the federal court. The portions of the opinion included here dealt with the above-quoted questions regarding strict liability.

Ternus, Justice

The Iowa Supreme Court first applied strict liability in tort for a product defect in 1970, adopting *Restatement (Second) of Torts* § 402A (1965). Section 402A provides:

(1) One who sells any product in a defective condition unreasonably dangerous to the user or consumer or to his property is subject to liability for physical harm thereby caused to the ultimate user or consumer, or to his property, if
  (a) the seller is engaged in the business of selling such a product, and
  (b) it is expected to and does reach the user or consumer without substantial change in the condition in which it is sold.

(2) The rule stated in Subsection (1) applies although
  (a) the seller has exercised all possible care in the preparation and sale of his product, and
  (b) the user or consumer has not bought the product from or entered into any contractual relation with the seller.

Our purpose in adopting this provision was to relieve injured plaintiffs of the burden of proving the elements of warranty or negligence theories, thereby insuring "that the costs of injuries resulting from defective products are borne by the manufacturers that put such products on the market." *Hawkeye-Security Insurance Co. v. Ford Motor Co.* (Iowa 1970). Consistent with this purpose, we held that a plaintiff seeking to recover under a strict liability theory need not prove the manufacturer's negligence. Moreover, we concluded that application of strict liability in tort was not exclusive and did not preclude liability based on the alternative ground of negligence, when negligence could be proved. Although *Hawkeye-Security* was a manufacturing defect case, our opinion implied that strict liability in tort was applicable to design defects as well.

In *Aller v. Rodgers Machinery Manufacturing Co.* (Iowa 1978), a design defect case, our court discussed in more detail the test to be applied in strict liability cases. In that case, the plaintiff asked the court to eliminate the "unreasonably dangerous" element of strict products liability, arguing that to require proof that the product was *unreasonably* dangerous injected considerations of negligence into strict liability, thwarting the purpose of adopting a strict liability theory. We rejected the plaintiff's request to eliminate the "unreasonably dangerous" element, concluding the theories of strict liability and negligence were distinguishable: "In strict liability the plaintiff's proof concerns the condition (dangerous) of a product which is designed or manufactured in a particular way. In negligence the proof concerns the reasonableness of the manufacturer's conduct in designing and selling the product as he did."

[This articulated distinction was], however, somewhat obscured by [*Aller*'s] explanation of the proof required in a strict liability case. Relying on comment *i* to § 402A, we held that a plaintiff seeking to prove a product was in a "defective condition unreasonably dangerous" must show that the product was "dangerous to an extent beyond that which would be contemplated by the ordinary consumer who purchases it, with the ordinary knowledge common to the community as to its characteristics." We went on, however, to discuss *how* the plaintiff is to prove the defective condition was unreasonably dangerous:

> In order to prove that a product is unreasonably dangerous, the injured plaintiff must prove the product is dangerous and that it was unreasonable for such a danger to exist. Proof of unreasonableness involves a balancing process. On one side of the scale is the utility of the product and on the other is the risk of its use. Whether the doctrine of negligence or strict liability is being used to impose liability *the same process is going on in each instance,* i.e., weighing the utility of the article against the risk of its use.

Two conclusions can be drawn from [the above] discussion in *Aller:* (1) the legal principles applied in a strict liability case

include both a consumer expectation or consumer contemplation test and a risk/benefit or risk/utility analysis; and (2) the risk/benefit analysis employed in a strict liability design defect case is the same weighing process as that used in a negligence case.

Since *Aller,* this court has varied in its application of the tests set forth in that decision, sometimes applying both tests and sometimes applying only the consumer expectation test. On the other hand, we have continued to equate the strict liability risk/benefit analysis used in a design defect case with that applied in a [negligent] design case.

One final development in product liability law in Iowa is worth mentioning before we address the precise issue in this case. In *Olson v. Prosoco* (Iowa 1994), this court rejected the distinction between negligence and strict liability claims first articulated in *Aller.* Examining a failure-to-warn case, we abandoned the analysis that differentiated strict liability from negligence on the basis that negligence focuses on the defendant's conduct while strict liability focuses on the condition of the product. We concluded that "inevitably the conduct of the defendant in a failure-to-warn case becomes the issue," and [that as a result], the product/conduct distinction had "little practical significance." Our acknowledgment that the test for negligence and strict liability were in essence the same led this court to discard the theory of strict liability in failure-to-warn cases and hold that such claims should be submitted under a theory of negligence only.

[W]e turn now to the parties' arguments on the question of the applicable test for determining whether cigarettes are unreasonably dangerous. The parties disagree as to whether the consumer contemplation test and the risk/benefit analysis are alternative tests or whether both apply in all product defect cases. The defendants assert that only the consumer contemplation test . . . should be used to determine whether cigarettes are unreasonably dangerous. Their desire for this test stems from their related argument that common knowledge of the risks of cigarette smoking precludes a finding that cigarettes are dangerous "to an extent beyond that which would be contemplated by the ordinary consumer." *Restatement (Second) of Torts* § 402A, comment *i*. The defendants argue that the risk/utility test should not be applied because it was designed for those products, unlike cigarettes, "about which the ordinary consumer would not normally have an expectation of safety or dangerousness."

The plaintiffs contend that both the consumer contemplation and risk/utility tests apply in design defect cases to determine whether a product is unreasonably dangerous. Alternatively, [the plaintiffs suggest that] this case presents an appropriate opportunity for the court to adopt the principles . . . set forth in § 2 of *Restatement (Third) of Torts: Product Liability* [hereinafter "Products Restatement"].

In determining what test should be applied in assessing whether cigarettes are unreasonably dangerous, we are confronted with the anomaly of using a risk/benefit analysis for purposes of strict liability based on defective design that is identical to the test employed in proving negligence in product design. This incongruity has drawn our attention once again to the "debate over whether the distinction between strict liability and negligence theories should be maintained when applied to a design defect case." *Lovick v. Wil-Rich* (Iowa 1999). We are convinced such a distinction is illusory, just as we found[, in *Olson*,] no real difference between strict liability and negligence principles in failure-to-warn cases. Because the Products Restatement is consistent with our conclusion, we think it sets forth an intellectually sound set of legal principles for product defect cases.

Before we discuss these principles, we first explain our dissatisfaction with the consumer expectation test advocated by the defendants. As one writer has suggested, the consumer expectation test in reality does little to distinguish strict liability from ordinary negligence:

The consumer expectations test for strict liability operates effectively when the product defect is a construction or manufacturing defect. . . . An internal standard exists against which to measure the product's condition—the manufacturer's own design standard. In essence, a product flawed in manufacture frustrates the manufacturer's own design objectives. Liability is imposed on manufacturers in these cases even if the manufacturer shows it acted reasonably in making the product. . . . When the claim of defect is based on the product's plan or design, however, the consumer expectations test is inadequate. The test seems to function as a negligence test because a consumer would likely expect the manufacturer to exercise reasonable care in designing the product and using the technology available at that time. . . . Although the consumer expectations test purports to establish [that] the manufacturer's conduct is unimportant, it does not explain what truly converts it into a standard of strict liability.

Keith Miller, *Design Defect Litigation in Iowa: The Myths of Strict Liability,* 40 Drake L. Rev. 465, 473–74 (1991). We agree that the consumer contemplation test is inadequate to differentiate a strict liability design defect claim from a negligent design case. Consequently, any attempts to distinguish the two theories in the context of a defective design are in vain. That brings us to the Products Restatement, which reflects a similar conclusion by its drafters.

The Products Restatement demonstrates a recognition that strict liability is appropriate in manufacturing defect cases, but negligence principles are more suitable for other defective product cases. Accordingly, it "establishes separate standards of liability for manufacturing defects, design defects, and defects based on inadequate instructions or warnings." Products Restatement § 2, comment *a*. Initially, § 1 of the Products Restatement provides: "One engaged in the business of selling or otherwise distributing products who sells or distributes a defective product is subject to liability for harm to persons or property caused by the defect." The "unreasonably dangerous" element of § 402A has been eliminated and has been replaced with a multifaceted definition of defective product. This definition is set out in § 2:

A product is defective when, at the time of sale or distribution, it contains a manufacturing defect, is defective in design, or is defective because of inadequate instructions or warning. A product:

(a) contains a manufacturing defect when the product departs from its intended design even though all possible care was exercised in the preparation and marketing of the product;

(b) is defective in design when the foreseeable risks of harm posed by the product could have been reduced or avoided by the adoption of a reasonable alternative design by the seller or other distributor, or a predecessor in the commercial chain of distribution, and the omission of the alternative design renders the product not reasonably safe;

(c) defective because of inadequate instructions or warnings when the foreseeable risks of harm posed by the product could have been reduced or avoided by the provision of reasonable instructions or warnings by the seller or other distributor, or a predecessor in the commercial chain of distribution, and the omission of the instructions or warnings renders the product not reasonably safe.

The commentators give the following explanation for the analytical framework adopted in the Products Restatement:

In contrast to manufacturing defects, design defects and defects based on inadequate instructions or warnings are predicated on a different concept of responsibility. In the first place, such defects cannot be determined by reference to the manufacturer's own design or marketing standards because those standards are the very ones that the plaintiffs attack as unreasonable. Some sort of independent assessment of advantages and disadvantages, to which some attach the label "risk-utility balancing," is necessary. Products are not generically defective merely because they are dangerous. Many product-related accident costs can be eliminated only by excessively sacrificing product features that make products useful and desirable. Thus, the various trade-offs need to be considered in determining whether accident costs are more fairly and efficiently borne by accident victims, on the one hand, or, on the other hand, by consumers generally through the mechanism of higher product prices attributable to liability costs imposed by the courts on product sellers.

Products Restatement § 2, comment *a*. [T]he Products Restatement has essentially dropped the consumer expectation test traditionally used in the strict liability analysis and adopted a risk-utility analysis traditionally found in the negligence standard. The Products Restatement[, however,] does not place a conventional label, such as negligence or strict liability, on design defect cases. We question the need for or usefulness of *any* traditional doctrinal label in design defect cases because, as [a Products Restatement comment indicates], a court should not submit both a negligence claim and a strict liability claim based on the same design defect since both claims rest on an identical risk-utility evaluation. Moreover, to persist in using two names for the same claim only continues the dysfunction engendered by § 402A. Therefore, we prefer to label a claim based on a defective product design as a design defect claim without reference to strict liability or negligence.

In summary, we now adopt *Restatement (Third) of Torts: Product Liability* §§ 1 and 2 for product defect cases. Under these sections, a plaintiff seeking to recover damages on the basis of a design defect must prove "the foreseeable risks of harm posed by the product could have been reduced or avoided by the adoption of a reasonable alternative design by the seller or other distributor, or a predecessor in the commercial chain of distribution, and the omission of the alternative design renders the product not reasonably safe." Products Restatement § 2(b); *accord Hawkeye Bank v. State* (Iowa 1994) (requiring "proof of an alternative safer design that is practicable under the circumstances" in negligent design case).

Certified questions answered through Iowa Supreme Court's holding that design defect cases will be governed by the test and requirements of* Restatement (Third) of Torts: Product Liability, *§§ 1 and 2.

Other Theories of Recovery

The Magnuson-Moss Act   The relevant civil-recovery provisions of the federal Magnuson-Moss Warranty Act apply to sales of *consumer products* costing more than *$10 per item*. A consumer product is tangible personal property normally used for personal, family, or household purposes. If a seller gives a *written warranty* for such a product to a *consumer,* the warranty must be designated as full or limited. A seller who gives a full warranty promises to (1) *remedy* any defects in the product and (2) *replace* the product or *refund* its purchase price if, after a reasonable number of attempts, it cannot be repaired.[4] A seller who gives a limited warranty is bound to whatever promises it actually makes. However, neither warranty applies if the seller simply declines to give a written warranty.

Misrepresentation   Product liability law has long allowed recoveries for misrepresentations made by sellers of goods. The *Restatement (Third)* does likewise. Its rule applies to merchantlike sellers engaged in the business of selling the product in question. The rule includes fraudulent, negligent, or innocent misrepresentations made by such sellers. The misrepresentation must involve a *material fact* about the product—a fact that would matter to a reasonable buyer. This means that sellers are not liable for inconsequential misstatements, sales talk, and statements of opinion. However, the product need not be defective. Unlike past law, moreover, the misrepresentation need not be made to the public, and the plaintiff need not have justifiably relied upon it. However, it must have made the plaintiff suffer personal injury or property damage.

Industrywide Liability   The legal theory we call **industrywide liability** is a way for plaintiffs to bypass problems of causation that exist where several firms within an industry have manufactured a harmful standardized product, and it is impossible for the plaintiff to prove which firm produced the product that injured her. The main reasons for these proof problems are the number of firms producing the product and the time lag between exposure to the product and the appearance of the injury. Most of the cases presenting such problems have involved DES (an antimiscarriage drug that has produced

---

[4]Also, many states have enacted so-called "lemon laws" that may apply only to motor vehicles or to various other consumer products as well. The versions applying to motor vehicles generally require the manufacturer to replace the vehicle or refund its purchase price once certain conditions are met. These conditions may include the following: a serious defect covered by warranty; a certain number of unsuccessful attempts at repair or a certain amount of downtime because of attempted repairs; and the manufacturer's failure to show that the defect is curable.

Ethics in Action

Litigation against tobacco companies has proliferated in recent years. Many cases have been brought by cigarette smokers or the estates of deceased smokers in an effort to obtain damages for the adverse health effects resulting from their years of smoking cigarettes. Sometimes class action suits brought by groups of smokers or persons exposed to secondhand smoke have been instituted. The federal government and many state governments have also sued tobacco companies in an effort to recoup health care costs incurred by those governments in regard to citizens whose health problems allegedly resulted from smoking.

The cases against tobacco firms—particularly those brought by private parties—have been pursued on a wide variety of legal theories that initially included breach of express or implied warranty, negligent design, negligent failure to warn, and strict liability. Results have been mixed, with tobacco companies frequently prevailing but plaintiffs occasionally receiving jury verdicts for very large amounts of damages (some of which have been subject to reduction or outright elimination by the trial judge or an appellate court). During the past few years, plaintiffs have had greater success in cases against tobacco companies than they once did, in large part because plaintiffs have acquired access to old tobacco industry documents they previously did not have. Some of these documents have helped plaintiffs augment the traditional product liability claims referred to above with claims for fraudulent concealment of, and conspiracy to conceal, the full extent of the health risks of smoking during a time when tobacco firms' public pronouncements allegedly minimized or soft-pedaled those risks. Although plaintiffs' cases against tobacco companies remain far from surefire winners, there is no doubt that plaintiffs' chances of winning such cases are somewhat better today than they were 15 years ago.

In addition to the many legal issues spawned by cases against tobacco companies, various ethical issues come to mind. Consider, for instance, the questions set forth below. Some of them pertain to tobacco litigation, whereas others pertain to related issues for business and society. In considering these questions, you may wish to employ the ethical theories outlined in Chapter 4, as well as that chapter's suggested process for making decisions that carry potential ethical implications.

- Given what is now known about the dangers of tobacco use, are the production and sale of tobacco products ethically justifiable business activities? What are the arguments each way? Does it make a difference whether the health hazards of smoking have, or have not, been fully disclosed by the tobacco companies?

- Would the federal government be acting ethically if it took the step of outlawing the production and sale of tobacco products? Why or why not?

- If a company that produces a product—whether tobacco or another product—acquires information indicating that its product may be or is harmful to users of it, does the company owe an ethical duty to disclose this actual or potential danger? If so, at what point? What considerations should be taken into account?

- If a manufacturer's product—whether tobacco or another product—is well received by users but poses a significant risk of harm when used as intended by the manufacturer, does the manufacturer owe an ethical duty to take steps to redesign the product so as to lessen the risk or severity of the harm? Justify your conclusion, noting the considerations you have taken into account.

- When tobacco companies comply with federal law by placing the mandated health warnings on packages of their cigarettes and in their cigarette advertisements, have they simultaneously taken care of any ethical obligations they may have regarding disclosure of health risks? Why or why not?

- Are smokers' (or smokers' estates') lawsuits against tobacco companies ethically justifiable? If so, is this true of all of them or only some of them, and why? If only some are ethically justifiable, which ones, and why? If you believe that such lawsuits are not ethically justifiable, why do you hold that view?

- Some critics have taken the position that health care cost–recouping litigation brought by the federal government and state governments against tobacco companies reflects hypocrisy, because our governments extend support to tobacco farmers and collect considerable tax revenue from parties involved in tobacco growing, tobacco product manufacturing, and tobacco product sales. How do you weigh in on this issue? Are there ethical dimensions here? If our federal and state governments are "in bed" with the tobacco industry, did our governments act unethically in pursuing this litigation, or would our governments have been acting unethically if they had not pursued this litigation? Be prepared to justify your conclusions.

various ailments in daughters of the women to whom it was administered) or diseases resulting from long-term exposure to asbestos. In such cases, each manufacturer of the product can argue that the plaintiff should lose because she cannot show that its product harmed her.

How do courts handle these cases? Most of the time, they continue to deny recovery under traditional causation rules because the special circumstances necessary to trigger application of industrywide liability are found not to be present. However, using various approaches whose many details are beyond the scope of this text, other courts have made it easier for plaintiffs to recover in appropriate cases. Where recovery is allowed, some of these courts have apportioned damages among the firms that might have produced the harm-causing product. Such an apportionment is typically based on market share at some chosen time.

Time Limitations

We now turn to several problems that are common to each major product liability theory but that may be resolved differently from theory to theory. One such problem is the time within which the plaintiff must sue or else lose the case. Traditionally, the main time limits on product liability suits have been the applicable contract and tort **statutes of limitations.** The usual UCC statute of limitations for express and implied warranty claims is four years after the seller offers the defective goods to the buyer (usually, four years after the sale). In tort cases, the applicable statute of limitations may be shorter, depending upon applicable state law. It begins to run, however, only when the defect was or should have been discovered—often, the time of the injury.

In part because of tort reform, some states now impose various other limitations on the time within which product liability suits must be brought. Among these additional time limitations are (1) special statutes of limitations for product liability cases involving death, personal injury, or property damage (e.g., from one to three years after the time the death or injury occurred or should have been discovered); (2) special time limits for "delayed manifestation" injuries such as those resulting from exposure to asbestos; (3) useful safe life defenses (which prevent plaintiffs from suing once the product's "useful safe life" has passed); and (4) statutes of repose (whose aim is similar). Statutes of repose usually run for a 10- to 12-year period that begins when the product is sold to the first buyer not purchasing for resale—usually an ordinary consumer. In a state with a 10-year statute of repose, for example, such parties cannot recover for injuries that occur more than 10 years after they purchased the product causing the harm. This is true even when the suit is begun quickly enough to satisfy the applicable statute of limitations.

Damages in Product Liability Cases

The damages obtainable under each theory of product liability recovery strongly influence a plaintiff's strategy. Here, we describe the major kinds of damages awarded in product liability cases, along with the theories under which each can be recovered. One lawsuit may involve claims for all these sorts of damages.

1. *Basis-of-the-bargain damages.* Buyers of defective goods have not received full value for the goods' purchase price. The resulting loss, usually called basis-of-the-bargain damages or **direct economic loss,** is the value of the goods as promised under the contract, minus the value of the goods as received.

Basis-of-the-bargain damages are almost never awarded in tort cases. In express and implied warranty cases, however, basis-of-the-bargain damages are recoverable where there was *privity of contract* (a direct contractual relation) between the plaintiff and the defendant. As discussed in the next section, however, only occasionally will a warranty plaintiff who lacks privity with the defendant obtain basis-of-the-bargain damages. Such recoveries most often occur where an express warranty was made to a remote plaintiff through advertising, brochures, or labels.

2. *Consequential damages.* Consequential damages include **personal injury, property damage** (damage to the plaintiff's other property), and **indirect economic loss** (e.g., lost profits or lost business reputation) resulting from a product defect. The *Simo* case, which appeared earlier in the chapter, illustrates consequential damages of the sort just noted. Consequential damages also include **noneconomic loss**—for example, pain and suffering, physical impairment, mental distress, loss of enjoyment of life, loss of companionship or consortium, inconvenience, and disfigurement. Noneconomic loss usually is part of the plaintiff's personal injury claim. Recently, some states have limited noneconomic loss recoveries, typically by imposing a dollar cap on them.

Plaintiffs in tort cases normally can recover for personal injury and property damage. Recoveries for foreseeable indirect economic loss sometimes are allowed.

In express and implied warranty cases where *privity exists* between the plaintiff and the defendant, the plaintiff can recover for (1) personal injury and property damage, if either proximately resulted from the breach of warranty; and (2) indirect economic loss, if the defendant had reason to know that this was likely. As discussed in the next section, a UCC plaintiff who *lacks privity* with the defendant has a reasonably good chance of recovering for personal injury or property damage. Recovery for indirect economic loss is rare because remote sellers usually cannot foresee such losses.

3. *Punitive damages.* Unlike the compensatory damages discussed above, punitive damages are not designed to compensate the plaintiff for harms suffered (even though the plaintiff typically becomes entitled to collect any punitive damages assessed against the defendant). Punitive damages are intended to punish defendants who have acted in an especially outrageous fashion, and to deter them and others from so acting in the future. Of the various standards for awarding punitive damages, probably the most common is the defendant's conscious or reckless disregard for the safety of those likely to be affected by the goods. Examples include concealment of known product hazards, knowing violation of government or industry product safety standards, failure to correct known dangerous defects, and grossly inadequate product testing or quality control procedures.

In view of their perceived frequency, size, and effect on business and the economy, punitive damages were targeted for some states' tort reform efforts during the 1980s and 1990s. The approaches taken by the resulting statutes vary. Some set the standards for punitive damage assessment and the plaintiff's burden of proof; some articulate factors courts should consider when ruling on punitive damage awards; and some create special procedures for punitive damage determinations. A number of states have also limited the size of punitive damage recoveries, usually by restricting them to some multiple of the plaintiff's compensatory damages or by putting a flat dollar cap on them. Moreover, decisions of the U.S. Supreme Court have revealed that constitutional concerns may be implicated by a punitive damages award that does not bear a reasonable relation to the amount of compensatory damages awarded.

Assuming that the standards just described have been met, punitive damages are recoverable in tort cases. Because of the traditional rule that punitive damages are not available in contract cases, they seldom are awarded in express and implied warranty cases.

The No-Privity Defense

Today, defective products often move through long chains of distribution before reaching the person they harm. This means that a product liability plaintiff often has not dealt directly with the party ultimately responsible for her losses. For example, in a chain of distribution involving defective component parts, the parts may move *vertically* from their manufacturer to the manufacturer of a product in which those parts are used, and then to a wholesaler and a retailer before reaching the eventual buyer. The defect's consequences may move *horizontally* as well, affecting members of the buyer's family, guests in her home, and even bystanders. If the buyer or one of these

parties suffers loss because of the defect in the component parts, may she successfully sue the component parts manufacturer or any other party in the vertical chain of distribution with whom she did not directly deal?

Such cases were unlikely to succeed under 19th-century law. At that time, there was no recovery for defective goods without privity of contract between the plaintiff and the defendant. In many such cases, a buyer would have been required to sue his dealer. If the buyer was successful, the retailer might have sued the wholesaler, and so on up the chain. For various reasons, the party ultimately responsible for the defect often escaped liability.

Tort Cases By now, the old no-liability-outside-privity rule effectively has been eliminated in tort cases. It has no effect in strict liability cases, where even bystanders can recover against remote manufacturers. In negligence cases, a plaintiff generally recovers against a remote defendant if the plaintiff's loss was a reasonably foreseeable consequence of the defect. Depending on the circumstances, therefore, bystanders and other distant parties may recover in a negligence case against a manufacturer. The *Restatement (Third)* suggests that tort principles should govern the privity determination. This should mean a test of reasonable foreseeability in most instances.

Warranty Cases The no-privity defense retains some vitality in UCC cases. Unfortunately, the law on this subject is complex and confusing. Under the Code, the privity question is formally governed by section 2–318, which comes in three alternative versions. Section 2–318's language, however, is a less-than-reliable guide to the courts' actual behavior in UCC privity cases.

UCC Section 2–318 Alternative A to section 2–318 states that a seller's express or implied warranty runs to natural persons in the family or household of *his* (the seller's) buyer and to guests in his buyer's home, if they suffer personal injury and if it was reasonable to expect that they might use, consume, or be affected by the goods sold. On its face, Alternative A does little to undermine the traditional no-privity defense.

Alternatives B and C go much further. Alternative B extends the seller's express or implied warranty to any natural person who has suffered personal injury, if it was reasonable to expect that this person would use, consume, or be affected by the goods. Alternative C is much the same, but it extends the warranty to any person (not just natural persons) and to those suffering injury in general (not just personal injury). If the reasonable-to-expect test is met, these two provisions should extend the warranty to many remote parties, including bystanders.

Departures from Section 2–318 For various reasons, section 2–318's literal language sometimes has little relevance in UCC privity cases. Some states have adopted privity statutes that differ from any version of 2–318. One of the comments to section 2–318, moreover, allows courts to extend liability beyond what the section expressly permits. Finally, versions B and C are fairly open-ended as written. The plaintiff's ability to recover outside privity in warranty cases thus varies from state to state and situation to situation. The most important factors affecting resolution of this question are:

1. Whether it is *reasonably foreseeable* that a party such as the plaintiff would be harmed by the product defect in question.

2. The *status of the plaintiff*. On average, consumers and other natural persons fare better outside privity than do corporations and other business concerns.

3. The *type of damages* the plaintiff has suffered. In general, remote plaintiffs are (*a*) most likely to recover for personal injury, (*b*) somewhat less likely to recover for property damage, (*c*) occasionally able to obtain basis-of-the-bargain damages, and (*d*) seldom able to recover for indirect economic loss. Recall from the previous section that a remote plaintiff is most likely to receive basis-of-the-bargain damages where an express warranty was made to him through advertising, brochures, or labels.

In the *Hyundai* case, which follows, the court discusses the privity requirement's history and the alternative versions of section 2–318 before rejecting the defendant's argument that the absence of privity should bar the plaintiff's implied warranty claim.

Hyundai Motor America, Inc. v. Goodin   822 N.E.2d 947 (Ind. Sup. Ct. 2005)

Sandra Goodin purchased a new Hyundai Sonata automobile in November 2000 from an Evansville, Indiana, dealer. The Sonata's manufacturer, Hyundai Motor America, Inc., provided a written express warranty of a limited nature, but the dealer did not furnish an express warranty. The contract of sale between the dealer and Goodin contained the dealer's disclaimer of the implied warranty of merchantability. (Disclaimers will be discussed later in the chapter.) Because Hyundai provided a written warranty, the federal Magnuson-Moss Warranty Act prohibited Hyundai from disclaiming the implied warranty of merchantability. (This aspect of the Magnuson-Moss Act will be addressed later in the chapter.)

For a two-year period that ran essentially from the time of purchase, Goodin complained that the car vibrated excessively and that its brakes groaned, squeaked, and made a grinding noise when applied. Various repairs were performed by the dealer that sold Goodin the car and by another Hyundai dealer. Hyundai Motor America, Inc.'s limited warranty covered most of these repairs. Goodin incurred the cost of other repairs conducted after the expiration of Hyundai's limited warranty. None of the repairs, however, completely took care of the problems Goodin had consistently pointed out.

In April 2002, Goodin's attorney retained an expert to examine the car. The expert noted the brake-related problems and the excessive vibration, and expressed the view that the car was "defective and unmerchantable at the time of manufacture and unfit for operation on public roadways." In October 2002, a district service manager for Hyundai inspected and test-drove Goodin's car. Although he did not notice excessive vibration or the brake-related noises about which Goodin complained, he heard "a droning noise" that probably resulted from a failed wheel bearing. The district service manager said he regarded the wheel bearing problem as a serious one that should have been covered by Hyundai's limited warranty.

Goodin later sued Hyundai in an Indiana court for breach of express warranty and breach of the implied warranty of merchantability. Over Hyundai's objection, the trial judge's instructions to the jury on the implied warranty of merchantability claim made no mention of any privity requirement. The jury returned a verdict for Hyundai on Goodin's breach of express warranty claim, but awarded Goodin $3,000 on her claim for breach of the implied warranty of merchantability. (Goodin's counsel was later awarded attorney's fees of $19,237.50 pursuant to fee-shifting provisions in the Magnuson-Moss Warranty Act.)

Hyundai appealed, asserting that a lack of privity between Goodin and Hyundai barred Goodin's recovery for breach of the implied warranty of merchantability. The Indiana Court of Appeals reversed the lower court's decision. In holding that the absence of privity barred Goodin's claim, the Court of Appeals regarded itself as bound by language in a footnote in a 1993 decision of the Supreme Court of Indiana. Goodin appealed to the state Supreme Court.

Boehm, Justice

Goodin's claim . . . for breach of the implied warranty of merchantability . . . lives or dies on the resolution of [this issue:] whether Indiana requires privity between buyer and manufacturer for a claim of breach of implied warranty.

Indiana has adopted the Uniform Commercial Code, notably its provision that "[a] warranty that the goods shall be merchantable is implied in a contract for their sale if the seller is a merchant with respect to goods of that kind. . . ." Hyundai asserts [that] Indiana law requires vertical privity between manufacturer and consumer when economic damages are sought. In this case, Goodin seeks only direct economic damages for the decreased value of the Sonata by reason of [its] allegedly defective [nature]. Goodin argues that traditional privity of contract between the consumer and manufacturer is not required for a claim against a manufacturer for breach of the implied warranty of merchantability.

Privity originated as a doctrine limiting tort relief for breach of warranties. The lack of privity defense was first recognized in [an English case in the 1840s]. [H]owever, *MacPherson v. Buick Motor Co.,* 111 N.E.2d 150 (N.Y. Ct. App. 1916), and *Henningsen v. Bloomfield Motors, Inc.,* 161 A.2d 69 (N.J. Sup. Ct. 1960), established that lack of privity between an automobile manufacturer and a consumer would not preclude the consumer's action for personal injuries and property damage caused by the negligent manufacture of an automobile. "Vertical" privity typically becomes an issue when a purchaser files a breach of warranty action against a vendor in the purchaser's distribution chain who is not the purchaser's immediate seller. Simply put, vertical privity exists only between immediate links in a distribution chain. A buyer in the same chain who did not purchase directly from a seller is "remote" as to that seller. "Horizontal" privity, in contrast, refers to claims by nonpurchasers, typically someone who did not purchase the product but who was injured while using it. Goodin[, who] purchased her car from a dealership and is thus remote from the manufacturer[,] . . . lacks "vertical" privity with Hyundai.

"Although warranty liability originated as a tort doctrine, it was assimilated by the law of contracts and ultimately became part of the law of sales." [Citation of authority omitted.] But "privity is more than an accident of history. It permitted manufacturers and distributors to control in some measure their risks of doing business." [Citation of authority omitted.] Because vertical privity involves a claim by a purchaser who voluntarily acquired the goods, it enjoys a stronger claim to justification on the basis of freedom of contract or consensual relationship. It nevertheless has come under criticism in recent years, and this is the first opportunity for this court to give full consideration to this issue.

This court has mentioned the common law privity requirement in the context of actions sounding in contract only once, and that in a footnote. *Martin Rispens & Son v. Hall Farms, Inc.,* 621 N.E.2d 1078 (Ind. Sup. Ct. 1993), addressed negligence and express and implied warranty claims by a farmer against both the direct seller and the grower of seed that allegedly damaged the farmer's crops. The footnote cited the UCC and two Court of Appeals decisions, and other courts have taken the footnote as settled Indiana law on this issue. As the Court of Appeals put it in its decision in this case:

The [footnote] indicates our Supreme Court's unequivocal acceptance that privity between a consumer and a manufacturer is required in order to maintain a cause of action for breach of an implied warranty of merchantability. . . . To the extent Goodin argues that this result is inequitable, we are not entirely unsympathetic. Whether the cons of the vertical privity rule outweigh the pros is something for either our Supreme Court or the General Assembly [the Indiana legislature] to address.

In *Martin Rispens,* the implied warranty claims were rejected based on an effective disclaimer of implied warranty, under [an Indiana statute that] permits parties to agree to exclude or modify implied warranties if [the disclaimer meets certain requirements]. The farmer did not present privity as an issue on [appeal] to this court and neither party briefed it. It was not necessary to the decision. Accordingly, the language in *Martin Rispens,* though often cited, is dicta and we accept the invitation from the Court of Appeals to reconsider it.

Indiana law, as developed in the Court of Appeals, has already eroded the privity requirement to some degree. In [a 1977 case], the Court of Appeals permitted the plaintiff to recover on an implied warranty where it was shown that the contractual arrangements between the manufacturer and the dealer who sold to the plaintiff created an agency relationship; and the manufacturer's agents participated significantly in the sale both through advertising and personal contact with the buyer. Under those circumstances the Court of Appeals held that the manufacturer was a [merchant seller for purposes of the plaintiff's implied warranty claim]. [A later decision of the Court of Appeals] involved a defective boat sold by a dealer. . . . [The facts showed that] the manufacturer's agents engaged in personal contact with the buyer by giving demonstrations and [by] attempting to adjust the loss after the sale. The Court of Appeals . . . held that the participation in the sale by the manufacturer was sufficient to bring it into the transaction as a [potentially liable party for purposes of the plaintiff's implied warranty claim]. However, if the plaintiff could not show perfect vertical privity or an exception to the rule [because of the manufacturer's participation in the sale], then the plaintiff could not prove the claim. [Case citations omitted.]

[Indiana's] Product Liability Act does not require a personal injury plaintiff to prove vertical privity in order to assert a product liability claim against the manufacturer. Even before the [enactment of the] Product Liability Act in 1978, the requirement of privity of contract in warranty actions in Indiana began to erode in 1963 with the passage of the Uniform Commercial Code [and its] section 2–318:

> A seller's warranty whether express or implied extends to any natural person who is in the family or household of his buyer or who is a guest in his home if it is reasonable to expect that such person may use, consume or be affected by the goods and who is injured in person by breach of the warranty. A seller may not exclude or limit the operation of this section.

Section 2–318 was taken verbatim from the UCC as [drafted] in 1952. It eliminated "horizontal" privity as a requirement for warranty actions. However, that version of section 2–318 took no position on the requirement of vertical privity.

The purpose of the original version of section 2–318, which remains unchanged in Indiana today, was to give standing to certain nonprivity plaintiffs to sue as third-party beneficiaries of the warranties that a buyer received under a sales contract. That version of section 2–318 provided only that the benefit of a warranty automatically extended to the buyer's family, household, and houseguests. It was intended to, and did, accomplish its goal of "freeing any such beneficiaries from any technical rules as to [horizontal] privity." [Quoting an official comment of the UCC drafters.] Some states refused to enact this version of section 2–318, and others adopted nonuniform versions of the statute. In 1966, in response to this proliferation of deviant versions of a purportedly uniform code, the drafters proposed three alternative versions of section 2–318. [All but three states chose an alternative to enact from among the three alternative versions.]

The majority of states, including Indiana, retained or adopted the 1952 version of section 2–318, which now appears in the Uniform Commercial Code as "Alternative A." Alternative B provides that "any natural person who may reasonably be expected to use, consume or be affected by the goods and who is injured in person by breach of warranty" may institute a breach of warranty action against the seller. Alternative B expands the class of potential plaintiffs beyond family, household, and guests, and also implicitly abolishes the requirement of vertical privity because the seller's warranty is not limited to "his buyer" and persons closely associated with that buyer.

[Although] Alternatives A and B of 2–318 are limited to cases where the plaintiff is "injured in person," they do not [contain language barring] a nonprivity plaintiff from recovery against a remote manufacturer for direct economic loss.

[Accordingly], Alternatives A and B do not prevent a court from [eliminating] the *vertical* privity requirement [when] a nonprivity buyer [sues to recover] direct economic loss.

Alternative C is the most expansive in eliminating the lack-of-privity defense. It provides that "[a] seller's warranty whether express or implied extends to any person who may reasonably be expected to use, consume, or be affected by the goods and who is injured by breach of the warranty." Alternative C expands the class of plaintiffs to include other nonpurchasers such as the buyer's employees and invitees, and bystanders. Alternative C also eliminates the vertical privity requirement, but is not restricted to "personal" injury. Because Alternative C refers simply to "injury," plaintiffs sustaining only property damage or economic loss in some states have been held to have standing to sue under this language.

The commentaries to the UCC . . . explain that the three alternatives were not to be taken as excluding the development of the common law on the issue of vertical privity. There is a split of authority in other jurisdictions with similar or identical versions of section 2–318 on the availability of implied warranty claims by remote purchasers, particularly if only economic loss is claimed, as in the present case. Courts of other [states] that have retained or adopted Alternative A note that the statute speaks only to horizontal privity, and is silent as to vertical privity. As the Pennsylvania Supreme Court put it: "Merely to read the language [of § 2–318] is to demonstrate that the code simply fails to treat this problem. . . . There thus is nothing to prevent this court from joining in the growing number of jurisdictions which, although bound by the code, have nevertheless abolished vertical privity in breach of warranty cases." [Case citation omitted.] Indiana has not legislated on this issue since 1966 when the UCC adopted these three alternatives. In short, the General Assembly, in keeping Alternative A, left to this court the issue of [the] extent [to which] vertical privity of contract will be required.

Several jurisdictions that have adopted Alternative A have abolished [vertical] privity. Others have retained the common law privity rule. Courts that have abolished vertical privity have cited a variety of reasons. Principal among these is the view that, in today's economy, manufactured products typically reach the consuming public through one or more intermediaries. As a result, any loss from an unmerchantable product is likely to be identified only after the product is attempted to be used or consumed. Others have cited the concern that privity encourages thinly capitalized manufacturers by insulating them from responsibility for inferior products. Yet others have focused on the point that if implied warranties are effective against remote sellers, it produces a chain of lawsuits or cross-claims against those up the distribution chain. And some focus on the reality . . . that manufacturers focus on the consumer in communications promoting the product.

Finally, some jurisdictions have abolished privity in warranty actions where only economic losses were sought based on the notion that there is "no reason to distinguish between recovery for personal and property injury, on the one hand, and economic loss on the other." [Case citation omitted.] A variance on this theme is the view that abolishing privity "simply recognizes that economic loss is potentially devastating to the buyer of an unmerchantable product and that it is unjust to preclude any recovery from the manufacturer for such loss because of a lack of privity, when the slightest physical injury can give rise to strict liability under the same circumstances." [Case citation omitted.] One court preserving the privity requirement expressed the view that "there may be cases where the plaintiff may be unfairly prejudiced by the operation of the economic loss rule in combination with the privity requirement." [Case citation omitted.]

In Indiana, the economic loss rule applies to bar recovery in tort "where a negligence claim is based upon the failure of a product to perform as expected and the plaintiff suffers only economic damages." [Quoting *Martin Rispens.*] Possibly because of the economic loss rule, Goodin did not raise a negligence claim here. Furthermore, at oral argument, Goodin's attorney pointed to the warranty disclaimer in the [contract between Goodin and the dealer] as a bar to Goodin's ability to sue her direct seller, AutoChoice, which could then have sued Hyundai for reimbursement. This disclaimer, Goodin contends, precluded a chain of claims ultimately reaching the manufacturer. Therefore, Goodin claims that if this court does not abolish the vertical privity requirement, she will be left without a remedy for Hyundai's breach of its implied warranty of merchantability, and Hyundai's implied warranty becomes nonexistent in practical terms.

The basis for the privity requirement in a contract claim is essentially the idea that the parties to a sale of goods are free to bargain for themselves, and thus allocation of risk of failure of a product is best left to the private sector. The Indiana Court of Appeals summarized this view [in a 1979 decision]:

> Generally privity extends to the parties to the contract of sale. It relates to the bargained-for expectations of the buyer and seller. Accordingly, when the cause of action arises out of economic loss related to the loss of the bargain or profits and consequential damages related hereto, the bargained-for expectations of buyer and seller are relevant and privity between them is still required. Implied warranties of merchantability and fitness for a particular use, as they relate to economic loss from the bargain, cannot then ordinarily be sustained between the buyer and a remote manufacturer.

We think that this rationale has eroded to the point of invisibility as applied to many types of consumer goods in today's economy. The UCC recognizes an implied warranty of merchantability if "goods" are sold to "consumers" by one who ordinarily deals in this product. Warranties are often explicitly promoted as marketing tools, as was true in this case of the Hyundai warranties. Consumer expectations are framed by these legal developments to the point where technically advanced consumer goods are virtually always sold under express warranties, which, as a matter of federal law run to the consumer without regard to privity. [The federal] Magnuson-Moss Warranty Act precludes a disclaimer of the implied warranty of merchantability as to consumer goods where an express warranty is given. Given this framework, we think ordinary consumers are entitled to, and do, expect that a consumer product sold under a warranty is merchantable, at least at the modest level of merchantability set by UCC section 2–314, where hazards common to the type of product do not render the product unfit for normal use.

Even if one party to the contract—the manufacturer—intends to extend an implied warranty only to the immediate purchaser, . . . doing away with the privity requirement for a [consumer] product subject to the Magnuson-Moss Warranty Act, rather than rewriting the deal, simply gives the consumer the contract the consumer expected. The manufacturer, on the other hand, is encouraged to build quality into its products. To the extent there is a cost of adding uniform or standard quality in all products, the risk of a lemon is passed to all buyers in the form of pricing and not randomly distributed among those unfortunate enough to have acquired one of the lemons. [E]limination of the privity requirement gives consumers such as Goodin the value of their expected bargain. . . . The remedy for breach of implied warranty of merchantability is in most cases, including this one, the difference between "the value of the goods accepted and the value they would have had if they had been as warranted." [Citation of Indiana statute omitted.] This gives the buyer the benefit of the bargain. In most cases, however, if any additional damages are available under the UCC as the result of abolishing privity, Indiana law would award the same damages under the Product Liability Act as personal injury or damage to "other property" from a "defective" product. [Case citation omitted.]

For the reasons given above, we conclude that Indiana law does not require vertical privity between a consumer and a manufacturer as a condition to a claim by the consumer against the manufacturer for breach of the manufacturer's implied warranty of merchantability.

Judgment of Court of Appeals reversed.

Disclaimers and Remedy Limitations

A product liability **disclaimer** is a clause in the sales contract whereby the seller attempts to eliminate *liability* it might otherwise have under the theories of recovery described earlier in the chapter. A **remedy limitation** is a clause attempting to block recovery of certain *damages*. If a disclaimer is effective, no damages of any sort are recoverable under the legal theory attacked by the disclaimer. A successful remedy limitation prevents the plaintiff from recovering certain types of damages but does not attack the plaintiff's theory of recovery. Damages not excluded still may be recovered because the theory is left intact.

The main justification for enforcing disclaimers and remedy limitations is freedom of contract. Why, however, would any rational contracting party freely accept a disclaimer or remedy limitation? Because sellers need not insure against lawsuits for defective goods accompanied by an effective disclaimer or remedy limitation, they should be able to sell those goods more cheaply. Thus, enforcing such clauses allows buyers to obtain a lower price by accepting the economic risk of a product defect. For purchases by ordinary consumers and other unsophisticated buyers, however, this argument often is illusory. Sellers normally present the disclaimer or remedy limitation in a standardized, take-it-or-leave-it fashion. It is also doubtful whether many consumers read disclaimers and remedy limitations at the time of purchase, or would comprehend them if they did read them. As a result, there is little or no genuine bargaining over disclaimers or remedy limitations in consumer situations. Instead, they are effectively dictated by a seller with superior size and organization. These observations, however, are less valid when the buyer is a business entity with the capability to engage in genuine bargaining with sellers.

Because the realities surrounding the sale differ from situation to situation, and because some theories of recovery are more hospitable to contractual limitation than others, the law on product liability disclaimers and remedy limitations is complicated. We begin by discussing implied warranty disclaimers. Then we examine disclaimers of express warranty liability, negligence liability, 402A liability, and liability under the *Restatement (Third),* before considering remedy limitations separately.

Implied Warranty Disclaimers

The Basic Tests of UCC Section 2–316(2) UCC section 2–316(2) makes it relatively easy for sellers to disclaim the implied warranties of merchantability and fitness for a particular purpose. The section states that to exclude or modify the implied warranty of merchantability, a seller must (1) use the word *merchantability,* and (2) make the disclaimer conspicuous if it is written. To exclude or modify the implied warranty of fitness, a seller must (1) use a writing, and (2) make the disclaimer conspicuous. A disclaimer is conspicuous if it is written so that a reasonable person ought to have noticed it. Capital letters, larger type, contrasting type, and contrasting colors usually suffice.

Unlike the fitness warranty disclaimer, a disclaimer of the implied warranty of merchantability can be oral. Although disclaimers of the latter warranty must use the word *merchantability,* no special language is needed to disclaim the implied warranty of fitness. For example, a conspicuous written statement that "THERE ARE NO WARRANTIES THAT EXTEND BEYOND THE DESCRIPTION ON THE FACE HEREOF" disclaims the implied warranty of fitness but not the implied warranty of merchantability.

Other Ways to Disclaim Implied Warranties: Section 2–316(3) According to UCC section 2–316(3)(a), sellers may also disclaim either implied warranty by using such terms as "with all faults," "as is," and "as they stand." Some courts have held that these terms must be conspicuous to be effective as disclaimers. Other courts have allowed such terms to be effective disclaimers only in sales of used goods.

UCC section 2–316(3)(b) describes two situations in which the buyer's *inspection* of the goods or her *refusal to inspect* may operate as a disclaimer. If a buyer examines the goods before the sale and fails to discover a defect that should have been reasonably apparent to her, there can be no implied warranty claim based on that defect. Also, if a seller requests that the buyer examine the goods and the buyer refuses, the buyer cannot base an implied warranty claim on a defect that would have been reasonably apparent had she made the inspection. The definition of a reasonably apparent defect varies with the buyer's expertise. Unless the defect is blatantly obvious, ordinary consumers may have little to fear from section 2–316(3)(b).

Finally, UCC section 2–316(3)(c) says that an implied warranty may be excluded or modified by *course of dealing* (the parties' previous conduct), *course of performance* (the parties' previous conduct under the same contract), or *usage of trade* (any practice regularly observed in the trade). For example, if it is accepted in the local cattle trade that buyers who inspect the seller's cattle and reject certain animals must accept all defects in the cattle actually purchased, such buyers cannot mount an implied warranty claim regarding those defects.

Unconscionable Disclaimers   From the previous discussion, it seems that any seller who retains a competent attorney can escape implied warranty liability at will. In fact, however, a seller's ability to disclaim implied warranties sometimes is restricted by the doctrine of **unconscionability** established by UCC section 2–302 and discussed in Chapter 15. In appropriate instances, courts may apply section 2–302's unconscionability standards to implied warranty disclaimers even though those disclaimers satisfy UCC section 2–316(2). Despite a growing willingness to protect smaller firms that deal with corporate giants, however, courts still tend to reject unconscionability claims where business parties have contracted in a commercial context. Implied warranty disclaimers often are declared unconscionable, however, in personal injury cases brought by ordinary consumers.

The Impact of Magnuson-Moss   The Magnuson-Moss Act also limits a seller's ability to disclaim implied warranties. If a seller gives a consumer a full warranty on consumer goods whose price exceeds $10, the seller may not disclaim, modify, or limit the duration of any implied warranty. If a limited warranty is given, the seller may not disclaim or modify any implied warranty but may limit its duration to the duration of the limited warranty if this is done conspicuously and if the limitation is not unconscionable. These are significant limitations on a seller's power to disclaim implied warranties. Presumably, however, a seller still can disclaim by refusing to give a written warranty while placing the disclaimer on some other writing.

Express Warranty Disclaimers   UCC section 2–316(1) says that an express warranty and a disclaimer should be read consistently if possible, but that the disclaimer must yield if such a reading is unreasonable. Because it normally is unreasonable for a seller to exclude with one hand what he has freely and openly promised with the other, it is quite difficult to disclaim an express warranty.

Disclaimers of Tort Liability   Disclaimers of negligence liability and strict liability are usually ineffective in cases involving ordinary consumers. However, some courts enforce such disclaimers where both parties are business entities that (1) dealt in a commercial setting, (2) had relatively equal bargaining power, (3) bargained over the product's specifications, and (4) negotiated the risk of loss from product defects (e.g., the disclaimer itself). Even though it has a provision that seems to bar all disclaimers, the same should be true under the *Restatement (Third)*.

Limitation of Remedies   In view of the expense they can create for sellers, consequential damages are the usual target of remedy limitations. When a limitation of consequential damages succeeds, buyers of the product may suffer. For example, suppose that Dillman buys a computer system for $20,000 under a contract that excludes consequential damages and limits the buyer's remedies to the repair or replacement of defective parts. Suppose also that the system never works properly, causing Dillman to suffer $10,000 in lost profits. If the remedy limitation is enforceable, Dillman could only have the system replaced or repaired by the seller and could not recover his $10,000 in consequential damages.

In tort cases, the tests for the enforceability of remedy limitations resemble the previous tests for disclaimers. Under the UCC, however, the standards for remedy limitations differ from those for disclaimers. UCC section 2–719 allows the limitation of consequential damages in express and implied warranty cases unless the limitation of remedy "fails of its essential purpose" or is unconscionable. The section adds that a limitation of consequential damages is very likely to be unconscionable where the sale is for *consumer goods* and the plaintiff has suffered *personal injury*. Where the loss is "commercial," however, the limitation may or may not be unconscionable.

Whether a limitation of remedy "fails of its essential purpose" depends on all of the relevant facts and circumstances. In a fairly recent case, for instance, the court concluded that a limitation of remedy in a contract for the sale of a motor home failed of its essential purpose when a collection of problems caused the motor home to be out of service for 162 days during the first year after the buyer purchased it.[5]

Defenses

Various matters—for example, the absence of privity or a valid disclaimer—can be considered defenses to a product liability suit. Here, however, our initial concern is with product liability defenses that involve the plaintiff's behavior. Although the *Restatement (Third)* has a "comparative responsibility" provision that apportions liability among the plaintiff, the seller, and distributors, and various states have similar rules, the following discussion is limited to two-party situations.

---

[5]*Pack v. Damon Corp.,* 2006 U.S. App. LEXIS 2303 (6th Cir. 2006).

CYBERLAW IN ACTION

In Chapters 9 and 11, you read about shrinkwrap and clickwrap contracts, which are often used in sales of computer hardware and licenses of software and in establishing terms of use for access to networks and Web sites. It is extremely common for these shrinkwrap or clickwrap contracts to contain **warranty disclaimers** and **limitation of remedy** clauses. For some examples of how these disclaimers and limitations of remedy look, see *Warranty and Liability Disclaimer Clauses in Current Shrinkwrap and Clickwrap Contracts,* www.cptech .org/ecom/ucita/licenses/liability.html.

The courts that have considered the enforceability of click-wrap or shrinkwrap warranty disclaimers or limitations of remedy have upheld them. For example, in *M. A. Mortenson Company, Inc. v. Timberline Software Corp.,* 998 P.2d 305 (Wash. Sup. Ct. 2000), Mortenson, a general contractor, purchased Timberline's licensed software and used it to prepare a

construction bid. Mortenson later discovered that its bid was $1.95 million too low because of a malfunction of the software. When Mortenson sued Timberline and others for breach of warranty, Timberline asserted that the limitation of remedies clause contained in the software license, which limited Mortenson's remedies to the purchase price of the software, prevented Mortenson from recovering any consequential damages caused by a defect in the software. Although Mortenson contended that it never saw or agreed to the terms of the license agreement, the Washington Supreme Court held that the terms of the license became part of the parties' contract. The terms were set forth or referenced in various places, such as the shrinkwrap packaging for the program disks, the software manuals, and the protection devices for the software. Applying the principle that limitations of remedy are generally enforceable unless they are unconscionable, the court found the limitation of remedies clause to be conscionable and enforceable.

The Traditional Defenses Traditionally, the three main defenses in a product liability suit have been the overlapping trio of product misuse, assumption of risk, and contributory negligence. **Product misuse** (or abnormal use) occurs when the plaintiff uses the product in some unusual, unforeseeable way, and this causes the loss for which he sues. Examples include ignoring the manufacturer's instructions, mishandling the product, and using the product for purposes for which it was not intended. If, however, the defendant had reason to foresee the misuse and failed to take reasonable precautions against it, there is no defense. Product misuse traditionally has been a defense in warranty, negligence, and strict liability cases.

Assumption of risk, discussed in Chapter 7, is the plaintiff's voluntary consent to a known danger. It can occur anytime the plaintiff willingly exposes herself to a known product hazard—for example, by consuming obviously adulterated food. As with product misuse, assumption of risk ordinarily has been a defense in warranty, negligence, and strict liability cases.

Contributory negligence, also discussed in Chapter 7, is the plaintiff's failure to act reasonably and prudently. In the product liability context, perhaps the most common example is the simple failure to notice a hazardous product defect. Contributory negligence is a defense in a negligence case (if state law has not replaced the contributory negligence defense with the comparative rules discussed below), but courts have disagreed about whether

or when it should be a defense in warranty and strict liability cases.

Comparative Principles Where they are allowed and proven, the three traditional product liability defenses completely absolve the defendant from liability. Dissatisfaction with this all-or-nothing situation has spurred the increasing use of comparative principles in product liability cases.[6] Rather than letting the traditional defenses completely absolve the defendant, nearly all states now require apportionment of damages on the basis of relative fault. They do so by requiring that the fact-finder establish the plaintiff's and the defendant's percentage shares of the total fault for the injury and then award the plaintiff his total provable damages times the defendant's percentage share of the fault.

Unsettled questions persist among the states that have adopted comparative principles. First, it is not always clear what kinds of fault will reduce the plaintiff's recovery. Some state comparative negligence statutes, however, have been read as embracing assumption of risk and product misuse, and state comparative fault statutes usually define fault broadly. Second, comparative

---

[6]Comparative negligence and comparative fault are discussed in Chapter 7. Although courts and commentators often use the terms comparative fault and comparative negligence interchangeably, comparative fault usually includes forms of blameworthiness other than negligence.

principles may assume either the *pure* or the *mixed* forms described in Chapter 7. In "mixed" states, for example, the defendant has a complete defense when the plaintiff was more at fault than the defendant. There is also some uncertainty about the theories of recovery and the types of damage claims to which comparative principles apply.

Preemption and Regulatory Compliance?

What if Congress—or an administrative agency acting within the scope of power delegated to it by Congress—enacts legislation or promulgates regulations dealing with safety standards for a certain type of product, and the product's manufacturer has met those standards? Does the manufacturer's compliance with the federal standards serve as a defense when a plaintiff brings state law claims such as negligence, strict liability, or breach of implied warranty in an effort to hold the manufacturer liable for supposed defects in product? The answer: *Sometimes*. The questions just posed, and the indefinite answer just offered, pertain to two potential defenses: the *preemption* defense, and the *regulatory compliance* defense.

The preemption defense rests on a federal supremacy premise—the notion that federal law overrides state law when the two conflict or when state law stands in the way of the objectives underlying federal law. Sometimes a federal statute dealing with a certain type of product may contain a provision that calls for preemption of state law–based claims under circumstances specified in the federal law's preemption provision. In that event, courts must determine whether the plaintiff's state law–based claim (e.g., negligence, strict liability, or breach of implied warranty) is preempted. Such a determination depends heavily upon the language used in the statute and the specific nature of the plaintiff's claim. When preemption occurs, the federal law controls and the state law–based claim cannot serve as a basis for relief—meaning that the plaintiff loses. For instance, in *Riegel v. Medtronic, Inc.,* an almost certainly influential 2008 decision that follows shortly, the Supreme Court interpreted a preemption provision in the federal statute dealing with medical devices as barring the plaintiffs' state law–based claims against the manufacturer of an allegedly defective medical device.

Even when a federal law dealing with product safety does not contain a preemption section, it is conceivable that courts could interpret the statute as having a preemptive effect if the federal law sets up a highly specific regulatory regime that the court believes would be undermined by allowance of liability claims brought under state law. The absence of a specific preemption section from the relevant federal statute, however, makes it less likely that a court would consider a plaintiff's state law–based claims to be preempted. For example, there is no preemption provision in the federal statute requiring Food and Drug Administration (FDA) approval of new drugs before they go to the marketplace (in contrast with the preemption section in the medical device approval statute interpreted in *Riegel*). Accordingly, in a case involving a plaintiff's state law–based claim regarding an allegedly defective drug, the court presumably might not be as likely to order preemption as it would be in a case regarding an allegedly defective medical device. Portions of *Riegel*, however, can be read as supporting a wide berth for the preemption defense—suggesting that defendants in product liability cases will be likely to argue for preemption even when the relevant federal law does not contain a preemption section. When this book went to press, a then-pending Supreme Court case called for a decision on such a preemption question in the context of a negligence law-suit concerning an FDA–approved drug.

A controversial recent development has suggested potential for added litigation over preemption issues. In the waning months of the Bush Administration, certain federal agencies indicated an intent to promulgate regulations whose content would call for preemption of state law–based claims, even in instances where there was no preemption clause in the relevant federal statute from which the agencies derived their authority to regulate. Proponents of such action saw it as a sensible way to underscore the federal control that they believed should be present when a detailed federal regulatory regime existed, whether in regard to product safety or some other subject. Critics derided such action as overreaching attempts by federal agencies to go beyond the authority extended to them by Congress, and as back-door devices for achieving, through regulations promulgated by unelected agency personnel, what could not be achieved in the political give-and-take of the congressional arena. Given the controversy, litigation over the preemption-by-agency-regulation issue seems inevitable.

Regulatory compliance is the other potential defense connected with the questions asked earlier. Even if outright preemption of the plaintiff's negligence, strict liability, or breach-of-warranty claim is not appropriate, defendants in product liability cases have become increasingly likely in recent years to argue that their products complied with applicable federal safety standards and that this compliance should shield them from liability. This defense becomes highly fact-specific, with its potential for success depending upon the particular product and product defect at issue and the specific content of the federal standards.

In some cases, courts may not treat regulatory compliance as a full-fledged defense, but may still allow it to be considered as a factor in determining whether the defendant should be held liable. For instance, in a negligence case, the court may regard the defendant's compliance with federal standards as being among the relevant factors in a determination of whether the defendant failed to use reasonable care in the design or manufacturing of the product or in not issuing a warning about a supposed danger presented by the product. Similarly, in a strict liability case, the court may decide to take the defendant's compliance with federal standards into account in determining whether the product was both defective and unreasonably dangerous.

Riegel v. Medtronic, Inc.   128 S. Ct. 999 (U.S. Sup. Ct. 2008)

The case referred to below centered around an allegedly defective medical device—a balloon catheter—that was produced by Medtronic, Inc., and was inserted into Charles Riegel's right coronary artery during an angioplasty procedure. Before further discussion of the case's facts and identification of the key issues presented, explanation of the federal regulatory process regarding medical devices is necessary.

A federal statute, the Food, Drug, and Cosmetic Act, has long required Food and Drug Administration (FDA) approval prior to the introduction of new drugs into the marketplace. Until the Medical Device Amendments of 1976 (MDA), however, the introduction of new medical devices was left largely for the states to supervise as they saw fit. The regulatory landscape changed in the 1960s and 1970s, as complex devices proliferated and some failed. In the absence of federal regulation, several states adopted regulatory measures requiring premarket approval of medical devices. In 1976, Congress federalized the medical device approval requirement by enacting the MDA, 21 U.S.C. § 360(c) et seq., which imposed a regime of detailed federal oversight of medical devices.

The new regulatory regime established by the MDA set differing levels of oversight for medical devices, depending on the risks they present. Class I, which includes such devices as elastic bandages and examination gloves, is subject to the lowest level of oversight: "general controls" such as labeling requirements. Class II, which includes such devices as powered wheelchairs and surgical drapes, is subject in addition to "special controls" such as performance standards and postmarket surveillance measures. Class III devices receive the most federal oversight. That class includes such devices as replacement heart valves, implanted cerebella stimulators, and pacemaker pulse generators. In general, a device is assigned to Class III if it cannot be established that a less stringent classification would provide reasonable assurance of safety and effectiveness, and the device is "purported or represented to be for a use in supporting or sustaining human life or for a use which is of substantial importance in preventing impairment of human health," or the device "presents a potential unreasonable risk of illness or injury." 21 U.S.C. § 360c(a)(1)(C)(ii).

Although the MDA established a rigorous regime of premarket approval for new Class III devices, it grandfathered many that were already on the market. Devices sold before the MDA's effective date may remain on the market until the FDA promulgates a regulation requiring premarket approval. A related provision seeks to limit the competitive advantage grandfathered devices thus would appear to receive. According to that provision, a new device need not undergo premarket approval if the FDA finds it is "substantially equivalent" to another device exempt from premarket approval. The FDA's review of devices for substantial equivalence is known as the § 510(k) process, named after the section of the MDA describing the review. Most new Class III devices enter the market through § 510(k). In 2005, for example, the FDA authorized the marketing of 3,148 devices under § 510(k) and granted premarket approval to just 32 devices.

Premarket approval is a rigorous process involving the device manufacturer's submission of a multivolume application, detailed explanations of the device's components, ingredients, and properties, and detailed reports regarding studies and investigations into the device's safety and effectiveness. Before deciding whether to approve the application, the FDA may refer it to a panel of outside experts and may request additional data from the manufacturer. The FDA spends an average of 1,200 hours reviewing each application for premarket approval (as opposed to roughly 20 hours for the typical § 510(k) substantial equivalence application). The premarket approval process also includes review of the device's proposed labeling. The FDA evaluates safety and effectiveness under the conditions of use set forth on the label, and must determine that the proposed labeling is neither false nor misleading.

After completing its review, the FDA may grant or deny premarket approval, or may also condition approval on adherence to performance standards or other specific conditions or requirements. Premarket approval is to be granted only if the

FDA concludes there is a "reasonable assurance" of the device's "safety and effectiveness." § 360e(d). The agency must "weig[h] any probable benefit to health from the use of the device against any probable risk of injury or illness from such use." § 360c(a)(2)(C).

The MDA includes an express preemption provision, § 360k(a), which states, in pertinent part:

[N]o State or political subdivision of a State may establish or continue in effect with respect to a device intended for human use any requirement—

(1) which is different from, or in addition to, any requirement applicable under this chapter to the device, and

(2) which relates to the safety or effectiveness of the device or to any other matter included in a requirement applicable to the device under this chapter.

Inclusion of the preemption provision causes the MDA to differ from the Food, Drug, and Cosmetic Act's sections requiring FDA approval prior to the introduction of new drugs into the marketplace. No such preemption provision appears in the drug approval sections of the Food, Drug, and Cosmetic Act.

Medtronic's Evergreen Balloon Catheter Company Profile is a Class III device that received premarket approval from the FDA in 1994. Changes to its label received supplemental approvals in 1995 and 1996. Charles Riegel underwent coronary angioplasty in 1996, shortly after suffering a myocardial infarction. His right coronary artery was diffusely diseased and heavily calcified. Riegel's doctor inserted the Evergreen Balloon Catheter into his patient's coronary artery in an attempt to dilate the artery, even though the device's labeling stated that use was contraindicated for patients with diffuse or calcified stenoses. The label also warned that the catheter should not be inflated beyond its rated burst pressure of eight atmospheres. Riegel's doctor inflated the catheter five times, to a pressure of 10 atmospheres. On its fifth inflation, the catheter ruptured. Riegel developed a heart block, was placed on life support, and underwent emergency coronary bypass surgery.

In 1999, Riegel and his wife, Donna, sued Medtronic in the United States District Court for the Northern District of New York. Their complaint raised various claims centering around the allegations that Medtronic's catheter was designed, labeled, and manufactured in a manner that violated New York common law, and that these defects caused Riegel to suffer severe and permanent injuries. The district court held that the MDA preempted the Riegels' claims of strict liability, breach of implied warranty, and negligence in the design, testing, manufacturing, inspection, distribution, labeling, marketing, and sale of the catheter. After the U.S. Court of Appeals for the Second Circuit affirmed, the U.S. Supreme Court granted the Riegels' petition for a writ of certiorari.

Scalia, Justice

We consider whether the pre-emption clause enacted in the MDA, 21 U.S.C. § 360k, bars common-law claims challenging the safety and effectiveness of a medical device given premarket approval by the Food and Drug Administration (FDA). Since the MDA expressly pre-empts only state requirements "different from, or in addition to, any requirement applicable . . . to the device" under federal law, § 360k(a)(1), we must determine whether the federal government has established requirements applicable to Medtronic's catheter. If so, we must then determine whether the Riegels' common-law claims are based upon New York requirements with respect to the device that are "different from, or in addition to" the federal ones, and that relate to safety and effectiveness. § 360k(a).

We turn to the first question. In *Medtronic, Inc. v. Lohr,* 518 U.S. 470 (1996), . . . this Court interpreted the MDA's pre-emption provision [and] concluded that federal manufacturing and labeling requirements applicable across the board to almost all medical devices did not pre-empt the common-law claims of negligence and strict liability at issue in [the case]. The federal requirements, we said, were not requirements specific to the device in question—they reflected "entirely generic concerns about device regulation generally." While we disclaimed a conclusion that general federal requirements could never pre-empt, or [that] general state duties [could] never be pre-empted, we held that no pre-emption occurred in the case at hand based on a careful comparison between the state and federal duties at issue.

Even though substantial-equivalence review under § 510(k) is device specific, *Lohr* also rejected the manufacturer's contention that § 510(k) approval [(which the device at issue in the case had received)] imposed device-specific "requirements." We regarded the fact that products entering the market through § 510(k) may be marketed only so long as they remain substantial equivalents of the relevant pre-1976 devices as a qualification for an exemption rather than a requirement.

Premarket approval, in contrast, imposes "requirements" under the MDA as we interpreted it in *Lohr.* Unlike general labeling duties, premarket approval is specific to individual devices. And it is in no sense an exemption from federal safety review—it is federal safety review. Thus, the attributes that

Lohr found lacking in § 510(k) review are present here. While § 510(k) is "focused on equivalence, not safety" (quoting *Lohr*), premarket approval is focused on safety, not equivalence. While devices that enter the market through § 510(k) have "never been formally reviewed under the MDA for safety or efficacy" (quoting *Lohr*), the FDA may grant premarket approval only after it determines that a device offers a reasonable assurance of safety and effectiveness. § 360e(d). And while the FDA does not require that a device allowed to enter the market as a substantial equivalent "take any particular form for any particular reason" (quoting *Lohr*), the FDA requires a device that has received premarket approval to be made with almost no deviations from the specifications in its approval application, for the reason that the FDA has determined that the approved form provides a reasonable assurance of safety and effectiveness.

We turn, then, to the second question: whether the Riegels' common-law claims rely upon "any requirement" of New York law applicable to the catheter that is "different from, or in addition to" federal requirements and that "relates to the safety or effectiveness of the device or to any other matter included in a requirement applicable to the device." § 360k(a). Safety and effectiveness are the very subjects of the Riegels' common-law claims, so the critical issue is whether New York's tort duties constitute "requirements" under the MDA.

In *Lohr*, five Justices [expressed the view] that common-law causes of action for negligence and strict liability do impose "requirement[s]" and would be pre-empted by federal requirements specific to a medical device [if such device-specific requirements, not present in *Lohr,* were present in an appropriate case]. We adhere to that view. In interpreting two other statutes we have likewise held that a provision pre-empting state "requirements" pre-empted common-law duties. *Bates v. Dow Agrosciences LLC,* 544 U.S. 431 (2005), found common-law actions to be pre-empted by a provision of the Federal Insecticide, Fungicide, and Rodenticide Act that said certain states "shall not impose or continue in effect any requirements for labeling or packaging in addition to or different from those required under this subchapter." *Cipollone v. Liggett Group, Inc.,* 505 U.S. 504 (1992), held [certain] common-law [claims] pre-empted by a provision of the Public Health Cigarette Smoking Act of 1969, which said that "[n]o requirement or prohibition based on smoking and health shall be imposed under state law with respect to the advertising or promotion of any cigarettes" whose packages were labeled in accordance with federal law.

Congress is entitled to know what meaning this Court will assign to terms regularly used in its enactments. Absent other indication, reference to a state's "requirements" includes its common-law duties. As the plurality opinion said in *Cipollone*, common-law liability is "premised on the existence of a legal duty," and a tort judgment therefore establishes that the defendant has violated a state-law obligation. And while the common-law remedy is limited to damages, a liability award[, as noted in *Cipollone,*] "can be, indeed is designed to be, a potent method of governing conduct and controlling policy."

In the present case, there is nothing to contradict this normal meaning. To the contrary, in the context of this legislation excluding common-law duties from the scope of pre-emption would make little sense. State tort law that requires a manufacturer's catheters to be safer, but hence less effective, than the model the FDA has approved disrupts the federal scheme no less than state regulatory law to the same effect. Indeed, one would think that tort law, applied by juries under a negligence or strict-liability standard, is less deserving of preservation. A state statute, or a regulation adopted by a state agency, could at least be expected to apply cost-benefit analysis similar to that applied by the experts at the FDA: How many more lives will be saved by a device which, along with its greater effectiveness, brings a greater risk of harm? A jury, on the other hand, sees only the cost of a more dangerous design, and is not concerned with its benefits; the patients who reaped those benefits are not represented in court. As Justice Breyer explained in [his concurring opinion in] *Lohr,* it is implausible that the MDA was meant to "grant greater power (to set state standards different from, or in addition to, federal standards) to a single state jury than to state officials acting through state administrative or legislative lawmaking processes." That perverse distinction is not required or even suggested by the broad language Congress chose in the MDA, and we will not turn somersaults to create it.

The dissent would narrow the pre-emptive scope of the term "requirement" on the ground that it is "difficult to believe that Congress would, without comment, remove all means of judicial recourse" for consumers injured by FDA-approved devices (quoting Justice Ginsburg's dissent). But, as we have explained, this is exactly what a pre-emption clause for medical devices does by its terms. It is not our job to speculate upon congressional motives. If we were to do so, however, the only indication available—the text of the statute—suggests that the solicitude for those injured by FDA-approved devices, which the dissent finds controlling, was overcome in Congress's estimation by solicitude for those who would suffer without new medical devices if juries were allowed to apply the tort law of 50 states to all innovations.

The dissent also describes at great length the experience under the FDCA with respect to drugs and food and color additives. Two points render the conclusion the dissent seeks to draw from that experience—that the pre-emption clause permits tort suits—unreliable. (1) It has not been established (as the dissent assumes) that no tort lawsuits are pre-empted by drug or additive approval under the FDCA. (2) If, as the dissent believes, the pre-emption clause permits tort lawsuits for medical devices just as they are (by hypothesis) permitted for drugs and additives; and if, as the dissent believes, Congress wanted the two regimes to be alike, Congress could have applied the pre-emption clause to the entire FDCA. It did not do so, but instead wrote a pre-emption clause that applies only to medical devices.

The Riegels contend that the duties underlying negligence, strict-liability, and implied-warranty claims are not pre-empted even if they impose "requirements," because general common-law duties are not requirements maintained "'with respect to devices.'" Again, a majority of [the justices] suggested otherwise in *Lohr*. And with good reason. The language of the statute does not bear the Riegels' reading. The MDA provides that no state "may establish or continue in effect with respect to a device . . . any requirement" relating to safety or effectiveness that is different from, or in addition to, federal requirements. § 360k(a). The Riegels' suit depends upon New York's "continu[ing] in effect" general tort duties "with respect to" Medtronic's catheter. Nothing in the statutory text suggests that the pre-empted state requirement must apply only to the relevant device, or only to medical devices and not to all products and all actions in general.

State requirements are pre-empted under the MDA only to the extent that they are "different from, or in addition to" the requirements imposed by federal law. § 360k(a)(1). Thus, § 360k does not prevent a state from providing a damages remedy for claims premised on a violation of FDA regulations; the state duties in such a case parallel, rather than add to, federal requirements.

Court of Appeals judgment in favor of Medtronic affirmed.

Problems and Problem Cases

1. Hall Farms, Inc., ordered 40 pounds of Prince Charles watermelon seed from Martin Rispens & Son, a seed dealer. Rispens had obtained the seed from Petoseed Company, Inc., a seed producer. The label on Petoseed's can stated that the seeds are "top quality seeds with high vitality, vigor and germination." Hall Farms germinated the seeds in a greenhouse, before transplanting the small watermelon plants to its fields. Although the plants had a few abnormalities, they grew rapidly. By mid-July, however, purple blotches had spread over most of the crop, and by the end of July the crop was ruined. It was later determined that the crop had been destroyed by "watermelon fruit blotch." Hall Farms' lost profits on the crop came to $180,000. Hall Farms sued Petoseed for, among other things, breach of express warranty. Petoseed moved for summary judgment, but the trial court denied the motion. Petoseed appealed. Was Petoseed entitled to summary judgment in its favor?

2. Hilda Forbes was the driver in an accident in which the front end of her car struck another vehicle. The driver's airbag did not deploy, and she sustained serious injuries. She later filed suit against the car's manufacturer because of the failure of the airbag to deploy. The owner's manual for the car—a manual prepared by the manufacturer—contained a statement that if a front-end collision was "hard enough," the air bag would deploy. Although Forbes did not read the manual before buying the car, she told the salesman with whom she negotiated the purchase that a working air bag was important to her. The salesman informed Forbes of the gist of what the owner's manual said about a functioning air bag. In her lawsuit, Forbes presented the testimony of an expert witness who offered the opinion that the collision in which she was involved was severe enough to cause a properly functioning airbag to deploy. Under the circumstances, did the owner's manual's "hard enough" statement constitute an express warranty concerning the airbag. If so, why? If not, why not? If the "hard enough" statement constituted an express warranty, was the warranty breached?

3. Steven Taterka purchased a 1972 Ford Mustang from a Ford dealer in January 1972. In October 1974, after Taterka had put 75,000 miles on the car and Ford's express warranty had expired, he discovered that the taillight assembly gaskets on his Mustang had been installed in such a way that water was permitted to enter the taillight assembly, causing rust to form. Even though the rusting problem was a recurrent one of which Ford was aware, Ford did nothing for Taterka. Was Ford liable to Taterka under the implied warranty of merchantability?

4. Yong Cha Hong bought take-out fried chicken from a Roy Rogers Family Restaurant owned by the

Marriott Corporation. While eating a chicken wing from her order, she bit into an object that she perceived to be a worm. Claiming permanent injuries and great physical and emotional upset from this incident, Hong sued Marriott in federal district court. She claimed that Marriott had breached the implied warranty of merchantability. After introducing an expert's report opining that the object in the chicken wing was not a worm but was instead the chicken's aorta or trachea, Marriott moved for summary judgment. What two alternative tests might the court have applied in deciding whether the chicken wing was merchantable? Which of the two alternative tests did the court decide to apply? Under that test, was Marriott entitled to summary judgment?

5. In 1994, David and Corrine Bako signed a contract with Don Walter Kitchen Distributors, Inc. (DW), for the purchase and installation of cabinets in their new home. DW ordered the cabinets from a manufacturer, Crystal Cabinet Works, Inc. Crystal shipped the cabinets to DW, which installed them in the Bakos' residence. Soon after the installation, Corrine Bako contacted a DW employee, Neil Mann, and asked whether DW could provide a stain to match the kitchen cabinets. She informed Mann that the stain would be applied to the wood trim primarily on the first floor of the house. Mann ordered two one-gallon cans of stain from Crystal, which shipped the stain to DW in unmarked cans. There were no labels, instructions, or warnings regarding improper use or application of the stain. The cans arrived at DW's store in unmarked cardboard boxes and were delivered to the Bakos in this manner. The stain in the cans turned out to be lacquer-based. Shortly thereafter, Corrine Bako again contacted Mann about purchasing additional stain in a slightly different color to apply to a hardwood floor. At Mann's suggestion, she contacted Crystal's paint lab and spoke with a Crystal employee. The Crystal employee shipped the Bakos a series of samples from which Corrine ordered two gallons of stain. This stain was also a lacquer-based stain and was shipped directly from Crystal to the Bakos in unmarked cans. Once again, there were no instructions for use, no warning regarding improper use or application of the product, no label indicating that it was a lacquer-based stain, and no label indicating that a special topcoat was required because it was a lacquer-based stain. The Bakos applied the stain to their floor.

The Bakos then obtained a polyurethane topcoat sealant and applied it to the wood surfaces they had stained with the stain purchased from DW and Crystal. Following this application of the sealant, all of the stained and sealed areas suffered severe and permanent damage as a result of the nonadherence of the polyurethane sealant to the lacquer-based stain. Evidence adduced at the trial of the case referred to below established that lacquer-based stains are incompatible with the polyurethane topcoat that the Bakos applied to their home's wood surfaces. In October 1996, the Bakos filed suit against Crystal and DW for breach of the implied warranty of merchantability and breach of the implied warranty of fitness for a particular purpose. They also claimed that the defendants had been negligent. An Ohio trial court found for the Bakos and held the defendants liable for approximately $25,000 in compensatory damages. Contending that the Bakos should not have prevailed on any of their claims, Crystal appealed to the Court of Appeals of Ohio. How did the appellate court rule on the Bakos' two breach of implied warranty claims?

6. Connie Daniell attempted to commit suicide by locking herself inside the trunk of her 1973 Ford LTD. She remained in the trunk for nine days, but survived after finally being rescued. Later, Daniell brought a negligence action against Ford in an effort to recover for her resulting physical and psychological injuries. She contended that the LTD was defectively designed because its trunk did not have an internal release or opening mechanism. She also argued that Ford was liable for negligently failing to warn her that the trunk could not be unlocked from within. Was Ford liable for negligent design and/or negligent failure to warn?

7. A six-day-old 1991 Ford Aerostar driven by Kathleen Jarvis suddenly accelerated, resulting in an accident in which Jarvis sustained severe injuries. Jarvis contended that the Aerostar "took off" even though she had not depressed the accelerator and that she was unable to stop the van by pumping the brakes. She sued Ford Motor Company in a federal district court, claiming that Ford's negligence in designing the Aerostar's cruise control system led to the sudden acceleration and her accident. The injury sustained by Jarvis in the accident prevented her from returning to her previous employment. Jarvis testified at trial that she started the Aerostar in the driveway of her home with her right foot "lightly on the

brake." After she turned on the ignition, the engine suddenly revved and the vehicle "took off." As the van accelerated, Jarvis pumped the brake with both feet. The van would not stop. She steered to avoid people walking in the road and then heard saplings brushing against the side of the van before she blacked out.

George Pope, an accident reconstruction specialist who testified for Jarvis, stated that the van traveled approximately 330 feet and did some braking that slowed it to 15 to 20 miles per hour before it entered a ditch and turned over. Pope testified that the Aerostar had vacuum power brakes that draw their vacuum from the engine, but that the engine does not create the necessary vacuum when accelerating full throttle. Even though a check valve traps a reservoir of vacuum for use when the engine vacuum is low, this reserve can be depleted after one-and-a-half hard brake applications. Therefore, according to Pope, if Jarvis pumped the brakes in an effort to stop the Aerostar after it began accelerating at full throttle, she would have lost approximately 1,000 pounds of additional force that the booster normally could have supplied to the brakes. Pope concluded that "under those circumstances . . . , it will feel to a person like they've lost their brakes, [because] they're pushing and nothing is happening." In support of her claim that the Aerostar had suddenly accelerated even though she did not press the accelerator, Jarvis presented testimony from five Aerostar owners who recounted having had similar problems with their 1989 or 1990 Aerostars. In addition, the jury was presented with evidence that Ford had received reports of incidents of sudden acceleration in a total of 560 Aerostars. Samuel J. Sero, an electrical engineer, also testified as an expert for Jarvis. He offered a theory noting possible electrical malfunctions and mechanical reasons that could have caused the sudden acceleration to occur. This theory focused on the design and workings of Aerostar's cruise control system. Sero also testified concerning a possible alternative design of the Aerostar's cruise control system—a design that he believed would have prevented the sudden acceleration problem if the design had been implemented by Ford.

In its defense, Ford claimed principally that the acceleration was the result of a driver error by Jarvis. Ford contended that Jarvis must have been unaware that the parking brake had been set and must have mistaken the accelerator pedal for the brake pedal.

Ford also presented expert testimony that the Aerostar would not have malfunctioned in the manner suggested by Jarvis's expert. In addition, Ford maintained that the existence of the Aerostar's dump valve, a spring-loaded plunger designed to open when the brake pedal is depressed, would have effectively stopped the Aerostar from accelerating when Jarvis applied the brakes, even if the cruise control had malfunctioned as Sero suggested. Ford's expert testified that he tested the dump valve after the accident and found that it had no leaks.

The jury concluded that Ford negligently designed the Aerostar's cruise control system, that this was a substantial factor in causing the accident, and that Jarvis's negligence was also a substantial factor in causing the accident. It apportioned 65 percent of the fault to Ford and 35 percent to Jarvis, presumably because of evidence that the Aerostar owner's manual directs drivers to apply the brakes firmly with one stoke and not in a pumping action. The jury awarded Jarvis more than $1 million in damages for past and future medical insurance premiums, lost earnings, and pain and suffering. Asserting that the only logical conclusion to be drawn from the evidence was that Jarvis never applied the brake pedal and mistakenly applied the accelerator instead, Ford moved for judgment as a matter of law (judgment notwithstanding the verdict). The trial judge granted Ford's motion, set aside the verdict, and entered judgment in Ford's favor. Jarvis appealed to the United States Court of Appeals for the Second Circuit. Did the trial court rule correctly in setting aside the jury's verdict and entering judgment in Ford's favor?

8. Robyn Williams placed her purse on top of the refrigerator at her family's apartment. Later, her two-year-old son, Jerome, managed to pull the purse down. Jerome then retrieved a Cricket disposable butane cigarette lighter from the purse. The lighter lacked any child-resistant feature. Jerome's five-year-old brother, Neil, saw Jerome use the lighter to ignite some linens. As the fire spread throughout the apartment, Neil unsuccessfully attempted to rouse his mother. Neil then made his way to a window and began screaming. A neighbor rescued him, but Robyn, Jerome, and another one of Robyn's children, Alphonso, died in the fire.

Acting as Neil's guardian and as administrator of the estates of Robyn, Jerome, and Alphonso, Gwendolyn Phillips filed suit against the manufacturers and distributors of the Cricket lighter. Her complaint included strict liability and negligence claims. These claims were predicated on the basic contention that the defendants' lighter was defectively designed because it did not have childproof features. The defendants moved for summary judgment. Concerning the design defect claim brought on strict liability grounds, the trial court noted that the plaintiff was required to establish that the Cricket lighter was unsafe for its intended use. Observing that "intended use . . . necessarily entails the participation of the intended user" and that a two-year-old child was not the intended user of a cigarette lighter, the trial court concluded that the defendants could not be held strictly liable. In addition, the court reasoned that if a product is found to be nondefective for strict liability purposes, a design defect claim brought on negligence grounds must also fail. Therefore, the trial court granted summary judgment in favor of the defendants.

Phillips appealed to the Superior Court of Pennsylvania, the state's intermediate appellate court. That court reversed the lower court's grant of summary judgment. The appellate court held that for strict liability purposes, a product must be safe for its intended use—here, to create a flame—when used by any user, whether intended or unintended. Concerning the negligent design claim, the Superior Court concluded that summary judgment had been improperly granted in favor of the defendants because the trial court had made the erroneous assumption that if a strict liability claim for defective design fails, a negligence claim dealing with design issues must also fail. The defendants appealed to the Supreme Court of Pennsylvania. How did that court rule on the strict liability claim, and how did it rule on the negligent design claim?

9. Arlyn and Rose Spindler were dairy farmers who leased a feed storage silo from Agristor Leasing. The silo was supposed to limit the oxygen reaching the feed and thus to hinder its spoilage. The Spindlers alleged that the silo was defective and that the dairy feed it contained was spoiled as a result. They further alleged that due to the spoilage of the feed, their dairy herd suffered medically and reproductively, and their milk production dropped. The Spindlers sued Agristor in negligence and under section 402A for their resulting lost income. What *type* of damages are they claiming? Under the majority rule, can

they recover for such damages in negligence or under section 402A? Would your answer be different if the Spindlers had sued for the damage to the *dairy feed* itself? Assume for purposes of argument that both section 402A and negligence claims are possible under this equipment lease.

10. Matthew Kovach, a nine-year-old child, was admitted to Surgicare, LLC (Surgicare), to undergo a scheduled adenoidectomy. While he recovered in the ambulatory surgery center, a nurse administered Capital of Codeine, an opiate, to him. To administer the drug, the nurse used a graduated medicine cup (the Cup), manufactured and/or sold by various parties that later became defendants in the case described below. (Those defendants will be referred to here as the Cup Defendants.) The Cup is made of flexible translucent plastic which is not completely clear and denotes various volume measurement graduation markings, including milliliters (ml), drams, ounces, teaspoons, tablespoons, and cubic centimeters. These measurement markers are located on the interior surface of the Cup and have a similar translucency as the Cup. The vertical distance between the ml volume graduation markings varies: the smallest volume of ml measurement for the graduations between empty and 10 ml is 2.5 ml; while the smallest volume of ml measurement for the graduations between 10 ml and 30 ml is 15 ml. The Cup holds 30 ml or more of medicine when full. Matthew was prescribed 15 ml, or one-half of the Cup's volume, of Capital of Codeine. Although the nurse stated that she gave Matthew only 15 ml of Codeine, Matthew's father, Jim Kovach, who was in the room at the time, testified that the Cup was completely full. Matthew drank all of the medicine in the Cup. After being discharged from Surgicare and arriving home, Matthew went into respiratory arrest. He was transported to a hospital, where he was pronounced dead of asphyxia due to an opiate overdose. The autopsy revealed that Matthew's blood contained between 280 and 344 nanograms per ml of codeine, more than double the recommended therapeutic level of the drug.

Jim and Jill Kovach (Matthew's mother) filed suit in an Indiana trial court against the Cup Defendants, asserting claims for (1) breach of the implied warranty of merchantability; (2) breach of the implied warranty of fitness for a particular purpose; (3) negligent design; and (4) strict liability. Their claims centered around contentions that the design of the

Cup was defective, largely because its translucency and lack of clear, easily distinguishable measurement markings led to a danger of measurement errors, and because the Cup Defendants issued no warning to the effect that the Cup should not be used when a precise measurement of medication quantity was important. By way of affidavit, the Kovaches' expert witness, a pharmacy professor with many years of experience, offered an opinion consistent with the above contentions regarding the Cup's design and lack of warning. The trial court granted the Cup Defendants' motion for summary judgment on each of the claims filed against them by the Kovaches. Did the trial court rule correctly in doing so? In your answer, consider each of the four claims brought by the plaintiffs.

11. Duane Martin, a small farmer, placed an order for cabbage seed with the Joseph Harris Company, a large national producer and distributor of seed. Harris's order form included the following language:

> NOTICE TO BUYER: Joseph Harris Company, Inc. warrants that seeds and plants it sells conform to the label descriptions as required by Federal and State seed laws. IT MAKES NO OTHER WARRANTIES, EXPRESS OR IMPLIED, OF MERCHANTABILITY, FITNESS FOR PURPOSE, OR OTHERWISE, AND IN ANY EVENT ITS LIABILITY FOR BREACH OF ANY WARRANTY OR CONTRACT WITH RESPECT TO SUCH SEEDS OR PLANTS IS LIMITED TO THE PURCHASE PRICE OF SUCH SEEDS OR PLANTS.

All of Harris's competitors used similar clauses in their contracts.

After Martin placed his order, and unknown to Martin, Harris stopped using a cabbage seed treatment that had been effective in preventing a certain cabbage fungus. Later, Martin planted the seed he had ordered from Harris, but a large portion of the resulting crop was destroyed by fungus because the seed did not contain the treatment Harris had previously used. Martin sued Harris for his losses under the implied warranty of merchantability.

Which portion of the notice quoted above is an attempted disclaimer of implied warranty liability, and which is an attempted limitation of remedies? Will the disclaimer language disclaim the implied warranty of merchantability under UCC section 2–316(2)? If Martin had sued under the implied warranty of fitness for a particular purpose, would the

disclaimer language disclaim that implied warranty as well? Assuming that the disclaimer and the remedy limitation contained the correct legal boilerplate needed to make them effective, what argument could Martin still make to block their operation? What are his chances of success with this argument?

12. McKinnon Bridge Company was a general contractor primarily involved in heavy construction and bridge construction. Trinity Industries, Inc., a steel fabricator, was the supplier of structural steel to McKinnon for use in building the bridge at issue in the case described below. The relationship between the parties began after the state of Tennessee awarded McKinnon a contract to build a bridge over the Tennessee River. Soon after McKinnon was awarded this contract, Trinity presented McKinnon with a bid (i.e., an offer) to supply fabricated steel for the bridge in return for payments totaling $2,535,000 from McKinnon. McKinnon's president, acting on behalf of the firm, accepted Trinity's offer and thereby caused the parties' contract to come into being. During construction, McKinnon discovered that several girders and cross-frame stiffeners supplied by Trinity contained misaligned holes, which prevented proper construction and assembly of the bridge. After McKinnon notified Trinity of the problem, the parties agreed on a remedial plan that was approved by the state. Trinity's representatives went to the job site and redrilled the holes. The redrilled holes were approved by McKinnon. In the litigation described below, McKinnon claimed that it later encountered other problems with the steel such as incorrect length, lack of proper curvature, dimensional and fitting errors, and poor quality. None of the steel received from Trinity had been rejected by McKinnon, however, as of May 16, 1995. On that date, the partially constructed bridge collapsed.

After the collapse of the bridge, McKinnon Bridge retained experts, some of whom concluded that the steel provided by Trinity was defective and caused or contributed to the structure's collapse. McKinnon therefore ceased payment on the contract for that steel. At approximately the same time, the state informed McKinnon's president that the firm could reconstruct the bridge with Trinity-supplied steel that was in storage, as long as certain modifications were made to the steel. The state agreed to pay for these changes. McKinnon, however, ordered replacement steel from another supplier without asking Trinity to repair or replace the allegedly defective steel. When asked why his company did not use the steel from Trinity, McKinnon's president stated that it would have been necessary for the steel

> to have been picked up [and] taken to Carolina . . . where it was fabricated—and all that freight and allowance, and I made a decision not to use it. . . . Cost was some consideration. It just wasn't worth it, to get in all of the trouble you could have if it didn't work. I would be responsible. They have already put the responsibility on McKinnon Bridge Company's back for that to work, and I didn't want the responsibility.

Trinity filed suit in a Tennessee state court against McKinnon, seeking the remaining $1.6 million due under the steel subcontract. McKinnon counterclaimed and sought damages from Trinity because of Trinity's alleged breach of contract in furnishing steel that did not conform to the contract terms and specifications. Trinity moved for summary judgment on McKinnon's counterclaim. Trinity asserted that the parties' contract expressly limited McKinnon's remedies to repair or replacement of any defective goods (and thus, in Trinity's view, eliminated money damages as a possible remedy). The court granted Trinity summary judgment on McKinnon's counterclaim. A trial was later held on Trinity's breach of contract claim against McKinnon. After concluding that none of the nonconformities or defects in the Trinity-supplied steel caused or contributed to the collapse of the bridge, the court held in favor of Trinity for all sums still owed by McKinnon under the contract. McKinnon appealed to the Tennessee Court of Appeals, arguing that it should have prevailed on its counterclaim because, in its view, the contract's limitation of remedy clause—the repair-or-replace clause—should have been treated by the lower court as unconscionable or as having failed of its essential purpose. Was the limited remedy clause unconscionable? Did it fail of its essential purpose?

13. Richard Jimenez was injured when a disc for the handheld electric disc grinder he had purchased from Sears Roebuck shattered while he used the grinder to smooth down a steel weld. When Jimenez brought a strict liability lawsuit against Sears, the defendant argued that he had misused the grinder, and that this misuse caused his injury. Assuming that

Sears was right, what effect would this have in a state that has not adopted comparative negligence or comparative fault? What effect would it have in a comparative fault state?

14. On June 25, 1986, a general contractor completed the Oceanside at Pine Point Condominium. In the construction, the contractor used windows manufactured by Peachtree Doors, Inc. Peachtree delivered the windows to the contractor in December 1985. After sale of the condominium units to the public, the condominium building suffered significant water damage around the windows. Thus, Pine Point's owners' association brought a class action product liability suit against Peachtree on December 31, 1991. The suit included claims based on Article 2 of the UCC. Have the plaintiffs satisfied Article 2's statute of limitations?

15. James Bainbridge and Daniel Fingarette formulated a plan for a three-dimensional photography business through four independent companies. In January 1988, Bainbridge met with officials of the Minnesota Mining & Manufacturing Company (3M) to seek assistance with the three-dimensional film development process. In mid-1989, 3M formulated a new emulsion that it claimed would work well with the film development process. 3M apparently understood that this emulsion would be used in combination with a backcoat sauce that 3M had also developed. In December 1989, 3M began selling the new emulsion and backcoat sauce to two of the claimants' four companies, but not to the two others. After Bainbridge and Fingarette began using 3M's new emulsion, they encountered a problem with the film development process: the photographs faded, losing their three-dimensional effect. By early 1990, the claimants experienced a significant decline in camera sales. 3M eventually solved the problem, but the claimants' business ultimately failed.

The four companies established by Bainbridge and Fingarette sued 3M in a Texas trial court for breach of express and implied warranties. They argued that the photographic fading was caused by the incompatibility of 3M's new emulsion and its old backcoat sauce. The jury concluded that 3M breached an express warranty for the emulsion and implied warranties for the emulsion and the backcoat sauce. Applying Minnesota law, the trial court awarded the four firms $29,873,599 in lost profits. An intermediate appellate court upheld this award. The Supreme Court of Texas withheld final judgment and certified the following question to the Supreme Court of Minnesota: "For breach of warranty under [Minnesota's version of UCC section 2–318], is a seller liable to a person who never acquired any goods from the seller, directly or indirectly, for pure economic damages (e.g., lost profits), unaccompanied by any injury to the person or the person's property?" This question arose because two of the plaintiff companies, while suffering losses due to 3M's breaches of warranty, had not dealt directly with 3M. How did the Supreme Court of Minnesota answer the certified question?

Online Research

Parked Vehicles and Fire Risks

Media reports in recent years told the stories of consumers who claimed that well after they parked their Ford Motor Co. vehicle and turned off the ignition, the vehicle had caught fire. Some consumers suffered serious burns and experienced property damage to their garages and houses as a result of such fires.

Using at least two online sources, find out more information about incidents of the sort described above, including what experts believe was the probable reason why the vehicles caught fire. Then prepare a two-page essay in which you (1) identify the legal theories that affected consumers could use if they pursued litigation against Ford regarding the vehicles' fires, and (2) explain what the key issues would be in regard to each of the theories you identified.

Consider completing the case "WARRANTY: Who's Distorting What?" from the You Be the Judge Web site element after you have read this chapter. Visit our Web site at www.mhhe.com/mallor14e for more information and activities regarding this case segment.

chapter 21

PERFORMANCE OF SALES CONTRACTS

Sarah Saunders was interested in purchasing a new hybrid-fueled vehicle. Using the Web page of a large volume dealer in a nearby city, she provided the dealer with the make, model, color, and primary options for the vehicle she was seeking. The dealer indicated that he could obtain a vehicle meeting Sarah's specifications, quoted her a very favorable price, and offered to deliver the vehicle to her at the apartment house where she lived. Sarah accepted the offer and wired a deposit to the dealer. When the vehicle arrived, the truck driver refused to unload it from the car carrier or let Sarah inspect it until she had given him a certified check for the balance due. Then he gave her the title to the vehicle, unloaded it, and drove away. Sarah subsequently discovered a number of scratches in the paint and that some of the options she had bargained for—such as a CD player—were not on the vehicle. When she complained to the dealer, he offered her a monetary "allowance" to cover the defects. She also discovered that the vehicle had a tendency to stall and have to be restarted when she stopped at intersections. Despite repeated trips to the nearby city to have the dealer remedy the problem, those efforts have been unavailing. Sarah has indicated that she wants to return the vehicle to the dealer and get a vehicle that performs properly, but the dealer insists that she has to give him additional time to try to fix it. This situation raises a number of legal questions that, among others, will be discussed in this chapter, including:

- Did Sarah have the right to inspect the vehicle before she paid the balance of the purchase price?
- When Sarah discovered the scratches on the vehicle and that it did not conform to the contract specifications, could she have refused to accept the car and required the dealer to provide one that met the contract?
- Does Sarah have the right to return the defective vehicle to the dealer and obtain either a new vehicle or her money back, or must she give the dealer the opportunities he wants to try to remedy the defect?
- If the dealer knew the vehicle he was delivering to Sarah did not conform to the contract and was damaged, was it ethical for him to deliver it anyway?

IN THE TWO PREVIOUS chapters, we discussed the formation and terms of sales contracts, including those terms concerning express and implied warranties. In this chapter, the focus is on the legal rules that govern the performance of contracts. Among the topics covered are the basic obligations of the buyer and seller with respect to delivery and payment, the rights of the parties when the goods delivered do not conform to the contract, and the circumstances that may excuse the performance of a party's contractual obligations.

General Rules

The parties to a contract for the sale of goods are obligated to perform the contract according to its terms. The Uniform Commercial Code (UCC or Code) gives the parties great flexibility in deciding between themselves how they will perform a contract. The practices in the trade or business as well as any past dealings between the parties may supplement or explain the contract. The Code gives both the buyer and the seller certain rights,

Ethics in Action

What Should You Do When the Price Rises—or Falls?

When goods that are the subject of a contract are in significantly shorter supply than when the agreement was made and the price has risen, the seller may be tempted to look for an excuse so that he can sell to someone else and realize a greater profit. This situation often arises in the sale of commodities, such as crops, fuel oil, gasoline, and natural gas. Similarly, if goods are in significantly more plentiful supply than when a contract was made, a buyer might be tempted to create an excuse to cancel so that she could buy elsewhere at a lower price. When, if ever, is a seller or buyer ethically justified in trying to find a way out of a contractual obligation because the supply or market conditions have so changed that he or she can make a much better deal elsewhere? Concomitantly, are there circumstances under which the other party, acting in an ethically responsible manner, should voluntarily release the disadvantaged party from his or her contractual commitment?

and it also sets out what is expected of them on points that they did not deal with in their contract. It should be kept in mind that the Code changes basic contract law in a number of respects.

Good Faith
The buyer and seller must act in good faith in the performance of a sales contract [1–203].[1] Good faith is defined to mean "honesty in fact" in performing the duties assumed in the contract or in carrying out the transaction [1–201(19)]. And, in the case of a merchant, **good faith,** means honesty in fact as well as the observance of reasonable commercial standards of fair dealing in the trade [2–103(1)(b)]. Thus, if the contract requires the seller to select an assortment of goods for the buyer, the selection must be made in good faith; the seller should pick out a reasonable assortment [2–311]. It would not, for example, be good faith to include only unusual sizes or colors.

Course of Dealing
The terms in the contract between the parties are the primary means for determining the obligations of the buyer and seller. The meaning of those terms may be explained by looking at any performance that has already taken place. For example, a contract may call for periodic deliveries of goods. If the seller has made a number of deliveries without objection by the buyer, the way the deliveries were made shows

how the parties intended them to be made. Similarly, if there were any past contracts between the parties, the way the parties interpreted those contracts is relevant to the interpretation of the present contract. If there is a conflict between the express terms of the contract and the past course of dealing between the parties, the express terms of the contract prevail [1–205(4)].

In the case below, *Grace Label, Inc. v. Kliff,* the court looked to the prior dealing between the parties to explain or supplement the terms of a current contract between the parties.

Usage of Trade
In many kinds of businesses, there are customs and practices of the trade that are known by people in the business and that are usually assumed by parties to a contract for goods of that type. Under the Code, the parties and courts may use these trade customs and practices—known as usage of trade—in interpreting a contract [2–202; 1–205]. If there is a conflict between the express terms of the contract and trade usage, the express terms prevail [1–205(4)].

An example of usage of trade comes from the building supply business where one common lumber item is referred to as a "two-by-four" and might be assumed to measure two inches by four inches by someone not familiar with trade practice. If you were to buy two-by-fours of varying lengths from your local lumberyard or building supply store, you would find that they in fact measure 1⅞ inches by 3¼ inches.

---

[1]The numbers in brackets refer to sections of the Uniform Commercial Code.

Grace Label, Inc. v. Kliff   355 F.Supp.2d 965 (S.D. Iowa 2005)

Steve Kliff, a citizen of California, is a sole proprietor in the business of brokering printing projects. On May 24, 2002, Barcel S.A. de C.V. (Barcel), a Mexican company, by purchase order contracted with Kliff for at least 47,250,000 foil trading cards bearing the likeness of Britney Spears. Barcel is a large, multinational corporation which sells a variety of food products. It indicated that the cards would be placed in snack food packaging and would come in direct contact with the food contents.

On May 30, Kliff by purchase order contracted with Grace Label to produce the Spears cards. Grace is an Iowa corporation engaged in the business of manufacturing pressure-sensitive labels and flexible packaging. The purchase order described the product as a "Foil Trading Card (Direct Food Contact Compatible)." It also specified the printing process was to use "FDA Varnish," which Grace Label understood it was to use to accomplish the food contact compatibility requirement. Grace Label did not have any direct communication with Barcel because Kliff did not want it to be in touch with his customer.

The Spears job was the third or fourth Barcel job Grace Label had worked on with Kliff in about a year's time. Two of the jobs were arranged while Kliff was employed by Chromium Graphics; together they involved 58,000,000 "scratch off" game piece cards where customers rubbed off a coating to determine if they had won a prize. In February 2002, Kliff arranged for Grace Label to do the "Ponte Sobre Ruedas Job," which involved printing about 42,000,000 "peel apart" game piece cards whereby consumers peeled off a top layer to see if they had won a prize. The Spears card was simply a trading card with no "scratch off" or "peel apart" feature. The Spears card was varnished on both sides, the others were varnished on one side. The "direct food compatible" description appeared only in the Spears card purchase order. All of the cards manufactured by Grace Label for the various Barcel projects were inserted in packages of Barcel's snack food products. On several occasions Kliff advised Grace Label that he wanted the same materials used for the Spears cards as had been used on the prior jobs.

The adhesive used on the Chromium Graphics cards was Rad-Cure 12PSFLV, as specified by Chromium Graphics. This particular adhesive is not listed on the Rad-Cure Web site as being among Rad-Cure's FDA (Food & Drug Administration) food grade adhesives—but Grace Label was unaware of this. Other than ordering the FDA-approved varnish, Grace Label did nothing to determine if the other materials used to produce the Spears cards were compatible for direct contact with food items. Before its work for Barcel, Grace Label had not produced a product intended to be in direct contact with food—and it assumed that the materials it was told to use had been approved by Chromium Graphics or Barcel.

Grace Label produced prototype cards, using leftover materials from the past Barcel jobs (except for the foil, which has no odor), and submitted them to Barcel, through Kliff, for approval. Grace Label understood that Barcel was interested in the size and weight of the cards to make sure they would fit in the Barcel dispensing units. Kliff was on the Grace Label premises during the first week of production and had many boxes of cards brought to him for inspection. He raised no issues concerning the cards.

On June 28, 2002, Grace Label shipped 17,138,000 production cards directly to Barcel. An additional 7,500,000 cards were shipped to Barcel on July 5, 2002. After receipt of the production cars, Barcel complained to Kliff that the cards emitted a foul odor and were not fit for use in the potato chip bags for which they were intended. Grace Label suggested they be aired out to eliminate the odor. Barcel attempted to do this—but the odor persisted despite Grace Label's contention that the Spears production cards smelled the same as the cards for the other Barcel jobs that Grace Label had printed and which had been accepted by Kliff and Barcel.

Barcel rejected the cards under its contact with Kliff before the final production of cards was shipped from Grace Label. Kliff thereupon canceled the remaining order with Grace Label. Beyond a $90,000 down payment, Kliff did not pay Grace Label the contract amount for the cards. Grace Label then brought suit against Kliff for breach of contract. Kliff contended that the cards smelled bad and that the smell was caused by a chemical (beta-phenoxyethyl acrylate [BPA]) in the adhesive, which was not direct food compatible. Kliff's expert stated that the BPA was undetectable in the prototype cards but that in the production cards, the concentration of BPA far exceeded that in uncured or cured Rad-Cure. Grace Label's response was that Kliff specified and approved of the material components of the cards and it relied on Kliff and Barcel to select appropriate material as it had no expertise in the area. This argument would require the court to consider the course of dealing between the parties; Kliff objected to the introduction of this evidence.

Walters, Chief United States Magistrate Judge

The parol evidence rule does not bar the course of dealing between the parties. The UCC codifies a commercial version of the rule:

Terms with respect to which the confirmatory memoranda of the parties agree or which are otherwise set forth in a writing intended as a final expression of their agreement with respect to such terms as are included therein and may not be contradicted by evidence of any prior agreement or of a contemporaneous oral agreement but may be explained or supplemented (a) by a course of dealing or usage of trade . . . or by course of performance.

[2–202(a)]. "Course of dealing" is a defined term meaning "a sequence of previous conduct between the parties to a particular transaction which is fairly to be regarded as establishing a common basis for interpreting their expressions and other conduct." [1–205(3)]. A course of dealing "gives particular meaning to and supplements or qualifies terms of an agreement." [1–205(3)]. "Whenever reasonable" express terms and the course of dealing are to be construed consistent with each other. The rule incorporated in the UCC reflects the common-sense assumption that the course of prior dealings between the parties and usages of trade were taken for granted when the contract document was phrased.

[Author's note: The court then held that the written contract could be explained or supplemented by "course of dealing"

between the parties. Such evidence would be intended not to change or vary the contract terms, but rather to explain what the parties meant by them. At the same time, the court concluded that there were genuine issues of material fact that precluded giving summary judgment at this time. These included (1) whether the parties intended, on the basis of successful use of adhesive and other material on prior jobs, that the trading cards made with the same materials would be "direct food compatible" within the meaning of the contract and (2) whether the odor on the cards was worse than what had been accepted before.]

Motion for summary judgment denied.

Modification

Under the Code, consideration is not required to support a modification or rescission of a contract for the sale of goods. However, the parties may specify in their agreement that modification or rescission must be in writing, in which case a signed writing is necessary for enforcement of any modification to the contract or its rescission [2–209].

Waiver

In a contract that entails a number of instances of partial performance (such as deliveries or payments) by one party, the other party must be careful to object to any late deliveries or payments. If the other party does not object, it may waive its rights to cancel the contract if other deliveries or payments are late [2–208(3), 2–209(4)]. For example, a contract calls for a

---

CYBERLAW IN ACTION

The Internet and E-Commerce Facilitate Contract Modifications

Buyers and sellers sometimes change parts of their contracts after formation. For example, the buyer may need the goods slightly sooner or somewhat later than originally planned. Or the seller may only be able to supply yellow life jackets instead of the buyer's preferred blue and red mix of life jackets. So long as the parties agree to change the particulars of the performance contracted for, an event that Article 2 calls a "modification," they may change their contract. Modifications are quite common in deals between two merchants and are not uncommon in sales in which one lay buyer and one merchant participate.

Let's assume that the buyer decides that her customers like the first shipment of goods under a contract so much that she should order more. To change the quantity in her office, she can do several things—call the seller, send a telegram, or send a revised contract for the seller to sign and return.

E-commerce makes this easier—the buyer can send an e-mail asking the seller to send more of the same goods, preferably by specifying the number above that provided in the earlier agreement that the buyer now wishes to buy. If the buyer bought three $60 life jackets for her own use, Article 2

allows a court to enforce the seller's commitment to sell three at $60 each even without worrying about the statute of frauds in Section 2–201. However, if the buyer wanted to increase her order from three to 15 life jackets, the dollar amount of the purchase would rise above $500—and courts would not enforce the larger purchase unless the deal met the statute of frauds. How does the Internet help buyers and sellers who want to be able to enforce their agreements in court if the other party does not perform? Using either the federal E-Sign law or state-enacted versions of the Uniform Electronic Transactions Act (UETA), the party seeking to enforce the larger quantity could send an e-mail or message using a click-through form provided by a seller's Web site, and could use that e-mail or other electronically revised order to show the fact of the revision to the "order" and, as applicable, the existence of a reply message from the seller confirming the seller's agreement to the change.

As a further example of how e-mail and the Internet assist sales transactions, sellers now routinely send or post confirmations that shipment has occurred. These messages help buyers plan for the arrival of goods, otherwise keep track of delays in orders that they may need to act upon, and also check that their insurance is effective for a particular purchase or that their warehouse is ready to receive the goods sent.

fish wholesaler to deliver fish to a supermarket every Thursday and for the supermarket to pay on delivery. If the fish wholesaler regularly delivers the fish on Friday and the supermarket does not object, the supermarket will be unable to cancel the contract for that reason. Similarly, if the supermarket does not pay cash but sends a check the following week, then unless the fish wholesaler objects, it will not be able to assert the late payments as grounds for later canceling the contract. A party that has waived rights to a portion of the contract not yet performed may retract the waiver by giving reasonable notice to the other party that strict performance will be required. The retraction of the waiver is effective unless it would be unjust because of a material change of position by the other party in reliance on the waiver [2–209(5)].

Assignment

Under the Code, the buyer and/or the seller may delegate their duties to someone else. If there is a strong reason for having the original party perform the duties, perhaps because the quality of the performance might differ otherwise, the parties may not delegate their duties. Also, they may not delegate their duties if the parties agree in the contract that there is to be no assignment of duties. However, they may assign rights to receive performance—for example, the right to receive goods or payment [2–210].

Delivery

Basic Obligation

The basic duty of the seller is to deliver the goods called for by the contract. The basic duty of the buyer is to accept and pay for the goods if they conform to the contract [2–301]. The buyer and seller may agree that the goods are to be delivered in several lots or installments. If there is no such agreement, then a single delivery of all the goods must be made. Where delivery is to be made in lots, the seller may demand the price of each lot upon delivery unless there has been an agreement for the extension of credit [2–307].

Place of Delivery

The buyer and seller may agree on the place where the goods will be delivered. If no such agreement is made, then the goods are to be delivered at the seller's place of business. If the seller does not have a place of business, then delivery is to be made at his home. If the goods are located elsewhere than the seller's place of business or home, the place of delivery is the place where the goods are located [2–308].

Seller's Duty of Delivery

The seller's basic obligation is to tender delivery of goods that conform to the contract with the buyer. Tender of delivery means that the seller must make the goods available to the buyer. This must be done during reasonable hours and for a reasonable period of time, so that the buyer can take possession of the goods [2–503]. The contract of sale may require the seller merely to ship the goods to the buyer but not to deliver the goods to the buyer's place of business. If this is the case, the seller must put the goods into the possession of a carrier, such as a trucking company or a railroad. The seller must also make a reasonable contract with the carrier to take the goods to the buyer. Then, the seller must notify the buyer that the goods have been shipped [2–504]. Shipment terms were discussed in Chapter 19, Formation and Terms of Sales Contracts.

If the seller does not make a reasonable contract for delivery or notify the buyer and a material delay or loss results, the buyer has the right to reject the shipment. Suppose the goods are perishable, such as fresh produce, and the seller does not ship them in a refrigerated truck or railroad car. If the produce deteriorates in transit, the buyer can reject the produce on the ground that the seller did not make a reasonable contract for shipping it.

In some situations, the goods sold may be in the possession of a bailee such as a warehouse. If the goods are covered by a negotiable warehouse receipt, the seller must endorse the receipt and give it to the buyer [2–503(4)(a)]. This enables the buyer to obtain the goods from the warehouse. Such a situation exists when grain being sold is stored at a grain elevator. The law of negotiable documents of title, including warehouse receipts, is discussed in Chapter 23, Personal Property and Bailments.

If the goods in the possession of a bailee are not covered by a negotiable warehouse receipt, then the seller must notify the bailee that it has sold the goods to the buyer and must obtain the bailee's consent to hold the goods for delivery to the buyer or release the goods to the buyer. The risk of loss as to the goods remains with the seller until the bailee agrees to hold them for the buyer [2–503(4)(b)].

Inspection and Payment

Buyer's Right of Inspection

Normally, the buyer has the right to inspect the goods before he accepts or pays for them. The buyer and seller may agree on the time, place, and manner in which the buyer will inspect the goods. If no agreement is made, then the buyer may inspect the goods at any reasonable time and place and in any reasonable manner [2–513(1)].

If the shipping terms are cash on delivery (COD), then the buyer must pay for the goods before inspecting them unless they are marked "Inspection Allowed." However, if it is obvious even without inspection that the goods do not conform to the contract, the buyer may reject them without paying for them first [2–512(1)(a)]. For example, if a farmer contracted to buy a bull and the seller delivered a cow, the farmer would not have to pay for it. The fact that a buyer may have to pay for goods before inspecting them does not deprive the buyer of remedies against the seller if the goods do not conform to the contract [2–512(2)].

The Global Business Environment

Assurance of Payment

Perhaps the most important provisions in the international sales contract cover the manner by which the buyer pays the seller. Frequently, a foreign buyer's contractual promise to pay when the goods arrive does not provide the seller with sufficient assurance of payment. The seller may not know the overseas buyer well enough to determine the buyer's financial condition or inclination to refuse payment if the buyer no longer wants the goods when they arrive. When the buyer fails to make payment, the seller will find it difficult and expensive to pursue its legal rights under the contract. Even if the seller is assured that the buyer will pay for the goods on arrival, the time required for shipping the goods often means that payment is not received until months after shipment.

To solve these problems, the seller often insists on receiving an **irrevocable letter of credit.** The buyer obtains a letter of credit from a bank in the buyer's country. The letter of credit obligates the buyer's bank to pay the amount of the sales contract to the seller. To obtain payment, the seller must produce a **negotiable bill of lading** and other documents proving that it shipped the goods required by the sales contract in conformity with the terms of the letter of credit.[1] A letter of credit is irrevocable when the buyer's bank cannot withdraw its obligation to pay without the consent of the seller and the buyer.

Letters of credit may be confirmed or advised. Under a **confirmed letter of credit,** the seller's bank agrees to assume liability on the letter of credit. Typically, under a confirmed letter of credit, the buyer's bank issues a letter of credit to the seller; the seller's bank confirms the letter of credit; the seller delivers the goods to a carrier; the carrier issues a negotiable bill of lading to the seller; the seller delivers the bill of lading to the seller's bank and presents a draft[2] drawn on the buyer demanding payment for the goods; the seller's bank pays the seller for the goods; the buyer's bank reimburses the seller's bank; and the buyer reimburses its bank.

With an **advised letter of credit,** the seller's bank merely acts as an agent for collection of the amount owed to the seller. The seller's bank acts as agent for the seller by collecting from the buyer's bank and giving the payment to the seller. The buyer's bank is reimbursed by the buyer.

The confirmed letter of credit is the least risky payment method for sellers. The confirmation is needed because the seller, unlike the confirming bank, may not know any more about the financial integrity of the issuing bank than it knows about that of the buyer. The seller has a promise of immediate payment from an entity it knows to be financially solvent—the confirming bank. If the draft drawn pursuant to the letter of credit is not paid, the seller may sue the confirming bank, which is a bank in his home country.

Under the confirmed letter of credit, payment is made to the seller well before the goods arrive. Thus, the buyer cannot claim that the goods are defective and refuse to pay for them. When the goods are truly defective on arrival, however, the customer can commence an action for damages against the seller based on their original sales contract.

Figure 1 (page 552) summarizes the confirmed letter of credit transaction.

Conforming and Nonconforming Documents

In a letter of credit transaction, the promises made by the buyer's and seller's banks are independent of the underlying sales contract between the seller and the buyer. Therefore, when the seller presents a bill of lading and other documents that *conform* to the terms of the letter of credit, the issuing bank and the confirming bank are required to pay, even if the buyer refuses to pay its bank or even, generally, if the buyer claims to know that the goods are defective. However, if the bill of lading or other required documents do not conform to the terms of the letter of credit, a bank may properly refuse to pay. A bill of lading is *nonconforming* when, for example, it indicates the wrong goods were shipped, states the wrong person to receive the goods, or states a buyer's address differently than the letter of credit.

---

[1] A bill of lading is a document issued by a carrier acknowledging that the seller has delivered particular goods to it and entitling the holder of the bill of lading to receive these goods at the place of destination. Bills of lading are discussed in Chapter 23.

[2] A draft is a negotiable instrument by which the drawer (in this case, the seller) orders the drawee (the buyer) to pay the payee (the seller). Drafts are discussed in Chapter 31.

Figure 1   *Confirmed Letter of Credit Transaction*

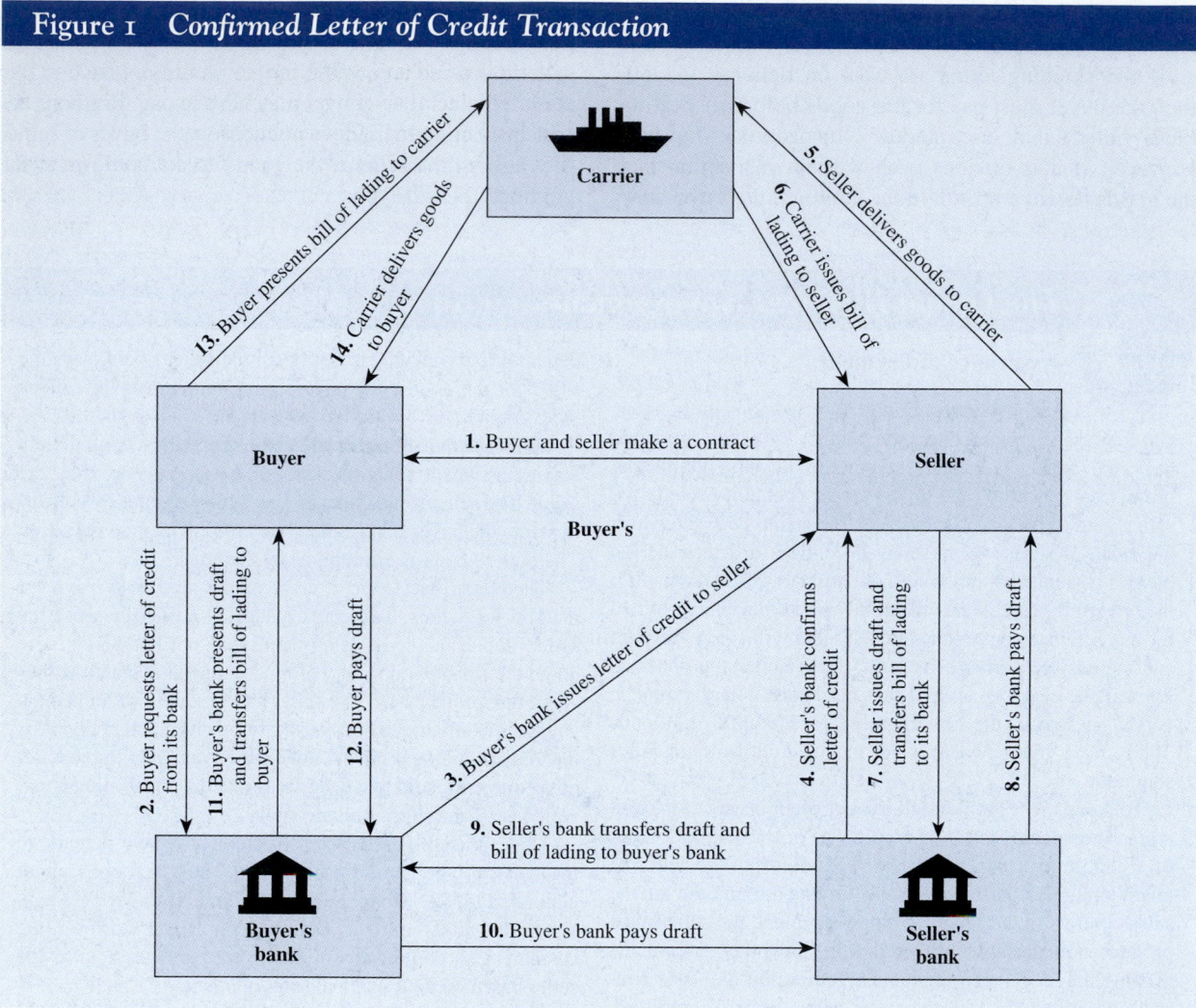

If the goods conform to the contract, the buyer must pay the expenses of inspection. However, if the goods are nonconforming, he may recover his inspection expenses from the seller [2–513(2); 2–715(1)].

Payment   The buyer and seller may agree in their contract that the price of the goods is to be paid in money or in other goods, services, or real property. If all or part of the price of goods is payable in real property, then only the transfer of goods is covered by the law of sales of goods. The transfer of the real property is covered by the law of real property [2–304].

The contract may provide that the goods are sold on credit to the buyer and that the buyer has a period of time to pay for them. If there is no agreement for extending

credit to the buyer, the buyer must pay for them upon delivery. The buyer usually can inspect goods before payment except where the goods are shipped COD, in which case the buyer must pay for them before inspecting them.

Unless the seller demands cash, the buyer may pay for the goods by personal check or by any other method used in the ordinary course of business. If the seller demands cash, the seller must give the buyer a reasonable amount of time to obtain it. If payment is made by check, the payment is conditional on the check's being honored by the bank when it is presented for payment [2–511(3)]. If the bank refuses to pay the check, the buyer has not satisfied the duty to pay for the goods. In that case, the buyer does not have the right to retain the goods and must give them back to the seller.

Acceptance, Revocation, and Rejection

Acceptance

Acceptance of goods occurs when a buyer, after having a reasonable opportunity to inspect them, either indicates that he will take them or fails to reject them. To **reject** goods, the buyer must notify the seller of the rejection and specify the defect or nonconformity. If a buyer treats the goods as if he owns them, the buyer is considered to have accepted them [2–606].

For example, Ace Appliance delivers a new large flat screen television set to Baldwin. Baldwin has accepted the set if, after trying it and finding it to be in working order, she says nothing to Ace or tells Ace that she will keep it. Even if the set is defective, Baldwin is considered to have accepted it if she does not give Ace timely notice that she does not want to keep it because it is not in working order. If she takes the set to her vacation home even though she knows that it does not work properly, this is also an acceptance. In the latter case, her use of the television set would be inconsistent with its rejection and the return of ownership to the seller.

If a buyer accepts any part of a **commercial unit** of goods, he is considered to have accepted the whole unit [2–606(2)]. A commercial unit is any unit of goods that is treated by commercial usage as a single whole. It can be a single article (such as a machine), a set or quantity of articles (such as a dozen, bale, gross, or carload), or any other unit treated as a single whole [2–105(6)]. Thus, if a bushel of apples is a commercial unit, then a buyer purchasing 10 bushels of apples who accepts 8½ bushels is considered to have accepted 9 bushels.

In the *Weil v. Murray* case, which follows, the buyer was considered to have accepted goods that it had handled inconsistently with a claim of rejection and return of ownership of the goods to the seller.

Weil v. Murray   2001 WL 345222 (U.S.D.C. S.D.N.Y. 2001)

On October 19, 1997, Mark Murray, a New York art dealer and gallery owner, traveled to Montgomery, Alabama, to view various paintings in the art collection owned by Robert Weil. Murray examined one of the paintings under ultraviolet light—a painting by Edgar Degas entitled Aux Courses. *Murray discussed the Degas with Ian Peck, another art dealer, who indicated an interest in buying it and asked Murray to arrange to have it brought to New York.*

Murray and Weil executed an agreement which provided for consignment of the Degas to Murray's gallery "for a private inspection in New York for a period of a week from November 3" to be extended only with the express permission of the consignor. The director of Murray's Gallery picked up the painting, which was subsequently shown by Murray to Peck. Peck agreed to purchase the painting for $1,225,000 with Murray acting as a broker. On November 8, Murray advised Weil that he had a buyer for the Degas and they orally agreed to the sale. Subsequently, they entered into a written agreement for the sale of the painting for $1 million that indicated, among other things, that if Weil did not receive full payment by December 8, Murray would disclose the name of the undisclosed principal on whose behalf he was acting.

Neither Murray nor anyone else ever paid Weil the $1 million. Nonetheless, Murray maintained possession of the Degas from November 3, 1997, through March 25, 1998, when Weil requested its return. At some point in mid-November, Weil and Peck took the Degas to an art conservator. A condition report prepared by the conservator and dated December 3, 1997, showed that the conservator had cleaned the painting and sought to correct some deterioration. Weil brought an action to recover the price of the painting from Murray.

Mukasey, District Judge

The undisputed facts establish also that Murray accepted the Degas. "Goods that a buyer has in its possession necessarily are accepted or rejected by the time a reasonable opportunity for inspecting them passes." Murray first inspected the Degas under an ultraviolet light when he viewed it at the Weils' home in late October. Murray had the opportunity to further examine the Degas at his gallery in New York pursuant to the consignment agreement and his continued possession of the painting following the expiration of the consignment agreement. It is also undisputed that Murray was present when Simon Parkes assessed the condition of the painting sometime between November 3 and November 19, 1997. Not only did Murray have a reasonable time to inspect the goods, but also it is undisputed that he actually did inspect the Degas. There is no evidence that Murray found the painting unsatisfactory or nonconforming. See *Integrated Circuits Unltd. v. E. F. Johnson Co.,* (2d Cir. 1989) (discussing acceptance as the failure to make an effective rejection after a reasonable time to inspect). Although the question of whether the buyer has had a reasonable time to inspect is generally a question for the trier of fact, no reasonable jury could find that Murray did not accept the Degas in light of the undisputed facts that he inspected the Degas on at least two occasions, signed the written agreement, and continued to retain possession of the Degas. See *Sessa v. Riegle*, (D.C. Pa. 1977) (finding acceptance when buyer was permitted unlimited inspection of a horse and then indicated that he would buy the horse).

Moreover, it is undisputed that, without Weil's consent, Murray, at a minimum, permitted the painting to be cleaned and restored in late November or early December. Murray's participation in the alteration of the painting, regardless of whether such alteration increased its value, was an act inconsistent with Weils' ownership. See *In re Fran Char Press, Inc.,* (Bankr. E.D.N.Y. 1985) (finding that buyer had accepted posters by taking possession of them and mounting them on cardboard); *Industria De Calcados Martini Ltd. v. Maxwell Shoe Co.,* (Mass. App. Ct. 1994) (finding acceptance where buyer had shoes refinished). The Weils have established that Murray agreed to purchase the Degas, accepted it, and nonetheless failed to pay the purchase price.

Summary judgment granted in favor of the Weils.

Effect of Acceptance

Effect of Acceptance Once a buyer has accepted goods, he cannot later reject them unless at the time they were accepted, the buyer had reason to believe that the nonconformity would be cured. By accepting goods, the buyer does not forfeit or waive all remedies against the seller for any nonconformities in the goods. However, if the buyer wishes to hold the seller responsible, he must give the seller timely notice that the goods are nonconforming.

The buyer is obligated to pay for goods that are accepted. If the buyer accepts all of the goods sold, she is, of course, responsible for the full purchase price. If the buyer accepts only part of the goods, she must pay for that part at the contract rate [2–607(1)].

Revocation of Acceptance

Revocation of Acceptance Under certain circumstances, a buyer may **revoke** or undo the acceptance. A buyer may revoke acceptance of nonconforming goods where (1) the nonconformity substantially impairs the value of the goods and (2) the buyer accepted them without knowledge of the nonconformity because of the difficulty of discovering the nonconformity, or the buyer accepted the goods because of the seller's assurances that it would cure the defect [2–608(1)].

The buyer must exercise her right to revoke acceptance within a reasonable time after the buyer discovers or should have discovered the nonconformity. Revocation is not effective until the buyer notifies the seller of the intention to revoke acceptance. After a buyer revokes acceptance, her rights are the same as they would have been if the goods had been rejected when delivery was offered [2–608].

The right to revoke acceptance could arise, for example, where Arnold buys a new car from Dealer. While driving the car home, Arnold discovers that it has a seriously defective transmission. When she returns the car to Dealer, Dealer promises to repair it, so Arnold decides to keep the car. If the dealer does not fix the transmission after repeated efforts to fix it, Arnold could revoke her acceptance on the grounds that the nonconformity substantially impairs the value of the car, that she took delivery of the car without knowledge of the nonconformity, and that her acceptance was based on Dealer's assurances that he would fix the car. Similarly, revocation of acceptance might be involved where a serious problem with the car not discoverable by inspection shows up in the first month's use.

Revocation must occur prior to any substantial change in the goods, however, such as serious damage in an accident or wear and tear from using them for a period of time. What constitutes a "substantial impairment in value" and when there has been a "substantial change in the goods" are questions that courts frequently have to decide when an attempted revocation of acceptance results in a lawsuit. The *Waddell* case illustrates a number of the issues that arise in situations where a buyer is seeking to revoke her acceptance.

Waddell v. L.V.R.V. Inc.   58 UCC Rep.2d 654 (Sup. Ct. Nev. 2006)

In 1996, Arthur and Roswitha Waddell served jointly as president of the Las Vegas area Coachmen Association Camping Club. During the course of one of the group's meetings, they spoke with Tom Pender, the sales manager of Wheeler's Las Vegas RV (Wheeler's), about upgrading the motor home they owned to a "diesel pusher" motor coach. Pender took the Waddells to the Wheeler's lot and showed them a 1996 Coachmen Santara model diesel pusher coach. The Waddells test-drove and eventually agreed to purchase the RV and an extended warranty. Before they took possession of the RV, they requested that Wheeler's perform various repairs including service on the RV's engine cooling system, new batteries, and alignment of the door frames. Wheeler's told the Waddells that the repairs had been performed as requested, and they took delivery of the RV on September 1, 1997.

The Waddells first noticed a problem with the RV's engine shortly after taking possession of it. They drove the RV from Las Vegas to Hemet, California. On the return trip, the entry door popped open, and the RV's engine overheated while ascending a moderate grade to such a degree that Mr. Waddell had to pull over to the side of the road and wait for the engine to cool down.

When the Waddells returned from California, they took the RV back to Wheeler's for repairs. Despite Wheeler's attempts to repair the RV, the Waddells continually experienced more problems with the RV, including further episodes of the engine overheating. Between September 1997 and March 1999, Wheeler's service department spent a total of seven months during different periods of time attempting to repair the RV.

On June 9, 2000, the Waddells brought suit against Wheeler's seeking both equitable relief and monetary damages. The trial court concluded that the RV's nonconformities substantially impaired its value to the Waddells and allowed them to revoke their acceptance of the RV. The court also ordered Wheeler's to return all of the Waddells' out-of-pocket expenses. Wheeler's appealed the judgment.

Gibbons, Justice

The district court found that despite Wheeler's good-faith attempts to repair the RV, the nonconformities persisted and rendered the RV unfit for its intended use. Some of those nonconformities included: the bedroom air conditioning does not cool, the front air conditioning does not cool, the dash heater does not blow hot air, RV batteries do not stay charged, and chronic engine overheating. The district court concluded that these nonconformities and others substantially impaired the RV's value to the Waddells and that the Waddells had revoked their acceptance of the RV within a reasonable time.

We have never before determined when a nonconformity substantially impairs the value of a good to the buyer. Other jurisdictions treat this determination as an issue of fact, which is made in light of the totality of the circumstances of each particular case, including the number of deficiencies and type of nonconformity and the time and inconvenience spent in downtime and attempts at repair.

The Supreme Court of Oregon has established a two-part test to determine whether a nonconformity, under the totality of the circumstances, substantially impairs the value of the goods to the buyer. The test has both an objective and a subjective prong:

Since the statute provides that the buyer may revoke acceptance of goods "whose nonconformity substantially impairs its value *to him*," the value of the conforming goods *to the plaintiff* must first be determined. This is a subjective question in the sense it calls for a consideration of the needs and circumstances of the plaintiff who seeks to revoke, not the needs and circumstances of an average buyer. The second inquiry is whether the nonconformity in fact substantially impairs the value of the goods to the buyer, having in mind his particular needs. This is an objective question in the sense that it calls for evidence of something more than

plaintiff's assertion that the nonconformity impaired the value to him; it requires evidence from which it can be inferred that plaintiff's needs were not met because of the nonconformity.

Subjective value to the Waddells

Arthur Waddell testified that he purchased the RV to enjoy the RV lifestyle. Before purchasing the RV, the Waddells owned similar vehicles that they used both as a residence and for camping trips. In fact, Mr. Waddell testified that he and his wife intended to sell their house and spend two to three years traveling around the country.

Mr. Waddell further testified that he shopped at Wheeler's based on Wheeler's advertisements. Marlene Wheeler, president and chief operating officer, testified that Wheeler's advertising encouraged the purchase of an RV to find unlimited freedom. When Mr. Waddell spoke with Tom Pender, sales manager at Wheeler's about upgrading to an RV for those purposes, Pender told him that he had an RV on the lot that would meet his needs.

Mr. Waddell's testimony demonstrates that the RV's subjective value to the Waddells was based on their ability to spend two or three years driving the RV around the country. Thus, we must consider whether the RV's nonconformity substantially impaired the value of the RV based on the Waddells' particular needs.

Objective impairment

Mr. Waddell testified that as a result of the RV's defects, he and his wife were unable to enjoy the RV as they had intended. Mr. Waddell further testified that the RV's engine would overheat within ten miles of embarking if the travel involved any climbing.

****

Consequently, the RV spent a total of 213 days, or seven months and one day, at Wheeler's service department during the eighteen months immediately following the purchase. This testimony is sufficient to demonstrate an objective, substantial impairment of value.

The Supreme Court of Ohio has stated that a nonconformity effects a substantial impairment of value if it "shakes the buyer's faith or undermines his confidence in the reliability of the purchased item." The Supreme Judicial Court of Massachusetts has recognized that "even cosmetic or minor defects that go unrepaired . . . or defects which do not totally prevent the buyer from using the goods, but circumscribe that use . . . can substantially impair the goods' value to the buyer." The United States District Court for the District of Nevada recently reiterated that " the seller's inability to correct defects in motor vehicles creates a major hardship and an unacceptable economic burden on the consumer."

In this case, the chronic engine overheating shook the Waddells' faith in the RV and undermined their confidence in the RV's reliability and integrity. Not only did this problem make travel in the RV unreliable and stressful to the Waddells, the overheating made travel in the vehicle objectively unsafe.

Reasonable time for revoking acceptance

Wheeler's argues that the Waddells should not have been allowed to revoke their acceptance when they did not attempt to revoke within a reasonable time after purchasing the RV. We disagree.

Under section 2–608(2), "revocation of acceptance must occur within a reasonable time after the buyer discovers or should have discovered the ground for it and before any substantial change in the condition of goods which is not caused by their own defects." The statute further provides that revocation "is not effective until the buyer notifies the seller of it." We have never before determined a reasonable timeline for revocation of acceptance. However, other jurisdictions have held that the reasonable time determination "depends upon the nature, purpose and circumstances of the transaction."

Here, the district court found that the Waddells were entitled to revoke their acceptance since they notified Wheeler's of their intent to revoke within a reasonable time.

Mr. Waddell testified that he first notified the RV's defects immediately after his purchase. Mr. Waddell took the RV to Wheeler's service department whenever he noticed a defect and Wheeler's always attempted, often unsuccessfully, to repair the RV. As a result of those defects, Wheeler's service department kept the RV for approximately seven months of the eighteen months that the Waddells owned the RV. Roger Beauchemin, a former employee of Wheeler's service department, testified that Wheeler's was unable to repair some of the defects, including the engine's chronic overheating problems. In January 1999, the Waddells again brought the RV to Wheeler's complaining of persistent engine overheating. The Waddells demanded a full refund of the purchase price in March 1999 and sought legal counsel. Through counsel, the Waddells wrote to Wheeler's during the summer of 1999 to resolve the matter. Wheeler's did not respond to those inquiries until early 2000. Unable to resolve the dispute with Wheeler's, the Waddells revoked their acceptance of the RV in June 2000.

The seller of nonconforming goods must generally receive an opportunity to cure the deformity before the buyer may revoke his acceptance. However, the seller may not postpone revocation in perpetuity by fixing everything that goes wrong. Rather there comes a time when the buyer is entitled to say, "that's all," and revoke, not withstanding the seller's repeated good faith to cure.

Furthermore, the seller's attempts to cure do not count against the buyer regarding timely revocation. The United States District Court for the District of Nevada has held that the "time for revocation of acceptance will be tolled while the seller attempts repairs." Tolling the reasonable time for revocation of acceptance is appropriate given the buyer's obligation to act in good faith and to afford the seller a reasonable opportunity to cure any defect in the goods.

The Waddells gave Wheeler's several opportunities to repair the defects before revoking their acceptance. Because Wheeler's was unable to repair the defects after a total of seven months, the Waddells were entitled to say "that's all" and revoke their acceptance, notwithstanding Wheeler's good-faith efforts to repair the RV. Also the reasonable time for revocation was tolled during the seven months that Wheeler's kept the RV and attempted to repair the defects.

Judgment affirmed in favor of the Waddells.

Buyer's Rights on Improper Delivery

If the goods delivered by the seller do not conform to the contract, the buyer has several options. The buyer can (1) reject all of the goods, (2) accept all of them, or (3) accept any commercial units and reject the rest [2–601]. The buyer, however, cannot accept only part of a commercial unit and reject the rest. The buyer must pay for the units accepted at the price per unit provided in the contract.

CYBERLAW IN ACTION

Providing Notice

Sections 2–602 and 2–607 require that the buyer notify the seller if the buyer wishes to reject goods the seller has tendered to the buyer, or if the buyer decides to revoke acceptance of goods that the seller has promised to repair or replace and has neither repaired nor replaced the goods as promised—or where the buyer gets goods that have a latent (hard-to-find) defect. "Notice" does not have to be in writing to be effective under 2–602 or 2–607, but many buyers prefer to have a record that they gave notice to the seller and the time of the notice given. This reduces the risk that a court will find that the buyer's failure to give notice deprives the buyer of her right to a remedy (see Section 2–607(3)(a)). Electronic commerce tools, including e-mail, allow buyers to provide speedy and reliable information to sellers in cases such as these. Buyers whose e-mail systems provide confirmation that the seller recipient actually has received the message about the buyer's concerns about the goods, or who show the time and date that the intended recipient opened the e-mail, should make providing notice easier and less expensive than using traditional means of communication.

Where the contract calls for delivery of the goods in separate installments, the buyer's options are more limited. The buyer may reject an installment delivery only if the nonconformity *substantially affects the value* of that delivery and *cannot be corrected* by the seller in a timely fashion. If the nonconformity is relatively minor, the buyer must accept the installment. The seller may offer to replace the defective goods or give the buyer an allowance in the price to make up for the nonconformity [2–612].

Where the nonconformity or defect in one installment impairs the value of the whole contract, the buyer may treat it as a breach of the whole contract but must proceed carefully so as not to reinstate the remainder of the contract [2–612(3)].

Rejection
If a buyer has a basis for rejecting a delivery of goods, the buyer must act within a *reasonable time* after delivery. The buyer must also give the seller *notice* of the rejection, preferably in writing [2–602]. The buyer should be careful to state all of the defects on which he is basing the rejection, including all of the defects that a reasonable inspection would disclose. This is particularly important if these are defects that the seller might cure (remedy) and the time for delivery has not expired. In that case, the seller may notify the buyer that he intends to redeliver conforming goods.

If the buyer fails to state in connection with his rejection a particular defect that is ascertainable by reasonable inspection, he cannot use the defect to justify his rejection if the seller could have cured the defect had he been given reasonable notice of it. In a transaction taking place between merchants, the seller has, after rejection, a right to a written statement of all the defects in the goods on which the buyer bases his right to reject, and the buyer may not later assert defects not listed in justification of his rejection [2–605].

If the buyer wrongfully rejects goods, she is liable to the seller for breach of the sales contract [2–602(3)].

In the case that follows, *Fitl v. Strek,* the court addressed the question of whether a buyer had acted in a timely fashion to notify the seller of a significant defect in an otherwise very valuable baseball trading card.

Fitl v. Strek   690 N.W.2d 605 (Sup. Ct. Neb. 2005)

In September 1995, James Fitl attended a sports card show in San Francisco where Mark Stek, doing business as Star Cards of San Francisco, was an exhibitor. Fitl purchased from Strek a 1952 Mickey Mantle Topps baseball card for $17,750. According to Fitl, Strek represented that the card was in near mint condition. After Stek delivered the card to Fitl in Omaha, Nebraska, Fitl placed it in a safe-deposit box.

In May 1997, Fitl sent the baseball card to Professional Sports Authenticators (PSA), a leading grading service for sports cards that is located in Newport, California. PSA reported to Fitl that the card was ungradable because it had been discolored and doctored. The expert from the firm stated that any alteration of a card, including the touchup or trimming of a card would render it valueless. In this case, the edges of the card had been trimmed and reglued. One spot on the front of the card and a larger spot on the back had been repainted, which left the card with no value. He also said that the standard for sports memorabilia was a lifetime guarantee and that a reputable dealer would stand behind what he sold and refund the money if an item were fake or had been altered.

On May 29, 1997, Fitl wrote to Strek and indicated that he planned to pursue "legal methods" to resolve the matter. Strek replied that Fitl should have initiated a return of the baseball card in a timely fashion so that Strek could have confronted his source and remedied the situation. Strek asserted that a typical grace period for the unconditional return of a card was from seven days to one month.

In August 1997, Fitl sent the baseball card to ASA Accugrade, Inc. (ASA) in Longwood, Florida, for a second opinion. ASA also concluded that the baseball card had been refinished and trimmed.

On September 8, 1997, Fitl sued Stek, alleging that Strek knew the baseball card had been recolored or otherwise altered and concealed this fact from him. Fitl claimed he had relied on Strek's status as a reputable dealer. The trial court entered judgment for Fitl in the amount of $17,750 and costs. The court found that Fitl notified Strek as soon as he realized the baseball card was altered and worthless and that Fitl had notified Strek of the defect within a reasonable time after its discovery. The court rejected Strek's theory that Fitl should have determined the authenticity of the baseball card immediately after it had been purchased.

Wright, Justice

Strek claims that the court erred in determining that notification of the defective condition of the baseball card two years after the date of purchase was timely pursuant to UCC section 2–607(3)(a).

Section 2–607(3)(a) states: "Where a tender has been accepted . . . the buyer must within a reasonable time after he discovers or should have discovered any breach notify the seller of breach or be barred from any remedy." "What is a reasonable time for taking any action depends on the nature, purpose and circumstances of such action." [2–204(2)].

The notice requirement set forth in section 2–697(3)(a) serves three purposes. It provides the seller with an opportunity to correct any defect, to prepare for negotiation and litigation, and to protect itself against stale claims before it is too late for the seller to investigate. Whether the notice given is satisfactory and whether it is given within reasonable time are generally questions of fact to be measured by all the circumstances of the case.

Fitl purchased the baseball card in 1995 and immediately placed it in a safe-deposit box. Two years later, he retrieved the baseball card, had it appraised, and learned that it was of no value. Fitl testified that he had relied on Strek's position as a dealer of sports cards and on his representation that the baseball card was authentic. In *Cao v. Nguyen* (2000), we stated a party is justified in relying upon a representation made to the party as a positive statement of fact when an investigation would be required to ascertain its falsity. In order for Fitl to have determined that the baseball card had been altered, he would have been required to conduct an investigation. We find that he was not required to do so. Once Fitl

learned that the baseball card had been altered, he gave notice to Strek.

As the court noted in *Maybank v. Kresge Co.* (1981), one of the most important policies behind the notice requirement of 2–607(3)(a) is to allow the seller to cure the breach by making adjustments or replacements to minimize the buyer's damages and the seller's liability. However, even if Fitl had learned immediately upon taking possession of the baseball card that it was not authentic and had notified Strek at that time, there is no evidence that Strek could have made any adjustment or taken any action that would have minimized his liability. In its altered condition, the baseball card was worthless.

Strek claimed via his correspondence to Fitl that if Strek had received notice earlier, he could have contacted the person who sold him the baseball card to determine the source of the alteration, but there is no evidence to support this allegation. Earlier notification would not have helped Strek prepare for negotiation in a suit because the damage to Fitl could not be repaired. Thus, the policies behind the notice requirement, to allow the seller to repair a defect, to prepare for negotiation and litigation, and to protect against stale claims at a time beyond which an investigation can be completed, were not unfairly prejudiced by the lack of an earlier notice to Strek. Any problem Strek may have had with the party from whom he obtained the baseball card was a separate matter from his transaction with Fitl, and an investigation into the source of the altered card would not have minimized Fitl's damages.

Judgment affirmed in favor of Fitl.

Right to Cure

If the seller has some reason to believe that the buyer would accept nonconforming goods, then the seller can take a reasonable time to re-ship conforming goods. The seller has this opportunity even if the original time for delivery has expired. For example, Ace Manufacturing contracts to sell 200 red, white, and blue soccer balls to Sam's Sporting Goods, with delivery to be made by April 1. On March 1, Sam's receives a package from Ace containing 200 all-white soccer balls and refuses to accept them. Ace can notify Sam's that it intends to cure the improper delivery by supplying 200 red, white, and blue soccer balls, and it has until April 1 to deliver the correct balls to Sam's. If Ace thought that Sam's would accept the all-white soccer balls because on past shipments Sam's did not object to the substitution of white balls for red,

white, and blue balls, then Ace has a reasonable time even after April 1 to deliver the red, white, and blue soccer balls [2–508].

Buyer's Duties after Rejection

If the buyer is a merchant, then the buyer owes certain duties concerning the goods that he rejects. First, the buyer must follow any reasonable instructions that the seller gives concerning disposition of the goods. The seller, for example, might request that the rejected goods be shipped back to the seller. If the goods are perishable or may deteriorate rapidly, then the buyer must make a reasonable effort to sell the goods. The seller must reimburse the buyer for any expenses that the buyer incurs in carrying out the seller's instructions or in trying to resell perishable goods. In reselling goods, the

---

CONCEPT REVIEW

Acceptance, Revocation, and Rejection

Acceptance	1. Occurs when buyer, having had a reasonable opportunity to inspect goods, either (a) indicates he will take them or (b) fails to reject them.
	2. If buyer accepts any part of a commercial unit, he is considered to have accepted the whole unit.
	3. If buyer accepts goods, he cannot later reject them *unless* at the time they were accepted the buyer had reason to believe that the nonconformity would be cured.
	4. Buyer is obligated to pay for goods that are accepted.
Revocation	1. Buyer may revoke acceptance of nonconforming goods where (a) the nonconformity *substantially impairs the value* of the goods and (b) buyer accepted the goods without knowledge of the nonconformity because of the difficulty of discovering the nonconformity *or* buyer accepted because of assurances by the seller.
	2. Right to revoke must be exercised within a *reasonable* time after buyer discovers *or* should have discovered the nonconformity.
	3. Revocation must be invoked before there is any *substantial* change in the goods.
	4. Revocation is not effective until buyer notifies seller of his intent to revoke acceptance.
Rejection	1. Where the goods delivered do not conform to the contract, buyer may (a) reject all of the goods, (b) accept all of the goods, or (c) accept any commercial unit and reject the rest. Buyer must pay for goods accepted.
	2. Where the goods are to be delivered in installments, an installment delivery may be rejected *only if* the nonconformity substantially affects the value of that delivery and cannot be corrected by the seller.
	3. Buyer must act within a reasonable time after delivery.

buyer must act reasonably and in good faith [2–603(2) and (3)].

If the rejected goods are not perishable or if the seller does not give the buyer instructions, then the buyer has several options. First, the buyer can store the goods for the seller. Second, the buyer can reship them to the seller. Third, the buyer can resell them for the seller's benefit. If the buyer resells the goods, the buyer may keep his expenses and a reasonable commission on the sale. If the buyer stores the goods, the buyer should exercise care in handling them. The buyer also must give the seller a reasonable time to remove the goods [2–604].

If the buyer is not a merchant, then her obligation after rejection is to hold the goods with reasonable care for a sufficient time to give the seller an opportunity to remove them. The buyer is not obligated to ship the goods back to the seller [2–602].

Assurance, Repudiation, and Excuse

Assurance The buyer or seller may become concerned that the other party may not be able to perform his contract obligations. If there is a reasonable basis for that concern, the buyer or seller can demand **assurance** from the other party that the contract will be performed. If such assurances are not given within a reasonable time not exceeding 30 days, the party is considered to have repudiated the contract [2–609].

In the case that follows, *Koch Materials Co. v. Shore Slurry Seal, Inc.,* the court held that a party obligated on a contract failed to provide adequate assurance that its commitments would be met and was found to have repudiated the contract.

Koch Materials Co. v. Shore Slurry Seal, Inc.   205 F.Supp.2d 324 (D.N.J. 2002)

Koch Materials Company is a manufacturer of asphalt and other road surfacing materials. In February 1998, Koch bought from Shore Slurry Seal, Inc., an asphalt plant in New Jersey as well the domestic license rights to a specialty road surfacing substance known as "Novachip." Koch's purchase price was $5 million, payable in three installments. The last and smallest of the three installments in the amount of $500,000 was not due until 2004.

As part of the sale, Shore entered into two side contracts with Koch. First, Shore and Koch signed an Exclusive Supply Agreement, under which Shore agreed that for the seven years following the sale it would purchase all of its asphalt requirements from Koch, and in any event at least two million gallons of asphalt per year. The Agreement provided that, in the event Shore purchased less than six million gallons over the first three years of the contract, the $500,000 installment payment would be reduced by the same percentage by which Shore missed the six million gallon mark. Second, Shore promised to utilize at least 2.5 million square yards of Novachip annually, either in its own business or through sublicense agreements in certain permitted regions, and to pay royalties to Koch accordingly.

For the first three years of the contract, Shore met or exceeded its two million gallon minimum under the Exclusive Supply contract, but sold somewhat less than the 7.5 million square yards of Novachip the Sublicense Agreement called for. As the contracts provided, the parties adjusted the third-year installment payment to account for the shortfall.

On March 16, 2001, Robert Capoferri ("Capoferri"), the president and sole shareholder of Shore, sent a letter to Koch's general manager. The letter provided in relevant part that:

I have decided to retire from the road construction business. . . .

The attorney for the buyer purchasing my assets has been in contact with our legal counsel, and they are close to having drafts prepared for the proposed purchase agreement. In addition to the sale of all balance sheet assets, it is also intended that 100% of any and all existing Shore Slurry Seal, Inc., contracts will be assigned and/or sold to the prospective buyer.

Given that the Nova Chip Sublicense Agreement is not part of this proposed asset sale, Shore Slurry Seal, Inc., will continue to exist beyond the closing date in order to primarily collect and remit Nova Chip royalties on behalf of Koch Pavement Solutions.

Koch responded on April 3, 2001, with a letter from its attorney to the attorney for Shore. After referencing the Capoferri letter, Koch's missive stated:

We have concerns about the sale because, during the next four years, Koch is owed a substantial amount of money from Shore under the February, 1998, Sale and Purchase Agreement, namely under the two schedules providing for exclusive supply and for Novachip royalties. In particular, we are concerned as to Shore's continued capacity to live up to its two million gallon per year commitment to buy asphalt emulsions and cutbacks and to meet its minimum square yardage requirements for Novachip.

Mr. Capoferri's secrecy surrounding Shore's negotiations and the terms and conditions of sale are adding to our discomfort. We do not know the prospective purchaser, the closing date or what, if any, arrangements have been made to provide for an assignment of Shore's obligations to the new purchaser. Further, we have no indication that Shore is providing, or is willing to provide any type of security to satisfy its obligations to Koch. To date we know only that the sign in front of Shore's current offices has been changed to read "Asphalt Paving Systems" and that several company vehicles are now bearing this new moniker.

Of course, once Shore has provided Koch with adequate assurance of performance of its obligations to Koch the process which we began with this letter can be terminated.

Shore's answer, on April 6, 2001, was again a letter from Capoferri to Koch's general manager. Capoferri noted that he had conferred with his attorney, and went on to argue that:

There has not been a failure to pay amounts due or to comply with requirements under any of the agreements we have with Koch. Nothing in any of the agreements drafted by Koch prohibit me from retiring business, nor do they require me to provide any type of security, collateral, or personal guarantee of payments similar to those we imposed upon our Nova Chip sublicensees.

Regarding the assertion of secrecy contained in Mr. Hull's letter of April 3, 2001, I am not aware of provisions within our agreements requiring me to notify Koch of any business negotiations that I may be involved in.

Finding little comfort in Shore's response, Koch filed a lawsuit seeking recognition of its right to treat Shore's failure to give adequate assurances as a repudiation of the contract, pursuant to New Jersey's Uniform Commercial Code, 2–609(1) (1962), and the common law of contracts.

Orlofsky, District Judge

When, in a contract for the sale of goods, one party has reasonable grounds to doubt that the other party will be able to perform, the doubting party may demand of its counterpart assurance that performance will occur. Section 2–609 (1). If no adequate assurance is forthcoming within a commercially reasonable time, or in any event within 30 days, the doubting party may treat its counterparty as having repudiated the contract. Section 609(3), (4). A party need not wait for an actual material breach to demand assurances; it need only show that it reasonably believed that such an event might be in the offing.

Turning then, to the pertinent facts, I conclude that no reasonable fact-finder could fail to conclude that Koch had a commercially reasonable basis for demanding assurances on both the Exclusive Supply and Sublicense Agreements. The Sublicense Agreement analysis is straightforward. Shore reported that it planned to sell all of its "balance-sheet assets," but retain, rather than assign, the Sublicense Agreement. Even assuming that historically, Shore had met most of its Novachip obligations by selling sublicenses to third parties, rather than laying its own road surfacing, any reasonable person would wonder how Shore planned to sell *anything* with no telephones, no computers, and no office furniture. That Shore might well have leased these items only prompts further questions: Would Shore have had the financial capacity to obtain leases and hire a sales staff? Or were the proceeds of the sale going directly to Capoferri?

The Exclusive Supply Agreement is a bit more complex, but no less certain. In entering the ESA, Shore promised Koch not only a minimum annual purchase, but also all of the potential upside of Shore's requirements over and above the minimum should Shore's demand for asphalt grow over time. Thus, the identity of the purchaser, its future business plans, and its anticipated need for Koch's product could all affect significantly the amount of money that Koch would realize under the ESA, not only from the two million gallon minimum, but also from the potential upside. Capoferri's letter, it is true, promised that Shore's contracts, presumably including the ESA, would be assigned to the purchaser. Start-up construction businesses, however, begin unbonded, unable to win any bid for their first year and unable to secure sufficient bonding for large construction bids for several years. Koch had no way of knowing whether Asphalt was already a going business, and, if not, whether it would be able to win sufficient subcontracting bids even to meet the minimum requirements, let alone approach the potential upside of an established enterprise like Shore.

Even aside from the particular facts of the construction industry, counterparty risk is an important feature of any requirements contract. Courts have often refused to permit assignment or delegation of duties under requirements or "best efforts" contracts where the assignment or delegation would be contrary to the justified expectations of the opposite contracting party.

Indeed, the ESA protected Koch against the risk of assignment of contract rights to unknown third parties, by requiring Koch's "prior written consent" before assignment. At the time of the April 3 letter, Koch knew that some of Shore's offices and assets were now under the control of an unknown new party, Asphalt. Koch also knew that it had certainly never agreed to any assignment of the contract. Koch could reasonably have believed that a sale had already happened, either with no assignment of the ESA, or with an assignment in violation of the ESA's terms. Given the importance of the identity of the counterparty to the contract, the possibility that requirement might have been in danger of breach would alone have been reasonable grounds at least to seek assurances otherwise.

Shore also argues that, regardless of whether Koch had reasonable grounds for doubt, the April 3, 2001, letter was insufficient, as a matter of law, to trigger any obligation on the part of Shore to respond. Koch's letter tracked closely the language of section 609, and was sent from one attorney to another. In Shore's view, Koch should have not only quoted from the U.C.C., but also actually cited section 609. Yet courts have routinely accepted as sufficient under section 609 requests for assurances of a far less formal nature. I conclude, therefore, that Shore was required to give Koch adequate assurances that it would perform the contracts.

The remaining question, then, is whether it did so. Based on the summary judgment record, it appears that any reasonable fact-finder would determine that Shore did not. Far from assuring Koch that Shore would secure Koch's permission before assigning the ESA, Capoferri's April 6 letter asserted that "I am not aware of provisions within our agreements requiring me to notify Koch of any business negotiations that I may be involved in." This evasive answer not only failed to give Koch any information about the potential successor party to the contract, but also raised a new inference that Shore might be actively planning to *evade* the exclusive supply aspects of the ESA. It was, furthermore, close to a vow to breach P 14 of the ESA. Nor did Shore give any indication about its ability to meet the Sublicense Agreement volume requirements.

I conclude, therefore, that Shore repudiated the ESA and Sublicense Agreement as of May 3, 2001.

Judgment for Koch on its motion for partial summary judgment on the question of whether Shore had repudiated the contract.

The Global Business Environment

Insecurity in International Transactions

The Convention on Contracts for the International Sale of Goods (CISG) has provisions concerning insecurity, assurance, and anticipatory repudiation that parallel those in the UCC. Under Article 71 of CISG, a party may suspend performance of his obligations if after the contract is entered it "becomes apparent that the other party will not perform a substantial part of his obligations as a result of: (a) a serious deficiency in his ability to perform or his creditworthiness; or (b) his conduct in preparing to perform or in performing the contact." The party suspending performance must immediately give notice to the other party and must continue with performance if the other party provides adequate assurance of its performance.

Under Article 72 of CISG, if prior to the date of performance of a contract, it is clear that one of the parties will "commit a fundamental breach of contract," the other party may declare the contract avoided. If time allows, the party intending to declare the contract avoided must give reasonable notice to the other party in order to permit him to provide adequate assurance of his performance. However, such notice need not be provided if the other party has declared that he will not perform the contract.

In a recent case a German court[1] upheld an Italian shoe manufacturer's decision to avoid a contract and awarded damages against the German buyer. The German company had ordered 140 pairs of winter shoes from the Italian manufacturer. After the shoes were manufactured, the Italian seller demanded security for the sales price as the buyer had other accounts payable to the seller still outstanding. When the buyer neither paid nor provided security, the seller declared the contract avoided and resold the shoes to other retailers. The court allowed the seller to recover the difference between the contract price and the price it obtained in the substitute transactions.

[1]*Oberlandesgericht Dusseldorf,* 17 U 146/93, Jan. 14, 1994 (Germany), 1 UNILEX D. 1994-1 (M. J. Bonnell, ed.)

Anticipatory Repudiation

Sometimes, one of the parties to a contract repudiates the contract by advising the other party that he does not intend to perform his obligations. When one party repudiates the contract, the other party may suspend his performance. In addition, he may either await performance for a reasonable time or use the remedies for breach of contract that are discussed in Chapter 22 [2–610].

Suppose the party who repudiated the contract changes his mind. Repudiation can be withdrawn by clearly indicating that the person intends to perform his obligations. The repudiating party must do this before the other party has canceled the contract or has materially changed position, for example, by buying the goods elsewhere [2–611].

Excuse

Unforeseen events may make it difficult or impossible for a person to perform his contractual obligations. The Code rules for determining when a person is excused from performing are similar to the general contract rules. General contract law uses the test of **impossibility.** In most situations, however, the Code uses the test of **commercial impracticability.**

The Code attempts to differentiate events that are unforeseeable or uncontrollable from events that were part of the risk borne by a party. If the goods required for the performance of a contract are destroyed without fault of either party prior to the time that the risk of loss passed to the buyer, the contract is voided [2–613]. Suppose Jones agrees to sell and deliver an antique table to Brown. The table is damaged when Jones's antiques store is struck by lightning and catches fire. The specific table covered by the contract was damaged without fault of either party prior to the time that the risk of loss was to pass to Brown. Under the Code, Brown has the option of either canceling the contract or accepting the table with an allowance in the purchase price to compensate for the damaged condition [2–613].

If unforeseen conditions cause a delay or the inability to make delivery of the goods and thus make performance impracticable, the seller is excused from making delivery. However, if a seller's capacity to deliver is only partially affected, the seller must allocate production in any fair and reasonable manner among his customers. The seller has the option of including any regular customer not then under contract in his allocation scheme. When the seller allocates production, he must notify the buyers [2–615]. When a buyer receives this notice, the buyer may either terminate the contract or agree to accept the allocation [2–616].

For example, United Nuclear contracts to sell certain quantities of fuel rods for nuclear power plants to a number of electric utilities. If the federal government limits the amount of uranium that United has access to, so that United is unable to fill all of its contracts, United is excused from full performance on the grounds of commercial impracticability. However, United may allocate its production of fuel rods among its customers by reducing each customer's share by a certain percentage and giving the customers notice of the allocation. Then, each utility can decide whether to cancel the contract or accept the partial allocation of fuel rods.

In the absence of compelling circumstances, courts do not readily excuse parties from their contractual obligations, particularly where it is clear that the parties anticipated a problem and sought to provide for it in the contract.

Problems and Problem Cases

1. Baker was a buyer and distributor of popcorn. Ratzlaff was a farmer who grew popcorn. Baker and Ratzlaff entered into a written contract pursuant to which Ratzlaff agreed that in the current year he would raise 380 acres of popcorn and sell the popcorn to Baker. Baker agreed to furnish the seed popcorn and to pay $4.75 per hundred pounds of popcorn. The popcorn was to be delivered to Baker as he ordered it, and Baker was to pay for the popcorn as it was delivered. At Baker's request, the first delivery was made on February 2 of the following year and the second on February 4. On neither occasion did Ratzlaff ask Baker to pay or Baker offer to pay. During that week, Ratzlaff and Baker had several phone conversations about further deliveries, but there was no discussion about payments. On February 11, Ratzlaff sent written notice to Baker that he was terminating the contract because Baker had not paid for the two loads of popcorn that had been delivered. In the meantime, Ratzlaff sold his remaining 1.6 million pounds of popcorn to another buyer at $8 per hundred pounds. Baker then sued Ratzlaff for breach of contract. Did Ratzlaff act in good faith in terminating the contract?

2. Harold Ledford agreed to purchase three used Mustang automobiles (a 1966 Mustang coupe, a 1965 fastback, and a 1966 convertible) from J. L. Cowan for $3,000. Ledford gave Cowan a cashier's check for $1,500 when he took possession of the coupe, with the understanding he would pay the remaining $1,500 on the delivery of the fastback and the convertible. Cowan arranged for Charles Canterberry to deliver the remaining vehicles to Ledford. Canterberry dropped the convertible off at a lot owned by Ledford and proceeded to Ledford's residence to deliver the fastback. He refused to unload it until Ledford paid him $1,500. Ledford refused to make the payment until he had an opportunity to inspect the convertible, which he suspected was not in the same condition that it had been in when he purchased it. Canterberry refused this request and returned both the fastback and the convertible to Cowan. Cowan then brought suit against Ledford to recover the balance of the purchase price. Was Ledford entitled to inspect the car before he paid the balance due on it?

3. Spada, an Oregon corporation, agreed to sell Belson, who operated a business in Chicago, Illinois, two carloads of potatoes at "$4.40 per sack, FOB Oregon shipping point." Spada had the potatoes put aboard the railroad cars; however, he did not have floor racks used in the cars under the potatoes as is customary during winter months. As a result, there was no warm air circulating and the potatoes were frozen while in transit. Spada claims that his obligations ended with the delivery to the carrier and that the risk of loss was on Belson. What argument would you make for Belson?

4. James Shelton is an experienced musician who operates the University Music Center in Seattle, Washington. On Saturday, Barbara Farkas and her 22-year-old daughter, Penny, went to Shelton's store to look at violins. Penny had been studying violin in college for approximately nine months. Mrs. Farkas and Penny advised Shelton of the price range in which they were interested, and Penny told him she was relying on his expertise. He selected a violin for $368.90, including case and sales tax. Shelton claimed that the instrument was originally priced at $465 but that he discounted it because Mrs. Farkas was willing to take it on an "as is" basis. Mrs. Farkas and Penny alleged that Shelton represented that the violin was "the best" and "a perfect violin for you" and that it was of high quality. Mrs. Farkas paid for it by check. On the following Monday, Penny took the violin to her college music teacher, who immediately told her that it had poor tone and a crack in the body and that it was not the right instrument for her. Mrs. Farkas telephoned Shelton and asked for a refund. He refused, saying that she had purchased and accepted the violin on an "as is" basis. Had Farkas "accepted" the violin so that it was too late for her to "reject" it?

5. In the spring of 1991 Vince Ford, a retailer, contracted with a wholesaler, Starr Fireworks, for the purchase of various types of fireworks at an agreed price of $6,748.86. In May 1991, Starr delivered the 138 cases of fireworks in one lot to Ford's warehouse in Lusk, Wyoming. Ford did not immediately inspect the fireworks; instead, he distributed them to his retail outlets throughout Wyoming for resale to the public.

Approximately 10 days after the fireworks were distributed to the retail outlets, Ford discovered that some fireworks were unsalable because of water damage and packaging problems. However, Ford did not inspect the remainder of the fireworks from the shipment. Ford telephoned Starr's representative to report the problems. Although Ford claimed that he instructed his employees not to sell any products received from Starr, a month later one of his stores sold several cases of the fireworks that had been purchased from Starr to another fireworks retailer. The buyer reported no problem with those fireworks, and they were subsequently resold to customers without reported problems.

After several unsuccessful attempts by Starr representatives to pick up the fireworks, they did pick up 10 cases of fireworks, worth $1,476.87, on August 3, 1991; at that time Ford signed an acknowledgment that he still owed $5,251.99 to Starr. Ford claimed to have returned the remaining fireworks to Starr's Denver office on August 13, 1991. He said that no one was available in the office so he left the fireworks outside a side door; Starr never received those fireworks.

Starr brought suit to recover the balance due on the fireworks that Ford had acknowledged retaining. Ford claimed that he had rejected the entire shipment on the grounds they were unmerchantable and counterclaimed for damages he asserted he had sustained. Ford contended that his inspection of some of the fireworks disclosed packages with torn wrappings, mold or mildew on some fireworks, and paper wrapping that fell apart exposing the fireworks. Ford argued that from this sampling it was reasonable to assume all the goods delivered by Starr were unmerchantable. Did Ford make an effective rejection of the entire shipment?

6. On August 20, 1983, Elmer and Martha Bosarge purchased from J & J Mobile Home Sales a furnished mobile home manufactured by North River Homes. The mobile home, described by a J & J salesman as the "Cadillac" of mobile homes, cost $23,900. Upon moving into their new home, the Bosarges immediately discovered defect after defect. The defects included a bad water leak that caused water to run all over the trailer and into the insulation, causing the trailer's underside to balloon downward; loose moldings; warped dishwasher door; warped bathroom door; holes in the walls; defective heating and cooling system; cabinets with chips and holes in them; furniture that fell apart; rooms that remained moldy and mildewed; a closet that leaked rainwater; and spaces between the doors and windows and their frames that allowed the elements to come in. The Bosarges had not been able to spot the defects before taking delivery because they had viewed the mobile home at night on J & J's lot and there was no light on in the mobile home.

  The Bosarges immediately and repeatedly notified North River Homes of the defects, but it failed to satisfactorily repair the home. In November 1983 the Bosarges informed North River of their decision to revoke their acceptance of the defective home. On some occasions, repairmen came but did not attempt to make repairs, saying they would come back. Other times, the repairs were inadequate. For example, while looking for the water leak, a repairman cut open the bottom of the mobile home and then taped it back together with masking tape which failed to hold and resulted in the floor bowing out. Another inadvertently punctured a septic line and did not properly repair the puncture, resulting in a permanent stench. Other repairmen simply left things off at the home, like a new dishwasher door and a countertop, saying they did not have time to make the repairs.

  In June 1984 the Bosarges provided North River with an extensive list of problems that had not been corrected. When they did not receive a satisfactory response, they send a letter on October 4, 1984, saying they would make no further payments. North River made no further efforts to correct the problems. In March 1986 the Bosarges' attorney wrote to North River, formally revoking acceptance of the mobile home because of its substantially impaired value, tendering the mobile home back to it, and advising North River that it could pick the home up at its earliest convenience. They then brought a lawsuit requesting return of the purchase price and seeking damages for breach of various warranties. Did the Bosarges effectively revoke their acceptance of the mobile home and were they barred from revoking acceptance because of their continued use?

7. Walters, a grower of Christmas trees, contracted to supply Traynor with "top-quality trees." When the shipment arrived and was inspected, Traynor discovered that some of the trees were not top quality. Within 24 hours, Traynor notified Walters that he was rejecting the trees that were not top quality. Walters did not have a place of business or an agent in the town where Traynor was. Christmas was only a short time away. The trees were perishable and would decline in value to zero by Christmas Eve. Walters did not give Traynor any instructions, so Traynor sold the trees for Walters's account. Traynor then tried to recover from Walters the expenses he incurred in caring for and selling the trees. Did the buyer act properly in rejecting the trees and reselling them for the seller?

8. Haralambos Fekkos purchased from Lykins Sales & Service a Yammar Model 165D, 16-horsepower diesel tractor and various implements. On Saturday, April 27, Fekkos gave Lykins a check for the agreed-on purchase price, less trade-in of $6,596, and the items were delivered to his residence. The next day, while attempting to use the tractor for the first time, Fekkos discovered it was defective. The defects included a dead battery requiring jump starts, overheating while pulling either the mower or tiller, missing safety shields over the muffler and the power takeoff, and a missing water pump. On Monday, Fekkos contacted Lykins's sales representative, who believed his claims to be true and agreed to have the tractor picked up from Fekkos's residence; Fekkos also stopped payment on his check. Fekkos placed the tractor with the tiller attached in his front yard as

near as possible to the front door without driving it onto the landscaped area closest to the house. Fekkos left the tractor on the lawn because his driveway was broken up for renovation and his garage was inaccessible, and because the tractor would have to be jump-started by Lykins's employees when they picked it up. On Tuesday, Fekkos went back to Lykins's store to purchase an Allis-Chalmers tractor and reminded Lykins's employees that the Yammar tractor had not been picked up and remained on his lawn. On Wednesday, May 1, at 6:00 AM, Fekkos discovered that the tractor was missing although the tiller had been unhitched and remained in the yard. Later that day, Lykins picked up the remaining implements. The theft was reported to the police. On several occasions, Fekkos was assured that Lykins's insurance would cover the stolen tractor, that it was Lykins's fault for not picking it up, and that Fekkos had nothing to worry about. However, Lykins subsequently brought suit against Fekkos to recover the purchase price of the Yammar tractor. Was Fekkos liable for the purchase price of the tractor that had been rejected and was stolen while awaiting pickup by the seller?

9. Creusot-Loire, a French manufacturing and engineering concern, was the project engineer to construct ammonia plants in Yugoslavia and Syria. The design process engineer for the two plants—as well as a plant being constructed in Sri Lanka—specified burners manufactured by Coppus Engineering Corporation. After the burner specifications were provided to Coppus, it sent technical and service information to Creusot-Loire.

Coppus expressly warranted that the burners were capable of continuous operation using heavy fuel oil with combustion air preheated to 260 degrees Celsius. The warranty extended for one year from the start-up of the plant but not exceeding three years from the date of shipment. In January 1989, Creusot-Loire ordered the burners for the Yugoslavia plant and paid for them; in November 1989, the burners were shipped to Yugoslavia. Due to construction delays, the plant was not to become operational until the end of 1993. In 1991, however, Creusot-Loire became aware that there had been operational difficulties with the Coppus burners at the Sri Lanka and Syria plants and that efforts to modify the burners had been futile. Creusot-Loire wrote to Coppus expressing concern

that the burners purchased for the Yugoslavia plant, like those in the other plants, would prove unsatisfactory and asking for proof that the burners would meet contract specifications. When subsequent discussions failed to satisfy Creusot-Loire, it requested that Coppus take back the burners and refund the purchase price. Coppus refused. Finally, Creusot-Loire indicated that it would accept the burners only if Coppus extended its contractual guarantee to cover the delay in the start-up of the Yugoslavia plant and if Coppus posted an irrevocable letter of credit for the purchase price of the burners. When Coppus refused, Creusot-Loire brought an action for breach of contract, seeking a return of the purchase price. Coppus claimed that Creusot-Loire's request for assurance was unreasonable. How should the court rule?

10. In July 1980, Alimenta (U.S.A.), Inc., and Gibbs, Nathaniel (Canada), Ltd., each an international dealer in agricultural commodities, entered into three separate contracts in advance of the 1980 peanut harvest. Each contract called for the delivery in installments by Gibbs to Alimenta of "1980 crop U.S. runner split peanuts." When Gibbs failed to make delivery of the quantities specified in the contract, and made some deliveries later than the scheduled dates, Alimenta brought suit against Gibbs seeking damages for breach of contract. Gibbs claimed that it was excused from full performance by the recurrence of a drought in the peanut-growing areas. The 1980 peanut crop had been planted in April and May. Rainfall was adequate in April, May, and June, and the crop came up in good condition. In the 25 years preceding 1980, the nation's peanut industry had experienced a steady growth in total production, with yield per acre increasing 250 percent over that period. In addition to Alimenta, Gibbs sold 1980 crop peanuts to 75 other customers and had contracted to purchase peanuts from 15 shellers in quantities 7 percent in excess of its sales. In early July, a hot and dry spell developed and became a full-fledged drought that did not break until late September. July and August were among the hottest and driest months on record in the last 100 years. In October, Gibbs received notices from 13 of its 15 shellers stating that because of the crop shortage, they were invoking section 2–615 of the UCC and would be delivering only a portion of the peanuts they had

contracted to deliver. Gibbs expected to receive only 52 percent of the peanuts it had contracted for, and in turn notified its customers, including Alimenta, to expect reduced quantities. Alimenta ultimately received 87 percent of the contract quantity from Gibbs. Was Gibbs excused from full performance of its contract by the occurrence of the drought?

Online Research

Using the Internet to Check Out an eBay Seller

Go to the eBay Web site (www.ebay.com), select a category of goods being auctioned, and identify an item for which you might consider bidding. Assume that you would like to ascertain the experience other buyers have had dealing with that seller, including whether the seller has a reputation for (1) fairly describing the goods she puts up for auction, (2) properly preparing the goods for shipment to the winning bidder, and (3) promptly shipping the goods once payment is received. You also would like to know if other buyers have complained about this particular seller. How would you go about ascertaining this information through the eBay Web site? What information do you find concerning the seller of the item you chose?

chapter 22

REMEDIES FOR BREACH
OF SALES CONTRACTS

Kathy is engaged to be married. She contracts with the Bridal Shop for a custom-designed bridal gown in size 6 with delivery to be made by the weekend before the wedding. Kathy makes a $500 deposit against the contract price of $2,500. If the dress is completed in conformance with the specifications and on time, then Kathy is obligated to pay the balance of the agreed-on price. But what happens if either Kathy or the Bridal Shop breaches the contract? For example:

- If Kathy breaks her engagement and tells the Bridal Shop that she is no longer interested in having the dress before the shop has completed making it, what options are open to the Bridal Shop? Can it complete the dress or should it stop work on it?
- If the Bridal Shop completes the dress but Kathy does not like it and refuses to accept it, what can the Bridal Shop do? Can it collect the balance of the contract price from Kathy, or must it first try to sell the dress to someone else?
- If the Bridal Shop advises Kathy that it will be unable to complete the dress in time for the wedding, what options are open to Kathy? If she has another dress made by someone else, or purchases a ready-made one, what, if any, damages can she collect from the Bridal Shop?
- If the Bridal Shop completes the dress but advises Kathy it plans to sell it to someone else who is willing to pay more money for it, does Kathy have any recourse?
- Would it be ethical for the Bridal Shop to sell the dress to someone else who offers more money for it?

USUALLY, BOTH PARTIES TO a contract for the sale of goods perform the obligations that they assumed in the contract. Occasionally, however, one of the parties to a contract fails to perform his obligations. When this happens, the Uniform Commercial Code (UCC or Code) provides the injured party with a variety of remedies for breach of contract. This chapter will set forth and explain the remedies available to an injured party, as well as the Code's rules that govern buyer-seller agreements as to remedies and the Code's statute of limitations. The objective of the Code remedies is to put the injured person in the same position that he would have been in if the contract had been performed. Under the Code, an injured party may not recover consequential or punitive damages unless such damages are specifically provided for in the Code or in another statute [1–106].[1]

---

[1]The numbers in brackets refer to sections of the Uniform Commercial Code.

Agreements as to Remedies

The buyer and seller may provide their own remedies in the contract, to be applied in the event that one of the parties fails to perform. They may also limit either the remedies that the law makes available or the damages that can be covered [2–719(1)]. If the parties agree on the amount of damages that will be paid to the injured party, this amount is known as **liquidated damages.** An agreement for liquidated damages is enforced if the amount is reasonable and if actual damages would be difficult to prove in the event of a breach of the contract. The amount is considered reasonable if it is not so large as to be a penalty or so small as to be unconscionable [2–718(1)].

For example, Carl Carpenter contracts to build and sell a display booth for $5,000 to Hank Hawker for Hawker to use at the state fair. Delivery is to be made to Hawker by September 1. If the booth is not delivered on time, Hawker will not be able to sell his wares at the fair. Carpenter and Hawker might agree that if delivery is not made by September 1, Carpenter will pay Hawker $2,750 as liquidated damages. The actual sales that Hawker might lose without a booth would be very hard to prove, so Hawker and Carpenter can provide some certainty through the liquidated damages agreement. Carpenter then knows what he will be liable for if he does not perform his obligation. Similarly, Hawker knows what he can recover if the booth is not delivered on time. The $2,750 amount is probably reasonable. If

the amount were $500,000, it likely would be void as a penalty because it is way out of line with the damages that Hawker would reasonably be expected to sustain. And if the amount were too small, say $1, it might be considered unconscionable and therefore not enforceable.

If a liquidated damages clause is not enforceable because it is a penalty or unconscionable, the injured party can recover the actual damages that he suffered. The following *Baker* case illustrates a situation where a court enforced a liquidated damages clause in a contract.

Baker v. International Record Syndicate, Inc.
812 S.W.2d 53 (Tex. Ct. App. 1991)

International Record Syndicate (IRS) hired Jeff Baker to take photographs of the musical group Timbuk-3. Baker mailed 37 "chromes" (negatives) to IRS via the business agent of Timbuk-3. When the chromes were returned to Baker, holes had been punched in 34 of them. Baker brought an action for breach of contract to recover for the damage done to the chromes.

A provision printed on Baker's invoice to IRS stated: "[r]eimbursement for loss or damage shall be determined by a photograph's reasonable value which shall be no less than $1,500 per transparency."

Enoch, Chief Judge

The Uniform Commercial Code provides:

> Damages for breach by either party may be liquidated in the agreement but only at an amount which is reasonable in light of the anticipated harm caused by the breach, the difficulties of proof of loss, and the inconvenience or nonfeasibility of otherwise obtaining an adequate remedy. A term fixing unreasonably large liquidated damages is void as a penalty.

Under Texas law a liquidated damages provision will be enforced when the court finds (1) the harm caused by the breach is incapable of estimation, and (2) the amount of liquidated damages is a reasonable forecast of just compensation. This might be termed the "anticipated harm" test. The party asserting that a liquidated damages clause is, in fact, a penalty provision has the burden of proof. Evidence related to the difficulty of estimation and the reasonable forecast must be viewed as of the time the contract was executed.

Baker testified that he had been paid as much as $14,000 for a photo session, which resulted in 24 photographs and that several of these photographs had also been resold. Baker further testified that he had received as little as $125 for a single photograph. Baker also testified that he once sold a photograph for $500. Subsequently, he sold reproductions of the same photograph three additional times at various prices; the total income from this one photograph was $1,500. This particular photo-

graph was taken in 1986 and was still producing income in 1990. Baker demonstrated, therefore, that an accurate demonstration of the damages from a single photograph is virtually impossible.

Timbuk-3's potential for fame was also an important factor in the valuation of the chromes. At the time of the photo session, Timbuk-3's potential was unknown. In view of the difficulty in determining the value of a piece of art, the broad range of values and long-term earning power of photographs, and the unknown potential for fame of the subject, $1,500 is not an unreasonable estimate of Baker's actual damages.

Additionally, liquidated damages must not be disproportionate to actual damages. If the liquidated damages are shown to be disproportionate to the actual damages, then the liquidated damages can be declared a penalty and recovery limited to actual damages proven. This might be called the "actual harm" test. The burden of proving this defense is upon the party seeking to invalidate the clause. The party asserting this defense is required to prove the amount of the other party's actual damages, if any, to show that the actual loss was not an approximation of the stipulated sum.

While evidence was presented that showed the value of several of Baker's other projects, this was not evidence of the photographs in question. The evidence clearly shows that photographs are unique items with many factors bearing on their actual value. Each of the 34 chromes may have had a different value. Proof of this loss is difficult; where damages are real but difficult to prove, injustice will be done the injured party if the court substitutes the requirements of judicial proof for the parties' own informed agreement as to what is a reasonable measure of damages. The evidence offered to prove Baker's actual damages lacks probative force. IRS failed to establish Baker's actual damages as to these particular photographs.

Judgment reversed in favor of Baker.

Liability for consequential damages resulting from a breach of contract (such as lost profits or damage to property) may also be limited or excluded by agreement. The limitation or exclusion is not enforced if it would be unconscionable. Any attempt to limit consequential damages for injury caused to a person by consumer goods is considered prima facie unconscionable [2–719(3)].

Suppose an automobile manufacturer makes a warranty as to the quality of an automobile that is purchased as a consumer good. It then tries to disclaim responsibility for any person injured if the car does not conform to the warranty and to limit its liability to replacing any defective parts. The disclaimer of consequential injuries in this case would be unconscionable and therefore would not be enforced. Exclusion of or limitation on consequential damages is permitted where the loss is commercial, as long as the exclusion or limitation is not unconscionable. Where circumstances cause a limited remedy agreed to by the parties to fail in its essential purpose, the limited remedy is not enforced and the general Code remedies are available to the injured party.

The *Star-Shadow Productions* case involves the enforcement of a limitation of liability clause.

Star-Shadow Productions, Inc. v. Super 8 Sync Sound System
38 UCC Rep. 2d 1128 (R.I. Sup.Ct. 1999)

Star-Shadow Productions, Inc., and Bruce J. Haas produce and film low-budget movies. One of their projects, The Night of the Beast, *was scheduled for filming from March 12 through 18, 1994, at the General Stanton Inn in Charlestown, Rhode Island. In preparation for the filming, Star-Shadow rented a Beaulieu 7008 Pro 8-millimeter camera and bought 108 rolls of Super 8 Sound high-resolution color negative film from Super 8 Sync Sound System. Unfortunately, on the first day of filming, Star-Shadow's cameraman was unable to use the Super 8 film because of loading and jamming problems. A representative of Super 8, Lisa Mattei, offered advice by phone and subsequently traveled to Charlestown with a replacement camera and Kodak Reverse film. When her troubleshooting efforts proved fruitless, she replaced the Super 8 film with Kodak Reverse film and the camera operated successfully. On March 22, 1994, Star-Shadow returned the camera and Star-Shadow's account was credited for the unused film.*

Star-Shadow subsequently sued Super 8 for damages allegedly caused by the Super 8 film's inability to operate correctly. Super 8 filed a motion for summary judgment arguing that it had complied with all the terms of the contract by replacing the defective film and crediting Star-Shadow's account for the unused film. Super 8 pointed to the limitation of liability clause contained on price sheets and film boxes provided to Star-Shadow to show that Super 8 could not be subject to any additional liabilities. The limitation of liability clause's pertinent part reads: "Limitation of Liability: This product will be repaired if defective in manufacture or packing. Except for such replacement this product is sold without warranty or liability even though defect, damage, or loss is caused by negligence or other fault. . . ."

The trial court granted the motion for summary judgment. The judge found that the limitation of liability clause contained on the Super 8 film package was valid; therefore, Super 8 could not be held liable for damages beyond the value of replacement film. Star-Shadow appealed.

Per Curiam

Star-Shadow maintains that the limitation of liability clause failed its essential purpose—to adequately protect the filmmakers from damages arising from defective film. They point to the fact that the limitation of liability clause leaves them without recourse against Super 8 for the thousands of dollars of damages caused by the defective film. We have held in an analogous situation that the purchase price of goods is "not a premium for . . . insurance," and consequently, limitation of liability clauses are not unconscionable merely because buyers are not fully protected for damages that may arise from the malfunction of their purchased goods or service. In the case of defective film, the commercial film maker is not abandoned without protection [by limitation of liability clauses] but is free to purchase raw stock insurance.

The fact that Star-Shadow in this case has no protection other than their bargained-for remedy of replacement film does not make the limitation of liability clause unconscionable. "In an industry where the undertaking may vary from a multi-million dollar extravaganza to a low-budget instructional film," plaintiffs were in the better position to assess their risks and "mold the protection to the scope of [the] project" than defendant who was unaware of the breadth of plaintiffs' undertaking. Thus, Star-Shadow received what it bargained for, and the risk of equipment failure properly lay on them, not Super 8.

Judgment for Super 8 affirmed.

Statute of Limitations

The Code provides that a lawsuit for breach of a sales contract must be filed within four years after the breach occurs. The parties to a contract may shorten this period to one year, but they may not extend it for longer than four years [2–725]. Normally, a breach of warranty is considered to have occurred when the goods are delivered to the buyer. However, if the warranty covers future performance of goods (for example, a warranty on a tire for four years or 40,000 miles), then the breach occurs at the time the buyer should have discovered the defect in the product. If, for example, the buyer of the tire discovers the defect after driving 25,000 miles on the tire over a three-year period, he would have four years from that time to bring any lawsuit to remedy the breach.

Seller's Remedies

Remedies Available to an Injured Seller

A buyer may breach a contract in a number of ways. The most common are (1) by wrongfully refusing to accept goods, (2) by wrongfully returning goods, (3) by failing to pay for goods when payment is due, and (4) by indicating an unwillingness to go ahead with the contract. When a buyer breaches a contract, the seller has a number of remedies under the Code, including the right to:

- Cancel the contract [2–703(f)].
- Withhold delivery of undelivered goods [2–703(a)].
- Complete manufacture of unfinished goods and identify them as to the contract or cease manufacture and sell for scraps [2–704].
- Resell the goods covered by the contract and recover damages from the buyer [2–706].
- Recover from the buyer the profit that the seller would have made on the sale or the damages that the seller sustained [2–708].
- Recover the purchase price of goods delivered to or accepted by the buyer [2–709].

In addition, a buyer may become insolvent and thus unable to pay the seller for goods already delivered or for goods that the seller is obligated to deliver. When a seller learns of a buyer's insolvency, the seller has a number of remedies, including the right to:

- Withhold delivery of undelivered goods [2–703(a)].
- Recover goods from a buyer upon the buyer's insolvency [2–702].
- Stop delivery of goods that are in the possession of a carrier or other bailee before they reach the buyer [2–705].

Cancellation and Withholding of Delivery

When a buyer breaches a contract, the seller has the right to cancel the contract and to hold up her own performance of the contract. The seller may then set aside any goods that were intended to fill her obligations under the contract [2–704].

If the seller is in the process of manufacturing the goods, she has two choices. She may complete manufacture of the goods, or she may stop manufacturing and sell the uncompleted goods for their scrap or salvage value. In choosing between these alternatives, the seller should select the alternative that will minimize the loss [2–704(2)]. Thus, a seller would be justified in completing the manufacture of goods that could be resold readily at the contract price. However, a seller would not be justified in completing specially manufactured goods that could not be sold to anyone other than the buyer who ordered them. The purpose of this rule is to permit the seller to follow a reasonable course of action to mitigate (minimize) the damages.

The hypothetical case at the beginning of the chapter posits a customer who contracts with the Bridal Shop for the creation of a custom-designed bridal gown in size 6 and then seeks to cancel the order before the Bridal Shop has completed it. What options are open to the Bridal Shop? Can it complete the dress and recover the full contract price from the customer, or should it stop work on it? What facts would be important to your decision? As you reflect on these questions, you might consider the facts set out in problem case number 3 at the end of this chapter where a manufacturer of pool tables stopped work on some customized pool tables. What considerations does it suggest that the Bridal Shop might be advised to take into account in deciding whether or not to continue work on the bridal gown?

Resale of Goods

Resale of Goods If the seller sets aside goods intended for the contract or completes the manufacture of such goods, he is not obligated to try to resell the goods to someone else. However, he may resell them and recover damages. The seller must make any resale in good faith and in a commercially reasonable manner. If the seller does so, he is entitled to recover from the buyer as damages the difference between the resale price and the price the buyer agreed to pay in the contract [2–706].

If the seller resells, he may also recover incidental damages, but the seller must give the buyer credit for any expenses that the seller saved because of the buyer's breach of contract. Incidental damages include storage charges and sales commissions paid when the goods were resold [2–710]. Expenses saved might be the cost of packaging the goods and/or shipping them to the buyer.

If the buyer and seller have agreed as to the manner in which the resale is to be made, the courts will enforce the agreement unless it is found to be unconscionable [2–302]. If the parties have not entered into an agreement as to the resale of the goods, they may be resold at public or private sale, but in all events the resale must be made in good faith and in a commercially reasonable manner. The seller should make it clear that the goods he is selling are those related to the broken contract.

If the goods are resold at private sale, the seller must give the buyer reasonable notification of his intention to resell [2–706(3)]. If the resale is a public sale, such as an auction, the seller must give the buyer notice of the time and place of the sale unless the goods are perishable or threaten to decline in value rapidly. The sale must be made at a usual place or market for public sales if one is reasonably available; and if the goods are not within the view of those attending the sale, the notification of the sale must state the place where the goods are located and provide for reasonable inspection by prospective bidders. The seller may bid at a public sale [2–706(4)].

The purchaser at a public sale who buys in good faith takes free from any rights of the original buyer even though the seller has failed to conduct the sale in compliance with the rules set out in the Code [2–706(5)]. The seller is not accountable to the buyer for any profit that the seller makes on a resale [2–706(6)].

Recovery of the Purchase Price

Recovery of the Purchase Price In the normal performance of a contract, the seller delivers conforming goods (goods that meet the contract specifications) to the buyer. The buyer accepts the goods and pays for them. The seller is entitled to the purchase price of all goods accepted by the buyer. She also is entitled to the purchase price of all goods that conformed to the contract and were lost or damaged after the buyer assumed the risk for their loss [2–709].

For example, a contract calls for Frank, a farmer, to ship 1,000 dozen eggs to Sutton, a grocer, with shipment "FOB Frank's Farm." If the eggs are lost or damaged while on their way to Sutton, she is responsible for paying Frank for them. Risk of loss is discussed in Chapter 19, Formation and Terms of Sales Contracts.

In one other situation, the seller may recover the purchase or contract price from the buyer. This is where the seller has made an honest effort to resell the goods and was unsuccessful or where it is apparent that any such effort to resell would be unsuccessful. This might happen where the seller manufactured goods especially for the buyer and the goods are not usable by anyone else. Assume that Sarton's Supermarket sponsors a bowling team. Sarton's orders six green-and-red bowling shirts to be embroidered with "Sarton's Supermarket" on the back and the names of the team members on the pocket. After the shirts are completed, Sarton's wrongfully refuses to accept them. The seller will be able to recover the agreed purchase price if it cannot sell the shirts to someone else.

If the seller sues the buyer for the contract price of the goods, she must hold the goods for the buyer. Then, the seller must turn the goods over to the buyer if the buyer pays for them. However, if resale becomes possible before the buyer pays for the goods, the seller may resell them. Then, the seller must give the buyer credit for the proceeds of the resale [2–709(2)].

Damages for Rejection or Repudiation

Damages for Rejection or Repudiation When the buyer refuses to accept goods that conform to the contract or repudiates the contract, the seller does not have to resell the goods. The seller has two other ways of determining the damages that the buyer is liable for because of the breach of contract: (1) the difference between the contract price and the market price at which the goods are currently selling and (2) the "profit" that

The Global Business Environment

Seller's Remedies in International Transactions

Under the Convention on Contracts for the International Sale of Goods (CISG), an aggrieved seller has five potential remedies when the buyer breaches the contract: (1) suspension of the seller's performance; (2) "avoidance" of the contract; (3) reclamation of the goods in the buyer's possession; (4) an action for the price; and (5) an action for damages. The last two remedies can be pursued only in a judicial proceeding.

As noted in Chapter 21 (see The Global Business Environment box entitled "Insecurity" on page 562), the seller may "suspend its performance" when it is apparent the other party to the contract will not be performing its obligations, for example, if the buyer was insolvent and unable to pay for any goods delivered to it.

Avoidance of a contract—which under the CISG essentially means canceling the contract—is a remedy most commonly utilized by buyers because the initial performance

called for in contracts typically rests with the seller—for example, to deliver specified goods. When a seller has not been paid for goods, it may "avoid" the contract and seek their return from the buyer. If the buyer has possession of the goods when the contract is avoided, he must take reasonable steps to preserve them. Where the goods are perishable, the buyer might try to sell them for the seller's account but is not required to follow a seller's instructions to resell.

Where the seller has performed its obligations, the seller has the right to require the buyer to pay the contract price unless the seller has pursued an inconsistent remedy—such as reclaiming the goods. An aggrieved seller may also pursue an action for damages based on either (1) the difference between the contract price and the resale price (where the seller resold the goods) or (2) the difference between the contract price and the market price at the time the contract was avoided. The CISG also permits a measure of damages based on lost profits. Thus, in a number of respects, the UCC and CISG offer similar remedies to sellers.

---

the seller lost when the buyer did not go through with the contract [2–708].

The seller may recover as damages the difference between the contract price and the market price at the time and place the goods were to be delivered to the buyer. The seller also may recover any incidental damages, but must give the buyer credit for any expenses that the seller has saved [2–708(1)]. This measure of damages most commonly is sought by a seller when the market price of the goods dropped substantially between the time the contract was made and the time the buyer repudiated the contract.

For example, on October 1, Wan Ho Manufacturing contracts with Sports Properties, Inc., to sell the company 100,000 New England Patriot bobble heads at $6.50 each with delivery to be made in Boston on December 1. By December 1, the market for New England Patriot bobble heads has softened considerably because a competitor flooded the market with them first and the bobble heads are selling for $3 each in Boston. If Sports Properties repudiates the contract on December 1 and refuses to accept delivery of the 100,000 bobble heads, Wan Ho is entitled to the difference between the contract price of $6.50 and the December 1 market price in Boston of $300,000. Thus, Wan Ho could recover $350,000 in damages plus any incidental expenses, but

less any expenses saved by it not having to ship the bobble heads to Sports Properties (such as packaging and transportation costs).

If getting the difference between the contract price and the market price would not put the seller in as good a financial position as the seller would have been in if the contract had been performed, the seller may choose an alternative measure of damages based on the lost profit and overhead that the seller would have made if the sale had gone through. The seller can recover this lost profit and overhead plus any incidental expenses. However, the seller must give the buyer credit for any expenses saved as a result of the buyer's breach of contract [2–708(2)].

Using the bobble head example, assume that the direct labor and material costs to Wan Ho Manufacturing of making the bobble heads was $2.75 each. Wan Ho could recover as damages from Sports Properties the profit Wan Ho lost when Sports Properties defaulted on the contract. Wan Ho would be entitled to the difference between the contract price of $650,000 and its direct cost of $275,000. Thus, Wan Ho could recover $375,000 plus any incidental expenses and less any expenses saved, such as the shipping costs to Boston.

This measure of damages is illustrated in the case that follows below, *Jewish Federation of Greater Des Moines v. Cedar Forrest Products Co.*

Jewish Federation of Greater Des Moines v. Cedar Forrest Products Co.
52 UCC Rep.2d 422 (Iowa Ct. App. 2003)

Cedar Forrest Products Company (CFP) manufactures precut building packages for shelters, pavilions, gazebos, and other structures typically utilized in park, camp, and recreational facilities. The Jewish Federation of Greater Des Moines (Jewish Federation) contracted with CFP for the manufacture of a 3,500 square foot building with unique and customized features. With the signing of the Purchase and Sales Agreement, Jewish Federation sent CFP a deposit of $53,605; shortly thereafter it prematurely sent the remaining balance of $160,813 for a total contract price of $214,418. After a series of redesign discussions and change orders, Jewish Federation informed CFP it was rescinding the contract and requesting return of all monies paid. CFP returned $160,530.54, but retained $53,887.46 as lost profits it would have made had Jewish Federation not breached the contract.

In anticipation of the building project, CFP purchased cedar paneling, insulation, floor plywood, and cedar timber. It had not begun to assemble the building when Jewish Federation breached the contract. After the breach, CFB was able to sell the purchased items to other customers for the same price as called for in the Jewish Federation contract.

Jewish Federation filed an action for the return of the remaining $53,887.46, claiming there had been no meeting of the minds and the agreement was merely a quote based on a preliminary schematic drawing; CFP counterclaimed for breach of contract. The trial court found the agreement was a completely integrated contract which Jewish Federation had breached and determined that CFP was only entitled to retain $13,470.13 for "incidental damages." CFP appealed.

Vogel, Presiding Judge

The primary issue on appeal is the proper measure of damages for a lost volume seller under these particular circumstances. The Illinois Uniform Commercial Code, like the Uniform Commercial Code (UCC), provides for liberal administration such that "the aggrieved party may be put in as good a position as if the other party had fully performed . . ." According to the Illinois Code,

> [T]he measure of damages for non-acceptance or repudiation by the buyer is the difference between the market price at the time and place for tender and the unpaid contact price together with any incidental damages provided in this Article (Section 2–710), but less expenses saved in consequence of the buyer's breach.

Section 2–708(1). However, if this amount is

> inadequate to put the seller in as good a position as performance would have done then the measure of damages is the profit (including reasonable overhead) which the seller would have made from full performance by the buyer, together with any incidental damages provided in this Article (Section 2–710), due allowance for costs reasonably incurred and due credit for payments or proceeds of resale.

Section 2–708(2).

To resolve this issue, we look to case law construing the Illinois statute or similar statutory law in other jurisdictions. In *R. E. Davis Chem. Corp. v. Diasonics, Inc.* (N.D. Ill. 1987), the court used lost profits as the measure of damages pursuant to section 2–708(2) after the buyer repudiated. For the seller to recover lost profits, the court reasoned that the seller must establish that (1) it had the capacity to make the sale to the buyer as well as the sale to the resale buyer and (2) it would have been profitable for it to make both sales. Applying this test to the present case, the record reflects CFP was capable of manufacturing the building for Jewish Federation as well as its numerous other customers and it would have been profitable to do so.

Jewish Federation argues that CFP had not begun to assemble the purchased items into the contracted for building at the time of breach, therefore incidental damages were sufficient. However, this position is not supported by case law. Lost profits may be awarded for items *yet to be manufactured.* [Citations omitted.]

The rationale for these holdings appears to be that a lost volume seller can handle a certain number of sales during the year and when one negotiated sale is lost, the seller simply cannot recoup that anticipated profit. Instead, the seller is one sale short of normal capacity. So to put the seller in the position he would have been but for the breach, the Illinois statute provides the seller a remedy which includes the anticipated profit as well as incidental expenses and costs incurred. As a lost volume seller, CFP is entitled to its lost profits of $53,887.46 pursuant to Section 2–708(2) which includes the incidental damages of $13,470.17 awarded by the district court.

Judgment reversed in favor of CFP.

Seller's Remedies Where Buyer Is Insolvent

If the seller has not agreed to extend credit to the buyer for the purchase price of goods, the buyer must make payment on delivery of the goods. If the seller tenders delivery of the goods, he may withhold delivery unless the agreed payment is made. Where the seller has agreed to extend credit to the buyer for the purchase price of the goods, but discovers before delivery that the buyer is insolvent, the seller may refuse delivery unless the buyer pays cash for the goods together with the unpaid balance for all goods previously delivered under the contract [2–702(1)].

At common law, a seller had the right to rescind a sales contract induced by fraud and to recover the goods unless they had been resold to a bona fide purchaser for value. Based on this general legal principle, the Code provides that where the seller discovers that the buyer has received goods while insolvent, the seller may reclaim the goods upon demand made within 10 days after their receipt. This right granted to the seller is based on constructive deceit on the part of the buyer. Receiving goods while insolvent is equivalent to a false representation of solvency. To protect his rights, all the seller must do is to make a demand within the 10-day period; he need not actually repossess the goods.

If the buyer has misrepresented his solvency to this particular seller in writing within three months before the delivery of the goods, the 10-day limitation on the seller's right to reclaim the goods does not apply. However, the seller's right to reclaim the goods is subject to the rights of prior purchasers in the ordinary course of the buyer's business, good faith purchasers for value, creditors with a perfected lien on the buyer's inventory [2–702(2) and (3)], and of a trustee in bankruptcy. The relative rights of creditors to their debtor's collateral are discussed in Chapter 29, Security Interests in Personal Property.

Seller's Right to Stop Delivery

If the seller discovers that the buyer is insolvent, he has the right to stop the delivery of any goods that he has shipped to the buyer, regardless of the size of the shipment. If a buyer repudiates a sales contract or fails to make a payment due before delivery, the seller has the right to stop delivery of any large shipment of goods, such as a carload, a truckload, or a planeload [2–705].

To stop delivery, the seller must notify the carrier or other bailee in time for the bailee to prevent delivery of the goods. After receiving notice to stop delivery, the carrier or other bailee owes a duty to hold the goods and deliver them as directed by the seller. The seller is liable to the carrier or other bailee for expenses incurred or damages resulting from compliance with his order to stop delivery. If a nonnegotiable document of title has been

<table>
<tr><td colspan="2">CONCEPT REVIEW</td></tr>
<tr><td>Problem</td><td>Seller's Remedy</td></tr>
<tr><td>Buyer Refuses to Go Ahead with Contract and Seller Has Goods</td><td>1. Seller may cancel contract, suspend performance, and set aside goods intended to fill the contract.
a. If seller is in the process of manufacturing, he may complete manufacture or stop and sell for scrap, picking alternative that in his judgment at the time will minimize the seller's loss.
b. Seller can resell goods covered by contract and recover difference between contract price and proceeds of resale.
c. Seller may recover purchase price where resale is not possible.
d. Seller may recover damages for breach based on difference between contract price and market price, or in some cases based on lost profits.</td></tr>
<tr><td>Goods Are in Buyer's Possession</td><td>1. Seller may recover purchase price.
2. Seller may reclaim goods in possession of insolvent buyer by making a demand within 10 days after their receipt. If the buyer represented solvency to the seller in writing within three months before delivery, the 10-day limitation does not apply.</td></tr>
<tr><td>Goods Are in Transit</td><td>1. Seller may stop any size shipment if buyer is insolvent.
2. Seller may stop carload, truckload, planeload, or other large shipment for reasons other than buyer's insolvency.</td></tr>
</table>

issued for the goods, the carrier or other bailee does not have a duty to obey a stop-delivery order issued by any person other than the person who consigned the goods to him [2–705(3)].

Liquidated Damages

If the seller has justifiably withheld delivery of the goods because of the buyer's breach, the buyer may recover any money or goods he has delivered to the seller over and above the agreed amount of liquidated damages. If there is no such agreement, the seller may not retain an amount in excess of $500 or 20 percent of the value of the total performance for which the buyer is obligated under the contract, whichever is smaller. This right of restitution is subject to the seller's right to recover damages under other provisions of the Code and to recover the amount of value of benefits received by the buyer directly or indirectly by reason of the contract [2–718].

Buyer's Remedies

Buyer's Remedies in General

A seller may breach a contract in a number of ways. The most common are (1) failing to make an agreed delivery, (2) delivering goods that do not conform to the contract, and (3) indicating that he does not intend to fulfill the obligations under the contract.

A buyer whose seller breaks the contract is given a number of alternative remedies. These include:

- Buying other goods (covering) and recovering damages from the seller based on any additional expense that the buyer incurs in obtaining the goods [2–712].
- Recovering damages based on the difference between the contract price and the current market price of the goods [2–713].
- Recovering damages for any nonconforming goods accepted by the buyer based on the difference in value between what the buyer got and what he should have gotten [2–714].
- Obtaining specific performance of the contract where the goods are unique and cannot be obtained elsewhere [2–716].

In addition, the buyer can in some cases recover consequential damages (such as lost profits) and incidental damages (such as expenses incurred in buying substitute goods).

CYBERLAW IN ACTION

E-Commerce Aids Buyers

Electronic commerce helps solve two of the most important concerns for buyers of goods in enforcing their rights under Article 2. The first of these relates to means by which the buyer may learn—from the seller or otherwise—of a recall that affects the goods purchased. For example, sellers could notify merchant buyers that it is notifying consumer buyers that they will need to take their cars in to a dealership to have a seatbelt replaced. This early e-mail or posting on the seller's Web site can alert the merchant buyer to the need to train personnel how to handle recall questions from the buyers and also how to make the needed replacement. Buyers also may be able to determine in advance of their purchases whether the goods they plan to buy have been the subject of a recall and whether the recall was voluntary (a problem found by the seller) or required by the federal government, for example. Information about earlier recalls may be especially helpful to buyers of used goods, such as cars and trucks, to baby items, and anything where personal safety is critically important.

The second involves the buyer's duty to give the seller "notice" if the buyer needs a remedy from the seller. As noted in Chapter 21, Sections 2–602 and 2–607 require that the buyer notify the seller if the buyer wishes to reject goods the seller has tendered, or if the buyer decides to revoke acceptance of goods that the seller has promised to repair or replace and has neither repaired nor replaced the goods as promised—or where the buyer gets goods that have a latent defect. "Notice" does not have to be in writing to be effective, but it usually is preferable to have a record that the buyer gave notice to the seller and the time of the notice given. This reduces the risk that a court will find that the buyer's failure to give notice deprives the buyer of her right to a remedy (see Section 2–607(3)(a)). Electronic commerce tools, including e-mail, allow buyers to provide speedy and reliable information to sellers in cases such as these. Buyers whose e-mail systems provide confirmation that the seller recipient actually has received the message about the buyer's concerns about the goods, or who show the time and date that the intended recipient opened the e-mail, make providing notice easier and easier to document than using traditional methods of communication.

Buyer's Right to Cover If the seller fails or refuses to deliver the goods called for in the contract, the buyer can purchase substitute goods; this is known as **cover.** If the buyer does purchase substitute goods, the buyer can recover as damages from the seller the difference between the contract price and the cost of the substitute goods [2–712]. For example, Frank Farmer agrees to sell Ann's Cider Mill 1,000 bushels of apples at $10 a bushel. Farmer then refuses to deliver the apples. Cider Mill can purchase 1,000 bushels of similar apples, and if it has to pay $15 a bushel, it can recover the difference ($5 a bushel) between what it paid ($15)

and the contract price ($10). Thus, Cider Mill could recover $5,000 from Farmer.

The buyer can also recover any incidental damages sustained, but must give the seller credit for any expenses saved. In addition, he may be able to obtain consequential damages. The buyer is not required to cover, however. If he does not cover, the other remedies under the Code are still available [2–712].

The case that follows, *KGM Harvesting Co.,* illustrates a situation where the aggrieved buyer chose to seek damages based on its cost of cover from the defaulting seller.

KGM Harvesting Co. v. Fresh Network   26 UCC Rep.2d 1028 (Cal. App. 1995)

KGM Harvesting Company, a California lettuce grower and distributor, and Fresh Network, an Ohio lettuce broker, began dealing with each other in 1989, and over the years the terms of the agreement were modified. As of May 1991, their agreement called for KGM to deliver 14 "loads" of lettuce a week at a price of 9 cents a pound. A load of lettuce consists of 40 bins, each of which weighs 1,000 to 1,200 pounds. At an average bin weight of 1,100 pounds, one load would equal 44,000 pounds, and the 14 loads called for in the contract would weigh 616,000 pounds. At 9 cents per pound, the cost would be approximately $55,440 per week.

Fresh Network, in turn, resold all of the lettuce to another broker (Castellani Company) who sold it to Club Chef, a company that chopped and shredded it for the fast food industry (specifically, Burger King, Taco Bell, and Pizza Hut). The transactions between Fresh Network and Castellani, and in turn between Castellani and Club Chef, were on a cost-plus basis. This meant each paid its buyer its actual cost plus a small commission.

In May and June 1991, when the price of lettuce went up dramatically, KGM refused to supply Fresh Network with lettuce at the contract price of 9 cents per pound. Instead, it sold the lettuce to others at a profit between $800,000 and $1,100,000.

Fresh Network then went out on the open market and purchased lettuce to satisfy its obligations to Castellani Company. Castellani covered all of Fresh Network's extra expense except for $70,000. Fresh Network then sought to recover from KGM as damages the difference between what it was forced to spend to buy replacement lettuce and the contract price of 9 cents a pound (approximately $700,000). KGM objected on the grounds that Fresh Network had been able to pass some of the increased cost along to Castellani.

Cottle, Presiding Judge

Section 2–711 of the California Uniform Commercial Code provides a buyer with several alternative remedies for a seller's breach of contract. The buyer can "'cover' by making in good faith and without unreasonable delay any reasonable purchase of . . . goods in substitution for those due from the seller." Section 2–712(1). In that case, the buyer "may recover from the seller as damages the difference between the cost of cover and the contract price." Section 2–712(2). If the buyer is unable to cover or chooses not to cover, the measure of damages is the difference between the market price and the contract price. Section 2–713.

In the instant case, buyer "covered" in order to fulfill its own contractual obligations to the Castellani Company. Accordingly, it was awarded the damages called for in cover cases—the difference between the contract price and the cover price.

In appeals from judgments rendered pursuant to section 2–712, the dispute typically centers on whether the buyer

acted in "good faith," whether the "goods in substitution" differed substantially from the contracted for goods, whether the buyer unreasonably delayed in purchasing substitute goods in the mistaken belief the price would go down, or whether the buyer paid too much for the substitute goods.

In this case, however, none of these typical issues is in dispute. Seller does *not* contend that buyer paid too much for the substitute lettuce or that buyer was guilty of "unreasonable delay" or lack of "good faith" in its attempt to obtain substitute lettuce. Nor does seller contend that the lettuce purchased was of a higher quality or grade and therefore not a reasonable substitute.

Instead, seller takes issue with section 2–712 itself, contending that despite the unequivocal language of section 2–712, a buyer who covers should not *necessarily* recover the difference between the cover price and the contract price. Seller points out that because of buyer's "cost plus" contract with Castellani Company, buyer was eventually able to pass on the extra expenses (except for $70,000) occasioned by seller's breach and buyer's consequent purchase of substitute lettuce on the open market. It urges this court under these circumstances not to allow buyer to obtain a "windfall."

The basic premise of contract law is to effectuate the expectations of the parties to the agreement, to give them the "benefit of the bargain" they struck when they entered into the agreement. In this case, the damage formula of section 2–712 put buyer in the identical position performance would have: it gave buyer the contracted for 14 loads of lettuce with which to carry on its business at the contracted for price of 9 cents per pound.

Despite the obvious applicability and appropriateness of section 2–712, seller argues in this appeal that the contract-cover differential of section 2–712 is inappropriate in cases, as here, where the aggrieved buyer is ultimately able to pass on its additional costs to other parties. Seller contends that section

1–106's remedial injunction to put the aggrieved party "in as good a position as if the other party had fully performed" demands that all subsequent events impacting on *buyer's* ultimate profit or loss be taken into consideration (specifically, that buyer passed on all but $70,000 of its loss to Castellani Company, which passed on all of its loss to Club Chef, which passed on most of its loss to its fast food customers).

No section 2–712 case has ever held that cover damages must be limited by section 1–106. The obvious reason is that the cover-contract differential puts a buyer who covers in the exact same position as performance would have done. This is precisely what is called for in section 1–106. In this respect, the cover/contract differential of section 2–712 is very different than the market/contract differential of section 2–713, which need bear no close relation to the buyer's actual loss.

Judgment affirmed for Fresh Network.

Incidental Damages

Incidental damages include expenses that the buyer incurs in receiving, inspecting, transporting, and storing goods shipped by the seller that do not conform to those called for in the contract. Incidental damages also include any reasonable expenses or charges that the buyer has to pay in obtaining substitute goods [2–715(1)].

Consequential Damages

In certain situations, an injured buyer is able to recover consequential damages, such as the buyer's lost profits caused by the seller's breach of contract. The buyer must be able to show that the seller knew or should have known at the time the contract was made that the buyer would suffer special damages if the seller did not perform his obligations. In case of commercial loss, the buyer must also show that he could not have prevented the damage by obtaining substitute goods [2–715(2)(a)].

Suppose Knitting Mill promises to deliver 15,000 yards of a special fabric to Dorsey by September 1. Knitting Mill knows that Dorsey wants to acquire the material to make garments suitable for the Christmas season. Knitting Mill also knows that in reliance on the contract with it, Dorsey will enter into contracts with stores to deliver the finished garments by October 1. If Knitting Mill fails to deliver the fabric or delivers the fabric after September 1, it may be liable to Dorsey for any consequential damages that she sustains if she is unable to acquire the same material elsewhere in time to fulfill her October 1 contracts.

Consequential damages can also include an injury to a person or property caused by a breach of warranty

[2–715(2)(b)]. For example, an electric saw is defective. Hanson purchases the saw, and while he is using it, the blade comes off and severely cuts his arm. The injury to Hanson is consequential damage resulting from a nonconforming or defective product.

In the hypothetical case presented at the beginning of this chapter, a customer contracts with Bridal Shop to make a custom-designed bridal gown in size 6 in time for her wedding. The case posits the Bridal Shop advising the customer that it will not be able to complete the production of the gown in time for the wedding. If the customer "covers" by buying a gown from another wedding shop, what is the measure of damages that the customer would be entitled to? Can you think of "incidental damages" or "consequential damages" that might be incurred in this situation and that might be claimed?

Damages for Nondelivery

If the seller fails or refuses to deliver the goods called for by the contract, the buyer has the option of recovering damages for the nondelivery. Thus, instead of covering, the buyer can get the difference between the contract price of the goods and their market price at the time he learns of the seller's breach. In addition, the buyer may recover any incidental damages and consequential damages, but must give the seller credit for any expenses saved [2–713].

Suppose Biddle agreed on June 1 to sell and deliver 1,500 bushels of wheat to a grain elevator on September 1 for $7 per bushel and then refused to deliver on September 1 because the market price was then $10 per bushel. The grain elevator could recover $4,500 damages from Biddle, plus incidental damages that could not have been prevented by cover.

The case that follows, *Green Wood Industrial Company v. Forceman International Development Group,* *Inc.,* involves an award of damages in connection with a contract to sell scrap metal to a buyer in China where the goods were never shipped even though the seller fraudulently represented they had been shipped.

Green Wood Industrial Company v. Forceman International Development Group, Inc.   64 UCC Rep.2d 378 (Ct. App. Cal. 2007)

Green Wood, a sole proprietorship owned and operated by Joseph Li in Hong Kong, is primarily in the business of buying scrap from sellers in the United States for resale to buyers in China. Richshine Metals, Inc. (Richshine), owned and operated by its president, Christine Fan, was in the business in California of selling scrap metal for export. In the summer of 2003, Green Wood purchased approximately 680 metric tons of scrap plate metal from Richshine. Green Wood sold the scrap plate to a buyer in China. Green Wood's buyer was very pleased with the material supplied by Richshine and wanted more.

In November 2003, Green Wood placed a purchase order with Richshine to acquire 2,100 metric tons of scrap plate metal and 10,650 metric tons of scrap iron for a total purchase price of $1.89 million. Richshine was to deliver the goods directly to Green Wood's buyer at Guangxi Port in southern China by the end of November. Green Wood was to pay a $200,000 deposit, $340,000 cash on delivery, and the balance by letter of credit.

By the beginning of January 2004, Richshine had not shipped the goods. During this time frame the price of scrap metal was rising in the world market. Li and Green Wood's buyer were concerned that Richline might have sold the goods to another buyer at a higher price. They agreed to make some changes in the shipping terms and to wire additional money to Richshine's account. Green Wood ultimately paid Richshine $1,074,548 in advance toward the purchase price of the goods. Green Wood's Chinese buyer funded $862,500 of that amount.

Thereafter, Richshine provided packing lists, invoices, and bills of lading as well as certain certificates required by the Chinese government that the goods had been inspected (China Certification and Inspection Corporation or "CCIC" certificates). The certificates had been obtained by Forceman International Development Group, Inc. (Forceman), and purported to represent they had been issued by CCIC South America and indicated that the containers with the scrap had been inspected in Tijuana, Mexico. The goods allegedly were awaiting shipment to China.

Unbeknownst to Li, the packing lists provided by Richshine with respect to the purchase order were fake, the CN Link bills of lading were forgeries, and the CCIC certificates were obtained fraudulently. The goods that Richshine had purported to ship pursuant to the purchase order never existed.

When the goods did not arrive, Li mounted an investigation to track down Fan and her confederates. They were eventually found in Nevada where they had moved and were doing business under the name of Moundhouse Metals. When Li confronted Fan, telling her that if the goods did not arrive soon, Li would sue Fan, she, in essence, dared Li to do so.

When further investigation made it clear the goods had never existed, Li brought suit against Richline, Fan, and Forceman for fraud and negligence. Li sought to recover, as out-of pocket damages, $1,074,548 paid to Richline and Fan; $159,000 in lost profits that Green Wood lost as a result of the nondelivery of the goods; and $274,868 for a claim Green Wood's buyer had made against Green Wood, apparently for its lost profits, which Green Wood had agreed to pay but had not yet paid. A jury awarded Green Wood compensatory damages of $1,508,416 plus punitive damages of $5,000, and the defendants appealed.

Mosk, Judge

The fraud in this case related to the purchase order. The purchase order was a contract for the sale of goods subject to Article 2 of the Uniform Commercial Code. Accordingly, the damages available to Green Wood from the fraud are governed by UCC section 2–721, which provides for recovery on a basis-of-the-bargain basis. That section provides: "Remedies for material misrepresentation or fraud include all remedies available under this section for nonfraudulent breach. Neither rescission or a claim for rescission of the contract for sale nor rejection or return of the goods shall bar or be deemed inconsistent with a claim for damage or other remedy." Section 2–721 represents an exception to the general rule in California that a plaintiff defrauded in the purchase or sale of property may recover only out-of-pocket loss.

Where, as here, a seller fails to deliver goods pursuant to a contract governed by the UCC and the buyer does not cover, the buyer's remedy is set forth in section 2–713(1). That section provides, in pertinent part, "the measure of damages for nondelivery or repudiation by the seller is the difference between the market price at the time when the buyer learned of the breach and the contract price *together with any incidental and consequential damages provided in this division* (2–715), but less expenses saved in consequence of the seller's breach" (italics added). Green Wood did not seek damages based on the difference between contract price and market price, but rather sought its out-of-pocket damages and consequential damages based on its lost profits. Pursuant to section 2–715(2)(a), a buyer of goods for resale may generally recover its lost profits as consequential damages, provided such damage "could not reasonably be prevented by cover or otherwise. . . ."

In this case, none of the defendants offered evidence that Green Wood had failed to mitigate its consequential damages. Green Wood, however, introduced substantial evidence to sustain an award of lost profits. Green Wood presented evidence of its purchase price from Richshine, which included the cost of shipping the goods to China. Li of Green Wood testified that Green Wood sold the plate scrap to its buyer for $25 per ton more than Green Wood paid, and sold the scrap iron at $10 per ton more than Green Wood paid. Forceman had a full and fair opportunity to test Green Wood's damage calculation through cross-examination or rebuttal. On appeal, Forceman does not identify any specific manner in which Li's calculation was erroneous, and Forceman provides no argument or authority that the amount of lost profits awarded was excessive. Accordingly, substantial evidence supports the $159,000 award for Green Wood's lost profits.

Forceman asserts that the trial court erred in awarding Green Wood $274,868 for a claim made against Green Wood by its Chinese buyer, or an obligation of Green Wood to that buyer, for damages suffered by that buyer resulting from Green Wood's failure to deliver the goods. We agree that as to this item, the damage award was improper. A plaintiff may not recover damages for unpaid liabilities to a third party, unless the plaintiff proves to a reasonable certainty that the liability could and would be enforced by the third party against the plaintiff or that the plaintiff otherwise could and would satisfy the obligation.

Under California law, a plaintiff—whether the plaintiff's claim sounds in contract or tort—generally cannot recover damages alleged to arise from a third-party claim against the plaintiff when caused by the defendant's misconduct. It is clear that the mere possibility, or even probability, that an event causing damage will result from a wrongful act, does not render the act actionable. Accordingly, the existence of a mere liability is not the equivalent of actual damage. This is because the *fact* of damage is inherently uncertain in such circumstances. The facts that a third party has demanded payment by the plaintiff of a particular liability and plaintiff has admitted such liability are not, by themselves, sufficient to support an award of damages for that liability, because that third party may never attempt to force the plaintiff to satisfy the alleged obligation, and plaintiff may never pay the obligation.

California law does, however, recognize that a plaintiff in a tort action may recover for a "loss reasonably certain to occur in the future." A similar concept has been recognized by some authorities in the context of contract damages. For example, an authority states, "Indeed, in a resale situation, the buyer has been permitted to claim as consequential damages from the seller the amount of the buyer's potential liability to its customer; if the buyer establishes the probability that the buyer will be sued by the customer, it is immaterial that the buyer has not yet been sued and made to bear the loss, and recovery is measured by the probable liability of the buyer to the customer. Other authorities note that a plaintiff may recover for future losses if there is an appropriate showing that those losses will in fact be incurred in the future.

It may be that existing California authorities generally require payment of the liability in order to include the liability as damages. But even if a liability to a third party might be included as damages without actual payment, more certainty is required than just evidence of an obligation to pay a third party.

In this case, the evidence established that, at the time of trial, Green Wood has not paid any portion of its Chinese buyer's $274,868 claim. Although there is evidence that Green Wood had, in effect, settled the claim by agreeing to pay it, Green Wood presented no evidence that any such agreement would be enforceable in China, or that the liability could and would be enforced by the buyer in the United States or elsewhere, or that the claim will otherwise be paid. There was no evidence from which the jury could conclude that it was reasonably certain that Green Wood would ever have to pay the money.

Furthermore, it appears that the Chinese buyer's claim against Green Wood was for the buyer's own lost profits. The only evidence regarding the Chinese buyer's business, however, was that the buyer is a manufacturer of some kind, not a reseller. Green Wood presented no evidence to establish the fact or amount of the Chinese buyer's lost profits other than the Chinese buyer's mere claim. This illustrates another problem with allowing damages based on a third-party claim. If a defendant is liable for any sum a plaintiff *agreed* to pay a third party, that sum could be subject to unfair manipulation.

Accordingly, the evidence is insufficient to sustain the award of $274,868 for the Chinese buyer's claim.

Ethics in Action

Should the Buyer Get an Honest Answer?

Problem case number 7 at the end of this chapter is based on the following situation: Barr purchased from Crow's Nest Yacht Sales a 31-foot tiara pleasure yacht manufactured by S-2 Yachts. He had gone to Crow's Nest knowing the style and type yacht he wanted. He was told that the retail price was $102,000 but that he could purchase the model it had for $80,000. When he asked about the reduction in price, he was told that Crow's Nest had to move it because there was a change in the model and it had new ones coming in. He was assured that the yacht was new, that there was nothing wrong with it, and there was only 20 hours on the engine. When Barr began to use the boat, he experienced tremendous difficulties with equipment malfunctions. On examination by an expert, it was determined that the yacht had earlier been sunk in salt water, resulting in significant rusting and deterioration in the engine, equipment, and fixtures. How would you assess the ethicality of the representations made by the salesperson in response to his question? In a case like this, should it be incumbent on the buyer to ask the "right" question in order to protect himself or herself, or should there be an ethical obligation on the seller to disclose voluntarily material facts that may be relevant to the buyer making an informed decision?

Damages for Defective Goods

If a buyer accepts defective goods and wants to hold the seller liable, the buyer must give the seller notice of the defect within a reasonable time after the buyer discovers the defect [2–607(3)]. Where goods are defective or not as warranted and the buyer gives the required notice, he can recover damages. The buyer is entitled to recover the difference between the value of the goods received and the value the goods would have had if they had been as warranted. He may also be entitled to incidental and consequential damages [2–714].

For example, Al's Auto Store sells Anders an automobile tire, warranting it to be four-ply construction. The tire goes flat when it is punctured by a nail, and Anders discovers that the tire is really only two-ply. If Anders gives the store prompt notice of the breach, she can keep

The Global Business Environment

Buyer's Remedies in International Transactions

Under the Convention on Contracts for the International Sale of Goods (CISG), an aggrieved buyer has four potential types of remedies against a seller who has breached the contract: (1) "avoidance" of the contract; (2) an adjustment in the price; (3) specific performance; and (4) an action for damages. The first two remedies can be pursued without involving a court, and the last two require the buyer to initiate a judicial proceeding.

As noted in Chapter 21 (see The Global Business Environment box entitled "Insecurity" on page 562), a buyer has the right to suspend its performance and/or to "avoid" a contract where the seller appears unable to perform its obligations and does not provide adequate assurances that it can and will perform. A buyer may also "avoid" the contract—which under the CISG essentially means "cancel" the contract—and refuse to accept and pay for goods that are so defective or nonconforming as to constitute a "fundamental breach" of the contract.

Aggrieved buyers who receive nonconforming goods "may reduce the price" paid to the seller. The CISG provides a formula for calculating the reduction that involves comparing the value of the goods actually delivered at the time they were delivered to the value that conforming goods would have had at the time of delivery.

The CISG gives the aggrieved buyer a right to "require performance" by the seller. This follows the civil law principle that the best relief to the buyer is not damages but rather having the seller perform as promised. Thus, the CISG does not require that the goods must be "unique"—as the UCC does—in order for the buyer to be entitled to specific performance.

While the buyer has the right to seek specific performance with the assistance of a court, the buyer also has the option of seeking damages, including consequential damages. Such damages can be based either on (1) the difference between the cost of cover and the contract price or (2) on the difference between the market price and the contract price. However, unlike the UCC, the CISG requires the buyer to use the "cover" formula for calculating damages if the buyer does cover by obtaining substitute goods.

the tire and recover from Al's the difference in value between a two-ply and a four-ply tire.

Buyer's Right to Specific Performance

Sometimes, the goods covered by a contract are unique and it is not possible for a buyer to obtain substitute goods. When this is the case, the buyer is entitled to specific performance of the contract.

Specific performance means that the buyer can require the seller to give the buyer the goods covered by the contract [2–716]. Thus, the buyer of an antique automobile such as a 1910 Ford might have a court order the seller to deliver the specified automobile to the buyer because it was one of a kind. On the other hand, the buyer of grain in a particular storage bin could not get specific performance if he could buy the same kind of grain elsewhere.

Buyer and Seller Agreements as to Remedies

As mentioned earlier in this chapter, the parties to a contract may provide remedies in addition to or as substitution for those expressly provided in the Code [2–719]. For example, the buyer's remedies may be limited by the contract to the return of the goods and the repayment of the price or to the replacement of nonconforming goods or parts. However, a court looks to see whether such a limitation was freely agreed to or whether it is unconscionable. In the latter case, the court does not enforce the limitation and the buyer has all the rights given to an injured buyer by the Code.

The *Baker* case, which follows below, involves a situation where a merchant was unsuccessful in seeking to restrict an aggrieved buyer's efforts to recover the purchase price paid for defective goods.

Baker v. Burlington Coat Factory Warehouse
34 UCC Rep.2d 1052 (N.Y. City Ct. 1998)

Catherine Baker purchased a fake fur coat from the Burlington Coat Factory Warehouse store in Scarsdale, New York, paying $127.99 in cash. The coat began shedding profusely, rendering the coat unwearable. The shedding was so severe that Baker's allergies were exacerbated, necessitating a visit to her doctor and to the drugstore for a prescription.

She returned the coat to the store within two days and demanded that Burlington refund her $127.99 cash payment. Burlington refused, indicating that it would give her a store credit or a new coat of equal value, but no cash refund. Baker searched the store for a fake fur of equal value and found none. She refused the store credit, repeated her demand for a cash refund, and brought a lawsuit against Burlington when it again refused to make a cash refund.

In its store, Burlington displayed several large signs which stated, in part,

WAREHOUSE POLICY

Merchandise, in New Condition, May be Exchanged Within 7 Days of Purchase for Store Credit and Must be Accompanied by a Ticket and Receipt. No Cash Refunds or Charge Credits.

On the front of Baker's sales receipt was the following language:

Holiday Purchases May be Exchanged Through January 11th, 1998, In House Store Credit Only No Cash Refunds or Charge Card Credits.

On the back of the sales receipt was the following language:

We will be Happy to Exchange Merchandise in New Condition Within 7 Days When Accompanied By Ticket and Receipt. However, Because of Our Unusually Low Prices: No Cash Refunds or Charge Card Credits Will Be Issued. In House Store Credit Only.

At the trial, Baker claimed that she had not read the language on the receipt and was unaware of Burlington's No Cash Refunds policy.

Dickerson, Judge

Under most circumstances retail stores in New York State are permitted to establish a no cash and no credit card charge refund policy and enforce it. Retail Store refund policies are governed, in part, by New York General Business Law section 218–a, Disclosure of Refund Policies, which requires conspicuous signs on the item or at the cash register or on signs visible from the cash register or at each store entrance, setting forth its refund policy including whether it is "in cash, or as credit or store credit only." If the store violates GBL section 218–a, the consumer has twenty days to return "merchandise (which) has not been used or damaged."

Baker returned the undamaged and unworn, albeit shedding, Fake Fur to Burlington Coat within two days of purchase thus coming within Burlington Coat's "7 Days of Purchase" policy and within the twenty-day claim filing period in GBL 218–a(3). Although Baker professed ignorance of Burlington Coat's refund policy, the Court finds that Burlington Coat's signs and the front and back of its sales receipt reasonably inform consumers of its no cash and no credit card charge refund policy.

Notwithstanding its visibility Burlington Coat's no cash and no credit card charge refund policy as against Baker is unenforceable. Stated simply, when a product is defective as was Baker's common and, hardly unique, shedding Fake Fur, Burlington Coat cannot refuse to return the consumer's payment whether made in cash or with a credit card.

UCC section 2–314 mandates that "a warranty that the goods shall be merchantable is implied in a contract of their sale if the seller is a merchant with respect to goods of that kind . . . (2) Goods to be merchantable must be . . . fit for the ordinary purposes for which such goods are used" [UCC section 2–314]. Should there be a breach of the implied warranty of merchantability then consumers may recover all appropriate damages including the purchase price in cash [UCC section 2–714]. The Court finds that Burlington Coat sold Baker a defective and unwearable Fake Fur and breached the implied warranty of merchantability. Baker is entitled to the return of her purchase price of $127.99 in cash and all other appropriate damages. However, Baker's claim for the $15.00 co-pay for visiting her doctor and the cost of allergy medicine is denied. Baker admitted having allergies, but it is not clear that the Fake Fur exacerbated those allergies.

As between the implicit cash refund policy contained in UCC sections 2–314 and 2–714, the no cash refund policy explicitly authorized in GBL section 218–a(2), the UCC provisions are paramount and preempt any contrary provisions in GBL 218–a. To hold otherwise would allow a merchant whether in good faith or otherwise, to place in commerce a defective product and merely give credit exchange upon the product's return.

Judgment for Baker.

CONCEPT REVIEW

Buyer's Remedies (on breach by seller)

Problems	Buyer's Remedy
Seller Fails to Deliver Goods or Delivers Nonconforming Goods That Buyer Rightfully Rejects or Justifiably Revokes Acceptance Of	1. Buyer may cancel the contract and recover damages. 2. Buyer may "cover" by obtaining substitute goods and recover difference between contract price and cost of cover. 3. Buyer may recover damages for breach based on difference between contract price and market price.
Seller Delivers Nonconforming Goods That Are Accepted by Buyer	Buyer may recover damages based on difference between value of goods received and value of goods if they had been as warranted.
Seller Has the Goods but Refuses to Deliver Them and Buyer Wants Them	Buyer may seek specific performance if goods are unique and cannot be obtained elsewhere, or buyer may replevy (obtain from the seller) goods identified to contract if buyer cannot obtain cover.

Problems and Problem Cases

1. Lobianco contracted with Property Protection, Inc., for the installation of a burglar alarm system. The contract provided in part:

> Alarm system equipment installed by Property Protection, Inc., is guaranteed against improper function due to manufacturing defects of workmanship for a period of 12 months. The installation of the above equipment carries a 90-day warranty. The liability of Property Protection, Inc., is limited to repair or replacement of security alarm equipment and does not include loss or damage to possessions, persons, or property.

As installed, the alarm system included a standby battery source of power in the event that the regular source of power failed. During the 90-day warranty period, burglars broke into Lobianco's house and stole $35,815 worth of jewelry. First, they destroyed the electric meter so that there was no electric source to operate the system, and then they entered the house. The batteries in the standby system were dead, and thus the standby system failed to operate. Accordingly, no outside siren was activated and a telephone call that was supposed to be triggered was not made. Lobianco brought suit, claiming damage in the amount of her stolen jewelry because of the failure of the alarm system to work properly. Did the disclaimer effectively eliminate any liability on the alarm company's part for consequential damages?

2. On March 23, 1993, Poli purchased a new 1992 Dodge Spirit manufactured by DaimlerChrysler Corporation. When he made the purchase Poli elected to obtain a seven-year, seventy-thousand-mile "powertrain" warranty from DaimlerChrysler. Over the next few years, the car required a series of repairs and replacements to the engine timing belt, which was one of the parts covered by the powertrain warranty. On December 16, 1993, after the car had been driven 16,408 miles, Poli had the timing belt replaced. More than three years later, on March 21, 1997, after the car had been driven 36,149 miles, the timing belt was repaired. Poli then had to replace the timing belt on May 16, 1997, on January 5, 1998, and on July 6, 1998. The timing belt again failed on July 31, 1998, causing the destruction of the "short block" of the engine which the dealer took six months to repair. All of the timing belt repairs and replacements were undertaken by the dealer in accordance with the seven-year, seventy-thousand-mile powertrain warranty. On December 15, 1998, Poli brought an action against DaimlerChrysler for breach of warranty. The company moved for summary judgment on the grounds that the breach of warranty claim was barred by the four-year statute of limitations in the UCC because it was brought more than four years after the car had been purchased and that is when the breach occurred. Poli claimed that the breach of warranty claim was timely because the seven-year, seventy-thousand-mile powertrain warranty was a "guarantee of performance" which DaimlerChrysler breached by failing to properly repair the timing belt. Was Poli's breach of warranty claim barred by the four-year statute of limitations?

3. Murrey & Sons Company, Inc. (Murrey), was engaged in the business of manufacturing and selling pool tables. Erik Madsen was working on an idea to develop a pool table that, through the use of electronic devices installed in the rails of the table, would produce lighting and sound effects in a fashion similar to a pinball machine. Murrey and Madsen entered into a written contract whereby Murrey agreed to manufacture 100 of its M1 4-foot by 8-foot six-pocket coin-operated pool tables with customized rails capable of incorporating the electronic lighting and sound effects desired by Madsen. Under the agreement, Madsen would design the rails and provide the drawings to Murrey, which would manufacture them to Madsen's specifications. Madsen was to design, manufacture, and install the electronic components for the tables. Madsen agreed to pay $550 per table or a total of $55,000 for the 100 tables and made a $42,500 deposit on the contract.

Murrey began the manufacture of the tables while Madsen continued to work on the design of the rails and electronics. Madsen encountered significant difficulties and notified Murrey that he would be unable to take delivery of the 100 tables. Madsen then brought suit to recover the $42,500 he had paid Murrey.

Following Madsen's repudiation of the contract, Murrey dismantled the pool tables and used salvageable materials to manufacture other pool tables. A good portion of the material was simply used as firewood. Murrey made no attempt to market the 100 pool tables at a discount or at any other price in order to mitigate its damages. It claimed the salvage value of the materials it reused was $7,488. There was evidence that if Murrey had completed the tables, they would have had a value of at least $21,250 and could have been sold for at least that much, and that the changes made in the frame to accommodate the electrical wiring would not have adversely affected the quality or marketability of the pool tables. Murrey said it had not completed manufacture because its reputation for quality might be hurt if it dealt in "seconds," and that the changes in the frame might weaken it and subject it to potential liability. Was Murrey justified in not completing manufacture of the pool tables?

4. Precision Mirror & Glass is a manufacturer of custom-made glass products, such as shower doors, mirrors, and glass table tops. On July 9, Bobby Nelms brought Precision a pattern drawn on paper for a glass table top cover for an antique table he owned. He advised the sales representative that he wanted to cover his table with ¾-inch glass conforming to the pattern. After some discussion, it was decided that the table top would be made with ⅜-inch glass at a cost, including sales tax, of $684.33. Nelms left a $100 deposit, leaving a balance of $584.33 payable upon pickup of the table top. At that time Nelms signed a contract that set out the specifications and price and that also included a noncancellation clause indicating "ALL ORDERS ARE FINAL SALE" and "personally guaranteed . . . I waive my right to cancellation." Precision's practice was to allow a customer to cancel an order as long as it occurs prior to the start of production. However, once a custom item is made to a customer's unique specifications, it rarely has any resale value. On July 11, Nelms called Precision and stated that he wanted to cancel the order because he believed that the ⅜-inch glass ordered would not be suitable for his purposes. Precision responded that the glass had already been cut and was awaiting his pickup. When Nelms failed to pick up the glass despite a demand that he do so, Precision brought suit against him to seek money damages in the amount owed on the contract. Is Precision entitled to recover the full contract price from Nelms?

5. Cohn advertised a 30-foot sailboat for sale in *The New York Times*. Fisher saw the ad, inspected the sailboat, and offered Cohn $4,650 for the boat. Cohn accepted the offer. Fisher gave Cohn a check for $2,535 as a deposit on the boat. He wrote on the check, "Deposit on aux sloop, D'arc Wind, full amount $4,650." Fisher later refused to go through with the purchase and stopped payment on the deposit check. Cohn readvertised the boat and sold it for the highest offer he received, which was $3,000. Cohn then sued Fisher for breach of contract. He asked for damages of $1,679.50. This represented the $1,650 difference between the contract price and the sale price plus $29.50 in incidental expenses in reselling the boat. Is Cohn entitled to this measure of damages?

6. McCain Foods sold on credit and delivered a quantity of frozen french fries to Flagstaff Food Service Company. Several days later, when the potatoes had not yet been paid for, McCain discovered that Flagstaff was insolvent and had just filed a petition in bankruptcy. What would you advise McCain Foods to do?

7. Barr purchased from Crow's Nest Yacht Sales a 31-foot Tiara pleasure yacht manufactured by S-2 Yachts. He had gone to Crow's Nest knowing the style and type yacht he wanted. He was told that the retail price was $102,000 but that he could purchase the model it had for $80,000. When he asked about the reduction in price he was told that Crow's Nest had to move it because there was a change in the model and it had new ones coming in. He was assured that the yacht was new, that there was nothing wrong with it, and that it had only 20 hours on the engines. Barr installed a considerable amount of electronic equipment on the boat. When he began to use it, he experienced tremendous difficulties with equipment malfunctions. On examination by a marine expert it was determined that the yacht had earlier been sunk in salt water, resulting in significant rusting and deterioration in the engine, equipment, and fixtures. Other experts concluded that significant replacement and repair was required, that the engines would have only 25 percent of their normal expected life, and that following its sinking, the yacht would have only half of its original value. Barr then brought suit against Crow's Nest and S-2 Yachts for breach of warranty. To what measure of damages is Barr entitled to recover for breach of warranty?

8. De La Hoya bought a used handgun for $140 from Slim's Gun Shop, a licensed firearms dealer. At the time, neither De La Hoya nor Slim's knew that the gun had been stolen prior to the time Slim's bought it. While De La Hoya was using the gun for target shooting, he was questioned by a police officer. The officer traced the serial number of the gun, determined that it had been stolen, and arrested De La Hoya. De La Hoya had to hire an attorney to defend himself against

the criminal charges. De La Hoya then brought a lawsuit against Slim's Gun Shop for breach of warranty of title. He sought to recover the purchase price of the gun plus $8,000, the amount of his attorney's fees, as "consequential damages." Can a buyer who does not get good title to the goods he purchased recover from the seller consequential damages caused by the breach of warranty of title?

9. On February 5, 2004, Michael Taylor entered into a retail purchase order agreement with Hoffman Ford for the first new 2005 Ford GT 40 allotted and/or delivered to Hoffman Ford. The sales price was listed "MSRP Dealer Prep." MSRP is the manufacturer's suggested retail price, and dealer preparation charges are charges associated with getting the car ready for delivery and usually run between $100 and $500. The dealer preparation charge is about the same for all new cars. On March 4, 2004, Taylor paid, and Hoffman accepted, a $5,000 deposit on the purchase. The Ford GT 40 is a limited edition car, a re-creation of a 1960s race car and was first being produced in 2005. There is an extra value associated with the first year of a limited edition automobile, as well as with being the original owner, and scarcity also affects market price. Hoffman Ford was allotted one 2005 Ford GT with delivery some time in September 2004. The manufacturer's suggested retail price for the car is $156,945. The price necessary to purchase a GT 40 on the open market is substantially greater than the manufacturer's suggested retail price. At the time some cars were available for sale on the Internet at prices starting at $250,000. The open-market price of such a car was likely to be double the manufacturer's suggested retail price. However, the Ford GT 40 was not readily available on the open market, and it was highly unlikely that the car could be purchased from another dealer.

In November 2004, Taylor's lawyer inquired of counsel for Hoffman Ford whether Hoffman would duly perform the contract between them. Hoffman Ford's counsel replied that it stood ready, willing, and able to perform under the contract and that the price of the car, including "dealer prep" is $300,000. Hoffman Ford normally did not charge a "dealer prep" but claimed in this case it was an "availability" surcharge. As a result of this response, Taylor filed a lawsuit against Hoffman Ford for breach of contract and seeking an injunction against transferring ownership or possession of the first 2005 GT allotted to Hoffman Ford to anyone else, as well as specific performance and damages. Subsequently, Hoffman Ford received an offer from another buyer to purchase the car. Is Taylor entitled to seek specific performance of the contract?

Online Research

Use the Internet to Check for Product Recalls

Use the Internet to locate the Web site for the U.S. Consumer Product Safety Commission (CPSC) (www.cpsc .gov). Use it to find five products that the Commission recently has either ordered recalled or for which it has entered into voluntary settlements with manufacturers to issue recall notices. Then go to the Web site for one of the manufacturers and compare the information concerning the product on the manufacturer's Web site with the information posted on the CPSC site. What, if any, differences do you discern?

Part Five

Property

chapter 23
Personal Property and Bailments

chapter 24
Real Property

chapter 25
Landlord and Tenant

chapter 26
Estates and Trusts

chapter 27
Insurance Law

PERSONAL PROPERTY AND BAILMENTS

Claudio is a skilled craftsman employed by the Goldcasters Jewelry to make handcrafted jewelry. Working after his normal working hours and using materials he paid for himself, Claudio crafts a fine ring by skillfully weaving together strands of gold wire. He presents the ring to his fiancé, Cheryl, as an engagement ring in anticipation of their forthcoming marriage. While visiting the restroom in a steak and ribs restaurant, Cheryl removes the ring so she can wash some barbecue sauce from her hands. In her haste to get back to her table, she leaves the ring on the washstand when she exits the restroom. Sandra, a part-time janitor for the restaurant, finds the ring and slips it into her purse. When Cheryl realizes she is missing the ring and returns to the restroom to look for it, neither the ring nor Sandra is still there. Later that evening Sandra sells the ring to her cousin, Gloria, who gives her $200 for it. Several days later, Cheryl breaks her engagement to Claudio, telling him that she no longer loves him. Claudio asks Cheryl to return the ring, indicating that he only intended for her to have it if their engagement led to marriage. This situation raises a number of questions concerning rights and interests in personal property that will be discussed in this chapter. They include:

- Between Claudio and Goldcasters, who was the owner of the ring at the time Claudio created it?
- Did Claudio make an effective gift of the ring to Cheryl? Or was it a conditional gift that he could revoke when Cheryl decided to call off the marriage?
- What was Sandra's responsibility when she found the ring? Between Sandra and the restaurant, who had the better right to the ring?
- Did Gloria become the owner of the ring when she paid the $200 to Sandra? Does Cheryl have the right to recover the ring from Gloria if she finds that Gloria has it?
- Was it ethical for Claudio to use this employer's tools and facilities for a personal project?

Nature of Property

The concept of property is crucial to the organization of society. The essential nature of a particular society is often reflected in the way it views property, including the degree to which property ownership is concentrated in the state, the extent to which it permits individual ownership of property, and the rules that govern such ownership. History is replete with wars and revolutions that arose out of conflicting claims to, or views concerning, property. Significant documents in our Anglo-American legal tradition, such as the Magna Carta and the Constitution, deal explicitly with property rights.

The word **property** is used to refer to something that is capable of being owned. It is also used to refer to a right or interest that allows a person to exercise dominion over a thing that may be owned or possessed.

When we talk about property ownership, we are speaking of a *bundle of rights* that the law recognizes and enforces. For example, ownership of a building includes the exclusive right to use, enjoy, sell, mortgage, or rent the building. If someone else tries to use the property without the owner's consent, the owner may use the courts and legal procedures to eject that person. Ownership of a patent includes the rights to produce, use, and sell the patented item, and to license others to do those things.

In the United States, private ownership of property is protected by the Constitution, which provides that the government shall deprive no person of "life, liberty or property without due process of law." We recognize and encourage the rights of individuals to acquire, enjoy, and use property. These rights, however, are not unlimited. For example, a person cannot use property in an unreasonable manner that injures others. Also, the state has **police power** through which it can impose reasonable regulations on the use of property, tax it, and take it for public use by paying the owner compensation for it.

Property is divided into a number of categories based on its characteristics. The same piece of property may fall into more than one class. The following discussion explores the meaning of **personal property** and the numerous ways of classifying property.

Classifications of Property

Personal Property versus Real Property

Personal property is defined by process of exclusion. The term *personal property* is used in contrast to *real property.* Real property is the earth's crust and all things firmly attached to it.[1] For example, land, office buildings, and houses are considered to be real property. All other objects and rights that may be owned are personal property. Clothing, books, and stock in a corporation are examples of personal property.

Real property may be turned into personal property if it is detached from the earth. Personal property, if attached to the earth, becomes real property. For example, marble in the ground is real property. When the marble is quarried, it becomes personal property, but if it is used in constructing a building, it becomes real property again. Perennial vegetation that does not have to be seeded every year, such as trees, shrubs, and grass, is usually treated as part of the real property on which it is growing. When trees and shrubs are severed from the land, they become personal property. Crops that must be planted each year, such as corn, oats, and potatoes, are usually treated as personal property. However, if the real property on which they are growing is sold, the new owner of the real property also becomes the owner of the crops.

When personal property is attached to, or used in conjunction with, real property in such a way as to be treated as part of the real property, it is known as a **fixture.** The law concerning fixtures is discussed in the next chapter.

Tangible versus Intangible Personal Property

Personal property may be either tangible or intangible. Tangible property has a physical existence. Cars, animals, and computers are examples. Property that has no physical existence is called intangible property. For example, rights under a patent, copyright, or trademark would be intangible property.[2]

The distinction between tangible and intangible property is important primarily for tax and estate planning purposes. Generally, tangible property is subject to tax in the state in which it is located, whereas intangible property is usually taxable in the state where its owner lives.

Public and Private Property

Property is also classified as public or private, based on the ownership of the property. If the property is owned by the government or a governmental unit, it is public property. If it is owned by an individual, a group of individuals, a corporation, or some other business organization, it is private property.

Acquiring Ownership of Personal Property

Production or Purchase

The most common ways of obtaining ownership of property are by producing it or purchasing it. A person owns the property that she makes unless the person has agreed to do the work for another party. In that case, the other party is the owner of the product of the work. For example, a person who creates a painting, knits a sweater, or develops a computer program is the owner unless she has been retained by someone to create the painting, knit the sweater, or develop the program. Another major way of acquiring property is by purchase. The law regarding the purchase of tangible personal property (that is, sale of goods) is discussed in Chapter 19.

The scenario set out at the start of this chapter posits that Claudio, a skilled craftsman employed by Goldcasters to make handcrafted jewelry, works after his normal working hours and uses materials he paid for himself to make a gold ring. Who should be considered to be the owner of the ring at the time Claudio created it, Claudio or Goldcasters? What are the critical factors that lead you to this conclusion?

[1]The law of real property is treated in Chapter 24.

[2]These important types of intangible property are discussed in Chapter 8.

Possession of Unowned Property

In very early times, the most common way of obtaining ownership of personal property was simply by taking possession of unowned property. For example, the first person to take possession of a wild animal became its owner. Today, one may still acquire ownership of personal property by possessing it if the property is unowned. The two major examples of unowned property that may be acquired by possession are wild animals and abandoned property. Abandoned property will be discussed in the next section, which focuses on the rights of finders.

The first person to take possession of a wild animal normally becomes the owner.[3] To acquire ownership of a wild animal by taking possession, a person must obtain enough control over it to deprive it of its freedom. If a person fatally wounds a wild animal, the person becomes the owner. Wild animals caught in a trap or fish caught in a net are usually considered to be the property of the person who set the trap or net. If a captured wild animal escapes and is caught by another person, that person generally becomes the owner. However, if that person knows that the animal is an escaped animal and that the prior owner is chasing it to recapture it, then he does not become the owner.

Rights of Finders of Lost, Mislaid, and Abandoned Property

The old saying "finders keepers, losers weepers" is not a reliable way of predicting the legal rights of those who find personal property that originally belonged—or still belongs—to another. The rights of the finder will be determined according to whether the property he finds is classified as abandoned, lost, or mislaid.

1. *Abandoned property.* Property is considered to be abandoned if the owner intentionally placed the property out of his possession with the intent to relinquish ownership of it. For example, Norris takes his TV set to the city dump and leaves it there. The finder who takes possession of abandoned property with intent to claim ownership becomes the owner of the property. This means he acquires better rights to the property than anyone else in the world, including the original owner. For example, if Fox finds the TV set, puts it in his car, and takes it home, Fox becomes the owner of the TV set.

2. *Lost property.* Property is considered to be lost when the owner did not intend to part with possession of the property. For example, if Barber's camera fell out of her handbag while she was walking down the street, it would be considered lost property. The person who finds lost property does not acquire ownership of it, but he acquires better rights to the lost property than anyone other than the true owner. For example, suppose Lawrence finds Barber's camera in the grass where it fell. Jones then steals the camera from Lawrence's bookbag. Under these facts, Barber is still the owner of the camera. She has the right to have it returned to her if she discovers where it is—or if Lawrence knows that it belongs to Barber. As the finder of lost property, however, Lawrence has a better right to the camera than anyone else except Barber. This means that Lawrence has the right to require Jones to return it to him if he finds out that Jones has it.

If the finder does not know who the true owner is or cannot easily find out, the finder must still return the property when the real owner shows up and asks for the property. If the finder of lost property knows who the owner is and refuses to return it, the finder is guilty of **conversion** and must pay the owner the fair value of the property.[4] A finder who sells the property that he has found can pass to the purchaser only those rights that he has; he cannot pass any better title to the property than he himself has. Thus, the true owner could recover the property from the purchaser.

3. *Mislaid property.* Property is considered to be mislaid if the owner intentionally placed the property somewhere and accidentally left it there, not intending to relinquish ownership of the property. For example, Fields places her backpack on a coatrack at Campus Bookstore while shopping for textbooks. Forgetting the backpack, Fields leaves the store and goes home. The backpack would be considered mislaid rather than lost because Fields intentionally and voluntarily placed it on the coatrack. If property is classified as mislaid, the finder acquires no rights to the property. Rather, the person in possession of the real property on which the personal property was mislaid has the right to hold the property for the true owner and has better rights to the property than anyone other than the true owner. For example, if Stevens found Fields's backpack in Campus Bookstore, Campus Bookstore would have the right to hold the mislaid property for

---

[3]As wildlife is increasingly protected by law, however, some wild animals cannot be owned because it is illegal to capture them (e.g., endangered species).

[4]The tort of conversion is discussed in Chapter 6.

Fields. Stevens would acquire neither possession nor ownership of the backpack.

The rationale for this rule is that it increases the chances that the property will be returned to its real owner. A person who knowingly placed the property somewhere but forgot to pick it up might well remember later where she left the property and return for it.

In the scenario set out at the start of this chapter, Cheryl visits the restroom in a steak and ribs restaurant in order to wash some barbecue sauce from her hands. She removes her engagement ring and places it on the washstand, but in her haste to get back to her table, she leaves the ring on the washstand when she exits the washroom. Sandra, a part-time janitor for the restaurant, finds the ring, slips it in her purse, and later sells the ring to her cousin, Gloria, for $200. When Cheryl returns to the restroom to look for the ring, neither the ring nor Sandra is still there.

At the time Sandra discovers the ring, should it be considered abandoned, lost, or mislaid property? What factors lead you to this conclusion? What should Sandra do with the ring at that point? Between Sandra and the owner of the restaurant, who has the best claim to the ring? Between the restaurant owner, Sandra, and Cheryl, who has the best claim to it? Why? If Cheryl discovers that Gloria has the ring, does she have the right to recover it from her? Why?

Some states have a statute that allows finders of property to clear their title to the property. The statutes, known as **estray statutes,** generally provide that the person must give public notice of the fact that the property has been found, perhaps by putting an ad in a local newspaper. All states have statutes of limitations that require the true owner of property to claim it or bring a legal action to recover possession of it within a certain number of years. A person who keeps possession of lost or unclaimed property for longer than that period of time will become its owner.

The *Corliss* case, which follows, discusses the relative rights of a person who finds property on land owned by someone else.

Corliss v. Wenner and Anderson   2001 Ida. App. LEXIS 79 (Ct. App. Idaho 2001)

In the fall of 1996, Jann Wenner hired Anderson Asphalt Paving to construct a driveway on his ranch. Larry Anderson, the owner of Anderson Asphalt Paving, and his employee, Gregory Corliss, were excavating soil for the driveway when they unearthed a glass jar containing paper-wrapped rolls of gold coins. Anderson and Corliss collected, cleaned, and inventoried the gold pieces dating from 1857 to 1914. The 96 coins weighed about four pounds. Initially, Anderson and Corliss agreed to split the coins among themselves, with Anderson retaining possession of all the coins. Subsequently, Anderson and Corliss argued over ownership of the coins, and Anderson fired Corliss. Anderson later gave possession of the coins to Wenner in exchange for indemnification on any claim Corliss might have against him regarding the coins.

Corliss sued Anderson and Wenner for possession of some or all of the coins. Corliss contended that the coins should be considered "treasure trove" and awarded to him pursuant to the "finders keepers" rule of treasure trove. Wenner, defending both himself and Anderson, contended that he had the better right to possession of the gold coins. The trial court held Idaho did not recognize "treasure trove" and that the coins, having been carefully concealed for safekeeping, fit within the legal classification of mislaid property, to which the right of possession goes to the landowner. Alternatively, the court ruled that the coins, like the topsoil being excavated, were a part of the property owned by Wenner and that Anderson and Corliss were merely Wenner's employees. Corliss appealed.

Schwartzman, Chief Judge

At common law all found property is generally categorized in one of five ways. Those categories are:

ABANDONED PROPERTY—that which the owner has discarded or voluntarily forsaken with the intention of terminating his ownership, but without vesting ownership in any other person.

LOST PROPERTY—that property which the owner has involuntarily and unintentionally parted with through neglect, carelessness, or inadvertence and does not know the whereabouts.

MISLAID PROPERTY—that which the owner has intentionally set down in a place where he can again resort to it, and then forgets where he put it.

TREASURE TROVE—a category exclusively for gold or silver in coin, plate, bullion, and sometimes its paper money equivalents, found concealed in the earth or in a house or other private place. Treasure trove carries with it the thought of antiquity, i.e., that the treasure has been concealed for so long as to indicate that the owner is probably dead or unknown.

EMBEDDED PROPERTY—that personal property which has become a part of the natural earth, such as pottery, the sunken wreck of a steamship, or a rotted-away sack of gold-bearing quartz rock buried or partially buried in the ground.

Under these doctrines, the finder of lost or abandoned property and treasure trove acquires a right to possess the property against the entire world but the rightful owner regardless of the place of finding. The finder of mislaid property is required to turn it over to the owner of the premises who has the duty to safeguard the property for the true owner. Possession of embedded property goes to owner of the land on which the property was found.

One of the major distinctions between these various categories is that only lost property necessarily involves an element of involuntariness. The four remaining categories involve voluntary and intentional acts by the true owner in placing the property where another eventually finds it. However, treasure trove, despite not being lost or abandoned property, is treated as such in that the right to possession is recognized to be in the finder rather than the premises owner.

On appeal, Corliss argues that the district court should have interpreted the undisputed facts and circumstances surrounding of the placement of the coins in the ground to indicate that the gold coins were either lost, abandoned, or treasure trove. Wenner argues that the property was properly categorized as either embedded or mislaid property.

As with most accidentally discovered buried treasure, the history of the original ownership of the coins is shrouded in mystery and obscured by time. The coins had been wrapped in paper, like coins from a bank, and buried in a glass jar, apparently for safekeeping. Based on these circumstances, the district court determined that the coins were not abandoned because the condition in which the coins were found evidenced an intent to keep them safe, not an intent to voluntarily relinquish all possessory interest in them. The district court also implicitly rejected the notion that the coins were lost, noting that the coins were secreted with care in a specific place to protect them from the elements and from other people until such time as the original owner might return for them. There is no indication that the coins came to be buried through neglect, carelessness, or inadvertence. Accordingly, the district court properly concluded, as a matter of law, that the coins were neither lost nor abandoned.

The district court then determined that the modern trend favored characterizing the coins as property either embedded in the earth or mislaid—under which the right of possession goes to the landowner—rather than treasure trove—under which the right of possession goes to the finder. Although accepted by a number of states prior to 1950, the modern trend since then, as illustrated by decisions of the state and federal courts, is decidedly against recognizing the "finders keepers" rule of treasure trove.

We conclude that the rule of treasure trove is of dubious heritage and misunderstood application, inconsistent with our values and traditions. The danger of adopting the doctrine of treasure trove is laid out in *Morgan v. Wiser* (Tenn. 1985).

> [We] find the rule with respect to treasure-trove to be out of harmony with modern notions of fair play. The common-law rule of treasure-trove invites trespassers to roam at large over the property of others with their metal detecting devices and to dig wherever such devices tell them property might be found. If the discovery happens to fit the definition of treasure-trove, the trespasser may claim it as his own. To paraphrase another court: The mind refuses consent to the proposition that one may go upon the lands of another and dig up and take away anything he discovers there which does not belong to the owner of the land.

The invitation to trespassers inherent in the rule with respect to treasure trove is repugnant to the common law rules dealing with trespassers in general. The common law made a trespass an actionable wrong without the necessity of showing any damage therefrom. Because a trespass often involved a breach of the peace and because the law was designed to keep the peace, the common law dealt severely with trespassers.

Recognizing the validity of the idea that the discouragement of trespassers contributes to the preservation of the peace in the community, we think this state should not follow the common law rule with respect to treasure trove. Rather, we adopt the rule suggested in the concurring opinion in *Schley v. Couch* . . . which we restate as follows:

> Where property is found embedded in the soil under circumstances repelling the idea that it has been lost, the finder acquires no title thereto, for the presumption is that the possession of the article found is in the owner of the locus in quo.

Landownership includes control over crops on the land, buildings and appurtenances, soils, minerals buried under those soils. The average Idaho landowner would expect to have a possessory interest in any object uncovered on his or her property. And certainly the notion that a trespassing treasure hunter, or a hired handyman or employee, could or might have greater possessory rights than a landowner in objects uncovered on his or her property runs counter to the reasonable expectations of present-day landownership.

There is no reason for a special rule for gold and silver coins, bullion, or plate as opposed to other property. Insofar as personal property (money and the like) buried or secreted on privately owned realty is concerned, the distinctions between treasure trove, lost property, and mislaid property are anachronistic and of little value. The principal point of such distinctions is the intent of the true owner which, absent some written declaration indicating such, is obscured in the mists of time and subject to a great deal of speculation.

By holding that property classed as treasure trove (gold or silver coins, bullion, plate) in other jurisdictions is classed in Idaho as personal property embedded in the soil, subject to the same limitations as mislaid property, possession will be awarded to the owner of the soil as a matter of law. Thus, we craft a simple and reasonable solution to the problem, discourage trespass, and avoid the risk of speculating about the true owner's intent

when attempting to infer such from the manner and circumstances in which an object is found. Additionally, the true owner, if any, will have the opportunity to recover the property.

We hold that the owner of the land has constructive possession of all personal property secreted in, on, or under his or her land. Accordingly, we adopt the district court's reasoning and conclusion melding the law of mislaid property with that of embedded property and conclude, as a matter of law, that the landowner is entitled to possession to the exclusion of all but the true owner, absence a contract between the landowner and finder.

Judgment for Wenner affirmed.

Legal Responsibilities of Finders

Some states go further and make it a criminal offense for a person who comes into control of property that he knows or learns has been lost or mislaid to appropriate the property to his own use without first taking reasonable measures to restore the property to the owner. For example under the Georgia Code, "A person commits the offense of theft of lost or mislaid property that he knows or learns to have been lost or mislaid property when he comes into control of property that he knows or learns to have been lost or mislaid and appropriates the property to his own use without first taking reasonable measures to restore the property to the owner" (O.C.G. A. section 16-8-6).

In a recent case[5] under that statute, an individual was convicted of the offense when she found a bank deposit bag containing checks, deposit slips, and over $500 in cash and subsequently attempted to cash one of the checks at a local check cashing business. The deposit bag had been misplaced while the victim was transporting it from her business located in a shopping mall to a car parked outside the mall. Some of the checks contained the victim's phone number and address, and the finder admitted that she never contacted the victim to restore the property to her.

Leasing

A lease of personal property is a transfer of the right to possess and use personal property belonging to another.[6] Although the rights of one who leases personal property (a lessee) do not constitute ownership

of personal property, leasing is mentioned here because it is becoming an increasingly important way of acquiring the use of many kinds of personal property, from automobiles to farm equipment.

Articles 2 and 9 of the UCC may sometimes be applied to personal-property leases by analogy. However, rules contained in these articles are sometimes inadequate to resolve special problems presented by leasing. For this reason, a new article of the UCC dealing exclusively with leases of goods, Article 2A, was written in 1987. Forty-seven states and the District of Columbia have adopted Article 2A.

Gifts

Title to personal property may be obtained by **gift.** A gift is a voluntary transfer of property to the **donee** (the person who receives a gift), for which the **donor** (the person who gives the gift) gets no consideration in return. To have a valid gift, all three of the following elements are necessary:

1. The donor must *intend* to make a gift.

2. The donor must make *delivery* of the gift.

3. The donee must *accept* the gift.

The most critical requirement is delivery. The donor must actually give up possession and control of the property either to the donee or to a third person who is to hold it for the donee. Delivery is important because it makes clear to the donor that he is voluntarily giving up ownership without getting something in exchange. A promise to make a gift is usually not enforceable;[7] the person must actually part with the property. In some cases, the

---

[5]*Shannon v. The State,* 574 S.E.2d 889 (Ct. App. Ga. 2002).

[6]A lease of personal property is a form of bailment, a "bailment for hire." Bailments are discussed later in this chapter.

[7]The idea is discussed in Chapter 12.

Ethics in Action

Finders Keepers: It May Be Legal, But Is It Ethical?

You're walking along the beach, and you find a toilet kit washed ashore. It contains some sodden cosmetics and a few dollars in change, but no identification. What should you do? The ordinarily ethical person probably tosses the potions and keeps the cash, persuaded by three arguments: Whatever drifts ashore falls under the heading of "finders, keepers," whatever has no identification is difficult to return, and whatever has trivial value would cost more to advertise for the proper owner than it's worth.

The next day on the same beach you find a dinghy with a small outboard motor attached, but no name or registration number. What should you do? While the finders-keepers and anonymity tests still hold, the triviality test does not: The dinghy clearly has significant value. The ordinarily ethical person probably, at the very least, contacts nearby harbormasters to see if anyone is missing a boat, leaving a phone number in case the owner calls.

The third day, astonishingly, you find 40 shipping containers that have washed off the deck of a vessel grounded on a sandbar in plain view a mile offshore. One contains a dozen brand-new BMW motorcycles, each worth more than $20,000. What should you do?

This third case is not hypothetical. The ship was the *Napoli,* a 62,000-ton cargo ship. On January 19, she encountered a terrific storm and was abandoned by her crew off the coast of Devon, England. As she was being towed to a nearby port, she began to list and was deliberately grounded. When the containers came loose, scores of people came from miles around, swarmed across Branscombe Beach under the eyes of helpless police, opened the containers, and made off with everything of value, including the motorcycles.

Why? They apparently saw this opportunity as somewhere between winning a lottery and finding money in a hollow tree. "It's great, isn't it?" one man told the *Guardian* newspaper, "a cross between a bomb site and a car boot [trunk] sale." Another said it was like finding "Aladdin's cave." In their view, the stuff was there for the taking, and they were in the right place at the right time.

To call these people "looters" gives the wrong impression. These weren't professional second-story men, cat burglars, or back-alley thugs. By all accounts (and there were many in the news here last week), they were ordinary people. Two questions, then: Were their actions legal, and were they ethical?

What they did clearly fails the triviality test. As for anonymity, there's no doubt about the source of their loot, and no difficulty tracing its ownership. The finders-keepers test, however, is more complex. In fact, the police were legitimately flummoxed. English law allows salvagers to take whatever marine wreckage they find, as long as they fill out a form and take it to the Maritime and Coastguard Agency within 28 days. That entitles them to a reward if the property is claimed—and to legal ownership if, after a year, it is not. So the police felt they could do little more than hand out forms. By day's end, some of the items began showing up for sale on eBay, brazenly described as coming from the *Napoli,* suggesting that even the pretense of legality had been breached by some of these collectors.

What's being tested here, then, is not simply the law but the ethics underlying the law. Given the circumstances, would we expect a reasonably ethical person to remove objects clearly belonging to someone else, or would we want them to help restore lost property to its owners? Surely the latter. Cynics, of course, will yawp that if you don't take it, others will— a line of reasoning so thin that it also would permit you to slaughter your obnoxious neighbor if you thought others were also upset with him. Cynics also will argue that the shipper's insurance will recompense the owner for anything removed— an argument that, along with driving up insurance costs for everyone else, fails to account for one woman's loss of a collection of letters and pictures, personal and irreplaceable, that disappeared from Branscombe Beach as she was moving her home to South Africa.

So suppose we grant that, except for those who fenced their wares on eBay, the rest intended to behave legally by filing proper forms. Even so, does that make them ethical?

Source: Excerpted from the January 29, 2007, issue of **Ethics Newsline** (www.glopalethics.org/newsline/). A publication of the Institute for Global Ethics.

---

delivery may be symbolic or constructive. For example, handing over the key to a strongbox may be symbolic delivery of the property in the strongbox.

There are two kinds of gifts: gifts *inter vivos* and gifts *causa mortis*. A gift *inter vivos* is a gift between two living persons. For example, when Melissa's parents give her a car for her 21st birthday, that is a gift *inter vivos*. A gift *causa mortis* is a gift made in contemplation of death. For example, Uncle Earl, who is about to undergo a serious heart operation, gives his watch to his nephew, Bart, and says that he wants Bart to have it if he does not survive the operation.

CONCEPT REVIEW

Rights of Finders of Personal Property

Character of Property	Description	Rights of Finder	Rights of Original Owner
Lost	Owner unintentionally parted with possession	Rights superior to everyone except the owner	Retains ownership; has the right to the return of the property
Mislaid	Owner intentionally put property in a place but unintentionally left it there	None; person in possession of real property on which mislaid property was found holds it for the owner, and has rights superior to everyone except owner	Retains ownership; has the right to the return of the property
Abandoned	Owner intentionally placed property out of his possession with intent to relinquish ownership of it	Finder who takes possession with intent to claim ownership acquires ownership of property	None

A gift *causa mortis* is a conditional gift and is effective unless any of the following occurs:

1. The donor recovers from the peril or sickness under fear of which the gift was made, or

2. The donor revokes or withdraws the gift before he dies, or

3. The donee dies before the donor.

If one of these events takes place, ownership of the property goes back to the donor.

Conditional Gifts Sometimes a gift is made on condition that the donee comply with certain restrictions or perform certain actions. A conditional gift is not a completed gift. It may be revoked by the donor before the donee complies with the conditions. Gifts in contemplation of marriage, such as engagement rings, are a primary example of a conditional gift. Such gifts are generally considered to have been made on an implied condition that marriage between the donor and donee will take place. The traditional rule applied in many states provides that if the donee breaks the engagement without legal justification or the engagement is broken by mutual consent, the donor will be able to recover the ring or other engagement gift. However, if the engagement is unjustifiably broken by the donor, the traditional rule generally bars the donor from recovering gifts made in contemplation of marriage. As illustrated by the *Lindh* case, which follows, a growing number of courts have rejected the traditional approach and its focus on fault. Some states have enacted legislation prescribing the rules applicable to the return of engagement presents.

Lindh v. Surman   742 A.2d 643 (Sup. Ct. Pa. 1999)

In August 1993, Rodger Lindh (Rodger) proposed marriage to Janis Surman (Janis). Rodger presented her with a diamond engagement ring that he had purchased for $17,400. Janis accepted the marriage proposal and the ring. Two months later, Rodger broke the engagement and asked Janis to return the ring. She did so. Rodger and Janis later reconciled, with Rodger again proposing marriage and again presenting Janis with the engagement ring. Janis accepted the proposal and the ring. In March 1994, Rodger again broke the engagement and asked Janis to return the ring. This time, however, she refused. Rodger sued her, seeking recovery of the ring or a judgment for its value. The trial court held in Rodger's favor and awarded him damages in the amount of the ring's value. When Janis appealed, the Pennsylvania Superior Court affirmed the award of damages and held that when an engagement is broken, the engagement ring must be returned even if the donor broke the engagement. Janis appealed to the Supreme Court of Pennsylvania.

Newman, Justice

We are asked to decide whether a donee of an engagement ring must return the ring or its equivalent value when the donor breaks the engagement. We begin our analysis with the only principle on which the parties agree: that Pennsylvania law treats the giving of an engagement ring as a conditional gift. In *Pavlicic v. Vogtsberger* (Sup. Ct. Pa. 1957), the plaintiff supplied his ostensible fiancée with numerous gifts, including money for the purchase of engagement and wedding rings, with the understanding that they were given on the condition that she marry him. When the defendant left him for another man, the plaintiff sued her for recovery of these gifts. Justice Musmanno explained the conditional gift principle:

> A gift given by a man to a woman on condition that she embark on the sea of matrimony with him is no different from a gift based on the condition that the donee sail on any other sea. If, after receiving the provisional gift, the donee refuses to leave the harbor—if the anchor of contractual performance sticks in the sands of irresolution and procrastination—the gift must be restored to the donor.

The parties disagree, however, over whether fault [on the part of the donor] is relevant to determining return of the ring. Janis contends that Pennsylvania law . . . has never recognized a right of recovery in a donor who severs the engagement. She maintains that if the condition of the gift is performance of the marriage ceremony, [a rule allowing a recovery of the ring] would reward a donor who prevents the occurrence of the condition, which the donee was ready, willing, and eagerly waiting to perform. Janis's argument that . . . the donor should not be allowed to recover the ring where the donor terminates the engagement has some basis in [decisions from Pennsylvania's lower courts and in treatises]. This Court, however, has not decided the question of whether the donor is entitled to return of the ring where the donor admittedly ended the engagement.

The issue we must resolve is whether we will follow the fault-based theory argued by Janis, or the no-fault rule advocated by Rodger. Under a fault-based analysis, return of the rings depends on an assessment of who broke the engagement, which necessarily entails a determination of why that person broke the engagement. A no-fault approach, however, involves no investigation into the motives or reasons for the cessation of the engagement and requires the return of the engagement ring simply upon the nonoccurence of the marriage.

The rule concerning the return of a ring founded on fault principles has superficial appeal because, in the most outrageous instances of unfair behavior, it appeals to our sense of equity. Where one of the formerly engaged persons has truly "wronged" the other, justice appears to dictate that the wronged individual should be allowed to keep the ring or have it returned, depending on whether the wronged person was the donor . . . or the donee. However, the process of determining who is "wrong" and who is "right," when most modern relationships are complex circumstances, makes the fault-based approach less desirable. A thorough fault-based inquiry would not . . . end with the question of who terminated the engagement, but would also examine that person's reasons. In some instances the person who terminated the engagement may have been entirely justified in his or her actions. This kind of inquiry would invite the parties to stage the most bitter and unpleasant accusations against those whom they nearly made their spouse. A ring-return rule based on fault principles will inevitably invite acrimony and encourage parties to portray their ex-fiancées in the worst possible light. Furthermore, it is unlikely that trial courts would be presented with situations where fault was clear and easily ascertained.

The approach that has been described as the modern trend is to apply a no-fault rule to engagement ring cases. Courts that have applied this rule have borrowed from the policies of their respective legislatures that have moved away from the notion of fault in their divorce statutes. All fifty states have adopted some form of no-fault divorce. We agree with those jurisdictions that have looked toward the development of no-fault divorce law for a principle to decide engagement ring cases. In addition, the inherent weaknesses in any fault-based system lead us to adopt a no-fault approach to resolution of engagement ring disputes.

Decision of Superior Court in favor of Rodger Lindh affirmed.

Cappy, Justice, dissenting

The majority urges adoption of the no-fault rule to relieve trial courts from having the onerous task of sifting through the debris of the broken engagement in order to ascertain who is truly at fault. Are broken engagements truly more disturbing than cases where we ask judges and juries to discern possible abuses in nursing homes, day care centers, dependency proceedings involving abused children, and criminal cases involving horrific, irrational injuries to innocent victims? The subject matter our able trial courts address on a daily basis is certainly of equal sordidness as any fact pattern they may need to address in a simple case of who broke the engagement and why.

I can envision a scenario whereby the prospective bride and her family have expended thousands of dollars in preparation for the culminating event of matrimony and she is, through no fault of her own, left standing at the altar holding the caterer's bill. To add insult to injury, the majority would also strip her of her engagement ring. Why the majority feels compelled to modernize this relatively simple and ancient legal concept is beyond the understanding of this poor man. As I see no valid reason to forego the [fault-based rule] for determining possession of the engagement ring under the simple concept of conditional gift law, I cannot endorse the modern trend advocated by the majority.

In the scenario set out at the beginning of this chapter, Claudio gave the ring to Cheryl as an engagement ring in anticipation of their forthcoming marriage. Later, Cheryl breaks off the engagement, telling Claudio that she no longer loves him. Claudio then asks Cheryl to return the ring to him.

What argument would Claudio make to support his claim that he has the legal right to have the ring returned to him? What argument might Cheryl make to support her contention that she should have the legal right to retain the ring? If Claudio and Cheryl lived in Pennsylvania, where the *Lindh v. Surman* case was decided, would Claudio be entitled to recover the ring from Cheryl? Why or why not? Would it make a difference if they lived in a state that used a fault-based approach concerning gifts given in anticipation of marriage?

Uniform Transfers to Minors Act

The Uniform Transfers to Minors Act, which has been adopted in one form or another in every state, provides a fairly simple and flexible method for making gifts and other transfers of property to minors.[8] As defined in this act, a minor is anyone under the age of 21. Under the act, an adult may transfer money, securities, real property, insurance policies, and other property. The specific ways of doing this vary according to the type of property transferred. In general, however, the transferor (the person who gives or otherwise transfers the property) delivers, pays, or assigns the property to, or registers the property with, a custodian who acts for the benefit of the minor "under the Uniform Transfers to Minors Act." The custodian is given fairly broad discretion to use the gift for the minor's benefit and may not use it for the custodian's personal benefit. The custodian may be the transferor himself, another adult, or a trust company, depending again on the type of property transferred. If the donor or other transferor fully complies with the Uniform Transfers to Minors Act, the transfer is considered to be irrevocable.

Will or Inheritance

Ownership of personal property may also be transferred upon the death of the former owner. The property may pass under the terms of a will if the will was validly executed. If there is no valid will, the property is transferred to the heirs of the owner according to state laws. Transfer of property at the death of the owner will be discussed in Chapter 26.

---

[8]This statute was formerly called, and is still called in some states, the Uniform Gift to Minors Act.

Confusion

Title to personal property may be obtained by **confusion**. Confusion is the intermixing of different owners' goods in such a way that they cannot later be separated. For example, suppose wheat belonging to several different people is mixed in a grain elevator. If the mixing was by agreement or if it resulted from an accident without negligence on anyone's part, each person owns his proportionate share of the entire quantity of wheat. However, a different result would be reached if the wheat was wrongfully or negligently mixed. Suppose a thief steals a truckload of Grade #1 wheat worth $8.50 a bushel from a farmer. The thief dumps the wheat into his storage bin, which contains a lower-grade wheat worth $4.50 a bushel, with the result that the mixture is worth only $4.50 a bushel. The farmer has first claim against the entire mixture to recover the value of the higher-grade wheat that was mixed with the lower-grade wheat. The thief, or any other person whose intentional or negligent act results in confusion of goods, must bear any loss caused by the confusion.

Accession

Ownership of personal property may also be acquired by **accession**. Accession means increasing the value of property by adding materials, labor, or both. As a general rule, the owner of the original property becomes the owner of the improvements. This is particularly likely to be true if the improvement was done with the permission of the owner. For example, Hudson takes his automobile to a shop that replaces the engine with a larger engine and puts in a new four-speed transmission. Hudson is still the owner of the automobile as well as the owner of the parts added by the auto shop.

Problems may arise if materials are added or work is performed on personal property without the consent of the owner. If property is stolen from one person and improved by the thief, the original owner can get it back and does not have to reimburse the thief for the work done or the materials used in improving it. For example, a thief steals Rourke's used car, puts a new engine in it, replaces the tires, and repairs the brakes. Rourke is entitled to get his car back from the thief and does not have to pay him for the engine, tires, and brakes.

The result is less easy to predict, however, if property is mistakenly improved in good faith by someone who believes that he owns the property. In such a case, a court must weigh the respective interests of two innocent parties: the original owner and the improver.

For example, Johnson, a stonecarver, finds a block of limestone by the side of the road. Assuming that it has been abandoned, he takes it home and carves it into a sculpture. In fact, the block was owned by Hayes. Having fallen off a flatbed truck during transportation, the block is merely lost property, which Hayes ordinarily could recover from the finder. In a case such as this, a court could decide the case in either of two ways. The first alternative would be to give the original owner (Hayes) ownership of the improved property, but to allow the person who has improved the property in good faith (Johnson) to recover the cost of the improvements. The second alternative would be to hold that the improver, Johnson, has acquired ownership of the sculpture, but that he is required to pay the original owner the value of the property as of the time he obtained it. The greater the extent to which the improvements have increased the value of the property, the more likely it is that the court will choose the second alternative and permit the improver to acquire ownership of the improved property.

Bailments

Nature of Bailments
A **bailment** is the delivery of personal property by its owner or someone holding the right to possess it (the **bailor**) to another person (the **bailee**) who accepts it and is under an express or implied agreement to return it to the bailor or to someone designated by the bailor. Only personal property can be the subject of bailments.

Although the legal terminology used to describe bailments might be unfamiliar to most people, everyone is familiar with transactions that constitute bailments. For example, Lincoln takes his car to a parking garage where the attendant gives Lincoln a claim check and then drives the car down the ramp to park it. Charles borrows his neighbor's lawn mower to cut his grass. Tara, who lives next door to Kyle, agrees to take care of Kyle's cat while Kyle goes on a vacation. These are just a few of the everyday situations that involve bailments.

Elements of a Bailment
The essential elements of a bailment are:

1. The bailor owns personal property or holds the right to possess it.
2. The bailor delivers exclusive possession of and control over the personal property to the bailee.
3. The bailee knowingly accepts the personal property with the understanding that he owes a duty to return the property, or to dispose of it, as directed by the bailor.

Creation of a Bailment
A bailment is created by an express or implied contract. Whether the elements of a bailment have been fulfilled is determined by examining all the facts and circumstances of the particular situation. For example, a patron goes into a restaurant and hangs his hat and coat on an unattended rack. It is unlikely that this created a bailment, because the restaurant owner never assumed exclusive control over the hat and coat. However, if there is a checkroom and the hat and coat are checked with the attendant, a bailment will arise.

If a customer parks her car in a parking lot, keeps the keys, and may drive the car out herself whenever she wishes, a bailment has not been created. The courts treat this situation as a lease of space. Suppose, however, that she takes her car to a parking garage where an attendant, after giving her a claim check, parks the car. There is a bailment of the car because the parking garage has accepted delivery and possession of the car. However, a distinction is made between the car and packages locked in the trunk. If the parking garage was not aware of the packages, it probably would not be a bailee of them as it did not knowingly accept possession of them. The creation of a bailment is illustrated in Figure 1.

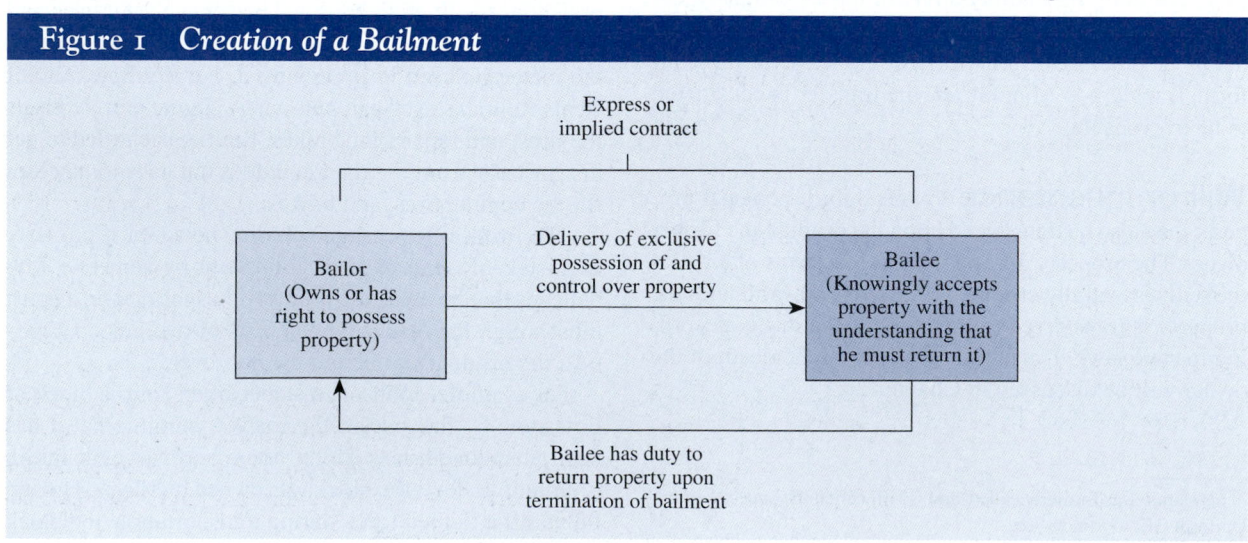

Figure 1   Creation of a Bailment

Express or implied contract

Bailor (Owns or has right to possess property)

Delivery of exclusive possession of and control over property

Bailee (Knowingly accepts property with the understanding that he must return it)

Bailee has duty to return property upon termination of bailment

Types of Bailments

Types of Bailments Bailments are commonly divided into three different categories:

1. Bailments for the sole benefit of the bailor.
2. Bailments for the sole benefit of the bailee.
3. Bailments for mutual benefit.

The type of bailment involved in a case can be important in determining the liability of the bailee for loss of or damage to the property. As will be discussed later, however, some courts no longer rely on these distinctions when they determine whether the bailee is liable.

Bailments for Benefit of Bailor A bailment for the sole benefit of the bailor is one in which the bailee renders some service but does not receive a benefit in return. For example, Brown allows his neighbor, Reston, to park her car in Brown's garage while she is on vacation. Brown does not ask for any compensation. Here, Reston, the bailor, has received a benefit from the bailee, Brown, but Brown has not received a benefit in return.

Bailments for Benefit of Bailee A bailment for the sole benefit of the bailee is one in which the owner of the goods allows someone else to use them free of charge. For example, Anderson lends a lawn mower to her neighbor, Moss, so he can cut his grass.

Bailments for Mutual Benefit If both the bailee and the bailor receive benefits from the bailment, it is a bailment for mutual benefit. For example, Sutton rents china for his daughter's wedding from E-Z Party Supplies for an agreed-on price. Sutton, the bailee, benefits by being able to use the china; E-Z benefits from his payment of the rental charge. On some occasions, the benefit to the bailee is less tangible. For example, a customer checks a coat at an attended coatroom at a restaurant. Even if no charge is made for the service, it is likely to be treated as a bailment for mutual benefit because the restaurant is benefiting from the customer's patronage.

Special Bailments

Special Bailments Certain professional bailees, such as innkeepers and common carriers, are treated somewhat differently by the law and are held to a higher level of responsibility than is the ordinary bailee. The rules applicable to common carriers and innkeepers are detailed later in this chapter.

Duties of the Bailee

Duties of the Bailee The bailee has two basic duties:

1. To take care of the property that has been entrusted to her.

2. To return the property at the termination of the bailment.

The following discussion examines the scope of these duties.

Duty of Bailee to Take Care of Property

Duty of Bailee to Take Care of Property The bailee is responsible for taking steps to protect the property during the time she has possession of it. If the bailee does not exercise proper care and the property is lost or damaged, the bailee is liable for negligence. The bailee would then be required to reimburse the bailor for the amount of loss or damage. If the property is lost or damaged without the fault or negligence of the bailee, however, the bailee is not liable to the bailor. The degree of care required of the bailee traditionally has depended in large part on the type of bailment involved.

1. *Bailment for the benefit of the bailor.* If the bailment is solely for the benefit of the bailor, the bailee is expected to exercise only a minimal, or slight, degree of care for the protection of the bailed property. He would be liable, then, only if he were grossly negligent in his care of the bailed property. The rationale for this rule is that if the bailee is doing the bailor a favor, it is not reasonable to expect him to be as careful as when he is deriving some benefit from keeping the goods.

2. *Bailment for mutual benefit.* When the bailment is a bailment for mutual benefit, the bailee is expected to exercise ordinary or reasonable care. This degree of care requires the bailee to use the same care a reasonable person would use to protect his own property in the relevant situation. If the bailee is a professional that holds itself out as a professional bailee, such as a warehouse, it must use the degree of care that would be used by a person in the same profession. This is likely to be more care than the ordinary person would use. In addition, a professional bailee usually has the obligation to explain any loss of or damage to property—that is, to show it was not negligent. If it cannot do so, it will be liable to the bailor.

3. *Bailment for the benefit of the bailee.* If the bailment is solely for the benefit of the bailee, the bailee is expected to exercise a high degree of care. For instance a person who lends a sailboat to a neighbor would probably expect the neighbor to be even more careful with the sailboat than the owner might be. In such a case, the bailee would be liable for damage to the property if his action reflected a relatively small degree of negligence.

A number of courts today view the type of bailment involved in a case as just one factor to be considered in determining whether the bailee should be liable for loss of or damage to bailed goods. The modern trend appears to be moving in the direction of imposing a duty of reasonable care on bailees, regardless of the type of bailment. This flexible standard of care permits courts to take into account a variety of factors such as the nature and value of the property, the provisions of the parties' agreement, the payment of consideration for the bailment, and the experience of the bailee. In addition, the bailee is required to use the property only as was agreed between the parties. For example, Jones borrows Morrow's lawn mower to mow his lawn. If Jones uses the mower to cut the weeds on a trash-filled vacant lot and the mower is damaged, he would be liable because he was exceeding the agreed purpose of the bailment—to cut his lawn.

Bailee's Duty to Return the Property

An essential element of a bailment is the duty of the bailee to return the property at the termination of the bailment. If the bailed property is taken from the bailee by legal process, the bailee should notify the bailor and must take whatever action is necessary to protect the bailor's interest. In most instances, the bailee must return the identical property that was bailed. A person who lends a 1999 Mercury Sable to a friend expects to have that particular car returned. In some cases, the bailor does not expect the return of the identical goods. For example, a farmer who stores 1,500 bushels of Grade #1 wheat at a local grain elevator expects to get back 1,500 bushels of Grade #1 wheat when the bailment is terminated, but not the identical wheat he deposited.

The bailee must return the goods in an undamaged condition to the bailor or to someone designated by the bailor. If the goods have been damaged, destroyed, or lost, there is a rebuttable presumption of negligence on the part of the bailee. To overcome the presumption, the bailee must come forward with evidence showing that he exercised the relevant level of care.

The *Detroit Institute of Arts* case, which follows, illustrates the duty a bailee has to return the property at the termination of the bailment.

Detroit Institute of Arts v. Rose and Smith
127 F. Supp.2d 117 (U.S.D.C. D.Conn. 2001)

The Howdy Doody Show *was a television program beloved by millions of children in what is now known as "the baby boom generation." It was produced and broadcast by the National Broadcasting Company, Inc. (NBC), from 1947 to 1960. Hosted by Robert "Buffalo Bob" Smith, the show's main character was Howdy Doody, a puppet in the image of a freckled-faced boy in cowboy clothing.*

Beginning in 1952, Rufus Rose served as the puppet master, puppeteer, and caretaker for many of the puppets that appeared on the show. While the show was on the air, he created, stored, and made repairs to the puppets in his workshop in Waterford, Connecticut—and was compensated accordingly. When the show ended in 1960, Rose, pursuant to an informal agreement, kept possession of the puppets at this workshop until final arrangements were made for them. Rose acknowledged that the puppets belonged to NBC.

In 1965, Rose began a series of correspondence with NBC about payment for his maintenance and storage of the puppets, including Howdy Doody, since the end of the show in 1960. In a letter to NBC, Rose proposed that (1) NBC pay him for storage and upkeep of all the puppets since the end of the show; (2) he be allowed to keep the minor puppets but with the understanding he would not use them as Howdy Doody Show *characters; and (3) the main puppets from the show, including Howdy Doody, would be turned over to a museum, the Detroit Institute of Arts (DIA), that housed the recognized museum of puppetry in America. Subsequently, he signed a release acknowledging payment for past fees and indicating his agreement to send Howdy Doody to the DIA.*

In 1970, Rose, in response to a request from his friend Buffalo Bob who was making personal appearances throughout the country, sent Howdy Doody to Buffalo Bob. In an accompanying letter, Rose explained to Buffalo Bob that he had agreed with NBC that the puppet would "eventually" be placed in the DIA and that it would never be used in a commercial manner—and that the original Howdy Doody was being sent to Buffalo Bob "with this mutual understanding and responsibility." For the next 15 years, Buffalo Bob kept Howdy Doody and used him in personal appearances.

In 1992, Buffalo Bob's attorney contacted Rose's widow, NBC, and DIA, requesting that they waive the requirement that Howdy Doody be placed in the DIA. He indicated that Buffalo Bob had fallen on difficult financial times and now wished to sell the puppet and keep the proceeds. Rose's son, Christopher, replied on behalf of his mother, stating that it was his father's intention that Buffalo Bob honor the "condition" that Howdy Doody be given to the DIA. NBC refused to release Howdy Doody to him, and the DIA declined to let him sell the puppet. Buffalo Bob then informed the DIA that he would transfer Howdy Doody to the museum "when he no longer wished to keep the puppet."

In 1998, Buffalo Bob and Christopher executed an agreement to sell the puppet and split the proceeds 50-50. They "certified" that Christopher had received the puppet from Buffalo Bob, and Christopher entered into a consignment agreement with an auction house to sell the "original Howdy Doody." A few days later Buffalo Bob died, and the DIA brought a lawsuit to prevent the Rose family from selling the puppet and also to gain possession of it. One of the questions in the lawsuit was whether the 1970 letter created a bailment to Buffalo Bob that obligated him to turn the puppet over to the DIA.

Droney, District Judge

A bailment arises when the owner or bailor "delivers personal property to another for some particular purpose with an express or implied contract to redeliver the goods when the purpose has been fulfilled, or to otherwise deal with the goods according to the bailor's directions." The bailor has a property interest in the goods bailed, while the bailee merely possesses them. The bailee's possession must be exclusive, so that he or she has sole custody and control of the property.

There are two types of bailments: those that are for the mutual benefit of the parties involved and those that are for the sole benefit of either the bailee or bailor. The latter variety, known as gratuitous bailments, typically involve no actual consideration. Instead, it is enough that the bailor suffers a detriment by giving up the present possession or custody of the property bailed on the bailee's promise that the latter will redeliver or otherwise account for it.

Bailments involve certain implied obligations, but these obligations generally are implied only in the absence of an express provision to the contrary. For example, while the law of bailment implies a general obligation to redeliver the property bailed to the owner, the parties are able to stipulate the time, place, and manner of delivery. "The general principle that the manner of a bailee's redelivery should be in accordance with the contract stipulations is too well settled to belabor." Similarly, a bailee may become liable to a third party when the bailment contract includes provisions that were incorporated for the third party's special benefit and interest.

The evidence establishes that Rufus Rose's 1970 letter to Buffalo Bob created an enforceable bailment whereby Buffalo Bob assumed a duty to turn over Howdy Doody to the DIA.

Rufus Rose delivered Howdy Doody to Buffalo Bob with an express term of the bailment that Buffalo Bob would be allowed to possess Howdy Doody "for as long as [he] personally wished to have him," but specifically conditioned Buffalo Bob's use on the same two requirements that NBC imposed upon Rufus Rose: that Howdy Doody would not be used in a commercial manner and that the puppet would "eventually be placed in the care of the Detroit Institute of Arts." These statements indicate that the bailment was express, and that Buffalo Bob, as bailee, was bound to deal with Howdy Doody according to the instructions of Rufus Rose, the bailor.

The defendants first argue that this agreement between Rufus Rose and Buffalo Bob is unenforceable as a bailment because it lacks consideration. However, actual consideration is not required for a bailment to be enforceable. As stated above, gratuitous bailments are generally not supported by actual consideration, but are still binding on the bailee. Here, it appears that the bailment was gratuitous: it was undertaken for the sole benefit of one of the parties, in this case, the bailee, Buffalo Bob. Thus, it is enough that Rufus Rose, as bailor, gave up custody of Howdy Doody based upon Buffalo Bob's promise that he would redeliver the puppet. As a result, the bailment agreement between Rufus Rose and Buffalo Bob is enforceable without actual consideration.

The defendants maintain that the 1970 agreement between Rose and Smith was satisfied by his return of Howdy Doody to the Rose family in 1998. They also argue that the 1966–1967 agreement is satisfied by "eventually" giving the puppet to the DIA. In other words, other members of the Rose or Smith family may keep the puppet so long as one day it is turned over to the DIA. However, these interpretations of Rufus Rose's words are unsupported by the language of the bailment letter itself; it states that the puppet could only be kept by Smith "personally" and does not mention that the puppet could be passed along by Buffalo Bob after the death of Rufus Rose to anyone else, other than giving it to the DIA. Also, delaying delivery of Howdy Doody through the latter interpretation would undermine the terms of the 1966–1967 agreement between Rufus Rose and NBC: it would allow Howdy Doody to be passed indefinitely, perhaps never to be sent to the DIA.

Thus, the DIA has shown that there is no genuine issue of material fact that the DIA is entitled to possession of Howdy Doody based on the agreement between NBC and Rufus Rose from 1966–1967 and the obligations of Buffalo Bob under the Rufus Rose–Buffalo Bob agreement from 1970.

Judgment in favor of Detroit Institute of Arts.

Bailee's Liability for Misdelivery

The bailee is also liable to the bailor if he misdelivers the bailed property at the termination of the bailment. The property must be returned to the bailor or to someone specified by the bailor.

The bailee is in a dilemma if a third person, claiming to have rights superior to those of the bailor, demands possession of the bailed property. If the bailee refuses to deliver the bailed property to the third-party claimant and the claimant is entitled to possession, the bailee is liable to the claimant. If the bailee delivers the bailed property to the third-party claimant and the claimant is not entitled to possession, the bailee is liable to the bailor. The circumstances may be such that the conflicting claims of the bailor and the third-party claimant can be determined only by judicial decision. In some cases, the bailee may protect himself by bringing the third-party claimant into a lawsuit along with the bailor so that all the competing claims can be adjudicated by the court before the bailee releases the property. This remedy is not always available, however.

Limits on Liability

Bailees may try to limit or relieve themselves of liability for the bailed property. Some examples include the storage receipts purporting to limit liability to a fixed amount such as $100, signs near checkrooms such as "Not responsible for loss of or damage to checked property," and disclaimers on claim checks such as "Goods left at owner's risk." The standards used to determine whether such limitations and disclaimers are enforceable are discussed in Chapter 15.

Any attempt by the bailee to be relieved of liability for intentional wrongful acts is against public policy and will not be enforced. A bailee's ability to be relieved of liability for negligence is also limited. Courts look to see whether the disclaimer or limitation of liability was communicated to the bailor at the time of the bailment. When the customer handed her coat to the checkroom attendant, did the attendant point out the "not responsible for loss or damage" sign? Did the parking lot attendant call the car owner's attention to the disclaimer on the back of the claim check?

If not, the court may hold that the disclaimer was not communicated to the bailor and did not become part of the bailment contract. Even if the bailor was aware of the disclaimer, it still may not be enforced on the ground that it is contrary to public policy.

If the disclaimer was offered on a take-it-or-leave-it basis and was not the subject of arm's-length bargaining, it is less likely to be enforced than if it was negotiated and voluntarily agreed to by the parties. A bailee may be able to limit liability to a certain amount or to relieve himself of liability for certain perils. Ideally, the bailee will give the bailor a chance to declare a higher value and to pay an additional charge in order to be protected up to the declared value of the goods. Common carriers, such as railroads and trucking companies, often take this approach. Courts do not look with favor on efforts by a person to be relieved of liability for negligence. For this reason, terms limiting the liability of a bailee stand a better chance of being enforced than do terms completely relieving the bailee of liability.

An implied agreement as to the bailee's duties may arise from a prior course of dealing between the bailor and the bailee, or from the bailor's knowledge of the bailee's facilities or method of doing business. The bailee may, if he wishes, assume all risks incident to the bailment and contract to return the bailed property undamaged or to pay for any damage to or loss of the property.

Right to Compensation

The express or implied contract creating the bailment controls whether the bailee has the right to receive compensation for keeping the property or must pay for having the right to use it. If the bailment is made as a favor, then the bailee is not entitled to compensation even though the bailment is for the bailor's sole benefit. If the bailment involves the rental of property, the bailee must pay the agreed rental rate. If the bailment is for the storage or repair of property, the bailee is entitled to the contract price for the storage or repair services. When no specific price was agreed on but compensation was contemplated by the parties, the bailee is entitled to the reasonable value of the services provided.

In many instances, the bailee will have a lien (a charge against property to secure the payment of a debt) on the bailed property for the reasonable value of the services. For example, Silver takes a chair to Ace Upholstery to have it recovered. When the chair has been recovered, Ace has the right to keep it until the agreed price—or, if no price was set, the reasonable value of the work—is paid. This is an example of an **artisan's lien,** which is discussed in Chapter 29.

Bailor's Liability for Defects in the Bailed Property

When personal property is rented or loaned, the bailor makes an implied warranty that the property has no hidden defects that make it unsafe for use. If the bailment is for the bailee's sole benefit, the bailor is liable for injuries that result from defects in the bailed property only if the bailor knew about the defects and did not tell the bailee. For example, Price lends his car, which he knows has bad brakes, to Sloan. If Price does not tell Sloan about the bad brakes and Sloan is injured in an accident because the brakes fail, Price is liable for Sloan's injuries.

If the bailment is a bailment for mutual benefit, the bailor has a greater obligation. The bailor must use reasonable care in inspecting the property and seeing that it is safe for the purpose for which it is intended. The bailor is liable for injuries suffered by the bailee because of defects that the bailor either knew about or should have discovered through reasonable inspection. For example, Acme Rent-All, which rents trailers, does not inspect the trailers after they are returned. A wheel has come loose on a trailer that Acme rents to Hirsch. If the wheel comes off while Hirsch is using the trailer and the goods Hirsch is carrying in it are damaged, Acme is liable to Hirsch.

In addition, product liability doctrines that apply a higher standard of legal responsibility have been applied to bailors who are commercial lessors of personal property.[9] Express or implied warranties of quality under either Article 2 or Article 2A of the UCC may apply. Liability under these warranties does not depend on whether the bailor knew about or should have discovered the defect. The only question is whether the property's condition complied with the warranty. Some courts have also imposed strict liability on the commercial lessor-bailor of defective, unreasonably dangerous goods that cause personal injury or property damage to the lessee-bailee. This liability is imposed regardless of whether the lessor was negligent.

Special Bailments

Common Carriers
Bailees that are common carriers are held to a higher level of responsibility than are bailees that are private carriers. Common carriers are licensed by governmental agencies to carry the property of anyone who requests the service. Private contract carriers carry goods only for persons selected by the carrier.

Both common carriers and private contract carriers are bailees. However, the law makes the common carrier a near-absolute insurer of the goods it carries. The common carrier is responsible for virtually any loss of or

damage to the entrusted goods, unless the common carrier shows that the loss or damage was caused by one of the following:

1. An act of God.
2. An act of a public enemy.
3. An act or order of the government.
4. An act of the person who shipped the goods.
5. The nature of the goods themselves.

Therefore, the common carrier is liable if goods entrusted to it are stolen by some unknown person, but not if the goods are destroyed when the warehouse is damaged by a hurricane.

If goods are damaged because the shipper improperly packaged or crated them, the carrier is not liable. Similarly, if perishable goods are not in suitable condition to be shipped and therefore deteriorate in the course of shipment, the carrier is not liable so long as it used reasonable care in handling them.

Common carriers are usually permitted to limit their liability to a stated value unless the bailor declares a higher value for the property and pays an additional fee.

Hotelkeepers
Hotelkeepers are engaged in the business of offering food and/or lodging to transient persons. They hold themselves out to serve the public and are obligated to do so. As is the common carrier, the hotelkeeper is held to a higher standard of care than that of the ordinary bailee. The hotelkeeper, however, is not a bailee in the strict sense of the word. The guest does not usually surrender the exclusive possession of his property to the hotelkeeper. Even so, the hotelkeeper is treated as the virtual insurer of the guest's property. The hotelkeeper is not liable for loss of or damage to property if she shows that it was caused by one of the following:

1. An act of God.
2. An act of a public enemy.
3. An act of a governmental authority.
4. The fault of a member of the guest's party.
5. The nature of the goods.

Most states have passed laws that limit the hotelkeeper's liability, however. Commonly, the law requires the hotel owner to post a notice advising guests that any valuables should be checked into the hotel vault. The hotelkeeper's liability is then limited, usually to a fixed amount, for valuables that are not so checked.

---

[9]Product liability doctrines are discussed in Chapter 20.

CYBERLAW IN ACTION

Online Tracking of Bailments

To lower package loss and increase consumer confidence, many large shipping companies such as UPS and FedEx provide an online tracking system. The tracking system is used by companies to identify and trace all packages as they move through the company's system to their destination. Often a package is assigned a tracking code or number that the customer can use to locate the package using an online mapping system. If a package is feared to be lost, Internet access to the tracking system allows customers immediate confirmation of its location en route, or place and time of delivery. The confidence that Internet tracking systems gives consumers increases the possibility that they will become repeat customers. Furthermore, the tracking system reveals the company's internal systems of operation to the consumer. This transparency of operation creates a forcing function that encourages companies to be certain that their shipping system is in smooth working order. Also, companies can view the tracking system to determine what shipping routes their competitors are using. Finally, the online tracking system saves a company money by lowering the cost of paying for representatives to deal with customer inquiries.

CONCEPT REVIEW

Duties of Bailees and Bailors

Type of Bailment	Duties of Bailee	Duties of Bailor
Sole Benefit of Bailee	1. Must use great care; liable for even slight negligence. 2. Must return goods to bailor or dispose of them at his direction. 3. May have duty to compensate bailor.	1. Must notify the bailee of any known defects.
Mutual Benefit	1. Must use reasonable care; liable for ordinary negligence. 2. Must return goods to bailor or dispose of them at his direction. 3. May have duty to compensate bailor.	1. Must notify bailee of all known defects and any defects that could be discovered on reasonable inspection. 2. Commercial lessors may be subject to warranties of quality and/or strict liability in tort. 3. May have duty to compensate bailee.
Sole Benefit of Bailor	1. Must use at least slight care; liable for gross negligence. 2. Must return goods to bailor or dispose of them at his direction.	1. Must notify bailee of all known defects and any hidden defects that are known or could be discovered on reasonable inspection. 2. May have duty to compensate bailee.

Safe-Deposit Boxes

If a person rents a safe-deposit box at a local bank and places property in the box, the box and the property are in the physical possession of the bank. However, it takes both the renter's key and the key held by the bank to open the box. In most cases, the bank does not know the nature, amount, or value of the goods in the box. Although a few courts have held that the rental of a safe-deposit box does not create a bailment, most courts have concluded that the renter of the box is a bailor and the bank is a bailee. As such, the bank is not an insurer of the contents of the box. It is obligated, however, to use due care and to come forward and explain loss of or damage to the property entrusted to it.

Involuntary Bailments

Suppose a person owns a cottage on a beach. After a violent storm, a sailboat washed up on his beach. As the finder of lost or misplaced property, he may be considered the **involuntary bailee** or **constructive bailee** of the sailboat. This relationship may arise when a person finds himself in possession of someone else's property without having agreed to accept possession.

The duties of the involuntary bailee are not well defined. The involuntary bailee does not have the right to destroy or use the property. If the true owner shows up, the property must be returned to him. Under some circumstances, the involuntary bailee may be under an obligation to assume control of the property or to take some minimal steps to ascertain the owner's identity, or both.

Documents of Title

Storing or shipping goods, giving a warehouse receipt or bill of lading representing the goods, and transferring such a receipt or bill of lading as representing the goods are practices of ancient origin. The warehouseman or the common carrier is a bailee of the goods who contracts to store or transport the goods and to deliver them to the owner or to act otherwise in accordance with the lawful directions of the owner. The warehouse receipt or the bill of lading may be either negotiable or nonnegotiable. To be negotiable, a warehouse receipt, bill of lading, or other document of title must provide that the goods are to be delivered to the bearer or to the order of a named person [7–104(1)]. The primary differences between the law of negotiable instruments and the law of negotiable documents of title are based on the differences between the obligation to pay money and the obligation to deliver specific goods.

Warehouse Receipts

A warehouse receipt, to be valid, need not be in any particular form, but if it does not embody within its written or printed form each of the following, the warehouseman is liable for damages caused by the omission to a person injured as a result of it: (1) the location of the warehouse where the goods are stored; (2) the date of issue; (3) the consecutive number of the receipt; (4) whether the goods are to be delivered to the bearer or to the order of a named person; (5) the rate of storage and handling charges; (6) a description of the goods or of the packages containing them; (7) the signature of the warehouseman or his agent; (8) whether the warehouseman is the owner of the goods, solely, jointly, or in common with others; and (9) a statement of the amount of the advances made and of the liabilities incurred for which the warehouseman claims a lien or security interest. Other terms may be inserted [7–202].

A warehouseman is liable to a purchaser for value in good faith of a warehouse receipt for nonreceipt or misdescription of goods. The receipt may conspicuously qualify the description by a statement such as "contents, condition, and quantity unknown" [7–203].

Because a warehouseman is a bailee of the goods, he owes to the holder of the warehouse receipt the duties of a mutual benefit bailee and must exercise reasonable care [7–204]. The warehouseman may terminate the relation by notification where, for example, the goods are about to deteriorate or where they constitute a threat to other goods in the warehouse [7–206]. Unless the warehouse receipt provides otherwise, the warehouseman must keep separate the goods covered by each receipt; however, different lots of fungible goods such as grain may be mingled [7–207].

A warehouseman has a lien against the bailor on the goods covered by his receipt for his storage and other charges incurred in handling the goods [7–209]. The Code sets out a detailed procedure for enforcing this lien [7–210].

Bills of Lading

In many respects, the rights and liabilities of the parties to a negotiable bill of lading are the same as the rights and liabilities of the parties to a negotiable warehouse receipt. The contract of the issuer of a bill of lading is to transport goods, whereas the contract of the issuer of a warehouse receipt is to store goods. Like the issuer of a warehouse receipt, the issuer of a bill of lading is liable for nonreceipt or misdescription of the goods, but he may protect himself from liability where he does not know the contents of packages by marking the bill of lading "contents or condition of packages unknown" or similar language. Such terms are ineffective when the

The Global Business Environment

Liability of Carriers of Goods

When an American firm ships goods to a foreign buyer, the goods may be shipped by ground, air, or water carrier. The duties and extent of liability of these various carriers is largely determined by domestic statutes and international law.

Ground Carriers

American trucking and railroad companies are regulated by the Interstate Commerce Act. American carriers are liable for any loss or damage to the goods with few exceptions—for example, damage caused by acts of God and acts of the shipper (usually the seller of the goods), such as poorly packaging the goods. An American carrier may limit its liability by contract, provided it allows the shipper to obtain full liability by paying a higher shipping charge.

Most European trucking companies and railroads are covered by EU rules, which place liability on carriers for damages to goods they carry with few exceptions—for example, defective packaging by the shipper and circumstances beyond the carrier's control. EU rules also limit a carrier's liability unless the shipper agrees to pay for greater liability.

Air Carriers

The Warsaw Convention governs the liability of international air carriers. Most nations have ratified the Warsaw Convention in its original or amended form. Under the Convention, an air carrier is liable to the shipper for damages to goods with few exceptions, including that it was impossible for the carrier to prevent the loss or that the damage was caused by the negligence of the shipper. The Warsaw Convention limits a carrier's liability to a stated amount per pound, unless the shipper pays for greater liability.

Water Carriers

The Hague Rules govern the liability of international water carriers. The Hague Rules were amended in Vishy, Sweden, in 1968. The United States codified the Hague Rules in the Carriage of Goods by Sea Act (COGSA), but has not ratified the Visby amendments, which do not substantially change the liability of international water carriers.

The Hague–Visby Rules and the COGSA impose on international water carriers the duties to (1) furnish a seaworthy ship and (2) stow the cargo carefully to prevent it from breaking loose during storms at sea. When these duties are met, a water carrier will not usually be liable for damages to cargo. Water carriers have no liability for damages caused by circumstances beyond their control—such as poor packaging, piracy, or acts of war. Under COGSA, liability is limited to $500 per package, unless the shipper agrees to pay a higher shipping fee. Under the Hague–Visby Rules, liability will be the value of the goods declared by the shipper. Sometimes a carrier will attempt to reduce or eliminate its liability in the shipping contract. However, COGSA does not permit a carrier to eliminate its liability for loss or damages to goods resulting from the carrier's negligence or other fault.

Under COGSA or the Hague–Visby Rules, the owner of cargo will be liable for damage his cargo does to other cargo. Also, under the ancient **maritime doctrine of general average,** when a carrier sacrifices an owner's cargo, such as throwing it overboard in order to save the ship and the other cargo, the other owners have liability to the owner whose cargo was sacrificed; liability is prorated to each owner according to the value of each owner's goods in relation to the value of the voyage (the value of the ship plus the value of the other owners' goods plus the carrier's total shipping fees).

The doctrine of general average is commonly expanded by the contract between the carrier and cargo owners in **New Jason clauses.** Typically, a New Jason clause provides that in *all* cases when goods are damaged and the carrier is not liable under COGSA, the goods owner is entitled to general average contributions from all other cargo owners. The doctrine of general average, bolstered by a New Jason clause, also requires cargo owners to pay for damages to the ship when not the result of the carrier's fault.

Ethics in Action

Is It Ethical?

Suppose that you own and operate a warehouse. A local liquor store owner occasionally uses your facilities to store shipments of wine from France until he has room for the wine in his store. You are aware that from time to time your warehouse employees "borrow" a bottle from the crates of wine being stored in your warehouse. After a number of crates with a total of four bottles missing are delivered to the liquor store, the store owner queries you about the missing bottles and you tell him that they must have been broken in transit to your warehouse. Have you acted ethically?

goods are loaded by an issuer who is a common carrier unless the goods are concealed by packages [7–301].

Duty of Care

A carrier who issues a bill of lading, or a warehouse operator who issues a warehouse receipt, must exercise the same degree of care in relation to the goods as a reasonably careful person would exercise under similar circumstances. Liability for damages not caused by the negligence of the carrier may be imposed on him by a special law or rule of law. Under tariff rules, a common carrier may limit her liability to a shipper's declaration of value, provided that the rates are dependent on value [7–309].

In the case that follows, *Gyamfoah v. EG&G Dynatrend,* a warehouseman who was unable to return goods that had been entrusted to it for safekeeping or to account for their disappearance was held liable to the bailor for the value of the goods.

Gyamfoah v. EG&G Dynatrend (now EG&G Technical Services)
51 U.C.C. Rep. 2d 805 (E.D. Penn. 2003)

On May 7, 1999, Yaa Gyamfoah, a citizen of Ghana, arrived at JFK International Airport with two suitcases containing a number of watches she had purchased in Hong Kong. The suitcases were seized by U.S. Customs because it suspected the watches were counterfeit. Gyamfoah was given a receipt for 3,520 watches. The watches were transported to a warehouse operated by EG&G Dynatrend (EG&G), now known as EG&G Technical Services, under contract with the U.S. Department of Treasury to provide seized management services for all agencies of the department. The warehouse accepted and signed for the watches on June 2, 1999.

On October 13, U.S. Customs advised Gyamfoah's agent that the nonviolative (ones that were not counterfeit) portion of the seizure (2,940 watches) would be released upon payment of $1,470. On November 18, a Customs agent, observed by EG&G's warehouse supervisor, separated the watches into a group of 580 "violative" watches, which were placed in a carton, and 2,940 "nonviolative" watches, which were placed back in the suitcases. The carton and the suitcases were then returned to the custody of EG&G. When the Customs agent returned on November 24 to again, under the observation of the warehouse supervisor, examine the watches, there were only 1,002 watches in the carton and suitcases; some 2,518 were missing.

Gyamfoah subsequently brought suit against the United States and EG&G. The claim against the United States was dismissed, and the case went to trial on the claim against EG&G.

O'Neil, Jr., Judge

The duties of a warehouseman that existed under New Jersey common law have now been codified in *N.J.S.A. 12A: 7–101.* EG&G is a warehouseman under the definition in the statute: "a person engaged in the business of storing goods for hire." New Jersey requires that a warehouseman exercise reasonable care when storing bailed items. The statute imposes the following liability, in a provision adopted from the Uniform Commercial Code:

> A warehouseman is liable for damages for loss of or injury to the goods caused by his failure to exercise such care in regard to them as a reasonably careful man would exercise under like circumstances but unless otherwise agreed he is not liable for damages which could not have been avoided by the exercise of such care.

N.J.S.A. 12A: 7–204(1).

The warehouseman's statute has been interpreted to involve a burden-shifting scheme that reflects that common law of bailment. The bailor must present *a prima facie* case of conversion by proving (1) delivery of the bailed goods to the bailee; (2) demand for return of the bailed goods from the bailee; and (3) failure of the bailee to return the bailed goods. Once the bailee has proved these three points, the burden shifts to the bailee to show how the bailed goods were lost. If the bailee cannot prove how the bailed goods were lost it is liable under the New Jersey statute for conversion. Although the burden of proof regarding how the goods were lost shifts to the defendant, the burden of proving conversion rests at all times on the bailor as plaintiff.

The tort of conversion that can be proved under the statute is not necessarily an intentional tort. In this instance "[a] conversion can occur even when a bailee has not stolen the merchandise but has acted negligently in permitting the loss of the merchandise from its premises." In other words, if a bailor establishes that the bailed goods had disappeared while in the care of the bailee, there is a rebuttable presumption of conversion based either on the bailee's negligent conduct in permitting third parties to steal the goods, or by the negligent or intentional conduct of the bailee's employees or agents.

As established earlier, I find that Gyamfoah showed by a preponderance of the evidence that: (1) 3,520 watches were delivered to EG&G's warehouse; (2) when Gyamfoah's agent presented the papers entitling Gyamfoah to return of the watches 2,518 watches were missing; and (3) the U.S. Customs officers who manipulated the watches did not remove the missing watches.

Therefore, Gyamfoah has established delivery to EG&G and EG&G's failure to redeliver all of the items on Gyamfoah's demand. Under New Jersey law this creates a rebuttable presumption of conversion by EG&G.

EG&G produced evidence at trial of reasonable precautions against loss. Mr. Wenzcel testified that the watches were shrink-wrapped to a pallet and stored in a secured area on a high shelf that required a forklift to be reached. Paul Hehir, the EG&G district manager who oversaw operations in the New York district of the company, also testified about security. He testified that the area in which the watches were stored was armed and within a gated area that only EG&G employees could enter.

EG&G does not provide any evidence, however, regarding what happened to the missing watches. EG&G mentions the possibility that the missing watches were never delivered to the warehouse. This possibility is refuted, however, by evidence that U.S. Customs officers left the warehouse on November 18 thinking that there were 3,520 watches in storage. As I stated earlier, I find that Gyamfoah has proved by a preponderance of the evidence that there were 3,520 watches in the suitcases when the suitcases were delivered to EG&G's warehouse. There is no explanation for the disappearance of the watches other than EG&G's negligence. In fact, when asked "so it's fair to say that sitting here today, EG&G can offer no explanation of the loss of the majority of the contents of those two suitcases?" EG&G employee Mr. Herir testified "I cannot offer any explanation, no."

EG&G has not met its burden to rebut the presumption of negligence created by plaintiff's case. Gyamfoah has met her burden of proving by a preponderance of the evidence that EG&G is liable to her under New Jersey's law of bailment, as found in Section *7–204(1)* and the common law. EG&G is liable for the value of the lost watches.

Gyamfoah has proved by a preponderance of the evidence that EG&G is liable for the loss of 2,518 watches. For negligence, the measure of damages is the value of the lost goods.

The only evidence presented at trial regarding the value of the missing watches is a receipt from Andex Trading Limited. The receipt lists ten models of watches, the quantity bought by Gyamfoah, the unit price and the amount paid for the number of watches of each model bought. Because Gyamfoah has not shown which models the 2,518 missing watches were, I will calculate damages as if the least expensive 2,518 watches are missing.

The cost of the least expensive 2,518 watches is $3,781.30. That includes 300 watches at $0.90 each, 100 watches at $1.40 each, 350 watches at $1.55 each and 1,768 watches at $1.60 each.

Judgment in favor of Yaa Gyamfoah and against EG&G Dynatrend in the amount of $3,781.30.

Negotiation of Document of Title

A negotiable document of title and a negotiable instrument are negotiated in substantially the same manner. If the document of title provides for the delivery of the goods to bearer, it may be negotiated by delivery. If it provides for delivery of the goods to the order of a named person, it must be endorsed by that person and delivered. If an order document of title is endorsed in blank, it may be negotiated by delivery unless it bears a special endorsement following the blank endorsement, in which event it must be endorsed by the special endorsee and delivered [7–501].

A person taking a negotiable document of title takes as a bona fide holder if she takes in good faith and in the regular course of business. The bona fide holder of a negotiable document of title has substantially the same advantages over a holder who is not a bona fide holder or over a holder of a nonnegotiable document of title as does a holder in due course of a negotiable instrument over a holder who is not a holder in due course or over a holder of a nonnegotiable instrument.

Rights Acquired by Negotiation

A person who acquires a negotiable document of title by due negotiation acquires (1) title to the document, (2) title to the goods, (3) the right to the goods delivered to the bailee after the issuance of the document, and (4) the direct obligation of the issuer to hold or deliver the goods according to the terms of the document [7–502(1)].

Under the broad general principle that a person cannot transfer title to goods he does not own, a thief—or the owner of goods subject to a perfected security interest—cannot, by warehousing or shipping the goods on a negotiable document of title and then negotiating the document of title, transfer to the purchaser of the document of title a better title than he has [7–503].

Warranties of Transferor of Document of Title The transferor of a negotiable document of title warrants to his immediate transferee, in addition to any warranty of goods, only that the document is genuine, that he has no knowledge of any facts that would impair its validity or worth, and that his negotiation or transfer is rightful and fully effective with respect to the title to the document and the goods it represents [7–507].

Problems and Problem Cases

1. Leonard Charrier was an amateur archeologist. After researching colonial maps and records, he concluded that the Trudeau Plantation near Angola, Louisiana, was the possible site of an ancient village of the Tunica Indians. Charrier obtained the permission of the caretaker of the Trudeau Plantation to survey the property with a metal detector for possible burial locations. At the time, he mistakenly believed that the caretaker was the Plantation's owner. He located and, over the next three years, excavated approximately 150 burial sites containing beads, European ceramics, stoneware and glass bottles; iron kettles, vessels, and skillets; knives, muskets, gunflints, balls, and shots; crucifixes, rings, and bracelets; and native pottery. He began discussions with Harvard University to sell the collection to its Peabody Museum. While the University inventoried, cataloged, and displayed the items pursuant to a lease agreement, it was unwilling to go through with a sale unless Charrier could establish title to the artifacts. He then brought suit against the owners of the Trudeau Plantation seeking a declaratory judgment that he was the owner of the artifacts. The state of Louisiana intervened in the litigation to assert the rights of the lawful heirs of the artifacts. Charrier argued that the Indians abandoned the artifacts when they moved from the Trudeau Plantation in 1764. He contended that they were unowned property until he found them and reduced them to his possession. He compared them to wild game and fish, which are unowned until someone takes possession of them. Were the artifacts abandoned property of which Charrier could become the owner by taking possession?

2. Alex Franks was staying at a Comfort Inn in Searcy, Arkansas, while working on a highway project. He checked into the hotel on Monday, September 10. Two days later, after he had checked out and returned to his room to retrieve some laundry, he discovered $14,200 in plain view in a drawer of the dresser in the room. It was wrapped tightly with masking tape, like a brick, with some of the money showing. Franks notified the hotel manager, who in turn notified the police. The police determined that there were two bundles of money separated by denominations and then bundled together. The bundle contained 46 one hundred dollar bills and 480 twenty dollar bills. The officer who took custody of the money testified that the money appeared to be intentionally and meticulously wrapped because all the bills faced in the same direction. Franks brought suit against the City of Searcy claiming the money. The city joined the owners of the hotel as third-party defendants and then withdrew any claim on its part to the money. Should the court hold that the money is abandoned, lost, or mislaid? Between Franks and the owner of the hotel, who has the best right to it? Why?

3. Rick Kenyon purchased a painting by a noted Western artist, Bill Gollings, valued between $8,000 and $15,000 for $25 at a Salvation Army thrift store. Claude Abel filed suit against Kenyon seeking the return of the painting, which had belonged to his late aunt. Abel claimed that the Salvation Army mistakenly took the painting from his aunt's house when the box in which it was packed was mixed with items being donated to the thrift store. Abel's aunt, Billie Taylor, was a friend of the artist whose works were known for their accurate portrayal of the Old West. Sometime before his death in 1932, Gollings gave a painting to Taylor depicting a Native American on a white horse in the foreground with several other Native Americans on horses in the background traveling through a traditional Western prairie landscape. The painting remained in Taylor's possession at her home in Sheridan, Wyoming, until her death on August 31, 1999. After Taylor's death, Abel traveled from his home in Idaho to Sheridan for the funeral and to settle the estate. Abel was the sole heir of Taylor's estate, so he inherited all of her personal belongings, including the Gollings painting. Abel and his wife sorted through Taylor's belongings, selecting various items they would keep for themselves. Abel and his wife, with the help of a local moving company, packed those items into boxes marked for delivery to their home in Idaho. Items not being

retained by Abel were either packed for donation to the Salvation Army or, if they had sufficient value, were taken by an antiques dealer for auction. The scene at the house was one of some confusion as Abel tried to vacate the residence as quickly as possible while attempting to make sure all of the items went to their designated destinations. The painting was packed by Abel's wife in a box marked for delivery to Idaho. However, in the confusion and unbeknown to Abel, the box containing Gollings's painting was inadvertently picked up with the donated items by the Salvation Army. It was priced at $25 in its thrift store and sold to Kenyon. After returning to Idaho, Abel discovered that the box containing the painting was not among those delivered by the moving company. He also learned that the painting had gone to the Salvation Army and had been sold to Kenyon. When Kenyon refused to acknowledge he had the painting, Abel brought suit seeking its return. Kenyon claimed that he was a good faith purchaser of the painting that had been given to the Salvation Army. Was Abel entitled to have the painting returned to him on the grounds that not having made a gift of the painting, he was still the owner, and that its sale by the Salvation Army was a conversion of his property?

4. Chad Clippard and Jamie Pfefferkorn dated for four or five months in late 2002. On December 23, Chad proposed marriage to Jamie and presented her with a 2.02-carat diamond engagement ring valued at approximately $13,500. Jamie accepted the proposal and the ring. Several days later, they exchanged Christmas gifts. During the weeks following Christmas 2002, the couple experienced difficulties in their relationship. On February 8, 2003, Chad terminated the engagement. He attributed the decision not to go forward with marriage to a belief that Jamie was not the "right" person and to the influence of his brother, sisters, and parents. There were times during the engagement when it was "off" and Jamie returned the ring to Chad, but when the parties renewed the engagement he gave it back to her. When the couple finally broke up, Chad asked Jamie to return the ring, but she refused. In July 2003, Chad filed a petition in court seeking a court order to have Jamie return the ring or, in the alternative, to pay damages in the amount of $13,500, the approximate value of the ring. Jamie took the position that she was entitled to keep the ring because the ring

constituted either (1) a Christmas gift that as an *inter vivos* gift was absolute when she received it; or (2) a conditional gift, which became absolute when Chad terminated the engagement. Chad denied that it was a Christmas gift. He claimed that it was a gift in contemplation of marriage and thus a conditional gift that had to be returned upon the termination of the engagement. Is Jamie entitled to retain the ring?

5. Faith Ballard's Corvette was substantially damaged in an accident and was being stored in her garage. Her son, Tyrone Ballard, told her that he would take the vehicle and have it restored. Instead he sold it to Lambert Auto Parts. Johnny Wetzel purchased the Corvette "hull" for $900 from Lambert, whose regular business is selling parts. Wetzel obtained a receipt documenting the purchase of the parts. He also checked the VIN numbers through the county clerk's office to make sure the parts were not stolen. Wetzel spent approximately $5,000 and 100 hours of labor restoring the vehicle. When completed, the restoration had a market value of $7,950. George Martin, an employee of Lambert, testified that he purchased only a "hull" of a car—rather than a whole vehicle—from Tyrone Ballard. Martin also testified that he usually received a title when he bought a "whole" vehicle but had not received one in this case where he had purchased only part of one. Under Tennessee law, a certificate of title is not required to pass ownership of a motor vehicle, but any owner dismantling a registered vehicle is to send the certificate of title back to the state. Faith Ballard brought suit against Wetzel to recover possession of the Corvette. Wetzel contended that he was a good faith purchaser for value and had become the owner of the restored auto hull by accession. Did Wetzel become the owner of the Corvette by accession?

6. R. B. Bewley and his family drove to Kansas City to attend a week-long church convention. When they arrived at the hotel where they had reservations, they were unable to park their car and unload their luggage because of a long line of cars. They then drove to a nearby parking lot where they took a ticket, causing the gate arm to open, and drove in 15 or 20 feet. A parking attendant told them that the lot was full, that they should leave the keys with him, and that he would park the car. They told the attendant that they had reservations at the nearby hotel and that after they checked in they would come back for their luggage. Subsequently, someone broke into

the Bewley's car and stole their personal property from the car and its trunk. Was the parking lot a bailee of the property?

7. On March 27, 2001, Felice Jasphy brought three fur coats to Illana Osinsky's establishment trading as Cedar Lane Furs in Teaneck, New Jersey, for storage and cleaning. The three coats included a ranch mink coat, a Shearling, and a blush mink. In addition to storage of the three coats, Jasphy also sought cleaning of the ranch mink. In 1997, the ranch mink had been appraised for $11,500; the Shearling for $3,500; and the blush mink for $3,995. Jasphy signed a written agreement, labeled "fur storage sales receipt," which included Jasphy's name and address, and the price of the storage and cleaning. On the back of the receipt, the following preprinted provision limiting Cedar Lane Furs' liability read:

> This receipt is a storage contract, articles listed are accepted for storage until December 31, of dated year, subject to the terms and conditions hereof, in accepting this receipt, the depositor agrees to be bound by all its terms and conditions and acknowledges that this receipt is the entire agreement with the furrier, which cannot be changed except by endorsement herein signed by the furrier. If no value is specified, or if no separate insurance covering the garment is declared at the time of issuance of this receipt, insurance in the amount of $1.00 will be placed on the garment.

Immediately above the location on the receipt for a customer's signature, the following was printed: "I understand and agree that Cedar Lane Furs' liability for loss or damage from any cause whatsoever, including their own negligence or that of employees and others, is limited to the declared valuation." Jasphy did not state the value of the coats or declare whether she had separate insurance coverage when the receipt was issued. There is no identifiable room provided on the receipt to specify such information. The limitation of the furrier's liability was not brought to Jasphy's attention, nor was she asked to furnish the value of her coats for storage. The following day, March 28, 2001, a fire swept through Cedar Lane Furs, causing Jasphy's furs to be completely destroyed. A hot iron, which Cedar Lane Furs' employees apparently forgot to unplug overnight, caused the fire. Jasphy subsequently learned that her furs had not been placed in the fur vault before the fire and were destroyed in the fire.

Jasphy filed a claim form with Cedar Lane Furs' insurance company but never received any reimbursement. She then brought suit against Osinsky and Cedar Lane Furs. They contended that their liability was limited by the contract provision to $1 per garment. Should the court enforce the contractual provision limiting the furrier's liability to $1 per garment?

8. In early 1991, William Seebold, the president of Eagle Boats, Ltd., was approached by a boating magazine, *Trailer Boats,* about doing a feature on a motorboat manufactured by Eagle Boats. The magazine feature would include a written article and photographs of the boat on Grand Lake near Ketchum, Oklahoma. Seebold expressed interest in the idea to the magazine's representative. At the time, a motorboat owned by Hoppies Village Marina was at Eagle Boat's facility in Fenton, Missouri, undergoing minor paint repairs. The motorboat was a 1991 Seebold Eagle 265 Limited Edition: a 26-foot, 4,000- to 4,500-pound, 600-horsepower supercharged motorboat capable of attaining a speed of 80 mph. It was considered to be the "Cadillac" of motorboats in its class. Seebold called Hoppies about using its motorboat for the magazine article, which would include information not only about the motorboat and Eagle Boats, but also about Hoppies Village Marina. Hoppies agreed. The arrangement was for Seebold to transport the boat to Ketchum and then return it to Hoppies' custody. After the touch-up work on the motorboat was finished, the boat was loaded onto a custom-built trailer owned by Hoppies. The trailer did not have a locking device on it—a device capable of locking the trailer to the truck. The trailer was then hooked up to an Eagle Boats truck, and Seebold drove it to Ketchum. He arrived at the Grand Lodge Inn about 9:30 PM. The demonstration for the magazine was scheduled lor 6:00 AM the next morning.

Seebold parked the truck, boat, and trailer on the motel's parking lot, parallel to a fence at the end of the lot, facing away from the highway. There was one dusk-to-dawn light shining in front of the motel, and the boat was parked across the lot from this light. The parking lot was small and narrow, making it difficult for the boat and trailer to be turned around. There were other boats parked on the lot, but this was the closest to the road and also the most expensive. Behind the motel were storage units. Seebold was awakened about 4:30 the next morning with the news that the boat and trailer were missing. At the time of the theft, the motorboat and trailer had a combined fair market value of more than $60,000. Hoppies' insurance carrier, Institute of London Underwriters, paid Hoppies' insurance claim. Then as the subrogee of Hoppies' claim against Eagle Boats, it brought suit against Eagle and Seebold for their failure to use reasonable care of the bailed motorboat and trailer to prevent their theft. Were Eagle Boats and Seebold, as bailees, liable to Hoppies Village Marina for their failure to use reasonable care to prevent the theft of the motorboat and trailer?

9. Marvin Gooden checked into a Day's Inn in Atlanta, paying in advance for two days' lodging. The next day he temporarily left his room. He left behind, in the room, a paper bag filled with approximately $9,000. Shortly after Gooden left, housekeeper Mary Carter entered his room to clean it. Carter found the bag of money. Because she saw no other personal effects, Carter assumed that Gooden had checked out. She therefore turned the bag of money over to her supervisor, Vivian Clark. Clark gave the bag to Dempsey Wilson, who was responsible for general supervision and maintenance of the grounds. During the three years he had worked for Day's Inn, Wilson had occasionally been given items of value to turn in at the hotel's office. In the past, he had always turned in the items. This time, however, he absconded with the bag of money. There was a safe on the Day's Inn premises. Day's Inn had posted, on the door of Gooden's room, a notice concerning the safe's availability for use by guests who had valuables with them. Gooden, who had never sought the use of the safe, brought a tort action against Day's Inn, Clark, and Carter in an effort to collect $9,000 in damages. Day's Inn argued that it was protected against liability by the following Georgia statute: "The innkeeper may provide a safe or other place of deposit for valuable articles and, by posting a notice thereof, may require the guests of the innkeeper to place such valuable articles therein or the innkeeper shall be relieved from responsibility for such articles." Gooden contended, however, that the statute could not insulate an innkeeper from liability when the loss of a guest's valuables is occasioned by the negligent (or other tortious) conduct of the innkeeper's employees.

Should Gooden prevail against Day Inn, Clark, and Carter?

10. Griswold and Bateman Warehouse Company stored 337 cases of Chivas Regal Scotch Whiskey for Joseph H. Reinfeld, Inc., in its bonded warehouse. The warehouse receipt issued to Reinfeld limited Griswold and Bateman's liability for negligence to 250 times the monthly storage rate, a total of $1,925. When Reinfeld sent its truck to pick up the whiskey, 40 cases were missing. Reinfeld then brought suit seeking the wholesale market value of the whiskey, $6,417.60. Reinfeld presented evidence of the delivery of the whiskey, the demand for its return, and the failure of Griswold and Bateman to return it. Reinfeld claimed that the burden was on Griswold and Bateman to explain the disappearance of the whiskey. Griswold and Bateman admitted that it had been negligent, but sought to limit its liability to $1,925: Is Griswold and Bateman's liability limited to $1,925?

Online Research

What Should You Do If You Find Valuable Property?

Use the Internet to determine whether your state has a law dealing with unclaimed or estray property. If you find a valuable item that appears to have been lost, what steps are you legally obligated to take in your state? What procedures does your state have for trying to locate the owner of such property?

Consider completing the case "PROPERTY: Subtracting the Addition" from the You Be the Judge Web site element after you have read this chapter. Visit our Web site at www.mhhe.com/mallor14e for more information and activities regarding this case segment.

chapter 24

REAL PROPERTY

Joyce and John, a married couple with two young children, are in the process of buying a house. They made an offer on a single-family house in Greenwood, a new subdivision. The house has four bedrooms, one with custom-built bunk beds in it, four bathrooms, a swimming pool, and a large basement. There is a well-equipped kitchen and a large dining room with a vintage Tiffany lamp over the dining room table. The basement is perfect for Joyce, who plans to operate a small day care center in the house. Joyce and John notice that the next-door neighbors, the Fieldings, have been dumping their garden refuse in a ravine at the back of the property that they have offered to buy, but they assume that they will be able to stop that practice once they move in.

- Are the bunk beds and Tiffany lamp considered to be part of the real property that Joyce and John have offered to buy?
- If their offer is accepted, how will Joyce and John share ownership of the property? What form of ownership will they have?
- What are the steps involved in purchasing this property?
- What rights might others, such as the Fieldings, have in the property?
- What liability might John and Joyce have to others who are injured on their property?
- What controls does the legal system place on the use of property?
- Is it ethical for the Fieldings to dump their garden refuse on this property?

LAND'S SPECIAL IMPORTANCE IN the law has long been recognized. In the agrarian society of previous eras, land served as the basic measure and source of wealth. In today's society, land functions not only as a source of food, clothing, and shelter but also as an instrument of commercial and industrial development. It is not surprising, then, that a complex body of law—the law of *real property*—exists regarding the ownership, acquisition, and use of land.

This chapter discusses the scope of real property and the various legal interests in it. In addition, the chapter examines the ways in which real property is transferred and the controls society places on an owner's use of real property.

Scope of Real Property

Real property includes not only land but also things firmly attached to or embedded in land. Buildings and other permanent structures thus are considered real property. The owner of a tract of real property also owns the air above it, the minerals below its surface, and any trees or other vegetation growing on the property.[1]

Unlike readily movable personal property, real property is immovable or attached to something immovable. Distinguishing between real and personal property is important because rules of law governing real property transactions such as sale, taxation, and inheritance are frequently different from those applied to personal property transactions.

Fixtures
An item of personal property may, however, be attached to or used in conjunction with real property in such a way that it ceases being personal property and instead becomes part of the real property. This type of property is called a **fixture.**

---

[1] Ownership of air above one's property is not an unlimited interest, however. Courts have held that the flight of aircraft above property does not violate the property owner's rights, so long as it does not unduly interfere with the owner's enjoyment of her land.

Fixtures belong to the owner of the real property. One who provides or attaches fixtures to real property without a request to that effect from the owner of the real property is normally not entitled to compensation from the owner. A conveyance (transfer of ownership) of real property also transfers the fixtures associated with that property, even if the fixtures are not specifically mentioned.

People commonly install items of personal property on the real property they own or rent. Disputes may arise regarding rights to such property. Suppose that Jacobsen buys an elaborate ceiling fan and installs it in his home. When he sells the house to Orr, may Jacobsen remove the ceiling fan, or is it part of the home Orr has bought? Suppose that Luther, a commercial tenant, installs showcases and tracklights in the store she leases from Nelson. May Luther remove the showcases and the lights when her lease expires, or do the items now belong to Nelson? If the parties' contracts are silent on these matters, courts will resolve the cases by applying the law of fixtures. As later discussion will reveal, Jacobsen probably cannot remove the ceiling fan because it is likely to be considered part of the real property purchased by Orr. Luther, on the other hand, may be entitled to remove the showcases and the lights under the special rules governing trade fixtures.

Factors Indicating Whether an Item Is a Fixture

There is no mechanical formula for determining whether an item has become a fixture. Courts tend to consider these factors:

1. *Attachment.* One factor helping to indicate whether an item is a fixture is the degree to which the item is **attached** or **annexed** to real property. If firmly attached to real property so that it cannot be removed without damaging the property, the item is likely to be considered a fixture. An item of personal property that may be removed with little or no injury to the property is less likely to be considered a fixture.

Actual physical attachment to real property is not necessary, however. A close physical connection between an item of personal property and certain real property may enable a court to conclude that the item is **constructively annexed.** For example, heavy machinery or remote control devices for automatic garage doors may be considered fixtures even though they are not physically attached to real property.

2. *Adaptation.* Another factor to be considered is **adaptation**—the degree to which the item's use is necessary or beneficial to the use of the real property. Adaptation is a particularly relevant factor when the item is not physically attached to the real property or is only slightly attached. When an item would be of little value except for use with certain real property, the item is likely to be considered a fixture even if it is unattached or could easily be removed. For example, keys and custom-sized window screens and storm windows have been held to be fixtures.

3. *Intent.* The third factor to be considered is the **intent** of the person who installed the item. Intent is judged not by what that person subjectively intended, but by what the circumstances indicate he intended. To a great extent, intent is indicated by the annexation and adaptation factors. An owner of real property who improves it by attaching items of personal property presumably intended those items to become part of the real estate. If the owner does not want an attached item to be considered a fixture, he must specifically reserve the right to keep the item. For instance, if a seller of a house wants to keep an antique chandelier that has been installed in the house, she should either replace the chandelier before the house is shown to prospective purchasers or specify in the contract of sale that the chandelier will be excluded from the sale.

The following *Olbekson v. Huber* case illustrates the characteristics of a fixture.

Olbekson v. Huber   2002 Mont. Dist. LEXIS 2935 (Dist. Ct. Montana 2002)

In May 1994, Leo and Emelia Huber rented a house to Lois Olbekson, who was the daughter of their friends, Loren and Alice May Olbekson. Lois hoped to be able to purchase the house from the Hubers one day. The primary source of heat for the rental house was a wood furnace located in the basement. At around the time the Hubers entered into their rental agreement with Lois, they hired a local contractor to reline the brick chimney. Lois was not happy with the wood furnace. In the fall of 1995, she persuaded her parents to buy an oil furnace to replace the wood furnace in the rental house. During the process of installing the new oil furnace, the old wood furnace was removed from the rental house at the Olbeksons' direction and hauled to the landfill. Installation of the oil furnace required wiring in a thermostat and drilling a hole in the wall to accommodate the fuel line from the outside oil tank, and the Olbeksons had to widen an existing doorway into the basement in order to accommodate the new oil furnace. The Olbeksons paid $2,525 to have the new oil furnace installed. The Hubers acquiesced in the installation of the new furnace, but would not have done so if they had believed that they would be required to purchase it.

During the time that Lois lived in the Hubers' rental house, the Hubers spent approximately $28,000 remodeling it, yet collected only $175 per month in rent. Lois admitted that before the remodeling was complete, the reasonable rental value of the house was probably $250 per month. In order to placate her husband about the rent, Emelia prepared an agreement which purported to tie the low rent to compensation for the cost of the furnace. The agreement, which Emelia and Lois signed, read as follows:

> During October 1995, a fuel furnace for $2,525.00 was installed at 317 W. Lincoln and paid for by Loren and Alice May Olbekson. To compensate for the expense of this heating device, rent on this residence will remain at $175.00 per month thru the duration of Nov. 1st, 1995 thru Dec. 31st 1997.

Lois continued to rent the house until September 2000. Even though the written agreement provided that Lois would enjoy reduced rent only until December 31, 1997, the Hubers did not raise the rent at any time prior to the termination of the tenancy. At the end of Lois's tenancy, the Olbeksons removed the outside oil tank. Claiming the right to remove the oil furnace, they brought a claim against the Hubers for conversion of the oil furnace.

Prezeau, District Judge

The Olbeksons' claim is for conversion. A claim of conversion requires: ownership of property, a right of possession, and unauthorized dominion over the property by another resulting in damages. Whether or not the Olbeksons owned the oil furnace and had a right to possess it when Lois left premises depends upon real property law pertaining to fixtures. Montana law states that in the absence of an agreement otherwise, as between the property owner and the person who installed the fixture, the fixture belongs to the owner of the property.

> 70-18-101. Fixture attached by other—accession by owner. When a person affixes his property to the land of another, without an agreement permitting him to remove it, the thing affixed . . . belongs to the owner of the land unless he chooses to require the former to remove it.

There was no agreement between the parties that the Olbeksons could remove the oil furnace. Thus, if the furnace is a fixture, it belongs to the Hubers. A fixture is defined by Montana law as something that is permanently attached to real property by means of cement, plaster, nails, bolts, or screws. Ultimately, however, whether something is a fixture depends upon several factors. To determine whether an object has become a fixture or not, we consider the following factors: (1) annexation to the realty, (2) an adaptation to the use to which the realty is devoted, and (3) intent that the object become a permanent accession to the land.

Of those three, the intent of the parties has the most weight and is the controlling factor. The second two factors are particularly relevant to this case. The oil furnace was installed through a doorway that had to be enlarged to accommodate the new furnace. The furnace had to be wired to a thermostat, and a hole had to be drilled into a wall of the house to attach the furnace to the outside oil tank. Clearly, the oil furnace was adapted to use as the rental house's primary heat source. As to the intent of the parties, the evidence is that Lois was hoping when she moved into the rental house that she might one day be in a position to purchase the house from the Hubers. Obviously, the Olbeksons would not be intending to install a temporary heat source into the house, which is born out by the fact that they not only disconnected the previous furnace, but they had it removed from the house with a backhoe and hauled away to the dump.

Even the Olbeksons admit that their alleged intention to remove the oil furnace was conditioned upon Lois not eventually purchasing the house. No reasonable person could believe that a tenant would have the right to remove the furnace from a rental house, replace it with a new furnace, and take the furnace with them years later (in this case, five years later) when the tenant vacates the premises, leaving the rental house without its primary heating system.

In addition to the definition of a fixture contained in § 70-15-103 (4), MCA, a fixture is defined as "anything affixed [to real property] for purposes of trade, manufacture, ornament, or domestic use if the removal can be effected without injury to the premises unless the thing has, by the manner in which it is affixed, become an integral part of the premises." Section 70-18-102, MCA. The oil furnace satisfies the definition on both counts; it is affixed to the house for domestic use and cannot be removed without injury to the premises, and it is affixed in such a manner that it is an integral part of the premises.

Judgment in favor of the Hubers.

Express Agreement If the parties to an express agreement have clearly stated their intent about whether a particular item is to be considered a fixture, a court will generally enforce that agreement. For example, the buyer and seller of a house might agree to permit the seller to remove a fence or shrubbery that would otherwise be considered a fixture.

Trade Fixtures An exception to the usual fixture rules is recognized when a tenant attaches personal property to leased premises for the purpose of carrying on her trade or business. Such fixtures, called **trade fixtures,** remain the tenant's personal property and may normally be removed at the termination of the lease. This trade fixtures exception encourages commerce and industry. It recognizes that the commercial tenant who affixed the item of personal property did not intend a permanent improvement of the leased premises.

The tenant's right to remove trade fixtures is subject to two limitations. First, the tenant cannot remove the fixtures if doing so would cause substantial damage to the landlord's realty. Second, the tenant must remove the fixtures by the end of the lease if the lease is for a definite period. If the lease is for an indefinite period, the tenant usually has a reasonable time after the expiration of the lease to remove the fixtures. Trade fixtures not removed within the appropriate time become the landlord's property.

Leases may contain terms expressly addressing the parties' rights in any fixtures. A lease might give the tenant the right to attach items or make other improvements, and to remove them later. The reverse may also be true. The lease could state that any improvements made or fixtures attached will become the landlord's property at the termination of the lease. Courts generally enforce parties' agreements on fixture ownership.

Security Interests in Fixtures Special rules apply to personal property subject to a lien or security interest at the time it is attached to real property. Assume, for example, that a person buys a dishwasher on a time-payment plan from an appliance store and has it installed in his kitchen. To protect itself, the appliance store takes a security interest in the dishwasher and perfects that interest by filing a

---

CONCEPT REVIEW

Fixtures

Concept	A *fixture* is an item of personal property attached to or used in conjunction with real property in such a way that it is treated as being part of the real property.
Significance	A transfer of the real property will also convey the fixtures on that property.
Factors Considered in Determining Whether Property Is a Fixture	1. Attachment: Is the item physically attached or closely connected to the real property? 2. Adaptation: How necessary or beneficial is the item to the use of the real property? 3. Intent: Did the person who installed the item manifest intent for the property to become part of the real property?
Express Agreement	Express agreements clearly stating intent about whether property is a fixture are generally enforceable.
Trade Fixtures (Tenants' Fixtures)	Definition of *trade fixture:* personal property attached to leased real property by a tenant for the purpose of carrying on his trade or business. Trade fixtures can be removed and retained by the tenant at the termination of the lease except when any of the following applies: 1. Removal would cause substantial damage to the landlord's real property. 2. The tenant fails to remove the fixtures by the end of the lease (or within a reasonable time, if the lease is for an indefinite period of time). 3. An express agreement between the landlord and tenant provides otherwise.

financing statement in the appropriate real estate records office within the period of time specified by the Uniform Commercial Code. The appliance store then is able to remove the dishwasher if the buyer defaults in his payments. The store could be liable, however, to third parties such as prior real estate mortgagees for any damage removal of the dishwasher caused to the real estate. The rules governing security interests in personal property that will become fixtures are explained more fully in Chapter 29.

Rights and Interests in Real Property

When we think of real property ownership, we normally envision one person owning all of the rights in a particular piece of land. Real property, however, involves a bundle of rights subject to ownership—sometimes by different people. This discussion examines the most common forms of present *possessory interests* (rights to exclusive possession of real property): *fee simple absolute* and *life estate*. It also explores the ways in which two or more persons may share ownership of a possessory interest. Finally, it discusses the interests and rights one may have in another person's real property, such as the right to use the property or restrict the way the owner uses it.

Estates in Land   The term **estate** is used to describe the nature of a person's ownership interest in real property. Estates in land are classified as either **freehold estates** or **nonfreehold estates.** Nonfreehold (or leasehold) estates are those held by persons who lease real property. They will be discussed in the next chapter, which deals with landlord–tenant law. Freehold estates are ownership interests of uncertain duration. The most common types of freehold estates are fee simple absolute and life estates.

Fee Simple Absolute   The **fee simple absolute** is what we normally think of as "full ownership" of land. One who owns real property in fee simple absolute has the right to possess and use the property for an unlimited period of time, subject only to governmental regulations or private restrictions. She also has the unconditional power to dispose of the property during her lifetime or upon her death. A person who owns land in fee simple absolute may grant many rights to others without giving up ownership. For example, she may grant a mortgage on the property to a party who has loaned her money, lease the property to a tenant, or grant rights such as those to be discussed later in this section.

Life Estate   The property interest known as a **life estate** gives a person the right to possess and use property for a time measured by his or another person's lifetime. For example, if Haney has a life estate (measured by his life) in a tract of land known as Greenacre, he has the right to use Greenacre for the remainder of his life. At Haney's death, the property will revert to the person who conveyed the estate to him or will pass to some other designated person. Although a life tenant has the right to use the property, he is obligated not to commit acts that would result in permanent injury to the property.

Co-ownership of Real Property   Co-ownership of real property exists when two or more persons share the same ownership interest in certain property. The co-owners do not have separate rights to any portion of the real property; each has a share in the whole property. Seven types of co-ownership are recognized in the United States.

Tenancy in Common   Persons who own property under a **tenancy in common** have undivided interests in the property and equal rights to possess it. When property is transferred to two or more persons without specification of their co-ownership form, it is presumed that they acquire the property as tenants in common. The respective ownership interests of tenants in common may be, but need not be, equal. One tenant, for example, could have a two-thirds ownership interest in the property, with the other tenant having a one-third interest.

Each tenant in common has the right to possess and use the property. Individual tenants, however, cannot exclude the other tenants in common from also possessing and using the property. If the property is rented or otherwise produces income, each tenant is entitled to share in the income in proportion to her ownership share. Similarly, each tenant must pay her proportionate share of property taxes and necessary repair costs. If a tenant in sole possession of the property receives no rents or profits from the property, she is not required to pay rent to her cotenant unless her possession is adverse to or inconsistent with her cotenant's property interests.

A tenant in common may dispose of his interest in the property during life and at death. Similarly, his interest is subject to his creditors' claims. When a tenant dies, his interest passes to his heirs or, if he has made a will, to the person or persons specified in the will. Suppose Peterson and Sievers own Blackacre as tenants in common. Sievers dies, having executed a valid will in which he leaves his Blackacre interest to Johanns. In this situation, Peterson and Johanns become tenants in common.

Tenants in common may sever the cotenancy by agreeing to divide the property or, if they are unable to agree, by petitioning a court for *partition.* The court will physically divide the property if that is feasible, so that each tenant receives her proportionate share. If physical division is not feasible, the court will order that the property be sold and that the proceeds be appropriately divided.

Joint Tenancy A **joint tenancy** is created when equal interests in real property are conveyed to two or more persons by means of a document clearly specifying that they are to own the property as joint tenants. The rights of use, possession, contribution, and partition are the same for a joint tenancy as for a tenancy in common. The joint tenancy's distinguishing feature is that it gives the owners the **right of survivorship,** which means that upon the death of a joint tenant, the deceased tenant's interest automatically passes to the surviving joint tenant(s). The right of survivorship makes it easy for a person to transfer property at death without the need for a will. For example, Devaney and Osborne purchase Redacre and take title as joint tenants. At Devaney's death, his Redacre interest will pass to Osborne even if Devaney did not have a will setting forth such an intent. Moreover, even if Devaney had a will that purported to leave his Redacre interest to someone other than Osborne, the will's Redacre provision would be ineffective.

When the document of conveyance contains ambiguous language, a court may be faced with determining whether persons acquired ownership of real property as joint tenants or, instead, as tenants in common.

A joint tenant may mortgage, sell, or give away her interest in the property during her lifetime. Her interest in the property is subject to her creditors' claims. When a joint tenant transfers her interest, the joint tenancy is severed and a tenancy in common is created as to the share affected by the transaction. When a joint tenant sells her interest to a third person, the purchaser becomes a tenant in common with the remaining joint tenant(s).

Tenancy by the Entirety Approximately half of the states permit married couples to own real property under a **tenancy by the entirety.** This tenancy is essentially a joint tenancy with the added requirement that the owners be married. As does the joint tenancy, the tenancy by the entirety features the right of survivorship. Neither spouse can transfer the property by will if the other is still living. Upon the death of the husband or wife, the property passes automatically to the surviving spouse.[2]

A tenancy by the entirety cannot be severed by the act of only one of the parties. Neither spouse can transfer the property unless the other also signs the deed. Thus, a creditor of one tenant cannot claim an interest in that person's share of property held in tenancy by the entirety. Divorce, however, severs a tenancy by the entirety and transforms it into a tenancy in common. Figure 1 compares the features of tenancy in common, joint tenancy, and tenancy by the entirety.

Community Property A number of western and southern states recognize the **community property** system of co-ownership of property by married couples. This type of co-ownership assumes that marriage is a partnership in which each spouse contributes to the family's property base. Property acquired during the marriage through a spouse's industry or efforts is classified as *community* property. Each spouse has an equal interest in such property regardless of who produced or earned the property. Because each spouse has an equal share in community property, neither can convey community property without the other's joining in the transaction. Various community property states permit the parties to dispose of their interests in community property at death. The details of each state's community property system vary, depending on the specific provisions of that state's statutes.

Not all property owned by a married person is community property, however. Property a spouse owned before marriage or acquired during marriage by gift or inheritance is *separate* property. Neither spouse owns a legal interest in the other's separate property. Property exchanged for separate property also remains separately owned.

Tenancy in Partnership When a partnership takes title to property in the partnership's name, the co-ownership form is called **tenancy in partnership.** This form of co-ownership is discussed in Chapter 37.

Condominium Ownership Under condominium ownership, a purchaser takes title to her individual unit and becomes a tenant in common with other unit owners in shared facilities such as hallways, elevators, swimming pools, and parking areas. The condominium owner pays property taxes on her individual unit and makes a monthly

---

[2]In states that do not recognize the tenancy by the entirety, married couples often own real property in joint tenancy, but they are not required to elect that co-ownership form.

Figure 1   *Tenancy in Common, Joint Tenancy, and Tenancy by the Entirety*

	Tenancy in Common	Joint Tenancy	Tenancy by the Entirety
Equal Possession and Use?	Yes	Yes	Yes
Share Income?	Yes	Yes	Presumably
Contribution Requirement?	Generally	Generally	Generally
Free Conveyance of Interest?	Yes; transferee becomes tenant in common	Yes, but joint tenancy is severed on conveyance and reverts to tenancy in common	Both must agree; divorce severs tenancy
Effect of Death?	Interest transferable at death by will or inheritance	Right of survivorship; surviving joint tenant takes decedent's share	Right of survivorship; surviving spouse takes decedent's share

payment for the maintenance of the common areas. She may generally mortgage or sell her unit without the other unit owners' approval. For federal income tax purposes, the condominium owner is treated as if she owned a single-family home, and is thus allowed to deduct her property taxes and mortgage interest expenses.

Cooperative Ownership In a cooperative, a building is owned by a corporation or group of persons. One who wants to buy an apartment in the building purchases stock in the corporation and holds his apartment under a long-term, renewable lease called a *proprietary lease.* Frequently, the cooperative owner must obtain the other owners' approval to sell or sublease his unit.

Interests in Real Property Owned by Others

In various situations, a person may hold a legally protected interest in someone else's real property. Such interests, to be discussed below, are not possessory because they do not give their holder the right to complete dominion over the land. Rather, they give him the right to use another person's property or to limit the way in which the owner uses the property.

Easements

An **easement** is the right to make certain uses of another person's property (*affirmative easement*) or the right to prevent another person from making certain uses of his own property (*negative easement*). The right to run a sewer line across someone else's property would be an affirmative easement. Suppose an easement prevents Rogers from erecting, on his land, a structure that would block his neighbor McFeely's solar collector. Such an easement would be negative in nature.

If an easement qualifies as an **easement appurtenant,** it will pass with the land. This means that if the owner of the land benefited by an easement appurtenant sells or otherwise conveys the property, the new owner also acquires the right contemplated by the easement. An easement appurtenant is primarily designed to benefit a certain tract of land, rather than merely giving an individual a personal right. For example, Agnew and Nixon are next-door neighbors. They share a common driveway that runs along the borderline of their respective properties. Each has an easement in the portion of the driveway that lies on the other's property. If Agnew sells his property to Ford, Ford also obtains the easement in the driveway portion on Nixon's land. Nixon, of course, still has an easement in the driveway portion on Ford's land.

Creation of Easements

Easements may be acquired in the following ways:

1. *By grant.* When an owner of property expressly provides an easement to another while retaining ownership of the property, he is said to **grant** an easement. For example, Monroe may sell or give Madison, who owns adjoining property, the right to go across Monroe's land to reach an alley behind that land.

2. *By reservation.* When one transfers ownership of her land but retains the right to use it for some specified purpose, she is said to **reserve** an easement in the land. For example, Smythe sells land to Jones but reserves the mineral rights to the property as well as an easement to enter the land to remove the minerals.

3. *By prescription.* An easement by **prescription** is created when one person uses another's land openly, continuously, and in a manner adverse to the owner's rights for a period of time specified by state statute. The necessary period of time varies from state to state. In such a situation, the property owner presumably is on notice that someone else is acting as if she possesses rights to use the property. If the property owner does not take action during the statutory period to stop the other person from making use of his property, he may lose his right to stop that use. Suppose, for instance, that State X allows easements by prescription to be obtained through 15 years of prescriptive use. Tara, who lives in State X, uses the driveway of her next-door neighbor, Kyle. Tara does this openly, on a daily basis, and without Kyle's permission. If this use by Tara continues for the 15-year period established by statute and Kyle takes no action to stop Tara within that time span, Tara will obtain an easement by prescription. In that event, Tara will have the right to use the driveway not only while Kyle owns the property but also when Kyle sells the property to another party. Easements by prescription resemble *adverse possession,* a concept discussed later in this chapter.

4. *By implication.* Sometimes, easements are implied by the nature of the transaction rather than created by express agreement of the parties. Such easements, called **easements by implication,** take either of two forms: easements by prior use and easements by necessity.

An *easement by prior use* may be created when land is subdivided and a path, road, or other apparent and beneficial use exists as of the time that a portion of the land is conveyed to another person. In this situation, the new owner of the conveyed portion of the land has an easement to continue using the path, road, or other prior use running across the nonconveyed portion of the land. Assume, for example, that a private road runs through Greenacre from north to south, linking the house located on Greenacre's northern portion to the public highway that lies south of Greenacre. Douglas, the owner of Greenacre, sells the northern portion to Kimball. On these facts, Kimball has an easement by implication to continue using the private road even where it runs across the portion of Greenacre retained by Douglas. To prevent such an easement from arising, Douglas and Kimball would need to have specified in their contract of sale that the easement would not exist.

An *easement by necessity* is created when real property once held in common ownership is subdivided in such a fashion that the only reasonable way a new owner can gain access to her land is through passage over another's land that was once part of the same tract. Such an easement is based on the necessity of obtaining access to property. Assume, for instance, that Tinker, the owner of Blackacre, sells Blackacre's northern 25 acres to Evers and its southern 25 acres to Chance. In order to have any reasonable access to her property, Chance must use a public road that runs alongside and just beyond the northern border of the land now owned by Evers; Chance must then go across Evers's property to reach hers. On these facts, Chance is entitled to an easement by necessity to cross Evers's land in order to go to and from her property.

Easements and the Statute of Frauds As interests in land, easements are potentially within the coverage of the statute of frauds. To be enforceable, an express agreement granting or reserving an easement must be evidenced by a suitable writing signed by the party to be charged.[3] An express grant of an easement normally must be executed with the same formalities observed in executing the grant of a fee simple interest. However, easements not granted expressly (such as easements by prior use, necessity, or prescription) are enforceable despite the lack of a writing.

Profits

A **profit** is a right to enter another person's land and remove some product or part of the land. Timber, gravel, minerals, and oil are among the products and parts frequently made the subject of profits. Generally governed by the same rules applicable to easements, profits are sometimes called *easements with a profit.*

Licenses

A **license** is a temporary right to enter another's land for a specific purpose. Ordinarily, licenses are more informal than easements. Licenses may be created orally or in any other manner indicating the landowner's permission for the licensee to enter the property. Because licenses are considered to be personal rights, they are not true interests in land. The licensor normally may revoke a license at his will. Exceptions to this general rule of revocability arise when the license is coupled with an interest (such as the licensee's ownership of personal property located on the licensor's land) or when the licensee has paid money or provided something else of value either for the license or in reliance on its existence. For example, Branch pays Leif $900 for certain trees on Leif's land. Branch is to dig up the trees and haul them to her own property for transplanting. Branch has an irrevocable license to enter Leif's land to dig up and haul away the trees.

Restrictive Covenants

Within certain limitations, real estate owners may create enforceable agreements that restrict the use of real property. These private

---

[3]Chapter 16 discusses the statute of frauds and compliance with the writing requirement it imposes when it is applicable.

agreements are called **restrictive covenants.** For example, Grant owns two adjacent lots. She sells one to Lee subject to the parties' agreement that Lee will not operate any liquor-selling business on the property. This use restriction appears in the deed Grant furnishes Lee. As another illustration, a subdivision developer sells lots in the subdivision and places a provision in each lot's deed regarding the minimum size of house to be built on the property.

The validity and enforceability of such private restrictions on the use of real property depend on the purpose, nature, and scope of the restrictions. A restraint that violates a statute or other expression of public policy will not be enforced. For example, the federal Fair Housing Act (discussed later in this chapter) would make unlawful an attempt by a seller or lessor of residential property to refuse to sell or rent to certain persons because of an existing restrictive covenant that purports to disqualify those prospective buyers or renters on the basis of their race, color, religion, sex, handicap, familial status, or national origin.

Public policy generally favors the unlimited use and transfer of land. A restrictive covenant therefore is unenforceable if it effectively prevents the sale or transfer of the property. Similarly, ambiguous language in a restrictive covenant is construed in favor of the less restrictive interpretation. A restraint is enforceable, however, if it is clearly expressed and neither unduly restrictive of the use and transfer of the property nor otherwise violative of public policy. Restrictions usually held enforceable include those relating to minimum lot size, building design and size, and maintenance of an area as a residential community.

An important and frequently arising question is whether subsequent owners of property are bound by a restrictive covenant even though they were not parties to the original agreement that established the covenant. Under certain circumstances, restrictive covenants are said to "run with the land" and thus bind subsequent owners of the restricted property. For a covenant to run with the land, it must have been *binding* on the original parties to it, and those parties must have *intended that the covenant bind their successors.* The covenant must also *"touch and concern"* the restricted land. This means that the covenant must involve the use, value, or character of the land, rather than being merely a personal obligation of one of the original parties. The *Gardner* case, which follows, involves the analysis of whether a restrictive covenant runs with the land. In addition, a covenant will not bind a subsequent purchaser unless she had notice of the covenant's existence when she took her interest. This notice would commonly be provided by the recording of the deed (a subject discussed later in this chapter) or other document containing the covenant.

Restrictive covenants may be enforced by the parties to them, by persons meant to benefit from them, and—if the covenants run with the land—by successors of the original parties to them. If restrictive covenants amounting to a general building scheme are contained in a subdivision plat (recorded description of a subdivision), property owners in the subdivision may be able to enforce them against noncomplying property owners.

Gardner v. Jefferys   2005 Vt. LEXIS 86 (Vt. Sup. Ct. 2005)

In 1957, William Jefferys Jr. and his wife, Ena, the parents of William Jefferys III, purchased approximately 200 acres of farm land in Fayston, Vermont, known as the Strong Farm. Beginning in 1966, the elderly Jefferys began selling off parcels of the farm. In 1969, Sheldon and Carin Gardner purchased a 10-acre parcel of undeveloped land from the Jefferys. The deed contains a restrictive covenant providing that a specified part of the premises "shall forever be and remain open and free of all buildings and structures, except the right to construct on said open land a private swimming pool, and/or tennis court, and, the usual fences and structures appurtenant thereto and such other buildings and structures as meet the approval, in writing of the Grantors herein, their heirs and assigns." The provision further states that rights secured therein are "to be enjoyed by the Grantors, their heirs and assigns." In 1975, the Jefferys conveyed a five-acre parcel of land to Karin Souminen, who, in turn, sold the parcel to George and Janice Soules in 1987. The Soules built a house on the land and lived there. Their property is located above the Gardners' land. In 1979, the elderly Jefferys conveyed the remainder of their Fayston property to their son, William Jefferys III, and his wife, Susan.

In the late summer and early fall of 1999, the Gardners wrote to William and Susan Jefferys twice requesting approval to build a two-story structure within the area restricted by the covenant. The Jefferys gave the Soules a copy of the request. In June 2000, the Soules wrote the Gardners a letter stating that they were interested parties to the restrictive covenant. In September 2000, the Gardners filed a declaratory judgment action asking the court to determine the effect of the restrictive covenant in their deed. The Soules filed a counterclaim. In May 2001, the Gardners began building a shed in the restricted area. Shortly thereafter, the superior court granted the Soules' request for a preliminary injunction stopping the construction. In the fall of 2001, the Gardners began planting white pines in the restricted area directly in the Soules' view.

In July 2003, the superior court ruled that the benefit of the restrictive covenant ran with the land and was enforceable by both the Soules and the Jefferys, and that the Gardners had violated the covenant by beginning construction of the proposed shed and by planting trees in the restricted area. Accordingly, the court enjoined the continued existence of the shed and the trees. Further, the court prohibited the Gardners from allowing plants or crops in the restricted area to exceed six feet in height. The Gardners appealed.

Per Curiam

On appeal, Sheldon Gardner first contends that the restrictive covenant does not run with the land to the benefit of the Soules because the parties intended the covenant to bind only the grantors, their heirs and assigns, and neither the Soules nor the Jefferys are heirs or assigns of the grantors. We do not find this argument persuasive. Four requirements must be met for a restrictive covenant to "run with the land" so that successor property owners may enforce its burdens and benefits: (1) the covenant must be in writing; (2) the parties to the covenant must have intended that the covenant run with the land; (3) the covenant must "touch and concern" the land; and (4) privity of estate must exist between the parties.

Gardner argues only that the second requirement is not met in this case. Intent that a restrictive covenant is to run with the land may be either express or implied, and may be shown by extraneous circumstances. In some instances, a covenant is so intimately connected with the land as to require the conclusion that the necessary intention for the running of the benefit is present absent language clearly negating that intent. For example, we have held that a covenant prohibiting placing a particular type of structure on a property is such a restriction. Indeed, unless the terms of a restrictive covenant provide otherwise, when a property benefited by a restrictive covenant is divided into separately owned parcels, "each separately owned parcel is entitled to enforce [the] . . . covenant benefiting the property." *Restatement (Third) of the Law of Property* § 5.7(2) (2000).

Here, Gardner argues that the restrictive covenant in his deed does not run with the land because it expressly benefits only the grantors and their heirs and assigns, thereby implying an intent not to allow the covenant to be enforced by successors to the land who are not heirs or assigns. Gardner further states that neither the Soules' deed nor the Jefferys' deed includes an assignment from the elderly Jefferys, and that the Jefferys are not heirs because Ena Jefferys is still alive, and they did not obtain the land through inheritance. According to Gardner, they would never have purchased the property with the restrictive covenant if they thought that an indefinite number of successors could dictate how they used their property.

We conclude that the record in this case overwhelmingly demonstrates that the parties intended the restrictive covenant to run with the land. The testimony of several witnesses, including Ena Jefferys, unequivocally demonstrated that the covenant was intended to keep the restricted area, which had always been an open meadow, "forever" open and free of any obstructions that would diminish the view from the grantors' remaining lands located above the meadow. Moreover, the record, including evidence of negotiations surrounding the covenant and of the Gardners' subsequent conduct, demonstrates that the Gardners were aware of this intent. Notwithstanding Gardner's argument to the contrary, use of the term "assigns" rather than "successors" does not suggest that the parties intended to preclude subsequent owners of the dominant estate from enforcing the covenant. To the contrary, it is well settled that where a restrictive covenant contains words of succession, i.e., heirs and assigns, a presumption is created that the parties intended the restrictive covenant to run with the land.

Next, Gardner argues that the superior court erred by construing the restrictive covenant to prohibit him from planting trees in the restricted area, and that, by doing so, the court imposed a burden on his property greater than that imposed by the restrictive covenant. We disagree. We conclude that both the language of the covenant and evidence of the circumstances surrounding the making of the covenant support the court's determination. The word "open" refers to the land that had historically been maintained as an open field. The question, then, is what the parties meant by "open." The record demonstrates that most of the restricted area had been mowed or hayed for several decades or more when the restrictive covenant was signed. Ena Jefferys, one of the original grantors, testified that she always assumed that the phrase "open and free of all buildings and structures" meant that nothing would interfere with the view, which was "everything up there" and the reason why people bought property there. Indeed, Gardner himself acknowledged that he bought his property, at least in part, for the view, and that the word "open" in the covenant did not necessarily refer to buildings and structures. In short, there was overwhelming evidence that the intent underlying the restrictive covenant at issue here was to maintain the restricted area as an open meadow, thereby allowing unobstructed views to the south for the benefit of adjoining neighbors.

Affirmed in favor of the Jefferys and Soules.

Termination of Restrictive Covenants Restrictive covenants may be terminated in a variety of ways, including voluntary relinquishment or *waiver*. They may also be terminated *by their own terms* (such as when the covenant specifies that it is to exist for a certain length of time) or *by dramatically changed circumstances*. If Oldcodger's property is subject, for instance, to a restrictive covenant allowing only residential use, the fact that all of the surrounding property has come to be used for industrial purposes may operate to terminate the covenant. When a restrictive covenant has been terminated or held invalid, the deed containing the restriction remains a valid instrument of transfer but is treated as if the restriction had been removed from the document.

Acquisition of Real Property

Title to real property may be obtained in various ways, including purchase, gift, will or inheritance, tax sale, and adverse possession. Original title to land in the United States was acquired either from the federal government or from a country that held the land prior to its acquisition by the United States. The land in the 13 original colonies had been granted by the king of England either to the colonies or to certain individuals. The states ceded the land in the Northwest Territory to the federal government, which in turn issued grants or patents of land. Original ownership of much of the land in Florida and the Southwest came by grants from Spain's rulers.

Acquisition by Purchase Selling one's real property is a basic ownership right. Unreasonable restrictions on an owner's right to sell her property are considered unenforceable because they violate public policy. Most owners of real property acquired title by purchasing the property. Each state sets the requirements for proper conveyances of real property located in that state. The various elements of selling and buying real property are discussed later in this chapter.

Acquisition by Gift Real property ownership may be acquired by gift. For a gift of real property to be valid, the donor must deliver a properly executed deed to the donee or to some third person who is to hold it for the donee. Neither the donee nor the third person needs to take actual possession of the property. The gift's essential element is delivery of the deed. Suppose that Fields executes a deed to the family farm and leaves it in his safe-deposit box for delivery to his daughter (the intended donee) when he dies. The attempted gift will not be valid, because Fields did not deliver the gift during his lifetime.

Acquisition by Will or Inheritance The owner of real property generally has the right to dispose of the property by will. The requirements for a valid will are discussed in Chapter 26. If the owner of real property dies without a valid will, the property passes to his heirs as determined under the laws of the state in which the property is located.

Acquisition by Tax Sale If taxes assessed on real property are not paid when due, they become a *lien* on the property. This lien has priority over other claims to the land. If the taxes remain unpaid, the government may sell the land at a tax sale. Although the purchaser at the tax sale acquires title to the property, a number of states have statutes giving the original owner a limited time (such as a year) within which to buy the property from the tax sale purchaser for the price paid by the purchaser, plus interest.

Acquisition by Adverse Possession

Each state has a statute of limitations that gives an owner of land a specific number of years within which to bring suit to regain possession of her land from someone who is trespassing on it. This period varies from state to state, generally ranging from 5 to 20 years. If someone wrongfully possesses land and acts as if he were the owner, the actual owner must take steps to have the possessor ejected from the land. If the owner fails to do this within the statutory period, she loses her right to eject the possessor.

Assume, for example, that Titus owns a vacant lot next to Holdeman's house. Holdeman frequently uses the vacant lot for a variety of activities and appears to be the property's only user. In addition, Holdeman regularly mows and otherwise maintains the vacant lot. He has also placed a fence around it. By continuing such actions and thus staying in possession of Titus's property for the statutory period (and by meeting each other requirement about to be discussed), Holdeman may position himself to acquire title to the land by **adverse possession.**

To acquire title by adverse possession, one must possess land in a manner that puts the true owner on notice of the owner's cause of action against the possessor. The adverse possessor's acts of possession must be (1) *open,* (2) *actual,* (3) *continuous,* (4) *exclusive,* and (5) *hostile* (or adverse) *to the owner's rights*. The hostility element is not a matter of subjective intent. Rather, it means that the adverse possessor's acts of possession must be inconsistent with the owner's rights. If a person is in possession of another's property under a lease, as a cotenant, or with the permission of the owner, his possession is not hostile.

In some states, the possessor of land must also pay the property taxes in order to gain title by adverse possession.

It is not necessary that the same person occupy the land for the statutory period. The periods of possession of several adverse possessors may be "tacked" together when calculating the period of possession if each possessor claimed rights from another possessor. The possession must, however, be continuous for the requisite time.

The following *Schlichting* case applies these criteria for adverse possession.

Schlichting v. Cotter
2007 Conn. Super. LEXIS 461 (Conn. Super. Ct. 2007)

Angela Schlichting and her husband Walter acquired title to a piece of real estate in 1979. They had a cordial, neighborly relationship with their adjoining property owners, Fethon and Dorothy Nitsos. There had been no survey of the boundaries of the two properties, but it was believed that a certain section of the woods between the two houses contained the boundary line. The Schlichtings took care of an area that they believed was theirs. In 1993, Walter conveyed his interest in the Schlichtings' property to Angela. In 2005, the Nitsos conveyed their property to the Cotters. A dispute arose between Angela and the Cotters about whether Angela was encroaching on the Cotters property. The Cotters cut down trees, removed part of a stone wall, dug up the lawn, cut up the driveway, erected a fence, and otherwise disturbed part of the property that Angela claimed as hers. Angela applied for a temporary injunction against the Cotters.

Moraghan, Judge Trial Referee

Essentially, the elements of adverse possession are rather simple and uncomplicated. They are that the owners shall be ousted from possession and kept out uninterruptedly for a period of fifteen years under a claim of right by an open, visible and exclusive possession of the claimant without license or consent of the owner. At this point there seems to be little question that the "mutual agreement" non-memorialized and not marked with any type of surveying device was the product of a mutual mistake. In order to comprehend the concept of adverse possession, it might be appropriate to discuss and, to a degree, analyze the hostility of the taking.

> *Powell on Real Property,* Sec. 91.05 et seq. In order to establish adverse possession, the possession must be openly hostile. Hostile possession can be understood as possession that is opposed and antagonistic to all other claims, and that conveys the clear message that the possessor intends to possess the land as his or her own. . . . It is not necessary that the possessor intend to take away from the true owner something which he knows belongs to another, or even that he be indifferent as to the facts of the legal title. It is the intent to possess, and not the intent to take irrespective of his right, which governs.

The word "hostile," as employed in the law of adverse possession, is a term of art; it does not imply animosity, ill will or bad faith. Nor is the claimant required to make express declarations of adverse intent during the possessory period. "Hostile" use has been defined as use that is "inconsistent with the right of the owner, without permission asked or given, [to] use such as would entitle the owner to a cause of action against the intruder."

The modern position of American courts is that possession of land under the mistaken belief of legal ownership usually satisfies the hostility requirements, as long as the possessor does not hold in subordination to another and has no conscious doubt as to his or her rights. A large number of adverse possession disputes involve a mistaken belief on the part of a landowner as to the true boundary line between adjoining properties.

An occupation of land by a defendant as his own under an "owner" plaintiff's eye to what is supposed to be the dividing line between him and the "owner" plaintiff and which for many years the "owner" plaintiff permitted without any question challenging such action which flows from the mutual assent of the parties is strong presumptive evidence of the true place of the line. The very act itself has to be an assertion of his own title and thus equivalent to a denial of the title of all others and it does not matter that he was mistaken and if he had been better informed he would not have entered upon the land.

The testimony at trial and as set forth in the Nitsos' deposition clearly shows the Schlichtings continuously used the disputed area as their own from 1979 to March of 2006 in many ways in an open and visible fashion. Open and visible possession is a use calculated to let others know that the land is owned and occupied by the claimant. The use must be notorious and unconcealed so as to give the owner or any other claimant knowledge and the full opportunity to assert his rights, if any.

With respect to the open and visible ouster of the defendants there seems to be no evidence that contradicts Mrs. Nitsos concerning the action between 1979 and 2006. Suffice it to say that the fifteen-year limitation is satisfied. Use by the plaintiff in an open and visible possession consisted of spraying, pruning and removal of trees; planting and maintenance of pachysandra, German ferns, berry bushes, rhododendron; removal of poison ivy from the trees and the removal of sumac from the foliage in the area; utilization of gypsy moth traps and spraying; and the dumping, blowing and raking of leaves; the mowing and fertilizing and maintenance of the lawn area; the planting, cultivating and maintenance of the garden; and the paving, plowing, sealing and use of the driveway from 1979 to 2006 to the exclusion of others was open and notorious and put the Nitsos on notice that the property area was being occupied by the Schlichtings. Generally speaking, exclusive possession can and more often than not will be established by acts which at the time considering the state of the land comport with ownership, dominion and control such acts as would ordinarily be exercised by an owner in appropriating land to his own use to the exclusion of others.

Testimony unrefuted shows the Schlichtings maintained that they exclusively used up to the middle of the wooded area, and Mrs. Nitsos also testified that the Schlichtlings used that area exclusively as their own. There is a pond behind these two adjoining lots which was certainly attractive to children in terms of skating at least. The Nitsos would call the Schlichtings each time that one of their children or children's guests wanted to go skating. Permission was never denied but permission was always sought and granted. The reason for that was that the area behind the Nitsos' property tended to be swampy and muddy and the area behind the Schlichtings' property was more solid, less difficult to walk in and generally a cleaner path to the pond. The attitude of the abutting neighbor who enjoyed a friendly neighborly relationship with the Schlichtings lends strength to the recognition of the fact that they recognized the plaintiffs as the owners of the property.

The court finds by clear and convincing evidence that the plaintiff has proven her claim for adverse possession and is entitled to the property which she claims. The defendants are ordered to remove their fence, their piles of stone and to replace the ground cover and flowering bushes and shrubs and wall that they have destroyed within sixty (60) days of the date of this decision.

Judgment for Schlichtling.

Transfer by Sale

Steps in a Sale
The major steps normally involved in the sale of real property are:

1. Contracting with a real estate broker to locate a buyer.

2. Negotiating and signing a contract of sale.

3. Arranging for the financing of the purchase and satisfying other requirements, such as having a survey conducted or acquiring title insurance.

4. Closing the sale, which involves payment of the purchase price and transfer of the deed, as well as other matters.

5. Recording the deed.

LOG ON

For a variety of articles about practical aspects of buying, selling, or owning real estate, see Nolo.com Real Estate Law Center at **www.nolo.com/resource .cfm/catID/912DD28B-1329-4CEB-9E4FF25438CB52DF/ 213/243/217/.**

Contracting with a Real Estate Broker
Although engaging a real estate broker is not a legal requirement for the sale of real property, it is common for one who wishes to sell his property to "list" the property with a broker. A listing contract empowers the broker to act as the seller's agent in procuring a ready, willing, and able buyer and in managing details of the property transfer. A number of states' statutes of frauds require listing contracts to be evidenced by a writing and signed by the party to be charged.

Real estate brokers are regulated by state and federal law. They owe *fiduciary duties* (duties of trust and confidence) to their clients. Chapter 35 contains additional information regarding the duties imposed on such agents.

Types of Listing Contracts Listing contracts specify such matters as the listing period's duration, the terms on which the seller will sell, and the amount and terms of the broker's commission. There are different types of listing contracts.

1. *Open listing.* Under an open listing contract, the broker receives a *nonexclusive* right to sell the property. This means that the seller and third parties (for example, other brokers) also are entitled to find a buyer for the property.

The broker operating under an open listing is entitled to a commission only if he was the first to find a ready, willing, and able buyer.

2. *Exclusive agency listing.* Under an exclusive agency listing, the broker earns a commission if he *or any other agent* finds a ready, willing, and able buyer during the period of time specified in the contract. Thus, the broker operating under such a listing would have the right to a commission even if another broker actually procured the buyer. Under the exclusive agency listing, however, the seller has the right to sell the property himself without being obligated to pay the broker a commission.

3. *Exclusive right to sell.* An exclusive right to sell contract provides the broker the exclusive right to sell the property for a specified period of time and entitles her to a commission no matter who procured the buyer. Under this type of listing, a seller must pay the broker her commission even if it was the seller or some third party who found the buyer during the duration of the listing contract.

Contract of Sale

The contract formation, performance, assignment, and remedies principles about which you read in earlier chapters apply to real estate sales contracts. Such contracts identify the parties and subject property, and set forth the purchase price, the type of deed the purchaser will receive, the items of personal property (if any) included in the sale, and other important aspects of the parties' transaction. Real estate sales contracts often make the closing of the sale contingent on the buyer's obtaining financing at a specified rate of interest, on the seller's procurement of a survey and title insurance, and on the property's passing a termite inspection. Because they are within the statute of frauds, real estate sales contracts must be evidenced by a suitable writing signed by the party to be charged in order to be enforceable.

Financing the Purchase

The various arrangements for financing the purchase of real property—such as mortgages, land contracts, and deeds of trust—are discussed in Chapter 28.

Fair Housing Act

The Fair Housing Act, enacted by Congress in 1968 and substantially revised in 1988, is designed to prevent discrimination in the housing market. Its provisions apply to real estate brokers, sellers (other than those selling their own single-family dwellings without the use of a broker), lenders, lessors, and appraisers. Originally, the act prohibited discrimination on the basis of race, color, religion, sex, and national origin. The 1988 amendments added handicap and "familial status" to this list. The familial status category was intended to prevent discrimination in the housing market against pregnant women and families with children.[4] "Adult" or "senior citizen" communities restricting residents' age do not violate the Fair Housing Act even though they exclude families with children, so long as the housing meets the requirements of the act's "housing for older persons" exemption.[5]

The act prohibits discrimination on the above-listed bases in a wide range of matters relating to the sale or rental of housing. These matters include refusals to sell or rent, representations that housing is not available for sale or rental when in fact it is, and discriminatory actions regarding terms, conditions, or privileges of sale or rental or regarding the provision of services and facilities involved in sale or rental.[6] The act also prohibits discrimination in connection with brokerage services, appraisals, and financing of dwellings.

Prohibited discrimination on the basis of handicap includes refusals to permit a handicapped person to make (at his own expense) reasonable modifications to the property. It also includes refusals to make reasonable accommodations in property-related rules, policies, practices, or services when such modifications or accommodations are necessary to afford the handicapped person full enjoyment of the property. The act also outlaws the building of multifamily housing that is inaccessible to persons with handicaps.

A violation of the Fair Housing Act may result in a civil action brought by the government or the aggrieved individual. If the aggrieved individual sues and prevails, the court may issue injunctions, award actual and punitive damages, assess attorney's fees and costs, and grant other appropriate relief. Finally, the Fair Housing Act invalidates any state or municipal law requiring or permitting an action that would be a discriminatory housing practice under federal law.

---

[4]"Familial status" is defined as an individual or individuals under the age of 18 who is/are domiciled with a parent, some other person who has custody over him/her/them, or the designee of the parent or custodial individual. The familial status classification also applies to one who is pregnant or in the process of attempting to secure custody of a child or children under the age of 18.

[5]The Fair Housing Act defines "housing for older persons" as housing provided under any state or federal program found by the Secretary of HUD to be specifically designed to assist elderly persons, housing intended for and solely occupied by persons 62 years old or older, or housing that meets the requirements of federal regulations and is intended for occupancy by at least one person 55 years old or older.

[6]Chapter 25 discusses the Fair Housing Act's application to rentals of residential property.

CYBERLAW IN ACTION

How does the Fair Housing Act apply to Web sites that permit users to post advertisements about the sale or rental of real estate? Advertisements about property for sale or lease that are posted by individuals sometimes make statements indicating a "preference, limitation, or discrimination, or an intention to make a preference, limitations, or discrimination, on the basis of race, color, national origin, sex, religion, and familial status" that could violate the Fair Housing Act if the statements were made offline. For example, in *Chicago Lawyers' Committee for Civil Rights under the Law, Inc. v. Craigslist, Inc.*, 519 F.3d 666 (7th Cir. 2008), the plaintiff alleged that Craigslist.com posted notices in violation of the Fair Housing Act such as "Apt. too small for families with small children," "NO MINORITIES," and "Christian single straight female needed." The content of advertisements on the Web site is created by Craigslist.com users, not by Craigslist, Inc. This is a legally significant point, because a federal statute, § 230 of the Communications Decency Act, states that "No provider or user of an interactive computer service shall be treated as the publisher or speaker of any information provided by another information content provider." This statute has been interpreted in many cases to immunize Web sites, ISPs, and other interactive computer services for liability for third-party content. In the *Craigslist* case, the Seventh Circuit held that under § 230 of the Communications Decency Act, Craigslist could not be treated as the publisher of information provided by others and, therefore, that § 230 shielded Craigslist from liability.

In *Fair Housing Council of San Fernando Valley v. Roommate.com, LLC,* 521 F.3d 1157 (9th Cir. 2008), however, the Ninth Circuit held that § 230 of the Communications Decency Act immunized Roommate for some but not all of its activities. Roommate.com operates a roommate-matching Web site. Prior to searching or posting listings, subscribers were required to disclose their sex, sexual orientation, and to indicate whether children would live with them. Subscribers also described their preferences in roommates with regard to the same three criteria and were encouraged to provide additional comments. Roommate.com would then compile information provided in the questionnaires into a profile for each user, which would be used to match subscribers with listings and which could be viewed by other subscribers. The plaintiffs alleged that these practices constituted Fair Housing Act violations. The Ninth Circuit emphasized that § 230 provides a shield for an interactive computer service for content created by third parties, but not for content developed by the interactive computer service itself. It characterized Roommate.com's creation and required use of the questionnaires as being "entirely its own" and the profiles created and displayed from the information provided in the questionnaire as information developed by Roommate.com. Since these practices involved content developed by Roommate.com and not a third party, they were not shielded from potential Fair Housing Act liability. However, § 230 did immunize Roommate.com from liability for discriminatory content authored by subscribers in the open-ended "additional comments" section of the questionnaire.

Deeds Each state's statutes set out the formalities necessary to accomplish a valid conveyance of land. As a general rule, a valid conveyance is brought about by the execution and delivery of a **deed,** a written instrument that transfers title from one person (the grantor) to another (the grantee). Three types of deeds are in general use in the United States: *quitclaim deeds, warranty deeds,* and *deeds of bargain and sale* (also called *grant deeds*). The precise rights contemplated by a deed depend on the type of deed the parties have used.

Quitclaim Deeds A **quitclaim deed** conveys whatever title the grantor has at the time he executes the deed. It does not, however, contain warranties of title. The grantor who executes a quitclaim deed does not claim to have good title—or any title, for that matter. The grantee has no action against the grantor under a quitclaim deed if the grantee does not acquire good title. Quitclaim

deeds are frequently used to cure technical defects in the chain of title to property.

Warranty Deeds A **warranty deed,** unlike a quitclaim deed, contains covenants of warranty. Besides conveying title to the property, the grantor who executes a warranty deed guarantees the title she has conveyed. There are two types of warranty deeds.

1. *General warranty deed.* Under a general warranty deed, the grantor warrants against (and agrees to defend against) all title defects and encumbrances (such as liens and easements), including those that arose before the grantor received her title.

2. *Special warranty deed.* Under a special warranty deed, the grantor warrants against (and agrees to defend against) title defects and encumbrances that arose after she acquired the property. If the property conveyed is subject to an encumbrance such as a mortgage, a long-term lease, or an easement, the grantor frequently provides a special warranty deed that contains a provision excepting those specific encumbrances from the warranty.

Deeds of Bargain and Sale In a **deed of bargain and sale** (also known as a **grant deed**), the grantor makes no covenants. The grantor uses language such as "I grant" or "I bargain and sell" or "I convey" property. Such a deed does contain, however, the grantor's implicit representation that he owns the land and has not previously encumbered it or conveyed it to another party.

Form and Execution of Deed
Some states' statutes suggest a form for deeds. Although the requirements for execution of deeds are not uniform, they do follow a similar pattern. As a general rule, a deed states the *name of the grantee,* contains a *recitation of consideration and a description of the property conveyed,* and is *signed by the grantor.* Most states require that the deed be notarized (acknowledged by the grantor before a notary public or other authorized officer) in order to be eligible for recording in public records.

No technical words of conveyance are necessary for a valid deed. Any language is sufficient if it indicates with reasonable certainty the grantor's intent to transfer ownership of the property. The phrases "grant, bargain, and sell" and "convey and warrant" are commonly used. Deeds contain recitations of consideration primarily for historical reasons. The consideration recited is not necessarily the purchase price of the property. Deeds often state that the consideration for the conveyance is "one dollar and other valuable consideration."

The property conveyed must be described in such a manner that it can be identified. This usually means that the legal description of the property must be used. Several methods of legal description are used in the United States. In urban areas, descriptions are usually by lot, block, and plat. In rural areas where the land has been surveyed by the government, property is usually described by reference to the government survey. It may also be described by a metes and bounds description that specifies the boundaries of the tract of land.

Recording Deeds
Delivery of a valid deed conveys title from a grantor to a grantee. Even so, the grantee should promptly **record** the deed in order to prevent his interest from being defeated by third parties who may claim interests in the property. The grantee must pay a fee to have the deed recorded, a process that involves depositing and indexing the deed in the files of a government office designated by state law. A recorded deed operates to provide the public at large with notice of the grantee's property interest.

Recording Statutes Each state has a **recording statute** that establishes a system for the recording of all transactions affecting real property ownership. These statutes are not uniform in their provisions. In general, however, they provide for the recording of all deeds, mortgages, land contracts, and similar documents.

Types of Recording Statutes State recording statutes also provide for priority among competing claimants to rights in real property, in case conflicting rights or interests in property should be deeded to (or otherwise claimed by) more than one person. (Obviously, a grantor has no right to issue two different grantees separate deeds to the same property, but if this should occur, recording statutes provide rules to decide which grantee has superior title.) These priority rules apply only to grantees who have given value for their deeds or other interest-creating documents (primarily purchasers and lenders), and not to donees. A given state's recording law will set up one of three basic types of priority systems: race statutes, notice statutes, and race-notice statutes. Figure 2 explains these priority systems. Although the examples used in Figure 2 deal with recorded and unrecorded deeds, recording statutes apply to other documents that create interests in real estate. Chapter 28 discusses the recording of mortgages, as well as the adverse security interest–related consequences a mortgagee may experience if its mortgage goes unrecorded.

Methods of Assuring Title
In purchasing real property, the buyer is really acquiring the seller's ownership interests. Because the buyer does not want to pay a large sum of money for something that proves to be of little or no value, it is important for her to obtain assurance that the seller has good title to the property. This is commonly done in one of three ways:

1. *Title opinion.* In some states, it is customary to have an attorney examine an **abstract of title.** An abstract of title is a history of what the public records show regarding the passage of title to, and other interests in, a parcel of real property. It is not a guarantee of good title. After examining the abstract, the attorney renders an opinion about whether the grantor has **marketable title,** which is title free from defects or reasonable doubt about its validity. If the grantor's title is defective, the nature of the defects will be stated in the attorney's title opinion.

Figure 2   Three Basic Types of Priority Systems for Recording Deeds

Race Statutes	Under a race statute—so named because the person who wins the race to the courthouse wins the property ownership "competition"—the first grantee who records a deed to a tract of land has superior title. For example, if Grantor deeds Blackacre to Kerr on March 1 and to Templin on April 1, Templin will have superior title to Blackacre if she records her deed before Kerr's is recorded. Race statutes are relatively uncommon today.
Notice Statutes	Under a notice system of priority, a later grantee of property has superior title if he acquired his interest without notice of an earlier grantee's claim to the property under an unrecorded deed. For example, Grantor deeds Greenacre to Jonson on June 1, but Jonson does not record his deed. On July 1, Marlowe purchases Greenacre without knowledge of Jonson's competing claim. Grantor executes and delivers a deed to Marlowe. In this situation, Marlowe would have superior rights to Greenacre even if Jonson ultimately records his deed before Marlowe's is recorded.
Race-Notice Statutes	The race-notice priority system combines elements of the systems just discussed. Under race-notice statutes, the grantee having priority is the one who both *takes his interest without notice* of any prior unrecorded claim and *records first*. For example, Grantor deeds Redacre to Frazier on September 1. On October 1 (at which time Frazier has not yet recorded his deed), Grantor deeds Redacre to Gill, who is then unaware of any claim by Frazier to Redacre. If Gill records his deed before Frazier's is recorded, Gill has superior rights to Redacre.

2. *Torrens system.* A method of title assurance available in a few states is the **Torrens system** of title registration. Under this system, one who owns land in fee simple obtains a certificate of title. When the property is sold, the grantor delivers a deed and a certificate of title to the grantee. All liens and encumbrances against the title are noted on the certificate, thus assuring the purchaser that the title is good except as to the liens and encumbrances noted on the certificate. However, some claims or encumbrances, such as those arising from adverse possession, do not appear on the records and must be discovered through an inspection of the property. In some Torrens states, encumbrances such as tax liens, short-term leases, and highway rights are valid against the purchaser even though they do not appear on the certificate.

3. *Title insurance.* Purchasing a policy of **title insurance** provides the preferred and most common means of protecting title to real property. Title insurance obligates the insurer to reimburse the insured grantee for loss if the title proves to be defective. In addition, title insurance covers litigation costs if the insured grantee must go to court in a title dispute. Lenders commonly require that a separate policy of title insurance be obtained for the lender's protection. Title insurance may be obtained in combination with the other previously discussed methods of ensuring title.

Seller's Responsibilities regarding the Quality of Residential Property

Buyers of real estate normally consider it important that any structures on the property be in good condition. This factor becomes especially significant if the buyer intends to use the property for residential purposes. The rule of **caveat emptor** (let the buyer beware) traditionally applied to the sale of real property unless the seller committed misrepresentation or fraud or made express warranties about the property's condition. In addition, sellers had no duty to disclose hidden defects in the property. In recent years, however, the legal environment for sellers—especially real estate professionals such as developers and builder-vendors of residential property—has changed substantially. This section examines two important sources of liability for sellers of real property.

Implied Warranty of Habitability Historically, sellers of residential property were not regarded as making any **implied warranty** that the property was habitable or suitable for the buyer's use. The law's attitude toward the buyer–seller relationship in residential property sales began to shift, however, as product liability law underwent rapid change in the late 1960s. Courts began to see that the same policies favoring the creation of implied warranties in the sale of goods applied with equal force to the sale of residential real estate.[7] Both goods and housing are frequently mass-produced. The disparity of knowledge and bargaining power often existing between a buyer of goods and a professional seller is also likely to exist between a buyer of a house and a builder-vendor (one who builds and sells houses). Moreover, many defects in houses are not readily discoverable during a buyer's inspection. This creates the possibility of serious loss, because the purchase of a home is often the largest single investment a person ever makes.

For these reasons, courts in most states now hold that builders, builder-vendors, and developers make an implied warranty of habitability when they build or sell real property for residential purposes. An ordinary owner who sells her house—in other words, a seller who was neither the builder nor the developer of the residential property—does not make an implied warranty of habitability.

The implied warranty of habitability amounts to a guarantee that the house is free of latent (hidden) defects that would render it unsafe or unsuitable for human habitation. A breach of this warranty subjects the defendant to liability for damages, measured by either the cost of repairs or the loss in value of the house.[8]

A related issue that has led to considerable litigation is whether the implied warranty of habitability extends to subsequent purchasers of the house. For example, PDQ Development Co. builds a house and sells it to Johnson, who later sells the house to McClure. May McClure successfully sue PDQ for breach of warranty if a serious defect renders the house uninhabitable? Although some courts have rejected implied warranty actions brought by subsequent purchasers, many courts today hold that an implied warranty made by a builder-vendor or developer would extend to a subsequent purchaser.

May the implied warranty of habitability be *disclaimed* or *limited* in the contract of sale? It appears at least possible to disclaim or limit the warranty through a contract provision, subject to limitations imposed by the unconscionability doctrine, public policy concerns, and contract interpretation principles.[9] Courts construe attempted disclaimers very strictly against the builder-vendor or developer, and often reject disclaimers that are not specific regarding rights supposedly waived by the purchaser.

Duty to Disclose Hidden Defects

Traditional contract law provided that a seller had no duty to disclose to the buyer defects in the property being sold, even if the seller knew about the defects and the buyer could not reasonably find out about them on his own. The seller's failure to volunteer information, therefore, could not constitute misrepresentation or fraud. This traditional rule of nondisclosure was another expression of the prevailing *caveat emptor* notion. Although the nondisclosure rule was subject to certain exceptions,[10] the exceptions seldom applied. Thus, there was no duty to disclose in most sales of real property.

Today, courts in many jurisdictions have substantially eroded the traditional nondisclosure rule and have placed a duty on the seller to disclose any known defect that materially affects the property's value and is not reasonably observable by the buyer. The seller's failure to disclose such defects effectively amounts to an assertion that the defects do not exist—an assertion on which a judicial finding of misrepresentation or fraud may be based.[11]

Other Property Condition–Related Obligations of Real Property Owners and Possessors

In recent years, the law has increasingly required real property owners and possessors to take steps to further the safety of persons on the property and to make the property more accessible to disabled individuals. This section discusses two legal developments along these lines: the trend toward expansion of *premises liability* and the inclusion of property-related provisions in the *Americans with Disabilities Act*.

Expansion of Premises Liability

Premises liability is the name sometimes used for negligence cases in which property owners or possessors (such as business operators leasing commercial real estate) are held liable to persons injured while on the property. As explained in Chapter 7, property owners and possessors face liability when their *failures to exercise*

---

[7]See Chapter 20 for a discussion of the development of similar doctrines in the law of product liability.
[8]Measures of damages are discussed in Chapter 18.
[9]The unconscionability doctrine and public policy concerns are discussed in Chapter 15. Chapter 16 addresses contract interpretation.

[10]These exceptions are discussed in Chapter 13.
[11]Misrepresentation and fraud are discussed in Chapter 13.

reasonable care to keep their property reasonably safe result in injuries to persons lawfully on the property.[12] The traditional premises liability case was one in which a property owner's or possessor's negligence led to the existence of a potentially hazardous condition on the property (e.g., a dangerously slick floor or similar physical condition at a business premises), and a person justifiably on the premises (e.g., a business customer) sustained personal injury upon encountering that unexpected condition (e.g., by slipping and falling).

Security Precautions against Foreseeable Criminal Acts

Recent years have witnessed a judicial inclination to expand premises liability to cover other situations in addition to the traditional scenario. A key component of this expansion has been many courts' willingness to reconsider the once-customary holding that a property owner or possessor had no legal obligation to implement security measures to protect persons on the property from the wrongful acts of third parties lacking any connection with the owner or possessor. Today, courts frequently hold that a property owner's or possessor's duty to exercise reasonable care includes the obligation to take *reasonable security precautions* designed to protect persons lawfully on the premises from *foreseeable* wrongful (including criminal) acts by third parties.

This expansion has caused hotel, apartment building, and convenience store owners and operators to be among the defendants held liable—sometimes in very large damage amounts—to guests, tenants, and customers on whom third-party attackers inflicted severe physical injuries. In such cases, the property owners' or possessors' negligent failures to take security precautions restricting such wrongdoers' access to the premises served as at least a *substantial factor* leading to the plaintiffs' injuries.[13] The security lapses amounting to a lack of reasonable care in a particular case may have been, for instance, failures to install deadbolt locks, provide adequate locking devices on sliding glass doors, maintain sufficient lighting, or employ security guards.

Determining Foreseeability

The security precautions component of the reasonable care duty is triggered only when criminal activity on the premises is foreseeable. It therefore becomes important to determine whether the foreseeability standard has been met. In making this determination, courts look at such factors as whether previous crimes had occurred on or near the subject property (and if so, the nature and frequency of those crimes), whether the property owner or possessor knew or should have known of those prior occurrences, and whether the property was located in a high-crime area. The fact-specific nature of the foreseeability and reasonable care determinations makes the outcome of a given premises liability case difficult to predict in advance. Nevertheless, there is no doubt that the current premises liability climate gives property owners and possessors more reason than ever before to be concerned about security measures.

Americans with Disabilities Act

In 1990, Congress enacted the broad-ranging Americans with Disabilities Act (ADA). This statute was designed to eliminate long-standing patterns of discrimination against disabled persons in matters such as employment, access to public services, and access to business establishments and similar facilities open to the public. The ADA's Title III focuses on places of *public accommodation*.[14] It imposes on certain property owners and possessors the obligation to take reasonable steps to make their property accessible to disabled persons (individuals with a physical or mental impairment that substantially limits one or more major life activities).

Places of Public Accommodation

Title III of the ADA classifies numerous businesses and nonbusiness enterprises as places of **public accommodation.** These include hotels, restaurants, bars, theaters, concert halls, auditoriums, stadiums, shopping centers, stores at which goods are sold or rented, service-oriented businesses (running the gamut from gas stations to law firm offices), museums, parks, schools, social services establishments (day care centers, senior citizen centers, homeless shelters, and the like), places of recreation, and various other enterprises, facilities, and establishments. Private clubs and religious organizations, however, are not treated as places of public accommodation for purposes of the statute.

[12]Chapter 7 explains the law's traditional view that real property owners and possessors owe persons who come on the property certain duties that vary depending on those persons' invitee, licensee, or trespasser status. It also discusses courts' increasing tendency to merge the traditional invitee and licensee classifications and to hold that property owners and possessors owe invitees and licensees the duty to exercise reasonable care to keep the premises reasonably safe.

[13]See Chapter 7's discussion of the *causation* element of a negligence claim.

[14]42 U.S.C. §§ 12181–12189. These sections examine only Title III of the ADA. Chapter 51 discusses the employment-related provisions set forth elsewhere in the statute.

Modifications of Property Under the ADA, the owner or operator of a place of public accommodation cannot exclude disabled persons from the premises or otherwise discriminate against them in terms of their ability to enjoy the public accommodation. Avoiding such exclusion or other discrimination may require alteration of the business or nonbusiness enterprise's practices, policies, and procedures. Moreover, using language contemplating the possible need for physical modifications of property serving as a place of public accommodation, the ADA includes within prohibited discrimination the property owner's or possessor's "failure to take such steps as may be necessary to ensure that no individual with a disability is excluded" or otherwise discriminated against in terms of access to what nondisabled persons are provided. The failure to take these steps does not violate the ADA, however, if the property owner or possessor demonstrates that implementing such steps would "fundamentally alter the nature" of the enterprise or would "result in an undue burden."

Prohibited discrimination may also include the "failure to remove architectural barriers and communication barriers that are structural in nature," if removal is "readily achievable." When the removal of such a barrier is not readily achievable, the property owner or possessor nonetheless engages in prohibited discrimination if he, she, or it does not adopt "alternative methods" to ensure access to the premises and what it has to offer (assuming that the alternative methods are themselves readily achievable). The ADA defines *readily achievable* as "easily accomplishable and able to be carried out without much difficulty or expense." The determination of whether an action is readily achievable involves consideration of factors such as the action's nature and cost, the nature of the enterprise conducted on the property, the financial resources of the affected property owner or possessor, and the effect the action would have on expenses and resources of the property owner or possessor.

New Construction Newly constructed buildings on property used as a place of public accommodation must contain physical features making the buildings *readily accessible* to disabled persons. The same is true of additions built on to previous structures. The ADA is supplemented by federal regulations setting forth property accessibility guidelines designed to lend substance and specificity to the broad legal standards stated in the statute. In addition, the federal government has issued technical assistance manuals and materials in an effort to educate public accommodation owners and operators regarding their obligations under the ADA.

Remedies A person subjected to disability-based discrimination in any of the respects discussed above may bring a civil suit for injunctive relief. An injunction issued by a court must include "an order to alter facilities" to make the facilities "readily accessible to and usable by individuals with disabilities to the extent required" by the ADA. The court has discretion to award attorney's fees to the prevailing party. The U.S. Attorney General also has the legal authority to institute a civil action alleging a violation of Title III of the ADA. In such a case, the court may choose to grant injunctive and other appropriate equitable relief, award compensatory damages to aggrieved persons (when the Attorney General so requests), and assess civil penalties (up to $50,000 for a first violation and up to $100,000 for any subsequent violation) "to vindicate the public interest." When determining the amount of any such penalty, the court is to give consideration to any good faith effort by the property owner or possessor to comply with the law. The court must also consider whether the owner or possessor could reasonably have anticipated the need to accommodate disabled persons.

Land Use Control

Although a real property owner generally has the right to use his property as he desires, society has placed certain limitations on this right. This section examines the property use limitations imposed by nuisance law and by zoning and subdivision ordinances. It also discusses the ultimate land use restriction—the eminent domain power—which enables the government to deprive property owners of their land.

Nuisance Law One's enjoyment of her land depends to a great extent on the uses her neighbors make of their land. When the uses of neighboring landowners conflict, the aggrieved party sometimes institutes litigation to resolve the conflict. A property use that unreasonably interferes with another person's ability to use or enjoy her own property may lead to an action for **nuisance** against the landowner or possessor engaging in the objectionable use.

The term *nuisance* has no set definition. It is often regarded, however, as encompassing any property-related use or activity that unreasonably interferes with the rights of others. Property uses potentially constituting nuisances include uses that are inappropriate to the neighborhood (such as using a vacant lot in a residential neighborhood as a garbage dump), bothersome to neighbors (such as keeping a pack of barking dogs in one's backyard), dangerous to others (such as storing large quantities of gasoline in 50-gallon drums in one's garage), or of questionable morality (such as operating a house of prostitution). To amount to a nuisance, a use need not be illegal. The fact that relevant zoning laws allow a given use does not mean that the use cannot be a nuisance. The use's having been in existence before complaining neighbors acquired their property does not mean that the use cannot be a nuisance, though it does lessen the likelihood that the use would be held a nuisance.

The test for determining the presence or absence of a nuisance is necessarily flexible and highly dependent on the individual case's facts. Courts balance a number of factors, such as the social importance of the parties' respective uses, the extent and duration of harm experienced by the aggrieved party, and the feasibility of abating (stopping) the nuisance.

Nuisances may be private or public. To bring a *private nuisance* action, the plaintiff must be a landowner or occupier whose enjoyment of her own land is substantially lessened by the alleged nuisance. The remedies for private nuisance include damages and injunctive relief designed to stop the offending use. A *public nuisance* occurs when a nuisance harms members of the public, who need not be injured in their use of property. For example, if a power plant creates noise and emissions posing a health hazard to pedestrians and workers in nearby buildings, a public nuisance may exist even though the nature of the harm has nothing to do with any loss of enjoyment of property. Public nuisances involve a broader class of affected parties than do private nuisances. The action to abate a public nuisance must usually be brought by the government. Remedies generally include injunctive relief and civil penalties that resemble fines. On occasion, constitutional issues may arise in public nuisance cases brought by the government. Private parties may sue for abatement of a public nuisance or for damages caused by one only when they suffered unique harm different from that experienced by the general public.

Eminent Domain

The Fifth Amendment to the Constitution provides that private property shall not be taken for public use without "just compensation." Implicit in this provision is the principle that the government has the power to take property for public use if it pays "just compensation" to the owner of the property. This power, called the power of **eminent domain,** makes it possible for the government to acquire private property for highways, water control projects, municipal and civic centers, public housing, urban renewal, and other public uses. Governmental units may delegate their eminent domain power to private corporations such as railroads and utility companies.

Although the eminent domain power is a useful tool of efficient government, there are problems inherent in its use. Determining when the power can be properly exercised presents an initial problem. When the governmental unit itself uses the property taken, as would be the case with property acquired for construction of a municipal building or a public highway, the exercise of the power is proper. The use of eminent domain is controversial, however, when the government acquires the property and transfers it to a private developer.[15] In the *Kelo* case, which follows shortly, the U.S. Supreme Court grappled with this issue.

Determining *just compensation* in a given case poses a second and frequently encountered eminent domain problem. The property owner is entitled to receive the "fair market value" of his property. Critics assert, however, that this measure of compensation falls short of adequately compensating the owner for her loss, because *fair market value* does not cover such matters as the lost goodwill of a business or one's emotional attachment to his home.

A third problem sometimes encountered is determining when there has been a "taking" that triggers the government's just compensation obligation. The answer is easy when the government institutes a formal legal action to exercise the eminent domain power (often called an action to *condemn* property). In some instances, however, the government causes or permits a serious physical invasion of a landowner's property without having instituted formal condemnation proceedings. For example, the government's dam-building project results in persistent flooding of a private party's land. Courts have recognized the right of property owners in such cases to institute litigation seeking compensation from the governmental unit whose actions effectively amounted to a physical taking of their land. In these so-called **inverse condemnation** cases, the property owner sends the message that "you have taken my land; now pay for it."

---

[15]This issue is discussed further in Chapter 3, as are other issues relating to eminent domain.

Kelo v. City of New London   125 S. Ct. 2655 (U.S. Sup. Ct. 2005)

The city of New London, Connecticut, had experienced decades of economic decline. In 1990, a state agency designated the city a "distressed municipality." In 1996, the federal government closed a U.S. naval facility in the Fort Trumbull area of the city that had employed over 1,500 people. In 1998, the city's unemployment rate was nearly double that of the rest of the state and its population of just under 24,000 residents was at its lowest since 1920. These conditions prompted state and local officials to target New London, and particularly its Fort Trumbull area, for economic revitalization.

To this end, New London Development Corporation (NLDC), a private nonprofit entity established some years earlier to assist the city in planning economic development, was reactivated. In January 1998, the state authorized a $5.35 million bond issue to support the NLDC's planning activities. In February, the pharmaceutical company Pfizer Inc. announced that it would build a $300 million research facility on a site immediately adjacent to Fort Trumbull; local planners hoped that Pfizer would draw new business to the area, thereby serving as a catalyst to the area's rejuvenation. In May, the city council authorized the NLDC to formally submit its plans to the relevant state agencies for review. Upon obtaining state-level approval, the NLDC finalized an integrated development plan focused on 90 acres of the Fort Trumbull area, which comprises approximately 115 privately owned properties, as well as the 32 acres of land formerly occupied by the naval facility.

The development plan called for the creation of restaurants, shops, marinas for both recreational and commercial uses, a pedestrian "riverwalk," 80 new residences, a new U.S. Coast Guard Museum, research and development office space, and parking. The NLDC intended the development plan to capitalize on the arrival of the Pfizer facility and the new commerce it was expected to attract. In addition to creating jobs, generating tax revenue, and helping to build momentum for the revitalization of downtown New London, the plan was also designed to make the city more attractive and to create leisure and recreational opportunities on the waterfront and in the park. The city council approved the plan in January 2000, and designated the NLDC as its development agent in charge of implementation. The city council also authorized the NLDC to purchase property or to acquire property by exercising eminent domain in the city's name.

The NLDC successfully negotiated the purchase of most of the real estate in the 90-acre area, but its negotiations with nine property owners, including the petitioners Susette Kelo, Wilhelmina Dery, and Charles Dery, failed. As a result, in November 2000, the NLDC initiated condemnation proceedings. Kelo had lived in the Fort Trumbull area since 1997. She had made extensive improvements to her house, which she prizes for its water view. Wilhelmina Dery was born in her Fort Trumbull house in 1918 and had lived there her entire life. Her husband, Charles, had lived in the house since they married some 60 years ago. In all, the nine petitioners own 15 properties in Fort Trumbull. There is no allegation that any of these properties is blighted or otherwise in poor condition; rather, they were condemned only because they happen to be located in the development area.

In December 2000, the petitioners brought this action claiming, among other things, that the taking of their properties would violate the "public use" restriction in the Fifth Amendment. The trial court granted a permanent restraining order prohibiting the taking of properties in one area of Fort Trumbull, but denied the order for properties in another area. Both sides appealed to the Supreme Court of Connecticut. That court held that all of the city's proposed takings were valid. The petitioners then appealed to the U.S. Supreme Court.

Stevens, Justice

Two polar propositions are perfectly clear. On the one hand, it has long been accepted that the sovereign may not take the property of *A* for the sole purpose of transferring it to another private party *B,* even though *A* is paid just compensation. On the other hand, it is equally clear that a State may transfer property from one private party to another if future "use by the public" is the purpose of the taking; the condemnation of land for a railroad with common-carrier duties is a familiar example. Neither of these propositions, however, determines the disposition of this case.

As for the first proposition, the City would no doubt be forbidden from taking petitioners' land for the purpose of conferring a private benefit on a particular private party. Nor would the City be allowed to take property under the mere pretext of a public purpose, when its actual purpose was to bestow a private benefit. The takings before us, however, would be executed pursuant to a carefully considered development plan. The trial judge and all the members of the Supreme Court of Connecticut agreed that there was no evidence of an illegitimate purpose in this case. On the other hand, this is not a case in which the City is planning to open the condemned land—at least not in its entirety—to use by the general public. Nor will the private lessees of the land in any sense be required to operate like common carriers, making their services available to all comers. But although such a projected use would be sufficient to satisfy the public use requirement, this Court long ago rejected any literal requirement that condemned property be put into use for the general public. Indeed, while many state courts in the mid-19th century endorsed "use by the public" as the proper definition of public use, that narrow view steadily eroded over time. Not only was the "use by the public" test difficult to administer (e.g., what proportion of the public need have access to the property? at what price?), but it proved to be impractical given the diverse and always evolving needs of society. Accordingly, when this Court began applying the Fifth Amendment to the States at the close of the 19th century, it embraced the broader and more natural interpretation of public use as "public purpose." The disposition of this case therefore turns on the question whether the City's development plan serves a "public purpose."

Without exception, our cases have defined that concept broadly, reflecting our long-standing policy of deference to legislative judgments in this field. Viewed as a whole, our jurisprudence has recognized that the needs of society have varied between different parts of the Nation, just as they have evolved over time in response to changed circumstances. For more than a century, our public use jurisprudence has wisely eschewed rigid formulas and intrusive scrutiny in favor of affording legislatures broad latitude in determining what public needs justify the use of the takings power.

Those who govern the City were not confronted with the need to remove blight in the Fort Trumbull area, but their determination that the area was sufficiently distressed to justify a program of economic rejuvenation is entitled to our deference. The City has carefully formulated an economic development plan that it believes will provide appreciable benefits to the community, including—but by no means limited to—new jobs and increased tax revenue. As with other exercises in urban planning and development, the City is endeavoring to coordinate a variety of commercial, residential, and recreational uses of land, with the hope that they will form a whole greater than the sum of its parts. To effectuate this plan, the City has invoked a state statute that specifically authorizes the use of eminent domain to promote economic development. Given the comprehensive character of the plan, the thorough deliberation that preceded its adoption, and the limited scope of our review, it is appropriate for us to resolve the challenges of the individual owners, not on a piecemeal basis, but rather in light of the entire plan. Because that plan unquestionably serves a public purpose, the takings challenged here satisfy the public use requirement of the Fifth Amendment.

To avoid this result, petitioners urge us to adopt a new bright-line rule that economic development does not qualify as a public use. Putting aside the unpersuasive suggestion that the City's plan will provide only purely economic benefits, neither precedent nor logic supports petitioners' proposal. Promoting economic development is a traditional and long-accepted function of government. There is, moreover, no principled way of distinguishing economic development from the other public purposes that we have recognized. In our cases upholding takings that facilitated agriculture and mining, for example, we emphasized the importance of those industries to the welfare of the States in question. It would be incongruous to hold that the City's interest in the economic benefits to be derived from the development of the Fort Trumbull area has less of a public character than any of those other interests. Clearly, there is no basis for exempting economic development from our traditionally broad understanding of public purpose.

Petitioners contend that using eminent domain for economic development impermissibly blurs the boundary between public and private takings. Again, our cases foreclose this objection. Quite simply, the government's pursuit of a public purpose will often benefit individual private parties. It is further argued that without a bright-line rule nothing would stop a city from transferring citizen A's property to citizen B for the sole reason that citizen B will put the property to a more productive use and thus pay more taxes. Such a one-to-one transfer of property, executed outside the confines of an integrated development plan, is not presented in this case. While such an unusual exercise of government power would certainly raise a suspicion that a private purpose was afoot, the hypothetical cases posited by petitioners can be confronted if and when they arise. They do not warrant the crafting of an artificial restriction on the concept of public use.

Alternatively, petitioners maintain that for takings of this kind we should require a "reasonable certainty" that the expected public benefits will actually accrue. Such a rule, however, would represent an even greater departure from our precedent. The disadvantages of a heightened form of review are especially pronounced in this type of case. Orderly implementation of a comprehensive redevelopment plan obviously requires that the legal rights of all interested parties be established before new construction can be commenced. A constitutional rule that required postponement of the judicial approval of every condemnation until the likelihood of success of the plan had been assured would unquestionably impose a significant impediment to the successful consummation of many such plans.

Just as we decline to second-guess the City's considered judgments about the efficacy of its development plan, we also decline to second-guess the City's determinations as to what lands it needs to acquire in order to effectuate the project. In affirming the City's authority to take petitioners' properties, we do not minimize the hardship that condemnations may entail, notwithstanding the payment of just compensation. We emphasize that nothing in our opinion precludes any State from placing further restrictions on its exercise of the takings power. Indeed, many States already impose "public use" requirements that are stricter than the federal baseline. Some of these requirements have been established as a matter of state constitutional law, while others are expressed in state eminent domain statutes that carefully limit the grounds upon which takings may be exercised. As the submissions of the parties make clear, the necessity and wisdom of using eminent domain to promote economic development are certainly matters of legitimate public debate. This Court's authority, however, extends only to determining whether the City's proposed condemnations are for a "public use" within the meaning of the Fifth Amendment to the Federal Constitution.

Affirmed in favor of the City.

Zoning and Subdivision Laws

State legislatures commonly delegate to cities and other political subdivisions the power to impose reasonable regulations designed to promote the public health, safety, and welfare (often called the *police power*). Zoning ordinances, which regulate real property use, stem from the exercise of the police power. Normally, zoning ordinances divide a city or town into various districts and specify or limit the uses to which property in those districts may be put. They also contain requirements and restrictions regarding improvements built on the land.

Zoning ordinances frequently contain direct restrictions on land use, such as by limiting property use in a given area to single-family or high-density residential uses, or to commercial, light industry, or heavy industry uses. Other sorts of use-related provisions commonly found in zoning ordinances include restrictions on building height, limitations on the portion of a lot that can be covered by a building, and specifications of the distance buildings must be from lot lines (usually called *setback* requirements). Zoning ordinances also commonly restrict property use by establishing population density limitations. Such restrictions specify the maximum number of persons who can be housed on property in a given area and dictate the amount of living space that must be provided for each person occupying residential property. In addition, zoning ordinances often establish restrictions designed to maintain or create a certain aesthetic character in the community. Examples of this type of restriction include specifications of buildings' architectural style, limitations on billboard and sign use, and designations of special zones for historic buildings.

Many local governments also have ordinances dealing with proposed subdivisions. These ordinances often require the subdivision developer to meet certain requirements regarding lot size, street and sidewalk layout, and sanitary facilities. They also require that the city or town approve the proposed development. Such ordinances are designed to further general community interests and to protect prospective buyers of property in the subdivision by ensuring that the developer meets minimum standards of suitability.

Nonconforming Uses A zoning ordinance has *prospective* effect. This means that the uses and buildings already existing when the ordinance is passed (**nonconforming uses**) are permitted to continue. The ordinance may provide, however, for the gradual phasing out of nonconforming uses and buildings that do not fit the general zoning plan.

Relief from Zoning Ordinances A property owner who wishes to use his property in a manner prohibited by a zoning ordinance has more than one potential avenue of relief from the ordinance. He may, for instance, seek to have the ordinance **amended**—in other words, attempt to get the law changed—on the ground that the proposed amendment is consistent with the essence of the overall zoning plan.

A different approach would be to seek permission from the city or political subdivision to deviate from the zoning law. This permission is called a **variance.** A person seeking a variance usually claims that the ordinance works an undue hardship on her by denying her the opportunity to make reasonable use of her land. Examples of typical variance requests include a property owner's seeking permission to make a commercial use of her property even though it is located in an area zoned for residential purposes, or permission to deviate from normal setback or building size requirements.

Attempts to obtain variances and zoning ordinance amendments frequently clash with the interests of other owners of property in the same area—owners who have a vested interest in maintaining the status quo. As a result, variance and amendment requests often produce heated battles before local zoning authorities.

Ethics in Action

The Jesus Center rented a two-story building in the City of Farmington Hills in a district zoned for single-family dwellings as well as churches and "other facilities normally incidental thereto." In its leased property, the church held services, Bible study, and prayer meetings as well as providing for collection and distribution of food, clothing, and other essentials for needy people. In 1991, The Jesus Center began to operate a homeless shelter.

After being notified that zoning approval was needed for this use of the property, The Jesus Center sought such approval, but it was denied on the ground that the provision of shelter services was not a permissible accessible use. What are the major ethical considerations suggested by such uses of zoning ordinances and restrictive covenants? What are the major ethical considerations suggested by attempts to place homeless shelters in primarily single-family residential locations?

Challenges to the Validity of the Zoning Ordinance

A disgruntled property owner might also attack the zoning ordinance's validity on constitutional grounds. Litigation challenging zoning ordinances has become frequent in recent years, as cities and towns have used their zoning power to achieve social control. For example, assume that a city creates special zoning requirements for adult bookstores or other uses considered moral threats to the community. Such uses of the zoning power have been challenged as unconstitutional restrictions on freedom of speech. In *City of Renton v. Playtime Theatres, Inc.,* however, the Supreme Court upheld a zoning ordinance that prohibited the operation of adult bookstores within 1,000 feet of specified uses such as residential areas and schools.[16] The Court established that the First Amendment rights of operators of adult businesses would not be violated by such an ordinance so long as the city provided them a "reasonable opportunity to open and operate" their businesses within the city. The reasonable opportunity test was satisfied in *City of Renton* even though the ordinance at issue effectively restricted adult bookstores to a small area of the community in which no property was then available to buy or rent. Lower court cases reveal, however, that the fact-specific nature of the inquiry contemplated by the reasonable opportunity test means that the government is not guaranteed of passing the test in every case.

Other litigation has stemmed from ordinances by which municipalities have attempted to "zone out" resi-

dential facilities such as group homes for mentally retarded adults. In a leading case, the Supreme Court held that the Constitution's Equal Protection Clause was violated by a zoning ordinance that required a special use permit for a group home for the mentally retarded.[17] The Fair Housing Act, which forbids discrimination on the basis of handicap and familial status, has also been used as a basis for challenging decisions that zone out group homes. Such a challenge has a chance of success when the plaintiff demonstrates that the zoning board's actions were a mere pretext for discrimination.[18] Certain applications of zoning ordinances that establish single-family residential areas may also raise Fair Housing Act–based claims of handicap discrimination.

Many cities and towns have attempted to restrict single-family residential zones to living units of traditional families related by blood or marriage. In enacting ordinances along those lines, municipalities have sought to prevent the presence of groups of unrelated students, commune members, or religious cult adherents by specifically defining the term *family* in a way that excludes these groups. In *Belle Terre v. Boraas,*[19] the Supreme Court upheld such an ordinance as applied to a group of unrelated students. The Court later held, however, that an ordinance defining *family* so as to prohibit a grandmother from living with her grandsons was an unconstitutional intrusion on personal freedom regarding family life.[20] Restrictive definitions of *family* have been held unconstitutional under state constitutions in some cases but narrowly construed by courts in other cases.

---

[16]475 U.S. 41 (U.S. Sup. Ct. 1986). A later case, *FW/PBS, Inc. v. City of Dallas,* 493 U.S. 215 (U.S. Sup. Ct. 1990), presented a different sort of restriction on adult businesses and resulted in a different outcome. There, the Court held that a comprehensive ordinance requiring licensing of adult cabarets and other adult entertainment establishments violated the First Amendment because the ordinance did not have appropriate procedural safeguards against arbitrary denials of licenses. The ordinance's chief defect was its failure to establish a time limit within which city authorities were required to act on license applications.

[17]*City of Cleburne v. Cleburne Living Centers,* 473 U.S. 432 (U.S. Sup. Ct. 1985).
[18]See, for example, *Baxter v. City of Nashville,* 720 F. Supp. 720 (S.D. Ill. 1989), which involves a challenge by a hospice for AIDS patients to a city's denial of a special use permit.
[19]416 U.S. 1 (U.S. Sup. Ct. 1974).
[20]*Moore v. City of East Cleveland,* 431 U.S. 494 (U.S. Sup. Ct. 1977).

Land Use Regulation and Taking

Another type of litigation seen with increasing frequency in recent years centers around zoning laws and other land use regulations that make the use of property less profitable.[21] Affected property owners have challenged the application of such regulations as unconstitutional takings of property without just compensation, even though these cases do not involve the actual physical invasions present in the inverse condemnation cases discussed earlier in this chapter.

States normally have broad discretion to use their police power for the public benefit, even when that means interfering to some extent with an owner's right to develop her property as she desires. Some regulations, however, may interfere with an owner's use of his property to such an extent that they constitute a taking.

For instance, in *Nollan v. California Coastal Commission,*[22] the owners of a beach-front lot (the Nollans) wished to tear down a small house on the lot and replace that structure with a larger house. The California Coastal Commission conditioned the grant of the necessary coastal development permit on the Nollans' agreeing to allow the public an easement across their property. This easement would have allowed the public to reach certain nearby public beaches more easily. The Nollans challenged the validity of the Coastal Commission's action.

Ultimately, the Supreme Court concluded that the Coastal Commission's placing the easement condition on the issuance of the permit amounted to an impermissible regulatory taking of the Nollans' property. In reaching this conclusion, the Court held that the state could not avoid paying compensation to the Nollans by choosing to do by way of the regulatory route what it would have had to pay for if it had followed the formal eminent domain route.

Regulations Denying Economically Beneficial Uses

What about a land use regulation that allows the property owner no *economically beneficial use* of his property? *Lucas v. South Carolina Coastal Commission*[23] was brought by a property owner, Lucas, who had paid nearly $1 million for two residential beach-front lots before South Carolina enacted a coastal protection statute. This statute's effect was to bar Lucas from building any permanent habitable structures on the lots. The trial court held that the statute rendered Lucas's property "valueless" and that an unconstitutional taking had occurred, but the South

Carolina Supreme Court reversed. The U.S. Supreme Court, however, held that when a land use regulation denies "all economically beneficial use" of property, there normally has been a taking for which just compensation must be paid. The exception to this rule, according to the Court, would be when the economically productive use being prohibited by the land use regulation was already disallowed by nuisance law or other comparable property law principles. The Court therefore reversed and remanded the case for determination of whether there had been a taking under the rule crafted by the Court, or instead an instance in which the "nuisance" exception applied. On remand, the South Carolina Supreme Court concluded that a taking calling for compensation had occurred (and, necessarily, that the nuisance exception did not apply to Lucas's intended residential use).[24]

The mere fact that a land use regulation deprives the owner of the *highest and most profitable use* of his property does not mean, however, that there has been a taking. If the regulation still allows a use that is economically beneficial in a meaningful sense—even though not the most profitable use—the *Lucas* analysis would seem to indicate that an unconstitutional taking probably did not occur. At the same time, *Lucas* offered hints that less-than-total takings (in terms of restrictions on economically beneficial uses) may sometimes trigger a right of compensation on the landowner's part. Thus, it appears that even as to land use regulations that restrict some but not all economically beneficial uses, property owners are likely to continue arguing (as they have in recent years) that the regulations go "too far" and amount to a taking.

There is no set formula for determining whether a regulation has gone too far. Courts look at the relevant facts and circumstances and weigh a variety of factors, such as the economic impact of the regulation, the degree to which the regulation interferes with the property owner's reasonable expectations, and the character of the government's invasion. The weighing of these factors occurs against the backdrop of a general presumption that state and local governments should have reasonably broad discretion to develop land use restrictions pursuant to the police power. As a result, the outcome of a case in which *regulatory taking* allegations are made is less certain than when a *physical taking* (a physical invasion of the sort addressed in the earlier discussion of inverse condemnation cases) appears to have occurred.

The following *Lingle v. Chevron U.S.A., Inc.* case clarifies the legal standard that should be used in determining if a regulation constitutes a taking.

---

[21]This issue is also discussed in Chapter 3.
[22]483 U.S. 825 (U.S. Sup. Ct. 1987).
[23]505 U.S. 1003 (U.S. Sup. Ct. 1992).

[24]424 S.E. 2d 484 (S.C. Sup. Ct. 1992).

Lingle v. Chevron U.S.A., Inc.   544 U.S. 528 (U.S. Sup. Ct. 2005)

Chevron was the largest refiner and marketer of gasoline in Hawaii. It sold most of its products through 64 independent lessee-dealer stations. In a typical lessee-dealer arrangement, Chevron would buy or lease land from a third party, build a service station, and then lease the station to a dealer. Chevron charged the lessee-dealer a monthly rent, defined as a percentage of the dealer's margin on retail sales of gasoline and other goods.

In June 1997, the Hawaii Legislature enacted Act 257, apparently in response to concerns about the effects of market concentration on retail gasoline prices. The statute sought to protect independent dealers by imposing certain restrictions on the ownership and leasing of service stations by oil companies. Among other provisions, Act 257 limited the amount of rent that an oil company may charge a lessee-dealer to 15 percent of the dealer's gross profits from gasoline sales plus 15 percent of gross sales of products other than gasoline. Act 257 reduced by about $207,000 per year the aggregate rent that Chevron would otherwise charge on 11 of its 64 lessee-dealer stations. On the other hand, the statute allowed Chevron to collect more rent than it would otherwise charge at its remaining 53 lessee-dealer stations, such that Chevron could increase its overall rental income from all 64 stations by nearly $1.1 million per year. Over the past 20 years, Chevron has not fully recovered the costs of maintaining lessee-dealer stations in any state through rent alone. Rather, the company recoups its expenses through a combination of rent and product sales.

Chevron sued the Governor and Attorney General of Hawaii in their official capacities, claiming that the statute's rent cap provision, on its face, was a taking of Chevron's property in violation of the Fifth and Fourteenth Amendments. Chevron sought a declaration to this effect as well as an injunction against the application of the rent cap to its stations. Chevron moved for summary judgment on its takings claim, and Hawaii filed a cross-motion for summary judgment on all of Chevron's claims. The District Court granted summary judgment to Chevron, and Hawaii appealed. The Court of Appeals for the Ninth Circuit reversed and remanded the case. On remand, the District Court entered judgment for Chevron after a one-day bench trial. The Ninth Circuit affirmed this judgment, and Hawaii appealed.

O'Connor, Justice

The Takings Clause of the Fifth Amendment provides that private property shall not "be taken for public use, without just compensation." As its text makes plain, the Takings Clause does not prohibit the taking of private property, but instead places a condition on the exercise of that power. In other words, it is designed not to limit the governmental interference with property rights per se, but rather to secure compensation in the event of otherwise proper interference amounting to a taking. While scholars have offered various justifications for this regime, we have emphasized its role in barring Government from forcing some people alone to bear public burdens which, in all fairness and justice, should be borne by the public as a whole.

The paradigmatic taking requiring just compensation is a direct government appropriation or physical invasion of private property. However, the Court recognized that government regulation of private property may, in some instances, be so onerous that its effect is tantamount to a direct appropriation or ouster—and that such "regulatory takings" may be compensable under the Fifth Amendment. In Justice Holmes' storied but cryptic formulation, "while property may be regulated to a certain extent, if regulation goes too far it will be recognized as a taking." The rub, of course, has been—and remains—how to discern how far is "too far."

Our precedents stake out two categories of regulatory action that generally will be deemed per se takings for Fifth

Amendment purposes. First, where government requires an owner to suffer a permanent physical invasion of her property—however minor—it must provide just compensation. A second categorical rule applies to regulations that completely deprive an owner of "all economically beneficial use" of her property. We held in *Lucas* [*v. South Carolina Coastal Council*] that the government must pay just compensation for such "total regulatory takings." Outside these two relatively narrow categories, regulatory takings challenges are governed by the standards set forth in *Penn Central Transp. Co. v. New York City*. The Court in *Penn Central* identified "several factors that have particular significance." Primary among those factors are "the economic impact of the regulation on the claimant and, particularly, the extent to which the regulation has interfered with distinct investment-backed expectations." In addition, the "character of the governmental action"—for instance whether it amounts to a physical invasion or instead merely affects property interests through "some public program adjusting the benefits and burdens of economic life to promote the common good"—may be relevant in discerning whether a taking has occurred. The *Penn Central* factors have served as the principal guidelines for resolving regulatory takings claims that do not fall within the physical takings or *Lucas* rules.

In *Agins v. City of Tiburon,* the Court declared that "the application of a general zoning law to particular property effects a taking if the ordinance does not substantially advance legitimate state interests or denies an owner economically viable use of his land." Because this statement is phrased in the disjunctive, *Agins'* "substantially advances" language has been read to announce a stand-alone regulatory takings test that is wholly independent of *Penn Central* or any other test. Indeed, the lower courts in this case struck down Hawaii's rent control statute based solely upon their findings that it does not substantially advance a legitimate state interest. We conclude that this formula has no proper place in our takings jurisprudence. The "substantially advances" formula asks, in essence, whether a regulation of private property is effective in achieving some legitimate public purpose.

An inquiry of this nature has some logic in the context of a due process challenge, for a regulation that fails to serve any legitimate governmental objective may be so arbitrary or irrational that it runs afoul of the Due Process Clause. But such a test is not a valid method of discerning whether private property has been "taken" for purposes of the Fifth Amendment. In stark contrast to the regulatory takings tests discussed above, the "substantially advances" inquiry reveals nothing about the magnitude or character of the burden a particular regulation imposes upon private property rights. Nor does it provide any information about how any regulatory burden is distributed among property owners. In consequence, this test does not help to identify those regulations whose effects are functionally comparable to government appropriation or invasion of private property; it is tethered neither to the text of the Takings Clause nor to the basic justification for allowing regulatory actions to be challenged under the Clause.

Chevron appeals to the general principle that the Takings Clause is meant to bar Government from forcing some people alone to bear public burdens which, in all fairness and justice, should be borne by the public as a whole. But that appeal is clearly misplaced, for the reasons just indicated. A test that tells us nothing about the actual burden imposed on property rights, or how that burden is allocated, cannot tell us when justice might require that the burden be spread among taxpayers through the payment of compensation. The owner of a property subject to a regulation that effectively serves a legitimate state interest may be just as singled out and just as burdened as the owner of a property subject to an ineffective regulation. It would make little sense to say that the second owner has suffered a taking while the first has not. Likewise, an ineffective regulation may not significantly burden property rights at all, and it may distribute any burden broadly and evenly among property owners. The notion that such a regulation nevertheless "takes" private property for public use merely by virtue of its ineffectiveness or foolishness is untenable.

Chevron's challenge to the Hawaii statute in this case illustrates the flaws in the "substantially advances" theory. To begin with, it is unclear how significantly Hawaii's rent cap actually burdens Chevron's property rights. The cap would reduce Chevron's aggregate rental income on 11 of its 64 lessee-dealer stations by about $207,000 per year, but that Chevron nevertheless expects to receive a return on its investment in these stations that satisfies any constitutional standard. Moreover, Chevron asserted below, and the District Court found, that Chevron would recoup any reductions in its rental income by raising wholesale gasoline prices. In short, Chevron has not clearly argued—let alone established—that it has been singled out to bear any particularly severe regulatory burden. Rather, the gravamen of Chevron's claim is simply that Hawaii's rent cap will not actually serve the State's legitimate interest in protecting consumers against high gasoline prices. Whatever the merits of that claim, it does not sound under the Takings Clause. Chevron plainly does not seek compensation for a taking of its property for a legitimate public use, but rather an injunction against the enforcement of a regulation that it alleges to be fundamentally arbitrary and irrational.

We conclude that the "substantially advances" formula announced in *Agins* is not a valid method of identifying regulatory takings for which the Fifth Amendment requires just compensation. Since Chevron argued only a "substantially advances" theory in support of its takings claim, it was not entitled to summary judgment on that claim.

Reversed in favor of Hawaii.

Problems and Problem Cases

1. Perrone Realty leased approximately 2,500 square feet of its 8,500 square foot building to J & P on a four-year lease with options to extend the lease to 2019. The structure was a pre-engineered steel building on cement. Although it was always intended for commercial retail use, the building was not constructed for any particular type of business. Wiring and insulation and the construction of walls were needed. J & P undertook the finishing of the interior of the premises to serve an intended use as a delicatessen. In addition to overseeing the installation of walls, drop ceiling components, lighting, flooring,

and other necessary parts of its new business, J & P installed a hood system over the grill and stove to exhaust smoke and grease-laden vapors. The hood was stainless steel and approximately two feet high, four and one-half feet deep and twelve feet wide. It hung from eight threaded steel rods, one-half inch in diameter, which were bolted to bar joists in the rafters of the building and welded to the top of the hood. Air ducts were constructed through the back wall of the building. The system hooked up to electricity, natural gas, and water, so removal of the hood system would require the capping of electrical, plumbing, and gas conduits. The life expectancy of the hood was about 25 years. It was resalable and transferable to another business involving the cooking of food, and J & P intended it to be portable to another site. J & P had operated delicatessens or restaurants at other locations in the past and intended to do so in the future. The written rental agreement was silent on the status of the range hood. The type of business that will occupy the premises in the future is uncertain. Perrone brought an action against J & P for possession of the property. A question arose whether the range hood was personal property or a fixture. Could J & P remove the hood at the termination of its lease?

2. In 1982, Green's grandmother, Billie Harrild, offered Green a piece of the family's land. Green selected a parcel of land on a bluff, across a creek from her grandparents' house. The alleged gift was not recorded, and Green's grandparents and cousin remained the owners of record. However, according to Green's testimony, in the 10 years following her entry onto the property, all three "absolutely" recognized the land as hers. Neighbors testified that Billie consistently referred to the land as Green's property. Between 1982 and 1992, Green gradually built a house and cultivated grounds on the bluff. She worked on the property over the summers, and worked as a nurse and glassmaker in California for the rest of the year. In 1982, she planned the site of her house and cleared trees on the lot. In the summers of 1983 and 1984, she lived in a camper on the property, cleared more trees and stumps, and oversaw hand excavation for the foundation of the house. In the following summers, she gradually expanded the cultivated section of the property, planting lilac bushes and fruit trees and installing a coop for chickens and turkeys. She and a neighbor worked on building the house itself, and beginning in 1987, Green lived in the nearly complete house during the summers. In 1986, Green worked in Fairbanks the whole year and visited the property by snow machine during the winter. In 1989 she lived on the property for eight or nine months. Green left trees standing on much of the property, but cleared undergrowth and planted native plants over an area of several acres. She also cut trees from a wide area on the southern hillside in order to clear the view from the cabin. She posted "No Trespassing" signs and built benches in some areas away from the house. She put up a chain across the road entering the property, but did not fence the entire area. In 1990, the house was considerably damaged by vandalism, and Green repaired the damage when she returned to Alaska in the spring. Green arranged with her grandparents that, for the remainder of their lives, they could extract and sell small quantities of rock from the property, but she strongly opposed use of such equipment on the property. Sometime between 1988 and 1991, the Harrilds signed a contract with an extraction company, Earthmovers, allowing them to excavate rock from the family property, including the bluff. Earthmovers excavated a trench on the bluff on a day when Green was not at home. When Green returned and found the workers and equipment on the property, however, she told them that they were not allowed to excavate there. Green granted the workers permission to finish the task at hand, insisted that they arrange to repair a telephone line that they had damaged, and ordered them to leave the property. In 1988, Vezey became interested in properties in this area. Vezey approached the Harrilds about purchasing their land. In 1994, while Vezey was still in negotiations with the Harrilds, Green called him, and, according to Green, she told Vezey that the land belonged to her. In the winter of 1994–1995, Vezey purchased property that included the bluff area claimed by Green. Green brought suit, asserting that she owned the bluff area property. Will she win?

3. Aidinoff purchased land in 1979. It is adjacent to Sterling City Road but can only be reached by crossing land formerly owned by Rand. Other routes of access are impossible because of wetlands and a brook. A gravel driveway crosses the Rand land to Aidinoff's land. The person from whom Aidinoff purchased her land used the driveway for access to her land, and Aidinoff used the driveway from 1979 until 2003. She drove vehicles, walked, and brought

animals across the driveway. She also used the power coming in over utility lines serving the property. After Aidinoff had begun using the driveway, she and Rand had had a conversation about the driveway, and Rand had told her that he owned it and he had no problem with her using it but it was not "an open way for everybody to go through." In 2003, Rand sold his property to the Lathrops. After buying the property, the Lathrops blocked the driveway and prevented Aidinoff from using it to access her property. Aidinoff claimed that she had the right to use the driveway because she had acquired an easement by prescription and an easement by necessity. Did she?

4. A declaration of restrictive covenants for the Mains Farm subdivision was recorded in 1962. Worthington purchased a residential lot in Mains Farm in 1987. A house already existed on the property. Before the purchase, Worthington obtained and read a copy of the restrictive covenants, which stated in part that all lots in Mains Farms "shall be designated as 'Residence Lots' and shall be used for single-family residential purposes only." Worthington later began occupying the residence along with four adults who paid her for 24-hour protective supervision and care. These four adults, who were not related to Worthington, were unable to do their own housekeeping, prepare their own meals, or attend to their personal hygiene. In providing this supervision and care on a for-profit basis, Worthington complied with the licensing and inspection requirements established by state law, but she obtained the permit by stating that only her family would be living with her. The Mains Farm Homeowners Association, which consisted of owners of property in the subdivision, filed suit against Worthington, asserting that her use of her property violated the restrictive covenant. Will the association prevail?

5. In 1968, JEP bought a fully functioning theater in the Lake of the Ozarks. The building was designed and constructed as a live theater. It contained a raked concrete floor, 1,000 seats bolted to the floor, stage and backstage areas, a concession stand, and a ticket booth. In 1970, the building was converted to a movie theater. On April 1, 1973, JEP agreed to a 20-year lease with Jablonow-Komm Theatres. Shortly thereafter, and with the approval of JEP, Jablonow removed the old wooden seats and installed 733 fabric-covered plastic theater seats. Jablonow then transferred its interest in the lease and property to RKO Mid-America Theatres, Inc. In May 1982, JEP and RKO amended the 1973 lease, giving RKO the right to remodel the theater so that it had two screens instead of one for an increase in monthly rent. Two years later, RKO transferred its interest in the lease and property to Commonwealth Theatres of Missouri. As part of this transfer, RKO gave Commonwealth a "Bill of Sale and Assignment" that purported to transfer to Commonwealth 654 theater seats, "free and clear of all liens, encumbrances, claims, clouds, charges, equities, or imperfections of any kind or nature. . . ." In May 1985, Commonwealth transferred its interest in the lease and property to Wehrenberg. In April 1993, after the lease had expired and without JEP's approval, Wehrenberg uprooted the theater seats from the floor, breaking sections of concrete and leaving behind only the inclined floor, pocked with 2,600 holes. Were these seats fixtures?

6. Manor Ridge is a development consisting of 118 one-family residential lots on a 50-acre tract. When the tract was developed in the late 1920s, the developer established various deed restrictions "to run with the land." In addition to the covenant prohibiting "outbuildings," the Manor Ridge deeds provide that (1) "no more than one house intended for not more than one family shall be built on any plot," and (2) "no house shall be erected on any property . . . costing less than Fourteen thousand ($14,000) dollars based on the cost of construction of January 1st 1926." The deeds also require any residence to be set back 40 feet from the street and any detached garage to be set back 75 feet. The evident objective of this set of deed restrictions was to establish an exclusive residential community. The Lenocis bought their home in Manor Ridge in the summer of 1994. Shortly thereafter, they contracted to do extensive renovations to the home and to construct a "pool cabana" next to an existing in-ground swimming pool. The Lenocis began construction of the cabana in late March of 1995. Sneirson, who lives two houses away, observed the construction and promptly notified the municipal building department that the structure violated the restrictive covenant prohibiting "outbuildings." The building department issued a stop work order, but later rescinded the order. The Lenocis completed construction of the cabana. It is a substantial structure that covers more than 600 square feet, and has a cathedral ceiling, bathroom, refrigerator, dryer, wet bar, and heating system. It is located only five feet from the rear boundary line

between the Lenocis' property and the property of the Steigers, close to the Steigers' swimming pool. Fifteen of the 118 properties located in Manor Ridge are occupied by ancillary structures. Ten of those structures are small sheds for the storage of pool or lawn mowing equipment, one is a dollhouse, and the other four are pool cabanas. The Lenocis' cabana is the largest in Manor Ridge; the only other one nearly as large is located on a two-and-a-half-acre lot, which is five times larger than the Lenocis' half-acre lot. Should the Lenocis be compelled to remove the cabana?

7. The Buzby Landfill was operated from 1966 to 1978. Although it was not licensed to receive liquid industrial or chemical wastes, large amounts of hazardous materials and chemicals were dumped there. Toxic wastes began to escape from the landfill because it had no liner or cap. Tests performed by a state environmental protection agency revealed ground water contamination caused by hazardous waste seepage from the landfill. The federal Environmental Protection Agency investigated the situation and recommended that the Buzby Landfill site be considered for cleanup under the federal Superfund law, but the cleanup did not take place. During the 1980s, Canetic Corp. and Canuso Management Corp. developed a housing subdivision near the closed Buzby Landfill. Some of the homes in the subdivision were within half a mile of the old landfill. Some of the homeowners filed a class action lawsuit alleging that Canetic and Canuso had substantial information about the dangers of placing a subdivision near the landfill, but they had not disclosed to buyers the fact that the subdivision was located near a hazardous waste dump. The defendants claimed that they did not have the duty to disclose conditions that happened on someone else's property. Will the defendants win?

8. Voyeur Dorm operates an Internet-based Web site that provides a 24-hour-a-day Internet transmission portraying the lives of the residents of 2312 West Farwell Drive, Tampa, Florida. Throughout its existence, Voyeur Dorm has employed 25 to 30 different women, most of whom entered into a contract that specifies, among other things, that they are "employees," on a "stage and filming location," with "no reasonable expectation of privacy," for "entertainment purposes." Subscribers to voyeurdorm.com pay a subscription fee of $34.95 a month to watch the women employed at the premises and pay an added

fee of $16.00 per month to "chat" with the women. At a zoning hearing, Voyeur Dorm's counsel conceded that five women live in the house, that there are cameras in the corners of all the rooms of the house, that for a fee a person can join a membership to a Web site wherein a member can view the women 24 hours a day, seven days a week, that a member, at times, can see someone disrobed, that the women receive free room and board, and that the women are paid as part of a business enterprise. From August 1998 to June 2000, Voyeur Dorm generated subscriptions and sales totaling $3,166,551.35.

Section 27–523 of Tampa's City Code defines adult entertainment establishments as:

> any premises . . . on which is offered to members of the public or any person, for a consideration, entertainment featuring or in any way including specified sexual activities . . . or entertainment featuring the displaying or depicting of specified anatomical areas . . . ; "entertainment" as used in this definition shall include, but not be limited to, books, magazines, films, newspapers, photographs, paintings, drawings, sketches or other publications or graphic media, filmed or live plays, dances or other performances either by single individuals or groups, distinguished by their display or depiction of specified anatomical areas or specified sexual activities.

The City of Tampa argues that Voyeur Dorm is an adult use business pursuant to the express and unambiguous language of section 27–523 and, as such, cannot operate in a residential neighborhood. Is the city correct?

9. In 1973, the Feests purchased real property from Renak and several co-owners. Included on the property was a building, "the shop," in which three generations of the Renak family had operated a blacksmith, wagon repair, and machine repair business. The real estate purchase agreement gave Renak the right to exclusive use and occupancy of the shop for the rest of his life. The agreement also provided:

> Included in the purchase price is all tangible personalty now on the property, except the following:
>
> . . . .
>
> B. Any item of personalty owned by Delmar Renak alone as distinguished from personalty which is owned by him and the other sellers in common. The statement of Delmar Renak that he owns alone any item of personalty shall be binding upon all parties to this agreement.

After the sale of the property to the Feests, Renak continued to use the shop until sometime in 2000.

Various equipment in the shop was powered by a gasoline Pierce Engine which had been installed in the shop by Renak's grandfather and father. The Pierce Engine, approximately six and one-half feet long, three and one-half feet tall, and weighing more than a ton, was attached to a brick foundation within the shop's "engine room" by four large bolts. It had been in the shop for nearly 100 years. Although large, it was detachable and, with a hoist, easily movable. In the fall of 2000, the Feests removed the Pierce Engine from the shop and stored it elsewhere on their property. The Feests had no interest in operating the business, and in fact, tore the shop down. In November 2000, Renak agreed to donate the Pierce Engine to the Racine County Historical Society and Museum. The Feests claimed ownership of the Pierce Engine and refused to permit its removal from their property. Was the Pierce Engine a fixture that belonged to the Feests?

10. Emma Yocum was married to James Yocum as of the time of her death in 1990. She and James had begun living together in March 1959. In July 1959, by way of a warranty deed that referred to them as "husband and wife," Emma and James took ownership of a home. She and James, however, were not yet married. Emma was still married to Joseph Perez, from whom she was divorced in April 1960. Emma and James were married in July 1960. When they acquired their home in 1959, James had provided the down payment. A mortgage executed by Emma and James at that time also referred to them as husband and wife even though they were not then married. After Emma's death in 1990, her children by her marriage to Joseph Perez filed suit in an effort to have the court determine present ownership of the home Emma and James had owned during her lifetime. Had Emma and James owned the home as *tenants in common* (meaning that Emma's interest in the property would pass to her estate, in which her children were entitled to share), or instead as either *tenants by the entirety* or *joint tenants* (meaning that James would then solely own the home by virtue of the right of survivorship)?

Online Research

Researching Real Property on the Web

1. Using your favorite search engine, locate a Web site that lists real estate for sale. Find a property listing on one of these sites. Using the concepts discussed in this chapter, identify the property features on the listing that would be considered fixtures.

2. Find an example online of each of the following kinds of deeds: quitclaim deed, general warranty deed, and special warranty deed.

chapter 25

LANDLORD AND TENANT

Frank Johnson and Sonia Miller, along with several other friends, were looking to rent a house near campus for the following school year. In June, they orally agreed with a landlord on a one-year lease to begin the following August 15 with a monthly rent of $1,250 and provided a $1,500 security deposit. When they arrived at school in August, the current tenants were still in possession and did not move out until September 1, leaving the house a mess. The landlord told Frank and Sonia to move in and that he would clean it up later; however, he never did so despite repeated requests. They complained to the city housing department, which conducted an inspection and found numerous violations of the city's housing code. The city gave the landlord 15 days to make the necessary repairs. Before any of the repairs were made, a friend who was visiting was injured when she fell through some rotten floorboards on the porch. At the end of September, Frank, Sonia and the other tenants moved out, but the landlord refused to return their security deposit.

Among the legal issues raised by this scenario are:

- Did the oral agreement create an enforceable lease?
- Were the tenants' rights violated when they were unable to take possession on August 15?
- Does the landlord have any liability to the injured friend?
- Are the tenants entitled to cancel the lease on the grounds the house is not habitable and obtain the return of their security deposit?
- If the landlord never intended to clean up the house, was it ethical for him to tell the tenants he would do so?

LANDLORD–TENANT LAW HAS undergone dramatic change during the past four decades, owing in large part to the changing nature of the relationship between landlords and tenants. In England and in early America, farms were the usual subjects of leases. The tenant sought to lease land on which to grow crops or graze cattle. Accordingly, traditional landlord–tenant law viewed the lease as primarily a conveyance of land and paid relatively little attention to its contractual aspects.

In today's society, however, the landlord–tenant relationship is typified by the lease of property for residential or commercial purposes. A residential tenant commonly occupies only a small portion of the total property. He bargains primarily for the use of structures on the land rather than for the land itself. He is likely to have signed a landlord-provided form lease, the terms of which he may have had little or no opportunity to negotiate. In areas with a shortage of affordable housing, a residential tenant's ability to bargain for favorable lease provisions is further hampered. Because the typical landlord–tenant relationship can no longer fairly be characterized as one in which the parties have equal knowledge and bargaining power, it is not always realistic to presume that tenants are capable of negotiating to protect their own interests.

Although it was initially slow to recognize the changing nature of the landlord–tenant relationship, the law now places greater emphasis than it once did on the contract components of the relationship. As a result, modern contract doctrines such as unconscionability, constructive conditions, the duty to mitigate damages, and implied warranties are commonly applied to leases. Such doctrines may operate to compensate for tenants' lack of bargaining power. In addition, state legislatures and city councils have enacted statutes and ordinances that increasingly regulate leased property and the landlord–tenant relationship.

This chapter's discussion of landlord–tenant law will focus on the nature of leasehold interests, the traditional rights and duties of landlords and tenants, and recent statutory and judicial developments affecting those rights and duties.

Leases and Tenancies

Nature of Leases A **lease** is a contract under which an owner of property, the **landlord** (also called the *lessor*), conveys to the **tenant** (also called the *lessee*) the exclusive right to possess property for a period of time. The property interest conveyed to the tenant is called a **leasehold estate.**

Types of Tenancies The duration of the tenant's possessory right depends upon the type of **tenancy** established by or resulting from the lease. There are four main types of tenancies.

1. *Tenancy for a term.* In a **tenancy for a term** (also called a *tenancy for years*), the landlord and tenant have agreed on a specific duration of the lease and have fixed the date on which the tenancy will terminate. For example, if Dudley, a college student, leases an apartment for the academic year ending May 25, 2010, a tenancy for a term will have been created. The tenant's right to possess the property ends on the date agreed upon without any further notice, unless the lease contains a provision permitting extension.

2. *Periodic tenancy.* A **periodic tenancy** is created when the parties agree that rent will be paid in regular successive intervals until notice to terminate is given, but do not agree on a specific lease duration. If the tenant pays rent monthly, the tenancy is from month to month; if the tenant pays yearly, as is sometimes done under agricultural leases, the tenancy is from year to year. (Periodic tenancies therefore are sometimes called *tenancies from month to month* or *tenancies from year to year.*) To terminate a periodic tenancy, either party must give advance notice to the other. The precise amount of notice required is often defined by state statutes. For example, to terminate a tenancy from month to month, most states require that the notice be given at least one month in advance.

3. *Tenancy at will.* A **tenancy at will** occurs when property is leased for an indefinite period of time and either party may choose to conclude the tenancy at any time. Generally, tenancies at will involve situations in which the tenant either does not pay rent or does not pay it at regular intervals. For example, Landon allows her friend Trumbull to live in the apartment over her garage. Although this tenancy's name indicates that it is terminable "at [the] will" of either party, most states require that the landlord give reasonable advance notice to the tenant before exercising the right to terminate the tenancy.

4. *Tenancy at sufferance.* A **tenancy at sufferance** occurs when a tenant remains in possession of the property (holds over) after a lease has expired. In this situation, the landlord has two options: (1) treating the holdover tenant as a trespasser and bringing an action to eject him; or (2) continuing to treat him as a tenant and collecting rent from him. Until the landlord makes her election, the tenant is a tenant at sufferance. Suppose that Templeton has leased an apartment for one year from Larson. At the end of the year, Templeton holds over and does not move out. Templeton is a tenant at sufferance. Larson may have him ejected or may continue treating him as a tenant. If Larson elects the latter alternative, a new tenancy is created. The new tenancy will be either a tenancy for a term or a periodic tenancy, depending on the facts of the case and any presumptions established by state law. Thus, a tenant who holds over for even a few days runs the risk of creating a new tenancy he might not want.

Execution of a Lease As transfers of interests in land, leases may be covered by the statute of frauds. In most states, a lease for a term of more than one year from the date it is made is unenforceable unless it is evidenced by a

---

CYBERLAW IN ACTION

The Internet Facilitates Leasing Property

E-commerce has eased the sometimes challenging and time-consuming task of finding an apartment or rental property. Now in many cities and resort communities a person can search for a suitable rental using the Internet. There are numerous Internet portals that provide databases of available rental properties. While some are nationwide, most focus on a specific region or city. These Web sites allow prospective renters to list their particular requirements such as size, location, price range, and amenities. Then the site operator provides available options to the prospective renter and may periodically update the list. Some companies even provide virtual tours of apartment or house layouts that allow the prospective renter to view the property online. In some cases, a rental application may be submitted and the rental arrangements finalized via the Internet. The Internet portal sites also commonly provide links that allow customers to turn on their gas, water, telephone, and other desired utilities over the Internet.

Types of Tenancies

Type of Lease	Characteristics	Termination
Tenancy for a Term	Landlord and tenant agree on a specific duration of the lease and fix the date on which the tenancy will end.	Ends automatically on the date agreed upon; no additional notice necessary.
Periodic Tenancy	Landlord and tenant agree that tenant will pay rent at regular, successive intervals (e.g., month to month).	Either party may terminate by giving the amount of advance notice required by state law.
Tenancy at Will	Landlord and tenant agree that tenant may possess property for an indefinite amount of time, with no agreement to pay rent at regular, successive intervals.	May be terminated "at will" by either party, but state law requires advance notice.
Tenancy at Sufferance	Tenant remains in possession after the termination of one of the leaseholds described above, until landlord brings ejectment action against tenant or collects rent from him.	Landlord has choice of: 1. Treating tenant as a trespasser and bringing ejectment action against him, *or* 2. Accepting rent from tenant, thus creating a new leasehold.

suitable writing signed by the party to be charged. A few states, however, require leases to be evidenced by a writing only when they are for a term of more than three years.

Good business practice demands that leases be carefully drafted to make clear the parties' respective rights and obligations. Care in drafting leases is especially important in cases of long-term and commercial leases. Lease provisions normally cover such essential matters as the term of the lease, the rent to be paid, the uses the tenant may make of the property, the circumstances under which the landlord may enter the property, the parties' respective obligations regarding the condition of the property, and the responsibility (as between landlord and tenant) for making repairs. In addition, leases often contain provisions allowing a possible extension of the term of the lease and purporting to limit the parties' rights to assign the lease or sublet the property. State or local law often regulates lease terms. For example, the Uniform Residential Landlord and Tenant Act (URLTA) has been enacted in a substantial minority of states. The URLTA prohibits the inclusion of certain lease provisions, such as a clause by which the tenant supposedly agrees to pay the landlord's attorney's fees in an action to enforce the lease. In states that have not enacted the URLTA, lease terms are likely to be regulated at least to a moderate degree by some combination of state statutes, common law principles, and local housing codes.

Rights, Duties, and Liabilities of the Landlord

Landlord's Rights The landlord is entitled to receive the *agreed rent* for the term of the lease. Upon expiration of the lease, the landlord has the right to the *return of the property in as good a condition as it was when leased,* except for normal wear and tear and any destruction caused by an act of God.

Security Deposits Landlords commonly require tenants to make security deposits or advance payments of rent. Such deposits operate to protect the landlord's right to receive rent as well as her right to reversion of the property in good condition. In recent years, many cities and states have enacted statutes or ordinances designed to prevent landlord abuse of security deposits. These laws typically limit the amount a landlord may demand and require that the security deposit be refundable, except for portions withheld by the landlord because of the tenant's nonpayment of rent or tenant-caused property damage beyond ordinary wear and tear. Some statutes or ordinances also require the landlord to place the funds in interest-bearing accounts when the lease is for more than a minimal period of time. As a general rule, these laws require landlords to provide tenants a written accounting regarding their security deposits and any portions being withheld. Such an accounting normally must be provided within a specified period of time (30 days, for example) after the termination of the lease. The landlord's failure to comply with statutes and ordinances regarding security deposits may cause the landlord to experience adverse consequences that vary state by state.

Landlord's Duties

Fair Housing Act   As explained in Chapter 24, the Fair Housing Act prohibits housing discrimination on the basis of race, color, sex, religion, national origin, handicap, and familial status.[1] The Fair Housing Act prohibits discriminatory practices in various transactions affecting housing, including the rental of dwellings.[2] Included within the act's prohibited instances of discrimination against a protected person are refusals to rent property to such a person; discrimination against him or her in the terms, conditions, or privileges of rental; publication of any advertisement or statement indicating any preference, limitation, or discrimination operating to the disadvantage of a protected person; and representations that a dwelling is not available for rental to such a person when, in fact, it is available.

The act also makes it a discriminatory practice for a landlord to refuse to permit a tenant with a handicap to make—at his own expense—reasonable modifications to leased property. The landlord may, however, make this permission conditional on the tenant's agreement to restore the property to its previous condition upon termination of the lease, reasonable wear and tear excepted. In addition, landlords are prohibited from refusing to make reasonable accommodations in rules, policies, practices, or services if such accommodations are necessary to afford a handicapped tenant equal opportunity to use and

enjoy the leased premises. When constructing certain types of multifamily housing for first occupancy, property owners and developers risk violating the act if they fail to make the housing accessible to persons with handicaps.

Because of a perceived increase in the frequency with which landlords refused to rent to families with children, the act prohibits landlords from excluding families with children. If, however, the dwelling falls within the act's "housing for older persons" exception, this prohibition does not apply.[3]

Implied Warranty of Possession   Landlords have certain obligations that are imposed by law whenever property is leased. One of these obligations stems from the landlord's **implied warranty of possession.** This warranty guarantees the tenant's right to possess the property for the term of the lease. Suppose that Turner rents an apartment from Long for a term to begin on September 1, 2009, and to end on August 31, 2010. When Turner attempts to move in on September 1, 2009, she finds that Carlson, the previous tenant, is still in possession of the property. In this case, Long has breached the implied warranty of possession.

Implied Warranty of Quiet Enjoyment   By leasing property, the landlord also makes an **implied warranty of quiet enjoyment** (or *covenant of quiet enjoyment*). This covenant guarantees that the tenant's possession will not be interfered with as a result of the landlord's act or omission. In the absence of a contrary provision in the lease or an emergency that threatens the property, the landlord may not enter the leased property during the term of the lease. If he does, he will be liable for trespass. In some cases, courts have held that the covenant of quiet enjoyment was violated when the landlord failed to stop third parties, such as trespassers or other tenants who make excessive noise, from interfering with the tenant's enjoyment of the leased premises.

Constructive Eviction   The doctrine of **constructive eviction** may aid a tenant when property becomes unsuitable for the purposes for which it was leased because of the landlord's act or omission, such as the breach of a duty to repair or the covenant of quiet enjoyment. Under this doctrine, which applies both to residential and commercial property, the tenant may terminate the lease because she has effectively been evicted as a result of the

---

[1]Familial status is defined in Chapter 24.

[2]The act provides an exemption for certain persons who own and rent single-family houses. To qualify for this exemption, owners must not use a real estate broker or an illegal advertisement and cannot own more than three such houses at one time. It also exempts owners who rent rooms or units in dwellings in which they themselves reside, if those dwellings house no more than four families.

[3]The "housing for older persons" exception is described in Chapter 24.

poor condition or the objectionable circumstances there. Constructive eviction gives a tenant the right to vacate the property without further rent obligation if she does so *promptly* after giving the landlord reasonable notice and an opportunity to correct the problem. Because constructive eviction requires the tenant to vacate the leased premises, it is an unattractive option, however, for tenants who cannot afford to move or do not have a suitable alternative place to live.

Landlord's Responsibility for Condition of Leased Property

The common law historically held that landlords made no implied warranties regarding the *condition* or *quality* of leased premises. As an adjunct to the landlord's right to receive the leased property in good condition at the termination of the lease, the common law imposed on the *tenant* the duty to make repairs. Even when the lease contained a landlord's express warranty or express promise to make repairs, a tenant was not entitled to withhold rent if the landlord failed to carry out his obligations. This was because a fundamental contract performance principle—that a party is not obligated to perform if the other party fails to perform—was considered inapplicable to leases. In recent years, however, changing views of the landlord–tenant relationship have resulted in dramatically increased legal responsibility on the part of landlords for the condition of leased residential property.

Implied Warranty of Habitability

The legal principle that landlords made no implied warranty regarding the condition of leased property arose during an era when tenants used land primarily for agricultural purposes. Buildings existing on the property were frequently of secondary importance. They also tended to be simple structures, lacking modern conveniences such as plumbing and wiring. These buildings were fairly easily inspected and repaired by the tenant, who was generally more self-sufficient than today's typical tenant. In view of the relative simplicity of the structures, landlord and tenant were considered to have equal knowledge of the property's condition upon commencement of the lease. Thus, a rule requiring the tenant to make repairs seemed reasonable.

The position of modern residential tenants differs greatly from that of an earlier era's agricultural tenants. The modern residential tenant bargains not for the use of the ground itself but for the use of a building (or portion thereof) as a dwelling. The structures on land today are complex, frequently involving systems (such as plumbing and electrical systems) to which the tenant does not have physical access. Besides decreasing the likelihood of perceiving defects during inspection, this complexity compounds the difficulty of making repairs—something at which today's tenant already tends to be less adept than his grandparents were. Moreover, placing a duty on tenants to negotiate for express warranties and duties to repair is no longer feasible. Residential leases are now routinely executed on standard forms provided by landlords.

For these reasons, statutes or judicial decisions in most states now impose an **implied warranty of habitability** on many landlords who lease residential property. According to the vast majority of cases, this warranty is applicable only to *residential* property, and not to property leased for commercial uses. The implied warranty of habitability's content in lease settings is basically the same as in the sale of real estate: the property must be safe and suitable for human habitation. In lease settings, however, the landlord not only must deliver a habitable dwelling at the beginning of the lease but also must *maintain* the property in a habitable condition during the term of the lease. Various statutes and judicial decisions provide that the warranty includes an obligation that the leased property comply with any applicable housing codes.

Remedies for Breach of Implied Warranty of Habitability

From a tenant's point of view, the implied warranty of habitability is superior to constructive eviction because a tenant does not have to vacate the leased premises in order to seek a remedy for breach of the warranty. The particular remedies for breach of the implied warranty of habitability differ from state to state. Some of the remedies a tenant may pursue include:

1. *Action for damages.* The breach of the implied warranty of habitability violates the lease and renders the landlord liable for damages. The damages generally are measured by the diminished value of the leasehold. The landlord's breach of the implied warranty of habitability may also be asserted by the tenant as a counterclaim and defense in the landlord's action for eviction and/or nonpayment of rent.

2. *Termination of lease.* In extreme cases, the landlord's breach of the implied warranty of habitability may justify the tenant's termination of the lease. For this remedy to be appropriate, the landlord's breach must have been substantial enough to constitute a material breach.

3. *Rent abatement.* Some states permit rent abatement, a remedy under which the tenant withholds part of the rent for the period during which the landlord was in breach of the implied warranty of habitability. Where authorized by law, this approach allows the tenant to pay a reduced rent that reflects the *actual* value of the leasehold in its defective condition. There are different ways of computing this value. State law determines the amount by which the rent will be reduced.

4. *Repair-and-deduct.* A number of states have statutes permitting the tenant to have defects repaired and to deduct the repair costs from her rent. The repairs authorized in these statutes are usually limited to essential services such as electricity and plumbing. They also require that the tenant give the landlord notice of the defect and an adequate opportunity to make the repairs himself.

Housing Codes Many cities and states have enacted housing codes that impose duties on property owners with respect to the condition of leased property. Typical of these provisions is Section 2304 of the District of Columbia Housing Code, which provides: "No person shall rent or offer to rent any habitation or the furnishing thereof unless such habitation and its furnishings are in a clean, safe and sanitary condition, in repair and free from rodents or vermin." Such codes commonly call for the provision and maintenance of necessary services such as heat, water, and electricity, as well as suitable bathroom and kitchen facilities. Housing codes also tend to require that specified minimum space–per-tenant standards be met; that windows, doors, floors, and screens be kept in repair; that the property be painted and free of lead paint; that keys and locks meet certain specifications; and that the landlord issue written receipts for rent payments. A landlord's failure to comply with an applicable housing code may result in a fine or in liability for injuries resulting from the property's disrepair. The noncompliance may also result in the landlord's losing part or all of his claim to the agreed-upon rent. Some housing codes establish that tenants have the right to withhold rent until necessary repairs have been made and the right to move out in cases of particularly egregious violations of housing code requirements.

In the case that follows, *Brooks v. Lewin Realty III, Inc.,* the court held that a landlord could be liable for injuries to a child that were caused by the landlord's failure to comply with the city's housing code.

Brooks v. Lewin Realty III, Inc.   835 A.2d 616 (Md. Ct. App. 2003)

In August 1988, Shirley Parker rented a house in Baltimore City. Fresh paint was applied to the interior of the house at the beginning of the tenancy. Sharon Parker, Shirley's daughter, moved into the house shortly after her mother rented it. On December 6, 1989, Sharon gave birth to Sean, who then also lived there. Early in 1991, when Sean was slightly more than a year old, Lewin Realty purchased the house at an auction. Before the purchase, one of the owners of Lewin Realty walked through the house accompanied by Sharon as he inspected it. At the time of the walk-through there was peeling, chipping, and flaking paint present in numerous areas of the interior of the house, including in Sean's bedroom. After Lewin Realty purchased the house, it entered into a new lease with Shirley but did not paint its interior at that time.

In February 1992, Sean was diagnosed with an elevated blood lead level. In May 1992, the house was inspected and found to contain 56 areas of peeling, chipping, and flaking lead paint, and the Baltimore City Health Department (BCHD) issued a lead paint violation notice to Lewin Realty.

Section 702 (a) of the Baltimore City Housing Code requires that a dwelling be kept in "good repair" and "safe condition" and prohibits a landlord from leasing a dwelling that violates the Housing Code. The Housing Code further provides that maintaining a dwelling in good repair and safe condition includes keeping all interior walls, ceilings, woodwork, doors, and windows clean and free of any flaking, loose, or peeling paint. It also mandates the removal of loose and peeling paint from interior surfaces and requires that any new paint be free of lead. The Housing Code also grants the landlord the right of access to rental dwellings at reasonable times for purpose of making inspections and such repairs as are necessary to comply with the Code.

Sharon Parker brought a lawsuit on behalf of her son, alleging, among other things, negligence. The negligence claim was founded on several grounds, including (a) Lewin Realty's violation of the Baltimore City Code; (b) Sean's exposure to an unreasonable risk of harm from the lead-based paint while Lewin Realty knew that its dangerous properties were not known to Sean and not discoverable in the exercise of reasonable care; (c) Lewin Realty's failure to exercise reasonable care in properly maintaining the walls, doors, and ceilings after Lewin Realty had actual and constructive knowledge of the flaking paint condition; and (d) Lewin Realty's failure to exercise reasonable care to inspect the dwelling's paint when a reasonable inspection would have revealed the flaking paint condition.

One of the questions in the litigation was whether the tenants were required to show that the landlord had notice of the violation in order to establish a prima facie *case of negligence. Lewin Realty argued that because the tenant had control over the property and neither the common law nor any statute expressly required inspections during the tenancy, the court should not impose such a duty. Lewin Realty further argued it should not be held liable unless it had actual knowledge of the violation and that landlords who do not perform periodic inspections should not be charged with knowledge of what such inspections would reveal.*

Eldridge, Justice

As the parties point out, under the common law and in the absence of a statute, a landlord ordinarily has no duty to keep rental premises in repair, or to inspect the rental premises either at the inception of the lease or during the lease term. There are, however, exceptions to this general rule.

Moreover, where there is an applicable statutory scheme designed to protect a class of persons which includes the plaintiff, another well-settled Maryland common law rule has long been applied by this Court in negligence actions. That rule states that the defendant's duty ordinarily "is prescribed by the statute" or ordinance and that the violation of the statute or ordinance is itself evidence of negligence.

Under this principle, in order to make out a *prima facie* case in a negligence action, all that a plaintiff must show is: (a) the violation of a statute or ordinance designed to protect a specific class of persons which includes the plaintiff, and (b) that the violation proximately caused the injury complained of. "Proximate cause is established by determining whether the plaintiff is within the class of persons sought to be protected, and the harm suffered is of a kind which the drafters intended the statute to prevent. . . . It is the existence of this cause and effect relationship that makes the violation of a statute *prima facie* evidence of negligence."

We stress that none of the cases we cite impose upon the plaintiff the additional burden of proving that the defendant was aware that he or she was violating the statute or ordinance. Depending upon the statute and the particular sanction involved, knowledge, and the type thereof, may or may not be pertinent in establishing whether or not there was a statutory violation. Nevertheless, once it is established that there was a statutory violation, the tort defendant's knowledge that he or she violated the statute is not part of the tort plaintiff's burden of proof. It is the violation of the statute or ordinance alone which is evidence of negligence.

This rule has been stated in the context of landlords and tenants in the *Restatement (Second) of Property, Landlord and Tenant* Section *17.6* (1977), and cited with approval by this Court in lead paint premises liability cases. Section 17.6 of the *Restatement (Second) of Property* provides (emphasis added):

A landlord is subject to liability for physical harm caused to the tenant . . . by a dangerous condition existing before or

arising after the tenant has taken possession, if he has failed to exercise reasonable care to repair the condition and the existence of the condition is in violation of:
    (1) an implied warranty of habitability; or
    (2) *a duty created by statute or administrative regulation.*

In the instant case, the Housing Code, Baltimore City Code imposes numerous duties and obligations upon landlords who rent residential property to tenants. The plaintiffs are obviously within a class of persons which the Housing Code was designed to protect. *Brown v. Dermer* ("Patently, by enacting Sections 702 and 703 of the Housing Code, the City Council sought to protect children from lead paint poisoning by putting landlords on notice of conditions which could enhance the risk of such injuries"). Under the established principles of Maryland tort law set forth in the previously cited cases, if the plaintiffs can establish a violation of the Housing Code which proximately caused Sean's injuries, then the plaintiffs are entitled to have count one of their complaint submitted to the trier of facts. Under the above-cited cases, the plaintiffs need not prove that Lewin Realty had notice of the Housing Code violation.

* * *

Thus, under the plain meaning of the Code's language, it is clear that the Mayor and City Council of Baltimore mandated a *continuing* duty to keep the dwelling free of flaking, loose, or peeling paint, *at all times* "while [the dwelling is] in use," in order for the landlord to remain in compliance with the Housing Code. The nature of the landlord's duty is continuous. The Housing Code does not limit the landlord's duty to keep the premises free of flaking paint to a one-time duty at the inception of the lease. The landlord must take whatever measures are necessary during the pendency of the lease to ensure the dwelling's continued compliance with the Code.

To facilitate such continuous maintenance of the leased premises, Section 909 explicitly grants a right of entry to the landlord to ensure that he or she can "make such inspections and such repairs as are necessary" to comply with the Housing Code. It states:

Every occupant of a dwelling . . . shall give the owner thereof . . . access to any part of such dwelling . . . at all reasonable times for the purpose of making such inspection and such repairs or alterations as are necessary to effect compliance with the provisions of this Code. . . .

Although this section may not explicitly require the landlord to perform periodic inspections, it grants such right to the landlord and shows that the City anticipated that periodic inspections might be necessary to comply with the Code.

Lewin Realty urges that "during a tenancy . . . the landlord surrenders control of the property and, in doing so, surrenders the ability, at least in some respects, to prevent a violation of the housing code during the tenancy." Lewin Realty's principal argument is that the landlord has no ability to control the condition of the interior surfaces of the premises during the tenancy. We disagree. Contrary to Lewin Realty's argument, Section 909 vests the landlord with sufficient control of the leased premises during the tenancy to inspect and to rectify a condition of flaking, loose, or peeling paint.

Furthermore, contrary to Lewin Realty's statements in its brief, our holding in the instant case does not impose a strict liability regime upon landlords. Whether Lewin Realty is held liable for an injury to a child, based on lead paint poisoning, will depend on the jury's evaluation of the reasonableness of Lewin Realty's actions under all the circumstances.

Lewin Realty also contends that "the imposition of a duty to inspect during [the] tenancy would create a minefield of difficulties." The respondent's concerns that a landlord will be required to "inspect the property every day, three times a week, twice a week, twice a month, once a month . . ." are without basis. The nature of the defective condition in question—a flaking, loose, or peeling paint condition—is a slow, prolonged process which is easily detected in the course of reasonable periodic inspections. As Lewin Realty concedes, "we know that paint in a property will chip—it is just a matter of time." It does not occur overnight.

In addition, Lewin Realty raises doubts about the ability to quantify the dangerousness of a lead paint condition: "Is one area in a far corner of a property a 'dangerous condition'? . . . Is the presence of lead-based paint in the eighth layer of paint, covered by seven non-leaded layers of paint, a hazardous condition when present on a windowsill as opposed to the upper far corner of a wall?" In a negligence case, such as the case at bar, the simple answer to these questions is that it will be the duty of the trier of fact to determine whether the steps taken by the landlord to ensure continued compliance with the Code, i.e., the frequency and thoroughness of inspections, and the maintenance of the interior surfaces of the dwelling, were reasonable under all the circumstances. The test is what a reasonable and prudent landlord would have done under the same circumstances.

Finally, Lewin Realty suggests that a tenant might object to the landlord's need to inspect the premises. That concern is allayed by the fact that the Housing Code *requires* the tenant to give the owner access to the premises "at all reasonable times for the purpose of making such inspections . . . as are necessary to effect compliance with the provisions of this Code." Section 909.

Raker, Judge, dissenting

I respectfully dissent. The majority explicitly overrules *Richwind v. Brunson (1994)*—a case that, until today, had never had any doubt cast upon it by this Court or any other—and holds that by enacting the Baltimore City Housing Code, the City Council intended to abolish the element of notice in a common law negligence action for injuries resulting from flaking, loose or peeling paint. In the process of overruling *Richwind,* the majority also reads into the Code an ongoing, affirmative duty by landlords to inspect periodically each of their housing units for loose or flaking paint for as long as they retain ownership of the premises. I disagree with the majority's conclusion that the ordinance does away with the traditional, common law notice requirement to the landlord as a precursor to liability for negligence.

It is helpful to understand first what the majority's holding actually means and its implications for landlords and tenants in Baltimore. A violation of Baltimore's Housing Code occurs when the landlord does not comply with Section 703, which mandates, in relevant part, that "all walls, ceilings, woodwork, doors and windows shall be kept clean and free of any flaking, loose or peeling paint. . . ." The majority asserts that "if the plaintiffs can establish a violation of the Housing Code which proximately caused [their] injuries, then the plaintiffs are entitled to have . . . their complaint submitted to the trier of facts." Read together, the result of the majority's holding is astounding: *Any* flaking, loose or peeling paint in a leased premises, combined with an injury from lead paint, automatically gives rise to a cognizable action, worthy of a jury trial. The majority admits as much in summarizing its holding:

> In sum, the presence of flaking, loose, or peeling paint is a violation of the Housing Code. As earlier pointed out, certain provisions of the Housing Code were clearly enacted to prevent lead poisoning in children. Therefore, the plaintiff Sean is in the class of people intended to be protected by the Housing Code, and his injury, lead poisoning, is the kind of injury intended to be prevented by the Code. *This is all the plaintiffs must show to establish a* prima facie *case sounding in negligence.*

The majority's new rule means that the landlord will be forced to defend the case in court even if the plaintiff concedes that the landlord behaved reasonably in not knowing about a

Code violation. Without any express instruction, the majority reads into the statute the dramatic institution of a wholly new regulatory scheme that essentially imposes strict liability upon landlords and makes landlords the insurers of litigants for injuries sustained by a minor plaintiff due to exposure to lead-based paint. Furthermore, the majority's new rule means that plaintiff tenants will no longer be required to notify landlords of hazards in their dwelling home, hazards that they, not the landlord, are in the best position to identify.

The common law used to deal with such unfairness by providing that a landlord who had a valid excuse, such as lack of notice, for not remedying the violation would not be held liable, *see Restatement (Second) of Torts* Section 288A (2)(b) (1965) (excusing liability for violation of a legislative enactment or administrative regulation when defendant neither knows nor should know of the occasion for compliance). But under the majority's new rule, no such excuse is relevant.

Americans with Disabilities Act Landlords leasing property constituting a *place of public accommodation* (primarily commercial property as opposed to private residential property) must pay heed to Title III of the Americans with Disabilities Act. Under Title III, owners and possessors of real property that is a place of public accommodation may be expected to make reasonable accommodations, including physical modifications of the property, in order to allow disabled persons to have access to the property. Chapter 24 contains a detailed discussion of Title III's provisions.

Landlord's Tort Liability

Traditional No-Liability Rule   There were two major effects of the traditional rule that a landlord had no legal responsibility for the condition of the leased property. The first effect—that the uninhabitability of the premises traditionally did not give a tenant the right to withhold rent, assert a defense to nonpayment, or terminate a lease—has already been discussed. The second effect was that landlords normally could not be held liable in tort for injuries suffered by tenants on leased property. This state of affairs stemmed from the notion that the tenant had the ability and responsibility to inspect the property for defects before leasing it. By leasing the property, the tenant was presumed to take it as it was, with any existing defects. As to any defects that might arise during the term of the lease, the landlord's tort immunity was seen as justified by his lack of control over the leased property once he had surrendered it to the tenant.

Traditional Exceptions to No-Liability Rule   Even before the current era's protenant legal developments, however, courts created exceptions to the no-liability rule. In the following situations, landlords have traditionally

owed the tenant (or an appropriate third party) a duty the breach of which could constitute a tort:

1. *Duty to maintain common areas.* Landlords have a duty to use reasonable care to *maintain the common areas* (such as stairways, parking lots, and elevators) over which they retain control. If a tenant or a tenant's guest sustains injury as a result of the landlord's negligent maintenance of a common area, the landlord is liable.

2. *Duty to disclose hidden defects.* Landlords have the duty to disclose hidden defects about which they know, if the defects are not reasonably discoverable by the tenant. The landlord is liable if a tenant or appropriate third party suffers injury because of a hidden danger that was known to the landlord but went undisclosed.

3. *Duty to use reasonable care in performing repairs.* If a landlord repairs leased property, he must *exercise reasonable care in making the repairs.* The landlord may be liable for the consequences stemming from negligently performed repairs, even if he was not obligated to perform them.

4. *Duty to maintain property leased for admission to the public.* The landlord has a duty to suitably maintain property that is leased for *admission to the public.* A theater would be an example.

5. *Duty to maintain furnished dwellings.* The landlord who rents a *fully furnished dwelling* for a short time impliedly warrants that the premises are safe and habitable.

Except for the above circumstances, the landlord traditionally was not liable for injuries suffered by the tenant on leased property. Note that none of these exceptions would apply to one of the most common injury scenarios—when the tenant was injured by a defect in her own apartment and the defect resulted from the landlord's failure to repair, rather than from negligently performed repairs.

Current Trends in Landlord's Tort Liability Today, there is a strong trend toward abolition of the traditional rule of landlord tort immunity. The proliferation of housing codes and the development of the implied warranty of habitability have persuaded a sizable number of courts to impose on landlords the duty to use *reasonable care* in their maintenance of the leased property. As discussed earlier, a landlord's duty to keep the property in repair may be based on an express clause in the lease, the implied warranty of habitability, or provisions of a housing code or statute. The landlord now may be liable if injury results from her negligent failure to carry out her duty to make repairs. As a general rule, a landlord will not be liable unless she had *notice* of the defect and a reasonable opportunity to make repairs.

The duty of care landlords owe tenants has been held to include the duty to take reasonable steps to protect tenants from substantial risks of harm created by other tenants. Courts have held landlords liable for tenants' injuries resulting from dangerous conditions (such as vicious animals) maintained by other tenants when the landlord knew or had reason to know of the danger.

It is not unusual for landlords to attempt to insulate themselves from negligence liability to tenants by including an *exculpatory clause* in the standard form leases they expect tenants to sign. An exculpatory clause purports to relieve the landlord from legal responsibility that the landlord could otherwise face (on negligence or other grounds) in certain instances of premises-related injuries suffered by tenants. In recent years, a number of state legislatures and courts have frowned upon exculpatory clauses when they are included in leases of residential property. There has been an increasing judicial tendency to limit the effect of exculpatory clauses or declare them unenforceable on public policy grounds when they appear in residential leases.

In the case that follows, *Matthews v. Amberwood Associates Limited Partnership, Inc.,* the Maryland Court of Appeals, on a split vote, held that a landlord had a duty to protect a social visitor to the apartment of a tenant from a Pit Bull the tenant kept in the apartment where the landlord knew of the dog's viciousness, the presence of the dog was in violation of the lease, and where the landlord could have taken steps to abate the danger.

Matthews v. Amberwood Associates Limited Partnership, Inc.
719 A.2d 119 (Maryland Ct. App. 1998)

Shelly Morton leased an apartment building in Baltimore, Maryland, from October 9, 1993, through October 31, 1994. The apartment building was managed by Monocle Management, Ltd. and owned by Amberwood Associates Limited Partnership, Inc. The lease Morton signed contained the following provisions:

The resident agrees to comply with the following rules and regulations which shall be deemed to be part of the lease. Breach of these rules and regulations shall be deemed to be a default of the lease.

* * *

18. Not to have any pets on the premises.

Morton kept her boyfriend's dog, a Pit Bull named Rampage, in her apartment. Sometimes she kept the dog chained outside, on the grounds of the apartment complex. The dog was not normally aggressive toward persons when Morton was present, but, when she was absent, Rampage would attempt to attack people in his vicinity. Several employees of the building's management had dangerous encounters involving the dog; they considered the dog to be "vicious," and reported incidents involving the dog to the resident manager.

On February 9, 1994, Shanita Matthews and her 16-month-old son, Tevin Williams, visited Morton and Morton's 5-year-old son, Darnell, at Morton's apartment. The children were playing together in the living room, and the adults were seated at the dining room table putting together a puzzle when Morton was called away from the apartment. Shortly after Morton left the apartment, Rampage attacked Tevin. Rampage grabbed Tevin by the neck and was shaking him back and forth. Matthews was unable to free Tevin from Rampage's jaws. Matthews then called 911 and yelled for Morton to assist her.

Morton reentered the apartment and was also unable to free Tevin. She grabbed a knife, and, while Matthews held Tevin in her arms, Morton repeatedly stabbed Rampage causing the animal temporarily to release Tevin. Rampage continued to bite Tevin, however, until Morton finally was able to put the dog out of the apartment through the back door. By this time the ambulance had arrived, and Morton took Tevin from Matthews and ran with him to the ambulance. Approximately one hour after arriving at the hospital, Tevin died from his injuries.

Matthews and Tevin's father, Andre Williams, filed a wrongful death action against Monocle and Amberwood Associates. They alleged that the landlord owed a duty to social guests of a tenant who, while in the tenant's apartment, are injured or killed by a highly dangerous Pit Bull dog kept by the tenant, when the landlord knew of the dog's dangerousness, when the presence of the dog was in violation of the lease, and where the landlord could have taken steps to abate the danger.

A jury found Amberwood and Monocle liable and awarded damages including $5,018,750 to Matthews and $562,100 to Williams for the wrongful death of Tevin. Both sides appealed to the Maryland Court of Special Appeals, which held that, under the circumstances, Amberwood and Monocle owed no duty to social invitees of a tenant. Both parties again sought review in the Maryland Court of Appeals.

Eldridge, Judge

In order to state a cause of action in negligence, the plaintiff must show the following: (1) that the defendant was under a duty to protect the plaintiff from injury, (2) that the defendant breached that duty, (3) that the plaintiff suffered actual injury or loss, and (4) that the loss or injury proximately resulted from the defendant's breach of the duty. The question in the instant case focuses upon the first of these factors, namely, whether Amberwood and Monocle owed Matthews and Tevin a duty of abating the dangerous condition consisting of a vicious pit bull dog being in the apartment. The plaintiffs contend that Rampage constituted a known dangerous condition upon the property and that the defendants retained control over the presence of the pit bull within the leased premises through the "no pets" clause in the lease. Thus, the plaintiffs argue that the defendants had a duty of care to protect Matthews and her son from that extremely dangerous animal.

Under our cases, whether a landlord owes a duty to his or her tenants and their guests with respect to dangerous or defective conditions on the property, of which the landlord has notice, depends upon the circumstances presented. In a multi-unit facility, the landlord ordinarily has a duty to maintain the common areas in a reasonably safe condition. Our recognition of landlord liability in common areas is generally premised on the control a landlord maintains over the common areas. The duty to maintain these areas in a reasonably safe condition extends not only to the tenant but includes the members of his family, his guests, his invitees, and others on the land in the right of the tenant.

On the other hand, the duty which a landlord owes to a tenant, and the tenant's guests, within the tenant's apartment or other leased premises, is constrained by the general common law principle that where property is demised, and at the time of the demise it is not a nuisance, and becomes so *only* by the act of the tenant while in his possession, and injury happens during such possession, the owner is not liable. But, that where the owner leases premises which are a nuisance, or must in the nature of things become so by their use, and receives rent, then, whether in or out of possession, he is liable. Thus, a landlord is not ordinarily liable to a tenant or guest of a tenant for injuries from a hazardous condition in the leased premises that comes into existence after the tenant has taken possession.

As with most general principles of law, however, this principle, that a landlord is not responsible for dangerous conditions in the leased premises, is not absolute and has exceptions. For example, where a landlord agrees to rectify a dangerous condition in the leased premises, and fails to do so, he may be liable for injuries caused by the condition. If a landlord, although not contractually obligated to do so, voluntarily undertakes to rectify a dangerous or defective condition within the leased premises, and does so negligently, the landlord is liable for resulting injuries. Defective or dangerous conditions in the leased premises which violate statutes or ordinances may also be the basis for a negligence action against the landlord.

Just last month, in *Shields v. Wagman,* this Court held that landlords of a strip shopping center may be liable for injuries sustained by a business invitee and a tenant when they were attacked by a pit bull dog owned by another tenant and kept on the leased premises. The injuries in *Shields* occurred in a common area, the parking lot of the shopping center, on two occasions when the pit bull escaped from the leased premises. Stating that "our recognition of landlord liability in common areas is generally premised on the control a landlord maintains over the common areas," this Court reversed a judgment for the landlords.

The principal rationale for the general rule that the landlord is not ordinarily liable for injuries caused by defects or dangerous conditions in the leased premises is that the landlord "has parted with control." Moreover, as illustrated by the *Shields* opinion, a common thread running through many of our cases involving circumstances in which landlords have been liable (i.e., common areas, pre-existing defective conditions in the leased premises, a contract under which the landlord and tenant agree that the landlord shall rectify a defective condition) is the landlord's ability to exercise a degree of control over the defective or dangerous condition and to take steps to prevent injuries arising therefrom. Moreover, the principle that the landlord may have a duty with regard to matters within his control extends beyond common areas; it may be applicable to conditions in the leased premises.

Turning to the case at bar, the landlord also retained control with respect to the extremely dangerous condition in Morton's apartment. The tenant Morton did not have exclusive control over the leased premises because the lease gave the landlord a degree of control. The landlord retained control over the presence of a dog in the leased premises by virtue of the "no pets" clause in the lease. The lease plainly stated that breach of the "no pets" clause was a "default of the lease." Such a default would enable the landlord to bring a breach of lease action to terminate the tenancy pursuant to Code *Section 8–402.1 of the Real Property Article.*

Even before bringing such an action, the landlord, when it first received notice of the dangerous incidents involving Rampage, could have informed Morton that harboring the pit bull was in violation of her lease, could have told her to get rid of the aggressive animal, and could have threatened legal action if she failed to do so. If the landlord had taken these steps, it would have been likely that Morton would have gotten rid of the pit bull, particularly because she did not own him. If she refused to get rid of the dog, the landlord could then have instituted legal action. The record in this case, however, shows that the landlord did nothing. In fact, the defendants acknowledge that the landlord "did not take steps to enforce the no pets clause."

It is true that the conduct of the tenant Morton may also have been negligent, that Morton may have breached a duty owed to Matthews and Tevin, and that the landlord may not have affirmatively approved of Morton's harboring the pit bull. Morton's conduct in keeping a vicious animal in her apartment was also a cause of Tevin's death. Nonetheless, as Judge Wilner, writing for the Court of Special Appeals in another context, stated (*Bocchini v. Gorn Management Co., (1986)*), our concern in this case should be

> not so much on whether the landlord has approved the conduct of the tenant as whether he is in a position to correct or terminate it. *Where, through lease provisions or otherwise, he has that ability, the thought is that he ought not to be able to escape his obligation under a covenant of quiet enjoyment by steadfastly refusing to exercise his authority.*

* * *

The insertion in a lease of a restriction against excessive noise or other offensive conduct is precisely for the purpose of enabling the landlord to control that conduct. (Emphasis omitted and added.)

The tenant Morton was maintaining an extremely dangerous instrumentality, both in the leased premises and at times in the common areas. The landlord knew about the dangerous pit bull dog for a considerable period of time. By the terms of the lease, the landlord had retained a large measure of control over the presence of such an animal in the leased premises. Under the circumstances here, and the prior cases in this Court emphasizing the factor of a landlord's control, it is not unreasonable to impose upon the landlord a duty owed to guests who are either on the leased premises or the common areas.

In addition to the landlord's control and ability to abate the danger of a vicious pit bull in the leased premises, the foreseeability of the harm supports the imposition of a duty on the landlord. The facts here unequivocally indicate that harm to a tenant's guest by Rampage was entirely foreseeable. Numerous employees of Monocle testified that they knew of the pit bull, were afraid of the pit bull, witnessed attacks by the dog, and were unable to carry out their duties, both in the leased premises and in the common areas, because of the presence of the pit bull.

Thus, the foreseeability of harm in the present case was clear. The extreme dangerousness of this breed, as it has evolved today, is well recognized. Pit bulls as a breed are known to be extremely aggressive and have been bred as attack animals. Indeed, it has been judicially noted that pit bull dogs "bite to kill without signal," are selectively bred to have very powerful jaws, high insensitivity to pain, extreme aggressiveness, a natural tendency to refuse to terminate an attack, and a greater propensity to bite humans than other breeds. The Pit Bull's massive canine jaws can crush a victim with up to two thousand pounds (2,000) of pressure per square inch—three times that of a German Shepard or Doberman Pinscher.

We do not hold that a landlord's retention in the lease of some control over particular matters in the leased premises is, standing alone, a sufficient basis to impose a duty upon the landlord which is owed to a guest on the premises. This Court has employed a balancing test to determine whether a duty of reasonable care should be imposed in particular circumstances. Ultimately, the determination of whether a duty should be imposed is made by weighing the various policy considerations and reaching a conclusion that the plaintiff's interests are, or are not, entitled to legal protection against the conduct of the defendant. In the instant case, the various policy considerations that need to be weighed are the general understanding that a tenant is primarily in control of the leased premises and the sanctity of a tenant's home, including her ability generally to do as she sees fit within the privacy thereof, against the public safety concerns of permitting that same tenant to harbor an extremely dangerous animal that will foreseeably endanger individuals inside and outside the walls of the leased premises, the degree of control maintained by the landlord, the landlord's knowledge of the dangerous condition, and the landlord's ability to abate the condition. We, like the majority of courts addressing this issue in other states, believe that the balance should be struck on the side of imposing a duty on the landlord which is owed to guests on the premises.

To reiterate, we do not suggest that a landlord is responsible for most negligent conditions in leased apartments including conditions covered by provisions in a lease. Under the present circumstances, however, where a landlord retained control over the matter of animals in the tenant's apartment, coupled with the knowledge of past vicious behavior by the animal, the extremely dangerous nature of pit bull dogs, and the foreseeability of harm to persons and property in the apartment complex, the jury was justified in finding that the landlord had a duty to the plaintiffs and that the duty was breached. The following principle set forth in *Prosser and Keeton on The Law of Torts,* Section 4 at 25-26 (5th ed. 1984), is applicable here:

> The "aprophylactic" factor of preventing future harm has been quite important in the field of torts. The courts are concerned not only with the compensation of the victim, but with admonition of the wrongdoer. When the decisions of the courts become known, and defendants realize that they may be held liable, there is of course a strong incentive to prevent the occurrence of the harm. Not infrequently one reason for imposing liability is the deliberate purpose of providing that incentive.

Judgment for Matthews affirmed.

Rodowsky, Judge, dissenting

Tragic cases may have tragic consequences when sympathy for a plaintiff interferes with a court's ability to analyze the facts and apply the law. Sympathy for the victim of a tragedy should not serve as a substitute for evidence of duty, culpability, and proximate cause. The legal issue in this case is whether a landlord should have to pay over five million dollars solely because the landlord did not make a futile attempt to evict a tenant whose dog barked and growled at maintenance men trying to enter the dog's residence when its owner was not home.

Ms. Matthews suffered a grievous loss as a result of her son playing with a pit bull in a friend's apartment where she and her son were weekly social guests. The effect of affirming this five million dollar judgment in favor of Ms. Matthews

may ultimately have severe repercussions for lessees with dogs. Landlords wishing to avoid multimillion dollar lawsuits may be forced to initiate eviction proceedings to terminate leases whenever a tenant's dog acts aggressively toward maintenance personnel who attempt to enter the tenant's dwelling when the tenants are not home, and I doubt very many dogs would not bark and growl at a stranger trying to enter a dwelling when the dog's owner is absent. The case will certainly have tragic consequences for pit bulls because the majority opinion, in effect, makes ownership of a pit bull per se negligence, and the Court seems to advocate that the entire breed should be eradicated.

Perhaps the worst tragedy is the implication that rich landlords and sympathetic victims are judged by totally different standards. Ms. Matthews knew this pit bull and its temperament far, far better than the landlord; yet, under the majority's ruling, the landlord was negligent for not safeguarding Ms. Matthews' son from the dog, and Ms. Matthews was neither contributorily negligent for not safeguarding her son nor an intervening superseding cause for allowing her son to play with the dog. On that same issue, the majority discusses at great length the widespread general knowledge that pit bulls are extremely dangerous, but apparently only the landlord, not Ms. Matthews, could be chargeable with that knowledge since her contributory negligence is held not to be an issue to be submitted to the jury. Under the majority's reasoning, the young child's injury by the dog was foreseeable by the landlord, but not by his mother. The landlord was a cause of the child's injuries because it did not make a futile attempt to evict the dog's caretaker, but Ms. Matthews could not be found to be an intervening superseding cause even though she brought her young child to the dog's home and permitted the infant's unsupervised play with the dog. It does not seem as if the rules of the law of negligence are being applied equally.

In holding that there was insufficient evidence to permit a jury to find Ms. Matthews was contributorily negligent or that her actions were an intervening superseding cause, the majority may be losing sight of its obligation to look at the facts in the light most favorable to the landlord. These facts indicate Ms. Matthews had far, far greater knowledge of Rampage and his temperament than the landlord, and if the landlord could be found negligent for not evicting the dog, how could Ms. Matthews not also be negligent for letting her infant son play throughout this two-bedroom apartment with this dog?

On the issue of superseding cause, it seems a reasonable conclusion that 16-month-old Tevin did something to enrage Rampage. On this occasion, while Ms. Matthews was working on a puzzle, the two children were playing in Darnelle's room, the hallway, and the living room along with the dog. It is reasonable to assume Tevin unwittingly did something that injured or tormented Rampage. Rampage's hostility was only directed at young Tevin, and even after the dog was repeatedly stabbed, it continued to attack Tevin. Keeping in mind that this was the first time Rampage had bitten anyone, if the landlord was a cause of the injuries for not evicting the tenant, could not a reasonable jury find that Ms. Matthews was a superseding cause for letting a 16-month-old child play throughout the apartment with the dog?

Ms. Matthews knew Rampage better than anyone except the dog's owner. She and her child had visited with the dog on dozens and dozens of occasions, at least weekly, for the entire time her friend was caring for the dog. Even if the landlord's negligence was an issue for the jury, the jury also should have been permitted to consider whether Ms. Matthews' own conduct in failing to safeguard her infant son from the dog, which is what she claims the landlord did, as well as that her conduct in permitting this 16-month-old child's unsupervised play throughout a two-bedroom apartment with and around the dog

could be an intervening, superseding cause or contributory negligence as to her cause of action.

In the instant case, the tenant was in sole control of the premises where the injury occurred, and the tenant had the sole opportunity to protect her guests from the dog and failed to do so. Even if the landlord knew the dog had vicious tendencies, the landlord should be able to assume that when the dog was confined within the tenant's apartment that the tenant would take reasonable precautions to protect guests in her home. Moreover, there may be tenants who have a legitimate desire to keep watch dogs or guard dogs for the protection of their person or property, and this practice is not necessarily to be discouraged if the tenant keeps the dog controlled whenever it is off the tenant's premises or confined to the tenant's premises.

Thus, for the reasons set forth above, I would conclude that under the circumstances of this case there was no special duty on the part of the landlord to act affirmatively to protect Tevin or other social guests of the tenant, and therefore, the landlord may not be held liable for failing to take measures to enforce the "no pets" clause in the lease.

Ethics in Action

Disclosing Possible Hazards to Tenants

Suppose you own an older home that in the past was painted with lead-based paint. You rent it to a family with three small children. A state law forbids using lead-based paint on residential property after the effective date of the statute, but it does not require owners of property with residues of lead-based paint to remove it. Should you disclose the presence of the lead-based paint to your tenants?

Landlord's Liability for Injuries Resulting from Others' Criminal Conduct Another aspect of the trend toward increasing landlords' legal accountability is that many courts have imposed on landlords the duty to take reasonable steps to protect tenants and others on their property from foreseeable criminal conduct.[4] Although landlords are not insurers of the safety of persons on their property, an increasing number of courts have found them liable for injuries sustained by individuals who were criminally attacked on the landlord's

property if the attack was facilitated by the landlord's failure to comply with housing codes or maintain reasonable security. This liability has been imposed on residential and commercial landlords (such as shopping mall owners). Some courts have held that the implied warranty of habitability includes the obligation to provide reasonable security. In most states that have imposed this type of liability, however, principles of negligence or negligence per se furnish the controlling rationale.[5]

---

[4]Chapter 24 contains a more extensive discussion of courts' recent inclination to impose this duty on owners and possessors of property.

[5]The law of negligence is covered in detail in Chapter 7.

Rights, Duties, and Liabilities of the Tenant

Rights of the Tenant

The tenant has the right to *exclusive possession* and *quiet enjoyment* of the property during the term of the lease. The landlord is not entitled to enter the leased property without the tenant's consent, unless an emergency threatens the property or the landlord is acting under an express lease provision giving her the right to enter. The tenant may use the leased premises for any lawful purpose that is reasonable and appropriate, unless the purpose for which it may be used is expressly limited in the lease. Furthermore, the tenant has both the right to receive leased residential property in a habitable condition at the beginning of the lease and the right to have the property maintained in a habitable condition for the duration of the lease.

Duty to Pay Rent

The tenant, of course, has the duty to pay rent in the agreed amount and at the agreed times. If two or more persons are cotenants, their liability under the lease is *joint and several*. This means that each cotenant has complete responsibility—not just partial responsibility—for performing the tenants' duties under the lease. For example, Alberts and Baker rent an apartment from Caldwell, with both Alberts and Baker signing a one-year lease. If Alberts moves out after three months, Caldwell may hold Baker responsible for the entire rent, not just half of it. Naturally, Alberts remains liable on the lease—as well as to Baker under any rent-sharing agreement the two of them had—but Caldwell is free to proceed against Baker solely if Caldwell so chooses.

Duty Not to Commit Waste

The tenant also has the duty not to commit **waste** on the property. This means that the tenant is responsible for the routine care and upkeep of the property and that he has the duty not to commit any act that would harm the property. In the past, fulfillment of this duty required that the tenant perform necessary repairs. Today, the duty to make repairs has generally been shifted to the landlord by court ruling, statute, or lease provision. The tenant now has no duty to make major repairs unless the relevant damage was caused by his own negligence. When damage exists through no fault of the tenant and the tenant therefore is not obligated to make the actual repairs, the tenant nonetheless has the duty to take reasonable interim steps to prevent further damage from the elements. This duty would include, but not necessarily be limited to, informing the landlord of the problem. The duty would be triggered, for instance, when a window breaks or the roof leaks.

Assignment and Subleasing

As with rights and duties under most other types of contracts, the rights and duties under a lease may generally be assigned and delegated to third parties. **Assignment** occurs when the landlord or the tenant transfers all of her remaining rights under the lease to another person. For example, a landlord may sell an apartment building and assign the relevant leases to the buyer, who will then become the new landlord. A tenant may assign the remainder of her lease to someone else, who then acquires whatever rights the original tenant had under the lease (including, of course, the right to exclusive possession of the leased premises).

Subleasing occurs when the tenant transfers to another person some, but not all, of his remaining right to possess the property. The relationship of tenant to sublessee then becomes one of landlord and tenant. For example, Dorfman, a college student whose 18-month lease on an apartment is to terminate on December 31, 2010, sublets his apartment to Wembley for the summer months of 2010. This is a sublease rather than an assignment, because Dorfman has not transferred all of his remaining rights under the lease.

The significance of the assignment–sublease distinction is that an assignee acquires rights and duties under the lease between the landlord and the original tenant, but a sublessee does not. An assignee steps into the shoes of the original tenant and acquires any rights she had under the lease.[6] For example, if the lease contained an option to renew, the assignee would have the right to exercise this option. The assignee, of course, becomes personally liable to the landlord for the payment of rent.

Under both an assignment and a sublease, the original tenant remains liable to the landlord for the commitments made in the lease. If the assignee or sublessee fails to pay rent, for example, the tenant has the legal obligation to pay it. Figure 1 compares the characteristics of assignments and subleases.

Lease Provisions Limiting Assignment   Leases commonly contain limitations on assignment and subleasing.

---

[6]Assignment is discussed in detail in Chapter 17.

Figure 1 Comparison of Assignment and Sublease

	Sublease	Assignment
Does the tenant transfer to the third party *all* his remaining rights under the lease?	No	Yes
Does the tenant remain liable on the lease?	Yes	Yes
Does the third party (assignee or sublessee) acquire rights and duties under the tenant's lease with the landlord?	No	Yes

This is especially true of commercial leases. Such provisions typically require the landlord's consent to any assignment or sublease, or purport to prohibit such a transfer of the tenant's interests. Provisions requiring the landlord's consent are upheld by the courts, although some courts hold that the landlord cannot withhold consent unreasonably. Total prohibitions against assignment may be enforced as well, but they are disfavored in the law. Courts usually construe them narrowly, resolving ambiguities against the landlord.

Tenant's Liability for Injuries to Third Persons

The tenant is normally liable to persons who suffer harm while on the portion of the property over which the tenant has control, *if the injuries resulted from the tenant's negligence.*

Termination of the Leasehold

A leasehold typically terminates because the lease term has expired. Sometimes, however, the lease is terminated early because of a party's material breach of the lease or because of mutual agreement.

Eviction

If a tenant breaches the lease (most commonly, by nonpayment of rent), the landlord may take action to **evict** the tenant. State statutes usually establish a relatively speedy eviction procedure. The landlord who desires to evict a tenant must be careful to comply with any applicable state or city regulations governing evictions. These regulations usually forbid self-help measures on the landlord's part, such as forcible entry to change locks. At common law, a landlord had a lien on the tenant's personal property. The landlord therefore could remove and hold such property as security for the rent obligation. This lien has been abolished in many states. Where the lien still exists, it is subject to constitutional limitations requiring that the tenant be given notice of the lien, as well as an opportunity to defend and protect his belongings before they can be sold to satisfy the rent obligation.

Agreement to Surrender

A lease may terminate prematurely by mutual agreement between landlord and tenant to **surrender** the lease (i.e., return the property to the landlord prior to the end of the lease). A valid surrender discharges the tenant from further liability under the lease.

Abandonment

Abandonment occurs when the tenant unjustifiably and permanently vacates the leased premises before the end of the lease term, and defaults in the payment of rent. If a tenant abandons the leased property, he is making an offer to surrender the leasehold. As shown in Figure 2, the landlord must make a decision at this point. If the landlord's conduct shows acceptance of the tenant's offer of surrender, the tenant is relieved of the obligation to pay rent for the remaining period of the lease. If the landlord does not accept the surrender, she may sue the tenant for the rent due until such time as she rents the property to someone else, or, if she cannot find a new tenant, for the rent due for the remainder of the term.

At common law, the landlord had no obligation to mitigate (decrease) the damages caused by the abandonment by attempting to rent the leased property to a new tenant. In fact, taking possession of the property for the purpose of trying to rent it to someone else was a risky move for the landlord—her retaking of possession might be construed as acceptance of the surrender. As the *Sylva Shops Limited Partnership v. Hibbard* case illustrates, some states still adhere to the rule that the nonbreaching landlord has no duty to mitigate damages. Many states, however, now place the duty on the landlord to attempt to mitigate damages by making a reasonable effort to rerent the property. These states also hold that the landlord's retaking of possession for the purpose of rerenting does not constitute a waiver of her right to pursue an action to collect unpaid rent.

Figure 2   *Termination of a Leasehold by Abandonment*

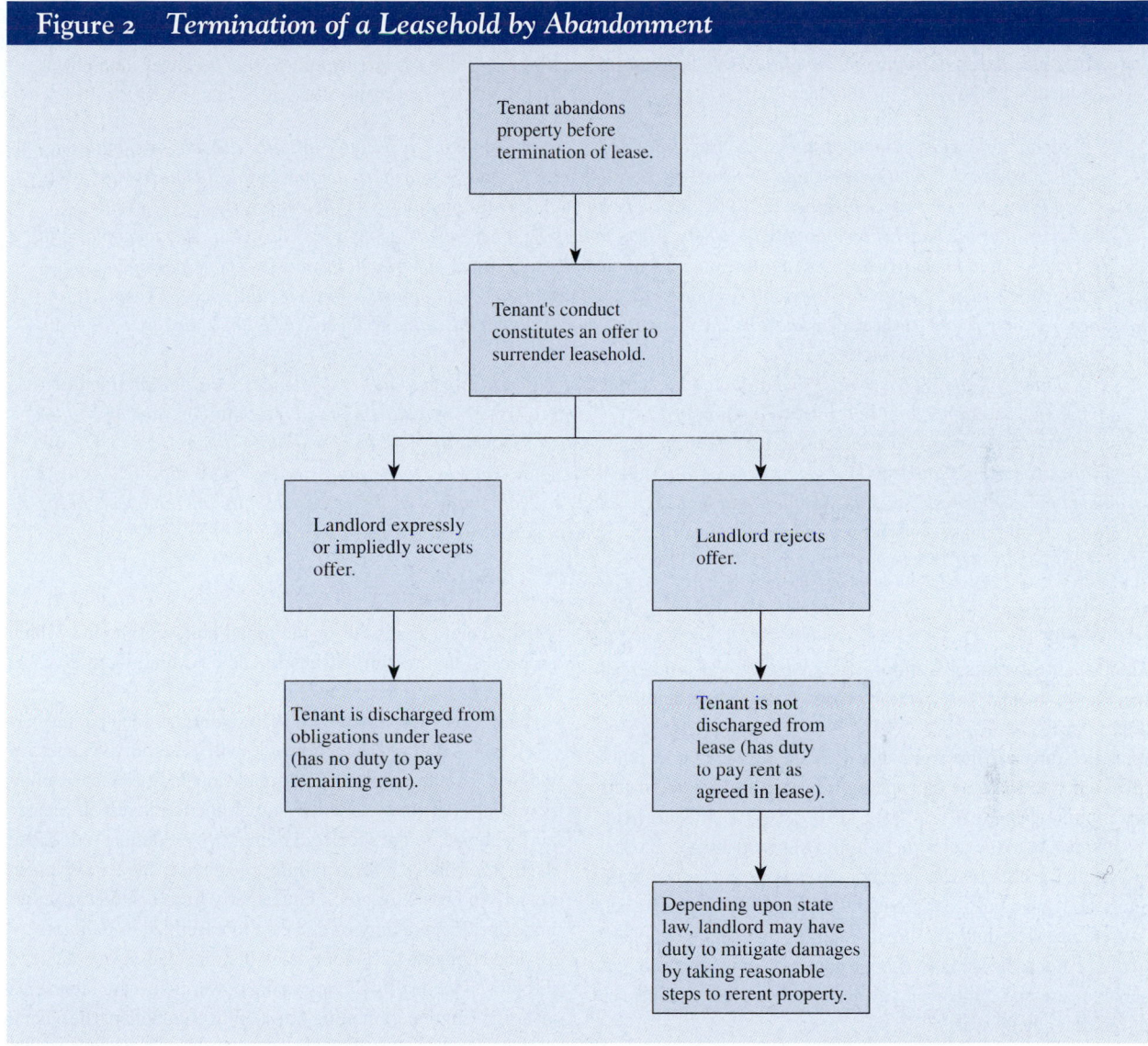

Tenant abandons property before termination of lease.

Tenant's conduct constitutes an offer to surrender leasehold.

Landlord expressly or impliedly accepts offer.

Landlord rejects offer.

Tenant is discharged from obligations under lease (has no duty to pay remaining rent).

Tenant is not discharged from lease (has duty to pay rent as agreed in lease).

Depending upon state law, landlord may have duty to mitigate damages by taking reasonable steps to rerent property.

Sylva Shops Limited Partnership v. Hibbard
623 S.E.2d 785 (Ct. App. N.C. 2005)

On January 2, 2002, Loanne and Stanley Hibbard entered into a lease agreement for space at the Sylva Shopping Center in Sylva, North Carolina, owned by the Sylva Shops Limited Partnership. They signed a five-year lease for an out-parcel space that had good visibility from the road. An out-parcel space is normally more expensive than other locations in the rest of the shopping center. The lease contained the following clause:

In no event shall Landlord's termination of this Lease and/or Tenant's right to possession of the Premises abrogate Tenant's agreement to pay rent and additional charges due hereunder for the full term hereof. Following re-entry of the Demised Premises by the Landlord, Tenant shall continue to pay all such rent and additional charges as same become due under the terms of this Lease, together with all other expenses incurred by Landlord in regaining possession until such time, if any, as Landlord relets same and the Demised Premises are occupied by such successor, *it being understood that Landlord shall have no obligations to mitigate Tenant's damages by reletting the Demised Premises.* (Emphasis added.)

The Hibbard's opened their business, the Bagel Bin and Sandwich Shop, in April 2002. Initially, the shop was quite successful, but when the summer came and the local college students left, there was a sharp decline in sales. The Hibbards were forced to close the shop on September 30, 2002, with four and a half years remaining on their lease.

Shortly after the bagel shop closed Sylva Shops began to look for a new tenant using a leasing agent. The agent placed a "For Lease" sign in the window, sent mailings to national tenants, and called other local businesses about leasing the space. She ultimately negotiated with a Mexican restaurant, but the restaurant never signed a lease for the space. Eventually, the space was rented to a sandwich restaurant. The Hibbards contended that the difficulty in releasing the space was due to an unwillingness to agree to a lower rent.

In January 2003, Sylva Shops filed a complaint against the Hibbards for unpaid rent, late fees, common area maintenance fees, insurance, and taxes in the amount of $14,170. On August 27, Sylva Shops filed a motion for summary judgment, attaching an affidavit indicating that their damages totaled $35,511.70 (rent, fees, and interest equaled $44,515.40, but a payment of $9,003.70 had been received from the bankruptcy court in connection with the bagel shop's Chapter 7 bankruptcy). A jury subsequently determined that Sylva Shops had failed to use ordinary care to mitigate the effects of the Hibbards' breach of contract, and the judge awarded judgment against the Hibbards in the amount of $13,110. Both parties appealed.

Geer, Judge

The question for this Court is whether parties to a commercial lease may, in this state, validly contract away the landlord's duty to mitigate.

The Hibbards first argue that a clause relieving a landlord of its duty to mitigate damages is contrary to the law of this state, citing *Isbey v. Crews* (1981). In *Isbey,* this Court held: "With respect to the question of mitigation of damages, the law in North Carolina is that the non-breaching party to a lease agreement has a duty to mitigate his damages upon such breach of contract." The duty to mitigate requires that an injured plaintiff, whether his case is in tort or contract, must exercise reasonable care and diligence to avoid or lessen the consequences of the defendant's wrong.

The Hibbards assert that because this Court has held that a landlord has a duty to mitigate upon a tenant's default, a provision that relieves the landlord of this duty is contrary to the law and not allowed. The existence of a common law duty of care does not, however, absolutely preclude parties from agreeing in a contract to relieve a party of that duty. As our Supreme Court has explained in discussing clauses exculpating parties from liability for their own negligence:

While contracts exempting persons from liability for negligence are not favored by the law, and are strictly construed against those relying on thereon, nevertheless, the majority rule, to which we adhere, is that, subject to certain limitations hereinafter discussed, a person may effectively bargain against liability for harm caused by his ordinary negligence in the performance of a legal duty arising out of a contractual relation.

This principle arises out of the broad policy of the law which accords to contracting parties freedom to bind themselves as they see fit.

This Court has since held that a contract exculpating persons from liability for negligence will be enforced unless it violates a statute, is gained through inequality of bargaining power, or is contrary to a substantial public interest. If a party may—subject to the specified limitations—contract to insulate itself from liability for a failure to exercise due care, we can perceive no basis for precluding a party from contracting to relieve itself from a duty of due care to minimize its damages.

The Hibbards have not argued that the clause was obtained through an inequality of bargaining power. The lease represents an arm's-length commercial transaction with both parties using brokers or advisors to assist them in obtaining the best possible bargain. The Hibbards were not forced to lease this particular space. They picked the space because it was the best location and admitted that "nobody was holding a gun to our head" to sign the lease.

The question remains whether the mitigation clause violates the public policy of this state or is otherwise contrary to a substantial public interest. Public policy has been defined as the principle of law that holds that no citizen can lawfully do that which has a tendency to be injurious to the public or against the public good. This lease involves a private contract between businesses relating to a bagel shop. The clause does not create a risk of injury to the public or the rights of third parties.

The Hibbards argue that allowing such clauses "would cripple the small business and residential tenant." We emphasize that this opinion does not address the viability of such a clause in a residential lease, which presents an entirely different situation. With respect to risk to the business community, we note that a number of states do not impose any duty to mitigate. In examining commercial real estate lease transactions in light of public policy considerations, we recognize that negotiations generally involve relatively equal bargaining power due to the availability of other space and the fact that neither party is compelled to make a deal. Each lessee has to determine whether the lease offered is acceptable in business terms. Through negotiations, the parties to a commercial lease often include specific provisions for almost every contingency that could arise from their agreement and exact from each other concessions in order to obtain the desired provisions. Ultimately, if the rent is too high or the provisions unacceptable to the lessee, a prospective commercial tenant can always look for another location.

Other jurisdictions have relied on these considerations in determining that provisions relieving a landlord of duty to mitigate do not violate public policy and should be enforced based upon ordinary contract principles. [Cases omitted.] Although not controlling, we find these decisions persuasive. Accordingly, we hold that a clause in a commercial lease that relieves the landlord from its duty to mitigate damages is not against public policy and is enforceable.

Judgment vacated and remanded for entry of judgment in favor of Sylva Shops Limited Partnership for $35,511.70.

Problems and Problem Cases

1. In October 1981, Mary Elizabeth Cook entered into an oral lease to rent a residence to Rivard Melson. Melson agreed to pay $400 per month, in advance, as rent. In November 1987, Cook sent Melson a letter advising that the rent would be increased to $525 per month, effective January 1, 1988, and asking whether Melson was going to pay. On December 10, 1987, Melson replied that he would not pay the increased rent. On January 2, 1988, Melson sent Cook a check for $400 as rent for January. Cook returned the check and stated that the rent was now $525. Melson did not vacate the premises until February 1, 1988. Cook brought a suit against Melson for $525, allegedly the unpaid rent for the month of January. Was Melson liable for the $525?

2. A tenant rented an apartment from the landlord pursuant to a lease that required her to surrender the premises in "as good a state and condition as reasonable use and wear and tear will permit," and also required her to make a refundable security deposit. After the lease was executed, the landlord notified the tenants in the building that no tenant was to shampoo the wall-to-wall carpet on surrender of the lease because the landlord had retained a professional carpet cleaner to do it. The cost of the carpet cleaner's services was to be automatically deducted from the security deposit. When the tenant left the building, a portion of her security deposit was withheld to cover carpet cleaning and she sued for a refund of the full deposit. Is the tenant entitled to a refund?

3. Pines was a student at the University of Wisconsin. In May, he and some other students asked Perssion if he had a house they could rent for the next school year. Perssion showed them a house that was in filthy condition, saying he would clean and fix it up, provide the necessary furniture, and have it in good condition by September. Pines agreed to rent the house. When Pines and the other tenants arrived in the fall, the house was still filthy and there were no student furnishings. They began to clean up the house themselves and to paint it using some paint supplied by Perssion. However, they became discouraged with their progress. They contacted an attorney who advised them to request the city building inspector to check the building. The inspector found numerous violations of the building code, including inadequate electric wiring and the kitchen sink and toilet in need of repair. The inspector gave Perssion two weeks to make the repairs. Pines and the others moved out of the house. They then sued Perssion to get their deposit returned to them along with payment for the work they had done in cleaning the house. Was there an implied warranty of habitability that was breached in the lease of the house?

4. Sheldon Solow, doing business as Solovieff Gallery Company, was the owner of a 300-unit luxury apartment building on the upper east side of Manhattan that had received awards for architectural design. Rents, which were subject to a city rent-stabilization law, ranged from $1,064.89 per month for a 4th-floor studio apartment to $5,379.92 per month for a two-bedroom on the 44th floor. A brochure shown to

prospective tenants before they signed a lease touted the high-quality features in the building and apartments, including the roof-top pool club, 24-hour-attended lobby, video-monitored service and garage entrances, four high-speed elevators with direct access to the attended underground garage, 46th-floor laundry with spectacular city view, and a four-pipe heating and air conditioning system in the public areas as well as individual apartments.

In 1987, approximately 80 tenants joined in a rent strike to protest against what they viewed as deteriorating conditions and services. Among their complaints were (1) malfunctioning elevators that consistently skipped floors, opened on the wrong floors, and were often out of service, causing interminable delays, lateness, and missed appointments; (2) stench of garbage stored between the package room and the garage as well as rodent and roach infestation; (3) frequently inoperative lobby air conditioning; (4) fire alarms that did not function; (5) a dirty laundry room with overflowing sinks, a collapsed ceiling, and missing floor tiles; (6) soiled carpets in the lobby and other public areas; (7) unlocked door separating the garage and the building; (8) exposed wiring in public areas; (9) several floods that made ingress and egress to the building difficult, caused floors to buckle, and seeped into mailboxes and the package room; (10) missing caulking that allowed water to seep into apartments; (11) standing water in the boiler room; and (12) graffiti on some walls. Solow brought suit against the tenants to recover rent, and the tenants sought an abatement of rent for breach of warranty of habitability.

The Real Property Law of New York creates an implied warranty of habitability in residential housing and provides, in pertinent part, that "in every written or oral lease or rental agreement for residential premises the landlord or lessor shall be deemed to covenant and warrant that the premises so leased or rented and all areas used in connection therewith, in common with other tenants or residents, are fit for human habitation and for the uses reasonably intended by the parties and that the occupants of such premises shall not be subjected to any conditions which would be dangerous, hazardous, or detrimental to their life, health or safety." Did the conditions present in the apartment building constitute a breach of the implied warranty of habitability?

5. On June 1, 2003, James Welsch, as owner, entered into a written agreement with Michael Groat, as tenant, for a one-year lease of a single-family residence located in Old Saybrook, Connecticut, at a monthly rent of $1,500 due on the first day of each month. At the execution of the lease, Groat paid the June rental of $1,500 and a security deposit of $3,000. He made an additional payment of $1,500 for a total of $6,000, but ended up only occupying the premises for three months. When Groat began occupancy along with his children, he discovered leaks and water damage in the basement of the premises. In early July, Groat advised Welsch that, in addition to water damage and the presence of mold and mildew, the premises contained many other deficiencies. Groat had intended to use a basement room as a bedroom for his children, but the water damage made such use impossible.

In response to Groat's notification of the poor condition of the premises, Welsch's attorney referred Groat to section 12 of the lease he had signed which stated he had inspected the premises and accepted them as he found them. By letter dated August 1, 2003, Groat outlined the defects in the premises including gutters clogged, spilling over; driveway severely cracked and crumbling; side storm door falling apart, missing screen; front storm door pump broken, missing screen; faucet leaks from stem when on; oven temperature gauge off; sink drain does not work; tub drain does not work; cold water handle is stripped; water ends up on basement floor; small bedroom closet door does not clear carpet; large bedroom entry door does not close; basement is constantly wet; there are puddles when it rains and a constant wet slime along the east wall; the paneling and trim is badly rotted, obviously a long-term problem; paint is peeing from concrete walls; latex floor is bubbling and peeling from wetness; only one basement window is operational; there are significant mold and mildew issues with the entire basement, especially the finished living area. Groat moved out in August. On October 11, 2003, Welsch brought an action against Groat for breach of the lease. Groat filed a counterclaim claiming, among other things, constructive eviction. Did the conditions at the house and the landlord's failure to make the necessary repairs in a timely fashion constitute a breach of the lease and justify termination of the lease on the grounds of constructive eviction?

6. DeEtte Junker leased an apartment from F. L. Cappaert in the Pecan Ridge Apartment Complex, which consisted of six buildings, each with 12 apartments. Junker's apartment was upstairs, and she and the

tenants in two other apartments used a common stairway for access to their apartments. Junker slipped on the stairway and was injured. She sued Cappaert for damages on the grounds that he had been negligent in maintaining the stairway. Junker's lease contained an exculpatory clause in which Cappaert disclaimed any liability for injury due to his negligence. Did the exculpatory clause immunize the landlord against damages caused by his own negligence in maintaining a common area in leased residential property?

7. On November 25, 1997, Suzette and Howard Hemmings entered into an agreement with the Pelham Wood Limited Liability Limited Partnership (the Landlord) to lease a two-bedroom apartment at Pelham Wood, a multibuilding apartment complex consisting of 400 units in Baltimore County, Maryland. The provisions in the lease include the following:

- The Landlord has the right to enter the apartment at any time by master key or force to make repairs/alterations in the apartment or elsewhere on the property;
- The Landlord has the responsibility for repairs to the apartment, its equipment and the appliances furnished by the Landlord;
- The apartment will be made available such that it will not contain conditions that constitute, or if not properly corrected, would constitute a fire hazard or a serious and substantial threat to the life, health or safety of occupants;
- The tenant agrees that the Landlord shall not be liable for an injury, damage, or loss to person or property caused by other tenants or other persons or caused by theft, vandalism, fire, water, smoke, explosion, or other causes unless the same is exclusively the omission, fault, negligence or other misconduct of the Landlord;
- The tenant will not change the locks on the doors of the Premises or install additional locks, door knockers, chains or other fasteners without the prior written permission of the Landlord.

The Hemmings's apartment was located on the second floor, just above a ground-level apartment. A sliding glass door in the Hemmings's apartment allowed access to a rear patio balcony overlooking a wooded area. In an attempt to deter criminal activity at or around the apartment complex, the Landlord testified that it had installed exterior lighting around the property, each apartment had a regular lock as well as a dead bolt on the front door, patio apartments had a Charlie Bar (a horizontally mounted bar securing the sliding glass doors), and the ground floor apartments had an alarm system.

At approximately 1:17 AM one morning in June, an unidentified intruder entered the Hemmings's apartment through the sliding glass door, and, upon encountering Howard Hemmings, shot him twice in the abdomen. He died later that morning from the wounds. The contractor, hired by the Landlord to come in and repair the sliding glass door, noted that the whole left side of the sliding glass door frame had been mutilated and the frame around the door was twisted, mangled, and destroyed. The locking mechanism no longer worked and had to be replaced. He found the cradle in which the Charlie Bar would rest still attached to the door—but no evidence of a Charlie Bar. Others living in the same building as the Hemmings, including the tenants living immediately below their apartment, testified that there were no light fixtures at the rear of that building at that time and that it was pitch black and really dark at night. They said it improved only when the Landlord installed additional lights after the Hemmings incident. Police Department logs indicated there had been numerous tenant complaints of criminal activity in and around the complex, but the Landlord did not keep any records of criminal activity there. Suzette Hemmings filed a wrongful death action against the Landlord. Does a landlord have a duty to repair a known dangerous or defective condition under its control to prevent a foreseeable third-party attack upon a tenant within leased premises?

8. On March 1, Sharon Fitzgerald entered into an oral lease of a house owned by Parkin. The lease was on a month-to-month basis, and the rent was set at $290 per month. Parkin also agreed to make certain repairs to the house. On July 1, Fitzgerald notified Parkin by mail of the repairs that needed to be made. These included repairs of leaky pipes, the kitchen ceiling, and the back porch. Fitzgerald also said she would withhold the rent if the repairs were not made within 30 days. On July 13, Fitzgerald had the premises inspected by a city housing inspector who found eight violations of the city code. Parkin was given notice of these violations. On July 29, Parkin served Fitzgerald with a formally correct notice to vacate the premises within 30 days. In September, he brought a lawsuit to have Fitzgerald evicted. A Minnesota statute gives a tenant a defense to an eviction action if the eviction is in retaliation for the reporting of a housing violation in good faith to city officials. Could the landlord evict the tenant from the house under these circumstances?

9. Kridel entered into a lease with Sommer, owner of the Pierre Apartments, to lease apartment 6-L for two years. Kridel, who was to be married in June, planned to move into the apartment in May. His parents and future parents-in-law had agreed to assume responsibility for the rent because Kridel was a full-time student who had no funds of his own. Shortly before Kridel was to have moved in, his engagement was broken. He wrote Sommer a letter explaining his situation and stating that he could not take the apartment. Sommer did not answer the letter. When another party inquired about renting apartment 6-L, the person in charge told her that the apartment was already rented to Kridel.

Sommer did not enter the apartment or show it to anyone until he rented apartment 6-L to someone else when there were approximately eight months left on Kridel's lease. He sued Kridel for the full rent for the period of approximately 16 months before the new tenant's lease took effect. Kridel argued that Sommer should not be able to collect rent for the first 16 months of the lease because he did not take reasonable steps to rerent the apartment. Was Sommer entitled to collect the rent he sought?

Online Research

Check Out Your Housing Code

Use the Internet to ascertain whether the city or county in which you reside has a housing code that covers the lease of residential property. If it does not, then locate the housing code of New York City. What obligations does the code place on landlords? What rights does it give to landlords? What rights does it give to tenants? What obligations, if any, does it place on tenants?

Consider completing the case "TENANT RIGHTS: When the Lessee Leaves" from the You Be the Judge Web site element after you have read this chapter. Visit our Web site at www.mhhe.com/mallor14e for more information and activities regarding this case segment.

chapter 26

ESTATES AND TRUSTS

George, an elderly widower, has no children of his own but enjoys a very close relationship with his two stepdaughters, his late wife's children by her first marriage. George's only living blood relative is his brother, from whom he has been estranged for many years. George has a substantial amount of property—his home, two cars, stocks and bonds, rental property, bank accounts, and a valuable collection of baseball cards. Though retired, George is an active volunteer for, and supporter of, several community charities and organizations. Presently, George does not have a will, but he is considering writing one.

- What will happen to George's property upon his death if he does not have a will at that time?
- What are the requirements for executing a valid will?
- What can cause a will to be invalid?
- After George's death, how would his estate be probated?
- If George decided to create a trust to benefit his stepdaughters, what is required to create a trust, and what are the legal duties of a trustee? What are the *ethical* duties of a trustee?

ONE OF THE BASIC features of the ownership of property is the right to dispose of the property during life and at death. You have already learned about the ways in which property is transferred during the owner's life. The owner's death is another major event for the transfer of property. Most people want to be able to choose who will get their property when they die. There are a variety of ways in which a person may control the ultimate disposition of his property. He may take title to the property in a form of joint ownership that gives his co-owner a right of survivorship. He may create a trust and transfer property to it to be used for the benefit of a spouse, child, elderly parent, or other beneficiary. He may execute a will in which he directs that his real and personal property be distributed to persons named in the will. If, however, a person makes no provision for the disposition of his property at his death, his property will be distributed to his heirs as defined by state law. This chapter focuses on the transfer of property at death and on the use of trusts for the transfer and management of property, both during life and at death.

The Law of Estates and Trusts

Each state has its own statutes and common law regulating the distribution of property upon death. Legal requirements and procedures may vary from state to state, but many general principles can be stated. The **Uniform Probate Code (UPC)** is a comprehensive, uniform law that has been enacted in 16 states. It is intended to update and unify state law concerning the disposition and administration of property at death. Several relevant UPC provisions will be discussed in this chapter.

Estate Planning A person's **estate** is all of the property owned by that person. **Estate planning** is the popular name for the complicated process of planning for the transfer of a person's estate in later life and at death. Estate planning also concerns planning for the possibility of prolonged illness or disability. An attorney who is creating an estate plan will take an inventory of the client's assets, learn the client's objectives, and draft the instruments necessary to carry out the plan. This plan is normally guided by the desire to reduce the amount of tax liability and to provide for the orderly disposition of the estate.

Wills

Right of Disposition by Will The right to control the disposition of property at death has not always existed. In the English feudal system, the king owned all land. The lords and knights had only the right to use land for their lifetime. A landholder's rights in land terminated upon his death, and no rights descended to his heirs. In 1215, the king granted the nobility the right to pass their interest in the land they held to their heirs. Later, that right was extended to all property owners. In the United States, each state has enacted statutes that establish the requirements for a valid will, including the formalities that must be met to pass property by will.

Nature of a Will A **will** is a document executed with specific legal formalities by a **testator** (person making a will) that contains his instructions about the way his property will be disposed of at his death. A will can dispose only of property belonging to the testator at the time of his death. Furthermore, wills do not control property that goes to others through other planning devices (such as life insurance policies) or by operation of law (such as by right of survivorship). For example, property held in joint tenancy or tenancy by the entirety is not controlled by a will, because the property passes automatically to the surviving cotenant by right of survivorship. In addition, life insurance proceeds are controlled by the insured's designation of beneficiaries, not by any provision of a will. (Because joint tenancy and life insurance are ways of directing the disposition of property, they are sometimes referred to as "will substitutes.")

LOG ON

For discussion of why it is important to have a will, see Peter Weaver, *10 Good Reasons Why You Should Have a Will,*
www.thirdage.com/features/money/goodwill/ and
Rebecca Berlin, *Wills: Why You Need One,*
www.alllaw.com/articles/wills_and_trusts/
article2.asp.

Common Will Terminology Some legal terms commonly used in wills include the following:

1. *Bequest.* A **bequest** (also called **legacy**) is a gift of personal property or money. For example, a will might provide for a bequest of a family heirloom to the testator's daughter. Since a will can direct only property that is owned by the testator at the time of his death, a specific bequest of property that the testator has disposed of before his death is ineffective. This is called **ademption.** For example, Samuel's will states that Warren is to

receive Samuel's collection of antique guns. If the guns are destroyed before Warren's death, however, the bequest is ineffective because of ademption.

2. *Devise.* A **devise** is a gift of real property. For example, the testator might devise his family farm to his grandson.

3. *Residuary.* The **residuary** is the balance of the estate that is left after specific devises and bequests are made by the will. After providing for the disposition of specific personal and real property, a testator might provide that the residuary of his estate is to go to his spouse or be divided among his descendants.

4. *Issue.* A person's **issue** are his lineal descendants (children, grandchildren, great-grandchildren, and so forth). This category of persons includes adopted children.

5. *Per capita.* This term and the next one, *per stirpes,* are used to describe the way in which a group of persons are to share a gift. **Per capita** means that each of that group of persons will share equally. For example, Grandfather dies, leaving a will that provides that the residuary of his estate is to go to his issue or descendants *per capita.* Grandfather had two children, Mary and Bill. Mary has two children, John and James. Bill has one child, Margaret. Mary and Bill die before Grandfather (in legal terms, *predecease* him), but all three of Grandfather's grandchildren are living at the time of his death. In this case, John, James, and Margaret would each take one-third of the residuary of Grandfather's estate.

6. *Per stirpes.* When a gift is given to the testator's issue or descendants **per stirpes** (also called **by right of representation**), each surviving descendant divides the share that his or her parent would have taken if the parent had survived. In the preceding example, if Grandfather's will had stated that the residuary of his estate was to go to his issue or descendants *per stirpes,* Margaret would take one-half and John and James would take one-quarter each (that is, they would divide the share that would have gone to their mother).

Testamentary Capacity The capacity to make a valid will is called **testamentary capacity.** To have testamentary capacity, a person must be *of sound mind* and *of legal age,* which is 18 in most states. A person does not have to be in perfect mental health to have testamentary capacity. Because people often delay executing wills until they are weak and in ill health, the standard for mental capacity to make a will is fairly low. To be of "sound mind," a person need only be sufficiently rational to be capable of understanding the nature and character of his property, of realizing that he is making a will, and of knowing the persons who would normally be the beneficiaries of his affection. A person could move in and out of periods of lucidity and still have testamentary capacity if he executed his will during a lucid period.

Lack of testamentary capacity is a common ground upon which wills are challenged by persons who were excluded from a will. *Fraud* and *undue influence* are also common grounds for challenging the validity of a will.[1]

Execution of a Will

Unless a will is executed with the formalities required by state law, it is *void*. The courts are strict in interpreting statutes concerning the execution of wills. If a will is declared void, the property of the deceased person will be distributed according to the provisions of state laws that will be discussed later.

The formalities required for a valid will differ from state to state. For that reason, an individual should consult the laws of his state before making a will. If he should move to another state after having executed a will, he should consult a lawyer in his new state to determine whether a new will needs to be executed. All states require that a will be *in writing.* State law also requires that a formal will be *witnessed,* generally by two or three *disinterested* witnesses (persons who do not stand to inherit any property under the will), and that it be *signed* by the testator or by someone else at the testator's direction. Most states also require that the testator *publish* the will—that is, declare or indicate at the time of signing that the instrument is his will. Another formality required by most states is that the testator sign the will in the presence and the sight of the witnesses and that the witnesses sign in the presence and the sight of each other. As a general rule, an **attestation clause,** which states the formalities that have been followed in the execution of the will, is written following the testator's signature. These detailed formalities are designed to prevent fraud. Section 2–502 of the UPC requires that a will must be in writing, signed by the testator (or in the testator's name by some other individual in the testator's conscious presence and by the testator's direction), and signed by at least two individuals, each of whom signed within a reasonable time after he witnessed either the signing of the will or the testator's acknowledgment of that signature or will. Also, under the UPC, any individual who is generally competent to be a witness may witness a will, and the fact that the witness is an interested party does not invalidate the will [2–505]. When a testator has made a technical error in executing a

will, however, the UPC permits the document to be treated as if it had been executed properly if it can be proven by clear and convincing evidence that the testator intended the document to constitute his will [2–503].

In some situations, a lawyer might arrange to have the execution of a will *videotaped* to provide evidence relating to the testator's capacity and the use of proper formalities. (Note that the will is executed in the normal way; the videotape merely records the execution of the will.) Some state probate codes specifically provide that videotapes of the executions of wills are admissible into evidence.

Incorporation by Reference

In some situations, a testator might want his will to refer to and incorporate an existing writing. For example, the testator may have created a list of specific gifts of personal property that he wants to incorporate in the will. A writing such as this is called an **extrinsic document**—that is, a writing apart from the will. In most states, the contents of extrinsic documents can be essentially incorporated into the will when the circumstances satisfy rules that have been designed to ensure that the document is genuine and that it was intended by the testator to be incorporated in the will. This is called **incorporation by reference.** For an extrinsic document to be incorporated by reference, it must have been *in existence at the time the will was executed.* In addition, the writing and the will must refer to each other so that the extrinsic document can be identified and so that it is clear that the testator intended the extrinsic document to be incorporated in the will. Under the UPC, incorporation by reference is allowed when the extrinsic document was in existence when the will was executed, the language of the will manifests the intent to incorporate the writing, and the will describes the writing sufficiently to identify it [2–510].

Informal Wills

Some states recognize certain types of wills that are not executed with these formalities. These are:

1. *Nuncupative wills.* A **nuncupative** will is an oral will. Such wills are recognized as valid in some states, but only under limited circumstances and to a limited extent. In a number of states, for example, nuncupative wills are valid only when made by soldiers in military service and sailors at sea, and even then they will be effective only to dispose of personal property that was in the actual possession of the person at the time the oral will was made. Other states place low dollar limits on the amount of property that can be passed by a nuncupative will.

---

[1]Fraud and undue influence are discussed in detail in Chapter 13.

2. Holographic wills. **Holographic wills** are wills that are written and signed in the testator's handwriting. You will see an example of a holographic will in *Estate of Shelly,* which appears below. The fact that holographic wills are not properly witnessed makes them suspect. They are recognized in about half of the states and by section 2–502(b) of the UPC, even though they are not executed with the formalities usually required of valid wills. For a holographic will to be valid in the states that recognize them, it must evidence testamentary intent and must actually be *handwritten* by the testator. A typed holographic will would be invalid. Some states require that the holographic will be *entirely* handwritten—although the UPC requires only that the signature and material portions of the will be handwritten by the testator [2–502(b)]—and some also require that the will be dated.

Joint and Mutual Wills

In some circumstances, two or more people—a married couple, for example—decide together on a plan for the disposition of their property at death. To carry out this plan, they may execute a **joint will** (a single instrument that constitutes the will of both or all of the testators and is executed by both or all) or they may execute **mutual wills** (joint or separate, individual wills that reflect the common plan of distribution).

Underlying a joint or mutual will is an agreement on a common plan. This common plan often includes an express or implied contract (a contract to make a will or not to revoke the will). One issue that sometimes arises is whether a testator who has made a joint or mutual will can later change his will. Whether joint and mutual wills are revocable depends on the language of the will, on state law, and on the timing of the revocation. For example, a testator who made a joint will with his spouse may be able to revoke his will during the life of his spouse, because the spouse still has a chance to change her own will, but he may be unable to revoke or change the will after the death of his spouse. The UPC provides that the mere fact that a joint or mutual will has been executed does *not* create the presumption of a contract not to revoke the will or wills [2–514].

Construction of Wills

Even in carefully drafted wills, questions sometimes arise as to the meaning or legal effect of a term or provision. Disputes about the meaning of the will are even more likely to occur in wills drafted by the testator himself, such as holographic wills. To interpret a will, a court will examine the entire instrument in an attempt to determine the testator's intent. The following *Estate of Shelly* case provides a good example of the methods and principles courts use to interpret wills.

Estate of Shelly   2008 Pa. Super. LEXIS 1099 (Pa. Super. Ct. 2008)

Norman Shelly died on July 27, 1999. After his death, a cardboard panel of a cigarette carton that purported to be a will was submitted for probate. The cigarette carton was labeled:

FIRST AND LAST ONLY WILL
OF "DRAFT ?"
NORMAN F SHELLY

It was signed and dated by Shelly, but was not witnessed or notarized. None of the people named as beneficiaries of the estate would have been intestate heirs of Shelly. In August 1999, the Register of Wills issued letters of administration.

Between 2000 and 2006, a number of individuals who stood to inherit from Shelly if he had died intestate challenged the cigarette carton document. Some of these individuals ("the Four Heirs") filed a motion for summary judgment seeking a declaration by the orphans' court (the court that has jurisdiction of this type of case in Pennsylvania) that if the cigarette carton were held to be a will, then a partial intestacy results because not all assets of the estate were disposed of by the cigarette carton document. The beneficiaries named in the cigarette carton document ("the beneficiaries") also filed a motion for summary judgment requesting that it be declared Shelly's valid Last Will and Testament and the appeal of the heirs dismissed. The orphans' court granted the Four Heirs' motion for summary judgment and denied the beneficiaries' motion for summary judgment. The beneficiaries appealed.

Popovich, Judge

In order to determine whether a particular writing constitutes a will, no formal words are necessary, the form of the instrument is immaterial if its substance is testamentary. A gift or bequest after death is of the very essence of a will, and determines a writing, whatever its form, to be testamentary. Therefore, our first inquiry is whether the cigarette carton provides for a positive disposition of assets.

The beneficiaries argue that a positive disposition of assets is evidenced by the writing labeled "FIRST AND LAST ONLY WILL" and signed and dated by the decedent. Specifically, they argue that the orphans' court erred in finding the cigarette carton did not evidence testamentary intent due to the absence of a positive disposition of assets. They contend that the term "will" is a dispositive term and the fact that the decedent signed and dated the cigarette carton resulted in a determination that it was a will written with testamentary intent. No rule regarding wills is more settled than the general rule that the testator's intent, if it is not unlawful, must prevail. Moreover, the testator's intention must be ascertained from the language and scheme of his will; it is not what the Court thinks he might or would have said in the existing circumstances, or even what the Court thinks he meant to say, but is what is the meaning of his words.

As found by the orphans' court, this document did not make a disposition of property. Rather the document contained a list of items accompanied by the names of individuals. The only term that could have been construed to dispose of property is "DEVIDE," which the orphans' court presumed to be "divide." The context of the placement of the word "DEVIDE" was as follows:

MONEY. DEVIDE

MICHAEL COOKS SONS

However, the decedent also placed an arrow leading from the previous section of the document which read: "FARM MACH + MACHINES AND TOOLS MICHAEL COOK SR LIVING MY AGE" into this section. The beneficiaries contend that "DEVIDE" written in this context indicated that Michael Cook, Sr., was the father of the two sons and that the decedent intended the money to be divided equally between the two sons. We disagree.

There is no indication of what money was to be divided, into what shares it was to be divided, or if it was to be divisible by three including Michael Cook, Sr., or divisible by two including only his two sons. There was no specificity as to the proposed beneficiaries or to the subject matter to be distributed. Therefore, this was not a positive disposition of property nor can a positive disposition of property be inferred from the cigarette carton. Accordingly, because the cigarette carton does not include the one essential element for the creation of a will, a disposition of property, it cannot be considered as such.

The beneficiaries' next argument is that the writing on the cigarette carton evidenced the testamentary intent of the decedent. Specifically, the beneficiaries contend that the orphans' court erred in determining the decedent lacked testamentary intent due to the insertion of the term "DRAFT ?" at the top of the cigarette carton. The beneficiaries argue that because the will was otherwise valid, the insertion of the term "DRAFT ?" did not destroy the presence of testamentary intent inherent in the writing. The term "DRAFT ?" was distinguished from the other writing on the cigarette carton in that it was set inside a box and was inserted into the heading of the writing, which appeared as follows:

FIRST AND LAST ONLY WILL
OF "DRAFT ?"
NORMAN F SHELLY

Our determination focuses on whether we are faced with a document that is testamentary as a matter of law, nontestamentary as a matter of law, or ambiguous, in which case extrinsic evidence is to be considered to resolve the ambiguity. With regard to a court's consideration of testamentary intent, we note if a testator intends to make a testamentary gift, it can be done in many ways and in many forms, and the intent, as we have often said, is the polestar. Papers—holographic and otherwise—have been sustained as wills where a testamentary disposition of property was clearly contained in a letter or a deed or a certificate of deposit or a power of attorney or an agreement or a check or a note or an assignment, and even in a letter of instructions to an attorney where it was later proved that the writer intended such letter to be a will. Moreover, if a further or additional act or writing is contemplated by an alleged testator in order to make a written document his will or codicil, the writing is nontestamentary in nature.

Black's Law Dictionary defines the term "draft" as, inter alia, "[a]n initial or preliminary version." The obvious connotation of the term "draft" is that it is a contemplation of a further or additional act or writing. The beneficiaries' arguments to the contrary are unavailing. The fact that the decedent did not strike out the word "Will" but included it on the cigarette carton in addition to "DRAFT ?" was not an indication of testamentary intent but rather an indication that the decedent contemplated a final document to be created at a later time. The beneficiaries' contention that labeling a document a "Will" is determinative of the character of the writing itself is illogical, in that, if this were the case, then any writing labeled "Will" would be a valid will despite the lack of a positive disposition of assets or testamentary intent. Simply labeling a document "Will" does not end our inquiry into the validity of the document itself. The beneficiaries' argue that the decedent did not strike out his signature or give any other indication that he was revoking his will written on the cigarette carton. This argument is misplaced under these circumstances because the issue to be determined is whether the cigarette carton was a valid will and not whether the decedent revoked a prior valid will.

The beneficiaries contend that the definition of "draft" as set forth in the dictionary does not encompass the term "DRAFT ?" as indicated on a will. This is an unreasonable limitation on the definition of "draft" because a dictionary does not include an exhaustive list of each context in which the word may be used in the English language. Further, *Black's Law Dictionary* defines a "drafter" as "[a] person who draws or frames a legal document, such as a will, contract, or legislative bill."

The beneficiaries argue that the signing and dating of the cigarette carton was conclusive as to the decedent's testamentary intent. We reiterate that there is no special form of words necessary to constitute a will, however, it must include one essential element, that is, the document must dispose of property. As noted above, the decedent's words do not constitute a plain and clear meaning by which this Court can decipher his intention. The fact that the cigarette carton itself is labeled a "Will"

and that it was signed and dated by the decedent is of no consequence when the contents of the writing do not amount to a disposition of property.

The beneficiaries aver that if there was real doubt as to whether "DRAFT ?" destroyed testamentary intent, then extrinsic evidence should have been admitted to aid in this determination. As noted above, extrinsic evidence is only admissible when a writing by its terms clearly constitutes a testamentary disposition. Extrinsic evidence is not admissible to prove testamentary intent because this writing did not constitute a testamentary disposition by decedent. In conclusion, the cigarette carton was not a will because it lacked both a positive disposition of property and the testamentary intent of the decedent.

Judgment affirmed in favor of the Four Heirs.

Limitations on Disposition by Will

A person who takes property by will takes it subject to all outstanding claims against the property. For example, if real property is subject to a mortgage or other lien, the beneficiary who takes the property gets it subject to the mortgage or lien. In addition, the rights of the testator's creditors are superior to the rights of beneficiaries under his will. Thus, if the testator was insolvent (his debts exceeded his assets), persons named as beneficiaries do not receive any property by virtue of the will.

Under the laws of most states, the surviving spouse of the testator has statutory rights in property owned solely by the testator that cannot be defeated by a contrary will provision. This means that a husband cannot effectively disinherit his wife, and vice versa. Even if the will provides for the surviving spouse, he or she can elect to take the share of the decedent's estate that would

be provided by state law rather than the amount specified in the will. In some states, personal property, such as furniture, passes automatically to the surviving spouse.

At common law, a widow had the right to a life estate in one-third of the lands owned by her husband during their marriage. This was known as a widow's **dower right.** A similar right for a widower was known as **curtesy.** A number of states have changed the right by statute to give a surviving spouse a one-third interest in fee simple in the real and personal property owned by the deceased spouse at the time of his or her death. (Naturally, a testator can leave his spouse more than this if he desires.) Under UPC 2–201, the surviving spouse's elective share varies depending on the length of the surviving spouse's marriage to the testator—the elective share increases with the length of marriage.

Ethics in Action

Dr. Coggins died in 1963. In his last will, Dr. Coggins gave the residue of his estate to the Mercantile–Safe Deposit & Trust Company, to be held by it as trustee under the will. The trust provided for monthly payments to four income beneficiaries until the death of the last of them. The last of these annuitants was Dr. Coggins's widow, who died in 1998. A provision of the will stated that, upon the death of the survivor of the four annuitants, the trust would terminate and the assets and all unpaid income shall be paid over "free of trust unto the Keswick Home, formerly Home for Incurables of Baltimore City, with the request that said Home use the estate and property thus passing to it for the acquisition or construction of a new building to provide additional housing accommodations to be known as the 'Coggins Building,' to house white patients who need physical rehabilitation. If not acceptable to the Keswick Home, then this bequest shall go to the University of Maryland Hospital to be used for physical rehabilitation." What are the major ethical considerations involved in determining whether this will provision should be enforced?

As a general rule, a surviving spouse is given the right to use the family home for a stated period as well as a portion of the deceased spouse's estate. In community property states, each spouse has a one-half interest in community property that cannot be defeated by a contrary will provision. (Note that the surviving spouse will obtain *full* ownership of any property owned by the testator and the surviving spouse as joint tenants or tenants by the entirety.)

Children of the testator who were born or adopted after the will was executed are called **pretermitted** children. There is a presumption that the testator intended to provide for such a child, unless there is evidence to the contrary. State law gives pretermitted children the right to a share of the testator's estate. For example, under section 2–302 of the Uniform Probate Code, a pretermitted child has the right to receive the share he would have received under the state intestacy statute unless it appears that the omission of this child was intentional, the testator gave substantially all of his estate to the child's other parent, or the testator provided for the child outside of the will.

Revocation of Wills One important feature of a will is that it is *revocable* until the moment of the testator's death. For this reason, a will confers *no present interest* in the testator's property. A person is free to revoke a prior will and, if she wishes, to make a new will. Wills can be revoked in a variety of ways. Physical destruction and mutilation done with intent to revoke a will constitute revocation, as do other acts such as crossing out the will or creating a writing that expressly cancels the will.

In addition, a will is revoked if the testator later executes a valid will that expressly revokes the earlier will. A later will that does not *expressly* revoke an earlier will operates to revoke only those portions of the earlier will that are inconsistent with the later will. Under the UPC, a later will that does not expressly revoke a prior will operates to revoke it by inconsistency if the testator intended the subsequent will to *replace* rather than *supplement* the prior will [2–507(b)]. Furthermore, the UPC presumes that the testator intended the subsequent will to replace rather than supplement the prior will if the subsequent one makes a complete disposition of her estate, but it presumes that the testator intended merely to supplement and not replace the prior will if the subsequent will disposes of only part of her estate [2–507(c), 2–507(d)]. In some states, a will is presumed to have been revoked if it cannot be located after the testator's death, although this presumption can be rebutted with contrary evidence.

Wills can also be revoked by operation of law without any act on the part of the testator signifying revocation. State statutes provide that certain changes in relationships operate as revocations of a will. In some states, marriage will operate to revoke a will that was made when the testator was single. Similarly, a divorce may revoke provisions in a will made during marriage that leave property to the divorced spouse. Under the laws of some states, the birth of a child after the execution of a will may operate as a partial revocation of the will.

Codicils A **codicil** is an amendment of a will. If a person wants to change a provision of a will without making an entirely new will, she may amend the will by executing a codicil. One may *not* amend a will by merely striking out objectionable provisions and inserting new provisions. The same formalities are required for the creation of a valid codicil as for the creation of a valid will.

Advance Directives: Planning for Disability

Advances in medical technology now permit a person to be kept alive by artificial means, even in many cases in which there is no hope of the person being able to function without life support. Many people are opposed to their lives being prolonged with no chance of recovery. In response to these concerns, almost all states have enacted statutes permitting individuals to state their choices about the medical procedures that should be administered or withheld if they should become incapacitated in the future and cannot recover. Collectively, these devices are called **advance directives.** An advance directive is a written document (such as a living will or durable power of attorney) that directs others how future health care decisions should be made in the event that the individual becomes incapacitated.

Living Wills **Living wills** are documents in which a person states in advance his intention to forgo or obtain certain life-prolonging medical procedures. Almost all states have enacted statutes recognizing living wills. These statutes also establish the elements and formalities required to create a valid living will and describe the legal effect of living wills. Currently, the law concerning living wills is primarily a matter of state law and differs from state to state. Living wills are typically included with a patient's medical records. Many states require physicians and other health care providers to follow the provisions of a valid living will. Because living wills are

Figure 1   *Living Will*

LIVING WILL DECLARATION*

Declaration made this _____ day of _____ (month, year). I, _____, being at least eighteen (18) years of age and of sound mind, willfully and voluntarily make known my desires that my dying shall not be artificially prolonged under the circumstances set forth below, and I declare:

If at any time my attending physician certifies in writing that: (1) I have an incurable injury, disease, or illness; (2) my death will occur within a short time; and (3) the use of life prolonging procedures would serve only to artificially prolong the dying process, I direct that such procedures be withheld or withdrawn, and that I be permitted to die naturally with only the performance or provision of any medical procedure or medication necessary to provide me with comfort care or to alleviate pain, and, if I have so indicated below, the provision of artificially supplied nutrition and hydration. (Indicate your choice by initialing or making your mark before signing this declaration):

__I wish to receive artificially supplied nutrition and hydration, even if the effort to sustain life is futile or excessively burdensome to me.

__I do not wish to receive artificially supplied nutrition and hydration, if the effort to sustain life is futile or excessively burdensome to me.

__I intentionally make no decision concerning artificially supplied nutrition and hydration, leaving the decision to my health care representative appointed under IC 16–36–1–7 or my attorney in fact with health care powers under IC 30–5–5.

In the absence of my ability to give directions regarding the use of life prolonging procedures, it is my intention that this declaration be honored by my family and physician as the final expression of my legal right to refuse medical or surgical treatment and accept the consequences of the refusal.

I understand the full import of this declaration.

Signed: _____

City, County, and State of Residence

The declarant has been personally known to me, and I believe (him/her) to be of sound mind. I did not sign the declarant's signature above for or at the direction of the declarant. I am not a parent, spouse, or child of the declarant. I am not entitled to any part of the declarant's estate or directly financially responsible for the declarant's medical care. I am competent and at least eighteen (18) years of age.

Witness _____   Date _____

Witness _____   Date _____

*From Ind. Code § 16–36 4–10 (1999).

created by statute, it is important that all terms and conditions of one's state statute be followed. Figure 1 shows an example of a living will form.

Durable Power of Attorney
Another technique of planning for the eventuality that one may be unable to make decisions for oneself is to execute a document that gives another person the legal authority to act on one's behalf in the case of mental or physical incapacity. This document is called a **durable power of attorney.**

A *power of attorney* is an express statement in which one person (the **principal**) gives another person (the **attorney in fact**) the authority to do an act or series of acts on his behalf. For example, Andrews enters into a contract to sell his house to Willis, but he must be out of state on the date of the real estate closing. He gives Paulsen a power of attorney to attend the closing and execute the deed on his behalf. Ordinary powers of attorney terminate upon the principal's incapacity. By contrast, the *durable power of attorney* is not affected if the principal becomes incompetent.

A durable power of attorney permits a person to give someone else extremely broad powers to make decisions and enter transactions such as those involving real and personal property, bank accounts, and health care, and to specify that those powers will not terminate upon incapacity. The durable power of attorney is an extremely important planning device. For example, a durable power of attorney executed by an elderly parent to an adult child at a time in which the parent is competent would permit the child to take care of matters such as investments, property, bank accounts, and hospital admission. Without the durable power of attorney, the child would be forced to apply to a court for a guardianship, which is a more expensive and often less efficient manner in which to handle personal and business affairs.

Durable Power of Attorney for Health Care
The majority of states have enacted statutes specifically providing for **durable powers of attorney for health care** (sometimes called **health care representatives**). This is a type of durable power of attorney in which the principal specifically gives the attorney in fact the authority to make certain health care decisions for him if the principal should become incompetent. Depending on state law and the instructions given by the principal to the attorney in fact, this could include decisions such as consenting or withholding consent to surgery, admitting the principal to a nursing home, and possibly withdrawing or prolonging life support. Note that the durable power of attorney becomes relevant only in the event that the principal becomes incompetent. So long as the principal is competent, he retains the ability to make his own health care decisions. This power of attorney is also revocable at the will of the principal. The precise requirements for creation of the durable power of attorney differ from state to state, but all states require a written and signed document executed with specified formalities, such as witnessing by disinterested witnesses.

Federal Law and Advance Directives
A federal statute, The Patient Self-Determination Act,[2] requires health care providers to take active steps to educate people about the opportunity to make advance decisions about medical care and the prolonging of life and to record the choices that they make. This statute, which became effective in 1991, requires health care providers such as hospitals, nursing homes, hospices, and home health agencies, to provide written information to adults receiving medical care about their rights concerning the ability to accept or refuse medical or surgical treatment, the health care provider's policies concerning those rights, and their right to formulate advance directives.

The act also requires the provider to document in the patient's medical record whether the patient has executed an advance directive, and it forbids discrimination against the patient based on the individual's choice regarding an advance directive. In addition, the provider is required to ensure compliance with the requirements of state law concerning advance directives and to educate its staff and the community on issues concerning advance directives.

Intestacy

If a person dies without making a will, or if he makes a will that is declared invalid, he is said to have died **intestate.** When that occurs, his property will be distributed to the persons designated as the intestate's heirs under the appropriate state's **intestacy** or **intestate succession** statute. The intestate's real property will be distributed according to the intestacy statute of the state in which the property is located. His personal property will be distributed according to the intestacy statute of the state in which he was **domiciled** at the time of his death. A domicile is a person's permanent home. A person can have only one domicile at a time. Determinations of a person's domicile turn on facts that tend to show that person's intent to make a specific state his permanent home.

Characteristics of Intestacy Statutes
The provisions of intestacy statutes are not uniform. Their purpose, however, is to distribute property in a way that reflects the *presumed intent* of the deceased—that is, to distribute it to the persons most closely related to him. In general, such statutes first provide for the distribution of most or all of a person's estate to his surviving spouse, children, or grandchildren. If no such survivors exist, the statutes typically provide for the distribution of the estate to parents, siblings, or nieces and nephews. If no relatives at this level are living, the property may be distributed to surviving grandparents, uncles, aunts, or cousins. Generally, persons with the same degree of relationship to the deceased person take equal shares. If the deceased had no surviving relatives, the property **escheats** (goes) to the state.

Figure 2 shows an example of a distribution scheme under an intestacy statute.

In the following *Estate of McDaniel v. McDaniel* case, you will see a court's determination of who should inherit from a person who died intestate.

---

[2]42 U.S.C. section 1395cc (1990).

Figure 2 Example of a Distribution Scheme under an Intestacy Statute

Person Dying Intestate Is Survived By	Result
1. Spouse* and child or issue of a deceased child	Spouse ½, Child ½
2. Spouse and parent(s) but no issue	Spouse ¾, Parent ¼
3. Spouse but no parent or issue	All of the estate to spouse
4. Issue but no spouse	Estate is divided among issue
5. Parent(s), brothers, sisters, and/or issue of deceased brothers and sisters but no spouse or issue	Estate is divided among parent(s), brothers, sisters, and issue of deceased brothers and sisters
6. Issue of brothers and sisters but no spouse, issue, parents, brothers, and sisters	Estate is divided among issue of deceased brothers and sisters
7. Grandparents, but no spouse, issue, parents, brothers, sisters, or issue of deceased brothers and sisters	All of the estate goes to grandparents
8. None of the above	Estate goes to the state

*Note, however, second and subsequent spouses who had no children by the decedent may be assigned a smaller share.

Estate of McDaniel v. McDaniel   73 Cal. Rptr. 3d 907 (Cal. Ct. App. 2008)

Troy and Marie McDaniel were married in August 2003. Their marriage was troubled, and Marie filed a petition for dissolution of the marriage in October 2004. Troy filed his response to the petition in April 2005. In May 2005, Marie and Troy each executed an "Interspousal Transfer Grant Deed," in which they released their interest in the other party's property. They also waived their right to appeal. On July 25, 2005, the court entered a stipulated judgment dissolving the marriage and ordering that the marital partnership be terminated and the parties be restored to the status of single persons effective October 29, 2005.

Nevertheless, Marie and Troy were apparently attempting to reconcile and end the dissolution proceedings before the marital partnership finally terminated on October 29, 2005. Both Marie and Troy attended counseling, and Marie attended Alcoholics Anonymous meetings with Troy. In April 2005, they each signed a private agreement providing that Marie would seek to vacate a restraining order against Troy, that they would attend counseling, that they would continue their marriage, and that they would keep their dissolution action open, "both knowing that we can cancel and dismiss anytime before the final date of termination." Troy and Marie also signed, but did not date or file, a request for dismissal of the dissolution action. According to Marie, they had intended to file the request after Troy attended a hearing on a criminal matter related to their marital differences on September 29.

Troy died in a motorcycle accident on September 23; however, and the request for dismissal of the dissolution action was never filed. Troy's mother, Marianne, filed a petition for entitlement of distribution of Troy's estate. Her petition alleged that Troy had died intestate, that he did not have and had not had any children, and that Marianne and Troy's father, Lyle, were entitled to have Troy's estate distributed equally between them. Marie opposed this position, arguing that, despite the dissolution proceeding, she was still Troy's wife at the time of his death and therefore entitled to inherit his estate.

The trial court held that Marie was not Troy's "surviving spouse" within the meaning of the Probate Code at the time of his death, and she was not entitled to inherit from his estate. The court granted Marianne's petition for distribution. Marie appealed.

Hull, Judge

Section 78, subdivision (d) provides that a "surviving spouse" for purposes of the Probate Code does not include "[a] person who was a party to a valid proceeding concluded by an order purporting to terminate all marital property rights." It is apparent that the parties divided their community property, confirmed their individual share of what was formerly community property as separate property, and waived spousal support, thus accounting for and terminating their marital property rights. It is equally apparent that, given the waiver of their right to appeal, the judgment dividing their marital property became final when entered by the court on July 25, 2005, and that the proceedings regarding their marital property were then concluded. Under the circumstances, we find that Marie was, by the time of Troy's death, "a party to a valid proceeding concluded by an order purporting to terminate all marital property rights" within the meaning of section 78, subdivision (d).

We find support for our holding in *Estate of Lahey.* In *Lahey,* Frances and Clarence Lahey were married in 1984 and they separated in March 1995. In April 1995 Frances petitioned for a legal separation alleging that there were no community debts or assets, waiving spousal support, and requesting that the court terminate any right of spousal support for Clarence. The court entered an order to that effect in July 1995. Clarence died intestate in December 1996 and Frances claimed one-half of his estate as the surviving spouse. While recognizing that a judgment of legal separation left the bonds of marriage intact, the Court of Appeal pointed out that a surviving spouse for purposes of intestate succession is different from a husband or wife of a decedent. The question before the *Lahey* court was whether the judgment of legal separation constituted an order purporting to terminate marital property rights within the meaning of section 78, subdivision (d). The court, noting that a judgment of legal separation is a final adjudication of the parties' property rights and is conclusive as to those rights, held that it did. There is no principled basis to reach a different result here.

Marie concedes that to the extent the judgment expressly divided marital property rights and recited the parties' agreement to waive spousal support, the judgment was final as to those matters at the time it was entered. But she attempts to avoid the effect of section 78, subdivision (d) by arguing that, although the July 25 judgment may have settled property rights, it did not settle inheritance rights. She enlists the support of a number of older cases—all of which were decided before the enactment of section 78, subdivision (d)—that construe the breadth of marital settlement agreements and decide whether those agreements were intended by the parties to determine inheritance rights. In this, Marie misses the mark. "Nothing in the language or meaning of [section 78, subdivision (d)] requires . . . an express termination of inheritance rights, for the obvious effect of the statute itself is to terminate the inheritance rights of such a spouse." *Lahey, supra.*

We agree with that reading of the statute. In whatever manner spousal inheritance rights might be determined under other circumstances, under the circumstances presented here, section 78, subdivision (d) determines such rights, denying them to a person in Marie's position because she is not deemed a surviving spouse within the meaning of the Probate Code and is therefore ineligible to inherit all or any of Troy's estate.

To the extent that Marie relies for relief on the provisions of Family Code section 2339, we must reject that argument also. That section provides that "no judgment of dissolution is final for the purpose of terminating the marriage relationship of the parties until six months have expired from the date of service of a copy of summons and petition or the date of appearance of the respondent, whichever occurs first." Both parties agree, and the judgment states, that Marie and Troy's marital status did not terminate, nor were they to be restored to the status of single persons until October 29, 2005. But Marie's reliance on Family Code section 2339 ignores the difference between her legal status as Troy's wife at the time of his death and her legal status as a "surviving spouse" at the time of his death. She was at that time legally his wife but she was not his surviving spouse.

Having been a party to a valid proceeding concluded by an order terminating all marital property rights, Marie was not Troy's surviving spouse at the time of his death and she could not share in his estate.

Affirmed in favor of Marianne.

Special Rules Under intestacy statutes, a person must have a relationship to the deceased person through blood or marriage in order to inherit any part of his property. State law includes adopted children within the definition of "children," and treats adopted children in the same way as it treats biological children. Normally adopted children inherit from their adoptive families and not from their biological families, although some state's laws may allow them to inherit from both. Half brothers and half sisters are usually treated in the same way as brothers and sisters related by whole blood. An illegitimate child may inherit from his mother, but as a general rule, illegitimate children do not inherit from their fathers unless paternity has been either acknowledged or established in a legal proceeding.

A person must be alive at the time the decedent dies to claim a share of the decedent's estate. An exception may be made for pretermitted children or other descendants who are born *after* the decedent's death. If a person who is entitled to a share of the decedent's estate survives the decedent but dies before receiving his share, his share in the decedent's estate becomes part of his own estate.

Simultaneous Death A statute known as the Uniform Simultaneous Death Act provides that where two persons who would inherit from each other (such as husband and wife) die under circumstances that make it difficult or impossible to determine who died first, each person's property is to be distributed as though he or she survived. This means, for example, that the husband's property will go to his relatives and the wife's property to her relatives.

Administration of Estates

When a person dies, an orderly procedure is needed to collect his property, settle his debts, and distribute any remaining property to those who will inherit it under his will or by intestate succession. This process occurs under the supervision of a probate court and is known as the **administration process** or the **probate process.** Summary (simple) procedures are sometimes available when an estate is relatively small—for example, when it has assets of less than $7,500.

The Probate Estate   The probate process operates only on the decedent's property that is considered to be part of his **probate estate.** The probate estate is that property belonging to the decedent at the time of his death other than property held in joint ownership with right of survivorship, proceeds of insurance policies payable to a trust or a third party, property held in a revocable trust during the decedent's lifetime in which a third party is the beneficiary, or retirement benefits, such as pensions, payable to a third party. Assets that pass by operation of law and assets that are transferred by other devices such as trusts or life insurance policies do not pass through probate.

Note that the decedent's probate estate and his *taxable estate* for purposes of federal estate tax are two different concepts. The taxable estate includes all property owned or controlled by the decedent at the time of his death. For example, if a person purchased a $1 million life insurance policy made payable to his spouse or children, the policy would be included in his taxable estate, but not in his probate estate.

Determining the Existence of a Will

The first step in the probate process is to determine whether the deceased left a will. This may require a search of the deceased person's personal papers and safe-deposit box. If a will is found, it must be *proved* to be admitted to probate. This involves the testimony of the persons who witnessed the will, if they are still alive. If the witnesses are no longer alive, the signatures of the witnesses and the testator will have to be established in some other way. In many states and under UPC section 2–504,

a will may be proved by an affidavit (declaration under oath) sworn to and signed by the testator and the witnesses at the time the will was executed. This is called a **self-proving affidavit.** If a will is located and proved, it will be admitted to probate and govern many of the decisions that must be made in the administration of the estate.

Selecting a Personal Representative

Another early step in the administration of an estate is the selection of a personal representative to administer the estate. If the deceased left a will, it is likely that he designated his personal representative in the will. The personal representative under a will is also known as the **executor.** Almost anyone could serve as an executor. The testator may have chosen, for example, his spouse, a grown child, a close friend, an attorney, or the trust department of a bank.

If the decedent died intestate, or if the personal representative named in a will is unable to serve, the probate court will name a personal representative to administer the estate. In the case of an intestate estate, the personal representative is called an **administrator.** A preference is usually accorded to a surviving spouse, child, or other close relative. If no relative is available and qualified to serve, a creditor, bank, or other person may be appointed by the court.

Most states require that the personal representative *post a bond* in an amount in excess of the estimated value of the estate to ensure that her duties will be properly and faithfully performed. A person making a will often directs that his executor may serve without posting a bond, and this exemption may be accepted by the court.

Responsibilities of the Personal Representative

The personal representative has a number of important tasks in the administration of the estate. She must see that an inventory is taken of the estate's assets and that the assets are appraised. Notice must then be given to creditors or potential claimants against the estate so that they can file and prove their claims within a specified time, normally five months. As a general rule, the surviving spouse of the deceased person is entitled to be paid an allowance during the time the estate is being settled. This allowance has priority over other debts of the estate. The personal representative must see that any properly payable funeral or burial expenses are paid and that the creditors' claims are satisfied.

Both federal and state governments impose estate or inheritance taxes on estates of a certain size. The personal representative is responsible for filing estate tax returns. The federal tax is a tax on the deceased's estate, with provisions for deducting items such as debts, expenses of administration, and charitable gifts. In addition, an amount equal to the amount left to the surviving spouse may be deducted from the gross estate before the tax is computed. State inheritance taxes are imposed on the person who receives a gift or statutory share from an estate. It is common, however, for wills to provide that the estate will pay all taxes, including inheritance taxes, so that the beneficiaries will not have to do so. The personal representative must also make provisions for filing an income tax return and for paying any income tax due for the partial year prior to the decedent's death.

When the debts, expenses, and taxes have been taken care of, the remaining assets of the estate are distributed to the decedent's heirs (if there was no will) or to the beneficiaries of the decedent's will. Special rules apply when the estate is too small to satisfy all of the bequests made in a will or when some or all of the designated beneficiaries are no longer living.

When the personal representative has completed all of these duties, the probate court will close the estate and discharge the personal representative.

Trusts

Nature of a Trust
A **trust** is a legal relationship in which a person who has legal title to property has the duty to hold it for the use or benefit of another person. The person benefited by a trust is considered to have **equitable title** to the property, because it is being maintained for his benefit. This means that he is the real owner even though the trustee has the legal title in his or her name. A trust can be created in a number of ways. An owner of property may *declare* that he is holding certain property in trust. For example, a mother might state that she is holding 100 shares of General Motors stock in trust for her daughter. A trust may also arise *by operation of law.* For example, when a lawyer representing a client injured in an automobile accident receives a settlement payment from an insurance company, the lawyer holds the settlement payment as trustee for the client. Most commonly, however, trusts are created through *express instruments* whereby an owner of property transfers title to the property to a trustee who is to hold, manage, and invest the property for the benefit of either the original owner or a third person. For example, Long transfers certain stock to First Trust Bank with instructions to pay the income to his daughter during her lifetime and to distribute the stock to her children after her death.

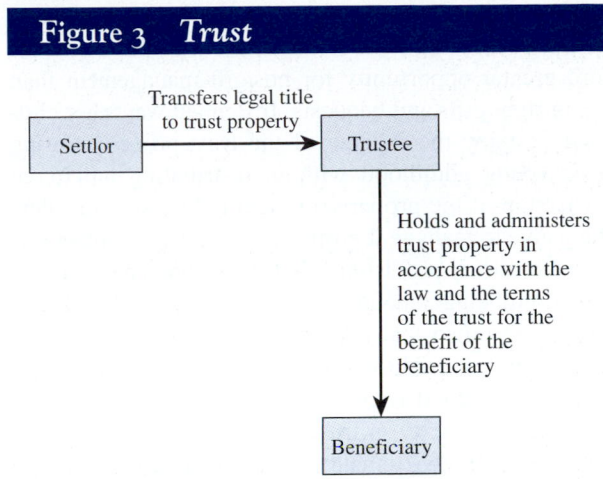

Figure 3   Trust

Settlor → *Transfers legal title to trust property* → Trustee

Trustee → Holds and administers trust property in accordance with the law and the terms of the trust for the benefit of the beneficiary → Beneficiary

Trust Terminology
A person who creates a trust is known as a **settlor** or **trustor.** The person who holds the property for the benefit of another person is called the **trustee.** The person for whose benefit the property is held in trust is the **beneficiary.** Figure 3 illustrates the relationship between these parties. A single person may occupy more than one of these positions; however, if there is only one beneficiary, he cannot be the sole trustee. The property held in trust is called the **corpus** or **res.** A distinction is made between the property in trust, which is the principal, and the income that is produced by the principal.

A trust that is established and effective during the settlor's lifetime is known as an **inter vivos trust.** A trust can also be established in a person's will. Such trusts take effect only at the death of the settlor. They are called **testamentary trusts.**

Why People Create Trusts
Bennett owns a portfolio of valuable stock. Her husband has predeceased her. She has two children and an elderly father for whom she would like to provide. Why might it be advantageous to Bennett to transfer the stock to a trust for the benefit of the members of her family?

First, there may be income tax or estate tax advantages in doing so, depending on the type of trust she establishes and the provisions of that trust. For example, she can establish an irrevocable trust for her children and remove the property transferred to her trust from her estate so that it is not taxable at her death. In addition, the trust property can be used for the benefit of others and may even pass to others after the settlor's death without the necessity of having a will. Many people prefer to pass their property by trust rather than by will because trusts afford more privacy: unlike a probated will, they do not become an item of public record. Trusts also afford greater opportunity for postgift management than do outright gifts and bequests. If Bennett wants her children to enjoy the income of the trust property during their young adulthood without distributing unfettered ownership of the property to them before she considers them able to manage it properly, she can accomplish this through a trust provision. A trust can prevent the property from being squandered or spent too quickly. Trusts can be set up so that a beneficiary's interest cannot be reached by his creditors in many situations. Such trusts, called **spendthrift trusts,** will be discussed later.

Placing property in trust can operate to increase the amount of property held for the beneficiaries if the trustee makes good investment decisions. Another important consideration is that a trust can be used to provide for the needs of disabled beneficiaries who are not capable of managing funds.

Creation of Express Trusts

There are five basic requirements for the creation of a valid express trust, although special and somewhat less restrictive rules govern the establishment of charitable trusts. The requirements for forming an express trust are:

1. *Capacity.* The settlor must have had the **legal capacity** to convey the property to the trust. This means that the settlor must have had the capacity needed to make a valid contract if the trust is an *inter vivos* trust or the capacity to make a will if the trust is a testamentary trust. For example, a trust would fail under this requirement if at the time the trust was created, the settlor had not attained the age required by state law for the creation of valid wills and contracts (age 18 in most states).

2. *Intent and formalities.* The settlor must *intend* to create a trust at the present time. To impose enforceable duties on the trustee, the settlor must meet certain formalities. Under the laws of most states, for example, the trustee must accept the trust by signing the trust instrument. In the case of a trust of land, the trust must be in writing so as to meet the statute of frauds. If the trust is a testamentary trust, it must satisfy the formal requirements for wills.

3. *Conveyance of specific property.* The settlor must convey *specific property* to the trust. The property conveyed must be property that the settlor has the *right to convey.*

4. *Proper purpose.* The trust must be created for a *proper purpose.* It cannot be created for a reason that is contrary to public policy, such as the commission of a crime.

5. *Identity of the beneficiaries.* The *beneficiaries* of the trust must be described clearly enough so that their identities can be ascertained. Sometimes, beneficiaries may be members of a specific class, such as "my children."

Charitable Trusts

A distinction is made between private trusts and trusts created for charitable purposes. In a private trust, property is devoted to the benefit of specific persons, whereas in a charitable trust, property is devoted to a charitable organization or to some other purposes beneficial to society. While some of the rules governing private and charitable trusts are the same, a number of these rules are different. For example, when a private trust is created, the beneficiary must be known at the time or ascertainable within a certain time (established by a legal rule known as the **rule against perpetuities**). However, a charitable trust is valid even though no definitely ascertainable beneficiary is named and even though it is to continue for an indefinite or unlimited period.

Doctrine of Cy Pres

A doctrine known as **cy pres** is applicable to charitable trusts when property is given in trust to be applied to a particular charitable purpose that becomes impossible, impracticable, or illegal to carry out. Under the doctrine of *cy pres,* the trust will not fail if the settlor indicated a general intention to devote the property to charitable purposes. If the settlor has not specifically provided for a substitute beneficiary, the court will direct the application of the property to some charitable purpose that falls within the settlor's general charitable intention.

Totten Trusts

A **Totten trust** is a deposit of money in a bank or other financial institution in the name of the depositor *as trustee* for a named beneficiary. For example, Bliss deposits money in First Bank in trust for his daughter, Bessie. The Totten trust creates a revocable living trust. At Bliss's death, if he has not revoked this trust, the money in the account will belong to Bessie.

Powers and Duties of the Trustee

In most express trusts, the settlor names a specific person to act as trustee. If the settlor does not name a trustee, the court will appoint one. Similarly, a court will replace a trustee who resigns, is incompetent, or refuses to act.

The trust codes of most states contain provisions giving trustees broad management powers over trust property. These provisions can be limited or expanded by express provisions in the trust instrument. The trustee must use a *reasonable degree of skill, judgment, and care* in the exercise of his duties unless he holds himself out as having a greater degree of skill, in which case he will be held to a higher standard. Section 7–302 of the UPC provides that the trustee is held to the standard of a prudent person dealing with the property of another, and if he has special skills or is named trustee based on a representation of special skills, he is required to use those special skills. He *may not commingle* the property he holds in trust with his own property or with that of another trust.

A trustee owes a *duty of loyalty* (fiduciary duty) to the beneficiaries. This means that he must administer the trust for the benefit of the beneficiaries and avoid any conflict between his personal interests and the interest of the trust. For example, a trustee cannot do business with a trust that he administers without express permission in the trust agreement. He must not prefer one beneficiary's interest to another's, and he must account to the beneficiaries for all transactions. Unless the trust agreement provides otherwise, the trustee must make the trust productive. He may not delegate the performance of discretionary duties (such as the duty to select investments) to another, but he may delegate the performance of ministerial duties (such as the preparation of statements of account).

A trust may give the trustee discretion as to the amount of principal or income paid to a beneficiary. In such a case, the beneficiary cannot require the trustee to exercise his discretion in the manner desired by the beneficiary.

Allocating between Principal and Income

One of the duties of the trustee is to distribute the principal and income of the trust in accordance with the terms of the trust instrument. Suppose Wheeler's will created a testamentary trust providing that his wife was to receive the income from the trust for life, and at her death, the trust property was to be distributed to his children. During the duration of the trust, the trust earns profits, such as interest or rents, and has expenses, such as taxes or repairs. How should the trustee allocate these items as between Wheeler's surviving spouse, who is an **income beneficiary,** and his children, who are **remaindermen**?

The terms of the trust and state law bind the trustee in making this determination. As a general rule, ordinary profits received from the investment of trust property are allocated to income. For example, interest on trust property or rents earned from leasing real property held in trust would be allocated to income. Ordinary expenses such as insurance premiums, the cost of ordinary maintenance and repairs of trust property, and property taxes, would be chargeable to income. The principal of the trust includes the trust property itself and any extraordinary receipts, such as proceeds or gains derived from the sale of trust property. Extraordinary expenses—for example,

the cost of long-term permanent improvements to real property or expenses relating to the sale of property— would ordinarily be charged against principal.

Liability of Trustee

A trustee who breaches any of the duties of a trustee or whose conduct falls below the standard of care applicable to trustees may incur personal liability. For example, if the trustee invests unwisely and imprudently, the trustee may be personally liable to reimburse the trust estate for the shortfall. The language of the trust affects the trustee's liability and the level of care owed by the trustee. A settlor might, for example, include language lowering the trustee's duty of care or relieving the trustee of some liability that he might otherwise incur.

The trustee can also have liability to third persons who are injured by the operation of the trust. Because a trust is not in itself a legal entity that can be sued, a third party who has a claim (such as a tort claim or a claim for breach of contract) must file his claim against the trustee of the trust. The trustee's actual personal liability to a third party depends on the language of the trust and of any contracts he might enter on behalf of the trust as well as the extent to which the injury complained of by the third party was a result of the personal fault or omission of the trustee.

Spendthrift Trusts

Generally, the beneficiary of a trust may voluntarily assign his rights to the principal or income of the trust to another person. In addition, any distributions to the beneficiary are subject to the claims of his creditors. Sometimes, however, trusts contain provisions known as **spendthrift clauses,** which restrict the voluntary or involuntary transfer of a beneficiary's interest. Such clauses are generally enforced, and they preclude assignees or creditors from compelling a trustee to recognize their claims to the trust. The enforceability of such clauses is subject to four exceptions, however:

1. A person cannot put his own property beyond the claims of his own creditors. Thus, a spendthrift clause is not effective in a trust when the settlor makes himself a beneficiary.

2. Divorced spouses and minor children of the beneficiary can compel payment for alimony and child support.

3. Creditors of the beneficiary who have furnished necessaries can compel payment.

4. Once the trustee distributes property to a beneficiary, it can be subject to valid claims of others.

The following *Kulp* case illustrates a situation in which a court holds a spendthrift trust subject to a creditor's claims.

Kulp v. Timmons　　2002 Del. Ch. LEXIS 94 (Del. Ct. of Chancery 2002)

Before 1985, Franklin Timmons and his wife, Kathryn, owned property adjacent to Pepper Creek in Sussex County, Delaware. The property included farmland, the Timmonses' residence, and a marina called the "Boatyard," where Timmons operated the family business. The above-described land was the only real property that Timmons owned, and was the only capital asset that supported the family business. Timmons's primary income was derived from the Boatyard. At the Boatyard, Timmons rented out boat slips, assessed dry dock fees, maintained and repaired boats, and performed the day-to-day operations of the marina. According to Timmons, the business operated at a loss, but there are no records to prove that. In 1977, Timmons was sued by Charles Cannon on transactions that involved the Boatyard. Cannon was awarded a $7,700 judgment against Timmons in 1980, but Timmons never paid the judgment, claiming that he lacked sufficient funds. In 1985, Timmons and Kathryn established a Joint Irrevocable Living Trust. Timmons and Kathryn conveyed to the Trust the farm and the Boatyard, which comprised all the real property that they owned and the only significant assets that were capable of responding to a creditor judgment. Under the terms of the Trust, Timmons, Kathryn, and their son, Jimmy, were named as trustees. The Trust instrument gave trustees discretion to invade the trust principal and to sell the land for their own benefit.

Although his property was now held by the Trust, Timmons never viewed the Trust as limiting his ability to use the land for himself or to rent it to others. Timmons believed that he could continue to live on the land, operate his business on it, and use the land as his own, as he had done in the past. Two additional documents were executed in connection with the Trust instrument. The first was a partnership agreement, which created a partnership between Timmons and his son, Jimmy, for the purpose of operating the Boatyard. The Partnership Agreement identified Kathryn and Jimmy—but not Timmons—as partners. The second document was a lease that called for the payment of a monthly rent for using the Boatyard, but left the specific rental amount blank. Although it was understood that the rental amount would be inserted after Timmons secured an appraisal of the Boatyard's fair market value, no rental amount was ever inserted and no rent was ever paid. Nor, insofar as the record shows, did the Trust engage in any trust activity after it was formed. Other than filing tax returns, the Trust had no financial records for any year other than 1988, or any checking or banking account; and it received no rent or other income from Timmons's use of the land. In addition, although Kathryn was the Boatyard's bookkeeper, the Trust never took any action evidenced by a formal writing.

In 1985, six months after the Trust was created, Norman Kulp, Timmons's employee, was severely injured while working at the Boatyard when Timmons instructed him to remove a gas tank from a boat docked at the Boatyard. Timmons told Kulp that he, Timmons, had personally ventilated the tank and that Jimmy would help Kulp remove it. In fact, the tank had not been emptied and Kulp was left to perform that task alone. The tank exploded and Kulp was burned over one-third of his body. Timmons did not carry workers' compensation insurance, and he did not reimburse any of Kulp's medical expenses. Kulp filed a petition for compensation due with the Industrial Accident Board (IAB) under the Delaware Workers' Compensation Act, and the IAB ordered Timmons to post a $150,000 bond and to pay Kulp's medical expenses and other benefits. Timmons did not comply with the IAB order, and several years of litigation ensued.

Timmons's son, Jimmy, died in October 1994, and Timmons's wife, Kathryn, died two years later. As a consequence, Timmons became the sole settlor, trustee, and lifetime beneficiary of the Trust. Kulp's IAB award still remained unpaid, which prompted the filing of a Superior Court proceeding to enforce payment of that award. In 1997, the Superior Court entered a money judgment in favor of Kulp, doubling the initial IAB award to $194,316.74 to compensate Kulp for the delay in payment. The Superior Court concluded, however, that it did not have the power to compel Timmons to pledge, sell, or encumber the assets held by the Trust to satisfy the judgment. In response to the Court's suggestion that Kulp's remedy would lie in equity, Kulp brought this action in this Court for a determination that the Trust was invalid and that its assets were subject to execution process. Less than one month after this action was filed, Timmons conveyed all his personal property to his daughter-in-law, Beverly, and his granddaughter, Brandi. Thereafter, Beverly and Brandi conveyed a life estate in the conveyed property to Timmons. Timmons argued that as a consequence of that conveyance, and the transfer of his (and his wife's) assets to the Trust in 1985, he has no assets from which to satisfy the judgment. Kulp moved for summary judgment.

Jacobs, Vice Chancellor

As a general matter, creditors may not reach property held in a spendthrift trust to satisfy their claims against the beneficial owner. That rule, however, is not absolute. The Court first considers whether the Trust is invalid under Delaware's spendthrift trust statute. Section 3536 (a) articulates the rights of creditors to reach assets held in spendthrift trusts as follows: The creditors of a beneficiary of a trust shall have only such rights against such beneficiary's interest in the trust property or the income therefrom as shall not be denied to them by the terms of the instrument creating or defining the trust or by the laws of this State. *If such beneficiary has transferred property to the trust in defraud of the beneficiary's creditors the foregoing shall in no way limit the rights of such creditors with respect to the property so transferred.* Thus, the statute expressly permits a trust to be invalidated if it is shown that the transfer of the property to the trust operated as a fraud on the beneficiary's creditors. If a fraud is shown, the trust is void, and a creditor of the beneficiary may reach its assets to satisfy the creditor's judgment claim.

Delaware courts have held that the test of a fraudulent conveyance of property involves a two-step analysis: first, a determination of whether the transfer was made for less than fair consideration; and second, a determination of whether the transferor was rendered insolvent as a result of the transfer. Del. C. Section 1302, as it existed when the Trust was created in 1985, stated that a person is insolvent "when the fair salable value of his assets is less than the amount that will be required to pay his probable liability on his existing debts as they become absolute and matured." In this case, the absence of financial records and other documentation precludes the Court from determining, as an evidentiary matter, whether in fact Timmons was insolvent at the time of the asset transfer. Nor does the record evidence show whether the Boatyard was transferred to the Trust for fair consideration. All the record does show is that Timmons transferred the Boatyard to a Trust controlled by himself, his wife, and his son. Where, as here, a transfer of assets occurs between relatives, collusion is difficult to prove, and therefore "a rebuttable presumption of fraud arises." That presumption requires the party asserting the validity of the transfer to show either that he was solvent after the transfer or that fair consideration was paid. Timmons has not shown either, nor has he offered any evidence on either of those issues. What evidence there is shows an intent to defraud past and future creditors. At the time the Trust was created, Cannon's judgment was outstanding and Timmons had never paid it, even though he had the resources to do so. Moreover, the Trust served no discernable economic purpose. The Trust engaged in no recorded economic activity; no rent was paid to the Trust for the use of the Boatyard; and no formal action evidenced by a writing by the Trust was ever taken. In short, Timmons has presented no evidence that rebuts the presumption that the creation and the transfer of his (and his wife's) assets to the Trust was a fraud. I conclude therefore that the Trust is invalid and has been from the outset, and must be set aside, on the basis of the fraud exception of Section 3536 (a).

In addition to, and apart from, the statute, the Trust is void because the statute does not displace the applicable principles of common law, and because under those principles the Trust is void as well. The Delaware case law has not delineated in any comprehensive "bright line" fashion the universe of common law grounds upon which a trust can be invalidated and made subject to claims of the beneficiary's creditors. The decisions do, however, clearly reflect a basic principle: our courts will not give effect to a spendthrift trust that has no economic reality and whose only function is to enable the settlor to control and enjoy the trust property without limitations or restraints, as was done before the trust was created. Apart from cases involving fraud, that principle has found expression under at least two different doctrines. Some cases express that result in terms of public policy. In such cases, our courts have denied effect to a trust agreement provision that prohibits the beneficiary's alienation of trust income or assets, where the beneficiary is also the settlor. Where, as here, the settlor or trustee is also the beneficiary, the spendthrift trust will be invalidated, because public policy does not permit one to create a spendthrift trust with his own property for his own benefit. That is because where (as here) the trustee controls the assets and income of the trust for his own benefit, unconstrained by any fiduciary duties owed to others, the purpose of a spendthrift trust—to protect the beneficiary from his or her own improvidence—is lost. The evidence of record—undisputed by Timmons—amply supports the conclusion that at all times Timmons had—and exercised—the power to use the Trust assets as his own. The Trust instruments authorize Timmons to expend the entire corpus of the Trust at his discretion, for his own benefit and without any limitation or restriction. Timmons acknowledged that after he conveyed the property to the Trust he expected to continue to use the land as he had in the past. Timmons also admitted that he did not believe the Trust limited in any way his ability to rent the property to someone else. Further supportive of the invalidity of the Trust on public policy grounds is the fact that the Trust has no economic reality and from the outset was a sham. Most telling is the fact that the mortgage payments were made from Timmons's *personal* income (not from Trust assets), and the income from boat maintenance and repairs was reported as income to Timmons *personally*, rather than as income to the Trust. That shows that Timmons never intended for the Trust to have any economic function other than as a vehicle to avoid paying his debts. On this basis alone, the Trust is void and the Trust assets are subject to Kulp's claim as a judgment. On all of these grounds, the Trust is void under the principles of Delaware common law, and Kulp may reach the Trust's assets to satisfy his judgment claim.

Summary judgment granted in favor of Kulp.

Termination and Modification of a Trust

Normally, a settlor cannot revoke or modify a trust unless he reserves the power to do so at the time he establishes the trust. However, a trust may be modified or terminated with the consent of the settlor and all of the beneficiaries. When the settlor is dead or otherwise unable to consent, a trust can be modified or terminated by consent of all the persons with a beneficial interest, but only when this would not frustrate a material purpose of the trust. Because trusts are under the supervisory jurisdiction of a court, the court can permit a deviation from the terms of a trust when unanticipated changes in circumstances threaten accomplishment of the settlor's purpose.

Implied and Constructive Trusts

Under exceptional circumstances in which the creation of a trust is necessary to effectuate a settlor's intent or avoid unjust enrichment, the law *implies* or imposes a trust even though no express trust exists or an express trust exists but has failed. One trust of this type is a **resulting trust,** which arises when there has been an incomplete disposition of trust property. For example, if Hess transferred property to Wickes as trustee to provide for the needs of Hess's grandfather and the grandfather died before the trust funds were exhausted, Wickes will be deemed to hold the property in a resulting trust for Hess or Hess's heirs. Similarly, if Hess had transferred the property to Wickes as trustee and the trust had failed because Hess did not meet one of the requirements of a valid trust, Wickes would not be permitted to keep the trust property as his own. A resulting trust would be implied.

A **constructive trust** is a trust created by operation of law to avoid fraud, injustice, or unjust enrichment. This type of trust imposes on the constructive trustee a duty to convey property he holds to another person on the ground that the constructive trustee would be unjustly enriched if he were allowed to retain it. For example, when a person procures the transfer of property by means of fraud or duress, he becomes a constructive trustee and is under an obligation to return the property to its original owner.

Problems and Problem Cases

1. On March 23, 1994, Evelyn Foster died, leaving a house and nearly 400 acres of land in Mercer County along with personal property. She had executed a holographic will, which was offered for probate. The will stated in part:

   I—Evelyn Foster—being of sound Mind and Body—do hereby declare—In the event of my death—I herby [sic] will the farm-house + contents to go to Judy Foster Monk—any Monies shall be divided equally—after the funeral Expenses—between Greg Foster + Judy Foster Monk—also I do herby [sic] request that the Farm *not be sold!* Any personal items shall be equally divided—
   Sincerely—
   Evelyn Foster

   Foster's son claims that Foster willed only a "farm-house + contents" to his sister (Judy) and not the farmland. Is he correct?

2. Meade, a widow with no children, died on May 4, 2002. In March 2001, Meade had executed a typewritten will prepared by an attorney. After Meade's death, the executor named in the will presented it for probate. Gilliam was Meade's niece and had cared for her during the months of her last illness. Gilliam offered for probate a handwritten will that Meade had written and signed subsequent to the typewritten will. It provided:

Will

Jo and Ron Gilliam, my (niece) & her husband said they would take care of me, and not put me in a rest home. They have said if they had to they would move in my home and take care of me.

Grady Lee (brother) $ 20.00 and my car. Jo Gilliam (niece) & (Ron) husband the rest of my house & furniture except a few items.

Cecil Lee (brother) the rest of my life ins. After burial is pd.

Bertha Mae Cox (niece) mama's old sewing machine, pink wash bowl and pitcher (Xmas dishes), to Jo red ruby ring & diamond necklas [spelling?] ear rings.

Jo Gilliam (niece) all my gold chains, lg. Diamond ring & holder.

Kimberly Dalton (niece) white luggage, sewing machine, pink iron, glasses, stone dishes, & pink crystal. Paul Revere stainless ware, punch bowl, & lg. dimon [spelling?] ring & band.

David Lee (nephew) rocking chair, luggage, camester [spelling?] & grand ma Lee's quilt. Leslie Tinter (great niece) blue safire [spelling] rg.

Gary Vicars (gardner) $ 500.00.

I'll divide the rest of my clothes & jewelry. I want my house to keep in the family & don't change the way it's brick. Just keep it up.

Kathleen (Lee) Meade.

There is no dispute about the authenticity of this document. Gilliam claims that the handwritten will should be received as Meade's last will. Is this a good argument?

3. Roy and Icie Johnson established two revocable *inter vivos* trusts in 1966. The trusts provided that upon Roy's and Icie's deaths, income from the trusts was to be paid in equal shares to their two sons, James and Robert, for life. Upon the death of the survivor of the sons, the trust was to be *"divided equally between all of my grandchildren, per stirpes."* James had two daughters, Barbara and Elizabeth. Robert had four children, David, Rosalyn, Catherine, and Elizabeth. James and Robert disclaimed their interest in the trust in 1979, and a dispute arose about how the trust should be distributed to the grandchildren. The trustee filed an action seeking instructions on how the trusts should be distributed. What should the court hold?

4. Opal Gefon died in November 2005, and a typewritten will that had been properly witnessed and executed in May 6, 2005, was submitted for probate. Johnson, a great-niece of Gefon, filed a contest of the May 6 instrument, claiming that a holographic will had been executed in October 2005. The court admitted the holographic will for probate, but confusion arose about the meaning of two provisions in the will. One provision used the words "savings and checking account" in the First Team Bank in Heber Springs to the Lost Cherokee of Arkansas and Missouri, Inc., and another referred to "the remainder of my savings and checking to the Native American Indians." At the time of Gefon's death, she had approximately $205,000 in savings accounts at First Arkansas Bank and Trust and $226,000 in cash in a safety deposit box at the same bank. Following a hearing, the court entered an order in which it found that Gefon intended that the $226,000 in cash located in her safety deposit box at the time of her death was part of her "savings" so that the references to "savings and checking account" and "remainder of my savings and checking" in the will included the $226,000 in cash. The court further found that the phrase "Native American Indians" referred to the Lost Cherokee of Arkansas and Missouri, Inc., and that the phrase, "remainder of my savings and checking" was a residual clause with respect to those funds, and that after any specific bequests were made, the remaining amounts were to be distributed to the Lost Cherokee of Arkansas and Missouri, Inc. Was this a correct ruling?

5. Crawshaw bequeathed the bulk of his estate to two residuary beneficiaries, the Salvation Army and Marymount College. Crawshaw's will provided for 15 percent of the residue to go to the Salvation Army outright and 85 percent to Marymount College in trust. The stated purpose of this trust was to provide loans to nursing and other students at Marymount. Marymount ceased operation on June 30, 1989. It sought to have the trust funds directed to Marymount Memorial Educational Trust Fund. The Salvation Army challenged this, arguing that Crawshaw did not intend to benefit students attending colleges other than Marymount. It asked that the court distribute the trust funds to the Salvation Army as the remaining beneficiary of Crawshaw's residuary estate. What should the court do?

6. Almost a century ago, Henry and Martha Kolb started a family-owned floral business in Storm Lake, Iowa. Both the business and the family grew into prominence. After their grandson, Robert, was tragically killed in a hunting accident, the Kolbs established an agreement with the City of Storm Lake to establish a flower garden in the memory of Robert. The agreement provided for the "establishment, installation and maintenance of a formal flower garden" at a specific location within the city park on the north shore of Storm Lake. The agreement made it clear that the garden was a gift to the city, and that the agreement was to "continue during the period of the trust as created in [Henry's] Will . . . providing for the continued maintenance of said formal flower garden." The trust was later supplemented for the addition of a water fountain in the garden. The Robert James Kolb Memorial Trust Fund was finally established in 1970. Henry and Martha established the trust by deeding a quarter section of farmland they owned to their sons "Robert H. Kolb and Norman J. Kolb, as Trustees for the use and benefit of the City of Storm Lake." The warranty deed stated in pertinent part:

> It is the purpose of the grantors to hereby establish the Robert James Kolb Memorial Trust Fund out of the real estate above described and the proceeds derived from the sale thereof and/or the income derived therefrom, or any investments created by said trust fund. . . .

> The said trust fund shall be used in connection with improvements needed for the planting and upkeep of flower beds, such as annuals and perennials of all kinds, also flowering bulbs and rose bushes as may be put upon the tract of real estate hereinafter described.

In 1973, Henry and Martha deeded another quarter section of their farmland to their sons, Robert and

Norman, as trustees, "for the use and benefit of the City of Storm Lake" to become a "part of the Robert James Kolb Memorial Trust Fund established by the grantors in the year 1970, in order that this trust and the previously established trust may be handled as a single trust." Neither warranty deed stated when the trust terminated. The trust operated without much trouble or question for over 30 years under the direction of Robert and Norman as trustees. The reports indicated the income produced from the farmland was more than enough to pay for the trust expenses. The trust disbursements mainly consisted of farm, garden, and fountain expenses, which often equaled $20,000–$30,000. On one occasion, however, the trustees used surplus trust funds to help the Storm Lake School District purchase additional school property. This transaction was memorialized in a 1980 agreement between Norman and the school district.

Henry died testate in 1978 and Martha died a short time later. Despite their deaths, the garden and fountain survived for many years with the help of the city's maintenance and funds provided by the trust. It was a cherished location in Storm Lake, and often provided an ideal spot for weddings and celebrations. In 2003, however, the existence of the garden and fountain was placed in jeopardy. At this time the city was developing plans for an economic revitalization project called "Project Awaysis," funded with Vision Iowa grant money. The plans sought to turn the city's park on the north shore of Storm Lake and surrounding areas into a Midwest vacation destination. Among other things, the project was to provide a new public beach, a lighthouse, a family playground, a lodge, and an indoor/outdoor water park. Most importantly, the plans called for relocating the memorial gardens and fountain within the city's park. The project was viewed by its planners, and others, as a vital and necessary move for the city to grow and compete for jobs and residents in the future. Norman, as trustee of the Kolb trust, filed a petition for an injunction preventing the removal of the garden and fountain. The trial court ruled against Norman on the injunction and the city began the removal of the garden and fountain. After a later trial, however, the court found that the trust's purpose had been destroyed and that it therefore became a resulting trust to benefit the Kolbs' successors. Was this ruling correct?

7. John Henry Kirkpatrick was born Gion Rosetti to Joseph and Beatrice Rosetti in 1914. He had 10 siblings. On January 25, 1927, Edgar and Margaret Kirkpatrick adopted Gion and his brother, Leo. The Kirkpatricks changed Gion's name to John Henry Kirkpatrick and Leo's name to Edward Watson Kirkpatrick. The other nine birth siblings were either adopted away or remained with their birth parents. John Kirkpatrick was married briefly, divorced, and had no children. Edward Kirkpatrick married and, with his wife, raised a daughter, Karen Shippey. John and Edward Kirkpatrick's nine biological siblings produced eight children (the cousins). John Kirkpatrick died intestate on August 4, 2000, leaving a substantial estate consisting of stocks, bonds, real estate, and personal property. Shippey and Rick Rogers were appointed co-personal representatives of John Kirkpatrick's estate. Shippey and Rogers filed a document asking the court to determine the proper heirs for distribution of the estate. Shippey argued that she was John Kirkpatrick's sole heir because his adoption terminated the rights of any biological relative not adopted by his adoptive family. *Wyo. Stat. Ann.* §§ 2-4-101 and 2-4-107 establish the rules of intestate succession and, specifically, those that apply to persons in an adoptive family. The pertinent parts are:

Except in cases above enumerated, the estate of any intestate shall descend and be distributed as follows:

(ii) If there are no children, nor their descendents, then to his father, mother, brothers and sisters, and to the descendents of brothers and sisters who are dead, the descendents collectively taking the share which their parents would have taken if living, in equal parts[.]

An adopted person is the child of an adopting parent *and of the natural parents for inheritance purposes only.*

An adopted person shall inherit from all other relatives of an adoptive parent as though he was the natural child of the adoptive parent and the relatives shall inherit from the adoptive person's estate as if they were his relatives[.]

Will Karen prevail?

Online Research

Living Wills

Using your favorite search engine, find an example of a living will other than the form that appears in Figure 1 of this chapter.

chapter 27

INSURANCE LAW

Hurricane Katrina struck Louisiana, Mississippi, and Alabama with overwhelming force in late August 2005. For many weeks thereafter, media coverage focused on the tragic personal consequences produced by Katrina and the tremendous devastation the storm inflicted on the Gulf Coast. Billions of dollars of property damage resulted from the hurricane and the flooding it spawned. Large numbers of homeowners simply did not have a property insurance policy. To their dismay, homeowners and commercial property owners who did have property insurance policies discovered that their particular losses may not have been covered by their policies. This was so even though damage from wind is a typical covered peril in a property insurance policy.

   Coverage disputes between property owners and insurance companies began to spring up with frequency not long after the extensive damage stemming from Hurricane Katrina became apparent. Property owners filed numerous cases against their insurers in an effort to convince courts to rule that typical property insurance policies' coverage of wind damage would cover a broad range of Katrina-related losses, including those directly related to post-hurricane flooding. In general, however, the plaintiffs had little success. As you read this chapter, consider the hurricane aftermath and think about the following questions:

- If wind is a typical covered peril in property insurance policies, how is it possible that losses stemming from Hurricane Katrina might not be covered under such policies?
- Is there a typical exclusion from coverage that property insurers could credibly argue as a basis for denying coverage of certain Katrina-connected losses?
- Why might a policyholder whose home or building was flattened by the powerful storm be in a stronger position to collect under her insurance policy than, say, a New Orleans insured whose home was destroyed or rendered uninhabitable by the flooding that engulfed the city when the powerful hurricane caused the city's levee system to fail?

   Think, too, about these broader questions:

- What is the nature of the relationship between an insurer and the insured? Is it collaborative, adversarial, or some of each?
- What legal obligations does an insurer owe to an insured? Do ethical obligations also attend the insurer–insured relationship?
- When a disaster of Hurricane Katrina's magnitude strikes, should the terms of an insurance policy be interpreted any differently from how they would have been interpreted in the event of more ordinary losses?
- What role do courts play in resolving insurance policy disputes?
- Should legislatures and government agencies regulate the terms of insurance policies, or should the content of policies be left to the market?

INSURANCE SERVES AS a frequent topic of discussion in various contexts in today's society. Advertisements for companies offering life, automobile, and property insurance appear daily on television and in the print media. Journalists report on issues of health insurance coverage and movements for reform. Persons engaged in business lament the excessive (from their perspective) costs of obtaining liability insurance. Insurance companies and insurance industry critics offer differing explanations for why those costs have reached their present levels.

Despite the frequency with which insurance matters receive public discussion and the perceived importance of insurance coverage, major legal aspects of insurance relationships remain unfamiliar to many persons. This chapter, therefore, examines important components of insurance law. We begin by discussing the nature of insurance relationships and exploring contract law's application to insurance policies in general. We then discuss other legal concepts and issues associated with specific types of insurance, most notably property insurance and liability insurance. The chapter concludes with an examination of an important judicial trend: allowing insurers to be held liable for compensatory and punitive damages if they refuse in bad faith to perform their policy obligations.

Nature and Benefits of Insurance Relationships

Insurance relationships arise from an agreement under which a risk of loss that one party (normally the **insured**) otherwise would have to bear is shifted to another party (the **insurer**). The ability to obtain insurance enables the insured to lessen or avoid the adverse financial effects that would be likely if certain happenings were to take place. In return for the insured's payment of necessary consideration (the **premium**), the insurer agrees to shoulder the financial consequences stemming from particular risks if those risks materialize in the form of actual events.

Each party benefits from the insurance relationship. The insured obtains a promise of coverage for losses that, if they occur, could easily exceed the amounts of the premiums paid. Along with this promise, the insured acquires the "peace of mind" that insurance companies and agents like to emphasize. By collecting premiums from many insureds over a substantial period of time, the insurer stands to profit despite its obligation to make payments covering financial losses that stem from insured-against risks. The insured-against risks, after all, are just that—risks. In some instances, events triggering the insurer's payment obligation to a particular insured

may never occur (e.g., the insured's property never sustains damage from a cause contemplated by the property insurance policy). The insurer nonetheless remains entitled to the premiums collected during the policy period. Other times, events that call the insurer's payment obligation into play in a given situation may occur infrequently (e.g., a particular insured under an automobile insurance policy has an accident only every few years) or only after many years of premium collection (e.g., an insured paid premiums on his life insurance policy for 35 years prior to his death).

Insurance Policies as Contracts

Interested Parties Regardless of the type of insurance involved, the insurance relationship is contractual. This relationship involves at least two—and frequently more than two—interested parties. As noted earlier, the insurer, in exchange for the payment of consideration (the premium), agrees to pay for losses caused by specific events (sometimes called *perils*). The insured is the person who acquires insurance on real or personal property or insurance against liability, or, in the case of life or health insurance, the person whose life or health is the focus of the policy. The person to whom the insurance proceeds are payable is the **beneficiary.** Except in the case of life insurance, the insured and the beneficiary will often be the same person. In most but not all instances, the insured will also be the policy's **owner** (the person entitled to exercise the contract rights set out in the insurance policy and in applicable law). In view of the contractual nature of the insurance relationship, insurance policies must satisfy all of the elements required for a binding contract.

Offer, Acceptance, and Consideration

The insurance industry's standard practice is to have the potential insured make an offer for an insurance contract by completing and submitting an application (provided by the insurer's agent), along with the appropriate premium, to the insurer. The insurer may then either accept or reject this offer. If the insurer accepts, the parties have an insurance contract under which the insured's initial premium payment and future premium payments furnish consideration for the insurer's promises of coverage for designated risks, and vice versa.

What constitutes acceptance of the offer set forth in the application may vary somewhat, depending on the type of insurance requested and the language of the application. As a general rule, however, acceptance occurs when the insurer (or agent, if authorized to do so) indicates to the insured an intent to accept the application. It is important to know the precise time when acceptance occurs, because the insurer's contractual obligations to the insured do not commence until acceptance has taken place. If the insured sustains losses after the submission of the application (the making of the offer) but prior to acceptance by the insurer, those losses normally must be borne by the insured rather than the insurer.

With property insurance and sometimes other types of insurance, the application may be worded so that insurance coverage begins when the insured signs the application. This arrangement provides temporary coverage until the insurer either accepts or rejects the offer contained in the application. The same result may also be achieved by the use of a *binder*, an agreement for temporary insurance pending the insurer's decision to accept or reject the risk. The *World Trade Center Properties* case, which follows, deals with interpretation of property insurance binders issued shortly before the September 11, 2001, plane attacks on the World Trade Center towers.

World Trade Center Properties, LLC v. Hartford Fire Insurance Co.
345 F.3d 154 (2d Cir. 2003)

Prior to the September 11, 2001, attacks that destroyed the World Trade Center (WTC) towers, 22 insurance companies had issued property insurance binders covering the WTC complex. These binders were issued to Silverstein Properties, Inc., the holder of a 99-year lease of the WTC complex under an agreement with the Port Authority of New York and New Jersey. A binder is a temporary contract of insurance that is in force until a formal insurance policy is issued by the insurer. The 22 insurers intended to issue formal insurance policies to Silverstein, but very few had done so as of 9/11. Therefore, the binders established and limited their obligations to pay Silverstein after the destruction of the WTC complex.

Property insurance binders and policies often provide that the insurer's obligation to pay is triggered when a covered "occurrence" results in damage to or destruction of the relevant real estate. Binders and policies also have policy limits, which are both the amount of insurance coverage purchased and the maximum sum that the insurer can be obligated to pay for a covered claim. The policy limits in a property insurance binder or policy typically apply on a per-occurrence basis. For example, if the policy limits are $200,000, the insurer may become obligated to pay up to a maximum of $200,000 for losses resulting from one occurrence and up to another $200,000 on losses stemming from a separate occurrence.

Various ones of the 22 insurers that had issued binders regarding the WTC complex prior to 9/11 became involved in litigation with Silverstein over the amounts they were obligated to pay after the events of 9/11. Three of the insurers that were parties to the litigation—Hartford Fire Insurance Company, Royal Indemnity Company, and St. Paul Fire and Marine Insurance Company—had issued binders whose combined policy limits totaled approximately $112 million dollars, out of a total of approximately $3.5 billion in insurance coverage contemplated by the binders and policies issued by all 22 insurers. Another party to the litigation was Travelers Indemnity Co., which also promised millions of dollars of coverage under a binder that differed in a key respect from the Hartford, Royal, and St. Paul binders. The estimated cost of rebuilding the complex was $5 billion or more.

In the litigation referred to above, a federal court agreed with an argument made by Hartford, Royal, and St. Paul: that their binders should be interpreted as containing the terms set forth in a form binder known as the "WilProp form," which had been circulated among many of the various insurers. The WilProp form made the insurance coverage applicable on a per-occurrence basis and contained a specific definition of occurrence. (The definition will be quoted later, in the edited version of the decision ultimately issued by a federal court of appeals.)

The court then addressed the critical issue: whether, for purposes of the binders at issue, the two plane attacks that destroyed the WTC towers on 9/11 were one occurrence or, instead, two occurrences. If, as argued by Hartford, Royal, and St. Paul, the two plane attacks were one occurrence, those three insurers would be obligated to pay Silverstein a total of $112 million. If, as argued by Silverstein, the two plane attacks were two occurrences, the three insurers would be obligated to pay Silverstein a total of $224 million. Although most of the remaining insurers were not parties to the case, a determination of the extent of their liabilities to Silverstein was likely to be heavily influenced by the court's decision because it seemed reasonably likely that various ones of the other insurers would be viewed as having agreed to the same form binder terms to which Hartford, Royal, and St. Paul had agreed. Thus, although the actual amount in controversy under the Hartford, Royal, and St. Paul binders ranged from a minimum of $112 million to a maximum of $224 million, the practical economic stakes appeared to be much higher. Ruling on a motion for partial summary judgment filed by Hartford, Royal, and St. Paul, the *district court held that in view of the WilProp form's definition of occurrence, the two plane attacks on the WTC were one occurrence for purposes of those companies' binders.*

Travelers, however, had issued a binder that differed from the form binder employed by Hartford, Royal, and St. Paul. The Travelers binder called for coverage on a per-occurrence basis but did not contain a definition of occurrence. Silverstein moved for partial summary judgment, asking the court to rule that under the Travelers binder, the two plane attacks constituted two occurrences. Concluding that there were genuine issues of material fact to be resolved by a jury in regard to the plane attacks on the WTC, the district court denied Silverstein's motion.

Appealing to the U.S. Court of Appeals for the Second Circuit, Silverstein asked the appellate court to overturn the district court's grant of partial summary judgment to Hartford, Royal, and St. Paul. Silverstein also appealed the district court's denial of its (Silverstein's) motion for partial summary judgment against Travelers.

Walker, Chief Judge

This case arises out of the devastating tragedy that occurred at the World Trade Center ("WTC") in lower Manhattan, New York, on the morning of September 11, 2001. At issue in this case is the amount of insurance that is recoverable for the total destruction of the WTC that occurred after the buildings were struck by two fuel-laden aircraft that had been hijacked by terrorists. In the spring of 2001, Silverstein Properties, Inc., was the successful bidder on a 99-year lease for the [WTC Complex] from the Port Authority of New York and New Jersey. In July 2001, Silverstein obtained primary and excess insurance coverage for the WTC complex from about two dozen insurers . . . in the total amount of approximately $3.5 billion "per occurrence."

The parties do not dispute that the destruction of the WTC resulted in a loss that greatly exceeded $3.5 billion. The broad question presented in this case is whether the events of September 11, 2001, constituted one or two "occurrences." The answer will determine whether Silverstein can recover once, up to $3.5 billion, or twice, up to $7 billion, under the insurance coverage. Complicating the resolution of this question is the fact that as of September 11, 2001, only one of the many insurers that bound coverage on the WTC had issued a final policy, necessitating an individualized inquiry to determine the terms of the insurance binders issued by each insurer.

[*Note:* In portions of the opinion not included here, the Second Circuit upheld two important rulings of the district court: first, that the binders of Hartford, Royal, and St. Paul should be interpreted as including the WilProp form's specific definition of *occurrence;* and second, that the obligation of Travelers should be determined according to the binder it issued prior to September 11, 2001, rather than on the basis of the insurance policy Travelers actually issued on September 14, 2001. The Second Circuit then went on to address the one occurrence versus two occurrences issue in regard to the binders of Hartford, Royal, and St. Paul and the different binder issued by Travelers.]

Of the four insurers in these appeals, Travelers was the only insurer to submit its own [binder]. Whereas the Travelers [binder contemplated per-occurrence coverage but] did not define the term *occurrence,* the WilProp form[—used by Hartford, Royal, and St. Paul as the basis of their per-occurrence binders—]defined *occurrence.* Our conclusion that [Hartford, Royal, and St. Paul] bound coverage on the basis of the WilProp form leaves only Silverstein's claim that there are issues of fact as to whether there were one or two occurrences on September 11th under the WilProp form's definition. [T]he WilProp form contain[ed] the following definition:

> *Occurrence* shall mean all losses or damages that are attributable directly or indirectly to one cause or to one series of similar causes. All such losses will be added together and the total amount of such losses will be treated as one occurrence irrespective of the period of time or area over which such losses occur.

Although Silverstein attempts to argue that this definition is ambiguous, [it is not]. [N]o finder of fact could reasonably fail to find that the intentional crashes into the WTC of two hijacked airplanes sixteen minutes apart as a result of a single, coordinated plan of attack was, at the least, a "series of similar causes." Accordingly, we agree with the district court that under the WilProp definition [and the Hartford, Royal, and St. Paul binders that employed it], the events of September 11th constitute a single occurrence as a matter of law.

Silverstein's appeal from the denial of the motion for summary judgment against Travelers raises a different set of issues from those just discussed. This motion was based chiefly on [Silverstein's] argument that where an insurance policy uses the term *occurrence* without defining the term, then, as a matter of law, the term's meaning is not ambiguous and must be decided by reference to well-established New York legal precedent. Silverstein further argues that under the definition of *occurrence* established by New York law, the events of September 11th constituted two occurrences as a matter of law.

Because nothing in the documents that constitute the Travelers binder defined *occurrence,* we must decide whether the undefined term *occurrence* when used in a . . . property damage contract is ambiguous. Whether a contract is ambiguous is a question of law for a court to determine as a threshold matter.

[A]n ambiguity exists where a contract term "could suggest more than one meaning when viewed objectively by a reasonably intelligent person who has examined the context of the entire integrated agreement and who is cognizant of the customs, practices, usages and terminology as generally understood in the particular trade or business." *Morgan Stanley Group, Inc. v. New England Insurance Co.,* 225 F.3d 270 (2d Cir. 2000).

Once a court finds that a contract is ambiguous, it may look to extrinsic evidence to determine the parties' intended meaning. If factfinding is necessary to determine the parties' intent, however, the matter must be submitted to the finder of fact, [a jury unless the parties have agreed to a bench trial rather than a jury trial].

Silverstein [argues] that the undefined term *occurrence* is not ambiguous because it is typical for insurance policies not to define *occurrence* and . . . that the WilProp definition is atypically broad. [This argument] is undercut by the policy forms of two other insurers [(not parties to this litigation) that] provided their own forms for coverage, each of which defined *occurrence.* In addition, in order to demonstrate the ambiguity of the undefined term *occurrence,* Travelers has proffered evidence of industry custom and usage concerning the meaning of occurrence that differs from the definition asserted by the Silverstein Parties. For example, [an insurance forms specialist] testified that she did not believe that the WilProp form definition . . . deviated from the commonly understood meaning of *occurrence.* Similarly, . . . an underwriter at Travelers testified that "it's recognized that multiple causes of loss can be involved in a single occurrence, and it's recognized that all loss arising out of an overriding cause or group of causes is considered a single occurrence. It's never been a question."

Finally, Silverstein asserts that the mere fact that the word *occurrence* was not defined in the binder is not enough to render it ambiguous. [Silverstein contends] that in the absence of a definition in the binder, a court seeking to construe the meaning of *occurrence* must first turn to well-established New York precedent. If there is a clear and uniform meaning of the term under the law, [Silverstein argues], then a court must reject a claim of ambiguity and apply that definition. This argument fails because its underlying premise—that there is a uniform meaning of *occurrence* under New York law—is erroneous.

[Silverstein] maintains that under New York law, there is but one meaning of *occurrence,* which is the direct, physical cause of a loss and not more remote causes. [According to Silverstein,] this definition is so accepted and well settled . . . that it must be implied into the Travelers binder as a matter of law. Applying this definition to the facts of this case, it follows [according to Silverstein,] that because the destruction of the WTC was the result of two physical impacts from two separate planes, there were two occurrences as a matter of law. To support [this] argument, Silverstein [relies] on a string of [New York cases that deal mainly with liability insurance]. [Other cases—most notably property insurance cases—reveal, however, that there is no single set meaning of *occurrence* under New York law.]

[W]e are not called upon here to decide whether there was one occurrence or two [for purposes of the Travelers binder]. [Instead, we must determine] only whether the district court properly concluded that because there is no well-settled definition of the term *occurrence* under New York law, the Travelers binder was sufficiently ambiguous to preclude summary judgment and to permit the factfinder to consider extrinsic evidence of the parties' intent. [We agree with the district court and hold that] the meaning of the undefined term *occurrence* is an open question as to which reasonable finders of fact could reach different conclusions.

District court's grant of summary judgment for Hartford, Royal, and St. Paul affirmed; district court's denial of Silverstein's motion for summary judgment against Travelers affirmed; case remanded for further proceedings.

[*Note:* Because of the Second Circuit's decision that the plane attacks on the WTC were one occurrence for purposes of their binders, Hartford, Royal, and St. Paul had to pay the amount of their policy limits only once. Because the Second Circuit's decision that the Travelers binder's undefined reference to occurrence was ambiguous, the stage was set for a later trial on the extent of the insurance obligation owed by Travelers and other insurers whose binders also did not define *occurrence.* In December 2004, a federal court jury concluded that for purposes of the Travelers binder and eight other companies' binders that did not define *occurrence,* the plane attacks on the WTC were two occurrences, not one. Therefore, those nine companies, unlike Hartford, Royal, and St. Paul, were held liable to Silverstein for damages equaling their respective policy limits times two—a total of approximately $2.2 billion. The affected insurers appealed to the Second Circuit, which issued a 2006 decision affirming the lower court's decision.]

Insurer's Delay in Acting on Application   A common insurance law problem is the effect of the insurer's delay in acting on the application. If the applicant suffers a loss after applying but before a delaying insurer formally accepts, who must bear the loss? As a general rule, the insurer's delay does not constitute acceptance. Some states, however, have held that an insurer's retention of the premium for an unreasonable time constitutes acceptance and hence obligates the insurer to cover the insured's loss.

Other states have allowed negligence suits against insurers for delaying unreasonably in acting on an application. The theory of these cases is that insurance companies have a public duty to insure qualified applicants and that an unreasonable delay prevents applicants from obtaining insurance protection from another source. A few states have enacted statutes establishing that insurers are bound to the insurance contract unless they reject the prospective insured's application within a specified period of time.

Effect of Insured's Misrepresentation

Applicants for insurance have a duty to reveal to insurers all the material (significant) facts about the nature of the risk so that the insurer may make an intelligent decision about whether to accept the risk. When an application for property, liability, or health insurance includes an insured's false statement regarding a material matter, the insured's misrepresentation, if relied on by the insurer, has the same effect produced by misrepresentation in connection with other contracts—the contract becomes voidable at the election of the insurer. This means that the insurer may avoid its obligations under the policy. The same result is possible if the insured failed, in the application, to disclose known material facts to the insurer, which issued a policy it would not have issued if the disclosures had been made. However, special rules applicable to misrepresentations in life insurance applications may sometimes limit the life insurer's ability to use the insured's misrepresentation as a way of avoiding all obligations under the policy.

Warranty/Representation Distinction It sometimes becomes important to distinguish between **warranties** and representations that the insured makes (usually in the application) to induce the insurer to issue an insurance policy. Warranties are *express terms in the insurance policy.* They are intended to operate as conditions on which the insurer's liability is based. The insured's breach of warranty terminates the insurer's duty to perform under the policy. For example, a property insurance policy on a commercial office building specifies that the insured must install and maintain a working sprinkler system in the building, but the insured never installs the sprinkler system. The sprinkler system requirement is a warranty, which the insured breached by failing to install the system. This means that the insurer may not be obligated to perform its obligations under the policy.

Traditionally, an insured's breach of warranty has been seen as terminating the insurer's duty to perform *regardless of whether the condition set forth in the breached warranty was actually material to the insurer's risk* (unlike the treatment given to the insured's misrepresentations, which do not make the insurance policy voidable unless they pertained to a material matter). In view of the potential harshness of the traditional rule concerning the effect of a breach of warranty, some states have refused to allow insurers to escape liability on breach of warranty grounds unless the condition contemplated by the breached warranty was indeed material.

Legality The law distinguishes between unlawful wagering contracts and valid insurance contracts. A wagering contract creates a new risk that did not previously exist. Such a contract is contrary to public policy and therefore illegal. An insurance contract, however, *transfers existing risks*—a permissible, even desirable, economic activity. A major means by which insurance law separates insurance contracts from wagering contracts is the typical requirement that the party who purchases a policy of property or life insurance must possess an **insurable interest** in the property or life being insured. Specific discussion of the insurable interest requirement appears later in the chapter.

Form and Content of Insurance Contracts

Writing State law governs whether insurance contracts are within the statute of frauds and must be evidenced by a writing. Some states require specific types of insurance contracts to be in writing. Contracts for property insurance are not usually within the statute of frauds, meaning that they may be either written or oral unless they come within some general provision of the statute of frauds— for example, the "one-year" provision.[1] Even when a writing is not legally required, however, wisdom dictates that the parties reduce their agreement to written form whenever possible.

Reformation of Written Policy As one would expect, insurance companies' customary practice is to issue written policies of insurance regardless of whether the applicable statute of frauds requires a writing. An argument sometimes raised by insureds is that the written policy issued by the insurer did not accurately reflect the content of the parties' actual agreement. For instance, after the occurrence of a loss for which the insured thought there was coverage under the insurance contract, the insured learns that the loss-causing event was excluded from coverage by the terms expressly stated in the written policy. In such a situation, the insured may be

---

[1]The usual provisions of the statute of frauds are discussed in detail in Chapter 16.

inclined to argue that the written policy should be judicially **reformed,** so as to make it conform to the parties' supposed actual agreement.

Although reformation is available in appropriate cases, courts normally presume that the written policy of insurance should be treated as the embodiment of the parties' actual agreement. Courts consider reformation an extreme remedy. Hence, they usually refuse to grant reformation unless either of two circumstances is present. The first reformation-triggering circumstance exists when the insured and the insurer, through its agent or agents, were *mutually mistaken* about a supposedly covered event or other supposed contract term (i.e., both parties believed an event was covered by, or some other term was part of, the parties' insurance agreement but the written policy indicated otherwise). The alternative route to reformation calls for proof that the insurer committed fraud as to the terms contained in the policy or otherwise engaged in inequitable conduct.

Interpretation of Insurance Contracts

Modern courts realize that many persons who buy insurance do not have the training or background to fully understand the technical language often contained in insurance policies. As a result, courts interpret insurance policy provisions as they would be understood by an average person. In addition, courts construe ambiguities in an insurance contract against the insurer, the drafter of the contract (and hence the user of the ambiguous language). This rule of construction means that if a word or phrase used in an insurance policy is equally subject to two possible interpretations, one of which favors the insurer and the other of which favors the insured, the court will adopt the interpretation that favors the insured. *Auto-Owners Insurance Co. v. Harvey,* which appears later in the chapter, illustrates the application of this rule of construction to an ambiguous provision in a liability insurance policy.

A number of states purport to follow the *reasonable expectations of the insured* approach to interpretation of insurance policies. Analysis of judicial decisions reveals, however, that this approach's content and effect vary among the states ostensibly subscribing to it. Some states do little more than attach the reasonable expectations label to the familiar principles of interpretation set forth in the preceding paragraph. A few states give the reasonable expectations approach a much more significant effect by allowing courts to effectively read clauses into or out of an insurance policy, depending on whether reasonable persons in the position of the insured would have expected such clauses to be in a policy of the sort at issue. When applied in the latter manner, the reasonable expectations approach tends to resemble reformation in its effect.

Clauses Required by Law

The insurance business is highly regulated by the states, which recognize the importance of the interests protected by insurance and the difference in bargaining power that often exists between insurers and their insureds. In an attempt to remedy this imbalance, many states' statutes and insurance regulations require the inclusion of certain standard clauses in insurance policies. Many states also regulate such matters as the size and style of the print used in insurance policies. Laws in a growing number of states encourage or require the use of plain, straightforward language—rather than insurance jargon and legal terms of art—whenever such language is possible to use.

Notice and Proof of Loss-Causing Event

The insured (or, in the case of life insurance, the beneficiary) who seeks to obtain the benefits or protection provided by an insurance policy must notify the insurer that an event covered by the policy has occurred. In addition, the insured (or the beneficiary) must furnish reasonable proof of the loss-causing event. Property insurance policies, for instance, ordinarily require the insured to furnish a sworn statement (called a *proof of loss*) in which the covered event and the resulting damage to the insured's property are described. Under life insurance policies, the beneficiary is usually expected to provide suitable documentation of the fact that the insured person has died. Liability insurance policies call for the insured to give the insurer copies of liability claims made against the insured.

Time Limits

Insurance policies commonly specify that notice and proof of loss must be given within a specified time. Policies sometimes state that compliance with these requirements is a condition of the insured's recovery and that failure to comply terminates the insurer's obligation. Other times, policies merely provide that failure to comply suspends the insurer's duty to pay until compliance occurs. Some courts require the insurer to prove it was harmed by the insured's failure to give notice before allowing the insurer to avoid liability on the ground of tardy notice.

Cancellation and Lapse

When a party with the power to terminate an insurance policy (extinguish all rights under the policy) exercises that power, **cancellation** has occurred. **Lapse** occurs at the end of the term specified in a policy written for a stated duration, unless the parties take action to renew the policy for an additional period of time. Alternatively, lapse may occur as a result of the insured's failure to pay premiums or some other significant default on the part of the insured.

Performance and Breach by Insurer

The insurer performs its obligations by paying out the sums (and taking other related actions) contemplated by the policy's terms within a reasonable time after the occurrence of an event that triggers the duty to perform. If the insurer fails or refuses to pay despite the occurrence of such an event, the insured may sue the insurer for breach of contract. By proving that the insurer's denial of the insured's claim for payment constituted a breach, the insured becomes entitled to recover compensatory damages in at least the amount that the insurer would have had to pay under the policy if the insurer had not breached.

What if the insurer's breach caused the insured to incur consequential damages that, when added to the amount due under the policy, would lead to a damages claim exceeding the dollar limits set forth in the policy? Assume that XYZ Computer Sales, Inc.'s store building is covered by a property insurance policy with Secure Insurance Co., that the building is destroyed by an accidental fire (a covered peril), and that the extent of the destruction makes the full $500,000 policy limit due from Secure to XYZ. Secure, however, denies payment because it believes—erroneously—that XYZ officials committed arson (a cause, if it had been the actual one, that would have relieved Secure from any duty to pay). Because it needs to rebuild and take other related steps to stay in business but is short on available funds as a result of Secure's denial of its claim, XYZ borrows the necessary funds from a bank. XYZ thereby incurs substantial interest costs, which are consequential damages XYZ would not have incurred if Secure had performed its obligation under the policy. Assuming that XYZ's consequential damages would have been foreseeable to Secure, most states would allow XYZ to recover the consequential damages in addition to the amount due from Secure under the policy.[2] This is so even though the addition of the consequential damages would cause XYZ's damages recovery to exceed the dollar limit set forth in the parties' insurance policy. The breaching insurer's liability may exceed the policy limits despite the insurer's good faith (though incorrect) basis for denying the claim, because a good faith but erroneous refusal to pay is nonetheless a breach of contract. If the insurer could point to the policy limits as a maximum recovery in this type of situation, it would have an all-too-convenient means of avoiding responsibility for harms that logically flowed from its breach of contract.

Many states' laws provide that if an insured successfully sues her insurer for amounts due under the policy, the insured may recover interest on those amounts (amounts that, after all, should have been paid by the insurer much sooner and without litigation). Some states also have statutes providing that insureds who successfully sue insurers are entitled to awards of attorney's fees. Punitive damages are *not* allowed, however, when the insurer's breach of contract consisted of a *good faith (though erroneous) denial* of the insured's claim. Later in this chapter, we will explore the trend toward allowing punitive damages when the insurer's breach was in *bad faith* and thus amounted to the tort of bad faith breach of contract.

Property Insurance

Owners of residential and commercial property always face the possibility that their property might be damaged or destroyed by causes beyond their control. These causes include, to name a few notable ones, fire, lightning, hail, and wind. Although property owners may not be able to prevent harm to their property, they can secure some protection against resulting financial loss by contracting for property insurance and thereby transferring certain risks of loss to the insurer. Persons holding property interests that fall short of ownership may likewise seek to benefit, as will be seen, from the risk-shifting feature of property insurance.

The Insurable Interest Requirement As noted earlier in this chapter, in order for a property insurance contract not to be considered an illegal wagering contract, the person who purchases the policy (the policy owner) must have an **insurable interest** in the property being insured. One has an insurable interest if he, she, or it possesses a legal or equitable interest in the property and that interest translates into an economic stake in the continued existence of the property and the preservation of its condition. In other words, a person has an insurable interest if he would suffer a financial loss in the event of harm to the subject property. If no insurable interest is present, the policy is void.

---

[2]Even though the terms of the insurance policy almost certainly would state that Secure's payment obligation is limited to costs of repair or replacement or to the property's actual cash value—that is, without any coverage for consequential harms experienced by the insured— Secure cannot invoke this policy language as a defense. If Secure had performed its contract obligation, its payment obligation would have been restricted to what the policy provided in that regard. Having breached the insurance contract, however, Secure stands potentially liable for consequential damages to the full extent provided for by general contract law. For additional discussion of damages for breach of contract, see Chapter 18.

The Global Business Environment

A California statute, the Holocaust Victim Insurance Relief Act of 1999 (HVIRA), provided that if an insurer doing business in California sold insurance policies to persons in Europe between 1920 and 1945 (Holocaust-era policies), the insurer was to file certain information about those policies with the California insurance commissioner. The reporting requirement also applied to insurance companies that did business in California and were "related" to a company that sold Holocaust-era policies, even if the relationship arose after the policies were issued. A "related company" was defined as any "parent, subsidiary, reinsurer, successor in interest, managing general agent, or affiliate company of the insurer."

Insurance companies subject to HVIRA were expected to provide this information: (1) the number of Holocaust-era insurance policies; (2) the holder, beneficiary, and current status of each such policy; and (3) the city of origin, domicile, or address for each policyholder listed in the policies. In addition, HVIRA required the insurers to certify whichever one of the following was accurate: (1) that the proceeds of the policies were paid; (2) that the beneficiaries or heirs could not, after diligent search, be located, and the proceeds were distributed to Holocaust survivors or charities; (3) that a court of law had certified a plan for the distribution of the proceeds; or (4) that the proceeds had not been distributed. HVIRA instructed the California insurance commissioner to store the information disclosed under the statute in a Holocaust Era Insurance Registry, which was available to the public. In addition, HVIRA required the insurance commissioner to "suspend the certificate of authority to conduct insurance business in the state of any insurer that fails to comply" with HVIRA's reporting requirements.

Various U.S.-based, German, and Italian insurance companies filed suit in a federal district court in an effort to have HVIRA invalidated on constitutional grounds. The district court held the statute unconstitutional on various grounds, but the U.S. Court of Appeals for the Ninth Circuit reversed. Seeing no constitutional obstacle, the Ninth Circuit regarded HVIRA as legitimate, state-related legislative action that fit within the customary authority of states to regulate regarding insurance-related matters. The U.S. Supreme Court granted the insurers' petition for certiorari.

In *American Insurance Association v. Garamendi*, 539 U.S. 396 (2003), the Supreme Court identified Article II of the U.S. Constitution as the key constitutional provision at issue in the case. Article II reserves to the federal executive branch the power to conduct foreign policy.

Pointing to relevant history as necessary background, the Court observed that after a 1990 treaty lifted a previous moratorium on certain claims related to the Holocaust, various class action lawsuits were filed in U.S. courts against non-U.S. firms that allegedly had done business in Germany during the Nazi era. These cases drew protests from the defendant firms and from various foreign governments. Following these protests, the executive branch of the U.S. government entered into agreements with the governments of Germany, Austria, and France during 2000 and 2001. The agreements outlined a Holocaust-related claims resolution process under which the foreign governments were to create foundations that would be funded by those governments and certain foreign firms. Foundation funds would satisfy valid Holocaust-related claims. The claims to be covered by the agreements included insurance claims the resolution of which was to be eased by agreement provisions calling for the foundations to negotiate with European insurers. The agreements stated that the claims resolution process was in the foreign policy interest of the United States. In addition, the federal government agreed to use its "best efforts" to have Holocaust-related claims go through the process rather than through the courts or other mechanisms set up by state and local governments.

After taking into account the history, purposes, and content of the 2000 and 2001 agreements entered into by the executive branch and the governments of Germany, Austria, and France, the Court concluded that HVIRA posed a significant obstacle to, if not an outright conflict with, the foreign policy objectives articulated in the agreements. This meant that the federal government's Article II foreign policy power must preempt—that is, take precedence over—HVIRA. Therefore, the Court reversed the Ninth Circuit's decision and held HVIRA unconstitutional.

Examples of Insurable Interest The legal owner of the insured property would obviously have an insurable interest. So might other parties whose legal or equitable interests in the property do not rise to the level of an ownership interest. For example, mortgagees and other lienholders would have insurable interests in the property on which they hold liens. A nonexhaustive list of other examples would also include holders of life estates in real property, buyers under as-yet unperformed

contracts for the sale of real property, and lessees of real estate.[3] In the types of situations just noted, the interested

---

[3]Chapter 28 contains a detailed discussion of security interests in real property. Chapter 29 addresses security interests in personal property. Chapter 24 contains a discussion of life estates and an examination of contracts for the sale of real property. Leases of real estate are explored in Chapter 25.

party stands to lose financially if the property is damaged or destroyed.

Timing and Extent of Insurable Interest A sensible and important corollary of the insurable interest principle is that the requisite insurable interest must exist *at the time of the loss* (i.e., at the time the subject property was damaged). If an insurable interest existed when the holder thereof purchased the property insurance but the interest was no longer present when the loss occurred, the policy owner is not entitled to payment for the loss. This would mean, for example, that a property owner who purchased property insurance would not be entitled to collect from the insurer for property damage that occurred after she had transferred ownership to someone else. Similarly, a lienholder who purchased property insurance could not collect under the policy if the loss took place after his lien had been extinguished by payment of the underlying debt or by another means.[4]

The extent of a person's insurable interest in property is limited to the value of that interest. For example, Fidelity Savings & Loan extends Williams a $250,000 loan to purchase a home and takes a mortgage on the home as security. In order to protect this investment, Fidelity obtains a $250,000 insurance policy on the property. Several years later, the house is destroyed by fire, a cause triggering the insurer's payment obligation. At the time of the fire, the balance due on the loan is $220,000. Fidelity's recovery under the insurance policy is limited to $220,000, because that amount is the full extent of its insurable interest. (An alternative way by which mortgagees protect their interest is to insist that the property owner list the mortgagee as the *loss payee* under the property owner's policy. This means that if the property is destroyed, the insurer will pay the policy proceeds to the mortgagee. Once again, however, the mortgagee's entitlement to payment under this approach would be limited to the dollar value of its insurable interest, with surplus proceeds going to the insured property owner.)

Covered and Excluded Perils

Property insurers usually do not undertake to provide coverage for losses stemming from any and all causes of harm to property. Instead, property insurers tend to either specify certain causes (**covered perils**) as to which the insured *will* receive payment for resulting losses—meaning that there is no coverage regarding a peril not specified—or set forth a seemingly broad statement of coverage but then specify certain perils concerning which there will be *no* payment for losses (**excluded perils**). Sometimes, property insurers employ a combination of these two approaches by specifying certain covered perils and certain excluded perils. For an example, see *Shelter Mutual Insurance Co. v. Maples,* which follows shortly.

Typical Covered Perils The effects of these approaches are essentially the same, as most property insurers tend to provide coverage for the same sorts of causes of harm to property. The perils concerning which property insurance policies typically provide benefits include fire, lightning, hail, and wind. In addition, property insurance policies often cover harms to property resulting from causes such as the impact of an automobile or aircraft (e.g., an automobile or aircraft crashes into an insured building), vandalism, certain collapses of buildings, and certain accidental discharges or overflows from pipes or heating and air-conditioning systems.

Fire as a Covered Peril Historically, the importance of coverage against the peril of fire made *fire insurance* a commonly used term. Various insurance companies incorporated the term into their official firm name; the policies these companies issued came to be called *fire insurance policies* even when they covered perils in addition to fire (as policies increasingly have done in this century). As a result, judges, commentators, and persons affiliated with the insurance industry will sometimes refer to today's policies as fire insurance policies despite the usual property insurer's tendency to cover not only fire but also some combination of the other perils mentioned in the preceding paragraph. Whether the term used is *property insurance* (generally employed in this chapter) or *fire insurance,* reference is being made to the same type of policy.

Fire-related losses covered by property insurance policies are those resulting from accidental fires. An accidental fire is one other than a fire deliberately set by, or

---

[4]In the life insurance context, the requisite insurable interest *must exist at the time the policy was issued* but need not exist at the time of the insured's death. Persons who stand to suffer a financial loss in the event of the insured's death have the insurable interest necessary to support the purchase of a life insurance policy on the insured. The insured and his or her spouse, parents, children, and other dependents thus possess an insurable interest in the insured's life. In addition, the business associates of the insured may also have an insurable interest in his or her life. Such persons would include the insured's employer, business partners, or shareholders in a closely held corporation with which the insured is connected. Creditors of the insured also have an insurable interest, but only to the extent of the debt owed by the insured.

at the direction of, the insured for the purpose of damaging the property. In other words, the insured obtains no coverage for losses stemming from the insured's act of arson. This commonsense restriction on an insurer's duty to pay for losses also applies to other harms the insured deliberately caused to his property.

For purposes of fire coverage, insurance contracts often distinguish between *friendly fires,* which are those contained in a place intended for a fire (such as fires in a woodstove or fireplace), and *hostile fires,* which burn where no fire is intended to be (such as fires caused by lightning, outside sources, or electrical shorts, or those that began as friendly fires but escaped their boundaries). Losses caused by hostile fires are covered; those stemming from friendly fires tend not to be. As a general rule, covered fire losses may extend beyond direct damage caused by the fire. Indirect damage caused by smoke and heat is usually covered, as is damage caused by firefighters in their attempts to put out the fire.

Typical Excluded Perils   Although flood-related harm to property may seem similar to harm stemming from some of the weather-related causes listed earlier among the typical covered perils, it does not usually receive the same treatment. Property insurance policies frequently exclude coverage for flood damage. On this point, however, as with other questions regarding perils covered or excluded, the actual language of the policy at issue must always be consulted before a coverage issue is resolved in any given case.[5] Other typical exclusions include earthquake damage and harm to property stemming from war or nuclear reaction, radiation, or contamination. As previously indicated, property insurance policies exclude coverage for losses caused by the insured's deliberate actions that were intended to cause harm to the property.

Additional Coverages   Even as to perils for which there may not be coverage in the typical property insurance policy, the property owner may sometimes be able to purchase a specialized policy (e.g., a flood insurance policy) that does afford coverage for such perils. Other

times, even if coverage for a given peril is not provided by the terms of most standard property insurance policies, it may nonetheless be possible for the property owner to have coverage for that peril added to the policy by paying an additional premium. This is sometimes done, for example, by policy owners who desire earthquake coverage.

Personal Property Insurance   Although the broad term *property insurance* is what has been employed, the discussion so far in this section has centered around policies providing coverage for harm to *real* property. Items of *personal* property are, of course, insurable as well. Property insurance policies commonly known as homeowners' policies—because the real property serving as the policy's primary subject is the insured's dwelling—cover not only harm to the dwelling but also to personal property located inside the dwelling or otherwise on the subject real property. (Sometimes, depending on the policy language, there may be coverage even when the item of personal property was not located at the designated real property when the item was damaged.) Property insurance policies covering office buildings and other commercial real estate often provide some level of personal property coverage as well. When personal property coverage is included in a policy primarily concerned with real property coverage, the perils insured against in the personal property coverage tend to be largely the same as, though not necessarily identical to, those applicable to the real property coverage.

Lessees of residential or commercial real estate may obtain insurance policies to cover their items of personal property that are on the leased premises. Such policies are highly advisable, because the apartment or office building owner's insurance policy on the real property is likely to furnish little or no coverage for the tenant's personal property.

Automobile insurance policies are in part personal property insurance policies because they provide coverage (under what are usually called the *comprehensive* and *collision* sections) for car damage resulting from such causes as fire, wind, hail, vandalism, or collision with an animal or tree. As will be seen, automobile insurance policies also contain significant features of another major type of insurance policy to be discussed later— liability insurance. Other specialized types of personal property insurance are also available. For example, many farmers purchase crop insurance in order to guard against the adverse financial effects that would result if a hailstorm or other covered peril severely damaged a season's crop.

---

[5]It may be that a type of peril frequently excluded in property insurance policies is in fact a covered peril under the language of the policy at issue. Alternatively, losses that at first glance appear to have resulted from an excluded peril may sometimes be characterized as having resulted, at least in part, from a covered peril. In the latter event, there may be some coverage for the losses.

Shelter Mutual Insurance Co. v. Maples   309 F.3d 1068 (8th Cir. 2002)

Shelter Mutual Insurance Co. brought a declaratory judgment action against Tommy and Bessie Maples (referred to collectively as "Maples") in the United States District Court for the Western District of Arkansas. Shelter asked the court to declare that Shelter had no obligation to pay a claim made by Maples under a homeowner's insurance policy issued by Shelter. The facts set forth in the following paragraph were as stipulated (i.e., as agreed to) by the parties.

While residing in Saudi Arabia, Maples contracted for the construction of a single-family retirement home in Arkansas. Maples purchased homeowner's insurance from Shelter, whose policy, issued in November 2000, was in full effect at all times relevant to the case. The two-story residence, which had a wooden frame and a basement made of concrete, was largely complete as of November 2000. Maples, who remained in Saudi Arabia, took reasonable precautions for winter weather by leaving a key with the contractor and asking him to winterize the residence. At some unknown time, a water pipe froze and burst. As a result, between four to six inches of water stood continuously in the basement until the contractor discovered the problem in April 2001. The standing water caused only minimal structural damage to the basement, but the humidity from the standing water caused mold to form on all of the interior surfaces of the residence. As a result of the mold, the residence became uninhabitable and had to be demolished.

Maples reported the loss to Shelter, which instituted the declaratory judgment action referred to above. After the federal district court granted summary judgment in favor of Shelter, Maples appealed to the United States Court of Appeals for the Eighth Circuit.

Riley, Circuit Judge

As relevant, the insurance policy provided:

PERILS WE INSURE AGAINST—SECTION I

We cover accidental direct physical loss to property covered under Dwelling and Other Structures Coverages except for losses excluded in this section.

Under Dwelling and Other Structures Coverages, we do not cover loss caused by:

1. wear and tear; marring or scratching; deterioration; inherent vice; latent defect; mechanical breakdown; rust; mold; wet or dry rot; contamination; smog, smoke from agricultural smudging or industrial operations; settling, cracking, shrinkage, bulging or expansion of pavement, patios, foundations, walls, floors, roofs, or ceilings; birds, vermin, rodents, insects or domestic animals. If, because of any of these, water escapes from a plumbing, heating, or air conditioning system or domestic appliance, we cover loss caused by the water. We also cover the cost of tearing out and replacing any part of the covered building necessary to repair the system or appliance. We do cover loss to the system or appliance from which the water escapes.

[T]he district court concluded that Shelter was entitled to summary judgment, reasoning that the policy language clearly provided that any loss due to mold was not covered. This court reviews de novo the district court's grant of summary judgment, as well as its interpretation of Arkansas law. Under Arkansas law, insurance policies are to be construed liberally in favor of the insured, and exclusionary language that is susceptible to more than one reasonable interpretation should be construed in favor of the insured. The insurer bears the burden of proving as a matter of law that the insured's claim was excluded under the policy.

Here, a covered peril, frozen pipes, caused an excluded peril, mold, which resulted in the loss. The district court concluded that the policy precluded coverage for mold damage regardless of its cause, relying on the following lead-in language from the policy:

We do not cover loss:
  (a) resulting directly or indirectly from any of the following events;
  (b) which would not have occurred in the absence of any of the following events;
  (c) which occurs regardless of the cause of any of the following events; or
  (d) if loss occurs concurrently or in any sequence with any of the events.

We disagree with the court's reading of the policy, because we find this language leads into a list of ten specified items not including mold, while the mold-exclusion paragraph is separately numbered and follows the lead-in clause "Under Dwelling and Other Structures Coverages, we do not cover loss caused by." Thus, the plain language of the policy does not automatically preclude coverage. Compare *Cooper v. American Family Mutual Insurance Co.*, 184 F. Supp. 2d 960, 961–63 (D. Ariz. 2002) (no coverage for mold damage from plumbing leak where lead-in clause excluded losses regardless of any other contributing cause or event), with *West v. Umialik Insurance Co.*, 8 P.3d 1135, 1137–41 (Alaska 2000) (settling of house from broken plumbing was covered loss, where no lead-in clause precluded coverage regardless of cause).

It appears to us, then, that the determinative question is a factual one: whether the frozen pipe or the mold was the dominant and efficient cause of the loss. See 10 LEE R. RUSS & THOMAS F. SEGALLA, COUCH ON INSURANCE §§ 148:60, 148:61 (3d ed. 1998) (where covered and non-covered perils join to cause a loss, and the covered peril is the efficient and dominant cause, there is coverage under the policy);

11 COUCH ON INSURANCE § 153:96 (mold exclusions do not necessarily apply where "efficient proximate cause" of loss was a covered risk). Because the parties' factual stipulation does not answer this question, we conclude [that] a material issue of fact remains, and [that] summary judgment was improper.

District court's grant of summary judgment in favor of Shelter reversed; case remanded for consideration of causation issue.

Nature and Extent of Insurer's Payment Obligation

Property insurance policies are **indemnity** contracts. This means that the insurer is obligated to reimburse the insured for his actual losses associated with a covered harm to the insured property. The insured's recovery under the policy thus cannot exceed the extent of the loss sustained. Neither may it exceed the extent of the insured's insurable interest or the amount of coverage that the insured purchased (the **policy limits**).[6]

Policy provisions other than the policy limits also help define the extent of the insurer's obligation to pay. When covered real property is damaged but not destroyed, the **cost of repair** is normally the relevant measure. Many policies provide that when covered real property is destroyed, the insurer must pay the **actual cash value** (or *fair market value*) of the property. Some policies, however, establish **cost of replacement** as the payment obligation in this situation. The policies that call for payment of the actual cash value frequently give the insurer the option to pay the cost of replacement, however, if that amount would be less than the actual cash value. As to covered personal property, the controlling standard is typically the least of the following: cost of repair, cost of replacement, or actual cash value.[7]

Many property insurance policies supplement the above provisions by obligating the insurer to pay the insured's reasonable costs of temporarily living elsewhere if the insured property was her residence and the damage to the residence made it uninhabitable pending completion of repairs or replacement. Comparable benefits may sometimes be provided in policies covering business property. Lost profits and similar consequential losses resulting from harm to or destruction of one's insured property, however, do not normally fall within the insurer's payment obligation unless a specific provision obligates the insurer along those lines.[8] Regardless of whether the damaged or destroyed property is real or personal in nature, the particular language of the policy at issue must always be consulted before a definite determination can be made concerning what is and is not within the insurer's duty to pay.

Valued and Open Policies When insured real property is destroyed as a result of fire or another covered peril, the amount to be paid by the insurer may be further influenced by the type of policy involved. Some property insurance contracts are **valued policies.** If real property insured under a valued policy is destroyed, the insured is entitled to recover the face amount of the policy regardless of the property's fair market value. For example, in 1985, Douglas purchased a home with a fair market value of $90,000. Douglas also purchased a valued policy with a face amount of $90,000 to insure the house against various risks, including fire. The home's fair market value decreased in later years because of deterioration in the surrounding neighborhood. In 2008, when the home had a fair market value of only $75,000, it was destroyed by fire. Douglas is entitled to $90,000 (the

---

[6]Some insurers, however, provide, in exchange for a more substantial premium than would be charged for a policy without this feature, a homeowner's policy under which the insurer could become obligated to pay *more* than the policy limits if the insured's home was destroyed and the cost to replace it would actually exceed the policy limits.
[7]Concerning certain designated items of personal property such as furs or jewelry, policies often set forth a maximum insurer payout (such as $1,000) that is less than the general policy limits applicable to personal property. Such a payout limitation would operate as a further restriction on the extent of the insurer's obligation.

[8]Recall, however, that if the insurer violates its payment obligation by wrongfully failing or refusing to pay what the policy contemplates, the insurer has committed a breach of contract. As noted in this chapter's earlier discussion of insurance policies as contracts, fundamental breach of contract principles dictate that the breaching insurer is potentially liable for consequential damages.

face amount of the valued policy) despite the reduction in the home's fair market value.

Most property insurance policies, however, are open policies. Open policies allow the insured to recover the fair market value (actual cash value) of the property at the time it was destroyed, up to the limits stated in the policy. Thus, if Douglas had had an open policy in the example presented in the previous paragraph, he would have been entitled to only $75,000 when the home was destroyed by fire. Suppose instead that Douglas's home had increased in value, so that at the time of the fire its fair market value was $150,000. In that event, it would not matter what type of policy (valued or open) Douglas had. Under either type of policy, his recovery would be limited to the $90,000 face amount of the policy.

Coinsurance Clause Some property insurance policies contain a **coinsurance clause,** which may operate as a further limit on the insurer's payment obligation and the insured's right to recovery. A coinsurance clause provides that in order for the insured to be able to recover the full cost of partial losses, the insured must obtain insurance on the property in an amount equal to a specified percentage (often 80 percent) of the property's fair market value.

For example, PDQ Corporation has a fire insurance policy on its warehouse with Cooperative Mutual Insurance Group. The policy has an 80 percent coinsurance clause. The warehouse had a fair market value of $400,000, meaning that PDQ was required to carry at least $320,000 of insurance on the building. PDQ, however, purchased a policy with a face amount of only $240,000. A fire partially destroyed the warehouse, causing $200,000 worth of damage to the structure. Because of the coinsurance clause, PDQ will recover only $150,000 from Cooperative. This figure was arrived at by taking the amount of insurance carried ($240,000) divided by the amount of insurance required ($320,000) times the loss ($200,000).

The coinsurance formula for recovery for partial losses is stated as follows:

$$\frac{\text{Amount of insurance carried}}{\text{Coinsurance percent} \times \text{Fair market value}} \times \text{Loss} = \text{Recovery}$$

Remember that the coinsurance formula applies only to *partial* losses (i.e., damage to, but not complete destruction of, property). If PDQ's warehouse had been totally destroyed by the fire, the formula would not have been used. PDQ would have recovered $240,000—the

face amount of the policy—for the total loss. If the formula had been used, it would have indicated that Cooperative owed PDQ $300,000—more than the face amount of the policy. This result would be neither logical nor in keeping with the parties' insurance contract. Whether the loss is total or partial, the insured is not entitled to recover more than the face amount of the policy.

Pro Rata Clause With the limited exception of the valued policy (discussed above), the insured cannot recover more than the amount of the actual loss. A rule allowing the insured to recover more than the actual loss could encourage unscrupulous persons to purchase policies from more than one insurer on the same property—thus substantially overinsuring it—and then intentionally to destroy the property in a way that appeared to be a covered peril (e.g., committing arson but making the fire look accidental). In order to make certain that the insured does not obtain a recovery that exceeds the actual loss, property insurance policies commonly contain a *pro rata clause*, which applies when the insured has purchased insurance policies from more than one insurer. The effect of the pro rata clause is to apportion the loss among the insurance companies. (Applicable state law sometimes contains a rule having this same effect.)

Under the pro rata clause, the amount any particular insurer must pay the insured depends on the percentage of total insurance coverage represented by that insurer's policy. For example, Mumford purchases two insurance policies to cover his home against fire and other risks. His policy from Security Mutual Insurance Corp. has a face amount of $50,000; his policy from Reliable Insurance Co. is for $100,000. Mumford's home is partially destroyed by an accidental fire, with a resulting loss of $30,000. Security Mutual must pay Mumford $10,000, with Reliable having to pay the remaining $20,000 of the loss.

The formula for determining each insurer's liability under a pro rata clause is stated as follows:

$$\frac{\text{Amount of insurance policy}}{\text{Total coverage by all insurers}} \times \text{Loss} = \text{Liability of insurer}$$

Thus, Security Mutual's payment amount was calculated as follows:

$$\frac{\$50,000 \text{ (Security Mutual's policy)}}{\$150,000 \text{ (Total of both policies)}} \times \$30,000 \text{ (Loss)} = \$10,000$$

Reliable's payment amount could be similarly calculated by substituting $100,000 (Reliable's policy amount) for the $50,000 (Security Mutual's policy amount) in the numerator of the equation. This formula may be used for both partial and total losses. However, each company's payment obligation is limited by the face amount of its policy. Thus, Security Mutual could never be liable for more than $50,000. Similarly, Reliable's liability is limited to a maximum of $100,000.

Right of Subrogation
The insurer may be able in some instances to exercise a **right of subrogation** if it is required to pay for a loss under a property insurance contract. Under the right of subrogation, the insurer obtains all of the insured's rights to pursue legal remedies against anyone who negligently or intentionally caused the harm to the property. For example, Arnett purchased a property insurance policy on her home from Benevolent Insurance Company. Arnett's home was completely destroyed by a fire that spread to her property when her neighbor, Clifton, was burning leaves and negligently failed to control the fire. After Benevolent pays Arnett for her loss, Benevolent's right of subrogation entitles it to sue Clifton to recover the amount Benevolent paid Arnett. Arnett will be obligated to cooperate with Benevolent and furnish assistance to it in connection with the subrogation claim.

If the insured provides the liable third party a general release from liability, the insurer will be released from his payment obligation to the insured. Suppose that in the above scenario, Clifton persuaded Arnett to sign an agreement releasing him from liability for the fire. Because this action by Arnett would interfere with Benevolent's right of subrogation, Benevolent would not have to pay Arnett for the loss. A partial release of Clifton by Arnett would relieve Benevolent of responsibility to Arnett to the extent of her release.

Duration and Cancellation of Policy
Property insurance policies are usually effective for a designated period such as six months or a year. They are then extended for consecutive periods of like duration if the insured continues to pay the necessary premium and neither the insured nor the insurer elects to cancel the policy. The insured is normally entitled to cancel the policy at any time by providing the insurer written notice to that effect or by surrendering the policy to the insurer. Although property insurers usually have some right to cancel policies, terms of the policies themselves and/or governing law typically limit the grounds on which property insurers may do so. Permitted grounds for cancellation

include the insured's nonpayment of the premium and, as a general rule, the insured's misrepresentation or fraud (see this chapter's discussion of contract law's applicability to insurance policies). Policy provisions and/or applicable law typically provide that if the property insurer intends to cancel the policy, the insured must be given meaningful advance written notice (often 30 days) of this intent before cancellation takes effect.

Another cancellation basis exists by virtue of the **increase of hazard** clauses that appear in many property insurance policies. An increase of hazard clause provides that the insurer's liability will be terminated if the insured takes any action materially increasing the insurer's risk. Some increase of hazard provisions also specify certain types of behavior that will cause termination. Common examples of such behavior include keeping highly explosive material on the property and allowing the premises to remain vacant for a lengthy period of time.

Liability Insurance

As its name suggests, liability insurance provides the insured the ability to transfer liability risks to the insurer. Under policies of liability insurance, the insurer agrees, among other things, to pay sums the insured becomes legally obligated to pay to another party. This enables the insured to minimize the troublesome or even devastating financial effects that he could experience in the event of his liability to someone else.

Types of Liability Insurance Policies
Liability insurance policies come in various types. These include, but are not limited to, **personal liability policies** designed to cover a range of liabilities an individual person could face; **business liability policies** (sometimes called *comprehensive general liability policies*) meant to apply to various liabilities that sole proprietors, partnerships, and corporations might encounter in their business operations; **professional liability policies** (sometimes called *malpractice insurance policies*) that cover physicians, attorneys, accountants, and members of other professions against liabilities to clients and sometimes other persons; and **workers' compensation policies** under which insurers agree to cover employers' statutorily required obligation to pay benefits to injured workers.

Some policies combine property insurance features with liability insurance components. Automobile insurance policies, for instance, afford property insurance when they cover designated automobiles owned by the insured against perils such as vandalism, hail, and collisions with animals, telephone poles, and the like. Other sections of automobile insurance policies provide liability insurance to the insured (the policy owner), members of her household, and sometimes other authorized drivers when their use of a covered automobile leads to an accident in which they face liability to another party. Typical homeowners' policies also combine property and liability insurance features. Besides covering the insured's home and contents against perils of the types discussed earlier in this chapter, these policies normally provide the insured coverage for a range of liabilities he may face as an individual.

Liabilities Insured Against

Although the different types of liability insurance policies discussed above contain different terms setting forth the liabilities covered and not covered, liability policies commonly afford coverage against the insured's liability for negligence but not against the insured's liability stemming from deliberate wrongful acts (most intentional torts and most behavior constituting a crime). Liability policies tend to reach this common ground in the same sorts of ways property insurance policies define the scope of coverage—by listing particular liabilities that are covered and stating that an unlisted liability is not covered, by setting forth a seemingly broad statement of coverage and then specifying exclusions from coverage, or by employing a combination of the previous approaches (e.g., specifying certain covered liabilities and certain excluded liabilities).

Personal Liability and Homeowners' Policies Personal liability policies and the liability sections of homeowners' policies often state that coverage is restricted to instances of "bodily injury" and "property damage" experienced by a third party as a result of an "occurrence" for which the insured faces liability. These sorts of policies normally define *occurrence* as an "accident" resulting in bodily injury or property damage. The provisions just noted often lead to the conclusion that intentional torts and most criminal behavior, if committed or engaged in by the insured, would fall outside the coverage of the policy at issue because they are not accidents (whereas instances of the insured's negligence would be). This conclusion is underscored by typical clauses purporting to exclude coverage for bodily injury or property damage the insured intended to cause. However, as illustrated by *Auto-Owners Insurance Co. v. Harvey,* which follows shortly, ambiguity in a liability policy's occurrence provision may sometimes lead to a conclusion that the policy covers an intentional action whose particular consequences were not intended.

The occurrence, bodily injury, and property damage references in liability policies also indicate that harms stemming from, for example, breach of contract would not be covered either (no accident, no bodily injury, no property damage). In addition, personal liability policies and liability sections of homeowners' policies tend to specify that if bodily injury or property damage results from the insured's business or professional pursuits, it is not covered.

Auto-Owners Insurance Co. v. Harvey   842 N.E.2d 1279 (Ind. Sup. Ct. 2006)

Brandy Harvey, age 16, and Toby Gearheart, age 19, were at a Wabash River boat ramp one evening. When a disagreement arose, Brandy moved toward Gearheart and pushed him toward the water more than once. When she again approached Gearheart, he put his hands on her shoulders and pushed her. Brandy lost her balance and fell off the boat ramp, down a rocky embankment, and into the river, where she drowned. In a criminal proceeding concerning the incident, Gearheart pleaded guilty to involuntary manslaughter.

Acting as co-personal representatives of Brandy's estate, her parents, Jon Harvey and Misty Johnson, filed a wrongful death action against Gearheart in an Indiana trial court. They contended in their complaint that Gearheart's "negligence and recklessness" had caused Brandy's death. Harvey and Johnson also named Auto-Owners Insurance Co. as a defendant on the theory that because of the liability insurance portion of a homeowners' insurance policy issued to Gearheart's parents, Auto-Owners would be obligated to pay any judgment entered against Gearheart (who still lived in his parents' home and was therefore an insured person under the policy). The insurance policy at issue stated that Auto-Owners "will pay all sums any Insured becomes legally obligated to pay as damages because of or arising out of bodily injury or property damage caused by an occurrence *to which this coverage applies." The policy also defined "occurrence" to mean "an accident that results in bodily injury or property damage and includes, as one occurrence, all continuous or repeated exposure to substantially the same generally harmful conditions." The word "accident" was not defined in the policy. In addition, an exclusion set forth in the policy indicated that there was no coverage for "bodily injury or property damage reasonably expected or intended by the insured."*

Auto-Owners moved for summary judgment, asserting that in view of the facts and the above-quoted provisions, the policy furnished no coverage in regard to Gearheart's actions. The trial court denied Auto-Owners' motion, but the Court of Appeals of Indiana reversed. Harvey and Johnson appealed to the Supreme Court of Indiana.

Dickson, Justice

Auto-Owners contends that it was entitled to summary judgment on two separate grounds, which [allegedly] establish as a matter of law that there is no coverage under its policy: (1) Gearheart's conduct does not constitute an "occurrence" as required by the policy's insuring agreement; and (2) Gearheart's conduct falls under the [policy's exclusion for] intended or expected harm.

To support its contention that Brandy's death did not result from an "occurrence" as defined in the policy, Auto-Owners first argues that it was not an "accident" because Gearheart, though insisting that he did not intend to harm Brandy, admitted that he intended to push her. Auto-Owners asserts that because Gearheart's conduct was intentional, the incident was not an accident. It urges [in its brief] that Gearheart's testimony regarding whether he intended harm to result from his intentional act of pushing "is not relevant as to whether there was an 'occurrence.'" Rather, Auto-Owners urges that Brandy's death was the natural and probable result of Gearheart's voluntary and intentional act of pushing, and thus her death should not be considered an "accident" for insurance purposes.

Certain disparity in bargaining power, which is characteristic of the parties to insurance contracts, has led courts to develop distinct rules of construction for those contracts. If a contract is clear and unambiguous, its language is given its plain meaning. But if there is ambiguity, the contract is construed strictly against the insurer, and the language of the policy is viewed from the insured's perspective. "An ambiguity exists where a provision is susceptible to more than one interpretation and reasonable persons would differ as to its meaning." [Case citation omitted.]

Indiana case law has held that, "in the context of insurance coverage, an accident means an unexpected happening without an intention or design." [Case citation omitted.] This description is consistent with the plain meaning of "accident," as indicated by the primary definition provided in several modern dictionaries. We agree with Auto-Owners that implicit in the meaning of "accident" is the lack of intentionality.

In the present case, the policy states that Auto-Owners will pay for its insured's legal liability for "damages because of or arising out of bodily injury or property damage caused by an occurrence." Under the facts of this case, however, the meaning and application of this provision is unclear. The language used by Auto-Owners can reasonably be understood in two different ways, depending on whether "occurrence" means Gearheart's push or Brandy's drowning. The policy language does not require that the "occurrence" or "accident" be limited to the actions of the insured. The claimed damages clearly arise out of Brandy's death, and the coverage ambiguity thus is whether the death should be considered to have been caused by the event of Gearheart's pushing or by the event of Brandy's drowning. If the required "accident" refers to Gearheart's push, then it is undisputed that it did not occur unexpectedly or unintentionally. If it applies to Brandy's slip, fall, and drowning, however, it is not clear that the drowning was clearly unexpected and unintentional. It was obviously unexpected and unintentional from Brandy's perspective, and possibly so from Gearheart's point of view. We thus find the policy language ambiguous and must construe it against Auto-Owners, holding that the term "occurrence" applies to Brandy's slip, fall, and drowning, and not to Gearheart's push.

Auto-Owners further contends that Brandy's death did not result from an "accident" (and thus was not an "occurrence" covered by the policy) because of Gearheart's plea of guilty to involuntary manslaughter, which it asserts conclusively establishes that Gearheart battered Brandy by pushing her, resulting in her death. It argues [in its brief] that "intentional conduct is not accidental and thus not an occurrence for purposes of insurance coverage," and that the intentionality of Gearheart's conduct was conclusively established in the criminal proceedings and may not be relitigated in this case. Auto-Owners urges that by this guilty plea, Gearheart admitted that pushing Brandy posed a serious risk of injury and that he intended to batter her.

The crime of battery, which [Indiana law establishes as] the knowing or intentional touching of another person in a rude, insolent, or angry manner, is among the crimes that, if resulting in death, can constitute the crime of involuntary manslaughter. Involuntary manslaughter is distinguished from the crime of murder by whether the defendant intended to batter or kill. The intent that must be shown to prove involuntary manslaughter is the intent required by the predicate offense, which in this case was battery.

The [record in this case contains] the plea agreement and the judgment of conviction, but not the charging information, the contents of which are not reflected in the plea agreement or judgment. These documents show that Gearheart pleaded guilty to, and was convicted of and sentenced for, involuntary manslaughter, a felony. The plea agreement also reflects that Gearheart acknowledged "that entry of a guilty plea pursuant to this Agreement constitutes an admission of the truth of all facts alleged in the charge."

Auto-Owners asserts [in its brief] that Gearheart pleaded guilty to the charge that he "did kill another human being, to wit: Brandy Nicole Harvey, while committing or attempting to commit battery." But the quoted language does not appear in the plea agreement, and we do not find it elsewhere in the record. [Harvey and Johnson concede in their brief] that the acceptance of Gearheart's guilty plea constituted a judicial determination "that [Gearheart] committed a 'knowing' touching of Brandy in a rude, insolent or angry manner, resulting in her death, and that there was a factual basis for the plea." They argue, however, that Gearheart's plea judicially admitted only the unlawful touching, but nothing concerning his "motive, mental operations, intentions or purpose in pushing Brandy."

We are not persuaded by the claim of Auto-Owners that Gearheart's guilty plea conclusively establishes that there is no coverage under the "occurrence" clause. At most, the guilty plea shows only that Gearheart intended the battery (improper touching by pushing Brandy), and that her death resulted. But it does not establish that he intended Brandy's slip, fall, and drowning, and thus does not preclude the assertion that her death was accidental, and thus an "occurrence." And, as discussed above, the "occurrence" language of the Auto-Owners policy must be construed to refer not to Gearheart's push, but to Brandy's slip, fall, and drowning. The push was not accidental, but a genuine issue exists whether the drowning and resulting death were. We conclude that the trial court did not err in denying Auto-Owners' motion for summary judgment as to its claim that the plaintiffs' claims fall outside the "occurrence" requirement of its liability insurance coverage.

In addition to claiming no coverage as a matter of law due to the requirement of an "occurrence" in its insuring agreement, Auto-Owners also contends that there is no coverage because of a policy exclusion declaring that the personal liability coverage does not apply to "bodily injury or property damage reasonably expected or intended by the insured." In contrast to the insurance policy's insuring agreement that requires the occurrence to be accidental, this exclusion more narrowly considers whether the resulting injury or damage was intentional or reasonably expected by the insured.

Auto-Owners argues that the exclusion for intended injury or damage applies because the nature and character of Gearheart's conduct was such that his intent to harm Brandy must be inferred as a matter of law, regardless of his subjective intent, and because of his guilty plea to involuntary manslaughter. It urges that from the physical circumstances of the boat ramp, Gearheart's knowledge of Brandy's proximity to its edge, and the comparative size and strength of Gearheart and Brandy, his intent to harm her should be inferred as a matter of law, arguing [in its brief] that the chance she would be harmed was "not only reasonable, . . . it was a certainty."

Auto-Owners does not assert that the presence or force of Gearheart's hands on Brandy's shoulders, standing alone, directly caused a "bodily injury" under the policy exclusion. Rather, it "contends that under the circumstances, the only reasonable conclusion or inference to be drawn . . . is that [Brandy] would fall into the Wabash River and be harmed if Gearheart pushed her." We initially observe that, as discussed above, Gearheart's plea to involuntary manslaughter at most shows that he intended to push Brandy, but it does not establish that he intended or expected her to fall into the river and drown. His plea therefore is not conclusive upon whether Brandy's death was "reasonably expected or intended by the insured," as required for the coverage exclusion to apply.

Basic summary judgment jurisprudence [also] suggests [that Gearheart's intent to harm Brandy should not be inferred as a matter of law]. Auto-Owners acknowledges that Gearheart insists that he did not intend to harm Brandy. Gearheart testified [in his deposition] that when he pushed Brandy, he did not intend or expect for her to fall into the water or to be physically injured. In ruling on a motion for summary judgment, not only all facts but also all reasonable inferences drawn from those facts are construed in favor of the nonmoving party. The court must accept as true those facts alleged by the nonmoving party and resolve all doubts against the moving party. Application of these principles requires us to accept for summary judgment purposes Gearheart's statements and to reject the claim that Brandy's death was "intended" by the insured.

[In an effort to overcome] Gearheart's statements expressly denying any intent or expectation to cause bodily injury to Brandy and explaining the circumstances of his push of Brandy, . . . Auto-Owners emphasizes evidence regarding the physical dimensions of the boat ramp, Gearheart's knowledge of Brandy's proximity to its edge, Gearheart's awareness of his own size and strength as compared to Brandy, and [the fact] that Gearheart's push of Brandy caused her to slip and fall into the river. This evidence is definitely not so overwhelming as to mandate us to conclude that Gearheart must have intended to harm Brandy. Because Auto-Owners has failed to demonstrate the absence of a genuine issue of material fact regarding Gearheart's intent to harm Brandy, the trial court was correct to deny summary judgment on Auto-Owners' claimed application of the coverage exclusion. [We therefore conclude that the Court of Appeals erred in reversing the trial court's decision.]

Decision of Court of Appeals reversed, and case remanded for further proceedings.

Business Liability Policies   Business liability policies also feature coverage for bodily injury and property damage stemming from the insured's actions. The relevant range of actions, of course, is broadened to include the insured's business pursuits or "conduct of business." A major focus remains on unintentional wrongful conduct (usually negligence) of the insured, with the insured's deliberate wrongful acts normally being specifically excluded from coverage. Another typical exclusion is the pollution exclusion, which deprives the insured of coverage for actions that lead to pollution of other parties' property, unless the pollution occurs suddenly and accidentally.

Business liability policies also tend to provide the insured coverage in instances where the insured would be liable for certain torts of his employees (normally under the *respondeat superior* doctrine).[9] In addition, business liability policies sometimes afford coverage broader than instances of tortious conduct producing physical injury or property damage. Some policies, for instance, contain a clause that contemplates coverage for the insured's defamation of another person or invasion of that person's privacy (though other policies specifically exclude coverage for those same torts). Furthermore, the broad "conduct of business" language in certain policies, as well as specialized clauses (in some policies) referring to liability stemming from advertising or unfair competition, may contemplate coverage for the insured's legal wrongs that cause others to experience economic harm. In the end, the particular liabilities covered by a business liability policy cannot be determined without a close examination of the provisions in the policy at issue. It may become necessary for a court to interpret a policy provision whose meaning is unclear or scope is uncertain.

Other Liability Policies   Professional liability policies also afford coverage for the insured's tortious conduct, this time in the practice of his or her profession. Negligent professional conduct producing harm to a third party (normally bodily injury in the medical malpractice setting but usually economic harm in the legal or other professional malpractice context) would be a covered liability. Wrongful professional conduct of an intentional nature typically would not be covered.

Automobile liability policies cover liability for physical injury and property damage stemming from the insured's (and certain other drivers') negligent driving. Once again, however, there is no coverage for liability arising from the insured's (or another driver's) deliberate vehicle operation acts of a wrongful nature.

Workers' compensation policies tend to approach coverage questions somewhat differently, primarily because injured employees need not prove negligence on the part of their employer in order to be entitled to benefits. Therefore, the insurer's obligation under a workers' compensation policy is phrased in terms of the liability the insured employer would face under state law.

Insurer's Obligations

Duty to Defend   When another party makes a legal claim against the insured and the nature and allegations of the claim are such that the insurer would be obligated to cover the insured's liability if the claim were proven, the insurer has a **duty to defend** the insured. A commonsense precondition of this duty's being triggered is that the insured must notify the insurer that the claim has been made against her. The duty to defend means that the insurer must furnish, at its expense, an attorney to represent the insured in litigation resulting from the claim against her. If the insurer fails to perform its duty to defend in an instance where the duty arose, the insurer has breached the insurance contract. Depending on the facts, the breaching insurer would at least be liable for compensatory damages (as indicated in this chapter's earlier discussion of insurance policies as contracts)[10] and potentially for punitive damages as well under the *bad faith* doctrine examined later in this chapter.

Sometimes it is quite clear that the insurer's duty to defend applies or does not apply, given the nature of the claim made against the insured. Other times, however, there may be uncertainty as to whether the claim alleged against the insured would fall within the scope of the liability insurance policy. Such uncertainty, of course, means that it is not clear whether the insurer has a duty to defend. Insurers tend to take one of two approaches

---

[9]The *respondeat superior* doctrine is discussed in Chapter 36. Although the insured's own intentional torts would not normally be covered, business liability policies sometimes provide that if the insured is liable on *respondeat superior* grounds for an employee's intentional tort such as battery, the insured will be covered unless the insured directed the employee to commit the intentional tort.

[10]The compensatory damages in such an instance would normally be the reasonable costs incurred by the insured in retaining an attorney and paying him to represent her. Of course, if the insured ended up being held liable in the third party's suit and the insurer wrongfully refused to pay the damages assessed against the insured in that case, the insured's compensatory damages claim against the breaching insurer would be increased substantially.

in an effort to resolve this uncertainty. Under the first approach, the insurer files a declaratory judgment action against the insured. In this suit, the insurer asks the court to determine whether the insurer owes obligations to the insured under the policy in connection with the particular liability claim made against the insured by the injured third party. The other option insurers often pursue when it is unclear whether the liability policy applies is to retain an attorney to represent the insured in the litigation filed by the third party—thus fulfilling any duty to defend that may be owed—but to do so under a *reservation of rights* notice. By providing the reservation of rights notice to the insured, the insurer indicates that it reserves the right, upon acquisition of additional information, to conclude (or seek a later judicial determination) that it does not have the obligation to pay any damages that may be assessed against the insured as a result of the third party's claim. The insurer's reservation of rights also serves to eliminate an argument that by proceeding to defend the insured, the insurer waived the ability to argue that any actual liability would not be covered.

Duty to Pay Sums Owed by Insured If a third party's claim against the insured falls within the liabilities covered by the policy, the insurer is obligated to pay the compensatory damages held by a judge or jury to be due and owing from the insured to the third party. In addition, the insured's obligation to pay such expenses as court costs would also be covered. These payment obligations are subject, of course, to the policy limits of the insurance contract involved. For example, if the insured is held liable for compensatory damages and court costs totaling $150,000 but the policy limits of the relevant liability policy are $100,000, the insurer's contractual obligation to pay sums owed by the insured is restricted to $100,000.

Is the insurer also obligated to pay any *punitive damages* assessed against the insured as a result of a covered claim? As a general rule, the insurer will have no such obligation, either because of an insurance contract provision to that effect or because of judicial decisions holding that notions of public policy forbid arrangements by which one could transfer his punitive damages liability to an insurer. Not all courts facing this issue have so held, however, meaning that in occasional instances the insured's punitive damages liability may also be covered if the insurance policy's terms specifically contemplate such a result.

The liability insurer need not wait until litigation has been concluded to attempt to dispose of a liability claim made against the insured. Insurance policy provisions, consistent with our legal system's tendency to encourage voluntary settlements of claims, allow insurers to negotiate settlements with third parties who have made liability claims against the insured. These settlements involve payment of an agreed sum of money to the third party, in exchange for the third party's giving up her legal right to proceed with litigation against the insured. Settlements may occur regardless of whether litigation has been formally instituted by the third party or whether the claim against the insured consists of the third party's prelitigation demand for payment by the insured. If settlements are reached—and they are reached much more often than not—the substantial costs involved in taking a case all the way to trial may be avoided. The same is also true, from the insurer's perspective, of the damages that might have been assessed against the insured if the case had been tried. Note, however, that even if the defendant (the insured) wins a suit that does proceed to trial, the costs to the insurer are still substantial even though there is no award of damages to pay. Those costs include a considerable amount for attorney's fees for the insured (the insurer's obligation regardless of the outcome of the case) as well as other substantial expenses associated with protracted litigation. Accordingly, even when the insurer thinks that the insured probably would prevail if the case went to trial, the insurer may be interested in pursuing a settlement with the third-party claimant if a reasonable amount—an amount less than what it would cost the insurer to defend the case—can be agreed upon.

Is There a Liability Insurance Crisis?

Since the mid-1980s, the necessary premiums for liability insurance policies of various types (particularly business and professional liability policies) have risen considerably. Sometimes, the premiums charged by liability insurers have become so substantial that would-be insureds have concluded that they cannot afford liability insurance and therefore must go without it despite its importance. In addition, some insurers have ceased offering certain types of liability policies and/or have become much more restrictive in their decisions about which persons or firms to insure.

Insurance companies tend to blame the above state of affairs on what they see as a tort law regime under which plaintiffs win lawsuits too frequently and recover very large damage awards too often. As a result, insurers have been among the most outspoken parties calling for tort reform, a subject discussed in earlier chapters in this book. Plaintiffs' attorneys and critics of the insurance industry blame rising liability insurance premiums on, primarily, another alleged cause: questionable investment practices and other unsound business practices

CYBERLAW IN ACTION

So-called bugs in Version 5.0 of America Online's Inc.'s Internet access software ("AOL 5.0") drew the ire of large numbers of disgruntled customers. In numerous cases that were later consolidated, these customers sued AOL. Relying on a variety of legal theories, the plaintiffs contended that AOL 5.0 was defective and that as a result, their computers crashed or they experienced other loss of use of their computers, computer systems, and computer software and data.

AOL called upon its liability insurer, St. Paul Mercury Insurance Co., to defend it against the customers' claims. St. Paul refused, contending that the claims did not fall within the coverage obligations St. Paul had assumed. AOL retained legal counsel to defend it against the customers' claims and then sued St. Paul for an alleged breach of the contract of insurance. Concluding that the claims against AOL were not covered by the policy St. Paul issued, a federal district court granted summary judgment in favor of St. Paul. AOL appealed.

In *America Online, Inc. v. St. Paul Mercury Insurance Co.*, 347 F.3d 89 (4th Cir. 2003), the U.S. Court of Appeals for the Fourth Circuit considered AOL's appeal. The court began its analysis by noting basic rules applicable to insurance policy interpretation and determinations of whether a liability insurer must defend its policyholder against third parties' claims. First, if the language of the policy is unambiguous, the court will "give the words their ordinary meaning and enforce the policy as written." Second, "if the language of the policy is subject to different interpretations, [the court] will construe it in favor of coverage." Third, the insurer's "obligation to defend arises whenever the complaint against the insured alleges facts and circumstances, some of which, if proved, would fall within the risk covered by the policy."

The St. Paul policy at issue included a coverage provision stating that St. Paul would "pay amounts [AOL] is legally required to pay as damages for covered bodily injury, property damage, or premises damage." The policy defined *property damage* as "physical damage to tangible property of others, including all resulting loss of use of that property . . . or loss of use of tangible property of others that isn't physically damaged."

In addition, the St. Paul policy excluded certain events or harms from coverage. Among these exclusions was a provision stating that St. Paul would not cover "property damage to impaired property, or to property which isn't physically damaged, that results from [AOL's] faulty or dangerous products or completed work [or from] a delay or failure in fulfilling the terms of a contract or agreement." The policy defined *impaired property* as "tangible property, other than [AOL's] products or completed work, that can be restored to use by nothing more than . . . an adjustment, repair, replacement, or

removal of [AOL's] products or completed work which forms a part of it, [or AOL's] fulfilling the terms of a contract or agreement."

Proceeding to interpret the St. Paul policy in light of the rules noted earlier, the court paid careful attention to the types of damages sought by the AOL customers. The court reasoned that claims seeking damages from AOL for harm to or loss of use of computer systems or computer software or data were not covered claims because systems, software, and data are not "tangible" since they are not "'capable of being touched [and] able to be perceived as materially existent . . . by the sense of touch'" [quoting definition of "tangible" in *Webster's New Third International Dictionary of the English Language* (1993)]. Systems, software, and data thus would not appear to be "tangible property" for purposes of St. Paul's policy. The Fourth Circuit also noted that computer systems, software, and data are customarily classified by courts as *intangible* property. In view of the St. Paul policy's *property damage* definition (quoted above) and its references to "tangible property," the court held that any harm to or loss of use of computer data, software, and systems would not be covered by the policy.

The claims brought against AOL, however, also alleged loss of use of the customers' computers. The court concluded that the computers themselves would be tangible property under the definition set forth above and that the claims alleging loss of use of computers might therefore appear, at first glance, to be covered by the policy. However, the Fourth Circuit noted, the AOL customers were not actually alleging that their computers were physically harmed. Instead, the AOL customers were contending that AOL 5.0 interfered with the proper operation of their computers and that loss of use of the computers resulted. The claimants' allegations that their computers crashed were substantively allegations of system failure rather than of physical harm to the computers themselves. The absence of a claim of physical damage to the computers meant that harm consisting of loss of use would not be covered by the portion of the *property damage* definition that referred to "physical damage to tangible property of others, including all resulting loss of use of that property."

Still potentially applicable, though again at first glance only, was the portion of the *property damage* definition that appeared to cover "loss of use of tangible property of others that isn't physically damaged." That possible avenue to coverage was blocked, according to the court, by the St. Paul policy's "impaired property" exclusion. The plaintiffs, after all, premised their claim on the notion that AOL 5.0 was defective and that as a result, their computers were rendered inoperable. The court observed that "the straightforward meaning of [the impaired property] exclusion bars coverage for loss of use of tangible property of others that is not phys- ically damaged by the insured's defective product." The Fourth Circuit stressed that even though AOL 5.0 allegedly "caused damage to other software, including operating sys- tems[, . . .] there has been no demonstration or claim that the physical or tangible components of any computer were damaged. In the absence of property that is physically damaged, AOL's arguments for covering loss of use must be rejected."

Having concluded that none of the customers' claims against AOL came within the terms of the St. Paul policy, the Fourth Circuit affirmed the district court's grant of summary judgment to St. Paul and held that the insurer owed AOL no duty to defend it against those claims.

Ethics in Action

With the costs of medical treatment, hospitaliza- tion, and medications having increased dramati- cally in recent years, health insurance has become a critical means by which insured persons minimize the adverse financial consequences associated with illness and injury. The costs of serious illness or injury may be finan- cially crippling unless insurance coverage exists. Often this coverage comes in the form of a group policy that is made available to employees of a certain company or to persons affiliated with a particular organization. Subject to certain exclusions and other contractual restrictions, group policies tend to cover a significant portion of the costs of obtaining health care services.

Although a very large percentage of the U.S. population has some form of health insurance, many millions of U.S. res- idents do not. Public policy questions regarding health insur- ance availability and costs have been debated extensively in political arenas during the past two decades, but sweeping legislative proposals to increase access to health coverage had not been enacted into law at the federal level as of the time this book went to press in 2008. Congress has opted for more limited measures, such as the Health Insurance Portability and Accountability Act of 1996, which allows most employees who had health insurance in connection with their employment to change jobs without fear of losing health coverage. This statute followed the lead of the earlier COBRA statute, under which persons who end an employment status that had entitled them to group policy coverage may continue that coverage for a limited time.

Much of the debate over whether health insurance "reform" is desirable tends to have an ethical flavor. For instance, con- sider the questions set forth below. In doing so, you may wish to employ the ethical theories discussed in Chapter 4.

- Is there a "right," in an ethical sense, to health insurance coverage? If so, why? If not, why not?
- Do employers have an ethical obligation to make group health insurance available to their employees? If so, why? If so, does this obligation always exist, or does it exist only under certain circumstances? If employers do not have such an obligation, why don't they?
- Would Congress be acting ethically if it enacted a law re- quiring the vast majority of employers in the United States to make health insurance available to their employees? Be prepared to justify your position.
- Does the U.S. government have an ethical duty to furnish health coverage to all U.S. residents? Be prepared to justify your position.

supposedly engaged in by insurance companies. The parties making these assertions thus oppose tort reform efforts as being unnecessary and unwise.

Liability insurance premiums in general may not be increasing as rapidly today as they once did, but they re- main substantial in amount. So long as liability insurance remains unaffordable or otherwise difficult to obtain, there is a "crisis," given the adverse financial conse- quences that could beset an uninsured person. This is so regardless of which of the competing explanations set forth above bears greater legitimacy.

Bad Faith Breach of Insurance Contract

Earlier in this chapter, we discussed the liability that an insurer will face if it breaches its policy obligations by means of a good faith but erroneous denial of coverage. That liability is for compensatory damages—damages designed to compensate the insured for the losses stem- ming from the insurer's breach—just as in breach of contract cases outside the insurance setting. Punitive damages are not available, however, when the insurer's wrongful failure or refusal to perform stemmed from a good faith (though erroneous) coverage denial. What if the insurer's failure or refusal to perform exhibited a lack of good faith? In this section, we examine the recent judicial tendency to go beyond the conventional remedy of compensatory damages and to assess punitive damages against the insurer when the insurer's refusal to perform its policy obligations amounted to the tort of **bad faith breach of contract.**

The special nature of the insurer–insured relationship tends to involve a "we'll take care of you" message that insurers communicate to insureds—at least at the outset of the relationship. Recognizing this, courts have displayed little tolerance in recent years for insurers' unjustifiable refusals to take care of insureds when taking care of them is clearly called for by the relevant policy's terms. When an insurer refuses to perform obvious policy obligations without a plausible, legitimate explanation for the refusal, the insurer risks more than being held liable for compensatory damages. If the facts and circumstances indicate that the insurer's refusal to perform stemmed not from a reasonable argument over coverage but from an intent to "stonewall," deny or unreasonably delay paying a meritorious claim, or otherwise create hardship for the insured, the insurer's breach may be of the bad faith variety. Because bad faith breach is considered an independent tort of a flagrantly wrongful nature, punitive damages—in addition to compensatory damages—have been held to be appropriate. The purposes of punitive damages in this context are the same as in other types of cases that call for punitive damages: to punish the flagrant wrongdoer and to deter the wrongdoer

(as well as other potential wrongdoers) from repeating such an action.

The past 25 years have witnessed bad faith cases in which many millions of dollars in punitive damages have been assessed against insurers. The types of situations in which bad faith liability has been found have included a liability insurer's unjustifiable refusal to defend its insured and/or pay damages awarded against the insured in litigation that clearly triggered the policy obligations. Various cases involving very large punitive damages assessments for bad faith liability have stemmed from property insurers' refusals to pay for the insured's destroyed property when the cause was clearly a covered peril and the insurer had no plausible rationale for denying coverage. Still other bad faith cases in which liability was held to exist have included malpractice or other liability insurers' refusals to settle certain meritorious claims against the insured within the policy limits. Bad faith liability in these cases tends to involve a situation in which the insured is held legally liable to a plaintiff for an amount well in excess of the dollar limits of the liability policy (meaning that the insured would be personally responsible for the amount of the judgment in excess of the policy limits), after the liability insurer, without reasonable justification, refused the plaintiff's offer to settle the case for an amount less than or equal to the policy limits. The *Vining* case, which follows, furnishes another example of behavior that triggers bad faith liability.

Whether bad faith liability exists in a given case depends, of course, on all of the relevant facts and circumstances. Although bad faith liability is not established in every case in which insureds allege it, cases raising a bad faith claim are of particular concern to insurers.

Vining v. Enterprise Financial Group, Inc.   148 F.3d 1206 (10th Cir. 1998)

Enterprise Financial Group, Inc., provided financing and credit life insurance to consumers who bought automobiles at Crown Auto World in Tulsa, Oklahoma. If purchased by a car buyer, the credit life insurance would pay off the customer's car loan in the event of his death. In March 1992, Milford Vining (Milford) purchased a jeep at Crown Auto World. Nancy Sidler, an Enterprise employee whose office was at the dealership, sold a credit life insurance policy to Milford when he purchased the jeep.

In late May 1993, Milford suffered a heart attack and died. His surviving spouse, Billie Vining (Vining), filed a claim with Enterprise for death benefits of approximately $10,000 under Milford's credit life policy. Enterprise refused to pay the claim and rescinded the policy on the supposed ground that Milford had misrepresented his health history in his application for the credit life policy. After unsuccessfully contesting the rescission, Vining sued Enterprise for breach of contract and for rescinding the policy in bad faith. In defense, Enterprise maintained that it had a legitimate basis for contesting the claim and that Milford had made material misrepresentations in his application for the credit life policy.

The evidence adduced at trial showed that in 1983, Milford suffered from coronary artery disease and underwent a triple bypass operation. After the surgery and follow-up tests, Milford began taking heart maintenance medication to prevent the occurrence of angina. From the time immediately following the 1983 surgery until the time of his death, Milford led an active life. He did not complain of chest pain or related symptoms.

In February 1992, Milford visited Dr. Michael Sullivan. This visit took place because Milford, who had recently moved, wanted to find a doctor closer to home. Milford's visit to Dr. Sullivan was not brought on by illness or physical symptoms. At the general time of this visit, Milford suffered from little, if any, angina. Dr. Sullivan continued Milford on his heart maintenance medications as a preventive measure. When Milford applied for the credit life policy in March 1992, he signed an application that contained the following statement:

I HEREBY CERTIFY THAT I AM IN GOOD HEALTH AS OF THE EFFECTIVE DATE ABOVE. I FURTHER CERTIFY THAT I DO NOT PRESENTLY HAVE, NOR HAVE I EVER HAD, NOR HAVE I BEEN TOLD I HAVE, NOR HAVE I BEEN TREATED WITHIN THE PRECEDING 12 MONTHS FOR ANY OF THE FOLLOWING: ANY HEART DISEASE, OR OTHER CARDIOVASCULAR DISEASES.

Vining presented evidence designed to show that Enterprise routinely rescinded credit life policies after insureds' deaths and that the rescission of Milford's policy fit into this pattern. The jury returned a verdict in Vining's favor, awarding her $400,000 in compensatory damages for financial losses, emotional distress, and related harms. In addition, the jury assessed $400,000 in punitive damages against Enterprise, which appealed to the U.S. Court of Appeals for the Tenth Circuit.

Ebel, Circuit Judge

Both parties agree that Milford did not intentionally attempt to mislead Enterprise [when he signed the insurance application containing the statement about his health], that Milford's appointment with Dr. Sullivan was his only medical visit in the 12 months preceding the policy purchase date, and that under Oklahoma Insurance Regulations, an insurance company may consider only the last 12 months of an applicant's medical history [when evaluating] an insurance application.

After Milford's death, Enterprise sought all of Milford's medical records, including Dr. Sullivan's notes. On the same day it received Dr. Sullivan's notes, Enterprise rescinded the policy. Enterprise routinely contests all claims on life insurance policies made within two years of a policy's effective date and investigates to find misrepresentations in the insurance application. [U]nder Oklahoma law, a claim made more than two years after the effective date of a life insurance policy is generally incontestable by the insurer. Debbie Cluck, Enterprise's claims examiner, denies four out of every ten claims that she reviews. Enterprise does not have a claims manual or any written guidelines specifying when a claim is payable or not, and it never informed Cluck of any applicable Oklahoma law or regulation pertaining to when a policy may be rescinded.

Cluck felt it appropriate to rescind a policy even if the agent issued the policy with full knowledge of an applicant's medical history. Cluck's beliefs comport with Enterprise company philosophy. Cluck never paid a claim if she had any reason to doubt whether a person's medical history was inconsistent with the health [statement] included on the insurance application. Cluck rescinded Milford's policy because she considered the office visit with Dr. Sullivan and the continuation of his angina medication by Dr. Sullivan [as] constitut[ing] treatment for triple bypass surgery. Cluck did not investigate whether Sidler

[the Enterprise employee who dealt with Milford] was informed of Milford's medical history, did not contact either Sidler or Vining, and did not contact Dr. Sullivan to discuss his notes before rescinding the policy.

Enterprise's training manual for its agents emphasizes that applicants only need to be between the ages of 18 and 65 to purchase insurance. The manual does not discuss the health [statement on the application] or in any way suggest that the agent is supposed to ask the customer about his health. [It does not suggest] that health is relevant [to a decision to issue] the policy. The manual also encourages agents to maximize profit by overstating the actual monthly premium that should be charged and by secretly increasing the actual amount of monthly payments the customer agrees to pay—for example, raising a payment from $78.22 to $78.99 because customers look more closely at dollars than cents. The manual informs agents that the life insurance policies they sell are guaranteed issue policies, which means that the coverage is in force immediately as compared to ordinary life insurance [policies, applicants for which] must be approved by the insurer before coverage takes effect.

John Myerson was Enterprise's representative to agents at automobile dealerships that sell Enterprise life insurance policies. [These agents included Sidler.] Myerson testified that he did not know what the terms used in the health [statement on the application] meant and that he did not know how Enterprise processed claims. Myerson also testified that he does not train agents to ask about doctor visits or medication. Sidler [was] never . . . trained . . . by Enterprise . . . on what constituted "good health" [for purposes of the application's health statement].

In response to numerous complaints against Enterprise for improper rescission of life insurance policies, the Oklahoma

Insurance Department conducted an investigation of Enterprise's business practices. The Department [issued a 1992 report that] criticized Enterprise for requiring applicants to sign a disclaimer stating that they had never had any health problems. The report sharply criticized Enterprise's loss ratio, the ratio of benefits paid to premiums received, as being unreasonably below accepted levels due to a large number of policy rescissions. Enterprise paid out in benefits only about 16 percent of premiums received. Oklahoma Insurance Department regulations require a 50 percent loss ratio for credit life insurance companies. Based on the report, the Oklahoma Insurance Commissioner issued an order levying a $15,000 fine against Enterprise for various violations and mandating that Enterprise lower its premiums to produce an acceptable loss ratio level. Enterprise made no changes in light of the report's criticism. In fact, loss ratios for the two years following the report continued to remain below 18 percent. Enterprise's rescission conduct and loss ratios bear some resemblance to those of the fictional insurance company portrayed in John Grisham's novel *The Rainmaker* and in the motion picture of the same name.

Numerous witnesses testified that their decedent spouses had bought life insurance from Enterprise in circumstances similar to [those of] the Vinings. Enterprise summarily rescinded those life insurance policies after the survivors made claims on the policies. In each case, Enterprise cited evidence of an insured's health problems that existed at the time the insured signed a health disclaimer statement in the insurance application as the grounds for rescission.

Finally, John Hammond testified as an expert on the handling and management of insurance claims. Hammond expressed his opinion that Enterprise's conduct was "completely inappropriate." He stated that Enterprise investigated Vining's claim by looking for a reason to rescind the policy. Hammond added that Enterprise erred by not contacting either Sidler, the agent who sold the policy, or Vining before rescinding the policy. Hammond also criticized Enterprise for not providing claims manuals detailing credit life insurance policy eligibility requirements to its claims examiners who were charged with investigating claims on those policies.

Under Oklahoma law, an insurer has a legal duty to "deal fairly and act in good faith with its insured." *Christian v. American Home Assurance Co.* (Okla. Sup. Ct. 1977). An insured may bring a cause of action in tort for bad faith if the insurer breaches this duty. The essence of a bad faith claim centers on the unreasonableness of the insurer's conduct. An insurer does not breach the duty of good faith to pay a claim "by litigating a dispute with its insured if there is a legitimate dispute as to coverage or amount of the claim, and the insurer's position is reasonable and legitimate." *Oulds v. Principal Mutual Life Insurance Co.* (10th Cir. 1993).

Enterprise argues on appeal that because it in fact had a legitimate reason for rescinding Milford's policy based on his medical history and heart condition, Enterprise is entitled as a matter of law to a verdict in its favor on the claim of bad faith. An insurer does not act in bad faith if it had a "good faith belief, at the time its performance was requested, that it had justifiable reason for withholding payment under the policy." *Buzzard v. Farmers Insurance Co.* (Okla Sup. Ct. 1991). An insurer may legitimately and in good faith dispute a claim based on material misrepresentations in the insured's application for insurance.

Vining does not dispute that her husband had a heart condition and that the insurance application he signed included a disclaimer . . . certifying that he was in good health and had not been treated within the preceding 12 months for heart disease or any other cardiovascular disease. As a result, Enterprise could contest liability on the basis of a misrepresentation if it had a good faith belief that the misrepresentation was intentional. Here, Enterprise reasonably could have determined that by signing the disclaimer, Milford materially misrepresented the condition of his health. However, even a "legitimate dispute as to coverage will not act as an impenetrable shield against a valid claim of bad faith" where the insured presents "sufficient evidence reasonably tending to show bad faith" or unreasonable conduct. *Timberlake Construction Co. v. U.S. Fidelity & Guaranty Co.* (10th Cir. 1995). That is, a plaintiff may bring a bad faith cause of action even though a legitimate defense to a breach of contract claim exists if the defendant did not actually rely on that defense to deny payment under the policy.

Vining demonstrated at trial a deliberate, willful pattern of abusive conduct by Enterprise in handling claims under its life insurance policies. Vining offered evidence that as a matter of course Enterprise would rescind life insurance policies issued on a guaranteed basis as soon as claims were made. Enterprise based these rescissions on the grounds that the insured had made material misrepresentations on the insurance application regardless of whether Enterprise in fact would have declined to write the policy had it known of that information at the time the policy was written. Vining presented evidence that Enterprise engaged in a systematic, bad faith scheme of canceling policies without determining whether it had good cause to do so. Such conduct constitutes bad faith regardless of whether Enterprise legitimately might have been able to contest Vining's claim based on Milford's heart condition, because the evidence showed that Enterprise, in fact, did not dispute coverage in good faith based on Milford's heart condition.

Enterprise also raises the affirmative defense of rescission. Under [an Oklahoma statute], an insurer properly may rescind an insurance policy when the application contains a misrepresentation that (1) is fraudulent; (2) is material to the insurance company's acceptance of the risk; or (3) induced the insurer to issue the policy where it would not have done so had it known the true facts. However, Enterprise concedes that [the statute does not allow an insurer to rescind unless the insured had an intent to deceive]. Because Enterprise . . . admits that Milford did not willfully or intentionally misrepresent his health history on the application, Enterprise cannot rely on the affirmative defense of rescission.

Enterprise complains that [the district court erred in] the jury instruction [concerning what Vining needed to prove in order to establish bad faith]. Bad faith may be established by showing an unreasonable refusal to pay a claim, and the instruction set forth three alternative scenarios which are deemed to be unreasonable: (1) the insurance company "had no basis for the refusal," (2) the insurance company did not perform a proper investigation, or (3) the insurance company did not evaluate the results of the investigation properly. As we pointed out earlier, merely because there is a reasonable basis that an insurance company could invoke to deny a claim does not necessarily

immunize the insurer from a bad faith claim if, in fact, it did not actually rely on that supposed reasonable basis and instead took action in bad faith. [T]he jury instruction correctly stated the applicable law.

Enterprise challenges the damages awarded to Vining as excessive and as lacking sufficient evidentiary support. Vining testified at trial regarding the distress she experienced as a result of Enterprise's conduct toward her during the three years she spent fighting the insurance company over the claim. Such evidence is sufficient in a bad faith claim to support an award for emotional distress. In addition, $400,000 for mental pain and suffering, financial losses, embarrassment, and loss of reputation in the context of bad faith insurance claims is not excessive on this record. [The award of] $400,000 in punitive damages [was also appropriate] and need not be adjusted.

Judgment in favor of Vining affirmed.

Problems and Problem Cases

1. Eighteen-year-old Arthur Smith became intoxicated at a New Year's Eve party. At 11:00 PM, Smith left the party and began walking home. Police officer Don Czopek saw Smith walking down the center of a road and weaving from side to side. Because Smith was interfering with traffic and placing himself at risk of physical harm, Czopek pulled his patrol car alongside Smith and attempted to talk him into getting off the road. Smith refused, became argumentative, and started shouting. Czopek parked his patrol car, got out, and approached Smith in an effort to calm him down. Smith became increasingly hostile and grabbed Czopek by the lapels of his coat. Officer Herdis Petty then arrived on the scene to assist Czopek. A struggle occurred as the two officers attempted to handcuff Smith and put him into a patrol car. Smith kicked, hit, and bit the officers during this struggle, which continued for a substantial length of time. Czopek suffered frostbite on one of his hands. Petty sustained broken ribs as a result of being kicked by Smith (plus other less serious injuries). Smith was later convicted of assault and battery. He admitted that he intentionally resisted arrest but said that he did not recall hitting or kicking anyone. Officers Czopek and Petty filed a civil suit against Smith's parents, whose homeowners' policy with Group Insurance Company of Michigan

(GICOM) provided liability coverage to the insureds—a status that, under the policy's terms, included Arthur Smith—for third parties' personal injury claims resulting from an "occurrence." The policy defined "occurrence" as "an accident, including injurious exposure to conditions, which results . . . in bodily injury or property damage." The policy contained an exclusion from coverage for "bodily injury or property damage which is either expected or intended from the standpoint of the insured." GICOM filed a declaratory judgment suit in which it asked the court to declare that it had no duty to defend or indemnify Arthur Smith and his parents in connection with the litigation brought by Czopek and Petty. Was GICOM entitled to such a ruling by the court?

2. Don Davis owned a lumber mill that was subject to a $248,000 mortgage held by Diversified Financial Systems, Inc. Early in 1995, Aaron Harber became interested in forming a partnership with Davis for ownership and operation of the mill. Harber and Davis orally agreed upon the terms of a partnership. Harber contended that these terms included a purchase by Harber of Diversified's interest in the mortgage on the mill. Davis later informed Harber that he (Davis) would not proceed with the partnership. Nevertheless, Harber purchased Diversified's mortgage interest in April 1995. Harber did this in reliance on the oral

partnership agreement with Davis—an agreement Harber intended to enforce despite Davis's refusal to proceed.

During Harber's negotiations with Davis concerning their supposed partnership and with Diversified for purchase of its mortgage interest, Harber discovered that the mill was not covered by property insurance. Harber therefore purchased a policy from Underwriters at Lloyd's of London (Lloyd's). The policy, whose one-year term began in late May 1995, named Harber and U.S.A. Properties, Inc., a corporation set up and wholly owned by Harber, as insureds.

In mid-June 1995, one of the buildings at the mill was destroyed by fire. Approximately two weeks later, in an effort to prompt negotiations in the dispute with Davis over whether a partnership existed or would be pursued, Harber filed suit to foreclose the Diversified mortgage. The mortgage was in default at that time. Harber and Davis soon entered into a settlement agreement that provided in part for the transfer of the mill property to Harber, in exchange for Harber's giving up all of his claims against Davis. The agreement also conveyed, to Harber, whatever interest Davis had in insurance proceeds related to the building that had been destroyed by fire.

Harber and U.S.A. Properties submitted a claim to Lloyd's concerning the destroyed building. After Lloyd's denied the claim, Harber and U.S.A. Properties sued Lloyd's for payment according to the terms of the policy. A federal district court held that the plaintiffs lacked an insurable interest and that Lloyd's was therefore entitled to summary judgment. Harber and U.S.A. Properties appealed. Was the district court's holding correct?

3. Property Owners Insurance Co. (POI) was the insurer and Thomas Cope was the insured under a liability policy that excluded liability except in cases of liability "with respect to the conduct of a business" owned by Cope. Cope's business was a roofing company. While the policy was in force, Cope traveled to Montana with Edward Urbanski, a person with whom Cope did significant business. While on the trip, Cope snowmobiled with a group of persons that included Gregory Johnson, who died in a snowmobiling accident. Johnson's estate brought a wrongful death lawsuit against Cope. After Cope notified POI of the case brought against him, POI filed a declaratory judgment action against Cope and Johnson's estate. In the declaratory judgment action, POI sought a judicial determination that it had no obligations to Cope and

Johnson's estate under the liability policy. POI took the position that Cope's trip to Montana was a personal trip for recreation purposes and that it therefore was not a trip "with respect to the conduct of [Cope's] business." Cope maintained that even if the trip was largely recreational, it was at least incidental to his business because Urbanski, who also was on the trip, was a business associate of Cope's. POI moved for summary judgment. Was POI entitled to summary judgment?

4. In a class action suit against Aamco Transmissions, Inc., consumers Joseph R. Tracy and Joseph P. Tracy claimed that Aamco and its network of franchisees used deceptive advertising that inaccurately described Aamco's services and lured many consumer purchasers of transmission services into paying excessively and for unnecessary repairs. The Tracys asserted that Aamco was liable under the Pennsylvania Unfair Trade Practices and Consumer Protection Law. Aamco was the insured under a comprehensive general liability insurance policy issued by Granite State Insurance Co. This policy provided liability coverage to Aamco "for personal injury or advertising injury . . . arising out of the conduct of" Aamco's business. The policy defined *advertising injury* as "injury arising . . . in the course of [Aamco's] advertising activities, if such injury arises out of libel, slander, defamation, violation of right of privacy, piracy, unfair competition, or infringement of copyright, title or slogan."

Contending that it had coverage under the "unfair competition" category of the advertising injury coverage, Aamco demanded that Granite defend and indemnify it in connection with the consumer class action case described above. When Granite declined to do so, Aamco settled the case on its own. Granite then brought a declaratory judgment action against Aamco in federal district court. Granite sought a ruling that it was not obligated to provide coverage for Aamco in the class action case brought by the Tracys. A federal district court concluded that the *unfair competition* term in the policy contemplated coverage only for common law–based claims against Aamco, not for any claims based on a state or federal statute. Because the Tracys' class action case was based on a supposed violation of a Pennsylvania statute, the district court held that Granite's policy did not furnish coverage to Aamco. In addition, the court held that the term *unfair competition* was not ambiguous and that Aamco could not have had a reasonable expectation that consumers' claims against it would be covered. Aamco appealed. Did Aamco win its appeal?

5. Sims and Dorothy Good purchased a property insurance policy on their home from Continental Insurance Co. Fire was among the covered perils. The policy contained an "increase of hazard" clause stating that Continental would not be obligated under the policy if the risk of fire was increased "by any means within the control or knowledge of the insured." After the policy took effect, a fire destroyed much of the Goods' home. While putting out the fire, firefighters discovered an illegal liquor still concealed in a false closet under the eaves of the roof. The still, encased by bricks and mortar, consisted of a 90-gallon copper vat over a butane gas burner. Firefighters also discovered 22 half-gallons of "moonshine" and many 55-gallon drums full or partially full of mash. A police detective who dismantled and examined the still's burner after the fire concluded that the still was in operation when the fire occurred. The Goods denied this, though Sims Good admitted having installed the still two years earlier, after the Continental insurance policy became effective. Continental refused to pay the Goods' claim, so the Goods sued Continental to recover proceeds under the policy. After the trial court awarded damages to the Goods, Continental appealed. Were the Goods entitled to recover damages from Continental?

6. The Plummers owned a commercial building in which they operated two businesses. The building and its contents were insured by Indiana Insurance Company (IIC). After an explosion and fire destroyed the building, the Plummers filed a claim and proof of loss with IIC. After an investigation, IIC denied the claim due to its conclusion that the Plummers had intentionally set the fire. IIC then filed a declaratory judgment action in which it asked for a determination that it had no obligation to cover losses stemming from the fire. The Plummers counterclaimed, seeking damages for breach of contract as well as punitive damages. The jury returned a verdict in favor of the Plummers on all issues. The jury awarded the Plummers approximately $700,000 in compensatory damages (an amount that exceeded the policy limits set forth in the insurance policy at issue), plus $3.5 million in punitive damages. The $700,000 compensatory damages award included not only the value of the destroyed building and its contents (what would have been due under the policy) but also $200,000 in consequential damages allegedly incurred by the Plummers as a

result of IIC's lengthy investigation of the fire and ultimate denial of the Plummers' claim. For the most part, the consequential damages represented interest costs and similar expenses incurred by the Plummers—costs and expenses they would not have incurred if IIC had paid their claim. Although the evidence IIC adduced at trial included experts' testimony that the fire had been intentionally set, the jury rejected that testimony and accepted the Plummers' contrary evidence. IIC appealed, arguing that its denial of the Plummers' claim was in good faith, that it therefore should have no liability for consequential damages and punitive damages, and that the damages awarded for breach of an insurance contract cannot exceed the policy limits set forth in the contract. Was IIC correct in these arguments?

7. In August 1982, a hog confinement building owned by Charles Ridenour collapsed and was rendered a total loss. Some of Ridenour's hogs were killed as a further result of the collapse. Ridenour made a claim for these losses with his property insurer, Farm Bureau Insurance Company, whose Country Squire policy had been issued on Ridenour's property in July 1977 and had been renewed on a yearly basis after that. Farm Bureau denied the claim because the policy did not provide coverage for the collapse of farm buildings such as the hog confinement structure. Moreover, though the policy provided coverage for hog deaths resulting from certain designated causes, collapse of a building was not among the causes listed. Asserting that the parties' insurance contract was to have covered the peril of building collapse notwithstanding the terms of the written policy, Ridenour sued Farm Bureau. He asked the court to order reformation of the written policy so that it would conform to the parties' supposed agreement regarding coverage. At trial, Ridenour testified about a February 1982 meeting in which he, his wife, and their son discussed insurance coverage with Farm Bureau agent Tim Moomey. Ridenour testified that he wanted to be certain there was insurance coverage if the hog confinement building collapsed because he had heard about the collapse of a similar structure owned by someone else. Therefore, he asked Moomey whether the Country Squire policy then in force provided such coverage. According to Ridenour, Moomey said that it did. Ridenour's wife, Thelma, testified that she asked Moomey (during the same meeting) whether there would be coverage if the floor slats of the hog confinement building collapsed and caused hogs to

fall into the pit below the building. According to her testimony, Moomey responded affirmatively. The Ridenours' son, Tom, testified to the same effect. Mr. and Mrs. Ridenour both testified that they had not completely read the Country Squire policy and that because they did not understand the wording, they relied on Moomey to interpret the policy for them.

Moomey, who had ended his relationship with Farm Bureau by the time the case came to trial, testified that at no time did the Ridenours request that the hogs and the confinement building be insured so as to provide coverage for losses resulting from collapse of the building. Moomey knew that collapse coverage was not available from Farm Bureau for hog confinement buildings. In addition, Moomey testified that he met with Ridenour in April 1982 and conducted a "farm review" in which he discussed a coverage checklist and the Country Squire policy's declarations pages (which set forth the policy limits). This checklist, which Ridenour signed after Moomey reviewed it with him, made no reference to coverage for collapse losses. (Ridenour admitted in his testimony that he had signed the checklist after Moomey read off the listed items to him.) When Moomey was contacted by the Ridenours on the day the building collapsed, he had his secretary prepare a notice of loss report for submission to Farm Bureau. He also assigned an adjuster to inspect the property. Moomey and the adjuster discussed the fact that the Country Squire policy did not provide coverage for Ridenour's losses. Ridenour further testified that the day after the collapse occurred, Moomey told him he was sorry but that Farm Bureau's home office had said there was no coverage.

The trial court granted reformation, as Ridenour had requested. Farm Bureau appealed. Was the trial court's decision correct?

8. Robert Baer and Dareen Dahlstrom had been close friends for more than 20 years. Dahlstrom, who was in the process of separating from her husband, went to visit Baer in July 1988. On various occasions, Baer had used a recreational drug known as Ecstasy. For several years after its discovery, Ecstasy was not an illegal drug. It was, however, designated by federal law as a prohibited controlled substance beginning in March 1988. Baer believed that the use of Ecstasy had certain psychological and emotional benefits, and that using it might help Dahlstrom cope with the personal problems she was experiencing at the time of her July 1988 visit. After she and Baer discussed his

beliefs regarding Ecstasy, Dahlstrom told him that she wanted to use the drug. Baer and Dahlstrom went through various rituals in preparation for use of the drug and recited a prayer that "this [may] bring harm to no one and blessing to all." Baer then removed some Ecstasy from his personal supply, which he had purchased prior to March 1988. Baer dissolved approximately one-half of his usual dose in a glass of water and gave it to Dahlstrom. She drank the mixture. Within approximately 30 minutes, she was dead. Dahlstrom's survivors filed a wrongful death suit against Baer, who asserted that the claim fell within the liability coverage provided to him by State Farm Insurance Company as part of his homeowner's policy. The policy afforded coverage for third parties' claims for physical injury resulting from an "occurrence," which was defined in terms of an "accident" that caused injury. The policy also contained an exclusion from coverage for injury that was either intended or expected by the insured. State Farm filed a declaratory judgment action in which it asked for a judicial determination that in light of the above provisions in the parties' insurance contract as well as public policy considerations, it owed Baer no coverage duties regarding the suit that stemmed from Dahlstrom's death. Was State Farm entitled to the relief it sought?

9. Jeffrey Lane was employed by Memtek, Inc., at its Arby's Restaurant. He was being trained as a cook. After 11:00 one evening, Lane finished work and clocked out. He remained in the restaurant's lobby, however, because he was waiting for the manager to complete her duties. As Lane waited, friends of other restaurant employees came to a door of the restaurant. Lane and the other employees became involved in a conversation with these persons, who included John Taylor. Lane told Taylor that he could not enter the restaurant because it was closed. Taylor did not attempt to force his way into the restaurant. Instead, he "dared" Lane to come outside. Lane left the restaurant "of [his] own will" (according to Lane's deposition) for what he assumed would be a fight with Taylor. In the fight that transpired, Lane broke Taylor's nose and knocked out three of his teeth. Lane later pleaded guilty to a criminal battery charge. Taylor filed a civil suit against Lane and Memtek in an effort to collect damages stemming from the altercation with Lane. American Family Mutual Insurance Company provided liability insurance for Memtek in connection with its restaurant. The policy stated that for purposes

of American Family's duties to defend and indemnify, "the insured" included not only Memtek but also Memtek's "employees, . . . but only for acts within the scope of their employment." American Family filed a declaratory judgment action in which it asked the court to determine that it owed Lane neither a duty to defend nor a duty to indemnify in connection with the incident giving rise to Taylor's lawsuit. American Family's theory was that for purposes of that incident, Lane was not an insured within the above-quoted policy provision. Was American Family correct?

10. Earl and Vonette Crowell owned a farm in Minnesota. In 1980, they mortgaged the farm to Farm Credit Services and purchased a property insurance policy on the farm (including the farmhouse) from Delafield Farmers Mutual Insurance Co. Fire was among the perils covered by this policy, which ran from October 1985 to October 1988. When the Crowells fell behind on their mortgage payments, Farm Credit began foreclosure proceedings. Upon foreclosure, mortgagors such as the Crowells have a right of redemption for a specified time. The right of redemption allows the defaulting mortgagors to buy back their property after it has been sold to someone else in the foreclosure proceedings. In November 1987, the Crowells' right of redemption expired. Minnesota law provides, however, that farmers who lose their farms to corporate lenders are given an additional opportunity to repurchase their farms under a "right of first refusal." This right meant that Farm Credit was forbidden to sell the farm to anyone else before offering it to the Crowells at a price no higher than the highest price offered by a third party. Farm Credit allowed the Crowells to remain on the farm while they attempted to secure financing to buy the property under their right of first refusal. In November 1987, a fire substantially damaged the farmhouse. The Crowells filed a claim for the loss with Delafield. Although Delafield paid the claim concerning the Crowells' personal effects that were located inside the farmhouse and were destroyed in the fire, it denied the claim on the farmhouse itself. Delafield took the position that because the time period for the Crowells' right of redemption had expired, they no longer had an insurable interest in the farmhouse. The Crowells therefore sued Delafield. Concluding that the Crowells had an insurable interest in the farmhouse, the trial court granted summary judgment in their favor. Was the trial court correct?

Online Research

State Regulation of Insurance

Most insurance regulation is done by the individual states. Typically, a state agency named the "Department of Insurance" (or something similar) will have significant supervisory and regulatory powers with regard to insurance companies, their business practices, and the policies they issue.

Locate the Web site of the insurance department of a state of your choice. After reviewing information and material available on that Web site, prepare a brief report summarizing the insurance department's role in addressing complaints from consumers regarding insurance company practices.

Part Six

Credit

chapter 28
Introduction to Credit and
Secured Transactions

chapter 29
Security Interests in
Personal Property

chapter 30
Bankruptcy

INTRODUCTION TO CREDIT AND SECURED TRANSACTIONS

E ric Richards decided to go into the commercial laundry and dry-cleaning business. He began by agreeing to buy the land, building, and equipment of a small dry cleaner. Richards agreed to pay the owner $200,000 in cash and "to assume" a $50,000 existing mortgage on the property. He next entered into a contract with a local contractor to build, within five months, a large addition to the building for $150,000 with $40,000 payable with the signing of the contract and the balance to be paid in periodic installments as the construction progressed. Because Richards had heard some horror stories from friends in the local Chamber of Commerce about contractors who walked away from jobs without completing them, he asked the contractor to post a security bond or provide a surety to ensure the contract would be completed in a timely manner. Richards also had some of the existing dry-cleaning equipment picked up for repair and refurbishment. When the work was completed, the repairman refused to redeliver it until Richards paid in full for the work, claiming he had a lien on the equipment until he was paid.

Among the questions that will be addressed in this chapter are:

- What legal rights and obligations accompany the "assumption" of a mortgage?
- Would Richards risk losing any of his rights to recover against the surety if he granted the contractor additional time to complete the construction?
- If the contractor does not pay subcontractors or companies who provide construction material for the job, would they be able to assert a lien against the property until they are paid?
- Would the person who repaired and refurbished the dry-cleaning equipment be able to asset a lien until Richards paid for it? Would it make a difference if the repair work had been done on-site?
- Whether it would be ethical for a person who has sold a parcel of real property on a land contract to declare a default of the contract when there is a minor default in making the payments called for in the contract and to reclaim possession of the property with the purchaser losing all the equity he might have built up in the property?

IN THE UNITED STATES, a substantial portion of business transactions involves the extension of credit. The term *credit* has many meanings. In this chapter, it will be used to mean transactions in which goods are sold, services are rendered, or money is loaned in exchange for a promise to repay the debt at some future date.

In some of these transactions, a creditor is willing to rely on the debtor's promise to pay at a later time; in others, the creditor wants some further assurance or security that the debtor will make good on his promise to pay. This chapter will discuss the differences between secured and unsecured credit and will detail various mechanisms that are available to the creditor who wants to obtain security. These mechanisms include obtaining liens or security interests in personal or real property, sureties, and guarantors. Security interests in real property, sureties and guarantors, and common law liens on personal property will be covered in this chapter, and the Uniform Commercial Code (UCC or Code) rules concerning security interests in personal property will be covered in Chapter 29, Security

Interests in Personal Property. The last chapter in Part 6 deals with bankruptcy law, which may come into play when a debtor is unable to fulfill his obligation to pay his debts when they are due.

Credit

Unsecured Credit

Many common transactions are based on unsecured credit. For example, a person may have a charge account at a department store or a Master-Card account. If the person buys a sweater and charges it to his charge account or MasterCard account, unsecured credit has been extended to him. He has received goods in return for his promise to pay for them later. Similarly, if a person goes to a dentist to have a tooth filled and the dentist sends her a bill payable by the end of the month, services have been rendered on the basis of unsecured credit. Consumers are not the only people who use unsecured credit. Many transactions between businesspeople utilize it. For example, a retailer buys merchandise or a manufacturer buys raw materials, promising to pay for the merchandise or materials within 30 days after receipt.

The unsecured credit transaction involves a maximum of risk to the creditor—the person who extends the credit. When goods are delivered, services are rendered, or money is loaned on unsecured credit, the creditor gives up all rights in the goods, services, or money. In return, the creditor gets a promise by the debtor to pay or to perform the promised act. If the debtor does not pay or keep the promise, the creditor's options are more limited than if he had obtained security to ensure the debtor's performance. One course of action is to bring a lawsuit against the debtor and obtain a judgment. The creditor might then have the sheriff execute the judgment on any property owned by the debtor that is subject to execution. The creditor might also try to **garnish** the wages or other moneys to which the debtor is entitled. However, the debtor might be **judgment-proof;** that is, the debtor may not have any property subject to execution or may not have a steady job. Under these circumstances, execution or garnishment would be of little aid to the creditor in collecting the judgment.

A businessperson may obtain credit insurance to stabilize the credit risk of doing business on an unsecured credit basis. However, he passes the costs of the insurance to the business, or of the unsecured credit losses that the business sustains, on to the consumer. The consumer pays a higher price for goods or services purchased, or a higher interest rate on any money borrowed, from a business that has high credit losses.

Secured Credit

To minimize his credit risk, a creditor may contract for security. The creditor may require the debtor to convey to the creditor a security interest or lien on the debtor's property. Suppose a person borrows $3,000 from a credit union. The credit union might require her to put up her car as security for the loan or might ask that some other person agree to be liable if she defaults. For example, if a student who does not have a regular job goes to a bank to borrow money, the bank might ask that the student's father or mother cosign the note for the loan.

When the creditor has security for the credit he extends and the debtor defaults, the creditor can go against the security to collect the obligation. Assume that a person borrows $18,000 from a bank to buy a new car and that the bank takes a security interest (lien) on the car. If the person fails to make his monthly payments, the bank has the right to repossess the car and have it sold so that it can recover its money. Similarly, if the borrower's father cosigned for the car loan and the borrower defaults, the bank can sue the father to collect the balance due on the loan.

Development of Security

Various types of security devices have been developed as social and economic need for them has arisen. The rights and liabilities of the parties to a secured transaction depend on the nature of the security—that is, on whether (1) the security pledged is the promise of another person to pay if the debtor does not, or (2) a security interest in goods, intangibles, or real estate is conveyed as security for the payment of a debt or obligation.

If personal credit is pledged, the other person may guarantee the payment of the debt—that is, become a guarantor—or the other person may join the debtor in the debtor's promise to pay, in which case the other person would become surety for the debt.

The oldest and simplest security device was the pledge. To have a pledge valid against third persons with an interest in the goods, such as subsequent purchasers or creditors, it was necessary that the property used as security be delivered to the pledgee or a pledge holder. Upon default by the pledger, the pledgee had the right to sell the property and apply the proceeds to the payment of the debt.

Situations arose in which it was desirable to leave the property used as security in the possession of the debtor. To accomplish this objective, the debtor would give the creditor a bill of sale to the property, thus passing title to the creditor. The bill of sale would provide that if the debtor performed his promise, the bill of sale would become null and void, thus revesting title to the property in the debtor. A secret lien on the goods was created by this device, and the early courts held that such a transaction was a fraud on third-party claimants and void as to them. An undisclosed or secret lien is unfair to creditors who might extend credit to the debtor on the strength of property that they see in the debtor's possession but that in fact is subject to the prior claim of another creditor. Statutes were enacted providing for the recording or filing of the bill of sale, which was later designated as a chattel mortgage. These statutes were not uniform in their provisions. Most of them set up formal requirements for the execution of the chattel mortgage and also stated the effect of recording or filing on the rights of third-party claimants.

To avoid the requirements for the execution and filing of the chattel mortgage, sellers of goods would sell the goods on a "conditional sales contract" under which the seller retained title to the goods until their purchase price had been paid in full. Upon default by the buyer, the seller could (a) repossess the goods or (b) pass title and recover a judgment for the unpaid balance of the purchase price. Abuses of this security device gave rise to some regulatory statutes. About one-half of the states enacted statutes providing that the conditional sales contract was void as to third parties unless it was filed or recorded.

No satisfactory device was developed whereby inventory could be used as security. The inherent difficulty is that inventory is intended to be sold and turned into cash and the creditor is interested in protecting his interest in the cash rather than in maintaining a lien on the sold goods. Field warehousing was used under the pledge, and an after-acquired property clause in a chattel mortgage on a stock of goods held for resale partially fulfilled this need. One of the devices used was the trust receipt. This short-term marketing security arrangement had its origin in the export–import trade. It was later used extensively as a means of financing retailers of consumer goods having a high unit value.

Security Interests in Personal Property

Chapter 29, Security Interests in Personal Property, will discuss how a creditor can obtain a security interest in the personal property or fixtures of a debtor. It will also explain the rights to the debtor's property of the creditor, the debtor, and other creditors of the debtor. These security interests are covered by Article 9 of the Uniform Commercial Code, which sets out a comprehensive scheme for regulating security interests in personal property and fixtures. The Code abolishes the old formal distinctions between different types of security devices used to create security interests in personal property.

Security Interests in Real Property Three types of contractual security devices have been developed by which real estate may be used as security: (1) the real estate mortgage, (2) the trust deed, and (3) the land contract. In addition to these contract security devices, all of the states have enacted statutes granting the right to mechanic's liens on real estate. Security interests in real property are covered later in this chapter.

Suretyship and Guaranty

Sureties and Guarantors

As a condition of making a loan, granting credit, or employing someone (particularly as a fiduciary), a creditor may demand that the debtor, contractor, or employee provide as security for his performance the liability of a third person as surety or guarantor. The purpose of the contract of suretyship or guaranty is to provide the creditor with additional protection against loss in the event of default by the debtor, contractor, or employee.

A **surety** is a person who is *liable for the payment of another person's debt or for the performance of another person's duty.* The surety joins with the person primarily liable in promising to make the payment or to perform the duty. For example, Kathleen Kelly, who is 17 years old, buys a used car on credit from Harry's Used Cars. She signs a promissory note, agreeing to pay $200 a month on the note until the note is paid in full. Harry's has Kathleen's father cosign the note; thus, her father is a surety. Similarly, the city of Chicago hires the B&B Construction Company to build a new sewage treatment plant. The city will probably require B&B to have a surety agree to be liable for B&B's performance of its contract. There are insurance companies that, for a fee, will agree to be a surety on the contract of a company such as B&B.

The surety is *primarily liable* for the debtor's obligation, and the debtor can demand performance from the surety at the time the debt is due. The creditor does not need to establish a default by the debtor or proceed first against the debtor on his obligation.

A guaranty contract is similar to a suretyship contract in that the promisor agrees to answer for the obligation of another. However, a guarantor does not join the principal in making a promise; rather, a guarantor makes a separate promise and agrees to be liable upon the happening of a certain event. For example, a father tells a merchant, "I will guarantee payment of my daughter Rachel's debt to you if she does not pay it," or "If Rachel becomes bankrupt, I will guarantee payment of her debt to you." While a surety is *primarily liable,* a guarantor is *secondarily liable* and can be held to his guarantee only after the principal defaults and cannot be held to his promise or payment. Generally, a guarantor's promise must be made in writing to be enforceable under the statute of frauds.

The rights and liabilities of the surety and the guarantor are substantially the same. No distinction will be made between them in this chapter except where the distinction is of basic importance. Moreover, most commercial contracts and promissory notes today that are to be signed by multiple parties provide for the parties to be "jointly and severally" liable, thus making the surety relationship the predominate one.

Creation of Principal and Surety Relation

The relationship of principal and surety, or that of principal and guarantor, is created by contract. The basic rules of contract law apply in determining the existence and nature of the relationship as well as the rights and duties of the parties.

Defenses of a Surety

Suppose Jeffrey's mother agrees to be a surety for Jeffrey on his purchase of a motorcycle. If the motorcycle was defectively made and Jeffrey refuses to make further payments on it, the dealer might try to collect the balance due from Jeffrey's mother. As a surety, Jeffrey's mother can use any defenses against the dealer that Jeffrey has if they go to the merits of the primary contract. Thus, if Jeffrey has a valid defense of breach of warranty against the dealer, his mother can use it as a basis for not paying the dealer.

Other defenses that go to the merits include (1) lack or failure of consideration, (2) inducement of the contract by fraud or duress, and (3) breach of contract by the other party. Certain defenses of the principal cannot be used by the surety. These defenses include lack of capacity, such as minority or insanity, and bankruptcy. Thus, if Jeffrey is only 17 years old, the fact that he is a minor cannot be used by Jeffrey's mother to defend against the dealer. This defense of Jeffrey's lack of capacity to contract does not go to the merits of the contract between Jeffrey and the dealer and cannot be used by Jeffrey's mother.

A surety contracts to be responsible for the performance of the principal's obligation. If the principal and the creditor change that obligation by agreement, the surety is relieved of responsibility unless the surety agrees to the change. This is because the surety's obligation cannot be changed without his consent.

For example, Fredericks cosigns a note for his friend Kato, which she has given to Credit Union to secure a loan. Suppose the note was originally for $2,500 and payable in 12 months with interest at 11 percent a year. Credit Union and Kato later agree that Kato will have 24 months to repay the note but that the interest will be 13 percent per year. Unless Fredericks consents to this change, he is discharged from his responsibility as surety. The obligation he agreed to assume was altered by the changes in the repayment period and the interest rate.

The most common kind of change affecting a surety is an extension of time to perform the contract. If the creditor merely allows the principal more time without the surety's consent, this does not relieve the surety of responsibility. The surety's consent is required only where there is an actual binding agreement between the creditor and the principal as to the extension of time.

In addition, the courts usually make a distinction between **accommodation sureties** and **compensated sureties.** An accommodation surety is a person who acts as a surety without compensation, such as a friend who cosigns a note as a favor. A compensated surety is a person, usually a professional such as a bonding company, who is paid for serving as a surety.

The courts are more protective of accommodation sureties than of compensated sureties. Accommodation sureties are relieved of liability unless they consent to an extension of time. Compensated sureties, on the other hand, must show that they will be harmed by an extension of time before they are relieved of responsibility because of a binding extension without their consent. A compensated surety must show that a change in the contract was both material and prejudicial to him if he is to be relieved of his obligation as surety.

Creditor's Duties to Surety

The creditor is required to disclose any material facts about the risk involved to the surety. If he does not do so, the surety is relieved of liability. For example, a bank (creditor) knows that an employee, Arthur, has been guilty of criminal conduct in the past. If the bank applies to a bonding company to obtain a bond on Arthur, the bank must disclose this information about Arthur. Similarly, suppose the bank has an employee, Alison, covered by a bond and discovers that Alison is embezzling money. If the bank agrees to give Alison another chance but does not report her actions to the bonding company, the bonding company is relieved of responsibility for further wrongful acts by Alison.

If the debtor posts security for the performance of an obligation, the creditor must not surrender the security without the consent of the surety. If the creditor does so, the surety is relieved of liability to the extent of the value surrendered.

In the following *New Jersey Economic Development Authority* case, the court rejected a claim by sureties that the creditors had violated their duty to the sureties.

New Jersey Economic Development Authority v. Pavonia Restaurant, Inc.
725 A.2d 1133 (N.J. Super. Ct., App. Div. 1998)

In June 1992, the New Jersey Economic Development Authority (EDA) and the Banque Nationale de Paris loaned $1,470,000 to Pavonia Restaurant, Inc. Pavonia was established to open and operate a new restaurant known as "Hudson's," to be located in a newly constructed eight-story office building in downtown Jersey City. Repayment of the loan was individually guaranteed by a number of individuals who were mostly professional and local businesspeople and, with one exception, were also stockholders in Pavonia.

To acquire the funds necessary to make the loan, the EDA issued and sold Economic Growth Bonds to investors. In order to encourage investment in the bonds, at the request of Pavonia and the guarantors, the bank issued an irrevocable letter of credit pursuant to which it agreed to repay the bondholders in the event Pavonia defaulted.

On June 1, 1992, Pavonia executed a loan agreement, a promissory note, financing statements, and a security agreement pledging its leasehold improvements and restaurant equipment as security for repayment of the loan (the loan documents). On the same date, the guarantors executed a Personal Guaranty Agreement under which they each agreed individually to guarantee repayment of the loan to EDA and the Bank.

Because of a four-month delay in the opening of the restaurant, insufficient advertising, a high-priced menu, staffing problems, and the shareholders' failure to make the necessary capital contributions, Pavonia ran into financial difficulty and the loan went into default. Consequently, as of August 19, 1994, the arrearages due from Pavonia to the EDA equaled $24,207.71, and EDA and the Bank sought payment from the guarantors in accordance with their guarantees.

Thereafter, Pavonia and the guarantors requested EDA and the Bank to forebear enforcement of their rights under the loan agreement and guarantees. EDA and the Bank agreed, and, on October 17, 1994, the parties entered into a "Loan Forbearance Agreement." The agreement essentially provided that EDA and the Bank would not accelerate the loan balance for a period of time if Pavonia and the guarantors paid the delinquent amounts due and advanced monthly payments through December 1, 1994, totaling $312,970.19. In the agreement Pavonia and the guarantors acknowledged that Pavonia had defaulted on the loan, that they had not cured the default, and that they had no defenses to EDA's and the Bank's claims under the loan documents or individual guarantees.

On February 1, 1995, Pavonia again defaulted, and EDA and the Bank accelerated the loan balance. In a letter dated June 22, 1995, their counsel made a demand upon the guarantors for full payment of the loan or possession of the assets Pavonia had pledged as collateral. When the guarantors failed to respond, on July 2, 1995, EDA and the Bank filed suit against Pavonia and the guarantors seeking possession of the pledged assets and judgment in the amount of the loan balance, interest, counsel fees, and costs.

EDA and the Bank moved for summary judgment. The guarantors opposed the motion and asserted defenses grounded in fraud, bad faith, and allegations that EDA and the Bank had failed to disclose material facts at the inception of the loan that materially increased their risk under the guarantees rendering them unenforceable. Specifically, guarantors alleged that from the inception of the loan, EDA and the Bank knew and failed to disclose (1) that Pavonia's assets were insufficient to secure the loan and (2) that EDA and the Bank were relying principally, if not exclusively, upon the guarantees as the source of repayment of the loan.

Eichen, Judge

The guarantors claim that EDA and the Bank placed sole reliance on their individual guarantees for repayment of the loan. The record does not support that assertion. Rather, it reflects that both EDA and the Bank and the guarantors anticipated that the revenues from the restaurant would support repayment of the loan. The information concerning the anticipated revenues, was, in fact, derived form Pavonia's accountant, Sobel & Company. Although the guarantors maintain that the loan review document concluded that "no reliance could be placed on the 'collateral or cash flow generating ability of the restaurant,'" the record clearly belies this assertion. The record discloses that

EDA and the Bank believed, based on the projections made by Pavonia's accountant, that the restaurant would generate sufficient cash flow to repay the loan. As Lloyd Cox, vice president of the Bank, indicated, the Bank never would have included the loan to Pavonia in the composite bond issue if it did not believe that Pavonia would be successful. Despite the guarantors' attempts to make it appear as though plaintiffs knew Pavonia would be unable to repay the loan and therefore insisted on the guarantees, nothing in the record supports this proposition. The guarantors have not pointed to any evidence that even suggests EDA and the Bank had information about Pavonia's ability to repay the loan which the guarantors did not have. Indeed, everyone understood that opening a restaurant in a new location was inherently risky business. EDA and the Bank hoped that the restaurant's success would comport with the financial projections of Pavonia's accountant just as the guarantors did. The obvious fact is that the external factors impeded Pavonia's success, factors which were completely unrelated to EDA and the Bank's evaluation of the loan agreements. Although Pavonia was unsuccessful in establishing a viable restaurant business, its successor, Laico's of Journal Square, has been successful.

In sum, the guarantors have utterly failed to demonstrate what facts EDA and the Bank had, but guarantors lacked, that materially increased the risk beyond that which EDA and the Bank knew the guarantors intended to assume.

Impliedly recognizing that they could not prove their case under these theories the guarantors argue that their claims are viable under the principles of law contained in the *Restatement of Security: Suretyship* section 124 (1941) (the *Restatement*). That section provides in relevant part:

> Where before [a] surety has undertaken his obligation the creditor knows facts unknown to the surety that materially increase the risk beyond that which the creditor has reason to believe the surety intends to assume, and the creditor also has reason to believe that these facts are unknown to the surety and has a reasonable opportunity to communicate them to the surety, failure of the creditor to notify the surety of such facts is a defense to the surety.

The guarantors argue that EDA and the Bank violated these principles of law by failing to disclose facts to them that materially increased their risk under the guarantees, specifically, that unbeknownst to the Guarantors, EDA and the Bank were relying on their guarantees as the primary security for repayment of the loan and failed to disclose this fact to them. They maintain they would not have undertaken the risk if they had known the guarantees were the principal security for the loan.

Section 124 prescribed three conditions precedent to imposing a duty on a creditor to disclose facts it knows about the debtor to the surety: (1) the creditor must have reason to believe that those facts materially increase the risk beyond that which the surety intends to assume; (2) the creditor must have reason to believe that the facts are unknown to the surety; and (3) the creditor must have a reasonable opportunity to notify the surety of such facts.

However, the comments to section 124 of the *Restatement* explain that:

> [this rule] does not place any burden on the creditor to investigate for the surety's benefit. It does not require the creditor to take any unusual steps to assure himself that the surety is acquainted with facts which he may assume are known to both of them.
>
> . . .
>
> Every surety by the nature of his obligation undertakes risks which are the inevitable concomitants of the transactions involved. Circumstances of the transactions vary the risks which will be regarded as normal and comtemplated by the surety.

For the reasons previously stated in our rejection of the guarantors' claims of fraud and bad faith, we are satisfied that the guarantors failed to raise any factual issue applying the principles derived from the *Restatement*. Suffice it to say, EDA and the Bank were not in possession of any facts that the guarantors were not aware of; both parties hoped the restaurant would generate sufficient cash flow to repay the loan. Regrettably, it did not.

Judgment affirmed for EDA and the Bank.

Subrogation, Reimbursement, and Contribution

If the surety has to perform or pay the principal's obligation, then the surety acquires all of the rights that the creditor had against the principal. This is known as the surety's **right of subrogation.** The rights acquired could include the right to any collateral in the possession of the creditor, any judgment right the creditor had against the principal on the obligation, and the rights of a creditor in bankruptcy proceedings.

If the surety performs or pays the principal's obligation, she is entitled to recover her costs from the principal; this is known as the surety's **right to reimbursement.** For example, Amado cosigns a promissory note for $2,500 at the credit union for her friend Anders. Anders defaults on the note, and the credit union collects $2,500 from Amado on her suretyship obligation. Amado then not only gets the credit union's rights against Anders under the right of subrogation, but also the right to collect $2,500 from Anders under the right of reimbursement.

Suppose several persons (Tom, Dick, and Harry) are cosureties of their friend Sam. When Sam defaults, Tom pays the whole obligation. Tom is entitled to collect one-third from both Dick and Harry since he paid more than his prorated share. This is known as the cosurety's **right to contribution.** The relative shares of cosureties, as well as any limitations on their liability, are normally set out in the contract of suretyship.

A surety also has what is known as **a right of exoneration,** which is the right of the surety or guarantor to require the debtor to make good on his commitment to the creditor when he (1) is able to do so and (2) does not have a valid defense against payment. The right is exercised when the creditor is pursuing the surety or guarantor to make good on their liability. The surety or guarantor then sues the debtor to force him to pay the creditor, automatically staying the creditor's action against the surety or guarantor. The surety or guarantor uses this right to prevent its having to pay the creditor (which may require liquidation of some of the surety's or guarantor's assets) and then having to sue the debtor under the right of subrogation or reimbursement.

Liens on Personal Property

Common Law Liens Under the common—or judge-made—law, artisans, innkeepers, and common carriers (such as airlines and trucking companies) were entitled to liens to secure the reasonable value of the services they performed. An artisan such as a furniture upholsterer or an auto mechanic uses his labor or materials to improve personal property that belongs to someone else. The improvement becomes part of the property and belongs to the owner of the property. Therefore, the artisan who made the improvement is given a **lien** on the property until he is paid.

For example, the upholsterer who recovers a sofa for a customer is entitled to a lien on the sofa. The innkeeper and common carrier are in business to serve the public and are required by law to do so. Under the common law, the innkeeper, to secure payment for his reasonable charges for food and lodging, was allowed to claim a lien on the property that the guest brought to the hotel or inn. Similarly, the common carrier, such as a trucking company, was allowed to claim a lien on the goods carried for the reasonable charges for the service. The justification for such liens was that the innkeeper and common carrier were entitled to the protection of a lien because they were required by law to provide the service to anyone seeking it.

Statutory Liens While common law liens are still generally recognized today, many states have incorporated this concept into statutes. Some of the state statutes have created additional liens, while others have modified the common law liens to some extent. The statutes commonly provide a procedure for foreclosing the lien. **Foreclosure** is the method by which the rights of the property owner are cut off so that the lienholder can realize her security interest. Typically, the statutes provide for a court to authorize the sale of the personal property subject to the lien so that the creditor can obtain the money to which she is entitled.

Carriers' liens and warehousemen's liens are provided for in Article 7, Documents of Title, of the Uniform Commercial Code. They are covered in Chapter 23, Personal Property and Bailments.

Characteristics of Liens The common law lien and most of the statutory liens are known as **possessory liens.** They give the artisan or other lienholder the right to keep possession of the debtor's property until the reasonable charges for services have been paid. For the lien to come into play, possession of the goods must have been entrusted to the artisan. Suppose a person takes a chair to an upholsterer to have it repaired. The upholsterer can keep possession of the chair until the person pays the reasonable value of the repair work. However, if the upholsterer comes to the person's home to make the repair, the upholsterer would not have a lien on the chair as the person did not give up possession of it.

Ethics in Action

What Is the Ethical Thing to Do?

Suppose you own and operate a small loan business. A young man applies for a $1,000 loan. When you run a credit check on him, you find that he has had difficulty holding a job and has a terrible credit record. You conclude that he is a poor credit risk and inform him that you are willing to make the requested loan only if he can find someone who has a good credit rating to cosign a promissory note with him. The next day he comes by the office with a young woman who meets your criteria for a good credit rating and who indicates she is willing to cosign the note. Do you have any ethical obligation to share with the young woman the information you have about the young man's employment and credit history?

The two essential elements of the lien are (1) possession by the improver or the provider of services and (2) a debt created by the improvement or the provision of services concerning the goods. If the artisan or other lienholder gives up the goods voluntarily, he loses the lien. For example, if a person has a new engine put in his car and the mechanic gives the car back to him before he pays for the engine, the mechanic loses the lien on the car to secure the person's payment for the work and materials. However, if the person uses a spare set of keys to regain possession, or does so by fraud or another illegal act, the lien is not lost. Once the debt has been paid, the lien is terminated and the artisan or other lienholder no longer has the right to retain the goods. If the artisan keeps the goods after the debt has been paid, or keeps the goods without the right to a lien, he is liable for conversion or unlawful detention of goods.

Another important aspect of common law liens is that the work or service must have been performed at the request of the owner of the property. If the work or service is performed without the consent of the owner, no lien is created.

In the case that follows, *In re Borden,* the court had to decide whether an artisan lost its priority claim to some farming equipment it had repaired when the owner of the equipment removed it from the artisan without permission and without paying for it.

In re Borden
361 B.R. 489 (U.S. Bankruptcy Appellate Panel for the Eighth Circuit 2007)

On June 25, 2002, Michael Borden and his wife granted the Genoa National Bank a blanket security interest on all of their personal property, including machinery and equipment then owned and thereafter acquired. The lender perfected its security interest by filing a UCC financing statement with the Nebraska Secretary of State on June 26, 2002. [These concepts are covered in the next chapter, Chapter 29, Security Interests in Personal Property.]

On separate occasions in late 2004, Borden took a cornhead and a tractor to Bellamy's, Inc., for repairs. Bellamy's performed the repairs and in February 2005 sent the Bordens a bill in the amount of $3,811.46 for the work performed on the cornhead and in March 2005 sent a bill in the amount of $1,281.34 for the work performed on the tractor. Borden did not have the money to pay for the repairs, and Bellamy's refused to release the tractor and cornhead to Borden without payment, so they remained in Bellamy's possession.

On April 1, Borden and his wife filed a voluntary petition for relief under Chapter 12 of the Bankruptcy Code. [Bankruptcy is discussed in Chapter 30 of this textbook.] On this date the tractor and cornhead were in Bellamy's possession. In June 2005, Borden took the tractor from Bellamy's lot without permission and used it in connection with his farming operation. Bellamy's discovered the tractor was missing and contacted Borden to inquire if he had it in his possession. Borden admitted he had taken the tractor, explained that he needed it for his farming operation, and agreed to return it to Bellamy's as soon as he was finished using it. The tractor broke down while he was using it, and he returned it to Bellamy's in the fall of 2005.

In September 2005, Borden took the cornhead from Bellamy's without permission. Bellamy's became aware that the cornhead was missing and contacted Borden. He admitted that he had taken the cornhead, explained that he needed it to harvest corn, and agreed to return it as soon as he completed harvesting the crop. Borden returned the cornhead to Bellamy's in November 2005.

In 2006, Genoa National Bank filed a motion with the bankruptcy court to determine the priority of the respective liens claimed by it and by Bellamy's. The bankruptcy court determined that no controlling authority existed in Nebraska concerning the situation of competing liens where an artisan loses possession of the personal property through action of the property owner. The bankruptcy court looked to other jurisdictions for guidance and found that other courts faced with the issue had reached conflicting results. The bankruptcy court decided that Genoa National Bank's lien had priority over the lien asserted by the artisan, Bellamy's. In reaching its decision, the bankruptcy court concluded that continuous possession is required to maintain an artisan's lien. Bellamy's appealed.

Schermer, Bankruptcy Judge

Nebraska law provides a lien to any person who repairs a vehicle, machinery, or a farm implement while in such person's possession for the reasonable or agreed charges for the work done or materials furnished on or to such vehicle, machinery, or farm implement and authorizes the artisan to retain possession of the property until the charges are paid. Such a lien is referred to as an artisan's lien. Nebraska law also recognizes a possessory lien as an interest, other than a security interest or an agricultural lien, which secures payment or performance of an obligation for services or materials furnished with respect to goods by a person in the ordinary course of such person's business which is created by statute or rule in favor of the person and whose effectiveness depends on the person's possession of the goods. An artisan's lien falls within this definition of possessory lien under Nebraska law. A possessory lien on goods, such as an artisan's lien, has priority over a security interest in the goods unless the possessory lien is created by a statute that expressly provides otherwise. The artisan's lien statute does not provide otherwise; accordingly, an artisan's lien has priority over a previously perfected security interest in the same goods.

In order to determine the respective rights of the Lender and the Artisan in the Equipment, we must determine if the Artisan has an artisan's lien in the Equipment under Nebraska law. If the Artisan does, its lien has priority over the Lender's security interest in the Equipment. In making this determination, we must answer the difficult question of whether the Artisan has a possessory lien where it involuntarily lost and later regained possession of the Equipment without court authority following the Debtor's bankruptcy filing. The statute is silent on this situation and no Nebraska court has addressed this situation other than the trial court below.

Courts from other jurisdictions have addressed various situations where artisans have lost possession of the personal property to which they provided services yet asserted a lien thereon either without possession or after regaining possession. Some general rules can be gleaned from the case law. First, possession is generally required for a possessory lien. If an artisan surrenders possession, the artisan no longer has a possessory lien with priority over pre-existing security interests. Some courts recognize a continuing lien as between the artisan and the owner after return of possession to the owner; however, such lien lacks priority over pre-existing security interests. Other courts relegate the lien to a state of suspended animation upon release of the goods to the owner; the artisan cannot enforce the lien while it is in a state of suspended animation. In this situation, if the artisan regains possession lawfully, the ability to enforce the artisan's lien is once again available to the artisan.

Where the artisan loses possession involuntarily, the artisan does not necessarily lose the artisan's lien. Likewise, a conditional release of goods does not necessarily defeat the artisan's lien. This result follows at least with respect to holders of prior security interests who are not impaired by the conditional release. Some courts hold that an artisan's lien lost when possession is lost is revived upon resumption of possession. Such a lien retains its priority as before the release except that the lien

is subordinate to the interests of a bona fide purchaser or a creditor who attached or levied on the property while it was in the possession of the owner.

We conclude that the Artisan did not lose its artisan's lien in the Equipment when the Debtor took the Equipment without the Artisan's knowledge or consent. Such involuntary loss of possession does not defeat the Artisan's lien. Furthermore, even if the Artisan's failure to take action to regain possession of the Equipment can be deemed consent to the Debtor's prior wrongful taking of the Equipment, such after-the-fact consent could not have been more than a conditional consent to the Debtor's temporary use of the Equipment with an agreement to return it to the Artisan. A conditional consent to a prior wrongful taking likewise does not defeat the Artisan's lien.

This result is consistent with the policy underlying the creation and priority of security interests. A lien or security interest must be perfected. The purpose of perfection is to give the world notice of the lien or security interest. Notice is generally accomplished in one of three ways: by registering the lien with an agency (usually a local government entity or a secretary of state's office), by noting the lien on the title, or by possession. Third parties can learn of any liens or security interests in any particular property by searching the records of the appropriate authority or by viewing the title. If no lien or security interest is disclosed, the third party may rely on the assumption that the property is owned free and clear of any liens if the property is in the owner's possession.

An artisan's lien does not require registration with any entity. Therefore, in order to give notice of the lien, the artisan is permitted to retain the property until receiving payment for the services provided to the property. Upon payment the lien is satisfied and the artisan releases the property. A third party interested in the property can easily learn that the property is not in the owner's possession and is then put on inquiry notice to determine why the owner does not have possession of the property. If the owner cannot produce the property, the third party has notice that another entity, including an artisan, may assert an interest in such property. A third party who continues to deal with the property owner after learning the owner lacks possession of the property does so at his or her peril.

With respect to competing holders of liens or security interests in the same property, notice of the various liens and security interests allows each interested party to know where he or she falls in the pecking order. With respect to recorded interests, the general rule is that first in time has priority. However, artisan's liens are not recorded and invariably are created after security interests have been granted. Courts and legislatures generally recognize that a party who provides labor and materials to property enhances the value of the property. Therefore, the principles of natural justice and commercial necessity dictate that the entity who enhances the value of property should be entitled to payment for such services and may retain the property until receipt of payment therefore. Indeed, the Nebraska statute at issue in this case provides exactly that. Artisan's lien laws are to be liberally construed to accomplish their equitable purpose of aiding materialmen and laborers to obtain compensation for materials used and services bestowed upon property of another which thereby enhances the value of such property.

A lender who advances funds to acquire certain property or who loans money secured by existing property does so on the basis of the property at the time of the loan. The lender generally assumes the owner will maintain the property after the loan is made and often mandates such maintenance in the loan documentation. If the property later breaks or is in need of maintenance, the owner takes the property to an artisan for repair or maintenance. Such repair or maintenance enhances the value of the property, thus enhancing the value of the lender's collateral. The lender thus benefits from the repair.

This was the case with the Equipment. The Lender took the security interest in the Equipment long before the Artisan performed the repairs to it. Immediately prior to the repairs, the Equipment was not working properly and therefore its value was diminished. By performing the repairs, the Artisan enhanced the value of the Equipment, thus benefitting the Lender by increasing the value of its collateral. Recognizing the superiority of the Artisan's lien over the Lender's security interest is consistent with the policy underlying artisan lien law.

The bankruptcy court was troubled by the lack of certainty where an artisan is permitted to retain a lien without maintaining possession of the property. By requiring continuous possession in order to maintain an artisan's lien, the court limited uncertainty. While certainty is a valid goal in statutory interpretation, it should not come at the expense of the

purpose behind the statute. Artisan's liens are designed to be equitable in nature and to protect the rights of artisans. If the artisan voluntarily surrenders possession, the artisan loses its lien. However, if the artisan loses possession through no action of his or her own, the artisan should not be punished. This is especially true where the Lender benefitted from the repairs to its collateral and its interests in the Equipment were in no way impaired when the Debtor took the Equipment from the Artisan nor when he later returned the Equipment to the Artisan.

Conclusion

The Artisan had an artisan's lien in the Equipment on the date the Debtor filed bankruptcy which had priority over the Lender's security interest under Nebraska law. The Artisan did not lose its artisan's lien nor its priority over the Lender's security interest when the Debtor took the Equipment from the Artisan's possession postpetition without authority. **Accordingly, under these circumstances we REVERSE the bankruptcy court's order determining that the Lender's security interest in the Equipment takes priority over the Artisan's lien therein.**

Kressel, Chief Judge, dissenting

The majority has done an admirable job of reviewing the split of authority on the issue presented here, none of which admittedly is binding, and picking the line of cases which it feels provides the fair result for this case. I concede that the result reached is appealing. I think that in reaching it, the majority has departed from well-established principles of interpretation and, as a result, has essentially engaged in the legislative process.

Since I think the Nebraska statute unequivocally provides for a first priority possessory lien only until possession is lost, I would hold that the bankruptcy court correctly held that Genoa National Bank's perfected security interest has priority over Bellamy's lien and would affirm.

Foreclosure of Lien The right of a lienholder to possess goods does not automatically give the lienholder the right to sell the goods or to claim ownership if his charges are not paid. Commonly, there is a procedure provided by statute for selling property once it has been held for a certain period of time. The lienholder is required to give notice to the debtor and to advertise the proposed sale by posting or publishing notices. If there is no statutory procedure, the lienholder must first bring a lawsuit against the debtor. After obtaining a judgment for

his charges, the lienholder can have the sheriff seize the property and have it sold at a judicial sale.

Security Interests in Real Property

There are three basic contract devices for using real estate as security for an obligation: (1) the real estate mortgage, (2) the deed of trust, and (3) the land contract. In addition, the states have enacted statutes giving mechanics, such as carpenters and plumbers, and materialmen, such as lumberyards, a right to a lien on real property into which their labor or materials have been incorporated.

Historical Developments of Mortgages

A **mortgage** is a security interest in real property or a deed to real property that is given by the owner (the **mortgagor**) as security for a debt owed to the creditor (the **mortgagee**). The real estate mortgage was used as a form of security in England as early as the middle of the 12th century, but our present-day mortgage law developed from the common law mortgage of the 15th century. The common law mortgage was a deed that conveyed the land to the mortgagee, with the title to the land to return to the mortgagor upon payment of the debt secured by the mortgage. The mortgagee was given possession of the land during the term of the mortgage. If the mortgagor defaulted on the debt, the mortgagee's title to the land became absolute. The land was forfeited as a penalty, but the forfeiture did not discharge the debt. In addition to keeping the land, the mortgagee could sue on the debt, recover a judgment, and seek to collect the debt.

The early equity courts did not favor the imposition of penalties and would relieve mortgagors from such forfeitures, provided that the mortgagor's default was minor and was due to causes beyond his control. Gradually, the courts became more lenient in permitting redemptions and allowed the mortgagor to **redeem** (reclaim his property) if he tendered performance without unreasonable delay. Finally, the courts of equity recognized the mortgagor's right to redeem as an absolute right that would continue until the mortgagee asked the court of equity to decree that the mortgagor's right to redeem be foreclosed and cut off. Our present law regarding the foreclosure of mortgages developed from this practice.

Today, the mortgage is generally viewed as a lien on land rather than a conveyance of title to the land. There are still some states where the mortgagor goes through the process of giving the mortgagee some sort of legal title to the property. Even in these states, however, the mortgagee's title is minimal and the real ownership of the property remains in the mortgagor.

Form, Execution, and Recording

Because the real estate mortgage conveys an interest in real property, it must be executed with the same formality as a deed. As a general rule, the mortgage must contain the name of the secured party, the legal description of the property, and the terms and conditions of the security interest in the property—and it must be signed by the debtor/owner of record of the property. In addition, most states require a mortgage to be notarized, that is acknowledged by the debtor/owner before a notary public or other authorized officer. Unless it is executed with the required formalities, it will not be eligible for recording in the local land records. Recordation of the mortgage does not affect its validity as between the mortgagor and the mortgagee. However, if it is not recorded, it will not be effective against subsequent purchasers of the property or creditors, including other mortgagees, who have no notice of the earlier mortgage. It is important to the mortgagee that the mortgage be recorded so that the world will be on notice of the mortgagee's interest in the property.

CYBERLAW IN ACTION

Real Estate Finance on the Internet

Recently it has become quite easy to search for financing, to compare options from multiple possible funding sources, and to apply for mortgages online when purchasing, refinancing, or remodeling a home. Many mortgage companies have developed interactive Web sites that allow their full array of services to be conducted over the Internet. Shopping for a mortgage on the Internet allows consumers to broaden their search to include companies outside of their city or region and to determine the best rates and options available to them. By using the Internet, consumers have the ability to search for mortgage options whenever and wherever they want without the need to visit multiple possible funding sources. Also, consumers can quickly check the status of an existing account online. Mortgage companies that offer services online significantly expand their pool of potential customers to include persons across the country, rather than just those in their immediate vicinity. Conducting transactions online can reduce their cost of doing business by reducing the number of agents they need to interact with potential customers. In addition, a customer can often fill out one online informational form that the company can make multiple uses of, thus cutting down on the need for duplicate paperwork.

Rights and Liabilities

The owner (mortgagor) of property subject to a mortgage can sell the interest in the property without the consent of the mortgagee. However, the sale does not affect the mortgagee's interest in the property or the mortgagee's claim against the mortgagor. In some cases, the mortgage may provide that if the property is sold, then any remaining balance becomes immediately due and payable. This is known as a "due on sale" clause.

Suppose Erica Smith owns a lot on a lake. She wants to build a cottage on the land, so she borrows $55,000 from First National Bank. She signs a note for $55,000 and gives the bank a $55,000 mortgage on the land and cottage as security for her repayment of the loan. Several years later, Smith sells her land and cottage to Melinda Mason. The mortgage she gave First National might make the unpaid balance due on the mortgage payable on sale. If it does not, Smith can sell the property with the mortgage on it. If Mason defaults on making the mortgage payments, the bank can foreclose on the mortgage. If at the foreclosure sale the property does not bring enough money to cover the costs, interest, and balance due on the mortgage, First National is entitled to a deficiency judgment against Smith. However, some courts are reluctant to give deficiency judgments where real property is used as security for a debt. If on foreclosure the property sells for more than the debt, Mason is entitled to the surplus.

A purchaser of mortgaged property may buy it **subject to** the mortgage or may **assume** the mortgage. If she buys subject to the mortgage and there is a default and foreclosure, the purchaser is not personally liable for any deficiency. The property is liable for the mortgage debt and can be sold to satisfy it in case of default; in addition, the original mortgagor remains liable for its payment. If the buyer assumes the mortgage, then she becomes personally liable for the debt and for any deficiency on default and foreclosure.

The creditor (mortgagee) may assign his interest in the mortgaged property. To do this, the mortgagee must assign the mortgage as well as the debt for which the mortgage is security. In most jurisdictions, the negotiation of the note carries with it the right to the security and the holder of the note is entitled to the benefits of the mortgage.

Foreclosure

Foreclosure is the process by which any rights of the mortgagor or the current property owner are cut off. Foreclosure proceedings are regulated by statute in the state in which the property is located. In many states, two or more alternative methods of foreclosure are available to the mortgagee or his assignee. The methods in common use today are (1) strict foreclosure, (2) action and sale, and (3) power of sale.

A small number of states permit what is called **strict foreclosure**. The creditor keeps the property in satisfaction of the debt, and the owner's rights are cut off. This means that the creditor has no right to a deficiency and the debtor has no right to any surplus. Strict foreclosure is normally limited to situations where the amount of the debt exceeds the value of the property.

Foreclosure by **action and sale** is permitted in all states, and it is the only method of foreclosure permitted in some states. Although the state statutes are not uniform, they are alike in their basic requirements. In a foreclosure by action and sale, suit is brought in a court having jurisdiction. Any party having a property interest that would be cut off by the foreclosure must be made a defendant, and if any such party has a defense, he must enter his appearance and set up his defense. After the case is tried, a judgment is entered and a sale of the property ordered. The proceeds of the sale are applied to the payment of the mortgage debt, and any surplus is paid over to the mortgagor. If there is a deficiency, a deficiency judgment is, as a general rule, entered against the mortgagor and such other persons as are liable on the debt. Deficiency judgments are generally not permitted where the property sold is the residence of the debtor.

The right to foreclose under a **power of sale** must be expressly conferred on the mortgagee by the terms of the mortgage. If the procedure for the exercise of the power is set out in the mortgage, that procedure must be followed. Several states have enacted statutes that set out the procedure to be followed in the exercise of a power of sale. No court action is required. As a general rule, notice of the default and sale must be given to the mortgagor. After the statutory period, the sale may be held. The sale must be advertised, and it must be at auction. The sale must be conducted fairly, and an effort must be made to sell the property at the highest price obtainable. The proceeds of the sale are applied to the payment of costs, interest, and the principal of the debt. Any surplus must be paid to the mortgagor. If there is a deficiency and the mortgagee wishes to recover a judgment for the deficiency, she must bring suit on the debt.

Right of Redemption

At common law and under existing statutes, the mortgagor or an assignee of the mortgagor has what is called an **equity of redemption** in the mortgaged real estate. This means that he has the absolute right to discharge the mortgage when due and to have title to the mortgaged property restored free and clear of the mortgage debt. Under the statutes of all states, the mortgagor or any party having an interest in the mortgaged property that will be cut off by the foreclosure may redeem the property after default and before the mortgagee forecloses the mortgage. In several states, the mortgagor or any other party in interest is given by statute what is known as a redemption period (usually six months or one year, beginning either after the foreclosure proceedings are started or after a foreclosure sale of the mortgaged property has been made) in which to pay the mortgaged debt, costs, and interest and to redeem the property.

As a general rule, if a party in interest wishes to redeem, he must, if the redemption period runs after the foreclosure sale, pay to the purchaser at the foreclosure sale the amount that the purchaser has paid plus interest up to the time of redemption. If the redemption period runs before the sale, the party in interest must pay the amount of the debt plus the costs and interest. The person who wishes to redeem from a mortgage foreclosure sale must redeem the entire mortgage interest; he cannot redeem a partial interest by paying a proportionate amount of the debt or by paying a proportionate amount of the price bid at the foreclosure sale.

Recent Development Concerning Foreclosures
As the subprime lending crisis unfolded during 2007, the number of defaults and foreclosure actions on both subprime and conventional mortgages increased significantly and the trend continued into 2008 when this book went to press. In November 2007 there were 202,000 foreclosure filings in the country, an almost 70 percent increase over the 120,000 filed the previous November. Historically, mortgage lenders were local banks that lent money to a homeowner who then paid the money back to the bank. If the loan was in

difficulty, the borrower and his local lender would work through the matter directly. Over time, local lenders began to resell or assign the loans they originated to others. And, in recent years, the practice of bundling loans together as mortgage-backed securities became commonplace.

Securitization takes the role of the lender and breaks it down into different components. The loan is sold to a third party, the issuer, that bundles the loan into a security and then sells it to investors who are entitled to a share of the cash paid by the borrowers on their mortgages. Another party—the trustee—is created to represent the interests of the investors. And, another party—the servicer—collects the payments, distributes them to the issuer, and also deals with any delinquencies on the part of borrowers.

Thus, these arrangements involving bundles of hundreds or thousands of mortgages are much more complex than the simple assignment of a single mortgage, and concomitantly the paperwork involved is much more complicated—and the documentation sometimes incomplete when there was/is pressure to get deals done.

As some of the collateralized loans fell into default and the owners of the securities—often large banks—brought foreclosure actions, judges began to scrutinize the cases to make sure that the parties bringing the foreclosure actions actually were the legal holders of the mortgage obligation and to dismiss the cases where that showing had not been made. The opinion that follows by Judge Boyko in *In re Foreclosure Cases* generated a lot of attention in the media and in the financial and legal communities when it was issued in October 2007 and served as a warning to would-be foreclosers that they needed to have their paperwork in order before they sought to put a homeowner out of his house.

In re Foreclosure Cases   2007 U.S. Dist. LEXIS 84011 (N.D. Ohio 2007)

Boyko, U.S. District Judge

On October 10, 2007, this court issued an Order requiring Plaintiff-Lenders in a number of pending foreclosure cases to file a copy of the executed Assignment demonstrating Plaintiff was the holder and owner of the Note and Mortgage *as of the date the Complaint was filed,* or the Court would order a dismissal. After considering the submissions along with all the documents filed of record, the Court dismisses the captioned cases without prejudice.

To satisfy the requirements of Article III of the United States Constitution, the plaintiff must show he has personally suffered some actual injury as a result of the illegal conduct of the defendant. In each of the (Complaints, the named Plaintiff alleges that it is the holder and owner of the) Note and Mortgage. However, the attached Note and Mortgage identify the mortgagee and promise as the original lending institution—one other than the named Plaintiff. Further the Preliminary Judicial Report attached as an exhibit to the complaint makes no reference to the named Plaintiff in the recorded chain of title/interest. The Court's Amended General Order requires Plaintiff to submit an affidavit along with the complaint, which identifies Plaintiff either as the original mortgage holder, or as an assignee, trustee, or successor-in-interest. Once again, the affidavits submitted in all these cases recite the averment that Plaintiff is the owner of the Note and Mortgage, without any mention of an assignment or trust or successor interest. Consequently, the very filings and submissions of the Plaintiff create a conflict. In every instance, then, Plaintiff has not satisfied its burden of demonstrating standing at the time of the filing of the Complaint.

Understandably, the Court requested clarification by requiring each Plaintiff to submit a copy of the Assignment of the Note and Mortgage, executed as of the date of the Foreclosure Complaint. In the above captioned cases, **none** of the Assignments show the named Plaintiff to be the owner of the rights, title, and interest under the Mortgage at issue as of the date of the Foreclosure Complaint. The Assignments, in every instance, express a present intent to convey all rights, title and interest in the Mortgage and the accompanying Note to the Plaintiff named in the Foreclosure Complaint upon receipt of sufficient consideration on the date the Assignment was signed and notarized. Those preferred documents belie Plaintiffs' assertion they own the Note and Mortgage by means of a purchase which pre-dated the Complaint by days, months or years.

This Court is obligated to carefully scrutinize all filings and pleadings in foreclosure actions, since the unique nature of real property requires contracts and transactions concerning real property to be in writing. Ohio law holds that when a mortgage is assigned, moreover, the assignment is subject to the recording requirements. Thus, with regards to real property, before an entity assigned an interest in that property would be entitled to receive a distribution from the sale of the property, their interest therein must have been recorded in accordance with Ohio law.[1]

This Court acknowledges the right of banks, holding valid mortgages, to receive timely payments. And, if they do not receive timely payments, banks have the right to properly file actions on the defaulted notes—seeking foreclosure on the property securing the notes. Yet, this Court possesses the independent obligations to preserve the judicial integrity of the federal court and to jealously guard federal jurisdiction. Neither the fluidity of the secondary mortgage market, nor monetary or economic considerations of the parties, nor the convenience of the litigants supersede those obligations.

Despite Plaintiffs' counsel's belief that "there appears to be some level of disagreement and/or misunderstanding amongst professionals, borrowers, attorneys and members of the judiciary," the Court does not require instruction and is not operating under any misapprehension. Plaintiff's, "Judge, you just don't understand how things work," argument reveals a condescending mindset and quasi-monopolistic system where financial institutions have traditionally controlled, and still control, the foreclosure process. Typically, the homeowner who finds himself/herself in financial straits, fails to make the required mortgage payments and faces a foreclosure suit, is not interested in testing state or federal jurisdictional requirements, either *pro se* or through counsel. Their focus is either, "how do I save my home," or "if I have to give it up, I'll simply leave and find somewhere else to live."

In the meantime, the financial institutions or successors/assignees rush to foreclose, obtain a default judgment and then sit on the deed, avoiding responsibility for maintaining the property while reaping the financial benefits of interest running on a judgment. The financial institutions know the law charges the one with title (still the homeowner) with maintaining the property.

There is no doubt every decision made by a financial institution in the foreclosure process is driven by money. And the legal work which flows from winning the financial institution's favor is highly lucrative. There is nothing improper or wrong with financial institutions or law firms making a profit—to the contrary, they should be rewarded for sound business and legal practices. However, unchallenged by underfinanced opponents, the institutions worry less about jurisdictional requirements and more about maximizing returns. Unlike the focus of financial institutions, the federal courts must act as gatekeepers, assuring that only those who meet diversity and standing requirements are allowed to pass through. Counsel for the institutions are not without legal argument to support their position, but their arguments fall woefully short of justifying their premature filings, and utterly fail to satisfy their standing and jurisdictional burdens. The institutions seem to adopt the attitude that since they have been doing this for so long, unchallenged, this practice equates with legal compliance. Finally put to the test, their weak legal arguments compel the Court to stop them at the gate.

The Court will illustrate in simple terms its decision: "Fluidity of the market"—"X" dollars, "contractual arrangements between institutions and counsel"—"X" dollars, "purchasing mortgages in bulk and securitizing"—"X" dollars, "rush to file, slow to record after judgment"—"X" dollars, "the jurisdictional integrity of United States District Court"—"Priceless."

For all the foregoing reasons, the above-captioned Foreclosure Complaints are dismissed without prejudice.

---

[1]Astoundingly, counsel at oral argument stated that his client, the purchaser from the original mortgagee, acquired complete legal and equitable interest in land when money changed hands, even before the purchase agreement, let alone a proper assignment, made its way into his client's possession.

Deed of Trust States typically use either the mortgage or the **deed of trust** as the primary mechanism for holding a security interest in real property. There are three parties to a deed of trust: (1) the owner of the property who borrows the money (the debtor), (2) the trustee who holds legal title to the property put up as security, and (3) the lender who is the beneficiary of the trust. The trustee serves as a fiduciary for both the creditor and the debtor. The purpose of the deed of trust is to make it easy for the security to be liquidated. However, most states treat the deed of trust like a mortgage in giving the borrower a relatively long period of time to redeem the property, thereby defeating this rationale for the arrangement.

In a deed of trust transaction, the borrower deeds to the trustee the property that is to be put up as security. The trust agreement usually gives the trustee the right to foreclose or sell the property if the debtor fails to make a required payment on the debt. Normally, the trustee does not sell the property until the lender notifies him that the borrower is in default and demands that the property be sold. The trustee must notify the debtor that he is in default and that the land will be sold. The trustee advertises the property for sale. After the statutory period, the trustee will sell the property at a public or private sale. The proceeds are applied to the costs of the foreclosure, interest, and debt. If there is a surplus, it is paid to the borrower. If there is a deficiency, the lender has to sue the borrower on the debt and recover a judgment.

Land Contracts The **land contract** is a device for securing the balance due the seller on the purchase price of real estate. Essentially, it is an installment contract for the purchase of land. The buyer agrees to pay the purchase price over a period of time. The seller agrees to convey title to the property to the buyer when the full price is paid. Usually, the buyer takes possession of the property, pays the taxes, insures the property, and assumes the other obligations of an owner. However, the seller keeps legal title and does not turn over the deed until the purchase price is paid.

If the buyer defaults, the seller usually has the right to declare a forfeiture and take over possession of the property. The buyer's rights to the property are cut off at that point. Most states give the buyer on a land contract a limited period of time to redeem his interest. Moreover, some states require the seller to go through a foreclosure proceeding. Generally, the procedure for declaring a forfeiture and recovering property sold on a land contract is simpler and less time-consuming than foreclosure of a mortgage. In most states, the procedure in case of default is set out by statute. If the buyer, after default, voluntarily surrenders possession to the seller, no court procedure is necessary; the seller's title will become absolute, and the buyer's equity will be cut off.

Purchases of farm property are commonly financed through the use of land contracts. As an interest in real estate, a land contract should be in writing and recorded in the local land records so as to protect the interests of both parties.

However, some courts have invoked the equitable doctrine against forfeitures and have required that the seller on a land contract must foreclose on the property in order to avoid injustice to a defaulting buyer.

Mechanic's and Materialman's Liens

Each state has a statute that permits persons who contract to furnish labor or materials to improve real estate to claim a lien on the property until they are paid. There are many differences among states as to exactly who can claim such a lien and the requirements that must be met to do so.

Rights of Subcontractors and Materialmen
A general contractor is a person who has contracted with the owner to build, remodel, or improve real property. A subcontractor is a person who has

---

Ethics in Action

What Is the Right Thing to Do?

Suppose you have sold a farm to a young couple on a land contract that calls for them to pay off the purchase price over a 10-year period. After the couple has paid about a third of the purchase price, a serious drought damages their crop and they miss several payments, triggering your right to declare a default and reclaim possession of the property. Are there any ethical considerations involved in your taking such an action that you are otherwise legally entitled to take? If you proceed with a forfeiture action in court, what policy considerations should the court take into account in deciding whether to grant your request?

Security Interests in Real Property

Type of Security Instrument	Parties	Features
Mortgage	1. Mortgagor (property owner/debtor) 2. Mortgagee (creditor)	1. Mortgagee holds a security interest (and in some states, title) in real property as security for a debt. 2. If mortgagor defaults on her obligation, mortgagee must *foreclose* on property to realize on his security interest. 3. Mortgagor has a limited time after foreclosure to *redeem* her interest.
Deed of Trust	1. Owner/debtor 2. Lender/creditor 3. Trustee	1. Trustee holds legal title to the real property put up as security. 2. If debt is satisfied, the trustee conveys property back to owner/debtor. 3. If debt is not paid as agreed, creditor notifies trustee to sell the property. 4. While intended to make foreclosure easier, most states treat it like a mortgage for purposes of foreclosure.
Land Contract	1. Buyer 2. Seller	1. Seller agrees to convey title when full price is paid. 2. Buyer usually takes possession, pays property taxes and insurance, and maintains the property. 3. If buyer defaults, seller may declare a forfeiture and retake possession (most states) after buyer has limited time to redeem; some states require foreclosure.

contracted with the general contractor to perform a stipulated portion of the general contract. A materialman is a person who has contracted to furnish certain materials needed to perform a designated general contract.

Two distinct systems—the New York system and the Pennsylvania system—are followed by the states in allowing mechanic's liens on real estate to subcontractors and materialmen. The New York system is based on the theory of subrogation, and the subcontractors or materialmen cannot recover more than is owed to the contractor at the time they file a lien or give notice of a lien to the owner. Under the Pennsylvania system, the subcontractors or materialmen have direct liens and are entitled to liens for the value of labor and materials furnished, irrespective of the amount due from the owner to the contractor. Under the New York system, the general contractor's failure to perform his contract or his abandonment of the work has a direct effect on the lien rights of subcontractors and materialmen, whereas under the Pennsylvania system, such breach or abandonment by

the general contractor does not directly affect the lien rights of subcontractors and materialmen.

Basis for Mechanic's or Materialman's Lien

Some state statutes provide that no lien shall be claimed unless the contract for the improvement is in writing and embodies a statement of the materials to be furnished and a description of the land on which the improvement is to take place and of the work to be done. Other states permit the contract to be oral, but in no state is a licensee or volunteer entitled to a lien. No lien can be claimed unless the work is done or the materials are furnished in the performance of a contract to improve specific real property. A sale of materials without reference to the improvement of specific real property does not entitle the person furnishing the materials to a lien on real property that is, in fact, improved by the use of the materials at some time after the sale.

Unless the state statute specifically includes submaterialmen, they are not entitled to a lien. For example, if a lumber dealer contracts to furnish the lumber for the erection of a specific building and orders from a sawmill a carload of lumber that is needed to fulfill the contract, the sawmill will not be entitled to a lien on the building in which the lumber is used unless the state statute expressly provides that submaterialmen are entitled to a lien.

At times, the question has arisen as to whether materials have been furnished. Some courts have held that the materialman must prove that the material furnished was actually incorporated into the structure. Under this ruling, if material delivered on the job is diverted by the general contractor or others and not incorporated into the structure, the materialman will not be entitled to a lien. Other courts have held that the materialman is entitled to a lien if he can provide proof that the material was delivered on the job under a contract to furnish the material.

Requirements for Obtaining Lien The requirements for obtaining a mechanic's or materialman's lien must be complied with strictly. Although there is no uniformity in the statutes as to the requirements for obtaining a lien, the statutes generally require the filing of a notice of lien with a county official such as the register of deeds or the county clerk, which notice sets forth the amount claimed, the name of the owner, the names of the contractor and the claimant, and a description of the property. Frequently, the notice of lien must be verified by an affidavit of the claimant. In some states, a copy of the notice must be served on the owner or be posted on the property.

The notice of lien must be filed within a stipulated time. The time varies from 30 to 90 days, but the favored time is 60 days after the last work performed or after the last materials furnished. Some statutes distinguish between labor claims, materialmen's claims, and claims of general contractors as to time of filing. The lien, when filed, must be foreclosed within a specified time, which generally varies from six months to two years.

Priorities and Foreclosure The provisions for priorities vary widely, but most of the statutes provide that a mechanic's lien has priority over all liens attaching after the first work is performed or after the first materials are furnished. This statutory provision creates a hidden lien on the property, in that a mechanic's lien, filed within the allotted period of time after completion of the work, attaches as of the time the first work is done or the first material is furnished, but no notice of lien need be filed during this period. And if no notice of lien is filed during this period, third persons would have no means of knowing of the existence of a lien. There are no priorities among lien claimants under the majority of the statutes.

The case that follows, *Mutual Savings Association v. Res/Com Properties, L.L.C.,* illustrates a situation where subcontractors were able to obtain a preferred position through compliance with a state lien statute.

Mutual Savings Association v. Res/Com Properties, L.L.C.
79 P.3d 184 (Ct. App. Kansas 2003)

In July 1999, George Kritos contracted with the Peridian Group to provide design and engineering services on a property known as the Whispering Meadows development in Eudora, Kansas. The work included boundary verification, topographical surveying, preparing preliminary and final site development plans, platting, storm water drainage studies, sanitary sewer design, street and storm sewer design, and water line design. The on-site work consisted of surveying, staking the boundary corners, staking of preliminary layouts for utilities and streets, plus horizontal and vertical control benchmark staking used for sewer, street, and storm water designs. Peridian's work began prior to May 22, 2000.

On May 22, 2000, Res/Com Properties, L.L.C., purchased the property from Kritos. That same day, Res/Com signed a promissory note and related mortgage in favor of Mutual Savings Association (Mutual). Mutual recorded its mortgage on May 24, 2000. Res/Com used the money it borrowed from Mutual to purchase the property from Kritos. Peridian then contracted with Res/Com to continue its design and engineering services.

On July 2, 2000, Modern Engineering Utilities Company, Inc. (Modern), began installing the sanitary sewers on the property under a subcontract with Heartland Building and Development Company, Res/Com's general contractor on the project. On July 19, Res/Com executed and delivered to Mutual a second mortgage to secure a further loan on the property; the mortgage was filed the following day, July 20, 2000. On August 30, LRM Industries, Inc. (LRM), entered into two contracts with Heartland to construct improvements on the property. LRM worked on the property from September through November 2000.

On October 26, 2000, Peridian filed its mechanic's lien. LRM filed its mechanic's lien on December 18, 2000, and Modern filed a lien on December 19, 2000. In March 2001, Mutual paid Peridian for its work, took an assignment of its lien, and filed a release of the lien. Res/Com subsequently defaulted on both of the notes it owed to Mutual. Mutual brought suit to foreclose its mortgages, and one of the issues in the litigation was the relative priority of the mechanic's liens held by LRM and Modern. LRM and Modern argued that their liens were entitled to priority by "relating back" to Peridian's preliminary staking of the property and its off-site design and engineering work.

Kansas statutes—K.S.A. section 60–1101 entitled "Liens of contractors; priority" states:

Any person furnishing labor, equipment, material, or supplies used or consumed for the improvement of real property, under a contract or with the trustee, agent or spouse of the owner, shall have a lien upon the property for the labor, equipment, material or supplies furnished, and for the cost of transporting the same. The lien shall be preferred to all other liens or encumbrances which are subsequent to the furnishing of such labor, equipment, material or supplies at the site of the property subject to the lien. When two or more such contracts are entered into applicable to the same improvement, the liens of all claimants shall be similarly preferred to the date of the earliest unsatisfied lien of any of them.

K.S.A. 2002 Supp. 60–1103 entitled "Liens of subcontractors; procedure, recording and notice, owner's liability" states in part:

(a) *Procedure.* Any supplier, subcontractor or other person furnishing labor, equipment, material or supplies, used or consumed at the site of the property subject to the lien, under an agreement with the contractor, subcontractor or owner contractor may obtain a lien for the amount due in the same manner and to the same extent as the original contractor.

Rulon, Chief Justice

Our Supreme Court in *Haz-Mat Response, Inc. v. Certified Waste Services Ltd.* (1996), noted:

Our mechanic's lien law is remedial in nature, enacted for the purpose of providing effective security to any persons furnishing labor, equipment, material, or supplies used or consumed for the improvement of real property under a contract with the owner. The theory underlying the granting of a lien against the property is that the property improved by the labor, equipment, material, or supplies should be charged with the payment of the labor, equipment, material, or supplies.

At the same time, a mechanic's lien is purely a creation of statute, and those claiming a mechanic's lien must bring themselves clearly within the provisions of the authorizing statute. The statute must be followed strictly with regard to the requirements upon which the right to lien depends. However, because the statute is remedial and designed for the benefit and protection of persons designated by the act, once a lien has been found to have attached, the law is to be liberally construed in favor of such claimant.

Subcontractors' liens attach at the time the general contractor began work or construction. Contractors' liens attach when there has been a furnishing of labor, equipment, material, or supplies used or consumed for the improvement of the property. The liens of all contractors and subcontractors are similarly preferred to the date of the earliest unsatisfied lien.

Under the facts before us, the status of Peridian as a subcontractor or contractor is immaterial. The central issue on appeal is when and if Peridian's work, done prior to Mutual's mortgage, became lienable and attached. If Peridian's on-site surveying and staking and off-site designing and planning, done prior to Mutual's mortgage being filed, were not lienable or had not attached, LRM and Modern's liens could only relate back to when Modern began work, which was subsequent to Mutual's mortgage. The effect of such would be that Mutual would have priority.

Initially, a mechanic's lien which has attached is superior to any subsequent purchaser for value and without notice, even if no lien statement is filed until after the conveyance. The work itself constitutes notice to the world of the existence of the lien. As such, the fact Peridian's work was done prior to Res/Com actually becoming the owner of the property is not in and of itself a bar to LRM's and Modern's claims of priority. However, for LRM and Modern to prevail, Peridian's "permortgage" work must have attached to the property. Under *K.S.A. 60–1101,* "in order for a mechanic's lien for labor and materials to attach, such items must be used or consumed for the improvement of real property, and thus become part of the realty itself."

Our Supreme Court, in *Haz-Mat Response, Inc.,* clarified the test to be used in determining what types of activity were and were not lienable. After reviewing a number of prior Kansas cases as well as cases from other states dealing generally with the meaning of the phrase "improvement of real property," the *Haz-Mat* court devised seven (7) considerations for determining if an activity is considered to improve real property.

(1) What is or is not an improvement of real property must necessarily be based upon the circumstances of each case;

(2) improvement of the property does not require the actual

construction of a physical improvement on the real property; (3) the improvement of real property need not necessarily be visible, although in most instances it is; (4) the improvement of the real property must enhance the value of the real property, although it need not enhance the selling value of the property; (5) for labor, equipment, material, or supplies to be lienable items, they must be used or consumed and thus become part of the real property; (6) the nature of the activity performed is not necessarily a determining factor of whether there is an improvement of real property within the meaning of the statute; rather, the purpose of the activity is more directly concerned in the determination of whether there is an improvement of property which is thus lienable; and (7) the furnishing of labor, equipment, material, or supplies used or consumed for the improvement of real property may become lienable if established to be part of an overall plan to enhance the value of the property, its beauty or utility, or to adapt it for a new or further purpose, or if the furnishing of labor, equipment, material, or supplies is a necessary feature of a plan of construction of a physical improvement to the real property.

Finally, the *Haz-Mat* court adopted the *Black's Law Dictionary* definition of the phrase "improvement of real property" as it is used in *K.S.A. 60–1101:* "A valuable addition made to real property (usually real estate) or an amelioration in its condition, amounting to more than mere repairs or replacement, costing labor or capital, and intended to enhance its value, beauty or utility or to adapt it for new or further purposes."

Here, the first issue is whether Peridian's preliminary staking and surveying, done prior to Mutual's mortgage, constituted an "improvement" as used in *K.S.A. 60–1101.* Applying the considerations set out in *Haz-Mat,* we conclude Peridian's efforts were lienable. It is undisputed that the labor and capital expended in the surveying and staking work done by Peridian were actually used in the development of the property. This record is silent as to whether stakes installed by Peridian were still on the property at the time Mutual's mortgages were filed, but this is irrelevant under the *Haz-Mat* test. If they were in fact visible, this lends further support to the subcontractors' claim.

The next issue is, if Peridian's work is lienable, when did that lien attach. Once again *K.S.A. 60–1101* reads in relevant part:

The lien shall be preferred to all other liens or encumbrances which are subsequent to the *commencement of the furnishing of such labor, equipment, material or supplies at the site of the property subject to the lien.* When two or more such contracts are entered into applicable to the same improvement, the liens of all claimants shall be similarly preferred to the date of the earliest unsatisfied lien of any of them. (Emphasis added.)

K.S.A. 2002 Supp. 60–1103 reads:

(a) *Procedure.* Any supplier, subcontractor or other person *furnishing labor, equipment, material or supplies, used or consumed at the site of the property subject to the lien,* under an agreement with the contractor, subcontractor or owner contractor *may obtain a lien for the amount due in the same manner and to the same extent as the original contractor. . . .* (Emphasis added.)

The question is what is meant by *commencement of the furnishing of such labor, equipment, material, or supplies at the site of the property subject to the lien.* Here, the district court properly found that under the reasoning in *Haz-Mat,* the off-site engineering and design work done by Peridian was no doubt lienable. However, the district court went on to find that the lien did not attach until the plans drawn up by Peridian were actually "used or consumed" at the site, i.e., the lien did not attach until Modern used the plans to install the sanitary sewers. The district court further found that the preliminary surveying and/or staking done at the site by Peridian before May 22, 2000, was used for preparation of plats, designs, and other paperwork and was not sufficient to be deemed work used or consumed at the site because the work did not become "part of the real property" until the plans and drawings were actually used by Modern to begin construction. The district court appeared to draw a distinction between the staking Peridian completed and the more precise construction staking which subcontractors like Modern used in locating actual physical improvements. We disagree with such a distinction.

Once it is determined that the work performed is lienable, the plain language of *K.S.A. 60–1101* only requires that for priority purposes, the subcontractor or contractor commence the furnishing of such labor, equipment, material, or supplies *at the site* of the property subject to the lien.

It is undisputed that Peridian's work was used in the construction at the site. The question remains whether the surveying and staking Peridian did at the site was sufficient to cause its lien to attach.

In Kansas, "The theory underlying the granting of a lien against the property is that the property improved by the labor, equipment, material, or supplies should be charged with the payment of the labor, equipment, material, or supplies."

Based on the plain language of the Kansas statute, it is irrelevant at what point in the construction process that work was used or consumed. Further, it is undisputed that Peridian did staking work at the site. Again, the record is silent as to whether these stakes were still on the property when Mutual's mortgages were filed. While this may not have been as substantial as the staking required to pour footings and foundation walls, the statute makes no such distinction. Peridian's work was just as necessary in the development of the project as the work of the dirt contractor digging the trenches for the foundation. We are convinced there is no reason to give preference to one type of subcontractor over another based on an arbitrary distinction of the relative worth of each.

. . .

On the date Mutual filed its first mortgage securing the note from Res/Com, Peridian was an unsatisfied lienholder. As such, all contractors' and subcontractors' liens were perfected as of the date Peridian started work. If Mutual wanted to ensure that its mortgages had priority over all other liens, Mutual could have paid off any contractor or subcontractor with potential outstanding liens and obtained lien waivers.

Reversed and remanded for further proceedings.

The procedure followed in the foreclosure of a mechanic's lien on real estate follows closely the procedure followed in a court foreclosure of a real estate mortgage. The rights acquired by the filing of a lien and the extent of the property covered by the lien are set out in some of the mechanic's lien statutes. In general, the lien attaches only to the interest that the person has in the property that has been improved at the time the notice is filed. Some statutes provide that the lien attaches to the building and to the city lot on which the building stands, or if the improvement is to farm property, the lien attaches to a specified amount of land.

Waiver of Lien
The question often arises as to the effect of an express provision in a contract for the improvement of real estate that no lien shall attach to the property for the cost of the improvement. In some states, there is a statute requiring the recording or filing of the contract and making such a provision ineffective if the statute is not complied with. In some states, courts have held that such a provision is effective against everyone; in other states, courts have held that the provision is ineffective against everyone except the contractor; and in still other states, courts have held that such a provision is ineffective as to subcontractors, materialmen, and laborers. Whether the parties to the contract have notice of the waiver of lien provision plays an important part in several states in determining their right to a lien.

It is common practice that before a person who is having improvements made to his property makes final payment, he requires the contractor to sign an affidavit that all materialmen and subcontractors have been paid and to supply him with a release of lien signed by the subcontractors and materialmen.

Problems and Problem Cases

1. Rusty Jones, a used car dealer, applied to First Financial Federal Savings and Loan Association for a $50,000 line of credit to purchase an inventory of used cars. First Financial refused to make the loan to Jones alone but agreed to do so if Worth Camp, an attorney and friend of Jones, would cosign the note. Camp agreed to cosign as an accommodation maker or surety. The expectation of the parties was that the loans cosigned by Camp would be repaid from the proceeds of the car inventory. The original note for $25,000 was signed on August 2, 1994, and renewals were executed on January 25, 1995, September 11, 1995, and March 15, 1996, and the amount was eventually increased to $50,000. In August 1995, as Camp was considering whether to sign the September renewal note, he was advised by First Financial's loan officer that the interest on the loan had not been paid. In fact, interest payments were four months delinquent. In addition, unknown to Camp, as the $50,000 credit limit was approached, First Financial began making side, or personal, loans to Jones totaling about $25,000, which were also payable out of the used car inventory. Camp knew nothing of these loans and thought that Jones's used car business was making payments only on the loans he had cosigned. Jones defaulted on the $50,000 note cosigned by Camp, and First Financial brought suit against Camp on his obligation as surety on the note. Was Camp relieved of his obligation as surety by First Financial's failure to disclose material facts to him?

2. Bayer was the general contractor on a Massachusetts state highway contract. He hired Deschenes as a subcontractor to do certain excavation work. Deschenes was to start the job by November 24, 1988, and to complete it on or before March 1, 1989. Deschenes was required to furnish a bond of $91,000 to ensure his faithful performance of the subcontract, and he

purchased such a bond from Aetna Insurance Company. Deschenes began the work on December 1, 1988, and quit on June 22, 1989, after completing only about half of the work. Bayer had made numerous efforts to get Deschenes to do the work and then completed the job himself when Deschenes walked off the job. Bayer then brought a lawsuit against Aetna on the bond, and Aetna claimed that it was discharged by the extension of the time given to Deschenes. Should Bayer recover on the bond?

3. During May and June, John Shumate regularly parked his automobile on a vacant lot in downtown Philadelphia. At that time, no signs were posted prohibiting parking on the lot or indicating that vehicles parked there without authorization would be towed. On July 7, Shumate again left his car on the lot. When he returned two days later, the car was gone and the lot was posted with signs warning that parking was prohibited. Shumate learned that his car had been towed away by Ruffie's Towing Service and that the car was being held by Ruffie's at its place of business. Ruffie's refused to release the car until Shumate paid a towing fee of $44.50 plus storage charges of $4 per day. Shumate refused to pay the fee, and Ruffie's kept possession of the car. Did Ruffie's have a common law possessory lien on the car?

4. Philip and Edith Beh purchased some property from Alfred M. Gromer and his wife. Sometime earlier, the Gromers had borrowed money from City Mortgage. They had signed a note and had given City Mortgage a second deed of trust on the property. There was also a first deed of trust on the property at the time the Behs purchased it. In the contract of sale between the Behs and the Gromers, the Behs promised to "assume" the second deed of trust of approximately $5,000 at 6 percent interest. The Behs later defaulted on the first deed of trust. Foreclosure was held on the first deed of trust, but the proceeds of the sale left nothing for City Mortgage on its second deed of trust. City Mortgage then brought a lawsuit against the Behs to collect the balance due on the second deed of trust. When the Behs "assumed" the second deed of trust, did they become personally liable for it?

5. Pope agreed to sell certain land to Pelz and retained a mortgage on the property to secure payment of the purchase price. The mortgage contained a clause providing that if Pelz defaulted, Pope had the "right to enter upon the above-described premises and sell the same at public sale" to pay the balance of the purchase price, accounting to Pelz for any surplus realized on the sale. What type of foreclosure does this provision contemplate: (1) strict foreclosure, (2) action and sale, or (3) private power of sale?

6. Betty Nelson signed a promissory note payable to Family Bank in return for a loan the bank had made to her. The note was secured by a deed of trust on a duplex owned by Nelson. When the note was signed, the duplex was rented to third parties. Nelson defaulted on the note, and Family Bank filed a complaint to foreclose the trust deed. Nelson advised the bank that she and her son were occupying the duplex as their residence. Under Orgeon law, a lender can obtain a deficiency judgment in connection with the foreclosure of a commercial deed of trust; however, a deficiency judgment is not available in connection with the foreclosure of a noncommercial (residential) deed of trust. If Family Bank went forward with foreclosure of the deed of trust, could it obtain a deficiency judgment against Nelson if the sale of the property produced less than the amount of the debt?

7. In October 1992, Verda Miller sold her 107-acre farm for $30,000 to Donald Kimball, who was acting on behalf of his own closely held corporation, American Wonderlands. Under the agreement, Miller retained title and Kimball was given possession pending full payment of all installments of the purchase price. The contract provided that Kimball was to pay all real estate taxes. If he did not pay them, Miller could discharge them and either add the amounts to the unpaid principal or demand immediate payment of the delinquencies plus interest. Miller also had the right to declare a forfeiture of the contract and regain possession if the terms of the agreement were not met. In 1995, Miller had to pay the real estate taxes on the property in the amount of $672.78. She demanded payment of this amount plus interest from Kimball. She also served a notice of forfeiture on him that he had 30 days to pay. Kimball paid the taxes but refused to pay interest of $10.48. Miller made continued demands on Kimball for two months, then filed notice of forfeiture with the county recorder in August 1995. She also advised Kimball of this. Was Miller justified in declaring a forfeiture and taking back possession of the land?

8. Edwin Bull was the owner of an 80-foot fishing trawler named the *Bull Head* that had been leased for

use in dismantling a bridge over the Illinois River at Pekin, Illinois. At the termination of the lease, the *Bull Head* was towed upriver to Morris, Illinois, not operating on its own power. At Morris, a tugboat owned by Iowa Marine Repair Corporation was used to remove the *Bull Head* from the tow and to move it to the south bank of the river where it was tied up. Several months later, the *Bull Head* was moved across the river by Iowa Marine and moored at a place on the north bank where it maintained its fleeting operations. The *Bull Head* remained there for several years and greatly deteriorated. Iowa Marine sent Bull a bill for switching, fleeting, and other services. Bull refused to pay and brought suit against Iowa Marine to recover possession of the boat. In turn, Iowa Marine claimed that it had a mechanic's lien on the *Bull Head* and that the boat should be sold to satisfy the lien. Illinois law provides that

> any architect, contractor, subcontractor, materialman, or other person furnishing services, labor, or material for the purpose of, or in constructing, building, altering, repairing or ornamenting a boat, barge, or watercraft shall have a lien on such boat for the value of such services, labor, or material in the same manner as in this act provided for the purpose of building, altering, repairing, or ornamenting a house or other building.

Does Iowa Marine have a valid mechanic's lien on the boat for its switching, fleeting, and storage services?

9. Bowen-Rodgers Hardware Company was engaged in the business of furnishing materials for the construction of buildings. It delivered a quantity of materials to property owned by Ronald and Carol Collins. The materials were for the use of a contractor who was building a home for the Collinses as well as several other houses in the area. The hardware company was not paid for the materials by the contractor, and it sought to obtain a mechanic's lien against the Collinses' property. The Collinses claimed that even though the materials were delivered to their home, they were actually used to build other houses in the area. Was the Collinses' property subject to a mechanic's lien because payment had not been made for materials delivered to it?

Online Research

What Protection Does Your State Give Artisans?

Use the Internet to research your state law to determine what (a) an artisan who improves personal property or (b) a contractor or supplier of materials for the improvement of real property must do to claim a lien on the property until he is paid. What steps must the lienholder do to foreclose on his lien? If your state's laws are not accessible online, then look at the law in New York or California.

Consider completing the case "DEBT COLLECTION: Overdue or Overdone?" from the You Be the Judge Web site element after you have read this chapter. Visit our Web site at www.mhhe.com/mallor14e for more information and activities regarding this case segment.

chapter 29

SECURITY INTERESTS
IN PERSONAL PROPERTY

laine Stanley decides that she will start a card and gift shop in leased space in a shopping mall. Her personal assets are not sufficient to finance the business so she borrows some initial working capital from a bank. She purchases some display fixtures from a local supplier, making a small down payment and agreeing to pay the balance of the purchase price over the next two years. She purchases her initial inventory from several suppliers, agreeing to either pay for the goods within 60 days or to pay interest at the rate of 15 percent per year on any unpaid balance. To attract customers, she plans to offer both a layaway plan and store charge accounts. Among the questions raised by this hypothetical are:

- How can the creditors of the business, such as the bank, the supplier of the display fixtures, and the suppliers of the inventory, obtain security for the credit they have extended to Elaine?
- What steps must the creditors take to obtain maximum protection against Elaine and against her other creditors in the event she defaults on her obligations?
- What relative rights will the creditors have against each other in the event Elaine defaults on her obligations to them?
- How can Elaine protect herself when she extends credit to her customers?
- If a customer has paid Elaine a significant amount of the agreed-upon price for an item Elaine is holding for her on layaway and then defaults on paying the balance of the purchase price, would it be ethical for Elaine to retain all of the money she has received as well as the item, or should she return some of the money paid to the customer?

IN MANY CREDIT TRANSACTIONS the creditor, in order to protect his investment, takes a security interest, or lien, in personal property belonging to the debtor. The law covering security interests in personal property is set forth in Article 9 of the Uniform Commercial Code. Article 9, entitled Secured Transactions, applies to situations that consumers and businesspeople commonly face; for example, the financing of an automobile, the purchase of a refrigerator on a time-payment plan, or the financing of business inventory.

Article 9

If a creditor wants to obtain a security interest in the personal property of the debtor, he also wants to be sure that his interest is superior to the claims of other creditors. To do so, the creditor must carefully comply with Article 9. In Part 4 of this text, Sales, we pointed out that businesspersons sometimes leave out important terms in a contract or insert vague terms to be worked out later. Such looseness is a luxury that is not permitted in secured transactions. If a debtor gets into financial difficulties and cannot meet her obligations, even a minor noncompliance with Article 9 may cause the creditor to lose his preferred claim to the personal property of the debtor. A creditor who loses his secured interest is only a general creditor if the debtor is declared bankrupt. As a general creditor in bankruptcy proceedings, he may have little chance of recovering the money owed by the debtor because of the relatively low priority of such claims. Chapter 30, Bankruptcy, covers this in detail.

In 1998, the National Conference on Uniform State Laws adopted a "Revised Article 9" that has now been adopted by all 50 states with effective dates ranging from 2001 to 2002. Because Revised Article 9 is much more complex than the old Article 9 and because Article 9 has not been adopted in exactly the same form in every state, the law must be examined very carefully to determine the procedure in a particular state for obtaining a security interest and for ascertaining the rights of the creditors and debtors. However, the general concepts are the same in each state and will be the basis of our discussion in this chapter.

Security Interests under the Code

Security Interests Basic to a discussion of secured consumer and commercial transactions is the term **security interest.** A security interest is an interest in personal property or fixtures obtained by a creditor to secure payment or performance of an obligation [1–201(37)].[1] For example, when a person borrows money from a bank to buy a new car, the bank takes a security interest in, or puts a lien on, the car until the loan is repaid. If the person defaults on the loan, the bank can repossess the car and have it sold to cover the unpaid balance. A security interest is a property interest in the collateral.

Types of Collateral Goods—tangible items such as automobiles and business computers—are commonly used as collateral for loans. Article 9 of the Uniform Commercial Code also covers security interests in a much broader grouping of personal property. The Code breaks down personal property into a number of different classifications, which are important in determining how a creditor obtains an enforceable security interest in a particular kind of collateral.

The Code classifications include:

1. *Instruments.* This includes checks, notes, drafts, and certificates of deposit [9–102(a)(47)].
2. *Documents of title.* This includes bills of lading, dock warrants, dock receipts, and warehouse receipts [9–102(a)(30)].
3. *Accounts.* This includes the rights to payment of a monetary obligation for goods sold or leased or

for services rendered that are not evidenced by instruments or chattel paper but are carried on open accounts, including lottery winnings and health care–insurance receivables. Items in the "accounts" category include such rights to payment whether or not the rights have been earned by performance [9–102(a)(2)].

4. *Chattel paper.* This includes written documents that evidence both an obligation to pay money and a security interest in specific goods [9–102(a)(11)]. A typical example of chattel paper is what is commonly known as a *conditional sales contract.* This is the type of contract that a consumer might sign when she buys a large appliance such as a refrigerator on a time-payment plan.

5. *General intangibles.* This is a catchall category that includes, among other things, patents, copyrights, software, and franchises [9–102(a)(42)].

6. *Goods.* Goods [9–102(a)(44)] are divided into several classes; the same item of collateral may fall into different classes at different times, depending on its use:

   a. *Consumer goods.* Goods used or bought primarily for personal, family, or household use, such as automobiles, furniture, and appliances [9–102(a)[23)].

   b. *Equipment.* Goods other than inventory, farm products, or consumer goods [9–102(a)(33)].

   c. *Farm products.* Crops, livestock, or supplies used or produced in farming operations as long as they are still in the possession of a debtor who is engaged in farming [9–102(a)(34)].

   d. *Inventory.* Goods held for sale or lease or to be used under contracts of service, as well as raw materials, work in process, or materials used or consumed in a business [9–102(a)(48)].

   e. *Fixtures.* Goods that will be so affixed to real property that they are considered a part of the real property [9–102(a)(41)].

7. *Investment property.* This includes securities such as stocks, bonds, and commodity contracts [9–102(a)(49)].

8. *Deposit accounts.* This includes demand, time, savings, passbook, and similar accounts maintained with a bank [9–102(a)(29)].

It is important to note that an item such as a stove could in different situations be classified as inventory, equipment, or consumer goods. In the hands of the manufacturer or an appliance store, the stove is *inventory.* If it is being used in a restaurant, it is *equipment.* In a home, it is classified as *consumer goods.*

---

[1]The numbers in brackets refer to sections of the Uniform Commercial Code.

Obtaining a Security Interest

Obtaining a Security Interest The goal of a creditor is to obtain a security interest in certain personal property that will be good against (1) the debtor, (2) other creditors of the debtor, and (3) a person who might purchase the property from the debtor. In case the debtor defaults on the debt, the creditor wants to have a better right to claim the property than anyone else. Obtaining an enforceable security interest is a two-step process—attachment and perfection.

Attachment of the Security Interest

Attachment A security interest is not legally enforceable against a debtor until it is attached to one or more particular items of the debtor's property. The **attachment** of the security interest takes place in a legal sense rather than in a physical sense. There are three basic requirements for a security interest to be attached to the goods of a debtor [9–203]. First is an *agreement* in which the debtor grants the creditor a security interest in particular property (collateral) in which the debtor has an interest. Second, the debtor must have *rights in the collateral.* Third, the creditor must give *value* to the debtor. The creditor must, for example, lend money or advance goods on credit to the debtor. Unless the debtor owes a debt to the creditor, there can be no security interest. The purpose of obtaining a security interest is to secure a debt.

The Security Agreement The agreement in which a debtor grants a creditor a security interest in the debtor's property must generally be authenticated by the debtor. An authenticated agreement is required in all cases except where the creditor has possession or control of the collateral [9–203]. Suppose Cole borrows $50 from Fox and gives Fox her wristwatch as a security for the loan. The agreement whereby Cole put up her watch as collateral does not have to be authenticated by Cole to be enforceable. Because the creditor (Fox) is in possession of the collateral, an oral agreement is sufficient.

The security agreement must reasonably describe the collateral so that it can readily be identified. For example, it should list the year, make, and serial number of an automobile. The security agreement usually spells out the terms of the arrangement between the creditor and the debtor. Also, it normally contains a promise by the debtor to pay certain amounts of money in a certain way. The agreement specifies which events, such as nonpayment by the buyer, constitute a default. In addition, it may contain provisions that the creditor feels are necessary to protect his security interest. For example, the debtor may be required to keep the collateral insured, not to move it without the creditor's consent, or to periodically report sales of secured inventory goods. In the case that follows, *In re Shirel,* the court found that the information contained in a credit application did not meet the requirements for a security agreement.

In re Shirel   251 BR 157 (Bankr., W.D. Oklahoma 2000)

Kevin Shirel applied for a credit card from Sight'N Sound Appliance Centers, Inc. The credit application, which constituted the agreement between the parties, was a barely legible, seven-page, single-spaced, small-print document. Shirel signed it on the first page. The form contained a statement that Sight'N Sound would have a "security interest" in all "merchandise" purchased with the credit card. The statement was located approximately four pages into the application.

Shirel's credit was approved, and he purchased a new refrigerator using the credit card. Several months later, Shirel filed a bankruptcy petition listing the remaining credit card debt as unsecured and the refrigerator as exempt from the claims of creditors. Subsequently, Sight'N Sound objected to the claim of exemption. It contended that Shirel had improperly listed the debt as unsecured and asserted that it held a secured interest in the refrigerator.

Bohanon, Bankruptcy Judge

The central issue here is whether the language included in the credit application is sufficient to grant a security interest under the Oklahoma Uniform Commercial Code. Neither the Oklahoma Supreme Court, nor the Court of Appeals for this Circuit, has indicated what precise language is required to create a security interst in goods purchased with a credit card.

Therefore, I will evaluate the plain language of the Uniform Commercial Code and determine whether or not this credit card application is a security agreement.

This statute defines a security interest as "an agreement which creates or provides for a security interest." Section 9–105(h). The formal requirements are set forth in section 9–203. The relevant provision states that, "a security agreement is not enforceable against the debtor or third parties . . . unless . . . the debtor has signed a security agreement which contains a description of the collateral."

Section 9–110 of the UCC clarifies how the word "description" should be interpreted. It states that, "for the purposes of this Article any description of personal property . . . sufficient whether or not it is specific if it reasonably identifies what is described." While the UCC encourages courts to interpret "description" liberally so as to avoid requiring a precise detailed description such as a serial number, the agreement must at a minimum "do the job assigned." That job is to sufficiently describe the collateral so that a third party would reasonably identify the items which are subject to the security interest.

The credit application here states that the card issuer, "will have a purchase money security interest in all merchandise purchased on [the] account until such merchandise is paid in full." The description "all merchandise" is vague, broad, and fails to sufficiently identify a refrigerator.

It is understandable for a creditor to desire one catchall-phrase which creates a security agreement in every possible situation. However, in doing so, it may not ignore one of the primary reasons for creating a security interest which is to give notice to a third party. This can only be achieved by describing what property is subject to the security interest.

Oklahoma courts have held that the following were sufficient descriptions for section 9–110 purposes: "laundry equipment" when referring to a washing machine; "all machinery," and "paving equipment" to describe a wheel loader; and the words "pickup truck" were sufficient even though the borrower owned two pickup trucks. A reasonable party would understand those descriptions alone, with no need to inquire further. One could be reasonably certain, based on those descriptions, of what collateral is secured. This is not so with the description "all merchandise." This description could conceivably cover any type of item.

In conclusion, no reasonable party would understand that a security interest was created by merely looking to the description itself. This court can only conclude that the word "merchandise" does not sufficiently describe the collateral at issue here. Accordingly, it is determined that Sight'N Sound does not have a security interest in the refrigerator.

Judgment against Sight'N Sound.

Note: Although this case was decided under the 1972 version of Article 9, the same result would be expected under Revised Article 9, which places more emphasis on the nature of the description.

CYBERLAW IN ACTION

Revised Article 9 Is E-Commerce Friendly

The revision to Article 9 that became effective in most states on July 1, 2001, is friendlier to e-commerce than the version it replaced. It no longer requires that the debtor "sign" a "security agreement" to create an enforceable interest in the collateral that supports the loan or performance obligation. Instead, it allows an "authenticated record"—one produced by the consumer online—to substitute for the signed "writing" of the earlier versions of Article 9 and the earlier state laws that Article 9 replaced. This is very advantageous for the buyer who wants to finance, for example, the purchase of an expensive computer or camera without using a credit card to pay for the purchase. The buyer will be able to complete the purchase transaction using an Internet seller of the type of merchandise desired and also finalize the secured transaction at the same time and using the same Internet-based system provided on the seller's Web site. If the seller is providing financing, in a "purchase-money" transaction, the seller can obtain an enforceable sales contract and an enforceable security agreement, and get the goods heading toward the consumer from the seller's warehouse without delay. The seller in many states also will be able to file an "authenticated record" in substitution for a paper "financing statement" and can complete the filing (and perhaps even pay the filing fee) using e-commerce applications.

Like the "click-through" method of forming a contract described in Chapter 9, click-through secured transactions give the buyer and seller the time- and money-saving advantages of other online transactions. They have similar risks to those present in the pure sales portion of the transaction—of unscrupulous persons trying to take advantage of either the buyer or seller, or both. But the speed and convenience are likely to outweigh the risks for many consumers and many sellers as well.

Purchase Money Security Interests. When the seller of goods retains a security interest in goods until they are paid for, or when money is loaned for the purpose of acquiring certain goods and the lender takes a security interest in those goods, the security interest that is created and attached to the goods is known as a **purchase money security interest (PMSI).** Creditors who hold PMSIs are considered important creditors because they help the economy by financing the purchase of property and are given certain advantages vis-à-vis other creditors. These advantages are discussed later in this chapter in the sections concerning Perfection of Security Interests and Priorities.

Future Advances

A security agreement may stipulate that it covers advances of credit to be made at some time in the future [9–204(3)]. Such later extensions of credit are known as **future advances.** Future advances would be involved where, for example, a bank grants a business a line of credit for $100,000 but initially advances only $20,000. When the business draws further against its line of credit, it has received a future advance and the bank is considered to have given additional "value" at that time. The security interest that the creditor obtained earlier also covers these later advances of money.

After-Acquired Property

A security agreement may be drafted to grant a creditor a security interest in the **after-acquired property** of the debtor. After-acquired property is property that the debtor does not currently own or have rights in but that he may acquire in the future. However, the security interest does not attach until the debtor actually obtains some rights to the new property [9–203(b)(2)].[2] For example, Dan's Diner borrows $25,000 from the bank and gives it a security interest in all of its present restaurant equipment as well as all of the restaurant equipment that it may "hereafter acquire." If Dan's owns only a stove at the time, then the bank has a security interest only in the stove. However, if a month later Dan's buys a refrigerator, the bank's security interest would "attach" to the refrigerator when Dan's acquires some rights to it.

A security interest in after-acquired property may not have priority over certain other creditors if the debtor acquires his new property subject to what is known as a *purchase money security interest.* When the seller of goods retains a security interest in goods until they are paid for, or when money is loaned for the purpose of acquiring certain goods and the lender takes a security interest in those goods, the security interest is a purchase money security interest. Later in this chapter, the section entitled Priority Rules discusses the rights of the holder of a purchase money security interest versus the rights of another creditor who filed earlier on after-acquired property of the debtor.

Proceeds

The creditor is commonly interested in having his security interest cover not only the collateral described in the agreement but also the **proceeds** on the disposal of the collateral by the debtor. For example, if a bank lends money to Dealer to enable Dealer to finance its inventory of new automobiles and the bank takes a security interest in the inventory, the bank wants its interest to continue in any cash proceeds obtained by Dealer when the automobiles are sold to customers. Under the 1998 amendments to Article 9, these proceeds are automatically covered as of the time the security interest attaches to the collateral [9–203(f)].

Perfecting the Security Interest

Perfection

While attachment of a security interest to collateral owned by the debtor gives the creditor rights vis-à-vis the debtor, a creditor is also concerned about making sure that she has a better right to the collateral than any other creditor if the debtor defaults. In addition, a creditor may be concerned about protecting her interest in the collateral if the debtor sells it to someone else. The creditor gets protection against other creditors or purchasers of the collateral by perfecting her security interest. Perfection is not effective without an attachment of the security interest [9–308(a)].

Under the Code, there are three main ways of perfecting a security interest:

1. By filing a public notice of the security interest.

2. By the creditor's taking possession or control of the collateral.

3. In certain transactions, by mere attachment of the security interest; this is known as automatic perfection.

Perfection by Public Filing

The most common way of perfecting a security interest is to file a **financing statement** in the appropriate public office. The financing statement serves as constructive notice to

---

[2]The Code imposes an additional requirement as to security interests in after-acquired consumer goods. Security interests do not attach to consumer goods other than "accessions" unless the consumer acquires them within 10 days after the secured party gave value [9–203(b)].

CONCEPT REVIEW

Attachment

A security interest is not legally enforceable against a debtor until it is attached to one or more particular items of the debtor's property; the attachment takes place in a legal, rather than physical, sense.

There are three requirements for a security interest to attach to the goods of the debtor:

1. There must be an *agreement* in which the debtor grants the creditor a security interest in the debtor's property.
2. The debtor must have *rights in the collateral*.
3. The creditor must give value to the debtor, for example, by lending him money or advancing goods on credit.

Future Advances. A security may provide for the advance of credit to a debtor at some time in the future. At the time the debtor actually draws on the future extension of credit, the creditor is considered to have given additional value for purposes of attachment of a security interest.

After-Acquired Property. A security agreement may be drafted to grant a creditor a security interest in property that the debtor does not currently own but which she may acquire at some time in the future. However, the security interest does not attach until the debtor actually obtains some rights in the new property.

Proceeds. Proceeds on the sale or other disposition of collateral to which a security interest has been attached are automatically covered as of the time the security interest attaches to the collateral.

---

the world that the creditor claims an interest in collateral that belongs to a certain named debtor. The financing statement usually consists of a multicopy form that is available from the office of the secretary of state (see Figure 1). However, the security agreement can be filed as the financing statement if it contains the required information and has been signed by the debtor.

To be sufficient, the financing statement must (1) contain the names of the debtor; (2) give the name of the secured party; and (3) contain a statement indicating or describing the collateral covered by the financing statement. If the financing statement covers goods that are to become fixtures, a description of the real estate must be included.

Each state specifies by statute where the financing statement has to be filed. In all states, a financing statement that covers fixtures must be filed in the office where a mortgage on real estate would be filed [9–501]. To obtain maximum security, the secured party acquiring a security interest in property that is a fixture or is to become a fixture should double file—that is, file the security interest as a fixture and as a nonfixture.

In regard to collateral other than fixtures, most states require only central filing, usually in the office of the secretary of state. However, if you are a creditor taking a security interest, it is important to check the law in your state to determine where to file the financing statement [9–501].

A financing statement is effective for a period of five years from the date of filing, and it lapses then unless a continuation statement has been filed before that time. An exception is made for real estate mortgages that are effective as fixture filings—they are effective until the mortgage is released or terminates [9–515].

A **continuation statement** may be filed within six months before the five-year expiration date. The continuation statement must be signed by the secured party, identify the original statement by file number, and state that the original statement is still effective. Successive continuation statements may be filed [9–403(3)].

When a consumer debtor completely fulfills all debts and obligations secured by a financing statement, she is entitled to a **termination statement** signed by the secured party or an assignee of record [9–513].

Possession by Secured Party as Public Notice

Public filing of a security interest is intended to put any interested members of the public on notice of the security interest. A potential creditor of the debtor, or a potential buyer of the collateral, can check the records to see whether anyone else claims an interest in the debtor's collateral. The same objective can be reached if the debtor

Figure 1　A Financing Statement

UCC FINANCING STATEMENT
FOLLOW INSTRUCTIONS (front and back) CAREFULLY

A. NAME & TELEPHONE OF CONTACT AT FILER (optional)

B. SEND ACKNOWLEDGMENT TO: (Name and Address)

THE ABOVE SPACE IS FOR FILING OFFICE USE ONLY

1. DEBTOR'S EXACT FULL LEGAL NAME -insert only <u>one</u> debtor name (1a or 1b) - do not abbreviate or combine names

1a ORGANIZATION'S NAME			
OR			
1b INDIVIDUAL'S LAST NAME	FIRST NAME	MIDDLE NAME	SUFFIX

1c MAILING ADDRESS	CITY	STATE	POSTAL CODE	COUNTRY

1d TAX ID　SSN OR EIN	ADD'L INFO RE ORGANIZATION DEBTOR	1e TYPE OF ORGANIZATION	1f JURISDICTION OF ORGANIZATION	1g ORGANIZATIONAL ID #, if any	□ NONE

2. ADDITIONAL DEBTOR'S EXACT FULL LEGAL NAME - insert only <u>one</u> debtor name (2a or 2b) - do not abbreviate or combine names

2a ORGANIZATION'S NAME			
OR			
2b INDIVIDUAL'S LAST NAME	FIRST NAME	MIDDLE NAME	SUFFIX

2c MAILING ADDRESS	CITY	STATE	POSTAL CODE	COUNTRY

2d TAX ID　SSN OR EIN	ADD'L INFO RE ORGANIZATION DEBTOR	2e TYPE OF ORGANIZATION	2f JURISDICTION OF ORGANIZATION	2g ORGANIZATIONAL ID #, if any	□ NONE

3. SECURED PARTY'S NAME (or NAME of TOTAL ASSIGNEE of ASSIGNOR S/P) - insert only <u>one</u> secured party name (3a or 3b)

3a ORGANIZATION'S NAME			
OR			
3b INDIVIDUAL'S LAST NAME	FIRST NAME	MIDDLE NAME	SUFFIX

3c MAILING ADDRESS	CITY	STATE	POSTAL CODE	COUNTRY

4. This FINANCING STATEMENT covers the following collateral

5. ALTERNATIVE DESIGNATION (if applicable) □ LESEE/LESSOR □ CONSIGNEE/CONSIGNOR □ BAILEE/BAILOR □ SELLER/BUYER □ AG LIEN □ NON-UCC FILING

6. □ This FINANCING STATEMENT is to be filed (for record)(or recorded) in the REAL ESTATE RECORDS　Attach Addendum　If applicable | 7. Check to REQUEST SEARCH REPORT(S) on Debtor(s) [ADDITIONAL FEE]　(optional)　□ ALL DEBTORS　□ DEBTOR 1　□ DEBTOR 2

8. OPTIONAL FILER REFERENCE DATA

FILING OFFICE COPY—NATIONAL UCC FINANCING STATEMENT (FORM UCC1) (REV. 07/29/98)

Figure 1   A Financing Statement (continued)

UCC FINANCING STATEMENT **ADDENDUM**
FOLLOW INSTRUCTIONS (front and back) CAREFULLY

9. NAME OF FIRST DEBTOR (1a or 1b) ON RELATED FINANCING STATEMENT

	9a ORGANIZATION'S NAME
OR	9b INDIVIDUAL'S LAST NAME

9b INDIVIDUAL'S LAST NAME	FIRST NAME	MIDDLE NAME SUFFIX

10. MISCELLANEOUS:

THE ABOVE SPACE IS FOR FILING OFFICE USE ONLY

11. ADDITIONAL DEBTOR'S EXACT LEGAL NAME -insert only one name (11a or 11b) - do no abbreviate or combine names

	11a ORGANIZATION'S NAME			
OR	11b INDIVIDUAL'S LAST NAME	FIRST NAME	MIDDLE NAME	SUFFIX

11c MAILING ADDRESS	CITY	STATE	POSTAL CODE	COUNTRY

11d TAX ID SSN OR EIN	ADD'L INFO RE ORGANIZATION DEBTOR	11e TYPE OF ORGANIZATION	11f JURISDICTION OF ORGANIZATION	11g ORGANIZATIONAL ID #, if any	NONE

12. ☐ ADDITIONAL SECURED PARTY'S or ☐ ASSIGNOR S/P'S   NAME -insert only <u>one</u> name (12a or 12b)

	12a ORGANIZATION'S NAME			
OR	12b INDIVIDUAL'S LAST NAME	FIRST NAME	MIDDLE NAME	SUFFIX

12c MAILING ADDRESS	CITY	STATE	POSTAL CODE	COUNTRY

13. This FINANCING STATEMENT covers ☐ timber to be cut or ☐ as extracted collateral, or is filed as a ☐ future filing.

14. Description of real estate

15. Name and address of a RECORD OWNER of above-described real estate (if Debtor does not have a record interest):

16. Additional collateral description

17. Check <u>only</u> if applicable and Check <u>only</u> one box

Debtor is a ☐ Trust or ☐ Trustee acting with respect to property held in trust or ☐ Decedent's estate

18. Check <u>only</u> if applicable and check <u>only</u> one box.
☐ Debtor is a TRANSMITTING UTILITY
☐ Filed in connection with a Manufacturing-Home Transaction—effective 30 years
☐ Filed in connection with a Public Finance Transaction—effective 30 years

FILING OFFICE COPY—NATIONAL UCC FINANCING STATEMENT ADDENDUM (FORM UCC1Ad) (REV. 07/29/98) gives up possession of the collateral to the creditor or to a third person who holds the collateral for the creditor. If a debtor does not have possession of collateral that he claims to own, then a potential creditor or debtor is on notice that someone else may claim an interest in it. Thus, a security interest is perfected by change of possession of collateral from the debtor to the creditor/secured party or his agent [9–313(a)]. For example, Simpson borrows $150 from a pawnbroker and leaves his guitar as collateral for the loan. The pawnbroker's security interest in the guitar is perfected by virtue of her possession of the guitar.

Change of possession is not a common or convenient way for perfecting most security interests in consumer goods. It is more practicable for perfecting security interests in commercial collateral. In fact, it is the only way to perfect a security interest in money [9–312(b)].

Possession of collateral by the creditor is often the best way to perfect a security interest in chattel paper and negotiable documents of title. Possession is also a possible way of perfecting a security interest in inventory. This is sometimes achieved through a **field warehousing arrangement**. For example, a finance company makes a large loan to a peanut warehouse to enable it to buy peanuts from local farmers. The finance company takes a security interest in the inventory of peanuts. It sets up a field warehousing arrangement under which a representative of the finance company takes physical control over the peanuts. This representative might actually fence off the peanut storage area and control access to it. When the peanut warehouse wants to sell part of the inventory to a food processor, it must make a payment to the finance company. Then the finance company's representative will allow the peanut warehouse to take some of the peanuts out of the fenced-off area and deliver them to the processor. In this way the finance company controls the collateral in which it has a security interest until the loan is repaid.

Possession by the creditor is usually not a practicable way of perfecting a security interest in equipment or farm products. In the case of equipment, the debtor needs to use it in the business. For example, if a creditor kept possession of a stove that was sold on credit to a restaurant, it would defeat the purpose for which the restaurant was buying the stove, that is, to use it in its business.

The person to whom the collateral is delivered holds it as bailee, and he owes the duties of a bailee to the parties in interest [9–207].

Control
A secured party can provide a similar form of public notice by controlling the collateral [9–314].

Control is the only perfection method if the collateral is a deposit account [9–312(b)(1)]. A secured party obtains control by one of three means: (1) the secured party is the bank with which the deposit account is maintained; (2) the debtor, secured party, and the bank have agreed that the bank will comply with the secured party's instructions regarding funds in the account; or (3) the secured party becomes the bank's customer for the deposit account.

Perfection by Attachment/Automatic Perfection
Perfection by mere attachment of the security interest, sometimes known as automatic perfection, is the only form of perfection that occurs without the giving of public notice. It occurs automatically when all the requirements of attachment are complete. This form of perfection is limited to certain classes of collateral; in addition, it may be only a temporary perfection in some situations.

A creditor who sells goods to a consumer on credit, or who lends money to enable a consumer to buy goods, can obtain limited perfection of a security interest merely by attaching the security interest to the goods. A creditor under these circumstances has what is called a **purchase money security interest in consumer goods**. For example, an appliance store sells a television set to Margaret Morse on a conditional sales contract, or time-payment plan. The store does not have to file its purchase money security interest in the set. The security interest is considered perfected just by virtue of its attachment to the set in the hands of the consumer.

Perfection by attachment is not effective if the consumer goods are motor vehicles for which the state issues certificates of title and has only limited effectiveness if the goods are fixtures [9–303]. A later section of this chapter discusses the special rules covering these kinds of collateral.

There are also major limitations to the perfection by attachment principle. As discussed later in the Priority section of this chapter, relying on attachment for perfection does not, in some instances, provide as much protection to the creditor as does public filing.

One potential concern for a creditor is that the use of the collateral will change from that anticipated when the security interest was obtained. It is important that the creditor properly perfect the security interest initially so that it will not be adversely affected by a subsequent change in use and will continue to have the benefit of its initial perfection.

Automatic perfection by attachment of the security interest is illustrated in the following case, *Meskell v. Bertone.*

In this case, the bank that provided funds for the purchase of a boat obtained a purchase money security interest that was automatically perfected; however, because the bank did not file the security interest, when the original purchaser sold it to another consumer who intended to use it for household purposes and had no knowledge of the bank's purchase money security interest, the subsequent purchaser took free of the bank's security interest.

Meskell v. Bertone   55 UCC Rep.2d 179 (Super. Ct. Mass. 2004)

On September 28, 2001, John Meskell borrowed $31,601.75 from Key Bank to finance his purchase of a 66-foot Chapparral boat. That same day, he executed a "Note, Security Agreement, and Disclosure Statement" in connection with the loan. The security agreement lists the boat as collateral for the loan. The terms of the note prohibited Meskell from transferring ownership or possession of the boat by sale, lease, or other means without first obtaining Key Bank's written permission. In addition, the note terms defined default as including breach of any significant term or condition. In the event of a default, Key Bank was entitled to repossess the boat and to require Meskell to repay the entire loan balance. The bank did not file a financing statement documenting its security interest.

In late 2002, Meskell advertised the boat for sale in the Boston Globe. *Kimberly Friedman contacted Meskell in response to the advertisement and indicated that her husband, Dale Friedman of Sea Dog Yacht Sales, would be willing to procure a buyer for a commission of 10 percent of the purchase price. Meskell towed his boat to Sea Dog's yard where a "For Sale" sign was placed on it with an asking price of $49,000.*

In the spring of 2003, John Bertone made an offer to purchase the boat for $44,000, which was accepted by Meskell. Bertone tendered a refundable deposit check to Sea Dog in the amount of $4,400; signed a purchase and sales agreement that stated the obligation of the seller to deliver the yacht free and clear of any liens, mortgages, or applicable bills; and agreed that the broker could deduct the applicable funds from the proceeds of the mortgage. Bertone tendered a check for $39,695, payable to the Sea Dog, and other checks payable to the Commonwealth of Massachusetts to cover the boat sales tax, title, and registration. On July 12, 2003, Bertone took possession of the boat.

On July 18, Meskell approved a final accounting that listed the sales price, Friedman's commission, the payoff of the amount owed to Key Bank, and the amount due to Meskell. Meskell received a check in the amount of $7,084.69 from Friedman. In August, Friedman absconded with the remaining sales proceeds without having satisfied the lien held by Key Bank; he subsequently was indicted for embezzlement.

Key Bank filed a complaint against Meskell and Bertone. The claim against Meskell was based on breach of contract and contended that as a result of the breach of the sales agreement by the sale to Bertone, the full amount owing on the note was due and payable. The bank asserted an equitable claim against Bertone, alleging that it was the rightful owner of the boat and seeking its repossession.

Cratsley, Justice

Article 9 guides the resolution of the competing ownership claims presented in these two cases. A sweeping revision of Article 9 became effective in Massachusetts on July 1, 2001, but many historical secured transactions principles remain relevant to the resolution of this dispute.

The Bank's Security Interest in the Boat

The Bank seeks replevin of the boat from the Bertones, claiming that under Article 9 it is the rightful possessor of the boat. By placing the boat for sale without the Bank's express written permission, Meskell breached the security agreement and the promissory note. Consequently, the Bank was entitled to immediate possession of the collateral, unless the Bertones took free of the Bank's security interest in the boat.

The security agreement and note executed by Meskell and the Bank gave the Bank a security interest in the boat. A security interest is "effective according to its terms between the parties, against purchasers of the collateral and against creditors" unless the secured party is required to file a financing statement in order to perfect the interest. The secured party must file a financing statement to perfect the security interest in all cases except, among others, that of a purchase money security interest (PMSI). Therefore, the Bank was required to file a financing statement to perfect its interest in the boat unless the interest constituted a PMSI. Article 9 defines a PMSI as follows: "a security interest in goods is a [PMSI] . . . to the extent that the goods are purchase-money collateral with respect to that security interest." Purchase-money collateral are goods used to secure an "obligation of an obligor incurred as all or part of the purchase price of the collateral."

Meskell borrowed funds from the Bank to finance the sale of the boat and, in turn, granted the Bank a security interest in the boat to secure the purchase price. Therefore, the Bank's security interest in the boat constituted a PMSI and the Bank was not required to file a financing statement to perfect its security interest in the collateral.

A PMSI is automatically perfected upon attachment. The Bank's security interest attached when the following events occurred: (1) Meskell signed the security agreement describing the boat as collateral, (2) the Bank gave Meskell value in the form of a loan, and (3) Meskell used the loan funds to obtain rights in the boat. The Bank's interest is therefore enforceable according to its terms between the parties, any purchasers of the collateral, and any creditors, subject to the buyer of consumer goods exception set forth in § 9–320(b). The Bank's interest in the boat takes priority over the Bertones' interest, unless the Bertones demonstrate that they meet the requirements of the buyer of consumer goods exception as described below.

Buyer of Consumer Goods

The buyer of consumer goods exception in revised Article 9 mirrors the historical notion of buyer in ordinary course. The aim of both provisions may be summarized as follows: "one who buys consumer goods *from another consumer* for his own personal use without knowledge of a perfected security interest takes the goods free of such interest unless the secured party has previously filed." Under § 9–320(b), "a buyer of goods from a person who used or bought the goods for use primarily for personal, family, or household purposes takes free of a security interest, even if perfected, if the buyer buys: (1) without knowledge of the security interest; (2) for value; (3) primarily for the buyer's personal, family, or household purposes; and (4) before the filing of a financing statement covering the goods."

To invoke the protection of 9–320(b), both the buyer and seller of the goods must be consumers. To hold § 9–320(b) applicable, this Court must decide whether Meskell's sale of the boat through his selling agents, Friedman and Sea Dog, constitutes a consumer-to-consumer sale. Agency principles guide this analysis. In a contractual context, any negotiation undertaken on behalf of the principal is deemed to be the act of the principal himself. Indeed, "whatever one does by another, he does so by himself so far as concerns legal responsibility." In this case, title never passed from Meskell to Friedman or Sea Dog. The agency relationship was disclosed to the Bertones,

and they were aware that they were purchasing the boat from the owner, a consumer. Although negotiated by Meskell's agent, the Final P&S and Bill of Sale evidenced an agreement between the Bertones and Meskell for the sale of consumer goods. I am therefore persuaded by a preponderance of the evidence that the transaction in question falls within the buyer of consumer goods exception in § 9–320(b).

Knowledge, Good Faith, and Title

To defeat the Bank's PMSI on the basis of the buyer of consumer goods exception, the Bertones must also meet additional criteria. The Bank and Meskell argue that the Bertones cannot claim the protection of § 9–320(b) because (1) they had notice of Key Bank's lien, and (2) they did not approach the transaction in good faith. The Bank and Meskell further argue that the Bertones are not the rightful possessors of the boat because they did not obtain title as required by the state statutory scheme.

The Bank's lien is clearly marked on the state title. The Bank and Meskell argue that the Bertones were on notice of the Bank's lien because they did not receive the state Certificate of Title at closing. The Article 9 provision regarding buyer of consumer goods, however, concerns knowledge, not notice. Whereas notice places a duty of inquiry on the party, "knowledge," as defined in § 1–201(25), requires that the party have "actual knowledge" of the fact. Based on all of the facts previously developed about the transaction in question, and finding John Bertone's trial testimony credible, I am persuaded by a preponderance of the evidence that the Bertones did not have actual knowledge of the Bank's security interest in the boat.

Similar to their arguments on knowledge, the Bank and Meskell contend that the Bertones are not good-faith purchasers because they did not receive title when they tendered payment to Friedman at closing. The Bank and Meskell assert that by taking possession of the boat without title, the Bertones acted at their peril and were on notice that further inquiry into the state of title was necessary. Consequently, the Bank and Meskell argue, the Bertones' failure to further inquire into the state of title at that time evidences the Bertones' lack of good faith. The definition of good faith, however, does not place the buyer on a duty of inquiry. Good faith means "honesty in fact in the conduct of the transaction concerned." § 1–201(19).

The preponderance of the trial evidence demonstrates that on July 11, 2003, the Bertones had a genuine belief that they were purchasing the boat in a legitimate transaction free of liens. At all times during the transaction, the Bertones negotiated with Friedman, not Meskell. They had previously tendered a deposit to Friedman without incident. The Bill of Sale stated that all liens and encumbrances on the boat had been revealed. Moreover, both the initial P&S and the Final P&S

conspicuously and unambiguously stated that the boat would be sold free of liens, or that any outstanding liens would be satisfied by the sale proceeds. Lastly, Sea Dog's employee, Thurman, represented to John Bertone that the Bill of Sale was the most important aspect of the transaction, and that title and registration were ancillary to the sale. The Bertones obtained a Bill of Sale that they used to document the boat through the Coast Guard pursuant to the federal vessel documentation regime.

Under Massachusetts law, a boat owner may choose to register the vessel within the state system or to document the vessel with the United States Coast Guard. The Bertones reasonably pursued federal documentation because, as John Bertone testified, he believed the federal approach afforded greater protection of their property. All of this evidence supports my conclusion that the Bertones acted honestly and in good faith with respect to the closing on July 11, 2004.

The Bank and Meskell also argue that the state boat title statute nullifies transactions involving titled motorboats where, as here, the owner does not deliver title to the transferee. Indeed, the boat title statute not only requires buyers of registered vessels to obtain a certificate of title, but also requires sellers of such vessels to provide a certificate of title upon transfer or sale. Here, a sale occurred even though Meskell did not furnish the Bertones with the state title. Article 2 of the Code notes the Code's "departure from the title or property concept for deciding sales controversies." The Code provisions with respect to passing of title note that "title passes to the buyer at the time and place at which the seller completes his performance with reference to the physical delivery of the goods, . . . even though a document of title is to be delivered at a different time or place," unless the parties contract otherwise. The Bertones tendered the full contract price and took possession of the boat, thereby completing delivery.

The boat title statute does not displace or supersede § 9–320(b) but imposes additional requirements upon boat owners and dealers regarding the title and registration of vessels. The statute does not vitiate the transfer of ownership that occurred when the Bertones, without knowledge and in good faith, furnished consideration for the boat according to the parties' agreement.

Because the Bertones purchased the boat for value from another consumer, intended to use the boat for household purposes, and did not have knowledge of the Bank's security interest, their ownership rights are superior to those of the Bank. Article 9 imposes the burden on the party most able to insulate itself from risk. Here, the Bank had the option of filing a financing statement to ensure its priority in this factual situation, even though it was not required to file to perfect its PMSI. The Bank chose not to avail itself of the additional protection afforded by filing a financing statement. In addition, Meskell enlisted Friedman as his agent to represent him in the boat sale and accepted the benefits of that transaction. Therefore, Meskell bears the loss resulting from Friedman's apparent malfeasance.

Motor Vehicles If state law requires a certificate of title for motor vehicles, then a creditor who takes a security interest in a motor vehicle (other than a creditor holding a security interest in inventory held for sale by a person in the business of selling goods of that kind) must have the security interest noted on the title [9–302]. Suppose a credit union lends Carlson money to buy a new car in a state that requires certificates of title for cars. The credit union cannot rely on filing or on attachment of its security interest in the car to perfect that interest; rather, it must have its security interest noted on the certificate of title.

This requirement protects the would-be buyer of the car or another creditor who might extend credit based on Carlson's ownership of the car. By checking the certificate of title to Carlson's car, a potential buyer or creditor would learn about the credit union's security interest in the car. If no security interest is noted on the certificate of title, the buyer can buy—or the creditor can extend credit—with confidence that there are no undisclosed security interests that would be effective against him.

Fixtures The Code also provides special rules for perfecting security interests in consumer goods that become fixtures by virtue of their attachment to or use with real property. A creditor with a security interest in consumer goods (including consumer goods that will become fixtures) obtains perfection merely by attachment of her security interest to a consumer good. However, as discussed in the Priority section of this chapter, a creditor who relies on attachment for perfection will not, in some instances, prevail against other creditors who hold an interest in the real estate to which the consumer good is attached unless a special financing statement known as a fixture filing is filed with the real estate records to perfect the security interest [9–102(40); 9–334].

Perfection

Perfection is the mechanism by which a creditor who has attached his security interest to collateral obtains protection for his interest in the collateral against other creditors or against purchasers of the collateral from the debtor. As will be seen in the section on Priorities, the amount of protection obtained by perfection can vary depending on the nature of any competing security interests, whether and how the security interests were perfected, and the nature of the buyer.

The primary ways of perfecting a security interest are:

1. Perfection by public filing of a financing statement with the appropriate government office.
   * To be sufficient a financing statement must:
     a. Contain the name(s) of the debtor.
     b. Provide the name of the secured party.
     c. Contain a statement describing the collateral covered by the financing statement.
     d. If the financing statement covers goods that are to become fixtures, a description of the real estate must be included.
   * Filing a financing statement can be used to perfect a security interest in most kinds of collateral except for (1) money, (2) noninventory motor vehicles where the security interest must be noted on the title, and (3) letters of credit.
   * Filing a financing statement is the only way to perfect a security interest in accounts receivable and general intangibles.
2. Perfection by the secured party taking possession of the collateral.
   * Possession works for most kinds of collateral except for accounts receivable and general intangibles.
   * Possession is the only way to perfect a security interest in money.
3. Perfection by the secured party taking control of the security.
   * Taking control works for security interests in securities (such as stocks), letter of credit rights, and electronic chattel paper.
   * Taking control is the only way for letter of credit rights.
   * There are two ways for a creditor to take control of a security entitlement:
     a. The security intermediary lists the creditor/secured party as a beneficial owner of the security.
     b. The security intermediary agrees to act on the instructions of the creditor/secured party.
4. Attachment of the security interest/automatic perfection.
   * This method of perfection, whereby the security interest is perfected automatically when it attaches to the collateral, is available only for purchase money security interests in consumer goods (other than motor vehicles for which the state issues titles).
5. Notation of the security interest on Certificate of Title of Motor Vehicles.
   * This method is only appropriate for motor vehicles for which the state issues titles.

Priority Rules

Importance of Determining Priority

Because several creditors may claim a security interest in the same collateral of a debtor, the Code establishes a set of rules for determining which of the conflicting security interests has priority. Determining which creditor has priority or the best claim takes on particular importance in bankruptcy situations, where, unless a creditor has a perfected secured interest in collateral that fully protects the obligation owed to him, the creditor may realize nothing or only a few cents on every dollar owed to him.

General Priority Rules

The basic rule established by the Code is that when more than one security interest in the same collateral has been filed (or otherwise perfected), the first security interest to be filed (or perfected) has priority over any that is filed (or perfected) later [9–322(a)(1)]. If only one security interest has been perfected, for example, by filing, then that security interest has priority. However, if none of the conflicting security interests has been perfected, then the first security interest to be *attached* to the collateral has priority [9–322(a)(3)].

Thus, if Bank A filed a financing statement covering a retailer's inventory on February 1, 2009, and Bank B filed a financing statement on March 1, 2009, covering that same inventory, Bank A would have priority over Bank B. This is true even though Bank B might have made its loan and attached its security interest to the inventory prior to the time that Bank A did so. However, if Bank A neglected to perfect its security interest by filing and Bank B did perfect, then Bank B would prevail, as it has the only perfected security interest in the inventory.

If both creditors neglected to perfect their security interest, then the first security interest that attached would have priority [9–322(a)(3)]. For example, if Loan Company Y has a security agreement covering a dealer's equipment dated June 1, 2009, and advances money to the dealer on that date, whereas Bank Z does not obtain a security agreement covering that equipment or advance money to the dealer until July 1, 2009, then Loan Company Y has priority over Bank Z. In connection with the last situation, it is important to note that unperfected secured creditors do not enjoy a preferred position in bankruptcy proceedings, thus giving additional importance to filing or otherwise perfecting a security interest.

Purchase Money Security Interest in Inventory

There are several very important exceptions to the general priority rules. First, a **perfected purchase money security interest in inventory** has priority over a conflicting security interest in the same inventory *if* all four of these requirements are met: (1) the purchase money security interest is perfected at the time the debtor receives possession of the inventory, (2) the purchase money secured party gives notification in writing to the prior secured creditor before the debtor receives the inventory, (3) the holder of the competing security interest received notification within five years before the debtor receives the inventory, and (4) the notification states that the person expects to acquire a purchase money security interest in inventory of the debtor and describes the inventory [9–324(b)].

Assume that Bank A takes and perfects a security interest in "all present and after-acquired inventory" of a debtor. Then the debtor acquires some additional inventory from a wholesaler, which retains a security interest in the inventory until the debtor pays for it. The wholesaler perfects this security interest. The wholesaler has a *purchase money security interest* in inventory goods and will have priority over the prior secured creditor (Bank A) if the wholesaler has perfected the security interest by the time the collateral reaches the debtor and if the wholesaler sends notice of its purchase money security interest to Bank A before the wholesaler ships the goods. Thus, to protect itself, the wholesaler must check the public records to see whether any of the debtor's creditors are claiming an interest in the debtor's inventory. When it discovers that some are claiming an interest, it should file its own security interest and give notice of that security interest to the existing creditors [9–324(b) and (c)].

As the following *General Electric Capital Commercial Automotive Finance* case illustrates, the subsequent seller of inventory can obtain a priority position if it files a financing statement and notifies the prior secured party in a timely fashion.

General Electric Capital Commercial Automotive Finance, Inc. v. Spartan Motors, Inc.
675 N.Y.S. 2d 626 (New York Sup. Ct., App. Div. 1998)

On September 28, 1983, a predecessor of General Electric Capital Commercial Automotive Finance (GECC) entered into an "Inventory Security Agreement" with Spartan Motors, in connection with its "floor plan" financing of the dealership's inventory. By assignment of that agreement, GECC acquired a blanket lien (otherwise known as a "dragnet" lien) on Spartan's inventory to secure a debt in excess of $1,000,000. "Inventory" was defined in the agreement as "[a]ll inventory, of whatever kind or nature, wherever located, now owned or hereafter acquired, and all returns, repossessions, exchanges, substitutions, *replacements, attachments, parts, accessories and accessions thereto and thereof, and all other goods used or intended to be used in conjunction therewith, and all proceeds thereof (whether in the form of cash, instruments, chattel paper, general intangibles, accounts or otherwise)." This security agreement was duly filed in the office of the Dutchess County Clerk and with Secretary of State for New York State.*

On July 19, 1991, Spartan signed a new Wholesale Security Agreement with General Motors Acceptance Corporation (GMAC), in which the latter agreed to finance or "floor-plan" Spartan's inventory. According to its terms, Spartan agreed, inter alia, *as follows:*

In the course of our business, we acquire new and used cars, trucks and chassis ("Vehicles") from manufacturers or distributors. We desire you to finance the acquisition of such vehicles and to pay the manufacturers or distributors therefore.

We agree upon demand to pay to GMAC the amount it advances or is obligated to advance to the manufacturer or distributor for each vehicle with interest at the rate per annum designated by GMAC from time to time and then in force under the GMAC Wholesale Plan.

We also agree that to secure collectively the payment by us of the amounts of all advances and obligations to advance made by GMAC to the manufacturer, distributor or other sellers, and the interest due thereon, GMAC is hereby granted a security interest in the vehicles and the proceeds of sale thereof ("Collateral") as more fully described herein.

The collateral subject to this Wholesale Security Agreement is new vehicles held for sale or lease and used vehicles acquired from manufacturers or distributors and held for sale or lease.

We understand that we may sell and lease the vehicles at retail in the ordinary course of business. We further agree that as each vehicle is sold, or leased, we will faithfully and promptly remit to you the amount you advanced or have become obligated to advance on our behalf to the manufacturer, distributor or seller.

GMAC'S Security Agreement was duly filed. In addition, by certified letter dated July 17, 1991, GMAC officially notified GECC of its competing security interest in Spartan's inventory, as follows:

This is to notify you that General Motors Acceptance Corporation holds or expects to acquire purchase money security interests in inventory collateral which will from time to time hereafter be delivered to Spartan Motors Ltd. of Poughkeepsie, New York, and in the proceeds thereof.

Such inventory collateral consists, or will consist, of the types of collateral described in a financing statement, a true copy of which is annexed hereto and made a part hereof.

On May 7, 1992, Spartan paid $121,500 of its own money to European Auto Wholesalers, Ltd., to acquire a 1992 600 SEL Mercedes-Benz. Six days later, on May 13, 1992, GMAC reimbursed Spartan and the vehicle was placed on GMAC's floor plan.

On July 7, 1992, Spartan paid $120,000 of its own money to the same seller to acquire a second 1992 600 SEL Mercedes. Two days later, on July 9, 1992, GMAC reimbursed Spartan for that amount and placed the second vehicle on its floor plan. The two vehicles remained unsold in Spartan's showroom.

A few months later, on or about October 2, 1992, GECC commenced an action against Spartan, seeking $1,180,999.98, representing money then due to GECC under its agreement with Spartan. Claims were also made against the principals of Spartan, upon their guarantees, as well as against GMAC and Mercedes-Benz of North America, Inc. (MBNA), to determine lien priority in the collateral.

After commencement of the litigation, Spartan filed a bankruptcy petition and ceased doing business. GECC, GMAC, and MBNA took possession of and liquidated their respective collateral pursuant to a prior agreement between the parties. Among the assets appropriated and sold by GMAC were two Mercedes-Benz automobiles, which were auctioned for $194,500. GECC settled its claims against all of the defendants except GMAC, which it accused of converting the two Mercedes-Benz vehicles in violation of GECC's earlier security interest.

The trial court granted GECC's motion for summary judgment, finding persuasive GECC's argument that a literal reading of GMAC's security agreement with Spartan, in conjunction with the wording of Uniform Commercial Code section 9–107(b), required a holding that GMAC had a purchase-money secured interest only to the extent that it paid funds directly to "manufacturers, distributors and sellers" of Spartan's inventory in advance of the transfer of the merchandise to the car dealership. The court reasoned that because "[n]owhere in the contracts of adhesion signed by Spartan with GMAC is there an obligation by GMAC to reimburse Spartan for funds used to purchase automobiles," GECC's previously perfected security interest in all of Spartan's inventory should prevail. GMAC appealed.

Friedman, Judge

A perfected purchase-money security interest provides an exception to the general first-in-time, first-in-right rule of conflicting security interest. Thus, a perfected purchase money security interest in inventory has priority over a conflicting prior security interest in the same inventory (see, UCC 9–312 (3)). However, the purported purchase-money security interest must fit within the Uniform Commercial Code definition to qualify for the exception.

Uniform Commercial Code section 9–107 defines a "purchase money security interest" as a security interest:

(a) taken or retained by the seller of the collateral to secure all or part of its price; or
(b) taken by a person who by making advances or incurring an obligation gives value to enable the debtor to acquire rights in or the use of collateral if such value is in fact so used.

The issue here is therefore whether GMAC's payment as reimbursement to Spartan after it had acquired the two Mercedes-Benz vehicles on two different occasions qualifies as an "advance" or "obligation" that enabled Spartan to purchase the cars, such that GMAC acquired a purchase-money security interest in the vehicles. The arguments *against* finding a purchase-money security interest under these circumstances are basically twofold: Firstly, of the few courts to construe Uniform Commercial Code section 9–107 (b), many have been reluctant to decide that a purchase-money security interest has been created where, as here, title to and possession of the merchandise have passed to the debtor before the loan is advanced. Secondly, the literal wording of the agreement between GMAC and Spartan appears to accord GMAC purchase-money secured status only when the finance company paid Spartan's "manufacturer, distributor or other seller" directly. As the Supreme Court noted, nothing in GMAC's contract with Spartan appears to contemplate any obligation on the part of the financier to "reimburse" the auto dealership for funds that the latter had already expended to purchase merchandise. These two interrelated arguments will be discussed *seriatim*.

(1) Whether after-advanced funds may qualify for purchase-money security status under Uniform Commercial Code section 9–107(b).

Research indicates that there is no judicial authority in New York construing the application of UCC 9–107(b) to a creditor's subsequent reimbursement of a debtor for an antecedent purchase of collateral.

One factor that courts have considered is simple temporal proximity—that is, whether the value is given by the creditor "more or less contemporaneously with the debtor's acquisition of the property."

The authorities are agreed that the critical inquiry, as in all contract matters, is into the intention of the parties. In determining whether a security interest exists, the intent of the parties controls, and that intent may best be determined by examining the language used and considering the conditions and circumstances confronting the parties when the contract was made. In assessing the relationship of the transactions, the test should be whether the availability of the loan was a factor in negotiating the sale, and/or whether the lender was committed at the time of the sale to advance the amount required to pay for the items purchased.

Applying these principles to the matter before us: (1) The record establishes that GMAC's reimbursements to Spartan following its two Mercedes-Benz purchases were only six and two days apart, respectively. (2) GECC does not dispute GMAC's contention that a postpurchase reimbursement arrangement was common in the trade, as well as routine in Spartan's course of dealing with GMAC and its other financiers, depending upon the circumstances of the purchase. For example, GMAC employee Philip Canterino, who handled GMAC's account with Spartan, has averred without contradiction by GECC that although it was customary for GMAC to prepay a car manufacturer before it delivered new vehicles to Spartan's showroom, in a case of the sort at issue here—where the vehicles were difficult to obtain from the manufacturer but were readily available from a distributor—it was not uncommon for GMAC to reimburse Spartan after the cars had been delivered to Spartan's showroom, upon Spartan's presentation of proof of clear title. In the language of Uniform Commercial Code UCC 9–107(b): GMAC was committed to give value to enable the car dealership to acquire rights in the collateral. The value so extended was intended to and in fact did enable Spartan to acquire the two Mercedes-Benzes, as GECC does not seriously suggest that without GMAC's backing Spartan could have afforded to purchase the expensive vehicles. Accordingly, the literal requirements of Uniform Commercial Code section 9–107 (b) are satisfied, notwithstanding the inverted purchase-loan. Because GMAC's loans were "closely allied" with Spartan's inventory acquisitions, GMAC enjoys a purchase-money security interest in the contested merchandise.

(2) Whether GMAC's lien is circumscribed by the precise language of its agreement with Spartan.

It is well established that the terms of a written security agreement may be amplified by "other circumstances including course of dealing or usage of trade or course of performance" (UCC 1–201 (3)). Here, GECC does not deny that, although the written terms of GMAC's contract with Spartan appeared to contemplate a single method of inventory financing (i.e., GMAC's payment to Spartan's sellers in advance of the purchase transaction), in fact it was not at all unusual for the parties to pursue the same end by somewhat different means (i.e., GMAC's posttransaction reimbursement to Spartan for its inventory purchases), as GMAC employee Canterino repeatedly explained.

Generally, the express terms of an agreement and a differing course of performance, course of dealing, and/or usage of trade "shall be construed whenever reasonable as consistent with each other" (UCC 1–215 (4); 2–208 (2)). Only when a consistent construction would be "unreasonable" must express terms control over course of performance, and course of performance prevail over course of dealing and usage of trade. GMAC's election on some occasions to fund Spartan's floor planning by reimbursing the car dealership for its purchases can hardly be considered inconsistent with its decision on other occasions to accomplish the same goal by following the strict wording of the contract and prepaying the supplier directly. Rather, it is only reasonable to consider these two methods of financing to be entirely compatible with one another. Here, GMAC's security agreement and its timely notice to GECC adequately specified the precise nature of the vehicular inventory to which its lien attached, such that GECC should have been alerted to GMAC's claim to the two Mercedes-Benzes; and, as discussed above, it

is clear that GMAC and Spartan intended these vehicles to be covered by their financing agreement.

Accordingly, the Supreme Court erred when it found that, having financed the two vehicles at issue here by way of reimbursements—"the very opposite of an advance"—GMAC did not acquire a purchase-money security interest pursuant to Uniform Commercial Code 9–107(b). Rather, since GMAC has established—and GECC does not deny—that GMAC was "obligated" to give value to enable Spartan to acquire rights in the two Mercedes-Benzes, and the purchase and loan transactions were only days apart, it is clear that Spartan's purchase and GMAC's subsequent reimbursement were sufficiently "closely allied" to give GMAC a purchase-money security interest in the subject vehicles. Under these circumstances, we conclude, upon searching the records, that GMAC is entitled to retain the proceeds of the sale of the two contested vehicles and to summary judgment against GECC.

Judgment in favor of GECC reversed and summary judgment granted in favor of GMAC.

Note: Although this case was decided under the 1972 version of Article 9, the same result would be expected under Revised Article 9.

Purchase Money Security Interest in Noninventory Collateral

The second exception to the general priority rule is that a purchase money security interest in collateral other than inventory has priority over a conflicting security interest in the same collateral if the purchase money security interest is perfected at the time the debtor receives the collateral or within 20 days afterward [9–324(a)].

Assume that Bank B takes and perfects a security interest in all the present and after-acquired equipment belonging to a debtor. Then, a supplier sells some equipment to the debtor, reserving a security interest in the

equipment until it is paid for. If the supplier perfects the purchase money security interest by filing at the time the debtor obtains the collateral or within 20 days thereafter, it has priority over Bank B. This is because its purchase money security interest in noninventory collateral prevails over a prior perfected security interest if the purchase money security interest is perfected at the time the debtor takes possession or within 20 days afterward.

In the following case, *In re McAllister,* the court applied the rule concerning the priority of purchase money security interests in collateral other than inventory over a prior perfected conflicting security interest.

In re McAllister   267 B.R. 614 (U.S.B.C. N.D. Iowa 2001)

In May 1985, Michael and Pamela McAllister executed a security agreement in favor of First Southeast Bank, granting it a security interest in all equipment owned and thereafter acquired. The bank filed a Financing Statement with the Iowa Secretary of State on May 28, 1985, and filed proper Continuation Statements thereafter that kept the perfection current.

On January 16, 1998, the McAllisters and Ag Services of America entered into an Agricultural Security Agreement for the production of crops. In addition to granting Ag Services a security interest in the crops, the McAllisters also granted Ag Services a security interest in "All of Debtors' equipment and motorized vehicles, whether or not required to be licensed or registered, whether now owned or hereafter acquired, including, but not limited to, machinery and tools, together with all accessories, parts, accessions and repairs or hereafter attached and affixed thereto."

The Ag Services security agreement with the McAllisters contained a future advances clause. Ag Services perfected its security interest by filing a Financing Statement on January 23, 1998.

Ag Services advanced funds to the McAllisters that enabled them to acquire an auger in November 1999 and a planter and trailer in January 2000. The current value of the auger is $2,500 and the value of the planter and trailer is $3,500. Subsequently, the McAllisters filed a petition in bankruptcy. One of the issues in the bankruptcy proceeding was whether Ag Services' lien on the auger, planter, and trailer was a perfected purchase money security interest that had priority over the earlier filed and perfected security interest of the bank.

Kilburg. Chief Judge

This dispute focuses on the conflicting rights of secured creditors First Southeast Bank and Ag Services. Article 9 of the Uniform Commercial Code governs the attachment and perfection of security interests in goods. *Iowa Code sec. 9–203(1)* provides that "a security interest is not enforceable against the debtor or third parties with respect to the collateral and does not attach unless: (1) the collateral is in the possession of the secured party pursuant to agreement, or the debtor has signed a security agreement which contains a description of the collateral . . . ; (2) value has been given; and (3) the debtor has rights in the collateral."

A security interest is perfected when it has attached and a financing statement has been filed or the security interest is otherwise perfected. *Section 9–303(1), 9–302(1).* "If such steps are taken before the security interest attaches, it is perfected at the time when it attaches." *§ 9–303(1).* The term "attached" is used to describe the point at which property becomes subject to a security interest. *§ 9–303* comment.

Where the funds are delivered by the lender for the specific purpose of purchasing equipment that is described in a prior, perfected financing statement between the parties, that security interest is a purchase money security interest when and to the extent the funds are so used. *§ 9–107 (b);* section 9–204 comment 2. Ag Services' earlier-filed financing statement perfects the subsequent security agreements. The filed financing statement gives notice to other creditors that Ag Services may claim a security interest in Debtors' equipment.

Article 9 is a notice filing system. When a conflict exists between secured creditors, the general rule provides that between creditors who perfected their security interests in the same collateral by filing a financing statement, the first in time to file their security interest has priority. *§ 9–312 (5).* Section *9–312* governs the priority of security interests in the same collateral. In this case both parties have perfected their security interests by filing financing statements. It is undisputed that, unless Ag Services has a purchase money security interest, the Bank is entitled to priority under this section.

The paramount exception to the first-to-file rule is the superpriority arising from a purchase money security interest (PMSI). By definition, a security interest is a "purchase money security interest" to the extent that it is "taken by a person who by making advances or incurring an obligation gives value to enable the debtor to acquire rights in or the use of collateral if such value is in fact so used. *§ 9–107(b).* The Iowa Supreme Court simply describes a PMSI as "a secured loan for the price of new collateral."

Debtors claim that Ag Services has a PMSI and, therefore, *§ 9–312(4)* controls the priority of the conflicting security interests. Section 9–312(4) provides that a purchase money security interest in collateral has priority if it was perfected at the time the debtor receives possession of the collateral or within 20 days thereafter. *§ 9–107(b).* Debtors must establish Ag Services' superpriority status.

The court ordered an evidentiary hearing to determine the extent of the PMSI held by Ag Services.

Note: While Iowa has adopted Revised Article effective July 1, 2001, the court applied the prior version of the Article (and the section references are to that version) because the matters in controversy occurred prior to the effective date of the new Article 9. However, the same result would be expected under the new version of Article 9.

Rationale for Protecting Purchase Money Security Interests

The preference given to purchase money security interests, provided that their holders comply with the statutory procedure in a timely manner, serves several ends. First, it prevents a single creditor from closing off all other sources of credit to a particular debtor and thus possibly preventing the debtor from obtaining additional inventory or equipment needed to maintain his business. Second, the preference makes it possible for a supplier to have first claim on inventory or equipment until it is paid for, at which time it may become subject to the after-acquired property clause of another creditor's security agreement. By requiring that the first perfected creditor be given notice of a purchase money security interest at the time the new inventory comes into the debtor's inventory, the Code serves to alert the first creditor to the fact that some of the inventory on which it may be relying for security is subject to a prior secured interest until the inventory is paid for.

Buyers in the Ordinary Course of Business

A third exception to the general priority rule is that a **buyer in the ordinary course of business** (other than a person buying farm products from a person engaged in farming operations) takes free from a security interest created by his seller even though the security interest is perfected and even though the buyer knows of its existence [9–320(a)]. For example, a bank loans money to a dealership to finance that dealership's inventory of new automobiles and takes a security interest in the inventory, which it perfects by filing. Then, the dealership sells an automobile out of inventory to a customer. The customer takes the automobile free of the bank's security interest even though the dealership may be in default on its loan agreement and even if the customer knows about the bank's interest. As long as the customer is a buyer in the ordinary course of business, she is protected. The reasons for this rule are that a bank really expects to be paid from the proceeds of the dealership's automobile sales and that the rule is necessary to the smooth conduct of commerce. Customers would be very reluctant to buy goods if they could not be sure they were getting clear title to them from the merchants from whom they buy.

Artisan's and Mechanic's Liens

The Code also provides that certain liens arising by operation of law (such as an artisan's lien) have priority over a perfected security interest in the collateral [9–333]. For example, Marshall takes her automobile, on which a credit union has a perfected security interest, to Frank's Garage to have it repaired. Under common or statutory law, Frank's may have a lien on the car to secure payment for the repair work; such a lien permits Frank's to keep the car until it receives payment. If Marshall defaults on her loan to the credit union, refuses to pay Frank's for the repair work, and the car is sold to satisfy the liens, Frank's is entitled to its share of the proceeds before the credit union gets anything.

Liens on Consumer Goods Perfected by Attachment/Automatic Perfection

A retailer of consumer goods who relies on attachment of a security interest to perfect it prevails over other creditors of the debtor-buyer. However, the retailer does not prevail over someone who buys the collateral from the debtor if the buyer (1) has no knowledge of the security interest; (2) gives value for the goods; and (3) buys the goods for his personal, family, or household use [9–320(b)]. The retailer does not have priority over such a **bona fide purchaser** unless it filed its security interest.

For example, an appliance store sells a television set to Arthur for $750 on a conditional sales contract, reserving a security interest in the set until Arthur has paid for it. The store does not file a financing statement, but relies on attachment for perfection. Arthur later borrows money from a credit union and gives it a security interest in the television set. When Arthur defaults on his loans and the credit union tries to claim the set, the appliance store has a better claim to the set than does the credit union. The credit union then has the rights of an unsecured creditor against Arthur. The first to attach has priority if neither security interest is perfected [9–322(a)(2)].

Now, suppose Arthur sells the television set for $500 to his neighbor Andrews. Andrews is not aware that Arthur still owes money on the set to the appliance store. Andrews buys it to use in her home. If Arthur defaults on his obligation to the store, it cannot recover the television set from Andrews. To be protected against such a purchaser from its debtor, the appliance store must file a financing statement rather than relying on attachment for perfection [9–320(b)].

Fixtures

A separate set of problems is raised when the collateral is goods that become fixtures by being so related to particular real estate that an interest in them arises under real estate law. Determining the priorities among a secured party with an interest in the fixtures, subsequent purchasers of the real estate, and those persons who have a secured interest such as a mortgage on the real property, can involve both real estate law and the Code. The general rule is that the interest of an encumbrancer of real estate (such as a mortgagor) or the interest of the owner of real estate (other than the debtor) has priority over a security interest in fixtures [9–334(c)]. However, a perfected security interest in fixtures has priority over the conflicting interest of an encumbrancer or owner of the real property if (1) the debtor has an interest of record in the real property or is in possession of it, (2) the security interest is a purchase money security interest, (3) the interest of the encumbrancer arose before the goods became fixtures, and (4) the fixtures' security interest is perfected by a "fixtures filing" either before the goods became fixtures or within 20 days after the goods became fixtures [9–334(d)].

For example, Restaurant Supply sells Arnie's Diner a new stove on a conditional sales contract, reserving a security interest until Arnie's pays for it. The stove is to be installed in a restaurant where Arnie's is in possession under a 10-year lease. Restaurant Supply can ensure that its purchase money security interest in the stove will have priority over a conflicting claim to the stove by the owner of the restaurant and anyone holding a mortgage on the restaurant if Restaurant Supply (1) enters into a security agreement with Arnie's prior to the time the stove is delivered to him and (2) perfects its security interest by fixture filing before the stove is hooked up by a plumber or within 20 days of that time. The case below, *Yeadon Fabric Domes, Inc. v. Maine Sports Complex, LLC,* illustrates this principle.

The Code contains several other rules concerning the relative priority of a security interest in fixtures [9–334(e)–(h)]. For example, the secured party whose interest in fixtures is perfected will have priority where (1) the fixtures are removable factory or office machines or readily removable replacements of domestic appliances that are consumer goods and (2) the security interest is perfected *prior* to the time the goods become fixtures. Suppose Harriet's dishwasher breaks and she contracts with an appliance store to buy a new one on a time-payment plan. The mortgage on Harriet's house provides that it covers the real property along with all kitchen appliances or their replacements. The appliance store's security interest will have priority on the dishwasher over the interest of the mortgage if the appliance store perfects its security interest prior to the time the new dishwasher is installed in Harriet's home

[9–334(e)(2)]. Perfection in consumer goods can, of course, be obtained merely by attaching the security interest through the signing of a valid security agreement.

Note that a creditor holding a security interest in consumer goods that become fixtures who relies on attachment for perfection prevails over other creditors with an interest in the real property *only* where the consumer goods are "readily removable replacements for domestic appliances."

Suppose a hardware store takes a security interest in some storm windows. Because the storm windows are likely to become fixtures through their use with the homeowner's home, the hardware store cannot rely merely on attachment to protect its security interest. It should file a financing statement to protect that security interest against other creditors of the homeowner with an interest in his home. This rule helps protect a person interested in buying the real property or a person considering lending money based on the real property. By checking the real estate records, the potential buyer or creditor would learn of the hardware store's security interest in the storm windows.

Once a secured party has filed his security interest as a fixture filing, he has priority over purchasers or encumbrances whose interests are filed after that of the secured party [9–334(e)(1)].

Where the secured party has priority over all owners and encumbrancers of the real estate, he generally has the right on default to remove the collateral from the real estate. However, he must make reimbursement for the cost of any physical injury caused to the property by the removal.

Yeadon Fabric Domes, Inc. v. Maine Sports Complex, LLC
60 UCC Rep.2d 367 (Sup. Jud. Ct. Maine 2006)

In 2001, the Maine Sports Complex entered into a series of business transactions to build a sports complex in Hampden, Maine. It purchased real estate and gave a mortgage to the seller, H.O. Bouchard, Inc. It engaged Kiser & Kiser Company to provide engineering services for construction of the complex and Harriman Brothers to provide groundwork for the sports complex. Subsequently, both Kiser and Harriman filed mechanic's liens on the property in 2002. Maine Sports Complex entered into a contract to purchase an inflatable fabric dome from Yeadon Fabric Domes, along with the materials and equipment to erect and operate the dome. It also obtained a loan from Bangor Savings Bank, giving the bank a mortgage.

Maine Sports Complex defaulted on its obligations to each of these entities, and litigation resulted as they attempted to realize on the security for their competing claims. Yeadon had filed a financing statement for the dome and equipment with the Secretary of State on July 22, 2002. It brought an action seeking the right to enter the property and to recover the dome. The court dismissed the action after concluding that the dome was a fixture and not personal property. Subsequently, on February 27, 2004, Yeadon recorded a financing statement in the Penobscot County Registry of Deeds.

Yeadon filed a collection action against Maine Sports Complex which was consolidated with other collection actions that had been filed by Harrison and Kiser to enforce their lien claims. The court found that Kiser began its work for Maine Sports

Complex on December 3, 2001, and that Harriman began its work on December 7, 2001. The court put Yeadon last in the order of priority. Yeadon appealed, contending that its security interest should have priority.

Calkins, Justice

The issue in this case is whether the court erred in determining the order of priority afforded to Harriman's and Kiser's mechanic's liens and to Yeadon's security interest in the dome.

Maine's version of the U.C.C. sets out requirements concerning security interests and how to perfect them. Generally speaking, a financing statement must be filed to perfect a security interest. A security interest is perfected by filing unless certain exceptions apply, none of which are applicable here. A security interest in fixtures may be perfected by filing the financing statement in either of two places: in the registry of deeds for the county where the related real property is located, or in the Secretary of State's office. The relevant portions of *section 9–501(1)* provide:

> [T]he office in which to file a financing statement to perfect the security interest . . . is:
>
> (a) The registry of deeds for the county in which the related real property is located, if:
>
> . . . .
>
> (ii) The financing statement is recorded as a fixture filing and the collateral is goods that are or are to become fixtures; or
>
> (b) The office of the Secretary of State, in all other cases, including a case in which the collateral is goods that are or are to become fixtures and the financing statement is not filed as a fixture filing.

Thus, for goods that are, or are to become, fixtures, the secured party who wishes to perfect a security interest should file the financing statement in the county registry of deeds if the filing is to be a fixture filing, or with the Secretary of State.

A fixture filing is defined as "the filing of a financing statement covering goods that are or are to become fixtures and satisfying *section 9–502, subsections (1)* and *(2)*." Section 9–502 lists the information that a financing statement must contain to qualify as a fixture filing.

The provision in Maine's version of the U.C.C. dealing with the priority of security interests in fixtures is *§ 9–334*. The general rule is that "a security interest in fixtures is subordinate to a conflicting interest of an encumbrancer or owner of the related real property other than the debtor." An encumbrance is defined as "a right, other than an ownership interest, in real property." The term "includes mortgages and other liens on real property."

There are exceptions to the general rule and several alternatives by which a security interest in fixtures has priority over conflicting interests. The alternatives that are most likely to fit the factual situation of this case are found in *§ 9–334(4)* and

(5). The first of these alternatives is in *section 9–334(4)*, which gives a perfected security interest in fixtures priority when the debtor has an interest of record in, or is in possession of, the real property; the security interest in fixtures is a purchase-money security interest; the encumbrancer's interest arose before the goods became fixtures; and the security interest was perfected by a fixture filing before or within twenty days of the time the goods became fixtures. Another alternative is *section 9–334(5)(a)*, which states that a perfected security interest in fixtures has priority if:

> (a) The debtor has an interest of record in the real property or is in possession of the real property and the security interest:
>
> (i) Is perfected by a fixture filing before the interest of the encumbrancer or owner is of record; and
>
> (ii) Has priority over any conflicting interest of a predecessor in title of the encumbrancer or owner. . . .

Application of the Statutes to the Facts

Yeadon filed a financing statement covering the dome and equipment with the Secretary of State on July 22, 2002, and with the registry of deeds on February 27, 2004. The court determined that the dome with its equipment is a fixture. The claims of Kiser and Harriman are pursuant to the mechanic's lien statute. Kiser began work on December 3, 2001, filed its lien on November 18, 2002, and filed its enforcement action on February 10, 2003. Harriman began work on December 7, 2001, filed its lien on August 27, 2002, and filed the enforcement action on October 17, 2002.

The issue is whether the District Court correctly placed Yeadon's priority after Harriman and Kiser. The determination of the correct priority requires an interpretation and application of the statutes. Yeadon perfected its security interest when it filed a financing statement with the Secretary of State on July 22, 2002. This filing did not qualify as a fixture filing, but *§ 9–501(1)(b)* provides that a security interest in goods that are, or are to become, fixtures can be perfected by filing with the Secretary of State. There is no requirement that a fixture filing be made in order to perfect a security interest in fixtures. Yeadon's later filing with the registry of deeds on February 27, 2004, qualified as a fixture filing.

The significance of a fixture filing, as compared to a filing with the Secretary of State, is shown in *§ 9–334*. A fixture filing is necessary for a security interest in fixtures to obtain priority pursuant to *sections 9–334(4)* and *(5)(a)*. In order for Yeadon to obtain priority over Harriman and Kiser pursuant to *section 9–334(4)*, which is one of the exceptions to the general rule that security interests in fixtures are subordinate, Yeadon's security interest had to be perfected by a fixture filing before the dome became a fixture or within twenty days thereafter. The record is not clear as to when the dome became a fixture, but it had obviously become a fixture before July 21, 2003, the date of the forcible entry and detainer hearing. As Yeadon's fixture filing was not made until February 2004, it was not made within twenty days of the time the dome became a fixture. Thus, *section 9–334(4)* is of no help to Yeadon.

To obtain priority over Harriman and Kiser pursuant to *section 9–334(5)(a)*, Yeadon's security interest had to be perfected by a fixture filing before the Harriman or Kiser interests became of record. Because Yeadon's fixture filing was not made until 2004 and both Harriman's and Kiser's title 10 liens were of record in 2002, Yeadon does not have priority over Harriman and Kiser pursuant to *section 9–334(5)(a)*.

Judgment affirmed.

Default and Foreclosure

Default   The Code does not define what constitutes default. Usually the creditor and debtor state in their agreement what events constitute a default by the buyer, subject to the Code requirement that the parties act in "good faith" in doing so. If the debtor defaults, the secured creditor has several options:

1. Forget the collateral, and sue the debtor on his note or promise to pay.
2. Repossess the collateral, and use strict foreclosure—in some cases—to keep the collateral in satisfaction of the remaining debt.
3. Repossess and sell the collateral, and then, depending on the circumstances, either sue for any deficiency or return the surplus to the debtor.

Right to Possession   The agreement between the creditor and the debtor may authorize the creditor to repossess the collateral in case of default. If the debtor does default, the creditor is entitled under the Code to possession of the collateral. If through self-help the creditor can obtain possession peaceably, he may do so. However, if the collateral is in the possession of the debtor and cannot be obtained without disturbing the peace, then the creditor must take court action to repossess the collateral [9–609]. See the *Giles v. First Virginia Credit Services* case, which follows shortly, for a discussion of what constitutes repossession without breach of the peace.

If the collateral is intangible, such as accounts, chattel paper, instruments, or documents, *and performance has been rendered to the debtor,* the secured party may give notice and have payments made or performance rendered to her [9–607].

Sale of the Collateral   The secured party may dispose of the collateral by sale or lease or in any manner calculated to produce the greatest benefit to all parties concerned. However, the method of disposal must be commercially reasonable [9–610; 9–627]. Notice of the time and place of a public sale must be given to the debtor, as must notice of a private sale. If the creditor decides to sell the collateral at a public sale such as an auction, then the creditor must give the debtor accurate advance notice of the time and place of the public sale. Similarly, if the creditor proposes to make a private sale of the collateral, notice must be given to the debtor. This gives the debtor a chance to object to the proposed private sale if she considers it not to be commercially reasonable or to otherwise protect her interests [9–613].

Until the collateral is actually disposed of by the creditor, the buyer has the right to *redeem* it. This means that if the buyer tenders fulfillment of all obligations secured by the collateral as well as of the expenses incurred by the secured party in retaking, holding, and preparing the collateral for disposition, she can recover the collateral from the creditor [9–623].

Consumer Goods   If the creditor has a security interest in consumer goods and the debtor has paid 60 percent or more of the purchase price or debt (and has not agreed in writing to a strict foreclosure), the creditor must sell the repossessed collateral. If less than 60 percent of the purchase price or debt related to consumer goods has been paid, and as to any other security interest, the creditor may propose to the debtor that the seller keep the collateral in satisfaction of the debt. The consumer-debtor has 20 days to object in writing. If the consumer objects, the creditor must sell the collateral. Otherwise, the creditor may keep the collateral in satisfaction of the debt [9–620].

Distribution of Proceeds

The Code sets out the order in which any proceeds are to be distributed after the sale of collateral by the creditor. First, any expenses of repossessing, storing, and selling the collateral, including reasonable attorney's fees, are paid. Second, the proceeds are used to satisfy the debt of the creditor who conducts the sale. Third, any junior interests or liens are paid. Finally, if any proceeds remain, the debtor is entitled to them. If the proceeds are not sufficient to satisfy the debt, then the creditor is usually entitled to a **deficiency judgment.** This means that the debtor remains personally liable for any debt remaining after the sale of the collateral [9–615(d)(2)].

For example, suppose a loan company lends Christy $5,000 to purchase a car and takes a security interest. After making several payments and reducing the debt to

---

CONCEPT REVIEW

Priority Rules

Priority between Two or More Secured Creditors Claiming an Interest in the Same Collateral

General rule. The *first creditor to file or to perfect* his security interests has priority over other creditors who filed or perfected later. If no secured creditor has perfected, then the *first security interest to attach* has priority.

Exceptions to the general rule. These secured creditors have higher priorities:

- A *purchase money security interest (PMSI) in inventory* has priority over a conflicting security interest if the PMSI in inventory is perfected and written notice is given to the conflicting secured creditor no later than when the collateral is delivered to the debtor.
- A *PMSI in noninventory* collateral has priority over a conflicting security interest if the PMSI in noninventory collateral is perfected not later than 20 days after the collateral is delivered to the debtor.
- A *PMSI in fixtures* has priority over a security interest in the real property to which the fixtures are affixed if the PMSI in fixtures is perfected not later than 20 days after the time the goods are attached to the real property.
- A *security interest in fixtures that are removable equipment or readily removable replacements of domestic appliance consumer goods* has priority over a security interest in the real property if the security interest in such fixtures is perfected prior to the time the fixtures are attached to the real property.
- A *security interest in securities perfected by possession or control* has priority over a security interest in the securities perfected by filing.
- *Artisan's liens*—and other possessory liens arising by operation of law—generally have priority over other security interests.

Between Secured Creditors and a Buyer of the Collateral from the Debtor

General rule. Buyer has priority over an unperfected security interest that is unknown to the buyer.

Exceptions to the general rule. These buyers have higher priorities:

- A *buyer in the ordinary course of business (BITOCOB) of his seller* has priority over any security interest created by his seller.
- A *bona fide purchaser of consumer goods for value* has priority over an unfiled, unknown *PMSI in consumer goods.*
- A *bona fide purchaser of a negotiable instrument* has a priority over a secured interest in the negotiable instrument perfected other than by possession if the bona fide purchaser takes possession of the negotiable instrument.

$4,800, Christy defaults. The loan company pays $50 to have the car repossessed and then has it sold at an auction, where it brings $4,500, thus incurring a sales commission of 10 percent ($450) and attorney's fees of $150. The repossession charges, sales commission, and attorney's fees, totaling $650, are paid first from the $4,500 proceeds. The remaining $3,850 is applied to the $4,800 debt, leaving a balance due of $950. Christy remains liable to the loan company for the $950 unless Christy challenges the amount of the deficiency claimed [9–626(a)].

Liability of Creditor A creditor who holds a security interest in collateral must be careful to comply with the provisions of Article 9 of the Code. A creditor acting improperly in repossessing collateral or in its foreclosure and sale is liable to the parties injured. Thus, a creditor can be liable to a debtor if she acts improperly in repossessing or selling collateral [9–625; 9–627].

In the case that follows, *Giles v. First Virginia Credit Services, Inc.*, the court rejected a claim for wrongful repossession of an automobile.

Giles v. First Virginia Credit Services, Inc.
46 UCC Rep. 2d 913 (N.C. Ct. App. 2002)

On January 18, 1997, Joann Giles entered into an installment sale contract for the purchase of an automobile. The contract was assigned to First Virginia, which obtained a senior perfected purchase money security interest in the automobile. The terms of the contract required Joann Giles to make 60 regular monthly payments to First Virginia. The contract stated that Joann Giles's failure to make any payment due under the contract within 10 days after its due date would be a default. The contract contained an additional provision agreed to by Joann Giles that stated:

> If I am in default, you may consider all my remaining payments to be due and payable, without giving me notice. I agree that your rights of possession will be greater than mine. I will deliver the property to you at your request, or you may use lawful means to take it yourself without notice or other legal action. . . . If you excuse one default by me, that will not excuse later defaults.

During the early morning hours of June 27, 1999, Professional Auto Recovery, at the request of First Virginia, repossessed the locked automobile from Giles's front driveway. At the time Giles was in arrears for payments due on May 2, 1999, and June 2, 1999. Giles's neighbor, Glenn Mosteller, testified that he was awakened around 4:00 AM by the running of a loud diesel truck engine on the road outside his house. When he went to the window to look, he saw a large rollback diesel with a little pickup on the bed behind it. He saw a man jump out of the truck and run up the driveway to Giles's house. Then the car came flying out of the driveway and started screeching down the street. About the same time, the rollback truck also took off at a high rate of speed making a loud diesel noise. The neighbor then called Giles and told her someone was stealing her car. Giles's husband came out of the house and hollered back and forth with the neighbor. Then the neighbor jumped in his truck and contacted the police. Eventually three police cars came to the scene, producing a great commotion in the neighborhood. The Gileses testified that neither of them saw the car being repossessed and were only awakened by the neighbor after it was gone. During the actual repossession there was no contact between Professional Auto Recovery and the Gileses or their neighbor.

Giles brought suit against First Virginia and Professional Auto Recovery for wrongful repossession of an automobile, alleging among other things, that she had mailed a payment on the account just prior to the repossession, which First Virginia had accepted and applied to their account after the repossession, and that the removal of the automobile constituted breach of the peace in violation of UCC section 9–503.

McGee, Judge

Our courts have long recognized the right of secured parties to repossess collateral from a defaulting debtor without resort to judicial process, so long as the repossession is effected peaceably. Our General Assembly codified procedures for self-help repossessions, including this common law restriction, in the North Carolina Uniform Commercial Code (UCC). N.C. Gen. Stat. § 9–503 (1999), in effect at the time of the repossession in this case, reads in part,

> Unless otherwise agreed a secured party has on default the right to take possession of the collateral. In taking possession a secured party may proceed without judicial process if this can be done without breach of the peace or may proceed by action.

The General Assembly did not define breach of the peace but instead left this task to our courts, and although a number of our appellate decisions have considered this self-help right of secured parties, none have clarified what actions constitute a breach of the peace.

Section 9–503, at issue in this appeal, has been replaced by section 9–609 (Effective July 1, 2001), which states that a secured party, after default, may take possession of the collateral without judicial process, if the secured party proceeds without breach of the peace. In Number 3 of the Official Comment to the new statutory provision, our General Assembly continued to state that, "like former Section 9–503, this section does not define or explain the conduct that will constitute a breach of the peace, leaving that matter for continuing development by the courts." The General Assembly clearly may further define and/or limit the time, place and conditions under which a repossession is permitted, but it has not yet done so.

In a case addressing the issue of whether prior notice of repossession is required under section 9–503, our Supreme Court stated that repossession can be accomplished under the statute without prior notice so long as the repossession is peaceable. Without specifically defining breach of the peace, our Supreme Court explained that "of course, if there is confrontation at the time of the attempted repossession, the secured party must cease the attempted repossession and proceed by court action in order to avoid a 'breach of the peace.' " This indicates, as argued by First Virginia, that confrontation is at least an element of a breach of the peace analysis.

In a criminal case, our Supreme Court defined breach of the peace as "a disturbance of public order and tranquility by act or conduct not merely amounting to unlawfulness but tending also to create public tumult and incite others to break the peace."

We must also consider the nature and purpose of Chapter 25 of the North Carolina General Statutes, the UCC, which is to be "liberally construed and applied to promote its underlying purposes and policies." Section 1–102 (1999). Its stated purposes are:

(a) to simplify, clarify and modernize the law governing commercial transactions;
(b) to permit the continued expansion of commercial practices through custom, usage and agreement of the parties;
(c) to make uniform the law among the various jurisdictions.

In carrying out the policy of uniformity with other jurisdictions, we consider their treatment of the term of breach of the peace. While cases from other jurisdictions are not binding on our courts, they provide insight into how this term has been analyzed by other courts and therefore are instructive.

The courts in many states have examined whether a breach of the peace in the context of the UCC has occurred. Courts have found a breach of the peace when actions by a creditor incite violence or are likely to incite violence. Other courts have expanded the phrase "breach of the peace" beyond the criminal law context to include occurrences where a debtor or his family protest the repossession. Some courts, however, have determined that a mere oral protest is not sufficient to constitute a breach of the peace. Removal of collateral from a private driveway, without more, however, has been found not to constitute a breach of the peace. Additionally, noise alone has been determined to not rise to the level of a breach of the peace.

Many courts have used a balancing test to determine if a repossession was undertaken at a reasonable time and in a reasonable manner, and to balance the interests of debtors and creditors. Five relevant factors considered in this balancing test are: "(1) where the repossession took place, (2) the debtor's express or constructive consent, (3) the reactions of third parties, (4) the type of premises entered, and (5) the creditor's use of deception." The Gileses argue that the "guiding star" in determining whether a breach of the peace occurred should be whether or not the public peace was preserved during the repossession. The Gileses contend "the elements as to what constitutes a breach of the peace should be liberally construed" and urge our Court to adopt a subjective standard considering the totality of the circumstances as to whether a breach of the peace occurred.

The Gileses claim that adopting a subjective standard for section 9–503 cases will protect unwitting consumers from the "widespread use of no notice repossessions, clandestine and after midnight repossessions" and will protect "our State's commitment to law and order and opposition to vigilante policies, opposition to violence and acts from which violence could reasonably flow." If a lender is not held to such a high subjective standard, the Gileses contend that self-help repossessions should be disallowed altogether.

First Virginia, in contrast, argues that a breach of the peace did not occur in this case, as a matter of law, because there was no confrontation between the parties. Therefore, because the facts in this case are undisputed concerning the events during the actual repossession of the automobile, the trial court did not err in its partial grant of summary judgment.

First Virginia disputes the Giles's contention that a determination of whether a breach of the peace occurred should be a wholly subjective standard, because if such a standard is adopted, every determination of whether a breach of the peace occurred would hereafter be a jury question and "would run directly contrary to the fundamental purpose of the Uniform Commercial Code, which is to provide some degree of certainty to the parties engaging in various commercial transactions." Further, First Virginia argues that applying a subjective standard to a breach of the peace analysis could be detrimental to borrowers, with lenders likely increasing the price of credit to borrowers to cover the costs of having to resort to the courts in every instance to recover their collateral upon default. The standard advocated by the Gileses would "eviscerate" the self-help rights granted to lenders by the General Assembly, leaving lenders "with no safe choice except to simply abandon their 'self help' rights altogether, since every repossession case could [result] in the time and expense of a jury trial on the issue of 'breach of the peace.' " Finally, First Virginia argues that a subjective standard would be detrimental to the judicial system as a whole because "with a case-by-case, wholly subjective standard . . . the number of lawsuits being filed over property repossessions could increase dramatically."

Based upon our review of our appellate courts' treatment of breach of the peace in pre-UCC and UCC cases, as well as in other areas of the law, the purposes and policies of the UCC, and the treatment other jurisdictions have given the phrase, we find that a breach of the peace, when used in the context of section 9–503, is broader than the criminal law definition. A confrontation is not always required, but we do not agree with the Giles that every repossession should be analyzed subjectively, thus bringing every repossession into the purview of the jury so as to eviscerate the self-help rights duly given to creditors by the General Assembly. Rather, a breach of the peace analysis should be based upon the reasonableness of the time and manner of the repossession. We therefore adopt a balancing test using the five factors discussed above to determine whether a breach of the peace occurs when there is no confrontation.

In applying these factors to the undisputed evidence in the case before us, we affirm the trial court's determination that there was no breach of the peace, as a matter of law. Professional Auto Recovery went onto the Giles's driveway in the early morning hours, when presumably no one would be outside, thus decreasing the possibility of confrontation. Professional Auto Recovery did not enter into the Giles's home or any enclosed area. Consent to repossession was expressly given in the contract with First Virginia signed by Joann Giles. Although a third party, Mr. Mosteller, was awakened by the noise of Professional Auto Recovery's truck, Mr. Mosteller did not speak with anyone from Professional Auto Recovery, nor did he go outside until Professional Auto Recovery had departed with the Giles's automobile. Further, neither of the Gileses were awakened by the noise of the truck, and there was no confrontation between either of them with any representative of Professional Auto Recovery. By the time Mr. Mosteller and plaintiffs went outside, the automobile was gone. Finally, there is no evidence, nor did the Gileses allege, that First Virginia or Professional Auto Recovery employed any type of deception when repossessing the automobile.

There is no factual dispute as to what happened during the repossession in this case, and the trial court did not err in granting summary judgment to First Virginia on this issue.

Partial summary judgment for First Virginia affirmed.

Ethics in Action

What Is the Ethical Thing to Do?

Suppose you own an appliance business in a working-class neighborhood that makes most of its sales on credit. What considerations would you take into account in determining whether and when to foreclose or repossess items on which customers have fallen behind in making their payments?

Should you be swayed by the personal circumstances of your debtors or look only to protecting your financial interests? For example, would you consider the value of the item to the debtor—such as whether it is a necessity for her life, such as a refrigerator, or a luxury? Would you consider the reason the person had fallen behind—that is, whether she had been ill or recently lost her job?

Problems and Problem Cases

1. Symons, a full-time insurance salesperson, bought a set of drums and cymbals from Grinnel Brothers. A security agreement was executed between them but was never filed. Symons purchased the drums to supplement his income by playing with a band. He had done this before, and his income from his two jobs was about equal. He also played several other instruments. Symons became bankrupt, and the trustee tried to acquire the drums and cymbals as part of his bankruptcy estate. Grinnel's claimed that the drums and cymbals were consumer goods and thus it had a perfected security interest merely by attachment of the security interest. Were the drums and cymbals consumer goods?

2. Richard Silch purchased a camcorder at Sears Roe-buck by charging it to his Sears charge account. Printed on the face of the sales ticket made at that time was the following:

> This credit purchase is subject to the terms of my Sears Charge Agreement which is incorporated herein by reference and identified by the above account number. I grant Sears a security interest or lien in this merchan-dise, unless prohibited by law, until paid in full.

Silch's signature appeared immediately below that language on the sales ticket. The ticket also con-tained the brand name of the camcorder and a stock number.

Silch subsequently filed a Chapter 7 bankruptcy proceeding and was eventually discharged. Sears filed a petition to recover the camcorder from Silch, contending that it had a valid and enforceable security interest in the camcorder. Silch, in turn, contended that the sales ticket did not constitute a valid and en-forceable security agreement. Does the sales ticket constitute a valid security agreement?

3. On June 10, 1994, 4-R Management, by and through its officers, Chris and Lucretia Ryan, executed a promissory note to the First Bank of Eva. The Ryans signed the note both personally and as officers of 4-R Management. The Ryans also executed a security agreement dated June 10, 1994, pledging one "book coin collection" and various other items, including a tractor, bush hog, farm products, and cattle, as secu-rity for the note. The promissory note incorporated by reference this separate security agreement. The coin collection was the property of 4-R Management, and the bank took possession of the coins on June 10. In subsequent renewal notes, 4-R Management, in its corporate capacity, expressly granted the bank a secu-rity interest in the coin collection.

On November 8, 1995, 4-R Management filed a voluntary petition for relief under the Bankruptcy Code. Subsequently, the bankruptcy trustee sought to recover for the bankruptcy estate the coin collection being held by the bank as security. The question of whether the bank or the bankruptcy trustee had the better right to the coin collection turned on whether the bank had a perfected security interest in the collection. When the bank has possession of collat-eral pursuant to a security agreement but has not filed a financing statement on the public record, does the bank hold a perfected security interest in the collateral?

4. Nicolosi bought a diamond ring on credit from Rike-Kumber as an engagement present for his fiancé. He signed a purchase money security agreement giving Rike-Kumber a security interest in the ring until it was paid for. Rike-Kumber did not file a financing statement covering its security interest. Nicolosi filed for bankruptcy. The bankruptcy trustee claimed that the diamond ring was part of the bankruptcy estate because Rike-Kumber did not perfect its security in-terest. Rike-Kumber claimed that it had a perfected security interest in the ring. Did Rike-Kumber have to file a financing statement to perfect its security inter-est in the diamond ring?

5. On October 28, 1983, Steve Gresham, doing business as Midway Cycle Sales, entered into a Wholesale Financing Agreement with ITT Commercial Finance Corporation. The agreement was to finance the purchase of new motorcycles from Suzuki Motor Corporation. ITT filed a financing statement with the Indiana secretary of state on December 16, 1983. The description of the collateral in which ITT asserted a security interest included "all inventory . . . replacements and proceeds." On January 9, 1984, Union Bank filed a financing statement with the Indiana secretary of state claiming it was engaged in "floor planning of new motorcycles" for Midway Cycle Sales. In August 1984, ITT began paying Suzuki invoices for Gresham. In July 1985, ITT sent a letter to Union Bank notifying it that it expected to acquire purchase money security interests in the in-ventory of Stephan Gresham d/b/a Midway Cycle Sales. In early 1986, Union Bank began loaning money to Gresham under its floor planning agree-ment with him. Actually, Gresham was "double floor planning"—that is, he was taking invoices for motor-cycles that had been paid for by ITT to the Union Bank and claiming that he had paid for the motorcy-cles but had decided to floor plan them. When Union Bank advanced money to him, he used the money to make payments on the loans to ITT. He made no pay-ments to Union Bank and did not pay off all of his loan to ITT. Midway Cycle Sales went bankrupt when Union Bank repossessed 22 new Suzuki motor-cycles. ITT brought suit against Union Bank, claim-ing it had paid for the motorcycles and had a perfected security interest in the motorcycles that had priority over Union Bank's security interest in them. Did ITT's security interest have priority over Union Bank's security interest?

6. On November 18, Firestone & Company made a loan to Edmund Carroll, doing business as Kozy Kitchen. To secure the loan, a security agreement was executed, which listed the items of property included, and concluded as follows: "together with all property and articles now, and which may hereafter be, used or mixed with, added or attached to, and/or substituted for any of the described property." A financing statement that included all the items listed in the security agreement was filed with the town clerk on November 18 and with the secretary of state on November 22. On November 25, National Cash Register Company delivered a cash register to Carroll on a conditional sales contract. National Cash Register filed a financing statement on the cash register with the town clerk on December 20 and with the secretary of state on December 21. Carroll defaulted in his payments to both Firestone and National Cash Register. Firestone repossessed all of Carroll's fixtures and equipment covered by its security agreement, including the cash register, and then sold the cash register. National Cash Register claimed that it was the title owner of the cash register and brought suit against Firestone for conversion. Did Firestone or National Cash Register have the better right to the cash register?

7. On February 19, 1988, DBC Capital Fund, Inc., entered into an agreement with the owner of Devers Auto Sales under which it loaned money to Devers and DBC obtained a security interest in the automotive inventory maintained by Devers. This security interest was perfected by filing with the secretary of state on February 25, 1988. On March 24, 1989, Cheryl Snodgrass purchased a 1984 Oldsmobile from Devers for $5,000 in cash. The automobile was taken from the inventory covered by DBC's security interest, although Snodgrass was not made aware of the financing agreement between Devers and DBC. When Snodgrass took possession of the Oldsmobile, Devers told her that the certificate of title would be mailed to her. In the meantime, she was issued a temporary registration. On April 28, 1989, Snodgrass was informed by letter that DBC had physical possession of the title and that DBC considered itself to have a valid lien on the automobile. In a later telephone conversation, DBC's attorney informed Snodgrass that DBC would not release the certificate of title until she paid DBC $4,200. On April 25, 1989, the temporary registration issued to Snodgrass by Devers had expired. Because she was not in possession of the certificate of title, she was unable to obtain proper licensing for the car and, therefore, could not use it. In an effort to obtain the certificate of title, Snodgrass brought suit against DBC. Does Snodgrass have a better right than DBC to the certificate of title?

8. Inkas Coffee Distribution Realty and Equipment LLC (Inkas) purchased a 2001 Ford F250 for $36,340 which was to be paid in 60 months. The retail installment agreement signed by Inkas was assigned to Charter One Auto Finance. Charter One Auto Finance was granted a security interest in the motor vehicle on September 20, 2000, and the security interest was noted on the title to the vehicle. On May 10, 2001, Inkas delivered the vehicle to Connecticut International Parking, LLC, which was in the business of storing motor vehicles at its open-air parking lot in East Granby, Connecticut. Pursuant to an oral agreement, Connecticut International agreed to store the automobile at the rate of $9.25 per day and to care for it by regularly starting and moving the car on a monthly basis so that its engine, mechanical system, and tires would remain in operating condition. Between May 10, 2001, and May 16, 2004, Inkas incurred $9,851 in storage fees. Inkas defaulted on its obligations under the installment agreement by not making payments due from July 4, 2001, until March 2005. On April 16, Charter, claiming that it had rights in the motor vehicle, demanded that Connecticut International deliver it to Charter. Connecticut International offered to do so upon proof of Charter's rights, but demanded that it be paid for the storage charges owed to it. Charter refused, and brought suit to recover the car. Inkas filed for bankruptcy in 2001. While that action was dismissed, both Charter and Connecticut International concluded that Inkas was not in a position to pay either of them. By virtue of its prior perfected security interest in the motor vehicle, does Charter have the right to recover the vehicle without first reimbursing Connecticut International for its storage fees?

9. In August, Norma Wade purchased a Ford Thunderbird automobile and gave Ford Motor Credit a security interest in it to secure her payment of the $7,000 balance of the purchase price. When Wade fell behind on her monthly payments, Ford engaged the Kansas Recovery Bureau to repossess the car. On the following February 10, an employee of the Recovery Bureau located the car in Wade's driveway, unlocked the door,

got in, and started it. He then noticed a discrepancy between the serial number of the car and the number listed in his papers. He shut off the engine, got out, and locked the car. When Wade appeared at the door of her house, he advised her that he had been sent by Ford to repossess the car but would not do so until he had straightened out the serial number. She said that she had been making payments, that he was not going to take the car, and that she had a gun, which she would use. He suggested that Wade contact Ford to straighten out the problem. She called Ford and advised its representative that if she caught anybody on her property again trying to take her car, she would use her gun to "leave him laying right where I saw him." Wade made several more payments, but Ford again contracted to have the car repossessed. At 2:00 AM on March 5, the employee of the Kansas Recovery Bureau successfully took the car from Wade's driveway. She said that she heard a car burning rubber, looked out of her window, and saw that her car was missing. There was no confrontation between Wade and the employee since he had safely left the area before she discovered that the car had been taken. Wade then brought lawsuit against Ford claiming that the car had been wrongfully repossessed. She sought actual and punitive damages, plus attorney's fees. Should Ford be held liable for wrongful repossession?

10. Gibson, a collector of rare old Indian jewelry, took two of his pieces to Hagberg, a pawnbroker. The two pieces, a silver belt and a silver necklace, were worth $500 each. Hagberg loaned only $45 on the belt and $50 on the necklace. Gibson defaulted on both loans, and immediately and without notice, the necklace was sold for $240. A short time later, the belt was sold for $80. At the time of their sale, Gibson owed interest on the loans of $22. Gibson sued Hagberg to recover damages for improperly disposing of the collateral. Is Gibson entitled to damages because of Hagberg's actions in disposing of the collateral?

Online Research

Using the Internet to Search for Preexisting Security Interests

The company you work for wants to save money by using the Internet to search for Article 9 filings against persons it may sell goods to on credit. It knows that some states have all of the filings in computer databases and that some also allow searches from the Internet. Your employer asks you to search the Arizona statewide system and tell him whether you can find everything you need concerning possible Article 9 filings against a prospective customer whose business name is John J. [for Joseph] Smith.

chapter 30

BANKRUPTCY

B ob and Sue Brown are a young couple with two small children. Within the past three years they stretched themselves financially in the course of acquiring and furnishing their first home and starting their family. Recently, Bob was laid off from his job managing computer technology operations for a telecom company. Then, Sue was injured in an automobile accident and has been unable to continue substitute teaching. Bob's unemployment benefits are insufficient to provide for the ordinary family expenses, much less meet the heavy financial obligations the family has taken on. The bank has filed a notice of intent to foreclose the mortgage on their home, and other creditors have sent letters threatening to repossess their car and furnishings. A friend has suggested that Bob and Sue consult with an attorney who specializes in bankruptcy matters who may be able to get them some relief from their creditors and gain a new start financially.

This situation raises a number of questions that will be addressed in this chapter. They include:

- If the Browns file a petition in bankruptcy, what assets would they be able to retain as exempt from the claims of their creditors?
- Which of their debts could be discharged in a bankruptcy proceeding?
- What advantages and disadvantages would the Browns have if they filed under Chapter 7 (liquidations) as opposed to filing under Chapter 13 (consumer debt adjustments)?
- Under the 2005 amendments to the Bankruptcy Code, are they eligible to file for Chapter 7 liquidation or must they file under Chapter 13, which will require them to continue to make payments on their debts?

WHEN AN INDIVIDUAL, a partnership, or a corporation is unable to pay its debts to creditors, problems can arise. Some creditors may demand security for past debts or start court actions on their claims in an effort to protect themselves. Such actions may adversely affect other creditors by depriving them of their fair share of the debtor's assets. Also, quick depletion of the debtor's assets may effectively prevent the debtor who needs additional time to pay off his debts from having an opportunity to do so.

At the same time, creditors need to be protected against the actions a debtor in financial difficulty might be tempted to take to their detriment. For example, the debtor might run off with his remaining assets or might use them to pay certain favored creditors, leaving nothing for the other creditors. Finally, a means is needed by which a debtor can get a fresh start financially and not continue to be saddled with debts beyond his ability to pay. This chapter focuses on the body of law and procedure that has developed to deal with the competing interests when a debtor is unable to pay his debts in a timely manner.

The Bankruptcy Code

The Bankruptcy Code is a federal law that provides an organized procedure under the supervision of a federal court for dealing with insolvent debtors. Debtors are considered insolvent if they are unable or fail to pay their debts as they become due. The power of Congress to enact bankruptcy legislation is provided in the Constitution. Through the years, there have been many amendments to the Bankruptcy Code. Congress completely revised the code in 1978 and then passed significant amendments to it in 1984, 1986, and 1994. On April 20, 2005, President Bush signed the "Bankruptcy Abuse, Prevention and Consumer Protection Act of 2005," the most substantial revision of the bankruptcy law since the 1978 Bankruptcy Code was adopted. With a few exceptions, the revisions are effective for cases filed after October 17, 2005.

The Bankruptcy Code has several major purposes. One is to ensure that the debtor's property is fairly distributed to the creditors and that some creditors do not obtain unfair advantage over the others. At the same time, the code protects all of the creditors against actions by the debtor that would unreasonably diminish the debtor's assets to which they are entitled. The code also provides the honest debtor with a measure of protection against the demands for payment by his creditors. Under some circumstances, the debtor is given additional time to pay the creditors, freeing him of those pressures creditors might otherwise exert. If the debtor makes a full and honest accounting of his assets and liabilities and deals fairly with his creditors, the debtor may have most—if not all—of the debts discharged so as to have a fresh start.

At one time, **bankruptcy** carried a strong stigma for the debtors who became involved in it. Today, this is less true. It is still desirable that a person conduct her financial affairs in a responsible manner. However, there is a greater understanding that such events as accidents, natural disasters, illness, divorce, and severe economic dislocations are often beyond the ability of individuals to control and may lead to financial difficulty and bankruptcy.

Bankruptcy Proceedings

The Bankruptcy Code covers a number of bankruptcy proceedings. In this chapter, our focus will be on:

1. Straight bankruptcy (liquidations).
2. Reorganizations.
3. Family farms and commercial fishing operations.
4. Consumer debt adjustments.

The Bankruptcy Code also contains provisions regarding municipal bankruptcies, which are not covered in this chapter.

Liquidations

A liquidation proceeding, traditionally called **straight bankruptcy,** is brought under Chapter 7 of the Bankruptcy Code. Individuals, as well as businesses, may file under Chapter 11. The debtor must disclose all of the property she owns and surrender this bankruptcy estate to the **bankruptcy trustee.** The trustee separates out certain property that the debtor is permitted to keep and then administers, liquidates, and distributes the remainder of the bankrupt debtor's estate.

There is a mechanism for determining the relative rights of the creditors, for recovering any preferential payments made to creditors, and for disallowing any preferential liens obtained by creditors. If the bankrupt person has been honest in her business transactions and in the bankruptcy proceedings, she is usually given a **discharge** (relieved) of her debts.

Reorganizations

Chapter 11 of the Bankruptcy Code provides a proceeding whereby a debtor can work out a plan to solve its financial problems under the supervision of a federal court. A reorganization plan is essentially a contract between a debtor and its creditors. The proceeding is intended for debtors, particularly businesses, whose financial problems may be solvable if they are given some time and guidance and if they are relieved of some pressure from creditors.

Family Farms

Historically, farmers have been accorded special attention in the Bankruptcy Code. Chapter 12 of the Bankruptcy Code provides a special proceeding whereby a debtor involved in a family farming operation or a family-owned commercial fishing operation can develop a plan to work out his financial difficulties. Generally, the debtor remains in possession of the farm or fishing operations and continues to operate it while the plan is developed and implemented.

Consumer Debt Adjustments

Under Chapter 13 of the Bankruptcy Code, individuals with regular incomes who are in financial difficulty can develop plans under court supervision to satisfy their creditors. Chapter 13 permits compositions (reductions) of debts and/or extensions of time to pay debts out of the debtor's future earnings.

The Bankruptcy Courts

Bankruptcy cases and proceedings are filed in federal district courts. The district courts have the authority to refer the cases and proceedings to bankruptcy judges, who are considered to be units of the district court. If a dispute falls within what is known as a **core proceeding,** the bankruptcy judge can hear and determine the controversy. Core proceedings include a broad list of matters related to the administration of a bankruptcy estate. However, if a dispute is not a core proceeding but rather involves a state law claim, then the bankruptcy judge can only hear the case and prepare draft findings and conclusions for review by the district court judge.

Certain proceedings affecting interstate commerce have to be heard by the district court judge if any party requests that this be done. Moreover, even the district courts are precluded from deciding certain state law claims that could not normally be brought in federal court, even if those claims are related to the bankruptcy matter. Bankruptcy judges are appointed by the president for terms of 14 years.

Chapter 7: Liquidation Proceedings

Petitions All bankruptcy proceedings, including liquidation proceedings, are begun by the filing of a petition. The petition may be either a **voluntary petition** filed by the debtor or an **involuntary petition** filed by a creditor or creditors of the debtor. A voluntary petition in bankruptcy may be filed by an individual, a partnership, or a corporation. However, municipal, railroad, insurance, and banking corporations and savings or building and loan associations are not permitted to file for straight bankruptcy proceedings. A person filing a voluntary petition need not be insolvent—that is, her debts need not be greater than her assets. However, the person must be able to allege that she has debts. The primary purpose for filing a voluntary petition is to obtain a discharge from some or all of the debts.

The 2005 revisions establish a new "means test" for consumer debtors to be eligible for relief under Chapter 7. The purpose of the test is to ensure that individuals who will have income in the future that might be used to pay off at least a portion of their debts must pursue relief under Chapter 13 as opposed to pursuing relief and a discharge of liabilities through the liquidation provisions of Chapter 7. In general, debtors who earn more than the median income in their state and who can repay at least $6,575 of their debt over five years are required to use Chapter 13. This means test is discussed in detail later in this section under the subsection entitled "Substantial Abuse."

Involuntary Petitions

An involuntary petition is a petition filed by creditors of a debtor. By filing it, they seek to have the debtor declared bankrupt and his assets distributed to the creditors. Involuntary petitions may be filed against many debtors. However, involuntary petitions in straight bankruptcy cannot be filed against (1) farmers; (2) ranchers; (3) nonprofit organizations; (4) municipal, railroad, insurance, and banking corporations; (5) credit unions; and (6) savings or building and loan associations.

If a debtor has 12 or more creditors, an involuntary petition to declare him bankrupt must be signed by at least 3 creditors. If there are fewer than 12 creditors, then an involuntary petition can be filed by a single creditor. The creditor or creditors must have valid claims against the debtor exceeding the value of any security they hold by $13,475 or more. To be forced into involuntary bankruptcy, the debtor must be generally not paying his debts as they become due—or have had a custodian for his property appointed within the previous 120 days.

If an involuntary petition is filed against a debtor engaged in business, the debtor may be permitted to continue to operate the business. However, the court may appoint an **interim trustee** if this is necessary to preserve the bankruptcy estate or to prevent loss of the estate. A creditor who suspects that a debtor may dismantle her business or dispose of its assets at less than fair value may apply to the court for protection.

Requirement for Credit Counseling and Debtor Education Under the 2005 revisions, individuals are ineligible for relief under any chapter of the Code unless within 180 days preceding their bankruptcy filing they received individual or group credit counseling from an approved nonprofit budget and credit counseling agency or obtain an exemption from the requirement. The required briefing, which may take place by telephone or on the Internet, must "outline" the opportunities for credit counseling and assist the debtor in performing a budget analysis. The debtor is required to file a certificate from the credit counseling agency that describes the services that were provided to the debtor and also to file any debt repayment plan developed by the agency. Because individuals who have not received the required briefing are not eligible for relief under the Bankruptcy Code, it is difficult for a creditor to force an individual debtor into bankruptcy by filing an involuntary petition against the debtor.

Attorney Certification The 2005 act increases the legal responsibilities for an attorney who signs a bankruptcy petition. The attorney's signature constitutes a certification that the attorney, after inquiry, has no knowledge that the information contained in the schedules filed by the debtor is incorrect. In addition, the attorney's signature on a petition, motion, or other written pleading constitutes a certification that the attorney, after inquiry, has determined that the pleading is well grounded in fact and is either warranted by existing law or is based on a good faith argument for extending existing law. In cases where the trustee files a motion to dismiss a case for substantial abuse, the court may order the debtor's attorney to reimburse the trustee for the reasonable costs, including attorney fees, for prosecuting the motion and may also order the attorney to pay a civil penalty to the trustee or the United States Trustee.

These provisions have raised concerns that bankruptcy practice will be less attractive to bankruptcy attorneys that handle a large volume of cases because the provisions will increase their costs and risks—and they operate on relatively thin margins.

Automatic Stay Provisions

The filing of a bankruptcy petition operates as an **automatic stay,** holding in abeyance various forms of creditor action against a debtor or her property. These actions include (1) beginning or continuing judicial proceedings against the debtor; (2) actions to obtain possession of the debtor's property; (3) actions to create, perfect, or enforce a lien against the debtor's property; and (4) setoff of indebtedness owed to the debtor before commencement of the bankruptcy proceeding. A court may give a creditor relief from the stay if the creditor can show that the stay does not give her "adequate protection" and jeopardizes her interest in certain property. The relief to the creditor might take the form of periodic cash payments or the granting of a replacement lien or an additional lien on property.

Concerned that debtors were taking advantage of the automatic stay provisions to the substantial detriment of some creditors, such as creditors whose claims were secured by an interest in a single real estate asset, in 1994 Congress provided specific relief from the automatic stay for such creditors. Debtors must either file a plan of reorganization that has a reasonable chance of being confirmed within a reasonable time or must be making monthly payments to each such secured creditor that are in an amount equal to interest at a current fair market rate on the value of the creditor's interest in the real estate.

The automatic stay provisions are not applicable to actions to establish paternity, to establish or modify orders for domestic support obligations, for the collection of domestic support obligations from property that is not the property of the bankruptcy estate, or to withhold, suspend, or restrict a driver's license or professional, occupational, or recreational license.

In 2005, Congress added two additional exceptions from the automatic stay provisions for the benefit of landlords seeking to evict tenants. First, any eviction proceedings in which the landlord obtained a judgment of possession prior to the filing of the bankruptcy petition can be continued. Second, in cases where the landlord's claim for eviction is based on the use of illegal substances

on the property or "endangerment" of the property, the eviction proceedings are exempt from the stay even if they are initiated after the bankruptcy proceeding was filed so long as the endangerment or illegal use occurred within 30 days before the filing. Debtors are able to keep the stay in effect by filing certifications that certain nonbankruptcy laws allow the lease to remain in effect and that they have cured any defaults within 30 days of the bankruptcy filing.

The 2005 revisions also include a number of provisions dealing with serial filings for bankruptcy that are designed to keep debtors from abusing the automatic stay provisions to the detriment of creditors.

Order of Relief

Once a bankruptcy petition has been filed, the first step is a court determination that relief should be ordered. If a voluntary petition is filed by the debtor, or if the debtor does not contest an involuntary petition, this step is automatic. If the debtor contests an involuntary petition, then a trial is held on the question of whether the court should order relief. The court orders relief only (1) if the debtor is generally not paying his debts as they become due, or (2) if within 120 days of the filing of the petition a custodian was appointed or took possession of the debtor's property. The court also appoints an interim trustee pending election of a trustee by the creditors.

Meeting of Creditors and Election of Trustee

The bankrupt person is required to file a list of her assets, liabilities, and creditors and a statement of her financial affairs. The 2005 revisions impose a number of new production requirements on debtors. Now, individual debtors must file, along with their schedules of assets and liabilities:

- A certificate that they have received and/or have read the notice from the Clerk of the Bankruptcy Court that they must receive credit counseling to be eligible for relief under the Bankruptcy Code;
- Copies of all payment advices and other evidence of payments they have received from any employer within 60 days before the filing of the petition;
- A statement of the amount of monthly net income, itemized to show how the amount is calculated; and
- A statement showing any anticipated increase in income or expenditures over the 12-month period following the date of filing the petition.

Should an individual debtor in a voluntary Chapter 7 case or in a Chapter 13 case fail to file the required information within 45 days of the filing of the petition, the case is to be automatically dismissed. A court, upon finding that an extension is justified, can extend the time period to file for up to an additional 45 days.

Individual debtors also must provide copies of their most recent tax returns to the trustee and to creditors making a timely request; failure to do so can result in dismissal of the case. Debtors also must, at the request of the judge or a party in interest, file at the same time they file with the IRS copies of federal tax returns due while the bankruptcy case is pending and also file copies of tax returns (including any amended returns) for tax years that ended within the three years before the bankruptcy petition was filed.

Once the court receives the bankruptcy filing and the required schedules and certifications, the U.S. Trustee calls a meeting of the creditors. At the meeting, the U.S. Trustee is required to examine the debtor to make sure she is aware of (1) the potential consequences of seeking a discharge in bankruptcy, including the effects on credit history; (2) the debtor's ability to file a petition under other chapters (such as 11, 12, or 13) of the Bankruptcy Code; (3) the effect of receiving a discharge of debts; and (4) the effect of reaffirming a debt (discussed later in this chapter).

The creditors also elect a **trustee** who, if approved by the judge, takes over administration of the bankrupt's estate. The **trustee** represents the creditors in handling the estate. At the meeting, the creditors have a chance to ask the debtor questions about her assets, liabilities, and financial difficulties. These questions commonly focus on whether the debtor has concealed or improperly disposed of assets.

Duties of the Trustee
The trustee takes possession of the debtor's property and has it appraised. The debtor must also turn over her records to the trustee. For a time, the trustee may operate the debtor's business. The trustee sets aside the items of property that a debtor is permitted to keep under state exemption statutes or federal law.

The 2005 act places restrictions on the authority of the trustee to sell personally identifiable information about individuals to persons who are not affiliated with the debtor. Congress was concerned about situations where individuals had provided information to persons and entities on the understanding and commitment that the information would remain in confidence with the recipient. These data files often are a valuable asset of a debtor involved in bankruptcy proceedings, but Congress concluded it was not reasonable to allow that information to be sold to a third party that was not in their contemplation when the individuals provided the information to the debtor under a promise of confidentiality.

The trustee examines the claims filed by various creditors and objects to those that are improper in any way. The trustee separates the unsecured property from the secured and otherwise exempt property. He also sells the bankrupt's nonexempt property as soon as possible, consistent with the best interest of the creditors.

The trustee is required to keep an accurate account of all the property and money he receives and to promptly deposit moneys into the estate's accounts. The trustee files a final report with the court, with notice to all creditors who then may file objections to the report.

Health Care Businesses The 2005 revisions reflect Congress's concern with what happens if a petition for bankruptcy is filed by a health care business and contain a number of provisions concerning that possibility. First, the trustee is instructed to use his reasonable best efforts to transfer patients in a health care business that is in the process of being closed to an appropriate health care business in the vicinity of the one being closed that offers similar services and maintains a reasonable quality of care. Second, the actual, necessary costs of closing a health care business are considered administrative expenses entitled to priority. Third, the automatic stay provisions do not apply to actions by the Secretary of Health and Human Services to exclude the debtor from participating in Medicare and other federal health care programs. Finally, the act sets out requirements for the disposal of patient records where there are insufficient funds to continue to store them as required by law. The requirements include giving notice to the affected patients and specifying the manner of disposal for unclaimed records.

Liquidation of Financial Firms The Bankruptcy Code contains special provisions for the liquidation of stockbrokers, commodity brokers, and clearing banks that are designed to protect the interests of customers of the entities who have assets on deposit with the bankrupt debtor. These responsibilities are overseen by the trustee.

The Bankruptcy Estate
The commencement of a Chapter 7 bankruptcy case by the filing of a voluntary or involuntary petition creates a bankruptcy estate. The estate is composed of all of the debtor's legal and equitable interests in property, including certain community property. Certain property is exempted (see "Exemptions" section below). The estate also includes:

1. Profits, royalties, rents and revenue, along with the proceeds from the debtor's estate, received during the Chapter 7 proceeding.

2. Property received by the debtor in any of the following ways within 180 days of the filing of the Chapter 7 petition: (*a*) by bequest or inheritance; (*b*) as a settlement with a divorced spouse or as a result of a divorce decree; or (*c*) as proceeds of a life insurance policy.

3. Property recovered by the bankruptcy trustee because (*a*) creditor of the debtor received a voidable preferential transfer or (*b*) the debtor made a fraudulent transfer of her assets to another person. Preferential and fraudulent transfers are discussed later in this chapter.

Exemptions Even in a liquidation proceeding, the bankrupt is generally not required to give up all of his property; he is permitted to **exempt** certain items of property. Under the Bankruptcy Code, the debtor may choose to keep certain items or property either exempted by state law, or exempt under federal law unless state law specifically forbids use of the federal exemptions. However, any such property concealed or fraudulently transferred by the debtor may not be retained.

The 2005 revisions specify that the state or local law governing the debtor's exemptions is the law of the place where the debtor was domiciled for 730 days before filing. If the debtor did not maintain a domicile in a single state for that period, then the law governing the exemptions is the law of the place of the debtor's domicile for the majority of the 180-day period preceding the filing of the petition that is between two and two and one-half years before the filing. For example, on January 1, 2007, Alex Smith was living in Florida. In March 2007 he moved to Georgia and in November 2007 he moved again and took up residence in Alabama. On July 1, 2009, Smith filed a petition in bankruptcy. Because Smith had not lived in Alabama for the 2 years (730 days) before he filed, he would not be able to claim the exemptions that Alabama provides. Rather, he would be entitled to claim the exemptions provided by Georgia where he lived for the majority of the 180 days between January 1, 2007 and July 1, 2007.

The debtor must elect to use *either* the set of exemptions provided by the state or the set provided by the federal bankruptcy law; she may not pick and choose between them. A husband and wife involved in bankruptcy proceedings must both elect either the federal or the state exemptions; where they cannot agree, the federal exemptions are deemed elected.

The **exemptions** permit the bankrupt person to retain a minimum amount of the assets considered necessary to life and to his ability to continue to earn a living. They are part of the fresh start philosophy that is one of the purposes of the Bankruptcy Code. The general effect of the federal exemptions is to make at least a minimum exemption available to debtors in all states. States that wish to be more generous to debtors can provide more liberal exemptions.

The specific items that are exempt under state statutes vary from state to state. Some states provide fairly liberal exemptions and are considered "debtors' havens." For example, in Florida none of the equity in the debtor's homestead can be used to pay off unsecured creditors, thus allowing even relatively well-off individuals to shield significant assets from creditors. Items that are commonly made exempt from sale to pay debts owed creditors include the family Bible; tools or books of the trade; life insurance policies; health aids, such as wheelchairs and hearing aids; personal and household goods; and jewelry, furniture, and motor vehicles worth up to a certain amount.

The case that follows, *In re Kyllogen,* illustrates a claim by a debtor for an exemption under a state statute.

In re Kyllogen   264 B.R.17 (U.S.D.C. D.Minn. 2001)

Patricia Kyllogen owns a five-acre lot with a home and pole barn located on it; the property has an estimated value of $350,000 and is subject to a $90,000 mortgage. She purchased the property from her parents in 1974 and built the home after she married in 1980. The couple has two daughters. She and her husband David also own an adjacent unimproved lot of approximately five acres located behind the lot with their home. The second lot, which is valued at $45,000, was purchased in 1988. Both lots are heavily wooded with mature oak trees and used to be part of Patricia Kyllogen's parents' family farm.

Much of the surrounding area that once had constituted the family farm has been subdivided into residential parcels of at least two and a half acres or more; many of the parcels contain large, expensive, and upscale homes. Three or four nearby properties are occupied by individuals who have full-time outside jobs but who also grow farm crops, primarily hay, on a part-time basis.

In 1996 Kyllogen and her husband cleared one-tenth of an acre of land on the front lot and planted ginseng seeds. Ginseng is a small herbal plant harvested for its roots. The longer the root grows before it is harvested, the more valuable it is, *and the earliest one can harvest ginseng root is about five to seven years after it is planted. The ginseng is planted under the shade of mature hardwood trees, and, once an area is cleared and the ginseng planted, it requires relatively little care except for periodic weeding. Kyllogen was employed full-time at a Burlington Coat Factory; her husband did not have a regular full-time job, although he described himself as a ginseng farmer. In five years of operation (1996–2000), the ginseng "farm" had no income and approximately $28,000 in tax deductible losses.*

Kyllogen filed a petition in bankruptcy. She claimed her home and the two contiguous five-acre parcels as "exempt" assets of the bankruptcy estate. The Bankruptcy Trustee objected to the claimed exemption, asserting that Kyllogen was entitled to exempt a homestead of no more than one-half of an acre of land in area with a value of no more than $200,000.

Dreher, Bankruptcy Judge

A debtor may exempt from her bankruptcy estate certain property which is exempt under applicable state law on the petition filing date.

Section 510.01 of the Minnesota Statutes specifically provides:

The house owned and occupied by a debtor as the debtor's dwelling place, together with the land upon which it is situated to the amount hereinafter limited and defined, shall constitute the homestead of such debtor and debtor's family, and be exempt from seizure or sale under legal process on account of any debt . . . charged thereon in writing, except such as are incurred for work or materials furnished in the construction, repair, or improvement of such homestead, or for services performed by laborers or servants.

Section 510.02, in turn, defines the area limits of the homestead:

The homestead may include any quantity of land not exceeding 160 acres, and not included in the laid out or platted portion of any city. If the homestead is within the laid out or platted portion of a city, its area must not exceed one-half of an acre. The value of the homestead exemption, whether the exemption is claimed jointly or individually, may not exceed $200,000, or, if the homestead is used primarily for agricultural purposes, $500,000, exclusive of the limitations set forth in section 510.05.

Generally speaking, exemption laws work in tandem with debt discharge to effectuate a debtor's fresh start. The intent of the homestead exemption is to secure a debtor's home against uncertainties and misfortunes of life and to preserve the home as a dwelling place for the debtor and his or her family. However, the area limitations and other requirements ensure that the debtor does not unfairly retain assets.

* * *

This case is unlike others in which the debtors are clearly family farmers who live and work on the land and use it for agricultural purposes. *Cf. In re Becker* (finding debtors who had farmed for three-plus decades a 58-acre parcel which contained a barn and several outbuildings were entitled to larger homestead exemption). While Debtor testified that she and her family always wanted to farm, nothing in this record shows that they have farmed or are farming. Debtor and, to a lesser extent, her spouse have always been principally employed off the "farm." Moreover, what little "farming" they have engaged in—a fish farm in Wisconsin, one year's worth of failed mushrooms, and upstart wood-cultivated ginseng operations—is not farming in the traditional sense, was and is small-scale, and undertaken even as they maintained outside employment. These farming operations have never provided support for Debtor and her family but instead have merely given them healthy tax write-offs year after year.

Ginseng "farming," which can be done on small plots of wooded property, can be conducted with little or no land. In five years, Debtor and her spouse have planted less than one-half of an acre of land and never expect to harvest more than one-tenth of an acre of crop per year. Debtor and her spouse do not, and never will in their lifetime, need such expansive acreage for their operations even if they stay with wood-cultivated ginseng. What they do can be termed "farming," but it is clearly not agricultural as that term is traditionally understood and is not the sort of "farm" the homestead exemption statute was designed to protect.

Debtor and her spouse fervently testified that they are ginseng farmers, but in actuality, they are a couple who own a very large house on a very large lot, which is virtually surrounded by other very large houses on very large lots, or in a few instances, some smaller houses on sizeable vacant lots, in the country. Debtor has a full-time day job and spends her evenings and weekends pulling weeds and tending small plots of ginseng, akin to a city resident who maintains a backyard vegetable garden. Her spouse likewise has historically had a full-time day job, usually as an electrical contractor, with his various "farming" operations being secondary or on the side. Debtor and her spouse are not farming their parcels in any true sense, and there is nothing inherently agricultural about what they are doing. In short, ginseng "farming" is their hobby. Therefore, given the conclusively urban use and nature of Debtor's two contiguous parcels, Debtor is only entitled to a homestead exemption of one-half of an acre up to $200,000.

Judgment affirmed in favor of Bankruptcy Trustee.

Limits on State Homestead Exemptions Concerns that very generous homestead exemptions in a number of states were leading to abuses by debtors who transferred assets into large homes in those states and then filed for bankruptcy led Congress in 2005 to place some limits on state homestead exemptions. These limits include:

- The value of the debtor's homestead for purposes of a state homestead exemption is reduced to the extent that it reflects an increase in value on account of the disposition of nonexempt property by the debtor during the 10 years prior to the filing with the intent to hinder, delay, or defraud creditors.
- Any value in excess of $136,875—irrespective of the debtors intent—that is added to the value of a homestead during the 1,215 days (about 3 years, 4 months) preceding the bankruptcy filing may not be included in a state homestead exemption unless it was transferred from another homestead in the same state or the homestead is the principal residence of a family farmer.
- An absolute $136,875 homestead cap applies if either (*a*) the bankruptcy court determines that the debtor has been convicted of a felony demonstrating that the filing of the case was an abuse of the provisions of the Bankruptcy Code or (*b*) the debtor owes a debt arising from a violation of federal or state securities laws, fiduciary fraud, racketeering, or crimes or intentional torts that caused serious injury or death in the preceding five years. In certain cases, a discharge of a debtor under Chapters 7, 11, or 13 may be delayed where the debtor is subject to a proceeding that might lead to a limitation of a homestead exemption.

Federal Exemptions Twelve categories of property are exempt under the federal exemptions, which the debtor may elect in lieu of the state exemptions. The federal exemptions include:

1. The debtor's interest (not to exceed $20,200 in value) in real or personal property that the debtor or a dependent of the debtor uses as a residence.
2. The debtor's interest (not to exceed $3,225 in value) in one motor vehicle.
3. The debtor's interest (not to exceed $525 in value for any particular item) up to a total of $10,775 in household furnishings, household goods, wearing apparel, appliances, books, animals, crops, or musical instruments that are held primarily for the personal, family, or household use of the debtor or a dependent of the debtor.
4. The debtor's aggregate interest (not to exceed $1,350 in value) in jewelry held primarily for the personal,

family, or household use of the debtor or a dependent of the debtor.
5. $1,075 in value of any other property of the debtor's choosing, plus up to $10,125 of any unused homestead exemption.
6. The debtor's aggregate interest (not to exceed $2,025 in value) in any implements, professional books, or tools of the trade.
7. Life insurance contracts.
8. Interest up to $10,775 in specified kinds of dividends or interest in certain kinds of life insurance policies.
9. Professionally prescribed health aids.
10. Social Security, disability, alimony, and other benefits reasonably necessary for the support of the debtor or his dependents.
11. The debtor's right to receive certain insurance and liability payments.
12. Retirement funds that are in a fund or account that is exempt from taxation under the Internal Revenue Code. For certain individual retirement accounts, the aggregate amount exempted is limited to $1 million. Also protected are some contributions to certain education and college savings accounts made more than one year prior to bankruptcy.

The term **value** means "fair market value as of the date of the filing of the petition." In determining the debtor's interest in property, the amount of any liens against the property must be deducted.

Avoidance of Liens
The debtor is also permitted to **void** certain liens against exempt properties that impair her exemptions. Liens that can be voided on this basis are judicial liens or nonpossessory, nonpurchase money security interests in (1) household furnishings, household goods, wearing apparel, appliances, books, animals, crops, musical instruments, or jewelry that are held primarily for the personal, family, or household use of the debtor or a dependent of the debtor; (2) implements, professional books, or tools of the trade of the debtor or a dependent of the debtor; and (3) professionally prescribed health aids for the debtor or a dependent of the debtor.

Debtors are also permitted to **redeem** exempt personal property from secured creditors by paying them the full value of the collateral at the time the property is redeemed. Then, the creditor is an unsecured creditor as to any remaining debt owed by the debtor. Under the 2005 revisions, the value of personal property securing a claim of an individual debtor in a Chapter 7 proceeding is based on the cost to the debtor of replacing the property—without deduction for costs of sale or marketing—and if the property was acquired for personal, family, or household purposes, the replacement cost will be the retail price for property of similar age and condition. The debtor is not permitted to retain collateral without redemption or reaffirmation of the debt (discussed later in this chapter) by just continuing to make the payments on the secured debt.

Under the 2005 revisions, the "household goods" as to which a nonpossessory, nonpurchase–money security interest can be avoided have been limited. The new definition limits electronic equipment to one radio, one television, one VCR, and one computer with related equipment. Specifically excluded are works of art other than those created by the debtor or family member, jewelry worth more than $550 (except wedding rings), and motor vehicles (including lawn tractors, motorized vehicles such as ORVs (off-road vehicles), watercraft, and aircraft.

Preferential Payments

A major purpose of the Bankruptcy Code is to ensure equal treatment for the creditors of an insolvent debtor. The code also seeks to prevent an insolvent debtor from distributing her assets to a few favored creditors to the detriment of the other creditors. Thus, the trustee has the right to recover for the benefit of the estate **preferential payments** above a certain threshold that are made by the bankrupt debtor in advance of the bankruptcy. In the case of an individual debtor whose debts are primarily consumer debts, the trustee is not entitled to avoid preferences unless the aggregate value of the property is $600 or more. In the case of a corporate debtor, a transfer by a debtor of less than $5,475 in the aggregate is not subject to avoidance. A preferential payment is a payment made by an insolvent debtor within 90 days before the filing of the bankruptcy petition that enables a creditor to obtain a greater percentage of a preexisting debt than other similar creditors of the debtor. It is irrelevant whether the creditor knew that the debtor was insolvent. A debtor is presumed to have been insolvent on and during the 90 days immediately preceding the filing of a petition.

For example, Fredericks has $1,000 in cash and no other assets. He owes $650 to his friend Roberts, $1,500 to a credit union, and $2,000 to a finance company. If Fredericks pays $650 to Roberts and then files for bankruptcy, he has made a preferential payment to Roberts. Roberts has had his debt paid in full, whereas only $350 is left to satisfy the $3,500 owed to the credit union and finance company. They stand to recover only 10 cents on each dollar that Fredericks owes them. The trustee has the right to get the $650 back from Roberts.

If the favored creditor is an insider—a relative of an individual debtor or an officer, director, or related party of a company—who had reasonable cause to believe the debtor was insolvent at the time the transfer was made, then a preferential payment made to that creditor up to one year prior to the filing of the petition can be recovered by the trustee.

The 1994 amendments to the Bankruptcy Code provided that the trustee may not recover as preferential payments any bona fide payments of debts to a spouse, former spouse, or child of the debtor for alimony, maintenance, or support pursuant to a separation agreement, divorce decree, or other court order.

Preferential Liens

Preferential liens are treated in a similar manner. A creditor might try to obtain an advantage over other creditors by obtaining a lien on the debtor's property to secure an existing debt. The creditor might seek to get the debtor's consent to a lien or to obtain a lien by legal process. Such liens are considered *preferential* and are invalid if they are obtained on property of an insolvent debtor within 90 days before the filing of a bankruptcy petition and if their purpose is to secure a preexisting debt. A preferential lien obtained by an insider up to one year prior to the filing of the bankruptcy petition can be avoided.

Transactions in the Ordinary Course of Business

The Bankruptcy Code provides several exceptions to the trustee's avoiding power that are designed to allow a debtor and his creditors to engage in ordinary business transactions. The exceptions include (1) transfers that are intended by the debtor and creditor to be a contemporaneous exchange for new value or (2) the creation of a security interest in new property where new value was given by the secured party to enable the debtor to obtain the property and where the new value was in fact used by the debtor to obtain the property and perfected within 20 days after the debtor took possession of the collateral.

For example, George Grocer is insolvent. He is permitted to purchase and pay cash for new inventory, such as produce or meat, without the payment being considered preferential. His assets have not been reduced. He has simply traded money for goods to be sold in his business. Similarly, he could buy a new display counter and give the seller a security interest in the counter until he has paid for it. This would not be considered a preferential lien. The seller of the counter has not gained an

Ethics in Action

Should the Homestead Exemption Be Limited?

As of June 2002, six states, including Florida and Texas, provide an unlimited household exemption that allows bankrupt debtors to shield unlimited amounts of equity in a residential estate. The unlimited exemption has come under increased scrutiny in recent years as a number of public figures as well as noted wrongdoers have taken advantage of the unlimited exemption to shield significant amounts of wealth from creditors. For example, a prominent actor who was declared bankrupt in 1996 was allowed to keep a $2.5 million estate located in Hobe Sound, Florida, and a corporate executive convicted of securities fraud kept his Tampa, Florida, mansion from the claims of his creditors in bankruptcy, including federal regulators seeking to collect civil fines. When the Enron and WorldCom corporate scandals broke in 2001 and 2002, the media called attention to a $15 million mansion under construction in Boca Raton, Florida, for the former CFO of WorldCom and to a $7 million penthouse owned by the former CEO of Enron as well as to the fact that the liberal exemption laws in Florida and Texas might be utilized by them to protect a significant amount of their wealth against claims from creditors and regulators.

As noted above, in the 2005 act, Congress took some steps to limit the ability of debtors to shift assets into an expensive home in a state with an unlimited household exemption shortly before filing for bankruptcy and also to limit the exemption for debtors convicted of violations of the federal securities laws. While the act was pending in the conference committee, a group of about 80 law professors who teach bankruptcy and commercial law wrote to the committee urging that it adopt a hard cap on the homestead exemption contained in the Senate version of the bill. They pointed out the fundamental unfairness created when residents of one state can protect in a supposedly "uniform" federal bankruptcy proceeding an asset worth millions while residents in other states face sharp limitations on what they can protect. As an example, they noted that a wealthy investor in Texas could keep an unencumbered home worth $10 million while a factory worker in Virginia puts at risk anything over $10,000 in equity.

The law professors described various ways that the formulation the conference committee had adopted could be gamed. They also asserted that the provisions to limit the homestead exemption for those who violate securities laws, who commit fraud while in a fiduciary capacity, or who commit certain felonies or intentional torts were too tightly drawn and would create a "playground of loopholes for wealthy individuals and clever lawyers." They noted, for example, that the provisions "would not cap the homestead exemption for someone who finds a dozen ways to bilk the elderly out of their money, someone who takes advantage of first-time home buyers, or someone who deceives people trying to set up college funds for their children."

Should Congress adopt a uniform cap on the homestead exemption?

---

unfair advantage over other creditors, and Grocer's assets have not been reduced by the transaction. The unfair advantage comes where an existing creditor tries to take a lien or obtain a payment of more than his share of the debtor's assets. Then, the creditor has obtained a preference over other creditors, which is what the trustee is allowed to avoid.

The Bankruptcy Code also provides an exception for transfers made in payment of a debt incurred in the ordinary course of the business or financial affairs of the debtor and the transferee (a) made in the ordinary course of business or (b) made according to ordinary business terms. Thus, for example, a consumer could pay her monthly utility bills in a timely fashion without the creditor/utility being vulnerable to having the transfer of funds avoided by a trustee. The purpose of this exception is to leave undisturbed normal financial relations, and it is consistent with the general policy of the preference section of the code to discourage *unusual action* by either a debtor or her creditors when the debtor is moving toward bankruptcy.

Exceptions to the trustee's avoidance power are also made for certain statutory liens, certain other perfected security interests, and cases filed by individual debtors whose debts are primarily consumer debts and the aggregate value of all property affected by the transfer is less than $600, and cases filed by a debtor where debts are not primarily consumer debts and the aggregate value of all property affected by the transfer is less than $5,000.

Fraudulent Transfers If a debtor transfers property or incurs an obligation with *intent to hinder, delay, or defraud creditors,* the transfer is *voidable* by the trustee. Transfers of property for less than reasonable value are similarly voidable. Suppose Kasper is in financial difficulty. She "sells" her $15,000 car to her mother for $100 so that her creditors cannot claim it. Kasper did not receive fair consideration for this transfer. The transfer could be declared void by a trustee if it was made within two years before the filing of a bankruptcy petition against Kasper.

Some states provide longer periods of time; for example, New York allows trustees to avoid fraudulent transfers made in a six-year period before the bankruptcy filing.

Avoidance of Certain "Retention Bonuses" The 2005 revisions also explicitly authorize the trustee to avoid two types of transfers as fraudulent. First, he may avoid transfers to or for the benefit of an insider under an employment contract and not in the ordinary course of business. Specifically addressed are "retention bonuses" which Congress believed had been abused in some recent high-profile corporate bankruptcies. Retention bonuses can be paid to insiders only where they are made in response to bona fide outside offers, the individual's services are essential to the survival of the business, and the amount of the bonus is not more than 10 times the mean of similar bonuses paid to nonmanagement employees during the year.

Avoidance of Transfers to Certain Asset Protection Trusts The second type of transfer that the trustee was explicitly suthorized to avoid as fraudulent is transfers to a self-settled trust made within 10 years of the filing by a debtor where the debtor is a beneficiary and the transfer was made with actual intent to hinder or delay. There is a particular focus on transfers made in anticipation of any money judgment, settlement, civil penalty, equitable order, or criminal fine which the debtor believed would be incurred through any violation of federal or state securities laws or fraud, deceit or manipulation in a fiduciary capacity, or in connection with the purchase or sale of securities registered under the federal securities acts.

The provisions of law concerning **fraudulent transfers** are designed to prevent a debtor from concealing or disposing of his property in fraud of creditors. Such transfers may also subject the debtor to criminal penalties and prevent discharge of the debtor's unpaid liabilities.[1]

In the *Manhattan Investment Fund, Ltd.* case that follows, the court held that the trustee could recover margin payments transferred to a brokerage firm as transfers presumed to have been made with actual intent to hinder, delay, or defraud other creditors.

[1]Bulk sales of a debtor's materials, supplies, merchandise, or other inventory of the business in bulk and not in the ordinary course of business have the potential to defraud creditors.

In re Manhattan Investment Fund Ltd.
359 B.R. 510 (U.S.B.C., S.D. N.Y. 2007)

Michael Berger created the Manhattan Investment Fund through his wholly owned company, Manhattan Capital Management, Inc., and used the Fund as his vehicle to conduct a massive Ponzi scheme. On January, 14, 2000, following an investigation into the Fund's trading activities, the Securities and Exchange Commission (SEC), filed a complaint alleging securities fraud against the Fund, MCM, and Berger. The SEC obtained an asset freeze and the appointment of Helen Gredd as Receiver for the Fund. On March 7, 2000 (the "Petition Date"), the Receiver caused the Fund to file a voluntary petition for relief under Chapter 11 of the Bankruptcy Code, and on April 4, 2000, the Receiver was appointed Trustee of the Fund under Chapter 11.

On April 24, 2000, the Trustee commenced an adversary proceeding against Bear Stearns. In her complaint, the Trustee sought to avoid, pursuant to section 548(a)(1)(A) of the Bankruptcy Code, transfers that were made to Bear Stearns in connection with the Fund's short selling activities during the last 10 months of its operation. Count I of the complaint sought to avoid $141.1 million in margin payments which Berger transferred to Bear Stearns from the Fund's account with the Bank of Bermuda.

In the year prior to the Petition Date, the Fund made 18 separate transfers totaling $141.4 million from its account at Bank of Bermuda to an account maintained by Bear Stearns at Citibank. Those monies were then transferred to the Fund's Bear Stearns account. The monies in the Fund's Bear Stearns account were used by the Fund to engage in securities trading. The Bear Stearns account was subject to a Professional Account Agreement between Berger and Bear Stearns which provided, in relevant part, that (1) Bear Stearns had the right to set the level of maintenance margin; (2) Bear Stearns had a security interest in all monies held in the account; (3) Bear Stearns had sole discretion to prevent the Fund from withdrawing any money credited to its account as long as any short positions remained open; and (4) Bear Stearns had sole discretion to use any and all monies credited to the Fund's account to liquidate the Fund's open short positions with or without the Fund's consent. The agreement and the account itself were governed by SEC Rule 15c3-3 which expressly precluded Bear Stearns from using the funds in the account for any purpose other than those outlined in the agreement.

Lifland, U.S. Bankruptcy Judge

The Bankruptcy Code bestows broad powers upon a trustee to avoid certain transfers of property made by the debtor before the filing of the bankruptcy petition. In this way, the transferred property is returned to the estate for the benefit of all persons who have presented valid claims. Specifically, *section 548 of the Bankruptcy Code* provides for the avoidance of any transfer of an interest in property made by the debtor in the year prior to the filing of its bankruptcy petition as a fraudulent conveyance provided that the transfer was made with an actual fraudulent intent or with the badges of fraud constituting constructive fraud of the debtor's creditors. A fraudulent conveyance avoided under *section 548* is recoverable by the trustee under *section 550(a)* which provides, in relevant part, "the trustee may recover, . . . the property transferred, or, if the court so orders, the value of such property, from (1) the *initial transferee* of such transfer or the entity for whose benefit such transfer was made . . ." (emphasis added).

However, *section 546(e) of the Bankruptcy Code*, commonly known as the "stockbroker defense," prevents the trustee from avoiding margin payments made to a stockbroker except where there is actual fraud. Legislative history reveals that Congress was concerned about the volatile nature of the commodities and securities markets, and decided that certain protections were necessary to prevent the insolvency of one commodity or security firm from spreading to other firms and possibly threatening the collapse of the affected market. *Section 548(a)(1)(A),* referred to as the "actual fraud" provision, requires that in order to avoid a transfer, it must be made with actual intent to hinder, delay, or defraud any entity to which the debtor was or became, on or after the date that such transfer was made or such obligation was incurred or indebted.

The eighteen transfers at issue in this matter were deposited by the Fund in its account at Bear Stearns to allow it to continue short selling activities within the year prior to the Petition Date. To engage in short sales, federal securities regulations required the Fund to maintain its margin account with Bear Stearns at a specified level. Bear Stearns, in turn, could, and did, make those requirements more stringent based on the level of risk at which it perceived the Fund's trading to be. The transfers were made in order to open new short positions or to comply with the requirements of its margin account in order to continue trading. As such, the transfers fit squarely within the definition of a margin payment as defined in *the Bankruptcy Code*.

The Trustee argues that the transfers are within the exception to *section 546(e) of the Bankruptcy Code* because the transfers were made in furtherance of a "Ponzi" scheme. A "Ponzi" or "Pyramid" scheme is a fraudulent investment scheme in which money contributed by later investors is used to pay artificially high dividends to the original investors, creating an illusion of profitability, thus attracting new investors.

Actual intent to hinder, delay or defraud may be established as a matter of law in cases in which the debtor runs a Ponzi scheme or a similar illegitimate enterprise, because transfers made in the course of a Ponzi operation could have been made for no purpose other than to hinder, delay or defraud creditors. Thus, courts nationwide have recognized that establishing the existence of a Ponzi scheme is sufficient to prove a debtor's actual intent to defraud. Moreover, acts taken in furtherance of the Ponzi scheme, such as paying brokers commissions, are also fraudulent. Every payment made by the debtor to keep the scheme on-going was made with the actual intent to hinder, delay or defraud creditors, primarily the new investors.

Bear Stearns argues that there was no fraud. However, this Court, along with the District Court has already determined that issue. In ruling on Bear Stearns' motion to dismiss, this Court explained that, "[w]hen a debtor operating a Ponzi scheme makes a payment with the knowledge that future creditors will not be paid, that payment is presumed to have been made with actual intent to hinder, delay or defraud other creditors—regardless of whether payments were made to early investors, or whether the debtor was engaged in a strictly classic Ponzi scheme." In light of Berger's guilty plea and conviction coupled with the fact that the margin payments were made in connection with a massive Ponzi scheme, this Court finds sufficient evidence of actual fraudulent intent in connection with the Transfers. Similarly, the District Court found that "[t]his action arises out of a Ponzi scheme engineered by Michael Berger, the Fund's manager, who sought to cover losses from ill-advised short sales of technology stocks with deposits made by new investors. The results were disastrous; the Fund hemorrhaged hundreds of millions of dollars [in 1998, Berger collected nearly $200 million in investment principal, lost more than $197 million in trading while claiming gains of more than $33 million] and Mr. Berger was criminally prosecuted, pleading guilty to securities fraud. Accordingly, the issue is whether or not the payments may be recovered from Bear Stearns as an initial transferee under *section 550(a)(1).*"

Bear Stearns argues that it is a "mere conduit" and not an initial transferee. The Bankruptcy Code does not define the term "transferee" and as such the "mere conduit" defense has arisen as a defense to liability in avoidance actions. In order to be an initial transferee courts require something more than being the "first hands" to touch the asset, but rather that the entity have the requisite possession and control over the transferred asset.

Under the terms of the Fund's Agreement with Bear Stearns, Bear Sterns had a security interest in any monies transferred; held the monies transferred as collateral for short sales; had the right to and did prohibit the Fund from withdrawing any of the monies transferred as long as any short position remained open; and had the right to and did use the monies transferred to purchase covering securities, with or without the Fund's consent. Thus, Bear Stearns had the ability to exercise control and use the transfers to protect its own economic well-being and thus, is not a mere conduit with respect to those transfers.

Bear Stearns asserts that even should it be found to be an initial transferee within the meaning of *section 550(a) of the Bankruptcy Code,* that if Bear Stearns accepted the transfers from the Fund in good faith under *548(c),* without knowledge of the fraud, then the Trustee will not be permitted to recover these monies. The Trustee contends that Bear Stearns' knowledge of the Fund's questionable activity put it on notice of the Ponzi scheme more than a year before the Fund was shut down and investigated by the SEC. She contends that Bear Stearns had the opportunity to discover the Ponzi scheme and therefore was on constructive notice of the Fund's continued fraud.

Section 548(c) provides, in relevant part, that to the extent that a transfer is voidable, a transferee that takes for value and in good faith may retain any interest transferred to the extent that such transferee gave value to the debtor in exchange for such transfer or obligation. Under *section 548(c),* the transferee of a fraudulent transfer must prove his good faith in order to sustain his defense.

It is clear from the record that Bear Stearns was on inquiry notice of Berger's fraud from December 1998 and throughout the following year. Based upon the information it had, Bear Stearns was required to do more than simply ask the wrongdoer if he was doing wrong. Diligence requires consulting easily obtainable sources of information that would bear on the truth of any explanation received from the potential wrongdoer. The simple steps Bear Stearns finally performed one year later [it asked to see the Fund's financial statements, saw that it was the only broker the Fund had and that the moneys shown as present at Bears Stearns were substantially more than was actually there—and then notified the SEC], demonstrate that Bear Stearns failed to act diligently in a timely manner and accordingly, Bear Stearns cannot satisfy its burden of showing that it acted with the diligence required to establish good faith under *section 548(c) of the Bankruptcy Code.*

Trustee's motion for summary judgment granted.

Claims
If creditors wish to participate in the estate of a bankrupt debtor, they must file a **proof of claim** in the estate within a certain time, usually 90 days after the first meeting of creditors. Only unsecured creditors are required to file proofs of claims. However, a secured creditor whose secured claim exceeds the value of the collateral is an unsecured creditor to the extent of the deficiency. That creditor must file a proof of claim to support the recovery of the deficiency.

Allowable Claims
The fact that a proof of claim is filed does not ensure that a creditor can participate in the distribution of the assets of the bankruptcy estate. The claim must also be allowed. If the trustee has a valid defense to the claim, he can use the defense to disallow or reduce it. For example, if the claim is based on goods sold to the debtor and the seller breached a warranty, the trustee can assert the breach as a defense. All of the defenses available to the bankrupt person are available to the trustee.

Under the 2005 revisions, the court is authorized to reduce claims based on unsecured consumer debt by 20 percent on motion by the debtor and a showing that the creditor refused to negotiate a reasonable alternative repayment schedule proposed on behalf of the debtor by an approved nonprofit budget and credit counseling agency. The offer had to have been made at least 60 days before filing of the petition and to have provided for the payment of at least 60 percent of the debt over a period not to exceed the original period of the loan or a reasonable extension of the time.

Secured Claims
The trustee must also determine whether a creditor has a lien or secured interest to secure an allowable claim. If the debtor's property is subject to a secured claim of a creditor, that creditor has first claim to it. The property is available to satisfy claims of other creditors only to the extent that its value exceeds the amount of the debt secured.

Priority Claims
The Bankruptcy Code declares certain claims to have **priority** over other claims. The 10 classes of **priority** claims are:

1. Domestic support obligations of the debtor, including claims for debts to a spouse, former spouse, or child for alimony to, maintenance for, or support of such spouse or child in connection with a separation agreement, divorce decree, or other court order (but not if assigned to someone else other than a governmental unit). Expenses of a trustee in administering

assets that might otherwise be used to pay the support obligations have priority before the support obligations themselves. And, support obligations owed directly to, or recoverable by, spouses and children have priority over support obligations that have been assigned to or are owed directly to a governmental unit.

2. Expenses and fees incurred in administering the bankruptcy estate.

3. Unsecured claims in involuntary cases that arise in the ordinary course of the debtor's business after the filing of the petition but before the appointment of a trustee or the order of relief.

4. Unsecured claims of up to $10,950 per individual (including vacation, severance, and sick pay) for employee's wages earned within 180 days before the petition was filed or the debtor's business ceased.

5. Contributions to employee benefit plans up to $10,950 per person (moreover, the claim for wages plus pension contribution is limited to $10,950 per person).

6. Unsecured claims (*a*) for grain or the proceeds of grain against a debtor who owns or operates a grain storage facility or (*b*) up to $5,400 by a U.S. fisherman against a debtor who operates a fish produce storage or processing facility and who has acquired fish or fish produce from the fisherman.

7. Claims of up to $2,245 each by individuals for deposits made in connection with the purchase, lease, or rental of property or the purchase of goods or services for personal use that were not delivered or provided.

8. Certain taxes owed to governmental units.

9. Allowed unsecured claims based on a commitment by the debtor to a federal depository institution regulatory agency (such as the FDIC).

10. Allowed claims for liability for death or personal injury resulting from operation of a motor vehicle where the operator was unlawfully intoxicated from alcohol, drugs, or other substances.

The 2005 act adds as a category of administrative expenses (see priority 2 above) "the value of any goods received by a debtor within 20 days before the petition date in which the goods have been sold to the debtor in the ordinary course of the debtor's business" The expectation is that a very significant percentage of claims arising from goods sold and received will qualify as administrative expenses. The 2005 revisions also extend the right of vendors to reclaim goods shipped before the petition. Any goods sold in the ordinary course of business and received by a debtor while insolvent may be reclaimed by the seller provided that the seller demands reclamation in writing not later than 45 days after the receipt of the goods or, if the debtor filed its petition during the 45 days, then not later than 20 days after the commencement of the bankruptcy case.

Distribution of the Debtor's Estate The priority claims are paid *after* secured creditors realize on their collateral but *before* other unsecured creditors are paid. Payments are made to the 10 priority classes, in order, to the extent there are funds available. Each class must be paid in full before the next class is entitled to receive anything. To the extent there are insufficient funds to satisfy all the creditors within a class, each class member receives a pro rata share of his claim.

Unsecured creditors include (1) those creditors who had not taken any collateral to secure the debt owed to them; (2) secured creditors to the extent their debt was not satisfied by the collateral they held; and (3) priority claimholders to the extent their claims exceed the limits set for priority claims.

Unsecured creditors, to the extent any funds are available for them, share in proportion to their claims. Unsecured creditors frequently receive little or nothing on their claims. Secured claims, trustee's fees, and other priority claims often consume a large part of the bankruptcy estate.

Special rules are set out in the Bankruptcy Code for distribution of the property of a bankrupt stockbroker or commodities broker.

Discharge in Bankruptcy

Discharge A bankrupt person who has not been guilty of certain dishonest acts and has fulfilled his duties as a bankrupt is entitled to a **discharge in bankruptcy.** A discharge relieves the bankrupt person of further responsibility for dischargeable debts and gives him a fresh start. A corporation or a partnership is not eligible for a discharge in bankruptcy. A bankrupt person may file a written waiver of his right to a discharge. An individual may not be granted a discharge if she obtained one within the previous eight years.

Objections to Discharge After the bankrupt has paid all of the required fees, the court gives creditors and others a chance to file objections to the discharge of

Distribution of Debtor's Estate (Chapter 7)

Secured creditors proceed directly against the collateral. If debt is fully satisfied, they have no further interest; if debt is only partially satisfied, they are treated as general creditors for the balance.

↓

Debtor's Estate Is Liquidated and Distributed

↓

Priority Creditors (10 classes)

1. Domestic support obligations of the debtor and expenses of administration of assets used to pay support obligations.
2. Costs and expenses of administration.
3. If involuntary proceeding, expenses incurred in the ordinary course of business after petition filed but before appointment of trustee.
4. Claims for wages, salaries, and commissions earned within 180 days of petition; limited to $10,950 per person.
5. Contributions to employee benefit plans arising out of services performed within 180 days of petition; limit of $10,950 (including claims for wages, salaries, and commissions) per person.
6. Unsecured claims (a) for grain or the proceeds of grain against a debtor who owns or operates a grain storage facility or (b) up to $5,400 by a United States fisherman against a debtor who operates a fish produce or processing facility and who has acquired fish or fish produce from the fisherman.
7. Claims of individuals, up to $2,425 per person, for deposits made on consumer goods or services that were not received.
8. Government claims for certain taxes.
9. Allowed unsecured claims based on a commitment by the debtor to a federal depository institution regulatory agency.
10. Allowed claims for liability for death or personal injury resulting from operation of a motor vehicle where the operator was intoxicated.

    A. Distribution is made to 10 classes of priority claims in order.
    B. Each class must be fully paid before next class receives anything.
    C. If funds not sufficient to satisfy everyone in a class, then each member of the class receives same proportion of claim.

↓

General Creditors

1. General unsecured creditors.
2. Secured creditors for the portion of their debt that was not satisfied by collateral.
3. Priority creditors for amounts beyond priority limits.

If funds are not sufficient to satisfy all general creditors, then each receives the same proportion of their claims.

↓

Debtor

Debtor receives any remaining funds.

the bankrupt. Objections may be filed by the trustee, a creditor, or the U.S. attorney. If objections are filed, the court holds a hearing to listen to them. At the hearing, the court must determine whether the bankrupt person has committed any act that is a bar to discharge. If the bankrupt has not committed such an act, the court grants the discharge. If the bankrupt has committed an act that is a bar to discharge, the discharge is denied. The discharge is also denied if the bankrupt fails to appear at the hearing on objections or if he refused earlier to submit to the questioning of the creditors.

Acts That Bar Discharge

Discharges in bankruptcy are intended for honest debtors. Therefore, the following acts bar a debtor from being discharged: (1) the unjustified falsifying, concealing, or destroying of records; (2) making false statements, presenting false claims, or withholding recorded information relating to the debtor's property or financial affairs; (3) transferring, removing, or concealing property in order to hinder, delay, or defraud creditors; (4) failing to account satisfactorily for any loss or deficiency of assets; and (5) failing to obey court orders or to answer questions approved by the court.

Nondischargeable Debts

Certain debts are not affected by the discharge of a bankrupt debtor. The Bankruptcy Code provides that a discharge in bankruptcy releases a debtor from all provable debts except for certain specified debts. These include, among others, debts that:

1. Are due as a tax or fine to the United States or any state or local unit of government.
2. Result from liabilities for obtaining money by false pretenses or false representations.
3. Were incurred by the debtor's purchase of more than $500 in luxury goods or services on credit from a single creditor within 90 days of filing a petition (presumed to be nondischargeable).
4. Are cash advances in excess of $750 obtained by use of a credit card or a revolving line of credit at a credit union and obtained within 70 days of filing a bankruptcy petition (presumed to be nondischargeable).
5. Were not scheduled in time for proof and allowance because the creditor holding the debt did not have notification of the proceeding even though the debtor was aware that he owed money to that creditor.
6. Were created by the debtor's larceny or embezzlement or by the debtor's fraud while acting in a fiduciary capacity.
7. Were for a domestic support obligation (unless excepting it from discharge would impose an undue hardship on the debtor's dependents).
8. Are due for willful or malicious injury to a person or his property.
9. Are educational loans.
10. Are judgments arising out of a debtor's operation of a motor vehicle while legally intoxicated.
11. Are debts incurred to pay a tax to the United States that would not be dischargeable.
12. Are property settlements arising from divorce or separation proceedings *other than* support provisions that are priority claims.

All of these nondischargeable debts are provable debts. The creditor who owns these claims can participate in the distribution of the bankrupt's estate. However, the creditor has an additional advantage: His right to recover the unpaid balance is not cut off by the bankrupt's discharge. All other provable debts are dischargeable; that is, the right to recover them is cut off by the bankrupt's discharge.

In the case that follows, *In re Gerhardt*, the court denied the request of a debtor that his student loans be discharged because their repayment would constitute an undue hardship to him.

In re Gerhardt   348 F.3d 89 (5th Cir. 2003)

Jonathon Gerhardt was a professional cellist who had obtained over $77,000 in government-insured student loans to finance his education at the University of Southern California, the Eastman School of Music, the University of Rochester, and the New England Conservatory of Music. He was 43 years old, healthy, and had no dependants. He subsequently defaulted on each loan owed to the United States government, having paid a total of only $755 on those loans. In 1999, Gerhardt filed for Chapter 7 bankruptcy and subsequently sought discharge of his student loans.

At the time he filed for bankruptcy, Gerhardt was earning $1,680.47 per month as the principal cellist for the Louisiana Philharmonic Orchestra (LPO), including a small amount of supplemental income earned as a cello teacher for Tulane

University. His monthly expenses, which included a health club membership and Internet access, averaged $1,829.39. During the LPO off-season, Gerhardt collected unemployment.

The bankruptcy court discharged the student loans as causing undue hardship. On appeal, the district court reversed, holding that it would not be an undue hardship for Gerhardt to repay his loans. Gerhardt appealed that decision to the U.S. Circuit Court of Appeals.

Jones, Circuit Judge

This circuit has not explicitly articulated the appropriate test with which to evaluate the undue hardship determination. The Second Circuit in *Brunner v. New York State Higher Educational Service Corp.* (2nd Cir. 1987) crafted the most widely adopted test. To justify discharging the debtor's student loans, the *Brunner* test requires a three-part showing:

(1) that the debtor cannot maintain, based on current income and expenses, a "minimal" standard of living for himself and his dependents if forced to repay the loans; (2) that additional circumstances exist indicating this state of affairs is likely to persist for a significant portion of the repayment period of the student loans; and (3) that the debtor has made good faith efforts to pay the loans.

Because the Second Circuit presented a workable approach to evaluating the "undue hardship" determination, this court expressly adopts the *Brunner* test for purposes of evaluating a section claims of "undue hardship".

Under the first prong of the *Brunner* test, the bankruptcy court determined that Gerhardt could not maintain a minimal standard of living if forced to repay his student loans. Evidence was produced at trial that Gerhardt earned $1,680.47 as the principal cellist for the Louisiana Philharmonic Orchestra (LPO), including a small amount of supplemental income earned as a cello teacher for Tulane University. His monthly expenses, which included a health club membership and Internet access, averaged $1,829.39. The bankruptcy court's factual findings are not clearly erroneous. Consequently, we agree with the bankruptcy court conclusion of law that flows from these factual findings. Given that Gerhardt's monthly expenses exceed his monthly income, he has no ability at the present time to maintain a minimal standard of living if forced to repay his loans.

The second prong of the *Brunner* test asks if "additional circumstances exist that this state of affairs is likely to persist for

a significant period." "Additional circumstances" encompass "circumstances that impacted on the debtor's future earning potential but which were either not present when the debtor applied for the loans or have since been exacerbated." The second aspect of the test is meant to be a demanding requirement. Thus, proving that the debtor is currently in financial straights is not enough. Instead, the debtor must specifically prove "a total incapacity in the future to pay his debts for reasons not within his control."

Under the second prong of the test, the district court concluded that Gerhardt had not established persistent hardship entitling him to discharge his student loans. Gerhardt holds a masters degree in music from the New England Conservatory of Music. He is about 43 years old, healthy, well-educated, and has no dependants, yet has repaid only $755 of his over $77,000 debt. During the LPO's off-season, Gerhardt has collected unemployment, but he has somehow managed to attend the Colorado Music Festival. Although trial testimony tended to show that Gerhardt would likely not obtain a position at a higher-paying orchestra, he could obtain additional steady employment in a number of different arenas. For instance, he could attempt to teach full-time, obtain night-school teaching, or even work as a music store clerk. Thus, no reasons out of Gerhardt's control perpetuate his inability to repay his student loans.

In addition, nothing in the Bankruptcy Code suggests that a debtor may choose to work only in the field in which he was trained, obtain a low-paying job, and then claim that it would be an undue hardship to repay his student loans. Under the facts presented by Gerhardt, it is difficult to imagine a professional orchestra musician who would not qualify for an undue hardship discharge. Accordingly, Gerhardt has failed to demonstrate the type of exceptional circumstances that are necessary to meet his burden under the second prong of *Brunner*.

Judgment denying the discharge on the grounds of undue hardship affirmed.

Reaffirmation Agreements Sometimes, creditors put pressure on debtors to reaffirm, or to agree to pay, debts that have been discharged in bankruptcy. When the 1978 amendments to the Bankruptcy Code were under consideration, some individuals urged Congress to prohibit such agreements. They argued that reaffirmation agreements were inconsistent with the fresh start philosophy of the Bankruptcy Code. Congress did not agree to a total prohibition; instead, it set up a rather elaborate procedure for a creditor to go through to get a debt reaffirmed. Essentially, the agreement must be made *before* the discharge is granted and the debtor must receive certain specified disclosures at or before the time he signs the reaffirmation agreement. These disclosures include the "amount reaffirmed," the annual percentage rate of interest, the total of fees and costs accrued to date, that the agreement may be rescinded at any time prior to discharge or within 60 days after filing with the court, and a clear and conspicuous statement advising the debtor that the reaffirmation agreement is not required by the bankruptcy law or any other law.

The agreement must be filed with the court—and if the debtor is represented by an attorney, the agreement must be accompanied by a certification from the debtor's attorney that (1) it represents a voluntary agreement by the debtor, (2) that it does not impose an undue hardship on the debtor or any dependent of the debtor, and (3) the debtor was fully advised about the legal consequences of signing the agreement. Where the debtor is not represented by an attorney during the negotiation of the reaffirmation agreement, it is not effective unless approved by the court.

Until 60 days after a reaffirmation agreement is filed with the court, there is a presumption that the agreement will work an undue hardship on the debtor if the debtor's income less the monthly expenses as shown on the schedule she filed is less than the scheduled payments on the reaffirmed debt. The debtor has the opportunity to rebut the presumption, but where the debtor does not do so, the court may disapprove the reaffirmation agreement.

Dismissal for Substantial Abuse

In 1984, Congress, concerned that too many individuals with an ability to pay their debts over time pursuant to a Chapter 13 plan were filing petitions to obtain Chapter 7 discharges of liability, authorized the Bankruptcy Courts to dismiss cases that they determined were a **substantial abuse** of the bankruptcy process. The courts used this power to dismiss cases where it determined the debtor had acted in bad faith or had the present or future ability to pay a significant portion of her current debts. In the 2005 amendments Congress reduced the standard for dismissal from "substantial abuse" to just "abuse."

Means Testing In the 2005 act, Congress amended the Bankruptcy Code to provide for the dismissal of Chapter 7 cases—or with the debtor's consent their conversion to Chapter 13 cases—on a finding of abuse by an individual debtor with primarily consumer debts. The abuse can be established in two ways: (1) through an unrebutted finding of abuse based on a new "means test" that is included in the Code; or (2) on general grounds of abuse, including bad faith, determined under the totality of the circumstances.

The **means test** is designed to determine the debtor's ability to repay general unsecured claims. It has three elements: (1) a definition of "current monthly income"—which is the total income a debtor is presumed to have available; (2) a list of allowed deductions from the current monthly income for the purpose of supporting the debtor and his family and for repayment of higher priority debts; and (3) defined "trigger points" at which the income remaining after the allowed deductions would trigger the presumption of abuse. For example, if the debtor's current monthly income after the defined deductions is more than $166.66, the presumption of abuse arises irrespective of the amount of debt; and, if the debtor has at least $100 per month of current monthly income after the allowed deductions (which would amount to $6,000 over five years), then abuse is presumed if that income would be sufficient to pay at least 25 percent of the debtor's unsecured debts over 5 years. To rebut the presumption of abuse, the debtor must show "special circumstances" that would decrease the income or increase expected expenses so as to bring the debtor's income below the trigger points.

Debtors have to file a statement of their calculations under the means test as part of their schedule of current income and expenditures. If the presumption of abuse arises, then the court has to notify the creditors of this situation. While any party in interest generally has the right to bring a motion seeking dismissal of a Chapter 7 case for abuse, only the U.S. Trustee or bankruptcy administrator can bring the motion if the debtor's income is below the median income in the state. Moreover, the means test presumption is inapplicable to debtors whose income is below that state median and also to certain disabled veterans.

In the case that follows, *In re Siegenberg,* the court dismissed a Chapter 7 case on the grounds it was filed in bad faith.

| In re Siegenberg | 2007 LEXIS 2538 (U.S.B.C., C.D. Cal. 2007) |

Commencing in 2000, when she was hired by Mariah Carey, a prominent entertainer, Nicole Siegenberg worked as a costumer in the entertainment business. Her duties were to buy clothes for and costume her employer. In 2004, she lost her job with Carey and began looking for other similar employment in the entertainment industry. In order to do that she had to build *a portfolio which required purchases of clothing stock totaling $9,273 in 2004. Siegenberg's statement of financial affairs indicates that she earned $10,000 in 2004.*

Since 2004, Siegenberg was employed only sporadically on temporary jobs such as television pilots. When employed, she earned about $2,000 per week. Unfortunately, since 2004 she was usually unemployed. Thus, in 2005 she earned $12,648, and in 2006 she earned $35,253.

Siegenberg lived with her parents in her parents' condominium in Pacific Palisades. During the 2004 to 2006 period she incurred debts to, among other things, assist her parents with a property they had bought as an investment to provide income when her father was unable to continue his job; to assist a boyfriend who was a realtor with expenses on properties he was seeking to market; travel with her boyfriend and her mother to South Africa to visit her sick grandmother; assist her mother with medical expenses; and provide living expenses for herself. Some of the expenses were reimbursed to her, while others were not.

Siegenberg filed a Chapter 7 bankruptcy on November 29, 2006. Siegenberg owed $82,597.12 in unsecured debt and $27,664 in secured debt on her car and her boyfriend's car (a 2001 BMW and a 1999 Cadillac Escalade, respectively). The United States Trustee (UST) filed a motion to dismiss Siegenberg's Chapter 7 petition as filed in bad faith and sought a one-year bar against refiling.

Donovan, U.S. Bankruptcy Judge

In considering whether a Chapter 7 case should be dismissed because granting relief would be an abuse of the provisions of Chapter 7, courts may consider (a) whether the debtor filed the petition in bad faith; or (b) whether the totality of the circumstances of the debtor's financial situation demonstrates abuse.

A. Dismissal for Bad Faith under 707(b)(3)(A)

Section 707(b)(3) was added to the Bankruptcy Code by the Bankruptcy Abuse Prevention and Consumer Protection Act of 2005 (BAPCPA). Since BAPCPA, the Ninth Circuit has not established a standard for determining a finding of "bad faith" in Chapter 7 cases under *§ 707(b)(3)(A)*. However, a few bankruptcy courts have addressed the issue. The court in *In re Mitchell*, a Chapter 7 case, used a nine-part test borrowing both from the Ninth Circuit's pre-BAPCPA "substantial abuse" test and from Chapter 11 and 13 bad faith cases. The court in *Mitchell* considered the following nine factors in determining whether "the debtor's intention in filing bankruptcy is inconsistent with the Chapter 7 goals of providing a 'fresh start' to debtors and maximizing return to creditors" and whether the case should thus be dismissed under *§ 707(b)(3)(A)*:

1. Whether the Chapter 7 debtor has a likelihood of sufficient future income to fund a Chapter 11, 12, or 13 plan which would pay a substantial portion of the unsecured claims;

2. Whether debtor's petition was filed as a consequence of illness, disability, unemployment, or other calamity;

3. Whether debtor obtained cash advances and consumer goods on credit exceeding his or her ability to repay;

4. Whether debtor's proposed family budget is excessive or extravagant;

5. Whether debtor's statement of income and expenses misrepresents debtor's financial condition;

6. Whether debtor made eve of bankruptcy purchases;

7. Whether debtor has a history of bankruptcy petition filings and dismissals;

8. Whether debtor has invoked the automatic stay for improper purposes, such as to delay or defeat state court litigation;

9. Whether egregious behavior is present.

1. Likelihood that the Chapter 7 debtor will have sufficient future income to fund a Chapter 11 or 13 plan. Siegenberg does not currently have income to fund a Chapter 11 or 13 plan. According to the pleadings, such future income is not foreseeable. This fact supports Siegenberg's position.

2. Consequence of illness, disability, unemployment or other calamity. Siegenberg claims, in part, that the bankruptcy petition was filed as a consequence of the disability of her father. His disability and surgery in April 2006 caused financial panic in her family, in response to which her parents bought a house in the hope of remodeling it and selling it quickly at a profit. Siegenberg contributed $35,000 to remodel that investment property under an agreement that promised her 50% of the profit. However, her parents sold the home at a loss and Siegenberg received no money in return for her investment.

Siegenberg did not experience an illness, disability, new unemployment, or other calamity. On the contrary, she provides evidence of only modest improvement in her employment status for the year 2006, not enough to match her greater expenditures. There was no change in her health status after 2004.

Further Siegenberg incurred thousands of dollars of new credit card debt on plane tickets, a car for her boyfriend, hotel stays, and other consumer items that are not convincingly attributable to any reasonably, potentially revenue-producing activities during May 2006, the month after her father's surgery and the month during which her parents purchased a house as an investment property, the alleged period of financial distress.

3. Obtaining cash advances and consumer goods on credit exceeding Siegenberg's ability to repay. Much of the argument between the two parties revolves around the question of consumer spending. The UST argues that Siegenberg purchased luxury consumer items on credit beyond her ability to repay at the expense of her creditors. Siegenberg urges in response that various expenditures were either for business purposes or were repaid.

Siegenberg asserts that she spent approximately $35,000 on her parent's residential investment; she repaid pre-bankruptcy almost two-thirds of the cost of the plane tickets to South Africa ($5,500); her parents wrote a check that she forwarded to her credit card company to repay $12,500 for the credit card charges for her mother's surgery; her expenditures on clothing were (a) a legitimate business expense and (b) some of the clothing was returned for credit; and she traveled to Mexico for the purpose of attaining a job.

On the other hand, Siegenberg provides no detail to explain $42,775 in cash advances she received on her credit card accounts between May 2005 and October 2006. She does not provide evidence of contractor payments she claims to have made that exceeded $19,607. She does not provide corroborating detailed evidence that during the period covered by the UST's motion she used the clothing she bought for demonstrable business purposes. Regarding her Mexican expenditures, it appears that she incurred credit card debt of more than $6,000 before July 2006, but only about $2,000 between July and October 2006, the period during which she claims she was interviewing for employment in Mexico. The pre-July Mexican expenditures appear to be for consumer items such as plane tickets, hotels, and restaurants for the personal pleasure of Siegenberg and her boyfriend, and Siegenberg offers no convincing evidence to persuade me otherwise.

Similarly, Siegenberg does not persuasively explain the reasonable business purpose of about $5,500 in car-related credit card debt creating expenditures (including $2,500 on her boyfriend's Cadillac down payment), as well as $2,129 on restaurants, and about $900 on hotels in Southern California, among other consumer items.

The sum of Siegenberg's justified business or personal expenditures, including contractor expenses, reimbursed tickets to South Africa, her mother's surgery, returned clothing, and spending to pursue employment in Mexico is about $59,000. On the other hand, the sum of her unexplained and unjustified cash advances, and other credit card debt for Mexican travel spending prior to her Mexican job interviews, on cars, Southern California hotels, and unexplained clothing expenditures is about $58,000. Further, if only the $19,607 in contractor charges are included in her explained expenditures, instead of her uncorroborated claim that she incurred $35,000 for such contractor charges, then her adequately explained expenditures are about $44,000 while her unexplained expenditures would appear to be about $73,000.

Whatever Siegenberg's business-oriented goals, her very substantial credit card charges for consumer goods and cash advances were incurred without any reasonable or foreseeable ability to repay them. I conclude, on balance, that such charges, under the circumstances, are evidence of Siegenberg's bad faith.

4. Excessive or extravagant proposed family budget. Siegenberg's budget appears to be excessive. In Schedules I and J, she claims average monthly income of $2,466.58 and average monthly expenditures of $5,368.60, including $1,824 to support her parents and $560.43 for car payments, as well as $652 in regular business operating expenses. In light of the thousands of dollars Siegenberg charged on her credit cards monthly during 2006, as well as minimal credit card payments she was required to make, the gap between her monthly income and budget appears excessive and is suggestive of a lack of good faith on her part.

5. Statement of income and expenses misrepresenting financial condition. The UST has not alleged any misrepresentation in Siegenberg's statement of financial condition.

6. Eve of bankruptcy purchases. Siegenberg claims that in fact she made an eve of bankruptcy payment rather than purchases, $12,500 toward her mother's surgery, militating in favor of a finding of good faith.

On the other hand, according to her Schedule F, Siegenberg opened at least three of her 11 credit cards in 2006, one in January and two in July. She owes $7,670 on the one opened in January, $10,925 on one opened in July, and $6,522 on the other opened in July. Thus, in under four months of use, Siegenberg became indebted for $17,447 on two cards that she opened within five months of filing. Also, she charged at least $6,759 in September and October 2006, within about two months of her bankruptcy petition. These are instances of eve of bankruptcy purchases that suggest a lack of good faith under the circumstances, regardless of alleged business purpose, given the wide gaps between her earnings and her new credit card debt.

7. Bankruptcy history. Siegenberg does not have a history of bankruptcy petition filing and dismissals.

8. Improper purpose for automatic stay: state litigation. There is no evidence that Siegenberg has invoked the automatic stay for an improper purpose, such as to defeat state court litigation.

9. Egregious behavior. Siegenberg argues that rather than exhibiting egregious behavior, the facts illustrate bad financial luck. She points to the fact that she has had a hard time finding a job in the entertainment industry, though she has spent a lot of money trying; her family's real estate investment flopped; and the interviews for a job selling Mexican time shares turned out to be a waste of time. In the end, she claims that despite her honest efforts to improve her income, she has been unlucky and, thus, is unable to pay off her debts.

Even assuming all of what Siegenberg says is true, those factors do not justify the spending detailed above. In light of her low rate of income over a three-year period preceding bankruptcy, her sizeable consumer-oriented expenditures and unexplained cash advance debt appear to be egregious under the circumstances, rather than legitimate startup business expenses.

Thus, analysis pursuant to five of nine *Mitchell* factors, factors 2, 3, 4, 6, and 9 supports a finding of a lack of good faith.

B. Dismissal under *707(b)(3)(B):* Totality of the Circumstances

Additionally, dismissal would appear to be appropriate under *§ 707(b)(3)(B)*, considering the "totality of the circumstances" presented by the evidence. Bankruptcy courts that have addressed *§ 707(b)(3)* since the enactment of BAPCPA have found that the "totality of the circumstances" tests that were applicable under the former *§ 707(b)* remain applicable under BAPCPA. BAPCPA made changes, however, making it easier for the UST to prove a case for abuse because (a) there is no longer a presumption in favor of granting relief to a debtor, and (b) the standard for dismissal is reduced from "substantial abuse" to mere "abuse." The *In re Price* "totality of the circumstances" test includes the following six factors:

1. Whether there is a likelihood of future income to fund debtor's Chapter 11, 12, or 13 plan;

2. Whether the petition was filed as a consequence of illness, disability, unemployment, or other calamity;

3. Whether the schedules suggest debtor obtained cash advances and consumer goods without the ability to repay;

4. Whether debtor's proposed family budget is excessive or extravagant;

5. Whether debtor's papers misrepresent his or her financial condition; and

6. Whether debtor engaged in eve of bankruptcy purchases.

Here, *Price* factors 2, 3, 4, and 6 are unfavorable to Siegenberg, indicating a lack of good faith and supporting a conclusion of abuse under *§ 707(b)(3)(B)*.

1. Future income to fund a Chapter 11 or 13 plan. The UST has failed to establish that Siegenberg has a foreseeable likelihood of future income to fund a Chapter 11 or 13.

2. Consequence of illness, disability, unemployment, or calamity. This factor is unfavorable to Siegenberg because she does not present evidence that she herself experienced a grave illness, change in employment status, disability, or any other calamity that might explain the excess of her debt over her income.

3. Cash advances and consumer goods without ability to repay. As discussed above, Siegenberg incurred substantial credit card debt that might be considered business related or which may have been incurred in the attempt to improve her financial situation. However, a large portion of her credit card debt was incurred to acquire consumer goods and services and cash advances whose business purposes remain unexplained. Thus, on balance, this factor weighs against her.

4. Excessive or extravagant family budget. As discussed above, Siegenberg's monthly income is less than half of her monthly spending, which includes $560.43 on cars payments and $1,824 in support of her parents. Considering her high rate of debt accumulation, her budget is excessive and suggestive of a lack of good faith.

5. Misrepresentation of financial condition. The UST has not alleged any misrepresentation in Siegenberg's papers as to her financial condition.

6. Eve of bankruptcy purchases. As discussed above, Siegenberg opened two credit cards in July of 2006. During the four months in which those cards were in use she charged $17,447 on those two cards alone. Further, Siegenberg purchased at least $6,759 on various cards in September and October 2006. These facts are suggestive of a lack of good faith in her bankruptcy filing.

C. Dismissal with a One-Year Bar against Refiling

A bankruptcy court may, for cause, dismiss a bankruptcy case with a bar against later discharge of debt. A finding of bad faith based on egregious behavior can justify dismissal with prejudice. The bankruptcy court should consider the following factors when considering barring later discharge for bad faith:

1. Whether debtor misrepresented facts in her petition, unfairly manipulated the bankruptcy code, or otherwise filed in an inequitable manner;

2. Debtor's filing history;

3. Whether debtor only intended to defeat state court litigation;

4. Whether egregious behavior is present.

Here, while egregious behavior is present, the other three factors are not. There are no allegations of misrepresentation; Siegenberg has no bankruptcy history; and there has been no mention of state court litigation. Under the egregious circumstances outlined, it would appear to be appropriate to bar Siegenberg from refiling a bankruptcy petition for at least one year, as the UST has requested.

Conclusion

Siegenberg has used her credit cards in various efforts to extricate herself and her family from financial difficulties. She also used her credit cards for tens of thousands of dollars in personal expenditures, the purchase of consumer goods and services, and to obtain unexplained cash advances. The record contains significant evidence of these ostensibly excessive expenditures and contains only patchy, incomplete, and unconvincing evidence that most of these expenditures were made to further Siegenberg's business efforts. **I believe it is appropriate to grant the UST's motion to dismiss Siegenberg's Chapter 7 petition, and to impose a one-year bar on future bankruptcy filings by or against Siegenberg.**

Chapter 11: Reorganizations

Reorganization Proceeding
Sometimes, creditors benefit more from the continuation of a bankrupt debtor's business than from the liquidation of the debtor's property. Chapter 11 of the Bankruptcy Code provides a proceeding whereby, under the supervision of the Bankruptcy Court, the debtor's financial affairs can be reorganized rather than liquidated. Chapter 11 proceedings are available to individuals and to virtually all business enterprises, including individual proprietorships, partnerships, and corporations (except banks, savings and loan associations, insurance companies, commodities brokers, and stockbrokers). Chapter 11 cases for individuals look much like the Chapter 13 cases which are discussed later in this chapter but the amount of debt is usually much larger and it commonly is predominantly nonconsumer debt. The 2005 act created a special subclass of "small business debtors" debtors with less than $2 million in debts and provides special rules for them, including expedited decision making.

Petitions for reorganization proceedings can be filed voluntarily by the debtor or involuntarily by its creditors. Once a petition for a reorganization proceeding is filed and relief is ordered, the court usually appoints (1) a committee of creditors holding unsecured claims, and (2) a committee of equity security holders (shareholders). Normally, the debtor becomes the "Debtor in Possession" and the responsibility for running the debtor's business. It is also usually responsible for developing a plan for handling the various claims of creditors and the various interests of persons such as shareholders.

The reorganization plan is essentially a contract between a debtor and its creditors. This contract may involve recapitalizing a debtor corporation and/or giving creditors some equity, or shares, in the corporation in exchange for part or all of the debt owed to them. The plan must (1) divide the creditors into classes; (2) set forth how each creditor will be satisfied; (3) state which claims, or classes of claims, are impaired or adversely affected by the plan; and (4) provide the same treatment to each creditor in a particular class, unless the creditors in that class consent to different treatment.

For example, when Kmart's Chapter 11 reorganization plan was accepted by its creditors and approved by the bankruptcy court in 2003, the plan called for its banks who held secured claims to receive about 40 cents on each dollar they were owed and for the holders of unsecured claims to receive new stock valued at 14.4 percent of their claim.

The Bankruptcy Code provides for an initial 120-day period after the petition is filed during which only the debtor can file a reorganization plan, and a 180-day period within which only the debtor may solicit acceptances of the plan from creditors. The bankruptcy court, in its discretion, may extend these periods. The 2005 act limits the debtor's exclusive plan proposal period to 18 months and the exclusive solicitation period to 20 months. After the initial time periods pass, creditors are free to propose plans and seek acceptance of them by other creditors. In some cases, debtors develop what is known as a **prepackaged plan** whereby the debtor solicits acceptances of the plan prior to filing for bankruptcy. The 2005 act contains a number of provisions designed to facilitate the use of such plans.

A reorganization plan must be confirmed by the court before it becomes effective. Plans can be confirmed either through the voluntary agreement of creditors or alternatively through what is known as a "cram down" whereby the court forces dissenting creditors whose claims would be impaired by a proposed plan to accept the plan when the court can find that it is fair and equitable to the class of creditors whose claims are impaired. If the plan is confirmed, the debtor is responsible for carrying it out.

However, until a plan is confirmed, the bankruptcy court has no authority to distribute any portion of the bankruptcy assets to unsecured creditors.

Confirmation through Acceptance by Creditors
A court must confirm a plan if the following requirements, among others, are met:

1. Each class of creditors or interests has either accepted the plan or such class is not impaired under the plan.
2. Each impaired class of claimants has either unanimously accepted the plan or will receive or retain

under the plan property of a value not less than the holders of the claims would receive or retain if the debtor was liquidated under Chapter 7.

3. All secured creditors have either accepted the plan or their class of creditors is not impaired under the plan.

4. If any class of claims is impaired, then at least one class of impaired claims must have voted to accept the plan. A plan is deemed accepted by a class of creditors if more than one-half the number of creditors who vote to accept the plan represent at least two-thirds of the dollar amount of allowed claims in the class.

5. The plan must be feasible. The court must be able to conclude that confirmation of the plan is not likely to be followed by the liquidation or the need for further financial reorganization of the debtor or any successor to the debtor unless the reorganization is proposed in the plan.

In addition, where the debtor is an individual, the amount of property to be distributed under the plan must not be less than the projected disposable income of the individual to be received during the period for which payments are to be made or five years, whichever is longer. Also, the debtor must have paid all domestic support obligations that became payable after the filing of the petition.

In the case below, *In re Made In Detroit,* the court was unable to conclude that a proposed plan was feasible and declined to confirm it.

Confirmation of a Plan by a Cram Down Where a class of creditors whose claims or interests are impaired does not accept the proposed plan, then the plan has not been accepted but the court may still confirm the plan under a "cram down" if it concludes that the plan is fair and equitable to the impaired class. A plan is considered to be fair and equitable to an impaired class of *secured creditors* if the reorganization plan (1) allows the class to retain its liens securing the claims (even where the property is transferred to a third person) and each holder of a claim in the class receives deferred cash payments totaling at least the allowed amount of claim, of value of at least the value of the holder's interest in the bankruptcy estate's interest in the property; *or* (2) provides for the sale of any property subject to liens securing such claims free and clear of such liens with the liens to attach to the proceeds of the sale; *or* (3) provides for the realization by the holders of the "indubitable equivalent" of such claims.

A plan is considered to be fair and equitable to *a class of impaired claimants with unsecured claims* if the plan (1) provides that each holder of a claim will receive or retain on account of the claim property of a value equal to the allowed amount of such claim *or* (2) the holder of any claim that is junior to the claims of such class will not receive or retain any property on account of the junior claim or interest.

A plan is considered to be fair and equitable to a *class of interests* (such as equity holders) if (1) the plan provides that each holder of an interest in the class receives or retains property of a value equal to the greatest of the amount of any fixed liquidation preference to which the holder is entitled, any fixed redemption price to which the holder is entitled, or the value of such interest; or (2) the holder of any interest that is junior to the interests of such class will not receive any property on account of such junior claim.

In re Made In Detroit, Inc.   299 B.R. 170 U.S.B.C. (E.D. Mich. 2003)

In 1997, Made In Detroit, Inc., purchased approximately 410 acres of property for the purpose of development. The property is located on the Detroit River in Gibraltar and Trenton, Michigan, and is Made In Detroit's only significant asset. For the next five years, Made In Detroit attempted to develop the property. Due to problems obtaining permits, and because Made In Detroit was not generating income, it became delinquent to secured creditors. In 2002, the primary secured creditor, Standard Federal, commenced a foreclosure action against Made In Detroit. As a result, on October 23, 2002, Made In Detroit filed for bankruptcy protection under Chapter 11 of the Bankruptcy Code.

On July 15, 2003, Made In Detroit filed its Third Amended Combined Plan and Disclosure Statement (the "Debtor's Plan"). The Debtor's Plan provided that it would be funded with a $9 million loan from Kennedy Funding and that the Kennedy loan is contingent on certain conditions precedent, including the payment of a nonfundable $270,000 commitment fee and an appraisal of the property that indicated it would have a "quick sale" value of at least $15 million. The Kennedy commitment also provided a condition of its part; namely, that it intended to bring participants into the transaction and if it was unable to do so, it would only be obligated to refund the commitment fee less compensation for its time and expenses. The Debtor's Plan provided that once the $9 million loan was obtained, the secured creditors and administrative claimants would be paid in full, the unsecured creditors would receive an initial distribution of $750,000 (with the balance of the claims to be paid from the sale of lots), and equity shareholders would retain their interest.

The Official Committee of Unsecured Creditors (the "Committee") and the Wayne County Treasurer filed objections to confirmation of the Debtor's Plan. In addition, on July 9, 2003, the Committee filed its own plan of reorganization. The Committee's Plan provided that it would be financed by an "as is" immediate cash sale of the property to the Trust for Public Land for $4 million. Under the Plan, the Trust for Public Land would pay $4.8 million to the Debtor's Estate to settle all claims with respect to the real property and would receive title to the property free of all liens, claims, and other encumbrances. Under the terms of the Committee's Plan, the secured creditors would be paid in full, the unsecured creditors would receive a pro rata payment (after payment of the administrative claims and higher classes of claims), and the equity shareholders would not receive any distribution nor would they retain any property interest.

Made In Detroit objected to the Committees Plan, and the Bankruptcy Court held a hearing on confirmation of both the Debtor's and the Committee's Plans.

McIvor, Bankruptcy Judge

Debtor's Plan fails to meet the requirement that a plan must be feasible. Feasibility is a mandatory requirement for confirmation. Section 1129(a)(11) of the Bankruptcy Code provides that a plan can be confirmed only if "confirmation of the plan is not likely to be followed by the liquidation, or the need for further organization, of the debtor or any successor to the debtor under the plan, unless such liquidation or reorganization is proposed in the plan."

Section 1129(a)(11) prevents confirmation of visionary schemes which promise creditors more than the debtor can possibly attain after confirmation. A plan that is submitted on a conditional basis is not considered feasible, and thus confirmation of such a plan must be denied.

The plan does not need to guarantee success, but it must present reasonable assurance of success. To provide such reasonable assurance, a plan must provide a realistic and workable framework for reorganization. The plan cannot be based on "visionary promises"; it must be doable.

> Sincerity, honesty and willingness are not sufficient to make the plan feasible, and neither are visionary promises. The test is whether the things which are to be done after confirmation can be done as a practical matter under the facts.

In re Hoffman (Bankr. D.N.D. 1985).

In *Hoffman*, the debtor's plan proposed to pay creditors within two years from the sale of real property. However, there was no potential purchaser and the plan did not set forth the terms of the proposed sale. The court found that the plan was not feasible because the proposed sale of the real estate was not "sufficiently concrete to assure either consummation within the two-years, or that even if sold within the two-year period the price obtained would be sufficient" to pay the secured creditor.

Similarly, in *In re Walker* (E.D. Va. 1994), the court also found a plan based on funding through a speculative sale of real estate was not feasible. There, the district court reversed the bankruptcy court's confirmation of a plan because the plan was not feasible. The plan proposed to pay creditors from the sale of two parcels of real estate. However, the plan did not provide any time frame within which the properties would be sold, did not set forth the terms of the proposed sale, and did not set forth a plan for the liquidation of other properties if the proceeds from the sale of the two identified properties was insufficient to pay creditors. Based on these deficiencies, the court held that the proposed plan was not feasible.

Likewise, in *In re Thurmon* (Bankr. M.D. Fla. 1988), the court found that a plan conditioned on a sale of property which in turn was conditioned on financing was not feasible. In *Thurmon,* the plan proposed that funding would be obtained through a lease-purchase agreement. The lease-purchase agreement provided that a buyer would lease property from the debtor and would then purchase 147 acres from the debtor. The closing of the land sale was conditioned on the buyer's ability to obtain financing on favorable terms. The buyer had not yet applied for the financing but testified that he would do so within 30 days. The court found that the plan was not feasible because it was not reasonably likely that the money to fund the plan would come from the buyer.

While Debtor in this case is sincere, honest, and willing, the Debtor's Plan of Reorganization is not realistic, as it does not provide a reasonable assurance of success. The Plan is based on "wishful thinking" and "visionary promises." As a practical matter, the Debtor's Plan is not sufficiently concrete as to be feasible because it is contingent on exit financing from Kennedy and there is no reasonable assurance that the Kennedy loan will ever close or that the property will be appraised at a value high enough to provide a $9 million loan. Like in *Hoffman, Walker,* and *Thurmon,* it is not reasonably likely that Debtor's Plan will be funded. The conditions precedent to Kennedy's funding of the loan were not satisfied as of the date of the confirmation hearing. Further, the evidence did not show that the satisfaction of such conditions was reasonably likely in the foreseeable future.

The $270,000 loan commitment fee was never put into an escrow account or paid to Kennedy Funding. Even if Debtor had paid the commitment fee, there still were substantial obstacles to closing on the proposed Kennedy loan. First and foremost, in order for Kennedy to fund the required $9 million loan, it would need to value the property on an "as is" quick sale basis at $15 million. The evidence did not provide any reasonable assurance that the property would be valued at this amount; in fact, the evidence showed that the property, if sold "as is," was only worth approximately $4.2 million.

The best evidence of the value of the property, what a reasonable buyer would pay a reasonable seller for the property, is the Trust for Public Land's offer to purchase the property "as is" for $4.8 million. Additional evidence that the "as is" value of the property is well below the $15 million value needed to obtain the Kennedy financing was provided by a current appraisal prepared by Integra Realty Resources.

The Integra appraisal report, dated on September 5, 2003, indicates that the "as is" market value of the property, if marketed from nine to twelve months, was $5,260,000. The report also stated the "disposition value" of the property, if only marketed for three to six months, was $4,210,000. The "as is" quick sale value as defined in the Kennedy commitment letter was based on a marketing period of "90 to 120 days," i.e., three to six months. Thus, for Kennedy to fund the $9 million loan proposed in Debtor's Plan, the "disposition value" of the property would have to be at least, $15 million. The appraiser who prepared the Integra report, Kenneth Blondell, testified at the confirmation hearing. Blondell is a certified MAI appraiser, and he was qualified as an expert. The Integra report and Blondell's testimony provided a credible expert opinion that the disposition value of the property is only $4.2 million.

In summary, the Debtor failed to show at confirmation that it had exit financing to fund its plan. The proposed financing had so many contingencies that Debtor's Plan was conditional at best. Thus, the Debtor's Plan is not feasible under 1129(a)(11), and the Court must deny confirmation of Debtor's Plan.

The Court denied confirmation of Debtor's Plan.

Use of Chapter 11

During the 1980s, attempts by a number of corporations to seek refuge in Chapter 11 as a means of escaping problems they were facing received considerable public attention. Some of the most visible cases involved efforts to obtain some protection against massive product liability claims and judgments for damages for breach of contract and to escape from collective bargaining agreements. Thus, for example, Johns-Manville Corporation filed under Chapter 11 because of the claims against it arising out of its production and sale of asbestos years earlier, while A. H. Robins Company was concerned about a surfeit of claims arising out of its sale of the Dalkon Shield, an intrauterine birth control device. And, in 1987, Texaco, Inc., faced with a $10.3 billion judgment in favor of Pennzoil in a breach of contract action, filed a petition for reorganizational relief under Chapter 11. Companies such as LTV and Allegheny Industries sought changes in retirement and pension plans, and other companies such as Eastern Airlines sought refuge in Chapter 11 while embroiled in labor disputes.

In the 1990s, a number of companies that were the subject of highly leveraged buyouts (LBOs) financed with so-called junk bonds, including a number of retailers, resorted to Chapter 11 to seek restructuring and relief from their creditors. Similarly, companies such as Pan Am and TWA that were hurt by economic slowdown and increase in fuel prices filed Chapter 11 petitions. In 2001, Enron and Kmart filed for reorganization under Chapter 11 as did WorldCom and USAirways in 2002.

In recent years, Chapter 11 has been the subject of significant criticism and calls for its revision. Critics point out that many of the Chapter 11 cases are permitted to drag on for years, thus depleting the assets of the debtor through payments to trustees and lawyers involved in administration and diminishing the assets available to creditors. For example, *The Wall Street Journal* noted in a July 11, 2003, article, "The Chapter 11 restructuring of Enron, whose controversial collapse became a symbol of corporate malfeasance, has dragged on for 19 months, generating more than 11,000 court filings and nearly $500 million in professional fees." This took the case to the point where the company was about to file its proposed reorganization plan and seek acceptance from creditors and approval by the bankruptcy court.

In the 2005 act, Congress responded to some of these concerns by establishing tighter time frames and placing some limits or restrictions on the availability of extensions of time. Examples include the limitations on the time period in which the debtor has the exclusive right to develop a reorganization plan and special rules forcing debtors to make decisions as to whether to assume or reject unexpired leases of nonresidential property such as space in shopping centers and office buildings.

Special Rules for Nonresidential Real Property Lessors Under the pre-2005 act, courts were allowed to grant, and often granted, repeated extensions of the 60-day period that debtors in Chapter 11 proceedings have to either assume or reject unexpired leases of nonresidential real property. Under the 2005 revisions, debtors must assume or reject unexpired leases of nonresidential real property by the earlier of 120 days from the date the petition is filed or the date a plan is confirmed. Failure to do so in a timely way results in the lease being deemed rejected. Courts are permitted to extend the time for an additional 90 days on a showing of good cause, but any further extensions can be granted only if the lessor consents in writing. These provisions help protect landlords who have leased property to individuals or entities that subsequently filed for bankruptcy protection. They require the bankrupt to decide relatively quickly whether they will go forward with the lease and fullfill their obligation or whether they will surrender the property to the landlord so he can secure a new paying tenant.

Collective Bargaining Agreements

Collective bargaining contracts pose special problems. Prior to the 1984 amendments, there was concern that some companies would use Chapter 11 reorganizations as a vehicle to avoid executed collective bargaining agreements. The concern was heightened by the Supreme Court's 1984 decision in *NLRB v. Bildisco and Bildisco*. In that case, the Supreme Court held that a reorganizing debtor did not have to engage in collective bargaining before modifying or rejecting portions of a collective bargaining agreement and that such unilateral alterations by a debtor did not violate the National Labor Relations Act.

Congress then acted to try to prevent the misuse of bankruptcy proceedings for collective bargaining purposes. The act's 1984 amendments adopt a rigorous multistep process that must be complied with in determining whether a labor contract can be rejected or modified as part of a reorganization. Among other things that must be done before a debtor or trustee can seek to avoid a collective bargaining agreement are the submission of a proposal to the employees' representative that details the "necessary" modifications to the collective bargaining agreement and ensures that "all creditors, the debtor and all affected parties are fairly treated." Then, before the bankruptcy court can authorize a rejection of the original collective bargaining agreement, it must review the proposal and find that (1) the employees' representative refused to accept it without good cause, and (2) the balance of equities clearly favors the rejection of the original collective bargaining agreement.

Chapter 12: Family Farmers and Fishermen

Relief for Family Farmers and Fishermen

Historically, farmers have been accorded special treatment in the Bankruptcy Code. In the 1978 act, as in earlier versions, small farmers were exempted from involuntary proceedings. Thus, a small farmer who filed a voluntary Chapter 11 or 13 petition could not have the proceeding converted into a Chapter 7 liquidation over his objection so long as he complied with the act's requirements in a timely fashion. Additional protection was also accorded through the provision allowing states to opt out of the federal exemption scheme and to provide their own exemptions. A number of states used this flexibility to provide generous exemptions for farmers so they would be able to keep their tools and implements.

Despite these provisions, the serious stress on the agricultural sector in the mid-1980s led Congress in 1986 to further amend the Bankruptcy Code by adding a new Chapter 12 targeted to the financial problems of the family farm. During the 1970s and 1980s, farmland prices appreciated and many farmers borrowed heavily to expand their productive capacity, creating a large debt load in the agricultural sector. When land values subsequently dropped and excess production in the world kept farm product prices low, many farmers faced extreme financial difficulty. In the 2005 act, Chapter 12 proceedings were made available to family fishermen.

Chapter 12 is modeled after Chapter 13, which is discussed next. It is available only for family farmers and fishermen with regular income. To qualify, a farmer and spouse must have not less than 80 percent of their total noncontingent, liquidated debts arising out of their farming operations. The aggregate debt must be less than $3,544,525 and at least 50 percent of an individual's or couple's income during the year preceding the filing of the petition must have come from the farming operation and at least 80 percent of the assets must be related to the farming operation. A corporation or partnership can also qualify, provided that more than 50 percent of the stock or equity is held by one family or its relatives and they conduct the farming operation. Again, 80 percent of the

debt must arise from the farming operation; the aggregate debt ceiling is $3,544,525.

In the case of a family fisherman, the debtor and spouse engaged in a commercial fishing operation are eligible for relief under Chapter 12 if their aggregate debts do not exceed $1,642,500 and not less than 80 percent of their aggregate noncontingent liquidated debts (excluding a debt for their principal residence) arise out of the commercial fishing operation. Again, a corporation or partnership can qualify so long as at least 50 percent is held by the family and relatives that conduct the fishing operation, its aggregate debts do not exceed $1,642,500, and at least 80 percent of the aggregate noncontingent liquidated debts arise out of a commercial fishing operation.

The debtor is usually permitted to remain in possession to operate the farm or fishing vessel. Although the debtor in possession has many of the rights of a Chapter 11 trustee, a trustee is appointed under Chapter 12 and the debtor is subject to his supervision. The trustee is permitted to sell unnecessary assets, including farmland

The Global Business Environment

Transnational Insolvency Proceedings

As the volume of international trade and the number of multinational corporations have grown, there has been a concomitant increase in transnational insolvency cases. When a company engaged in international business transactions becomes insolvent, commonly some kind of insolvency proceeding will be initiated in each country where the company does business. Different laws and different national interests can produce a challenging—if not difficult—situation for creditors of the insolvent enterprise. Where and how should the creditor go about protecting its interests? Should it seek to have its claim allowed in any one—or more—of the various proceedings? What rights will it be accorded in those proceedings, particularly the foreign forums?

Historically, two different approaches have been used to deal with transnational insolvencies. The first uses the principle of "territoriality" where each country takes control of the enterprise's assets within that country and administers them according to the law of that country, giving little attention to what may be happening in other forums or to foreign interests. A second approach, often referred to as "universalism," seeks a cooperative or coordinated approach to transnational insolvency. This might be achieved through the identification of a single forum or proceeding where all assets of a company would be administered and all claims and interests addressed.

Another variant of this approach is to identify a primary proceeding that has the lead in conjunction with a number of coordinated ancillary proceedings in other countries.

In an effort to encourage cooperation among countries and to try to harmonize the competing and conflicting schemes, the United Nations Commission on International Trade Law has adopted a Model Law on Cross-Border Insolvency. On a regional level, the European Union has adopted a "Convention on Insolvency Proceedings" to coordinate and harmonize such proceedings in EU countries. And the American Law Institute has a Transnational Insolvency Project to develop principles of cooperation in transnational insolvency cases among the members (United States, Canada, and Mexico) of the North American Free Trade Agreement (NAFTA).

The 2005 Bankruptcy Act creates a new chapter of the Bankruptcy Code to deal with cross-border cases. The new sections incorporate the Model Code of Cross-Border Insolvency. The new chapter expands the scope of U.S. bankruptcy law and provides an explicit statutory mechanism for dealing with cross-border insolvency and for the U.S. courts, trustees, and debtors to cooperate with their foreign counterparts. It provides a framework for common cross-border situations such as providing access for foreign creditors to domestic cases and for the coordination of simultaneous domestic and foreign proceedings for the same debtor so that the relief afforded in different jurisdictions is consistent.

and farming or fishing equipment, without the consent of secured creditors and before a plan is approved. However, the secured creditor's interest attaches to the proceeds of the sale.

The debtor is required to file a plan within 90 days of the filing of the Chapter 12 petition–although the bankruptcy court has the discretion to extend the time. A hearing is held on the proposed plan, and it can be confirmed over the objection of creditors. The debtor may release to any secured party the collateral that secures the claim to obtain confirmation without the acceptance by that creditor.

Unsecured creditors are required to receive at least liquidation value under the Chapter 12 plan. If an unsecured creditor or the trustee objects to the plan, the court may still confirm the plan despite the objection so long as it calls for full payment of the unsecured creditor's claim or it provides that the debtor's disposable income for the duration of the plan is applied to making payments on it. A debtor who fulfills his plan, or is excused from full performance because of subsequent hardship, is entitled to a discharge.

Chapter 13: Consumer Debt Adjustments

Relief for Individuals Chapter 13 of the Bankruptcy Code, entitled Adjustments of Debts for Individuals, gives individuals who want to avoid the stigma of a Chapter 7 bankruptcy an opportunity to pay their debts in installments under the protection of a federal court. Under Chapter 13, the debtor has this opportunity free of such problems as garnishments and attachments of her property by creditors. Only individuals with regular incomes (including sole proprietors of businesses) who owe individually (or with their spouse) liquidated, unsecured debts of less than $336,900 and secured debts of less than $1,010,650 are eligible to file under Chapter 13.

Procedure Chapter 13 proceedings are initiated only by the voluntary petition of a debtor filed in the Bankruptcy Court. Creditors of the debtor may not file an involuntary petition for a Chapter 13 proceeding. Commonly, the debtor files at the same time a list of his creditors as well as a list of his assets, liabilities, and executory contracts. The court then appoints a trustee.

Following the filing of the petition, the trustee calls a meeting of creditors, at which time proofs of claims are received and allowed or disallowed. The debtor is examined, and she submits a plan of payment. If the court is satisfied that the plan is proposed in good faith, meets the legal requirements, and is in the interest of the creditors, the court approves the plan.

If the debtor's income is above the state median income for a family of the size of his family, then the plan must provide for payments over a period of five years unless all claims will be fully paid in a shorter period. In the case of a debtor whose income is less than the median income of the applicable state, the plan may not provide for payments over a period that is longer than three years unless the court, for cause, approves a longer period, which is no case can be more than five years.

The plan must provide that all of the debtor's disposable income during the applicable commitment period will be applied to make payments to unsecured creditors under the plan. Unsecured creditors must receive at least what they would receive under Chapter 7. All priority claims must be paid in full.

No plan may be approved if the trustee or an unsecured creditor objects, unless the plan provides for the objecting creditor to be paid the present value of what he is owed or provides for the debtor to commit all of his projected disposable income for the applicable period to pay his creditors.

In the case below, *In re Burt,* the court agreed with an objection raised by a creditor to confirmation of a proposed Chapter 13 plan that would cram down the creditor's secured interest.

Under the 1984 amendments, a Chapter 13 debtor must begin making the installment payments proposed in her plan within 30 days after the plan is filed. The interim payments must continue to be made until the plan is confirmed or denied. If the plan is denied, the money, less any administrative expenses, is returned to the debtor by the trustee. The interim payments give the trustee an opportunity to observe the debtor's performance and thus to be in a better position to make a recommendation about whether the plan should be approved.

Once approved, a plan may be subsequently modified on petition of a debtor or a creditor where there is a material change in the debtor's circumstances.

Suppose Curtis Brown has a monthly take-home pay of $1,000 and a few assets. He owes $1,500 to the credit union, borrowed for the purchase of furniture; he is supposed to repay the credit union $75 per month. He owes $1,800 to the finance company on the purchase of a used car; he is supposed to repay the company $90 a month. He has also run up charges of $1,200 on a MasterCard account, primarily for emergency repairs to his car; he must pay $60 per month to MasterCard. His rent is $350 per month, and food and other living expenses run him another $425 per month. Curtis was laid off from his job for a month and fell behind on his payments to his creditors. He then filed a Chapter 13 petition. In his plan, he might, for example, offer to repay the credit union $50 a month, the finance company $60 a month, and Master-Card $40 a month—with the payments spread over three years rather than the shorter time for which they are currently scheduled.

In re Burt	378 B.R. 352 (U.S.B.C., D. Utah 2007)

On December 31, 2005, Darin Burt purchased a 2006 Ford F-150, a pickup truck for his personal use, from LaPoint Automotive LLC. LaPoint financed the transaction through a Utah Simple Interest Retail Installment Contract. Under the contract, LaPoint retained a purchase money security interest (PMSI) in the truck. LaPoint later assigned its interest in the truck to Ford Motor Credit, which perfected its security interest by notation on the truck's title as required by the Utah Motor Vehicle Act.

The contract indicated that the cash price of the truck was $32,630 and the total amount financed was $45,628.14. The difference between the two amounts included charges of $2,425 for a service contract, $500 for gap insurance, $298 for document preparation fee, $1,149.46 for tax and license fees, and $11,021.68 to pay off the obligation owed on a trade-in vehicle (2004 Ford F-150). The negative equity rolled into the transaction, therefore, was the $11,021.68 payoff less the Burt's down payment of $1,800 and the manufacturer's rebate of $3,000, yielding a net negative equity of $6,221. Because of the Burt's marginal credit, he was required to trade-in his 2004 Ford F-150 in order to qualify for financing on the new vehicle. The dealer would not have financed the purchase had Burt not agreed to all the terms of the contract, including the refinancing of negative equity.

On July 13, 2007, Burt filed a petition under Chapter 13. On August 30, 2007, Ford Motor Credit filed a proof of secured claim for its security interest in the truck in the amount of $42,941.64. Burt filed his Chapter 13 plan on July 25, 2007, which proposed to bifurcate Ford Motor Credit's claim into a secured portion in the amount of $28,000 and an unsecured portion in the amount of the negative equity paid off by the financing transaction. Ford Motor Credit objected to confirmation of the debtor's plan, arguing that its entire claim qualified for treatment as a secured claim and could not be bifurcated.

Thurman, U.S. Bankruptcy Judge

In order to obtain confirmation of a Chapter 13 plan, the debtor must comply with provisions of *11 U.S.C. § 1325(a)*. Prior to the enactment of the Bankruptcy Abuse Prevention and Consumer Protection Act of 2005 (BAPCPA), *sections 506(a)(1)* and *1325(a)(5)(B)* allowed a Chapter 13 debtor to bifurcate an under-secured creditor's claim into secured and unsecured portions, with the result that a creditor's claim was allowed as secured only to the extent of the value of the collateral securing its debt. The portion of the creditor's claim allowed as secured would be paid in full with interest, whereas the unsecured portion of the claim would be paid pro-rata with all other general unsecured claims. This process of bifurcation is often referred to as "cram-down." BAPCPA, however, amended *§ 1325* to give special protection to creditors who finance automobile transactions that occur within 910 days prior to the debtors' filing for Chapter 13 relief.

Under BAPCPA, Congress added the "hanging paragraph" after *§ 1325(a)(9)*, which prevents the bifurcation of certain secured claims. It is commonly referred to as the "hanging paragraph" because it follows the numbered subsections of *§ 1325(a)* but has no numerical designation of its own. Specifically, the hanging paragraph states:

> For purposes of paragraph (5), section 506 shall not apply to a claim described in that paragraph if the creditor has a pur-chase money security interest securing the debt that is the subject of the claim, the debt was incurred within the 910-day [sic] preceding the date of the filing of the petition, and the collateral for that debt consists of a motor vehicle (as defined in section 30102 of title 49) acquired for the personal use of the debtor, or if collateral for that debt consists of any other thing of value, if the debt was incurred during the 1-year period preceding that filing.

Thus, in order to avoid a cram-down, four conditions must be satisfied: (1) the creditor has a purchase money security interest (PMSI); (2) the debt was incurred within 910 days preceding the filing of the petition; (3) the collateral for the debt is a motor vehicle; and (4) the motor vehicle was acquired for the personal use of the debtor. If these requirements are satisfied, "then the creditor's claim is deemed fully secured" and cannot be bifurcated. The parties do not dispute that the collateral in this case was a motor vehicle, purchased within 910 days of the debtor's petition, or that it was acquired for personal use. The only requirement that is in dispute is whether Ford Motor Credit's debt is secured by a purchase money security interest. To determine this issue, the Court must first decide whether the negative equity from the trade-in vehicle that was rolled into the financing for the Truck as well as the other costs associated with the purchase constitute a purchase money security interest as defined under Utah law.

In order to address the effect of the hanging paragraph, the Court must first determine the extent to which Ford Motor Credit's security interest is a purchase money security interest. The term "purchase money security interest," as used in the hanging paragraph, is not defined in the Bankruptcy Code. Therefore, courts uniformly refer to state law, and specifically to the state's version of the Uniform Commercial Code (UCC), to determine whether a creditor holds a purchase money security interest. The applicable statute in Utah is the *Utah Code Annotated §9a-103(2),* which provides that "[a] security interest in goods is a purchase-money security interest . . . to the extent that the goods are a purchase-money collateral with respect to that security interest. . . ." "Purchase-money collateral" is defined as "goods . . . that secures a purchase-money obligation incurred with respect to that collateral," and "purchase-money obligation" is defined as "an obligation of an obligor incurred as all or part of the *price of the collateral* or for *value given to enable* the debtor to acquire rights in or the use of the collateral if the value is in fact so used."

Whether a PMSI exists in this case, then, "turns on whether the negative equity on the debtor's trade-in vehicle constitutes 'part of the price of the collateral,' *i.e.* part of the price of the new vehicle, or whether it constitutes 'value given to enable the debtor to acquire rights in or the use of the collateral. . . .'" Although *§9a-103* does not define the terms "price" or "value given," Comment 3 to *§9a-103* states that "the 'price' of collateral or the 'value given to enable' includes obligations for expenses incurred in connection with acquiring rights in the collateral, sales, taxes, duties, finance charges, interest freight charges, costs of storage in transit, demurrage, administrative charges, expenses of collection and enforcement, attorney's fees, and other similar obligations."

The Court believes that this list is not exhaustive and the expenses identified in Comment 3 are merely examples or additional components of the "price of the collateral" or of "value given" by the debtor. Therefore, this Court cannot see how the refinancing of negative equity and the other transaction costs incurred in connection with the purchase of the debtor's new truck could not qualify as an "expense" within the meaning of Comment 3.

The debtor and the dealer in this case agreed that as part of the purchase of the truck and pursuant to the retail installment contract, the dealer would advance funds to payoff the lien on the debtor's trade-in vehicle and to cover tax, license and document preparation fees. Essentially, this was a package deal. Ford Motor Credit later stepped into the purchase-money lender shoes of the dealer. The Court concludes that the agreement and the dealings between the debtor and the dealer/creditor demonstrate that the costs of satisfying these outstanding obligations of the debtor were clearly incurred in connection with the purchase of the new vehicle.

Additionally, Comment 3 states that "[t]he concept of 'purchase money security interest' requires a close nexus between the acquisition of the collateral and the secured obligation." The Court finds that in the present case, there is a very close connection between the negative equity and the financing of the Debtor's new vehicle. As noted earlier, the financing transaction was a package deal where the negative equity in the trade-in was paid off by the dealer as part of its retail installment sale of the new vehicle and the related obligation was included in the Contract with the Debtor. All of the amounts financed in the contract, except the gap insurance and service contract, were directly connected to the Debtor's purchase of the new vehicle. In fact, the evidence before this Court shows that Ford Motor Credit would not have financed the total purchase price had the Debtor not agreed to all of the terms of the Contract including the negative equity and the add-on transaction costs. The Court, therefore, concludes that because of this close nexus between the negative equity and the financing of the Debtor's new vehicle, the entire transaction qualifies as a purchase money security interest.

Accordingly, Ford Motor Credit's entire claim including that portion of the claim attributable to the payoff of negative equity on the Debtor's trade-in vehicle and the other transaction costs, should be allowed as a fully secured claim that must be paid in full through the Debtor's Chapter 13 plan.

[Author's note—there is a split of authority concerning the issue in this case and at least one other court reached a different conclusion, allowing the claim to be bifurcated. See, *In re Mitchell,* 64 UCC Rep.2d 483 (U.S.B.C., M.D. Tenn. 2007).]

Discharge

Discharge As soon as practicable after the completion by the debtor of all payments under the plan, the court is required to grant the debtor a discharge of all debts provided for by the plan (or specifically disallowed) except:

- Debts covered by a waiver of discharge executed by the debtor and approved by the court;
- Debts that are for taxes required to be collected or paid and for which the debtor is liable;
- Certain debts that are not dischargeable under Chapter 7 such as those that result from liabilities for obtaining

Comparison of Major Forms of Bankruptcy Proceedings

Purpose	Chapter 7 Liquidation	Chapter 11 Reorganization	Chapter 12 Adjustments of Debts	Chapter 13 Adjustments of Debts
Eligible Debtors	Individuals, and partnerships, and corporations *except* municipal corporations, railroads, insurance companies, banks, and savings and loan associations. Farmers and ranchers are eligible only if they petition voluntarily.	Generally, same as Chapter 7 except a railroad may be a debtor, and a stockbroker and commodity broker may not be a debtor under Chapter 11.	Family farmer with regular income, at least 50 percent of which comes from farming, and less than $3,544,525 in debts, at least 80 percent of which is farm related. Family fishermen with regular income whose aggregate debts do not exceed $1,642,500 and at least 80 percent of which arose out of the fishing operation.	Individual with regular income with liquidated unsecured debts less than $336,900 and secured debts of less than $1,010,650.
Initiation of Proceeding	Petition by debtor (voluntary). Petition by creditors (involuntary).	Petition by debtor (voluntary). Petition by creditors (involuntary).	Petition by debtor.	Petition by debtor.
Basic Procedure	1. Appointment of trustee. 2. Debtor retains exempt property. 3. Nonexempt property is sold and proceeds distributed based on priority of claims. 4. Dischargeable debts are terminated.	1. Appointment of committees of creditors and equity security holders. 2. Debtor submits reorganization plan. 3. If plan is approved and implemented, debts are discharged.	1. Trustee is appointed but debtor usually remains in possession. 2. Debtor submits a plan in which unsecured creditors must receive at least liquidation value. 3. If plan is approved and fulfilled, debtor is entitled to a discharge.	1. Trustee is appointed but debtor usually remains in possession. 2. Debtor submits a plan in which unsecured creditors must receive at least liquidation value. 3. If plan is approved and fulfilled, debts covered by plan are discharged.
Advantages	After liquidation and distribution of assets, most or all debts may be discharged and debtor gets a fresh start.	Debtor remains in business and debts are liquidated through implementation of approved reorganization plan.	Debtor generally remains in possession and has opportunity to work out of financial difficulty over period of time (usually three years) through implementation of approved plan.	Debtor has opportunity to work out of financial difficulty over period of time (usually three–five years) through implementation of approved plan.

money by false pretenses or false representations (see page 784 for a more complete list)
- Debts for restitution or a criminal fine included in a sentence on the debtor's conviction of a crime; or

- For restitution or damages awarded in a civil action against the debtor as a result of willful or malicious injury by the debtor that caused personal injury to an individual or the death of an individual.

A debtor who is subject to a judicial or administrative order, or, by statute, to pay a domestic support obligation, must, in addition to making the payments pursuant to his plan, certify that all amounts under the order or statute have been paid up to the date of certification in order to be entitled to a discharge.

As is the situation under Chapter 7, the court is also prohibited from granting a discharge where there is reason to believe there is a pending proceeding in which the debtor may be found guilty of a violation of the federal securities laws or is liable for a debt based on the violation of those laws.

Repeat Bankruptcies The 2005 act prohibits a court from granting a discharge of the debts provided for in the plan (or disallowed) if the debtor received a discharge in a case filed under Chapter 7, 11, or 12 of the Bankruptcy Code in the four-year period preceding the date of the order for relief under Chapter 13—or in a case filed under Chapter 13 during the two-year period preceding the date of the order of relief in the current case.

Advantages of Chapter 13 A debtor may choose to file under Chapter 13 to avoid the stigma of bankruptcy or to retain more of his property than is exempt from bankruptcy under state or federal law. Nonexempt property would have to be surrendered to the trustee in a Chapter 7 liquidation proceeding. Chapter 13 can provide some financial discipline to a debtor as well as an opportunity to get his financial affairs back in good shape. It also gives him relief from the pressures of individual creditors so long as he makes the payments called for by the plan. The debtor's creditors may benefit by recovering a greater percentage of the debt owed to them than would be obtainable in straight bankruptcy.

Problems and Problem Cases

1. Gilbert and Kimberly Barnes filed a voluntary Chapter 7 petition in the U.S. Bankruptcy Court for the District of Maryland. Subsequently they moved to avoid a non–purchase money lien held by ITT Financial Services on their exempt "household goods." Among the goods that the Barneses were claiming as "household goods." were a videocassette recorder (VCR), a 12-gauge pump shotgun, a 20-gauge shotgun, a 30-06 rifle, and a 22 pistol. ITT contended that the VCR and the firearms were not household goods that they could exempt. Under Maryland law, household goods are items of personal property necessary for the day-to-day existence of people in the context of their homes. Should the court consider the VCR and firearms to be "household goods"?

2. In 1991 Joseph and Toni Trujillo bought a house in Las Vegas, Nevada. Subsequently, Joseph borrowed $20,000 of his wife's savings to invest in business ventures. On November 15, 1993, the Trujillos defaulted in payment on a promissory note to Richard Hart and then entered into a stipulated agreement with him that was entered as a judgment on August 8, 1994. In May of 1994, purportedly as security to his wife for the $20,000 loan, Joseph transferred the title to his Cadillac automobile to his son, Gilbert. Joseph instructed Gilbert to hold the title in trust until the loan was repaid. Later the Trujillos transferred to Gilbert the titles of two more vehicles, a Pontiac and a Volkswagen, purportedly to obtain a group insurance rate. No consideration was given for the transfer of any of the vehicles, and the Trujillos retained possession and control of all three vehicles.

    On August 22, 1994, the Trujillos deeded, by a quit claim deed, their house to their daughter, Valerie Aquino. The transfer was purportedly done to obtain a loan with Aquino's credit because Joseph's outstanding debts prevented him from obtaining credit in his own name. No consideration was given to the Trujillos for the transfer of the house, and the Trujillos retained both possession and control of the house. On May 16, 1995, within a year of transferring the vehicles and deeding the house, the Trujillos filed a petition for relief under Chapter 7 of the Bankruptcy Code. The Bankruptcy Trustee, Tom Grimmett, filed a complaint for fraudulent conveyance, requested denial of discharge against the Trujillos, and sought recovery of the fraudulently conveyed property from Gilbert and Aquino. Were the transfers of the vehicles and the house fraudulent transfers that could be recovered by the trustee?

3. David Hott was a college graduate with a degree in business administration who was employed as an insurance agent. He and his wife graduated from college in 1996. At the time he graduated, Hott had outstanding student loans of $14,500 for which he was given a grace period before he had to repay them. Hott became unemployed. Bills began to accumulate, and a number of his outstanding bills were near the

credit limits on his accounts. About that time, he received a promotional brochure by mail from Signal Consumer Discount Company, offering the opportunity to borrow several thousand dollars. The Hotts decided it appeared to be an attractive vehicle for them to use to consolidate their debts. Hott went to the Signal office and filled out a credit application. He did not list the student loan as a current debt. He later claimed that someone in the office told him he didn't have to list it if he owned an automobile, but there was significant doubt about the credibility of this claim. Had he listed it, he would not have met the debt-income ratio required by Signal, and it would not have made the loan. As it was, Signal agreed to make the loan on the condition Hott pay off a car debt in order to reduce his debt-income ratio and Hott agreed to do so. On March 30, 1997, Signal loaned the Hotts $3,458.01. On June 24, 1998, the Hotts filed for bankruptcy. Signal objected to discharge of the balance remaining on its loan on the ground it had been obtained through the use of a materially false financial statement. Was discharge of the debt barred on the ground it had been obtained through the use of a materially false financial statement?

4. In January 1990 Dr. Anthony Byrd, a dentist, applied to the Bank of Mississippi for an unsecured loan in the amount of $20,000. Prior to this time the bank had no relationship with Dr. Byrd. The bank requested and received from Dr. Byrd a 1988 individual income tax return along with a statement of his financial condition prepared by his accountant. The bank also obtained a credit report. After considering all the information, the bank granted the loan. The promissory note was renewed on a number of occasions, beginning in July 1990. On each occasion the bank requested, and was provided, a current financial statement.

The financial statement dated June 30, 1989, showed Dr. Byrd having a net worth of approximately $649,000. Listed in the financial statements was an asset consisting of 60 acres of real property with a value of $30,000. In fact Dr. Byrd did not own the property, nor did he ever pay the property taxes on it. He later explained that he had listed it because he believed that it had passed to him on his father-in-law's death. The property was farmed by his brother-in-law. The statement also listed as an asset a residence in Covington County, Mississippi, with an appraised value of $49,800. At the time the financial statement was submitted, the property had been sold to his brother on a conditional sale contract with a purchase price of $39,000; it also was encumbered with a deed of trust securing a $39,000 note to the Bank of Simpson County. However, neither the conditional sales contract nor the note and deed of trust was mentioned in the financial statement. Dr. Byrd later explained that this was an "oversight." The initial credit report obtained by the bank did not mention either of these elements, so the bank had no reason to disbelieve the assertion in the statement provided by Dr. Byrd.

The initial financial statement also listed as an asset a note receivable for $103,000 from Southern Outdoors, Inc., a company which the statement noted was 92 percent owned by Dr. Byrd. A subsequent statement listed the note receivable as $184,000. The last statement he submitted omitted this loan; Dr. Byrd indicated that he had been told by his accountant that it should be considered as a capital contribution to Southern Outdoors rather than as an account receivable.

Dr. Byrd filed for bankruptcy under Chapter 7. The Bank of Mississippi commenced an adversary proceeding to have its claim arising out of the $20,000 promissory note declared nondischargeable on the grounds that it had been obtained on the basis of a materially false statement in writing concerning the debtor's financial statement which the bank had relied on in granting the loan. Should the Bankruptcy Court declare the debt owed by Dr. Byrd to the Bank of Mississippi to be nondischargeable on the grounds it had been obtained on the basis of a materially false financial statement?

5. Brian Scholz was involved in an automobile collision with a person insured by The Travelers Insurance Company. At the time, Scholz was cited for, and pled no contest to, a criminal charge of driving under the influence of alcohol arising out of the accident. The Travelers paid its insured $4,303.68 and was subrogated to the rights of its insured against Scholz. Subsequently, The Travelers filed a civil action against Scholz to recover the amount it had paid, and a default judgment was entered against Scholz. Eleven months later, Scholz sought relief from the bankruptcy court by filing a voluntary petition under Chapter 7. One of the questions in the bankruptcy proceeding was whether the debt owing to The Travelers was nondischargeable. Is the debt dischargeable?

6. Bryant filed a Chapter 7 petition on January 7, 1984. On March 8, she filed an application to reaffirm an indebtedness owed to General Motors Acceptance Corporation (GMAC) on her 1980 Cadillac automobile.

Bryant was not married, and she supported two teenage daughters. She was not currently employed, and she collected $771 a month in unemployment benefits and $150 a month in rental income from her mother. Her monthly house payments were $259. The present value of the Cadillac was $9,175; she owed $7,956.37 on it, and her monthly payments were $345.93. Bryant indicated that she wanted to keep the vehicle because it was reliable. GMAC admitted that Bryant had been, and continued to be, current in her payments. GMAC said that the car was in no danger of being repossessed but that, absent reaffirmation, it might decide to repossess it. Under the law at the time, permission of the court was required for a reaffirmation agreement. Should the court grant Bryant's petition to reaffirm her indebtedness to GMAC?

7. During their 12 years of marriage, Roger and Georgianne Huckfeldt accumulated over $250,000 in debts while Roger completed college, medical school, and six years of residency in surgery and while Georgianne completed college and law school. These debts included $166,000 in student loans to Huckfeldt and $47,000 jointly borrowed from Georgianne's parents. The Huckfeldts divorced on March 26, 1992. The divorce decree ordered Roger to pay his student loans, one-half of the debt to Georgianne's parents, and other enumerated debts totaling some $241,000. The decree also ordered Roger to hold Georgianne harmless for these debts but otherwise denied Georgianne's request for maintenance.

On June 4, 1992, six months before Roger would complete his residency, he filed a voluntary Chapter 7 petition, listing assets of $1,250 and liabilities of $546,857. After filing the petition, Roger accepted a fellowship at Oregon Health Sciences University, a one- or two-year position paying $45,000 per year, substantially less than the income he could likely earn during the pendency of his Chapter 7 proceeding. Following Roger's petition, creditors of the debts assigned to him in the divorce decree began pursuing Georgianne for repayment. She filed for bankruptcy protection in March 1993.

In September 1992, Georgianne and her parents filed a motion to dismiss Roger's Chapter 7 petition on the ground that it was filed in bad faith. They alleged that Roger had threatened to file for bankruptcy during the divorce proceeding and had commenced the bankruptcy proceeding in defiance of the divorce decree for the purpose of shifting responsibility for assigned debts to Georgianne. They also alleged that

Roger had deliberately taken steps to reduce his annual income to avoid payment of his debts through the Chapter 7 liquidation.

After a hearing the bankruptcy court granted the motion to dismiss the proceeding on the grounds it was filed in bad faith, finding, among other things, that Roger could be earning $110,000 to $120,000 after expenses. The district court affirmed the decision, and Roger appealed to the court of appeals. Should Roger's Chapter 7 petition be dismissed on the grounds it was filed in bad faith?

8. The A. H. Robins Company is a publicly held company that filed a voluntary petition for relief under Chapter 11 of the Bankruptcy Code. Robins sought refuge in Chapter 11 because of a multitude of civil actions filed against it by women who alleged they were injured by use of the Dalkon Shield intrauterine device that it manufactured and sold as a birth control device. Approximately 325,000 notices of claim against Robins were received by the Bankruptcy Court.

In 1985, the court appointed the Official Committee of Security Holders to represent the interest of Robins' public shareholders. In April 1987, Robins filed a proposed plan of reorganization but no action was taken on the proposed plan because of a merger proposal submitted by Rorer Group, Inc. Under this plan, Dalkon Shield claimants would be compensated out of a $1.75 billion fund, all other creditors would be paid in full, and the Robins stockholders would receive stock of the merged corporation. However, it being a time of other critical activity in the bankruptcy proceeding, no revised plan incorporating the merger proposal had been filed or approved.

Earlier, in August 1986, the court had appointed Ralph Mabey as an examiner to evaluate and suggest proposed elements of a plan of reorganization. On Mabey's suggestion, a proposed order was put before the district court supervising the proceeding that would require Robins to establish a $15 million emergency treatment fund "for the purpose of assisting in providing tubal reconstructive surgery or in-vitro fertilization to eligible Dalkon Shield claimants." The purpose of the emergency fund was to assist those claimants who asserted that they had become infertile as a consequence of their use of the product. A program was proposed for administering the fund and for making the medical decisions required.

On May 21, 1987, the district court ordered that the emergency treatment fund be created. This action was challenged by the committee representing the equity security holders. Was the court justified in ordering the distribution of some of the bankrupt's assets on an emergency basis before a reorganization plan was approved?

9. Royal Composing Room, Inc., is an advertising typography company, and one of the last unionized shops in an industry that was subjected to considerable stress as computer technology replaced the Linotype machine. Royal was a party to a collective bargaining agreement with Typographical Union No. 6. Royal was a profitable company until 1982, when its gross revenues declined by $2 million; over the next four years, it sustained operating losses. Confronted with these difficulties, in 1983 Royal began to cut expenses by sharply cutting the compensation of its principal executives, freezing the salaries of salespeople and middle management foremen, eliminating company automobiles, and moving to a smaller location to save rent. At the start of 1986, Royal lost its largest customer, Doyle Dane Bernbach, Inc., and sought to convince the union, which theretofore had not made any sacrifices or concessions, to forgo a 3 percent wage increase agreed to earlier. When the union refused, Royal filed a petition for reorganization under Chapter 11 and sought to reject its collective bargaining agreement. Under section 1113(b) of the Bankruptcy Code, before it could reject the collective bargaining agreement. Royal was required to make a proposal to the union "which provides for those necessary modifications in the employees' benefits and protections that are necessary to permit the reorganization of the debtor and assures that all creditors, the debtor and all of the affected parties are treated fairly and equally." Royal held a meeting with officials of the union and offered a proposal that included a reduction of benefits, changes in work rules, the elimination of the scheduled wage increase, and the elimination of the union's right to arbitration as the way to change the contract. The union rejected the proposal and did not negotiate. Should the bankruptcy court approve the rejection of the collective bargaining agreement?

10. Paul Kelly was a graduate student at the University of Nebraska and had been working on his Ph.D. since 1991. He expected to complete it in 1999. He was also working as a clerk in a liquor store approximately 32 hours per week and earned $5.85 per hour. His monthly expenses were $743.00, and his monthly take-home pay was $761,00. Kelly borrowed money through student loans to enable him to pay tuition, fees, books, and other school-related expenses and expected to continue to do so until he finished his Ph.D.

On July 26, 1994, the U.S. District Court in Minnesota entered a judgment in the amount of $30,000 against Kelly and in favor of Capitol Indemnity Corporation. The judgment was based on a misappropriation of funds by Kelly from a bank insured by Capitol. The court's order provided that the judgment was not dischargeable in bankruptcy.

Kelly filed a Chapter 13 petition. In his Chapter 13 plan, Kelly proposed to pay a total of $7,080.00 by paying off $118.00 per month, $100.00 of which would come from student loans. In the proceeding, Kelly testified that, among other things, he was currently qualified to teach at the college or university level and could earn about $20,000 but he preferred to work part-time as a clerk while he completed graduate school. Capitol objected to the proposed plan on the grounds it was not proposed in good faith. Capitol contended that Kelly should not be allowed to languish in graduate school, remain underemployed, and obtain the benefit of a Chapter 13 discharge. Capitol asserted that Kelly was attempting to discharge a debt that was nondischargeable under Chapter 7, proposed to make payments primarily from his student loans, and would be paying a dividend to unsecured creditors of only 8½ percent. These factors, Capitol contended, demonstrated that the plan had not been proposed in good faith and that it should not be confirmed. Should confirmation of Kelly's plan be denied on the grounds it was not proposed in good faith?

Online Research

Current Corporate Reorganizations

Use the Internet to locate articles from *The Wall Street Journal* and other financial publications concerning one of the recent major corporate bankruptcies and ascertain the following information concerning the bankruptcy case: (1) When was the bankruptcy petition filed? (2) Was the petition filed under Chapter 7 (liquidation) or under Chapter 11 (reorganization)? (3) Who were/are the major creditors or holders of claims against the bankrupt entity? (4) If the matter is in Chapter 11, has a reorganization plan been filed and what were/are its major elements? (5) Has the bankruptcy proceeding been completed? (6) If it has been completed, how did the major creditors appear to fare?

Part Seven

Commercial Paper

chapter 31
Negotiable Instruments

chapter 32
Negotiation and Holder
in Due Course

chapter 33
Liability of Parties

chapter 34
Checks and Electronic Transfers

NEGOTIABLE INSTRUMENTS

Chances are that you are using a variety of negotiable instruments in your everyday life, perhaps without realizing the special qualities that have led to their widespread use in commerce and the rules that govern them. If you have a job, your employer probably pays you by check, and you likely have a checking account that you use to make purchases and pay your bills. If you have accumulated some savings, you may have invested them in a certificate of deposit at a bank. And, if you have borrowed money, you very likely were asked to sign a promissory note acknowledging the debt and committing to repay it on specified terms. This chapter introduces the law of negotiable instruments, including:

- The special qualities and benefits of negotiable instruments.
- The basic types of commercial paper and their defining characteristics.
- The formal requirements that must be met for instruments such as checks, notes, and certificates of deposit to qualify as negotiable instruments.
- What happens if you write or receive a check in which there is a conflict between the amount set forth in figures and the amount set out in words.
- Whether it was ethical for the purchaser of two engines to deliberately place two different amounts on a check (one figure using a check-writing machine and the other by writing numerals in handwriting) that was sent in payment for the engines.

AS COMMERCE AND TRADE developed, people moved beyond exclusive reliance on barter to the use of money and then to the use of substitutes for money. The term *commercial paper* encompasses substitutes in common usage today such as checks, promissory notes, and certificates of deposit.

History discloses that every civilization that engaged to an appreciable extent in commerce used some form of commercial paper. Probably the oldest commercial paper used in the carrying on of trade is the promissory note. Archaeologists found a promissory note made payable to bearer that dated from about 2100 B.C. The merchants of Europe used commercial paper—which, under the law merchant, was negotiable—in the 13th and 14th centuries. Commercial paper does not appear to have been used in England until about A.D. 1600.

This chapter and the three following chapters outline and discuss the body of law that governs commercial paper. Of particular interest are those kinds of commercial paper having the attribute of *negotiability*—that is,

they can generally be transferred from party to party and accepted as a substitute for money. This chapter discusses the nature and benefits of negotiable instruments and then outlines the requirements an instrument must meet to qualify as a negotiable instrument. Subsequent chapters discuss transfer and negotiation of instruments, the rights and liabilities of parties to negotiable instruments, and the special rules applicable to checks.

Nature of Negotiable Instruments

When a person buys a television set and gives the merchant a check drawn on his checking account, that person uses a form of negotiable commercial paper. Similarly, a person who goes to a bank or a credit union to borrow money might sign a promissory note agreeing to pay the money back in 90 days. Again, the bank and borrower use a form of negotiable commercial paper.

Commercial paper is basically a *contract for the payment of money*. It may serve as a substitute for money payable immediately, such as a check. Or, it can be used as a means of extending credit. When a television set is bought by giving the merchant a check, the check is a substitute for money. If a credit union loans a borrower money now in exchange for the borrower's promise to repay it later, the promissory note signed by the borrower is a means of extending credit.

Uniform Commercial Code The law of commercial paper is covered in Article 3 (Negotiable Instruments) and Article 4 (Bank Deposits and Collections) of the Uniform Commercial Code. Other negotiable documents, such as investment securities and documents of title, are treated in other articles of the Code. The original Code Articles 3 and 4, adopted initially in the 1960s, generally followed the basic, centuries-old rules governing the use of commercial paper; but at the same time they adopted modern terminology and coordinated, clarified, and simplified the law. However, business practices continued to evolve and new technological developments have changed the way that banks process checks. Accordingly, in 1990 a Revised Article 3, along with related amendments to Articles 1 and 4, were developed and have now been adopted by all states except New York. However, the reader should keep in mind that instruments may be interpreted under the version of the Code that was in effect when the instruments were issued.

Negotiable Instruments The two basic types of negotiable instruments are *promises to pay money* and *orders to pay money*. Promissory notes and certificates of deposit issued by banks are promises to pay someone money. Checks and drafts are orders to another person to pay money to a third person. A check, which is a type of draft, is an order directed to a certain kind of person, namely a bank, to pay money from a person's account to a third person.

Negotiability Negotiable instruments are a special kind of commercial paper that can pass readily through our financial system and is accepted in place of money. This gives negotiable instruments many advantages.

For example, Searle, the owner of a clothing store in New York, contracts with Amado, a swimsuit manufacturer in Los Angeles, for $10,000 worth of swimsuits. If negotiable instruments did not exist, Searle would have to send or carry $10,000 across the country, which would be both inconvenient and risky. If someone stole the money along the way, Searle would lose the $10,000

unless he could locate the thief. By using a check in which Searle orders his bank to pay $10,000 from his account to Amado, or to someone designated by Amado, Searle makes the payment in a far more convenient manner. He sends only a single piece of paper to Amado. If the check is properly prepared and sent, sending the check is less risky than sending money. Even if someone steals the check along the way, Searle's bank may not pay it to anyone but Amado or someone authorized by Amado. And, because the check gives Amado the right either to collect the $10,000 or to transfer the right to collect it to someone else, the check is a practical substitute for cash to Amado as well as to Searle.

In this chapter and in the three following chapters, we discuss the requirements necessary for a contract for the payment of money to qualify as a negotiable instrument. We also explain the features that not only distinguish a negotiable instrument from a simple contract but also led to the widespread use of negotiable instruments as a substitute for money.

Kinds of Negotiable Instruments

Promissory Notes The promissory note is the simplest form of commercial paper; it is simply a promise to pay money. A **promissory note** is a two-party instrument in which one person (known as the **maker**) makes an unconditional promise in writing to pay another person (the **payee**), a person specified by that person, or the bearer of the instrument, a fixed amount of money, with or without interest, either on demand or at a specified, future time [3–104].[1]

The promissory note, shown in Figures 1 and 2, is a credit instrument; it is used in a wide variety of transactions in which credit is extended. For example, if a person purchases an automobile using money borrowed from a bank, the bank has the person sign a promissory note for the unpaid balance of the purchase price. Similarly, if a person borrows money to purchase a house, the lender who makes the loan and takes a mortgage on the house has the person sign a promissory note for the amount due on the loan. The note probably states that it is secured by a mortgage. The terms of payment on the note should correspond with the terms of the sales contract for the purchase of the house.

---

[1]The numbers in brackets refer to the sections of the 1990 Revised Article 3 (and the conforming amendments to Articles 1 and 4) of the Uniform Commercial Code.

Figure 1   *Promissory Note*

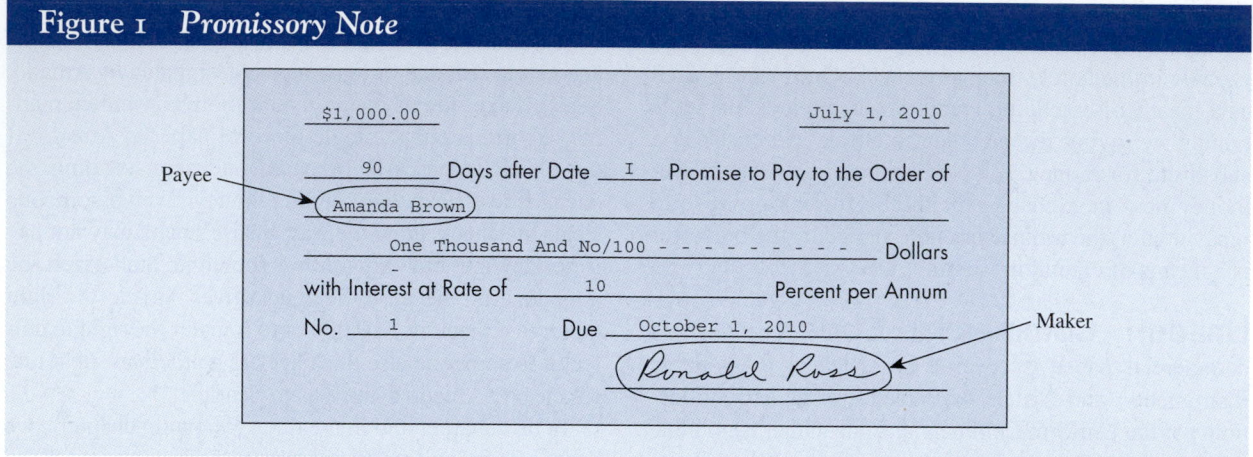

Payee → Amanda Brown

$1,000.00   July 1, 2010

        90   Days after Date ___I___ Promise to Pay to the Order of

Amanda Brown

        One Thousand And No/100 - - - - - - - - - - Dollars

with Interest at Rate of _____10_____ Percent per Annum

No. ___1___   Due ___October 1, 2010___

Ronald Ross ← Maker

Certificates of Deposit

The certificate of deposit given by a bank or a savings and loan association when a deposit of money is made is a type of note, namely a note of a bank. A **certificate of deposit** is an instrument containing (1) an acknowledgment by a bank that it has received a deposit of money and (2) a promise by the bank to repay the sum of money [3–104(j)].

Most banks no longer issue certificates of deposit (CD) in paper form. Rather, the bank maintains an electronic deposit and provides the customer with a statement indicating the amount of principal held on a CD basis and the terms of the CD, such as the maturity and interest rate. In these instances, the certificate of deposit is not in negotiable instrument form.

Drafts

A **draft** is a form of commercial paper that involves an *order* to pay money rather than a promise to pay money [3–104(e)]. The most common example of a draft is a check. A draft has three parties to it: one person (known as the **drawer**) orders a second person (the **drawee**) to pay a certain sum of money to a third person (the **payee**), to a person specified by that person, or to bearer.

Drafts other than checks are used in a variety of commercial transactions. If Brown owes Ames money, Ames may draw a draft for the amount of the debt, naming Brown as drawee and herself or her bank as payee, and send the draft to Brown's bank for payment. Alternatively, Ames might send a draft providing for payment on a certain day in the future to Brown for "acceptance." Brown could "accept" the draft by signing his name to it, thereby obligating himself to pay the amount specified in the draft on that day in the future to Ames or to someone specified by Ames. Automobile dealers selling to each other, or selling cars at auctions, commonly use drafts, as do sellers and buyers of livestock.

In freight shipments in which the terms are "cash on delivery," the seller commonly ships the goods to the buyer on an "order bill of lading" consigned to himself at the place of delivery. The seller then indorses the bill of lading and attaches a draft naming the buyer as drawee. He then sends the bill of lading and the draft through banking channels to the buyer's bank. A bank in the buyer's locale presents the draft to the buyer's bank for payment, and when the former bank receives payment, delivers the bill of lading to the buyer. Through this commercial transaction, the buyer gets the goods and the seller gets his money.

When credit is extended, the same procedure is followed, but the seller uses a time draft—a draft payable at some future time (see Figure 3). In such a transaction, the buyer "accepts" the draft (instead of paying it) and obligates herself to pay the amount of the draft when due. In these cases, the *drawee* (now called the **acceptor**) should date her signature so that the date at which payment is due is clear to all [3–409(c)].

As a consumer, you are most likely to encounter drafts when your insurance company pays a claim—you'll see that often it is denoted as a "DRAFT" and indicates that it is payable through a particular bank. This notation means that the bank will pay the draft to you only after it has checked with the insurance company (the drawer) and the insurance company authorizes the bank to pay the instrument.

Checks

A **check** is a *draft payable on demand* and drawn on a bank (i.e., a bank is the drawee or person to whom the order to pay is addressed). Checks are the most widely used form of commercial paper. The issuer of a check orders the bank at which she maintains an account to pay a specified person, or someone designated by that person, a fixed amount of money from the

Figure 2   *Promissory Note (Consumer Loan Note)*

The National BANK OF WASHINGTON

CONSUMER LOAN NOTE

Date___November 21,___, 20_10_

#___

The words I and me mean all borrowers who signed this note. The word bank means The National Bank of Washington._____

Promise to Pay

Payee →   30 months from today, I promise to pay to the order of (The National Bank of Washington)
Seventy-Eight Hundred Seventy Five and
no/100 - - - - - - - - - - - -dollars ($ 7,875.00).

Responsibility

Although this note may be signed below by more than one person, I understand that we are each as individuals responsible for paying back the full amount.

Breakdown of Loan

This is what I will pay:

Amount of loan	1.$	6,800.00
Credit Life Insurance (optional)	2.$	100.00
Other (describe) _____	3.$	-0-
Amount Financed (Add 1 and 2 and 3)	4.$	6,900
FINANCE CHARGE	5.$	975.00
Total of Payments (Add 4 and 5)	$	7,875.00
ANNUAL PERCENTAGE RATE		10.5%

Repayment

This is how I will repay:
I will repay the amount of this note in ___30___ equal uninterrupted monthly installments of $_262.50_ each on the _1st_ day of each month starting on the _1st_ day of _December_, 20_10_ and ending on ___May 1___, _____   _2013_

Prepayment

I have the right to prepay the whole outstanding amount of this note at any time. If I do, or if this loan is refinanced—that is, replaced by a new note—you will refund the unearned finance charge, figured by the rule of 78—a commonly used formula for figuring rebates on installment loans.

Late Charge

Any installment not paid within ten days of its due date shall be subject to a late charge of 5% of the payment, not to exceed $5.00 for any such late installment.

Security

To protect the National Bank of Washington, I give what is known as a security interest in my auto and/or other: (Describe) _Ford Thunderbird_____

_____# Serial #115117-12-_____

See the security agreement.

Credit Life Insurance

Credit life insurance is not required to obtain this loan. The bank need not provide it and I do not need to buy it unless I sign immediately below. The cost of credit life insurance is $_100.00_ for the term of the loan.

Signed: *A. J. Smith*_____

Date: _November 21, 2010_____

Default

If for any reason I fail to make any payment on time, I shall be in default. The bank can then demand immediate payment of the entire remaining unpaid balance of this loan, without giving anyone further notice. If I have not paid the full amount of the loan when the final payment is due, the bank will charge me interest on the unpaid balance at six percent (6%) per year.

Right of Offset

If this loan becomes past due, the bank will have the right to pay this loan from any deposit or security I have at this bank without telling me ahead of time. Even if the bank gives me an extension of time to pay this loan, I still must repay the entire loan.

Collection Fees

If this note is placed with an attorney for collection, then I agree to pay an attorney's fee of fifteen percent (15%) of the unpaid balance. This fee will be added to the unpaid balance of the loan.

Co-borrowers

If I am signing this note as a co-borrower, I agree to be equally responsible with the borrower for this loan. The bank does not have to notify me that this note has not been paid. The bank can change the terms of payment and release any security without notifying or releasing me from responsibility for this loan.

Copy Received

I received a completely filled in copy of this note. If I have signed for Credit Life Insurance, I received a copy of the Credit Life Insurance certificate.

Borrower: *A. J. Smith* ← Maker
          A. J. Smith
          3412 Brookdale, S. W. Washington D.C.
Address _____

Co-borrower: *Andrea H. Smith* ← Co-maker
          Andrea H. Smith
          3412 Brookdale, S. W. Washington D.C.
Address _____

Co-borrower: _____

Address _____

CONSUMER CREDIT HOTLINE: If you have any questions, please call us immediately at (202) 624-3450.

NBW 437 (Rev. 11-78)   1-Bank's copy   2-File copy   3-Customer's copy

Source: The National Bank of Washington.

account. For example, Elizabeth Brown has a checking account at the National Bank of Washington. She goes to Sears Roebuck and agrees to buy a washing machine priced at $459.95. If she writes a check to pay for it, she is the drawer of the check, the National Bank of Washington is the drawee, and Sears is the payee. By writing the check, Elizabeth is ordering her bank to pay $459.95 from her account to Sears or to Sears's order—that is, to whomever Sears asks the bank to pay the money (see Figure 4).

An instrument may qualify as a "check" and be governed by Article 3 even though it is described on its face

Figure 3   *Draft*

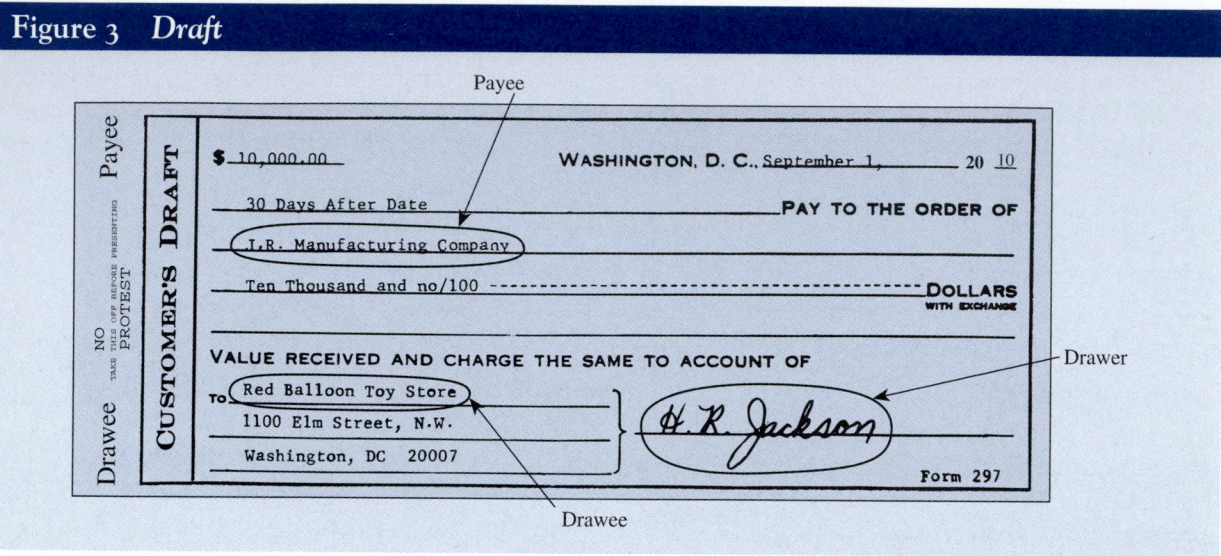

CYBERLAW IN ACTION

E-Checks

In addition to checks, electronic funds transfers through the use of ATMs or in retail stores, and telephone-initiated checks, larger retailers such as grocers and department stores use e-commerce instead of traditional paper checks. This process, called "check conversion," starts with the buyer giving the seller a paper check. The seller uses special equipment to gather information from the paper check; this information includes the buyer's bank account number, the "routing number" that identifies the buyer's bank, and the check's serial number. Then, the seller hands the paper check back to the buyer and completes the transaction by naming itself as the payee of the transaction and by coding in the amount of the purchase. Check conversion is one of the fastest-growing means of taking payments from consumer buyers and saves the seller time and money it otherwise would spend collecting the paper check from the buyer's bank. The legal rules concerning e-checks are discussed in Chapter 34—Checks and Electronic Transfers.

Figure 4   *Check*

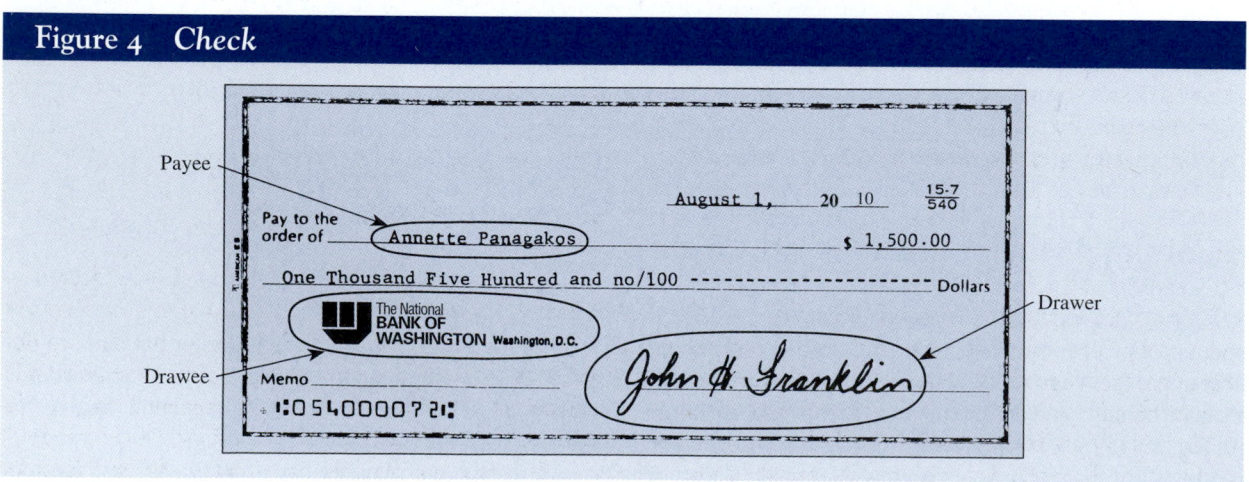

by another term, such as "money order." The Code definition of a "check" includes a "cashier's check" and a "teller's check." A **cashier's check** is a draft on which the drawer and drawee are the same bank (or branches of the same bank); a **teller's check** is a draft drawn by a bank (as drawer) on another bank or payable at or through a bank [3–104(g) and (h)]. For example, a check drawn by a credit union on its account at a federally insured bank would be a teller's check.

Benefits of Negotiable Instruments

Rights of an Assignee of a Contract
As we noted in Chapter 17, Rights of Third Parties, the assignee of a contract can obtain no greater rights than the assignor had at the time of the assignment. For example, Browning Construction Company agrees to build an in-ground swimming pool pursuant to plans provided by Geraldo Garcia. At the time the contract is signed by the two parties on March 1, Garcia makes a down payment of $5,000 and agrees to pay the balance of $20,000 when Browning Construction completes the pool. If on April 1, Browning Construction assigns its rights under the contract to First Bank—including the right to collect the money from Garcia—then First Bank will obtain whatever rights Browning Construction has at the time First Bank seeks to collect the balance due on the contract. If Browning Construction has completed its work consistent with the plans, then First Bank is entitled to be paid the $20,000. However, if the work has not been completed, or was not done consistent with the plans, then Garcia may have a valid defense or reason to avoid paying the full $20,000.

Taking an assignment of a contract involves assuming certain risks. The assignee (First Bank) may not be aware of the nature and extent of any defenses that the party liable on the contract (Garcia) might have against the assignor (Browning Construction). An assignee who does not know what rights he is getting, or which risks he is assuming, may be reluctant to take an assignment of the contract.

Rights of a Holder of a Negotiable Instrument
The object of a negotiable instrument is to have it accepted readily as a substitute for money. In order to accept it readily, a person must be able to take it free of many of the risks assumed by the assignee of a regular contract. Under the law of negotiable instruments, this is possible if two conditions are met: (1) the contract for the payment of money must meet the formal requirements to qualify as a negotiable instrument; and (2) the person who acquires the instrument must qualify as a holder in due course. Basically, a *holder in due course* is a person who has good title to the instrument, paid value for it, acquired it in good faith, and had no notice of certain claims or defenses against payment. In addition, the instrument cannot bear facial irregularities (evidence of forgery or alteration or questions concerning its authenticity).

The next section of this chapter discusses the formal requirements for a negotiable instrument. Chapter 32, Negotiation and Holder in Due Course, outlines the requirements that a person must meet to qualify as a holder in due course.

A holder in due course of a negotiable instrument takes the instrument free of all defenses and claims to the instrument except those that concern its validity. For example, a holder in due course of a note given in payment for goods may enforce the obligation in spite of the buyer's claim that the seller breached a warranty. However, if the maker of a note wrote it under duress, such as a threat of force, or was a minor, then even a holder in due course is subject to the defenses of duress or infancy to the extent other law (1) would nullify the obligation for duress or (2) would permit infancy as a defense to a simple contract. The person who holds the note could not obtain the payment from the maker but would have to recover from the person from whom he got the note.

The Federal Trade Commission (FTC) has adopted a regulation that alters the rights of a holder in due course in consumer purchase transactions. This regulation allows a consumer who gives a negotiable instrument to use additional defenses (breach of warranty or fraudulent inducement) against payment of the instrument against even a holder in due course. Similarly, some states have enacted the Uniform Consumer Credit Code (UCCC), which produces a similar result. Chapter 32, Negotiation and Holder in Due Course, discusses the rights of a holder in due course, as well as the FTC rule.

Formal Requirements for Negotiability

Basic Requirements
An instrument such as a check or a note must meet certain formal requirements to be a negotiable instrument. If the instrument does not meet these requirements, it is nonnegotiable; that is, it is treated as a simple contract and not as a negotiable instrument. A primary purpose for these formal requirements is to ensure the willingness of prospective

purchasers of the instrument, particularly financial institutions such as banks, to accept it as a substitute for money.

For an instrument to be negotiable, it must:

1. Be in writing.

2. Be signed by the issuer (the *maker* in the case of a person undertaking to pay or the *drawer* in the case of a person giving an order or instruction to pay).

3. Contain an unconditional promise or order to pay a fixed amount of money, with or without interest or other charges described in the promise or order.

4. Be payable to order or to bearer.

5. Be payable on demand or at a definite time.

6. Not state any other undertaking or instruction by the person promising or ordering to do any act in addition to the payment of money (however, it may contain (*a*) an undertaking or promise relative to collateral to secure payment, (*b*) an authorization for confession of judgment, or (*c*) a waiver of benefit of any law intended for the advantage or protection of an obligor) [3–103; 3–104].

In addition, an instrument that otherwise qualifies as a check can be negotiable even if it is not explicitly payable to order or to bearer [3–104(c)]. As explained later, this means that a check that reads "pay John Doe" could be negotiable even though the normal form for a check is "pay to the order of _____."

A promise or order other than a check is not a negotiable instrument if at the time it is issued or first comes into the possession of a holder it contains a conspicuous statement that the promise or order is not negotiable or is not an instrument governed by Article 3 [3–104(d)]. For example, if a promissory note contained the legend "NONNEGOTIABLE," it would not qualify as a negotiable instrument even if it otherwise met the formal requirements for one.

Importance of Form   Whether or not an instrument satisfies these formal requirements is important only for the purpose of determining whether an instrument is negotiable or nonnegotiable. Negotiability should not be confused with validity or collectibility. If an instrument is negotiable, the law of negotiable instruments in the Code controls in determining the rights and liabilities of the parties to the instrument. If an instrument is nonnegotiable, the general rules of contract law control. The purpose of determining negotiability is to ascertain whether a possessor of the instrument can become a holder in due course.

An instrument that meets all of the formal requirements is a negotiable instrument even though it is void, voidable, unenforceable, or uncollectible for other reasons. Negotiability is a matter of form and nothing else. Suppose a person gives an instrument in payment of a gambling debt in a state that has a statute declaring that any instrument or promise given in payment of a gambling debt is void. The instrument is a negotiable instrument if it is negotiable in form even though it is absolutely void. Also, an instrument that is negotiable in form is a negotiable instrument even though it is issued by a minor. The instrument is voidable at the option of the minor if state law makes infancy a defense to a simple contract, but it is negotiable.

In Writing

To be negotiable, an instrument must be in writing. An instrument that is handwritten, typed, or printed is considered to be in writing [1–201(46)]. The writing does not have to be on any particular material; all that is required is that the instrument be in writing. A person could create a negotiable instrument in pencil on a piece of wrapping paper. It would be poor business practice to do so, but the instrument would meet the statutory requirement that it be in writing.

Signed

To qualify as a negotiable instrument, an instrument in the form of a note must be signed by the person undertaking to pay (the maker) and an instrument in the form of a draft must be signed by the person giving the instruction to pay (the drawer) [3–103]. An instrument has been signed if the maker or drawer has put a name or other symbol on it with the intention of validating it [3–401(b)]. Normally, the maker or drawer signs an instrument by writing his name on it; however, this is not required. A person or company may authorize an agent to sign instruments for it. A typed or rubber-stamped signature is sufficient if it was put on the instrument to validate it. A person who cannot write her name might make an X or some other symbol and have it witnessed by someone else.

In the *Interbank of New York* case, which follows, the court considered whether preauthorized checks containing the notation "verbally authorized by your depositor" met the requirement that an instrument must be "signed," among other things, in order to qualify as a negotiable instrument.

Interbank of New York v. Fleet Bank
45 UCC Rep.2d 167 (New York Civ. Ct. 2001)

Interbank of New York brought an action against Fleet Bank to recover on four drafts in the total sum of $3,361.25 paid out by Interbank from the account of its customer Dimittrous Tasoulis. Two of the drafts were issued by and made payable to Sprint PCS, and two were issued by and made payable to Atlantic Mobile, Inc. The drafts are known commonly in the banking industry as preauthorized drafts or "telechecks." The drafts are created when a consumer has agreed to pay for goods or services by allowing a vendor to prepare and issue a preauthorized check drawn on the consumer's account at the consumer's designated financial institution. The consumer provides the vendor with the necessary account number and bank at which it is maintained, and the vendor then issues a check drawn on the consumer's account.

In this case, Sprint and Atlantic Mobile issued drafts on the account of Tasoulis to pay for telephone services. The drafts contained the typed notation "verbally authorized by your depositor." Bell and Atlantic Mobile deposited the drafts in their respective accounts at Fleet, and the drafts were ultimately paid by Interbank.

Thereafter, Tasoulis advised Interbank that he had never authorized Atlantic Mobile or Sprint to issue the drafts and executed affidavits to that effect as to each draft. Interbank then sued Fleet Bank to recover the amount of the drafts.

Fleet took the position that the preauthorized checks should be treated like any other check and that in accordance with the UCC a depository bank such as Fleet could not be held liable for accepting a check on which the signature of the drawer is forged, unless it knew the signature was forged (this will be discussed in Chapter 33, Liability). Interbank took the position that a preauthorized check cannot be treated as an ordinary check and is not a negotiable instrument.

Edmead, Judge

Section 3–104(a) of the UCC provides that for a writing to be a negotiable instrument it must be signed by the maker or drawer. Interbank argues that since the subject drafts are not signed by the maker, but merely contain the notation "verbally authorized by your depositor," the drafts do not constitute negotiable instruments.

UCC section 1–201(3) provides that "signed" includes any symbol executed or adopted by a party with a present intention to authenticate a writing. UCC section 3–401(2) provides that a signature is made by any word or mark used in lieu of a written signature.

In accordance with these sections of the UCC, if a drawer or maker intended the notation "verbally authorized by your depositor" to authenticate the checks and intended that the notation take the place of a written signature, then the check would be a negotiable instrument.

Clearly, if Tasoulis had authorized Atlantic Mobile to issue the check with the notation "verbally authorized by your depositor," in place of his written signature, the check would qualify

as a negotiable instrument. The only infirmity in the subject drafts is that Tasoulis did not authorize their issuance. Thus, the notation "verbally authorized by your depositor," which could constitute a signature under the UCC, is unauthorized.

The unauthorized use of a stamped printed signature constitutes a forgery. So too here the notation "verbally authorized by your depositor," which can constitute a signature under the UCC, when unauthorized, constitutes a forged signature. Accordingly, the preauthorized checks should be treated as any other check that contains a forged signature. These preauthorized checks constitute negotiable instruments.

Summary judgment granted to Fleet.

Note: The case did not address the issue of whether Atlantic Mobile and Sprint would be liable to Interbank if they did not have the proper authorization from Tasoulis. It should also be noted that this case was decided under the pre-1990 version of Articles 3 and 4 as New York has not adopted the 1990 Revision of Articles 3 and 4. However, the same result would be expected if it had adopted the Revised Articles.

Unconditional Promise or Order

Requirement of a Promise or Order
If an instrument is promissory in nature, such as a note or a certificate of deposit, it must contain an unconditional promise to pay or it cannot be negotiable. Merely acknowl-

edging a debt is not sufficient [3–103(9)]. For example, the statement "I owe you $100" does not constitute a promise to pay. An IOU in this form is not a negotiable instrument.

If an instrument is an order to pay, such as a check or a draft, it must contain an unconditional order. A simple request to pay as a favor is not sufficient; however, a politely phrased demand, such as "please pay," can meet the

CYBERLAW IN ACTION

E-Payments Compared to "Negotiable Instruments"

Article 3 has numerous requirements for the appearance and content of promises to pay (notes) and orders to pay (drafts/checks) if they are to qualify as negotiable instruments and be readily transferable. Two of these requirements contemplate paper-based transactions—the requirement that promises to pay and orders to pay be "in writing" (see 3–103) and be "signed" (see 3–104). For this reason, at present, it would be difficult to "electrify" negotiable instruments successfully.

In contrast, e-payments—more commonly substitutes for traditional "check" payments—are neither in writing or "signed" by affixing a signature in ink to a sheet of paper. Instead, the transaction is documented electronically—such as by sending an e-mail message or fax to a bank to direct them to pay a third-party seller of goods or services (such as the purchase of an online information product).

The buyer and seller using e-payments have many of the same concerns as buyers and sellers using traditional payments methods: they want to be certain that they are dealing with each other honestly and that it will not be easier for the seller to double-charge the buyer's account or to get away with taking payment but not delivering the goods or services that the buyer seeks from the transaction; and they want to guard against unscrupulous persons hacking into their records and stealing from either the buyer or seller. Because of legal uncertainty about which body of law—federal consumer protection laws designed to govern credit-card payments or "electronic funds transfers" or state-created laws such as Articles 3 and 4 of the Uniform Commercial Code—will govern the transaction, the majority of consumers have continued to use traditional, paper-based payments methods and credit cards that they understand better than newer e-payments methods of payment. For e-commerce to reach its fullest potential, more consumers will have to become comfortable with e-payments methods, in addition to better-known checks and credit cards.

requirement. Checks commonly use the language "Pay to the order of." This satisfies the requirement that the check contain an order to pay. The order is the word "pay," not the word "order." The word "order" has another function—that of designating the instrument as payable "to order" or "to bearer" for purposes of negotiability.

Promise or Order Must Be Unconditional

An instrument is not negotiable unless the promise or order is unconditional. For example, a note that provides, "I promise to pay to the order of Karl Adams $100 if he replaces the roof on my garage," is not negotiable because it is payable on a condition.

To be negotiable, an instrument must be written so that a person can tell from reading the instrument alone what the obligations of the parties are. If a note contains the statement "Payment is subject to the terms of a mortgage dated November 20, 2010," it is not negotiable. To determine the rights of the parties on the note, one would have to examine another document—the mortgage.

However, a reference to another document for a statement of rights with respect to collateral, prepayment, or acceleration does not destroy the negotiability of a note [3–106(b)]. For example, a note could contain this statement: "This note is secured by a mortgage dated August 30, 2010" without affecting its negotiability. In this case, the mortgage does not affect rights and duties of

the parties to the note. It would not be necessary to examine the mortgage document to determine the rights of the parties to the note; the parties need only examine the note.

The negotiability of an instrument is not affected by a statement of the consideration for which the instrument was given or by a statement of the transaction that gave rise to the instrument. For example, a negotiable instrument may state that it was given in payment of last month's rent or that it was given in payment of the purchase price of goods. The statement does not affect the negotiability of the instrument.

A check may reference the account to be debited without making the check conditional and thus nonnegotiable. For example, a check could contain the notation, "payroll account" or "petty cash." Similarly, the account number that appears on personal checks does not make the instrument payable only out of a specific fund. Under original Article 3, a check (other than a governmental check) that stated that it was payable only out of a specific fund or account was treated as a conditional order and thus was not negotiable. Revised Article 3 changed this rule so that limiting payment to a particular fund or source does not make the promise or order conditional [3–106(b)].

Revised Article 3 also addresses the negotiability of traveler's checks that commonly require, as a condition to payment, a countersignature of a person whose specimen signature appears on the draft. Under the revision, the condition does not prevent the instrument from meeting the "unconditional promise or order" requirement [3–106(c)]. However, if the person whose specimen signature appears on the instrument fails to countersign it, the failure to sign becomes a defense to the obligation of the issuer to pay. This concept will be discussed in the following chapter.

A conditional *indorsement* does not destroy the negotiability of an otherwise negotiable instrument. The Code determines negotiability at *issuance,* so that indorsements do not affect the underlying negotiability of the instrument. We discuss conditional indorsements in Chapter 32, Negotiation and Holder in Due Course.

Fixed Amount of Money

Fixed Amount The promise or order in an instrument must be to pay a fixed amount of money, with or without interest or other charges described in the promise or order. The requirement of a "fixed amount" applies only to principal; the amount of any interest payable is that described in the instrument. Interest may be stated in an instrument as a fixed or variable amount of money or it may be expressed as a fixed or variable rate or rates. If a variable rate of interest is prescribed, the amount of interest is calculated by reference to the formula or index referenced in the instrument. For example, a note might provide for interest at "three percent (3.00%) over JPMorgan Chase Prime Rate to be adjusted monthly." If the description of interest in the instrument does not allow the amount of interest to be ascertained, then interest is payable at the judgment rate in effect at the place of payment at the time interest first accrues [3–112]. The judgment rate is the rate of interest courts impose on losing parties until they pay the winning parties.

Under the original version of Article 3, a promise or order had to be to pay a "sum certain." Generally, to meet this requirement, a person had to be able to compute from the information in the instrument the amount required to discharge—or pay off—the instrument at any given time. Among other things, this caused problems when applied to variable rate instruments that came into common commercial usage in the United States after the original Article 3 was drafted. Some state courts held that instruments providing for variable interest rates ascertainable through reference to indexes outside the instrument were not negotiable; other courts sought to interpret the Code to accommodate this new commercial practice. As noted above, the negotiability of instruments that provide for variable interest rates has now been resolved in Revised Article 3.

Payable in Money The amount specified in the instrument must be payable in money. *Money* is a medium of exchange authorized or adopted by a domestic or foreign government and includes a monetary unit of account established by an intergovernmental organization or by agreement between two or more nations [1–201(24)]. Unless the instrument otherwise provides, an instrument that states the amount payable in foreign money may be paid in the foreign money or in an equivalent dollar amount [3–107]. If the person obligated to pay off an instrument can do something other than pay money, the instrument is not negotiable. For example, if a note reads, "I promise to pay to the order of Sarah Smith, at my option, $40 or five bushels of apples, John Jones," the note is not negotiable.

Payable on Demand or at a Definite Time

To be negotiable, the promise or order must be payable either on demand or at a specified time in the future. The reason for this requirement is that the time when the instrument is payable can be determined with some certainty. An instrument that is payable on the happening of some uncertain event is not negotiable. Thus, a note payable "when my son graduates from college" is not negotiable, even though the son does graduate subsequently.

Payable on Demand A promise or order is "payable on demand" if (1) it states that it is payable on "demand" or "sight" (or otherwise at the will of the holder of the instrument) or (2) does not state any time for payment [3–108(a)]. For example, if the maker forgets to state when a note is payable, it is payable immediately at the request of the holder of the note.

An instrument may be antedated or postdated, and normally an instrument payable on demand is not payable before the date of the instrument [3–113(a)]. However, revised Article 3 makes an important exception for checks: a payor bank (a bank that is the drawee of a draft) may pay a postdated check before the stated date *unless* the drawer has notified the bank of postdating pursuant to a procedure set out in the Code [3–113(a); 4–401(c)] that is similar to the process involved in stopping payment on a check. (See Chapter 34.)

Payable at a Definite Time A promise or order is "payable at a definite time" if it is payable at a fixed date or dates or at a time or times readily ascertainable at the time the promise or order is issued [3–108(b)]. Thus, a note dated March 25, 2010, might be made payable at a fixed time after a stated date, such as "30 days after date."

Under the Code, an instrument that names a fixed date or time for payment—without losing its negotiable character—also may contain a clause permitting the time for payment to be accelerated at the option of the maker. Similarly, an instrument may allow an extension of time at the option of the holder or allow a maker or acceptor to extend payment to a further definite time. Or, the due date of a note might be triggered by the happening of an event, such as the filing of a petition in bankruptcy against the maker. The Code permits these clauses so long as one can determine the time for payment with certainty [3–108].

A promise or order also is "payable at a definite time" if it is payable on elapse of a definite period of time after "sight" or "acceptance." A draft payable at a specified time—such as "15 days after sight"—is, in effect, payable at a fixed time after the draft is presented to the drawee for acceptance.

If an instrument is undated, its "date" is the date it is issued by the maker or drawer [3–113(b)].

Payable to Order or Bearer

Except for checks, to be negotiable an instrument must be "payable to order or to bearer." A note that provides, "I promise to pay to the order of Sarah Smith" or "I promise to pay to Sarah Smith or bearer" is negotiable. However, one that provides "I promise to pay to Sarah Smith" is not. The words "to the order of" or "to bearer" show that the drawer of a draft, or the maker of a note, intends to issue a negotiable instrument. The drawer or maker is not restricting payment of the instrument to just Sarah Smith but is willing to pay someone else designated by Sarah Smith. This is the essence of negotiability.

In the original version of Article 3, an order in the form of a check also had to be "payable to order or bearer" to qualify as a negotiable instrument. However, the drafters of Revised Article 3 created an exception for instruments that otherwise meet the requirements for a negotiable instrument as well as the definition of a check [3–104(c)]. Under the revised article, a check that reads "Pay John Doe" could qualify as a negotiable instrument. As a result, the Code treats checks, which are payment instruments, as negotiable instruments whether or not they contain the words "to the order of." The drafters explained that most checks are preprinted with these words

but that occasionally the drawer may strike out the words before issuing the check and that a few check forms have been in use that do not contain these words. In these instances, the drafters preferred not to limit the rights of holders of such checks who may pay money or give credit for a check without being aware that it is not in the conventional form for a negotiable instrument.

A promise or order is considered to be payable "to order" if it is payable (1) to the order of an identified person or (2) to an identified person or that person's order [3–109(b)]. Examples would include: "Pay to the order of Sandy Smith" and "Pay to Sandy Smith or order." The most common forms of a promise or order being payable to bearer use the words "pay to bearer," "pay to the order of bearer," "pay to cash," or "pay to the order of cash" [3–109(a)]. A check sent with the payee line blank is payable to bearer. However, it is also considered an incomplete instrument, the rules concerning which will be discussed in the following two chapters.

The original payee of a draft or a note can transfer the right to receive payment to someone else. By making the instrument payable "to the order of" or "to bearer," the drawer or maker is giving the payee the chance to negotiate the instrument to another person and to cut off certain defenses that the drawer or maker may have against payment of the instrument.

An instrument that is payable to the order of a specific person is known as "order paper." Order paper can be negotiated or transferred only by indorsement. An instrument payable "to bearer" or "to cash" is known as "bearer paper"; it can be negotiated or transferred by delivery of possession without indorsement [3–201(b)]. The rules governing negotiation of instruments will be detailed in the next chapter.

An instrument can be made payable to two or more payees. For example, a check could be drawn payable "to the order of John Jones and Henry Smith." Then, both Jones and Smith have to be involved in negotiating it or enforcing its payment. An instrument also can be made payable to alternative persons—for example, "to the order of Susan Clark or Betsy Brown." In this case, either Clark or Brown could negotiate it or enforce its payment [3–110(d)].

A number of recent cases have addressed the question of whether checks should be interpreted as being payable jointly, or whether they are payable in the alternative. Some of those cases have addressed the use of the virgule (/) punctuation mark to separate the names of the payees. One recent case involved a check made payable to "International Livestock/Purina Mills." The court reasoned that a virgule is used to separate alternatives and concluded that the check required only the indorsement of either International Livestock or Purina Mills. The following case, *Pelican National Bank,* involves a check where the payees were listed in a stacked formation without any grammatical connector or punctuation. The court concluded that the check was ambiguous and applied the default rule that treated the document as if it was payable in the alternative.

Pelican National Bank v. Provident Bank of Maryland
849 A.2d 475 (Maryland Ct. App. 2004)

Hartford Mutual Insurance Company issued a check drawn on Allfirst Bank in the amount of $60,150.00 to payees as follows:

> Andrew Michael Bogdan, Jr., Crystal Bodgan
> Oceanmark Bank FSB
> Goodman-Gable-Gould Company

The check was in payment of a casualty claim made by Bodgan on an insurance policy issued by Hartford Mutual on commercial property owned by Bodgan and his wife and on which Oceanmark Bank (Pelican National Bank's predecessor) held a mortgage. Thus, the payees on the check were the property owners, the mortgage holder, and the insurance agent who adjusted the casualty claim. In addition to the payees, the front of the check listed in small print the insurance policy number, claim identification number, the "loss date," and a small notation that read "MEMO Fire—building."

The check, indorsed only by the Bodgans and the adjuster, was presented for payment to Provident Bank, which cashed it. Michael Bodgan deposited the proceeds to a commercial account he held at Provident Bank. When Oceanmark Bank was unable to obtain reimbursement from Provident Bank for negotiating the check without Oceanmark Bank's indorsement, it brought suit against Provident Bank for conversion of the check by paying it without having obtained a required indorsement.

The trial court held that the check was ambiguous as to whether it was payable jointly and thus negotiable only with the indorsement of all of the payees. Accordingly, the court held that it could be negotiated with the indorsement of any of the named payees. Oceanmark Bank appealed.

Bell, Chief Judge

The issue in this case is whether a check made payable to multiple payees, listed in stacked formation on its face, without any grammatical connector or punctuation, is ambiguous as to whether it is negotiable only jointly, thus, requiring the indorsement of all of the named payees, or alternatively, requiring the indorsement of any one of the named payees.

Enacted as part of the 1996 revision to the Maryland Uniform Commercial Code, Section 3–110(d) enunciates the rules for determining, objectively, the intent of a drawer with respect to an instrument made payable to multiple payees. Therefore, we must first examine Section 3–110(d) to determine whether the stacked payee format in this case is an ambiguous multiple payee designation as contemplated by the Maryland Legislature when it enacted the statute. Section 3–110(d) provides:

(d) If an instrument is payable to two or more persons alternatively, it is payable to any of them and may be negotiated, discharged, or enforced by any or all of them in possession of the instrument. If an instrument is payable to two or more persons not alternatively, it is payable to all of them and may be negotiated, discharged, or enforced only by all of them. If an instrument payable to two or more persons is ambiguous as to whether it is payable to the persons alternatively, the instrument is payable to the persons alternatively.

The Official Comment to that section provides further guidance regarding how to treat a check with multiple payees:

An instrument payable to X or Y is governed by the first sentence of subsection (d). An instrument payable to X and Y is governed by the second sentence of subsection (d). If an instrument is payable to X or Y, either is the payee and if either is in possession that person is the holder and the person entitled to enforce the instrument. . . . If an instrument is payable to X and Y, neither X nor Y acting alone is the person to whom the instrument is payable. . . . The instrument is "payable to an identified person." The "identified person" is X and Y acting jointly.

* * *

The third sentence of subsection (d) is directed to cases in which it is not clear whether an instrument is payable to multiple payees alternatively. In the case of ambiguity, persons dealing with the instrument should be able to rely on the indorsement of a single payee. For example, an instrument payable to X and/or Y is treated like an instrument payable to X or Y.

Thus, Section 3–110(d), confirmed by the explanation in the Official Comment, clearly and unambiguously enunciates the default rule, that, unless checks payable to multiple payees are specifically and clearly made payable jointly or in the alternative, they are ambiguous with respect to how they are to be paid and, therefore, are payable alternatively. Indeed, that is precisely what the last sentence of the section states.

Applying Section 3–110(d) and this default rule to the facts of this case produces a clear result. The subject check was drawn to the order of three payees, listed in stacked format, with no grammatical connector, punctuation or symbol indicating their relationship or how the check was intended to be paid. Therefore, the check was neither clearly payable in the alternative, the payees not being connected by "or" or its equivalent, nor clearly payable jointly, the payees not being joined by "and" or its equivalent. It was, consequently, we hold, "ambiguous as to whether it is payable to the persons alternatively." Accordingly, we further hold, it was proper for Provident Bank to have negotiated the check without the indorsement of Oceanmark. The indorsement of any one of the payees was sufficient.

Judgment for Provident Bank affirmed.

Special Terms

Additional Terms
Generally, if an instrument is to qualify as a negotiable instrument, the person promising or ordering payment may not state undertakings or instructions in addition to the payment of money [3–104(a)(3)]. However, the instrument may include clauses concerning (1) giving, maintaining, or protecting collateral to secure payment; (2) an authorization to confess judgment or to realize on or dispose of collateral; and (3) waiving the benefit of any law intended for the protection or benefit of any person obligated on the instrument.

Thus, a term authorizing the confession of judgment on an instrument when it is due does not affect the negotiability of the instrument. A confession of judgment clause authorizes the creditor to go into court if the debtor defaults and, with the debtor's acquiescence, to have a judgment entered against the debtor. However, some states prohibit confessions of judgment.

Banks and other businesses often use forms of commercial paper that meet their particular needs. These forms may include certain other terms that do not affect the negotiability of an instrument. For example, a note may designate a place of payment without affecting the instrument's negotiability. Where the instrument does not specify a place of payment, the Code sets out rules for ascertaining where payment is to be made [3–111].

Ambiguous Terms
Occasionally, a person may write or receive a check on which the amount written in figures differs from the amount written in words. Or a note may have conflicting terms or an ambiguous term. Where a conflict or an ambiguous term exists, there are general rules of interpretation that are applied to resolve the conflict or ambiguity: Typewritten terms prevail over printed terms, handwritten terms prevail over printed and typewritten terms, and where words and numbers conflict, the words control the numbers [3–114].

The following *Galatia Community State Bank v. Kindy* case involves a check on which there was a difference between the numbers on the check placed there by a check-writing machine and the number written by hand.

Galatia Community State Bank v. Kindy   307 Ark. 467 (Ark. Sup. Ct. 1991)

Galatia Community State Bank honored a check it took for collection for $5,550, which was the amount imprinted by a check-writing machine in the center underlined section of the check commonly used for stating the amount in words. The imprint looked like this:

Registered
No. 497345 **5550 DOL'S 00 CTS

*The impression made by the check-writing machine could be felt on the front and back of the check, and "**5550 DOL'S 00 CTS" was imprinted in red ink. In the box on the right-hand side of the check commonly used for numbers, "6,550.00"* *appeared in handwriting. The check was in partial payment of the purchase price of two engines that Eugene Kindy was buying from the payee on the check, Tony Hicks. Kindy postdated the check by a month and deliberately placed two different amounts on the check because he thought the bank would check with him before paying it. Kindy wanted to be sure that the engines had been delivered to Canada before he paid the $6,550 balance of the purchase price.*

After the check was deposited in the Galatia Bank and Hicks was given $5,550, an employee of the bank altered the "6" by hand to read "5." Because Kindy had stopped payment on the check, the drawee bank refused to pay it to Galatia Bank. Galatia Bank then brought suit against Kindy as the drawer of the check. One of the issues in the lawsuit was how the check should be constructed. The trial court found that the rules on construction provided in the Code were not helpful because they were contradictory. The trial court held in favor of Kindy, and Galatia Bank appealed.

Newbern, Justice

The trial court reviewed Code section 3–118(b) and (c) (1987) which has since been superseded by section 3–114 (1991) but which was in effect at the time in question in this case. The statute provided in relevant part:

3–118. Ambiguous terms and rules of construction. The following rules apply to every instrument:

* * *

(b) Handwritten terms control typewritten and printed terms, and typewritten control printed.

(c) Words control figures except that if the words are ambiguous figures control.

The frustration expressed by the trial court with respect to section 3–118 which stated the applicable rules of construction for negotiable instruments is understandable.

The $5550.00 amount imprinted by the check-writing machine upon the line customarily used for words is expressed in figures and not in words. One question is whether imprinted numbers located where words are customarily placed on a check control figures placed where figures are customarily placed. Another question is whether handwritten figures control printing.

We find both questions satisfactorily answered in *St. Paul Fire & Marine Ins. Co. v. Bank of Salem.* In that case, there was a conflict between an amount imprinted by a check-imprinting machine and numbers expressed in typewritten figures. The court recognized the imprinted amount was not expressed in words but held "the purposes of the UCC are best served by considering an amount imprinted by a check-writing machine as 'words' for the purpose of resolving an ambiguity between an amount and an amount entered upon the line usually used to express the amount in figures." The court quoted from a pre-UCC case, *United States Fidelity and Guaranty Co. v. First National Bank of South Carolina* (1964), as follows:

A prime purpose, as we see it, of making a sum payable when expressed in words controlling over the sum payable expressed in figures is the very fact that words are much

more difficult to alter. The perforated imprinting by a check-writing machine, while fully expressing the sum payable in figures, is even more difficult to successfully alter than a sum payable in written words.

Because a check-imprinting machine's purpose is to protect against alterations, the amount shown on the imprint should control whether the number is in words or figures.

Turning to the question of whether typewriting controls printing, the court in *United States Fidelity and Guaranty Co.* stated:

As the section makes clear, in the event of an ambiguity between printed terms and typewritten terms, the latter would control. We do not consider the impression made by the check imprinter to be "printed terms" under this section.

A conflict between the two amounts on a check would be resolved by section 3–118 which states that words control figures. Arguably, the amount imprinted by the check-writing machine upon the line customarily expressing the amount in words, is expressed in figures. . . . We think, however, that the purposes of the UCC are best served by considering an amount imprinted by a check-writing machine as "words" for the purpose of resolving an ambiguity between that amount and an amount entered upon the line usually used to express the amount in figures.

Although the court did not say specifically that it regarded the portion written by the check-writing machine as the equivalent of handwriting, that is the clear effect of the decision.

In *United States v. Hibernia National Bank*, a typed numerical amount was located in the place customarily used for words. The amount conflicted with the amount located in the place customarily used for figures. The court found the typed amount controlling despite the fact it was not expressed in words.

Judgment for Kindy reversed on other grounds.

———

Note: Although, as the court notes, this case was decided under the original version of Article 3, the dilemma posed, and the conclusion reached by the court on the construction of the check, would likely be the same under Revised Article 3.

CONCEPT REVIEW

Requirements for Negotiability

Requirement	Basic Rules
Must Be in Writing	1. The instrument may be handwritten, typed, or printed.
Must Be Signed by the Maker or Drawer	1. Person issuing the instrument must sign with intent of validating his or her obligation. 2. Person issuing may affix the signature in a variety of ways–for example, by word, mark, or rubber stamp. 3. Agent or authorized representative may supply the "signature."
Must Contain a Promise or Order to Pay	1. Promise must be more than acknowledgment of a debt. 2. Order requirement is met if the drawer issues an instruction to "pay."
Promise or Order Must Be Unconditional	1. Entire obligation must be found in the instrument itself and not in another document or documents. 2. Payment cannot be conditioned on the occurrence of an event.
Must Call for Payment of a Fixed Amount of Money	1. Must be able to ascertain the principal from the face of the instrument. 2. May contain a clause providing for payment of interest or other charges such as collection or attorney's fees.
Must Be Payable in Money	1. Obligation must be payable in a medium of exchange authorized or adopted by a government or by an international organization or agreement between two or more nations. 2. Maker or drawer cannot have the option to pay in something other than money.
Must Be Payable on Demand or at a Definite Time	1. Requirement is met if instrument says it is payable on demand or, if no time for payment is stated, it is payable on demand. 2. Requirement is met if it is payable on a stated date, at a fixed time after a stated date, or a fixed time "after sight." 3. Instrument may contain an acceleration clause or a clause allowing maker or holder to extend the payment date.
Generally Must Be Payable to Bearer or to Order	1. Bearer requirement is met if instrument is payable "to bearer" or "to cash." 2. Order requirement is met if instrument is payable "to the order of" a specified person or persons. 3. Exception from requirement is made for instruments meeting both the definition of a check and all the other requirements for a negotiable instrument.
May Not State Any Other Undertaking or Instruction by the Person Promising or Ordering Payment to Do Any Act in Addition to the Payment of Money	1. However, it may contain (*a*) an undertaking or power to give, maintain, or protect collateral to secure payment, (*b*) an authorization or power to the holder to confess judgment or realize on or dispose of collateral, or (*c*) a waiver of the benefit of any law intended for the advantage or protection of an obligor on the instrument.

Problems and Problem Cases

1. Is the following instrument a note, a check, or a draft? Why? If it is not a check, how would you have to change it to make it a check?

   To: Arthur Adams January 1, 2010
   TEN DAYS AFTER DATE PAY TO THE ORDER OF:

   Bernie Brown
   THE SUM OF: Ten thousand and no/100 DOLLARS
   SIGNED: Carl Clark

2. Frank agrees to build a garage for Sarah for $15,000. Sarah offers either to sign a contract showing her obligation to pay Frank $15,000 or to sign a negotiable promissory note for $15,000 payable to the order of

Frank. Would you advise Frank to ask for the contract or the promissory note? Explain.

3. Wiley, Tate & Irby, buyers and sellers of used cars, sold several autos to Houston Auto Sales. Houston wrote out the order for payment on the outside of several envelopes. He signed them and they were drawn on his bank, Peoples Bank & Trust Co., to be paid on the demand of Wiley, Tate & Irby. Can the envelopes qualify as negotiable instruments?

4. A handwritten note provided as follows:

> I, Robert Harrison, owe Peter Jacob $25,000 (twenty-five thousand dollars) as of 3/27/10 for the following:
>   (1) $15,000 for Caterpillar loader
>   (2) $5,000 for a loan
>   (3) $5,000 for a tag-a-long trailer.

Would this instrument qualify as a negotiable instrument?

5. Holly Hill Acres, Ltd., executed a promissory note and mortgage and delivered them to Rogers. The note contained the following stipulation:

> This note with interest is secured by a mortgage on real estate of even herewith, made by the maker hereof in favor of the said payee, and shall be construed and enforced according to the laws of the State of Florida. The terms of said mortgage are by this reference made a part hereof.

Is the note a negotiable instrument?

6. Strickland ordered a swimming pool from Kafko Manufacturing and gave it a check for the purchase price that included the following words in the space following the word *memo*: "for pool kit to be delivered." Is the check negotiable?

7. Holliday made out a promissory note to Anderson, leaving the date of payment of the note blank. Anderson filled in the words "on demand" in the blank without Holliday's knowledge. Does this alter the rights or obligations of the parties?

8. Darryl Young presented five photocopied checks to the Lynnwood Check-X-Change on five different days between June 13 and June 21. Lynwood cashed the first four checks presented. The fifth check, which was presented on a Saturday, was drawn on a different account from the first four checks and was payable on the following Monday. Lynnwood's practice was to cash checks on Saturday that are dated the following Monday. Young was convicted of five counts of forgery. On appeal, Young argued that the postdated check was not a legal instrument for purposes of the forgery statute. The crime of forgery requires an instrument that, if genuine, may have legal effect or be the foundation of legal liability. Young argued that the postdated check did not meet this requirement "because the time for payment had not arrived and thus the check could not have created any legal liability on the part of any person at that time." If a check is postdated, can it qualify as a negotiable instrument and create legal liability?

9. Emmett McDonald, acting as the personal representative of the estate of Marion Cahill, wrote a check payable to himself, individually, on the estate checking account in the Commercial Bank & Trust Company. The instrument contained an obvious variance between the numbers and the written words that indicated the amount of the check. It said: "Pay to the order of Emmett E. McDonald $10075.00 Ten hundred seventy five . . . Dollars." The bank paid the $10,075 sum stated by the numerals to McDonald, who absconded with the funds. Yates, the successor representative, sued the bank on behalf of the estate to recover the $9,000 difference between that amount and the $1,075 that was written out. Did the bank pay the correct amount on the check?

Online Research

Accessing Information from Your Bank

Use the Internet to locate the Web site for the bank or financial institution where you maintain a checking account. From the Web site ascertain the following information: (1) what is the monthly fee (if any) for maintaining the type of checking account you maintain? (2) does the institution charge a fee for each check you use or if you exceed a certain number of transactions per month? (3) what rate of interest does the institution pay on a $10,000, five-year certificate of deposit (CD)? and (4) what rate of interest does the institution charge on secured personal loans such as a loan for the purchase of a new car?

chapter 32

NEGOTIATION AND HOLDER IN DUE COURSE

Rachel Allen purchases a used Honda from Friendly Fred's Used Cars, paying $1,500 down and signing a promissory note in which she promises to pay $2,000 to Fred or to his order 12 months from the date of the note with interest at 8.5 percent. Fred assures Rachel that the car is in good condition and has never been involved in an accident. Fred indorses (signs) his name on the back of the promissory note and discounts (assigns) the note to Factors, Inc. Subsequently, Rachel discovers that, contrary to Fred's assurance, the Honda had in fact been involved in an accident that caused a front-end alignment problem. When Factors notifies her of the assignment to it of the note and asks for payment on the due date, Rachel wants to assert a defense of failure of consideration or breach of contract (warranty) against full payment of the note.

Among the legal issues raised in this scenario are:

- When Fred transferred the promissory note to Factors after signing his name to the back of it, what rights did Factors obtain?
- Will Rachel be able to assert a defense of failure of consideration or breach of contract against full payment of the note to Factors?
- If the promissory note contained the clause required by the Federal Trade Commission in consumer notes or installment sales contracts, would it change Rachel's rights?

THE PRECEDING CHAPTER DISCUSSED the nature and benefits of negotiable instruments. It also outlined the requirements an instrument must meet to qualify as a negotiable instrument and thus possess the qualities that allow it to be accepted as a substitute for money.

This chapter focuses on negotiation—the process by which rights to a negotiable instrument pass from one person to another. Commonly, this involves an indorsement and transfer of the instrument. This chapter also develops the requirements that a transferee of a negotiable instrument must meet to qualify as a holder in due course and thus attain special rights under negotiable instruments law. These rights, which put a holder in due course in an enhanced position compared to an assignee of a contract, are discussed in some detail.

In this chapter, you also will consider whether it would be ethical to incur a gambling debt, to issue a check or other negotiable instrument in satisfaction of the debt, and then assert the defense of illegality against payment of the instrument.

Negotiation

Nature of Negotiation
Under Revised Article 3, **negotiation** is the transfer of possession (whether voluntary or involuntary) of a negotiable instrument by a person (other than the issuer) to another person who becomes its *holder* [3–201]. A person is a **holder** if she is in possession of an instrument (1) that is payable to bearer or (2) made payable to an identified person and she is that identified person [1–201(20)].[1]

For example, when an employer gives an employee, Susan Adams, a paycheck payable "to the order of Susan Adams," she is the holder of the check because she is in possession of an instrument payable to an identified person (Susan Adams) and she is that person. When she indorses (writes her name) on the back of the check and

---

[1]The numbers in brackets refer to sections of the Uniform Commercial Code (UCC), which is reproduced in the appendix.

exchanges it for cash and merchandise at Ace Grocery, she has negotiated the check to the grocery store and the store is now the holder because it is in possession by transfer of a check and unless she specifies the grocery store by name, the check now is payable to bearer. Similarly, if Susan Adams indorsed the check "Pay to the Order of Ace Grocery, Susan Adams" and transferred it to the grocery store, it would be a holder through the negotiation of the order check to it. The grocery store would be in possession of an instrument payable to an identified person (Ace Grocery) and is the person identified in the check.

In certain circumstances, Revised Article 3 allows a person to become a holder by negotiation even though the transfer of possession is involuntary. For example, if a negotiable instrument is payable to bearer and is stolen by Tom Thief or found by Fred Finder, Thief or Finder becomes the holder when he obtains possession. The involuntary transfer of possession of a bearer instrument results in a negotiation to Thief or Finder.

Formal Requirements for Negotiation

The formal requirements for negotiation are very simple. If an instrument is payable to the order of a specific payee, it is called **order paper** and it can be negotiated by transfer of possession of the instrument after indorsement by the person specified [3–201(b)].

For example, if Rachel's father gives her a check payable "to the order of Rachel Stern," then Rachel can negotiate the check by indorsing her name on the back of the check and giving it to the person to whom she wants to transfer it. Note that the check is order paper, not because the word *order* appears on the check but rather because it named a specific payee, Rachel Stern.

If an instrument is payable "to bearer" or "to cash," it is called **bearer paper** and negotiating it is even simpler. An instrument payable to bearer may be negotiated by transfer of possession alone [3–201(b)]. Thus, if someone gives you a check that is made payable "to the order of cash," you can negotiate it simply by giving it to the person to whom you wish to transfer it. No indorsement is necessary to negotiate an instrument payable to bearer. However, the person who takes the instrument may ask for an indorsement for her protection. By indorsing the check, you agree to be liable for its payment to that person if it is not paid by the drawee bank when it is presented for payment. This liability will be discussed in Chapter 33, Liability of Parties.

Nature of Indorsement An indorsement is made by adding the signature of the holder of the instru-

ment to the instrument, usually on the back of it, either alone or with other words. **Indorsement** is defined to mean "a signature (other than that of a maker, drawer or acceptor) that alone or accompanied by other words, is made on an instrument for purpose of (i) negotiating the instrument, (ii) restricting payment of the instrument, or (iii) incurring indorser's liability on the instrument" [3–204(a)]. The negotiation and restriction of payment aspects of indorsements will be discussed below; indorser's liability will be covered in the next chapter.

The signature constituting an indorsement can be supplied or written either by the holder or by someone who is authorized to sign on behalf of the holder. For example, a check payable to "H&H Meat Market" might be indorsed "H&H Meat Market by Jane Frank, President," if Jane is authorized to do this on behalf of the market.

Wrong or Misspelled Name When indorsing an instrument, the holder should spell his name in the same way as it appears on the instrument. If the holder's name is misspelled or wrong, then legally the indorsement can be made either in his name or in the name that is on the instrument. However, any person who pays the instrument or otherwise gives value for it may require the indorser to sign both names [3–204(d)].

Suppose Joan Ash is issued a check payable to the order of "Joanne Ashe." She may indorse the check as either "Joan Ash" or "Joanne Ashe." However, if she takes the check to a bank to cash, the bank may require her to sign both "Joanne Ashe" and "Joan Ash."

Checks Deposited without Indorsement Occasionally, when a customer deposits a check to her account with a bank, she may forget to indorse the check. It is common practice for depositary banks to receive unindorsed checks under what are known as "lock-box" arrangements with customers who receive a high volume of checks. Normally, a check payable to the order of an identified person would require the indorsement of that person in order for a negotiation to the depositary bank to take place and for it to become a holder. Under the original Article 3, the depositary bank, in most cases, had the right to supply the customer's indorsement. Instead of actually signing the customer's name to the check as the indorsement, the bank might just stamp on it that it was deposited by the customer or credited to her account. Banks did not have the right to put the customer's indorsement on a check that the customer has deposited if the check specifically required the payee's signature. Insurance and government checks commonly require the payee's signature.

The revision to Article 3 and the conforming amendments to Articles 1 and 4 address the situation where a check is deposited in a depository bank without indorsement differently. The depository bank becomes a holder of an item delivered to it for collection, whether or not it is indorsed by the customer, if the customer at the time of delivery qualified as a holder [4–205]. Concomitantly, the depository bank warrants to other collecting banks, the payor bank (drawee), and the drawer that it paid the amount of the item to the customer or deposited the amount to the customer's account.

Transfer of Order Instrument

Except for the special provisions concerning depository banks, if an order instrument is transferred without indorsement, the instrument has not been negotiated and the transferee cannot qualify as a holder. For example, Sue Brown gives a check payable "to the order of Susan Brown" to a drugstore in payment for some cosmetics. Until Sue indorses the check, she has not "negotiated" it and the druggist could not qualify as a "holder" of the check.

Transfer of an instrument, whether or not the transfer is a negotiation, vests in the transferee, such as the drugstore, any right of Sue, the transferor, to enforce the instrument. However, the transferee cannot obtain the rights of a holder in due course (discussed later in this chapter) if he is engaged in any fraud or illegality affecting the instrument. Unless otherwise agreed, if an instrument is transferred for value but without a required indorsement, the transferee has the right to obtain the unqualified indorsement of the transferor; however, the "negotiation" takes place only when the transferor applies her indorsement [3–203(c)].

The *Town of Freeport* case, which follows, illustrates these principles.

Town of Freeport v. Ring   727 A.2d 901 (Maine Sup. Jud. Ct. 1999)

Thornton Ring was the owner of real property located on Main Street in Freeport, Maine. In August 1994, the Town sent Ring a letter noting that his 1993–1994 real estate taxes were unpaid and notified him of the Town's intent to file a lien on the property if payment was not received within 30 days. The taxes remained unpaid and a tax lien was filed on the property. On January 26, 1996, because a portion of the taxes still remained unpaid, the Town sent a Notice of Impending Foreclosure of the Tax Lien Certificate to Ring by certified mail, advising him that the tax lien would be deemed to be foreclosed on February 27, 1996. Ring subsequently was in default for his 1994–1995 taxes and similar notices were sent.

In January 1997, Ring delivered to the Town a check in the amount of $11,347.09. The check was issued by Advest, Inc., and made payable to the order of Thornton D. Ring. The back of the check was inscribed as follows:

Payable to Town of Freeport
Property Taxes
2 Main St[.]

The check was accompanied by a letter, signed by Ring and dated January 20, 1997, which reads, "I have paid $11,347.09 of real estate taxes and request the appropriate action to redeem the corresponding property." On February 3, 1997, Ring received a letter from the Town which explained that the Town was returning the check because the 1994 tax lien on the property had matured in 1996.

The Town filed suit seeking a declaratory judgment that it had good title to the Main Street property. One of the issues was whether the delivery of the check by Ring constituted payment of his outstanding taxes.

Clifford, Justice

With respect to a check that is made payable to the order of a specific person, negotiation occurs, and the person receiving the check becomes a holder of a negotiable instrument, if possession of the check is transferred and the check is indorsed by the transferor. An indorsement is a signature of someone other than the maker, or some other designation identifying the indorser, that is made on an instrument for the purpose of negotiating the instrument. *Kelly v. Central Bank & Trust Co.* (writing on back of check which reads "For deposit only" to an account other than the payee's and without payee's signature is not an effective indorsement). If negotiation occurs and the holder qualifies as a holder in due course, the holder can demand payment of the instrument subject only to real defenses.

The check Ring sent to the Town was issued by Advest, Inc., payable to the order of Thornton D. Ring. Because it was payable to Ring's order, the check could only be negotiated by Ring through indorsement and transfer of possession. Ring's signature, however, does not appear on the back of the check. The words that do appear on the back of the check—"Payable to Town of Freeport[/]Property Taxes[/]2 Main St[.]"—do not identify Ring. The words only indicate to whom the instrument should have been payable had the check been properly indorsed. Thus, the writing is an incomplete attempt to create a special indorsement. A special indorsement is an indorsement that identifies a person to whom the indorser is making the check payable.

The statement included within the letter accompanying the check does not serve as a valid indorsement either. In determining whether an instrument is properly indorsed, any papers affixed to the instrument are considered part of the instrument. See section 3–204(1). This language specifically references only "affixed" documents. Courts interpreting this language have concluded that a signature on a separate, unattached piece of paper is not an indorsement of the instrument. Ring does not dispute that there is no evidence on record to suggest that the letter was physically attached to the check.

Relying on sections 3–203(3) and 3–203(2), Ring also contends that even in the absence of an indorsement, the check should have been accepted as payment of his outstanding taxes because the Town (1) had a statutory right to demand an indorsement of the check, or (2) was entitled to enforce the instrument without the indorsement. Section 3–203(3) provides that "if an instrument is transferred for value and the transferee does not become a holder because of lack of indorsement by the transferor, the transferee has a specifically enforceable right to the unqualified indorsement of the transferor. . . ." Section 3–203(2) provides "Transfer of an instrument, whether or not the transfer is a negotiation, vests in the transferee any right of the transferor to enforce the instrument."

Even if the Town could demand an indorsement pursuant to section 3–203(3), negotiation does not occur until the indorsement is made. See section 3–203(3). Thus, at the time the check was received, the Town had a right to demand an indorsement, but could not go to the bank to demand payment of the check. Pursuant to section 3–203(2), the bank also had the right to enforce the instrument as the transferee of an instrument from a holder. That right, however, could be enforced only through a judicial proceeding. Such contingent rights to receive payment are not sufficient to redeem property subject to a municipal tax lien. Checks are meant to be the functional equivalent of cash when they are properly issued and negotiated. If the Town has to institute a judicial proceeding to receive the cash equivalent of the check, the check has not served its purpose. The unindorsed check presented to the Town is not the type of payment the redemption option of the tax lien statute contemplates.

Judgment for Town affirmed.

Indorsements

Effects of an Indorsement
There are three functions to an indorsement. First, an indorsement is necessary in order for the negotiation of an instrument that is payable to the order of a specified person. Thus, if a check is payable "to the order of James Lee," James must indorse the check before it can be negotiated. Second, the form of the indorsement that the indorser uses also affects future attempts to negotiate the instrument. For example, if James indorses it "Pay to the order of Sarah Hill," Sarah must indorse it before it can be negotiated further.

Third, an indorsement generally makes a person liable on the instrument. By indorsing an instrument, a person incurs an obligation to pay the instrument if the person primarily liable on it (for example, the maker of a note) does not pay it. We discuss the contractual liability of indorsers in Chapter 33. In this chapter, we discuss the effect of an indorsement on further negotiation of an instrument.

Kinds of Indorsements
There are three basic kinds of indorsements: (1) special, (2) blank, and (3) restrictive. In addition, an indorsement may be "qualified."

Special Indorsement A **special indorsement** contains the signature of the indorser along with words indicating to whom, or to whose order, the instrument is payable. For example, if a check is drawn "Pay to the Order of Marcia Morse" and Marcia indorses it "Pay to the Order of Sam Smith, Marcia Morse," or "Pay to Sam Smith, Marcia Morse," it has been indorsed with a special indorsement. An instrument that is indorsed with a special indorsement remains "order paper." It can be negotiated only with the indorsement of the person specified [3–205(a)]. In this example, Sam Smith must indorse the check before he can negotiate it to someone else.

Blank Indorsement If an indorser merely signs his name and does not specify to whom the instrument is payable, he has indorsed the instrument **in blank.** For example, if a check drawn "Pay to the Order of Natalie

Owens" is indorsed "Natalie Owens" by Natalie, Natalie has indorsed it in blank. An instrument indorsed in blank is payable to the bearer (person in possession of it) and from that act is "bearer paper." As such, the bearer negotiates it by transfer alone and no further indorsement is necessary for negotiation [3–205(b)].

If Natalie indorsed the check in blank and gave it to Kevin Foley, Kevin would have the right to convert the blank indorsement into a special indorsement [3–205(c)]. He could do this by writing the words "Pay to the Order of Kevin Foley" above Natalie's indorsement. Then Kevin would have to indorse the check before it could be further negotiated.

If Kevin took the check indorsed in blank to a bank and presented it for payment or for collection, the bank normally would ask him to indorse the check. It asks not because it needs his indorsement for the check to be negotiated to it; the check indorsed in blank can be negotiated merely by delivering it to the bank cashier. Rather, the bank asks for his indorsement because it wants to make him liable on the check if it is not paid when the bank sends it to the drawee bank for payment. Chapter 33, Liability of Parties, discusses the liability of indorsers.

Restrictive Indorsement A **restrictive indorsement** is one that specifies the purpose of the indorsement or specifies the use to be made of the instrument. Among the more common restrictive indorsements are:

1. Indorsements for deposit. For example, "For Deposit Only" or "For Deposit to My Account at First National Bank."

2. Indorsements for collection, which are commonly put on by banks involved in the collection process. For example, "Pay any bank, banker, or trust company" or "For collection only."

3. Indorsements indicating that the indorsement is for the benefit of someone other than the person to whom it is payable. For example, "Pay to Arthur Attorney in Trust for Mark Minor."

Generally, the person who takes an instrument with a restrictive indorsement must pay or apply any money or other value he gives for the instrument consistently with the indorsement. In the case of a check indorsed "for deposit" or "for collection," any person other than a bank who purchases the check is considered to have **converted** the check unless (1) the indorser received the amount paid for it or (2) the bank applied the amount of the check consistently with the indorsement (e.g., deposited it to the indorser's account). Similarly, a depositary bank (a bank that takes an item for collection) or payor bank (the drawee bank) that takes an instrument for deposit or for immediate payment over the counter that has been indorsed "for deposit" or "for collection" will be liable for conversion unless the indorser received the amount paid for the instrument or the proceeds or the bank applied the amount consistently with the indorsement [3–206(c)].[2]

By way of illustration, assume that Robert Franks has indorsed his paycheck "For Deposit to My Account No. 4068933 at First Bank." While on his way to the bank he loses the check, and Fred Finder finds it. If Finder tries to cash the check at a check-cashing service, the service must ensure that any value it gives for the check either is deposited to Franks's account at First Bank or is received by Franks. If it gives the money to Finder, it will be liable to Franks for converting his check. This principle is illustrated in *Lehigh Presbytery,* which involves a bank that failed to apply value given for checks consistently with restrictive indorsements on the checks.

[2]Otherwise, a payor bank as well as an intermediary bank may disregard the indorsement and is not liable if the proceeds of the instrument are not received by the indorser or applied consistently with the indorsement [3–206(c)(4)].

Lehigh Presbytery v. Merchants Bancorp. Inc.
17 UCC Rep. 2d 163 (Penn. Super. Ct. 1991)

Mary Ann Hunsberger was hired by the Lehigh Presbytery as a secretary/bookkeeper. In this capacity, she was responsible for opening the Presbytery's mail, affixing a rubber-stamp indorsement to checks received by the Presbytery, and depositing the checks into the Presbytery's account at Merchants Bancorp, Inc. Over a period of more than five years, Hunsberger deposited into her own account 153 of these checks. Each check was indorsed: "For Deposit Only To The Credit of Presbytery of Lehigh, Ernest Hutcheson, Treas." The bank credited the checks to Hunsberger's account, despite the rubber stamp restrictive indorsement, because it relied solely on the account number handwritten on the deposit slips submitted by Hunsberger with the checks at the time of deposit. Hunsberger obtained the deposit slips in the lobby of the bank, wrote the proper account title, "Lehigh Presbytery," but inserted her own account number rather than the account number of her employer.

When Lehigh Presbytery discovered the diversionary scheme, it sued the bank to recover the funds credited to Hunsberger's account. The primary issue in the case was whether the bank was bound to follow the restrictive indorsements on the 153 checks that it instead had deposited to the personal account of Hunsberger. The trial court ruled in favor of the bank and Lehigh Presbytery appealed.

McEwen, Judge

UCC Section 3–205 provides:

An indorsement is restrictive which either:

. . .

(3) includes the words "for collection," "for deposit," "pay any bank," or like terms signifying a purpose of deposit or collection; or

. . .

It is undisputed that the indorsement stamped on each check by Ms. Hunsberger is a restrictive indorsement within the meaning of section 3–205.

Section 3–206 of the UCC addresses the effect of such an indorsement and provides, in pertinent part:

(c) Conditional or specified purpose indorsement.—Except for an intermediary bank, any transferee under an indorsement which is conditional or includes the words "for collection," "for deposit," "Pay any bank," or like terms (section 3–205(1) and (3) (relating to restrictive indorsements) must

pay or apply any value given by him for or on the security of the instrument consistently with the indorsement and to the extent he does he becomes a holder for value.

Thus, the UCC mandates application of the value of the checks consistently with the indorsement, that is, for deposit to Lehigh Presbytery's account.

Courts considering the significance of a restrictive indorsement have consistently concluded that the UCC imposes an unwaivable obligation upon the bank to follow the indorsement. New York State's highest court has held that "[t]he presence of a restriction imposes upon the depositary bank an obligation not to accept that item other than in accord with the restriction. By disregarding the restriction, it not only subjects itself to liability for any losses resulting from its actions, but it also passes up what may be the best opportunity to prevent the fraud."

Judgment reversed in favor of Lehigh Presbytery.

Note: Although this case was decided under the original version of Article 3, the same result would be expected under Revised Article 3.

Some indorsements indicate payment to the indorsee as an agent, trustee, or fiduciary. A person who takes an instrument containing such an indorsement from the indorsee may pay the proceeds to the indorsee without regard to whether the indorsee violates a fiduciary duty to the indorser *unless* he is on *notice* of any breach of fiduciary duty that the indorser may be committing [3–206(d)]. A person would have such notice if he took the instrument in any transaction that benefited the indorsee personally [3–307]. Suppose a person takes a check indorsed to "Arthur Attorney in Trust for Mark Minor." The money given for the check should be put in Mark Minor's trust account. A person would not be justified in taking the check in exchange for a television set that he knew Attorney was acquiring for his own—rather than Minor's—use.

There are two other kinds of indorsements that the original Article 3 treated as restrictive indorsements but that the revised Article 3 no longer considers as restrictive indorsements. They are:

1. Indorsements purporting to prohibit further negotiation. For example, "Pay to Carl Clark Only."

2. Conditional indorsements, which indicate that they are effective only if the payee satisfies a certain condition. For example, "Pay to Bernard Builder Only if He Completes Construction on My House by November 1, 2010."

Under Revised Article 3, any indorsement that purports to limit payment to a particular person, or to prohibit further transfer or negotiation of the instrument, is not effective to prevent further transfer or negotiation [3–206(a)]. Thus, if a note is indorsed "Pay to Carl Clark Only" and given to Clark, he may negotiate the note to subsequent holders who may ignore the restriction on the indorsement.

Indorsements that state a condition to the right of the indorsee to receive payment do not affect the right of the indorsee to enforce the instrument. Any person who pays the instrument or takes it for value or for collection may disregard the condition. Moreover, the rights and liabilities of the person are not affected by whether the condition has been fulfilled [3–206(b)].

Qualified Indorsement A **qualified indorsement** is one where the indorser disclaims her liability to make the

The Global Business Environment

Convention on International Bills of Exchange and International Promissory Notes

In 1988 the Convention on International Bills of Exchange and International Promissory Notes was adopted by the United Nations. The Convention is applicable to drafts and notes but not to checks. Under the Convention, a bill of exchange is an order to pay money while a promissory note is a promise to pay money. To be covered, they must have the attributes of negotiability. They also must be international in nature in that at least two of the places where their operations occur—such as the address of the drawer or promissory, the address of the payee, or the place of payment—must be in different countries. The Convention also requires that the parties must affirmatively elect to be covered by the Convention by placing a specified legend on the instrument.

In drafting the Convention, the drafters had to try to accommodate or harmonize differences between civil and common law countries concerning negotiable instruments. A major difference between the two systems is how they deal with forged indorsements. Under the common law and UCC Articles 3 and 4, a forged indorsement is not effective to negotiate an instrument to the indorsee while under the civil law it is. Under the civil law, the indorsee takes title to the instrument and acquires the rights of a holder, and payment to the indorsee discharges makers and drawers. As discussed in this and the following chapter, under the UCC, an indorsee taking an instrument with a forged indorsement does not gain these rights and a maker or drawer is not discharged by making payment to that indorsee. The resolution of these differences in the Convention is too complex to discuss in this textbook.

---

instrument good if the maker or drawer defaults on it. Words such as "Without Recourse" are used to qualify an indorsement. They can be used with either a blank indorsement or a special indorsement and thus make it a qualified blank indorsement or a qualified special indorsement. The use of a qualified indorsement does not change the negotiable nature of the instrument. Its effect is to eliminate the contractual liability of the particular indorser. Chapter 33, Liability of Parties, will discuss this liability in detail.

Rescission of Indorsement Negotiation is effective to transfer an instrument even if the negotiation is (1) made by a minor, a corporation exceeding its powers, or any other person without contractual capacity; (2) obtained by fraud, duress, or mistake of any kind; (3) made in breach of duty; or (4) part of an illegal transaction. A negotiation made under the preceding circumstances is subject to **rescission** before the instrument has been negotiated to a transferee who can qualify as a holder in due course or a person paying the instrument in good faith and without knowledge of the factual basis for rescission or other remedy [3–202]. The situation in such instances is analogous to a sale of goods where the sale has been induced by fraud or misrepresentation. In such a case, the seller may rescind the sale and recover the goods, provided that the seller acts before the goods are resold to a bona fide purchaser for value.

Holder in Due Course

A person who qualifies as a holder in due course of a negotiable instrument gets special rights. Normally, the transferee of an instrument—like the assignee of a contract—gets only those rights in the instrument that are held by the person from whom he got the instrument. But a holder in due course can get better rights. A holder in due course takes a negotiable instrument free of all **personal defenses, claims to the instrument,** and **claims in recoupment** either of the obligor or of a third party. A holder in due course does not take free of the **real defenses,** which go to the validity of the instrument or of claims that develop after he becomes a holder. We develop the differences between "personal" and "real defenses" in more detail later in this chapter and also explain claims to the instrument and claims in recoupment. The following example illustrates the advantage that a holder in due course of a negotiable instrument may have.

Assume that Carl Carpenter contracts with Helen Hawkins to build her a garage for $18,500, payable on October 1 when he expects to complete the garage. Assume further that Carpenter assigns his right to the $18,500 to First National Bank in order to obtain money for materials. If the bank tries to collect the money from Hawkins on October 1 but Carpenter has not finished building the garage, then Hawkins may assert the fact that the garage is

CONCEPT REVIEW

Indorsements (Assume a check is payable "To The Order of Mark Smith.")

Type	Example	Consequences
Blank	Mark Smith	1. Satisfies the indorsement requirement for the negotiation of order paper.
		2. The instrument becomes bearer paper and can be negotiated by delivery alone.
		3. The indorser becomes obligated on the instrument. (See Chapter 33, Liability of Parties.)
Special	Pay to the Order of Joan Brown, Mark Smith	1. Satisfies the indorsement requirement for the negotiation of order paper.
		2. The instrument remains order paper and Joan Brown's indorsement is required for further negotiation.
		3. The indorser becomes obligated on the instrument. (See Chapter 33.)
Restrictive	For deposit only to my account in First American Bank, Mark Smith	1. Satisfies the indorsement requirement for the negotiation of order paper.
		2. The person who pays value for the instrument is obligated to pay it consistent with the indorsement (i.e., to pay it into Mark Smith's account at First American Bank).
		3. The indorser becomes obligated on the instrument. (See Chapter 33.)
Qualified	Mark Smith (without recourse)	1. Satisfies the indorsement requirement for negotiation of order paper.
		2. Eliminates the indorser's obligation. (See Chapter 33.)

not complete as a defense to paying the bank. As assignee of a simple contract, the bank has only those rights that its assignor, Carpenter, has and is subject to all claims and defenses that Hawkins has against Carpenter.

Now assume that instead of simply signing a contract with Hawkins, Carpenter had Homeowner give him a negotiable promissory note in the amount of $18,500 payable to the order of Carpenter on October 1 and that Carpenter then negotiated the note to the bank. If the bank is able to qualify as a holder in due course, it may collect the $18,500 from Hawkins on October 1 even though she might have a personal defense against payment of the note because Carpenter had not completed the work on the garage. Hawkins cannot assert that personal defense against a holder in due course. She would have to pay the note to the bank and then independently seek to recover from Carpenter for breach of their agreement. The bank's improved position is due to its status as a holder in due course of a negotiable instrument. If the instrument in question was not negotiable, or if the bank could not qualify as a holder in due course, then it would be in the same position as the assignee of a simple contract and would be subject to Homeowner's personal defense.

We turn now to a discussion of the requirements that must be met for the possessor of a negotiable instrument to qualify as a holder in due course.

General Requirements   In order to become a **holder in due course,** a person who takes a negotiable instrument must be a *holder,* and take the instrument:

1. For *value.*

2. In *good faith.*

3. *Without notice* that is *overdue* or has been *dishonored* or that there is any uncured default with respect to payment of another instrument issued as part of the same series.

4. *Without notice that the instrument contains an unauthorized signature or has been altered.*

5. *Without notice of any claim of a property or possessory interest in it.*

6. *Without notice* that any party has any *defense against it* or claim in *recoupment to it* (3–302[a][2]).

In addition, revised Article 3 requires "that the instrument when issued or negotiated to the holder does not bear such *apparent evidence of forgery or alteration* or is not otherwise so *irregular* or *incomplete* as to call into question its authenticity" [3–302(a)(1)].

If a person who takes a negotiable instrument does not meet these requirements, he is not a holder in due course. Then the person is in the same position as an assignee of a contract.

Holder

To be a **holder** of a negotiable instrument, a person must have possession of an instrument that is either payable to "bearer" or that is payable to him. For example, if Teresa Gonzales is given a check by her grandmother that is made payable "to the order of Teresa Gonzales," Teresa is a holder of the check because it is made out to her. If Teresa indorses the check "Pay to the order of Ames Hardware, Teresa Gonzales" and gives it to Ames Hardware in payment for some merchandise, then Ames Hardware is the holder of the check. Ames Hardware is a holder because it is in possession of a check that is indorsed to its order. If Ames Hardware indorses the check "Ames Hardware" and deposits it in its account at First National Bank, the bank becomes the holder. The bank is in possession of an instrument that is indorsed in blank and thus is payable to bearer.

It is important that all indorsements on the instrument at the time it is payable to the order of someone are *authorized indorsements*. With limited exceptions (discussed later), a forged indorsement is not an effective indorsement and prevents a person from becoming a holder.

To be a holder, a person must have a complete chain of authorized indorsements. Suppose the Internal Revenue Service mails to Robert Washington an income tax refund check payable to him. Tom Turner steals the check from Washington's mailbox, signs (indorses) "Robert Washington" on the back of the check, and cashes it at a shoe store. The shoe store is not a holder of the check because its transferor, Turner, was not a holder and because it needs Washington's signature to have a good chain of authorized indorsements. Robert Washington has to indorse the check in order for there to be a valid chain of indorsements. Turner's signature is not effective for this purpose because Washington did not authorize him to sign Washington's name to the check [1–201(20); 3–403(a); 3–416(a)(2)].

The *Golden Years Nursing Home* case illustrates that a party in possession of a check indorsed in blank is a holder of the instrument.

Golden Years Nursing Home, Inc. v. Gabbard
682 N.E. 2d 731 (Ohio Ct. App. 1996)

From 1972 until 1991, Nancy Gabbard, the office manager for the Golden Years Nursing Home, received at the nursing home Social Security checks drawn on the United States Treasury and made payable either to individual patients or to "Golden Years Nursing Home for [an individual patient]." From 1986 until 1991, Gabbard engaged in an embezzling scheme whereby she would have certain patients indorse their own checks in blank; that is, each patient would sign his own name on the back of the check placing no restrictions on the manner in which the check could subsequently be negotiated. Gabbard would then cash the checks and either keep the cash or deposit the funds into her personal bank account.

In 1992, after Gabbard's scheme was discovered, Golden Years brought suit against Gabbard and also against the Star Bank Corporation where the checks had been cashed. The patients had in other documents assigned their interests in the checks to Golden Years, and the claim against the bank alleged that it had converted Golden Years' property by cashing checks with forged indorsements. One of the issues in the lawsuit was whether the checks had been properly negotiated to Star Bank. The trial court granted summary judgment to Golden Years, finding that the bank was not a holder in due course because the checks contained "forged indorsements." Star Bank appealed.

Per Curiam

The Star Bank argues that the genuine indorsement of the individual payee designated on face of an instrument cannot constitute an unauthorized signature or a forged indorsement. Under the circumstances presented in this case, we agree.

Under the Ohio Uniform Commercial Code, the term "unauthorized signature" "includes both a forgery and a signature made by an agent exceeding his actual or apparent authority," i.e., it occurs in the context of an agency relationship. Golden Years does not argue that the patients forged their own signatures as that term is commonly understood. Rather, it contends that the signatures constitute unauthorized indorsements and, thus, were also forged indorsements because "for purposes of a [section 3–419] conversion action, a forged indorsement and an unauthorized indorsement are synonymous." In addition, Golden Years does not argue that the patients were agents of the nursing home who signed the checks without actual or apparent authority. Rather, Golden Years contends that because the patients had assigned their beneficial interest in the checks to Golden Years, any signature other than Golden Years' corporate stamp was "unauthorized."

We note that Golden Years use of the term "unauthorized signature" does not fall within the scope of the UCC definition of that term, i.e., "made without actual, implied or apparent authority." More important, assuming that the patients had assigned their interest in the checks to Golden Years, any separate agreement between the patient-payees and Golden Years would not affect the negotiability of patients' checks bearing the patients' genuine indorsements.

UCC section 3–119(2) provides that a "separate agreement does not affect the negotiability of an instrument." Negotiability "is always to be determined by what appears on the face of the instrument alone. . . ." A separate writing may affect the terms of an instrument but the Official Comment makes clear that the inquiry is controlled by what *the instrument itself* states or reflects, not, what the collateral agreement says.

If an instrument is payable to order it is negotiated by delivery with any necessary indorsement. (UCC 3–202). "However, once a payee indorses the check in blank, it becomes bearer paper which can be 'negotiated by delivery alone'" (UCC 3–204). "Negotiation is the transfer of an instrument in such form that the transferee becomes a holder" (UCC 3–202). Thus, in this case, Gabbard became a holder of the checks when the checks, indorsed in blank by the patient-payees, were delivered to her. When Star Bank accepted the checks that were indorsed with the genuine signatures of the payees, the checks bore no indication that they had been assigned to Golden Years. Star Bank cashed the checks in good faith without notice of any defenses and thus became a holder in due course.

This analysis does not change even if Gabbard presented the checks to the payees for their indorsement with the intent to embezzle the funds eventually:

> Assuming that the stolen bearer instrument does not bear a restrictive indorsement, the thief will himself be a holder and whether or not he is a holder, he can constitute his transferee a holder simply by transfer. If his transferee then cashes the check and so gives value in good faith and without notice of any defense, that transferee will be a holder in due course under 3–302, free of all claims to the instrument on the part of any person and free of all defenses to it.

Judgment for Star Bank.

Note: Ohio's adoption of Revised Articles 3 and 4 was not effective until Aug. 19, 1994, after the events that gave rise to this action. However, the same result would be expected under Revised Articles 3 and 4.

Value To qualify as a holder in due course of a negotiable instrument, a person must give **value** for it. Value is not identical to simple consideration. Under the provisions of the Revised Article 3, a holder takes for value if (1) the agreed-upon promise of performance has been performed—for example, if the instrument was given in exchange for a promise to deliver a refrigerator and the refrigerator has been delivered; (2) he acquires a security interest in, or a lien on, the instrument; (3) he takes the instrument in payment of, or as security for, an antecedent claim; (4) he gives a negotiable instrument for it; or (5) he makes an irrevocable commitment to a third person [3–303]. Thus, a person who gets a check as a gift or merely makes an executory promise in return for a check has not given value for it and cannot qualify as a holder in due course.

A bank or any person who discounts an instrument in the *regular course of trade* has given value for it. In this context the discount essentially is a means for increasing the return or the rate of interest on the instrument. Likewise, if a loan is made and an instrument is pledged as security for the repayment of the loan, the secured party has given value for the instrument to the amount of the loan. If Axe, who owes Bell a past-due debt, indorses and delivers to Bell, in payment of the debt or as security for its repayment, an instrument issued to Axe, Bell has given value for the instrument. If a bank allows a customer to draw against a check deposited for collection, it has given value to the extent of the credit drawn against.

If the promise of performance that is the consideration for an instrument has been partially performed, the holder may assert rights as a holder in due course of the instrument only to the fraction of the amount payable under the instrument equal to the partial performance divided by the value of the promised performance [3–302(d)]. For example, Arthur Wells agrees to purchase a note payable to the order of Helda Parks. The note is for the sum of $5,000. Wells pays Parks $1,000 on the negotiation of the note to him and agrees to pay the balance of $4,000 in 10 days. Initially, Wells is a holder in due course for one-fifth of the amount of the note. If he later pays the $4,000 due he may become a holder in due course for the full amount.

Good Faith To qualify as a holder in due course of a negotiable instrument, a person must take it in **good faith,** which means that the person obtained it honestly and in the observance of reasonable commercial standards of fair dealing [3–103(a)(4)]. If a person obtains a check by trickery or with knowledge that it has been stolen, the person has not obtained the check in good faith and cannot be a holder in due course. A person who pays too little for an instrument, perhaps because she suspects that something may be wrong with the way it was obtained, may have trouble meeting the good faith test. Suppose a finance company works closely with a door-to-door sales company that engages in shoddy practices. If the finance company buys the consumers' notes from the sales company, it will not be able to meet the good faith test and qualify as a holder in due course of the notes.

Overdue or Dishonored
In order to qualify as a holder in due course, a person must take a negotiable instrument before he has notice that it either is **overdue** or has been **dishonored.** The reason for this is that one should perform obligations when they are due. If a negotiable instrument is not paid when it is due, the Code considers the person taking it to be on notice that there may be defenses to the payment of it.

Overdue Instruments If a negotiable instrument is payable on demand, it is overdue (1) the day after demand for payment has been made in a proper manner and form; (2) 90 days after its date if it is a check; and (3) if it is an instrument other than a check, when it has been outstanding for an unreasonably long period of time in light of the nature of the instrument and trade practice [3–304(a)]. Thus, a check becomes **stale** after 90 days. For other kinds of instruments, one must consider trade practices and the facts of the particular case. In a farming community, the normal period for loans to farmers may be six months. A demand note might be outstanding for six or seven months before it is considered overdue. On the other hand, a demand note issued in an industrial city where the normal period of such loans is 30 to 60 days would be considered overdue in a much shorter period of time.

If a negotiable instrument due on a certain date is not paid by that date, normally then it will be overdue at the beginning of the next day after the due date. For example, if a promissory note dated January 1 is payable "30 days after date," it is due on January 31. If it is not paid by January 31, it is overdue beginning on February 1.

As to instruments payable at a definite time, Revised Article 3 sets out the following rules: (1) if the principal is not payable in installments and the due date has not been accelerated, the instrument is overdue on the day after the due date; (2) if the principal is due in installments and a due date has not been accelerated, the instrument is overdue upon default for nonpayment of an installment and remains overdue until the default is cured; (3) if a due date for the principal has been accelerated, the instrument is overdue on the day after the accelerated due date; and (4) unless the due date of the principal has been accelerated, an instrument does not become overdue if there is a default in payment of interest but no default in payment of principal [3–304(b)].

Dishonored Instruments To be a holder in due course, a person not only must take a negotiable instrument before he has notice that it is overdue but also must take it before it has been dishonored. A negotiable instrument has been *dishonored* when the holder has *presented* it for payment (or acceptance) and payment (or acceptance) has been refused.

For example, Susan writes a check on her account at First National Bank that is payable "to the order of Sven Sorensen." Sven takes the check to First National Bank to cash it but the bank refuses to pay it because Susan has insufficient funds in her account to cover it. The check has been dishonored. If Sven then takes Susan's check to Harry's Hardware and uses it to pay for some paint, Harry's cannot be a holder in due course of the check if it is on notice that the check has been dishonored. Harry's would have such notice if First National had stamped the check "Payment Refused NSF" (not sufficient funds).

Similarly, suppose Carol Carson signs a 30-day note payable to Ace Appliance for $500 and gives it to Ace as payment for a stereo set. When Ace asks Carol for payment, she refuses to pay because the stereo does not work properly. If Ace negotiates the note to First National Bank, First National cannot be a holder in due course if it knows about Carol's refusal to pay.

Notice of Unauthorized Signature or Alteration
A holder who has notice that an instrument contains an unauthorized signature or has been altered cannot qualify as a holder in due course of the instrument. For example, Frank makes out a check in the amount of $5 payable to George Grocer and gives it to his daughter, Jane, to take to the grocery store to purchase some groceries. The groceries Frank wants cost $20 and Jane changes the check to read $25, giving it to Grocer in exchange for the groceries and $5 in cash. Grocer cannot qualify as a holder in due course if he sees Jane make the alteration to the check or otherwise is on notice of it. [See 3–302(a)(1).]

Notice of Claims
If a person taking a negotiable instrument is *on notice of an adverse claim* to the instrument by someone else (for example, that a third person is the rightful owner of the instrument) or that someone earlier sought to rescind a prior negotiation of the instrument, the current holder cannot qualify as a holder in due course. For example, a U.S. Treasury check is payable to Susan Samuels. Samuels loses the check and it is found by Robert Burns. Burns takes the check to a hardware

store, signs "Susan Samuels" on the back of the check in the view of a clerk, and seeks to use it in payment of merchandise. The hardware store cannot be a holder in due course because it is on notice of a potential claim to the instrument by Susan Samuels.

Notice of Breach of Fiduciary Duty

One situation in which the Code considers a person to be on notice of a claim is if she is taking a negotiable instrument from a fiduciary, such as a trustee. If a negotiable instrument is payable to a person as a trustee or an attorney for someone, then any attempt by that person to negotiate it for his own behalf or for his use (or benefit) or to deposit it in an account other than that of the fiduciary puts the person on notice that the beneficiary of the trust may have a claim [3–307].

For example, a check is drawn "Pay to the order of Arthur Adams, Trustee for Mary Minor." Adams takes the check to Credit Union, indorses his name to it, and uses it to pay off the balance on a loan Adams had from Credit Union. Credit Union cannot be a holder in due course because it should know that the negotiation of the check is in violation of the fiduciary duty Adams owes to Mary Minor. Ace should know this because Adams is negotiating the check for his own benefit, not Mary's.

Notice of Defenses and Claims in Recoupment

To qualify as a holder in due course, a person must also acquire a negotiable instrument without notice that any party to it has any **defenses** or **claims in recoupment.** Potential defenses include infancy, duress, fraud, and failure of consideration. Thus, if a person knows that a signature on the instrument was obtained by fraud, misrepresentation, or duress, the person cannot be a holder in due course.

A *claim in recoupment* is a claim of the person obligated on the instrument against the original payee of the instrument. The claim must arise from the transaction that gave rise to the instrument. An example of a claim in recoupment would be as follows: Buyer purchases a used automobile from Dealer for $8,000, giving the dealer a note for $8,000 payable in one year. Because the automobile is not as warranted, Buyer has a breach of warranty claim that could be asserted against Dealer as counter-claim or "claim in recoupment" to offset the amount owing on the note.

Irregular and Incomplete Instruments

A person cannot be a holder in due course of a negotiable instrument if, when she takes it, the instrument is irregular or some important or material term is blank. If the negotiable instrument contains a facial irregularity, such as an obvious alteration in the amount, then it is considered to be **irregular paper.** If you take an irregular instrument, you are considered to be on notice of any possible defenses to it. For example, Kevin writes a check for "one dollar" payable to Karen. Karen inserts the word "hundred" in the amount, changes the figure "$1" to "$100," and gives the check to a druggist in exchange for a purchase of goods. If the alterations in the amount should be obvious to the druggist, perhaps because there are erasures, different handwritings, or different inks, then the druggist cannot be a holder in due course. She would have taken irregular paper and would be on notice that there might be defenses to it. These defenses include Kevin's defense that he is liable for only $1 because that is the amount for which he made the check.

Similarly, if someone receives a check that has been signed but the space where the amount of the check is to be written is blank, then the person cannot be a holder in due course of that check. The fact that a material term is blank means that the instrument is **incomplete** and should put the person on notice that the drawer may have a defense to payment of it. To be material, the omitted term must be one that affects the legal obligation of the parties to the negotiable instrument. Material terms include the amount of the instrument and the name of the payee. If a negotiable instrument is unauthorizedly completed after the obligor signed it but before a person acquires it, the person can qualify as a holder in due course if she had no notice about the unauthorized completion. A person has notice if she knows or should know of the unauthorized completion.

In the case that follows, *Firstar Bank, N.A. v. First Service Title Agency, Inc.,* the court concluded that a bank could not qualify as a holder in due course of three instruments because it took them with obvious irregularities that called their authenticity into question.

Firstar Bank, N.A. v. First Service Title Agency, Inc.
54 UCC Rep.2d 701 (Ct. App. Ohio 2004)

On January 22, 2002, as a result of a real estate transaction, First Service Title Agency issued three checks drawn on its account with Key Bank. The first check was for $850 and was payable to the order of "Richard G. Knostman, Atty. and Mark F. Foster, Atty. and Resa Kermani & Badri Kermani." The second check was for $36,295.80 and was made payable to "JD Properties and Resa Kermani & Badri Kermani." The third check was for $4,010 and payable to "Knab Mortgage."

First Service Title subsequently learned that the underlying real estate transaction had been fraudulent. Consequently, on January 23, 2002, it put stop payment orders on all three checks and refunded the monies it had received in the transaction. First Service Title notified the parties and the payees of the stop payment orders.

On the same day that First Service Title Agency placed the stop payment orders on the checks, Randall Davis, who had various accounts at Firstar Bank, presented all three checks to Firstar Bank. Firstar Bank paid the checks to Davis even though Davis was not a party to any of the checks, the checks contained multiple indorsements that appeared to be in the same handwriting, and they all were marked "for deposit only."

Key Bank subsequently returned the checks to Firstar Bank with the notation "Payment stopped." Firstar Bank then filed suit against First Services Title Agency and Davis. One of the issues in the suit against First Services Title Agency was whether Firstar Bank was a holder in due course of the three checks.

Per Curiam

A holder becomes a holder in due course if the holder takes the instrument (1) for value; (2) in good faith; (3) and without notice of any claims or defenses otherwise available to the person obligated on the instrument or of various defects in the instrument. A person has notice of a fact when (1) the person has actual knowledge of it; (2) the person has received a notice or notification of it; or (3) from all the facts and circumstances known to the person at the time in question, the person has reason to know that it exists. Additionally, an instrument when issued or negotiated to the holder, cannot bear any evidence of forgery or alteration that is so apparent or cannot otherwise be so irregular or incomplete as to call into question its authenticity.

The trial court held that Firstar was not a holder in due course because "it failed to exercise ordinary care having knowledge that the checks were forged or otherwise deficient." The checks in question bore evidence of forgery and were so irregular on their face as to call into question their authenticity and to give notice to a reasonably prudent person exercising ordinary care of defects in the checks.

Judgment affirmed in favor of First Service Title Agency, Inc.

Shelter Rule The transferee of an instrument—whether or not the transfer is a negotiation—obtains those rights that the transferor had, including (1) the transferor's right to enforce the instrument and (2) any right as a holder in due course [3–203(b)]. This means that any person who can trace his title to an instrument back to a holder in due course receives rights like those of a holder in due course even if he cannot meet the requirements himself. This is known as the **shelter rule** in Article 3. For example, Archer makes a note payable to Bryant. Bryant negotiates the note to Carlyle, who qualifies as a holder in due course. Carlyle then negotiates the note to Darby, who cannot qualify as a holder in due course because she knows the note is overdue. Because Darby can trace her title back to a holder in due course (Carlyle), Darby has rights like a holder in due course when she seeks payment of the note from Archer.

There is, however, a limitation on the shelter rule. A transferee who has himself been a party to any fraud or illegality affecting the instrument cannot improve his position by taking, directly or indirectly, from a later holder in due course [3–203(b)]. For example, Archer, through fraudulent representations, induced Bryant to execute a negotiable note payable to Archer and then negotiated the instrument to Carlyle, who took as a holder in due course. If Archer thereafter took the note for value from Carlyle, Archer could not acquire Carlyle's rights as a holder in due course. Archer was a party to the fraud that induced the note, and, accordingly, cannot improve his position by negotiating the instrument and then reacquiring it.

Rights of a Holder in Due Course

Claims and Defenses Generally
Revised Article 3 establishes four categories of claims and defenses. They are:

1. *Real defenses*—which go to the validity of the instrument.
2. *Personal defenses*—which generally arise out of the transaction that gave rise to the instrument.
3. *Claims to an instrument*—which generally concern property or possessory rights in an instrument or its proceeds.
4. *Claims in recoupment*—which also arise out of the transaction that gave rise to the instrument.

Requirements for a Holder in Due Course

Requirement	Rule
1. Must be a *holder*.	A holder is a person in possession of an instrument payable to bearer or payable to an identified person and he is that person.
2. Must take *for value*.	A holder has given value: *a.* To the extent the agreed-on consideration has been paid or performed. *b.* To the extent a security interest or lien has been obtained in the negotiable instrument. *c.* By taking the negotiable instrument in payment of—or as security for—an antecedent claim. *d.* By giving a negotiable instrument for it. *e.* By making an irrevocable commitment to a third person.
3. Must take in *good faith*.	Good faith means honesty in fact and the observance of reasonable commercial standards of fair dealing.
4. Must take *without notice* that the instrument is *overdue*.	An instrument payable on demand is overdue the day after demand for payment has been duly made. A check is overdue 90 days after its date. If it is an instrument other than a check and payable on demand, then it is overdue when it has been outstanding for an unreasonably long period of time in light of nature of the instrument and trade practice. If it is an instrument due on a certain date, then it is overdue at the beginning of the next day after the due date.
5. Must take *without notice* that the instrument has been *dishonored*.	An instrument has been dishonored when the holder has presented it for payment (or acceptance) and payment (or acceptance) has been refused.
6. Must take *without notice* of any *uncured default* with respect to payment of another instrument issued as part of the same series.	If there is a series of notes, holder must take without notice that there is an uncured default as to any other notes in the series.
7. Must take *without notice* that the instrument contains an *unauthorized signature* or has been *altered*.	Notice of unauthorized signature or alteration—that is, a change in a material term—prevents holder from obtaining HDC status.
8. Must take *without notice* of any *claim of a property* or possessory *interest* in it.	Claims of property or possessory interest include: *a.* Claim by someone that she is the rightful owner of the instrument. *b.* Person seeking to rescind a prior negotiation of the instrument. *c.* Claim by a beneficiary that a fiduciary negotiated the instrument for his own benefit.
9. Must take *without notice* that any party has a *defense* against it.	Defenses include real defenses that go to the validity of the instrument and personal defenses that commonly are defenses to a simple contract.
10. Must take *without notice* of a *claim in recoupment* to it.	A claim in recoupment is a claim of the obligor on the instrument against the original payee that arises from the transaction that gave rise to the instrument.
11. The instrument must not bear *apparent evidence of forgery or alteration* or be *irregular* or *incomplete*.	The instrument must not contain obvious reasons to question its authenticity.

These defenses and claims are discussed in some detail below.

Importance of Being a Holder in Due Course

In the preceding chapter, we explained that one advantage of negotiable instruments over other kinds of contracts is that they are accepted as substitutes for money. People are willing to accept them as substitutes for money because, generally, they can take them free of claims or defenses to payment between the original parties to the instrument. On the other hand, a person who takes an assignment of a simple contract gets only the same rights as the person had who assigned the contract.

There are two qualifications to the ability of a person who acquires a negotiable instrument to be free of claims or defenses between the original parties. First, the person in possession of a negotiable instrument must be a *person entitled to enforce the instrument* as well as a *holder in due course* (or must be a holder who has the rights of a holder in due course through the shelter rule). If the person is neither, then she is subject to all claims or defenses to payment that any party to it has. Second, the only claims or defenses that the holder in due course has to worry about are so-called real defenses—those that affect the validity of the instrument—or claims that arose after she became a holder. For example, if the maker or drawer did not have legal capacity because she was a minor, the maker or drawer has a real defense. The holder in due course does not have to worry about other defenses and claims that do not go to the validity of the instrument—the so-called personal defenses.

Real Defenses

There are some claims and defenses to payment of an instrument that go to the validity of the instrument. These claims and defenses are known as **real defenses.** They can be used as reasons against payment of a negotiable instrument to any holder, including a holder in due course (or a person who has the rights of a holder in due course). Real defenses include:

1. *Minority or infancy* that under state law makes the instrument void or voidable. For example, if Mark Miller, age 17, signs a promissory note as maker, he can use his lack of capacity to contract as a defense against paying it even to a holder in due course.

2. *Incapacity* that under state law makes the instrument void. For example, if a person has been declared mentally incompetent by a court, then the person has a real defense if state law declares all contracts entered into by the person after the adjudication of incompetency to be void.

3. *Duress* that voids or nullifies the obligation of a party liable to pay the instrument. For example, if Harold points a gun at his grandmother and forces her to execute a promissory note, the grandmother can use duress as a defense against paying it even to a holder in due course.

4. *Illegality* that under state law renders the obligation void. For example, in some states, checks and notes given in payment of gambling debts are void.

5. *Fraud in the essence (or fraud in the factum).* This occurs where a person signs a negotiable instrument without knowing or having a reasonable opportunity to know that it is a negotiable instrument or of its essential terms. For example, Amy Jones is an illiterate person who lives alone. She signs a document that is actually a promissory note but is told that it is a grant of permission for a television set to be left in her house on a trial basis. Amy has a real defense against payment of the note even to a holder in due course. Fraud in the essence is distinguished from fraud in the inducement, discussed below, which is only a personal defense.

6. *Discharge in bankruptcy.* For example, if the maker of a promissory note has had the debt discharged in a bankruptcy proceeding, she no longer is liable on it and has a real defense against payment [3–305(a)(1)].

Real defenses can be asserted even against a holder in due course of a negotiable instrument because it is more desirable to protect people who have signed negotiable instruments in these situations than it is to protect persons who have taken negotiable instruments in the ordinary course of business.

In the case that follows, *General Credit Corp. v. New York Linen,* the court held that a holder in due course of a check was not subject to the personal defense of failure of consideration that the drawer of the check had against the payee of the check.

General Credit Corp. v. New York Linen Co., Inc.
46 UCC Rep.2d 1055 (New York Civ. Ct., Kings County 2002)

On February 25, 2001, New York Linen Co., a party rental company, agreed to purchase approximately 550 chairs from Elite Products, a company owned by Meir Schmeltzer. A deposit was given for the chairs and upon their delivery, a final check dated February 27, 2001, was issued for $13,300. After a final count of the chairs was made, New York Linen discovered that *the delivery was not complete. New York Linen then contacted its bank and asked that the bank stop payment of the check. A second check, dated February 28, 2001, for $11,275, was drafted and delivered to New York Linen the next day. This check reflected the adjusted amount due for the chairs that had actually been delivered.*

Unbeknownst to New York Linen, the original check for $13,300 was sold by Meir Schmeltzer to General Credit Corp., a company in the business of purchasing instruments from payees in exchange for immediate cash. When New York Linen's bank refused to pay the check to General Credit because of the stop-payment order that had been placed on it, General Credit Corp. brought suit against New York Linen to collect on the check.

Baily-Schiffman, Judge

Pursuant to UCC section 3–302 [pre-1990 version inasmuch as New York has not yet adopted Revised Article 3] General Credit is a holder in due course since it took the instrument for value and claims to have all the rights of a holder in due course. General Credit seeks to force New York Linen to pay on the check.

Pursuant to Article 3 of the Uniform Commercial Code, a holder in due course has significant rights vis-à-vis the negotiable instrument being held. A holder of an instrument becomes the holder in due course if the instrument is taken for value, in good faith, and without notice of defect or defense (UCC section 3–302). An indorsed check, as in this case, is a negotiable instrument as defined in this section of the UCC. In this case, pursuant to the applicable sections of Article 3 (sections 3–303 and 3–304), General Credit was a good faith purchaser without notice. As a holder in due course, General Credit is protected by section 3–305, taking the check free of all defenses and claims, except those enumerated by the section. Thus, any defense New York Linen had which related to its purchase of the chairs was not a defense against General Credit.

New York Linen contends that it would not have drafted a second check if it had known that Elite had already been paid by General Credit. While to the casual observer, the potential double payment by New York Linen may seem an unfair result, it is specifically mandated by the Uniform Commercial Code. New York Linen has offered no legal defense to General Credit's claim as a holder in due course pursuant to Article 3 of the UCC. By tradition the defenses from which a holder in due course takes free are called "personal defenses" and they include failure for lack of consideration, which is New York Linen's defense in this case.

Summary judgment granted in favor of General Credit on its claim against New York Linen.

Note: While this case was decided under the pre-1990 version of Article 3 because New York is the one state that has not yet adopted Revised Article 3, the same result would result from application of Revised Article 3 to the facts of this case.

In addition to the real defenses discussed above, there are several other reasons why a person otherwise liable to pay an instrument would have a defense against payment that would be effective even against a holder in due course. They include:

1. *Forgery.* For example, if a maker's signature has been put on the instrument without his authorization and without his negligence, the maker has a defense against payment of the note.

2. *Alteration of a completed instrument.* This is a partial defense against a holder in due course (or a person having the rights of a holder in due course) and a complete defense against a nonholder in due course. A holder in due course can enforce an altered instrument against the maker or drawer according to its original tenor (terms).

3. *Discharge.* If a person takes an instrument with knowledge that the obligation of any party obligated on the instrument has been discharged, the person takes subject to the discharge even if the person is a holder in due course.

Personal Defenses   **Personal defenses** are legal

reasons for avoiding or reducing liability of a person who is liable on a negotiable instrument. Generally, personal defenses arise out of the transaction in which the negotiable instrument was issued and are based on negotiable instruments law or contract law. A holder in due course of a negotiable instrument (or one who can claim the rights of one) is not subject to any personal defenses or claims that may exist between the original parties to the instrument. Personal defenses include:

1. *Lack or failure of consideration.* For example, a promissory note for $100 was given to someone without intent to make a gift and without receiving anything in return [3–303(b)].

2. *Breach of contract, including breach of warranty.* For example, a check was given in payment for repairs to an automobile but the repair work was defective.

3. *Fraud in the inducement of any underlying contract.* For example, an art dealer sells a lithograph to Cheryl, telling her that it is a Picasso, and takes Cheryl's check for $500 in payment. The art dealer knows that the lithograph is not a genuine Picasso but a forgery. Cheryl has been induced to make the purchase and to give her check by the art dealer's fraudulent representation. Because of this fraud, Cheryl has a personal defense against having to honor her check to the art dealer.

4. *Incapacity to the extent that state law makes the obligation voidable, as opposed to void.* For example, where state law makes the contract of a person of limited mental capacity but who has not been adjudicated incompetent voidable, the person has a personal defense to payment.

5. *Illegality that makes a contract voidable, as opposed to void.* For example, where the payee of a check given for certain professional services was required to have a license from the state but did not have one.

6. *Duress, to the extent it is not so severe as to make the obligation void but rather only voidable.* For example, if the instrument was signed under a threat to prosecute the maker's son if it was not signed, the maker might have a personal defense.

7. *Unauthorized completion or alteration of the instrument.* For example, the instrument was completed in an unauthorized manner, or was altered after it left the maker's or drawer's possession.

8. *Nonissuance of the instrument, conditional issuance, and issuance for a special purpose.* For example, the person in possession of the instrument obtained it by theft or by finding it, rather than through an intentional delivery of the instrument to him [3–105(b)].

9. *Failure to countersign a traveler's check* [3–106(c)].

10. *Modification of the obligation by a separate agreement* [3–117].

11. *Payment that violates a restrictive indorsement* [3–206(f)].

12. *Breach of warranty when a draft is accepted* (discussed in following chapter) [3–417(b)].

The following example illustrates the limited extent to which a maker or drawer can use personal defenses as a reason for not paying a negotiable instrument he signed. Suppose Tucker Trucking bought a used truck from Honest Harry's and gave Harry a 60-day promissory note for $32,750 in payment for the truck. Honest Harry's "guaranteed" the truck to be in "good working condition," but in fact the truck had a cracked engine block. If Harry tries to collect the $32,750 from Tucker Trucking, Tucker Trucking could claim breach of warranty as a reason for not paying Harry the full $32,750 because Harry is not a holder in due course. However, if Harry negotiated the note to First National Bank and the bank was a holder in due course, the situation would be changed. If the bank tried to collect the $32,750 from Tucker Trucking, Tucker Trucking would have to pay the bank. Tucker Trucking cannot use its defense or claim of breach of warranty as a reason for not paying the bank, which qualified as a holder in due course. It is a personal defense. Tucker Trucking must pay the bank the $32,750 and then pursue its breach of warranty claim against Harry.

The rule that a holder in due course takes a negotiable instrument free of any personal defenses or claims to it has been modified to some extent, particularly in relation to certain instruments given by consumers. These modifications will be discussed in the next section of this chapter.

Claims to the Instrument
For purposes of Revised Article 3, the term *claims* to an instrument can include:

1. A claim to ownership of the instrument by one who asserts that he is the owner and was wrongfully deprived of possession.

2. A claim of a lien on the instrument.

3. A claim for rescission of an indorsement.

A holder in due course takes free of claims that arose before he became a holder but is subject to those arising

---

Ethics in Action

Asserting the Defense of Illegality against Payment of a Gambling Debt

Assume that in the course of a vacation you drop by the casino in the hotel where you were staying. You decide to play a few hands of blackjack. After winning your first few hands, you then go on a sustained losing streak. Believing your luck is about to change, you keep going until you have lost $10,000,

much more than you intended or could readily afford. At the end of the evening, you write the casino a check. Later in the hotel bar, you tell your sad tale to a fellow drinker who is a local lawyer and who informs you that a state law makes gambling obligations void. Would it be ethical for you to stop payment on the check and then assert the defense of illegality against the holder of the check?

when or after she becomes a holder in due course. For example, if a holder impairs the collateral given for an obligation, he may be creating a defense for an obligor.

Claims in Recoupment

A *claim in recoupment* is not actually a defense to an instrument but rather an *offset to liability*. For example, Ann Adams purchases a new automobile from Dealership, giving it a note for the balance of the purchase price beyond her down payment. After accepting delivery, she discovers a breach of warranty that the dealer fails to remedy. If Dealer has sold the note to a bank that subsequently seeks payment on the note from Adams, she has a claim in recoupment for breach of warranty. If the bank is a holder in due course, the claim in recoupment cannot be asserted against it. However, if the bank is not a holder in due course, then Adams can assert the claim in recoupment to reduce the amount owing on the instrument at the time the action is brought against her on the note. Her claim could serve only to reduce the amount owing and not as a basis for a net recovery from the bank. However, if Dealer was the person bringing an action to collect the note, Adams could assert the breach of warranty claim as a counterclaim and potentially might recover from Dealer any difference between the claim and the damages due for breach of warranty.

The obligor may assert a claim up to the amount of the instrument if the holder is the original payee but cannot assert claims in recoupment against a holder in due course. In addition, the obligor may assert a claim against a transferee who does not qualify as a holder in due course, but only to reduce the amount owing on the instrument at the time it brought the claim in recoupment.

Changes in the Holder in Due Course Rule for Consumer Credit Transactions

Consumer Disadvantages

The rule that a holder in due course of a negotiable instrument is not subject to personal defenses between the original parties to it makes negotiable instruments a readily accepted substitute for money. This rule can also result in serious disadvantages to consumers. Consumers sometimes buy goods or services on credit and give the seller a negotiable instrument such as a promissory note. They often do this without knowing the consequences of their signing a negotiable instrument. If the goods or services are defective or not delivered, the consumer would like to withhold payment of the note until the seller corrects the problem or makes the delivery. Where the note is still held by the seller, the consumer can do this because any defenses of breach of warranty or nonperformance are good against the seller.

However, the seller may have negotiated the note at a discount to a third party such as a bank. If the bank qualifies as a holder in due course, the consumer must pay the note in full to the bank. The consumer's personal defenses are not valid against a holder in due course. The consumer must pay the holder in due course and then try to get her money back from the seller. This may be difficult if the seller cannot be found or will not accept responsibility. The consumer would be in a much stronger position if she could just withhold payment, even against the bank, until the goods or services are delivered or the performance is corrected.

State Consumer Protection Legislation

Some state legislatures and courts have limited the holder in due course rule, particularly as it affects consumers. State legislation limiting the doctrine typically amended state laws dealing with consumer credit transactions. For example, some state laws prohibit a seller from taking a negotiable instrument other than a check from a consumer in payment for consumer goods and services. Other states require promissory notes given by consumers in payment for goods and services to carry the words *consumer paper*. Holders of instruments with the legend "consumer paper" are not eligible to be holders in due course[3] [3–106(d)].

Federal Trade Commission Regulation

The Federal Trade Commission (FTC) has promulgated a regulation designed to protect consumers against operation of the holder in due course rule. The FTC rule applies to persons who sell to consumers on credit and have the consumer sign a note or an installment sale contract or arrange third-party financing of the purchase. The seller must ensure that the note or the contract contains the following clause:

> NOTICE: ANY HOLDER OF THIS CONSUMER CREDIT CONTRACT IS SUBJECT TO ALL CLAIMS AND DEFENSES WHICH THE DEBTOR COULD ASSERT AGAINST THE SELLER OF THE GOODS OR SERVICES OBTAINED PURSUANT HERETO OR

---

[3] Revised Article 3 expressly deals with these state variations in section 3–106(d) and Official Comments 3 to 3–106 and Comments 3 to 3–305. Section 3–106(d) permits instruments containing legends or statements required by statutory or administrative law that preserve the obligator's right to assert claims or defenses against subsequent holders as within Article 3 except that no holder can be a holder in due course.

CONCEPT REVIEW

Claims and Defenses against Payment of Negotiable Instruments

Claim or Defense	Examples
Real Defense Valid against all holders, including holders in due course and holders who have the rights of holders in due course.	1. Minority that under state law makes the contract void or voidable. 2. Other lack of capacity that makes the contract void. 3. Duress that makes the contract void. 4. Illegality that makes the contract void. 5. Fraud in the essence (fraud in the factum). 6. Discharge in bankruptcy.
Personal Defense Valid against plain holders of instruments—but not against holders in due course or holders who have the rights of in due course holders through the shelter rule.	1. Lack or failure of consideration. 2. Breach of contract (including breach of warranty). 3. Fraud in the inducement. 4. Lack of capacity that makes the contract voidable (except minority). 5. Illegality that makes the contract voidable. 6. Duress that makes the contract voidable. 7. Unauthorized completion of an incomplete instrument, or material alteration of the instrument. 8. Nonissuance of the instrument. 9. Failure to countersign a traveler's check. 10. Modification of the obligation by a separate agreement. 11. Payment that violates a restrictive indorsement. 12. Breach of warranty when a draft is accepted.
Claim to an Instrument	1. Claim of ownership by someone who claims to be the owner and that he was wrongfully deprived of possession. 2. Claim of a lien on the instrument. 3. Claim for rescission of an indorsement.
Claims in Recoupment	1. Breach of warranty in the sale of goods for which the instrument was issued.

WITH THE PROCEEDS HEREOF. RECOVERY HEREUNDER BY THE DEBTOR SHALL NOT EXCEED AMOUNTS PAID BY THE DEBTOR HEREUNDER.

The effect of the notice is to make a potential holder of the note or contract subject to all claims and defenses of the consumer. This is illustrated in *Music Acceptance Corp.*, which follows.

In the hypothetical case set out at the start of this chapter, Rachel buys a used car and gives the seller a negotiable promissory note in which she promises to pay the balance in 12 months. The seller then negotiates the promissory note to a third party. When Rachel discovers that, contrary to the seller's assurances, the car had previously been involved in an accident, Rachel would like to assert a defense of failure of consideration or breach of contract (warranty) against payment. You know that normally, if the person to whom the note was assigned can qualify as a holder in due course, then the maker of a note will not be

able to assert those particular defenses against payment because they are considered to be "personal defenses," and a holder in due course of an instrument takes the instrument free of such defenses against payment. However, the introductory hypothetical goes on to pose the question of whether it would make a difference if the promissory note contained the clause required by the Federal Trade Commission in consumer notes. You are now in a position to know that it would make a difference in Rachel's rights and that she would be able to assert such defenses against payment of the note to the current holder, even if he could qualify as holder in due course. If the note or contract does not include the clause required by the FTC rule, the consumer does not gain any rights that he would not otherwise have under state law, and a subsequent holder may qualify as a holder in due course. However, the FTC does have the right to seek a fine of as much as $10,000 against the seller who failed to include the clause.

Music Acceptance Corp. v. Lofing   39 Cal. Rptr. 159 (Cal. Ct. App. 1995)

Dan Lofing purchased a Steinway grand piano from Sherman Clay & Co., Steinway & Sons' Sacramento dealer, and received financing through Sherman Clay's finance company, Music Acceptance Corporation (MAC). The consumer note for $19,650.94 prepared by MAC and signed by Lofing included the following in boldface type:

NOTICE

ANY HOLDER OF THIS CONSUMER CREDIT CONTRACT IS SUBJECT TO ALL CLAIMS AND DEFENSES WHICH THE DEBTOR COULD ASSERT AGAINST THE SELLER OF GOODS OR SERVICES OBTAINED PURSUANT HEREIN OR WITH THE PROCEEDS HEREOF. RECOVERY HEREUNDER SHALL NOT EXCEED AMOUNTS PAID BY THE DEBTOR HEREUNDER.

Lofing received a warranty from Steinway that provided the company "will promptly repair or replace without charge any part of this piano which is found to have a defect in material or workmanship within five years" from the date of sale.

Lofing became disenchanted with the piano after experiencing a variety of problems with it. There was a significant deterioration in the action and tonal quality of the piano which the Sherman Clay piano technician was unable to remedy despite lengthy and repeated efforts. A Steinway representative who was called in to inspect the piano concluded that it was in "terrible condition" and expressed surprise that it had ever left the factory. He concluded that the piano would have to be completely rebuilt at the factory.

Because the piano was impossible to play and was ruining his technique, Lofing stopped making payments on the piano. To mitigate his damages, Lofing sold the piano for $7,000 and purchased a Kawai piano from another dealer. He brought suit against Sherman Clay, Steinway, and MAC for, among other things, breach of warranty. One of the issues in the litigation was whether the Notice in the note allowed him to assert the breach of warranty as a grounds for not continuing to pay off the note to MAC.

Sparks, Associate Justice

The FTC adopted a rule which makes it an unfair or deceptive act or practice for a seller to take or receive a consumer credit application which does not contain the following provision in large boldface type:

NOTICE

ANY HOLDER OF THIS CONSUMER CREDIT CONTRACT IS SUBJECT TO ALL CLAIMS AND DEFENSES WHICH THE DEBTOR COULD ASSERT AGAINST THE SELLER OF GOODS OR SERVICES OBTAINED PURSUANT HEREIN OR WITH THE PROCEEDS HEREOF. RECOVERY HEREUNDER SHALL NOT EXCEED AMOUNTS PAID BY THE DEBTOR HEREUNDER.

This notice is identical to that included in Lofing's sales contract.

The FTC enacted this rule because it believed it was "an unfair practice for a seller to employ procedures in the course of arranging the financing of a consumer deal which separate[d] the buyer's duty to pay for goods or services from the seller's reciprocal duty to perform as promised." The FTC explained: "Our primary concern . . . has been the distribution or allocation of costs occasioned by seller misconduct in credit sale transactions. These costs arise from breaches of contract, breaches of warranty, misrepresentation, and even fraud. The current commercial system which enables sellers and creditors to divorce a consumer's obligation to pay for goods and services from the seller's obligation to perform as promised, allocates all of these costs to the consumer/buyer."

In its "Guidelines on Trade Regulation Rule Concerning Preservation of Consumers' Claims and Defenses," the FTC explained further:

[The] dramatic increase in consumer credit over the past thirty years has caused certain problems. Evolving doctrines and principles of contract law have not kept pace with changing social needs. One such legal doctrine which has worked to deprive consumers of the protection needed in credit sales is the so-called "holder in due course doctrine." Under this doctrine, the obligation to pay for goods or services is not conditioned upon the seller's corresponding duty to keep his promises.

Typically, the circumstances are as follows: A consumer relying in good faith on what the seller has represented to be a product's characteristics, service warranty, etc., makes a purchase on credit terms. The consumer then finds the product unsatisfactory; it fails to measure up to the claims made on its behalf by the seller, or the seller refuses to provide promised maintenance. The consumer, therefore, seeks relief from his debt obligations only to find that no relief is possible. His debt obligation, he is told, is not to the seller but to a third party whose claim to payment is legally unrelated to any promise made about the product.

The seller may, prior to the sale, have arranged to have the debt instrument held by someone other than himself; he may have sold the debt instrument at a discount after the purchase.

From the consumer's point of view, the timing and means by which the transfer was effected are irrelevant. He has been left without ready recourse. He must pay the full amount of his obligation. He has a product that yields less than its promised value. And he has been robbed of the only realistic leverage he possessed that might have forced the seller to provide satisfaction—his power to withhold payment.

As one court noted, before this rule was adopted "[t]he reciprocal duties of the buyer and seller which were mutually dependent under ordinary contract law became independent of one another. Thus, the buyer's duty to pay the creditor was not excused upon the seller's failure to perform. In abrogating the holder in due course rule in consumer credit transactions, the FTC preserved the consumer's claims and defenses against the creditor-assignee. The FTC rule was therefore designed to reallocate the cost of seller misconduct to the creditor. The commission felt the creditor was in a better position to absorb the loss or recover the cost from the guilty party—the seller."

MAC contends the FTC rule is inapplicable here. MAC cites comments in the FTC guidelines discussing possible limitations on the rule. Specifically, the FTC points out that because the regulation's definition of "Financing a Sale" expressly refers to the Truth-in-Lending Act, it "thus incorporate[s] the limitations contained in these laws. As a result, even with respect to transactions involving a sale of consumer goods or services, a purchase involving an expenditure of more than $25,000 is not affected by the Rule." MAC argues that since the cash price of the piano, including sales tax, was $25,650.94, the transaction is exempt from these requirements.

MAC's argument is unavailing as it is based on the guideline's unfortunate use of the phrase "expenditure of more than $25,000." As Lofing points out, the exemption referred to in the Truth-in-Lending Act does not speak of expenditures of more than $25,000, but of transactions in which the "total amount financed exceeds $25,000." Here, because Lofing traded in his piano, the total amount financed was $19,650.94, well below the exemption level.

More importantly, it is irrelevant whether the FTC rule applies. Even if such a notice was not required to be given, the fact remains that it was: Lofing's contract included the precise language mandated by the FTC rule. Put simply, Lofing is in the same position whether we apply the FTC rule or the language of his particular contract. The jury's finding that Sherman Clay breached its warranties mandates that the judgment in favor of MAC and against Lofing be reversed.

Judgment in favor of Lofing.

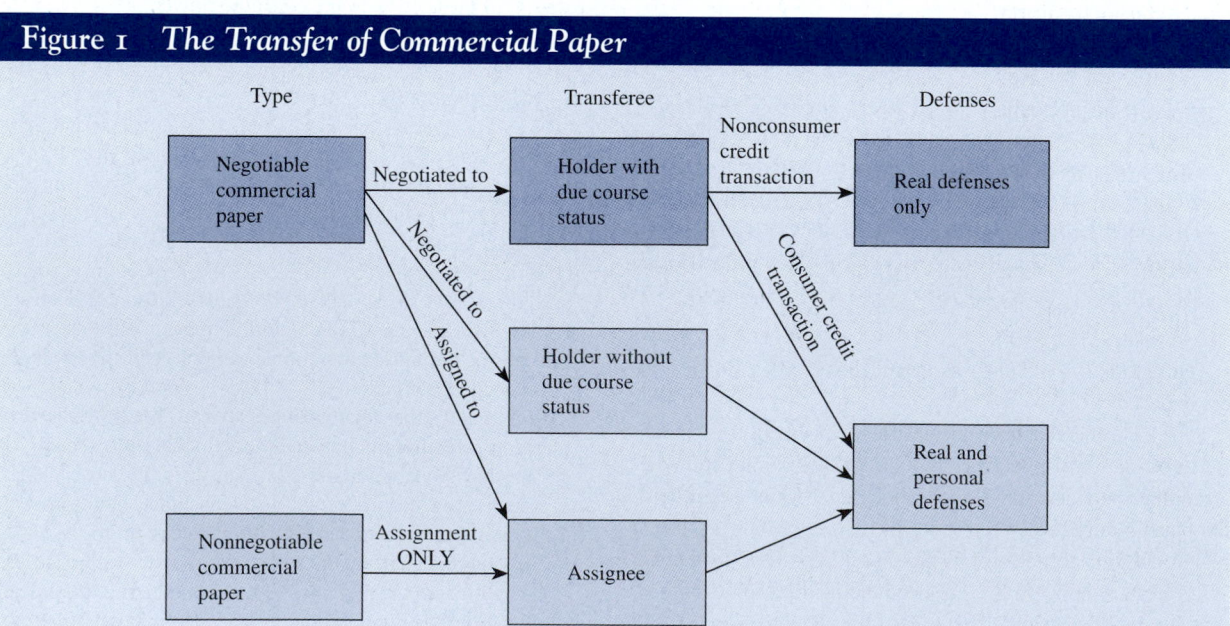

Figure 1   *The Transfer of Commercial Paper*

Source: "Charting the Way through the Transfer of Commercial Paper," Janell Kurtz and Wayne Wells, *Journal of Legal Studies Education* 13 (1995), p. 191.

Problems and Problem Cases

1. From 1999 through 2003 Christina Cidoni, individually and as president of Spectrum Settlement Group, Inc., maintained bank accounts at the Bay Shore branch of NSBC Bank USA (NSBC). On August 30, 2003, Cidoni appeared at a real estate closing for the purchase and sale of residential property as an independent title closer. At the closing, a check drawn on the Fleet Bank Boston account of Laura Hamel, the attorney handling the closing, and payable to "ABN Amro Mortgage" was issued in the amount of $207,530.14. The check was intended to satisfy the existing mortgage of the sellers of the residential property. One of Spectrum's responsibilities was to see that the check was delivered to a representative of ABN Amro Mortgage. Instead, Cidoni indorsed the check on the back "for deposit" and deposited it into Spectrum's account at NSBC. Was the check negotiated to the bank?

2. A bank cashed the checks of its customer, Dental Supply, Inc., presented to the bank by an employee of Dental Supply named Wilson. The checks were indorsed in blank with a rubber stamp of Dental Supply, Inc. Wilson had been stealing the checks by taking cash rather than depositing them to Dental Supply, Inc.'s account. What could Dental Supply have done to avoid this situation?

3. Reliable Janitorial Service, Inc., maintained a bank account with AmSouth Bank. Rosa Pennington was employed by Reliable as a bookkeeper/office manager. She deposited checks made payable to Reliable but did not have authority to write checks on Reliable's account. Beginning in January, Pennington obtained counter deposit slips from AmSouth. She wrote on the deposit slips that the depositor was "Reliable Janitorial Services, Inc.," but in the space for the account number, Pennington wrote the account number for her own personal account with AmSouth. She stamped the checks that were made payable to "Reliable Janitorial Service, Inc." with the indorsement "For Deposit Only, Reliable Carpet Cleaning, Inc." Over an 11-month period, Pennington was able to deposit 169 checks so indorsed. AmSouth credited the deposits to Pennington, not Reliable. Pennington spent all the funds that she diverted to her account. When Reliable discovered the fraud, it brought suit against AmSouth for conversion and sought to have its account credited with the improperly paid checks. Was AmSouth Bank liable to Reliable for the value of the restrictively indorsed checks that it paid inconsistently with the indorsement?

4. Reggie Bluiett worked at the Silver Slipper Gambling Hall and Saloon. She received her weekly paycheck made out to her from the Silver Slipper. She indorsed the check in blank and left it on her dresser at home. Fred Watkins broke into Bluiett's house and stole the check. Watkins took the check to the local auto store, where he bought two tires at a cost of $71.21. He obtained the balance of the check in cash. Could the auto store qualify as a holder in due course?

5. While cleaning out his self-storage locker in Largo, Florida, in late January 2001, Kim Griffith found a certificate of deposit issued by Mellon Bank, N.A., of Pittsburgh, Pennsylvania, on July 3, 1975, for the amount of $530,000. The certificate was entitled "Negotiable Certificate of Deposit, No. I-48346" and stated as follows:

> This certifies that there has been deposited with this Bank the sum of FIVE HUNDRED AND THIRTY THOUSAND AND 00/100 * * DOLLARS $530,000* which will be paid to bearer on August 4, 1975 with interest at the rate of 5.75% per annum on presentation of this certificate at any office of this Bank in Pennsylvania. This deposit is not subject to check, draft, or any form of withdrawal prior to the above maturity date.

Griffith and his wife found the certificate in one of several books stored in their storage locker as he and his wife were shaking out all of the books in the locker. Griffith purchased the books in the locker from some unnamed person and was unable to recall how much he had paid for them. On its face, the certificate of deposit had not been marked paid. On August 15, 2002, Griffith presented the certificate for payment in person at a Mellon Bank office in Pennsylvania. Mellon refused to honor the certificate of deposit, and Griffith brought suit against Mellon seeking payment of the certificate, seeking to recover $2.5 million dollars in principal and interest. Among the issues in the case were whether Griffith was a holder in due course or a person entitled to enforce the instrument.

Pennsylvania law provides that:

> After the lapse of twenty years, all debts . . . not within the orbit of the Statue of Limitations are presumed to have been paid. . . . Until the passage of twenty years it is the burden of the debtor to prove payment; after the passage of twenty years, it is the burden of the creditor to prove non-payment and for the satisfaction of such

burden the evidence must be clear and convincing and must consist of proof other than the specialty itself.

Griffith presented evidence that the certificate had not been marked paid and it was the policy of Mellon Bank to mark certificates paid or to destroy them when they are redeemed. Was Griffith a holder in due course or a person otherwise entitled to enforce the certificate of deposit?

6. Charles Alcombrack was appointed guardian for his son, Chad Alcombrack, who was seven years old and the beneficiary of his grandfather's life insurance policy. The insurance company issued a check for $30,588.39 made payable to "Charles Alcombrack, Guardian of the Estate of Chad Stephen Alcombrack, a Minor." The attorney for the son's estate directed the father to take the check, along with the letters of guardianship issued to the father, to the bank and open up a guardianship savings and checking account. Instead, the father took the check, without the letters of guardianship, to the Olympic Bank and opened a personal checking and a personal savings account. Despite the fact that the check was payable to the father in his guardianship capacity, the bank allowed the father to place the entire amount in his newly opened personal accounts. The father used all but $320.60 of the trust money for his personal benefit. A new guardian, J. David Smith, was appointed for Chad. Smith brought suit against the Olympic Bank, on Chad's behalf, to recover the amount of the check. Was the bank a holder in due course of the check?

7. On December 11, 1990, two American Express money orders in the amounts of $550 and $650, respectively, which were payable to Stacey Anne Dillabough, were presented to Chuckie Enterprise, Inc. (Chuckie's), a check-cashing operation in Philadelphia. The money orders were duly indorsed, and photo identifications were provided by the payee, whereupon Chuckie's paid the face amounts minus a 2 percent fee. Dillabough was a previous customer of Chuckie's and was recognized as such by the president of Chuckie's, Charles Giunta, who handled the transaction. The two money orders had been stolen from the premises of an American Express agent. When stolen, the money orders were signed with the preprinted signature of the chairman of American Express but were blank as to payee, date, sender, and amount. When presented to Chuckie's, however, they had been completed by

persons unknown. Dillabough's role is not clear from the case. She could have been an accomplice of the thief, the thief, or even someone who bought it from the thief, but the court does not say, and it is not critical to the issue here.

The money orders were passed through the usual banking channels and were presented for payment at United Bank of Grand Junction, Colorado. American Express, having noted on its "fraud log" that the money orders were stolen, returned the money orders marked "Reported Lost or Stolen Do Not Redeposit." American Express refused to pay the amounts of the money orders.

Triffin, a commercial discounter, purchased the dishonored money orders for cash from Chuckie's and took an assignment of all of Chuckie's rights, claims, and interests in the money orders. Triffin brought suit against Dillabough and American Express, demanding payment of the stolen money orders. Judgment was entered against Dillabough by default. Where blank money orders were stolen and completed without authorization prior to their negotiation, can the transferee enforce the instruments as completed if he qualifies as a holder in due course?

8. Panlick, the owner of an apartment building, entered into a written contract with Bucci, a paving contractor, whereby Bucci was to install asphalt paving on the parking lot of the building. When Bucci finished the job, Panlick gave Bucci a check for $6,500 and a promissory note for $7,593 with interest at 10 percent due six months from its date. When the note came due, Panlick refused to pay it. Bucci brought suit to collect the note, and Panlick claimed that there had been a failure of consideration because the asphalt was defectively installed. Can Panlick assert this defense against Bucci?

9. Ralph Herrmann wrote a check for $10,000 payable to Ormsby House, a hotel-casino in Carson City, Nevada, and exchanged it for three counterchecks he had written earlier that evening to acquire gaming chips. Ormsby House was unable to collect the proceeds from the check because Herrmann had insufficient funds in his account. The debt evidenced by the check was assigned to Sea Air Support, Inc., d/b/a Automated Accounts Associates, for collection. Sea Air was also unsuccessful in its attempts to collect and filed a lawsuit against Herrmann to recover on the dishonored check. Nevada law then provided that all

instruments drawn for the purpose of reimbursing or repaying any money knowingly lent or advanced for gaming are "utterly void, frustrate, and of none effect." Is Herrmann still liable to Sea Air?

10. Pedro and Paula de la Fuente were visited by a representative of Aluminum Industries, Inc., who was seeking to sell them aluminum siding for their home. They agreed to purchase the siding and signed a number of documents, including a retail installment contract and a promissory note for $9,137.24. The contract granted Aluminum Industries, Inc., a first lien on the de la Fuentes' residence; this was in violation of the Texas Civil Code, which prohibited such provisions. The promissory note contained a notice in bold type as required by the Federal Trade Commission. It read in part:

NOTICE: ANY HOLDER OF THIS CONSUMER CREDIT CONTACT IS SUBJECT TO ALL CLAIMS AND DEFENSES WHICH THE DEBTOR COULD ASSERT AGAINST THE SELLER OF GOODS OR SERVICES OBTAINED PURSUANT HERETO WITH THE PROCEEDS THEREOF.

Aluminum Industries assigned the promissory note and first lien to Home Savings Association. Aluminum Industries subsequently went out of business. Home Savings brought suit against the de la Fuentes to collect the balance due on the note. Home Savings contended that it was a holder in due course and that the de la Fuentes could not assert any defense against it that they had against Aluminum Industries. Can an assignee of a consumer promissory note that includes the notice required by the FTC qualify as a holder in due course?

Online Research

Does Your State Void Instruments Given for Gambling Debts?

Use the Internet to locate the statutes for your state. Ascertain whether in your state checks and notes given in satisfaction of gambling debts are void.

LIABILITY OF PARTIES

hen you sign a promissory note, you expect that you will be liable for paying the note on the day it is due. Similarly, when you sign a check and mail it off to pay a bill, you expect that it will be paid by your bank out of your checking account and that if there are not sufficient funds in the account to cover it, you will have to make it good out of other funds you have. The liability of the maker of a note and of the drawer of a check is commonly understood.

However, there are other ways a person can become liable on a negotiable instrument. Moreover, some of the usual liability rules are modified when a party is negligent in issuing or paying a negotiable instrument—or otherwise contributes to a potential loss.

The issues that will be discussed in this chapter include:

- Suppose you indorse a check that is payable to your order and "cash" it at a check-cashing service. What liability have you assumed by indorsing and transferring the check?
- Suppose you make out a check in such a way that someone is able to raise (change) the amount of the check from $1 to $1,000 and then obtain payment of the check from the drawee bank. Will your bank be entitled to charge your account for $1,000 or can you limit the charge to $1, the original amount of the check?
- Suppose one of your employees who has responsibility for writing checks makes some of them payable to people you normally do business with and then keeps the checks, indorses the checks in the name of the named payee, and obtains payment of the checks for her own purposes. Are you entitled to have your account recredited for the amount of the checks on the grounds they were paid over a forged indorsement?
- Whether, in some circumstances, it is ethical to use a qualified indorsement to avoid the contractual liability of an indorser.

THUS FAR IN PART 7, Commercial Paper, the focus has been on the nature of, and requirements for, negotiable instruments as well as the rights that an owner of an instrument can obtain and how to obtain them. Another important aspect to negotiable instruments concerns how a person becomes liable on a negotiable instrument and the nature of the liability incurred.

Liability in General

Liability on negotiable instruments flows from signatures on the instruments as well as actions taken concerning them. It can arise from the fact that a person has signed a negotiable instrument or has authorized someone else to sign it. The liability depends on the capacity in which the person signs the instrument. Liability also arises from (1) transfer or presentment of an instrument; (2) negligence relating to the issuance, alteration, or indorsement of the instrument; (3) improper payment; or (4) conversion of an instrument.

Contractual Liability

When a person signs a negotiable instrument, whether as maker, drawer, indorser, or in some other capacity, she generally becomes contractually liable on the instrument. As mentioned above, this contractual liability depends on the capacity in which the person signed the instrument. The terms of the contract of the parties to a negotiable instrument are not set out in the text of the instrument. Rather, Article 3 of the Uniform Commercial Code supplies the terms, which are as much a part of the instrument as they would be as part of its text.

Primary and Secondary Liability
A party to a negotiable instrument may be either *primarily liable or secondarily liable* for payment of it. A person who is primarily liable has agreed to pay the negotiable instrument. For example, the maker of a promissory note is the person who is primarily liable on the note.

A person who is secondarily liable is like a guarantor on a contract; Article 3 requires a secondary party to pay the negotiable instrument only if a person who is primarily liable defaults on that obligation. Chapter 28, Introduction to Credit and Secured Transactions, discusses guarantors of contracts.

Secondary liability is a contingent liability. To trigger it, the instrument must be properly *presented* for payment or acceptance, the instrument must be *dishonored* (that is, the payment or acceptance must be refused or not obtained within the prescribed time), and *notice of the dishonor* must be given to the person secondarily liable. The notice may be given in any reasonable manner, such as orally, in writing, or by e-mail, and must be given to any party other than a bank (which has a very limited time to provide the notice) within 30 days following the day of the dishonor.

Obligation of a Maker
The **maker** of a promissory note is primarily liable for payment of it. The maker makes an unconditional promise to pay a fixed amount of money and is responsible for making good on that promise. The obligation of the maker is to pay the negotiable instrument according to its terms at the time he issues it or, if it is not issued, then according to its terms at the time it first came into possession of a holder [3–412].[1] If the material terms of the note are not complete when the maker signs it, then the maker's obligation is to pay the note as it is completed, provided that the terms filled in are as authorized. If the instrument is incomplete when the maker signs it and it is completed in an unauthorized manner, then the maker's liability will depend on whether the person seeking to enforce the instrument can qualify as a holder in due course.

The obligation of the maker is owed to (1) a *person entitled to enforce the instrument* or (2) any indorser who paid the instrument pursuant to her indorser's liability (discussed below). A person entitled to enforce an instrument includes (1) the holder of the instrument; (2) a nonholder in possession of the instrument who has the rights of a holder; and (3) a person not in possession of the instrument who has the right to enforce the instrument under section 3–309, which deals with lost, destroyed, or stolen instruments.

Revised Article 3 provides that the *drawer of a cashier's check* has the same obligation as the maker or issuer of a note. Thus, it treats the bank drawer of a draft drawn on a bank the same as a note for purposes of the issuer's liability rather than treating the issuer as a drawer of a draft [3–412].

Obligation of a Drawee or an Acceptor
The **acceptor** of a draft is obligated to pay the draft according to the terms at the time of its acceptance. As was discussed in Chapter 31, acceptance is the drawee's signed engagement to honor the draft as presented—and is commonly indicated by the signature of the acceptor on the instrument itself. The acceptor's obligation extends to (1) a person entitled to enforce the draft, (2) the drawer, and (3) an indorser who paid the instrument pursuant to her indorser's liability [3–413].

If the certification of a check or other acceptance of a draft states the amount certified or accepted, the obligation of the acceptor is that amount. If the certification or acceptance does not state an amount, if the amount of the instrument is subsequently raised and then the instrument is negotiated to a holder in due course, the obligation of the acceptor is the amount of the instrument at the time a holder in due course takes it [3–413(b)].

At the time a payee receives possession of a check or other draft, the payee gets the drawer's contract to pay the instrument if the drawee—bank or buyer of goods—does not pay. (This liability is discussed in the next section of this chapter.) *Issuance* of the check or draft, however, does not obligate the *drawee* to pay it. Like other Article 3 contracts discussed in this chapter, the drawee does not have liability on the instrument until it *signs* the instrument.

The drawer or a holder of the check may ask the drawee bank to accept or certify the check. The drawee bank certifies the check by signing its name to the check and, with that act, accepts liability as acceptor. The drawee bank debits, or takes the money out of, the drawer's account and holds the money to pay the check. If the drawee bank certifies the check, it becomes primarily, or absolutely, liable for paying the check as it reads at the time of its acceptance [3–413], and its acceptance discharges the drawer and indorsers who indorsed before the acceptance. Similarly, when a trade draft is presented

---

[1]The numbers in brackets refer to sections of the Uniform Commercial Code (UCC), which is reproduced in the appendix.

for acceptance or payment, and the named drawee accepts it, then the drawee accepts the obligation set forth in the instrument and the drawer and earlier indorsers are discharged.

A drawee has no liability on a check or other draft unless it certifies or accepts the check or draft—that is, agrees to be liable on it. However, a drawee bank that refuses to pay a check when it is presented for payment may be liable to the drawer for wrongfully refusing payment, assuming the drawer had sufficient funds in his checking account to cover it. The next chapter discusses this liability of a drawee bank.

The principle that a drawee has no liability on an instrument to a holder unless it has certified or accepted the instrument is illustrated in the following case, *Harrington v. MacNab*.

Harrington v. MacNab   45 UCC Rep.2d 698 (U.S.D.C.D. Maryland 2001)

Harrington, an experienced attorney, conducted a settlement on a piece of property in Cambridge, Maryland, being purchased by a couple named MacNab. They showed up for the settlement without certified funds, but rather with a personal check drawn on their Merrill Lynch cash management account for $150,128.70. Instead of refusing to go forward with the settlement, Harrington phoned the Merrill Lynch office in Delaware where the MacNabs had their account. He was told by a Ms. Ruark of Merrill Lynch, in response to his inquiry, that there were sufficient funds in the MacNabs' account to cover the check and that she would put a hold on the account in the amount of the check. When asked to confirm this in writing, Ms. Ruark sent a fax to Harrington that read as follows: "This letter is to verify that the funds are available in the Merrill Lynch account. There is a pend on the funds for the check that was given to you."

Harrington interpreted "pend" to mean that a hold would be placed on the MacNabs' account to cover the check in question. Merrill Lynch later claimed it meant that the funds deposited to cover that check were not themselves yet cleared. In fact, the MacNabs' account did not contain sufficient cleared funds to cover the check, which bounced. Subsequent promises by the MacNabs to make the check good came to naught. Harrington obtained a judgment against the MacNabs, but it was never satisfied in full. Harrington then brought suit against Merrill Lynch for negligent misrepresentation.

Smalkin, District Judge

There are no reported cases in Maryland in which a payee on a check has recovered against the drawee (or one, like Merrill Lynch, in the position of a drawee) for a negligent statement that there were sufficient (cleared) funds in the drawee's account to cover a check and/or that a hold would correspondingly be placed on the account. This court is of the opinion that the Court of Appeals of Maryland would not recognize a cause of action on these facts.

Here, there is no contractual privity or its equivalent between Mr. Harrington and Merrill Lynch which was in a position equivalent to that of the drawee on the MacNabs' check (a check is a species of draft, see section 3–104[f]), nor can any argument be made that Mr. Harrington was a third-party beneficiary of the MacNab cash management account agreement any more than the Baltimore Gas and Electric Company is, by virtue of the fact I draw it a check to cover my utility bill, the third party beneficiary of my checking-account contract with my bank.

To hold that such a relationship existed in this case would lead to the result that any payee on a check who makes inquiry is in the equivalent of contractual privity with the drawee, a proposition that would place substantial and potential unlimited liability on drawees for uncertified checks in contravention of the basic policies underlying the checking system in the United States as codified in the Uniform Commercial Code. For example, the UCC section 3–408 specifically provides that a drawee is not liable as an assignee of the drawer on a check. Even more to the point, a drawee has no contract liability on a check to a payee unless and until it has accepted the check, viz, certified it. See UCC sections 3–408 and 3–409. Acceptance requires the formality of the drawee's signature on the check. See UCC section 3–409(a).

To recognize a cause of action under the circumstances of this case essentially would create a tort remedy allowing suit to be brought for oral certification of checks, in clear violation of the policies of the Uniform Commercial Code and hundreds of years of commercial law.

Furthermore . . . it can hardly be claimed that reliance by an experienced real estate attorney on the statements in this case in lieu of adhering to the sound practice of requiring the buyer to pay with an accepted draft (certified check) or bank draft is justifiable. Indeed, the reason for the practice of requiring certified or bank checks is that in the eyes of the UCC, such instruments are the equivalent of cash as far as satisfying the underlying obligation. See UCC section 3–310(a).

Summary judgment granted for Merrill Lynch.

Obligation of a Drawer

The **drawer's** obligation is that if the drawee dishonors an unaccepted check (or draft), the drawer will pay the check (or draft) according to its terms at the time he issued it or, if it was not issued, according to its terms at the time it first came into possession of a holder. If the draft was not complete when issued but was completed as authorized, then the obligation is to pay it as completed. If any completion is not authorized, then the obligation will depend on whether the person seeking to enforce the instrument can qualify as a holder in due course. A person entitled to enforce the draft or an indorser who paid the draft pursuant to his indorser's liability may enforce the drawer's obligation [3–414(b)].

For example, Janis draws a check on her account at First National Bank payable to the order of Collbert. If First National does not pay the check when Collbert presents it for payment, then Janis is liable to Collbert on the basis of her drawer's obligation.

If a draft is accepted by a bank—for example, if the drawee bank certifies a check—the drawer is discharged of her drawer's obligation. If someone other than a bank accepts a draft, then the obligation of the drawer to pay the draft, if the draft is dishonored, is the same as an indorser (discussed next) [3–414(c) and (d)].

Obligation of an Indorser

A person who indorses a negotiable instrument usually is secondarily liable. An indorser is liable upon the *dishonor* by the maker (of a note), drawer (of an unaccepted draft) or the drawee (of an accepted draft), and the indorser's *receipt of notice of the dishonor.* Unless the indorser qualifies or otherwise disclaims liability, the **indorser**'s obligation on dishonor of the instrument is to pay the amount due on the instrument according to its terms at the time he indorsed it or if he indorsed it when incomplete, then according to its terms when completed, provided that it is completed as authorized. The **indorser** owes the obligation to a person entitled to enforce the instrument or to any subsequent indorser who had to pay it [3–415].

The indorser can avoid this liability only by qualifying his indorsement, such as "without recourse," on the instrument when he indorses it [3–415(b)].

Indorsers are liable to each other in the chronological order in which they indorse, from the last indorser back to the first. For example, Mark Maker gives a promissory note to Paul Payee. Payee indorses it and negotiates it to Fred First, who indorses it and negotiates it to Shirley Second. If Maker does not pay the note when Second takes it to him for payment, then Second can require First to pay it to her. First is secondarily liable on the basis of his indorsement. First, in turn, can require Payee to pay him because Payee also became secondarily liable when he indorsed it. Then, Payee is left to try to collect the note from Maker. Second also could have skipped over First and proceeded directly against Payee on his indorsement. First has no liability to Payee, however, because First indorsed after Payee indorsed the note.

If a bank accepts a draft (for example, by certifying a check) after an indorsement is made, the acceptance discharges the liability of the indorser [3–415(d)]. If notice of dishonor is required and proper notice is not given to the indorser, she is discharged of liability [3–415(c)]. And, where no one presents a check or gives it to a depositary bank for collection within 30 days after the date of an indorsement, the indorser's liability is discharged [3–415(e)].

Obligation of an Accommodation Party

An **accommodation party** is a person who signs a negotiable instrument for the purpose of lending her credit to another party to the instrument but is not a direct beneficiary of the value given for the instrument. For example, a bank might be reluctant to lend money to—and take a note from—Payee because of his shaky financial condition. However, the bank may be willing to lend money to Payee if he signs the note and has a relative or a friend also sign the note as an accommodation maker.

The obligation of an accommodation party depends on the capacity in which the party signs the instrument [3–419]. If Maker has his brother Sam sign a note as an

CYBERLAW IN ACTION

With the advent of high-resolution scanners, sophisticated desktop publishing programs, and laser printers that print in color, forgery of negotiable instruments has become increasingly easier and more common with significant financial risks for those who may unwittingly accept such instruments in payment for goods and services and/or pass them along to others.

The April 26, 2005, edition of *The New York Times* carried a story headlined "A Common Currency for Online Fraud: Forgers of U.S. Postal Money Orders Grow in Numbers and Skill." The story begins:

> Fake checks have been the stock in trade of online fraud artists for years. Now authorities are noting a surge in schemes involving sophisticated counterfeiting of a different form of payment: United States postal money orders. And the fleecing of victims often begins in an e-mail in box.

After noting a very significant increase in counterfeit postal money orders that have been intercepted by federal law enforcement officials, the article details how the scams, often involving international forgers, work. Historically, postal money orders have been considered very difficult to forge, and sellers of goods view them as the same as cash and preferable to personal checks. In the recent scams, online buyers send money orders in payment for goods which are then shipped. By the time the seller becomes aware that the postal money order was counterfeit, the buyer has the goods and the seller has no way of getting the money or the goods back from the erstwhile buyer. Sometimes the purchases are of expensive items like computers. In another variant of the scam, the buyer sends a postal money order for much more than the cost of the item—and requests that the seller send the item and remit cash for the difference between the cost of the item and the amount of the money order. Thus the "buyer"

gains both cash and merchandise in exchange for a worthless piece of paper.

In addition to the scrutiny from law enforcement officials that may come from being in possession of counterfeit postal money orders, or from trying to pass—or actually passing—them on to others, the person who takes and passes along a counterfeit order may well incur some of the liability discussed in this chapter. For example, Ralph has taken a postal money order in payment for a computer he sold and then shipped to a purchaser in Nigeria. When he deposits the postal money order in his account at his bank—or takes it to the post office to seek payment of it—he will be asked to indorse his name on the back of the order. You may recall from Chapter 31, Negotiable Instruments, that money orders are commonly in a form that meets the requirements for being a negotiable instrument. When the bank—or the post office—discovers that the postal money order given to them by Ralph is a forgery, they will go back against him to recoup the money they credited to his account or paid to him. They can do so on the basis of his contractual liability as an indorser. By indorsing the instrument, he obligated himself to make the instrument good if it was dishonored. Ralph, in turn, is left with what may be a fairly worthless right to recoup the money from the person in Nigeria who sent him the counterfeit instrument.

As bank and other officials are alerted to counterfeiting of particularly kinds of negotiable instruments, we can expect that the scam artists will change their targets or increase the sophistication of their forgeries so as to more readily pass without detection. Legitimate negotiable instruments offer lots of advantages to those who use them. But in a world where things may not be what they appear to be, it can be important to your financial well-being to know the person you are taking an instrument from and be confident that if it turns out that there is something wrong with it, you will be able to recoup what you paid or gave for it.

---

accommodation maker, then Sam has the same contractual liability as a maker. Sam is primarily liable on the note. The bank may ask Sam to pay the note before asking Maker to pay. However, if Sam pays the note to the bank, he has the right to recover his payment from Maker, the person on whose behalf he signed.

Similarly, if a person signs a check as an accommodation indorser, his contractual liability is that of an indorser. If the accommodation indorser has to make good on that liability, he can collect in turn from the person on whose behalf he signed.

Signing an Instrument
No person is contractually liable on a negotiable instrument unless she or her

authorized agent has signed it and the signature is binding on the represented person. A signature can be any name, word, or mark used in place of a written signature [3–401]. As discussed earlier, the capacity in which a person signs an instrument determines his liability on the instrument.

Signature by an Authorized Agent
An authorized agent can sign a negotiable instrument. If Sandra Smith authorized her attorney to sign checks as her agent, then she is liable on any checks properly signed by the attorney as her agent. All negotiable instruments signed by corporations have to be signed by an agent of the corporation who is authorized to sign negotiable instruments.

If a person purporting to act as a representative signs an instrument by signing either the name of the represented person or the name of the signer, that signature binds the represented person to the same extent she would be bound if the signature were on a simple contract. If the represented person has authorized the signature of the representative, it is the "authorized signature of the represented person" and the represented person is liable on the instrument, whether or not identified in the instrument. This brings the Code in line with the general principle of agency law that binds an undisclosed principal on a simple contract. For example, if Principal authorizes Agent to borrow money on Principal's behalf and Agent signs her name to a note without disclosing that the signature was on behalf of Principal, Agent is liable on the note. In addition, if the person entitled to enforce the note can show that Principal authorized Agent to sign on his behalf, then Principal is liable on the note as well.

When a representative signs an authorized signature to an instrument, then the representative is not bound provided the signature shows "unambiguously" that the signature was made on behalf of the represented person who is named in the instrument [3–402(b)(1)]. For example, if a note is signed "XYZ, Inc. by Flanigan, Treasurer," Flanigan is not liable on the instrument in his own right but XYZ, Inc., is liable.

If an authorized representative signs his name as the representative of a drawer of a check without noting his representative status but the check is payable from an account of the represented person who is identified on the check, the signer is not liable on the check as long as his signature was authorized [3–402(c)]. The rationale for this provision is that because most checks today identify the person on whose account the check is drawn, no one is deceived into thinking that the person signing the check is meant to be liable.

Except for the check situation noted above, a representative is personally liable to a holder in due course that took the instrument without notice that the representative was not intended to be liable if (1) the form of the signature does not show unambiguously that the signature was made in a representative capacity or (2) the instrument does not identify the represented person. As to persons other than a holder in due course without notice of the representative nature of the signature, the representative is liable *unless* she can prove that the original parties did not intend her to be liable on the instrument [3–402(b)(2)].

Thus, if an agent or a representative signs a negotiable instrument on behalf of someone else, the agent should indicate clearly that he is signing as the representative of someone else. For example, Kim Darby, the president of Swimwear, Inc., is authorized to sign negotiable instruments for the company. If Swimwear borrows money from the bank and the bank asks her to sign a 90-day promissory note, Darby should sign it either "Swimwear, Inc., by Kim Darby, President" or "Kim Darby, President, for Swimwear, Inc." If Kim Darby signed the promissory note merely "Kim Darby," she could be personally liable on the note. Similarly, if Clara Carson authorizes Arthur Anderson, an attorney, to sign checks for her, Anderson should make sure either that the checks identify Clara Carson as the account involved or should sign them "Clara Carson by Arthur Anderson, Agent." Otherwise, he risks being personally liable on them.

Unauthorized Signature

If someone signs a person's name to a negotiable instrument without that person's authorization or approval, the signature does not bind the person whose name appears. However, the signature is effective as the signature of the unauthorized signer in favor of any person who in good faith pays the instrument or takes it for value [3–403(a)]. For example, if Tom Thorne steals Ben Brown's checkbook and signs Brown's name to a check, Brown is not liable on the check because Brown had not authorized Thorne to sign Brown's name. Thorne can be liable on the check, however, because he did sign it, even though he did not sign it in his own name. Thorne's forgery of Brown's signature operates as Thorne's signature. Thus, if Thorne cashed the check at the bank, Thorne would be liable to it or if he negotiated it to a store for value, he would be liable to the store to make it good.

Even though a signature is not "authorized" when it is put on an instrument initially, it can be ratified later by the person represented [3–403(a)]. It also should be noted that if more than one person must sign to constitute the authorized signature of an organization, the signature of the organization is unauthorized if one of the required signatures is lacking [3–403(b)]. Corporate and other accounts sometimes require multiple signatures as a matter of maintaining sound financial control.

Contractual Liability in Operation

To bring the contractual liability of the various parties to a negotiable instrument into play, generally it is necessary that the instrument be *presented for payment*. In addition, to hold the parties that are secondarily liable on the instrument to their contractual liability, generally it is necessary that the instrument be *presented for payment* and *dishonored*.

Presentment of a Note

The maker of a note is primarily liable to pay it when it is due. Normally, the holder takes the note to the maker at the time it is due and asks the maker to pay it. Sometimes, the note may provide for payment to be made at a bank or the maker sends the payment to the holder at the due date. The party to whom the holder presents the instrument, without dishonoring the instrument, may (1) require the exhibition of the instrument, (2) ask for reasonable identification of the person making presentment, (3) ask for evidence of his authority to make it if he is making it for another person, or (4) return the instrument for lack of any necessary indorsement, (5) ask that a receipt be signed for any payment made, and (6) surrender the instrument if full payment is made [3–501].

Dishonor of a note occurs if the maker does not pay the amount due when (1) it is presented in the case of (*a*) a demand note or (*b*) a note payable at or through a bank on a definite date that is presented on or after that date, or (2) if it is not paid on the date payable in the case of a note payable on a definite date but not payable at or through a bank [3–502]. If the maker or payor dishonors the note, the holder can seek payment from any persons who indorsed the note before the holder took it. The basis for going after the indorsers is that they are secondarily liable. To hold the indorsers to their contractual obligation, the holder must give them notice of the dishonor. The notice can be either written or oral [3–503].

For example, Susan Strong borrows $1,000 from Jack Jones and gives him a promissory note for $1,000 at 9 percent annual interest payable in 90 days. Jones indorses the note "Pay to the order of Ralph Smith" and negotiates the note to Ralph Smith. At the end of the 90 days, Smith takes the note to Strong and presents it for payment. If Strong pays Smith the $1,000 and accrued interest, she can have Smith mark it "paid" and give it back to her. If Strong does not pay the note to Smith when he presents it for payment, then she has dishonored the note. Smith should give notice of the dishonor to Jones and advise him that he intends to hold Jones secondarily liable on his indorsement. Smith may collect payment of the note from Jones. Jones, after making the note good to Smith, can try to collect the note from Strong on the ground that she defaulted on the contract she made as maker of the note. Of course, Smith also could sue Strong directly on the basis of her maker's obligation.

Presentment of a Check or a Draft

The holder should present a check or draft to the drawee. The presentment can be either for payment or for acceptance (certification) of the check or draft. Under Revised Article 3, the presentment may be made by any commercially reasonable means, including a written, oral, or electronic communication [3–501]. The drawee is not obligated on a check or draft unless it accepts (certifies) it [3–408]. An acceptance of a draft is the drawee's signed commitment to honor the draft as presented. The acceptance must be written on the draft, and it may consist of the drawee's signature alone [3–409].

A drawer who writes a check issues an order to the drawee to pay a certain amount out of the drawer's account to the payee (or to someone authorized by the payee). This order is not an assignment of the funds in the drawer's account [3–408]. The drawee bank does not have an obligation to the payee to pay the check unless it certifies the check. However, the drawee bank usually does have a separate contractual obligation (apart from Article 3) to the drawer to pay any properly payable checks for which funds are available in the drawer's account.

For example, Janet Payne has $850 in a checking account at First National Bank and writes a check for $100 drawn on First National and payable to Ralph Smith. The writing of the check is the issuance of an order by Payne to First National to pay $100 from her account to Smith or to whomever Smith requests it to be paid. First National owes no obligation to Smith to pay the $100 unless it has certified the check. However, if Smith presents the check for payment and First National refuses to pay it even though there are sufficient funds in Payne's account, then First National is liable to Payne for breaching its contractual obligation to her to pay items properly payable from existing funds in her account. Chapter 34, Checks and Electronic Transfers, discusses the liability of a bank for wrongful dishonor of checks in more detail.

If the drawee bank does not pay or certify a check when it is properly presented for payment or acceptance (certification), the drawee bank has dishonored the check [3–502]. Similarly, if a draft is not paid on the date it is due (or accepted by the drawee on the due date for acceptance), it has been dishonored. The holder of the draft or check then can proceed against either the drawer or any indorsers on their liability. To do so, the holder must give them notice of the dishonor [3–503]. Notice of dishonor, like presentment, can be by any commercially reasonable means, including oral, written, or electronic communication. Under certain circumstances, set out in section 3–504, presentment or notice of dishonor may be excused.

Suppose Matthews draws a check for $200 on her account at a bank payable to the order of Williams.

Contract Liability Based on Signature on a Negotiable Instrument

Concept	Contractual Liability

Primary and Secondary Liability	Every party (other than an indorser who qualifies his/her indorsement) who *signs a negotiable instrument* is either primarily or secondarily liable for payment of the instrument when it comes due.
	
	1. *Primary liability*—Makers and acceptors (a drawee that promises to pay the instrument when it is presented for payment at a later time) are primarily liable.
	2. *Secondary liability*—Drawers and indorsers are secondarily liable. Parties who are secondarily liable on an instrument promise to pay the instrument only if the following events occur:
	   a. The instrument is properly presented for payment.
	   b. The instrument is dishonored.
	   c. Timely notice of the dishonor is given to the party who is secondarily liable.

Accommodation Parties	An accommodation party is one who signs an instrument for the purpose of lending his credit to another party to the instrument but is not a direct beneficiary of the value given for the instrument. The obligation of the accommodation party depends on the capacity in which the party signs the instrument. Thus, an accommodation maker has the same obligation as a maker and is primarily liable while an accommodation indorser is secondarily liable on the instrument.
Signature by Agent	An authorized agent can sign an instrument on behalf of the principal and create liability for the principal on the instrument. 1. If the represented person authorized the signature, then the represented person is liable on the instrument whether or not identified in the instrument. 2. If the agent signs an authorized signature to an instrument, the agent is not personally bound on the instrument provided the signature shows unambiguously that the signature was made on behalf of the represented person. 3. If the agent does not identify the represented party in the instrument, then the agent is liable as well unless the instrument is a check drawn on an account for which the agent is an authorized signature.
Unauthorized Signature	An unauthorized signature operates as the signature of the unauthorized signer in favor of a person who in good faith pays the instrument or takes it for value—but it is wholly inoperative as the signature of the person whose name is signed unless: 1. The person whose name is signed ratifies (affirms) the signature. 2. The person whose signature is signed is precluded from denying it.

Williams indorses the check "Pay to the order of Clark, Williams" and negotiates it to Clark. When Clark takes the check to the bank, it refuses to pay the check because there are insufficient funds in Matthews's account to cover the check. The check has been presented and dishonored. Clark has two options: He can proceed against Williams on Williams's secondary liability as an indorser (because by putting an unqualified indorsement on the check, Williams is obligated to make the check good if it was not honored by the drawee). Or, he can proceed against Matthews on Matthews's obligation as drawer because in drawing the check, Matthews must pay any person entitled to enforce the check if it is dishonored. Because Clark dealt with Williams, Clark is probably more likely to return the check to Williams for payment. Williams then has to go against Matthews on Matthews's liability as drawer.

Time of Presentment
If an instrument is payable at a definite time, the holder should present it for payment on the due date. In the case of a demand instrument, the nature of the instrument, trade or bank usage,

and the facts of the particular case determine a reasonable time for presentment for acceptance or payment. In a farming community, for example, a reasonable time to present a promissory note that is payable on demand may be six months or within a short time after the crops are ready for sale, because the holder commonly expects payment from the proceeds of the crops.

Warranty Liability

Whether or not a person signs a negotiable instrument, a person who transfers such an instrument or presents it for payment or acceptance may incur liability on the basis of certain implied warranties. These warranties are (1) **transfer warranties,** which persons who transfer negotiable instruments make to their transferees; and (2) **presentment warranties,** which persons who present negotiable instruments for payment or acceptance (certification) make to those who pay or accept the instruments.

Transfer Warranties A person who transfers a negotiable instrument to someone else and for consideration makes five warranties to his immediate transferee. If the transfer is by indorsement, the transferor makes these warranties to all subsequent transferees. The five transfer warranties are:

1. The warrantor is a person entitled to enforce the instrument. (In essence the transferor warrants that there are no unauthorized or missing indorsements that prevent the transferor from making the transferee a holder or a person entitled to enforce the instrument.)

2. All signatures on the instrument are authentic or authorized.

3. The instrument has not been altered.

4. The instrument is not subject to a defense or a claim in recoupment that any party can assert against the warrantor.

5. The warrantor has no knowledge of any insolvency proceedings commenced with respect to the maker or acceptor or, in the case of an unaccepted draft, the drawer [3–416(a)]. Note that this is not a warranty against difficulty in collection or insolvency—the warranty stops with the warrantor's knowledge.

Revised Article 3 provides that in the event of a breach of a transfer warranty, a beneficiary of the transfer warranties who took the instrument in good faith may recover from the warrantor an amount equal to the loss suffered as a result of the breach. However, the damages recoverable may not be more than the amount of the instrument plus expenses and loss of interest incurred as a result of the breach [3–416(b)].

Transferors of instruments other than checks may disclaim the transfer warranties. Unless the warrantor receives notice of a claim for breach of warranty within 30 days after the claimant has reason to know of the breach and the identity of the warrantor, the delay in giving notice of the claim may discharge the warrantor's liability to the extent of any loss the warrantor suffers from the delay, such as the opportunity to proceed against the transferor [3–416(c)].

Although contractual liability often furnishes a sufficient basis for suing a transferor when the party primarily obligated does not pay, warranties are still important. First, they apply even when the transferor did not indorse. Second, unlike contractual liability, they do not depend on presentment, dishonor, and notice, but may be utilized before presentment has been made or after the time for giving notice has expired. Third, a holder may find it easier to return the instrument to a transferor on the ground of breach of warranty than to prove her status as a holder in due course against a maker or drawer.

In the case that follows, *Bank One, N.A. v. Streeter,* the court found that an individual who deposited checks to his account on which the payee's name had been altered breached transfer warranties and was not a person entitled to enforce the instruments.

Bank One, N.A. v. Streeter   58 UCC Rep.2d 1 (U.S.D.C. N.D. Ind. 2005)

On August 20, 2003, Dennis Streeter deposited a check drawn by Economy Gas Company in the amount of $117,469.80 into his Bank One account. On August 22, 2003, Streeter deposited a check drawn by Newspaper Services of America in the amount of $137,374.08 into his Bank One account. Also, on August 22, 2003, Streeter deposited a money order issued by Kroger in the amount of $100,447.05 into his Bank One account. Bank One credited Streeter's account for the three checks. At this time, Bank One did not believe that the checks had been altered. However, after the deposits were made, Bank One received notice from the banks on which the three checks had been drawn that the checks had been altered.

When Economy Gas Company originally issued its check, the payee was "B.P. Products." The name of the payee was altered to "Dennis Streeter." This alteration was made without Economy Gas's knowledge or consent. When Newspaper Services of America originally issued its check, the payee was "N.Y. Times Co." The payee was changed to "Dennis Streeter," and the alteration was made without the knowledge or consent of Newspaper Services of America. When Kroger issued its money order, the initial payee was "SlimFast Foods Co." The payee was altered to "Dennis Streeter," and made without Kroger's knowledge.

Bank One brought suit against Streeter to recover the funds it had credited to his account. The bank asserted that the transfer warranties as set forth in Indiana's Uniform Commercial Code dictate that Streeter is liable to Bank One for its damages stemming from the altered checks. In response, Streeter argued that he had not breached any warranty because he was the person entitled to enforce the instruments and that there was no evidence that the checks were altered by him or that he had any knowledge of any alterations. Bank One moved for summary judgment on the issue of whether Streeter was liable to it for breach of the transfer warranties that (1) he was a person entitled to enforce the instrument and (2) the instrument had not been altered.

Lozano, Judge

Altered checks are governed by Indiana's Uniform Commercial Code ("UCC") Article 3, entitled "Negotiable Instruments," and Article 4, entitled "Bank Deposits and Collections." *Section 3–416(a)* states that "[a] person who transfers an instrument for consideration warrants to the transferee . . . that: (1) the warrantor is a person entitled to enforce the instrument . . . (3) the instrument has not been altered. . . ." Similarly, *section 4–207(a)* provides "[a] customer . . . that transfers an item and receives a settlement or other consideration warrants to the transferee . . . that: (1) the warrantor is a person entitled to enforce the item . . . (3) the item has not been altered. . . ." Both statutes provide "the warranties stated in subsection (a) cannot be disclaimed with respect to checks."

The undisputed evidence shows that Streeter issued these transfer warranties to Bank One when he transferred the Economy Gas check, the Newspaper Services check, and the Kroger money order to Bank One for consideration. Streeter does not deny the general applicability of these warranties, and the Court finds that they apply to this case.

Bank One argues that Streeter breached the warranty of no material alteration. "Alteration" is defined as "an unauthorized change in an instrument that purports to modify in any respect the obligation of a party." *§3–407(a)(1)*.

Initially, Streeter argues that Bank One presented insufficient evidence that the instruments had been altered by Streeter, or that Streeter had any knowledge of any alteration. He contends that the affiants of the affidavits submitted by Bank One did not have personal knowledge of the payee of the check.

Bank One replies that each affidavit submitted by Bank One was signed by an authorized representative of the company that issued the check. After reviewing the affidavits at issue, the Court agrees with Bank One that each affidavit was submitted by an authorized representative of the company that issued the check in question. Moreover, the affidavits establish that the checks were altered by someone without permission from the drawers. Because each individual has attested, in a sworn affidavit, that the respective checks were altered without authorization, this Court refuses to grant Streeter's request to strike.

Streeter also states that at most he was negligent in detecting any alterations in the checks, and that both Bank One and Streeter were not in a position to determine that the checks were altered. Essentially, Streeter argues that because he did not alter the checks himself or have knowledge of the alterations, he could not breach the transfer warranties. Bank One correctly points out that there is no requirement that the party transferring the instrument either alter it or have knowledge of the alteration in order for the transfer warranty to be breached. Since there is no knowledge or notice requirement with respect to the material alteration warranties, the question of whether or not a party breached these warranties is simply a question of whether or not the checks were materially altered. The parties do not dispute the materiality requirement, and it is clear that an alteration adding an alternative payee is a material alteration as the term is used in the UCC.

It is clear that Streeter breached the transfer warranty of material alteration. He issued a non-disclaimable warranty to Bank One that the checks had not been altered. Because there is unrefuted evidence that the checks were in fact altered by someone without authority from the drawers (whether that person was Streeter or someone else is immaterial), Streeter breached the warranty as a matter of law.

Bank One also argues that Streeter was not entitled to enforce the checks because he was not the proper payee of the instruments. Bank One contends that without endorsements of the intended payees, Streeter could not obtain good title to the checks. Bank One argues that because the checks were altered without the endorsements of the intended payees, Streeter was not entitled to enforce the checks, and Streeter breached the warranty that he was entitled to enforce the instrument.

In response, Streeter baldly contends that he was the person entitled to enforce the instruments because the checks were delivered to him as partial payment on his contract. Aside from Streeter's affidavit, he cites to nothing in the record or any other authority to support this assertion. Nor does Streeter present any case law or authority for the proposition that if he did not alter the checks himself, he cannot be held liable for breach of warranty.

Streeter does not dispute that Bank One accepted the checks in good faith. *Section 3–416(b)* establishes that:

> A person to whom the [transfer warranties] are made and who took the instrument in good faith may recover from the warrantor as damages for breach of warranty an

amount equal to the loss suffered as a result of the breach, but not more than the amount of the instrument plus expenses and loss of interest incurred as a result of the breach.

Consequently, because it is undisputed that the checks were altered and Streeter was not entitled to enforce the checks, the Court finds that Streeter breached the warranty of entitlement to enforce the checks.

Summary judgment granted to Bank One on the issue of liability.

Presentment Warranties

Persons who present negotiable instruments for payment or drafts for acceptance also make warranties, but their warranties differ from those transferors make. If an unaccepted draft (such as a check) is presented to the drawee for payment or acceptance and the drawee pays or accepts the draft, then the person obtaining payment or acceptance warrants to the drawee making payment or accepting the draft in good faith that:

1. The warrantor is, or was, at the time the warrantor transferred the draft, a person entitled to enforce the draft or authorized to obtain payment or acceptance of the draft on behalf of a person entitled to enforce the draft.

2. The draft has not been altered.

3. The warrantor has no knowledge that the signature of the drawer of the draft has not been authorized [3–417(a)].

These warranties also are made by any prior transferor of the instrument at the time the person transfers the instrument; the warranties run to the drawee who makes payment or accepts the draft in good faith. Such a drawee would include a drawee bank paying a check presented to it for payment directly or through the bank collection process.

The effect of the third presentment warranty is to leave with the drawee the risk that the drawer's signature is unauthorized, unless the person presenting the draft for payment, or a prior transferor, had knowledge of any lack of authorization.

A drawee who makes payment may recover as damages for any breach of a presentment warranty an amount equal to the amount paid by the drawee less the amount the drawee received or is entitled to receive from the

drawer because of the payment. In addition, the drawee is entitled to compensation for expenses and loss of interest resulting from the breach [3–417(b)]. The drawee's right to recover damages for breach of warranty is not affected by any failure on the part of the drawee to exercise ordinary care in making payment.

If a drawee asserts a claim for breach of a presentment warranty based on an unauthorized indorsement of the draft or an alteration of the draft, the warrantor may defend by showing that the indorsement is effective under the *impostor* or *fictitious payee* rules (discussed later in this chapter) or that the drawer's negligence precludes him from asserting against the drawee the unauthorized indorsement or alteration (also discussed below) [3–417(c)].

If (1) a *dishonored draft* is presented for payment to the drawer or an indorser or (2) any other instrument (such as a note) is presented for payment to a party obligated to pay the instrument and the presenter receives payment, the presenter makes the following presentment warranty:

> The person obtaining payment is a person entitled to enforce the instrument or authorized to obtain payment on behalf of a person entitled to enforce the instrument [3–417(d)].

On breach of this warranty, the person making the payment may recover from the warrantor an amount equal to the amount paid plus expenses and loss of interest resulting from the breach.

With respect to checks, the party presenting the check for payment cannot disclaim the presentment warranties [3–417(e)]. Unless the payor or drawee provides notice of a claim for breach of a presentment warranty to the warrantor within 30 days after the claimant has reason to know of the breach and the identity of the warrantor, the

CONCEPT REVIEW

Transfer Warranties

The five transfer warranties made by a person who transfers a negotiable instrument to someone else for consideration are:

1. The warrantor is entitled to enforce the instrument.
2. All signatures on the instrument are authentic or authorized.
3. The instrument has not been altered.
4. The instrument is not subject to a defense or a claim in recoupment that any party can assert against the warrantor.
5. The warrantor has no knowledge of any insolvency proceedings commenced with respect to the maker or acceptor or, in the case of an unaccepted draft, the drawer.

Who	What Warranties	To Whom
Nonindorsing Transferor	Makes all five transfer warranties	To his immediate transferee only
Indorsing Transferor	Makes all five transfer warranties	To his immediate transferee and all subsequent transferees

warrantor is discharged to the extent of any loss caused by the delay in giving notice of the claim of breach.

Payment or Acceptance by Mistake

A long-standing general rule of negotiable instruments law is that payment or acceptance is final in favor of a holder in due course or payee who changes his position in reliance on the payment or acceptance. Revised Article 3 retains this concept by making payment final in favor of a person who took the instrument in good faith and for value.

However, payment is not final—and may be recovered from—a person who does not meet these criteria where the drawee acted on the mistaken belief that (1) payment of a draft or check has not been stopped, and (2) the signature of the purported drawer of the draft was authorized [3–418(a)]. In some jurisdictions, the drawee's mistaken belief that the account held available funds also could serve as a basis for recovery of the payment [3–418(b)].

As a result, this means that if the drawee bank mistakenly paid a check over a stop-payment order, paid a check with a forged or unauthorized drawer's signature on it, or paid despite the lack of sufficient funds in the drawer's account to cover the check, the bank cannot recover if it paid the check to a presenter who had taken the instrument in good faith and for value. In that case, the drawee bank would have to pursue someone else, such as the forger or unauthorized signer, or seller

whose goods proved to be defective. On the other hand, if the presenter had not taken in good faith or for value, the bank could, in these enumerated instances, recover from the presenter the payment it made by mistake.

Operation of Warranties

Following are three scenarios that show how the transfer and presentment warranties shift the liability back to a wrongdoer or to the person who dealt immediately with a wrongdoer and thus was in the best position to avert the wrongdoing.

Scenario 1 Arthur makes a promissory note for $2,000 payable to the order of Betts. Carlson steals the note from Betts, indorses her (Betts's) name on the back, and gives it to Davidson in exchange for a television set. Davidson negotiates the note for value to Earle, who presents the note to Arthur for payment. Assume that Arthur refuses to pay the note because Betts has advised him that it has been stolen and that he is the person entitled to enforce the instrument. Earle then can proceed to recover the face amount of the note from Davidson on the grounds that as a transferor Davidson has warranted that he is a person entitled to enforce the note and that all signatures were authentic. Davidson, in turn, can proceed against Carlson on the same basis—if he can find Carlson. If he cannot, then Davidson must bear the loss caused by Carlson's wrongdoing. Davidson was in the best position to ascertain whether Carlson was the owner of the note and

Presentment Warranties

If an unaccepted draft (such as a check) is presented for payment or acceptance and the drawee pays or accepts the draft, then the person obtaining payment or acceptance and prior transferors warrant to the drawee:

1. The warrantor is a person entitled to enforce payment or authorized to obtain payment or acceptance on behalf of a person entitled to enforce the draft.

2. The draft has not been altered.

3. The warrantor has no knowledge that the signature of the drawer of the draft has not been authorized.

If (*a*) a dishonored draft is presented for payment to the drawer or indorser or (*b*) any other instrument (such as a note) is presented for payment to a party obligated to pay the instrument and the presenter receives payment, the presenter (as well as a prior transferor of the instrument) makes the following warranty to the person making payment in good faith:

The person obtaining payment is a person entitled to enforce the instrument or authorized to obtain payment on behalf of a person entitled to enforce the instrument.

whether the indorsement in the name of Betts was genuine. Of course, even though Arthur does not have to pay the note to Earle, Arthur remains liable for his underlying obligation to Betts.

Scenario 2 Anderson draws a check for $10 on her checking account at First Bank payable to the order of Brown. Brown cleverly raises the check to $110, indorses it, and negotiates it to Carroll. Carroll then presents the check for payment to First Bank, which pays her $110 and charges Anderson's account for $110. Anderson then asks the bank to recredit her account for the altered check, and it does so. The bank can proceed against Carroll for breach of the presentment warranty that the instrument had not been altered, which she made to the bank when she presented the check for payment. Carroll in turn can proceed against Brown for breach of her transfer warranty that the check had not been altered—if she can find her. Unless she was negligent in drawing the check, Article 3 limits Anderson's liability to $10 because her obligation is to pay the amount in the instrument at the time she issued it.

Scenario 3 Bates steals Albers's checkbook and forges Albers's signature to a check for $100 payable to "cash," which he uses to buy $100 worth of groceries from a grocer. The grocer presents the check to Albers's bank. The bank pays the amount of the check to the grocer and charges Albers's account. Albers then demands that the

bank recredit his account. The bank can recover against the grocer only if the grocer knew that Albers's signature had been forged. Otherwise, the bank must look for Bates. The bank had the responsibility to recognize the true signature of its drawer, Albers, and not to pay the check that contained an unauthorized signature. The bank may be able to resist recrediting Albers's account if it can show he was negligent. The next section of this chapter discusses negligence.

Other Liability Rules

Normally, a bank may not charge against (debit from) the drawer's account a check that has a forged payee's indorsement. Similarly, a maker does not have to pay a note to the person who currently possesses the note if the payee's signature has been forged. If a check or note has been altered—for example, by raising the amount—the drawer or maker usually is liable only for the instrument in the amount for which he originally issued it. However, there are a number of exceptions to these usual rules. These exceptions, as well as liability based on conversion of an instrument, are discussed below.

Negligence A person can be so negligent in writing or signing a negotiable instrument that she in effect invites an alteration or an unauthorized signature on it. If a person has been negligent, Article 3 precludes her from using the alteration or lack of authorization as a reason for not paying a person that in good faith pays the instrument or takes it for value [3–406]. For example, Mary Maker makes out a note for $10 in such a way that someone could alter it to read $10,000. Someone alters the note and negotiates it to Katherine Smith, who can qualify as a holder in due course. Smith can collect $10,000 from Maker. Maker's negligence precludes her from claiming alteration as a defense to paying it. Maker then has to find the person who "raised" her note and try to collect the $9,990 from him.

Where the person asserting the preclusion failed to exercise ordinary care in taking or paying the instrument and that failure substantially contributed to the loss, Article 3 allocates the loss between the two parties based on their comparative negligence [3–406(b)]. Thus, if a drawer was so negligent in drafting a check that he made it possible for the check to be altered and the bank that paid the check, in the exercise of ordinary care, should have noticed the alteration, then any loss occasioned by the fact that the person who made the alteration could not be found would be split between the drawer and the bank based on their comparative fault.

Impostor Rule

Article 3 establishes special rules for negotiable instruments made payable to impostors and fictitious persons. An impostor is a person who poses as someone else and convinces a drawer to make a check payable to the person being impersonated—or to an organization the person purports to be authorized to represent. When this happens, the Code makes any indorsement "substantially similar" to that of the named payee effective [3–404(a)]. Where the impostor has impersonated a person authorized to act for a payee, such as claiming to be Jack Jones, the president of Jones Enterprises, the impostor has the power to negotiate a check drawn payable to Jones Enterprises.

An example of a situation involving the impostor rule would be the following: Arthur steals Paulsen's automobile and finds the certificate of title in the automobile. Then, representing himself as Paulsen, he sells the automobile to Berger Used Car Company. The car dealership draws its check payable to Paulsen for the agreed purchase price of the automobile and delivers the check to Arthur. Any person can negotiate the check by indorsing it in the name of Paulsen.

The rationale for the impostor rule is to put the responsibility for determining the true identity of the payee on the drawer or maker of a negotiable instrument. The drawer is in a better position to do this than some later holder of the check who may be entirely innocent. The impostor rule allows that later holder to have good

title to the check by making the payee's signature valid although it is not the signature of the person with whom the drawer or maker thought he was dealing. It forces the drawer or maker to find the wrongdoer who tricked him into signing the negotiable instrument or to bear the loss himself.

Fictitious Payee Rule

A fictitious payee commonly arises in one of the two following situations: (1) a dishonest employee makes a check payable to a "fictitious payee"—someone who does not exist, or (2) the dishonest employee makes the check payable to a real person who does business with the employer—but the employee does not intend to send the check to that person. If the employee has the authority to sign checks, he may sign the check himself. Where the employee does not have the authority to sign checks for the employer, the dishonest employee gives the check with the fictitious payee to the employer for signature and represents to the employer that the employer owes money to the person named as the payee. The dishonest employee then takes the check, indorses it in the name of the payee, presents it for payment, and pockets the money. The employee may be in a position to cover up the wrongdoing by intercepting the canceled checks or juggling the company's books.

The Code allows any indorsement in the name of the fictitious payee to be effective as the payee's indorsement in favor of any person that pays the instrument in good faith or takes it for value or for collection [3–404(b) and (c)]. For example, Anderson, an accountant in charge of accounts payable at Moore Corporation, prepares a false invoice naming Parks, Inc., a supplier of Moore Corporation, as having supplied Moore Corporation with goods, and draws a check payable to Parks, Inc., for the amount of the invoice. Anderson then presents the check to Temple, treasurer of Moore Corporation, together with other checks with invoices attached. Temple signs all of these checks and returns them to Anderson for mailing. Anderson then withdraws the check payable to Parks, Inc. Anyone, including Anderson, can negotiate the check by indorsing it in the name of Parks, Inc.

The rationale for the fictitious payee rule is similar to that for the impostor rule. If someone has a dishonest employee or agent who is responsible for the forgery of some checks, the employer of the wrongdoer should bear the immediate loss of those checks rather than some other innocent party. In turn, the employer must locate the unfaithful employee or agent and try to recover from him.

Comparative Negligence Rule concerning Impostors and Fictitious Payees

Revised Article 3 also establishes a comparative negligence rule if (1) the person, in a situation covered by the impostor or fictitious payee rule, pays the instrument or takes it for value or collection without exercising ordinary care in paying or taking the instrument, and (2) that failure substantially contributes to the loss resulting from payment of the instrument. In these instances, the person bearing the loss may recover an allocable share of the loss from the person who did not exercise ordinary care [3–404(d)].

Fraudulent Indorsements by Employees

Revised Article 3 specifically addresses employer responsibility for fraudulent indorsements by employees and adopts the principle that the risk of loss for such indorsements by employees who are entrusted with responsibilities for instruments (primarily checks) should fall on the employer rather than on the bank that takes the check or pays it [3–405]. As to any person who in good faith pays an instrument or takes it for value, a fraudulent indorsement by a responsible employee is effective as the indorsement of the payee if it is made in the name of the payee or in a substantially similar name [3–405(b)]. If the person taking or paying the instrument failed to exercise ordinary care and that failure substantially contributed to loss resulting from the fraud, the comparative negligence doctrine guides the allocation of the loss.

A fraudulent indorsement includes a forged indorsement purporting to be that of the employer on an instrument payable to the employer; it also includes a forged indorsement purporting to be that of the payee of an instrument on which the employer is drawer or maker [3–405(a)(2)]. "Responsibility" with respect to instruments means the authority to (1) sign or indorse instruments on behalf of the employer, (2) process instruments received by the employer, (3) prepare or process instruments for issue in the name of the employer, (4) control the disposition of instruments to be issued in the name of the employer, or (5) otherwise act with respect to instruments in a responsible capacity. "Responsibility" does not cover those who simply have access to instruments as they are stored or transported, or that are in incoming or outgoing mail [3–405(a)(3)].

In the case that follows, *Victory Clothing Co., Inc. v. Wachovia Bank, N.A.*, the court applied comparative negligence principles to split the loss between a company whose employee forged checks and a depositary bank that allowed the forger to deposit the checks to her own personal account in violation of its own rules. As you read the case and note the reasons the court gave for assigning 30 percent of the risk to the employer, you might ask yourself whether the answer would be different today when many banks no longer return copies of canceled checks—or even photocopies of them—regularly to the customer. You might also ask, what steps would you take to prevent something like this from happening without your being aware of the fact an employee was forging checks on the company's account.

Victory Clothing Co., Inc. v. Wachovia Bank, N.A.
59 UCC Rep.2d 376 (Ct. Common Pleas Penn. 2006)

Victory Clothing Company maintained a corporate checking account at Hudson Bank. Jeannette Lunny was employed by Victory as its office manager and bookkeeper for approximately 24 years until she resigned in May 2003. From August 2001 through May 2003, Lunny deposited approximately 200 checks drawn on Victory's corporate account totaling $188,273 into her personal checking account at Wachovia Bank.

Lunny's scheme involved double forgeries. She prepared checks in the company's computer system and made them payable to known vendors of Victory (e.g., Adidas) to whom no money was actually owed. The checks were for dollar amounts that were consistent with the legitimate checks to those vendors. She then would forge the signature of Victory's owner, Mark Rosenfeld, as drawer on the front of the check, and then forge the indorsement of the unintended payee (Victory's various vendors) on the reverse of the check. After forging the indorsement of the payee, Lunny either indorsed the check with her name followed by her account number, or referenced her account number following the forged indorsement. She then deposited the checks into her personal account at Wachovia Bank.

At the time of the fraud by Lunny, Wachovia's policies and regulations regarding the acceptance of checks for deposit provided that "checks payable to a non-personal payee can be deposited ONLY into a non-personal account with the same name."

Rosenfeld reviewed the bank statements from Hudson Bank on a monthly basis. However, among other observable irregularities, he failed to detect that Lunny had forged his signature on approximately 200 checks. Nor did he have a procedure to match checks to invoices.

Victory brought suit against Wachovia pursuant to the Pennsylvania Commercial Code claiming that Wachovia should be liable to it for the entire amount of the losses it sustained by virtue of Lunny's forgery scheme. Victory contended that Wachovia had failed to exercise ordinary care in taking the instruments that were payable to various businesses and allowing them to be deposited into Lunny's personal account. It asserted that this was commercially unreasonable, contrary to Wachovia's own internal rules and regulations, and exhibited a lack of ordinary care, substantially contributing to the loss resulting from the fraud. Under section 3–405 of the Code, in such circumstances, the person bearing the loss can recover from the person failing to exercise ordinary care to the extent the failure to exercise ordinary care contributed to the loss.

Wachovia, in turn, argued that because Lunny made the fraudulent checks payable to actual vendors of Victory with the intention that the vendors not get paid, Victory's action against it should be barred by the fictitious payee rule set out in section 3–404. Because section 3–404 contains a comparative negligence provision, the court also needed to decide whether it should be applied in this case.

Abrahamson, Judge

In 1990, new revisions to Articles 3 and 4 of the UCC were implemented (the "revisions"). The new revisions made a major change in the area of double forgeries. Before the revisions, the case law was uniform in treating a double forgery case as a forged drawer's signature case, with the loss falling on the drawee bank. The revisions, however, changed this rule by shifting to a comparative fault approach. Under the revised version of the UCC, the loss in double forgery cases is allocated between the depositary and drawee banks based on the extent that each contributed to the loss. "By adopting a comparative fault approach, classification of the double forgery as either a forged signature or forged indorsement case is no longer necessarily determinative." Thus, under the revised Code, a depositary bank may not necessarily escape liability in double forgery situations, as they did under the prior law.

Specifically, revised § 3–405 of the UCC, entitled "Employer's Responsibility for Fraudulent Indorsement by Employee," introduced the concept of comparative fault as between the employer of the dishonest employee/embezzler and the bank(s). This is the section under which Victory sued Wachovia. Section 3–405(b) states, in relevant part:

> If the person paying the instrument or taking it for value or for collection fails to exercise ordinary care in paying or taking the instrument and that failure substantially contributes to loss resulting from the fraud, the person bearing the loss may recover from the person failing to exercise ordinary care to the extent the failure to exercise ordinary care contributed to the loss.

The Fictitious Payee Rule

Lunny made the fraudulent checks payable to actual vendors of Victory with the intention that the vendors not get paid. Wachovia therefore argues that Victory's action against it should be barred by the fictitious payee rule under § 3–404. Section 3–404 states, in relevant part:

> § 3–404. Impostors; fictitious payees
>
> (b) FICTITIOUS PAYEE.—If a person whose intent determines to whom an instrument is payable (section 3–110(a) or (b)) does not intend the person identified as payee to have any interest in the instrument or the person identified as payee of an instrument is a fictitious person, the following rules apply until the instrument is negotiated by special indorsement:
>
> (1.) Any person in possession of the instrument is its holder.
>
> (2.) An indorsement by any person in the name of the payee stated in the instrument is effective as the indorsement of the payee in favor of a person who, in good faith, pays the instrument or takes it for value or for collection.

The fictitious payee rule applies when a dishonest employee writes checks to a company's actual vendors, but intends that the vendors never receive the money; instead, the employee forges the names of the payees and deposits the checks at another bank. Under section 3–404(b) of the UCC, the indorsement is deemed to be "effective" since the employee did not intend for the payees to receive payment. The theory under the rule is that since the indorsement is "effective," the drawee bank was justified in debiting the company's account. Therefore, the loss should fall on the company whose employee committed the fraud.

Revised UCC § 3–404 changed the prior law by introducing a comparative fault principle. Subsection (d) of 3–404 provides that if the person taking the checks fails to exercise ordinary care, "the person bearing the loss may recover from the person failing to exercise ordinary care to the extent the failure to exercise ordinary care contributed to the loss." Therefore, "although the fictitious payee rule makes the indorsement 'effective,' the corporate drawer can shift the loss to any negligent bank, to the extent that the bank's negligence substantially contributed to the loss." Under the revised Code, the drawer now has the right to sue the depositary bank directly based on the bank's negligence. Under the Old Code, the fictitious payee rule was a "jackpot" defense for depositary banks because most courts held that the depositary bank's own negligence was irrelevant. However, under revised UCC §§ 3–404 and 3–405, the fictitious payee defense triggers principles of comparative fault, so a depositary bank's own negligence may be considered by the trier of fact. Therefore, based on the foregoing reasons, the fictitious payee defense does not help Wachovia in this case.

Allocation of Liability

As stated, comparative negligence applies in this case because of the revisions in the Code. In determining the liability of the parties, the Court has considered, *inter alia,* the following factors:

- At the time of the fraud by Lunny, Wachovia's policies and regulations regarding the acceptance of checks for deposit provided that "checks payable to a non-personal payee can be deposited ONLY into a non-personal account with the same name."
- Approximately two hundred (200) checks drawn on Victory's corporate account were deposited into Lunny's personal account at Wachovia.
- The first twenty-three (23) fraudulent checks were made payable to entities that were not readily distinguishable as businesses, such as "Sean John." The check dated December 17, 2001, was the first fraudulent check made payable to a payee that was clearly a business, specifically "Beverly Hills Shoes, Inc."
- Lunny had been a bookkeeper for Victory from approximately 1982 until she resigned in May 2003. Rosenfeld never had any problems with Lunny's bookkeeping before she resigned.
- Lunny exercised primary control over Victory's bank accounts.
- Between 2001 and 2003, the checks that were generated to make payments to Victory's vendors were all computerized checks generated by Lunny. No other Victory employee, other than Lunny, knew how to generate the computerized checks, including Rosenfeld.
- The fraudulent checks were made payable to known vendors of Victory in amounts that were consistent with previous legitimate checks to those vendors.
- After forging the indorsement of the payee, Lunny either indorsed the check with her name followed by her account number, or referenced her account number following the forged indorsement. All of the checks that were misappropriated had the same exact account number, which was shown on the back side of the checks.

- About ten (10) out of approximately three hundred (300) checks each month were forged by Lunny and deposited into her personal account.
- Rosenfeld reviewed his bank statements from Hudson Bank on a monthly basis. Rosenfeld received copies of Victory's cancelled checks from Hudson Bank on a monthly basis. However, the copies of the cancelled checks were not in their normal size; instead, they were smaller, with six checks (front and back side) on each page.
- The forged indorsements were written out in longhand, i.e., Lunny's own handwriting, rather than a corporate stamped signature.
- Victory did not match its invoices for each check at the end of each month.
- An outside accounting firm performed quarterly reviews of Victory's bookkeeping records, and then met with Rosenfeld. This review was not designed to pick up fraud or misappropriation.

Based on the foregoing, the Court finds that Victory and Wachovia are comparatively negligent. With regard to Wachovia's negligence, it is clear that Wachovia was negligent in violating its own rules in repeatedly depositing corporate checks into Lunny's personal account at Wachovia. Standard commercial bank procedures dictate that a check made payable to a business be accepted only into a business checking account with the same title as the business. Had a single teller at Wachovia followed Wachovia's rules, the fraud would have been detected as early as December 17, 2001, when the first fraudulently created non-personal payee check was presented for deposit into Lunny's personal checking account. Instead, Wachovia permitted another one hundred and seventy-six (176) checks to be deposited into Lunny's account after December 17, 2001. The Court finds that Wachovia failed to exercise ordinary care, and that failure substantially contributed to Victory's loss resulting from the fraud. Therefore, the Court concludes that Wachovia is seventy (70) percent liable for Victory's loss.

Victory, on the other hand, was also negligent in its supervision of Lunny, and for not discovering the fraud for almost a two-year period. Rosenfeld received copies of the cancelled checks, albeit smaller in size, on a monthly basis from Hudson Bank. The copies of the checks displayed both the front and back of the checks. Rosenfeld was negligent in not recognizing his own forged signature on the front of the checks, as well as not spotting his own bookkeeper's name and/or account number on the back of the checks (which appeared far too many times and on various "payees" checks to be seen as regular by a non-negligent business owner).

Further, there were inadequate checks and balances in Victory's record keeping process. For example, Victory could have ensured that it had an adequate segregation of duties, meaning that more than one person would be involved in any control activity. Here, Lunny exercised primary control over Victory's bank accounts. Another Victory employee, or Rosenfeld himself, could have reviewed Lunny's work. In addition, Victory could have increased the amount of authorization that was needed to perform certain transactions. For example, any check that was over a threshold monetary amount would have to be authorized by more than one individual. This would ensure an additional control on checks that were larger in amounts. Furthermore, Victory did not match its invoices for each check at the end of each month. When any check was created by Victory's computer system, the value of the check was automatically assigned to a general ledger account before the check could be printed. The values in the general ledger account could have been reconciled at the end of each month with the actual checks and invoices. This would not have been overly burdensome or costly because Victory already had the computer system that could do this in place. Based on the foregoing, the Court concludes that Victory is also thirty (30) percent liable for the loss.

For all the foregoing reasons, the Court finds that Wachovia is 70 percent liable and Victory is 30 percent liable for the $188,273.00 loss. Therefore, Victory Clothing Company, Inc. is awarded $131,791.10.

Conversion Conversion of an instrument is an unauthorized assumption and exercise of ownership over it. A negotiable instrument can be converted in a number of ways. For example, it might be presented for payment or acceptance, and the person to whom it is presented might refuse to pay or accept and refuse to return it. An instrument also is converted if a person pays an instrument to a person not entitled to payment—for example, if it contains a forged indorsement.

Revised Article 3 modifies and then expands the previous treatment of conversion and provides that the law applicable to conversion of personal property applies to instruments. It also specifically provides that conversion occurs if (1) an instrument lacks an indorsement necessary for negotiation; and (2) it is (*a*) purchased, (*b*) taken for collection, or (*c*) paid by a drawee to a person not entitled to payment. An action for conversion may not be brought by (1) the maker, drawer, or acceptor of the instrument; or (2) a payee or an indorsee who did not receive delivery of the instrument either directly or through delivery to an agent or copayee [3–420].

Thus, if a bank pays a check that contains a forged indorsement, the bank has converted the check by wrongfully paying it. The bank then becomes liable for the face amount of the check to the person whose indorsement was forged [3–420]. For example, Arthur Able draws a check for $500 on his account at First Bank, payable to the order of Bernard Barker. Carol Collins steals the check, forges Barker's indorsement on it, and cashes it at First Bank. First Bank has converted Barker's property, because it had no right to pay the check without Barker's valid indorsement. First Bank must pay Barker $500 and then it can try to locate Collins to get the $500 back from her.

As is true under the original version of Article 3, if a check contains a restrictive indorsement (such as "for deposit" or "for collection") that shows a purpose of having the check collected for the benefit of a particular account, then any person who purchases the check or any depositary bank or payor bank that takes it for immediate payment converts the check unless the indorser receives the proceeds or the bank applies them consistent with the indorsement [3–206].

Discharge of Negotiable Instruments

Discharge of Liability The obligation of a party to pay an instrument is discharged (1) if he meets the requirements set out in Revised Article 3 or (2) by any act or agreement that would discharge an obligation to pay money on a simple contract. Discharge of an obligation is not effective against a person who has the rights of a holder in due course of the instrument and took the instrument without notice of the discharge [3–601].

The most common ways that an obligor is discharged from his liability are:

1. Payment of the instrument.
2. Cancellation of the instrument.
3. Alteration of the instrument.
4. Modification of the principal's obligation that causes loss to a surety or impairs the collateral.
5. Unexcused delay in presentment or notice of dishonor with respect to a check (discussed earlier in this chapter).
6. Acceptance of a draft [3–414(c) or (d); 3–415(d)]; as noted earlier in the chapter, a drawer is discharged of liability of a draft that is accepted by a bank (e.g., if a

check is certified by a bank) because at that point the holder is looking to the bank to make the instrument good.

Discharge by Payment

Generally, payment in full discharges liability on an instrument to the extent payment is (1) by or on behalf of a party obligated to pay the instrument and (2) to a person entitled to enforce the instrument. For example, Arthur makes a note of $1,000 payable to the order of Bryan. Bryan indorses the note "Pay to the order of my account no. 16154 at First Bank, Bryan." Bryan then gives the note to his employee, Clark, to take to the bank. Clark takes the note to Arthur, who pays Clark the $1,000. Clark then runs off with the money. Arthur is not discharged of his primary liability on the note because he did not make his payment consistent with the restrictive indorsement. To be discharged, Arthur has to pay the $1,000 into Bryan's account at First Bank.

To the extent of payment, the obligation of a party to pay the instrument is discharged even though payment is made with knowledge of a claim to the instrument by some other person. However, the obligation is not discharged if: (1) there is a claim enforceable against the person making payment and payment is made with knowledge of the fact that payment is prohibited by an injunction or similar legal process; or (2) in the case of an instrument other than a cashier's, certified, or teller's check, the person making the payment had accepted from the person making the claim indemnity against loss for refusing to make payment to the person entitled to enforce payment. The obligation also is not discharged if he knows the instrument is a stolen instrument and pays someone he knows is in wrongful possession of the instrument [3–602].

Discharge by Cancellation

A person entitled to enforce a negotiable instrument may discharge the liability of the parties to the instrument by canceling or renouncing it. If the holder mutilates or destroys a negotiable instrument with the intent that it no longer evidences an obligation to pay money, the holder has canceled it [3–604]. For example, a grandfather lends $5,000 to his grandson for college expenses. The grandson gives his grandfather a promissory note for $5,000. If the grandfather later tears up the note with the intent that the grandson no longer owes him $5,000, the grandfather has canceled the note.

An accidental destruction or mutilation of a negotiable instrument is not a cancellation and does not discharge the parties to it. If an instrument is lost, mutilated accidentally, or destroyed, the person entitled to enforce it still can enforce the instrument. In such a case, the person must prove that the instrument existed and that she was its holder when it was lost, mutilated, or destroyed.

Altered Instruments; Discharge by Alteration

A person paying a fraudulently altered instrument, or taking it for value, in good faith and without notice of the alteration, may enforce the instrument (1) according to its original terms or (2) in the case of an incomplete instrument later completed in an unauthorized manner, according to its terms as completed [3–407(c)]. An alteration occurs if there is (1) an unauthorized change that modifies the obligation of a party to the instrument or (2) an unauthorized addition of words or numbers or other change to an incomplete instrument that changes the obligation of any party [3–407]. A change that does not affect the obligation of one of the parties, such as dotting an *i* or correcting the grammar, is not considered to be an alteration.

Two examples illustrate the situations in which Revised Article 3 allows fraudulently altered instruments to be enforced. First, assume the amount due on a note is fraudulently raised from $10 to $10,000. The contract of the maker has been changed: the maker promised to pay $10, but after the change has been made, he would be promising to pay much more. If the note is negotiated to or paid by a person who was without notice of the alteration, that person can enforce the note against the maker only according to its original terms. It would pursue the alterer or the person taking from the alterer for the balance on a presentment or transfer warranty [3–417; 3–416]. If the maker's negligence substantially contributed to the alteration, then the maker would be responsible for as much as the entire $10,000 [3–407(c); 3–406].

Second, assume Swanson draws a check payable to Frank's Nursery, leaving the amount blank. He gives it to his gardener with instructions to purchase some fertilizer at Frank's and to fill in the purchase price of the fertilizer when it is known. The gardener fills in the check for $100 and gives it to Frank's in exchange for the fertilizer ($17.25) and the difference in cash ($82.75). The gardener then leaves town with the cash. If Frank's had no knowledge of the unauthorized completion, it could enforce the check for $100 against Swanson. A similar situation is illustrated in *American Federal Bank, FSB v. Parker.*

American Federal Bank, FSB v. Parker   392 SE.2d 798 (S.C. Ct. App. 1990)

Thomas Kirkman was involved in the horse business and was a friend of John Roundtree, a loan officer for American Federal Bank. Kirkman and Roundtree conceived a business arrangement in which Kirkman would locate buyers for horses and the buyers could seek financing from American Federal. Roundtree gave Kirkman blank promissory notes and security agreements from American Federal. Kirkman was to locate the potential purchaser, take care of the paperwork, and bring the documents to the bank for approval of the purchaser's loan.

Kirkman entered into a purchase agreement with Gene Parker, a horse dealer, to copurchase for $35,000 a horse named Wills Hightime that Kirkman represented he owned. Parker signed the American Federal promissory note in blank and also executed in blank a security agreement that authorized the bank to disburse the funds to the seller of the collateral. Kirkman told Parker he would cosign the note and fill in the details of the transaction with the bank. While Kirkman did not cosign the note, he did complete it for $85,000 as opposed to $35,000. Kirkman took the note with Parker's signature to Roundtree at American Federal and received two checks from the bank payable to him in the amounts of $35,000 and $50,000. Kirkman took the $35,000 and gave it to the real owner of the horse. Parker then received the horse.

Parker began making payments to the bank and called on Kirkman to assist in making the payments pursuant to their agreement. However, Kirkman skipped town, taking the additional $50,000 with him. Parker repaid the $35,000 but refused to pay any more. He argued that he agreed to borrow only $35,000 and the other $50,000 was unauthorized by him. American Federal Bank filed suit to recover the balance due on the note. The trial court held in favor of the bank and Parker appealed.

Cureton, Judge

Parker executed a promissory note in blank. Under the Uniform Commercial Code, the maker of a note agrees to pay the instrument according to its tenor at the time of engagement "or as completed pursuant to section 3–115 on incomplete instruments." Under section 3–115(2) if the completion of an instrument is unauthorized the rules as to material alteration apply. Under section 3–407(1)(b) the completion of an incomplete instrument otherwise than as authorized is considered an alteration. However, under section 3–407(3) a subsequent holder in due course may enforce an incomplete instrument as completed. Official comment 4 indicates that where blanks are filled or an incomplete instrument is otherwise completed, the loss is placed upon the party who left the instrument incomplete and the holder is permitted to enforce it according to its completed form.

We agree with the trial court that the bank was entitled to the directed verdicts. The responsibility for the situation rests with Parker. He and Kirkman negotiated their deal. Parker signed a blank promissory note. He relied upon Kirkman to cosign the note and fill it in for $35,000. Parker's negligence substantially contributed to the material alteration as a matter of law.

Parker argues that it was not reasonable commercial practice for American Federal to give Kirkman possession of blank promissory notes. After the fact, Parker argues the bank should have contacted him or checked to be sure everything was correct before disbursing the proceeds of the loan to Kirkman. There is no evidence in the record to establish the bank had any reason to inquire into the facial validity of the note. The note was complete when presented to the bank and there were no obvious alterations on it.

The record establishes American Federal took the note in good faith and without notice of any defense to it by Parker. American Federal gave value for the note when it disbursed the funds to Kirkman. As a holder in due course, American Federal may enforce the note against Parker as completed. Sections 3–302; 3–407(3).

Judgment for American Federal affirmed.

Note: Although this case was decided under the original version of Article 3, the same result would be reached under Revised Article 3 so long as the court found Kirkman's completion (alteration) to be fraudulent.

In any other case, a fraudulent alteration **discharges** any party whose obligation is affected by the alteration *unless* (1) the party assents or (2) is precluded from asserting the alteration (e.g., because of the party's negligence). Assume that Anderson signs a promissory note for $100 payable to Bond. Bond indorses the note "Pay to the order of Connolly, Bond" and negotiates it to Connolly. Connolly changes the $100 to read $100,000. Connolly's change is unauthorized and fraudulent. As a result, Anderson is discharged from her liability as maker of the note and Bond is discharged from her liability as indorser. Neither of them has to pay Connolly. The obligations of both Anderson and Bond were changed because the amount for which they are liable was altered.

No other alteration—that is, one that is not fraudulent—discharges any party and a holder may enforce the instrument according to its *original* terms. Thus, there would be no discharge if a blank is filled in the honest belief that it is authorized or if a change is made, without any fraudulent intent, to give the maker on a note the benefit of a lower interest rate.

Discharge of Indorsers and Accommodation Parties

If a person entitled to enforce an instrument agrees, with or without consideration, to a material modification of the obligation of a party to the instrument, including an extension of the due date, then any accommodation party or indorser who has a right of recourse against the person whose obligation is modified is discharged *to the extent the modification causes a loss to the indorser or accommodation party.* Similarly, if collateral secures the obligation of a party to an instrument and a person entitled to enforce the instrument impairs the value of the collateral, the obligation of the indorser or accommodation party having the right of recourse against the obligor is discharged to the extent of the impairment. These discharges are not effective unless the person agreeing to the modification or causing the impairment knows of the accommodation or has notice of it. Also, no discharge occurs if the obligor assented to the event or conduct, or if the obligor has waived the discharge [3–605].

For example, Frank goes to Credit Union to borrow $4,000 to purchase a used automobile. The credit union has Frank sign a promissory note and takes a security interest in the automobile (i.e., takes it as collateral for the loan). It also asks Frank's brother, Bob, to sign the note as an accommodation maker. Subsequently, Frank tells the credit union he wants to sell the automobile and it releases its security interest. Because release of the collateral adversely affects Bob's obligation as accommodation maker, he is discharged from his obligation as accommodation maker in the amount of the value of the automobile.

Problems and Problem Cases

1. Terance Fitzgerald drew a check for $4,000 payable to New Look Auto Trim and Upholstery and delivered it to Yuvonne Goss and Benii Arrazza, the owners of New Look. Goss and Arrazza each indorsed the check in blank and deposited it in Goss's personal account at the Cincinnati Central Credit Union. When the Credit Union presented the check to Fitzgerald's bank, the check was dishonored for insufficient funds. The credit union then demanded that Goss and Arrazza honor the check. Are Goss and Arrazza obligated to make the check good to the credit union?

2. Janota's signature appeared on a note under the name of a corporation acknowledging a $1,000 debt. No other wording appeared other than Janota's name and the corporate name. The holder of the note sues Janota on the note. What will Janota argue and what will be the result?

3. In 1997, Maryellen Peterson was a part-time employee of Textiles Specialties & Chemicals doing business as CS Industries. On April 17, 1997, Peterson signed a check in the amount of $13,789.80 on the account of CS Industries and payable to Holtrachem, Inc. The check was imprinted with name of CS Industries. However, Peterson signed only her name and did not indicate she was signing in her representative capacity behalf of CS industries. The drawee bank returned the check to Holtrachem due to insufficient funds in CS Industries' account. Holtrachem filed suit against Peterson, seeking to hold her liable in her personal capacity as the drawer of the check. Is an individual who signs a check drawn on a corporate account without indicating she is signing in representative capacity personally liable on the instrument?

4. In November 2005, Michele Fehl, an administrative assistant recently hired by AFT Trucking stole eight company checks from the company's offices. She made out the checks to herself in various amounts. Fehl was not authorized to sign checks on behalf of the company. Over the next three weeks, Fehl presented the checks at Money Stop, a check-cashing service, which gave her cash for the checks. Subsequently, the checks were dishonored by AFT Trucking. It fired Fehl, who was arrested and criminally prosecuted. Money Stop brought suit against AFT Trucking to recover the funds it had disbursed. AFT Trucking asserted that Money Stop's only recourse was against Fehl, the person who had signed the checks. Is Money Stop entitled to recover from AFT Trucking?

5. First National Bank certified Smith's check in the amount of $29. After certification, Smith altered the

check so that it read $2,900. He presented the check to a merchant in payment for goods. The merchant then submitted the check to the bank for payment. The bank refused, saying it had certified the instrument for only $29. Can the merchant recover the $2,900 from the bank?

6. A check was drawn on First National Bank and made payable to Howard. It came into the possession of Carson, who forged Howard's indorsement and cashed it at Merchant's Bank. Merchant's Bank then indorsed it and collected payment from First National. Assuming that Carson is nowhere to be found, who bears the loss caused by Carson's forgery?

7. From May through August 1992, Adrenetti Collins, an employee of the Professional Golfers Association (PGA), forged and negotiated 18 PGA checks totaling $22,699.81. The PGA brought action against Whitney National Bank of New Orleans, which paid the checks, to recover the monies paid out of the PGA account. The bank contended that PGA should be precluded from recovering because its negligence substantially contributed to the forgeries.

Collins was hired as a temporary employee sometime in February or March 1992 by Robert Brown, the executive director of the Gulf States Section of the PGA, and then was hired as a full-time employee in May. Brown had known Collins when he hired her but was not aware that in 1982 she had been convicted of the theft of $5,445.07 from a previous employer, which she obtained by forging and negotiating 20 company checks. She also had a 1985 conviction for issuing worthless checks.

Brown had the primary responsibility in the office for signing checks, paying bills, and handling the bank accounts. The checks came in lots of 2,000, were made to be tractor-fed through a printer, and were prenumbered. They were kept in a box under the printer in Brown's office. Collins had access to the office. Brown wrote approximately 150 to 200 checks a month using a computer program, Quicken, to write and record the checks. Occasionally, there were alignment problems with the printer and checks were not printed correctly and had to be destroyed. Brown did not account for checks that he destroyed during the alignment process, but simply overrode the computer program and printed whatever check number was next in line.

Collins apparently took the first group of checks numbered 6365–6370 from Brown's office in late April, and Brown did not take note of them when he

wrote check number 6371 on May 1. The computer had no record of them—and Brown overrode the computer and went on to print the next check in line. The first of the forged checks was cashed on May 4. Collins intercepted both the May and June 1992 bank statements sent by Whitney to Brown. She prepared forged statements leaving out the numbers of those checks she had stolen. The forged statements were crude replicas of the usual Whitney statements. However, when Brown received them, he simply reconciled them; they contained canceled checks, but not the ones Collins had forged and negotiated. Brown did not receive any statements for July and August. On August 31, 1992, Collins asked for a leave of absence. On September 18, 1992, Brown received an overdraft notice from Whitney; this was the first inkling he had that something was wrong. He asked for copies of the July and August statements, discovered the unauthorized use, and notified Whitney.

The forgeries would have been very difficult for the bank to detect. Brown's signature on the account signature card consisted of a semi-legible letter or two and a long loop. The signature on the forged checks contained a very similar semi-legible letter or two followed by a long loop. Whitney's practice was to verify checks in the amount of $5,000 and over; one check fell into this category. The evidence established that Whitney had followed reasonable commercial standards in the banking industry in paying the checks. Was the PGA precluded from recovering the amount of the forged checks from Whitney National Bank because its negligence substantially contributed to the forgery?

8. C & M Contractors is a construction and general contracting company in Gardendale, Alabama, that performs work at job sites throughout the southeastern United States. Mary Bivens was employed by C & N and performed general administrative duties for it.

Each Wednesday morning, the foreman at each job site telephoned Bivens and gave her the names of the employees working on the job site and the number of hours they had worked. Bivens then conveyed this information to Automatic Data Processing (ADP), whose offices are in Atlanta, Georgia. ADP prepared payroll checks based on the information given by Bivens and sent the checks to the offices of C & N in Gardendale for authorized signatures. Bivens was not an authorized signatory. After the checks were signed, Bivens sent the checks to the job site foreman for delivery to the employees.

In 1991, Bivens began conveying false information to ADP about employees and hours worked. On the basis of this false information, ADP prepared payroll checks payable to persons who were actual employees but had not worked the hours Bivens had indicated. After obtaining authorized signatures from C & N, Bivens intercepted the checks, forged the indorsement of the payees, and either cashed the checks at Community Bancshares or deposited them into her account at Community Bancshares, often presenting numerous checks at one time. Bivens continued this practice for almost a year, forging over 100 checks, until Jimmy Nation, vice president of C & N, discovered the embezzlement after noticing payroll checks payable to employees who had not recently performed services for the corporation. Bivens subsequently admitted to forging the indorsements.

C & N brought suit against Community Bancshares for conversion when it cashed or accepted for deposit the numerous payroll checks containing forged payee indorsements. Was Community Bancshares, as the depositary bank, liable to the drawer, C & N, for conversion because it accepted the checks containing forged payee indorsements?

9. Stockton's housekeeper stole some of his checks, forged his name as drawer, and cashed them at Gristedes Supermarket where Stockton maintained check-cashing privileges. The checks were presented to Stockton's bank and honored by it. Over the course of 18 months, the scheme netted the housekeeper in excess of $147,000 on approximately 285 forged checks. Stockton brought suit against Gristedes Supermarket for conversion, seeking to recover the value of the checks it accepted and for which it obtained payment from the drawee bank. Was Gristedes Supermarket liable to Stockton for conversion for accepting and obtaining payment of the stolen and forged checks?

10. Charles Peterson, a farmer and rancher, was indebted to Crown Financial Corporation on a $4,450,000 promissory note that was due on December 29, 1992. Shortly before the note was due, Crown sent Peterson a statement of interest due on the note ($499,658.85). Petersen paid the interest and executed a new note in the amount of $4,450,000 that was to mature in December 1995. The old note was then marked "canceled" and returned to Peterson. In 1995, Crown billed Peterson for $363,800 in interest that had been due on the first note but apparently not included in the statement. Peterson claimed that the interest had been forgiven and that he was not obligated to pay it. Was Peterson still obligated to pay interest on the note that had been returned to him marked "canceled"?

Online Research

The FTC's Holder in Due Course Rule

Use the Internet to locate the site for the Federal Trade Commission. Review the FTC's presentation of the holder in due course rule, and note when someone taking a negotiable instrument from a consumer needs to be concerned with its implications.

chapter 34

CHECKS AND ELECTRONIC TRANSFERS

Susan Williams opened a checking account at the First National Bank. She made an initial deposit of $1,800, signed a signature card that indicated to the bank that she was the authorized signator on the account, and was given a supply of blank checks. She also received an ATM card that, when used along with an assigned PIN (personal identification number), allowed her to make deposits to her account as well as to obtain cash from it. Each month the bank sent her a statement reflecting the activity in the account during the previous month along with the canceled checks. Several months after she opened the account, the bank erroneously refused to pay a check she had written to a clothing store even though she had sufficient funds in her account. As a result, the store filed a complaint with the local prosecutor indicating she had written a "bad check." On one occasion, Susan called the bank to stop payment on a check she had written to cover repairs to her automobile because while driving the car home, she discovered the requested repair had not been made. However, the bank paid the check later that day despite the stop-payment order she had given the bank. Another time, Susan's wallet fell out of her purse while she was shopping at a mall. She received a call the next morning indicating the wallet had been found and she retrieved it at that time. However, when she received her next monthly statement from the bank, she discovered that someone had apparently used her ATM card to withdraw $200 from her account on the day her wallet had been lost. Susan's experience raises a number of legal issues that will be covered in this chapter, including:

- What rights does Susan have against the bank for refusing to pay the check to the clothing store despite the fact she had sufficient funds on deposit to cover it?
- What rights does Susan have against the bank for failing to honor the stop-payment order she placed on the check she had written to the repair shop?
- What rights does Susan have against the bank because of the unauthorized use of her ATM card? What must she do to preserve those rights?
- If a repair shop refuses to release your automobile unless you pay it more than the repair shop had advised you it would charge you for the the work, would it be ethical to give the repair shop a check for the larger amount knowing you intend to immediately go to your bank and stop payment on it?

FOR MOST PEOPLE, a checking account provides the majority of their contact with negotiable instruments. This chapter focuses on the relationship between the drawer with a checking account and the drawer's bank, known as the drawee bank.

The Drawer–Drawee Relationship

There are two sources that govern the relationship between the depositor and the drawee bank: the deposit agreement and Articles 3 and 4 of the Code. Article 4, which governs Bank Deposits and Collections, allows the depositor and drawee bank (which Article 4 calls the "payor bank") to vary Article 4's provisions with a few important exceptions. The deposit agreement cannot disclaim the bank's responsibility for its own lack of good faith or failure to exercise ordinary care or limit the measure of damages for the lack or failure; however, the parties may determine by agreement the standards by which to measure the bank's responsibility so long as the standards are not manifestly unreasonable [4–103].

The deposit agreement establishes many important relationships between the depositor and drawee/payor bank. The first of these is their relationship as creditor and debtor, respectively, so that when a person deposits money in an account at the bank, the law no longer considers him the owner of the money. Instead, he is a creditor of the bank to the extent of his deposits and the bank becomes his debtor. Also, when the depositor deposits a check to a checking account, the bank also becomes his agent for collection of the check. The bank as the person's agent owes a duty to him to follow his reasonable instructions concerning payment of checks and other items from his account and a duty of ordinary care in collecting checks and other items deposited to the account.

Bank's Duty to Pay

When a bank receives a properly drawn and payable check on a person's account and there are sufficient funds to cover the check, the bank is under a duty to pay it. If the person has sufficient funds in the account and the bank refuses to pay, or dishonors, the check, the bank is liable for the actual damages proximately caused by its wrongful dishonor as well as consequential damages [4–402]. Actual damages may include charges imposed by retailers for returned checks as well as damages for arrest or prosecution of the customer. Consequential damages include injury to the depositor's credit rating that results from the dishonor.

For example, Donald Dodson writes a check for $1,500 to Ames Auto Sales in payment for a used car. At the time that Ames Auto presents the check for payment at Dodson's bank, First National Bank, Dodson has $1,800 in his account. However, a teller mistakenly refuses to pay the check and stamps it NSF (not sufficient funds). Ames Auto then goes to the local prosecutor and signs a complaint against Dodson for writing a bad check. As a result, Dodson is arrested. Dodson can recover from First National the damages that he sustained because the bank wrongfully dishonored his check, including the damages involved in his arrest, such as his attorney's fees.

Bank's Right to Charge to Customer's Account

The drawee bank has the right to charge any properly payable check to the account of the customer or drawer. The bank has this right even though payment of the check creates an overdraft in the account [4–401]. If an account is overdrawn, the customer owes the bank the amount of the overdraft and the bank may take that amount out of the next deposit that the customer

---

CYBERLAW IN ACTION

Account Aggregation

"Account aggregation" is a financial management tool offered by banks and by third-party, Internet-based companies. Consumers who want to use this tool will allow a bank or third party to gather information from many accounts (checking, savings, pension funds, certificates of deposit, securities firms, and insurance companies) by giving the account aggregator key information such as the account numbers and passwords for the consumer's various accounts. The aggregator then gathers information from the Web sites of the different financial services firms (insurance companies, banks, investment planners, securities brokers, etc.) and makes it possible for the consumer to view all of this information on one screen, and in some cases to transfer funds between accounts.

Some consumer advocates argue that "account aggregation"—also known as "screen scraping"—is more risky for consumers than accessing each financial service provider's Web site separately. They worry that the possibility of hacking into such an information-heavy account increases the chance that a criminal could wipe out the entire holdings of one consumer or a group of consumers. Consumers like "account aggregation" because it gives them all of their financial accounts essentially on one "page" on their computer screens. Other consumers like it because "account aggregation" allows them to move funds between their various accounts quickly from their computers without waiting to speak to each specific financial services provider to complete transactions.

makes or from another account that the depositor maintains with the bank. Alternatively, the bank might seek to collect the amount directly from the customer. If there is more than one customer who can draw from an account, only that customer—or those customers—who sign the item or who benefit from the proceeds of an overdraft are liable for the overdraft.

Stale Checks   The bank does not owe a duty to its customer to pay any checks out of the account that are more than six months old. Such checks are called **stale checks.** However, the bank acting in good faith may pay a check that is more than six months old and charge it to the drawer-depositor's account [4–404].

Altered and Incomplete Items   If the bank in good faith pays a check drawn by the drawer-depositor but subsequently altered, it may charge the customer's account with the amount of the check as originally drawn. Also, if an incomplete check of a customer gets into circulation, is completed, and is presented to the drawee bank for payment, and the bank pays the check, the bank can charge the amount as completed to the customer's account even though it knows that the check has been completed, unless it has notice that the completion was improper [4–401(d)]. The respective rights, obligations, and liabilities of drawee banks and their drawer-customers concerning forged and altered checks are discussed in more detail later in this chapter.

Limitations on Bank's Right or Duty   Article 4 recognizes that the bank's right or duty to pay a check or to charge the depositor's account for the check (including exercising its right to set off an amount due to it by the depositor) may be terminated, suspended, or modified by the depositor's order to stop payment (which is discussed in the next section of this chapter). In addition, it may be stopped by events external to the relationship between the depositor and the bank. These external events include the filing of a bankruptcy petition by the depositor or by the depositor's creditors, and the garnishment of the account by a creditor of the depositor. The bank must receive the stop-payment order from its depositor or the notice of the bankruptcy filing or garnishment before the bank has certified the check, paid it in cash, settled with another bank for the amount of the item without a right to revoke the settlement, or otherwise become accountable for the amount of the check under Article 4, or the cut-off hour on the banking day after the check is received if the bank established a cut-off hour [4–303]. These restrictions on the bank's right or duty to pay are discussed in later sections of this chapter.

Postdated Checks   Under original Articles 3 and 4, a postdated check was not properly payable by the drawee bank until the date on the check. The recent amendments to Article 4 change this. Under the revision, an otherwise properly payable postdated check that is presented for payment before the date on the check may be paid and charged to the customer's account *unless* the customer has given notice of it to the bank. The customer must give notice of the postdating in a way that describes the check with reasonable certainty. It is effective for the same time periods as Article 4 provides for stop-payment orders (discussed below). The customer must give notice to the bank at such time and in such a manner as to give the bank an opportunity to act on it before the bank takes any action with respect to paying the check. If the bank charges the customer's account for a postdated check before the date stated in the notice given to the bank, the bank is liable for damages for any loss that results. Such damages might include those associated with the dishonor of subsequent items [3–113(a); 4–401(c)].

There are a variety of reasons why a person might want to postdate a check. For example, a person might have a mortgage payment due on the first of the month at a bank located in another state. To make sure that the check arrives on time, the customer may send the payment by mail several days before the due date. However, if the person is depending on a deposit of her next monthly paycheck on the first of the month to cover the mortgage payment, she might postdate the check to the first of the following month. Under the original version of Articles 3 and 4, the bank could not properly pay the check until the first of the month. However, under the revisions it could be properly paid by the bank before that date if presented earlier. To avoid the risk that the bank would dishonor the check for insufficient funds if presented before the first, the customer should notify the drawee bank in a manner similar to that required for stop payment of checks.

Stop-Payment Order

A stop-payment order is a request made by a customer of a drawee bank instructing it not to pay or certify a specified check. As the drawer's agent in the payment of checks, the drawee bank must follow the reasonable orders of the drawer-customer about payments made on the drawer's behalf. Any person authorized to draw a check may stop payment of it. Thus, any person authorized to sign a check on the account may stop payment even if she did not sign the check in question [4–403(a)].

To be effective, a payor bank must receive the stop-payment order in time to give the bank a reasonable opportunity to act on the order. This means that the bank must receive the stop-payment order before it has paid or certified the check. In addition, the stop-payment order must come soon enough to give the bank time to instruct its tellers and other employees that they should not pay or certify the check [4–403(a)]. The stop-payment order also must describe the check with "reasonable certainty" so as to provide the bank's employees the ability to recognize it as the check corresponding to the stop-payment order.

The customer may give a stop-payment order orally to the bank, but it is valid for only 14 days unless the customer confirms it in writing during that time. A written stop-payment order is valid for six months and the customer can extend it for an additional six months by giving the bank instructions in writing to continue the order [4–403(b)]. (See Figure 1.)

Sometimes the information given the bank by the customer concerning the check on which payment is to be stopped is incorrect. For example, there may be an error in the payee's name, the amount of the check, or the number of the check. The question then arises whether the customer has accorded the bank a reasonable opportunity to act on his request. A common issue is whether the stop-payment order must have the dollar amount correct to the penny. Banks often take the position that the stop-payment order must be correct to the penny because they program and rely on computers to focus on the customer's account number and the amount of the check in question to avoid paying an item subject to a stop-payment order. The

amendments to Article 4 do not resolve this question. In the Official Comments, the drafters indicate that "in describing an item, the customer, in the absence of a contrary agreement, must meet the standard of what information allows the bank under the technology then existing to identify the check with reasonable certainty." In the Stop-Payment Order in Figure 1, the bank takes a more lenient approach than some: it asks for the range of number or low and high dollar of the check the customer does not want the bank to pay.

Bank's Liability for Payment after Stop-Payment Order

While a stop-payment order is in effect, the drawee bank is liable to the drawer of a check that it pays for any loss that the drawer suffers by reason of such payment. However, the drawer-customer has the burden of establishing the fact and amount of the loss. To show a loss, the drawer must establish that the drawee bank paid a person against whom the drawer had a valid defense to payment. To the extent that the drawer has such a defense, he has suffered a loss due to the drawee's failure to honor the stop-payment order.

For example, Brown buys what is represented to be a new car from Foster Ford and gives Foster Ford his check for $16,280 drawn on First Bank. Brown then discovers that the car is in fact a used demonstrator model and calls First Bank, ordering it to stop payment on the check. If Foster Ford presents the check for payment the following day and First Bank pays the check despite the stop-payment order, Brown can require the bank to recredit his account. (The depositor-drawer bases her claim to recredit on the

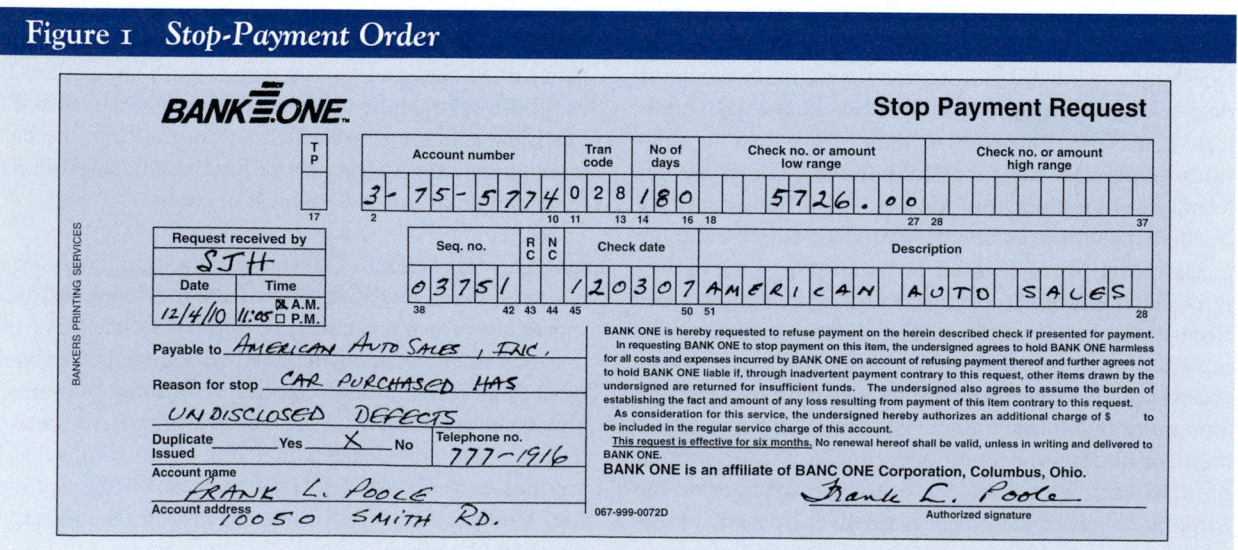

Figure 1   *Stop-Payment Order*

fact that the bank did not follow her final instruction—the instruction not to pay the check.) Brown had a valid defense of misrepresentation that she could have asserted against Foster Ford if it had sued her on the check. Foster Ford would have been required to sue on the check or on Brown's contractual obligation to pay for the car.

Assume, instead, that Foster Ford negotiated the check to Smith and that Smith qualified as a holder in due course. Then, if the bank paid the check to Smith over the stop-payment order, Brown would not be able to have her account recredited, because Brown would not be able to show that she sustained any loss. If the bank had refused to pay the check, so that Smith came against Brown on her drawer's liability, Brown could not use her personal defense of misrepresentation of the prior use of the car as a reason for not paying Smith. Brown's only recourse would be to pursue Foster Ford on her misrepresentation claim.

The bank may ask the customer to sign a form in which the bank tries to disclaim or limit its liability for the stop-payment order, or, as in Figure 1, for damages if it fails to obey the stop-payment order. As explained at the beginning of this chapter, the bank cannot disclaim its responsibility for its failure to act in good faith or to exercise ordinary care in paying a check over a stop-payment order [4–103].

If a bank pays a check after it has received a stop-payment order and has to reimburse its customer for the improperly paid check, it acquires all the rights of its customer against the person to whom it originally made payment, including rights arising from the transaction on which the check was based [4–407]. In the previous example involving Brown and Foster Ford, assume that Brown was able to have her account recredited because First Bank had paid the check to Foster Ford over her stop-payment order. Then, the bank would have any rights that Brown had against Foster Ford for the misrepresentation.

If a person stops payment on a check and the bank honors the stop-payment order, the person may still be liable to the holder of the check. Suppose Peters writes a check for $450 to Ace Auto Repair in payment for repairs to her automobile. While driving the car home, she concludes that the car was not repaired properly. She calls her bank and stops payment on the check. Ace Auto negotiated the check to Sam's Auto Parts, which took the check as a holder in due course. When Sam's takes the check to Peters's bank, the bank refuses to pay because of the stop-payment order. Sam's then comes after Peters on her drawer's liability. All Peters has is a personal defense against payment, which is not good against a holder in due course. So, Peters must pay Sam's the $450 and pursue her claim separately against Ace. If Ace were still the holder of the check, however, the situation would be different. Peters could use her personal defense concerning the faulty work against Ace to reduce or possibly to cancel her obligation to pay the check.

In the following case, *Seigel v. Merrill Lynch, Pierce, Fenner & Smith, Inc.,* the drawer was not entitled to have his account recredited for checks paid over a stop-payment order because he was unable to show he had suffered any loss.

Seigel v. Merrill Lynch, Pierce, Fenner & Smith, Inc.
745 A.2d 301 (D.C. Ct. App. 2000)

Walter Seigel, a Maryland resident, traveled to Atlantic City, New Jersey, to gamble. While there, Seigel wrote a number of checks to various casinos and, in exchange, received gambling chips with which to wager. The checks were drawn on Seigel's cash management account at Merrill, Lynch, Pierce, Fenner & Smith, which was established through its District of Columbia offices. There were sufficient funds in the accounts to cover all the checks.

Seigel eventually gambled away all the chips he had received for the checks. Upon returning to Maryland, Seigel discussed the outstanding checks with Merrill Lynch, informing his broker of the gambling nature of the transactions and his desire to avoid realizing the apparent losses. Merrill Lynch informed Seigel that it was possible to escape paying the checks by placing a stop-payment order and liquidating his cash management account. He took the advice and instructed Merrill Lynch to close his account, liquidate the assets, and to not honor any checks drawn on the account. Merrill Lynch agreed and confirmed Seigel's instructions.

Many of the checks were subsequently dishonored. However, Merrill Lynch accidentally paid several of the checks totaling $143,000, despite the stop-payment order and account closure. Merrill Lynch then debited Seigel's margin account to cover the payments.

Seigel brought suit in the District of Columbia against Merrill Lynch for paying the checks over his stop-payment order. He argued that the District of Columbia Code precluded enforcement of the checks as void gambling debts, or in the alternative that New Jersey law prohibited the enforcement of the check. Therefore, he contended, Merrill Lynch had no rights by way of subrogation as a defense to payment over the stop-payment order. Merrill lynch denied the applicability of the DC statute or any New Jersey law and contended that it stood in the shoes of the casinos to whom valid and enforceable checks had been given.

Steadman, Associate Judge

We begin with an examination of the statutory scheme relating to stop-payment orders, because we believe these provisions are determinative of this appeal. The relevant sections are found in the Uniform Commercial Code as enacted in the District of Columbia, and in particular §§ 4–403 and 4–407.

The basic right of the depositor to stop payment on any item drawn on the depositor's account is set forth in section 4–403(a). However, liability on the bank for payment over a stop-payment order is far from automatic. On the contrary, section 4–403(c) provides: "The burden of establishing the fact and amount of loss resulting from the payment of an item contrary to a stop-payment order or order to close an account is on the customer."

The provision, which places the burden on the customer to show actual loss, is reinforced by the extensive rights of subrogation given to the payor bank by section 4–407. Under that section, as to the drawer or make (that is, the depositor), the bank is subrogated both to the rights of "any holder in due course on the item" and to the rights of "the payee or any other holder of the item against the drawer or maker either on the item or under the transaction out of which the item arose." As a leading authority on the Uniform Commercial Code has noted, this section "contemplates that the bank will use its subrogation rights primarily to defend against a suit by the customer to recover payment." 2 WHITE & SUMMERS, UNIFORM COMMERCIAL CODE § 21–6, at 396 n.11 (4th ed. 1995).

As applied to the facts here, then, Seigel is required to bear the burden of establishing that he in fact suffered a loss as a result of the payment of the checks. In assessing whether any such loss was actually incurred, Merrill Lynch must be treated as the subrogee of any rights of the casino payees against Seigel. As a payee of a dishonored check, the casino would have a prima facie right to recover its amount from Seigel as drawer, § 3–414(b), and the burden would be on Seigel to establish any defense he might assert on the instrument. § 3–308(b). Seigel asserts two such defenses: duress and illegality. We turn to an examination of those defenses.

Seigel first argues that the casinos would have no right to enforce the checks even under New Jersey law because he is a compulsive gambler. He contends that enforcement of checks by a casino against a compulsive gambler would run counter to New Jersey's Casino Control Act, or against the common law, and therefore the checks are invalid. N.J.S.A. § 5:12–1 *et seq*

(1998). Nothing in the New Jersey Casino Control Act, however, specifically prohibits the cashing and redemption of checks made by "compulsive gamblers."

With regard to Seigel's common law argument, it appears to be true that intoxication, duress, and unconscionability may, in certain circumstances, be valid defenses to the enforcement of gambling contracts in New Jersey. However, compulsive gambling, in and of itself, is not a defense to a contract action in New Jersey. Rather, the facts of a particular transaction may reveal "some overreaching or imposition resulting from a bargaining disparity between the parties, or such patent unfairness in the contract that no reasonable person not acting under compulsion or out of necessity would accept its terms." The question, therefore, is whether Seigel has set forth adequate facts to raise a genuine issue regarding the enforceability of the checks in light of his alleged compulsion and duress flowing from that disorder.

The entirety of Seigel's duress argument emanates from a single sentence in his affidavit: "For years I have had [a] gambling problem." If not ambiguous, the statement is conclusory. Unlike the gambler in *Lomonaco v. Sands Hotel Casino,* Seigel fails to produce any evidence in the record, specific or otherwise, regarding his problem and its relation to any unconscionable duress in the transactions at issue. In *Lomonaco,* the gambler described an abusive and bizarre "marathon gambling session" that included unsolicited credit increases from the casino, the existence of an alleged psychological disorder, and the gambler's concomitant use of pain killers, during which he lost $285,000 in little over two days. The record—even when viewed in the light most favorable to Seigel on whom the burden of proof rests—simply does not present a genuine disputed issue of fact as to whether the contracts evidenced by the checks were made under duress, and therefore unenforceable. We therefore conclude that Seigel's assertion that the checks would be unenforceable in New Jersey fails.

Seigel also invokes the fact that these checks were given in order to obtain chips with which to gamble, and cites us in particular to D.C. Code § 16–1701(a) (1997 Repl.). Modeled after the English "Statute of Anne," 9 Anne, 14, § 1 (1710), that section provides that:

A thing in action, judgment, mortgage, or other security or conveyance made and executed by a person in which any part of the consideration is for money or other valuable things won by playing at any game whatsoever, or by betting on the sides or hands of persons who play, or for the reimbursement or payment of any money knowingly lent or advanced for the purpose, or lent or advanced at the time and place of the play or bet, to a person so playing or betting or who, during the play, so plays or bets, is void.

In substance, Seigel claims that this statute would serve as a defense if the casinos were to seek to enforce the checks in the first instance in a District of Columbia court, and therefore this same statute requires that he be entitled to affirmatively recover from Merrill Lynch the amount of the checks in a District of Columbia court, regardless of the checks' enforceability elsewhere.

We may assume for present purposes that this statute would prevent direct enforcement of the checks in the District of Columbia, a somewhat dubious proposition in itself given the validity of the checks where made. But that is not this case. Rather, the question is whether under the relevant provisions of the Uniform Commercial Code, Seigel has met his burden of proof to establish actual loss. We think he has not.

As already indicated, even if payment had been stopped, the casinos could have enforced the checks in New Jersey, where the transaction was entered into. Merrill Lynch therefore, under the Code scheme, conceptually has the same right. Furthermore, even if there were a problem in asserting jurisdiction over Seigel in New Jersey, Maryland would have provided an appropriate forum for enforcing the checks. The highest Maryland court has squarely held that because there is no longer a strong public policy against gambling per se, but only against illegal gambling, the doctrine of *lex loci contractus* prevails in full, and that therefore Maryland courts will enforce gambling debts if legally incurred in a foreign jurisdiction. Accordingly, the casinos, and hence derivatively Merrill Lynch, could enforce the checks directly against Seigel in the state of his residence—Maryland.

We conclude that Seigel failed to establish that he ultimately suffered any actual loss as a result of the payment of the checks by Merrill Lynch.

Judgment for Merrill Lynch affirmed.

Ethics in Action

What Is the Ethical Thing to Do?

Suppose you take your car to a body shop to have it repainted. When you go to pick it up, you are not happy with the quality of the work, but the body shop refuses to release the car to you unless you pay in full for the work. You give the shop a check in the amount requested, and on your way home you stop at your bank and request that the bank stop payment on the check you have just written, an action you decided to take when you were writing the check. Have you acted ethically?

Certified Check

Certified Check Normally, a drawee bank is not obligated to certify a check. When a drawee bank does certify a check, it substitutes its undertaking (promise) to pay the check for the drawer's undertaking and becomes obligated to pay the check. At the time the bank certifies a check, the bank usually debits the customer's account for the amount of the certified check and shifts the money to a special account at the bank. It also adds its signature to the check to show that it has accepted primary liability for paying it. The bank's signature is an essential part of the certification: the bank's signature must appear on the check [3–409]. If the holder of a check chooses to have it certified, rather than seeking to have it paid at that time, the holder has made a conscious decision to look to the certifying bank for payment and no longer may rely on the drawer or the indorsers to pay it. See Figure 2 for an example of a certified check.

If the drawee bank certifies a check, then the drawer and any persons who previously indorsed the check are discharged of their liability on the check [3–414(c); 3–415(d)].

Cashier's Check

Cashier's Check A cashier's check differs from a certified check. A check on which a bank is both the drawer and the drawee is a cashier's check. The bank is primarily liable on the cashier's check. See Figure 3 for an example of a cashier's check. A teller's check is similar to a cashier's check. It is a check on which one bank is the drawer and another bank is the drawee. An example of a teller's check is a check drawn by a credit union on its account at a bank.

Figure 2 Certified Check

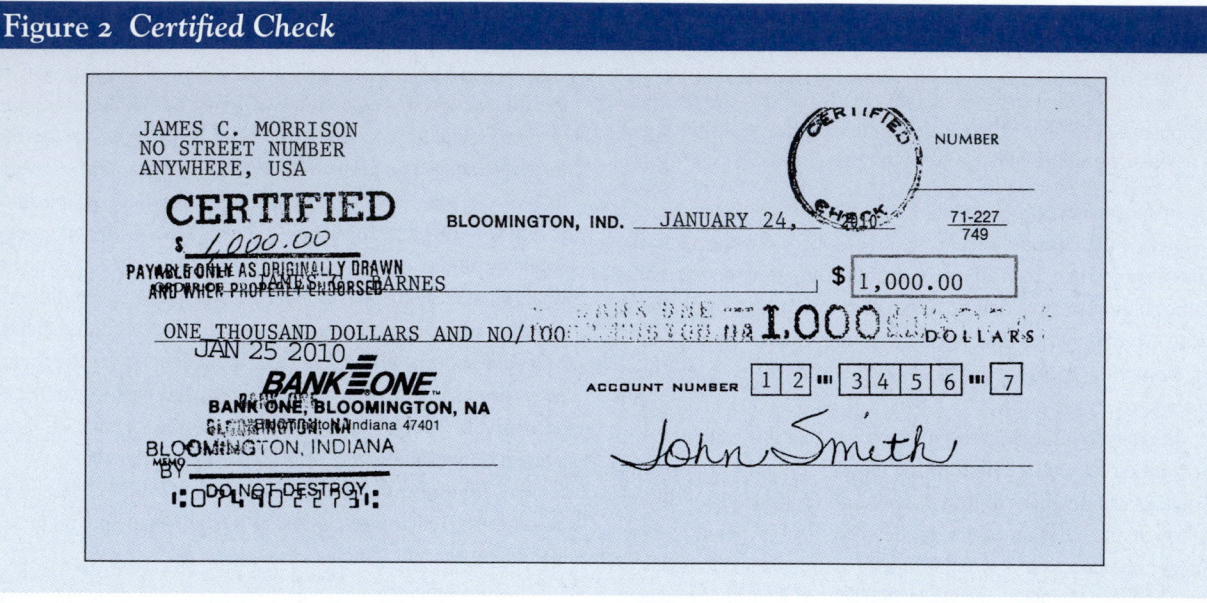

JAMES C. MORRISON
NO STREET NUMBER
ANYWHERE, USA

CERTIFIED
$ *1,000.00*

PAYABLE ONLY AS ORIGINALLY DRAWN
AND WHEN PROPERLY ENDORSED   BARNES

ONE THOUSAND DOLLARS AND NO/100

JAN 25 2010

BANK ONE.
BANK ONE, BLOOMINGTON, NA
BLOOMINGTON, Indiana 47401
BLOOMINGTON, INDIANA

MEMO

BY

DO NOT DESTROY

BLOOMINGTON, IND.   JANUARY 24, 2010   71-227 / 749

$ 1,000.00

1,000 DOLLARS

ACCOUNT NUMBER   1 2   3 4 5 6   7

John Smith

Figure 3   Cashier's Check

Bank of Homewood

OFFICIAL CHECK   10-86 / 220   418026913

DATE   MARCH 13, 2010

PAY   ONE THOUSAND AND NO/100   *Sample*

TO THE ORDER OF   HENRY JONES

NAME OF REMITTER   JACK ROBERTS

ADDRESS

DRAWER: BANK OF HOMEWOOD

BY *John Smith, Vice President*
AUTHORIZED SIGNATURE

Death or Incompetence of Customer

Under the general principles of agency law, the death or incompetence of the principal terminates the agent's authority to act for the principal. However, slightly different rules apply to the authority of a bank to pay checks out of the account of a deceased or incompetent person. The bank has the right to pay the checks of an incompetent person until it has notice that a court has determined that the person is incompetent. Once the bank learns of this fact, it loses its authority to pay that person's checks—because the depositor is not competent to issue instructions to pay.

Similarly, a bank has the right to pay the checks of a deceased customer until it has notice of the customer's death. Even if a bank knows of a customer's death, for a period of 10 days after the customer's death it can pay checks written by the customer prior to his death. However, the deceased person's heirs or other persons claiming an interest in the account can order the bank to stop payment [4–405].

Forged and Altered Checks

Bank's Right to Charge Account

A check that bears a forged signature of the drawer or payee is generally not properly payable from the customer's account because the bank is not following the instructions of the depositor precisely as he gave them. The bank is expected to be familiar with the authorized signature of its depositor. If it pays such a check, Article 4 will treat the transaction as one in which the bank paid out its own funds, rather than the depositor's funds.

Similarly, a check that was altered after the drawer made it out—for example, by increasing the amount of the check—is generally not properly payable from the customer's account. However, as noted earlier, if the drawer is negligent and contributes to the forgery or alteration, he may be barred from claiming it as the reason that a particular check should not be charged to his account.

For example, Barton makes a check for $1 in a way that makes it possible for someone to easily alter it to read $101, and it is so altered. If the drawee bank pays the check to a holder in good faith, it can charge the $101 to Barton's account if Barton's negligence contributed to the alteration. Similarly, if a company uses a mechanical check writer to write checks, it must use reasonable care to see that unauthorized persons do not have access to blank checks and to the check writer.

If the alteration is obvious, the bank should note that fact and refuse to pay the check when it is presented for payment. Occasionally, the alteration is so skillful that the bank cannot detect it. In that case, the bank is allowed to charge to the account the amount for which the check originally was written.

The bank has a duty to exercise "ordinary care" in the processing of negotiable instruments; it must observe the reasonable commercial standards prevailing among other banks in the area in which it does business. In the case of banks that take checks for collection or payment using automated means, it is important to note that reasonable commercial standards do not require the bank to examine every item *if* the failure to examine does not violate the bank's prescribed procedures and those procedures do not vary unreasonably from general banking practice or are not disapproved by the Code [3–107(a)(7); 4–103(c)]. For example, the bank's practice may be to examine those checks for more than $1,000 and a sample of smaller checks. Thus, if it did not examine a particular check in the amount of $250 for evidence of alteration or forgery, its action would be commercially reasonable so long as (1) it followed its own protocol, (2) that protocol was not a great variance from general banking usage, and (3) the procedure followed was not specifically disallowed in the Code.

In a case where both a bank and its customer fail to use ordinary care, a comparative negligence standard is used [4–406(e)].

Customer's Duty to Report Forgeries and Alterations

A bank must send a monthly (or quarterly) statement listing the transactions in an account, and it commonly returns the canceled checks to the customer. Revised Article 3 recognizes the modern bank practice of truncating (or retaining) checks and permits the bank to supply only a statement showing the item number, amount, and date of payment [4–406(a)]. When the bank does not return the paid items to the customer, the bank must either retain the items or maintain the capacity to furnish legible copies of the items for seven years after their receipt. The customer may request an item and the bank has a reasonable time to provide either the item or a legible copy of it [4–406(b)].

If the bank sends or makes available a statement of account or items, the customer must exercise reasonable promptness to examine the statement or items to determine whether payment was not authorized because of an alteration of any item or because a signature of the customer was not authorized. If, based on the statement or items provided, the customer should discover the unauthorized payment, the customer must notify the bank of the relevant facts promptly [4–406(c)].

Multiple Forgeries or Alterations Revised Article 3 provides a special rule to govern the situation in which the same wrongdoer makes a series of unauthorized drawer's signatures or alterations. The customer generally cannot hold the bank responsible for paying, in good faith, any such checks after the statement of account or item that contained the first unauthorized customer's signature or an alteration was available to the customer for a reasonable period, not exceeding 30 calendar days. This rule holds if (1) the customer did not notify the bank of the unauthorized signature or alteration, and (2) the bank proves it suffered a loss because of the customer's failure to examine his statement and notify the bank [4–406(d)]. Unless the customer has notified the bank about the forgeries or alterations that he should have discovered by reviewing the statement or item, the customer generally bears responsibility for any subsequent forgeries or alterations by the same wrongdoer.

Suppose that Allen employs Farnum as an accountant and that over a period of three months, Farnum forges Allen's signature to 10 checks and cashes them. One of the forged checks is included in the checks returned to Allen at the end of the first month. Within 30 calendar days after the return of these checks, Farnum forges two more checks and cashes them. Allen does not examine the returned checks until three months after the checks that included the first forged check were returned to her. The bank would be responsible for the first forged check and for the two checks forged and cashed within the 30-day period after it sent the first statement and the canceled checks (unless the bank proves that it suffered a loss because of the customer's failure to examine the checks and notify it more promptly). It would not be liable for the seven forged checks cashed after the expiration of the 30-day period.

Regardless of which party may have been negligent, a customer must discover and report to the bank any unauthorized customer's signature or any alteration within one year from the time after the statement or items are made available to him. If the customer does not do so, he cannot require the bank to recredit his account for such items. [4–406(f)].

In the case that follows, *Union Planters Bank, N.A. v. Rogers,* the court concluded that the bank's customer had not discovered and reported to the bank in a timely fashion a series of multiple forgeries on checks drawn against her account and thus was precluded from seeking to have her account recredited for the unauthorized items.

Union Planters Bank, N.A. v. Rogers
57 UCC Rep.2d 236 (Sup. Ct. Miss. 2005)

Neal and Helen Rogers maintained four checking accounts with the Union Planters Bank in Greenville, Mississippi. Each of the four accounts had originally been opened at other banks that later merged with Union Planters. The Rogers were both in their 80s when the events set out here took place. After Neal became bedridden, Helen hired Jackie Reese to help her take care of Neal and to do chores and errands.

In September 2000, Reese began writing checks on the Rogers' four accounts and forged Helen's name on the signature line. Some of the checks were made out to "cash," some to "Helen K. Rogers," and some to "Jackie Reese." Between September 2000 and August 2001, there were 168 checks totaling $58,398.00 written by Reese against the four accounts.

Neal died in late May 2001. Shortly thereafter, the Rogers' son, Neal, Jr., began helping Helen with financial matters. Together they discovered that many bank statements were missing and that there was not as much money in the accounts as they had thought. In June 2001, they contacted Union Planters and asked for copies of the missing bank statements. In September 2001, Helen was advised by Union Planters to contact the police due to the forgeries made on her account. Subsequently, criminal charges were brought against Reese. In the meantime, Helen filed suit against Union Planters seeking to have her account recredited for the checks charged to the account on which her signature as drawer had been forged.

Waller, Presiding Justice

The relationship between Rogers and Union Planters is governed by Article 4 of the Uniform Commercial Code. *Section 4–406(a) & (c)* provide that a bank customer has a duty to discover and report "unauthorized signatures"; i.e., forgeries. *Section 4–406 of the UCC* reflects an underlying policy decision that furthers the UCC's "objective of promoting certainty and predictability in commercial transactions." The UCC facilitates financial transactions, benefiting both consumers and financial institutions, by allocating responsibility among the parties according to whomever is best able to prevent a loss. Because the customer is more familiar with his own signature, and should know whether or not he authorized a particular withdrawal or check, he can prevent further unauthorized activity better than a financial institution which may process thousands of transactions in a single day. *Section 4–406* acknowledges that the customer is best situated to detect unauthorized transactions on his own account by placing the burden on the customer to exercise reasonable care to discover and report such transactions. The customer's duty to exercise this care is triggered when the bank satisfies its burden to provide sufficient information to the customer. As a result, if the bank provides sufficient information, the customer bears the loss when he fails to detect and notify the bank about unauthorized transactions.

Miss. Code Ann. § 4–406(a) & (c) provide as follows:

(a) A bank that sends or makes available to a customer a statement of account showing payment of items for the account shall either return or make available to the customer the items paid or provide information in the statement of account sufficient to allow the customer reasonable to identify the items paid. The statement of account provides sufficient information if the items is described by item number, amount, and date of payment.

* * *

(c) If a bank sends or makes available a statement of account or items pursuant to subsection (a), the customer must exercise reasonable promptness in examining the statement or the items to determine whether any payment was not authorized because of . . . a purported signature by or on behalf of the customer was not authorized. If, based on the statement or items provided, the customer should reasonably have discovered the unauthorized payment, the customer must promptly notify the bank of the relevant facts.

A. Union Planters' Duty to Provide Information under § 4–406(a)

The court admitted into evidence copies of all Union Planters statements sent to Rogers during the relevant time period. Enclosed with the bank statements were either the cancelled checks themselves or copies of the checks relating to the period of time of each statement. The evidence shows that all bank statements and cancelled checks were sent, via United States Mail, postage prepaid, to all customers at their "designated address" each month. Rogers introduced no evidence to the contrary. We therefore find that the bank fulfilled its duty of making the statements available to Rogers and that the remaining provisions of §4–406 are applicable to the case at bar.

In defense of her failure to inspect the bank statements, Rogers claims that she never received the bank statements and cancelled checks. Even if this allegation is true, it does not excuse Rogers from failing to fulfill her duties under § 75–4–406(a) & (c) because the statute clearly states a bank discharges its duty in providing the necessary information to a customer when it "sends . . . to a customer a statement of account showing payment of items." The word "receive" is absent. The customer's duty to inspect and report does not arise when the statement is received, as Rogers claims; the customer's duty to inspect and report arises when the bank sends the statement to the customer's address. A reasonable person who has not received a monthly statement from the bank would promptly ask the bank for a copy of the statement. Here, Rogers claims that she did not receive numerous statements. We find that she failed to act reasonably when she failed to take any action to replace the missing statements.

B. Rogers' Duty to Report the Forgeries under § 75–4–406(d)

A customer who has not promptly notified a bank of an irregularity may be precluded from bringing certain claims against the bank:

(d) If the bank proves that the customer failed, with respect to an item, to comply with the duties imposed on the customer by subsection (c), the customer is precluded from asserting against the bank:

(1) The customer's unauthorized signature . . . on the item, if the bank also proves that it suffered a loss by reason of the failure; . . .

§ 4–406(d)(1).

Also, when there is a series of forgeries, *§4–406(d)(2)* places additional duties on the customer:

(2) The customer's unauthorized signature . . . by the same wrongdoer on any other item paid in good faith by the bank if the payment was made before the bank received notice from the customer of the unauthorized signature . . . and after the customer had been afforded a reasonable period of time, not exceeding thirty (30) days, in which to examine the item or statement of account and notify the bank.

A bank may shorten the customer's thirty-day period for notifying the bank of a series of forgeries, and here, Union Planters shortened the thirty-day period to fifteen days. The statute states that a customer must report a series of forgeries within "a reasonable period of time, *not exceeding* thirty (30) days, . . ." "The 30-day period is an outside limit only. However 30 days is presumed to be reasonable and the bank bears the burden of proving otherwise."

Although there is no mention of a specific date, Rogers testified that she and her son began looking for the statements in late May or early June of 2001, after her husband had died. Her son felt that it was prudent to consolidate some of the five bank accounts. When they discovered that statements were missing, they notified Union Planters in June of 2001 to replace the statements. At this time, no mention of possible forgery was made, even though Neal, Jr., thought that "something was wrong." In fact, Neal, Jr., had felt that something was wrong as far back as December of 2000, but failed to do anything. Neal, Jr., testified that neither he nor his mother knew that Reese had been forging checks until September of 2001. Courts in Louisiana and Texas have held that, under similar circumstances, a customer's claims against a bank for paying forged checks are without merit.

Rogers is therefore precluded from making claims against Union Planters because (1) under *§ 4–406(a)*, Union Planters provided the statements to Rogers, and (2) under *§ 75–4–406(d)(2)*, Rogers failed to notify Union Planters of the forgeries within 15 and/or 30 days of the date she should have reasonably discovered the forgeries.

Judgment in favor of Union Planters Bank.

CONCEPT REVIEW

Liability for Multiple Forgeries or Alterations by the Same Person

Date First Statement Disclosing an Altered or Forged Check Is Available to Customer	Date 30 Days Later	Date Customer Gives Notice of Alteration or Forgery
Customer is not liable for forged/altered checks paid during this period unless bank suffers a loss from customer's unreasonable delay in notifying bank of forgery or alteration.	Customer is liable for forged or altered checks paid during this period unless customer gives bank notice of forgery or alteration within a reasonable time after date the first statement containing a forged or altered check was available to customer.	Customer is not liable for forged or altered checks paid during this period.

Check Collection and Funds Availability

Historically, the process of collecting a check that has been deposited or presented for payment has been a fairly complicated and time-consuming one. While the process is simplified if the check happens to be presented for payment at the drawee bank on which it is written, commonly checks are presented at other banks, often in other locations from the drawee bank where the drawer's account is maintained.. The historical process is explained below.

Because the bank where a check has been deposited for collection needs some time to make sure that the item is valid and will be paid, banks typically put a "hold" on the depositor's ability to access some or all of the funds represented by the instrument until it "clears" through the system. The current rules established by the Federal Reserve to govern funds availability are discussed in the section following the check collection process.

In the past few years, developments in electronic technology allow payments to be processed much more rapidly and efficiently than the old paper-based systems and are rapidly changing the way that goods and services are paid for and that money is transferred from one entity to another. In 2004, Congress enacted a federal law, known as "Check 21," that is designed to allow banks to handle more checks electronically and provides a federal overlay to some of the law that has previously been state-based in the form of Articles 3 and 4

of the Uniform Commercial Code. Check 21, along with various electronic substitutes for checks, will be covered later in this chapter.

Check Collection As Chapter 31, Negotiable Instruments, describes, checks and other drafts collected through the banking system usually have at least three parties—the drawer, the drawee bank, and the payee. If the payee deposits the check at the same bank as the drawee bank, the latter will take a series of steps necessary to reflect the deposit as a credit to the payee's account and to decide whether to pay the check from the drawer's account. In connection with its handling of the deposit for the payee's benefit, it will make one ledger entry showing the deposit as a credit to the payee's account. In connection with its decision to pay, the bank's employees and computers will perform several steps commonly referred to as the process of posting. These steps need not be taken in any particular order, but they customarily include determining whether there are sufficient funds to pay, debiting the drawer's account for the amount of the check, and placing the check into a folder for later return to the drawer (to satisfy its obligations under the "bank statement" rule) [4–406]. Banks in those states that have not enacted the 1990 amendments to Article 4 will also compare the drawer's signature on the check with that on the deposit agreement as part of this process.

If the payee deposits the check at a bank other than the drawee bank, the depositary bank, acting as the agent of the payee, will make the ledger entry showing the deposit as a credit to the payee's account. The next step of the collection process depends on where the depositary bank is located. If the drawee and depositary banks are in the same town or county, the depositary bank will indorse the check and deliver (present) it to the drawee bank for payment. It may deliver it by courier or through a local association of banks known as a "clearing house" [4–104(1)(d)]. Under Article 4, the drawee-payor bank must settle for the check before midnight of the banking day of its receipt of the check, which means that it must give the depositary bank funds or a credit equal to the amount of the check. Once it settles for the check, the drawee-payor bank has until midnight of the banking day after the banking day of receipt to pay the check or to return the check or send notice of dishonor. This deadline for the drawee-payor bank's action on the check is known as the bank's "midnight deadline" [4–104(1)(h)]. The drawee-payor bank's failure to settle by midnight of the banking day of receipt, or its failure to pay or return the check, or send notice of dishonor, results in the drawee-payor bank's becoming "accountable" for the amount of the check, which means it must pay the amount of the check [4–302(a)].

If the drawee and depositary banks are located in different counties, or in different states, the depositary bank will use an additional commercial bank, and one or more of the regional Federal Reserve Banks, in the collection of the check. In these cases, the depositary bank will send the check on to the drawee-payor bank through these "collecting banks." Each bank in the sequence must use ordinary care in presenting the check or sending it for presentment, and in sending notice of dishonor or returning the check after learning that the check has not been paid [4–202(a)]. The depositary and collecting banks have until their respective midnight deadlines—or, in some cases, a further reasonable time—to take the action required of them in the sequence of collection steps.

If the drawee-payor bank dishonors the check prior to its midnight deadline or shortly after the midnight deadline under circumstances specified in "Regulation CC" of the Federal Reserve Board (described in the next section of this chapter), it will send the check back to the depositary bank. Until September 1, 1988, the drawee-payor bank customarily sent the dishonored check back to the collecting bank from which it received the check, and the collecting bank sent it back to the bank from which it had received it, and through any other bank that handled the check in the "forward collection" process until the check again reached the depositary bank. The provisions of Article 4 still describe this sequence as the "return collection" process, although Regulation CC imposes new responsibilities on the payor bank and on any other "returning bank." Each bank in the return sequence adjusts its accounts to reflect the return and has until its midnight deadline to send the check back to the bank from which it originally had received the check. After September 1, 1988, the drawee-payor bank may return the check directly to the depositary bank—skipping all of the collecting banks and the delay represented by the midnight deadlines that each bank otherwise would have had.

Direct return also increases the likelihood that the depositary bank will know whether the check has been dishonored by the day on which Regulation CC requires the depositary bank to allow the payee to write checks or otherwise make withdrawals against the deposit. The next section of this chapter discusses the "funds availability" aspect of Regulation CC in more detail.

On receipt of the dishonored check, the depositary bank will return the check or otherwise notify its depositor (the payee) of the dishonor and will debit or charge back her account for the check it did not collect. The depositary bank may charge back the deposit even if it previously had allowed the payee-depositor to withdraw against the credit given for the deposit.

When the depositor receives the notice of dishonor and returned check it will take one of several steps, depending on whether it received the check directly from the drawer or took it by indorsement from another person. If the depositor was not the original payee of the check, it usually will prefer to return the check—giving notice of dishonor unless already given by the drawee bank or another collecting bank—to the person who negotiated the check to her, the prior indorser. Recall that an indorser is obligated to pay the check following dishonor and notice of dishonor [3–415].

If the depositor received the check directly from the drawer, for example as payee, the depositor normally will demand payment from the drawer. Recall that the drawer is obligated to pay the check upon dishonor [3–414]; alternatively, the payee may seek to enforce the underlying obligation for which the drawer originally issued the check, such as the purchase of groceries or an automobile.

The case that follows, *Valley Bank of Ronan v. Hughes*, involves the question of a bank's right to charge back a depositor's account for the amount of checks he had received and deposited in the course of being the victim of a scam.

Valley Bank of Ronan v. Hughes
61 UCC Rep.2d 277 (Sup. Ct. Montana 2006)

Lured by the promise of quick wealth, Charles Hughes was conned by a "Nigerian scam." The swindlers promised Hughes a $3 million to $4.5 million commission for his aid in procuring agricultural equipment for import into Africa and then proceeded to bilk him for hundreds of thousands of dollars in advanced fees. Some of the funds that Hughes advanced were wired via the services of Valley Bank of Ronan, resulting in a dispute over which party should bear the loss from the flimflam.

On Friday, March 22, 2002, Hughes received four checks from one of the con-artists and deposited them into accounts Hughes held at Valley Bank. Two of them were "official" checks, and the other two were personal checks. One official check, for $1 million, was drawn on Colonial Bank. The other official check, for $500,000, was drawn on Firstar. The personal checks were for $62,000—drawn on the account of Maximilian H. Miltzlaff—and for $70,000—drawn on a Capital One credit card account held by Sarah Briscoe and Mary Bullard.

Prior to depositing the checks, Hughes requested that Nancy Smith, a cashier and officer of Valley Bank, verify the validity of the official checks. In his deposition, Hughes described his conversation with Smith:

Well, my question was, how long do you have to hold money to have—how long do you have to hold these checks before they're sufficient funds; I think the bank calls them collected funds. And she said, these are official checks, Chuck. These two big ones are official checks. You will be transferring these? And I said I will be transferring a large sum. We'll have to determine next week what it will be. And she says, official checks, same as cash. You can do whatever you want to do.

Smith also assured Hughes that official checks were "just like" cashier's checks. Milanna Shear, another bank employee, told Hughes to believe whatever Smith said regarding the validity of the checks. According to the deposition testimony of Hughes's wife, Barbara, Hughes had told her that "everybody at the bank assured him that the checks would be good."

On Tuesday, March 26, 2002, Hughes delivered a written request to Valley Bank to wire $800,000 to Ali dh. Abbas, an accountholder at the Housing Bank for Trade and Finance in Amman, Jordan. Valley Bank executed the transfer no later than 1:51 PM on the same day. The transfer proceeded through two intermediary banks, Wells Fargo, near Denver, Colorado, and Citibank in New York, before being sent to Amman. Upon receipt in Amman, the funds were promptly withdrawn, never to be seen again.

At about 2:00 PM—approximately 10 minutes after initiation of the transfer—Valley Bank and Hughes learned that one of the personal checks was being returned marked "nonsufficient funds." Hughes immediately requested the wire to be stopped. No later than 3:26 PM, Valley Bank requested that Wells Fargo reverse the wire transfer. The record is unclear about what happened during the interim between Hughes's request for cancellation and Valley Bank's attempts to comply with the request. The efforts of the several banks involved in the transfer to reverse the transaction were unsuccessful, and the later discovery that the two official checks were counterfeit resulted in Hughes's account being overdrawn by $800,000.

Valley Bank subsequently exercised its right to charge back the account and collect the $800,000 from Hughes. Allen Buhr, Valley Bank's president, met with Hughes on March 29, 2002, to discuss Hughes's liability and suggested at that time that Hughes could be involved in a criminal prosecution for fraud. On April 11, 2002, Hughes deposited $607,838, which he had withdrawn from his retirement account, into the Valley Bank account. Also, on April 30, 2002, Hughes executed a promissory note to Valley Bank on behalf of his trust in the amount of $400,000, secured by mortgaged property. Of the $400,000 in proceeds generated by the secured note, $202,751.21 was used to pay off a previous loan against the mortgaged property, and the balance, $197,248.79, was applied to satisfy the charge-back liability in Hughes's account. Hughes was under the impression, given by Buhr, that the bank needed the note and loan agreement because it expected to be the subject of a government audit in the near future, and though Hughes thought that a new agreement might be reached after resolution of the "fraud situation," he understood that the loan may not be forgiven. The trust subsequently made the first interest payment on the note on August 1, 2002, though it was one month late. The trust made no other payments on the note, and Valley Bank sent a notice of default and acceleration on October 15, 2002. Hughes requested that the bank forebear foreclosure until the end of the year, and the bank complied.

However, when Hughes failed to make any more payments on the note, Valley Bank initiated an action for judicial foreclosure. Hughes asserted counterclaims of negligence, negligent misrepresentation, constructive fraud, unjust enrichment,

breach of contract, breach of the implied covenant of good faith and fair dealing, promissory estoppel, and intentional inflic-
tion of emotional distress (which was later abandoned). The district court granted Valley Bank summary judgment on its
claims regarding the promissory note. Hughes appealed.

Rice, Justice

A short introduction to the check settlement process will give context to our following legal analysis. When a customer deposits a check at a bank, the bank will sometimes (but not always) credit the customer's account immediately with the face amount of the check and permit the customer to draw on the deposited funds. This practice is known in Uniform Commercial Code parlance as "provisional settlement" because the bank has not yet presented the check to the drawee bank and received payment from the check maker's account (which would constitute "final settlement"). The depositary bank, however, may "charge back" the depositor's account in the event the check is subsequently dishonored by the drawee bank. Thus, the UCC encourages the provisional settlement process by protecting a depositary bank from fraudulent or otherwise unenforceable check deposits. With this overview of the check settlement process in mind, we turn now to the specifics of the case before us.

Hughes argues that the District Court erroneously concluded that the UCC preempts Hughes' equitable and common law claims. Hughes asserts that preemption does not occur because "[t]here *are* no regulations or UCC provisions which expressly regulate . . . promises and representations that bank personnel make to their customers." Further, Hughes contends that the "practical effect of the District Court's interpretation affords banks absolute immunity for negligence, fraud, misrepresentation and other acts which are not expressly addressed in the UCC. . . ."

The District Court rested its conclusion on its interpretation of *§ 1–103, MCA,* which reads as follows:

Unless displaced by the particular provisions of this code, the principles of law and equity, including the law merchant and the law relative to capacity to contract, principal and agent, estoppel, fraud, misrepresentation, duress, coercion, mistake, bankruptcy, or other validating or invalidating cause shall supplement its provisions.

We disagree with the District Court's interpretation of *§ 1–103.* A bank receiving checks from depositors must use "ordinary care"—as that term is defined and used in the UCC—in settling those checks. *See §§ 4–103(3), 4–103(5),* and *4–212, MCA.* Section *3–102(1)(g)* defines "ordinary care" as follows:

"Ordinary care" in the case of a person engaged in business means observance of reasonable commercial standards, prevailing in the area in which that person is located, with respect to the business in which that person is engaged. In the case of a bank that takes an instrument for processing for collection or payment by automated means, reasonable commercial standards do not require the bank to examine the instrument if the failure to examine does not violate the bank's prescribed procedures and the bank's procedures do not vary unreasonably from general banking usage not disapproved by this chapter or chapter 4.

In its order, the District Court examined the meaning of "ordinary care" but did not distinguish the term's application to the two different actions at issue here: the settlement of the deposited checks and the alleged representations about the check settlement process. The second sentence of the definition of ordinary care specifically states that, subject to certain exceptions, a bank does not have a duty to examine instruments, in this case, checks. Pursuant to *§ 1–103* and *UCC § 1–103, cmt. 2,* such specificity preempts any common law concepts that might otherwise supplement the UCC. Thus, to the extent that Hughes' common law claims relate to Valley Bank's processing of the checks, they are preempted by the UCC.

Indeed, Hughes presents a claim directed toward the UCC-defined standard of ordinary care with respect to check processing. Hughes asserts that, by failing to comply with its own policies and the applicable federal regulations, Valley Bank inappropriately charged back his account after the dishonor of the deposited checks. However, *§ 4–212(4)* states, "[t]he right to charge back is not affected by . . . failure by any bank to exercise ordinary care with respect to the item but any bank so failing remains liable." Official Comment 5 to *§ 4–212(4)* expounds on this point, stating that "charge-back is permitted *even where non-payment results from the depositary bank's own negligence.*" (Emphasis added.) Accordingly, in evaluating the propriety of Valley Bank's actions with regard to check processing, it is irrelevant whether Valley Bank exercised ordinary care in exercising its charge back rights, and the claims are preempted.

Note: The court went on to hold that Hughes could assert common law claims of negligence against the bank as to the communications the bank made to him about the process on which he claimed to have relied. Thus, while the bank had an absolute right to charge back the fraudulent checks to Hughes's account and he had the obligation to repay the bank, it nonetheless was possible for Hughes to obtain a judgment against the bank to compensate him for the charge-back debt.

CYBERLAW IN ACTION

Banks Honor Bogus Checks and Scam Victims Pay

Trying to sell his 1968 Mustang online, John Schaefer received what appeared to be a firm offer from an overseas classic-car dealer. The buyer sent Schaefer a check for $14,000 even though Schaefer was asking only $8,000. The buyer said the extra money was to cover shipping and directed Schaefer to wire him the difference.

"It seemed kind of funny, and I had some hesitation," said Schaefer, who deposited the check in his bank's ATM over the weekend. On Monday, he asked a teller to see if the check was good. She left her perch, went to the backroom and returned assuring him "there was no problem," Schaefer recalled.

On Wednesday, "still not feeling quite right," Schaefer asked the same teller to make sure the check was good. That time, the teller told him the check had been cleared and he was "all set." Schaefer withdrew $5,000 and wired the money to the buyer.

Four days later, as he reviewed his account online, he discovered the check was not good. Even worse, the bank was demanding that he repay the $5,000.

"Had I made the deposit and not tried to make sure it was legitimate, I *should* have full obligation to make good on it," said Schaefer, 34, a facilities manager in Brattleboro, Vermont. "But I checked with the bank twice, and now I find out they have no accountability."

Schaefer is one of thousands of consumers who have been victimized by an increasingly common check scam that relies on the vagaries of the banking system to take advantage of unsuspecting consumers. Federal rules require banks to release funds from a consumer's deposit quickly, usually within one to five business days, depending on the kind of check. However, it can take weeks before a bank discovers a check is fraudulent.

So when a teller says "the check has cleared," the teller is "usually thinking in terms of bank rules, that the hold time is over, and the consumer now has access to the funds," said Susan Grant, director of the National Fraud Information Center. But the average consumer thinks that phrase means "the check is not fraudulent," Grant added. When that happens, it is depositors who are responsible for the money, she said. As the American Bankers Association explains in a "Fraud Alert!" statement insert it distributes to banks to send to customers: The consumer is the one dealing directly with the person who sent the money and therefore is "in the best position to determine how risky the transaction is."

To facilitate the flow of funds behind the 40 billion checks processed each year, banks are required to release funds within a few days, said Nessa Feddis, senior federal counsel for American Bankers Association. If tellers start asking a lot of questions or start holding checks until they are determined to be good, banks "might be perceived as trying to circumvent the rules entitling people to withdraw funds," Feddis added. And if the banks are wrong, it will only be a matter of time before they are hauled before Congress and "accused of trying to hold on to people's funds," she said.

That provides no comfort to those who have gotten caught in scams. "I want security more than fast check-cashing and money flying all over the place," said Toni Gaston, a New Jersey administrative assistant who was the victim of an Internet work-at-home scam earlier this year.

In February, about a year after Gaston had posted her résumé on a job-search Web site, she received an e-mail about a part-time opportunity: to work as a courier for money for an international charity that builds homes for people in disaster areas. Her assignment was to deposit local donations into her own bank account, wait for the checks to clear and then wire the money to another address. She was told she would be paid 7 percent of every donation check, with a guarantee of $500 the first week on the job.

Gaston received a $4,500 cashier's check on Saturday, February 26, and immediately deposited it in her Bank of America account. The teller told her it would take three days for the check to clear. On Wednesday, Gaston reviewed her account online and saw the funds were in her account. "I assumed, since it was a cashier's check, that Bank of America had actually gotten money from the other bank and put it into my account," she said.

On Thursday, Gaston withdrew $2,000 and wired it to a Ukrainian address. That's not unusual since most of these scams direct money outside the United States, often to Canada or Nigeria. The next day, Gaston followed instructions from another e-mail directing her to wire $1,900 to a different Ukrainian address.

"I couldn't believe I could make this much from this little bit of work," Gaston said. It was only a few days later that Gatson's euphoria wore off, when she caught a snippet of a TV news story about a person who had been scammed by an identical work-at-home scheme. "My face turned completely green," said Gaston, who called the bank immediately. Bank officials told her there was nothing the bank could do and warned her that she would have to repay the $3,900 when the counterfeit cashier's check was finally returned to the bank.

It took another month before that happened. By that time, Gaston had surfed the Internet and learned there were hundreds of other victims around the country. She was furious. "The banks know this is going on. They know people are compromising the bank system, so why don't they upgrade their security, train their tellers to spot the counterfeit checks?"

According to Gaston: "A bank vice president told me that the bank cashes so many checks a day it doesn't have time to do that. I thought my money was safe. . . . I should have stashed it in a mattress."

Bank of America spokeswoman Diane Wagner said privacy rules prohibit talking about Gaston's case. However, in general terms, she said, "We advise customers to know with whom they're doing business. We also tell them they should never agree to wire back funds to a person they're not familiar with."

Wagner and other bank officials around the country all note that both the deposit receipt and the initial agreement customers sign when setting up an account make it clear that if any deposit item is returned, for any reason, the customer is responsible. Bank of America's deposit receipt, for example, says: "All items are credited subject to verification, collection, and conditions of the Rules and Regulations of this Bank and as otherwise provided by law."

For most consumers, that language is clearly not enough, said Shawn Mosch, who launched a "Scam Victims United" Web site after she and her husband fell victim to a counterfeit check scam when they tried to sell a 1961 Buick online. Begun in 2003, Scam Victims United now has 2,616 members registered to its message board of 4,000 postings.

"There ought to be a law that says banks can't release the money until the check is guaranteed to have cleared—or the customer is willing to sign a release realizing it is his/her responsibility if the check turns out bad," Mosch said. "Had there been something like that for me when I was a victim, I would have said, 'Oh wait, you mean we're not guaranteed here?'. . . We didn't trust the guy we were selling the car to, but we trusted our bank to tell us the truth. . . . I specifically asked the teller, 'I want to make sure if I do anything with this check it won't come back and bite me,' and the same teller assured me three times there was no problem."

Bank officials say it is not possible to warn each and every consumer about potential scams. "Everybody is in a hurry, so if we made such a disclosure with each transaction about every responsibility the depositor has, we'd be there all day,"

the ABA's Feddis said. Besides, Feddis added, the proportion of fraudulent checks is very small, fewer than 100,000 out of the 40 billion checks processed annually. But the numbers are growing. According to the suspicious-activity reports banks file with the federal government, the number of fraudulent and counterfeit checks totaled 88,986 in 2005. That's more than triple the 28,670 reported in 2000. Between 2004 and 2005 alone, the number of reports of fraudulent and counterfeit checks grew by 45 percent.

Driving this increase is the Internet, which has made it easy for scammers to reach an ever-widening circle of susceptible consumers. "Because you're on the Internet in the comfort of your home, you may not realize the dark alleys you're dealing with," said John Hambrick, the FBI's unit chief at the Internet Crime Complaint Center.

Banks say they are trying to be more proactive, alerting their customers to those dark fraud-filled alleys through statement inserts and posters. "Banks could do a better job," added Grant of the National Fraud Information Center. Among other things, she said, they could improve technology to catch fraudulent checks faster and be more upfront with customers about the risks.

"For example, when a customer says, 'Has this check cleared?' it's an opportunity to say the hold period is over and now you can have access to the money, but that doesn't mean the check or money order is good. If it bounces, you will still be responsible." Even so, Grant added, consumers need to be vigilant, too. "And there's one sure way consumers can avoid a scam: Anytime anyone asks you to wire them money, that's all you need to know."

Schaefer learned that lesson the expensive way with his Mustang. He eventually sold it "to a gentlemen in Massachusetts," he said, adding, "He paid cash."

Source: C. Mayer, "Banks Honor Bogus Checks and Scam Victims Pay," *Washington Post*, June 1, 2006, p. A1. © 2006 The Washington Post Company.

Funds Availability

When a bank takes a check for deposit to a customer's account, it typically places a hold on the funds represented by the deposited check because it runs a number of risks in allowing a customer to withdraw deposits that it has not collected from the drawee bank. The risks that the check may be returned include (1) there may be insufficient funds in the drawer's account or the account may have been closed; (2) the check may contain a forged drawer's or indorser's signature, or there may have been a material alteration of the check; (3) the possibility that the drawer is kiting checks or playing two accounts off against each other; or (4) a stop-payment order may have been placed against the check. These are real concerns to a depositary bank, and it has a significant interest in protecting itself against these possibilities.

Until recently, the risks run by a depositary bank were complicated by a very slow process used by drawee-payor banks in returning a dishonored check or notifying the bank of the dishonor. Moreover, depositary banks did not get direct notice from drawee-payor banks when they paid checks. Accordingly, banks often restricted the depositor's use of the deposit by placing relatively long holds on checks deposited with them for collection; these sometimes ran 15 to 20 days for items drawn on other than local banks.

The extensive use of holds, and a growing public sentiment that they were excessive and often unfair, led to the passage by Congress in 1987 of the Expedited Funds Availability Act. In the act, Congress set out mandatory schedules limiting check holds and specifying when funds are to be made available to customers by depositary institutions. The act also delegated to the Federal Reserve Board the authority to speed up the check-processing system. The regulations adopted by the Board to speed up check processing supersede the provisions of Article 4 of the UCC (Bank Deposits and Collections) in a number of respects but will not be covered in this text.

The key elements of the mandatory funds availability schedules, which are set out in Federal Reserve Board Regulation CC, are:

1. Local checks (those drawn on banks in the same Federal Reserve check region as the depositary bank) must be made available for the depositor to draw against by the second business day following deposit.

2. Nonlocal checks (those drawn on banks located in the United States but outside the Federal Reserve check-processing region in which the depositary bank is located) must be made available by the fifth business day following deposit.

3. Certain items must be made available by the next day after the day of deposit. These include:

   a. Cash deposits where the deposit is made in person to an employee of the depositary bank (i.e., not at an ATM).

   b. Electronic payments.

   c. Checks drawn on the U.S. Treasury.

   d. U.S. Postal Service money orders.

   e. Checks drawn on a Federal Reserve Bank or Federal Home Loan Bank.

   f. Checks drawn by a state or a unit of local government (under certain conditions).

   g. Cashier's, certified, or teller's checks.

   h. Checks drawn on the depositary bank.

   i. The lesser of $100 or the aggregate deposit on any one banking day.

4. If the next-day items are not deposited in person with an employee of the depositary institution but rather are deposited in an ATM machine or by mail, then the deposit does not have to be made available for withdrawal until the second business day after deposit.

5. Generally, the depositary bank must begin accruing interest to a depositor's interest-bearing account from the day it receives credit for cash and check deposits to an interest-bearing account.

There are six major exceptions to the mandatory availability schedules set out above that are designed to safeguard depositary banks against higher risk situations. The exceptions are:

1. *New account exception.* The depositary bank may suspend the availability rules for new accounts and can limit the next-day and second-day availability to the first $5,000 deposited.

2. *Large deposit exception.* The hold periods can be extended to the extent the aggregate deposit on any banking day exceeds $5,000.

3. *Redeposited check exception.* The hold period can be extended where a check has been returned one or more times.

4. *Repeated overdraft exception.* A longer hold period may be required for deposits to accounts that have been overdrawn repeatedly.

5. *Reasonable cause exception.* The scheduled availability may be extended where the bank has reasonable cause to believe the check is uncollectible.

6. *Emergency conditions exception.* The scheduled availability may be extended under certain emergency conditions such as a communications interruption or a computer failure.

Banks are required to disclose their funds availability policy to all of their customers; they may provide different policies to different classes or categories of customers.

Check 21

The Check Clearing for the 21st Century Act, commonly known as "Check 21," a federal law that is designed to enable banks to handle more checks electronically, became effective on October 28, 2004. As detailed in the previous section, for many years banks had to physically move checks from the bank where they are deposited to the drawee bank that pays them—a time-consuming, inefficient, and costly process. And, for many years, banks then returned the canceled checks to their customers along with their monthly account statement. In recent years, however, many banks have stopped providing canceled checks to their customers; you may have noticed this change in the way your own checking account was handled by your bank. Instead, they provide images of the checks with multiple pictures of canceled checks appearing on pages of a paper or electronic bank statement. If the drawee bank keeps the original checks, this is called "check truncation." Credit unions and an increasing number of commercial banks have been truncating checks for quite a while. Check 21 allows "check truncation" to happen at an earlier stage of the check collection process—as early as the payee if the bank the payee uses as a depositary bank will let the payee keep the checks.

For many years, banks have had the capacity to capture information from the MICR lines of checks and to transmit that information electronically to collecting banks as well as the drawee bank if the banks later in the collection chain had electronic capabilities. But, in order for a bank to send only the electronic image forward (as opposed to the paper check drawn by the drawer of the check), each bank had to have an "electronic presentment agreement" with the other banks in the collection chain. If one bank in the chain of collection or the drawee bank did not have electronic processing ability, then the use of electronic processing was ended. One bank could hold up the use of electronic innovations simply by refusing to take electronic items.

Check 21 authorizes banks to transform information they receive in electronic form back into a paper copy of the check. It grants legal status to paper copies that meet specific standards and so qualify as "substitute checks," that is, the equivalent as against all persons and for all purposes of the paper check drawn by the drawer. As a result, if a bank with electronic capacity encountered a drawee bank that did not have electronic capacity, the first bank could use its electronic information file to create a substitute check (assuming it met the standards) and to present that substitute check for payment. Similarly, if all the banks in a check collection chain used electronic presentment processing, but the payee or drawer needed a paper copy of the check to prove it had paid an obligation, its bank could create and deliver a substitute check to the payee or drawer. In both cases, the resulting substitute check is legally the same as the original check if it accurately represents the information on the original check and includes the following statement: "This is a legal copy of your check. You can use it the same way you would use the original check." The substitute check must also have been handled by a bank.

Banks are not required to keep your original check for any specific period of time. Existing state law requires that banks retain a legible copy of checks for seven years, but does not require that the copies returned to customers with statements be legible. Check 21 does not add any new retention requirements. Under the new law, original checks are more likely to be destroyed. If you request your original check from your bank, your bank may provide you with the original check, a substitute check, or a copy of the check.

Articles 3 and 4 of the Uniform Commercial Code continue to provide protection against erroneous and unauthorized checks. In addition, Check 21 contains a number of new protections for customers. For example, Check 21 contains a special refund procedure, called expedited recredit, for a customer who suffers a loss because of a substitute check.

Because checks are now transmitted electronically from one bank to another, customers must make sure they have funds in their account to cover them and no longer anticipate a "float" based on the time it would take the check to be physically transmitted back to the drawee bank. Consumer groups warn consumers to be aware that there is an increased risk that a check will bounce if funds are not in the account when the check is written. At the same time, customers may not get access to the funds from checks that they deposit to their account any sooner because Check 21 does not shorten the check hold times set out in the Federal Funds Availability Act.

Electronic Transfers

Over the past three decades, many new mechanisms have emerged for transferring money electronically without the need for paper money or the use of paper-based negotiable instruments such as checks. Concomitantly, financial institutions. merchants, and providers of service are encouraging customers to use these mechanisms in order to expedite the movement of money in a more cost-effective manner, to the benefit of all parties involved in financial transactions. The electronic funds transfer systems (EFTs) utilized by consumers include (1) automated teller machines; (2) point-of-sale terminals, which allow consumers to use their EFT cards like checks to transfer money from their checking account to the merchant; (3) preauthorized payments, such as automatic deposit of paychecks and government benefits, or the payment of mortgage, credit card, and utility bills; and (4) telephone transfers between accounts or authorization to pay specific bills. And, for large business and financial institutions, wire transfers of funds are commonly used to move large sums of money very quickly across the country or around the world.

As these mechanisms have emerged and are increasingly supplanting the traditional methods for transferring money, they have required new legal constructs to deal with the issues and problems they present that do not fit well in existing legal regimes such as Articles 3 (Negotiable Instruments) and 4 (Bank Deposits and Collections) of the Uniform Commercial Code. The Electronic Funds Transfer Act (EFTA) now addresses many of the issues that arise out of consumer use of EFTs while Article 4A (Funds Transfers) of the Uniform Commercial Code deals with the funds transfers that are outside of the overage of the EFTA.

Electronic Funds Transfer Act

The consumer who used electronic funds transfer systems (EFTs), the so-called cash machines or electronic tellers, in the early years often experienced problems in identifying and resolving mechanical errors resulting from malfunctioning EFTs. In response to these problems, Congress passed the Electronic Funds Transfer Act in 1978 to provide "a basic framework, establishing the rights, liabilities, and responsibilities of participants in electronic funds transfer systems" and especially to provide "individual consumer rights."

Similar to the Truth in Lending Act and the Fair Credit Billing Act (FCBA) discussed in Chapter 48, the EFT Act requires disclosure of the terms and conditions of electronic funds transfers at the time the consumer contracts for the EFT service. Among the nine disclosures required are the following: the consumer's liability for unauthorized electronic funds transfers (those resulting from loss or theft), the nature of the EFT services under the consumer's account, any pertinent dollar or frequency limitations, any charges for the right to make EFTs, the consumer's right to stop payment of a preauthorized transfer, the financial institution's liability to the consumer for failure to make or stop payments, and the consumer's right to receive documentation of transfers both at the point or time of transfer and periodically. The act also requires 21 days' notice prior to the effective date of any change in the terms or conditions of the consumer's account that pertains to the required disclosures.

The EFT Act does differ from the Fair Credit Billing Act in a number of important respects. For example, under the EFT Act, the operators of EFT systems have a maximum of 10 working days to investigate errors or provisionally recredit the consumer's account, whereas issuers of credit cards have a maximum of 60 days under the FCBA. The liability of the consumer also is different if an EFT card is lost or stolen than it is if a credit card is lost or stolen.

The *Kruser* case illustrates the application of the EFT Act's provisions that require a customer to provide timely notification of any unauthorized use of his card in order to limit his liability for the unauthorized use of the card.

Kruser v. Bank of America NT & SA   281 Cal.Rptr. 463 (Cal. Ct. App. 1991)

Lawrence and Georgene Kruser maintained a joint checking account with the Bank of America. The bank issued each of them a "Versatel" card and separate personal identification numbers that would allow access to funds in their account from automatic teller machines. The Krusers also received with their cards a "Disclosure Booklet" that provided to the Krusers a summary of consumer liability, the bank's business hours, and the address and telephone number by which they could notify the bank in the event they believed an unauthorized transfer had been made.

The Krusers believed Mr. Kruser's card had been destroyed in September 1986. The December 1986 account statement mailed to the Krusers by the bank reflected a $20 unauthorized withdrawal of funds by someone using Mr. Kruser's card at an automatic teller machine. The Krusers reported this unauthorized transaction to the bank when they discovered it in August or September 1987.

Mrs. Kruser underwent surgery in late 1986 or early 1987 and remained hospitalized for 11 days. She then spent a period of six or seven months recuperating at home. During this time, she reviewed the statements the Krusers received from the bank.

In September 1987, the Krusers received bank statements for July and August 1987 that reflected 47 unauthorized withdrawals totaling $9,020 made from an automatic teller machine, again by someone using Mr. Kruser's card. They notified the bank of these withdrawals within a few days of receiving the statements. The bank refused to credit the Kruser's account with the amount of the unauthorized withdrawals. The Krusers sued the bank claiming damages for the unauthorized withdrawals from their account. The trial court ruled in favor of the bank on the grounds that the Krusers had failed to comply with the note and reporting requirements of the Electronic Funds Transfer Act (EFTA). The Krusers appealed.

Stone, Associate Justice

The ultimate issue we address is whether, as a matter of law, the unauthorized $20 withdrawal which appeared on the December 1986 statement barred the Krusers from recovery for the losses incurred in July and August 1987. Resolution of the issue requires the interpretation of the EFTA and section 205.6 of Regulation E, one of the regulations prescribed by the Board of Governors of the Federal Reserve System in order to carry out the EFTA.

Section 205.6 of Regulation E mirrors [the EFTA] and in particular provides:

(b) Limitations on the amount of liability. The amount of a consumer's liability for an unauthorized electronic fund transfer or a series of related unauthorized transfers shall not exceed $50 or the amount of unauthorized transfers that occur before notice to the financial institution . . . whichever is less, unless one of the following exceptions apply:

. . .

(2) If the consumer fails to report within 60 days of transmittal of the periodic statement any unauthorized electronic fund transfer that appears on the statement, the consumer's liability shall not exceed the sum of (i) The lesser of $50 or the amount of unauthorized electronic fund transfers that appear on the periodic statement during the 60-day period and (ii) The amount of unauthorized electronic fund transfers that occur after the close of the 60 days and before notice to the financial institution and that the financial institution establishes would not have occurred but for the failure of the consumer to notify the financial institution within that time.

. . .

(4) If a delay in notifying the financial statements was due to extenuating circumstances, such as extended travel or hospitalization, the time periods specified above shall be extended to a reasonable time.

The trial court concluded the Bank was entitled to judgment as a matter of law because the unauthorized withdrawals of July and August 1987 occurred more than 60 days after the Krusers received a statement which reflected an unauthorized transfer in December 1986. The court relied upon section 205.6(b)(2) of Regulation E.

The Krusers contend the December withdrawal of $20 was so isolated in time and minimal in an amount that it cannot be considered in connection with the July and August withdrawals. They assert the court's interpretation of section 205.6(b)(2) of Regulation E would have absurd results which would be inconsistent with the primary objective of the EFTA—to protect the consumer. They argue that if a consumer receives a bank statement which reflects an unauthorized minimal electronic transfer and fails to report the transaction to the bank within 60 days of transmission of the bank statement, unauthorized transfers many years later, perhaps totaling thousands of dollars, would remain the responsibility of the consumer.

The result the Krusers fear is avoided by the requirement that the bank establish the subsequent unauthorized transfers could have been prevented had the consumer notified the bank of the first unauthorized transfer. Here, although the unauthorized transfer of $20 occurred approximately seven months before the unauthorized transfers totaling $9,020, it is undisputed that all transfers were made by using Mr. Kruser's card which the Krusers believed had been destroyed prior to December 1986. According to the declaration of Yvonne Maloon, the Bank's Versatel risk manager, the Bank could have and would have canceled Mr. Kruser's card had it been timely notified of the December unauthorized transfer. In that event Mr. Kruser's card could not have been used to accomplish the unauthorized transactions in July and August.

In the alternative, the Krusers contend the facts establish that Mrs. Kruser, who was solely responsible for reconciling the bank statements, was severely ill and was also caring for a terminally ill relative when the December withdrawal occurred. Therefore they claim they were entitled to an extension of time within which to notify the bank.

The evidence the Krusers rely upon indicates in late 1986 or early 1987 Mrs. Kruser underwent surgery and remained in the hospital for 11 days. She left her house infrequently during the first six or seven months of 1987 during which she was recuperating. Mrs. Kruser admits, however, she received and reviewed bank statements during her recuperation. Therefore, we need not consider whether Mrs. Kruser's illness created circumstances which might have excused her failure to notice the unauthorized withdrawal pursuant to the applicable sections. She in fact did review the statements in question.

Judgment for Bank of America affirmed.

Wire Transfers While consumers increasingly are using various methods to transfer funds electronically, for some time electronic transfer has been an important part of the banking system and the commercial sector.

The Federal Reserve operates a domestic wire transfer system known as *Fedwire*. International wire transfers can be made through the New York Clearinghouse Interbank Payments System (CHIPS). The volume of

CYBERLAW IN ACTION

E-Checks

Chapter 31—Negotiable Instruments—notes that the process known as "check conversion" is utilized by a number of large retailers. The process begins with the buyer giving the seller a paper check. The seller uses special equipment to gather information from the paper check; this information includes the buyer's bank account number, the bank routing number, and the serial number of the check. The retailer then names itself as the payee, codes in the amount of the purchase, and forwards it for collection through an automated clearing house (ACH) transaction instead of the collection route for paper checks.

The Federal Reserve Board recently decided that the Electronic Funds Transfer Act (EFTA) and Regulation E would govern "check conversion" transactions. The EFTA will govern even if the consumer gives a blank and unsigned check to the merchant. The act also governs if the merchant uses a paper check as a "source document" (source of critical account- and bank-related information) and then uses an electronic fund transfer rather than the ACH transfer mentioned above in the section entitled "Check Collection."

payments over these two systems exceeds one trillion dollars per day.

Electronic funds transfers between business and financial institutions—generally referred to as *wholesale wire transfers*—are covered by Article 4A (Funds Transfers) of the Uniform Commercial Code. Article 4A explicitly excludes consumer payments that are covered by the Electronic Funds Transfer Act (EFTA), which includes the payments made through automated clearing houses.

In the Prefatory Note to Article 4A, the National Commissioners on Uniform State Laws note that the typical transfer covered by the Article is not a complex transaction and provide the following example, which also illustrates the terminology used in wire transfers:

> X, a debtor, wants to pay an obligation owed to Y. Instead of delivering to Y a negotiable instrument such as a check or other writing such as a credit card slip that enables Y to obtain payment from a bank, X transmits an instruction to X's bank to credit a sum of money to the bank account of Y. In most cases X's bank and Y's bank are different banks. X's bank may carry out X's bank by instructing Y's bank to credit Y's account by the amount that X has requested. The instruction that X issues to its bank is a "payment order." X is the "sender" of the payment order and X's bank is the "receiving bank" with respect to X's order. Y is the "beneficiary" of X's order. When X's bank issues an instruction to Y's bank to carry out X's payment order, X's bank "executes" X's order. With respect to that order, X's bank is the sender, Y's bank is the receiving bank, and Y is the beneficiary. The entire series of transactions is known as the "funds transfer." With respect to the funds transfer, X is the "originator," X's bank is the "originator's bank," Y is the "beneficiary" and Y's bank is the "beneficiary's bank." In more complex transactions there are one or more additional banks known as "intermediary banks" between X's bank and Y's bank.

Funds transfers have a number of advantages for those who utilize them, typically sophisticated business or financial organizations. They allow significant sums of money to move at high speed so that transactions can be completed in a very short period of time and are an effective substitute for payments made by the delivery of paper instruments. And, the cost of the transfers is very low compared to the amount of money being transferred. At the same time, the risk of loss can be very large if something goes wrong in the transaction. Among the possibilities are (1) a bank fails to execute the payment order of a customer; (2) a bank is late in executing a payment order; (3) a bank makes an error in executing the payment order, either as to the amount to be paid or the identity of the person to be paid. A major policy issue in the drafting of Article 4A was the allocation of risk to the various parties in light of the price structure in the industry.

For example, if a receiving bank executes a payment order by paying more than the order calls for, or makes a duplicative payment, the bank is entitled to the amount of the payment order but is left to recover any excess or duplicative payment from the beneficiary under the law governing mistake and restitution. Where banks carry out a funds transfer but are late in executing it, the banks are obligated to pay interest to either the originator or the beneficiary of the funds transfer for the period of delay caused by the improper execution. For other types of improper execution or failure to execute payment orders, banks can be liable to the originator or sender for their expenses in the transaction along with incidental expenses and interest losses due to improper execution or failure to execute; however, consequential damages are recoverable only to the extent provided in an express written agreement of the receiving bank and are not otherwise recoverable.

The Global Business Environment

International Electronic Funds Transfers

The Model Law on International Credit Transfers, adopted in 1992 by the United Nations Commission on International Trade Law, is the major international legal document concerning electronic funds transfers. The Model Law covers basically the same kind of transactions as Article 4A does, but it does require the funds transferred to have an international component and is not identical in its treatment of certain issues.

Problems and Problem Cases

1. James Drumm and Debra Brading were dating and lived together on and off for several years. Drumm was providing financial support to Brading. Brading had written numerous checks on Drumm's checking account and had access to his corporate credit cards. However, she was not an authorized signator on either his checking or savings accounts. After one particularly ugly fight between the two on July 3, 2000, Brading went to the National City Bank and withdrew $314,000 from Drumm's individual savings account. She did so by approaching a teller, giving her Drumm's account number and electronic personal identification number (PIN), and providing the teller with a driver's license bearing the name Debra Brading along with a Racquet Club membership identifying her as Debra Drumm. She was also wearing a $20,000 diamond ring, which appeared to be an engagement ring. On the basis of these facts, a teller allowed the transaction. Drumm brought suit against National City Bank for breach of contract for allowing an unauthorized transfer of funds from his account. Is National City Bank liable to Drumm?

2. Louise Kalbe drew a check in the amount of $7,260 payable to the "order of cash" on her account at the Pulaski State Bank. The check was lost or stolen, but Kalbe did not report this to the bank, nor did she attempt to stop payment on it. When the check was received by the Pulaski State Bank, Kalbe had only about $700 in her checking account. However, the bank paid the check, creating an overdraft in her account of $6,542.12. The bank then sued Kalbe to recover the amount of the overdraft. Kalbe asserted that the check was not properly payable from her account. Was the bank legally entitled to pay a check that exceeded the balance in the drawer's account and to recover the overdraft from the drawer?

3. RPM Pizza, Inc., a Domino's Pizza franchisee, maintained a checking account at Bank One–Cambridge. On May 29, 1992, RPM erroneously issued a $96,000 check drawn on its account at the bank and payable to a computer broker, Systems Marketing. After mailing the check, RPM realized its error, and on June 2, 1992, RPM placed a stop-payment order on the check. As stated in its account agreement with Bank One (and in the UCC as adopted in Ohio), written stop-payment orders are effective for six months. The stop-payment order expired on December 6, 1992, and RPM failed to renew it.

   On December 22, 1992, Systems Marketing deposited the check in its account at the Bank of Tampa, Florida. When the Bank of Tampa received the check, it was more than six months old and was therefore "stale" according to standard banking procedures. The Bank of Tampa credited the check to Systems Marketing's account and sent it forward to Bank One–Cambridge, which charged it against RPM's checking account.

   RPM brought suit against Bank One, claiming that the bank had not exercised ordinary care or acted in good faith in paying the stale check. The bank established that it routinely paid stale checks and that its internal operating procedures simply required it to perform a signature authorization on checks of more than $50,000, which it did in this case. Did the bank violate the duty it owed to its customer, RPM, when it paid a check that was more than six months old?

4. Dr. Sherrill purchased a Buick Skylark from Frank Morris Buick. He gave the auto dealer a check for $4,960.61 drawn on his account at First Alabama Bank. The check was dated "2/6/1976," was payable "to the order of Frank Morris Buick," and was not numbered. After buying the Skylark, Sherrill became concerned about whether he had gotten valid title to it. The day after he gave the dealer the check, he called in an oral stop-payment order on it. He later confirmed the stop-payment order in writing. In the stop-payment order, Sherrill stated that the check was not numbered, was payable to "Walter Morris Buick,"

was dated "6/3/76," and was in the amount of $4,960.61. The bank paid the check when it was presented for payment. Sherrill then claimed that the bank should recredit his account for $4,960.61 because it paid the check over a valid stop-payment order. Did the stop-payment order describe the check accurately enough to constitute a valid stop-payment order?

5. Brenda Jones, who did business as Country Kitchen, purchased some cookware from an itinerant salesman, giving him a check in the amount of $200 for the purchase price. The salesman cashed the check at the First National Bank before noon on May 22, the day of the sale. Jones later became concerned about the lack of documentation from the salesman, thinking that the cookware might be stolen, and placed a stop-payment order with her bank, the State Bank of Conway Springs, at 3:30 that afternoon. State Bank refused to honor the check when it was presented for payment through banking channels. First National Bank, claiming to be a holder in due course, then brought suit against Jones to recover the $200 value of the check. Is the drawer of a check on which a stop-payment order was placed and honored by the bank liable to pay the check to a holder in due course?

6. John Doe had a checking account at Highland National Bank in New York. Two days after John Doe died in Florida, but before Highland National knew of his death, John's sister appeared at the bank. She had a check signed by John Doe but with the amount and name of the payee left blank. She told the bank that her brother wanted to close his account. She asked how much was in the account, filled the check in for that amount, and made the check payable to herself. The bank checked her identification and verified the signature of John Doe. Then it paid the check to the sister. The executor of John Doe's estate sued Highland National Bank to recover the amount of money that was in John's account on the day he died. The executor claimed that the bank had no authority to pay checks from John Doe's account after his death. May a bank pay checks drawn on the account of a deceased customer?

7. In December, Whalley Company hired Nancy Cherauka as its bookkeeper. Her duties included preparing checks, taking deposits to the bank, and reconciling the monthly checking account statements. She was not authorized to sign or cash checks. Between the following January 24 and May 31, Cherauka forged 49 checks on the Whalley account at National City Bank. Each month, National City Bank sent Whalley a statement and the canceled checks (including the forgeries) it had paid the previous month. The president of Whalley looked at the statement to see the balance in the account, but he did not look at the individual checks. Then he gave the statement and checks to the bookkeeper. The January 24 forged check was sent to Whalley on February 3. In June, Whalley discovered that Cherauka was forging checks and fired her. It then brought a lawsuit against National City Bank to force it to recredit Whalley's account with the total amount of the 49 checks. Whalley claimed that the checks were not properly payable from the account. Is National City required to recredit Whalley's account?

8. Lor-Mar/Toto, Inc., maintained a business checking account at the First Constitution Bank. The corporate banking resolution between Lor-Mar and the bank provided that checks drawn on the checking account could be honored upon one authorized signature of the four named officers stated in the resolution, including Loretta A. Van Middlesworth and Louis J. Toto, Jr., its president and vice president respectively. On May 28, 1997, Lor-Mar notified the bank that the signatures of Van Middlesworth and Toto would be "stamped" on Lor-Mar's checks and provided the bank with samples of its stamped facsimile signatures. Thus, from May 1997 forward, the bank was authorized by Lor-Mar to honor checks bearing a stamped facsimile of either Van Middlesworth or Toto.

Beginning in June 2002 a series of five allegedly unauthorized checks totaling $24,350.00 were drawn against the Lor-Mar account. All five checks bore what appeared to be the stamped facsimile signature of Van Middlesworth as provided to the bank on May 28, 1997, and another signature which is illegible. However, the unauthorized checks were a different stock and color than Lor-Mar's regular checks, which were light yellow in color and the type routinely purchased from banks. On the front, under the preprinted check number, they contained a numerical bank designation of "55-715/21201." The back of the authentic checks contained a repetitive pattern and the words "ORIGINAL DOCUMENT" with a security message stating: "IMPORTANT: The back of this document has been printed with a patented security process in order to deter check fraud. If you do not clearly see the words 'Original Document' and the Security

Weave pattern, or the word VOID appears to the right of this message, do not cash." Sample checks provided by the company contained the facsimile signature of Toto and the actual signature of another corporate signatory, Maureen E. Zaleck.

In comparison, the challenged checks were computer-generated and laser-printed on light blue paper and contained no bank designation number under the preprinted check number. Their purported security features are different from the legitimate checks; they contain the words "ORIGINAL DOCUMENT" in large letters once on the back with a boxed designation:

THIS DOCUMENT INCLUDES THE FOLLOWING VALUGUARD SECURITY FEATURES; EXCEEDING FSA GUIDELINES:

- INVISBLE FLUORESCENT FIBERS
- TWO SOLVENT STAINS
- BROWNSTAIN
- UV DULL

ATTEMPTS TO COPY OR CHEMICALLY ALTER THIS DOCUMENT WILL ACTIVATE VALUGUARD SECURITY FEATURES.

Significantly, the unauthorized checks contained repeated duplicate numbers from legitimate checks that had already been issued by Lor-Mar. The five checks were debited to Lor-Mar's account from June 24 to July 1, 2002, and appeared on Lor-Mar's statements covering the periods May 31, 2002, through June 28, 2002, and June 28, 2002, through July 31, 2002. Upon receiving the statements, Lor-Mar discovered and reported the unauthorized checks to the bank in July 2002. For each of the five checks, Toto executed an "Affidavit For Forged or Lost Check/Money Order" to the bank attesting that he never signed his name on the check, authorized any person to indorse his name, the indorsement of his name that appears on the check is a forgery, and he never received any of the funds the check represented. Lor-Mar brought suit seeking to have its account recredited for the amount of the unauthorized checks. Is Lor-Mar entitled to have its account recredited for the amount of the unauthorized checks on the grounds the checks were not properly payable from the account?

9. On August 16, Frederick Ognibene went to the ATM area at a Citibank branch and activated one of the machines with his Citibank card, provided his personal identification code, and withdrew $20. When he approached the machine a person was using the customer service telephone located between two ATM machines and appeared to be telling customer service that one of the machines was malfunctioning. As Ognibene was making his withdrawal, the person said into the telephone, "I'll see if his card works in my machine." He then asked Ognibene if he could use his card to see if the other machine was working. Ognibene handed his card to him and saw him insert it into the adjoining machine at least two times while saying into the telephone, "Yes, it seems to be working." When Ognibene received his Citibank statement, it showed that two withdrawals of $200 each from his account were made at 5:42 PM and 5:43 PM, respectively, on August 16. His own $20 withdrawal was made at 5:41 PM. At the time, Ognibene was unaware that any withdrawals from his account were being made from the adjoining machine. Ognibene sought to have his account recredited for $400, claiming that the withdrawals had been unauthorized. Citibank had been aware for some time of a scam being perpetrated against its customers by persons who observed the customer inserting his personal identification number into an ATM and then obtained access to the customer's ATM card in the same manner as Ognibene's card was obtained. After learning about the scam, Citibank posted signs in ATM areas containing a red circle approximately 2½ inches in diameter in which was written "Do Not Let Your Citicard Be Used For Any Transaction But Your Own." Was Citibank required under the Electronic Fund Transfer Act to recredit Ognibene's account on the grounds that the withdrawal of the $400 was unauthorized?

Online Research

How Does Your Bank Handle Stop-Payment Orders?

Use the Internet to locate the Web site for the bank or other financial institution where you maintain a checking account. Ascertain from the Web site what the bank's policy is concerning stopping payment on checks, including (1) the means by which the bank will accept a stop-payment order, (2) the information it requires, (3) the charge it imposes for entering a stop-payment order, and (4) any qualifications or limitations it makes to its responsibility to follow your instruction to stop payment.

Part Eight

Agency Law

chapter 35
The Agency Relationship

chapter 36
Third-Party Relations of the
Principal and the Agent

chapter 35

THE AGENCY RELATIONSHIP

Upon graduating from college, Rita Morales was hired as a software consultant by IPQ Company, a large computer manufacturing and services company. Rita negotiated a high salary and even a nice signing bonus, yet after a few years of work she found that her spending often outstripped her earnings and savings. As her credit card bills piled up, Rita started her own consulting firm. Initially, Rita provided software consulting for her clients only on nights and weekends after she had finished her IPQ work for the day. As her business grew, she began seeing clients during normal weekday working hours and calling them from her office at IPQ. To find new clients, Rita downloaded IPQ's client information from IPQ's database. She contacted over 200 IPQ clients and asked them to switch from IPQ to Rita's business. Over two dozen IPQ clients switched to Rita.

- Do you see any potential problems with Rita's actions?
- What legally and practically can IPQ do to prevent Rita from taking its clients?
- What would an ethical employee in Rita's position do if her income did not meet her expenses?

OFTEN, BUSINESSES ARE LEGALLY bound by the actions of their employees or other representatives. For example, corporations frequently are liable on contracts their employees make or for torts their employees commit. We take such liability for granted, but why should we? A corporation is an artificial legal person distinct from the officers, employees, and other representatives who contract on its behalf and who may commit torts while on the job. Similarly, a sole proprietor is distinct from the people she may employ. How can these and other business actors be bound on contracts they did not make or for torts they did not commit? The reason is the law of **agency.**

Agency is a two-party relationship in which one party (the **agent**) is authorized to act on behalf of, and under the control of, the other party (the **principal**). Examples include a Toyota dealership hiring a salesman to sell cars, Google employing a software engineer to write computer code, and you engaging a real estate agent to sell your home. Agency law's most important social function has been to stimulate commercial activity. It does so by enabling businesses to increase the number of transactions they can complete within a given time. Without agency, for instance, a sole proprietor's ability to engage in trade would be limited by the need to make

each of her purchase or sale contracts in person. As artificial persons, moreover, corporations can act only through their agents.

Agency law divides into two rough categories. The first involves legal relations between the principal and the agent. These include the rules governing formation of an agency, the duties the principal and the agent owe each other, and the ways an agency can be terminated. These topics are the main concern of this chapter. Chapter 36 discusses the principal's and the agent's relations with third parties. In that chapter, our main concerns are the principal's and the agent's liability on contracts the agent makes and for torts the agent commits.

Much of the law of agency, which is largely state law in the United States, has been codified or adopted by the state legislatures or their courts in the form of the *Restatement (Second) of Agency,* a project of the American Law Institute (ALI). The *Restatement (Third) of Agency* was adopted by the ALI in 2006, and in the next several years, we expect states gradually to adopt this new *Restatement,* which is not appreciably different from the *Restatement (Second).* The material in Chapters 35 and 36 mostly covers the common features of the two versions, with differences, such as new terminology, noted as necessary.

Creation of an Agency

Formation   Agency is the fiduciary relationship that arises when one person (a principal) manifests assent to another person (an agent) that the agent will act on the principal's behalf and be subject to the principal's control. Agency is a fiduciary relationship because the principal entrusts the agent with power to make contracts for the principal and to possess and use the principal's property. As a fiduciary, the agent must use the entrusted power and property in the best interest of the principal.

As the term *manifested* suggests, the test for an agency's existence is *objective*. If the parties' behavior and the surrounding facts and circumstances indicate an agreement that one person is to act for the benefit and under the control of another, the relationship exists. The *MDM* case, which appears after this section, applies the *Restatement (Third)* definition of agency. That case shows that an agent is a fiduciary of the principal and not vice versa.

If the facts establish an agency, neither party need know about the agency's existence or subjectively desire that it exist. In fact, an agency may be present even when the parties expressly say that they do not intend to create it, or intend to create some other legal relationship instead.

Often, parties create an agency by a written contract. But an agency contract may be oral unless state law provides otherwise. Some states, for example, require written evidence of contracts to pay an agent a commission for the sale of real estate. More important, the agency relation need not be contractual at all. Thus, consideration required to form a contract is not necessary to form an agency.

Capacity   A principal or agent who lacks the necessary mental capacity when the agency is formed ordinarily can release himself from the agency at his option. Examples include those who are minors or are mentally incapacitated when the agency is created. Of course, incapacity may occur during the agency relationship also. Terminations of an agency due to subsequent lack of capacity are discussed later in this chapter.

Corporations can and must appoint agents. In a partnership, each partner normally acts as the agent of the partnership in transacting partnership business, and a partnership can appoint nonpartner agents as well. In addition, corporations, partnerships, and other business organizations themselves can act as agents for other business organizations as well as individuals.

Nondelegable Obligations   Certain duties or acts must be performed personally and cannot be delegated to an agent. Examples include making statements under oath, voting in public elections, and signing a will. The same is true for service contracts in which the principal's personal performance is crucial, for example, certain contracts by lawyers, doctors, athletes, and entertainers.

MDM Group Associates, Inc. v. CX Reinsurance Company Ltd.
165 P.3d 882 (Colo. Ct. App. 2007)

MDM Group is an insurance broker. Joseph McNasby, its president, developed an insurance program for insuring ski resorts against the risk that the number of "paid skier days" during a ski season would fall below a specified minimum. CX Reinsurance Co. and others agreed to underwrite insurance policies covering the risk for a year, starting with the 1997–1998 ski season, and issued policies to a number of ski resorts in exchange for premium payments. For the first two years, the policies generated premiums of about $550,000 and $476,000, from which MDM received a commission of 12.5 percent. No claims were submitted under the policies during the first and second seasons.

Before the 1999–2000 ski season, several underwriters declined to renew their involvement. However, CX issued policies for that year, which, because more ski resorts purchased the coverage, generated total premiums of approximately $3 million. MDM received commissions totaling approximately $378,000. Unfortunately, the 1999–2000 ski season was not a good one for the insured resorts. There was little snowfall in the United States until well after the Christmas and New Year's ski holidays, and vacation travel was reduced because of concerns related to the millennium change. All the insured resorts, including Vail and Mammoth, submitted claims. CX negotiated, mediated, and litigated the claims, ultimately paying in excess of $23 million to settle them. As was its right, CX declined to renew the insurance policies after their one-year term expired in May 2000.

MDM initiated this action against CX asserting several grounds for liability, including a breach of fiduciary duty claim. MDM contended that CX, as the principal in an agency relationship with MDM, owed it a fiduciary duty and breached its *duty by handling the ski resorts' claims improperly and in bad faith, thereby causing the resorts not to renew their policies and causing MDM to lose renewal commissions. The jury found for MDM and awarded it $6,750,783 in damages. CX appealed to a Colorado appeals court.*

Casebolt, Judge

CX contends that MDM's breach of fiduciary duty claim must fail because a principal cannot owe a fiduciary duty to an agent as a matter of law.

A fiduciary duty arises among parties through a relationship of trust, confidence, and reliance. Certain types of relationships give rise to general fiduciary duties as a matter of law, such as attorney-client, principal-agent, and trustee-beneficiary. However, fiduciary duties are owed by only one of the parties in these relationships.

A fiduciary duty arises when one party has a high degree of control over the property or subject matter of another, or when the benefiting party places a high level of trust and confidence in the fiduciary to look out for the beneficiary's best interest.

In the principal-agent context, it is the *agent* who owes a fiduciary duty to the principal as a matter of law. "An agent has a fiduciary duty to act loyally for the principal's benefit in all matters connected with the agency relationship." *Restatement (Third) of Agency,* § 8.01 (2006).

A principal does owe *some* duties to an agent. *See Restatement (Third) of Agency,* §§ 8.13–8.15. However, the "obligations that a principal owes an agent, specified in §§ 8.13–8.15, *are not fiduciary*." *Restatement (Third) of Agency,* § 1.01 comment e (emphasis supplied).

The jury was wrongly instructed that there was a fiduciary duty as a matter of law if it found that an agency relationship existed. As a matter of law, a principal is not a fiduciary of an agent. The principal is not "entrusted to act for the benefit of or in the interest of another." It is the principal who entrusts business to the agent to act for the principal's benefit. Any duties owed by a principal to an agent are not fiduciary. *Restatement (Third) of Agency,* § 1.01 comment e.

Judgment reversed in favor of CX.

Agency Concepts, Definitions, and Types

Agency law includes various concepts, definitions, and distinctions. These matters often determine the rights, duties, and liabilities of the principal, the agent, and third parties. In addition, they sometimes are important outside agency law. Because these basic topics are crucial in many different situations, we outline them together here.

Authority   Although agency law lets people multiply their dealings by employing agents, a principal is not always liable for his agent's acts. Normally, an agent can bind his principal on a contract or other matter only when the agent has **authority** to do so. Authority is an agent's ability to affect his principal's legal relations. It comes in two main forms: **actual authority** and **apparent authority.** Each is based on the principal's manifested consent that the agent may act for and bind the principal. For actual authority this consent must be communicated to the *agent,* while for apparent authority it must be communicated to the *third party.*

Actual authority comes in two forms: **express authority** and **implied authority.** *Express authority* is created by the principal's *actual words* (whether written or oral). Thus, an agent has express authority to bind her principal on a contract or other matter only when the principal has made a fairly precise statement to that effect.

However, it is often impractical for a principal to specify the agent's authority fully and exactly. To avoid unnecessarily restricting an agent's ability to represent her principal, agency law also gives agents *implied authority* to bind their principals. An agent generally has implied authority to do whatever it is reasonable to assume that the principal wanted him to do. Relevant factors include the principal's express statements, the nature of the agency, the acts reasonably necessary to carry on the agency business, and the acts customarily done when conducting that business.

Sometimes an agent who lacks actual authority may still *appear* to have such authority, and third parties may reasonably rely on this appearance of authority. To protect third parties in such situations, agency law lets agents bind the principal on the basis of their apparent authority. *Apparent authority* arises when the *principal's* behavior causes a third party to believe reasonably that the agent is authorized to act in a certain way.

Apparent authority depends on what the *principal* communicates to the third party—either directly or through the agent. A principal might clothe an agent with apparent authority by making direct statements to the third party, telling an agent to do so, or allowing an agent to behave in a way that creates an appearance of authority. The principal's communications to the agent are irrelevant unless they become known to the third party or affect the agent's behavior. Also, agents cannot give themselves apparent authority, and apparent authority does not exist where an agent creates an appearance of authority without the principal's consent. Finally, the third party must *reasonably* believe in the agent's authority. Trade customs and business practices can help courts determine whether such a belief is reasonable.

Authority is important in a number of agency contexts. Chapter 36 examines its most important agency application—determining a principal's liability on contracts made by his agent.

General and Special Agents

Although it may be falling out of favor with courts, the blurred distinction between general agents and special agents still has some importance. A **general agent** is continuously employed to conduct a series of transactions, while a **special agent** is employed to conduct a single transaction or a small, simple group of transactions. Thus, a continuously employed general manager of a McDonald's restaurant, a construction project supervisor for homebuilder Pulte, or a buyer of women's clothing for Macy's normally is a general agent. A person employed to buy or sell a few objects on a one-shot basis usually is a special agent. General agents often serve for longer periods, perform more acts, and deal with more parties than do special agents.

Gratuitous Agents

An agent who receives no compensation for his services is called a **gratuitous agent.** Gratuitous agents have the same power to bind their principals as do paid agents with the same authority. However, the fact that an agent is gratuitous sometimes lowers the duties principal and agent owe each other and also may increase the parties' ability to terminate the agency without incurring liability.

Subagents

A **subagent** basically is an agent of an agent. More precisely, a subagent is a person appointed by an agent to perform tasks that the agent has undertaken to perform for his principal. For example, if you retain accounting firm PricewaterhouseCoopers as your agent, the accountant actually handling your affairs is PWC's agent and your subagent. For a subagency to exist, an agent must have the authority to make the

subagent *his agent* for conducting the principal's business. Sometimes, however, a party appointed by an agent is not a subagent because the appointing agent only had authority to appoint agents *for the principal.* For instance, sales agents appointed by a corporation's sales manager are agents of the corporation, not agents of the sales manager.

When an agent appoints a true subagent, the agent becomes a principal with respect to the subagent, his agent. Thus, the legal relations between agent and subagent closely parallel the legal relations between principal and agent. But a subagent is also the *original principal's* agent. Here, though, the normal rules governing principals and agents do not always apply. We occasionally refer to such situations in the pages ahead.

Employees and Independent Contractors

Many legal questions depend on whether an agent or some other party who contracts with the principal is classed as an **employee** (or servant) or as an **independent contractor.** No sharp line separates employees from independent contractors; the following *Eisenberg* case lists the factors considered in making such determinations. The most important of these factors is the principal's *right to control the manner and means* of the agent's performance or work. Employees typically are subject to such control. Independent contractors, on the other hand, generally contract with the principal to produce a result, and determine for themselves how that result will be accomplished.

Although many employees perform physical labor or are paid on an hourly basis, corporate officers who do no physical work and receive salaries usually are employees as well. Professionals such as brokers, accountants, and attorneys often are independent contractors of their clients, although they are employees of the brokerage, accounting, or law firms that pay their salaries. Consider the difference between a corporation represented by an attorney engaged in her own practice (an independent contractor) and a corporation that maintains a staff of salaried in-house counsel (employees). Finally, franchisees, like a KFC restaurant, usually are independent contractors of their franchisors, like YUM! Brands.

As Chapter 36 makes clear, the employee–independent contractor distinction often is crucial in determining the principal's liability for an agent's torts. The distinction also helps define the coverage of some employment laws discussed in Chapter 51. Unemployment compensation, the Fair Labor Standards Act (the subject of *Eisenberg*), and workers' compensation are clear examples.

Eisenberg v. Advance Relocation & Storage, Inc.
237 F.3d 111 (2d. Cir. 2000)

In July 1998, Julianne Eisenberg discussed with Peter White and Mike Ewing working for Advance Relocation & Storage, Inc., a Danbury, Connecticut warehouse. White was involved in Advance's hiring process, and Ewing was the warehouse manager. The men discussed with Eisenberg the possibility of her working on a "permanent full-time" basis at Advance. They did not inquire into any special skills that Eisenberg may have had, and they did not ask about her prior work experiences. Instead, Eisenberg believed, the men were interested in her working at the warehouse because White knew that she was strong, having played football with her, and that she had been doing carpentry work for many years.

Eisenberg started work at Advance, where she and her co-workers were responsible for loading and unloading furniture from trucks at the warehouse and at residences. They were paid on an hourly basis, and were required to punch in and out. Eisenberg and her co-workers were occasionally sent home early if there was little to do, and they were sometimes asked to work on the weekend.

At the warehouse, Ewing gave Eisenberg orders, and if he was not going to be at the warehouse on a particular day, he told her on the prior day where to go and what to do. At job sites, an Advance representative told the crew what objects each crew member, including Eisenberg, was to move.

Eisenberg claimed that during much of the time that she worked at Advance, she was sexually harassed. She asserts that on September 16, 1998, she complained about this alleged sexual harassment to Joan Isaacson, the Advance office manager. Eisenberg also alleges that she told Isaacson that she had seen several Advance employees using cocaine in the warehouse.

The warehouse was closed by management the next day. Eisenberg then met again with Isaacson, at which point Isaacson allegedly told her that she would receive a job when the warehouse reopened and would be contacted and told when to return to work. However, Isaacson then told Eisenberg that she would not be called back to work at Advance if, based on her allegations of sexual harassment, she sought legal counsel or filed a complaint. Undeterred, Eisenberg hired an attorney and initiated an action against Advance on the grounds that she was sexually harassed in violation of the Civil Rights Act of 1964 (Title VII) and the New York Human Rights Law (NYHRL). After doing so, Eisenberg claimed that she was not called back to work at Advance by Isaacson or anyone else. Eisenberg alleged that she was subjected to a hostile work environment at Advance, that her termination from the firm was discriminatory, and that Advance retaliated against her for complaining about the violation of her right to be free of sexual harassment—all in violation of Title VII and the NYHRL.

The district court granted Advance's motion for summary judgment on the grounds that Eisenberg was not an Advance employee, and thus could not invoke the protections of Title VII or the NYHRL. Eisenberg appealed to the Court of Appeals, arguing that she was an Advance employee.

Cabranes, Circuit Judge

Title VII and the NYHRL cover "employees," not independent contractors. For the purposes of these statutes, a decision on whether a worker is an "employee"—or whether he or she is merely an independent contractor—requires the application of the common law of agency. In turn, whether a hired person is an employee under the common law of agency depends largely on the thirteen factors articulated by the Supreme Court in *Community for Creative Non-Violence v. Reid*, 490 U.S. 730 (1989). These so-called "*Reid* factors," which are culled from the federal common law of agency, are as follows:

[1] the hiring party's right to control the manner and means by which the product is accomplished . . . ; [2] the skill required; [3] the source of the instrumentalities and tools; [4] the location of the work; [5] the duration of the relationship between the parties; [6] whether the hiring party has the right to assign additional projects to the hired party; [7] the extent of the hired party's discretion over when and how

long to work; [8] the method of payment; [9] the hired party's role in hiring and paying assistants; [10] whether the work is part of the regular business of the hiring party; [11] whether the hiring party is in business; [12] the provision of employee benefits; and [13] the tax treatment of the hired party.

Though no single factor is dispositive, the "greatest emphasis" should be placed on the first factor—that is, on the extent to which the hiring party controls the "manner and means" by which the worker completes his or her assigned tasks. The first factor is entitled to this added weight because, under the common law of agency, an employer–employee relationship exists if the purported employer controls or has the right to control both the result to be accomplished and the "manner and means" by which the purported employee brings about that result.

Turning to the individual *Reid* factors, it is plain that the fifth, seventh, and ninth factors must be disregarded. As to the fifth factor, it is not disputed that Eisenberg worked at Advance for only 28–35 days. A relatively short tenure such as Eisenberg's ordinarily implies that a worker is an independent contractor. Here, however, the brevity of Eisenberg's stint at Advance does not suggest much of anything—her job lasted only 28–35 days because of the closing of the warehouse, not because of the nature of her work or her relationship to Advance. As to the seventh factor, the District Court found that Eisenberg had "some" control over her schedule, but not full control over it. Because this ambivalent finding does not seem to cut in any particular direction, we disregard it. Finally, the ninth factor is irrelevant to this case: Eisenberg hired no one to assist her with her work at Advance, and Advance hired no assistants for Eisenberg.

The remaining factors are the dispositive ones. As noted above, Eisenberg did not receive benefits such as medical insurance or vacation days, and Advance treated her as an independent contractor for tax purposes, giving her a "1099" tax form rather than a "W-2" form, and not deducting or withholding taxes from her wages. These factors favor characterizing Eisenberg as an independent contractor.

The remaining factors, however, suggest that Eisenberg was an Advance employee. As to the first factor, Advance exercised a great deal of control over the "manner and means" by which Eisenberg accomplished her assigned tasks. As we noted above, at the warehouse White gave Eisenberg "orders" on a daily basis; if he was not going to be at the warehouse on a particular day, he told her on the prior day "where . . . to go and what . . . to do." Moreover, at job sites, an Advance representative—White, Ewing, or someone else—would direct the crew as to what objects each crew member, including Eisenberg was to move.

As to the second factor, Eisenberg's job at Advance—loading and unloading trucks—was not one that required relatively specialized skills. Other courts have held that the level of skill associated with being an architect, computer programmer, graphic artist, photographer, or treasurer suggests that workers who perform these jobs are independent contractors. In terms of the level of skill that it required, Eisenberg's moving work was not analogous to any of these jobs. Indeed, in this case White and Ewing all but offered Eisenberg a job without first asking her about moving-related work that she had done in the past, or about relevant skills that she might have developed over the years. That White seemed to view Eisenberg as qualified for the job solely on the basis of her football and carpentry abilities only emphasizes the point: While simple moving of the sort Eisenberg performed certainly requires skills—strength, for example, and agility—it does not demand *specialized* skills of the sort typically acquired through experience and/or education.

As to the third and fourth factors, the District Court found that "Advance supplied all of the [necessary] instrumentalities," including "trucks and other supplies," and that "the majority of plaintiff's work took place at Advance's warehouse or on Advance's trucks." Each of these findings suggests that Eisenberg was an Advance employee.

As to the sixth factor, the District Court found that Eisenberg "was not hired for a specific move or project." Instead, the District Court found that Eisenberg "was assigned to numerous moves or projects," and was required "to perform work on Advance's trucks and in its warehouse, on whatever moves or projects Advance undertook while she was there." This finding bolsters the conclusion that Eisenberg was an employee.

As to the eighth factor, the District Court found that Eisenberg was paid on an hourly basis. Compensation primarily or exclusively on the basis of time worked (rather than on the basis of projects completed) suggests that a worker is an employee. As to the ninth and tenth factors, the District Court found that Advance is "in the business of moving and storage" so that Eisenberg's work was "in the regular business of Advance," and that, "obviously, Advance is a business." Each of these findings favors characterizing Eisenberg as an employee.

Therefore, we conclude that Eisenberg was an "employee" within the meaning of Title VII and the NYHRL.

Judgment reversed in favor of Eisenberg.

Duties of Agent to Principal

Agency law establishes certain **fiduciary duties** that the agent owes the principal. These duties supplement the duties created by an agency contract. They exist because agency is a relationship of trust and confidence. The principal's many remedies for an agent's breach of her fiduciary duties include termination of the agency and recovery of damages from the agent.

A gratuitous agent usually has the same fiduciary duties as a paid agent, but need not perform as promised. She normally can terminate the agency without incurring liability. However, a gratuitous agent *is* liable for failing to perform as promised when her promise causes the principal to rely upon her to undertake certain acts, and the principal suffers losses because he refrained from performing those acts himself.

A subagent owes the agent (his principal) all the duties agents owe their principals. A subagent who knows of the original principal's existence also owes that principal all the duties agents owe their principals, except for duties arising solely from the original principal's contract with the agent. Finally, the agent who appointed the subagent generally is liable to the original principal when the principal is harmed by the subagent's conduct.

Agent's Duty of Loyalty
Because agency is a relationship of trust and confidence, an agent has a **duty of loyalty** to his principal. Thus, an agent must subordinate his personal concerns by (1) avoiding conflicts of interest with the principal, and (2) not disclosing confidential information received from the principal.

Conflicts of Interest
An agent whose interests conflict with the principal's interests may be unable to represent his principal effectively. Therefore, an agent may not *acquire a material benefit* from a third party in connection with an agency transaction. When conducting the principal's business, an agent may **not deal with himself.** For example, an agent authorized to sell property cannot sell that property to himself. Many courts extend the rule to include transactions with the agent's relatives or business associates or with business organizations in which the agent has an interest. However, an agent may engage in self-dealing transactions if the principal consents. For this consent to be effective, the agent must disclose all relevant facts to the principal before dealing with the principal on his own behalf.

Unless the principal agrees otherwise, an agent also may *not* **compete with the principal** regarding the agency business so long as he remains an agent. Thus, an agent employed to purchase specific property may not buy it himself if the principal desires it. Furthermore, an agent ordinarily may not solicit customers for a planned competing business while still employed by the principal.

Finally, an agent who is authorized to make a certain transaction may **not act on behalf of the other party** to the transaction unless the principal knowingly consents. Thus, one ordinarily may **not act as agent for both parties** to a transaction without first disclosing the double role to, and obtaining the consent of, both principals. Here, the agent must disclose to each principal all the factors reasonably affecting that principal's decision. Occasionally, though, an agent who acts merely as a middleman may serve both parties to a transaction without notifying either. For instance, an agent may simultaneously be employed as a "finder" by a firm seeking suitable businesses to acquire and a firm looking for prospective buyers, so long as neither principal expects the agent to advise it or negotiate for it.

An agent will not breach her duty of loyalty, however, if she acts in good faith, discloses to the principal all material facts regarding her conflict of interest, and deals fairly with the principal.

Confidentiality
Unless otherwise agreed, an agent may not **use or disclose confidential information** acquired through the agency. Confidential information is the principal's information *entrusted* by the principal to the agent for purposes of the agent carrying out her duties. Confidential information includes facts that are valuable to the principal because they are not widely known or that would harm the principal's business if they became widely known. Examples include the principal's business plans, financial condition, contract bids, technological discoveries, manufacturing methods, customer files, and other trade secrets.

In the absence of an agreement to the contrary, after the agency ends almost all fiduciary duties terminate. For example, an agent may compete with her principal after termination of the agency. As the following *ABKCO* case illustrates, however, the duty not to use or disclose confidential information continues after the agency ends. The former agent may, however, utilize general knowledge and skills acquired during the agency.

ABKCO Music Inc. v. Harrisongs Music, Ltd.   722 F.2d 988 (2d Cir. 1983)

In 1963, a song called "He's So Fine" was a huge hit in the United States and Great Britain. In February 1971, Bright Tunes Music Corporation, the copyright holder of "He's So Fine," sued ex-Beatle George Harrison and Harrisongs, Music, Ltd. in federal district court. Bright Tunes claimed that the Harrison composition "My Sweet Lord" infringed its copyright to "He's So Fine." At this time, Harrison's business affairs were handled by ABKCO Music, Inc., and Allen B. Klein, its president. Shortly after the suit began, Klein unsuccessfully tried to settle it by having ABKCO purchase Bright Tunes.

Shortly thereafter, Bright Tunes went into receivership, and it did not resume the suit until 1973. At this time, coincidentally, ABKCO's management contract with Harrison expired. In late 1975 and early 1976, however, Klein continued his efforts to have ABKCO purchase Bright Tunes. As part of these efforts, he gave Bright Tunes three schedules summarizing Harrison's royalty income from "My Sweet Lord," information he possessed because of his previous service to Harrison.

Throughout the 1973–76 period, Harrison's attorneys had been trying to settle the copyright infringement suit with Bright Tunes. Because Klein's activities not only gave Bright Tunes information about the economic potential of its suit but also gave it an economic alternative to settling with Harrison, Klein may have impeded Harrison's efforts to settle.

When the copyright infringement suit finally came to trial in 1976, the court found that Harrison had infringed Bright Tunes' copyright. The issue of damages was scheduled for trial at a later date, and this trial was delayed for some time. In 1978, ABKCO purchased the "He's So Fine" copyright and all rights to the infringement suit from Bright Tunes. This made ABKCO the plaintiff in the 1979 trial for damages on the infringement suit. At trial, Harrison counterclaimed for damages resulting from Klein's and ABKCO's alleged breaches of the duty of loyalty. Finding a breach of duty, the district judge issued a complex order reducing ABKCO's recovery. ABKCO appealed.

Pierce, Circuit Judge

The relationship between Harrison and ABKCO prior to termination of the management agreement in 1973 was that of principal and agent. An agent has a duty not to use confidential knowledge acquired in his employment in competition with his principal. This duty exists as well after the employment as during its continuance. On the other hand, use of information based on general business knowledge is not covered by the rule, and the former agent is permitted to compete with his former principal in reliance on such publicly available information. The principal issue before us, then, is whether Klein (hence, ABKCO) improperly used confidential information, gained as Harrison's former agent, in negotiating for the purchase of Bright Tunes' stock in 1975–76.

One aspect of this inquiry concerns the nature of the schedules of "My Sweet Lord" earnings which Klein furnished to Bright Tunes in connection with the 1975–76 negotiations. It appears that at least some of [this] information was confidential. The evidence is not at all convincing that the information was publicly available.

Another aspect of the breach of duty issue concerns the timing and nature of Klein's entry into the negotiation picture and the manner in which he became a plaintiff in this action. We find this case analogous to those where an employee, with the use of information acquired through his former employment, completes for his own benefit a transaction originally undertaken on the former employer's behalf. Klein had commenced a purchase transaction with Bright Tunes in 1971 on behalf of Harrison, which he pursued on his own account after termination of his fiduciary relationship with Harrison. Klein pursued the later discussions armed with the intimate knowledge not only of Harrison's business affairs, but also of the value of this lawsuit. Taking all of these circumstances together, we agree that Klein's conduct during the period 1975–78 did not meet the standard required of him as a former fiduciary.

Judgment in favor of Harrison affirmed.

Agent's Duty to Obey Instructions

Because an agent acts under the principal's control and for the principal's benefit, she has a duty to obey the principal's reasonable instructions for carrying out the agency business.

There are exceptions to the duty to obey instructions. A gratuitous agent need not obey his principal's order to continue to act as an agent. Also, agents generally have no duty to obey orders to behave illegally or unethically. Thus, a sales agent need not follow directions to misrepresent the quality of the principal's goods, and professionals such as attorneys and accountants are not obligated to obey directions that conflict with the ethical rules of their professions.

Usually a principal's instructions are clear and can be easily followed. Sometimes, however, the instructions are ambiguous. For example, an instruction may have terms an agent does not understand. Or perhaps a cell phone conversation may be garbled due to poor signal strength. When a principal's instructions are unclear, the agent has a duty to communicate with the principal to clarify the instructions.

Agent's Duty to Act with Care and Skill

A paid agent must **act with the care, competence, and diligence** normally exercised by agents in similar circumstances. A gratuitous agent need only exercise the care and skill required of nonagents who perform similar gratuitous undertakings. Paid agents who represent that they possess a higher than customary level of skill may be held to a correspondingly higher standard of performance. Similarly, an agent's duty may change if the principal and the agent agree that the agent must possess and exercise greater or lesser than customary care and skill.

Ethics in Action

Corporations give special attention to rooting out conflicts of interests that result from kickbacks, bribes, and gifts to the corporations' employees. To ensure independence of auditors, auditing firms commonly have rules banning their audit staff from receiving anything of value from clients. In other contexts, most corporations permit their employees to receive items or services of nominal value only. Most firms have detailed rules, such as the following from Google's code of ethics:

Gifts, Entertainment, and Payments

Accepting gifts or entertainment from a Google customer, supplier, partner or competitor can easily create the appearance of a conflict of interest, especially if the value of the gift or entertainment is significant. Don't accept significant gifts, entertainment or any other business courtesy (including discounts or benefits that are not made available to all Googlers) from any of our customers, suppliers, partners or competitors if the gift would likely be perceived as influencing your business decisions or otherwise creating a conflict of interest. It's just not how we want to do business.

That said, we understand that not all gifts and entertainment represent conflicts of interest: Inexpensive "token" non-cash gifts, infrequent and moderate business meals and entertainment, and infrequent invitations to local sporting events and celebratory meals can be acceptable aspects of many Google business relationships, provided that they aren't excessive and don't create the appearance of impropriety. Accepting an invitation to a cocktail party thrown by an advertising partner, for instance, might be considered not only an acceptable business activity, but a necessary one for an AdWords sales employee. Similarly, accepting a company T-shirt or coffee mug isn't likely to change your assessment of a potential business relationship. However, accepting tickets to something like the Olympics, Super Bowl or World Cup, especially if travel and lodging are included, can create at least the appearance of a conflict of interest. You should get the approval of your manager and Ethics & Compliance for significant gifts and entertainment like that.

Gifts from customers, suppliers, partners or competitors of cash or cash equivalents (e.g., gift certificates or prepaid gift cards) should never be accepted.

Agent's Duty to Notify the Principal An agent must promptly communicate to the principal matters within the agent's knowledge that are relevant and material to the agency business and that he knows or should know are of concern to the principal. The basis for the duty to notify is the principal's interest in being informed of matters that are important to the agency business.

However, there is no duty to notify when the agent receives privileged or confidential information. For example, a consultant may acquire confidential information from a client and thus be obligated not to disclose it to a second client. If the consultant cannot properly represent the second client without revealing this information, he should refuse to represent that client.

Agent's Duties to Account An agent's duties of loyalty and care require that she give the principal any money or property received in the course of the agency business. This includes profits resulting from the agent's breach of the duty of loyalty, or other duties. It also includes incidental benefits received through the agency business. Examples include bribes, kickbacks, and gifts

from parties with whom the agent deals on the principal's behalf. However, the principal and the agent may agree that the agent can retain certain benefits received during the agency. Courts may imply such an agreement when it is customary for agents to retain tips or accept entertainment while doing the principal's business.

Another type of **duty to account** concerns agents whose business involves collections, receipts, or expenditures. Such agents must keep accurate records and accounts of all transactions and disclose these to the principal once the principal makes a reasonable demand for them. Also, an agent who obtains or holds property for the principal usually may not commingle that property with her own property. For example, an agent ordinarily cannot deposit the principal's funds in her own name or in her own bank account.

Ordinarily, if a principal suffers no monetary damages from the agent's breach of duty, it is not entitled to any recovery from the agent, although termination of the agency may be justified. The following *Sanders* case shows how Madison Square Garden tried to circumvent the damage requirement by using the faithless servant doctrine.

Sanders v. Madison Square Garden L.P.
2007 U.S. Dist. LEXIS 48126 (S.D.N.Y. 2007)

Anuche Browne Sanders was vice president of marketing for the New York Knickerbockers, an NBA basketball team owned by Madison Square Garden (MSG). She was responsible for all aspects of the Knicks' marketing and media efforts, and she had access to confidential MSG financial and business proprietary material. When she was hired, Browne Sanders signed a copy of MSG's Confidentiality, Code of Business Conduct and Proprietary Property Agreement, which provided that during her employment, she may not engage in activities or have personal or financial interests that may impair, or appear to impair, her independence or judgment or otherwise conflict with her responsibilities to MSG. She also signed MSG's Employee Code of Conduct, which stated that "public trust and confidence are the greatest assets held by MSG."

In 2002, Browne Sanders was promoted to senior vice president, marketing and business operations, and her responsibilities expanded to include, among other things, oversight of the marketing and business operations budget. Browne Sanders remained in that position until she was fired in January 2006. Her total compensation for just over five years of employment with the Knicks exceeded $1,100,000. Shortly after being fired, Browne Sanders sued MSG and Knicks head coach and president, Isiah Thomas, among others, alleging that she was discriminated against on the basis of her sex and terminated in retaliation for her sexual harassment complaint against MSG and Thomas.

MSG obtained copies of Browne Sanders's federal, New York, and New Jersey tax returns for 2000–2005. The 2001–2004 returns included Schedule C deductions for the expenses of a "direct marketing" business, totaling approximately $73,000, seeming to indicate that she had conducted her own business on the side while working for the Knicks or that she had illegally deducted personal expenses as business expenses on her tax returns. Browne Sanders denied that she operated her own direct marketing business while working for the Knicks and claimed that the Schedule C deductions were due to accountant error and not a deliberate attempt to commit tax fraud. She filed amended tax returns for 2003 and 2004 that removed the Schedule C deductions. She did not amend the 2000 and 2001 tax returns on the advice of her current accountant, who informed her that there is a three-year statute of limitations for amending tax returns.

MSG counterclaimed against Browne Sanders for breach of fiduciary duty, claiming that she had breached her duty either by operating an outside business or by committing tax fraud while employed at MSG. MSG argued that under the faithless servant doctrine, it may recover all compensation paid to Browne Sanders while she was committing tax fraud or secretly operating an unauthorized direct marketing business while employed by MSG. MSG sought to amend its answer to Browne Sanders's complaint to include the faithless servant claim.

Lynch, District Judge

The faithless servant doctrine provides that an agent is obligated to be loyal to his employer and is prohibited from acting in any manner inconsistent with his agency or trust and is at all times bound to exercise the utmost good faith and loyalty in the performance of his duties. To show a violation of the faithless servant doctrine, an employer must show (1) that the employee's disloyal activity was related to the performance of his duties, and (2) that the disloyalty permeated the employee's service in its most material and substantial part.

Thus, the faithless servant doctrine, like the traditional fiduciary duty standard, is limited to matters relevant to affairs entrusted to the employee. However, unlike a traditional breach of fiduciary duty claim, which requires a showing of actual damages, to prove a violation of the faithless servant doctrine, an employer is not required to show that it suffered provable damage as a result of the breach of fidelity by the agent.

Here, MSG claims that Browne Sanders's tax returns show that she was either operating an outside business or that she committed tax fraud while employed at MSG. However, neither operating an outside business nor unethical conduct unrelated to employment violates the faithless servant doctrine unless such business or behavior adversely affects the employee's job performance. MSG neither claims nor has provided any evidence that Browne Sanders's alleged misconduct hurt her job performance.

Under MSG's interpretation of the faithless servant doctrine, an employee breaches her duty of loyalty any time she engages in conduct that is not condoned by her employer or that violates her employer's ethical standards, regardless of whether the employee's conduct was related to her job performance. However, the purpose of the doctrine is not to dissolve the well-established boundaries of an employee's fiduciary duty, but to provide a remedy for an employer if an employee breaches that duty and it is difficult to prove that harm resulted from the breach or the employee realizes no profit through the breach. *Restatement (Third) of Agency,* § 8.01 (2006). While employers may contractually obligate employees to act in an ethical manner, and condition continued employment on compliance with that requirement, an employee's alleged violation of that requirement does not result in a violation of the faithless servant doctrine unless the employee's unethical conduct materially and substantially infringed on her job performance. A faithless servant doctrine read as broadly as urged by MSG would allow an employer to sue an employee if the employee engaged in any conduct that fell short of the employer's ethical standards, no matter how disconnected to the employer's business the employee's misconduct might have been, simply because the employee's private misbehavior might reflect poorly on her employer.

MSG conspicuously fails to identify any way in which it suffered any such damage. As noted, it does not identify any way in which her alleged derelictions affected Browne Sanders's performance of her duties. Nevertheless, having ac-

cepted the fruits of Browne Sanders's labor for five years, MSG argues that it is entitled to obtain those fruits for free by forcing the forfeiture of all of Browne Sanders's pay for her entire period of employment. The remedies of the faithless servant doctrine are drastic, and appropriately so where the doctrine applies. An employee who works to undermine or covertly compete with her employer cannot be permitted to retain the benefits of an agency relationship she has betrayed. An employee who violates an incidental work rule, however, or who cheats the government out of taxes due, may have to respond in damages for breach of contract, but need not forfeit her entire salary.

MSG's motion to amend its answer denied.

Duties of Principal to Agent

If an agency is formed by a written contract, the contract normally states the duties the principal owes the agent. In addition, the law implies certain duties from the existence of an agency relationship, however formed. The most important of these duties are the principal's obligations to **compensate** the agent, to **reimburse** the agent for money spent in the principal's service, and to **indemnify** the agent for losses suffered in conducting the principal's business. These duties generally can be eliminated or modified by agreement between the parties.

Duty to Compensate Agent

If the agency contract states the compensation the agent is to receive, it usually controls questions about the agent's pay. In other cases, the relationship of the parties and the sur-

rounding circumstances determine whether and in what amount the agent is to be compensated. Where compensation is due but its amount is not expressly stated, the amount is the market price or the customary price for the agent's services or, if neither is available, their reasonable value.

Sometimes an agent's compensation depends on the accomplishment of a specific result. For instance, an investment banker may be retained on a contingent fee basis to find a buyer for its client's product line and be compensated with a percentage of the purchase price. In such cases, the agent is not entitled to compensation unless he achieves the result within the time stated or, if no time is stated, within a reasonable time. This is true no matter how much effort or money the agent expends. However, the principal must cooperate with the agent in achieving the result and must not do anything to frustrate

The Global Business Environment

While all modern nations regulate the relationship of agents and principals, associations of professional agents often reinforce or augment these legal duties with codes of ethics. For the real estate industry, you can find codes of ethics in 23 countries at the Web site of the International Consortium of Real Estate Associations, www.worldproperties.com.

Excerpts from the Code of Ethics of the Italian Federation of Real Estate Agents are below. Note how the listed rules relate to the agent's fiduciary duties we have studied.

• The Professional Real Estate Agent must know the real estate market and its development as well as the laws and regulations that govern his own activity.

• The Real Estate Agent must gather for any of his assignments all useful information in order to accomplish his task.
• The Real Estate Agent must not intermingle his own assets with the money received by a third party.
• The Real Estate Agent entrusted with the task of managing property must agree with the Client in advance on the amount of the compensation to be given to him and may not accept any amount of money from a third party at any time.
• The Real Estate Agent must examine the assignment entrusted to him and inform the Client of all the difficulties of the transaction.

the agent's efforts. Otherwise, the agent is entitled to compensation despite the failure to perform as specified.

A principal generally is not required to pay for undertakings that she did not request, services to which she did not consent, and tasks that typically are undertaken without pay. Also, a principal usually need not compensate an agent who has materially breached the agency contract or has committed a serious breach of a fiduciary duty, as the *Sanders* case on page 905 pointed out. Of course, there is no duty to compensate a gratuitous agent.

An agent's duties to a subagent are the same as a principal's duties to an agent. If there is no agreement to the contrary, however, the original principal has no contractual liability to a subagent. For example, such a principal normally is not obligated to compensate a subagent. But a principal must reimburse and indemnify subagents as he would agents.

Duties of Reimbursement and Indemnity

If an agent makes expressly or impliedly authorized expenditures while acting on the principal's behalf, the agent normally is entitled to **reimbursement** for those expenditures. Unless otherwise agreed, for example, an agent requested to make overnight trips as part of his agency duties can recover reasonable transportation and hotel expenses.

A principal's duty of reimbursement overlaps with her duty of **indemnity.** Agency law implies a promise by the principal to indemnify an agent for losses that result from the agent's authorized activities. These include authorized payments made on the principal's behalf and payments on contracts on which the agent was authorized to become liable. A principal may also have to indemnify an agent if the agent's authorized acts constitute a breach of contract or a tort for which the agent is required to pay damages to a third party.

So long as the principal did not benefit from such behavior, however, he is *not* required to indemnify an agent for losses resulting (1) from unauthorized acts, or (2) solely from the agent's negligence or other fault. Even where the principal directed the agent to commit a tortious act, moreover, there is no duty to indemnify if the agent knew the act was tortious. But the principal must indemnify the agent for tort damages resulting from authorized conduct that the agent did not believe was tortious. For example, if a principal directs his agent to repossess goods located on another's property and the agent, believing her acts legal, becomes liable for conversion or trespass, the principal must indemnify the agent for the damages the agent pays.

Termination of an Agency

An agency can terminate in many ways that fall under two general headings: (1) termination by act of the parties, and (2) termination by operation of law.

Termination by Act of the Parties
Termination by act of the principal and/or agent occurs:

1. *At a time or upon the happening of an event stated in the agreement.* If no such time or event is stated, the agency terminates after a reasonable time.

2. *When a specified result has been accomplished, if the agency was created to accomplish a specified result.* For example, if an agency's only objective is to sell certain property, the agency terminates when the property is sold.

3. *By mutual agreement of the principal and the agent,* at any time.

4. *At the option of either party.* This is called **revocation** when done by the principal and **renunciation** when done by the agent. Revocation or renunciation occurs when either party manifests to the other that he does not wish the agency to continue. This includes conduct inconsistent with the agency's continuance. For example, an agent may learn that his principal has hired another agent to perform the same job.

A party can revoke or renounce even if doing so violates the agency agreement. Although either party has the *power* to terminate in such cases, there is no *right* to do so. This means that where one party terminates in violation of the agreement, she need not perform any further, but she may be liable for damages to the other party. A gratuitous agency normally is terminable by either party without liability. Also, the terminating party is not liable when the revocation or renunciation is justified by the other party's serious breach of a fiduciary duty.

Termination by Operation of Law
Termination by operation of law usually involves situations where it is reasonable to believe that the principal would not wish the agent to act further, or where accomplishment of the agency objectives has become impossible or illegal. Although courts may recognize exceptions in certain cases, an agency relationship usually is terminated by:

1. *The death of an individual principal.* Under the *Restatement (Third) of Agency,* this termination is effective only when the agent has notice of the principal's death.

2. *The death of an individual agent.*

3. *The principal's permanent loss of capacity.* This is a *permanent* loss of capacity occurring *after* creation of the agency—most often, due to the principal's insanity. The principal's permanent incapacity ends the agency even without notice to the agent. The *Trepanier* case, which follows, presents one approach to a related problem: the principal's *temporary* incapacity.

4. *The agent's loss of capacity to perform the agency business.* The scope of this basis for termination is unclear. As Chapter 36 states, an agent who becomes insane or otherwise incapacitated after the agency is formed still can bind his principal to contracts with third parties. Thus, it probably makes little sense to treat the agency as terminated in such cases. As a result, termination under this heading may be limited to such situations as the loss of a license needed to perform agency duties.

5. The *cessation of existence or suspension of power* of an agent or principal that is not an individual, such as the dissolution of a corporation or partnership.

6. Under the *Restatement (Third) of Agency,* upon the *occurrence of circumstances* from which the agent should reasonably conclude that the *principal no longer would want the agent to take action* for the principal.

7. *Changes in the value of the agency property or subject matter* (e.g., a significant decline in the value of land to be sold by an agent).

8. *Changes in business conditions* (e.g., a much lower supply and a much increased price for goods to be purchased by an agent).

9. *The loss or destruction of the agency property or subject matter or the termination of the principal's interest therein* (e.g., when a house to be sold by a real estate broker burns down or is taken by a mortgage holder to satisfy a debt owed by the principal).

10. *Changes in the law that make the agency business illegal* (e.g., when drugs to be sold by an agent are banned by the government).

11. *The principal's bankruptcy*—as to transactions the agent should realize the principal no longer desires. For example, consider the likely effect of the principal's bankruptcy on an agency to purchase antiques for the principal's home versus its likely effect on an agency to purchase necessities of life for the principal.

12. *The agent's bankruptcy*—where the agent's financial condition affects his ability to serve the principal. This could occur when an agent is employed to purchase goods on his own credit for the principal.

13. *Impossibility of performance by the agent.* This covers various events, some of which fall within the categories just stated. The *Restatement's* definition of impossibility, for example, includes (*a*) destruction of the agency subject matter, (*b*) termination of the principal's interest in the agency subject matter (as, for example, by the principal's bankruptcy), and (*c*) changes in the law or in other circumstances that make it impossible for the agent to accomplish the agency's aims.

14. *A serious breach of the agent's duty of loyalty.*

15. *The outbreak of war*—when this leads the agent to the reasonable belief that his services are no longer desired. An example might be the outbreak of war between the principal's country and the agent's country.

Termination of Agency Powers Given as Security

An agency power given as security for a duty owed by the principal, sometimes called an **agency coupled with an interest,** is an exception to some of the termination rules just discussed. Here, the agent has an interest in the subject matter of the agency that is distinct from the principal's interest and that is not exercised for the principal's benefit. This interest exists to benefit the agent or a third person by securing performance of an obligation owed by the principal. A common example is a **power of sale,** a secured loan agreement authorizing a lender (the agent) to sell property used as security if the borrower (the principal) defaults. For instance, suppose that Allen lends Peters $500,000 and Peters gives Allen a lien or security interest on Peters's land to secure the loan. The agreement might authorize Allen to act as Peters's "agent" to sell the land if Peters fails to repay the loan.

Because the power given the "agent" in such cases is not for the principal's benefit, it sometimes is said that an agency coupled with an interest is not truly an agency. In any event, courts distinguish it from genuine agency relations in which the agent is compensated from the profits or proceeds of property held for the principal's benefit. For example, if an agent is promised a commission for selling the principal's property, the relationship is not an agency coupled with an interest. Here, the power exercised by the agent (selling the principal's property) benefits the principal.

Why is the agency coupled with an interest important? The main reason is that it is not terminated by (1) the principal's revocation, (2) the principal's or the agent's loss of capacity, (3) the agent's death, and (4) (usually) the principal's death. However, unless an agency coupled with an interest is held for the benefit of a third party, the agent can voluntarily surrender it. Of course, an agency coupled with an interest terminates when the principal performs her obligation.

Trepanier v. Bankers Life & Casualty Co.   706 A.2d 943 (Vt. Sup. Ct. 1997)

On March 2, 1993, Bankers Life & Casualty Co. proposed in a letter addressed to Gaston Trepanier that he accept a lump sum settlement of $20,000 in exchange for release from a disability income policy that paid him a $400-a-month benefit. The letter stated that should Mr. Trepanier decide "to accept our offer," he could "jot a note at the bottom of this letter and return it." According to Mrs. Clemence Trepanier, she discussed the idea with her husband, who decided to accept the offer and directed her to write a note on the bottom of the March letter as directed. She did so on April 6, and placed the letter in an envelope, intending to send it the following day. On April 7, Mr. Trepanier was hospitalized and the letter was not mailed. Mr. Trepanier fell into a coma on April 8. On April 12, Mrs. Trepanier tried to accept the offer by mailing the letter to Bankers Life. On April 14, Mr. Trepanier died. Bankers Life subsequently revoked its offer and issued a final disability payment.

Clemence Trepanier then filed a breach-of-contract action against Bankers Life on behalf of her husband's estate, alleging that a valid contract had been formed when she accepted the $20,000 offer on her husband's behalf. Mrs. Trepanier moved for partial summary judgment on the issue of whether a binding contract had been formed. In response, Bankers Life filed a cross-motion for summary judgment, arguing that Clemence Trepanier's authority to act as agent for her husband terminated when he lapsed into a coma on April 8, four days before she mailed the acceptance. The trial court denied Clemence's motion and entered a summary judgment in favor of Bankers Life. Clemence appealed, eventually to the Supreme Court of Vermont.

By the Court

The sole issue on appeal is whether Mrs. Trepanier's agency terminated when Mr. Trepanier lapsed into a coma on April 8. The general rule is that an agency terminates with the death or permanent incapacity of the principal. Mrs. Trepanier argues that her power of agency was coupled with an interest, an exception to the general rule which allows the agency to survive the death or permanent incapacity of the principal. We need not decide whether Mrs. Trepanier's agency fits within this exception, however, for an individual in a comatose state is generally not considered to be permanently incapacitated under general agency principles. The rule has been stated as follows: "A comatose person is mentally incompetent while his coma continues and . . . when an agent under a power of attorney acts during the mental incapacity of a principal who has not been adjudicated incompetent and for whom no court-appointed committee or conservator has been designated, the act is at most voidable,

and not void." This rule is predicated on the view that comatose individuals are only temporarily incapacitated, as they may recover, and acts by individuals temporarily incapacitated are at most voidable. With respect to such voidable contracts, the power to affirm or disaffirm rests solely with the principal or an authorized representative, which can include the estate of the principal. The contract here was not voided by Mr. Trepanier, and there is no claim or evidence that he would have done so prior to his death.

We hold, therefore, that the trial court erred in concluding as a matter of law that Mrs. Trepanier's agency terminated when Mr. Trepanier lapsed into a coma, and in entering summary judgment on this basis.

Summary judgment in favor of Bankers Life reversed; case remanded to the trial court.

Effect of Termination on Agent's Authority
Sometimes former agents continue to act on their ex-principals' behalf even though the agency has ended. Once an agency terminates by any of the means just described, the agent's *express* and *implied* authority end as well. Nonetheless, such "ex-agents" may retain *apparent authority* to bind their former principals.

Third parties who are unaware of the termination may reasonably believe that an ex-agent still has authority. To protect third parties who rely on such a reasonable appearance of authority, an agent's *apparent authority* often persists after termination. Thus, a former agent may be able to bind the principal under his apparent authority even though the agency has ended. But apparent authority ends where the termination was caused by (1) the principal's death, (2) the principal's loss of capacity, or (3) impossibility. Note from the previous discussion that certain other bases for termination may also end the agent's apparent authority because they fit within the broad category of impossibility.

Notice to Third Parties Apparent authority also ends when the third party receives appropriate notice of the termination. In general, any facts known to the third party that reasonably indicate the agency's termination constitute suitable notice. Some bases for termination by operation of law (e.g., changed business conditions) may provide such notice.

To protect themselves against unwanted liability, however, prudent principals may want to notify third parties themselves. The required type of notification varies with the third party in question.

1. *For third parties who have previously dealt with the agent or who have begun to deal with the agent,* **actual notification** is necessary. This can be accomplished by (1) a direct personal statement to the third party; or (2) a writing delivered to the third party personally, to his place of business, or to some other place reasonably believed to be appropriate.

2. *For all other parties,* **constructive notification** suffices. Usually, these other parties are aware of the agency but did no business with the agent. Constructive notification normally can be accomplished by advertising the agency's termination in a newspaper of general circulation in the place where the agency business regularly was carried on. If no suitable publication exists, notification by other means reasonably likely to inform third parties—for example, posting a notice in public places or at a Web site—may be enough.

LOG ON

Go to
www.wma.com

You can check out a career in the agency industry at the William Morris Agency Web site. WMA is the oldest and largest talent and literary agency in the world. Its business includes securing concert gigs for musicians and speaking engagements for authors. WMA clients include actor Tommy Lee Jones, director Spike Lee, musician Alicia Keys, and comedienne Margaret Cho.

Problems and Problem Cases

1. When Del-Mar Development Corp. failed to pay real estate taxes on an office building it owned, the building was seized by tax authorities and sold to pay the taxes. The purchaser was Euclid Plaza Associates, LLC. The sale was not valid, however, until approved by a court. After the sale and before the court's approval of the sale, Del-Mar agreed to a three-year lease of the building with African American Law Firm LLC (AALF), which immediately began paying rent of $1,500 per month to Del-Mar. After the court approved the sale, Euclid claimed it was not bound by the lease made by Del-Mar with AALF. Euclid wanted to evict AALF unless it paid $2,033 in monthly rent. Was Del-Mar acting as Euclid's agent within Del-Mar's actual and apparent authority when Del-Mar leased the building to AALF?

2. Karsten was hired as a outside sales agent by Ling Company, a manufacturer of golf equipment and accessories. Karsten's duties required him to visit golf pro shops at golf courses and other golf equipment and accessory retailers. It was common for an outside sales agent in Karsten's position to have the power to make contracts to sell any item in his employer's line of products. However, Ling Company instructed Karsten that he could not contract to sell any Ling golf shoes without first getting permission from Ling's vice president of sales, Perez. Ling imposed this limit on Karsten's authority, because Ling was temporarily having problems getting shipments of golf shoes from its supplier in China. Neither Ling nor Karsten, however, had informed pro shops or retailers of the limitation on Karsten's authority. Nonetheless, Karsten, anxious to make a big sale, made a contract to sell 700 pairs of Ling golf shoes to Pro Golf Company. Was Ling bound to this contract with Pro Golf Company?

3. Circle C Investments operated two nightclubs featuring topless dancers. The secretary of labor sued to compel Circle C to comply with the minimum-wage and maximum-hours provisions of the Fair Labor Standards Act, which applies only to employees, not independent contractors. Circle C required the

dancers to comply with weekly work schedules, to charge at least $10 for table dances and $20 for couch dances, and to mingle with customers when not dancing. Circle C enforced the rules by fining infringing dancers. Dancers supplied their own costumes and padlocks for personal lockers. One dancer spent $600 per month on costumes, but another spent only $40 per month. A dancer's initiative, hustle, and costume contributed significantly to her tips. Circle C was responsible for advertising the club, choosing its location, and business hours, creating club aesthetics, and establishing a food and beverage menu, all of which attracted customers to the club. Dancers did not need long training or highly developed skills to dance at the club. Most dancers had a short-term relationship with Circle C. Were the dancers employees or independent contractors for purposes of the Fair Labor Standards Act?

4. Merrill Lynch, the investment firm, hired Elliot Jarvin as Director of Wealth Management Services. His duties included managing a team of 10 wealth managers who advised Merrill Lynch clients regarding their investment portfolios. When Jarvin joined Merrill Lynch, he brought with him 15 very wealthy clients to whom he provided investment services on behalf of Merrill Lynch. Unknown to Merrill Lynch, Jarvin had five additional clients, the five wealthiest of his clients. Jarvin continued to advise these clients on his own, retaining for himself all fees he charged for services provided to the five clients. In addition, to help him service the five personal clients, two members of his Merrill Lynch wealth management team frequently met with Jarvin's five personal clients to create investments plans for them. Has Jarvin breached a fiduciary duty owed to Merrill Lynch?

5. In July 1987, Marsha Levin bought her daughter a round-trip plane ticket from New York City to Paris from Kasmir World Travel, Inc. Upon arriving in Paris, Mrs. Levin's daughter was denied entry and was placed on the next return flight to the United States because she did not have a visa. The apparent reason for the visa requirement was the French government's effort to deal with terrorist activities directed at Americans abroad. Neither Mrs. Levin nor her daughter was aware of the requirement; indeed, a few years earlier Mrs. Levin had traveled to France without being required to present a visa. Did Kasmir breach its duty to notify the Levins about matters relevant to the agency business?

6. When Perry Olsen died, his children placed his ranch in Vail, Colorado, for sale. Perry's children retained Vail Associates Real Estate, a real estate broker, to sell the land for them. Vail Associates introduced the children to Magnus Lindholm, who wanted to buy Perry's ranch along with adjacent land owned by Perry's children. The children eventually decided to sell only Perry's ranch and not the children's land. Their asking price for Perry's ranch was $400 per acre. Before committing to buying Perry's ranch (because he needed more land), Lindholm asked Vail Associates to introduce him to Del Rickstrew, whose land also abutted Perry's ranch. Rickstrew refused to negotiate the sale through a real estate agent, so Lindholm negotiated directly with Rickstrew. Vail Associates did, however, introduce Rickstrew to Lindholm and provide a model contract to Lindholm. A month later, Lindholm agreed to buy Rickstrew's land for $6,000 per acre, subject to his buying Perry's ranch also. Vail Associates was not aware that Lindholm and Rickstrew had a contract or that the price was $6,000 per acre. Two months later, with Vail Associates' assistance, the children sold Perry's ranch to Lindholm for $400 per acre. Vail Associates received a commission from the sale. When the children discovered later that Rickstrew received 15 times as much for his acreage as did they for Perry's ranch, they sued Vail Associates for failing to disclose material information, that is, that Lindholm was negotiating with Rickstrew. Did Vail Associates breach a fiduciary duty?

7. When Nitrogen Media was acquired by General Electric's NBC Universal unit, Nitrogen's Vice President of Finance, Babs Grogan, was terminated as a Nitrogen employee, but hired by NBCU as an outside consultant. The term of Grogan's contract was three months, and her engagement with NBCU required her to assess business opportunities presented to NBCU, such as the financial value of newly created television shows. Grogan represented to NBCU that she had an MBA degree in finance and six years of experience in financial analysis. In fact, Grogan had falsified her academic record and possessed only an undergraduate degree in political science. In addition, she had no experience as a financial analyst, having delegated such work to co-workers for the past six years, although she took credit for their work. When NBCU asked Grogan to value the new TV show *Car Shop,* she delegated the task in part to

a new MBA graduate, Roger Harvey, who was recently hired by NBCU and had virtually no on-the-job experience. As a result, Grogan and Harvey failed to perform a reasonable investigation into the facts regarding the TV show's value and to use appropriate valuations tools. Did Grogan and Harvey breach their fiduciary duty?

8. Lawrence is a clothing buyer for Federal Department Stores, a general merchandise retailer. Over the past five years, Lawrence has bought 75 percent of Federal's inventory of men's and women's denim pants from Worldwide Jeans Co. and 15 percent from Oskash Corp. Wanting to increase its sales of denim pants to Federal, Oskash contacts Lawrence and offers to sell 40,000 pairs of jeans to Federal for $320,000 and to make a contribution of $5,000 to the college education fund that Lawrence has established for his children. Should Lawrence accept this offer from Oskash?

9. Marjorie and Randall Bender owned a ranch they wished to sell, so they hired Johnson Realty as the listing agent. Johnson Realty found a buyer of the ranch, who relied on a brochure describing the ranch and its historic crop yields. The Benders authorized the production and distribution of the brochure by Johnson Realty. The buyer later sued Johnson Realty and the Benders on the grounds that the crop yields in the brochure were inflated. Although Johnson Realty and the Benders won that case, Johnson Realty suffered the expense of legal fees and other legal costs amounting to $45,000. On what grounds did Johnson Realty attempt to recover those costs from the Benders?

10. Brenda Smith was injured by a falling ceiling in a building owned by the Cynfax Corporation. She retained Floyd Goldsman as her attorney, and Goldsman sued Cynfax on her behalf. On February 4, Cynfax's insurer, the Cumberland Mutual Fire Insurance Company, made Smith a $7,000 settlement offer through Goldsman. Goldsman immediately tried to inform Smith of the offer, but learned that she had died two days earlier on February 2. Later, Goldsman accepted Cumberland's offer to Smith. Did he have authority to do so? In answering this question, consider whether we have an agency coupled with an interest here, and why it would matter if we did.

Online Research

Investment Advisers' Fiduciary Duty

Conflicts of interest are a concern in the securities industry when securities brokers and investments advisers create investment plans and recommend securities purchases to their customers. Search the Internet for the Web site of the North American Securities Administrators Association. Find the Investment Adviser Guide. Scroll down and read the Fiduciary Duty section. Note how these duties reflect the fiduciary duties you studied in this chapter.

Consider completing the case "AGENCY: Duped by Duplication" from the You Be the Judge Web site element after you have read this chapter. Visit our Web site at www.mhhe.com/mallor14e for more information and activities regarding this case segment.

chapter 36

THIRD-PARTY RELATIONS
OF THE PRINCIPAL
AND THE AGENT

You are vice president of acquisitions for a medium-sized consumer food products company, Bon Vivant Foods, Inc. The company's board of directors has given you authority to negotiate acquisitions of consumer food brands on behalf of Bon Vivant. The board has told you in written and oral instructions that you have the power to acquire any consumer products brand if the acquisition price is not greater than $30,000,000, which is the authority typically held by most vice presidents of acquisitions for businesses like yours. The board's written instructions also indicate, however, that you have no authority to purchase or negotiate the purchase of a cola drink brand. Others in your position in the consumer food industry typically have authority to purchase a cola drink brand for their companies. The board also tells you that the company wants to buy the Eddie's ice cream brand from its owner, Eddie Ghahraman, at a price not greater than $28,000,000. The board is fearful, however, that if Eddie knows the company wants to buy the Eddie's ice cream brand, he will demand a higher price. The board tells you, therefore, not to disclose to Eddie that you are buying for Bon Vivant, and instead to make it appear that you are buying for your own company. They suggest you make up a name for this fictitious company. You decide to use the name LHIW, Inc.

Assess the risks to you and Bon Vivant. Consider the following questions:

- If you make a contract in the name of Bon Vivant to buy a snack-cracker brand for $15,000,000, will Bon Vivant be bound on that contract?
- If you make a contract in the name of Bon Vivant to buy a cola brand for $13,500,000, will Bon Vivant be bound on that contract?
- If you make a contract in the name of Bon Vivant to buy an organic canned soup brand for $40,000,000, will Bon Vivant be bound on that contract? Will Bon Vivant be bound on that contract if you present the contract to the board, the board decides to accept the contract, and then the board later rejects the contract as too costly?
- Suppose you make a contract for Bon Vivant to purchase the Eddie's ice cream brand for $26,200,000. The contract is signed by Eddie. You sign LHIW's name and also your own name as agent for LHIW. Who is liable on that contract?

BY LETTING PRINCIPALS CONTRACT through their agents and thereby multiply their dealings, agency law stimulates business activity. For this process to succeed, there must be rules for determining when the principal and the agent are liable on the agent's contracts. Principals need to predict and control their liability on agreements their agents make. Also, third parties need assurance that such agreements really bind the principal. Furthermore, both agents and third parties have an interest in knowing when an agent is bound on these contracts. The first half of this chapter discusses the principal's and the agent's contract liability.

While acting on the principal's behalf, agents sometimes harm third parties. Normally, this makes the agent liable to the injured party in tort. Sometimes, moreover, a principal is liable for his agent's torts. Because tort judgments can be expensive, the rules for determining the principal's and the agent's tort liability are of great concern to principals, their agents, and third parties. Thus, we examine these subjects in this chapter's second half.

The law in this chapter, as in Chapter 35, reflects the rules of the *Restatement (Second) of Agency* and the *Restatement (Third) of Agency*. Adopted in 2006, the *Restatement (Third)* will soon be the dominant law of agency in the United States. The two versions of the *Restatement* are largely similar. When they differ, the rule of the *Restatement (Third)* will usually be the only rule discussed in this chapter.

Contract Liability of the Principal

A principal normally is liable on a contract made by his agent if the agent had **express, implied,** or **apparent authority** to make the contract. Yet even when the agent lacks authority to contract, a principal may bind herself by later **ratifying** a contract made by an unauthorized agent.

Express Authority
Express authority is created by a principal's *words* to his agent, whether written or spoken, and by the principal's other conduct. Thus, an agent has express authority to bind her principal to a contract if the principal clearly told the agent that she could make that contract on the principal's behalf. Express authority is part of an agent's **actual authority.** For example, suppose that Microsoft instructs its agent Gates to contract to sell a Windows XT software license for $400 or more. If Gates contracts to sell the software license to Dell for $425, Microsoft is liable to Dell on the basis of Gates's express authority. However, Gates would not have express authority to sell the software license for $375 or to sell a different software license.

Implied Authority
Implied Authority Often it is difficult for a principal to specify his agent's authority completely and precisely. Thus, agents can also bind their principals on the basis of the agent's **implied authority.** An agent generally has implied authority to do whatever it is reasonable to assume that his principal wanted him to do, in light of the principal's manifestations to the agent and the principal's objectives of the agency. Relevant factors include the principal's express statements, the nature of the agency, the acts reasonably necessary to carry on the agency business, the acts customarily done when conducting that business, and the relations between principal and agent.

Implied authority usually derives from a grant of express authority by the principal and is part of an agent's actual authority. On occasion, however, implied authority may exist even though there is no relevant grant of express authority. Courts generally derive implied authority from the nature of the agency business, the relations between principal and agent, customs in the trade, and other facts and circumstances. There may be implied authority to make a certain contract if the agent has made similar past contracts with the principal's knowledge and without his objection or if the agent's position usually gives an agent the power to make a certain contract.

No matter what its source, an agent's implied authority cannot contradict the principal's express statements. Thus, there is no implied authority to contract when a principal has limited her agent's authority by express statement or clear implication and the contract would conflict with that limitation. But as we will see, apparent authority may still exist in such cases.

Examples of Implied Authority Courts have created general rules or presumptions for determining the implied authority of certain agents in certain situations. For example:

1. An agent hired to *manage a business* normally has implied authority to make contracts that are reasonably necessary for conducting the business or that are customary in the business. These include contracts for obtaining equipment and supplies, making repairs, employing employees, and selling goods or services. However, a manager ordinarily has no power to borrow money or issue negotiable instruments in the principal's name unless the principal is a banking or financial concern regularly performing such activities.

2. An agent given *full control over real property* has implied authority to contract for repairs and insurance and may rent the property if this is customary. But such an agent may not sell the property or allow any third-party liens or other interests to be taken on it.

3. Agents appointed to *sell the principal's goods* may have implied authority to make customary warranties on those goods. In states that still recognize the distinction, a general agent described in Chapter 35 is more likely to have such authority than a special agent.

Apparent Authority
Apparent authority arises when the principal's behavior causes a third party to form a reasonable belief that the agent is authorized to

The Global Business Environment

Electronic Agents

In the Internet Age, evolving business practices show an increasing use of software programs known as electronic agents in e-commerce transactions. A common definition of an electronic agent is a computer program or an electronic or other automated means used to initiate an action or to respond to electronic messages without review by an individual.

In the legal context, an electronic agent can be an automated means for making or performing contracts. In automated transactions, an individual does not deal with another individual, but one or both parties are represented by electronic agents. You have probably dealt with an electronic agent if you have ordered books, CDs, airline tickets, and other goods and services from an Internet site like Amazon.com.

The legal relationship between the principal and the automated agent is not fully equivalent to common law agency, but takes into account that the electronic agent is not a human actor. Nonetheless, parties who employ or deal with electronic agents are ordinarily bound by the results of their operations.

Most modern countries have laws that indicate when a person can be bound by the action of its electronic agent. In the United States, the Uniform Computer Information Transactions Act (2002) recognizes the ability of electronic agents to bind their principals, even if no individual is aware of or reviews the agent's operation or the results of the operation. Under the Philippines' Electronic Commerce Act, a contract may not be denied legal validity solely because it was created using an electronic agent, provided the electronic agent is under the control of or its actions attributable to the person sought to be bound. India's Electronic Commerce Act states that a contract may be formed between an individual and an electronic agent if the individual has reason to know she is dealing with an electronic agent. In Canada, the Uniform Electronic Commerce Act permits contracts to be formed by electronic agents, but if an individual deals with an electronic agent and makes an error, the individual will not be bound on the contract if the electronic agent provided no opportunity to correct the error and the individual immediately notifies the other party of the error.

act in a certain way. In other words, apparent authority is based on (1) *manifestations by the principal* to the third party (2) that cause the *third party* to *believe reasonably* that the agent has such authority. Background factors such as trade customs and established business practices often determine whether it is reasonable for the third party to believe that the agent has authority. In other words, apparent authority exists because it *appears* that the agent may act for the principal, based on what the principal has manifested to the third party.

Principals can give their agents apparent authority through the statements they make, or tell their agents to make, *to third parties* and through the actions they knowingly allow their agents to take *with third parties.* Thus, a principal might create apparent authority by telling a third party that the agent has certain authority or by directing the agent to do the same. A principal might also create apparent authority by appointing his agent to a position that customarily involves the authority to make certain contracts. For instance, if Exxon makes Alba its gasoline sales agent, and if that position customarily involves the power to sell gasoline, Alba would have apparent authority to sell gasoline. Here, Exxon's behavior in appointing Alba to the position of gasoline sales agent, as reasonably interpreted in light of business customs, gives Alba apparent authority. However, because agents cannot give themselves apparent authority, there would

be no such authority if, without Exxon's knowledge or permission, Alba falsely told third parties that he had been promoted to gasoline sales agent.

Apparent authority protects third parties who reasonably rely on the principal's manifestations that the agent has authority. It assumes special importance in cases where the principal has told the agent not to make certain contracts that the agent ordinarily would have actual authority to make, but the third party knows nothing about this limitation and has no reason to know about it. Suppose that Prince employs Arthur as general sales agent for its tennis racquet manufacturing business. Certain warranties customarily accompany the racquets Prince sells, and agents like Arthur ordinarily are empowered to give these warranties. But Prince tells Arthur not to make any such warranties to buyers, thus cutting off Arthur's express and implied authority. Despite Prince's orders, however, Arthur makes the usual warranties in a sale to Modell, who is familiar with customs in the trade. If Modell did not know about the limitation on Arthur's authority, Prince is bound by Arthur's warranties.

The following *Opp* case discusses whether an agent has express, implied, or apparent authority. Although decided under the *Restatement (Second) of Agency,* the case would have been resolved the same under the *Restatement (Third) of Agency.*

Opp v. Wheaton Van Lines, Inc.   231 F.3d 1060 (7th Cir. 2000)

Shelley Opp lived in California with her husband, Richard Opp, until they sought a divorce in August 1996. In June 1997, Ms. Opp contacted Soraghan Moving and Storage, an agent of Wheaton Van Lines, to move her personal property from California to Illinois. Ms. Opp told Soraghan she wanted to insure her property for its full value of $10,000. Soraghan faxed to Ms. Opp an "Estimate/Order for Service" form which stated that Ms. Opp intended to declare that the value of the goods shipped was $10,000. Ms. Opp signed the form. According to Soraghan, it explained to Ms. Opp that she or her representative must advise the mover at the time the shipment was picked up whether Ms. Opp would like full replacement coverage of $10,000. According to Ms. Opp, she was never informed that the person releasing her property in California would have to sign anything, declare any value for her property, or do anything other than give the movers access to her belongings. The estimate form also provided a location where Ms. Opp could designate someone as her "true and lawful representative," but she made no such designation.

On the day of the move, the movers in California called Ms. Opp in Illinois to tell her they would be late arriving at the California home due to a flat tire. Ms. Opp then phoned Mr. Opp at his office and asked him to go to the house, open the door, and let the movers in. Ms. Opp also told Soraghan that "someone" would be at the California home to give the movers access to her property. Mr. Opp met the movers at the house, and he signed the bill of lading on a line that indicated that he was Ms. Opp's authorized agent, and he allegedly agreed to limit the carriers' liability for her property at 60 cents per pound. Mr. Opp also signed an inventory of the property that indicated that he was its "owner or authorized agent."

On July 8, 1997, the truck carrying Ms. Opp's belongings was struck by a train, damaging most of her property. Ms. Opp inspected her damaged property and estimated its full replacement value to be over $10,000. Soraghan claimed that its liability was limited by the bill of lading to $2,625. Ms. Opp sued Sorghan and Wheaton to recover $10,000 for property damage. The carriers moved for summary judgment, which the district court granted, finding that Mr. Opp had the actual and apparent authority to sign the bill of lading as Ms. Opp's agent. Ms. Opp appealed.

Manion, Circuit Judge

An agent's authority may be either actual or apparent, and actual authority may be express or implied. Only the words or conduct of the alleged principal, not the alleged agent, establish the actual or apparent authority of an agent. We first note that Mr. Opp never received the express authority to represent Ms. Opp and to limit the carriers' liability. An agent has express authority when the principal explicitly grants the agent the authority to perform a particular act. There is no evidence that Ms. Opp explicitly granted authority to Mr. Opp to bind her to an agreement that limited the carriers' liability for her goods. Ms. Opp never requested or intended Mr. Opp to do anything other than to open the door and allow the movers to remove her property.

We next determine whether Mr. Opp had the implied authority to limit the carriers' liability. An agent has implied authority for the performance or transaction of anything reasonably necessary to effective execution of his express authority. *Restatement (Second) of Agency* § 35. Thus we must determine whether it was reasonably necessary for Mr. Opp to sign the bill of lading in order to execute his express authority to open the door to give the movers access to Ms. Opp's property.

The carriers argue that because Ms. Opp allegedly knew that the bill of lading had to be signed when her property was picked up, but she arranged for Mr. Opp to be the only person present in California for the move, Ms. Opp's request for

Mr. Opp to tender the goods to the movers also included the necessary authority for him to sign the bill of lading. But as noted above, Ms. Opp only told Mr. Opp to open the door. She made no request for him to sign anything, or to make any agreement as to the carriers' liability. Ms. Opp also testified that she was never informed that the person releasing her property in California would have to sign a bill of lading and declare a value for her property. Moreover, it is unclear whether Mr. Opp ever inferred from Ms. Opp's request that he was also authorized to limit the carriers' liability, or whether he merely thought that he was signing forms to confirm that Ms. Opp's goods were taken from the home. Thus we conclude that there is insufficient evidence to support a grant of summary judgment for the carriers on this issue.

We must then consider whether Mr. Opp had the apparent authority to sign the bill of lading and limit the carriers' liability. Under the doctrine of apparent authority, a principal will be bound not only by the authority that it actually gives to another, but also by the authority that it appears to give. Apparent authority arises when a principal creates, by its words or conduct, the reasonable impression in a third party that the agent has the authority to perform a certain act on its behalf. Thus we must determine whether the evidence demonstrates that Ms. Opp's words or conduct created a reasonable impression in the carriers that Mr. Opp had the authority to sign the bill of lading and limit their liability.

The carriers argue that they reasonably believed that Mr. Opp had the authority to sign the bill of lading because Ms. Opp allegedly knew that a bill of lading had to be signed when her goods were picked up, and she had also arranged for Mr. Opp to be the only person present at the California home to tender the goods. But material facts in the record also justify a reasonable inference that Mr. Opp did not have the apparent authority to limit the carriers' liability. It is undisputed that Ms. Opp told Soraghan that she wanted the full replacement value of $10,000 on her goods, which is reflected on the Estimate/Order for Service form. Ms. Opp never designated a "lawful representative" on the space provided on the estimate form, and thus Soraghan's own form lacked any indication that Mr. Opp was her agent. And when the movers were delayed by a flat tire on their moving truck, they called to notify Ms. Opp in Illinois, not Mr. Opp in California. Additionally, Ms. Opp

testified that the carriers never informed her that the person releasing her property in California would have to sign anything, declare any value for her property, or do anything other than to give the movers access to her belongings, which indicates that the carriers could not reasonably conclude that she knew that the bill of lading had to be signed in California, and that Mr. Opp had that authority. And there is no evidence in the record that the carriers had any knowledge that Ms. Opp ever discussed the valuation of her property with Mr. Opp. We conclude, therefore, that summary judgment is precluded because the record provides sufficient evidence to enable a reasonable jury to find that Mr. Opp lacked the apparent authority to limit the carriers' liability.

Judgment reversed in favor of Ms. Opp. Remanded to the district court.

Agent's Notification and Knowledge

Sometimes the general agency rules regarding *notification* and *knowledge* affect a principal's contract liability. If a third party gives proper notification to an agent with actual or apparent authority to receive it, the principal is bound as if the notification had been given directly to him. Similarly, notification to a third party by an agent with the necessary authority is considered notification by the principal.

In certain circumstances, an agent's knowledge of facts is *imputed* to the principal. This means that the principal's rights and liabilities are what they would have been if the principal had known what the agent knew. Generally, an agent's knowledge is imputed to a principal when it is relevant to activities that the agent is authorized to undertake, or when the agent is under a duty to disclose the knowledge to the principal. Suppose that Ames, acting on behalf of Sony, contracts with Target. Ames knows that Target is completely mistaken about a matter material to the contract to purchase TVs. Even though Sony knew nothing about Target's unilateral mistake, Target probably can avoid its contract with Sony.

Ratification

Ratification is a process whereby a principal binds himself to an unauthorized act done by an agent, or by a person purporting to act as an agent. Usually, the act in question is a contract. Ratification relates back to the time when the contract was made. It binds the principal as if the agent had possessed authority at that time.

Conduct Amounting to Ratification Ratification can be express or implied. An *express ratification* occurs when the principal communicates an intent to ratify by words, whether written or oral. *Implied ratification* arises when the principal's behavior evidences an intent to ratify. Examples include the principal's part performance of a contract made by an agent, or the principal's acceptance of benefits under such a contract. Sometimes even a principal's silence, acquiescence, or failure to repudiate the transaction may constitute ratification. This can occur when the principal would be expected to object if he did not consent to the contract, the principal's silence leads the third party to believe that he does consent, and the principal is aware of all relevant facts.

Additional Requirements Even if a principal's words or behavior indicate an intent to ratify, other requirements must be met before ratification occurs. These requirements have been variously stated; the following list is typical.

1. The act ratified must be one that was *valid* at the time it was performed. For example, an agent's illegal contract cannot be made binding by the principal's subsequent ratification. However, a contract that was voidable when made due to the principal's incapacity may be ratified by a principal who has later attained or regained capacity.

2. The principal must have been *in existence* at the time the agent acted. However, as discussed in Chapter 42, corporations may bind themselves to their promoters' *preincorporation* contracts by *adopting* such contracts.

3. When the contract or other act occurred, the agent must have indicated to the third party that she was acting for a principal and not for herself. The agent need not, however, have disclosed the principal's identity.

4. The principal must be *legally competent* at the time of ratification. For instance, an insane principal cannot ratify.

5. As the following *Work Connection* case makes clear, the principal must have *knowledge of all material facts* regarding the prior act or contract at the time it is ratified. Here, an agent's knowledge is not imputed to the principal.

6. The principal must ratify the *entire* act or contract. He cannot ratify the beneficial parts of a contract and reject those that are detrimental.

7. In ratifying, the principal must use the *same formalities* required to give the agent authority to execute the

transaction. As Chapter 35 stated, few formalities normally are needed to give an agent authority. But when the original agency contract requires a writing, ratification likewise must be written.

Note that a principal's ratification is binding even if not communicated to the third party. Also, once a principal has ratified a contract, the principal may not revoke the ratification.

Intervening Events Certain events occurring after an agent's contract but before the principal's ratification may cut off the principal's power to ratify. These include (1) the third party's *withdrawal* from the contract; (2) the third party's *death or loss of capacity;* (3) the principal's *failure to ratify within a reasonable time* (assuming that the principal's silence did not already work a ratification); and (4) *changed circumstances* (especially where the change places a greater burden on the third party than he assumed when the contract was made).

The Work Connection, Inc. v. Universal Forest Products, Inc.
2002 Minn. App. LEXIS 659 (Minn. Ct. App. 2002)

The Work Connection, Inc. (Connection) is a temporary employment agency that provides workers to customers for a fee. In February 1995, Doyle Olson, a sales representative for Connection, contacted Universal Forest Products, Inc. (Universal). Olson spoke with Ken Von Bank, Universal's production manager who had direct supervisory authority over temporary workers. Universal hired some of Connection's employees, including Wayne DeLage, to construct fence panels at its Shakopee plant.

Olson gave to Universal work verification forms that were used as employee timecards. Universal filled out and signed the forms, which contained the worker's name, date, and hours worked. Submission of a completed, signed form was required for an employee to be paid, and Connection processed the forms through its payroll department. The work verification forms contained the following language:

CUSTOMER AGREES TO THE TERMS AND CONDITIONS SET FORTH ON THE REVERSE SIDE HEREOF AND CERTIFIES THAT THE LISTED EMPLOYEES HAVE SATISFACTORILY PERFORMED SERVICES FOR THE HOURS SHOWN ABOVE.

The back of the verification form stated the following:

CONDITIONS OF UNDERTAKING

* * * *

3. CUSTOMER agrees to indemnify, hold harmless and defend THE WORK CONNECTION against claims, damages, or penalties under the following circumstances:

* * * *

(b) From any claims for bodily injury (including death), or loss of, and loss of use of, or damage to, property arising out of the use of or operation of CUSTOMER'S owned, nonowned, or leased vehicles, machinery or equipment by

THE WORK CONNECTION employees.

The parties never discussed the language on the back of the work verification form. The parties' oral agreement did not include a term that required Universal to provide workers' compensation insurance for Connection's employees. Nonetheless, Von Bank signed the verification forms for Universal from March 1995 through July 1995, when the office manager, Yvonne

Kohout, took over signing duties. At some point, Universal ran out of original work verification forms. Kohout simply photocopied the front side of the form and, thereafter, submitted forms that were blank on the back.

In August 1995, DeLage severed three of his fingers while operating a radial arm saw. DeLage received $75,000 in workers' compensation benefits from Connection. Connection then asked Universal to indemnify it pursuant to the language on the back of the verification form. Universal refused to pay, and Connection sued Universal for breach of contract. The trial court granted Universal's motion for a directed verdict. Connection appealed.

The Minnesota Court of Appeals held that Von Bank and Kohout had no actual or apparent authority to bind Universal to the indemnification clause. The court then considered whether Universal had ratified the indemnification clause by accepting the benefits of the employment contract for DeLage's labors.

Halbrooks, Judge

Connection contends that Universal agreed to be liable for workers' compensation costs based on a theory of ratification. Ratification occurs when a principal retains the benefits of an agent's unauthorized act. Once the principal has received the benefit, it is estopped from disclaiming liability based on the fact that the act was unauthorized. Connection contends that because Universal received the benefit of the temporary worker's labor, it also accepted the associated burden of the indemnification clause on the back of the verification form.

This argument is not viable. Ratification does not occur if the principal is ignorant of material facts surrounding the transaction. Ratification by a party of another's unauthorized acts occurs where the party with full knowledge of all material facts confirms, approves, or sanctions the other's acts. Where a principal accepts and retains the benefits of an unauthorized act of an agent with full knowledge of all the facts he thereby ratifies the act.

Here Universal lacked knowledge of a material fact: that the original timecards that Kohout signed contained language committing Universal to indemnify Connection for a workers' compensation claim. Given that Universal lacked full information regarding Kohout's actions, it did not ratify her conduct.

Judgment for Universal affirmed.

Contracts Made by Subagents

The rules governing a principal's liability for her agent's contracts generally apply to contracts made by her subagents. If an agent has authorized his subagent to make a certain contract and this authorization is within the authority granted the agent by his principal, the principal is bound to the subagent's contract.

Also, a subagent contracting within the authority conferred by her principal (the agent) binds the *agent* in an appropriate case. In addition, both the principal and the agent probably can ratify the contracts of subagents.

LOG ON

www.lexmercatoria.net/international.economic .law/itl

European Union Agency Law

Lex Mercatoria, the international trade and commercial law monitor, posts online the law of agency of the European Union. Go to the URL above and you'll find links for both "Agency" and "Contract Principles." Follow the "Agency" link to the "Unidroit Convention on Agency in the International Sale of Goods (1983)." Follow the "Contract Principles" link to view the "Principles of European Contract Law." Chapter 3 covers agent's authority.

Contract Liability of the Agent

When are *agents* liable on contracts they make on their principals' behalf? For the most part, this question depends on a different set of variables than those determining the principal's liability. The most important of these variables is the *nature of the principal*. Thus, this section first examines the liability of agents who contract for several different kinds of principals. Then it discusses two ways that an agent can be bound after contracting for any type of principal.

The Nature of the Principal

Disclosed Principal A principal is **disclosed** if a third party knows or has reason to know (1) that the agent is acting for a principal, and (2) the principal's identity. Unless he agrees otherwise, an agent who represents a disclosed principal is *not liable* on authorized contracts made for such a principal. Suppose that Adkins, a sales agent for Google, calls on Toyota and presents a business card clearly identifying her as Google's agent. If Adkins contracts to sell Google's advertising space to Toyota with authority to do so, Adkins is not bound because Google is a disclosed principal. This rule usually is consistent with the third party's intention to contract only with the principal.

Unidentified Principal A principal is **unidentified** or **partially disclosed** if the third party (1) knows or has reason to know that the agent is acting for *a* principal, but (2) lacks knowledge or reason to know the principal's *identity*. This can occur when an agent simply neglects to disclose his principal's identity. Also, a principal may tell her agent to keep her identity secret to preserve her bargaining position, such as when a national retailer tries to buy land on which to build a large store.

Among the factors affecting anyone's decision to contract are the integrity, reliability, and creditworthiness of the other party to the contract. When the principal is unidentified or partially disclosed, the third party ordinarily cannot judge these matters. As a result, he usually depends on the agent's reliability to some degree. For this reason, and to give the third party additional protection, an agent is liable on contracts made for an unidentified or partially disclosed principal unless the agent and the third party agree otherwise.

Undisclosed Principal A principal is **undisclosed** when the third party lacks knowledge or reason to know both the principal's existence *and* the principal's identity. This can occur when a principal judges that he will get a better deal if his existence and identity remain secret, or when the agent neglects to make adequate disclosure.

A third party who deals with an agent for an undisclosed principal obviously cannot assess the principal's reliability, integrity, and creditworthiness. Indeed, here the third party reasonably believes that the *agent* is the other party to the contract. Thus, the third party may hold an agent liable on contracts made for an undisclosed principal.

The undisclosed principal is also a party to the contract. The third party may not usually refuse to perform the contract merely because the principal was undisclosed, unless the contract excluded the possibility of an undisclosed principal.

Nonexistent Principal Unless there is an agreement to the contrary, an agent who purports to act for a **legally nonexistent** principal, such as an unincorporated association, is personally liable when the agent knows or has reason to know the principal does not exist. This is true even when the third party knows that the principal is nonexistent. See Chapter 42 for a more detailed discussion of the liability of those who transact on behalf of nonexistent corporations.

In the *Treadwell* case that follows, the court found that an agent acted for an unidentified principal when he disclosed he was transacting for a corporation, but gave the wrong corporate name to the third party with whom he transacted.

Treadwell v. J.D. Construction Co.   938 A.2d 794 (Me. Sup. Jud. Ct. 2007)

In the early 1990s, Jesse Derr created a corporation, JCDER, Inc., to operate his construction business. At some point, Derr began referring to the corporation as J.D. Construction Co., Inc., but no corporation by that name was ever created. JCDER, Inc., remained the official name for purposes of organization and filing with Maine's Secretary of State. Derr never filed with the Secretary of State a statement of intention to do business under the assumed name J.D. Construction Co., Inc.

In 2003, when Leah and William Treadwell decided to build a home, they were referred to Derr. The Treadwells brought their home plans to Derr's office to get a quote and left them with an employee, Jane Veinot. They did not meet with Derr, but received a quote from him in the mail. Soon after, the Treadwells signed a contract with J.D. Construction, with work to start in May 2003. Derr signed the contract, and his signature appeared on the contract as follows:

J.D. Construction Co., Inc.
By: Jesse Derr

The name JCDER, Inc., was nowhere in the contract, and the Treadwells were unaware of the existence of JCDER, Inc., when they signed the agreement. None of the documents the Treadwells received from J.D. Construction indicated that the company's real name was JCDER, Inc.

Mr. Treadwell testified that he spoke with Derr twice at the worksite, just as they were breaking ground. The Treadwells, who visited the site almost daily, never saw Derr again, even though they tried many times to contact him. They spoke to Veinot often, but she would tell them that Derr was at another construction site. Derr had hired subcontractors to do the work on the Treadwells' property. Around Thanksgiving 2003, the Treadwells visited the site and found that Derr had abandoned the job with the house unfinished because the company was not making any money on the job. The Treadwells had paid Derr approximately $91,000 before construction halted.

The Treadwells found many problems with the structure, including twisted studs and other lumber that had to be replaced. The Treadwells hired new contractors to fix and finish the project, for which they paid a significant sum.

To recover the additional costs, the Treadwells sued J.D. Construction Co., JCDER, Inc., and Derr for breach of contract and other grounds. The trial court awarded the Treadwells damages against J.D. Construction Co., Inc., and JCDER, Inc., but found that Derr was not personally liable for the damages. The Treadwells appealed to the Supreme Judicial Court of Maine, asking that Derr also be held liable.

Alexander, Judge

The Treadwells argue that the trial court should have awarded damages against Derr individually since he signed the contract for a non-existent corporation. In the alternative, they contend that the trial court should have pierced the corporate veil and held Derr responsible because he failed to disclose the existence of JCDER, Inc.

The question presented to us is whether, as a matter of law, an individual who signs a contract, purporting to act on behalf of a corporate entity that he knows does not exist, becomes personally liable for damages arising from failure to properly perform under that contract.

An agent who makes a contract for an undisclosed principal or a partially disclosed principal will be liable as a party to the contract. In order for an agent to avoid personal liability on a contract negotiated in his principal's behalf, he must disclose not only that he is an agent but also the identity of the principal. The term "partially disclosed" principal is synonymous with "unidentified" principal. *Restatement (Third) of Agency,* § 1.04 comment b (2006). "A principal is unidentified if, when an agent and a third party interact, the third party has notice that the agent is acting for a principal but does not have notice of the principal's identity." *Restatement (Third) of Agency,* § 1.04(2)(c) (2006). To avoid liability for the agent, the third party must have *actual* knowledge of the identity of the principal, and does not have a duty to investigate.

In *Maine Farmers Exch. v. McGillicuddy,* 697 A.2d 1266 (Me. 1996), the son of a potato seller signed a contract with a distributor for a certain grade potato. The father/seller furnished the potatoes, which turned out to be the wrong grade. In an action by the distributor against the father and son, the trial court found them to be jointly and severally liable. They appealed the finding of joint and several liability, arguing that the distributor should have been aware that the son was acting as an agent for his father. We affirmed that finding because the son did not disclose that he was an agent for his father, and the distributor believed he was buying potatoes from the son.

In the present case, Derr organized a corporation called JCDER, Inc., which he used to operate his construction business. Both Derr and JCDER, Inc., acted under the assumed name J.D. Construction Co., Inc., Derr signed the contract on behalf of J.D. Construction, hired the subcontractors, and was purported to be the contact-person for the project, although he was not available to the Treadwells. Derr's use of an assumed trade name was not sufficient to disclose his agency relationship with JCDER, Inc. JCDER, Inc., was therefore an unidentified or partially disclosed principal. As a matter of law, Derr is personally liable for performance of contracts entered into as agent for the non-existent J.D. Construction, Co., Inc., or the undisclosed principal JCDER, Inc.

Judgment reversed in favor of the Treadwells.

Liability of Agent by Agreement

An agent may bind herself to contracts she makes for a principal by *expressly agreeing* to be liable. This is true regardless of the principal's nature. An agent may expressly bind herself by (1) making the contract in her own name rather than in the principal's name, (2) joining the principal as an obligor on the contract, or (3) acting as surety or guarantor for the principal.

Problems of contract interpretation can arise when it is claimed that an agent has expressly promised to be bound. The two most important factors affecting the agent's liability are the wording of the contract and the way the agent has signed it. An agent who wishes to avoid liability should make no express promises in her own name and should try to ensure that the agreement obligates only the principal. In addition, the agent should use a signature form that clearly identifies the principal and indicates the agent's representative capacity—for example, "Parker, by Adkins," or "Adkins, for Parker." Simply adding the word "agent" when signing her name ("Adkins, Agent") or signing without any indication of her status ("Adkins") could subject the agent to liability. Sometimes, the body of the contract suggests one result and the signature form another. In such contexts, oral evidence or other extrinsic evidence of the parties' understanding may help resolve the uncertainty.

Implied Warranty of Authority

An agent also may be liable to a third party if he contracts for a legally existing and competent principal while lacking authority to do so. Here, the principal is not bound on the contract. Yet it is arguably unfair to leave the third party without any recovery. Thus, an agent normally is bound on the theory that he made an implied warranty of his authority to contract. This liability exists regardless of whether the agent is otherwise bound to the third party.

To illustrate, suppose that Allen is a salesman for Prine, a seller of furs. Allen has actual authority to receive offers for the sale of Prine's furs but not to make sale contracts, which must be approved by Prine himself. Prine has long followed this practice, and it is customary in the markets where his agents work. Representing himself as Prine's agent but saying nothing about his authority, Allen contracts to sell Prine's furs to Thatcher on Prine's behalf. Thatcher, who should have known better, honestly believes that Allen has authority to contract to sell Prine's furs. Prine is not liable on Allen's contract because Allen lacked actual or apparent authority to bind him. But Allen is liable to Thatcher for breaching his implied warranty of authority.

However, an agent is *not* liable for making an unauthorized contract if any of the following applies:

1. The third party *actually knows* that the agent lacks authority. Note from the previous example, however, that the agent still is liable where the third party merely had *reason to know* that authority was lacking.

2. The principal subsequently *ratifies* the contract. Here, the principal is bound, and there is no reason to bind the agent.

3. The agent adequately *notifies* the third party that he does not warrant his authority to contract.

In the following *Interbank Funding* case, the court found the president of a dissolved corporation liable for breaching the agent's implied warranty of authority.

In re Interbank Funding Corp. v. Chadmoore Wireless Group Inc.
2007 Bankr. LEXIS 3422 (Bank. Ct. S.D.N.Y. 2007)

Chadmoore Wireless Group was a Colorado corporation that sold substantially all of its assets to another company in early 2002. It was dissolved under Colorado law on February 23, 2002. Following Chadmoore's dissolution, there were only three remaining members on its board of directors. Robert Moore was president, CEO, and a director of the Chadmoore Board.

Purporting to act on behalf of Chadmoore, Moore signed the "Chadmoore Put," by which Chadmoore guaranteed the payment of the purchase price for the sale of US Mills, Inc., to Sunset Brands, Inc. The value of the Chadmoore Put was $2,500,000. One beneficiary of the Chadmoore Put was Fund LLC. The Chadmoore Put included a representation that Chadmoore had "full power, right and authority" to execute, deliver, and perform under the Chadmoore Put; that the execution, delivery, and performance by Chadmoore under the Chadmoore Put was "duly and validly authorized by all necessary actions on the part of Chadmoore" and would not conflict with Chadmoore's corporate formation documents or any applicable law; and that no further approvals, consents, or other actions by Chadmoore or any other person or entity were required. The Chadmoore Put included a representation that Moore was authorized to execute and deliver the Chadmoore Put, that Moore had obtained all required approvals, and that the Chadmoore Put was a binding obligation on Chadmoore.

Moore signed the Chadmoore Put on Chadmoore's behalf without approval of Chadmoore's board of directors. When Moore executed the Chadmoore Put, he inserted by hand the term "President" on the title line of the Chadmoore Put. Moore admits that he signed the Chadmoore Put intending that it would not be enforceable against Chadmoore. Moore concedes that he signed the Chadmoore Put to protect his friend, Todd Sanders, who allegedly led Moore to believe he would have serious financial difficulty and possibly be subject to physical harm if Moore did not sign the Chadmoore Put.

After the Chadmoore Put matured in November 2006, Fund LLC demanded that Chadmoore perform. Chadmoore refused to honor the Chadmoore Put and claimed that the two directors other than Moore had no prior knowledge of the Chadmoore Put. Fund LLC moved for summary judgment, asking the bankruptcy court to award it damages on the grounds that Moore breached an agent's implied warranty of authority.

Lifland, Judge

An action may lie in breach of implied warranty of authority when an agent executes an agreement purportedly on behalf of a principal; without authority from the principal; and damages result. The *Restatement of Agency* provides,

A person who purports to make a contract, representation, or conveyance to or with a third party on behalf of another person, lacking power to bind that person, gives an implied warranty of authority to the third party and is subject to liability to the third party for damages for loss caused by breach of that warranty, including loss of the benefit expected from performance by the principal.

Restatement (Third) of Agency, § 6.10 (2006). New York courts recognize that a purported agent who signs a contract on behalf of his principal makes an implied warranty of authority to the other party to the contract.

Moore acknowledged that he signed the Chadmoore Put as President of Chadmoore and that he knew he did not have authority from the Board of Directors of Chadmoore at the time he executed the Chadmoore Put. In fact, Moore indicated that he signed the Chadmoore Put intending that it would never be enforceable. Yet he did sign the Chadmoore Put, and all of its accompanying representations and warranties.

Moore cites cases holding that an agent can only be held liable for contracts signed without authority to the extent the contract would have been enforceable against the principal but for the lack of authority of the agent. However, New York courts have specifically ruled that in the case of agents executing contracts on behalf of dissolved corporations, those agents are personally liable for the contracts. Fund LLC's motion for summary judgment on implied warranty of authority is granted. There are simply no facts asserted by Moore that would lead to a different result. Moore does not deny that he signed the Chadmoore Put as President of Chadmoore without actually having authority to do so. Moore does not deny that as a result of his signing the Chadmoore Put, Chadmoore defaulted on its obligation on the Chadmoore Put.

The damages resulting from Moore's breach of the implied warranty of authority include the third-party financial accommodations owed under the Chadmoore Put and all injury resulting from his want of power, including the costs of an unsuccessful action against the alleged principal.

Summary judgment granted in favor of Fund LLC.

Figure 1   *Liability of Principal and Agent: The Major Possibilities*

Principal	Agent's Authority		
	Actual	Apparent	None
Disclosed	P liable on the contract; A not liable on the contract unless agrees to be liable	P liable on the contract; A not liable on the contract unless agrees to be liable	P not liable on the contract; A usually liable for breach of the implied warranty of authority
Unidentified (Partially Disclosed)	P liable on the contract; A liable on the contract	P liable on the contract; A liable on the contract	P not liable on the contract; A liable on the contract or for breach of the implied warranty of authority
Undisclosed	P liable on the contract; A liable on the contract	Impossible	P not liable on the contract; A liable on the contract

Tort Liability of the Principal

Besides contracting on the principal's behalf, an agent may also commit torts while acting for the principal. A principal's liability for an agent's torts may be found on any one or more of four bases.

Respondeat Superior* Liability**   Under the doctrine of ***respondeat superior (let the master answer), a principal who is an **employer** is liable for torts committed by agents (1) who are **employees** and (2) who commit the tort while acting within the **scope of their employment.** *Respondeat superior* makes the principal liable both for an employee's negligence and for her intentional torts. Chapter 35 outlined the main factors courts consider when determining whether an agent is an employee. The most important of these factors is a principal's right to control the manner and means of an agent's performance of work.

Respondeat superior is a rule of *imputed* or *vicarious* liability because it bases an employer's liability on her relationship with the employee rather than her own fault.

This imputation of liability reflects the following beliefs: (1) that the economic burdens of employee torts can best be borne by employers; (2) that employers often can protect themselves against such burdens by self-insuring or purchasing insurance; and (3) that the resulting costs frequently can be passed on to consumers, thus "socializing" the economic risk posed by employee torts. *Respondeat superior* also motivates employers to ensure that their employees avoid tortious behavior. Because they typically control the physical details of the work, employers are fairly well positioned to do so.

Scope of Employment *Respondeat superior*'s scope-of-employment requirement has been stated in many ways and is notoriously ambiguous. Some courts considering this question asked whether the employee was on a "frolic" of his own, or merely made a "detour" from his assigned activity. According to the *Restatement,* an employee's conduct is within the scope of his employment if it meets each of the following four tests:

1. It was of the *kind* that the employee was employed to perform. To meet this test, an employee's conduct need only be of the same general nature as work expressly authorized or be incidental to its performance.

2. It occurred substantially within the authorized *time* period. This is simply the employee's assigned time of work. Beyond this, there is an extra period of time during which the employment may continue. For instance, a security guard whose regular quitting time is 5:00 probably meets the time test if he unjustifiably injures an intruder at 5:15. Doing the same thing three hours later, however, would probably put the guard outside the scope of employment.

3. It occurred substantially within the *location* authorized by the employer. This includes locations not unreasonably distant from the authorized location. For example, a salesperson told to limit her activities to New York City probably would satisfy the location requirement while pursuing the employer's business in New Rochelle just north of the city limits but not while pursuing the same business in Philadelphia. Generally, the smaller the authorized area of activity, the smaller the departure from that area needed to put the employee outside the scope of employment. For example, consider the different physical distance limitations that should apply to a factory worker assigned to a single building and a traveling salesperson assigned to a five-state territory.

4. It was motivated *at least in part* by the *purpose* of serving the employer. This test is met when the employee's conduct was motivated *to any appreciable extent* by the desire to serve the employer. Thus, an employee's tort may be within the scope of employment even if the motives for committing it were partly personal. For example, suppose that a delivery employee is behind schedule and for that reason has an accident while speeding to make a delivery in his employer's truck. The employee would be within the scope of employment even if another reason for his speeding was to finish work quickly so he could watch his daughter's soccer game.

Direct Liability A principal's **direct liability** for an agent's torts differs considerably from *respondeat superior* liability. Here, the principal himself is at fault, and there is no need to impute liability to him. Also, no scope-of-employment requirement exists in direct liability cases, and the agent need not be an employee. Of course, a principal might incur both direct liability and *respondeat superior* liability in cases where due to the principal's fault, an employee commits a tort within the scope of her employment.

Ethics in Action

Principal's Liability for Agent's Torts

We have covered the reasons the law makes employers liable for the torts of employees under *respondeat superior,* including the ability of employers to bear the burden or to socialize the cost of paying for damages caused by an employee's tort.

- Do you think those are good reasons to make someone liable for the actions of another person? What kind of behavior is the rule of *respondeat superior* likely to foster? Does the rule encourage employers to train and supervise their employees better?

- Do you think *respondeat superior* makes employers liable for too many acts of their employees? Does the rule discourage some businesses from using employees? Does any discouragement affect both prospective employers and prospective employees?

- Do you think the law should make employers liable for all the torts of their employees?

- Do you think it is right for an employer to pay for all damages caused to others by the tort of an employee? When forming your answers, consider the ethical theories we covered in Chapter 4.

A principal is directly liable for an agent's tortious conduct if the agent acts within her actual authority or the principal ratifies the agent's conduct. Usually this means the principal directs the agent's conduct and intends that it occur. In such cases, the *agent's* behavior might be intentional, reckless, or negligent. For instance if Lawn Mower Company directs its agent Agnew to sell defective lawn mowers to Landscape Company, Lawn Mower Company is directly liable to Landscape Company. Likewise, Procenture Consulting Company would be liable for harm to clients caused by its ordering its consulting employees to complete an engagement in an unreasonable, substandard manner.

The typical direct liability case, however, involves harm caused by the principal's negligence regarding the agent. Examples of direct liability for negligence include (1) giving the agent improper or unclear instructions;

LOG ON

www.toolkit.com

The CCH Business Owners Toolkit is a font of information on managing the liability of employers for the acts of employees. One article, "Negligent Hiring or Supervision," gives advice on how an employer may avoid vicarious and direct liability for the torts of employees.

(2) failing to make and enforce appropriate regulations to govern the agent's conduct; (3) hiring an unsuitable agent; (4) failing to discharge an unsuitable agent; (5) furnishing an agent with improper tools, instruments, or materials; and (6) carelessly supervising an agent. Today, suits for negligent hiring are common.

The next case, *Millan,* covers both direct liability and *respondeat superior.*

Millan v. Dean Witter Reynolds, Inc.   90 S.W. 3d 760 (Tex. Ct. App 2002)

Maria Millan opened two brokerage accounts at Dean Witter Reynolds, Inc. One was for herself and the other for her as trustee for her son James. The broker for both accounts was her other son Miguel, an employee of Dean Witter. Over the course of the next three years, Miguel systematically looted his mother's account, ultimately stealing from her more than $287,000. He managed to do this by forging her signature on an account application form and opening an additional account in her name. This account had check-writing privileges and a credit card attached to it that Miguel used liberally. Dean Witter did not verify Millan's signature, as its policy required, when the bogus account was opened.

Miguel took his mother's periodic deposits, usually consisting of several thousand dollars, deposited these checks into this fictitious account, and wrote himself checks from the account, usually made out to "cash." Miguel covered his tracks by opening a post office box, filing a false change of address form on which he forged his mother's signature, and creating false account statements purporting to be from Dean Witter. In one instance, Miguel forged a check he stole from his mother's checkbook and made it payable to "cash" in the amount of $35,000. Disregarding Dean Witter written policy, a Dean Witter supervisor did not verify the check despite the high amount, the payment to "cash," and the concerns of a Dean Witter employee who first handled the check.

Millan sued her son and Dean Witter for unauthorized transactions, negligence, and gross negligence. The trial court directed a verdict for Dean Witter on the issues of vicarious liability. The jury was given the issue regarding Dean Witter's direct liability to Millan, and it found Dean Witter negligent and liable for 15 percent of her damages. Millan was found responsible for 85 percent of her damages on the grounds that she should have discovered the fraud earlier than she did. Millan appealed the trial court's decision to a Texas court of appeals. The court of appeals upheld the jury verdict that Dean Witter was only 15 percent responsible for Millan's damages under direct liability. The court then considered the vicarious liability issue using the doctrine of respondeat superior.

Angelini, Justice

Under the doctrine of *respondeat superior,* an employer is vicariously liable for the negligence of an agent or employee acting within the scope of his or her agency or employment. To determine whether an employee's acts are within the scope of his or her employment, we ask whether the employee's actions fall within the scope of the employee's general authority, are in furtherance of the employer's business, and are for the accom-

plishment of the object for which the employee was hired. In cases involving serious criminal activity, an employer is not liable for intentional and malicious acts that are unforeseeable considering the employee's duties. Our inquiry, therefore, must first focus on the scope of Miguel's general authority.

Miguel, in the course and scope of his employment for Dean Witter opened a brokerage account for his mother. It was within Miguel's general authority to open such accounts for clients, receive deposits to these accounts, and purchase and sell securities as directed by clients. Miguel's activities, however, went far beyond these general brokerage duties. Miguel greatly exceeded the scope of his authority when, through a litany of deceitful acts, he stole money from his mother. Those acts include stealing checks from his mother's bathroom drawer, writing checks on his mother's account, depositing his mother's checks into his own account, forging his mother's signature on numerous occasions, stealing statements from his mother's mailbox, creating and sending bogus statements to his mother, and opening a post office box so he could receive his mother's actual statements. These acts were not related to Miguel's duties and were not within his general scope of authority as a broker for Dean Witter.

We hold there was no evidence that Miguel acted within the scope of his authority as a broker at Dean Witter. Accordingly, there is no evidence to support the submission of the issue of Dean Witter's vicarious liability for fraud to the jury.

Judgment in favor of Dean Witter affirmed.

Liability for Torts of Independent Contractors

A principal ordinarily is *not* liable for torts committed by **independent contractors.** As compared with employees, independent contractors are more likely to have the size and resources to insure against tort liability and to pass on the resulting costs themselves. Sometimes, therefore, the risk still can be socialized if only the independent contractor is held responsible. Because the principal does not control the manner in which an independent contractor's work is performed, moreover, he has less ability to prevent a contractor's torts than an employer has to prevent an employee's torts. Thus, imposing liability on principals for the torts of independent contractors may do little to eliminate the contractor's torts.

However, the rule that principals are not liable for torts committed by independent contractors has exceptions. For example:

1. A principal can be *directly* liable for tortious behavior connected with the retention of an independent contractor. One example is the hiring of a dangerously incompetent independent contractor.

2. A principal is liable for harm resulting from the independent contractor's failure to perform a *nondelegable duty.* A nondelegable duty is a duty whose proper performance is so important that a principal cannot avoid liability by contracting it away. Examples include a carrier's duty to transport its passengers safely, a municipality's duty to keep its streets in repair, a railroad's duty to maintain safe crossings, and a landlord's duties to make repairs and to use care in doing so. Thus, a landlord who retains an independent contractor to repair the stairs in an apartment building is liable for injuries caused by the contractor's failure to repair the stairs properly.

3. A principal is liable for an independent contractor's negligent failure to take the special precautions needed to conduct certain *highly dangerous* or *inherently dangerous* activities. Examples of such activities include excavations in publicly traveled areas, the clearing of land by fire, the construction of a dam, and the demolition of a building. For example, a contractor engaged in demolishing a building presumably has duties to warn pedestrians and to keep them at a safe distance. If injury results from the independent contractor's failure to meet these duties, the principal is liable.

Liability for Agent's Misrepresentations

Special rules apply when a third party sues a principal for **misrepresentations** made by her agent. In most cases where the principal is liable under these rules, the third party can elect to recover in tort, or to rescind the transaction.

A principal is *directly* liable for misrepresentations made by her agent during authorized transactions if she *intended* that the agent make the misrepresentations. In some states, a principal also may be directly liable if she *negligently* allows the agent to make misrepresentations. Even where a principal is not directly at fault, she may be liable for an agent's misrepresentations if the agent had *actual or apparent authority to make true statements on the subject.* Suppose that an agent authorized to sell farmland falsely states that a stream on the land has never flooded the property when in fact it does so almost every year, and that this statement induces a third party to buy the land. The principal is directly liable if she intended that the agent make this false statement. Even if the principal is personally blameless, she is liable if the agent had actual or apparent authority to make true statements about the stream.

After contemplating their potential liability under the rules just discussed, both honest and dishonest principals may try to escape liability for an agent's misrepresentations by including an **exculpatory clause** in contracts the

An Outline of the Principal's Tort Liability

Respondeat Superior	1. Agent must be an employee, *and*
	2. Employee must act within scope of employment while committing the tort
Direct Liability	1. Principal intends and directs agent's intentional tort, recklessness, or negligence, *or*
	2. Principal is negligent regarding hiring or training of agent
Torts of Independent Contractors	1. Principal generally is *not* liable
	2. Exceptions exist for direct liability, highly dangerous activities, and nondelegable duties
Misrepresentation	1. Direct liability
	2. Vicarious liability when agent has authority to make true statements on the subject of the misrepresentation
	3. An exculpatory clause may eliminate the principal's tort liability, but the third party still can rescind the contract

agent makes with third parties. Such clauses typically state that the agent has authority only to make the representations contained in the contract and that only those representations bind the principal. Exculpatory clauses do not protect a principal who intends or expects that an agent will make false statements. Otherwise, though, they insulate the principal from *tort* liability if the agent misrepresents a material fact. But the third party still may rescind the transaction, because it would be unjust to let the principal benefit from the transaction while disclaiming responsibility for it.

Tort Liability of the Agent

Agents are usually liable for their own torts. Normally, they are not absolved from tort liability just because they acted at the principal's command. However, there are exceptions to this generalization.

1. An agent can escape liability if she is *exercising a privilege of the principal.* Suppose that Tingle grants Parkham a right-of-way to transport his farm products over a private road crossing Tingle's land. Parkham's agent Adams would not be liable in trespass for driving across Tingle's land to transport farm products if she did so at Parkham's command. However, an agent must not exceed the scope of the privilege and must act for the purpose for which the privilege was given. Thus, Adams would not be protected if she took her Jeep on a midnight joyride across Tingle's land. Also, the privilege given the agent must be delegable in the first place. If Tingle had given the easement to Parkham exclusively,

Adams would not be privileged to drive across Tingle's land.

2. A principal who is *privileged to take certain actions in defense of his person or property* may often authorize an agent to do the same. In such cases, the agent escapes liability if the principal could have done so. For example, a WalMart warehouse guard may use force to protect the property in WalMart's warehouse.

3. An agent who makes *misrepresentations* while conducting the principal's business is not liable in tort unless he either *knew or had reason to know* their falsity. Suppose Parker authorizes Arnold to sell his house, falsely telling Arnold that the house is fully insulated. Arnold does not know that the statement is false and could not discover its falsity through a reasonable inspection. If Arnold tells Thomas that the house is fully insulated and Thomas relies on this statement in purchasing the house, Parker is directly liable to Thomas, but Arnold is not liable.

4. An agent is not liable for injuries to third persons caused by *defective tools or instrumentalities* furnished by the principal unless the agent had actual knowledge or reason to know of the defect.

Tort Suits against Principal and Agent

Sometimes both principal and agent are liable for an agent's torts. Here, the parties are *jointly and severally* liable. This means that a third party may join the principal and the agent in one suit and get a judgment against each, or may sue either or both individually and get a judgment against either or both. However, once a third party actually collects in full from either the principal or the agent, no further recovery is possible.

In some cases, therefore, either the principal or the agent has to satisfy the judgment alone despite the other party's liability. Here, the other party sometimes is required to *indemnify* the party who has satisfied the judgment. As discussed in Chapter 35, for example, sometimes a principal is required to indemnify an agent for tort liability the agent incurs. On the other hand, some torts committed by agents may involve a breach of duty to their principal, and the principal may be able to recover from an agent on this basis.

LOG ON

www.ncaa.org

Agents and College Athletes

The National Collegiate Athletic Association (NCAA) is the largest organization regulating competition in intercollegiate athletics. One of the NCAA's objectives is to protect the amateur standing of college athletics. The NCAA Web site has links to state statutes that regulate contacts between agents and college athletes. Click on "Academics & Athletics"; then click "Eligibility and Recruiting." You will see a link for "Agents." Click on your state to find your state's laws. Note that if an agent causes a college athlete to lose his eligibility to participate in college athletics, the agent may have tort liability to the college and face criminal penalties as well.

Problems and Problem Cases

1. Jonas Bravario hires Suzanne Hermano, a securities broker, to manage his $700,000 portfolio of securities. When Bravario managed his own investments, his investment strategy was to own a large number of different companies, with no one company representing more than 5 percent of his total investments. Bravario also purchased all his investments for cash and did not borrow money to finance the purchase of any investment. Hermano is aware of Bravario's historical investment strategy, which Bravario informed Hermano that he wanted to continue in the future. Nonetheless, Hermano opts to purchase 1 million shares of Enron Corporation for $70,000. To finance the purchase, Hermano sells $40,000 of Bravario's current investments and borrows $30,000 from Wells Fargo Bank in the name of Bravario. The interest rate on the loan is 10 percent. When Bravario discovers the purchase and the loan, he attempts to repudiate both contracts. Is Bravario liable on the Enron purchase and loan contracts?

2. Kamitra Smith was a catering specialist for TLC Catering, a food service business. TLC's catering specialists were authorized to make catering contracts with customers and to serve food in compliance with those contacts. On behalf of TLC, Smith made a contract with Miller Clandon & Associates, a law firm, to cater a holiday party in Miller Clandon's office. Smith signed a contract that was drafted by Miller Clandon. The contract provided that TLC would be liable for all damages suffered by Miller Clandon and its staff in connection with TLC's performance of the contract. Smith and three other TLC employees catered the Miller Clandon party for TLC. One of Miller Clandon's staff attorneys slipped on coffee spilled by a TLC employee during the catered party. The attorney sued TLC, arguing that TLC was bound by the contact signed by Smith. Did Smith have express, implied, or apparent authority to sign the contact that imposed liability on TLC?

3. Harry Tighe opened an investment securities account with Legg Mason Wood Walker, Inc. Legg Mason could make no investments for Tighe's account without Tighe's authorization. When Tighe received his first monthly statement from Legg Mason, he saw that his broker had made an unauthorized $220,000 purchase of limited partnership units. Tighe called the broker and objected to the purchase. Later, the broker persuaded Tighe to hold the units to see how well the investment performed. Tighe decided to hold onto the units only because the broker told him that they were not readily marketable. In fact, the units were readily marketable. For more than two years, Tighe continued to invest in his Legg Mason account through the broker. He finally complained to a Legg Mason compliance officer, but even then did not revoke the purchase of the limited partnership units. Has Tighe ratified the broker's unauthorized purchase of the units?

4. Sally Leiner was the sole shareholder, director, and president of Ecco Bella, Inc., a New Jersey corporation. On various occasions, African Bio-Botanica, Inc., sold Leiner and/or Ecco Bella merchandise. African gave little thought to the party with whom it

was dealing. Initially, its records listed Sally Leiner as the customer; later, this was changed to Ecco Bella, but without any indication that Ecco Bella was a corporation. The checks with which Leiner paid for her orders and her firm's stationery bore the name Ecco Bella, but likewise did not indicate that the firm was a corporation.

Eventually, Leiner did not pay for a shipment from African, and African sued her personally for damages in a New Jersey trial court. Leiner's defense was that only the corporation, and not herself personally, was liable. Is Leiner correct?

5. A sales representative of Wired Music, Inc., sold Frank Pierson, president of the Great River Steamboat Company, a five-year Muzak Program Service for a riverboat and restaurant owned by Great River. Pierson signed a form contract drafted by Wired Music in the following manner:

By /s/ Frank C. Pierson, Pres.
Title

The Great River Steamboat Co.
~~Port of St. Louis Investment, Inc.~~
For the Corporation

In signing, Pierson crossed out "Port of St. Louis Investments, Inc.," which had been incorrectly listed as the name of the corporation, and inserted the proper name. The contract included the following clause arguably making Pierson a surety or guarantor for Great River: "The individual signing this agreement for the subscriber guarantees that all of the above provisions shall be complied with."

Great River made approximately four payments under the contract and then ceased to pay. Wired Music brought an action for contract damages against Pierson personally. Is Pierson liable?

6. Jerome Cohen was a youth counselor for Mellon Community Center (MCC). Needing paper supplies for a project he had planned for the youths he was counseling, Cohen went to a local Staples supplies store and selected $150 of paper goods. He paid for the goods with his personal credit card. He did not tell Staples that he was buying the paper goods for MCC. Cohen asked MCC to reimburse him for the cost of the paper goods, but it refused on the grounds that Cohen should have asked for permission in advance. Cohen then refused to pay the credit card bill for the paper purchase. He argued that since he bought the goods for MCC, only MCC was liable on the contract to buy the goods. Was Cohen right?

7. James Thurn and Deryl Hines incorporated their feedlot business as Hines & Thurn Feedlot, Inc., a corporation. The corporation made three livestock purchases from Zumbrota Livestock Auction Market totaling over $540,000. Zumbrota sent invoices addressed to "Thurn-Hines Lvstk" or "Thurn Hines Livst." The corporation paid for the livestock with three checks. Printed on each check was "Thurn-Hines Livestock, Hines-Thurn Feedlot, Inc., Box 555, Edgewood, IA 52042." The checks were signed by Jean Offerman, a corporation employee, but did not indicate the capacity in which Offerman signed. When the corporation stopped payment on the checks, Zumbrota sued Thurn and Hines individually for the amount of the livestock purchases, claiming that Thurn and Hines were agents for an undisclosed principal. Zumbrota's vice president argued that he knew the business only as "Thurn & Hines." Were Thurn and Hines liable to Zumbrota?

8. Mark Bradshaw, an agent for National Foundation Life Insurance Co. (NFLIC), tried to sell a health insurance policy to Bobby Reed. Bradshaw told Reed that his health insurance coverage would begin upon signing some forms and paying the first premium. On January 7, Reed signed but did not read the forms, which included language stating that Reed understood that Bradshaw could not change any NFLIC policy or make any policy effective, that the policy would not be effective until actually issued by NFLIC, and that it could take up to two weeks for Reed's application to be processed and the policy issued. NFLIC received Reed's application, including his payment for the first premium, on January 12. On January 19, NFLIC called Reed's home and was informed he had a heart attack on January 15. NFLIC declined to issue the policy to Reed. On what grounds did Reed sue Bradshaw? Was Reed's suit against Bradshaw successful?

9. Redford had been a backhoe operator for five years. Although he had worked for other sign companies, he had spent 90 percent of his time during the past three years working for Tube Art Display, Inc. Redford generally dug holes exactly as directed by the sign company employing him. He did, however, pay his own business taxes, and he did not participate in any of the fringe benefits available to Tube Art employees.

Tube Art obtained a permit to install a sign in the parking lot of a combination commercial and apartment building. Telling Redford how to proceed, Tube Art's service manager laid out the exact location of a

4 × 4 foot square on the asphalt surface with yellow paint and directed that the hole be 6 feet deep. After Redford began the job, he negligently struck a small natural gas pipeline with the backhoe. He examined the pipe, and, finding no indication of a leak or break, concluded that the line was not in use and left the worksite. Later, an explosion and fire occurred in the building serviced by the line. As a result, a business owned by Massey was destroyed. Massey sued Tube Art for Redford's negligence under the doctrine of *respondeat superior*. Will Massey recover?

10. LaVar Johnson was a retail representative for the Wheaton Company, a processor of consumer packaged goods like cereals and canned goods. Johnson's job was to visit grocery stores in his territory to ensure that each store gave adequate shelf space to all Wheaton products sold by the store. Wheaton told Johnson that maintaining good relations with the general manager and assistant manager of each store was essential. It was important, Wheaton told him, to accommodate the managers to ensure that Wheaton got the shelf space it wanted in each store.

While visiting a store in Springfield, Illinois, Johnson chatted for a few minutes with the manager, who got a phone call that his wife was in an auto accident while on her way to pick up the manager at the store. While the wife was not seriously injured, Johnson offered to take the manager to the scene of the accident, and the manager accepted. On the way to the accident scene, Johnson negligently ran a red light, resulting in his car being struck by another car. The grocery store manager received a broken leg, arm, and pelvis. Is Wheaton liable for the manager's injuries under the doctrine of *respondeat superior*?

11. Gary McCoy ordered a pizza from a Papa John's restaurant. The restaurant was owned by RWT, Inc., a franchisee of Papa John's International, Inc. RWT did business as Papa John's Pizza. Wendell Burke, an employee of RWT, Inc., delivered the pizza and obtained payment from McCoy at his place of business. Burke lingered for almost two hours after being paid, asking McCoy for a job and viewing a hunting videotape. When Burke returned to the Papa John's restaurant, to avoid criticism for being late he concocted the story that McCoy held him against his will. The police arrested McCoy for false imprisonment, which charges were eventually dropped. McCoy sued Burke, RWT, and Papa John's International for malicious prosecution based on Burke's false statements. Does the doctrine of *respondeat superior* impose liability on the franchisor, Papa John's International, in this case?

12. Tammy Bauer hires consulting firm Accent Pointe LLP to find a buyer for the formula and trade name of her pest repellent, NO BUGGZ. Bauer tells Accent Pointe to tell prospective buyers that NO BUGGZ is organic and has no health risks to humans. Bauer knows that NO BUGGZ has serious negative health effects on humans even when used as directed. Consequently, Accent Pointe tells Scotts Company that NO BUGGZ has no serious negative health risks to humans when used as directed. The written purchase contract that Scotts signs with Bauer does not represent that NO BUGGZ has no health risks to humans; the contract contains an exculpatory clause stating that Bauer is not bound by Accent Pointe's representations, unless they also appear in the written contract. Two years after Scotts buys NO BUGGZ, Scotts is subjected to consumer lawsuits claiming that NO BUGGZ is causing health problems for its users. Is Bauer liable to Scotts for misrepresentation?

Online Research

Workplace Violence Research Institute

The Workplace Violence Research Institute is a provider of workplace violence prevention programs. In part a response to employers' risk exposure due to violent employees, the Institute has resources that help an employer identify potentially dangerous employees.

- Find the Workplace Violence Research Institute Web site.
- Find the article by Steve Kaufer, "Corporate Liability: Sharing the Blame for Workplace Violence." Create a list of steps that an employer should take to protect its employees from violent fellow workers and thereby reduce the employer's risk of liability for the violent acts of employees.

Part Nine

Partnerships

chapter 37
Introduction to Forms of Business
and Formation of Partnerships

chapter 38
Operation of Partnerships
and Related Forms

chapter 39
Partners' Dissociation and
Partnerships' Dissolution
and Winding Up

chapter 40
Limited Liability Companies,
Limited Partnerships,
and Limited Liability
Limited Partnerships

INTRODUCTION TO FORMS OF BUSINESS AND FORMATION OF PARTNERSHIPS

After working for a large company for 10 years, you decide to give expression to your entrepreneurial urges and start a business. Your business plan is to help small firms that are struggling with finding ways to make new information technologies affordable and effective for their business. You envision that your business will need a capital infusion of $500,000 for the first year, during which you project the business will have a net loss of $200,000, which reflects in part your salary of $80,000. Beginning with the second year, you believe that the business will generate enough cash flow to finance internally all its normal capital expenditures. You expect second-year losses to be $100,000. Beginning with the third year, the business will be profitable.

You have $120,000 of savings that you are willing to invest in the business. You hope to obtain the remaining $380,000 of initial capital from investors. While you are willing to give a portion of the equity of the business to the investors, you want to control the business, including day-to-day operations. It is especially important that the other investors not be able to expel you from the business or its management.

- What business forms are best for your business?
- How will you modify the default rules of some business forms to make those forms work best for you?

IN THIS CHAPTER, YOU begin your study of business organizations. Early in this chapter, you will preview the basic characteristics of the most important forms of business and learn how to select an appropriate form for a business venture. Following that introduction, you will begin your in-depth study of partnerships, learning their characteristics and the formalities for their creation.

Choosing a Form of Business

One of the most important decisions made by a person beginning a business is choosing a **form of business.** This decision is important because the business owner's liability and control of the business vary greatly among the many forms of business. In addition, some business forms offer significant tax advantages to their owners.

Although other forms of business exist, usually a person starting a business will wish to organize the business as a sole proprietorship, partnership, limited liability partnership, limited partnership, limited liability limited partnership, corporation, or limited liability company.

Sole Proprietorship
A **sole proprietorship** has only one owner. The sole proprietorship is merely an extension of its only owner, the **sole proprietor.**

As the only owner, the sole proprietor has the right to make all the management decisions of the business. In addition, all the profits of the business are his. A sole proprietor assumes great liability: He is personally liable for all the obligations of the business. All the debts of the business, including debts on contracts signed only in the name of the business, are his debts. If the assets of the business are insufficient to pay the claims of its creditors, the creditors may require the sole proprietor to pay the claims using his individual, nonbusiness assets such as money from his bank account and the proceeds from the sale of his house. A sole proprietor may lose everything if his business becomes insolvent. Hence, the sole proprietorship is a risky form of business for its owner.

Despite this risk, there are two reasons why a person may organize a business as a sole proprietorship. First, the sole proprietorship is formed very easily and inexpensively. No formalities are necessary. Second, few people consider the business form decision. They merely begin their businesses. Thus, by default, a person going into business by herself automatically creates a sole proprietorship when she fails to choose another business form. These two reasons explain why the sole proprietorship is the most common form of business in the United States.

Because the sole proprietorship is merely an extension of its owner, it has no life apart from its owner. Therefore, while the business of a sole proprietorship may be freely sold to someone else, legally the sole proprietorship as a form of business cannot be transferred to another person. The buyer of the business must create his own form of business to continue the business.

A sole proprietorship is not a legal entity. It cannot sue or be sued. Instead, creditors must sue the owner. The sole proprietor—in his own name—must sue those who harm the business.

A sole proprietor may hire employees for the business, but they are employees of the sole proprietor. Under the law of agency, the sole proprietor is responsible for her employees' authorized contracts and for the torts they commit in the course of their employment. Also, a sole proprietorship is not a tax-paying entity for federal income tax purposes. All of the income of a sole proprietorship is income to its owner and must be reported on the sole proprietor's individual federal income tax return. Likewise, any business losses are deductible without limit on the sole proprietor's individual tax return. This loss-deduction advantage explains why some wealthier taxpayers use the sole proprietorship for selected business investments—when losses are expected in the early years of the business, yet the risk of liability is low. Such an investor may form a sole proprietorship and hire a professional manager to operate the business.

Many sole proprietorships have trade names. For example, Caryl Stanley may operate her bagel shop under the name Caryl's Bagel Shop. Caryl would be required to file the trade name under a state statute requiring the registration of fictitious business names. If she were sued by a creditor, the creditor would address his complaint to "Caryl Stanley, doing business as Caryl's Bagel Shop."

Partnership   A **partnership** has two or more owners, called **partners.** The partners have the right to make all the management decisions for the business. In addition, all the profits of the business are shared equally by the partners.

The partners assume personal liability for all the obligations of the business. All the debts of the business are the debts of all the partners. Likewise, partners are liable for the torts committed in the course of business by their partners or by partnership employees. If the assets of the business are insufficient to pay the claims of its creditors, the creditors may require one or more of the partners to pay the claims using their individual, nonbusiness assets. Thus, a partner may have to pay more than his share of partnership liabilities.

Like the sole proprietorship, the partnership is not a tax-paying entity for federal income tax purposes. All of the income of the partnership is income to its partners and must be reported on the individual partner's federal income tax return whether or not it is distributed to the partners. Likewise, any business losses are deductible without limit on the partner's individual tax return.

The partnership has a life apart from its owners. When a partner dies or otherwise leaves the business, the partnership usually continues. A partner's ownership interest in a partnership is not freely transferable: A purchaser of the partner's interest is not a partner of the partnership, unless the other partners agree to admit the purchaser as a partner.

Why would persons organize a business as a partnership? Formation of a partnership requires no formalities and may be formed by default. A partnership is created automatically when two or more persons own a business together without selecting another form. Also, each partner's right to manage the business and the deductibility of partnership losses on individual tax returns are attractive features.

Limited Liability Partnership   A limited liability partnership is a partnership whose partners have elected limited liability status. Reacting to the large personal liability sometimes imposed on accountants and lawyers for the professional malpractice of their partners, Texas enacted in 1991 the first statute permitting the formation of **limited liability partnerships (LLPs).** An LLP is identical to a partnership except that an LLP partner has no liability for most LLP obligations; however, an LLP partner retains unlimited liability for his *own* wrongful acts, such as his malpractice liability to a client.

LLP partners may elect to have the LLP taxed like a partnership or a corporation. If an LLP is taxed like a corporation, it pays federal income tax on its income, but the partners pay federal income tax only on the compensation paid and the partnership profits distributed to the partners.

The formation of an LLP requires filing a form with the secretary of state; some states require LLPs to maintain adequate professional insurance or have a high net worth.

The LLP is an especially good form of business for professionals such as consultants and auditors, allowing them management flexibility while insulating them mostly from personal liability. The LLP is the preferred form of business for professionals.

Limited Partnership A **limited partnership**

has one or more general partners and one or more limited partners. General partners have rights and liabilities similar to partners in a partnership. They manage the business of the limited partnership and have unlimited liability for the obligations of the limited partnership. Typically, however, the only general partner is a corporation, thereby protecting the human managers from unlimited liability.

Limited partners usually have no liability for the obligations of the limited partnership once they have paid their capital contributions to the limited partnership. Limited partners have no right to manage the business, but if they do manage, they nonetheless retain their limited liability.

Like an LLP, a limited partnership may elect to be taxed either as a partnership or as a corporation. If a limited partnership is taxed like a partnership, general partners report their shares of the limited partnership's income and losses on their individual federal income tax returns. For general partners, losses of the business are deductible without limit. A limited partner must pay federal income tax on his share of the profits of the business, but he may deduct his share of losses only to the extent of his investment in the business. As a passive investor, a limited partner may use the losses only to offset income from other passive investments.

If a limited partnership is taxed like a corporation, the limited partnership pays federal income tax on its net income. The partners pay federal income tax only on compensation paid and profits distributed to them.

A limited partnership may have a life apart from its owners. When a limited partner dies or otherwise leaves the business, the limited partnership is not dissolved. When a general partner dies or withdraws, however, the limited partnership may be dissolved if there is no remaining general partner. A general or limited partner's rights may not be wholly transferred to another person unless the other partners agree to admit the new person as a partner.

Unlike a sole proprietorship or partnership—but like an LLP—a limited partnership may be created only by complying with a state statute permitting limited partnerships. Thus, no limited partnership may be created by default.

There are three main reasons why persons organize a business as a limited partnership. First, by using a corporate general partner, no human will have unlimited liability for the debts of the business. Second, if the limited partnership is taxed like a partnership, losses of the business are deductible on the owners' federal income tax returns. Third, investors may contribute capital to the business yet avoid unlimited liability and the obligation to manage the business. Thus, the limited partnership has the ability to attract large amounts of capital, much more than the sole proprietorship, which has only one owner, or the partnership, whose partners' fear of unlimited liability restricts the size of the business. Hence, for a business needing millions of dollars of capital, wanting only a few owners to manage the business, and expecting to lose money in its early years, the limited partnership is a particularly good form of business.

Limited Liability Limited Partnership A **limited liability limited partnership (LLLP)** is a limited partnership whose partners have elected limited liability status for all the partners. An LLLP is created by making a filing with the secretary of state. The LLLP is designed to give the same limited liability advantages to general partners in a limited partnership as have been granted to partners who manage an LLP or a limited liability company (LLC). The LLC is explained below.

The LLLP is identical to a limited partnership in its management and the rights and duties of its partners. However, by electing LLLP status, both the limited partners and the general partners in a limited partnership will have no liability for most obligations of the LLLP. Nonetheless, a general partner will have unlimited liability for any torts he commits while acting for the LLLP.

Corporation A **corporation** is owned by shareholders who elect a board of directors to manage the business. The board of directors often selects officers to run the day-to-day affairs of the business. Consequently, ownership and management of a corporation may be completely separate: No shareholder has the right to manage, and no officer or director needs to be a shareholder.

Shareholders have limited liability for the obligations of the corporation, even if a shareholder is elected as a director or selected as an officer. Directors and officers have no liability for the contracts they or the corporation's employees sign only in the name of the corporation. While managers have liability for their own misconduct, they have no liability for corporate torts committed by other corporate managers or employees. Therefore, shareholders, officers, and directors have limited liability for the obligations of the business.

The usual corporation is a tax-paying entity for federal income tax purposes. The corporation pays taxes on its profits. Shareholders do not report their shares of corporation profits on their individual federal income tax returns. Instead, only when the corporation distributes its profits to the shareholders in the form of dividends or the shareholders sell their investments at a profit do the shareholders report income on their individual returns. This creates a double-tax possibility, as profits are taxed once at the corporation level and again at the shareholder level when dividends are paid.

Also, shareholders do not deduct corporate losses on their individual returns. They may, however, deduct their investment losses after they have sold their shares of the corporation.

There is one important exception to these corporate tax rules. The shareholders may elect to have the corporation and its shareholders taxed under Subchapter S of the Internal Revenue Code. By electing **S Corporation** status, the corporation and its shareholders are taxed nearly entirely like a partnership: Income and losses of the business are reported on the shareholders' individual federal income tax returns. A corporation electing S Corporation status may have no more than 100 shareholders, have only one class of shares, and be owned only by individuals and trusts.

A corporation has a life separate from its owners and its managers. When a shareholder or manager dies or otherwise leaves the business, the corporation is not dissolved. A shareholder may sell his shares of the corporation to other persons without limitation unless there is a contrary agreement. The purchaser becomes a shareholder with all the rights of the selling shareholder.

There are several reasons why persons organize a business as a corporation. First, no human has unlimited liability for the debts of the business. As a result, businesses in the riskiest industries—such as manufacturing—incorporate. Second, because investors may contribute capital to the business, avoid unlimited liability, escape the obligation to manage the business, and easily liquidate their investments by selling their shares, the corporation has the ability to attract large amounts of capital, even more than the limited partnership, or LLLP, whose partnership interests are not as freely transferable. Thus, the corporation has the capacity to raise the largest amount of capital.

The S Corporation has an additional advantage: Losses of the business are deductible on individual federal income tax returns. However, because the S Corporation is limited to 100 shareholders, its ability to raise capital is severely limited. Also, while legally permitted to sell their shares, S Corporation shareholders may be unable to find investors willing to buy their shares or may be restricted from selling their shares pursuant to an agreement between the shareholders.

Professional Corporation
All states permit professionals such as accountants, physicians, and dentists to incorporate their professional practices. The **professional corporation** is identical to a business corporation in most respects. It is formed only by a filing with the secretary of state, and it is managed by a board of directors, unless a statute permits it to be managed like a partnership. The rigid management structure makes the professional corporation inappropriate for some smaller professional practices.

While professional shareholders have no personal liability for the obligations of the professional corporation, such as a building lease, they retain unlimited liability to their clients for their professional malpractice. A professional will have no personal liability, however, for the malpractice of a fellow shareholder or associate.

Typically, only professionals holding the same type of license to practice a profession may be shareholders of a professional corporation. For example, only physicians licensed to practice medicine may be shareholders of a professional corporation that practices medicine.

Professional corporation shareholders may elect for the corporation to be taxed like a corporation, or they may elect S Corporation tax treatment.

Fewer and fewer professionals incorporate each year. All of the liability and taxation advantages of the professional corporation have been assumed by the LLP. In addition, most professionals like the flexible management structure of the LLP better.

Limited Liability Company
A **limited liability company** (LLC) is a business form intended to combine the nontax advantages of corporations with the favorable tax treatment of partnerships. An LLC is owned by members, who may manage the LLC themselves or elect the manager or managers who will operate the business. Members have limited liability for the obligations of the LLC.

All states except California permit professionals to organize as LLCs. Professionals in a professional LLC have unlimited liability, however, for their own malpractice. Like an LLP or LLLP, members of an LLC may elect to have the LLC taxed like a partnership or a corporation.

There is limited free transferability of the LLC members' ownership interests. Transfer of a membership interest entitles the transferee to receive only the member's distributions from the LLC, unless all members or the LLC agreement permits the transferee to become a member. The death, retirement, or bankruptcy of any member usually does not dissolve or cause the liquidation of the LLC.

What are the advantages of the LLC? The LLC has the limited liability advantage and, if manager-managed, the management advantage of the corporation. The LLC and its members may elect to receive federal tax treatment similar to the S Corporation and its shareholders,

yet the LLC has no limit on the number or type of owners, as does an S Corporation.

See Figure 1 for a summary of the general characteristics of business forms.

LOG ON

www.sba.gov/smallbusinessplanner/index.html
The Small Business Association has valuable resources for anyone starting a business. Under "Start Your Business" you will find a link to "Choose a Structure." Listed under "Forms of Ownership" is a section describing some forms of business and listing the tax forms necessary to those business forms.

The Global Business Environment

Globally, businesses have a wide choice of business forms, and many of them are forms shared by many countries. For example, the partnership is recognized not only in the United States but also in Australia, Canada, Cyprus, England, India, Israel, Russia, South Africa, Turkey, Zimbabwe, and many other nations. In the Chinese province of Hong Kong, the sole proprietorship, partnership, limited partnership, and company are the typical business forms. Limited liability partnerships and limited liability limited partnerships do not exist in Hong Kong as yet, or much of the world for that matter. Limited liability companies in Hong Kong are like American corporations.

German law recognizes the public stock corporation (*AG* or *Aktiengesellschaft*). Its shares are freely transferable like

those of American corporations, so it may have an unlimited number of shareholders. More common is the limited liability company (*GmbH* or *Gesellschaft mit beschrankter Haftung*), first created in 1892. It permits the owners to restrict the transfer of its shares. The majority of German subsidiaries of foreign corporations are *GmbHs* rather than *AGs*. Owners of *AGs* and *GmbHs* have liability limited to their capital contributions. The German general commercial partnership (*OHG* or *offene Handelsgesellschaft*) and the limited commercial partnership (*KG* or *Kommanditgesellschaft*) are essentially the same as the general and limited partnerships in the United States.

To find examples of forms of business in 60 countries, go to www.wikipedia.org/wiki/types_of_companies.

Ethics in Action

Two people who carefully consider which American business form to use for their business can achieve nearly any combination of attributes. For example, by choosing LLP status, they can limit their personal liability, totally control the business, and deduct business losses on their individual federal income tax returns. They can do the same with an LLC or S Corporation. They will have no liability for the contracts of the business, even though they make all business decisions and make all contracts for the business. When the business becomes profitable, they can elect to have the business form taxed like a

corporation, and if the corporate tax rate is lower than their individual tax rate, they will derive tax savings by retaining earnings in the business.

- Is it ethical for a business owner who controls the business to escape liability for the business's contracts and torts by hiding behind the veil of the business organization?
- Would you ever choose to use the partnership form when the LLP form is available?
- Is it ethical for a business owner to select a business form and elect a tax treatment that minimizes her tax liability?

Figure 1 General Characteristics of Forms of Business

	Sole Proprietorship	Partnership	Limited Liability Partnership	Limited Partnership	Limited Liability Limited Partnership	Corporation	S Corporation	Limited Liability Company
Formation	When one person owns a business without forming a corporation or LLC	By agreement of owners or by default when two or more owners conduct business together without creating another business form	By agreement of owners; must comply with limited liability partnership statute	By agreement of owners; must comply with limited partnership statute	By agreement of owners; must comply with limited liability limited partnership statute	By agreement of owners; must comply with corporation statute	By agreement of owners; must comply with corporation statute; must elect S Corporation status under Internal Revenue Code	By agreement of owners; must comply with limited liability company statute
Duration	Terminates on death or withdrawal of sole proprietor	Usually unaffected by death or withdrawal of partner	Usually unaffected by death or withdrawal of partner	Unaffected by death or withdrawal of partner, unless sole general partner dissociates	Unaffected by death or withdrawal of partner, unless sole general partner dissociates	Unaffected by death or withdrawal of shareholder	Unaffected by death or withdrawal of shareholder	Usually unaffected by death or withdrawal of member
Management	By sole proprietor	By partners	By partners	By general partners	By general partners	By board of directors	By board of directors	By members, unless choose to be manager-managed
Owner Liability	Unlimited	Unlimited	Limited to capital contribution, except for owner's individual torts	Unlimited for general partners; limited to capital contribution for limited partners	Limited to capital contribution, except for owner's individual torts	Limited to capital contribution, except for owner's individual torts	Limited to capital contribution, except for owner's individual torts	Limited to capital contribution, except for owner's individual torts
Transferability of Owners' Interest	None	Limited	Limited	Limited, unless agreed otherwise	Limited, unless agreed otherwise	Freely transferable, although shareholders may agree otherwise	Freely transferable, although shareholders usually agree otherwise	Limited, unless agreed otherwise
Federal Income Taxation	Only sole proprietor taxed	Only partners taxed	Usually only partners taxed; may elect to be taxed like a corporation	Usually only partners taxed; may elect to be taxed like a corporation	Usually only partners taxed; may elect to be taxed like a corporation	Corporation taxed; shareholders taxed on dividends (double tax)	Only shareholders taxed	Usually only members taxed; may elect to be taxed like a corporation

Partnerships

The basic concept of partnership is as ancient as the history of collective human activity. Partnerships were known in ancient Babylonia, ancient Greece, and the Roman Empire. Hammurabi's Code of 2300 B.C. regulated partnerships. The definition of a partnership in the 6th-century Justinian Code of the Roman Empire does not differ materially from that in our laws today. The partnership was likewise known in Asian countries, including China. During the Middle Ages, much trade between nations was carried on by partnerships.

By the close of the 17th century, the partnership was recognized in the English common law. When the United States became an independent nation and adopted the English common law in 1776, the English law of partnerships became a part of American law. In the early part of the 19th century, the partnership became the most important form of association in the United States.

Today, the American common law of partnership has been largely replaced by statutory law. Every state has a statute on partnership law. The Revised Uniform Partnership Act (RUPA) of 1994, with the 1997 amendments, is a model partnership statute that is the product of the National Conference of Commissioners on Uniform State Laws, a group of practicing lawyers, judges, and law professors. The aims of the RUPA are to codify partnership law in one document, to make that law more nearly consistent with itself, and to attain uniformity throughout the country.

In recent years, the RUPA has supplanted the Uniform Partnership Act (UPA) of 1914 as the dominant source of partnership law in the United States. As of October 2008, 36 states plus the District of Columbia, Puerto Rico, and the Virgin Islands have adopted the RUPA. The RUPA is the framework of your study of partnerships and limited liability partnerships. (See Figure 2.)

Creation of Partnership

No formalities are necessary to create a partnership. Two or more persons may become partners in accordance

---

Figure 2   *Principal Characteristics of Partnerships under the RUPA*

1. A partnership may be created with no formalities. Two or more people merely need to agree to own and conduct a business together in order to create a partnership.

2. Partners have unlimited liability for the obligations of the business.

3. Each partner, merely by being an owner of the business, has a right to manage the business of the partnership. He is an agent of the partnership and may make the partnership liable for contracts, torts, and crimes. Because partners are liable for all obligations of the partnership, in effect each partner is an agent of the other partners. Each partner may hire agents, and every partner is liable for the agents' authorized contracts and for torts that the agents commit in the course of their employments.

4. A partnership is not an employer of the partners, for most purposes. As a result, for example, a partner who leaves a partnership is not entitled to unemployment benefits.

5. Partners are fiduciaries of the partnership. They must act in the best interests of the partnership, not in their individual best interests.

6. The profits or losses of the business are shared by the partners, who report their shares of the profits or losses on their individual federal income tax returns, because the partnership does not pay federal income taxes. Nonetheless, a partnership does keep its own financial records and must file an information return with the Internal Revenue Service.*

7. A partnership may own property in its own name.

8. A partnership may sue or be sued in its own name. The partners may also be sued on a partnership obligation.

9. A partner may sue her partners during the operation of the partnership.

10. A partner's ownership interest in a partnership is not freely transferable. A purchaser of a partner's interest does not become a partner, but is entitled to receive only the partner's share of the partnership's profits.

11. Generally, a partnership has a life apart from its owners. If a partner dies, the partnership usually continues.

*The federal income tax return filed by a partnership, Schedule K-1, is merely an information return in which the partnership indicates its gross income and deductions and the names and addresses of its partners (IRC Sec. 6031). The information return allows the Internal Revenue Service to determine whether the partners accurately report partnership income on their individual returns.

with a written partnership agreement (articles of partnership), they may agree orally to be partners, or they may become partners merely by arranging their affairs as if they were partners. If partners conduct business under a trade name, they must file the name with the secretary of state in compliance with state statutes requiring the registration of fictitious business names.

When people decide to become partners, they should employ a lawyer to prepare a written partnership agreement. Although a partnership agreement is not required to form a partnership, it is highly desirable for the same reasons that written contracts are generally preferred. In addition, the statute of frauds requires a writing for a partnership having a term of a year or more.

More importantly, when partners do not define their relationship as partners, the default rules of the RUPA determine the rights of the partners vis-á-vis each other. While the RUPA rules are sensible and meet the needs of many partners, they may not meet the specific interests of other partners. Thus, having a written partnership agreement will allow the partners to define their rights and duties appropriately for them.

When there is no written partnership agreement, a dispute may arise over whether persons who are associated in some enterprise are partners. For example, someone may assert that she is a partner and, therefore, claim a share of the value of a successful enterprise. More frequently, an unpaid creditor may seek to hold a person liable for a debt incurred by another person in the same enterprise. To determine whether there is a partnership in the absence of an express agreement, the courts use the definition of partnership in the RUPA.

RUPA Definition of Partnership

The RUPA defines a partnership as an "association of two or more persons to carry on as co-owners a business for profit." If the definition is satisfied, then the courts will treat those involved as partners. A relationship may meet the RUPA definition of partnership even when a person does not believe he is a partner, and occasionally, even if the parties agree that they are not partners.

Association of Two or More Persons As an association, a partnership is a *voluntary and consensual relationship*. It cannot be imposed on a person; a person must agree expressly or impliedly to have a person associate with her. For example, a partner cannot force her partners to accept her daughter into the partnership.

No person can be a partner with herself—a partnership must have *at least two partners*. A person may be a partner with her spouse.

Nearly everyone or everything may be a partner. An individual, trust, partnership, limited partnership, corporation, or other association may be a partner.

Carrying On a Business Any trade, occupation, or profession may qualify as a business. Carrying on a business usually requires a series of transactions conducted over a period of time. For example, a group of farmers that buys supplies in quantity to get lower prices is not carrying on a business but only part of one. If the group buys harvesting equipment with which it intends to harvest crops for others for a fee for many years, it is carrying on a business.

Co-ownership Partners must *co-own the business* in which they associate. There is no requirement that the capital contributions or the assets of the business be co-owned.

Also, by itself, co-ownership of assets does not establish a partnership. For example, two persons who own a building as joint tenants are not necessarily partners. To be partners, they must co-own a business.

The two most important factors in establishing co-ownership of the business are the sharing of profits and the sharing of management of the business. The RUPA declares that a person's **sharing the profits** of a business is presumptive evidence that she is a partner in the business. This means that persons sharing profits are partners, unless other evidence exists to disprove they are partners. The rationale for this rule is that a person ordinarily would not be sharing the profits of a business unless she were a co-owner. This rule brings under partnership law many persons who fail to realize that they are partners. For example, two college students who purchase college basketball tickets, resell them, and split the profits are partners.

Sharing the gross revenues of a business does not create a presumption of partnership. The profits, not the gross receipts, must be shared. For example, a broker who receives a commission on a sale of land is not a partner of the seller of that land.

Although sharing profits usually is presumptive proof of a partnership, the RUPA provides that no presumption of partnership is made when a share of profits is received in payment

1. of a debt,
2. of wages to an employee or services to an independent contractor,
3. of rent,

4. of an annuity or other retirement or health benefit to a beneficiary or representative of a deceased partner,

5. interest on a loan, or

6. for the sale of the goodwill of a business or other property.

These exceptions reflect the normal expectations of the parties that no partnership exists in such situations.

Sharing management of a business is additional evidence tending to prove the existence of a partnership. However, by itself, participation in management is not conclusive proof of the existence of a partnership. For example, a creditor may be granted considerable control in a business, such as a veto power over partnership decisions and the right of consultation, without becoming a partner. Also, a sole proprietor may hire someone to manage his business, yet the manager will not be a partner of the sole proprietor.

However, when the parties claim that they share profits for one of the six reasons above, the sharing of management may overcome the presumption that they are not partners. When the parties arrange their affairs in a manner that otherwise establishes an objective intent to create a partnership, the courts find that a partnership exists. For example, when a nonmanagerial employee initially shares profits as a form of employment compensation, the employee is not a partner of his employer. But when the employer and employee modify their relationship by having the employee exercise the managerial control of a partner and fail to reaffirm that the manager is merely an employee, a partnership may exist.

Creditors occupy a special position. Many cases have permitted creditors to share profits and to exercise considerable control over a business without becoming partners. Creditor control is often justified on the grounds that it is merely reasonable protection for the creditor's risk.

For Profit The owners of an enterprise must *intend to make a profit* to create a partnership. If the enterprise suffers losses, yet the owners intend to make a profit, a partnership may result. When an endeavor is carried on by several people for charitable or other nonprofit objectives, it is not a partnership. For example, Alex and Geri operate a restaurant booth at a county fair each year to raise money for a Boy Scout troop. Their relationship is not a partnership but merely an association. (Nonetheless, like partners, they may be individually liable for the debts of the enterprise.)

Intent Frequently, courts say that there must be intent to form a partnership. This rule is more correctly stated as follows: *The parties must intend to create a relationship that the law recognizes as a partnership.* A partnership may exist even if the parties entered it inadvertently, without considering whether they had created a partnership. A written agreement to the effect that the parties do not intend to form a partnership is not conclusive if their actions provide evidence of their intent to form a relationship that meets the RUPA partnership test.

There are several important consequences of being a partner. See Figure 3 for a summary of the most important consequences.

The *Southex* case, which follows the next section, considers whether two businesses are partners.

Creation of Joint Ventures
Courts frequently distinguish **joint ventures** from partnerships. A joint venture may be found when a court is reluctant to call an arrangement a partnership because the purpose of the arrangement is not to establish an ongoing business involving many transactions; instead, it is limited to a single project. For example, an agreement to buy, develop, and

---

Figure 3   *Important Consequences of Being a Partner*

1. You share ownership of the business. For example, you want to bring an employee into your business, which is worth $250,000. If you and the employee conduct your affairs like partners, your employee will become your partner and own half of your business.

2. You share the profits of the business.

3. You share management of the business. Your partner must be allowed to participate in management decisions.

4. Your partner is an agent of the partnership. You are liable for your partner's torts and contracts made in the ordinary course of business.

5. You owe fiduciary duties to your partnership and your partner, such as the duties not to compete with the business, not to self-deal, and not to disclose confidential matters.

6. You have unlimited personal liability for all the obligations of the partnership.

resell for profit a particular piece of real estate is likely to be viewed as a joint venture rather than a partnership. In all other respects, joint ventures are created just as partnerships are created. The joint venturers may have a formal written agreement. In its absence, a court applies the RUPA definition of partnership—modified so as not to require the carrying on of a business—to determine whether a joint venture has been created.

The legal implications of the distinction between a partnership and a joint venture are not entirely clear.

Generally, partnership law applies to joint ventures. For example, all of the participants in a joint venture are personally liable for its debts, and joint venturers owe each other the fiduciary duties imposed on partners. Joint ventures are treated as partnerships for federal income tax purposes. The most significant difference between joint venturers and partners is that joint venturers are usually held to have *less implied and apparent authority* to make contracts for the joint venture than partners, because of the limited scope of the enterprise.

Southex Exhibitions, Inc. v. Rhode Island Builders Association, Inc.
279 F. 3d 94 (1st Cir. 2002)

The Rhode Island Builder's Association, Inc. (RIBA), is an association of home construction companies. In 1974, RIBA's executive director, Ross Dagata, made an agreement with Sherman Exposition Management, Inc. (SEM), a professional show owner and producer, regarding future productions of the RIBA home shows at the Providence Civic Center. The preamble in the 1974 Agreement announced that "RIBA wishes to participate in such shows as sponsors and partners." The term of the 1974 Agreement was five years, renewable by mutual agreement.

RIBA also agreed to sponsor and endorse only shows produced by SEM, to persuade RIBA members to exhibit at those shows, and to permit SEM to use RIBA's name for promotional purposes. In turn, SEM promised to obtain all necessary leases, licenses, permits and insurance, to indemnify RIBA for show-related losses, to grant RIBA the right to accept or reject any exhibitor, to audit show income, and to advance all the capital required to finance the shows. Net show profits were to be shared: 55 percent to SEM; 45 percent to RIBA.

The 1974 Agreement provided that all show dates and admission prices, as well as the Rhode Island bank at which show-related business would be transacted, required agreement by both parties. If the Civic Center became unavailable for reasons beyond SEM's control, SEM was to be excused from its production duties, provided that SEM promoted no other home show in Rhode Island. RIBA retained the right to conduct a home show at another venue, after notice to SEM.

When the 1974 Agreement was being negotiated, SEM and RIBA had conversations relating to the meaning of the term "partners" in the agreement. Manual Sherman, SEM's president, informed RIBA's Ross Dagata that he "wanted no ownership of the show" because he was uncertain about the financial prospects for home shows in the Rhode Island market. Sherman advised Dagata: "After the first year, if I'm not happy, we can't produce the show properly or make any money, we'll give you back the show." Although SEM owned other home shows which it produced outside Rhode Island, Sherman consistently described himself simply as the "producer" of the RIBA shows.

In 1994, Southex Exhibitions, Inc., acquired SEM's interest under the 1974 Agreement. By 1998, Southex determined that in order to maintain its financial stake in the RIBA home shows, the 1974 Agreement either needed to be renegotiated or allowed to expire according to its terms in 1999. RIBA in turn expressed dissatisfaction with Southex's performance, and eventually entered into a management contract with another producer, Yoffee Exposition Services, Inc.

Southex sued RIBA to enjoin the RIBA 2000 home show on the grounds that the 1974 Agreement established a partnership between RIBA and Southex's predecessor, SEM. Southex argued that RIBA breached its fiduciary duties to Southex by its dissolution of their partnership and its subsequent appointment of another producer. The federal district court denied Southex's request for a preliminary injunction and found that the 1974 Agreement did not create a partnership. Southex appealed.

Cyr, Senior Circuit Judge

Under Rhode Island law, a partnership is an association of two or more persons to carry on as co-owners a business for profit. The receipt by a person of a share of the profits of a business is prima facie evidence that he or she is a partner in the business.

Southex insists that the 1974 Agreement contains ample indicia that a partnership was formed, including: (1) a 55–45 percent sharing of profits; (2) mutual control over designated business operations, such as show dates, admission prices, choice of exhibitors, and "partnership" bank accounts; and (3) the respective contributions of valuable property to the partnership by the partners. In our view, the evidence indicating a nonpartner relationship cannot be dismissed as insubstantial.

First, the 1974 Agreement is simply entitled "Agreement," rather than "Partnership Agreement." Second, rather than an agreement for an indefinite duration, it prescribed a fixed (albeit renewable) term. Third, rather than undertake to share operating costs with RIBA, SEM not only agreed to advance all monies required to produce the shows, but to indemnify RIBA for all show-related losses as well. State law normally presumes that partners share equally or at least proportionately in partnership losses. Although partners may agree to override such statutory "default" provisions, there is no evidence that SEM and RIBA meant to do so, notwithstanding an intent to form a partnership.

Similarly, although RIBA involved itself in some management decisions, SEM was responsible for the lion's share. Partners normally share equal rights in management. Furthermore, Southex not only entered into contracts but conducted business with third parties, in its own name, rather than in the name of the putative partnership. As a matter of fact, their mutual association was never given a name. It is noteworthy as well that Southex never filed either a federal or state partnership tax return.

Similarly, the evidence as to whether either SEM or RIBA contributed any corporate property with the intent that it become jointly-owned partnership property is highly speculative, particularly since their mutual endeavor simply involved a periodic event, i.e., an annual home show, which neither generated, nor necessitated, ownership interests in significant tangible properties, aside from cash receipts. Unlike tangible real and personal property, whose ownership is more readily established, the intangible intellectual property involved here, such as clientele lists, goodwill, and business expertise, did not so readily lend itself to evidentiary establishment. As a consequence, in the present circumstances the requisite mutual intent to convert intangible intellectual properties into partnership assets may well depend much more importantly upon a clear contractual expression of mutual intention to form a partnership.

Finally, even assuming that the 1974 Agreement, as a whole, is ambiguous, (i) Manual Sherman testified that he regarded SEM as simply the producer of the annual RIBA shows; and (ii) Dagata testified that SEM specifically disclaimed any ownership interest in the home shows in 1974.

Southex urges that the 1974 Agreement necessitated a finding of partnership formation, in that it unambiguously describes the contracting parties as "partners." The labels the parties assign to their intended legal relationship, while probative of partnership formation, are not necessarily dispositive as a matter of law, particularly in the presence of countervailing evidence—e.g., the provision in the 1974 Agreement indemnifying RIBA for all show-related losses—which would tend to refute the partnership characterization. Although the manner in which the parties themselves characterize the relationship is probative, the question ultimately is objective intent.

Although the courts should refrain from resorting to extrinsic evidence where a contract is utterly unambiguous, the lone reference to "partners" in the 1974 Agreement's prefatory clause is so inconclusive as to carry minimal interpretive weight, especially since it arguably conflicted with other contract provisions. Had the parties intended otherwise, it would seem entirely reasonable to expect the 1974 Agreement to have been entitled "Partnership Agreement," rather than simply "Agreement."

Judgment for RIBA affirmed.

Creation of Mining Partnerships

Although similar to an ordinary partnership or a joint venture, a mining partnership is recognized as a distinct relationship in a number of states. Persons who cooperate in the working of either a mine or an oil or gas well are treated as mining partners if there is (1) joint ownership of a mineral interest, (2) joint operation of the property, and (3) sharing of profits and losses. Joint operation requires more than merely financing the development of a mineral interest, but it does not require active physical participation in operations; it may be proved by furnishing labor, supplies, services, or advice. The delegation of sole operating responsibility to one of the participants does not bar treatment as a mining partnership.

Creation of Limited Liability Partnerships

Unlike an ordinary partnership, a limited liability partnership (LLP) may not be created merely by partners conducting a business together. The partners must expressly agree to create an LLP by complying with a limited liability partnership statute. The formation of an LLP requires filing a form with the secretary of state, paying an annual fee, and adding the words "Registered Limited Liability Partnership," "Limited Liability Partnership," or the acronym "RLLP" or "LLP" to the partnership's name. Some states also require an LLP to maintain a minimum level of professional liability insurance or net worth.

Purported Partners

Two persons may not be partners, yet in the eyes of a third person they may **appear** to be partners. If the third person deals with one of the apparent partners, he may be harmed and seek to recover damages from both of the apparent partners. The question, then, is whether the third person may collect damages from both of the apparent partners, even though they are not partners in fact.

For example, Thomas thinks that Wilson, a wealthy person, is a partner of Porter, a poor person. Thomas decides to do business with Porter on the grounds that if Porter does not perform as agreed, he can recover damages from Wilson. If Thomas is wrong and Wilson is not Porter's partner, Thomas ordinarily has no recourse against Wilson. RUPA Section 308(e) states that "persons who are not partners as to each other are not liable as partners to other persons." However, if Thomas can prove that Wilson misled him to believe that Wilson and Porter were partners, he may sue Wilson for damages suffered when Porter failed to perform as agreed. This is an application of the doctrine of **purported partners.**

The liability of a purported partner is based on substantial, detrimental reliance on the appearance of partnership. A person will be a purported partner and have liability when the three elements of RUPA Section 308(a) are met:

1. A person purports to be or consents to being represented as a partner of another person or partnership.

2. A third party relies on the representation.

3. The third party transacts with the actual or purported partnership.

The third party may hold liable the persons who purported to be partners or consented to being represented as the partner of the actual or purported partnership.

Purporting to Be a Partner

A person may purport to be a partner by referring to himself as another person's partner. Or he might appear frequently in the office of a purported partner and confer with him. Perhaps he and another person share office space, have one door to an office with both of their names on it, have one telephone number, and share a receptionist who answers the phone giving the names of both persons.

More difficult is determining when a person *consents* to being represented as another's partner. Mere knowledge that one is being held out as a partner is not consent. But a person's silence in response to a statement that the person is another's partner is consent.

For example, suppose Chavez tells Eaton that Gold is a partner in Birt's new restaurant. In fact, Gold is not Birt's partner. Later, Gold learns of the conversation between Chavez and Eaton. Gold does not have to seek out Chavez and Eaton to tell them that he is not Birt's partner

in order to avoid being held liable as a partner for Birt's business debts. Had Chavez made the statement to Eaton in Gold's presence, however, Gold must deny the partnership relation or he will be held liable for Eaton's subsequent reliance on Gold's silence.

Note also that if a person makes a public representation that she is a partner of another, the purported partner is liable to any third person who relies on the representation, even if the purported partner is not aware of the reliance.

Reliance Resulting in a Transaction with the Partnership

A purported partner is liable only to those persons who rely on the representation and enter into a transaction with the actual or purported partnership. This means that purported partnership is determined on a case-by-case basis. The third party must in fact rely on the appearance of partnership. For example, when Trump transacts with Doby based on Crabb's representation that Doby and Crabb are partners, Trump is able to hold both Doby and Crabb liable. If however, Trump had dealt with Doby believing Doby was in business by herself and later discovers that Crabb had purported to be Doby's partner, only Doby would be liable to Trump, because there was no reliance on Crabb's purporting to be Doby's partner when Trump transacted with Doby.

Effect of Purported Partnership

Once persons are proved to be purported partners, a person who purported to be the others' partner or who consented to being represented as the others' partner is liable as though he were a partner of those persons. He is liable on contracts entered into by third parties on their belief that he was a partner. He is liable for torts committed during the course of relationships entered by third parties who believed he was a partner. In addition, a partnership that represents that a person is a partner endows the purported partner with the apparent authority to make contracts for the partnership.

Although two persons are purported partners to a person who knows of the representation and who relies on it, the purported partners are not partners in fact and do not share the profits, management, or value of the business of the purported partnership. Purported partnership is merely a device to allow creditors to sue persons who mislead the creditors into believing that a partnership exists. It does not create an actual partnership.

In the following *Palmer* case, the court found that there was a factual dispute whether the two lawyers were purported partners under the RUPA.

Palmer v. Claydon   1999 Conn. Super. LEXIS 2661 (Conn. Super. Ct. 1999)

Linda Palmer sued John Claydon, an attorney, for legal malpractice in connection with legal services he provided her in several land transactions. Palmer also sued George Lawler. Lawler was not a partner of Claydon, did not provide any services to Palmer, and did not participate in Claydon's services provided to Palmer. Palmer alleged, however, that Lawler was liable for Claydon's malpractice because he was a purported partner of Claydon. Lawler asked the court to grant him summary judgment.

Hodgson, Justice

Lawler asserts as a first ground that he was not a law partner of Claydon and did not hold himself out to be. He states that he and Claydon were never partners but that they shared space and expenses. He states that he and Claydon "never shared clients, nor employed each other to represent our clients" and did not commingle their funds received from the practice of law nor share profits or losses from the practice of law.

Palmer asserts that the two attorneys held themselves out to be a partnership by identifying their practice as "Claydon & Lawler" on a sign at their law office and on their stationery and in their telephone directory listing. She further avers that Claydon introduced Lawler to her as his law partner; and that Lawler, in a telephone conversation with her, identified himself as Claydon's law partner. The plaintiff further avers in her affidavit that she relied on the status of the entity as a partnership:

> I relied upon Attorney Claydon's and Attorney Lawler's representations that they did business as a law partnership. I believed that I would have the benefits of working with a partnership, including adequate resources and legal coverage for the real estate transactions.

Lawler states that "the only way in which Palmer can hold Lawler liable in this action is if she can prevail that there was a partnership between Lawler and Claydon." The court does not agree with this statement. While Palmer does not allege that there was an actual partnership, she alleges that Claydon and Lawler held themselves out as partners and that she relied on that representation.

Pursuant to Conn. Gen. Stat. 34–329(a), a party who purports, by words or conduct, to be a partner or consents to being represented by another as a partner in a partnership is liable to persons who rely on the representation in entering "into a transaction with the actual or purported partnership" either to the same extent as a partner for partnership liability or "jointly and severally" with any other person consenting to the representation that a partnership existed, depending on the situation.

The affidavits submitted plainly establish that there are disputed issues of material fact concerning (a) whether defendant Lawler held himself out as a participant in a partnership or allowed that impression to be created by defendant Claydon and (b) whether Palmer relied on the representation that a partnership existed. The existence of these disputed issues of material fact precludes summary judgment on the first ground raised by Lawler.

Lawler has failed to establish entitlement to summary judgment on this ground; however, he asserts a separate and distinct ground based on Palmer's release of Claydon. Lawler claims that even if he is assumed to have held himself out as a partner of Claydon, the release and withdrawal of Palmer's claims against Claydon serves to release him from liability.

In the absence of any express provision in the Act limiting the effect of releases of purported partners, the common law principles apply. The release of Claydon, about which there is no genuine dispute of material fact, as a matter of law releases Lawler from the vicarious liability imposed on him by Conn. Gen. Stat. 34–329(a).

Motion for summary judgment granted to Lawler.

Ethics in Action

Consider the ethical basis of the doctrine of purported partnership.

• Why does Kant's categorical imperative, which we studied in Chapter 4, suggest the rule of purported partnership is the right one?

• What steps will you take to avoid being a purported partner when you carry on business with an associate who is not your partner? Are those not only legal, but also ethical acts? Is there any distinction between law and ethics in this context?

Partnership Capital

When a partnership or limited liability partnership is formed, partners contribute cash or other property to the partnership. The partners' contribution is called **partnership capital.** To supplement beginning capital, other property may be contributed to the partnership as needed, such as by the partners permitting the partnership to retain some of its profits. Partnership capital is the equity of the business.

Loans made by partners to a partnership are not partnership capital but instead are liabilities of the business. Partners who make loans to a partnership are both owners and creditors.

Partnership Property

A partnership or limited liability partnership may own all or only a part of the property it uses. For example, it may own the business and perhaps a small amount of working capital in the form of cash or a checking account, yet own no other assets. All other tangible and intangible property used by the partnership may be individually or jointly owned by one or more of the partners or rented by the partnership from third parties. A determination of what is partnership property becomes essential when the partnership is dissolved and the assets are being distributed and when third persons claim that partnership property has been sold to them.

The RUPA provides that all property actually acquired by a partnership by transfer or otherwise is partnership property and, therefore, belongs to the partnership as an entity rather than to the partners. The RUPA has several rules that help determine when property is acquired by a partnership.

Property belongs to the partnership if the property is transferred (1) to the partnership in its name, (2) to any partner acting as a partner by a transfer document that names the partnership, or (3) to any partner by a transfer document indicating the partner's status as a partner or that a partnership exists. In addition, property acquired with partnership funds is presumed to be partnership property.

The presumption is very strong that property purchased with partnership funds and used in the partnership belongs to the partnership. On the other hand, property used by the partnership is presumed to belong to an individual partner when the property is purchased by a partner with her own funds and in her own name with no indication in the transfer document of the partner's status as a partner or the existence of a partnership. However, in both situations, other factors such as an agreement among the partners may rebut the RUPA presumption of ownership.

The intent of the partners controls whether the partnership or an individual partner owns the property. It is best to have a written record of the partners' intent as to ownership of all property used by the partnership, such as a partnership agreement and partnership accounting records.

Examples   A tax accountant discovers that a partnership is using a building to which a partner, Jacob Smith, holds title. The partnership pays rent monthly to Smith, but the partnership pays for all maintenance and repairs on the building. The accountant wants to know whether the partnership or Smith should be paying real property taxes on the building. Smith is the owner and should be paying taxes on it because his partners' intent to allow Smith to retain ownership is evidenced by the partnership's paying rent to Smith.

Changing the facts, suppose the partnership pays no rent to Smith, the partnership maintains and repairs the building, and the partnership pays real property taxes on the building, but the title is in Smith's name. Who owns the building? The property belongs to the partnership, because all the objective criteria of ownership point toward partnership ownership, especially the payment of taxes. Therefore, when the partnership is liquidated, the building will be sold along with other partnership assets, and the proceeds of its sale will be distributed to partnership creditors and to all of the partners.

Need for Partnership Agreement   It would be best for the partnership agreement to remove all ambiguity regarding ownership of property used by a partnership. For example, if the partnership is using a partner's building and the partners want the owning partner to retain ownership, it would be best to have a lease agreement between themselves and the partner stating that the partner owns the building, the monthly rent, and who is responsible for property taxes, maintenance, and improvements to the building.

In the following case, *Brevig,* the court held that property listed on a partnership's tax returns was nonetheless property of a partner, not the partnership.

McCormick v. Brevig   96 P. 3d 697 (Mont. Sup. Ct. 2004)

Joan Brevig McCormick and Clark Brevig were sister and brother. Clark had been a partner with his father, Charles, until Charles's death in 1982. At that time, Joan became a partner with her brother in the Brevig Ranch, and eventually they were 50–50 partners.

Disagreements concerning management of the ranch caused Clark and Joan's relationship to deteriorate. By the early 1990s, cooperation between Clark and Joan had essentially ceased, and they began looking for ways to dissolve the partnership. In 1995, Joan brought suit against Clark and the partnership, alleging that Clark had converted partnership assets to his own personal use. The source of the dispute was cattle purchased by their mother, Helen.

In 1990, Helen Brevig purchased 10 head of Charolais cattle to live on the ranch. The following year, Helen transferred ownership of the cattle to Clark and his two sons. Thereafter, these cattle were listed and treated as partnership property for all tax purposes, and proceeds from the sale of the cattle's offspring were placed into a partnership account. At the time of Helen's lawsuit against Clark, all the Charolais cattle residing on the ranch were offspring of those cattle originally purchased by Helen in 1990.

At the district court trial, Clark argued that the Charolais cattle should be regarded as separate property due to the fact that his mother, who was not a partner, had given the cattle to Clark and his two sons, neither of whom were partners. The district court concluded, however, that since Clark had signed tax returns indicating that the cattle were partnership property, and had placed proceeds from the sale of calves into partnership accounts, the cattle should be treated as partnership assets.

Clark appealed, arguing that the mere inclusion of the cattle in the partnership tax returns is legally insufficient to transfer title of the cattle to the partnership.

Rice, Justice

Section 35–10–203, Montana Code, pertains to partnership property and provides as follows:

(1) Property transferred to or otherwise acquired by a partnership is property of the partnership and not of the partners individually.

(2) Property is partnership property if acquired in the name of:

    (a) the partnership; or

    (b) one or more partners with an indication in the instrument transferring title to the property of the person's capacity as a partner or of the existence of a partnership but without an indication of the name of the partnership.

(3) Property is acquired in the name of the partnership by a transfer to:

    (a) the partnership in its name; or

    (b) one or more partners in their capacity as partners in the partnership if the name of the partnership is indicated in the instrument transferring title to the property.

(4) Property is presumed to be partnership property if purchased with partnership assets even if not acquired in the name of the partnership or of one or more partners with an indication in the instrument transferring title to the property of the person's capacity as a partner or of the existence of a partnership.

(5) *Property acquired in the name of one or more of the partners without an indication in the instrument transferring title to the property of the person's capacity as a partner or of the existence of a partnership and without use of partnership assets is presumed to be separate property even if used for partnership purposes.*

(Emphasis added.) As reflected in the statute, property purchased with partnership assets, or transferred in the partnership's name, or to one or more of the partners in their capacity as partners of the partnership, is presumed to be partnership property. On the other hand, property acquired in the name of a partner without an indication that the property is being transferred to that person in his or her capacity as a partner of the partnership is presumed to be separate property, even if used for partnership purposes.

In the present case, the district court included the cattle as partnership assets in its accounting because they were listed on the partnership tax returns. However, nothing in the record suggests that the Charolais cattle were purchased with partnership assets or transferred to Clark and his two sons in their capacity as partners of the partnership. Nor has there been any assignment of the cattle to the partnership. Therefore, despite the fact that the cattle were included in the partnership tax returns, and proceeds from the sale of the cattle's offspring placed in partnership accounts, the cattle are to be presumed separate property.

As Joan correctly points out, this presumption is a rebuttable one. Nonetheless, Joan did not introduce any evidence to overcome the presumption but, rather, has relied upon the District Court's findings that money from the sale of calves had been placed into partnership accounts, and that the cattle had been listed on partnership tax returns. However, we have previously considered and rejected arguments that a third party acquires an interest in cattle simply by feeding, watering, and pasturing them.

Here proceeds from the sale of calves had been deposited in partnership accounts and used for partnership purposes. Joan has not demonstrated any equitable interest in the cattle by virtue of the partnership's care and feeding of the cattle, nor has she provided any authority which would compel the conclusion that ownership of the cattle passed to the partnership. Because the presumption established by § 35–10–203(5), MCA, has not been overcome by evidence to the contrary, we conclude the District Court erred in categorizing the Charolais cattle as partnership assets, and reverse the court's determination in that regard.

Judgment reversed in favor of Clark Brevig.

Partner's Partnership Interest

As an owner of a partnership or LLP, a partner has an ownership interest in the partnership. A partner's ownership interest is called a **partnership interest,** which embodies all a partner's rights in a partnership:

1. The partner's transferable interest.
2. The partner's management and other rights.

The first right is discussed in this section. Partners' management and other rights are discussed in Chapter 38, Operation of Partnerships and Related Forms.

Note that a partner has no individual ownership rights in partnership property. The RUPA gives ownership of partnership property to the partnership only. Partners do, however, have the right to *use* partnership property for partnership purposes.

Partner's Transferable Interest

Like a shareholder owning stock in a corporation, a partner owns his partnership interest. The only part of the partnership interest, however, that may be transferred to another person is the partner's **transferable interest:** the partner's share of profits and losses and his right to receive partnership distributions. The transferable interest may be transferred or sold to any other person. It may also be used as collateral to secure a partner's debt.

Transfer The sale or transfer of a partner's transferable interest is a voluntary act of the partner. It entitles the buyer or transferee to receive the partner's distributions from the partnership, such as a share of profits. Although the transferee is the owner of the transferable interest, the transferee does not become a partner of the partnership. The transferee has no right to inspect the partnership's books and records or to manage the partnership. The transferee's only other right is to ask a court to dissolve and wind up the partnership, but only if the partnership is at will (i.e., has no term or objective). If the partnership dissolves and is wound up, the transferee will obtain the partner's claim against the partnership's assets.

By itself a partner's transfer of his transferable interest does not dissociate the partner from the partnership or effect a dissolution; the transferring partner remains a partner and may continue to manage the partnership.

The nontransferring partners may vote to expel the transferring partner from the partnership by their unanimous agreement (unless the partner merely granted a lien in the transferable interest to the partner's creditor), even if the term or objective of the partnership has not yet been met.

Charging Order A partner's personal creditor with a judgment against the partner may ask a court to issue a **charging order**—that is, an order charging all or part of the partner's transferable partnership interest with payment of the unsatisfied amount of the judgment. Unlike a transfer, a charging order is obtained without the partner's consent. As with a transfer, however, the partner remains a partner and may manage the partnership. The charging-order creditor is a lien creditor and is entitled to receive only the partner's share of the partnership distributions. If the distributions are insufficient to pay the debt, the creditor may ask the court to order foreclosure and to sell the partner's interest to satisfy the charging order.

Neither the issuance of a charging order nor the purchase of a transferable interest at a foreclosure sale dissociates the transferring partner from the partnership. But the purchaser of a transferable interest at the foreclosure sale becomes a transferee and therefore may ask a court to dissolve and wind up a partnership at will. The other partners may eliminate this potential threat to the continuation of the partnership by **redeeming the charging order.** To redeem a charging order, the other partners must pay the creditor the amount due on the judgment against the partner. If the other partners so choose, however, they may expel the partner suffering the charging order by their unanimous agreement, even if the term or objective of the partnership has not been met.

Effect of Partnership Agreement
The partners may believe that a partner's transferring her transferable partnership interest or suffering a charging order threatens the partnership. For example, they may believe that a partner may be less motivated to work for the partnership if the partner has transferred her partnership interest to a personal creditor, because she will not receive distributions from the partnership.

Consequently, the partners may restrict the transfer of a partner's transferable interest or impose negative consequences on a partner who transfers her transferable interest or suffers a charging order. For example, the partnership agreement may require a partner to offer to sell her partnership interest to the partnership prior to transferring it to any other person. Or the partnership agreement may effect a dissociation of any partner who suffers

a charging order and fails to redeem the charging order within 30 days.

Note that any transfer restriction must not unreasonably limit the ability of a partner to transfer her property interest. For example, a transfer restriction that bans the transfer of a partner's interest would be unreasonable and therefore unenforceable against a partner. In addition, a transfer restriction will not be enforceable against a transferee who does not have notice of the restriction.

Joint Venturers and Mining Partners Transfers of interests in joint ventures are treated in the same way as transfers of partnership interests. However, a mining partner's interest is *freely transferable.* The transferee becomes a partner with all the rights of ownership and management, and the transferor loses all of his partnership rights. The other mining partners cannot object to the transfer, and their consent to a transfer is not required.

Problems and Problem Cases

1. One of your clients, a motion picture producer, has asked your firm to invest $2 million in her latest motion picture production, a movie based on the life of 1960s singing star Janis Joplin. In return for the contribution, your firm will receive a 10 percent interest in the limited partnership that will produce and own the movie. The movie is expected to be in preproduction for four years as rights to the subject matter, script, actors, and director are obtained. Production is expected to take three months, and postproduction editing and promotion will last another six months, after which the movie will be released into theaters domestically. Three months after its theater release, the movie will be released on pay-per-view and premium television channels like HBO. Six months after the theatrical release, the movie will be sold on DVD. As a consequence, the production company is not expected to make a profit for at least five years. Your client wants to form the production company as a limited partnership. Do you believe that the limited partnership is the right business form? What business form may be better? How would you set up that business form to make sure your firm's interests are best protected?

2. You and nine of your wealthy friends decide to purchase a local minor league baseball team. The purchase price is $15 million, 60 percent of which you contribute to the business as capital. Your nine friends will contribute the remaining $6 million. All 10 of you agree that you will be the sole general manager of the business, making all business and baseball decisions, except as you delegate them to employees of the business, such as a team manager or vice president of baseball operations. Due to the way you will account for the purchase of the team and player salaries, you expect the business not to make a profit until year four. You expect that all 10 of you will remain owners of the business for at least 10 years, at which time you expect to sell the team at a profit. Which business form do you believe is best for this business?

3. Rick Yurko frequently purchased lottery tickets from Phyllis Huisel at the coffee shop she operated. In February 1990, Yurko bought 100 scratch-off lottery tickets, which revealed instant winners when a film covering was scratched off. Yurko asked Phyllis, Judy Fitchie, and Frances Vincent to help him scratch off the tickets. Yurko stated that if they helped him, they would be his partners and share in any winnings. Judy uncovered a ticket that gave its owner a chance to be on television and win $100,000. The owner had to complete a form on the back of the ticket and submit it for a drawing. Six tickets would be drawn for the TV appearance. Judy and Yurko urged Phyllis to fill out the ticket, but she did not want to appear on TV, so Yurko said he would.

After a discussion, Frances, Judy, Phyllis, and Yurko agreed that Yurko would represent them on TV. Yurko then printed on the back of the ticket "F. J. P. Rick Yurko." F.J.P. stood for the first initials of Frances, Judy, and Phyllis. As Yurko completed the tickets, he told Phyllis that he was going to put all their initials and his name on the ticket and that they would be partners no matter what they might win.

You can predict what happened next. The ticket was drawn for the TV show, and Yurko appeared on the show and won the $100,000 prize. He did not share the winnings with the three women. Were the three women able to share the winnings by proving they were partners with Yurko?

4. In August 2003, Tammy Duncan began working as a waitress at Bynum's Diner, which was owned by her mother, Hazel Bynum, and stepfather, Eddie Bynum. Tammy, Hazel, and Eddie signed an agreement stating the following:

> As of September 6th, 2003, I, Eddie Bynum, lease Bynum's Diner to Hazel Bynum and Tammy Duncan for $800 a month. I am completely out of it for 6 months, at which time they (Hazel Bynum and Tammy) have the option of renewing this contract for another 6 months. They are responsible for all repairs, taxes and expenses for Bynum's Diner.

Tammy began doing paperwork and bookkeeping for the diner in addition to occasionally waiting tables and performing other duties. Tammy and Hazel's intention in their agreement was to make Tammy a co-manager and not a co-owner of the business. Tammy understood that she would take over her stepfather's duties as manager. She received wages for the performance of her duties. Although Tammy had no agreement to share in the diner's profits, Hazel believed that she and Tammy were to split half of any profit. Hazel's intent, however, was not to transfer ownership of the business to Tammy before Hazel retired, whenever that might be. On October 30, 2003, Tammy was injured when she slipped off a ladder and fell onto both knees. The diner's insurer, Cypress Insurance Company, paid Tammy temporary total disability benefits beginning in November 2003. On April 2, 2004, however, Cypress notified Tammy that it would refuse to pay her disability claim on the grounds that she was not an employee of the diner, but a co-owner. Under the diner's insurance policy with Cypress, if Duncan were an owner of the diner, she would not have been entitled to

workers' compensation benefits, because she did not notify Cypress that she elected to be included under the policy's coverage as a partner. Was Tammy a partner in the diner?

5. Ritesh Amani and Omur Ganesh purchased and operated two coin-operated car wash businesses, a self-storage warehouse facility, and two coin-operated laundromats. Amani contributed $250,000 to the business venture, and Ganesh contributed $50,000. Ganesh conducted the day-to-day management of the venture, including maintaining the facilities and collecting the coins from the car washes and laundromats. Before changing prices or signage for the businesses, however, Ganesh obtained Amani's approval. Amani and Ganesh agreed that each would pay 50 percent of the expenses of the business, such as electricity, water, detergent, telephone, heat, and parts for repairs, with each paying his half by personal check. They also agreed to split 50–50 the cash receipts generated by the business. After two years, Amani and Ganesh had disagreements, and Ganesh chose to leave the business. At the time, the business's net worth was $740,000. Amani argued he owned the business and that Ganesh was only an employee. Ganesh argued that he was Amani's partner and was entitled to 50 percent of the value of the business. Were Amani and Ganesh partners? Was Ganesh entitled to 50 percent of the value of the business?

6. John Williams was an assistant manager of a restaurant operated by Pizzaville, Inc. He was promoted to manager and later designated a managing partner with business cards describing him so. Williams's compensation was a salary of $270 per week plus 70 percent of the restaurant's gross sales less the cost of food purchases and employees' wages. Pizzaville fired Williams. Williams sued Pizzaville to receive a portion of the value of the restaurant business on the ground that he was a partner with Pizzaville. Was Williams a partner?

7. The parents of Michael Milano sought medical care from The Freed Group, including Dr. Jay Freed, Dr. Mitchell Kleinberg, and Dr. Stephanie Citerman. The three doctors were not, however, partners in fact. For several months after his birth, Michael was examined by all three doctors. His parents received a bill from the Freed group in which all three names were prominently displayed. When Dr. Freed and Dr. Kleinberg examined Michael, they misdiagnosed a serious

medical condition. On behalf of Michael, his parents sued all three doctors, including Dr. Citerman, even though she had not committed malpractice herself. Was Dr. Citerman held liable to Michael?

8. Karlsen Carmody and Estelle Reboloff were partners in a retail furniture store. Carmody contributed $150,000 cash to the business, and Reboloff contributed $100,000. Carmody purchased a delivery truck for the business using $50,000 of partnership funds. The truck's certificate of title listed Carmody as the owner of the truck. The partnership used the truck for two years, during which time the partnership paid all property taxes and maintenance expenses on the truck. When the business became unprofitable, Carmody and Reboloff dissolved the partnership and sold its assets. Carmody argued that he owned the truck, and refused to share the proceeds of its sale with Reboloff. Was the truck a partnership asset?

9. Steve Holmes and his son Mike were partners in a construction business. Steve also owned a ranch, which he contributed to the partnership, even though Steve was still listed as the owner of record. Steve learned of a low-interest loan available for the purchase of property from a parent. Solely to obtain the benefits of the low-interest loan, Steve deeded the ranch to Mike. No money exchanged hands, however, and Mike never paid Steve or the partnership for the ranch. The transfer was not treated as a sale on Steve's or Mike's books, Mike did not claim ranch income as his own, and there were no changes in ranch operation. When Steve and Mike had disagreements, Steve asked a court to dissolve the partnership and to distribute its assets. Was the ranch an asset of the partnership or Mike?

10. Demas Yan and Dong Fu made an agreement to build condominiums on Yan's land in the Chinatown section of San Francisco. Their agreement provided that Yan would own 75 percent and Fu 25 percent of the property. Yan was responsible for the initial $300,000 construction cost, and Fu the remainder. They agreed to share the proceeds of the sale or rental of the condominiums according to the ownership percentage. Fu, however, had sole power to decide whether to sell or to rent the property. Afterward, Fu assigned his interest under the agreement to Wei Suen. Thereafter, the condominiums were sold for a combined price of $2.3 million. Was Suen entitled to a share of the condominium sale proceeds?

Online Research

The Revised Uniform Partnership Act and Your State

The National Conference of Commissioners on Uniform State Laws is the author of uniform state laws on forms of business.

- Find the Web site for the National Conference of Commissioners on Uniform State Laws.
- Find the link to the listing of the uniform state acts. This link will take you to the full text of the acts including the drafters' comments, which can help you understand why the acts were written as they are. Find the text of the Revised Uniform Partnership Act and its comments. Read section 202, which has the definition of partnership.
- Find the link to the "Legislative Fact Sheet" for the RUPA. Has your state adopted the RUPA?

chapter 38

OPERATION OF PARTNERSHIPS
AND RELATED FORMS

After many years working with a large consulting partnership, you and several of your business associates and friends decide to form your own consulting business as a limited liability partnership. You and five of your close friends have 20 to 25 years' experience in the consulting field. Each of you plans to contribute capital of $400,000 to the business. Each of you has a strong national reputation and expects to attract most of the firm's clients, at least in the first few years. You six partners will manage only a few of the firm's consulting engagements, but you six will bring to the firm clients generating $40,000,000 of annual revenue for the firm. Each of you also has experience managing consulting businesses, including expertise in personnel, financial, and marketing matters.

In addition, 15 other partners with 10 to 15 years' experience will join the new firm. Each of these 15 partners will contribute capital of $200,000. They are expected to bring few clients to the firm at this time, but they are expected to service the firm's clients and to bring in new clients as their reputations and skills expand and as the six older partners retire. Chiefly, these 15 partners will take charge of consulting engagements. They will directly supervise the firm's 50 associate consultants. The associate consultants will not be partners when the partnership is formed, but some expect to be offered partnership status within 5 to 10 years.

- What are the default rules regarding how the partnership will be managed?
- Why are those default rules inappropriate for this partnership?
- Write the management section of the partnership agreement. Accommodate the interests of all partners.
- What are the default rules regarding how the partners are compensated?
- Why are those default rules inappropriate for this partnership?
- Write the compensation section of the partnership agreement. Accommodate the interests of all partners.

TWO RELATIONSHIPS ARE IMPORTANT during the operation of a partnership or limited liability partnership (LLP) business: (1) the relation of the partners to each other and the partnership; and (2) the relation of the partners to third parties who are affected by the business of the partnership. In the examination of the first relationship, partners owe duties to each other and the partnership and they share the management and profits of the partnership. As for the second relation, partners have the ability to make the partnership liable to third parties for contracts and torts.

Duties of Partners to the Partnership and Each Other

The relation between partners and the partnership is a fiduciary relation of the highest order. It is one of mutual trust, confidence, and honesty. Therefore, under the Revised Uniform Partnership Act (RUPA) partners owe to the partnership and each other the highest degree of *loyalty*. In addition, partners must act consistently with the obligation of *good faith and fair dealing.* The duties partners owe each other are the same in ordinary partnerships and in limited liability partnerships.

Having Interest Adverse to Partnership

Unless there is a contrary agreement, a partner's sole compensation from partnership affairs is a share of partnership profits. Therefore, a partner may not deal with the partnership when the partner has an interest adverse to the partnership or acts on behalf of another person with any adverse interest. For example, a partner may not profit personally by receiving an undisclosed kickback from a partnership supplier. In addition, a partner may not profit secretly when she makes a contract with her partnership, such as selling a building she owns to her partnership without disclosing her ownership and her profit to her partners.

When a partner receives a secret profit, she has a conflict of interests, and there is a risk that she may prefer her own interests over those of the partnership. Therefore, the law permits a partner to profit personally from partnership transactions only if she deals in good faith, makes a full disclosure of all material facts affecting the transaction, and obtains approval from her partners. The remedy for a breach of this duty not to make a secret profit is a return of the profit that she made in the transaction with the partnership.

Competing against the Partnership

A partner may not compete against his partnership unless he obtains consent from the other partners. For example, a partner of a retail clothing store may not open a clothing store nearby. However, he may open a grocery store and not breach his fiduciary duty. The partnership has the remedy of recovering the profits of the partner's competing venture.

Partnership agreements often define what conduct constitutes competing with the partnership. For example, a partnership agreement of a large auditing firm may state that no partner may provide auditing services except on behalf of the partnership. It may also state that a partner may provide other accounting services not offered by the partnership after disclosure to and approval by the partnership's managing partners.

Duty to Serve

The duty to serve requires a partner to undertake his share of responsibility for running the day-to-day operations of the partnership business. The basis of this duty is the expectation that all partners will work. Sometimes, this duty is termed the duty to devote full time to the partnership.

Partners may agree to relieve a partner of the duty to serve. So-called *silent partners* merely contribute capital to the partnership. Silent partners do not have the duty to serve, but they have the same liability for partnership debts as any other partner.

The remedies for breach of the duty to serve include assessing the partner for the cost of hiring a person to do his work and paying the other partners additional compensation.

Duty of Care

In transacting partnership business, each partner owes **a duty of care.** A partner is not liable to her partnership for losses resulting from honest errors in judgment, but a partner is liable for losses resulting from her gross negligence, reckless conduct, intentional misconduct, or knowing violation of the law. A partner also has an obligation of good faith and fair dealing when acting for the partnership. Collectively, these duties mean that a partner must make an **investigation** before making a decision so that she has an adequate basis for making the decision. The decision she makes must be one she has **grounds to believe is in the best interests of the partnership.**

In the partnership agreement, the partners may reduce or increase the duty of care owed to the partnership. They may not, however, eliminate the duty of care. It is common for partnership agreements to excuse partners from liability if they act in good faith and with the honest belief that their actions are in the best interests of the partnership. Such a provision is designed to encourage honest partners to take reasonable business risks without fearing liability.

Duty to Act within Actual Authority

A partner has the duty not to exceed the authority granted him by the partnership agreement or, if there is no agreement, the authority normally held by partners in his position. He is responsible to the partnership for losses resulting from unauthorized transactions negotiated in the name of the partnership. For example, suppose partners agree that no partner shall purchase supplies from Jasper Supply Company, which is unaware of the limitation on the partners' authority. When one partner purchases supplies from Jasper and the partnership suffers a loss because the supplies are of low quality, the wrongdoing partner must bear the loss caused by her breach of the partnership agreement.

Duty to Account

Partners have a duty to account for their use or disposal of partnership funds and partnership property, as well as their receipt of any property, benefit, or profit, without the consent of the other partners. Partnership property should be used for partnership purposes, not for a partner's personal use. In addition, a partner may not misappropriate a business opportunity in which the partnership had an interest or expectancy.

For example, when a partner of a firm that leases residential property to college students allows his daughter to live in a partnership-owned apartment, the partner must collect rent for the partnership from his daughter or risk breaching the duty to account.

Each partner owes a duty to keep a reasonable record of all business transacted by him for the partnership and to make such records available to the person keeping the partnership books. The books must be kept at the partnership's chief executive office. Every partner must at all times have access to them and may inspect and copy them.

Closely related to the duty to account is the right of a partner to be **indemnified** for payments made from personal funds and for personal liabilities incurred during the ordinary conduct of the business. For example, a partner uses her own truck to pick up some partnership supplies, which she pays for with her personal check. The partner is entitled to be reimbursed for the cost of the supplies and for her cost of picking up the supplies, including fuel.

Other Duties A partner must maintain the **confidentiality** of partnership information such as a trade secret or a customer list. This means a partner should not disclose to third parties confidential information of the partnership unless disclosure benefits the partnership.

On the other hand, each partner owes a duty to disclose to the other partners all information that is material to the partnership business. She also owes a duty to inform the partners of notices she has received that affect the rights of the partnership. For example, Gordon Gekko, a partner of a stock brokerage firm, learns that National Motors Corporation is projecting a loss for the current year. The projection reduces the value of National stock, which the firm has been recommending that its customers buy. Gekko has a duty to disclose the projection to his partners to allow them to advise customers of the brokerage.

In *Spector v. Konover,* a case you'll read after the next section, the court found a managing partner liable for misusing partnership funds, self-dealing, and failing to disclose material information.

Joint Ventures and Mining Partnerships The fiduciary duties of partners also exist in joint ventures and mining partnerships, although there are a few special rules regarding their enforcement. For example, a joint venturer may seek an accounting in a court to settle claims between the joint venturers, or he may sue his joint venturers to recover joint property or to be indemnified for expenditures that he has made on behalf of the joint venture. A mining partner's remedy against his partners is an accounting; however, a mining partner has a lien against his partners' shares in the mining partnership for his expenditures on behalf of the mining partnership. The lien can be enforced against purchasers of his partners' shares.

Compensation of Partners

A partner's compensation for working for a partnership or limited liability partnership is a share of the profits of the business. The RUPA continues the UPA rule that a partner is not entitled to a salary or wages, even if he spends a disproportionate amount of time conducting the business of the partnership.

Profits and Losses Unless there is an agreement to the contrary, partners share partnership profits equally, according to the number of partners, and not according to their capital contributions or the amount of time that each devotes to the partnership. For example, a partnership has two partners, Juarez, who contributes $85,000 of capital to the partnership and does 35 percent of the work, and Easton, who contributes $15,000 and does 65 percent of the work. If they have made no agreement how to share profits, when the partnership makes a $50,000 profit in the first year, each partner is credited with $25,000, half of the profits.

Although the default RUPA rule allocates profits equally to partners, the partners do not necessarily *receive* profits earned by the partnership or LLP. Profits are *allocated* to each partner's capital account as profits are recognized by the business. Profits are *distributed* to partners in an amount and at a time determined by a majority of the partners. Consequently, in a partnership or LLP that is taxed like a partnership for federal income tax purposes, a partner may have taxable income despite not receiving a distribution from the partnership.

Losses When the partnership agreement is silent on how to share losses, losses are shared in the same proportion that profits are shared. The basis of this rule is the presumption that partners want to share benefits and detriments in the same proportions. Nonetheless, the presumption does not work in reverse. If a partnership agreement specifies how losses are shared but does not specify how profits are shared, profits are shared equally by the partners, not as losses are shared.

Examples   For example, when there is no agreement regarding how profits or losses are shared, profits are shared equally, and because losses are shared like profits, losses are shared equally as well. When two partners agree to share profits 70–30 and make no agreement on losses, both profits and losses are shared 70–30.

However, when two partners make no agreement how to share profits but agree to share losses 60–40, losses are shared in that proportion but profits are shared equally.

Partners may agree to split profits on one basis and losses on another basis for many reasons, including their making different capital and personal service contributions or a partner's having higher outside income than the other partners, which better enables him to use a partnership loss as a tax deduction.

Effect of Agreement on Creditors' Rights   Each partner has unlimited personal liability to partnership creditors. Loss-sharing agreements between partners do not bind partnership creditors unless the creditors agree to be bound. For example, two partners agree to share losses 60–40, the same proportion in which they contributed capital to the partnership. After the partnership assets have been distributed to the creditors, $50,000 is still owed to them. The creditors may collect the entire $50,000 from the partner who agreed to assume only 60 percent of the losses. That partner may, however, collect $20,000—40 percent of the amount—from the other partner.

Compensation in Large Partnerships   In a large accounting or other partnership that has thousands of partners, the partnership agreement often has a detailed section on the amount of partners' compensation and when it is paid. Usually, each partner is entitled to a monthly draw or salary. The amount of each partner's draw may be established yearly by the partnership's compensation committee or be determined by a rigid formula that takes into account a partner's capital contribution to the partnership, years of service as a partner, level of partner (such as managing partner, senior partner, or junior partner), area of practice (such as consulting, auditing, or tax), and other factors.

In addition, the compensation article will state how partners share profits and when profits are distributed to partners. While partners in a small partnership usually share profits according to each partner's capital contribution, in a large partnership the calculation may be very complex, including also the partner's area of practice, level of partner, and revenue received from a partner's clients. Usually, the profits are distributed four times a year, in January, April, June, and September, coinciding with the quarterly payment dates for estimated federal and state income taxes. In addition, the compensation articles will provide for partners' expense accounts, vacations and leaves, and other fringe benefits, such as health insurance.

In the following case, involving all-too-common overreaching and misconduct in a partnership with active and passive partners, the court found that the managing partner was not entitled to receive special compensation for managing the business, absent agreement of the other partners. The court also found that the managing partner breached several fiduciary duties, including by refusing to distribute a higher amount of partnership profits.

Spector v. Konover   747 A.2d 39 (Conn. Ct. App. 2000)

Martin Spector, Abner Rosenberg, Marvin Patron, and Simon Konover agreed to build a shopping plaza in Seymour, Connecticut. There was no written partnership agreement. The four orally formed Tri Town Realty Co., a partnership in which each partner received a 25 percent interest. Spector and Rosenberg contributed a land lease, while Patron and Konover were charged with building, operating, and managing the shopping plaza.

Konover and Patron initially managed the shopping plaza themselves, charging the partnership for any out-of-pocket expenses they incurred. Over time, as Konover and Patron amassed 20 or 30 shopping centers, they formed K and P Management Company. K and P Management hired managers and leasing agents to manage all of Konover and Patron's properties and charged management fees and leasing commissions to all of their properties, including Tri Town. Eventually, K and P Management was replaced by the Konover Management Corporation, which managed the Tri Town plaza for the last 10 years of the partnership.

Konover's duties in managing Tri Town included the preparation and distribution of monthly reports to each of the partners. In the early 1980s, Spector believed that Konover's reports did not adequately explain the finances of the partnership. Konover also determined the amount of money that was to be distributed to the partners as profit, and Spector felt that the amount being distributed was too low.

In June 1985, Spector requested an increase in the distributions. In September 1985, Konover increased the distributions from $500 per month to $1,200 per month. In February 1989, Spector again requested an increase in the distribution of profits and an explanation of various expenses appearing on the monthly report. Spector did not receive a response from Konover, and, in May 1989, Spector demanded that the partnership be terminated. Konover did not respond.

In April 1990, Konover stopped making profit distributions to Spector. In 1994, Spector hired a certified public accountant to review the financial records of the partnership. The accountant's review revealed that Konover did not maintain any account dedicated solely to the Tri Town partnership. Rather, the Tri Town partnership funds were commingled with funds from several other Konover entities, and all the funds were commingled in one account called the K and R Associates Trust Fund (K and R). The accountant further discovered that not only were the funds commingled in one account, but also the Tri Town funds were used by other properties owned by Konover. Even though Tri Town funds supposedly were kept in the K and R checking account, the balance of the entire K and R checking account actually was far less than the amount purported to be in the Tri Town partnership account. Additionally, interest earned on Tri Town funds was not credited to Tri Town's account.

Konover admitted to diverting funds between his various entities. He and several of his employees said that by sharing the funds in the K and R account, Konover could use one property's funds to cover expenses incurred by another property. For instance, if one property needed repairs but did not have enough cash to pay for the repairs, Konover would use cash from another property to pay for those repairs. It was, therefore, advantageous for him to commingle the funds of different Konover entities so that one property's funds could be used to cover an overdraft of another entity.

Spector sued Konover seeking damages stemming from Konover's alleged breaches of his fiduciary duties in managing the Tri Town partnership. The trial court found that Konover proved that he dealt with Spector fairly and breached no fiduciary duty. Spector appealed to the Appellate Court of Connecticut.

Foti, Judge

Konover's practice of diverting Tri Town funds to other entities and retaining interest earned on Tri Town partnership funds constitutes a breach of fiduciary duty. It is a thoroughly well-settled equitable rule that any one acting in a fiduciary relation shall not be permitted to make use of that relation to benefit his own personal interest. This rule is strict in its requirements and in its operation. It extends to all transactions where the individual's personal interests may be brought into conflict with his acts in the fiduciary capacity, and it works independently of the question whether there was fraud or whether there was good intention.

Konover's misuse of partnership property is a clear case of self-dealing and a violation of his fiduciary duty to Spector. As managing partner, Konover held a unique position of responsibility within the partnership. Spector trusted Konover to act in the best interest of the partnership. Instead, he used partnership funds to finance other entities owned by Konover and retained interest generated by Tri Town funds. This misuse of partnership funds for Konover's personal financial gain clearly constitutes a breach of fiduciary duty.

Spector also claims that Konover's commingling scheme affected his decisions regarding the disbursement of profits to the Tri Town partners. We agree with Spector and conclude that Konover's failure to make greater distributions of profits was a breach of his fiduciary duty. His proffered reason for withholding disbursements was that he wanted to create a large cash reserve to cover any expenses that might have arisen from the bankruptcy of one of Tri Town's largest tenants, Ames. According to the facts presented at trial, however, Konover did not actually maintain a reserve account dedicated to potential expenses related to Ames' bankruptcy. Rather, he continued the practice of diverting Tri Town funds to cover the expenses of other Konover properties. It is clear that his decision to withhold the disbursement of profits was, at least in part, motivated by his desire to use Tri Town funds to finance other Konover entities. This, too, was a breach of his fiduciary duty.

Spector also claims that Konover breached his fiduciary duty by billing the Tri Town partnership for management fees, leasing commissions, payroll maintenance fees, and undisclosed overhead charges included in Tri Town's insurance premiums. We agree. One of the factors to consider in determining whether a particular transaction is fair is whether the principal had competent and independent advice before completing that transaction. Implicit in this factor is the idea that the principal must consent to the transaction. With regard to the management fees and leasing commissions that Konover charged the partnership, the court found that there never were any meetings or partnership votes giving them the right to receive such compensation. In the absence of any agreement to the contrary,

Konover and his management company were not entitled to any compensation, other than reimbursement for out-of-pocket expenses, for managing Tri Town. General Statutes § 34-335(c) provides that a partner is to be reimbursed for out-of-pocket partnership expenses. General Statutes § 34-335(h) provides in relevant part that "[a] partner is not entitled to remuneration for services performed for the partnership. . . ."

Even after Spector complained to Konover about the management fees, Konover began charging the partnership an additional "payroll maintenance fee." These new fees were clearly not authorized by Spector. Additionally, the insurance premiums charged to Tri Town included undisclosed overhead costs that were paid to another Konover entity. Thus, Konover did not make a free and frank disclosure of all the relevant information.

Konover, without the formal consent of his partners, compensated himself for managing Tri Town. He also added hidden charges to the insurance premiums charged to Tri Town. These acts of self-dealing were in breach of his fiduciary duty. Thus, we conclude that the trial court's finding that Konover proved fair dealing by clear and convincing evidence was clearly erroneous.

Judgment reversed in favor of Spector.

Management Powers of Partners

Individual Authority of Partners In a partnership or limited liability partnership, every partner is a general manager of the business and may make contracts that bind the partnership. This power is expressed in the RUPA, which states that a partnership is bound by the act of every partner for apparently carrying on in the ordinary course the business of the partnership or business of the kind carried on by the partnership. Such authority to make contracts derives from the nature of the business. It permits a partner to bind the partnership and his partners for acts within the ordinary course of business. The scope of this **implied authority** is determined with reference to what is usual business for partnerships of the same general type.

Implied authority of a partner may not contradict a partner's **express authority,** which is created by agreement of the partners. An agreement among the partners can expand, restrict, or even completely eliminate the implied authority of a partner. For example, the partners in an online publishing business may agree that one

partner shall have the authority to purchase a magazine business for the partnership and that another partner shall not have the authority to sell advertising space. The partners may agree also that all partners must consent to borrow money for the partnership. The partners' implied authority to be general managers is modified in accordance with these express agreements.

Express authority may be stated orally or in writing, or it may be obtained by acquiescence. Regardless of the method of agreement, all of the partners must agree to the modification of implied authority. Partners may give everyone notice of a partner's authority or limitation on a partner's authority by filing a **Statement of Partnership Authority** or **Statement of Denial** with the secretary of state or the real estate recording office. Together, a partner's express and implied authority constitute her **actual authority.**

Apparent Authority Apparent authority exists because it reasonably appears to a third party that a partner has authority to do an act. Often, the implied authority and apparent authority of a partner are coincident. However, when a partner's implied authority is restricted or eliminated, the partnership risks the possibility that **apparent**

authority to do a denied act will remain. To prevent apparent authority from continuing when there is a limitation of a partner's actual authority, third persons with whom the partner deals must have knowledge of the limitation of his actual authority or have received notification of the limitation, such as receiving an e-mail or fax or otherwise having the limitation brought to their attention. Filing a Statement of Partnership Authority or Statement of Denial may help notify third parties of a partner's limited authority. Just as a principal must notify third persons of limitations of an agent's authority, so must a partnership notify its customers, suppliers, and others of express limitations of the actual authority of partners.

Suppose that Carroll, Melton, and Ramirez are partners and that they agree that Carroll will be the only purchasing agent for the partnership. This agreement must be communicated to third parties selling goods to the partnership, or Melton and Ramirez will have apparent authority to bind the partnership on purchase contracts. Melton and Ramirez do not have express authority to purchase goods, because they have agreed to such a restriction on their authority. They do not have implied authority to purchase, because implied authority may not contradict express authority.

Ratification   A partnership may ratify the unauthorized acts of partners. Essentially, **ratification** occurs when the partners accept an act of a partner who had no actual or apparent authority to do the act when it was done.

For example, suppose Cabrillo and Boeglin are partners in an accounting firm. They agree that only Cabrillo has authority to make contracts to perform audits of clients, an agreement known by Mantron Company. Nonetheless, Boeglin and Mantron contract for the partnership to audit Mantron's financial statements. At this point, the partnership is not liable on the contract, because Boeglin has no express, implied, or apparent authority to make the contract. But suppose Boeglin takes the contract to Cabrillo, who reads it and says, "OK, we'll do this audit." Cabrillo, as the partner with express authority to make audit contracts, has ratified the contract and thereby bound the partnership to the contract.

Special Transactions
The validity of some partner's actions is affected by special partnership rules that reflect a concern for protecting important property and the credit standing of partners. This concern is especially evident in the rules for conveying the partnership's real property and for borrowing money in the name of the partnership.

Power to Convey Partnership Real Property   To bind the partnership, an individual partner's conveyance of a partnership's real property must be expressly, impliedly, or apparently authorized or be ratified by the partnership. For example, the partners may expressly agree that a partner may sell the partnership's real property.

The more difficult determination is whether a partner has *implied* and *apparent* authority to convey real property. A partner has implied and apparent authority to sell real property if a partnership sells real property in the usual course of the partnership business. Such would be the case with the partner of a real estate investment partnership that buys and sells land as its regular business. By contrast, a partner has no implied or apparent authority to sell the building in which the partnership's retail business is conducted. Here, unanimous agreement of the partners is required, since the sale of the building may affect the ability of the firm to continue. In addition, a partner has no implied or apparent authority to sell land held for investment not in the usual course of business. A sale of such land would be authorized only if the partners concurred.

When title to partnership real property is recorded in the name of the partners and not the partnership, those partners in whose name title is recorded have apparent authority to convey title to a bona fide purchaser unaware of the partnership's interest in the real property. However, purchasers are deemed to have knowledge of a limitation on a partner's authority to convey real property that is contained in a Statement of Partnership Authority or Statement of Denial that is filed in the real estate recording office.

Borrowing Money   Partnership law restricts the ability of a partner to borrow money in the name of a partnership. Essentially, a partner must possess express, implied, or apparent authority to borrow. Express authority presents few problems. Finding implied and apparent authority to borrow is more difficult.

Although the RUPA does not explicitly recognize the distinction, a number of courts have distinguished between trading and nontrading partnerships for purposes of determining whether a partner has implied or apparent authority to borrow money on behalf of the partnership. A **trading partnership** has an inventory; that is, its regular business is buying and selling merchandise, such as retailing, wholesaling, importing, or exporting. For example, a toy store and a clothing store are trading partnerships. Since there is a time lag between the date they pay for their inventory and the date they sell inventory to their customers, these firms ordinarily need to borrow to avoid cash flow problems. Therefore, a partner of a trading partnership has implied and apparent authority to borrow money for the partnership.

A **nontrading partnership** has no substantial inventory and is usually engaged in providing services—for example, accounting services or real estate brokerage. Such partnerships have no normal borrowing needs. Therefore, a partner of a nontrading partnership has no implied or apparent authority to borrow money for the partnership.

The distinction between trading and nontrading partnerships is not always clear. Businesses such as general contracting, manufacturing, and dairy farming, although not exclusively devoted to buying and selling inventory, have been held to be trading partnerships. The rationale for their inclusion in this category is that borrowing is necessary in the ordinary course of business to augment their working capital.

This suggests why the distinction between trading partnerships and nontrading partnerships is useless or misleading. There is no necessary connection between borrowing money and buying and selling. The more important inquiry should be whether a partner's borrowing is in the ordinary course of business. When borrowing is in the ordinary course of business, a partner has implied and apparent authority to borrow money. If borrowing is not in the ordinary course of business, then no individual partner has implied or apparent authority to borrow money.

If a court finds that a partner has authority to borrow money, the partnership is liable for his borrowings on behalf of the partnership. There is a limit, however, to a partner's capacity to borrow. A partner may have authority to borrow, yet borrow beyond the ordinary needs of the business. A partnership will not be liable for any loan whose amount exceeds the ordinary needs of the business, unless otherwise agreed by the partners.

The power to borrow money on the firm's credit will ordinarily carry with it the power to grant the lender a lien or security interest in firm assets to secure the repayment of the borrowed money. Security interests are a normal part of business loan transactions.

Issuing Negotiable Instruments A partner who has the authority to borrow money also has authority to issue negotiable instruments such as promissory notes for that purpose. When a partnership has a checking account and a partner's name appears on the signature card filed with the bank, the partner has express authority to draw checks. A partner whose name is not on the signature card filed with the bank has apparent authority to issue checks, but only in respect to a third person who has no knowledge or notification of the limitation on the partner's authority.

Negotiating Instruments A partnership receives many negotiable instruments during the course of its business. For example, an accounting firm's clients often pay fees by check. Even though borrowing money and issuing negotiable instruments may be beyond a partner's implied and apparent authority, a partner usually has implied and apparent authority to transfer or negotiate instruments on behalf of the partnership.

For example, when a partnership has a bank account, a partner has implied and apparent authority to indorse and deposit in the account checks drawn payable to the partnership. As a general rule, a partner also has implied and apparent authority to indorse and cash checks drawn payable to the order of the partnership. Likewise, partners have implied authority to indorse drafts and notes payable to the order of the partnership and to sell them at a discount.

Admissions and Notice A partnership is bound by admissions or representations made by a partner concerning partnership affairs that are within her express, implied, or apparent authority. Likewise, notice to a partner is considered to be received by the partnership. Also, a partner's knowledge of material information relating to partnership affairs is **imputed** to the partnership. These rules reflect the reality that a partnership speaks, sees, and hears through its partners.

Disagreement among Partners: Ordinary Course of Business
Usually, partners will discuss management decisions among themselves before taking action, even when doing so is not required by a partnership agreement and even when a partner has the implied authority to take the action by herself. When partners discuss a prospective action, they will usually vote on what action to take. Under the default RUPA rules, each partner has one vote, regardless of the relative sizes of their partnership interests or their shares of the profits. On matters in the ordinary course of business, the vote of a majority of the partners controls ordinary business decisions and, thereby, limits the actual authority of the partners. Nonetheless, the apparent authority of the partners to bind the partnership on contracts in the ordinary course of business is unaffected by the majority vote of partners, unless the limitation on the partners' actual authority is communicated to third parties.

When Unanimous Partners' Agreement Required
Some partnership actions are so important that one partner should not be able to do them by himself. To make clear that no single partner has

implied or apparent authority to do certain acts, in the absence of a contrary agreement, the UPA requires unanimity for several actions. The RUPA, however, deletes such a list. Instead, the RUPA requires that any partnership act not in the ordinary course of business be approved by all partners, absent a contrary agreement of the partners.

For example, a decision to build a new executive office complex must be approved by all partners. Similarly, the decision of a small accounting partnership in Sacramento to open a second office in San Jose would require unanimity. When other actions, such as submitting a partnership claim to arbitration, are in the ordinary course of business, any partner has authority to do the actions.

Joint Ventures and Mining Partnerships
Most of the authority rules of partnerships apply to joint ventures and mining partnerships. These business organizations are in essence partnerships with limited purposes. Therefore, their members have less implied and apparent authority than do partners. Joint venturers have considerable apparent authority if third persons are unaware of the limited scope of the joint venture. A mining partner has no implied authority to borrow money or issue negotiable instruments. As with partners, joint venturers and mining partners may by agreement expand or restrict each other's agency powers.

Effect of Partnership Agreement
The partners may modify the rules of management by their unanimous agreement. They may agree that a partner will relinquish his management right, thus removing the partner's express and implied authority to manage the partnership. They may grant sole authority to manage the business to one or more partners. Such removals or delegations of management powers will not, however, eliminate a partner's apparent authority to bind the partnership for his acts within the usual course of business unless a third party has knowledge or notification of the limitation.

A partnership agreement may create classes of partners, some of which will have the power to veto certain actions. Some classes of partners may be given greater voting rights. Unequal voting rights are often found in very large partnerships, such as an accounting firm with hundreds or thousands of partners.

For example, in a large accounting partnership, the partnership agreement will have a management section. This section usually begins with a restatement of the RUPA fiduciary duties that partners owe to the partnership, with exceptions or revisions, such as changes in the duty of care. The section also lists the duties of the partnership to the partners, such as the duty to indemnify.

Regarding the authority of partners, the management articles may give a managing partner or a managing partners' committee control over much of the firm's day-to-day management, such as the hiring, firing, and promotion of employees, investing the firm's excess cash, and drawing and indorsing partnership checks. The managing partners or a compensation committee may be given power to determine the partners' draws or salaries. Individual partners may have most of their management powers taken away but may be granted the power to hire a personal assistant or to make expenditures within limits from an expense account, such as buying a laptop computer. Other matters may require approval of all the partners (such as selling the partnership's real property and moving the partnership's place of business), a super-majority of partners (such as 75 percent approval to bind the partnership to a bank loan), a majority of partners (such as installing new carpeting), or the partners in a particular area of practice (such as requiring approval of a majority of consulting partners for a consulting engagement over $1,000,000).

In small partnerships of 10 or fewer partners, the partnership agreement often requires unanimous partners' agreement for many actions, such as hiring employees and making large contracts. In small partnerships, these and other actions have a greater impact on each partner. This impact is evident in the next case, *NBN Broadcasting,* in which a partnership agreement that was designed to prevent and resolve conflicts between the two partners eventually caused serious disagreements. The partners wanted to be equal essentially, but a deadlock provision allowed one partner to dominate, eventually causing a breakdown of the partners' relationship. It illustrates the necessity for careful drafting of partnership agreements, including anticipating that a part of the agreement may cause an undesired result.

NBN Broadcasting, Inc. v. Sheridan Broadcasting Networks, Inc.
105 F.3d 72 (2d Cir. 1997)

NBN Broadcasting, Inc., and Sheridan Broadcasting Networks, Inc., operated competing radio networks. In 1991, NBN and Sheridan agreed to form American Urban Radio Network (AURN), a Pennsylvania partnership that combined NBN's and Sheridan's networks. Sheridan owned 51 percent of the partnership; NBN owned 49 percent. They agreed to maintain NBN's offices in New York and Sheridan's offices in Pittsburgh to allow direct oversight and input by AURN's cochairmen and co-CEOs, Sydney Small (chairman of NBN) and Ronald R. Davenport (chairman of Sheridan). NBN and Sheridan wanted equal rights in management of the partnership. The partners' equal right to manage AURN was modified by the partnership agreement in sections 5.2 and 5.3. Section 5.2 created a five-member Management Committee comprising two members selected by NBN and two by Sheridan; a seat on the Management Committee was to be vacant and would be filled only when the Management Committee was deadlocked. Section 5.2 also provided:

The Management Committee shall be responsible for the following functions of the partnership and contractual arrangements relating thereto:

   (i) Sales and marketing;

  (ii) Promotions and public relations;

 (iii) Affiliate relations and compensation;

 (iv) Network programming;

  (v) Personnel administration; and

 (vi) Budgeting, accounting, and finance.

Section 5.3 provides:

(a) In the event that three of the four members of the Management Committee are unable to reach agreement on any issue or issues relating to items (i) through (v) above and remain so unable for a period of thirty days, then Ronald R. Davenport, Chairman of Sheridan, shall have the right to fill the vacant seat on the Management Committee for the purpose of reaching an agreement, and only until an agreement is reached, on such issue or issues.

Section 5.3 did not authorize appointment of a fifth member of the Management Committee when there was a deadlock regarding budgeting, accounting, or finance or any matter other than those listed in Section 5.2(i) through (v). As to budgeting, accounting, and finance and matters not listed in Section 5.2(i) through (v), NBN and Sheridan were equal partners, and all decisions on such matters required their agreement.

At a Management Committee meeting on September 14, 1995, Davenport proposed that AURN open an expensive new office in Washington, D.C., hire Skip Finley as chief operating officer, and employ Richard Boland. When NBN's representatives opposed opening the new office and hiring Finley and Boland, Davenport scheduled a meeting solely to appoint a fifth member to break the deadlock. On September 15, NBN asked a Pennsylvania state trial court to grant a preliminary injunction and a permanent injunction against Sheridan's opening a new AURN office in Washington and hiring Finley and Boland, on the grounds that the proposals related to budgeting, accounting, and finance and were, therefore, not subject to the deadlock voting provision. On October 13, the state trial court denied NBN's motion for a preliminary injunction. The state trial court held that Sheridan had the right to invoke the deadlock provision to "make additions to personnel" by hiring Finley and Boland. The trial court did not rule on NBN's request for a permanent injunction.

At an October 16 Management Committee meeting, Davenport appointed a fifth member of the committee. By a 3–2 vote, the Management Committee voted to hire Finley and Boland, with NBN's representatives opposing. At that meeting, Davenport also proposed to relocate AURN's New York offices from NBN's office space in New York to other office space in the New York area; to transfer to Pittsburgh from New York AURN's traffic, billing, and collection functions; and to require Finley to make cuts in AURN's New York–based marketing and research personnel. NBN's representatives opposed the proposals, and Davenport scheduled a meeting on November 28 to break the deadlock.

Sensing that the Pennsylvania state trial court would dismiss its request for a permanent injunction and hoping to litigate the issues at a later time, NBN sought to withdraw its motion for a permanent injunction. On November 28, 1995, while the state trial court judge was considering NBN's request to withdraw its lawsuit, a meeting of AURN's Management Committee was held. Davenport again invoked the deadlock provision and appointed his son as fifth member of the Management Committee. By a 3–2 vote, the Management Committee agreed to relocate AURN's New York offices from NBN's office space, to transfer AURN functions to Pittsburgh from New York, and to authorize Finley to make cuts in AURN's New York–based marketing and research personnel. Davenport also proposed to promote Finley to chief executive officer and Boland to vice president of administration. NBN Chairman Small objected, and Davenport scheduled another meeting to break the deadlock.

On November 29 and 30, the state trial court, wanting to put "a final end to this unnecessary litigation," ordered the discontinuance of NBN's lawsuit with prejudice, meaning that NBN could appeal the ruling to an appellate court but would not be permitted to have another trial court litigate the same issues. NBN chose not to appeal the decision of the Pennsylvania state trial court.

After the November 28 meeting, Sheridan located new office space for AURN in New York and entered a new lease with a minimum annual liability of $900,000, yet Sheridan never revealed the location of the space to NBN or sought NBN approval of the relocation or new lease. On January 18, 1996, at the next Management Committee meeting, Davenport again appointed his son as the fifth member. By a 3–2 vote, with NBN's representatives opposing, the Management Committee appointed Finley as CEO and Boland as vice president of administration.

On January 31, 1996, NBN filed a federal lawsuit seeking an injunction against Sheridan's alleged violations of the equal management rights of the partners by hiring Finley and Boland, interfering with AURN's personnel and customer relations, and relocating AURN's New York offices. Sheridan asked the federal district court to dismiss the suit on the grounds of res judicata; that is, Sheridan argued that NBN was raising legal issues that the Pennsylvania state trial court had already considered or that NBN should have brought to the Pennsylvania trial court. Thus, Sheridan argued, because the Pennsylvania trial court had already dismissed NBN's request for an injunction with prejudice, the federal district court should not reconsider these issues. The federal district court agreed with Sheridan and dismissed NBN's lawsuit. NBN appealed to the federal court of appeal.

Pollack, Judge

A discontinuance with prejudice is deemed a final adjudication on the merits for res judicata purposes on the claims asserted or which could have been asserted in the suit. Any issue concerning the relocation of the New York Office could not have been raised in the State Court suit commenced on September 15, 1995, or until the voting deadlock thereon on November 28, 1995. The NBN claim on the relocation of the New York Office was a claim based on new conduct that could have only arisen long after the filing of NBN's State Court suit. Since a plaintiff has no obligation to expand its suit in order to add a claim that it could not have asserted at the time the suit was commenced, a later suit based on subsequent conduct is not barred by res judicata.

The res judicata effect is limited to those claims that had arisen at the time that NBN brought the State Court action.

They did not include the relocation of the New York Office, which had not yet even been brought to an initial vote. There was no submission to the State Court of NBN's equal right to decide whether the New York Office should be moved from its existing location as part of NBN's premises.

The doctrine of res judicata embraces all claims of NBN, excluding those claims relating to the relocation of the New York Office, which were passed on by the Management Committee prior to the filing of NBN's State Court action; the claims asserted therein and the dismissal thereof on the grounds of res judicata is affirmed.

Judgment for Sheridan affirmed in part; judgment in part reversed in favor of NBN. Remanded to the district court.

LOG ON

Model Partnership Agreements
www.mhhe.com/mallor14e

Go to your textbook's Web site above to find a model partnership agreement. Note that the agreement repeats the fiduciary duties we studied. A well-drafted partnership agreement will expand that section to make clear what each duty covers, such as stating what activities constitute competition with the partnership. In England and India, partnership agreements are called partnership deeds. See an example at **www.thebharat.com/legal/agreements/partnershipdeed. html.**
There are several commercial Web sites that sell model partnership agreements. One is FindLegalForms.com. See a list of partnership agreements for sale at **www.findlegalforms.com/forms/partnership.**

Liability for Torts and Crimes

Torts The standards and principles of agency law's *respondeat superior* are applied in determining the liability of the partnership and of the other partners for the torts of a partner and other partnership employees. See Chapter 36. In addition, the partnership and the other partners are liable jointly and severally for the torts of a partner committed within the ordinary course of partnership business or within the authority of that partner. Finally, when a partner commits a breach of trust, the partnership and all of the partners are liable. For example, all of the partners in a stock brokerage firm are liable for a partner's embezzlement of a customer's securities and funds.

Intentional Torts While a partnership and its partners are usually liable for a partner's negligence, they usually have no liability for a partner's intentional torts. The reason for this rule is that intentional torts are not usually within the ordinary scope of business or within the ordinary authority of a partner.

A few intentional torts impose liability on a partnership and its partners. For example, a partner who repossesses consumer goods from debtors of the partnership may trespass on consumer property or batter a consumer. Such activities have been held to be in the ordinary course of business. Also, a partner who authorizes a partner to commit an intentional tort is liable for such torts.

Partners' Remedies When a partnership and the other partners are held liable for a partner's tort, they may recover the amount of their vicarious liability from the wrongdoing partner, but only if the partner fails to comply with the fiduciary duty of care. For example, in the *Moren* case, which follows the next section, although a partner caused the harm for which the partnership was liable, she was not grossly negligent or reckless in causing the harm. Therefore, it was appropriate to deny the partnership a recovery against the partner and to require the partnership to assume ultimate liability to the victim.

Tort Liability and Limited Liability Partnerships

State legislatures created the limited liability partnership (LLP) as a means of reducing the personal liability of professional partners, such as accountants. Consequently, an innocent partner of an LLP has no liability for the professional malpractice of his partners. LLP statutes grant partners broad protection, eliminating an innocent partner's liability for errors, omissions, negligence, incompetence, or malfeasance of his partners or employees.

Under the RUPA, the protection afforded LLP partners is even broader. LLP partners have no liability for other debts of the business, such as a supplier's bill, lease obligations, and bank loans.

That is the limit of protection, however. The LLP itself is liable for the tort of a wrongdoing partner or employee under the doctrine of *respondeat superior*. In addition, a wrongdoing partner is liable for his own malpractice or negligence. Also, the partner supervising the work of the wrongdoing partner may have unlimited liability for the wrongdoing partner's tort. Thus, the LLP's assets, the wrongdoing partner's personal assets, and the supervising partner's personal assets are at risk.

Crimes

When a partner commits a crime in the course and scope of transacting partnership business, rarely are his partners criminally liable. But when the partners have participated in the criminal act or authorized its commission, they are liable. They may also be liable when they know of a partner's criminal tendencies yet place him in a position in which he may commit a crime.

Until recent times, a partnership could not be held liable for a crime in most states because it was not viewed as a legal entity. However, modern criminal codes usually define a partnership as a "person" that may commit a crime when a partner, acting within the scope of his authority, engages in a criminal act.

Lawsuits by and against Partnerships and Partners

Under the RUPA, a partnership may sue in its own name. Since suing someone is usually an ordinary business decision, ordinarily any partner has authority to initiate a lawsuit.

The RUPA also permits a partnership to be sued in its own name. Partners may also be sued individually on partnership obligations. Partners are jointly and severally liable for partnership obligations, whether based in contract or tort. This means that in addition to suing the partnership, a creditor may sue all of the partners (jointly) or sue fewer than all the partners (severally). If a creditor sues the partnership and all of the partners, the judgment may be satisfied from the assets of the partnership and, if partnership assets are exhausted, from the assets of the partners. If the partnership and fewer than all the partners are sued severally, the judgment may be satisfied only from the assets of the partnership and the assets of the partners sued. Again, partners cannot be required to pay until partnership assets have been exhausted.

When fewer than all the partners are sued and made to pay a partnership obligation, the partners paying may seek **indemnification** and **contribution** from the other partners for their shares of the liability.

Limited Liability Partnerships For LLP partners, only the LLP is liable on a contractual obligation, and only the LLP may be sued on such a claim. For tort obligations, the LLP is liable as well as the partner who committed the tort. LLP partners who had no role in the commission of the tort have no liability.

The following case, *Moren v. JAX Restaurant,* found a partnership liable to a partner's child who was injured as a result of the parent-partner's negligence.

Moren v. JAX Restaurant   679 N.W.2d 165 (Minn. Sup. Ct. 2004)

Nicole Moren and her sister Amy Benedetti were partners in the JAX Restaurant in Foley, Minnesota. One afternoon in October 2000, Nicole completed her day shift at JAX and left to pick up her two-year-old son, Remington, from day care. She returned to the restaurant with Remington after learning that Amy needed help. Nicole called her husband, Martin, who told her that he would pick Remington up in about 20 minutes. Because Nicole did not want Remington running around the restaurant, she brought him into the kitchen with her, set him on top of the counter, and began rolling out pizza dough using the dough-pressing machine. As she was making pizzas, Remington reached his hand into the dough press. His hand was crushed, and he sustained permanent injuries.

On behalf of his son, Martin sued the partnership for damages, alleging that it negligently caused Remington's injuries. The partnership then brought a legal action against Nicole, claiming that if it was obligated to compensate Remington, the partnership was entitled to indemnity or contribution from Nicole for her negligence in allowing Remington to be on the counter where he could be injured by the pizza press.

The district court issued a summary judgment for Nicole on the grounds that she had no obligation to indemnify JAX Restaurant so long as the injury occurred while she was engaged in ordinary business conduct. The district court also rejected JAX Partnership's argument that its obligation to compensate Remington was reduced by the negligence of Nicole as a mother. JAX Partnership appealed to the Minnesota Supreme Court.

Crippen, Judge

Under Minnesota's Revised Uniform Partnership Act of 1994, a partnership is an entity distinct from its partners, and as such, a partnership may sue and be sued in the name of the partnership. Minn. Stat. § 323A.3–07; RUPA § 307. "A partnership is liable for loss or injury caused to a person . . . as a result of a wrongful act or omission, or other actionable conduct, of a partner acting in the ordinary course of business of the partnership or with authority of the partnership." Minn. Stat. § 323A.3–05(a); RUPA § 305(a). Accordingly, a "partnership shall . . . indemnify a partner for liabilities incurred by the partner in the ordinary course of the business of the partnership. . . ." Minn. Stat. § 323A.4–01(c); RUPA § 401(c). Stated conversely, an "act of a partner which is not apparently for carrying on in the ordinary course the partnership business or business of the kind carried

on by the partnership binds the partnership only if the act was authorized by the other partners." Minn. Stat. § 323A.3–01(2) (2002); RUPA § 301(2). Thus, under the plain language of the RUPA, a partner has a right to indemnity from the partnership, but the partnership's claim of indemnity from a partner is not authorized or required.

The district court correctly concluded that Nicole Moren's conduct was in the ordinary course of business of the partnership and, as a result, indemnity by the partner to the partnership was inappropriate. It is undisputed that one of the cooks scheduled to work that evening did not come in, and that Moren's partner asked her to help in the kitchen. It also is undisputed that Moren was making pizzas for the partnership when her son was injured. Because her conduct at the time of the injury was in the ordinary course of business of the partnership, under the

RUPA, her conduct bound the partnership and it owes indemnity to her for her negligence.

JAX Partnership heavily relies on one foreign case for the proposition that a partnership is entitled to a contribution or indemnity from a partner who is negligent. *See Flynn v. Reaves,* 135 Ga. App. 651, 218 S.E.2d.661 (Ga. Ct. App. 1975). In *Flynn,* the Georgia Court of Appeals held that "where a partner is sued individually by a plaintiff injured by the partner's sole negligence, the partner cannot seek contribution from his co-partners even though the negligent act occurred in the course of the partnership business." But this case is inapplicable because the Georgia court applied common law partnership and agency principles and makes no mention of the RUPA, which is the law in Minnesota.

JAX Partnership also claims that because Nicole Moren's action of bringing Remington into the kitchen was partly motivated by personal reasons, her conduct was outside the ordinary course of business. There is no Minnesota authority regarding this issue. But there are two cases from outside of Minnesota that address the issue in a persuasive fashion. *Grotelueschen v. Am. Family Ins. Co.,* 171 Wis. 2d 437, 492 N.W.2d 131, 137 (Wis. 1992) (An "act can further part personal and part business purposes and still occur in the ordinary course of the partnership."); *Wolfe v. Harms,* 413 S.W.2d 204, 215 (Mo. 1967) ("Even if the predominant motive of the partner was to benefit himself or third persons, such does not prevent the concurrent business purpose from being within the scope of the partnership."). Adopting this rationale, we conclude that the conduct of Nicole Moren was no less in the ordinary course of business because it also served personal purposes. It is undisputed that Moren was acting for the benefit of the partnership by making pizzas when her son was injured, and even though she was simultaneously acting in her role as a mother, her conduct remained in the ordinary course of the partnership business.

Judgment for Nicole Moren affirmed.

Problems and Problem Cases

1. Kyle Jauretz and Galina Marvano formed JM Solutions, a partnership that managed events for business clients. Jauretz had been an event manager for several years, and he insisted before the partnership was formed that Marvano agree that Jauretz could keep several clients to himself and not share the revenue or profits from those clients with Marvano. One such client was Bay Shores LLC, a golf community for which Jauretz had managed an annual golf tournament. When Jauretz was working for Bay Shores LLC, his personal client, he needed additional staff to manage the event. Jauretz directed two JM Solutions employees to work full-time on the Bay Shores event, which they did for three weeks. JM Solutions continued to pay the employees' wages while they worked on the Bay Shores event. Jauretz also used JM Solutions assets, including stakes and ropes, in the course of managing the Bay Shores event. He did not pay JM Solutions for the use of the stakes and ropes. Has Jauretz breached a fiduciary duty to JM Solutions?

2. Larry Rose, Paul G. Veale Sr., Paul G. Veale Jr., Gary Gibson, and James Parker offered professional accounting services as partners under the firm name of Paul G. Veale and Co. Their written partnership agreement expressed the general duties of the partners, but it recognized that Veale Sr. and Rose had outside investments and a number of other business commitments. All of the partners were allowed to pursue other business activities so long as the activities did not conflict with the partnership practice of public accounting or materially interfere with the partners' duties to the partnership. While a partner, Larry Rose performed accounting services for Right Away Foods and Ed Payne. He was paid personally by those clients. Rose was an officer and shareholder of Right Away. In addition, Rose used the partnership's employees and computers to service those clients. Has Rose breached a fiduciary duty owed to his partners?

3. Dennis Ranzau and William Brosseau formed a partnership to purchase the Casa T, a house in Acapulco. Their intent was to use the Casa T as a vacation home for a few weeks each year, to lease it for the remainder of each year, and to share the rental income after expenses. Ranzau soon became concerned that Brosseau was not accounting for the expenses and income of the Casa T. Brosseau refused Ranzau's requests to provide receipts for expenses Brosseau claimed to have incurred on the house. Brosseau also let his friend have "total run of the house" over Ranzau's objection. On another occasion, Ranzau's

wife and her friends were locked out of the house by an agent of Brosseau and had to make other accommodation arrangements. Has Brosseau breached his fiduciary duty to Ranzau?

4. Brothers Harold and Ray Warren formed a partnership to operate a funeral home. A year later, they created a second partnerhip, The Warren Yard and Tree Service. Although their partnership agreements were oral only, they adopted a system by which each partner drew from the two partnerships' funds a reasonable compensation for his actual services rendered to the two businesses. After a few years, Harold—a licensed embalmer and funeral director—spent an increasing amount of time in the funeral home, performing all the lab and specialized mortuary services. Ray—licensed only as a funeral director—devoted most his time to the tree services partnership, spending only a few hours each week assisting with funerals. Consequently during the term of the partnership, Harold drew large sums of compensation from the funeral home partnership and only about $400 from the tree service partnership. Ray drew his primary compensation from the tree service partnership and smaller compensation from the funeral home partnership. Because the funeral home was the more profitable business, Harold's total compensation exceeded Ray's by a considerable amount. Ray sued Harold claiming he was entitled to the same compensation as Harold over the entire lives of the partnerships. Was Ray successful?

5. Nicolas Marsch and Ronald Williams formed a partnership, Horizon Properties, to develop a golf course and luxury home sites in Rancho Santa Fe, California. The partnership was a disaster. When the partnership ended, its assets were $27 million less than the claims against the partnership. Williams demanded that Marsch pay half of the $27 million loss by contributing $13,500,000 to the partnership. Marsch objected on the grounds that section 2.02 of their partnership agreement stated: "Additional capital contributions to the Partnership shall only be by prior mutual agreement of the Partners." Also section 2.03 stated: "No Partner may make any voluntary contribution of capital to the Partnership without the prior consent of the other Partner." Is Marsch liable for half of the $27 million partnership loss?

6. Eric Wilmot and Renee Harmeau form WH & Associates Properties LLP, a limited liability partnership in Rochester, Minnesota, to purchase and manage commercial and residential real estate in the Rochester area. WH & Associates owns five residential apartment buildings, the largest of which has 32 units on two floors and has a value of $3 million. WH & Associates also owns seven strip shopping centers, of which the biggest has 12 stores and a value of $6 million. The total value of all the apartment buildings and shopping centers owned by WH & Associates is $31 million. Most of the residential buildings and shopping centers have been purchased partly with loans for which the properties are collateral.

To escape the harsh Minnesota winters, Wilmot wants to move his home to Jacksonville, Florida. He also wants to move WH Associates' management office to Jacksonville. In additional, he has identified a mall in Jacksonville that he wants to buy for the LLP. The mall has 32 stores, and the asking price is $29 million. To purchase the mall, Wilmot wants to borrow $27 million. Does Wilmot have the authority to move WH Associates' office, to purchase the mall, and to borrow money to fund the purchase?

7. Jake Coombs, Yemi Ogarra, and Wade Stram formed a financial services consulting partnership. The partnership's ordinary business was to provide investment advice to businesses with assets between $500,000 and $40,000,000. The partnership operated from a small building that was owned by the partnership, even though title was held in the name of Yemi Ogarra, who had transferred the building to the partnership as her capital contribution. Because the partnership quickly became profitable, the partners chose to retain some of the earnings of the business and to invest it in commercial real estate in the community. Such investments, however, were not part of the partnership's regular business, which remained financial consulting. Title to investment property purchased by the partnership was held in the partnership's name. After a few years, the partners had a falling out. Ogarra wanted the partnership to move its offices to a bigger, more impressive building. She also believed that the commercial real estate market was in a bubble and that the partnership should sell some of its investment property. Without obtaining approval from her partners, Ogarra sold the building in which the partnership did its business to CFC Financial LLC. Because the building was titled only in Ogarra's name, CFC believed that she was the only person with an interest in the building.

Ogarra also sold to CFC a commercial shopping mall that had been held by the partnership for investment. Title in the mall had been recorded in the partnership's name. Coombs and Stram sued to void the sales of the building and mall to CFC on the grounds that Ogarra had no authority to sell the properties. Were they right?

8. Roberto Frientas and Herman Graham formed an IT consulting business, which they organized as a limited liability partnership, Accent Pointe LLP. For the most part, each LLP client was assigned either to Frientas or Graham, but not both. On behalf of the LLP, Graham did an IT audit for Bemus, Inc., which required Graham to ensure that Bemus's IT controls complied with section 404 of the Sarbanes–Oxley Act. Graham failed to check whether the client had an off-site backup system for critical records like accounts receivable information, an omission that resulted in Bemus's failure to comply with section 404. As a result, when Bemus's system crashed internally, Bemus was unable to verify some of its receivables, resulting in a loss of $500,000. Bemus sued Graham, Accent Pointe LLP, and Frientas to recover its damages. Who is liable to Bemus?

9. Upon his release from prison, Michael Clott, convicted of securities fraud and racketeering, retained a law firm partnership, Ross & Hardies, to provide Clott's company, Capital Financial Group, Inc., a legal framework to do financial, securities, and banking business in Maryland. Steven Kersner was the Ross & Hardies partner primarily assigned to Clott's account. Clott created the 7.5% Program, a mortgage program designed to provide lines of credit to minority homeowners. The 7.5% Program was a fraud by which Clott stole money that was borrowed by the homeowners participating in the program. Kersner helped perpetuate the fraud by assuring homeowners that the program was legitimate, aiding Clott in transferring borrowed funds to bank accounts, opening empty accounts in the name of homeowners to deceive them that lines of credit had been opened for them, preparing false statements to make it appear that the homeowners were no longer liable on the mortgages, telling lenders with questions to contact Kersner instead of homeowners, and forging and altering checks. Did Kersner's actions make his partnership liable to homeowners under the Racketeering Influenced Corrupt Organization Act?

10. Florence and Michael Acri were married and also partners in the Acri Café, which they jointly managed. For the first 15 years of their marriage, Michael had been in and out of sanitaria for the treatment of mental disorders. Although he had beaten Florence when they had marital problems, he had not attacked anyone else. Michael and Florence separated, and Michael assumed full control and management of the café. A few months after the Acris' separation, Stephen Vrabel and a friend went into the Acri Café. Without provocation, Michael shot and killed Vrabel's companion and seriously injured Vrabel while they were seated and drinking at the café's bar. Was Florence liable for Vrabel's injuries?

Online Research

Complex Partnership Agreements

The NBN case on page 959 is an example of a complex partnership agreement that attempts to anticipate all future issues that partners may face. Often, but not always, these complex agreements are between two or more businesses. There are many other interesting examples you can find online at www.onecle.com. Under "Business Contracts from SEC Filings," find the link for "Partnership Agreements" and click on it. You will find partnership agreements involving Time Warner, Trump Hotels, and many others. You will also see an Accenture partnership agreement between its human partners.

Examine these agreements. Note to whom management is entrusted and how management succession is planned. Determine the manner in which profits and other compensation are paid to the partners and the timing of payments. Note the statement of fiduciary duties, especially in the Accenture partnership agreement.

Consider completing the case "PARTNERSHIP: You Sunk My Partnership" from the You Be the Judge Web site element after you have read this chapter. Visit our Web site at www.mhhe.com/mallor14e for more information and activities regarding this case segment.

chapter 39

PARTNERS' DISSOCIATION AND PARTNERSHIPS' DISSOLUTION AND WINDING UP

You are planning the formation of a 50-partner venture capital limited liability partnership. Knowing the attributes, weaknesses, and faults of humans, you expect that some partners will die, become ill, and act irresponsibly during the term of the partnership. You know that some partners will want to leave the partnership for good reasons and some for bad reasons. You know that when a partner leaves the partnership, the leaving partner will want to be paid the value of her partnership interest. You also know it is human nature for partners to disagree about the value of a partnership interest. You are also concerned about how the partnership will fund its repurchase of the leaving partner's interest without causing severe liquidity problems for the firm. You know that some of the firm's clients have strong business and personal attachments to one or more firm partners; therefore, when those partners leave the partnership, the firm may lose the business of those partners' clients. Finally, you know that the firm will need to add new partners from time to time to ensure the firm's survival.

- What are the default rules that apply when partners leave and enter a partnership?
- Why may the default rules be unacceptable to you?
- Write the sections of your partnership agreement regarding partners' leaving and entering the partnership.

THIS CHAPTER IS ABOUT the death of partnerships. Four terms are important in this connection: dissociation, dissolution, winding up, and termination. Dissociation of a partner is a change in the relation of the partners, as when a partner dies or retires from the firm. Dissolution of a partnership is the commencement of the winding up process. Winding up is the orderly liquidation of the partnership assets and the distribution of the proceeds to those having claims against the partnership. Termination, the end of the partnership's existence, automatically follows winding up. A partner in a limited liability partnership dissociates from the LLP and the LLP is dissolved, wound up, and terminated in the same manner as an ordinary partnership.

Dissociation

Dissociation is defined in the Revised Uniform Partnership Act (RUPA) as a change in the relation of the partners caused by any partner's ceasing to be associated in the carrying on of the business. A dissociation may be caused by a partner's retirement, death, expulsion, or bankruptcy filing, among other things. Whatever the cause of dissociation, however, it is characterized by a partner's **ceasing to take part in the carrying on of the partnership's business.**

Dissociation is the starting place for the dissolution, winding up (liquidation), and termination of a partnership. Although dissolution and winding up do not always follow dissociation, they often do. Winding up usually has a severe effect on a business: It usually ends the business, because the assets of the business are sold and the proceeds of the sale are distributed to creditors and partners.

A partner has the *power* to dissociate from the partnership *at any time,* such as by withdrawing from the partnership. A partner does not, however, always have the *right* to dissociate.

When a partner's dissociation does not violate the partnership agreement and otherwise is nonwrongful, the partner has the right to dissociate from the partnership: Such a dissociation is **nonwrongful.** When a partner's dissociation violates the partnership agreement or otherwise is wrongful, the partner has the power—but not the right—to dissociate from the partnership: Such a dissociation is **wrongful.** The consequences that follow a nonwrongful dissocation may differ from those that follow a wrongful dissociation.

Nonwrongful Dissociation

A dissociation is nonwrongful when the dissociation does not violate the partnership agreement and is not otherwise wrongful. The following events are nonwrongful dissociations:

1. Death of a partner.

2. Withdrawal of a partner at any time from a partnership at will. A partnership at will is a partnership whose partnership agreement does not specify any term or undertaking to be accomplished.

3. In a partnership for a term or completion of an undertaking, withdrawal of a partner within 90 days after another partner's death, adjudicated incapacity, appointment of a custodion over his property, or wrongful dissociation. This dissociation is deemed nonwrongful to protect a partner who may think her interests are impaired by the premature departure of an important partner.

4. Withdrawal of a partner in accordance with the partnership agreement. For example, a partnership agreement allows the partners to retire at age 55. A partner who retires at age 60 has dissociated from the partnership nonwrongfully.

5. Automatic dissociation by the occurrence of an event agreed to in the partnership agreement. For example, a partnership may require a partner to retire at age 70.

6. Expulsion of a partner in accordance with the partnership agreement. For example, the removal of a partner who has been convicted of a crime causes a dissociation from the partnership if the partnership agreement allows removal on such grounds.

7. Expulsion of a partner who has transferred his transferable partnership interest or suffered a charging order against his transferable interest. Under the RUPA, such an expulsion must be approved by all the other partners, absent a contrary partnership agreement.

8. Expulsion of a partner with whom it is unlawful for the partnership to carry on its business. Under the RUPA, this expulsion must be approved by all the other partners, absent a contrary agreement.

9. A partner's assigning his assets for the benefit of creditors or consenting to the appointment of a custodian over his assets.

10. Appointment of a guardian over a partner or a judicial determination that a partner is incapable of performing as a partner. For example, a court rules that a partner who has suffered a stroke and has permanent brain damage is unable to continue as a partner of a consulting partnership.

In addition, there are a few special rules for nonwrongful dissociations of nonhuman partners, such as corporations.

Consequences of Nonwrongful Dissociation

A partner who nonwrongfully dissociates from the partnership is entitled to be paid the value of her partnership interest. The partner or her representative has no power, however, to dissolve the partnership and to force winding up, unless it is a partnership at will, that is, a partnership with no term. If the partnership is not at will, the partnership will continue. If dissociation was caused by a partner's retirement in compliance with the partnership agreement, a partnership for a term may be dissolved only by all remaining partners agreeing to the dissolution. Dissociation caused by a partner's death, however, permits as few as 50 percent of the partners to dissolve a partnership for a term. See the Concept Review at the end of this chapter for a comprehensive summary of the consequences of dissociation due to death or retirement.

Wrongful Dissociation

A partner wrongfully dissociates from a partnership when she dissociates in violation of the partnership agreement or in any other wrongful way. The following are wrongful dissociations:

1. Withdrawal of a partner that breaches an express provision in the partnership agreement.

2. Withdrawal of a partner before the end of the partnership's term or completion of its undertaking, unless the partner withdraws within 90 days after another partner's death, adjudicated incapacity, appointment of a custodion over his property, or wrongful dissociation.

3. A partner's filing a bankruptcy petition or being a debtor in bankruptcy.

4. Expulsion of a partner by a court at the request of the partnership or another partner. The grounds for judicial dissociation are when

a. A partner's wrongful conduct adversely and materially affects the partnership business,

b. A partner willfully and persistently breaches the partnership agreement or her fiduciary duties, or

c. A partner's conduct makes it not reasonably practicable to conduct partnership business with the partner.

For example, a partner may persistently and substantially use partnership property for his own benefit. Or three partners may refuse to allow two other partners to manage the partnership's business. The harmed partners may seek judicial dissociation. For the expelled, wrongdoing partners, the dissociation is wrongful.

In addition, there are a few wrongful dissociations that apply only to nonhuman partners, such as a corporation.

Consequences of Wrongful Dissociation A partner who wrongfully dissociates from a partnership has no right to demand that the partnership be dissolved and its business wound up. That means the remaining partners may continue the partnership and its business. If at least 50 percent of the remaining partners so choose, however, the partnership will be wound up.

Should the other partners choose to wind up the business, the wrongfully dissociated partner has no right to perform the winding up. Nonetheless, a wrongfully dissociated partner is entitled to his share of the value of his partnership interest, minus the damages he caused the partnership. Damages may include the cost of obtaining new financing and the harm to the partnership goodwill caused by the loss of a valuable partner. Moreover, the wrongfully dissociated partner is not entitled to receive the buyout price until the term of the partnership has expired.

Acts Not Causing Dissociation
Many events that you think may cause a dissociation in fact do not. For example, a partner's transfer of his transferable partnership interest, by itself, does not cause a dissociation from the partnership, and neither does a creditor's obtaining a charging order. Also, the addition of a partner to a partnership is not a dissociation, because no one ceases to be associated in the business.

Mere disagreements, even irreconcilable differences, between partners are expectable, and therefore by themselves are not grounds for dissociation. If the disagreements threaten the economic viability of the partnership, however, a court may order a dissolution, as will be discussed below.

Effect of Partnership Agreement
The dissociations listed in the RUPA are merely default rules. The partners may limit or expand the definition of dissociation and those dissociations that are wrongful,

and they may change the effects of nonwrongful and wrongful dissociations. For example, the partners may require dissociation if a partner transfers his transferable partnership interest, if a partner does not redeem a charging order within 15 days of the order, or if a partner fails to make a capital contribution required by the partnership agreement. The partnership agreement may also reduce the number of partners that must approve the expulsion of a partner, such as a two-thirds vote, and expand the grounds for expulsion. If one partner is very powerful, the partnership agreement might allow that partner to dissociate at any time without penalty.

Dissolution and Winding Up the Partnership Business

When a partner dissociates from a partnership, the next step may be dissolution and **winding up** of the partnership's business. This involves the orderly liquidation—or sale—of the assets of the business. Liquidation may be accomplished asset by asset; that is, each asset may be sold separately. It may also be accomplished by a sale of the business as a whole. Or it may be accomplished by a means somewhere between these two extremes.

Winding up does not always require the sale of the assets or the business. When a partnership has valuable assets, the partners may wish to receive the assets rather than the proceeds from their sale. Such *distributions-in-kind* are rarely permitted.

During winding up, the partners continue as fiduciaries to each other, especially in negotiating sales or making distributions of partnership assets to members of the partnership. Nonetheless, there is a termination of the fiduciary duties unrelated to winding up. For example, a partner who is not winding up the business may compete with his partnership during winding up.

Events Causing Dissolution and Winding Up
Recognizing that a partnership business is worth more as a going concern, the RUPA contemplates that the partnership business will usually continue after a partner's dissociation. Many dissociations, such as one caused by a partner's death or retirement, will *not* automatically result in the dissolution and winding up of a partnership.

Nonetheless, the RUPA provides that a partnership will be dissolved and wound up in the following situations:

1. When the partnership's term has expired.

2. When the partnership has completed the undertaking for which it was created.

3. When all the partners agree to wind up the business.

4. When an event occurs that the partnership agreement states will cause a winding up of the partnership.

5. For a partnership at will, when any partner expressly withdraws from the partnership, other than a partner who is deceased, was expelled, is a debtor in bankruptcy, assigned his assets for the benefit of creditors, had a custodian appointed over his assets, or was automatically dissociated by the occurrence of an event agreed to in the partnership agreement.

6. For a partnership for a term or completion of an undertaking, when at least half the remaining partners vote to dissolve and wind up the partnership within 90 days after a partner dies, wrongfully dissociates, assigns his property for the benefit of his creditors, or consents to the appointment of a custodian over his property.

7. When the business of the partnership is unlawful.

8. Upon the request by a partner, when a court determines that the economic purpose of the partnership is likely to be unreasonably frustrated, a partner's conduct makes it not reasonably practicable to carry on the business with that partner, or it is not reasonably practicable to conform with the partnership agreement.

9. Upon the request of a transferee of a partner's transferable interest in a partnership at will or a partnership whose term or undertaking has been completed, when a court determines that it is equitable to wind up the partnership business.

Effect of Partnership Agreement The above causes of winding up are the RUPA's default rules, which except for the last three may be changed by the partnership agreement. For example, the partnership agreement may provide that at any time two-thirds of the partners may cause a winding up or that upon the death or retirement of a partner no partner has the right to force a winding up. Partners will frequently want to limit the events that cause dissolution and winding up, because they believe the business will be worth more as a going concern than by being liquidated.

In addition, if dissolution has occurred, the partners may agree to avoid winding up and to continue the business. To avoid winding up after dissolution has occurred, under the RUPA all the partners who have not wrongfully dissociated must consent to continuing the business. That means that any partner who has not wrongfully dissociated may force winding up if dissolution has occurred. That RUPA rule gives great power to one partner who wants to wind up the business when all other partners want to continue the business. Many partnership agreements, therefore, prohibit a single partner from forcing not only dissolution but also winding up of the partnership's business.

In the following *Schwartz* case, we return to a recurrent theme: the importance of carefully drafting partnership agreements to make sure that the partners' intent is clearly expressed. In this case, the court interpreted the partnership agreement to allow two partners to expel a third partner from the partnership without cause.

Schwartz v. Family Dental Group, P.C.
943 A.2d 1122 (Conn. App. Ct. 2008)

In 1996, Steven Schwartz, Ken Epstein, and Peter Munk entered into a partnership agreement. All were dentists by profession. Under the partnership agreement, they formed Family Dental Group–Clinton Associates in Bridgeport, Connecticut. Their partnership agreement provided the following: The partnership was to continue until the year 2051, unless the partners agreed to an early dissolution. The partners wanted the partnership to survive their deaths. The partners were to devote full professional time and attention to the partnership during the first five years of its inception. The two practicing partners, Schwartz and Munk, were to receive 35 percent of their collections from patients. Additionally, any profit beyond expenses would be put into a profit pool of which the first 20 percent would be divided equally between all three partners and the remaining, if any, would be divided equally between Schwartz and Munk.

In 1997, Schwartz reduced his workload, decreasing his hours on Wednesdays and Thursdays, and eliminating Fridays. Munk, however, maintained a consistent, full-time work schedule. When Munk became aware of Schwartz's schedule change, he became upset and ceased communicating with Schwartz. Munk was dissatisfied with Schwartz's management style and the way he conducted his practice. Schwartz also refused to accept HMOs, take emergencies, and work on Saturdays. In addition, Munk was unhappy with Schwartz's appearance, the condition of his work space, and the amount of vacation time he took. He expressed his dissatisfaction to Epstein through letters he wrote to him over the course of several years; however, he did not approach Schwartz directly. Despite Munk's unhappiness, Schwartz was able to function normally in the office and interact appropriately with the remaining staff.

Munk was also dissatisfied with both his compensation and Schwartz's refusal to expand the partnership's dental facilities. Munk wanted to change the agreement to alter his compensation or alternatively terminate Schwartz as a partner. Schwartz did not accept either proposal and insisted that the parties submit to mediation pursuant to the agreement. The mediation resulted in an award of a management fee for Munk in the amount of two-thirds of 1 percent of the gross revenue.

In 2002, Epstein and Munk offered to buy out Schwartz's interest in the practice, or alternatively, to keep him as a partner while eliminating his management responsibilities and his share of the profits. Schwartz rejected the offer. On February 26, 2003, at a special meeting of the partners, Ken Epstein and Munk voted to terminate Schwartz from the practice "without cause" and provided him with 90 days notice pursuant to §12(a)(i) in the partnership agreement.

Section 12 of the partnership agreement is entitled "Other withdrawal from practice." Section 12(a)(i) states:

In the event that any Partner's association with the Partnership is terminated for any reason other than death or total disability, either party shall give the other not less than ninety (90) days written notice of such termination and the Partnership shall have the first option to retire the interest of the departing Partner by paying the departing Partner deferred compensation at the Formula Amount.

As a result of the termination, Schwartz sued Munk and Epstein seeking restoration of his partnership status. The trial court found that the partnership's termination date of December 31, 2051, implied that a reduction in workload was contemplated. The court rejected Munk and Epstein's argument that §12(a)(i) of the agreement provides for termination without cause, as long as a 90-day notice is provided. Instead, the court found the provision unenforceable on the ground that "no reasonable, educated person would sign an agreement whereby they could be stripped of their equitable interest in a business without a reasonable basis. Simply put, it is something a reasonably prudent person would not do." The trial court also found that §12(a)(i) of the agreement does not clearly state a majority of the partners can terminate another partner without any reasonable basis. The court concluded that Munk and Epstein did not provide a reasonable basis for Schwartz's termination. Munk and Epstein appealed to the Court of Appeals of Connecticut.

McLachlan, Judge

Munk and Epstein first claim that the court improperly concluded that §12(a)(i) of the parties' partnership agreement is unenforceable.

There is a strong public policy in Connecticut favoring freedom of contract. It is established well beyond the need for citation that parties are free to contract for whatever terms on which they may agree. This freedom includes the right to contract for the assumption of known or unknown hazards and risks that may arise as a consequence of the execution of the contract. Accordingly, in private disputes, a court must enforce the contract as drafted by the parties and may not relieve a contracting party from anticipated or actual difficulties undertaken pursuant to the contract, unless the contract is voidable on grounds such as mistake, fraud or unconscionability. If a contract violates public policy, this would be a ground not to enforce the contract. A contract, or in this instance, a partnership agreement, however, does not violate public policy just because the contract was made unwisely. Moreover, our Supreme Court has opined: "A provision of a partnership agreement does not violate public policy simply because it is susceptible of an application that is advantageous to one partner and disadvantageous to another." *Konover Development Corp. v. Zeller,* 228 Conn. 206, 231, 635 A.2d 798 (1994).

In the present case, it is clear that the provision in §12(a)(i) does not violate public policy and is enforceable. This provision was entered into by sophisticated and highly educated professionals.

Moreover, this provision, which Munk and Epstein argue is an involuntary termination clause, does not favor one partner over another because the majority of the parties voted to terminate Schwartz's association with the partnership. If the circumstances were different, Schwartz would have been able to rely on the same provision to terminate one of the other partners. Thus, this provision is not against public policy just because in the present case it was a disadvantage to Schwartz.

Munk and Epstein next claim that the court improperly concluded that §12(a)(i) of the parties' partnership agreement does not provide that a majority of the partners can terminate another partner without cause. Munk and Epstein maintain that, as the provision is written, the language refers to "termination resulting from any possible circumstance, excluding death or total disability, except as otherwise modified by another provision in the agreement." In opposition, Schwartz argues that this provision is not a termination without cause provision; rather, it provides only the right of any partner to withdraw from the practice and voluntarily terminate his association in the event that a partner moved or relocated or for some other reason decided to terminate his association with the partnership. We disagree with Schwartz's assertion.

A contract must be construed to effectuate the intent of the parties, which is determined from the language used interpreted in the light of the situation of the parties and the circumstances connected with the transaction. The intent of the parties is to be ascertained by a fair and reasonable construction of the written words and the language used must be accorded its common, natural, and ordinary meaning and usage where it can be sensibly applied to the subject matter of the contract.

Munk and Epstein assert that the language in §12(a)(i) is clear and unambiguous and permits the partners to terminate another partner without cause. Under §12(a)(i), "[i]n the event that any Partner's association with the Partnership is terminated for any reason other than death or total disability, *either party shall give the other not less than ninety (90) days written notice. . . .*" (Emphasis added.) Munk and Epstein argue that if the parties intended that §12(a)(i) would refer only to voluntary termination, they could have stated such intent. Munk and Epstein also refer to §9(a), which provides that "[a]ll decisions concerning the conduct of the Partnership business shall be made by a majority of the Partnership shares, except as otherwise expressly agreed to by the Partners."

The language of §12(a)(i), specifically, that *either party shall give the other* ninety days notice, clearly indicates that this provision does not simply apply to voluntary withdrawal. The term used in the provision, "either party," evidences the intent of the parties that this provision be a termination without cause provision. Furthermore, §12(a)(i) coupled with §9(a) permits the very action taken by Munk and Epstein: the majority of shares acting to terminate a partner without cause. Most significantly, Schwartz himself testified that §12(a)(i) permitted termination for reasons other than death, disability and termination for cause. Thus, we conclude that the provision is enforceable and that it permits the termination of Schwartz's association with the partnership in the manner taken by Munk and Epstein. Accordingly, we disagree with the conclusion of the trial court.

Judgment reversed in favor of Munk and Espstein.

Joint Ventures and Mining Partnerships

The partnership rules of dissociation and dissolution apply to joint ventures. Mining partnerships are difficult to dissolve, because of the free transferability of mining partnership interests. The death of a mining partner does not effect a dissolution. In addition, a mining partner may sell his interest to another person and dissociate from the carrying on of the mining partnership business without causing a dissolution.

Performing Winding Up

For the well-planned partnership, the partnership agreement will indicate who may perform the process of winding up for the partnership, what is the power of the persons performing winding up, and what their compensation is for performing the service.

In the absence of a partnership agreement, the RUPA provides that any partner who has not wrongfully dissociated from the partnership may perform the winding up. A winding-up partner is entitled to reasonable compensation for her winding-up services, in addition to her usual share of profits.

Partner's Authority during Winding Up

Express and Implied Authority During winding up, a partner has the express authority to act as the partners have agreed. The implied authority of a winding up partner is the power to do those acts *appropriate for winding up* the partnership business. That is, he has the power to bind the partnership in any transaction necessary to the liquidation of the assets. He may collect money due, sue

to enforce partnership rights, prepare assets for sale, sell partnership assets, pay partnership creditors, and do whatever else is appropriate to wind up the business. He may maintain and preserve assets or enhance them for sale, for example, by painting a building or by paying a debt to prevent foreclosure on partnership land. A winding-up partner may temporarily continue the business when the effect is to preserve the value of the partnership.

Performing Executory Contracts The implied authority of a winding up partner includes the power to perform executory contracts (made before dissolution but not yet performed). A partner may not enter into *new* contracts unless the contracts aid the liquidation of the partnership's assets. For example, a partner may fulfill a contract to deliver wind turbines if the contract was made before dissolution. She may not make a new contract to deliver wind turbines unless doing so disposes of wind turbines that the partnership owns or has contracted to purchase.

Borrowing Money Usually, the implied authority of a winding up partner includes no power to borrow money in the name of the partnership. Nonetheless, when a partner can preserve the assets of the partnership or enhance them for sale by borrowing money, he has implied authority to engage in new borrowing. For example, a partnership may have a valuable machine repossessed and sold far below its value at a foreclosure sale unless it can refinance a loan. A partner may borrow the money needed to refinance the loan, thereby preserving the asset. A partner may also borrow money to perform executory contracts.

Apparent Authority

Winding-up partners have apparent authority to conduct business as they did before dissolution, when notice of dissolution is not given to those persons who knew of the partnership prior to its dissolution. For example, a construction partnership dissolves and begins winding up but does not notify anyone of its dissolution. After dissolution, a partner makes a contract with a customer to remodel the customer's building. The partner would have no implied authority to make the contract, because the contract is new business and does not help liquidate assets. Nonetheless, the contract may be within the partner's apparent authority, because to persons unaware of the dissolution, it appears that a partner may continue to make contracts that have been in the ordinary course of business.

To eliminate the apparent authority of a winding-up partner to conduct business in the ordinary way, the partnership must ensure that one of the following occurs:

1. A third party knows or has reason to know that the partnership has been dissolved.

2. A third party has received notification of the dissolution by delivery of a communication to the third party's place of business. For example, an e-mail message is sent to a creditor of the partnership.

3. The dissolution has come to the attention of the third party. For example, a partnership creditor was told of the dissolution by another creditor.

4. A partner has filed a Statement of Dissolution with the secretary of state, which limits the partners' authority during winding up. A third party is deemed to have notice of a limitation on a partner's authority 90 days after the filing of a Statement of Dissolution.

To be safe, a dissolved partnership should eliminate its partners' apparent authority to conduct business in the ordinary way by directly informing parties with whom it has previously conducted business, such as by e-mail, fax, or a phone call. The partnership should be able to identify such parties from its records. As for parties that may know about the partnership but with whom the partnership has not done business, the partnership should post notice of the dissolution at its place of business and in newspapers of general circulation in its area, increasing the chance that third parties will know of the dissolution. Also, the partnership should file a Statement of Dissolution: 90 days after its filing, no one should be able to rely on the apparent authority of a partner to conduct any business that is not appropriate to winding up. The partnership agreement of a well-planned partnership will require the partnership to take these steps when dissolution occurs.

Disputes among Winding-Up Partners

When more than one partner has the right to wind up the partnership, the partners may disagree concerning which steps should be taken during winding up. For decisions in the ordinary course of winding up, the decision of a majority of the partners controls. When the decision is an extraordinary one, such as continuing the business for an extended period of time, unanimous partner approval is required.

In the following case, *Paciaroni v. Crane,* the court found that the business of the partnership to train and race a horse should continue during winding up. The drafters of the RUPA expressly noted that this case is a model for continuing a business during winding up.

Paciaroni v. Crane   408 A.2d 946 (Del. Ct. Ch. 1979)

Black Ace, a harness racehorse of exceptional speed, was the fourth best pacer in the United States in 1979. He was owned by a partnership: Richard Paciaroni owned 50 percent; James Cassidy, 25 percent; and James Crane, 25 percent. Crane, a professional trainer, was in charge of the daily supervision of Black Ace, including training. It was understood that all of the partners would be consulted on the races in which Black Ace would be entered, the selection of drivers, and other major decisions; however, the recommendations of Crane were always followed by the other partners because of his superior knowledge of harness racing.

In 1979, Black Ace won $96,969 through mid-August. Seven other races remained in 1979, including the prestigious Little Brown Jug and the Messenger at Roosevelt Raceway. The purse for these races was $600,000.

A disagreement among the partners arose when Black Ace developed a ringbone condition and Crane followed the advice of a veterinarian not selected by Paciaroni and Cassidy. The ringbone condition disappeared, but later Black Ace became uncontrollable by his driver, and in a subsequent race he fell and failed to finish the race. Soon thereafter, Paciaroni and

Cassidy sent a telegram to Crane dissolving the partnership and directing him to deliver Black Ace to another trainer they had selected. Crane refused to relinquish control of Black Ace, so Paciaroni and Cassidy sued him in August 1979, asking the court to appoint a receiver who would race Black Ace in the remaining 1979 stakes races and then sell the horse. Crane objected to allowing anyone other than himself to enter the horse in races. Before the trial court issued the following decision, Black Ace had entered three additional races and won $40,000.

Brown, Vice Chancellor

It is generally accepted that once dissolution occurs, the partnership continues only to the extent necessary to close out affairs and complete transactions begun but not then finished. It is not generally contemplated that new business will be generated or that new contractual commitments will be made. This, in principle, would work against permitting Black Ace to participate in the remaining few races for which he is eligible.

However, in Delaware, there have been exceptions to this. Where, because of the nature of the partnership business, a better price upon final liquidation is likely to be obtained by the temporary continuation of the business, it is permissible, during the winding up process, to have the business continue to the degree necessary to preserve or enhance its value upon liquidation, provided that such continuation is done in good faith with the intent to bring affairs to a conclusion as soon as reasonably possible. And one way to accomplish this is through an application to the Court for a winding up, which carries with it the power of the Court to appoint a receiver for that purpose.

The business purpose of the partnership was to own and race Black Ace for profit. The horse was bred to race. He has the ability to be competitive with the top pacers in the country. He is currently "racing fit" according to the evidence. He has at best only seven more races to go over a period of the next six weeks, after which time there are established horse sales at which he can be disposed of to the highest bidder. The purse for these remaining stake races is substantial. The fact that he could possibly sustain a disabling injury during this six-week period appears to be no greater than it was when the season commenced. Admittedly, an injury could occur at any time. But this is a fact of racing life which all owners and trainers are forced to accept. And the remaining stake races are races in which all three partners originally intended that he would compete, if able.

Under these circumstances, I conclude that the winding up of the partnership affairs should include the right to race Black Ace in some or all of the remaining 1979 stakes races for which he is now eligible. The final question, then, is who shall be in charge of racing him.

On this point, I rule in favor of Paciaroni and Cassidy. They may, on behalf of the partnership, continue to race the horse through their new trainer, subject, however, to the conditions hereafter set forth. Crane does have a monetary interest in the partnership assets that must be protected if Paciaroni and Cassidy are to be permitted to test the whims of providence in the name of the partnership during the next six weeks. Accordingly, I make the following ruling:

1. Paciaroni and Cassidy shall first post security in the sum of $100,000 so as to secure to Crane his share of the value of Black Ace.

2. If Paciaroni and Cassidy are unable or unwilling to meet this condition, then they shall forgo the right to act as liquidating partners. In that event, each party, within seven days, shall submit to the Court the names of two persons who they believe to be qualified, and who they know to be willing, to act as receiver for the winding up of partnership affairs.

3. In the event that no suitable person can be found to act as receiver, or in the event that the Court should deem it unwise to appoint any person from the names so submitted, then the Court reserves the power to terminate any further racing by Black Ace and to require that he simply be maintained and cared for until such time as he can be sold as a part of the final liquidation of the partnership.

Judgment for Paciaroni and Cassidy.

Distribution of Dissolved Partnership's Assets

After the partnership's assets have been sold during winding up, the proceeds are distributed to those persons who have claims against the partnership. Not only creditors but also partners have claims against the proceeds. As you might expect, the claims of creditors must be satisfied first, yet a partner who is also a creditor of the partnership is entitled to the same priority as other creditors of the partnership. Thus a partner who has loaned money to the partnership is paid when other creditors of the partnership are paid.

After the claims of creditors have been paid, the remaining proceeds from the sale of partnership assets will be distributed to the partners according to the net amounts in their capital accounts. Over the life of a partnership, a partner's capital account is credited (increased) for any capital contributions the partner has made to the partnership plus the partner's share of partnership profits, including profits from the sale of partnership assets during winding up. The partner's capital account is charged (decreased) for the partner's share of partnership losses, including losses from the sale of partnership assets during winding up, and any distributions made to the partners, such as a distribution of profits or a return of capital. The net amount in the partner's account is distributed to the partner.

If the net amount in a partner's capital account is negative, the partner is obligated to contribute to the partnership an amount equal to the excess of charges over credits in the partner's account. Some partners may have a positive capital account balance and other partners may have a negative capital account balance. This means that during winding up, some partners may be required to contribute to enable the partnership to pay the claim of another partner.

In many partnerships that have been unprofitable, all the partners will have negative capital accounts. This means that the partnership assets have been exhausted and yet some of the partnership creditors have not been paid their claims. If partnership creditors cannot be paid from the partnership assets, the creditors may proceed against the partners, including a partner who may have already received a portion of partnership assets on account of her being a creditor also.

Since partners have liability for all the obligations of a partnership, if one partner fails to contribute the amount equal to her negative capital account balance, the other partners are obligated to contribute to the partnership in the proportions in which they share the losses of the partnership. The partner who fails to contribute as required is liable, however, to the partners who pay the defaulting partner's contribution.

The RUPA eliminates the old UPA's concept of marshaling of assets. While partnership creditors still have a priority over a partner's creditors with regard to partnership assets, partnership and partners' creditors share pro rata in the assets of individual partners.

Asset Distributions in a Limited Liability Partnership

The asset distribution rules are modified for a limited liability partnership, because in an LLP most partners have no liability for partnership obligations beyond the partnership's assets. If the LLP has been profitable, each partner will receive the net amount in her capital account. If creditors' claims exceed the LLP's assets, however, an LLP partner is not ordinarily required to contribute an amount equal to the negative balance in her account, and the creditors may not sue the partner to force the partner to pay the debt. This result is necessary to protect the limited liability of innocent partners who did not commit a wrong against the creditors.

If, however, a partner has committed malpractice or another wrong for which LLP statutes do not provide protection from liability, that wrongdoing partner must contribute to the LLP an amount equal to her share of the unpaid liability. Creditors may sue such a partner when the LLP fails to pay the liability. If more than one partner has liability, they must contribute to the LLP in proportion in which they share liability. If one is unable to pay, the other liable partners must contribute the shortfall. The partners who are not liable for the obligation cannot be forced to pay the debt.

Termination After the assets of a partnership have been distributed, **termination** of the partnership occurs automatically.

When the Business Is Continued

Dissolution and winding up need not follow a partner's dissociation from a partnership. The partners may choose not to seek dissolution and winding up, or the partnership agreement may provide that the business may be continued by the remaining partners.

When there is no winding up and the business is continued, the claims of creditors against the partnership and the partners may be affected, because old partners are no longer with the business and new partners may enter the business.

Successor's Liability for Predecessor's Obligations

When the business of a partnership is continued after dissociation, creditors of the partnership are creditors of the person or partnership continuing the business. In addition, the original partners remain liable for obligations incurred prior to dissociation unless there is agreement with the creditors to the contrary. Thus, partners may not usually escape liability by forming a new partnership or a corporation to carry on the business of the partnership.

Dissociated Partner's Liability for Obligations Incurred While a Partner

Dissociated partners remain liable to partnership creditors for partnership liabilities incurred while they were partners; however, a dissociated partner's liability may be eliminated by the process of **novation.** Novation occurs when the following two conditions are met:

1. The continuing partners release a dissociated partner from liability on a partnership debt, and

2. A partnership creditor releases the dissociated partner from liability on the same obligation.

Continuing partners are required to indemnify dissociated partners from liability on partnership obligations. To complete the requirements for novation, a dissociated partner must also secure his release by the partnership's creditors. A creditor's agreement to release an outgoing partner from liability may be express, but usually it is implied. *Implied* novation may be proved by a creditor's knowledge of a partner's withdrawal and his continued extension of credit to the partnership. In addition, a *material modification* in the nature or time of payment of an obligation operates as a novation for an outgoing partner, when the creditor has knowledge of the partner's dissociation.

When former partners release a dissociated partner from liability but creditors do not, there is not a novation. As a result, creditors may enforce a partnership liability against a dissociated partner. However, the outgoing partner may recover from his former partners who have indemnified him from liability.

Dissociated Partner's Liability for Obligations Incurred after Leaving the Partnership

Ordinarily, a dissociated partner has no liability for partnership obligations incurred after he leaves the partnership. Nonetheless, a third party may believe that a dissociated partner is still a partner of the continuing partnership and transact with the partnership while holding that belief. In such a context, a dissociated partner could be liable to the third party even though the dissociated partner will not benefit from the transaction between the partnership and the third party.

The RUPA makes a dissociated partner liable as a partner to a party that entered into a transaction with the continuing partnership, unless:

1. The other party did not reasonably believe the dissociated partner was still a partner.

2. The other party knew or should have known or has received notification of the partner's dissociation.

3. The transaction was entered into more than 90 days after the filing of a Statement of Dissociation with the secretary of state, or

4. The transaction was entered into more than two years after the partner has dissociated.

Moreover, although a dissociated partner's right to manage the partnership has terminated upon his dissociation,

The Global Business Environment

Dissolutions around the Globe

For most nations, partnership law on dissolutions is more like the old Uniform Partnership Act than the RUPA, which was drafted to create better default rules when partners leave a partnership. In countries other than the United States, dissolution is defined much like dissociation is defined under the RUPA, a change in the partners' relation. Unlike dissociation in the United States, dissolution in those countries (and in American states that still follow the UPA) often results in the end of the partnership and its business, absent a contrary agreement of the partners. Well-planned partnerships, however, have partnership agreements that in many situations provide for continuation of the partnership and its business by the remaining partners, despite dissolution.

In India, dissolution may be caused by a court, by agreement of the partners, automatically by operation of law, upon the happening of certain contingencies, and by notice. An Indian court may dissolve a partnership due to a partner's insanity, permanent incapacity, conduct that prejudicially affects carrying on the business of the firm, willful or persistent breach of the partnership agreement, and transfer of his partnership interest, or if the partnership cannot be carried on except as a loss. Partners in an Indian partnership may dissolve the partnership by their unanimous agreement. An Indian partnership dissolves automatically if its term ends or undertaking is accomplished, if a partner dies or is insolvent, or if the partnership's business is illegal. Finally, a partnership at will in India may be dissolved by action of any partner.

In Austria, a partnership is dissolved by expiration of the period for which it was entered into, by resolution of the partners, by institution of bankruptcy proceedings against the partnership assets or the assets of a partner, by death of a partner, by notice of termination by a partner, and by judicial decision.

unless one of the above can be proved the dissociated partner retains his apparent authority to bind the partnership on matters in the ordinary course of business.

This means that when dissociation occurs, a partnership should take steps similar to those it took to reduce the apparent authority of a winding-up partner: that is, the partnership should directly inform parties with whom it has previously conducted business, such as by e-mail, fax, or a phone call, that the partner has dissociated. It should also post notice of the dissociation at its place of business and in newspapers of general circulation in its area. Finally, the partnership should cause the filing of a Statement of Dissociation, limiting the authority of the dissociated partner and notifying the public that the partner is no longer a partner. Taking these steps will reduce the risk that the dissociated partner will be liable for future obligations of the partnership, and it will help eliminate the apparent authority of the dissociated partner to act on behalf of the partnership. The partnership agreement of a well-planned partnership will require that these steps be taken by the partnership immediately upon the dissociation of a partner.

Effect of LLP Status

In an LLP, a dissociated partner has less risk of continuing liability for contracts and torts occurring before or after the partner leaves the LLP, since the partner's liability is limited to the LLP's assets. However, a buyout payment made to a dissociated LLP partner may not impair the ability of the LLP to pay its creditors. If so, the dissociated partner will be required to return some or all of the buyout payment to creditors.

In the following case, *In re Labrum & Doak,* the court considered both the UPA and RUPA rules regarding liability of dissociated partners.

In re Labrum & Doak, LLP   237 B.R. 275 (Bank. Ct. E. Pa. 1999)

Labrum & Doak, LLP, was a law partnership that began in 1904 in Pennsylvania. In 1997, its partners dissolved the partnership. The partnership entered reorganization under Chapter 11 of the federal Bankruptcy Code in January 1998. A reorganization plan was confirmed in December 1998, which authorized the reorganization administrator to bring a deficiency proceeding against the partners of Labrum & Doak, seeking to hold individual partners liable on obligations of the partnership.

John Seehousen, Jonathan Herbst, and James Hilly were former partners of Labrum & Doak. Seehousen withdrew from the partnership in 1992, Herbst resigned from the partnership in early 1996, and James Hilly resigned in late 1995. They argued that because of their dissociations from Labrum & Doak, they were not liable for partnership obligations—in particular, liability for the malpractice of other partners—that were incurred after their resignations. The bankruptcy court was asked to rule on the matter.

Scholl, Justice

A very difficult issue is presented in ascertaining whether withdrawing former partners of the Debtor partnership are liable for all of the Debtor's deficiency, even those obligations which arose after their withdrawal. The determination of this issue requires interpretation of several principles of general partnership law.

We note that Pennsylvania Uniform Partnership Act (PAUPA) does not address the effect of dissociation on future liabilities. PAUPA was modeled after the Uniform Partnership Act of 1914. The UPA also does not address the effects of dissociation. At the most, the UPA, section 36, suggests that dissolution does not have any effect on the existing liability of any given partner. Accordingly, under these strictures, Seehousen, Herbst, and Hilly would be liable for the deficiencies incurred regardless of the fact that some of the deficiency claims at issue arose after their dissociation from the Debtor partnership.

The reasoning behind this conclusion is as follows. A partner may be discharged from any existing liability upon dissolution by an agreement to that effect between himself, the partnership creditor, and the person or partnership continuing the business. UPA section 36(2). None of the partners submitted into evidence, nor testified of the existence of, any such agreement. As a result, we can only conclude that no such agreement existed, and that therefore Seehousen, Herbst, and Hilly are liable for all of the deficiencies at hand.

Conscious of these consequences, the drafters of the Revised Uniform Partnership Act (RUPA) tried to clarify the effects of dissociation of partners from a partnership. For this reason, RUPA section 703, which corresponds somewhat to the UPA, section 36, provides as follows:

SECTION 703. DISSOCIATED PARTNER'S LIABILITY TO OTHER PERSONS.

(a) A partner's dissociation does not of itself discharge the partner's liability for a partnership obligation incurred before dissociation. A dissociated partner is not liable for a partnership obligation incurred after dissociation, except as otherwise provided in subsection (b).

(b) A partner who dissociates without resulting in a dissolution and winding up of the partnership business is liable as a partner to the other party in a transaction entered into by the partnership, or a surviving partnership under Article 9, within two years after the partner's dissociation, only if at the time of entering into the transaction the other party:

(1) reasonably believed that the dissociated partner was then a partner;

(2) did not have notice of the partner's dissociation; and,

(3) is not deemed to have had knowledge under Section 303(e) or notice under Section 704 (c).

However, as of this date, RUPA has been only adopted in nineteen jurisdictions. Pennsylvania is not one of them. Moreover, assuming arguendo that RUPA did indeed apply in this jurisdiction, we would be forced to arrive at the same conclusion. Section 703(b) of RUPA simply states that a dissociated partner is not liable for partnership obligations incurred after dissociation, only if at the time the partnership enters into a given trans-

action with a third party, the party in question had notice of the dissociation. See RUPA, section 703(b)(2).

Although Pennsylvania case law is scarce on these issues, it is important to note that dated, but viable and therefore controlling, Pennsylvania cases arrived at similar conclusions when facing analogous problems.

In the instant factual setting the Defendant Partners presented no evidence of their having provided any notice of their dissociation from the Debtor to any of the Debtor's creditors. Moreover, no evidence was submitted to support the conclusion that any of these parties were discharged from any liability by an agreement to that effect between themselves, the partnership creditors, and/or the Debtor. Accordingly, they remain liable for all of the deficiencies at issue, even those which arose after they withdrew as partners from the Debtor.

Judgment for the bankruptcy reorganization administrator.

Buyout of Dissociated Partners

When the partnership is continued, the partnership is required to purchase the dissociated partner's partnership interest. In well-planned partnerships, the purchase price and timing of the buyout will be included in the partnership agreement. For example, the partnership agreement may require the payment of an amount equal to the current value of the partnership multiplied by the partner's proportionate share of profits or capital. The partnership agreement may specify how to value the partnership, such as average annual profits plus partners' salaries for the last three years multiplied by seven. Many professional partnerships, however, pay a dissociated partner only his capital contribution plus his share of undistributed profits. The agreement may also permit deductions against the value of the partnership interest if the dissociated partner acted wrongly.

The agreement will state when the buyout is effected; for example, it may require the payment in a lump sum 30 days after dissociation, or it may allow the partnership to pay the amount in monthly installments over the course of three years.

In the absence of a partnership agreement, the RUPA spells outs the amount and timing of the buyout of the dissociated partner's interest. The buyout price is the greater of the amount that would have been in the dissociated partner's capital account had the partnership liquidated all its assets on the dissociation date *or* the amount in the capital account had it sold the entire business as a going concern on that date. If the partner has wrongfully

dissociated from the partnership, the buyout price is reduced by any damages caused by the wrongfully dissociated partner, such as the reduction in the goodwill of the business caused by the loss of a valuable partner.

When the dissociated partner has not wrongfully dissociated and there is no partnership agreement on the issue, the RUPA requires the partnership to pay the dissociated partner in cash within 120 days after he has demanded payment in writing. The buyout amount must include interest from the date of dissociation. If the dissociated partner and the partnership cannot agree on the buyout price, the partnership must, within 120 days of the written demand for payment, pay in cash to the partner the partnership's estimate of the buyout price, plus interest. The partner may challenge the sufficiency of the buyout price tendered by the partnership by asking a court to determine the buyout price.

If a partner has wrongfully dissociated, the partnership may wait to buy out the partner until the end of the partnership's term, unless the partner shows that the partnership will suffer no undue hardship by paying earlier. The buyout price must include interest from the date of the dissociation.

In the following *Warnick* case between a son and his parents, we see again the risks of relying on the RUPA to resolve partnership issues. The case shows that the RUPA's less than unambiguous provision for valuing a partner's interest should be replaced in the partnership agreement by a concrete valuation method that covers every aspect of valuation the partners want to consider.

Warnick v. Warnick   133 P. 3d 997 (Wyo. S. Ct. 2006)

In 1978, Wilbur and Dee Warnick and their son Randall Warnick formed Warnick Ranches general partnership to operate a ranch in Sheridan County, Wyoming. The initial capital contributions of the partners totaled $60,000, paid 36 percent by Wilbur, 30 percent by Dee, and 34 percent by Randall. The partners over the years each contributed additional funds to the operation of the ranch and received cash distributions from the partnership. After 1983, Randall contributed very little new money. Almost all of the additional funds to pay off the mortgage on the ranch came from Wilbur and Dee Warnick. Wilbur also left in the partnership account two $12,000 cash distributions that were otherwise payable to him. The net cash contributions of the partners through 1999, considering the initial contributions, payments to or on behalf of the partnership, draws not taken, and distributions from the partnership were:

Wilbur $170,112.60 (51%)
Dee $138,834.63 (41%)
Randall $25,406.28 (8%)

After a dispute among the partners arose in 1999, Randall's lawyer sent a letter to Warnick Ranches stating:

I have been asked to contact you regarding [Randall's] desire either to sell his interest in the ranch to a third party or the partnership or to liquidate the partnership under Paragraph 12 of the partnership agreement. It would appear that it would be in the best interests of all to agree amicably to a selling price of his interest either to a third party or to the partnership as provided in the partnership agreement.

Warnick Ranches responded, treating the letter as Randall's intent to dissociate from the partnership. The partnership's response included an offer for Randall's interest, as provided under Wyo. Stat. Ann. § 17-21-701(e) and (g) [RUPA section 701(f) and (g)] in the case of a dissociating partner. Randall in turn exercised his right under § 17-21-701(j) [RUPA section 701(i)] to reject the offer and bring a lawsuit against the partnership to determine his interest in the partnership, including a buyout price if he was dissociated from the partnership.

A Wyoming district court found that dissociation of Randall as a partner was the appropriate remedy and awarded to Randall the amount of his cash contributions, plus 34 percent of the partnership assets' increase in value above all partners' cash contributions. As a result of that calculation, $230,819, or 25.24 percent, of the undisputed value of the partnership was awarded to Randall, without provision of interest for any partner in the calculation.

Warnick Ranch disputed the valuation and appealed to the Wyoming Supreme Court, which remanded the case to the district court, ordering it to take into account advances made by each partner to the partnership. Back in the district court again, Warnick Ranches asserted that for purposes of calculating the buyout price, the value of ranch assets should be less than the amount reflected in its appraisal. Specifically, it requested that the district court deduct $50,000 for real estate commissions and expenses of sale, including those associated with selling livestock and equipment. The district court rejected the deduction, ruling that possible costs associated with selling the assets of the partnership are too speculative.

The district court determined the amount to be paid to Randall by first valuing the partnership assets and deducting advances made to the partnership by each partner to arrive at a net value of the partnership of $133,901.68. Randall's percentage of ownership (34 percent) was then applied to the net value, to arrive at his proportionate share of the partnership of $45,526.57. Adding this amount to the amount of Randall's loan to the partnership, $70,256.56, the district court determined a buyout price of $115,783.13. Warnick Ranches appealed once more to the Wyoming Supreme Court.

Burke, Justice

The statute at issue is part of the Wyoming Revised Uniform Partnership Act (RUPA), Wyo. Stat. Ann. §§ 17-21-101 *et seq.* (2003). The district court was charged with calculating the amount owed to Randall Warnick pursuant to the applicable provisions of RUPA, Wyo. Stat. Ann. § 17-21-603(a) (2003) and Wyo. Stat. Ann. § 17-21-701. That amount, or the buyout price, is the amount that would have been paid to the dissociating partner following a settlement of partnership accounts upon the winding up of the partnership, if, on the date of dissociation, the assets of the partnership were sold at a price equal to the greater of the liquidation value or the value based on a sale of the business as a going concern without the dissociating partner. Wyo. Stat. Ann. § 17-21-701(b).

"[P]artnership assets must first be applied to discharge partnership liabilities to creditors, including partners who are creditors." Wyo. Stat. Ann. § 17-21-808(b) [RUPA section 807(a)]. The interplay between RUPA § 701(b) and § 808(b) requires that obligations to known creditors must be deducted before a partner distribution can be determined. Stated another way, in computing the buyout price, the amount the dissociating partner receives is reduced by his or her share of partnership liabilities.

Warnick Ranches claims that the district court erred in the first step of its calculation of the buyout price by overvaluing the ranch assets. The asserted error is the district court's failure to deduct estimated sales expenses of $50,000 from the value of the partnership assets. A common understanding of liquidation is the act or process of converting assets into cash. Warnick Ranches appears to assume that the liquidation value of the ranch is the amount of cash that would remain following a sale. This assumption is not supported by the pertinent statutory language and the circumstances of this case.

Critical to our determination in this case is the recognition that the assets of this partnership were not, in fact, liquidated. Instead, the record reflects that the assets were retained by Warnick Ranches. Randall Warnick's dissociation from the partnership did not require the winding up of the partnership. The partnership's ranching operations had continued following Randall Warnick's departure. There was no evidence of any actual, intended, or pending sale before the district court at the time of dissociation, and, therefore, asset liquidation was only hypothetical. Accordingly, the deduction urged by Warnick Ranches is for *hypothetical* costs. Because of the hypothetical nature of the urged $50,000 deduction, we find that the district court's calculation was not erroneous.

If, in applying Wyo. Stat. Ann. § 17-21-701(b), we were to interpret the term "liquidation value" in isolation, we might envision an amount representing the net proceeds resulting from a distress sale. However, that interpretation is precluded by the language contained in the statute. The full text of Wyo. Stat. Ann. § 17-21-701(b) provides:

> The buyout price of a dissociated partner's interest is the amount that would have been distributable to the dissociating partbner under W.S. 17-21-808(b) if, on the date of dissociation, the assets of the partnership were sold at a price equal to the greater of the liquidation value or the value based on a sale of the entire business as a going concern without the dissociated partner and the partnership were wound up as of that date. In either case, the sale price of the partnership assets shall be determined on the basis of the amount that would be paid by a willing buyer to a willing seller, neither being under any compulsion to buy or sell, and with knowledge of all relevant facts. Interest shall be paid from the date of dissociation to the date of payment.

Wyo. Stat. Ann. § 17-21-701(b) differs somewhat from the Uniform Laws version of the same provision, which does not include the second to last sentence. Revised Uniform Partnership Act § 701.

Liquidation value is one of two identified methods for valuing the partnership assets. Application of the two methods to the same partnership may yield two distinct values. The liquidation value looks to the value of the partnership's assets less its liabilities and determines each partner's appropriate share. When valuing a going concern, however, the market value of the partnership interest itself is what is at stake, rather than the percentage of net assets it represents.

Significantly, the buyout price under Wyo. Stat. Ann. § 17-21-701(b) involves use of the *greater* value resulting from the alternate valuation methods. Warnick Ranches' argument seems to assume that the district court's calculation incorporated the liquidation value of the partnership assets. We see room for disagreement based upon the record. The district court did not specify which valuation method was selected, and it was therefore possible that the value used in the buyout price calculation represented the going concern value of the ranch. Warnick Ranches makes no argument that costs of sale should also be deducted from the going concern value because, under its rationale, the $50,000 deduction is required only as part and parcel of liquidation value. Were we to conclude that the district court used a figure which represented the going concern value, our analysis could end here without further discussion of hypothetical costs of sale.

However, even if the district court valued the partnership assets using liquidation value, the deduction for costs associated with a hypothetical sale would not be warranted. Contrary to the interpretation asserted by Warnick Ranches, liquidation value is not the amount of the seller's residual cash following a sale. We find that the meaning of liquidation value in the statute is best understood by comparing it to the other method provided. When contrasted with "going concern value" it is clear that "liquidation value" simply means the sale of the separate assets rather than the value of the business as a whole.

Additionally, under either valuation method, Wyo. Stat. Ann. § 17-21-701(b) directs that the sale price be determined "on the basis of the amount that would be paid by a willing buyer to a willing seller, neither being under any compulsion to buy or sell, and with knowledge of all relevant facts." The legislature chose to supplement the Uniform Laws version of this provision by adding this sentence, lending added significance to this language. This "willing buyer" and "willing seller" language does not present a novel legal concept, as it sets forth precisely what has long been the legal definition or test of "fair market value." *Black's Law Dictionary* 1587 (8th ed. 2004). This language is similar to that found in commentary to RUPA, § 701(b).

Warnick Ranches does not provide any analysis concerning the fair market value language contained in Wyo. Stat. Ann. § 17-21-701(b) and does not explain how it can be reconciled with its urged meaning of liquidation value as involving a deduction for costs of sale. That reconciliation may be difficult. Simply stated, a deduction from fair market value yields an amount which is, by definition, less than fair market value.

Considering the language of RUPA § 701(b) as a whole, we conclude that "liquidation value" does not have the meaning that Warnick Ranches desires, i.e., the amount a seller would "net" upon liquidation. Rather, "liquidation value" represents the sale price of the assets based upon fair market value. Where it is con-

templated that a business will continue, it is not appropriate to assume an immediate liquidation with its attendant transactional costs and taxes. We therefore hold that, under Wyo. Stat. Ann. § 17-21-701(b), purely hypothetical costs of sale are not a required deduction in valuing partnership assets. We find no error in the district court rejecting the $50,000 deduction urged by Warnick Ranches in calculating the buyout price.

Judgment for Randall Warnick affirmed.

Partners Joining an Existing Partnership

Frequently, a partnership will admit new partners. For example, many of you hope to be admitted to a well-established consulting or accounting partnership after you graduate and have practiced for several years. The terms under which a new partner is admitted to a partnership are usually clearly stated in the partnership agreement and in the partner's admission agreement. The terms usually include the procedure for admission as well as the new partner's capital contribution, compensation including salary and share of profits, and power to manage the business. In the absence of a partnership agreement, the RUPA sets the rules for the partner's admission and rights and duties upon admission. For example, a new partner is admitted to a partnership only if all partners consent.

Liability of New Partners An important question is what level of liability a new partner should

have for obligations of the new partnership. It makes sense for a new partner to be fully liable for all partnership obligations incurred *after* he becomes a partner, for he clearly benefits from the partnership during that time. This is the RUPA rule.

What should be his liability for partnership obligations incurred *before* he became a partner? The RUPA states that a new partner has no liability for partnership obligations incurred before he became a partner. However, many

LOG ON

www.nccusl.org

At the Web site for the National Conference of Commissioners on Uniform State Laws, you can find the complete text and comments of the RUPA. You can find the complex default rules regarding dissociation, dissolution, and buyouts of partners in Articles 6, 7, and 8. Pay particular attention to sections 601, 701, 801, and 802. Knowing the content of these sections will help you draft the partnership agreement dealing with a partner leaving the partnership.

Ethics in Action

The default rules of the RUPA provide that any partner who leaves the partnership is entitled to the value of her partnership interest. The default valuation method uses the greater of the partnership's liquidation or going concern value. If a partner wrongfully dissociates, however, damages are deducted from the partner's interest and the partner need not be paid until the partnership ends.

- Why would partners want a partnership agreement that sets out a different valuation method than the default rule?
- What risk is taken by relying on the default rule? Among other things, under the default rule a court will value a part-

nership interest when partners cannot agree on the valuation. Why would partners not want a court to valuate a partnership interest?

- Using profit maximization analysis, is it ethical to delay payment to a wrongfully dissociating partner for the value of her partnership interest until the partnership terminates? Does utilitarian analysis change your answer? What are the costs and benefits of delaying payment?
- When do you propose your partnership should pay a partner who dissociates due to death, disability, retirement at an expected age, and unexpected dissociations? What ethical arguments would you make to justify the rules you propose?

Consequences of Partner's Death or Retirement under the RUPA's Default Rules

Death of Partner

A. Is a nonwrongful dissociation

B. Does not by itself effect a dissolution

C. Rights of estate of deceased partner

   1. Receive the amount in the deceased partner's capital account at the time of death, valuing the partnership or its assets at the greater of

      a. liquidation value or

      b. going concern value.

   2. Payment must be made not later than 120 days after a written demand by the estate

D. Rights of other partners

   1. In a partnership at will: any partner may dissociate at any time and effect a dissolution

   2. In a partnership for a term

      a. Any partner may dissociate within 90 days of death:

         1) that dissociation will not dissolve the partnership

         2) that dissociated partner must be paid the amount in her capital account (see calculation in C.1 above) within 120 days after a written demand by the partner

      b. By a vote of at least 50 percent of partners within 90 days of death, the partnership may be dissolved and its business wound up

Retirement (Withdrawal) of Partner

A. Is a dissociation

   1. Is a nonwrongful dissociation if the partnership is at will

   2. Is a wrongful dissociation if the partnership is for a term, the term has not expired, and the partnership agreement does not permit the partner's withdrawal

B. Automatically effects a dissolution if the partnership is at will

C. Rights of dissociated partner

   1. If nonwrongful dissociation, dissociated partner

      a. may wind up the business, if a partnership at will, or

      b. receives the amount in the dissociated partner's capital account (see calculation in C.1 above) within 120 days after a written demand

   2. If wrongful dissociation, dissociated partner

      a. may not dissolve the partnership and

      b. receives the amount in the dissociated partner's capital account (see calculation in C.1 above) less damages, at the end of the partnership's term, unless no undue hardship to partnership by paying earlier

D. Rights of other partners

   1. In a partnership at will, any partner may dissociate at any time and effect a dissolution

   2. In a partnership for a term if the retirement is a wrongful dissociation,

      a. any partner may dissociate within 90 days of the retirement and be paid the amount in her capital account (see calculation in C.1 above) within 120 days after a written demand by the partner;

      b. by a vote of at least 50 percent of partners within 90 days of the retirement, the partnership may be dissolved and its business wound up

   3. In a partnership for a term if the retirement is a nonwrongful dissociation, the remaining partners have no rights created by the retirement

partnership agreements modify this rule by requiring a partner to assume liability for all the obligations of the business as a condition of being admitted to the partnership.

Effect of LLP Statutes   If a new partner enters an LLP, however, the RUPA provides that the partner has no lia-

bility for the obligations of the LLP beyond his capital contribution, whether incurred before or after his admission, unless the new partner has committed malpractice or other wrong for which he is personally responsible. LLP partnership agreements should not change this rule.

Problems and Problem Cases

1. Horizon/CMS Healthcare Corp., a large provider of both nursing home facilities and management for nursing homes, expanded into the Kissimmee, Florida, market by entering several 20-year partnerships with Southern Oaks Health Care, Inc. Within a few years, Horizon claimed that the partners had irreconcilable differences regarding how profits were to be determined and divided, resulting in the partners incapacity to operate in business together. Horizon asked a court to dissolve the partnership on these grounds. Did the court grant Horizon's request? Has Horizon wrongly dissociated by seeking judicial dissolution on these grounds?

2. Byron Bennett and Louis Gagliardi were partners in a law practice. Gagliardi received 60 percent of partnership profits and Bennett received 40 percent. When Gagliardi died, Bennett continued to practice law at the partnership location in Philadelphia, Pennsylvania. While winding up partnership cases, Bennett commingled all of the revenue generated from partnership case files with his own personal funds. In addition, he spent all but approximately $2,000 of the partnership's revenue for personal and other nonpartnership purposes. Bennett expended 563.5 hours and incurred costs of $2,938 in winding up the partnership cases. Bennett paid $750 to a CPA for preparation of the partnership's 1993 tax return. He spent 73.5 hours and paid $618.87 to produce the accountings of the partnerships affairs. Did Bennett do anything wrong? Was Bennett entitled to compensation for his time and reimbursement of expenses for winding up the affairs of the partnership?

3. In 1968, Hal Bolinger and his son Bud Bolinger created a partnership that operated a ranch. The partnership agreement set a value of $48,000 for the partnership and stated that the value controlled in the event of a sale or dissolution of the partnership. The terms also stated that each year the partners would update

the value, which will serve for the following year as the value of the partnership. In the event of Hal's or Bud's death, the agreement gave the surviving partner the right to purchase the deceased partner's interest at the value established in the agreement. Despite this agreement, Hal and Bud never updated the valuation of the partnership. In 1995, Bud died and was survived by his children. The partnership dissolved, but Hal continued the business. Bud's estate sought the value of his partnership interest. The fair value of the partnership was over $400,000, far above the 1968 valuation of $48,000 that was never updated. To determine the value of Bud's partnership interest, did the court use the 1968 valuation or did it determine the fair value of the partnership?

4. Pietra Korda and Anna Kim were partners in an IT consulting business, K2 Solutions. They operated the business in a building owned by the partnership. The partnership purchased the building with the proceeds of a loan from Commerce Bank of Brunswick, which held a mortgage in the building. When Korda dissociated from the partnership, Kim paid Korda the value of her partnership interest, and Korda gave up all her claims against the partnership and its assets. Korda filed a Statement of Dissociation with the secretary of state, and she gave notice by a letter to Commerce Bank that she had left the partnership. Commerce Bank did not respond to the letter. Kim dissolved the partnership, filing a Statement of Dissolution, and continued the business under the name K-One Solutions LLC. For two years, Kim made monthly payments to Commerce Bank on the mortgage, paying with checks drawn on K-One Solutions' checking account at Commerce Bank. When Kim defaulted on the mortgage obligation, Commerce Bank sued K2 Solutions, Kim, and Korda. Was Korda liable on the mortgage obligation to Commerce Bank?

5. Robert Weiss was a partner in the Hillman Group, which operated a hotel in Tampa, Florida. Weiss was the manager of the hotel and received 50 percent of

its profits. The hotel became unprofitable because of Weiss's mismanagement. The partners were asked to make an additional capital contribution to the partnership, but Weiss failed to contribute as required by the partnership agreement. Pursuant to the partnership agreement, Weiss was expelled from the partnership. The partners continuing the partnership agreed to relieve Weiss from liability on the partnership's obligations. Did the partners' agreement relieve Weiss from liability to partnership creditors on obligations incurred prior to his explusion?

6. Bertrand Barnes was one of three partners of NMB Associates, LLP, a limited liability partnership in the consulting and investment banking industries. When Barnes retired from the LLP, he sought to be released from liability on the $5,438,000 of outstanding bank loans the LLP had incurred during his tenure at NMB. Neither the partners nor the LLP nor the banks have agreed to release Barnes from liability on the loans. What is the extent of Barnes's liability on the bank loans? Would his liability be different if NMB were a partnership and not an LLP?

7. Marc Senatre and Jacob Lewellen were partners in a business, Tavern Associates, which operated a bar in Des Moines, Iowa. The bar was located in a building that Tavern Associates leased from Graham Financial Corp. The term of the lease was five years. After two years, Senatre and Lewellen found a different building in a better location, and they moved the bar to the new location. They also reorganized the business as a limited liability company, named Tavern Associates II LLC. They transferred all the assets of Tavern Associates to Tavern Associates II. When Graham Financial sued Senatre, Lewellen, and Tavern Associates II for breaching the lease on the original building, Senatre and Lewellen argued that only Tavern Associates was liable on that lease. Were they right?

8. Joe Creel owned a NASCAR collectibles business named Joe's Racing Collectibles. In 1994, Creel brought Arnold Lilly and Roy Altizer into the business, which they reformed as a partnership named Joe's Racing. Creel contributed as capital to the partnership inventory and supplies of the old business, valued at $15,000. Lilly and Altizer each contributed $6,666 in cash to the partnership, and each paid $3,333 to Creel for his rights in the existing business. The partners agreed to share profits and losses with 52 percent going to Creel and 24 percent each

to Lilly and Altizer. Less than a year later, Creel died and his wife sought to receive the value of his interest in the partnership. An accountant valued the partnership at $44,589.44. The partnership's creditors were the accountant for $875, Mrs. Creel $495, Lilly $2,187, and Altizer $900. What was the value of the Creel's partnership interest?

9. Simon Weinberg and his brother were the only partners in Times Square Stationers LLP. The partners signed a 20-year lease with Tisch Leasing. After 12 years, Simon retired from the business and was replaced as a partner by his son, Seth. A year later, the business defaulted on its lease with Tisch Leasing. What is Seth's liability on the lease with Tisch? Would your answer change if the business were an ordinary partnership, not an LLP?

10. Herbert Lemon, Greg Clarkson, Adrienne Boysen, and five other marketing professionals decide to create a marketing consulting partnership. They expect the business will add partners from time to time, and they also know that it is likely one of the original partners will retire before the partnership is dissolved. They want to ensure that no partner entering the partnership is liable for obligations of the business that were incurred prior to the partner's entering the partnership. They also want to ensure that no partner leaving the partnership is liable for any obligation of the partnership that was incurred after she leaves. What should they do?

Online Research

Complex Partnership Agreements Redux

This research task continues the task you started at the end of Chapter 38. Return to the Web site www.onecle.com. Find the link for "Partnership Agreements" and click on it. Also click on the link "All Partnership Agreements by Industry." As before, you will find many partnership agreements involving companies like Intel, Micron Technologies, and stamps.com.

Examine these agreements. Note how they resolve the issues regarding partners leaving and entering a partnership. Compare the lists of grounds for dissociation and dissolution in the agreements with those in the RUPA. Note the dissociations that are wrongful. Read the provisions regarding the valuation of a partner's interest. Do you find that the partners' agreed upon valuations methods are less ambiguous than the RUPA's valuation method?

chapter 40

LIMITED LIABILITY COMPANIES, LIMITED PARTNERSHIPS, AND LIMITED LIABILITY LIMITED PARTNERSHIPS

You are planning two business ventures. The first venture is a business that will own self-service businesses, such as laundromats, car washes, and warehouse storage. Due to start-up costs and accelerated write-offs of expenses and assets, you expect the business to generate losses in the first year or two, after which it should earn a yearly return on equity of over 20 percent. You prefer to own this business entirely yourself, yet you want to hire someone with experience in the business to do most of the day-to-day operations of the business. While you prefer that person not be an owner of the business, you may be willing to grant a small amount of ownership or a share of profits to her.

The other business venture will purchase and develop 320 acres of land on the outskirts of your city. You plan to construct several commercial buildings on the site and to lease the building space to several tenants. The venture will generate losses during the first four or five years of construction prior to full occupancy of the buildings. You want the business to be owned by members of your family. You want to be the only manager of the business; other family members will be passive owners only. You hope that this business will generate enough income to provide a moderate level of income to every member of your family in perpetuity.

- Why is the limited liability company an especially good business form for the first venture?
- Why should you choose the limited liability limited partnership for the family-owned commercial development?

STATE LEGISLATURES AND THE Internal Revenue Service have cooperated to permit the creation of three business forms that offer taxation advantages similar to the sole proprietorship and the partnership, yet have simple default rules that promote management of the business by fewer than all the owners and extend limited liability to some or all of the owners. These forms are the limited liability company (LLC), limited partnership, and limited liability limited partnership (LLLP).

Limited Liability Companies

The limited liability company (LLC) is the product of attempts by state legislators to create a new business organization that combines the nontax advantages of the corporation and the favorable tax status of the partnership. Wyoming, in 1977, passed the first LLC statute. Every state and the District of Columbia have adopted an LLC statute. The National Commissioners on Uniform

State Laws has adopted the **Revised Uniform Limited Liability Company Act of 2006 (RULLCA).** The RULLCA provides default rules that govern an LLC in the absence of a contrary agreement of its owners. The RULLCA treats LLCs and their owners similarly to the way the Revised Uniform Partnership Act (RUPA) treats limited liability partnerships (LLPs) and their partners, with exceptions noted in this chapter. In general, the RULLCA has fewer rules than the RUPA, leaving more decisions to its members.

LOG ON

www.nccusl.org
You can find the Revised Uniform Limited Liability Company Act of 2006 at the Web site for the National Conference of Commissioners on Uniform State Laws.

The popularity of the LLC has grown dramatically since 2000. It is the preferred form for businesses with few owners, including high-profile sports firms such as Yankee Global Enterprises LLC. Many families use LLCs for estate planning purposes. Major corporations also form some of their subsidiaries as LLCs.

Tax Treatment of LLCs
An LLC may elect to be taxed like a partnership or a corporation for federal income tax purposes. LLC members usually elect for the LLC to be recognized as a partnership for federal income tax purposes. As a result, the LLC pays no federal income tax. Instead, all income and losses of the LLC are reported by the LLC's owners on their individual income tax returns. Sometimes, the LLC is a tax shelter for wealthy investors, allowing such investors to reduce their taxable income by deducting LLC losses on their federal income tax returns to the extent they are *at risk,* that is, their capital contributions to the LLC. Moreover, passive investors in an LLC, like limited partners in a limited partnership, may use their shares of LLC losses to offset only income from other *passive* investments.

Formation of LLCs
To create an LLC, one or more persons must file a **certificate of organization** with the secretary of state. The certificate must include the name of the LLC, and the name and address of its registered agent. The name of the LLC must include the words "limited liability company," "limited company," or an abbreviation such as "LLC" or "L.L.C.," indicating that the liability of its owners is limited.

The owners of an LLC are called **members.** An individual, partnership, corporation, and even another LLC may be a member of an LLC.

Although not required, an LLC will typically have an **operating agreement,** which is an agreement of the members. The operating agreement will usually state whether the LLC is member-managed or manager-managed. It also will cover how members share profits, manage the LLC, and withdraw from the LLC, among other things. Well-planned LLCs have detailed operating agreements that cover all aspects of the LLC's operation and members' relations, often restating much of what is contained in the RULLCA but with changes to suit the members' needs.

Once formed, an LLC has a perpetual existence and is an entity separate from its members. It may sue and be sued in its own name. It can buy, hold, and sell property. It can make contracts and incur liabilities.

LOG ON

www.medlawplus.com/legalforms/instruct/sample-llc.pdf
It is easy to find model and even actual LLC operating agreements on the Web. The link above is typical. You can find others by typing "LLC operating agreement" in a search engine. There are also Web sites that charge for downloads of LLC operating agreements. One such site is **www.uslegalforms.com.**

Members' Rights and Liabilities

Limited Liability An LLC member has no individual liability on LLC contracts, unless she also signs LLC contracts in her personal capacity. Therefore, a member's liability is usually limited to her capital contributions to the LLC. She is, however, liable for torts she commits while acting for the LLC.

In addition, a member must make capital contributions to the LLC as she has agreed. This includes the initial capital she agreed to contribute and additional calls for capital that can be made on members according to the operating agreement.

Management Rights Under the RULLCA, an LLC may choose to be member-managed or manager-managed. If it fails to make that choice in its operating agreement, the LCC is member-managed. Each member in a **member-managed LLC** shares equal rights in the management of the business merely by being a member of the LLC.

Figure 1   *Principal Characteristics of LLCs under the RULLCA of 2006*

1. An LLC may be created only *in accordance with a statute.*

2. An LLC is owned by *members.* Members usually have *liability limited to their capital contributions* to the business.

3. LLC members *share equally in the profits* of the business, unless members agree otherwise.

4. An LLC may be *member-managed or manager-managed.* If it is member-managed, each member has an equal right to manage the business.

5. A member who manages the LLC owes *fiduciary duties* to the LLC and its members.

6. A member's ownership interest in an LLC is *not freely transferable.* A transferee of a member's distributional interest receives only the member's share of LLC distributions.

7. The death or other withdrawal of a member *does not usually dissolve an LLC.*

8. Members of an LLC may choose to have the LLC *taxed as a partnership or as a corporation.*

Each member is an agent of the LLC with implied authority to carry on its ordinary business. If a member-managed LLC has limited the implied authority of one of its members, that member will retain apparent authority to transact for the LLC with a third party who did not know and had no notice that the member's authority was restricted.

The LLC operating agreement may modify the default rules of the RULLCA by granting more power to some members, such as creating a class of members whose approval is required for certain contracts. The agreement could also provide that members share power in relation to their capital contributions.

Managers in a **manager-managed LLC** may be elected and removed *at any time* by a vote of a majority of LLC members. The powers of a manager to act for the LLC are similar to the power of members in a member-managed LLC. Each manager in a manager-managed LLC shares equal rights in the management of the business as an agent of the LLC with implied authority to carry on the LLC's ordinary business. If a manager-managed LLC has limited the implied authority of one of its managers, that manager retains apparent authority to transact for the LLC with a third party who did not know and had no notice that the manager's authority was restricted.

Under the RULLCA, most matters in an LLC may be conducted by individual managing members or managers, or by a vote of a majority of managing members or managers. This facilitates the conduct of ordinary business. Some matters, however, require the consent of all members, including amendment of the operating agreement, admission of new members, the redemption of a member's interest, and the sale of substantially all the LLC's assets.

In addition to being contractually liable for the acts of its members or managers acting within their express, implied, or apparent authority, the LLC is also liable for the torts and other wrongful acts of managing members and other managers acting within their authority. The LLC is not ordinarily liable for the wrongful acts of members not designated as managers in a manager-managed LLC.

Duties Each member in a member-managed LLC and each manager in a manager-managed LLC is a fiduciary of the LLC and its members. The managing member or manager must account for LLC property and funds and not compete with the LLC. They owe a duty to act with the care that a person in a like position would reasonably exercise and with a reasonable belief that the act is in the best interest of the LLC. Managers must comply with the business judgment rule, a rule we cover in detail in our treatment of corporation law in Chapter 43. This duty of care can be increased or it can be decreased within limits set by the RULLCA.

Nonmanaging members of a manager-managed LLC owe no fiduciary duties to the LLC. Nonetheless, whether or not they are managers, all members owe a duty of good faith and fair dealing when exercising their rights as members. This means all members must act honestly and treat each other fairly.

In the following *Katris* case, the court held that while managers of an LLC owe fiduciary duties, a nonmanaging member of an LLC had no fiduciary duty, even when the LLC's manager delegated considerable power to him.

Katris v. Carroll   842 N.E. 2d 221 (Ill. Ct. App. 2005)

In the 1990s, Stephen Doherty wrote for Lester Szlendak a software program called Viper. On February 14, 1997, Doherty and Szlendak, along with Peter Katris and William Hamburg (both employees of Ernst & Company), formed Viper Execution Systems L.L.C. to exploit the software. Each member held a 25 percent interest in the LLC. Szlendak and Doherty assigned all their rights in Viper to the LLC. The operating agreement provided that the "business and affairs of the LLC shall be managed by its managers" and that the members agreed to elect Katris and Hamburg as the "sole managers" of the LLC. The operating agreement also listed the powers of the managers and the rights and obligations of the members. None of the rights and obligations of the members provided the members with any managerial authority. The operating agreement also stated it could "not be amended except by the affirmative vote of members holding a majority of the participating percentages."

Also on February 14, 1997, Katris and Hamburg, as managers of the LLC, adopted resolutions naming Hamburg as chief executive officer, Katris as chief financial officer, Szlendak as director of marketing, and Doherty as director of technical services. The written consent to the resolution contained signature lines for Hamburg and Katris, who were identified as "all of the managers" of the LLC.

Prior to and at the time of the LLC's formation, Doherty worked as an independent contractor for Hamburg and Patrick Carroll (also an Ernst employee). In late 1997, Ernst hired Doherty to work for Carroll. Working for Carroll and Ernst, Doherty helped to adapt a software program, Worldwide Options Web (WWOW).

By 2002, Katris came to believe that WWOW was functionally similar to Viper. He sued Doherty, Carroll, and Ernst arguing that Doherty usurped a corporate opportunity of the LLC by working in secret with Carroll to develop competing software for Ernst. He further contended that Carroll and Ernst colluded with Doherty in the breach of Doherty's fiduciary duties to the LLC. Doherty subsequently settled the case with Katris, leaving only Carroll and Ernst as defendants.

Carroll and Ernst filed a motion for summary judgment asserting that Katris's collusion claim failed because Doherty, as a nonmanaging member of the manager-managed LLC, did not owe Katris or the LLC a fiduciary duty under the Illinois Limited Liability Company Act; thus, Carroll and Ernst could not collude with Doherty to breach a fiduciary duty under that statute. Katris argued that the 1997 resolution of the managers amended the operating agreement to name Doherty as named Director of Technology and gave Doherty "sole management responsibility for developing, writing, revising and implementing the Viper software." Katris contended, therefore, that pursuant to the Illinois LLC Act, Doherty was subject to the standards of conduct imposed on managers by the act. The Illinois trial court disagreed with Katris, granting Carroll and Ernst's motion for summary judgment. Katris appealed to the Appellate Court of Illinois.

NcNulty, Justice

Summary judgment is appropriate where the pleadings, depositions, affidavits, admissions, and exhibits on file, when viewed in the light most favorable to the nonmoving party, show that there is no genuine issue as to any material fact and the moving party is entitled to judgment as a matter of law.

Katris' claim against Carroll and Ernst depended upon a finding that Doherty owed Katris and the LLC a fiduciary duty. We look to the applicable provisions of the Illinois Limited Liability Company Act in determining the fiduciary duties owed by the managers and members of the LLC. The parties here agree that section 15-3(g) of the Act (805 ILCS 180/15-3(g)) applies to determine Doherty's fiduciary duties.

Katris acknowledges that theirs was a manager-managed LLC and that, pursuant to the Act, a member of a manager-managed LLC "who is not also a manager owes no duties to the company or to the other members solely by reason of being a member." 805 ILCS 180/15-3(g)(1). Katris thus concedes that Doherty did not owe any fiduciary duties solely by reason of being a member of the LLC.

Katris contends, however, that Doherty owed fiduciary duties to the LLC pursuant to section 15-3(g)(3) of the Act. Section 15-3(g)(3) provides:

> [A] member who pursuant to the operating agreement exercises some or all of the authority of a manager in the management and conduct of the company's business is held to the standards of conduct in subsections (b), (c), (d), and (e) of this Section to the extent that the member exercises the managerial authority vested in a manager by this Act[.]" 805 ILCS 180/15-3(g)(3).

Looking at the plain language of section 15-3(g)(3) of the Act, Doherty was subject to fiduciary duties if he exercised some or all of the authority of a manager pursuant to the LLC's operating agreement. 805 ILCS 180/15-3(g)(3). Looking to that operating agreement, it specifically provides that the business and affairs of the LLC "shall be managed by its managers," provides for the election of Katris and Hamburg as the "sole managers" of the LLC, and sets forth the powers of the managers of the LLC. Although the operating agreement also sets forth the rights and obligations of the members, these provisions do not provide for any managerial authority. Accordingly, Doherty did not exercise any managerial authority pursuant to the LLC's operating agreement.

Katris contends, however, that the managers amended the operating agreement by passing the February 14, 1997 written consent wherein they elected Doherty "Director of Technology." He contends that Doherty's designation as "Director of Technology" elevated him to a position beyond that of a mere member of the LLC and was sufficient to impart on him some managerial authority. This argument fails for two reasons.

First, Katris has provided no authority for his contention that the written consent constituted an amendment to the operating agreement. Pursuant to its own terms, an amendment to the operating agreement required the "affirmative vote of members holding a majority of the participating percentages." Katris and Hamburg were the sole participants to the February 14, 1997, written consent and held only a combined 50% interest in the LLC. They thus could not amend the operating agreement without an additional vote. Accordingly, the facts do not support Katris' contention that the written consent constituted an amendment to the operating agreement.

Second, even if the written consent were viewed as part of the operating agreement, it did not change and, indeed, it reaffirmed the terms of the operating agreement. Katris and Hamburg executed the written consent in their capacities as the managers of the LLC. In it, they specifically resolved to adopt the operating agreement the four members had executed that day as the operating agreement of the LLC. In the signature lines to the written consent, Katris and Hamburg designated themselves as "all of the managers" of the LLC. In light of these facts, something more than the managers' designation of Doherty as "Director of Technology" was required to change the terms of the operating agreement and grant Doherty managerial authority pursuant to it.

We find Katris' contentions inapposite under section 15-3(g)(3) of the Act. By its terms, that section applies where the nonmanager member exercises some or all of the authority of a manager *pursuant to the operating agreement*. To look beyond the operating agreement to Katris' affidavit would be to ignore the plain meaning of the statute and to render the express words used therein superfluous or meaningless. This we cannot do.

The undisputed facts of this case show that Doherty was a member of a manager-managed LLC and exercised no managerial authority pursuant to the LLC's operating agreement. Accordingly, the undisputed facts show that Doherty owed no fiduciary duties to Katris or the LLC pursuant to the Act. Katris's collusion claim against Carroll and Ernst fails as a matter of law.

Summary Judgment for Carroll and Ernst & Company affirmed.

Member's Distributions A member's most important right in an LLC is to receive distributions (usually profits) from the LLC. The RULLCA provides that members share profits and other distributions equally, regardless of differences in their capital contributions. No member, however, is entitled to a distribution of profits prior to the dissolution of the LLC, unless the LLC decides to make an interim distribution. The LLC members will usually state in the LLC operating agreement how and when profits are distributed. For example, the operating agreement may simply state that managing members are entitled to salaries and that all members share profits after salaries in proportion to their capital contributions to the LLC. At the other extreme, the LLC operating agreement may have complex rules determining how profits are allocated, including factors such as hours a member works for the LLC, the revenue from clients acquired for the LLC by a member, and a member's capital contribution.

Member's Ownership Interest An LLC member's ownership interest in an LLC is the personal property of the member. However, unlike a corporation in which a shareholder may freely transfer her shares and all her rights to another person, a member has limited ability to sell or transfer her rights in the LLC. Under the RULLCA, a member may transfer her **transferable interest** in the LLC to another person; however, the transferee is not a member of the LLC. The transferee's most important right is to receive the transferring member's right to distributions from the partnership; that is, a share of profits and the value of the member's interest when the LLC is liquidated. A transferee has no right to manage the business and has only a limited right to information about the LLC's accounts.

The LLC operating agreement may provide that a transferee of a member's transferable interest becomes an LLC member. If so, the transferee has the rights, powers, and liabilities of the transferring member, which may include the right to manage the LLC, the right to access LLC records, and the duty to make additional capital contributions.

A personal creditor of a member may obtain from a court a charging order that charges the member's transferable interest with the payment of the debt owed to the creditor. The creditor with a charging order receives, therefore, the member's share of distributions for the life of the charging order. The creditor does not own the transferable interest, but instead only has a lien or security interest against it. To own the transferable interest and acquire all the rights of a transferee, the creditor must foreclose against the interest and purchase it at a foreclosure sale.

Members' Dissociations and LLC Dissolution

Under the RULLCA, members dissociate from an LLC in ways similar to those by which a partner dissociates from a partnership or LLP under the RUPA. Dissolution of an LLC is also similar to that of a partnership or LLP. Therefore, generally, when an LLC member dies or otherwise withdraws from the LLC, the LLC's business will continue, preserving its going concern value.

Member Dissociations A member's dissociation is a change in the relationship among the dissociated member, the LLC, and the other members caused by a member's ceasing to be associated in the carrying on of the business. Under the RULLCA, a partner has the power to dissociate by withdrawing from the LLC at any time. Dissociations are also caused by a member's death, having a guardian appointed over her affairs, being adjudged legally incompetent by a court, being a debtor in bankruptcy, or being expelled by the other members. The other members may expel a member if it is unlawful to carry on business with her, she has suffered a charging order against her transferable interest, or she has transferred all her transferable interest in the LLC. At the request of the LLC or a member, a court may also expel a member because she has harmed the LLC's business, breached the LLC operating agreement, or engaged in conduct that makes it not practicable to carry on business with her. Judicial expulsion would be appropriate when a member persistently breaches the duty of good faith or competes against the LLC. There are also other causes of dissociation for nonhuman members.

A member's dissociation may be wrongful or nonwrongful. Wrongful dissociations breach the LLC operating agreement. Under the RULLCA, a member has wrongfully dissociated by withdrawing before an LLC's term expires, being a debtor in bankruptcy, or being expelled by a court. When dissolution is wrongful, the dissociating member is liable to the LLC for damages caused by the dissociation, such as the loss of business due to the member's withdrawal.

When a member dissociates, his right to manage the business terminates, as do his duties to the LLC, for the most part. He may, however, have apparent authority to transact for the LLC, unless notice of his dissociation is given to third parties. This apparent authority can be eliminated by giving personal notice to LLC creditors that a member has dissociated or by filing a Statement of Dissociation with the secretary of state.

Dissociation also terminates a member's status as a member. A dissociated member is treated as a transferee of a member's transferable interest.

Payment to a Dissociated Member Under the RULLCA, the dissociated member has no right after her dissociation to force the LLC to dissolve and to liquidate its assets. The RULLCA leaves such decisions to the operating agreement. In addition, a dissociated member is not entitled to receive the value of her LLC interest until the LLC dissolves, unless the members agree otherwise. The RULLCA expects members to resolve buyout issues in the operating agreement.

There is one exception. If the LLC is *at will* and is not dissolved, the LLC must purchase his interest at fair value within 120 days after the member's dissociation. If the LLC *has a term,* however, and is not dissolved, the LLC may continue its business and pay the dissociated member the value of his interest within 120 days after the end of the LLC's term.

LLC Dissolution When an LLC is dissolved, ordinarily it must be wound up. Since a business usually is worth more as a going concern, the RULLCA has few events that automatically cause dissolution of an LLC. For example, death and withdrawal of members do not by themselves cause dissolution of an LLC. Instead, the RULLCA mostly lets members decide the causes of dissolution.

The few grounds for dissolution in the RULLCA include an event making it unlawful for the LLC business to continue, judicial dissolution at the request of a member or transferee of a member's transferable interest, and administrative dissolution by the secretary of state. A member or dissociated member may ask for a judicial dissolution if, for example, the LLC cannot practicably carry on its business, the LLC is being managed illegally or oppressively, or the LLC failed to purchase a dissociated member's transferable interest on the date required. The RULLCA allows the members to state in the operating agreement the events that will dissolve the LLC. The operating agreement may also allow the members to dissolve the LLC by their vote, which may be any percentage of members that the members choose.

When an LLC dissolves, any member who has not wrongly dissociated may wind up the business. Winding-up members should liquidate the assets, yet they may preserve the LLC's assets or business as a going concern for a reasonable time in order to optimize the proceeds from the liquidation.

The LLC is bound by the reasonable acts of its members during winding up, and may be liable for actions that continue the business and are inconsistent with winding up, unless the LLC gives third parties notice of dissolution. Notice can be given in a reasonable manner, such as by e-mail, letter, or phone call, and by filing a Notice of Dissociation with the secretary of state, which is effective against all parties 90 days after filing.

Distribution of Dissolved LLC's Assets After all the LLC assets have been sold, the proceeds will be distributed first to LLC creditors, including members who are creditors. If there are excess proceeds, members' contributions are returned next. Any remaining proceeds are distributed in proportion to how they share profits.

If the LLC's assets are insufficient to pay all creditors' claims, ordinarily creditors have no recourse, because the LLC's members have liability limited to the assets of the LLC. If an LLC member has not paid in all the capital she was required to pay, however, creditors may sue the member to force the member to contribute the additional capital.

Effect of Operating Agreement The default dissociation and dissolution rules of the RULLCA may be unacceptable to members of an LLC. Therefore, a well-drafted operating agreement will cover this area completely, defining the grounds for dissociation, such as death, withdrawal, and disability of a member. The agreement should also state when a member may be expelled by the other members and a court. The RULLCA gives the members much flexibility to arrange their affairs the way they want.

The operating agreement may state the amount and timing of payments to a dissociated member for the value of her ownership interest. For example, the operating agreement may provide for a lump-sum payment within 90 days after a member dies, becomes disabled, or withdraws at age 55 or later. If a member withdraws before age 55, the agreement may provide for payment in quarterly installments over a five-year period.

The agreement may also state when dissolution and winding up occur. For example, the agreement may provide that no member has the power to seek dissolution at any time. Instead, the agreement may permit a vote of 75 percent of the members to commence winding up if any member dies or withdraws before the time permitted in the LLC operating agreement. It may require unanimous approval by the members in all other contexts. The agreement should also stipulate which members will have the right to participate in winding up.

The LLC operating agreement may also modify how proceeds are distributed to members during winding up after creditors are paid. For example, the agreement may state that all proceeds beyond creditors' claims are distributed equally to members, regardless of their capital contributions.

The following case considers both the effects of a member's dissociation and the management rights of a member in an LLC. It contains a good example of an LLC operating agreement that details the management powers of a managing member.

In re Garrison-Ashburn, LC   253 B.R. 700 (E. D. Va. 2000)

Cralle Comer and Stephen Chapman formed two manager-managed limited liability companies, Garrison-Ashburn, L. C. and Garrison-Woods, L. C. Comer and Chapman each owned a 50 percent membership interest in each LLC. While Chapman was the initial operating manager, Comer later replaced him as operating manager.

In 1999, Chapman filed a voluntary petition in bankruptcy under Chapter 11 of the United States Bankruptcy Code. In the course of the bankruptcy proceeding, Comer wished to sell a parcel of land owned by Garrison-Woods. Chapman argued that Garrison-Woods could not sell the land without his consent on the grounds that the LLC's operating agreement required all deeds and sales contracts be executed by both members. He refused to sign the contract of sale or the deed. Comer argued that as operating manager he was fully authorized to execute the contract. The bankruptcy court ruled in favor of Comer, and Chapman moved for the court to reconsider its judgment.

Mayer, Judge

The court is satisfied that Comer can bind Garrison-Woods and consummate the contract without Chapman's consent or participation.

The heart of Chapman's argument is Article IV, Section 6 of the Operating Agreement which addresses the powers of the Operating Manager. This section states in part:

Operating Manager. The Operating Manager shall be the chief executive officer of the Company and shall have the general charge of the business and affairs of the Company, subject, however, to the right of the Members to confer specified powers on officers and subject generally to the direction of Members. . . . The Operating Manager shall also have the sole and complete control of the management and operation of the affairs and business of the Company. Without limiting the foregoing, the Operating Manager shall have full and complete authority in his sole and exclusive discretion to execute on behalf of the company, any listing agreement, contract or other paper.

Article IV, Section 11 of the Operating Agreement states in part:

Signature Authority. Without limiting the foregoing, the signatures of both the Operating Manager and the Assistant Operating Manager shall be required for, and they shall have full and complete authority in their sole and exclusive discretion to:

a. Execute on behalf of the Company, any bond or deed, execute or endorse promissory notes and renew the same from time to time;

b. Draw upon any bank or banks or any corporations, associations, or individuals for any sum or sums of money that may be to the credit of the Company, or which the Company may be entitled to receive;

c. Make all necessary deeds and conveyances thereof of Company real and/or personal property, wheresoever located, with all necessary covenants, warranties, and assurances, and to sign, seal, and acknowledge and deliver the same;

Chapman argues that pursuant to Article IV, Section 11, he along with Comer must also sign such a contract for it to be legally binding. This argument is contrary to the plain meaning of the Operating Agreement. The Operating Agreement plainly vests in the Operating Manager "the sole and complete control of the management and operation of the affairs and business of the Company" and the "full and complete authority . . . to execute on behalf of the Company" any contract. Operating Agreement, Article IV, Section 6. The Operating Manager controls the business affairs of the company pursuant to Section 6. This

includes the ability to sell the principal property of the company thereby realizing the company's objective. Section 11 by its express terms does not limit this authority. Moreover, it does not require both members to execute a deed, as suggested in the Motion, but rather two officers, the Operating Manager and the Assistant Operating Manager. At best, if Chapman is the Assistant Operating Manager, Section 11 requires the deed that would be necessary to consummate the contract be signed by Comer as Operating Manager and Chapman as Assistant Operating Manager.

Chapman fails to consider the effect of the filing of his voluntary petition in bankruptcy on his rights in the limited liability company. The Code of Virginia provides that a member is "dissociated" from a limited liability company upon the occurrence of certain events, one of which is filing a petition in bankruptcy.

Dissociation of a member does not dissolve the company. The company continues in existence. The effect on a member of becoming dissociated from a limited liability company is to divest the member of all rights as a member to participate in the management or operation of the company. The only rights remaining are the dissociated member's economic rights, his membership interest. That is to say, the dissociated member is expelled from the company, but does not forfeit the value of his ownership interest.

The question presented by Chapman is whether Garrison-Woods can lawfully execute and consummate a contract for the sale of its real estate. Under present Virginia law, when Chapman filed his voluntary petition, he ceased to be a member and had no further voice or vote in the management of Garrison-Woods. Comer, as the sole remaining member, has the unilateral power to remove Chapman as Assistant Operating Manager at any time and elect a new Assistant Operating Manager. The new Assistant Operating Manager need not be a member of the company. In any event, Comer could elect himself the new Assistant Operating Manager. Article IV, Section 1 of the Operating Agreement provides that any two or more offices may be held by the same person. The restriction Chapman raises in his motion to reconsider would not prevent Garrison-Woods from executing the sales contract for its parcel or from consummating the sale. The legal authority, and the intention, to execute the contract and consummate it are both present. The contract approved by the court can be fully consummated.

Chapman's motion to reconsider is denied. Judgment for Comer.

The Global Business Environment

The limited liability company is known in many countries throughout the world. However, LLCs formed under the laws of other nations are a bit different from American LLCs.

In Germany, which claims to be the first nation to permit them, in 1892, LLCs are known as *Gesellschaft mit beschrankter Haftung* (GmbH). Other countries soon followed Germany's lead, including Portugal (1917), Brazil (1919), Chile (1923), Turkey (1926), Uruguay (1933), Mexico (1934), and Belgium (1935). In France, the *societes de responsabilite limitee* is more popular than the more traditional stock corporation.

In these countries, LLC law confers limited liability on the members, requires use of the word *limited* in the entity's name, permits members to control admission of new members to the entity, and allows the entity to be dissolved by death of a member, unless otherwise expressly stated in the articles of association. Most countries provide for management of LLCs by one or more managing directors. Many countries also limit the number of members in an LLC, making the LLC an entity inappropriate for a publicly held company. Some experts refer to these LLCs as private limited companies, which more accurately describes what they are: corporations with a limited number of owners.

Limited Partnerships and Limited Liability Limited Partnerships

The partnership form—with managerial control and unlimited liability for all partners—is not acceptable for all business arrangements. Often, business managers want an infusion of capital into a business yet are reluctant to surrender managerial control to those contributing capital. Investors wish to contribute capital to a business and share in its profits yet limit their liability to the amount of their investment and be relieved of the obligation to manage the business.

As you have already seen in this chapter and the other partnership chapters, an LLC may have an operating agreement and a limited liability partnership (LLP) may have a partnership agreement that accomplishes these objectives by limiting the management right to fewer than all of the LLC's members or LLP's partners. The **limited partnership,** however, has a basic, default structure that serves these needs. The limited partnership has two classes of owners: **general partners,** who contribute capital to the business, manage it, share in its profits, and possess unlimited liability for its obligations; and **limited partners,** who contribute capital and share profits, but possess no management powers and have liability limited to their investments in the business.

A variant of the limited partnership is the **limited liability limited partnership (LLLP).** An LLLP is a limited partnership that has elected limited liability status for all its partners, including general partners. Except for the liability of general partners, limited partnerships and LLLPs are identical. For that reason, every well-planned limited partnership should eliminate the unlimited liability

of its human managers by having a corporate general partner or electing LLLP status, when available. Today, every state recognizes limited partnerships and many recognize LLLPs as well.

The Uniform Limited Partnership Acts

In 2001 the National Conference of Commissioners on Uniform State Laws drafted a new Uniform Limited Partnership Act (ULPA) to replace the Revised Uniform Partnership Act of 1976 and its 1985 amendments. The ULPA of 2001 is the first comprehensive statement of American limited partnership law. As shown in Figure 2, many characteristics of a limited partnership under the ULPA are similar to those of a partnership or LLP under the Revised Uniform Partnership Act. While the ULPA copies much of the law of the RUPA, only the ULPA applies to limited partnerships.

Although most states at this time have enacted the RULPA, we will study the ULPA of 2001, which will soon be the dominant limited partnership law in the United States. As of October 2008, 17 states have adopted or introduced the ULPA. The ULPA governs both limited partnerships and LLLPs. Under the ULPA, limited partnerships and LLLPs are identical except for the liability of general partners. Therefore, when this chapter addresses limited partnership law (other than the rules regarding the liability of general partners), the law applies to LLLPs as well.

Use of Limited Partnerships and LLLPs
The limited partnership (or LLLP) form is used primarily in tax shelter ventures and activities such as real estate investment, oil and gas drilling, and professional sports. When the limited partnership elects to be taxed as a partnership, it operates as a tax shelter by allowing

Figure 2   Principal Characteristics of Limited Partnerships and LLLPs

1. A limited partnership or LLLP may be *created only in accordance with a statute.*

2. A limited partnership or LLLP has two types of partners: *general partners* and *limited partners.* It must have one or more of each type.

3. All partners, limited and general, *share the profits* of the business *in relation to their capital contributions.*

4. Each limited partner has *liability limited to his capital contribution* to the business. Each general partner of a limited partnership has *unlimited liability* for the obligations of the business. A general partner in an LLLP, however, has *liability limited to his capital contribution.*

5. Each general partner has a *right to manage* the business, and she is an agent of the limited partnership or LLLP. A limited partner has *no right to manage* the business or to act as its agent, but he does have the right to vote on fundamental matters. A limited partner may manage the business, yet retain limited liability for partnership obligations.

6. General partners, as agents, are *fiduciaries* of the business. Limited partners are not fiduciaries.

7. A partner's rights in a limited partnership or LLLP *are not freely transferable.* A transferee of a general or limited partnership interest is not a partner, but is entitled only to the transferring partner's share of capital and profits, absent a contrary agreement.

8. The death or other withdrawal of a partner does not usually dissolve a limited partnership or LLLP, unless there is no surviving general partner.

9. Usually, a limited partnership or LLLP is taxed like a partnership. However, a limited partnership or LLLP may elect to be taxed like a corporation.

partners to reduce their personal federal income tax liability by deducting limited partnership losses on their individual income tax returns. General partners, however, receive a greater tax shelter advantage than do limited partners. Losses of the business allocated to a general partner offset his income from any other sources. Losses of the business allocated to limited partners may be used to offset only income from other *passive* investments and only to the extent limited partners are *at risk,* that is, to the extent of their capital contributions to the limited partnership. If a limited partner has sold her limited partnership interest or the limited partnership has terminated, her loss offsets any income. Limited partnerships are also used by family businesses for estate planning purposes. The *Moser* case after the next section concerns a family limited partnership. Regardless of the use, the ULPA presumes that its partners want a highly centralized, strongly entrenched management (general partners) and passive investors with little control and little right to exit the limited partnership (limited partners).

LOG ON

www.nccusl.org
You can find the Uniform Limited Partnership Act of 2001 at the Web site for the National Conference of Commissioners on Uniform State Laws.

Creation of Limited Partnerships and LLLPs

A limited partnership (or LLLP) may be created only by complying with the applicable state statute. Yet the statutory requirements of the ULPA are minimal. A **certificate of limited partnership** must be executed and submitted to the secretary of state. The certificate must be signed by all general partners. A limited partnership begins its existence at the time the certificate is filed by the office of the secretary of state. The limited partnership may ask the secretary of state to issue a Certificate of Existence, which is conclusive proof the limited partnership exists.

The ULPA requires that the limited partnership certificate submitted by the limited partnership include its address, its registered agent for service of process, its general partners' names and addresses, and whether it is a limited partnership or an LLLP. The name of a limited partnership must include the words *limited partnership* or the letters *L.P.* or *LP.* The name of a limited liability limited partnership must contain the words *limited liability limited partnership* or the letters *L.L.L.P.* or *LLLP.* The name of a limited partnership or LLLP may include the name of any partner, general or limited.

It is expected that many limited partnerships (or LLLPs) will have unlimited duration. Therefore, the

ULPA provides for the perpetual life of a limited partnership (or LLLP). The limited partnership certificate or limited partnership agreement, however, may place a limit on the limited partnership's duration.

The certificate is not required to address many other matters that are essential to the limited partnership, such as the limited partners' names, the partners' capital contributions, the partners' shares of profits and other distributions, or the acts that cause a dissolution of the limited partnership. A well-planned limited partnership will usually include those and other matters in the certificate or in a separate **limited partnership agreement.**

Any *person* may be a general or limited partner. Persons include a natural person, partnership, LLC, trust, estate, association, or corporation. Hence, as commonly occurs, a corporation may be the sole general partner of a limited partnership.

Creation of LLLPs
A well-planned limited partnership should shield all its partners from liability by electing LLLP status, when available. This election is simple, requiring no special filing. LLLP status is elected by making a statement in the limited partnership certificate submitted to the secretary of state that the business is an LLLP.

Defective Compliance with Limited Partnership Statute
The ULPA requires at least *substantial compliance* with the previously listed requirements to create a limited partnership. If the persons attempting to create a limited partnership do not substantially comply with the ULPA, a limited partnership does not exist; therefore, a limited partner may lose her limited liability and have unlimited liability for limited partnership obligations. A general partner in an LLLP will have unlimited liability if the LLLP was formed defectively.

A lack of substantial compliance might result from failing to file a certificate of limited partnership or from filing a defective certificate. A defective certificate might, for example, misstate the name of the limited partnership or erroneously identify the business form as a limited partnership when an LLLP was intended.

Limited Partners Infrequently, a person will believe that she is a limited partner but discover later that she has been designated a general partner or that the general partners have not filed a certificate of limited partnership. In such circumstances and others, she may be liable as a general partner unless she in good faith believes she is a limited partner and upon discovering she is not a limited partner she either:

1. Causes a proper certificate of limited partnership (or an amendment thereto) to be filed with the secretary of state, or
2. Withdraws from future equity participation in the firm by filing a certificate declaring such withdrawal with the secretary of state.

However, such a person remains liable as a general partner to third parties who previously believed in good faith that the person was a general partner.

General Partners The ULPA of 2001 has no provision protecting general partners who erroneously believe an LLLP has been formed. Consequently, a general partner in a limited partnership who believes wrongly that an LLLP has been created has unlimited liability for the obligations of the limited partnership.

In the following *Moser v. Moser* case, a husband and wife tried to use a family limited partnership to reduce taxes. Although they properly formed the limited partnership, they failed to comply with tax law and otherwise to keep the limited partnership's assets separate from themselves. Consequently, the court ruled that the husband and wife had not made a gift of the limited partnership's property to their children.

Moser v. Moser	2007 Ohio 4109 (Ohio Ct. App. 2007)

Terrance and Barbara Moser were married on October 11, 1980. Over the next 16 years, they had two children, Shannon and Joshua, and accumulated assets in excess of $2 million. On December 31, 1996, Terrance and Barbara signed a document creating the Moser Family Limited Partnership. A family limited partnership is an estate planning device designed to minimize tax liabilities. The Moser Family Limited Partnership was set up with Terrance, as trustee of a revocable trust holding his assets, as general partner; Barbara, as trustee of a revocable trust holding her assets, as a limited partner; Shannon and Joshua as limited partners, with Barbara as their custodian. Typically, a family partnership is funded with assets having a high potential for appreciation. Parents will then give to their children a certain number of units or a percentage interest in the limited partnership, without tax liability, taking advantage of the gift tax exclusion. At the time the Moser Family Limited

Partnership was created, the annual gift tax exclusion was $10,000. In order to function properly as an estate planning device, the gifts of partnership interest to the children had to be completed, irrevocable gifts. In this way, wealth could be transferred to children during the parents' lifetime, thus avoiding estate taxes, while the parents would be able to maintain a certain amount of control of the wealth, by virtue of the general partner's control of the partnership. After its creation, the Moser Family Limited Partnership, in conjunction with Moser Construction and other business entities previously owned and operated by the Mosers, successfully oversaw several land development ventures.

Unfortunately, Terrance and Barbara had marital problems. On January 17, 2003, Barbara filed for divorce. In addition to naming Terrance as a defendant, she also named the Moser Family Limited Partnership as an additional defendant, arguing that its assets were part of the marital estate and that she should receive a portion of the limited partnership's assets. The trial court agreed with Barbara. The court determined the total value of the marital estate to be $3,778,764, of which $1,507,663 represented the net value of the Moser Family Limited Partnership. Terrance appealed the decision to an Ohio appellate court.

Grendell, Judge

Terrance raises two arguments. The first is that the trial court erred by invalidating the gifts of partnership interest to the Moser children. The second is that the trial court erred by treating partnership assets as marital property.

As any initial assets of the Partnership were marital, Terrance and Barbara were deemed to be equal partners, *i.e.*, fifty percent owners of the partnership shares. The trial court found that transfers of interest in the Moser Family Limited Partnership to the Moser children did not occur on December 31, 1996, and January 1, 1997, as purported in the federal gift tax returns. Leslie D. Smeach is a certified public accountant who did work for Terrrance. Smeach testified that the valuation of the partnership units allegedly given to the Moser children on December 31, 1996, and January 1, 1997, did not occur until April 1997. Prior to this valuation, it would have been impossible to determine the number of partnership units that could be given in accordance with the gift tax exclusion.

The trial court also found that Terrance operated the Moser Family Limited Partnership and its subsidiary companies as his own personal assets. The court noted the free transfer of funds between business entities that were part of, or associated with, the Moser Family Limited Partnership. For example, although the tax returns indicated the Moser Family Limited Partnership possessed a 50% interest in Rootstown Storage Partnership, Terrance continued to list Rootstown Storage as an asset on his personal financial statements. In April 2000, Terrance received a personal distribution of $55,000 from Rootstown Storage.

The trial court determined that Terrance and Barbara had not made valid, *inter vivos* gifts of their interests in the Moser Family Limited Partnership to the Moser children. In Barbara's case, the court relied upon her testimony that she did not intend to relinquish ownership interest in the Partnership until her death.

In Terrance's case, the court found the intent to make such a gift in the Memoranda of Gifts signed by Terrance on December 31, 1997. However, the court also found that there was no delivery of the Memorandum of Gift letters to the Moser children or to Barbara as their custodian. The court also concluded that Terrance had not relinquished control over his ownership interest in the Partnership in a manner consistent with the intent to make a gift.

There was considerable testimony from various witnesses at the hearings which likened Terrance's powers under the Moser Family Limited Partnership to those of "a benevolent dictator." There was also evidence at the hearings that Terrance exercised this power freely. When the marital residence was inadvertently transferred into the Partnership, Terrance transferred it out. Terrance used Partnership funds to meet the expenses of other businesses owned by him. As noted above, there was considerable "cash flow" between entities existing both within and without the Partnership.

Accordingly, the trial court had jurisdiction over the Moser Family Limited Partnership and its partners and could exercise that jurisdiction to order Terrance to assign specific partnership properties so as to effectuate a fair and equitable division of property.

Judgment for Barbara Moser affirmed.

Rights and Liabilities of Partners in Limited Partnerships or LLLPs

The partners of a limited partnership (or LLLP) have many rights and liabilities. Some are common to both general and limited partners, while others are not shared.

Rights and Liabilities Shared by General and Limited Partners

Capital Contributions A partner may contribute any property or other benefit to the limited partnership. This includes cash, tangible or intangible property, services rendered, a promissory note, or a promise to contribute cash, property, or services. A partner is obligated to contribute as he promised. This obligation may be enforced by the limited partnership or by any of its creditors.

Share of Profits and Losses

Under the ULPA, profits and losses are shared on the basis of the value of each partner's capital contribution unless there is a written agreement to the contrary. For example, if 2 general partners contribute $100,000 each and 20 limited partners contribute $2,000,000 each, and the profit is $40,200,000, each general partner's share of the profits is $100,000 and each limited partner's share is $2,000,000.

Because most limited partnerships are tax shelters, partnership agreements often provide for limited partners to take all the losses of the business, up to the limit of their capital contributions.

Voting Rights

The ULPA of 2001 requires few actions to be approved by all the partners. Only amendment of the limited partnership agreement, amendment of the limited partnership certificate, and sale or other transfer of substantially all the limited partnership's assets outside the ordinary course of business require approval of all the partners. In a well-planned limited partnership, the limited partnership agreement may require that certain transactions be approved by general partners, by limited partners, or by all the partners. The agreement may give each general partner more votes than it grants limited partners, or vice versa.

The ULPA makes it clear that limited partners have no inherent right to vote on any matter as a class. They may receive such a right only by agreement of the partners.

Admission of New Partners

Under the ULPA, the default rule is that no new partner may be admitted unless each partner has consented to the admission. The limited partnership agreement may provide for other admission procedures. For example, the general partners may be given the power to admit new limited partners without the consent of existing limited partners. Usually, this power is given to general partners to facilitate the ability of the limited partnership to raise capital, but the power should be restricted to prevent any significant dilution of the ownership interests of existing limited partners.

The limited partnership agreement may also provide for the election of new general partners, such as when a general partner dies or retires. Instead of requiring approval of all partners, the agreement may provide that a majority of the partners may elect a replacement general partner. Another option is to give to limited partners the power to replace a general partner. Another alternative is to grant such power to the partners owning a majority

of the limited partnership, measured by their capital contributions.

In general, the ULPA does not grant partners much power to expel other partners from the partnership. When we discuss partners' dissociations later in the chapter, we will examine the few grounds for expulsion.

Partner's Transferable Interest

Each partner in a limited partnership owns a transferable interest in the limited partnership. It is his personal property. He may sell or transfer it to others, such as his personal creditors. Or his personal creditor may obtain a charging order against it. Generally, a buyer or transferee—or a creditor with a charging order—is entitled to receive only the partner's share of distributions. The ULPA treats charging orders like ordinary partnership law does.

When the limited partnership agreement so provides or all the partners consent, a buyer or transferee of a partner's transferable interest may become a partner. The new partner then assumes all the rights and liabilities of a partner, except for liabilities unknown to her at the time she became a partner.

A partner's transfer of his transferable interest has no effect on his status as a partner, absent a contrary agreement. The partner has not dissociated and the limited partnership has not dissolved merely as a result of the transfer. However, the limited partnership agreement may create consequences, such as expulsion of the transferring partner.

Power and Right to Withdraw

Partners have the power to withdraw from the limited partnership at any time. The expectation, however, is that a limited partnership will have perpetual duration. Consequently, the ULPA gives the partners no right to withdraw, absent a contrary provision in the limited partnership agreement.

One result, therefore, under the ULPA, is that a withdrawing partner has no right to receive the value of her partnership interest. This means that a partner who withdraws from a limited partnership will not receive a return of her investment, unless the limited partnership agreement provides for a buyout of the withdrawing partner or the limited partnership dissolves and liquidates.

Other Rights of General Partners

A general partner of a limited partnership or an LLLP has the same right to manage and the same agency powers as a partner in an ordinary partnership. He has the express authority to act as the partners have agreed he should and the implied authority to do what is in the ordinary course of business. In addition, he may have apparent authority to bind the partnership to contracts when his implied authority is limited yet no notice of the limitation has been given to third parties.

A general partner has no right to compensation beyond his share of the profits, absent an agreement to the contrary. Since most limited partnerships are tax shelters that are designed to lose money during their early years of operation, most limited partnership agreements provide for the payment of salaries to general partners.

Other Liabilities of General Partners

Liability A general partner in a limited partnership has unlimited liability to the creditors of the limited partnership. In an LLLP, however, a general partner's liability is limited to his capital contribution to the business.

Even so, in an LLLP a general partner may not escape liability for torts he commits in the course of the LLLP's business. Suppose a general partner drives a car on LLLP business and negligently injures a pedestrian. Not only may the LLLP be liable, but also the general partner will have personal liability to the pedestrian. Yet the LLLP form does protect the general partner from most torts of the business. For example, the general partner in an LLLP will not have personal liability for the torts of her fellow general partners or employees.

Fiduciary Duties Any general partner, whether in a limited partnership or an LLLP, is in a position of trust when she manages the business and therefore owes fiduciary duties to the limited partnership and the other partners. The general partner must account for limited partnership property, not compete against the partnership, and not self-deal with the partnership.

In addition, a general partner owes a duty of care when transacting for the partnership. The ULPA provides considerable protection for general partners under the duty of care, imposing liability to the limited partnership only if she engages in grossly negligent or reckless conduct, intentional misconduct, or knowing violations of the law. The limited partnership agreement may increase the general partners' duty of care, although that is not typical. The ULPA permits the partners to reduce the general partners' duty of care, if not unreasonable, but gives no clue to what is reasonable or unreasonable. The *Lach* case, which appears near the end of this chapter, found general partners breached their fiduciary duty by attempting to circumvent a limited partner's right to approve new general partners.

Other Rights of Limited Partners

Limited partners have the right to be informed about partnership affairs. The ULPA obligates the general partners to provide financial information and tax returns to the limited partners on demand. In addition, a limited partner may inspect and copy a list of the partners, information concerning contributions by partners, the certificate of limited partnership, tax returns, and partnership agreements.

Other Liabilities of Limited Partners

Liability Once a limited partner has contributed all of his promised capital contribution, generally he has no further liability for partnership losses or obligations.

Under the RULPA of 1976, a limited partner who participates in the control of the business may be liable to creditors of the limited partnership. Under the RULPA, a limited partner who participates in control is liable only to those persons who transact with the limited partnership reasonably believing, based on the limited partner's conduct, that the limited partner is a general partner.

The ULPA of 2001 eliminates this liability risk. The ULPA extends to limited partners the same protection given to owners who manage LLCs and LLPs: liability limited to their capital contributions, regardless whether they manage the business.

Duties No limited partner owes fiduciary duties to the limited partnership or his partners solely by being a limited partner. That means, for example, a limited partner in an oil and gas limited partnership may also invest as a limited partner in other oil and gas limited partnerships. However, all limited partners owe a duty to act in good faith and to deal fairly with the limited partnership. For example, a limited partner who lends money to the partnership is expected to disclose his interest and to transact fairly with the limited partnership. In addition, a limited partner who is an agent of the limited partnership owes the fiduciary duties imposed by agency law. For example, a limited partner who is a leasing agent for a limited partnership that owns apartment buildings owes the duty to account for rental income and a duty of skill and care.

Partner Who Is Both a General Partner and a Limited Partner

Although unusual, a person may be both a general partner and a limited partner in a limited partnership or LLLP. A general partner may wish to be a limited partner to increase his share of limited partnership profits. A partner who is both a general and limited partner has the duties of a general partner when acting as a general partner and the duties of a limited partner when acting as a limited partner.

A general partner's liability in a limited partnership is not reduced merely because he is also a limited partner, but a limited partner who becomes a general partner would lose his limited liability. In an LLLP, liability is unaffected by whether a partner is both a general and limited partner, as the liability is the same for both types of partners in an LLLP.

Note, however, that ULPA section 102(11) indicates that the *only* limited partner and *only* general partner may *not* be the same person.

Partners' Dissociations and Limited Partnership Dissolution

The ULPA of 2001 greatly changed the law regarding dissolutions of limited partnerships and LLLPs. The ULPA adopts much of the terminology and framework of partnership law in the RUPA. Reflecting the intent that limited partnerships and LLLPs are for long-term businesses, the ULPA makes it harder for a limited partnership to dissolve and provides few rights for partners who dissociate from the limited partnership before the partners expect.

Partners' Dissociations Because the roles of limited partners and general partners are different in a limited partnership or LLLP, the ULPA's default rules for dissociations by a limited partner are in part different from the default rules for dissociations by a general partner.

Limited Partner Dissociations A limited partner will dissociate upon the limited partner's death, withdrawal, or expulsion from the partnership.

A limited partner may be expelled by the other partners or by a court. The other partners may expel a limited partner if she has transferred all of her transferable interest or suffered a charging order against her partnership interest. She can also be expelled if it is illegal to conduct business with the limited partner, such as a securities investment firm limited partner who has been convicted of securities fraud. The other partners' vote to expel must be unanimous.

At the request of the limited partnership, a court may also expel a limited partner if she has engaged in wrongful conduct that negatively affects the business or if she has willfully and persistently breached the partnership agreement or the limited partner's duty of good faith and fair dealing.

The ULPA also defines dissociations for nonhuman limited partners, such as corporations, LLCs, and trusts. For example, the other partners may expel an LLC that has been dissolved and is winding up its business.

A dissociated limited partner is not a limited partner, has no rights as a limited partner, and is treated as a mere transferee of the dissociated limited partner's transferable interest. That means the dissociated limited partner has no right to vote or exercise any other partners' powers, but does have the right to receive distributions (profits) from the limited partnership and has the right to receive the liquidation value of her transferable interest at the termination of the limited partnership.

General Partner Dissociations The ULPA treats general partners' dissociations the same as the RUPA treats partners' dissociations in a partnership. A general partner's death, withdrawal, or expulsion causes dissociation, just as with limited partners. In addition, a general partner dissociates if he becomes mentally or physically unable to care for himself (such as when a court appoints a guardian over his affairs) or he is unable to perform as a general partner (as determined by a court). A general partner also dissociates if he is a debtor in bankruptcy, assigns his assets for the benefit of creditors, or has a custodian appointed over his property. In addition, a general partner may be expelled by a vote of all the other partners or by a court for the same grounds that limited partners may be expelled. The ULPA also provides for dissociation of nonhuman general partners, such as the termination of a corporation that is a general partner.

Like a dissociated limited partner, a dissociated general partner is treated as a transferee of the dissociated general partner's transferable interest. He will receive the liquidation value of the partnership interest at the termination of the partnership.

While a general partner always has the power to dissociate, his dissociation may be wrongful. A general partner wrongfully dissociates by leaving the partnership before it terminates, violating the limited partnership agreement, being a debtor in bankruptcy, or being expelled by a court. A general partner who has wrongfully dissociated is liable to the limited partnership and other partners for damages caused by his dissociation.

Authority and Liability of Dissociated General Partners Dissociation ends a general partner's right to manage the limited partnership. The dissociated general partner is released from most of his fiduciary duties. For example, the duty not to compete would no longer apply, so the dissociated general partner could set up a competing business. The duty of confidentiality, however, exists after dissociation to protect the limited partnership's trade secrets and other proprietary information.

While a general partner's express and implied authority to act for the limited partnership terminates upon his dissociation, he may retain apparent authority to transact for the limited partnership. Moreover, his liability for partnership obligations does not terminate merely due to his dissociation. Therefore, the dissociated general partner and the limited partnership must take steps to notify creditors and other parties of the dissociation to protect the limited partnership and the dissociated general partner from liability.

The best way is for the limited partnership to give notice of the dissociation, such as by e-mail or phone calls. To give notice of a dissociation that is effective against everyone, the ULPA permits the filing of a Notice of Dissociation, which is effective 90 days after filing. In addition, two years after the dissociation, the apparent authority of a dissociated general partner automatically ends.

A dissociated general partner will remain liable on a limited partnership obligation incurred while he was a partner unless the creditor agrees to release him from liability. The dissociated general partner will not be liable for limited partnership obligations incurred after he dissociated, if notice has been given of his association or more than two years have passed since his dissociation.

In an LLLP, however, there is no need for the dissociated general partner to be released from liability by existing creditors or to give notice of the dissolution, because a general partner in an LLLP has liability limited to his contribution to the LLLP.

Effect of Limited Partnership Agreement The partners may agree to modify the default dissociation rules in the ULPA. For example, the partners may agree that no limited partner may withdraw from the limited partnership. While such a provision will not prevent dissociation upon a limited partner's death, it would otherwise require a limited partner to remain with the limited partnership until its term ends. The partnership agreement may also state the events that cause dissociation, such as a general partner becoming a manager of a competing business. The partners may also provide grounds to expel a partner, such as when a partner fails to contribute additional capital as required by the partnership agreement. The agreement may also reduce the percentage of partners required to expel a partner, such as requiring only 80 percent approval or giving expulsion power to general partners.

While a limited partner's power to withdraw may be eliminated, the limited partnership agreement may not restrict a general partner's right to withdraw. The grounds

for this distinction is that a general partner should be able to withdraw from his duties to manage the limited partnership, while the limited partner as a passive investor has no such need to be relieved of that burden.

It may be unacceptable to the partners in a limited partnership that the dissociated partners do not receive the value of their partnership interests until the partnership terminates. Therefore, the limited partnership agreement may provide for the buyout of a partner's interest. A well-written buyout agreement should state the events that trigger a buyout, the valuation method, and when and how the dissociated partner will be paid (for example, in a lump sum 120 days after dissociation or in quarterly installments for five years). To protect creditors, the ULPA prohibits any payment to a dissociated partner if the limited partnership is insolvent.

To protect the limited partnership's competitive position, the partners' agreement may also limit a dissociated general partner's ability to compete against the partnership. For example, a noncompete agreement may prohibit a dissociated general partner from competing for five years in the geographic area served by the limited partnership.

Limited Partnership Dissolutions

Recognizing that a limited partnership is usually worth more as a going concern, the ULPA provides that a limited partnership (or LLLP) is not dissolved, its business is not wound up, and it does not terminate merely because a partner has dissociated from the limited partnership. The ULPA provides that a limited partnership is dissolved and its business wound up only if all general partners and limited partners owning a majority of the claims to limited partner distributions (such as profits) vote for dissolution, if a general partner dissociates and partners owning a majority of the claims to partners' distributions vote for dissolution, if the last general or limited partner dissociates and is not replaced within 90 days, or if a court dissolves the limited partnership because it is not reasonably practicable to carry on the business of the limited partnership. Administrative dissolution by the secretary of state is also possible if the limited partnership fails to pay fees and taxes due to the secretary of state or fails to deliver an annual report to the secretary.

When a limited partnership dissolves, winding up of its business follows automatically. The general partners have the power to wind up the business. Dissociated general partners have no right to wind up.

If there is no remaining general partner, the limited partners may appoint a general partner to conduct the winding up. The limited partnership is bound by the acts of a general partner that are appropriate to winding up, such as selling assets of the business and completing contracts. No new business should be conducted by the winding-up general partners.

After dissolution, a general partner has no express or implied authority to continue the business, except as necessary to liquidation. The general partners may have apparent authority to continue business in the usual way, however, and therefore bind the limited partnership. To avoid liability for the act of a general partner outside the scope of winding up, the limited partnership should give notice of its dissolution to all parties. One way to give notice is by filing a certificate of dissolution, which is effective against everyone after 90 days.

Distribution of Assets   After the general partners have liquidated the assets of the limited partnership, the proceeds are distributed to those having claims against the limited partnership. First paid are creditors, which may include partners who, for example, have sold goods or made loans to the limited partnership.

If the proceeds from the sale of limited partnership assets exceed creditors' claims, the remainder is paid to the partners in the same proportions that they share distributions. This modifies the RULPA rule that repaid partners' capital contributions prior to distributing the remainder according to how partners share distributions. The ULPA rule may result in a wealth transfer from partners who have disproportionately larger contributions than their shares of distributions to partners who have disproportionately larger shares of distributions in relation to their capital contributions. If this is unacceptable, the partners may modify the ULPA rule in the limited partnership agreement, such as by requiring a return of capital contributions before distributing the remaining proceeds in the manner that partners share profits.

If a limited partnership's assets are insufficient to pay a creditor's claim, the persons who were general partners when the obligation was incurred must contribute cash to allow the limited partnership to pay the obligation. The general partners contribute in the same proportions that they shared distributions (considering only distributions to general partners) when the obligation was incurred.

In an LLLP, general partners are not required to contribute additional cash when the LLLP's assets are insufficient to pay creditors' claims because the liability of general partners in an LLLP is limited to their capital contributions.

Mergers and Conversions

The ULPA and the RULLCA permit limited partnerships and LLCs to merge with other businesses, including other limited partnerships, LLCs, and corporations. All partners of a limited partnership and all members of an LLC must consent to the plan of **merger.**

In addition, those statutes also permit a limited partnership or an LLC to convert easily into another business form. For example, some limited partnerships will want to become LLCs in order to enjoy all the limited liability advantages of the LLC. By executing a plan of **conversion** to an LLC, the partners can change the form of business without the more expensive and time-consuming process of forming a new business to take over the old business and then dissolving the old one. All the owners need to do is adopt a plan of conversion to which all partners consent.

In the following *Lach* case, the court held that the general partners were not required to comply with the requirements for conversion, because a new LLC was formed and the limited partnership dissolved. However, the court found that the general partners breached their fiduciary duty by transferring the assets of the limited partnership to the LLC without the consent of a limited partner.

Lach v. Man O'War, LLC   256 S.W. 3d 563 (Ky. S. Ct. 2008)

In 1986, Shirley Lach and her then husband, Lynwood Wiseman, formed Man O'War Limited Partnership for the purpose of leasing real property and developing and operating shopping centers. Robert Miller became a general partner along with Wiseman. Lach was one of eight limited partners. The partners' ownership percentages were Miller, 1 percent, Wiseman, 32 percent, Lach, 27 percent, Jonathan Miller, 9 percent, Harry B. Miller, 12 percent, Harvey Morgan, 1 percent, Penny Miller, 3 percent, Jeffery Mullens, 1 percent, Jennifer Miller, 9 percent, and Sophie Wiseman, 5 percent. Wiseman, Lach, and Robert Miller also formed M.O.W. Place, Ltd., to lease a shopping center from the joint venture. In 1988, Wiseman and Lach were divorced, but continued in business together.

In the spring of 2002, Robert Miller became ill with cancer. With his approaching death, he met with Lach concerning the shopping center. Miller asked Lach to agree to naming Wiseman, Jeffery Mullens (brother-in-law of Robert Miller), and Jonathan Miller (son of Robert Miller), as the new general partners of the Partnership. Under the original Partnership agreement, new general partners could not be added without the consent of all the partners. Robert Miller also asked Lach to agree that when Wiseman died, the two remaining general partners will select a new general partner. Lach objected because it would allow the Miller family, which owned less than Lach's individual interest, to manage and control the shopping center. The Millers' would have two of the three general partners while Wiseman, who was then of advancing age, was alive. Upon his death, Jonathan Miller and Jeffery Mullens would then select the third general partner. Lach proposed substituting her daughter, Sherri McVay, an attorney, as a general partner in place of Jeffery Mullens. Her proposal was rejected.

Miller and Wiseman then sought to restructure the business form of the partnership to eliminate the need for Lach's consent to the proposed management change. They formed a new business entity, Man O'War Limited Liability Company. When operational, the LLC would be manager-managed and controlled only by a majority vote of the owners. The initial managers were to be Wiseman, Jonathan Miller, and Jeffery Mullens.

After forming the LLC, Robert Miller and Wiseman dissolved the Partnership, distributing its assets (the ownership of the LLC) to the partners in identical proportions to their previous ownership of the Partnership, that is—with one catch. Unless a partner signed the documents validating the restructuring, that partner would have no voting rights in the LLC. All the partners except Lach signed the agreement, leaving only Lach without any voting rights.

Lach then sued the LLC and Wiseman, among others. She asked the court to set aside the transfer of Partnership assets to the LLC on the grounds that the transfer and the Partnership's subsequent termination was a violation of KRS 362.490 and a breach by the general partners of their fiduciary duty to the Partnership and Lach. The trial court found for the LLC and Wiseman, granting them summary judgment. The Kentucky appellate court affirmed the trial court's decision. Lach appealed to the Supreme Court of Kentucky.

Scott, Justice

Lach argues that the restructuring of the Partnership business form was invalid without her consent for two reasons: (1) the restructuring was a conversion in violation of KRS 275.370, and (2) the restructuring made it impossible for the Partnership to carry on its business in violation of KRS 362.490.

KRS 275.370 provides, in pertinent part:

(1) A partnership or limited partnership may be converted to a limited liability company pursuant to this section.

(2) The terms and conditions of a conversion of a partnership or limited partnership to a limited liability company shall, in the case of a partnership, be approved by all the partners or by a number or percentage specified for conversion in the partnership agreement or, in the case of a limited partnership, by all the partners, notwithstanding any provision to the contrary in the limited partnership agreement.

While conceding that the statute, in this instance, requires the approval of all the limited partners before a limited partnership can be converted into a limited liability company, the LLC and Wiseman argue that the transformation constituted a "reorganization," not a "conversion" as envisioned under KRS 275.370(1). They illustrate their distinction of the word "conversion," by pointing out that the statute envisions a limited partnership *redesignating itself* as a limited liability company, whereas, in this instance, the limited liability company was created separately and existed concurrently with the Partnership (albeit without any assets). Thus, the fact that the LLC acquired all the assets of the Partnership and the Partnership then dissolved is simply immaterial.

KRS 275.375(1) acknowledges that "[a] partnership or limited partnership that has been converted pursuant to this chapter shall be for all purposes the same entity that existed before the conversion." KRS 275.375(2) recognizes that the property "*shall remain* vested in the converted [business entity] . . . [and] [a]ll obligations of the converting . . . limited partnership *shall continue* as obligations of the converted [business entity]." (Emphasis added.) All of which seem to confirm the LLC and Wiseman's argument that a "conversion" involves only one entity changing its legal form pursuant to statutory authorizations, rather than through interaction between *two* entities.

Looking at subsequent statutes for what light they cast on the question, we note that the Kentucky Legislature adopted the *new* Kentucky Uniform Limited Partnership Act in 2006. KRS 362.2-102, et. seq. This Act was adopted, with some changes, from the Uniform Limited Partnership Act (2001). The Act specifically provides "[i]n applying and construing this uniform act, consideration shall be given to the need to promote uniformity of the law with respect to its subject matter among states that enact it." KRS 362.2-1201.

When the need for uniformity is acknowledged, courts may consider the "Official Comments" to a Uniform Act, even where they have not been officially adopted. Looking at the

Official Comments to §1102 of the Uniform Limited Partnership Act, which, with changes, corresponds to KRS 362.2-1102, the Comment acknowledges, "[i]n contrast to a merger, which involves at least two entities, a conversion involves only one. The converting and converted organizations are the same entity." Unif. Limited Partnership Act §1102–1105, GA U.L.A. 107 (2006).

Having thus considered the statutory scheme, its particular language, the subsequent statute and Official Comments, we answer the question that was presented to us—that the restructuring of the business form of the Partnership, to that of the LLC, in this instance, was not a conversion under, or subject to, KRS 275.370, for reasons that a conversion deals only with one entity. We have not been asked, nor have we considered, whether the restructuring of the Partnership into the LLC constituted a merger, pursuant to KRS 362.531.

Under Kentucky law, partners owe the utmost good faith to each and every other partner. The scope of the fiduciary duty has been variously defined as one requiring utter good faith or honesty, loyalty or obedience, as well as candor, due care, and fair dealing. Indeed, it has often been said, there is no relation of trust or confidence known to law that requires of the parties a higher degree of good faith than that of a partnership. Thus, the doing of an act proscribed by law is a breach of that duty.

KRS 362.490 provides, in pertinent part:

A general partner shall have all the rights and powers and be subject to all the restrictions and liabilities of a partner in a partnership without limited partners, except that without the written consent or ratification of the specific act by all the limited partners, a general partner or all the general partners have no authority to

* * *

(2) do any act which would make it impossible to carry on the ordinary business of the partnership.

The LCC and Wiseman argue that Miller and Wiseman had the authority to perform all the acts constituting the restructuring without Lach's consent because they did not make it impossible to carry on the business of the partnership. They assert, *it was the only act which made it possible* to carry on the business of the partnership; suggesting that Lach would, by virtue of her right of rejection, have destroyed the partnership's business, something she hadn't done for the previous sixteen years. Moreover, the fact that a limited partner with significant ownership interests in a limited partnership would object to a transaction which would deprive her of her say in who might be able to successfully manage her business interest as a general partner, in return for a minority voting, or for that fact, a non-voting interest, in a limited liability company controlled by a majority vote, is not evidence that such limited partner has an interest in destroying the business, including the value of her interest therein.

They further argue that under the certificate of partnership and partnership agreement, the general partners had the absolute right to "(1) terminate the partnership, (2) execute documents agreements, contracts, leases, etc., on behalf of the partnership, and (3) to manage the partnership business in all aspects, which should include, but should not be limited to . . . take such other action, execute and deliver such other documents, and perform such other acts as the general partners may deem necessary, appropriate, or incidental to carrying out the business and affairs of the partnership." In this regard, they seek to distinguish *Mist Properties, Inc. v. Fitzsimmons Realty Co.,* 228 N.Y.S.2d 406 (Sup. Ct. 1962), in which the court approved the general partner's transfer of title to property owned by the limited partnership as against the claim of the receiver, because the limited partnership agreement allowed the general partners to do so.

Mist Properties, Inc., however, had a partnership agreement that gave the general partners the specific power to sell all of the partnership's property, subject to written approval of sixty-five percent of the limited partners. "There clearly appears to have been no violation of the statute since the conveyance was not without the written consent of the limited partners but was specifically contemplated and provided for by the agreement." *Id.* at 410. As the court recognized therein, the agreement the partners had made with themselves through their partnership agreement controlled. "There is no intervening public policy which prevents persons dealing at arm's length from entering into an agreement such as set forth above. It has been repeatedly held that where a limited partnership agreement has been entered into the partners cannot, *inter se,* set up that their rights are not governed thereby. . . ." *Id.* at 410.

Simply put, we find that the general partners' rights under the partnership agreement to (1) terminate the partnership at any time upon agreement of the general partners, and (2) to act upon behalf of the Partnership in matters that are "necessary, appropriate, or incidental to carry out its business," can be not construed to allow them the power to transform the partnership into a limited liability company, in order to favor a majority of the partners in their selection, or substitution, of the general partners/managers of the business, without the approval of all the limited partners.

We therefore conclude that the transfer of the partnership assets to the LLC was in violation of KRS 362.490 and thus a breach of the general partners' fiduciary duty to the nonconsenting limited partner.

Judgment reversed in favor of Lach.

The Global Business Environment

Limited Partnerships in Other Countries

All modern commercial countries permit the creation of limited partnerships, but almost none allow the creation of LLLPs. England and its former colonies, including the United States, Canada, Singapore, and Australia, use the term *limited partnership*. In Italy, the limited partnership form is named *Societa in accomandita semplice* (S.a.s.); in Latin American countries, the *Sociedad en comandita;* in Austria the *Kommanditgesellschaft* (Kg).

These business forms are mostly identical to American limited partnerships, having general partners who manage the business and possess unlimited liability and limited partners who may not manage and are granted limited liability. Most countries also permit the partners to restrict the transfer of a partner's interest and usually provide for the continuation of the business despite the death of a limited partner.

Ethics in Action

You now know the characteristics and default rules of LLCs, limited partnerships, and LLLPs. If you are a profit maximizer, which one of these forms would you find less desirable than the others? The answer is that the limited partnership is less desirable, because a limited partnership, LLLP, and LLC may have the same tax and management benefits, yet only the LLLP and LLC extend limited liability to all the owners. General partners in a limited partnership have unlimited liability for the limited partnership's obligations. Therefore, you reduce your risk and increase your return relative to risk by choosing the LLLP or LLC.

If you believe in utilitarianism, rights theory, or justice theory, does the distinction between limited partnerships and LLLPs and LLCs make sense to you? Why grant limited liability only to owners who know enough to create an LLLP or LLC? Is the business of an LLLP or LLC more important to society than the business of a limited partnership merely because the managers in a limited partnership have failed to acquire limited liability status? Is it fair for the law to protect someone better than others merely because she is more knowledgeable about the law?

Problems and Problem Cases

1. Eric Stratum and Terese Brown formed ESTB, L.L.C., a member-managed limited liability company created for the purpose of owning and leasing a residential apartment building. The term of the LLC was 25 years. Their operating agreement provided that each owned 50 percent of the LLC. Stratum contributed $120,000 cash as his contribution to the business. Brown contributed $10,000 cash at the time of the LLC's creation, with the expectation that she would contribute to the LLC with services to be performed in the future. The agreement, however, listed Brown's capital contribution as $10,000 and did not stipulate by how much it should be increased as Brown continued to manage the business. Although Brown was expected to be the primary manager of the business, nothing in the operating agreement gave more power to Brown or removed power from Stratum. For the first two years, Brown did most of the day-to-day management of the LLC. She and Stratum agreed on other actions, including replacing carpeting in apartments and reroofing the building. After two years, Brown claimed she was entitled to a larger share of the LLC's profits. Is she?

    Suppose that Stratum responded by appointing his son to manage the LLC along with Brown. May Brown object to Stratum's son managing the LLC?

    Suppose the relationship between Stratum and Brown has so deteriorated that she withdraws from the LLC. She demands to receive the value of her interest in the LLC. The LLC has a current value of $500,000. How much must Brown receive? When?

    Suppose after she leaves the LLC, Brown purchases a residential apartment building that competes against the LLC. May Stratum prevent Brown from competing with the LLC?

2. Bonnie Strickland and her husband Jake formed the Strickland Family Limited Liability Company as part of their estate plan. They transferred 83 percent

of the equity shares of the LLC to their daughter Suzy Strickland Harbison. The Stricklands retained a 17 percent interest in the LLC and acted as co-managers of the LLC for the next two years. When Jake died, Bonnie became the only manager of the LLC. In 2002, Bonnie conveyed three parcels of real property belonging to the LLC to her son David Strickland. David was not a member of the LLC. Bonnie transferred the parcels of real property for an amount Suzy believed was less than fair market value. Suzy sued Bonnie, claiming that Strickland had breached her fiduciary duty to the LLC under the Alabama Limited Liability Company Act and that she had violated the terms of the operating agreement when she failed to make managerial decisions based on the best interests of the LLC and the equity owners. Bonnie defended by referring to the LLC's operating agreement, which clearly stated that the LLC was not formed for profit purposes:

> The managers do not, in any way guarantee a profit for the Equity Owners from the operations of the Company. Decisions with respect to the conduct, dissolution and winding up of the business of the company shall be made in the sole discretion of the Equity Owners and such other matters as the Managers consider relevant. There shall be no obligation on the part of the Managers to maximize financial gain or to make any or all of the Company Property productive.

Has Bonnie breached her fiduciary duty?

3. In 1994, Steven Mossbrook, Sandra Mossbrook, and Michael Lieberman created Wyoming.com LLC. Lieberman contributed initial capital of $20,000 consisting of services rendered and to be rendered. He was given a 40 percent ownership interest in the LLC. The Mossbrooks contributed $30,000 and received a 60 percent ownership interest. In 1995, two new members were added to the LLC, each contributing $25,000 and receiving a 2.5 percent ownership interest. Lieberman's ownership interest and his stated capital contribution remained the same.

   In 1998, Lieberman was terminated as vice president of Wyoming.com by the other members of Wyoming. Two weeks later, Lieberman withdrew from the LLC and demanded the immediate return of his share of the current value of the company, which he estimated at $400,000. The other members accepted Lieberman's withdrawal, chose to continue the LLC's business, and approved the return of Lieberman's $20,000 capital contribution, which

Lieberman refused to accept. Is Lieberman entitled to the fair market value of his ownership interest?

4. Nabil Gamez was a member of Rock Angus LLC, a member-managed LLC that bred and sold beef cattle. Gamez was the most active of the member-managers, negotiating contracts with breeders, feedlots, and banks on behalf of the LLC. One contract obligated Rock Angus LLC to purchase two Angus bulls for $624,000 from Shirlynne Farms, Inc. The contract was signed by Gamez as general manager acting on behalf of Rock Angus. Rock Angus defaulted on the contract with Shirlynne Farms, which sued Rock Angus LLC and Gamez. Was Gamez personally liable on the contract with Shirlynne Farms?

5. Tim Everest and Quinn Rider formed an LLC for the purpose of investing and managing commercial real estate properties. Everest drafted articles of organization for the LLC and gave the articles to Rider, who read them briefly. Rider told Everest "Everything looks OK to me," and signed the agreement. Everest submitted the LLC articles to the secretary of state, who filed the articles. After the LLC was formed, Everest operated the LLC as if he were the primary manager, excluding Rider from most of the day-to-day investment and management decisions of the LLC. When Rider protested, Everett showed him the LLC's articles of organization, which clearly stated that the LLC was manager-managed, with Everest listed as the sole manager. Rider argued that as a member of the LLC, he had the inherent right to manage the LLC. Was Rider correct?

6. Harlan Nesbitt was a member of Oak Creek Golf LLC, a limited liability company that owned and operated a golf course. Nesbitt wanted to dissociate from the LLC, but neither the LLC nor any other LLC member was willing to purchase his LLC interest. Nesbitt gave his LLC interest to his daughter, Eliza Portraro, and he notified the LLC that he was withdrawing from the LLC. Portraro sought to assert rights as a member of the LLC, including voting on matters submitted to LLC members, demanding a share of LLC profits, and inspecting the financial records of the LLC. The LLC operating agreement was silent on whether a transferee of a member's interest had those rights. Did Portraro have those rights?

7. Judith Carpenter was an experienced businesswoman and served on the board of directors of a bank. In 1984, Carpenter invested in Briargate

Homes, a business that owned several condominiums. She believed that Briargate was a limited partnership and that she was a limited partner. In fact, Briargate was a partnership and she was a general partner. No attempt had been made to comply with the North Carolina limited partnership statute. By 1987, Carpenter had possession of documents stating that Briargate was a partnership and she a partner. As an owner of condominiums, the partnership was liable to the condominium association for assessments for maintenance, repairs, and replacement of common areas in the complex. In 1988, the partnership failed to pay $85,000 in assessments. The partnership and its partners were sued by the condominium association. May Carpenter escape liability on the assessment because she thought she was a limited partner?

8. Virginia Partners, Ltd., a limited partnership organized in Florida, was in the business of drilling oil wells. When Virginia Partners injected acid into an oil well in Kentucky, a bystander, Robert Day, was injured by acid that sprayed on him from a ruptured hose. Virginia Partners had failed to register as a foreign limited partnership in Kentucky. Are the limited partners of Virginia Partners liable to Day for his injuries?

9. Brookside Realty, Ltd., was a limited partnership. In the limited partnership certificate filed with the secretary of state, four of its limited partners agreed to make capital contributions and be liable for future assessments in amounts ranging between $36,000 and $145,000. Brookside failed to pay for material Builders Steel sold to Brookside. Because the limited partners had not paid all the assessments required by the limited partnership certificate, Builders Steel claimed that it was entitled to require the limited partners to pay those assessments to the extent of the debt to Builders Steel. Did the court agree?

10. Blinder, Robinson & Co., as limited partner, and Combat Promotions, Inc., as general partner, created Combat Associates to promote an eight-round exhibition match between Muhammad Ali and Lyle Alzado, the pro football player. Combat Associates promised to pay Alzado $100,000 for his participation in the match.

Combat Promotions was owned entirely by Alzado, his accountant, and his professional agent. Alzado was also vice president of Combat Promotions. Blinder, Robinson used its Denver office as a ticket outlet for the match, gave two parties to promote the match, and provided a meeting room for Combat Associates' meetings. Meyer Blinder, president of Blinder, Robinson, personally appeared on a TV talk show and gave TV interviews to promote the match.

Few tickets were sold, and the match was a financial debacle. Alzado received no payments for participating in the match. Alzado sued Blinder, Robinson claiming that since it acted like a general partner it had the liability of a general partner. The case was decided under the law of the RULPA. Was Blinder, Robinson liable to Alzado? Would Blinder, Robinson be liable to Alzado under the ULPA of 2001?

11. Virgina Mattson decides to form a limited partnership with herself as the sole general partner and with 10 friends and associates as the limited partners. She chooses the limited partnership form, because its default rules clearly grant sole management rights to her, the only general partner. Mattson is concerned, however, about having personal liability on contracts she signs on behalf of the limited partnership. What should she do to limit her personal liability for the obligations of the business to the amount of her capital contribution?

Online Research

Your State and the RULLCA and the ULPA

Go to the Web site of the National Conference of Commissioners on Uniform State Laws.

- Check the legislative update to see whether your state has adopted the RULLCA and the ULPA.
- If your state has not adopted the RULLCA, find your state law for LLCs. Find the differences between the RULLCA and your state's LLC law.
- If your state has not adopted the ULPA, find the Revised Uniform Limited Partnership Act as amended in 1985. Note the differences between the RULPA and the ULPA of 2001, which are summarized in a table in the ULPA's Prefatory Note.

Part Ten

Corporations

chapter 41
History and Nature
of Corporations

chapter 42
Organization and Financial
Structure of Corporations

chapter 43
Management of Corporations

chapter 44
Shareholders' Rights
and Liabilities

chapter 45
Securities Regulation

chapter 46
Legal and Professional
Responsibilities of
Auditors, Consultants, and
Securities Professionals

HISTORY AND NATURE OF CORPORATIONS

You and three friends create an online retailer, which is incorporated in California under the name Gifts&Awards.com, Inc. The Web site will sell awards, clocks, desk sets, and other merchandise that businesses want as gifts for their clients and as promotional items for their employees. Physically, Gifts&Awards.com, Inc. will be located exclusively in San Jose, California. All its shareholders, employees, and assets will be in California. As an online retailer, however, Gifts&Awards.com's merchandise will be available to anyone anywhere in the world. Businesses worldwide will place orders through the Web site, which will be filled by the Gifts&Awards.com's staff. Gifts&Awards.com will ship about 20 percent of the merchandise ordered from a warehouse it leases in California. The other 80 percent will be shipped directly from the manufacturers or importers of the items. For that 80 percent, Gifts&Awards.com will take orders from customers and direct the orders to the appropriate manufacturers or importers, some of which will be in California but most of which will be dispersed throughout the United States.

You estimate that Gifts&Awards.com will have $4,000,000 in annual sales, $60,000 of which is to customers resident in Arizona. The goods will be delivered to customers by UPS, a third-party carrier whose fee will be added to the price of the goods. Some of the goods will be shipped from Gifts&Awards.com's warehouse in California, and some from manufacturers in other states, including Arizona. Consider the following questions regarding the State of Arizona's regulation of Gifts&Awards.com, Inc., a California corporation:

- May the State of Arizona require Gifts&Awards.com, Inc., to obtain a certificate of authority to do business in Arizona and collect a fee from Gifts&Awards.com for the privilege of doing business in the state?
- May the State of Arizona impose its state income tax on a portion of Gifts&Awards.com's worldwide income?
- May the State of Arizona require Gifts&Awards.com to collect the Arizona sales tax on sales to Arizona residents?
- If Gifts&Awards.com sells defective awards to a customer in Arizona, may the customer sue Gifts&Awards.com in an Arizona trial court? Will your answer affect Gifts&Awards.com policy on customers' returns and refunds?

THE MODERN CORPORATION HAS facilitated the rapid economic development of the last 200 years by permitting businesses to attain economies of scale. Businesses organized as corporations can attain such economies because they have a greater capacity to raise capital than do other business forms. This capital-raising advantage is ensured by corporation law, which allows persons to invest their money in a corporation and become owners without imposing unlimited liability or management responsibilities on themselves. Many people are willing to invest their savings in a large, risky business if they have limited liability and no management responsibilities. Far fewer are willing to invest in a partnership or other business form in which owners have unlimited liability and management duties.

History of Corporations

Although modern corporation law emerged only in the last 200 years, ancestors of the modern corporation existed in the times of Hammurabi, ancient Greece, and the Roman Empire. As early as 1248 in France, privileges of incorporation were given to mercantile ventures to encourage investment for the benefit of society. In England, the corporate form was used extensively before the 16th century.

The famous British trading companies—such as the Massachusetts Bay Company—were the forerunners of the modern corporation. The British government gave these companies monopolies in trade and granted them powers to govern in the areas they colonized. They were permitted to operate as corporations because of the benefits they would confer on the British empire, such as the development of natural resources. Although these trading companies were among the few corporations of the time whose owners were granted limited liability, they sought corporate status primarily because the government granted them monopolies and governmental powers.

American Corporation Law Beginning in 1776, corporation law in the United States evolved independently of English corporation law. Early American corporations received **special charters** from state legislatures. These charters were granted one at a time by special action of the legislatures; few special charters were granted.

In the late 18th century, general incorporation statutes emerged in the United States. Initially, these statutes permitted incorporation only for limited purposes beneficial to the public, such as operating toll bridges and water systems. Incorporation was still viewed as a privilege, and many restrictions were placed on corporations: incorporation was permitted for only short periods of time; maximum limits on capitalization were low; ownership of real and personal property was often restricted.

During the last 150 years, such restrictive provisions have disappeared in most states. Today, modern incorporation statutes are mostly enabling, granting the persons who control a corporation great flexibility in establishing, financing, and operating it.

See Figure 1 for a statement of the characteristics of corporations.

Figure 1   *Principal Characteristics of Corporations*

1. *Creation.* A corporation may be created only by *permission of a government.*

2. *Legal status.* A corporation is a legal person and a legal entity independent of its owners (*shareholders*) and its managers (officers and the *board of directors*). Its life is unaffected by the retirement or death of its shareholders, officers, and directors. A corporation is a person under the Constitution of the United States.

3. *Powers.* A corporation may *acquire, hold, and convey property* in its own name. A corporation may *sue and be sued* in its own name. Harm to a corporation is not harm to the shareholders; therefore, with few exceptions, a shareholder may not sue to enforce a claim of the corporation.

4. *Management.* Shareholders elect a board of directors, which manages the corporation. The board of directors may delegate management duties to officers. A shareholder has *no right or duty to manage* the business of a corporation, unless he is elected to the board of directors or is appointed an officer. The directors and officers need not be shareholders.

5. *Owners' liability.* The shareholders have *limited liability.* With few exceptions, they are not liable for the debts of a corporation after they have paid their promised capital contributions to the corporation.

6. *Transferability of owner's interest.* Generally, the ownership interest in a corporation is *freely transferable.* A shareholder may sell her shares to whomever she wants whenever she wants. The purchaser becomes a shareholder with the same rights that the seller had.

7. *Taxation.* Usually, a corporation pays *federal income taxes* on its income. Shareholders have personal income from the corporation only when the corporation makes a distribution of its income to them. For example, a shareholder would have personal income from the corporation when the corporation pays him a dividend. This creates a *double-taxation* possibility: The corporation pays income tax on its profits, and when the corporation distributes the after-tax profits as dividends, the shareholders pay tax on the dividends.

Classifications of Corporations

Corporations may be divided into three classes: (1) corporations **for profit,** (2) corporations **not for profit,** and (3) **government-owned** corporations. State and federal corporation statutes establish procedures for the incorporation of each of these classes and for their operation. In addition, a large body of common law applies to all corporations.

Most business corporations are **for-profit corporations.** For-profit corporations issue stock to their shareholders, who invest in the corporation with the expectation that they will earn a profit on their investment. That profit may take the form of dividends paid by the corporation or increased market value of their shares.

Nearly all for-profit corporations are incorporated under the **general incorporation law** of a state. All of the states require professionals who wish to incorporate, such as physicians, dentists, lawyers, and accountants, to incorporate under **professional corporation acts.** In addition, for-profit corporations that especially affect the public interest, such as banks, insurance companies, and savings and loan associations, are usually required to incorporate under special statutes.

For-profit corporations range from huge international organizations such as General Motors Corporation to small, one-owner businesses. GM is an example of a **publicly held corporation** because its shares are generally available to public investors. The publicly held corporation tends to be managed by professional managers who own small percentages of the corporation. Nearly all the shareholders of the typical publicly held corporation are merely investors who are not concerned in the management of the corporation.

Corporations with very few shareholders whose shares are not available to the general public are called **close corporations.** In the typical close corporation, the controlling shareholders are the only managers of the business.

Usually, close corporations and publicly held corporations are subject to the same rules under state corporation law. Many states, however, allow close corporations greater latitude in the operation of their internal affairs than is granted to public corporations. For example, the shareholders of a close corporation may be permitted to dispense with the board of directors and manage the close corporation as if it were a partnership.

A Subchapter S corporation, or **S corporation,** is a special type of close corporation. It is treated nearly like a partnership for federal income tax purposes. Its shareholders report the earnings or losses of the business on their individual federal income tax returns. This means that an S corporation's profits are taxed only once—at the shareholder level, eliminating the double-taxation penalty of incorporation. All shareholders must consent to an S corporation election. The Internal Revenue Code requires an S corporation to have only one class of shares and 100 or fewer shareholders. Shareholders may be only individuals or trusts.

Not-for-profit corporations do not issue stock and do not expect to make a profit. Instead, they provide services to their members under a plan that eliminates any profit motive. These corporations have **members** rather than shareholders, and none of the surplus revenue from their operations may be distributed to their members. Since they generally pay no income tax, nonprofit corporations can reinvest a larger share of their incomes in the business than can for-profit corporations. Examples of nonprofit corporations are charities, churches, fraternal organizations, community arts councils, cooperative grocery stores, and cooperative farmers' feed and supplies stores.

Some corporations are owned by governments and perform governmental and business functions. A municipality (city) is one type of **government-owned corporation.** Other types are created to furnish more specific services—for example, school corporations and water companies. Others—such as the Tennessee Valley Authority and the Federal Deposit Insurance Corporation—operate much like for-profit corporations except that at least some of their directors are appointed by governmental officials, and some or all of their financing frequently comes from government. The TVA and the FDIC are chartered by Congress, but government-owned corporations may also be authorized by states. Government-operated businesses seek corporate status to free themselves from governmental operating procedures, which are more cumbersome than business operating procedures.

Regulation of For-Profit Corporations

To become a corporation, a business must **incorporate** by complying with an incorporation statute. Incorporation is a fairly simple process usually requiring little more than paying a fee and filing a document with a designated government official—usually the secretary of state of the state of incorporation. Incorporation of for-profit businesses has been entrusted primarily to the governments of the 50 states.

The Global Business Environment

Corporations around the Globe

The corporate form of business is recognized throughout the world, and, regardless of the country, the form has essentially the same characteristics: limited liability for its owners, free transferability of shares, and separation of management from ownership. In Italy, the name is *Societa per azioni*. In Zimbabwe and England, corporations are called limited companies. In Germany, the term is *Aktiengesellschaft* (AG). In Brazil, the name is *sociedade anonima*. You can learn a lot about Canadian corporations at www.corporationscanada.ic.gc.ca. This site has links to federal, provincial, and territorial Web sites that facilitate the incorporation process.

State Incorporation Statutes

State incorporation statutes set out the basic rules regarding the relationship between the corporation, its shareholders, and its managers. For example, an incorporation statute sets the requirements for a business to incorporate, the procedures for shareholders' election of directors, and the duties directors and officers owe to the corporation. Although a corporation may do business in several states, usually the relationship between the corporation, its shareholders, and its managers is regulated only by the state of incorporation.

The American Bar Association's Committee on Corporate Laws has prepared a *model* statute for adoption by state legislatures. The purpose of the model statute is to improve the rationality of corporation law. It is called the **Model Business Corporation Act (MBCA).** It was last revised in 2002.

The revised MBCA is the basis of corporation law in most states. Your study of statutory corporation law in this book concentrates on the revised MBCA. Delaware and several major commercial and industrial states such as New York and California do not follow the MBCA. Therefore, selected provisions of the Delaware and other acts will be addressed.

Several states have special provisions or statutes that are applicable only to close corporations. The ABA's Committee on Corporate Laws has adopted the *Statutory Close Corporation Supplement to the Model Business Corporation Act.* The Supplement is designed to provide a rational, statutory solution to the special problems facing close corporations.

LOG ON

Go to
www.abanet.org/buslaw/library/onlinepublications/ mbca2002.pdf
You can view the MBCA at the Web site of the American Bar Association.

State Common Law of Corporations

Although nearly all of corporation law is statutory law, including the courts' interpretation of the statutes, there is a substantial body of common law of corporations (judge-made law). Most of this common law deals with creditor and shareholder rights. For example, the law of piercing the corporate veil, which you will study later in this chapter, is common law protecting creditors of corporations.

Regulation of Nonprofit Corporations

Nonprofit corporations are regulated primarily by the states. Nonprofit corporations may be created only by complying with a nonprofit incorporation statute. Incorporation under state law requires delivering articles of incorporation to the secretary of state. The existence of a nonprofit corporation begins when the secretary of state files the articles. Most states have statutes based on the revised **Model Nonprofit Corporation Act (MNCA).** Because of constitutional protection of freedom of religion, many states have special statutes regulating nonprofit religious organizations.

The law applied to nonprofit corporations is substantially similar to for-profit corporation law. At various points in the corporations chapters of this book, you will study the law of nonprofit corporations and examine how this form of business and its laws differ from the for-profit corporation and its laws. The Model Nonprofit Corporation Act will be the basis of your study of nonprofit corporation law.

Regulation of Foreign and Alien Corporations

A corporation may be incorporated in one state yet do business in many other states in which it is not incorporated. The corporation's contacts with other persons in those states may permit the states to regulate the corporation's transactions with their citizens, to subject the corporation to suits in their courts, or to tax the corporation. The circumstances under which states may impose their laws on a business incorporated in another state is determined by the law of foreign corporations.

A corporation is a **domestic corporation** in the state that has granted its charter; it is a **foreign corporation** in all the other states in which it does business. For example, a corporation organized in Delaware and doing business in Florida is domestic in Delaware and foreign in Florida. Note that a corporation domiciled in one country is an **alien corporation** in other countries in which it does business. Many of the rules that apply to foreign corporations apply as well to alien corporations.

Generally, a state may impose its laws on a foreign corporation if such imposition does not violate the Constitution of the United States, notably the Due Process Clause of the Fourteenth Amendment and the Commerce Clause. The law discussed here also applies to foreign partnerships, LLPs, LLCs, limited partnerships, and LLLPs, forms of business discussed in Chapters 37–40.

Due Process Clause

The Due Process Clause requires that a foreign corporation have sufficient contacts with a state before a state may exercise jurisdiction over the corporation. The leading case in this area is the *International Shoe* case.[1] In that case, the Supreme Court ruled that a foreign corporation must have "certain minimum contacts" with the state such that asserting jurisdiction over the corporation does not offend "traditional notions of fair play and substantial justice." The Supreme Court justified its holding with a **benefit theory:** When a foreign corporation avails itself of the protection of a state's laws, it should suffer any reasonable burden that the state imposes as a consequence of such benefit. In other words, a foreign corporation should be required to pay for the benefits that it receives from the state.

Commerce Clause

Under the Commerce Clause, the power to regulate interstate commerce is given to the federal government. The states have no power to exclude or to discriminate against foreign corporations that are engaged solely in *interstate* commerce. Nevertheless, a state may require a foreign corporation doing interstate business in the state to comply with its laws if the application of these laws does not unduly burden interstate commerce. When a foreign corporation

enters interstate commerce to do *intrastate* business in a state, the state may regulate the corporation's activities, provided again that the regulation does not unduly burden interstate commerce.

A state law regulating the activities of a foreign corporation does not unduly burden interstate commerce if (1) the law serves a legitimate state interest, (2) the state has chosen the least burdensome means of promoting that interest, and (3) that legitimate state interest outweighs the statute's burden on interstate commerce. Because conducting intrastate business increases a corporation's contact with a state, it is easier to prove that the state has a legitimate interest and that there is no undue burden on interstate commerce when the state regulates a corporation that is conducting intrastate business.

Doing Business To aid their determination of whether a state may constitutionally impose its laws on a foreign corporation, courts have traditionally used the concept of **doing business.** Courts have generally held that a foreign corporation is subject to the laws of a state when it is doing business in the state. The activities that constitute doing business differ, however, depending on the purpose of the determination. There are four such purposes: (1) to determine whether a corporation is subject to a lawsuit in a state's courts, (2) to determine whether the corporation's activities are subject to taxation, (3) to determine whether the corporation must qualify to carry on its activities in the state, and (4) to determine whether the state may regulate the internal affairs of the corporation.

Subjecting Foreign Corporations to Suit

The Supreme Court of the United States has held that a foreign corporation may be brought into a state's court in connection with its activities within the state, provided that the state does not violate the corporation's due process rights under the Fourteenth Amendment of the Constitution and its rights under the Commerce Clause.

The *International Shoe* minimum contacts test must be met. Subjecting the corporation to suit cannot offend "traditional notions of fair play and substantial justice." A court must weigh the corporation's contacts within the state against the inconvenience to the corporation of requiring it to defend a suit within the state. The burden on the corporation must be reasonable in relation to the benefit that it receives from conducting activities in the state.

Under the minimum contacts test, even an isolated event may be sufficient to confer jurisdiction on a state's courts. For example, driving a truck from Arizona through New Mexico toward a final destination in

---

[1]*International Shoe Co. v. State of Washington*, 326 U.S. 310 (1945).

Florida provides sufficient contacts with New Mexico to permit a suit in New Mexico's courts against the foreign corporation for its driver's negligently causing an accident within New Mexico.

Most of the states have passed **long-arm statutes** to permit their courts to exercise jurisdiction under the decision of the *International Shoe* case. These statutes frequently specify several kinds of corporate activities that make foreign corporations subject to suit within the state, such as the commission of a tort, the making of a con-

tract, or the ownership of property. Most of the long-arm statutes grant jurisdiction over causes of action growing out of any transaction within the state. Later in this chapter, the court in *Ryan v. Cerullo* looks at Connecticut's long-arm statute.

In the following Global Business Environment box, the court considers whether a Liechtenstein corporation may be sued in a New Hampshire court. The law that applies to foreign corporations also applies to alien corporations.

The Global Business Environment

Jet Wine & Spirits, Inc. v. Bacardi & Co., Ltd., 298 F.3d 1 (1st Cir. 2002)

Bacardi & Co., a Liechtenstein corporation, was sued in a New Hampshire court by a New Hampshire liquor distributor, Jet Wine & Spirits, Inc. Bacardi & Co. (BACO) has its primary place of business in the Bahamas and is wholly owned by Bacardi International Limited, which is almost wholly owned by Bacardi Limited, a Bermuda corporation with its primary place of business in Bermuda. Bacardi Limited also wholly owns Bacardi U.S.A. (BUSA), a Delaware corporation with its primary place of business in Florida.

BACO owns several brands of Dewar's Scotch and Bombay Gin, which it acquired from Diageo, which had a relationship with Jet Wine & Spirits. Jet Wine had previously distributed Dewar's in several New England states, including New Hampshire, under a contract it had with subsidiaries of the companies that merged to form Diageo, including Schieffelin. BACO assumed Schieffelin's contract with Jet Wine when it acquired the Dewar's brand from Diageo.

BACO does no business directly in New Hampshire, except possibly through its Web site. From November 1998 to September 1999, www.bacardi.com sold some Bacardi promotional items (clothing and keychains, not alcohol), including two sales to New Hampshire addresses for a total of $30.75. This money went to National Corporate Services Unlimited, an unrelated company that buys merchandise from BUSA and sells it over the Web site. BACO owns one trademark, "Havana Club," that is registered in New Hampshire.

Acting under authority given it by BACO, BUSA terminated Jet Wine as distributor. Jet Wine then sued a number of members of the Bacardi corporate family, including BACO, under breach of contract and the tort of interfering with a contractual relation. BACO argued it had nothing to do with New Hampshire and moved to dismiss for lack of personal jurisdiction. The District Court granted BACO's motion, and Jet Wine appealed.

Lynch, Judge Jet Wine bears the burden of establishing personal jurisdiction. To do that, it must show that BACO has had "certain minimum contacts" with New Hampshire "such

that maintenance of the suit does not offend traditional notions of fair play and substantial justice." *Int'l Shoe Co. v. Washington,* 326 U.S. 310, 316 (1945).

The most important contact that Jet Wine alleges between BACO and New Hampshire is BACO's alleged assumption of Schieffelin's obligations under the Dewar's contract when BACO and Diageo signed the Dewar's Agreement. The primary fact produced is the provision in the Dewar's Agreement by which BACO assumed "all liabilities and obligations that arise out of or relate to the Transferred Assets (including under any Contract) [or] the Dewar's Business." Jet Wine argues that its contract with Schieffelin creates an obligation that arises out of, and relates to, the Dewar's Business, defined as "the marketing, sales and distribution of Scotch whisky" under the trade names here at issue. We agree that is a quite plausible interpretation, sufficient for a prima facie showing of jurisdiction.

The second significant contact that Jet Wine alleges between BACO and New Hampshire is BUSA's termination of Jet Wine as the distributor of Dewar's in New Hampshire and BUSA's subsequent use of another distributor for Dewar's in New Hampshire. Jet Wine claims that the district court should have imputed these actions to BACO for jurisdictional purposes because BUSA acted as BACO's agent.

Jet Wine has argued that BUSA was BACO's agent for the purpose of distributing Dewar's in New Hampshire, because [a June 16 letter from BACO to BUSA] identifies BUSA as BACO's "exclusive brand agent and distributor" and authorizes BUSA "to take all legal steps necessary to effectuate the sale of our products in the United States of America." The existence of the letter satisfies Jet Wine's burden to support its allegation that BUSA acted as BACO's agent in terminating Jet Wine as the Dewar's distributor for New Hampshire.

We must consider whether Jet Wine's claims against BACO arise out of or are related to BACO's contacts with New Hampshire. For the contract claim, the answer is a straightforward yes. Jet Wine's action against BACO for breach of contract arises out of BACO's alleged assumption of Jet Wine's contract with Schieffelin. That assumption was a contact with the state of New Hampshire that relates intimately to Jet Wine's claim.

Jet Wine must also demonstrate that BACO purposefully availed itself of the privilege of doing business in New Hampshire. There must be some voluntary action that BACO has taken that should have put it fairly on notice that it might one day be called to defend itself in a New Hampshire court. If BACO assumed the various obligations of Diageo to its distributors in the Dewar's Agreement, including Schieffelin's to Jet Wine, that was a voluntary act from which BACO should have known that it was rendering itself liable to suit in many places throughout the world. From the schedules attached to the Agreement, it knew that one of those places was New Hampshire.

We acknowledge that there is some burden on BACO if it must appear in New Hampshire's courts. New Hampshire is far removed from Liechtenstein, where BACO is incorporated, and also far from the Bahamas, BACO's primary place of business. BACO is, however, an international corporation that does business in the United States, including through its purported agent, BUSA. It cannot wholly expect to escape the reach of United States courts.

We add a final note addressing an argument made by BACO. BACO says that because the agreements between Schieffelin and Jet Wine contain clauses consenting to the jurisdiction of the federal district courts within New York as the fora for resolving disputes, it is unreasonable to subject BACO to the jurisdiction of New Hampshire. Contractual language consenting to the jurisdiction of one forum, however, is not the same as language specifying one forum and excluding all others.

Judgment reversed in favor of Jet Wine. Remanded to the district court.

Taxation

A state may tax a foreign corporation if such taxation does not violate the Due Process Clause or the Commerce Clause. Generally, a state's imposition of a tax must serve a legitimate state interest and be reasonable in relation to a foreign corporation's contacts with the state. For example, a North Carolina corporation's property located in Pennsylvania is subject to property tax in Pennsylvania. The corporation enjoys Pennsylvania's protection of private property. It may be required to pay its share of the cost of such protection.

Greater contacts are needed to subject a corporation to state income and sales taxation in a state than are needed to subject it to property taxation. A state tax does not violate the commerce clause when the tax (1) is applied to an activity with a substantial connection with the taxing state, (2) is fairly apportioned, (3) does not discriminate against interstate commerce, and (4) is fairly related to the services provided by the state.[2]

For example, New Jersey has been permitted to tax a portion of the entire net income of a corporation for the privilege of doing business, employing or owning capital or property, or maintaining an office in New Jersey when the portion of entire net income taxed is determined by an average of three ratios: in-state property to total property, in-state to total receipts, and in-state to total wages, salaries, and other employee compensation.[3] However, Pennsylvania could not assess a flat tax on the operation of all trucks on Pennsylvania highways. The flat tax imposed a disproportionate burden on interstate trucks as compared with intrastate trucks because interstate trucks traveled fewer miles per year on Pennsylvania highways.[4] Nonetheless, the Supreme Court upheld a $100 fee levied by the state of Michigan on all trucks, whether or not owned by in-state or out-of-state companies, that made point-to-point hauls between Michigan cities, on the grounds that the fee taxed purely local activity and did not tax an interstate truck's entry into Michigan or transactions spanning multiple states.[5] Regarding sales and use taxes, the *Quill* case allows a state to tax an interstate sale by a foreign corporation to an in-state consumer if the seller has a physical presence in the state, such as a retail outlet.[6]

State taxation of interstate Internet transactions has become a potential source for state revenue. However, in 1998 the federal Congress placed a moratorium on new Internet access taxes. That moritorium has been extended to 2014. The states and Congress are currently debating whether states should be allowed to tax interstate Internet sales. Some states have been very aggressive in finding *Quill*-approved presences that allow them to tax Internet sales.

Qualifying to Do Business

A state may require that foreign corporations **qualify** to conduct **intrastate** business in the state, that is, conducting business transaction *within* the state. The level of doing

---

[2]*Complete Auto Transit, Inc. v. Brady,* 430 U.S. 274 (1977).
[3]*Amerada Hess Corp. v. Director of Taxation,* 490 U.S. 66 (1989).

[4]*American Trucking Assns., Inc. v. Scheiner,* 483 U.S. 266 (1987).
[5]*American Trucking Assns., Inc. v. Mich. Pub. Serv. Comm.* 545 U.S. 429 (2005).
[6]*Quill Corp. v. North Dakota,* 504 U.S. 298 (1992).

The Global Business Environment

Offshore Tax Havens

In recent years, a few large American companies have reincorporated in Caribbean countries that offer favorable tax treatment compared to American law. For example, consulting firm Accenture incorporated in Bermuda in 2001, as did Ingersoll-Rand. Tyco in 1997 and Fruit of the Loom in 1999 also incorporated in Bermuda. The Cayman Islands are another popular tax haven.

Offshore reincorporation is a response to U.S. federal income tax law, which taxes all of an American corporation's income, regardless where it is earned. Bermuda, by contrast, does not tax corporate profits. Instead, a Bermuda corporation doing business in many countries—as is typical for the multinational corporations organized there—pays income tax in each country only on the amount of income earned there.

Fewer than 30 of the thousands of publicly traded American corporations have reincorporated in the Caribbean. Yet in three-fourths of the mergers between U.S. and foreign firms from 1998 to 2000, the resulting companies chose to incorporate in the foreign country because of American tax law. Proponents point to these and other examples of corporate flight as proof that American tax law must be revised to assess income taxes based on where profits are earned, not merely where the company is incorporated.

Opponents brand fleeing businesses as corporate traitors. Already, efforts are under way to restrict or prohibit offshore reincorporation or to punish firms that reincorporate offshore. One proposal would ban offshore companies from receiving lucrative federal government contracts. The 10 biggest companies that have relocated to Bermuda did over one billion dollars of federal contract business in 2002. Consulting firm Accenture alone had over $600 million of federal contracts.

---

business that constitutes intrastate business for qualification purposes has been difficult to define. To help clarify the confusion in this area, the MBCA lists several activities that do *not* require qualification. For example, soliciting—by mail or through employees—orders that require acceptance outside the state is not doing intrastate business requiring qualification. That exception, for example, allows Amazon.com to make Internet sales in many states outside its home state of Washington without needing to qualify in those states. In addition, selling through independent contractors or owning real or personal property does not require qualification.

Also classified as not doing business for qualification purposes is conducting an **isolated transaction** that is completed within 30 days and is not one in the course of repeated transactions of a like nature. This isolated transaction safe harbor allows a tree grower to bring Christmas trees into a state in order to sell them to one retailer. However, a Christmas tree retailer who comes into a state for 29 days before Christmas and sells to consumers from a street corner is required to qualify. Although both merchants have consummated their transactions within 30 days, the grower has engaged in only one transaction, but the retailer has engaged in a series of transactions.

Maintaining an office to conduct intrastate business, selling personal property not in interstate commerce, entering into contracts relating to local business or sales, or owning or using real estate for general corporate purposes does constitute doing intrastate business. Passive ownership of real estate for investment, however, is not doing intrastate business.

Maintaining a stock of goods within a state from which to fill orders, even if the orders are taken or accepted outside the state, is doing intrastate business requiring qualification. Performing service activities such as machinery repair and construction work may be doing intrastate business.

Qualification Requirements If required to qualify to do intrastate business in a state, a foreign corporation must apply for a **certificate of authority** from the secretary of state, pay an application fee, maintain a registered office and a registered agent in the state, file an annual report with the secretary of state, and pay an annual fee.

Doing intrastate business without qualifying usually subjects a foreign corporation to a fine, in some states as much as $10,000. The MBCA disables the corporation to use the state's courts to bring a lawsuit until it obtains a certificate of authority. The corporation may defend itself in the state's courts, however, even if it has no certificate of authority.

LOG ON

Go to
www.usregisteredagents.com

Several online businesses have been created to relieve corporations of the burden of qualifying to do business and maintaining a registered agent in each state in which it does business. US Registered Agents is one such business. Can you find the cost of hiring US Registered Agents to be a corporation's registered agent?

In the following case, *Ryan v. Cerullo,* the court found that a New York professional accounting corporation was not required to qualify to do business in Connecticut despite providing tax services to a Connecticut resident. Consequently, the New York corporation was not properly subject to a lawsuit in a Connecticut court.

Ryan v. Cerullo   918 A.2d 867 (Conn. S. Ct. 2007)

Thomas Ryan, a resident of Westport, Connecticut, was an investment banker in New York City. He also had an apartment in New York City. John Cerullo was a resident of New York. His accounting firm, Cerullo & Company, was a New York corporation with its principal office in Tarrytown, New York, and a satellite office in New York City.

Ryan retained Cerullo and his firm to prepare Ryan's 1998 and 1999 federal, Connecticut, and New York personal income tax returns. The New York tax returns Cerullo prepared for Ryan claimed that Ryan was a nonresident of New York. Because Ryan had an apartment in New York, the State of New York ruled that Ryan was not a nonresident and, therefore, assessed him an additional $149,654 in taxes, penalties, and interest.

To recover the penalties assessed by the New York tax department, Ryan sued Cerullo and his firm in a Connecticut court, alleging breach of contract and malpractice. Cerullo and his firm moved to dismiss Ryan's legal action, claiming that Connecticut lacked personal jurisdiction over them because they had insufficient contact with the State of Connecticut. Cerrulo argued that all meetings between Ryan and Cerullo took place in New York, the tax services provided by Cerullo and his firm for Ryan included communications exclusively with New York tax department personnel, and the vast majority of the Cerullo's revenues were derived from persons residing or doing business in New York.

Ryan pointed out that Cerullo & Company had not obtained a certificate of authority to conduct intrastate business in Connecticut. Therefore, Ryan claimed that Connecticut's courts had jurisdiction over Cerullo & Company under Connecticut General Statutes § 33-929(e). General Statutes § 33-929(e) provides:

Every foreign corporation which transacts business in this state in violation of section 33-920 shall be subject to suit in this state upon any cause of action arising out of such business. . . .

General Statutes § 33-920 provides:

(a) A foreign corporation, other than an insurance, surety or indemnity company, may not transact business in this state until it obtains a certificate of authority from the Secretary of the State. . . .

(b) The following activities, among others, do not constitute transacting business within the meaning of subsection (a) of this section: (1) Maintaining, defending or settling any proceeding; (2) holding meetings of the board of directors or shareholders or carrying on other activities concerning internal corporate affairs; (3) maintaining bank accounts; (4) maintaining offices or agencies for the transfer, exchange and registration of the corporation's own securities or maintaining trustees or depositaries with respect to those securities; (5) selling through independent contractors; (6) soliciting or obtaining orders, whether by mail or through employees or agents or otherwise, if the orders require acceptance outside this state before they become contracts; (7) creating or acquiring indebtedness, mortgages and security interests in real or personal property; (8) securing or collecting debts or enforcing mortgages and security interests in property securing the debts; (9) owning, without more, real or personal property; (10) conducting an isolated transaction that is completed within thirty days and that is not one in the course of repeated transactions of a like nature; (11) transacting business in interstate commerce.

The trial court concluded that it lacked personal jurisdiction over Cerullo and Cerullo & Company under the applicable long-arm statutes on the grounds that the case involved preparation of New York state income tax returns by a New York firm for an individual who worked in New York. Ryan appealed to the Supreme Court of Connecticut. The Supreme Court first concluded that the trial court had no grounds for personal jurisdiction over Cerullo. The court then considered whether there were grounds for jurisdiction over Cerullo & Company.

Palmer, Judge

Cerullo and his firm derived only minimal income from Connecticut residents, did not solicit business in Connecticut and did not promote themselves as a national accounting firm. With respect to the professional accounting services that Ryan retained Cerullo and his firm to provide, they performed those services exclusively in New York, met with Ryan exclusively in New York, and corresponded exclusively with New York tax officials. Moreover, Ryan had retained them to prepare federal and state tax returns on income earned in New York. Although it is true, of course, that Ryan resides in Connecticut and that Cerullo prepared Ryan's Connecticut income tax returns, we agree with the trial court that those facts alone are insufficient to warrant a determination that the professional services rendered by Cerullo constituted the transacting of business in this state.

We next turn to Ryan's contention that the trial court incorrectly concluded that it lacks jurisdiction over Cerullo & Company under the corporate long-arm statute, namely, § 33-929(e), which vests our courts with jurisdiction over any foreign corporation that transacts business in this state without first having obtained a certificate of authority from the secretary of the state in accordance with § 33-920(a) when the cause of action arises out of such business. Our analysis under § 33-929(e) is twofold. We first must determine whether Cerullo & Company transacted business in this state without authorization to do so as required by § 33-920(a), and, if so, we then must determine whether Ryan's claim against Cerullo & Company arose out of such business.

We disagree with both prongs of Ryan's argument. With respect to his claim that Cerullo & Company transacted business in this state, this court previously has observed that the phrase "transacts any business" in General Statutes § 52-59b has a broader meaning than the phrases "transact business" or "transacts business" in the corporate long-arm statutes. In the absence of any claim or showing by Ryan that Cerullo & Company has a different, more substantial relationship to this state than Cerullo, and because we already have concluded that the trial court properly determined that it lacks personal jurisdiction over Cerullo under § 52-59b, it follows, a fortiori, that Cerullo & Company did not transact business in this state within the meaning of § 33-929(e).

Even if we assume, arguendo, that Cerullo & Company did transact business in this state within the meaning of § 33-929(e), Ryan cannot satisfy the second requirement of § 33-929(e), namely, that his claim against Cerullo arose out of that business. It is abundantly clear that Ryan's cause of action arises out of the allegedly negligent preparation of his New York income tax returns, not from the preparation of his Connecticut income tax returns. Indeed, Ryan's cause of action has no connection with or relationship to the preparation of his Connecticut income tax returns. Ryan, therefore, has failed to demonstrate that his claim arises out of any business that Cerullo & Company conducted in this state, as required by § 33-929(e).

Judgment affirmed for Cerullo & Company.

Regulation of a Corporation's Internal Affairs

Regulation of the internal affairs of a corporation—that is, the relation between the corporation and its directors, officers, and shareholders—is usually exercised only by the state of incorporation. Nonetheless, a foreign corporation may conduct most of its business in a state other than the one in which it is incorporated. Such a corporation is called a **pseudo-foreign corporation** in the state in which it conducts most of its business.

A few states subject pseudo-foreign corporations to extensive regulation of their internal affairs, regulation similar to that imposed on their domestic corporations. California's statute requires corporations that have more than 50 percent of their business and ownership in California to elect directors by cumulative voting, to hold annual directors' elections, and to comply with California's dividend payment restrictions. Foreign corporations raise many constitutional objections to the California statute, including violations of the Commerce Clause and the Due Process Clause.

Regulation of Foreign Nonprofit Corporations

The Model Nonprofit Corporation Act and other laws impose the same requirements and penalties on nonprofit corporations as are imposed on for-profit corporations. For example, the MNCA requires a foreign nonprofit corporation to qualify to do intrastate business in a state. The failure to qualify prevents the foreign nonprofit corporation from using the state's courts to bring lawsuits and subjects it to fines for each day it transacts intrastate business without a certificate of authority.

Piercing the Corporate Veil

A corporation is a legal entity separate from its shareholders. Corporation law erects an imaginary wall between a corporation and its shareholders that protects shareholders from liability for a corporation's actions. Once shareholders have made their promised capital contributions to the corporation, they have no further financial liability. This means that contracts of a corporation are not contracts of its shareholders, and debts of a corporation are not debts of its shareholders.

Nonetheless, in order *to promote justice and to prevent inequity,* courts will sometimes ignore the separateness of a corporation and its shareholders by **piercing the corporate veil.** The primary consequence of piercing the corporate veil is that a corporation's shareholders may lose their limited liability.

Two requirements must exist for a court to pierce the corporate veil: (1) **domination** of a corporation by its shareholders; and (2) use of that domination for an **improper purpose.**

As an entity separate from its shareholders, a corporation should act for itself, not for its shareholders. If a shareholder causes a corporation to act to the personal benefit of the shareholder, *domination*—the first requirement for piercing the corporate veil—is proved. For example, a majority shareholder's directing a corporation to pay the shareholder's personal expenses is domination. Domination is also proved if the controlling shareholders cause the corporation to fail to observe corporate formalities (such as failing to hold shareholder and director meetings or to maintain separate accounting records). Some courts say that shareholder domination makes the corporation the *alter ego* (other self) of the shareholders. Other courts say that domination makes the corporation an *instrumentality* of the shareholders.

To prove domination, it is not sufficient, or even necessary, to show that there is only one shareholder. Many one-shareholder corporations will never have their veils pierced. However, nearly all corporations whose veils are pierced are close corporations, since domination is more easily accomplished in a close corporation than in a publicly held one.

In addition to domination, there must be an *improper use* of the corporation. The improper use may be any of three types: defrauding creditors, circumventing a statute, or evading an existing obligation.

Defrauding Creditors Shareholders must organize a corporation with sufficient capital to meet the initial capital needs of the business. Inadequate capitalization, called **thin capitalization,** is proved when capitalization is very small in relation to the nature of the business of the corporation and the risks the business necessarily entails.

Thin capitalization defrauds creditors of a corporation. An example of thin capitalization is forming a business with a high debt-to-equity ratio, such as a $10 million–asset business with only $1,000 of equity capital, with the shareholders sometimes contributing the remainder of the needed capital as secured creditors. By doing so, the shareholders elevate a portion of their bankruptcy repayment priority to a level above that of general creditors, thereby reducing the shareholders' risk. The high debt-to-equity ratio harms nonshareholder-creditors by failing to provide an equity cushion sufficient to protect their claims. In such a situation, either the shareholders will be liable for the corporation's debts or the shareholders' loans to the corporation will be subordinated to the claims of other creditors. As a result, the nonshareholder-creditors are repaid all of their claims prior to the shareholder-creditors receiving payment from the corporation.

Transfers of corporate assets to shareholders for less than fair market value (called **looting**) also defraud creditors. For example, shareholder-managers loot a corporation by paying themselves excessively high salaries or by having the corporation pay their personal credit card bills. When such payments leave insufficient assets in the corporation to pay creditors' claims, a court will hold the shareholders liable to the creditors.

Frequently, the same shareholders may own two corporations that transact with each other. The shareholders may cause one corporation to loot the other. When such looting occurs between corporations of common ownership, courts pierce the veils of these corporations. This makes each corporation liable to the creditors of the other corporation. For example, a shareholder-manager operates two corporations from the same office. Corporation 1 transfers inventory to Corporation 2, but it receives less than fair market value for the inventory. Also, both corporations employ the same workers, but all of the wages are paid by Corporation 1. In such a situation, the veils of the corporations will be pierced, allowing the creditors of Corporation 1 to satisfy their claims against the assets of Corporation 2.

Looting may occur also when one corporation (called the **parent corporation**) owns at least a majority of the shares of another corporation (called the **subsidiary corporation**). Ordinarily, the parent is liable for its own obligations and the subsidiary is liable for its own obligations, but the parent is not liable for its subsidiary's debts and the subsidiary is not liable for the parent's debts. Nonetheless, because a parent corporation is able to elect the directors of its subsidiary and therefore can control the management of the subsidiary, the parent may cause its subsidiary to transact with the parent in a manner that benefits the parent but harms the subsidiary.

For example, a parent corporation may direct its subsidiary to sell its assets to the parent for less than fair value. Because the subsidiary has given more assets to the parent than it has received from the parent, creditors of the subsidiary have been defrauded. Consequently, a court will pierce the veil between the parent and its subsidiary and hold the parent liable to the creditors of the subsidiary.

To prevent the piercing of veils between them, affiliated corporations must not commingle their assets. Each corporation must have its own books of accounts. Transactions between affiliated corporations must be recorded on the books of both corporations, and such transactions must be executed at fair value.

Circumventing a Statute A corporation should not engage in a course of conduct that is prohibited by a statute. For example, a city ordinance may prohibit retail businesses from being open on consecutive Sundays. To avoid the statute, a retail corporation forms a subsidiary owned entirely by the retail corporation; on alternate weeks, it leases its building and inventory to the subsidiary. A court will pierce the veil because the purpose of creating the subsidiary corporation is to circumvent the statutory prohibition. Consequently, both the parent and the subsidiary will be liable for violating the statute.

Evading an Existing Obligation Sometimes, a corporation will attempt to escape liability on a contract by reincorporating or by forming a subsidiary corporation. The new corporation will claim that it is not bound by the contract, even though it is doing the same business as was done by the old corporation. In such a situation, courts pierce the corporate veil and hold the new corporation liable on the contract.

For example, to avoid an onerous labor union contract, a corporation creates a wholly owned subsidiary and sells its entire business to the subsidiary. The subsidiary will claim that it is not a party to the labor contract and may hire nonunion labor. A court will pierce the veil between the two corporations because the subsidiary was created only to avoid the union contract.

Nonprofit Corporations

Like a for-profit corporation, a nonprofit corporation is an entity separate and distinct from its members. A member is not personally liable for a nonprofit corporation's acts or liabilities merely by being a member. However, a court may pierce the veil of a nonprofit corporation if it is used to defraud creditors, circumvent a statute, or evade an existing obligation, the same grounds on which a for-profit corporation's veil may be pierced.

For a summary of the law of piercing the corporate veil, see Figure 2. Note that the law of veil piercing also applies to other business forms we studied in Chapters 37–40, including LLCs and LLPs.

In the next case, the Maryland Court of Appeals refused to pierce the corporate veil when the corporation was not used to defraud the creditor and the shareholder was not its alter ego. The court also held that the New Jersey corporation's failure to register to do business in Maryland did not impose personal liability on the foreign corporation's sole shareholder.

Hildreth v. Tidewater Equipment Co.   838 A.2d 1204 (Md. Ct. App. 2003)

John Hildreth was the sole shareholder, director, and officer of a New Jersey corporation, HCE, Inc., also referred to as HCE-NJ. Engaged in the construction business, in late 1996 or early 1997, HCE-NJ began to do business in Maryland, opening an office in Columbia. However, Hildreth did not register HCE-NJ in Maryland, as required by Maryland Code, sections 7–202, 7–202.1, or 7–203 of the Corporations and Associations Article. Those sections require that foreign corporations register with the Maryland Department of Assessments and Taxation before doing any intrastate business in Maryland. Registration requires that the corporation have a resident agent in Maryland.

In February 1998, HCE-NJ rented a 20-ton capacity crane from Tidewater Equipment Company, Inc., for one or two days and paid the rental charge as agreed. In September 1998, HCE-NJ and Tidewater commenced negotiations for the long-term rental of a crane that HCE-NJ intended to use in connection with a construction project in Alexandria, Virginia.

Hildreth made clear he was acting for HCE, Inc., but neither said nor was asked where that company was incorporated. He informed Frank Kolbe, a Tidewater representative, that the company had an office in Columbia, Maryland. Kolbe visited both the Columbia office and a job site. He testified that the company "didn't appear to be a fly-by-night operation," but had "a nice office suite" and "numerous employees." The job site was also substantial, with "a huge warehouse," a rail siding, and "hundreds of metal building panels." Kolbe assumed that HCE-NJ was a Maryland corporation because it had an office in Columbia.

Tidewater and HCE-NJ signed a series of daily contracts. Hildreth did not sign the contracts, which were signed on behalf of HCE-NJ by some other employee. The charges for September, October, and November 1998, were paid in January and February 1999. When payments were not received thereafter, Tidewater repossessed the equipment. At the time, Tidewater was owed $47,246 for the months of December, January, February, and March, and for a few days in April.

Tidewater sued Hildreth on the grounds Hildreth was personally liable for the debts incurred by HCE-NJ. The court entered judgment against Hildreth for the entire corporate debt. Hildreth appealed to the Court of Special Appeals, arguing that officers and directors of a foreign corporation are not personally liable for corporate debts solely because the corporation fails to qualify to do business in Maryland and that Tidewater knew that it was dealing with a corporation.

On appeal, the intermediate appellate court pointed out that the only thing that was not disclosed to Tidewater was the fact that HCE-NJ was a foreign corporation that had not registered to do business in Maryland. Tidewater knew that it was dealing with a corporation engaged in the construction business; it knew the actual name of the corporation and that it had offices not just in Maryland but in New Jersey and New York as well.

The Court of Special Appeals also concluded that, as a general rule, officers and directors of a valid foreign corporation are not personally liable on corporate debts merely because the corporation fails to register to do business in the forum state, but held that the court could impose such liability "when justice requires." Although acknowledging that the traditional factors justifying veil piercing were not present, the court determined that the case presented a situation in which the corporate form must be disregarded to "enforce a paramount equity." After the court affirmed Hildreth's liability to Tidewater, Hildreth asked the Maryland Court of Appeals to review the decision.

Wilner, Judge

The only issue before us is whether there was a basis for piercing the corporate veil of HCE-NJ and imposing personal liability for the corporate obligation on Hildreth.

As the Court of Special Appeals recognized, there was no allegation here of fraud on the part of either Hildreth or HCE-NJ; nor was there any evidence or finding of fraud. Personal liability rested solely upon the notion of "paramount equity," which, in that court's view, arose from a combination of the following circumstances:

(1) Hildreth was the sole shareholder of HCE-NJ;
(2) Hildreth was "personally involved" in the business transaction with Tidewater, which the court viewed as "Hildreth's dirty hands";
(3) * * *
(4) Contracts made by unregistered foreign corporations, though valid, nonetheless constitute "illegal business transactions on the part of the unregistered foreign corporation, for which that corporation and its agents, officers, directors, and shareholders may be penalized," which the court characterized as "the public policy against illegal business transactions;"
(5) Maryland law precludes unregistered corporations doing business in Maryland from seeking relief in Maryland courts, which the court regarded as "the public policy against unregistered corporations using Maryland courts to protect their illegal business transactions."

Although we have not heretofore given any generic definition of "paramount equity" in this context, it is abundantly clear from our actual holdings in cases where attempts were made to pierce a corporate veil—to hold stockholders personally liable for corporate obligations—that those circumstances, individually or in combination, do not suffice.

In a number of cases, we made favorable reference to the synthesis supplied in the 1953 edition of Herbert Brune's work, *Maryland Corporation Law and Practice,* § 371, as to when a corporate entity will be disregarded:

First. Where the corporation is used *as a mere shield for the perpetration of a fraud,* the courts will disregard the fiction of separate corporate entity.
Second. The courts may consider a corporation as unencumbered by the fiction of corporate entity and deal with substance rather than form as though the corporation did not exist, *in order to prevent evasion of legal obligations.*
Third. Where the stockholders themselves, or a parent corporation owning the stock of a subsidiary corporation, *fail to observe the corporate entity, operating the business or dealing with the corporation's property as if it were their own,* the courts will also disregard the corporate entity for the protection of third persons.
(Emphasis added).

There is nothing in this record that could possibly justify the first of these circumstances. As already noted, there is no claim, no evidence, and no finding that Hildreth used HCE-NJ as "a mere shield for the perpetration of a fraud."

The third circumstance embodies what is sometimes called the "alter ego" doctrine. Fletcher observes that the "alter ego" doctrine has been applied "where the corporate entity has been used as a subterfuge and to observe it would work an injustice," the rationale being that "if the shareholders or the corporations themselves disregard the proper formalities of a corporation, then the law will do likewise as necessary to protect individual and corporate creditors." William Meade Fletcher, *1 Fletcher Cyclopedia of the Law of Private Corporations,* § 41.10 at 574–76 (1999 Rev. Vol.). Courts will apply the doctrine when the plaintiff shows (1) "complete domination, not only of the finances, but of policy and business practice in respect to the transaction so that the corporate entity as to this transaction had at the time no separate mind, will or existence of its own," (2) that "such control [was] used by the defendant to commit fraud or wrong, to perpetrate the violation of the statutory or other positive legal duty, or dishonest and unjust act in contravention of the plaintiff's legal rights," and (3) that such "control and breach of duty proximately caused the injury or unjust loss." *Id.* at 583–86. Because piercing the corporate veil is founded on equity, "where no fraud is shown, the plaintiff must show that an inequitable result, involving fundamental unfairness, will result from a failure to disregard the corporate form." *Id.* at 605.

Although there appears to be no universal rule as to the specific criteria that courts will consider in determining whether to apply the doctrine, Fletcher observes that some of the factors commonly considered, when dealing with a single corporation, are (1) whether the corporation is inadequately capitalized, fails to observe corporate formalities, fails to issue stock or pay dividends, or operates without a profit; (2) whether there is commingling of corporate and personal assets; (3) whether there are nonfunctioning officers or directors; (4) whether the corporation is insolvent at the time of the transaction; and (5) the absence of corporate records.

There is no support in this record for basing personal liability on the "alter ego" doctrine. There is no evidence that Hildreth exercised such complete domination over HCE-NJ to warrant a conclusion that the corporation had no separate mind, will, or existence of its own. There is no evidence that HCE-NJ was undercapitalized, that corporate formalities were not observed, that the corporation operated without a profit, that there were non-functioning officers or directors, that the company was insolvent when it entered into the arrangement with Tidewater, that there were no or inadequate corporate records.

What the record does show is that HCE-NJ was a valid, subsisting corporation which, until it suffered a reversal of fortunes, had substantial assets and business prospects. The relevant contracts, with the general contractor and with Tidewater, were in its name, and, indeed, the contracts with Tidewater were signed on its behalf not by Hildreth but by another employee. Although the conclusion is certainly warranted that Hildreth deliberately permitted HCE-NJ to operate in Maryland without benefit of registration, there is no evidence that that conduct in any way influenced Tidewater to enter into the contractual arrangement from which this debt arose. Tidewater knew that it was dealing with a corporation, and it had satisfied itself that the corporation had substantial contracts and assets, that it had two business locations in the state, that it had numerous employees, and that it was not a "one man show." Kolbe's assumption that HCE-NJ was a Maryland corporation did not come from anything Hildreth said. Indeed, much of the information apparently relied upon by Kolbe in agreeing to the contract came from another HCE-NJ employee, not Hildreth.

In sustaining liability on Hildreth's part, the Court of Special Appeals seemed to be applying the second in Brune's trilogy of circumstances, disregarding the corporate existence "in order to prevent the evasion of legal obligations." That, in turn, appears to rest on Hildreth's failure to register the corporation. Tidewater sees that set of circumstances as an independent basis for "paramount equity," urging that "paramount equity" need not rest solely on the "alter ego" doctrine.

Hildreth's conduct may have subjected him to a $1,000 fine pursuant to § 7–302(b) of the Corporations and Associations Article; it would have served as well to preclude the corporation from filing suit in Maryland, *see* § 7–301. Section 7–305 makes clear, however, that the failure of a foreign corporation to comply with the registration requirements "does not affect the validity of any contract to which the corporation is a party," and there is nothing in the registration statutes that permits a court to invade the corporate entity simply because of a failure to register.

We do not regard Brune's second proposition as a separate basis for piercing a corporate veil. It is, at best, subsumed, along with the "alter ego" doctrine, in the notion of paramount equity, and has no application in this case. The record here reveals nothing more than the fact that a valid, subsisting corporation entered into a commercial contract and later became unable to satisfy its obligation under that contract. That is unfortunate, but it is not a basis for making someone else liable for the corporate debt.

Judgment reversed in favor of Hildreth.

Figure 2   *Examples of Piercing the Corporate Veil*

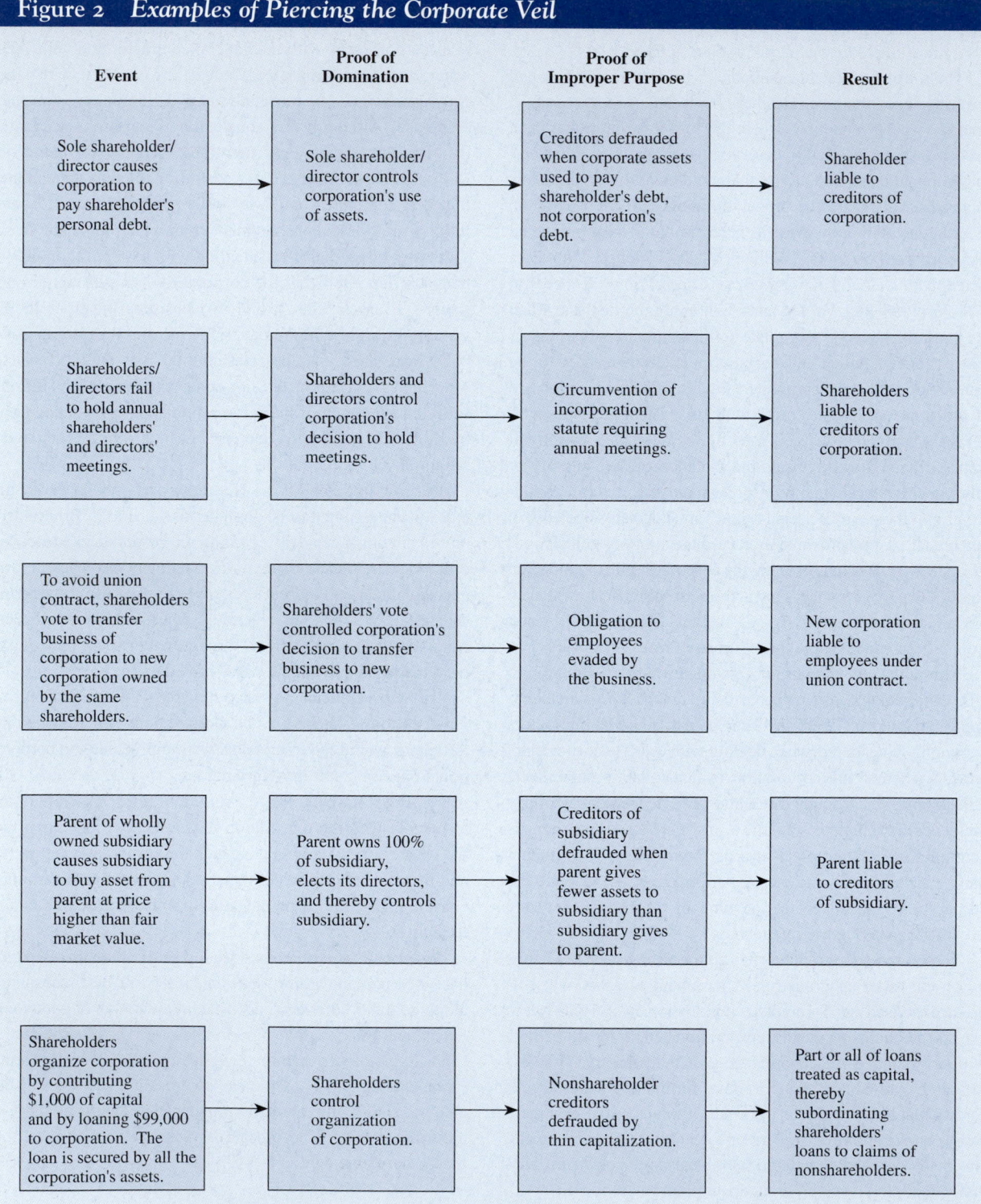

Event	Proof of Domination	Proof of Improper Purpose	Result
Sole shareholder/director causes corporation to pay shareholder's personal debt.	Sole shareholder/director controls corporation's use of assets.	Creditors defrauded when corporate assets used to pay shareholder's debt, not corporation's debt.	Shareholder liable to creditors of corporation.
Shareholders/directors fail to hold annual shareholders' and directors' meetings.	Shareholders and directors control corporation's decision to hold meetings.	Circumvention of incorporation statute requiring annual meetings.	Shareholders liable to creditors of corporation.
To avoid union contract, shareholders vote to transfer business of corporation to new corporation owned by the same shareholders.	Shareholders' vote controlled corporation's decision to transfer business to new corporation.	Obligation to employees evaded by the business.	New corporation liable to employees under union contract.
Parent of wholly owned subsidiary causes subsidiary to buy asset from parent at price higher than fair market value.	Parent owns 100% of subsidiary, elects its directors, and thereby controls subsidiary.	Creditors of subsidiary defrauded when parent gives fewer assets to subsidiary than subsidiary gives to parent.	Parent liable to creditors of subsidiary.
Shareholders organize corporation by contributing $1,000 of capital and by loaning $99,000 to corporation. The loan is secured by all the corporation's assets.	Shareholders control organization of corporation.	Nonshareholder creditors defrauded by thin capitalization.	Part or all of loans treated as capital, thereby subordinating shareholders' loans to claims of nonshareholders.

Ethics in Action

Large multinational corporations and smaller closely held corporations use multiple corporations (and sometimes LLCs and limited partnerships) to manage their tax, contract, and tort liability. As we will learn in Chapter 42, American corporations set up subsidiaries in Delaware to take advantage of its low taxes. Also, if a corporation wants to engage in a risky new venture in a country with a volatile political climate, the corporation will almost always conduct the business in a wholly owned subsidiary.

Even in the absence of an abnormal risk, many corporations create a structure like the following, in which parts of the corporation's business, such as finance, sales, and manufacturing, are placed in separate corporations, each wholly owned by the parent corporation:

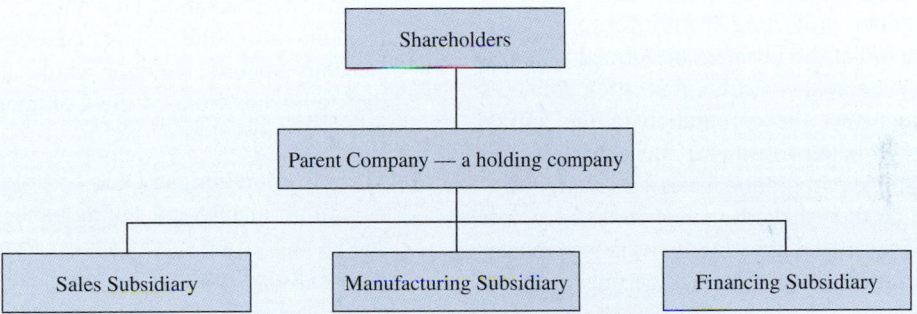

The parent company is a holding company that owns all the shares of the subsidiaries. Commonly, it also provides management services to the subsidiaries; in such cases, usually many employees working for the subsidiaries are actually employees of the parent, because the employees often work for more than one subsidiary. Employees are assigned by the parent holding company, which receives a management fee from the subsidiaries and allocates employees to the subsidiaries as needed. The holding company will also be the capital-raising arm of the business because its cost of capital is usually lower than the individual subsidiaries' costs of capital due to diversification of risk.

As far as corporation law is concerned, this parent–subsidiary structure allows the business to isolate liability. Thus, if one subsidiary is unable to pay its obligations and its assets lost, the assets of the other subsidiaries are preserved.

- Is it ethical for a business to set up such a parent–subsidiary structure? Would a profit maximizer be likely to set up such a structure?
- If a subsidiary becomes insolvent and is unable to pay its debts, would its creditors appreciate that neither the parent nor the other subsidiaries are liable to the creditors? Is it important that a creditor chose to do business with the subsidiary and could have examined its financial position before extending credit to the subsidiary?
- Would a tort victim who was injured by a product sold by the sales subsidiary appreciate that only its assets are available to pay his tort claim? Is it important that the victim is ignorant of corporation law and is not aware that the parent and subsidiaries are separate corporations? Does a tort victim have the same ability as a contract creditor to check out the corporate structure of the business before being injured by the product? Would a believer in justice theory see a difference between a contract creditor and a tort victim?

Problems and Problem Cases

1. You and four of your closest friends have decided to start a business that will purchase from banks and other financial institutions high-risk, subprime mortgage loans that are in default. You believe that you will be able to purchase the loans for no more than 40 percent of their face value. The plan is that the business will buy the loans by paying half the purchase amount in cash and the other half by issuing promissory notes due in six months to two years. You expect to turn a profit by restructuring the loans with the debtors, foreclosing against the real property securing the loans, or aggregating the loans and reselling them. You and your four friends are willing to invest $2 million each in the business. Needing an

additional $10 million to start the venture, you and your four friends agree to allow 10 other investors to contribute equity of $1 million each to the business. Only you and the four friends will be the managers of the business. The five of you want to share equally all decisions regarding the acquisition, management, and sale of the loans. You want the other 10 investors to be passive investors only with no say in the management of the business. However, the 10 other investors, who are contributing half the equity of the business, are concerned about protecting their investments. You have proposed that the business be formed as a limited liability company (LLC), but some of your friends believe that the corporation or the limited partnership is a better form. One friend says that the advantages of the corporation make it a superior business form. List the usual advantages of the corporate form of business. Explain why the usual advantages of the corporation are not likely to be fully available in this context.

2. Sculptchair, Inc., a Florida corporation, owned a patent to chair covers. It signed a contract with Century Arts, Ltd., a Canadian corporation, giving Century Arts exclusive rights under the patent to manufacture and sell chair covers. Century Arts was owned entirely by Mary Bien and Phyllis Rich. Almost immediately, Century Arts failed to make payments under the contract to Sculptchair, which terminated the contract. Century Arts went out of business. Bien and Rich formed a new Canadian corporation, Chair Décor, Inc., which carried on the business of Century Arts. Soon after, Sculptchair sued Chair Décor in a Florida court on the grounds that it was infringing Sculptchair's patent. Chair Décor argued that it could not be sued in a Florida court. Was Chair Décor right?

3. Dayton Furniture Fashions, Inc. (DFF), is incorporated in Ohio and operates three retail furniture stores in Dayton, Ohio. DFF advertises its stores on radio stations and in newspapers in Richmond, Indiana, a city near the Indiana border with Ohio. In response to DFF's advertisements, Greta Hammond, a resident of Richmond, drives to a DFF store in Dayton and purchases a sofa bed for $956. DFF agrees to deliver the sofa bed to Hammond's home in Richmond in three days. DFF's employees deliver the sofa bed to Hammond as promised, driving a delivery truck owned by DFF from its warehouse in

Huber Heights, Ohio. A few days later, when Hammond attempts to use the sofa bed for the first time, she discovers the sofa bed is defective and is not usable. When DFF refuses to replace the sofa bed, Hammond sues DFF in an Indiana state court. Does the Indiana court have jurisdiction over DFF?

4. A Hawaiian statute imposed a 20 percent wholesale excise tax on liquor sold in Hawaii. To encourage the development of Hawaiian liquor, the statute exempted from taxation Okolehao, a brandy distilled from the root of the ti plant, a native Hawaiian shrub. Bacchus Imports, a liquor wholesaler, claimed that the excise tax violated the Commerce Clause. Was Bacchus correct?

5. Mead Corporation, an Ohio corporation in the business of producing and selling paper, packaging, and school and office supplies, also owned Lexis/Nexis, the electronic research service. Either as a separate subsidiary or as a division of Mead, Lexis was subject to Mead's oversight, but Mead did not manage its day-to-day affairs. Mead was headquartered in Ohio, while a separate management team ran Lexis out of its headquarters in Illinois. The two businesses maintained separate manufacturing, sales, and distribution facilities, as well as separate accounting, legal, human resources, credit and collections, purchasing, and marketing departments. Mead's involvement was generally limited to approving Lexis's annual business plan and any significant corporate transactions that Lexis wished to undertake. Mead managed Lexis's free cash, which was swept nightly from Lexis's bank accounts into an account maintained by Mead. The cash was reinvested in Lexis's business, but Mead decided how to invest it. Neither business was required to purchase goods or services from the other. Lexis, for example, was not required to purchase its paper supply from Mead and in fact purchased most of its paper from other suppliers. Neither received any discount on goods or services purchased from the other, and neither was a significant customer of the other.

In 1994, Mead sold Lexis for $1.5 billion, realizing a capital gain of over $1 billion. Mead did not report any of this gain as business income on its 1994 Illinois tax return, taking the position that it was nonbusiness income and should be allocated entirely to Mead's domestic state, Ohio. Did the Supreme Court of the United States agree with Mead?

6. B & D Shrimp, Inc., a Delaware corporation, made a contract in Texas to sell a commercial shrimp boat to Donald Gosch and Jesse Bach. Gosch and Bach paid $5,000 down and received immediate possession of the boat in Texas, where they would shrimp in the coastal waters. The contract stated that Gosch and Bach would get title to the boat after transferring a cabin cruiser to Shrimp, Inc., and paying 15 percent of the cash proceeds from the boat's daily shrimp catches for the next calendar year. When Gosch and Bach defaulted on the contract, Shrimp, Inc., sued Gosch and won the case. Shrimp, Inc., however, had not obtained a certificate of authority to do business in Texas. Twenty days after the judgment was entered, Gosch contested the judgment on the grounds that Shrimp, Inc., by failing to qualify to do business, could not use Texas's courts to obtain a judgment against Gosch. Shrimp, Inc., decided at that time, therefore, to obtain a certificate of authority. Is the judgment for Shrimp, Inc., against Gosch valid?

7. The National Collegiate Athletic Association (NCAA) is a corporation organized in the State of Indiana. The NCAA conducts several championship events throughout the United States. The 2011 Men's Basketball Final Four will be held at Reliant Stadium in Houston, Texas. The NCAA has contracted to lease Reliant Stadium for two weeks up to and including the championship. The NCAA has also leased over 200 hotel rooms in Houston. To plan and conduct the championship event in Houston, over 20 NCAA employees will visit Houston over a two-year period, some of them spending over 75 days in Texas. Should the NCAA qualify to do business in Texas?

8. Eric Dahlbeck incorporated Viking Construction, Inc., with an initial capital of $3,000. Dahlbeck also made a $7,000 loan to Viking. Viking had as assets 65 lots of land held for development. The lots cost $430,000. Viking became unable to pay its creditors, who sought to pierce the corporate veil and hold Dahlbeck liable. Were the creditors successful?

9. New York law required that every taxicab company carry $10,000 of accident liability insurance for each cab in its fleet. The purpose of the law was to ensure that passengers and pedestrians injured by cabs operated by these companies would be adequately compensated for their injuries. Carlton organized 10 corporations, each owning and operating two taxicabs in New York City. Each of these corporations carried $20,000 of liability insurance. Carlton was the principal shareholder of each corporation. The vehicles, the only freely transferable assets of these corporations, were collateral for claims of secured creditors. The 10 corporations were operated more or less as a unit with respect to supplies, repairs, and employees. Walkovszky was severely injured when he was run down by one of the taxicabs. He sued Carlton personally, alleging that the multiple corporate structure amounted to fraud upon those who might be injured by the taxicabs. Should the court pierce the corporate veil to reach Carlton individually?

10. REIS, Inc., owns, constructs, and manages 25 shopping malls throughout the United States and Canada. REIS is concerned that the failure of any one mall will be a substantial financial loss that will cause the entire business to fail. What parent-subsidiary structure do you recommend REIS, Inc., create to solve the liability risks of operating 25 malls? What roles will the parent corporation undertake after the subsidiary structure has been established? List the dos or don'ts that will help prevent a piercing of the veils between the subsidiaries and between the parent company and its subsidiaries.

11. Castleberry, Branscum, and Byboth each owned one-third of the shares of a furniture-moving business, Texan Transfer, Inc. Branscum formed Elite Moving Company, a business that competed with Texan Transfer. Castleberry objected and sued to claim part ownership of Elite Moving. Branscum threatened Castleberry that he would not receive any return on his investment in Texan Transfer unless he abandoned his claim of ownership of Elite Moving. Consequently, Castleberry sold his shares back to Texan Transfer for a $42,000 promissory note. Gradually, Elite Moving took over more and more of the business of Texan Transfer. Texan Transfer allowed Elite Moving to use its employees and trucks. Elite Moving advertised for business, while Texan Transfer did not. Elite Moving prospered, while Texan Transfer's business declined. As a result, Castleberry was paid only $1,000 of the $42,000 promissory note. Did Castleberry have any grounds to hold Branscum liable for the unpaid portion of the note?

12. Rachel Romano owns 90 percent of the stock of RRC, Inc. Romano is the president and CEO and the only voting member of the board of directors. Her husband and daughter each own 5 percent of the

shares of RRC, and each is also an officer and non-voting director. When Romano receives payments from RRC's clients, she deposits the payments in her personal checking and savings accounts. She also pays all RRC's creditors with checks written on her personal account. She also pays all her personal expenses from the personal checking account into which she deposits RRC funds. For three years, Romano has not held a shareholders meeting or a meeting of the board of directors. Is Romano risking being held liable for the obligations of RRC?

Online Research

Your State's or Country's Corporation Law

Find a Web site that posts the corporation law of your state or country. All state governments have online access to their statutes, and a few countries do as well. When you find the statute, determine what a foreign or alien corporation must do in your state or country to qualify to do business.

chapter 42

ORGANIZATION AND FINANCIAL STRUCTURE OF CORPORATIONS

A client has sought your assistance before incorporating a business that will buy and sell fine art. The client will enter the business with three other associates, all about 35 years old. They plan to own equal shares of the business and to manage it together. The business has not yet been incorporated.

- Your client and her associates identify five valuable paintings they want to purchase. To reduce their personal liability on the contracts to purchase the paintings, what do you recommend they do prior to signing the purchase contracts?
- Your client states that she wants to incorporate the business because a corporation's shares are freely transferable, making it easy for shareholders to liquidate their investments. You know better. Explain to your client why free transferability of the shares as a legal matter is a problem for her and her associates. Also explain to your client why free transferability of the shares as a practical matter does not exist. What should your client do to address the share transferability issues? Sketch the contents of a buy-sell agreement that addresses all the transferability issues.

A PERSON DESIRING TO incorporate a business must comply with the applicable state or federal corporation law. Failing to comply can create various problems. For example, a person may make a contract on behalf of the corporation before it is incorporated. Is the corporation liable on this contract? Is the person who made the contract on behalf of the prospective corporation liable on the contract? Do the people who thought that they were shareholders of a corporation have limited liability, or do they have unlimited liability as partners of a partnership?

Promoters and Preincorporation Transactions

A **promoter** of a corporation incorporates a business, organizes its initial management, and raises its initial capital. Typically, a promoter creates or discovers a business or an idea to be developed, finds people who are willing to invest in the business, negotiates the contracts necessary for the initial operation of the proposed venture, incorporates the business, and helps management start the operation of the business. Consequently, a promoter may engage in many acts prior to the incorporation of the business. As a result, the promoter may have liability on the contracts he negotiates on behalf of the prospective corporation. In addition, the corporation may *not* be liable on the contracts the promoter makes on its behalf.

Corporation's Liability on Preincorporation Contracts

A nonexistent corporation has no liability on contracts made by a promoter prior to its incorporation. This is because the corporation does not exist.

Even when the corporation comes into existence, it does not automatically become liable on a preincorporation contract made by a promoter on its behalf. It cannot be held liable as a principal whose agent made the contracts because the promoter was not its agent and the corporation was not in existence when the contracts were made.

The only way a corporation may become bound on a promoter's preincorporation contracts is by the corporation's **adoption** of the promoter's contracts. Adoption is similar to the agency concept of ratification, which is covered in Chapter 36. For a corporation to adopt a promoter's contract, the corporation must accept the contract with knowledge of all its material facts.

Acceptance may be express or implied. The corporation's knowing receipt of the benefits of the contract is sufficient for acceptance. For example, a promoter makes a preincorporation contract with a genetic engineer, requiring the engineer to work for a prospective corporation for 10 years. After incorporation, the promoter presents the contract to the board of directors. Although the board takes no formal action to accept the contract, the board allows the engineer to work for the corporation for one year as the contract provides and pays him the salary required by the contract. The board's actions constitute an acceptance of the contract, binding the corporation to the contract for its 10-year term. The *SmithStearn* case is another example of a corporation adopting a preincorporation contract.

Promoter's Liability on Preincorporation Contracts

A promoter and her copromoters are jointly and severally liable on preincorporation contracts the promoter negotiates in the name of the nonexistent corporation. This liability exists even when the promoters' names do not appear on the contract. Promoters are also jointly and severally liable for torts committed by their copromoters prior to incorporation.

A promoter retains liability on a preincorporation contract until **novation** occurs. For novation to occur, the corporation and the third party must agree to release the promoter from liability and to substitute the corporation for the promoter as the party liable on the contract. Usually, novation will occur by express or implied agreement of all the parties.

If the corporation is not formed, a promoter remains liable on a preincorporation contract unless the third party releases the promoter from liability. In addition, the mere formation of the corporation does not release a promoter from liability. A promoter remains liable on a preincorporation contract even after the corporation's adoption of the contract, since adoption does not automatically release the promoter. The corporation cannot by itself relieve the promoter of liability to the third party; the third party must also agree, expressly or impliedly, to release the promoter from liability.

A few courts have held that a promoter is not liable on preincorporation contracts if the third party *knew of the nonexistence* of the corporation yet insisted that the promoter sign the contract on behalf of the nonexistent corporation. Other courts have found that the promoter is not liable if the third party clearly stated that he would *look only to the prospective corporation* for performance.

Recently, courts have held that the Model Business Corporation Act (MBCA) permits a promoter to escape liability for preincorporation contracts when the promoter has made some effort to incorporate the business and believes the corporation is in existence. The MBCA rule is discussed below in the section titled Defective Attempts to Incorporate.

Obtaining a Binding Preincorporation Contract

While it may be desirable for the promoter to escape liability on a preincorporation contract, there is one disadvantage: Only when the promoter is liable on the preincorporation contract is the other party liable on the contract. This means that when the promoter is not liable on the contract, the other party to the contract may rescind the contract at any time prior to adoption by the corporation. Once the corporation has adopted the contract, the corporation and the third party are liable on it, and the contract cannot be rescinded without the consent of both parties.

To maintain the enforceability of a preincorporation contract prior to adoption, a promoter may want to be liable on a preincorporation contract at least until the corporation comes into existence and adopts the contract. To limit his liability, however, the promoter may wish to have his liability cease automatically upon adoption. The promoter should ensure that the contract has an **automatic novation clause.** For example, a preincorporation contract may read that "the promoter's liability on this contract shall terminate upon the corporation's adoption of this contract."

Instead of using automatic novation clauses, today most well-advised promoters incorporate the business prior to making any contracts for the corporation. That is, the well-advised promoter makes *no* preincorporation contracts. Instead, she makes contracts only for existing corporations. As a result, only the corporation and the third party—and not the promoter—have liability on the contract.

SmithStearn Yachts, Inc. v. Gyrographic Communications, Inc.
2006 Conn. Super. LEXIS 1927 (Ct. Super. Ct. 2006)

SmithStearn Yachts, Inc., a Delaware corporation providing luxury yachting services in Connecticut, agreed to a contract with Gyrographic Communications, Inc., a California company, by which Gyrographic would provide advertising, marketing, and promotional services to SmithStearn. When SmithStearn sued Gyrographic for breaching the contract, Gyrographic countered that SmithStearn was not a party to the contact, because the contract was purportedly made with a limited liability corporation, SmithStearn Yachts, LLC, not the corporation that was suing Gyrographic.

Rodiquez, Judge

Leathern Stearn, the purported promoter and president of SmithStearn Yachts, Inc., executed the agreement with Gyrographic on behalf of SmithStearn, LLC, an entity that never came into existence. Rather, the plaintiff, SmithStearn Yachts, Inc. was formed. SmithStearn Yachts, Inc. contends that it has standing to bring this action because it assumed and ratified, both explicitly and implicitly, the agreement that was made on its behalf, prior to its formation.

Generally, a corporation is not bound by contracts entered into on its behalf prior to its existence. A corporation can, however, acquire rights and subject itself to duties with respect to preincorporation matters. A contract made in the name of an inchoate corporation can be enforced after the corporation is organized on the principle of ratification. Ratification is defined as the affirmance by a person of a prior act which did not bind him but which was done or professedly done on his account. Ratification requires acceptance of the results of the act with an intent to ratify, and with full knowledge of all the material circumstances.

A corporation may after its organization become liable on preliminary contracts made by its promoters by expressly adopting such contracts or by receiving the benefits from them. Although SmithStearn Yachts, Inc. was formed after the execution of the agreement, it received the benefit of the services pursuant to the agreement. Gyrographic worked toward developing letterheads, business cards, and other marketing material for SmithStearn Yachts, Inc. SmithStearn Yachts, Inc. made payments to Gyrographic, which SmithStearn Yachts, Inc. then recorded in its books. Thus, SmithStearn Yachts, Inc. received the benefits of the agreement and also fulfilled the obligations under it, thereby ratifying the agreement.

Furthermore, ratification, adoption, or acceptance of a preincorporation contract by a promoter need not be expressed, but may be implied from acts or acquiescence on the part of the corporation or its authorized agents. Thus, a corporation's act of suing on a preincorporation contract is in itself an adoption of the contract. SmithStearn Yachts, Inc. implicitly ratified the agreement when it brought this action. By suing under the agreement, SmithStearn Yachts, Inc. is also assuming the liabilities under it, thereby enforcing and adopting the agreement.

Judgment for SmithStearn Yachts, Inc.

Preincorporation Share Subscriptions

Promoters sometimes use **preincorporation share subscriptions** to ensure that the corporation will have adequate capital when it begins its business. Under the terms of a share subscription, a prospective shareholder offers to buy a specific number of the corporation's shares at a stated price. Under the Model Business Corporation Act (MBCA), a prospective shareholder may not revoke a preincorporation subscription for a six-month period, in the absence of a contrary provision in the subscription. Generally, corporate acceptance of preincorporation subscriptions occurs by action of the board of directors after incorporation.

Promoters have no liability on preincorporation share subscriptions. They have a duty, however, to make a good faith effort to bring the corporation into existence. When a corporation fails to accept a preincorporation subscription or becomes insolvent, the promoter is not liable to the disappointed subscriber, in the absence of fraud or other wrongdoing by the promoter.

Today, most promoters incorporate the business and obtain promises to buy shares from prospective shareholders. These promises, which may take the form of postincorporation subscriptions, are discussed later in this chapter.

Relation of Promoter and Prospective Corporation

A promoter of a nonexistent corporation is not an agent of the prospective corporation. A promoter is not an agent of prospective investors in the business because they did not appoint him and they have no power to control him.

Although not an agent of the proposed corporation or its investors, a promoter owes a **fiduciary duty** to the corporation and to its prospective investors. A promoter owes such parties a duty of full disclosure and honesty. For example, a promoter breaches this duty when he diverts money received from prospective shareholders to pay his expenses, unless the shareholders agree to such payment. The fiduciary duty also prevents a promoter from diverting a business opportunity from the corporation and giving it to himself instead. In addition, the promoter may not purchase shares of the corporation at a price lower than that paid by the public shareholders.

A promoter may not profit personally by transacting secretly with the corporation in his personal capacity.

The promoter's failure to disclose his interest in the transaction and the material facts permits the corporation to rescind the transaction or to recover the promoter's secret profit. On the other hand, the promoter's full disclosure of his interest and the material facts of the transaction to an independent board of directors that approves the transaction prevents the corporation from recovering the promoter's profit. Note, however, that when a promoter is a director, approval of the transaction by the board of directors may not be sufficient; the transaction may need to be intrinsically fair to the corporation.

Liability of Corporation to Promoter

Valuable as the services of a promoter may be to a prospective corporation and to society, a corporation is generally not required to compensate a promoter for her promotional services, or even her expenses, unless the corporation has agreed expressly to compensate the promoter. The justification for this rule is that the promoter is self-appointed and acts for a corporation that is not in existence.

Nonetheless, a corporation may choose to reimburse the promoter for her reasonable expenses and to pay her the value of her services to the corporation. Corporations often compensate their promoters with shares. The MBCA permits the issuance of shares for a promoter's preincorporation services.

To ensure that she is compensated for her services, a promoter may tie herself to a person or property that the corporation needs to succeed. For example, a promoter may purchase the invention that the corporation was formed to exploit. Another way to ensure compensation is by the promoter's dominating the board of directors during the early months of its life. By doing so, the promoter may direct the corporation to compensate her, but only if the compensation is reasonable and, therefore, fair to the corporation.

Incorporation

Anyone seeking to incorporate a business must decide where to do so. If the business of a proposed corporation is to be primarily *intrastate,* it is usually cheaper to incorporate in the state where the corporation's business is to be conducted. For the business that is primarily *interstate,* however, the business may benefit by incorporating in a state different from the state in which it has its principal place of business. Because few businesses qualify to incorporate under federal law, that option is rarely exercised.

Incorporation fees and taxes, annual fees, and other fees such as those on the transfer of shares or the dissolution of the corporation vary considerably from state to state. Delaware has been a popular state in which to incorporate because its fees and taxes tend to be low. It also has judges experienced in resolving corporate disputes.

Promoters frequently choose to incorporate in a state whose corporation statute and court decisions grant managers broad management discretion. For example, it is easier to pay a large dividend and to effect a merger in Delaware than in many other states.

Steps in Incorporation There are only a few requirements for incorporation. It is a fairly simple process and can be accomplished inexpensively in most cases. The steps prescribed by the incorporation statutes of the different states vary, but they generally include the following, which appear in the MBCA:

1. Preparation of articles of incorporation.

2. Signing and authenticating the articles by one or more incorporators.

3. Filing the articles with the secretary of state, accompanied by the payment of specified fees.

4. Receipt of a copy of the articles of incorporation stamped "Filed" by the secretary of state, accompanied by a fee receipt. (Some states retain the old MBCA rule requiring receipt of a certificate of incorporation issued by the secretary of state.)

5. Holding an organization meeting for the purpose of adopting bylaws, electing officers, and transacting other business.

Articles of Incorporation The basic governing document of the corporation is the **articles of incorporation** (sometimes called the charter). The articles are similar to a constitution. They state many of the rights and responsibilities of the corporation, its management, and its shareholders. Figure 1 lists the contents of the articles.

The corporation must have a name that is distinguishable from the name of any other corporation incorporated or qualified to do business in the state. The name must include the word *corporation, incorporated, company,* or *limited,* or the abbreviation *corp., inc., co.,* or *ltd.*

The MBCA does not require the inclusion of a statement of purpose in the articles. When a purpose is stated, it is sufficient to state, alone or together with specific purposes, that the corporation may engage in "any lawful activity."

The MBCA permits a corporation to have perpetual existence. If desired, the articles of incorporation may provide for a shorter duration.

Figure 1   *Contents of Articles of Incorporation (pursuant to MBCA)*

The following *must* be in the articles:

1. The name of the corporation.

2. The number of shares that the corporation has authority to issue.

3. The address of the initial registered office of the corporation and the name of its registered agent.

4. The name and address of each incorporator.

The following *may* be included in the articles:

1. The names and addresses of the individuals who are to serve as the initial directors.

2. The purpose of the corporation.

3. The duration of the corporation.

4. The par value of shares of the corporation.

5. Additional provisions not inconsistent with law for managing the corporation, regulating the internal affairs of the corporation, and establishing the powers of the corporation and its directors and shareholders.

Most of the state corporation statutes require the articles to recite the initial capitalization of the business. Usually, the statutes require that there be a minimum amount of initial capital, such as $1,000. Since such a small amount of capital is rarely enough to protect creditors adequately, the MBCA dispenses with the need to recite a minimum amount of capital. Instead, the thin capitalization rule we studied in Chapter 41 protects creditors.

The articles may contain additional provisions not inconsistent with law for managing the corporation, regulating the internal affairs of the corporation, and establishing the powers of the corporation and its directors and shareholders. For example, these additional provisions may contain the procedures for electing directors, the quorum requirements for shareholders' and directors' meetings, and the dividend rights of shareholders.

The MBCA specifies that one or more persons, including corporations, partnerships, and unincorporated associations, may serve as the **incorporators.** Incorporators have no function beyond lending their names and signatures to the process of bringing the corporation into existence. No special liability attaches to a person merely because she serves as an incorporator.

Filing Articles of Incorporation   The articles of incorporation must be delivered to the office of the secretary of state, and a filing fee must be paid. The office of the secretary of state reviews the articles of incorporation that are delivered to it. If the articles contain everything

Ethics in Action

Domestic Tax Havens

In the last 20 years, some American companies have reincorporated all or part of their businesses in states that offer favorable tax treatment. For example, Limited Brands Inc., the owner of the Limited, Bath & Body Works, and Victoria's Secret chains, has incorporated seven subsidiaries in Delaware. The primary function of the subsidiaries is to own the chains' trademarks. The subsidiaries charge the retail chains high fees to use the trademarks. This parent–subsidiary structure allows the business to transfer hundreds of millions of dollars each year from retail outlets in high-tax states like New York into Delaware subsidiaries that pay no state tax. Delaware is the most used domestic tax haven, but Nevada and Florida also provide favorable tax treatment for corporations.

- Is it ethical and socially responsible for an American corporation to incorporate its business wholly or in part in states that have low tax rates? Would a profit maximizer incorporate where tax rates are lowest? Would a believer in rights theory?
- If you were a state legislator in a state with high income taxes that is losing incorporations to Delaware, what legislation would you introduce? Would your answer depend on whether you were a utilitarian or a believer in justice theory?

that is required, the secretary of state stamps the articles "Filed" and returns a copy of the stamped articles to the corporation along with a receipt for payment of incorporation fees. Some states require a duplicate filing of the articles with an office—usually the county recorder's office—in the county in which the corporation has its principal place of business.

The existence of the corporation begins when the articles are filed by the secretary of state. Filing of the articles by the secretary of state is conclusive proof of the existence of the corporation.

Because the articles of incorporation embody the basic contract between a corporation and its shareholders, shareholders must approve most changes in the articles. For example, when the articles are amended to increase the number of authorized shares, shareholder approval is required.

The Organization Meeting After the articles of incorporation have been filed by the secretary of state, an organization meeting is held. Usually, it is the first formal meeting of the directors. Frequently, only bylaws are adopted and officers elected. The function of the bylaws is to supplement the articles of incorporation by defining more precisely the powers, rights, and responsibilities of the corporation, its managers, and its shareholders and by stating other rules under which the corporation and its activities will be governed. Its common contents are listed in Figure 2.

The MBCA gives the incorporators or the initial directors the power to adopt the initial bylaws. The board

of directors holds the power to repeal and to amend the bylaws, unless the articles reserve this power to the shareholders. Under the MBCA, the shareholders, as the ultimate owners of the corporation, always retain the power to amend the bylaws, even if the directors also have such power. To be valid, bylaws must be consistent with the law and with the articles of incorporation.

If the organization meeting is the first meeting of the board of directors, the board may adopt a corporate seal for use on corporate documents, approve the form of share certificates, accept share subscriptions, authorize the issuance of shares, adopt preincorporation contracts, authorize reimbursement for promoters' expenses, and fix the salaries of officers.

Filing Annual Report To retain its status as a corporation in good standing, a corporation must file an annual report with the secretary of state of the state of incorporation and pay an annual franchise fee or tax. The amount of annual franchise tax varies greatly from state to state. While the annual report includes very little information and repeats information already filed in the articles of incorporation, failure to file an annual report or pay the annual fee or tax may result in a dissolution of the corporation and an imposition of monetary penalties.

Close Corporation Elections
Close corporations face problems that normally do not affect publicly held corporations. In recognition of these problems, 20 states and the District of Columbia have statutes that attend to the special needs of close corporations. For example, some corporation statutes allow a close corporation to be managed by its shareholders.

To take advantage of these close corporation statutes, most statutes require that a corporation make an *election* to be treated as a close corporation. The Statutory Close Corporation Supplement to the MBCA permits a corporation with *fewer than 50 shareholders* to elect to become a close corporation. The Close Corporation Supplement requires the articles of incorporation to state that the corporation is a statutory close corporation.

There is no penalty for a corporation's failure to make a close corporation election. The only consequence of a failure to meet the requirements is that the close corporation statutory provisions are inapplicable. Instead, statutory corporation law will treat the corporation as it treats any other general corporation.

Note, however, that even when a corporation fails to meet the statutory requirements for treatment as a close corporation, a court may decide to apply special *common law* rules applicable only to close corporations.

Figure 2   *Contents of the Bylaws*

1. The authority of the officers and the directors, specifying what they may or may not do.

2. The time and place at which the annual shareholders' meetings will be held.

3. The procedure for calling special meetings of shareholders.

4. The procedures for shareholders' and directors' meetings, including whether more than a majority is required for approval of specified actions.

5. Provisions for special committees of the board, defining their membership and the scope of their activities.

6. The procedures for the maintenance of share records.

7. The machinery for the transfer of shares.

8. The procedures and standards for the declaration and payment of dividends.

Defective Attempts to Incorporate

When business managers attempt to incorporate a business, sometimes they fail to comply with all the conditions for incorporation. For example, the incorporators may not have filed articles of incorporation or the directors may not have held an organization meeting. These are examples of **defective attempts to incorporate.**

One possible consequence of defective incorporation is to make the managers and the purported shareholders *personally liable* for the obligations of the defectively formed corporation. For example, an employee of an insolvent corporation drives the corporation's truck over a pedestrian. If the pedestrian proves that the corporation was defectively formed, he may be able to recover damages for his injuries from the managers and the shareholders.

A second possible consequence of defective incorporation is that a party to a contract involving the purported corporation may claim nonexistence of the corporation in order to avoid a contract made in the name of the corporation. For example, a person makes an ill-advised contract with a corporation. If the person proves that the corporation was defectively formed, he may escape liability on the contract because he made a contract with a nonexistent person, the defectively formed corporation. As an alternative, the defectively formed corporation may escape liability on the contract on the grounds that its nonexistence makes it impossible for it to have liability.

The courts have tried to determine when these two consequences should arise by making a distinction between de jure corporations, de facto corporations, corporations by estoppel, and corporations so defectively formed that they are treated as being nonexistent.

De Jure Corporation

A de jure corporation is formed when the promoters substantially comply with each of the **mandatory conditions precedent** to the incorporation of the business. *Mandatory* provisions are distinguished from *directory* provisions by statutory language

and the purpose of the provision. Mandatory provisions are those that the corporation statute states "shall" or "must" be done or those that are necessary to protect the public interest. Directory provisions are those that "may" be done and that are unnecessary to protect the public interest.

For example, statutes provide that the incorporators shall file the articles of incorporation with the secretary of state. This is a mandatory provision, not only because of the use of the word *shall* but also because of the importance of a filing to protect the public interest by informing the public that a business has shareholders with limited liability. Other mandatory provisions include conducting an organization meeting. Directory provisions include minor matters such as the inclusion of the incorporators' addresses in the articles of incorporation.

If a corporation has complied with each mandatory provision, it is a de jure corporation and is treated as a corporation for all purposes. The validity of a de jure corporation cannot be attacked, except in a few states in which the state, in a *quo warranto* proceeding, may attack the corporation for noncompliance with a condition subsequent to incorporation, such as a failure to file an annual report with the secretary of state.

De Facto Corporation

A de facto corporation exists when the incorporators fail in some material respect to comply with all of the mandatory provisions of the incorporation statute yet comply with most mandatory provisions. There are three requirements for a de facto corporation:

1. There is a valid statute under which the corporation could be organized.

2. The promoters or managers make an honest attempt to organize under the statute. This requires substantial compliance with the mandatory provisions taken as a whole.

3. The promoters or managers exercise corporate powers. That is, they act as if they were acting for a corporation.

Generally, failing to file the articles of incorporation with the secretary of state will prevent the creation of a de facto corporation. However, a de facto corporation will exist despite the lack of an organization meeting or the failure to make a duplicate filing of the articles with a county recorder.

A de facto corporation is treated as a corporation against either an attack by a third party or an attempt of the business itself to deny that it is a corporation. The state, however, may attack the claimed corporate status of the business in a *quo warranto* action.

Corporation by Estoppel

When people hold themselves out as representing a corporation or believe themselves to be dealing with a corporation, a court will estop those people from denying the existence of a corporation. This is called **corporation by estoppel.** For example, a manager states that a business has been incorporated and induces a third person to contract with the purported corporation. The manager will not be permitted to use a failure to incorporate as a defense to the contract because he has misled others to believe reasonably that a corporation exists.

Under the doctrine of estoppel, each contract must be considered individually to determine whether either party to the contract is estopped from denying the corporation's existence.

Liability for Defective Incorporation

If people attempt to organize a corporation but their efforts are so defective that not even a corporation by estoppel is found to exist, the courts have generally held such persons to be partners with unlimited liability for the contracts and torts of the business. However, most courts impose the unlimited *contractual* liability of a partner only on those who are *actively engaged in the management* of the business or who are responsible for the defects in its organization. *Tort* liability, however, is generally imposed on everyone—the managers and the purported shareholders of the defectively formed corporation.

Modern Approaches to the Defective Incorporation Problem

As you can see, the law of defective incorporation is confusing. It becomes even more confusing when you consider that many of the defective incorporation cases look like promoter liability cases, and vice versa. A court may have difficulty deciding whether to apply the law of promoter liability or the law of defective incorporation to preincorporation contracts. It is not surprising, therefore, that modern corpo-ration statutes have attempted to eliminate this confusion by adopting simple rules for determining the existence of a corporation and the liability of its promoters, managers, and shareholders.

The MBCA states that incorporation occurs when the articles are filed by the secretary of state. The **filing** of the articles is **conclusive proof** of the existence of the corporation, except in a proceeding brought by the state. Consequently, the incorporators may omit even a mandatory provision, yet create a corporation, provided that the secretary of state has filed the articles of incorporation. Conversely, courts have held that a failure to obtain a filing of the articles is conclusive proof of the nonexistence of the corporation, on the grounds that the MBCA eliminates the concepts of de facto corporation and corporation by estoppel.

Liability for Defective Incorporation under the MBCA The MBCA imposes joint and several liability on those persons who purport to act on behalf of a corporation and know that there has been no incorporation. Thus, managers and shareholders who both (1) *participate* in the operational decisions of the business and (2) *know* that the corporation does not exist are liable for the purported corporation's contracts and torts.

The MBCA releases from liability shareholders and others who either (1) take no part in the management of the defectively formed corporation *or* (2) mistakenly believe that the corporation is in existence. Consequently, *passive* shareholders have no liability for the obligations of a defectively formed corporation even when they know that the corporation has not been formed. Likewise, managers of a defectively formed corporation have no liability when they believe that the corporation exists.

The following case found two owners of a business liable as partners when they failed to comply with Tennessee's corporation statute.

Christmas Lumber Co., Inc. v. Valiga   99 S.W.3d 585 (Tenn. Ct. App. 2002)

Robert Waddell decided to go into the home construction business. He entered into a contract with Robert Valiga on September 12, 1988. When he entered into the contract with Valiga, Waddell signed the contract on behalf of R. H. Waddell Construction, Inc. At the time the contract was entered into with Valiga, Waddell had no knowledge that the corporation's articles of incorporation had not been filed. Although Waddell had signed the articles of incorporation as the incorporator on August 19, 1988, the articles were not filed by the Secretary of State's office until December 9, 1988, and by the Registrar's Office in Knox County until January 12, 1989.

On September 12, 1988, the same day Waddell entered into the contract with Valiga, John Graves opened an account at Christmas Lumber Company in order to obtain building materials for the Valiga house. Graves opened the account in

Waddell's name, and where the account information stated "type of customer," Graves marked "individual." Graves signed the document on behalf of Waddell.

In a letter from Valiga to Waddell dated November 9, 1988, Valiga made several requests about the construction of the house. In a letter dated the next day, Valiga terminated Waddell's services. Sensing potential litigation, Waddell and Graves on November 11, 1988, entered into a Joint Venture Agreement. The only parties to the Agreement were Waddell and Graves. R. H. Waddell Construction, Inc., was not a party to the agreement. Pursuant to the terms of the Agreement, Waddell and Graves divided funds received from Heritage Federal Credit Union for construction of the Valiga home.

After Waddell patched things up with Valiga, he returned to work on the project from November until February of the next year. On February 11, 1989, Waddell received a letter from Valiga expressing his shock regarding the cost of the construction job. Three days later, Waddell quit as Valiga's contractor.

On January 10, 1990, Christmas Lumber Company filed a lawsuit against Valiga, Waddell, and others seeking to enforce a materialmen's lien for building materials purchased by Waddell to be used on the house being built for Valiga. On December 2, 1992, Valiga filed a separate lawsuit against Waddell and Graves claiming there was no corporation chartered by the State of Tennessee named R. H. Waddell Construction, Inc., when the contract was entered into on September 12, 1988.

After the two lawsuits were consolidated, the trial court found that Waddell and Graves were liable as partners on the construction contract signed in the name of R. H. Waddell Construction, Inc., and awarded Valiga damages of $80,045.79. Waddell and Graves appealed to the Tennessee Court of Appeals. The court considered Waddell's argument that he did not know that the corporation was not formed at the time the construction contract was signed.

Swiney, Judge

Waddell relies on Tenn. Code Ann. § 48-12-104, which provides as follows:

48-12-104. Liability for preincorporation transactions. All persons purporting to act as or on behalf of a corporation, knowing there was no incorporation under chapters 11–27 of this title, are jointly and severally liable for all liabilities created while so acting except for any liability to any person who knew or reasonably should have known that there was no incorporation.

Waddell argues he signed the necessary paperwork to have his business incorporated and was unaware of the delay in filing the charter with the Secretary of State's office. He claims, therefore, he did not "know" there was no incorporation.

Pursuant to Tenn. Code Ann. § 48-12-103, absent a delayed effective date, the "corporate existence begins when the charter is filed by the secretary of state."

Waddell apparently signed the charter on August 19, 1988. On September 12, 1988, the contract was signed between Valiga and R. H. Waddell Construction, Inc. Two months later, on November 11, 1988, Waddell and Graves entered into the Joint Venture Agreement. On December 9, 1988, the charter was filed with the Secretary of State's office. Waddell's claim he did not "know" the corporate charter had not been filed with the Secretary of State is belied by the fact he and Graves essentially memorialized their relationship in writing with the Joint Venture Agreement which was signed after Waddell claims he "thought" there was a corporation and before the corporation actually was formed. Waddell's assertion is made further suspect by his deposition testimony that he and Graves were "partners."

Based on the roles occupied by Waddell and Graves during the construction of Valiga's house, coupled with: (1) the terms of Joint Venture Agreement; (2) Waddell's deposition testimony he and Graves were "partners;" (3) Graves' testimony that he spent a significant amount of time at the work site; and (4) Waddell and Graves dividing the contractor's fee, we conclude the evidence does not preponderate against the Trial Court's findings leading to its conclusion that Waddell and Graves were partners.

Judgment for Valiga affirmed.

Incorporation of Nonprofit Corporations

Nonprofit corporations are incorporated in substantially the same manner as for-profit corporations. One or more persons serve as incorporators and deliver articles of incorporation to the secretary of state for filing. A nonprofit corporation's articles must include the name and address of the corporation and state its registered agent. Unlike a for-profit corporation, a nonprofit corporation must state that it is either a public benefit corporation, a mutual benefit corporation, or a religious corporation. A public benefit corporation is incorporated primarily for the benefit of the public—for example, a community arts council that promotes the arts. A mutual benefit corporation is designed to benefit its members—for example, a golf country club. An example of a religious corporation is a church.

A nonprofit corporation's articles must also state whether it will have members. While it is typical for nonprofit corporations to have members, the Model Nonprofit Corporation Act (MNCA) does not require a nonprofit corporation to have members. An example of a nonprofit corporation having no members is a public benefit corporation established to promote business development in a city, whose directors are appointed by the city's mayor.

A nonprofit corporation's articles may include the purpose of the corporation, its initial directors, and any matter regarding the rights and duties of the corporation and its directors and members. Each incorporator and director named in the articles must sign the articles.

A nonprofit corporation's existence begins when the secretary of state files the articles. After incorporation, the initial directors or incorporators hold an organization meeting to adopt bylaws and conduct other business.

Liability for Preincorporation Transactions

Nonprofit corporation status normally protects the members and managers from personal liability. However, when a nonprofit corporation is not formed or is defectively formed, promoters and others who transact for the nonexistent nonprofit corporation have the same liability as promoters and others who transact for a nonexistent for-profit corporation. The MNCA states the same rule as the MBCA: Persons who act on behalf of a corporation knowing there is no corporation are jointly and severally liable for all liabilities created while so acting.

Similarly, promoters have no authority to make contracts for a nonexistent nonprofit corporation. The corporation becomes liable on preincorporation contracts when its board of directors adopts the contracts.

Financing For-Profit Corporations

Any business needs money to operate and to grow. One advantage of incorporation is the large number of sources of funds that are available to businesses that incorporate. One such source is the sale of corporate **securities,** including shares, debentures, bonds, and long-term notes payable.

In addition to obtaining funds from the sale of securities, a corporation may be financed by other sources. A bank may lend money to the corporation in exchange for the corporation's short-term promissory notes, called commercial paper. Earnings provide a source of funds once the corporation is operating profitably. In addition, the corporation may use normal short-term financing, such as accounts receivable financing and inventory financing, that is, borrowing from banks or other financial institutions and using the corporation's receivables or inventory as collateral.

In this section, you will study only one source of corporate funds—a corporation's sale of securities. A corporate security may be either (1) a share in the corporation or (2) an obligation of the corporation. These two kinds of securities are called equity securities and debt securities.

Equity Securities

Every business corporation issues equity securities, which are commonly called stock or **shares.** The issuance of shares creates an ownership relationship: the holders of the shares—called stockholders or **shareholders**—are the owners of the corporation.

Modern statutes permit corporations to issue several classes of shares and to determine the rights of the various classes. Subject to minimum guarantees contained in the state business corporation law, the shareholders' rights are a matter of contract and appear in the articles of incorporation, in the bylaws, in a shareholder agreement, and on the share certificates.

Common Shares

Common shares (or common stock) are a type of equity security. Ordinarily, the owners of common shares—called **common shareholders**—have the exclusive right to elect the directors, who manage the corporation.

The common shareholders often occupy a position inferior to that of other investors, notably creditors and preferred shareholders. The claims of common shareholders are subordinate to the claims of creditors and other classes of shareholders when liabilities and dividends are paid and when assets are distributed upon liquidation.

In return for this subordination, however, the common shareholders have an exclusive claim to the corporate earnings and assets that exceed the claims of creditors and other shareholders. Therefore, the common shareholders bear the major risks of the corporate venture, yet stand to profit the most if it is successful.

Preferred Shares

Shares that have preferences with regard to assets or dividends over other classes of shares are called preferred shares (or preferred stock). **Preferred shareholders** are customarily given liquidation and dividend preferences over common shareholders. A corporation may have several classes of preferred shares. In such a situation, one class of preferred shares may be given preferences over another class of preferred shares. Under the MBCA, the preferences of preferred shareholders must be set out in the articles of incorporation.

The **liquidation preference** of preferred shares is usually a stated dollar amount. During a liquidation, this amount must be paid to each preferred shareholder before any common shareholder or other shareholder subordinated to the preferred class may receive his share of the corporation's assets.

Dividend preferences may vary greatly. For example, the dividends may be cumulative or noncumulative. Dividends on **cumulative** preferred shares, if not paid in any year, accumulate until paid. The entire accumulation must be paid before any dividends may be paid to common shareholders. Dividends on **noncumulative** preferred shares do not accumulate if unpaid. For such shares, only the current year's dividends must be paid to preferred shareholders prior to the payment of dividends to common shareholders.

Participating preferred shares have priority up to a stated amount or percentage of the dividends to be paid by the corporation. Then, the preferred shareholders participate with the common shareholders in additional dividends paid.

Some close corporations attempt to create preferred shares with a **mandatory dividend** right. These mandatory dividend provisions have generally been held illegal as unduly restricting the powers of the board of directors. Today, a few courts and some special close corporation statutes permit mandatory dividends for shareholders of close corporations.

A **redemption** or **call** provision in the articles allows a corporation at its option to repurchase preferred shareholders' shares at a price stated in the articles, despite the shareholders' unwillingness to sell. Some statutes permit the articles to give the shareholders the right to force the corporation to redeem preferred shares.

Preferred shares may be **convertible** into another class of shares, usually common shares. A **conversion** right allows a preferred shareholder to exchange her preferred shares for another class of shares, usually common shares. The conversion rate or price is stated in the articles.

Preferred shares have **voting rights** unless the articles provide otherwise. Usually, most voting rights are taken from preferred shares, except for important matters such as voting for a merger or a change in preferred shareholders' dividend rights. Rarely are preferred shareholders given the right to vote for directors, except in the event of a corporation's default in the payment of dividends.

Authorized, Issued, and Outstanding Shares

Authorized shares are shares that a corporation is permitted to issue by its articles of incorporation. A corporation may not issue more shares than are authorized. **Issued** shares are shares that have been sold to shareholders. **Outstanding** shares are shares that are currently held by shareholders. The distinctions between these terms are important. For example, a corporation pays cash, property, and share dividends only on outstanding shares. Only outstanding shares may be voted at a shareholders' meeting.

Canceled Shares Sometimes, a corporation will purchase its own shares. A corporation may cancel repurchased shares. Canceled shares do not exist: They are neither authorized, issued, nor outstanding. Since canceled shares do not exist, they cannot be reissued.

Shares Restored to Unissued Status Repurchased shares may be restored to unissued status instead of being canceled. If this is done, the shares are merely authorized and they may be reissued at a later time.

Treasury Shares If repurchased shares are neither canceled nor restored to unissued status, they are called **treasury shares.** Such shares are authorized and issued, but not outstanding. They may be sold by the corporation at a later time. The corporation may not vote them at shareholders' meetings, and it may not pay a cash or property dividend on them.

The MBCA abolishes the concept of treasury shares. It provides that repurchased shares are restored to unissued status and may be reissued, unless the articles of incorporation require cancellation.

Options, Warrants, and Rights

Equity securities include options to purchase common shares and preferred shares. The MBCA expressly permits the board of directors to issue **options** for the purchase of the corporation's shares. Options permit their holders to purchase a specific number of shares at a specified price during a specified time period, usually beginning months or years after the option is issued. Share options are often issued to top level managers as an incentive to increase the profitability of the corporation. An increase in profitability should increase the market value of the corporation's shares, resulting in increased compensation to the employees who own and exercise share options.

Warrants are options evidenced by certificates. They are sometimes part of a package of securities sold as a unit. For example, they may be sold along with notes, bonds, or even shares. Underwriters may receive warrants as part of their compensation for aiding a corporation in selling its shares to the public.

Rights are short-term certificated options that are usually transferable. Rights are used to give present security holders an option to subscribe to a proportional quantity of the same or a different security of the corporation. They are most often issued in connection with a **preemptive right** requirement, which obligates a corporation to offer each existing shareholder the opportunity to buy the corporation's newly issued shares in the same proportion as the shareholder's current ownership of the corporation's shares.

Debt Securities

Corporations have inherent power to borrow money necessary for their operations by issuing debt securities. Debt securities create a debtor–creditor relationship between the corporation and the security holder. With the typical debt security, the corporation is obligated to pay interest periodically and to pay the amount of the debt (the principal) on the maturity date. Debt securities include debentures, bonds, and promissory notes.

Debentures are long-term, unsecured debt securities. Typically, a debenture has a term of 10 to 30 years. Debentures usually have indentures. An **indenture** is a contract that states the rights of the debenture holders. For example, an indenture defines what acts constitute default by the corporation and what rights the debenture holders have upon default. It may place restrictions on the corporation's right to issue other debt securities.

Bonds are long-term, secured debt securities that usually have indentures. They are identical to debentures except that bonds are secured by collateral. The collateral for bonds may be real property such as a building, or personal property such as a commercial airplane. If the debt is not paid, the bondholders may force the sale of the collateral and take the proceeds of the sale.

Generally, **notes** have a shorter duration than debentures or bonds. They seldom have terms exceeding five years. Notes may be secured or unsecured.

It is not uncommon for notes or debentures to be **convertible** into other securities, usually preferred or common shares. The right to convert belongs to the holder of the convertible note or debenture. This conversion right permits an investor to receive interest as a debt holder and, after conversion, to share in the increased value of the corporation as a shareholder.

Consideration for Shares

The board of directors has the power to issue shares on behalf of the corporation. The board must decide at what *price* and for what *type of consideration* it will issue the shares. Corporation statutes restrict the discretion of the board in accepting specified kinds of consideration and in determining the value of the shares it issues.

Quality of Consideration for Shares

Not all kinds of consideration in contract law are acceptable as legal consideration for shares in corporation law. To protect creditors and other shareholders, the statutes require legal consideration to have *real value.* Modern statutes, however, place few limits on the type of consideration that may be received for shares. The MBCA permits shares to be issued in return for any tangible or intangible *property* or *benefit to the corporation,* including cash, promissory notes, services performed for the corporation, contracts for services *to be performed* for the corporation, and securities of the corporation or another corporation. The rationale for the MBCA rule is a recognition that future services and promises of future services have value that is as real as that of tangible property. Consequently, for example, a corporation may issue common shares to its president in exchange for the president's commitment to work for the corporation for three years or in exchange for bonds of the corporation or debentures issued by another corporation. In addition, the MBCA permits corporations to issue shares to their promoters in consideration for their promoters' preincorporation services. This rule acknowledges that a corporation benefits from a promoter's preincorporation services.

Several states' constitutions place stricter limits on permissible consideration for shares. They provide that shares may be issued only for money paid to the corporation, labor done for the corporation, or property actually received by the corporation. Such a rule prohibits a corporation from issuing its shares for a promise to pay money or a promise to provide services to the corporation in the future.

Quantity of Consideration for Shares

The board is required to issue shares for an adequate dollar amount of consideration. Whether shares have been issued for an adequate amount of consideration depends in part on the *par value* of the shares. The more important concern, however, is whether the shares have been issued for *fair value.*

Par Value   Par value is an arbitrary dollar amount that may be assigned to the shares by the articles of incorporation. Par value does not reflect the fair market value of the shares, but par value is the minimum amount of consideration for which the shares may be issued.

Shares issued for less than par value are called **discount shares.** The board of directors is liable to the corporation for issuing shares for less than par value. A shareholder who purchases shares from the corporation for less than par value is liable to the corporation for the difference between the par value and the amount she paid.

Fair Value   It is not always enough, however, for the board to issue shares for their par value. Many times, shares are worth more than their par value. In addition, many shares today do not have a par value. In fact, the MBCA purports to eliminate the concept of par value as it affects the issuance of shares. In all cases, the board must exercise care to ensure that the corporation receives the *fair value* of the shares it issues. If there are no par value problems, the board's judgment as to the amount of consideration that is received for the shares is *conclusive* when the board acts in good faith, exercises the care of ordinarily prudent directors, and acts in the best interests of the corporation.

Disputes may arise concerning the value of property that the corporation receives for its shares. The board's valuation of the consideration is conclusive if it acts in good faith with the care of prudent directors and in a manner it reasonably believes to be in the best interests of the corporation. When the board impermissibly overvalues the consideration for shares, the shareholder receives **watered shares.** Both the board and the shareholder are liable to the corporation when there is a watered shares problem.

When a shareholder pays less than the amount of consideration determined by the board of directors, the corporation or its creditors may sue the shareholder to recover the deficit. When a shareholder has paid the proper amount of consideration, the shares are said to be *fully paid and nonassessable.*

Accounting for Consideration Received   The consideration received by a corporation for its equity securities appears in the equity or capital accounts in the shareholders' equity section of the corporation's balance sheet. The **stated capital** account records the product of the number of shares outstanding multiplied by the par value of each share. When the shares are sold for more than par value, the excess or surplus consideration received by the corporation is **capital surplus.**

Under the MBCA, the terms *stated capital* and *capital surplus* have been eliminated. All consideration received for shares is lumped under one accounting entry for that class of shares, such as common equity.

Resales of Shares   The par value of shares is important *only when the shares are issued* by the corporation. Since

---

The Global Business Environment

Corporation Law Worldwide: Proper Consideration for Shares

There is substantial similarity in corporation laws from country to country. Even in many countries where corporation law is different from American law, there are legislative attempts to modernize the law by making it more nearly consistent with U.S. law. One example is Israel, whose Knesset has adopted a corporation law in line with Western law, especially American law.

Examining the requirements to incorporate and the limits on consideration for shares, there are some differences globally, but generally not much more than one sees from state to state in the United States. For example, although the MBCA permits corporate shares to be issued for any benefit to the corporation, the laws of many countries retain the historic American rule (which is still law in many states) that certain types of benefits are improper consideration. For example, the corporate law of the Dominion of Melchizedek (which comprises a slice of Antarctica and five Pacific islands) states that consideration for the issuance of shares shall consist of money or other property, tangible or intangible, or labor or services actually received by or performed for the corporation or for its benefit or in its formation or reorganization. Its law prohibits the issuance of shares for future payments or future services.

Chinese law is bit more restrictive, allowing shareholders to make their investments only in cash, in kind, in industrial property rights, in nonpatented technology, or land use rights. The Kingdom of Bhutan is more limiting, however, forbidding share issuances for consideration other than cash, unless shareholders approve.

treasury shares are issued but not outstanding, the corporation does not issue treasury shares when it resells them. Therefore, the board may sell treasury shares for less than par, provided that it sells the shares for an amount equal to their fair value.

Because par value and fair value are designed to ensure only that the corporation receives adequate consideration for its shares, a shareholder may buy shares from another shareholder for less than par value or fair value and incur no liability. However, if the purchasing shareholder *knows* that the selling shareholder bought the shares from the corporation for less than par value, the purchasing shareholder is liable to the corporation for the difference between the par value and the amount paid by the selling shareholder.

Share Subscriptions

Under the terms of a **share subscription,** a prospective shareholder promises to buy a specific number of shares of a corporation at a stated price. If the subscription is accepted by the corporation and the subscriber has paid for the shares, the subscriber is a shareholder of the corporation, even if the shares have not been issued. Under the MBCA, subscriptions need not be in writing to be enforceable. Usually, however, subscriptions are written.

Promoters use written share subscriptions in the course of selling shares of a proposed corporation to ensure that equity capital will be provided once the corporation comes into existence. These are called **preincorporation subscriptions,** which were covered in this chapter's discussion of promoters. Preincorporation subscriptions are not contracts binding on the corporation and the shareholders until the corporation comes into existence and its board of directors accepts the share subscriptions.

Close corporations may use share subscriptions when they seek to sell additional shares after incorporation. These are examples of **postincorporation subscriptions,** subscription agreements made *after* incorporation. A postincorporation subscription is a contract between the corporation and the subscriber at the time the subscription agreement is made.

A subscription may provide for payment of the price of the shares on a specified day, in installments, or upon the demand of the board of directors. The board may not discriminate when it demands payment: It must demand payment from all the subscribers of a class of shares or from none of them.

A share certificate may not be issued to a share subscriber until the price of the shares has been fully paid. If the subscriber fails to pay as agreed, the corporation may sue the subscriber for the amount owed.

Issuance of Shares

Uniform Commercial Code (UCC) Article 8 regulates the issuance of securities. Under Article 8, a corporation has a duty to issue only the number of shares authorized by its articles. Overissued shares are void.

When a person is entitled to overissued shares, the corporation may not issue the shares. However, the person has two remedies. The corporation must obtain identical shares and deliver or register them to the person entitled to issuance or the corporation must reimburse the person for the value paid for the shares plus interest.

The directors may incur liability, including criminal liability, for an overissuance of shares. To prevent overissuance through error in the issuance or transfer of their shares, corporations often employ a bank or a trust company as a registrar.

A share certificate is evidence that a person has been issued shares, owns the shares, and is a shareholder. The certificate states the corporation's name, the shareholder's name, and the number and class of shares. A person can be a shareholder without receiving a share certificate, such as a holder of a share subscription.

Under the MBCA, a corporation is not required to issue share certificates. If a corporation does not issue share certificates, it must register the security in the name of its owner or his agent, usually a stockbroker. Today, most shareholders of public companies never receive certificates, especially those who have brokerage accounts at online brokers like E*TRADE.

Transfer of Shares

Because share certificates are evidence of the ownership of shares, their transfer is evidence of the transfer of the ownership of shares. The MBCA and UCC Article 8 cover the registration and transfer of shares, both certificated and uncertificated.

Shares are issued in *registered* form; that is, they are registered with the corporation in the name of a specific person. The indorsement of a share certificate on its back by its registered owner and the delivery of the certificate to another person transfers ownership of the shares to the other person. The transfer of a share certificate without naming a transferee creates a *street certificate.* The transfer of a street certificate may be made by delivery without indorsement. Any holder of a street certificate is presumed to be the owner of the shares it represents. Therefore, a transferee should ask the corporation to reregister the shares in his name.

Ownership of uncertificated securities is transferred by a corporation's registering the security in the new owner's name.

Under the UCC, a corporation owes a duty to register the transfer of any registered shares presented to it for registration, provided that the shares have been properly indorsed, or in the case of uncertificated shares, the corporation has received an **instruction** notifying it of the transfer of ownership. If the corporation refuses to make the transfer, it is liable to the transferee for either conversion or specific performance.

When an owner of shares claims that his registration or certificate has been lost, destroyed, or stolen, the corporation must register new shares to the owner if the corporation has not received notice that the shares have been acquired by a bona fide purchaser, the owner files with the corporation a sufficient indemnity bond, and the owner meets any other reasonable requirements of the corporation. A **bona fide purchaser** is a purchaser of the shares for value in good faith with no notice of any adverse claim against the shares.

If, after the issuance of the new certificated shares or registration of new uncertificated shares, a bona fide purchaser of the original shares presents them for registration, the corporation must register the transfer, unless overissuance would result. In addition, the corporation may recover the new certificated shares from the original owner or revoke the new registration.

Restrictions on Transferability of Shares

Historically, a shareholder has been free to sell her shares to whomever she wants whenever she wants. Such free transferability is important to shareholders in a publicly held corporation. Because shares in a publicly held corporation are freely transferable, shareholders know that they can easily liquidate their investment by selling their shares, often on a stock exchange.

In close corporations, however, free transferability as a legal matter is a threat to the balance of power among shareholders. For example, if one of three shareholders owning a third of a corporation sells his shares to one of the other shareholders, the buying shareholder will own two-thirds of the corporation and may be able to dominate the third shareholder. In addition, as a practical matter, free transferability of close corporation shares is illusory, as few people other than existing shareholders are willing to purchase shares in a close corporation.

Consequently, many close corporations restrict the transfer of shares to ensure those in control of a corporation will continue in control. Share transfer restrictions can also be used to guarantee a market for the shares when a shareholder dies or retires from the corporation.

The courts have been reluctant to allow restrictions on the free transferability of shares, even if the shareholder agreed to a restriction on the transfer of her shares. Gradually, the courts and the legislatures have recognized that there are good reasons to permit the use of some restrictions on the transfer of shares. Today, modern corporation statutes allow most transfer restrictions, especially for close corporations.

Types of Restrictions on Transfer There are four categories of transfer restrictions: (1) rights of first refusal and option agreements, (2) buy-and-sell agreements, (3) consent restraints, and (4) provisions disqualifying purchasers.

A **right of first refusal** grants to the corporation or the other shareholders the right to match the offer that a selling shareholder receives for her shares. An **option agreement** grants the corporation or the other shareholders an option to buy the selling shareholder's shares at a price determined by the agreement. An option agreement will usually state a formula used to calculate the price of the shares.

A **buy-and-sell agreement** compels a shareholder to sell his shares to the corporation or to the other shareholders at the price stated in the agreement. It also obligates the corporation or the other shareholders to buy the selling shareholder's shares at that price. The price of the shares is usually determined by a stated formula.

A **consent restraint** requires a selling shareholder to obtain the consent of the corporation or the other shareholders before she may sell her shares. A **provision disqualifying purchasers** may be used in rare situations to exclude unwanted persons from the corporation. For example, a transfer restriction may prohibit the shareholders from selling to a competitor of the business.

Uses of Transfer Restrictions A corporation and its shareholders may use transfer restrictions to maintain the balance of shareholder power in the corporation. For example, four persons may own 25 shares each in a corporation. No single person can control such a corporation. If one of the four can buy 26 additional shares from the other shareholders, he will acquire control. The shareholders may therefore agree that each shareholder is entitled or required to buy an equal amount of any shares sold by any selling shareholder. The right of first refusal, option agreement, or buy-and-sell agreement may serve this purpose.

A buy-and-sell agreement is the preferred transfer restriction for nearly every context in well-planned close corporations, because certainty is obtained by both sides being obligated, one required to buy and the other to sell. For example, a buy-and-sell agreement may be used to guarantee a shareholder a market for his shares. In a close corporation, there may be no ready market for the shares of the corporation. To ensure that a shareholder can obtain the value of her investment when she leaves the corporation, the shareholders or the corporation may be required to buy a shareholder's shares upon the occurrence of a specific event, such as death, disability, or retirement.

A buy-and-sell agreement may also be used to determine who should be required to sell and who should be required to buy shares when there is a severe disagreement between shareholders that threatens the profitability of the corporation. It could also be worded to require majority shareholders to buy the shares of minority shareholders when a lucrative merger offer for the corporation is rejected by the majority but favored by the minority. The agreement could, but rarely does, set the buyout price as the price offered in the merger.

If minority shareholders are afraid of being frozen in a close corporation that will never go public and give shareholders a chance to sell their shares on the market and get a return on investment, a buy-and-sell agreement could require the corporation to repurchase the minority's shares if the corporation has not gone public after a specified number of years.

In a close corporation, the shareholders may want only themselves or other approved persons as shareholders. A buy-and-sell agreement or right of first refusal may be used to prevent unwanted persons from becoming shareholders.

A provision disqualifying purchasers may be used in limited situations only, such as when the purchaser is a competitor of the business or has a criminal background.

A consent restraint is used to preserve a close corporation or Subchapter S taxation election. Close corporation statutes and Subchapter S of the Internal Revenue Code limit the number of shareholders that a close corporation or S corporation may have. A transfer restriction may prohibit the shareholders from selling shares if, as a result of the sale, there would be too many shareholders to preserve a close corporation or S corporation election. A consent restraint is also used to preserve an exemption from registration of a securities offering. Under the Securities Act of 1933 and the state securities acts, an offering of securities is exempt from registration if the offering is to a limited number of qualified investors, usually 35 financially sophisticated investors. A transfer restriction may require a selling shareholder to obtain permission from the corporation's legal counsel, which permission will be granted upon proof that the shareholder's sale of the shares does not cause the corporation to lose its registration exemption.

Legality of Transfer Restrictions Corporation statutes permit the use of option agreements, rights of first refusal, and buy-and-sell agreements with virtually no restrictions. The MBCA authorizes transfer restrictions for any reasonable purpose. The reasonableness of a restraint is judged in light of the character and needs of the corporation.

Consent restraints and provisions disqualifying purchasers may be used if they are not *manifestly unreasonable.* The MBCA makes per se reasonable any consent restraint that maintains a corporation's status when that status is dependent on the number or identity of shareholders, as with close corporation or S corporation status. The MBCA also makes per se reasonable any restriction that preserves registration exemptions under the Securities Act of 1933 and state securities laws.

Enforceability To be enforceable against a shareholder, a transfer restriction must be contained in the articles of incorporation, the bylaws, an agreement among the shareholders, or an agreement between the corporation and the shareholders. In addition, the shareholder must either agree to the restriction or purchase the shares with notice of the restriction. Under the MBCA, a purchaser of the shares has notice of a restriction if it is noted conspicuously on the face or the back of a share certificate or a written statement provided to shareholders if no certificates were issued. A purchaser also has notice if he knows of the restriction when he buys the shares or otherwise has been notified.

In the next case, *Coyle v. Schwartz,* the court enforced a buy-sell agreement in which the shareholders were to agree from time to time on the price to be paid for the shares. It is a good example of a poorly drafted buy-sell agreement that failed to attain the objectives of all the shareholders.

Coyle v. Schwartz   2004 Ky. App. LEXIS 75 (Ky. Ct. App. 2004)

American Scale Corporation, a closely held Kentucky corporation with its principal place of business in Louisville, Kentucky, was incorporated in February 1985 to engage in the sale and repair of industrial and commercial scales. Daniel Coyle was president and Steven Schwartz was vice president. They were the sole shareholders. At the time of incorporation, Coyle and Schwartz each received 200 shares of stock in exchange for their capital contributions of $10,000.

In early March 1986 Schwartz had an automobile accident in which his passenger was seriously injured. Schwartz's passenger filed suit against American Scale, since it had provided insurance coverage on Schwartz's vehicle. Coyle became concerned that Schwartz's activities would expose American Scale to further liability. He was particularly displeased with Schwartz's actions in transporting an underage female, who was purportedly Schwartz's girlfriend, in a vehicle insured by American Scale.

As a result, Coyle informed Schwartz that he no longer desired to be in a 50–50 shareholder with him. Coyle told Schwartz that unless Schwartz agreed to transfer l percent of his shares to Coyle, thereby permitting Coyle to assume majority control of American Scale, Coyle would either seek dissolution of American Scale, or withdraw and begin operating a business in competition with American Scale. On March 21, 1986, Coyle and Schwartz executed a share-transfer agreement wherein Schwartz transferred 1 percent of his American Scale shares to Coyle. The agreement specifically stated that Coyle would thereafter own a 51 percent interest in American Scale, leaving Schwartz as owner of the remaining 49 percent of American Scale's shares.

About two years later, on August 25, 1988, Coyle and Schwartz made a buy-sell agreement that they titled, "Stockholders' Cross-Purchase Agreement." The agreement provided for the repurchase of a shareholder's stock in the event of death, disability, or voluntary withdrawal of that shareholder. Specifically, the agreement stated that if Coyle or Schwartz died, or otherwise attempted to dispose of his shares, the other shareholder would have the right to purchase those shares. In addition, the agreement gave the majority shareholder an option to purchase all of the minority shareholder's stock at any time upon a 60-day written notice.

The agreement provided a stock-valuation method for determining a per share price in the event either of the provisions was triggered:

> Unless altered as herein provided, for the purpose of determining the purchase price to be paid for the stock of a Stockholder, the fair market value of each share of stock shall be, as of August 25, 1988, $250.
>
> The Stockholders shall redetermine the value of the stock within 60 days following the end of each fiscal year. If the Stockholders fail to make the required annual redetermination of value for a particular year, the last previously recorded value shall control.

Over the course of the next 12 years, neither Coyle nor Schwartz attempted to revaluate the price of American Scale's shares as provided in the agreement. Hence, the initial buyout price of $250 per share was never changed.

In a letter dated November 20, 2000, Coyle informed Schwartz that he was exercising his option as majority shareholder to purchase Schwartz's stock for $250 per share. Schwartz refused to tender his shares to Coyle and filed suit against Coyle seeking to invalidate the buyout agreement. Schwartz argued that the shareholders had abandoned the agreement by not changing the buyout price for 12 years. Schwartz also argued that the buyout price was so low as to constitute a penalty. In response to Coyle's motion for summary judgment, the trial court ruled that the shareholders had not abandoned the agreement. However, the court agreed with Schwartz that forcing him to sell all of his stock at the price of $250 per share was a penalty and, therefore, unenforceable. The trial court ordered a current valuation of the stock be undertaken before Schwartz could be compelled to transfer his shares. Coyle appealed to the Kentucky Court of Appeals.

Johnson, Judge

In his appeal, Coyle argues that the trial court erred by finding that the stock-valuation provision was unenforceable as a penalty.

While Coyle and Schwartz never revaluated the stock, this fact alone does not render the provision unenforceable. Schwartz, as owner of 49% of American Scale's outstanding shares, had the right under the corporation's bylaws to call for a special meeting to revaluate the listed price of American

Scale's shares. Schwartz has admitted in his deposition testimony that he never made such a request. Hence, by sitting on his rights for over 12 years, Schwartz took the risk that Coyle would exercise the majority-purchase option at a time when the actual value of American Scale's shares was in excess of the $250 price originally listed in the stock-valuation provision. Schwartz is not entitled to have the courts rewrite the parties' agreement simply because he believes he is receiving the short end of the bargain. Accordingly, we reverse the trial court's finding that the stock-valuation provision listing a price of $250 per share was unenforceable.

The terms of the stock-valuation provision listed an original price of $250 per share. The provision further stated that the fair market value shall be $250 "unless altered as herein provided" via the "mutual agreement" revaluation method. Since the parties failed to revaluate the price of American Scale's shares, $250 is the "last recorded value" with respect to the price of the corporation's shares. Therefore, the majority-purchase option and the stock-valuation provision entitle Coyle to purchase all of Schwartz's stock at a price of $250 per share.

Finally, we address Schwartz's claim in his cross-appeal that the trial court erred by finding that Schwartz and Coyle did not abandon the stock-valuation provision of the cross-purchase agreement. Specifically, Schwartz argues that by completely ignoring the cross-purchase agreement's requirement that both shareholders "shall re-determine the value of the stock within 60 days following the end of each fiscal year" and record the same, as well as their intention to revalue their shares in American Scale, Schwartz and Coyle unequivocally acted in a manner inconsistent with the existence of the cross-purchase agreement.

We disagree and hold that the trial court did not err by finding that Coyle and Schwartz did not abandon their rights under the stock-valuation provision. A contract may be rescinded or discharged by acts or conduct of the parties inconsistent with the continued existence of the contract, and mutual assent to abandon a contract may be inferred from the attendant circumstances and conduct of the parties. While as a general rule a contract will be treated as abandoned or rescinded where the acts and conduct of one party inconsistent with its existence are acquiesced in by the other party, to be sufficient the acts and conduct must be positive and unequivocal.

In the instant case, while Coyle and Schwartz never revaluated American Scale's stock in the years following the execution of the cross-purchase agreement, this fact, standing alone, does not constitute "positive and unequivocal" acts which could lead to a finding of abandonment. The stock-valuation provision itself provided a default price for the stock in the event the parties failed to revaluate the shares. Therefore, Coyle and Schwartz contemplated that they might not always conduct a revaluation. Accordingly, the failure of Coyle and Schwartz to conduct an annual revaluation of American Scale's shares did not constitute an abandonment of the stock-valuation provision.

Judgment reversed in favor of Coyle.

Statutory Solution to Close Corporation Share Transfer Problems Although transfer restrictions are important to close corporations, many close corporation shareholders fail to address the share transferability problem. Therefore, a few states provide statutory resolution of the close corporation transferability problem. In these states, statutes offer solutions to the transferability problem that are similar to the solutions that the shareholders would have provided had they thought about the problem. Not all transferability problems are settled by the Close Corporation Supplement, however. For example, there is no statutory buy-and-sell provision.

Financing Nonprofit Corporations

Nonprofit corporations are financed differently from for-profit corporations. This is especially true of a public benefit corporation such as a public television station, which obtains annual financing from government sources, private foundations, members, and public contributors. A religious corporation such as a church receives weekly offerings from its congregation and may occasionally conduct capital drives to obtain additional funding from its members. A mutual benefit corporation, such as a fraternal or social organization like an Elks Club or golf country club, obtains initial funding from its original members to build facilities and assesses its members annually and monthly to pay operating expenses. In addition, nonprofit corporations have the power to obtain debt financing, such as borrowing from a bank or issuing notes and debentures.

A nonprofit corporation may admit members whether or not they pay consideration for their memberships. There is no statutory limit on the number of members a nonprofit corporation may admit, although the articles may place a limit on the number of members. Social clubs typically limit the number of members. Members must be admitted in compliance with procedures stated in the articles or the bylaws.

Generally, memberships in a nonpublic corporation are not freely transferable. No member of a public benefit corporation or religious corporation may transfer her membership or any rights she possesses as a member. A member of a mutual benefit corporation may transfer her membership and rights only if the articles or bylaws permit. When transfer rights are permitted, restrictions on transfer are valid only if approved by the members, including the affected member.

Problems and Problem Cases

1. You and three of your friends have entered negotiations with Toyota Motor Sales USA to acquire a Lexus automobile dealership. You plan to operate the dealership as a corporation, to be named Community Lexus, Inc. You and your three friends have not yet formed the corporation. You will be the president and CEO of the corporation. Among the many agreements that will be signed are a contract to purchase automobiles from Toyota, joint advertising agreements with Toyota, and loan contracts with Genesee National Bank. What should you do before you sign any of these contracts on behalf of Community Lexus, Inc.?

2. Roy Rose signed articles of incorporation for R&F Capital Corporation in December 1989, but Flaherty, who had been entrusted by Rose to create R&F, failed to file the articles until February 9, 1990. On January 12, 1990, purporting to act on behalf of R&F as its chairman, Rose signed a contract to lease a warehouse owned by Dennis Sivers. When R&F breached the lease, Sivers claimed that Rose was liable on the lease because he should have known on the basis of his vast experience as a businessman that R&F was not incorporated. Rose and another R&F director testified that they both believed R&F had been incorporated in December 1989, and Rose said he would not have invested in R&F or signed a document on its behalf if he had known that R&F was not incorporated. Was Rose found liable on the lease?

3. Garry Fox met with Coopers & Lybrand to request a tax opinion and other accounting services. Fox told Coopers that he was acting on behalf of a corporation that he was in the process of forming, to be named G. Fox and Partners, Inc. Coopers knew that the corporation was not in existence. Fox and Coopers had no agreement regarding Fox's personal liability for payment of the fee for the services. G. Fox and Partners, Inc., was incorporated, and a few weeks later Coopers completed its work. The corporation did not pay for the work, so Coopers sued Fox. Is Fox liable to Coopers?

4. George Richert agreed to retain Crye-Leike Realtors, Inc., as his sole and exclusive real estate agent to find a building for Richert's business. The agency contract was signed by Richert and by Colman Borosky for Crye-Leike. All parties understood that Richert would soon form a corporation that would be the actual party to lease the building found by Crye-Leike. A month later, Richert formed WDM, Inc. Richert was president and CEO. WDM never formally adopted the agency contract with Crye-Leike. However, Crye-Leike contacted various landlords for WDM, showed several properties to WDM, and prepared an offer to lease space on behalf of WDM. All these efforts were done with Richert's full knowledge. When WDM hired another real estate agent, Crye-Leike sued for breach of the exclusive agency contract. WDM claimed that it was not a party to the contract between Richert and Crye-Leike. Was WDM correct?

5. Two colleagues decide to incorporate their Internet social networking business. They want complete control of the business, yet they need additional capital to expand the business. The two colleagues enter negotiations with eight friends willing to provide capital to the corporation. The friends agree that they will not be allowed to elect directors, but they want to make sure that they will receive a return on their investments by receiving payments from the corporation quarterly or semiannually. What securities with what rights should the corporation create to achieve the objectives of the friends and colleagues? For each security you create, sketch the rights of the holders.

6. Eastern Oklahoma Television Corporation was incorporated to operate KTEN, a television station. To

assist the station's start-up, Bill Hoover, an owner and operator of a radio station, pledged his radio station as collateral for KTEN's obligations, personally guaranteed the new corporation's obligations for the purchase of equipment, designed the television studio, planned operations, and hired and trained personnel. Hoover also became a director of the corporation. By action of the board of directors, the corporation issued some of the common shares to Hoover in consideration for his experience in broadcasting, his standing with the Federal Communications Commission, and his personal guarantee of the station's debt. Has Hoover paid a proper type of consideration for the shares?

7. Miranda Juarez is hired as the CEO of Spanata Corporation. Spanata's board of directors issues to Juarez 100,000 common shares of Spanata as part of her compensation package. Jaurez receives the shares in return for her giving a contractual promise to be Spanata's CEO for five years and her issuing to Spanata a promissory note in which Jaurez promises to pay $500,000 in five years. Has the board of directors issued the shares for a proper type of consideration?

8. Bruce Bowman received 1,500 shares of Ling and Company Class A common shares. The shares were the subject of an option agreement contained in the articles of incorporation requiring Bowman to offer the shares to the corporation before selling them to any other person. On the front of Bowman's share certificate, in small print, it was stated that transfer of the shares was subject to the provisions of the articles, that a copy of the articles could be obtained from Ling or from the secretary of state, and that the back of the share certificate stated which sections of the articles contained the content of the option agreement. On the back of the share certificate, in small print, the reference to the restriction was again made, and specific reference was given to Article 4 of the articles of incorporation, in which the restriction was contained. Bowman borrowed money from Trinity Savings and Loan. When Bowman defaulted on the loan, Trinity attempted to sell the shares, but Ling objected, invoking the option agreement. Is the option agreement enforceable against Trinity?

9. Stufft Farms, Inc., was a Montana corporation that owned and operated a family farm. The only shareholders were five family members. The bylaws included a share-transfer restriction stating that no shareholder had the right to sell her shares without first offering the shares to the corporation and shareholders at book value. Neil Johnson offered to purchase all of Stufft Farm's shares. His offer was contingent upon all of the shares being tendered to him. When four shareholders accepted Johnson's offer, the fifth shareholder, David Stufft, who did not accept the offer, argued that he had the right to buy the shares of the tendering four shareholders at book value. Was he correct?

10. Rhiann Legath, Cortney Renoir, and Bornett McGann create a corporation to develop satellite software. Each will contribute $160,000 initial capital to the business. They want to be equal owners and share equal management of the corporation. They do not expect the business to go public at any time, but they would not be averse to selling the business at a huge profit to a large textile company after five years. They are concerned that they will not receive a return on their investment because there will be no market for their shares. What agreement do they use to ensure that they may obtain a return on their investment through capital appreciation of their shares? Sketch the contents of that agreement. How do you suggest the agreement determine the value of the shares?

Online Research

Pricing Incorporation

Type "incorporate" in your Internet search engine and you will obtain a list of companies that assist persons who wish to incorporate a business. Most incorporation Web sites quote their fees for assisting incorporation and also fees assessed by the state of incorporation. Find which Web site offers the most services at the best price.

Note that some Web sites sell corporate kits. A corporate kit is a notebook with sample bylaws, organization meeting minutes, stock certificates, and a stock transfer ledger. Corporate kits usually include a corporate seal, which is used to emboss the corporation's name on official documents. Banks and other institutions may require that all documents signed by a corporation bear the corporate seal.

chapter 43

MANAGEMENT OF CORPORATIONS

Clestra Corporation is a manufacturer of consumer products ranging from canned and packaged foods like spaghetti sauce and popcorn to over-the-counter health aids like toothpaste and mouthwash. Its annual worldwide revenues are just under $6 billion. Clestra brands are not among the top two in the industry in any of its product lines, each brand ranking from fourth to sixth in annual sales in countries in which it markets its products. Clestra's CEO has been discussing the company's future with its consultant, KRNP Consulting LLP. KRNP has suggested that Clestra consider acquiring Ballmax, Inc., a consumer products company with two billion dollars annual sales. Ballmax's brands are complementary to Clestra's brands, and while smaller than Clestra, Ballmax has a distribution system that will give Clestra access to markets in which Clestra is not currently a significant seller.

Clestra's CEO also wants to improve consumer recognition of the Clestra brand. She suggests that Clestra acquire naming rights to a stadium being built for a baseball team in northern Virginia, the Virginia Hatchets. The CEO thinks that Clestra has the inside track to acquire naming rights because the family of one of Clestra's board members owns the baseball team that will own and operate the stadium.

- What legal standard will determine whether Clestra's board of directors has acted properly when approving Clestra's acquisition of Ballmax, Inc.? What role may KRNP Consulting take in helping Clestra's board of directors meet its duties under that legal standard?
- What legal standard will judge whether Clestra's board of directors has acted properly when acquiring naming rights to the Virginia Hatchets' stadium? What role may KRNP Consulting take in helping Clestra's board of directors meet its duties under that legal standard?
- Suppose Clestra's CEO is concerned that Clestra may be a target for a takeover by one of the larger consumer goods companies. If Clestra wants to remain an independent company, what should Clestra's board of directors do now to increase the chances that it may fend off a hostile takeover? What legal standard will judge whether Clestra's board has acted properly in adopting defenses against a hostile takeover? What should Clestra's board do now to increase the likelihood that the board will comply with that legal standard when it opposes a hostile takeover?

ALTHOUGH SHAREHOLDERS OWN a corporation, they traditionally have possessed no right to manage the business of the corporation. Instead, shareholders elect individuals to a *board of directors,* to which management is entrusted. Often, the board delegates much of its management responsibilities to *officers.*

This chapter explains the legal aspects of the board's and officers' management of the corporation. Their management of the corporation must be consistent with the objectives and powers of the corporation, and they owe duties to the corporation to manage it prudently and in the best interests of the corporation and the shareholders as a whole.

Corporate Objectives

The traditional objective of the business corporation has been to *enhance corporate profits and shareholder gain.* According to this objective, the managers of a corporation must seek the accomplishment of the profit objective to the exclusion of all inconsistent goals. Interests other than profit maximization may be considered, provided that they do not hinder the ultimate profit objective.

Nonetheless, some courts have permitted corporations to take *socially responsible actions* that are *beyond the profit maximization requirement.* In addition, every state recognizes corporate powers that are not economically inspired. For example, corporations may make contributions to colleges, political campaigns, child abuse prevention centers, literary associations, and employee benefit plans, regardless of economic benefit to the corporations. Also, every state expressly recognizes the right of shareholders to choose freely the extent to which profit maximization captures all of their interests and all of their sense of responsibility.

Most states have enacted **corporate constituency statutes,** which broaden the legal objectives of corporations. Such statutes permit or require directors to take into account the interests of constituencies other than shareholders, including employees, suppliers, and customers. These statutes direct the board to act in the best interests of the corporation, not just the interests of the shareholders, and to maximize corporate profits *over the long term.* The new laws promote the view that a corporation is a collection of interests working together for the purpose of producing goods and services at a profit, and that the goal of corporate profit maximization over the long term is not necessarily the same as the goal of stock price maximization over the short term.

Corporate Powers

The actions of management are limited not only by the objectives of business corporations but also by the *powers* granted to business corporations. Such limitations may appear in the state statute, the articles of incorporation, and the bylaws.

The primary source of a corporation's powers is the corporation statute of the state in which it is incorporated. Some state corporation statutes expressly specify the powers of corporations. These powers include making gifts for charitable and educational purposes, lending money to corporate officers and directors, and purchasing and disposing of the corporation's shares. Other state corporation statutes limit the powers of corporations, such as prohibiting the acquisition of agricultural land by corporations.

Modern statutes attempt to authorize corporations to engage in any activity. The Model Business Corporation Act (MBCA) states that a corporation has the power to do *anything that an individual may do.*

Purpose Clauses in Articles of Incorporation

Most corporations state their purposes in the articles of incorporation. The purpose is usually phrased in broad terms, even if the corporation has been formed with only one type of business in mind. Most corporations have purpose clauses stating that they may engage in any lawful business.

Under the MBCA, the inclusion of a purpose clause in the articles is optional. Any corporation incorporated under the MBCA has the purpose of engaging in any lawful business, unless the articles state a narrower purpose.

The Ultra Vires Doctrine

Historically, an act of a corporation beyond its powers was a nullity, as it was *ultra vires,* which is Latin for "beyond the powers." Therefore, any act not permitted by the corporation statute or by the corporation's articles of incorporation was void due to lack of capacity.

This lack of capacity or power of the corporation was a defense to a contract assertable either by the corporation or by the other party that dealt with the corporation.

Often, *ultra vires* was merely a convenient justification for reneging on an agreement that was no longer considered desirable. This misuse of the doctrine has led to its near abandonment.

Today, the *ultra vires* doctrine is of small importance for two reasons. First, nearly all corporations have broad purpose clauses, thereby preventing any *ultra vires* problem. Second, the MBCA and most other statutes do not permit a corporation or the other party to an agreement to avoid an obligation on the ground that the corporate action is *ultra vires*.

Under the MBCA, *ultra vires* may be asserted by only three types of persons: (1) by a shareholder seeking to enjoin a corporation from executing a proposed action that is *ultra vires;* (2) by the corporation suing its management for damages caused by exceeding the corporation's powers; and (3) by the state's attorney general, who may have the power to enjoin an *ultra vires* act or to dissolve a corporation that exceeds its powers.

Powers of Nonprofit Corporations

Nonprofit corporations, like for-profit corporations, have the power to transact business granted by the incorporation statute, the articles, and the bylaws. The Model Nonprofit Corporation Act (MNCA), like the MBCA, grants nonprofit corporations the power to engage in any lawful activity and to do anything an individual may do. Thus, a nonprofit corporation may sue and be sued, purchase, hold, and sell real property, lend and borrow money, and make charitable and other donations, among its many powers.

Commonly, a nonprofit corporation's articles will limit its powers pursuant to a purpose clause. For example, a nonprofit corporation established to operate a junior baseball league may limit its powers to that business and matters reasonably connected to it. When a nonprofit corporation limits its powers, a risk arises that the corporation may commit an *ultra vires* act. The MNCA adopts the same rules for *ultra vires* contracts as does the MBCA: Generally, neither the corporation nor the other party may use *ultra vires* as a defense to a contract.

The Board of Directors

Traditionally, the **board of directors** has had the authority and the duty to manage the corporation. Yet in a large publicly held corporation, it is impossible for the board to manage the corporation on a day-to-day basis, because many of the directors are high-level executives in other corporations and devote most of their time to their other business interests. Therefore, the MBCA permits a corporation to be managed *under the direction of* the board of directors. Consequently, the board of directors delegates major responsibility for management to committees of the board such as an executive committee, to individual board members such as the chairman of the board, and to the officers of the corporation, especially the chief executive officer (CEO). In theory, the board supervises the actions of its committees, the chairman, and the officers to ensure that the board's policies are being carried out and that the delegatees are managing the corporation prudently.

Board Authority under Corporation Statutes
A corporation's board of directors has the authority to do almost everything within the powers of the corporation. The board's authority includes not only the general power to manage or direct the corporation in the ordinary course of its business but also the power to issue shares of stock and to set the price of shares. Among its other powers, the board may repurchase shares, declare dividends, adopt and amend bylaws, elect and remove officers, and fill vacancies on the board.

Some corporate actions require *board initiative* and shareholder approval. That is, board approval is necessary to *propose such actions to the shareholders,* who then must approve the action. Board initiative is required for important changes in the corporation, such as amendment of the articles of incorporation, merger of the corporation, the sale of all or substantially all of the corporation's assets, and voluntary dissolution.

Committees of the Board
Most publicly held corporations have committees of the board of directors. These committees, which have fewer members than the board has, can more efficiently handle management decisions and exercise board powers than can a large board. Only directors may serve on board committees.

Although many board powers may be delegated to committees of the board, some decisions are so important that corporation statutes require their *approval by the board as a whole.* Under the MBCA, the powers that may not be delegated concern important corporate actions such as declaring dividends, filling vacancies on the board or its committees, adopting and amending bylaws, approving issuances of shares, and approving repurchases of the corporation's shares.

The most common board committee is the **executive committee.** It is usually given authority to act for the board on most matters when the board is not in session. Generally, it consists of the inside directors and perhaps one or two outside directors who can attend a meeting on short notice. An inside director is an officer of the corporation who devotes substantially full time to the corporation. Outside directors have no such affiliation with the corporation.

Audit committees are directly responsible for the appointment, compensation, and oversight of independent public accountants. They supervise the public accountants' audit of the corporate financial records. The Sarbanes–Oxley Act requires that all publicly held firms have audit committees comprising independent directors. That act was a response to allegations of unethical and criminal conduct by corporate CEOs and auditors at firms like Enron, WorldCom, and Arthur Andersen in the 1990s and early 2000s. Rules of the New York Stock Exchange (NYSE) and the National Association of Securities Dealers (NASD), which apply to firms listed on the NYSE or NASDAQ, require that independent directors approve audit committee nominations.

Nominating committees choose management's slate of directors that is to be submitted to shareholders at the annual election of directors. Nominating committees also often plan generally for management succession. Nominating committees wholly or largely comprise outside directors.

Compensation committees review and approve the salaries, bonuses, stock options, and other benefits of high-level corporate executives. Although compensation committees usually comprise directors who have no affiliation with the executives or directors whose compensation is being approved, compensation committees may also set the compensation of their members. Directors of a typical corporation receive annual compensation between $30,000 to $60,000.

In the early 2000s, the public and Congress criticized board approvals of large compensation packages to CEOs and other top level officers, including stock options and bonus plans that sometimes allowed individual officers to earn more than $100 million in a single year. Hoping that board independence would rein in such compensation, in 2003 the Securities and Exchange Commission (SEC) approved NYSE and NASD rules that require independent directors to approve executive compensation.

A **shareholder litigation committee** is given the task of determining whether a corporation should sue someone who has allegedly harmed the corporation. Usually, this committee of disinterested directors is formed when a shareholder asks the board of directors to cause the corporation to sue some or all of the directors for mismanaging the corporation.

Powers, Rights, and Liabilities of Directors as Individuals

A director is not an agent of the corporation *merely* by being a director. The directors may manage the corporation only when they act as a board, unless the board of directors grants agency powers to the directors individually.

A director has the *right to inspect* corporate books and records that contain corporate information essential to the director's performance of her duties. The director's right of inspection is denied when the director has an interest adverse to the corporation, as in the case of a director who plans to sell a corporation's trade secrets to a competitor.

Normally, a director does not have any personal liability for the contracts and torts of the corporation.

Election of Directors

Generally, any individual may serve as a director of a corporation. A director need not even be a shareholder. Nonetheless, a corporation is permitted to specify qualifications for directors in the articles of incorporation.

A corporation must have the number of directors required by the state corporation law. The MBCA and several state corporation statutes require a minimum of one director, recognizing that in close corporations with a single shareholder-manager, additional board members are superfluous. Several statutes, including the New York statute, require at least three directors, unless there are fewer than three shareholders, in which case the corporation may have no fewer directors than it has shareholders.

A corporation may have more than the minimum number of directors required by the corporation statute. The articles of incorporation or bylaws will state the number of directors of the corporation. Most large publicly held corporations have boards with more than 10 members.

Directors are elected by the shareholders at the annual shareholder meeting. Usually, each shareholder is permitted to vote for as many nominees as there are directors to be elected. The shareholder may cast as many votes for each nominee as he has shares. The top votegetters among the nominees are elected as directors. This voting process, called **straight voting,** permits a holder of more than 50 percent of the shares of a corporation to dominate the corporation by electing a board of directors that will manage the corporation as he wants it to be managed.

To avoid domination by a large shareholder, some corporations allow class voting or cumulative voting.

Class voting may give certain classes of shareholders the right to elect a specified number of directors. **Cumulative voting** permits shareholders to multiply the number of their shares by the number of directors to be elected and to cast the resulting total of votes for one or more directors. As a result, cumulative voting may permit minority shareholders to obtain representation on the board of directors.

Directors usually hold office for only one year, but they may have longer terms. The MBCA permits **staggered terms** for directors. A corporation having a board of nine or more members may establish either two or three approximately equal classes of directors, with only one class of directors coming up for election at each annual shareholders' meeting. If there are two classes of directors, the directors serve two-year terms; if there are three classes, they serve three-year terms.

The original purpose of staggered terms was to permit continuity of management. Staggered terms also frustrate the ability of minority shareholders to use cumulative voting to elect their representatives to the board of directors.

The Proxy Solicitation Process   Most individual investors purchase corporate shares in the public market to increase their wealth, not to elect or to influence the directors of corporations. Nearly all institutional investors—such as pension funds, mutual funds, and bank trust departments—have the same profit motive. Generally, they are passive investors with little interest in exercising their shareholder right to elect directors by attending shareholder meetings.

Once public ownership of the corporation's shares exceeds 50 percent, the corporation cannot conduct any business at its shareholder meetings unless some of the shares of these passive investors are voted. This is because the corporation will have a shareholder quorum requirement, which usually requires that 50 percent or more of the shares be voted for a shareholder vote to be valid. Since passive investors rarely attend shareholder meetings, the management of the corporation must solicit **proxies** if it wishes to have a valid shareholder vote. Shareholders who will not attend a shareholder meeting must be asked to appoint someone else to vote their shares for them. This is done by furnishing each such shareholder with a proxy form to sign. The proxy designates a person who may vote the shares for the shareholder.

Management Solicitation of Proxies   To ensure its perpetuation in office and the approval of other matters submitted for a shareholder vote, the corporation's management solicits proxies from shareholders for directors' elections and other important matters on which shareholders vote, such as mergers. The management designates an officer, a director, or some other person to vote the proxies received. The person who is designated to vote for the shareholder is also called a proxy. Typically, the chief executive officer (CEO) of the corporation, the president, or the chairman of the board of directors names the person who serves as the proxy.

Usually, the proxies are merely signed and returned by the public shareholders, including the institutional shareholders. Passive investors follow the **Wall Street rule:** Either support management or sell the shares. As a result, management almost always receives enough votes from its proxy solicitation to ensure the reelection of directors and the approval of other matters submitted to the shareholders, even when other parties solicit proxies in opposition to management.

Management's solicitation of proxies may produce a result quite different from the theory of corporate management that directors serve as representatives of the shareholders. The CEO usually nominates directors of his choice, and they are almost always elected. The directors appoint officers chosen by the CEO. The CEO's nominees for director are not unduly critical of his programs or of his methods for carrying them out. This is particularly true if a large proportion of the directors are officers of the company and thus are more likely to be dominated by the CEO. In such situations, the board of directors may not function effectively as a representative of the shareholders in supervising and evaluating the CEO and the other officers of the corporation. The board members and the other officers are subordinates of the CEO, even though the CEO is not a major shareholder of the corporation.

Proposals for improving corporate governance in public-issue corporations seek to develop a board that is capable of functioning independently of the CEO by changing the composition or operation of the board of directors. Some corporate governance critics propose that a federal agency such as the SEC appoint one or more directors to serve as watchdogs of the public interest. Other critics would require that shareholders elect at least a majority of directors without prior ties to the corporation, thus excluding shareholders, suppliers, and customers from the board.

Other proposals recommend changing the method by which directors are nominated for election. One proposal would encourage shareholders to make nominations for directors. Supporters of this proposal argue that in addition to reducing the influence of the CEO, it would also broaden the range of backgrounds represented on the board. The SEC recommends that publicly held corporations establish a nominating committee composed of outside directors. Many publicly held corporations have nomination committees.

Due to pressure from the public and Congress after the corporate scandals of the 1990s and early 2000s, the SEC, in 2003, approved NYSE and NASD corporate governance rules that make corporate boards more nearly independent of the CEO in structure, if not in action. One rule requires boards to comprise mostly independent directors. Equally important, the independent directors must meet from time to time by themselves in executive session independent of the CEO. In addition, institutional investors—including mutual funds and hedge funds—are taking increasingly active roles in director elections

For a complete treatment of the corporate social responsibility debate, including proposals to improve corporate governance, see Chapter 4.

LOG ON

www.riskmetrics.com/knowledge
Check out the Knowledge Center of RiskMetrics Group for trends and best practices in corporate governance.

In the following case, *Grimes v. Donald,* the court considered whether a board of directors abdicated its duty to direct the corporation by delegating unlimited power to the CEO.

Grimes v. Donald   673 A.2d 1207 (Del. Sup. Ct. 1996)

James Donald was the chief executive officer of DSC Communications, a Delaware corporation headquartered in Plano, Texas. In 1990, DSC's board of directors entered an employment agreement with Donald that ran until his 75th birthday. The employment agreement provided that Donald "shall be responsible for the general management of the affairs of the company and report to the Board." Donald's employment could be terminated by death, disability, for cause, and without cause. The agreement provided, however, that Donald could declare a "Constructive Termination Without Cause" by DSC, if there was "unreasonable interference, in the good faith judgment of Donald, by the Board or a substantial stockholder of DSC, in Donald's carrying out of his duties and responsibilities." When there was termination without cause, the employment agreement provided that Donald was entitled to payment of his annual base salary ($650,000) for the remainder of the contract, his annual incentive award ($300,000), and other benefits. The total amount of payments and benefits for the term of the contract was about $20,000,000.

C. L. Grimes, a DSC shareholder, sued Donald on behalf of the corporation asking the court to invalidate the employment agreement between Donald and DSC on the grounds that the agreement illegally delegated the duties and responsibilities of DSC's board of directors to Donald. The Delaware Chancery Court dismissed the case, and Grimes appealed to the Supreme Court of Delaware.

Veasey, Chief Justice

Grimes claims that the potentially severe financial penalties which DSC would incur in the event that the Board attempts to interfere in Donald's management will inhibit and deter the Board from exercising its duties. We disagree.

Grimes has pleaded, at most, that Donald would be entitled to $20 million in the event of a Constructive Termination. In light of the financial size of DSC, this amount would not constitute a *de facto* abdication.

Directors may not delegate duties which lie at the heart of the management of the corporation. A court cannot give legal sanction to agreements which have the effect of removing from directors in a very substantial way their duty to use their own best judgment on management matters. The Donald agreement

does not formally preclude the DSC board from exercising its statutory powers and fulfilling its fiduciary duty.

With certain exceptions, an informed decision to delegate a task is as much an exercise of business judgment as any other. Likewise, business decisions are not an abdication of directorial authority merely because they limit a board's freedom of future action. A board which has decided to manufacture bricks has less freedom to decide to make bottles. In a world of scarcity, a decision to do one thing will commit a board to a certain course of action and make it costly and difficult to change course and do another. This is an inevitable fact of life and is not an abdication of directorial duty.

If the market for senior management, in the business judgment of the board, demands significant severance packages, boards will inevitably limit their future range of action by entering into employment agreements. Large severance payments will deter boards, to some extent, from dismissing senior officers. If an independent and informed board, acting in good faith, determines that the services of a particular individual warrant large amounts of money, whether in the form of current salary or severance provisions, the board has made a business judgment. That judgment normally will receive the protection of the business judgment rule unless the facts show that such amounts, compared with services to be received in exchange,

constitute waste or could not otherwise be the product of a valid exercise of business judgment.

The Board of DSC retains the ultimate freedom to direct the strategy and affairs of DSC. If Donald disagrees with the Board, DSC may or may not be required to pay a substantial amount of money in order to pursue its chosen course of action. So far, we have only a rather unusual contract, but not a case of abdication.

Judgment for Donald affirmed.

The Global Business Environment

Corporate Governance in Germany

Corporate governance varies somewhat from country to country. In Germany, for example, the *Aktiengesellschaft* (AG) has a **management board** and a **supervisory board.** The AG's management board represents and manages the company. Its members are not directly answerable to shareholders, but are appointed by the AG's supervisory board. All members of the management board manage the company together. However, the articles may provide that the company may be represented by two members of the management board.

The members of the AG's supervisory board are like the outside directors of an American company. They are elected by the AG's shareholders and, if German co-determination

rules apply, by the employees. The supervisory board is charged with protecting the interests of the company, which may not coincide with those of the shareholders. To enable the supervisory board to carry out its oversight function, the management board is required to report regularly on the current status of the company's business and corporate planning. However, the supervisory board has no say in the day-to-day management of the company.

The Shop Constitution Act (*Betriebsverfassungsgesetz*) covers AGs with more than 500 employees. It provides that one-third of supervisory board members be employee representatives. Under the Co-determination Act (*Mitbestimmungsgesetz*), the supervisory boards of AGs with more than 2,000 employees must have equal numbers of shareholder and employee representatives.

Vacancies on the Board   The MBCA permits the directors to fill vacancies on the board. A majority vote of the remaining directors is sufficient to select persons to serve out unexpired terms, even though the remaining directors are less than a quorum.

Removal of Directors   Modern corporation statutes permit shareholders to remove directors *with or without cause.* The rationale for the modern rule is that the shareholders should have the power to judge the fitness of directors at any time.

However, most corporations have provisions in their articles authorizing the shareholders to remove directors *only for cause.* Cause for removal would include mismanagement or conflicts of interest. Before removal for cause, the director must be given notice and an opportunity for a hearing.

A director elected by a class of shareholders may be removed only by that class of shareholders, thereby protecting the voting rights of the class. A director elected by cumulative voting may not be removed if the votes cast against her removal would have been sufficient to elect her to the board, thereby protecting the voting rights of minority shareholders.

Directors' Meetings

For the directors to act, a *quorum* of the directors must be present. The quorum requirement ensures that the decision of the board will represent the views of a substantial portion of the directors. A quorum is usually a *majority* of the number of directors.

Each director has *one vote.* If a quorum is present, a vote of a majority of the directors present is an act of the board, unless the articles or the bylaws require the vote of a greater number of directors. Such *supermajority voting provisions* are common in close corporations but not in publicly held corporations. The use of supermajority voting provisions by close corporations is covered later in this chapter.

Directors are entitled to reasonable notice of all *special meetings,* but not of regularly scheduled meetings. The MBCA does not require the notice for a special meeting to state the purpose of the meeting. A director's attendance at a meeting waives any required notice, unless at the beginning of the meeting the director objects to the lack of notice.

Traditionally, directors could act only when they were properly convened as a board. They could not vote by proxy or informally, as by telephone. This rule was based on a belief in the value of consultation and collective judgment.

Today, the corporation laws of a majority of the states and the MBCA specifically permit action by the directors without a meeting if all of the directors consent in writing to the action taken. Such authorization is useful for dealing with routine matters or for formally approving an action based on an earlier policy decision made after full discussion.

The MBCA also permits a board to meet by telephone, television, or Internet hookup. This section permits a meeting of directors who may otherwise be unable to convene. The only requirement is that the directors be able to hear one another simultaneously.

Officers of the Corporation

The board of directors has the authority to appoint the officers of the corporation. Many corporation statutes provide that the officers of a corporation shall be the *president,* one or more *vice presidents,* a *secretary,* and a *treasurer.* Usually, any two or more offices may be held by the same person, except for the offices of president and secretary.

The MBCA requires only that there be an officer performing the duties normally granted to a corporate secretary. Under the MBCA, one person may hold several offices, including the offices of president and secretary.

The officers are agents of the corporation. As agents, officers have *express authority* conferred on them by the bylaws or the board of directors. In addition, officers have *implied authority* to do the things that are reasonably necessary to accomplish their express duties. Also, officers have *apparent authority* when the corporation leads third parties to believe reasonably that the officers have authority to act for the corporation. Like any principal, the corporation may *ratify* the unauthorized acts of its officers. This may be done expressly by a resolution of the board of directors or impliedly by the board's acceptance of the benefits of the officer's acts.

The most perplexing issue with regard to the authority of officers is whether an officer has *inherent authority* merely by virtue of the title of his office. Courts have held that certain official titles confer authority on officers, but such powers are much more restricted than you might expect.

Traditionally, a *president* possesses no power to bind the corporation by virtue of the office. Instead, she serves merely as the presiding officer at shareholder meetings and directors' meetings. A president with an additional title such as *general manager* or *chief executive officer* has broad implied authority to make contracts and to do other acts in the ordinary business of the corporation.

A *vice president* has no authority by virtue of that office. An executive who is vice president of a specified department, however, such as a vice president of marketing, will have the authority to transact the normal corporate business falling within the function of the department.

The *secretary* usually keeps the minutes of directors' and shareholder meetings, maintains other corporate records, retains custody of the corporate seal, and certifies corporate records as being authentic. Although the secretary has no authority to make contracts for the corporation by virtue of that office, the corporation is bound by documents certified by the secretary.

The *treasurer* has custody of the corporation's funds. He is the proper officer to receive payments to the corporation and to disburse corporate funds for authorized purposes. The treasurer binds the corporation by his receipts, checks, and indorsements, but he does not by virtue of that office alone have authority to borrow money, to issue negotiable instruments, or to make other contracts on behalf of the corporation.

Like any agent, a corporate officer ordinarily has *no liability on contracts* that he makes on behalf of his principal, the corporation, if he signs for the corporation and not in his personal capacity.

Officers serve the corporation at the pleasure of the board of directors, which may remove an officer at any time with or without cause. An officer who has been removed without cause has no recourse against the corporation, unless the removal violates an employment contract between the officer and the corporation.

Managing Close Corporations

Many of the management formalities that you have studied in this chapter are appropriate for publicly held corporations yet inappropriate for close corporations. For example, each close corporation shareholder may want to be *involved in management* of the corporation. If a close corporation shareholder is not involved in management, he may want to protect his interest by placing *restrictions on the managerial discretion* of those who do manage the corporation.

Modern close corporation statutes permit close corporations to dispense with most, if not all, management formalities. The Statutory Close Corporation Supplement to the MBCA permits a close corporation to *dispense with a board of directors* and to be *managed by the shareholders*. The California General Corporation Law permits the close corporation to be managed *as if it were a partnership*.

LOG ON

www.sos.ca.gov/business/corp/pdf/
articles/corp_artsclose.pdf

This Web site for California's secretary of state will show you how to create a close corporation in California.

When a close corporation chooses to have a traditional board of directors, a minority shareholder may be dominated by the shareholders who control the board of directors. To protect minority shareholders, close corporations may impose **supermajority voting** requirements for board actions and **restrictions on the managerial discretion** of the board of directors.

Any corporation may require that board action be possible only with the approval of more than a majority of the directors, such as three-fourths or unanimous approval. A supermajority vote is often required to terminate the employment contract of an employee-shareholder, to reduce the level of dividends, and to change the corporation's line of business. Supermajority votes are rarely required for ordinary business matters, such as deciding with which suppliers the corporation should deal.

Traditionally, shareholders could not restrict the managerial discretion of directors. This rule recognized the traditional roles of the board as manager and of the shareholders as passive owners. Modern close corporation statutes permit shareholders to intrude into the sanctity of the boardroom. The Statutory Close Corporation Supplement grants the shareholders *unlimited* power to restrict the discretion of the board of directors. For example, the shareholders may agree that the directors may not terminate or reduce the salaries of employee-shareholders and must pay a mandatory dividend, if earned. And, as was stated above, close corporation statutes even permit the shareholders to dispense with a board of directors altogether and to manage the close corporation as if it were a partnership.

Of course, any article or bylaw protecting the rights of minority shareholders should not be changeable, unless the minority shareholders consent.

Managing Nonprofit Corporations

A nonprofit corporation is managed under the direction of a board of directors. The board of directors must have at least three directors. All corporate powers are exercised by or under the authority of the board of directors. Any person may serve as a director; however, the Model Nonprofit Corporation Act has an optional provision stating that no more than 49 percent of directors of a public service corporation may be financially interested in the business of the public service corporation. An interested person is, for example, the musical director of a city's symphony orchestra who receives a salary from the nonprofit corporation operating the orchestra.

If a nonprofit corporation has members, typically the members elect the directors. However, the articles may provide for the directors to be appointed or elected by other persons. Directors serve for one year, unless the articles or bylaws provide otherwise. Directors who are elected may not serve terms longer than five years, but appointed directors may serve longer terms.

Directors may be elected by straight or cumulative voting and by class voting. Members may elect directors in person or by proxy. Directors may be removed at any time with or without cause by the members or other persons who elected or appointed the directors. When a director engages in fraudulent or dishonest conduct or breaches a fiduciary duty, members holding at least 10 percent of the voting power may petition a court to remove the wrongdoing director. Generally, a vacancy may be filled by the members or the board of directors; however, if a removed director was elected by a class of members or appointed by another person, only the class or person electing or appointing the director may fill the vacancy.

The board is permitted to set directors' compensation. Typically, directors of public benefit corporations and religious corporations are volunteers and receive no compensation.

Directors of a nonprofit corporation usually act at a meeting at which all directors may simultaneously hear each other, such as a meeting in person or by telephone conference call. The board may also act without a meeting if all directors consent in writing to the action. The board has the power to do most actions that are within the powers of the corporation, although some actions, such as mergers and amendments of the articles, require member action also. Ordinarily, an individual director has no authority to transact for a nonprofit corporation.

The board of directors of a nonprofit corporation may delegate some of its authority to committees of the board and to officers. A nonprofit corporation is not required to have officers, except for an officer performing the duties of corporate secretary. If a corporation chooses to have more officers, one person may hold more than one office. The board may remove an officer at any time with or without cause.

Officers have the authority granted them by the bylaws or by board resolution. However, a nonprofit corporation is bound by a contract signed by both the presiding officer of the board and the president, when the other party had no knowledge that the signing officers had no authority. The corporation is also bound to a contract signed by either the presiding officer or the president which is also signed by either a vice president, the secretary, the treasurer, or the executive director.

Directors' and Officers' Duties to the Corporation

Directors and officers are in positions of trust; they are entrusted with property belonging to the corporation and with power to act for the corporation. Therefore, directors and officers owe **fiduciary duties** to the corporation. They are the duties to act within the authority of the position and within the objectives and powers of the corporation, to act with due care in conducting the affairs of the corporation, and to act with loyalty to the corporation.

Acting within Authority   An officer or director has a duty to **act within the authority** conferred on her by the articles of incorporation, the bylaws, and the board of directors. The directors and officers must act within the scope of the powers of the corporation. An officer or a director may be liable to the corporation if it is damaged by an act exceeding that person's or the corporation's authority.

Duty of Care   Directors and officers are liable for losses to the corporation resulting from their lack of *care or diligence*. The MBCA expressly states the standard of care that must be exercised by directors and officers. MBCA section 8.30 states:

(a) Each member of the board of directors . . . shall act:
 (1) in good faith, and
 (2) in a manner the director reasonably believes to be in the best interests of the corporation.
(b) The members of the board of directors or a committee of the board, when becoming informed in connection with their decision-making function or devoting attention to their oversight function, shall discharge their duties with the care that a person in a like position would reasonably believe appropriate under similar circumstances.

The MBCA section 8.42 imposes almost the same duty on corporate officers:

(a) An officer . . . shall act:
 (1) in good faith;
 (2) with the care that a person in a like position would reasonably exercise under similar circumstances; and
 (3) in a manner the officer reasonably believes to be in the best interests of the corporation.

Managers need merely meet the standard of the **ordinarily prudent person in the same circumstances,** a standard focusing on the basic manager attributes of common sense, practical wisdom, and informed judgment. The duty of care does not hold directors and officers to the standard of a prudent businessperson, a person of some undefined level of business skill. A director or officer's performance is evaluated at the time of the decision, thereby preventing the application of hindsight in judging her performance.

The MBCA duty of care test requires that a director or officer make a **reasonable investigation** and **honestly believe** that her decision is in the **best interests of the corporation.** For example, the board of directors decides to purchase an existing manufacturing business for $15 million without inquiring into the value of the business or examining its past financial performance. Although the directors may believe that they made a prudent decision, they have no reasonable basis for that belief. Therefore, if the plant is worth only $5 million, the directors will be liable to the corporation for its damages—$10 million—for breaching the duty of care.

The Business Judgment Rule   The directors' and officers' duty of care is sometimes expressed as the **business judgment rule:** Absent bad faith, fraud, or breach of fiduciary duty, the judgment of the board of directors is conclusive. When directors and officers have complied with the business judgment rule, they are protected from liability to the corporation for their harmful decisions. The business judgment rule precludes the courts from substituting their business judgment for that of the corporation's managers. The business judgment rule recognizes that the directors and officers—not the shareholders and the courts—are best able to make business judgments and should not ordinarily be vulnerable to second-guessing. Shareholders and the courts are ill equipped to make better business decisions than those made by the officers and directors of a corporation, who have more business experience and are more familiar with the needs, strengths, and limitations of the corporation.

Three requirements must be met for the business judgment rule to protect managers from liability:

1. The managers must make an **informed decision.** They must take the steps necessary to become informed about the relevant facts by making a **reasonable investigation** before making a decision.

2. The managers may have **no conflicts of interest.** The managers may not benefit personally—other than as shareholders—when they transact on behalf of the corporation.

3. The managers must have a **rational basis** for believing that the decision is in the best interests of the corporation. The rational basis element requires only that the managers' decision have a *logical connection to the facts* revealed by a reasonable investigation or that the decision *not be manifestly unreasonable.* Some courts have held that the managers' wrongdoing must amount to *gross negligence* for the directors to lose the protection of the business judgment rule.

If the business judgment rule does not apply because one or more of its elements are missing, a court may *substitute its judgment* for that of the managers.

Nonetheless, courts rarely refuse to apply the business judgment rule. As a result, the rule has been criticized frequently as providing too much protection for the managers of corporations. In one famous case, the court applied the business judgment rule to protect a 1965 decision made by the board of directors of the Chicago Cubs not to install lights and not to hold night baseball games at Wrigley Field.[1] Yet the business judgment rule is so flexible that it protected the decision of the Cubs' board of directors to install lights in 1988.

The *Trans Union* case[2] is one of the few cases that has held directors liable for failing to comply with the business judgment rule. The Supreme Court of Delaware found that the business judgment rule was not satisfied by the board's approval of an acquisition of the corporation for $55 per share. The board approved the acquisition after only two hours' consideration. The board received no documentation to support the adequacy of the $55 price. Instead, it relied entirely on a 20-minute *oral* report of the chairman of the board. No written summary of the acquisition was presented to the board. The directors failed to obtain an investment banker's report, prepared after careful consideration, that the acquisition price was fair.

In addition, the court held that the mere fact that the acquisition price exceeded the market price by $17 per share did not legitimize the board's decision. The board had frequently made statements prior to the acquisition that the market had undervalued the shares, yet the board took no steps to determine the intrinsic value of the shares. Consequently, the court found that at a minimum, the directors had been grossly negligent.

Complying with the Business Judgment Rule
While the *Trans Union* case created some fear among directors that they could easily be held liable for making a decision that harms the corporation, nothing could be further from the truth. The *Trans Union* case and the business judgment rule provide a blueprint for how directors, with the assistance of investment bankers and other consultants, can avoid liability. First, to make an informed decision, the board must perform a reasonable investigation or reasonably rely on someone who has made a reasonable investigation, such as consultants, corporate officers, and employees. For example, few boards have the financial skills to value a product line that the corporation wants to sell, yet investment bankers are skilled at valuations. Therefore, a board will make an informed decision when an investment banker makes a reasonable investigation, informs the board of its finding in a written report delivered to the board several days prior to the board meeting, makes a presentation at the board meeting, and takes questions from the board, provided the board makes its decision after giving sufficient time and care to its deliberation of the facts.

Second, the business judgment rule will not apply unless the board has no conflicts of interest. By compiling a list of questions and quizzing the board members, consultants can help the board determine whether any

---

[1]*Shlensky v. Wrigley,* 237 N.E.2d 776 (Ill. Ct. App. 1968).

[2]*Smith v. Van Gorkom,* 488 A.2d 858 (Del. Sup. Ct. 1985).

member has a financial or other improper interest in the matter before the board.

Third, for the board to have a rational basis to believe that the decision is in the best interests of the corporation, the decision must fit with the firm's corporate strategy and the facts revealed by a reasonable investigation. Investment bankers and consultants can help, first by defining the corporation's strategy and second by demonstrating the fit between the course of action, the facts, and the corporate strategy.

Changes in the Duty of Care Despite the low risk of liability, many state legislatures have changed the wording of the duty of care, typically imposing liability only for willful or wanton misconduct or for gross negligence. Some states allow corporations to reduce the duty of care in their articles of incorporation. For example, the MBCA allows corporations to reduce or eliminate directors' liability for monetary damages, unless a director has received an improper financial benefit or intended to violate the law or harm the corporation.

In the following case involving Disney's hiring and firing of Michael Ovitz, the Delaware court applied the business judgment rule. This case has a good explanation of the diligence directors should exercise in acquiring information before making a decision.

Brehm v. Eisner   906 A. 2d 27 (Del. S. Ct. 2006)

From the mid-1980s to the mid-1990s, The Walt Disney Company enjoyed remarkable success under the guidance of Chairman and CEO Michael Eisner and President and Chief Operating Officer Frank Wells. In 1994, Wells died in a helicopter crash, prematurely forcing the company to consider his replacement. Eisner promoted the candidacy of his long-time friend, Michael Ovitz. Ovitz was the head of Creative Artists Agency (CAA), which he and four others had founded in 1974. By 1995, CAA had grown to be the premier Hollywood talent agency. CAA had 550 employees and an impressive roster of about 1,400 of Hollywood's top actors, directors, writers, and musicians, clients that generated $150 million in annual revenues for CAA. Ovitz drew an annual income of $20 million from CAA. He was regarded as one of the most powerful figures in Hollywood.

To leave CAA and join Disney as its president, Ovitz insisted on an employment agreement that would provide him downside risk protection if he was terminated by Disney or if he was interfered with in his performance of his duties as president. After protracted negotiations, Ovitz accepted an employment package that would provide him $23.6 million per year for the first five years of the deal, plus bonuses and stock options. The agreement guaranteed that the stock options would appreciate at least $50 million in five years or Disney would make up the difference. The Ovitz employment agreement (OEA) also provided that if Disney fired Ovitz for any reason other than gross negligence or malfeasance, Ovitz would be entitled to a Non-Fault Termination payment (NFT), which consisted of his remaining salary, $7.5 million a year for any unaccrued bonuses, the immediate vesting of some stock options, and a $10 million cash out payment for other stock options. While there was some opposition to the employment agreement among directors and upper management at Disney, Ovitz was hired in October 1995 largely due to Eisner's insistence.

At the end of 1995, Eisner's attitude with respect to Ovitz was positive. Eisner wrote, "1996 is going to be a great year— We are going to be a great team—We every day are working better together—Time will be on our side—We will be strong, smart, and unstoppable!!!" Eisner also wrote that Ovitz performed well during 1995, notwithstanding the difficulties Ovitz was experiencing assimilating to Disney's culture.

Unfortunately, such optimism did not last long. In January 1996, a corporate retreat was held at Walt Disney World in Orlando. At that retreat, Ovitz failed to integrate himself in the group of executives by declining to participate in group activities, insisting on a limousine when the other executives—including Eisner—were taking a bus, and making inappropriate demands of the park employees. In short, Ovitz was a little elitist for the egalitarian Disney and a poor fit with his fellow executives.

By the summer of 1996, Eisner had spoken with several directors about Ovitz's failure to adapt to the company's culture. In the fall of 1996, directors began discussing that the disconnect between Ovitz and Disney was likely irreparable, and that Ovitz would have to be terminated. In December 1996, Ovitz was officially terminated by action of Eisner alone. Eisner concluded that Ovitz was terminated without cause, requiring Disney to make the costly NFT payment.

Shareholders of Disney brought a derivative action on behalf of Disney against Eisner and other Disney directors. The shareholders alleged breaches of fiduciary duty in the hiring and firing of Ovitz. Eisner and the other directors defended on the grounds that they had complied with the business judgment rule. Because Disney was incorporated in Delaware, the case was brought in the Delaware Court of Chancery. The chancery court found that Eisner and the other directors had complied with the business judgment rule. The Disney shareholders appealed to the Delaware Supreme Court.

Jacobs, Justice

The shareholders' claims are subdivisible into two groups: (A) claims arising out of the approval of the OEA and of Ovitz's election as President; and (B) claims arising out of the NFT severance payment to Ovitz upon his termination.

A. Claims Arising from the Approval of the OEA and Ovitz's Election as President

The shareholders' core argument in the trial court was that the Disney directors' approval of the OEA and election of Ovitz as President were not entitled to business judgment rule protection, because those actions were either grossly negligent or not performed in good faith. The Court of Chancery rejected these arguments, and held that the shareholders had failed to prove that the Disney defendants had breached any fiduciary duty.

The shareholders advance five contentions to support their claim that the Chancellor reversibly erred by concluding that the shareholders had failed to establish a violation of the Disney defendants' duty of care. The shareholders claim that the Chancellor erred by: (1) treating as distinct questions whether the shareholders had established by a preponderance of the evidence either gross negligence or a lack of good faith; (2) ruling that the board was not required to approve the OEA; (3) determining whether the board had breached its duty of care on a director-by-director basis rather than collectively; (4) concluding that the compensation committee members did not breach their duty of care in approving the NFT provisions of the OEA; and (5) holding that the remaining members of the board (*i.e.,* the directors who were not members of the compensation committee) had not breached their duty of care in electing Ovitz as Disney's President.

Our law presumes that in making a business decision the directors of a corporation acted on an informed basis, in good faith, and in the honest belief that the action taken was in the best interests of the company. Those presumptions can be rebutted if the shareholder shows that the directors breached their fiduciary duty of care or of loyalty or acted in bad faith. If that is shown, the burden then shifts to the director defendants to demonstrate that the challenged act or transaction was entirely fair to the corporation and its shareholders.

Because no duty of loyalty claim was asserted against the Disney defendants, the only way to rebut the business judgment rule presumptions would be to show that the Disney defendants had either breached their duty of care or had not acted in good faith. The Chancellor determined that the shareholders had failed to prove either. [The Delaware Supreme Court affirmed the Chancellor's finding.]

The shareholders next challenge the Court of Chancery's determination that the full Disney board was not required to consider and approve the OEA, because the Company's governing instruments allocated that decision to the compensation committee. This challenge also cannot survive scrutiny.

Under the Company's governing documents the board of directors was responsible for selecting the corporation's officers, but under the compensation committee charter, the committee was responsible for establishing and approving the salaries, together with benefits and stock options, of the Company's CEO and President. The compensation committee also had the charter-imposed duty to "approve employment contracts, or contracts at will" for "all corporate officers who are members of the Board of Directors regardless of salary." That is exactly what occurred here. The full board ultimately selected Ovitz as President, and the compensation committee considered and ultimately approved the OEA, which embodied the terms of Ovitz's employment, including his compensation.

The Delaware General Corporation Law (DGCL) expressly empowers a board of directors to appoint committees and to delegate to them a broad range of responsibilities, which may include setting executive compensation. Nothing in the DGCL mandates that the entire board must make those decisions. At Disney, the responsibility to consider and approve executive compensation was allocated to the compensation committee, as distinguished from the full board. The Chancellor's ruling—that executive compensation was to be fixed by the compensation committee—is legally correct.

In the Court of Chancery the shareholders argued that the board had failed to exercise due care, using a director-by-director, rather than a collective analysis. In this Court, however, the shareholders argue that the Chancellor erred in following that very approach. An about-face, the shareholders now claim that in determining whether the board breached its duty of care, the Chancellor was legally required to evaluate the actions of the old board collectively.

We reject this argument, without reaching its merits, for two separate reasons. To begin with, the argument is precluded by Rule 8 of this Court, which provides that arguments not fairly presented to the trial court will not be considered by this Court. The argument also fails because nowhere do shareholders identify how this supposed error caused them any prejudice. The Chancellor viewed the conduct of each director individually, and found that no director had breached his or her fiduciary duty of care (as members of the full board) in electing Ovitz as President or (as members of the compensation committee) in determining Ovitz's compensation. If, as shareholders now argue, a due care analysis of the board's conduct must be made collectively, it is incumbent upon them to show how such a collective analysis would yield a different result. The shareholders' failure to do that dooms their argument on this basis as well.

The shareholders next challenge the Chancellor's determination that although the compensation committee's decision-making process fell far short of corporate governance "best practices," the committee members breached no duty of care in considering and approving the NFT terms of the OEA. That conclusion is reversible error, the shareholders claim, because the record establishes that the compensation committee members did not properly inform themselves of the material facts and, hence, were grossly negligent in approving the NFT provisions of the OEA.

The overall thrust of that claim is that the compensation committee approved the OEA with NFT provisions that could potentially result in an enormous payout, without informing themselves of what the full magnitude of that payout could be. The Court of Chancery found that the compensation committee members were adequately informed.

In our view, a helpful approach is to compare what actually happened here to what would have occurred had the committee followed a "best practices" (or "best case") scenario, from a process standpoint. In a "best case" scenario, all committee members would have received, before or at the committee's first meeting on September 26, 1995, a spreadsheet or similar document prepared by (or with the assistance of) a compensation expert (in this case, Graef Crystal). Making different, alternative assumptions, the spreadsheet would disclose the amounts that Ovitz could receive under the OEA in each circumstance that might foreseeably arise. One variable in that matrix of possibilities would be the cost to Disney of a non-fault termination for each of the five years of the initial term of the OEA. The contents of the spreadsheet would be explained to the committee members, either by the expert who prepared it or by a fellow committee member similarly knowledgeable about the subject. That spreadsheet, which ultimately would become an exhibit to the minutes of the compensation committee meeting, would form the basis of the committee's deliberations and decision.

Had that scenario been followed, there would be no dispute (and no basis for litigation) over what information was furnished to the committee members or when it was furnished. Regrettably, the committee's informational and decision-making process used here was not so tidy. That is one reason why the Chancellor found that although the committee's process did not fall below the level required for a proper exercise of due care, it did fall short of what best practices would have counseled.

The Disney compensation committee met twice: on September 26 and October 16, 1995. The minutes of the September 26 meeting reflect that the committee approved the terms of the OEA (at that time embodied in the form of a letter agreement), except for the option grants, which were not approved until October 16—after the Disney stock incentive plan had been amended to provide for those options. At the September 26 meeting, the compensation committee considered a "term sheet" which, in summarizing the material terms of the OEA, relevantly disclosed that in the event of a non-fault termination, Ovitz would receive: (i) the present value of his salary ($1 million per year) for the balance of the contract term, (ii) the present value of his annual bonus payments (computed at $7.5 million) for the balance of the contract term, (iii) a $10 million termination fee, and (iv) the acceleration of his options for 3 million shares, which would become immediately exercisable at market price.

Thus, the compensation committee knew that in the event of an NFT, Ovitz's severance payment alone could be in the range of $40 million cash, plus the value of the accelerated options. Because the actual payout to Ovitz was approximately $130 million, of which roughly $38.5 million was cash, the value of the options at the time of the NFT payout would have been about $91.5 million. Thus, the issue may be framed as whether the compensation committee members knew, at the time they approved the OEA, that the value of the option component of the severance package could reach the $92 million order of magnitude if they terminated Ovitz without cause after one year. The evidentiary record shows that the committee members were so informed.

On this question the documentation is far less than what best practices would have dictated. There is no exhibit to the minutes that discloses, in a single document, the estimated value of the accelerated options in the event of an NFT termination after one year. The information imparted to the committee members on that subject is, however, supported by other evidence, most notably the trial testimony of various witnesses about spreadsheets that were prepared for the compensation committee meetings.

The compensation committee members derived their information about the potential magnitude of an NFT payout from two sources. The first was the value of the "benchmark" options previously granted to Eisner and Wells and the valuations by Raymond Watson [a Disney director, member of Disney's compensation committee, and past Disney board chairman who had helped structure Wells's and Eisner's compensation packages] of the proposed Ovitz options. Ovitz's options were set at 75% of parity with the options previously granted to Eisner and to Frank Wells. Because the compensation committee had established those earlier benchmark option grants to Eisner and Wells and were aware of their value, a simple mathematical calculation would have informed them of the potential value range of Ovitz's options. Also, in August and September 1995, Watson and Irwin Russell [a Disney director and chairman of the compensation committee] met with Crystal to determine (among other things) the value of the potential Ovitz options, assuming different scenarios. Crystal valued the options under the Black-Scholes method, while Watson used a different valuation metric. Watson recorded his calculations and the resulting values on a set of spreadsheets that reflected what option profits Ovitz might receive, based upon a range of different assumptions about stock market price increases. Those spreadsheets were shared with, and explained to, the committee members at the September meeting.

The committee's second source of information was the amount of "downside protection" that Ovitz was demanding. Ovitz required financial protection from the risk of leaving a very lucrative and secure position at CAA, of which he was a controlling partner, to join a publicly held corporation to which Ovitz was a stranger, and that had a very different culture and an environment which prevented him from completely controlling his destiny. The committee members knew that by leaving CAA and coming to Disney, Ovitz would be sacrificing "booked" CAA commissions of $150 to $200 million—an amount that Ovitz demanded as protection against the risk that his employment relationship with Disney might not work out. Ovitz wanted at least $50 million of that compensation to take the form of an "up-front" signing bonus. Had the $50 million bonus been paid, the size of the option grant would have been lower. Because it was contrary to Disney policy, the compensation committee rejected the up-front signing bonus demand, and elected instead to compensate Ovitz at the "back end," by awarding him options that would be phased in over the five-year term of the OEA.

It is on this record that the Chancellor found that the compensation committee was informed of the material facts relating to an NFT payout. If measured in terms of the documentation that would have been generated if "best practices" had been followed, that record leaves much to be desired. The Chancellor acknowledged that, and so do we. But, the Chancellor also found that despite its imperfections, the evidentiary record was sufficient to support the conclusion that the compensation committee had adequately informed itself of the potential magnitude of the entire severance package, including the options, that Ovitz would receive in the event of an early NFT.

The OEA was specifically structured to compensate Ovitz for walking away from $150 million to $200 million of anticipated commissions from CAA over the five-year OEA contract term. This meant that if Ovitz was terminated without cause, the earlier in the contract term the termination occurred the larger the severance amount would be to replace the lost commissions. Indeed, because Ovitz was terminated after only one year, the total amount of his severance payment (about $130 million) closely approximated the lower end of the range of Ovitz's forfeited commissions ($150 million), less the compensation Ovitz received during his first and only year as Disney's President. Accordingly, the Court of Chancery had a sufficient evidentiary basis in the record from which to find that, at the time they approved the OEA, the compensation committee members were adequately informed of the potential magnitude of an early NFT severance payout.

The shareholders' final claim in this category is that the Court of Chancery erroneously held that the remaining members of the old Disney board had not breached their duty of care in electing Ovitz as President of Disney. This claim lacks merit, because the arguments shareholders advance in this context relate to a different subject—the approval of the OEA, which was the responsibility delegated to the compensation committee, not the full board.

The Chancellor found and the record shows the following: well in advance of the September 26, 1995 board meeting the directors were fully aware that the Company needed—especially in light of Wells' death and Eisner's medical problems—to hire a "number two" executive and potential successor to Eisner. There had been many discussions about that need and about potential candidates who could fill that role even before Eisner decided to try to recruit Ovitz. Before the September 26 board meeting Eisner had individually discussed with each director the possibility of hiring Ovitz, and Ovitz's background and qualifications. The directors thus knew of Ovitz's skills, reputation and experience, all of which they believed would be highly valuable to the Company. The directors also knew that to accept a position at Disney, Ovitz would have to walk away from a very successful business—a reality that would lead a reasonable person to believe that Ovitz would likely succeed in similar pursuits elsewhere in the industry. The directors also knew of the public's highly positive reaction to the Ovitz announcement, and that Eisner and senior management had supported the Ovitz hiring. Indeed, Eisner, who had long desired to bring Ovitz within the Disney fold, consistently vouched for Ovitz's qualifications and told the directors that he could work well with Ovitz.

The board was also informed of the key terms of the OEA (including Ovitz's salary, bonus and options). Russell reported this information to them at the September 26, 1995 executive session, which was attended by Eisner and all non-executive directors. Russell also reported on the compensation committee meeting that had immediately preceded the executive session. And, both Russell and Watson responded to questions from the board. Relying upon the compensation committee's approval of the OEA and the other information furnished to them, the Disney directors, after further deliberating, unanimously elected Ovitz as President.

Based upon this record, we uphold the Chancellor's conclusion that, when electing Ovitz to the Disney presidency the remaining Disney directors were fully informed of all material facts, and that the shareholders failed to establish any lack of due care on the directors' part.

B. Claims Arising from the Payment of the NFT Severance Payout to Ovitz

The shareholders contend that: (1) only the full Disney board with the concurrence of the compensation committee—but not Eisner alone—was authorized to terminate Ovitz; (2) because Ovitz could have been terminated for cause, Sanford Litvack [Disney's general counsel and member of the Disney board] and Eisner acted without due care and in bad faith in reaching the contrary conclusion; and (3) the business judgment rule presumptions did not protect the new Disney board's acquiescence in the NFT payout, because the new board was not entitled to rely upon Eisner's and Litvack's contrary advice.

The Chancellor determined that although the board as constituted upon Ovitz's termination (the "new board") had the authority to terminate Ovitz, neither that board nor the compensation committee was required to act, because Eisner also had, and properly exercised, that authority. The new board, the Chancellor found, was not required to terminate Ovitz under the company's internal documents. Without such a duty to act, the new board's failure to vote on the termination could not give rise to a breach of the duty of care or the duty to act in good faith.

Article Tenth of the Company's certificate of incorporation in effect at the termination plainly states that:

> The officers of the Corporation shall be chosen in such a manner, shall hold their offices for such terms and shall carry out such duties as are determined solely by the Board of Directors, subject to the right of the Board of Directors to remove any officer or officers at any time with or without cause.

Article IV of Disney's bylaws provided that the Board Chairman/CEO "shall, subject to the provisions of the Bylaws and the control of the Board of Directors, have general and active management, direction, and supervision over the business of the Corporation and over its officers. . . ."

Read together, the governing instruments do not yield a single, indisputably clear answer, and could reasonably be interpreted either way. For that reason, with respect to this specific issue, the governing instruments are ambiguous.

Here, the extrinsic evidence clearly supports the conclusion that the board and Eisner understood that Eisner, as Board Chairman/CEO had concurrent power with the board to terminate Ovitz as President. Because Eisner possessed, and exercised, the power to terminate Ovitz unilaterally, we find that the Chancellor correctly concluded that the new board was not

required to act in connection with that termination, and, therefore, the board did not violate any fiduciary duty to act with due care or in good faith.

As the Chancellor correctly held, the same conclusion is equally applicable to the compensation committee. The only role delegated to the compensation committee was "to establish and approve compensation for Eisner, Ovitz and other applicable Company executives and high paid employees." The committee's September 26, 1995 approval of Ovitz's compensation arrangements "included approval for the termination provisions of the OEA, obviating any need to meet and approve the payment of the NFT upon Ovitz's termination."

Because neither the new board nor the compensation committee was required to take any action that was subject to fiduciary standards, that leaves only the actions of Eisner and Litvack for our consideration. The shareholders claim that in concluding that Ovitz could not be terminated "for cause," these defendants did not act with due care or in good faith. We next address that claim.

After considering the OEA and Ovitz's conduct, Litvack concluded, and advised Eisner, that Disney had no basis to terminate Ovitz for cause and that Disney should comply with its contractual obligations. Even though Litvack personally did not want to grant a NFT to Ovitz, he concluded that for Disney to assert falsely that there was cause would be both unethical and harmful to Disney's reputation. In conclusion, Litvack gave the proper advice and came to the proper conclusions when it was necessary. He was adequately informed in his decisions, and he acted in good faith for what he believed were the best interests of the Company.

With respect to Eisner, the Chancellor found that faced with a situation where he was unable to work well with Ovitz, who required close and constant supervision, Eisner had three options: 1) keep Ovitz as President and continue trying to make things work; 2) keep Ovitz at Disney, but in a role other than as President; or 3) terminate Ovitz. The first option was unacceptable, and the second would have entitled Ovitz to the NFT, or at the very least would have resulted in a costly lawsuit to determine whether Ovitz was so entitled. After an unsuccessful effort to "trade" Ovitz to Sony, that left only the third option, which was to terminate Ovitz and pay the NFT. The Chancellor found that in choosing this alternative, Eisner had breached no duty and had exercised his business judgment:

> . . . I conclude that Eisner's actions in connection with the termination are, for the most part, consistent with what is expected of a faithful fiduciary. Eisner unexpectedly found himself confronted with a situation that did not have an easy solution. He weighed the alternatives, received advice from counsel and then exercised his business judgment in the manner he thought best for the corporation. Eisner knew all

the material information reasonably available when making the decision, he did not neglect an affirmative duty to act (or fail to cause the board to act) and he acted in what he believed were the best interests of the Company, taking into account the cost to the Company of the decision and the potential alternatives. Eisner was not personally interested in the transaction in any way that would make him incapable of exercising business judgment, and I conclude that the shareholders have not demonstrated by a preponderance of the evidence that Eisner breached his fiduciary duties or acted in bad faith in connection with Ovitz's termination and receipt of the NFT.

These determinations rest squarely on factual findings that, in turn, are based upon the Chancellor's assessment of the credibility of Eisner and other witnesses. Even though the Chancellor found much to criticize in Eisner's "imperial CEO" style of governance, nothing has been shown to overturn the factual basis for the Court's conclusion that, in the end, Eisner's conduct satisfied the standards required of him as a fiduciary.

The shareholders' third claim of error challenges the Chancellor's conclusion that the remaining new board members could rely upon Litvack's and Eisner's advice that Ovitz could be terminated only without cause. The short answer to that challenge is that, for the reasons previously discussed, the advice the remaining directors received and relied upon was accurate. Moreover, the directors' reliance on that advice was found to be in good faith. Although formal board action was not necessary, the remaining directors all supported the decision to terminate Ovitz based on the information given by Eisner and Litvack. The Chancellor found credible the directors' testimony that they believed that Disney would be better off without Ovitz, and the shareholders offer no basis to overturn that finding.

To summarize, the Court of Chancery correctly determined that the decisions of the Disney defendants to approve the OEA, to hire Ovitz as President, and then to terminate him on an NFT basis, were protected business judgments, made without any violations of fiduciary duty. Having so concluded, it is unnecessary for the Court to reach the shareholders' contention that the Disney defendants were required to prove that the payment of the NFT severance to Ovitz was entirely fair.

Judgment for Eisner and the other directors affirmed.

Board Opposition to Acquisition of Control of a Corporation

In the last 45 years, many outsiders have attempted to acquire control of publicly held corporations. Typically, these outsiders (called **raiders**) will make a **tender offer** for the shares of a corporation (called the **target**). A tender offer is an offer to the shareholders to buy their shares at a price above the current market price. The raider hopes to acquire a majority of the shares, which will give it control of the target corporation.

Most tender offers are opposed by the target corporation's management. The defenses to tender offers are many and varied, and they carry colorful names, such as the Pac-Man defense, the white knight, greenmail, the poison pill, and the lock-up option. See Figure 1 for definitions of these and other defenses.

When takeover defenses are successful, shareholders of the target may lose the opportunity to sell their shares at a price up to twice the market price of the shares prior to the announcement of the hostile bid. Frequently, the loss of this opportunity upsets shareholders, who then decide to sue the directors who have opposed the tender offer. Shareholders contend that the directors have opposed the tender offer only to preserve their corporate jobs. Shareholders also argue that the target corporation's interests would have been better served if the tender offer had succeeded.

Generally, courts have refused to find directors liable for opposing a tender offer because the business judgment rule applies to a board's decision to oppose a tender offer.

Nonetheless, the business judgment rule will not apply when the directors make a decision to oppose the tender offer before they have carefully studied it. In addition, if the directors' actions indicate that they opposed the tender offer in order to preserve their jobs, they will be liable to the corporation.

Court decisions have seemingly modified the business judgment rule as it is applied in the tender offer context. For example, in *Unocal Corp. v. Mesa Petroleum Co.*,[3] the Supreme Court of Delaware upheld the application of the business judgment rule to a board's decision to block a hostile tender offer by making a tender offer for its own shares that excluded the raider.[4] But in so ruling, the court held that the board may use only those defense tactics that are *reasonable* compared to the takeover threat. The board

---

[3]493 A.2d 946 (Del. Sup. Ct. 1985).
[4]Discriminatory tender offers are now illegal pursuant to Securities Exchange Act Rule 13e-4.

Figure 1   *Tender Offer Defenses*

Greenmail

The target's repurchase of its shares from the raider at a substantial profit to the raider, upon the condition that the raider sign a standstill agreement in which it promises not to buy additional shares of the target for a stated period of time.

White Knight

A friendly tender offeror whom management prefers over the original tender offeror — called a black knight. The white knight rescues the corporation from the black knight (the raider) by offering more money for the corporation's shares.

Pac-Man

The target corporation turns the tables on the tender offeror or raider (which is often another publicly held corporation) by making a tender offer for the raider's shares. As a result, two tender offerors are trying to buy each other's shares. This is similar to the Pac-Man video game, in which Pac-Man and his enemies chase each other.

Golden Parachutes

An incentive to attract top managers, a golden parachute requires a corporation to make a large severance payment to a top level executive such as the CEO when there is a change in control of the corporation. Payments to an individual executive may exceed $500 million. The severance agreement in *Grimes v. Donald* on page 1052 was a golden parachute.

Scorched Earth Tactics

Borrowed from a war tactic, scorched earth tactics attack the raider and its management directly and indiscriminately, like a tank with a flame thrower. These tactics include public relations campaigns in which the target points out the business, legal, and ethical failings of the raider and its management. The target typically warns its employees and communities that the raider will close the target's business in its current locations and move the jobs to another state or country. Finally, the target sues the raider alleging that the hostile takeover violates state corporation law, federal and state securities law, and antitrust law.

Long-Range Acquisition Strategy

A corporation should have a long-run strategy for expansion of its business, including by acquisition. That strategy may be to maintain a narrow business plan that allows the corporation and its management to focus on its core competencies. Or the strategy may be to seek new business opportunities that complement current business operations. An acquisition strategy allows the board of directors to oppose a hostile takeover that threatens the strategy, in accordance with the *Unocal* test. In the *Paramount* case on page 1065, Time, Inc., was better set to oppose Paramount's bid because Time's board had a long-range acquisition strategy requiring protection of the editorial integrity of Time's magazine.

Lock-Up Option

Used in conjunction with a white knight to ensure the success of the white knight's bid. The target and the white knight agree that the white knight will buy a highly valuable asset of the target at a very attractive price for the white knight (usually a below-market price) if the raider succeeds in taking over the target. For example, a movie company may agree to sell its film library to the white knight.

Friendly Shareholders

Establishing employee stock option plans (ESOPs), by which employees of the corporation purchase the corporation's shares, and selling the corporation's shares to other shareholders likely to be loyal to management, such as employee pension funds and people in the community in which the corporation conducts its business, may create a significant percentage of friendly shareholders that are not likely to tender their shares to a raider who may be perceived as hostile to the continuation of the corporation's business in the local community. Thus, building and maintaining a base of friendly shareholders make it easier to defeat a raider.

Poison Pill

Also called a shareholders' rights plan. There are many types, but the typical poison pill involves the target's issuance of a new class of preferred shares to its common share-holders. The preferred shares have rights (share options) attached to them. These rights allow the target's shareholders to purchase shares of the raider or shares of the target at less than fair market value. The poison pill deters hostile takeover attempts by threatening the raider and its shareholders with severe dilutions in the value of the shares they hold.

Stock Trading Surveillance Program

A target should watch the volume of trading in its stock, looking for unexplained spikes in volume that would indicate a future hostile bidder is acquiring a toe-hold in the target's stock prior to announcing a hostile takeover. By detecting abnormal trading in its stock, the target obtains advance knowledge of an impending hostile bid and will have additional time to implement its antitakeover strategy.

Control Share Law

A target company may incorporate in a state with a so-called Control Share Law. When a raider acquires 20 percent of the target's shares in a short period of time (say 90 days), the control share law renders the shares nonvoting, unless the target's board of directors opts out of the control share law or the target's shareholders vote to allow the raider to vote the shares. The effect is to diminish the ability of a raider to acquire voting control of the target without the consent of the target. Since most raiders are unwilling to risk that shareholders will deny them voting power, hostile takeovers of companies incorporated in control share law states are mostly deterred.

may consider a variety of concerns, including the inadequacy of the price offered, nature and timing of the offer, questions of illegality, the impact on constituencies other than shareholders (i.e., creditors, customers, employees, and perhaps even the community generally), the risk of nonconsummation, and the quality of securities being offered in the exchange.

In *Unocal,* the threat was a two-tier, highly coercive tender offer. In the typical two-tier offer, the raider first offers cash for a majority of the shares. After acquiring a majority of the shares, the offeror initiates the second tier, in which the remaining shareholders are forced to sell their shares for a package of securities less attractive than the first tier. Because shareholders fear that they will be forced to take the less attractive second-tier securities if they fail to tender during the first tier, shareholders—including those who oppose the offer—are coerced into tendering during the first tier. *Unocal* and later cases specifically authorize the use of defenses to defeat a coercive two-tier tender offer.

Since its decision in *Unocal,* the Supreme Court of Delaware has applied this modified business judgment rule to validate a poison pill tender offer defense tactic in *Moran v. Household Int'l, Inc.*[5] and to invalidate a lock-up option tender offer defense in the *Revlon*[6] case. These

---

[5]500 A.2d 346 (Del. Sup. Ct. 1985).
[6]*Revlon Inc. v. MacAndrews & Forbes Holdings, Inc.,* 506 A.2d 173 (Del. S. Ct. 1986).

cases confirmed the *Unocal* holding that the board of directors must show that:

1. It had reasonable grounds to believe that a danger to corporate policy and effectiveness was posed by the takeover attempt.

2. It acted primarily to protect the corporation and its shareholders from that danger.

3. The defense tactic was reasonable in relation to the threat posed to the corporation.

Such a standard appeared to impose a higher standard on directors than the rational basis requirement of the business judgment rule, which historically has been interpreted to require only that a decision of a board not be manifestly unreasonable. In addition, the *Revlon* case required the board to establish an auction market for the company and to sell it to the highest bidder when the directors have abandoned the long-term business objectives of the company by embracing a bust-up of the company.

In the following *Paramount v. Time* case, the Supreme Court of Delaware expanded board discretion in fighting hostile takeovers, holding that a board may oppose a hostile takeover provided the board had a *preexisting, deliberately conceived corporate plan* justifying its opposition. The existence of such a plan enabled Time's board to meet the reasonable-tactic element of the *Unocal* test.

Paramount Communications, Inc. v. Time, Inc.
571 A.2d 1140 (Del. Sup. Ct. 1989)

Since 1983, Time, Inc., had considered expanding its business beyond publishing magazines and books, owning Home Box Office and Cinemax, and operating television stations. In 1988, Time's board approved in principle a strategic plan for Time's acquisition of an entertainment company. The board gave management permission to negotiate a merger with Warner Communications, Inc. The board's consensus was that a merger of Time and Warner was feasible, but only if Time controlled the resulting corporation, preserving the editorial integrity of Time's magazines. The board concluded that Warner was the superior candidate because Warner could make movies and TV shows for HBO, Warner had an international distribution system, Warner was a giant in the music business, Time and Warner would control half of New York City's cable TV system, and the Time network could promote Warner's movies.

Negotiations with Warner broke down when Warner refused to agree to Time's dominating the combined companies. Time continued to seek expansion, but informal discussions with other companies terminated when it was suggested the other companies purchase Time or control the resulting board. In January 1989, Warner and Time resumed negotiations, and on March 4, 1989, they agreed to a combination by which Warner shareholders would own 62 percent of the resulting corporation, to be named Time-Warner. To retain the editorial integrity of Time, the merger agreement provided for a board committee dominated by Time representatives.

On June 7, 1989, Paramount Communications, Inc., announced a cash tender offer for all of Time's shares at $175 per share. (The day before, Time shares traded at $126 per share.) Time's financial advisers informed the outside *directors that Time's auction value was materially higher than $175 per share. The board concluded that Paramount's $175 offer was inadequate. Also, the board viewed the Paramount offer as a threat to Time's control of its own destiny and retention of the Time editorial policy; the board found that a combination with Warner offered greater potential for Time.*

In addition, concerned that shareholders would not comprehend the long-term benefits of the merger with Warner, on June 16, 1989, Time's board recast its acquisition with Warner into a two-tier acquisition, in which it would make a tender offer to buy 51 percent of Warner's shares for cash immediately and later buy the remaining 49 percent for cash and securities. The tender offer would eliminate the need for Time to obtain shareholder approval of the transaction.

On June 23, 1989, Paramount raised its offer to $200 per Time share. Three days later, Time's board rejected the offer as a threat to Time's survival and its editorial integrity; the board viewed the Warner acquisition as offering greater long-term value for the shareholders. Time shareholders and Paramount then sued Time and its board to enjoin Time's acquisition of Warner. The trial court held for Time. Paramount and other Time shareholders appealed to the Supreme Court of Delaware.

Horsey, Justice

Our decision does not require us to pass on the wisdom of the board's decision. That is not a court's task. Our task is simply to determine whether there is sufficient evidence to support the initial Time-Warner agreement as the product of a proper exercise of business judgment.

We have purposely detailed the evidence of the Time board's deliberative approach, beginning in 1983–84, to expand itself. Time's decision in 1988 to combine with Warner was made only after what could be fairly characterized as an exhaustive appraisal of Time's future as a corporation. Time's board was convinced that Warner would provide the best fit for Time to achieve its strategic objectives. The record attests to the zealousness of Time's executives, fully supported by their directors, in seeing to the preservation of Time's perceived editorial integrity in journalism. The Time board's decision to expand the business of the company through its March 4 merger with Warner was entitled to the protection of the business judgment rule.

The revised June 16 agreement was defense-motivated and designed to avoid the potentially disruptive effect that Paramount's offer would have had on consummation of the proposed merger were it put to a shareholder vote. Thus, we decline to apply the traditional business judgment rule to the revised transaction and instead analyze the Time board's June 16 decision under *Unocal*.

In *Unocal,* we held that before the business judgment rule is applied to a board's adoption of a defensive measure, the burden will lie with the board to prove (a) reasonable grounds for believing that a danger to corporate policy and effectiveness existed; and (b) that the defensive measure adopted was reasonable in relation to the threat posed.

Paramount argues a hostile tender offer can pose only two types of threats: the threat of coercion that results from a two-tier offer promising unequal treatment for nontendering shareholders; and the threat of inadequate value from an all-shares, all-cash offer at a price below what a target board in good faith deems to be the present value of its shares.

Paramount would have us hold that only if the value of Paramount's offer were determined to be clearly inferior to the value created by management's plan to merge with Warner could the offer be viewed—objectively—as a threat.

Paramount's position represents a fundamental misconception of our standard of review under *Unocal* principally because it would involve the court in substituting its judgment as to what is a "better" deal for that of a corporation's board of directors. The usefulness of *Unocal* as an analytical tool is precisely its flexibility in the face of a variety of fact scenarios. Thus, directors may consider, when evaluating the threat posed by a takeover bid, the inadequacy of the price offered, nature and timing of the offer, questions of illegality, the impact on constituencies other than shareholders, the risk of nonconsummation, and the quality of securities being offered in the exchange.

The Time board reasonably determined that inadequate value was not the only threat that Paramount's all-cash, all-shares offer could present. Time's board concluded that Paramount's offer posed other threats. One concern was that Time shareholders might elect to tender into Paramount's cash offer in ignorance or a mistaken belief of the strategic benefit which a business combination with Warner might produce.

Paramount also contends that Time's board had not duly investigated Paramount's offer. We find that Time explored the available entertainment companies, including Paramount, before determining that Warner provided the best strategic "fit." In addition, Time's board rejected Paramount's offer because Paramount did not serve Time's objectives or meet Time's needs. Time's board was adequately informed of the potential benefits of a transaction with Paramount. Time's failure to negotiate cannot be fairly found to have been uninformed. The evidence supporting this finding is materially enhanced by the fact that 12 of Time's 16 board members were outside independent directors.

We turn to the second part of the *Unocal* analysis. The obvious requisite to determining the reasonableness of a defensive action is a clear identification of the nature of the threat. This requires an evaluation of the importance of the corporate objective threatened; alternative methods of protecting that objective; impacts of the defensive action; and other relevant factors.

The fiduciary duty to manage a corporate enterprise includes the selection of a time frame for achievement of corporate goals. Directors are not obliged to abandon a deliberately conceived corporate plan for a short-term shareholder profit unless there is clearly no basis to sustain the corporate strategy. Time's responsive action to Paramount's tender offer was not aimed at "cramming down" on its shareholders a management-sponsored alternative, but rather had as its goal the carrying forward of a preexisting transaction in an altered form. Thus, the response was reasonably related to the threat. The revised agreement did not preclude Paramount from making an offer for the combined Time-Warner company or from changing the conditions of its offer so as not to make the offer dependent upon the nullification of the Time-Warner agreement. Thus, the response was proportionate.

Judgment for Time affirmed

Complying with the Unocal *Test* To avoid liability when opposing a takeover of the corporation, the board of directors must act in a manner similar to which it complies with the business judgment rule. First, the board must make a reasonable investigation into the threats the takeover poses to the corporation's policies and effectiveness. Having a preexisting acquisition and expansion plan, as Time, Inc., had in the *Paramount* case, will provide a basis for determining whether there is an threat to the company's policies. An investment banker can help the company investigate the facts that reveal threats to the corporation and help define an acquisition strategy, if one does not currently exist.

Second, the board must be motivated primarily to protect the company from the raider's threat, not to save their positions as directors, including the compensation and power that go with the position of director. The *Unocal* test recognizes that directors may be conflicted by their interest in saving their jobs, yet it allows directors to oppose the takeover if they mostly are concerned about protecting the company from the takeover's threat to the company's policies, such as a preexisting acquisition or expansion strategy that would be frustrated by the takeover.

Third, the board may adopt only those takeover defenses that are reasonable in relation to the threat. While this requirement seems to limit board discretion, in practice once the board has identified a credible threat to the corporation's policies, the board may engage in nearly any legal maneuver to stop that threat. That is especially true if the threat is to a preexisting acquisition or expansion strategy, such as a long-existing corporate strategy to remain an independent company or to grow by purchasing smaller competitors.

Duties of Loyalty Directors and officers owe a duty of **utmost loyalty and fidelity** to the corporation. Judge Benjamin Cardozo stated this duty of trust. He declared that a director:

> owes loyalty and allegiance to the corporation—a loyalty that is undivided and an allegiance that is influenced by no consideration other than the welfare of the corporation. Any adverse interest of a director will be subjected to a scrutiny rigid and uncompromising. He may not profit at the expense of his corporation and in conflict with its rights; he may not for personal gain divert unto himself the opportunities which in equity and fairness belong to his corporation.[7]

Directors and officers owe the corporation the same duties of loyalty that agents owe their principals, though many of these duties have special names in corporation law. The most important of these duties of loyalty are the duties not to *self-deal,* not to *usurp a corporate opportunity,* not to *oppress minority shareholders,* and not to *trade on inside information.*

Conflicting Interest Transactions A director or officer has a conflicting interest when a director or officer deals with his corporation. The director or officer with a **conflict of interest** may prefer his own interests over those of the corporation. The director's or officer's interest may be *direct,* such as his interest in selling his land to the corporation, or it may be *indirect,* such as his interest in having another business of which he or his family is an owner, director, or officer supply

---

[7]*Meinhard v. Salmon,* 164 N.E.2d 545, 546 (N.Y. Ct. App. 1928).

goods to the corporation. When a director has a conflict of interest, the director's transaction with the corporation may be voided or rescinded.

Under the MBCA, a director's conflicting interest transaction will not be voided merely on the grounds of a director's conflict of interest when *any one* of the following is true:

1. The transaction has been approved by a majority of informed, disinterested directors,

2. The transaction has been approved by a majority of the shares held by informed, disinterested shareholders, or

3. The transaction is fair to the corporation.

Nonetheless, even when disinterested directors' or shareholders' approval has been obtained, courts will void a conflict-of-interest transaction that is unfair to the corporation. Therefore, every corporate transaction in which a director has a conflict of interest must be fair to the corporation. If the transaction is fair, the interested director is excused from liability to the corporation. A transaction is fair if reasonable persons in an *arm's-length bargain* would have bound the corporation to it. This standard is often called the **intrinsic fairness standard.**

The function of disinterested director or disinterested shareholder approval of a conflict-of-interest transaction is merely to shift the burden of proving unfairness. The burden of proving fairness lies initially on the interested director. The burden of proof shifts to the corporation that is suing the interested officer or director if the transaction was approved by the board of directors or the shareholders. Nonetheless, when disinterested directors approve an interested person transaction, substantial deference is given to the decision in accordance with the business judgment rule, especially when the disinterested directors compose a majority of the board.

Generally, *unanimous* approval of an interested person transaction by informed shareholders *conclusively* releases an interested director or officer from liability even if the transaction is unfair to the corporation. The rationale for this rule is that fully informed shareholders should know what is best for themselves and their corporation.

Complying with the Intrinsic Fairness Standard
Complying with the intrinsic fairness standard is not much different than complying with the business judgment rule, despite the higher standard of conduct. The board must make a reasonable investigation to discover facts that will permit an informed decision. Almost always, the board will be aided in its investigation by officers and other employees of the corporation and by investment bankers, other consultants, and legal counsel. When relying on others' investigations, the board must receive written and oral reports in sufficient time to absorb the information, to ask questions of those who made the investigation, and to debate and to deliberate after receiving all relevant information.

Ethics in Action

Sarbanes–Oxley Act of 2002 Prohibits Loans to Management

Early corporation law prohibited loans by a corporation to its officers or directors, on the grounds that such loans may result in looting of corporate assets. Today, however, the MBCA and most other general corporation statutes allow loans to directors and officers, although they require either shareholder approval or compliance with conflicting interest transaction rules.

In 2002, Congress took steps to return to the past. After it was revealed that several executives of public companies were using their corporations as personal banks to fund extravagant lifestyles—some of which loans were never repaid and some of which corporations became bankrupt—Congress included in the Sarbanes–Oxley Act of 2002 a section generally prohibiting public companies from making loans to their directors or executive officers. This includes the company's CEO and CFO, any vice president in charge of a principal business unit or function, and any other officer or other person who performs a policy-making function. If the corporation is not a public company or if the loan is made to a nonexecutive, the Sarbanes–Oxley Act does not prohibit the corporate loan.

- Do you think the Congress has gone too far in banning loans to directors and officers? What are the ethical justifications to ban loans? What would a rights theorist argue? What would a utilitarian argue? What would a profit maximizer argue?

- Do you think that the Sarbanes–Oxley Act should have banned all corporation loans to its employees? Would you prohibit a bank from making loans to its employees, officers, and directors?

Investment bankers, other consultants, and legal counsel are especially helpful in ascertaining and disclosing any director's conflict of interest. By compiling a list of questions and quizzing the board members, consultants can help the board determine the extent of a director's conflict and ensure that the conflict is fully disclosed to the board. They should also make sure that only board members who are independent of the conflicted directors approve the conflicting interest transaction.

Finally, the board must make a decision that is fair to the corporation. Investment bankers and other consultants can help with this determination by demonstrating the decision's close fit with the firm's corporate strategy and the facts revealed by a reasonable investigation. They must ensure the decision is one that a reasonable person would make acting at arm's length.

Parent–Subsidiary Transactions Self-dealing is a concern when a parent corporation *dominates* a subsidiary corporation. Often, the subsidiary's directors will be directors or officers of the parent also. When persons with dual directorships approve transactions between the parent and the subsidiary, the opportunity for *overreaching* arises. There may be *no arm's-length bargaining* between the two corporations. Hence, such transactions must meet the *intrinsic fairness* test.

Usurpation of a Corporate Opportunity

Directors and officers may steal not only assets of their corporations (such as computer hardware and software) but also *opportunities* that their corporations could have exploited. Both types of theft are equally wrongful.

As fiduciaries, directors and officers are liable to their corporation for **usurping corporate opportunities.**

The opportunity must come to the director or officer *in her corporate capacity.* Clearly, opportunities received at the corporate offices are received by the manager in her corporate capacity. In addition, courts hold that CEOs and other high level officers are nearly always acting in their corporate capacities, even when they are away from their corporate offices.

The opportunity must have a *relation or connection* to an *existing or prospective* corporate activity. Some courts apply the *line of business test,* considering how closely related the opportunity is to the lines of business in which the corporation is engaged. Other courts use the *interest or expectancy test,* requiring the opportunity to relate to property in which the corporation has an existing interest or in which it has an expectancy growing out of an existing right.

The corporation must be *able financially* to take advantage of the opportunity. Managers are required to make a good faith effort to obtain external financing for the corporation, but they are not required to use their personal funds to enable the corporation to take advantage of the opportunity.

A director or officer is free to exploit an opportunity that has been rejected by the corporation.

In the following case, *Guth v. Loft,* the court found that an opportunity to become the manufacturer of Pepsi-Cola syrup was usurped by the president of a corporation that manufactured beverage syrups and operated soda fountains. Note that the court ordered the typical remedy for usurpation: the officers forfeiture to the corporation of all benefits the officer received.

Guth v. Loft, Inc.   5 A. 2d 503 (Del. Sup. Ct. 1939)

Loft, Inc., manufactured and sold candies, syrups, and beverages and operated 115 retail candy and soda fountain stores. Loft sold Coca-Cola at all of its stores, but it did not manufacture Coca-Cola syrup. Instead, it purchased its 30,000-gallon annual requirement of syrup and mixed it with carbonated water at its various soda fountains.

In May 1931, Charles Guth, the president and general manager of Loft, became dissatisfied with the price of Coca-Cola syrup and suggested to Loft's vice president that Loft buy Pepsi-Cola syrup from National Pepsi-Cola Company, the owner of the secret formula and trademark for Pepsi-Cola. The vice president said he was investigating the purchase of Pepsi syrup.

Before being employed by Loft, Guth had been asked by the controlling shareholder of National Pepsi, Megargel, to acquire the assets of National Pepsi. Guth refused at that time. However, a few months after Guth had suggested that Loft purchase Pepsi syrup, Megargel again contacted Guth about buying National Pepsi's secret formula and trademark for only $10,000. This time, Guth agreed to the purchase, and Guth and Megargel organized a new corporation, Pepsi-Cola Company, to acquire the Pepsi-Cola secret formula and trademark from National Pepsi. Eventually, Guth and his family's corporation owned a majority of the shares of Pepsi-Cola Company.

Very little of Megargel's or Guth's funds were used to develop the business of Pepsi-Cola. Instead, without the knowledge or consent of Loft's board of directors, Guth used Loft's working capital, credit, plant and equipment, and executives and employees to produce Pepsi-Cola syrup. In addition, Guth's domination of Loft's board of directors ensured that Loft would become Pepsi-Cola's chief customer.

By 1935, the value of Pepsi-Cola's business was several million dollars. Loft sued Guth, asking the court to order Guth to transfer to Loft his shares of Pepsi-Cola Company and to pay Loft the dividends he had received from Pepsi-Cola Company. The trial court found that Guth had usurped a corporate opportunity and ordered Guth to transfer the shares and to pay Loft the dividends. Guth appealed.

Layton, Chief Justice

Public policy demands of a corporate officer or director the most scrupulous observance of his duty to refrain from doing anything that would deprive the corporation of profit or advantage. The rule that requires an undivided and unselfish loyalty to the corporation demands that there shall be no conflict between duty and self-interest.

The real issue is whether the opportunity to secure a very substantial stock interest in a corporation to be formed for the purpose of exploiting a cola beverage on a wholesale scale was so closely associated with the existing business activities of Loft, and so essential thereto, as to bring the transaction within that class of cases where the acquisition of the property would throw the corporate officer purchasing it into competition with his company.

Guth suggests a doubt whether Loft would have been able to finance the project. The answer to this suggestion is two-fold. Loft's net asset position was amply sufficient to finance the enterprise, and its plant, equipment, executives, personnel and facilities were adequate. The second answer is that Loft's resources were found to be sufficient, for Guth made use of no other resources to any important extent.

Guth asserts that Loft's primary business was the manufacturing and selling of candy in its own chain of retail stores, and that it never had the idea of turning a subsidiary product into a highly advertised, nationwide specialty. It is contended that the Pepsi-Cola opportunity was not in the line of Loft's activities, which essentially were of a retail nature.

Loft, however, had many wholesale activities. Its wholesale business in 1931 amounted to over $800,000. It was a large company by any standard, with assets exceeding $9 million, excluding goodwill. It had an enormous plant. It paid enormous rentals. Guth, himself, said that Loft's success depended upon the fullest utilization of its large plant facilities. Moreover, it was a manufacturer of syrups and, with the exception of cola syrup, it supplied its own extensive needs. Guth, president of Loft, was an able and experienced man in that field. Loft, then, through its own personnel, possessed the technical knowledge, the practical business experience, and the resources necessary for the development of the Pepsi-Cola enterprise. Conceding that the essential of an opportunity is reasonably within the scope of a corporation's activities, latitude should be allowed for development and expansion. To deny this would be to deny the history of industrial development.

We cannot agree that Loft had no concern or expectancy in the opportunity. Loft had a practical and essential concern with respect to some cola syrup with an established formula and trademark. A cola beverage has come to be a business necessity for soft drink establishments; and it was essential to the success of Loft to serve at its soda fountains an acceptable five-cent cola drink in order to attract into its stores the great multitude of people who have formed the habit of drinking cola beverages.

When Guth determined to discontinue the sale of Coca-Cola in the Loft stores, it became, by his own act, a matter of urgent necessity for Loft to acquire a constant supply of some satisfactory cola syrup, secure against probable attack, as a replacement; and when the Pepsi-Cola opportunity presented itself, Guth having already considered the availability of the syrup, it became impressed with a Loft interest and expectancy arising out of the circumstances and the urgent and practical need created by him as the directing head of Loft.

The fiduciary relation demands something more than the morals of the marketplace. Guth did not offer the Pepsi-Cola opportunity to Loft, but captured it for himself. He invested little or no money of his own in the venture, but commandeered for his own benefit and advantage the money, resources, and facilities of his corporation and the services of his officials. He thrust upon Loft the hazard, while he reaped the benefit. In such a manner he acquired for himself 91 percent of the capital stock of Pepsi-Cola, now worth many millions. A genius in his line he may be, but the law makes no distinction between the wrongdoing genius and the one less endowed.

Judgment for Loft affirmed.

Oppression of Minority Shareholders

Directors and officers owe a duty to manage a corporation in the best interests of the corporation and the shareholders as a whole. When, however, a group of shareholders has been isolated for beneficial treatment to the detriment of another isolated group of shareholders, the disadvantaged group may complain of **oppression.**

For example, oppression may occur when directors of a close corporation who are also the majority shareholders pay themselves high salaries yet refuse to pay dividends or to hire minority shareholders as employees of the corporation. Since there is no market for the shares of a close corporation (apart from selling to the other shareholders), these oppressed minority shareholders have investments that provide them no return. They receive no dividends or salaries, and they can sell their shares only to the other shareholders, who are usually unwilling to pay the true value of the shares.

Generally, courts treat oppression of minority shareholders the same way courts treat director self-dealing: The transaction must be intrinsically fair to the corporation and the minority shareholders.

A special form of oppression is the **freeze-out.** A freeze-out is usually accomplished by merging a corporation with a newly formed corporation under terms by which the minority shareholders do not receive shares of the new corporation but instead receive only cash or other securities. The minority shareholders are thereby *frozen out as shareholders.*

Going private is a special term for a freeze-out of shareholders of *publicly owned corporations.* Some public corporations discover that the burdens of public ownership exceed the benefits of being public. For example, the SEC requires public companies to provide to shareholders annual reports that include audited financial statements. The Sarbanes–Oxley Act has increased the cost of being public by requiring, in section 404, that annual reports include an internal control report acknowledging management's responsibility to maintain "an adequate internal control structure and procedures for financial reports." For some firms, section 404 compliance consumes as much as 3 percent of profits. Today, therefore, some publicly owned companies choose to freeze out their minority shareholders to avoid such burdens.

Freeze-Out Methods   The two easiest ways to freeze out minority shareholders are the freeze-out merger and the reverse share split. With the freeze-out merger, the majority shareholders form a new corporation owned only by the majority shareholders. Articles of merger are drafted that will merge the old corporation into the new corporation. Under the merger terms, only shareholders of the new corporation will survive as shareholders of the surviving new corporation; the shareholders of the old corporation will receive cash only. Since the majority shareholders control both corporations, the articles of merger will be approved by the directors and shareholders of both corporations. The freeze-out merger was used in the *Coggins* case, which follows at the end of this section.

Using a reverse share split to freeze out the minority shareholders is simpler. Here the articles are amended to reduce the number of outstanding shares by a multiplier, say 1/50,000, that will result in the majority shareholders having whole shares but the minority shareholders having only fractional shares. The articles amendment will be approved by directors and shareholders since the majority shareholder controls the corporation. After the reverse share split, corporation law permits the corporation to repurchase any fractional shares, even if the shareholders don't consent. The corporation buys the minority shareholders' fractional shares for cash, leaving only the majority shareholder owning the corporation.

Legal Standard   Often, going private transactions appear abusive because the corporation goes public at a high price and goes private at a much lower price. Some courts have adopted a fairness test and a business purpose test for freeze-outs. Most states apply the **total fairness test** to freeze-outs. In the freeze-out context, total fairness has two basic aspects: *fair dealing* and *fair price.* Fair dealing requires disclosing material information to directors and shareholders and providing an opportunity for negotiation. A determination of fair value requires the consideration of all the factors relevant to the value of the shares, except speculative projections.

Some states apply the **business purpose test** to freeze-outs. This test requires that the freeze-out accomplish some legitimate business purpose and not serve the special interests of the majority shareholders or the managers.

Other states place no restrictions on freeze-outs provided a shareholder has a **right of appraisal,** which permits a shareholder to require the corporation to purchase his shares at a fair price.

In addition, the SEC requires a *publicly held* company to make a statement on the fairness of its proposed going private transaction and to discuss in detail the material facts on which the statement is based.

In the *Coggins* case, the court required that a freeze-out of minority shareholders of the New England Patriots football team meet both the business purpose and intrinsic fairness tests. The court held that freezing out the minority shareholders merely to allow the corporation to repay the majority shareholder's personal debts was not a proper business purpose.

Coggins v. New England Patriots Football Club, Inc.
492 N.E.2d 1112 (Mass. Sup. Jud. Ct. 1986)

In 1959, the New England Patriots Football Club, Inc. (Old Patriots), was formed with one class of voting shares and one class of nonvoting shares. Each of the original 10 voting shareholders, including William H. Sullivan, purchased 10,000 voting shares for $2.50 per share. The 120,000 nonvoting shares were sold for $5 per share to the general public in order to generate loyalty to the Patriots football team. In 1974, Sullivan was ousted as president of Old Patriots. In November 1975, Sullivan succeeded in regaining control of Old Patriots by purchasing all 100,000 voting shares for $102 per share. He again became a director and president of Old Patriots.

To finance his purchase of the voting shares, Sullivan borrowed $5,350,000 from two banks. The banks insisted that Sullivan reorganize Old Patriots so that its income could be used to repay the loans made to Sullivan and its assets used to secure the loans. To make the use of Old Patriots' income and assets legal, it was necessary to freeze out the nonvoting shareholders. In November 1976, Sullivan organized a new corporation called the New Patriots Football Club, Inc. (New Patriots). Sullivan was the sole shareholder of New Patriots. In December 1976, the shareholders of Old Patriots approved a merger of Old Patriots and New Patriots. Under the terms of the merger, Old Patriots went out of business, New Patriots assumed the business of Old Patriots, Sullivan became the only owner of New Patriots, and the nonvoting shareholders of Old Patriots received $15 for each share they owned.

David A. Coggins, a Patriots fan from the time of its formation and owner of 10 Old Patriots nonvoting shares, objected to the merger and refused to accept the $15 per share payment for his shares. Coggins sued Sullivan and Old Patriots to obtain rescission of the merger. The trial judge found the merger to be illegal and ordered the payment of damages to Coggins and all other Old Patriots shareholders who voted against the merger and had not accepted the $15 per share merger payment. Sullivan and Old Patriots appealed to the Massachusetts Supreme Judicial Court.

Liacos, Justice

When the director's duty of loyalty to the corporation is in conflict with his self-interest, the court will vigorously scrutinize the situation. The dangers of self-dealing and abuse of fiduciary duty are greatest in freeze-out situations like the Patriots merger, when a controlling shareholder and corporate director chooses to eliminate public ownership. Because the danger of abuse of fiduciary duty is especially great in a freeze-out merger, the court must be satisfied that the freeze-out was for the advancement of a legitimate corporate purpose. If satisfied that elimination of public ownership is in furtherance of a business purpose, the court should then proceed to determine if the transaction was fair by examining the totality of the circumstances. Consequently, Sullivan and Old Patriots bear the burden of proving, first, that the merger was for a legitimate business purpose, and second, that, considering the totality of circumstances, it was fair to the minority.

Sullivan and Old Patriots have failed to demonstrate that the merger served any valid corporate objective unrelated to the personal interests of Sullivan, the majority shareholder. The sole reason for the merger was to effectuate a restructuring of Old Patriots that would enable the repayment of the personal indebtedness incurred by Sullivan. Under the approach we set forth above, there is no need to consider further the elements of fairness of a transaction that is not related to a valid corporate purpose.

Judgment for Coggins affirmed as modified.

Trading on Inside Information
Officers and directors have *confidential access* to nonpublic information about the corporation. Sometimes, directors and officers purchase their corporation's securities with knowledge of confidential information. Often, disclosure of previously nonpublic, **inside information** affects the value of the corporation's securities. Therefore, directors and officers may make a profit when the prices of the securities increase after the inside information has been disclosed publicly. Shareholders of the corporation claim that they have been harmed by such activity, either because the directors and officers misused confidential information that should have been used only for corporate purposes or because the directors and officers had an unfair informational advantage over the shareholders.

In this century, there has been a judicial trend toward finding a duty of directors and officers to disclose information that they have received confidentially from the corporation before they buy or sell the corporation's securities. As will be discussed fully in Chapter 45,

Securities Regulation, the illegality of insider trading is already federal law under the Securities Exchange Act; however, it remains only a minority rule under state corporation law.

Director's Right to Dissent

A director who assents to an action of the board of directors may be held liable for the board's exceeding its authority or its failing to meet its duty of due care or loyalty. A director who attends a board meeting is deemed to have assented to any action taken at the meeting, unless he dissents.

Under the MBCA, to register his **dissent** to a board action, and thereby to protect himself from liability, the director must **not vote in favor** of the action and **must make his position clear** to the other board members. His position is made clear either by requesting that his dissent appear in the minutes or by giving written notice of his dissent to the chairman of the board at the meeting or to the secretary immediately after the meeting. These procedures ensure that the dissenting director will attempt to dissuade the board from approving an imprudent action.

Generally, directors are not liable for failing to attend meetings. However, a director is liable for *continually failing* to attend meetings, with the result that the director is unable to prevent the board from harming the corporation by its self-dealing.

Duties of Directors and Officers of Nonprofit Corporations

Directors and officers of nonprofit corporations owe fiduciary duties to their corporations that are similar to the duties owed by managers of for-profit corporations. Directors and officers owe a duty of care and duties of loyalty to the nonprofit corporation. They must act in good faith, with the care of an ordinarily prudent person, and with a reasonable belief that they are acting in the best interests of the corporation. In addition, a director should not have a conflict of interest in any transaction of the nonprofit corporation. As with for-profit corporations, conflict-of-interest transactions must meet the intrinsic fairness standard. Finally, a nonprofit corporation may not lend money to a director.

Liability concerns of directors of nonprofit corporations, especially public benefit corporations in which directors typically receive no compensation, have made it difficult for some nonprofit corporations to find and retain directors. Therefore, the Model Nonprofit Corporation Act permits nonprofit corporations to limit or eliminate the liability of directors for breach of the duty of care. The articles may not limit or eliminate a director's liability for failing to act in good faith, engaging in intentional misconduct, breaching the duty of loyalty, or having a conflict of interest.

Ethics in Action

Sarbanes–Oxley Act Imposes Duties and Liabilities on Corporate Management

In the early 2000s, it was revealed that some high-level officers of public corporations reaped millions of dollars of bonuses and profits from their sale of their corporations' stock during periods in which the corporations' profits were fraudulently inflated. In the Sarbanes–Oxley Act, Congress took a two-barreled approach, increasing top management's responsibility for the accuracy of financial statements and eliminating management's ability to profit personally from misstated financial data.

First, the Sarbanes–Oxley Act requires the CEO and the CFO of public companies to certify that to their knowledge all financial information in annual and quarterly reports filed with the Securities and Exchange Commission fairly presents the financial condition of the company and does not include untrue or misleading material statements. The purpose of the certification requirement is to protect shareholders and investors who rely on corporate financial statements. If a CEO or CFO certified materially false financial statements that she knew were false or misleading, she is subject to a fine of $5 million and 20 years' imprisonment. In addition, the officer could have civil liability to shareholders far exceeding the fine limitation.

Second, the act requires the CEO and the CFO of a public company to disgorge any bonus, incentive-based or equity-based compensation, and the profit from the sale of corporate securities received during any period in which the corporation was required to restate a financial statement due to a wrongful material noncompliance with a financial reporting requirement. This reimbursement of the corporation applies to the CEO and the CFO even if the wrongdoing was by some other officer or employee. In addition, the act expands the disgorgement remedy available against any wrongdoing officer who receives bonuses or stock profits during the period of time the stock price is inflated by false financial information. The act permits recovery of not only improper gains but also any other relief necessary to protect and to mitigate harm to investors.

Corporate and Management Liability for Torts and Crimes

When directors, officers, and other employees of the corporation commit torts and crimes while conducting corporate affairs, the issue arises concerning who has liability. Should the individuals committing the torts and crimes be held liable, the corporation, or both?

Liability of the Corporation
For **torts,** the vicarious liability rule of *respondeat superior* applies to corporations. The only issue is whether an employee acted within the scope of her employment, which encompasses not only acts the employee is authorized to commit but may also include acts that the employee is expressly instructed to avoid. Generally, under the doctrine of *respondeat superior,* a corporation is liable for an employee's tort that is reasonably connected to the authorized conduct of the employee.

The traditional view was that a corporation could not be guilty of a **crime** because criminal guilt required intent. A corporation, not having a mind, could form no intent. Other courts held that a corporation was not a person for purposes of criminal liability.

Today, few courts have difficulty holding corporations liable for crimes. Modern criminal statutes either expressly provide that corporations may commit crimes or define the term *person* to include corporations. In addition, some criminal statutes designed to protect the public welfare do not require intent as an element of some crimes, thereby removing the grounds used by early courts to justify relieving corporations of criminal liability.

Courts are especially likely to impose criminal liability on a corporation when the criminal act is requested, authorized, or performed by:

1. The board of directors,
2. An officer,
3. Another person having responsibility for formulating company policy, or
4. A high level administrator having supervisory responsibility over the subject matter of the offense and acting within the scope of his employment.

In addition, courts hold a corporation liable for crimes of its agent or employee committed within the scope of his authority, even if a higher corporate official has no knowledge of the act and has not ratified it.

Directors' and Officers' Liability for Torts and Crimes
A person is always *liable for his own torts and crimes,* even when committed on behalf of his principal. Every person in our society is expected to exercise independent judgment and not merely to follow orders. Therefore, directors and officers are personally liable when they commit torts or crimes during the performance of their corporate duties.

A director or officer is usually not liable for the torts of employees of the corporation, since the corporation, not the director or the officer, is the principal. He will have **tort** liability, however, if he *authorizes* the tort or *participates* in its commission. A director or officer has **criminal** liability if she *requests, authorizes, conspires,* or *aids and abets* the commission of a crime by an employee.

The early 21st century has been a busy time for verdicts in criminal cases against CEOs accused of acceding to accounting irregularities or looting their companies in the late 1990s and early 2000s. Bernard Ebbers, former CEO of WorldCom, was found guilty of helping to mastermind the $11 billion accounting fraud that saw the firm seek bankruptcy. Ebbers received a 25-year prison sentence. The jury rejected his defense that he knew nothing of the fraud that was orchestrated by WorldCom CFO Scott Sullivan. The jury believed that as CEO Ebbers must have known of the fraud and was motivated to prop up the price of WorldCom stock to increase the value of stock options he held. Sullivan, who pled guilty and testified against Ebbers, cooperated with the prosecution and received a five-year prison sentence, despite his central role in the fraud.

Also in 2005, Adelphia founder and former CEO John Rigas received a 15-year prison sentence and his son and former CFO Scott, 20 years, after being found guilty of looting Adelphia. According to prosecutors, the Rigases used Adelphia as their "private ATM" to provide $50 million in cash advances, buy $1.6 billion in securities, and repay $252 million in margin loans. Also, Tyco's former CEO Dennis Kozlowski received up to 25 years in prison for looting Tyco, including using company funds for his wife's $2 million birthday party. Kozlowski was also fined $70 million and ordered to repay $134 million to Tyco.

The following *Jensen* case involves one of the most highly publicized options backdating cases. The case is a primer on why corporations backdated options for their top executives and how courts determine an appropriate sentence, including imprisonment, for executives who willingly violate the law.

United States v. Jensen 537 F. Supp. 2d 1069 (N.D. Cal. 2008)

On March 18, 2006, The Wall Street Journal *published an article analyzing how some companies were granting stock options to their executives. According to the article, companies issued a suspiciously high number of options at times when the stock price hit a periodic low, followed by a sharp price increase. The odds of these well-timed grants occurring by chance alone were astronomical—less likely than winning the lottery. Eventually it was determined that such buy-low, sell-high returns simply could not be the product of chance. In testimony before Congress, Professor Erik Lie identified three potential strategies to account for these well-timed stock option grants. The first strategy included techniques called "spring-loading" and "bullet-dodging." The practice of "spring-loading" involved timing a stock option grant to precede an announcement of good news. The practice of "bullet-dodging" involved timing a stock option grant to follow an announcement of bad news. A second strategy included manipulating the flow of information—timing corporate announcements to match known future grant dates. A third strategy, backdating, involved cherry-picking past, and relatively low, stock prices to be the official grant date. Backdating occurs when the option's grant date is altered to an earlier date with a lower, more favorable price to the recipient.*

A company grants stock options to its officers, directors, and employees at a certain "exercise price," giving the recipient the right to buy shares of the stock at that price, once the option vests. If the stock price rises after the date of the grant, the options have value. If the stock price falls after the date of the grant, the options have no value. Options with an exercise price equal to the stock's market price are called "at-the-money" options. Options with an exercise price lower than the stock's market price are called "in-the-money" options. By granting in-the-money, backdated options, a company effectively grants an employee an instant opportunity for profit.

Granting backdated options has important accounting consequences for the issuing company. For financial reporting purposes, companies granting in-the-money options have to recognize compensation expenses equal to the difference between the market price and the exercise price. APB 25 is the accounting rule that governed stock-based compensation through June 2005; it required companies to recognize this compensation expense for backdated options. For options granted at-the-money, a company did not have to recognize any compensation expenses under APB 25.

Backdating stock options by itself is not illegal. Purposefully backdated options that are properly accounted for and disclosed are legal. On the other hand, the backdating of options that is not disclosed or does not result in the recognition of a compensation expense is fraud.

A motive for fraudulent backdating may be to avoid recognizing a compensation expense, or a hit to the earnings, while awarding in-the-money options. To accomplish the fraud, those responsible assign an earlier date to the stock options—a date where the stock price was attractively low—and pretend the option was awarded on that earlier date, rather than the real date. In other words, fraudulent backdating disguises in-the-money options (which require recognizing compensation expenses) as at-the-money options (which do not require recognizing compensation expenses). The paperwork and phony grant dates allow the company to avoid compensation expenses, while aware that the price on the true grant date is higher than the price on the phony grant date.

A company's failure to account properly for in-the-money options would inflate the bottom line such that the company's net income would be higher than it should have been from an accounting perspective. As a result, the company would report excessive earnings per share, one of the more important metrics that investors used to evaluate a company's performance.

After 2002, a company's ability to backdate fraudulently option grants became much more difficult. On August 29, 2002, Congress passed the Sarbanes–Oxley Act, which instituted new reporting requirements for stock option grants. Before Sarbanes–Oxley, an employee who received a stock option grant had to file financial forms with the SEC within 45 days after the company's fiscal year-end. After Sarbanes–Oxley, an employee must file financial forms with the SEC within two days of receiving the stock option grant. After Sarbanes–Oxley, a company fraudulently backdating stock options by a few weeks or months would not filed have the required SEC forms on time, raising red flags with the SEC.

There have been several highly publicized options backdating cases involving American corporations. One involved Brocade Communications issuing backdated options to its CEO Gregory Reyes. Not only were Brocade Communications and Reyes prosecuted for violating federal securities laws, but also Stephanie Jensen, a Brocade vice president and director of its human resources department. At their trial, Dr. John Garvey, an expert witness for the prosecution, provided testimony about the size of the compensation expenses that went unstated as a result of Brocade's options pricing practices. Dr. Garvey testified that Brocade failed to recognize more than $173 million of compensation expenses in 2001 and more than $161 million in 2002. He further testified that, if Brocade had properly accounted for the stock options it had backdated, then the company would have recorded a loss of $110 million in 2001, rather than the profit of $3 million it actually reported, and would have recorded a loss of $45 million in 2002, rather than the profit of nearly $60 million it actually reported.

In December 2007, a federal district court jury convicted Jensen of willingly and knowingly falsifying Brocade's records over a three-year period to conceal the actual date when stock options were granted to Reyes. The district court judge next considered whether a proper sentence for Jensen included imprisonment.

Breyer, Judge

The Securities Exchange Act's penalty provision, 15 U.S.C. § 78ff, precludes imprisonment "for the violation of any rule or regulation if [the defendant] proves that he had no knowledge of such rule or regulation." Concerned that a great mass of rules and regulations would be issued by the SEC in the wake of the Securities Act and Securities Exchange Act, Congress enacted the No Knowledge Clause, thereby rendering ludicrous a strict adherence to the fiction of presumed knowledge of the law.

The No Knowledge Clause is an affirmative defense to a sentence of imprisonment. As such, the defendant bears the burden of proving no knowledge by a preponderance of the evidence. To be more specific, Jensen bears the burden of proving that she did not know there was any applicable SEC rule prohibiting the falsification of books and records. It is not a defense for Jensen to argue that she did not know, for example, the precise number or common name of the rule, the book and page where it was to be found, or the date upon which it was promulgated.

Accordingly, the question becomes whether Jensen has satisfied her burden of proving by a preponderance that she was unaware of an SEC rule or regulation prohibiting the falsification of books and records. In the Court's opinion, she has not. Jensen argues that: (1) her background and experience are in areas that have nothing to do with SEC rules and regulations; (2) her job responsibilities had nothing to do with SEC rules or regulations; (3) Jensen had nothing to do with the SEC reporting process; (4) none of the individuals who worked with Jensen drew any connection between their work on options grants and SEC regulations; and (5) none of the more than 50 deponents in the SEC action recall discussing anything connected to any SEC rule with Jensen.

There is no smoking gun conclusively demonstrating that Jensen was aware that falsification of books was outlawed by SEC regulation. However, the circumstantial evidence that Jensen offers up is insufficient to carry her burden in light of the evidence established at trial. There is substantial evidence that Jensen knew her conduct was wrongful, including the fact that Jensen attempted to minimize the obviousness of backdated options, concealed the way options were actually dated, and directed employees not to communicate about options over the phone or email. To be sure, Jensen can only be imprisoned if she knew her conduct was unlawful *and* knew that it was prohibited by SEC rule or regulation. But in light of the evidence demonstrating that Jensen knew her conduct affected Brocade finances, the Court is assured that Jensen also knew she was violating an SEC rule or regulation.

For example, Jensen received emails establishing that options had an effect on Brocade financials and audits. On January 28, 2002, Jensen received an email from Brocade comptroller Bob Bossi, asking for the stock grant list to support an upcoming quarter-end audit from Arthur Andersen. Similarly, Jensen received an email confirming that the stock options grant lists and compensation committee meetings would be used in Brocade's year-end audit. The only reasonable conclusion to draw is that Jensen knew that stock options, and how they were priced, affected the audited results of the company.

Moreover, there was evidence at trial that after Jensen shepherded options through the pricing process, the forms were then given to the finance department so that finance could ensure that the grants were accurate. It can be reasonably assumed that as director of human resources, Jensen understood the chain for processing option grants and that stock options went from human resources directly to finance. A reasonably intelligent corporate official would understand that if the options forms went directly to finance, that was so because the forms had an effect on Brocade's financials. Falsifying options grants would therefore impair the integrity of the company's financials, which a reasonable official would know is illegal under SEC rule and regulation.

In short, the Court does not believe that Jensen was so far removed from the financial side of the process that she would not know her conduct was prohibited by the SEC. Jensen clearly knew her conduct was unlawful and, the Court believes, knew that her conduct affected Brocade's finances and audits. Under the circumstances, Jensen has not persuasively established that she was unaware her conduct violated any SEC rule or regulation.

In determining the sentence of co-defendant Gregory Reyes, the Court concluded that it would be inappropriate to enhance the sentence for loss, number of victims, and sophisticated means. The Court reaches the same conclusion with respect to Jensen's sentence. As to other enhancements, the Court will impose a two-level abuse of trust enhancement and a two-level enhancement for obstruction of justice, but rejects the government's request for an aggravating role enhancement and a public officer enhancement.

In general, the government bears the burden of proving, by a preponderance of the evidence, the facts necessary to enhance a defendant's offense level under the Sentencing Guidelines. However, when a sentencing factor has an extremely disproportionate effect on the sentence relative to the offense of conviction, due process requires that the government prove the facts underlying the enhancement by clear and convincing evidence.

The government has *not* demonstrated—at least not by clear and convincing evidence—that Jensen was the kind of Vice President who owed a heightened fiduciary duty to shareholders. Brocade proxy statements, 10-Qs, and 10-Ks frequently listed corporate officers, including the Vice Presidents in charge of Engineering, Operations, and Sales— core decisional and policy-making roles—but never Jensen. In addition, the government has identified no securities law that imposes heightened duties on executives in divisions such as human resources, as opposed to divisions more closely connected to the operational functions of the company.

To be sure, Jensen played an important *internal* role in the organization. Jensen was one of only nine executives who reported directly to Reyes, in contrast to sixteen Vice Presidents who did not. But the government has not pointed to persuasive evidence demonstrating that Jensen played the kind of role in relation to *shareholders* such that as head of Human Resources, she owed them a heightened fiduciary duty. Accordingly, the Court will not impose the four-level public officer enhancement.

Because the Court will not impose the public officer enhancement, it may consider whether to impose an enhancement for abuse of trust. To impose an enhancement for abuse of trust, the government must establish by clear and convincing evidence that: (1) Jensen occupied a position of trust; and (2) Jensen abused her position in a manner that significantly facilitated the commission or concealment of the offense.

Jensen used her managerial position to escort the backdated stock option grants through the necessary processes. It was Jensen who involved and oversaw employees in the human resources department tasked with the picking of lower dates, Jensen who ordered her employees to conceal the picking of past dates by not using email or phones, and Jensen who coordinated the signing of falsified dates by Reyes, providing the CEO with an array of earlier dates from which he could select. A lesser employee of the firm could not have accomplished these things which significantly facilitated the scheme's success and concealment.

Even if Jensen did not owe a heightened fiduciary duty to shareholders, she was entrusted with accurately maintaining books and records that affected the financials of the company. Thus, there can be no doubt that shareholders were obligated to trust that Jensen would properly maintain any books and records bearing on Brocade's assets. Because Jensen occupied a position of trust and abused that position to commit and conceal the falsification of books and records, a two-level enhancement is appropriate.

The Court will enhance Jensen's sentence by two levels because she impeded justice by proffering—through counsel—a false declaration in support of her motion to sever. Jensen's arguments that the declaration was truthful and that she should not be punished for the conduct of her attorney are unpersuasive.

In his declaration, Reyes declared, "I told Ms. Jensen that the option grant dates were the dates that I made the granting decisions. *Options were priced at the fair market value on the grant dates.*" (Emphasis added.) Jensen argues that no one obstructed justice because the declaration did not provide false information to the Court. According to Jensen, Reyes' declaration intended to convey that he *sometimes* priced grant dates on the same day he made granting decisions, but was not intended to deny that on other occasions, Reyes did backdate option grants with Jensen's help.

Even if Jensen is correct that, technically speaking, Reyes' statement was not per se false, the Court still finds that the declaration impeded justice because it was seriously misleading. Reyes' declaration, in combination with the statements of counsel, misled the Court into believing that Reyes' declaration related to *all* stock option grants. Whether or not Reyes and Jensen's counsel subjectively believed that the declaration only related to some grants, there was no way for the Court to discern that subtle distinction.

Jensen sat in court while her lawyer argued that Reyes' declaration provided "absolutely exculpatory" evidence that precluded the jury from convicting Jensen for backdating options. Jensen also sat idly by while her lawyer argued that there was no evidence Jensen actually knew that Reyes was backdating. But at the time, Jensen did know that Reyes had backdated, and therefore knew that Reyes' declaration was not "absolutely exculpatory."

Because Jensen knew that Reyes' declaration was not accurate, the Court is also unpersuaded by her assertion that any obstruction was not willful. There can be no doubt that Jensen acted with the intent to mislead the Court. Jensen *knew* that Reyes backdated, but she nonetheless sat idly by while her lawyer represented to the court that a severance was justified because Reyes would testify otherwise. Put simply, that kind of conduct is not permitted, because when a defendant's lawyer proffers misleading evidence to the court, which the defendant knows to be inaccurate, the failure to act can form the basis of an enhancement for obstruction.

Because Jensen has not carried her burden of proving that the No Knowledge Clause controls her sentence, the Court will impose a sentence with an eye towards—among other factors—the Sentencing Guidelines. With a base offense level of six, plus two-level enhancements for abuse of trust and obstruction of justice, the Guidelines recommend a sentence of 6–12 months. The minimum term may be satisfied by a sentence of imprisonment that includes a term of supervised release with a condition that substitutes community confinement or home detention, provided that at least one month is satisfied by imprisonment.

Order entered sentencing Jensen to imprisonment.

Insurance and Indemnification

The extensive potential liability of directors deters many persons from becoming directors. They fear that their liability for their actions as directors may far exceed their fees as directors. To encourage persons to become directors, corporations **indemnify** them for their outlays associated with defending lawsuits brought against them and paying judgments and settlement amounts. In addition, or as an alternative, corporations purchase **insurance** that will make such payments for the directors. Indemnification and insurance are provided for officers, also.

Mandatory Indemnification of Directors Under the MBCA, a director is entitled to *mandatory indemnification* of her reasonable litigation expenses when she is sued and *wins completely* (is *wholly successful*). The greatest part of such expenses is attorney's fees. Because indemnification is mandatory in this context, when the corporation refuses to indemnify a director who has won completely, she may ask a court to order the corporation to indemnify her.

Permissible Indemnification of Directors Under the MBCA, a director who loses a lawsuit

Ethics in Action

Expanding Indemnification

The MBCA permits a corporation to expand the grounds on which it may indemnify a director, within limits. For example, the corporation may provide for indemnification of a director's liability (including a judgment paid to the corporation) when the director acted carelessly and in bad faith, but did not intend to harm the corporation or its shareholders and did not receive an improper financial benefit.

- Do you think it is ethical for a corporation to indemnify a careless director for the amount for which she was liable to the corporation? Would a rights theorist support indemnification in that context? Would a utilitarian? Would a profit maximizer?
- Would you be a shareholder in a corporation that permits indemnification in the context above?
- Would you be a director in a corporation if it did not indemnify you in that context?

---

may be indemnified by the corporation. This is called *permissible indemnification,* because the corporation is permitted to indemnify the director but is not required to do so.

The corporation must establish that the director acted in *good faith* and reasonably believed that she acted in the *best interests* of the corporation. When a director seeks indemnification for a *criminal* fine, the corporation must establish a third requirement—that the director had no reasonable cause to believe that her conduct was unlawful. Finally, any permissible indemnification must be approved by someone independent of the director receiving indemnification—a disinterested board of directors, disinterested shareholders, or independent legal counsel. Permissible indemnification may cover not only the director's reasonable expenses but also fines and damages that the director has been ordered to pay.

A corporation may not elect to indemnify a director who was found to have received a *financial benefit* to which he was not entitled. Such a rule tends to prevent indemnification of directors who acted from self-interest. If a director received no financial benefit but was held liable to his corporation or paid an amount to the corporation as part of a *settlement,* the director may be indemnified only for his reasonable expenses, not for the amount that he paid to the corporation. The purpose of these rules is to avoid the circularity of having the director pay damages to the corporation and then having the corporation indemnify the director for the same amount of money.

Advances   A director may not be able to afford to make payments to her lawyer prior to the end of a lawsuit. More important, a lawyer may refuse to defend a director who cannot pay legal fees. Therefore, the MBCA permits a corporation to make advances to a director to allow the director to afford a lawyer, if the director affirms that she meets the requirements for permissible indemnification and she promises to repay the advances if she is found not entitled to indemnification.

Court-Ordered Indemnification   A court may order a corporation to indemnify a director if it determines that the director meets the standard for *mandatory* indemnification or if the director is *fairly and reasonably* entitled to indemnification in view of all the relevant circumstances.

Indemnification of Nondirectors   Under the MBCA, officers and employees who are not directors are entitled to the same mandatory indemnification rights as directors.

Insurance

The MBCA does not limit the ability of a corporation to purchase insurance on behalf of its directors, officers, and employees. Insurance companies, however, are unwilling to insure all risks. In addition, some risks are *legally uninsurable as against public policy.* Therefore, liability for misconduct such as self-dealing, usurpation, and securities fraud is uninsurable.

Nonprofit Corporations

A nonprofit corporation may obtain insurance and indemnify its officers and directors for liabilities incurred in the course of their performance of their official duties. The MNCA requires indemnification when the director or officer wins the lawsuit completely. A corporation is permitted to indemnify an officer or director who is found liable if he acted in good faith and reasonably believed he acted in the best interests of the corporation.

Problems and Problem Cases

1. Pantry Pride, Inc., made a hostile tender offer to acquire the shares of Revlon, Inc., for $47.50 per share. Pantry Pride's plan thereafter was to sell Revlon's various lines of business individually. Recognizing that a takeover was inevitable, Revlon's board negotiated a friendly acquisition with Forstmann Little & Co. for $56 per share. Revlon's board also agreed to break up the company by selling its cosmetic division. Forstmann wanted to sell two other Revlon divisions after the purchase. Eventually, Forstmann upped its offer price to $57.25. In return, Revlon's board gave Forstmann a lock-up option, promising to sell two valuable divisions to Forstmann at nearly $200 million below their market value if Pantry Pride took over Revlon instead of Forstmann. The purpose and effect of the lock-up option was to prevent any other bidder, including Pantry Pride, from being willing to purchase Revlon. What standard or test judges whether Revlon's board acted properly in giving a lock-up option to Forstmann? Did Revlon's board comply with that test?

2. Deborah Goode, Thomas Goode, Cynthia Mann, and Hodges Mann were the only shareholders and directors of Star Communications, Inc. Each owned 25 shares. The Goodes were married to each other, as were the Manns. When the Goodes had marital problems, notice was given for a directors' meeting, the stated purpose of which was to oust Mrs. Goode as a director. The Goodes and Manns attended the meeting. There was some discussion whether the meeting was a directors' or shareholders' meeting, but the issue was never clearly resolved. Nonetheless, a vote was taken to remove Mrs. Goode as a director. The Manns voted for removal, Mrs. Goode voted against, and Mr. Goode abstained. May Mrs. Goode invalidate her removal on grounds that she was removed without cause and that she was removed by action of the directors, not the shareholders?

3. Countrywide Financial Corporation created for its employees a pension plan that allowed employees to select how their pension plan amounts are invested, including investing in the common stock of Countrywide. When the value of the common stock of Countrywide Financial Corporation declined from over $40 per share to $6 in a six-month period in 2007 and 2008 due to the collapse of the sub-prime lending market, Countrywide employees sued Countrywide and its directors for breaching a fiduciary duty to the employees by not exercising its discretion to suspend both offering Countrywide stock as a plan investment and matching employees' investment in Countrywide stock. Has the board of directors breached a fiduciary duty to the employees?

4. Lillian Pritchard was a director of Pritchard & Baird Corporation, a business founded by her husband. After the death of her husband, her sons took control of the corporation. For two years, they looted the assets of the corporation through theft and improper payments. The corporation's financial statements revealed the improper payments to the sons, but Mrs. Pritchard did not read the financial statements. She did not know what her sons were doing to the corporation or that what they were doing was unlawful. When Mrs. Pritchard was sued for failing to protect the assets of the corporation, she argued that she was a figurehead director, a simple housewife who served as a director as an accommodation to her husband and sons. Was Mrs. Pritchard held liable?

5. The Chicago National League Ball Club, Inc. (Chicago Cubs), operated Wrigley Field, the Cubs' home park. Through the 1965 baseball season, the Cubs were the only major league baseball team that played no home games at night because Wrigley Field had no lights for nighttime baseball. Philip K. Wrigley, director and president of the corporation, refused to install lights because of his personal opinion that baseball was a daytime sport and that installing lights and scheduling night baseball games would result in the deterioration of the surrounding neighborhood. The other directors assented to this policy. From 1961 to 1965, the Cubs suffered losses from their baseball operations. The Chicago White Sox, whose weekday games were generally played at night, drew many more fans than did the Cubs. A shareholder sued the board of directors to force them to install lights at Wrigley Field and to schedule night games. What did the court rule? Why?

6. James Gray was the president and managing officer of Peoples Bank and Trust Company. Frank Piecara was an old customer of the bank. Piecara was president of Mirage Construction, Inc. Gray directed Peoples Bank to make a $536,000 loan to a trust

managed by Piecara, the loan proceeds to be used to provide working capital for Mirage. Gray obtained a security interest in Mirage's accounts receivable and contract rights for work Mirage was to perform for Rogers Construction. Gray did not perfect the security interest or notify Rogers that it should remit payments for Mirage's work directly to Peoples Bank. Piecara and Mirage defaulted on the loan to Peoples Bank. Gray was sued by his employer for breaching his fiduciary duty. Has Gray complied with the business judgment rule?

7. Paramount Communications, Inc., was the target of an unsolicited $90 per share takeover bid by QVC Network, Inc. To thwart QVC's bid, Paramount's board of directors adopted defense tactics to facilitate a friendly takeover by Viacom, Inc., at a price of $85 per share. Paramount agreed to grant Viacom a lock-up option to purchase almost 20 percent of Paramount's shares at a bargain price. In addition, Paramount promised to pay Viacom a termination fee of $100 million, which was about 10 percent of Paramount's assets, if Paramount terminated the merger because of a competing transaction or if its shareholders voted against the merger. Has Paramount's board of directors acted legally?

8. Nook Pharmacies, Inc., is a small public company that operates 50 pharmacies in six states. Nook's board of directors is aware that CVS and Walgreen, the dominant companies in the pharmacy industry, are buying many of the remaining small pharmacy companies. Nook's directors prefer that Nook remain an independent company that will grow internally as it embraces new markets near its current pharmacies. The board wants to oppose any attempt by CVS or Walgreen to take over Nook. Nook's board has consulted you for advice on how to oppose a hostile takeover bid. In anticipation of a hostile bid, with what standard of conduct do you advise Nook's board to plan to comply? What do you advise Nook's board to do now to help Nook's board comply with that standard of conduct?

9. Lymon Properties Group, Inc., is a developer and operator of retail shopping malls. Lymon owns 75 percent of the shares of LDC, Inc., whose business is investing in undeveloped land. All of LDC's directors are appointed by Lymon. LDC owns 320 acres of land that Lymon wants to purchase for mall construction. LDC purchased the land two years ago for $6.4 million. Lymon has offered to purchase the land for $8.2 million. When approving the purchase, with what standard of conduct must Lymon's board comply? What should LDC's board of directors do before accepting the offer in order to reduce the likelihood that LDC's minority shareholders will be able to sue LDC's board successfully for selling the land for too low a price?

10. Gimble Hardt Corporation (GHC) is a manufacturer of aluminum wiring. Jason Gimble owns 82 percent of the 2 million outstanding shares of GHC. The remaining 360,000 shares are owned by 832 minority shareholders, none of whom owns more than 1,200 shares. Gimble wants to freeze out the minority shareholders using a reverse share split. Describe that procedure, including a statement of who must approve the transaction. What legal standard must the freeze-out transaction meet? Does it matter that Gimble wants to freeze out the minority shareholders so that GHC is no longer a public company that has to comply with the costly rules of the Sarbanes–Oxley Act?

11. In 1997, Peter Zaccagnino sold to investors historical bonds—issued by railroad and foreign governments—that he claimed were high-yield securities. In reality, the bonds had no value to anyone other than to collectors of historical documents. Peter obtained over $6.8 million from the sale of these bonds. During this time, his wife, Gigi, attended meetings where her husband represented to investors that the bonds could yield 7 to 30 percent of their valuation within a year. Zaccagnino sold the historical bonds through two corporate entities and deposited most of the sales proceeds into the corporations' accounts. One of those corporations was Wonder Glass Products, of which Gigi was the secretary, treasurer, and director. She received $5,200 a month from her employment with Wonder Glass. In March 1998, Gigi incorporated a business called Diamond in the Rough (DIR) in the British Virgin Islands, of which she was president, secretary, and director. Peter promoted DIR as a firm that placed client funds into high-yield offshore investment programs, promising investors substantial earnings. At one DIR meeting with prospective purchasers, Gigi sat at a table and made prospective investors promise that they would not record the meeting. Meanwhile, Peter told them that they could make huge sums of money with the

proposed investments and that he had been arranging similar investments successfully for so long that he was ready to retire. This foreign investment scheme earned Peter millions in addition to the money from the historical bond sales. When the federal government prosecuted Peter and Gigi for conspiracy and racketeering, Gigi claimed that she became aware of the criminal conduct only in December 1999, when she overheard her husband and one of his business partners laughing about the falsity of the statements they sent to investors. Did the court accept Gigi's argument or was she found to have willfully engaged in criminal conduct while acting for the corporations?

12. Shareholders of Barney Slaney, Inc., brought a derivative suit against the corporation's board of directors for failing to supervise adequately the corporation's loan officers, who made several high-risk loans to substandard borrowers. Almost 40 percent of the high-risk borrowers defaulted on the loans, resulting in a loss of $55 million to Barney Slaney. The directors asked the corporation to advance to them the cost of legal fees for defending themselves against the charges. Under what conditions may the corporation make advances of legal fees to the directors?

Online Research

The Credit Crisis and Directors' Fiduciary Duties

The credit crunch of 2008 and 2009 was caused in part by decisions of banks like Countrywide Financial to make loans to borrowers who had insufficient income to repay the loans, as well as by investment banks like Bear Stearns which purchased many of those loans from banks in the secondary market. Check online to see how shareholders of banks and investment banks are faring in their lawsuits against the officers and directors who owed a fiduciary duty to make prudent decisions when issuing and purchasing loans.

Consider completing the case "LIABILITY: Office Party Blame Game" from the You Be the Judge Web site element after you have read this chapter. Visit our Web site at **www.mhhe.com/mallor14e** for more information and activities regarding this case segment.

chapter 44

SHAREHOLDERS' RIGHTS AND LIABILITIES

Four business associates create a business that will develop and sell information technology software. The business will be incorporated. The four will provide 90 percent of the initial capital needs of the business, but none of them has the IT skills to develop marketable software. In addition, none of the four wants to be involved in the day-to-day management of the business. The four associates have found, however, an IT engineer to develop software and another person who is willing to manage the business. The engineer and the general manager each want a 5 percent equity interest in the corporation, which the four associates are willing to grant to them. Although the engineer and the GM would each like to elect a representative to the corporation's board of directors, the four associates want to control the business absolutely, with each associate owning an equal share of the corporation and sitting on the board.

- Using classes of shares, create an equity structure for the corporation that meets the wants of the four associates, the engineer, and the GM.
- In this context, why is using classes of shares preferable to using one class of shares with cumulative voting for directors?

THE SHAREHOLDERS ARE THE owners of a corporation, but a shareholder has *no right to manage* the corporation. Instead, a corporation is managed by its board of directors and its officers for the benefit of its shareholders.

The shareholders' role in a corporation is limited to electing and removing directors, approving certain important matters, and ensuring that the actions of the corporation's managers are consistent with the applicable state corporation statute, the articles of incorporation, and the bylaws.

Shareholders also assume a few responsibilities. For example, all shareholders are required to pay the promised consideration for shares. Shareholders are liable for receiving dividends beyond the lawful amount. In addition, controlling shareholders may owe special duties to minority shareholders.

Close corporation shareholders enjoy rights and owe duties beyond the rights and duties of shareholders of publicly owned corporations. In addition, some courts have found close corporation shareholders to be fiduciaries of each other.

This chapter's study of the rights and responsibilities of shareholders begins with an examination of shareholders' meetings and voting rights.

Shareholders' Meetings

The general corporation statutes of most states and the Model Business Corporation Act (MBCA) provide that an **annual meeting of shareholders** shall be held. The purpose of an annual shareholders' meeting is to elect new directors and to conduct other necessary business. Often, the shareholders are asked to approve the corporation's independent auditors and to vote on shareholders' proposals.

Special meetings of shareholders may be held whenever a corporate matter arises that requires immediate shareholders' action, such as the approval of a merger that cannot wait until the next annual shareholders' meeting. Under the MBCA, a special shareholders' meeting may be called by the board of directors or by a person authorized to do so by the bylaws, usually the president or the chairman of the board. In addition, the holders of at least 10 percent of the shares entitled to vote at the meeting may call a special meeting.

Notice of Meetings

To permit shareholders to arrange their schedules for attendance at shareholders' meetings, the MBCA requires the corporation to give shareholders **notice** of annual and special meetings of shareholders. Notice of a *special meeting* must list the purpose of the meeting. Under the MBCA, notice of an *annual meeting* need not include the purpose of the meeting unless shareholders will be asked to approve extraordinary corporate changes—for example, amendments to the articles of incorporation and mergers.

Notice need be given only to shareholders entitled to vote who are **shareholders of record** on a date fixed by the board of directors. Shareholders of record are those whose names appear on the share-transfer book of the corporation. Usually, only shareholders of record are entitled to vote at shareholders' meetings.

Conduct of Meetings

To conduct business at a shareholders' meeting, a **quorum** of the outstanding shares must be represented at the meeting. If the approval of more than one class of shares is required, a quorum of each class of shares must be present. A quorum is a majority of shares outstanding, unless a greater percentage is established in the articles. The president or the chairman of the board usually presides at shareholders' meetings. Minutes of shareholders' meetings are usually kept by the secretary.

A majority of the votes cast at the shareholders' meeting will decide issues that are put to a vote. If the approval of more than one class of shares is required, a majority of the votes cast by each class must favor the issue. The articles may require a greater than majority vote. Ordinarily, a shareholder is entitled to cast as many votes as he has shares.

Shareholders have a right of *full participation* in shareholders' meetings. This includes the right to offer resolutions, to speak for and against proposed resolutions, and to ask questions of the officers of the corporation.

Typical shareholder resolutions are aimed at protecting or enhancing the interests of minority shareholders and promoting current social issues. Proposals have included limiting corporate charitable contributions, restricting the production of nuclear power, banning the manufacture of weapons, and requiring the protection of the environment.

Shareholder Action without a Meeting

Generally, shareholders can act only at a properly called meeting. However, the MBCA permits shareholders to act without a meeting if *all of the shareholders entitled to vote consent in writing* to the action.

Shareholders' Election of Directors

Straight Voting

The most important shareholder voting right exercised at a shareholder meeting is the right to elect the directors. Normally, directors are elected by a single class of shareholders in **straight voting,** in which each share has one vote for each new director to be elected. With straight voting, a shareholder may vote for as many nominees as there are directors to be elected; a shareholder may cast for each such nominee as many votes as she has shares. For example, in a director election in which 15 people have been nominated for 5 director positions, a shareholder with 100 shares can vote for up to 5 nominees and can cast up to 100 votes for each of those 5 nominees.

Under straight voting, the nominees with the most votes are elected. Consequently, straight voting allows a majority shareholder to elect the entire board of directors. Thus, minority shareholders are unable to elect any representatives to the board without the cooperation of the majority shareholder.

Straight voting is also a problem in close corporations in which a few shareholders own equal numbers of shares. In such corporations, no shareholder individually controls the corporation, yet if the holders of a majority of the shares act together, those holders will elect all of the directors and control the corporation. Such control may be exercised to the detriment of the other shareholders.

Two alternatives to straight voting aid minority shareholders' attempts to gain representation on the board and prevent harmful coalitions in close corporations: cumulative voting and classes of shares.

Cumulative Voting

With cumulative voting, a corporation allows a shareholder to cumulate her votes by multiplying the number of directors to be elected by the shareholder's number of shares. A shareholder may then allocate her votes among the nominees as she chooses. She may vote for only as many nominees as there are directors to be elected, but she may vote for fewer nominees. For example, she may choose to cast all of her votes for only one nominee.

See Figure 1 for a further explanation of the mechanics of cumulative voting.

Figure 1   *Cumulative Voting Formula*

The formula for determining the minimum number of shares required to elect a desired number of directors under cumulative voting is:

$$X = \frac{S \times R}{D + 1} + 1$$

X = Number of shares needed to elect the desired number of directors

S = Total number of shares voting at the shareholders' meeting

R = Number of director representatives desired

D = Total number of directors to be elected at the meeting

Example: Sarah Smiles wants to elect two of the five directors of Oates Corporation. One thousand shares will be voted. In this case:

$S = 1,000$

$R = 2$

$D = 5$

Therefore:

$$X = 333.33$$

Fractions are ignored; thus, Sarah will need to hold at least 333 shares to be able to elect two directors.

Classes of Shares

A corporation may have several classes of shares. The two most common classes are *common shares* and *preferred shares,* but a corporation may have several classes of common shares and several classes of preferred shares. Many close corporations have two or more classes of common shares with different voting rights. Each class may be entitled to elect one or more directors, in order to balance power in a corporation.

For example, suppose a corporation has four directors and 100 shares held by four shareholders—each of whom owns 25 shares. With straight voting and no classes of shares, no shareholder owns enough shares to elect himself as a director, because 51 shares are necessary to elect a director. Suppose, however, that the corporation has four classes of shares, each with the right to elect one of the directors. Each class of shares is issued to only one shareholder. Now, as the sole owner of a class of shares entitling the class to elect one director, each shareholder can elect himself to the board.

Using classes of shares is the cleanest way to allocate among shareholders the power to elect directors, as well as allocate equity ownership of the corporation. To protect such allocations, however, the articles should require approval of every class of shares to change the rights of any class or to create a new class of shares.

Shareholder Control Devices

While cumulative voting and class voting are two useful methods by which shareholders can allocate or acquire voting control of a corporation, there are other devices that may also be used for these purposes: voting trusts; shareholder voting agreements; and proxies, especially irrevocable proxies.

Voting Trusts   With a **voting trust,** shareholders transfer their shares to one or more voting trustees and receive voting trust certificates in exchange. The shareholders retain many of their rights, including the right to receive dividends, but the voting trustees vote for directors and other matters submitted to shareholders.

The purpose of a voting trust is to control the corporation through the concentration of shareholder voting power in the voting trustees, who often are participating shareholders. If several minority shareholders collectively own a majority of the shares of a corporation, they may create a voting trust and thereby control the corporation. You may ask why shareholders need a voting trust when they are in apparent agreement on how to vote their shares. The reason is that they may have disputes in the future that could prevent the shareholders from agreeing how to vote. The voting trust ensures that the shareholder group will control the corporation despite the emergence of differences.

The MBCA limits the duration of voting trusts to 10 years, though all or part of the participating shareholders may agree to extend the term for another 10 years. Also, a voting trust must be made public, with copies of the voting trust document available for inspection at the corporation's offices.

Shareholder Voting Agreements   As an alternative to a voting trust, shareholders may merely agree how they will vote their shares. For example, shareholders collectively owning a majority of the shares may agree to vote for each other as directors, resulting in each being elected to the board of directors.

A shareholder voting agreement must be written; only shareholders signing the agreement are bound by it. When a shareholder refuses to vote as agreed, courts specifically enforce the agreement.

Shareholder voting agreements have two advantages over voting trusts. First, their duration may be *perpetual.* Second, they may be kept secret from the other shareholders; they usually do not have to be filed in the corporation's offices.

Proxies A shareholder may appoint a **proxy** to vote his shares. If several minority shareholders collectively own a majority of the shares of a corporation, they may appoint a proxy to vote their shares and thereby control the corporation. The ordinary proxy has only a limited duration—11 months under the MBCA—unless a longer term is specified. Also, the ordinary proxy is *revocable* at any time. As a result, there is no guarantee that control agreements accomplished through the use of revocable proxies will survive future shareholder disputes.

However, a proxy is *irrevocable* if it is coupled with an interest. A proxy is coupled with an interest when, among other things, the person holding the proxy is a party to a shareholder voting agreement or a buy-and-sell agreement. The principal use of irrevocable proxies is in conjunction with shareholder voting agreements.

In the *RHCS* case, the court found that the parties created only a revocable proxy when they wanted a long-term shareholder voting agreement. The case is a good example of the need for careful drafting of corporate documents.

Reynolds Health Care Services, Inc. v. HMNH, Inc.
217 S.W.3d 797 (Ark. Sup. Ct. 2005)

John Reynolds was the sole shareholder and manager of his family's longtime business, the Hillsboro Manor Nursing Home, Inc., in El Dorado, Arkansas. In 1993, Reynolds needed capital to expand the nursing home, so he approached Dr. James Sheppard, who contacted three additional investors: Sheppard's two brothers, Andrew and Courtney Sheppard, and his brother-in-law, Eugene Bilo. The Sheppards and Bilo formed a corporation called HMNH, Inc., to acquire 80 percent ownership of Hillsboro Manor. HMNH, Inc., made a contract with Reynolds Health Care Services, Inc. (RHCS), a corporation in which Reynolds was the sole shareholder. Under the contract, RHCS agreed to manage the nursing home in return for 6 percent of HMNH's gross revenues. HMNH agreed to provide adequate working capital and oversight on budgets, policies, and personnel. Of course, RHCS hired Reynolds as administrator of the facility.

To buy the nursing home, HMNH and Hillsboro Manor Nursing Home, Inc., entered into a stock purchase agreement by which HMNH purchased all of the stock of Hillsboro Manor Nursing Home, Inc., for $1,804,000. Hillsboro Manor Nursing Home, Inc., was merged into HMNH, Inc., with the three Sheppards, Bilo, and RHCS each receiving 20 shares of stock of the 100 outstanding shares of stock in HMNH. The Sheppards and Bilo also agreed to give RHCS the power to vote 7.5 of each of their shares on any matter submitted to shareholders in the next 20 years. The affect of the voting agreement was to give RHCS 50 percent voting control, which meant that Reynolds, who owned RHCS, could veto any matter submitted to HMNH's shareholders.

By 1999, HMNH had become concerned with the way Reynolds was running the nursing home. The shareholders held a meeting on September 14, 2000, at which the Sheppards and Bilo were present, but Reynolds was absent. The Sheppards voted their combined 60 shares to elect a new board of directors comprising the three Sheppards, Bilo, and Reynolds. At the directors' meeting, held immediately thereafter, all five men were elected as officers of HMNH, although Reynolds—while now present—abstained from the vote. Andrew Sheppard then made a motion that the board of directors authorize its attorney to institute a lawsuit in the name of HMNH against Reynolds and RHCS to recover damages caused by RHCS's breach of the management contract. The Sheppards and Bilo voted to adopt the resolution. On January 19, 2001, HMNH filed suit against RHCS and Reynolds, alleging that RHCS had breached the management contract. Reynolds and RHCS asked the trial court to dismiss the lawsuit on the grounds that HMNH's board had no authority to bring the lawsuit. Reynolds and RHCS argued that the directors were not properly elected, because the Sheppards voted all their shares to elect the new directors, a violation of the shareholder voting agreement that gave RHCS the power to vote 7.5 of each of their shares. The trial court disagreed, ruling that the voting agreement was merely a revocable proxy, which the Sheppards revoked at the September 2000 shareholder meeting, and therefore, the Sheppards could vote all of their shares. Reynolds and RHCS appealed to the Arkansas Supreme Court.

Glaze, Justice

On appeal, RHCS argues that the trial court erred in refusing to enforce the parties' voting agreement. Ark. Code Ann. §4-27-731 provides as follows:

(a) Two (2) or more shareholders may provide for the manner in which they will vote their shares by signing an agreement

for that purpose. A voting agreement created under this section is not subject to the provisions of §4-27-730.

(b) A voting agreement created under this section is specifically enforceable.

This statute was adopted as part of the Arkansas Business Corporation Act, and the language used therein was taken from the

Model Business Corporation Act. The "Historical Background" information that accompanies the Model Act provides the following discussion:

> A voting agreement (sometimes called a pooling agreement) is an agreement among shareholders relating to the voting of shares; it is primarily used as a means to effect a specific allocation of representation on the board of directors of a closely held corporation. It differs fundamentally from a voting trust, which involves a transfer of the legal title of shares to the trustees and a change in the record ownership of the shares. *Model Bus. Corp. Act* §7.31 (Supp. 1996).

A voting agreement is also distinguished from an irrevocable proxy in that it does not necessarily result in the creation of an agency relationship, and need not involve the use of a proxy to effectuate it. However, the line of demarcation is not always clear, and some voting agreements have been treated as irrevocable proxies.

In a broad sense, the term "shareholders' agreement" refers to any agreement among two or more shareholders regarding their conduct in relation to the corporation whose shares they own. Such agreements are generally utilized in closely held corporations, and they may be used to guarantee to a minority shareholder such things as restrictions on the transfer of stock; a veto power over hiring and decisions concerning salaries, corporate policies or distribution of earnings; or procedures for resolving disputes or making fundamental changes in the corporate charter.

Shareholder or voting agreements differ from proxies in that a proxy is simply an authority given by the holder of the stock who has the right to vote it to another to exercise the holder's voting rights. Thus, a proxy differs from a voting agreement in that the former gives another person the authority to vote one's shares, while the latter purports to direct how the other person is to vote.

RHCS argues that it entered into a voting agreement with the Sheppards and Bilo when they signed a document titled "Option to Purchase Stock." In particular, RHCS points to the following language in support of its contention that a voting agreement was created:

> [HMNH] shall grant to [RHCS] a proxy to vote one-half of the issued and outstanding shares of stock of HMNH, Inc. pending the term of this option to purchase stock, which proxy shall be reduced to twenty-five percent of the issued and outstanding shares of stock of the corporation for a period of twenty years from the effective date of the Agreement to Provide Management Services to a Health Care Facility executed the 8th day of January, 1993, as set forth in paragraph IV thereof, by and between Reynolds Health Care Services, Inc., and HMNH, Inc., upon the exercise of this option and transfer to [RHCS] of the shares of stock subject to this option.

A subsequent agreement among the shareholders, dated September 19, 1996, provided that the Sheppards and Bilo "shall execute a proxy to Reynolds Health Care Services, Inc., appointing Reynolds Health Care Services, Inc. as [their] proxy to vote 7.5 shares of each of the said shareholder's stock held in HMNH, Inc." Those proxies were executed by each of the Sheppards and Bilo on October 21, 1996; the proxy agreements provided as follows:

> I, the undersigned shareholder of HMNH, Inc., an Arkansas corporation, do hereby appoint Reynolds Health Care Services, Inc., an Arkansas corporation, my true and lawful attorney and agent, for me and in my name, place and stead to vote as my proxy 7.5 shares of stock held by me in HMNH, Inc. at any stockholders' meetings to be held between the date of this proxy and 20 years from the effective date of the Agreement to Provide Management Services to a Health Care Facility dated January 7, 1993, as set forth in Paragraph IV thereof, by and between Reynolds Health Care Services, Inc., and HMNH, Inc., and I authorize Reynolds Health Care Services, Inc. to act for me and in my name and stead as fully as I could act if I were personally present, giving to Reynolds Health Care Services, Inc., attorney and agent, full power of substitution.

The trial court found that these agreements were not voting agreements, but rather were revocable proxies. Under Ark. Code Ann. §4-27-722 (Repl. 2001), proxies are revocable by a shareholder "unless the appointment form conspicuously states that it is irrevocable and the appointment is coupled with an interest." An appointment coupled with an interest includes the appointment of "a party to a voting agreement created under §4-27-731." None of the proxy agreements stated conspicuously on its face that it was irrevocable; indeed, in its reply brief, RHCS abandons its argument that the proxies were irrevocable. Nonetheless, RHCS maintains that the proxies "were merely the means of implementing the parties' foundational voting agreement," by which the Sheppards and Bilo gave RHCS the right to vote fifty percent of their shares in HMNH for twenty years.

However, we conclude that the document that RHCS calls a "voting agreement" is nothing more than a revocable appointment of proxy. The plain language of the agreement says nothing about how the stock is to be voted; it merely gives RHCS the right to vote a percentage of the stock. Because the agreement does not "provide for the manner in which" the shares are to be voted, it is not a voting agreement; it is a proxy.

Further, the proxies assigned to RHCS were revocable. Thus, the Sheppards and Bilo were acting within their rights as shareholders when they voted to revoke their proxies at the September 2000 shareholders' meeting. Accordingly, the trial court did not err when it concluded that the actions of the duly elected board of directors in voting to authorize the instant lawsuit were valid.

Judgment for HMNH affirmed.

Ethics in Action

By using classes of shares (or a perpetual shareholder voting agreement), shareholders that individually are minority shareholders but collectively control a majority of the corporation's shares may control the corporation absolutely. For example, suppose five shareholders create a corporation and decide at incorporation that it will have five classes of shares, one for each of the five shareholders. They decide that each of the five classes will elect its own director to the board of directors and that the consent of each class is required to amend the articles of incorporation, such as to increase the number of authorized shares of a class or to create a new class of shares. They also could agree that no shares may be issued without the consent of each class of shares. In the future, if they want to issue shares to employees of the corporation or public investors, by a vote of the five classes of shareholders they could create a class of shares that has a small (say, 20 percent) equity interest in the corporation,

either has no right to vote for directors or elects a nonvoting director, has a preferential right to dividends, and has no right to veto any action the five original classes of shares approve. The creation of the new share class would permit the five original shareholders to continue their control of the corporation while receiving an infusion of capital into the company.

- Do you think it is ethical for the five original shareholders to dominate the corporation in this way? If you were one of the five original shareholders, would you set up a different equity structure? Would you give more rights to the shareholders of the class with limited rights?
- Would you buy shares of the class that has limited rights? After you buy those shares, would it be ethical for you to argue for greater rights?
- Would your answers change if the corporation became a public company with over 2,000 shareholders?

Fundamental Corporate Changes

Other matters besides the election of directors require shareholder action, some because they make fundamental changes in the structure or business of the corporation.

Because the articles of incorporation embody the basic contract between a corporation and its shareholders, shareholders must approve most **amendments of the articles of incorporation.** For example, when the articles are amended to increase the number of authorized shares or reduce the dividend rights of preferred shareholders, shareholder approval is needed.

A **merger** is a transaction in which one corporation merges into a second corporation. Usually, the first corporation dissolves; the second corporation takes all the business and assets of both corporations and becomes liable for the debts of both corporations. Usually, the shareholders of the dissolved corporation become shareholders of the surviving corporation. Ordinarily, both corporations' shareholders must approve a merger.

Corporation law allows great flexibility in the terms of a merger. For example, a merger may freeze out minority shareholders by paying them cash only while allowing majority shareholders to remain as shareholders of the surviving corporation. Freeze-outs are covered in Chapter 43.

A **consolidation** is similar to a merger except that both old corporations go out of existence and a new corporation takes the business, assets, and liabilities of the old corporations. Both corporations' shareholders must approve the

consolidation. Modern corporate practice makes consolidations obsolete, since it is usually desirable to have one of the old corporations survive. The MBCA does not recognize consolidations. However, the effect of a consolidation can be achieved by creating a new corporation and merging the two old corporations into it.

A **share exchange** is a transaction by which one corporation becomes the owner of all of the outstanding shares of a second corporation through a *compulsory* exchange of shares: The shareholders of the second corporation are compelled to exchange their shares for shares of the first corporation. The second corporation remains in existence and becomes a wholly owned subsidiary of the first corporation. Only the selling shareholders must approve the share exchange.

A **sale of all or substantially all of the assets** of the business other than in the regular course of business must be approved by the shareholders of the selling corporation, since it drastically changes the shareholders' investment. Thus, a corporation's sale of all its real property and equipment is a sale of substantially all its assets, even though the corporation continues its business by leasing the assets back from the purchaser. However, a corporation that sells its building, but retains its machinery with the intent of continuing operations at another location, has not sold all or substantially all of its assets. Under the MBCA, a corporation that retains at least 25 percent of its business activity and either its income or revenue has not disposed of substantially all its assets.

A **dissolution** is the first step in the termination of the corporation's business. The typical dissolution requires

The Global Business Environment

In recent years, shareholder activism and discontent has been exported from the United States to affect corporations based in other nations. In some cases, American shareholders of non-American corporations have exercised their rights by attempting to oppose management through the ballot box or takeovers. In other cases, citizens of other nations have taken cues from their American cousins and attempted to assert their rights as shareholders.

For example, in late 2005, VNU NV, the Netherlands-based publishing and market research firm, faced pressure from a shareholder group that included Boston-based Fidelity Investments. The shareholder group, which held 40 percent of VNU's shares, opposed VNU's bid to acquire IMS Health, Inc., a Connecticut-based corporation. When shareholders first announced their opposition to the acquisition, VNU attempted to placate them by selling some assets, increasing a share buyback, and eventually replacing its CEO. Refusing to be appeased, the shareholders continued their opposition to VNU's acquisition of IMS Health.

Earlier in 2005, shareholders in Deutsche Borse AG, the German stock exchange company, prevented the company from completing an attempt to acquire London Stock Exchange PLC. The shareholders eventually forced the resignation of longtime CEO Werner Seifert. Despite Seifert's turning Deutsche Borse into the largest stock exchange during his 12-year tenure, his misjudgment of shareholder opposition to what he thought was the best strategy for the company ultimately led to his downfall.

In 2007 and 2008, U.S. activist investor Knight Vinke Asset Management engaged U.K.-based HSBC in a review of strategy in light of HSBC's significant losses in the U.S. subprime loan market. Knight Vinke has called on HSBC's board to appoint independent financial advisers to review future subprime loan business, criticized its new executive compensation plan, and expressed concern about the independence of its board of directors.

---

shareholder approval. Dissolution of corporations is covered more fully at the end of this chapter.

The articles of incorporation and the bylaws may require or permit other matters to be submitted for shareholder approval. For example, loans to officers, self-dealing transactions, and indemnifications of managers for litigation expenses may be approved by shareholders. Also, many of the states require shareholder approval of share option plans for high level executive officers, but the MBCA does not.

Procedures Required

Similar procedures must be met to effect each of the above fundamental changes. The procedures include approval of the board of directors, notice to all of the shareholders whether or not they are entitled to vote, and majority approval of the votes held by shareholders entitled to vote under the statute, articles, or bylaws. Majority approval will be insufficient if a corporation has a supermajority shareholder voting requirement, such as one requiring two-thirds approval.

If there are two or more classes of shares, the articles may provide that matters voted on by shareholders must be approved by each class substantially affected by the proposed transaction. For example, a merger may have to be approved by a majority of the preferred shareholders and a majority of the common shareholders. As an alternative, the articles may require only the approval of the shareholders as a whole.

Under the MBCA, voting by classes is required for mergers, share exchanges, and amendments of the articles if these would substantially affect the rights of the classes. For example, the approval of preferred shareholders is required if a merger would change the dividend rights of preferred shareholders.

In many states, no approval of shareholders of the *surviving corporation* is required for a merger *if* the merger does not fundamentally alter the character of the business or substantially reduce the shareholders' voting or dividend rights.

Also, many statutes, including the MBCA, permit a merger between a parent corporation and its subsidiary without the approval of the shareholders of either corporation. Instead, the board of directors of the parent approves the merger and sends a copy of the merger plan to the subsidiary's shareholders. This simplified merger is called a **short-form merger.** It is available only if the parent owns a high percentage of the subsidiary's shares—90 percent under the MBCA and the Delaware statute.

Dissenters' Rights

Many times, shareholders approve a corporate action by less than a unanimous vote, indicating that some shareholders oppose the action. For the most part, the dissenting shareholders have little recourse. Their choice is to remain shareholders or to sell their shares. For close corporation shareholders, there is no choice—the dissenting close corporation shareholder has no ready market for her shares, so she will remain a shareholder.

Some corporate transactions, however, so materially change a shareholder's investment in the corporation or have such an adverse effect on the value of a shareholder's shares that it has been deemed unfair to require the dissenting shareholder either to remain a shareholder (because there is no fair market for the shares) or to suffer a loss in value when he sells his shares on a market that has been adversely affected by the news of the corporate action. Corporate law has therefore responded by creating **dissenters' rights** (right of appraisal) for shareholders who disagree with specified fundamental corporate transactions. Dissenters' rights require the corporation to pay dissenting shareholders the *fair value* of their shares.

Under the MBCA, the dissenters' rights cover mergers, short-form mergers, share exchanges, significant amendments of the articles of incorporation, and sales of all or substantially all the assets other than in the ordinary course of business. Some statutes cover consolidations also.

A dissenting shareholder seeking payment of the fair value of his shares must have the *right to vote* on the action to which he objects; however, a shareholder of a subsidiary in a short-form merger has dissenters' rights despite his lack of voting power. In addition, the shareholder must *not vote in favor* of the transaction. The shareholder may either vote against the action or abstain from voting.

The MBCA and many states' statutes exclude from dissenters' rights shares that are traded on a recognized securities exchange such as the New York Stock Exchange. Instead, these statutes expect a shareholder to sell his shares on the stock exchange if he dissents to the corporate action. The MBCA also excludes shares held by at least 2,000 holders or having a market value of at least $20 million.

Generally, a shareholder must notify the corporation of his intent to seek payment before the shareholders have voted on the action. Next, the corporation informs a dissenting shareholder how to demand payment. After the dissenting shareholder demands payment, the corporation and the shareholder negotiate a mutually acceptable price. If they cannot agree, a court will determine the fair value of the shares and order the corporation to pay that amount.

To determine fair value, most judges use the **Delaware Block Method,** a weighted average of several valuation techniques—such as market value, comparisons with other similar companies, net present value of future cash flows, and book value. Ironically, the Supreme Court of Delaware has abandoned the Delaware Block Method, recognizing the need for courts to value shares by methods generally considered acceptable to the financial community. The MBCA values shares using "customary and current valuation concepts and techniques generally employed for similar businesses."

The Delaware appraisal statute provides that a court:

> shall appraise the shares, determining their fair value exclusive of any element of value arising from the accomplishment or expectation of the merger or consolidation, together with a fair rate of interest, if any, to be paid upon the amount determined to be the fair value. In determining such fair value, the Court shall take into account all relevant factors. 8 Del. Code § 262(h).

In *Weinberger v. UOP,*[1] the Delaware Supreme Court reconciled the dual mandates of section 262(h), which direct a court to determine fair value based upon all relevant factors, yet exclude any element of value arising from the accomplishment or expectation of the merger. In making that reconciliation, the *Weinberger* court wrote:

> Only the speculative elements of value that may arise from the "accomplishment or expectation" of the merger are excluded. We take this to be a very narrow exception to the appraisal process, designed to eliminate use of *pro forma* data and projections of a speculative variety relating to the completion of a merger. But elements of future value, including the nature of the enterprise, which are known or susceptible of proof as of the date of the merger and not the product of speculation, may be considered. When the trial court deems it appropriate, fair value also includes any damages, resulting from the taking, which the stockholders sustain as a class. If that was not the case, then the obligation to consider "all relevant factors" in the valuation process would be eroded.[2]

In the following case, the court applied the *Weinberger* test when reviewing competing valuations of minority shares. The case is a model for sophisticated financial valuations in litigation.

[1]457 A.2d 701 (Del. S. Ct. 1983)
[2]457 A.2d at 713.

Montgomery Cellular Holding Co., Inc. v. Dobler
880 A.2d 206 (Del. S. Ct. 2005)

Price Communications Corporation (Price) owned all the shares of Price Communications Wireless (PCW). PCW owned all the shares of Palmer Wireless Holdings Inc. (Palmer). Palmer owned controlling interests in 16 cellular telephone systems in Georgia, Florida, and Alabama, including Montgomery Cellular Holding Company (MCHC). Palmer owned 94.6 percent of MCHC stock. MCHC was a holding company with no operating assets. MCHC's sole asset was 100 percent of the stock of

Montgomery Cellular Telephone Co. (Montgomery). Montgomery was a cellular telephone system located in the area around Montgomery, Alabama.

As a group, Palmer's holdings formed a valuable cluster of cellular systems in the southeastern United States. Price entered into discussions with various cellular telecommunications system operators about a possible sale of Palmer's cellular systems. Price hired the investment bank, Donaldson, Lufkin & Jenrette (DLJ), to solicit interest in acquiring Palmer. Verizon emerged as the potential acquirer.

In 2000, Price agreed to sell Palmer to Verizon for $2.06 billion. Because Palmer did not control 100 percent of the stock in MCHC and other subsidiaries, the agreement obligated Price to acquire those minority shareholder interests. If Palmer failed to acquire the minority interests, the agreement allowed Verizon to reduce the purchase price by an amount equal to the minority shareholders' pro rata share of fiscal year 2000 EBITDA multiplied by 13.5. To receive the full $2.06 billion purchase price, Price would have to freeze out all the minority shareholders of MCHC. As a result of the agreement, Price had a strong incentive to squeeze out all the minority shareholders at a price that was lower than Verizon's corresponding price reduction.

On June 30, 2001, Price caused Palmer to buy out MCHC's minority shareholders by a short-form merger under Delaware law. In determining the price to be paid to MCHC's minority shareholders, Price made no effort to obtain an independent valuation, which its CEO viewed as "very costly." Instead, Palmer relied on Price's settlement of an appraisal action with the dissenting minority shareholders of a different Palmer subsidiary, Cellular Dynamics (CD).

CD, like MCHC, was the operator of a cellular telephone company in the southeastern United States and, like MCHC, was majority-owned by Price. In 1999, Price bought out the minority shareholders of CD by a short-form merger. After a lengthy negotiation using POPs as the valuation tool, the minority shareholders agreed to a settlement based upon a value of CD derived by multiplying the estimated population by $470 per POP. POP is a shorthand reference to the census population of a specific geographic area. POPs are a common cellular industry metric for valuing cellular systems.

Despite overwhelming evidence that the CD settlement was negotiated using POPs and not EBITDA, Price claimed that it had valued CD's stock using an EBITDA multiplier of 10.05 to arrive at the $8,102.23 per share price that was offered to MCHC minority shareholders as fair value. In contrast, multiplying the $470 per POP metric by MCHC's POPs (323,675) would have yielded a value of $15,212.74 per share.

Although Price had bought out MCHC minority shareholders and was entitled to receive the full agreed merger price of $2.06 billion, the initial Verizon deal was not consummated. Later, Price and Verizon agreed to a reduced purchase price of $1.7 billion. That second transaction was consummated on August 15, 2002.

Gerhard Dobler and other minority MCHC shareholders challenged the buyout price of $8,102.23 per share, and they sued Price, Palmer, and MCHC in the Delaware Court of Chancery. At the trial, the minority shareholders' expert, Marc Sherman, previously a KPMG partner in charge of its corporate transactions practice, valued MCHC at $21,346 per share. MCHC's expert, Kenneth D. Gartrell, previously an Ernst & Young auditor, testified that the stand-alone value of MCHC was $7,840 per share.

Although both experts used similar methods to value MCHC, Sherman looked to third-party experts to create his forecasts, whereas Gartrell did not consult outside appraisers or other sources of relevant information. Moreover, only Sherman performed a comparable transaction analysis.

MCHC's expert, Gartrell, employed two valuation methodologies: a comparable company analysis and a discounted cash flow (DCF) analysis. The Court of Chancery found that Gartrell's valuation approach was legally and factually flawed, and must be disregarded in its entirety, for three reasons. First, Gartrell's overall theoretical framework was invalid as a matter of law, because Gartrell valued MCHC as if it were not a going concern that had contractual relationships with other cellular providers. Second, Gartrell's DCF analysis was flawed because he used a generic growth rate (the long-term growth rate of GNP) as his growth rate for MCHC without any valid, credible explanation and despite his having had access to industry-specific growth rates; Gartrell used a constant growth rate, which would yield the same value for MCHC regardless of the time frame; and Gartrell created the financial projections based entirely on his own judgment, without reference to other available sources of relevant information. Third, the Court of Chancery found that Gartrell's comparable company analysis was invalid because of his methodology and his data. Gartrell switched between the mean and the median at critical points. Had Gartrell used the mean numbers consistently throughout, the value of MCHC based on EBITDA would be over $163 million, which when added to the nonoperating assets, would be $183 million—a figure much closer to the value reached by the shareholders' expert.

The Court of Chancery accepted the shareholders' expert, Sherman's, valuation of MCHC with some modification, and it valued the minority shares at $19,621.74. MCHC asked the Delaware Supreme Court to review the chancery court's nearly full acceptance of Sherman's valuation. MCHC did not appeal the court's rejection of MCHC's expert's valuation.

Jacobs, Justice

The shareholders' expert, Marc Sherman, performed three different financial analyses of MCHC: a comparable transactions analysis, a DCF analysis, and a comparable company analysis. In his comparable transactions analysis, Sherman split the selected comparable transactions into three categories: similar sized transactions, the initial Verizon transaction, and the CD settlement. For the similar sized transactions category, Sherman considered five transactions that occurred between May 2000 and January 2001, each involving a cellular company with approximately the same number of POPs. The remaining two categories (the initial Verizon transaction and the CD settlement) involved single transactions that were included in the analysis because they were related to the sale of MCHC.

Sherman then analyzed each category using his four cellular system metrics (POPs, subscribers, EBITDA, and revenue). For each metric, Sherman computed a value of MCHC based on the category of comparable transactions, and then weighted these values to derive his final overall valuation. Sherman did that as follows: he first weighted the metrics based on their importance in valuing cellular companies. He then weighted the category of comparable transactions within each metric. The result of that process is shown *infra* on the table:

Category	Valuation	Metric Weighting	Category Weighting
POPs		45%	
Verizon Transaction	$199,278,316		20%
CD Settlement	$199,286,698		10%
Similar Sized Transactions	$136,352,297		15%
Subscribers		20%	
Verizon Transaction	$226,758,135		15%
CD Settlement	$225,865,136		5%
Operating Cash Flows		25%	
Verizon Transaction	$160,650,176		20%
CD Settlement	$226,738,142		5%
Revenue		10%	
Verizon Transaction	$236,517,971		7% (sic)
CD Settlement	$224,240,681		7% (sic)
Total		100%	100%

Multiplying the valuations by their respective weightings, Sherman computed a value of $192 million based on comparable transactions. To that figure he added the $20 million value of the non–operating assets to arrive at a comparable transactions value for MCHC of $212 million.

Sherman also performed a DCF analysis. Because of the lack of management projections, Sherman created forecasts of MCHC's cash flows based on predictions by others for the cellular industry and the economy. Sherman relied primarily on Paul Kagan, an outside industry expert. Sherman also looked to industry growth reports that showed an annual growth rate for the wireless industry of 16 percent.

The next step in Sherman's DCF analysis was to determine the discount rate using a weighted average cost of capital (WACC) approach. Applying that approach to the inputs he determined for each component of the WACC formula, Sherman arrived at a discount rate of 13.25 percent.

For his DCF projection period, Sherman used a ten-year period from June 1, 2001 to May 31, 2011. Before projecting the cash flows, however, Sherman first adjusted them by removing two "irregularities": (i) a nonrecurring $861,000 bad debt expense resulting from Montgomery having installed a new billing system, and (ii) the rent of $638,000 MCHC paid annually to Old North, a wholly owned subsidiary of Palmer. Lastly, using a capitalization rate of 9.25 percent and a growth rate of 4 percent, Sherman calculated a terminal value of $258 million.

From these inputs, Sherman arrived at a final enterprise (DCF) valuation of $150 million for Montgomery as a going concern, operating asset of MCHC. To that figure Sherman added the value of Montgomery's non–operating assets, which increased his valuation to $170 million. Finally, to that sum, Sherman applied a control premium of 31 percent, thereby increasing his DCF valuation to $216 million.

In his third (comparable company) analysis, Sherman found only two comparable companies, neither of which was similar in size to Montgomery. Sherman excluded companies that had international operations, multiple lines of business, or prepaid customers, as well as companies that used PCS technology. After selecting his comparable companies, Sherman applied the same metrics that he used in his comparable transactions analysis and gave them the same weight. That approach resulted in a valuation of $206 million. After adding in the value of the non–operating assets, Sherman's ultimate comparable company valuation of MCHC was $226 million.

Thus, Sherman's three analyses valued MCHC within a range of from $212 million to $226 million. Sherman derived his final fair value by combining the results of his three analyses into a weighted average, giving 80 percent weight to the comparable transactions value, 15 percent weight to the DCF value, and 5 percent weight to the comparable company value. Sherman's heavy weighting of the comparable transactions analysis reflected his judgment that the transaction data, particularly the initial Verizon transaction price, were the best indication of value for MCHC. In contrast, Sherman gave little weight to the DCF analysis because of his concerns about the reliability of MCHC's financial data and the lack of management projections. He gave even less weight to the comparable company valuation because of the scarcity of publicly traded companies to which MCHC could reliably be compared. Combining the results of the three analyses into a weighted average yielded a fair value for MCHC of $213,455,619, or $21,346 per share.

In making its independent determination of MCHC's fair value, the Court of Chancery adopted Sherman's overall valuation framework, and most of Sherman's inputs. The Court made adjustments to some of the inputs that it did not adopt. The result was to reduce Sherman's valuation of $213,455,619 ($21,346 per share) to a final valuation of MCHC of $196,217,373, or $19,621.74 per share.

First, with respect to the comparable transaction analysis, the Vice Chancellor determined that the Verizon transaction price and the CD settlement price were valid inputs. But, the Court adjusted Sherman's CD settlement price by eliminating what Sherman perceived (incorrectly, the Court determined) to be a minority discount. The Court then independently increased the CD settlement figure ($470 per POP) by 15 percent to eliminate a so-called "settlement haircut," to arrive at a value of $540.50 per POP.

Second, the Court adjusted Sherman's DCF valuation by eliminating the 31 percent control premium that Sherman had added to his DCF value. That adjustment reduced Sherman's DCF valuation of MCHC from $216 million to $170 million.

Third, and most significant, the Court adjusted the weights that Sherman had accorded to the values derived by his three valuation methods. Sherman had weighted the comparable transaction value at 80 percent of total fair value. Because the effect of that weighting was to give the Verizon transaction an overall weight of 50 percent—a weight the Court found to be "too significant"—the Vice Chancellor reduced the weight accorded to the comparable transactions valuation from 80 percent to 65 percent.

Finally, because Sherman had corrected the figures derived from MCHC's financial statements in a reasonable manner, and also had looked to third party authority for guidance on other inputs, the Court determined that the 15 percent weight Sherman had accorded to the DCF valuation should be increased to 30 percent.

On appeal, MCHC does not challenge the Court of Chancery's adoption of Sherman's overall valuation framework. Instead, MCHC limits its attack to selected inputs to the valuation model that Sherman used.

Specifically, MCHC contends that the Court of Chancery erred in three different respects, namely by: (1) including in its comparable transactions analysis the price that Verizon Wireless initially agreed to pay to acquire Palmer; (2) adding a 15 percent premium to the price that the minority shareholders of CD, a separate Palmer subsidiary, had agreed to accept to settle their appraisal action; (3) subtracting the management fees that Palmer charged to MCHC, as reported in MCHC's financial statement.

We conclude that none of the challenged findings is clearly wrong, and indeed, all have firm support in the evidentiary record.

1. The Verizon Transaction

MCHC argues that the Court of Chancery erroneously included the Verizon transaction, because the transaction price contained synergistic elements of value whose inclusion is proscribed by 8 *Del. C.* § 262. That statute requires the Court of Chancery to appraise the subject shares by "determining their fair value exclusive of any element of value arising from the accomplishment or expectation of the merger or consolidation." In determining statutory "fair value," the Court must value the appraisal company as a "going concern." In performing its valuation, the Court of Chancery is free to consider the price actually derived from the sale of the company being valued, but only after the synergistic elements of value are excluded from that price.

The Court found Palmer offered *no business-related* combinatorial value to MCHC, and MCHC was probably the most valuable company in Palmer's cluster. Thus, the Vice Chancellor concluded, the only synergies included in the purchase price were dealmaking—not business-related—synergies.

That conclusion is supported by the evidence. The Verizon merger with Palmer did not add any synergistic business value to MCHC because Montgomery was a metropolitan statistical area (MSA), which is generally more valuable than a rural service area (RSA), and Montgomery had superior demographics relative to Palmer's other cellular holdings. Therefore, the only synergies required to be eliminated from the Verizon transaction price were the Palmer-related "deal-making" synergies. The question became how to determine the value of those synergies.

The Court of Chancery was unable precisely to quantify those "deal-making" synergies, because MCHC did not present any reliable evidence at trial of what those synergies were worth. Having received no helpful evidence from MCHC, the

Court of Chancery had to—and did—account for the synergies in a different way, namely, by reducing the total weight accorded to the comparable transactions component of the overall valuation, from 80 percent to 65 percent. Although in a perfect world that may not have been the ideal solution, in this world it was the only one permitted by the record evidence, given MCHC's failure to obtain a pre–merger valuation and to present legally reliable expert valuation testimony during the trial.

MCHC next contends that including the Verizon transaction in its comparable transaction analysis led the Court of Chancery to commit reversible error by not valuing MCHC as a going concern. Delaware law requires that in an appraisal action, a corporation must be valued as a going concern based on the "operative reality" of the company as of the time of the merger. In determining a corporation's "operative reality," the use of "speculative" elements of future value arising from the expectation or accomplishment of a merger is proscribed, but elements of future value that are known or susceptible of proof as of the date of the merger may be considered. Any facts which were known or which could be ascertained as of the date of the merger and which throw any light on future prospects of the merged corporation are not only pertinent to an inquiry as to the value of the dissenting stockholder's interest, but must be considered by the agency fixing the value.

MCHC argues that the Verizon transaction was not part of MCHC's "operative reality." At the time of the MCHC–Palmer merger, the transaction was not expected to close. MCHC characterizes the Verizon transaction as a mere "option" whose exercise was entirely within Verizon's control and which neither Price nor Verizon realistically expected to close at the time the MCHC–Palmer merger occurred.

The Vice Chancellor rejected MCHC's argument that because the Verizon–Price agreement was conditional, it was impermissibly "speculative" and did not reflect MCHC's going concern value. The Court of Chancery found that the Verizon transaction was more than an offer. Rather, it was a validly executed enforceable transaction agreement which bound Verizon to the implied covenant of good faith and fair dealing that inheres in every contract.

2. Adjustment of the CD Settlement Price to Eliminate the Settlement Discount

MCHC's second claim of error is that the Court of Chancery improperly adjusted the "CD settlement" price to eliminate what the Court regarded as a "settlement haircut."

The CD settlement was a settlement of litigation that arose out of Price's elimination, in a short form merger, of the minority shareholders of Cellular Dynamics (CD), a cellular company located in the southeastern United States. The minority shareholders of CD sued, and after protracted negotiations the

parties agreed to a settlement price of $470 per POP. For purposes of valuing MCHC, both parties agreed that the CD settlement was a comparable transaction. Accordingly, Sherman utilized the $470 per POP metric in performing his comparable transactions analysis.

The Vice Chancellor upheld Sherman's use of the CD settlement price, but adjusted that price to reflect what the Court described as a "settlement haircut"; that is, a discount that reflected factors unrelated to CD's fair value, such as the costs of litigation and the uncertainty of the appraisal action's outcome. To eliminate that settlement discount, the Court of Chancery increased the CD settlement price by 15 percent, thereby reaching a value of $540.50 per POP as more fairly reflective of the value of CD. The Court then included that upwardly–adjusted CD settlement value in the comparable transactions analysis.

There was ample evidence to support the Court of Chancery's finding that the CD settlement reflected a discount from CD's fair value. The record included an exchange of several letters between Price and CD during settlement negotiations. Those letters included an offer by CD, on December 19, 2000, to settle the litigation for $500 per POP. In that December 19 letter, the CD minority shareholders specifically stated that the $500 per POP offer was less than CD's fair value, but was being made in an effort to resolve the matter quickly. That letter evidences that CD's minority shareholders were willing to settle for an amount below fair value to avoid the costs and delays of litigation.

Although there was no evidence of the precise magnitude of the actual CD settlement discount, the Court of Chancery did not err by selecting 15 percent as a reasonable measure. That percentage was based on evidence that the CD minority shareholders had accepted a price lower than CD's fair value, as well as the Court of Chancery's extensive expertise in the appraisal of corporate enterprises—an expertise that this Court has recognized on several occasions. To reiterate, where, as here, one side of the litigation presents no competent evidence to aid the Court in discharging its duty to make an independent valuation, we will defer to the Vice Chancellor's valuation approach unless it is manifestly unreasonable, *i.e.,* on its face is outside a range of reasonable values.

3. Eliminating the Management Fees Paid by MCHC to Palmer as an Input to the DCF Valuation

MCHC's third claim of error challenges the Court of Chancery's adjustment of MCHC's financial statements to eliminate from the DCF valuation the management fees Palmer had charged MCHC. The Court found that those fees were essentially a pretext, unrelated to the actual furnishing of management services.

Because there were no management projections upon which Sherman could rely to project MCHC's future cash flows,

Sherman had to create his own forecasts. To do that he relied upon various sources, including MCHC's financial statements. But Sherman did not accept MCHC's financial statements at face value. In his review of those statements, he identified several irregularities. The management fees that Palmer charged to MCHC represented one of those irregularities. The evidence established that since 1998, Palmer had charged MCHC more than $3 million in management fees, and that in the first five months of 2001 alone, those fees totaled $603,000. To determine MCHC's future cash flows more accurately, Sherman eliminated those fees.

None of Price's officers who testified were able to explain what management services Palmer had provided to MCHC, or how those management fees were calculated. Indeed, Price's CEO characterized the fees (under oath) as "accounting bullshit." The Court was also troubled by the fact that Palmer charged management fees only to its subsidiaries that had minority shareholders, but not to those subsidiaries that Palmer wholly owned. Tellingly, after Palmer eliminated MCHC's minority shareholders in the merger, Palmer stopped charging management fees to MCHC. That evidence strongly supports the elimination of the management fees as an expense.

Judgment for Dobler affirmed in part and reversed in part. Remanded to the Chancery Court.

Shareholders' Inspection and Information Rights

Inspecting a corporation's books and records is sometimes essential to the exercise of a shareholder's rights. For example, a shareholder may be able to decide how to vote in a director election only after examining corporate financial records that reveal whether the present directors are managing the corporation profitably. Also, a close corporation shareholder may need to look at the books to determine the value of his shares.

Many corporate managers are resistant to shareholders' inspecting the corporation's books and records, charging that shareholders are nuisances or that shareholders often have improper purposes for making such an inspection. Sometimes, management objects solely on the ground that it desires secrecy.

Most of the state corporation statutes specifically grant shareholders inspection rights. The purpose of these statutes is to facilitate the shareholder's inspection of the books and records of corporations whose managements resist or delay proper requests by shareholders. A shareholder's lawyer or accountant may assist the shareholder's exercise of his inspection rights.

The MBCA grants shareholders an **absolute right of inspection** of an alphabetical listing of the shareholders entitled to notice of a meeting, including the number of shares owned. Access to a shareholder list allows a shareholder to contact other shareholders about important matters such as shareholder proposals.

The MBCA also grants an absolute right of inspection of, among other things, the articles, bylaws, and minutes of shareholder meetings within the past three years.

Shareholders have a **qualified right to inspect** other records, however. To inspect accounting records, board and committee minutes, and shareholder minutes more than three years old, a shareholder must make the demand in *good faith* and have a *proper purpose*. Proper purposes include inspecting the books of account to determine the value of shares or the propriety of dividends. On the other hand, learning business secrets and aiding a competitor are clearly improper purposes.

Shareholders also have the right to receive from the corporation **information** that is important to their voting and investing decisions. The MBCA requires a corporation to furnish its shareholders *financial statements,* including a balance sheet, an income statement, and a statement of changes in shareholders' equity. The Securities Exchange Act of 1934 also requires publicly held companies to furnish such statements, as well as other information that is important to shareholders' voting and investing decisions. To protect shareholders of public companies, the Sarbanes–Oxley Act requires the CEO and the CFO of public companies to certify that to their knowledge all financial information filed with the Securities and Exchange Commission fairly presents the financial condition of the company and does not include untrue or misleading material statements.

Preemptive Right

The market price of a shareholder's shares will be reduced if a corporation issues additional shares at a price less than the market price. In addition, a shareholder's proportionate voting, dividend, and liquidation rights may be adversely affected by the issuance of additional shares. For example, if a corporation's only four shareholders each own 100 shares worth $10 per share, then each shareholder has shares worth $1,000, a 25 percent interest in any dividends declared, 25 percent of the voting power, and a claim against 25 percent of the corporation's assets after creditors' claims have been satisfied. If the corporation subsequently issues 100 shares to another person for only $5 per share, the value of each shareholder's shares falls to $900 and his dividend, voting, and liquidation rights are reduced to 20 percent. In a worst-case scenario, the corporation issues 201 shares to one of the existing shareholders, giving that shareholder majority control of the corporation and reducing the other shareholders' interests to less than 17 percent each. As a result, the minority shareholders will be dominated by the majority shareholder and will receive a greatly reduced share of the corporation's dividends.

Such harmful effects of an issuance could have been prevented if the corporation had been required to offer each existing shareholder a percentage of the new shares equal to her current proportionate ownership. If, for example, in the situation described above, the corporation had offered 50 shares to each shareholder, each shareholder could have remained a 25 percent owner of the corporation: her interest in the corporation would not have been reduced, and her total wealth would not have been decreased.

Corporation law recognizes the importance of giving a shareholder the option of maintaining the value of his shares and retaining his proportionate interest in the corporation. This is the shareholder's **preemptive right,** an option to subscribe to a new issuance of shares in proportion to the shareholder's current interest in the corporation.

The MBCA adopts a comprehensive scheme for determining preemptive rights. It provides that the preemptive right does not exist except to the extent provided by the articles. The MBCA permits the corporation to state expressly when the preemptive right arises.

When the preemptive right exists, the corporation must notify a shareholder of her option to buy shares, the number of shares that she is entitled to buy, the price of the shares, and when the option must be exercised. Usually, the shareholder is issued a **right,** a written option that she may exercise herself or sell to a person who wishes to buy the shares.

Distributions to Shareholders

During the life of a corporation, shareholders may receive distributions of the corporation's assets. Most people are familiar with one type of distribution—dividends—but there are other important types of distributions to shareholders, including payments to shareholders upon the corporation's repurchase of its shares.

There is one crucial similarity among all the types of distributions to shareholders: Corporate assets are transferred to shareholders. Consequently, an asset transfer to shareholders may harm the corporation's creditors and others with claims against the corporation's assets. For example, a distribution of assets may impair a corporation's ability to pay its creditors. In addition, a distribution to one class of shareholders may harm another class of shareholders that has a liquidation priority over the class of shareholders receiving the distribution. The existence of these potential harms compels corporation law to restrict the ability of corporations to make distributions to shareholders.

Dividends   One important objective of a business corporation is to make a profit. Shareholders invest in a corporation primarily to share in the expected profit either through appreciation of the value of their shares or through dividends. There are two types of dividends: *cash or property dividends* and *share dividends.* Only cash or property dividends are distributions of the corporation's assets. Share dividends are *not* distributions.

Cash or Property Dividends   Dividends are usually paid in cash. However, other assets of the corporation—such as airline discount coupons or shares of another corporation—may also be distributed as dividends. Cash or property dividends are declared by the board of directors and paid by the corporation on the date stated by the directors. Once declared, dividends are *debts* of the corporation, and shareholders may sue to force payment of the dividends. The board's dividend declaration, including the amount of dividend and whether to declare a dividend, is protected by the business judgment rule.

Preferred shares nearly always have a set dividend rate stated in the articles of incorporation. Even so, unless the preferred dividend is mandatory, the board has discretion to determine whether to pay a preferred dividend and what amount to pay. Most preferred shares are *cumulative preferred shares,* on which unpaid dividends cumulate. The entire accumulation must be paid before common shareholders may receive any dividend. Even when preferred shares are noncumulative, the current dividend must be paid to preferred shareholders before any dividend may be paid to common shareholders.

The following *Dodge v. Ford* case is one of the few cases in which a court ordered the payment of a dividend to common shareholders. The court found that Henry Ford had the wrong motives for causing Ford Motor Company to refuse to pay a dividend.

Dodge v. Ford Motor Co.   170 N.W. 668 (Mich. Sup. Ct. 1919)

In 1916, brothers John and Horace Dodge owned 10 percent of the common shares of the Ford Motor Company. Henry Ford owned 58 percent of the outstanding common shares and controlled the corporation and its board of directors. Starting in 1911, the corporation paid a regular annual dividend of $1.2 million, which was 60 percent of its capital stock of $2 million but only about 1 percent of its total equity of $114 million. In addition, from 1911 to 1915, the corporation paid special dividends totaling $41 million.

The policy of the corporation was to reduce the selling price of its cars each year. In June 1915, the board and officers agreed to increase production by constructing new plants for $10 million, acquiring land for $3 million, and erecting an $11 million smelter. To finance the planned expansion, the board decided not to reduce the selling price of cars beginning in August 1915 and to accumulate a large surplus.

A year later, the board reduced the selling price of cars by $80 per car. The corporation was able to produce 600,000 cars annually, all of which, and more, could have been sold for $440 instead of the new $360 price, a forgone revenue of $48 million. At the same time, the corporation announced a new dividend policy of paying no special dividend. Instead, it would reinvest all earnings except the regular dividend of $1.2 million.

Henry Ford announced his justification for the new dividend policy in a press release: "My ambition is to employ still more men, to spread the benefits of this industrial system to the greatest possible number, to help them build up their lives and their homes." The corporation had a $112 million surplus, expected profits of $60 million, total liabilities of $18 million, $52.5 million in cash on hand, and municipal bonds worth $1.3 million.

The Dodge brothers sued the corporation and the directors to force them to declare a special dividend. The trial court ordered the board to declare a dividend of $19.3 million. Ford Motor Company appealed.

Ostrander, Chief Justice

It is a well-recognized principle of law that the directors of a corporation, and they alone, have the power to declare a dividend of the earnings of the corporation, and to determine its amount. Courts will not interfere in the management of the directors unless it is clearly made to appear that they are guilty of fraud or misappropriation of the corporate funds, or they refuse to declare a dividend when the corporation has a surplus of net profits which it can, without detriment to the business, divide among its stockholders, and when a refusal to do so would amount to such an abuse of discretion as would constitute a fraud, or breach of that good faith that they are bound to exercise towards the shareholders.

The testimony of Mr. Ford convinces this court that he has to some extent the attitude towards shareholders of one who has dispensed and distributed to them large gains and that they should be content to take what he chooses to give. His testimony creates the impression that he thinks the Ford Motor Company has made too much money, has had too large profits, and that, although large profits might be still earned, a sharing of them with the public, by reducing the price of the output of the company, ought to be undertaken. We have no doubt that certain sentiments, philanthropic and altruistic, creditable to Mr. Ford, had large influence in determining the policy to be pursued by the Ford Motor Company.

There should be no confusion of the duties that Mr. Ford conceives that he and the shareholders owe to the general public and the duties that in law he and his co-directors owe to protest-

ing, minority shareholders. A business corporation is organized and carried on primarily for the profit of the shareholders. The powers of the directors are to be employed for that end.

We are not, however, persuaded that we should interfere with the proposed expansion of the Ford Motor Company. In view of the fact that the selling price of products may be increased at any time, the ultimate results of the larger business cannot be certainly estimated. The judges are not business experts. It is recognized that plans must often be made for a long future, for expected competition, for a continuing as well as an immediately profitable venture. We are not satisfied that the alleged motives of the directors, in so far as they are reflected in the conduct of the business, menace the interests of shareholders.

Assuming the general plan and policy of expansion were for the best ultimate interest of the company and therefore of its shareholders, what does it amount to in justification of a refusal to declare and pay a special dividend? The Ford Motor Company was able to estimate with nicety its income and profit. It could sell more cars than it could make. The profit upon each car depended upon the selling price. That being fixed, the yearly income and profit was determinable, and, within slight variations, was certain.

There was appropriated for the smelter $11 million. Assuming that the plans required an expenditure sooner or later of $10 million for duplication of the plant, and for land $3 million, the total is $24 million. The company was a cash business. If the total cost of proposed expenditures had been withdrawn in cash from the cash surplus on hand August 1, 1916, there would have remained $30 million.

The directors of Ford Motor Company say, and it is true, that a considerable cash balance must be at all times carried by such a concern. But there was a large daily, weekly, monthly receipt of cash. The output was practically continuous and was continuously, and within a few days, turned into cash. Moreover, the contemplated expenditures were not to be immediately made. The large sum appropriated for the smelter plant was payable over a considerable period of time. So that, without going further, it would appear that, accepting and approving the plan of the directors, it was their duty to distribute on and near the 1st of August 1916, a very large sum of money to stockholders.

Judgment for the Dodge brothers affirmed.

To protect the claims of the corporation's creditors, all of the corporation statutes limit the extent to which dividends may be paid. The MBCA imposes two limits: (1) the *solvency test* and (2) the *balance sheet test.*

Solvency Test A dividend may not make a corporation insolvent; that is, unable to pay its debts as they come due in the usual course of business. This means that a corporation may pay a dividend to the extent it has *excess solvency*—that is, liquidity that it does not need to pay its currently maturing obligations. This requirement protects creditors, who are concerned primarily with the corporation's ability to pay debts as they mature.

Balance Sheet Test After the dividend has been paid, the corporation's assets must be sufficient to cover its liabilities and the liquidation preference of shareholders having a priority in liquidation over the shareholders receiving the dividend. This means that a corporation may pay a dividend to the extent it has *excess assets*—that is, assets it does not need to cover its liabilities and the liquidation preferences of shareholders having a priority in liquidation over the shareholders receiving the dividends. This requirement protects not only creditors but also preferred shareholders. It prevents a corporation from paying to common shareholders a dividend that will impair the liquidation rights of preferred shareholders.

Example Batt Company has $27,000 in excess liquidity that it does not need to pay its currently maturing obligations. It has assets of $200,000 and liabilities of $160,000. It has one class of common shareholders. Its one class of preferred shareholders has a liquidation preference of $15,000. Examining these facts, we find that Batt's excess solvency is $27,000, but its excess assets are only $25,000 ($200,000 − 160,000 − 15,000). Therefore, Batt's shareholders may receive a maximum cash or property dividend of $25,000, which will eliminate all of Batt's excess assets and leave Batt with $2,000 of excess solvency.

Share Dividends and Share Splits Corporations sometimes distribute additional shares of the corporation to their shareholders. Often, this is done in order to give shareholders something instead of a cash dividend so that the cash can be retained and reinvested in the business. Such an action may be called either a *share dividend* or a *share split.*

A **share dividend** of a *specified percentage of outstanding shares* is declared by the board of directors. For example, the board may declare a 10 percent share dividend. As a result, each shareholder will receive 10 percent more shares than she currently owns. A share dividend is paid on outstanding shares only. Unlike a cash or property dividend, a share dividend may be revoked by the board after it has been declared.

A **share split** results in shareholders receiving a specified number of shares in exchange for each share that they currently own. For example, shares may be split two for one. Each shareholder will now have two shares for each share that he previously owned. A holder of 50 shares will now have 100 shares instead of 50.

The MBCA recognizes that a share split or a share dividend in the same class of shares does not affect the value of the corporation or the shareholders' wealth, because no assets have been transferred from the corporation to the shareholders. The effect is like that produced by taking a pie with four pieces and dividing each piece in half. Each person may receive twice as many pieces of the pie, but each piece is worth only half as much. The total amount received by each person is unchanged.

Therefore, the MBCA permits share splits and share dividends of the same class of shares to be made merely by action of the directors. The directors merely have the corporation issue to the shareholders the number of shares needed to effect the share dividend or split. The corporation must have a sufficient number of authorized, unissued shares to effect the share split or dividend; when it does not, its articles must be amended to create the required number of additional authorized shares.

Reverse Share Split A *reverse share split* is a decrease in the number of shares of a class such that, for example, two shares become one share. Most of the state corporation statutes require shareholder action to amend the articles to effect a reverse share split because the number of authorized shares is reduced. The purpose of a reverse share split is usually to increase the market price of the shares.

A reverse share split may also be used to freeze out minority shareholders. By the setting of a high reverse split ratio, a majority shareholder will be left with whole shares while minority shareholders will have only fractional shares. Corporation law allows a corporation to repurchase fractional shares without the consent of the fractional shareholders. Freeze-outs are discussed in Chapter 43.

Share Repurchases
Declaring a cash or property dividend is only one of the ways in which a corporation may distribute its assets. A corporation may also distribute its assets by repurchasing its shares from its shareholders. Such a repurchase may be either a *redemption* or an *open-market repurchase.*

The right of **redemption** (or a call) is usually a right of the corporation to force an *involuntary* sale by a shareholder at a fixed price. The shareholder must sell the shares to the corporation at the corporation's request; in most states, the shareholder cannot force the corporation to redeem the shares.

Under the MBCA, the right of redemption must appear in the articles of incorporation. It is common for a corporation to issue preferred shares subject to redemption at the corporation's option. Usually, common shares are not redeemable.

In addition, a corporation may repurchase its shares **on the open market.** A corporation is empowered to purchase its shares from any shareholder who is willing to sell them. Such repurchases are usually *voluntary* on the shareholder's part, requiring the corporation to pay a current market price to entice the shareholder to sell. However, a corporation may force a shareholder with a fractional share to sell that fractional share back to the corporation.

A corporation's repurchase of its shares may harm creditors and other shareholders. The MBCA requires a corporation repurchasing shares to meet tests that are the same as its cash and property dividend rules, recognizing that financially a repurchase of shares is no different from a dividend or any other distribution of assets to shareholders.

Ensuring a Shareholder's Return on Investment

Obtaining a return on her investment in a corporation is important to every shareholder. In a publicly held corporation, a shareholder may receive a return in the form of dividends and more significantly an increase in the value of her shares, which she may sell in the public securities markets.

For a shareholder in a close corporation, obtaining a return on his investment is often a problem, especially for minority shareholders. The majority shareholders dominate the board of directors, who usually choose not to pay any dividend to shareholders. And since the close corporation has no publicly traded shares, minority shareholders have little if any ability to sell their shares. The majority shareholders in a close corporation don't suffer the same effect, because they are usually officers and employees of the corporation and receive a return on their investment in the form of salaries.

What can a minority shareholder do? Rarely will a court, as in *Dodge v. Ford,* require the payment of a dividend. The only way a minority shareholder can protect himself is to bargain well prior to becoming a shareholder. For example, a prospective minority shareholder may insist on a mandatory dividend, that he be employed by the corporation at a salary, or that the corporation or majority shareholders be required to repurchase his shares upon the occurrence of certain events, such as the failure of the corporation to go public after five years. There is a limit to what a minority shareholder may demand, however, for the majority shareholders may refuse to sell shares to a prospective shareholder who asks too much.

Shareholders' Lawsuits

Shareholders' Individual Lawsuits
A shareholder has the right to sue in his own name to prevent or redress a breach of the shareholder's contract. For example, a shareholder may sue to recover dividends declared but not paid or dividends that should have been declared, to enjoin the corporation from committing an *ultra vires* act, to enforce the shareholder's right of inspection, and to enforce preemptive rights.

Shareholder Class Action Suits
When several people have been injured similarly by the same

persons in similar situations, one of the injured people may sue for the benefit of all the people injured. Likewise, if several shareholders have been similarly affected by a wrongful act of another, one of these shareholders may bring a **class action** on behalf of all the affected shareholders.

An appropriate class action under state corporation law would be an action seeking a dividend payment that has been brought by a preferred shareholder for all of the preferred shareholders. Any recovery is prorated to all members of the class.

A shareholder who successfully brings a class action is entitled to be reimbursed from the award amount for his *reasonable expenses,* including attorney's fees. If the class action suit is unsuccessful and has no reasonable foundation, the court may order the suing shareholder to pay the defendants' reasonable litigation expenses, including attorney's fees.

LOG ON

http://securities.stanford.edu
Stanford Law School maintains the Securities Class Action Clearinghouse. It provides detailed information relating to the prosecution, defense, and settlement of federal class action securities litigation.

Shareholders' Derivative Actions

When a corporation has been harmed by the actions of another person, the right to sue belongs to the corporation and any damages awarded by a court belong to the corporation. Hence, as a general rule, a shareholder has no right to sue in his own name when someone has harmed the corporation, and he may not recover for himself damages from that person. This is the rule even when the value of the shareholder's investment in the corporation has been impaired.

Nonetheless, one or more shareholders are permitted under certain circumstances to bring an action for the benefit of the corporation when the directors have failed to pursue a corporate cause of action. For example, if the corporation has a claim against its chief executive for wrongfully diverting corporate assets to her personal use, the corporation may not sue the chief executive because she controls the board of directors. Clearly, the CEO should not go unpunished. Consequently, corporation law authorizes a shareholder to bring a **derivative action** (or derivative suit) against the CEO on behalf of the corporation and for its benefit. Such a suit may also be used to bring a corporate claim against an outsider.

If the derivative action succeeds and damages are awarded, the damages ordinarily go to the corporate treasury for the benefit of the corporation. The suing shareholder is entitled only to reimbursement of his reasonable attorney's fees that he incurred in bringing the action.

Eligible Shareholders Although allowing shareholders to bring derivative suits creates a viable procedure for suing wrongdoing officers and directors, this procedure is also susceptible to abuse. **Strike suits** (lawsuits brought to gain out-of-court settlements for the complaining shareholders personally or to earn large attorney's fees, rather than to obtain a recovery for the corporation) have not been uncommon. To discourage strike suits, the person bringing the action must be a current shareholder who also held his shares at the time the alleged wrong occurred. In addition, the shareholder must fairly and adequately represent the interests of shareholders similarly situated in enforcing the right of the corporation.

One exception to these rules is the **double derivative suit,** a suit brought by a shareholder of a parent corporation on behalf of a subsidiary corporation owned by the parent. Courts regularly permit double derivative suits.

Demand on Directors Since a corporation's decision to sue someone is ordinarily made by its managers, a shareholder must first **demand** that the board of directors bring the suit. A demand informs the board that the corporation may have a right of action against a person that the board, in its business judgment, may decide to pursue. Therefore, if a demand is made and the board decides to bring the suit, the shareholder may not institute a derivative suit.

Ordinarily, a shareholder's failure to make a demand on the board prevents her from bringing a derivative suit. Nonetheless, the shareholder may initiate the suit if she proves that a demand on the board would have been useless or **futile.** Demand is futile, and therefore **excused,** if the board is unable to make a disinterested decision regarding whether to sue. Futility may be proved when all or a majority of the directors are interested in the challenged transaction, such as in a suit alleging that the directors issued shares to themselves at below-market prices.

If a shareholder makes a demand on the board and it **refuses** the shareholder's demand to bring a suit, ordinarily the shareholder is not permitted to continue the derivative action. The decision to bring a lawsuit is an ordinary business decision appropriate for a board of directors to make. The business judgment rule, therefore, is available to insulate from court review a board's decision not to bring a suit.

Of course, if a shareholder derivative suit accuses the board of harming the corporation, such as by misappropriating the corporation's assets, the board's refusal will not be protected by the business judgment rule because the board has a conflict of interest in its decision to sue. In such a situation, the shareholder may sue the directors despite the board's refusal.

Shareholder Litigation Committees In an attempt to ensure the application of the business judgment rule in demand refusal and demand futility situations, interested directors have tried to isolate themselves from the decision whether to sue by creating a special committee of the board, called a *shareholder* or *special litigation committee* (SLC) (or independent investigation committee) whose purpose is to decide whether to sue. The SLC should consist of directors who are not defendants in the derivative suit, who are not interested in the challenged action, are independent of the defendant directors, and, if possible, were not directors at the time the wrong occurred. Usually, the SLC has independent legal counsel that assists its determination whether to sue. Because the SLC is a committee of the board, its decision may be protected by the business judgment rule. Therefore, an SLC's decision not to sue may prevent a shareholder from suing.

Shareholders have challenged the application of the business judgment rule to an SLC's decision to dismiss a shareholder derivative suit against some of the directors. The suing shareholders argue that it is improper for an SLC to dismiss a shareholder derivative suit because there is a *structural bias.* That is, the SLC members are motivated by a desire to avoid hurting their fellow directors and adversely affecting future working relationships within the board.

When demand is **not futile,** most of the courts that have been faced with this question have upheld the decisions of special litigation committees that comply with the business judgment rule. The courts require that the SLC members be *independent* of the defendant directors, be *disinterested* with regard to the subject matter of the suit, make a *reasonable investigation* into whether to dismiss the suit, and act in *good faith.*

When demand is **futile or excused,** most courts faced with the decision of an SLC have applied the rule of the *Zapata* case, which follows.

The MBCA has adopted the *Zapata* rule in all contexts, whether or not an SLC is used. When a majority of directors are not independent, the corporation has the burden of proving that the *Zapata* test has been met: good faith and reasonable investigation by the directors making the decision to dismiss the action and a determination by those directors that the best interests of the corporation are served by dismissal. If, however, a majority of the directors are independent, the shareholders bringing the derivative action have the burden of proving that there was bad faith or no reasonable investigation or that bringing the action is in the best interest of the corporation.

Zapata Corp. v. Maldonado   430 A.2d 779 (Del. Sup. Ct. 1981)

Zapata Corporation had a share option plan that permitted its executives to purchase Zapata shares at a below-market price. Most of the directors participated in the share option plan. In 1974, the directors voted to advance the share option exercise date in order to reduce the federal income tax liability of the executives who exercised the share options, including the directors. An additional effect, however, was to increase the corporation's federal tax liability.

William Maldonado, a Zapata shareholder, believed that the board action was a breach of a fiduciary duty and that it harmed the corporation. In 1975, he instituted a derivative suit in a Delaware court on behalf of Zapata against all of the directors. He failed to make a demand on the directors to sue themselves, alleging that this would be futile since they were all defendants.

The derivative suit was still pending in 1979, when four of the defendants were no longer directors. The remaining directors then appointed two new outside directors to the board and created an Independent Investigation Committee consisting solely of the two new directors. The board authorized the committee to make a final and binding decision regarding whether the derivative suit should be brought on behalf of the corporation. Following a three-month investigation, the committee concluded that Maldonado's derivative suit should be dismissed as against Zapata's best interests.

Zapata asked the Delaware court to dismiss the derivative suit. The court refused, holding that Maldonado possessed an individual right to maintain the derivative action and that the business judgment rule did not apply. Zapata appealed to the Supreme Court of Delaware.

Quillen, Justice

We find that the trial court's determination that a shareholder, once demand is made and refused, possesses an independent, individual right to continue a derivative suit for breaches of fiduciary duty over objection by the corporation, as an absolute rule, is erroneous.

Derivative suits enforce corporate rights, and any recovery obtained goes to the corporation. We see no inherent reason why a derivative suit should automatically place in the hands of the litigating shareholder sole control of the corporate right throughout the litigation. Such an inflexible rule would recognize the interest of one person or group to the exclusion of all others within the corporate entity.

When, if at all, should an authorized board committee be permitted to cause litigation, properly initiated by a derivative stockholder in his own right, to be dismissed? The problem is relatively simple. If, on the one hand, corporations can consistently wrest bona fide derivative actions away from well-meaning derivative plaintiffs through the use of the committee mechanism, the derivative suit will lose much, if not all, of its effectiveness as an intracorporate means of policing boards of directors. If, on the other hand, corporations are unable to rid themselves of meritless or harmful litigation and strike suits, the derivative action, created to benefit the corporation, will produce the opposite, unintended result. It thus appears desirable to us to find a balancing point where bona fide shareholder power to bring corporate causes of action cannot be unfairly trampled on by the board of directors, but the corporation can rid itself of detrimental litigation.

We are not satisfied that acceptance of the business judgment rationale at this stage of derivative litigation is a proper balancing point. We must be mindful that directors are passing judgment on fellow directors in the same corporation and fellow directors, in this instance, who designated them to serve both as directors and committee members. The question naturally arises whether a "there but for the grace of God go I" empathy might not play a role. And the further question arises whether inquiry as to independence, good faith and reasonable investigation is sufficient safeguard against abuse, perhaps subconscious abuse.

We thus steer a middle course between those cases that yield to the independent business judgment of a board committee and this case as determined below, which would yield to unbridled shareholder control.

We recognize that the final substantive judgment whether a particular lawsuit should be maintained requires a balance of many factors—ethical, commercial, promotional, public relations, employee relations, fiscal, as well as legal. We recognize the danger of judicial overreaching but the alternatives seem to us to be outweighed by the fresh view of a judicial outsider.

After an objective and thorough investigation of a derivative suit, an independent committee may cause its corporation to file a motion to dismiss the derivative suit. The Court should apply a two-step test to the motion. First, the Court should inquire into the independence and good faith of the committee and the bases supporting its conclusions. The corporation should have the burden of proving independence, good faith, and reasonable investigation, rather than presuming independence, good faith, and reasonableness. If the Court determines either that the committee is not independent or has not shown reasonable bases for its conclusions, or if the Court is not satisfied for other reasons relating to the process, including but not limited to the good faith of the committee, the Court shall deny the corporation's motion to dismiss the derivative suit.

The second step provides the essential key in striking the balance between legitimate corporate claims as expressed in a derivative stockholder suit and a corporation's best interests as expressed by an independent investigating committee. The Court should determine, applying its own independent business judgment, whether the motion should be granted. The second step is intended to thwart instances where corporate actions meet the criteria of step one, but the result does not appear to satisfy its spirit, or where corporate actions would simply prematurely terminate a stockholder grievance deserving of further consideration in the corporation's interest. The Court of course must carefully consider and weigh how compelling the corporate interest in dismissal is when faced with a non-frivolous lawsuit. The Court should, when appropriate, give special consideration to matters of law and public policy in addition to the corporation's best interests.

The second step shares some of the same spirit and philosophy of the statement of the trial court: "Under our system of law, courts and not litigants should decide the merits of litigation."

Judgment reversed in favor of Zapata. Case remanded to the trial court.

Litigation Expenses If a shareholder is successful in a derivative suit, she is entitled to a reimbursement of her reasonable litigation expenses out of the corporation's

damage award. On the other hand, if the suit is unsuccessful and has been brought without reasonable cause, the shareholder must pay the defendants' expenses,

Ethics in Action

After reading *Zapata Corp. v. Maldonado* and the MBCA rules for dismissal of shareholder derivative actions, you may predict that a court will almost always respect the recommendation of a special litigation committee, even when a former or existing board member is a defendant. That is not always the case because the corporation does not have a valid right of action against a director, but often because an SLC has adopted the right process (good faith and reasonable inquiry) and easily can justify that the expense of litigation and the distraction of current management outweigh the likely recovery to the corporation from the wrongdoing director.

• Do you think is it ethical for an SLC to recommend dismissal of an action against a director who has harmed the corporation? Is that sending the right message to other directors and officers? Are there other ways to discipline a director or officer than by suing him? Are those alternatives sufficient deterrents or punishments?

• Do you think it would be justifiable for an SLC to recommend dismissal of an action against former officers who, like some top officers in Adelphia, Tyco, and Enron, either looted the corporation or caused it to overstate its earnings or understate its liabilities? Is it justifiable for a corporation not to sue directors and officers of corporations, like Apple Inc. and The Home Depot, Inc., who authorized or permitted the backdating of options given to the CEO and other officers, which nearly guaranteed that the officers would profit from the options? Is it clear that options backdating is unethical? Or is options backdating merely an alternative way of guaranteeing compensation to high quality officers? Would a utilitarian or profit maximizer be more likely to recommend dismissal than a rights theorist?

including attorney's fees. The purpose of this rule is to deter strike suits by punishing shareholders who litigate in bad faith.

Defense of Corporation by Shareholder

Occasionally, the officers or managers will refuse to defend a suit brought against a corporation. If a shareholder shows that the corporation has a valid defense to the suit and that the refusal or failure of the directors to defend is a breach of their fiduciary duty to the corporation, the courts will permit the shareholder to defend for the benefit of the corporation, its shareholders, and its creditors.

Shareholder Liability

Shareholders have many responsibilities and liabilities in addition to their many rights. In Chapters 41 and 42, we studied shareholder liability when a shareholder pays too little consideration for shares, when a corporation is defectively formed, and when a corporation's veil is pierced. In this section, four other grounds for shareholder liability are discussed.

Shareholder Liability for Illegal Distributions

Dividends and other distributions of a corporation's assets received by a shareholder with *knowledge of their illegality* may be recovered on behalf of the corporation. Under the MBCA, primary liability is placed on the directors who, failing to comply with the business judgment rule, authorized the unlawful distribution. However, the directors are entitled to contribution from shareholders who received an asset distribution knowing that it was illegally made. These liability rules enforce the limits on asset distributions that were discussed earlier in this chapter.

Shareholder Liability for Corporate Debts

One of the chief attributes of a shareholder is his *limited liability:* Ordinarily, he has no liability for corporate obligations beyond his capital contribution. Defective attempts to incorporate (in Chapter 42) and piercing the corporate veil (in Chapter 41) are grounds on which a shareholder may be held liable for corporate debts beyond his capital contribution. In addition, a few states impose personal liability on shareholders for *wages owed to corporate employees,* even if the shareholders have fully paid for their shares.

Sale of a Control Block of Shares

The per share value of the shares of a majority shareholder of a corporation is greater than the per share value of the shares of a minority shareholder. This difference in value is due to the majority shareholder's ability to control the corporation and to cause it to hire her as an employee at a high salary. Therefore, a majority shareholder can sell her shares for a *premium* over the fair market value of minority shares.

Majority ownership is not always required for control of a corporation. In a close corporation it is required, but in a publicly held corporation with a widely dispersed, hard-to-mobilize shareholder group, minority ownership of from 5 to 30 percent may be enough to obtain control. Therefore, a holder of minority control in such a corporation will also be able to receive a premium.

Current corporation law imposes no liability on any shareholder, whether or not the shareholder is a controlling shareholder, *merely* because she is able to sell her shares for a premium. Nonetheless, if the premium is accompanied by wrongdoing, controlling shareholders have been held liable either for the amount of the premium or for the damages suffered by the corporation.

For example, a seller of control shares is liable for selling to a purchaser who harms the corporation if the seller had or should have had a *reasonable suspicion* that the purchaser would mismanage or loot the corporation. A seller may be placed on notice of a purchaser's bad motives by facts indicating the purchaser's history of *mismanagement and personal use of corporate assets,* by the purchaser's *lack of interest in the physical facilities* of the corporation, or the purchaser's great *interest in the liquid assets* of the corporation. These factors tend to indicate that the purchaser has a short-term interest in the corporation.

The mere payment of a premium is not enough to put the seller on notice. If the *premium is unduly high,* however, such as a $50 offer for shares traded for $10, a seller must doubt whether the purchaser will be able to recoup his investment without looting the corporation.

When a seller has, or should have, a reasonable suspicion that a purchaser will mismanage or loot the corporation, he must not sell to the purchaser unless a *reasonable investigation* shows there is no reasonable risk of wrongdoing.

A few courts find liability when a selling shareholder takes or sells a *corporate asset.* For example, if a purchaser wants to buy the corporation's assets and the controlling shareholder proposes that the purchaser buy her shares instead, the controlling shareholder is liable for usurping a corporate opportunity.

A more unusual situation existed in *Perlman v. Feldman.*[3] In that case, Newport Steel Corporation had excess demand for its steel production, due to the Korean War. Another corporation, in order to guarantee a steady supply of steel, bought at a premium a minority yet controlling block of shares of Newport from Feldman, its chairman and president. The court ruled that Feldman was required to share the premium with the other share-

holders because he had sold a corporate asset—the ability to exploit an excess demand for steel. The court reasoned that Newport could have exploited that asset to its advantage.

Shareholders as Fiduciaries

A few courts have recognized a fiduciary duty of controlling shareholders to use their ability to control the corporation in a fair, just, and equitable manner that benefits all of the shareholders proportionately. This is a duty to be **impartial**—that is, not to prefer themselves over the minority shareholders. For example, controlling shareholders have a fiduciary duty not to cause the corporation to repurchase their own shares or to pay themselves a dividend unless the same offer is made to the minority shareholder.

One of the most common examples of impartiality is the **freeze-out** or *squeeze-out* of minority shareholders, which is wrongful because of its **oppression** of minority shareholders. It occurs in close corporations when controlling shareholders pay themselves high salaries while not employing or paying dividends to noncontrolling shareholders. Since there is usually no liquid market for the shares of the noncontrolling shareholders, they have an investment that provides them no return, while the controlling shareholders reap large gains. Such actions by the majority are especially wrongful when the controlling shareholders follow with an offer to buy the minority's shares at an unreasonably low price.

Some courts have held that all close corporation shareholders—whether majority or minority owners—are fiduciaries of each other and the corporation, on the grounds that the close corporation is an incorporated partnership. Thus, like partners, the shareholders owe fiduciary duties to act in the best interests of the corporation and the shareholders as a whole.

Some statutes, such as the Statutory Close Corporation Supplement to the MBCA, permit close corporation shareholders to dispense with a board of directors or to arrange corporate affairs as if the corporation were a partnership. The effect of these statutes is to impose management responsibilities, including the fiduciary duties of directors, on the shareholders. In essence, the shareholders are partners and owe each other fiduciary duties similar to those owed between partners of a partnership.

The next case, *Brodie v. Jordan,* is a decision of the Supreme Judicial Court of Massachusetts, a leading court in fashioning rights for minority shareholders in close corporations. The court found that the majority shareholders who oppressed a minority shareholder by

---

[3]219 F.2d 173 (2d Cir. 1955).

excluding her from the business operations were required to permit the minority shareholder to enjoy the financial or other benefits from the business to the extent that her ownership interest justified. The court refused, however, to order the majority shareholders to repurchase the minority shareholder's shares.

Brodie v. Jordan   857 N.E.2d 1076 (Mass. Sup. Jud. Ct. 2006)

Mary Brodie, Robert Jordan, and David Barbuto were the only shareholders of Malden Centerless Grinding Co., Inc., a Massachusetts corporation that operated a small machine shop. Mary's deceased husband, Walter Brodie, was one of the founding members of the company and served as its president from 1979 to 1992. Barbuto was a shareholder, director, and treasurer of the company since its formation. Jordan was an employee of the company since 1975 and a shareholder, director, and officer since 1984; he was in charge of the day-to-day operation of the business.

Beginning in 1984, Walter, Barbuto, and Jordan each held one-third of the shares of the corporation, and all three served as directors. By 1988, however, Walter was no longer involved in the company's day-to-day operation and only met with Barbuto and Jordan two to three times each year. After Walter disagreed with Barbuto and Jordan over management issues, Walter requested that the company purchase his shares, but those requests were rejected. Neither the articles of incorporation nor any corporate bylaw obligated Malden, Barbuto, or Jordan to purchase the stock of a shareholder.

The corporation had not paid any dividends to shareholders since 1989. As an employee, Jordan received a salary at a rate set by the board of directors (Barbuto and himself). Jordan participated in a profit-sharing plan made available by the corporation and had the use of a company vehicle. Barbuto received director's fees from the corporation until 1998. He owned the building that housed Malden's corporate offices and received rent from the corporation. Barbuto also owned a separate corporation, Barco Engineering, Inc., which was a customer of Malden and for which Malden regularly performed services. Walter received compensation from the company prior to 1992, when he was voted out as president and director of Malden. Walter was paid a consultant's fee in 1994 and 1995. He died in 1997, and Mary inherited his one-third interest in Malden. Neither Walter nor Mary received any compensation or other money from the corporation after 1995.

In July 1997, Mary attended a Malden shareholders' meeting, at which she nominated herself as a director; she was not elected as Barbuto and Jordan voted against her. At this same meeting, Mary asked Barbuto and Jordan to perform a valuation of the company so that she could value her shares, but a valuation was never performed.

In 1998, Mary sued Barbuto and Jordan claiming that they breached a fiduciary duty by freezing her out of the corporation. By the time the case came to trial, Barbuto and Jordan had failed to hold an annual shareholder's meeting for the previous five years, and Mary had not participated in any company decision making. The trial court found that Barbuto and Jordan had breached a fiduciary duty and oppressed Mary. The court ordered Barbuto and Jordan to purchase Mary's shares. After a court of appeals affirmed, Barbuto and Jordan appealed to the Massachusetts Supreme Judicial Court.

Cowin, Judge

The parties do not dispute that Malden is a close corporation, in that it has (1) a small number of stockholders; (2) no ready market for the corporate stock; and (3) substantial majority stockholder participation in the management, direction and operations of the corporation. "Stockholders in a close corporation owe one another substantially the same fiduciary duty in the operation of the enterprise that partners owe to one another" that is, a duty of "utmost good faith and loyalty." *Donahue v. Rodd Electrotype Co. of New England, Inc.,* 367 Mass. 578, 593, 328 N.E.2d 505 (1975).

Majority shareholders in a close corporation violate this duty when they act to "freeze out" the minority. We have defined freeze-outs by way of example: The squeezers (those who employ the freeze-out techniques) may refuse to declare dividends; they may drain off the corporation's earnings in the form of exorbitant salaries and bonuses to the majority shareholder-officers and perhaps to their relatives, or in the form of high rent by the corporation for property leased from majority shareholders; they may deprive minority shareholders of corporate offices and of employment by the company; they may cause the corporation to sell its assets at an inadequate price to the majority shareholders. What these examples have in common is that, in each, the majority frustrates the minority's reasonable expectations of benefit from their ownership of shares.

We have previously analyzed freeze-outs in terms of shareholders' "reasonable expectations" both explicitly and implicitly. See *Bodio v. Ellis,* 401 Mass. 1, 10, 513 N.E.2d 684 (1987) (thwarting minority shareholder's "rightful expectation" as to control of close corporation was breach of fiduciary duty); *Wilkes v. Springside Nursing Home, Inc.,* 370 Mass. 842, 850, 353 N.E.2d 657 (1976) (denying minority shareholders employment in corporation may "effectively frustrate their purposes in entering on the corporate venture").

In the present case, the Superior Court judge properly analyzed the defendants' liability in terms of the plaintiff's reasonable expectations of benefit. The judge found that the defendants had interfered with the plaintiffs reasonable expectations by excluding her from corporate decision-making, denying her access to company information, and hindering her ability to sell her shares in the open market. In addition, the judge's findings reflect a state of affairs in which the defendants were the only ones receiving any financial benefit from the corporation. The Appeals Court determined that the findings were warranted, and the defendants have not sought further appellate review with respect to liability. Thus, the only question before us is whether, on this record, the plaintiff was entitled to the remedy of a forced buyout of her shares by the majority. We conclude that she was not so entitled.

The proper remedy for a freeze-out is to restore the minority shareholder as nearly as possible to the position she would have been in had there been no wrongdoing. Because the wrongdoing in a freeze-out is the denial by the majority of the minority's reasonable expectations of benefit, it follows that the remedy should, to the extent possible, restore to the minority shareholder those benefits which she reasonably expected, but has not received because of the fiduciary breach.

If, for example, a minority shareholder had a reasonable expectation of employment by the corporation and was terminated wrongfully, the remedy may be reinstatement, back pay, or both. Similarly, if a minority shareholder has a reasonable expectation of sharing in company profits and has been denied this opportunity, she may be entitled to participate in the favorable results of operations to the extent that those results have been wrongly appropriated by the majority. The remedy should neither grant the minority a windfall nor excessively penalize the majority. Rather, it should attempt to reset the proper balance between the majority's conceded rights to what has been termed "selfish ownership" and the minority's reasonable expectations of benefit from its shares.

Courts have broad equitable powers to fashion remedies for breaches of fiduciary duty in a close corporation. Here, the Superior Court judge ordered the defendants to buy out the plaintiff at the price of an expert's estimate of her share of the corporation, a remedy that no Massachusetts appellate court has previously authorized. The problem with this remedy is that it placed the plaintiff in a significantly *better* position

than she would have enjoyed absent the wrongdoing, and well exceeded her reasonable expectations of benefit from her shares.

The remedy in *Donahue v. Rodd Electrotype Co. of New England, Inc.,* 367 Mass. 578, 603, 328 N.E.2d 505 (1975), is readily distinguishable. There, the majority had caused the corporation to purchase majority shareholders' stock at a favorable price while denying minority shareholders the same opportunity. We held that, to comply with its fiduciary duties, the majority had to either rescind the sale of its own shares to the corporation or cause the corporation to purchase the minority's shares on the same terms. Here, there is no allegation that Malden purchased the defendants' shares without giving the plaintiff a similar opportunity.

One of the defining aspects of a close corporation is the absence of a ready market for corporate stock. It is well established that in the absence of an agreement among shareholders or between the corporation and the shareholder, or a provision in the corporation's articles of organization or by-laws, neither the corporation nor a majority of shareholders is under any obligation to purchase the shares of minority shareholders when minority shareholders wish to dispose of their interest in the corporation. In this case, it is undisputed that neither the articles of organization nor any corporate bylaw obligates Malden or the defendants to purchase the plaintiff's shares. Thus, there is nothing in the background law, the governing rules of this particular close corporation, or any other circumstance that could have given the plaintiff a reasonable expectation of having her shares bought out.

In ordering the defendants to purchase the plaintiffs stock at the price of her share of the company, the judge created an artificial market for the plaintiff's minority share of a close corporation—an asset that, by definition, has little or no market value. Thus, the remedy had the perverse effect of placing the plaintiff in a position superior to that which she would have enjoyed had there been no wrongdoing.

The remedy for the defendants' breach of fiduciary duty is one that protects the plaintiff's reasonable expectations of benefit from the corporation and that compensates her for their denial in the past. An evidentiary hearing is appropriate to determine her reasonable expectations of ownership; whether such expectations have been frustrated; and, if so, the means by which to vindicate the plaintiff's interests. For breaches visited upon the plaintiff resulting in deprivations that can be quantified, money damages will be the appropriate remedy. Prospective injunctive relief may be granted to ensure that the plaintiff is allowed to participate in company governance, and to enjoy financial or other benefits from the business, to the extent that her ownership interest justifies.

In devising a remedy that grants the plaintiff her reasonable expectations of benefit from stock ownership in Malden, the judge may consider the fact that the plaintiff has received no economic benefit from her shares. If the defendants have denied the plaintiff any return on her investment while draining off the corporation's earnings for themselves, the judge may consider, among other possibilities, the propriety of compelling the declaration of dividends.

Judgment for Mary Brodie affirmed in part and reversed in part. Remanded to the trial court.

Members' Rights and Duties in Nonprofit Corporations

In a for-profit corporation, the shareholders' rights to elect directors and to receive dividends are their most important rights. The shareholders' duty to contribute capital as promised is the most important responsibility. By contrast, in a nonprofit corporation, the members' rights and duties—especially in a mutual benefit corporation—are defined by the ability of the members to use the facilities of the corporation (as in a social club) or to consume its output (as in a cooperative grocery store) and by their obligations to support the enterprise periodically with their money (such as dues paid to a social club) or with their labor (such as the duty to work a specified number of hours in a cooperative grocery store).

Nonprofit corporation law grants a corporation and its members considerable flexibility in determining the rights and liabilities of its members. The Model Nonprofit Corporation Act (MNCA) provides that all members of a nonprofit corporation have equal rights and obligations with respect to voting, dissolution, redemption of membership, and transfer of membership, unless the articles or bylaws establish classes of membership with different rights and obligations. For other rights and obligations, the MNCA provides that all members have the same rights and obligations, unless the articles or bylaws provide otherwise.

For example, a mutual benefit corporation that operates a golf country club may have two classes of membership. A full membership may entitle a full member to use all the club's facilities (including the swimming pool and tennis courts), grant the full member two votes on all matters submitted to members, and require the full member to pay monthly dues of $500. A limited membership may give a limited member the right to play the golf course only, grant the limited member one vote on all matters submitted to members, and require the limited members to pay monthly dues of $300 per month.

While members are primarily concerned about their consumption rights and financial obligations—such as those addressed above—that are embodied in the articles and the bylaws, they have other rights and obligations as well, including voting, inspection, and information rights similar to those held by shareholders of for-profit corporations.

Members' Meeting and Voting Rights

A nonprofit corporation must hold an annual meeting of its members and may hold meetings at other times as well. Members holding at least 5 percent of the voting power may call for a special meeting of members at any time.

All members of record have one vote on all matters submitted to members, unless the articles or bylaws grant lesser or greater voting power. The articles or bylaws may provide for different classes of members. Members of one class may be given greater voting rights than the members of another class. The articles or bylaws may provide that a class has no voting power.

Members may not act at a meeting unless a quorum is present. Under the MNCA, a quorum is 10 percent of the votes entitled to be cast on a matter. However, unless at least one-third of the voting power is present at the meeting, the only matters that may be voted on are matters listed in the meeting notice sent to members. The articles or bylaws may require higher percentages.

Members may elect directors by straight or cumulative voting and by class voting. The articles or bylaws may also permit members to elect directors on the basis of chapter or other organizational unit, by region or other geographical unit, or by any other reasonable method. For example, a national humanitarian fraternity such as Lions Club may divide the United States into seven regions whose members are entitled to elect one director. Members also have the right to remove directors they have elected with or without cause.

In addition to the rights to elect and to remove directors, members have the right to vote on most amendments of the articles and bylaws, merger of the corporation with another corporation, sale of substantially all the corporation's assets, and dissolution of the corporation. Ordinarily, members must approve such matters by two thirds of the votes cast or a majority of the voting power, whichever is less. This requirement is more lenient than the rule applied to for-profit corporations. Combined with the 10 percent quorum requirement, members with less than 7 percent of the voting power may approve matters submitted to members.

However, the unfairness of such voting rules is offset by the MNCA's notice requirement. A members' meeting may not consider important matters such as mergers and articles amendments unless the corporation gave members fair and reasonable notice that such matters were to be submitted to the members for a vote.

In addition, the MNCA requires approval of each class of members whose rights are substantially affected by the matter. This requirement may increase the difficulty of obtaining member approval. For example, full members of a golf country club may not change the rights of limited members without the approval of the limited members. In addition, the articles or bylaws may require third-person approval as well. For example, a city industrial development board may not be permitted to amend its articles without the consent of the mayor.

Members may vote in person or by proxy. They may also have written voting agreements. However, member voting agreements may not have a term exceeding 10 years. Members may act without a meeting if the action is approved in writing by at least 80 percent of the voting power.

Member Inspection and Information Rights

A member may not be able to exercise his voting and other rights unless he is informed. Moreover, a member must be able to communicate with other members to be able to influence the way they vote on matters submitted to members. Consequently, the MNCA grants members inspection and information rights.

Members have an absolute right to inspect and copy the articles, bylaws, board resolutions, and minutes of members' meetings. Members have a qualified right to inspect and copy a list of the members. The member's demand to inspect the members' list must be in good faith and for a proper purpose—that is, a purpose related to the member's interest as a member. Improper purposes include selling the list or using the list to solicit money. Members also have a qualified right to inspect minutes of board meetings and records of actions taken by committees of the board.

A nonprofit corporation is required to maintain appropriate accounting records, and members have a qualified right to inspect them. Upon demand, the corporation must provide to a member its latest annual financial statements, including a balance sheet and statement of operations. However, the MNCA permits a religious corporation to abolish or limit the right of a member to inspect any corporate record.

Distributions of Assets

Because it is not intended to make a profit, a nonprofit corporation does not pay dividends to its members. In fact, a nonprofit corporation is generally prohibited from making any distribution of its assets to its members.

Nonetheless, a mutual benefit corporation may purchase a membership and thereby distribute its assets to the selling member, but only if the corporation is able to pay its currently maturing obligations and has assets at least equal to its liabilities. For example, when a farmer joins a farmers' purchasing cooperative, he purchases a membership interest having economic value—it entitles him to purchase supplies from the cooperative at a bargain price. The mutual benefit corporation may repurchase the farmer's membership when he retires from farming. Religious and public benefit corporations may not repurchase their memberships.

Resignation and Expulsion of Members

A member may resign at any time from a nonprofit corporation. When a member resigns, generally a member may not sell or transfer her membership to any other person. A member of a mutual benefit corporation may transfer her interest to a buyer if the articles or bylaws permit.

It is fairly easy for a nonprofit corporation to expel a member or terminate her membership. The corporation must follow procedures that are fair and reasonable and carried out in good faith. The MNCA does not require the corporation to have a proper purpose to expel or terminate a member but only to follow proper procedures. The MNCA places no limits on a religious corporation's expulsion of its members.

The MNCA does not require a nonprofit corporation to purchase the membership of an expelled member, and—as explained above—permits only a mutual benefit corporation to purchase a membership. Members of mutual benefit corporations who fear expulsion should provide for repurchase rights in the articles or bylaws.

Derivative Suits

Members of a nonprofit corporation have a limited right to bring derivative actions on

The Global Business Environment

Chapter 43 covered some of the corporate governance differences between the United States and other countries, specifically Germany, including the makeup of corporate boards. There are many similarities but also quite a few differences in the powers of shareholders, including matters that must be submitted for shareholder approval. In Germany, the management board must obtain the approval of the shareholders to create new shares of the corporation, to transfer major assets, and to liquidate the company. The differences include German law requiring shareholder approval to declare dividends, issue new shares, and waive shareholders' preemptive right. In addition, many matters that in the United States may be included by director action in the bylaws must be included in German articles of incorporation, which cannot be modified without shareholder approval.

Shareholders of German companies have limited power to force a corporate right of action against someone who has harmed the corporation. A German corporation must sue members of the management board if a shareholders' meeting decides or if shareholders holding at least 10 percent of the shares demand the action. Beyond that, German law rarely permits an *actio pro socio,* the equivalent of an American derivative action. Moreover, German corporation law does not provide for direct actions by shareholders against members of the management board for breach of duty, such as wrongfully providing false financial information to shareholders.

behalf of the corporation. A derivative action may be brought by members having at least 5 percent of the voting power or by 50 members, whichever is less. Members must first demand that the directors bring the suit or establish that demand is futile. If the action is successful, a court may require the corporation to pay the suing members' reasonable expenses. When the action is unsuccessful and has been commenced frivolously or in bad faith, a court may require the suing members to pay the other party's expenses.

LOG ON

www.csd.bg/en/cgi

The Corporate Governance Initiative for Bulgaria is a coalition of Bulgarian nongovernmental organizations established to facilitate the adoption of relevant corporate governance standards and procedures in Bulgaria's maturing market-based economy. Visit the Web site above to find CGI's recommendations to improve shareholder rights in Bulgarian corporations.

www.cipe.org

The Center for International Private Enterprise is a nonprofit affiliate of the U.S. Chamber of Commerce and one of the four core institutes of the National Endowment for Democracy. CIPE advocates for market-based democratic systems in foreign countries and has adopted Corporate Governance Initiatives in the Middle East and North Africa to help countries and territories like Bahrain, Yemen, and the Palestinian Territories advance their efforts to establish strong norms for corporate governance. Click on **www.cipe.org/regional/menacg/index.php.**

Dissolution and Termination of Corporations

The MBCA provides that a corporation doing business may be dissolved by action of its directors and shareholders. The directors must adopt a dissolution resolution, and a majority of the shares outstanding must be cast in favor of dissolution at a shareholders' meeting. For a **voluntary dissolution** to be effective, the corporation must submit articles of dissolution to the secretary of state. The dissolution is effective when the articles are filed by the secretary of state.

A corporation may also be dissolved **without its consent** by administrative action of the secretary of state or by judicial action of a court. The secretary of state may commence an administrative proceeding to dissolve a corporation that has not filed its annual report, paid its annual franchise tax, appointed or maintained a registered office or agent in the state, or whose period of duration has expired. **Administrative dissolution** requires that the secretary of state give written notice to the corporation of the grounds for dissolution. If, within 60 days, the corporation has not corrected the default or demonstrated that the default does not exist, the secretary dissolves the corporation by signing a certificate of dissolution.

The shareholders, secretary of state, or the creditors of a corporation may ask a court to order the involuntary dissolution of a corporation. Any **shareholder** may obtain judicial dissolution when there is a deadlock of the directors that is harmful to the corporation, when the shareholders are deadlocked and cannot elect directors for two years, or when the directors act illegally, oppressively, or

Roles of Shareholders and the Board of Directors

Corporate Action	Board's Role	Shareholders' Role
Day-to-Day Management	Selects officers; supervises management	Elect and remove directors
Issuance of Shares	Issues shares	Protected by preemptive right
Merger and Share Exchange	Adopts articles of merger or share exchange	Vote to approve merger or share exchange; protected by dissenters' rights
Amendment of Articles of Incorporation	Proposes amendment	Vote to approve amendment
Dissolution	Proposes dissolution	Vote to approve dissolution
Dividends	Declares dividends	Receive dividends
Board of Directors Harms Individual Shareholder Rights	Has harmed shareholders	Bring individual or class action against directors or the corporation
Directors Harm Corporation	Sues wrongdoing directors	Bring derivative action against wrongdoing directors

fraudulently. The **secretary of state** may obtain judicial dissolution if it is proved that a corporation obtained its articles of incorporation by fraud or exceeded or abused its legal authority. **Creditors** may request dissolution if the corporation is insolvent.

Under the MBCA, a corporation that has not issued shares or commenced business may be dissolved by the vote of a majority of its incorporators or initial directors.

Many close corporations are nothing more than incorporated partnerships, in which all the shareholders are managers and friends or relatives. Corporation law reflects the special needs of those shareholders of close corporations who want to arrange their affairs to make the close corporation more like a partnership. The Close Corporation Supplement to the MBCA recognizes that a **close corporation shareholder** should have more dissolution power, like a partner had under the Uniform Partnership Act. This section, like similar provisions in many states, permits the articles of incorporation to empower any shareholder to dissolve the corporation at will or upon the occurrence of a specified event such as the death of a shareholder.

Winding Up and Termination
A dissolved corporation continues its corporate existence but may not carry on any business except that appropriate to winding up its affairs. Therefore, winding up (liquidation) must follow dissolution. Winding up is the orderly collection and disposal of the corporation's assets and the distribution of the proceeds of the sale of assets. From these proceeds, the claims of creditors will be paid first. Next, the liquidation preferences of preferred shareholders will be paid. Then, common shareholders receive any proceeds that remain.

After winding up has been completed, the corporation's existence terminates. A person who purports to act on behalf of a terminated corporation has the liability of a person acting for a corporation prior to its incorporation. See Chapter 42. Some courts impose similar liability on a person acting on behalf of a dissolved corporation, especially when dissolution is obtained by the secretary of state, such as for the failure to file an annual report or to pay annual taxes.

Dissolution of Nonprofit Corporations
A nonprofit corporation may be dissolved voluntarily, administratively, or judicially. Voluntary dissolution will usually require approval of both the directors and the members. However, a nonprofit corporation may include a provision in its articles requiring the approval of a third

person also. For example, such a third person might be a state governor who appointed some of the directors to the board of a nonprofit corporation organized to encourage industrial development in the state. The dissolution is effective when the corporation delivers articles of dissolution to the secretary of state and the secretary of state files them. The dissolved corporation continues its existence, but only for the purpose of liquidating its assets and winding up its affairs.

The secretary of state may administratively dissolve a nonprofit corporation that fails to pay incorporation taxes or to deliver its annual report to the secretary of state, among other things. Minority members or directors may obtain judicial dissolution by a court if the directors are deadlocked, the directors in control are acting illegally or fraudulently, or the members are deadlocked and cannot elect directors for two successive elections, among other reasons.

Problems and Problem Cases

1. At the annual shareholders' meeting of Levisa Oil Corporation, management proposed to increase the number of directors to five from four. Quigley and one other shareholder owning together more than 50 percent of the outstanding shares objected to the proposal. When Quigley was ruled out of order by the chairman of the board, Quigley and the other opposing shareholder stormed out of the meeting. The remaining shareholders voted to elect a five-member board. The new board then voted to issue new shares, which were issued to the minority shareholders. The effect of the issuance was to give the minority shareholders majority ownership of the corporation. Quigley later objected to the actions taken at the meeting. Were the actions taken after Quigley left invalid due to the lack of a quorum?

2. Kinetic Solutions, LLC, is an Internet software business with 15 members. Five members are the only managers of the business; the other 10 members are only investors. The five managing members want to sell part of the business to public investors. Before doing so, they opt to organize the business as a corporation. The five controlling shareholders want to be able to manage the corporation with little interference from other shareholders, and they want to continue to be compensated as managers of the business. The other 10 shareholders want some management control because of their sizable investments, especially if the business is not profitable. They are also concerned about being able to sell their shares at some point in the future. All 15 shareholders plan to raise an additional $50 million in capital by selling shares in the corporation to 1,000 wealthy public shareholders. The 15 original shareholders are unwilling to give the new investors any power to control the corporation or its management. The original shareholders expect that by having 1,000

new shareholders, a public market will be created in their shares. Sketch an ownership control structure (a structure that determines how shareholders own and control the corporation through their rights as shareholders) that serves the ownership control interests of the five controlling shareholders and the 10 other shareholders. What is the best way for the five controlling shareholders to receive returns on their investment in the corporation? What is the best way for the 10 other shareholders to receive returns on their investment in the corporation?

3. The Eliason family owned a majority (5,238) of the 9,990 shares of Brosius-Eliason Co., a building and materials company, with James Eliason (3,928 shares) and his sister Sarah Englehart (1,260) holding the controlling block. The Brosius family owned a total of 3,690 shares. Frank Hewlett owned the remaining 1,062 shares. On July 31, James Eliason executed a proxy giving his daughter, Louise Eliason, authority to vote his shares. Only in the notary public's acknowledgement verifying James's signature did the proxy state that it was irrevocable. The body of the proxy, the part signed by James, did not state it was irrevocable. Two weeks later, James and his sister Sarah made a voting agreement that ensured Eliason family control over the corporation by requiring their shares to be voted as provided in the agreement. The voting agreement was irrevocable, because it was coupled with an interest in each other's shares. Soon after, Sarah and Louise had a falling out when Louise tried to assert her family's control of the company. Consequently, Sarah voted her shares with the Brosiuses and Hewlett in violation of the agreement with James. She argued that she was not bound by the voting agreement with James on the grounds that James could not make the agreement, because he had given Louise an irrevocable proxy two weeks earlier. Was Sarah right?

4. Myron Lasky was a shareholder in Kramett, Inc., a manufacturer of novelty candies. When Kramett's business declined, its board of directors chose to save the business by selling it to a larger candy company, Narron Confectioners, Inc. Narron's shares were trading on the market at $9.25 per share, while Kramett's shares traded at $0.50 per share. Kramett's and Narron's boards of directors approved a merger in which each Kramett shareholder would receive one share of Narron for each 20 shares of Kramett. Both the shareholders of Kramett and Narron approved the merger. What right should Lasky exercise if he objects to the merger terms? What must he do to exercise that right?

5. Karen Shaw, a dairy farmer in Vermont, was a member of a cooperative stock corporation, Agri-Mark, Inc., which was formed to process and market milk and other dairy products for its member farmers in New England and New York. Agri-Mark's equity consisted of contributions from its members. Its members, however, were not shareholders. The only shareholders were directors, who were elected by regional delegates, who in turn were elected by members. If Shaw had a proper purpose, did she have the right to inspect Agri-Mark's member list and the compensation of the corporation's five highest paid executives?

6. For 22 consecutive years, Marston Corporation, a steel producer, has paid a quarterly dividend to its common shareholders. The annual dividend amount has ranged from 1 percent to 4 percent of the market price of Marston's common shares. Marston's board of directors decides not to declare a common dividend for the next three years. Its steel plants are over 40 years old, and several need to be updated or replaced. The board estimates the cost of updating or replacing its steel plants at $2.3 billion. Eliminating the common share dividend will result in Marston retaining an additional $634 million over a three-year period. Marston currently has retained earnings of $1.2 billion. Marston's minority shareholders sue Marton's to force the board of directors to declare the dividend. Will their action be successful?

7. Pomeroy Carnivals Co., Inc. (PCC), is a family-owned corporation that operates carnival rides at fairs and festivals. The founders of the business, Les and Clara Pomeroy, own 79 percent of the shares, and their three children own 21 percent. Les and Clara are the only members of the board of directors of PCC. Acting as directors of PCC, Les and Clara decide to sell 40 percent of its carnival rides and to reduce by 30 percent the number of fairs and festivals in which PCC will operate rides. The sale will result in a one-time cash infusion of $34,000,000, which Les and Clara plan to invest for PCC in commercial real estate. PCC's annual net income from carnivals will drop by $1,650,000, about 55 percent of current annual net income. The children want to sue PCC's board of directors to stop the sale of the carnival rides and the investment of the proceeds in real estate. What is the process by which the children will sue the directors? Can Les and Clara stop the suit?

8. Water Works, Inc., was a closely held corporation operating an automatic car wash in Wisconsin Rapids. Its 204 shares were issued to Duane and Sharon Jorgensen; their daughter, Doreen Barber, and her husband, James; and two family friends, Gary and Mary Tesch. Each received 34 shares, and each was a director. Duane was president; Sharon, Gary, and James were vice presidents; Mary was treasurer; and Doreen was secretary. The corporation's written business plan stated that Duane would be in charge of management and that the six shareholders would be permanent directors. An oral agreement of shareholders stated that Duane would oversee management as long as he lived. Each shareholder received weekly payments from the corporation, the amount of which was determined by the shareholders agreement. In 1995, Duane discovered that some of the officers and directors were engaged in illegal activity on property owned by the corporation and using the corporation's property for their own personal benefit. When Duane demanded the activities stop, the Barbers and Tesches removed the Jorgensens from the board of directors and stopped making payments to them. The Jorgensen's sued the Barbers and Tesches for breach of fiduciary duty. The Barbers and Tesches claimed they owed fiduciary duties only to the corporation and, therefore, the Jorgensens, as shareholders, could not sue in their own names. Were they right?

9. H. F. Ahmanson & Co. was the controlling shareholder of United Savings and Loan Association. There was very little trading in the Association's shares, however. To create a public market for their shares, Ahmanson and a few other shareholders of

the Association incorporated United Financial Corporation and exchanged each of their Association shares for United shares. United then owned more than 85 percent of the shares of the Association. The minority shareholders of the Association were not given an opportunity to exchange their shares. United made two public offerings of its shares. As a result, trading in United shares was very active, while sales of Association shares decreased to half of the formerly low level, with United as virtually the only purchaser. United offered to purchase Association shares from the minority shareholders for $1,100 per share. Some of the minority shareholders accepted this offer. At that time, the shares held by the majority shareholders were worth $3,700. United also caused the Association to decrease its dividend payments. Has Ahmanson done anything wrong?

10. Rexford Rand Corporation had three shareholders, Selwyn Ancel, who owned 50 percent of the shares, and his sons Gregory and Albert who owned 25 percent each. It sold over 200 products to 5,800 customers in many states. In 1991, Gregory was fired as vice president and treasurer, but remained a shareholder. From that point, he received no salary from the corporation, and the corporation never paid dividends. In 1993, Rexford Rand failed to file its annual report with the state of Illinois and, as a result, was administratively dissolved. The dissolution resulted in the name Rexford Rand becoming available for other businesses. Gregory learned of the dissolution but did not inform the other shareholders. Will Gregory act wrongly if he reserves the name Rexford Rand for his own corporation?

11. Jerry Yarmouth was the sole shareholder, director, and officer of J & R Interiors, Inc. The corporation's registered agent was its lawyer. Because the corporation's lawyer closed his office, when the secretary of state mailed a notice for payment of the annual fee and filing of the annual report, Yarmouth never received the notice. Consequently, the secretary of state administratively dissolved the corporation. Believing the corporation was still in existence, Yarmouth continued to transact on behalf of J & R Interiors, including making a contract to buy a $20,000 workbench from Equipto Division Aurora Equipment. Is Yarmouth personally liabile on the contract with Equipto?

Online Research

Corporate Governance Policies

The Council of Institutional Investors is an organization of large pension funds that addresses investment issues. As the representative of pension funds that are significant shareholders in public corporations, the council takes a strong stance in favor of shareholder rights. Log on to the CII's Web site, click on "Learn More" under "Council Policies" to find the CII's positions on shareholder voting rights, shareholder meeting rights, and board accountability to shareholders.

chapter 45

SECURITIES REGULATION

You are the CEO of L'Malle LLC, a nonpublic company that builds and manages shopping malls. L'Malle plans to raise $4,400,000 for construction of L'Malle's newest shopping center complex, Grande L'Malle Geneva. In an effort to avoid the application of the Securities Act of 1933, L'Malle's CFO has proposed that L'Malle issue 22 Profit Participation Plans (PPPs) to two insurance companies, four mutual funds, and 16 individual investors. Under the PPPs, each owner will contribute $200,000 cash to finance the construction of Grande L'Malle Geneva (GLG) and receive 3 percent of the profits generated by GLG. L'Malle will be the exclusive manager of GLG, making all decisions regarding its construction and operation, for which L'Malle will receive a fee equal to 34 percent of GLG's profits.

- Are the PPPs securities under the Securities Act of 1933?
- If the PPPs are securities, may L'Malle sell them pursuant to a registration exemption from the Securities Act of 1933 under Regulation A, Rule 504, Rule 505, or 506?

L'Malle decides to sell the PPPs directly to investors by making a Regulation A offering. As CEO, you will accompany L'Malle's CFO and communications vice president when they visit prospective investors. During those visits, you and the other L'Malle's executives will present copies of the offering circular to prospective investors and make oral reports about the offering, GLG, and L'Malle's business and prospects. You will also answer the investors' questions about L'Malle and GLG.

- Should you be fearful about having liability to the investors under Section 12(a)(2) of the 1933 Act and Rule 10b–5 of the Securities Exchange Act of 1934?

L'Malle decides to make a public offering of its common shares by registering the offering under the Securities Act of 1933 and complying with the requirements of Section 5 of the 1933 Act. The shares will be sold by a firm commitment underwriting.

- Under what legal conditions may L'Malle release earnings reports and make other normal communications with its shareholders and other investors?
- After L'Malle has filed its 1933 Act registration statement with the Securities and Exchange Commission and before the SEC has declared the registration statement effective, under what legal conditions may you (the CEO) and L'Malle's CFO conduct a road show where you pitch the shares to mutual fund investment managers in several cities?
- During that waiting period, may L'Malle post its preliminary prospectus and have an FAQ page for prospective investors at the offering's Web site?
- After the SEC has declared the registration statement effective, under what legal conditions may L'Malle confirm the sale of shares to an investor?
- During that post-effective period, under what legal conditions may L'Malle direct prospective investors from the offering's Web site to L'Malle's corporate Web site, where investors may obtain additional information about L'Malle?

MODERN SECURITIES REGULATION AROSE from the rubble of the great stock market crash of October 1929. After the crash, Congress studied its causes and discovered several common problems in securities transactions, the most important ones being:

1. Investors lacked the necessary information to make intelligent decisions whether to buy, sell, or hold securities.

2. Disreputable sellers of securities made outlandish claims about the expected performance of securities and sold securities in nonexistent companies.

Faced with these perceived problems, Congress chose to require securities sellers to disclose the information that investors need to make intelligent investment decisions. Congress found that investors are able to make intelligent investment decisions if they are given sufficient information about the company whose securities they are to buy. This **disclosure scheme** assumes that investors need assistance from government in acquiring information but that they need no help in evaluating information.

Purposes of Securities Regulation

To implement its disclosure scheme, in the early 1930s Congress passed two major statutes, which are the hub of federal securities regulation in the United States today. These two statutes, the **Securities Act of 1933** and the **Securities Exchange Act of 1934,** have three basic purposes:

1. To require the disclosure of meaningful information about a security and its issuer to allow investors to make intelligent investment decisions.

2. To impose liability on those persons who make inadequate and erroneous disclosures of information.

3. To regulate insiders, professional sellers of securities, securities exchanges, and other self-regulatory securities organizations.

The crux of the securities acts is to impose on issuers of securities, other sellers of securities, and selected buyers of securities the affirmative duty to disclose important information, even if they are not asked by investors to make the disclosures. By requiring disclosure, Congress hoped to restore investor confidence in the securities markets. Congress wanted to bolster investor confidence in the honesty of the stock market and thus encourage more investors to invest in securities. Build-

ing investor confidence would increase capital formation and, it was hoped, help the American economy emerge from the Great Depression of the 1930s.

Congress has reaffirmed the purposes of the securities law many times since the 1930s by passing laws that expand investor protections. Most recent is the enactment of the Sarbanes–Oxley Act of 2002, a response to widespread misstatements and omissions in corporate financial statements. Many public investors lost most of their life savings in the collapses of firms like Enron, while insiders profited. As we learned in Chapters 4 and 43 and will learn in this chapter and Chapter 46, the Sarbanes–Oxley Act imposes duties on corporations, their officers, and their auditors and provides for a Public Company Accounting Oversight Board to establish auditing standards.

LOG ON

www.law.uc.edu/CCL/index.html
The Securities Lawyer's Deskbook is maintained by the Center for Corporate Law at the University of Cincinnati College of Law. You can find the text of all the federal securities statutes and SEC regulations.

Securities and Exchange Commission

The Securities and Exchange Commission (SEC) was created by the 1934 Act. Its responsibility is to administer the 1933 Act, 1934 Act, and other securities statutes. Like other federal administrative agencies, the SEC has legislative, executive, and judicial functions. Its legislative branch promulgates rules and regulations; its executive branch brings enforcement actions against alleged violators of the securities statutes and their rules and regulations; its judicial branch decides whether a person has violated the securities laws.

SEC Actions
The SEC is empowered to investigate violations of the 1933 Act and 1934 Act and to hold hearings to determine whether the acts have been violated. Such hearings are held before an administrative law judge (ALJ), who is an employee of the SEC. The administrative law judge is a finder of both fact and law. Decisions of the ALJ are reviewed by the commissioners of the SEC. Decisions of the commissioners are appealed to the U.S. court of appeals. Most SEC actions are

not litigated. Instead, the SEC issues consent orders, by which the defendant promises not to violate the securities laws in the future but does not admit to having violated them in the past.

The SEC has the power to impose civil penalties (fines) up to $500,000 and to issue **cease and desist orders.** A cease and desist order directs a defendant to stop violating the securities laws and to desist from future violations. Nonetheless, the SEC does not have the power to issue injunctions; only courts may issue injunctions. The 1933 Act and the 1934 Act empower the SEC only to ask federal district courts for injunctions against persons who have violated or are about to violate either act. The SEC may also ask the courts to grant ancillary relief, a remedy in addition to an injunction. Ancillary relief may include, for example, the disgorgement of profits that a defendant has made in a fraudulent sale or in an illegal insider trading transaction.

To reduce the risk that a securities issuer's or other person's behavior will violate the securities law and result in an SEC action, anyone may contact the SEC's staff in advance, propose a transaction or course of action, and ask the SEC to issue a **no-action letter.** In the no-action letter, the SEC's staff states it will take no legal action against the issuer or other person if the issuer or other person acts as indicated in the no-action letter. Issuers often seek no-action letters before making exempted offerings of securities and excluding shareholder proposals from their proxy statements, issues we discuss later in the chapter. Since a no-action letter is issued by the SEC's staff and not the commissioners, it is not binding on the commissioners. Nonetheless, issuers that comply with no-action letters rarely face SEC action.

LOG ON

www.sec.gov
You can read more about the SEC at the SEC Web site.

What Is a Security?

The first issue in securities regulation is the definition of a security. If a transaction involves no security, then the law of securities regulation does not apply. The 1933 Act defines the term **security** broadly:

> Unless the context otherwise requires the term "security" means any note, stock, treasury stock, security future, bond, debenture, evidence of indebtedness, certificate of inter-

est or participation in any profit-sharing agreement, . . . preorganization certificate or subscription, . . . investment contract, voting trust certificate, . . . fractional undivided interest in oil, gas, or mineral rights, any put, call, straddle, option, or privilege on any security, . . . or, in general, any interest or instrument commonly known as a "security."

The 1934 Act definition of security is similar, but excludes notes and drafts that mature not more than nine months from the date of issuance.

While typical securities like common shares, preferred shares, bonds, and debentures are defined as securities, the definition of a security also includes many contracts that the general public may believe are not securities. This is because the term **investment contract** is broadly defined by the courts. The Supreme Court's three-part test for an investment contract, called the *Howey* test, has been the guiding beacon in the area for more than 50 years.[1] The *Howey* test states that an investment contract is an **investment of money** in a **common enterprise** with an expectation of **profits solely from the efforts of others.**

In the *Howey* case, the sales of plots in an orange grove along with a management contract were held to be sales of securities. The purchasers had investment motives (they intended to make a profit from, not to consume, the oranges produced by the trees). There was a common enterprise, because the investors provided the capital to finance the orange grove business and shared in its earnings. The sellers, not the buyers, did all of the work needed to make the plots profitable.

In other cases, sales of limited partnership interests, Scotch whisky receipts, and restaurant franchises have been held to constitute investment contracts and, therefore, securities.

Courts define in two ways the common enterprise element of the *Howey* test. All courts permit horizontal commonality to satisfy the common enterprise requirement. Horizontal commonality requires that investors' funds be pooled and that profits of the enterprise be shared pro rata by investors. Some courts accept vertical commonality, in which the investors are similarly affected by the efforts of the person who is promoting the investment.

Courts have used the *Howey* test to hold that some contracts with typical security names are not securities. The courts point out that some of these contracts possess few of the typical characteristics of a security. For example, in *United Housing Foundation, Inc. v. Forman,*[2] the

---

[1]*SEC v. W. J. Howey Co.,* 328 U.S. 293 (U.S. Sup. Ct. 1946).
[2]*United Housing Foundation Inc. v. Forman,* 421 U.S. 837 (U.S. Sup. Ct. 1975).

Supreme Court held that although tenants in a cooperative apartment building purchased contracts labeled as stock, the contracts were not securities. The "stock" possessed few of the typical characteristics of stock and the economic realities of the transaction bore few similarities to those of the typical stock sale: The stock gave tenants no dividend rights or voting rights in proportion to the number of shares owned, it was not negotiable, and it could not appreciate in value. More important, tenants bought the stock not for the purpose of investment but to acquire suitable living space.

However, when investors are misled to believe that the securities laws apply because a seller sold a contract bearing both the name of a typical security and significant characteristics of that security, the securities laws do apply to the sale of the security. The application of this doctrine led to the Supreme Court's rejection of the sale-of-business doctrine, which had held that the sale of 100 percent of the shares of a corporation to a single purchaser who would manage the corporation was not a security. The rationale for the sale-of-business doctrine was that the purchaser failed to meet element 3 of the *Howey* test because he expected to make a profit from his own efforts in managing the business. Today, when a business sale is effected by the sale of stock, the transaction is covered by the securities acts if the stock possesses the characteristics of stock.

In 1990, the Supreme Court further extended this rationale in *Reves v. Ernst & Young*,[3] adopting the **family resemblance test** to determine whether promissory notes were securities. The Supreme Court held that it is inappropriate to apply the *Howey* test to notes. Instead, applying the family resemblance test, the Court held that notes are presumed to be securities unless they bear a "strong family resemblance" to a type of note that is not a security.

The five characteristics of notes that are not securities are:

1. There is no recognized market for the notes.
2. The note is not part of a series of notes.
3. The buyer of the note does not need the protection of the securities laws.
4. The buyer of the note has no investment intent.
5. The buyer has no expectation that the securities laws apply to the sale of the note.

Types of notes that are not securities include consumer notes, mortgage notes, short-term notes secured by a lien on a small business, short-term notes secured by accounts receivable, and notes evidencing loans by commercial banks for current operations.

In the following case, the Supreme Court applied the *Howey* test.

[3]494 U.S. 56 (U.S. Sup. Ct. 1990).

SEC v. Edwards   540 U.S. 389 (U.S. S. Ct. 2004)

Charles Edwards was the chairman, chief executive officer, and sole shareholder of ETS Payphones, Inc. ETS sold pay telephones to the public. The payphones were offered with a site lease, a five-year leaseback and management agreement, and a buyback agreement. All but a tiny fraction of purchasers chose this package, although other management options were offered. The purchase price for the payphone packages was approximately $7,000. Under the leaseback and management agreement, purchasers were promised $82 per month, which was a 14 percent annual return on the purchase price. Purchasers were not involved in the day-to-day operation of the payphones they owned. ETS selected the site for the phone, installed the equipment, arranged for connection and long-distance service, collected coin revenues, and maintained and repaired the phone. Under the buyback agreement, ETS promised to refund the full purchase price of the package at the end of the lease or within 180 days of a purchaser's request.

In its marketing materials and on its Web site, ETS trumpeted the "incomparable payphone" as "an exciting business opportunity," in which recent deregulation had "opened the door for profits for individual payphone owners and operators." According to ETS, "very few business opportunities can offer the potential for ongoing revenue generation that is available in today's pay telephone industry."

In reality, the payphones did not generate enough revenue for ETS to make the payments required by the leaseback agreements, so the company depended on funds from new investors to meet its obligations. In September 2000, ETS filed for bankruptcy protection. The SEC brought a civil enforcement action alleging that Edwards and ETS had violated the registration requirements of Section 5 of the Securities Act of 1933 and the antifraud provisions of the 1933 and 1934 securities acts. The district court concluded that the payphone sale-and-leaseback arrangement was an investment contract within the meaning of the federal securities laws. Edwards and ETS appealed to the court of appeals, which reversed the district court's decision. It held that ETS's scheme did not offer either capital appreciation or a participation in the earnings of the enterprise and that the purchasers' returns on their investments was not derived solely from the efforts of others because the purchasers had a contractual entitlement to the return. The SEC asked the Supreme Court of the United States to review the decision of the court of appeals.

O'Connor, Justice

"Opportunity doesn't always knock . . . sometimes it rings." And sometimes it hangs up. So it did for the 10,000 people who invested a total of $300 million in the payphone sale-and-leaseback arrangements touted by ETS under that slogan. In this case, we must decide whether a moneymaking scheme is excluded from the term "investment contract" simply because the scheme offered a contractual entitlement to a fixed, rather than a variable, return.

Congress' purpose in enacting the securities laws was to regulate *investments,* in whatever form they are made and by whatever name they are called. To that end, it enacted a broad definition of "security," sufficient to encompass virtually any instrument that might be sold as an investment. Section 2(a)(1) of the 1933 Act and § 3(a)(10) of the 1934 Act define "security" to include "any note, stock, treasury stock, security future, bond, debenture, . . . investment contract, . . . [or any] instrument commonly known as a 'security.'" "Investment contract" is not itself defined.

The test for whether a particular scheme is an investment contract was established in our decision in *SEC v. W. J. Howey Co.,* 328 U.S. 293 (1946). We look to whether the scheme involves an investment of money in a common enterprise with profits to come solely from the efforts of others.

When Congress included "investment contract" in the definition of security, it was using a term the meaning of which had been crystallized by the state courts' interpretation of their "blue sky" laws. The state courts had defined an investment contract as a contract or scheme for the placing of capital or laying out of money in a way intended to secure income or profit from its employment, and had uniformly applied that definition to a variety of situations where individuals were led to invest money in a common enterprise with the expectation that they would earn a profit solely through the efforts of the promoter or a third party. Thus, when we held that "profits" must "come solely from the efforts of others," we were speaking of the profits that investors seek on their investment, not the profits of the scheme in which they invest. We used "profits" in the sense of income or return, to include, for example, dividends, other periodic payments, or the increased value of the investment.

There is no reason to distinguish between promises of fixed returns and promises of variable returns for purposes of the test, so understood. In both cases, the investing public is attracted by representations of investment income, as purchasers were in this case by ETS's invitation to watch the profits add up. More-

over, investments pitched as low-risk (such as those offering a "guaranteed" fixed return) are particularly attractive to individuals more vulnerable to investment fraud, including older and less sophisticated investors. Under the reading Edwards advances, unscrupulous marketers of investments could evade the securities laws by picking a rate of return to promise. We will not read into the securities laws a limitation not compelled by the language that would so undermine the laws' purposes.

Edwards protests that including investment schemes promising a fixed return among investment contracts conflicts with our precedent. We disagree. No distinction between fixed and variable returns was drawn in the blue sky law cases that the *Howey* Court used, in formulating the test. Indeed, two of those cases involved an investment contract in which a fixed return was promised. *People v. White,* 12 P.2d 1078 (Cal. 1932) (agreement between defendant and investors stated that investor would give defendant $5,000, and would receive $7,500 from defendant one year later); *Stevens v. Liberty Packing Corp.,* 161 A. 193 (N.J. 1932) ("ironclad contract" offered by defendant to investors entitled investors to $56 per year for 10 years on initial investment of $175, ostensibly in sale-and-leaseback of breeding rabbits).

None of our post-*Howey* decisions is to the contrary. In *United Housing Foundation, Inc. v. Forman,* 421 U.S. 837 (1975), we considered whether "shares" in a nonprofit housing cooperative were investment contracts under the securities laws. We identified the "touchstone" of an investment contract as "the presence of an investment in a common venture premised on a reasonable expectation of profits to be derived from the entrepreneurial or managerial efforts of others," and then laid out two examples of investor interests that we had previously found to be "profits." Those were "capital appreciation resulting from the development of the initial investment" and "participation in earnings resulting from the use of investors' funds." We contrasted those examples, in which "the investor is attracted solely by the prospects of a return on the investment," with housing cooperative shares, regarding which the purchaser "is motivated by a desire to use or consume the item purchased." Thus, *Forman* supports the commonsense understanding of "profits" in the *Howey* test as simply financial returns on investments.

The Eleventh Circuit's perfunctory alternative holding, that respondent's scheme falls outside the definition because purchasers had a contractual entitlement to a return, is incorrect and inconsistent with our precedent. We are considering investment *contracts*. The fact that investors have bargained for a return on their investment does not mean that the return is not also expected to come solely from the efforts of others. Any other conclusion would conflict with our holding that an investment contract was offered in *Howey* itself.

We hold that an investment scheme promising a fixed rate of return can be an "investment contract" and thus a "security" subject to the federal securities laws.

Judgment reversed in favor of the SEC; remanded to the Court of Appeals.

Securities Act of 1933

The Securities Act of 1933 (1933 Act) is concerned primarily with public distributions of securities. That is, the 1933 Act regulates the sale of securities while they are passing from the hands of the issuer into the hands of public investors. An issuer selling securities publicly must make necessary disclosures at the time the issuer sells the securities to the public.

The 1933 Act has two principal regulatory components: (1) registration provisions and (2) liability provisions. The registration requirements of the 1933 Act are designed to give investors the information they need to make intelligent decisions whether to purchase securities when an issuer sells its securities to the public. The various liability provisions in the 1933 Act impose liability on sellers of securities for misstating or omitting facts of material significance to investors.

Registration of Securities under the 1933 Act

The Securities Act of 1933 is primarily concerned with protecting investors when securities are sold by an issuer to investors. That is, the 1933 Act regulates the process during which issuers offer and sell their securities to investors, primarily public investors.

Therefore, the 1933 Act requires that *every* offering of securities be registered with the SEC prior to any offer or sale of the securities, unless the offering or the securities are exempt from registration. That is, an issuer and its underwriters may not offer or sell securities unless the securities are registered with the SEC or exempt from registration. Over the next few pages, we will cover the registration process. Then the exemptions from registration will be addressed.

Mechanics of a Registered Offering

When an issuer makes a decision to raise money by a public offering of securities, the issuer needs to obtain the assistance of securities market professionals. The issuer will contact a managing underwriter, the primary person assisting the issuer in selling the securities. The managing underwriter will review the issuer's operations and financial statements and reach an agreement with the issuer regarding the type of securities to sell, the offering price, and the compensation to be paid to the underwriters. The issuer and the managing underwriter will determine what type of underwriting to use.

In a **standby underwriting,** the underwriters obtain subscriptions from prospective investors, but the issuer sells the securities only if there is sufficient investor interest in the securities. The underwriters receive warrants—options to purchase the issuer's securities at a bargain price—as compensation for their efforts. The standby underwriting is typically used only to sell common shares to existing shareholders pursuant to a preemptive rights offering.

With a **best efforts underwriting,** the underwriters are merely agents making their best efforts to sell the issuer's securities. The underwriters receive a commission for their selling efforts. The best efforts underwriting is used when an issuer is not well established and the underwriter is unwilling to risk being unable to sell the securities.

The classic underwriting arrangement is a **firm commitment underwriting.** Here the managing underwriter forms an underwriting group and a selling group. The underwriting group agrees to purchase the securities from the issuer at a discount from the public offering price— for example, 25 cents per share below the offering price. The selling group agrees to buy the securities from the underwriters also at a discount—for example, 12½ cents per share below the offering price. Consequently, the underwriters and selling group bear much of the risk with a firm commitment underwriting, but they also stand to make the most profit under such an arrangement.

Securities Offerings on the Internet Increasingly, issuers are using the Internet to make public securities offerings, especially initial public offerings (IPOs) of companies' securities. The Internet provides issuers and underwriters the advantage of making direct offerings to all investors simultaneously, that is, selling directly to investors without the need for a selling group. The first

Internet securities offering that was approved by the SEC was a firm commitment underwriting. Internet offerings have increased dramatically since 1998. In the future, the Internet will become the dominant medium for marketing securities directly to investors.

Registration Statement and Prospectus

The 1933 Act requires the issuer of securities to register the securities with the SEC before the issuer or underwriters may offer or sell the securities. Registration requires filing a **registration statement** with the SEC. Historical and current data about the issuer, its business, its officers and directors, full details about the securities to be offered, and the use of the proceeds of the issuance, among other information, must be included in the registration statement prepared by the issuer of the securities with the assistance of the managing underwriter, securities lawyers, and independent accountants. Generally, the registration statement must include audited balance sheets as of the end of each of the two most recent fiscal years, in addition to audited income statements and audited statements of changes in financial position for each of the last three fiscal years.

The registration statement becomes effective after it has been reviewed by the SEC. The 1933 Act provides that the registration statement becomes effective automatically on the 20th day after its filing, unless the SEC delays or advances the effective date.

The **prospectus** is the basic selling document of an offering registered under the 1933 Act. Most of the information in the registration statement must be included in the prospectus. It must be furnished to every purchaser of the registered security prior to or concurrently with the sale of the security to the purchaser. The prospectus enables an investor to base his investment decision on all of the relevant data concerning the issuer, not merely on the favorable information that the issuer may be inclined to disclose voluntarily.

Although most prospectuses are delivered in person or by mail, the growth of the Internet as a communication tool has resulted in many issuers transmitting their prospectuses in their Web pages.

Section 5: Timing, Manner, and Content of Offers and Sales

The 1933 Act restricts the issuer's and underwriter's ability to communicate with prospective purchasers of the securities. Section 5 of the 1933 Act states the basic rules regarding the timing, manner, and content of offers and sales. It creates three important periods of time in the life of a securities offering: (1) the pre-filing period, (2) the waiting period, and (3) the post-effective period.

The Pre-filing Period Prior to the filing of the registration statement (the pre-filing period), the issuer and any other person may **not offer or sell** the securities to be registered. The purpose of the pre-filing period is to prevent premature communications about an issuer and its securities, which may encourage an investor to make a decision to purchase the security before all the information she needs is available. The pre-filing period also marks the start of what is sometimes called the **quiet period,** which continues for the full duration of the securities offering. A prospective issuer, its directors and officers, and its underwriters must avoid publicity about the issuer and the prospective issuance of securities during the pre-filing period and the rest of the quiet period.

The SEC has created a few nonexclusive safe harbors that allow issuers about to make public offerings to continue to release information to the public yet not violate Section 5. Under Rule 168, public issuers are permitted to continue to release regularly released factual business and forward-looking information. The type of information, as well as the timing, manner, and form, must be similar to past releases by the public issuer. Under Rule 169, nonpublic issuers may release only factual business information of the type they have previously released. For both types of issuers, the information may not mention the offering or be a part of it.

In addition, Rule 163A now allows any issuer to communicate *any* information about itself more than 30 days prior to the filing of a registration statement, provided the issuer does not reference the upcoming securities offering.

During the 30 days prior to the filing date, however, Rule 163 allows only well-known, seasoned issuers to use a **free-writing prospectus.** Well-known seasoned issuers are public issuers with at least $700 million of public float, that is, the value of its common shares held by non-affiliates of the issuer, which excludes officers and directors. A free-writing prospectus is a written offer that may contain any information about the issuer or its securities that does not conflict with the registration statement. It must include a legend that indicates an investor may obtain a prospectus at the SEC Web site. The free-writing prospectus must usually be filed with the SEC not later than the filing date of the registration statement.

SEC Rule 135 permits the issuer to publish a notice about a prospective offering during the pre-filing period. The notice may contain only the name of the issuer, the amount of the securities offered, and a basic description of the securities and the offering. It may not name the underwriters or state the price at which the securities will be offered.

The Waiting Period   The waiting period is the time between the filing date and the effective date of the registration statement, when the issuer is waiting for the SEC to declare the registration statement effective. During the waiting period, Section 5 permits the securities to be **offered but not sold.** However, not all kinds of offers are permitted. Face-to-face oral offers (including personal phone calls) are allowed during the waiting period. However, written offers may be made only by a statutory prospectus, usually a **preliminary prospectus,** or a free-writing prospectus. During the waiting period, the preliminary prospectus often omits the price of the securities. (A final prospectus will be available after the registration statement becomes effective. It will contain the price of the securities.) Other so-called free writings are not permitted during the waiting period.

The waiting period is part of the quiet period, but the issuer may continue to disclose regularly released factual business and forward looking information about itself.

In addition, one type of general advertisement, called the **tombstone ad,** is permitted during the waiting period and thereafter. The tombstone ad, which appears in financial publications, is permitted by SEC Rule 134, which allows disclosure of the same information as is allowed by Rule 135 plus the general business of the issuer, the price of the securities, and the names of the underwriters who are helping the issuer to sell the securities. In addition, Rule 134 requires the tombstone ad to state where a hard copy of a prospectus may be obtained or downloaded from the Internet. See Figure 1.

Under Rules 433 and 164, well-known seasoned issuers may continue to use a free-writing prospectus with few limitations after the waiting period, including a legend that the investor may obtain a prospectus at the SEC Web site. Other issuers may use a free-writing prospectus only after the filing date and only after the investor receiving it has also received a prospectus or an e-mail with a hyperlink to the prospectus. Although the free-writing prospectus may include information not in the registration statement, it may not conflict with information in the registration statement or other documents filed with the SEC

under the 1934 Act. All issuers must file the free-writing prospectus with SEC by the date of its first use.

Issuers making public offerings will typically send their CEOs and other top officers on the road to talk to securities analysts and institutional investors during the waiting period. These road shows are permissible, whether an investor attends in person or watches a Web cast, provided it is a live, real-time road show to a live audience.

Road shows that are not viewed live in real-time by a live audience are considered written offers, but are permitted during the waiting period if they meet the requirements of free-writing prospectuses. That means that issuers other than well-known seasoned issuers must provide a prospectus to investors who view an electronic road show that is not live. Such issuers must also make a copy of the electronic road show available to any investor or file a copy of the electronic road show with the SEC.

The Internet is an exceptional medium to communicate with investors during the waiting period. Investors may easily view a tombstone ad, watch a road show, and download a prospectus from an offering Web page.

The waiting period is an important part of the regulatory scheme of the 1933 Act. It provides an investor with adequate time (at least 20 days) to judge the wisdom of buying the security during a period when he cannot be pressured to buy it. Not even a contract to buy the security may be made during the waiting period.

The Post-effective Period   After the effective date (the date on which the SEC declares the registration effective), Section 5 permits the security to be **offered and also to be sold,** provided that the buyer has received a **final prospectus** (a preliminary prospectus is not acceptable for this purpose). Road shows and free-writing prospectuses may continue to be used. Other written offers not previously allowed are permitted during the post-effective period, but only if the offeree has received a final prospectus.

The Internet can be used extensively during the post-effective period. From the issuer's Web page, an investor may be required to download a final prospectus in order to obtain access to other written information about the issuer and the offering. Since the final prospectus download would be a delivery of the final prospectus to the investor, all communications thereafter would be legal even if they were written.

Liability for Violating Section 5   Section 12(a)(1) of the 1933 Act imposes liability on any person who violates the provisions of Section 5. Liability extends to any *purchaser* to whom an illegal offer or sale was made. The purchaser's remedy is *rescission* or damages.

Figure 1   *Rule 134 Tombstone Ad*

September 14, 2005

$4,353,983,175

Google™

Google Inc.

14,759,265 Shares

Class A Common Stock

Price $295 Per Share

Morgan Stanley   Credit Suisse First Boston

Allen & Company LLC

Citigroup   JPMorgan

Lehman Brothers   UBS Investment Bank

Thomas Weisel Partners LLC   Blaylock & Company, Inc.

M.R. Beal & Company   William Blair & Company   CIBC World Markets

Capital Management Group Securities LLC   Deutsche Bank Securities

Lazard Capital Markets   Loop Capital Markets, LLC   Needham & Company, LLC

Piper Jaffray   Siebert Capital Markets   The Williams Capital Group, L.P.

Communications and Information That an Issuer or Underwriter May Provide to the Public or to Investors during a Registered Offering

Pre-filing Period		Waiting Period	Post-effective Period
More than 30 days prior to the filing date of the registration statement	Less than 30 days prior to the filing date of the registration statement	After the filing date of the registration statement and before the SEC has declared the registration statement effective	After the SEC has declared the registration statement effective
• Any information about the issuer, provided the information does not reference the prospective securities offering	• Negotiations between the issuer and underwriters who are in privity of contract with the issuer • Formation of the Selling Group, if every member of the Selling Group is also a retail division of a member of the Underwriting Group (that is, in privity of contract with the issuer) • Rule 135 Notice of a Prospective Offering • Regularly released factual business information about the issuer, provided it is released at the regular time and with regular emphasis and is not intended for investors or prospective investors • If the issuer is a public issuer, regularly released forward looking information about the issuer, provided it is released at the regular time and with regular emphasis and is not intended for investors or prospective investors • If the issuer is a well-known seasoned issuer, a free-writing prospectus that contains any information that does not conflict with the registration statement and contains a legend indicating that a prospectus will be available at the SEC Web site when the filing date arrives.	• Formation of the Selling Group whether or not every member is also a member of the Underwriting Group (that is, in privity of contract with the issuer) • Rule 135 Notice of a Prospective Offering • Rule 134 Tombstone Ad • Oral offers (face-to-face either in person or on the phone) • Preliminary Prospectus • Regularly released factual business information about the issuer, provided it is released at the regular time and with regular emphasis and is not intended for investors or prospective investors • If the issuer is a public issuer, regularly released forward looking information about the issuer, provided it is released at the regular time and with regular emphasis and is not intended for investors or prospective investors • A free-writing prospectus that contains any information that does not conflict with the registration statement, if investors have a preliminary prospectus or an e-mail with a hyperlink to the preliminary prospectus • If the issuer is a well-known seasoned issuer, a free-writing prospectus that contains any information that does not conflict with the registration statement, if it contains a legend indicating that a prospectus is available at the SEC Web site. • Road show, if it is provided live to a live audience, the attendees have a copy of the preliminary prospectus, or it meets the requirements of a free-writing prospectus	• Rule 135 Notice of a Prospective Offering • Rule 134 Tombstone Ad • Oral offers (face-to-face either in person or on the phone) • Final Prospectus • Sales of securities, if a final prospectus is delivered to the buyer prior to or simultaneous with the confirmation of sale • Any written offer, if the offeree has received a final prospectus. • Regularly released factual business information about the issuer, provided it is released at the regular time and with regular emphasis and is not intended for investors or prospective investors • If the issuer is a public issuer, regularly released forward looking information about the issuer, provided it is released at the regular time and with regular emphasis and is not intended for investors or prospective investors • A free-writing prospectus that contains any information that does not conflict with the registration statement, if investors have a final prospectus or an e-mail with a hyperlink to the final prospectus • If the issuer is a well-known seasoned issuer, a free-writing prospectus that contains any information that does not conflict with the registration statement, if it contains a legend indicating that a prospectus is available at the SEC Web site. • Road show, if it is provided live to a live audience, the attendees have a copy of a final prospectus, or it meets the requirements of a free-writing prospectus

Exemptions from the Registration Requirements of the 1933 Act

Complying with the registration requirements of the 1933 Act, including the restrictions of Section 5, is a burdensome, time-consuming, and expensive process. Planning and executing an issuer's first public offering may consume six months and cost in excess of $1 million. Consequently, some issuers prefer to avoid registration when they sell securities. There are two types of exemptions from the registration requirements of the 1933 Act: securities exemptions and transaction exemptions.

Securities Exemptions
Exempt securities never need to be registered, regardless who sells the securities, how they are sold, or to whom they are sold. The following are the most important securities exemptions.[4]

1. Securities issued or guaranteed by any government in the United States and its territories.
2. A note or draft that has a maturity date not more than nine months after its date of issuance.
3. A security issued by a nonprofit religious, charitable, educational, benevolent, or fraternal organization.
4. Securities issued by banks and by savings and loan associations.
5. Securities issued by railroads and trucking companies regulated by the Surface Transportation Board.
6. An insurance policy or an annuity contract.

Although the types of securities listed above are exempt from the registration provisions of the 1933 Act, they are not exempt from the general antifraud provisions of the securities acts. For example, any fraud committed in the course of selling such securities can be attacked by the SEC and by the persons who were defrauded under Section 17(a) of the 1933 Act and Section 10(b) of the 1934 Act.

Transaction Exemptions
The most important 1933 Act registration exemptions are the transaction

exemptions. If a security is sold pursuant to a transaction exemption, that sale is exempt from registration. Subsequent sales, however, are not automatically exempt. Future sales must be made pursuant to a registration or another exemption.

The transaction exemptions are exemptions from the registration provisions. The general antifraud provisions of the 1933 Act and the 1934 Act apply to exempted and nonexempted transactions.

The most important transaction exemptions are those available to issuers of securities. These exemptions are the intrastate offering exemption, the private offering exemption, and the small offering exemptions.

Intrastate Offering Exemption
Under Section 3(a)(11), an offering of securities solely to investors in one state by an issuer resident and doing business in that state is exempt from the 1933 Act's registration requirements. The reason for the exemption is that there is little federal government interest in an offering that occurs in only one state. Although the offering may be exempt from SEC regulation, state securities law may require a registration. The expectation is that state securities regulation will adequately protect investors.

The SEC has defined the intrastate offering exemption more precisely in Rule 147. An issuer must have at least 80 percent of its gross revenues and 80 percent of its assets in the state and use at least 80 percent of the proceeds of the offering in the state. Resale of the securities is limited to persons within the state for nine months.

Although Rule 147 is not an exclusive rule, the SEC scrutinizes closely an intrastate offering that does not comply with it.

Private Offering Exemption
Section 4(2) of the 1933 Act provides that the registration requirements of the 1933 Act "shall not apply to transactions by an issuer not involving any public offering." A private offering is an offering to a small number of purchasers who can protect themselves because they are wealthy or because they are sophisticated in investment matters and have access to the information that they need to make intelligent investment decisions.

To create greater certainty about what a private offering is, the SEC adopted Rule 506. Although an issuer may exempt a private offering under either the courts' interpretation of Section 4(2) or Rule 506, the SEC tends to treat Rule 506 as the exclusive way to obtain the exemption.

Rule 506 Under Rule 506, which is part of Securities Act Regulation D, investors must be qualified to purchase the securities. The issuer must reasonably believe

---

[4]Excluded from the list of securities exemptions are the intrastate offering and small offering exemptions. Although the 1933 Act denotes them (except for the section 4(6) exemption) as securities exemptions, they are in practice transaction exemptions. An exempt security is exempt from registration forever. But when securities originally sold pursuant to an intrastate or small offering exemption are resold at a later date, the subsequent sales may have to be registered. The exemption of the earlier offering does not exempt a future offering. The SEC treats these two exemptions as transaction exemptions. Consequently, this chapter also treats them as transaction exemptions.

that each purchaser is either (a) an accredited investor or (b) an unaccredited investor who "has such knowledge and experience in financial and business matters that he is capable of evaluating the merits and risks of the prospective investment." Accredited investors include institutional investors (such as banks and mutual funds), wealthy investors, and high-level insiders of the issuer (such as executive officers, directors, and partners). Issuers should have purchasers sign a suitability or **investment letter** verifying that they are qualified.

An issuer may sell to no more than 35 unaccredited purchasers who have sufficient investment knowledge and experience; it may sell to an unlimited number of accredited purchasers, regardless of their investment sophistication.

Each purchaser must be given or have access to the information she needs to make an informed investment decision. For a public company making a nonpublic offering under Rule 506 (such as General Motors sellings $5 billion of its notes to 25 mutual funds plus 5 other, unaccredited investors), purchasers must receive information in a form required by the 1934 Act, such as a 10-K or annual report. The issuer must provide the following audited financial statements: two years' balance sheets, three years' income statements, and three years' statements of changes in financial position.

For a nonpublic company making a nonpublic offering under Rule 506, the issuer must provide much of the same nonfinancial information required in a registered offering. A nonpublic company may, however, obtain some relief from the burden of providing audited financial statements to investors. When the amount of the issuance is $2 million or less, only one year's balance sheet need be audited. If the amount issued exceeds $2 million but not $7.5 million, only one year's balance sheet, one year's income statement, and one year's statement of changes in financial position need be audited. When the amount issued exceeds $7.5 million, the issuer must provide two years' balance sheets, three years' income statements, and three years' statements of changes in financial position. In any offering of any amount by a nonpublic issuer, when auditing would involve unreasonable effort or expense, only an audited balance sheet is needed. When a limited partnership issuer finds that auditing involves unreasonable effort or expense, the limited partnership may use financial statements prepared by an independent accountant in conformance with the requirements of federal tax law.

Rule 506 prohibits the issuer from making any general public selling effort. This prevents the issuer from using the radio, newspapers, and television. However, offers to an individual one-on-one are permitted.

In addition, the issuer must take reasonable steps to ensure that the purchasers do not resell the securities in a manner that makes the issuance a public distribution rather than a private one. Usually, the investor must hold the security for a minimum of six months.

In the *Mark* case, the issuer failed to prove it was entitled to a private offering exemption under Rule 506. The case features the improper use of an investment letter.

Mark v. FSC Securities Corp.   870 F.2d 331 (6th Cir. 1989)

FSC Securities Corp., a securities brokerage, sold limited partnership interests in the Malaga Arabian Limited Partnership to Mr. and Mrs. Mark. A total of 28 investors purchased limited partnership interests in Malaga. All investors were asked to execute subscription documents, including a suitability or investment letter in which the purchaser stated his income level, that he had an opportunity to obtain relevant information, and that he had sufficient knowledge and experience in business affairs to evaluate the risks of the investment.

When the value of the limited partnership interests fell, the Marks sued FSC to rescind their purchase on the grounds that FSC sold unregistered securities in violation of the Securities Act of 1933. The jury held that the offering was exempt as an offering not involving a public offering. The Marks appealed.

Simpson, Judge

Section 4(2) of the Securities Act exempts from registration with the SEC "transactions by an issuer not involving any public offering." There are no hard and fast rules for determining whether a securities offering is exempt from registration under the general language of Section 4(2).

However, the "safe harbor" provision of Regulation D, Rule 506, deems certain transactions to be not involving any public offering within the meaning of Section 4(2). FSC had to prove that certain objective tests were met. These conditions include the general conditions not in dispute here, and the following specific conditions:

(i) Limitation on number of purchasers. The issuer shall reasonably believe that there are no more than thirty-five purchasers of securities in any offering under this Section.

(ii) Nature of purchasers. The issuer shall reasonably believe immediately prior to making any sale that each purchaser who is not an accredited investor either alone or with his purchaser representative(s) has such knowledge and experience in financial and business matters that he is capable of evaluating the merits and risks of the prospective investment.

In this case, we take the issuer to be the general partners of Malaga. FSC is required to offer evidence of the issuer's reasonable belief as to the nature of each purchaser. The only testimony at trial competent to establish the issuer's belief as to the nature of the purchasers was that of Laurence Leafer, a general partner in Malaga. By his own admission, he had no knowledge about any purchaser, much less any belief, reasonable or not, as to the purchasers' knowledge and experience in financial and business matters.

Q: What was done to determine if investors were, in fact, reasonably sophisticated?

A: Well, there were two things. Number one, we had investor suitability standards that had to be met. You had to have a certain income, be in a certain tax bracket, this kind of thing. Then in the subscription documents themselves, they, when they sign it, supposedly represented that they had received information necessary to make an informed investment decision, and that they were sophisticated. And if they were not, they relied on an offering representative who was.

Q: Did you review the subscription documents that came in for the Malaga offering?

A: No.

Q: So do you know whether all of the investors in the Malaga offering met the suitability and sophistication requirements?

A: I don't.

FSC also offered as evidence the Marks' executed subscription documents, as well as a set of documents in blank, to establish the procedure it followed in the Malaga sales offering. Although the Marks' executed documents may have been sufficient to establish the reasonableness of any belief the issuer may have had as to the Marks' particular qualifications, that does not satisfy Rule 506. The documents offered no evidence from which a jury could conclude the issuer reasonably believed each purchaser was suitable. Instead, all that was proved was the sale of 28 limited partnership interests, and the circumstances under which those sales were intended to have been made. The blank subscriptions documents simply do not amount to probative evidence, when it is the answers and information received from purchasers that determine whether the conditions of Rule 506 have been met.

Having concluded that the Malaga limited-partnership offering did not meet the registration exemption requirement of Rule 506 of Regulation D, we conclude that the Marks are entitled to the remedy of rescission.

Judgment reversed in favor of the Marks; remanded to the trial court.

Small Offering Exemptions
Sections 3(b) and 4(6) of the 1933 Act permit the SEC to exempt from registration any offering by an issuer not exceeding $5 million. Several SEC rules and regulations permit an issuer to sell small amounts of securities and avoid registration. The rationale for these exemptions is that the dollar amount of the securities offered or the number of purchasers is too small for the federal government to be concerned with registration. State securities law may require registration, however.

Rule 504 SEC Rule 504 of Regulation D allows a nonpublic issuer to sell up to $1 million of securities in a 12-month period and avoid registration. Rule 504 sets no limits on the number of offerees or purchasers. The purchasers need not be sophisticated in investment matters, and the issuer need disclose information only as required by state securities law. Rule 504 permits general selling efforts, and purchasers are free to resell the securities at any time but only if the issuer either registers the securities under state securities law or sells only to accredited investors pursuant to a state securities law exemption.

Rule 505 Rule 505 of Regulation D allows any issuer to sell up to $5 million of securities in a 12-month period and avoid registration. No general selling efforts are allowed, and purchasers may not resell the securities for at least six months or one year, depending on the type of issuer. Like Rule 506, the issuer may sell to no more than 35 unaccredited purchasers, and there is no limit on the number of accredited purchasers. The purchasers, however, need not be sophisticated in investment matters. Rule 505 has the same disclosure requirements as Rule 506.

Regulation A Regulation A permits a nonpublic issuer to sell up to $5 million of securities in a one-year period. There is no limit on the number of purchasers, no purchaser sophistication requirement, and no purchaser resale restriction.

The Regulation A disclosure document is the offering circular, which must be filed with the SEC. The offering circular is required to contain a balance sheet dated within 90 days before the filing date of the offering circular. It must also contain two years' income statements, cash flow statements, and statements of shareholder equity. Ordinarily, the financial statements need not be audited unless the issuer is otherwise required to have audited financial statements.

There is a 20-day waiting period after the filing of the offering circular, during which offers may be made. Oral offers are permitted, as are brief advertisements and written offers by an offering circular. Sales are permitted after the waiting period.

Regulation A also permits issuers to determine investors' interest in a planned offering prior to undertaking the expense of preparing an offering circular.

Securities Offerings on the Internet

With the emergence of the Internet as a significant communication tool, small issuers have sought to make offerings to investors over the Internet. Such offerings can easily run afoul of Rules 505 and 506 of Regulation D, which prohibit public solicitations of investors. Spring Street Brewing Company, the first issuer to offer securities via the Web in 1995, avoided registration by using the Regulation A exemption. Other issuers have used Rule 504, and some have made registered offerings exclusively over the Internet.

Transaction Exemptions for Nonissuers

Although it is true that the registration provisions apply primarily to issuers and those who help issuers sell their securities publicly, the 1933 Act states that every person who sells a security is potentially subject to Section 5's restrictions on the timing of offers and sales. You must learn the most important rule of the 1933 Act: **Every transaction in securities must be registered with the SEC or be exempt from registration.**

This rule applies to every person, including the small investor who, through the New York Stock Exchange, sells securities that may have been registered by the issuer 15 years earlier. The small investor must either have the issuer register her sale of securities or find an exemption from registration that applies to the situation. Fortunately, most small investors who resell securities will have an exemption from the registration requirements of the 1933 Act. The transaction ordinarily used by these resellers is Section 4(1) of the 1933 Act. It provides an exemption for "transactions by any person other than an issuer, underwriter, or dealer."

For example, if you buy GM common shares on the New York Stock Exchange, you may freely resell them without a registration. You are not an issuer (GM is). You are not a dealer (because you are not in the business of selling securities). And you are not an underwriter (because you are not helping GM distribute the shares to the public).

Application of this exemption when an investor sells shares that are already publicly traded is easy; however, it is more difficult to determine whether an investor can use this exemption when the investor sells **restricted securities.**

Sale of Restricted Securities

Restricted securities are securities issued pursuant to Rules 505 and 506 and sometimes under Rule 504. Restricted securities are supposed to be held by a purchaser unaffiliated with the issuer for at least six months if the issuer is a public company and one year if the issuer is not public. If they are sold earlier, the investor may be deemed an underwriter who has assisted the issuer in selling the securities to the general public. Consequently, both the issuer and the investor may have violated Section 5 of the 1933 Act by selling nonexempted securities prior to a registration of the securities with the SEC. As a result, all investors who purchased securities from the issuer in the exempted offering may have the remedy of rescission under Section 12(a)(1), resulting in the issuer being required to return to investors all the proceeds of the issuance.

For example, an investor buys 10,000 common shares issued by Arcom Corporation pursuant to a Rule 506 private offering exemption. One month later, the investor sells the securities to 40 other investors. The original investor has acted as an underwriter because he has helped Arcom distribute the shares to the public. The original investor may not use the issuer's private offering exemption because it exempted only the issuer's sale to him. As a result, both the original investor and Arcom have violated Section 5. The 40 investors who purchased the securities from the original investor—and all other investors who purchased common shares from the issuer in the Rule 506 offering—may rescind their purchases under Section 12(a)(1) of the 1933 Act, receiving from their seller the return of their investment.

SEC Rule 144 allows purchasers of restricted securities to resell the securities and not be deemed underwriters. The resellers must hold the securities for at least six months if the securities issuer is a public company and for one year if the issuer is nonpublic, after which the investors may sell all or part of the restricted securities. After the passage of those time periods, investors not affiliated with the issuer may sell all or part of the restricted securities they hold. For investors affiliated with the issuers, such as an officer or director, the rules are more complex. In any three-month period, the affiliated reseller may sell only a limited number of securities—the greater of 1 percent of the outstanding securities or the average weekly volume of trading. The reseller must file a notice (Form 144) with the SEC.

Issuer's Exemptions from the Registration Requirements of the Securities Act of 1933

	Type of Issuer	Amount of Securities Sold	Number of Purchasers	Purchaser Qualifications
Rule 504	Nonpublic issuer	$1,000,000 in a 12-month period	No limit	None
Rule 505	Any issuer	$5,000,000 in a 12-month period	Same number of purchasers as Rule 506	None

Rule 506	Any issuer	Unlimited	• 35 unaccredited purchasers and
			• Unlimited accredited purchasers
			  • High-level insiders,
			  • Income > $200,000,
			  • NW > $1,000,000, or
			  • Institutional investors
				Issuer must reasonably believe that each purchaser is either
				• accredited or
				• alone or with his purchaser representative has such knowledge and experience in financial and business matters to be capable of evaluating the merits and risks of the investment

Regulation A	Nonpublic issuer	$5,000,000 in a one-year period	No limit	None
Rule 147	• Issuer organized and doing business in the offerees' and purchasers' state • Issuer has 80% of its assets in the state • Issuer generates 80% of its gross revenues from the state • Issuer uses 80% of the offering's proceeds in the state	Unlimited	No limit	All offerees and purchasers must reside in the issuer's state

Consequence of Obtaining a Securities or Transaction Exemption

When an issuer has obtained an exemption from the registration provisions of the 1933 Act, the Section 5 limits on when and how offers and sales may be made do not apply. Consequently, Section 12(a)(1)'s remedy of rescission is unavailable to an investor who has purchased securities in an exempt offering.

When an issuer has attempted to comply with a registration exemption and has failed to do so, any offer or sale of securities by the issuer may violate Section 5. Because the issuer has offered or sold nonexempted securities prior to filing a registration statement with the SEC, any purchaser may sue the issuer under Section 12(a)(1) of the 1933 Act.

Although the registration provisions of the 1933 Act do not apply to an exempt offering, the antifraud

Disclosure Requirements	General Solicitations	Resale Restrictions
None	Permitted, if the issuer registered the securities under state law or sold the securities only to accredited investors pursuant to a state securities exemption	No resale restrictions, if the issuer registered the securities under state law or sold the securities only to accredited investors pursuant to a state securities exemption
Same disclosure requirements as Rule 506	Not permitted	Same resale restrictions as Rule 506

If issuer sells only to accredited purchasers: the issuer must give the investors only the information requested by investors. If issuer sells to any unaccredited purchasers, the issuer must give investors:
• the same nonfinancial information as required for a registered offering
• audited financial statements
  • Public issuer: 2 balance sheets, 3 income statements, 3 statements of changes in financial position
  • Nonpublic issuer: if amount of securities sold is
    • ≤$2,000,000: 1 balance sheet
    • >$2,000,000 but ≤$7,500,000: 1 balance sheet, 1 income statement, 1 statement of changes in financial position
    • >$7,500,000: 2 balance sheets, 3 income statements, 3 statements of changes in financial position
  • Nonpublic issuer, if auditing involves unreasonable effort or expense:
    • 1 balance sheet
Any information given to one investor must be given to all investors.
	Not permitted	• Investors may not sell securities of a public issuers for at least six months
		• Investors may not sell securities of a nonpublic issuer for at least one year
		• After the passage of the time periods above, a nonaffiliated investor may sell the securities without volume restrictions
		• After the passage of the time periods above, an affiliated investor may sell in any three-month period the greater of
		  • 1% of the issuer's outstanding shares or
		  • the average weekly volume of the issuer's shares

The issuer must use an Offering Circular. Financial statements in the Offering Circular: • Need not be audited unless otherwise required • 1 balance sheet, 2 income statements, 2 cash flow statements, 2 statements of shareholder equity	Permitted	No resale restrictions
None	Permitted	Investors may not sell the securities outside the issuer's state for nine months

provisions of the 1933 Act and 1934 Act, which are discussed later, are applicable. For example, when an issuer gives false information to a purchaser in a Rule 504 offering, the issuer may have violated the antifraud provisions of the two acts. The purchaser may obtain damages from the issuer under the antifraud rules even though the transaction is exempt from registration.

Liability Provisions of the 1933 Act

To deter fraud, deception, and manipulation and to provide remedies to the victims of such practices, Congress included a number of liability provisions in the Securities Act of 1933.

Ethics in Action

Section 5 of the 1933 Act and many of the exemptions from registration put severe limits on an issuer's ability to inform prospective investors during a registered or exempted offering. For example, during the quiet period of a registered offering, the SEC takes a dim view of an issuer's attempt to publicize itself and its business. Rules 505 and 506 prohibit general solicitations.

- Are those limitations consistent with the principles of a country that has a market-based economy and elevates freedom of speech to a constitutional right? Would a rights theorist support American securities law? How about a profit maximizer?
- Might a believer in justice theory view be more likely to support American law regulating issuances of securities? Whom would a justice theorist want to see protected?
- Who is the typical securities purchaser? Is it not someone from the wealthier classes of citizens? Is securities regulation welfare for the wealthy?

Note that Section 5 of the 1933 Act does not require that investors receive a preliminary prospectus during the waiting period. In fact, an issuer can completely avoid giving investors a prospectus until a sale is confirmed during the post-effective period. That means an investor may not receive a prospectus until he has made his purchase decision. Moreover, many investors find the prospectus overwhelming to read, and if they do read it, it is often couched in legalese that is difficult to understand. Finally, the prospectus mostly comprises historical information. It is more correctly a "retrospectus," not a prospectus, and contains information that is already in the marketplace. Yet professionals like auditors and investment bankers make millions of dollars by being involved in the preparation of the prospectus, which is not received by investors at the right time, not read, not readable, and not relevant to investment decisions.

- Is it ethical for professionals to profit enormously from their role of putting together a prospectus that provides little real value to investors?

Liability for Defective Registration Statements

Section 11 of the 1933 Act provides civil liabilities for damages when a 1933 Act registration statement on its effective date misstates or omits a material fact. A purchaser of securities issued pursuant to the defective registration statement may sue certain classes of persons that are listed in Section 11—the issuer, its chief executive officer, its chief accounting officer, its chief financial officer, the directors, other signers of the registration statement, the underwriter, and experts who contributed to the registration statement (such as auditors who issued opinions regarding the financial statements or lawyers who issued an opinion concerning the tax aspects of a limited partnership). The purchaser's remedy under Section 11 is for damages caused by the misstatement or omission. Damages are presumed to be equal to the difference between the purchase price of the securities less the price of the securities at the time of the lawsuit.

Section 11 is a radical liability section for three reasons. First, reliance is usually not required; that is, the purchaser need not show that she relied on the misstatement or omission in the registration statement. In fact, the purchaser need not have read the registration statement or have seen it. Second, privity is not required; that is, the purchaser need not prove that she purchased the securities from the defendant. All she has to prove is that the defendant is in one of the classes of persons liable under Section 11. Third, the purchaser need not prove that the defendant negligently or intentionally misstated or omitted a material fact. Instead, a defendant who

otherwise would be liable under Section 11 may escape liability by proving that he exercised due diligence.

Section 11 Defenses A defendant can escape liability under Section 11 by proving that the purchaser knew of the misstatement or omission when she purchased the security. In addition, a defendant may raise the **due diligence defense.** It is the more important of the two defenses.

Any defendant except the issuer may escape liability under Section 11 by proving that he acted with due diligence in determining the accuracy of the registration statement. The due diligence defense basically requires the defendant to prove that he was not negligent. The exact defense varies, however, according to the class of defendant and the portion of the registration statement that is defective. Most defendants must prove that after a **reasonable investigation** they had **reasonable grounds to believe** and **did believe** that the registration statement was true and contained no omission of material fact.

Experts need to prove due diligence only in respect to the parts that they have contributed. For example, independent auditors must prove due diligence in ascertaining the accuracy of financial statements for which they issue opinions. Due diligence requires that an auditor at least comply with generally accepted auditing standards (GAAS). Experts are those who issue an opinion regarding information in the registration statement. For example, auditors of financial statements are experts under Section 11 because they issue opinions regarding the ability of the financial statements to present fairly the financial position of the companies they have audited. A geologist who issues an opinion regarding the amount of oil reserves held by an energy company is a Section 11 expert if her opinion is included in a registration statement filed by the limited partnership.

Nonexperts meet their due diligence defense for parts contributed by experts if they had no reason to believe and did not believe that the expertised parts misstated or omitted any material fact. This defense does not require the nonexpert to investigate the accuracy of expertised portions, unless something alerted the nonexpert to problems with the expertised portions.

The *BarChris* case is the most famous case construing the due diligence defense of Section 11.

Escott v. BarChris Construction Corp.   283 F.Supp. 643 (S.D.N.Y. 1968)

BarChris Construction Corporation was in the business of constructing bowling centers. With the introduction of automatic pinsetters in 1952, there was a rapid growth in the popularity of bowling, and BarChris's sales increased from $800,000 in 1956 to over $9 million in 1960. By 1960, it was building about 3 percent of the lanes constructed, while Brunswick Corporation and AMF were building 97 percent. BarChris contracted with its customers to construct and equip bowling alleys for them. Under the contracts, a customer was required to make a small down payment in cash. After the alleys were constructed, customers gave BarChris promissory notes for the balance of the purchase price. BarChris discounted the notes with a factor. The factor kept part of the face value of the notes as a reserve until the customer paid the notes. BarChris was obligated to repurchase the notes if the customer defaulted.

In 1960, BarChris offered its customers an alternative financing method in which BarChris sold the interior of a bowling alley to a factor, James Talcott, Inc. Talcott then leased the alley either to a BarChris customer (Type A financing) or to a BarChris subsidiary that then subleased to the customer (Type B financing). Under Type A financing, BarChris guaranteed 25 percent of the customer's obligation under the lease. With Type B financing, BarChris was liable for 100 percent of its subsidiaries' lease obligations. Under either financing method, BarChris made substantial expenditures before receiving payment from customers and, therefore, experienced a constant need of cash.

In early 1961, BarChris decided to issue debentures and to use part of the proceeds to help its cash position. In March 1961, BarChris filed with the SEC a registration statement covering the debentures. The registration statement became effective on May 16. The proceeds of the offering were received by BarChris on May 24, 1961. By that time, BarChris had difficulty collecting from some of its customers, and other customers were in arrears on their payments to the factors of the discounted notes. Due to overexpansion in the bowling alley industry, many BarChris customers failed. On October 29, 1962, BarChris filed a petition for bankruptcy. On November 1, it defaulted on the payment of interest on the debentures.

Escott and other purchasers of the debentures sued BarChris and its officers, directors, and auditors, among others, under Section 11 of the Securities Act of 1933. BarChris's registration statement contained material misstatements and omitted material facts. It overstated current assets by $609,689 (15.6 percent), sales by $653,900 (7.7 percent), and earnings per share by 10 cents (15.4 percent) in the 1960 balance sheet and income statement audited by Peat, Marwick, Mitchell & Co. The registration statement also understated BarChris's contingent liabilities by $618,853 (42.8 percent) as of April 30, 1961. It overstated gross profit for the first quarter of 1961 by $230,755 (92 percent) and sales for the first quarter of 1961 by $519,810 (32.1 percent). The March 31, 1961, backlog was overstated by $4,490,000 (186 percent). The 1961 figures were not audited by Peat, Marwick.

In addition, the registration statement reported that prior loans from officers had been repaid, but failed to disclose that officers had made new loans to BarChris totaling $386,615. BarChris had used $1,160,000 of the proceeds of the debentures to pay old debts, a use not disclosed in the registration statement. BarChris's potential liability of $1,350,000 to factors due to customer delinquencies on factored notes was not disclosed. The registration statement represented BarChris's contingent liability on Type B financings as 25 percent instead of 100 percent. It misrepresented the nature of BarChris's business by failing to disclose that BarChris was already engaged and was about to become more heavily engaged in the operation of bowling alleys, including one called Capitol Lanes, as a way of minimizing its losses from customer defaults.

Trilling, BarChris's controller, signed the registration statement. Auslander, a director, signed the registration statement. Peat, Marwick consented to being named as an expert in the registration statement. All three would be liable to Escott unless they could meet the due diligence defense of Section 11.

McLean, District Judge

The question is whether Trilling, Auslander, and Peat, Marwick have proved their due diligence defenses. The position of each defendant will be separately considered.

Trilling

Trilling was BarChris's controller. He signed the registration statement in that capacity. Trilling entered BarChris's employ in October 1960. He was Kircher's [BarChris's treasurer] subordinate. When Kircher asked him for information, he furnished it.

Trilling was not a member of the executive committee. He was a comparatively minor figure in BarChris. The description of BarChris's management in the prospectus does not mention him. He was not considered to be an executive officer.

Trilling may well have been unaware of several of the inaccuracies in the prospectus. But he must have known of some of them. As a financial officer, he was familiar with BarChris's finances and with its books of account. He knew that part of the cash on deposit on December 31, 1960, had been procured temporarily by Russo [BarChris's executive vice president] for window-dressing purposes. He knew that BarChris was operating Capitol Lanes in 1960. He should have known, although perhaps through carelessness he did not know at the time, that BarChris's contingent liability on Type B lease transactions was greater than the prospectus stated. In the light of these facts, I cannot find that Trilling believed the entire prospectus to be true.

But even if he did, he still did not establish his due diligence defenses. He did not prove that as to the parts of the prospectus expertised by Peat, Marwick he had no reasonable ground to believe that it was untrue. He also failed to prove, as to the parts of the prospectus not expertised by Peat, Marwick, that he made a reasonable investigation which afforded him a reasonable ground to believe that it was true. As far as appears, he made no investigation. He did what was asked of him and assumed that others would properly take care of supplying accurate data as to the other aspects of the company's business. This would have been well enough but for the fact that he signed the registration statement. As a signer, he could not avoid responsibility by leaving it up to others to make it accurate. Trilling did not sustain the burden of proving his due diligence defenses.

Auslander

Auslander was an outside director, i.e., one who was not an officer of BarChris. He was chairman of the board of Valley Stream National Bank in Valley Stream, Long Island. In February 1961, Vitolo [BarChris's president] asked him to become a director of BarChris. In February and early March 1961, before accepting Vitolo's invitation, Auslander made some investigation of BarChris. He obtained Dun & Bradstreet reports that contained sales and earnings figures for periods earlier than December 31, 1960. He caused inquiry to be made of certain of BarChris's banks and was advised that they regarded BarChris favorably. He was informed that inquiry of Talcott had also produced a favorable response.

On March 3, 1961, Auslander indicated his willingness to accept a place on the board. Shortly thereafter, on March 14, Kircher sent him a copy of BarChris's annual report for 1960. Auslander observed that BarChris's auditors were Peat, Marwick. They were also the auditors for the Valley Stream National Bank. He thought well of them.

Auslander was elected a director on April 17, 1961. The registration statement in its original form had already been filed, of course without his signature. On May 10, 1961, he signed a signature page for the first amendment to the registration statement which was filed on May 11, 1961. This was a separate sheet without any document attached. Auslander did not know that it was a signature page for a registration statement. He vaguely understood that it was something "for the SEC."

At the May 15 directors' meeting, however, Auslander did realize that what he was signing was a signature sheet to a registration statement. This was the first time that he had appreciated the fact. A copy of the registration statement in its earlier form as amended on May 11, 1961, was passed around at the meeting. Auslander glanced at it briefly. He did not read it thoroughly. At the May 15 meeting, Russo and Vitolo stated that everything was in order and that the prospectus was correct. Auslander believed this statement.

In considering Auslander's due diligence defenses, a distinction must be drawn between the expertised and nonexpertised portions of the prospectus. As to the former, Auslander knew that Peat, Marwick had audited the 1960 figures. He believed them to be correct because he had confidence in Peat, Marwick. He had no reasonable ground to believe otherwise.

As to the nonexpertised portions, however, Auslander is in a different position. He seems to have been under the impression that Peat, Marwick was responsible for all the figures. This impression was not correct, as he would have realized if he had read the prospectus carefully. Auslander made no investigation of the accuracy of the prospectus. He relied on the assurance of Vitolo and Russo, and upon the information he had received in answer to his inquiries back in February and early March. These inquiries were general ones, in the nature of a credit check. The information which he received in answer to them was also general, without specific reference to the statements in the prospectus, which was not prepared until some time thereafter.

It is true that Auslander became a director on the eve of the financing. He had little opportunity to familiarize himself with the company's affairs. The question is whether, under such circumstances, Auslander did enough to establish his due diligence.

Section 11 imposes liability upon a director, no matter how new he is. He is presumed to know his responsibility when he becomes a director. He can escape liability only by using that reasonable care to investigate the facts that a prudent man would employ in the management of his own property. In my opinion, a prudent man would not act in an important matter without any knowledge of the relevant facts, in sole reliance upon general information which does not purport to cover the particular case. To say that such minimal conduct measures up to the statutory standard would, to all intents and purposes, absolve new directors from responsibility merely because they are new. This is not a sensible construction of Section 11, when one bears in mind its fundamental purpose of requiring full and truthful disclosure for the protection of investors.

Auslander has not established his due diligence defense with respect to the misstatements and omissions in those portions of the prospectus other than the audited 1960 figures.

Peat, Marwick

The part of the registration statement purporting to be made upon the authority of Peat, Marwick as an expert was the 1960 figures. But because the statute requires the court to determine Peat, Marwick's belief, and the grounds thereof, "at the time such part of the registration statement became effective," for the purposes of this affirmative defense, the matter must be viewed as of May 16, 1961, and the question is whether at that time Peat, Marwick, after reasonable investigation, had reasonable ground to believe and did believe that the 1960 figures were true and that no material fact had been omitted from the registration statement which should have been included in order to make the 1960 figures not misleading. In deciding this issue, the court must consider not only what Peat, Marwick did in its 1960 audit, but also what it did in its subsequent S–1 review. The proper scope of that review must also be determined.

The 1960 Audit

Peat, Marwick's work was in general charge of a member of the firm, Cummings, and more immediately in charge of Peat, Marwick's manager, Logan. Most of the actual work was performed by a senior accountant, Berardi, who had junior assistants, one of whom was Kennedy.

Berardi was then about 30 years old. He was not yet a CPA. He had had no previous experience with the bowling industry. This was his first job as a senior accountant. He could hardly have been given a more difficult assignment.

It is unnecessary to recount everything that Berardi did in the course of the audit. We are concerned only with the

evidence relating to what Berardi did or did not do with respect to those items which I have found to have been incorrectly reported in the 1960 figures in the prospectus. More narrowly, we are directly concerned only with such of those items as I have found to be material.

First and foremost is Berardi's failure to discover that Capitol Lanes had not been sold. This error affected both the sales figure and the liability side of the balance sheet. Fundamentally, the error stemmed from the fact that Berardi never realized that Heavenly Lanes and Capitol were two different names for the same alley. Berardi assumed that Heavenly was to be treated like any other completed job.

Berardi read the minutes of the board of directors meeting of November 22, 1960, which recited that "the Chairman recommended that the Corporation operate Capitol Lanes." Berardi knew from various BarChris records that Capitol Lanes, Inc., was paying rentals to Talcott. Also, a Peat, Marwick work paper bearing Kennedy's initials recorded that Capitol Lanes, Inc., held certain insurance policies.

Berardi testified that he inquired of Russo about Capitol Lanes and that Russo told him that Capitol Lanes, Inc., was going to operate an alley someday but as yet it had no alley. Berardi testified that he understood that the alley had not been built and that he believed that the rental payments were on vacant land.

I am not satisfied with this testimony. If Berardi did hold this belief, he should not have held it. The entries as to insurance and as to "operation of alley" should have alerted him to the fact that an alley existed. He should have made further inquiry on the subject. It is apparent that Berardi did not understand this transaction.

He never identified this mysterious Capitol with the Heavenly Lanes which he had included in his sales and profit figures. The vital question is whether he failed to make a reasonable investigation which, if he had made it, would have revealed the truth.

Certain accounting records of BarChris, which Berardi testified he did not see, would have put him on inquiry. One was a job cost ledger card for job no. 6036, the job number which Berardi put on his own sheet for Heavenly Lanes. This card read "Capitol Theatre (Heavenly)." In addition, two accounts receivable cards each showed both names on the same card, Capitol and Heavenly. Berardi testified that he looked at the accounts receivable records but that he did not see these particular cards. He testified that he did not look on the job cost ledger cards because he took the costs from another record, the costs register.

The burden of proof on this issue is on Peat, Marwick. Although the question is a rather close one, I find that Peat, Marwick has not sustained that burden. Peat, Marwick has not proved that Berardi made a reasonable investigation as far as

Capitol Lanes was concerned and that his ignorance of the true facts was justified.

I turn now to the errors in the current assets. As to cash, Berardi properly obtained a confirmation from the bank as to BarChris's cash balance on December 31, 1960. He did not know that part of this balance had been temporarily increased by the deposit of reserves returned by Talcott to BarChris conditionally for a limited time. I do not believe that Berardi reasonably should have known this. It would not be reasonable to require Berardi to examine all of BarChris's correspondence files [which contained correspondence indicating that BarChris was to return the cash to Talcott] when he had no reason to suspect any irregularity.

The S–1 Review

The purpose of reviewing events subsequent to the date of a certified balance sheet (referred to as an S–1 review when made with reference to a registration statement) is to ascertain whether any material change has occurred in the company's financial position which should be disclosed in order to prevent the balance sheet figures from being misleading. The scope of such a review, under generally accepted auditing standards, is limited. It does not amount to a complete audit.

Berardi made the S–1 review in May 1961. He devoted a little over two days to it, a total of 20½ hours. He did not discover any of the errors or omissions pertaining to the state of affairs in 1961, all of which were material. The question is whether, despite his failure to find out anything, his investigation was reasonable within the meaning of the statute.

What Berardi did was to look at a consolidating trial balance as of March 31, 1961, which had been prepared by BarChris, compare it with the audited December 31, 1960, figures, discuss with Trilling certain unfavorable developments which the comparison disclosed, and read certain minutes. He did not examine any important financial records other than the trial balance.

In substance, Berardi asked questions, he got answers which he considered satisfactory, and he did nothing to verify them. Since he never read the prospectus, he was not even aware that there had ever been any problem about loans from officers. He made no inquiry of factors about delinquent notes in his S–1 review. Since he knew nothing about Kircher's notes of the executive committee meetings, he did not learn that the delinquency situation had grown worse. He was content with Trilling's assurance that no liability theretofore contingent had become direct. Apparently the only BarChris officer with whom Berardi communicated was Trilling. He could not recall making any inquiries of Russo, Vitolo, or Pugliese [a BarChris vice president].

There had been a material change for the worse in BarChris's financial position. That change was sufficiently serious so that the failure to disclose it made the 1960 figures misleading. Berardi did not discover it. As far as results were concerned, his S–1 review was useless.

Accountants should not be held to a standard higher than that recognized in their profession. I do not do so here. Berardi's review did not come up to that standard. He did not take some of the steps which Peat, Marwick's written program prescribed. He did not spend an adequate amount of time on a task of this magnitude. Most important of all, he was too easily satisfied with glib answers to his inquiries.

This is not to say that he should have made a complete audit. But there were enough danger signals in the materials which he did examine to require some further investigation on his part. Generally accepted auditing standards require such further investigation under these circumstances. It is not always sufficient merely to ask questions.

Here again, the burden of proof is on Peat, Marwick. I find that burden has not been satisfied. I conclude that Peat, Marwick has not established its due diligence defense.

Judgment for Escott and the other purchasers.

Due Diligence Meeting Officers, directors, underwriters, accountants, and other experts attempt to reduce their Section 11 liability by holding a due diligence meeting at the end of the waiting period, just prior to the effective date of a registration statement. At the due diligence meeting, the participants obtain assurances and demand proof from each other that the registration statement contains no misstatements or omissions of material fact. If it appears from the meeting that there are inadequacies in the investigation of the information in the reg-

istration statement, the issuer will delay the effective date until an appropriate investigation is undertaken.

Statute of Limitations Under Section 11, a defendant has liability for only a limited period of time, pursuant to a statute of limitations. A purchaser must sue the defendant within one year after the misstatement or omission was or should have been discovered by the purchaser. In addition, the purchaser may sue the defendant not more than three years after the securities were offered to the

Due Diligence Defenses under Section 11 of the 1933 Act

	For Expertised Portion of the Registration Statement	For Nonexpertised Portion of the Registration Statement
Expert Liable only for the expertised portion of the registration statement contributed by the expert. Examples: Auditor that issues an audit opinion regarding financial statements; Geologist that issues an opinion regarding mineral reserves; Lawyer that issues a tax opinion regarding the tax deductibility of losses	After a reasonable investigation, had reason to believe and did believe that there were no misstatements or omissions of material fact in the expertised portion of the registration statement contributed by the expert.	Not liable for this portion of the registration statement.
Nonexpert Liable for the entire registration statement. Examples: Directors of the issuer; CEO, CFO, and CAO of the issuer; Underwriters who assist in the sale of the securities and help prepare the registration statement	Had no reason to believe and did not believe that there were any misstatements or omissions of material fact in the expertised portions of the registration statement.	After a reasonable investigation, had reason to believe and did believe that there were no misstatements or omissions of material fact in the nonexpertised portion of the registration statement.

public. Although the word "offered" is used in the statute, the three-year period does not usually begin until after the registered securities are first delivered to a purchaser. The Sarbanes–Oxley Act of 2002 arguably extends the statute of limitations to two years after discovery of facts constituting a violation of Section 11 and five years after the violation.

Other Liability Provisions
Section 12(a)(2) of the 1933 Act prohibits misstatements or omissions of material fact in any written or oral communication in connection with the general distribution of any security by an issuer (except government-issued or government-guaranteed securities). Section 17(a) prohibits the use of any device or artifice to defraud, or the use of any untrue or misleading statement, in connection with the offer or sale of any security. Two of the subsections of Section 17(a) require that the defendant merely act negligently, while the third subsection requires proof of scienter. Scienter is the intent to deceive, manipulate, or defraud the purchaser. Some courts have held that scienter also includes recklessness.

Since these liability sections are part of federal law, there must be some connection between the illegal activity and interstate commerce for liability to exist. Section 11 merely requires the filing of a registration statement with the SEC. Sections 12(a)(1), 12(a)(2), and 17(a) require the use of the mails or other instrumentality or means of interstate communication or transportation. Chapter 46 has more information on liability under Sections 11, 12(a)(2), and 17(a).

Criminal Liability
Section 24 of the 1933 Act provides for criminal liability for any person who willfully

violates the Act or its rules and regulations. The maximum penalty is a $10,000 fine and five years' imprisonment. Criminal actions under the 1933 Act are brought by the attorney general of the United States, not by the SEC.

Securities Exchange Act of 1934

The Securities Exchange Act of 1934 is chiefly concerned with requiring the disclosure of material information to investors. Unlike the 1933 Act, which is primarily a one-time disclosure statute concerned with protecting investors when an issuer sells its shares to investors, the 1934 Act requires **periodic disclosure** by issuers with publicly held equity securities. That is, the 1934 Act is primarily concerned with protecting investors after the issuer becomes a public company. An issuer with publicly traded equity securities must report annually to its shareholders and submit annual and quarterly reports to the SEC. Also, any material information about the issuer must be disclosed as the issuer obtains it, unless the issuer has a valid business purpose for withholding disclosure.

In addition, the 1934 Act regulates insiders' transactions in securities, proxy solicitations, tender offers, brokers and dealers, and securities exchanges. The 1934 Act also has several sections prohibiting fraud and manipulation in securities transactions. The ultimate purpose of the 1934 Act is to keep investors fully informed to allow them to make intelligent investment decisions at any time.

Registration of Securities under the 1934 Act

Under the 1934 Act, issuers must **register classes of securities.** This is different from the 1933 Act, which requires issuers to register issuances of securities. Under the 1933 Act, securities are registered only for the term of an issuance. Under the 1934 Act, registered classes of securities remain registered until the issuer takes steps to deregister the securities. The chief consequence of having securities registered under the 1934 Act is that the issuer is required periodically to disclose information about itself to its owners and the SEC.

Registration Requirement   Two types of issuers must register securities with the SEC under the 1934 Act.

1. An issuer whose total assets exceed $10 million must register a class of equity securities held by at least 500 holders if the securities are traded in interstate commerce.
2. An issuer must register any security traded on a national security exchange, such as common shares traded on the New York Stock Exchange or NASDAQ.

To register the securities, the issuer must file a 1934 Act **registration statement** with the SEC. The information required in the 1934 Act registration statement is similar to that required in the 1933 Act registration statement, except that offering information is omitted.

Termination of Registration   An issuer may avoid the expense and burden of complying with the periodic disclosure and other requirements of the 1934 Act if the issuer terminates its registration. A 1934 Act registration

---

The Global Business Environment

Securities Regulation of Global Issuers

All market-based economies have securities laws regulating the issuance and trading of securities. Even the Republic of China, which allows limited capitalism, has a comprehensive securities law, although not as extensive as United States law. All foreign laws regulate the issuance of securities, securities exchanges, and securities professionals.

Most countries' securities law applies equally to domestic and foreign issuers of securities. In the United States, for example, foreign issuers must register an issuance with the SEC in the same way a domestic company registers, under Regulation C.

Canadian securities law is similar to American law, although primarily enacted by the provinces and territories instead of the national government. Nonetheless, Canadian securities law is substantially similar throughout Canada. In general, domestic and foreign issuers must make securities offerings with a prospectus that has been filed with a securities commissioner. One exemption from registration is the private issuer exemption, which may be used by a nonpublic company with no more than 50 security holders. Another exemption is for offerings to a purchaser not exceeding C$150,000. While securities qualified by a prospectus may generally be freely traded in the secondary market, securities sold through an exemption must be held by the initial purchasers for 6 to 18 months, depending on the exemption.

For more information on international securities law, visit the Web site of the International Organization of Securities Commissions at www.iosco.org.

of a class of securities may be terminated if the issuer has fewer than 300 shareholders of that class. In addition, a registration may be terminated if the issuer has fewer than 500 shareholders of the registered class of equity securities and assets of no more than $10 million for each of the last three years. However, an issuer with securities listed on a national securities exchange would not be able to terminate a registration of the listed securities.

Periodic Reporting Requirement To maintain a steady flow of material information to investors, the 1934 Act requires public issuers to file periodic reports with the SEC. Three types of issuers must file such reports:

1. An issuer whose total assets exceed $10 million and who has a class of equity securities held by at least 500 holders, if the securities are traded in interstate commerce.

2. An issuer whose securities are traded on a national securities exchange.

3. An issuer who has made a registered offering of securities under the 1933 Act.

The first two types of issuers—which are issuers that must also register securities under the 1934 Act—must file several periodic reports, including an annual report (Form 10-K) and a quarterly report (Form 10-Q). They must file a current report (Form 8-K) when material events occur. Comparable reports must also be sent to their shareholders. The third type of issuer—an issuer who must disclose under the 1934 Act only because it has made a registered offering under the 1933 Act—must file the same reports as the other issuers, except that it need not provide an annual report to its shareholders. 1934 Act disclosure required of the third type of issuer is in addition to the disclosure required by the 1933 Act.

The 10-K annual report must include audited financial statements plus current information about the conduct of the business, its management, and the status of its securities. It includes management's description and analysis of the issuer's financial condition (the so-called MDA section) and the names of directors and executive officers, including their compensation (such as salary and stock options). The 10-K auditing requirements are the same as for a 1933 Act registration statement—two years' audited balance sheets, three years' audited income statements, and three years' audited statements of changes in financial position.

The quarterly report, the 10-Q, requires only a summarized, unaudited operating statement and unaudited figures on capitalization and shareholders' equity. The 8-K current report must be filed within four business days of the occurrence of the event, such as a change in the amount of securities, an acquisition or disposition of assets, a change in control of the company, a revaluation of assets, or "any materially important event."

The SEC permits issuers to file reports electronically, transmitting them by telephone or by sending computer tapes or disks to the SEC. These electronic filings are made with the SEC's Electronic Data Gathering, Analysis, and Retrieval system (EDGAR).

LOG ON

www.sec.gov/edgar.shtml
The SEC's Internet homepage gives anyone access to the EDGAR database.

Issuers have historically mailed to their shareholders written copies of their annual reports and other periodic disclosure statements. Today, issuers are able to transmit such reports over the Internet. The Internet increases investors' access to information and can reduce the issuer's costs as well.

Suspension of Duty to File Reports An issuer's duty to file periodic reports with regard to a class of securities is suspended if the issuer has fewer than 300 holders of that class. In addition, a suspension occurs if the issuer has fewer than 500 holders of that class of securities and assets of no more than $10 million. However, an issuer with securities traded on a national securities exchange would remain obligated to file periodic reports with respect to those securities.

Holdings and Trading by Insiders Section 16 of the 1934 Act is designed to promote investor confidence in the integrity of the securities markets by limiting the ability of insiders to profit from trading in the shares of their issuers. Section 16(a) requires statutory insiders to disclose their ownership of their company's securities within 10 days of becoming owners. In addition, statutory insiders must report any subsequent transaction in such securities within two business days after the trade.

A statutory insider is a person who falls into any of the following categories:

1. An officer of a corporation having equity securities registered under the 1934 Act.

2. A director of such a corporation.

3. An owner of more than 10 percent of a class of equity securities registered under the 1934 Act.

Section 16(b) prevents an insider from profiting from short-swing trading in his company's shares. Any profit made by a statutory insider is recoverable by the issuer if the profit resulted from the purchase and sale (or the sale and purchase) of any class of the issuer's equity securities within less than a six-month period. This provision was designed to stop speculative insider trading on the basis of information that "may have been obtained by such owner, director, or officer by reason of his relationship to the issuer." The application of the provision is without regard to intent to use or actual use of inside information. However, a few cases have held that sales made by a statutory insider without actual access to inside information do not violate Section 16(b).

Proxy Solicitation Regulation

In a public corporation, shareholders rarely attend and vote at shareholder meetings. Many shareholders are able to vote at shareholder meetings only by **proxy,** a document by which shareholders direct other persons to vote their shares. Just as investors need information to be able to make intelligent investment decisions, shareholders need information to make intelligent voting and proxy decisions.

The 1934 Act regulates the solicitation of proxies. Regulation 14A requires any person soliciting proxies from holders of securities registered under the 1934 Act to furnish each holder with a **proxy statement** containing voting information. Usually, the only party soliciting proxies is the corporation's management, which is seeking proxies from common shareholders to enable it to reelect itself to the board of directors.

If the management of the corporation does not solicit proxies, it must nevertheless inform the shareholders of material information affecting matters that are to be put to a vote of the shareholders. This **information statement,** which contains about the same information as a proxy statement, must be sent to all shareholders that are entitled to vote at the meeting.

The primary purpose of the SEC rules concerning information that must be included in the proxy or information statement is to permit shareholders to make informed decisions while voting for directors and considering any resolutions proposed by the management or shareholders. Information on each director nominee must include the candidate's principal occupation, his shareholdings in the corporation, his previous service as a director of the corporation, his material transactions with the corporation (such as goods or services provided), and his directorships in other corporations. The total remuneration of the five directors or officers who are highest paid, including bonuses, grants under stock option plans, fringe benefits, and other perquisites, must also be included in the proxy statement.

SEC rules regarding the content of proxies ensure that the shareholder understands how his proxy will be voted. The proxy form must indicate in boldface type on whose behalf it is being solicited—for example, the corporation's management. Generally, the proxy must permit the shareholder to vote for or against the proposal or to abstain from voting on any resolutions on the meeting's agenda. The proxy form may ask for discretionary voting authority if the proxy indicates in bold print how the shares will be voted. For directors' elections, the shareholders must be provided with a means for withholding approval for each nominee.

Modern technology has greatly increased the ease with which shareholders may participate in shareholder votes and meetings, as well as reducing the cost of counting shareholder votes. Shareholders can vote electronically by phone and on the Internet. Some companies broadcast their shareholder meetings by satellite, and others webcast their shareholder meetings.

SEC Rule 14a–9 prohibits misstatements or omissions of material fact in the course of a proxy solicitation. If a violation is proved, a court may enjoin the holding of the shareholders' meeting, void the proxies that were illegally obtained, or rescind the action taken at the shareholders' meeting.

Proxy Contests   A shareholder may decide to solicit proxies in competition with management. Such a competition is called a proxy contest, and a solicitation of this kind is also subject to SEC rules. To facilitate proxy contests, the SEC requires the corporation either to furnish a shareholder list to shareholders who desire to wage a proxy contest or to mail the competing proxy material for them.

Perhaps the most hotly contested proxy battle ever was fought in 2002 between the management of Hewlett-Packard, which wanted to merge with Compaq, and Walter Hewitt, the son of H-P's co-founder and leader of shareholders opposed to the merger. Both sides were well organized, and each deluged shareholders with proxy solicitation material. A mere 51 percent of H-P shareholders gave the merger a narrow victory. By contrast, about 90 percent of Compaq shareholders approved the merger.

Ethics in Action

Sarbanes–Oxley Act of 2002

In 2001 and 2002, the discovery of financial irregularities in financial statements of nearly two dozen companies–notably Enron, Global Crossing, and World-Com—led to the bankruptcy of some companies, cost investors billions of dollars, and contributed to the bear stock market of 2001 and 2002. While many ordinary investors lost a lifetime of savings, corporate insiders received and profited from lucrative stock options, bonuses, and favorable loans that were sometimes not repaid.

Consequently, Congress passed the Sarbanes–Oxley Act of 2002 (SOX), which was designed to restore integrity to corporate financial statements and revive investor confidence in the securities markets. The Sarbanes–Oxley Act attempts to accomplish these objectives by imposing a wide array of new responsibilities on public corporations and their executives and auditors. All the provisions result from the crisis of ethics, in which some corporate officers and auditors preferred their selfish interests over those of the corporation and its shareholders, creditors, and other stakeholders.

Because some public companies were manipulating their balance sheets by omitting liabilities of certain affiliate entities, SOX requires that 10-Ks and 10-Qs filed with the SEC disclose material off-balance sheet transactions. To increase the likelihood that auditors will not give in to corporate executives' pressure to account improperly for corporate transactions, SOX requires greater independence between the auditor and the corporation by prohibiting the audit firm from performing most types of consulting services for the corporation. Moreover, officers and directors are prohibited from coercing auditors into creating misleading financial statements. To ensure that auditors are serving the interests of shareholders and not those of corporate managers, SOX requires auditors to be hired and overseen by an audit committee whose members are independent of the CEO and other corporate executives.

In addition, the CEO and CFO of a public company must certify that the corporation's financial reports fairly present the company's operations and financial condition. To eliminate the CEO and CFO's incentive to manipulate earnings, the CEO and CFO must disgorge bonuses, other incentive-based compensation, and profits on stock sales that were received during the 12-month period before financial statements are restated due to material misstatements or omissions. Public corporations are also generally prohibited from making loans to officers and directors. To encourage the use of ethics codes, SOX requires public companies to disclose whether they have ethics codes for senior financial officers.

Finally, SOX gives the SEC several new powers, including the authority to freeze payments to officers and directors during any lawful investigation. The SEC may also bar "unfit" persons from serving as directors and officers of public companies. The previous standard was "substantial unfitness."

SOX Section 404

The most controversial part of the Sarbanes–Oxley Act has been Section 404, which requires that annual reports include an "internal control report" acknowledging management's responsibility to maintain "an adequate internal control structure and procedures for financial reports." The benefits of Section 404 are evident and substantial, yet the costs are as well. The benefits include more active participation by the board, audit committee, and management in internal controls; increased embedding of control concepts including a better understanding by operating personnel and management of their control responsibilities; improvements in the adequacy of audit trails; and a revival of basic controls such as segregation of duties and reconciliation of accounts that have been eroded as businesses downsized and consolidated.

The cost of initial compliance with Section 404 averaged about $3 million per company in 2004. That cost included an increase in employee hours, averaging about 26,000, when the SEC had estimated that only 383 staff hours would be required. In addition, companies paid higher fees to auditors, who have the additional Section 404 burden of attesting to the assessment made by management. At one extreme, General Electric estimated it spent $30 million to comply with Section 404. One study concluded that the total private cost of Section 404 compliance was $1.4 trillion. Another study found that only 14 percent of firms believed that the benefits of Section 404 exceeded the up-front costs of Section 404 compliance. By 2007, the cost of complying with Section 404 was an average of $1.7 million for companies with a market capitalization above $75 million. Nonetheless, Financial Executives International found that 69 percent of financial executives agreed that compliance with SOX Section 404 resulted in more investor confidence in their companies' financial reporting. Fifty percent agreed that financial reports were more accurate.

Go to www.sec.gov/news/testimony/2007/tsl21207cc.htm, where you will find the congressional testimony of SEC Chairman Christopher Cox concerning the benefits and costs of SOX Section 404.

Shareholder Proposals In a large public corporation, it is very expensive for a shareholder to solicit proxies in support of a proposal for corporate action that she will offer at a shareholders' meeting. Therefore, she usually asks the management to include her proposal in its proxy statement. SEC Rule 14a–8 covers proposals by shareholders.

Under SEC Rule 14a–8, the corporation must include a shareholder's proposal in its proxy statement if, among other things, the shareholder owns at least 1 percent or $2,000 of the securities to be voted at the shareholders' meeting. A shareholder may submit only one proposal per meeting. The proposal and its supporting statement may not exceed 500 words.

Under Rule 14a–8, a corporation's management may exclude many types of shareholder proposals from its proxy statement. For example, a proposal is excludable if:

1. The proposal deals with the ordinary business operations of the corporation. For example, Pacific Telesis Group was permitted on this ground to omit a proposal that the board consider adding an environmentalist director and designate a vice president for environmental matters for each subsidiary. However, TRW, Inc., was required to include in its proxy statement a proposal that it establish a shareholder advisory committee that would advise the board of directors on the interests of shareholders.

2. The proposal relates to operations that account for less than 5 percent of a corporation's total assets and is not otherwise significantly related to the company's business. For example, Harsco Corp. could not omit a proposal that it sell its 50 percent interest in a South African firm even though the investment was arguably economically insignificant—only 4.5 percent of net earnings—because the issues raised by the proposal were significantly related to Harsco's business.

3. The proposal requires the issuer to violate a state or federal law. For example, one shareholder asked North American Bank to put a lesbian on the board of directors. The proposal was excludable because it may have required the bank to violate antidiscrimination laws.

4. The proposal relates to a personal claim or grievance. A proposal that the corporation pay the shareholder $1 million for damages that she suffered from using one of the corporation's products would be excludable.

In addition, Rule 14a–8 prevents a shareholder from submitting a proposal similar to recent proposals that have been overwhelmingly rejected by shareholders in recent years.

Liability Provisions of the 1934 Act

To prevent fraud, deception, or manipulation in securities transactions and to provide remedies to the victims of such practices, Congress included provisions in the 1934 Act that impose liability on persons who engage in wrongful conduct.

Liability for False Statements in Filed Documents
Section 18 is the 1934 Act counterpart to Section 11 of the 1933 Act. Section 18 imposes liability on any person responsible for a false or misleading statement of material fact in any document filed with the SEC under the 1934 Act. (Filed documents include the 10-K report, 8-K report, and proxy statements, but the 10-Q report is not considered filed for Section 18 purposes.) Any person who relies on a false or misleading statement in such a filed document may sue for damages. The purchaser need not prove that the defendant was at fault. Instead, the defendant has a defense that he acted in good faith and had no knowledge that the statement was false or misleading. This defense requires only that the defendant prove that he did not act with scienter.

Section 10(b) and Rule 10b–5
The most important liability section in the 1934 Act is Section 10(b), an extremely broad provision prohibiting the use of any manipulative or deceptive device in contravention of any rules that the SEC prescribes as "necessary or appropriate in the public interest or for the protection of investors." Rule 10b–5 was adopted by the SEC under Section 10(b). The rule states:

> It shall be unlawful for any person, directly or indirectly, by use of any means or instrumentality of interstate commerce or of the mails, or of any facility of any national securities exchange,
>
> (a) to employ any device, scheme, or artifice to defraud,
>
> (b) to make any untrue statement of a material fact or to omit to state a material fact necessary in order to make the statements made, in the light of the circumstances under which they were made, not misleading, or
>
> (c) to engage in any act, practice, or course of business which operates or would operate as a fraud or deceit upon any person, in connection with the purchase or sale of any security.

Rule 10b–5 applies to all transactions in all securities, whether or not registered under the 1933 Act or the 1934 Act.

Elements of a Rule 10b–5 Violation The

most important elements of a Rule 10b–5 violation are a misstatement or omission of material fact and scienter. In addition, private persons suing under the rule must be purchasers or sellers of securities who relied on the misstatement or omission.

Misstatement or Omission of Material Fact Rule 10b–5 prohibits only *misstatements or omissions of material fact.* A person **misstates** material facts, for example, when a manager of an unprofitable business induces shareholders to sell their stock to him by stating that the business will fail, although he knows that the business has become potentially profitable.

Liability for an **omission of a material fact** arises when a person fails to disclose material facts when he has a duty to disclose. For example, a securities broker is liable to his customer for not disclosing that he owns the shares that he recommends to the customer. As an agent of the customer, he owes a fiduciary duty to his customer to disclose his conflict of interest. In addition, a person is liable for omitting to tell all of the material facts after he has chosen to disclose some of them. His incomplete disclosure creates the duty to disclose all of the material facts.

Materiality Under Rule 10b–5, the misstated or omitted fact must be **material.** In essence, material information is any information that is likely to have an impact on the price of a security in the market. A fact is material if there is a substantial likelihood that a reasonable investor would consider it important to his decision, that the fact would have assumed actual significance in the deliberations of the reasonable investor, and that the disclosure of the fact would have been viewed by the reasonable investor as having significantly altered the total mix of information made available.

When there is doubt whether an important event will occur, the *Texas Gulf Sulphur*[5] case holds that materiality of the doubtful event can be determined by "a balancing of both the indicated probability that the event will occur and the anticipated magnitude of the event in light of the totality of the company activity."

Scienter Under Rule 10b–5, the defendant is not liable unless he acted with **scienter.** Scienter is an intent to deceive, manipulate, or defraud. Scienter includes gross recklessness of the defendant in ascertaining the truth of his statements. Mere negligence is not scienter, but some courts hold that simple recklessness is sufficient proof of scienter.

Other Elements Rule 10b–5 requires that private plaintiffs seeking damages be **actual purchasers or sellers** of securities. Persons who were deterred from purchasing securities by fraudulent statements may not recover lost profits under Rule 10b–5.

Under Rule 10b–5, private plaintiffs alleging damages caused by misstatements by the defendant must prove that they **relied** on the misstatement of material fact. The SEC as plaintiff need not prove reliance. For private plaintiffs, reliance is not usually required in omission cases; the investor need merely prove that the omitted fact was material. In addition, the misstatement or omission must **cause the investor's loss.**

The following *Carr* case considers whether an investor was entitled to rely on the misstatements of a securities salesman that contradicted a writing disclosing the risks of an investment.

---

[5]*SEC v. Texas Gulf Sulphur Co.,* 401 F.2d 833 (2d Cir.1968).

Carr v. CIGNA Securities, Inc.   95 F.3d 544 (7th Cir. 1996)

Kenny Carr was a professional basketball player in the National Basketball Association (NBA) when in 1984 he paid CIGNA Securities, Inc., $450,000 for limited partner interests in two commercial real estate limited partnerships that CIGNA had created. Carr said that the CIGNA salesman told him the limited partnerships were safe, conservative investments. The CIGNA salesman gave Carr documents that disclosed the riskiness of the investment, but Carr did not read or understand them. Carr also said that the salesman "knew that I didn't understand them. He said they were boilerplate kind of stuff, and breezed through them. He just explained them in his own words. He didn't say they were contrary to what he had told me. What I understood was what he told me."

When the commercial real estate market collapsed in the late 1980s, Carr lost his entire investment. Carr sued CIGNA for fraudulently selling securities in violation of Securities Exchange Act Rule 10b–5. The district court dismissed the action, and Carr appealed.

Posner, Chief Judge

We are going to come directly to the merits of the fraud claim. Carr's claim is barred by a very simple, very basic, very sensible principle of the law of fraud. If a literate, competent adult is given a document that in readable and comprehensive prose says X (X might be, "this is a risky investment"), and the person who hands it to him tells him orally, not-X ("this is a safe investment"), our literate, competent adult cannot maintain an action for fraud against the issuer of the document. This principle is necessary to provide sellers of goods and services, including investments, with a safe harbor against groundless, or at least indeterminate, claims of fraud by their customers. Without such a principle, sellers would have no protection against plausible liars and gullible jurors. The sale of risky investments would be itself a very risky enterprise. Risky investments by definition often fizzle. If the documents an investor was given, warning him in capitals and bold face that it was a **RISKY** investment, do not preclude a suit, it will simply be his word against the seller's concerning the content of an unrecorded conversation.

Carr was a fully literate, fully competent adult investing $450,000, which even to an NBA player is not such chicken feed that a busy person could not realistically be expected to take the time to read a lot of fine-print legal mumbo-jumbo. Carr points out that he was not in 1984 a sophisticated investor, knowledgeable about limited partnerships or commercial real estate. He argues that CIGNA's salesman invited him to repose trust in the salesman's advice and by doing so created a fiduciary relationship. The general rule, however, is that a broker is not the fiduciary of his customer unless the customer entrusts him with discretion to select the customer's investments, which Carr did not do. But it hardly matters. A fiduciary relationship places on the fiduciary a duty of candor, and concomitantly excuses the principal from having to take the same degree of care that is expected of a participant in an arm's-length contractual relationship. But the fiduciary relationship does not excuse the principal from taking the most elementary precautions against a salesman's pitch, such as the precaution of reading a short and plain statement of what one is buying for one's $450,000.

We do not say that a written disclaimer provides a safe harbor in every fiduciary case. Not all principals of fiduciaries are competent adults; not all disclaimers are clear; and the relationship may involve such a degree of trust as to dispel any duty of self-protection by the principal. But we are dealing here with a case in which, if there is a fiduciary duty—and probably there is not—it lies at the outer limits of the fiduciary principle. In so attenuated a fiduciary relation, and with so much money at stake, the principal has a duty to read.

Carr points out that CIGNA handed him 427 pages of documents when he bought the shares of the limited partnerships. We agree that it would be unreasonable to expect Carr to pore through 427 pages of legal and accounting mumbo-jumbo looking for nuggets of intelligible warnings. But the subscription agreements for each of the limited partnerships were only eight pages long and rich in lucid warnings, such as: "the Units are speculative investments which involve a high degree of risk of loss by the undersigned of his entire investment in the Partnership."

Professional athletes may be a common prey of financial predators. But their vulnerability does not justify a rule that would have the effect of making financial advisors the guarantors of risky investments.

Judgment for CIGNA affirmed.

Several courts have held that an investor's reliance on the availability of the securities on the market satisfies the reliance requirement of Rule 10b–5 because the securities market is defrauded as to the value of the securities. This **fraud-on-the-market theory** is based on the hypothesis that, in an open and developed securities market, the price of a company's stock is determined by the available material information regarding the company and its business. With the presence of a market, the market is interposed between seller and buyer and, ideally, transmits information to the investor in the processed form of a market price. Thus, the market is performing a substantial part of the valuation process performed by the investor in a face-to-face transaction. The market is acting as the unpaid agent of the investor, informing him that given all the information available to it, the value of the stock is the same as the market price. Misleading statements will therefore defraud purchasers of stock even if the purchasers do not directly rely on the misstatements and even if the defendants never communicated with the plaintiffs.

In *Basic, Inc. v. Levinson,*[6] the Supreme Court held that the fraud-on-the-market theory permits a court to presume an investor's reliance merely from the public availability of material misrepresentations. That presumption, however, is rebuttable, such as by evidence that an investor knew the market price was incorrect.

---

[6]*Basic, Inc. v. Levinson,* 485 U.S. 224 (1988).

For Rule 10b–5 to apply, the wrongful action must be accomplished *by the mails, with any means or instrumentality of interstate commerce,* or *on a national securities exchange.* This element satisfies the federal jurisdiction requirement. Use of the mails or a telephone within one state has been held to meet this element.

The scope of activities proscribed by Rule 10b–5 is not immediately obvious. While it is easy to understand that actual fraud and price manipulation are covered by the rule, two other areas are less easily mastered—the corporation's continuous disclosure obligation and insider trading.

Continuous Disclosure Obligation The purpose of the 1934 Act is to ensure that investors have the information they need in order to make intelligent investment decisions at all times. The periodic reporting requirements of the 1934 Act are especially designed to accomplish this result. If important developments arise between the disclosure dates of reports, however, investors will not have all of the information they need to make intelligent decisions unless the corporation discloses the material information immediately. Rule 10b–5 requires a corporation to disclose material information immediately, unless the corporation has a valid business purpose for withholding disclosure. When a corporation chooses to disclose information or to comment on information that it has no duty to disclose, it must do so accurately.

Until 1988, courts had disagreed on whether Rule 10b–5 requires disclosure of merger and other acquisition negotiations prior to an agreement in principle. In *Basic, Inc. v. Levinson,* the Supreme Court of the United States held that materiality of merger negotiations is to be determined on a case-by-case basis. The Court held that materiality depends on the probability that the transaction will be consummated and on its significance to the issuer of the securities. In addition, the Court stated that a corporation that chooses to comment on acquisition negotiations must do so truthfully.

In response to the *Basic* decision, the SEC released guidelines to help public companies decide whether they must disclose merger negotiations. A company is not required to disclose merger negotiations if all three of the following requirements are met:

1. The company did not make any prior disclosures about the merger negotiations,

2. Disclosure is not compelled by other SEC rules.

3. Management determines that disclosure would jeopardize completion of the merger transaction.

Trading on Inside Information One of the greatest destroyers of public confidence in the integrity of the securities market is the belief that insiders can trade securities while possessing corporate information that is not available to the general public.

Rule 10b–5 prohibits **insider trading** on nonpublic corporate information. A person with nonpublic, confidential, inside information may not use that information when trading with a person who does not possess that information. He must either disclose the information before trading or refrain from trading. The difficult task in the insider trading area is determining when a person is subject to this **disclose-or-refrain** rule.

In *United States v. Chiarella,*[7] the Supreme Court laid down the test for determining an insider's liability for trading on nonpublic, corporate information:

> The duty to disclose arises when one party has information that the other party is entitled to know because of a fiduciary or similar relation of trust and confidence between them. A relationship of trust and confidence exists between the shareholders of a corporation and those insiders who have obtained confidential information by reason of their position with that corporation. This relationship gives rise to a duty to disclose because of the necessity of preventing a corporate insider from taking unfair advantage of the uninformed stockholders.

Under this test, **insiders** include not only officers and directors of the corporation, but also anyone who is *entrusted with corporate information for a corporate purpose.* Insiders include outside consultants, lawyers, independent auditors, engineers, investment bankers, public relations advisers, news reporters, and personnel of government agencies who are given confidential corporate information for a corporate purpose.

Tippees are recipients of inside information (tips) from insiders. Tippees of insiders—such as relatives and friends of insiders, stockbrokers, and security analysts—are forbidden to trade on inside information and are subject to recovery of their profits if they do.

In *Dirks v. SEC,* the Supreme Court stated the applicability of Rule 10b–5 to tippees. The Court held that a tippee has liability if (1) an insider has breached a fiduciary duty of trust and confidence to the shareholders by disclosing to the tippee and (2) the tippee knows or should know of the insider's breach. In addition, the Court held that an insider has not breached her fiduciary duty to the shareholders unless she has received a personal benefit by disclosing to the tippee. See the Concept Review after the *Dirks* case for a comprehensive explanation of insider and tippee liability.

---

[7]445 U.S. 222 (U.S. Sup. Ct. 1980).

Dirks v. SEC   463 U.S. 646 (U.S. Sup. Ct. 1983)

On March 6, 1973, Raymond Dirks, a security analyst in a New York brokerage firm, received nonpublic information from Ronald Secrist, a former officer of Equity Funding of America, a seller of life insurance and mutual funds. Secrist alleged that the assets of Equity Funding were vastly overstated as the result of fraudulent corporate practices. He also stated that the SEC and state insurance departments had failed to act on similar charges of fraud made by Equity Funding employees. Secrist urged Dirks to verify the fraud and to disclose it publicly.

Dirks visited Equity Funding's headquarters in Los Angeles and interviewed several officers and employees of the corporation. The senior management denied any wrongdoing, but certain employees corroborated the charges of fraud. Dirks openly discussed the information he had obtained with a number of his clients and investors. Some of these persons sold their holdings of Equity Funding securities.

Dirks urged a Wall Street Journal *reporter to write a story on the fraud allegations. The reporter, fearing libel, declined to write the story.*

During the two-week period in which Dirks investigated the fraud and spread the word of Secrist's charges, the price of Equity Funding stock fell from $26 per share to less than $15 per share. The New York Stock Exchange halted trading in Equity Funding stock on March 27. On that date, Dirks voluntarily presented his information on the fraud to the SEC. Only then did the SEC bring an action for fraud against Equity Funding. Shortly thereafter, California insurance authorities impounded Equity Funding's records and uncovered evidence of the fraud. On April 2, The Wall Street Journal *published a front-page story based largely on information assembled by Dirks. Equity Funding immediately went into receivership.*

The SEC brought an administrative proceeding against Dirks for violating Rule 10b–5 by passing along confidential inside information to his clients. The SEC found that he had violated Rule 10b–5, but it merely censured him, since he had played an important role in bringing the fraud to light. Dirks appealed to the Court of Appeals, which affirmed the judgment. Dirks then appealed to the Supreme Court.

Powell, Justice

In *U.S. v. Chiarella* (1980), we accepted the two elements set out in *In Re Cady, Roberts,* 40 S.E.C. 907 (1961) for establishing a Rule 10b–5 violation: (i) the existence of a relationship affording access to inside information intended to be available only for a corporate purpose, and (ii) the unfairness of allowing a corporate insider to take advantage of that information by trading without disclosure. The Court found that a duty to disclose under Section 10(b) does not arise from the mere possession of nonpublic market information. Such a duty arises from the existence of a fiduciary relationship.

There can be no duty to disclose when the person who has traded on inside information was not the corporation's agent, was not a fiduciary, or was not a person in whom the sellers of the securities had placed their trust and confidence.

This requirement of a specific relationship between the shareholders and the individual trading on inside information has created analytical difficulties for the SEC and courts in policing tippees who trade on inside information. Unlike insiders who have independent fiduciary duties to both the corporation and its shareholders, the typical tippee has no such relationship. In view of this absence, it has been unclear how a tippee acquires the duty to refrain from trading on inside information.

Not only are insiders forbidden by their fiduciary relationship from personally using undisclosed corporate information to their advantage, but also they may not give such information to an outsider for the same improper purpose of exploiting the information for their personal gain. The transactions of those who knowingly participate with the fiduciary in such a breach are as forbidden as transactions on behalf of the trustee himself. Thus, the tippee's duty to disclose or abstain is derivative from that of the insider's duty. The tippee's obligation has been viewed as arising from his role as a participant after the fact in the insider's breach of a fiduciary duty.

A tippee assumes a fiduciary duty to the shareholders of a corporation not to trade on material nonpublic information only when the insider has breached his fiduciary duty to the shareholders by disclosing the information to the tippee and the tippee knows or should know that there has been a breach.

In determining whether a tippee is under an obligation to disclose or abstain, it thus is necessary to determine whether the insider's tip constituted a breach of the insider's fiduciary duty. Whether disclosure is a breach of duty therefore depends in large part on the purpose of the disclosure. Thus, the test is whether the insider personally will benefit, directly or indirectly, from his disclosure. Absent some personal gain, there has been no breach of duty to stockholders. And absent a breach by the insider, there is no derivative breach.

This requires courts to focus on objective criteria, i.e., whether the insider receives a direct or indirect personal benefit from the disclosure, such as a pecuniary gain or a reputational benefit that will translate into future earnings. For example, there may be a relationship between the insider and the recipient that suggests a *quid pro quo* from the latter, or an intention to benefit the particular recipient. The elements of fiduciary duty and exploitation of nonpublic information also exist when an insider makes a gift of confidential information to a relative or friend who trades. The tip and trade resemble trading by the insider himself followed by a gift of the profits to the recipient.

Under the inside-trading and tipping rules set forth above, we find that there was no violation by Dirks. Dirks was a stranger to Equity Funding, with no pre-existing fiduciary duty to its shareholders. He took no action, directly or indirectly, that induced the shareholders or officers of Equity Funding to repose trust or confidence in him. There was no expectation by Dirks's sources that he would keep their information in confidence. Nor did Dirks misappropriate or illegally obtain the information about Equity Funding. Unless the insiders breached their *Cady, Roberts* duty to shareholders in disclosing the nonpublic information to Dirks, he breached no duty when he passed it on to investors as well as to *The Wall Street Journal*.

It is clear that neither Secrist nor the other Equity Funding employees violated their *Cady, Roberts* duty to the corporation's shareholders by providing information to Dirks. Secrist intended to convey relevant information that management was unlawfully concealing, and he believed that persuading Dirks to investigate was the best way to disclose the fraud. The tippers received no monetary or personal benefit for revealing Equity Funding's secrets, nor was their purpose to make a gift of valuable information to Dirks. The tippers were motivated by a desire to expose the fraud. In the absence of a breach of duty to shareholders by the insiders, there was no derivative breach by Dirks. Dirks therefore could not have been a participant after the fact in an insider's breach of a fiduciary duty.

Judgment reversed in favor of Dirks.

CONCEPT REVIEW

Rule 10b–5 Liability for Trading on Inside Information

	For Trading by Insider	For Trading by Tippee
Insider-Tipper Liability	Liable if insider breached the fiduciary duty of confidentiality by using corporate information that was entrusted to insider solely for corporate purposes	Liable if insider breached the fiduciary duty of confidentiality (which breach requires that the tipper receive a personal benefit) by disclosing confidential corporate information to the tippee
Tippee Liability	Not liable	Liable if: 1. Insider-tipper breached the fiduciary duty of confidentiality by disclosing confidential corporate information to the tippee, and 2. The tippee knew or should have known of the insider-tipper's breach of the fiduciary duty of confidentiality

When is a person a corporate insider?
That is, when does a person owe a fiduciary duty of confidentiality to the corporation?
   1. The corporation entrusts corporate information to a person for corporate purposes, and
   2. The corporation has a proper business purpose for keeping the information confidential.

When does a person breach the fiduciary duty of confidentiality?
   1. When the person uses the entrusted corporate information for his personal benefit, or
   2. When the person discloses the entrusted corporate information to someone other than for corporate purposes and the person receives a personal benefit.

When does a person NOT breach the fiduciary duty of confidentiality?
   1. When the person discloses the entrusted corporate information to someone who needs the information for corporate purposes.
   2. When the person does not receive a personal benefit by disclosing or using the entrusted corporate information.
   3. When the corporation does not have a proper business purpose for keeping the information confidential.

In June 1997, the Supreme Court held that Rule 10b–5 liability attaches to anyone who trades in securities for personal profit using confidential information misappropriated in a breach of fiduciary duty owed to the *source of the information.* Under the **misappropriation theory,** a person violates Rule 10b–5 not only when he steals confidential information from his company and trades in its shares, but also, for example, if he steals confidential information about his firm's intent to make a tender offer for another firm and buys securities of the second firm.

Extent of Liability for Insider Trading Section 20A of the 1934 Act allows persons who traded in the securities at about the same time as the insider or tippee to recover damages from the insider or tippee. Although there may be several persons trading at about the same time, the insider or tippee's total liability cannot exceed the profit she has made or the loss she has avoided by trading on inside information.

This limitation, which merely requires disgorgement of profits, has been assailed as not adequately deterring insider trading, because the defendant may realize an enormous profit if her trading is not discovered, but lose nothing beyond her profits if it is. In response to this issue of liability, Congress passed an amendment to the 1934 Act permitting the SEC to seek a civil penalty of three times the profit gained or the loss avoided by trading on inside information. This treble penalty is paid to the Treasury of the United States. The penalty applies only to SEC actions; it does not affect the amount of damages that may be recovered by private plaintiffs. The 1934 Act also grants the SEC power to award up to 10 percent of any triple-damage penalty as a bounty to informants who helped the SEC uncover insider trading.

Liability for Aiding and Abetting Persons who are not the primary actors that violate Rule 10b–5 but merely aid and abet another's violation of the rule nonetheless may be prosecuted by the SEC. To have aiding and abetting liability, there must be (1) a primary violation by another person, (2) the aider and abettor's knowledge of that violation, and (3) substantial assistance by the aider and abettor in the achievement of the primary violation. Although the SEC may prosecute aiders and abettors, investors harmed by a primary violation may recover their damages only from primary violators, not from aiders and abettors.

In the *Stoneridge* case, the Supreme Court considered whether actors who were aiders and abettors could be liable otherwise under Rule 10b–5.

Stoneridge Investment Partners, LLC v. Scientific-Atlanta, Inc.
128 S. Ct. 761 (U.S. Sup. Ct. 2008)

Stoneridge Investment Partners, LLC, was a shareholder in Charter Communications, Inc., a television cable service provider. Stoneridge sued Charter for engaging in a variety of fraudulent practices so that its quarterly reports would meet Wall Street expectations for cable subscriber growth and operating cash flow. The fraud included misclassification of its customer base, delayed reporting of terminated customers, improper capitalization of costs that should have been shown as expenses, and manipulation of the company's billing cutoff dates to inflate reported revenues.

Despite these efforts, in late 2000 Charter executives realized that the company would miss projected operating cash flow numbers by $15 to $20 million. To help meet the shortfall, Charter decided to alter its existing arrangements with Scientific-Atlanta and Motorola, which supplied Charter with the digital cable converter boxes that Charter furnished to its customers. Charter arranged to overpay Scientific-Atlanta and Motorola $20 for each set top box it purchased until the end of the year, with the understanding that Scientific-Atlanta and Motorola would return the overpayment by purchasing advertising from Charter. The transactions, it is alleged, had no economic substance, but because Charter would then record the advertising purchases as revenue and capitalize its purchase of the set top boxes, in violation of generally accepted accounting principles, the transactions would enable Charter to fool its auditor into approving a financial statement showing it met projected revenue and operating cash flow numbers. Scientific-Atlanta and Motorola agreed to the arrangement.

So that Charter's independent auditor, Arthur Andersen LLP, would not discover the link between Charter's increased payments for the boxes and the advertising purchases, the companies drafted documents to make it appear the transactions were unrelated and conducted in the ordinary course of business. Following a request from Charter, Scientific-Atlanta sent documents to Charter stating falsely that it had increased production costs. It raised the price for set top boxes for the rest of 2000 by $20 per box. As for Motorola, in a written contract Charter agreed to purchase from Motorola a specific number of *set top boxes and pay liquidated damages of $20 for each unit it did not take. The contract was made with the expectation Charter would fail to purchase all the units and pay Motorola the liquidated damages.*

To return the additional money from the set top box sales, Scientific-Atlanta and Motorola signed contracts with Charter to purchase advertising time for a price higher than fair value. The new set top box agreements were backdated to make it appear that they were negotiated a month before the advertising agreements. The backdating was important to convey the impression that the negotiations were unconnected, a point Arthur Andersen considered necessary for separate treatment of the transactions. Charter recorded the advertising payments to inflate revenue and operating cash flow by approximately $17 million. The inflated number was shown on financial statements filed with the Securities and Exchange Commission and reported to the public.

Scientific-Atlanta and Motorola had no role in preparing or disseminating Charter's financial statements. Their own financial statements booked the transactions as a wash, under generally accepted accounting principles.

Nonetheless, Stoneridge filed a securities fraud class action against Scientific-Atlanta and Motorola on behalf of purchasers of Charter stock. Stoneridge alleged that Scientific-Atlanta and Motorola, by entering wash transactions with Charter, violated § 10(b) of the Securities Exchange Act of 1934 and SEC Rule 10b–5, because they knew or were in reckless disregard of Charter's intention to use the transactions to inflate its revenues and knew the resulting financial statements issued by Charter would be relied upon by research analysts and investors.

The district court granted Scientific-Atlanta and Motorola's motion to dismiss for failure to state a claim on which relief can be granted. The court of appeals affirmed on the grounds that the allegations did not show that Scientific-Atlanta and Motorola made misstatements relied upon by the public or that they violated a duty to disclose. At most, the court observed, Scientific-Atlanta and Motorola had aided and abetted Charter's misstatement of its financial results, but, it noted, there is no private right of action for aiding and abetting a § 10(b) violation. Stoneridge asked the United States Supreme Court to grant certiorari and review the decision.

Kennedy, Justice

Decisions of the Courts of Appeals are in conflict respecting when, if ever, an injured investor may rely upon §10(b) to recover from a party that neither makes a public misstatement nor violates a duty to disclose but does participate in a scheme to violate §10(b). Compare *Simpson v. AOL Time Warner Inc.*, 452 F.3d 1040 (9th Cir. 2006), with *Regents of Univ. of Cal. v. Credit Suisse First Boston (USA), Inc.*, 482 F.3d 372 (5th Cir. 2007). We granted certiorari.

Section 10(b) of the Securities Exchange Act makes it "unlawful for any person, directly or indirectly, by the use of any means or instrumentality of interstate commerce or of the mails, or of any facility of any national securities exchange . . . [t]o use or employ, in connection with the purchase or sale of any security . . . any manipulative or deceptive device or contrivance in contravention of such rules and regulations as the Commission may prescribe as necessary or appropriate in the public interest or for the protection of investors." 15 U.S.C. § 78j. The SEC, pursuant to this section, promulgated Rule 10b-5.

Rule 10b-5 encompasses only conduct already prohibited by §10(b). Though the text of the Securities Exchange Act does not provide for a private cause of action for §10(b) violations, the Court has found a right of action implied in the words of the statute and its implementing regulation. In a typical §10(b) private action a plaintiff must prove (1) a material misrepresentation or omission by the defendant; (2) scienter; (3) a connection between the misrepresentation or omission and the purchase or sale of a security; (4) reliance upon the misrepresentation or omission; (5) economic loss; and (6) loss causation.

In *Central Bank of Denver, N. A. v. First Interstate Bank of Denver, N. A.,* 511 U.S. 164 (1994), the Court determined that §10(b) liability did not extend to aiders and abettors. The Court found the scope of §10(b) to be delimited by the text, which makes no mention of aiding and abetting liability. The Court doubted the implied §10(b) action should extend to aiders and abettors when none of the express causes of action in the securities acts included that liability. It added the following: "Were we to allow the aiding and abetting action proposed in this case, the defendant could be liable without any showing that the plaintiff relied upon the aider and abettor's statements or actions. Allowing plaintiffs to circumvent the reliance requirement would disregard the careful limits on 10b-5 recovery mandated by our earlier cases." *Central Bank,* at 180.

The decision in *Central Bank* led to calls for Congress to create an express cause of action for aiding and abetting within the Securities Exchange Act. Then-SEC Chairman Arthur Levitt, testifying before the Senate Securities Subcommittee, cited *Central Bank* and recommended that aiding and abetting liability in private claims be established. Congress did not follow this course. Instead, in §104 of the Private Securities Litigation Reform Act of 1995 (PSLRA), it directed prosecution of aiders and abettors by the SEC.

The §10(b) implied private right of action does not extend to aiders and abettors. The conduct of a secondary actor must satisfy each of the elements or preconditions for liability; and we consider whether the allegations here are sufficient to do so.

The Court of Appeals concluded Stoneridge had not alleged that Scientific-Atlanta and Motorola engaged in a deceptive act within the reach of the §10(b) private right of action, noting that only misstatements, omissions by one who has a duty to disclose, and manipulative trading practices are deceptive within the meaning of the rule. If this conclusion were read to suggest there must be a specific oral or written statement before there could be liability under §10(b) or Rule 10b-5, it would be erroneous. Conduct itself can be deceptive, as Scientific-Atlanta and Motorola concede. In this case, moreover, Scientific-Atlanta's and Motorola's course of conduct included both oral and written statements, such as the backdated contracts agreed to by Charter and Scientific-Atlanta and Motorola.

A different interpretation of the holding from the Court of Appeals opinion is that the court was stating only that any deceptive statement or act Scientific-Atlanta and Motorola made was not actionable because it did not have the requisite proximate relation to the investors' harm. That conclusion is consistent with our own determination that Scientific-Atlanta's and Motorola's acts or statements were not relied upon by the investors and that, as a result, liability cannot be imposed upon Scientific-Atlanta and Motorola.

Reliance by the plaintiff upon the defendant's deceptive acts is an essential element of the §10(b) private cause of action. It ensures that, for liability to arise, the requisite causal connection between a defendant's misrepresentation and a plaintiffs injury exists as a predicate for liability. We have found a rebuttable presumption of reliance in two different circumstances. First, if there is an omission of a material fact by one with a duty to disclose, the investor to whom the duty was owed need not provide specific proof of reliance. Second, under the fraud-on-the-market doctrine, reliance is presumed when the statements at issue become public. The public information is reflected in the market price of the security. Then it can be assumed that an investor who buys or sells stock at the market price relies upon the statement.

Neither presumption applies here. Scientific-Atlanta and Motorola had no duty to disclose; and their deceptive acts were not communicated to the public. No member of the investing public had knowledge, either actual or presumed, of Scientific-Atlanta's and Motorola's deceptive acts during the relevant times. Stoneridge, as a result, cannot show reliance upon any of Scientific-Atlanta's and Motorola's actions except in an indirect chain that we find too remote for liability.

Invoking what some courts call "scheme liability," Stoneridge nonetheless seeks to impose liability on Scientific-Atlanta and Motorola even absent a public statement. In our view this approach does not answer the objection that Stoneridge did not in fact rely upon Scientific-Atlanta's and Motorola's own deceptive conduct.

Liability is appropriate, Stoneridge contends, because Scientific-Atlanta and Motorola engaged in conduct with the purpose and effect of creating a false appearance of material fact to further a scheme to misrepresent Charter's revenue. The argument is that the financial statement Charter released to the public was a natural and expected consequence of Scientific-Atlanta's and Motorola's deceptive acts; had Scientific-Atlanta and Motorola not assisted Charter, Charter's auditor would not have been fooled, and the financial statement would have been a more accurate reflection of Charter's financial condition.

In effect Stoneridge contends that in an efficient market investors rely not only upon the public statements relating to a security but also upon the transactions those statements reflect. Were this concept of reliance to be adopted, the implied cause of action would reach the whole marketplace in which the issuing company does business; and there is no authority for this rule.

As stated above, reliance is tied to causation, leading to the inquiry whether Scientific-Atlanta's and Motorola's acts were immediate or remote to the injury. In considering Stoneridge's arguments, we note §10(b) provides that the deceptive act must be "in connection with the purchase or sale of any security." Though this phrase in part defines the statute's coverage rather than causation, the emphasis on a purchase or sale of securities does provide some insight into the deceptive acts that concerned the enacting Congress. In all events we conclude Scientific-Atlanta's and Motorola's deceptive acts, which were not disclosed to the investing public, are too remote to satisfy the requirement of reliance. It was Charter, not Scientific-Atlanta and Motorola, that misled its auditor and filed fraudulent financial statements; nothing Scientific-Atlanta and Motorola did made it necessary or inevitable for Charter to record the transactions as it did.

Stoneridge's theory, moreover, would put an unsupportable interpretation on Congress' specific response to *Central Bank* in §104 of the PSLRA. Congress amended the securities laws to provide for limited coverage of aiders and abettors. Aiding and abetting liability is authorized in actions brought by the SEC but not by private parties. Stoneridge's view of primary liability makes any aider and abettor liable under §10(b) if he or she committed a deceptive act in the process of providing assistance. Were we to adopt this construction of §10(b), it would revive in substance the implied cause of action against all aiders and abettors except those who committed no deceptive act in the process of facilitating the fraud; and we would undermine Congress' determination that this class of defendants should be pursued by the SEC and not by private litigants.

The practical consequences of an expansion, which the Court has considered appropriate to examine in circumstances like these, see *Blue Chip Stamps v. Manor Drug Stores,* 421 U.S. 723, 737, n. 5 (1975), provide a further reason to reject Stoneridge's approach. In *Blue Chip,* the Court noted that extensive discovery and the potential for uncertainty and disruption in a lawsuit allow plaintiffs with weak claims to extort settlements from innocent companies. Adoption of Stoneridge's approach would expose a new class of defendants to these risks. As noted in *Central Bank,* contracting parties might find it necessary to protect against these threats, raising the costs of doing business. Overseas firms with no other exposure to our securities laws could be deterred from doing business here. This, in turn, may raise the cost of being a publicly traded company under our law and shift securities offerings away from domestic capital markets.

The history of the §10(b) private right and the careful approach the Court has taken before proceeding without congressional direction provide further reasons to find no liability here. The §10(b) private cause of action is a judicial construct that Congress did not enact in the text of the relevant statutes. It is settled that there is an implied cause of action only if the underlying statute can be interpreted to disclose the intent to create one. This is for good reason. In the absence of congressional intent the Judiciary's recognition of an implied private right of action necessarily extends its authority to embrace a dispute Congress has not assigned it to resolve. This runs contrary to the established principle that the jurisdiction of the federal courts is carefully guarded against expansion by judicial interpretation and conflicts with the authority of Congress under Art. III to set the limits of federal jurisdiction.

Concerns with the judicial creation of a private cause of action caution against its expansion. The decision to extend the cause of action is for Congress, not for us. Though it remains the law, the §10(b) private right should not be extended beyond its present boundaries.

Secondary actors are subject to criminal penalties and civil enforcement by the SEC. The enforcement power is not toothless. Since September 30, 2002, SEC enforcement actions have collected over $10 billion in disgorgement and penalties, much of it for distribution to injured investors. And in this case both parties agree that criminal penalties are a strong deterrent. In addition some state securities laws permit state authorities to seek fines and restitution from aiders and abettors. All secondary actors, furthermore, are not necessarily immune from private suit. The securities statutes provide an express private right of action against accountants and underwriters in certain circumstances and the implied right of action in §10(b) continues to cover secondary actors who commit primary violations. *Central Bank, supra,* at 191.

Here Scientific-Atlanta and Motorola were acting in concert with Charter in the ordinary course as suppliers and, as matters then evolved in the not so ordinary course, as customers. Unconventional as the arrangement was, it took place in the marketplace for goods and services, not in the investment sphere. Charter was free to do as it chose in preparing its books, conferring with its auditor, and preparing and then issuing its financial statements. In these circumstances the investors cannot be said to have relied upon any of Scientific-Atlanta's and Motorola's deceptive acts in the decision to purchase or sell securities; and as the requisite reliance cannot be shown, Scientific-Atlanta and Motorola have no liability to Stoneridge under the implied right of action. This conclusion is consistent with the narrow dimensions we must give to a right of action Congress did not authorize when it first enacted the statute and did not expand when it revisited the law.

Judgment for Scientific-Atlanta affirmed.

Securities Fraud and the Internet In recent years, the Internet has become a new source of securities fraud. In response, the SEC has included the investigation of Internet users in its antifraud arsenal. The SEC has announced that it will use search engines to conduct Internet searches of phrases such as "get high returns with low investment" to detect likely fraud. Some securities professionals have objected to the SEC tactics as an invasion of privacy.

Statute of Limitations A purchaser or seller bringing an action under Rule 10b–5 must file his suit in a timely fashion or else be precluded from litigating the issue. The Sarbanes–Oxley Act of 2002 extends the statute of limitation by requiring an action under Rule 10b–5 to be commenced within two years after discovery of the facts constituting a violation of Rule 10b–5 and within five years of the violation.

Regulation FD

Regulation FD (Fair Disclosure) was passed by the SEC to allow general investors to have more nearly equal access to information that in the past was selectively disclosed to institutional investors and securities analysts. The regulation, which applies only to public companies, provides that when an issuer or person acting for the issuer discloses material nonpublic information to securities market professionals and holders of the issuer's securities, it must make public disclosure of that information. An *intentional* selective disclosure occurs when the discloser knows or is reckless in not knowing that the information is material and nonpublic. In such a situation, the remedy is that the issuer must make public disclosure simultaneously, that is, at the same time it discloses the information selectively. When the disclosure of material nonpublic information is selective but *nonintentional,* the issuer must make the public disclosure promptly, that is, as soon as reasonably practical after a senior official learns of the disclosure and knows it is material and nonpublic. This must be no later than 24 hours after the selective disclosure or by the commencement of the next day's trading on the NYSE, whichever is later. The required public disclosure may be made by filing or furnishing a Form 8-K or by another method that is reasonably designed to effect broad, nonselective disclosure to the public.

The SEC has taken action against several firms under Regulation FD. Most make the same mistake: a material disclosure from corporate management to a select audience in private conversations or at an invitation-only meeting. In one case, the CEO said in a public conference call that the company had a negative business outlook. Three weeks later, at an invitation-only technology conference, he presented attendees with a positive view of the company's prospects, and the price of its stock immediately rose 20 percent. In fining the company $250,000, the SEC said the public did not have access to the technology conference and was unable to benefit from the information disclosed there. In another case, the SEC prosecuted one company for making material nonpublic disclosures to securities analysts following one of its investor conferences.

One other case shows the importance of taking quick action when an inadvertent selective disclosure is made. A company's CEO, working from his home, participated in a conference call with a portfolio manager and a salesperson from an investment advisory group. From her office, the company's director of investor relations also took part in the conversation. During the call, the director realized the CEO unwittingly disclosed nonpublic information, but she didn't interrupt him. As soon as the conference call ended, she tried to reach him by telephone but was able to leave him only a voice-mail message expressing her concern over his inadvertent selective disclosure. Not until an hour later did the CEO get her message. He then asked the other call participants to keep the information confidential, but took no further action. At the time the CEO learned of his disclosure error, he had 24 hours to publicly disseminate the material information. That much time was available because his selective release was unintentional. The next day, however, the CEO intentionally selectively disclosed the material information to analysts without issuing a press release. This intentionally selective disclosure invoked a different part of Regulation FD: it had to be accompanied by a simultaneous public announcement. The company did not meet this requirement, instead issuing a press release three hours later, thus violating the rule. By then its stock had risen nearly 15 percent since the CEO's first nonpublic disclosure.

How can companies comply with Regulations FD? They should

- Establish clear rules for the content of information that may be disclosed.
- Require previews of any material disclosure by a qualified team of executives, such as legal counsel and an investor relations officer.
- Use several mass communications outlets, including submissions to the SEC, press releases, and Internet-based sound and video presentations.
- Adopt procedures for appropriate corrective action as soon as possible after a selective disclosure occurs.

An issuer should adopt absolute rules that provide guidance to its CEO, CFO, and others who regularly communicate with securities analysts and institutional investors. Clear rules can help prevent errors in judgment that can lead to inadvertent violations during an unscripted conference call or presentation. For instance, a company may have a rule that after the CEO gives his outlook on the company earnings in a press release or conference call, the CEO does not update the earnings outlook unless the company finds that the earnings are so far off that another release is required.

As an example of a preview process, consider W. R. Grace & Co., which circulates draft press releases by e-mail to its financial, executive, and legal groups. For Grace, the process consumes only a few hours typically and only a few days when the release is about a complex subject such as quarterly earnings.

Criminal Liability Like the 1933 Act, the 1934 Act provides for liability for criminal violations of the act. Section 32 provides that individuals may be fined up to $5 million and imprisoned up to 20 years for willful violations of the 1934 Act or the related SEC rules. Businesses may be fined up to $25 million.

Tender Offer Regulation

Historically, the predominant procedure by which one corporation acquired another was the merger, a transaction requiring the cooperation of the acquired corporation's management. Since the early 1960s, the **tender offer** has become an often used acquisition device. A tender offer is a public offer by a **bidder** to purchase a **subject company's** equity securities directly from its shareholders at a specified price for a fixed period of time. The offering price is usually well above the market price of the shares. Such offers are often made even though there is opposition from the subject company's management. Opposed offers are called hostile tender offers. The legality of efforts opposing a tender offer is covered in Chapter 43.

The Williams Act amendments to the 1934 Act require bidders and subject companies to provide a shareholder with information on which to base his decision whether to sell his shares to a bidder. The aim of the Williams Act is to protect investors and to give the bidder and the subject company equal opportunities to present their cases to the shareholder. The intent is to encourage an auction of the shares with the highest bidder purchasing the shares. The Williams Act applies only when the subject company's equity securities are registered under the 1934 Act.

The Williams Act does not define a tender offer, but the courts have compiled a list of factors to determine whether a person has made a tender offer. The greater the number of people solicited and the lower their investment sophistication, the more likely it is that the bidder will be held to have made a tender offer. Also, the shorter the offering period, the more rigid the price, and the greater the publicity concerning the offer, the more likely it is that the purchase efforts of the bidder will be treated as a tender offer. Given these factors, a person who offers to purchase shares directly from several shareholders at a set price for only a few days risks having a court treat the offer like a tender offer. The Williams Act does not regulate a tender offer unless the bidder intends to become a holder of at least 5 percent of the subject company's shares.

A bidder making a tender offer must file a tender offer statement (Schedule TO) with the SEC when the offer commences. The information in this schedule includes the terms of the offer (for example, the price), the background of the bidder, and the purpose of the tender offer (including whether the bidder intends to control the subject company).

The SEC requires the bidder to keep the tender offer open for at least 20 business days and prohibits any purchase of shares during that time. This rule gives shareholders adequate time to make informed decisions regarding whether to tender their shares. Tendering shareholders may withdraw their tendered shares during the entire term of the offer. This rule allows the highest bidder to buy the shares, as in an auction.

All tender offers, whether made by the issuer or by a third-party bidder, must be made to all holders of the targeted class of shares. When a bidder increases the offering price during the term of the tender offer, all of the shareholders must be paid the higher price even if they tendered their shares at a lower price. If more shares are tendered than the bidder offered to buy, the bidder must prorate its purchases among all of the shares tendered. This proration rule is designed to foster careful shareholder decisions about whether to sell shares. Shareholders might rush to tender their shares if the bidder could accept shares on a first-come, first-served basis.

After an initial offering period has expired, a bidder is permitted to include a "subsequent offering period" during which shareholders who tender will have no withdrawal rights. The SEC created the new offering period to allow shareholders a last opportunity to tender into an offer.

The management of the subject company is required to inform the shareholders of its position on the tender offer, with its reasons, within 10 days after the offer has been made. It must also provide the bidder with a list of the holders of the equity securities that the bidder seeks to acquire or mail the materials for the bidder.

SEC Rule 14e–3 prohibits persons who have knowledge of an impending tender offer from using such information prior to its public disclosure. The rule limits insider trading in the tender offer context.

Private Acquisitions of Shares The Williams Act regulates private acquisitions of shares differently from tender offers. When the bidder privately seeks a controlling block of the subject company's shares on a stock exchange or in face-to-face negotiations with only a few shareholders, no advance notice to the SEC or disclosure to shareholders is required. However, a person making a private acquisition is required to file a Schedule 13D with the SEC and to send a copy to the subject company within 10 days after he becomes a holder of 5 percent of its shares. A Schedule 13G (which requires less disclosure than a 13D) must be filed when a 5 percent holder has purchased no more than 2 percent of the shares within the past 12 months.

State Regulation of Tender Offers

Statutes that apply to tender offers have been enacted by about two-thirds of the states. State statutes have become highly protective of subject companies. For example, the Indiana statute gives shareholders other than the bidder the right to determine whether the shares acquired by the bidder may be voted in directors' elections

---

The Global Business Environment

The Foreign Corrupt Practices Act

The Foreign Corrupt Practices Act (FCPA) was passed by Congress in 1977 as an amendment to the Securities Exchange Act of 1934. Its passage followed discoveries that more than 400 American corporations had given bribes or made other improper or questionable payments in connection with business abroad and within the United States. Many of these payments were bribes to high level officials of foreign governments for the purpose of obtaining contracts for the sale of goods or services. Officers of the companies that had made the payments argued that such payments were customary and necessary in business transactions in many countries. This argument was pressed forcefully with regard to facilitating payments. Such payments were said to be essential to get lower level government officials in a number of countries to perform their nondiscretionary or ministerial tasks, such as preparing or approving necessary import or export documents.

In a significant number of cases, bribes had been accounted for as commission payments, as normal transactions with foreign subsidiaries, or as payments for services rendered by professionals or other firms, or had in other ways been made to appear as normal business expenses. These bribes were then illegally deducted as normal business expenses in income tax returns filed with the Internal Revenue Service.

The Payments Prohibition

The FCPA makes it a crime for any American firm—whether or not it has securities registered under the 1934 Act—to offer, promise, or make payments or gifts of anything of value to foreign officials and certain others. Payments are prohibited if the person making the payment knows or should know that some or all of it will be used for the purpose of influencing a governmental decision, even if the offer is not accepted or the promise is not carried out. The FCPA prohibits offers or payments to foreign political parties and candidates for office as well as offers and payments to government officials. Payments of kickbacks to foreign businesses and their officers are not prohibited unless it is known or should be known that these payments will be passed on to government officials or other illegal recipients.

Facilitating or grease payments are not prohibited by the FCPA. For example, suppose a corporation applies for a radio license in Italy and makes a payment to the government official who issues the licenses. If the official grants licenses to every applicant and the payment merely speeds up the processing of the application, the FCPA is not violated.

Substantial penalties for violations may be imposed. A company may be fined up to $2 million. Directors, officers, employees, or agents participating in violations are liable for fines of up to $100,000 and prison terms of up to five years.

Record-Keeping and Internal Controls Requirements

The FCPA also establishes record-keeping and internal control requirements for firms subject to the periodic disclosure provisions of the Securities Exchange Act of 1934. The purpose of such controls is to prevent unauthorized payments and transactions and unauthorized access to company assets that may result in illegal payments.

The FCPA requires the making and keeping of records and accounts "which, in reasonable detail, accurately, and fairly reflect the transactions and dispositions of the assets of the issuer" of securities. It also requires the establishment and maintenance of a system of internal accounting controls that provides "reasonable assurances" that the firm's transactions are executed in accordance with management's authorization and that the firm's assets are used or disposed of only as authorized by management.

and other matters. The statute, which essentially gives a subject company the power to require shareholder approval of a hostile tender offer, has been copied by several states.

Other states, such as Delaware, have adopted business combination moratorium statutes. These statutes delay the effectuation of a merger of the corporation with a shareholder owning a large percentage of shares (such as 15 percent) unless the board of directors' approval is obtained. Because the typical large shareholder in a public company is a bidder who has made a tender offer, these state statutes primarily affect the ability of a bidder to effectuate a merger after a tender offer and, therefore, may have the effect of deterring hostile acquisitions.

State Securities Law

State securities laws are frequently referred to as blue-sky laws, since the early state securities statutes were designed to protect investors from promoters and security salespersons who would "sell building lots in the blue sky." The first state to enact a securities law was Kansas, in 1911. All of the states now have such legislation.

The National Conference of Commissioners on Uniform State Laws has adopted the Uniform Securities Act of 1956. The act contains antifraud provisions, requires the registration of securities, and demands broker-dealer registration. About two-thirds of the states have adopted the act, but many states have made significant changes in it.

All of the state securities statutes provide penalties for fraudulent sales and permit the issuance of injunctions to protect investors from additional or anticipated fraudulent acts. Most of the statutes grant broad power to investigate fraud to some state official—usually the attorney general or his appointee as securities administrator. All of the statutes provide criminal penalties for selling fraudulent securities and conducting fraudulent transactions.

LOG ON

www.com.ohio.gov/secu
Many state securities commissioners maintain Web sites that warn investors of risky or fraudulent securities. Visit the Ohio Division of Securities Web site. Click on links under "Alerts" to see examples of investor warnings.

Registration of Securities   Most of the state securities statutes adopt the philosophy of the 1933 Act that informed investors can make intelligent investment decisions. The states with such statutes have a registration scheme much like the 1933 Act, with required disclosures for public offerings and exemptions from registration for small and private offerings. Other states reject the contention that investors with full information can make intelligent investment decisions. The securities statutes in these states have a **merit registration** requirement, giving a securities administrator power to deny registration on the merits of the security and its issuer. Only securities that are not unduly risky and promise an adequate return to investors may receive administrator approval.

All state statutes have a limited number of exemptions from registration. Most statutes have private offering exemptions that are similar to Securities Act Rule 506 of Regulation D. In addition, a person may avoid the registration requirements of state securities laws by not offering or selling securities.

Registration by Coordination   The Uniform Securities Act permits an issuer to register its securities by coordination. Instead of filing a registration statement under the Securities Act of 1933 and a different one as required by state law, registration by coordination allows an issuer to file the 1933 Act registration statement with the state securities administrator. Registration by coordination decreases an issuer's expense of complying with state law when making an interstate offering of its securities.

Capital Markets Efficiency Act of 1996   Congress passed the Capital Markets Efficiency Act (CMEA) to facilitate offerings of securities by small investors. The CMEA preempts state registration of offers and sales of securities to "qualified purchasers," as defined by the SEC, as well as offerings exempt under Rule 506 of Regulation D. An issuance of securities listed on the New York Stock Exchange or NASDAQ is also exempted from state registration provisions. Nonetheless, states may apply their antifraud laws despite the preemption of their registration provisions.

Problems and Problem Cases

1. A viatical settlement is a contract by which an investor purchases the life insurance policy of a terminally ill patient—typically an AIDS victim—who is in need of immediate cash to pay mounting medical expenses. Depending on the insured's life expectancy, the buyer pays 60 to 80 percent of the death benefit. When the insured dies, the investor receives the death benefit. The investor's profit is the difference between the death benefit collected from the insurer and the discounted purchase price paid to the insured, less insurance premiums paid by the investor. Life Partners, Inc. (LPI), acts as a middleman between the insured and investors. LPI assembles the purchasers of each insurance policy, selling fractional interests to investors for as little as $650. Individual investors may receive as little as 3 percent of the death benefits of a policy. The investors become owners of the insurance policy. After the purchase, LPI monitors the insured's health, makes sure the policy does not lapse, collects on the policy when the insured dies, and disburses the proceeds to the investors. Is LPI selling a security?

2. Mickie Wenwoods, an outstanding collegiate golfer, graduates from college and decides to turn professional. To finance her effort to qualify for the LPGA Tour and to cover the cost of travel, housing, food, and a caddy, Wenwoods asks 20 of her family friends to contribute $10,000 each to her efforts. In return for their contributions, each friend will receive 1 percent of Wenwoods's revenues from her golfing efforts, including tournament prize money and endorsement fees from sponsors, less Wenwoods's expenses. Whether Wenwoods is able to generate revenue is dependent on how well she plays in golf tournaments and whether she is able to convince sponsors to sign her as an endorser. Wenwoods will also determine the amount of her expenses for travel, food, housing, and a caddy. Is Wenwoods selling a security when she asks for contributions from her friends?

3. AltaVerba, Inc., is a nonpublic company controlled by its majority shareholder, Robyn Streel. AltaVerba wants to make an initial public offering by selling 300 million Class B common shares in a firm commitment underwriting, with Goldman Sachs acting as the lead underwriter. AltaVerba is not a public

company required to file periodic reports with the SEC under the Securities Exchange Act of 1934. AltaVerba and Goldman are considering the communications they may have with existing and prospective investors and securities analysts before and during the registered offering and comply with Section 5 of the Securities Act of 1933. Seventy-two days before the 1933 Act registration statement will be filed with the SEC, AltaVerba wants to release historical information about its business and financial results. What are the restrictions on the release of such information at that time? Twenty-three days before the 1933 Act registration statement will be filed with the SEC, AltaVerba wants to release forward-looking information about its business and financial results. May AltaVerba do that? After the registration statement has been filed with the SEC, Streel and AltaVerba's vice president of finance want to speak on the phone about the issuance with an investment manager of Fidelity Magellan Fund. Is that communication legal at that time? At the same time, AltaVerba and Goldman want to conduct a road show in five cities. Selected very wealthy investors, securities analysts, and mutual fund managers will attend the road show in person. Under what conditions may AltaVerba and Goldman conduct a legal road show? After the registration statement has been declared effective by the SEC, AltaVerba wants to use a free-writing prospectus that includes historical and forward-looking information about AltaVerba. What conditions must the free-writing prospectus meet to be legal under Section 5?

4. EMG, Corp., a public corporation, decides to enter the Internet marketing business by creating a subsidiary corporation, GME, Inc., that will be 51 percent owned by EMG and 49 percent owned by other investors. The plan is that GME will not be not a public corporation required to file periodic reports with the Securities and Exchange Commission under the Securities Exchange Act of 1934. GME plans to sell 100 million shares for $20 each to EMG and to the following investors:

   - An investor who has annual income of $4,080,000 and a net worth of $12,200,000.
   - GME's chief operations officer, whose annual income is $175,000 and net worth is $350,000.
   - A pension fund established for EMG's employees.
   - 14 mutual funds, each of which has assets exceeding $20 billion.

GME wants to sell its common shares to the above investors in an exemption from the registration requirements of the Securities Act of 1933 under Rule 506. Is the $2 billion amount of the offering too large for Rule 506? Is the number of purchasers a problem under Rule 506? Are the listed investors qualified purchasers under Rule 506? Under Rule 506, for how long must GME restrict the purchasers' resales of the common shares? If GME is unsure whether the offering it proposes meets the requirements of Rule 506, what document should GME request from the staff of the SEC?

5. Real Options, Inc. (ROI), is a company not required to provide periodic reports to investors under the Securities Exchange Act of 1934. ROI wants to raise $700,000 by selling preferred shares to 150 investors, including its customers, suppliers, and employees. Is ROI eligible to make the offering under Rule 504 of the Securities Act of 1933? What must ROI do to comply with Rule 504?

6. Podcast Services Company is incorporated in Illinois. It has 200 employees that work in an office building leased by Podcast in Alton, Illinois. Most of Podcast's employees reside in Illinois, but a few reside in Missouri near St. Louis. All of Podcast's assets are in Illinois. It sells its services to clients in 20 states. About 35 percent of its business is conducted with clients in Missouri in the St. Louis area. Podcast wants to sell debentures to its employees, the proceeds of which will be used to purchase the building Podcast currently leases in Alton. May Podcast make the offering in compliance with Securities Act Rule 147? What must Podcast to do comply with Rule 147?

7. Commonwealth Edison Co. registered 3 million common shares with the SEC and sold the shares for about $28 per share. The price of the purchasers' stock dropped to $21 when the Atomic Safety and Licensing Board denied ComEd's application to license one of its reactors. It was the first and only time the Board had denied a license application. ComEd assumed that the license would be granted; therefore, its registration statement failed to disclose the pendency of the license application. Did ComEd violate Section 11 of the Securities Act?

8. Joseph Crotty was a vice president of United Artists Communications, Inc. (UA), a corporation with equity securities registered under the Securities Exchange Act of 1934. Crotty was the head film buyer of UA's western division. He had virtually complete and autonomous control of film buying for the 351 UA theaters in the western United States, including negotiating and signing movie acquisition agreements, supervising movie distribution, and settling contracts after the movies had been shown. Crotty knew how many contracts were being negotiated at any one time and the price UA was paying for the rental of each movie. Crotty was required to consult with higher officers only if he wanted to exceed a certain limit on the amount of the cash advance paid to a distributor for a movie. This occurred no more than two or three times a year. The gross revenue from Crotty's division was about 35 percent of UA's gross revenue from movie exhibitions and around 17 percent of its total gross revenue. During a six-month period, Crotty purchased 7,500 shares of UA and sold 3,500 shares, realizing a large profit. Has Crotty violated Section 16(b) of the 1934 Act?

9. Shareholders of General Electric Company have asked the board of directors to include several shareholder proposals in its annual proxy statement. One proposal is that GE's articles of incorporation be amended to provide that shareholders will elect directors by cumulative voting of their shares. A second proposal asks that no GE director be permitted to serve on more than three corporate boards of directors, including GE's board. A third proposal asks GE to prepare a report outlining the vulnerability and substantial radiation risks of storage of irradiated fuel rods at all GE-designed nuclear reactor sites. May GE omit these shareholder proposals from its proxy statement under Rule 14a–8?

10. Michael Broudo and other investors purchased stock in Dura Pharmaceuticals, Inc., on the public securities market between April 15, 1997, and February 24, 1998. During this period, they allege that Dura or its officers made false statements concerning both Dura's drug profits and future Food and Drug Administration approval of a new asthmatic spray device. They also allege that Dura falsely claimed that it expected that its drug sales would prove profitable. Regarding the asthmatic spray device, they allege Dura falsely claimed that it expected the FDA

would soon grant its approval. On February 24, 1998, Dura announced that its earnings would be lower than expected, principally due to slow drug sales. The next day Dura's shares lost almost half their value falling from about $39 per share to about $21. Eight months later in November 1998, Dura announced that the FDA would not approve Dura's new asthmatic spray device. Soon after, Broudo and the other investors sued Dura and its officers under Rule 10b–5 of the Securities Exchange Act of 1934. In their complaint, they stated that in reliance on the integrity of the market, they paid artificially inflated prices for Dura securities and suffered damages. They did not specify or attempt to calculate the amount of damages caused by the alleged misstatements made by Dura. Dura defended on the grounds that Broudo and the other investors failed adequately to allege loss causation. Did the U.S. Supreme Court agree with Dura?

11. The managements of Combustion Engineering, Inc. (CEI), and Basic, Inc., entered negotiations regarding CEI's acquiring Basic. Despite the secrecy of the merger negotiations, there were repeated instances of abnormal trading in Basic's shares, with trading volume rising from 7,000 per day to 29,000. Basic issued a public statement that "the company knew no reason for the stock's activity and that no negotiations were under way with any company for a merger." Did Basic's statement violate Securities Exchange Act Rule 10b–5?

12. When he was the Oklahoma Sooner football coach, Barry Switzer attended a track meet, where he spoke with friends and acquaintances, including G. Platt, a director of Phoenix Corporation and chief executive officer of Texas International Company (TIC), a business that sponsored Switzer's coach's television show. TIC owned more than 50 percent of Phoenix's shares. Switzer moved around the bleachers at the track meet in order to talk to various people. After speaking with Platt and his wife, Linda, for the last of five times, Switzer lay down to sunbathe on a row of bleachers behind the Platts. G. Platt, unaware that Switzer was behind him, carelessly spoke too loud while talking with his wife about his desire to sell or liquidate Phoenix. He also talked about several companies making bids to buy Phoenix. Switzer also overheard that an announcement of a possible liquidation of Phoenix might be made within a week.

Switzer used the information he obtained in deciding to purchase Phoenix shares. Did Switzer trade illegally on inside information?

13. First City Financial Corp., a Canadian company controlled by the Belzberg family, was engaged in the business of investing in publicly held American corporations. Marc Belzberg identified Ashland Oil Company as a potential target, and on February 11, 1986, he secretly purchased 61,000 shares of Ashland stock for First City. By February 26, additional secret purchases of Ashland shares pushed First City's holdings to just over 4.9 percent of Ashland's stock. These last two purchases were effected for First City by Alan "Ace" Greenberg, the chief executive officer of Bear Stearns, a large Wall Street brokerage. On March 4, Belzberg called Greenberg and told him, "It wouldn't be a bad idea if you bought Ashland Oil here." Immediately after the phone call, Greenberg purchased 20,500 Ashland shares for about $44 per share. If purchased for First City, those shares would have increased First City's Ashland holdings above 5 percent. Greenberg believed he was buying the shares for First City under a put and call agreement, under which First City had the right to buy the shares from Bear Stearns and Bear Stearns had the right to require First City to buy the shares from it. Between March 4 and 14, Greenberg purchased an additional 330,700 shares. On March 17, First City and Bear Stearns signed a formal put and call agreement covering all the shares Greenberg purchased. On March 25, First City announced publicly for the first time that it intended to make a tender offer for all of Ashland's shares. First City filed a Schedule 13D on March 26. Has First City violated the Williams Act?

14. Amenity, Inc., was incorporated with 1 million authorized shares, which were issued to Capital General Corporation (CGC) for $2,000. CGC distributed 90,000 of those shares to about 900 of its clients, business associates, and other contacts to create and maintain goodwill among its clients and contacts. CGC did not receive any monetary or other direct financial consideration from those receiving the stock. Amenity had no actual business function at this time, and its sole asset was the $2,000 CGC had paid for the 1 million shares. Through CGC's efforts, Amenity was acquired by another company,

which paid CGC $25,000 for its efforts. The Utah Securities Division sought to suspend the public trading of Amenity stock on the grounds that when CGC distributed the shares it had sold them in violation of the Utah Securities Act. Was CGC's distribution a sale of securities?

Online Research

Internet Offerings of Securities

Using the term *Internet Securities Offerings,* you can find several Web sites and publications that explain how an issuer may make an Internet offering of securities without violating state or federal securities law. These resources can help you answer the following questions:

- Why will an Internet offering create problems if the issuer is trying to exempt the offering under Rules 505 or 506?
- Why are Rule 504 and Regulation A good exemptions for Internet offerings?
- What are the dos and don'ts for communications during an Internet registered offering?

chapter 46

LEGAL AND PROFESSIONAL RESPONSIBILITIES OF AUDITORS, CONSULTANTS, AND SECURITIES PROFESSIONALS

Credit Deutsch First Chicago LLP (CDFC) is a financial consulting and investment banking firm. Angst & Yearn LLP (A&Y) is a public accounting firm. A client of both firms is Macrohard Corporation, a public issuer of securities required to file periodic reports with the Securities and Exchange Commission under the Securities Exchange Act of 1934. Because Macrohard has a short-term cash flow problem due to a downturn in the economy, CDFC advises Macrohard to issue 300 promissory notes, each with a face value of $10,000,000, interest of 9 percent, and a due date 11 months after issuance. CDFC recommends that the notes be sold to mutual funds, insurance companies, pension funds, and other institutional investors using the Rule 506 exemption from registration under the Securities Act of 1933.

The notes are offered in part by an offering circular, which includes financial statements audited by A&Y. A&Y's unqualified audit opinion is also included in the offering circular. A&Y receives a $6,500,000 fee for auditing Macrohard's financial statements and reviewing the financial statements for inclusion in the offering circular.

CDFC assists Macrohard with the offering of the notes by calling prospective investors on the phone, visiting investors in person, and sending e-mails to prospective investors urging them to buy the notes. In all three contacts, CDFC emphasizes that the notes carry an interest rate that is 3 percent higher than the 30-year Treasury bond rate and, therefore, offer an excellent return on investment. As compensation for its role in the notes offering, CDFC will receive 0.5 percent of the proceeds from the sale of the notes.

- What standard of care must CDFC meet when recommending that Marcrohard issue promissory notes as a solution to its liquidity problems?
- If one of CDFC's managing partners during the course of the offering negligently makes false statements about Macrohard's financial position to purchasers of the notes, does CDFC have potential liability to the purchasers under Section 12(a)(2) of the Securities Act of 1933? Especially consider whether CDFC is a proper type of defendant under that section.
- Is CDFC a proper type of defendant under Rule 10b–5 of the Securities Exchange Act of 1934 due to its communications with purchasers, if one of its partners negligently makes false statements?
- Should A&Y fear liability to the note purchasers under Section 12(a)(2) of the 1933 Act?
- If A&Y negligently audited Macrohard's financial statements and as a result the financial statements materially misstate Macrohard's financial position, does A&Y have potential liability to the purchasers under Rule 10b–5 of the 1934 Act? Especially consider whether A&Y is a proper type of defendant under that rule.

- Does CDFC have potential liability to any of the note purchasers under the state law of negligent misrepresentation in a state that has adopted the *Ultramares* test?
- If A&Y knows that the audited financial statements will be used in the offering circular to sell the notes, but it does not know to which institutional investors the notes will be sold, does A&Y have potential liability to any of the note purchasers under the state law of negligent misrepresentation in a state that adopted the *Ultramares* test? How about a state that has adopted the rule of the *Restatement (Second) of Torts*?

Suppose that instead of making a Rule 506 offering, Macrohard issues preferred stock in a public offering registered under the 1933 Act. CDFC is Macrohard's underwriter for the public offering, receiving a 25-cent spread for each share sold. The financial statements audited by A&Y and its audit opinion are included in the registration statement. Unknown to CDFC and A&Y, there are material misstatements of fact in the financial statements included in the registration statement, and there are also omissions of material facts in the portions of the registration statement that describe Macrohard's business and the material risks of investing in the preferred stock.

- Is CDFC a statutory defendant under Section 11 of the 1933 Act? For what portions of the registration statement is CDFC liable under Section 11? What is CDFC's due diligence defense for errors in the financial statements audited by A&Y? What is CDFC's due diligence defense for errors in the portions of the registration statement that describe Macrohard's business and material risks?
- Is A&Y a statutory defendant under Section 11 of the 1933 Act? For what portions of the registration statement is A&Y liable under Section 11? What is A&Y's due diligence defense?
- Compile a checklist that will help CDFC and A&Y meet their due diligence defenses under Section 11.

Each year, many accounting and finance students choose to become CPAs and seek jobs as auditors of public companies. Many students, however, opt for positions in consulting and other fields connected to the securities industry. Therefore, this chapter covers the legal responsibilities of not only accountants and auditors, but also consultants and securities professionals. The chapter's primary focus is on auditors of financial statements, tax accountants, consultants who provide management and financial advice to clients, investment bankers, securities underwriters, securities analysts, and securities brokers.

This chapter will first cover the general standard of performance required of professionals. Next, we will study professionals' liability to their clients, especially under state law. The largest part of this chapter comprises liability to nonclient third parties. We will also examine criminal liability of professionals and end the chapter with coverage of the law protecting the integrity of communications between professionals and their clients.

General Standard of Performance

The general duty that auditors, consultants, and securities professionals owe to their clients and to other persons who are affected by their actions is to exercise the skill and care of the ordinarily prudent professional in the same circumstances. Hence, professionals must act carefully and diligently; they are *not* guarantors of the accuracy of their work or that the advice they give to clients will work out well. The professional's duty to exercise reasonable care is a subset of the negligence standard of tort law. Two elements compose the general duty of performance: skill and care.

A professional must have the **skill of the ordinarily prudent person in her profession.** This element focuses on education or knowledge, whether acquired formally at school or by self-instruction. For example, to audit financial records, an accountant must know generally accepted auditing standards (GAAS) and generally accepted accounting principles (GAAP). GAAS and GAAP are standards and principles embodied in the rules, releases, and pronouncements of the Securities and Exchange Commission, the American Institute of Certified Public Accountants (AICPA), the Financial Accounting Standards Board (FASB), the Public Company Accounting Oversight Board (PCAOB), and the International Accounting Standards Board (IASB). To assist a corporate client's development of an expansion strategy, a consultant must be knowledgeable of similar businesses and the opportunities for expansion. To assist a securities issuer making an initial public offering (IPO), an investment banker must know the mechanics of a public offering and the market for securities. In recommending stocks to an investor, a broker or investment adviser must know fundamental investment analysis and portfolio theory.

The care element requires a professional to act **as carefully as the ordinarily prudent person in her profession.** For example, in preparing a tax return, a tax accountant must discover the income exclusions, the deductions, and the tax credits that the reasonably careful accountant would find are available to the client. When recommending a corporate acquisition to a client, an investment banker must investigate the value of the acquired firm and check the acquired firm's fit with the business and strategy of the acquiring firm. A broker recommending a security to his customer must carefully investigate the security and its fit with the customer's investment goals, securities portfolio, and financial status.

Courts and legislatures usually defer to the members of a profession in determining what the ordinarily prudent professional would do. Such deference recognizes the lawmakers' lack of understanding of the nuances of professional practice. However, a profession will not be permitted to establish a standard of conduct that is harmful to the interests of clients or other members of society.

Professionals' Liability to Clients

Professionals are sometimes sued by their clients. For example, an accountant may wrongfully claim deductions on a client's tax return. When the IRS discovers the wrongful deduction, the individual will have to pay the extra tax, interest, and perhaps a penalty. The individual may sue his accountant to recover the amount of the penalty. For another example, consider a securities broker who churns the securities account of a 92-year-old investor by executing daily trades in risky Internet stocks. When the value of the investor's portfolio declines from $500,000 to near zero as high commissions and capital losses mount, the investor may sue the broker for making imprudent investment decisions and for churning the account merely to earn the commissions.

When clients sue professionals, there are three principal bases of liability: contract, tort, and trust.

Contractual Liability   As a party to a contract with her client, a professional owes a duty to the client to perform as she has agreed to perform. This includes an implied duty to perform the contract as the ordinarily prudent person in the profession would perform it. If the professional fails to perform as agreed, ordinarily she is

---

Ethics in Action

Public Company Accounting Oversight Board

One of the main features of the Sarbanes–Oxley Act (SOX) is the creation of an independent board that oversees the audits of public companies. Congress's perception was that auditing firms were not sufficiently independent of the public companies they audited due in part to the audit firms' receiving sizable nonaudit consulting fees from their audit clients. Thus, SOX created a Public Company Accounting Oversight Board (PCAOB). Public accounting firms that audit financial statements of public companies are required to register with PCAOB and submit to its rules. The board is charged with adopting rules establishing auditing, quality control, ethics, and independence standards. It has the power to regulate the nonaudit services that audit firms may perform for their clients. The PCAOB has the power to inspect periodically public accounting firms and to issue reports of the results of the reviews. The purpose of inspections is to assess the degree of compliance with the requirements of SOX,

professional auditing standards, and the rules of the PCAOB and the SEC in the performance of audits and the issuance of audit reports of public companies. In addition, the PCAOB may investigate and discipline audit firms and their partners and employees.

The PCAOB is not a federal agency, but a nonprofit corporation with broad regulatory power like the National Association of Securities Dealers, a self-regulatory organization that regulates securities brokers and dealers. It has five members, only two of which may be CPAs. No board member may receive any share of profits or compensation from a public accounting firm.

- Do you think that the creation and work of the PCAOB results in greater independence of auditors of public companies?
- If auditing of financial statements is required primarily for the protection of public investors, should not all PCAOB members be taken from the investment community that uses audited financial statements?

The Global Business Environment

U.S. Moving to International Accounting Standards?

In 2008, the SEC announced that it would consider requiring American companies to comply with international accounting standards adopted by the International Accounting Standards Board (IASB). The SEC proposal is designed to move the world to one set of accounting standards and, thereby, permit investors to compare more easily companies operating in differing parts of the world. The proposal, it is claimed, would also make it easier for companies to raise capital by allowing them to sell securities in securities markets anywhere in the world.

Under the SEC proposal, a small number of very large American firms (about 110) would be permitted to use international accounting standards in 2010. The SEC would require large American companies to move to the international standards in 2014 with small companies making the move in either 2015 or 2016.

- From time to time, the SEC has exercised its power to block an accounting standard issued by the FASB when it deems inappropriate the treatment required or permitted by the rule. Do you think the SEC will exercise the same power when it views as wrong an IASB standard?
- Under the Securities Exchange Act of 1934, the SEC has the power to set accounting standards for U.S. public companies. Do you think the SEC abdicated its responsibility by allowing the FASB today and the IASB in the future to set American accounting standards? Whom do you trust more to adopt reasonable accounting standards: the SEC, the FASB, or the IASB?

---

liable only for compensatory damages and those consequential damages that are contemplated by the client and the professional at the time the contract was made, such as the client's cost of hiring another consultant or auditor to complete the work. For example, an auditor agrees to provide audited financial statements for inclusion in a client's bank loan application. The loan will be used to expand the client's business. When the auditor fails to complete the audit on time, the auditor will not ordinarily be liable for the client's lost profits from the unexecuted expansion, unless the auditor had agreed to be liable for such lost profits.

A professional is not liable for breach of contract if the client obstructs the performance of the contract. For example, an investment banker is not liable for failing to make a timely public offering of a client's securities if the client delays giving the investment banker the information it needs to complete the securities offering registration statement.

A professional may not delegate his duty to perform a contract without the consent of the client. Delegation is not permitted because the performance of a contract for professional services depends on the skill, training, and character of the professional. For example, PricewaterhouseCoopers, a public accounting firm, may not delegate to Ernst & Young, another public accounting firm, the contractual duty to audit the financial statements of Apple Inc., even though both firms are nearly equally skillful and careful.

Tort Liability
Professionals' tort liability to their clients may be based on the common law concepts of negligence and fraud or on the violation of a statute, including the federal and state securities laws.

Negligence   The essence of negligence is the failure of a professional to exercise the skill and care of the ordinarily prudent person in the profession. A professional is negligent when he breaches the duty to act skillfully and carefully and proximately causes damages to the client. For example, a corporate client may recover from an investment banker when the client overpays for an acquired firm due to the investment banker's careless valuation of the acquired firm.

Under the **suitability** and **know-your-customer rules** of the NASD and stock exchanges, a securities broker is required to know the financial circumstances and investment objectives of his client before recommending securities or executing securities transactions for the client. A broker who does not know his customer is negligent and may be liable for losses from securities transactions that are inappropriate for the client. A broker that warns a client of the risks and inappropriateness of an investment has met his duty and is not liable, for example, to a client that disregards the risk and authorizes trading in the risky investment. The suitability and know-your-customer rules may also justify a client's action on *contract* grounds when the customer signs an account agreement that requires a broker to handle the account in accordance with industry standards.

See *Millan v. Dean Witter Reynolds* on page 925 of Chapter 36 for a case in which a securities brokerage was held liable to its client for negligence and gross negligence.

Audit Duties Audit engagements are a unique area of professional liability. Sometimes, an accountant will audit a company, yet fail to uncover fraud, embezzlement, or other intentional wrongdoing by an employee of the company. Ordinarily, an accountant has no specific duty to uncover employee fraud or embezzlement. Nonetheless, an accountant must uncover employee fraud or embezzlement if an ordinarily prudent accountant would have discovered it. The accountant who fails to uncover such fraud or embezzlement is negligent and liable to his client. In addition, an accountant owes a duty to investigate suspicious circumstances that tend to indicate fraud, regardless of how he became aware of those circumstances. Also, an accountant has a duty to inform a proper party of his suspicions. It is *not enough* to inform or confront the person suspected of fraud.

When an accountant is hired to perform a fraud audit to investigate suspected fraud or embezzlement, she has a greater duty to investigate. She must be as skillful and careful as the ordinarily prudent auditor performing a fraud audit.

When an accountant negligently fails to discover embezzlement, generally he is liable to his client only for an amount equal to the embezzlement that occurred after he should have discovered the embezzlement. The accountant is usually not liable for any part of the embezzlement that occurred prior to the time he should have uncovered the embezzlement unless his tardy discovery prevented the client from recovering embezzled funds.

Contributory and Comparative Negligence of Client Courts are reluctant to permit a professional to escape liability to a client merely because the client was **contributorily negligent.** Since the accountant or consultant has skills superior to those of the client, courts generally allow clients to rely on an accountant's duty to discover employee fraud, a consultant's duty to make reasonable recommendations, and an underwriter's advice on what type of security to issue. The client is not required to exercise reasonable care to discover these things itself.

Nonetheless, some courts allow the defense of contributory negligence or the defense of **comparative negligence,** such as when clients negligently fail to follow a consultant's advice or when clients possess information that makes their reliance on an investment banker unwarranted.

In the following *Fehribach* case, the appeals court considered the scope of an auditor's duty when conducting an audit and the greater ability of the client to know its financial condition and, thereby, protect itself. Note also that the court, applying the *Ultramares* rule we will study later in this chapter, found that the bankruptcy trustee was a proper plaintiff only because he sued the auditor on behalf of the auditor's client.

Fehribach v. E&Y LLP　　　493 F.3d 905 (7th Cir. 2007)

In October 1995, Ernst & Young LLP (E&Y) issued an audit report for fiscal year 1995 regarding its client, Taurus Foods, Inc., a small company engaged in the distribution of frozen meats and other foods. American Institute of Certified Public Accountants, Statement on Auditing Standards No. 59 *(1988) requires an auditor report to indicate the auditor's substantial doubt about the audited company's ability to continue as a going concern for a reasonable period of time, not to exceed one year beyond the date of the financial statements being audited. E&Y's report on Taurus indicated that E&Y had "no substantial doubt" that Taurus would continue as a going concern until at least January 1996.*

Several months after E&Y's audit report was received by Taurus, its chief lender, Bank One, became alarmed by the deterioration in Taurus's financial condition. The bank imposed restrictions on Taurus that increased the company's business troubles. To stave off disaster, Lisa Corry, the company's chief financial officer (and the daughter of one of Taurus's two owners), started defrauding Bank One by inflating the company's sales and accounts receivable in daily reports that Taurus was required to make to the bank. She was eventually caught, prosecuted, convicted, and sent to prison. Soon after, in 1998, Taurus entered in a bankruptcy proceeding.

Taurus's bankruptcy trustee, Gregory Fehribach, asked the district court to require E&Y to pay damages for failing to include a going concern qualification in its audit report for the 1995 fiscal year. The trustee argued that if E&Y had issued the qualification, the owners of Taurus—who were active owners who managed the company—would have realized that the company had no future and would immediately have liquidated, averting costs of some $3 million that the company incurred as a result of its continued operation under the restrictions imposed by Bank One. E&Y moved for summary judgment, which the district court granted. Taurus's bankruptcy trustee appealed to the Seventh Circuit Court of Appeals.

Posner, Circuit Judge

The trustee's damages claim is based on the theory of "deepening insolvency." This controversial theory allows damages sometimes to be awarded to a bankrupt corporation that by delaying liquidation ran up additional debts that it would not have incurred had the plug been pulled sooner. As originally formulated, the theory was premised on the notion that borrowing after a company becomes insolvent would "ineluctably" hurt the shareholders. That was a puzzling suggestion because by hypothesis a company harmed by *deepening* insolvency was insolvent before the borrowing spree, so what had the shareholders to lose? But a corporation can be insolvent in the sense of being unable to pay its bills as they come due, yet be worth more liquidated than the sum of its liabilities and so be worth something to the shareholders.

The theory could also be invoked in a case in which management in cahoots with an auditor or other outsider concealed the corporation's perilous state which if disclosed earlier would have enabled the corporation to survive in reorganized form. However, the theory makes no sense when invoked to create a substantive duty of prompt liquidation that would punish corporate management for trying in the exercise of its business judgment to stave off a declaration of bankruptcy, even if there were no indication of fraud, breach of fiduciary duty, or other conventional wrongdoing. Nor would it do to fix liability on a third party for lending or otherwise investing in a firm and as a result keeping it going, when management misused the opportunity created by that investment. Management could have instead used that opportunity to turn the company around and transform it into a profitable business. They did not, and therein lies the harm to the company.

The owners of Taurus lost their entire investment when the company became insolvent. They had nothing more to lose. The only possible losers from the prolongation of the corporation's miserable existence were the corporation's creditors. In a state that allows creditors (or shareholders) of the audited firm to sue the auditor for negligent misrepresentation, provided that the creditors' reliance on the auditor's report was foreseeable—or, in some states, was actually foreseen—Taurus's creditors could sue E&Y directly. But Indiana adheres to a close approximation to *Ultramares Corp. v. Touche,* 255 N.Y. 170, 174 N.E. 441 (N.Y. 1931). And under the *Ultramares* doctrine, creditors in the position of Taurus's creditors, not having a contractual relation with the auditor, have no claim against it.

Taurus had the contractual relation, and thus could sue, though because it is in bankruptcy and has been liquidated the suit is really on behalf of the creditors; anything that reduces the liquidation value of the corporation hurts them. That doesn't make the suit an impermissible end run around Indiana's limitation of creditor (or shareholder) suits against auditors.

Remember that under Indiana law E&Y has no duty of care to the creditors. But it does of course have such a duty to its client, Taurus, and that duty, on which this suit is founded, does not evaporate just because the client is bankrupt and any benefits from suing will accrue to its creditors.

The trustee's claim fails nevertheless, but fails on the facts, though not because Taurus survived for more than a year (in fact three years) after the audit period. A going-concern qualification is just a prediction; if it should have been included in the audit report and harm resulted as a foreseeable consequence of its omission, the auditor is liable to the firm audited for that harm. Such cases are rare because it is unusual for the audited firm to be able to make a plausible contention that it could not have been expected to recognize its financial peril on its own even though it supplied the financial information on which the audit was based. The purpose of an audit report is to make sure the audited company's financial statements—which are prepared by the company, not by the auditor—correspond to reality, lest they either have been doctored by a defalcating employee or innocently misrepresent the company's financial situation. The auditor is therefore required to state whether, in his opinion, the financial statements are presented in conformity with generally accepted accounting principles and to identify those circumstances in which such principles have not been consistently observed in the preparation of the financial statements of the current period in relation to those of the preceding period. There is no contention that E&Y failed to notice discrepancies between the statements and the company's actual financial situation. There were no discrepancies. And no information that the report contained or should have contained if the audit was carefully done indicated that Taurus couldn't limp through another year—the report revealed positive though slight net income in the most recent fiscal year and no obligations that would mature in the next year and by doing so might drive the firm under.

It is true that the report failed to warn Taurus of ominous trends in the frozen-meat distribution business. Intensified competition from national firms was causing Taurus to lose customers, thus depressing the firm's revenues; at the same time, the company's costs were rising because of higher workers' compensation premiums and other untoward developments. But predicting Taurus's future cash flow on any basis other than the financial statements for the audit year (which would for example reveal existing loan-repayment obligations) was not the function of the audit report. E&Y had not contracted to provide Taurus with management-consulting services. An auditor's duty is not to give business advice; it is merely to paint an accurate picture of the audited firm's financial condition, insofar as that condition is revealed by the company's books and inventory and other sources of an auditor's opinion.

But there is need to qualify what we have just said. The requirement that the auditor disclose in its report any substantial doubt it has that the firm will still be a going concern in a year expands the auditor's duty beyond that of verifying the accuracy of the company's financial statements. The accounting standards require the auditor to be on the lookout for certain conditions or events that, when considered in the aggregate, indicate there could be substantial doubt about the entity's ability to continue as a going concern for a reasonable period of time. The following are examples of such conditions and events:

Negative trends—for example, recurring operating losses, working capital deficiencies, negative cash flows from operating activities, adverse key financial ratios.

Other indications of possible financial difficulties—for example, default on loan or similar agreements, arrearages in dividends, denial of usual trade credit from suppliers, restructuring of debt, non-compliance with statutory capital requirements, need to seek new sources or methods of financing or to dispose of substantial assets.

Internal matters—for example, work stoppages or other labor difficulties, substantial dependence on the success of a particular project, uneconomic long-term commitments, need to significantly revise operations.

External matters that have occurred—for example, legal proceedings, legislation, or similar matters that might jeopardize an entity's ability to operate; loss of a key franchise, license, or patent; loss of a principal customer or supplier; uninsured or underinsured catastrophe such as a drought, earthquake, or flood.

American Institute of Certified Public Accountants, "The Auditor's Consideration of an Entity's Ability to Continue as a Going Concern," in *Codification of Statements on Accounting Standards*, § 341.06 (2007). It is the last bullet point, referring to "external matters," that stretches the auditor's duty—especially, so far as bears on this case, the reference to "loss of a principal customer or supplier." Elsewhere the standards emphasize that the auditor must have "an appropriate understanding of the entity *and its environment*" *Id.,* §§ 314.01-.02 (emphasis added).

Yet nowhere is the auditor required to *investigate* external matters as distinct from discovering them during the engagement. An accounting firm that conducts an annual audit of a multitude of unrelated firms in a multitude of different industries cannot be expected to be expert in the firms' business environments. Large accounting firms like E&Y do divide their practice into industry groups, and the accountants assigned to a particular group doubtless know a lot about the companies. But the auditor is not hired to assess the supply and demand conditions facing the audited firm. If the auditor is told by the firm or otherwise learns from the information that it collects in conducting the audit that the firm's near-term prospects are endangered by pending legislation, the loss of a customer, or other "conditions or events," then it must factor the information into its assessment of the firm's risk of going under within a year. But it is not expected to duplicate the expertise assumed to reside in the firms themselves and in management consultants specializing in the firm's industry. E&Y could not have been expected to know more about trends in the frozen-meat distribution business than Taurus, which had been in that business for more than 20 years.

Judgment for E&Y affirmed.

Fraud A professional is liable to his client for fraud when he misstates or omits facts in communications with his client and acts with **scienter.** A person acts with scienter when he knows of the falsity of a statement or he recklessly disregards the truth. Thus, accountants are liable in fraud for their intentional or reckless disregard for accuracy in their work.

For example, an accountant chooses not to examine the current figures in a client's books of account, but relies on last year's figures because he is behind in his work for other clients. As a result, the accountant understates the client's income on an income statement that the client uses to apply for a loan. The client obtains a loan, but he has to pay a higher interest rate because his low stated income makes the loan a higher risk for the bank.

Such misconduct by the accountant proves scienter and, therefore, amounts to fraud.

Scienter also includes recklessly ignoring facts, such as an auditor's finding obvious evidence of embezzlement yet failing to notify a client of the embezzlement. An investment banker defrauds its client when it withholds information concerning the value of the client's shares and causes the client to issue the shares for too little consideration, perhaps to an affiliate of the investment banker who, therefore, profits unreasonably. As you can see, fraud is extremely reprehensible conduct, and a defrauder deserves to be punished. Fraud actions are not designed to impose liability on honest professionals who sometimes make careless errors.

The chief advantage of establishing fraud is that the client may get a higher damage award than when the accountant is merely negligent. Usually, a client may receive only compensatory damages for a breach of contract or negligence. By proving fraud, a client may be awarded punitive damages as well.

Breach of Trust A professional owes a duty of trust to his client. Information and assets that are entrusted to an accountant, broker, or investment banker, for example, may be used only to benefit the client. The duty of trust requires the professional to maintain the confidentiality of the client's information entrusted to the firm. Therefore, a professional may not disclose sensitive matters such as a client's income and wealth or use secret information about a client's new product to purchase the client's securities. In addition, for example, an accountant or securities broker may not use the assets of his client for his own benefit.

Securities Law Federal and state securities law creates several rights of action for persons harmed in connection with the purchase or sale of securities. These rights of action are based in tort. Although some securities law sections permit clients to sue professionals, they are rarely used for that purpose. Usually, only third parties (nonclients) sue under the securities law. Therefore, the securities law sections that apply to professionals are discussed later in this chapter.

LOG ON

www.securitieslaw.com
The Securities Fraud & Investor Protection Resource Center provides information on the investor–broker relationship, including investors' rights of actions against brokers.

Professionals' Liability to Third Persons: Common Law

Other persons besides a professional's clients may use her work product. Banks may use financial statements reviewed by a loan applicant's accountant in deciding whether to make a loan to the applicant. Investors may use financial statements audited by a company's auditors in deciding whether to buy or sell the company's securities. These documents prepared by an accountant may prove incorrect, resulting in damages to the nonclients who relied on them. For example, banks may lend money to a corporation only because an income statement

Ethics in Action

The Sarbanes–Oxley Act: Auditor Independence Standards

When Congress studied the causes of financial statement irregularities in 2002, it became convinced that some auditors failed to challenge their clients' financial reporting practices for fear that the audit firms would lose lucrative consulting contracts with the clients. The belief was that firms undercharged for audit services to acquire valuable consulting clients. To ensure that audit firms are free from conflict-of-interest and lack of independence charges that can undermine the quality of their audits, the Sarbanes–Oxley Act (SOX) bans most types of services by audit firms for audit clients, including:

- Bookkeeping.
- Financial information system design.
- Appraisal or valuation services.
- Actuarial services.
- Internal audit outsourcing.
- Management or human resource services.
- Broker, dealer, investment banker, and investment adviser services.
- Legal and expert services related to the audit.
- Other services as determined by the Public Company Accounting Oversight Board.

The PCAOB also has power on a case-by-case basis to exempt services performed by an audit firm for an audit client. An audit firm may provide permissible nonaudit services for an audit client, such as tax services, only if the client's audit committee approves the services in advance.

In addition, SOX requires that the audit partner-in-charge be rotated every five years at a minimum. SOX also charges the General Accounting Office to study whether all public companies should be required to rotate audit firms on a regular basis. Finally, no audit firm may audit a public company that within the past year has hired an audit firm employee as a CEO, CFO, or CAO.

prepared by an accountant overstated the corporation's income. When the corporation fails to repay the loan, the bank may sue the accountant to recover the damages it suffered.

Nonclient actions are rarer outside the accountant context because the work product of nonaccounting professionals is infrequently used by others in an expectable way. For example, consulting advice is almost never passed from a client to a third party. A securities broker's client rarely relays the broker's investment advice to a friend; when the friend attempts to sue the broker if the advice turns out to be bad, the friend usually is not able to recover damages from the broker.

However, investment bankers often prepare documents for their clients that are created expressly to sell securities to nonclients, that is, shareholders and other holders of the client's securities. Therefore, purchasers who buy the client's securities based on false statements in a document prepared for investors by an investment banker may sue the investment banker.

Nonclients may sue professionals for common law negligence, common law fraud, and violations of the securities laws. In this section, common law negligence and fraud are discussed.

Negligence and Negligent Misrepresentation

When a professional fails to perform as the ordinarily prudent professional would perform, she risks having liability for negligence. Many courts have restricted the ability of nonclients to sue a professional for damages proximately caused by the professional's negligent conduct. These courts limit nonclient suits on the grounds that nonclient users of a professional's work product have not contracted with the professional and, therefore, are not in **privity of contract** with her. Essentially, these courts hold that a professional owes no duty to nonclients to exercise ordinary skill and care.

This judicial stance conflicts with the usual principles of negligence law under which a negligent person is liable to all persons who are reasonably foreseeably damaged by his negligence. The rationale for the restrictive judicial stance was expressed in the *Ultramares* case,[1] a decision of the highest court in New York. In that case, Judge Benjamin Cardozo refused to hold an auditor liable to third parties for mere negligence. His rationale was stated as follows:

> If liability for negligence exists, a thoughtless slip or blunder, the failure to detect a theft or forgery beneath the cover

of deceptive entries, may expose accountants to a liability in an indeterminate amount for an indeterminate time to an indeterminate class.

The *Ultramares* privity requirement protects an auditor or other professional who does not know the user or the extent of use of its work product and, therefore, is unable to assess the potential dollar amount of liability or the user's propensity to sue. *Ultramares* allows auditors and other professionals to manage the known risks of their work product being used by nonclients either by insuring against the risk, increasing the client's engagement fee, or declining the engagement.

Ultramares dominated the thinking of judges for many years, and its impact is still felt today. However, many courts understand that many nonclients use and reasonably rely on the work product of professionals, especially accountants. To varying degrees, these courts have relaxed the privity requirement and expanded the class of persons who may sue an accountant or other professional for negligent conduct. Today, most courts adopt one of the following three tests to determine whether a nonclient may sue a professional for negligence.

Primary Benefit Test The *Ultramares* court adopted a primary benefit test for imposing liability for negligence. Under this test, a professional's duty of care extends only to those persons for whose primary benefit the professional audits or prepares financial reports and other documents. The professional must actually foresee the nonclient's use and prepare the document primarily for use by a specified nonclient. That is, the nonclient must be a **foreseen user** of the professional's work product. The professional must know three things: (1) the name of the person who will use her work product, (2) the particular purpose for which that person will use the work product, and (3) the extent of the use, such as the dollar amount of the nonclient's transaction.

Suppose an investment banker acts as a broker for a client issuing $100 million of securities to 10 mutual funds identified as prospective buyers. To assist the client's sale of the securities, the investment banker prepares an offering memorandum for the client. If due to the investment banker's negligence the offering memorandum misstates material facts, and the client gives the offering memorandum to the previously identified mutual funds, the investment banker may have liability to the mutual funds that relied on the misstated facts.

Foreseen Users and Foreseen Class of Users Test By 1965, a draft of the *Restatement (Second) of Torts* proposed that the law of professional negligence expand

---

[1] *Ultramares Corp. v. Touche,* 174 N.E. 441 (N.Y.Ct.App. 1931).

the class of protected persons to **foreseen users** and **users within a foreseen class of users** of reports. Under this test, the professional must know the use and extent of use to be made of the work product. The protected persons are (1) those persons who a professional knows will use the work product and (2) those persons who use the work product in a way the professional knew the work product would be used.

For example, an accountant prepares an income statement that he knows his client will use to obtain a $50 million loan at Bank X. Any bank to which the client supplies the statement to obtain a similar loan, including Bank Y, may sue the accountant for damages caused by a negligently prepared income statement. Bank X is a foreseen user, and Bank Y is in a foreseen class of users. On the other hand, if an accountant prepares an income statement for a tax return and the client, without the accountant's knowledge, uses the income statement to apply for a loan from a bank, the bank is not among the protected class of persons—the accountant did not know that the tax return would be used for that purpose.

Also, if the accountant prepared the client's income statement for the purpose of aiding the client to obtain a $50 million loan, but instead the client obtained a $200 million loan, the accountant would not be liable to the nonclient bank: the accountant did not know the extent of the bank's use, that is, the dollar amount of risk to which she was exposed.

In the securities professional context, when an underwriter prepares an offering document for a client issuing a known amount of securities, the *Restatement* test extends an underwriter's liability for negligence to any purchaser of the securities whether known or not to the underwriter. This is because the underwriter knows the type of person who will use the offering document, that is, buyers of the securities, the use, and the extent of the use, that is, the dollar amount of securities to be bought.

Nonetheless, when the *Restatement* test is applied to securities brokers, liability rarely extends past the broker's client. A broker who gives investment advice to a client is rarely found liable to a nonclient who receives the advice secondhand on the grounds that investment advice is crafted specifically for the broker's client. That rationale is generally followed even in the context of a published investment newsletter, where usually only subscribers to the newsletter are permitted to sue the publisher of the newsletter.

Foreseeable Users Test A very few courts have applied traditional negligence causation principles to professional negligence. They have extended liability to **foreseeable users** of an accountant's audit and other reports who suffered damages that were proximately caused by the accountant's negligence. To be liable to a nonclient under this test, an accountant need merely be reasonably able to expect or foresee the nonclient's use of the accountant's work product. It is not necessary for the nonclient to prove that the accountant actually expected or foresaw the nonclient's use.

In the next case against accounting giant PwC, the court reviewed the scope of *Ultramares* and other cases in the course of interpreting the Illinois statute defining those persons to whom a professional may be liable for negligent misrepresentation.

Tricontinental Industries, Ltd. v. PricewaterhouseCoopers, LLP
475 F.3d 824 (7th Cir. 2007)

Anicom, Inc., was a wire distribution company founded in the early 1990s. Its stock became publicly traded, and the company adopted a strategy to increase market share and to expand its operations. Between 1995 and 1997, Anicom acquired 12 companies. Each of these transactions involved some payment in the form of Anicom stock. During this time, PricewaterhouseCoopers, LLP, rendered accounting, audit, and various types of consulting services to Anicom.

In 1996, Anicom began engaging in improper accounting procedures to enable it to report that it had met sales and revenue goals. The procedures included the use of fictitious sales orders or prebills for goods that were not ordered. PwC became aware of these practices in July 1997 when it was asked to investigate Anicom's billing practices. After conducting its investigation, PwC reported to Donald C. Welchco, Anicom's vice president and CFO, that improper billing had occurred at Anicom branches and that, in the absence of controls, the practice might arise at other branches as well. No mention of these irregularities was made in PwC's audits of Anicom's 1998 and 1999 financial statements. Indeed, PwC issued opinions that Anicom's financial statements were accurate, complete, and conformed with GAAP and that its audits were performed according to GAAS.

In September 1998, Anicom made an Asset Purchase Agreement to acquire the wire and cable distribution assets of three companies: Texcan Cables Ltd. (known now as Tricontinental Distribution Ltd.), Texcan Cables, Inc., and Texcan Cables International, Inc. Anicom acquired those assets in exchange for cash and Anicom stock. After the transaction, Tricontinental Distribution and Texcan Cables, Inc., transferred their stock to Tricontinental Industries, Ltd.

On July 18, 2000, Anicom announced that it was investigating possible accounting irregularities that could result in revision of its 1998, 1999, and first quarter 2000 financial statements by as much as $35 million. Accordingly, Anicom announced that its 1998 and 1999 financial statements should no longer be relied upon. After conducting an internal investigation, Anicom further announced that, subject to audit, it believed that, for the period from the first quarter of 1998 to the first quarter of 2000, the company had overstated revenue by approximately $39.6 million. None of the company's announcements or disclosures ever stated that full-year 1997 revenue or net income had been materially misstated or that any of Anicom's prior financial results were inaccurate in any way. On January 5, 2001, Anicom filed for bankruptcy protection.

In July 2001, Tricontinental Industries filed an action against PwC for negligent misrepresentation. Tricontinental maintained that PwC knew that Tricontinental was relying on Anicom's audited financial statement for 1997 and, specifically, was relying on PwC's representation that the audit was performed in a manner consistent with GAAS and that Anicom's financial statements conformed with GAAP. These statements, Tricontinental alleged, were materially false, misleading, and without reasonable basis.

PwC moved to dismiss Tricontinental's complaint on the grounds that PwC owed no duty to Tricontinental, because the Illinois Public Accounting Act (IPAA) limited PwC's liability to persons who were either in privity of contract with PwC or for whose primary intent Anicom had secured PwC's services. The district court granted PwC's motion. Tricontinental appealed.

Ripple, Circuit Judge

In order to state a claim for negligent misrepresentation under Illinois law, a party must allege:

(1) a false statement of material fact; (2) carelessness or negligence in ascertaining the truth of the statement by the party making it; (3) an intention to induce the other party to act; (4) action by the other party in reliance on the truth of the statement; (5) damage to the other party resulting from such reliance; and (6) a duty on the party making the statement to communicate accurate information.

The Illinois courts have considered, on several occasions, the application of these requirements, specifically, the element of duty, as it applies to public accountants. The Illinois Appellate Court first spoke to this issue in *Brumley v. Touche, Ross & Co.,* 463 N.E.2d 195 (Ill. App. Ct. 1984) (*Brumley I*). In that case, the court reviewed the various approaches that courts around the country had adopted for accountant liability to third parties: (1) the standard set forth in *Ultramares Corp. v. Touche,* 174 N.E. 441 (N.Y. 1931), which held that public accountants could not be liable in negligence to third parties absent privity, (2) a reasonable foreseeability standard; and (3) a more limited foreseeability rule that public accountants may be liable to plaintiffs, who are not exactly identifiable, but who belong to a limited class of persons whose reliance on the accountant's representations is specifically foreseen. The appellate court held that the plaintiff's complaint was insufficient to set forth a duty on the part of defendant to plaintiff because "the complaint did not allege Touche Ross knew of plaintiff or that

the report was to be used by KPK to influence plaintiff's purchase decision nor does it allege that was *the primary purpose and intent* of the preparation of the report by Touche Ross for KPK." *Id.* (emphasis added).

In *Brumley v. Touche, Ross & Company,* 487 N.E.2d 641 (Ill. App. Ct. 1985) (*Brumley II*), the court revisited this standard. In *Brumley II,* the plaintiff had argued that the Supreme Court of Illinois had altered the standard for liability for attorneys, which necessitated a change by the appellate court with respect to accountant liability. The appellate court rejected this argument: it is apparent that to be sufficient plaintiff's complaint must allege facts showing that *the purpose and intent of the accountant-client relationship* was to benefit or influence the third-party plaintiff. 487 N.E.2d at 644–45 (emphasis added).

Shortly after *Brumley II,* the Illinois legislature enacted the Illinois Public Accounting Act, 225 ILCS 450/30.1, which provides:

No person, partnership, corporation, or other entity licensed or authorized to practice under this Act . . . shall be liable to persons not in privity of contract with such person, partnership, corporation, or other entity for civil damages resulting from acts, omissions, decisions or other conduct in connection with professional services performed by such person, partnership, corporation, or other entity, except for:

(1) such acts, omissions, decisions or conduct that constitute fraud or intentional misrepresentations, or

(2) such other acts, omissions, decisions or conduct, if such person, partnership or corporation was aware that a

primary intent of the client was for the professional services to benefit or influence the particular person bringing the action; provided, however, for the purposes of this subparagraph (2), if such person, partnership, corporation, or other entity (i) identifies in writing to the client those persons who are intended to rely on the services, and (ii) sends a copy of such writing or similar statement to those persons identified in the writing or statement, then such person, partnership, corporation, or other entity or any of its employees, partners, members, officers or shareholders may be held liable only to such persons intended to so rely, in addition to those persons in privity of contract with such person, partnership, corporation, or other entity.

Following IPAA's passage, there was some question regarding the effect of the IPAA on accountant liability. We are obliged, however, to follow the interpretation given the language by the state appellate court in *Chestnut Corp. v. Pestine, Brinati, Gamer, Ltd.,* 667 N.E.2d 543, 546-47 (Ill. App. Ct. 1996). The Illinois court took the view that the first clause of subparagraph (2) states the general rule of accountant liability as set out in *Brumley* while the second clause creates a legislative exception to the general rule. Continued the court:

[T]o adopt the defendants' interpretation of the statute would require us to hold, as a matter of law, that accountants are never liable to third parties, absent fraud or intentional misrepresentation, unless they agree in writing to expose themselves to liability. The law in Illinois would have come full circle then and returned to the rationale of *Ultramares* in 1931. Absent a clear signal from the legislature or the supreme court that such a return is intended, we believe the observation of the trial court and the evolution of the law since *Ultramares* provides a useful background as one measures the statute's meaning.

Id. at 547.

Although the Supreme Court of Illinois has not spoken to the issue, Illinois Appellate Courts seem to agree that the IPAA embodies the rule applied to accountants in *Brumley II:* The plaintiff must show that a primary purpose and intent of the accountant-client relationship was to benefit or influence the third-party plaintiff.

The primary intent rule, however, has proven to be somewhat difficult to define in practical terms. For instance, disputes have arisen regarding whether the "primary intent" of the client must be contemporaneous with the accountant's work product on which the third party relies. With respect to this issue, the Illinois Appellatße Court has stated:

In terms of timing, we do not read the statute to strictly require that an accountant be made aware of his client's intention to influence or benefit a third party only at the time the work product was created as defendant contends. The stan-

dard requires that a plaintiff prove that the primary purpose and intent of the client was to benefit or influence the third party. In *Brumley II,* we held that the plaintiff in that case met the standard because he alleged that the defendant knew of the plaintiff's reliance on the defendant's reports and that the defendant had subsequently verified its accuracy. We do not, however, read *Brumley II* as *per se requiring independent verification* in order to meet the standard in *Pelham. Other conduct* may be sufficient to satisfy *Pelham.*

Builders Bank v. Barry Finkel & Assocs., 790 N.E.2d 30, 37 (Ill. App. Ct. 2003) (emphasis added).

Further, although Illinois case law has established that "independent verification" is not a per se requirement, Illinois courts have not set forth in detail what "other conduct" may satisfy the "primary intent" standard. The cases, however, do establish that *some* affirmative action on behalf of the defendant-accountant is necessary. For instance, in *Builders Bank,* the record indicated that Finkel, the accountant, was told by Urkov, the company owner, that UMC was applying for a loan and requested that financial statements be furnished to UMC. The record further establishes that Finkel personally met with UMC on two occasions to discuss issues related to the loan. In at least one meeting, UMC was seeking an increase of $200,000 on a loan that had already been approved. In our view, it is reasonable to infer that Finkel played an active role in securing the loan or increasing the loan amount for UMC. From this evidence, a finder of fact could conclude, pursuant to the statute, that Finkel knew its work was being used to influence UMC at least at the time of the second meeting and that defendant, at minimum, presented its work as accurate. *Id.*

Similarly, in *Freeman, Freeman & Salzman, P.C. v. Lipper,* 812 N.E.2d 562 (Ill. App. Ct. 2004), the court held that the standard had been met by the allegation that the accountant to an investment fund had "issued clean audit opinions on each investment partner's capital accounts for those years"; had "addressed and sent its clean audit opinions to the partners who invested in those funds, including plaintiffs"; and had "prepared federal income tax Schedules K-l for plaintiffs and the limited partners each year." *Id.* at 566–67. Furthermore, "each Schedule K-1 purported to reflect each partner's proportionate share of the partnership's net income for the year, as well as each partner's capital account balance at the beginning and end of each year." *Id.* at 567.

Finally, in *Chestnut Corp.,* the court held that the plaintiffs had stated a claim for negligent misrepresentation by alleging that the plaintiff's representatives had gone to the offices of the defendant-accountants to discuss their possible investment in the client company and to review its financial condition. In response to specific inquiries by the plaintiff's representatives, the defendants "stated that the audit was accurately performed according to generally accepted auditing standards." *Chestnut Corp.*, 667 N.E.2d at 545.

In sum, the duty owed by a professional accountant to non-client third-parties is the standard articulated in *Brumley II* and codified in the IPAA. The IPAA provides that an individual accountant, partnership or firm will be liable to a third party for negligence only "if such person, partnership or corporation was aware that a primary intent of the client was for the professional services to benefit or influence the particular person." This "primary intent" may be demonstrated by "independent verification" or by other affirmative actions taken by the accountant and directed to the third party.

With this standard in mind, we turn to the allegations set forth in the Amended Complaint to determine whether they state a claim for relief.

With respect to the negligent misrepresentation claim, Tricontinental alleged as follows:

163. Prior to the time that PwC conducted its 1997 audit, PwC had assisted Anicom in raising money for acquisitions and finding acquisition candidates. And, in 1997, PwC well knew that Anicom was seeking to complete additional acquisitions. PwC most certainly knew that acquisition candidates, such as Plaintiffs, would rely on the 1997 Form 10-K in making their decisions on whether to invest in Anicom's securities.

164. PwC knew prior to the closing of the Texcan transaction that Plaintiffs were negotiating to sell significant assets to Anicom in exchange in part for Anicom securities. PwC was on the circulation lists for drafts of the Asset Purchase Agreement and PwC conducted due diligence of Texcan for Anicom. PwC knew that Plaintiffs had received and were relying on Anicom's Form 10-K for 1997 and, in particular, PwC's unqualified audit report, and that Anicom intended that Plaintiffs rely on the 10-K and PwC's audit report in assessing an investment in Anicom. Despite its awareness of these facts, and despite its knowledge from its own investigation and its involvement in the business of Anicom that Anicom was engaged in improper accounting practices and lacked

adequate controls to prevent these irregular practices, PwC intentionally or recklessly failed to withdraw its audit opinion on the 1997 financial statements. Instead, PwC allowed Plaintiffs to rely on the false and misleading information contained in Anicom's Form 10-K for 1997.

As noted by the district court, these allegations do not demonstrate any "independent verification" provided by PwC to Tricontinental. However, such verification to the third party is not a per se requirement. "Other conduct" by PwC directed to Tricontinental also may satisfy the "primary intent" requirement of the IPAA. Tricontinental alleges that PwC knew of its reliance on the 1997 audit opinion, knew of the misrepresentation contained in the statement and "allowed plaintiffs to rely on the false and misleading information." However, Illinois cases, fairly read, make clear that the IPAA requires more. In order to state a claim under the IPAA, Tricontinental must allege that it was a primary purpose "of the accountant-client relationship . . . to benefit or influence" Tricontinental. None of the allegations contained in the above-recited paragraphs support such an inference. Indeed, the opposite appears to be the case. The actions taken by PwC—assisting Anicom in raising money for acquisitions, conducting due diligence "for Anicom," and being included on the circulation lists during the transaction—are examples of Anicom's use of PwC's services for its own benefit, not that of Tricontinental. Consequently, although we agree with Tricontinental that neither privity nor independent verification need to be asserted or shown in order to state a claim, Tricontinental must set forth a short and plain statement of the claim showing that it is entitled to relief. Absent an allegation that fairly states that Anicom's primary intent in retaining and utilizing PwC's services and work product during the transaction was to influence Tricontinental, or absent factual allegations that support such an inference, Tricontinental has not stated a claim for negligent misrepresentation under Illinois law.

Judgment for PricewaterhouseCoopers affirmed.

Fraud Fraud is such reprehensible conduct that all courts have extended a professional's liability for fraud to all foreseeable users of his work product who suffered damages that were proximately caused by the fraud. Privity of contract, therefore, is not required when a person sues a professional for fraud, even in a state that has adopted the *Ultramares* test for negligence actions. To prove fraud, a nonclient must establish that a professional acted with scienter.

Some courts recognize a tort called constructive fraud that applies when a professional misstates a material fact. For a misstatement to amount to constructive fraud, the professional must have recklessly or grossly negligently failed to ascertain the truth of the statement. As with actual fraud, a professional's liability for constructive fraud extends to all persons who justifiably rely on the misstatement.

Common Law Bases of Liability of Professional to Nonclients for Use of Professional's Work Product

Privity Test Adopted by State	Basis of Liability	
	Negligence	Fraud
Primary Benefit Test (*Ultramares*)	Professional liable only to foreseen users (professional knew name of user, purpose of the user's use, and extent of the use)	Professional liable to all persons whose damages were caused by their reliance on professional's fraud
Restatement (*Second*) *of Torts* Test	Professional liable to foreseen users and users in a foreseen class of users (professional knew at least the purpose and extent of the user's use)	
Foreseeable Users Test	Professional liable to all reasonably foreseeable users (professional can reasonably expect or foresee the purpose and extent of the user's use)	

Professional's Liability to Third Parties: Securities Law

The slow reaction of the common law in creating a negligence remedy for third parties has led to an increased use of securities law by nonclients—that is, persons not in privity with a professional. Many liability sections in these statutes either eliminate the privity requirement or expansively define privity.

Securities Act of 1933 There are several liability sections under the Securities Act of 1933 (1933 Act). The most important liability section of the Securities Act of 1933 is Section 11, but Sections 12(a)(2) and 17(a) are also important, especially for securities professionals.

Section 11 Liability Section 11 imposes liability on underwriters and experts for misstatements or omissions of material fact in Securities Act registration statements. The 1933 Act registration statement must be filed with the Securities and Exchange Commission by an issuer making a public distribution of securities. The most common expert is an auditor who issues an opinion regarding financial statements. An underwriter, although knowledgeable, skillful, and experienced in securities offerings, is not an "expert" under Section 11.

An auditor or underwriter is liable to any purchaser of securities issued pursuant to a defective registration statement. The purchaser need not establish privity of contract with an underwriter or auditor. Because the underwriter is not an expert under Section 11, the underwriter is liable for errors in the *entire* registration statement. Since an auditor is an expert, the auditor is liable only for the part of the registration statement contributed by the auditor, that is, the auditor's opinion regarding the audited financial statements and those audited financial statements. Usually, the purchaser need not prove he relied on the misstated or omitted material fact; he need not even have read or seen the defective registration statement.

For example, an auditor issues an unqualified opinion regarding a client's income statement that overstates net income by 85 percent. The defective income statement is included in the client's registration statement pursuant to which the client sells its preferred shares. Without reading the registration statement or the income statement, a person buys from the client 1,000 preferred shares for $105 per share. After the correct income figure is released, the price of the shares drops to $25 per share. The auditor will most likely be liable to the purchaser for $80,000, unless the auditor proves the purchaser's damages were caused by other persons or factors.

Under Section 11, auditors and underwriters may escape liability by proving that they exercised due diligence. For auditors, who are experts, this **due diligence defense** requires that an auditor issuing an opinion regarding financial statements prove that she made a reasonable investigation and that she reasonably believed that there were no misstatements or omissions of material fact in the financial statements at the time the registration statement became effective. Because the effective date is often several months after an audit has been completed, an auditor must perform an additional review of the audited statements to ensure that the statements are accurate as of the effective date. In essence, due diligence means that an auditor was not negligent, which is usually proved by showing that she complied with GAAS and GAAP.

For underwriters, who are liable for the entire registration statement, the due diligence defense varies depending on the part of the registration statement. For parts of the registration statement contributed by experts (so-called expertised portions, such as an auditor's opinion and the financial statements covered by that opinion), underwriters are entitled to rely on the expert. Therefore, the underwriter's due diligence defense for errors in audited financial statements generally requires no independent investigation by the underwriter. The underwriter will have no liability for mistakes in an expertised portion if the underwriter had no reason to believe and did not believe that there were any misstatements or omissions of material fact in the audited financial statements. If, however, the underwriter has information leading her to believe that an audited financial statement misstates or omits material facts, she has a duty to investigate until she no longer has that belief and no longer has a reason to have that belief.

For errors in parts of the registration statement not contributed by experts (the nonexpertised portion), the underwriter's defense is that after a reasonable investigation, she had a reasonable belief that there were no misstatements or omissions of material fact in those parts. The nonexpertised portion constitutes the bulk of the registration statement and includes the description of the securities, the statement of the underwriter's compensation, the use of the proceeds of the securities issuance, the description of the issuer's business, the statement of the securities' material risks, and unaudited financial statements.

Standards for complying with the due diligence defense are explained more fully in *Escott v. BarChris Construction Corp.,* which appears in Chapter 45, Securities Regulation, at page 1131.

Section 12(a)(2) Section 12(a)(2) imposes liability on any person who misstates or omits a material fact in connection with an offer or sale of a security that is part of a general distribution of securities by an issuer. Privity of contract between the plaintiff and the defendant apparently is required, because Section 12(a)(2) states that the defendant is liable to the person *purchasing* the security *from him.*

Under Section 12(a)(2), a defendant must have direct contact with a buyer of a security to be liable. Merely performing professional services, such as auditing financial statements, is not enough for Section 12(a)(2) liability. A person must actively solicit the sale, motivated at least by a desire to serve his own financial interest. Such a financial interest is unlikely to be met by an auditor whose compensation is a fee unconnected to the proceeds of the securities sale. In addition, the *Central Bank* case[2] makes it fairly clear that auditors who merely *aid and abet* a client's Section 12(a)(2) violation will not have liability under Section 12(a)(2).

Securities professionals have a greater risk of liability under Section 12(a)(2), because they frequently have direct contact with purchasers. Underwriters helping clients with public offerings sell securities or at least actively solicit sales by speaking with investors and writing the prospectus or other offering document. Since underwriters receive compensation for their services in the form of a commission or a spread (the difference between the amount underwriters pay the issuer and the price they sell at), they have the requisite financial stake in the sale. Securities brokers and dealers also are sellers or actively solicit securities sales and have a financial stake in the sale when they assist issuer distributions of securities and receive a commission or spread.

In the event that a person has sufficient contact with a purchaser to incur Section 12(a)(2) liability, the defendant may escape liability by proving that she did not know and could not reasonably have known of the untruth or omission; that is, she must prove that she was not negligent.

Section 17(a) Under Section 17(a), a purchaser of a security must prove his reliance on a misstatement or omission of material fact for which an accountant or securities professional is responsible. Under two of the subsections of Section 17(a), the investor need prove only negligence by the accountant, underwriter, broker, or adviser. Under the third, the investor must prove the accountant or securities professional acted with scienter.

---

[2]*Central Bank of Denver, N.A. v. First Interstate Bank of Denver, N.A.,* 511 U.S. 164 (1994).

Whether there is a private right of action for damages under Section 17(a) is unclear. The courts of appeals are in disagreement, and the Supreme Court has not ruled on the issue.

Securities Exchange Act of 1934
Two sections of the 1934 Act—Section 18 and Section 10(b)—especially affect the liability of professionals to nonclients.

Section 18 Section 18 of the 1934 Act imposes liability on persons who furnish misleading and false statements of material fact in any report or document filed with the Securities and Exchange Commission under the 1934 Act. Such reports or documents include the annual 10-K report—which includes auditors' opinions regarding financial statements—the 8-K current report, and proxy statements.

Under Section 18, a purchaser or seller of a security may sue an auditor if he relied on the defective statement in the filed document and it caused his damages. Usually, this means that a plaintiff must have *read and relied* on the defective statement in the filed document. The purchaser or seller may sue the auditor even if they are not in privity of contract.

An auditor may escape Section 18 liability by proving that she acted in *good faith* and had *no knowledge* that the information was misleading. That is, she must show that she acted *without scienter*. For this reason, as well as the difficulty of proving reliance, Section 18 liability for auditors is extremely rare.

Although securities professionals, such as brokers and dealers, may file reports under the 1934 Act, those documents are not the type normally used by investors making investment decisions. Section 18 liability is, therefore, not an issue for securities professionals.

Section 10(b) and Rule 10b–5 Securities Exchange Act Rule 10b–5, pursuant to Section 10(b), has been the basis for most of the recent suits investors have brought against auditors and securities professionals. Rule 10b–5 prohibits any person from making a misstatement or omission of material fact in connection with the purchase or sale of any security. Rule 10b–5 applies to misstatements or omissions in any communications with investors, including the use of audited financial statements resulting in a purchase or sale of a security. The wrongful act must have a connection with interstate commerce, the mails, or a national securities exchange.

A purchaser or seller of a security may sue an auditor, underwriter, or broker who has misstated or omitted a material fact. Privity is not required. The purchaser or seller must rely on the misstatement or omission. In omission cases, reliance may be inferred from materiality.

In addition, the defendant must act with scienter. In this context, scienter is an intent to deceive, manipulate, or defraud. For some courts, reckless misconduct is sufficient to prove scienter. Negligence, however, is not enough.

In the next case, the court found that the allegations against auditor Ernst & Young did not establish that E&Y had acted with scienter. The court gives several examples of what does and does not constitute scienter.

Ferris, Baker Watts, Inc. v. Ernst & Young, LLP
395 F.3d 851 (8th Cir. 2005)

MJK Clearing, Inc. (MJK), was a broker-dealer engaged in the risky business of securities borrowing. In securities borrowing, a party lent a security to MJK, which paid cash collateral slightly exceeding the value of the security. The cash collateral was "marked to market" so that if the market price of the security rose, MJK paid additional cash to the lender of the security. If the market price of the security fell, however, the lender owed MJK cash. In addition to borrowing securities, MJK was also a lender and therefore subject to the risk that it would be required to pay additional cash if the securities fell in value. MJK had lent securities to Ferris, Baker, Watts, Inc. (FBW), another broker-dealer, and received cash collateral.

By March 31, 2001, MJK had paid $160 million cash—representing nearly one-half of its accounts receivable and 21 percent of its total assets—to another broker-dealer, Native Nations Securities, Inc., in exchange for borrowed securities. These securities were mostly from three thinly traded issuers, including GenesisIntermedia, Inc. In 2001, the price of GenesisIntermedia fell, and Native Nations did not pay the cash collateral it owed MJK. As a result, MJK collapsed, and the Securities Investor Protection Corporation began the liquidation of MJK.

Consequently, FBW was unable to reclaim $20 million of cash collateral it had paid MJK. To recover its loss, FBW sued MJK's independent auditor, Ernst & Young, LLP. FBW argued that it dealt with MJK relying on E&Y's audit of MJK's financial statements, as of year-end March 31, 2001. FBW alleged that E&Y's audit violated Section 10(b) of the Securities Act of

1934 and SEC Rule 10b–5 by recklessly misrepresenting that its audit met generally accepted auditing standards and that MJK's financial statements were fairly presented in accordance with generally accepted accounting principles. The district court dismissed the action, holding that the complaint insufficiently alleged that E&Y had acted with scienter. FBW appealed.

Benton, Circuit Judge

Section 10(b) and Rule 10b–5 prohibit fraudulent conduct in the sale and purchase of securities. Claims require four elements: (1) misrepresentations or omissions of material fact or acts that operated as a fraud or deceit in violation of the rule; (2) causation, often analyzed in terms of materiality and reliance; (3) scienter on the part of the defendants; and (4) economic harm caused by the fraudulent activity occurring in connection with the purchase and sale of a security. Only scienter—the intent to deceive, manipulate, or defraud—is at issue here.

Mere negligence does not violate Rule 10b–5. Severe recklessness, however, may. Recklessness is limited to those highly unreasonable omissions or misrepresentations that involve not merely simple or even inexcusable negligence, but an extreme departure from the standards of ordinary care, and that present a danger of misleading buyers or sellers which is either known to the defendant or is so obvious that the defendant must have been aware of it. This level of recklessness requires that defendants make statements that they know, or have access to information suggesting, are materially inaccurate.

FBW argues it pleaded that E&Y knew of, or had access to, facts that permit a strong inference that its audit opinion was knowingly or recklessly false or misleading. It claims E&Y falsely stated that it conducted the audit in accordance with GAAS, when: (1) E&Y's review of internal control of MJK's securities-borrowing department—the largest and most rapidly growing part of the company—revealed a complete absence of internal control, imposing a duty of heightened scrutiny that E&Y ignored; (2) E&Y failed to investigate whether the $160 million receivable from Native Nations was impaired; and (3) E&Y failed to investigate any subsequent events after the audit (but before issuance of the audit opinion) as to the collectibility of MJK's account receivable from Native Nations, which investigation would have revealed defaults.

FBW further alleges that E&Y disregarded GAAP, which a reasonable accountant follows. Thus, FBW says, a strong inference of scienter arises that E&Y's audit opinion that MJK's financial statements conformed with GAAP was a knowing or reckless misstatement of fact. Specifically, FBW alleges that the financial statements do not disclose as required by GAAP: (1) the concentration of credit risk in the $160 million receivable from Native Nations; (2) the risk that the Native Nations receivable was impaired or uncollectible; and (3) the "going concern" risk from the Native Nations receivable.

Finally, FBW alleges that E&Y failed to disclose—as required by SEC Rule 17a–5—material inadequacies in MJK's internal controls known to E&Y, permitting a strong inference that the nondisclosure was knowing or reckless.

"Allegations of GAAP violations are insufficient, standing alone, to raise an inference of scienter. Only where these allegations are coupled with evidence of corresponding fraudulent intent might they be sufficient." *In re Navarre Corp. Sec. Litig.,* 299 F.3d 735, 745 (8th Cir. 2002). *See also Kushner v. Beverly Enters., Inc.,* 317 F.3d 820, 827, 831 (8th Cir. 2003) (affirming dismissal of complaint alleging failure to establish accounting reserves); *In re K-Tel Int'l, Inc. Sec. Litig.,* 300 F.3d 881, 894–95 (8th Cir. 2002) (affirming dismissal of complaint based on overstatement of assets and "sheer magnitude" of GAAP violations).

Assuming GAAP and GAAS violations occurred here, FBW's catch-all and blanket assertions that E&Y acted recklessly or knowingly are not evidence of corresponding fraudulent intent. This is not a case like Green Tree, where a defendant published statements knowing that crucial information in them was based on discredited assumptions. *Florida State Bd. of Admin, v. Green Tree Fin. Corp.,* 270 F.3d 645, 665 (8th Cir. 2001).

FBW asserts that the district court misreads *Kushner, K-Tel,* and *Navarre.* In fact, the lower court follows not only this court's cases, but also those from other Circuits. *See, e.g., Novak v. Kasaks,* 216 F.3d 300, 309 (2d Cir. 2000) (Allegations of GAAP violations or accounting irregularities, standing alone, are insufficient to state a securities fraud claim.); *Stevelman v. Alias Research Inc.,* 174 F.3d 79, 84 (2d Cir. 1999) (Allegations of a violation of GAAP provisions or SEC regulations, without corresponding fraudulent intent, are not sufficient to state a securities fraud claim.); *Fidel v. Farley,* 392 F.3d 220, 230 (6th Cir. 2004) (The failure to follow generally accepted accounting procedures does not in and of itself lead to an inference of scienter.); *DSAM Global Value Fund v. Altris Software, Inc.,* 288 F.3d 385, 387 (9th Cir. 2002) (affirming dismissal of allegations of a "seriously botched audit" and "a compelling case of negligence—perhaps even gross negligence"); *In re Software Toolworks Inc. Sec. Litig.,* 50 F.3d 615, 627–28 (9th Cir. 1994) (affirming summary judgment for auditor, stating that "mere publication of inaccurate accounting figures, or a failure to follow GAAP, without more, does not establish scienter").

FBW repeatedly asserts that E&Y's audit was so cursory and superficial as to amount to "no audit at all." *See Software*

Toolworks, 50 F.3d at 628 (auditing that is "no audit at all" shows scienter). The facts alleged here show otherwise. FBW's complaint says that E&Y was fully aware of the risks associated with MJK's securities borrowing and lending operations, and had an audit plan that recognized the need for closer testing of securities borrowing. FBW states that E&Y did confirm the account receivable with Native Nations, noting its excess over the value of the collateral securities, and its concentration in three issuers. According to the complaint, E&Y did interview MJK's securities-borrowing department manager, who described the processes and procedures, and represented that he performed credit reviews "anywhere from monthly to annually by reviewing other Broker FOCUS reports." FBW pleads that E&Y examined five files of MJK's (approximately) 60 customers for the presence of signed agreements and annual credit evaluations, inquired as to deficiencies in the files, and verified that securities-borrowing personnel prepared numerous reports, including daily "Balance Order Fail Reports." According to FBW, E&Y conducted tests of internal control activities, and identified reconciliations of balance-sheet cash accounts to bank accounts, and balance-sheet securities ledgers to securities accounts. E&Y concluded that internal controls were effective, and could be relied upon to reduce the substantive audit procedures (and increase reliance on management's representation that no subsequent events occurred after fieldwork, but before issue of the opinion). In sum, FBW alleges a poor audit, not the intent to deceive, manipulate, or defraud required for securities fraud.

Judgment for Ernst & Young affirmed.

Aiding and Abetting   Until the mid-1990s, a common way investors held an auditor liable under Rule 10b–5 was to prove that the auditor aided and abetted a client's fraud. Most courts had recognized aiding and abetting liability under Rule 10b–5 by requiring (1) a primary violation by another person (such as a client fraudulently overstating its earnings), (2) the person's knowledge of the primary violation, and (3) the person's substantial assistance in the achievement of the primary violation (such as an auditor's failure to disclose a client's fraud known to the auditor).

In 1994 in the *Central Bank* case discussed earlier, the Supreme Court of the United States held that those who merely aid and abet Rule 10b–5 violations have no liability to those injured by the fraud. The court drew a distinction between those **primarily** responsible for the fraud—who retain Rule 10b–5 liability—and those **secondarily** responsible—who no longer have liability under Rule 10b–5. The distinction between primary and secondary responsibility is unclear. Issuing unqualified opinions regarding false financial statements is primary fault and would impose Rule 10b–5 liability on the auditor. However, an independent accountant's work in connection with false unaudited statements or other financial information released by a client may be only secondary and may not impose Rule 10b–5 liability on the accountant.

The Supreme Court affirmed and explained its *Central Bank* ruling in *Stoneridge Investment Partners.*[3] You can read that case in Chapter 45 on page 1146.

Although auditors are not liable to private litigants for merely secondary activities, Congress has made it clear that the SEC may prosecute accountants for aiding and abetting a client's violation of Rule 10b–5. Even so, the risk of liability is slight, because Rule 10b–5 liability is imposed only on those who act with scienter.

Securities professionals may be primarily responsible for misstatements or omissions of material facts in a variety of contexts, and therefore may have Rule 10b–5 liability to nonclients and clients. For example, an underwriter who drafts an offering memorandum for a client's Rule 506 securities offering is primarily responsible for that document, as well as oral statements the underwriter makes about the issuer and the securities to a prospective investor. Securities brokers may have Rule 10b–5 liability for churning their clients' accounts to generate high commissions for the broker. In addition, brokers may have liability under Rule 10b–5 for giving fraudulent advice to clients. Such cases are difficult to prove, as illustrated in *Carr v. CIGNA Securities, Inc.*, which appears in Chapter 45, Securities Regulation, on page 1141.

Extent of Liability   The Private Securities Litigation Reform Act limits the liability of most auditors and securities professionals to the amount of an investor's loss for which the defendant is responsible. This means that a defendant has *proportionate liability* and need no longer fear being liable for investors' entire losses when a fraudulent client is unable to pay its share of the damages. The determination of the percentage of the loss for which a defendant is responsible is a question for the jury. Note, however, the Reform Act provides that when a person knowingly commits a violation of the securities laws, the

---

[3]*Stoneridge Investment Partners, LLC v. Scientific-Atlanta, Inc.*, 128 S.Ct. 761 (2008).

Liability Sections of the 1933 Act and 1934 Act

	Wrongful Conduct	Covered Communications	Who May Sue?	Must the Plaintiff Prove Reliance on the Wrongful Conduct?
Securities Act of 1933 Section 11	Misstatement or omission of material fact	1933 Act registration statement only	Any purchaser of securities issued pursuant to the registration statement	No
Securities Act of 1933 Section 12(a)(2)	Misstatement or omission of material fact	Any communication in connection with a general distribution of securities by an issuer (except government issued or guaranteed securities)	Any purchaser of the securities offered or sold	No
Securities Act of 1933 Section 17(a)	Misstatement or omission of material fact	Any communication in connection with any offer to sell or sale of any security	Any purchaser of the securities offered or sold	Yes
Securities Exchange Act of 1934 Section 10(b) and Rule 10b–5	Misstatement or omission of material fact	Any communication in connection with a purchase or sale of any security	Any purchaser or seller of the securities	Yes
Securities Exchange Act of 1934 Section 18	False or misleading statement of material fact	Any document filed with the SEC under the 1934 Act (includes the 1934 Act registration statement, 10-K, 8-K, and proxy statements)	Any purchaser or seller of a security whose price was affected by the statement	Yes

defendant may be required to pay an investor's entire loss.

State Securities Law   All states have securities statutes with liability sections. Most of the states have a liability section similar to Section 12(a)(2) of the Securities Act.

Securities Analysts' Conflicts of Interest

For years, investors have known that stock recommendations and research reports by securities analysts in major investment banking firms are almost always overly

Liability Sections of the 1933 Act and 1934 Act

Who May Be Sued?	Must the Plaintiff and Defendant Be in Privity of Contract?	Defendant's Level of Fault	Who Has the Burden of Proving or Disproving Defendant's Level of Fault?
Issuer, underwriters, directors, signers (CEO, CFO, and CAO must sign), and experts who contribute to the registration statement (such as auditors of financial statements)	No	Negligence, except for the issuer. Issuer is liable without regard to fault.	Defendant, except issuer, may escape liability by proving due diligence. There are two defenses, but for most defendants for most parts of the registration statement, the defense is that he made a reasonable investigation and had reason to believe and did believe there were no misstatements or omissions of material fact.
Any person who sells a security or actively solicits a sale of a security	Yes (although met by a defendant who has a financial interest in a sale of securities)	Negligence	Defendant may escape liability by proving he did not know and could not reasonably have known of the misstatement or omission of material fact.
Any person responsible for the misstatement or omission	No	Negligence for some parts of Section 17(a); scienter for one part	Plaintiff must prove the defendant acted negligently or with scienter, depending on the subsection.
Any person primarily responsible for the misstatement or omission	No, but defendant must communicate with the plaintiff or know or should know plaintiff will receive the communication with the misstatement or omission	Scienter	Plaintiff must prove the defendant acted with scienter.
Any person who made or caused the statement to be made	No	Scienter	Defendant may escape liability by proving he acted in good faith with no knowledge that the statement was false or misleading.

optimistic. Few analysts have recommended that investors sell a stock. Almost all recommendations are strong buy, buy, accumulate, or hold, with a few sell recommendations sprinkled in. The reasons for such optimism vary from an unwillingness to say anything bad to a belief that a bull market will sustain rising securities prices. But the reason that caught the attention of securities regulators is that analysts may have a conflict of interest. The belief is that full-service investment firms that have securities research, brokerage, and investment banking departments discourage their securities analysts from giving poor recommendations for a public company's stock for

The Global Business Environment

Global Internet Offerings

In a world linked by e-mail and the Internet, local offerings of securities can become international and attract the interest of securities regulators in countries whose citizens access a foreign securities offering Web site. When a foreign issuer does not register its issuance with the SEC in the United States, the issuer or a securities broker must make sure that offering materials are not sent to American investors. When offering information is sent by e-mail, there is a clear violation. When a securities offering is made on a Web page, it may be difficult to determine whether the securities offering was sent to American investors. An SEC release attempts to clarify the matter by stating that Web offerings will not come under U.S. regulation as long as the broker takes precautionary measures that are "reasonably designed to ensure that offshore Internet offers are not targeted" at the American investors. In practice, the Internet makes it difficult to discern what constitutes targeting U.S. investors. However, the SEC provides a safe harbor for foreign brokers by allowing them to post a conspicuous disclaimer on the Web site either listing the countries in which the broker's services are available or stating that the services are not available to American investors.

In the United Kingdom, the Financial Services Authority (FSA) has strict provisions for the treatment of material on overseas Web sites that is accessible in the U.K. but not intended for U.K. investors. The law states that any Web offering will fall within the definition of restricted activities in the U.K. if it contains any unauthorized invitation to buy securities. Unlike U.S. law, U.K. law provides that conspicuous disclaimers by themselves are insufficient to stop an investment advertisement from being made available to U.K. investors. In Australia, the Securities and Investments Commission issued a policy statement that Australian law covers investments that target people in Australia or operate within Australia. Therefore, Australian securities law does not regulate offshore offerings that do not affect Australians.

---

fear that a poor recommendation will offend the company's management and cause the company to award valuable investment banking business to a more cooperative investment firm. Some investment firms even threatened to lower public companies' stock recommendations unless the companies awarded investment banking business to the firms.

The Sarbanes–Oxley Act (SOX) directed the SEC to adopt or to direct the national securities exchanges and NASD to adopt rules to address research analysts' conflicts of interest. SOX requires the rules to accomplish the following:

- Restrict prepublication approval of analysts' research reports by investment banking or other nonresearch personnel in the firm.
- Limit supervision and evaluation of securities analysts' compensation to persons not in the investment banking side of the firm.
- Prohibit investment banking personnel from retaliating against a securities analyst because of a negative research report.
- Set time periods during which firms involved in an underwriting of public issuances may not publish research reports about the issuer and its securities.
- Place information partitions to separate research analysts from review, pressure, or oversight by those whose investment banking activities might bias their judgment.
- Require securities analysts to disclose in public appearances and research reports any conflict of interest,

including whether the analyst owns the issuer's securities, whether compensation has been received by the firm or analyst, and whether the issuer is currently or has been a client of the firm in the last year.

The SEC has adopted Regulation AC (Analyst Certification). Although not designed to implement the requirements of SOX, Regulation AC requires an analyst's research report to include the analyst's certification that the views expressed in the report accurately reflect her personal views. Regulation AC also requires a securities analyst to certify whether or not any part of her compensation is related to her recommendation of a security or to her views contained in a company research report. The rule also restricts the relationship between research and investment banking departments of a securities firm, as well as their relationships with companies covered by a securities firm's research reports.

The SEC also has approved NYSE and NASD rules regarding analysts' conflicts of interest. The rules are substantially similar. They prohibit a securities firm from offering favorable research to a company in order to induce the company to use the securities firm's investment banking service. The rules increase analyst independence by prohibiting investment banking personnel from supervising analysts or approving research reports. Analyst compensation may not be tied to a specific investment banking services transaction. Also, an analyst is restricted in trading for his personal account in securities he recommends. The SEC release discussing and

Ethics in Action

Securities and Investment Banking Firms Lose and Settle Conflict of Interest Cases

In the past few years, several securities firms and investment companies have settled or lost actions brought by investors, the SEC, the NASD, and other government and regulatory bodies in the face of allegations of conflicts of interest.

In 2003, securities firm and investment bank Goldman, Sachs & Co. agreed with the SEC, NASD, NYSE, and state regulators to pay $25 million in restitution and an additional $25 million in penalties, plus $50 million to provide the firm's clients with independent research and $10 million for investor education. The settlement stemmed from allegations that Goldman's research analysts were subject to inappropriate influence by Goldman's investment banking services. For example, Goldman required its analysts to prepare business plans that discussed the steps analysts planned to take to assist investment banking efforts. In preparing these business plans, analysts were required to answer such questions as "How much of your time will be devoted to IBD [investment banking division]?" and "How can you work more effectively with IBD to exploit the opportunities available to the firm?" In response to the question "What are the three most important goals for you in 2000?" one analyst replied, "1. Get more investment banking revenue. 2. Get more investment banking revenue. 3. Get more investment banking revenue."

A NASD arbitration panel ordered securities firm Merrill Lynch to pay $1 million to a Florida couple for failing to disclose that its analysts were recommending companies to Merrill Lynch customers that they privately disparaged. The analysts gave the companies positive recommendations in order for Merrill Lynch to obtain the companies' investment banking business.

Securities firm Morgan Stanley was charged by the NASD with improperly rewarding its brokers with tickets to concerts and sporting events in an attempt to boost sales of Morgan Stanley's mutual funds. Morgan Stanley agreed to pay a fine of $2 million.

In settlements with the SEC and state prosecutors, several mutual fund sellers, including Bank of America, FleetBoston Financial, and Putnam Investments agreed to pay hefty fines and make restitution to investors in light of allegations their employees engaged in "market timing" of the firms' mutual funds. Market timing involves frequent trading, usually in international funds, to exploit "stale" mutual fund prices that exist due to time zone differences. The practice allegedly hurts the returns of long-term shareholders of the mutual funds. Bank of America agreed to pay $250 million in restitution and $125 million in fines; FleetBoston, $70 million in restitution and $70 million in fines; Putnam, $10 million in restitution and $100 million in fines.

approving the NYSE and NASD rules may be viewed at www.sec.gov/rules/sro/34-48252.htm.

The NASD and the NYSE also passed rules on analysts' conflicts of interest prior to passage of SOX. The rules are substantially similar. They ban favorable research for pay, prohibit analyst compensation based on specific investment banking services, and limit the submission of a research report to an issuer prior to publication of the report.

Limiting Professionals' Liability: Professional Corporations and Limited Liability Partnerships

Every state permits professionals to incorporate their business under a professional incorporation statute.

While there are significant taxation advantages to incorporation, the principal advantage of incorporation—*limited liability of the shareholders*—does not isolate

professionals from liability for professional misconduct. For example, an accountant who injures his client by failing to act as the ordinarily prudent accountant would act has liability to his client, despite the incorporation of the accountant's business.

When two or more professionals conduct business as co-owners, however, the corporation—unlike the partnership—does offer them limited liability. While partners in a partnership are jointly and severally liable for each other's negligence, states permit incorporated professionals to escape liability for their associate's torts, unless the professional actually supervised the wrongdoing associate or participated in the tort.

Reacting to the large personal liability sometimes imposed on lawyers and accountants for the professional malpractice of their partners, Texas enacted in 1991 the first statute permitting the formation of limited liability partnerships (LLP). An LLP is similar to a partnership, except that a partner's liability for his partners' professional malpractice is limited to the partnership's assets, unless the partner supervised the work of the wrongdoing partner. A partner retains unlimited liability for his *own* malpractice and, in some states, for all *non-*professional obligations of the partnership.

Nearly every state and the District of Columbia have passed LLP statutes. The LLP has become the preferred form of business for professionals who do not incorporate.

For more information on the limited liability partnership, see Chapters 37–39.

Qualified Opinions, Disclaimers of Opinion, Adverse Opinions, and Unaudited Statements

After performing an audit of financial statements, an independent auditor issues an opinion letter regarding the financial statements. The **opinion letter** expresses whether the audit has been performed in compliance with GAAS and whether, in the auditor's opinion, the financial statements fairly present the client's financial position and results of operations in conformity with GAAP. Usually, an auditor issues an **unqualified opinion**—that is, an opinion that there has been compliance with GAAS and GAAP. Sometimes, an auditor issues a qualified opinion, a disclaimer of opinion, or an adverse opinion. Up to this point, you have studied the liability of an auditor who has issued unqualified opinions yet has not complied with GAAS and GAAP.

What liability should be imposed on an auditor who discloses that he has not complied with GAAS and GAAP? An auditor is relieved of responsibility only to the extent that a qualification or disclaimer is specifically expressed in the opinion letter. Therefore, letters that purport to disclaim liability totally for false and misleading financial statements are too general to excuse an accountant from exercising ordinary skill and care.

For example, an auditor qualifies his opinion of the ability of financial statements to present the financial position of a company by indicating that there is uncertainty about how an antitrust suit against the company may be decided. He would not be held liable for damages resulting from an unfavorable verdict in the antitrust suit. He would remain liable, however, for failing to make an examination in compliance with GAAS that would have revealed other serious problems.

For another example, consider an auditor who, due to the limited scope of the audit, disclaims any opinion on the ability of the financial statements to present the financial position of the company. She would nonetheless be liable for the nondiscovery of problems that the limited audit should have revealed.

Likewise, an accountant who issued an adverse opinion that depreciation had not been calculated according to GAAP would not be liable for damages resulting from the wrongful accounting treatment of depreciation, but he would be liable for damages resulting from the wrongful treatment of receivables.

Merely preparing unaudited statements does not create a disclaimer as to their accuracy. The mere fact that the statements are unaudited only permits an accountant to exercise a lower level of inquiry. Even so, an accountant must act as the ordinarily prudent accountant would act under the same circumstances in preparing unaudited financial statements.

Criminal, Injunctive, and Administrative Proceedings

In addition to being held liable for damages to clients and third parties, a professional may be found criminally liable for his violations of securities, tax, and other laws. For criminal violations, he may be fined and imprisoned. His wrongful conduct may also result in the issuance of an injunction, which bars him from doing the same acts in the future. In addition, his wrongful conduct may be the subject of administrative proceedings by the Securities and Exchange Commission and state licensing boards. An administrative proceeding may result in the revocation of a professional's license to practice or the suspension from practice. Finally, disciplinary proceedings may be brought by professional societies and self-regulatory organizations such as the AICPA or NASD.

Criminal Liability under the Securities Laws   Both the Securities Act of 1933 and the Securities Exchange Act of 1934 have criminal provisions that can be applied to professionals. The 1933 Act imposes criminal liability for willful violations of any section of the 1933 Act, including Sections 11, 12(a)(2), and 17(a), or any 1933 Act rule or regulation. For example, willfully making an untrue statement or omitting any material fact in a 1933 Act registration statement imposes criminal liability on a person. The maximum penalty for a criminal violation of the 1933 Act is a $10,000 fine and five years' imprisonment.

The 1934 Act imposes criminal penalties for willful violations of any section of the 1934 Act, such as Sections 10(b) and 18, and any 1934 Act rule or regulation, such as Rule 10b–5. For example, willfully making false or misleading statements in reports that are required to be filed under the 1934 Act incurs criminal liability.

Such filings include 10-Ks, 8-Ks, and proxy statements. An individual may be fined up to $5 million and imprisoned for up to 20 years for a criminal violation of the 1934 Act; however, an individual who proves that he had no knowledge of an SEC rule or regulation may not be imprisoned for violating that rule or regulation. A professional firm may be fined up to $25 million.

Most of the states have statutes imposing criminal penalties on professionals who willfully falsify financial statements or other reports in filings under the state securities laws and who willfully violate the state securities laws or aid and abet criminal violations of these laws by others.

In *Natelli,* accountants permitting a client to book unbilled sales after the close of the fiscal period subjected the accountants to the criminal penalties of the 1934 Act.

United States v. Natelli   527 F.2d 311 (2d Cir. 1975)

Anthony Natelli was the partner in charge of the Washington, D.C., office of Peat, Marwick, Mitchell & Co., a large CPA firm. In August 1968, Peat, Marwick became the independent public auditor of National Student Marketing Corporation. Natelli was the engagement partner for the audit of Student Marketing. Joseph Scansaroli was Peat, Marwick's audit supervisor on that engagement.

Student Marketing provided its corporate clients with a wide range of marketing services to help them reach the lucrative youth market. In its financial statements for the nine months ended May 31, 1968, Student Marketing had counted as income the entire amount of oral customer commitments to pay fees in Student Marketing's "fixed-fee marketing programs," even though those fees had not yet been paid. They were to be paid for services that Student Marketing would provide over a period of several years. Standard accounting practice required that part of the unpaid fees be considered income in the present year but that part be deferred as income until the years when Student Marketing actually performed the services for which the fees were paid. Therefore, in making the year-end audit, Natelli concluded that he would use a percentage-of-completion approach on these commitments, taking as income in the present year only those fees that were to be paid for services in that year.

The customer fee commitments were oral only, making it difficult to verify whether they really existed. Natelli directed Scansaroli to try to verify the fee commitments by telephoning the customers but not by seeking written verification. However, Scansaroli never called Student Marketing's clients. Instead, Scansaroli accepted a schedule prepared by Student Marketing showing estimates of the percentage of completion of services for each corporate client and the amount of the fee commitment from each client. This resulted in an adjustment of $1.7 million for "unbilled accounts receivable." The adjustment turned a loss for the year into a profit twice that of the year before.

By May 1969, a total of $1 million of the customer fee commitments had been written off as uncollectible. The effect of the write-off was to reduce 1968 income by $209,750. However, Scansaroli, with Natelli's approval, offset this by reversing a deferred tax item of approximately the same amount.

Student Marketing issued a proxy statement in September 1969 in connection with a shareholders' meeting to consider merging six companies into Student Marketing. The proxy statement was filed with the Securities and Exchange Commission. It contained several financial statements, some of which had been audited by Peat, Marwick. Others had not been audited, but Peat, Marwick had aided in their preparation. In the proxy statement, a footnote to the financial statements failed to show that the write-off of customer fee commitments had affected Student Marketing's fiscal 1968 income.

The proxy statement required an unaudited statement of nine months' earnings through May 31, 1969. This statement was prepared by Student Marketing with Peat, Marwick's assistance. Student Marketing produced a $1.2 million commitment from the Pontiac Division of General Motors Corporation two months after the end of May, but it was dated April 28, 1969. At 3 AM on the day the proxy statement was to be printed, Natelli informed Randall, the chief executive officer and founder of Student Marketing, that this commitment could not be included because it was not a legally binding contract. Randall responded at once that he had "a commitment from Eastern Airlines" for a somewhat comparable amount attributable to the same period. Such a letter was produced at the printing plant a few hours later, and the Eastern commitment was substituted for the Pontiac sale in the proxy. Shortly thereafter, another Peat, Marwick accountant, Oberlander, discovered $177,547 in "bad" commitments from 1968. These were known to Scansaroli in May 1969 as being doubtful, but they had not been written off. Oberlander suggested to the company that these commitments plus others, for a total of $320,000, be written off, but Scansaroli, after consulting with Natelli, decided against the suggested write-off.

There was no disclosure in the proxy statement that Student Marketing had written off $1 million (20 percent) of its 1968 sales and over $2 million of the $3.3 million of unbilled sales booked in 1968 and 1969. A true disclosure would have shown that Student Marketing had made no profit for the first nine months of 1969.

Subsequently, it was revealed that many of Student Marketing's fee commitments were fictitious. The attorney general of the United States brought a criminal action against Natelli and Scansaroli for violating the Securities Exchange Act of 1934 by willfully and knowingly making false and misleading statements in a proxy statement. The district court jury convicted both Natelli and Scansaroli, and they appealed.

Gurfein, Circuit Judge

The original action of Natelli in permitting the booking of un-billed sales after the close of the fiscal period in an amount sufficient to convert a loss into a profit was contrary to sound accounting practice. When the uncollectibility, and indeed, the nonexistence of these large receivables was established in 1969, the revelation stood to cause Natelli severe criticism and possible liability. He had a motive, therefore, intentionally to conceal the write-offs that had to be made.

Honesty should have impelled Natelli and Scansaroli to disclose in the footnote that annotated their own audited statement for fiscal 1968 that substantial write-offs had been taken, after year-end, to reflect a loss for the year. A simple desire to right the wrong that had been perpetrated on the stockholders and others by the false audited financial statement should have dictated that course.

The accountant owes a duty to the public not to assert a privilege of silence until the next audited annual statement comes around in due time. Since companies were being acquired by Student Marketing for its shares in this period, Natelli had to know that the 1968 audited statement was being used continuously.

Natelli contends that he had no duty to verify the Eastern commitment because the earnings statement within which it was included was unaudited. This raises the issue of the duty of the CPA in relation to an unaudited financial statement contained within a proxy statement where the figures are reviewed and to some extent supplied by the auditors. The auditors were associated with the statement and were required to object to anything they actually knew to be materially false. In the ordinary case involving an unaudited statement, the auditor would not be chargeable simply because he failed to discover the invalidity of booked accounts receivable, inasmuch as he had not undertaken an audit with verification. In this case, however, Natelli knew the history of post-period bookings and the dismal consequences later discovered.

In terms of professional standards, the accountant may not shut his eyes in reckless disregard of his knowledge that highly suspicious figures, known to him to be suspicious, were being included in the unaudited earnings figures in the proxy statement with which he was associated.

There is some merit to Scansaroli's point that he was simply carrying out the judgments of his superior, Natelli. The defense of obedience to higher authority has always been troublesome. There is no sure yardstick to measure criminal responsibility except by measurement of the degree of awareness on the part of a defendant that he is participating in a criminal act, in the absence of physical coercion such as a soldier might face. Here the motivation to conceal undermines Scansaroli's argument that he was merely implementing Natelli's instructions, at least with respect to concealment of matters that were within his own ken. The jury could properly have found him guilty on the specification relating to the footnote.

With respect to the Eastern commitment, Scansaroli stands in a position different from that of Natelli. Natelli was his superior. He was the man to make the judgment whether or not to object to the last-minute inclusion of a new commitment in the nine-months statement. There is insufficient evidence that Scansaroli engaged in any conversations about the Eastern commitment or that he was a participant with Natelli in any check on its authenticity. Since in the hierarchy of the accounting firm it was not his responsibility to decide whether to book the Eastern contract, his mere adjustment of the figures to reflect it under orders was not a matter for his discretion.

Conviction of Natelli affirmed. Conviction of Scansaroli affirmed in part and reversed in part.

Other Criminal Law Violations

Tax Law Federal tax law imposes on professionals a wide range of penalties for a wide variety of wrongful conduct. At one end of the penalty spectrum is a $50 fine for an accountant's failing to furnish a client with a copy of his income tax return or failing to sign a client's re-turn. At the other end is a fine of $500,000 and imprisonment of five years for tax fraud. In between is the penalty for promoting abusive tax shelters. The fine is $1,000, or 100 percent of the defendant's income from her participation in the tax shelter, whichever is lesser. In addition, all of the states impose criminal penalties for specified violations of their tax laws.

Mail Fraud Several other federal statutes also impose criminal liability on professionals. The most notable of these statutes is the general mail fraud statute, which prohibits the use of the mails to commit fraud. To be held liable, a professional must know or foresee that the mails will be used to transmit materials containing fraudulent statements provided by her.

In addition, the general false-statement-to-government-personnel statute prohibits fraudulent statements to government personnel. The false-statement-to-bank statute proscribes fraudulent statements on a loan application to a bank or other financial institution.

RICO The Racketeer Influenced and Corrupt Organizations Act (RICO) makes it a federal crime to engage in a pattern of racketeering activity. Although RICO was designed to attack the activities of organized crime enterprises, it applies to professionals who conduct or participate in the affairs of an enterprise in almost any pattern of business fraud. A pattern of fraud is proved by the commission of two predicate offenses within a 10-year period. Predicate offenses include securities law violations, mail fraud, and bribery. Individuals convicted of a RICO violation may be fined up to $250,000 and imprisoned up to 20 years.

A person who is injured in his business or property by reason of a professional's conduct or participation, directly or indirectly, in an enterprise's affairs through a pattern of racketeering activity may recover treble damages (three times his actual damages) from the professional. In *Reves v. Ernst & Young*,[4] the Supreme Court held that merely by auditing financial statements that substantially overvalued a client's assets, an accounting firm was not conducting or participating in the affairs of the client's business. The Court held that the accounting firm must participate in the "operation or management" of the enterprise itself to be liable under RICO.

Other Criminal Laws While there are many other criminal laws that may be violated by professionals, one final law bears mentioning: laws against the destruction of evidence that may be used against a professional in a criminal trial. All accounting and securities firms have rules regarding document retention and destruction. For the most part, retaining documents helps a firm prove that it has met its duty to its clients. Retained documents can establish that the firm acted in a reasonable manner when it conducted an audit or made an investment recommendation, for example.

On the other hand, documents may show that the professional or her client has acted inappropriately or even illegally. In general, professionals are not compelled to retain documents that prove their or a client's guilt, provided they do not destroy documents with the intent to obstruct a criminal prosecution. The *Andersen* case, which appears near the end of this chapter, held that Arthur Andersen LLP could not be found guilty when its employees shredded evidence regarding the Enron fraud, unless it was proved that Andersen intended to impede the prosecution of a particular criminal action at the time the shredding occurred.

Injunctions Administrative agencies such as the SEC and the Internal Revenue Service may bring injunctive actions against an auditor or securities professional in a federal district court. The purpose of such an injunction is to prevent a defendant from committing a future violation of the securities or tax laws.

After an injunction has been issued by a court, violating the injunction may result in serious sanctions. Not only may penalties be imposed for contempt, but also a criminal violation may also be more easily proven.

Administrative Proceedings The SEC has the authority to bring administrative proceedings against persons who violate the provisions of the federal securities acts. In recent years, the SEC has stepped up enforcement of SEC Rule of Practice 102(e). Rule 102(e) permits the SEC to bar temporarily or permanently from practicing before the SEC a professional who has demonstrated a lack of the qualifications required to practice before it, such as an accountant who has prepared financial statements not complying with GAAP. In the Sarbanes–Oxley Act, Congress amended the 1934 Act to include the language of Rule 102(e) almost word for word.

The SEC may discipline accountants who engage in a single instance of highly unreasonable conduct that leads to a violation of professional accounting standards. The SEC may also discipline an accountant who engages in repeated, unreasonable conduct that results in a violation of professional accounting standards. For example, an auditor's conduct in reviewing a client's financial statements is unreasonable when the auditor knew or should have known that heightened scrutiny is warranted yet failed to exercise the additional scrutiny while conducting an audit.

Rule 102(e) also permits the SEC to take action against a professional who has willfully violated or aided and abetted another's violation of the securities acts. An SEC administrative law judge hears the case and makes

---

[4]507 U.S. 170 (1993).

an initial determination. The SEC commissioners then issue a final order, which may be appealed to a federal court of appeals.

Rule 102(e) administrative proceedings can impose severe penalties on an accountant. By suspending an accountant from practicing before it, the SEC may take away a substantial part of an accountant's practice. Also, the SEC may impose civil penalties up to $500,000.

In addition, state licensing boards may suspend or revoke an accountant's license to practice if she engages in illegal or unethical conduct. If such action is taken, an accountant may lose her entire ability to practice accounting.

Securities Exchange Act Audit Requirements

The Private Securities Litigation Reform Act of 1995 imposes significant public duties on independent auditors that audit the financial statements of public companies. In part added to the Securities Exchange Act as Section 10A, the Reform Act requires auditors to take specific steps if they learn during the course of an audit that a client may have committed an illegal act (that is, a violation of any law, rule, or regulation). First, the auditor is required to determine whether an illegal act has in fact occurred. If the auditor determines that the client has committed an illegal act, the auditor must calculate the prospective impact on the client's financial statements, including fines, penalties, and liability costs such as damage awards to persons harmed by the client. As soon as practical, the auditor must inform the client's management and audit committee of the auditor's determination, unless the illegal act is clearly inconsequential.

If the client's management does not take appropriate remedial action with respect to an illegal act that has a material effect on the financial statements of the client—and if the failure to take remedial action is reasonably expected to result in the auditor's issuance of a nonstandard report or resignation from the audit engagement—the auditor must make a report to the client's board of directors. The board of directors has one business day to inform the SEC of the auditor's report; if the board does not submit a report to the SEC, the auditor has one additional business day to furnish a copy of its report to the SEC, whether or not the auditor also resigns from the audit engagement.

Section 10A imposes a significant whistle-blowing duty on independent auditors, consistent with the watchdog function that Congress and the courts have continu-

ally assigned to auditors. To encourage auditors to make such reports, Section 10A also provides that an auditor will have no liability to a private litigant for any statement in the auditor's reports given to management, the board of directors, or the SEC.

Section 10A is also the repository of many of the new securities provisions enacted under the Sarbanes–Oxley Act, including the list of services audit firms may not provide for audit clients, the audit partner rotation requirement, and the standards and duties of audit committees.

SOX Section 404 The most controversial part of the Sarbanes–Oxley Act has been Section 404, which requires public issuers to include in their annual reports an "internal control report" acknowledging management's responsibility to maintain "an adequate internal control structure and procedures for financial reports." The purpose of Section 404 is to improve the quality of accounting records and financial statements, which had eroded in the 1990s as management and audit committees lost control of internal accounting processes.

SOX Section 404 requires management's internal control report to include:

- A statement of management's responsibility for establishing and maintaining adequate internal control over financial reporting for the company;
- Management's assessment of the effectiveness of the company's internal control over financial reporting;
- A statement identifying the framework used by management to evaluate the effectiveness of the company's internal control over financial reporting; and
- A statement that the public accounting firm that audited the company's financial statements has issued an attestation report on management's assessment of the company's internal control over financial reporting.

Thus, SOX Section 404 requires not only that management maintain adequate internal controls, but also that auditors attest to management's assessment of internal controls. This requirement imposes new duties on auditors, yet at the same time provides new opportunities for providing services at a fee.

Auditors are experienced in performing attestation engagements on a broad variety of subjects. It was not surprising, therefore, that the rulemaking body charged with setting standards for Section 404, the Public Company Accounting Oversight Board, adopted the standard used in other contexts, SSAE No. 10, as the appropriate standard for Section 404 assessments. See Chapters 4 and 45 at pages 104, 105, and 1139 for additional materials on Section 404, including the benefits and costs of compliance.

Ownership of Working Papers

The personal records that a client entrusts to a professional during an engagement, such as accounting records during an audit, remain the property of the client. A professional must return these records to his client. Nonetheless, material created by a professional, such as working papers produced by independent auditors, belong to the accountant, not the client.

Working papers are the records made during an audit. They include such items as work programs or plans for the audit, evidence of the testing of accounts, explanations of the handling of unusual matters, data reconciling the accountant's report with the client's records, and comments about the client's internal controls. The client has a right of access to the working papers. The accountant must obtain the client's permission before the working papers can be transferred to another accountant.

No doubt in reaction to the massive shredding of Enron-related documents by the Arthur Andersen audit firm, Congress included in the Sarbanes–Oxley Act a requirement that all audit or review working papers be retained for seven years. A knowing or willful violation of the document retention rule is subject to 10 years' imprisonment, and, if corruptly done, 20 years. The *Andersen* case follows the next section.

Professional–Client Privilege

The attorney–client privilege is well established as necessary to protect confidential communications between a lawyer and her client and to permit a lawyer to perform her professional duties for her client. The privilege protects communications between clients and their attorneys from the prying eyes of courts and government agencies. It also protects a lawyer's working papers from the discovery procedures available in a lawsuit.

Although other professionals owe a duty of confidentiality to their clients, in general communications between clients and nonlawyer professionals are not protected from judicial and administrative agency scrutiny when the professional's client is a party to legal or administrative action or the professional possesses evidence probative to an action. Thus, consultants, investment bankers, underwriters, brokers, and other securities professionals may be required to testify about client communications and produce documents concerning their clients, despite the objections of the client.

Accountants, however, enjoy a status somewhere between attorneys and other professionals. While the common law does not recognize an accountant–client privilege, a large number of states have granted such a privilege by statute. An accountant–client privilege of confidentiality protects communications between accountants and their clients as well as accountants' working papers. The provisions of the state statutes vary, but usually the privilege belongs to the client, and an accountant may not refuse to disclose the privileged material in a courtroom if the client consents to its disclosure.

Generally, the state-granted privileges are recognized in both state and federal courts deciding questions of state law. Nonetheless, federal courts do not recognize the privilege in matters involving federal questions, including antitrust, securities, and criminal matters.

In federal tax matters, for example, no privilege of confidentiality is recognized on the grounds that an accountant has a duty as a public watchdog to ensure that his client correctly reports his income tax liability. Consequently, an accountant can be required to bring his working papers into court and to testify as to matters involving the client's tax records and discussions with the client regarding tax matters. In addition, an accountant may be required by subpoena to make available his working papers involving a client who is being investigated by the IRS or who has been charged with tax irregularities. The same holds true for SEC investigations.

Although no accountant–client privilege exists in federal tax matters, an attorney–client privilege does exist. Moreover, the attorney–client privilege will protect communications between a client and a professional when the professional is assisting an attorney in rendering advice to the client.

As Enron Corporation's financial difficulties became public in 2001, Arthur Andersen LLP, Enron's auditor, instructed its employees to destroy Enron-related documents pursuant to its document retention policy, actions culminating in the following case. The Supreme Court mentions a concern regarding the professional–client privilege. The holding, however, focuses on when a professional can be found guilty for destroying working papers and other evidence.

Arthur Andersen LLP v. United States   544 U.S. 696 (U.S. S. Ct. 2005)

Enron Corporation, during the 1990s, switched its business from operation of natural gas pipelines to an energy conglomerate, a move that was accompanied by aggressive accounting practices and rapid growth. Arthur Andersen LLP audited Enron's publicly filed financial statements and provided internal audit and consulting services to it. Andersen's engagement team for Enron was headed by global managing partner David Duncan. Enron's financial performance began to suffer in 2000 and continued to worsen in 2001. On August 14, 2001, Jeffrey Skilling, Enron's CEO, unexpectedly resigned. Within days, Sherron Watkins, a senior accountant at Enron, warned Kenneth Lay, Enron's newly reappointed CEO, that Enron could "implode in a wave of accounting scandals." She also informed Duncan and Michael Odom, an Andersen partner who supervised Duncan, of the problems.

A key accounting problem involved Enron's use of "Raptors," which were special-purpose entities used to engage in "off-balance-sheet" activities. Andersen's engagement team had allowed Enron to "aggregate" the Raptors for accounting purposes so that they reflected a positive return. This was a clear violation of generally accepted accounting principles.

On August 28, 2001, an article in The Wall Street Journal *suggested improprieties at Enron, and the SEC opened an informal investigation. By early September, Andersen had formed an Enron "crisis-response" team, which included Nancy Temple, an in-house lawyer. On October 8, Andersen retained outside counsel to represent it in any litigation that might arise from the Enron matter. The next day, Temple discussed Enron with other in-house lawyers. Her notes from that meeting reflect that "some SEC investigation" is "highly probable."*

On October 10, Odom spoke at a general training meeting attended by 89 employees, including 10 from the Enron engagement team. Odom urged everyone to comply with the firm's document retention policy. He added: "If it's destroyed in the course of normal policy and litigation is filed the next day, that's great. . . . We've followed our own policy, and whatever there was that might have been of interest to somebody is gone and irretrievable." On October 12, Temple entered the Enron matter into her computer, designating the "Type of Potential Claim" as "Professional Practice—Government/Regulatory Investigation." Temple also e-mailed Odom, suggesting that he "remind the engagement team of our documentation and retention policy."

Andersen's policy called for a single central engagement file, which "should contain only that information which is relevant to supporting our work." The policy stated that, "in cases of threatened litigation, . . . no related information will be destroyed." It also separately provided that, if Andersen is "advised of litigation or subpoenas regarding a particular engagement, the related information should not be destroyed." The policy statement set forth "notification" procedures for whenever "professional practice litigation against Andersen or any of its personnel has been commenced, has been threatened or is judged likely to occur, or when governmental or professional investigations that may involve Andersen or any of its personnel have been commenced or are judged likely."

On October 16, Enron announced its third quarter results, disclosing a $1.01 billion charge to earnings. The following day, the SEC notified Enron by letter that it had opened an investigation and requested certain information and documents. On October 19, Enron forwarded a copy of that letter to Andersen.

On the same day, Temple also sent an e-mail to a member of Andersen's internal team of accounting experts and attached a copy of the document retention policy. On October 20, the Enron crisis-response team held a conference call, during which Temple instructed everyone to "make sure to follow the [document] policy." On October 23, Enron CEO Lay declined to answer questions during a call with analysts because of "potential lawsuits, as well as the SEC inquiry." After the call, Duncan met with other Andersen partners on the Enron engagement team and told them that they should ensure team members were complying with the document retention policy. Another meeting for all team members followed, during which Duncan distributed the policy and told everyone to comply. These, and other smaller meetings, were followed by substantial destruction of paper and electronic documents.

On October 26, one of Andersen's senior partners circulated a New York Times *article discussing the SEC's response to Enron. His e-mail commented that "the problems are just beginning and we will be in the cross hairs. The marketplace is going to keep the pressure on this and is going to force the SEC to be tough." On October 30, the SEC opened a formal investigation and sent Enron a letter that requested accounting documents.*

Throughout this time period, Andersen continued to destroy documents, despite reservations by some of Andersen's managers. For example, on October 26, John Riley, another Andersen partner, saw Duncan shredding documents and told him "this wouldn't be the best time in the world for you guys to be shredding a bunch of stuff." On October 31, David Stulb, a forensics investigator for Andersen, met with Duncan. During the meeting, Duncan picked up a document with the words "smoking gun" written on it and began to destroy it, adding "we don't need this." Stulb cautioned Duncan on the need to maintain documents and later informed Temple that Duncan needed advice on the document retention policy.

On November 8, Enron announced that it would issue a comprehensive restatement of its earnings and assets. Also on November 8, the SEC served Enron and Andersen with subpoenas for records. On November 9, Duncan's secretary sent an e-mail that stated: "Per Dave—No more shredding. . . . We have been officially served for our documents." Enron filed for bankruptcy less than a month later. Duncan was fired and later pleaded guilty to witness tampering.

In March 2002, Andersen was indicted in the Southern District of Texas on one count of violating witness tampering provisions 18 U.S.C. §§1512(b)(2)(A) and (B). The indictment alleged that, between October 10 and November 9, 2001, Andersen knowingly, intentionally, and corruptly persuaded Andersen's employees, with intent to cause them to withhold documents from, and alter documents for use in, an official proceeding. The case went to a jury, which deadlocked after deliberating for seven days. The district court instructed the jury that it could find Andersen guilty if Andersen intended to "subvert, undermine, or impede" governmental factfinding by suggesting to its employees that they enforce the document retention policy. After three more days of deliberation, the jury returned a guilty verdict. Andersen appealed to the court of appeals, which affirmed the conviction. The court of appeals held that the jury instructions properly conveyed the meaning of "corruptly persuades" and "official proceeding" and that the jury need not find any consciousness of wrongdoing. The Supreme Court granted Andersen's request to review the decision.

Rehnquist, Chief Justice

Chapter 73 of Title 18 of the United States Code provides criminal sanctions for those who obstruct justice. Sections 1512(b)(2)(A) and (B), part of the witness tampering provisions, provide in relevant part:

> Whoever knowingly uses intimidation or physical force, threatens, or corruptly persuades another person, or attempts to do so, or engages in misleading conduct toward another person, with intent to . . . cause or induce any person to . . . withhold testimony, or withhold a record, document, or other object, from an official proceeding [or] alter, destroy, mutilate, or conceal an object with intent to impair the object's integrity or availability for use in an official proceeding . . . shall be fined under this title or imprisoned not more than ten years, or both.

In this case, our attention is focused on what it means to "knowingly . . . corruptly persuade" another person "with intent to . . . cause" that person to "withhold" documents from, or "alter" documents for use in, an "official proceeding."

We have traditionally exercised restraint in assessing the reach of a federal criminal statute, both out of deference to the prerogatives of Congress and out of concern that a fair warning should be given to the world in language that the common world will understand, of what the law intends to do if a certain line is passed.

Such restraint is particularly appropriate here, where the act underlying the conviction—"persuasion"—is by itself innocuous. Indeed, "persuading" a person "with intent to . . . cause" that person to "withhold" testimony or documents from a Government proceeding or Government official is not inherently malign. Consider, for instance, a mother who suggests to her son that he invoke his right against compelled self-incrimination or a wife who persuades her husband not to disclose marital confidences.

Nor is it necessarily corrupt for an attorney to "persuade" a client "with intent to . . . cause" that client to "withhold" documents from the Government. In *Upjohn Co. v. United States,* 449 U.S. 383 (1981), for example, we held that Upjohn was justified in withholding documents that were covered by the attorney–client privilege from the Internal Revenue Service. No one would suggest that an attorney who "persuaded" Upjohn to take that step acted wrongfully, even though he surely intended that his client keep those documents out of the IRS' hands.

"Document retention policies," which are created in part to keep certain information from getting into the hands of others, including the Government, are common in business. It is, of course, not wrongful for a manager to instruct his employees to comply with a valid document retention policy under ordinary circumstances.

Acknowledging this point, the parties have largely focused their attention on the word "corruptly" as the key to what may or may not lawfully be done in the situation presented here. Section 1512(b) punishes not just "corruptly persuading" another, but *"knowingly* . . . corruptly persuading" another. The Government suggests that "knowingly" does not modify "corruptly persuades," but that is not how the statute most naturally reads. It provides the *mens rea*—"knowingly"—and then a list of acts—"uses intimidation or physical force, threatens, or corruptly persuades." The Government suggests that it is questionable whether Congress would employ such an inelegant formulation as "knowingly . . . corruptly persuades." Long experience has not taught us to share the Government's doubts on this score, and we must simply interpret the statute as written.

The parties have not pointed us to another interpretation of "knowingly . . . corruptly" to guide us here. In any event, the natural meaning of these terms provides a clear answer. "Knowledge" and "knowingly" are normally associated with awareness, understanding, or consciousness. "Corrupt" and "corruptly" are normally associated with wrongful, immoral, depraved, or evil. Joining these meanings together here makes sense both linguistically and in the statutory scheme. Only persons conscious of wrongdoing can be said to "knowingly . . . corruptly persuade." And limiting criminality to persuaders conscious of their wrongdoing sensibly allows §1512(b) to reach only those with the level of "culpability . . . we usually require in order to impose criminal liability."

The outer limits of this element need not be explored here because the jury instructions at issue simply failed to convey the requisite consciousness of wrongdoing. Indeed, it is striking how little culpability the instructions required. For example, the jury was told that, "even if Andersen honestly and sincerely believed that its conduct was lawful, you may find Andersen guilty." The instructions also diluted the meaning of "corruptly" so that it covered innocent conduct.

The District Court based its instruction on the definition of that term found in the Fifth Circuit Pattern Jury Instruction for §1503. This pattern instruction defined "corruptly" as "knowingly and dishonestly, with the specific intent to subvert or undermine the integrity" of a proceeding. The Government, however, insisted on excluding "dishonestly" and adding the term "impede" to the phrase "subvert or undermine." The District Court agreed over Andersen's objections, and the jury was told to convict if it found Andersen intended to "subvert, undermine, or impede" governmental factfinding by suggesting to its employees that they enforce the document retention policy.

These changes were significant. No longer was any type of "dishonesty" necessary to a finding of guilt, and it was enough for petitioner to have simply "impeded" the Government's factfinding ability. "Impede" has broader connotations than "subvert" or even "undermine," and many of these connotations do not incorporate any "corruptness" at all. The dictionary defines "impede" as "to interfere with or get in the way of the progress of" or "hold up" or "detract from." By definition, anyone who innocently persuades another to withhold information from the Government "gets in the way of the progress of" the Government.

The instructions also were infirm for another reason. They led the jury to believe that it did not have to find *any* nexus between the "persuasion" to destroy documents and any particular proceeding. In resisting any type of nexus element, the Government relies heavily on §1512(e)(1), which states that an official proceeding "need not be pending or about to be instituted at the time of the offense." It is, however, one thing to say that a proceeding "need not be pending or about to be instituted at the time of the offense," and quite another to say a proceeding need not even be foreseen. A "knowingly . . . corrupt persuader" cannot be someone who persuades others to shred documents under a document retention policy when he does not have in contemplation any particular official proceeding in which those documents might be material. If the defendant lacks knowledge that his actions are likely to affect the judicial proceeding, he lacks the requisite intent to obstruct.

For these reasons, the jury instructions here were flawed in important respects.

Judgment reversed in favor of Andersen.

Problems and Problem Cases

1. Lincoln Assurance Company engages audit firm Accent Pointe LLP to review its financial statements and internal controls. Accent Pointe examines Lincoln's expense ledger, which lists the creditors to whom Lincoln has made payments for supplies and services rendered to Lincoln, such as stationery, electricity, and phone. Accent Pointe makes no effort to verify that the payments were made to real creditors by randomly asking creditors to confirm that they had billed Lincoln and received payment. As a result, Accent Pointe fails to uncover an ongoing embezzlement by Lincoln's bookkeeper, who for the past six months has been writing checks to a fictitious creditor and then cashing the checks herself. The total amount of the checks is $155,000. When Lincoln uncovers the embezzlement scheme three months later, the bookkeeper has embezzled an additional $45,000. Is Accent Pointe liable to Lincoln for failing to uncover the embezzlement scheme?

2. Diversified Graphics, Ltd., hired Ernst & Whinney to assist it in obtaining a computer system to fit its data processing needs. DG had a long-standing relationship with E&W and developed great trust and reliance on E&W's services. Because DG lacked computer expertise, it decided to entrust E&W with the selection and implementation of an in-house

computer data processing system. E&W promised to locate a "turnkey" system, which would be fully operational without the need for extensive employee training. Instead, DG received a system that was difficult to operate and failed to meet its needs. Is E&W liable to DG?

3. Sonny Martinez opened a securities brokerage account with Edelstein & Co., depositing $680,000 in the account. Martinez was 10 years from his retirement and wanted his funds to be invested in blue chip stocks, which through capital appreciation and dividends would increase in value to $1,300,000 by the time of his retirement. Martinez's broker at Edelstein invested Martinez's funds in blue chip stocks like IBM, Procter & Gamble, and Merck, but he traded the account almost daily, sometimes holding a stock for only a matter of days and holding no stock for longer than 13 months. The broker executed over 4,000 trades in a two-year period, generating commissions of over $200,000. As a result of the broker's trading strategy, the value of Martinez's account declined to $300,000. During the same period, the Dow Jones Industrial Average increased 22 percent. May Martinez recover from the broker under contract law, the law of negligence, and Rule 10b–5 of the 1934 Act?

4. Scioto Memorial Hospital Association, Inc., planned the construction of Richmond Place, a 170-unit retirement center in Lexington, Kentucky. Scioto hired Price Waterhouse to review the work of the architect, the financial underwriter, and the marketing consultant and to recommend whether Scioto should proceed with the Richmond Place investment. PW's engagement letter represented that PW would issue a preliminary feasibility study and review a detailed financial forecast of the project. Financial forecasts represent management's judgment of the most likely set of conditions and management's most likely course of action. Instead of reviewing a financial forecast for Richmond Place, PW reviewed only a financial projection compiled by the underwriter of the construction. As PW explained in its letter to Scioto, a projection "represents management's estimate of its possible, but not necessarily most probable, future course of action." PW's final report to Scioto assumed an occupancy rate of 98 percent. Unfortunately, construction of Richmond Place was slow and delayed by a fire. While Scioto used insurance proceeds to rebuild, sales of the units were slow, and a year after opening, only 15 residents occupied

Richmond Place. Scioto sued PW for negligence and breach of contract. PW defended on the grounds that Scioto's delays in construction and its lack of business interruption insurance caused Scioto's damages. Was PW found liable to Scioto?

5. Piece Goods Shops Company, L.P., hired Price Waterhouse LLP to audit its 1992 financial statements. Piece Goods forwarded the audited 1992 financial statements to Marcus Brothers Textiles, Inc., which made several extensions of credit to Piece Goods up to April 1993 in reliance on the 1992 balance sheet. When Piece Goods filed for bankruptcy in April 1993, Piece Goods owed Marcus Brothers almost $300,000. Marcus Brothers sued PW for negligent misrepresentation under state law on the grounds PW negligently conducted the audit of the 1992 financial statements, which Marcus Brothers alleged contained several material misstatements. PW moved to dismiss the case on the grounds that PW did not know that Marcus Brothers would be using the financial statements to make credit extension to Piece Goods. Marcus Brothers produced evidence that PW had been Piece Goods's auditor since 1986. A PW internal memo stated that PW had historically reported on Piece Goods's financial statements and that its vendors were accustomed to receiving those financial statements. A PW audit partner signed a memo stating that some of PW's audit clients typically provided their audited financial statements to their trade creditors in reference to obtaining loans or extensions of credit. An audit manager who oversaw the audit of Piece Goods's 1992 financial statements testified that audited financial statements are used by management of the company and possibly outsiders and that such outsiders could include trade creditors such as Marcus Brothers. Piece Goods's bankruptcy filing revealed that 43 of its trade creditors had received the audited 1992 financial statements. Under the *Restatement (Second) of Torts,* is Marcus Brothers a proper plaintiff to whom PW owed a duty not to be negligent when conducting the audit?

6. Due to alleged overstatements of the value of loans held by First National Bank of Keystone (Keystone), the federal Office of the Comptroller of the Currency (OCC) began investigating Keystone. OCC required Keystone to retain an auditor to determine the appropriateness of Keystone's accounting treatments of its purchased loans and securitization of loans. Keystone hired Grant Thornton LLP to perform an audit

of Keystone's financial statements. In April 1999, Grant Thornton issued an audit opinion to Keystone stating that its 1998 financial statements—which showed shareholder equity of $84 million—were fairly stated in accordance with GAAP. In fact, Keystone was insolvent. Grant Thornton's audit report stated that "This report is intended for the information and use of the Board of Directors and Management of The First National Bank of Keystone and its regulatory agencies and should not be used by third parties for any other purpose." Gary Ellis, a candidate to become Keystone's next president, reviewed in April 1999 the 1998 financial statements audited by Grant Thornton. At the time, Ellis was president of another bank and not an employee of Keystone. He became a candidate for the Keystone presidency in late March 1999. Relying on the audit, Ellis decided to accept Keystone's offer to be its president at a base salary of $375,000. He also purchased $49,500 in Keystone stock. When Keystone failed, Ellis claimed he lost over $2 million in compensation he would have earned had he not taken the Keystone presidency, as well as losing the full amount of his investment in Keystone stock. He sued Grant Thornton for negligent misrepresentation. Under the *Restatement (Second) of Torts,* was Ellis a proper plaintiff to whom Grant Thornton owed a duty not to be negligent when conducting the audit?

7. Kibbmann & Co., an investment banking firm, acted as the underwriter for Vartarian Corporation's public issuance of common shares. Kibbmann prepared the 1933 Act registration statement that was filed with the SEC and the prospectus that investors received. Kibbmann also accompanied Vartarian's CEO and CFO to road shows where Kibbmann spoke with mutual funds and other institutional investors interested in purchasing Vartarian's stock. Kibbmann's compensation for assisting Vartarian was a 25-cent spread on each share sold. Due to its negligent investigation of Vartarian's business, Kibbmann made material misstatements of fact in the registration statement and prospectus and during the road show. Did Kibbmann have liability to purchasers of the shares who attended the road show under Section 12(a)(2) of the 1933 Act, Rule 10b–5 of the 1934 Act, and the common law of negligent misrepresentation? Did Kibbman have liability to purchasers of the shares under Section 11 of the 1933 Act?

8. Sonya Kwan, a 75-year-old retired factory worker, opened a securities account with Barton & Associates, a brokerage firm. She completed a customer account agreement form in which she disclosed her assets, liabilities, income, expenses, and investment objectives. That form indicated that it was important for her to maintain a steady income stream to augment her pension and Social Security income. Nonetheless, Kwan's broker advised her to purchase the stock of a high-risk company that paid no dividends to its shareholders. Kwan, who was not a sophisticated investor, followed her broker's advice and purchased the stock. Within two months, the company was dissolved and Kwan lost her entire investment. Kwan later discovered that her broker was a significant investor in the company. May Kwan recover from the analyst under Rule 10b–5 of the 1934 Act? Is Kwan able to recover under the common law of negligent misrepresentation, fraud, or breach of trust?

9. Norman Cross was the independent auditor for Home-Stakes Production Company, a company that offered investors interests in oil and gas drilling programs. The programs offered investors both income and tax deductions. Cross issued unqualified opinions regarding Home-Stakes's financial statements. He prepared consolidated financial statements and start-up balance sheets for two programs. All these documents were included, with Cross's consent, in 1933 Act registration statements filed with the SEC and included in prospectuses and program books distributed to investors. When Home-Stakes collapsed after it was discovered that the oil and gas drilling programs were a classic Ponzi scheme (with investments from new investors providing the "profits" to old investors), purchasers of the programs sued Cross under Securities Exchange Act Section 10(b) and Rule 10b–5. Was Cross found liable, or was he only an aider and abettor to Home-Stakes's fraud with no Rule 10b–5 liability?

10. Floogle, Inc., a provider of a variety of Internet services, decides to make a public offering of its common shares. It retains investment bank Sturm & Drang Company to underwrite the offering and assist in the marketing of the common shares. Accounting firm Barnes Jonson LLP audits the financial statements that will be included in the 1933 Act registration statement that will be filed with the SEC. Floogle's income statement for the last fiscal year materially overstates Floogle's earnings, indicating that earnings were $1.25 per share when in reality earnings were only $0.03 per share. The

earnings misstatement is known both to Sturm & Drang and Barnes Jonson. Nonetheless, when meeting with prospective investors, Sturm & Drang tells investors "last year's earnings were a robust $1.25 per share." Barnes Jonson also issues an opinion that Floogle's financial statements fairly present the financial position of Floogle. Investors purchase Floogle's common shares relying on Sturm & Drang's representation of Floogle's earnings and Barnes Jonson's audit opinion. When Floogle's real earnings are released three months later, the purchasers of Floogle's shares sue both Sturm & Drang and Barnes Jonson under Rule 10b–5 of the Securities Exchange Act of 1934. Both Strum & Drang and Barnes Jonson claim they are not liable under Rule 10b–5, because they merely aided and abetted Floogle's fraud. Are they correct?

11. Walter Piecyk, a broker and analyst with securities firm Fulcrum Global Partners, heard a rumor that Nokia Corp., the largest customer of RF Micro Devices Inc., was going to delay equipment orders from RF Micro. After short-selling RF Micro stock, Piecyk spread the rumor, which was highly sensational. RF Micro's stock fell 5 percent that day. The next day, when RF Micro publicly denied the rumor (which was completely false), the stock fell another 8 percent, apparently because the market believed the rumor, not RF Micro. The market price continued to fall, as the rumor persisted, and Piecyk eventually covered his short sale, making a profit of about $8,000. RF Micro asked the NASD to take disciplinary action against Piecyk on the grounds that he had not adequately investigated whether there was a reasonable basis for the rumor. Did the NASD discipline Piecyk?

12. Accounting firm Procenture LLP was hired to audit fiscal year 2008 financial statements of Bard-Gramercy Corporation, a public company with assets of $7.3 billion and a market value of $2.7 billion. Procenture completed the audit, and its audit opinion was included in Bard-Gramercy's annual report filed with the SEC. Because of time constraints, Procenture did a cursory review of Bard-Gramercy's internal financial controls, essentially asking management and receiving oral confirmation that management was satisfied with Bard-Gramercy's processes for recording financial transactions. Although Procenture's audit opinion made no mention of Bard-Gramercy's internal controls, Procenture was confident based on its inquiries that Bard-Gramercy's internal controls were adequate. Did Procenture meet its duty under the Sarbanes–Oxley Act of 2002?

13. Media personality Martha Stewart was investigated by the SEC for alleged insider trading in the stock of ImClone Systems. Stewart was a friend of Sam Waksal, founder and former chief executive of ImClone, who pleaded guilty in October 2002 to several counts of bank fraud, securities fraud, conspiracy to obstruct justice, and perjury. Stewart sold nearly 4,000 shares of ImClone stock in December 2001, just one day before the U.S. Food and Drug Administration announced it would reject ImClone's application for approval of its cancer-fighting drug Erbitux. That announcement sent the company's stock into a tailspin. The SEC believed Stewart may have been tipped off by Waksal about the looming FDA decision, but Waksal did not implicate Stewart. Stewart asserted that she told her broker, Peter Bacanovic of Merrill Lynch, to sell her shares if ImClone's stock dropped below $60 a share. The stock fell to $58 the day she sold. If the SEC wanted to know all communications between Stewart and her broker Bacanovic, may Stewart invoke a professional–client privilege to prevent the SEC's discovery of her confidential communications with Bacanovic?

Online Research

Sarbanes–Oxley Act Section 404

The cost of initial compliance with SOX Section 404 has made it a lightning rod for criticism by companies, especially small issuers. Keep abreast of the current status of SOX Section 404, especially these issues:

- Has the cost of complying with SOX 404 fallen as management and auditors have become more experienced at performing assessments and attestations?
- Have the expected benefits of SOX 404 been realized?
- In light of the credit crunch of 2008–2009, has Congress taken steps to lighten the burdens of SOX 404 or expand them?

Part Eleven

Regulation of Business

chapter 47
Administrative Agencies

chapter 48
The Federal Trade Commission Act
and Consumer Protection Laws

chapter 49
Antitrust: The Sherman Act

chapter 50
The Clayton Act,
The Robinson-Patman Act, and
Antitrust Exemptions and Immunities

chapter 51
Employment Law

chapter 52
Environmental Regulation

chapter 47

ADMINISTRATIVE AGENCIES

During the mid-1990s, the Food and Drug Administration (FDA) adopted various regulations that restricted advertising and other marketing practices regarding tobacco products. The FDA premised these regulations on the theory that nicotine was a "drug" and cigarettes were a drug-delivery "device" for purposes of the Food, Drug, and Cosmetic Act, which gives the FDA the authority to regulate such items.

Various tobacco companies and other parties challenged the regulations in federal court, arguing that Congress had not given the FDA authority to regulate tobacco products and that in any event, the advertising restrictions contemplated by the regulations violated the First Amendment. The litigation, which made its way to the ultimate forum—the United States Supreme Court—suggested fundamental questions that arise in the field of *administrative law:*

- In what subject matter area has the relevant administrative agency been granted authority to regulate by Congress or, at the state level, by the state legislature? What are the specific boundaries of that subject matter area?
- In what ways has the administrative agency been empowered by Congress or the state legislature to exercise its regulatory authority? What restrictions, if any, have been placed by Congress or the state legislature on the ways in which the agency may regulate?
- Do regulations (i.e., rules) adopted by an administrative agency have the same force of law that statutes have?
- How do constitutional provisions affect the regulatory actions that administrative agencies may take?

As you will see, the Supreme Court held in *FDA v. Brown & Williamson Tobacco Corp.,* 529 U.S. 120 (2000), that given a series of statutes enacted over the years, Congress did not intend for the FDA to have authority to regulate tobacco as part of its otherwise broad authority in the Food, Drug, and Cosmetic Act. Because the FDA did not have authority to regulate tobacco, the Court did not need to address the full list of questions set forth above. Your understanding of administrative law, however, will be enhanced if you consider the questions as you study this chapter.

Keep in mind, too, that changes in prevailing political winds may influence congressional decisions on whether to extend regulatory authority to an administrative agency. Authority not previously delegated by Congress can be delegated, and vice versa. For instance, the U.S. House of Representatives overwhelmingly passed a 2008 bill that, if enacted, would extend tobacco regulatory authority to the FDA. As this book went to press in 2008, the Senate appeared likely to pass the bill, though probably not by a veto-proof margin (an apparent problem because President Bush had promised a veto if both houses passed the bill). However, with President-Elect Obama having expressed support for the bill, prospects that the FDA would ultimately be granted authority to regulate tobacco appeared good.

TODAY'S BUSINESSES OPERATE IN a highly regulated environment. The *administrative agency* serves as a primary vehicle for the creation and enforcement of modern regulation. As governmental bodies that are neither courts nor legislatures, administrative agencies have the legal power to take actions affecting the rights of

Ethics in Action

Controversies over the roles and actions of administrative agencies often present both legal and ethical issues. Consider the example of the federal Food and Drug Administration (FDA), whose various legal responsibilities include issuing so-called *new drug approvals* before newly developed medications can lawfully be sold in the United States. A pharmaceutical maker seeking a new drug approval must provide the FDA with considerable documentary information, including clinical trial results, in order to enable the FDA to determine that the medication is likely to be effective for its intended purposes without posing undue dangers to consumers who will use it.

Although the determination just mentioned is of course a legal matter, ethical questions necessarily are present as well. For instance, in deciding whether to approve a new drug, how should decision makers at the FDA balance the health benefits many consumers would be likely to receive against the harm that other consumers could experience as a result of clinically documented side effects? What are the potential consequences for society if the new medication is approved and, alternatively, if it is not approved? If a new drug appears likely to produce tremendous health benefits for most users but potentially devastating health consequences for other users, has the FDA discharged any ethical obligations it may have if it allows the new drug to be sold but requires a warning on the product's label or in its package insert?

Other questions combining legal and ethical concerns may arise if, after FDA approval occurs and a medication becomes widely used and generally successful for its intended purpose, serious health dangers for some users come to light. Such a situation arose in recent years in regard to prescription pain relievers in the COX-2 inhibitor category. After Merck & Co.'s Vioxx brand pain reliever became heavily prescribed with largely positive results, the adverse experiences of some users led to concern over possible links between long-term Vioxx use and an increased risk of heart attacks or strokes. Merck eventually withdrew Vioxx from the market on a voluntary basis, but not before some commentators criticized the FDA for supposedly devoting too many FDA resources to the initial drug approval process and not enough resources to follow-ups designed to assess the postapproval track records of pharmaceutical products. Whether fair or not in the case of Vioxx, such criticisms suggest that there may be ethical dimensions to administrative agencies' decisions on how to allocate agency resources when the agency has various responsibilities to fulfill.

Of course, other legal and ethical questions arise in regard to private parties' dealings with administrative agencies. For instance, consider the concern expressed by some observers regarding alleged failures of some COX-2 inhibitor producers to disclose adverse health indications they supposedly learned of after receiving FDA approval to market their medications. If a pharmaceutical company receives reliable information of that nature after it wins FDA approval for a new drug and begins selling it, does that company owe the FDA or the public an obligation to disclose the information?

private individuals and organizations. The influence of administrative agencies has become so sweeping that they are sometimes referred to as the "fourth branch" of a government that officially consists of three branches (legislative, executive, and judicial).

This chapter focuses on federal administrative agencies. It is important to remember, however, that the past century's significant growth in *federal* regulation has been accompanied by a comparable growth in *state* and *local* regulation by agencies at those levels of government.

It is difficult to think of an area of modern individual life that is not somehow touched by the actions of administrative agencies. The energy that heats and lights your home and workplace, the clothes you wear, the food you eat, the medicines you take, the design of the car you drive, the programs you watch on television, and the contents of (and label on) the pillow on which you lay your head at night are all shaped in some way by regulation.

This observation is even more appropriate regarding corporations. Almost every significant aspect of contemporary corporate operations is regulated to the point that the *legal* consequences of a corporation's actions are nearly as important to its future success as the *business* consequences of its decisions.

Administrative agencies have always been objects of controversy. Are they protectors of the public or impediments to business efficiency? Are they guardians of competitive market structures or shields behind which noncompetitive firms have sought refuge from more vigorous competitors? Have they been impartial, efficient agents of the public interest or are they more often overzealous, or inept, or "captives" of the industries they supposedly regulate? At various times, and where various agencies are concerned, each of the above allegations is likely to have been true. Why, then, did we resort to such controversial entities to perform the regulatory function?

Origins of Administrative Agencies

In the 19th century's latter decades, the United States was in the midst of a dramatic transformation from an agrarian nation to a major industrial power. Improved means of transportation and communication facilitated dramatic market expansions. Large business organizations acquired unprecedented economic power, and new technologies promised additional social transformations.

The tremendous growth that resulted from these developments, however, was not attained without some cost. Large organizations sometimes abused their power at the expense of their customers, distributors, and competitors. New technologies often posed risks of harm to large numbers of citizens. Yet traditional institutions of legal control, such as courts and legislatures, were not particularly well suited to the regulatory needs of an increasingly complex, interdependent society in the throes of rapid change.

Courts, after all, are passive institutions that must await a genuine case or controversy before they can act. In addition, they are constrained by rules of procedure and evidence that make litigation a time-consuming and expensive process.

Legislatures, on the other hand, are theoretically able to anticipate social problems and to act in a comprehensive fashion to minimize social harm. In reality, however, legislatures rarely act until a problem has become severe enough to generate strong political support for a regulatory solution. Legislatures may also lack (as do courts) the expertise necessary to make rational policy regarding highly technical activities.

What was needed, therefore, was a new type of governmental entity: one that would be exclusively devoted to monitoring a particular area of activity; one that could, by its exclusive focus and specialized hiring practices, develop a reservoir of expertise concerning the relevant area; and one that could provide the continuous attention and constant policy development demanded by a rapidly changing environment. Such new entities, it was thought, could best perform their regulatory tasks if they were given considerable latitude in the approaches they utilized to achieve regulatory goals.

The modern regulatory era was born in 1887 when Congress, in response to complaints about discriminatory ratemaking practices by railroads, passed the Interstate Commerce Act. This statute created the Interstate Commerce Commission and empowered it to regulate transportation industry ratemaking practices. Since then, new administrative agencies have been added whenever *pressing social problems* (e.g., the threat to competition that led to the creation of the Federal Trade Commission) or *new technologies,* such as aviation (Federal Aviation Administration), communications (Federal Communications Commission), and nuclear power (Nuclear Regulatory Commission), have generated a political consensus in favor of regulation. More recently, developing scientific knowledge about the *dangers that modern technologies and industrial processes pose* to the environment and to industrial workers has led to the creation of new federal agencies empowered to regulate environmental pollution (Environmental Protection Agency) and promote workplace safety (Occupational Safety and Health Administration).

Sometimes, Congress may conclude that a new administrative agency need not be created to address a particular problem if an already existing agency's lines of authority and responsibility can be stepped up (something that tends to require an increase in the agency's budget). For example, following a series of horror stories about risks to children from large numbers of lead-contaminated toys that were being imported into the United States, Congress enacted—and the president signed into law—a 2008 statute that significantly increased the budget of the Consumer Product Safety Commission and charged the agency with taking a more active regulatory role.

The following sections examine the legal dimensions of the process by which administrative agencies are created.

Agency Creation

Enabling Legislation
Administrative agencies are created when Congress passes **enabling legislation** specifying the name, composition, and powers of the agency. For example, consider the following language from Section 1 of the Federal Trade Commission Act:

> A commission is created and established, to be known as the Federal Trade Commission [FTC], which shall be composed of five commissioners, who shall be appointed by the President, by and with the advice and consent of the Senate.

Section 5 of the FTC Act prohibits "unfair methods of competition" and "unfair or deceptive acts or practices in commerce," and empowers the FTC to prevent such practices.[1] Section 5 also describes the procedures the

---

[1]Section 5 of the FTC Act is discussed in detail in Chapter 48.

commission must follow to charge persons or organizations with violations of the act, and provides for judicial review of agency orders. Subsequent portions of the statute give the FTC the power "to make rules and regulations for the purpose of carrying out the provisions of the Act," to conduct investigations of business practices, to require reports from interstate corporations concerning their practices and operations, to investigate possible violations of the antitrust laws,[2] to publish reports concerning its findings and activities, and to recommend new legislation to Congress.

Thus, Congress has given the FTC powers typically associated with the three traditional branches of government. The FTC may, for instance, act in a legislative fashion by *promulgating rules* that have binding legal effect on future behavior. (As will be seen, however, an agency's regulations will not have binding effect if they go beyond the scope of the power delegated to the agency by Congress.) It may also take the executive branch–like actions of *investigating* and *prosecuting* alleged violations. Finally, the FTC may act much as courts do and *adjudicate* disputes concerning alleged violations of the law. Most other federal administrative agencies have a similarly broad mix of governmental powers, making these agencies potentially powerful agents of social control.

Great power to do good things, however, may also be great power to cause harm. Regulatory bias, zeal, insensitivity, or corruption, if left unchecked, may infringe on the basic freedoms that are the essence of our system of government. Accordingly, the fundamental problem in administrative law—a problem that will surface repeatedly in this chapter—is how to design a system of control over agency action that minimizes the potential for arbitrariness and harm yet preserves the power and flexibility that make administrative agencies uniquely valuable instruments of public policy.

Administrative Agencies and the Constitution Because administrative agencies are governmental bodies, administrative action is *governmental action* that is subject to the basic constitutional checks discussed in Chapter 3. This "fourth branch" of government is bound by basic constitutional guarantees such as *due process, equal protection,* and *freedom of speech,* just as the three traditional branches are. The *Pearson* case, which follows, deals with First Amendment limitations on the Food and Drug Administration's regulatory authority.

---

[2]The antitrust laws are discussed in detail in Chapters 49 and 50.

Pearson v. Shalala	164 F.3d 650 (D.C. Cir. 1999)

A federal statute prohibits marketers of dietary supplements from including on container labels any claim characterizing the relationship of the dietary supplement to the prevention or alleviation of a disease or health-related condition, unless the claim has been submitted to the Food and Drug Administration (FDA) for preapproval. According to one of its regulations, the FDA will authorize such a "health claim" only if the FDA finds "significant scientific agreement" among experts that the claim is supported by the available evidence. Dietary supplement marketers Durk Pearson and Sandy Shaw asked the FDA to authorize four separate health claims regarding their dietary supplements' preventative effects on health conditions such as cancer or heart disease.

The FDA refused to authorize any of the four health claims, not because there was a dearth of supporting evidence but because, in the FDA's view, the evidence was inconclusive and thus failed to give rise to "significant scientific agreement." The FDA declined to consider an alternative suggested by Pearson and Shaw: permitting the making of the health claims on the appropriate labels but requiring the use of a corrective disclaimer such as "The FDA has determined that the evidence supporting this claim is inconclusive."

Pearson, Shaw, and organizations representing health care practitioners and consumers of dietary supplements sought relief in the federal district court. The court rejected their arguments and upheld the FDA's action. Pearson, Shaw, and the organizations appealed to the U.S. Court of Appeals for the District of Columbia Circuit.

Silberman, Circuit Judge

Appellants raise a host of challenges to the [FDA's] action. [T]he most important are that their First Amendment rights have been impaired and that under the Administrative Procedure Act, the FDA was obliged . . . to articulate a standard a good deal more concrete than the undefined "significant scientific agreement." Normally we would discuss the non-constitutional argument first, particularly because we believe it has merit. We invert the normal order here to discuss [the argument] that the government has violated the First Amendment by declining to employ a less draconian method—the use of disclaimers—to serve the government's interests. [We do so because] even if "significant scientific agreement" were given a more concrete meaning, appellants might be entitled to make health claims that do not meet that standard—with proper disclaimers.

It is undisputed that the FDA's restrictions on appellants' health claims are [to be] evaluated under the commercial speech doctrine [and] that the FDA has unequivocally rejected the notion of requiring disclaimers to cure "misleading" health claims for dietary supplements. The government makes two alternative arguments in response to appellants' claim that it is unconstitutional for the government to refuse to entertain a disclaimer requirement for the proposed health claims: first, that health claims lacking "significant scientific agreement" are *inherently* misleading and thus entirely outside the protection of the First Amendment; and second, that even if the claims are only *potentially* misleading, . . . the government is not obliged to consider requiring disclaimers in lieu of an outright ban on all claims that lack significant scientific agreement.

If such health claims could be thought inherently misleading, that would be the end of the inquiry. [Although nonmisleading commercial speech about lawful activities receives an intermediate degree of First Amendment protection, misleading commercial speech goes wholly unprotected by the First Amendment.] [The government's] first argument runs along the following lines: that health claims lacking "significant scientific agreement" are inherently misleading because they have such an awesome impact on consumers as to make it virtually impossible for them to exercise any judgment *at the point of sale.* It would be as if the consumers were asked to buy something while hypnotized, and therefore they are bound to be misled. We think this contention is almost frivolous. We reject it. But the government's alternative argument is more substantial. It is asserted that health claims on dietary supplements should be thought at least potentially misleading because the consumer would have difficulty in independently verifying these claims. We are told, in addition, that consumers might actually assume that the government has approved these claims.

Under *Central Hudson Gas & Electric Corp. v. Public Service Commission* (U.S. Sup Ct. 1980), we are obliged to evaluate a government scheme to regulate potentially misleading commercial speech by applying a . . . test [that first asks] whether the asserted government interest is substantial. The FDA advanced two general concerns: protection of public health and prevention of consumer fraud. [In view of applicable precedent,] a substantial government interest is undeniable. The more significant questions under *Central Hudson* are the next two factors: "whether the regulation directly advances the governmental interest asserted," [quoting *Central Hudson,*] and whether the fit between the government's ends and the means chosen to accomplish those ends "is not necessarily perfect, but reasonable" [quoting *Board of Trustees v. Fox* (U.S. Sup. Ct. 1989)].

[Although any advancement of the underlying public health interest may seem more indirect than direct,] the government would appear to advance directly its interest in protecting against consumer fraud through its regulatory scheme. If it can be assumed—and we think it can—that some health claims on dietary supplements will mislead consumers, it cannot be denied that requiring FDA preapproval and setting the standard extremely, perhaps even impossibly, high will surely prevent any confusion among consumers. We also recognize that the government's interest in preventing consumer fraud/confusion may well take on added importance in the context of a product, such as dietary supplements, that can affect the public's health.

The difficulty with the government's consumer fraud justification comes at the final *Central Hudson* factor: Is there a reasonable fit between the government's goals and the means chosen to advance those goals? The government insists that it is never obliged to utilize the disclaimer approach, because the commercial speech doctrine does not embody a preference for disclosure over outright suppression. Our understanding of the doctrine is otherwise. [The Supreme Court has stated that when allegedly incomplete advertising is not inherently misleading,] "the preferred remedy is more disclosure, rather than less." *Bates v. State Bar of Arizona* (U.S. Sup. Ct. 1977). In more recent cases, the Court has reaffirmed this principle, repeatedly pointing to disclaimers as constitutionally preferable to outright suppression. [Moreover, when] government chooses a policy of suppression over disclosure—at least where there is no showing that disclosure would not suffice to [prevent or minimize] misleadingness—government disregards a far less restrictive means. [As a result, a reasonable fit between the regulatory scheme and the underlying government interest would be lacking.]

Our rejection of the government's position that there is no general First Amendment preference for disclosure over suppression . . . does not determine that any supposed weaknesses in the [health] claims at issue can be remedied by disclaimers. [We therefore examine the particular claims.] The FDA deemed the first three claims—(1) "Consumption of antioxidant vitamins may reduce the risk of certain kinds of cancers," (2) "Consumption of fiber may reduce the risk of colorectal cancer," and (3) "Consumption of omega-3 fatty acids may reduce the risk of coronary heart disease"—to lack significant scientific agreement because existing research had examined only the relationship between consumption of *foods* containing these components and the risk of these diseases. The FDA logically determined that the specific effect of the *component* of the food constituting the dietary supplement could not be determined with certainty. But certainly this concern could be accommodated, in the first claim for example, by adding a prominent disclaimer to the label along the following lines: "The evidence is inconclusive because existing studies have been performed with *foods* containing antioxidant vitamins, and the effect of those foods on reducing the risk of cancer may result from other components in those foods." A similar disclaimer would be equally effective for the latter two claims.

The FDA's concern regarding the fourth claim—".8mg of folic acid in a dietary supplement is more effective in reducing the risk of neural tube defects than a lower amount in foods in common form"—is different from its reservations regarding the first three claims: the agency simply concluded that "the scientific literature does not support the superiority of any one source over others." [W]e suspect that a clarifying disclaimer could be added to the effect that "the evidence in support of this claim is inconclusive."

The government's general concern that . . . consumers might assume that a claim on a supplement's label is approved by the government suggests an obvious answer. The agency could require the label to state that "The FDA does not approve this claim." Similarly, the government's interest in preventing the use of labels that are true but do not mention adverse effects would seem to be satisfied—at least ordinarily—by inclusion of a prominent disclaimer setting forth those adverse effects.

The government disputes that consumers would be able to comprehend appellants' proposed health claims in conjunction with the disclaimers we have suggested. [T]his mix of information would, in the government's view, create confusion among consumers. But all the government offers in support is the FDA's pronouncement that "consumers would be considerably confused by a multitude of claims with differing degrees of reliability." Although the government may have more leeway in choosing suppression over disclosure as a response to the problem of consumer confusion where the product affects health, it must still meet its burden of justifying a restriction on speech. [H]ere, the FDA's conclusory assertion falls far short.

We do not presume to draft precise disclaimers for each of appellants' four claims; we leave that task to the agency in the first instance. Nor do we rule out the possibility that where evidence in support of a claim is outweighed by evidence against the claim, the FDA could deem it incurable by a disclaimer and ban it outright. For example, if the weight of the evidence were against the hypothetical claim that "Consumption of Vitamin E reduces the risk of Alzheimer's disease," the agency might reasonably determine that adding a disclaimer such as "The FDA has determined that *no* evidence supports this claim" would not suffice to mitigate the claim's misleadingness. Finally, while we are skeptical that the government could demonstrate with empirical evidence that disclaimers similar to the ones we suggested above would bewilder consumers and fail to correct for deceptiveness, we do not rule out that possibility.

District court decision reversed; case remanded with instructions that FDA reconsider appellants' health claims.

Separation of Powers   One basic constitutional principle is uniquely important when the creation of administrative agencies is at issue: the principle of *separation of powers*. A fundamental attribute of our Constitution is its allocation of governmental power among the three branches of government. Lawmaking power is given to the legislative branch, law-enforcing power to the executive branch, and law-interpreting power to the judicial branch. By limiting the powers of each branch, and by giving each branch some checks on the exercise of power by the other branches, the Constitution seeks to ensure that governmental power remains accountable to the public will.

Administrative agencies, which exercise powers resembling those of each of the three branches of government, create obvious concerns about separation of powers. In particular, the congressional delegation of legislative power to an agency in its enabling legislation may be challenged as violating the separation of powers principle if the legislation is so broadly worded as to indicate that Congress has abdicated its lawmaking responsibilities. Early judicial decisions exploring the manner in which Congress could delegate its power tended to require enabling legislation to contain fairly specific guidelines and standards limiting the exercise of agency discretion.

More recently, courts have often sustained quite broad delegations of power to administrative agencies. Section 5 of the FTC Act contains such a delegation of power. A great range of unspecified behavior falls within the statute's prohibition of "unfair methods of competition" and "unfair or deceptive acts or practices." Courts tend to approve broad delegations of power when Congress has expressed an "intelligible principle" to guide the agency's actions.[3]

The *American Trucking Associations* decision, which follows, examines the delegation of power question.

---

[3]*J. W. Hampton, Jr. & Co. v. United States* (U.S. Sup. Ct. 1928).

Whitman v. American Trucking Associations
531 U.S. 457 (U.S. Sup. Ct. 2001)

The federal Clean Air Act requires the Environmental Protection Agency (EPA) to promulgate and periodically revise national ambient air quality standards (NAAQS) for each air pollutant that meets certain statutory criteria. Section 109 of the statute calls for the EPA to set, for each pollutant, a standard reflecting a concentration level "requisite to protect the public health" with an "adequate margin of safety." In July 1997, the EPA issued final rules revising the NAAQS for particulate matter and ozone. Various parties, including American Trucking Associations, Inc., filed petitions for review in the United States Court of Appeals for the District of Columbia Circuit. The D.C. Circuit held, among other things, that the Clean Air Act did not permit the EPA to consider costs of implementation in setting NAAQS, and that in any event, the challenged rules had been formulated pursuant to an unconstitutional delegation of power from Congress in § 109. However, the D.C. Circuit remanded the proceedings to the EPA, in order to allow the agency to construe § 109 in a way that would cure the delegation problem.

The U.S. Supreme Court granted the EPA's petition for certiorari. In a portion of the opinion not included here, the Supreme Court agreed with the D.C. Circuit's holding that costs of implementation could not be considered by the EPA in the setting of NAAQS. The Court then turned to the delegation of power issue.

Scalia, Justice

In a delegation challenge, the constitutional question is whether the statute has delegated legislative power to the agency. Article I, § 1, of the Constitution vests "all legislative Powers herein granted . . . in a Congress of the United States." This text permits no delegation of those powers, and so we repeatedly have said that when Congress confers decisionmaking authority upon agencies, *Congress* must "lay down by legislative act an intelligible principle to which the person or body authorized to [act] is directed to conform." *J. W. Hampton, Jr. & Co. v. United States* (1928). We have never suggested that an agency can cure an unlawful delegation of legislative power by adopting in its discretion a limiting construction of the statute. The idea that an agency can cure an unconstitutionally standardless delegation of power by declining to exercise some of that power seems to us internally contradictory. The very choice of which portion of the power to exercise—that is to say, the prescription of the standard that Congress had omitted—would *itself* be an exercise of the forbidden legislative authority. Whether the statute delegates legislative power is a question for the courts, and an agency's voluntary self-denial has no bearing upon the answer.

We agree with the Solicitor General[, who argued on behalf of the United States. According to the Solicitor General's argument,] the text of § 109 of the Clean Air Act at a minimum requires that "for a discrete set of pollutants and based on published air quality criteria that reflect the latest scientific knowledge, [the] EPA must establish uniform national standards at a level that is requisite to protect public health from the adverse effects of the pollutant in the ambient air." Requisite, in [the words of the Solicitor General], "means sufficient, but not more than necessary." These limits on the EPA's discretion are strikingly similar to the ones we approved in [a 1991 decision], which permitted the Attorney General to designate a drug as a controlled substance for purposes of criminal drug enforcement if doing so was "necessary to avoid an imminent hazard to the public safety." They also resemble the Occupational Health and Safety Act provision requiring the agency to "set the standard which most adequately assures, to the extent feasible, on the basis of the best available evidence, that no employee will suffer any impairment of health"—which the Court upheld in [a 1980 decision].

The scope of discretion § 109 allows is in fact well within the outer limits of our nondelegation precedents. In the history of the Court we have found the requisite "intelligible principle" lacking in only two statutes, one of which provided literally no guidance for the exercise of discretion, and the other of which conferred authority to regulate the entire economy on the basis of no more precise a standard than stimulating the economy by assuring "fair competition." We have, on the other hand, upheld the validity of [a section of] the Public Utility Holding Act of 1935, which gave the Securities and Exchange Commission authority to modify the structure of holding company systems so as to ensure that they are not "unduly or unnecessarily complicated" and do not "unfairly or inequitably distribute voting power among security holders." *American Power & Light Co. v. SEC* (1946). We have approved the wartime conferral of agency power to fix the prices of commodities at a level that "will be generally fair and equitable and will effectuate the purposes of [the relevant statute]." *Yakus v. United States* (1944). And we have found an "intelligible principle" in various statutes authorizing regulation in the "public interest." See, e.g., *National Broadcasting Co. v. United States* (1943). In short, we have "almost never felt qualified to second-guess Congress regarding the permissible degree of policy judgment that can be left to those executing or applying the law." *Mistretta v. United States* (1989) (Scalia, J., dissenting).

It is true enough that the degree of agency discretion that is acceptable varies according to the scope of the power congressionally conferred. While Congress need not provide any direction to the EPA regarding the manner in which it is to define "country elevators," which are to be exempt from new stationary-source regulations governing grain elevators, it must provide substantial guidance on setting air standards that affect the entire national economy. But even in sweeping regulatory schemes we have never demanded, as the Court of Appeals did here, that statutes provide a "determinate criterion" for saying "how much [of the regulated harm] is too much." [In the controlled substance designation case referred to above,] for example, we did not require the statute to decree how "imminent" was too imminent, or how "necessary" was necessary enough, or even—most relevant here—how "hazardous" was too hazardous. Similarly, the statute at issue in [another Supreme Court decision] authorized agencies to recoup "excess profits" paid under wartime government contracts, yet we did not insist that

Congress specify how much profit was too much. It is therefore not conclusive for delegation purposes that, as [American Trucking Associations and the other parties challenging the NAAQS] argue, ozone and particulate matter are "nonthreshold" pollutants that inflict a continuum of adverse health effects at any airborne concentration greater than zero, and hence require the EPA to make judgments of degree. "[A] certain degree of discretion, and thus of lawmaking, inheres in most executive or judicial action. *Mistretta* (Scalia, J., dissenting).

Section 109 (b) (1) of the CAA, which we interpret as requiring the EPA to set air quality standards at the level that is "requisite"—that is, not lower or higher than is necessary—to protect the public health with an adequate margin of safety, fits comfortably within the scope of discretion permitted by our precedent.

Court of Appeals decision reversed as to delegation of power issue.

Agency Types and Organization

Agency Types Administrative agencies may be found under a variety of labels. They may be called "administration," "agency," "authority," "board," "bureau," "commission," "department," "division," or "service." They sometimes have a governing body, which may be appointed or elected. They almost invariably have an administrative head (variously called "Chairman," "Commissioner," "Director," etc.), and a staff. Because our focus is on federal administrative agencies, it is important to distinguish between the two basic types of federal administrative agencies: executive agencies and independent agencies.

Executive Agencies Administrative agencies that reside within the Executive Office of the President or within the executive departments of the president's cabinet are called **executive agencies.** Examples of such agencies and their cabinet homes are the Food and Drug Administration (Department of Health and Human Services); the Nuclear Regulatory Agency and the Federal Energy Regulatory Agency (Department of Energy); the Occupational Safety and Health Administration (Department of Labor); and the Internal Revenue Service (Treasury Department). In addition to their executive home, such agencies share one other important attribute. Their

administrative heads serve "at the pleasure of the President," meaning that they are appointed and removable at his will.

Independent Agencies The Interstate Commerce Commission was the first independent administrative agency created by Congress. Much of the most significant regulation businesses face emanates from independent agencies such as the FTC, the National Labor Relations Board, the Consumer Product Safety Commission, the Equal Employment Opportunity Commission, the Environmental Protection Agency, and the Securities and Exchange Commission. Independent agencies are usually headed by a board or a commission (e.g., the FTC has five commissioners) whose members are appointed by the president "with the advice and consent of the Senate." Commissioners or board members are usually appointed for fixed terms (e.g., FTC commissioners serve seven-year, staggered terms) and are removable only for cause (e.g., FTC commissioners may be removed only for "inefficiency, neglect of duty, or malfeasance in office"). Enabling legislation often requires political balance in agency appointments (e.g., the FTC Act provides that "[n]ot more than three of the commissioners shall be members of the same political party").

Department of Homeland Security In 2002, Congress enacted legislation creating the cabinet-level Department of Homeland Security. This new department, whose creation had been proposed in various versions of House and Senate bills since shortly after the September 11, 2001, attacks on the United States, absorbed more than 20 different functions previously undertaken by other federal departments and agencies. The Department of Homeland Security employs roughly 170,000 workers, with the vast majority coming to that department by way of transfer from existing positions as federal government employees. With the creation of this new department and the resulting reassignments of employees and areas of responsibility, the 2002 enactment called for the most sweeping governmental reorganization in more than a half-century.

Agency Organization

An agency's organizational structure is largely a function of its regulatory mission. The FTC's operational side, for instance, is divided into three bureaus: the Bureau of Competition, which enforces the antitrust laws and unfair competitive practices; the Bureau of Consumer Protection, which focuses on unfair or deceptive trade practices; and the Bureau of Economics, which gathers data, compiles statistics, and furnishes technical assistance to the other bureaus. The commission is headquartered in Washington, D.C. It maintains regional offices in Atlanta, Boston, Chicago, Cleveland, Dallas, Denver, Los Angeles, New York, San Francisco, and Seattle. This regional office system enhances the commission's enforcement, investigative, and educational missions by locating commission staff closer to the public it serves.

Agency Powers and Procedures

Nature, Types, and Source of Powers

The powers administrative agencies possess may be classified in various ways. Some agencies' powers are largely *ministerial*—concerned primarily with the routine performance of duties imposed by law. The most important administrative agencies, however, have broad *discretionary* powers that necessitate the exercise of significant discretion and judgment when they are employed. The major discretionary powers agencies can possess are **investigative power, rulemaking power,** and **adjudicatory power.**

The formal powers an agency possesses are those granted by its enabling legislation. Important federal agencies such as the FTC normally enjoy significant

levels of each of the discretionary powers. However, even such powerful agencies face significant limitations on the exercise of their powers. In addition to explicit limits on agency proceedings contained in enabling legislation, basic constitutional provisions restrict agency action.

A federal agency's exercise of its rulemaking and adjudicatory powers is also constrained by the *Administrative Procedure Act (APA)*. The APA was enacted by Congress in 1946 in an attempt to standardize federal agency procedures and to respond to critics who said that administrative power was out of control. The APA applies to all federal agencies, although it will not displace stricter procedural requirements contained in a particular agency's enabling legislation. Besides specifying agency procedures, the APA plays a major role in shaping the conditions under which courts will review agency actions and the standards courts will use when conducting such a review. Most states have adopted "baby APAs" to govern the activities of state administrative agencies.

Finally, as later parts of this chapter will confirm, each of the three traditional branches of government possesses substantial powers to mold and constrain the powers of the "fourth branch." That being said, one final point should be made before we turn to a detailed examination of formal agency powers and procedures. An agency's formal powers also confer on it significant *informal* power. Agency "advice," "suggestions," or "guidelines," which technically lack the legal force of formal agency regulations or rulings, may nonetheless play a major role in shaping the behavior of regulated industries because they carry with them the implicit or explicit threat of formal agency action if they are ignored. Such gentle persuasion can be a highly effective regulatory tool, and one that is subject to far fewer constraints than formal agency action.

Investigative Power

Administrative agencies need accurate information about business practices and activities not only for the detection and prosecution of regulatory violations, but also to enable the agencies to identify areas in which new rules are needed or existing rules require modification. Much of the information agencies require to do their jobs is readily available. "Public interest" groups, complaints from customers or competitors, and other regulatory agencies are all important sources of information.

However, much of the information necessary to effective agency enforcement can come only from sources that may be strongly disinclined to provide it: the individuals and business organizations subject to regulation. This reluctance may stem from the desire to avoid or delay the regulatory action that disclosure would generate. It might also be the product, however, of more legitimate concerns, such as a desire to protect personal privacy, a desire to prevent competitors from acquiring trade secrets and other sensitive information from agency files, or a reluctance to incur the costs that may accompany compliance with substantial information demands. Agencies, therefore, need the means to compel unwilling possessors of information to comply with legitimate demands for information. The two most important (and most intrusive) investigative tools employed by administrative agencies are *subpoenas* and *searches and seizures.*

Subpoenas   There are two basic types of subpoena: the subpoena *ad testificandum* and the subpoena *duces tecum.* Subpoenas *ad testificandum* may be used by an agency to compel unwilling witnesses to appear and testify at agency hearings. Subpoenas *duces tecum* may be used by an agency to compel the production of most types of documentary evidence, such as accounting records and office memoranda.

Unlimited agency subpoena power risks sacrificing individual liberty and privacy in the name of regulatory efficiency. Accordingly, courts have formulated a number of limitations that seek to balance an agency's legitimate need to know against an investigatory target's legitimate privacy interests.

Agency investigations must be *authorized by law* and *conducted for a legitimate purpose.* The former requirement means that the agency's enabling legislation must have granted the agency the investigatory power it seeks to assert. The latter requirement prohibits bad faith investigations pursued for improper motives (e.g., Internal Revenue Service investigations undertaken solely to harass political opponents of an incumbent administration).

Even when the investigation is legally authorized and is undertaken for a legitimate purpose, the information sought must be *relevant to that purpose.* The Fourth Amendment to the Constitution provides this limitation on agency powers. However, an agency issuing an administrative subpoena need not possess the "probable cause" that the Fourth Amendment requires in support of regular search warrants.[4] In the words of the Supreme

Court, an agency "can investigate merely on the suspicion that the law is being violated, or even just because it wants assurance that it is not."[5] This lesser standard makes sense in the agency context, because the only evidence of many regulatory violations is documentary and "probable cause" might be demonstrable only after inspection of the target's records. In such cases, a probable cause requirement would effectively negate agency enforcement power.

Similarly, agency information demands must be *sufficiently specific* and *not unreasonably burdensome.* This requirement derives from the Fourth Amendment's prohibition against "unreasonable searches and seizures." It means that agency subpoenas must adequately describe the information the agency seeks. It also means that the cost to the target of complying with the agency's demand (e.g., the cost of assembling and reproducing the data, the disruption of business operations, or the risk that proprietary information will be indirectly disclosed to competitors) must not be unreasonably disproportionate to the agency's interest in obtaining the information.

Finally, the information sought *must not be privileged.* Various statutory and common law privileges may, at times, limit an agency's power to compel the production of information. By far the most important privilege in this respect is the Fifth Amendment *privilege against compelled testimonial self-incrimination,* or "the right to silence." As you learned in Chapter 5, however, this privilege is subject to serious limitations in the business context. The right to silence in the administrative context is further limited by the fact that it is only available in *criminal* proceedings. In some regulatory contexts, the potential sanctions for violation may be labeled "civil penalties" or "forfeitures." Only when such sanctions are essentially punitive in their intent or effect will they be considered "criminal" for the purpose of allowing the invocation of the privilege.

Public policy concerns provide another subpoena power limitation that may apply even if neither the Fifth Amendment nor another privilege bars production of the documents sought by an agency. As indicated in the *Collins* case, which follows, courts may conclude that an agency subpoena should not be enforced if its enforcement would tend to compromise important operations being conducted by another agency or arm of the government.

---

[4]The Fourth Amendment is discussed in Chapter 5.

[5]*United States v. Morton Salt* (U.S. Sup. Ct. 1950).

Commodity Futures Trading Commission v. Collins
997 F.2d 1230 (7th Cir. 1993)

The Commodity Futures Trading Commission (CFTC) was investigating Thomas Collins for possible civil violations of the Commodity Exchange Act. Among the violations of which Collins was suspected was the trading of commodities futures contracts other than on a commodities exchange. The CFTC's staff suspected that these trades were spurious trades, which (the staff theorized) were intended to enable Collins to reallocate losses to persons who would reap the maximum tax benefits from the losses. As part of this investigation, the CFTC issued a subpoena directing Collins to produce copies of his federal income tax returns for examination by the CFTC's staff. The staff's reasoning was that the presence of tax motives would be evidence of a likely violation of rules enforced by the CFTC.

Collins resisted the subpoena on the ground that it would force him to incriminate himself. Collins argued that the tax returns contained information that could be evidence—or could lead to evidence—of felony violations of federal law. The CFTC argued that the tax returns were required records and that compelling their disclosure therefore would not violate the Fifth Amendment. [See Chapter 5's discussion of the required-records doctrine, which operates to eliminate Fifth Amendment privilege claims regarding the contents of such records.] The district court agreed with the CFTC and entered an enforcement order requiring Collins to obey the subpoena. Collins appealed.

In a portion of its opinion not set forth here, the Seventh Circuit Court of Appeals concluded that the required-records doctrine was inapplicable because the subpoena sought a taxpayer's copies of his tax returns—copies that the taxpayer was not required by law to make—rather than the actual tax returns whose preparation and filing with the Internal Revenue Service were required by law. The Seventh Circuit then (as set forth below) continued its analysis of Collins's Fifth Amendment argument and addressed other policy concerns triggered by the CFTC's subpoena.

Posner, Judge

[The inapplicability of the required-records doctrine] does not end our inquiry. The [required-records] doctrine only comes into play if, were it not for the doctrine, the government would be forcing a person to incriminate himself. *Garner v. United States* (1976) holds that the taxpayer who includes incriminating information on his return is like the witness who blurts out incriminating testimony rather than invoking the Fifth Amendment and keeping mum: he has not been compelled to testify against himself, so he has no Fifth Amendment claim. *Garner* . . . is consistent with the cases which hold that there is no Fifth Amendment privilege in already created documents, because the disclosures in them were not compelled. *Garner* and [the cases dealing with already created documents] make the required-records exception to the Fifth Amendment privilege largely, perhaps entirely, superfluous, because records that are not required are by the same token not privileged. And those decisions suggest another reason for doubting that Collins has any Fifth Amendment claim: Collins created copies of his tax returns voluntarily, so any information in the copies, however incriminating, was not compelled by the government.

In light of all this it is doubtful that Collins has any constitutional leg to stand on. No matter. All constitutional concerns to one side, we think it was an abuse of discretion for the district judge to enforce this subpoena. Income tax returns are highly sensitive documents; that is why [federal law provides

that agencies such as the CFTC] cannot get Collins's tax returns directly from the Internal Revenue Service. The self-reporting, self-assessing character of the income tax system would be compromised were they promiscuously disclosed to agencies enforcing regulatory programs unrelated to tax collection itself. The CFTC made no showing that it needed Collins's tax returns. All it legitimately wants to know is whether Collins traded off the exchange and if so, why. It can ask him. If it doubts his answer, it can ask for substantiation. If he refuses to furnish it on the ground that it would compel him to incriminate himself, the CFTC can draw the appropriate inference—for example, that he was trading off the exchange in order to reap tax benefits. No law forbids a regulatory agency to draw the logical inference from a regulated entity's refusing on Fifth Amendment grounds to play ball with the agency. Should the government want to prosecute Collins criminally the Fifth Amendment would be a potential bar—but a very feeble one, in light of our previous discussion.

We are not experts in the investigation of violations of the commodity laws, so we may have overlooked reasons why, despite appearances, the effectiveness of the CFTC's investigation of Collins depends on its having access to his tax returns. The CFTC has not advanced any such reasons. It asked for and obtained the enforcement of the subpoena as a matter of rote, upon its bare representation that the tax returns might contain information germane to the investigation. That is not enough, if an appropriate balance is to be struck between the privacy of income tax returns and the needs of law enforcement. [L]arger interests are at stake than those of the immediate parties—namely the interest, unrepresented by . . . the parties to this case (for the CFTC is not represented by the Department of Justice, which might be assumed to be speaking for the Internal Revenue Service as well), in the effective administration of the federal tax laws.

District court order enforcing subpoena reversed in favor of Collins.

Searches and Seizures Sometimes the evidence necessary to prove a regulatory violation can be obtained only by entering private property such as a home, an office, or a factory. When administrative agencies seek to gather information by such an entry, the Fourth Amendment's prohibition against unreasonable searches and seizures and its warrant requirement come into play. Owners of commercial property, although afforded less Fourth Amendment protection than the owners of private dwellings, do have some legitimate expectations of privacy in their business premises.

Not all agency information-gathering efforts, however, will be considered so intrusive as to amount to a prohibited search and seizure. In *Dow Chemical Co. v. United States* (U.S. Sup. Ct. 1986), for instance, the Environmental Protection Agency's warrantless aerial photography of one of Dow's plants was upheld. Furthermore, in *State of New York v. Burger* (U.S. Sup. Ct. 1987), the Supreme Court upheld the constitutionality of warrantless administrative inspections of the premises of "closely regulated" businesses so long as three criteria are satisfied: (1) there must be a substantial government interest in the regulatory scheme in question, (2) the warrantless inspections must be necessary to further the scheme, and (3) the inspection program must provide a constitutionally adequate substitute for a warrant by giving owners of commercial property adequate notice that their property is subject to inspection and by limiting the discretion of inspecting officers.

Rulemaking Power An agency's rulemaking power derives from its enabling legislation. For example, the FTC Act gives the FTC the power "to make rules and regulations for the purpose of carrying out the provisions of this Act." The Administrative Procedure Act (APA) defines a rule as "an agency statement of general or particular applicability and future effect designed to complement, interpret or prescribe law or policy." All agency rules are compiled and published in the *Code of Federal Regulations*.

Types of Rules Administrative agencies create three types of rules: procedural, interpretive, and legislative. *Procedural rules* specify how the agency will conduct itself. For instance, agencies typically have procedural rules dealing with such matters as the manner in which advance notice of agency rulemaking proceedings will be communicated.

Interpretive rules are designed to advise regulated individuals and entities of the manner in which an agency interprets the statutes it enforces. For example, the FTC has promulgated a rule interpreting the term *consumer product,* as used in the Magnuson-Moss Warranty Act (a statute the FTC has the legal responsibility to enforce). Interpretive rules technically do not have the force of law. Therefore, they are not binding on businesses and the courts. Courts interpreting regulatory statutes often give agency interpretations substantial weight, however, in deference to the agency's familiarity with the statutes it administers and its presumed expertise in the general area being regulated. Business is also likely to pay attention to agency interpretive rules because such rules indicate the circumstances in which an agency is likely to take formal enforcement action.

If consistent with an agency's enabling legislation and the Constitution, and if created in accordance with the procedures dictated by the APA, *legislative rules* have the full force and effect of law. Legislative rules thus are binding on the courts, the public, and the agency. Federal agencies have promulgated very large numbers of legislative rules, many of which address highly specific matters. For example, an FTC legislative rule states that if a party sells a quick-freeze aerosol spray product designed for the frosting of beverage glasses and the product contains an ingredient known as Fluorocarbon 12, the seller must issue a warning (on the product label) that the product should not be inhaled in concentrated form, in view of the risk that such behavior may lead to severe harm or death.

Given the greater relative importance of legislative rules, you should not be surprised to learn that the process by which they are promulgated—unlike the process by which procedural and interpretive rules are created—is highly regulated by the APA and closely scrutinized by the courts. There are three basic types of agency rulemaking: informal, formal, and hybrid.

Informal Rulemaking

Informal rulemaking (or "notice and comment" rulemaking) is the method most commonly employed by administrative agencies that are not forced by their enabling legislation to follow the more stringent procedures of formal rulemaking. The informal rulemaking process commences with the publication of a "Notice of Proposed Rulemaking" in the *Federal Register.* The APA requires that such notices contain a statement of the time and place at which the proceedings will be held; a statement of the nature of the proceedings; a statement of the legal authority for the proceedings (usually the agency's enabling legislation); and either a statement of the terms of the proposed rule or a description of the matters to be addressed by the rule.

Publication of notice must then be followed by a *comment period* during which interested parties may submit written comments detailing their views about the proposed rule. After comments have been received and considered, the agency must publish the regulation in its final form in the *Federal Register.* As a general rule, the rule cannot become effective until at least 30 days after this final publication. The APA, however, recognizes a "good cause" exception to the 30-day waiting period requirement, and to the notice of rulemaking requirement as well, when notice would be impractical, unnecessary, or contrary to the public interest.

Agencies tend to favor the informal rulemaking process because it allows quick and efficient regulatory action. Such quickness and efficiency, however, are purchased at a significant cost—a minimal opportunity for interested parties to participate in the rule-formation process. Giving interested parties the opportunity to be heard may, ultimately, further regulatory goals. For example, the vigorous debate about a proposed rule that a public hearing can provide may contribute to the creation of more effective rules. Also, providing interested parties an adequate opportunity to participate in the rulemaking process lends credibility to that process and the rules it produces, thereby enhancing the chances of voluntary compliance.

Formal Rulemaking

Formal rulemaking is designed to give interested parties a far greater opportunity to make their views heard than that afforded by informal rulemaking. As does informal rulemaking, formal rulemak-

ing begins with publication of a "Notice of Proposed Rulemaking" in the *Federal Register.* Unlike the notice employed to announce informal rulemaking procedures, however, this notice must include notice of a time and place at which a public hearing will be held. Such hearings resemble trials in that the agency must produce evidence justifying the proposed regulation, and interested parties are allowed to present evidence in opposition to it. Both sides may examine each other's exhibits and cross-examine each other's witnesses. At the conclusion of the proceedings, the agency must prepare a formal, written document detailing its findings based on the evidence presented at the hearing.

Although the formal rulemaking process affords interested parties greatly enhanced opportunities to be heard, this greater access is purchased at significant expense and at the risk that some parties will abuse their access rights in an effort to impede the regulatory process. By tireless cross-examination of government witnesses and lengthy presentations of their own, opponents seeking to derail or delay regulation may consume months, or even years, of agency time. A classic example of such behavior would be the Food and Drug Administration's hearings on a proposed rule requiring that the minimum peanut content of peanut butter be set at 90 percent. Industry forces favored an 87 percent minimum and were able to delay regulation for almost 10 years.

Hybrid Rulemaking

Frustrated over the lack of access afforded by informal rulemaking and the potential for paralyzing the regulatory process that is inherent in formal rulemaking, some legislators have attempted to create a rulemaking process that combines some of the elements of informal and formal procedures. Although hybrid rulemaking procedures are insufficiently established and standardized at this point to permit a detailed discussion of them, some general tendencies are evident. Hybrid procedures bear some resemblance to those of formal rulemaking in that both involve some sort of hearing. Unlike formal rulemaking procedures, however, hybrid procedures tend to limit the right of interested parties to cross-examine agency witnesses.

Failure to Promulgate Rules

When Congress has granted an agency rulemaking authority without specifically requiring the promulgation of regulations on a given topic, the agency normally has considerable freedom to decide not to exercise its rulemaking authority in a particular context. Despite the deference usually paid to an agency's decision not to engage in rulemaking, failure-to-regulate decisions may sometimes be subject

The Global Business Environment

With the many administrative agencies that exist at the federal, state, and sometimes even local levels, the United States surely possesses more extensive and expansive administrative law than any other nation. (Whether this is viewed as a good or bad thing may have a great deal to do with one's philosophical and political perspectives.) Many nations that lack the vast administrative agency "infrastructure" present in the United States nevertheless tend to have some regulatory—or at least advisory—bodies charged with addressing certain types of issues that, in the United States, would fall within the regulatory authority of administrative agencies.

For instance, in the European Union (EU), individual countries typically have *ministries* that may help shape governmental policy on issues falling within their respective areas of responsibility. At the EU level, the European commission's primary responsibility is to propose legislation to the Council of Ministers. The commission, however, does have limited rulemaking authority that it may exercise on its own in a manner similar to—though clearly on a lesser scale than—administrative agencies' exercising of rulemaking authority in the United States. In fulfilling its responsibilities, the commission frequently relies on the research assistance, recommendations, and other input provided by subject matter–specific advisory bodies known as the Directorates General.

to judicial review. *Massachusetts v. Environmental Protection Agency*, a 2007 Supreme Court decision that appears later in the chapter, furnishes an illustration.

Adjudicatory Power

Most major federal agencies possess substantial adjudicatory powers. Besides having the authority to investigate alleged behaviors and to produce regulations that have legal effect, agencies often have the power to conduct proceedings to determine whether regulatory or statutory violations have occurred. The administrative adjudication process is at once similar to, but substantially different from, the judicial process you studied in Chapter 2.

The administrative adjudication process normally begins with a complaint filed by the agency. The party charged in the complaint (called the *respondent*) files an answer. Respondents are normally entitled to a hearing before the agency. At this hearing, they may confront and cross-examine agency witnesses and present evidence of their own. Respondents may be represented by legal counsel. No juries are present in administrative adjudications, however. The cases are heard by an agency employee usually called an **administrative law judge (ALJ).** Unlike criminal prosecutions, the burden of proof in administrative proceedings is normally the civil *preponderance of the evidence* standard. Constitutional procedural safeguards such as the exclusionary rule do not protect the respondent.[6]

The agency, in effect, functions as police officer, prosecutor, judge, and jury. The APA attempts to deal with the obvious potential for abuse inherent in this combination in a number of ways. First, the APA attempts to ensure that ALJs are as independent as possible by requiring internal separation between an agency's judges and its investigative and prosecutorial functions. The APA also prohibits ALJs from having private consultations with any party to an agency proceeding and shields them from agency disciplinary action other than for "good cause." Finally, insufficient separation between an agency's adjudication function and its other functions can be contrary to basic due process requirements.

After each party to the proceeding has been heard, the ALJ renders a decision stating her findings of fact and conclusions of law, and imposing whatever penalty she deems appropriate within the parameters established by the agency's enabling legislation (e.g., a fine or a cease-and-desist order). If neither party challenges the ALJ's decision, it becomes final. The losing party, however, may appeal an ALJ's decision, which will then be subjected to a *de novo* **review** by the governing body of the agency (e.g., appeals from FTC ALJ decisions are heard by the five FTC commissioners). *De novo review* means that the agency's governing body may treat the proceedings as if they were occurring for the first time and may ignore the ALJ's findings. Often, however, the agency's governing body will adopt the ALJ's findings. In any event, those findings will be part of the record if a disappointed respondent seeks judicial review of an agency's decision.

Finally, it is important to note that many agency proceedings are settled by a **consent order** before completion

---

[6]The exclusionary rule and the beyond a reasonable doubt standard employed in criminal cases are discussed in Chapter 5. The preponderance of the evidence standard is discussed in Chapter 6.

of the adjudication process. Consent orders are similar to the nolo contendere pleas discussed in Chapter 5. Respondents who sign consent orders do not admit wrongdoing, but they waive all rights to judicial review, agree to accept a specific sanction imposed by the agency, and commonly agree to discontinue the business practice that triggered the agency action.

Controlling Administrative Agencies

By this point in our discussion, we have already encountered certain legal controls on agency action, such as the terms of an agency's enabling legislation, the procedural requirements imposed by the APA, and the basic constraints that the Constitution places on all governmental action. The following sections continue to focus on agency control by examining the various devices through which the three traditional branches of government influence and control the actions of administrative agencies.

Presidential Controls The executive branch has at its disposal a number of tools that may be employed to shape agency action. The most obvious among them is the president's power to appoint and remove agency administrators. This presidential power is obviously more limited in the case of independent agencies than it is where executive agencies are concerned, but the president generally has the power to appoint the heads of independent agencies and demote the prior chairpersons without cause. Skillful use of the new chair's managerial powers, probably the most important of which is the power to influence agency hiring policies, can eventually effect substantial changes in agency policy. Also, significant and sustained policy differences between an independent agency and the executive branch often eventually trigger resignations by agency commissioners, thus providing the president with the opportunity to appoint new members whose philosophies are more congruent with his own.

The executive branch also exercises significant control over agency action through the Office of Management and Budget (OMB). The OMB plays a major role in the creation of the annual executive budget the president presents to Congress. In the process, the OMB reviews, and sometimes modifies, the budgetary requests of executive agencies. In addition, an executive order requires executive agencies to prepare cost-benefit and least-cost analyses for all major proposed rules and to submit this information to the OMB for review prior to seeking

public comments. This order and a subsequent executive order requiring agencies to give the OMB early warning of possible rule changes have made the OMB a powerful player in the rulemaking process.

Finally, the president's power to *veto* legislation concerning administrative agencies represents another point of executive influence over agency operations.

Congressional Controls The legislative branch possesses a number of devices, both formal and informal, by which it may influence agency action. Obvious avenues of congressional control include the Senate's "advice and consent" role in agency appointments, the power to amend an agency's enabling legislation (what Congress has given, Congress can take away), and the power to pass legislation that mandates changes in agency practices or procedures. Examples of the latter include the National Environmental Policy Act (NEPA), which dictated that administrative agencies file *environmental impact statements* for every agency action that could significantly affect the quality of the environment, and the Regulatory Flexibility Act, which ordered changes in agency rulemaking procedures designed to give small businesses improved notice of agency rulemaking activities that may have a substantial impact on them. Congress can also pass *sunset legislation* providing for the automatic expiration of an agency's authority unless Congress expressly extends it by a specified date. Such legislation ensures periodic congressional review of the initial decision to delegate legislative authority to an administrative agency.

Congress enjoys several other less obvious, but no less important, points of influence over agency action. For example, Congress must authorize agency budgetary appropriations. Thus, Congress may limit or deny funding for agency programs with which it disagrees. Also, the Governmental Operations Committees of both houses of Congress exercise significant oversight over agency activities. These committees review agency programs and conduct hearings concerning proposed agency appointments and appropriations. Finally, individual members of Congress may seek to influence agency action through "casework"—informal contacts with an agency on behalf of constituents who are involved with the agency.

Judicial Review As important as the roles of the executive and legislative branches are in controlling agency action, the courts exercise the greatest control over agency behavior, perhaps because they are the branch of government most accessible to members of the public aggrieved by agency action. The APA provides for judicial review of most agency action, which takes place either in one of the U.S. courts of appeals or a U.S. district court, depending on the nature of the agency action at issue. The Supreme Court, if it chooses to grant certiorari, is the court of last resort for review of agency action.

Not all agency actions are subject to judicial review. Moreover, only certain parties may challenge those that are reviewable. An individual or organization seeking judicial review must demonstrate that the agency action being challenged is *reviewable,* that the challenging party has *standing to sue,* that *necessary administrative remedies have been exhausted,* and that the dispute is *ripe for judicial review.* These requirements are discussed below.

Reviewability Only reviewable agency actions may be challenged by dissatisfied individuals and organizations. Normally, it is not difficult for aggrieved parties to show that the agency action is reviewable because the APA creates a strong presumption in favor of reviewability. This presumption may be overcome only by a showing that "statutes preclude review" or that the decision in question is "committed to agency discretion by law." These limitations on reviewability come from Congress's power to dictate the jurisdiction of the federal courts and from judicial deference to the proper functions of the other branches of government (e.g., a decision relating to matters of foreign policy is likely to be seen as outside the proper province of the judiciary).

Standing to Sue Once reviewability of an agency action has been established, the challenging party must demonstrate that he, she, or it has standing to sue. This means that the individual or organization seeking judicial review is "an aggrieved party" whose interests have been substantially affected by the agency action. Initially, courts took a relatively restrictive view of this basic requirement, requiring plaintiffs to show harm to a legally protected interest. More recently, however, courts have liberalized the standing requirement somewhat, requiring plaintiffs to demonstrate that they have suffered an "injury" to an interest that lies within the "zone of interests" protected by the statute or constitutional provision that serves as the basis of their challenge. Demonstrating an economic loss remains the surest way to satisfy the "injury" requirement, but emotional, aesthetic, and environmental injuries have been found sufficient on occasion.

Massachusetts v. Environmental Protection Agency, which follows, addresses issues presented by the standing requirement. The case also furnishes an illustration of judicial review of an agency decision not to take regulatory action.

Massachusetts v. Environmental Protection Agency   549 U.S. 497 (2007)

The federal Clean Air Act was enacted in 1970 and was later amended on more than one occasion. Section 202(a)(1) of the Act, 42 U.S.C. § 7521(a)(1), provides:

> The [Environmental Protection Agency (EPA)] Administrator shall by regulation prescribe (and from time to time revise) in accordance with the provisions of this section, standards applicable to the emission of any air pollutant from any class or classes of new motor vehicles or new motor vehicle engines, which in his judgment cause, or contribute to, air pollution which may reasonably be anticipated to endanger public health or welfare. . . .

The Act defines "air pollutant" to include "any air pollution agent or combination of such agents, including any physical, chemical, biological, radioactive . . . substance or matter which is emitted into or otherwise enters the ambient air."
§ 7602(g).

In 1999, a group of 19 private organizations filed a rulemaking petition asking EPA to regulate "greenhouse gas emissions from new motor vehicles under § 202 of the Clean Air Act." The petition alleged that 1998 was the "warmest year on record"; that carbon dioxide, methane, nitrous oxide, and hydrofluorocarbons are "heat trapping greenhouse gases"; that greenhouse gas emissions have significantly accelerated climate change; and that a 1995 report of the Intergovernmental Panel on Climate Change (IPCC), a multinational scientific body organized under the auspices of the United Nations, warned that "carbon dioxide remains the most important contributor to [man-made] forcing of climate change." The petition further alleged that climate change will have serious adverse effects on human health and the environment. In addition, the petition noted that in a 1998 legal opinion, EPA's general counsel concluded that "CO_2 emissions are within the scope of EPA's authority to regulate," even though EPA had so far declined to exercise that authority.

After requesting public comment on the issues raised in the petition, EPA received more than 50,000 comments. Before the close of the comment period, the White House requested that the National Research Council provide "assistance in identifying the areas in the science of climate change where there are the greatest certainties and uncertainties." The result was a 2001 report titled Climate Change: An Analysis of Some Key Questions (NRC Report), which, drawing heavily on the 1995 IPCC report, concluded that "[g]reenhouse gases are accumulating in Earth's atmosphere as a result of human activities, causing surface air temperatures and subsurface ocean temperatures to rise."

In 2003, EPA denied the rulemaking petition. The agency gave two reasons: (1) that contrary to the opinion of EPA's by-then former general counsel, the Clean Air Act did not authorize EPA to issue mandatory regulations to address global climate change; and (2) that even if the agency had the authority to set greenhouse gas emission standards, it would be unwise to do so. The organizations that had filed the rulemaking petition, various states (including Massachusetts), and various local governments sought review of EPA's order in the United States Court of Appeals for the District of Columbia Circuit. Two of the three judges on the D.C. Circuit panel agreed that the EPA administrator acted properly in denying the petition for rulemaking. The court therefore denied the petition for review. Of the two judges who concluded that denial was appropriate, one took the position that none of the parties seeking review had legal standing to challenge EPA's order. The other avoided making a clear statement on the standing issue, but reasoned that the EPA administrator had appropriately taken into account not only scientific evidence but also policy considerations. The U.S. Supreme Court granted the petitioners' certiorari request.

Stevens, Justice

A well-documented rise in global temperatures has coincided with a significant increase in the concentration of carbon dioxide in the atmosphere. Respected scientists believe the two trends are related. For when carbon dioxide is released into the atmosphere, it acts like the ceiling of a greenhouse, trapping solar energy and retarding the escape of reflected heat. It is therefore a species—the most important species—of a "greenhouse gas."

Calling global warming "the most pressing environmental challenge of our time," [the petitioners allege] that EPA has abdicated its responsibility under the Clean Air Act to regulate the emissions of four greenhouse gases, including carbon dioxide. Petitioners have asked us to answer two questions concerning the meaning of § 202(a)(1) of the Act: whether EPA has the statutory authority to regulate greenhouse gas emissions from new motor vehicles; and if so, whether its stated reasons for refusing to do so are consistent with the statute. In response, EPA [has] correctly argued that we may not address those two questions unless at least one petitioner has standing to invoke our jurisdiction under Article III of the Constitution.

Standing

Article III of the Constitution limits federal-court jurisdiction to "Cases" and "Controversies." Those two words confine "the business of federal courts to questions presented in an adversary context and in a form historically viewed as capable of resolution through the judicial process." [Case citation omitted.]

The parties' dispute turns on the proper construction of a congressional statute, a question eminently suitable to resolution in federal court. Congress has moreover authorized this type of challenge to EPA action. *See* 42 U.S.C. § 7607(b)(l). That authorization is of critical importance to the standing inquiry: "Congress has the power to define injuries and articulate chains of causation that will give rise to a case or controversy where none existed before." *Lujan v. Defenders of Wildlife,* 504 U.S. 555, 580 (1992) (Kennedy, J., concurring in part and concurring in judgment). "In exercising this power, however, Congress must at the very least identify the injury it seeks to vindicate and relate the injury to the class of persons entitled to bring suit." *Id.* We will not, therefore, "entertain citizen suits to vindicate the public's non-concrete interest in the proper administration of the laws." *Id.* at 581.

EPA maintains that because greenhouse gas emissions inflict widespread harm, the doctrine of standing presents an insuperable jurisdictional obstacle. We do not agree. At bottom, "the gist of the question of standing" is whether petitioners have "such a personal stake in the outcome of the controversy as to assure that concrete adverseness which sharpens the presentation of issues upon which the court so largely depends for illumination." *Baker v. Corr,* 369 U.S. 186, 204 (1962).

To ensure the proper adversarial presentation, *Lujan* holds that a litigant must demonstrate that it has suffered a concrete and particularized injury that is either actual or imminent, that the injury is fairly traceable to the defendant, and that it is likely that a favorable decision will redress that injury. *See Lujan,* 504 U.S. at 560–561. However, a litigant to whom Congress has "accorded a procedural right to protect his concrete interests,"—here, the right to challenge agency action unlawfully withheld—"can assert that right without meeting all the normal standards for redressability and immediacy." *Id.* at 572. When a litigant is vested with a procedural right, that litigant has standing if there is some possibility that the requested relief will prompt the injury-causing party to reconsider the decision that allegedly harmed the litigant. *Id.*

Only one of the petitioners needs to have standing to permit us to consider the petition for review. *See Rumsfeld v. Forum for Academic and Institutional Rights, Inc.,* 547 U.S. 47, 52 (2006). We stress here . . . the special position and interest of Massachusetts. It is of considerable relevance that the party seeking review here is a sovereign state and not, as it was in *Lujan,* a private individual. Well before the creation of the modern administrative state, we recognized that states are not normal litigants for the purposes of invoking federal jurisdiction. As Justice Holmes explained in *Georgia v. Tennessee Copper Co.,* 206 U.S. 230, 237 (1907), a case in which Georgia sought to protect its citizens from air pollution originating outside its borders:

> The case has been argued largely as if it were one between two private parties; but it is not. The very elements that would be relied upon in a suit between fellow-citizens as a ground for equitable relief are wanting here. The state owns very little of the territory alleged to be affected, and the damage to it capable of estimate in money, possibly, at least, is small. This is a suit by a state for an injury to it in its capacity of *quasi*-sovereign. In that capacity the state has an interest independent of and behind the titles of its citizens, in all the earth and air within its domain. It has the last word as to whether its mountains shall be stripped of their forests and its inhabitants shall breathe pure air.

Just as Georgia's "independent interest . . . in all the earth and air within its domain" supported federal jurisdiction a century ago, so too does Massachusetts' well-founded desire to preserve its sovereign territory today. That Massachusetts does in fact own a great deal of the "territory alleged to be affected" only reinforces the conclusion that its stake in the outcome of this case is sufficiently concrete to warrant the exercise of federal judicial power.

When a state enters the Union, it surrenders certain sovereign prerogatives. Massachusetts cannot invade Rhode Island to force reductions in greenhouse gas emissions, it cannot negotiate an emissions treaty with China or India, and in some circumstances the exercise of its police powers to reduce in-state motor-vehicle emissions might well be preempted. These sovereign prerogatives are now lodged in the federal government, and Congress has ordered EPA to protect Massachusetts (among others) by prescribing standards applicable to the "emission of any air pollutant from any class or classes of new motor vehicle engines, which in [the Administrator's] judgment cause, or contribute to, air pollution which may reasonably be anticipated to endanger public health or welfare." 42 U.S.C. § 7521(a)(1). Congress has moreover recognized a concomitant procedural right to challenge the rejection of its rulemaking petition as arbitrary and capricious. § 7607(b)(l). Given that procedural right and Massachusetts' stake in protecting its

quasi-sovereign interests, [Massachusetts] is entitled to special solicitude in our standing analysis.

With that in mind, it is clear that petitioners' submissions as they pertain to Massachusetts have satisfied the most demanding standards of the adversarial process. EPA's steadfast refusal to regulate greenhouse gas emissions presents a risk of harm to Massachusetts that is both "actual" and "imminent." *Lujan,* 504 U.S. at 560. There is, moreover, a "substantial likelihood that the judicial relief requested" will prompt EPA to take steps to reduce that risk. *Duke Power Co. v. Carolina Environmental Study Group, Inc.,* 438 U.S. 59, 79 (1978).

The harms associated with climate change are serious and well recognized. Indeed, the NRC Report itself—which EPA [has called] an "objective and independent assessment of the relevant science,"—identifies a number of environmental changes that have already inflicted significant harms, including "the global retreat of mountain glaciers, reduction in snow-cover extent, the earlier spring melting of rivers and lakes, [and] the accelerated rate of rise of sea levels during the 20th century relative to the past few thousand years. . . ." Petitioners allege that this only hints at the environmental damage yet to come. According to the [affidavit of] climate scientist Michael MacCracken, "qualified scientific experts involved in climate change research" have reached a "strong consensus" that global warming threatens (among other things) a precipitate rise in sea levels by the end of the century, "severe and irreversible changes to natural ecosystems," a "significant reduction in water storage in winter snowpack in mountainous regions with direct and important economic consequences," and an increase in the spread of disease. He also observes that rising ocean temperatures may contribute to the ferocity of hurricanes.

That these climate-change risks are widely shared does not minimize Massachusetts' interest in the outcome of this litigation. According to petitioners' unchallenged affidavits, global sea levels rose somewhere between 10 and 20 centimeters over the 20th century as a result of global warming. These rising seas have already begun to swallow Massachusetts' coastal land. Because [Massachusetts] owns a substantial portion of the state's coastal property, it has alleged a particularized injury in its capacity as a landowner. The severity of that injury will only increase over the course of the next century: If sea levels continue to rise as predicted, one Massachusetts official believes that a significant fraction of coastal property will be "either permanently lost through inundation or temporarily lost through periodic storm surge and flooding events." Remediation costs alone, petitioners allege, could run well into the hundreds of millions of dollars.

EPA does not dispute the existence of a causal connection between man-made greenhouse gas emissions and global warming. At a minimum, therefore, EPA's refusal to regulate such emissions "contributes" to Massachusetts' injuries. EPA nevertheless maintains that its decision not to regulate greenhouse gas emissions from new motor vehicles contributes so insignificantly to petitioners' injuries that the agency cannot be haled into federal court to answer for them. But EPA overstates its case. Its argument rests on the erroneous assumption that a small incremental step, because it is incremental, can never be attacked in a federal judicial forum. Yet . . . [a]gencies, like legislatures, do not generally resolve massive problems in one fell regulatory swoop. They instead whittle away at them over time, refining their preferred approach as circumstances change and as they develop a more-nuanced understanding of how best to proceed. That a first step might be tentative does not by itself support the notion that federal courts lack jurisdiction to determine whether that step conforms to law.

And reducing domestic automobile emissions is hardly a tentative step. Even leaving aside the other greenhouse gases, the United States transportation sector emits an enormous quantity of carbon dioxide into the atmosphere—according to the MacCracken affidavit, more than 1.7 billion metric tons in 1999 alone. That accounts for more than 6% of worldwide carbon dioxide emissions. To put this in perspective: Considering just emissions from the transportation sector, which represent less than one-third of this country's total carbon dioxide emissions, the United States would still rank as the third-largest emitter of carbon dioxide in the world, outpaced only by the European Union and China. Judged by any standard, U.S. motor-vehicle emissions make a meaningful contribution to greenhouse gas concentrations and hence, according to petitioners, to global warming. While it may be true that regulating motor-vehicle emissions will not by itself *reverse* global warming, it by no means follows that we lack jurisdiction to decide whether EPA has a duty to take steps to *slow* or *reduce* it.

In sum—at least according to petitioners' uncontested affidavits—the rise in sea levels associated with global warming has already harmed and will continue to harm Massachusetts. The risk of catastrophic harm, though remote, is nevertheless real. That risk would be reduced to some extent if petitioners received the relief they seek. We therefore hold that petitioners have standing to challenge the EPA's denial of their rulemaking petition.

The Merits

The scope of our review of the merits of the statutory issues is narrow. [A]n agency has broad discretion to choose how best to marshal its limited resources and personnel to carry out its delegated responsibilities. That discretion is at its height when the agency decides not to bring an enforcement action. Therefore, in *Heckler v. Chaney,* 470 U.S. 821, 105 S. Ct. 1649, 84 L. Ed. 2d 714 (1985), we held that an agency's refusal to initiate enforcement proceedings is not ordinarily subject to judicial review.

There are key differences[, however,] between a denial of a petition for rulemaking and an agency's decision not to initiate an enforcement action. In contrast to non-enforcement decisions, agency refusals to initiate rulemaking "are less frequent, more apt to involve legal as opposed to factual analysis, and subject to special formalities, including a public explanation." [Case citation omitted.] They moreover arise out of denials of petitions for rulemaking which (at least in the circumstances here) the affected party had an undoubted procedural right to file in the first instance. Refusals to promulgate rules are thus susceptible to judicial review, though such review is "extremely limited" and "highly deferential." [Case citation omitted.]

EPA concluded in its denial of the petition for rulemaking that it lacked authority under 42 U.S.C. § 7521(a)(l) to regulate new vehicle emissions because[, in its view,] carbon dioxide is not an "air pollutant" as that term is defined in § 7602. In the alternative, it concluded that even if it possessed authority, it would decline to do so because regulation would conflict with other administration priorities.

On the merits, the first question is whether § 202(a)(1) of the Clean Air Act authorizes EPA to regulate greenhouse gas emissions from new motor vehicles in the event that it forms a "judgment" that such emissions contribute to climate change. We have little trouble concluding that it does. In relevant part, § 202(a)(l) provides that EPA "shall by regulation prescribe . . . standards applicable to the emission of any air pollutant from any class or classes of new motor vehicles or new motor vehicle engines, which in [the Administrator's] judgment cause, or contribute to, air pollution which may reasonably be anticipated to endanger public health or welfare." 42 U.S.C. § 7521(a)(l). Because EPA believes that Congress did not intend it to regulate substances that contribute to climate change, the agency maintains that carbon dioxide is not an "air pollutant" within the meaning of the provision.

The statutory text forecloses EPA's reading. The Clean Air Act's sweeping definition of "air pollutant" includes "*any* air pollution agent or combination of such agents, including *any* physical, chemical . . . substance or matter which is emitted into or otherwise enters the ambient air. . . ." § 7602(g) (emphasis added). On its face, the definition embraces all airborne compounds of whatever stripe, and underscores that intent through the repeated use of the word "any." Carbon dioxide, methane, nitrous oxide, and hydrofluorocarbons are without a doubt "physical [and] chemical . . . substance[s] which [are] emitted into . . . the ambient air." The statute is unambiguous.

Rather than relying on statutory text, EPA invokes post-enactment congressional actions and deliberations it views as tantamount to a congressional command to refrain from regulating greenhouse gas emissions. Even if such post-enactment legislative history could shed light on the meaning of an otherwise-unambiguous statute, EPA never identifies any action remotely suggesting that Congress meant to curtail its power to treat greenhouse gases as air pollutants. That subsequent Congresses have eschewed enacting binding emissions limitations to combat global warming tells us nothing about what Congress meant when it amended § 202(a)(l) in 1970 and 1977. And unlike EPA, we have no difficulty reconciling Congress' various efforts to promote interagency collaboration and research to better understand climate change with the agency's pre-existing mandate to regulate "any air pollutant" that may endanger the public welfare. Collaboration and research do not conflict with any thoughtful regulatory effort; they complement it.

EPA's reliance on *FDA v. Brown & Williamson Tobacco Corp.*, 529 U.S. 120 (2000), is similarly misplaced. In holding that tobacco products are not "drugs" or "devices" subject to Food and Drug Administration (FDA) regulation pursuant to the Food, Drug and Cosmetic Act (FDCA), we found critical at least two considerations that have no counterpart in this case. First, we thought it unlikely that Congress meant to ban tobacco products, which the FDCA would have required had such products been classified as "drugs" or "devices." Here, in contrast, EPA jurisdiction would lead to no such extreme measures. EPA would only *regulate* emissions, and even then, it would have to delay any action "to permit the development and application of the requisite technology, giving appropriate consideration to the cost of compliance." § 7521(a)(2).

Second, in *Brown & Williamson* we pointed to an unbroken series of congressional enactments that made sense only if adopted "against the backdrop of the FDA's consistent and repeated statements that it lacked authority under the FDCA to regulate tobacco." We can point to no such enactments here: EPA has not identified any congressional action that conflicts in any way with the regulation of greenhouse gases from new motor vehicles. Even if it had, Congress could not have acted against a regulatory "backdrop" of disclaimers of regulatory authority. Prior to the order that provoked this litigation, EPA had never disavowed the authority to regulate greenhouse gases, and in 1998 it in fact affirmed that it *had* such authority. There is no reason, much less a compelling reason, to accept EPA's invitation to read ambiguity into a clear statute.

EPA finally argues that it cannot regulate carbon dioxide emissions from motor vehicles because doing so would require it to tighten mileage standards, a job (according to EPA) that Congress has assigned to the Department of Transportation (DOT). But that DOT sets mileage standards in no way licenses EPA to shirk its environmental responsibilities. EPA has been charged with protecting the public's "health" and "welfare," 42

U.S.C. § 7521(a)(1), a statutory obligation wholly independent of DOT's mandate to promote energy efficiency.

The alternative basis for EPA's decision—that even if it does have statutory authority to regulate greenhouse gases, it would be unwise to do so at this time—rests on reasoning divorced from the statutory text. While the statute does condition the exercise of EPA's authority on its formation of a "judgment," 42 U.S.C. § 7521(a)(l), that judgment must relate to whether an air pollutant "cause[s], or contribute[s] to, air pollution which may reasonably be anticipated to endanger public health or welfare." Put another way, the use of the word "judgment" is not a roving license to ignore the statutory text. It is but a direction to exercise discretion within defined statutory limits.

If EPA makes a finding of endangerment, the Clean Air Act requires the agency to regulate emissions of the deleterious pollutant from new motor vehicles. *Id.* (stating that "[EPA] shall by regulation prescribe . . . standards applicable to the emission of any air pollutant from any class of new motor vehicles"). EPA no doubt has significant latitude as to the manner, timing, content, and coordination of its regulations with those of other agencies. But once EPA has responded to a petition for rulemaking, its reasons for action or inaction must conform to the authorizing statute. Under the clear terms of the Clean Air Act, EPA can avoid taking further action only if it determines that greenhouse gases do not contribute to climate change or if it provides some reasonable explanation as to why it cannot or will not exercise its discretion to determine whether they do. To the extent that this constrains agency discretion to pursue other priorities of the Administrator or the President, this is the congressional design.

EPA has refused to comply with this clear statutory command. Instead, it has offered a laundry list of reasons not to regulate. For example, EPA said that a number of voluntary executive branch programs already provide an effective response to the threat of global warming, that regulating greenhouse gases might impair the President's ability to negotiate with key developing nations to reduce emissions, and that curtailing motor-vehicle emissions would reflect an inefficient, piecemeal approach to address the climate change issue. [T]hese policy judgments . . . have nothing to do with whether greenhouse gas emissions contribute to climate change. Still less do they amount to a reasoned justification for declining to form a scientific judgment. In particular, while the President has broad authority in foreign affairs, that authority does not extend to the refusal to execute domestic laws.

Nor can EPA avoid its statutory obligation by noting the uncertainty surrounding various features of climate change and concluding that it would therefore be better not to regulate at this time. If the scientific uncertainty is so profound that it precludes EPA from making a reasoned judgment as to whether greenhouse gases contribute to global warming, EPA must say so. That EPA would prefer not to regulate greenhouse gases because of some residual uncertainty . . . is irrelevant. The statutory question is whether sufficient information exists to make an endangerment finding.

In short, EPA has offered no reasoned explanation for its refusal to decide whether greenhouse gases cause or contribute to climate change. Its action was therefore "arbitrary, capricious, . . . or otherwise not in accordance with law." 42 U.S.C. § 7607(d)(9)(A). We need not and do not reach the question whether on remand EPA must make an endangerment finding, or whether policy concerns can inform EPA's actions in the event that it makes such a finding. We hold only that EPA must ground its reasons for action or inaction in the statute.

Court of Appeals decision reversed, and case remanded for further proceedings.

Exhaustion and Ripeness Once standing has been established, two further obstacles—exhaustion and ripeness—confront the party challenging an agency action. Courts do not want to allow regulated parties to short-circuit the regulatory process. They also want to give agencies the chance to correct their own mistakes and to develop fully their positions in disputed matters. Accordingly, they normally insist that aggrieved parties *exhaust necessary administrative remedies* before they will grant judicial review.[7] The requirement that a dispute be *ripe* for judicial review is a general requirement emanating from the Constitution's insistence that only "cases or controversies" are judicially resolvable. In determining ripeness, the courts weigh the hardship to the parties of withholding judicial review against the degree of refinement of the issues still possible.

Legal Bases for Challenging Agency Actions
Assuming that the above prerequisites to judicial review are met, there are various legal theories on which agency action may be attacked. It may be alleged that the agency's action was *ultra vires* (exceeded its authority as granted by its enabling legislation). For example, in a 2000 case, the Supreme Court struck down the Food and Drug Administration's 1996 regulations dealing with cigarettes and smokeless tobacco. The Court held that in the Food, Drug, and Cosmetic Act, Congress neither gave, nor intended to give, the FDA authority to regulate tobacco products.[8] (When this book went to press in 2008, however, Congress seemed poised to grant such authority to the FDA. See the discussion in this chapter's opening problem.) In a 2005 decision, *American Library Association v. Federal Communications Commission,* the U.S. Court of Appeals for the District of Columbia Circuit held that the Federal Communications Commission (FCC) exceeded the scope of its regulatory authority when it promulgated a regulation requiring makers of televisions and computers to install "broadcast flag" technology in order to impede consumers' ability to copy digitally distributed programs. Using unusually strong language as it invalidated the regulation, the court stressed that the FCC's assertion of authority was "strained and implausible" and that "nothing in [the relevant federal] statute, its legislative history, the applicable case law, or agency practice indicat[es] that Congress meant to provide the sweeping authority the FCC now claims."

Alternatively, it may be alleged that the agency *substantially deviated from procedural requirements* contained in the APA or in the agency's enabling legislation. Agency action may also be challenged as *unconstitutional* or as the product of an *erroneous interpretation of statutes.* Finally, agency action may be overturned if it is *unsubstantiated by the facts* before the agency when it acted.

Standards of Review The degree of scrutiny that courts will apply to agency action depends on the nature of issues in dispute and the type of agency proceedings that produced the challenged action. Courts are least likely to defer to agency action when *questions of law* are at issue. Although courts afford substantial consideration to an agency's interpretations of the statutes it enforces, the courts are still the ultimate arbiters of the meaning of statutes and constitutional provisions.

When *questions of fact or policy* are at issue, courts are more likely to defer to the agency because it presumably has superior expertise and because the agency fact finders who heard and viewed the evidence were better situated to judge its merit. When agency factual judgments

---

[7]Necessary administrative remedies are those a statute or regulation establishes as mandatory steps to be completed before judicial review can be sought.

[8]*Food and Drug Administration v. Brown & Williamson Tobacco Corp.,* 529 U.S. 120 (U.S. Sup. Ct. 2000).

CYBERLAW IN ACTION

Does a federal statute, the Telecommunications Act of 1996, require cable companies to allow other firms to use their systems in order to offer high-speed Internet access services? In answering that question "no" by enacting an agency regulation to that effect, did the Federal Communications Commission improperly interpret the federal statute? The U.S. Supreme Court took up that issue and related questions in *National Cable and Telecommunications Association v. Brand X Internet Services,* 545 U.S. 967 (2005).

The Telecommunications Act of 1996 regulates providers of telecommunications services in various ways. One provision of the statute labels firms that provide "telecommunications service" as common carriers and requires them to sell other companies access to their networks (including their basic telephone service networks and their DSL Internet access lines) on a nondiscriminatory basis. Cable Internet firms furnish broadband service, which provides faster Internet access than the dial-up Internet service offered by various providers. Dial-up service providers and consumer groups, hoping to increase competition in Internet access services—particularly concerning the faster broadband variety—began asserting that cable Internet firms were subject to the Telecommunications Act provision that required the provider of a "telecommunications service" to sell other interested parties access to that provider's network. The cable Internet firms, not wanting to be forced to open up their networks to other providers, maintained that they were not subject to the Telecommunications Act requirement.

The argument that cable Internet service is a "telecommunications service" for purposes of the federal statute rested on the notion that cable Internet service consists of two parts. One part—simple data communication—is supposedly a telecommunications service. The other part, which involves the providing of more elaborate information services, is not a telecommunications service. Dial-up firms and consumer groups argued that the telecommunications service aspect of cable Internet service fell within the Telecommunication Act's

section requiring the provider of a telecommunications service to allow, for a fee and on a nondiscriminatory basis, access to its networks.

In 2002, the Federal Communications Commission (FCC) rejected the position of the dial-up firms and consumer groups. The FCC did so by promulgating a regulation that interpreted the Telecommunications Act and its provision-of-access-to-networks provision as inapplicable to cable Internet service providers. In the FCC's view, as expressed in the regulation, cable Internet service providers were information service providers, not "telecommunications service" providers for purposes of the statute. Brand X Internet Services, a dial-up provider that believed it was entitled (for a fee) to obtain access to a cable Internet service provider's broadband network, filed suit alleging that the FCC's regulation was an invalid and incorrect interpretation of the Telecommunications Act. The U.S. Court of Appeals for the Ninth Circuit agreed with Brand X and held that the FCC regulation was invalid.

The Supreme Court, however, reversed the Ninth Circuit's decision. In an opinion authored by Justice Thomas, a six-justice majority stated that the Telecommunications Act provision at issue in the case was ambiguous and that when an appropriate administrative agency issues a reasonable interpretation of an ambiguous statute, courts must defer to the agency's interpretation. The majority noted that such deference is appropriate even if the Court thinks the agency's interpretation, though reasonable, is not necessarily the best interpretation. According to the Court, the FCC's 2002 regulation interpreting the Telecommunications Act qualified as a reasonable interpretation, so the Court deferred to it. In dissent, Justice Scalia called the FCC's interpretation of the statute implausible and contrary to the wishes of Congress. Parties disappointed by the Court's decision expressed concerns that competition among providers of broadband access would suffer, that concentration in the providing of such access would be restricted to a relatively small number of firms, and that such interests as enhanced consumer choice and low-cost Internet access were likely to be thwarted.

---

are at stake, the APA provides for three standards of review, the most rigorous of which is *de novo* review.

When conducting a *de novo* review, courts make an independent finding of the facts after conducting a new hearing. Efficiency considerations plainly favor limited judicial review of the facts. Accordingly, *de novo* review is employed only when required by statute, when inadequate fact-finding proceedings were used in an agency adjudicatory proceeding, or when new factual issues that

were not before the agency are raised in a proceeding to enforce a nonadjudicatory agency action.

When courts review formal agency adjudications or formal rulemaking, the APA calls for the application of a **substantial evidence** test. Only agency findings that are "unsupported by substantial evidence" will be overturned. In conducting substantial evidence reviews, courts look at the reasonableness of an agency's actions in relation to the facts before it rather than conducting an independent fact-finding hearing. The substantial evidence test also tends to be employed in hybrid rulemaking cases.

The judicial standard of review used in cases involving informal agency adjudications or rulemaking is the **arbitrary and capricious** test. (For an example of an application of this test, see the *Massachusetts v. EPA* case, which appears earlier in the chapter.) This is the least rigorous standard of judicial review, in view of the great degree of deference it accords agency decisions. In deciding whether an agency's action was arbitrary and capricious, a reviewing court should not substitute its judgment for that of the agency. Instead, it should ask whether there was an adequate factual basis for the agency's action, and should sustain actions that do not amount to a "clear error of judgment." Although the substantial evidence and arbitrary and capricious tests are separate and distinct in theory, the distinctions often tend to blur in actual practice.

Information Controls

Over roughly the last four decades, Congress has enacted three major statutes aimed at controlling administrative agencies through the regulation of information. Each of these statutes represents a compromise between competing social interests of significant importance. On one hand, we have a strong democratic preference for public disclosure of governmental operations, believing that "government in the dark" is less likely to be consistent with the public interest than is "government in the sunshine." On the other hand, we recognize that some sensitive governmental activities must be shielded from the scrutiny of unfriendly parties, and that disclosure of some information may unjustifiably invade personal privacy, hinder government law enforcement efforts, or provide the competitors of a company about which information is being disclosed with proprietary information that could be used unfairly to the competitors' advantage.

Freedom of Information Act

The *Freedom of Information Act* (FOIA) has existed for nearly 35 years. Congress enacted it to enable private citizens to obtain access to documents in the government's possession. Agencies must normally respond to public requests for documents within 10 days after such a request has been received. An agency bears the burden of justifying a denial of any FOIA request. Denials are appealable to an appropriate federal district court. Successful plaintiffs may recover their costs and attorney's fees.

Not all government-held documents are obtainable under the FOIA, however. The FOIA exempts from disclosure documents that:

1. Must be kept secret in the interest of national security.
2. Concern an agency's internal personnel practices.
3. Are specifically exempted from disclosure by statute.
4. Contain trade secrets or other confidential or privileged commercial or financial information.
5. Are interagency or intra-agency memos or letters that would not be subject to discovery in litigation.
6. Appear in individual personnel or medical files, or in similar files if disclosure would constitute a clearly unwarranted invasion of personal privacy.
7. Would threaten the integrity of a law enforcement agency's investigations or jeopardize an individual's right to a fair trial.
8. Relate to the supervision or regulation of financial institutions.
9. Contain geological or geophysical data.

Frequent users of the FOIA include the media, industry trade associations, public interest groups, and companies seeking to obtain useful information about their competitors. The *Klamath Water Users* case, which follows shortly, deals with the fifth exemption listed above. It is important to note that although the FOIA allows agencies to refuse to disclose exempted documents, it does not impose on them the affirmative duty to do so. The Supreme Court has held that individuals cannot compel an agency to deny an FOIA request for allegedly exempt documents that contain sensitive information about them.

FOIA compliance has recently been the focus of considerable controversy on three points. First, budgetary cutbacks have combined with growing numbers of requests for information to produce agency delays as long as two years in responding to information requests. Courts tend to tolerate agency delays if the agency can show that it made a "due diligence" effort to respond. Second, the dramatic increase in computerized information storage that has occurred since the passage of the FOIA has created problems not specifically contemplated by the statute, which focuses on information stored in documentary form. Do interested parties have the same rights of access to data stored in agency computers that they have to government documents? May the government destroy electronic mail messages, or must it save them? Future legislative or judicial action may be necessary for definitive resolution of such questions.

Third, some members of Congress, media organizations, and public interest groups have criticized the federal government for what they see as excessive and unreasonable

reliance on FOIA exemptions in order to keep documents under wraps. Legislation designed to deal with this supposed problem seems likely in the coming years.

Department of the Interior v. Klamath Water Users Protective Association
532 U.S. 1 (U.S. Sup. Ct. 2001)

The Department of the Interior's Bureau of Reclamation (Reclamation) administers the Klamath Irrigation Project, which uses water from the Klamath River Basin to irrigate parts of Oregon and California. After the Department began developing the Klamath Project Operation Plan (Plan) to provide water allocations among competing uses and users, the Department asked the Klamath and other Indian Tribes (Basin Tribes or Tribes) to consult with Reclamation on the matter. A memorandum of understanding between those parties called for assessment, in consultation with the Tribes, of the impacts of the Plan on tribal trust resources. During roughly the same period, the Department's Bureau of Indian Affairs (Bureau) filed claims on behalf of the Klamath Tribe in an Oregon state court proceeding intended to allocate water rights. Because the Bureau is responsible for administering land and water held in trust for Indian tribes, it consulted with the Klamath Tribe. The Bureau and the Klamath Tribe then exchanged written memos on the appropriate scope of the claims ultimately submitted by the government for the benefit of the Tribe.

The Klamath Water Users Protective Association (Water Users Association) is a nonprofit organization, most of whose members receive water from the Klamath Irrigation Project. Because of the scarcity of water, most Water Users Association members have interests adverse to the tribal interests. The Water Users Association filed a series of requests with the Bureau under the Freedom of Information Act (FOIA), seeking access to communications between the Bureau and the Basin Tribes. In response, the Bureau turned over several documents but withheld others on the basis of FOIA Exemption 5. The Water Users Association then sued the Bureau and the Department under FOIA to compel release of the documents. A federal district court granted the government summary judgment but the U.S. Court of Appeals for the Ninth Circuit reversed, holding that Exemption 5 did not apply. The U.S. Supreme Court granted the government's petition for certiorari.

Souter, Justice

Upon request, FOIA mandates disclosure of records held by a federal agency, unless the documents fall within enumerated exemptions. "[T]hese limited exemptions do not obscure the basic policy that disclosure, not secrecy, is the dominant objective [of FOIA]." *Department of Air Force v. Rose* (U.S. Sup. Ct. 1976). "Consistent with [FOIA's] goal of broad disclosure, these exemptions have been consistently given a narrow compass." *Department of Justice v. Tax Analysts* (U.S. Sup. Ct. 1989).

Exemption 5 protects from disclosure "inter-agency or intra-agency memorandums or letters which would not be available by law to a party other than an agency in litigation with the agency." To qualify, a document must thus satisfy two conditions: its source must be a government agency, and it must fall within the ambit of a privilege against discovery under judicial standards that would govern litigation against the agency that holds it.

Our prior cases on Exemption 5 have addressed the second condition, incorporating civil discovery privileges. So far as they might matter here, those privileges include the privilege for attorney work product and what is sometimes called the "deliberative process" privilege. Work product protects "mental processes of the attorney" [citation omitted], while deliberative

process covers "documents reflecting advisory opinions, recommendations, and deliberations comprising part of a process by which governmental decisions and policies are formulated" [citation omitted]. The deliberative process privilege rests on the obvious realization that officials will not communicate candidly among themselves if each remark is a potential item of discovery and front page news. [Its] object is to enhance the quality of agency decisions by protecting open and frank discussion among those who make them within the government.

The point is not to protect government secrecy pure and simple, however, and the first condition of Exemption 5 is no less important than the second; the communication must be "inter-agency or intra-agency." Statutory definitions underscore the apparent plainness of this text. With exceptions not relevant here, "agency" means "each authority of the Government of the United States," and "includes any executive department, military department, Government corporation, Government controlled corporation, or other establishment in the executive branch of the Government . . . , or any independent regulatory agency."

Although neither the terms of the exemption nor the statutory definitions say anything about communications with outsiders, some Courts of Appeals have held that in some circumstances a document prepared outside the government may nevertheless qualify as an "intra-agency" memorandum under Exemption 5. Typically, courts taking [this] view have held that the exemption extends to communications between government agencies and outside consultants hired by them. In such cases, the records submitted by outside consultants played essentially the same part in an agency's process of deliberation as documents prepared by agency personnel might have done. To be sure, the consultants in these cases were independent contractors and were not assumed to be subject to the degree of control that agency employment could have entailed; nor do we read the cases as necessarily assuming that an outside consultant must be devoid of a definite point of view when the agency contracts for its services. But the fact about the consultant that is constant in the typical cases is that the consultant does not represent an interest of its own, or the interest of any other client, when it advises the agency that hires it. Its only obligations are to truth and its sense of what good judgment calls for, and in those respects the consultant functions just as an employee would be expected to do.

The Department purports to rely on this consultant corollary to Exemption 5 in arguing for its application to the Klamath Tribe's communications to the Bureau in its capacity of fiduciary for the benefit of the Indian Tribes. The existence of a trust obligation is not, of course, in question. The fiduciary relationship has been described as "one of the primary cornerstones of Indian law," and has been compared to one existing under a common law trust, with the United States as trustee, the Indian tribes or individuals as beneficiaries, and the property and natural resources managed by the United States as the trust corpus. The Department is surely right in saying that confidentiality in communications with tribes is conducive to a proper discharge of its trust obligation.

From the recognition of this interest in frank communication . . . , the Department would have us infer a sufficient justification for applying Exemption 5 to communications with the Tribes, in the same fashion that Courts of Appeals have found sufficient reason to favor a consultant's advice that way. But the Department's argument skips a necessary step, for it ignores the first condition of Exemption 5, that the communication be "intra-agency or inter-agency." The Department seems to be saying that "intra-agency" is a purely conclusory term, just a label to be placed on any document the government would find it valuable to keep confidential.

There is, however, no textual justification for draining the first condition of independent vitality, and once the intraagency condition is applied, it rules out any application of Exemption 5 to tribal communications on analogy to consultants' reports (assuming, which we do not decide, that these reports may qualify

as intra-agency under Exemption 5). As mentioned already, consultants whose communications have typically been held exempt have not been communicating with the government in their own interest or on behalf of any person or group whose interests might be affected by the government action addressed by the consultant. In that regard, consultants may be enough like the agency's own personnel to justify calling their communications "intra-agency." The Tribes, on the contrary, necessarily communicate with the Bureau with their own, albeit entirely legitimate, interests in mind. While this fact alone distinguishes tribal communications from the consultants' examples recognized by several Courts of Appeals, the distinction is even sharper, in that the Tribes are self-advocates at the expense of others seeking benefits inadequate to satisfy everyone.

As to those documents bearing on the Plan, the Tribes are obviously in competition with nontribal claimants, including those irrigators represented by the Water Users Association. The record shows that documents submitted by the Tribes included, among others, "a position paper that discusses water law legal theories" and "addresses issues related to water rights of the tribes," a memorandum "containing views on policy the BIA could provide to other governmental agencies," "views concerning trust resources," and a letter "conveying the views of the Klamath Tribe concerning issues involved in the water rights adjudication." While these documents may not take the formally argumentative form of a brief, their function is quite apparently to support the tribal claims. The Tribes are thus urging a position necessarily adverse to the other claimants, the water being inadequate to satisfy the combined demand. As the Court of Appeals said, "the Tribes' demands, if satisfied, would lead to reduced water allocations to members of the [Water Users] Association and have been protested by [those] members who fear water shortages and economic injury in dry years." The position of the Klamath Tribe . . . is thus a far cry from the position of the paid consultant.

All of this boils down to requesting that we read an "Indian trust" exemption into the statute, a reading that is out of the question. There is simply no support for the exemption in the statutory text, which we have elsewhere insisted be read strictly. In FOIA, after all, a new conception of government conduct was enacted into law, "a general philosophy of full agency disclosure." *Department of Justice v. Tax Analysts* (1989) (quoting FOIA legislative history). "Congress believed that this philosophy, put into practice, would help ensure an informed citizenry, vital to the functioning of a democratic society." *Id.* Congress had to realize that not every secret under the old law would be secret under the new.

Judgment of Court of Appeals affirmed.

Privacy Act of 1974

The **Privacy Act of 1974** allows individuals to inspect files that agencies maintain on them and to request that erroneous or incomplete records be corrected. It also attempts to prevent agencies from gathering unnecessary information about individuals and forbids the disclosure of an individual's records without his written permission, except in certain specifically exempted circumstances. For example, records may be disclosed to employees of the agency that collected the information if those employees need the records to perform their duties (the "need to know" exception), to law enforcement agencies, to other agencies' personnel for "routine use" (uses for purposes compatible with the purpose for which the record was collected), and to persons filing legitimate FOIA requests. In addition, records may be disclosed if a court order requires disclosure.

Government in the Sunshine Act

The **Government in the Sunshine Act of 1976** was designed to ensure that "[e]very portion of every meeting of an agency shall be open to public observation." However, complete public access to all agency meetings could have the same negative consequences that unrestrained public access to agency records may sometimes produce. Accordingly, the Sunshine Act exempts certain agency meetings from public scrutiny under circumstances similar to those under which documents are exempt from disclosure under the FOIA.

Issues in Regulation

"Old" Regulation versus "New" Regulation

Some interested observers of regulatory developments over roughly the past 50 years have noted significant differences between the regulations that originated during the Progressive (1902 to 1914) and New Deal (1933 to 1938) eras and many regulations promulgated more recently. They argue not only that the number and scope of regulatory controls have increased substantially in recent years, but also that the focus and the impact of regulation have changed significantly.

Whereas earlier regulation often focused on business practices that harmed the economic interests of specific segments of society (e.g., workers, small-business owners, investors), many modern regulations focus on the health and safety of all citizens. Furthermore, whereas earlier regulations often focused on a particular industry or group of industries (e.g., the railroads or the securities industry), many modern regulations affect large segments of industry (e.g., Title VII of the Civil Rights Act of 1964 and regulations governing environmental pollution and workplace safety). Finally, whereas earlier congressional delegations of regulatory power tended to be quite broad, many more recent regulatory statutes have been extremely detailed.

What are the consequences of these changes in the nature of regulation? Far more businesses than ever before feel the impact of federal regulation, and far more areas of internal corporate decision-making are affected by regulation. These changes tend to erode the historic distinction between "regulated" and other industries, and to heighten the importance of business–government relations. Detailed regulatory statutes also increase Congress's role in shaping regulatory policy at the expense of administrative discretion, making regulatory policy arguably more vulnerable to legislative lobbying efforts.

"Captive" Agencies and Agencies' "Shadows"

Proponents of regulation have traditionally feared that regulatory agencies would become "captives" of the industries they were charged with regulating. Through "revolving door" appointments by which key figures move back and forth between government and the private sector, and through excessive reliance on "experts" beholden to industry, the independence of administrative agencies may be compromised and their effectiveness as regulators destroyed.

More recently, commentators sympathetic to business have argued that similar dangers to agency independence exist in the form of the nonindustry "shadow" groups that public interest organizations maintain to monitor agency actions (e.g., the Center for Auto Safety, which monitors the work of the Highway Transportation Safety Administration). Agencies may develop dependency relationships with their shadows or at least make decisions based in part on their shadows' anticipated reactions. Such informal means of shaping regulatory policy, when combined with the ability to challenge agency actions in court, have made public interest organizations important players in the contemporary regulatory process.

Deregulation versus Reregulation

A useful axiom for understanding the process of social and legal evolution is that *the cost of the status quo is easier to perceive than the cost of change.* Few things are more illustrative of the operation of this axiom than the history of regulation in the United States.

In the latter years of the 19th century, the social costs of living in an unregulated environment were readily apparent. Large business organizations often abused their power at the expense of their customers, suppliers,

Ethics in Action

As noted elsewhere on these pages, a long-standing concern about administrative agencies focuses on the prospect of a "revolving door" situation in which top agency personnel leave the agency to take positions in the industry regulated by the agency, or in which agency officials' desire for an eventual position in the industry causes them to go "soft" on businesses the agency is charged with regulating. The "revolving door" prospect may take other forms, such as where an industry executive philosophically opposed to the work of a certain administrative agency ends up being appointed to a prominent position in that agency when the White House would like to see the agency become less active. Consider these potential issues regarding the revolving door situation:

- What ethical obligations does an administrative agency official owe when she leaves her agency position to accept a job in the industry regulated by the agency?
- What ethical obligations does an executive of a corporation owe when he leaves his corporate position to accept a job

with an administrative agency that regulates the industry in which the corporation does business?

- Is it ethical for an official of an administrative agency to inquire about possible employment in the very industry the agency is charged with regulating? What about the reverse of this situation?
- If the prevailing political winds lead to circumstances in which an avowed opponent of a certain administrative agency's work is appointed to a high-level position in that agency, does this new agency official have an ethical obligation to "buy in" to the work of the agency? If so, to what extent? Does this new agency official, on the other hand, have an ethical obligation to make efforts to change the agency? If so, to what extent?
- Is a revolving door between an administrative agency and its regulated industry necessarily a bad thing? May it be beneficial for the agency, the industry, and society in general? If so, in what way or ways?

employees, and distributors, and sought to increase their power by acquiring their competitors or driving them out of business. Market forces, standing alone, were apparently unable to protect the public from defective, and in some cases dangerous, products. As a result of these and numerous other social and historical factors, the 20th century witnessed a tremendous growth in government and in government regulation of business.

Regulation, too, has its costs. Regulatory bureaucracies generate their own internal momentum and have their own interests to protect. They may become insensitive to the legitimate concerns of the industries they regulate and the public they supposedly serve. They may continue to seek higher and higher levels of safety, heedless of the fact that life necessarily involves some elements of risk and that the total elimination of risk in a modern technological society may be impossible—or if possible, obtainable at a cost that we cannot afford to pay. At a time when many Americans are legitimately concerned about economic efficiency, as well as the ability of U.S. companies to compete effectively in world markets against competitors who operate in less regulated environments, these and other costs of regulation are also readily apparent.

As a result, in the last 25 to 30 years, we have witnessed substantial deregulation in a number of industries such as the airline, banking, railroad, and trucking industries. The results of these efforts are, at best, mixed. The

case of airline regulation should suffice to make the point. Proponents of deregulation cite the generally lower fares that deregulation has produced. Opponents tend to point to increased airline overbooking practices, reduced or eliminated services to smaller communities, and increased safety problems, all of which, they argue, are products of deregulation. The costs of deregulation have generated predictable calls for reregulating the airline industry. The ultimate outcome of the deregulation versus reregulation debate will depend on which costs we as a society decide we would prefer to pay.

Regulations That Preempt Private Lawsuits?

As this book went to press in 2008, a controversial development suggested potential for litigation over whether agency regulations had gone too far. In the waning months of the Bush Administration, certain federal agencies expressed interest in promulgating regulations whose content would call for preemption of state law–based private lawsuits alleging negligence or other failures to comply with state law in instances in which the federal regulations arguably would have been satisfied. (When federal preemption occurs, a state law–based claim cannot serve as a basis for obtaining damages or other legal relief.)

What made this proposed action by certain agencies controversial? It was the frequent absence of a preemption clause in the relevant federal statute from which the agencies derived their authority to regulate. Proponents of such action by agencies saw it as an appropriate way to reinforce the federal control that they believed should be present when a detailed federal regulatory regime existed. Critics condemned such action as overreaching attempts by federal agencies to go beyond the authority extended to them by Congress, and as backdoor devices for achieving, through regulations promulgated by unelected agency personnel, what could not be achieved in the political give-and-take of the congressional arena. In view of the potentially high stakes associated with the controversy, it seems inevitable that we will see litigation over the appropriateness—or inappropriateness—of preemption by agency regulation.

Problems and Problem Cases

1. Title X of the Public Health Service Act provides federal funding for family-planning services. Section 1008 of the statute specifies that none of the federal funds provided under Title X are to be "used in programs where abortion is a method of family planning." In 1988, the Secretary of Health and Human Services issued new regulations that, among other things, prohibited family-planning services that receive Title X funds from engaging in counseling concerning the use of abortion as a method of family planning, referrals for abortion as a method of family planning, and activities amounting to encouragement or advocacy of abortion as a method of family planning. Various Title X grantees and physicians supervising Title X funds challenged the validity of the regulations and sought an injunction against their implementation. Were the regulations a permissible interpretation of Section 1008? Did the regulations violate constitutional guarantees?

2. Section 9 of the Endangered Species Act (ESA) makes it unlawful for any person to "take" an endangered or threatened species of fish or wildlife. A definition section in the ESA states that *take* means "to harass, harm, pursue, hunt, school, wound, kill, trap, capture, or collect, or to attempt to engage in any such conduct." The Secretary of the Department of the Interior (the Secretary) promulgated a regulation that defined the term *harm* for purposes of the statutory language just quoted. This regulation stated that *harm* "means an act which actually kills or injures wildlife" and that "[s]uch act may include significant habitat modification or degradation where it actually kills or injures wildlife by significantly impairing essential behavioral patterns, including breeding, feeding or sheltering." A declaratory judgment action attacking the validity of this regulation was brought against the Secretary by a group of landowners, logging companies, and families dependent on the forest products industries, and by organizations representing those parties' interests. The plaintiffs sought a judicial ruling that the regulation defining *harm* as including habitat modification or degradation was an unreasonable and erroneous interpretation of the ESA. The plaintiffs alleged that they had been injured economically by the government's application of the *harm* regulation to the red-cockaded woodpecker, an endangered species, and the northern spotted owl, a threatened species. Was the Department of the Interior's regulation a reasonable interpretation of the statute?

3. Small lodges in remote regions of Alaska cater to hunters and fishermen. These lodges provide food and shelter, guide services, and air transportation to and from the lodge and on side trips, all for a flat fee. Hunting and fishing guides employed by the lodges often pilot light aircraft as part of their guiding service. Beginning in 1963, the Federal Aviation Administration, through its Alaskan Region office, consistently advised guide pilots that they were not governed by FAA regulations dealing with commercial pilots. This advice stemmed from a 1963 Civil Aeronautics Board decision in a case in which the FAA had attempted to sanction a guide pilot who had not complied with FAA regulations applicable to commercial pilots. The Civil Aeronautics Board concluded that the guide pilot's flight with a hunter was merely incidental to the guiding business, that the guide pilot was not a commercial pilot, and that the FAA's commercial pilot regulations therefore did not apply. During the 1990s, officials at FAA headquarters in Washington, D.C., began expressing concern about the safety of guide pilots and their passengers. In 1998, the FAA published an announcement that was aimed at guide pilots. This announcement stated that guide pilots must abide by all FAA regulations applicable to commercial pilots. In a petition for judicial review of this FAA action, the Alaska Professional Hunters Association (APHA) attacked the

validity of the announcement and the new rule it purported to adopt. APHA contended that because the FAA sought to adopt a rule that was contrary to the long-standing interpretation of the FAA's regulations and contrary to the expectations of the guide pilots and the lodges for which they worked, the FAA at a minimum needed to follow the "notice and comment" (informal rulemaking) procedure before adopting a new rule. Simply announcing the new rule, APHA argued, was improper. Was APHA's contention correct?

4. On December 10, 1986, a federal grand jury indicted James Mallen for allegedly making false statements to the Federal Deposit Insurance Corporation (FDIC) and for allegedly making false statements to a bank for the purposes of influencing the actions of the FDIC. Mallen was the president and a director of a federally insured bank at the time he was indicted. On January 20, 1987, the FDIC issued an ex parte order stating that Mallen's continued service could "pose a threat to the interests of the bank's depositors or threaten to impair public confidence in the bank." The order suspended Mallen as president and as a director of the bank and prohibited him "from further participation in any manner in the conduct of the affairs of the bank, or any other bank insured by the FDIC." In issuing the suspension order without first holding a hearing on the matter, the FDIC acted pursuant to a section of the Financial Institutions Supervisory Act. A copy of the FDIC's order was served on Mallen on January 26, 1987. Four days later, his attorney filed a written request for an "immediate administrative hearing" to commence no later than February 9. The FDIC scheduled a hearing for February 18, but on February 6, Mallen filed suit against the FDIC. Arguing that the FDIC's action denied him due process, Mallen sought a preliminary injunction against the suspension order. Was Mallen denied due process?

5. John Doe began work at the Central Intelligence Agency (CIA) in 1973 as a clerk-typist. Periodic fitness reports consistently rated him as an excellent or outstanding employee. By 1977, he had been promoted to covert electronics technician. In January 1982, Doe voluntarily told a CIA security officer that he was a homosexual. Almost immediately, the CIA placed Doe on paid administrative leave and began an investigation of his sexual orientation and conduct. Doe submitted to an extensive polygraph examination during which he denied having sexual relations with foreign nationals and maintained that he had not disclosed classified information to any of his sexual partners. The polygraph officer told Doe that the test results indicated that his responses had been truthful. Nonetheless, a month later Doe was told that the CIA's Office of Security had determined that his homosexuality posed a threat to security. CIA officials declined, however, to explain the nature of the danger. Doe was asked to resign. When he refused to do so he was dismissed by CIA Director William Webster, who "deemed it necessary and advisable in the interests of the United States to terminate [Doe's] employment with this Agency pursuant to section 102(c) of the National Security Act." The statutory section cited by the director allows termination of a CIA employee whenever the director "shall deem such termination necessary or advisable in the interests of the United States." Doe filed suit against the CIA, arguing that his termination was unlawful under section 102(c) and various constitutional guarantees. The CIA moved to dismiss Doe's complaint, arguing that the director's decision was a decision committed to agency discretion by law and thus was not subject to judicial review. Was the CIA's argument correct?

6. Scott Armstrong submitted a Freedom of Information Act (FOIA) request that, among other things, called for the federal government to reveal a list of names of lower-level FBI agents who attended certain meetings at the White House during the mid-1980s. When the government refused to reveal the agents' names, Armstrong filed suit under the FOIA. Upholding this refusal, the district court agreed with the government's contention that the names of FBI agents should always be exempt from disclosure under the FOIA exemption for "personnel and medical files and similar files the disclosure of which would constitute a clearly unwarranted invasion of personal privacy." On appeal, Armstrong argued that the district court erred in concluding that the FOIA's privacy exemption justifies a categorical rule that FBI agents' names are exempt from disclosure. Was Armstrong correct?

7. For many years, section 109 of the Federal Credit Union Act provided that "[f]ederal credit union membership shall be limited to groups having a common bond of occupation or association, or to groups within a well-defined neighborhood, community, or

rural district." Until 1982, the National Credit Union Administration and its predecessor agencies consistently interpreted section 109 as requiring that the same common bond of occupation unite every member of an occupationally defined credit union. In 1982, however, the NCUA reversed its long-standing policy in order to permit credit unions to be composed of multiple unrelated employer groups. The NCUA thus began interpreting section 109's common bond requirement as applying only to each employer group in a multiple-group credit union, rather than to every member of that credit union. Several banks and the American Bankers Association sought judicial review of this action by the NCUA. They alleged that the NCUA's 1982 interpretation of section 109 was improper and impermissible. Were the banks and the Bankers Association correct?

8. Section 7(a)(2) of the federal Endangered Species Act of 1973 divides responsibilities concerning protection of endangered species between the secretary of the interior and the secretary of commerce. The statute also requires each federal agency to consult with the relevant secretary in order to ensure that any action funded by the agency would be unlikely to jeopardize the existence or habitat of an endangered or threatened species. In 1978, the two secretaries promulgated a joint resolution stating that the obligations imposed by § 7(a)(2) extended not only to actions taken in the United States but also to actions taken in foreign nations. A revised joint regulation, reinterpreting § 7(a)(2) to require consultation only for actions taken in the United States or on the high seas, was promulgated in 1986. Defenders of Wildlife (DOW), an organization dedicated to wildlife conservation and other environmental causes, sued the secretary of the interior, seeking a declaratory judgment that the 1986 regulation erroneously interpreted the geographic scope of § 7(a)(2). DOW also sought an injunction requiring the secretary to develop a new regulation restoring the interpretation set forth in the 1978 regulation. DOW took the position that it should be regarded as having standing to sue because the 1986 regulation's elimination of the consultation requirement concerning actions in foreign nations would hasten the endangerment and possible extinction of certain species, and would thus adversely affect DOW members' ability to observe animals of those species when the members made trips to nations elsewhere in the world. The federal

district court denied the secretary's motion for summary judgment on the issue of whether DOW had standing to sue, granted DOW's motion for summary judgment on all issues, and ordered the secretary to develop a revised regulation. After the U.S. Court of Appeals for the Eighth Circuit affirmed, the U.S. Supreme Court granted certiorari. Did DOW possess standing to sue?

9. An agent of the Pennsylvania Department of Environmental Resources saw Disposal Service's loaded trash truck backing into a building that was used to compact waste to be loaded onto tractor-trailers for transportation and final disposal. Knowing the building's purpose and that Disposal Service did not have a permit to operate it as a transfer station, as required by the state Solid Waste Management Act (SWMA), the agent entered the property, went into the building, and observed the operation. Disposal Service was later prosecuted for operating a transfer station without a permit. Disposal Service moved to suppress the agent's evidence, arguing that his warrantless entry onto the property violated the Fourth Amendment. The state argued that the SWMA's provisions allowing such warrantless inspections were constitutional. Should the evidence be suppressed?

10. Relying on the Freedom of Information Act (FOIA), Public Citizen Health Research Group asked the Food and Drug Administration (FDA) for documents relating to drug applications that had been abandoned for health or safety reasons. When the FDA denied this request, Public Citizen sued in federal court. Schering Corporation, which had submitted five investigational new drug applications (INDs) of the sort requested by Public Citizen, intervened as a defendant. The FDA and Schering contended that certain documents in the five INDs contained confidential commercial information and could therefore be withheld under Exemption 4 of the FOIA. Public Citizen argued that disclosure would prevent other drug companies "from repeating Schering's mistakes, thereby avoiding risk to human health." In addition, Public Citizen argued that under Exemption 4, the court should gauge whether the competitive harm done to the sponsor of an IND by the public disclosure of confidential information is outweighed by the strong public interest in safeguarding the health of human trial participants. Were Public Citizen's arguments regarding Exemption 4 legally correct?

Were the requested documents subject to being withheld under Exemption 4?

11. Section 203(a) of the federal Communications Act required communications common carriers to file tariffs with the Federal Communications Commission (FCC). Section 203(b) of the same statute authorized the FCC to "modify any requirement made by or under" section 203. Relying on its modification authority under section 203(b), the FCC issued a series of orders during the 1980s and early 1990s. These orders made tariff filing optional for all nondominant long-distance carriers. American Telephone and Telegraph Co. (AT&T), the only long-distance carrier classified as dominant, asked the U.S. Court of Appeals for the District of Columbia Circuit to reverse these FCC orders. AT&T contended that making tariff filing optional for nondominant long-distance carriers was not a valid exercise of the FCC's modification authority under section 203(b). Was AT&T correct in this contention?

Online Research

The FCC and the FOIA

Locate the Web site of the Federal Communications Commission (FCC). Review it to find an explanation of how to file Freedom of Information Act (FOIA) requests. Then prepare a brief description of the filing options available to a party who wishes to submit an FOIA request to the FCC.

chapter 48

THE FEDERAL TRADE COMMISSION ACT AND CONSUMER PROTECTION LAWS

*D*oan's is a brand name used for more than 90 years for back pain medication sold on an over-the-counter basis. Shortly after its 1987 purchase of the *Doan's* trademark and the right to produce the underlying product, Ciba-Geigy Corporation (Ciba) conducted a marketing study concerning consumer perceptions of the *Doan's* medication for back pain. The study revealed that this medication had a weak image in comparison to the leading brands of analgesics, and indicated that Ciba would benefit from positioning *Doan's* as a more effective product that was strong enough for the types of pain typically experienced by persons susceptible to backaches.

In an effort to strengthen the image of *Doan's,* Ciba mounted a television and newspaper advertising campaign that lasted from 1988 to 1996. The advertisements characterized *Doan's* as an effective remedy specifically for back pain and stated that the product contained a special ingredient (magnesium salicylate) not found in other over-the-counter analgesics. Some of the advertisements displayed images of competing over-the-counter pain remedies. In 1998, the Federal Trade Commission (FTC) instituted an administrative proceeding against Ciba's successor-in-interest, Novartis Corporation, on the ground that the 1988 to 1996 advertisements for *Doan's* were deceptive, in supposed violation of § 5 of the Federal Trade Commission Act. The FTC's theory was that even though the *Doan's* advertisements were truthful in stating that the product was effective for back pain and that it contained a special ingredient not present in other over-the-counter analgesics, the combination of the two literally true statements created an implied representation for which there was no substantiation: that because of its special ingredient, *Doan's* was superior to other analgesics in relieving back pain. It was this implied representation that the FTC alleged to be deceptive. Consider the following questions as you study this chapter:

- In FTC administrative proceedings, what legal test controls the determination of whether an advertisement was deceptive?
- May the FTC validly base a deceptive advertising proceeding on the theory that an advertisement consisting of literally true statements may nevertheless be deceptive in what it implies?
- If the theory just noted is valid, were the *Doan's* advertisements deceptive?
- If the *Doan's* advertisements were deceptive, what potential legal consequences could follow for Novartis? In particular, may that firm be ordered to engage in corrective advertising, or would a corrective advertising order violate the firm's right to freedom of speech?

DURING THE PAST several decades, *direct government regulation* of consumer matters has become a prominent feature of the legal landscape at the federal and state levels. This chapter addresses federal consumer protection regulation. It begins with a general discussion of America's main consumer watchdog, the Federal Trade Commission (FTC). After describing how the FTC operates, the chapter examines its regulation of anticompetitive, deceptive, and unfair business practices. Then we discuss various federal laws that deal with consumer credit and other consumer matters.

The Federal Trade Commission

The Federal Trade Commission (FTC) was formed shortly after the 1914 enactment of the Federal Trade Commission Act (FTC Act).[1] Because the FTC is an independent federal agency, it is outside the executive branch of the federal government and is less subject to political control than agencies that are executive departments. The FTC is headed by five commissioners appointed by the president and confirmed by the Senate for staggered seven-year terms. The president designates one of the commissioners as chairman of the FTC. The FTC has a Washington headquarters and several regional offices located throughout the United States.

The FTC's Powers The FTC's principal missions are to keep the U.S. economy both *free* and *fair.* Congress has given the commission many tools for accomplishing these missions. By far the most important, however, is § 5 of the FTC Act, which empowers the commission to prevent *unfair methods of competition* and *unfair or deceptive acts or practices.* We examine these bases of FTC authority later in this chapter. The commission also enforces the consumer protection and consumer credit measures discussed in the last half of the chapter. Finally, the FTC enforces numerous other federal laws relating to specific industries or lines of commerce.

FTC Enforcement Procedures The FTC has various legal means for ensuring compliance with the statutes it administers. The three most important FTC enforcement devices are its procedures for facilitating voluntary compliance, its issuance of trade regulation rules, and its adjudicative proceedings.

Voluntary Compliance The FTC promotes voluntary business behavior by issuing advisory opinions and industry guides. An **advisory opinion** is the commission's response to a private party's query about the legality of proposed business conduct. The FTC is not obligated to furnish advisory opinions. The commission may rescind a previously issued opinion when the public interest requires. When the FTC does so, however, it cannot proceed against the opinion's recipient for actions taken in good faith reliance on the opinion, unless it gives the recipient notice of the rescission and an opportunity to discontinue those actions.

Industry guides are FTC interpretations of the laws it administers. Their purpose is to encourage businesses to abandon certain unlawful practices. To further this end, industry guides are written in lay language. Although industry guides lack the force of law, behavior that violates an industry guide often violates one of the statutes or other rules the commission enforces.

Trade Regulation Rules Unlike industry guides, FTC **trade regulation rules** are written in legalistic language and have the force of law. Thus, the FTC can proceed directly against those who engage in practices forbidden by a trade regulation rule. This may occur through the *adjudicative proceedings* discussed immediately below. The commission may also obtain a federal district court *civil penalty* of up to $10,000 for each knowing violation of a rule. Furthermore, it may institute court proceedings to obtain various forms of *consumer redress,* including the payment of damages, the refund of money, the return of property, and the reformation or rescission of contracts.

FTC Adjudicative Proceedings Often, the FTC proceeds against violators of statutes or trade regulation rules by administrative action within the commission itself. The FTC obtains evidence of possible violations from private parties, government bodies, and its own investigations. If the FTC decides to proceed against the alleged offender (the *respondent*), it enters a formal complaint. The case is heard in a public administrative hearing called an *adjudicative proceeding.* An FTC administrative law judge presides over this proceeding.[2] The judge's decision can be appealed to the FTC's five commissioners and then to the federal courts of appeals and the U.S. Supreme Court.

The usual penalty resulting from a final decision against the respondent is an FTC **cease-and-desist**

---

[1] See Chapter 47 for further discussion of the FTC's creation, organization, powers, and status as an independent agency.

[2] Chapter 47 describes federal administrative proceedings.

order. This is a command ordering the respondent to stop its illegal behavior. As you will see later in the chapter, however, FTC orders may go beyond the command to cease and desist. The civil penalty for noncompliance with a cease-and-desist order is up to $10,000 per violation. Where there is a continuing failure to obey a final order, each day that the violation continues is considered a separate violation.

Many alleged violations are never adjudicated by the FTC. Instead, they are settled through a **consent order.** This is an order approving a negotiated agreement in which the respondent promises to cease certain activities. Consent orders normally provide that the respondent does not admit any violation of the law. The failure to observe a consent order is punishable by civil penalties.

> **LOG ON**
>
> The Federal Trade Commission's Web site, **www.ftc.gov,** contains a wealth of information regarding topics addressed in this chapter.

Anticompetitive Behavior

Section 5 of the FTC Act empowers the commission to prevent "unfair methods of competition." This language allows the FTC to regulate anticompetitive practices made unlawful by the Sherman Act. The commission also has statutory authority to enforce the Clayton and Robinson-Patman Acts.[3]

For the most part, § 5's application to anticompetitive behavior involves the orthodox antitrust violations discussed in the following two chapters. Section 5, however, also reaches anticompetitive behavior *not covered by other antitrust statutes.* In addition, § 5 enables the FTC to proceed against *potential* or *incipient* antitrust violations.

Deception and Unfairness

Section 5 of the FTC Act also prohibits "unfair or deceptive acts or practices" in commercial settings. This language enables the FTC to regulate a wide range of activities that disadvantage consumers. In doing so, the commission may seek to prove that the activity is *deceptive,* or that it is *unfair.* Here, we set out the general standards that the FTC uses to define each of these § 5

violations. Much of this discussion involves FTC regulation of advertising, but the standards we outline apply to many other misrepresentations, omissions, and practices. Although their details are beyond the scope of this text, the commission also has enacted numerous trade regulation rules defining specific deceptive or unfair practices.

Deception   The FTC determines the deceptiveness of advertising and other business practices on a case-by-case basis. Courts often defer to the commission's determinations. To be considered deceptive under the FTC's Policy Statement on Deception, an activity must (1) involve a *material* misrepresentation, omission, or practice; (2) that is *likely to mislead* a consumer; (3) who acts *reasonably* under the circumstances.

Representation, Omission, or Practice Likely to Mislead   Sometimes, sellers *expressly* make false or misleading claims in their advertisements or other representations. As revealed in the *Kraft* case, which follows shortly, an advertiser's false or misleading claims of an *implied* nature may also be challenged by the FTC. The same is true of a seller's deceptive *omissions.* Finally, certain deceptive *marketing practices* may violate § 5. In one such case, encyclopedia salespeople gained entry to the homes of potential customers by posing as surveyors engaged in advertising research.

In all of these situations, the statement, omission, or practice must be *likely to mislead* a consumer. Actual deception is not required. Determining whether an ad or practice is likely to mislead requires that the FTC evaluate the accuracy of the seller's claims. In some cases, moreover, the commission requires that sellers *substantiate* objective claims about their products by showing that they have a reasonable basis for making such claims.

The "Reasonable Consumer" Test   To be deceptive, the representation, omission, or practice must also be likely to mislead *reasonable consumers under the circumstances.* This requirement aims to protect sellers from liability for every foolish, ignorant, or outlandish misconception that some consumer might entertain. As the commission noted many years ago, advertising an American-made pastry as "Danish Pastry" does not violate § 5 just because "a few misguided souls believe . . . that all Danish Pastry is made in Denmark."[4] Also, § 5 normally is not violated by statements of opinion, sales talk, or "puffing," statements about matters that consumers can easily evaluate for themselves, and statements regarding subjective

---

[3]Chapter 49 discusses the Sherman Act. Chapter 50 discusses the Clayton and Robinson-Patman Acts.

[4]*Heinz v. W. Kirchner,* 63 F.T.C. 1282, 1290 (1963).

The Global Business Environment

In most developed nations, the problem of misleading advertising is addressed through self-regulation and through regulatory schemes established by law. Self-regulation includes voluntary action by companies and resolution of parties' advertising-related disputes under industry codes of conduct or other agreed procedures that exist outside the formal legal system.

Since the passage of a 1984 European Union (EU) Directive on Misleading Advertising, EU nations have been obligated to have domestic laws addressing misleading advertising. The domestic laws of EU nations typically have not contemplated a significant role for direct government regulation of the sort in which the Federal Trade Commission and other government agencies engage in the United States. Instead, EU countries depend more on litigation instituted by private parties—competitors and, in some countries, consumer organizations—as the chief legal means of dealing with misleading advertising. In this sense, the approach taken by EU nations resembles a different aspect of advertising regulation

in the United States: the indirect regulation that comes with private parties' false advertising lawsuits under § 43(a) of the Lanham Act. (Section 43(a) and the types of cases that may be brought under it are discussed in Chapter 8.)

Sweden and the other Scandinavian countries have established, by law, a consumer ombudsman who hears advertising complaints, resolves them when possible, and resorts to litigation if necessary. The ombudsman also has some power to promulgate advertising rules that carry legal force. In this sense, the ombudsman's role resembles that of the FTC in the United States.

Advertising laws contemplate significant regulatory roles for government agencies in New Zealand, Australia, and Japan, though industry self-regulation remains prominent in at least the latter two of those nations. In Great Britain, the traditional emphasis on self-regulation through the private Advertising Standards Authority has been supplemented during recent decades by government regulation through the office of the Director General of Fair Trading.

---

matters such as taste or smell. Such statements are unlikely to deceive reasonable consumers.

Materiality Finally, the representation, omission, or practice must be *material*. Material information is important to reasonable consumers and is likely to affect their choice of a product or service. Examples include statements or omissions regarding a product's cost,

safety, effectiveness, performance, durability, quality, or warranty protection. In addition, the commission presumes that express statements are material.

The *Kraft* case, which follows, illustrates the application of the FTC's deception test to an advertising claim of an implied nature. *Kraft* also reveals the commission's broad discretion in fashioning appropriate orders once deceptive advertising has been proven.

Kraft, Inc. v. Federal Trade Commission   970 F.2d 311 (7th Cir. 1992)

Individually wrapped slices of cheese and cheeselike products come in two major types: process cheese food slices, *which must contain at least 51 percent natural cheese according to a federal regulation; and* imitation slices, *which contain little or no natural cheese. Kraft, Inc.'s "Kraft Singles" are process cheese food slices. In the early 1980s, Kraft began losing market share to other firms' less expensive* imitation slices. *Kraft responded with its "Skimp" and "Class Picture" advertisements, which were designed to inform consumers that Kraft Singles cost more because each slice is made from 5 ounces of milk. These advertisements, which ran nationally in print and broadcast media between 1985 and 1987, also stressed the calcium content of Kraft Singles.*

In the broadcast version of the Skimp advertisements, a woman stated that she bought Kraft Singles for her daughter rather than "skimping" by purchasing imitation slices. *She noted that "[i]mitation slices* use hardly any milk. But Kraft has 5 ounces per slice. Five ounces. So her little bones get calcium they need to grow." *The commercial also showed milk being poured into a glass that bore the label "5 oz. milk slice." The glass was then transformed into part of the label on a package of Singles. In March 1987, Kraft added, as a subscript in the television commercial and as a footnote in the print media version, the disclosure that "one 3/4 ounce slice has 70% of the calcium of five ounces of milk."*

The televised version of the Class Picture advertisements cited a government study indicating that "half the school kids in America don't get all the calcium recommended for growing kids." According to the commercial, "[t]hat's why Kraft Singles are important. Kraft is made from five ounces of milk per slice. So they're concentrated with calcium. Calcium the government recommends for strong bones and healthy teeth." The commercial also included the subscript disclaimer mentioned above.

The Federal Trade Commission instituted a deceptive advertising proceeding against Kraft under § 5 of the FTC Act. According to the FTC's complaint, the Skimp and Class Picture advertisements made the false implied claim that a Singles slice contains the same amount of calcium as 5 ounces of milk (the milk equivalency *claim). The FTC regarded the milk equivalency claim as false even though Kraft actually uses 5 ounces of milk in making each Singles slice because roughly 30 percent of the calcium contained in the milk is lost during processing.*

The administrative law judge (ALJ) concluded that the Skimp and Class Picture advertisements made the milk equivalency claim, which was false and material. He concluded that Kraft's subscript and footnote disclosures of the calcium loss were inconspicuous and confusing and therefore insufficient to dispel the misleading impression created by the advertisements. The ALJ ordered Kraft to cease and desist making the milk equivalency claim regarding any of its individually wrapped process cheese food slices *or* imitation slices. *In addition, the ALJ ordered Kraft not to make other calcium or nutritional claims concerning its individually wrapped slices unless Kraft had reliable scientific evidence to support the claims.*

Kraft appealed to the FTC commissioners (referred to here as "the Commission"). The Commission affirmed the ALJ's decision but modified it. According to the Commission, the Skimp and Class Picture advertisements made the false and material milk equivalency claim. The Commission modified the ALJ's orders by extending their coverage from Kraft's individually wrapped slices to "any product that is a cheese, related cheese product, imitation cheese, or substitute cheese." Kraft appealed to the U.S. Court of Appeals for the Seventh Circuit. (In a portion of the opinion not set forth here, the Seventh Circuit concluded, as had the ALJ and the Commission, that some of the Kraft advertisements made a further false claim of an implied nature: that Kraft Singles slices contain more calcium than imitation slices. *The following portion of the Seventh Circuit's opinion addresses the milk equivalency claim.)*

Flaum, Circuit Judge

[A]n advertisement is deceptive under [§ 5 of the FTC Act] if it is likely to mislead consumers, acting reasonably under the circumstances, in a material respect.

In determining what claims are conveyed by a challenged advertisement, the Commission relies on two sources of information: its own viewing of the ad and extrinsic evidence. Its practice is to view the ad first and, if it is unable on its own to determine with confidence what claims are conveyed . . . , to turn to extrinsic evidence. The most convincing extrinsic evidence is a [consumer] survey . . . , but the Commission also relies on other forms of extrinsic evidence including consumer testimony, expert opinion, and copy tests of ads.

Kraft has no quarrel with this approach when it comes to determining whether an ad conveys *express* claims, but contends that the FTC should be required . . . to rely on extrinsic evidence rather than its own subjective analysis in all cases involving allegedly *implied* claims. The Commissioners, Kraft argues, are simply incapable of determining what implicit messages consumers are likely to perceive. Kraft [also] asserts that the Commissioners are predisposed to find implied claims because the claims have [already] been identified in the complaint.

Here, the Commission found implied claims based solely on its own intuitive reading of the ads (although it did reinforce

that conclusion by examining the proffered extrinsic evidence). Had the Commission fully and properly relied on available extrinsic evidence, Kraft argues it would have conclusively found that consumers do not perceive the milk equivalency . . . claim in the ads. Kraft's arguments . . . are unavailing as a matter of law. Courts, including the Supreme Court, have uniformly rejected imposing such a requirement on the FTC. We hold that the Commission may rely on its own reasoned analysis to determine what claims, including implied ones, are conveyed in a challenged advertisement, so long as those claims are reasonably clear from the face of the advertisement.

[Kraft relies on] the faulty premise that implied claims are inescapably subjective and unpredictable. In fact, implied claims fall on a continuum, ranging from the obvious to the barely discernible. The Commission does not have license to go on a fishing expedition to pin liability on advertisers for barely imaginable claims. However, when [implied] claims [are] conspicuous, extrinsic evidence is unnecessary because common sense and administrative experience provide the Commission with adequate tools to make its findings. The implied claims Kraft made are reasonably clear from the face of the advertisements, and hence the Commission was not required to utilize consumer surveys in reaching its decision.

Alternatively, Kraft argues that substantial evidence does not support the FTC's finding that the Class Picture ads convey a milk equivalency claim. We find substantial [supporting] evidence in the record. Although Kraft downplays the nexus in the ads between milk and calcium, the ads emphasize visually and verbally that five ounces of milk go into a slice of Kraft Singles; this image is linked to calcium content, strongly implying that the consumer gets the calcium found in five ounces of milk. Furthermore, the Class Picture ads contained one other element reinforcing the milk equivalency claim, the phrase "5 oz. milk slice" inside the image of a glass superimposed on the Singles package.

Kraft asserts that the literal truth of the . . . ads—[Kraft Singles] *are* made from five ounces of milk and they *do* have a high concentration of calcium—makes it illogical to render a finding of consumer deception. The difficulty with this argument is that even literally true statements can have misleading implications. Here, the average consumer is not likely to know that much of the calcium in five ounces of milk (30 percent) is lost in processing, which leaves consumers with a misleading impression about calcium content.

Kraft next asserts that the milk equivalency . . . claim, even if made, [is] not material to consumers. A claim is considered material if it involves information that is important to consumers and, hence, likely to affect their choice of, or conduct regarding, a product. In determining that the milk equivalency claim was material to consumers, the FTC cited Kraft surveys showing that 71 percent of respondents rated calcium content an extremely or very important factor in their decision to buy Kraft Singles, [and that a substantial percentage of respondents] reported significant personal concerns about adequate calcium consumption. [The Commission] rationally concluded that a 30 percent exaggeration of calcium content was a nutritionally significant claim that would affect consumer purchasing decisions. This finding was supported by expert witnesses who agreed that consumers would prefer a slice of cheese with 100 percent of the calcium in five ounces of milk over one with only 70 percent. [T]he FTC [also] found evidence in the record that Kraft designed the ads with the intent to capitalize on consumer calcium deficiency concerns.

Significantly, the FTC found further evidence of materiality in Kraft's conduct. Before the ads even ran, ABC television raised a red flag when it asked Kraft to substantiate the milk and calcium claims in the ads. Kraft's ad agency also warned Kraft in a legal memorandum to substantiate the claims before running the ads. Moreover, in October 1985, a consumer group warned Kraft that it believed the Skimp ads were potentially deceptive. Nonetheless, a high-level Kraft executive recommended that the ad copy remain unaltered because the "Singles business is growing for the first time in four years due in large part to the copy." Finally, the FTC and the California

Attorney General's Office independently notified the company in early 1986 that investigations had been initiated to determine whether the ads conveyed the milk equivalency claims. Notwithstanding these warnings, Kraft continued to run the ads and even rejected proposed alternatives that would have allayed concerns over their deceptive nature. From this, the FTC inferred—we believe, reasonably—that Kraft thought the challenged milk equivalency claim induced consumers to purchase Singles and hence that the claim was material to consumers.

The Commission's cease and desist order prohibits Kraft from running the Skimp and Class Picture ads, as well as from advertising any calcium or nutritional claims not supported by reliable scientific evidence. This order extends not only to the product contained in the deceptive advertisements (Kraft Singles), but to all Kraft cheeses and cheese-related products.

Kraft argues that the scope of the order is not reasonably related to Kraft's violation of the [FTC] Act because it extends to products that were not the subject of the challenged advertisements. The FTC has discretion to issue multi-product orders, so-called "fencing-in" orders, that extend beyond violations of the Act to prevent violators from engaging in similar deceptive practices in the future.

[The Commission] concluded that Kraft's violations were serious, deliberate, and easily transferable to other Kraft products, thus warranting a broad fencing-in order. We find substantial evidence to support the scope of the order. The Commission based its finding of seriousness on the size ($15 million annually) and duration (two and one-half years) of the ad campaign and on the difficulty most consumers would face in judging the truth or falsity of the calcium claims. [T]he FTC properly found that it is unreasonable to expect most consumers to perform the calculations necessary to compare the calcium content of Kraft Singles with five ounces of milk given the fact that the nutrient information given on milk cartons is not based on a five ounce serving.

As noted previously, the Commission [reasonably] found that Kraft's conduct was deliberate because it persisted in running the challenged ad copy despite repeated warnings from outside sources that the copy might be implicitly misleading. Kraft made three modifications to the ads, but two of them were implemented at the very end of the campaign, more than two years after it had begun. This dilatory response provided a sufficient basis for the Commission's conclusion. The Commission further [made the reasonable finding] that the violations were readily transferable to other Kraft cheese products given the general similarity between Singles and other Kraft cheeses.

Commission's order upheld and enforced.

Unfairness

Section 5's prohibition of *unfair* acts or practices enables the FTC to attack behavior that, while not necessarily deceptive, is objectionable for other reasons. As demonstrated by the case discussed in an Ethics in Action box that appears later in the chapter, the FTC focuses on *consumer harm* when it attacks unfair acts or practices. To violate § 5, this harm:

1. *Must be substantial.* Monetary loss and unwarranted health and safety risks usually constitute substantial harm, but emotional distress and the perceived offensiveness of certain advertisements generally do not.

2. *Must not be outweighed by any offsetting consumer or competitive benefits produced by the challenged practice.* This element requires the commission to balance the harm caused by the act or practice against its benefits to consumers and to competition generally. A seller's failure to give a consumer complex technical data about a product, for example, may disadvantage the consumer, but it may also reduce the product's price. Only when an act or practice is injurious in its *net effects* can it be unfair under § 5.

3. *Must be one that consumers could not reasonably have avoided.* An injury is considered reasonably unavoidable when a seller's actions significantly interfered with a consumer's ability to make informed decisions that would have prevented the injury. For example, a seller may have withheld otherwise unavailable information about important product features, or used high-pressure sales tactics on vulnerable consumers.

Remedies

Several types of orders may result from a successful FTC adjudicative proceeding attacking deceptive or unfair behavior. One possibility is an order telling the respondent to *cease* engaging in the deceptive or unfair conduct. Another is the *affirmative disclosure* of information whose absence made the advertisement deceptive or unfair. Yet another is *corrective advertising.* This requires the seller's future advertisements to correct false impressions created by its past advertisements. In certain cases, moreover, the FTC may issue an *all-products order* extending beyond the product or service whose advertisements violated § 5, and including future advertisements for other products or services marketed by the seller. The *Kraft* case, which appeared above, illustrates such an order. Finally, the FTC may sometimes go to court to seek injunctive relief or the civil penalties or consumer redress noted earlier.

Consumer Protection Laws

The term *consumer protection* includes everything from Chapter 20's product liability law to packaging and labeling regulations. Here, we examine federal regulation of telemarketing practices, product warranties, consumer credit, and product safety.

Telemarketing and Consumer Fraud and Abuse Prevention Act

In the Telemarketing and Consumer Fraud and Abuse Prevention Act (Telemarketing Act), Congress required the FTC to promulgate regulations defining and prohibiting *deceptive* and *abusive* telemarketing acts or practices. The FTC responded to this directive with the Telemarketing Sales Rule (TSR).

For purposes of the TSR, a *seller* is a party who (or which), in connection with a telemarketing transaction, offers or arranges to provide customers with goods or services in exchange for consideration. The TSR defines *telemarketer* as "any person who, in connection with telemarketing, initiates or receives telephone calls to or from a customer." It defines *telemarketing* as "a plan, program, or campaign which is conducted to induce the purchase of goods or services by use of one or more telephones and which involves more than one interstate telephone call." Exemptions from the telemarketing definition are provided for sellers that solicit sales through the mailing of a catalog and then receive customers' orders by telephone, and for sellers that make telephone calls of solicitation to a consumer but complete the transaction in a face-to-face meeting with the consumer.

A major feature of the TSR makes it a deceptive practice for telemarketers and sellers to fail to disclose certain information to a customer before she pays for the goods or services being telemarketed. The customer is regarded as having paid for goods or services once she provides information that may be used for billing purposes. The mandatory disclosures specified in the TSR include the total cost of the goods or services, any material restrictions or conditions on the purchase or use of the goods or services, and the terms of any refund or exchange policy mentioned in the solicitation (or, if the seller has a policy of not allowing refunds or exchanges, a disclosure of that policy). Various other disclosures are necessary if the telemarketing solicitation pertains to a prize promotion. The TSR also makes it a deceptive practice for a telemarketer or seller to misrepresent information required to be disclosed in the mandatory disclosures, or to misrepresent any other information

CYBERLAW IN ACTION

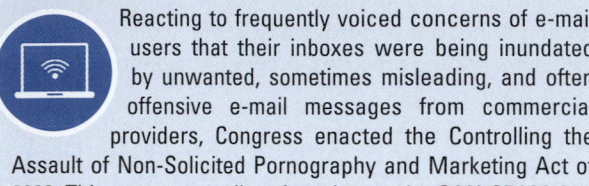

Reacting to frequently voiced concerns of e-mail users that their inboxes were being inundated by unwanted, sometimes misleading, and often offensive e-mail messages from commercial providers, Congress enacted the Controlling the Assault of Non-Solicited Pornography and Marketing Act of 2003. This statute, usually referred to as the CAN-SPAM Act, took effect on January 1, 2004.

In the CAN-SPAM Act, Congress outlawed various commercial e-mail practices, including the use of a false or misleading statement on the "from" line of a commercial message and the use of false or misleading subject headings in a commercial message. The CAN-SPAM Act also required that a sender of commercial e-mail use a functioning reply address or "opt-out" mechanism by which consumers could elect not to receive more messages from that sender, and that the sender send no further messages to a consumer more than ten days after the consumer has opted out. In addition, the CAN-SPAM Act required that commercial e-mail messages contain three components: clear identification that the message is an advertisement or solicitation; conspicuous notice that the recipient may decline to receive further messages from the sender; and a listing of the sender's postal address. A further CAN-SPAM Act provision required warning labels on commercial e-mail messages that feature sexually oriented material. Enforcement authority for violations of the CAN-SPAM Act was given to the FTC (which can launch adjudicative proceedings or initiate litigation in court), to state attorneys general (who can sue in federal court concerning certain violations), and to providers of Internet access services (which can sue in federal court concerning certain other violations).

The CAN-SPAM Act also required the FTC to promulgate regulations to implement the statute and further its purposes. The regulations promulgated by the FTC took effect in 2008. It is perhaps too early to make a full and fair assessment of the CAN-SPAM Act's effectiveness in dealing with the problem it was designed to address. Nevertheless, critics have lamented that the statute and the related regulations may not prove to be particularly effective. They have pointed to a continued proliferation of unwanted commercial e-mail as an indication that purveyors of such material have either ignored the legal requirements or have found it relatively easy to modify their e-mail techniques enough to comply with the law while still maintaining an ability to flood in-boxes with unsolicited messages.

concerning the performance, nature, or characteristics of the goods or services being offered for sale.

According to the TSR, a telemarketer or seller engages in an abusive practice if he directs threats, intimidation, or profane or obscene language toward a customer; causes the telephone to ring, or engages a person in a telephone conversation, repeatedly and with the intent to harass, abuse, or annoy a person at the called number; or initiates a call to a person who has previously stated that she does not wish to receive a call made by or on behalf of the seller whose goods or services are being offered.

The TSR also makes it an abusive practice for a telemarketer to call a person's residence at any time other than between 8:00 AM and 9:00 PM at the called person's location. In addition, the telemarketer engages in an abusive practice if, in a telephone call he initiated, he does not promptly and clearly disclose the identity of the seller, the sales purpose of the call, the nature of the goods or services, and the fact that no purchase or payment is necessary in order to win a prize or participate in a prize promotion (if a prize or prize promotion is being offered). Still other abusive practices are enumerated in the TSR.

The FTC and state attorneys general may bring enforcement proceedings against violators of the Telemarketing Act and the TSR. Civil penalties of up to $10,000 per violation are among the available remedies in government-initiated proceedings. Under some circumstances, private citizens may sue violators for damages and injunctive relief.

Do-Not-Call Registry Regulations promulgated in 2003 by the FTC and the Federal Communications Commission created a legal mechanism by which consumers who preferred not to receive telemarketing calls of a commercial nature could have their home telephone numbers listed on a national "do-not-call" registry. Commercial telemarketers became legally obligated not to place calls to the numbers listed. The do-not-call registry became popular among consumers, with many millions taking action to have their numbers placed on the list within the first several months of its existence. Affected commercial telemarketers initiated litigation questioning the legal validity of the do-not-call registry. In the *Mainstream Marketing* case, which follows, a federal court of appeals upheld the do-not-call registry against challenges brought on lack-of-statutory authority and First Amendment grounds. Additional information regarding the origins, purposes, and effect of the do-not-call registry appears in the statement of facts preceding the edited version of the *Mainstream Marketing* opinion.

Mainstream Marketing Services, Inc. v. Federal Trade Commission
358 F.3d 1228 (10th Cir. 2004)

In 2003, the Federal Trade Commission (FTC) and the Federal Communications Commission (FCC) promulgated rules that together created the national do-not-call registry. This registry is a list containing the personal telephone numbers of telephone subscribers who have voluntarily indicated that they do not wish to receive unsolicited calls from commercial telemarketers. Consumers can register their personal phone numbers for the do-not-call list either online or by phone. Commercial telemarketers are generally prohibited from calling phone numbers that have been placed on the do-not-call registry. As of early 2004, consumers had registered more than 50 million phone numbers.

The do-not-call registry's restrictions apply only to telemarketing calls made by or on behalf of sellers of goods or services, and not to charitable or political fundraising calls. Under exceptions to the general do-not-call rule, a seller may still call consumers who have signed up for the national registry if the seller has an established business relationship with the consumer or if the consumer has given that seller express written permission to call. Consumer listings on the do-not-call registry remain valid for five years.

Since the early 1990s, Congress, the FCC, and the FTC had been involved in a regulatory effort aimed at protecting the privacy rights of consumers and curbing the risk of telemarketing abuse. The do-not-call registry was the eventual product of this effort. In the Telephone Consumer Protection Act of 1991 (TCPA), under which the FCC enacted its do-not-call rules, Congress found that telemarketing sales calls constitute an intrusive invasion of the privacy of many consumers. Moreover, the TCPA's legislative history cited statistics indicating that "most unwanted telephone solicitations are commercial in nature" and that "unwanted commercial calls are a far bigger problem than unsolicited calls from political or charitable organizations." The TCPA therefore authorized the FCC to establish a national database of consumers who object to receiving "telephone solicitations," which the act defined as commercial sales calls.

In the Telemarketing and Consumer Fraud and Abuse Prevention Act of 1994 (Telemarketing Act), under which the FTC enacted its do-not-call rules, Congress found that consumers lose an estimated $40 billion each year as a result of telemarketing fraud. Therefore, Congress authorized the FTC to prohibit sales calls that a reasonable consumer would consider coercive or abusive of his or her right to privacy. The FCC and FTC initially sought to accomplish the goals of the TCPA and the Telemarketing Act by adopting rules that called for company-specific lists to be maintained by sellers. These lists were to contain the phone numbers of consumers who had requested not to be called by that particular solicitor. Telemarketers were obligated to honor those requests. The FCC and FTC later concluded that the company-specific lists had proven unworkable and had failed to achieve the objectives of Congress. Therefore, the agencies promulgated the regulations setting up a more expansive program: the national do-not-call registry.

Organizations engaged in commercial telemarketing filed various lawsuits that raised legal challenges to the do-not-call registry. In one of these cases, a federal district court held that the FTC lacked statutory authority to promulgate the regulations establishing the do-not-call registry. In another case, a federal district court held that the do-not-call registry violated the telemarketers' First Amendment right to freedom of speech. Those two cases, as well as others presenting challenges to parts of the regulations that established the do-not-call registry, were consolidated for purposes of appeal in the U.S. Court of Appeals for the Tenth Circuit. The following is an edited and reorganized version of the portions of the Tenth Circuit's opinion dealing with the statutory authority and First Amendment issues.

Ebel, Circuit Judge

The cases consolidated in this appeal involve challenges to the national do-not-call registry, which allows individuals to register their phone numbers on a national "do-not-call list" and prohibits most commercial telemarketers from calling the numbers on that list.

In [one of the consolidated cases], the district court held that the FTC lacked statutory authority to enact the do-not-call registry. In the Telemarketing Act, Congress authorized the FTC to "prescribe rules prohibiting deceptive telemarketing acts or practices and other abusive telemarketing acts or practices." More specifically, Congress directed the FTC to include "a requirement that telemarketers may not undertake a pattern of unsolicited telephone calls which the reasonable consumer would consider coercive or abusive of such consumer's right to privacy." The FTC's conclusion that this language authorized it to enact the national do-not-call registry is entitled to deference [from this court]. In light of this deference, we conclude that the FTC did have statutory authority to promulgate its do-not-call regulations because the agency's view that the Telemarketing Act authorized it to enact those rules is at least a permissible construction of that statute.

Moreover, even if some doubt once existed, Congress erased it through subsequent legislation. In the Do-Not-Call Implementation Act, Congress directed the FCC and FTC to maximize consistency between their respective do-not-call rules and . . . , in response to the district court's decision [regarding statutory authority,] expressly ratified the FTC's do-not-call regulations. The FTC's statutory authority is now unmistakably clear.

The primary issue [before the court] is whether the First Amendment prevents the government from establishing an opt-in telemarketing regulation that provides a mechanism for consumers to restrict commercial sales calls but does not provide a similar mechanism to limit charitable or political calls. [As we explain more fully below, we] hold that the do-not-call registry is a valid commercial speech regulation. . . . We express no opinion as to whether the do-not-call registry would be constitutional if it applied to political and charitable callers.

The national do-not-call registry's telemarketing restrictions apply only to commercial speech. Like most commercial speech regulations, the do-not-call rules draw a line between commercial and noncommercial speech on the basis of content. [Chapters 3 and 5 contain discussion of the distinction between commercial and noncommercial speech and of the Supreme Court's decisions establishing that commercial speech receives a lesser degree of First Amendment protection than noncommercial speech receives.] In reviewing commercial speech regulations, we apply the *Central Hudson* test. *Central Hudson Gas & Electric Corp. v. Public Service Commission,* 447 U.S. 557 (U.S. Sup. Ct. 1980), established a three-part test governing First Amendment challenges to regulations restricting non-misleading commercial speech that relates to lawful activity. First, the government must assert a substantial interest to be achieved by the regulation. Second, the regulation must directly advance that governmental interest, meaning that it must do more than provide "only ineffective or remote support for the government's purpose." Third, . . . the regulation . . . must be narrowly tailored not to restrict more speech than necessary. Together, these final two factors require that there be a reasonable fit between the government's objectives and the means it chooses to accomplish those ends.

The government bears the burden of asserting one or more substantial governmental interests and demonstrating a reasonable fit between those interests and the challenged regulation. The government asserts that the do-not-call regulations are justified by its interests in 1) protecting the privacy of individuals in their homes, and 2) protecting consumers against the risk of fraudulent and abusive solicitation. Both of these justifications are undisputedly substantial governmental interests.

In *Rowan v. United States Post Office Dept.,* 397 U.S. 728 (U.S. Sup. Ct. 1970), the Supreme Court upheld the right of a homeowner to restrict material that could be mailed to his or her house. The Court emphasized the importance of individual privacy, particularly in the context of the home, stating that "the ancient concept that 'a man's home is his castle' into which 'not even the king may enter' has lost none of its vitality." In *Frisby v. Schultz,* 487 U.S. 474 (U.S. Sup. Ct. 1988), the Court again stressed the unique nature of the home and recognized that "the State's interest in protecting the well-being, tranquility, and privacy of the home is certainly of the highest order in a free and civilized society." [According to the Court in *Frisby,*] "we have repeatedly held that individuals are not required to welcome unwanted speech into their own homes and that the government may protect this freedom." Additionally, the Supreme Court has recognized that the government has a substantial interest in preventing abusive and coercive sales practices. *Edenfield v. Fane,* 507 U.S. 761 (U.S. Sup. Ct. 1993) ("The First Amendment . . . does not prohibit the State from insuring that the stream of commercial information flows cleanly as well as freely.").

A reasonable fit exists between the do-not-call rules and the government's privacy and consumer protection interests if the regulation directly advances those interests and is narrowly tailored. See *Central Hudson.* In this context, the "narrowly tailored" standard does not require that the government's response to protect substantial interests be the least restrictive measure available. All that is required is a proportional response. In other words, the national do-not-call registry is valid if it is designed to provide effective support for the government's purposes and if the government did not suppress an excessive amount of speech when substantially narrower restrictions would have worked just as well. These criteria are plainly established in this case. The do-not-call registry directly advances the government's interests by effectively blocking a significant number of the calls that cause the problems the government sought to redress. It is narrowly tailored because its opt-in character ensures that it does not inhibit any speech directed at the home of a willing listener.

The telemarketers assert that the do-not-call registry is unconstitutionally underinclusive because it does not apply to charitable and political callers. First Amendment challenges based on underinclusiveness face an uphill battle in the commercial speech context. As a general rule, the First Amendment does not require that the government regulate all aspects of a problem before it can make progress on any front.

As discussed above, the national do-not-call registry is designed to reduce intrusions into personal privacy and the risk of telemarketing fraud and abuse that accompany unwanted telephone solicitation. The registry directly advances those goals. So far, more than 50 million telephone numbers have been registered on the do-not-call list, and the do-not-call regulations protect these households from receiving most unwanted telemarketing calls. According to the telemarketers' own estimate, 2.64 telemarketing calls per week—or more than 137 calls annually—were directed at an average consumer before the do-not-call list came into effect. Accordingly, absent the do-not-call registry, telemarketers would call those consumers who have already signed up for the registry an estimated total of 6.85 billion times each year. To be sure, the do-not-call list will not block all of these calls. Nevertheless, it will prohibit a substantial number of them, making it difficult to fathom how the registry could be called an ineffective means of stopping invasive or abusive calls, or a regulation that furnishes only speculative or marginal support for the government's interests.

[T]he type of unsolicited calls that the do-not-call list does prohibit—commercial sales calls—is the type that Congress, the FTC, and the FCC have all determined to be most to blame for the problems the government is seeking to redress. According to the legislative history accompanying the TCPA, "complaint statistics show that unwanted commercial calls are a far bigger problem than unsolicited calls from political or charitable organizations." Similarly, the FCC determined that calls from solicitors with an established business relationship with the recipient are less problematic than other commercial calls.

Additionally, the FTC has found that commercial callers are more likely than noncommercial callers to engage in deceptive and abusive practices. Specifically, the FTC concluded that in charitable and political calls, a significant purpose of the call is to sell a cause, not merely to receive a donation, and that noncommercial callers thus have stronger incentives not to alienate the people they call or to engage in abusive and deceptive practices. The speech regulated by the do-not-call list is therefore the speech most likely to cause the problems the government sought to alleviate in enacting that list, further demonstrating that the regulation directly advances the government's interests.

Although the least restrictive means test is not the test to be used in the commercial speech context, commercial speech regulations do at least have to be "narrowly tailored" and provide a "reasonable fit" between the problem and the solution. Whether or not there are numerous and obvious less-burdensome alternatives is a relevant consideration in our narrow tailoring analysis. A law is narrowly tailored if it "promotes a substantial government interest that would be achieved less effectively absent the regulation." [Case citation omitted.] Accordingly, we consider whether there are numerous and obvious alternatives that would restrict less speech and would serve the government's interest as effectively as the challenged law.

We hold that the national do-not-call registry is narrowly tailored because it does not overregulate protected speech; rather, it restricts only calls that are targeted at unwilling recipients. The do-not-call registry prohibits only telemarketing calls aimed at consumers who have affirmatively indicated that they do not want to receive such calls and for whom such calls would constitute an invasion of privacy.

The Supreme Court has repeatedly held that speech restrictions based on private choice (in other words, an opt-in feature) are less restrictive than laws that prohibit speech directly. In *Rowan*, for example, the Court approved a law under which an individual could require a mailer to stop all future mailings if he or she received advertisements that he or she believed to be erotically arousing or sexually provocative. Likewise, in rejecting direct prohibitions of speech (even fully protected speech), the Supreme Court has often reasoned that an opt-in regulation would have been a less restrictive alternative. In *Martin v. City of Struthers*, 319 U.S. 141 (U.S. Sup. Ct. 1943), [for instance,] the Court struck down a city ordinance prohibiting door-to-door canvassing, noting that the government's interest could have been achieved in a less restrictive manner by giving householders the choice of whether or not to receive visitors.

The idea that an opt-in regulation is less restrictive than a direct prohibition of speech applies not only to traditional door-to-door solicitation, but also to regulations seeking to protect the privacy of the home from unwanted intrusions via telephone, television, or the Internet. See *United States v. Playboy Entertainment Group, Inc.*, 529 U.S. 803 (U.S. Sup. Ct. 2000) (opt-in targeted blocking of offensive television programming "enables the Government to support parental authority without affecting the First Amendment interests of speakers and willing listeners. . . . Simply put, targeted blocking is less restrictive than banning. . . ."). Like the do-not-mail regulation approved in *Rowan*, the national do-not-call registry does not itself prohibit any speech. Instead, it merely "permits a citizen to erect a wall . . . that no advertiser may penetrate without his acquiescence." See *Rowan*. Almost by definition, the do-not-call regulations only block calls that would constitute unwanted intrusions into the privacy of consumers who have signed up for the list. Moreover, it allows consumers who feel susceptible to telephone fraud or abuse to ensure that most commercial callers will not have an opportunity to victimize them. Under the circumstances we address in this case, we conclude that the do-not-call registry's opt-in feature renders it a narrowly tailored commercial speech regulation.

The do-not-call registry's narrow tailoring is further demonstrated by the fact that it presents both sellers and consumers with a number of options to make and receive sales offers. From the seller's perspective, the do-not-call registry restricts only one avenue by which solicitors can communicate with consumers who have registered for the list. In particular, the do-not-call regulations do not prevent businesses from corresponding with potential customers by mail or by means of advertising through other media.

Finally, none of the telemarketers' proposed alternatives would serve the government's interests as effectively as the national do-not-call list. Primarily, the telemarketers suggest that company-specific rules effectively protected consumers. Yet as the FTC found, "the record in this matter overwhelmingly shows the contrary . . . it shows that the company-specific approach is seriously inadequate to protect consumers' privacy from an abusive pattern of calls placed by a seller or telemarketer."

First, the company-specific approach proved to be extremely burdensome to consumers, who had to repeat their do-not-call requests to every solicitor who called. In effect, this system gave solicitors one free chance to call each consumer, although many consumers find even an initial unsolicited sales call abusive and invasive of privacy. Second, the government's experience under the company-specific rules demonstrated that commercial solicitors often ignored consumers' requests to be placed on their company-specific lists. Third, consumers have no way to verify whether their numbers have been removed from a solicitor's calling list in response to a company-specific do-not-call request. Finally, company-specific rules are difficult to enforce because they require consumers to bear the evidentiary burden of keeping lists detailing which telemarketers have called them and what do-not-call requests they have made.

[T]he telemarketers [also] argue that it would have been less restrictive to let consumers rely on technological alternatives—such as caller ID, call rejection services, and electronic devices designed to block unwanted calls. Each of these alternatives puts the cost of avoiding unwanted telemarketing calls on consumers. Forcing consumers to compete in a technological arms race with the telemarketing industry is not an equally effective alternative to the do-not-call registry.

In sum, the do-not-call registry is narrowly tailored to restrict only speech that contributes to the problems the government seeks to redress, namely the intrusion into personal privacy and the risk of fraud and abuse caused by telephone calls that consumers do not welcome into their homes. No calls are restricted unless the recipient has affirmatively declared that he or she does not wish to receive them. Moreover, telemarketers still have the ability to contact consumers in other ways, and consumers have a number of different options in determining what telemarketing calls they will receive. Finally, there are not numerous and obvious less-burdensome alternatives that would restrict less speech while accomplishing the government's objectives equally as well.

The national do-not-call registry offers consumers a tool with which they can protect their homes against intrusions that Congress has determined to be particularly invasive. Just as a consumer can avoid door-to-door peddlers by placing a "No Solicitation" sign in his or her front yard, the do-not-call registry lets consumers avoid unwanted sales pitches that invade the home via telephone, if they choose to do so. We are convinced that the First Amendment does not prevent the government from giving consumers this option.

Judgment striking down do-not-call registry as being outside FTC's statutory authority reversed; judgment striking down do-not-call registry on First Amendment grounds also reversed.

Magnuson-Moss Warranty Act

The Magnuson-Moss Warranty Act of 1975 mainly applies to *written warranties* for *consumer products*. Nothing in the act requires sellers to give a written warranty. Sellers who decline to provide such a warranty generally escape coverage. A consumer product is personal property that is ordinarily used for personal, family, or household purposes. In addition, many Magnuson-Moss provisions apply only when a written warranty is given in connection with the sale of a consumer product to a *consumer.* A consumer is a buyer or transferee who does not use the product for resale or in his own business.

Chapter 20 discusses Magnuson-Moss's provisions giving consumers minimum warranty protection. Here, we examine its rules requiring that consumer warranties contain certain information and that this information be made available to buyers before the sale. Any failure to comply with these rules violates § 5 of the FTC Act and may trigger commission action. In addition, either the FTC or the attorney general may sue to obtain injunctive relief against such violations.

Required Warranty Information   The Magnuson-Moss Act and its regulations require the simple, clear, and conspicuous presentation of certain information in written warranties to consumers for consumer products costing more than $15. That information includes (1) the persons protected by the warranty when coverage is limited to the original purchaser or is otherwise limited; (2) the products, parts, characteristics, components, or properties covered by the warranty; (3) what the warrantor will do in case of a product defect or other failure to conform to the warranty; (4) the time the warranty begins (if different from the purchase date) and its duration; and (5) the procedure the consumer should follow to obtain the performance of warranty obligations. The act also requires that a warrantor disclose (1) any limitations on the duration of implied warranties; and (2) any attempt to limit consequential damages or other consumer remedies.

Presale Availability of Warranty Information The regulations accompanying Magnuson-Moss also contain detailed rules requiring that warranty terms be made available to a buyer before the sale. These rules generally govern sales to consumers of consumer products costing more than $15. They set out certain duties that must be met by sellers (usually retailers) and warrantors (usually manufacturers) of such products. For example:

1. *Sellers* must make the text of the warranty available for the prospective buyer's review before the sale, either by displaying the warranty in close proximity to the product or by furnishing the warranty upon request after posting signs informing buyers of its availability.

2. *Catalog or mail-order sellers* must clearly and conspicuously disclose in their catalog or solicitation either the full text of the warranty or the address from which a free copy can be obtained.

3. *Warrantors* must give sellers the warranty materials necessary for them to comply with the duties stated above.

Truth in Lending Act

When Congress passed the Truth in Lending Act (TILA) in 1968, its main aims were to increase consumer knowledge and understanding of credit terms by compelling their *disclosure,* and to help consumers shop for credit by commanding *uniform* disclosures. Now, however, the TILA protects consumers in other ways as well.

Coverage The TILA generally applies to creditors who extend consumer credit to a debtor in an amount not exceeding $25,000.[5] A *creditor* is a party who regularly

extends consumer credit. Examples include banks, credit card issuers, and savings and loan associations. Extending credit need not be a creditor's primary business. For instance, auto dealers and retail stores are creditors if they regularly extend credit. To qualify as a creditor, the party in question must also either impose a finance charge or by agreement require payment in more than four installments. *Consumer credit* is credit enabling the purchase of goods, services, or real estate used primarily for personal, family, or household purposes—not business or agricultural purposes. The TILA *debtor* must be a natural person; the act does not protect business organizations.

Disclosure Provisions The TILA's detailed disclosure provisions break down into three categories.

1. *Open-end credit.* The TILA defines an open-end credit plan as one that contemplates repeated transactions and involves a finance charge that may be computed on the unpaid balance. Examples include credit card plans and revolving charge accounts offered by retail stores. Open-end credit plans require two forms of disclosure: (1) an *initial statement* made before the first transaction under the plan; and (2) a series of *periodic statements* (usually, one for each billing cycle).

   Among the disclosures required in the initial statement are (1) when a finance charge is imposed and how it is determined; (2) the amount of any additional charges and the method for computing them; (3) the fact that the creditor has taken or will acquire a security interest in the debtor's property; and (4) the debtor's billing rights. Periodic statements require an even lengthier set of disclosures. Much of the information contained in a monthly credit card statement, for example, is compelled by the TILA.

2. *Closed-end credit.* The TILA requires a different set of disclosures for other credit plans, which generally involve closed-end credit. Closed-end credit such as a car loan or a consumer loan from a finance company is extended for a specific time period; the total amount financed, number of payments, and due dates are all agreed on at the time of the transaction. Examples of the disclosures necessary before the completion of a closed-end credit transaction include (1) the total finance charge; (2) the annual percentage rate (APR); (3) the amount financed; (4) the total number of payments, their due dates, and the amount of each payment; (5) the total dollar value of all payments; (6) any late charges imposed for past-due payments; and (7) any security interest taken by the creditor and the property that the security interest covers.

---

[5]The $25,000 maximum does not apply where a creditor takes a security interest in a debtor's real property or in personal property, such as a mobile home, used as the debtor's principal dwelling. Here, the disclosure rules differ slightly from the rules for closed-end credit discussed shortly. In certain transactions of this kind, moreover, the debtor has a three-day rescission right whose details are beyond the scope of this text.

3. *Credit card applications and solicitations.* The TILA imposes disclosure requirements on credit card applications and solicitations. These elaborate requirements differ depending on whether the application or solicitation is made by direct mail, telephone, or other means such as catalogs and magazines. To take just one example, direct mail applications and solicitations must include information about matters such as the APR, annual fees, the grace period for paying without incurring a finance charge, and the method for computing the balance on which the finance charge is based.

Other TILA Provisions The TILA has provisions dealing with *consumer credit advertising.* For example, the act prevents a creditor from "baiting" customers by advertising loan or down payment amounts that it does not usually make available. To help consumers put advertised terms in perspective, if ads for open-end consumer credit plans state any of the plan's specific terms, they must state various other terms as well. For instance, an advertisement using such terms as "$100 down payment," "6 percent interest," or "$99 per month" must also state other relevant terms such as the APR.

The TILA also regulates *open-end consumer credit plans involving an extension of credit secured by a consumer's principal dwelling*—e.g., the popular home equity loans. The act controls *advertisements* for such plans, requiring certain information such as the APR if the ad states any specific terms and forbidding misleading terms such as "free money." It also imposes elaborate disclosure requirements on *applications* for such plans. These include matters such as interest rates, fees, repayment options, minimum payments, and repayment periods. The act also controls the *terms* of such a plan and the *actions* a creditor may take under it. For example: (1) if the plan involves a variable interest rate, the "index rate" to which changes in the APR are pegged must be based on some publicly available rate and must not be under the creditor's control; and (2) a creditor cannot unilaterally terminate the plan and require immediate repayment of the outstanding balance unless a consumer has made material misrepresentations, has failed to repay the balance, or has adversely affected the creditor's security.

Finally, the TILA includes rules concerning *credit cards.* The most important such rule limits a cardholder's liability for unauthorized use of the card to a maximum of $50.

Enforcement Various federal agencies enforce the TILA. Except in areas committed to a particular agency, overall enforcement authority rests in the FTC. Those who willfully and knowingly violate the act may face criminal prosecution. Civil actions by private parties, including class actions, are also possible.

Fair Credit Reporting Act
The reports credit bureaus provide may significantly affect one's ability to obtain credit, insurance, employment, and many of life's other goods. Often, affected individuals are unaware of the influence that credit reports had on such decisions. The Fair Credit Reporting Act (FCRA) was enacted in 1970 to give people protection against abuses in the process of disseminating information about their creditworthiness.

Duties of Consumer Reporting Agencies The FCRA imposes certain duties on consumer reporting agencies—agencies that regularly compile credit-related information on individuals for the purpose of furnishing consumer credit reports to users. A consumer reporting agency must adopt *reasonable procedures* to:

1. Ensure that *users employ* the information only for the following purposes: consumer credit sales, employment evaluations, the underwriting of insurance, the granting of a government license or other benefit, or any other business transaction where the user has a legitimate business need for the information.

2. Avoid including in a report *obsolete information* predating the report by more than a stated period. This period usually is 7 years; for a prior bankruptcy, it is 10 years. This duty does not apply to credit reports used in connection with certain life insurance policies, large credit transactions, and applications for employment.

3. Ensure *maximum possible accuracy* regarding the personal information in credit reports. However, the act does little to limit the *types* of data included in credit reports. In fact, all kinds of information about a person's character, reputation, personal traits, and mode of living seemingly are permitted. However, medical information cannot be included without consent from the relevant consumer.

Duties of Users The FCRA also imposes disclosure duties on *users* of credit reports—mainly credit sellers, lenders, employers, and insurers. One of these duties applies to users who order an *investigative consumer report.* This is a credit report that includes information on a person's character, reputation, personal traits, or mode of living and is based on interviews with neighbors, friends, associates, and the like. If a user procures such a report on a person, it must inform him that the report has been requested, that the report may contain sensitive information, and that he has a right to obtain further disclosures about the user's investigation. If the person requests such disclosures within a reasonable time, the user must reveal the nature and scope of the investigation.

Another disclosure duty arises when, because of information contained in any credit report, a user (1) rejects an applicant for consumer credit, insurance, or employment; or (2) charges a higher rate for credit or insurance. Here, the user must maintain reasonable procedures for advising the affected individual that it relied on the credit report in making its decision and for stating the name and address of the consumer reporting agency that supplied the report. The *Safeco Insurance* case, which follows shortly, deals with issues surrounding this notice requirement.

Disclosure and Correction of Credit Report Information

After a request from a properly identified individual, a *consumer reporting agency* must normally disclose to that individual (1) the nature and substance of all its information about the individual; (2) the sources of this information; and (3) the recipients of any credit reports that it has furnished within certain time periods. Then, a person disputing the completeness or accuracy of the agency's information can compel it to reinvestigate.

The credit bureau must delete the information from the person's file if it finds the information to be inaccurate or unverifiable. An individual who is not satisfied with the agency's investigation may file a brief statement setting forth the nature of her dispute with the agency. If so, any subsequent credit report containing the disputed information must note that it is disputed and must provide either the individual's statement or a clear and accurate summary of it. An agency may also be required to notify certain prior recipients of deleted, unverifiable, or disputed information if the individual requests this. However, there is no duty to investigate or to include the consumer's version of the facts if the credit bureau has reason to believe that the individual's request is frivolous or irrelevant.

Enforcement

Violations of the FCRA are violations of FTC Act § 5; the commission may use its normal enforcement procedures in such cases. Other federal agencies may also enforce the FCRA in certain situations. The FCRA establishes criminal penalties for persons who knowingly and willfully obtain consumer information from a credit bureau under false pretenses. Criminal liability may also be imposed on credit bureau officers or employees who knowingly or willfully provide information to unauthorized persons. In addition, violations of the FCRA may trigger private civil suits against consumer reporting agencies and users.

Safeco Insurance Co. of America v. Burr
127 S. Ct. 2201 (U.S. Sup. Ct. 2007)

Congress enacted the Fair Credit Reporting Act (FCRA) in 1970 to ensure fair and accurate credit reporting, promote efficiency in the banking system, and protect consumer privacy. The FCRA requires, among other things, that "any person [who] takes any adverse action with respect to any consumer that is based in whole or in part on any information contained in a consumer report" must notify the affected consumer. 15 U.S.C. § 1681m(a). The FCRA defines "consumer report" as "any written, oral, or other communication of any information by a consumer reporting agency bearing on a consumer's credit worthiness, credit standing, [or] credit capacity . . . which is used or expected to be used or collected in whole or in part for the purpose of serving as a factor in establishing the consumer's eligibility for . . . credit or insurance to be used primarily for personal, family, or household purposes." § 1681a(d)(1). The notice of adverse action must point out that action, must explain how to reach the agency that reported on the consumer's credit, and must tell the consumer that he can get a free copy of the report and dispute its accuracy with the agency. § 1681m(a). As it applies to an insurance company, "adverse action" is "a denial or cancellation of, an increase in any charge for, or a reduction or other adverse or unfavorable change in the terms of coverage or amount of, any insurance, existing or applied for." § 1681a(k)(1)(B)(i).

The FCRA provides a private right of action against businesses that use consumer reports but fail to comply with the statute's requirements. If a violation is negligent in nature, the affected consumer is entitled to actual damages. § 1681o(a). If the violation is willful, however, the consumer may be entitled to added monetary relief, including punitive damages. § 1681n(a).

GEICO Corp. writes auto insurance through four subsidiaries: GEICO General, which sells "preferred" policies at low rates to low-risk customers; Government Employees, which also sells "preferred" policies, but only to government employees;

GEICO Indemnity, which sells standard policies to moderate-risk customers; and GEICO Casualty, which sells nonstandard policies at higher rates to high-risk customers. (For purposes of convenience, the four subsidiaries are referred to here as GEICO.) An applicant seeking insurance from GEICO calls a toll-free number answered by a GEICO employee, who takes information and, with the applicant's permission, obtains the applicant's credit score from a credit reporting firm. (The FCRA defines a "credit score" as "a numerical value or a categorization derived from a statistical tool or modeling system used by a person who makes or arranges a loan to predict the likelihood of certain credit behaviors, including default.") The information, including the credit score, goes into GEICO's computer system, which selects the appropriate company and the particular rate at which a policy may be issued.

For some time after the FCRA went into effect, GEICO sent adverse action notices to all applicants who were not offered "preferred" policies from GEICO General or Government Employees. GEICO changed its practice, however, after a method to "neutralize" an applicant's credit score was devised. Under the neutralization method, the applicant's company and tier placements are compared with the company and tier placements he would have been assigned with a "neutral" credit score—that is, one calculated without reliance on the applicant's credit history. Under this new scheme, GEICO sends an adverse action notice only if using a neutral credit score would have put the applicant in a lower-priced tier or company. The applicant is not otherwise told if he would have received better terms with a better credit score.

Ajene Edo applied for auto insurance with GEICO. After obtaining Edo's credit score, GEICO offered him a standard policy with GEICO Indemnity (at rates higher than the most favorable), which he accepted. Because Edo's company and tier placement would have been the same with a neutral score, GEICO did not give Edo an adverse action notice. Edo later sued GEICO, alleging willful failure to give notice in violation of § 1681m(a) and seeking damages—including punitive damages—under § 1681n(a). A federal district court granted summary judgment for GEICO, concluding that there was no adverse action when "the premium charged to [Edo] . . . would have been the same even if GEICO Indemnity did not consider information in [his] consumer credit history."

As does GEICO, Safeco Insurance Co of America relies on credit reports to set initial insurance premiums. After considering their credit reports, Safeco offered insurance applicants Charles Burr and Shannon Massey higher rates than the best rates possible. Safeco sent them no adverse action notices. Burr and Massey later sued Safeco, alleging willful violation of § 1681m(a) and seeking damages under § 1681n(a). A federal district court granted summary judgment to Safeco, reasoning that offering a single, initial rate for insurance cannot be "adverse action."

The U.S. Court of Appeals for the Ninth Circuit reversed the judgments in both of the cases described above. In the case against GEICO, the Ninth Circuit held that whenever a consumer "would have received a lower rate for his insurance had the information in his consumer report been more favorable, an adverse action has been taken against him." Because a better credit score would have placed Edo with GEICO General, not GEICO Indemnity, the appeals court held that GEICO's failure to give notice was an adverse action. The Ninth Circuit also held that an insurer "willfully" fails to comply with FCRA if it acts with "reckless disregard" of a consumer's rights under the statute—a conclusion inconsistent with the position taken by certain other federal courts of appeal. The Ninth Circuit remanded the case to the district court for further proceedings concerning whether GEICO acted with reckless disregard.

In the case against Safeco, the Ninth Circuit reversed the district court's decision by relying on its (the Ninth Circuit's) reasoning in the case against GEICO (where it had held that the notice requirement applies to a single statement of an initial charge for a new policy). The Ninth Circuit also remanded the case to the district court for further proceedings on the issue of whether Safeco willfully violated the FCRA. The Supreme Court granted the petitions for certiorari in both cases and consolidated the cases for purposes of disposition.

Souter, Justice

We . . . granted certiorari to resolve a conflict [among the various federal courts of appeal] as to whether § 1681n(a) reaches reckless disregard of the FCRA's obligations, and to clarify the notice requirement in § 1681m(a).

GEICO and Safeco argue that liability under § 1681n(a) for "willfully fail[ing] to comply" with the FCRA goes only to acts known to violate the Act, not to reckless disregard of statutory

duty, but we think they are wrong. [W]here willfulness is a statutory condition of civil liability, we have generally taken it to cover not only knowing violations of a standard, but reckless ones as well. [Case citations omitted.] This construction reflects common law usage, which treated actions in reckless disregard of the law as willful violations. The standard civil usage thus counsels reading the phrase "willfully fails to comply" in § 1681n(a) as reaching reckless FCRA violations.

Before getting to the claims that the companies acted reck-lessly, we have the antecedent question whether either company violated the adverse action notice requirement at all. In both cases, respondent-plaintiffs' claims are premised on initial rates charged for new insurance policies, which are not "adverse" actions unless quoting or charging a first-time pre-mium is "an increase in any charge for . . . any insurance, exist-ing or applied for." § 1681a(k)(1)(B)(i).

In Safeco's case, the district court held that the initial rate for a new insurance policy cannot be an "increase" because there is no prior dealing. The phrase "increase in any charge for . . . insurance" is readily understood to mean a change in treatment for an insured, which assumes a previous charge for comparison. Since the district court understood "increase" to speak of change just as much as of comparative size or quan-tity, it reasoned that the statute's "increase" never touches the initial rate offer, where there is no change.

The Government takes the [position] of the Court of Ap-peals in construing "increase" to reach a first-time rate. It says that regular usage of the term is not as narrow as the district court thought: the point from which to measure difference can just as easily be understood without referring to prior individ-ual dealing. The Government gives the example of a gas station owner who charges more than the posted price for gas to cus-tomers he doesn't like; it makes sense to say that the owner in-creases the price and that the driver pays an increased price, even if he never pulled in there for gas before. The Government implies, then, that reading "increase" requires a choice, and the chosen reading should be the broad one in order to conform to what Congress had in mind.

We think the Government's reading has the better fit with the ambitious objective set out in the FCRA's statement of purpose, which uses expansive terms to describe the adverse effects of unfair and inaccurate credit reporting and the responsibilities of consumer reporting agencies. The descriptions of systemic problem and systemic need as Congress saw them do nothing to suggest that remedies for consumers placed at a disadvantage by unsound credit ratings should be denied to first-time victims, and the legislative histories of FCRA's original enactment and [a 1996] amendment reveal no reason to confine attention to cus-tomers and businesses with prior dealings. Finally, there is noth-ing about insurance contracts to suggest that Congress might have meant to differentiate applicants from existing customers when it set the notice requirement; the newly insured who gets charged more owing to an erroneous report is in the same boat with the renewal applicant. We therefore hold that the "increase" required for "adverse action," 15 U.S.C. § 1681a(k)(1)(B)(i), speaks to a disadvantageous rate even with no prior dealing; the term reaches initial rates for new applicants.

Although offering the initial rate for new insurance can be an "adverse action," respondent-plaintiffs have another hurdle to clear, for § 1681m(a) calls for notice only when the adverse action is "based in whole or in part on" a credit report. GEICO argues that in order to have adverse action "based on" a credit report, consideration of the report must be a necessary condi-tion for the increased rate. The Government and respondent-plaintiffs do not explicitly take a position on this point.

To the extent there is any disagreement on the issue, we ac-cept GEICO's reading. In common talk, the phrase "based on" indicates a but-for causal relationship and thus a necessary log-ical condition. Under this most natural reading of § 1681m(a), then, an increased rate is not "based in whole or in part on" the credit report unless the report was a necessary condition of the increase.

To sum up [what has been determined so far], the difference required for an increase can be understood without reference to prior dealing (allowing a first-time applicant to sue), and con-sidering the credit report must be a necessary condition for the difference. The remaining step in determining a duty to notify in cases like these is identifying the benchmark for determining whether a first-time rate is a disadvantageous increase. The Government and respondent-plaintiffs argue that the baseline should be the rate that the applicant would have received with the best possible credit score, while GEICO contends it is what the applicant would have had if the company had not taken his credit score into account (the "neutral score" rate GEICO used in Edo's case). We think GEICO has the better position, prima-rily because its "increase" baseline is more comfortable with the understanding of causation just discussed, which requires notice under § 1681m(a) only when the effect of the credit re-port on the initial rate offered is necessary to put the consumer in a worse position than other relevant facts would have de-creed anyway. Congress was more likely concerned with the practical question whether the consumer's rate actually suf-fered when the company took his credit report into account than the theoretical question whether the consumer would have gotten a better rate with perfect credit.

The Government objects that this reading leaves a loophole, since it keeps first-time applicants who actually deserve better-than-neutral credit scores from getting notice, even when errors in credit reports saddle them with unfair rates. This is true; the neutral-score baseline will leave some consumers without a no-tice that might lead to discovering errors. But we do not know how often these cases will occur, whereas we see a more demonstrable and serious disadvantage inhering in the Govern-ment's position.

Since the best rates (the Government's preferred baseline) presumably go only to a minority of consumers, adopting the

Government's view would require insurers to send slews of adverse action notices; every young applicant who had yet to establish a gilt-edged credit report, for example, would get a notice that his charge had been "increased" based on his credit report. We think that the consequence of sending out notices on this scale would undercut the obvious policy behind the notice requirement, for notices as common as these would take on the character of formalities, and formalities tend to be ignored. It would get around that new insurance usually comes with an adverse action notice, owing to some legal quirk, and instead of piquing an applicant's interest about the accuracy of his credit record, the commonplace notices would mean just about nothing and go the way of junk mail. Assuming that Congress meant a notice of adverse action to get some attention, we think the cost of closing the loophole would be too high.

In GEICO's case, the initial rate offered to Edo was the one he would have received if his credit score had not been taken into account. GEICO [therefore] owed him no adverse action notice under § 1681m(a). Safeco did not give Burr and Massey any notice because it thought § 1681m(a) did not apply to initial applications, a mistake that left the company in violation of the statute if Burr and Massey received higher rates "based in whole or in part" on their credit reports; if they did, Safeco would be liable to them on a showing of reckless conduct (or worse). The first issue we can forget, however, for although the record does not reliably indicate what rates they would have obtained if their credit reports had not been considered, it is clear enough that if Safeco did violate the statute, the company was not reckless in falling down in its duty.

While "the term recklessness is not self-defining," the common law has generally understood it in the sphere of civil liability as conduct violating an objective standard: action entailing "an unjustifiably high risk of harm that is either known or so obvious that it should be known." [Case citation omitted.] The *Restatement (Second) of Torts,* for example, defines reckless disregard of a person's physical safety this way:

> The actor's conduct is in reckless disregard of the safety of another if he does an act or intentionally fails to do an act which it is his duty to the other to do, knowing or having reason to know of facts which would lead a reasonable man to realize, not only that his conduct creates an unreasonable risk of physical harm to another, but also that such risk is substantially greater than that which is necessary to make his conduct negligent.

It is this high risk of harm, objectively assessed, that is the essence of recklessness at common law.

There being no indication that Congress had something different in mind, we have no reason to deviate from the common law understanding in applying the statute. Thus, a company subject to the FCRA does not act in reckless disregard of it unless the action is not only a violation under a reasonable reading of the statute's terms, but shows that the company ran a risk of violating the law substantially greater than the risk associated with a reading that was merely careless.

Here, there is no need to pinpoint the negligence/recklessness line, for Safeco's reading of the statute, albeit erroneous, was not objectively unreasonable. On the rationale that "increase" presupposes prior dealing, Safeco took the definition as excluding initial rate offers for new insurance, and so sent no adverse action notices to Burr and Massey. While we disagree with Safeco's analysis, we recognize that its reading has a foundation in the statutory text, and a sufficiently convincing justification to have persuaded the district court to adopt it and rule in Safeco's favor.

This is not a case in which the business subject to the Act had the benefit of guidance from the courts of appeals or the Federal Trade Commission (FTC) that might have warned it away from the view it took. Before these cases, no court of appeals had spoken on the issue, and no authoritative guidance has yet come from the FTC. Given this dearth of guidance and the less-than-pellucid statutory text, Safeco's reading was not objectively unreasonable, and so falls well short of raising the "unjustifiably high risk" of violating the statute necessary for reckless liability.

The Court of Appeals correctly held that reckless disregard of a requirement of the FCRA would qualify as a willful violation within the meaning of § 1681n(a). But there was no need for that court to remand the cases for factual development. GEICO's decision to issue no adverse action notice to Edo was not a violation of § 1681m(a), and Safeco's misreading of the statute was not reckless.

Judgments of Court of Appeals reversed, and cases remanded for further proceedings consistent with Supreme Court's opinion.

FACT Act and the Identity Theft Problem

In recent years, the problem of so-called identity theft has become increasingly acute. Identity theft occurs when those who improperly obtain access to other persons' Social Security number and identifying information such as credit card numbers, bank account numbers, and the like use that information to commit financial fraud by making purchases or obtaining credit in the name of those other persons. A recent FTC estimate indicates that approximately 10 million persons per year may be victims of identity theft in at least one instance and sometimes an ongoing series of instances. Hundreds of thousands of persons have made formal complaints to the FTC regarding identity theft, which is behavior that falls under the FTC's regulatory authority to address deceptive or unfair practices in commercial settings.

Congress, federal agencies, and some state legislatures have attempted to deal with the identity theft problem through statutes and regulations. In late 2003, Congress enacted the Fair and Accurate Credit Transactions Act (usually called the FACT Act) as a series of amendments to the Fair Credit Reporting Act. The FACT Act aids victims of identity theft by allowing them to file identity theft reports with consumer reporting agencies and by requiring such agencies to include "fraud alerts" in their credit reports about consumers who believe they have been victimized by someone else's fraudulent use of their financial information. The FACT Act also required the FTC and various other government agencies to promulgate regulations setting standards for appropriate disposal of financial information about consumers by companies that possess such information. "Disposal," for purposes of the standards, would include not only discarding the information but also selling the information. This FACT Act requirement was designed to minimize the chances that consumers' financial information would fall into the hands of, or be purchased by, would-be identity thieves.

Recent years also witnessed a number of high-profile instances in which security breaches and other apparent lapses at prominent firms resulted in widespread disclosure of the private financial information of huge numbers of consumers. The publicity given to such breaches and lapses and the identity theft dangers they suggested have led to calls for further legislative action. With the identity theft concern seeming to intensify, additional statutory and regulatory efforts to deal with the problem seem likely.

Equal Credit Opportunity Act   The Equal

Credit Opportunity Act (ECOA) prohibits credit discrimination on the bases of sex, marital status, age, race, color, national origin, religion, and the obtaining of income from public assistance. The ECOA covers all entities that regularly arrange, extend, renew, or continue credit. Examples include banks, savings and loan associations, credit card issuers, and many retailers, auto dealers, and realtors. The act is not limited to consumer credit; it also covers business and commercial loans.

The ECOA governs all phases of a credit transaction. As authorized by the act, the Federal Reserve Board has promulgated regulations detailing permissible and impermissible creditor behavior at each stage. Even when the regulations do not specifically prohibit certain creditor behavior, that behavior may still violate the act itself. Moreover, a credit practice that is neutral on its face may result in an ECOA violation if the practice has an adverse statistical impact on one of the ECOA's protected classes.[6]

The ECOA also requires that creditors notify applicants of the action taken on a credit application within 30 days of its receipt or any longer reasonable time stated in the regulations. If the action is unfavorable, an applicant is entitled to a statement of reasons from the creditor.

The ECOA is enforced by several federal agencies, with overall enforcement resting in the FTC's hands. Which agency enforces the act depends on the type of creditor or credit involved. Civil actions by aggrieved private parties, including class actions, also are possible.

Fair Credit Billing Act   The Fair Credit Billing

Act is primarily aimed at credit card issuers. Although the act regulates the credit card business in other ways, its most important provisions involve billing disputes. To trigger these provisions, a cardholder must give the issuer written notice of an alleged error in a billing statement within 60 days of the time that the statement is sent to the cardholder. Then, within two complete billing cycles or 90 days (whichever is less), the issuer must either (1) correct the cardholder's account, or (2) send the cardholder a written statement justifying the statement's accuracy. Until the issuer takes one of these steps, it may not (1) restrict or close the cardholder's account because of her failure to pay the disputed amount; (2) try to collect the disputed amount; or (3) report or threaten to report the cardholder's failure to pay the disputed amount to a third party such as a consumer reporting agency.

Once an issuer has met the act's requirements, it must also give a cardholder at least 10 days to pay the disputed amount before making an unfavorable report to a third party. If the cardholder disputes the issuer's justification within the 10-day period allowed for payment, the issuer can make such a report only if it also tells the third party that the debt is disputed and gives the cardholder the third party's name and address. In addition, the issuer must report the final resolution of the dispute to the third party.

---

[6]This resembles the adverse impact or disparate impact method of proof used in employment discrimination cases under Title VII of the 1964 Civil Rights Act. See Chapter 51.

An issuer that fails to comply with any of these rules forfeits its right to collect $50 of the disputed amount from the cardholder. Because the issuer may still be able to collect the balance on large disputed debts, it is doubtful whether this provision does much to deter violations of the act.

Fair Debt Collection Practices Act

Concern over abusive, deceptive, and unfair practices by debt collectors led Congress to pass the Fair Debt Collection Practices Act (FDCPA) in 1977. The act applies to debts that involve money, property, insurance, or services obtained by a *consumer* for *consumer purposes*. Normally, the act covers only those who are in the business of collecting debts owed to *others*. However, creditors who collect their own debts are covered when, by using a name other than their own name, they indicate that a third party is collecting the debt.

Communication Rules Except when necessary to locate a debtor, the FDCPA generally prevents debt collectors from contacting third parties such as the debtor's employer, relatives, or friends. The act also limits a collector's contacts with the debtor himself. Unless the debtor consents, for instance, a collector cannot contact him at unusual or inconvenient times or places, or at his place of employment if the employer forbids such contacts. A collector cannot contact a debtor if it knows that the debtor is represented by an attorney, unless the attorney consents to such contact or fails to respond to the collector's communications. In addition, a collector must cease most communications with a debtor if the debtor gives the creditor written notification that he refuses to pay the debt or that he does not desire further communications.

The FDCPA also requires a collector to give a debtor certain information about the debt within five days of the collector's first communication with the debtor. The *Evory* case, which follows shortly, explains the content of this notice requirement and addresses various issues suggested by it. If the debtor disputes the debt in writing within 30 days after receiving this information, the collector must cease its collection efforts until it sends verification of the debt to the debtor.

Specific Forbidden Practices As explained in the *Evory* case, the FDCPA sets out categories of forbidden collector practices and lists specific examples of each category. The listed examples, however, do not exhaust the ways that debt collectors can violate the act. The categories are:

1. *Harassment, oppression, or abuse.* Examples include threats of violence, obscene or abusive language, and repeated phone calls.

2. *False or misleading misrepresentations.* Among the FDCPA's listed examples are statements that a debtor will be imprisoned for failure to pay, that a collector will take an action it is not legally entitled to take or does not intend to take, that a collector is affiliated with the government, and that misstate the amount of the debt.

3. *Unfair practices.* These include collecting from a debtor an amount not authorized by the agreement creating the debt, inducing a debtor to accept a collect call before revealing the call's true purpose, and falsely or unjustifiably threatening to take a debtor's property.

Enforcement The FTC is the main enforcement agency for the FDCPA, although other agencies enforce it in certain cases. The FDCPA also permits individual civil actions and class actions by the affected debtor or debtors.

Evory v. RJM Acquisitions Funding, L.L.C. 505 F.3d 769 (7th Cir. 2007)

Section 1692g of the Fair Debt Collection Practices Act (FDCPA) provides:

Within five days after the initial communication with a consumer in connection with the collection of any debt, a debt collector shall, unless the following information is contained in the initial communication or the consumer has paid the debt, send the consumer a written notice containing—

(1) the amount of the debt;
(2) the name of the creditor to whom the debt is owed;
(3) a statement that unless the consumer, within thirty days after receipt of the notice, disputes the validity of the debt, or any portion thereof, the debt will be assumed to be valid by the debt collector;

(4) a statement that if the consumer notifies the debt collector in writing within the thirty-day period that the debt, or any portion thereof, is disputed, the debt collector will obtain verification of the debt or a copy of a judgment against the consumer and a copy of such verification or judgment will be mailed to the consumer by the debt collector; and

(5) a statement that, upon the consumer's written request within the thirty-day period, the debt collector will provide the consumer with the name and address of the original creditor, if different from the current creditor.

Other sections of the FDCPA prohibit certain debt collection practices. Section 1692d forbids "any conduct the natural consequence of which is to harass, oppress, or abuse any person in connection with the collection of a debt." Section 1692e bars a debt collector from using "any false, deceptive, or misleading representation or means in connection with the collection of any debt." Section 1692f prohibits a debt collector's use of "any unfair or unconscionable means to collect or attempt to collect any debt."

Four appeals lodged in the U.S. Court of Appeals for the Seventh Circuit presented FDCPA questions regarding debt collectors' communications with attorneys for debtors and/or debt collectors' use of allegedly deceptive, abusive, or otherwise unfair settlement offers. The four cases were Evory v. RJM Acquisitions Funding, L.L.C.; Lauer v. Mason, Silver, Wenk & Mischlin, L.L.C.; Captain v. ARS National Services, Inc.; *and* Jackson v. National Action Financial Services, Inc. *In all four cases, the plaintiffs were debtors and the defendants were debt collectors. The Seventh Circuit consolidated the four cases for decision. Further facts concerning the cases are set forth in the following edited version of the Seventh Circuit's opinion.*

Posner, Circuit Judge

We have consolidated for decision four intertwined cases that present [various] questions under the FDCPA. We shall first answer the questions and then indicate the [appropriate] disposition[s] [of the cases]. Here are the questions:

1. Whether, if the consumer (as the statute refers to the putative debtor) is represented by a lawyer, a debt collector must give the same written notice to the lawyer that section 1692g would require were the consumer unrepresented and the notice sent directly to him.

2. Whether communications to lawyers are subject to sections 1692d through 1692f, which forbid harassing, deceptive, and unfair practices in debt collection. [Federal courts of appeal have split on this question.]

3. Whether, if the answer to question 2 is yes, the standard applicable to determining whether a representation is false, deceptive, or misleading under section 1692e is the same whether the representation is made to the lawyer or to his client.

4. Whether a settlement offer contained in a letter from the debt collector to a consumer is lawful per se under section 1692f. [Federal courts of appeal have also split on this question.]

5. If it is not per se lawful, whether its lawfulness should be affected by whether it is addressed to a lawyer, rather than to the consumer directly.

6. Whether there should be a safe harbor for a debt collector accused of violating section 1692e by making such an offer.

7. Again, if such a letter is not per se lawful, what type of evidence a plaintiff must present to prove that a settlement offer violates section 1692e.

8. Whether the determination that a representation is or is not false, deceptive, or misleading under section 1692 is always to be treated as a matter of law. [Federal courts of appeal have split on this question as well.]

. . . .

[Regarding the notice requirement set forth in § 1692g,] [i]t would be passing odd if the fact that a consumer was represented excused the debt collector from having to convey to the consumer the information to which the statute entitles him. For example, sections 1692g(a)(1) and (2) provide that the required notice must state the amount of the debt and the name of the creditor. Is it to be believed that by retaining a lawyer the debtor disentitles himself to the information? Or that the debt collector, though knowing that the debtor is represented, can communicate directly with him in defiance of the principle that once a party to a legal dispute is represented, the other party must deal with him through his lawyer, and not directly? We conclude that any written notice sent to the lawyer must contain the information that would be required by the Act if the notice were sent to the consumer directly.

The next question is whether debt collectors can, without liability, threaten, make false representations to, or commit other abusive, deceptive, or unconscionable acts against a consumer's lawyer, in violation of sections 1692d, e, or f. These sections[, which are quoted in the above statement of facts,] do not designate any class of persons, such as lawyers, who can be abused, misled, etc., by debt collectors with impunity. It is true that a lawyer is less likely to be deceived, intimidated, harassed, and so forth (for simplicity, we shall assume that only deception is alleged) than a consumer. But that is an argument not for immunizing practices forbidden by the statute when they are directed against a consumer's lawyer, but rather for recognizing that the standard for determining whether particular conduct violates the statute is different when the conduct is aimed at a lawyer than when it is aimed at a consumer.

The courts have ruled that the statute is intended for the protection of unsophisticated consumers (sophisticated consumers presumably do not need its protection), so that in deciding whether for example a representation made in a dunning letter is misleading, the court asks whether a person of modest education and limited commercial savvy would be likely to be deceived. The standpoint is not that of the *least* intelligent consumer in this nation of 300 million people, but that of the average consumer in the lowest quartile (or some other substantial bottom fraction) of consumer competence. But if the debt collector has targeted a particularly vulnerable group—say, consumers who he knows have a poor command of English—the benchmark for deciding whether the communication is deceptive would be the competence of the substantial bottom fraction of *that* group. [Case citations omitted.]

By the same token, the "unsophisticated consumer" standpoint is inappropriate for judging communications with lawyers, just as it is inappropriate to fix a physician's standard of care at the level of that of a medical orderly. But what should the standard be? Most lawyers who represent consumers in debt collection cases are familiar with debt collection law and therefore unlikely to be deceived. But sometimes a lawyer will find himself handling a debt collection case not because he's a specialist but because a friend or relative has asked him to handle it. His sophistication in collection matters would be less than that of the specialist practitioner but much greater than that of the average unsophisticated consumer. He would not have to be an expert on the FDCPA to be able to look it up and discover what information sections 1692g(a)(3)–(5) require be disclosed to the consumer, and then compare the requirements with the content of the communication that he has received on his client's behalf. Since, therefore, most lawyers who represent consumers in debt-collection cases are knowledgeable about the law and practices of debt collection, since those who are not should be able to inform themselves sufficiently to be able to represent their consumer clients competently, and since the debt collector cannot be expected to know how knowledgeable a particular consumer's lawyer is, we conclude that a representation by a debt collector that would be unlikely to deceive a competent lawyer, even if he is not a specialist in consumer debt law, should not be actionable.

We have assumed for the sake of simplicity that the communication to the lawyer is alleged to be *deceptive;* what if instead it is alleged to be false or misleading, terms also found in section 1692e? "Misleading" is similar to "deceptive," except that it can be innocent; one intends to deceive, but one can mislead through inadvertence. A sophisticated person is less likely to be either deceived or misled than an unsophisticated one. That is

less true if a statement is false. A false claim of fact in a dunning letter may be as difficult for a lawyer to see through as a consumer. Suppose the letter misrepresents the unpaid balance of the consumer's debt. The lawyer might be unable to discover the falsity of the representation without an investigation that he might be unable, depending on his client's resources, to undertake. Such a misrepresentation would be actionable whether made to the consumer directly, or indirectly through his lawyer.

We move now from the lawyer cases to the cases of settlement offers communicated directly to consumers, where there is no lawyer in the picture. But later we shall have to bring the lawyer back into the picture in order to round out our discussion of the difference between consumers and lawyers as recipients of potentially misleading statements from debt collectors.

It is apparently common for debt collectors to send letters to consumers that say such things as (these examples are all taken from the cases before us) "we would like to offer you a unique opportunity to satisfy your outstanding debt"—"a settlement of 25% OFF of your current balance. SO YOU ONLY PAY $[____] In ONE PAYMENT that must be received no later than 40 days from the date on this letter." Or "TIME'S A WASTIN'! . . . Act now and receive 30% off if you pay by March 31st." Or we are "currently able to offer you a substantial discount of *50% off* your Current Balance *if we receive payment by 05-14-2004*" (emphases in original). There is nothing improper about making a settlement offer. The concern is that unsophisticated consumers may think that if they don't pay by the deadline, they will have no further chance to settle their debt for less than the full amount; for the offers are in the idiom of limited-time or one-time sales offers, clearance sales, going-out-of-business sales, and other temporary discounts. In fact debt collectors, who naturally are averse to instituting actual collection proceedings for the often very modest sums involved in the consumer debt collection business, frequently renew their offers if the consumer fails to accept the initial offer.

The objection to allowing liability to be based on such offers is that the settlement process would disintegrate if the debt collector had to disclose the consequences of the consumer's rejecting his initial offer. If he has to say, "We'll give you 50 percent if you pay us by May 14, but if you don't, we'll probably offer you the same or even better deal later, and if you refuse that, we'll probably give up and you'll never have to pay a cent of the debt you owe," there will be no point in making offers. As in previous cases in which we have created safe-harbor language for use in cases under the FDCPA, [case citations omitted], we think the present concern can be adequately addressed yet the unsophisticated consumer still be protected against receiving a false impression of his options by the debt collector's including with the offer the following language: "We are not obligated to renew this offer." The word "obligated" is strong and even the unsophisticated consumer will realize that there is a renewal possibility but that it is not assured.

This is not to suggest that in the absence of safe-harbor language a debt collector is per se liable for violating section 1692 if he makes the kind of settlement offer that we quoted. We see a potential for deception of the unsophisticated in those offers but we have no way of determining whether a sufficiently large segment of the unsophisticated are likely to be deceived to enable us to conclude that the statute has been violated. For that, evidence is required, the most useful sort being [a suitable] consumer survey.

Other circuits, perhaps less kindly disposed to survey evidence than we, treat the deceptive character of a debt collector's communication as a question of law, so that if the communication is not deceptive on its face, the plaintiff is forbidden to try to show that it would be likely to deceive a substantial number of its intended recipients. We disagree with that position. The intended recipients of dunning letters are not federal judges, and judges are not experts in the knowledge and understanding of unsophisticated consumers facing demands by debt collectors. We are no more entitled to rely on our intuitions in this context than we are in deciding issues of consumer confusion in trademark cases, where the use of survey evidence is routine.

But we emphasize that survey evidence in debt-collection as in trademark cases must comply with the principles of professional survey research; if it does not, it is not even admissible, let alone probative of deception. We are exceedingly doubtful that any lawyer involved in representing debtors would be deceived by the settlement offers made by debt collectors, and doubt therefore that any cases based on such offers could survive summary judgment or even a motion to dismiss were the offer directed to the consumer's lawyer rather than to the consumer. This illustrates our earlier point about the importance of distinguishing between lawyers and unsophisticated consumers in applying section 1692e.

Having answered the questions that we listed at the beginning of our opinion, we can be brief in discussing our four cases. In *Lauer,* the consumer was represented by a lawyer. The defendant debt collector did not send either the lawyer or his client the written notice required by section 1692g, but instead sent the lawyer a letter that the plaintiff characterizes as coercive because it threatened to dispose of property of the plaintiff that had a purely sentimental value, such as scrapbooks, a wedding gown, and a videotape of the arrival of his adopted child from Korea. The plaintiff doesn't explain which subsection of section 1692 the threat violates, but it could well violate d, e, f, or indeed all three. The district court dismissed the complaint on the ground that communications with a consumer's lawyer are beyond the reach of the Fair Debt Collection Practices Act. That was error.

The defendant in *Lauer* also argues that if the initial communication from the debt collector is to the consumer's lawyer rather than to the consumer himself, the notice requirement is not triggered. If you glance back at section 1692g(a) you will see that it says that the written notice is required to be sent "five days after the initial communication with a consumer." The argument is that if there is no letter sent first ("initial communication") directly to the consumer, but instead the initial communication is to the consumer's lawyer, the condition for requiring the subsequent written notice containing specified information is not satisfied and therefore such a notice need never be sent either to the lawyer or to the consumer. All that this argument shows is how unsound it would be to suppose that a communication to a person's lawyer is not a communication to the person. It would make a consumer who had a lawyer worse off than one who did not, because neither he nor his lawyer would have a right to any of the information that the statute requires be disclosed to the consumer.

In *Captain,* before realizing that the consumer was represented, the defendant sent him a letter offering a 30 percent discount off the face amount of the debt, provided payment was received by a specified date. The plaintiff claims that the letter violated section 1692e. Shortly afterward, his lawyer called the defendant and was told that if the debt wasn't paid within two weeks of the date of the initial collection letter (a deadline that had already passed), a $15 daily charge would be added to the account balance until the debt was paid in full. Such a charge, equivalent to an interest rate of 730 percent a year on the unpaid balance of the debt, would violate Indiana law. Although a violation of state law is not in itself a violation of the FDCPA, a threat to impose a penalty that the threatener knows is improper because unlawful is a good candidate for a violation of sections 1692d and e. The district court dismissed the complaint for failure to state a claim: the settlement-offer charge on the ground that such offers are per se lawful under the Act and the challenge to the lawfulness of the $15 a day representation because it was made to a lawyer. Both rulings were erroneous.

Evory and *Jackson* . . . are pure settlement-offer cases—there were no communications to lawyers. But they are importantly different. In *Evory,* the district court dismissed the complaint, and that was error. But in *Jackson* the court granted summary judgment for the defendant. Much of the judge's opinion tracks the discussion in cases that hold that the kind of settlement offer involved in these cases is nondeceptive per se, and that is wrong. But the judge was willing to consider the survey evidence that the plaintiff had introduced. He concluded that it did not show that the settlement offer was deceptive. He was right and indeed should have ruled the evidence inadmissible. The plaintiffs lawyer at the argument of the appeal conceded that it was not a good survey. We would put the matter more strongly. The respondents in the survey were shown a letter similar to the one the plaintiff had received. The key question they were asked was, "Let's say the person getting this letter does not accept the settlement offer by the deadline date. Do you think that person would feel it is a limited-time offer, or it is not a limited-time offer?" By referring to "deadline date," the questioner signaled that it was a limited-time offer. Leading questions in surveys are improper. And "limited-time offer" was not defined. Nor should the respondents have been asked what they thought some *other* recipient of the letter would "feel," especially since they were given no information about the hypothetical recipient. They should simply have been asked, "What do you think would happen if you didn't accept the offer? Do you think it would be renewed or extended? Or do you think this would be your last chance to get a discount off the amount owed?"

There is compelling evidence that the offers in this and the other cases were not final offers. But that means only that if the offers were understood as such by the targeted recipients, they were deceptive. The anterior issue is whether they were likely to be understood as such by a substantial number of unsophisticated consumers. Maybe they were, but some evidence beyond the face of the offer was required to establish a prima facie case, and it was not presented.

District court's decision in* Jackson *affirmed; district courts' decisions in* Lauer, Captain, *and* Evory *reversed, and cases remanded for further proceedings.

Product Safety Regulation

Yet another facet of consumer protection law is federal regulation of product safety. As discussed in Chapter 20, sellers and manufacturers of dangerously defective products may be held civilly liable to those injured by such products. Damage recoveries, however, are at best an after-the-fact remedy for injuries caused by such products. Thus, federal law also seeks to promote product safety through *direct regulation* of consumer products.

The Consumer Product Safety Act

The most important federal product safety measure is the Consumer Product Safety Act (CPSA). The CPSA established the Consumer Product Safety Commission (CPSC), an independent regulatory agency that is the main federal body concerned with the safety of consumer products. Among the CPSC's activities are the following: (1) issuing *consumer product safety standards* (which normally pertain to the performance of consumer products or require product warnings or instructions); (2) issuing rules *banning* certain *hazardous products;* (3) bringing suit in federal district court to eliminate the dangers presented by *imminently hazardous* consumer products (products that pose an immediate and unreasonable risk of death, serious illness, or severe personal injury); and (4) *ordering private parties to address "substantial product hazards"* after receiving notice of such hazards. The CPSA's remedies and enforcement devices include injunctions, the seizure of products, civil penalties, criminal penalties, and private damage suits.

In 2008, widespread media reports highlighted the harms experienced by children as a result of being exposed to toys that contained dangerous chemical elements or other dangerous substances. Many of these toys had been imported into the United States. The intense attention to toy safety issues prompted Congress to enact the first major amendments to the CPSA in a number of years. Besides including a very significant increase in the CPSC budget, the 2008 amendments instructed the CPSC to study a variety of toy safety issues and other children's product safety issues, and to appoint a Chronic Hazard Advisory Panel to advise the CPSC on the children's health effects of certain chemicals in toys and child care products. The amendments also instructed the CPSC to follow up with appropriate new regulations to address major safety concerns.

The 2008 retooling of the CPSA furnished Congress an opportunity to address long-standing concerns over the numbers of rollover accidents in which users of all-terrain vehicles (ATVs) were injured or killed. Congress directed the CPSC to develop safety regulations regarding three-wheeled and four-wheeled ATVs, with the importation and sale of the three-wheeled ATVs being banned until the promulgation of the CPSC regulations concerning the three-wheeled variety.

Other Federal Product Safety Regulation

Other federal statutes besides the CPSA regulate various specific consumer products. Among the subjects so regulated are toys, cigarette labeling and advertising, eggs, meat, poultry, smokeless tobacco, flammable fabrics, drugs, cosmetics, pesticides, and motor vehicles. Some of these laws are enforced by the CPSC and some by other bodies.

Ethics in Action

Since at least the early 1950s, the International Harvester Company's gasoline-powered tractors had been subject to "fuel geysering." This was a phenomenon in which hot liquid gasoline would shoot from the tractor's gas tank when the filler cap was opened. The hot gasoline could cause severe burns and could ignite and cause a fire. Over the years, at least 90 fuel geysering incidents involving International Harvester tractors occurred. At least 12 of these involved significant burn injuries, and at least one caused a death.

International Harvester discovered the full dimensions of the fuel geysering problem in 1963. In that year, it revised its owner's manuals to warn buyers of new gas-powered tractors not to remove the gas cap from a hot or running tractor. In 1976, it produced a new fuel tank decal with a similar warning. Because of an industrywide shift to diesel-powered tractors, however, this warning had a very limited distribution to buyers of new tractors, and it rarely reached former buyers. International Harvester never specifically warned either new or old buyers about the geysering problem until 1980, when it voluntarily made a mass mailing to 630,000 customers.

In 1980, the FTC issued a complaint against International Harvester, alleging that its failure to warn buyers of the fuel geysering problem for 17 years violated FTC Act § 5. Agreeing with the initial decision of an administrative law judge, the full commission held that International Harvester's failure to warn was not deceptive but was unfair for purposes of § 5. *In the Matter of International Harvester,* 104 F.T.C. 949 (1984).

Applying the three-part analysis discussed earlier in this chapter, the commission weighed the consumer injury caused by fuel geysering against the costs of providing effective warnings about it. The commission concluded that the 12 instances of serious burns and the one death caused by fuel geysering were injuries that might have been avoided by a warning and were sufficient to outweigh the $2.8 million apparently required for an effective warning. However, the commission's method clearly left open the possibility that in some cases, a practice's benefits to consumers or to competition might outweigh the harm it causes.

- Is it morally right to balance personal injury and human life against economic gain? Isn't each human life valuable beyond measure? Can decision-making processes such as the FTC's ever be justified?
- On the other hand, if you think that the commission's balancing exercise *is* justifiable, how is one to strike the balance? How would you have decided *International Harvester* if ethical analysis, rather than legal standards, controlled the decision?

Problems and Problem Cases

1. For many years, advertisements for Listerine Antiseptic Mouthwash had impliedly claimed that Listerine was beneficial in the treatment of colds, cold symptoms, and sore throats. An FTC adjudicative proceeding concluded that these claims were false. Thus, the FTC ordered Warner-Lambert Company, the manufacturer of Listerine, to include the following statement in future Listerine advertisements: "Contrary to prior advertising, Listerine will not help prevent colds or sore throats or lessen their severity." Warner-Lambert argued that this order was invalid because it went beyond a command to simply cease and desist from illegal behavior. Was Warner-Lambert correct?

2. Pantron I Corp. sold a shampoo and conditioner known as the Helsinki Formula. Pantron promoted the Helsinki Formula as an aid in fighting male pattern baldness. According to Pantron, polysorbate was the main ingredient that made the Helsinki Formula effective in arresting hair loss and stimulating hair growth. The Federal Trade Commission filed suit against Pantron on the theory that Pantron's advertisements made deceptive representations about the effectiveness of the Helsinki Formula, as well as deceptive representations that scientific evidence supported the effectiveness claims. The FTC sought injunctive and monetary relief. The evidence showed that the Helsinki Formula was effective for some users with male pattern baldness but that this effectiveness was probably due to the "placebo effect" (i.e., the effectiveness for some users stemmed from psychological reasons rather than from the inherent merit of the product). Because there was no scientifically valid evidence indicating that polysorbate is effective in treating hair loss or in inducing hair growth, the district court concluded that Pantron's advertisements were deceptive in representing that *scientific evidence* supported a conclusion that the Helsinki Formula was effective. The district court therefore issued an injunction that barred Pantron

from representing, in its advertisements, that scientific evidence supports the alleged effectiveness of the Helsinki Formula in treating baldness or hair loss. However, because the Helsinki Formula did work for some users some of the time (whatever the reason), the district court concluded that the FTC had failed to carry its burden of proving that Pantron engaged in deceptive advertising when it represented that the Helsinki Formula was effective for persons with male pattern baldness. The court therefore refused to enjoin Pantron from making such a representation of effectiveness (i.e., a representation of effectiveness that did not go on to make the false claim of supporting scientific evidence). The court also refused to order monetary relief. In its appeal to the U.S. Court of Appeals for the Ninth Circuit, the FTC argued that when a product's effectiveness is due only to the placebo effect, an advertising claim of effectiveness is false and deceptive for purposes of the FTC Act. Was this FTC argument legally correct? Which party—the FTC or Pantron—was entitled to win the appeal?

3. Besides maintaining a private law practice, Keith Gill offered credit repair services to consumers in a business that he operated with a retired attorney, Richard Murkey. In various contexts, Gill and Murkey made representations to the effect that they could remove any accurate and nonobsolete information of a negative nature from the credit reports of consumers who used their credit repair services. The Federal Trade Commission filed suit against Gill and Murkey, alleging, among other things, that these representations violated § 5 of the Federal Trade Commission Act. Was § 5 violated?

4. Between 1966 and 1975, the Orkin Exterminating Company, the world's largest termite and pest control firm, offered its customers a "lifetime" guarantee that could be renewed each year by paying a definite amount specified in its contracts with the customers. The contracts gave no indication that the fees could be raised for any reasons other than certain narrowly specified ones. Beginning in 1980, Orkin unilaterally breached these contracts by imposing higher-than-agreed-upon annual renewal fees. Roughly 200,000 contracts were breached in this way. Orkin realized $7 million in additional revenues from customers who renewed at the higher fees. The additional fees did not purchase a higher level of service than that originally provided for in the contracts. Although

some of Orkin's competitors may have been willing to assume Orkin's pre-1975 contracts at the fees stated therein, they would not have offered a fixed, locked-in "lifetime" renewal fee such as the one Orkin originally provided. Under the three-part test stated in the text, did Orkin's behavior violate FTC Act § 5's prohibition against *unfair* acts or practices?

5. Patron Aviation, Inc., an aviation company, bought an airplane engine from L&M Aircraft. The engine was assembled and shipped to L&M by Teledyne Industries, Inc. L&M installed the engine in one of Patron's airplanes. The engine turned out to be defective, so Patron sued L&M and Teledyne. One of the issues presented by the case was whether the Magnuson-Moss Act was applicable. Does the Magnuson-Moss Act apply to this transaction?

6. National Financial Services, Inc., a debt collection agency that serves magazine subscriptions clearinghouses, handled roughly 2.2 million accounts during 1986 and 1987. It sent letters to debtors whose accounts were delinquent. The average unpaid balance owed on these accounts was approximately $20. One letter sent by National Financial to a large number of debtors stated that their account "Will Be Transferred To An Attorney If It Is Unpaid After The Deadline Date!!!" Debtors who did not pay after receiving this letter received one or more letters that bore the letterhead of "N. Frank Lanocha, Attorney at Law." Lanocha prepared the text of these form letters and gave copies to National Financial's president, Smith. Smith then arranged for the letters to be prepared and mailed out. One of these letters contained the following statements: "Please Note I Am The Collection Attorney Who Represents American Family Publishers. I Have The Authority To See That Suit Is Filed Against You In This Matter." The letter also stated: "Unless This Payment Is Received In This Office Within Five Days Of The Date Of This Notice, I Will Be Compelled To Consider The Use Of The Legal Remedies That May Be Available To Effect Collection." The Federal Trade Commission sued National Financial, Smith, and Lanocha, alleging violations of the Fair Debt Collection Practices Act. How should the court rule?

7. National Credit Management Group (NCMG) offered credit monitoring and credit card services to consumers throughout the United States. NCMG used the 1-800-YES-CREDIT toll-free telephone number as the central marketing focus of its business.

The company's advertisements on radio and cable television stated that persons with credit problems should call the toll-free number to receive a "confidential analysis" of their credit histories. Many of these advertisements also promised that NCMG would provide consumers with a complimentary application for a major credit card without a security deposit. In a number of the television advertisements, NCMG would flash the word "APPROVED" on the television screen or would otherwise highlight that word when the advertisement made reference to the credit card application.

NCMG received approximately 6,500 "inbound" calls per week from consumers who were responding to the radio and television advertisements. NCMG did not engage in "cold-calling" of consumers. When consumers called 1-800-YES-CREDIT, an NCMG representative offered them an initial credit analysis for an up-front fee of $95. During this phone conversation, the NCMG representative asked consumers for information—name, address, Social Security number, checking account number, employment information, and income information—that the representative stated was necessary to enable the credit analyst to gather information concerning the particular consumer's credit history. The NCMG representative also stated that the $95 fee was the charge associated with the accumulation and monitoring of the information contained in the credit profile of the consumer, and that the credit analyst would be telephoning the consumer in approximately two weeks to discuss the consumer's credit history. Between 5 and 9 percent of consumers who called the toll-free number purchased either the $95 initial credit analysis offered or other services (described below) that NCMG offered.

NCMG used the checking account information obtained by its representatives to set up an arrangement under which consumers' checking accounts would be debited in the amount of $95 if they accepted the initial credit analysis offer. Consumers who initially gave verbal authorization for the debiting arrangement later encountered great difficulty in attempting to cancel it. In the initial telephone conversation described above, the NCMG representatives did not tell consumers that when they used their "complimentary" application for a credit card (the application referred to in NCMG's advertisements), they could have to pay fees ranging from $50 to

$100 to sponsoring banks. Neither were consumers informed that they were not guaranteed of receiving a credit card. Although sponsoring banks approved a high percentage of consumers who used the NCMG-provided application, not all applicants were approved for a credit card.

NCMG did not actually perform a credit analysis for paying consumers, nor did NCMG check those consumers' credit reports. When the supposed credit analyst made the above-described follow-up telephone call to a consumer, he or she did not discuss the consumer's credit history. Instead, the credit analyst attempted to sell the consumer NCMG's two-year program designed for persons who wished to establish or reestablish their credit. The two-year program, which consisted largely of NCMG's furnishing certain educational materials, ranged in cost from several hundred dollars to well over $1,000, with the NCMG caller having the discretion to set the price at what seemed an appropriate level under the circumstances. The credit analyst typically did not disclose that the earlier check-debiting arrangement would be used as the payment mechanism for persons who agreed to subscribe to the two-year program.

The Federal Trade Commission (FTC) filed suit against NCMG. Among other things, the FTC alleged that NCMG violated § 5 of the FTC Act as well as the Telemarketing Sales Rule (TSR). Did NCMG violate § 5? Did NCMG violate the TSR?

8. The owners of a certain house had listed it for rental with Gatewood Realty, Inc. Ira Simonoff, a Gatewood broker, showed the house to brothers Jonathan and Robert Scott, who offered to rent the house at a lesser monthly rate than the owners had specified. Simonoff then asked the Scotts for certain background information. Jonathan Scott responded to Simonoff's request for his Social Security number by telling Simonoff that he (Simonoff) was not authorized to make a credit check. Robert Scott added that he did not want his credit checked. During the discovery phase of the litigation described below, Jonathan Scott testified that Simonoff assured him no credit check would be run. Both brothers testified that they understood Simonoff would not check their credit. Simonoff, however, testified that he informed the brothers of the house owners' requirement of a credit check and that one of the brothers had simply asked Simonoff not to have a credit check done "if at

all possible." When Simonoff relayed the Scotts' offer to the owners, they insisted that credit checks be conducted. Simonoff therefore asked Peter Visconti, who was affiliated with Real Estate Finance Group (REFG), to check the Scotts' credit. According to later testimony by Visconti, Simonoff represented that he had written authorizations from the Scotts. (The Scotts denied that any such authorizations existed.) Visconti obtained credit reports on the Scotts by falsely representing to a computerized credit reporting service that he needed the reports to evaluate a mortgage application. He then supplied the credit reports to Simonoff. When a real estate broker working on behalf of the Scotts learned that Simonoff had obtained their credit reports, she so informed the Scotts.

The Scotts filed suit against REFG, Gatewood, and Simonoff for alleged violations of the Fair Credit Reporting Act (FCRA). After discovery, the Scotts moved for partial summary judgment against all defendants on the theory that they had obtained the Scotts' credit reports by means of false pretenses, in violation of the FCRA. Gatewood and Simonoff moved for summary judgment in their favor. The district court granted the Scotts' summary judgment motion as to REFG but not as to Gatewood and Simonoff. Instead, the court granted summary judgment in favor of Gatewood Realty and Simonoff and ordered dismissal of the Scotts' FRCA claim against them. The Scotts appealed the dismissal of their FCRA claim against Gatewood and Simonoff. How did the appellate court rule?

9. When Samuel Grant sued his landlord, the landlord filed a counterclaim. Grant later was awarded a $608 judgment against the landlord, with the landlord receiving a $476.10 judgment against Grant on the counterclaim. This left Grant with a net judgment of $131.90. Approximately one year after the above case, Texaco denied Grant's application for a credit card. Texaco did so on the basis of a credit report prepared by TRW, Inc. This credit report stated that a judgment of approximately $400 had been entered against Grant in the above-described litigation between Grant and his landlord. Grant then informed TRW that the litigation involving his landlord had resulted in a net judgment in Grant's favor. TRW eventually sent Grant an "Updated Credit Profile" showing that the $400 judgment had been deleted from his file. Several months later, Grant again

applied for a Texaco credit card. Texaco again denied his application because a newly issued TRW credit report indicated that a $400 judgment had been entered against him in the case involving his landlord. Grant then sued TRW on the theory that TRW had violated the Fair Credit Reporting Act (FCRA). TRW moved to dismiss the case. Should Grant's FCRA case be dismissed?

10. Sylvia Miller, a married woman, wanted to buy a pair of loveseats from a retail furniture store. The store offered to arrange financing for her through the Public Industrial Loan Company. Public later refused to extend credit to Miller unless her husband cosigned the debt obligation. The reason was a consumer reporting agency's unfavorable credit report on Miller. Was Public's action forbidden sex discrimination under the Equal Credit Opportunity Act? In any event, what other legal remedy might Miller have?

11. John E. Koerner & Co., Inc., applied for a credit card account with the American Express Company. The application was for a company account designed for business customers. Koerner asked American Express to issue cards bearing the company's name to Louis Koerner and four other officers of the corporation. Koerner was required to sign a company account form, under which he agreed that he would be jointly and severally liable with the company for all charges incurred through use of the company card. American Express issued the cards requested by the company. Thereafter, the cards were used almost totally for business purposes, although Koerner occasionally used his card for personal expenses. Later, a dispute regarding charges appearing on the company account arose. Does the Fair Credit Billing Act apply to this dispute?

12. The Fair Debt Collection Practices Act (FDCPA) prohibits a creditor from giving a debtor the false impression that a third party is involved in efforts to collect the debt owed to the creditor. North Shore Agency, Inc., is a debt collection firm. For many years, North Shore and Book-of-the-Month Club (BOMC) had an arrangement under which BOMC would send North Shore the names and addresses of any BOMC customers from whom BOMC had been unable to collect payment. North Shore would then send these customers a letter demanding payment of the sums BOMC had reported to North Shore as due. The demand letters instructed the customers to pay

BOMC directly and stated that further collection efforts would be undertaken if payment was not made. If the demand letter to a given customer failed to elicit payment, BOMC would so notify North Shore, which would send a second demand letter. The process could be repeated a third time or even more times until either the customer paid BOMC or North Shore concluded that payment would not be forthcoming unless further collection efforts were made. BOMC paid North Shore a flat fee for every demand letter North Shore sent out. If a series of demand letters did not yield payment, it was up to North Shore whether to drop the matter—something it might often be likely to do because of the relatively small dollar amounts involved—or take other collection action. When North Shore took other collection action that resulted in payment, North Shore would keep 35 percent of the amount collected and remit the remainder to BOMC. Patricia White, a BOMC customer who had not made payment of $18.45, received a demand letter from North Shore. Alleging that BOMC and North Shore had violated the FDCPA, White brought a class action suit on behalf of herself and other similarly situated persons. In view of the frequent tendency of North Shore not to take legal action beyond sending demand letters,

did BOMC and North Shore violate the FDCPA prohibition on creating a false impression that a third party is involved in efforts to collect a debt?

Online Research

The FTC

Go to the Federal Trade Commission's Web site, www.ftc.gov, and review the information present there. Then briefly describe the respective responsibilities of the various offices and bureaus that exist within the FTC, and list the cities in which the FTC maintains regional offices.

Consider completing these two case segments from the You Be the Judge Web site element after you have read this chapter: "CONSUMER LAW: Misleading Menu Misery"
"CONSUMER LAW: The Not-So-Captive Audience"
Visit our Web site at www.mhhe.com/mallor14e for more information and activities regarding these case segments.

chapter 49

ANTITRUST: THE SHERMAN ACT

XYZ, Inc., manufactures widgets and sells them through various wholesale dealers. Several other firms also manufacture widgets. Of course, XYZ wishes to conduct its business within the bounds of the law, including the rules of antitrust law. As you study this chapter, consider the following questions regarding possible courses of action and their treatment under antitrust law:

- Would XYZ violate antitrust law if XYZ deliberately causes its prices to parallel those of a competing widget manufacturer?

- If XYZ and a competing widget manufacturer agree that each will charge no more than a certain agreed amount for their widgets (i.e., a maximum price), is there an antitrust violation? What if XYZ and its competitor agree to set a minimum price in order to avoid what each sees as the potentially ruinous consequences of a price-cutting war?

- Is there an antitrust violation if XYZ and its wholesale dealers agree that the dealers will adhere to an established maximum sale price when they sell to retailers? What if the agreement between XYZ and the dealers is that the dealers will adhere to a certain minimum price when they sell to retailers?

- If XYZ and its wholesale dealers agree on exclusive sales territories within which each dealer will operate, is there an antitrust violation?

- Is there an antitrust problem if XYZ informs its dealers that it will not sell them widgets unless they also buy a certain unrelated product from XYZ, and the dealers, wanting to preserve their widget dealerships, agree to this provision?

- Would there be an antitrust violation if XYZ and some of the other widget manufacturers agree that each manufacturer has an exclusive geographic area of business operation?

- Is there an antitrust violation if XYZ and some of the other widget manufacturers agree not to purchase, from a certain supplier, materials used in making widgets?

- If XYZ's widgets acquire a public reputation for being high in quality and this perception leads, over time, to XYZ's holding a market share so large that XYZ effectively holds monopoly status, has XYZ run afoul of antitrust law?

Regardless of the legal treatment given to the behaviors referred to in the above questions, consider the ethical questions suggested by such conduct.

THE POST–CIVIL WAR EMERGENCE and growth of large industrial combines and trusts significantly altered the business environment of earlier years. A major feature of this phenomenon was the tendency of various large business entities to acquire dominant positions in their industries by buying up smaller competitors or engaging in practices aimed at driving those competitors out of business. This behavior led to public demands for legislation to preserve competitive market structures and prevent the accumulation of great economic power in the hands of a few firms.

Congress responded in 1890 with the Sherman Act. It supplemented this response by enacting the Clayton Act in 1914 and the Robinson-Patman Act in 1936. In enacting the antitrust statutes, Congress adopted a public policy in favor of preserving and promoting free competition as the most efficient means of allocating social resources. The Supreme Court summarized, in *Times-Picayune Co. v. United States* (1953), the rationale for this faith in competition's positive effects:

> Basic to faith that a free economy best promotes the public weal is that goods must stand the cold test of competition; that the public, acting through the market's impersonal judgment, shall allocate the nation's resources and thus direct the course its economic development will take.

Congress thus presumed that competition was more likely to exist in an industrial structure characterized by a large number of competing firms than in concentrated industries dominated by a few large competitors.

Despite this long-standing policy in favor of competitive market structures, the antitrust laws have not been very successful in halting the trend toward concentration in American industry. Today's market structure in many important industries is *oligopolistic,* with the bulk of production accounted for by a few dominant firms. Traditional antitrust concepts are often difficult to apply to the behavior of firms in these highly concentrated markets. Recent years have witnessed the emergence of new ideas that challenge long-standing antitrust policy assumptions.

The Antitrust Policy Debate

Antitrust enforcement necessarily reflects fundamental public policy judgments about the economic activities to be allowed and the industrial structure best suited to foster desirable economic activity. Given the importance of such judgments to the future of the American economy, it is not surprising that antitrust policy spurs vigorous public debate.

Chicago School Theories
During the past four decades, traditional antitrust assumptions have faced an effective challenge from commentators and courts advocating the application of microeconomic theory to antitrust enforcement. These methods of antitrust analysis are commonly called **Chicago School theories** because many of their major premises were advanced by scholars affiliated with the University of Chicago.

Chicago School advocates view *economic efficiency* as the primary, if not sole, goal of antitrust enforcement. They are far less concerned with the supposed effects of industrial concentration than are traditional antitrust thinkers. Even highly concentrated industries, they argue, may engage in significant forms of nonprice competition, such as competition in advertising, styling, and warranties. They also point out that concentration in a particular industry does not necessarily preclude *interindustry competition*. For example, a concentrated glass container industry may still face significant competition from the makers of metal, plastic, and fiberboard containers. Chicago School advocates are also quick to point out that many markets today are international in scope, so that concentrated domestic industries may nonetheless face effective foreign competition. Moreover, they argue that the technological developments necessary for American industry to compete more effectively in international markets may require the great capital resources that result from domestic concentration.

According to the Chicago School viewpoint, the traditional antitrust focus on the structure of industry has improperly emphasized protecting *competitors* instead of protecting *competition*. Chicago School theorists argue that antitrust policy's primary thrust should feature *anticonspiracy* efforts rather than *anticoncentration* efforts. In addition, most of these theorists take a lenient view toward vertically imposed restrictions on price and distribution that have been traditionally seen as undesirable, because they believe that such restrictions can promote efficiencies in distribution. Thus, they tend to be tolerant of attempts by manufacturers to control resale prices or establish exclusive distribution systems for their products.

Traditional Antitrust Theories
Traditional antitrust thinkers, however, contend that even though economic efficiency is important, antitrust policy has historically embraced *political* as well as economic values. Concentrated economic power, they argue, is undesirable for a variety of noneconomic reasons. It may lead to antidemocratic concentrations of political power. Moreover, it may stimulate greater governmental intrusions into the economy in the same way that the post–Civil War activities of the trusts led to the passage of the antitrust laws. According to the traditional view, lessening concentration enhances individual freedom by reducing the barriers to entry that confront would-be competitors and by ensuring broader input into economic decisions having important social consequences. Judge Learned Hand summed up this perspective on antitrust policy:

> Great industrial consolidations are inherently undesirable, regardless of their economic results. Throughout the history of [the Sherman Act] it has been constantly assumed that one of [its] purposes was to perpetuate and preserve, for its own sake and in spite of possible cost, an organization of industry in small units which can effectively compete with each other.[1]

---

[1] *United States v. Aluminum Co. of America, Inc.* (2d Cir. 1945).

Effect of Chicago School Notions

Chicago School notions, however, have had a significant impact on the course of antitrust enforcement in recent decades. The Supreme Court and many presidential appointees to the lower federal courts, the Department of Justice, and the Federal Trade Commission have given credence to Chicago School economic arguments during the past 30-some years. The presence on the federal bench of so many judges embracing Chicago School ideas means that those views are likely to continue to have an impact on the shape of antitrust law.

Jurisdiction, Types of Cases, and Standing

Jurisdiction The Sherman Act outlaws monopolization, attempted monopolization, and agreements in restraint of trade. Because the federal government's power to regulate business originates in the Commerce Clause of the U.S. Constitution (discussed in Chapter 3), the federal antitrust laws apply only to behavior having some significant impact on *interstate* or *foreign* commerce. Given the interdependent nature of our national economy, it is normally fairly easy to demonstrate that a challenged activity either involves interstate commerce (the "in commerce" jurisdiction test) or has a substantial effect on interstate commerce (the "effect on commerce" jurisdiction test). Various cases indicate that a business activity may have a substantial effect on interstate commerce even if the activity occurs solely within the borders of one state. Activities that are purely *intrastate* in their effects, however, are outside the scope of federal antitrust jurisdiction and must be challenged under state law.

The federal antitrust laws have been extensively applied to activities affecting the international commerce of the United States. The conduct of American firms operating outside U.S. borders may be attacked under our antitrust laws if it has an intended effect on our foreign commerce. Likewise, foreign firms "continuously engaged" in our domestic commerce are subject to federal antitrust jurisdiction. An international transaction that has a direct, substantial, and reasonably foreseeable effect on domestic commerce may subject the firms involved to U.S. antitrust law and the jurisdiction of U.S. courts. Determining the full extent of the extraterritorial reach of our antitrust laws often involves courts in difficult questions of antitrust exemptions and immunities (to be discussed in Chapter 50). The extraterritorial reach issue also suggests the troubling political prospect that aggressive expansion of antitrust law's applicability may create tension between our antitrust policy and our foreign policy in general.

Types of Cases and the Role of Pretrial Settlements

Sherman Act violations may give rise to criminal prosecutions and civil litigation instituted by the federal government (through the Department of Justice), as well as to civil suits filed by private parties. A significant percentage of the antitrust cases brought by the Department of Justice are settled without trial through *nolo contendere* pleas in criminal cases and *consent decrees* in civil cases. Although a defendant who pleads nolo contendere technically has not admitted guilt, the sentencing court is free to impose the same penalty that would be appropriate in the case of a guilty plea or a conviction at trial. Consent decrees involve a defendant's consent to remedial measures aimed at remedying the competitive harm resulting from his actions. Because neither a nolo plea nor a consent decree is admissible as proof of a violation of the Sherman Act in a private plaintiff's later civil suit, these devices are often attractive to antitrust defendants.

LOG ON

For considerable background material dealing with antitrust law (including what is meant to be a consumer-friendly explanation of antitrust enforcement), go to the Web site of the United States Department of Justice, at **www.usdoj.gov**.

Criminal Prosecutions Individuals criminally convicted of Sherman Act violations may receive a fine of up to $1 million per violation and/or a term of imprisonment of up to 10 years. Corporations convicted of violating the Sherman Act may be fined up to $100 million per violation. The maximum punishments just noted reflect recent statutory amendments in which Congress significantly increased the previous maximum penalties.

Before an individual may be found criminally responsible under the Sherman Act, however, the government must prove an *anticompetitive effect* flowing from the challenged activity, as well as *criminal intent* on the defendant's part. The level of criminal intent required for a violation is a "knowledge of [the challenged activity's] probable consequences" rather than a specific intent to violate the antitrust laws.[2] Civil violations of the antitrust

---

[2]*United States v. U.S. Gypsum Co.* (U.S. Sup. Ct. 1978).

laws may be proved, however, through evidence of either an unlawful purpose or an anticompetitive effect.

Civil Litigation

The federal courts have broad injunctive powers to remedy civil antitrust violations. Courts may order convicted defendants to *divest* themselves of the stock or assets of acquired companies, to *divorce* themselves from a functional level of their operations (e.g., ordering a manufacturer to sell its captive retail outlets), to refrain from particular conduct in the future, and to cancel existing contracts. In extreme cases, courts may also enter a *dissolution decree* ordering a defendant to liquidate its assets and cease business operations. Private individuals and the Department of Justice may seek such injunctive relief regarding antitrust violations.

Treble Damages for Private Plaintiffs

Section 4 of the Clayton Act gives private parties a significant incentive to enforce the antitrust laws by providing that private plaintiffs injured by Sherman Act or Clayton Act violations are entitled to recover *treble damages* plus court costs and attorney's fees from the defendant. This means that once antitrust plaintiffs have demonstrated the amount of their actual losses (such as lost profits or increased costs) resulting from the challenged violation, this amount is tripled. The potential for treble damage liability plainly presents a significant deterrent threat to potential antitrust violators.

Standing

Private plaintiffs who seek to enforce the antitrust laws must first demonstrate that they have **standing** to sue. This means that they must show a *direct antitrust injury* as a result of the challenged behavior. An antitrust injury results from the unlawful aspects of the challenged behavior and is of the sort Congress sought to prevent. For example, in *Brunswick Corp. v. Pueblo Bowl-o-Mat, Inc.* (U.S. Sup. Ct. 1977), the operator of a chain of bowling centers (Pueblo) challenged a bowling equipment manufacturer's (Brunswick's) acquisition of various competing bowling centers that had defaulted on payments owed to Brunswick for equipment purchases. In essence, Pueblo asserted that if Brunswick had not acquired them, the failing bowling centers would have gone out of business—in which event Pueblo's profits would have increased. The Supreme Court rejected Pueblo's claim because its supposed losses flowed from Brunswick's having *preserved* competition by acquiring the failing centers. Allowing recovery for such losses would be contrary to the antitrust purpose of *promoting* competition.

Importance of Direct Injury

Proof that an antitrust injury is *direct* is critical because the Supreme Court has held that *indirect purchasers* lack standing to sue for antitrust violations. In *Illinois Brick Co. v. State of Illinois* (U.S. Sup. Ct. 1977), the state of Illinois and other governmental entities sought treble damages from concrete block suppliers who, they alleged, had illegally fixed the price of block used in the construction of public buildings. The plaintiffs acknowledged that the builders hired to construct the buildings had actually paid the inflated prices for the blocks, but argued that these illegal costs probably had been passed on to them in the form of higher prices for building construction. The Supreme Court refused to allow recovery, holding that granting standing to indirect purchasers would create a risk of duplicative recoveries by purchasers at various levels in a product's chain of distribution. The Court also observed that affording standing to indirect purchasers would lead to difficult problems of tracing competitive injuries through several levels of distribution and assessing the extent of an indirect purchaser's actual losses.

A number of state legislatures responded to *Illinois Brick* by enacting statutes allowing indirect purchasers to sue under *state* antitrust statutes. The Supreme Court has held that the *Illinois Brick* holding does not preempt such statutes.

Section 1—Restraints of Trade

Concerted Action

Section 1 of the Sherman Act states that "[e]very contract, combination in the form of trust or otherwise, or conspiracy, in restraint of trade or commerce among the several states, or with foreign nations is declared to be illegal." A **contract** is any agreement, express or implied, between *two or more* persons or business entities to restrain competition. A **combination** is a continuing *partnership* in restraint of trade. When *two or more* persons or business entities join for the purpose of restraining trade, a **conspiracy** occurs.

The above statutory language makes obvious the conclusion that § 1 of the Sherman Act is aimed at **concerted action** (i.e., *joint action*) in restraint of trade. *Purely unilateral action* by a competitor, on the other hand, cannot violate § 1. This statutory section reflects the public policy that businesspersons should make important competitive decisions on their own, rather than in conjunction with competitors. In his famous book *The Wealth of Nations* (1776), Adam Smith acknowledged both the danger to competition posed by concerted action and the tendencies of competitors to engage in such action. Smith observed that "[p]eople of the same trade seldom meet together, even for merriment and diversion, [without] the conversation end[ing] in a conspiracy against the public, or in some contrivance to raise prices."

Section 1's concerted action requirement poses two major problems. First, how separate must two business entities be before their joint activities are subject to the act's prohibitions? It has long been held that a corporation cannot conspire with itself or its employees and that a corporation's employees cannot be guilty of a conspiracy in the absence of some independent party. What about conspiracies, however, among related corporate entities? In decisions several decades ago, the Supreme Court appeared to hold that a corporation could violate the Sherman Act by conspiring with a wholly owned subsidiary. However, in *Copperweld Corp. v. Independence Tube Corp.* (U.S. Sup. Ct. 1984), the Court repudiated the "intra-enterprise conspiracy doctrine." The Court held that a parent company is legally incapable of conspiring with a wholly owned subsidiary for Sherman Act purposes, because an agreement between parent and subsidiary does not create the risk to competition that results when two independent entities act in concert. It remains to be seen whether this approach extends to corporate subsidiaries and affiliates that are not wholly owned. *Copperweld*'s logic would appear, however, to cover any subsidiary in which the parent firm has a controlling interest.

A second—and more difficult—problem frequently accompanies attempts to enforce § 1. This problem arises when courts are asked to *infer,* from the relevant circumstances, the existence of an agreement or conspiracy to restrain trade despite the lack of any *overt* agreement by the parties. Should parallel pricing behavior by several firms be enough, for instance, to justify the inference that a price-fixing conspiracy exists? Courts have consistently held that proof of pure *conscious parallelism,* standing alone, is *not* enough to establish a § 1 violation. Other evidence must be presented to show that the defendants' actions stemmed from an **agreement,** *express or implied,* rather than from independent business decisions. It therefore becomes quite difficult to attack *oligopolies* (a few large firms sharing one market) under § 1, because such firms may independently elect to follow the pricing policies of the industry "price leader" rather than risk their large market shares by engaging in vigorous price competition.

Per Se Analysis
Although § 1's language condemns "every" contract, combination, and conspiracy in

restraint of trade, the Supreme Court has long held that the Sherman Act applies only to behavior that *unreasonably* restrains competition. In addition, the Court has developed two fundamentally different approaches to analyzing behavior challenged under § 1. According to the Court, some actions always have a negative effect on competition—an effect that cannot be excused or justified. Such actions are classified as **per se** unlawful. If a particular behavior falls under the per se heading, it is conclusively presumed to violate § 1. Per se rules are thought to provide reliable guidance to business. They also simplify otherwise lengthy antitrust litigation, because if per se unlawful behavior is proven, the defendant cannot assert any supposed justifications in an attempt to avoid liability.

Per se rules, however, are frequently criticized on the ground that they oversimplify complex economic realities. Recent decisions reveal that for *various* economic activities, the Supreme Court is moving away from per se rules and instead adopting **rule of reason** analysis. This trend is consistent with the Court's increased inclination to consider economic theories that seek to justify behavior previously held to be per se unlawful.

"Rule of Reason" Analysis
Behavior not classified as per se unlawful is judged under the **rule of reason.** This approach requires a detailed inquiry into the actual competitive effects of the defendant's actions. It includes consideration of any justifications that the defendant may advance. If the court concludes that the challenged activity had a significant anticompetitive effect that was not offset by any positive effect on competition or other social benefit such as enhanced economic efficiency, the activity will be held to violate § 1. On the other hand, if the court concludes that the justifications advanced by the defendant outweigh the harm to competition resulting from the defendant's activity, there is no § 1 violation.

In recent years, courts have sometimes employed a so-called quick-look analysis instead of a full-fledged rule of reason analysis. Quick-look analysis may be described as an intermediate type of analysis that falls somewhere between the black-and-white per se approach and the more complicated rule of reason approach. Courts may be inclined to employ quick-look analysis when they believe the behavior at issue could have both anticompetitive and procompetitive effects that can be weighed against each other without the extensive market analyses that may be necessary under full rule of reason treatment. In this sense, quick-look analysis may be a toned-down version of the rule of reason approach.

The following subsections of this chapter examine some of the behaviors held to violate § 1. The legal analysis given to the respective behaviors is also considered.

Horizontal Price-Fixing

An essential attribute of a free market is that the price of goods and services is determined by the free play of the impersonal forces of the marketplace. Attempts by competitors to interfere with market forces and control prices—called **horizontal price-fixing**—have long been held per se unlawful under § 1. Horizontal price-fixing may take the form of direct agreements among competitors about the price at which they sell or buy a particular product or service. It may also be accomplished by agreements on the quantity of goods to be produced, offered for sale, or bought. In one famous case, an agreement by major oil refiners to purchase and store the excess production of small independent refiners was held to amount to price-fixing because the purpose of the agreement was to affect the market price for gasoline by artificially limiting the available supply.[3]

Some commentators have suggested that agreements among competitors to fix *maximum* prices should be treated under a rule of reason approach rather than the harsher per se standard because, in some instances, such agreements may result in savings to consumers. In addition, lower courts have occasionally sought to craft exceptions to the rule that horizontal price-fixing triggers per se treatment. It is important to note, however, that the Supreme Court continues to adhere to the long-standing rule of per se illegality for any form of horizontal price-fixing. In the *Denny's Marina* case, which follows, a federal court of appeals overturned a district court's attempt to limit the applicability of the per se rule in the horizontal price-fixing context.

---

[3]*United States v. Socony-Vacuum Oil Co.,* 310 U.S. 150 (U.S. Sup. Ct. 1940).

Denny's Marina, Inc. v. Renfro Productions, Inc.
8 F.3d 1217 (7th Cir. 1993)

Denny's Marina, Inc., filed an antitrust action, described more fully below, against various defendants: the "Renfro Defendants" (Renfro Productions, Inc., Indianapolis Boat, Sport, and Travel Show, Inc., and individuals connected with those firms); "CIMDA" (the Central Indiana Marine Dealers Association); and the "Dealer Defendants" (various boat dealers who competed with Denny's in the sale of fishing boats, motors, trailers, and marine accessories in the central Indiana market). The Renfro Defendants operate two boat shows each year, one in the spring and one in the fall, at the Indiana State Fairgrounds. The spring show has occurred annually for more than 30 years and is one of the top three boat shows in the United States. It attracts between 160,000 and 191,000 consumers each year. The fall show is a smaller operation that has occurred each year since 1987. Numerous boat dealers participate in the two shows.

Denny's participated in the fall show in 1988, 1989, and 1990. It participated in the spring show in 1989 and 1990. According to allegations made by Denny's in its antitrust complaint, Denny's was quite successful at each of these shows, apparently because it urged customers to shop the other dealers and then return to Denny's for a lower price. After the 1989 spring show, some of the Dealer Defendants began to complain (according to Denny's) to the Renfro Defendants about the sales methods used by Denny's. In addition, Denny's alleged, the Dealer Defendants spent a significant part of a CIMDA meeting venting frustration about similar sales tactics used by Denny's at the 1990 spring show. Denny's also asserted that the Dealer Defendants' complaints to the Renfro Defendants escalated, and that as a result, the Renfro Defendants informed Denny's after the 1990 fall show that Denny's could no longer participate in the boat shows.

Denny's claimed that the above-described conduct of the defendants amounted to a conspiracy, prohibited by Sherman Act § 1, to exclude Denny's from participating in the boat shows because its policy was to "meet or beat" its competitors' prices at the shows. When the district court granted the defendants' motions for summary judgment, Denny's appealed to the Seventh Circuit Court of Appeals.

Cummings, Circuit Judge

Because summary judgment was granted to the defendants, the facts alleged by Denny's and any inferences therefrom must be construed in its favor. Summary judgment will be denied if a reasonable jury could return a verdict for the plaintiff.

A successful claim under § 1 of the Sherman Act requires proof of three elements: (1) a contract, combination, or conspiracy; (2) a resultant unreasonable restraint of trade in the relevant market; and (3) an accompanying injury. The district court noted that [for purposes of a ruling on their summary judgment motions] defendants do not dispute the first and third elements of proof. Hence the parties' only argument is whether Denny's has made a sufficient showing of the second element, unreasonable restraint of trade, to withstand defendants' motions for summary judgment.

There are two standards for evaluating whether an alleged restraint of trade is unreasonable: the rule of reason and the per se rule. Because the restraint alleged by Denny's constitutes a horizontal price-fixing conspiracy, it is per se an unreasonable restraint of trade [under a long line of Supreme Court decisions]. The conspiracy in this case was horizontal because it . . . consisted of Denny's competitors and their association. That the conspiracy was joined by the operators of the . . . boat shows does not transform it into a vertical agreement.

Likewise, the conspiracy was to fix prices. Price-fixing agreements need not include "explicit agreement on prices to be charged or that one party have the right to be consulted about the other's prices." *Palmer v. BRG of Georgia, Inc.* (U.S. Sup. Ct. 1990). "Under the Sherman Act a combination formed for the purpose and with the effect of raising, depressing, fixing, pegging, or stabilizing the price of a commodity in interstate or foreign commerce is illegal per se." *United States v. Socony-Vacuum Oil Co.* (U.S. Sup. Ct. 1940). Concerted action by dealers to protect themselves from price competition by discounters constitutes horizontal price-fixing. Hence the actions of the Dealer Defendants and CIMDA, joined by the Renfro Defendants, to prevent Denny's from participating in the boat shows constitutes a horizontal price-fixing conspiracy notwithstanding the apparent lack of an explicit agreement to set prices.

So far, the position of this court is similar to that of the court below. Nevertheless, having essentially found that Denny's had adduced sufficient evidence of a horizontal price-fixing conspiracy to withstand a motion for summary judgment, the court below refused to apply the per se rule that would allow it to conclude that there had been an unreasonable restraint of trade in the relevant market. Instead, before it would apply the per se rule the court required Denny's to demonstrate a substantial potential for impact on competition in the central Indiana market as a whole. Such an exception to the per se rule against price-fixing is unwarranted by cited precedent . . . [and] would effectively require plaintiffs to make a rule of reason demonstration in order to invoke the per se rule! [In cases governed by the rule of reason], both parties are likely to present extensive economic analysis of the relevant market. It is in part to avoid such excessive costs of litigation that the per se rule is applied in cases where the anti-competitive effect of certain practices may be presumed.

As far back as 1940, it has been clear that horizontal price-fixing is illegal per se without requiring a showing of actual or likely impact on a market. *See Socony-Vacuum Oil.* This is because joint action by competitors to suppress price-cutting has the requisite "substantial potential for impact on competition" to warrant per se treatment. *Federal Trade Commission v. Superior Court Trial Lawyers Association* (U.S. Sup. Ct. 1990). The district court would require Denny's to demonstrate a particular potential for impact on the market, when one of the purposes of the per se rule is that in cases like this such a potential is so well-established as not to require individualized showings. The pernicious effects are conclusively presumed.

Since Denny's presented enough evidence for a court and jury to conclude that the defendants engaged in [per se behavior consisting of] a horizontal conspiracy to suppress price competition at boat shows, . . . the district court's grant of summary judgment to the defendants [was erroneous].

Summary judgment for defendants reversed; case remanded for trial.

Vertical Price-Fixing

Attempts by manufacturers to control the resale price of their products may also fall within the scope of § 1. This behavior is called **vertical price-fixing** or *resale price maintenance*. In determining whether vertical price-fixing occurred, the first question is whether there was only unilateral action on the part of the manufacturer or whether there was instead the concerted action contemplated by § 1. A manufacturer may lawfully state a suggested retail price for its products—an action that is unilateral and therefore not a violation of § 1. Illegality may be present, however, when there is a manufacturer-dealer agreement (express or implied) obligating the dealer to resell at a price dictated by the manufacturer.

Unilateral Refusals to Deal In *United States v. Colgate & Co.* (1919), the Supreme Court held that a manufacturer could *unilaterally refuse to deal* with those who failed to follow the manufacturer's suggested resale prices. The rationale underlying this rule was that a single firm may deal or not deal with whomever it chooses without violating § 1, because unilateral action is not the joint action prohibited by the statute. Subsequent decisions, however, have narrowly construed the *Colgate* doctrine. Depending upon the facts, circumstances, and effects, manufacturers may be held to have violated § 1 if they enlist the aid of dealers who are not price-cutting to help enforce their (the manufacturers') pricing policies, or if they engage in other concerted action to further those policies. "May be held to have violated § 1" is important language in the previous sentence, in view of the mode of analysis now required by the Supreme Court in cases of alleged resale price maintenance.

The Shift to Rule of Reason

Until relatively recently, Supreme Court decisions established that vertical price-fixing was a per se violation of § 1. With per se treatment being given to such cases, defendants were not permitted to offer justifications for their behavior. Chicago School theorists argued, however, that many of the same reasons held to justify rule of reason analysis of vertical *nonprice* restraints on distribution (discussed later in this chapter) were equally applicable to vertical price-fixing agreements. In particular, these critics argued that vertical restrictions limiting the *maximum* price at which a dealer can resell may prevent dealers with dominant market positions from exploiting consumers through price-gouging. In *State Oil Co. v. Khan,* a 1997 decision that follows shortly, the Supreme Court agreed with the critics, overruled a long-standing precedent that called for per se treatment of vertical maximum price-fixing, and held that such cases of vertical price-fixing should be analyzed under the rule of reason.

For 10 years after *Khan* was decided, vertical *minimum* price-fixing continued to be governed by the per se rule. Arguments for rule of reason analysis continued to resonate, however. In a 5–4 decision issued in 2007, the Supreme Court overruled a 96-year-old precedent and held that vertical minimum price-fixing would be judged under the rule of reason rather than the per se approach. The 2007 decision, *Leegin Creative Leather Products v. PSKS, Inc.,* appears below (immediately following the *Khan* case). After *Khan* and *Leegin,* all forms of vertical price-fixing now receive rule of reason analysis.

State Oil Co. v. Khan   522 U.S. 3 (U.S. Sup. Ct. 1997)

Barkat Khan operated a service station in Illinois under a contract with State Oil Co. The parties' contract called for State Oil to lease the station premises to Khan and for State Oil to supply him with gasoline and related products that he would sell at the station. According to the contract, State Oil would establish a suggested retail price for the gasoline it supplied Khan for resale under the "Union 76" brand name. State Oil would then sell the gasoline to Khan for 3.25 cents less than that price. If Khan regarded the suggested retail price as too low, he could ask State Oil to increase it. If State Oil refused to raise the suggested price and Khan increased his retail price anyway, the contract required Khan to rebate to State Oil the difference between his new price and the suggested price.

When Khan fell behind on his rent, State Oil terminated the contract. Khan then sued State Oil, alleging that the above provisions of the contract amounted to vertical maximum price-fixing in violation of § 1 of the Sherman Act. The district court held that the alleged price-fixing should be evaluated under the rule of reason approach rather than under the per se approach. When the court granted summary judgment in favor of State Oil, Khan appealed to the U.S. Court of Appeals for the Seventh Circuit. The Seventh Circuit reversed, holding that a Supreme Court precedent established the per se rule as controlling. The Supreme Court granted certiorari.

O'Connor, Justice

In *Albrecht v. Herald Co.* (U.S. Sup. Ct. 1968), this Court held that vertical maximum price-fixing is a per se violation of [§ 1 of the Sherman Act]. [W]e are asked to reconsider that decision.

The District Court found that [Khan's] allegations . . . did not establish the sort of "manifestly anticompetitive implications or pernicious effect on competition" that would justify per se prohibition of State Oil's conduct. The Court of Appeals for the Seventh Circuit reversed [the lower court's grant of summary judgment in favor of State Oil]. The [Seventh Circuit] first noted that the agreement between Khan and State Oil did indeed fix maximum gasoline prices by making it "worthless" for Khan to exceed the suggested retail prices. After reviewing legal and economic aspects of price-fixing, the court concluded that State Oil's pricing scheme was a per se antitrust violation under *Albrecht.* Although the [Seventh Circuit] characterized *Albrecht* as "unsound when decided" and "inconsistent with later decisions" of this Court, it felt constrained to follow that decision.

[M]ost antitrust claims are analyzed under a "rule of reason," according to which the finder of fact must decide whether the questioned practice imposes an unreasonable restraint on competition, taking into account a variety of factors, including specific information about the relevant business, its condition before and after the restraint was imposed, and the restraint's history, nature, and effect. Some types of restraints, however, have such predictable and pernicious anticompetitive effect, and such limited potential for procompetitive benefits, that they are deemed unlawful per se.

A review of this Court's decisions leading up to and beyond *Albrecht* is relevant to our assessment of the continuing validity of the per se rule established in *Albrecht*. Beginning with [a 1911 decision], the Court recognized the illegality of agreements under which manufacturers or suppliers set the minimum resale prices to be charged by their distributors. By 1940, the Court broadly declared all business combinations "formed for the purpose and with the effect of raising, depressing, fixing, pegging, or stabilizing the price of a commodity in interstate or foreign commerce" illegal per se. *United States v. Socony-Vacuum Oil Co.* (U.S. Sup. Ct. 1940). Accordingly, the Court condemned an agreement between two affiliated liquor distillers to limit the maximum price charged by retailers in *Kiefer-Stewart Co. v. Joseph E. Seagram & Sons, Inc.* (U.S. Sup. Ct. 1951).

In subsequent cases, the Court's attention turned to arrangements through which suppliers imposed restrictions on dealers with respect to matters other than resale price. In [a 1963 decision], the Court considered the validity of a manufacturer's assignment of exclusive territories to its distributors and dealers. The Court concluded that too little was known about the competitive impact of such vertical limitations to warrant treating them as per se unlawful. Four years later, in *United States v. Arnold, Schwinn & Co.* (U.S. Sup. Ct. 1967), the Court reconsidered the status of exclusive dealer territories and held that . . . a supplier's imposition of territorial restrictions on [a] distributor was "so obviously destructive of competition" as to constitute a per se violation of the Sherman Act.

Albrecht, decided [a year after *Schwinn*], involved a newspaper publisher who had granted exclusive territories to independent carriers subject to their adherence to a maximum price on resale of the newspapers to the public. Influenced by its decisions in *Socony-Vacuum, Kiefer-Stewart,* and *Schwinn,* the Court concluded that it was per se unlawful for the publisher to fix the maximum resale price of its newspapers. The Court acknowledged that "[m]aximum and minimum price-fixing may have different consequences in many situations," but nonetheless condemned maximum price-fixing for "substituting the perhaps erroneous judgment of a seller for the forces of the competitive market."

Nine years later, in *Continental T.V., Inc. v. GTE Sylvania, Inc.* (U.S. Sup. Ct. 1977), the Court overruled *Schwinn,* thereby rejecting application of a per se rule in the context of vertical nonprice restrictions. [The Court noted that *Schwinn*] neither explained the "sudden change in position," nor referred to the accepted requirements for per se violations set forth in [earlier cases]. The Court . . . reviewed scholarly works supporting the economic utility of vertical nonprice restraints. [It then] concluded that, because "departure from the rule-of-reason standard must be based upon demonstrable economic effect rather than—as in *Schwinn*—upon formalistic line-drawing," the appropriate course would be "to return to the rule of reason that governed vertical restrictions prior to *Schwinn*."

Subsequent decisions of the Court . . . have hinted that the analytical underpinnings of *Albrecht* were substantially weakened by *Sylvania*. We noted in [a 1982 decision] that vertical restraints are generally more defensible than horizontal restraints. [W]e explained in *324 Liquor Corp. v. Duffy* (U.S. Sup. Ct. 1987) that decisions such as *Sylvania* "recognize the possibility that a vertical restraint imposed by a single manufacturer or wholesaler may stimulate interbrand competition even as it reduces intrabrand competition."

[I]n *Atlantic Richfield Co. v. USA Petroleum Co. (ARCO)* (U.S. Sup. Ct. 1990), although *Albrecht*'s continuing validity was not squarely before the Court, some disfavor with that decision was signaled by our statement that we would "assume, *arguendo,* that *Albrecht* correctly held that vertical maximum price-fixing is subject to the per se rule." More significantly, we specifically acknowledged that vertical maximum price-fixing "may have procompetitive interbrand effects," and pointed out that, in the wake of *Sylvania,* "[t]he procompetitive potential of a vertical maximum price restraint is more evident . . . than it was when *Albrecht* was decided, because exclusive territorial arrangements and other nonprice restrictions were unlawful per se in 1968."

Thus, our reconsideration of *Albrecht*'s continuing validity is informed by several of our decisions, as well as a considerable body of scholarship discussing the effects of vertical restraints. Our analysis is also guided by our general view that the primary purpose of the antitrust laws is to protect interbrand competition. "Low prices," we . . . explained [in *ARCO*], "benefit consumers regardless of how those prices are set, and so long as they are above predatory levels, they do not threaten competition."

So informed, we find it difficult to maintain that vertically-imposed maximum prices could harm consumers or competition to the extent necessary to justify their per se invalidation. As Chief Judge Posner wrote for the Court of Appeals in this case:

As for maximum resale price fixing, . . . the supplier [usually] cannot squeeze his dealers' margins below a competitive level; the attempt to do so would just drive the dealers into the arms of a competing supplier. A supplier might, however, fix a maximum resale price in order to prevent his dealers from exploiting a monopoly position. . . . [S]uppose that State Oil, perhaps to encourage . . . dealer services . . ., has spaced its dealers sufficiently far apart to limit competition among them (or even given each of them an exclusive territory); and suppose further that Union 76 is a sufficiently distinctive and popular brand to give the dealers in it at least a modicum of monopoly power. Then State Oil might want to place a ceiling on the dealers' resale prices in order to prevent them from exploiting that monopoly power fully. It would do this not out of disinterested malice, but in its commercial self-interest. The higher the price at which gasoline is resold, the smaller the volume sold, and so the lower the profit to the supplier if the higher profit per gallon at the higher price is being snared by the dealer.

We recognize that the *Albrecht* decision presented a number of theoretical justifications for a per se rule against vertical maximum price-fixing. But criticism of those premises abounds. The *Albrecht* decision was grounded in the fear that maximum price-fixing by suppliers could interfere with dealer freedom. [However, as noted by Phillip Areeda in his treatise, *Antitrust Law,*] "the ban on maximum resale price limitations declared in *Albrecht* in the name of 'dealer freedom' has actually prompted many suppliers to integrate forward into distribution, thus eliminating the very independent trader for whom *Albrecht* professed solicitude."

The *Albrecht* Court also expressed the concern that maximum prices may be set too low for dealers to offer consumers essential or desired services. But such conduct, by driving away customers, would seem likely to harm manufacturers as well as dealers and consumers, making it unlikely that a supplier would set such a price as a matter of business judgment. In addition, *Albrecht* noted that vertical maximum price-fixing could effectively channel distribution through large or specially advantaged dealers. It is unclear, however, that a supplier would profit from limiting its market by excluding potential dealers. Further, although vertical maximum price-fixing might limit the viability of inefficient dealers, that consequence is not necessarily harmful to competition and consumers.

Finally, *Albrecht* reflected the Court's fear that maximum price-fixing could be used to disguise arrangements to fix minimum prices, which remains illegal per se. Although we have acknowledged the possibility that maximum pricing might mask minimum pricing, we believe that such conduct—as with the other concerns articulated in *Albrecht*—can be appropriately recognized and punished under the rule of reason. After reconsidering *Albrecht*'s rationale and the substantial criticisms the decision has received, . . . we conclude that there is insufficient economic justification for per se invalidation of vertical maximum price-fixing.

Despite what Chief Judge Posner aptly described as *Albrecht*'s "infirmities, [and] its increasingly wobbly, motheaten foundations," there remains the question whether *Albrecht* deserves continuing respect under the doctrine of *stare decisis*. The Court of Appeals was correct in applying that principle despite disagreement with *Albrecht,* for it is this Court's prerogative alone to overrule one of its precedents. We approach the reconsideration of decisions of this Court with the utmost caution. *Stare decisis* reflects "a policy judgment that in most matters it is more important that the applicable rule of law be settled than that it be settled right." *Agostini v. Felton* (U.S. Sup. Ct. 1997). But "[s]tare decisis is not an inexorable command." *Payne v. Tennessee* (U.S. Sup. Ct. 1991). In the area of antitrust law, there is a competing interest, well-represented in this Court's decisions, in recognizing and adapting to changed circumstances and the lessons of accumulated experience.

With the views underlying *Albrecht* eroded by this Court's precedent, there is not much of that decision to salvage. [W]e find its conceptual foundations gravely weakened. In overruling *Albrecht,* we of course do not hold that all vertical maximum price-fixing is per se lawful. Instead, vertical maximum price-fixing, like the majority of commercial arrangements subject to the antitrust laws, should be evaluated under the rule of reason.

Decision of Court of Appeals reversed; case remanded for further proceedings.

Leegin Creative Leather Products v. PSKS, Inc.
127 S. Ct. 2705 (U.S. Sup. Ct. 2007)

Leegin Creative Leather Products, Inc., designs, manufactures, and distributes leather goods and accessories. In 1991, Leegin began to sell belts under the "Brighton" brand name. The Brighton brand has since expanded into a variety of women's fashion accessories. It is sold across the United States in over 5,000 retail establishments. PSKS, Inc., operates Kay's Kloset, a women's apparel store that, in 1995, began purchasing Brighton goods from Leegin for retail sale. Brighton became the store's most important brand and once accounted for 40 to 50 percent of its profits.

In 1997, Leegin instituted the "Brighton Retail Pricing and Promotion Policy." Under this policy, Leegin refused to sell to retailers that discounted Brighton goods below suggested prices. Leegin adopted the policy to give its retailers sufficient margins to enable them to provide customers the service central to its distribution strategy. It also expressed concern that discounting harmed Brighton's brand image and reputation. In 1998, Leegin implemented a "Heart Stores" policy, under which retailers were given incentives to become Heart Stores and, in return, pledged to adhere to Leegin's suggested prices. Kay's Kloset became a Heart Store but later lost that status when a Leegin representative concluded that the store was physically unattractive. Kay's Kloset continued, however, to purchase Brighton products for resale at the store.

In December 2002, Leegin discovered that Kay's Kloset had been marking down the entire Brighton line by 20 percent. Kay's Kloset contended that it did so in order to compete with nearby retailers who also were undercutting Leegin's suggested prices. Leegin requested that Kay's Kloset cease discounting, but Kay's Kloset refused. Leegin then stopped selling to the store. The loss of the Brighton brand had a considerable negative impact on Kay's Kloset's revenues.

PSKS sued Leegin in federal district court, claiming that Leegin had violated Sherman Act § 1 by "enter[ing] into agreements with retailers to charge only those prices fixed by Leegin." Leegin planned to introduce expert testimony describing the procompetitive effects of its pricing policy. The district court excluded the testimony, however, because long-standing Supreme Court precedent extended per se treatment to vertical minimum price-fixing. At trial, PSKS argued that the Heart Store program, among other things, demonstrated that Leegin and its retailers had agreed to fix prices. Leegin responded that it had established a lawful unilateral pricing policy rather than engaging in the concerted action required for a violation of § 1. The jury agreed with PSKS and awarded it $1.2 million in damages. The district court trebled the damages and ordered reimbursement of PSKS for its attorney's fees. In its appeal to the U.S. Court of Appeals for the Fifth Circuit, Leegin did not dispute that it had entered into vertical price-fixing agreements with its retailers. Rather, it contended that the rule of reason should have been applied to those agreements. Rejecting this argument because it considered itself bound by Supreme Court precedent, the Fifth Circuit affirmed the district court's decision. The U.S. Supreme Court granted Leegin's petition for a writ of certiorari.

Kennedy, Justice

In *Dr. Miles Medical Co. v. John D. Park & Sons Co.*, 220 U.S. 373 (1911), the Court established the rule that it is per se illegal under § 1 of the Sherman Act for a manufacturer to agree with its distributor to set the minimum price the distributor can charge for the manufacturer's goods. The question presented by the instant case is whether the Court should overrule the per se rule and allow resale price maintenance agreements to be judged by the rule of reason, the usual standard applied to determine if there is a violation of § 1.

Section 1 prohibits "[e]very contract, combination in the form of trust or otherwise, or conspiracy, in restraint of trade or commerce among the several States." While § 1 could be interpreted to proscribe all contracts, . . . the Court has repeated time and again that § 1 "outlaw[s] only unreasonable restraints." *State Oil Co. v. Khan,* 522 U.S. 3, 10 (1997). The rule of reason is the accepted standard for testing whether a practice restrains trade in violation of § 1. "Under this rule, the factfinder weighs all of the circumstances of a case in deciding whether a restrictive practice should be prohibited as imposing an unreasonable restraint on competition." *Continental T.V., Inc. v. GTE Sylvania, Inc.,* 433 U.S. 36, 49 (1977). Appropriate factors to take into account include "specific information about the relevant business" and "the restraint's history, nature, and effect." *Khan,* at 10. Whether the businesses involved have market power is a further, significant consideration. In its design and function the rule distinguishes between restraints with anticompetitive effect that are harmful to the consumer and restraints stimulating competition that are in the consumer's best interest.

The rule of reason does not govern all restraints. Some types are deemed unlawful per se. The per se rule, treating categories of restraints as necessarily illegal, eliminates the need to study the reasonableness of an individual restraint in light of the real market forces at work. [I]t must be acknowledged [that] the per se rule can give clear guidance for certain conduct. Restraints that are per se unlawful include horizontal agreements among competitors to fix prices or to divide markets.

Resort to per se rules is confined to restraints, like those mentioned, "that would always or almost always tend to restrict competition and decrease output." [Case citation omitted.] To justify a per se prohibition a restraint must have "manifestly anticompetitive" effects and "lack . . . any redeeming virtue." [Case citations omitted.] As a consequence, the per se rule is appropriate only after courts have had considerable experience with the type of restraint at issue, and only if courts can predict with confidence that it would be invalidated in all or almost all instances under the rule of reason. It should come as no surprise, then, that "we have expressed reluctance to adopt per se rules with regard to restraints imposed in the context of business relationships where the economic impact of certain practices is not immediately obvious." *Khan,* at 10. [A]s we have stated, "a departure from the rule of reason standard must be based upon demonstrable economic effect rather than upon formalistic line-drawing." *GTE Sylvania,* at 58–59.

The Court has interpreted *Dr. Miles* as establishing a per se rule against a vertical agreement between a manufacturer and its distributor to set minimum resale prices. In *Dr. Miles,* the plaintiff, a manufacturer of medicines, sold its products only to distributors who agreed to resell them at set prices. The Court found the manufacturer's control of resale prices to be unlawful. It relied on the common-law rule that "a general restraint upon alienation is ordinarily invalid." The Court then explained that the agreements would advantage the distributors, not the manufacturer, and were analogous to a combination among competing distributors, which the law treated as void.

The reasoning of the Court's more recent jurisprudence has rejected the rationales on which *Dr. Miles* was based. By relying on the common-law rule against restraints on alienation, the Court justified its decision based on "formalistic" legal doctrine rather than "demonstrable economic effect" [quoting *GTE Sylvania*]. The Court in *Dr. Miles* relied on a treatise published in 1628, but failed to discuss in detail the business reasons that would motivate a manufacturer situated in 1911 to make use of vertical price restraints. The Court should be cautious about putting dispositive weight on doctrines from antiquity but of slight relevance. We reaffirm that "the state of the common law 400 or even 100 years ago is irrelevant to the issue before us: the effect of the antitrust laws upon vertical distributional restraints in the American economy today." *GTE Sylvania*, at 53.

Dr. Miles, furthermore, treated vertical agreements a manufacturer makes with its distributors as analogous to a horizontal combination among competing distributors. In later cases, however, the Court rejected the approach of reliance on rules governing horizontal restraints when defining rules applicable to vertical ones. Our recent cases formulate antitrust principles in accordance with the appreciated differences in economic effect between vertical and horizontal agreements, differences the *Dr. Miles* Court failed to consider. The reasons upon which *Dr. Miles* relied do not justify a per se rule. As a consequence, it is necessary to examine, in the first instance, the economic effects of vertical agreements to fix minimum resale prices, and to determine whether the per se rule is nonetheless appropriate.

Though each side of the debate can find sources to support its position, it suffices to say here that economics literature is replete with procompetitive justifications for a manufacturer's use of resale price maintenance. The few recent studies documenting the competitive effects of resale price maintenance also cast doubt on the conclusion that the practice meets the criteria for a per se rule. The justifications for vertical price restraints are similar to those for other vertical restraints. Minimum resale price maintenance can stimulate interbrand competition—the competition among manufacturers selling different brands of the same type of product—by reducing intrabrand competition—the competition among retailers selling the same brand. The promotion of interbrand competition is important because "the primary purpose of the antitrust laws is to protect [this type of] competition." *Khan*, at 15. A single manufacturer's use of vertical price restraints tends to eliminate intrabrand price competition; this in turn encourages retailers to invest in tangible or intangible services or promotional efforts that aid the manufacturer's position as against rival manufacturers. Resale price maintenance also has the potential to give consumers more options so that they can choose among low-price, low-service brands; high-price, high-service brands; and brands that fall in between.

Absent vertical price restraints, the retail services that enhance interbrand competition might be underprovided. This is because discounting retailers can free ride on retailers who furnish services and then capture some of the increased demand those services generate. Consumers might learn, for example, about the benefits of a manufacturer's product from a retailer that invests in fine showrooms, offers product demonstrations, or hires and trains knowledgeable employees. Or consumers might decide to buy the product because they see it in a retail establishment that has a reputation for selling high-quality merchandise. If the consumer can then buy the product from a retailer that discounts because it has not spent capital providing services or developing a quality reputation, the high-service retailer will lose sales to the discounter, forcing it to cut back its services to a level lower than consumers would otherwise prefer. Minimum resale price maintenance alleviates the problem because it prevents the discounter from undercutting the service provider. With price competition decreased, the manufacturer's retailers compete among themselves over services.

While vertical agreements setting minimum resale prices can have procompetitive justifications, they may have anticompetitive effects in other cases; and unlawful price fixing, designed solely to obtain monopoly profits, is an ever-present temptation. Notwithstanding the risks of unlawful conduct, it cannot be stated with any degree of confidence that resale price maintenance always or almost always tend[s] to restrict competition and decrease output. Vertical agreements establishing minimum resale prices can have either procompetitive or anticompetitive effects, depending upon the circumstances in which they are formed. And although the empirical evidence on the topic is limited, it does not suggest efficient uses of the agreements are infrequent or hypothetical. As the rule would proscribe a significant amount of procompetitive conduct, these agreements appear ill suited for per se condemnation.

PSKS contends, nonetheless, that vertical price restraints should be per se unlawful because of the administrative convenience of per se rules. That argument suggests per se illegality is the rule rather than the exception. This misinterprets our antitrust law. Per se rules may decrease administrative costs, but that is only part of the equation. Those rules can be counterproductive. They can increase the total cost of the antitrust system by prohibiting procompetitive conduct the antitrust laws should encourage. They also may increase litigation costs by promoting frivolous suits against legitimate practices. Were the Court now to conclude that vertical price restraints should be per se illegal based on administrative costs, we would undermine, if not overrule, the traditional demanding standards for adopting per se rules. Any possible reduction in administrative costs cannot alone justify the *Dr. Miles* rule.

PSKS also argues the per se rule is justified because a vertical price restraint can lead to higher prices for the manufacturer's goods. PSKS is mistaken in relying on pricing effects absent a further showing of anticompetitive conduct. For, as has been indicated already, the antitrust laws are designed primarily to protect interbrand competition, from which lower prices can later result. The Court, moreover, has evaluated other vertical restraints under the rule of reason even though prices can be increased in the course of promoting procompetitive effects.

The rule of reason is designed and used to eliminate anticompetitive transactions from the market. This standard principle applies to vertical price restraints. A party alleging injury from a vertical agreement setting minimum resale prices will have, as a general matter, the information and resources available to show the existence of the agreement and its scope of operation. As courts gain experience considering the effects of these restraints by applying the rule of reason over the course of decisions, they can establish the litigation structure to ensure the rule operates to eliminate anticompetitive restraints from the market and to provide more guidance to businesses.

For the foregoing reasons, we think that were the Court considering the issue as an original matter, the rule of reason, not a per se rule of unlawfulness, would be the appropriate standard to judge vertical price restraints. We do not write on a clean slate, [however,] for the decision in *Dr. Miles* is almost a century old. So there is an argument for its retention on the basis of stare decisis alone. Even if *Dr. Miles* established an erroneous rule, "[s]tare decisis reflects a policy judgment that in most matters it is more important that the applicable rule of law be settled than that it be settled right." *Khan,* at 20. And concerns about maintaining settled law are strong when the question is one of statutory interpretation.

Stare decisis is not as significant in this case, however, because the issue before us is the scope of the Sherman Act. *Khan,* at 20 ("[T]he general presumption that legislative changes should be left to Congress has less force with respect to the Sherman Act"). From the beginning the Court has treated the Sherman Act as [if it were common law]. Just as the common law adapts to modern understanding and greater experience, so too does the Sherman Act's prohibition on "restraint[s] of trade" evolve to meet the dynamics of present economic conditions. The case-by-case adjudication contemplated by the rule of reason has implemented this common-law approach. Likewise, the boundaries of the doctrine of per se illegality

should not be immovable. For "[i]t would make no sense to create out of the single term 'restraint of trade' a chronologically schizoid statute, in which a 'rule of reason' evolves with new circumstance and new wisdom, but a line of per se illegality remains forever fixed where it was." [Case citation omitted.]

Stare decisis, we conclude, does not compel our continued adherence to the per se rule against vertical price restraints. As discussed earlier, respected authorities in the economics literature suggest the per se rule is inappropriate, and there is now widespread agreement that resale price maintenance can have procompetitive effects. It is also significant that both the Department of Justice and the Federal Trade Commission—the antitrust enforcement agencies with the ability to assess the long-term impacts of resale price maintenance—have recommended that this Court replace the per se rule with the traditional rule of reason. In the antitrust context the fact that a decision has been "called into serious question" justifies our reevaluation of it. *Khan,* at 21.

Other considerations reinforce the conclusion that *Dr. Miles* should be overruled. Of most relevance, "we have overruled our precedents when subsequent cases have undermined their doctrinal underpinnings." [Case citation omitted.] The Court's treatment of vertical restraints has progressed away from *Dr. Miles'* strict approach. We have distanced ourselves from the opinion's rationales. This is unsurprising, for the case was decided not long after enactment of the Sherman Act when the Court had little experience with antitrust analysis.

In more recent cases the Court . . . has continued to temper, limit, or overrule once strict prohibitions on vertical restraints. In 1977, the Court overturned the per se rule for vertical nonprice restraints, adopting the rule of reason in its stead. *GTE Sylvania,* at 57–59. [I]n 1997, after examining the issue of vertical maximum price-fixing agreements in light of commentary and real experience, the Court overruled a 29-year-old precedent treating those agreements as per se illegal. It held instead that they should be evaluated under the traditional rule of reason. *Khan,* at 22. [O]ur recent treatment of other vertical restraints justif[ies] the conclusion that *Dr. Miles* should not be retained.

The *Dr. Miles* rule is also inconsistent with a principled framework, for it makes little economic sense when analyzed with our other cases on vertical restraints. If we were to decide the procompetitive effects of resale price maintenance were insufficient to overrule *Dr. Miles,* then cases such as . . . *GTE Sylvania* . . . would be called into question. There is yet another consideration. A manufacturer can impose territorial restrictions on distributors and allow only one distributor to sell its goods in a given region. Our cases have recognized, and the economics literature confirms, that these vertical nonprice restraints have impacts similar to those of vertical price restraints; both reduce intrabrand competition and can stimulate retailer services. The same legal standard (per se unlawfulness) applies to horizontal market division and horizontal price fixing because both have similar economic effect. There is likewise little economic justification for the current differential treatment of vertical price and nonprice restraints. Furthermore, vertical nonprice restraints may prove less efficient for inducing desired services, and they reduce intrabrand competition more than vertical price restraints by eliminating both price and service competition.

For these reasons, the Court's decision in *Dr. Miles* is now overruled. Vertical price restraints are to be judged according to the rule of reason.

Fifth Circuit decision reversed, and case remanded for further proceedings.

Breyer, Justice, dissenting

The only safe predictions to make about today's decision are that it will likely raise the price of goods at retail and that it will create considerable legal turbulence as lower courts seek to develop workable principles. I do not believe that the majority has shown new or changed conditions sufficient to warrant overruling a decision of such long standing. All ordinary stare decisis considerations indicate the contrary. For these reasons, with respect, I dissent.

Horizontal Divisions of Markets

It has traditionally been said that **horizontal division of markets** agreements—those agreements among competing firms to divide up the available market by assigning one another certain exclusive territories or certain customers—are illegal per se. Such agreements plainly represent agreements not to compete. They result in each firm being isolated from competition in the affected market.

In *United States v. Topco Associates, Inc.* (1972), the Supreme Court reaffirmed this long-standing principle by striking down a horizontal division of markets agreement among members of a cooperative association of local and regional supermarket chains. *Topco* was widely criticized, however, on the ground that its per se approach ignored an important point: that the defendants' joint activities in promoting Topco brand products were aimed at enabling them to compete more effectively with national supermarket chains. Critics argued that when such horizontal restraints were ancillary to *procompetitive* behavior, they should be judged under the rule of reason.

Naked Restraints and Ancillary Restraints

Such criticism has had an impact. Several decisions by lower federal courts have distinguished between "naked" horizontal restraints (those having no other purpose or effect except restraining competition) and "ancillary" horizontal restraints (those constituting a necessary part of a larger joint undertaking serving procompetitive ends). Although these courts continue to apply the per se rule to naked horizontal restraints, they give rule of reason (or at least quick-look) treatment to ancillary restraints. In determining whether ancillary restraints are lawful, courts weigh the harm to competition resulting from such restraints against the alleged offsetting benefits to competition.

Whether the Supreme Court ultimately will endorse such departures from *Topco* remains to be seen. However, the Court's post-*Topco* tendency to discard per se rules in favor of a rule of reason approach in other areas strongly suggests that *Topco*'s critics eventually will prevail with their arguments.

Vertical Restraints on Distribution

Vertical restraints on distribution (or *vertical nonprice restraints*) also fall within the scope of the Sherman Act. A manufacturer has always had the power to *unilaterally* assign exclusive territories to its dealers or to limit the dealerships it grants in a particular geographic area. However, manufacturers may run afoul of § 1 by causing dealers to *agree* not to sell outside their dealership territories or by placing other restrictions on their dealers' right to resell their products.

The Supreme Court once held that vertical restraints on distribution were per se illegal when applied to goods that the manufacturer had sold to its dealers. The Court changed course, however, in *Continental T.V., Inc. v. GTE Sylvania, Inc.* (1977) In *Sylvania,* the Court abandoned the per se rule in favor of a rule of reason approach to most vertical restraints on distribution. The Court accepted many Chicago School arguments concerning the potential *economic efficiencies* that could result from vertical restraints on distribution. Most notably, such restraints were alleged to offer a chance for increased *interbrand* competition among the product lines of competing manufacturers at the admitted cost of restraining *intrabrand* competition among dealers in a particular manufacturer's product. For further discussion of *Sylvania,* see the *Khan* and *Leegin* decisions, which appear earlier in the chapter.

Subsequent decisions on the legality of vertical restraints on distribution have emphasized the importance of the market share of the manufacturer imposing the restraints. Restraints imposed by manufacturers with large market shares are more likely to be found unlawful under the rule of reason because the resulting harm to intra-brand competition is unlikely to be offset by significant positive effects on interbrand competition.

Group Boycotts and Concerted Refusals to Deal

Under the *Colgate* doctrine, a single firm may lawfully refuse to deal with certain firms. The same is not true, however, of *agreements* by two or more business entities to refuse to deal with others, to deal with others only on certain terms and conditions, or to coerce suppliers or customers not to deal with one of their competitors. Such agreements are *joint* restraints on trade. Historically, they have been per se unlawful under § 1. For example, when a trade association of garment manufacturers agreed not to sell to retailers that sold clothing or fabrics with designs pirated from legitimate manufacturers, the agreement was held to be a per se violation of the Sherman Act.[4]

Vertical Boycotts Recent antitrust developments, however, indicate that not all concerted refusals to deal will receive per se treatment. If a manufacturer terminated a distributor in response to complaints from other distributors that the terminated distributor was selling to customers outside its prescribed sales territory, the manufacturer will be held to have violated § 1 only if the termination resulted in a significant harm to competition. This result follows logically from the *Sylvania* decision. If vertical restraints on distribution are judged under the rule of reason, the same standard should apply to a vertical boycott designed to enforce such restraints.

Even distributors claiming to have been terminated as part of a vertical price-fixing scheme have found recovery increasingly difficult to obtain in recent years. In *Monsanto v. Spray-Rite Service Corp.* (U.S. Sup. Ct. 1984), a manufacturer had terminated a discounting distributor after receiving complaints from its other distributors. The Supreme Court held that these facts would not trigger liability for vertical price-fixing in the absence of additional evidence tending to exclude the possibility that the manufacturer and the nonterminated distributors acted independently. In *Business Electronics Corp. v. Sharp Electronics Corp.* (U.S. Sup. Ct. 1988), the Court held that even proof of a conspiracy between a manufacturer and nonterminated distributors to terminate a price-cutter would not trigger liability unless it was accompanied by proof that the manufacturer and nonterminated dealers were also engaged in an unlawful vertical price-fixing conspiracy.

Horizontal Boycotts It also appears that the Supreme Court is willing to relax the per se rule for some *horizontal* boycotts. For instance, in *Northwest Wholesale Stationers, Inc. v. Pacific Stationery & Printing Co.* (U.S. Sup. Ct. 1985), members of an office supply retailers' purchasing cooperative had expelled a member retailer that engaged in some wholesale operations in addition to retail activities. The Court held that rule of reason treatment should be extended to the alleged boycott at issue, but declined to eliminate the per se rule for all horizontal boycotts. The Court has offered only general guidance for determining which horizontal boycotts trigger rule of reason analysis (or at least quick-look analysis) and which ones amount to per se violations. The appropriate legal treatment in a given case is therefore difficult to predict.

Tying Agreements

Tying agreements occur when a seller refuses to sell a buyer a certain product (the *tying product*) unless the buyer also agrees to purchase a different product (the *tied product*) from the seller. For example, a fertilizer manufacturer refuses to sell its dealers fertilizer (the tying product) unless they also agree to buy its line of pesticides (the tied product). The potential anticompetitive effect of a tying agreement is that the seller's competitors in the sale of the tied product may be foreclosed from competing with the seller for sales to customers that have entered into tying agreements with the seller. To the extent that tying agreements are coercively imposed, they also deprive buyers of the freedom to make independent decisions concerning their purchases of the tied product. Tying agreements may be challenged under both § 1 of the Sherman Act and § 3 of the Clayton Act.[5]

Elements of Prohibited Tying Agreements Tying agreements are often said to be per se illegal under § 1. However, because a tying agreement must meet certain criteria before it is subjected to per se analysis, and

---

[4]*Fashion Originators' Guild v. FTC* (U.S. Sup. Ct. 1941).

[5]Section 3 of the Clayton Act applies, however, only when both the tying and the tied products are commodities. Chapter 50 discusses Clayton Act standards for tying agreement legality.

because evidence of certain justifications is sometimes considered in tying cases, the rule against tying agreements is at best a "soft" per se rule.

Before a challenged tying agreement is held to violate § 1, these elements must be demonstrated: (1) the agreement involves *two* separate and distinct items rather than integrated components of a larger product, service, or system of doing business; (2) the tying product cannot be purchased unless the tied product is also purchased; (3) the seller has sufficient economic power in the market for the tying product (such as a large market share) to appreciably restrain competition in the tied product market; and (4) a "not insubstantial" amount of commerce in the tied product is affected by the seller's tying agreements.

Applying the above elements, a federal district court held in 2000 that Microsoft Corporation violated § 1 by tying its Internet Explorer Web browser to versions of its Windows operating system. In a 2001 decision, however, a federal court of appeals reversed that aspect of the district court's decision and remanded the tying claim for

reconsideration under the rule of reason. The appellate court concluded that in the context of software used as a platform for third-party applications, tying of the sort done by Microsoft should not necessarily be presumed to have a pernicious effect on competition. The court reasoned that in order to avoid discouraging platform software-related innovation, weighing and balancing of the tying arrangement's benefits and anticompetitive effects should be undertaken. Only the rule of reason would provide the opportunity for such weighing and balancing. The court stressed, however, that it was not changing the controlling rules for tying agreements generally or for such arrangements in computer-related settings not involving platform software. (Other aspects of the appellate court's *Microsoft* decision are addressed later in this chapter.)

The *Illinois Tool Works* case, which follows, contains a discussion of the elements of prohibited tying arrangements, with a focus on the third element: *market power as to the tying product.*

Illinois Tool Works, Inc. v. Independent Ink, Inc.
547 U.S. 28 (U.S. Sup. Ct. 2006)

Illinois Tool Works, Inc. (ITW), manufactures and markets printing systems that include three relevant components: (1) a patented piezoelectric impulse ink-jet printhead; (2) a patented ink container, consisting of a bottle and valved cap, which attaches to the printhead; and (3) specially designed, but unpatented, ink. ITW sells its systems to original equipment manufacturers (OEMs). The OEMS are licensed to incorporate the printheads and containers into printers that they sell to companies for use in printing bar codes on cartons and packaging materials. The OEMs agree that they will purchase their ink exclusively from ITW, and that neither they nor their customers will refill the patented containers with ink of any kind.

Independent Ink, Inc., which has developed an ink with the same chemical composition as the ink sold by ITW, was the target of patent infringement allegations by ITW. Independent therefore filed suit against ITW in order to seek a judgment of noninfringement and invalidity of ITW's patents. In addition, Independent's complaint alleged that ITW was engaged in illegal tying, in supposed violation of Sherman Act § 1. A federal district court granted ITW's motion for summary judgment on the § 1 claim. The court rejected Independent's contention that ITW's patent on the printhead system necessarily gave it market power regarding the tying product. Finding that Independent had submitted no affirmative evidence defining the relevant market or establishing ITW's power within it, the court held that Independent could not prevail on its tying claim. The U.S. Court of Appeals for the Federal Circuit reversed. The Federal Circuit concluded that the district court erred in not following U.S. Supreme Court precedents indicating that in a tying case, the fact that the tying product is patented gives rise to a presumption of market power concerning the tying product. The U.S. Supreme Court granted ITW's petition for a writ of certiorari.

Stevens, Justice

In [dictum in] *Jefferson Parish Hospital Dist. No. 2 v. Hyde,* 466 U.S. 2, 16 (1984), we repeated the well-settled proposition that "if the Government has granted the seller a patent or similar monopoly over a product, it is fair to presume that the inability to buy the product elsewhere gives the seller market power." This presumption of market power, applicable in the

antitrust context when a seller conditions its sale of a patented product (the "tying" product) on the purchase of a second product (the "tied" product), has its foundation in the judicially created patent misuse doctrine. *See United States v. Loew's, Inc.,* 371 U.S. 38, 46 (1962). In 1988, Congress substantially undermined that foundation, amending the Patent Act to eliminate the market power presumption in patent misuse cases. The question presented to us today is whether the presumption of market power in a patented product should survive as a matter of antitrust law despite its demise in patent law.

[During the past 75 years,] four different rules of law have supported challenges to tying arrangements. They have been condemned as improper extensions of the patent monopoly under the patent misuse doctrine, as unfair methods of competition under § 5 of the Federal Trade Commission Act, as contracts tending to create a monopoly under § 3 of the Clayton Act, and as contracts in restraint of trade under § 1 of the Sherman Act. In all of those instances, the justification for the challenge rested on either an assumption or a showing that the defendant's position of power in the market for the tying product was being used to restrain competition in the market for the tied product. As we explained in [an earlier decision], "[o]ur cases have concluded that the essential characteristic of an invalid tying arrangement lies in the seller's exploitation of its control over the tying product to force the buyer into the purchase of a tied product that the buyer either did not want at all, or might have preferred to purchase elsewhere on different terms." [Case citation omitted.]

Over the years, however, this Court's strong disapproval of tying arrangements has substantially diminished. Rather than relying on assumptions, in its more recent opinions the Court has required a showing of market power in the tying product. [For instance, in *United States Steel Corp. v. Fortner Enterprises, Inc.,* 429 U.S. 610, 622 (1977),] we unanimously held that the plaintiff's failure of proof on the issue of market power was fatal to its [tying] case. The assumption that "[t]ying arrangements serve hardly any purpose beyond the suppression of competition," rejected in *Fortner,* has not been endorsed in any opinion since. Instead, it was again rejected just seven years later in *Jefferson Parish,* where . . . we unanimously reversed a Court of Appeals judgment holding that an alleged tying arrangement constituted a per se violation of § 1 of the Sherman Act. Like the product at issue in the *Fortner* cases, the tying product in *Jefferson Parish*—hospital services—was unpatented, and our holding again rested on the conclusion that the plaintiff had failed to prove sufficient power in the tying product market to restrain competition in the market for the tied product—services of anesthesiologists. [The Court went on in *Jefferson Parish* to comment on the market power requirement and to cite *Loew's* for the proposition that a patent over a tying product would by itself indicate market power. This statement in *Jefferson Parish* was dictum, however, because the tying product in the case was unpatented and, in any event, market power evidence was lacking.]

[T]he presumption that a patent confers market power arose outside the antitrust context as part of the patent misuse doctrine. That doctrine had its origins in [a 1917 decision, in which

the Court] found no support in the patent laws for the proposition that a patentee may "prescribe by notice attached to a patented machine the conditions of its use and the supplies which must be used in the operation of it, under pain of infringement of the patent." [Case citation omitted.] [That decision] formed the basis for the Court's subsequent decisions creating a patent misuse defense to infringement claims when a patentee uses its patent "as the effective means of restraining competition with its sale of an unpatented article." *Morton Salt Co. v. G.S. Suppiger Co.,* 314 U.S. 488, 490 (1942). [Other case citations omitted.]

Without any analysis of actual market conditions, these patent misuse decisions assumed that, by tying the purchase of unpatented goods to the sale of the patented good, the patentee was restraining competition, or "secur[ing] a limited monopoly of an unpatented material" [Case citation omitted.] In other words, these decisions presumed "[t]he requisite economic power" over the tying product such that the patentee could "extend [its] economic control to unpatented products." *Loew's,* 371 U.S. at 45–46.

The presumption that a patent confers market power migrated from patent law to antitrust law in *International Salt Co. v. United States,* 332 U.S. 392 (1947). In that case, we affirmed a district court decision holding that leases of patented machines requiring the lessees to use the defendant's unpatented salt products violated § 1 of the Sherman Act and § 3 of the Clayton Act as a matter of law. Our opinion in *International Salt* clearly shows that we . . . import[ed] the presumption of market power in a patented product into our antitrust jurisprudence. [T]he rule adopted in *International Salt* necessarily accepted the Government's submission that the earlier patent misuse cases supported the broader proposition that this type of restraint is unlawful on its face under the Sherman Act. Indeed, later in the same term we cited *International Salt* for the proposition that the license of "a patented device on condition that unpatented materials be employed in conjunction with the patented device" is an example of a restraint that is "illegal per se." [Case citation omitted.]

Although the patent misuse doctrine and our antitrust jurisprudence became intertwined in *International Salt,* subsequent events initiated their untwining. This process has ultimately led to today's reexamination of the presumption of per se illegality of a tying arrangement involving a patented product, the first case since 1947 in which we have granted review to consider the presumption's continuing validity. [More than 50 years ago, Congress enacted a statute that narrowed somewhat the applicability of the misuse defense in patent infringement cases.] Thus, at the same time that our antitrust jurisprudence continued to rely on the assumption that tying arrangements generally serve no legitimate business purpose,

Congress began chipping away at the assumption in the patent misuse context from whence it came.

It is Congress' most recent narrowing of the patent misuse defense, however, that is directly relevant to this case. Four years after our decision in *Jefferson Parish,* [where the Court repeated in dictum] the patent-equals-market-power presumption, Congress amended the Patent Act to eliminate that presumption in the patent misuse context. The relevant provision reads:

> (d) No patent owner otherwise entitled to relief for infringement or contributory infringement of a patent shall be denied relief or deemed guilty of misuse or illegal extension of the patent right by reason of his having done one or more of the following: . . . (5) conditioned the license of any rights to the patent or the sale of the patented product on the acquisition of a license to rights in another patent or purchase of a separate product, unless, in view of the circumstances, the patent owner has market power in the relevant market for the patent or patented product on which the license or sale is conditioned.

35 U.S.C. § 271(d)(5).

The [above 1988 amendment] makes it clear that Congress did not intend the mere existence of a patent to constitute the requisite "market power." Indeed, fairly read, it provides that without proof that ITW had market power in the relevant market, its conduct at issue in this case was neither "misuse" nor an "illegal extension of the patent right." While the 1988 amendment does not expressly refer to the antitrust laws, it certainly invites a reappraisal of the per se rule announced in *International Salt.* [G]iven the fact that the patent misuse doctrine provided the basis for the market power presumption, it would be anomalous to preserve the presumption in antitrust after Congress has eliminated its foundation.

After considering the congressional judgment reflected in the 1988 amendment, we conclude that tying arrangements involving patented products should be evaluated under the standards applied in cases [such as] *Fortner* and *Jefferson Parish.* While some such arrangements are still unlawful, such as those that are the product of a true monopoly or a market-wide conspiracy, that conclusion must be supported by proof of power in the relevant market rather than by a mere presumption thereof. Our imposition of this requirement accords with the vast majority of academic literature on the subject.

[T]he lesson to be learned from *International Salt* and the academic commentary is the same: Many tying arrangements, even those involving patents and requirements ties, are fully consistent with a free, competitive market. It is no doubt the virtual consensus among economists that has persuaded the enforcement agencies to reject the position that the Government took when it supported the per se rule that the Court adopted in the 1940's. In antitrust guidelines issued jointly by the Department of Justice and the Federal Trade Commission in 1995, the enforcement agencies stated that in the exercise of their prosecutorial discretion they "will not presume that a patent, copyright, or trade secret necessarily confers market power upon its owner." While that choice is not binding on the Court, it would be unusual for the judiciary to replace the normal rule of lenity that is applied in criminal cases with a rule of severity for a special category of antitrust cases.

Congress, the antitrust enforcement agencies, and most economists have reached the conclusion that a patent does not necessarily confer market power upon the patentee. Today, we reach the same conclusion, and therefore hold that, in all cases involving a tying arrangement, the plaintiff must prove that the defendant has market power in the tying product.

Federal Circuit's decision vacated, and case remanded for further proceedings.

Possible Justifications for Tying Agreements The first two elements of a prohibited tying agreement have been particularly significant in cases involving franchisors and their franchised dealers. For example, a suit by a McDonald's franchisee alleged that McDonald's violated § 1 by requiring franchisees to lease their stores from McDonald's as a condition of acquiring a McDonald's franchise. A federal court of appeals, however, rejected the franchisee's claim and held that no tying agreement was involved. Instead, the franchise and the lease were integral components of a well-thought-out system of doing business.[6]

Courts have recognized two other possible justifications for tying agreements. First, tying arrangements that are instrumental in launching a new competitor with an otherwise uncertain future may be lawful until the new business has established itself in the marketplace. The rationale for this "new business" exception is that if a tying agreement enables a fledgling firm to become a viable competitor, the agreement's net effect on competition is positive. Second, some courts have recognized that tying agreements sometimes may be necessary to protect the reputation of the seller's product line. For example, one of the seller's products functions properly only if used in conjunction with another of its products. To qualify for this exception, however, the seller must convince the

---

[6]*Principe v. McDonald's Corp.,* 631 F.2d 303 (4th Cir. 1980).

court that a tying arrangement is the only viable means to protect its goodwill.

Chicago School Views on Tying Agreements

Chicago School thinkers have long criticized the traditional judicial approach to tying agreements because they do not believe that most tie-ins result in any significant economic harm. They argue that sellers who try to impose a tie-in in competitive markets gain no increased profits as a result. This is so because instead of participating in a tying agreement, buyers may turn to substitutes for the tying product or may purchase the tying product from competing sellers. The net effect of a tie-in may therefore be that any increase in the seller's sales in the tied product is offset by a loss in sales of the tying product. Only when the seller has substantial power in the tying product market is there potential that a tie-in may be used to increase the seller's power in the tied product market. However, even when the seller has such market power in the tying product, Chicago School thinkers argue that no harm to competition is likely to result if the seller faces strong competition in the tied product market. For these and other reasons, Chicago School thinkers favor a rule of reason approach to all tying agreements. A majority of the Supreme Court has yet to accept these arguments. Some justices, however, appear willing to do so. If other members of the Court are similarly persuaded in the future, a substantial change in the legal criteria applied to tying agreements will be the result.

Reciprocal Dealing Agreements

Under a **reciprocal dealing agreement,** a buyer attempts to exploit its purchasing power by conditioning its purchases from suppliers on reciprocal purchases of some product or service offered for sale by the buyer. For example, an oil company with a chain of wholly owned gas stations refuses to purchase the tires it sells in those stations unless the tire manufacturer (the would-be supplier of the tires) agrees to purchase, from the oil company, the petrochemicals used in the tire manufacturing process. Reciprocal dealing agreements are similar in motivation and effect to tying agreements. Courts therefore tend to treat them similarly. In seeking to impose the reciprocal dealing agreement on the tire manufacturer, the oil company is attempting to gain a competitive advantage over its competitors in the petrochemical market. A court judging the legality of such an agreement would examine the oil company's economic power as a purchaser of tires and the dollar amount of petrochemical sales involved.

Exclusive Dealing Agreements

Exclusive dealing agreements require buyers of a particular product or service to purchase that product or service exclusively from a particular seller. For example, Standard Lawnmower Corporation requires its retail dealers to sell only Standard brand mowers. A common variation of an exclusive dealing agreement is the *requirements contract,* under which the buyer of a particular product agrees to purchase all of its requirements for that product from a particular supplier. For example, a candy manufacturer agrees to buy all of its sugar requirements from one sugar refiner. Exclusive dealing contracts present a threat to competition similar to that involved in tying contracts—they may reduce interbrand competition by foreclosing a seller's competitors from the opportunity to compete for sales to its customers. Unlike tying contracts, however, exclusive dealing agreements may sometimes enhance efficiencies in distribution and stimulate interbrand competition. Exclusive dealing agreements reduce a manufacturer's sales costs and provide dealers with a secure source of supply. They may also encourage dealer efforts to market the manufacturer's products more effectively, because a dealer selling only one product line has a greater stake in the success of that line than does a dealer who sells the products of several competing manufacturers.

Because many exclusive dealing agreements involve commodities, they may also be challenged under § 3 of the Clayton Act. The legal tests applicable to exclusive dealing agreements under both acts are identical. Therefore, we defer discussing those tests until the next chapter.

Joint Ventures by Competitors

A **joint venture** is a combined effort by two or more business entities for a limited purpose such as research. Because joint ventures may yield enhanced efficiencies through integration of the resources of more than one firm, they are commonly judged under the rule of reason. Under this approach, courts tend to ask whether any competitive restraints that are incidental to the venture are necessary to accomplish its lawful objectives and, if so, whether those restraints are offset by the venture's positive effects. Joint ventures whose primary purpose is illegal per se, however, have been given per se treatment. An example of such a case would be two competing firms that form a joint sales agency and authorize it to fix the price of their products.

National Cooperative Research and Production Act

Antitrust critics have long argued that the threat of

antitrust prosecution seriously inhibits the formation of joint research and development ventures, and that American firms are placed at a competitive disadvantage in world markets as a result. Such arguments have enjoyed more acceptance during roughly the past two decades. In 1984, Congress passed the National Cooperative Research Act (NCRA). This act applies to *joint research and development ventures* (JRDVs), which are broadly defined to include basic and applied research and joint activities in the licensing of technologies developed by such research. The NCRA requires the application of a reasonableness standard, rather than a per se rule, when a JRDV's legality is determined. It also requires firms contemplating a JRDV to provide the Department of Justice and the Federal Trade Commission with advance notice of their intent to do so. The NCRA provides that only actual (not treble) damages may be recovered for losses flowing from a JRDV ultimately found to be in violation of § 1. In addition, the NCRA contains a provision allowing the parties to a challenged JRDV to recover attorney's fees from an unsuccessful challenger if the suit is shown to be "frivolous, unreasonable, without foundation, or in bad faith." Congress amended the statute in 1993 to extend its application to joint *production* ventures. In doing so, Congress renamed the statute the National Cooperative Research and Production Act.

Figure 1 summarizes the judicial treatment of potentially illegal practices under § 1 of the Sherman Act (as of 2008, when this book went to press).

Section 2—Monopolization

Firms that acquire **monopoly power** in a given market have defeated the antitrust laws' objective of promoting competitive market structures. Monopolists, by definition, have the power to fix prices unilaterally because they have no effective competition. Section 2 of the Sherman Act was designed to prevent the improper acquisition and abuse of monopoly power. It provides: "Every person who shall monopolize, or attempt to monopolize, or combine or conspire with any other person to monopolize any part of trade or commerce among the several states, or with foreign nations shall be deemed guilty of a felony." Section 2 does not outlaw monopolies. Instead, it outlaws the act of *monopolization*. Under § 2, a *single firm* can be guilty of monopolizing or attempting to monopolize a part of trade or commerce. The proof of joint action required for violations of § 1 is required only when two or more firms are charged with a conspiracy to monopolize under § 2.

Figure 1 *Potentially Illegal Practices and Their Treatment under Sherman Act § 1*

Potentially Illegal Practice	Judicial Treatment	
	Per Se	Rule of Reason or Quick-Look
Horizontal price-fixing	*	
Vertical price-fixing (nonmaximum)		*
Vertical maximum price-fixing		*
Horizontal division of markets	*?	*?
Vertical nonprice restraints on distribution		*
Horizontal boycotts	*	*
Vertical boycotts	*	*
Tying agreements	*?	*
Reciprocal dealing agreements	*?	*
Exclusive dealing agreements		*
Joint ventures	*	*

Note: An entry with an asterisk in both columns means the facts of the individual case determine the treatment. A question mark indicates that future treatment is in question.

Monopolization **Monopolization** is "the willful acquisition or maintenance of monopoly power in a relevant market as opposed to growth as a consequence of superior product, business acumen, or historical accident."[7] This means that to be liable for monopolization, a defendant must have possessed not only monopoly power but also an **intent to monopolize.**

Monopoly Power *Monopoly power* is usually defined for antitrust purposes as the power to *fix prices* or *exclude competitors* in a given market. Such power is generally inferred from the fact that a firm has captured a predominant share of the relevant market. Although the exact percentage share necessary to support an inference of monopoly power remains unclear and courts often look at other economic factors (such as the existence in

---

[7]*United States v. Grinnell Corp.* (U.S. Sup. Ct. 1966).

The Global Business Environment

United States–based firms that engage in international business activities must remember that they may be subject to the antitrust laws of other nations. In the European Union, for instance, the European Commission serves as chief antitrust regulator through the commission's Competition Directorate General. Articles in the Treaty of Rome contemplate bases of antitrust regulation similar, though not identical to, the legal bases in the United States under §§ 1 and 2 of the Sherman Act.

In 2004, the European Commission (EC) ruled against Microsoft in a case that dealt with some of the same types of business practices complained about in the high-profile case brought against the firm by the U.S. government and various states. (The U.S. case receives extensive treatment at various points in this chapter.) The European Union case also challenged other allegedly anticompetitive Microsoft practices that were not at issue in the U.S. case. In early 2004, the commission ruled that Microsoft held a dominant position in the European software market and had abused that position in various ways. The EC fined Microsoft an amount of euros equaling roughly $689 million. In addition, the EC ordered Microsoft to allow room for competitors by offering a version of its Windows operating system without the Media Player and by licensing confidential Windows-related information to other firms so that they could produce software compatible with Windows

In 2006, the EC levied a further fine equating to $357 million, after concluding that Microsoft had not complied with the EC's 2004 orders. The European Court of First Instance, in a 2007 ruling, rejected Microsoft's appeal of the EC's 2004 decision. In 2008, the EC again fined Microsoft—this time in an amount of euros equaling $1.3 billion—because, in the EC's judgment, Microsoft still was in violation of the 2004 orders.

---

the industry of barriers to the entry of new competitors), market shares in excess of 70 percent have historically justified an inference of monopoly power.

Before a court can determine a defendant's market share, it must first define the **relevant market.** This is a crucial issue in § 2 cases because a broad definition of the relevant market normally results in a smaller market share for the defendant and a resulting reduction in the likelihood that the defendant will be found to possess monopoly power. The two components of a relevant market determination are the relevant **geographic market** and the relevant **product market.**

Economic realities prevailing in the industry determine the relevant geographic market. In which parts of the country can the defendant effectively compete with other firms in the sale of the product in question? To whom may buyers turn for alternative sources of supply? Factors such as transportation costs may also play a critical role in relevant market determinations. Thus, the relevant market for coal may be regional in nature, but the relevant market for computer chips may be national in scope.

The relevant product market is composed of those products meeting the *functional interchangeability* test, which identifies the products "reasonably interchangeable by consumers for the same purposes." This test recognizes that a firm's ability to fix the price for its products is limited by the availability of competing products that buyers view as acceptable substitutes. In a famous antitrust case, for example, Du Pont was charged with monopolizing the national market for cellophane because it had a 75 percent share. The Supreme Court concluded, however, that the relevant market was all "flexible wrapping materials," including aluminum foil, waxed paper, and polyethylene. Du Pont's 20 percent share of that product market was far too small to amount to monopoly power.[8]

In the highly publicized *Microsoft* decision, a portion of which follows below, a federal court of appeals held that Microsoft Corporation possessed monopoly power in the worldwide market for Intel-compatible personal computer operating systems. The court concluded that Microsoft held a 95 percent share of the market.

Intent to Monopolize Proof of monopoly power standing alone, however, is never sufficient to prove a violation of § 2. The defendant's **intent to monopolize** must also be shown. Early cases required evidence that the defendant either acquired monopoly power by predatory or coercive means that violated antitrust rules (e.g., price-fixing or discriminatory pricing) or abused monopoly power in some way after acquiring it (such as by engaging in price-gouging). Contemporary courts focus on how the defendant acquired monopoly power. If the defendant *intentionally acquired it* or *attempted to maintain it* after acquiring it, the defendant possessed an intent to monopolize. Defendants are not in violation of § 2, however, if

---

[8]*United States v. E. I. du Pont de Nemours & Co.* (U.S. Sup. Ct. 1956).

their monopoly power resulted from the superiority of their products or business decisions, or from historical accident (e.g., the owner of a professional sports franchise in an area too small to support a competing franchise).

Purposeful acquisition or maintenance of monopoly power may be demonstrated in various ways. A famous monopolization case involved Alcoa, which had a 90 percent market share of the American market for virgin aluminum ingot. Alcoa was found liable for purposefully maintaining its monopoly power by acquiring every new opportunity relating to the production or marketing of aluminum, thereby excluding potential competitors.[9] As various cases indicate, firms that develop monopoly power by acquiring ownership or control of their competitors are likely to be held to have demonstrated an intent to monopolize.

In the following portion of the *Microsoft* decision, the court concluded that Microsoft Corporation was liable for monopolization because it possessed monopoly power in the relevant market and engaged in anticompetitive behavior in order to maintain its monopoly position.

---

[9]*United States v. Aluminum Co. of America, Inc.* (2d Cir. 1945).

United States v. Microsoft Corp.   253 F.3d 34 (D.C. Cir. 2001)

The United States, 19 individual states, and the District of Columbia brought civil antitrust actions against Microsoft Corporation. The cases were consolidated for trial. The plaintiffs charged, in essence, that Microsoft waged an unlawful campaign in defense of its monopoly position in the market for operating systems designed to run on Intel-compatible personal computers (PCs). More specifically, the plaintiffs claimed that Microsoft violated (1) § 2 of the Sherman Act by engaging in monopolization through a series of exclusionary and anticompetitive acts designed to maintain its monopoly power; (2) § 2 by engaging in attempted monopolization of the Web browser market; and (3) § 1 of the Sherman Act by unlawfully tying its browser to its operating system and by entering into exclusive dealing agreements that unreasonably restrained trade. The plaintiffs other than the United States alleged that Microsoft's behavior also violated their respective antitrust laws.

The United States District Court for the District of Columbia held that Microsoft violated § 1 through unlawful tying arrangements but that Microsoft's exclusive dealing agreements did not run afoul of § 1. The court also held that Microsoft engaged in monopolization with regard to the market for Intel-compatible PC operating systems, as well as attempted monopolization of the Web browser market, in violation of § 2 and comparable state laws. In a separate decision, the district court held that the appropriate remedy was a divestiture order splitting Microsoft into two separate companies, one for the operating systems business and the other for the applications business.

Microsoft appealed to the United States Court of Appeals for the District of Columbia Circuit. In portions of the opinion not included here, the D.C. Circuit affirmed the district court's holding that Microsoft's exclusive dealing agreements did not violate § 1; reversed the district court's holding that Microsoft violated § 1 through tying arrangements and remanded the case for reconsideration of that claim under different legal standards; and reversed the district court's holding that Microsoft violated § 2 by attempting to monopolize the Web browser market. The portions of the opinion set forth below deal with the D.C. Circuit's analysis of the claim that Microsoft violated § 2 by engaging in monopolization of the market for Intel-compatible PC operating systems. A nearby Cyberlaw in Action box examines the appellate court's treatment of the remedy issues and discusses later developments in the case

Per Curiam

Section 2 of the Sherman Act makes it unlawful for a firm to "monopolize." The offense of monopolization has two elements: "(1) the possession of monopoly power in the relevant market, and (2) the willful acquisition or maintenance of that power as distinguished from growth or development as a consequence of a superior product, business acumen, or historic accident." *United States v. Grinnell Corp.* (U.S. Sup. Ct. 1966).

1. Monopoly Power While merely possessing monopoly power is not itself an antitrust violation, it is a necessary element of a monopolization charge. The Supreme Court defines monopoly power as the power to control prices or exclude competition. [C]ourts . . . typically examine market structure in search of circumstantial evidence of monopoly power. [M]onopoly power may be inferred from a firm's possession of a dominant share of a relevant market that is protected by entry barriers. "Entry barriers" are factors . . . that prevent new rivals from timely responding to an increase in price above the competitive level.

Because the ability of consumers to turn to other suppliers restrains a firm from raising prices above the competitive level, the relevant market must include all products "reasonably inter-changeable by consumers for the same purposes." *United States v. E. I. du Pont de Nemours Co.* (U.S. Sup. Ct. 1956). [T]he district court defined the market as "the licensing of all Intel-compatible PC operating systems worldwide," finding that there are "currently no products—and . . . there are not likely to be any in the near future—that a significant percentage of computer users worldwide could substitute for [these operating systems] without incurring substantial costs." Calling this market definition far too narrow, Microsoft argues that the court improperly excluded . . . non-Intel compatible operating systems (primarily Apple's Macintosh operating system, Mac OS) . . . and "middleware" products.

The district court found that consumers would not switch from Windows to Mac OS in response to a substantial price increase because of the costs of acquiring the new hardware needed to run Mac OS and compatible software applications, . . . because of the effort involved in learning the new system and transferring files to its format, [and because] the Apple system . . . supports fewer applications. Microsoft . . . points to [no] evidence contradicting the district court's findings. [W]e have no basis for upsetting the court's decision to exclude Mac OS from the relevant market.

This brings us to Microsoft's main challenge to the district court's market definition: the exclusion of middleware. Because of the importance of middleware to this case, we [shall] explain what it is [and how it relates to operating systems]. Operating systems perform many functions, including allocating computer memory and . . . function[ing] as platforms for software applications. They do this by "exposing"—i.e., making available to software developers—routines or protocols that perform certain widely used functions. These are known as Application Programming Interfaces (APIs). For example, Windows contains an API that enables users to draw a box on the screen. Software developers wishing to include that function in an application need not duplicate it in their own code. Instead, they can "call"—i.e., use—the Windows API. Windows contains thousands of APIs.

"Middleware" refers to software products that expose their own APIs. Because of this, a middleware product written for Windows could take over some or all of Windows's valuable platform functions—that is, developers might begin to rely upon APIs exposed by the middleware for basic routines rather than relying upon the API set included in Windows. Ultimately, if developers could write applications relying exclusively on APIs exposed by middleware, their applications would run on any operating system on which the middleware was also present.

Microsoft argues that because middleware could usurp the operating system's platform function and might eventually take over other operating system functions . . . , the district court erred in excluding Navigator and Java from the relevant market. The court found, however, that neither Navigator, Java, nor any other middleware product could now, or would soon, expose enough APIs to serve as a platform for popular applications, much less take over all operating system functions. Whatever middleware's ultimate potential, the district court found that consumers could not now abandon their operating systems and switch to middleware in response to a sustained price for Windows above the competitive level. [B]ecause middleware is not now interchangeable with Windows, the district court had good reason for excluding middleware from the relevant market.

Having thus properly defined the relevant market, the district court found that Windows accounts for a greater than 95 percent share. The court also found that even if Mac OS were included, Microsoft's share would exceed 80 percent. [In addition], the court [properly] focused not only on Microsoft's present market share, but also on the structural barrier that protects the company's future position. That barrier—the applications barrier to entry—stems from two characteristics of the software market: (1) most consumers prefer operating systems for which a large number of applications have already been written; and (2) most developers prefer to write for operating systems that already have a substantial consumer base. This "chicken-and-egg" situation ensures that applications will continue to be written for the already dominant Windows, which in turn ensures that consumers will continue to prefer it over other operating systems.

2. Anticompetitive Conduct [After correctly] concluding that Microsoft had monopoly power, the district court held that Microsoft had violated § 2 by engaging in a variety of exclusionary acts . . . to maintain its monopoly. Whether any particular act of a monopolist is exclusionary, rather than merely a form of vigorous competition, can be difficult to discern. [T]o be condemned as exclusionary, a monopolist's act must have an anticompetitive effect. That is, it must harm the competitive *process* and thereby harm consumers. In contrast, harm to one or more *competitors* will not suffice. [Assuming that the plaintiff] establishes a *prima facie* case under § 2 by demonstrating anticompetitive effect, the monopolist may proffer a procompetitive justification. If the monopolist asserts a procompetitive justification—a nonpretextual claim that its conduct is indeed a form of competition on the merits because it involves, for example, greater efficiency or enhanced consumer appeal—then the burden shifts back to the plaintiff to rebut that claim. [I]f the monopolist's procompetitive justification stands unrebutted, then the plaintiff must demonstrate that the anticompetitive harm of the conduct outweighs the procompetitive benefit.

In cases arising under § 1 of the Sherman Act, the courts routinely apply a similar balancing approach under the rubric of the "rule of reason." With these principles in mind, we now [review] the district court's holding that Microsoft violated § 2 of the Sherman Act in a variety of ways.

a. Restrictions in Licenses Issued to Original Equipment Manufacturers (OEMs)

The district court condemned a number of provisions in Microsoft's agreements licensing Windows to OEMs, because it found that Microsoft's imposition of those provisions . . . serves to reduce usage share of Netscape's browser and, hence, protect Microsoft's operating system monopoly. Browser usage share is important because [a browser] must have a critical mass of users in order to attract software developers to write applications relying upon the APIs it exposes, and away from the APIs exposed by Windows. Applications written to a particular browser's APIs . . . would run on any computer with that browser, regardless of the underlying operating system. [The district court found that the] "overwhelming majority of consumers will only use a PC operating system for which there already exists a large and varied set of . . . applications, and for which it seems relatively certain that new types of applications and new versions of existing applications will continue to be marketed." If a consumer could have access to the applications he desired—regardless of the operating system he uses—simply by installing a particular browser on his computer, then he would no longer feel compelled to select Windows in order to have access to those applications; he could select an operating system other than Windows based solely upon its quality and price. In other words, the market for operating systems would be competitive.

The restrictions Microsoft places upon OEMs are of particular importance . . . because having an OEM pre-install a browser on a computer is one of the two most cost-effective methods by far of distributing browsing software. (The other is bundling the browser with Internet access software distributed by an Internet access provider (IAP).)

The district court concluded that [one Microsoft-imposed] license restriction—the prohibition upon the removal of desktop icons, folders, and Start menu entries—thwarts the distribution of a rival browser by preventing OEMs from removing visible means of user access to IE. The OEMs cannot practically install a second browser in addition to IE, the court found, in part because . . . a certain number of novice computer users, seeing two browser icons, will wonder which to use when and will call the OEM's support line. Support calls are extremely expensive and, in the highly competitive original equipment market, firms have a strong incentive to minimize costs. By preventing OEMs from removing visible means of user access

to IE, the license restriction prevents many OEMs from pre-installing a rival browser, and therefore, protects Microsoft's monopoly from the competition that middleware might otherwise present. Therefore, we conclude that the license restriction at issue is anticompetitive.

[A] second license provision [imposed by Microsoft] prohibits OEMs from modifying the initial boot sequence—the process that occurs the first time a consumer turns on the computer. [The district court found that prior to] the imposition of that restriction, "among the programs that many OEMs inserted into the boot sequence were Internet sign-up procedures that encouraged users to choose from a list of IAPs assembled by the OEM." Microsoft's prohibition on any alteration of the boot sequence thus prevents OEMs from using that process to promote the services of IAPs, many of which—at least at the time Microsoft imposed the restriction—used Navigator rather than IE in their Internet access software. Because this prohibition has a substantial effect in protecting Microsoft's market power, and does so through a means other than competition on the merits, it is anticompetitive.

Finally, Microsoft . . . prohibits OEMs from causing any user interface other than the Windows desktop to launch automatically, from adding icons or folders different in size or shape from those supplied by Microsoft, and from using the "Active Desktop" feature to promote third-party brands. These restrictions impose significant costs upon the OEMs; prior to Microsoft's prohibiting the practice, many OEMs would change the appearance of the desktop in ways they found beneficial. The anticompetitive effect of the license restrictions is . . . that OEMs are not able to promote rival browsers, which keeps developers focused upon the APIs in Windows. This kind of promotion is not a zero-sum game; but for the restrictions in their licenses to use Windows, OEMs could promote multiple IAPs and browsers. [T]his type of license restriction . . . is anticompetitive: Microsoft reduced rival browsers' usage share not by improving its own product but, rather, by preventing OEMs from taking actions that could increase rivals' share of usage.

Microsoft argues that the license restrictions are legally justified because . . . Microsoft is simply "exercising its rights as the holder of valid copyrights." The company claims an absolute and unfettered right to use its intellectual property as it wishes: "If intellectual property rights have been lawfully acquired," it says, then, "their subsequent exercise cannot give rise to antitrust liability." That is no more correct than the proposition that use of one's personal property, such as a baseball bat, cannot give rise to tort liability. As the Federal Circuit succinctly stated: "Intellectual property rights do not confer a privilege to violate the antitrust laws." *In re Independent Service Organizations Antitrust Litigation* (Fed Cir. 2000).

[Microsoft's copyright argument fails because the restrictions on OEMs are neither necessary to prevent substantial alteration of its copyrighted work nor necessary to preserve the stability of the Windows platform. Moreover,] Microsoft has not shown that the [actions OEMs otherwise would take would] reduce the value of Windows except in the sense that their promotion of rival browsers [would] undermine Microsoft's monopoly—and that is not a permissible justification for the license restrictions.

[W]e hold that . . . the OEM license restrictions represent uses of Microsoft's market power to protect its monopoly, unredeemed by any legitimate justification. The restrictions therefore violate § 2 of the Sherman Act.

b. Integration of Internet Explorer (IE) and Windows

[T]he district court found that "Microsoft's executives believed . . . its contractual restrictions placed on OEMs would not be sufficient in themselves to reverse the direction of Navigator's usage share. Consequently, . . . , Microsoft set out to bind [IE] more tightly to Windows 95." Technologically binding IE to Windows, the district court found, both prevented OEMs from pre-installing other browsers and deterred consumers from using them. [H]aving the IE software code as an irremovable part of Windows meant that pre-installing a second browser would increase an OEM's product testing costs, because an OEM must test and train its support staff to answer calls related to every software product pre-installed on the machine; moreover, pre-installing a browser in addition to IE would to many OEMs be "a questionable use of the scarce and valuable space on a PC's hard drive."

As a general rule, courts are properly very skeptical about claims that competition has been harmed by a dominant firm's product design changes. In a competitive market, firms routinely innovate in the hope of appealing to consumers, sometimes in the process making their products incompatible with those of rivals; the imposition of liability when a monopolist does the same thing will inevitably deter a certain amount of innovation. This is all the more true in a market, such as this one, in which the product itself is rapidly changing. Judicial deference to product innovation, however, does not mean that a monopolist's product design decisions are per se lawful.

The district court first condemned as anticompetitive Microsoft's decision to exclude IE from the "Add/Remove Programs" utility in Windows 98. Microsoft had included IE in the Add/Remove Programs utility in Windows 95, but when it modified Windows 95 to produce Windows 98, it took IE out of the Add/Remove Programs utility. This change reduces the usage share of rival browsers not by making Microsoft's own browser more attractive to consumers but by discouraging OEMs from distributing rival products. Because Microsoft's conduct, through something other than competition on the merits, has the effect of significantly reducing usage of rivals'

products and hence protecting its own operating system monopoly, it is anticompetitive.

[T]he district court [also] condemned Microsoft's decision to bind IE to Windows 98 "by placing code specific to Web browsing in the same files as code that provided operating system functions." Putting code supplying browsing functionality into a file with code supplying operating system functionality "ensures that the deletion of any file containing browsing-specific routines would also delete vital operating system routines and thus cripple Windows." [P]reventing an OEM from removing IE deters it from installing a second browser because doing so increases the OEM's product testing and support costs; by contrast, had OEMs been able to remove IE, they might have chosen to pre-install Navigator alone.

Microsoft denies . . . that it commingled browsing and non-browsing code, and it maintains the district court's findings to the contrary are clearly erroneous. In view of the contradictory testimony in the record, some of which supports the district court's finding that Microsoft commingled browsing and non-browsing code, we cannot conclude that the finding was clearly erroneous. Microsoft proffers no [procompetitive] justification for . . . excluding IE from the Add/Remove Programs utility [or for] commingling browser and operating systems code. Accordingly, we hold that [those actions] constitute exclusionary conduct, in violation of § 2.

c. Agreements with Internet Access Providers (IAPs)

Microsoft concluded exclusive agreements with all the leading IAPs, including [America Online and other] major online services. [The] plaintiffs allege that, by closing to rivals a substantial percentage of the available opportunities for browser distribution, Microsoft managed to preserve its monopoly in the market for operating systems. The IAPs constitute one of the two major channels by which browsers can be distributed. [The district court found that] Microsoft has exclusive deals with "14 of the top 15 access providers in North America[, which] account for a large majority of all Internet access subscriptions in this part of the world." By ensuring that the majority of all IAP subscribers are offered IE either as the default browser or as the only browser, Microsoft's deals with the IAPs clearly have a significant effect in preserving its monopoly.

[With the plaintiffs] having demonstrated a harm to competition, the burden falls upon Microsoft to [justify] its exclusive dealing contracts with IAPs. Microsoft's only explanation . . . is that it wants to keep developers focused upon its APIs—which is to say [that] it wants to preserve its power in the operating system market. That is not an unlawful end, but neither is it a procompetitive justification. Accordingly, we affirm the district court's holding that Microsoft's exclusive contracts with IAPs are exclusionary devices, in violation of § 2 of the Sherman Act.

d. Dealings with Independent Software Vendors (ISVs) and Apple Computer

The district court held that Microsoft engages in exclusionary conduct in its dealings with . . . ISVs, which develop software. The court described Microsoft's deals with ISVs as [including promises by Microsoft to provide] "preferential support, . . . technical information, and the right to use certain Microsoft seals of approval" if, in return, the ISVs agreed to "use Internet Explorer as the default browsing software for any software they develop with a hypertext-based user interface."

The court further found that the effect of these deals is to "increase the likelihood that the millions of consumers using [applications designed by ISVs subject to agreements with Microsoft] will use Internet Explorer rather than Navigator." Although the ISVs are a relatively small channel for browser distribution, they take on greater significance because[, as revealed above,] Microsoft had largely foreclosed the two primary channels to its rivals. In that light, one can tell from the record that by affecting the applications used by "millions" of consumers, Microsoft's exclusive deals with the ISVs had a substantial effect in further foreclosing rival browsers from the market. [T]he deals [thus] have an anticompetitive effect.

[In supposed justification of its ISV agreements,] Microsoft . . . states only that [the] agreements reflect an attempt "to persuade ISVs to utilize Internet-related system services in Windows rather than Navigator." [K]eeping developers focused upon Windows—that is, preserving the Windows monopoly—is a competitively neutral goal [rather than a] procompetitive justification for [Microsoft's] exclusive dealing arrangements with the ISVs. [We therefore] hold that those arrangements violate § 2.

[T]he district court [also] held that Microsoft's dealings with Apple Computer violated the Sherman Act. Apple . . . makes both software (including an operating system, Mac OS), and hardware (the Macintosh line of computers). Microsoft primarily makes software, including, in addition to its operating system, a number of popular applications. One, called "Office," is a suite of business productivity applications that Microsoft has ported to Mac OS. The district court found that "90 percent of Mac OS users running a suite of office productivity applications [use] Microsoft's Mac Office." Further, the court found that in 1997, "Apple's business was in steep decline" [and that] "many ISVs questioned the wisdom of continuing to spend time and money developing applications for the Mac OS. Had Microsoft announced in the midst of this atmosphere that it was ceasing to develop new versions of Mac Office, . . . ISVs, customers, developers, and investors would have interpreted the announcement as Apple's death notice."

Microsoft recognized the importance to Apple of its continued support of Mac Office. In June 1997 Microsoft Chairman Bill Gates [stated that] "Apple let us down on the browser by making Netscape the standard install" [and] that he had already called Apple's CEO to ask "how we should announce the cancellation of Mac Office." The district court further found that, within a month of Gates' call, Apple and Microsoft had reached an agreement pursuant to which [Microsoft promised] "to continue releasing up-to-date versions of Mac Office for at least five years" [and Apple] agreed to bundle the most current version [of IE] with Mac OS and make IE the default [browser]. The agreement also prohibit[ed] Apple from encouraging users to substitute another browser for IE, and state[d] that Apple [would] "encourage its employees to use [IE]."

This exclusive deal between Microsoft and Apple has a substantial effect upon the distribution of rival browsers. Preinstallation of a browser (which can be accomplished either by including the browser with the operating system or by the OEM installing the browser) is one of the two most important methods of browser distribution, and Apple had a not insignificant share of worldwide sales of operating systems. Because Microsoft's exclusive contract with Apple has a substantial effect in restricting distribution of rival browsers, and because [that effect] serves to protect Microsoft's monopoly, its deal with Apple must be regarded as anticompetitive. Microsoft offers no procompetitive justification for the exclusive dealing arrangement. It makes only the irrelevant claim that the IE-for-Mac Office deal is part of a multifaceted set of agreements between itself and Apple. Accordingly, we hold that the exclusive deal with Apple is exclusionary, in violation of § 2.

e. Java

Java, a set of technologies developed by Sun Microsystems, is another type of middleware posing a potential threat to Windows' position as the ubiquitous platform for software development. The Java technologies include: (1) a programming language; (2) a set of programs written in that language, called the "Java class libraries," which expose APIs; (3) a compiler, which translates code written by a developer into "bytecode"; and (4) a Java Virtual Machine ("JVM"), which translates bytecode into instructions to the operating system. Programs calling upon the Java APIs will run on any machine with a "Java runtime environment," that is, Java class libraries and a JVM.

In May 1995 Netscape agreed with Sun to distribute a copy of the Java runtime environment with every copy of Navigator. [The district court found that] "Navigator quickly became the principal vehicle by which Sun placed copies of its Java runtime environment on the PC systems of Windows users." Microsoft, too, agreed to promote the Java technologies—or so it seemed. For at the same time, [the district court concluded,] Microsoft took steps "to maximize the difficulty with which applications written in Java could be ported from Windows to other platforms, and vice versa." The court found that Microsoft took four steps to exclude Java from developing as a viable cross-platform threat: (a) designing a JVM incompatible with the one developed by Sun; (b) entering into contracts . . . requiring major ISVs to promote Microsoft's JVM exclusively; (c) deceiving Java developers about the Windows-specific nature of the tools it distributed to them; and (d) coercing Intel to stop aiding Sun in improving the Java technologies.

The district court [erred in holding] that Microsoft engaged in exclusionary conduct by developing and promoting its own JVM, [which was incompatible with Sun's.] A monopolist does not violate the antitrust laws simply by developing a product that is incompatible with those of its rivals. In order to violate the antitrust laws, the incompatible product must have an anti-competitive effect that outweighs any procompetitive justification for the design. Microsoft's JVM is not only incompatible with Sun's, it allows Java applications to run faster on Windows than does Sun's JVM. [Microsoft's JVM thus] does not itself have . . . anticompetitive effect.

To the extent Microsoft's [agreements] with the ISVs conditioned receipt of Windows technical information upon the ISVs' agreement to promote Microsoft's JVM exclusively, they raise a different competitive concern. The district court found that . . . the deals were exclusive in practice because they required developers to make Microsoft's JVM the default in the software they developed. [T]he record indicates that Microsoft's deals with the major ISVs had a significant effect upon JVM promotion. [T]he products of [these] ISVs reached millions of consumers. Because Microsoft's agreements foreclosed a substantial portion of the field for JVM distribution and because, in so doing, they protected Microsoft's monopoly from a middleware threat, they are anticompetitive. Because . . . Microsoft has no procompetitive justification for them, we hold that the provisions in the [ISV agreements] requiring use of Microsoft's JVM as the default are exclusionary, in violation of the Sherman Act.

Microsoft's "Java implementation" included, in addition to a JVM, a set of software development tools it created to assist ISVs in designing Java applications. The district court found that, not only were these tools incompatible with Sun's cross-platform aspirations for Java—no violation, to be sure—but Microsoft deceived Java developers regarding the Windows-specific nature of the tools. Microsoft's tools included "certain 'keywords' and 'compiler directives' that could only be executed properly by Microsoft's version of the Java runtime environment for Windows." As a result, even Java "developers who were opting for portability over performance . . . unwittingly

[wrote] Java applications that [ran] only on Windows." That is, developers who relied upon Microsoft's public commitment to cooperate with Sun and who used Microsoft's tools to develop what Microsoft led them to believe were cross-platform applications ended up producing applications that would run only on the Windows operating system.

Microsoft documents confirm that Microsoft intended to deceive Java developers, and predicted that the effect of its actions would be to generate Windows-dependent Java applications that their developers believed would be cross-platform; these documents also indicate that Microsoft's ultimate objective was to thwart Java's threat to Microsoft's monopoly in the market for operating systems. One Microsoft document, for example, states as a strategic goal: "Kill cross-platform Java by growing the polluted Java market." Microsoft's conduct related to its Java developer tools served to protect its monopoly of the operating system in a manner not attributable either to the superiority of the operating system or to the acumen of its makers, and therefore was anticompetitive. Unsurprisingly, Microsoft offers no procompetitive explanation for its campaign to deceive developers. [T]his conduct is exclusionary, in violation of § 2.

The district court [properly] held that Microsoft also acted unlawfully with respect to Java by using its "monopoly power to prevent firms such as Intel from aiding in the creation of cross-platform interfaces." [The record indicates that in 1995,] Intel was in the process of developing a high-performance, Windows-compatible JVM, [that] Microsoft wanted Intel to abandon [this] effort because a fast, cross-platform JVM would threaten Microsoft's monopoly in the operating system market, [and that Microsoft threatened to cease distributing] Intel technologies bundled with Windows [if Intel] did not stop aiding Sun on the multimedia front. Intel finally capitulated in 1997, after Microsoft [kept up the pressure]. Microsoft lamely characterizes its threat to Intel as "advice." The court, however, [properly concluded] that Microsoft's "advice" to Intel to stop aiding cross-platform Java was backed by the threat of retaliation. Therefore, we affirm the conclusion that Microsoft's threats to Intel were exclusionary, in violation of § 2.

District court's decision that Microsoft committed monopolization affirmed; other portions of decision affirmed in part, reversed in part, and remanded in part; remedial order of divestiture vacated and case remanded for further proceedings regarding appropriate remedies.

Attempted Monopolization

Firms that have not yet attained monopoly power may nonetheless be liable for an **attempt to monopolize** in violation of § 2 if they are dangerously close to acquiring monopoly power and are employing methods likely to result in monopoly power if left unchecked. As part of the required proof of a dangerous probability that monopoly power will be acquired, plaintiffs in attempted monopolization cases must furnish proof of the relevant market—as in monopolization cases. Attempt cases also require proof that the

CYBERLAW IN ACTION

As noted in the portion of the *Microsoft* decision included earlier, the federal district court (Thomas Penfield Jackson, District Judge) held that divestiture—in this instance, dividing Microsoft into two companies—was the appropriate remedy for Microsoft's Sherman Act violations. The D.C. Circuit Court of Appeals, however, reversed this determination and remanded the case for reconsideration of remedy-related issues.

The D.C. Circuit concluded that the district court erred in not holding a separate evidentiary hearing regarding remedies, and that because some of the bases of liability imposed by the district court had been reversed on appeal, the remedy of divestiture might no longer be the appropriate form of relief. Although the appellate court did not explicitly state that divestiture could not be ordered by the district court after it conducted further proceedings, the D.C. Circuit's opinion seemed to hint that divestiture was a more extreme remedy than was necessary. In remanding the case, the appellate court further ordered that the case be assigned to a district judge other than Judge Jackson, whose extensive participation in media interviews created the perception that he might not be impartial.

After the case was remanded, the United States, roughly half of the states that were plaintiffs, and Microsoft entered into a settlement agreement designed to resolve the case. District Judge Colleen Kollar-Kotelly held hearings on remedial and agreement-related issues, took under advisement the question whether to approve the agreement, and eventually issued her approval. Under the settlement agreement, Microsoft became obligated to allow computer manufacturers to add icons for Microsoft competitors' software to the desktop display for the Windows operating system. Microsoft must also employ uniform licensing agreements when dealing with software manufacturers, and must furnish technical information to Internet access providers and to software and hardware vendors so that their products will work with Windows.

Critics of the settlement agreement said it was not tough enough on Microsoft, that it would do little to benefit consumers or to curtail anticompetitive actions, and that it was, effectively, a victory for Microsoft. The U.S. Justice Department took a different view, calling the agreement a suitable and successful resolution of a case in which the plaintiffs had prevailed on their main claim of liability.

---

defendant possessed a specific intent to acquire monopoly power through anticompetitive means.

The *Microsoft* decision underscored the importance of the proof-of-relevant-market requirement in attempted monopolization cases. Although it affirmed the district court's holding that Microsoft had engaged in monopolization of the market for Intel-compatible PC operating systems, the United States Court of Appeals for the District of Columbia Circuit reversed the lower court's decision that Microsoft had attempted to monopolize the Web browser market. The D.C. Circuit stressed that the plaintiffs had failed to offer proof of—and that the district court had therefore made no appropriate finding regarding—the components and scope of any supposed browser market. Therefore, the lower court erred in basing its decision on conduct by Microsoft that, in the district court's view, seemed calculated to extend Microsoft's operating systems monopoly into another market. Whether Microsoft's conduct created a dangerous probability of monopoly power acquisition in that other market could not be determined without a definition of the latter market's boundaries—and no such definition had occurred.

A controversial issue that surfaces in many attempted monopolization cases concerns the role that *predatory pricing* may play in proving an intent to monopolize. The Supreme Court has defined predatory pricing as "pricing below an appropriate measure of cost for the purpose of eliminating competitors in the short run and reducing competition in the long run."[10] What constitutes "an appropriate measure of cost" in predatory pricing cases has long been a subject of debate among antitrust scholars. Although the Supreme Court has declined to resolve this debate definitively, it seems likely to take a skeptical view of predatory pricing claims in the future. The Court has described predatory pricing schemes as "rarely tried, and even more rarely successful."[11] As part of this characterization of predatory pricing schemes, the Court indicated that it agrees with economists who have argued that predatory pricing is often economically irrational because, to be successful, the predator must maintain monopoly power long enough after it has driven its competitors out of business to recoup the profits it lost through predatory pricing. The predator would be able to sustain monopoly power only if high barriers to entry prevented new competitors from being drawn into the market by the supracompetitive prices the predator would have to charge in order to recoup its losses.

---

[10]*Cargill, Inc. & Excel Corp. v. Monfort of Colorado, Inc.* (U.S. Sup. Ct. 1986).

[11]*Matsushita Electric Industrial Co., Ltd. v. Zenith Radio Corp.* (U.S. Sup. Ct. 1986).

Ethics in Action

Some of the cases in this chapter recite the statement that antitrust was designed to protect competition, not competitors. How is this statement consistent with the ethical justification of markets as the most efficient form of economic organization? Consider the case of a competitor who is driven out of business by another competitor's ultimately unsuccessful predatory pricing efforts (unsuccessful because the predator could not maintain monopoly power long enough to recoup the profits lost through predatory pricing).

- Although competition may not suffer in such a case, does the out-of-business competitor have any *ethical* or public policy–based claim to compensation?
- Should antitrust law recognize such a claim?

Conspiracy to Monopolize When two or more business entities **conspire to monopolize** a relevant market, § 2 may be violated. This portion of § 2 largely overlaps § 1, because it is difficult to conceive of a conspiracy to monopolize that would not also amount to a conspiracy in restraint of trade. The lower federal courts have differed on the elements necessary to prove a conspiracy to monopolize. In addition to requiring proof of the existence of a conspiracy, some courts insist on proof of the relevant market, a specific intent to acquire monopoly power, and overt action in furtherance of the conspiracy. Other courts do not require extensive proof of the relevant market. According to these courts, a violation is established through proof that the defendants conspired to exclude competitors from, or acquire control over prices in, some significant area of commerce. An approach that deemphasizes the requirement of proof of the relevant market, however, may not be consistent with Supreme Court precedent.

Problems and Problem Cases

1. Atlantic Richfield (ARCO) is an integrated oil company that sells gasoline to consumers both directly through its own stations and indirectly through ARCO-brand dealers. USA is an independent retail marketer of gasoline that buys gasoline from major petroleum companies for resale under its own brand name. USA competes directly with ARCO dealers at the retail level. Its outlets typically are low-overhead, high-volume "discount" stations that charge less than stations selling equivalent quality gasoline under major brand names. ARCO adopted a new marketing strategy in order to compete more effectively with independents such as USA. ARCO encouraged its dealers to match the retail gasoline prices offered by independents in various ways. These included making available to its dealers and distributors short-term discounts and reducing its dealers' costs by, for example, eliminating credit card sales. ARCO's strategy increased its sales and market share. When USA's sales dropped, it sued ARCO, charging that ARCO and its dealers were engaged in a per se illegal vertical price-fixing scheme. On these facts, could USA show an *antitrust injury* resulting from ARCO's actions (i.e., injury that flows from the unlawful aspects of the challenged behavior and is of a type that the antitrust laws were designed to prevent)? Does per se treatment apply to vertical price-fixing when the allegedly fixed price is of a *maximum* nature?

2. Co-Operative Theatres (Co-op), a Cleveland area movie theater booking agent, began seeking customers in southern Ohio. Shortly thereafter, Tri-State Theatre Services (Tri-State), a Cincinnati booking agent, began to solicit business in the Cleveland area. Later, however, Co-op and Tri-State allegedly entered into an agreement not to solicit each other's customers. The Justice Department prosecuted them for agreeing to restrain trade in violation of § 1 of the Sherman Act. Under a government grant of immunity, Tri-State's vice president testified that Co-op's vice president had approached him at a trade convention and threatened to start taking Tri-State's accounts if Tri-State did not stop calling on Co-op's accounts. He also testified that at a luncheon meeting he attended with officials from both firms, the

presidents of both firms said that it would be in the interests of both firms to stop calling on each other's accounts. Several Co-op customers testified that Tri-State had refused to accept their business because of the agreement with Co-op. The trial court found both firms guilty of a per se violation of the Sherman Act, rejecting their argument that the rule of reason should have been applied and refusing to allow them to introduce evidence that the agreement did not have a significant anticompetitive effect. Should the rule of reason have been applied?

3. Discon, Inc., specialized in providing the service of removing obsolete telephone equipment. New York Telephone Company was a subsidiary of NYNEX Corporation. Another NYNEX subsidiary, Materiel Enterprises Company, was a purchasing entity that arranged for Discon to provide removal services for New York Telephone. After regularly doing business with Discon, Materiel switched its purchases of removal services from Discon to a Discon competitor, AT&T Technologies. According to Discon, Materiel did this as part of an attempt to defraud local telephone customers and regulatory authorities. Discon contended that Materiel would pay AT&T Technologies more than Discon would have charged for similar removal services, that Materiel would then pass those higher prices on to New York Telephone, and that New York Telephone would in turn pass those prices on to consumers in the form of higher telephone service charges that were approved by the relevant regulatory authorities. Discon further contended that at the end of the year, Materiel would receive a special rebate from AT&T Technologies, and that Materiel would share this rebate with its corporate parent, NYNEX. Discon asserted that because it refused to participate in this fraudulent scheme, Materiel would not do business with Discon, which eventually went out of business. Discon sued Materiel, New York Telephone, and NYNEX, claiming that the above facts constituted a group boycott and thus a per se violation of § 1 of the Sherman Act. If Discon's allegations are true, did a per se group boycott take place?

4. The Maricopa Foundation for Medical Care was a nonprofit organization established by the Maricopa County Medical Society to promote fee-for-service medicine. Roughly 70 percent of the physicians in Maricopa County belonged to the foundation. The foundation's trustees set maximum fees that members could charge for medical services provided to policyholders of approved medical insurance plans. To obtain the foundation's approval, insurers had to agree to pay the fees of member physicians up to the prescribed maximum. Member physicians were free to charge less than the prescribed maximum, but had to agree not to seek additional payments in excess of the maximum from insured patients. The Arizona attorney general filed suit for injunctive relief against the Maricopa County Medical Society and the foundation, arguing that the fee agreement constituted per se illegal horizontal price-fixing. The district court denied the state's motion for a partial summary judgment. The Ninth Circuit Court of Appeals affirmed on the ground that the per se rule was not applicable to the case. Was the Ninth Circuit correct?

5. In 1986, Market Force, Inc. (MFI), began operating in the Milwaukee real estate market as a buyer's broker. MFI and prospective home buyers entered into exclusive contracts providing that MFI would receive a fee equal to 40 percent of the sales commission if it located a house that the buyer ultimately purchased. This 40 percent commission was the same commission selling brokers (those who ultimately produced a buyer, but whose duty of loyalty was to the seller) earned when they sold property placed on the local multiple listing service (MLS) by other brokers. MFI's contracts anticipated that the buyer would ask the listing broker (the one who had listed the property for sale on behalf of its owners and who received 60 percent of the commission when the property was sold) to pay MFI the commission at the time of the sale. If the listing broker agreed to do so, the buyer had no further obligation to MFI. For some time after MFI began operations, other real estate firms treated it inconsistently; some paid the full 40 percent commission but others paid nothing. In the fall of 1987, Wauwatosa Realty Co. and Coldwell Banker, the top two firms listing high quality homes in Milwaukee, issued formal policies on splitting commissions with buyer's brokers. Wauwatosa said it would pay 20 percent of the selling agent's 40 percent commission. Coldwell Banker said it would pay 20 percent of the total sales commission. Several other real estate firms followed suit, setting their rates at 10 or 20 percent of the total sales commission, with the result that firms accounting for 31 percent of the annual listings of the MLS adopted policies and disseminated them to other MLS

members. MFI filed suit against the brokers who had announced policies, arguing that they had conspired to restrain trade in violation of § 1 of the Sherman Act. At trial, the defendants introduced evidence of numerous business justifications for their policies and argued that their knowingly having adopted similar policies was not enough, standing alone, to justify a conclusion that the Sherman Act was violated. Was this argument correct?

6. Orson, Inc., owned and operated the Roxy, a movie theater located in downtown Center City, Philadelphia, from January 1992 until the permanent closing of the theater in October 1994. The Roxy exhibited art films—as opposed to movies that may be characterized as mainstream—on two screens. The total seating capacity at the Roxy was 260. The Ritz theaters, which competed with the Roxy in the showing of art films in the Center City area, consisted of two five-screen facilities with a total seating capacity of approximately 1,800. The ticket prices at the Roxy and at the Ritz theaters (referred to collectively as "the Ritz") were essentially the same. In addition to the Roxy and the Ritz, there were six other Center City area theaters that showed art films at least part of the time. Miramax Film Corp., a nationwide distributor of feature-length motion pictures (including art films), distributed movies to all of the theaters in Center City and elsewhere in the greater metropolitan Philadelphia area. Miramax licensed films for exhibition for a limited period of time. Consistent with the usual practice in the motion picture industry, these licenses normally were exclusive—meaning that during the time period established in the license, the film would not be licensed to other theaters located in a specified area. Such licenses, called clearances, contained compensation terms entitling Miramax to a portion of the exhibiting theater's box office gross.

In the motion picture industry, a *first run* is the initial exhibition of a film in a given geographic area. A *subsequent run* is an exhibition of that film in the same geographic area after the first run has expired. Between January 1992 and February 1994 (when discovery ended in the lawsuit described below), Miramax licensed 28 films on a first-run basis, as well as one on a subsequent-run basis, to the Ritz. During the same time period, Miramax granted the Roxy one first-run license and 14 subsequent-run licenses, and issued various first-run licenses to Center City area theaters other than the Roxy and the

Ritz. In addition, during the same time period, 59 distributors other than Miramax granted a total of 73 first-run licenses to the Roxy. All of the first-run licenses Miramax granted to the Ritz were exclusive in nature. On occasion, Orson sought a first-run nonexclusive license on a Miramax film and indicated that Orson would offer Miramax a higher percentage of the Roxy's box office receipts than the percentage the Ritz would pay. Nevertheless, Miramax did not grant Orson the licenses it had requested for the Roxy.

Orson sued Miramax in August 1993, alleging that it had violated § 1 of the Sherman Act by conspiring with the Ritz to exclude the Roxy from the art film market. According to Orson's complaint, this conspiracy involved an agreement to (1) make the Ritz Miramax's exclusive Philadelphia exhibitor for first-run art film features, and (2) grant the Ritz exclusive first-run rights to any Miramax film the Ritz wished to exhibit. The district court concluded that rule of reason analysis was appropriate because the supposed agreement between Miramax and the Ritz was "clearly a vertical agreement" between a distributor and an exhibitor. After undertaking such an analysis, the district court granted summary judgment in favor of Miramax. Orson appealed to the U.S. Court of Appeals for the Third Circuit. Was rule of reason treatment appropriate in this case? Did the trial court rule correctly in granting summary judgment to Miramax?

7. Eastman Kodak Co. (Kodak) manufactures and sells photocopiers and micrographic equipment. In addition, Kodak provides customers with service and replacement parts for its equipment. Kodak produces some of the parts itself. The other parts are made to order for Kodak by independent original equipment manufacturers (OEMs). Rather than selling a complete system of original equipment, lifetime parts, and lifetime service for a single price, Kodak furnishes service after an initial warranty period, either through annual service contracts or on a per-call basis. Kodak provides between 80 and 95 percent of the service for Kodak machines. In the early 1980s, independent service organizations (ISOs) began repairing and servicing Kodak equipment, as well as selling parts for it. ISOs kept an inventory of parts, purchased either from Kodak or from other sources (primarily OEMs). In 1985, Kodak adopted policies designed to limit ISOs' access to parts and to make it more difficult for ISOs to compete with

Kodak in servicing Kodak equipment. Kodak began selling replacement parts only to Kodak equipment buyers who used Kodak service or repaired their own machines (i.e., buyers who did not use ISOs for service). In addition, Kodak sought to limit ISO access to other sources of Kodak parts by working out agreements with OEMs that they would sell parts for Kodak equipment to no one other than Kodak, and by pressuring Kodak equipment owners and independent parts distributors not to sell Kodak parts to ISOs.

Eighteen ISOs sued Kodak, claiming that these policies amounted to unlawful tying of the sale of service for Kodak machines to the sale of parts, in violation of Sherman Act § 1. A federal district court granted summary judgment in favor of Kodak on each of these claims. The Ninth Circuit Court of Appeals reversed, holding that summary judgment was inappropriate because there were genuine issues of material fact regarding the ISOs' claims. The U.S. Supreme Court granted certiorari. For purposes of the § 1 tying claim presented in this case, are service and parts two distinct products? If so, do the facts make it reasonable to infer that Kodak possessed sufficient market power in the parts market to force unwanted purchases of service? How did the Supreme Court rule?

8. Grinnell Corporation manufactured plumbing supplies and fire sprinkler systems. It also owned 76 percent of the stock of ADT Co., 89 percent of the stock of AFA, Inc., and 100 percent of the stock of Holmes, Inc. ADT provided burglary-protection and fire-protection services. AFA provided only fire-protection services. Holmes provided only burglary-protection services. Each of the three firms offered a central station service under which hazard-detecting devices installed on the protected premises automatically transmitted an electronic signal to a central station. Other companies provided forms of protection service other than the central station variety. Subscribers to an accredited central station service (i.e., one approved by insurance underwriters) received substantially greater insurance premium reductions than the premium reductions received by users of other protection services. At the relevant time in question, ADT, AFA, and Holmes were the three largest central station service companies in terms of revenue. Together, they accounted for approximately 87 percent of the central station services provided. Contending that Grinnell, ADT, AFA, and Holmes had taken various anticompetitive actions that amounted to willful acquisition or maintenance of monopoly power, the U.S. government brought a monopolization action against Grinnell under § 2 of the Sherman Act. Concerning the first element of a monopolization claim (monopoly power in the relevant market), were fire-protection services and burglary-protection services too different to be part of the same market? What was the relevant market in this case? Were protection services other than those of the central station variety part of it?

9. Martindale Empowerment, a Virginia corporation, engaged in the business of providing commercial electronic-mail service to advertisers. Martindale regularly sent electronic advertising over the Internet in the form of e-mail to e-mail addresses throughout the United States. In September 1998, however, America Online, Inc., the largest commercial online service in the nation with more than 16,000,000 individual subscribers, implemented various mechanisms to block advertising messages that Martindale had been sending to AOL subscribers for nearly two years. AOL succeeded in blocking most of those transmissions by Martindale. Contending that Martindale was using deceptive practices in an effort to mask the source and quantity of its transmissions and thereby avoid AOL's blocking and filtering technologies, AOL sued Martindale on a variety of legal theories. AOL sought an injunction against Martindale's practice of sending unsolicited bulk e-mail advertisements to AOL subscribers. Martindale responded with a counterclaim in which it alleged that AOL had engaged in monopolization, in violation of § 2 of the Sherman Act. According to Martindale, AOL had established itself as the only entity that could advertise to AOL subscribers. For purposes of the first element of a monopolization claim—monopoly power in a relevant market—Martindale contended that the relevant product or service market was e-mail advertising. Was Martindale correct in this contention?

10. In July 1977, anesthesiologist Edwin G. Hyde applied for admission to the medical staff of East Jefferson Hospital in New Orleans. The credentials committee and the medical staff executive committee recommended approval, but the hospital board denied the application because the hospital was a party to a contract providing that all anesthesiological services required by the hospital's patients would be performed by Roux & Associates, a professional

medical corporation. Hyde filed suit against the board, arguing that the contract violated § 1 of the Sherman Act. The district court ruled in favor of the board, finding that the anticompetitive effects of the contract were minimal and outweighed by the benefits of improved patient care. It noted that there were at least 20 hospitals in the New Orleans metropolitan area and that roughly 70 percent of the patients residing in Jefferson Parish went to hospitals other than East Jefferson. It therefore concluded that East Jefferson lacked any significant market power and could not use the contract for anticompetitive ends. The Fifth Circuit Court of Appeals reversed, holding that the relevant market was the East Bank Jefferson Parish rather than the New Orleans metropolitan area. The court therefore concluded that because 30 percent of the parish residents used East Jefferson and "patients tend to choose hospitals by location rather than price or quality," East Jefferson possessed sufficient market power to make the contract a per se illegal tying contract. Was the Fifth Circuit correct?

11. For approximately three years, Larry and Shirley McQuillan had served as distributors of sorbothane products for a certain firm and its successor. After they lost their distributorship and their business failed, the McQuillans sued both firms, as well as other affiliated companies and individuals. The McQuillans raised various legal claims, including a claim that the defendants engaged in attempted monopolization, in violation of § 2 of the Sherman Act. The evidence produced at trial revealed various instances of unfair or predatory conduct engaged in by the defendants and directed toward the McQuillans. The jury awarded the McQuillans a very substantial damages award on their attempted monopolization claim. The defendants appealed. Relying on one of its own precedents (a 1964 decision), the U.S. Court of Appeals for the Ninth Circuit held that the evidence of the defendants' unfair or predatory conduct served to satisfy the *specific intent to monopolize* and *dangerous probability of achieving monopoly power* elements of the McQuillans' attempted monopolization claim, even though the McQuillans presented no proof of the relevant market or the defendants' market power therein. Was the Ninth Circuit's holding correct?

Online Research

U.S. Department of Justice, Antitrust Division

Visit the Web site of the United States Department of Justice, one of the major enforcers of antitrust law in the United States. Review the site's material and information regarding the Justice Department's Antitrust Division. Then prepare a brief description of the legal actions brought by the Antitrust Division against vitamin producers during the late 1990s.

chapter 50

THE CLAYTON ACT, THE ROBINSON–PATMAN ACT, AND ANTITRUST EXEMPTIONS AND IMMUNITIES

XYZ, Inc., the widget manufacturer referred to at the beginning of Chapter 49, may face antitrust issues that go beyond the ones addressed in that chapter. As you study this chapter, consider these questions regarding possible courses of action in which XYZ might engage:

- If XYZ, in selling its widgets, charges different prices to different wholesale dealers, is XYZ at risk of antitrust liability? What if XYZ charges a wholesale dealer a lower price than XYZ charges a *retailer* with whom XYZ deals directly?
- If XYZ has been charging a certain price for its widgets but XYZ learns that a competing widget manufacturer is offering its widgets at a lower price, would XYZ be at risk of violating antitrust law if it lowers its price for certain customers in order to *meet* the price offered by the competitor? What if XYZ lowers its price enough to *beat* the competitor's price?
- If XYZ and a competing widget manufacturer decide to merge, what potential hurdles might antitrust law present?
- If XYZ decides to acquire a company that produces a material used in making widgets (i.e., a noncompetitor), is antitrust law a potential obstacle to XYZ's ability to carry out the acquisition?
- If, through effective lobbying efforts, XYZ helps convince a state legislature to enact a statute that may benefit XYZ at the expense of competition in the widget market, has XYZ committed an antitrust violation?
- What ethical questions are suggested by the behaviors alluded to above?

CONCENTRATION IN THE AMERICAN economy continued despite the 1890 enactment of the Sherman Act. Restrictive judicial interpretations of section 2 of the Sherman Act limited its effectiveness against many monopolists. Critics therefore sought legislation to thwart would-be monopolists before they achieved full-blown restraint of trade or monopoly power. In 1914, Congress responded by passing the Clayton Act.

Congress envisioned the Clayton Act as a vehicle for attacking practices that monopolists historically employed to acquire monopoly power. These practices included tying and exclusive dealing arrangements designed to squeeze competitors out of the market, mergers and acquisitions aimed at reducing competition through the elimination of competitors, interlocking corporate directorates designed to reduce competition by placing competitors under common leadership, and predatory or discriminatory pricing intended to force competitors out of business. These practices will be discussed in the following pages.

In view of the congressional intent that the Clayton Act serve as a preventive measure, only a *probability* of a significant anticompetitive effect must be shown for most Clayton Act violations. Because the Clayton Act focuses on probable harms to competition, there are no criminal penalties for violating its provisions. Private plaintiffs, however, may sue for treble damages or injunctive relief if they are injured, or threatened with injury, by another party's violation of the statute. The Justice Department and the Federal Trade Commission (FTC) share responsibility for enforcing the Clayton Act. Each has the authority to seek injunctive relief to prevent or remedy violations of the statute. In addition, the FTC has the power to enforce the Clayton Act through cease and desist orders, which were discussed in Chapter 48.

Clayton Act Section 3

Section 3 of the Clayton Act makes it unlawful for any person engaged in interstate commerce to *lease or sell commodities,* or to *fix a price for commodities,* on the *condition, agreement, or understanding* that the lessee or buyer will not use or deal in the commodities of the lessor's or seller's competitors, if the effect of doing so *may be* to *substantially lessen competition* or *tend to create a monopoly* in any line of commerce. Section 3 primarily targets two potentially anticompetitive behaviors: **tying agreements** and **exclusive dealing agreements.** As you learned in Chapter 49, these types of contracts may amount to restraints of trade in violation of Sherman Act section 1. The language of section 3, however, contains limitations on the Clayton Act's application to such agreements.

A major limitation is that section 3 applies only to tying agreements and exclusive dealing contracts involving the leasing or sale of *commodities.* Any such agreements involving services, real estate, or intangibles must therefore be attacked under the Sherman Act. Although section 3 speaks of sales and leases on the "condition, agreement, or understanding" that the buyer or lessee not deal in the commodities of the seller's or lessor's competitors, no formal agreement is required. Whenever a seller or lessor uses its economic power to prevent its customers from dealing with its competitors, potential Clayton Act concerns are triggered.

Tying Agreements Many *tying agreements* plainly fall within at least the first portion of the section 3 language. Any agreement that requires a buyer to purchase one product (the *tied product*) from a seller as a condition of purchasing another product (the *tying product*) from the same seller necessarily prevents the buyer from purchasing the tied product from the seller's competitors.

Only tying agreements that may *"substantially lessen competition or tend to create a monopoly,"* however,

violate section 3. Several decades ago, the Supreme Court appeared to indicate that a tying agreement would violate the Clayton Act if the seller either had monopoly power over the tying product or restrained a substantial volume of commerce in the tied product. Most lower federal courts today, however, require essentially the same elements for a Clayton Act violation that they require for a Sherman Act violation: The challenged agreement must involve *two separate products; sale of the tying product must be conditioned* on an accompanying sale of the tied product; the seller must have *sufficient economic power in the market for the tying product* to appreciably restrain competition in the tied product market; and the seller's tying arrangements must restrain a *"not insubstantial" amount of commerce in the tied product market.* A few courts, however, continue to apply a less demanding standard for Clayton Act tying liability by dispensing with proof of the seller's economic power in the market for the tying product as long as the seller's tying arrangements involve a "not insubstantial" amount of commerce in the tied product. The defenses to tying liability under the Sherman Act (discussed in Chapter 49) are also applicable to tying claims brought under the Clayton Act.

Exclusive Dealing Agreements In the preceding chapter, we discussed the nature of *exclusive dealing agreements.* Such contracts clearly fall under the initial portion of the section 3 language because buyers who agree to handle one seller's product exclusively, or to purchase all of their requirements for a commodity from one seller, are also agreeing not to purchase similar items from the seller's competitors. However, not all exclusive dealing agreements are unlawful. Section 3 outlaws only those agreements that may "substantially lessen competition or tend to create a monopoly."

Exclusive dealing agreements initially were treated in much the same way as tying agreements. Courts looked at the dollar amount of commerce involved and declared illegal those agreements involving a "not insubstantial" amount of commerce. This *quantitative substantiality* test was employed by the Supreme Court in *Standard Oil Co. v. United States* (1949). Standard Oil was the largest refiner and supplier of gasoline in several western states, holding approximately 14 percent of the retail market. Roughly half of these sales were made by retail outlets owned by Standard. The remaining sales were made by independent dealers who had entered into exclusive dealing contracts with Standard. Standard's six major competitors had entered into similar contracts with their own independent dealers. The Court recognized that exclusive dealing contracts, unlike tying agreements, could benefit both buyers and sellers, but declared Standard's contracts unlawful on the ground that nearly $58 million in commerce was involved.

The *Standard Oil* decision prompted considerable criticism. In *Tampa Electric Co. v. Nashville Coal Co.* (1961), the Supreme Court applied a broader *qualitative substantiality* test to gauge the legality of a long-term requirements contract for the sale of coal to an electric utility. In *Tampa Electric,* the Court looked at the "area of effective competition," which was the total market for coal in the geographic region from which the utility could reasonably purchase its coal needs. The Court then examined the percentage of this region's coal sales accounted for by the challenged contract. Because that percentage share was less than 1 percent of the region's coal sales, the Court upheld the agreement even though it represented more than $100 million in coal sales.

Tampa Electric, however, is distinguishable from *Standard Oil,* which the Court has not overruled. Unlike *Standard Oil, Tampa Electric* involved parties with relatively equal bargaining power and an individual agreement, rather than an industrywide practice. In addition, there were obvious reasons why an electric utility such as Tampa Electric might want to lock in its coal costs by using a long-term requirements contract. Although lower court opinions employing each test may be found, the *qualitative* approach employed in *Tampa Electric* almost certainly is the one the current Court would employ.

Clayton Act Section 7

Introduction
Section 7 of the Clayton Act was designed to attack **mergers**—a term used broadly in this chapter to refer to the acquisition of one company by another. History indicates that one way monopolists acquired monopoly power was by acquiring control of their competitors. Section 7 prohibits any party engaged in commerce or in any activity affecting commerce from *acquiring the stock or assets* of another such party if the effect, in *any line of commerce* or *any activity affecting commerce* in any section of the country, *may be to substantially lessen competition* or *tend to create a monopoly.* Rather than adopting the Sherman Act approach of waiting until a would-be monopolist has acquired monopoly power or is dangerously close to doing so, section 7 attempts to "nip monopolies in the bud" by barring mergers that *may* have an anticompetitive effect.

Although section 7 is plainly an anticoncentration device, it has also been used (as the following text indicates) to attack mergers that have had no direct effect on concentration in a particular industry. Its future evolution, however, is uncertain, given the influence of Chicago School economic theories on contemporary antitrust law and the more tolerant stance those theories take toward mergers. During the 1980s, the Justice Department signaled a more permissive approach to merger activity than the government had previously adopted. Later, Justice Department and FTC officials undertook somewhat greater scrutiny of mergers in some industries, though clearly not on an across-the-board basis. As this book went to press in 2008, the federal government was again tending to allow considerable room for merger activity.

The Hart–Scott–Rodino Antitrust Improvement Act of 1976 requires that for planned mergers involving dollar values of stock or assets exceeding certain amounts, the parties to the merger agreement must provide advance notice to the FTC and the Justice Department. The purpose of this requirement is to provide the federal government a "heads-up" warning and to give regulators a reasonable opportunity to institute a legal challenge of the merger if a challenge seems warranted. Once the statutorily specified waiting period expires and the government has cleared the merger or at least has not taken legal action to block it, the merger may proceed. The normal waiting period is 30 days from the filing of the premerger notification form, though the waiting period is sometimes subject to extension. It should be remembered, however, that regardless of whether the government seeks to block a merger, private enforcement of section 7 is also possible.

Predictions regarding section 7's eventual judicial treatment are complicated considerably by the fact that many of the important merger cases in recent years have been settled out of court. This leaves interested observers of antitrust policy with few definitive expressions of the Supreme Court's current thinking on merger issues.

Relevant Market Determination
Regardless of the treatment section 7 ultimately receives in the courts, determining the **relevant market** affected by a merger is likely to remain a crucial component of any section 7 case. Before a court can determine whether a particular merger will have the *probable* anticompetitive effect required by the Clayton Act, it must first determine the *line of commerce* (or *relevant product market*) and the *section of the country* (or *relevant geographic market*) that are likely to be affected by the merger. The court's adoption of a broad relevant market definition will usually enhance the government's or private plaintiff's

difficulty in demonstrating the challenged merger's probable anticompetitive effect.

Relevant Product Market "Line of commerce" determinations under the Clayton Act have traditionally employed *functional interchangeability* tests similar to those employed in relevant product market determinations under the Sherman Act. Which products do the acquired and acquiring firms manufacture (assuming a merger between competitors), and which products are reasonably interchangeable by consumers to serve the same purposes? The federal government's merger guidelines indicate that the relevant market includes those products that consumers view as good substitutes at prevailing prices. The guidelines also state that the relevant market includes any products to which a significant percentage of current customers would shift in the event of a "small, but significant and non-transitory increase" in price of the merged firms' products. The *Olin* case, which follows, discusses the making of a relevant product market determination, as does the *Staples* case, which appears later in the chapter.

Olin Corporation v. Federal Trade Commission   986 F.2d 1295 (9th Cir. 1993)

Sanitizing agents are used to kill algae and bacteria in swimming pools. Pool owners may use any of three sanitizing agents. One is liquid pool bleach; the other two are chemicals sold in dry form. These dry sanitizers are isocyanurates (ISOS) and calcium hypochlorite (CAL/HYPO). The chemical cyanuric acid (CA) is a precursor in the manufacturing process of ISOS. When CAL/HYPO is used as a sanitizer, CA is used along with it as a stabilizer.

Olin Corporation was the market leader in CAL/HYPO production in the United States from 1980 through 1984, with a market share of 79 to 89 percent. Olin sought to increase its ability to produce and market ISOS. After technical problems doomed Olin's attempts to produce CA and ISOS during the late 1970s and early 1980s, Olin entered into a 1984 agreement with Monsanto Co. Under this agreement, Olin provided certain ISOS precursors to Monsanto, which then produced ISOS and provided them to Olin. Olin thus became a "repackager" of ISOS.

In 1985, Olin and FMC Corporation entered into an agreement under which Olin was to purchase FMC's swimming pool chemical business. The assets of that business included FMC's sanitizers manufacturing plant at South Charleston, West Virginia. The South Charleston plant produced both CA and ISOS. The Federal Trade Commission challenged the proposed acquisition on the theory that it would likely result in a substantial lessening of competition in the relevant markets, in violation of section 7 of the Clayton Act and section 5 of the FTC Act. To avoid a possible order that would have prohibited the acquisition, Olin agreed to maintain the acquired assets in such a way that divestiture would be possible if the FTC issued a final decision holding that the acquisition violated antitrust laws. In addition, Olin agreed to a graduated withdrawal from its agreement with Monsanto. Olin and FMC were therefore allowed to consummate their transaction, pending final review by the FTC.

After a hearing, the FTC administrative law judge (ALJ) concluded that the acquisition violated the Clayton and FTC Acts because it would likely result in a substantial lessening of competition in the relevant markets. The FTC commissioners (referred to below as "the Commission") upheld the ALJ's decision as well as the ALJ's proposed remedy of divestiture. The Commission therefore ordered Olin to divest itself of the South Charleston plant it had acquired from FMC. Olin petitioned the Ninth Circuit Court of Appeals for review of the Commission's decision and order.

Tang, Circuit Judge

Normally, "a delineation of proper geographic and product markets is a necessary precondition to assessment of the probabilities of a substantial effect on competition within them." *United States v. General Dynamics Corp.* (U.S. Sup. Ct. 1974). There is no dispute in this case that the [relevant] geographic market is the entire United States. The parties have further stipulated that one relevant United States product market consists solely of ISOS (the "ISOS-only" market). The Commission also identified over Olin's objection a second relevant United States product market, one comprised of both ISOS and CAL/HYPO (the "dry sanitizers" market). Olin contends that the finding of likely

anticompetitive effect is erroneous because it is premised on . . . a relevant dry sanitizers market [whose] existence is not supported by substantial evidence. In analyzing the post-acquisition dry sanitizers market [the existence of which Olin does not concede], the Commission concluded that Olin's production capacity would be 57 percent of a market in which the four-firm concentration ratio was 95 percent.

[In *California v. American Stores Co.* (9th Cir. 1989), we] described the process of product market definition as follows:

The outer boundaries of a product market are determined by the reasonable interchangeability of use or the cross-elasticity of demand between the product itself and substitutes for it" (quoting *Brown Shoe Co. v. United States* [U.S. Sup. Ct. 1962]). Where an increase in the price of one product leads to an increase in demand for another, both products should be included in the relevant product market.

In conducting its product market analysis for swimming pool sanitizers, the Commission discussed physical composition, usage, and technical characteristics of dry sanitizers. [T]he Commission observed that similarities in these categories "predominate over the minor [physical] differences between ISOS and CAL/HYPO. The following facts are particularly important: (1) both products are used to deliver chlorine to swimming pools; (2) each product is able to deliver chlorine with about the same efficiency—although a pool chlorinated with ISOS will remain chlorinated longer; (3) by virtue of both products' stability and other characteristics, "a pool owner can purchase a year's supply of either [product] in a single trip to the store"; and (4) both products are available to consumers in the same forms. In discussing these characteristics, the Commission apparently assumed that the relevant market is defined in terms of consumers who maintain their own pools. Although Olin challenged this assumption, we conclude there is substantial evidence in support of dealing with residential consumers as a distinct market.

Despite [the above] similarities, however, ISOS are perceived as more convenient than CAL/HYPO because, once applied, ISOS last longer than CAL/HYPO, and because CAL/HYPO requires use of a separate stabilizer (i.e., CA). Recognizing that the "convenience of [ISOS] is reflected in a price premium that [ISOS] maintain over [CAL/HYPO]," the Commission then analyzed whether this premium is sufficient to prevent inclusion of ISOS and CAL/HYPO in the same market. Ultimately, the Commission [applied a test set forth in the merger guidelines subscribed to by the Department of Justice and the FTC, and concluded that] "Olin could not profitably impose a small but significant and non-transitory increase in the price of [CAL/HYPO] because of the danger that consumers would then switch to [ISOS]." Given this indication of cross-elasticity of demand, the Commission concluded that ISOS and CAL/HYPO together compose a relevant product market (i.e., the dry sanitizers market).

Olin argues that it is inconsistent to recognize a larger, dry sanitizers market once a relevant ISOS-only market has been identified. However, relevant submarkets are common in merger analysis. Recognizing ISOS as a submarket of the dry sanitizers market is not inherently contradictory with recognizing a dry sanitizers market.

Olin charges that the Commission had no basis on which to conclude that any significant degree of elasticity existed between ISOS and CAL/HYPO. It is evident from its opinion that the Commission relied on a narrowing of the price gap between the two products in determining cross-elasticity. The opinion [stated that] "from 1977 to 1983, . . . the price of [CAL/HYPO] increased at a faster rate than that of [ISOS]." According to the opinion, this increase in the price of CAL/HYPO came about despite direct competition from Japanese CAL/HYPO, which was later the subject of an "antidumping" order. Olin argues that the narrowing of the price gap between CAL/HYPO and ISOS was artificial—and should not be used in determining cross-elasticity—because the Japanese were "dumping" ISOS on the American market. The Commission responds convincingly that, because CAL/HYPO was subject to the same pressures as the result of Japanese CAL/HYPO dumping, the narrowing in price was not artificial. Olin ignores this explanation and shifts its focus to the Commission concession that CAL/HYPO consumers would not switch to ISOS until the price of CAL/HYPO had risen at least 10 percent.

Olin . . . attempt[s] to emphasize the 5 percent factor normally used [by the Department of Justice and the FTC when they apply the merger guidelines' test that asks whether a "small but significant and nontransitory price increase" would cause consumers to switch to another product]. [However,] research has not disclosed a case that mandates [use of the 5 percent figure in] determining relevant product markets. Indeed, [the government's merger guidelines themselves acknowledge] that a higher percent increase in price is appropriate in determining the relevant product market in certain cases. Thus, a finding of cross-elasticity between ISOS and CAL/HYPO is not precluded by the fact that a higher price increase is necessary to induce a switch; a higher increase indicates only that the relationship between the two products is somewhat inelastic—but not necessarily so inelastic as to exclude the products from the same market, particularly under the substantial evidence standard of review.

[In making its cross-elasticity finding, the Commission also reasonably relied on] a statement Olin made to the International Trade Commission [in which Olin complained about Japanese "dumping" but appeared to acknowledge that CAL/HYPO faces competition from ISOS] and a statement made by an Olin competitor indicating a competitive relationship between CAL/HYPO and ISOS. [W]e find adequate support for the Commission's finding of cross-elasticity between ISOS and CAL/HYPO.

[The Ninth Circuit went on to hold that the divestiture remedy ordered by the Commission was an appropriate exercise of the Commission's discretion.]

Olin's petition for review denied; decision and order of Commission upheld.

Relevant Geographic Market To determine a particular merger's probable anticompetitive effect on a section of the country, courts have traditionally asked where the effects of the merger will be direct and immediate. This means that the relevant geographic market may not be as broad as the markets in which the acquiring and acquired firms actually operate or, in the case of a merger between competitors, the markets in which they actually compete. The focus of the relevant market inquiry is on those sections of the country in which competition is most likely to be injured by the merger. As a result, the relevant geographic market could be drawn as narrowly as one metropolitan area or as broadly as the entire nation. All that is necessary to satisfy this aspect of section 7 is proof that the challenged merger may have a significant negative effect on competition in any economically significant geographic market.

The federal government's merger guidelines adopt a somewhat different approach to determining the relevant geographic market. They define the relevant geographic market as the geographic area in which a sole supplier of the product in question could profitably raise its price without causing outside suppliers to begin selling in the area. The guidelines contemplate beginning with the existing markets in which the parties to a merger compete, and then adding the markets of those suppliers that would enter the market in response to a "small, but significant and non-transitory increase" in price.

Horizontal Mergers The analytical approach employed to gauge a merger's probable effect on competition varies according to the nature of the merger in question. **Horizontal mergers**—mergers among firms competing in the same product and geographic markets—have traditionally been subjected to the most rigorous scrutiny because they clearly lead to increased concentration in the relevant market.

Market Share of Resulting Firm To determine the legality of such a merger, courts look at the *market share of the resulting firm.* In *United States v. Philadelphia National Bank* (1963), the Supreme Court indicated that a horizontal merger producing a firm with an "undue percentage share" of the relevant market (33 percent in that case) and resulting in a "significant increase in concentration" of the firms in that market would be presumed illegal, absent convincing evidence that the merger would not have an anticompetitive effect.

In the past, mergers involving firms with smaller market shares than those involved in *Philadelphia National Bank* were also enjoined if other economic or historical

factors pointed toward a probable anticompetitive effect. Factors that courts have traditionally considered relevant include:

1. *A trend toward concentration in the relevant market.* Has the number of competing firms decreased over time?
2. *The competitive position of the merging firms.* Are the defendants dominant firms despite their relatively small market shares?
3. *A past history of acquisitions by the acquiring firm.* Are we dealing with a would-be empire builder?
4. *The nature of the acquired firm.* Is it an aggressive, innovative competitor despite its small market share?

Recent Assessments of Merger Effects Recent developments, however, indicate that the courts and federal antitrust enforcement agencies have become increasingly less willing to presume that anticompetitive effects will result from a merger that produces a firm with a relatively large market share. Instead, a more detailed inquiry is made into the nature of the relevant market and of the merging firms in order to ascertain the likelihood of probable harm to competition as a result of a challenged merger. The federal government's merger guidelines provide that when regulators assess a horizontal merger's probable effect, the focus is on the existing concentration in the relevant market, the increase in concentration as a result of the proposed merger, and other nonmarket share factors. The more concentrated the existing market and the greater the increase in concentration that would result from the proposed merger, the more likely the merger is to be challenged by the government.

The nonmarket share factors considered by federal regulators are more traditional. They include the existence (or absence) of barriers to the entry of new competitors into the relevant market; the prior conduct of the merging firms; and the probable future competitive strength of the acquired firm. The last factor is particularly important because courts have acknowledged that a firm's current market share may not reflect its ability to compete in the future. For example, courts have long recognized a "failing company" justification for some mergers. If the acquired firm is a failing company and no other purchasers are interested in acquiring it, its acquisition by a competitor may be lawful under section 7. Similarly, if an acquired firm has financial problems that reflect some underlying structural weakness, or if it lacks technologies that will be necessary if it is to compete effectively in the future, its current market share may overstate its future competitive importance.

Finally, given the increased weight being assigned to economic arguments in antitrust cases, two other merger justifications may be granted greater credence in the future. Some lower federal courts have recognized the notion that a merger between two small companies may be justifiable, despite the increase in concentration stemming from the merger, if the resulting firm is able to compete more effectively with larger competitors. In a similar vein, some commentators have argued that mergers resulting in cost savings or other enhanced economic efficiencies should sometimes be allowed even though they may have some anticompetitive impact. Though courts have not been very receptive to efficiency arguments in the past, the government's merger guidelines are flexible enough to allow the Justice Department and FTC to consider efficiency claims in deciding whether to challenge a merger.

The *Staples* case, which follows, illustrates a broad range of issues that arise in horizontal merger cases.

Federal Trade Commission v. Staples, Inc.   970 F. Supp. 1066 (D.D.C. 1997)

Office Depot, Inc., owned the nation's largest chain of retail outlets commonly known as "office supply superstores." Staples, Inc., owned the second-largest chain of this type. Each company operated more than 500 superstores, with Office Depot's outlets existing in 38 states and the District of Columbia and Staples' superstores appearing in 28 states and the District of Columbia. The only other office supply superstore firm in the United States was OfficeMax, Inc. In 1996, Staples and Office Depot entered into a merger agreement. As required by law, they filed a Premerger Notification and Report Form with the Federal Trade Commission (FTC) and the Department of Justice.

Following a lengthy investigation, the FTC initiated an adjudicative proceeding against Staples and Office Depot on the theory that the planned merger violated section 7 of the Clayton Act. (Adjudicative proceedings are discussed in Chapters 47 and 48.) In an effort to prevent the merger from taking place while its legality was being determined in the adjudicative proceeding, the FTC filed suit against Staples and Office Depot and requested a preliminary injunction against the merger. The federal district court conducted an extensive evidentiary hearing.

Hogan, District Judge

Section 7 of the Clayton Act makes it illegal for two companies to merge "where in any line of commerce or in any activity affecting commerce in any section of the country, the effect of such acquisition may be substantially to lessen competition, or to tend to create a monopoly." [The FTC Act provides that if] the Commission has reason to believe that a corporation is violating, or is about to violate, section 7 . . . , the FTC may seek a preliminary injunction to prevent a merger pending the Commission's adjudication of the merger's legality.

In order to determine whether the Commission has [made the required showing of] likelihood of success on the merits, . . . the court must consider the likely competitive effects of the merger. [This requires the court to determine the relevant product and geographic markets, as well as] the transaction's probable effect on competition in the product and geographic markets. [T]he parties . . . do not disagree . . . that [more than 40 different] metropolitan areas are the appropriate geographic markets for analyzing the competitive effects of the proposed merger. [However, the parties] sharply disagree with respect to the appropriate definition of the relevant product market. [T]o a great extent, this case hinges on the proper definition of the relevant product market.

The Commission defines the relevant product market as "the sale of consumable office supplies through office superstores," with "consumable" meaning products that consumers buy [on a recurring basis], i.e., items which "get used up" or discarded. [U]nder the Commission's definition, "consumable office supplies" would not include capital goods such as computers, fax machines, . . . or office furniture, but [would] include such products as paper, pens, file folders, post-it-notes, computer disks, and toner cartridges. The defendants . . . counter that the appropriate product market within which to assess the likely competitive consequences of a Staples–Office Depot combination is simply the overall sale of office products, of which a combined Staples–Office Depot accounted for 5.5% of total sales in North America in 1996.

The general rule when determining a relevant product market is that "the outer boundaries . . . are determined by the reasonable interchangeability of use [by consumers] or the cross-elasticity of demand between the product itself and substitutes for it." *Brown Shoe Co. v. United States* (U.S. Sup. Ct. 1962). This case . . . is an example of perfect interchangeability. The consumable office products at issue here are identical whether they are sold by Staples or Office Depot or another seller of office supplies [such as Wal-Mart or another retailer that is not an office supply superstore]. [A]s the government has argued, [however, the] functional interchangeability [of office supplies] should not end the court's analysis.

[In *United States v. E.I. Du Pont de Nemours and Co.* (U.S. Sup. Ct. 1956), the Court] did not stop after finding a high degree of functional interchangeability between cellophane and other wrapping materials. [T]he Court also found that "an element for consideration as to cross-elasticity of demand between products is the responsiveness of the sales of one product to price changes of the other." [T]he Court explained [that] "if a slight decrease in the price of cellophane causes a considerable number of customers of other flexible wrappings to switch to cellophane, it would be an indication that a high cross-elasticity of demand exists between [cellophane and other flexible wrappings, and] that the products compete in the same market." Following that reasoning . . . , the Commission has argued that a slight but significant increase in Staples–Office Depot's prices will not cause a considerable number of Staples–Office Depot's customers to purchase consumable office supplies from other non-superstore alternatives such as Wal-Mart [or] Best Buy. . . . On the other hand, the Commission has argued that an increase in price by Staples would result in consumers' turning to another office superstore, especially Office Depot, if the consumers had that option. Therefore, the Commission [contends] that the sale of consumable office supplies by office supply superstores is the . . . relevant product market in this case, and products sold by competitors such as Wal-Mart, Best Buy, . . . and others should be excluded.

The court acknowledges that there is . . . a broad market encompassing the sale of consumable office supplies by all sellers of such supplies, and that those sellers must, at some level, compete with one another. However, the mere fact that a firm may be termed a competitor in the overall marketplace does not necessarily require that it be included in the relevant product market for antitrust purposes. The Supreme Court . . . recognized [in *Brown Shoe*] that within a broad market, "well-defined submarkets may exist which, in themselves, constitute product markets for antitrust purposes." There is a possibility, therefore, that the sale of consumable office supplies by office superstores may qualify as a submarket within a large market of retailers of office supplies in general.

[T]he FTC presented evidence comparing Staples's prices in geographic markets where Staples is the only office superstore to markets where Staples competes with Office Depot or OfficeMax, or both. [I]n markets where Staples faces no office superstore competition . . . , something which was termed a one-firm market during the hearing, prices are 13 percent higher than in three-firm markets where it competes with both Office Depot and OfficeMax. Similarly, the evidence showed that Office Depot's prices are . . . well over 5 percent higher in Depot-only markets than they are in three-firm markets.

[The FTC's evidence] suggests that office superstore prices are affected primarily by other office superstores and not by non-superstore competitors such as . . . Wal-Mart, Kmart, or Target, wholesale clubs . . . , computer or electronic stores . . . , mail order firms . . . , and contract stationers. Though the FTC

did not present the court with evidence regarding the precise amount of non-superstore competition in each of Staples's and Office Depot's one-, two-, and three-firm markets, it is clear . . . that these competitors, albeit in different combinations and concentrations, are present in every one of these markets. For example, . . . the mail order competitors compete in all of the geographic markets at issue in this case. Despite this mail order competition, . . . Staples and Office Depot are still able to charge higher prices in their one-firm markets than they do in the two-firm markets and the three-firm markets without losing a significant number of customers to the mail order firms.

The same appears to be true with respect to Wal-Mart. [A Wal-Mart executive testified] that price-checking by Wal-Mart of Staples' prices in areas where both Staples and Wal-Mart exist showed that, on average, Staples's prices were higher than where there was a Staples and a Wal-Mart but no other superstore than where there was a Staples, a Wal-Mart, and another superstore. The evidence with respect to the wholesale club stores is consistent. There is also consistent evidence with respect to computer and/or consumer electronics stores. In addition, the] evidence shows that the defendants [lower their prices in a given geographic area] when faced with entry of another superstore [in that area], but do not do so for other retailers. There is no evidence that . . . prices fall when another non-superstore retailer enters a geographic market.

[The FTC made] a compelling showing that a small but significant increase in Staples's prices will not cause a significant number of consumers to turn to non-superstore alternatives for purchasing their consumable office supplies. Despite the high degree of functional interchangeability between consumable office supplies sold by the office superstores and other retailers of office supplies, the evidence . . . shows that even where Staples and Office Depot charge higher prices, certain consumers do not go elsewhere for their supplies.

[In addition,] both Staples and Office Depot focus primarily on competition from other superstores. [Staples's and Office Depot's own documents] show that the merging parties evaluate their "competition" as the other office superstore firms, without reference to other retailers, mail order firms, or independent stationers. When assessing key trends and making long-range plans, Staples and Office Depot focus on the plans of other superstores. [W]hen determining whether to enter a new metropolitan area, both Staples and Office Depot evaluate the extent of office superstore competition in the market and the number of office superstores the market can support. When selecting sites and markets for new store openings, the defendants repeatedly refer to markets without office superstores as "noncompetitive," even when the new store is adjacent to or near a warehouse club, consumer electronics store, or a mass-merchandiser such as Wal-Mart.

[T]he court finds that the sale of consumable office supplies through office supply superstores is the appropriate relevant product market for purposes of considering the possible anticompetitive effects of the proposed merger. [T]he court next must consider the probable effect of a merger between Staples and Office Depot in the geographic markets previously identified. [The evidence shows] that a merged Staples–Office Depot would have a dominant market share in 42 geographic markets across the country. The combined shares of Staples and Office Depot in the office superstore market would be 100 percent in 15 metropolitan areas. In 27 other metropolitan areas, where the number of office superstore competitors would drop from three to two, the post-merger market shares would range from 45 percent to 94 percent. [T]hough the Supreme Court has established that there is no fixed threshold at which an increase in market concentration triggers the antitrust laws, this is clearly not a borderline case.

[In addition to the] market concentration evidence, [there are other] indications that a merger between Staples and Office Depot may substantially lessen competition. Much of the evidence [concerning] the relevant product market also indicates that the merger would likely have an anticompetitive effect. The evidence of the defendant's current pricing practices, for example, shows that an office superstore chain facing no competition from other superstores has the ability to profitably raise prices for consumer office supplies above competitive levels. The evidence also shows that the defendants [lower their prices] when faced with entry of another office superstore [in a particular geographic area], but do not do so for other retailers. Since prices are significantly lower in markets where Staples and Office Depot compete, eliminating this competition with one another would free the parties to charge higher prices in those markets, especially those in which the combined entity would be the sole office superstore.

In addition, allowing the defendants to merge would eliminate . . . head-to-head competition between the two . . . lowest-priced firms in the superstore market. Thus, the merger would result in the elimination of a particularly aggressive competitor in a highly concentrated market, a factor which is certainly an important consideration when analyzing possible anticompetitive effects. It is based on all of this evidence that the court finds that the Commission has shown a likelihood of success on the merits and a reasonable probability that the proposed transaction will have an anticompetitive effect.

[T]he court finds it extremely unlikely that a new office superstore will enter the market and thereby avert the anticompetitive effects from Staples's acquisition of Office Depot. [Although the defendants also argued that] expansion [by] existing companies such as U.S. Office Products and Wal-Mart [would enhance competition in the sale of office supplies, the court]

finds it unlikely that expansion by U.S. Office Products and Wal-Mart would avert the anticompetitive effects which would result from the merger. The defendants' final argument with respect to entry was that existing retailers such as Sam's Club, Kmart, and Best Buy have the capability to reallocate their shelf space to include [greater quantities and varieties] of office supplies. While [such stores may] reallocate shelf space, there is no evidence that they will in fact do this if a combined Staples—Office Depot were to raise prices . . . following a merger. In fact, the evidence indicates that [they probably] would not.

[It is not clear] whether an efficiencies defense showing that the intended merger would create significant efficiencies in the relevant market, thereby offsetting any anticompetitive effects, may be used by a defendant to rebut the government's prima facie case. The newly revised efficiencies section of the [government's] Merger Guidelines recognizes that [some mergers may achieve efficiencies and that consideration of them may sometimes be relevant to a determination of whether an acquisition would substantially lessen competition]. [H]owever, in *FTC v. Procter & Gamble Co.* (U.S. Sup. Ct. 1967), [the Supreme Court] stated that "possible economies cannot be used as a defense to illegality in section 7 merger cases." There has been great disagreement regarding the meaning of this precedent and whether an efficiencies defense is permitted. Assuming that it is a viable defense, however, the court cannot find in this case that the defendants' efficiencies evidence rebuts the [FTC's showing] that the merger may substantially lessen competition.

The defendants submitted an "Efficiencies Analysis" which predicted that the combined company would achieve savings of between $4.9 and $6.5 billion over the next five years. In addition, the defendants argued that the merger would also generate dynamic efficiencies. For example, the defendants argued that as suppliers become more efficient due to their increased sales volume to the combined Staples–Office Depot, they would be able to lower prices to their other retailers. Moreover, the defendants argued that two-thirds of the savings realized by the combined company would be passed along to consumers.

[T]he court credits the testimony and report of the Commission's expert over the testimony and efficiencies study of the defendants' witness, [a] Senior Vice President of Integration at Staples. [The testimony of the Commission's expert] was compelling, and the court finds, based primarily on [that expert's] testimony, that the defendants' cost savings estimates are unreliable [and far in excess of estimates by the defendants in proxy statements and in presentations to the defendants' boards of directors]. [T]he court also finds that the defendants' projected pass-through rate—the amount of the projected savings that the combined company expects to pass on to customers in the form of lower prices—is unrealistic. Staples and Office Depot have a proven track record of achieving cost savings through efficiencies, and then passing those savings to customers in the form of lower prices. However, in this case the defendants have projected a pass-through rate of two-thirds of the savings while the evidence shows that, historically, Staples has passed through only 15–17 percent.

[T]he court cannot find that the defendants have rebutted [the FTC's showing] that the merger will subtantially lessen competition.

FTC's motion for preliminary injunction against merger granted.

Vertical Mergers

A **vertical merger** is a merger between firms that previously had, or could have had, a supplier–customer relationship. For example, a manufacturer may seek to vertically integrate its operations by acquiring a company that controls retail outlets at which the manufacturer's products could be sold. Alternatively, the manufacturer may vertically merge by acquiring a company that makes a product the manufacturer regularly uses in its production processes. Vertical mergers, unlike horizontal mergers, do not directly result in an increase in concentration. Nonetheless, they traditionally have been thought to threaten competition in various ways.

Foreclosing Competitors in Relevant Market

First, vertical mergers may *foreclose competitors* from a share of the relevant market. If a major customer for a product acquires a captive supplier of that product, the competitors of the acquired firm are foreclosed from competing with it for sales to the acquiring firm. Similarly, if a manufacturer acquires a captive retail outlet for its products, the manufacturer's competitors are foreclosed from competing for sales to that retail outlet. A vertical merger in the latter case may also result in reduced competition at the retail level. For instance, a shoe manufacturer acquires a retail shoe store chain that carries the brands of several competing manufacturers and has a dominant share of the retail market in certain geographic areas. If the retail chain carries only the acquiring manufacturer's brands after the merger occurs, competition among the acquiring manufacturer and its competitors is reduced in the retail market for shoes.

Creation of Increased Market Entry Barriers

A second way in which vertical mergers threaten competition is that they may lead to *increased barriers to market entry* for new competitors. For example, if a major purchaser of a product acquires a captive supplier of it, the merger-related contraction of the market for the product may discourage potential producers of it from commencing production.

Elimination of Potential Competition in Acquired Firm's Market

Some vertical mergers threaten competition by *eliminating potential competition* in one of two ways. First, an acquiring firm may be perceived by existing competitors in the acquired firm's market as a likely potential entrant into that market. The threat of such a potential entrant "waiting in the wings" may moderate the behavior of existing competitors because they fear that pursuing pricing policies that exploit their current market position might cause the potential entrant to react by entering the market. The acquiring firm's entry into the market by the acquisition of an existing competitor means the end of its moderating influence as a potential entrant. Second, a vertical merger may deprive the market of the potential benefits that would have resulted if the acquiring firm had entered the market in a more competitive manner, such as by creating its own entrant into the market through internal expansion or by making a toehold acquisition of a small existing competitor and then building it into a more significant competitor.

Historically, courts seeking to determine the legality of vertical mergers have tended to look at the *share of the relevant market foreclosed to competition.* If a more than insignificant market share is foreclosed to competition, courts consider other economic and historical factors. Factors viewed as aggravating the anticompetitive potential of a vertical merger include a trend toward concentration or vertical integration in the industry; a past history of vertical integration in the industry; a past history of vertical acquisitions by the acquiring company; and significant barriers to entry resulting from the merger. This approach to determining the legality of vertical mergers has been criticized by some commentators. They argue that vertical integration may yield efficiencies of distribution and that vertical integration by merger may be more economically efficient than vertical integration by internal expansion. The Justice Department generally affords greater weight to efficiency arguments in cases involving vertical mergers than in cases involving horizontal mergers. The department generally applies the same criteria to all nonhorizontal mergers.

We discuss these criteria in the upcoming section on conglomerate mergers.

Conglomerate Mergers

A **conglomerate merger** is a merger between two firms that neither compete with each other nor have a supplier–customer relationship with each other. Conglomerate mergers may be either *market extension* mergers or *product extension* mergers. In a market extension merger, the acquiring firm expands into a new geographic market by purchasing a firm already doing business in that market. For example, a conglomerate that owns an East Coast grocery chain buys a West Coast grocery chain. In a product extension merger, the acquiring firm diversifies its operations by purchasing a company in a new product market. For example, a conglomerate with interests in the aerospace and electronics industries purchases a department store chain.

There is considerable disagreement over the economic effects of conglomerate acquisitions. As later discussion will reveal, conglomerate mergers have been attacked with some degree of success under section 7 if they involve **potential reciprocity,** serve to **eliminate potential competition,** or give an acquired firm an **unfair advantage** over its competitors. Nevertheless, there is significant sentiment that the Clayton Act is not well suited to dealing with conglomerate mergers. This realization has produced calls for specific legislation on the subject. Such legislation has not been enacted, however.

Potential Reciprocity Conglomerate mergers that involve *potential reciprocity* are among those sometimes held to be prohibited by section 7. A conglomerate merger may create a risk of potential reciprocity if the acquired firm produces a product regularly purchased by the acquiring firm's suppliers. Such suppliers, eager to continue their relationship with the acquiring firm, may thereafter purchase the acquired firm's products rather than those of its competitors.

Elimination of Potential Competition Some conglomerate mergers may *eliminate potential competition* in ways similar to vertical mergers, and thus may be vulnerable to attack under section 7. If existing competitors perceive the acquiring company as a potential entrant in the acquired company's market, the acquiring company's entry by means of a conglomerate acquisition may result in the loss of the moderating influence that it had while waiting in the wings. In addition, when the acquiring company actually enters the new market by acquiring a well-established competitor rather than by starting a new competitor through internal expansion or by making a toehold acquisition, the market is deprived of the potential for increased competition flowing from the reduction in concentration that would have accompanied the latter strategies.

Supreme Court decisions suggest, however, that a high degree of proof is required before either of these potential competition arguments will be accepted. Arguments that a conglomerate merger eliminated a *perceived potential entrant* must be accompanied by proof that existing competitors actually perceived the acquiring firm as a potential entrant. Arguments that a conglomerate acquisition eliminated an *actual* potential entrant (and thereby deprived the market of the benefits of reduced concentration) must be accompanied by evidence that the acquiring firm had the ability to enter the market by internal expansion or a toehold acquisition and that doing so would have ultimately yielded a substantial reduction in concentration.

Unfair Advantage to Acquired Firm Finally, conglomerate mergers may violate section 7 in certain instances when the acquired firm obtains an *unfair advantage* over its competitors. When a large firm acquires a firm that already enjoys a significant market position, the acquired firm may gain an unfair advantage over its competitors through its ability to draw on the greater resources and expertise of its new owner. This advantage may entrench the acquired firm in its market by deterring existing competitors from actively competing with it for market share and by causing other potential competitors to be reluctant to enter the market.

Nearly all of the important conglomerate merger cases in recent years have been settled out of court. As a result, we do not have a clear indication of the Supreme Court's current thinking on conglomerate merger issues. The Justice Department takes the position that the primary theories to be used by the department in attacking all *nonhorizontal* mergers are the *elimination of perceived and actual potential competition* theories. In

The Global Business Environment

A planned merger involving firms whose business is international in scope may face scrutiny outside the United States even if the FTC and the Justice Department decide not to challenge the merger under U.S. law. Legal regimes for controlling mergers now exist in numerous nations, with applicable rules and enforcement approaches that do not always match those of the United States. Several years ago, for instance, legal objections lodged by the European Commission caused a highly publicized conglomerate merger-to-be involving the General Electric and Honeywell firms not to come about despite U.S. regulators' clearance of the deal.

The European Union's Merger Regulation, promulgated in furtherance of competition provisions in the Treaty of Rome, bars mergers that may "create or strengthen a [firm's] dominant position." As it has been applied, the Merger Regulation may focus somewhat more on protecting *competitors* than on preserving the *competitive process*. In this sense, the EU approach differs from the approach called for by the U.S.

rule—the Clayton Act provision prohibiting mergers that may "substantially lessen competition." The U.S. approach is also likely to allow greater ability to argue that a merger may produce economic efficiencies than does the EU's Merger Regulation.

In addition, the respective enforcement mechanisms in the U.S. and the EU differ. Under U.S. law, the FTC or the Justice Department normally must take legal action in court in order to block a planned merger, whereas in the EU, the commission has considerable authority to quash a merger through its own action.

Notwithstanding the differences noted above, U.S. regulators and the European Commission fairly often reach the same conclusions regarding proposed mergers—especially those of the horizontal variety. Recent years have witnessed the development of agreements under which the EU Commission, the FTC, and the Justice Department have committed to sharing information and strategies regarding the regulation of mergers.

---

employing these analytical tools, the department also considers other economic factors. These include the degree of concentration in the acquired firm's market; the existence of barriers to entry into the market and the presence or absence of other firms with a comparable ability to enter; and the market share of the acquired firm (with challenges being unlikely if this is 5 percent or less and likely if it is 20 percent or more). It remains to be seen whether the Supreme Court will accept this more restrictive view of the scope of section 7.

Clayton Act Section 8

If the same individuals control theoretically competing corporations, an obvious potential exists for anticompetitive conduct such as price-fixing or division of markets. Section 8 of the Clayton Act was designed to minimize the risks posed by such interlocks. Initially, section 8 prohibited any person from serving as a *director* of two or more corporations (other than banks or common carriers) if each corporation had "capital, surplus, and undivided profits aggregating more than $1,000,000" and the corporations were, or had been, competitors, "so that elimination of competition by agreement between them" would violate any of the antitrust laws. The Antitrust Amendments Act of 1990 amended section 8's original language to increase the amount required to trigger the statute from $1 million to $10 million (a figure to be

adjusted annually by an amount equal to the percentage increase or decrease in the gross national product).

Section 8 establishes a per se standard of liability in the sense that a violation may be demonstrated without proof that the interlock harmed competition. Until 1990, however, the statute's prohibition against interlocks was limited in scope because it barred only interlocking *directorates*. Nothing in the original language of section 8 prohibited a person from serving as an *officer* of two competing corporations, or as an officer of one firm and a director of its competitor. The Antitrust Amendments Act of 1990, however, expanded the scope of the statute by including senior "*officers*" (defined as officers elected or chosen by the board of directors) within its reach.

Although government enforcement of section 8 was historically lax, the past three decades have sometimes offered signs of growing government interest in the statute. Signs of renewed government interest in section 8 produced significant concern in an era of conglomerate merger activity. Given the wide diversification that characterizes many large corporations, it would be increasingly easy to demonstrate some degree of competitive overlap among a substantial number of large, diversified corporations. Critics alleged that section 8 has operated to discourage qualified persons from serving as directors when no potential for actual competitive harm exists. In response to such criticism, the Antitrust

Amendments Act of 1990 specified that individuals may serve as officers or directors of competing corporations when the "competitive overlap" between them is an insignificant part of either company's total sales. This exception took away some of section 8's potential bite.

The Robinson–Patman Act

Section 2 of the Clayton Act originally prohibited *local and territorial price discrimination* by sellers, a practice monopolists frequently used to destroy smaller competitors. A large company operating in a number of geographic markets would sell at or below cost in markets where it faced local competitors, and would then make up its losses by selling at higher prices in areas where it faced no competition. Faced with such tactics, the smaller local competitors might eventually be driven out of business. Section 2 was aimed at such **primary level** (or *first line*) price discrimination.

During the 1930s, Congress was confronted with complaints that large chain stores were using their buying power to induce manufacturers to sell to them at prices lower than those offered to their smaller, independent competitors. Chain stores were also inclined to seek and obtain other payments and services their smaller competitors did not receive. Being able to purchase at lower prices and to obtain discriminatory payments and services arguably gave large firms a competitive advantage over their smaller competitors. Such price discrimination in sales to the competing customers of a particular seller is known as **secondary level** (or *second line*) price discrimination. The *Volvo Trucks* decision, which appears later in the chapter, addresses issues that arise in secondary level price discrimination cases.

In addition, the customers of a manufacturer's favored customer (such as a wholesaler receiving a functional discount) may gain a competitive advantage over *their* competitors (for example, other retailers purchasing directly from the manufacturer at a higher price) if the favored customer passes on all or a portion of its discount to its customers. This form of price discrimination is known as **tertiary level** (or *third line*) price discrimination.

Congress responded to these problems by passing the Robinson–Patman Act in 1936. The Robinson–Patman Act preserved Clayton Act section 2's ban on primary level price discrimination. It also amended section 2 to outlaw secondary and tertiary level direct price discrimination, as well as indirect price discrimination in the form of discriminatory payments and services to a seller's customers. Since its enactment, the Robinson–Patman Act has been the subject of widespread dissatisfaction and

criticism. Critics have long charged that the act often protects competitors at the expense of promoting competition. Government enforcement of the act has been haphazard over the years, with prominent officials in the Justice Department and the Federal Trade Commission sometimes voicing disagreement with the act's underlying policies and assumptions. This government stance, when combined with Supreme Court decisions making private enforcement of the act difficult, raises questions about the act's future usefulness as a component of our antitrust laws.

Jurisdiction   The Robinson–Patman Act applies only to discriminatory acts that occur "in commerce." This test is narrower than the "affecting commerce" test employed under the Sherman Act. At least one of the discriminatory acts complained of must take place in interstate commerce. Thus, the act probably would not apply if a Texas manufacturer discriminated in price in sales to two Texas customers. Some lower federal courts have indicated, however, that even wholly intrastate sales may be deemed sufficiently "in commerce" if the nonfavored buyer bought the goods for resale to out-of-state customers.

Section 2(a)   Section 2(a) of the Robinson–Patman Act prohibits sellers, in certain instances, from *discriminating in price* "between different purchasers of commodities of like grade or quality." Such discrimination is prohibited when its effect may be to (1) "substantially . . . lessen competition or tend to create a monopoly in any line of commerce," or (2) "injure, destroy, or prevent competition with any person who either grants [*primary level*] or knowingly receives [*secondary level*] the benefit of such discrimination, or with the customers of either of them [*tertiary level*]."

Price Discrimination   To violate section 2(a), a seller must have made two or more sales to different purchasers at different prices. Merely quoting a discriminatory price or refusing to sell except at a discriminatory price does not violate the statute, because no actual purchase is involved. For the same reason, price discrimination in lease or consignment transactions is not covered by section 2(a). Actual sales at different prices to different purchasers will not be treated as discriminatory unless the sales were fairly close in time.

Section 2(a) does not directly address the legality of *functional discounts*. Such discounts are sometimes granted to buyers at various levels in a product's chain of distribution because of differences in the functions those buyers perform in the distribution system. The Supreme Court has indicated that the legality of such discounts depends on their competitive effect. If a seller charges wholesale customers lower prices than it charges retail customers, the Robinson–Patman Act is not violated unless the lower wholesale prices are somehow passed on to retailers in competition with the seller's retail customers.

Commodities of Like Grade and Quality Section 2(a) applies only to price discrimination in the sale of *commodities*. Price discrimination involving intangibles, real estate, or services must be challenged under the Sherman Act as a restraint of trade or an attempt to monopolize or under the FTC Act as an unfair method of competition. The essence of price discrimination is that two or more buyers are charged differing prices for the *same* commodity. Sales of commodities of varying grades or quality at varying prices, therefore, do not violate section 2(a) so long as uniform prices are charged for commodities of equal quality. Some *physical difference,* in the grade or quality of two products must be shown to justify a price differential between them. Differences solely in the brand name or label under which a product is sold—such as the seller's standard brand and a "house" brand sold to a large customer for resale under the customer's label—do not justify discriminatory pricing.

Anticompetitive Effect Only price discrimination having a *probable* anticompetitive effect is prohibited by section 2(a). Traditionally, courts have required a higher degree of proof of likely competitive injury in cases involving primary level price discrimination (which may damage the seller's competitors) than in cases involving secondary or tertiary level discrimination (which threatens competition among the seller's customers or its customers' customers). To prove a primary level violation, a market analysis must show that competitive harm has occurred as a result of the seller's engaging in significant and sustained price discrimination with the intent of punishing or disciplining a competitor. Proof of predatory pricing is often offered as evidence of a seller's anticompetitive intent. The *Brooke Group* case, which follows shortly, addresses predatory pricing claims under the Robinson–Patman Act and emphasizes that likely harm to competition—not merely to a competitor—remains the critical focus.

In secondary or tertiary level cases, courts tend to infer the existence of competitive injury from evidence of substantial price discrimination between competing purchasers over time. Some qualifications on this point are in order, however. Price discrimination for a short period of time ordinarily does not support an inference of competitive injury. Likewise, if the evidence indicates that nonfavored buyers could have purchased the same goods from other sellers at prices identical to those the defendant seller charged its favored customers, no competitive injury is inferred. Finally, buyers seeking treble damages for secondary or tertiary level harm must still prove that they suffered actual damages as a result of a violation of the act.

The *Volvo Trucks* decision, which appears immediately after the *Brooke Group* case, examines key issues presented in secondary level cases.

Brooke Group Ltd. v. Brown & Williamson Tobacco Corp.
509 U.S. 209 (U.S. Sup. Ct. 1993)

Brown & Williamson Tobacco Corp. (BW) and Brooke Group Ltd. (referred to here by its former corporate name, Liggett Corp.) are two of only six firms of significant consequence in the oligopolistic cigarette manufacturing industry. In 1980, BW's share of the national cigarette market was roughly 12 percent. This share placed BW a distant third behind market leaders Philip Morris and R. J. Reynolds. Liggett's share was less than half of BW's. Liggett pioneered the development of the economy segment of the national cigarette market in 1980 by introducing a popular line of "black and white" generic cigarettes (low-priced cigarettes sold in plain white packages with simple black lettering). As Liggett's sales of generic cigarettes became substantial, other cigarette manufacturers started introducing economy-priced cigarettes. In 1984, BW introduced a black and white cigarette whose net price was lower than Liggett's. BW achieved this lower price by offering volume rebates to wholesalers.

Liggett sued BW, claiming that BW's volume rebates amounted to price discrimination having a reasonable probability of injuring competition, in violation of section 2(a) of the Robinson–Patman Act. Specifically, Liggett alleged that BW's rebates were integral to a scheme of predatory pricing, under which BW reduced its net prices for generic cigarettes below average variable costs. Liggett further alleged that this pricing by BW was designed to pressure Liggett to raise its list prices on generic cigarettes, so that the percentage price difference between generic and branded cigarettes would narrow. As a result, according to Liggett, the growth of the economy segment would be restrained and BW would thereby be able to preserve its supracompetitive profits on branded cigarettes. Liggett further asserted that it could not afford to reduce its wholesale rebates without losing market share to BW. Therefore, Liggett claimed that its only choice, if it wished to avoid prolonged losses on the generic line that had become its principal product, was to raise retail prices.

After a 115-day trial, the jury returned a verdict in Liggett's favor for $49.6 million in damages. The district court trebled this amount. After reviewing the trial record, however, the district court concluded that BW was entitled to prevail as a matter of law. The court therefore set aside the jury's verdict and entered judgment in BW's favor. Liggett appealed. The Fourth Circuit Court of Appeals affirmed, holding that there cannot be liability for predatory price discrimination that allegedly takes place in the context of an oligopoly such as the cigarette industry. The Supreme Court granted certiorari.

Kennedy, Justice

Liggett contends that BW's discriminatory volume rebates to wholesalers threatened substantial competitive injury by furthering a predatory pricing scheme designed to purge competition from the economy segment of the cigarette market. This type of injury, which harms direct competitors of the discriminating seller, is known as primary-line injury. [P]rimary-line competitive injury under the Robinson–Patman Act is of the same general character as the injury inflicted by predatory pricing schemes actionable under section 2 of the Sherman Act. [T]he essence of the claim under either statute is the same.

Accordingly, whether the claim alleges predatory pricing under the Sherman Act or primary-line price discrimination under the Robinson–Patman Act, two prerequisites to recovery [exist]. First, a plaintiff seeking to establish competitive injury resulting from a rival's low prices must prove that the prices complained of are below an appropriate measure of its rival's costs. [Second, the plaintiff must demonstrate] that the competitor had a reasonable prospect [if the claim is brought under the Robinson–Patman Act], or . . . a dangerous probability [if the claim is brought under section 2 of the Sherman Act], of recouping its investment in below-cost prices. Recoupment is the ultimate object of an unlawful predatory-pricing scheme; it is the means by which a predator profits from predation. Without it, predatory pricing produces lower aggregate prices in the market, and consumer welfare is enhanced. That below-cost pricing may impose painful losses on its target is of no moment to the antitrust laws if competition is not injured.

For recoupment to occur, below-cost pricing must be capable . . . of producing the intended effects on the firm's rivals, whether driving them from the market, or, as was alleged to be the goal here, causing them to raise their prices to supracompetitive levels within a disciplined oligopoly. If circumstances indicate that below-cost pricing could likely produce its intended effect on the target, there is still the further question whether it would be likely to injure competition in the relevant market. The plaintiff must demonstrate that there is a likelihood that the predatory scheme alleged would cause a rise in prices above a competitive level that would be sufficient to compensate for the amounts expended on the predation. These prerequisites to recovery are not easy to establish, but . . . they are essential components of real market injury.

Liggett . . . allege[s] . . . that BW sought to preserve supracompetitive profits on branded cigarettes by pressuring Liggett to raise its generic cigarette prices through a process of tacit collusion with the other cigarette companies. Tacit collusion, sometimes called oligopolistic price coordination or conscious parallelism, describes the process, not in itself unlawful, by which firms in a concentrated market might in effect share monopoly power, setting their prices at a profit-maximizing, supracompetitive level by recognizing their shared economic interests and their interdependence with respect to price and output decisions.

In *Matsushita Electric Industrial Co. v. Zenith Radio Corp.* (U.S. Sup. Ct. 1986), we remarked upon the general implausibility of predatory pricing. *Matsushita* observed that such schemes are even more improbable when they require coordinated action among several firms. However unlikely predatory pricing by multiple firms may be when they conspire, it is even less likely when, as here, there is no express coordination. Firms that seek to recoup predatory losses through the conscious parallelism of oligopoly must rely on uncertain and ambiguous signals to achieve concerted action. The signals are subject to misinterpretation and are a blunt and imprecise means of ensuring smooth cooperation, especially in the context of changing or unprecedented market circumstances. This anticompetitive minuet is most difficult to compose and to perform, even for a disciplined oligopoly.

[O]n the whole, tacit cooperation among oligopolists must be considered the least likely means of recouping predatory losses. In addition to the difficulty of achieving effective tacit coordination and the high likelihood that any attempt to discipline will produce an outbreak of competition, the predator's present losses in a case like this fall on it alone, while the later supracompetitive profits must be shared with every other oligopolist in proportion to its market share, including the intended victim. In this case, for example, BW, with its 11–12 percent share of the cigarette market, would have had to generate around $9 in supracompetitive profits for each $1 invested in predation; the remaining $8 would belong to its competitors, who had taken no risk.

[However,] [t]o the extent that the Court of Appeals may have held that the interdependent pricing of an oligopoly may never provide a means for achieving recoupment and so may not form the basis of a primary-line injury claim, we disagree. A predatory pricing scheme designed to preserve or create a stable oligopoly, if successful, can injure consumers in the same way, and to the same extent, as one designed to bring about a monopoly. However unlikely that possibility may be as a general matter, when the realities of the market and the record facts indicate that it has occurred and was likely to have succeeded, theory will not stand in the way of liability. The Robinson–Patman Act . . . suggests no exclusion from coverage when primary-line injury occurs in an oligopoly setting. We decline to create a per se rule of nonliability [under the Robinson–Patman Act] for predatory price discrimination when recoupment is alleged to take place through supracompetitive oligopoly pricing.

Although Liggett's theory of liability, as an abstract matter, is within the reach of the statute, we agree with the [lower courts] that Liggett was not entitled to submit its case to the jury. Liggett . . . failed to demonstrate competitive injury as a matter of law. The evidence is inadequate to show that in pursuing [an alleged below-cost pricing] scheme, BW had a reasonable prospect of recovering its losses from below-cost pricing through slowing the growth of generics.

The only means by which BW is alleged to have established oligopoly pricing . . . is through tacit price coordination with the other cigarette firms. Yet the situation facing the cigarette companies in the 1980s would have made such tacit coordination unmanageable. Tacit coordination is facilitated by a stable market environment, fungible products, and a small number of variables upon which the firms seeking to coordinate their pricing may focus. By 1984, however, the cigarette market was in an obvious state of flux. The introduction of generic cigarettes in 1980 represented the first serious price competition in the cigarette market since the 1930s. This development was bound to unsettle previous expectations and patterns of market conduct and to reduce the cigarette firms' ability to predict each other's behavior. The larger number of product types and pricing variables also decreased the probability of effective parallel pricing.

Even if all the cigarette companies were willing to participate in a scheme to restrain the growth of the generic segment, they would not have been able to coordinate their actions and raise prices above a competitive level unless they understood that BW's entry into the [economy] segment was not a genuine effort to compete with Liggett. If even one other firm misinterpreted BW's entry as an effort to expand share, a chain reaction of competitive responses would almost certainly have resulted, and oligopoly discipline would have broken down, perhaps irretrievably. Liggett argues that [BW's] maintaining existing list prices while offering substantial rebates to wholesalers was a signal to the other cigarette firms that BW did not intend to attract additional smokers to the generic segment by its entry. But a reasonable jury could not conclude that this pricing structure eliminated or rendered insignificant the risk that the other firms might misunderstand BW's entry as a competitive move.

We hold that the evidence cannot support a finding that BW's alleged scheme was likely to result in oligopolistic price coordination and sustained supracompetitive pricing in the generic segment of the national cigarette market. Without this, BW had no reasonable prospect of recouping its predatory losses and could not inflict the injury to competition the antitrust laws prohibit.

Judgment for BW affirmed.

Volvo Trucks North America, Inc. v. Reeder-Simco GMC, Inc.
546 U.S. 164 (U.S. Sup. Ct. 2006)

Volvo Trucks North America, Inc. (Volvo), manufactures heavy-duty trucks. Reeder-Simco GMC, Inc. (Reeder), which became an authorized dealer of Volvo trucks in 1995, generally sold Volvo trucks through a competitive bidding process. In this process, the retail customer describes its specific product requirements and invites bids from several dealers. Once a Volvo dealer receives the customer's specifications, the dealer turns to Volvo and requests a discount or "concession" off the wholesale price (set at 80 percent of the published retail price). Volvo decides on a case-by-case basis whether to offer a discount and, if so, what the discount rate will be. The dealer then uses the discount offered by Volvo in preparing its bid, and purchases trucks from Volvo only if the retail customer accepts its bid.

Reeder was one of many Volvo dealers, each assigned by Volvo to a geographic territory. Although nothing prohibits a Volvo dealer from bidding outside its territory, Reeder seldom bid against another Volvo dealer. In the atypical event that the same retail customer solicited a bid from more than one Volvo dealer, Volvo's stated policy was to provide the same price concession to each dealer competing head-to-head for the same sale. After learning that Volvo had given another dealer a price concession greater than the concessions Reeder typically received, Reeder sued Volvo. Reeder claimed that Volvo violated the Robinson–Patman Act by providing other dealers more favorable price concessions than those offered to Reeder and, in the process, adversely affecting Reeder's sales and profits.

At trial, Reeder presented evidence concerning two instances when Reeder bid against another Volvo dealer for a particular sale. In one instance, each Volvo dealer received the same concession from Volvo, and neither Volvo dealer's bid was accepted by the retail customer. The other instance involved Hiland Dairy, which solicited bids from both Reeder and Southwest Missouri Truck Center (also a Volvo dealer). In accordance with its policy, Volvo initially offered the two dealers the same concession. Hiland selected Southwest Missouri, a dealer from which Hiland had previously purchased trucks. After a later price squabble between Southwest Missouri and Hiland, Volvo increased the size of the discount it had offered Southwest Missouri, in order to help make certain that the Southwest Missouri–Hiland deal would actually be accomplished.

For the most part, Reeder's evidence at trial focused on comparisons between concessions Volvo offered when Reeder bid against non-Volvo dealers and concessions accorded to other Volvo dealers similarly bidding against non-Volvo dealers for other sales. Reeder's evidence compared concessions Reeder received on four occasions when it bid successfully against non-Volvo dealers—meaning that Reeder therefore purchased Volvo trucks—with more favorable concessions than other successful Volvo dealers received in connection with bidding processes in which Reeder did not participate. In addition, Reeder identified concessions offered by Volvo on several occasions when Reeder bid unsuccessfully against non-Volvo dealers, and compared those concessions with more favorable concessions received by other Volvo dealers that gained contracts on which Reeder did not bid.

A federal district court jury found that there was a reasonable possibility that discriminatory pricing harmed competition between Reeder and other Volvo truck dealers, and that Volvo's discriminatory pricing injured Reeder to the extent of $1.3 million. The district judge tripled that amount in accordance with federal antitrust law and entered judgment accordingly. Volvo appealed, and the U.S. Court of Appeals for the Eighth Circuit affirmed. Rejecting Volvo's contention that competitive bidding situations do not give rise to claims under the Robinson–Patman Act, the Court of Appeals observed that Reeder was "more than an unsuccessful bidder." The instances in which Reeder "actually purchased Volvo trucks following successful bids on contracts," the court concluded, were sufficient to render Reeder a purchaser within the meaning of the statute. The Court of Appeals also determined that a jury could reasonably decide that Reeder was "in actual competition" with favored dealers, and that the jury could properly find from the evidence that Reeder had proven competitive injury resulting from price discrimination. The U.S. Supreme Court granted Volvo's petition for a writ of certiorari.

Ginsburg, Justice

We granted certiorari to resolve this question: May a manufacturer be held liable for secondary-line price discrimination under the Robinson–Patman Act in the absence of a showing that the manufacturer discriminated between dealers competing to resell its product to the same retail customer? Satisfied that the Court of Appeals erred in answering that question in the affirmative, we reverse the Eighth Circuit's judgment.

The Robinson–Patman Act, 15 U.S.C. § 13(a), provides, in relevant part:

It shall be unlawful for any person engaged in commerce . . . to discriminate in price between different purchasers of commodities of like grade and quality, . . . where the effect of such discrimination may be substantially to lessen competition or tend to create a monopoly in any line of commerce, or to injure, destroy, or prevent competition with any person who either grants or knowingly receives the benefit of such discrimination, or with customers of either of them . . . .

Mindful of the purposes of the Robinson–Patman Act and of the antitrust laws generally, we have explained that Robinson–Patman does not "ban all price differences charged to different purchasers of commodities of like grade and quality." *Brooke Group Ltd. v. Brown & Williamson Tobacco Corp.*, 509 U.S. 209, 220 (1993). Rather, the Act proscribes "price discrimination only to the extent that it threatens to injure competition." *Id.* Our decisions describe three categories of competitive injury that may give rise to a Robinson–Patman Act claim: primary line, secondary line, and tertiary line. Primary-line cases entail conduct—most conspicuously, predatory pricing—that injures competition at the level of the discriminating seller and its direct competitors. Secondary-line cases, of which this is one, involve price discrimination that injures competition among the discriminating seller's customers (here, Volvo's dealerships); cases in this category typically refer to "favored" and "disfavored" purchasers. Tertiary-line cases involve injury to competition at the level of the purchaser's customers.

To establish the secondary-line injury of which it complains, Reeder had to show that (1) the relevant Volvo truck sales were made in interstate commerce; (2) the trucks were of "like grade and quality"; (3) Volvo "discriminate[d] in price between" Reeder and another purchaser of Volvo trucks; and (4) "the effect of such discrimination may be . . . to injure, destroy, or prevent competition" to the advantage of a favored purchaser, i.e., one who "receive[d] the benefit of such discrimination." 15 U.S.C. § 13(a). It is undisputed that Reeder has satisfied the first and second requirements. Volvo maintains that Reeder cannot satisfy the third and fourth requirements, because Reeder has not identified any differentially priced transaction in which it was both a "purchaser" under the Act and "in actual competition" with a favored purchaser for the same customer.

A hallmark of the requisite competitive injury, our decisions indicate, is the diversion of sales or profits from a disfavored purchaser to a favored purchaser. We have also recognized that a permissible inference of competitive injury may arise from evidence that a favored competitor received a significant price reduction over a substantial period of time. Absent actual competition with a favored Volvo dealer, however, Reeder cannot establish the competitive injury required under the Act.

The evidence Reeder offered at trial falls into three categories: (1) comparisons of concessions Reeder received for four successful bids against non-Volvo dealers, with larger concessions other successful Volvo dealers received for different sales on which Reeder did not bid (purchase-to-purchase comparisons); (2) comparisons of concessions offered to Reeder in connection with several unsuccessful bids against non-Volvo dealers, with greater concessions accorded other Volvo dealers who competed successfully for different sales on which Reeder did not bid (offer-to-purchase comparisons); and (3) evidence of two occasions on which Reeder bid against another Volvo dealer (head-to-head comparisons). The Court of Appeals concluded that Reeder demonstrated competitive injury under the Act because Reeder competed with favored purchasers "at the same functional level . . . and within the same geographic market." As we see it, however, selective comparisons of the kind Reeder presented do not show the injury to competition targeted by the Robinson–Patman Act.

Both the purchase-to-purchase and the offer-to-purchase comparisons fall short, for in none of the discrete instances on which Reeder relied did Reeder compete with beneficiaries of the alleged discrimination for the same customer. Nor did Reeder even attempt to show that the compared dealers were consistently favored vis-à-vis Reeder. Reeder simply paired occasions on which it competed with non-Volvo dealers for a sale to Customer A with instances in which other Volvo dealers competed with non-Volvo dealers for a sale to Customer B. The compared incidents were tied to no systematic study and were separated in time by as many as seven months.

We decline to permit an inference of competitive injury from evidence of such a mix-and-match, manipulable quality. No similar risk of manipulation occurs in cases kin to the chainstore paradigm. Here, there is no discrete "favored" dealer comparable to a chainstore or a large independent department store—at least, Reeder's evidence is insufficient to support an inference of such a dealer or set of dealers. For all we know, Reeder, on occasion, might have gotten a better deal vis-à-vis one or more of the dealers in its comparisons.

Reeder may have competed with other Volvo dealers for the opportunity to bid on potential sales in a broad geographic area. At that initial stage, however, competition is not affected by differential pricing. A dealer in the competitive bidding process here at issue approaches Volvo for a price concession only after it has been selected by a retail customer to submit a bid. Competition for an opportunity to bid . . . is based on a variety of factors, including the existence of a relationship between the potential bidder and the customer, geography, and reputation. That Volvo dealers may bid for sales in the same geographic area does not import that they in fact competed for the same customer-tailored sales. In sum, the purchase-to-purchase and offer-to-purchase comparisons fail to show that Volvo sold at a lower price to Reeder's "competitors," hence those comparisons do not support an inference of competitive injury.

Reeder did offer evidence of two instances in which it competed head to head with another Volvo dealer. When multiple dealers bid for the business of the same customer, only one dealer will win the business and thereafter purchase the supplier's product to fulfill its contractual commitment. Because Robinson-Patman prohibits only discrimination between different purchasers, Volvo argues, the Act does not reach markets characterized by competitive bidding and special-order sales, as opposed to sales from inventory. We need not decide that question today. Assuming the Act applies to the head-to-head transactions, Reeder did not establish that it was disfavored vis-à-vis other Volvo dealers in the rare instances in which they competed for the same sale—let alone that the alleged discrimination was substantial.

Reeder's evidence showed loss of only one sale to another Volvo dealer, a sale of 12 trucks that would have generated $30,000 in gross profits for Reeder. Per its policy, Volvo initially offered Reeder and the other dealer the same concession. Volvo ultimately granted a larger concession to the other dealer, but only after it had won the bid. In the only other instance of head-to-head competition Reeder identified, Volvo increased Reeder's initial 17% discount to 18.9%, to match the discount offered to the other competing Volvo dealer; neither dealer won the bid. In short, if price discrimination between two purchasers existed at all, it was not of such magnitude as to affect substantially competition between Reeder and the "favored" Volvo dealer.

Interbrand competition, our opinions affirm, is the "primary concern of antitrust law." [Case citation omitted.] The Robinson–Patman Act signals no large departure from that main concern. Even if the Act's text could be construed in the manner urged by Reeder and embraced by the Court of Appeals, we would resist interpretation geared more to the protection of existing competitors than to the stimulation of competition. In the case before us, there is no evidence that any favored purchaser possesses market power, the allegedly favored purchasers are dealers with little resemblance to large independent department stores or chain operations, and the supplier's selective price discounting fosters competition among suppliers of different brands. By declining to extend Robinson–Patman's governance to such cases, we continue to construe the Act "consistently with broader policies of the antitrust laws." *Brooke Group,* at 220.

Court of Appeals decision reversed, and case remanded for further proceedings.

Defenses to Section 2(a) Liability
There are three major statutory defenses to liability under section 2(a): *cost justification, changing conditions,* and *meeting competition in good faith.*

Cost Justification
Section 2(a) legalizes price differentials that do no more than make an appropriate allowance for differences in the "cost of manufacture, sale, or delivery resulting from the differing methods or quantities" in which goods are sold or delivered to buyers. This defense recognizes the reality that it may be less costly for a seller to service some buyers than others. Sales to buyers purchasing large quantities may in some cases be more cost-effective than small-quantity sales to their competitors. Sellers are allowed to pass on such cost savings to their customers.

Utilizing this *cost justification* defense is difficult and expensive for sellers, however, because quantity discounts must be supported by *actual evidence of cost savings.* Sellers are allowed to average their costs and classify their customers into categories based on their average sales costs. The customers included in any particular classification, however, must be sufficiently similar to justify similar treatment.

Changing Conditions
Section 2(a) specifically exempts price discriminations that reflect "changing conditions in the market for or the marketability of the goods." The *changing conditions* defense has been narrowly confined to temporary situations caused by the physical nature of the goods. Examples include the deterioration of perishable goods and a declining market for seasonal goods. This defense also applies to forced judicial sales of the goods (such as during bankruptcy proceedings involving the seller) and to good faith sales by sellers that have decided to cease selling the goods in question.

Meeting Competition
Section 2(b) of the Robinson–Patman Act states that price discrimination may be lawful if the discriminatory lower price was charged "in good faith to meet an equally low price of a competitor." This *meeting competition* defense is necessary to prevent the act from stifling the very competition it was designed to preserve. For example, suppose Sony Corporation has been selling a particular model of DVD player to its customers for $100 per unit. Sony then learns that Sharp Electronics is offering a comparable DVD player to Acme Appliance Stores for $80 per unit. Acme, however, competes with Better Buy Video Stores, a Sony customer that has recently been charged the $100 price. Should Sony be forced to refrain from offering the lower competitive price to Acme for fear that Better Buy will charge Sony with price discrimination if it does so? If Sony cannot offer the lower competitive price to Acme, competition between Sony and Sharp will plainly suffer.

Section 2(b) avoids this undesirable result by allowing a seller to charge a lower price to certain customers if the seller has reasonable grounds for believing that the lower price is necessary to meet an equally low price offered by a competitor. Sellers may meet competition *offensively* (to gain a new customer) or *defensively* (to keep an existing customer). The meeting competition defense is subject to significant qualifications, however. First, the lower price must be necessary to meet a lower price charged by a competitor of the *seller,* not to enable a customer of the seller to compete more effectively with that customer's competitors. Second, the seller may lawfully seek only to *meet,* not *beat,* its competitor's price. A seller cannot, however, be held in violation of the act for beating a competitor's price if it did so unknowingly in a good faith attempt to meet competition. Third, the seller may reduce its price only to meet competitors' prices for products of *similar quality.*

Courts also have held that the discriminatory price must be a response to an individual competitive situation rather than the product of a seller's wholesale adoption of a competitor's discriminatory pricing system. However, a seller's competitive response need not be on a customer-by-customer basis, so long as the lower price is offered only to those customers that the seller reasonably believes are being offered a lower price by the seller's competitors.

Indirect Price Discrimination

When Congress enacted the Robinson–Patman Act, it also addressed **indirect price discrimination,** which takes the form of a seller's discriminating among competing buyers by making discriminatory payments to selected buyers or by furnishing certain buyers with services not made available to their competitors. Three sections of the act are designed to prevent such practices.

False Brokerage Section 2(c) prohibits sellers from granting, and buyers from receiving, any "commission, brokerage, or other compensation, or any allowance or discount in lieu thereof, except for services rendered in connection with the sale or purchase of goods." This provision prevents large buyers, either directly or through subsidiary brokerage agents, from receiving phony commissions or brokerage payments from their suppliers.

Section 2(c) establishes a per se standard of liability. No demonstration of probable anticompetitive effect is required for a violation. Neither the cost justification nor meeting competition defense is available in 2(c) cases. Individual plaintiffs still must prove that they have suffered some injury as a result of a 2(c) violation, however, before they are entitled to recover damages.

Discriminatory Payments and Services Sellers and their customers benefit from merchandising activities that customers employ to promote the sellers' products. Section 2(d) prohibits sellers from making *discriminatory payments* to competing customers for such customer-performed services as advertising and promotional activities or such customer-provided facilities as shelf space. Section 2(e) prohibits sellers from discriminating in the *services* they provide to competing customers, such as by providing favored customers with a display case or a demonstration kit.

A seller may lawfully make payments or provide services to customers only if the payments or services are made available to all competing customers on *proportionately equal terms.* This means that the seller must inform all customers of the availability of the payments or services and must distribute them on some rational basis, such as the quantity of goods bought by the customer. The seller must also devise a flexible plan that enables its various classes of customers to participate in the payment or services program in an appropriate way.

As does section 2(c), sections 2(d) and 2(e) create a per se liability standard. No proof of probable harm to competition is required for a violation; no cost justification defense is available. The meeting competition defense is applicable, however, to actions under sections 2(d) and 2(e).

Buyer Inducement of Discrimination

Section 2(f) of the Robinson–Patman Act makes it illegal for a buyer *knowingly to induce or receive* a discriminatory price in violation of section 2(a). The logic of the section is that buyers who are successful in demanding discriminatory prices should face liability along with the sellers charging discriminatory prices. To violate section 2(f), the buyer must know that the price the buyer received was unjustifiably discriminatory. This means that the price probably was neither cost-justified nor made in response to changing conditions. Section 2(f) does not apply to buyer inducements of discriminatory payments or services prohibited by sections 2(d) and 2(e). Such buyer actions may, however, be attacked as unfair methods of competition under section 5 of the FTC Act.

In *Great Atlantic and Pacific Tea Co. v. FTC* (1979), the Supreme Court further narrowed the effective reach of section 2(f) by holding that buyers who knowingly received a discriminatory price did not violate the act if their seller had a valid defense to the charge of violating section 2(a). The seller in *Great Atlantic* had a "meeting competition in good faith" defense. This fact was held to insulate the buyer from liability even though the buyer knew that the seller had beaten, rather than merely met, its competitor's price.

Antitrust Exceptions and Exemptions

Many economic activities occur outside the potential reach of the antitrust laws. This is so either because these activities have been specifically exempted by statute or because courts have carved out nonstatutory exceptions designed to balance our antitrust policy in favor of competition against other social policies.

Statutory Exemptions

Labor Unions and Certain Union Activities The Clayton Act and the Norris–LaGuardia Act of 1932 provide that *labor unions* are not combinations or conspiracies in restraint of trade and exempt certain union activities, including boycotts and secondary picketing, from antitrust scrutiny. This statutory exemption does not, however, exempt union combinations with nonlabor groups aimed at restraining trade or creating a monopoly. An example of such nonexempted activity would be a labor union's agreement with Employer A to call a strike at Employer B's plants. In an attempt to accommodate the strong public policy in favor of collective bargaining, courts have also created a limited nonstatutory exemption for legitimate union–employer agreements arising from the collective bargaining context.

Agricultural Cooperatives and Certain Cooperative Actions The Clayton Act and the Capper–Volstead Act exempt the formation and collective marketing activities of *agricultural cooperatives* from antitrust liability. Courts have narrowly construed this exemption, however. Cooperatives including members not engaged in the production of agricultural commodities have been denied exempt status. One such example would be a cooperative including retailers or wholesalers who do not also produce the commodity in question. The agricultural cooperatives exemption extends only to legitimate collective marketing activities. It does not legitimize coercive or predatory practices that are unnecessary to accomplish lawful cooperative goals. For example, this exemption would not prevent the antitrust laws from being applied to a boycott designed to force nonmembers of the cooperative to adopt a pricing policy established by the cooperative.

Joint Export Activities The Webb–Pomerene Act exempts the *joint export activities* of American companies, so long as those activities do not "artificially or intentionally enhance or depress prices within the United States." The purpose of the act is to encourage export activity by allowing the formation of combinations to enable domestic firms to compete more effectively with foreign cartels. Some critics assert that this exemption is no longer needed because there are fewer foreign cartels today and American firms often play a dominant role in foreign trade. Others question whether any group of American firms enjoying significant domestic market shares in the sale of a particular product could agree on an international marketing strategy, such as the amounts that they will export, without indirectly affecting domestic supplies and prices.

Business of Insurance The McCarran–Ferguson Act exempts from federal antitrust scrutiny those aspects of the *business of insurance* that are subject to state regulation. The act provides, however, that state law cannot legitimize any agreement to boycott, coerce, or intimidate others. Because the insurance industry is extensively regulated by the states, many practices in the industry are outside the reach of the federal antitrust laws.

In recent years, however, courts have tended to decrease the scope of this exemption by narrowly construing the meaning of "business of insurance." For example, in *Union Labor Life Insurance Co. v. Pireno* (1982), the Supreme Court held that the exemption did not insulate from antitrust scrutiny a peer review system in which an insurance company used a committee established by a state chiropractic association to review the reasonableness of particular chiropractors' charges. The Court stated that to qualify for the business of insurance exemption, a challenged practice must have the effect of transferring or spreading policyholders' risk and must be an integral part of the policy relationship between the insured and the insurer. Therefore, only practices related to traditional functions of the insurance business, such as underwriting and risk-spreading, are likely to be exempt.

Other Regulated Industries Many other *regulated industries* enjoy various degrees of antitrust immunity. The airline, banking, utility, railroad, shipping, and securities industries traditionally have been regulated in the public interest. The regulatory agencies supervising such industries have frequently been given the power to approve industry practices such as rate-setting and mergers that would otherwise violate antitrust laws. In recent years, there has been a distinct tendency to deregulate many regulated industries. If this trend continues, a greater portion of the economic activity in these industries could be subjected to antitrust scrutiny.

State Action Exemption In *Parker v. Brown* (1943), the Supreme Court held that a California state agency's regulation of the production and price of raisins was a state action exempt from the federal antitrust laws. The **state action exemption** developed in *Parker v. Brown* recognizes states' rights to regulate economic activity in the interest of their citizens. It also, however, may tempt business entities to seek "friendly" state regulation as a way of shielding anticompetitive activity from antitrust supervision. Recognizing this possibility, courts have placed important limitations on the scope of the state action exemption.

First, the exemption extends only to governmental actions by a state or to actions compelled by a state acting in its sovereign capacity. Second, various decisions indicate that challenged activity cannot qualify for immunity under this exemption unless the activity is affirmatively expressed as state policy and actively supervised by the state. In other words, the price of antitrust immunity is real regulation by the state. The Supreme Court placed a further limitation on the state action exemption by holding that it does not automatically confer immunity on the actions of municipalities. Municipal conduct is immune only if it was authorized by the state legislature and its anticompetitive effects were a foreseeable result of the authorization. The Court's decision caused concern that the threat of treble damage liability might inhibit legitimate regulatory action by municipal authorities. As a result, Congress passed the Local Government Antitrust Act of 1984. This statute eliminates damage actions against municipalities and their officers, agents, and employees for antitrust violations and makes injunctive relief the sole remedy in such cases.

The *Armstrong* case, which appears below, discusses the state action exemption and another key exemption, the *Noerr–Pennington* doctrine.

The Noerr–Pennington Doctrine

In the *Noerr* and *Pennington* cases, the Supreme Court held that "the Sherman Act does not prohibit two or more persons from associating together in an attempt to persuade the legislature or the executive to take particular action with respect to a law that would produce a restraint or a monopoly."[1] This exemption recognizes that the right to petition government provided by the Bill of Rights takes precedence over the antitrust policy favoring competition. In a later case, the Court made the *Noerr–Pennington* exemption applicable to a party's filing of a lawsuit. The exemption does not, however, extend to sham activities that are attempts to interfere with the business activities of competitors rather than legitimate attempts to influence governmental action. The *Armstrong* case, which follows, discusses the *Noerr–Pennington* doctrine and the relationship it may sometimes have to the state action exemption.

[1]*Eastern R. R. President's Conference v. Noerr Motor Freight, Inc.* (U.S. Sup. Ct. 1961): *United Mine Workers v. Pennington* (U.S. Sup. Ct. 1965).

Armstrong Surgical Center, Inc. v. Armstrong County Memorial Hospital
185 F.3d 154 (3d Cir. 1999)

Armstrong Surgical Center, Inc. (the "Surgical Center"), wished to establish an ambulatory surgery center in Armstrong County, Pennsylvania. At the time, Armstrong County Memorial Hospital (the "Hospital") was the only facility with operating rooms in Armstrong County. The Hospital's 19 staff physicians performed the vast majority of surgeries in the county. The Surgical Center's proposed facility, if it had been constructed, would have provided a variety of outpatient surgical services and would have competed with the Hospital.

Pennsylvania law provides that any party wishing to establish a new health care facility must first obtain a Certificate of Need ("CON") from Pennsylvania's Department of Health. The department reviews CON applications in an extensive proceeding consisting of an investigation, an evaluation of submitted materials, and a public hearing. Interested parties, including health care providers that supply similar services in the area, may submit information to the department regarding any CON application.

The Surgical Center filed an application for a CON. According to the Surgical Center, the Hospital and its staff physicians then conspired to subvert establishment of the new facility. The alleged conspiracy involved an announcement by the physicians that they would not use the facility, as well as the submission of false and misleading information by the Hospital and the staff physicians to the Department of Health. The false and misleading information, according to the Surgical Center, was to the effect that the Hospital intended to open its own outpatient center. Although construction had begun on such a center, the Hospital had stopped construction at a very early stage. The Surgical Center contended that even though the Hospital had made no commitment to resume construction, the Hospital and the staff physicians falsely represented to the department that the Hospital's center was either in use or very near completion.

The Department of Health denied the Surgical Center's CON application. The Surgical Center appealed to the Pennsylvania State Health Facility Hearing Board, which conducted its own hearing and received additional evidence. The board affirmed the department's denial of the CON after finding that (1) the Surgical Center's proposed facility would result in needless duplication of existing facilities and services; and (2) the Surgical Center would not be economically viable because the Hospital's staff physicians, who performed more than 90 percent of the surgeries in Armstrong County, would not use the Surgical Center's facility. The Surgical Center appealed to a Pennsylvania court, which affirmed the board's decision.

The Surgical Center then filed an antitrust action against the Hospital and its staff physicians (the "Hospital Defendants"). According to the Surgical Center's complaint, the Hospital Defendants' conspiracy to prevent the Surgical Center from establishing its surgery center restrained and monopolized trade, in violation of sections 1 and 2 of the Sherman Act. The federal district court dismissed the complaint after concluding that the Hospital Defendants' alleged conduct was immune from antitrust scrutiny. The Surgical Center appealed to the U.S. Court of Appeals for the Third Circuit.

Stapleton, Circuit Judge

The Hospital Defendants do not deny that [the Surgical Center's] complaint alleges a threat of a boycott that might under other circumstances constitute an antitrust violation. [T]hey contend, [however,] that their activities are insulated from antitrust scrutiny because their allegedly wrongful conduct occurred in the context of supplying information to the Pennsylvania Department of Health during the Surgical Center's CON application process and because the injuries alleged resulted solely from the Department's denial of the CON.

In *Parker v. Brown* (U.S. Sup. Ct. 1943), an agricultural producer challenged a marketing program adopted by California's Director of Agriculture as invalid under the Sherman Act. The program served to restrict competition among growers and maintain prices in commodity distribution. "Relying on principles of federalism and state sovereignty, [the Supreme Court] held [in *Parker*] that the Sherman Act did not apply to anticompetitive restraints imposed by the States 'as an act of government.'" *City of Columbia v. Omni Outdoor Advertising, Inc.* (U.S. Sup. Ct. 1991) (quoting *Parker*).

In *Eastern R. R. Presidents Conference v. Noerr Motor Freight, Inc.* (U.S. Sup. Ct. 1961) and *United Mine Workers v. Pennington* (U.S. Sup. Ct. 1965), the Supreme Court held that antitrust liability cannot be predicated solely on petitioning to secure government action even where those efforts are intended to eliminate competition. As the Court . . . observed [in *Omni*], "*Parker* and *Noerr* are complementary expressions of the principle that the antitrust laws regulate business, not politics; the former decision protects the States' acts of governing, and the latter the citizens' participation in government."

As the Surgical Center emphasizes, however, the immunity afforded to a private party under *Noerr* is not unlimited. Where the challenged private conduct is only "sham" petitioning—where it "is not genuinely aimed at procuring favorable government action as opposed to a valid effort to influence government action"—the *Noerr* immunity is not available. *Professional Real Estate Investors, Inc. v. Columbia Pictures,*

Inc. (U.S. Sup. Ct. 1993). In essence, sham petitioning entails, [as noted in *Professional Real Estate Investors*], "the use of the governmental process—as opposed to the outcome of that process—as an anticompetitive weapon." Accordingly, the sham petitioning exception does not apply in a case like the one before us, where the plaintiff has not alleged that the petitioning conduct was for any purpose other than obtaining favorable government action. [In this case,] the plaintiff affirmatively alleges that [the Hospital Defendants'] purpose was to secure the outcome of the process—denial of the CON. Thus, . . . the sham exception to *Noerr* immunity [is] inapplicable here.

It is also true that a private party can be held liable even for bona fide petitioning conduct where that conduct has caused direct antitrust injury in the marketplace. *FTC v. Superior Court Trial Lawyers Association* (U.S. Sup. Ct. 1990). In *Trial Lawyers,* for example, the public defenders of the District of Columbia engaged in a concerted refusal to represent indigent defendants in order to pressure the District into raising the hourly rate paid. The Court held that the defendants could be held liable under the Sherman Act for injuries that resulted directly from the boycott, even though the boycott was intended to secure government action. The limitation on *Noerr* immunity recognized in *Trial Lawyers* is inapplicable, however, to a case where the sole antitrust injury is caused directly by the government action that the private defendant has helped to secure. Thus, even where the same petitioning conduct might give rise to antitrust liability for injury directly caused to a competitor in the marketplace, if relief is sought solely for injury as to which the state would enjoy immunity under *Parker,* the private petitioner also enjoys immunity.

Here, looking to the source of the complained-of injuries, we find that all of the Surgical Center's alleged injuries arise solely from the denial of the CON: the denial of the ability to operate the proposed facility; the losses of the CON's value, the value of the facility, and the value of the operation's proceeds; the delay in securing the CON; and other related losses.

[W]here, as here, all of the plaintiff's alleged injuries result from state action, antitrust liability cannot be imposed on a private party who induced the state action by means of concerted anticompetitive activity. It follows that the complaint fails to state a boycott claim upon which relief can be granted.

The Surgical Center's second claim is that the Hospital Defendants, as part of their conspiracy, misled the Department [and] the Board . . . into believing that the Hospital's partially constructed facility would soon open and meet the needs of the relevant market, when the Hospital Defendants knew that the facility would not be completed. The Surgical Center would have us deny antitrust immunity to the Hospital Defendants on the [ground] that they successfully opposed the issuance of a CON using information known to be false.

Although the Supreme Court suggested in *California Motor Transport Co. v. Trucking Unlimited* (U.S. Sup. Ct. 1972) that petitioning activity involving knowingly false information submitted to an adjudicative tribunal might not enjoy antitrust immunity, the Court has never so held. Moreover, since *California Motor,* the Supreme Court decided [*City of Columbia v. Omni Outdoor Advertising, Inc.* (U.S. Sup Ct. 1991), which] casts doubt on whether such an exception exists under any circumstances and dictates that . . . we honor the Hospital Defendants' claim to immunity.

In *Omni,* [a relative newcomer to the outdoor sign business alleged that a competitor and a city council] conspired to restrain competition [through the adoption of] a zoning ordinance limiting the size, spacing, and location of billboards in the city. The Supreme Court . . . concluded that [the plaintiff's] alleged injury was the result of state action, [that *Parker* immunity would therefore protect the city against liability, and that the existence of a conspiracy between city officials and a private firm did not strip the city of its immunity]. It then observed that if "conspiracy" was taken to mean "nothing more than an agreement to impose the regulation in question," the purpose of *Parker* immunity would be defeated because "it is both inevitable and desirable that public officials often agree to do what one or another group of private citizens urges upon them."

The [*Omni*] Court next considered whether *Parker* immunity is lost when it is shown that an agreement between the defendants involved governmental corruption, bribery, or other violations of state or federal law. It held that *Parker* immunity remains in such circumstances. The Court found "impractical" the contention that *Parker* immunity is forfeited by governmental corruption. Such a rule would call upon antitrust courts to speculate as to whether state action purportedly taken in the public interest was the product of an honest judgment or desire for private gain. The Court stressed that *Parker* "was not meant to shift [judgments about the public interest] from elected officials to judges and juries." With respect to the contention that *Parker* immunity should be forfeited at least where bribery or other illegal activity may have subverted the state decision making process, the Court observed that this approach had "the virtue of practicality but the vice of being unrelated to" the purposes of the Sherman Act and *Parker.* [It noted that existing statutes] other than the Sherman Act [may be utilized] to discourage such behavior.

Turning to [whether the private firm that conspired with the city council could be held liable], the *Omni* Court addressed whether *Noerr*'s immunity for private parties was subject to any of the exceptions that had been urged in the context of *Parker* immunity. It declined to restrict *Noerr* immunity in this way for the same reason it had declined to so restrict *Parker* immunity. [In so concluding, the Court noted that] "[i]n *Noerr* . . . , where the private party 'deliberately deceived the public and public officials' in its successful lobbying campaign, we said that 'deception, reprehensible as it is, can be of no consequence so far as the Sherman Act is concerned.' "

The teachings of *Omni* are pertinent here. Considerations of federalism require an interpretation of the Sherman Act that forecloses liability predicated on anticompetitive injuries that are inflicted by states acting as regulators. Liability for injuries caused by such state action is precluded even where it is alleged that a private party urging the action did so by bribery, deceit, or other wrongful conduct that may have affected the decision making process. The remedy for such conduct rests with laws addressed to it and not with courts looking behind sovereign state action at the behest of antitrust plaintiffs. Federalism requires this result both with respect to state actors and with respect to private parties who have urged the state action.

On the facts alleged in the complaint, it is . . . clear that the state decision makers were disinterested, conducted their own investigation, and afforded all interested parties an opportunity to set the record straight. The initial decision was then twice reviewed. Finally, anyone who believed that a fraud was committed on the Department or Board could have moved to reopen the proceeding and attempted to persuade them that they were materially misled.

In these circumstances, *Omni* compels us to affirm the district court. Indeed, such a result seems to follow, a fortiori, from *Omni* given the conceded presence here of disinterested decision makers, an independent investigation, an open process, and extensive opportunities for error correction. The risk that the plaintiff's injury is not the result of a bona fide execution of state policy is far less substantial here than in *Omni* and there is, accordingly, far less justification for federal court review of the state's policy judgment.

District court's dismissal of complaint affirmed.

Ethics in Action

In the *Armstrong* case, which appeared earlier in this chapter, the court concluded that even if the defendants made false statements to state authorities, certain exemptions would protect them against antitrust liabil-ity. Assuming that the defendants made the false statements, how would deontologists view their behavior? How would utilitarians view their behavior? What about profit maximizers? (Refer to the discussion in Chapter 4, if necessary.)

Patent Licensing There is a basic tension between the antitrust objective of promoting competition and the purpose of the patent law, which, as noted in Chapter 8, seeks to promote innovation by granting a limited monopoly to those who develop new products or processes. In the early case of *United States v. General Electric Company* (1926), the Supreme Court allowed General Electric to control the price at which other manufacturers sold light bulbs they had manufactured under patent licensing agreements with General Electric. The Court recognized that an important part of holding a patent was the right to license others to manufacture the patented item. This right effectively would be negated if licensees were allowed to undercut the prices that patent holders charged for their own sales of patented products.

Patent holders cannot, however, lawfully control the price at which patented items are resold by distributors purchasing them from the patent holder. Nor can patent holders use their patents to impose tying agreements on their customers by conditioning the sale of patented items on the purchase of unpatented items, unless such agreements are otherwise lawful under the Sherman and Clayton Acts. Finally, firms that seek to monopolize by acquiring most or all of the patents related to an area of commerce may face liability for violating Sherman Act section 2 or Clayton Act section 7, because a patent has been held to be an asset within the meaning of section 7.

Foreign Commerce When foreign governments are involved in commercial activities affecting the domestic or international commerce of the United States, our antitrust policy may be at odds with our foreign policy. Congress and the courts have created a variety of antitrust exemptions aimed at reconciling this potential conflict. The Foreign Sovereign Immunities Act (FSIA) provides that the governmental actions of foreign sovereigns and their agents are exempt from antitrust liability. The commercial activities of foreign sovereigns, however, are not included within this **sovereign immunity** exemption. Significant international controversy exists concerning the proper criteria for determining whether a particular governmental act is commercial in nature. Under the FSIA, the courts employ a *nature of the act* test, holding that a commercial activity is one that an individual might customarily carry on for a profit.

The **act of state doctrine** provides that an American court cannot adjudicate a politically sensitive dispute whose resolution would require the court to judge the legality of a foreign government's sovereign act. This doctrine reflects judicial deference to the primary role of the executive and legislative branches in the adoption and execution of our foreign policy. The act of state doctrine recognizes (as does the doctrine of sovereign immunity) the importance of respecting the sovereignty of other nations. Unlike the doctrine of sovereign immunity, however, the act of state doctrine also reflects a fundamental attribute of our system of government: the principle of separation of powers.

Finally, the **sovereign compulsion doctrine** provides private parties a defense if they have been compelled by a foreign sovereign to commit, within that sovereign's territory, acts that would otherwise violate the antitrust laws because of their negative impact on our international commerce. To employ this defense successfully, a defendant must show that the challenged actions were the product of actual compulsion—as opposed to mere encouragement or approval—by a foreign sovereign.

Problems and Problem Cases

1. Mercedes-Benz of North America (MBNA), the exclusive U.S. distributor of Mercedes-Benz (Mercedes) automobiles, was a wholly owned subsidiary of Daimler-Benz Aktiengesellschaft (DBAG), the manufacturer of Mercedes automobiles. MBNA required its approximately 400 franchised Mercedes dealers to agree not to sell or use (in the repair or servicing of Mercedes automobiles) any parts other

than genuine Mercedes parts. Mozart, a wholesale automotive parts distributor, filed an antitrust suit against MBNA. Mozart alleged, among other things, that MBNA had violated section 1 of the Sherman Act and section 3 of the Clayton Act by tying the sale of Mercedes parts to the sale of Mercedes automobiles. The trial court ruled in favor of MBNA. Was the trial court's ruling correct?

2. Waste Management, Inc. (WMI), a company in the solid waste disposal business, acquired the stock of EMW Ventures, Inc. EMW was a diversified holding company, one of whose subsidiaries was Waste Resources. WMI and Waste Resources each had subsidiaries operating in or near Dallas, Texas. The government challenged the merger on the theory that it violated section 7 of the Clayton Act. The trial court agreed. In finding a section 7 violation, the trial court defined the relevant market as including all forms of trash collection (except at single-family or multiple-family residences or small apartment complexes) in Dallas County plus a small fringe area. The combined WMI and Waste Resources subsidiaries had a 48.8 percent share of the relevant market. The trial court held that this market share raised a presumption of illegality and that WMI had not rebutted the presumption. WMI appealed, arguing that new firms could easily enter the trash collection business in the relevant geographic area and that the trial court should have regarded this ease of entry as a sufficient rebuttal of the presumption of illegality. Was WMI correct?

3. In 1961, Ford Motor Company acquired Autolite, a manufacturer of spark plugs, in order to enter the profitable aftermarket for spark plugs sold as replacement parts. Ford and the other major automobile manufacturers had previously purchased original equipment spark plugs (those installed in new cars when they leave the factory) from independent producers such as Autolite and Champion, either at or below the producer's cost. The independents were willing to sell original equipment plugs so cheaply because aftermarket mechanics often replace original equipment plugs with the same brand of spark plug. GM had already moved into the spark plug market by developing its own division. Ford decided to do so by means of a vertical merger under which it acquired Autolite. Prior to the Autolite acquisition, Ford bought 10 percent of the total spark plug output. The merger left Champion as the only major independent spark plug producer. Champion's market

share thereafter declined because Chrysler was the only major original equipment spark plug purchaser remaining in the market. The government filed a divestiture suit against Ford, arguing that Ford's acquisition of Autolite violated section 7 of the Clayton Act. Should Ford have been ordered to divest itself of Autolite?

4. In 1975, Tenneco, Inc., was the 15th-largest industrial corporation in America. Tenneco's Walker Manufacturing Division produced and distributed a wide variety of automotive parts, the most important of which were exhaust system parts. Walker was the nation's leading seller of exhaust system parts in 1975 and 1976. Tenneco acquired control of Monroe Auto Equipment Company, a leading manufacturer of automotive shock absorbers. Monroe was the number two firm in the national market for replacement shock absorbers. Monroe and Gabriel, the industry leader, accounted for over 77 percent of replacement shock absorber sales in 1976. General Motors and Questor Corporation, the third- and fourth-largest firms, controlled another 15 percent of the market. The replacement shock absorber market exhibited significant barriers to the entry of new competitors. Economies of scale in the industry dictated manufacturing plants of substantial size. Furthermore, the nature of the industry required would-be entrants to acquire significant new technologies and marketing skills unique to the industry. The Federal Trade Commission (Commission) concluded that Tenneco's acquisition of Monroe violated section 7 of the Clayton Act by eliminating both perceived and actual potential competition in the replacement shock absorber market. The Commission therefore ordered Tenneco to divest itself of Monroe. Tenneco appealed. Was the Commission's decision correct?

5. The Federal Trade Commission filed an administrative complaint against six of the nation's title insurance companies. The complaint alleged that the title insurers engaged in horizontal price-fixing in their setting of uniform rates for title searches and title examinations. The challenged uniform rate-setting for title searches and title examinations occurred in various states through rating bureaus organized by the title insurers. These rating bureaus allegedly would set standard rates for search and examination services notwithstanding possible differences in efficiencies and costs as between individual title insurance companies. Though privately organized, these rating bureaus and the rates they set were potentially subject

to oversight by the various states in which they operated. In Wisconsin and Montana, two of the states in which price-fixing was alleged to have occurred, the rating bureaus filed rates with state agencies that operated under the so-called negative option rule. This rule provided that the rates became effective unless they were rejected by the appropriate Wisconsin or Montana agency within a set time. At most the state agencies checked the rate filings for mathematical accuracy. Some rates were unchecked altogether. Reviewing the administrative law judge's decision in the administrative proceeding, the FTC commissioners concluded that price-fixing occurred and that the state action exemption argued for by the title insurers did not apply. On appeal, the Third Circuit Court of Appeals held that the state action exemption shielded the title insurers' from antitrust liability for the price-fixing that occurred in Wisconsin and Montana. Was the Third Circuit correct?

6. Ricky Hasbrouck and 11 other plaintiffs were Texaco retail service station dealers in the Spokane area. They purchased gasoline directly from Texaco and resold it at retail under the Texaco trademark. Throughout the relevant time period (1972–81), Texaco also supplied gasoline to two gasoline distributors, Dompier Oil Company and Gull Oil Company, at a price that was at various times between 2.5 cents and 5.75 cents per gallon lower than the price Hasbrouck paid. Dompier and Gull sold the gasoline they purchased from Texaco to independent retail service stations. Dompier sold the gasoline to retailers under the Texaco trademark; Gull marketed it under private brand names. Gull's customers either sold their gasoline on consignment (in which case they set their own prices) or on commission (in which case Gull set their resale prices). Gull retained title until the gas was sold to a retail customer in either case. Some of the retail stations supplied by Dompier were owned and operated by Dompier's salaried employees. Both Dompier and Gull picked up gas at the Texaco bulk plant and delivered it to their retail customers, a service for which Dompier was compensated by Texaco at the common carrier rate.

Hasbrouck and the other dealers filed a price discrimination suit against Texaco under § 2(a) of the Robinson–Patman Act. At trial, Texaco argued that its lower prices to Gull and Dompier were lawful functional discounts. The jury awarded the plaintiffs $1,349,700 in treble damages. When the Ninth Circuit Court of Appeals affirmed the jury award, Texaco

appealed. The U.S. Supreme Court granted certiorari. How did the Supreme Court rule? Were the particular functional discounts provided by Texaco lawful?

7. Indian Coffee Company, a coffee roaster in Pittsburgh, Pennsylvania, sold its Breakfast Cheer coffee in the Pittsburgh area, where it had an 18 percent market share, and in Cleveland, Ohio, where it had a significant, but smaller, market share. Late in 1971, Folger Coffee Company, then the leading seller of branded coffee west of the Mississippi, entered the Pittsburgh market for the first time. In its effort to gain market share in Pittsburgh, Folger granted retailers high promotional allowances in the form of coupons. Retail customers could use these coupons to obtain price cuts. Redeeming retailers could use the coupons as credits against invoices from Folger. For a time, Indian tried to retain its market share by matching Folger's price concessions, but because Indian operated in only two areas, it could not subsidize such sales with profits from other areas. Indian, which finally was forced out of business in 1974, later filed a Robinson–Patman suit against Folger. At trial, Indian introduced evidence that Folger's Pittsburgh promotional allowances were far higher than its allowances in other geographic areas, and that Folger's Pittsburgh prices were below green (unroasted) coffee cost, below material and manufacturing costs, below total cost, and below marginal cost or average variable cost. Was the trial court's directed verdict in favor of Folger proper?

8. Bayer Corporation produced Bayferrox, a synthetic iron oxide pigment used to color paint, plastics, and building and concrete products. Hoover Color Corporation was one of several primary distributors of this pigment. Hoover therefore purchased Bayferrox from Bayer on a regular basis. For a number of years, Bayer had employed a volume-based incentive discount pricing system. Under this system, the price a distributor paid depended on the total amount of Bayferrox purchased by that distributor during the previous year. The quantities of Bayferrox purchased by Hoover were significantly smaller than those purchased by Hoover's competitors, Rockwood Industries and Landers-Segal Co. (Lansco). As a result, Hoover received smaller price discounts from Bayer than Rockwood and Lansco received. In 1992, for instance, Hoover received a 1 percent discount off Bayer's distributor market price for Bayferrox, whereas Lansco and Rockwood were given 6 percent and 10 percent discounts, respectively. Hoover sued

Bayer on the theory that Bayer's volume-based incentive discount pricing system involved price discrimination, in violation of section 2(a) of the Robinson–Patman Act. Bayer contended that it set its prices in a good faith attempt to meet competition in the marketplace, and that it was thus entitled to the protection of the affirmative defense set out in section 2(b) of the statute. Holding that Bayer was entitled to the protection of the "meeting competition" defense, the district court granted summary judgment in favor of Bayer. Was the district court's decision correct?

9. In 1982, a subsidiary of W. S. Kirkpatrick & Co. won a Nigerian Defense Ministry contract for the construction and equipment of an aeromedical center at a Nigerian Air Force base. Environmental Tectonics Corporation (Environmental), an unsuccessful bidder for the same contract, filed RICO and Robinson–Patman Act claims against Kirkpatrick. Environmental alleged that Kirkpatrick had won the contract by paying a 20 percent "commission" to bribe certain Nigerian officials. The parties agreed that the bribes, if paid, would violate Nigerian law. Was the trial court correct in holding that the act of state doctrine barred Environmental's claim?

10. Pocahontas Coal Company filed suit against a number of other companies engaged in the mining and production of coal in West Virginia. Pocahontas alleged that the defendants were involved in a conspiracy to control the production and pricing of coal. One of Pocahontas's specific claims was that the defendants had violated section 8 of the Clayton Act by "deputizing" various persons to sit on the boards of competing subsidiaries. The defendants moved for summary judgment, noting that Pocahontas's complaint contained no factual allegations that any of the defendants were competitors, failed to name any of the alleged "deputies," and was ambiguous because it alleged that certain persons were "officers and/or directors" of competing companies. The trial court offered Pocahontas the opportunity to clarify the complaint by bringing forth additional information on these points. Did the court properly grant the defendants summary judgment when Pocahontas declined to do so?

11. Professional Real Estate Investors, Inc. (PRE), operated a resort hotel in Palm Springs, California. Having installed videodisk players in the hotel's rooms and assembled a library of more than 200 motion picture titles, PRE rented videodisks to guests for in-room viewing. PRE also sought to develop a market for the sale of videodisk players to other hotels that wished to offer in-room viewing of prerecorded material. Columbia Pictures Industries, Inc., and seven other major motion picture studios (referred to collectively as "Columbia") owned the copyrights on the motion pictures that appeared on the videodisks PRE had purchased. Columbia also licensed the transmission of copyrighted motion pictures to hotel rooms through a wired cable system called Spectradyne. PRE therefore competed with Columbia not only for the viewing market at PRE's hotel but also for the broader market for in-room entertainment services in hotels. Columbia sued PRE for copyright infringement on the basis of PRE's rental of videodisks for viewing in hotel rooms. PRE counterclaimed, charging Columbia with violations of sections 1 and 2 of the Sherman Act. PRE alleged that Columbia's copyright action was a mere sham that cloaked underlying acts of monopolization and conspiracy to restrain trade. The district court granted summary judgment in favor of PRE on Columbia's copyright infringement claim. Columbia sought summary judgment on PRE's antitrust counterclaims. Columbia asserted that its copyright infringement claim had not been a sham and that the *Noerr–Pennington* doctrine therefore protected Columbia against antitrust attack. PRE opposed Columbia's motion for summary judgment on PRE's antitrust counterclaims by arguing that Columbia's copyright infringement claim was a sham because Columbia did not honestly believe that the claim was meritorious. If Columbia did not subjectively believe that the claim was meritorious but there was probable cause to bring the claim, was Columbia's claim a sham for purposes of the sham exception to the *Noerr–Pennington* doctrine's protection against liability?

Online Research

The *Heinz* Case

If your college or university allows students access to LEXIS or Westlaw, use one of those services to locate *Federal Trade Commission v. H. J. Heinz Co.,* 246 F.3d 708 (D.C. Cir. 2001). In that case, a federal court of appeals ruled on the FTC's request for a preliminary injunction to stop a planned merger of two manufacturers of baby food. Read the court's decision and prepare a written case brief. (For suggested guidelines regarding case briefs, see the Appendix to Chapter 1.)

chapter 51

EMPLOYMENT LAW

Westlawn Pediatric Center advertised a job opening for a pediatric nurse practitioner. Richard and Valerie, both of whom are licensed pediatric nurse practitioners and both of whom met the published qualifications for the job, applied for the position. Westlawn hired Valerie over Richard because "women are more nurturing." No verbal agreement was made between Westlawn and Valerie about the duration of her employment. Valerie performs well at her new job and receives glowing performance reviews.

- If Valerie is injured on the job, under what circumstances must Westlawn compensate her?
- What legal regulations must Westlawn meet with regard to workplace conditions, wages, and benefits?
- What criteria are permissible for employers to use in making hiring, firing, and promotion decisions? Was it legal for Westlawn to refuse to hire Richard on the basis of a stereotype?
- Does the fact that Valerie is doing a good job mean that she cannot legally be fired?
- Under what circumstances would Westlawn have the right to monitor Valerie's communications or require a search or drug test?
- Would it be ethical for Westlawn to monitor its employees' e-mail without giving them prior notice?

YEARS AGO, IT WAS unusual to see a separate employment law chapter in a business law text. At that time, the rights, duties, and liabilities accompanying employment usually were determined by basic legal institutions such as contract, tort, and agency. Today, these common law principles still control employer–employee relations unless displaced by government regulations or by new judge-made rules applying specifically to employment. By now, however, such rules and regulations are so numerous that they touch almost every facet of employment. This chapter discusses the most important of these modern legal controls on the employer–employee relation.

Modern American employment law is so vast and complex a subject that texts designed for lawyers seldom address it in its entirety. Indeed, specialized subjects like labor law and employment discrimination often get book-length treatment in their own right. This chapter's overview of employment law emphasizes three topics that have attracted much recent attention—employment discrimination, employee privacy, and common law claims for wrongful discharge. But no discussion of employment law is complete without outlining certain basic regulations that significantly affect the conditions of employment for most Americans. Figure 1 notes these regulations and briefly states the functions they perform.

LOG ON

For management tips about challenging personnel issues, information about employment law topics, and updates on employment cases, see Lawmemo.com
Employment Law:
http://www.lawmemo.com/default.htm;
Employment Law Infonet.com:
http://www.elinfonet.com/;
and Fair Measures:
http://www.fairmeasures.com/index.html.

Figure 1   *The Ends and Means of Modern Employment Law*

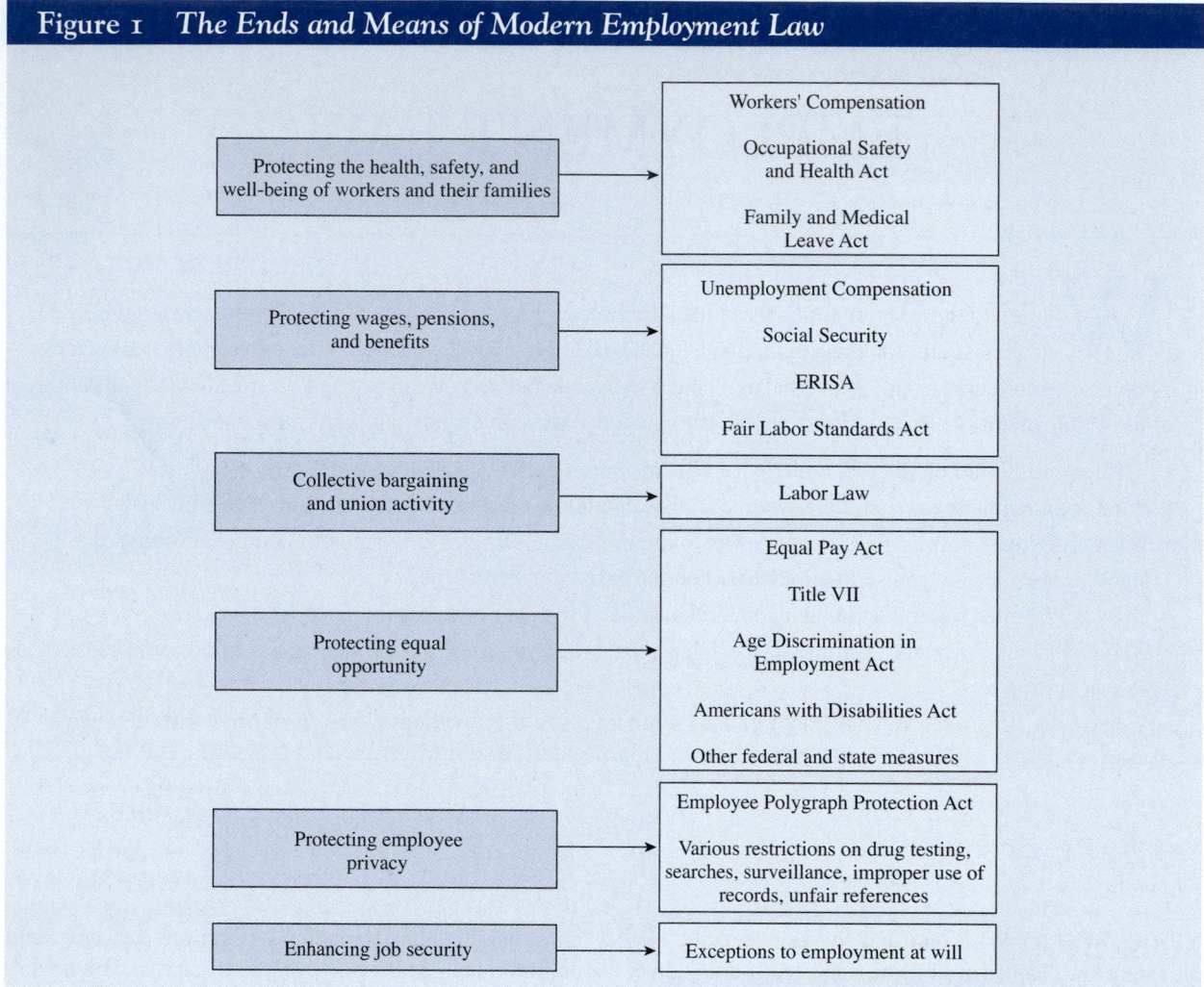

Protecting the health, safety, and well-being of workers and their families	Workers' Compensation Occupational Safety and Health Act Family and Medical Leave Act
Protecting wages, pensions, and benefits	Unemployment Compensation Social Security ERISA Fair Labor Standards Act
Collective bargaining and union activity	Labor Law
Protecting equal opportunity	Equal Pay Act Title VII Age Discrimination in Employment Act Americans with Disabilities Act Other federal and state measures
Protecting employee privacy	Employee Polygraph Protection Act Various restrictions on drug testing, searches, surveillance, improper use of records, unfair references
Enhancing job security	Exceptions to employment at will

Legislation Protecting Employee Health, Safety, and Well-Being

Workers' Compensation

Nineteenth-century law made it difficult for employees to recover when they sued their employer in negligence for on-the-job injuries.[1] At that time, employers had an implied assumption of risk defense under which an employee assumed all the normal and customary risks of his employment simply by taking the job. If an employee's own carelessness played some role in his injury, employers often could avoid negligence liability under the traditional rule that even a slight degree of contributory negligence is a complete defense. Another employer defense, the fellow-servant rule, said that where an employee's injury resulted from the negligence of a coemployee (or fellow servant), the employer was not liable. Finally, employees sometimes had problems proving the employer's negligence. State workers' compensation statutes, which first appeared early in the 20th century, were a response to all these problems. Today all 50 states have such systems.[2]

---

[1] Chapter 7 discusses negligence law and most of the negligence defenses noted below.

[2] In addition, various federal statutes regulate on-the-job injuries suffered by employees of the federal government and other employees such as railroad workers, seamen, longshoremen, and harbor workers.

Basic Features Workers' compensation protects only employees, and not independent contractors.[3] However, many states exempt casual, agricultural, and domestic employees, among others. State and local government employees may be covered by workers' compensation or by some alternative state system. Also, states usually exempt certain employers—for example, firms employing fewer than a stated number of employees (often three).

Where they apply, however, all workers' compensation systems share certain basic features. They allow injured employees to recover under *strict liability,* thus removing any need to prove employer negligence. They also eliminate the employer's three traditional defenses: contributory negligence, assumption of risk, and the fellow-servant rule. In addition, they make workers' compensation an employee's *exclusive remedy* against her employer for covered injuries. There are some exceptions to the exclusivity of worker's compensation, however. In cases in which an employer *intentionally* injures an employee, the injured employee can usually sue the employer outside of worker's compensation. In some states, this intentional injury exception has expanded beyond intentional torts to situations in which the employer did something or maintained a condition in the workplace that the employer knew was substantially certain to harm the employee. An example of this approach would be holding an employer responsible outside of worker's compensation when the employer knew that an employee was being sexually harassed but did nothing about it. In addition, in a number of states, an employee can sue outside of worker's compensation when the employer was acting in a *dual capacity* in relation to the employee. An example of this would be a case in which an employee is injured on the job by a defect in a product manufactured by the employer.

Workers' compensation basically is a social compromise. Because it involves strict liability and eliminates the three traditional employer defenses, workers' compensation greatly increases the probability that an injured employee will recover. Such recoveries usually include (1) hospital and medical expenses (including vocational rehabilitation), (2) disability benefits, (3) specified recoveries for the loss of certain body parts, and (4) death benefits to survivors and/or dependents. But the amount recoverable under each category of damages frequently is less than would be obtained in a negligence suit. Thus, injured employees sometimes deny that they are covered by workers' compensation so that they can pursue a tort suit against their employer instead.

Although workers' compensation is usually an injured employee's sole remedy against her employer, she may be able to sue other parties whose behavior helped cause her injury. One example is a product liability suit against a manufacturer who supplies an employer with defective machinery or raw materials that cause an on-the-job injury. However, many states immunize coemployees from ordinary tort liability for injuries they inflict on other employees. Complicated questions of contribution, indemnity, and subrogation can arise where an injured employee is able to recover against both an employer and a third party.

The Work-Related Injury Requirement Another basic feature of workers' compensation is that employees recover only for *work-related* injuries. To be work-related, the injury must (1) arise out of the employment, and (2) happen in the course of the employment. These tests have been variously interpreted.

The arising-out-of-the-employment test usually requires a sufficiently close relationship between the injury and the *nature* of the employment. Different states use different tests to define this relationship. Examples include:

1. *Increased risk.* Here, the employee recovers only if the nature of her job increases her risk of injury above the risk to which the general public is exposed. Under this test, a factory worker assaulted by a trespasser probably would not recover, while a security guard assaulted by the same trespasser probably would.

2. *Positional risk.* Under this more liberal test, an injured employee recovers if her employment caused her to be at the place and time where her injury occurred. Here, the factory worker probably would recover. The *Dulen* case that follows seems to adopt this test.

The in-the-course-of-the-employment requirement inquires whether the injury occurred within the *time, place,* and *circumstances* of the employment. Employees injured off the employer's premises generally are outside the course of the employment. For example, injuries suffered while traveling to or from work usually are not compensable. But an employee may be covered where the off-the-premises injury occurred while she was performing employment-related duties such as going on a business trip or running an employment-related errand.

Other work-related injury problems on which courts have disagreed include mental injuries allegedly arising from the employment and injuries resulting from employee horseplay. Virtually all states, however, regard

---

[3]Chapter 35 defines the terms *employee* and *independent contractor.*

intentionally self-inflicted injuries as outside workers' compensation. Recovery for occupational diseases, on the other hand, usually is allowed today. An employee whose preexisting diseased condition is aggravated by her employment sometimes recovers as well.

Administration and Funding Workers' compensation systems usually are administered by a state agency that adjudicates workers' claims and administers the system.

Its decisions on such claims normally are appealable to the state courts. The states fund workers' compensation by compelling covered employers to (1) purchase private insurance, (2) self-insure (e.g., by maintaining a contingency fund), or (3) make payments into a state insurance fund. Because employers generally pass on the costs of insurance to their customers, workers' compensation tends to spread the economic risk of workplace injuries throughout society.

Darco Transportation v. Dulen   922 P.2d 591 (Okla. Sup. Ct. 1996)

Elmer Dulen was injured and his codriver Polly Freeman was killed when a tractor-trailer rig driven by Dulen entered a railroad crossing and was struck by an oncoming train. Both Dulen and Freeman had been hired by Darco Transportation to transport goods cross-country to San Francisco. On the night of the accident, Dulen stopped his rig behind another truck when the signal arms at a railroad crossing lowered. The arms malfunctioned and came up before an oncoming train reached the intersection. The first truck proceeded across the tracks and Dulen followed. While the first truck avoided being hit, Dulen's rig was rammed by the train. The protective arms did not relower until Dulen's semi was on the tracks.

At the scene of the collision a female traffic investigator noticed that Freeman was clad only in a T-shirt. She also observed that Dulen's pants were unbuttoned, unzipped, and resting at mid-hip. After Dulen was admitted to the hospital, the investigator questioned Dulen about how the accident had happened. Dulen said, "I was f—ing her and now, oh, my God, I have killed her." According to the investigator, Dulen also told her that when the accident occurred, Freeman was sitting in his lap facing him. However, in later testimony Dulen explained that by his statement at the hospital he meant that he had been living in an intimate relationship with Freeman for five months before the accident and felt responsible for her death because she was driving with him. He also denied telling the officer that Freeman was sitting in his lap and that they were having sex when the accident occurred. Other evidence revealed that there was not enough room between the steering wheel and the seat for two people of Dulen's and Freeman's size physically to fit into that space together.

Dulen sought workers' compensation benefits for what he maintained were on-the-job injuries. After various Oklahoma courts ruled in Dulen's favor, Darco appealed to the Supreme Court of Oklahoma.

Opala, Judge

When examining the compensation tribunal's factual resolutions, this court applies the any-competent-evidence standard. The trial judge's findings may not be disturbed on review if supported by competent proof.

Oklahoma's jurisprudence has long recognized that a compensable work-related injury must both: (1) occur in the course of, and (2) arise out of the worker's employment. These two distinct elements are not to be understood as synonymous. The term "in the course of employment" relates to the time, place, or circumstances under which the injury is sustained. The term "arise out of employment" contemplates the causal connection between the injury and the risks incident to employment. We must be mindful that in this case we are applying workers' compensation law. The concept of a worker's contributory fault, which the compensation statute discarded, must not be resurrected obliquely as a defense against the employer's liability.

The Workers' Compensation Court was faced with the task of determining if Dulen, when injured, was performing work in

furtherance of his master's business—i.e., whether he was then "in the course of employment." If the trial tribunal tended to believe that Dulen and Freeman were having sex at the critical time, the question to be decided was whether the claimant's conduct is to be deemed horseplay—a complete departure from or abandonment of his employment. This issue concerns itself solely with the "course of employment" bounds—not with the risk incident to employment, i.e., the "arising out of" element.

Assuming as a fact that when the collision occurred, Dulen was having sex while also driving the rig, the trial judge could still find that this servant's acts constituted no more than a careless, negligent, or forbidden genre of performance, but did not amount to pure frolic which was tantamount to total abandonment of the master's business. On this record, such a finding would not be legally or factually incorrect. The record contains ample evidence reasonably supporting the notion that Dulen's injury was work-related, and occurred while he was en route to his assigned destination. Above all, uncontroverted is the stubborn fact that Dulen, when injured, occupied his assigned work station—the driver's seat behind the steering wheel of Darco's truck. The record offers no proof that Dulen had deviated from or abandoned his master's mission, transporting goods to San Francisco.

An injury is compensable if it arises out of the claimant's employment—i.e., was caused by a risk to which the employee was subjected by his work. Any other notion would impermissibly interject into this State's compensation regime concepts of common-law cause and foreseeability: the legal underpinnings of negligence. The only criterion for compensability is the statute's test of a connection-in-fact to the employment. The record is devoid of any proof that the protective arms were in good working order. The trial tribunal found the equipment's failure was the direct cause of the claimant's injuries. At the time of Dulen's injuries, he was employed as a Darco truck driver with an assigned task—transporting goods to the West Coast. This required his presence on the highways. A causal

connection between the act in which Dulen was engaged, when injured, and his job description is clear. Because the perils of this servant's travel for his master are co-extensive with the risks of employment, Dulen's injuries undeniably arose out of his work.

Two insuperable hurdles absolutely militate against overturning the trial tribunal's findings and exonerating the employer as a matter of law. Assuming Dulen and Freeman were engaged in sexual intercourse, (1) there is undisputed proof that, when the collision occurred, Dulen remained at the steering wheel and hence cannot be deemed to have then "abandoned" his assigned work station; and (2) there is competent evidence to support the trial judge's finding which ascribes the accident's cause, not to copulation-related inattention, but to defective railroad-crossing warning equipment.

Trial court order sustained; Dulen recovers.

The Occupational Safety and Health Act

Although it may stimulate employers to remedy hazardous working conditions, workers' compensation does not directly forbid such conditions. The most important measure directly regulating workplace safety is the federal Occupational Safety and Health Act of 1970. The Occupational Safety and Health Act imposes a duty on employers to provide their employees with a workplace and jobs free from recognized hazards that may cause death or serious physical harm. Employers are required to comply with many detailed regulations promulgated by the Occupational Safety and Health Administration (OSHA). One of these regulations, for example, requires employers to inform employees who could be exposed to hazardous chemicals in the workplace about the chemicals and to provide employees with training so that they can effectively protect themselves from harm. The act also requires employers to report to the secretary of labor any on-the-job injuries that require hospitalization. Because information about workplace dangers provided by employees themselves is important to the effectiveness of the act, employees who provide such information are protected from retaliation.

The Occupational Safety and Health Act applies to all employers engaged in a business affecting interstate commerce. Exempted, however, are the U.S. government, the states and their political subdivisions, and certain industries regulated by other federal safety legislation. The Occupational Safety and Health Act mainly is administered by the Occupational Safety and Health Administra-

tion (OSHA) of the Labor Department. It does not preempt state workplace safety regulation, but OSHA must approve any state regulatory plan.

OSHA can inspect places of employment for violations of the act and its regulations. If an employer is found to violate the act's general duty provision or any specific standard, OSHA issues a written citation.

The main sanctions for violations of the act and the regulations are various civil penalties. In addition, any employer who commits a willful violation resulting in death to an employee may suffer a fine, imprisonment, or both. Also, the secretary of labor may seek injunctive relief when an employment hazard presents an imminent danger of death or physical harm that cannot be promptly eliminated by normal citation procedures.

The Family and Medical Leave Act

After concluding that proper child-raising, family stability, and job security require that employees get reasonable work leave for family and medical reasons, Congress passed the Family and Medical Leave Act (FMLA) in 1993. In general, the act covers those employed for at least 12 months, and for 1,250 hours during those 12 months, by an employer employing 50 or more employees. Covered employers include federal, state, and local government agencies.

Under the FMLA, covered employees are entitled to a total of 12 workweeks of leave during any 12-month period for one or more of the following reasons: (1) the birth of a child and the need to care for that child; (2) the adoption of a child; (3) the need to care for a spouse, child, or parent with a serious health condition; and (4) the employee's own serious health condition. Usually, the leave is without pay. Upon the employee's return from leave, the employer ordinarily must put her in the same or an equivalent position and must not deny her any benefits accrued before the leave began. The National Defense Authorization Act of 2008 included provisions that revised the FMLA with respect to military families. The new provisions permit eligible employees who are employed by covered employers to take up to 12 weeks of leave because of any "qualifying exigency" arising from the fact that the employee's spouse, son, daughter, or parent is on active military duty or has been notified of an impending call to active duty status.

Employers who deny any of an employee's FMLA rights are civilly liable to the affected employee for resulting lost wages or, if no wages were lost, for any other resulting monetary losses not exceeding 12 weeks' wages. Employees may also recover an additional equal amount as liquidated damages, unless the employer acted in good faith and had reasonable grounds for believing that it was not violating the act. Like the Fair Labor Standards Act (FLSA), to be discussed later in this chapter, the FMLA permits civil actions by the secretary of labor, with any sums recovered distributed to affected employees. In such actions, employees may also obtain equitable relief, including reinstatement and promotion.

Legislation Protecting Wages, Pensions, and Benefits

Social Security

Today, the law requires that employers help ensure their employees' financial security after the employment ends. One example is the federal Social Security system. Social Security mainly is financed by the Federal Insurance Contributions Act (FICA). FICA imposes a flat percentage tax on all employee income below a certain base figure and requires employers to pay a matching amount. Self-employed people pay a different rate on a different wage base. FICA revenues finance various forms of financial assistance besides the old-age benefits that people usually call Social Security. These include survivors' benefits to family members of deceased workers, disability benefits, and medical and hospitalization benefits for the elderly (the Medicare system).

Unemployment Compensation

Another way that the law protects employees after their employment ends is by providing unemployment compensation for discharged workers. Since 1935, federal law has authorized joint federal–state efforts in this area. Today, each state administers its own unemployment compensation system under federal guidelines. The system's costs are met by subjecting employers to federal and state unemployment compensation taxes.

Unemployment insurance plans vary from state to state but usually share certain features. States often condition the receipt of benefits on the recipient's having worked for a covered employer for a specified time period, and/or having earned a certain minimum income over such a period. Generally, those who voluntarily quit work without good cause, are fired for bad conduct, fail to actively seek suitable new work, or refuse such work are ineligible for benefits. Benefit levels vary from state to state, as do the time periods during which benefits can be received.

ERISA

Many employers voluntarily contribute to their employees' postemployment income by maintaining pension plans. For years, pension plan abuses such as arbitrary termination of participation in the plan, arbitrary benefit reduction, and mismanagement of fund assets were not uncommon. The Employee Retirement Income Security Act of 1974 (ERISA) was a response to these problems. ERISA does not require employers to establish or fund pension plans and does not set benefit levels. Instead, it tries to check abuses and to protect employees' expectations that promised pension benefits will be paid.

ERISA imposes *fiduciary duties* on pension fund managers. For example, it requires that managers diversify the plan's investments to minimize the risk of large losses, unless this is clearly imprudent. ERISA also imposes *record-keeping, reporting,* and *disclosure* requirements. For instance, it requires that covered plans provide annual reports to their participants and specifies the contents of those reports. In addition, the act has a provision *guaranteeing employee participation* in the plan. For example, certain employees who complete one year of service with an employer cannot be denied plan participation. Furthermore, ERISA contains *funding* requirements for protecting plan participants against loss of pension income. Finally, ERISA contains complex *vesting requirements* that determine when an employee's right to receive pension benefits becomes nonforfeitable. These requirements help prevent employers from using a late vesting date to avoid pension obligations to employees who change jobs or are fired before that date. ERISA's remedies include civil suits by plan participants and beneficiaries, equitable relief, and criminal penalties.

The Fair Labor Standards Act

Although federal labor law regulates several aspects of labor–management relations, it still permits many terms of employment to be determined by private bargaining. Nonetheless, sometimes the law directly regulates such key terms of employment as wages and hours worked. The most important example is the Fair Labor Standards Act (FLSA) of 1938.

The FLSA regulates *wages and hours* by entitling covered employees to (1) a specified minimum wage whose amount changes over time, and (2) a time-and-a half rate for work exceeding 40 hours per week. The FLSA's complicated coverage provisions basically enable its wages-and-hours standards to reach most significantly sized businesses that are engaged in interstate commerce or produce goods for such commerce. Also covered are the federal, state, and local governments. The many exemptions from the FLSA's wages-and-hours provisions include executive, administrative, and professional personnel.

The FLSA also forbids oppressive *child labor* by any employer engaged in interstate commerce or in the production of goods for such commerce, and also forbids the interstate shipment of goods produced in an establishment where oppressive child labor occurs. Oppressive child labor includes (1) most employment of children below the age of 14; (2) employment of children aged 14–15, unless they work in an occupation specifically approved by the Department of Labor; and (3) employment of children aged 16–17 who work in occupations declared particularly hazardous by the Labor Department.

Both affected employees and the Labor Department can recover any unpaid minimum wages or overtime, plus an additional equal amount as liquidated damages, from an employer that has violated the FLSA's wages-and-hours provisions. A suit by the Labor Department terminates an employee's right to sue, but the department pays the amounts it recovers to the employee. Violations of the act's child labor provisions may result in civil penalties. Other FLSA remedies include injunctive relief and criminal liability for willful violations.

Collective Bargaining and Union Activity

Entire legal treatises are devoted to the topic of collective bargaining by unions. What follows is only a brief historical outline of the subject. Early in the 19th century, some courts treated labor unions as illegal criminal conspiracies. After this restriction disappeared around midcentury, organized labor began its lengthy—and sometimes violent—rise to power. During the late 19th and early 20th centuries, unions' growing influence and wage earners' increasing presence in the electorate spurred the passage of many laws benefiting labor. These included statutes outlawing "yellow-dog" contracts (under which employees agreed not to join or remain a union member), minimum wage and maximum hours legislation, laws regulating the employment of women and children, factory safety measures, and workers' compensation. But during this period, some say, the courts tended to represent business interests. Perhaps for this reason, some prolabor measures were struck down on constitutional grounds. Also, some courts were quick to issue temporary and permanent injunctions to restrain union picketing and boycotts and help quell strikes.

Organized labor's political power continued to grow during the first part of the 20th century. In 1926, Congress passed the Railway Labor Act, which regulates labor relations in the railroad industry, and which later included airlines. This was followed by the Norris-LaGuardia Act of 1932, which limited the circumstances in which federal courts could enjoin strikes and picketing in labor disputes, and also prohibited federal court enforcement of yellow-dog contracts.

The most important 20th-century American labor statute, however, was the National Labor Relations Act of 1935 (the NLRA or Wagner Act). The NLRA gave employees the *right to organize* by enabling them to form, join, and assist labor organizations. It also allowed them to *bargain collectively* through their own representatives. In addition, the Wagner Act prohibited certain *unfair labor practices* that were believed to discourage collective bargaining. These practices include (1) interfering with employees' rights to form, join, and assist labor unions; (2) dominating or interfering with the formation or administration of a labor union, or giving a union financial or other support; (3) discriminating against employees in hiring, tenure, or any term of employment due to their union membership; (4) discriminating against employees because they have filed charges or given testimony under the NLRA; and (5) refusing to bargain collectively with any duly designated employee representative. The NLRA also established the National Labor Relations Board (NLRB). The NLRB's main functions are (1) handling representation cases (which involve the process by which a union becomes the certified employee representative within a bargaining unit), and (2) deciding whether challenged employer or union activity is an unfair labor practice.

In 1947, Congress amended the NLRA by passing the Labor Management Relations Act (LMRA or Taft-Hartley Act). The act declared that certain acts by *unions* are unfair labor practices. These include (1) restraining or coercing employees in the exercise of their guaranteed bargaining rights (e.g., their right to refrain from joining a union); (2) causing an employer to discriminate against an employee who is not a union member; (3) refusing to bargain collectively with an employer; (4) conducting a secondary strike or a secondary boycott for a specified illegal purpose;[4] (5) requiring employees covered by union-shop contracts to pay excessive or discriminatory initiation fees or dues; and (6) featherbedding (forcing an employer to pay for work not actually performed). The LMRA also established an 80-day cooling-off period for strikes that the president finds likely to endanger national safety or health. In addition, it created a Federal Mediation and Conciliation Service to assist employers and unions in settling labor disputes.

Congressional investigations during the 1950s uncovered corruption in internal union affairs and also revealed that the internal procedures of many unions were undemocratic. In response, Congress enacted the Labor Management Reporting and Disclosure Act (or Landrum-Griffin Act) in 1959. The act established a "bill of rights" for union members and attempted to make internal union affairs more democratic. It also amended the NLRA by adding to the LMRA's list of unfair union labor practices. The proportion of U.S. workers who are members of labor unions has decreased fairly steadily over he past 40 years. Today, less than 13 percent of the workforce are members of labor unions.

Equal Opportunity Legislation

The Equal Pay Act
The Equal Pay Act (EPA), which forbids *sex* discrimination regarding *pay,* was a 1963 amendment to the FLSA. Its coverage resembles the coverage of the FLSA's minimum wage provisions. Unlike the FLSA, however, the EPA covers executive, administrative, and professional employees.

The typical EPA case involves a woman who claims that she has received lower pay than a male employee performing substantially equal work for the same employer. The substantially-equal-work requirement is met if the plaintiff's job and the higher-paid male employee's job involve *each* of the following: (1) equal effort, (2) equal skill, (3) equal responsibility, and (4) similar working conditions.

Effort basically means physical or mental exertion. *Skill* refers to the experience, training, education, and ability required for the positions being compared. Here, the question is not whether the employees being compared have equal skills but whether their jobs require or utilize substantially the same skills. *Responsibility* (or accountability) involves such factors as the degree of supervision each job requires and the importance of each job to the employer. For instance, a retail sales position in which an employee may not approve customer checks probably is not equal to a sales position in which an employee has this authority. *Working conditions* refers to such factors as temperature, weather, fumes, ventilation, toxic conditions, and risk of injury. These need only be *similar,* not equal.

If the two jobs are substantially equal and they are paid unequally, an employer must prove one of the EPA's four defenses or it will lose the case. The employer has a defense if it shows that the pay disparity is based on (1) seniority, (2) merit, (3) quality or quantity of production (e.g., a piecework system), or (4) any factor other than sex. The first three defenses require an employer to show some organized, systematic, structured, and communicated rating system with predetermined criteria that apply equally to employees of each sex. The any-factor-other-than-sex defense is a catchall category that includes shift differentials, bonuses paid because the job is part of a training program, and differences in the profitability of the products or services on which employees work.

The EPA's remedial scheme resembles the FLSA's scheme. Under the EPA, however, employee suits are for the amount of back pay lost because of an employer's discrimination, not for unpaid minimum wages or overtime. An employee may also recover an equal sum as liquidated damages. The EPA is enforced by the Equal Employment Opportunity Commission (EEOC) rather than the Labor Department.[5] Unlike some of the employment discrimination statutes described later, however, the EPA does not

---

[4]These are strikes or boycotts aimed at a third party with which the union has no real dispute. Their purpose is to coerce that party not to deal with an employer with which the union does have a dispute, and thus to gain some leverage over the employer.

[5]The EEOC is an independent federal agency with a sizable staff and many regional offices. Its functions include (1) enforcing most of the employment discrimination laws discussed in this chapter through lawsuits that it initiates or in which it intervenes, (2) conciliating employment discrimination charges (e.g., by encouraging their negotiated settlement), (3) investigating discrimination-related matters, and (4) interpreting the statutes it enforces through regulations and guidelines.

require that private plaintiffs submit their complaints to the EEOC or a state agency before mounting suit.

Title VII

Employment discrimination might be defined as employer behavior that penalizes certain individuals because of personal traits that they cannot control and that bear no relation to effective job performance. Of the many employment discrimination laws in force today, the most important is Title VII of the 1964 Civil Rights Act. Unlike the Equal Pay Act, which merely forbids sex discrimination regarding pay, Title VII is a wide-ranging employment discrimination provision. It prohibits discrimination based on *race, color, religion, sex,* and *national origin* in hiring, firing, job assignments, pay, access to training and apprenticeship programs, and most other employment decisions.

Basic Features of Title VII   In discussing Title VII, we first examine some general rules that govern all the kinds of discrimination it forbids. Then we examine each forbidden basis of discrimination in detail.

Covered Entities   Title VII covers all employers employing 15 or more employees and engaging in an industry affecting interstate commerce. Employers include individuals, partnerships, corporations, colleges and universities, labor unions and employment agencies (with respect to their own employees), and state and local governments.[6] Also, *referrals* by employment agencies are covered no matter what the size of the agency, if an employer serviced by the agency has 15 or more employees. In addition, Title VII covers certain unions—mainly those with 15 or more members—in their capacity as *employee representative.*

Procedures   Although the EEOC sometimes sues to enforce Title VII, the usual Title VII suit is a private claim. The complicated procedures governing private Title VII suits are beyond the scope of this text, but a few points should be kept in mind. Private parties with a Title VII claim have no automatic right to sue. Instead, they first must file a *charge* with the EEOC, or with a state agency in states having suitable fair employment laws and enforcement schemes. This allows the EEOC or the state agency to investigate the claim, attempt conciliation if the claim has substance, or sue the employer itself. If a plaintiff files with a state agency and the state fails to act, the plaintiff still can file a charge with the EEOC. Even if the EEOC fails to act on the claim, a plaintiff still may mount her own suit. Here, the EEOC issues a "right-to-sue letter" enabling the plaintiff to sue.

Proving Discrimination   The permissible methods for proving a Title VII violation are critical to its effectiveness against employment discrimination. Proof of discrimination is easy in cases where the employer had an **express policy** disfavoring one of Title VII's protected classes. **Direct evidence** of a discriminatory motive such as testimony or written evidence obviously is useful to plaintiffs as well. However, because employers can discriminate without leaving such obvious tracks, the courts have devised other methods of proving a Title VII violation.

Title VII **disparate treatment** suits involve situations in which an employer has treated an individual differently because of the person's race, sex, color, religion, or national origin. In such suits, the plaintiff first must show a *prima facie case:* a case strong enough to create a presumption of discrimination and to require a counterargument from the defendant. The proof needed for a prima facie case varies with the nature of the challenged employment decision (e.g., hiring or promotion), but ordinarily it gives plaintiffs few difficulties. Once the plaintiff establishes a prima facie case, the employer must produce evidence that the challenged employment decision was taken for *legitimate, nondiscriminatory reasons* or it will lose the lawsuit. To establish a prima facie case in a hiring situation, for example, the plaintiff must prove that she applied for the job and was qualified for it, that she is a member of a protected class, that she was rejected, and that the employer continued to attempt to fill the job. At that point, the employer might produce evidence that it rejected the plaintiff because she did not meet its hiring criteria or was not the best qualified applicant. If the employer produces satisfactory reasons, the plaintiff then must *show that discrimination actually occurred.* She might do so by showing that the employer's alleged nondiscriminatory reasons were a *pretext* for a decision that really involved discrimination. For example, she might show that the employer's alleged hiring criteria were not applied to similarly situated male job applicants. The *Becknell v. Board of Education* case, which follows later in this chapter, illustrates the process of proving discrimination in a case of disparate treatment.

Title VII's **disparate impact** (or adverse impact) method is most often used when the alleged discrimination

---

[6]Employment discrimination within the federal government is beyond the scope of this text.

affects many employees. Here, the plaintiffs ordinarily maintain that the employer uses a particular employment practice that causes a *disparate impact* on the basis of race, color, religion, sex, or national origin. Often, the practice is an employer rule that is neutral on its face but has a disproportionate adverse effect on one of Title VII's protected groups—for example, a height, weight, or high school diploma requirement for hiring, or a written test for hiring or promotion. If the plaintiffs show a disparate impact, the employer loses unless it demonstrates that the challenged practice is *job-related for the position in question and consistent with business necessity.* For example, the employer might show that its promotion test really predicts effective job performance, and that effective performance in the relevant job is necessary for its operations. Even if the employer makes this demonstration, the plaintiffs have another option: to show that the employer's legitimate business needs can be advanced by an *alternative employment practice* that is *less discriminatory than the challenged practice.* For example, the plaintiffs might show that the employer's legitimate needs can be met by a different promotion test that has less adverse impact on the protected group. If the employer refuses to adopt this practice, the plaintiffs win.

Defenses Even if a plaintiff proves a Title VII violation, the employer still prevails if it can establish one of Title VII's defenses. The most important such defenses are:

1. *Seniority.* Title VII is not violated if the employer treats employees differently pursuant to a *bona fide seniority system.* To be bona fide, such a system at least must treat all employees equally on its face, not have been created for discriminatory reasons, and not operate in a discriminatory fashion.

2. *The various "merit" defenses.* An employer also escapes Title VII liability if it acts pursuant to a *bona fide merit system,* a system basing earnings on *quantity or quality of production,* or the results of a *professionally developed ability test.* Presumably, such systems and tests at least must meet the general standards for seniority systems stated above. Also, the EEOC has promulgated lengthy *Uniform Guidelines on Employee Selection Procedures* that speak to these and other matters.

3. *The BFOQ Defense.* Finally, Title VII allows employers to discriminate on the bases of sex, religion, or national origin where one of those traits is a *bona fide occupational qualification (BFOQ) that is reasonably necessary to the business in question.* The BFOQ defense is applied to cases of disparate treatment, whereas the business necessity defense, which was discussed earlier, applies in disparate impact cases. The BFOQ defense does not protect race or color discrimination. As the *Becknell* case makes clear, moreover, the defense is a narrow one even where it applies. Generally, it is available only where a certain gender, religion, or national origin is necessary for effective job performance. For example, a BFOQ probably would exist where a female is employed to model women's clothing or to fit women's undergarments. But the BFOQ defense usually is unavailable where the discrimination is based on stereotypes (e.g., that women are less aggressive than men) or on the preferences of co-workers or customers (e.g., the preference of airline travelers for female rather than male flight attendants). The defense also is unavailable where the employer's discriminatory practice promotes goals, such as fetal protection, that do not concern effective job performance.

The following *Becknell* case provides a good example of BFOQ analysis.

Becknell v. Board of Education
2008 U.S. Dist. LEXIS 35075 (U.S. Dist. Ct. E.D. Ky. 2008)

Rhonda Becknell was a teacher at Owsley County Elementary School. Teresa Barrett was the principal of the Owsley County High School. In November 2005, Becknell applied for the vacant position of assistant principal at the high school. There were at least two other applicants: elementary school art teacher, Chad Mason, and high school agriculture teacher, Alan Dale Taylor.

The school's decision-making council, which included Barrett and five other members, met on December 13, 2005, to consider the applications. They decided to leave the choice up to Barrett. Barrett asserted that she had several concerns about Becknell, such as the principal of the elementary school having told Barrett that Becknell was unreliable. Council member Tina Cornwell testified that Barrett also stated at the council meeting, "I'd rather have a man than a woman because of disciplinary issues. When a male student gets in trouble, you know, a male teacher will have to be called out to be a witness or to help with the situation." Cornwell further testified that when she asked Barrett why she did not want to hire Becknell, Barrett stated, "I really prefer a male." Council member Kimberly Campbell testified that the council discussed the fact that the assistant principal would discipline students and that "with Mrs. Barrett being female, it would be helpful to have a male to discipline more with the male students and the female with the female students." Council member James Green testified that, when Barrett was discussing her preferences for the assistant principal position, she commented, "I really need a man." Barrett denies making these statements.

Barrett ultimately hired Mason, who is a male, for the position. Barrett had previously worked with Mason and was impressed with the way he handled disciplinary issues and other matters. During her interview of Mason, Barrett learned that he had not taken the tests necessary to obtain his principalship certification. However, he had taken all of the required classes to be assistant principal and he received his certification after having been hired by Barrett, and the school district had previously hired individuals on alternative or temporary certifications. Becknell, however, was already certified to serve as an assistant principal at the time that Barrett hired Mason.

Becknell sued the Board of Education of Owsley County, the superintendant of schools, and Barrett ("the defendants"), alleging sex discrimination in violation of Title VII and a violation of the Kentucky Civil Rights Act. The defendants filed a motion for summary judgment.

Caldwell, United States District Judge

Direct Evidence of Discrimination

The plaintiff can prove her claims through either direct evidence of discrimination, or through the *McDonnell Douglas* burden-shifting analysis. Under *McDonnell Douglas*—the circumstantial evidence approach—the plaintiff bears the initial burden of establishing a prima facie case of discrimination. To establish a prima facie case, the plaintiff must show that (1) she is a member of a protected class; (2) that she was qualified for the job; (3) that she suffered an adverse employment decision; and (4) that the job was given to a person outside the protected class. Establishment of the prima facie case creates a presumption that the employer unlawfully discriminated against the employee. Once a plaintiff proves her prima facie case, the burden shifts to the employer to articulate some legitimate, nondiscriminatory reason for the adverse employment action. If the defendant meets its burden, the burden shifts back to the plaintiff to show that the reason proffered by the defendant was not its true reason but merely a pretext for discrimination. A plaintiff can show pretext either directly by persuading the trier of fact that a discriminatory reason more likely motivated the employer or indirectly by showing that the employer's proffered explanation is unworthy of credence. The trier of fact simply proceeds to decide the ultimate question: whether the plaintiff has proved that the defendant intentionally discriminated against him. The *McDonnell Douglas* framework applies only when the plaintiff can produce only circumstantial evidence of discrimination. If a plaintiff can produce direct evidence of discrimination then the [*McDonnell Douglas*] paradigm is of no consequence. Where a plaintiff presents direct evidence of discriminatory intent in connection with a challenged employment action, the burden of both production and persuasion shifts to the employer to prove that it would have terminated the

employee even if it had not been motivated by impermissible discrimination.

Direct evidence is evidence that proves the existence of a fact without any inferences. Direct evidence of discrimination is that evidence, which, if believed, requires the conclusion that unlawful discrimination was at least a motivating factor in the employer's action. For example, a facially discriminatory employment policy or a corporate decision maker's express statement of a desire to remove employees in the protected group is direct evidence of discriminatory intent. However, isolated and ambiguous statements are too abstract to support a finding of discrimination. Barrett's alleged statements that she preferred to hire a male and really needed a man in the position of assistant principal is evidence which, if believed, requires the conclusion that discrimination was at least a motivating factor in her decision to hire Mason instead of Becknell. Thus, summary judgment on the issue of whether the defendants discriminated against Becknell is inappropriate.

Furthermore, even if Barrett's alleged statements regarding her preference for hiring a male were not regarded as direct evidence of discrimination, the defendants would nonetheless not be entitled to summary judgment under the *McDonnell Douglas* framework. Becknell has established a prima facie case of discrimination. The defendants have countered with a legitimate, nondiscriminatory reason for hiring Mason instead of Becknell, i.e., Becknell's alleged poor performance as assistant principal at the elementary school. Nevertheless, Becknell has responded with sufficient evidence of pretext to submit to a jury the issue of whether the defendants were motivated by a discriminatory purpose when they hired Mason instead of Becknell. This evidence includes Barrett's alleged statements regarding her preference for hiring a male and a letter written by the principal at the elementary school which positively evaluates Becknell's performance as assistant principal, stating, among other things, that "[a]ny task I have asked [Becknell] to do, she has completed the task with great precision and timeliness."

The Bona Fide Occupational Qualification Exception

The defendants argue that, even if gender motivated their decision to hire Mason instead of Becknell, their actions fall under the "bona fide occupational qualification," or BFOQ, exception to Title VII's prohibition against discrimination on the basis of sex found at 42 U.S.C. § 2000e-2(e). That provision permits gender-based discrimination "in those certain instances where . . . sex . . . is a bona fide occupational qualification reasonably necessary to the normal operation of that particular business or enterprise." [T]he BFOQ defense is written narrowly, and is to be read narrowly. In order to qualify for the defense, the defendants must establish (1) a basis in fact for its belief that gender discrimination is reasonably necessary—not merely reasonable or convenient—to the normal operation of its business. The employer can meet this requirement by showing that (a) all or substantially all members of one gender would be unable to perform safely and efficiently the duties of the job involved; (b) that it is impossible or highly impractical to determine on an individualized basis the fitness for employment of members of one gender; or (c) that the very womanhood or very manhood of the employee undermines his capacity to perform a job satisfactorily.

Second, the employer must establish that the gender qualification "relate[s] to the essence, or to the central mission of the employer's business." Third, the employer must establish that no reasonable alternatives exist to discrimination on the basis of sex. The defendants argue that it is "reasonably necessary" to the normal operation of the high school to hire only males for the assistant principal position. They argue that this is because the policies of the Owsley County School system require that a male at least be present when male students are being disciplined. It is not clear from the defendants' pleadings whether a male must also actually administer the discipline. The defendants state that, pursuant to the High School policy, administrators do all disciplining of students and that this is one of the "largest roles of administrators" at the school. They further argue that, if the assistant principal is not a male, then a male teacher would have to be called away from his teaching duties every time a male student had to be disciplined.

Based on the record before it, however, the Court cannot find as a matter of law that it is reasonably necessary to hire only males for the High School assistant principal position. The defendants assert that the Owsley County Board of Education requires that a male be present when male students are disciplined and they cite to Tina Cornwell's deposition as evidence of this policy. Cornwell testified that she "guessed" that two females couldn't discipline a male student in cases of corporal punishment. Chad Mason, the newly hired assistant principal, testified that a male must paddle male students and that a male witness must be present when that occurs. He testified that he is the person at the high school who paddles male students. He testified that this occurs "maybe once a month, once every three weeks. Maybe not . . . not very often." This does not establish as a matter of law that it is reasonably necessary that only males fill the position of assistant principal at the High School. Nor does this establish that the hiring of only males for the assistant principal position relates to the essence, or to the central mission of the employer's business. It appears that the only form of punishment implicated is paddling and it further appears that paddling is not done frequently.

Finally, the defendants have not established that there is no reasonable alternative to hiring only males for the position. Mason testified that, when he paddles male students, he generally asks both a police officer and a male teacher to be present. Thus, it appears that two males other than the assistant principal are generally available to both administer and witness the paddling of male students. Furthermore, the assistant principal position was vacant for nearly two years before Mason was hired. During that time period, the school must have had some alternative means of paddling male students that did not require a male assistant principal.

Further, neither the advertisement placed by the defendants in the local paper for the position nor the job posting on the Kentucky Department of Education website indicated that only males would be considered for the position. It is clear that, going into their December 13, 2005, meeting, at least some of the other members of the council did not believe that being male was a requirement for the position. At that meeting, some of the council members suggested Becknell for the position. Accordingly, based on the record before it, the Court cannot find that being male is a bona fide occupational qualification for the assistant principal position that is reasonably necessary to the normal operation of the High School.

Motion for summary judgment denied in favor of Becknell.

Remedies Various remedies are possible once private plaintiffs or the EEOC wins a Title VII suit. If intentional discrimination has caused lost wages, employees can obtain **back pay** accruing from a date two years before the filing of the charge. At the court's discretion, successful private plaintiffs also may recover reasonable **attorney's fees.** In addition, victims of intentional discrimination can recover **compensatory damages** for harms such as emotional distress, sickness, loss of reputation, or denial of credit. Victims of intentional discrimination also can recover **punitive damages** where the defendant discriminated with malice or with reckless indifference to the plaintiff's rights. However, the sum of the plaintiff's compensatory and punitive damages cannot exceed certain amounts that vary with the size of the employer. For example, they cannot total more than $300,000 for an employer with more than 500 employees.

Discrimination may also entitle successful plaintiffs to **equitable relief.** Examples include orders compelling hiring, reinstatement, or retroactive seniority. On occasion, moreover, the courts have ordered quotalike preferences in Title VII cases involving race and (occasionally) gender discrimination. For example, a court might order that whites and minorities be hired on a 50–50 basis until minority representation in the employer's work force reaches some specified percentage. Generally speaking, such orders are permissible if (1) an employer has engaged in severe, widespread, or long-standing discrimination; (2) the order does not unduly restrict the employment interests of white people; and (3) it does not force an employer to hire unqualified workers. Minority preferences also may appear in the **consent decrees** courts issue when approving the terms on which the parties have settled a Title VII case.[7]

Race or Color Discrimination

At this point, we consider each of Title VII's prohibited bases of discrimination in more detail. *Race or color* discrimination includes discrimination against blacks, other racial minorities, Eskimos, and American Indians, among others. Title VII also prohibits racial discrimination against whites. Nonetheless, voluntary racial preferences that favor minorities who are qualified for the job in question survive a Title VII attack if they (1) are intended to correct a racial imbalance involving underrepresentation of minorities in traditionally segregated job categories, (2) do not "unnecessarily trammel" the rights of white employees or create an absolute bar to their advancement, and (3) are only temporary. Note that here our concern is not the use of minority preferences as a *remedy* for a Title VII violation, but whether such preferences *themselves* violate Title VII when voluntarily established by an employer.

National Origin Discrimination

National origin discrimination includes discrimination based on (1) the country of one's or one's ancestors' origin; or (2) one's possession of physical, cultural, or linguistic characteristics identified with people of a particular nation. Thus, plaintiffs in national origin discrimination cases need not have been born in the country at issue. In fact, if the discrimination is based on physical, cultural, or linguistic traits identified with a particular nation, even the plaintiff's ancestors need not have been born there. Thus, a person of pure French ancestry may have a Title VII case if she suffers discrimination because she looks like, acts like, or talks like a German.

Certain formally neutral employment practices can also constitute national origin discrimination. Employers who hire only U.S. citizens may violate Title VII if their policy has the purpose or effect of discriminating against one or more national origin groups. This could happen where the employer is located in an area where aliens of a particular nationality are heavily concentrated. Also, employment criteria such as height, weight, and fluency in English may violate Title VII if they have a disparate impact on a national origin group and are not job-related.

Religious Discrimination

For Title VII purposes, the term *religion* is broadly defined. Although all courts may not agree, the EEOC says that it includes any set of moral beliefs that are sincerely held with the same strength as traditional religious views. In fact, Title VII forbids religious discrimination against atheists. It also forbids discrimination based on religious *observances or practices*—for example, grooming, clothing, or the refusal to work on the Sabbath. But such discrimination is permissible if an employer cannot reasonably accommodate the religious practice without suffering undue hardship. Undue hardship exists when the accommodation imposes more than a minimal burden on an employer.

Sex Discrimination

Title VII's ban on sex discrimination aims at *gender-based* discrimination and does not forbid discrimination on the basis of homosexuality or transsexuality.[8] Just as clearly, it applies to gender discrimination against both men and women. Still, voluntary employer programs favoring women in hiring

---

[7]As discussed in Chapter 3, the Supreme Court has held that federal government racial discrimination against whites gets the same full strict scrutiny as racial discrimination against blacks and other racial minorities. It remains to be seen whether this change will affect the courts' ability to order remedial minority preferences or to approve such preferences when they appear in consent decrees.

[8]However, a number of state and municipal fair employment practices laws forbid discrimination on the basis of sexual orientation. For a list of these states and municipalities, see Lambda Legal, http://lambdalegal .org/our-work/states (providing a summary of state laws that forbid discrimination on the basis of sexual orientation).

or promotion survive a Title VII attack if they meet the previous tests for voluntary racial preferences (reformulated in terms of gender). Title VII also forbids discrimination on the bases of pregnancy and childbirth, and requires employers to treat these conditions like any other condition similarly affecting working ability in their sick leave programs, medical benefit and disability plans, and so forth. Finally, sexual stereotyping violates Title VII. This is employer behavior that either (1) denies a woman employment opportunities by assuming that she must have traditionally "female" traits (e.g., unaggressiveness), or (2) penalizes her for lacking such traits (e.g., for acting aggressively).

Sexual Harassment Unwelcome sexual advances, requests for sexual favors, and other verbal or physical conduct of a sexual nature by supervisors, co-workers, or even nonemployees such as customers can violate Title VII. There are two basic forms of sexual harassment. The first, called *quid pro quo* sexual harassment, involves some express or implied linkage between an employee's submission to sexually oriented behavior and tangible job consequences. Quid pro quo cases usually arise when, due to an employee's refusal to submit, she suffers a *tangible job detriment* of an economic nature. Quid pro quo harassment is committed only by supervisory employees, because only supervisors have the power over hiring and firing. For example, suppose that a supervisor fires a secretary because she refuses to have sexual relations with him or refuses to go out on a date with him. Such conduct would violate Title VII whether or not the supervisor expressly told the secretary that she would be fired for refusing to submit. Title VII is also violated if a supervisor denies a subordinate a deserved promotion or other job benefit for refusing to submit.

The second form of harassment, called *hostile environment harassment,* occurs when an employee is subjected to unwelcome, sex-related behavior that is sufficiently severe or pervasive to change the conditions of the victim's employment and create an abusive working environment. Hostile environment sexual harassment can be inflicted by both supervisors and co-workers. Because such behavior must be *unwelcome,* however, an employee may have trouble recovering if she instigated or contributed to the sex-related behavior. Also, the offending behavior must be sufficiently *severe or pervasive* to create an environment that a *reasonable victim* would find hostile or abusive.

The reach of Title VII sexual harassment law continues to expand. Courts have long held that men can recover for sexual harassment by women. The U.S. Supreme Court, in

Oncale v. Sundowner,[9] confirmed that Title VII allows recovery when the harasser(s) and the harassee are of the same gender. Some courts have granted Title VII recoveries for "sexual favoritism"—discrimination in favor of employees who submit to sexual harassment, benefit from a sexual relationship with a superior, or trade sex for personal advancement. Finally, Title VII also forbids workplace harassment based on race, color, national origin, and religion.

Employer Liability for Sexual Harassment Committed by Its Employees Beyond the question of what is sexual harassment is the question whether a company will be held liable for sexual harassment committed by one of its employees. Is a company liable for sexual harassment committed by one of its employees against another one even if the harassment was not reported or otherwise known? The answer to that depends on whether the harasser was a coemployee or a supervisor of the victim, whether the victim suffered a tangible job detriment, and whether the company had sexual harassment policies, training, and grievance procedures. Generally, an employer will be liable for harassment by a *co-worker* of the victim only when the employer knew or should have known about the harassment.

Two 1998 Supreme Court cases[10] created a framework for deciding employer liability in cases of harassment by a *supervisor.* This framework distinguishes between situations in which sexual harassment by a supervisor ends in some tangible employment action, such as firing or demoting the employee, and those in which the victim suffers no tangible job consequence. When a supervisor with immediate or higher authority over the employee commits sexual harassment, the company is subject to vicarious liability. When no tangible employment action is taken, however, the employer may raise an affirmative defense to liability or damages. To prevail under this defense, the company, the employer must prove (1) that the employer exercised reasonable care to prevent and correct promptly any sexually harassing behavior, and (2) that the plaintiff unreasonably failed to take advantage of any preventive or corrective opportunities provided by the employer or to otherwise avoid harm. This framework is discussed in the following *Keeton v. Flying J* case.

---

[9]523 U.S. 75 (U.S. S. Ct. 1975).

[10]*Burlington Industries v. Ellerth,* 524 U.S. 742 (U.S. S. Ct. 1998), and *Faragher v. Boca Raton,* 524 U.S. 775 (U.S. S. Ct. 1998).

Keeton v. Flying J, Inc.   429 F.3d 259 (6th Cir. 2005)

Flying J operates travel plazas that cater to interstate plazas. Each plaza has a restaurant. Kyle Keeton applied to be an assistant restaurant manager at a Flying J plaza. On his employment application, he indicated a willingness to relocate to other Flying J plazas because he believed relocation would increase his chances for advancement. He lived in Georgia when Flying J hired him, but he agreed to relocate to Tennessee for training. After he completed his training in June of 2001, Flying J assigned Keeton to work as an associate manager at the Walton, Kentucky, plaza. Flying J orally committed to keep Keeton at the Walton store for five years. Judy Harrell was the general manager and his immediate supervisor.

In September, Harrell began making several sexual advances toward Keeton, which he rejected. Even though Keeton was not scheduled to work on December 4, 2001, Harrell called him at home and asked him to come to the restaurant so that she could speak to him in person. When Keeton arrived at the restaurant, Harrell told him that he was fired, explaining, "you're not supporting me." Prior to this meeting, Harrell had never disciplined Keeton formally or informally, had not criticized him at all during management meetings, and Keeton had no warning that his job was in jeopardy. After the meeting, an assistant manager escorted Keeton from the building.

Keeton returned home and phoned Jamal Abdalla, who had been the manager of the district encompassing Walton when Keeton was hired, but had changed jobs to be the district manager of another district that included Cannonsburg, a town 120 miles away from Walton. Keeton told Abdalla about the termination and that he thought it resulted from sexual harassment. Abdalla called Keeton back about one and a half hours later and told him that he could maintain his position as associate manager if he transferred to Cannonsburg. Later that same day, his termination was formally changed to a two-week suspension, then a one-week suspension, then "to however fast [Keeton] could get over to Cannonsburg." Abdalla told him that he was being "reinstated." It took Keeton one week to move to Cannonsburg, and he was paid for that week. Keeton maintained the same title, responsibilities, salary, and benefits in Cannonsburg that he had in Walton. Keeton's wife could not move with him to Cannonsburg because of a debilitating back problem that resulted in serious surgery. While he was working in Cannonsburg, Keeton maintained two residences—one for himself and one for his wife. Keeton worked at the Cannonsburg Flying J restaurant until mid-January, when he left for a position with another restaurant chain. Keeton sued Flying J for sexual harassment, retaliation, and constructive discharge in violation of Title VII. At trial, the jury found Flying J liable for supervisory sexual harassment resulting in a tangible employment action and it awarded Keeton $15,000 in compensatory damages for emotional suffering. Flying J appealed.

Guy, Circuit Judge

An employer's liability for supervisory sexual harassment depends on the consequences of the supervisor's actions. If proven sexual harassment by the supervisor did not result in a tangible employment action, then the employer may not be liable if it engaged in preventative or corrective measures and the plaintiff unreasonably failed to utilize the measures the employer provided. *Burlington Industries, Inc. v. Ellerth* (U.S. Sup. Ct. 1998). If the sexual harassment did result in a tangible employment action, the employer will be strictly liable for the supervisor's sexual harassment. When a plaintiff proves that a tangible employment action resulted from a refusal to submit to a supervisor's sexual demands, he or she establishes that the employment decision itself constitutes a change in the terms and conditions of employment that is actionable under Title VII. The *Ellerth* court defined a tangible employment action as "a significant change in employment status, such as hiring, firing, failing to promote, reassignment with significantly different responsibilities, or a decision causing a significant change in benefits." Accordingly, we have stated that an employment action must be materially adverse for an employer to be strictly liable for sexual harassment. Flying J argues on appeal that the termination was not a tangible employment action because it was too temporary, and that the transfer was not a tangible employment action because it was lateral.

A. The Termination

We have decided that when an employer imposes an employment action that would be an adverse employment action but then quickly reverses the action, the employee has not suffered an adverse employment action. In *Bowman v. Shawnee State University*, we determined that a temporary removal of responsibilities was not an adverse action. There, the plaintiff had been an instructor and the Coordinator of Sports Studies at a university, and he alleged that his supervisor, a woman, sexually harassed him, ultimately resulting in her removing him as Coordinator. Ten days later, he was restored to his previous position and the termination letter was removed from his file. We held that "even if we assume that the loss of the Coordinator position constitutes a significant change in employment status, there is no tangible employment action in this case because the very temporary nature of the employment action in question makes it a non-materially adverse employment action." Other courts have also held that when an otherwise adverse employment action is rescinded before the employee suffers a tangible harm, the employee has not suffered an adverse employment action. Therefore, the only reasonable conclusion the jury could have reached in this case is that Keeton's termination lasting only hours was not a tangible employment action.

B. The Transfer

Flying J maintains that a transfer without a change in status, benefits, or salary is not a tangible employment action. We have held that reassignments without salary or work hour changes do not ordinarily constitute adverse employment decisions in employment discrimination claims. In *Kocsis [v. Multi-Care Mgmt. Inc.]*, a nursing supervisor was reassigned as a unit nurse. There was no evidence that the new position held less prestige, earned a lower salary, demanded worse hours, or entitled her to any difference in employment related benefits of any kind. Therefore, we concluded that the reassignment was not an adverse action. In *White [v. Burlington N. & Santa Fe. Ry. Co.]*, a female railroad employee sued her employer for sex discrimination. After she had complained about sexual harassment committed by her immediate supervisor, she was removed from her forklift position and reassigned to a track laborer position. Her pay and benefits were the same, but the job was dirtier, more labor intensive, more difficult, required fewer qualifications, and was considered a worse job by the other employees. We concluded that even though there was no loss in salary or benefits, the factors listed above were unique to the plaintiff's situation and rendered the transfer a demotion.

In this case, Keeton's responsibilities in Cannonsburg were not different from his responsibilities in Walton. The only difference between the two positions was location, and Keeton did not present any evidence that Cannonsburg was objectively a worse location than Walton. Cannonsburg was, however, a substantial distance from Walton. Flying J correctly points out that *Koscis* and *White* focus on the differences in job duties and not other impacts on the employee. We have not precluded consideration of such factors as commuting distance or relocation, however. Flying J maintains that a dislike of a long commute or relocation is an example of the subjective desirability of a position to the employee and we therefore should disregard Keeton's dislike of his new location. If dislike of increased commute or relocation for a new position merely represents the subjective taste of the employee, then we would not have expressly stated that increased distance is a relevant consideration. In *Akers v. Alvey*, a state employee who complained about sexual harassment was transferred to a different county's office. We decided that the transfer was not an adverse employment action because there was no significant change in her pay or duties and the transfer actually reduced Aker's roundtrip commute from her home by 60 miles per day. While this jury found that Keeton was not constructively discharged, it could reasonably have found that Keeton's transfer, which increased his commute to the extent that he needed to consider relocation, was an adverse employment action.

Flying J also argues that the transfer could not have been an adverse employment action [because] Keeton had agreed to relocate on his employment application. Keeton's employment application does not negate the transfer's impact on Keeton because when he agreed to be transferred, he did so with the understanding that a transfer would be for advancement within the company and not as a result of unlawful sexual harassment. Having determined that the jury could have reasonably concluded that Keeton suffered an adverse employment action, we affirm.

Affirmed in favor of Keeton.

Section 1981
Where it applies, a post–Civil War civil rights statute called Section 1981 sets employment discrimination standards resembling those of Title VII. Section 1981 forbids public and private employment discrimination against blacks, people of certain racially characterized national origins such as Mexicans, and ethnic groups such as gypsies and Jews. Included within such discrimination are most of the ways that an employer might disadvantage an employee. A recent Supreme Court case held that 1981 also prohibits retaliation against employees who complain about racial discrimination.[11]

Section 1981 is important because it gives covered plaintiffs certain advantages that Title VII does not provide. Although courts often use Title VII's methods of proof in Section 1981 cases, Title VII's limitations on covered employers and its complex procedural requirements do not apply. Also, damages are apt to be greater under Section 1981; in particular, Title VII's limits on compensatory and punitive damages are inapplicable. For these reasons, covered plaintiffs often include a Section 1981 claim along with a Title VII claim in their complaint.

The Age Discrimination in Employment Act
The 1967 Age Discrimination in Employment Act (ADEA) prohibits age-based employment discrimination against employees who are *at least 40 years of age*. In

---

[11]*CBOCS West, Inc. v. Humphries*, 128 S. Ct. 1951 (U.S. Sup. Ct. 2008).

General Dynamics Land Systems v. Cline,[12] a recent U.S. Supreme Court case, the Court decided that it is not a violation of the ADEA for an employer to *favor* older employees over younger employees, even if the younger employees are in the 40-and-over age range. You can read the Court's opinion in *Cline* in Chapter 1.

Coverage   The ADEA covers individuals, partnerships, labor organizations and employment agencies (as to their employees), and corporations that (1) engage in an industry affecting interstate commerce, and (2) employ at least 20 persons. The act no longer regulates state and local governments.[13] *Referrals* by an employment agency to a covered employer are within the ADEA's scope regardless of the agency's size. In addition, the ADEA reaches labor union practices affecting *union members;* usually, unions with 25 or more members are covered. The ADEA protects against age discrimination in many employment contexts, including hiring, firing, pay, job assignment, and fringe benefits.

Procedural Requirements   The complex procedural requirements for an ADEA suit are beyond the scope of this text. Before she can sue in her own right, a private plaintiff must file a charge with the EEOC or with an appropriate state agency. The EEOC also may sue to enforce the ADEA; such a suit precludes private suits arising from the same alleged violation. For both government and private suits, the statute of limitations is three years from the date of an alleged *willful* violation and two years from the date of an alleged *nonwillful* violation.

Proof   Proving age discrimination is no problem where an employer uses an express age criterion, and may be easy where there is direct evidence of discrimination such as testimony or incriminating documents. The U.S. Supreme Court recently decided that the ADEA permits plaintiffs to prove discrimination through the disparate impact theory, just as Title VII does.[14]

Defenses   The ADEA allows employers to discharge or otherwise discipline an employee for *good cause,* and to use *reasonable factors other than age*[15] in their

employment decisions. It also allows employers to observe the terms of a *bona fide seniority system.* In addition, the ADEA has a *bona fide occupational qualification* (BFOQ) defense. As a very general statement, an employer seeking to use this defense must show that its age classification is reasonably necessary to the proper performance—usually the safe performance—of the job in question. For example, an employer that refuses to hire anyone over 60 as a helicopter pilot should have a BFOQ defense if it has a reasonable basis for concluding that 60-and-over helicopter pilots pose significant safety risks, or that it is not feasible to test older pilots individually.

Remedies   Remedies available after a successful ADEA suit include unpaid back wages and overtime pay resulting from the discrimination; an additional equal award of liquidated damages where the employer acted willfully; attorney's fees; and equitable relief, including hiring, reinstatement, and promotion. Most courts do not allow punitive damages and recoveries for pain, suffering, mental distress, and so forth.

The Americans with Disabilities Act

The Americans with Disabilities Act (the ADA) prohibits discrimination against people who have disabilities. Before the 1990s, federal regulation of employment discrimination against people with disabilities mainly was limited to certain federal contractors and recipients of federal financial assistance. By passing Title I of the ADA, however, Congress addressed this problem comprehensively. This portion of the ADA is primarily enforced by the EEOC, and its procedures and remedies are the same as for Title VII.

Covered Entities   Title I covers employers who have 15 or more employees and who are engaged in an industry affecting interstate commerce. Employers include individuals, partnerships, corporations, colleges and universities, labor unions and employment agencies (regarding their own employees), and state and local governments. The act also covers certain labor unions in their capacity as employee representative, as well as employment agencies' discrimination against their clients.

Substantive Protections   The ADA forbids covered entities from discriminating against *qualified individuals with a disability* because of that disability. It covers disability-related discrimination regarding hiring, firing, promotion, pay, and innumerable other employment decisions. The ADA protects both individuals who can perform their job despite their disability, and individuals

---

[12]540 U.S. 581 (U.S. S. Ct. 2004).

[13]Age discrimination in the federal government is beyond the scope of this text.

[14]*Smith v. City of Jackson,* 125 S. Ct. 1536 (U.S. S. Ct. 2005).

[15]According to a recent U.S. Supreme Court ruling, the employer who seeks to use the "reasonable factors other than age" defense in a disparate impact claim under the ADEA bears the burden of production and the burden of persuasion that its action was done for reasonable factors other than age. *Meacham v. Knolls Atomic Power Laboratory,* 128 S. Ct. 2395 (U.S. Sup. Ct. 2008).

Figure 2   A Map through the ADA

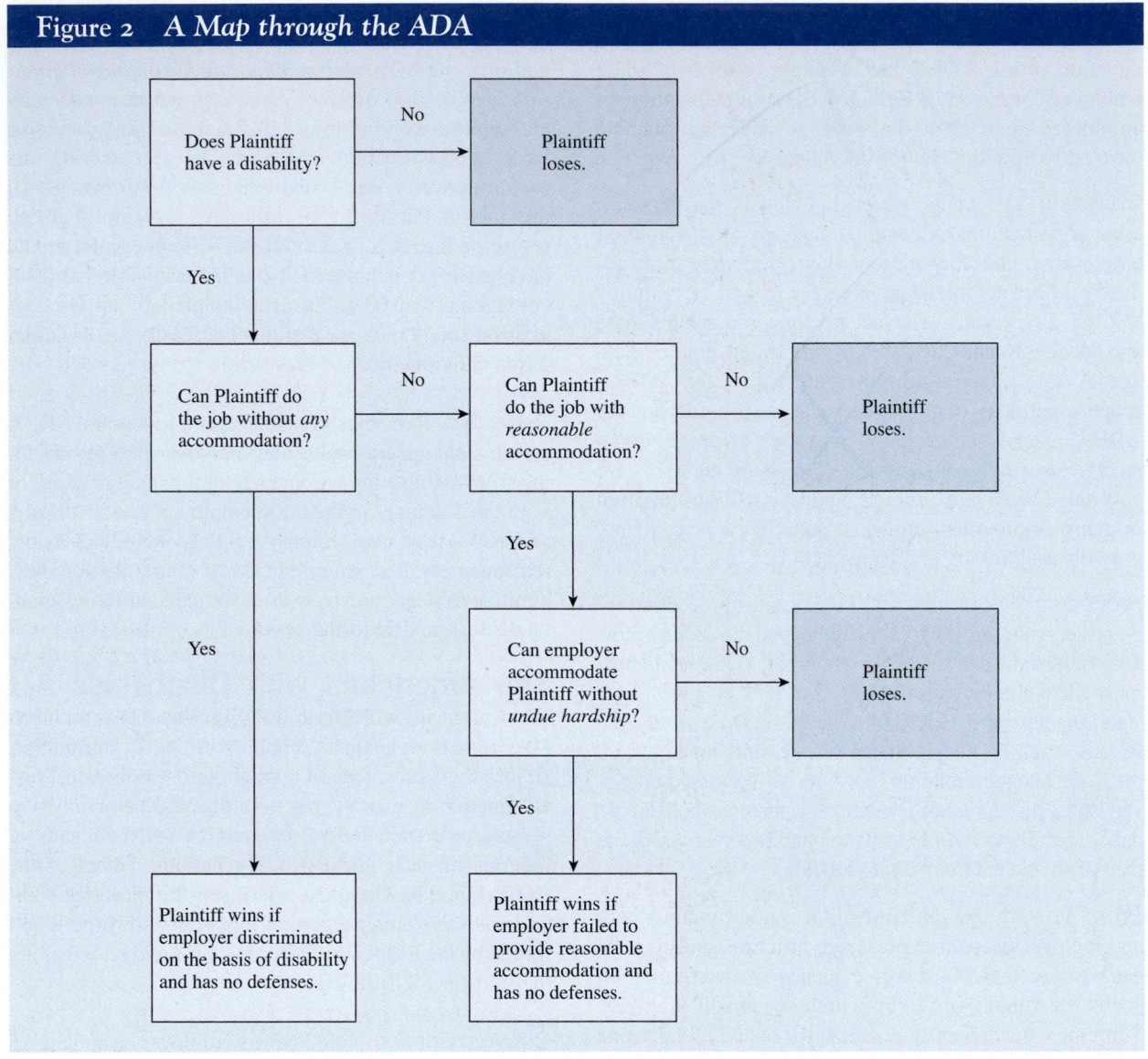

who could perform their job if reasonable accommodation is provided. In the later case, employers illegally discriminate if they do not provide such accommodation. *Reasonable accommodation* includes: making existing facilities readily accessible and usable, acquiring new equipment, restructuring jobs, modifying work schedules, and reassigning workers to vacant positions, among other options. Figure 2 displays the reasoning used in an ADA case.

However, employers need not make reasonable accommodation where such accommodation would cause them to suffer *undue hardship*. Undue hardship is an act

requiring significant difficulty or expense. Among the factors used to determine its existence are the cost of accommodation, the covered entity's overall financial resources, and the accommodation's effect on the covered entity's activities. The ADA also protects employers whose allegedly discriminatory decisions are based on *job-related criteria* and *business necessity,* so long as proper job performance cannot be accomplished by reasonable accommodation.

What Is a Disability? The ADA defines a *disability* as (1) a physical or mental impairment that substantially limits one or more major life activities, or (2) a record of such an impairment, or (3) one's being regarded as having such an impairment. (The last two categories protect those who have previously been misdiagnosed or who have recovered from earlier impairments.) Not protected, however, are those who suffer discrimination for currently engaging in the illegal use of drugs.

In the recent past, the U.S. Supreme court decided several cases interpreting the ADA's definition of disability in a way that narrowed the concept of disability. In *Sutton v. United Airlines,* a 1999 case, the Court decided that corrective measures must be taken into account in determining whether an impairment is a disability. There, severely nearsighted twin sisters whose vision was 20/20 with corrective lenses had been denied jobs as airline pilots because their corrected vision was worse than the airline's minimum vision requirement. The Court decided that their vision was not a disability within the meaning of the ADA. In the 2002 case of *Toyota Manufacturing Co. v. Williams,* the Court decided that for a physical impairment to constitute a disability, the life activity that it substantially limits must be one that is "central to daily life" as opposed to an activity that is used in a particular job.

The Americans with Disability Amendments Act of 2008 The reaction of Congress to the *Sutton* and *Toyota* decisions was that the Supreme Court had interpreted the definition of disability too narrowly, eliminating protections for people who Congress had intended to protect with the ADA. Congress's response was to enact the ADA Amendments Act of 2008, which clarifies the standards for determining disability. The amendments express Congress's intent that the ADA should be "construed in favor of broad coverage" and that "the question of whether an individual's impairment is a disability under the ADA should not demand extensive analysis."

The ADA amendments preserve the same broad language of the 1990 ADA that a disability is a physical or mental impairment that limits one or more major life activities or having a record of such an impairment or being regarded as having such an impairment. The amendments specify, however, that *major life activities* include (but are not limited to) tasks such as caring for oneself, performing manual tasks, seeing, hearing, eating, sleeping, walking, standing, lifting, bending, speaking, breathing, learning, reading, concentrating, thinking, communicating, and working. They also include the operation of major bodily functions, such as (but not limited to) the operation of the immune system, normal cell growth, digestive, bowel,

bladder, neurological, brain, respiratory, circulatory, endocrine, and reproductive functions.

As a response to the *Sutton* case, the amendments specifically state that the determination of whether an impairment limits a major life activity is to be made without regard to ameliorative effects of measures that people use to cope with their mental and physical conditions, such as medication, equipment, hearing aids, prosthetic limbs, mobility devices, and oxygen therapy. The ameliorative effect of ordinary eyeglasses and contact lenses can be considered in determining whether an impairment substantially limits a major life activity. However, an employer or other covered entity cannot use qualification standards, employment tests, or other selection criteria based on an individual's uncorrected vision unless the requirement is job related and consistent with business necessity.

As a response to the *Toyota* case, the amendments state that an impairment that substantially limits one major life activity need not limit other major life activities in order to be considered a disability. Furthermore, an impairment that is episodic or in remission is a disability if it would substantially limit a major life activity when active.

The ADA Amendment Act also states that a person meets the standard of "being regarded as having such an impairment" if he has been discriminated against because of an actual or perceived physical or mental impairment, whether or not the impairment limits or is perceived to limit a major life activity. A person is not "regarded as having such an impairment," however, if the impairment that he is perceived to have is one that is transitory or minor.

Executive Order 11246
Executive Order 11246, issued in 1965 and later amended, forbids race, color, national origin, religion, and sex discrimination by certain federal contractors. The order is enforced by the Labor Department's Office of Federal Contract Compliance Programs (OFCCP). In the past, OFCCP enforcement has included affirmative action requirements and occasionally quotalike preferences benefiting racial minorities.

State Antidiscrimination Laws
Most states have statutes that parallel Title VII, the EPA, the ADEA, and the ADA. These statutes sometimes provide more extensive protection than their federal counterparts. In addition, some states prohibit forms of discrimination not barred by federal law. Examples include discrimination

Ethics in Action

Bookworks, Inc., requires employees to sign an agreement that they will settle any dispute or claim concerning employment through binding arbitration. Catherine, a Bookworks employee, alleged that her supervisor fired her for refusing to go on a date with him. She wants to file a sexual harassment case under Title VII against Bookworks, and Bookworks asserts that this is a claim that must be arbitrated rather than adjudicated in court. What are the ethical considerations involved in mandatory arbitration agreements that require employees to arbitrate discrimination and other employment-related claims?

on the bases of one's marital status, physical appearance, sexual orientation, political affiliation, and off-the-job smoking.

Finally, some states and localities have adopted laws that adopt the employment discrimination theory called **comparable worth.** These laws, which typically apply only to public employees, often say that state governments should not discriminate in pay between female-dominated jobs and male-dominated jobs of comparable overall worth to the employer. The worth of different jobs may be determined by giving each job a point rating under factors such as skill, responsibility, effort, and working conditions; adding the ratings; and comparing the totals. It was once believed that comparable worth claims might find favor under Title VII, but that possibility has receded over the years.

Employee Privacy

The term employee privacy describes several employment issues that have assumed increasing importance recently. Uniting these issues is a concern with protecting employees' personal dignity and increasing their freedom from intrusions, surveillance, and the revelation of personal matters.

Polygraph Testing Over the years, employers have made increasing use of polygraph and other lie

CONCEPT REVIEW

The Employment Discrimination Laws Compared

	Protected Traits	Covered Employer Decisions	Need to File Charge in Private Suit?
Equal Pay Act	Sex only	Pay only	No
Title VII	Race, color, national origin, religion, sex	Wide range	Yes
Section 1981	Race, racially characterized national origin, perhaps alienage	Wide range	No
Age Discrimination in Employment Act	Age, if victim 40 or over	Wide range	Yes
Americans with Disabilities Act	Existence of disability, if person qualified to perform job with or without reasonable accommodation	Wide range	Yes
Executive Order 11246	Race, color, religion, national origin, sex	Wide range	Not applicable; enforced by OFCCP

detector tests—most often, to screen job applicants and to investigate employee thefts. This has led to concerns about the accuracy of such tests; the personal questions examiners sometimes ask; and the tests' impact on workers' job prospects, job security, and personal privacy. Besides provoking state restrictions on polygraph testing, such worries led Congress to pass the Employee Polygraph Protection Act in 1988.

The Employee Polygraph Protection Act mainly regulates lie detector tests, which include polygraph tests and certain other devices for assessing a person's honesty. Under the act, employers may not (1) require, suggest, request, or cause employees or prospective employees to take any lie detector test; (2) use, accept, refer to, or inquire about the results of any lie detector test administered to employees or prospective employees; and (3) discriminate or threaten to discriminate against employees or prospective employees because of the results of any lie detector test, or because such parties failed or refused to take such a test. The act also has an antiretaliation provision.

However, certain employers and tests are exempt from these provisions. They include (1) federal, state, and local government employers; (2) certain national defense and security-related tests by the federal government; (3) certain tests by security service firms; and (4) certain tests by firms manufacturing and distributing controlled substances. The act also contains a limited exemption for private employers that use polygraph tests when investigating economic losses caused by theft, embezzlement, industrial espionage, and so forth. Finally, the act restricts the disclosure of test results by examiners and by most employers.

The Polygraph Protection Act is enforced by the Labor Department, which has issued regulations in furtherance of that mission. It does not preempt state laws that prohibit lie detector tests or that set standards stricter than those imposed by federal law. Violations of the act or its regulations can result in civil penalties, suits for equitable relief by the Labor Department, and private suits for damages and equitable relief. Workers and job applicants who succeed in a private suit can obtain employment, reinstatement, promotion, and payment of lost wages and benefits.

Drug and Alcohol Testing

Due to their impact on employees' safe and effective job performance, employers have become increasingly concerned about both on-the-job and off-the-job drug and alcohol use. Thus, employers increasingly require employees and job applicants to undergo urine tests for drugs and/or alcohol. Because those who test positive may be either disciplined or induced to undergo treatment, and because the tests themselves can raise privacy concerns, some legal checks on their use have emerged.

Drug and alcohol testing by *public* employers can be attacked under the Fourth Amendment's search-and-seizure provisions. However, such tests generally are constitutional where there is a reasonable basis for suspecting that an employee is using drugs or alcohol, or drug use in a particular job could threaten the public interest or public safety. Due to the government action requirement discussed in Chapter 3, *private-sector* employees generally have no federal constitutional protection against drug and alcohol testing. Some state constitutions, however, lack a government action requirement. In addition, several states now regulate private drug and/or alcohol testing by statute. Tort suits for invasion of privacy or infliction of emotional distress may also be possible in some cases.[16]

Despite these protections, however, federal law *requires* private-sector drug testing in certain situations. Under a Defense Department rule, for example, employers who contract with the department must agree to establish a drug-testing program requiring, for instance, that employees who work in sensitive positions sometimes be tested. Also, Transportation Department regulations require random testing of public and private employees occupying safety-sensitive or security-related positions in industries such as aviation, trucking, railroads, mass transit, and others.

Employer Searches

Employers concerned about theft, drug use, and other misbehavior by their employees sometimes conduct searches of those employees' offices, desks, lockers, files, briefcases, packages, vehicles, and even bodies to confirm their suspicions. The Supreme Court has held that public employees sometimes have a reasonable expectation of privacy in areas such as their offices, desks, or files. But it also held that searches of those areas are constitutional under the Fourth Amendment when they are reasonable under the circumstances. Determining reasonableness generally means balancing the employee's legitimate privacy expectations against the government's need for supervision

---

[16]Invasion of privacy and intentional infliction of emotional distress are discussed in Chapter 6, and negligent infliction of emotional distress is discussed in Chapter 7.

and control of the workplace, with more intrusive searches demanding a higher degree of justification. Finally, the Court also said that neither probable cause nor a warrant is necessary for such searches to proceed.

As noted above, the U.S. Constitution ordinarily does not apply to private employment. Nonetheless, both private and public employees can mount common law invasion of privacy suits against employers who conduct searches. In such cases, courts usually try to weigh the intrusiveness of the search against the purposes justifying it and consider the availability of less intrusive alternatives that still would satisfy the employer's legitimate needs.

Records and References

Many states allow both public and private employees at least some access to personnel files maintained by their employers. Also, some states limit third-party access to such records. In addition, employers who transmit such data to third parties—for example, in letters of reference—may be civilly liable for defamation or invasion of privacy.[17] However, truth is a defense in defamation cases. In both defamation and invasion of privacy suits, moreover, the employer's actions may be conditionally privileged. This defense and these privileges can protect employers who are sued for truthful, accurate, relevant, good faith statements made in references concerning former employees. Finally, a few states have allowed defamation suits for so-called compelled self-disclosure by job-seeking, wrongfully discharged employees who have been required to tell potential employers their former employer's alleged reasons for firing them.

Employer Monitoring

Although employers have always monitored their employees' work, recent technological advances enable such monitoring to occur without those employees' knowledge. Examples include closed-circuit television, video monitoring, telephone monitoring, the monitoring of computer workstations (e.g., by counting keystrokes), and metal detectors at plant entrances. Such monitoring has encountered objections because employees often are unaware that it exists or may suffer stress when they do know or suspect its existence. Employers counter these objections by stressing that monitoring is highly useful in evaluating employee performance, improving efficiency, and reducing theft.

The amount of litigation and commentary about monitoring has grown as employers and employees are increasingly concerned about privacy. A variety of statutes exist on the federal and state levels concerning electronic privacy and security, and these may implicate some employer monitoring. Although employers have a significant amount of latitude in monitoring employees, telephone monitoring occasionally has been found illegal under federal wiretapping law. Although such claims have been uncommon, invasion of privacy suits may succeed in situations where an employer's need for surveillance is slight and it is conducted in areas, such as restrooms and lounges, in which employees have a reasonable expectation of privacy.

A growing number of companies have adopted specific policies regarding monitoring of employee communications and permissible use of company systems. Many companies have begun to inform their employees that their e-mail, voicemail, Internet usage, and other communications and transactions are subject to monitoring. Company policies may also limit the ways that employees can use company computer systems, and often subject employees who violate the policy to disciplinary penalties such as discharge. The following *TBG Insurance* case discusses the legal significance of these policies.

---

[17]Defamation and invasion of privacy are discussed in Chapter 6.

TBG Insurance Services Corp. v. Superior Court
No. B153400 (Cal. Ct. App. 2002)

For about 12 years, Robert Zieminski worked as a senior executive for TBG Insurance Services Corporation. In the course of his employment, Zieminski used two computers owned by TBG, one at the office, the other at his residence. Zieminski signed TBG's "electronic and telephone equipment policy statement" in which he agreed, among other things, that he would use the computers "for business purposes only and not for personal benefit or non-Company purposes, unless such use [was] expressly approved. Under no circumstances [could the] equipment or systems be used for improper, derogatory, defamatory, obscene or other inappropriate purposes." Zieminski consented to have his computer "use monitored by authorized company personnel" on an "as needed" basis, and agreed that communications transmitted by computer were not private. He acknowledged his understanding that his improper use of the computers could result in disciplinary action, including discharge.

In December 1998, Zieminski and TBG entered a "Shareholder Buy–Sell Agreement," pursuant to which TBG sold 4,000 shares of its stock to Zieminski at $.01 per share. One-third of the stock was to vest on December 1, 1999, one-third on December 1, 2000, and one-third on December 1, 2001, each vesting contingent upon Zieminski's continued employment. If Zieminski's employment terminated before all the shares had vested, TBG had the right to repurchase the nonvested shares at $.01 per share. One-third of Zieminski's shares vested on December 1, 1999. In March 2000, TBG's shareholders, including Zieminski, sold a portion of their TBG shares to Nationwide Insurance Company. Zieminski sold 1,230 of his 1,333 vested shares to Nationwide for $1,278,247. On November 28, 2000, three days before another 1,333 shares were to vest, TBG terminated Zieminski's employment. According to TBG, Zieminski was terminated for violating TBG's electronic policies by repeatedly accessing pornographic sites on the Internet while he was at work. According to Zieminski, the pornographic sites were not accessed intentionally but simply "popped up" on his computer.

Zieminski sued TBG, alleging that his employment had been wrongfully terminated as a pretext to prevent his substantial stock holdings in TBG from fully vesting and to allow TBG to repurchase his nonvested stock for $.01 per share. TBG asked Zieminski to return the home computer and cautioned Zieminski not to delete any information stored on the computer's hard drive. Zieminski responded that he would either return it or purchase it, but that it would be necessary for him to alter or delete some of the information on the hard drive, since "it contains personal information which is subject to a right of privacy." TBG refused to sell the computer to Zieminski and demanded its return without any deletions or alterations. TBG moved to compel production of the computer, contending it has the right to discover whether information on the hard drive proves that, as claimed by TBG, Zieminski violated his employer's policy statement. Zieminski opposed the motion and insisted that, notwithstanding the policy statement, he retained an expectation of privacy with regard to his home computer. According to Zieminski, the home computer was provided as a "perk" to all senior executives, and although it was provided so that business-related work could be done at home, it was "universally accepted and understood by all that the home computer would also be used for personal purposes as well." He said his home computer was used by his wife and children, and that it was primarily used for personal purposes and contained a significant amount of personal information and data such as details of his personal finances and income tax returns. The trial court denied TBG's motion, and TBG filed a petition for a writ of mandate, asking the appellate court to intervene.

Vogel, Justice

A party may obtain discovery regarding any matter, not privileged, that is relevant to the subject matter involved in the pending action. In the context of discovery, evidence is relevant if it might reasonably assist a party in evaluating its case, preparing for trial, or facilitating a settlement. Here, the home computer is indisputably relevant. The issue, therefore, is whether he has a protectible privacy interest in the information to be found on the computer.

Zieminski's privacy claim is based on article I, section I, of the California Constitution, which provides: "All people are by nature free and independent and have inalienable rights. Among these are enjoying and defending life and liberty, acquiring, possessing, and protecting property, and pursuing and obtaining safety, happiness, and privacy." Assuming the existence of a legally cognizable privacy interest, the extent of that interest is not independent of the circumstances and other factors (including advance notice) may affect a person's reasonable expectation of privacy. Accordingly, our decision about the reasonableness of Zieminski's claimed expectation of privacy must take into account any accepted community norms, advance notice to Zieminski about TBG's policy statement, and whether Zieminski had the opportunity to consent to or reject the very thing that constitutes the invasion.

We are concerned in this case with the "community norm" within 21st Century computer-dependent businesses. In 2001, the 700,000-member American Management Association reported that more than three-quarters of this country's major firms monitor, record, and review employee communications and activities on the job, including their telephone calls, e-mail, Internet connections, and computer files. Companies that engage in these practices do so for several reasons, including legal compliance, legal liability, performance review, productivity measures, and security concerns. It is hardly surprising therefore that employers are told they "should establish a policy for the use of [e-mail and the Internet], which every employee should have to read and sign. First, employers can diminish an individual employee's expectation of privacy by clearly stating in the policy that electronic communications are to be used solely for company business, and that the company reserves the right to monitor or access all employee Internet or e-mail usage." Fernandez, *Workplace Claims: Guiding Employers and Employees Safely In and Out of the Revolving Door* (1999), 614 Practicing Law Institute, Litigation and Administrative Practices Course Handbook Series, Litigation 725. For these reasons, the use of computers in the employment context carries with it social norms that effectively diminish the employee's reasonable expectation of privacy with regard to his use of his employer's computers.

TBG's advance notice to Zieminski (the company's policy statement) gave Zieminski the opportunity to consent to or reject the very thing that he now complains about, and that notice, combined with his written consent to the policy, defeats his claim that he had a reasonable expectation of privacy. Zieminski knew that TBG would monitor the files and messages stored on the computers he used at the office and at home. He had the opportunity to consent to TBG's policy or not, and had the opportunity to limit his use of his home computer to purely business matters. To state the obvious, no one compelled Zieminski or his wife or children to use the home computer for personal matters, and no one prevented him from purchasing his own computer for his personal use. With all the information he needed to make an intelligent decision, Zieminski agreed to the company's policy *and* chose to use his computer for personal matters. By any reasonable standard, Zieminski fully and voluntarily relin-quished his privacy rights in the information he stored on his home computer, and he will not now be heard to say that he nevertheless had a *reasonable* expectation of privacy.

Zieminski voluntarily waived whatever right of privacy he might otherwise have had in the information he stored on the home computer. But even assuming that Zieminski has some lingering privacy interest in the information he stored on the home computer, we do not view TBG's demand for production as a serious invasion of that interest. Appropriate protective orders can define the scope of TBG's inspection and copying of information to that which is directly relevant to this litigation, and can prohibit the unnecessary copying and dissemination of Zieminski's financial and other information that has no rational bearing on this case.

Petition granted and writ issued in favor of TBG.

Job Security

The Doctrine of Employment at Will

The traditional employment-at-will rule first appeared around 1870, and by the early 20th century most state courts had adopted it. The rule says that *either party can terminate an employment contract of indefinite duration.* The termination can occur at any time; and can be for good cause or no cause. (However, discharged employees can recover for work actually done.)

The Common Law Exceptions Because it allows employers to discharge indefinite-term employees with virtual impunity, employment at will has long been regarded as a force for economic efficiency but also as a threat to workers' job security. Although the doctrine remains important today, it has been eroded by many of the developments described in this chapter. For example, the NLRA forbids dismissal for union affiliation, and labor contracts frequently bar termination without just cause. Also, Title VII prohibits firings based on certain personal traits, the ADEA blocks discharges on the basis of age, and the ADA forbids terminations for covered disabilities.

Over the past 20 to 25 years, moreover, courts have been carving out common law exceptions to employment at will. Here we discuss the three most important such exceptions. Although a few states do not recognize any of these exceptions, most states have adopted one or more of them. In such states, a terminated employee sometimes can recover against her employer for **wrongful discharge** or **unjust dismissal.** The remedies in successful wrongful discharge suits depend heavily on whether the plaintiff's claim sounds in contract or in tort, with tort remedies being more advantageous for plaintiffs.

The Public Policy Exception The public policy exception to employment at will, which has been recognized by over four-fifths of the states, is the most common basis for a wrongful discharge suit. It usually is a tort claim. In public policy cases, the terminated employee argues that his discharge was unlawful because it violated the state's public policy. How do courts determine the content of this public policy? The mere fact that a discharge is unfounded or unfair does not mean that the public policy theory applies. Although there is some disagreement on the subject, most courts limit "public policy" to the policies furthered by existing laws such as constitutional provisions, statutes, and perhaps administrative regulations and common law rules. For this reason, employees often fail to recover where they are fired for ethical objections to job assignments or employer practices.

Successful suits under the public policy exception usually involve firings caused by an employee's (1) refusal to commit an unlawful act (e.g., committing perjury or violating the antitrust laws), (2) performance of an important public obligation (e.g., jury duty or whistle-blowing),[18] or (3) exercise of a legal right or privilege (e.g., making a workers' compensation claim or refusing

---

[18]Whistle-blowers are employees who publicly disclose dangerous, illegal, or improper behavior. Most states have passed statues protecting the employment rights of certain whistle-blowers.

to take an illegal polygraph test). In each case, the act (or refusal to act) that caused the firing is consistent with some public policy; for this reason, the firing frustrates the policy. For example, firing an employee for filing a workers' compensation claim undermines the public policies underlying state workers' compensation statutes.

The following *Franklin* case illustrates the application of the public policy theory.

Franklin v. The Monadnock Company
59 Cal. Rptr. 3d 692 (Cal. Ct. App. 2007)

The Monadnock Company hired Calvin Franklin as a "heat treater" in 2004. Franklin alleged that his co-worker, Richard Ventura, threatened his safety and that of three other Monadnock employees. The threatened employees elected Franklin to complain about Ventura's threats to Monadnock's human resources department, and Franklin did so. Monadnock did not take action to prevent Ventura from assaulting his co-workers. A week after Franklin made his complaint about Ventura to human resources, Ventura attempted to stab Franklin with a metal screwdriver. In response, Franklin complained to the police department that Ventura was endangering his safety and that of his co-workers. Monadnock discharged Franklin a week later. Franklin filed a wrongful discharge suit against Monadnock and others, alleging that he was fired because of his complaints about Ventura "internally" to defendants and "externally" to the police.

Monadnock filed a demurrer, and the trial court sustained it, dismissing Franklin's complaint. Franklin appealed.

Mosk, Judge

The vast majority of states have recognized that an at-will employee possesses a tort action when he or she is discharged for performing an act that public policy would encourage, or for refusing to do something that public policy would condemn. The difficulty, of course, lies in determining where and how to draw the line between claims that genuinely involve matters of public policy, and those that concern merely ordinary disputes between employer and employee. This determination depends in large part on whether the public policy alleged is sufficiently clear to provide the basis for such a potent remedy. In *Stevenson v. Superior Court*, the Supreme Court noted that a historical survey of tortuous discharge decisions established four requirements that a policy must meet in order to support a wrongful discharge claim: "First, the policy must be supported by either constitutional or statutory provisions. Second, the policy must be 'public' in the sense that it inures to the benefit of the public rather than serving merely the interests of the individual. Third, the policy must have been articulated at the time of the discharge. Fourth, the policy must be 'fundamental' and 'substantial.'" Monadnock contends that Franklin cannot state a wrongful termination cause of action because Franklin's complaint about Ventura's threats and his report of the assault to the police did not involve a fundamental public policy contained in a constitutional or statutory provision. We disagree.

Labor Code section 6400 et seq. and Code of Civil Procedure section 527.8, when read together, establish an explicit public policy requiring employers to provide a safe and secure workplace, including a requirement that an employer take reasonable steps to address credible threats of violence in the workplace.

Labor Code section 6400, subdivision (a) provides: "Every employer shall furnish employment and a place of employment that is safe and healthful for the employees therein."

Labor Code section 6401 provides: "Every employer shall do every other thing reasonably necessary to protect the life, safety, and health of employees."

Labor Code section 6402 provides: "No employer shall require, or permit any employee go or be in any employment or place of employment which is not safe and healthful."

Labor Code section 6403 to provides: "No employer shall fail or neglect to . . . (c) To do every other thing reasonably necessary to protect the life, safety, and health of employees."

Labor Code section 6404 provides: "No employer shall occupy or maintain any place of employment that is not safe and healthful."

Code of Civil Procedure section 527.8, subdivision (a) provides: "Any employer, whose employee has suffered unlawful violence or a credible threat of violence from any individual . . . may seek a temporary restraining order and an injunction on behalf of the employee. . . ."

A credible threat is one that an employee reasonably believes will be carried out, so as to cause the employee to fear for his or her safety or that of his or her family. And it is the policy of this state to protect an employee who complains in good faith about working conditions or practices which he reasonably believes to be unsafe.

Monadnock's position that there is no explicit public policy concerning the prevention of workplace violence would lead to the anomalous result that the Labor Code provisions to which we refer establish an express public policy requiring employers to take reasonable steps to protect employees from foreseeable occupational injuries and illnesses, but do not establish any corresponding policy concerning injuries in the workplace from foreseeable violence or credible threats of violence. There is no logic in drawing such an artificial distinction, and such a distinction ignores the reality of workplace violence that statutes were enacted to address. Moreover, it is self-evident that the policy expressed in the statutes upon which we rely that protects employees from violence or threats of violence in the workplace is a fundamental and substantial public policy. Threats can be crimes. The allegations in the instant case provide that Ventura made threats of violence in the workplace and thereafter criminally assaulted Franklin, such that Ventura posed a continuing risk of violence to fellow employees. The allegations here are sufficient to state a violation of the public policy that protects an employee against discharge for making a good faith complaint about working conditions that he or she reasonably believes to be unsafe.

Monadnock further contends that the policies upon which Franklin relies are not predicated on any duties that would benefit the public at large—a requirement for a claim of wrongful discharge in violation of public policy. According to Monadnock, Franklin's complaint to Monadnock and report to the police did not benefit the public, but rather only Franklin and his three coworkers. That is not a reasonable interpretation of Franklin's complaint. His complaint about Ventura's threats and report to the police served the public interest in promoting workplace safety, the interest in deterring workplace crime, and the interests of innocent coworkers who could have suffered harm. Thus, Franklin's conduct inured to the benefit of the public.

Reversed in favor of Franklin.

The Implied Covenant of Good Faith and Fair Dealing A wrongful discharge suit based on the implied covenant of good faith and fair dealing usually is a contract claim. Here, the employee argues that her discharge was unlawful because it was not made in good faith or did not amount to fair dealing, thus breaching the implied contract term. Only about 25 percent of the states have recognized this exception to employment at will, and most of these give it a narrow scope.

Promises by Employers Using various legal theories, courts have increasingly made employers liable for breaking promises to their employees regarding termination policy. Such promises typically are express statements made by employers during hiring or employee orientation, or in their employee manuals, handbooks, personnel policies, and benefit plans. You will see an example of this theory in the following *Cisco* case. Occasionally such promises are implied from business custom and usage as well. Here, our concern is with express or implied employer promises involving matters such as discharge policies and discharge procedures. If the employer fails to follow those promises when it fires an employee, it is liable for breach of contract. At least two-thirds of the states recognize this exception to employment at will. However, employers often succeed in avoiding liability under this theory by inserting disclaimers of job security in employment applications and employment manuals.

Cisco v. King   2005 Ark. App. LEXIS 264 (Ark. Ct. App. 2005)

In May 1991, St. Francis County, Arkansas, adopted an employment manual, which states in most relevant part:

Except as otherwise provided in these policies and procedures, the tenure of an employee with permanent status shall continue during good behavior and satisfactory performance of his duties except the Road Supervisor and Chief Deputies who are At Will Employees.

On January 4, 1999, these procedures were in full force and effect. On this same day, Jerry King, who was employed by the county for seven years as a bridge foreman, Louis Pugh, who was employed for two years as an equipment operator, and Herman Greenwood, who was employed for four and one-half years as an office manager, were called into a road-crew employee meeting by Carl Cisco, the newly elected St. Francis County Judge. At the meeting, the three employees were among six members of the road crew who were discharged from employment. The county, which had prearranged unemployment benefits for these dismissed employees, instructed them to proceed to the unemployment office to make their claims. Each of the them did as the county had instructed.

In April 2000, King, Pugh, and Cisco (the employees) filed a wrongful-termination action against the county. After their claim was denied, the employees filed an appeal in circuit court. The employees claimed that because they were permanent employees and exercised "good behavior and satisfactory performance of duties" and were not working in the excepted positions (road supervisor and chief deputy), they could only be terminated for cause. The county maintained that the language contained in its employment manual did not create a contract for employment and that it was free to terminate the employment relationship at any time and for any reason, in accordance with the doctrine of employment at will. The trial court concluded that the employees had a valid employment contract with the county and that each employee was entitled to compensation for lost wages because they "were fired without cause and in violation of the Employment Policies and Procedures Manual of St. Francis County, Arkansas." The county appealed.

Vaught, Judge

Our first and most fundamental inquiry is whether the language contained in the County's employment manual was of sufficient force to abrogate Arkansas's at-will doctrine and establish a contract for employment whereby the employees could be terminated only for cause. We begin our analysis with an examination of Arkansas's at-will doctrine. In Arkansas, an employer may fire an employee for good reason, bad reason, or no reason at all under the employment-at-will doctrine. An employment relationship remains terminable at the will of either an employer or employee, unless an agreement exists that provides otherwise. The employment-at-will doctrine does have exceptions, however.

We believe that a modification of the at-will rule is appropriate in two respects: where an employee relies upon a personnel manual that contains *an express provision* against termination except for cause he may not be arbitrarily discharged in violation of such a provision. Moreover, we reject as outmoded and untenable the premise announced in *St. Louis Iron Mt. Ry. Co. v. Matthews* that the at-will rule applies even where the employment agreement contains a provision that the employee will not be discharged except for cause, unless it is for a definite term. With those two modifications we reaffirm the at-will doctrine. In *Crain Industries, Inc. v. Cass,* our supreme court held that an express provision in an employment handbook could constitute a valid and enforceable contract assuming that (1) the handbook language is sufficiently definite to constitute an offer; (2) the offer has been communicated by dissemination of the handbook to the employee; (3) there has been acceptance of the offer; and (4) consideration has been furnished for its enforceability.

The County does not dispute that it intended for its manual to apply to its entire workforce and that it understood and expected that the manual would be read and considered by its employees. It argues instead that the specific provisions of the manual relating to job security are not sufficiently definite and comprehensive to be regarded by its workforce as enforceable. The County contends that "at no point does the manual state that the list is conclusive or that St. Francis County has a policy of termination 'for just cause only' or that employees could not be terminated 'without just cause.' " In our view, this argument amounts to nothing more than linguistic gymnastics; it would require moves of contortionistic proportion for us to find that language guaranteeing that "the tenure of an employee with permanent status shall continue during good behavior and satisfactory performance of his duties" is anything but an express promise not to terminate a permanent employee without cause. The logic of this conclusion is amplified when the promise is read in tandem with the exception to the promise, that the Road Supervisor and Chief Deputies remain "At-Will Employees."

Further, the employment manual distinguishes between probationary and permanent employees, indicating that a new employee must "serve a probationary period" and that no "appointment may be considered as permanent until the probationary period is completed." Further, the manual states that a probationary employee "may be terminated for any reason without recourse. . . ." Thus, it is reasonable for a County employee to expect that if he or she successfully completes the 180-day probationary period, he or she would then be considered a "permanent" employee subject to the duties and entitled to the benefits and safeguards of "permanent" employment. We hold that the breadth of coverage and dissemination of the County's manual coupled with the definiteness and comprehensiveness of its termination policy could reasonably lead an employee to expect that the manual created enforceable employment obligations. The continued employment of the employees as permanent employees completed the contract. Therefore, the County could only terminate the employees for cause. The undisputed evidence presented at trial showed that the employees had stellar and unblemished employment records. Based on these facts, we are convinced that the County denied their contractual right to continued employment by dismissing them without cause. Because the employees were terminated without cause, they are entitled to damages, and we affirm the judgment of the trial court.

Affirmed in favor of the employees.

Problems and Problem Cases

1. Brown was employed as a clerk in the shipping department at Pratt & Whitney. She did not take a standard lunch break. When she took a lunch break, however, she customarily took a walk around the grounds of the employer's campus. Pratt & Whitney acquiesced to walking during lunch hours, but did not promote or encourage employees to do so. Brown testified that she pursues walking for the betterment of her health. In July 2005, Brown had been released for lunch and was walking on a road on the grounds of Pratt & Whitney when she tripped while avoiding an oncoming car and fell on some gravel, injuring her right shoulder. She claimed workers' compensation, arguing that she was engaged in something "incidental" to her employment at the time of her injury. Is this a good argument?

2. In the early 1980s, D'Amato, acting as agent for the young Mike Tyson, agreed with Rooney that Rooney would be Tyson's trainer "for as long as [Tyson fights] professionally." The parties also agreed that Rooney would receive 10 percent of Tyson's boxing earnings. In 1986, Tyson orally reaffirmed the agreement, stating that Rooney "will be Mike Tyson's trainer as long as Mike Tyson is a professional fighter." In 1988, apparently in connection with Rooney's alleged comments about Tyson's divorce and other business litigation, Tyson formally terminated his boxer–trainer relationship with Rooney. In 1989, Rooney sued Tyson for breach of contract in federal district court. Should the doctrine of employment at will apply to this oral contract "for as long as the boxer fights professionally?"

3. Dianne Rawlinson, a female applicant who was rejected for employment as a prison guard in the Alabama prison system, challenged certain state rules restricting her employment prospects under Title VII. They were (1) requirements that all prison employees be at least 5 feet 2 inches tall and weigh at least 120 pounds, and (2) a rule expressly prohibiting women from assuming close-contact prison guard positions in maximum-security prisons (most of which were all male). What method of proving a Title VII case should Rawlinson use in attacking the height and weight requirements? Does she need to use one of these methods to attack the second rule? What argument should the state use if Rawlinson establishes that the height and weight requirements have an adverse impact? What Title VII defense might the state have for the second rule? With regard to the second rule, assume that at this time Alabama's maximum-security prisons housed their male prisoners barracks-style rather than putting them in cells, and that they did not separate sex offenders from other prisoners.

4. Johnson Controls, Inc., manufactures batteries. Lead is a primary ingredient in that manufacturing process. A pregnant female employee's occupational exposure to lead involves a risk of harm to a fetus that she is carrying. For this reason, Johnson Controls excluded women who are pregnant or *who are capable of bearing children* from jobs that involve exposure to lead. Numerous plaintiffs, including a woman who had chosen to be sterilized to avoid losing her job, filed a class action against Johnson Controls under Title VII. Is Johnson Controls entitled to use the BFOQ defense?

5. Azteca, which operates a chain of restaurants, employed Sanchez from October 1991 to July 1995. Throughout his tenure at Azteca, Sanchez was subjected to a relentless campaign of insults, name-calling, and vulgarities. Male co-workers and a supervisor repeatedly referred to Sanchez in Spanish and English as "she" and "her." Male co-workers mocked Sanchez for walking and carrying his serving tray "like a woman," and taunted him in Spanish and English as, among other things, a "faggot" and a "f--- female whore." The remarks were not stray or isolated. This conduct violated company policy. Since 1989, Azteca has expressly prohibited sexual harassment and retaliation and has directed its employees to bring complaints regarding such conduct directly to the attention of the corporate office. It also has sexual harassment training programs, in English and in Spanish. Although Sanchez attended Azteca's sexual harassment training and was familiar with the company's antiharassment policy and procedures, he never complained to the corporate EEO officer or the area manager about the harassment he experienced, as required by the corporate policy. He did, however, complain to the general manager of the Southcenter restaurant and an assistant manager as well as to Azteca's human resources director. Was this a case of sexual harassment?

6. Karen Bammert worked as the assistant manager at Don's Super Value in Menomonie, Wisconsin. Her husband is a Menomonie police officer. Don's is

owned by Don Williams, whose wife, Nona, was arrested for drunk driving. Bammert's husband assisted in the arrest by administering a breathalyzer test. Shortly thereafter, Bammert was fired, allegedly in retaliation for her husband's participation in the arrest of her boss's wife. Bammert sued Don's for wrongful discharge, invoking the public policy exception to the employment-at-will doctrine. Will she be successful in using this doctrine?

7. In 1993, Mohr sold his battery business to Batteries Plus, but he remained with the company as an employee, initially as a store manager and later as a commercial sales specialist. Mohr's compensation package included a base salary and a commission of a percentage of the gross profits on all sales. He used his own vehicle in his sales position, and he received reimbursement for mileage expenses. In 1996, Batteries Plus informed Mohr that it had mistakenly paid him for mileage expenses. It claims that it had been paying Mohr an extra 2 percent in commissions to accommodate his travel expenses and that he was not supposed to receive additional $11,500 reimbursement for mileage. Batteries Plus asked him to sign a note to pay back the money through deductions from future wages. Mohr refused and denied that he had been overpaid. Over a period of several months the parties discussed the company's claim of overpayment. There were sharp exchanges of words and letters, including a rejected request for an employment contract. Mohr claims that he was fired for refusing to sign the note to repay the money. Batteries Plus thereafter instituted a collection action against Mohr in circuit court to recover the alleged overpayment. Mohr counterclaimed, alleging wrongful discharge under the public policy theory. Will Mohr prevail?

8. In 1987, Nichols began working as a pressman for the Progress Printing Company. At the time of hiring, Nichols was presented with a copy of the company's employees' handbook. The handbook stated that Progress would not discharge or suspend an employee "without just cause" and that the company "shall give at least one warning notice in writing" before termination. Several weeks later, however, Progress's personnel director gave Nichols a form that stated in part, "The employment relationship between Progress Printing and the employee is *at will* and *may be terminated by either party at any time.*" Nichols and the personnel director both signed the form. In March 1989, Nichols became upset over Progress's failure to correct a recurring defect in a print job, and he refused to complete that job assignment as a result. Nichols was fired on the following day, without the prior written notice promised by the employee handbook. Does Nichols have a good case for wrongful discharge under the promises by employer theory?

9. Caldwell worked for Holland's Kentucky Fried Chicken restaurant, where she had an excellent record. On Saturday, her three-year-old son awoke with a high fever, pain in his ears, and congestion. Caldwell notified her manager that she would be absent because she had to take her son to the doctor. At the emergency clinic, the son was diagnosed with an acute ear infection and put on medication. Caldwell was also informed that he would need surgery to prevent permanent hearing loss. That night, Caldwell, a single mother, worked the night shift at another KFC owned by Holland, while her elderly mother cared for her son. When Caldwell reported to work on Monday, she was summarily fired. On a follow-up medical visit, the son had to have another course of antibiotics, and two weeks later, had surgery. Was Caldwell's leave covered by the FMLA?

10. In July 2005 Wal-Mart asked MSN, a health care staffing provider, for temporary assistance in its Onalaska, Wisconsin, pharmacy. MSN recommended Noesen. Noesen, a Roman Catholic, is licensed by the State of Wisconsin to practice pharmacy, but the state licensing authority restricted his license in 2004 because of his refusal to fill, or refer to another pharmacy, a woman's prescription for contraception. Under the restriction, Noesen must notify potential employers in writing of the pharmacy services he will not perform and the steps he will take to ensure that a patient's access to medication remains unimpeded. Before starting work at the Onalaska pharmacy, Noesen wrote to Wal-Mart and explained that, due to his religious convictions, he would "decline to perform the provision of, or any activity related to the provision of contraceptive articles," including "complete or partial cooperation with patient care situations which involve the provision of or counsel on contraceptive articles." Overton, a pharmacist and acting supervisor of the Onalaska pharmacy, understood Noesen's limitations to mean that he would not fill prescriptions for birth control, and agreed to accommodate that limitation. Overton relieved Noesen

from filling prescriptions for birth control, taking orders for birth control from customers or physicians, handing customers birth control medication, and performing checks on birth control orders. Overton also arranged for birth control prescriptions to be sorted into a separate basket so that Noesen would not have to touch the items and ensured that someone would be available to fill orders and respond to customer inquiries concerning birth control. Within days Overton realized that, even with these accommodations, Noesen refused to perform general customer-service duties if they involved even briefly talking to customers seeking contraception. For example, when Noesen answered telephone calls from customers or physicians attempting to place orders for birth control, Noesen put them on hold and refused to alert other pharmacy staff that someone was holding. Similarly, when customers came to the counter with birth control prescriptions, Noesen walked away and refused to tell anyone that a customer needed assistance. Noesen explained that if required to speak to customers seeking birth control, he would always counsel them against it and refuse to fill their prescriptions. Noesen rejected Overton's offer that Noesen assist only customers that were not of childbearing age or only male customers. He insisted that the only acceptable accommodation was to relieve him of all counter and telephone duties unless customers were first prescreened by some other employee to ensure that they were not seeking birth control. Overton agreed that he and the pharmacy intern could assist all walk-in customers but due to high caller volume Noesen, like all other staff, needed to answer the telephones, although he could refer callers with birth control issues to others. Noesen rejected this accommodation. On his fifth day at the Onalaska pharmacy, after Noesen refused his work assignment with the modified accommodations, Overton fired Noesen. But Noesen refused to leave the store. He began lecturing customers about Wal-Mart's discriminatory practices and had to be carried out by police. Based upon his conduct at Wal-Mart, MSN also fired Noesen. Noesen sued MSN and Wal-Mart, alleging discrimination on the basis of his religion. Will he prevail?

11. The Pillsbury Company maintained an electronic mail communication system. The company repeat-

edly assured its employees that all e-mail communications on the system would remain confidential. Pillsbury further assured its employees that it would not intercept e-mail communications and use them as grounds for terminating or reprimanding employees. Smyth, a Pillsbury employee, received e-mails from his supervisor over Pillsbury's e-mail system on his home computer. Relying on Pillsbury's assurances, Smyth exchanged some blunt e-mails with his supervisor. One of them apparently contained a threat to "kill the back-stabbing bastards," and another seemingly referred to a firm holiday party as the "Jim Jones Kool-aid affair." Later, Pillsbury retrieved or intercepted these messages, and fired Smyth for what it deemed inappropriate and unprofessional comments over the e-mail system. Smyth sued Pillsbury for wrongful discharge under the public policy theory, alleging that public policy precludes an employer from firing an employee in violation of his privacy. Will Smyth win?

Online Research

Researching Discrimination Charges

Access the EEOC's Web site (**www.eeoc.gov**), and find statistics about the numbers of discrimination charges filed in particular years. What trends do you see?

Consider completing these three case segments from the You Be the Judge Web site element after you have read this chapter:

"SEXUAL HARASSMENT: Did Sexy Prank Kill Promotion?"

"RELIGIOUS DISCRIMINATION: Dress Code Flips Burger Joint"

"PRIVACY/EMPLOYMENT AT WILL: Fired for Whistling?"

Visit our Web site at www.mhhe.com/mallor14e for more information and activities regarding these case segments.

chapter 52

ENVIRONMENTAL REGULATION

The B-P Paper Company is planning to build a new papermaking facility on property it owns in the Atlanta, Georgia, area that borders on the Chattahoochee River. The facility will have an industrial boiler that burns wood wastes to generate process steam for plant operation and will emit sulfur oxides, nitrogen oxides, and particulate emissions to the air. The company plans to draw water from the river to use in the papermaking process and will return it to the river after some in-house treatment to remove some of the pollutants that have been added by the process. Significant quantities of sludge from the papermaking process will have to be disposed of, as well as empty containers in which the chlorine used at the facility was delivered.

- What major requirements will the facility have to meet to control its anticipated air emissions?
- What major requirements will the facility have to meet to control its discharge of wastewater to the Chattahoochee River?
- What major requirements will the company have to meet in dealing with the waste sludge and containers?
- If the company realizes that some materials it releases into the environment pose a hazard to human health or the environment but are not currently subject to regulation, does the company have an ethical obligation to take steps to protect against those hazards?

TODAY'S BUSINESSPERSON MUST BE concerned not only with competing effectively against competitors but also with complying with a myriad of regulatory requirements. For many businesses, particularly those that manufacture goods or that generate wastes, the environmental laws and regulations loom large in terms of the requirements and costs they impose. They can have a significant effect on the way businesses have to be conducted as well as on their profitability. This area of the law has expanded dramatically over the last three decades, and environmental issues are a major concern of people and governments around the world. This chapter will briefly discuss the development of environmental law and will outline the major federal statutes that have been enacted to control pollution of air, water, and land.

Historical Perspective

Historically, people assumed that the air, water, and land around them would absorb their waste products. In recent times, however, it has become clear that nature's capacity to assimilate people's wastes is not infinite. Burgeoning population, economic growth, and the products of our industrial society can pose risks to human health and the environment. The societal challenge is to accommodate economic activity and growth and at the same time provide reasonable protection of human health and the environment.

Concern about the environment is not a recent phenomenon. In medieval England, Parliament passed smoke control acts making it illegal to burn soft coal at certain times of the year. Where the owner or operator of a piece of property is using it in such a manner as to unreasonably interfere with another owner's (or the public's) health or enjoyment of his property, the courts have long entertained suits to abate the nuisance. Nuisance actions, which are discussed in Chapter 24, Real Property, are frequently not ideal vehicles for dealing with widespread pollution problems. Rather than a hit-or-miss approach, a comprehensive across-the-board approach may be required.

Realizing this, the federal government, as well as many state and local governments, had passed laws to abate air and water pollution by the late 1950s and 1960s. As the 1970s began, concern over the quality and future of the environment produced new laws and fresh public demands for action. During the 1980s, these laws were refined and, in some cases, their coverage was extended. Environmental concerns continue to be prominent around the globe, and many countries, both individually and collectively, have programs in place to address them. Accordingly, it is increasingly important that the businessperson be cognizant of the legal requirements and the public's environmental concerns in operating a business. These requirements and concerns not only may pose challenges to businesses but can provide opportunities for them as well.

The Environmental Protection Agency

In 1970, the Environmental Protection Agency was created to consolidate the federal government's environmental responsibilities. This was an explicit recognition that the problems of air and water pollution, solid waste disposal, water supply, and pesticide and radiation control were interrelated and required a consolidated approach. Congress subsequently passed comprehensive new legislation covering, among other things, air and water pollution, pesticides, ocean dumping, and waste disposal. Among the considerations prompting these laws were protection of human health, aesthetics, economic costs of continued pollution, and protection of natural systems.

The initial efforts were aimed at problems that, by and large, could be seen, smelled, or tasted. As control requirements have been put in place and implemented by industry and government, and as significant progress has been noted in the form of cleaner air and water, attention has focused increasingly on problems that are somewhat less visible but potentially more threatening—the dangers posed by toxic substances. These dangers have come into more prominence as scientific research indicates the risks posed by some substances, as new detection technology has enabled the detection of suspect substances in ever more minute quantities in the world around us, and as increased monitoring and testing are conducted. Determination of the degree of risk posed by any particular substance or proposed action—and deciding the most appropriate control strategy—frequently triggers strong disagreements within society because of what is at stake in terms of economic costs and protection of health and the environment.

Concomitantly, with the fairly comprehensive environmental regulatory regime in the United States now more than 30 years old and having become very complex, considerable attention is being focused on whether parts of the regulatory regime that are based on command-and-control requirements can be replaced with alternative approaches that instead rely on economic incentives or allow the regulated community more flexibility in

addressing environmental concerns. The highly competitive world market places a premium on companies' ability to rapidly change their products and production methods—and this need can be frustrated by a cumbersome or slow regulatory regime. The tensions between protection of public health and the environment, the desire to be supportive of domestic companies in a global competitive business climate, and the costs of compliance with various environmental protection requirements will dominate the public policy debate in this area for years to come.

The National Environmental Policy Act

The National Environmental Policy Act (NEPA) was signed into law on January 1, 1970. The act required that an **environmental impact statement** be prepared for every recommendation or report on legislation and for every *major federal action significantly affecting the quality of the environment.* The environmental impact statement must (1) describe the environmental impact of the proposed action, (2) discuss impacts that cannot be avoided, (3) discuss the alternatives to the proposed action, (4) indicate differences between short- and long-term impacts, and (5) detail any irreversible commitments of resources.

NEPA requires a federal agency to consider the environmental impact of a project before the project is undertaken. Other federal, state, and local agencies, as well as interested citizens, have an opportunity to comment on the environmental impact of a project before the agency can proceed. Where the process is not followed, citizens can and have gone to court to force compliance with NEPA. A number of states and local governments have passed their own environmental impact laws requiring NEPA-type statements for major public and private developments.

While the federal and state laws requiring the preparation of environmental impact statements appear directed at government actions, it is important to note that the government actions covered often include the granting of permits to private parties. Thus, businesspeople may readily find themselves involved in the preparation of an environmental impact statement—for example, in connection with a marina to be built in a navigable waterway or a resort development that will impact wetlands, both of which require permits from the U.S. Army Corps of Engineers. Similarly, a developer seeking a local zoning change so she can build a major commercial or residential development may find that she is asked to finance a study of the potential environmental impact of her proposed project.

Air Pollution

Background

Fuel combustion, industrial processes, and solid waste disposal are the major contributors to air pollution. People's initial concern with air pollution related to what they could see—visible or smoke pollution. For instance, in the 1880s, Chicago and Cincinnati enacted smoke control ordinances. As the technology became available to deal with smoke and particulate emissions, attention focused on other, less visible gases that could adversely affect human health and vegetation or that could increase the acidity of lakes, thus making them unsuitable for fish.

Clean Air Act

The **Clean Air Act**—enacted in 1970 and amended in 1977 and 1990—provides the basis for the present approach to air pollution control.

Ambient Air Control Standards

The Clean Air Act established a comprehensive approach for dealing with air pollution. EPA is required to set **national ambient air quality standards** for the major pollutants that have an adverse impact on human health—that is, to regulate the amount of a given pollutant that may be present in the air around us. The ambient air quality standards are set at two levels: (1) **primary standards** are designed to protect the public's health from harm; and (2) **secondary standards** are designed to protect vegetation, materials, climate, visibility, and economic values. Pursuant to this statutory mandate, EPA has set national ambient air quality standards for carbon monoxide, nitrogen oxide, sulfur oxide, ozone, lead, and particulate matter.

Each state is required to develop a **state implementation plan** for meeting national ambient air quality standards. This necessitates an inventory of the various sources of air pollution and their contribution to the total air pollution in the air quality region. The major emitters of pollutants are then required to reduce their emissions to a level that ensures that overall air quality meets the national standards. For example, a factory may be required to limit its emissions of volatile organic compounds (a contributor to ozone or smog) to a certain amount per unit of production or hour of operation; similarly, a power plant might have its emissions of sulfur oxides and nitrogen oxides limited to so many pounds per Btu of energy produced. The states have the responsibility for selecting which activities must be regulated or curtailed so that air pollution at any point in the state or area does not exceed the national standards.

Because by the late 1980s many of the nation's major urban areas were still not in compliance with the health-based standards for ozone and carbon monoxide, Congress, in its 1990 amendments, imposed an additional set of requirements on the areas that were not in compliance. Thus, citizens living in the areas and existing businesses, as well as prospective businesses seeking to locate in the designated areas, face increasingly stringent control measures designed to bring the areas into attainment with the national standards. These new requirements mean that businesses such as bakeries that are generally not thought of as major polluters of the air have to further control their emissions, and that paints and other products that contain solvents may have to be reformulated.

Acid Rain Controls

Responding to the 1970 Clean Air Act, which sought to protect the air in the area near sources of air pollution, many electric generating facilities built tall smokestacks so that the emissions were dispersed over a broader area. Unwittingly, this contributed to long-range transport of some of the pollutants, which changed chemically en route and fell to earth many miles away in the form of acid rain, snow, fog, or dry deposition. For a number of years, a considerable debate ensued over acid rain, in particular as to whether it was a problem, what kind of damage it caused, whether anything should be done about it, and who should pay for the cost of limiting it. The 1990 amendments addressed acid deposition by among other things placing a cap on the overall emissions of the contributors to it (the oxides of sulfur and nitrogen) and requiring electric utilities to reduce their emissions to specified levels in two steps over the next decade. This required most electric generating facilities in the country to install large control devices known as scrubbers, to switch to lower sulfur coal, or to install so-called clean coal technologies. The 1990 amendments also provide an innovative system whereby companies whose emissions are cleaner than required by law can sell their rights to emit more sulfur oxide—known as *allowances*—to other companies that may be finding it more difficult to meet the standards. This emission trading scheme has worked well to achieve reductions in emissions in an economically efficient way.

Control of Toxic Air Pollutants

The 1970 Clean Air Act also required EPA to regulate the emission of toxic air pollutants. Under this authority, EPA set standards only for asbestos, beryllium, mercury, vinyl chloride, benzene, and radionuclides. Unhappy with the slow pace of regulation of toxic air pollutants, Congress in

1990 specified a list of 189 chemicals for which EPA is required to issue regulations requiring the installation of the maximum available control technology. The regulations are to be developed and the control technology installed by industry in phases. Thus, while many toxic emissions have largely gone unregulated, that situation has changed. In addition, a number of chemical companies have announced they are voluntarily reducing their emissions of toxic chemicals to levels below those they are required to meet by law.

New Source Controls

The Clean Air Act requires that new stationary sources such as factories and power plants install the best available technology for reducing air pollution. EPA is required to establish the standards to be met by new stationary sources and has done so for the major stationary sources of air pollution. This means that a new facility covered by the regulations must install state of the art control technology, even if it is locating in an area where the air quality is better than that required by law. Two major policy objectives underlie this requirement: (1) to provide a level playing field for new industry irrespective of where it locates and (2) to gradually improve air quality by requiring state of the art controls whenever a new facility is built.

The act also requires that facilities that undergo major modifications—defined as physical changes that result in significant increases in emissions of air pollutants—must go through a preconstruction review, obtain a permit, and meet the same new source performance standards or limits on emissions that must be met by new facilities. The rationale for imposing these standards when a new facility is built, or an existing facility undergoes a major modification, is that is the easiest time to design and incorporate state-of-the-art environmental controls into the facility. Routine maintenance, repair, and replacement activities, increases in hours of production, and physical changes that are not accompanied by increases in emissions are excluded from the definition of modification.

The preconstruction review process that is required—known as **new source review**—is the subject of very contentious debate and various proposals to modify it. Industry is concerned that the process slows down its ability to make changes to increase efficiency, take advantage of new technologies, or gain a competitive edge, while environmentalists claim that some companies are increasing emissions and avoiding the installation of required controls on emissions.

In the case that follows, *United States v. Ohio Edison Company,* the court rejected a utility's argument that its work on its coal-fired electric generating units was "routine maintenance, repair, and replacement" and thus exempt from the preconstruction review and permitting requirements applicable to facilities that are "modified" resulting in a significant increase in their emissions.

United States v. Ohio Edison Company   276 F. Supp.2d 829 (S.D. Ohio 2003)

The Sammis Plant is a coal-fired electric generating plant owned by the Ohio Edison Company and situated along the Ohio River in the Village of Stratton, Ohio. The plant consists of seven separate generating units, numbered 1 through 7. Units 1 through 4 were placed in service from 1959 to 1962, Unit 5 in 1967, Unit 6 in 1969, and Unit 7 in 1971.

Coal-fired power plants, such as the Sammis Plant, generate electricity using three major components: the boiler, turbine, and generator. The boiler is a large building-like structure (150–200 feet high) in which coal is burned inside the furnace and the energy from the combustion process is converted to water to produce steam. The steam is then directed to the turbine where it is further converted to mechanical energy in the form of a spinning turbine shaft, which in turn drives the generator that produces electricity. The walls, roof, and floor of the boiler are comprised of tubes, as are the other major components of the boiler, which are made up of densely packed assemblies of tubes that incrementally raise the temperature of the steam before it leaves the boiler to generate electricity.

The Sammis units are fueled by pulverized coal (coal that has been ground to a powdery consistency) that is fed through pipes to burners where it is ignited and combusts within the furnace area of the boiler. In the combustion of coal, chemical energy, gas by-products, and particulate matter are released. The gases are known as flue gas. The flue gases produced from the combustion process form carbon dioxide, carbon monoxide, sulfur dioxide, and nitrogen oxides. The flue gases are discharged to the atmosphere. At the time the seven units were built, Ohio Edison installed electrostatic precipitators to collect fly ash coming out of the boilers. At the time of installations, the precipitators were state-of-the-art technology. Over time the tubing that is in contact with the flue gases, combusting coal, and water inside the tubing deteriorates and periodically must be replaced.

Fossil fuel-fired generating stations have traditionally been built with an assumed nominal design and economic life of about 30 years. The implicit expectation was that these units would be replaced at the end of this period with new units that would meet load requirements and, through the use of technological improvements, produce power at lower cost, higher availability, and higher efficiency. For a number of reasons, these expectations have not been realized, and many utility companies have undertaken so-called "life extension" projects which offer the prospect of retaining units in service for 50 to 60 years or longer.

In the 1980s and 1990s Ohio Edison developed a program and undertook 11 projects at the Sammis with the purpose of extending the life of the seven units and making them more efficient. The projects went beyond the normal replacement of tubing and focused on other components that would require repair or replacement in the next 30 years. All of the projects involved replacement of major components that had never before been replaced on the particular units. The total cost of the projects was approximately $136.4 million. By replacing aging or deficient components, Ohio Edison intended and achieved a significant increase in the operation and output of the units. In turn, the amount of emission of sulfur dioxide, nitrogen oxides, and particulate matter also increased. The vast majority of the expenditures were treated for accounting purposes as capital, as opposed to maintenance, expenses. Most of the work was performed by outside contractors, as opposed to in-house maintenance crews.

Sargus, Judge

This case highlights an abysmal breakdown in the administrative process following the passage of the landmark Clean Air Act in 1970. For thirty-three years, various administrations have wrestled with and, to a great extent, have avoided a fundamental issue addressed in the Clean Air Act, that is, at what point plants built before 1970 must comply with new air pollution standards. The Clean Air Act requires plants constructed after 1970 to meet stringent air quality standards, but the Act exempts old facilities from compliance with the law, unless such sites undergo what the law identifies as a "modification." Decades later, the United States Environmental Protection Agency, together with the States of Connecticut, New Jersey, and New York, ask this Court to find that eleven construction projects undertaken between 1984 and 1998 on the seven electric generating units at the Sammis Plant constituted modifications, requiring Ohio Edison to bring the units into compliance with current ambient air quality standards.

By any standard, the enforcement of the Clean Air Act with regard to the Sammis Plant has been disastrous. From a public health perspective, thirty-three years after passage of the Act, the plant to this day emits on an annual basis 145,000 tons of sulphur dioxide, a pollutant injurious to the public health. From an employment perspective, Ohio Edison has chosen to meet other statewide and regional air quality standards by switching to out-of-state, low-sulphur coal, a strategy which in conjunction with other utilities has caused a huge loss of coal mining and related jobs in Ohio. From the standpoint of Ohio Edison, since 1970 the company has invested over $450 million to install pollution control devices on the Sammis units yet still fails to meet the new source pollution standards. Thirty-three years later, the air is still not clean, tens of thousands of jobs have been lost, and enforcement by the EPA has been highly inconsistent.

As is described in detail below, the original and current language of the Clean Air Act requires that an older plant undergoing a modification thereafter comply with new air quality standards. Regulations issued under the Clean Air Act by the U.S. EPA may not conflict with statutory language enacted into law by Congress. EPA regulations give further definition as to what types of projects are to be viewed as modifications which trigger the application of new air quality standards to an older facility. These statutory and regulatory definitions are at issue here.

With regard to this case, the parties have litigated at this juncture whether the eleven projects at the Sammis units have triggered application of the standards set forth in the 1977 amendments to the Clean Air Act. The questions resolved today by this Court are legal in nature. In contrast, in the next phase of this case, the remedies the Court may consider and impose involve a much broader, equitable analysis, requiring the Court to consider air quality, public health, economic impact, and employment consequences. The Court may also consider the less than consistent efforts of the EPA to apply and enforce the Clean Air Act.

The issues presented in this lawsuit turn on an interpretation of the term "modification." Congress provided in the Clean Air Act that any modification of a plant triggered application of the Act and later amendments. The Administrator of the EPA has refined, by regulation, the definition of modification to include only activities which involve both a physical change to a unit and a resulting significant increase in emissions. Excluded from the definition of modification are projects involving only "routine maintenance, repair or replacement."

In this case, Ohio Edison undertook eleven construction projects at the seven Sammis Units. The total cost of the projects was approximately $136.4 million. The documents prepared to justify the expenditures described the various purposes of the projects to include replacement of major components to increase both the life and the reliability of the units. A primary goal of the projects was to prevent or at least diminish the number and duration of outages, meaning unplanned periods of time when the unit was offline and unproductive.

By physically replacing aging or deficient components, Ohio Edison intended and achieved a significant increase in the operation and output of the units. In turn, the amount of emission of sulphur dioxide, nitrogen oxides, and particulate matter also increased.

If the projects were modifications, as used in the Clean Air Act, Ohio Edison was required prior to construction to project and calculate postconstruction emissions to determine if the new standards applied. Further, if the projects were modifications, Ohio Edison was required to obtain a preconstruction permit. Because the company contended the projects were not modifications but were instead "routine maintenance, repair and replacement," neither of those courses was pursued. The EPA and state plaintiffs contend that all eleven projects constituted modifications.

While the analysis required to distinguish between a modification sufficient to trigger compliance from routine maintenance, repair and replacement is complex, the distinction is hardly subtle. Routine maintenance, repair and replacement occurs regularly, involves no permanent improvements, is typically limited in expense, is usually performed in large plants by in-house employees, and is treated for accounting purposes as an expense. In contrast to routine maintenance stand capital improvements which generally involve more expense, are large in scope, often involve outside contractors, involve an increase of value to the unit, are usually not undertaken with regular frequency, and are treated for accounting purposes as capital expenditures on the balance sheet. The only two courts which have addressed this issue have essentially adopted this same analysis.

The projects were all intended to result in increased hours of operation as a result of a reduction in the number and length of forced outages, or shutdown for repair or maintenance. A significant decrease in outages results in a significant increase in both production and emissions. Given the actual goals placed on the construction projects by Ohio Edison, and the substantial increase in emissions certain to follow, the company was required to project future emissions. If those projected increases were substantial, as defined by regulations noted below, preconstruction approval, which was never sought, was required by law.

The eleven projects at issue in this case were extensive, involving a combined outlay of $136.4 million dollars. The vast majority of the expenditures were treated for accounting purposes as capital, as opposed to maintenance, expenses. Most of the work was performed by outside contractors, as opposed to in-house maintenance crews. The purpose of the projects was to extend the lives of units built before 1970, not simply to perform routine preventative care on components of the units. Finally, all of the projects involved replacement of major components which had never before been replaced on the particular units. As a result, the projects were not routine in any sense of the term, and could have been projected to significantly increase the emission of pollutants.

Congress expressly intended the Clean Air Act and the 1977 Amendments to become applicable to preexisting plants, as such facilities were modified. As noted by the United States Court of Appeals for the Seventh Circuit in *Wisconsin Electric Power Company v. Reilly* (1990):

> Congress did not permanently exempt existing plants from these requirements . . . existing plants that have been modified are subject to the Clean Air Act programs at issue here.

Further, as at least one member of the Sixth Circuit has observed:

> The purpose of the "modification" rule is to ensure that pollution control measures are undertaken when they can be most effective, at the time of new or modified construction.

National-Southwire Aluminum Co. v. EPA (6th Cir. 1988) (Boggs, J., dissenting).

The eleven projects at issue in this case were major modifications sufficient to trigger application of the Clean Air Act and subsequent amendments.

Judgment for United States and other plaintiffs.

Permits
In the 1990 amendments to the Clean Air Act, Congress established a permit system whereby major sources of air pollution—particularly those subject to the New Source Performance Standards, air toxics, nonattainment, and acid rain provisions of the act—as well as certain other sources have to obtain permits that specify the limits on emissions from the sources. The permits also contain monitoring and reporting requirements. Once a state permitting program is approved by EPA, the permits are issued by the state in which a facility is located. A controversial issue in the permitting regulations is when a source has to seek a modification of a permit because of process or operational changes that might increase emissions. If a modification to a permit

CYBERLAW IN ACTION

Online Permitting

The Clean Air Act, the Clean Water Act, and the Resource Conservation and Recovery Act, as well as a number of other federal and local environmental laws, require certain businesses to obtain permits and to periodically report their discharges and/or other information to administrative agencies by filing permits or monitoring reports. Now the EPA and most, if not all, states make permit applications and motoring report forms available online. In addition, some states make specific companies' reports, or permit files, available to the public on their Web sites. Online permit and report transactions can streamline the process of complying with environmental law and regulations.

Also, businesses can quickly access information on their competition's compliance with environmental standards by viewing, or ordering, their competitors' monitoring reports and permits on the Internet. Such information might provide insight into what materials another company is using in its processes—or how product volume may be changing over time. Moreover, the online permitting and reporting systems make environmental regulations more transparent, which helps ensure that businesses and regulatory agencies remain accountable to the public. (See, for example, **www.epa.gov/airmarkets/arp/permits/index.html, www.in.gov/idem/air/permits/Air-Permits-Online/index.html**)

---

is required by an anticipated change, this can greatly complicate the timely execution of business plans.

Enforcement   The primary responsibility for enforcing air quality standards lies with the states, but the federal government has the right to enforce the standards where the states fail to do so. The Clean Air Act also provides for suits by citizens to force industry or the government to fully comply with the act's provisions.

Automobile Pollution   The Clean Air Act provides specifically for air pollution controls on transportation sources such as automobiles. The major pollutants from automobiles are carbon monoxide, hydrocarbons, and nitrogen oxides. Carbon monoxide is a colorless, odorless gas that can dull mental performance and even cause death when inhaled in large quantities. Hydrocarbons, in the form of unburned fuel, are part of a category of air pollutants known as volatile organic compounds (VOCs). VOCs combine with nitrogen oxides under the influence of sunlight to become ozone—we know it as smog.

The 1970 Clean Air Act required a reduction of 90 percent of the carbon monoxide and hydrocarbons emitted by automobiles by 1975 and a 90 percent reduction in the nitrogen oxides emitted by 1976. At the time, these requirements were "technology forcing"; that is, the manufacturers could not rely on already existing technology to meet the standards but rather had to develop new technology. Ultimately, most manufacturers had to go beyond simply making changes in engine design and utilize pollution control devices known as catalytic converters.

Subsequently, Congress addressed the question of setting even more stringent limits on automobile emissions while at the same time requiring that the new automobiles get better gas mileage. The 1990 amendments require further limitations on emissions from tailpipes, the development of so-called clean-fueled vehicles (such as electric and natural gas fueled vehicles) for use in cities with dirty air, and the availability of oxygenated fuels (which are cleaner burning) in specified areas of the country that are having difficulty meeting the air quality limits at least part of the year. These new requirements have significant ramifications for the oil and automobile industries.

Under the Clean Air Act, no manufacturer may sell vehicles subject to emission standards without prior certification from EPA that the vehicles meet the required standards. The tests are performed on prototype vehicles and if they pass, a certificate of conformity covering that type of engine and vehicle is issued. EPA subsequently can test vehicles on the assembly line to make sure that the production vehicles covered by the certificate are meeting the standards. The manufacturers are required to warrant that the vehicle, if properly maintained, will comply with the emission standards for its useful life. If EPA discovers that vehicles in actual use exceed the emission standards, it may order the manufacturer to recall and repair the defective models; this is a power that EPA has exercised on a number of occasions.

The act also provides for the regulation and registration of fuel additives such as lead. In the 1980s, lead was largely phased out of use as an octane enhancer in gasoline. As indicated previously, the 1990 amendments

The Global Business Environment

International Air Problems

During the late 1970s and 1980s, concern developed that the release of chlorine-containing substances such as chlorofluorocarbons (CFCs) used in air conditioning, refrigeration, and certain foam products was depleting the stratospheric ozone layer. This could lead to more ultraviolet radiation reaching the earth and, in turn, more skin cancer. Subsequently, a number of nations, acting under the aegis of the United Nations, signed a treaty agreeing first to limit any increases in production of chlorine-containing substances and ultimately to significantly phase out their use. The 1990 amendments to the Clean Air Act implement the obligations of the United States under the treaty and provide for the phasedown and phaseout of a number of chlorofluorocarbons; accordingly, many businesses have developed or located substitutes for those chemicals that are available only in reduced quantities, if at all.

Other air pollution issues with international dimensions that may result in multinational control efforts are acid rain and global warming/climate change resulting, in part, from increased emissions of carbon dioxide to the atmosphere.

Currently, the issue of global warming/climate change is the focus of considerable debate, discussion, and some action by governments and private entities. The crux of the issue is whether human activity, primarily in the form of increased emissions of carbon dioxide to the atmosphere, is creating conditions that over time are resulting in the warming of the earth's atmosphere, a rise in sea level, an increase in number and severity of various weather events, and changes in the climate in many parts of the world. An international treaty known as the Koyoto Treaty was drafted with the intention of addressing this issue through collective international action. While it was signed by many nations, it has generated significant controversy in many countries, including the United States, and only recently was ratified by the required number of countries to bring it into effect. The issue raises important concerns for many kinds of businesses including insurance companies, producers and users of fossil fuels, and producers of products such as motor vehicles that emit carbon dioxide and may at some point be subjected to controls under either domestic or international regimes.

Ethics in Action

If It's Legal, Is It Ethical?

Suppose a manufacturing facility emits into the air a chemical that it has reason to believe is inadequately regulated by EPA and that poses a significant threat to nearby residents even at levels lower than permitted by EPA. As manager of the facility, would you be satisfied to meet the EPA required level or would you install the additional controls you believe necessary to achieve a reasonably safe level?

provide for the availability of alternative fuels based on ethanol and methanol.

Climate Change

As noted in the Global Business Environment box "International Air Problems," the issue of global warming/climate change is one of the major issues of our time with potentially significant implications for business. These implications turn on the extent, nature, pace, and location of possible warming-induced changes as well as on the reactions and the policy decisions of individuals, businesses, and governments to those changes. The issue also holds potential business opportunities for individuals and firms, and many are developing business plans to try to take advantage of the issue.

The next few years will likely see continued debate and discussion of global warming/climate change and the appropriate responses to it. As of 2009, the United States does not have a comprehensive legal regime in place to address the environmental and energy-related aspects of the issue. In the absence of such a federal response, a number of organizations and state and local governments have sought to use litigation to force the federal government to take some steps using existing authority. The case that follows, *Massachusetts v. EPA,* illustrates such an effort, which ended with the Supreme Court, on a 5–4 vote, agreeing that EPA had not provided sufficient legal justification to refuse to exercise legal authority it had to regulate greenhouse gas emissions from automobiles.

Massachusetts v. Environmental Protection Agency   127 S.Ct. 1438 (2007)

On October 20, 1999, a group of 19 private organizations filed a rulemaking petition asking EPA to regulate "greenhouse gas emissions from new motor vehicles under § 202 of the Clean Air Act." Petitioners maintained that 1998 was the "warmest year on record"; that carbon dioxide, methane, nitrous oxide, and hydrofluorocarbons are "heat trapping greenhouse gases"; and that greenhouse gas emissions have significantly accelerated climate change. They also noted that in a 1995 report the Intergovernmental Panel on Climate Change, a multinational scientific body organized under the auspices of the United Nations, warned that "carbon dioxide remains the most important contributor to [man-made] forcing of climate change." The petition further alleged that climate change will have serious adverse effects on human health and the environment. As to EPA's statutory authority, the petition observed that the agency itself had already confirmed that it had the power to regulate carbon dioxide. In 1998, Jonathan Z. Cannon, then EPA's general counsel, prepared a legal opinion concluding that "CO[2] emissions are within the scope of EPA's authority to regulate," even as he recognized that EPA had so far declined to exercise that authority. Cannon's successor, Gary S. Guzy, reiterated that opinion before a congressional committee just two weeks before the rulemaking petition was filed.

Fifteen months after the petition's submission, EPA requested public comment on "all the issues raised in [the] petition," adding a "particular" request for comments on "any scientific, technical, legal, economic or other aspect of these issues that may be relevant to EPA's consideration of this petition." EPA received more than 50,000 comments over the next five months.

Before the close of the comment period, the White House sought "assistance in identifying the areas in the science of climate change where there are the greatest certainties and uncertainties" from the National Research Council, asking for a response "as soon as possible." The result was a 2001 report titled Climate Change: An Analysis of Some Key Questions (NRC Report), which, drawing heavily on the 1995 IPCC report, concluded that "[g]reenhouse gases are accumulating in Earth's atmosphere as a result of human activities, causing surface air temperatures and subsurface ocean temperatures to rise. Temperatures are, in fact, rising."

On September 8, 2003, EPA entered an order denying the rulemaking petition. The agency gave two reasons for its decision: (1) that contrary to the opinions of its former general counsels, the Clean Air Act does not authorize EPA to issue mandatory regulations to address global climate change; and (2) that even if the agency had the authority to set greenhouse gas emission standards, it would be unwise to do so at this time.

The petitioners, joined by a number of states and local governments, sought review of EPA's order in the United States Court of Appeals for the District of Columbia Circuit. Although each of the three judges on the panel wrote a separate opinion, two judges agreed that the EPA administrator properly exercised his discretion under § 202(a)(1) in denying the petition for rulemaking. The court therefore denied the petition for review. The Supreme Court granted a petition for certiorari and agreed to hear the case.

Stevens, Justice

Section 202(a)(l) of the Clean Air Act provides:

The [EPA] Administrator shall by regulation prescribe (and from time to time revise) in accordance with the provisions of this section, standards applicable to the emission of any air pollutant from any class or classes of new motor vehicles or new motor vehicle engines, which in his judgment cause, or contribute to, air pollution which may reasonably be anticipated to endanger public health or welfare. . . .

The Act defines "air pollutant" to include "any air pollution agent or combination of such agents, including any physical, chemical, biological, radioactive . . . substance or matter which is emitted into or otherwise enters the ambient air." "Welfare" is also defined broadly: among other things, it includes "effects on . . . weather . . . and climate."

On the merits, the first question is whether § 202(a)(1) of the Clean Air Act authorizes EPA to regulate greenhouse gas emissions from new motor vehicles in the event that it forms a "judgment" that such emissions contribute to climate change. We have little trouble concluding that it does. In relevant part, § 202(a)(1) provides that EPA "shall by regulation prescribe . . . standards applicable to the emission of any air pollutant from any class or classes of new motor vehicles or new motor vehicle engines, which in [the Administrator's] judgment cause, or contribute to, air pollution which may reasonably be anticipated to endanger public health or welfare." Because EPA believes that Congress did not intend it to regulate substances that contribute to climate change, the agency maintains that carbon dioxide is not an "air pollutant" within the meaning of the provision.

The statutory text forecloses EPA's reading. The Clean Air Act's sweeping definition of "air pollutant" includes "*any* air pollution agent or combination of such agents, including *any* physical, chemical . . . substance or matter which is emitted into or otherwise enters the ambient air. . . ." (emphasis added).

On its face, the definition embraces all airborne compounds of whatever stripe, and underscores that intent through the repeated use of the word "any." Carbon dioxide, methane, nitrous oxide, and hydrofluorocarbons are without a doubt "physical [and] chemical . . . substance[s] which [are] emitted into . . . the ambient air." The statute is unambiguous.

Rather than relying on statutory text, EPA invokes postenactment congressional actions and deliberations it views as tantamount to a congressional command to refrain from regulating greenhouse gas emissions. Even if such postenactment legislative history could shed light on the meaning of an otherwise-unambiguous statute, EPA never identifies any action remotely suggesting that Congress meant to curtail its power to treat greenhouse gases as air pollutants. That subsequent Congresses have eschewed enacting binding emissions limitations to combat global warming tells us nothing about what Congress meant when it amended § 202(a)(1) in 1970 and 1977. And unlike EPA, we have no difficulty reconciling Congress' various efforts to promote interagency collaboration and research to better understand climate change with the agency's preexisting mandate to regulate "any air pollutant" that may endanger the public welfare. Collaboration and research do not conflict with any thoughtful regulatory effort; they complement it.

EPA finally argues that it cannot regulate carbon dioxide emissions from motor vehicles because doing so would require it to tighten mileage standards, a job (according to EPA) that Congress has assigned to DOT. But that DOT sets mileage standards in no way licenses EPA to shirk its environmental responsibilities. EPA has been charged with protecting the public's "health" and "welfare," a statutory obligation wholly independent of DOT's mandate to promote energy efficiency. The two obligations may overlap, but there is no reason to think the two agencies cannot both administer their obligations and yet avoid inconsistency.

While the Congresses that drafted § 202(a)(1) might not have appreciated the possibility that burning fossil fuels could lead to global warming, they did understand that without regulatory flexibility, changing circumstances and scientific developments would soon render the Clean Air Act obsolete. The broad language of § 202(a)(1) reflects an intentional effort to confer the flexibility necessary to forestall such obsolescence. Because greenhouse gases fit well within the Clean Air Act's capacious definition of "air pollutant," we hold that EPA has the statutory authority to regulate the emission of such gases from new motor vehicles.

The alternative basis for EPA's decision—that even if it does have statutory authority to regulate greenhouse gases, it would be unwise to do so at this time—rests on reasoning divorced from the statutory text. While the statute does condition the exercise of EPA's authority on its formation of a "judgment," that judgment must relate to whether an air pollutant "cause[s], or contribute[s] to, air pollution which may reasonably be anticipated to endanger public health or welfare," Put another way, the use of the word "judgment" is not a roving license to ignore the statutory text. It is but a direction to exercise discretion within defined statutory limits.

If EPA makes a finding of endangerment, the Clean Air Act requires the agency to regulate emissions of the deleterious pollutant from new motor vehicles. EPA no doubt has significant latitude as to the manner, timing, content, and coordination of its regulations with those of other agencies. But once EPA has responded to a petition for rulemaking, its reasons for action or inaction must conform to the authorizing statute. Under the clear terms of the Clean Air Act, EPA can avoid taking further action only if it determines that greenhouse gases do not contribute to climate change or if it provides some reasonable explanation as to why it cannot or will not exercise its discretion to determine whether they do. To the extent that this constrains agency discretion to pursue other priorities of the Administrator or the President, this is the congressional design.

EPA has refused to comply with this clear statutory command. Instead, it has offered a laundry list of reasons not to regulate. For example, EPA said that a number of voluntary executive branch programs already provide an effective response to the threat of global warming, that regulating greenhouse gases might impair the President's ability to negotiate with "key developing nations" to reduce emissions, and that curtailing motor-vehicle emissions would reflect "an inefficient, piecemeal approach to address the climate change issue."

Although we have neither the expertise nor the authority to evaluate these policy judgments, it is evident they have nothing to do with whether greenhouse gas emissions contribute to climate change. Still less do they amount to a reasoned justification for declining to form a scientific judgment. In particular, while the President has broad authority in foreign affairs, that authority does not extend to the refusal to execute domestic laws. In the Global Climate Protection Act of 1987, Congress authorized the State Department—not EPA—to formulate United States foreign policy with reference to environmental matters relating to climate. EPA has made no showing that it issued the ruling in question here after consultation with the State Department. Congress did direct EPA to consult with other agencies in the formulation of its policies and rules, but the State Department is absent from that list.

Nor can EPA avoid its statutory obligation by noting the uncertainty surrounding various features of climate change and concluding that it would therefore be better not to regulate at this time. If the scientific uncertainty is so profound that it precludes EPA from making a reasoned judgment as to whether greenhouse gases contribute to global warming, EPA must say so. That EPA would prefer not to regulate greenhouse gases because of some residual uncertainty is irrelevant. The statutory question is whether sufficient information exists to make an endangerment finding.

In short, EPA has offered no reasoned explanation for its refusal to decide whether greenhouse gases cause or contribute to climate change. Its action was therefore arbitrary, capricious, or otherwise not in accordance with law. We need not and do not reach the question whether on remand EPA must make an endangerment finding, or whether policy concerns can inform EPA's actions in the event that it makes such a finding. We hold only that EPA must ground its reasons for action or inaction in the statute.

The judgment of the Court of Appeals is reversed, and the case is remanded for further proceedings consistent with this opinion.

Water Pollution

Background
History is replete with plagues and epidemics brought on by poor sanitation and polluted water. Indeed, preventing waterborne disease has always been the major reason for combating water pollution. In the early 1970s, fishing and swimming were prohibited in many bodies of water, and game fish could no longer survive in some waters where they had formerly thrived. Lake Erie was becoming choked with algae and considered to be dying. The nation recognized that water pollution could affect public health, recreation, commercial fishing, agriculture, water supplies, and aesthetics. During the 1970s, Congress enacted three major statutes to protect our water resources: the Clean Water Act; the Marine Protection, Research, and Sanctuaries Act; and the Safe Drinking Water Act.

Early Federal Legislation
Federal water pollution legislation dates back to the 19th century when Congress enacted the River and Harbor Act of 1886. In fact, this statute, recodified in the River and Harbor Act of 1899, furnished the legal basis for EPA's initial enforcement actions against polluters. The act provided that people had to obtain a discharge permit from the Army Corps of Engineers to deposit or discharge refuse into a navigable waterway. Under some contemporary court decisions, even hot water discharged from nuclear power plants was considered refuse. The permit system established pursuant to the "Refuse Act" was replaced in 1972 by a more comprehensive permit system now administered by EPA.

Clean Water Act
The 1972 amendments to the Federal Water Pollution Control Act (FWPCA)—known as the Clean Water Act—were as comprehensive in the water pollution field as the 1970 Clean Air Act was in the air pollution field. They proclaimed two general goals for this country: (1) to achieve wherever possible by July 1, 1983, water clean enough for swimming and other recreational uses and clean enough for the protection and propagation of fish, shellfish, and wildlife; and (2) to have no discharges of pollutants into the nation's waters by 1985. These goals reflected a national frustration with the lack of progress in dealing with water pollution and a commitment to end such pollution. The new law set out a series of specific actions that federal, state, and local governments and industry were to take by certain dates and also provided strong enforcement provisions to back up the deadlines. In 1977 and again in 1987, Congress modified the 1972 act by adjusting some of the deadlines and otherwise fine-tuning the act.

Under the Clean Water Act, the states have the primary responsibility for preventing, reducing, and eliminating water pollution. The states have to do this within a national framework, and EPA is empowered to move in if the states do not fulfill their responsibilities.

Discharge Permits
The keystone of the Clean Water Act is a prohibition against persons discharging pollutants from "point sources" into "waters of the United States" except in compliance with the requirements of the act; these requirements normally include obtaining a permit from the federal or state government for the discharge. Thus anyone who discharges industrial wastewater (wastewater that contains pollutants) from a point source (such as a pipe or ditch) into a river must obtain a **National Pollution Discharge Elimination System (NPDES) permit** from the state where the discharge takes place or from EPA. Similarly, anyone who discharges wastewater, other than just domestic sewage, to a publicly owned treatment works (POTW) must obtain what is known as an **industrial discharge permit** from the local sewage treatment plant where the discharge is being sent or from the state.

Typically, these permits (1) establish limits on the concentration and amount of various pollutants that can be discharged; and (2) require the discharger to keep records, to install equipment to monitor the discharges, and report the monitoring results to the state environmental agency. All of the permits contain limits established by EPA in the form of **nationally applicable, technology-based effluent limits.** In the case of the industrial discharge permits, the limitations are known as **pretreatment standards** because they normally require the discharger to provide some on-site treatment of the wastewater before it enters the sewer system. For industries that discharge directly into rivers, the technology-based limits established by EPA can be tightened if necessary to ensure that the water quality standards established by the state for that body of water are met and the designated uses protected.

Water Quality Standards

The act continued and expanded the previously established system of setting *water quality standards* by designating, and establishing limits to protect, the uses of specific bodies of water for recreation, public water supply, propagation of fish and wildlife, and agricultural and industrial water supply.

Then, the maximum daily loads of various pollutants are set so that the water is suitable for the designated use. The final step is to establish limits on individual dischargers of pollutants so that the water quality standards will be met.

Enforcement

Both civil and criminal sanctions are included in the act. Criminal penalties for violating the law range from a minimum of $2,500 for a first offense up to $50,000 per day and two years in prison for subsequent violations. The act is enforced by federal and state governments. In addition, any citizen or group of citizens whose interests are adversely affected has the right to bring a court action against anyone violating an effluent standard, limitation, or order issued by EPA or a state. A significant number of cases have been brought by citizen-action groups against firms whose wastewater discharges exceeded the limits of their discharge permits. Citizens also have the right to take court action against EPA if it fails to carry out mandatory provisions of the law.

In the case that follows, *United States v. Hopkins,* a corporate officer was convicted and sentenced to prison for falsifying reports to the government concerning the discharge of pollutants.

| United States v. Hopkins | 53 F.3d 533 (2d Cir. 1995) |

Spirol International Corporation is a manufacturer of metal shims and fasteners located in northeastern Connecticut. Spirol's manufacturing operation involves a zinc-based plating process that generates substantial amounts of wastewater containing zinc and other toxic materials; this wastewater is discharged into the nearby Five Mile River. The U.S. Environmental Protection Agency (EPA) has delegated to the State of Connecticut's Department of Environmental Protection (DEP) the authority to administer the Clean Water Act provisions applicable to Spirol's discharges into the river. In 1987, Spirol entered into a consent order with DEP requiring Spirol to pay a $30,000 fine for past violations and to comply in the future with discharge limitations specified in the order. In February 1989, DEP issued a modified "wastewater discharge permit" imposing more restrictive limits on the quantity of zinc and other substances that Spirol was permitted to release into the river.

From 1987 through September 6, 1990, Robert Hopkins was Spirol's vice president for manufacturing. Hopkins signed the 1987 consent decree on behalf of Spirol and had the corporate responsibility for ensuring compliance with the order and the DEP permit. The DEP permit required Spirol each week to collect a sample of its wastewater and send it to an independent laboratory by Friday morning of that week. Spirol was required to report the laboratory results to DEP in a discharge monitoring report once a month. Under the DEP permit, the concentrations of zinc in Spirol's wastewater were not to exceed 2.0 milligrams per liter in any weekly sample, nor to average more than one milligram per liter in any month.

During the period March 1989 to September 1990, Spirol began its weekly sampling process on Monday. A composite sample was taken and analyzed in house. If it contained less than one milligram of zinc, it was sent to the independent laboratory with a "chain of custody" record signed by Hopkins. However, if it exceeded one milligram of zinc, it was discarded and another sample taken and tested the following day. In 54 of the 78 weeks, the samples were sent to the laboratory later than Tuesday. If the Wednesday sample also failed the in-house test, Hopkins would sometimes order that it be discarded and another taken on Thursday, but more often he instructed his subordinates doing the testing to dilute the sample with tap water or to reduce the zinc concentration using an ordinary coffee filter. Any Friday sample that failed the in-house test was always diluted or filtered so that a good sample could be sent to the laboratory by the Friday deadline. In some samples sent to the laboratory there was more tap water than wastewater.

During this period Hopkins filed with DEP monthly discharge monitoring reports consolidating the weekly tests from the independent laboratory. The reports showed no zinc concentrations above one milligram per liter. On each report, Hopkins signed the following certification.

> I certify under penalty of law that this document and all attachments were prepared under my direction or supervision in accordance with a system designed to assure that qualified personnel properly gather and evaluate the information submitted. Based on my inquiry of the person or persons who administer the system, or those persons directly responsible for gathering the information, the information is, to the best of my knowledge and belief, true, accurate and complete. I am aware that there are significant penalties for submitting false information, including the possibility of fine and imprisonment for knowing violations.

Contrary to Hopkins's certifications, his subordinates testified that he had caused the samples to be tampered with about 40 percent of the time. On some 25–30 occasions when he had been told that a satisfactory sample had finally been obtained by means of dilution or filtration, Hopkins responded, "I know nothing, I hear nothing." Hopkins was told that the testing procedures were improper, yet he continued to sign the certifications and Spirol continued its discharges into the river.

In December 1993, Hopkins was charged in a three-count indictment alleging (1) that he had knowingly falsified or tampered with Spirol's discharge sampling methods, (2) that he had knowingly violated the conditions of the permit, and (3) that he had conspired to commit those offenses. Hopkins was convicted following a jury trial and sentenced to 21 months in prison, with two years probation following that, and a $7,500 fine. Hopkins appealed, arguing that the government should have been required to prove that he intended to violate the law and that he had specific knowledge of the particular statutory, regulatory or permit requirements imposed under the Clean Water Act. The government contended that it was enough to prove that he had acted voluntarily or intentionally to falsify, tamper with, or render inaccurate a monitoring method—or to violate the permit—and that he did not do so by mistake, accident, or other innocent reason.

Kearse, Circuit Judge

Subsection (2) of section 1319(c), whose violation was alleged in count two of the indictment, establishes criminal penalties, including fines of up to $50,000 per day and imprisonment for up to three years, for "any person" who, inter alia, knowingly violates section 1311, 1312, 1316, 1317, 1318, 1321(b)(3), 1328, or 1345 of [Title 33], or any permit condition or limitation implementing any of such sections in a permit issued under [the Clean Water Act] by the Administrator or by a State.

Hopkins contends that the district court should have instructed the jury that it could not find him guilty of violating this section unless it found that he knew he was acting in violation of the CWA or the DEP permit. We disagree.

Section 1319(c)(2)(A) itself does not expressly state whether the adverb "knowingly" is intended to require proof that the defendant had actual knowledge that his conduct violated any of the statutory provisions that follow the phrase "knowingly violates" or had actual knowledge that his conduct violated a permit condition. As a matter of abstract logic, it would seem that a statute making it unlawful to "knowingly violate" a given statutory or permit provision would require proof that the defendant both violated and knew that he violated that provision. In defining the mental state required for conviction under a given statute, however, the courts must seek the proper "inference of the intent of Congress."

In *United States v. International Minerals & Chemical Corp.* ("International Minerals"), the Court construed a statute that authorized the Interstate Commerce Commission ("ICC") to promulgate regulations governing the transport of corrosive liquids and imposed criminal penalties on those who "knowingly violated any such regulation." The Court held that the quoted phrase required the government to prove only that the defendant knew the nature of his acts, not that he knew his acts violated an ICC regulation. The Court stated that "where . . . dangerous or deleterious devices or products or obnoxious waste materials are involved, the probability of regulation is so great that anyone who is aware that he is in possession of them or dealing with them must be presumed to be aware of the regulation." Applying this presumption of awareness, the Court concluded that the phrase "knowingly violated any [ICC] regulation" was meant to be a "shorthand" method of referring to the acts or omissions contemplated by the statute.

Noting the general rule that ignorance of the law is no excuse, the court declined to attribute to Congress the inaccurate view that use of the word "knowingly" would require proof of knowledge of the law, as well as the facts. The mens rea presumption requires knowledge only of the facts that make the defendant's conduct illegal, lest it conflict with the related presumption, deeply rooted in the American legal system, that ordinarily ignorance of the law or a mistake of law is no defense to criminal prosecution.

This court in *United States v. Laughlin* applied the *International Minerals* "presumption of awareness of regulation" in construing provisions of the Resource Conservation and Recovery Act ("RCRA") and the Comprehensive Environmental Response, Compensation and Liability Act ("CERCLA"). RCRA provides for the imposition of criminal penalties against any person who "knowingly treats, stores, or disposes of any hazardous waste identified or listed under [RCRA]" without a permit. We held that this provision did not require the government to prove that the defendant knew that the waste he dealt with was identified or listed under RCRA or that he lacked a disposal permit. Rather, we held that the government need prove only that the defendant knew the nature of the hazardous waste matter with which he dealt.

For several reasons, we view the presumption of awareness of regulation, applied to the ground-pollution offenses in *Laughlin,* to be equally applicable to the phrase "knowingly violates [the specified sections or permit]" in section 1319(c)(2)(A). Congress considered discharges of hazardous waste onto the ground, which are regulated in RCRA, as no less serious than such discharges into water. Further, the CWA sections to which section 1319(c)(2)(A) refers regulate a broad range of pollutant discharges, including "water quality related effluents," "toxic pollutants" listed in accordance with section 1317(a), "oil and hazardous substances," and "sewage sludge." The vast majority of these substances are of the type that would alert any ordinary user to the likelihood of stringent regulation. Moreover, the very fact that a governmental permit has been issued enhances the user's awareness of the existence of regulation.

Thus, we conclude that the purpose and legislative history of section 1319(c)(2)(A) indicate that Congress meant that that section would be violated if the defendant's acts were proscribed, even if the defendant was not aware of the proscription.

Judgment of conviction affirmed.

Wetlands Another aspect of the Clean Water Act having the potential to affect businesses as well as individual property owners is the wetlands provision. Commonly, wetlands are transition zones between land and open water. Under Section 404 of the act, any *dredging or filling* activity in a wetland that is connected to the waters of the United States—as well as in any water of the United States—requires a permit before any activity begins. The permit program is administered by the Army Corps of Engineers, with the involvement of the Environmental Protection Agency.

As can be seen in the *Bersani* case, which follows, the permit requirement can significantly limit a landowner's use of his property where the fill activity is viewed as injurious to the values protected by the act.

Bersani v. U.S. Environmental Protection Agency
674 F.Supp. 405 (N.D.N.Y. 1987) aff'd 395 F.2d 36 (2d Cir. 1988)

Pyramid Companies was an association of partnerships in the business of developing, constructing, and operating shopping centers; John Bersani was a principal in one of the partnerships. In 1983, Pyramid became interested in developing a shopping mall in the Attleboro, Massachusetts, area and focused its attention on an 82-acre site known as Sweden's Swamp along an interstate highway in South Attleboro. The project contemplated altering or filling some 32 acres of the 49.6 acres of wetlands on the property. At the same time, Pyramid planned to excavate 9 acres of uplands (nonwetlands) to create new wetlands and to alter some 13 acres of existing wetlands to enhance their value for fish and wildlife.

In 1984, Pyramid applied to the U.S. Army Corps of Engineers for a permit under Section 404 of the Clean Water Act to do the dredge and fill work in the wetlands. As part of its application, it was required to submit information on practicable alternative sites for its shopping mall. One site subsequently focused on by the Corps and the Environmental Protection Agency was about three miles north in North Attleboro. Pyramid relied on several factors in claiming that the site was not a practicable alternative to its proposed site: namely, the site lacked sufficient traffic volume and access from local roads, potential department store tenants had expressed doubts about the feasibility of the site, and previous attempts to develop the site had met with strong resistance from the surrounding community. However, after Pyramid examined the site, another major developer of shopping centers had taken an option to acquire the property.

The New England Division Engineer of the Corps recommended that the permit be denied because a practicable alternative with a less adverse effect on the environment existed. The Chief of Engineers directed that the permit be issued, noting that the alternative site was not available to Pyramid because it was owned by a competitor. He also believed that even if it was considered available, Pyramid had made a convincing case that the site would not fulfill its objectives for a successful project. EPA then exercised its prerogative under the Clean Water Act to veto the permit on the grounds that filling Sweden's Swamp to build the shopping mall would have an unacceptable adverse effect on the environment. In its view, another less environmentally damaging site had been available to Pyramid at the time it made its site selection; thus, any adverse effects on Sweden's Swamp were avoidable. Bersani and Pyramid then brought suit challenging the denial of its permit application.

McAvo, Judge

Section 404(a) authorizes the Secretary of the Army, acting through the Corps, to issue permits for the discharge of dredged or fill material at specified disposal sites. Criteria developed by the EPA in conjunction with the Corps govern these permitting decisions. Generally, the Corps must employ a "practicable alternative" analysis in determining whether to allow a proposed discharge. Section 230.10 of the regulations provides:

(a) . . . no discharge of dredged or fill material shall be permitted if there is a practicable alternative to the proposed discharge which would have less adverse impact on the aquatic ecosystem, so long as the alternative does not have other significant adverse environmental consequences. (2) An alternative is practicable if it is available and capable of being done, after taking into account cost, existing technology, and logistics in light of overall project purposes. If it is otherwise a practicable alternative, an area not presently owned by the applicant which could reasonably be obtained, utilized, expanded or managed in order to fulfill the basic purpose of the proposed activity may be considered. (3) Where the activity associated with a discharge which is proposed for a special aquatic site (including a wetland) does not require access or proximity to or siting within the special aquatic site in question to fulfill its basic purpose (i.e., is not "water dependent"), practicable alternatives that do not involve special aquatic sites are presumed to be available unless clearly demonstrated otherwise. In addition, where a discharge is proposed for a special aquatic site, all practicable alternatives to the proposed discharge which do not involve a discharge into a special aquatic site are presumed to have less adverse impact on the aquatic ecosystem, unless clearly demonstrated otherwise.

Where the proposed discharge involves a special aquatic site such as wetlands, a more stringent standard is imposed. Indeed Section 230.10(a)(3) creates a presumption that a practicable alternative exists when the discharge involves wetlands and the activity, here a shopping mall, is not "water dependent." Then the applicant must "clearly demonstrate" that no such alternative does in fact exist.

Pyramid argues that EPA's determination of feasibility was based on its erroneous conclusion that the marketplace considered the North Attleboro site suitable for a virtually identical regional shopping mall. Pyramid notes that six other shopping center developers over the past 15 years have tried and failed to develop the North Attleboro site as a shopping center. It contends that EPA has substituted its own judgment for that of the marketplace in an area in which it cannot claim expertise. The EPA, however, contends that it did not simply substitute its judgment for that of the developer. Instead, the EPA argues that the evidence on the record demonstrates that the North Attleboro site is suitable in fact for a regional shopping center mall virtually identical to that proposed by Pyramid. In this respect, the fact that a competing developer, the New England Development Company, had found the site suitable for a similar shopping mall and its own marketing analysis weighed in reaching this decision. The EPA also engaged in a review of the specific features that Pyramid found objectionable; namely, the distance from the primary trade area, lack of visibility from nearby highways, zoning, past failures of prior attempts to develop a shopping mall at the site, and various considerations. Consequently, the court finds that EPA's feasibility determination was not arbitrary.

Summary judgment granted for EPA.

Ocean Dumping The Marine Protection, Research, and Sanctuaries Act of 1972 set up a permit system regulating the dumping of all types of materials into ocean waters. EPA has the responsibility for designating disposal sites and for establishing the rules governing ocean disposal. The Ocean Dumping Ban Act of 1987 required that all ocean dumping of municipal sewage sludge and industrial wastes be terminated by December 31,

The Global Business Environment

International Voluntary Consensus Standards and Certification: ISO 14000 Environmental Management Standards

Today, national and international companies competing in a global economy face a daunting array of challenges, including complying with increasingly complex environmental regulations in those countries in which they operate or do business. And, differing national standards cannot only create nontariff trade barriers but also increase costs and the difficulty of doing business. Managers who want to be proactive in systematically improving the environmental performance of their organization can adopt and follow the ISO 14000 series of environmental management standards.

The ISO, located in Geneva, Switzerland, was founded in 1947 to promote the development of international manufacturing, trade, and communication standards. The ISO standards—which are international voluntary consensus standards—are developed with input from industry, government, and other interested parties. The standards have legal standing only if actually adopted by a country—but they have been utilized by many organizations on a voluntary basis. In addition to the performance enhancement that can be obtained by following the standards, in some instances certification of compliance with the standards can lead to competitive advantages and/or may be necessary to do certain types of business.

The most prominent of the ISO standards is the worldwide quality standard, ISO 9000. The standard provides organizations with a process for producing quality products through a systems approach that involves all phases of production. You may have encountered these standards in other business school classes. They have been adopted by many countries and utilized by many organizations—and more than 100,000 ISO 9000 certificates have been issued worldwide.

Development of the ISO 14000 series of standards began in 1993 and the initial set of standards were finalized in 1996. Theses include (1) ISO 14001 Environmental management systems—specification with guidance for use; (2) ISO 14004 Environmental management systems—general guidelines on principles, systems, and supporting techniques; (3) ISO 14010 Guidelines for environmental auditing—general principles; (4) ISO 14011 Guidelines for environmental auditing—audit procedures—Part 1: Auditing of environmental management programs; (5) ISO Guidelines for environmental auditing—qualification criteria for environmental auditors; (6) ISO 14024 Environmental labeling—guidance principles, practices, and criteria for multiple criteria-based practitioner programs (Type 1)—guide for certification procedures; (7) ISO 14040 Life-cycle assessment—principles and guidelines; and (8) ISO Guide for the inclusion of environmental aspects in product standards.

Organizations can be certified that they comply with ISO 14001. Certification is a procedure by which a third party gives written assurance that a product, process, or service conforms to the specific requirements of the ISO standard. An organization that obtains ISO certification can claim that it has an environmental management system (EMS) meeting the ISO standards that has been implemented and is being consistently followed. This certification would be based on an audit of the EMS system by the third-party certifier. It should be noted that the certification goes to the nature of the management system employed by the organization—and does not give it a basis for claiming that its products or services are environmentally superior to those of other organizations. However, such certification can be either a matter of competitive advantage—or of necessity—as some companies will only do business with ISO certified entities. In the United States, the American National Standards Institute (ANSI) is the organization responsible for certifying that an organization meets the requirements of ISO 14001.

1991. Thus, the major remaining questions of ocean dumping concern the disposal of dredge spoils from dredging to keep harbors open.

Drinking Water

In 1974, Congress passed, and in 1986 and in 1996 amended, the Safe Drinking Water Act that is designed to protect and enhance the quality of our drinking water. Under the act, EPA sets *primary drinking water standards,* minimum levels of quality for water consumed by humans. The act also establishes a program governing the injection of wastes into wells. The primary responsibility for complying with the federally established standards lies with the states. Where the states fail to enforce the drinking water standards, the federal government has the right to enforce them.

A significant number of suppliers of drinking water are privately owned—and they, as well as the publicly owned systems, have to be concerned with meeting the federal standards. In addition, factories, trailer parks, schools, and other entities that draw drinking water from wells and provide it within their facility can find that they are also subject to the drinking water regulations.

Waste Disposal

Background Historically, concern about the environment focused on decreasing air and water pollution as well as protecting natural resources and wildlife. People paid relatively little attention to the disposal of wastes on land. Until the early 1970s, much of the solid and hazardous waste generated was disposed of in open dumps and landfills. Although some of the waste we produce can be disposed of without presenting significant health or environmental problems, some industrial, agricultural, and mining wastes—and even some household wastes—are hazardous and can present serious problems. Unless wastes are properly disposed of, they can cause air, water, and land pollution as well as contamination of the underground aquifers from which much of our drinking water is drawn. Once aquifers have been contaminated, they can take a very long time to cleanse themselves of pollutants.

In the 1970s, the discovery of abandoned dump sites such as Love Canal in New York and the Valley of the Drums in Kentucky heightened public concern about the disposal of toxic and hazardous wastes. Congress has enacted several laws regulating the generation and disposal of hazardous waste: the Resource Conservation and Recovery Act mandates proper management and disposal of wastes currently generated; and the Comprehensive Environmental Response, Compensation, and Liability Act focuses on cleaning up past disposal sites threatening public health and the environment.

The Resource Conservation and Recovery Act

Congress originally enacted the Resource Conservation and Recovery Act (RCRA) in 1976 and significantly amended it in 1984. RCRA provides the federal government and the states with the authority to regulate facilities that generate, treat, store, and dispose of hazardous waste. Most of the wastes defined as hazardous are subject to a "cradle-to-the-grave" tracking system and must be handled and disposed of in defined ways. RCRA requires persons who generate, treat, store, or transport hazardous waste, to meet certain standards and follow specified procedures in the handling of the wastes, to keep records and, in some instances, to obtain permits. Figure 1 illustrates the form known as a *manifest*—that must accompany all shipments of hazardous waste from the point of generation until its final treatment or disposal.

In addition, operators of land waste disposal facilities must meet financial responsibility requirements and monitor groundwater quality. EPA determines whether certain wastes should be banned entirely from land disposal; a significant number of wastes must be treated before they can be disposed of in land disposal units.

Underground Storage Tanks

In 1984, Congress directed that EPA also regulate underground product storage tanks such as gasoline tanks to prevent and respond to leaks that might contaminate underground water. The regulations that EPA issued to implement these requirements impose significant costs on many businesses such as gasoline stations that utilize such storage tanks. Owners of such tanks have had to upgrade them or replace them with tanks that are corrosion resistant and can be monitored for leaks. New tanks must meet stringent standards, and any leaks must promptly be addressed.

State Responsibilities

EPA sets minimum requirements for state RCRA programs and then delegates the responsibility for conducting programs to the states when they have the legal ability and interest to administer them. Until a state assumes partial or complete responsibility for a RCRA program, the federal government administers the program.

Enforcement

Failure to comply with the hazardous waste regulations promulgated under RCRA can subject violators to civil and criminal penalties. In the *United States v. Dean* case, which follows, an employee of a company that disposed of hazardous waste without a RCRA permit was held criminally liable.

| United States v. Dean | 969 F.2d 187 (6th Cir. 1992) |

General Metal Fabricators, Inc. (GMF), owned and operated a facility in Erwin, Tennessee, which was engaged in metal stamping, plating, and painting. The facility utilized hazardous chemicals and generated hazardous waste but did not have a RCRA permit nor did it maintain the required records of the treatment, storage, and disposal of hazardous substances. The hazardous waste disposal practices at GMF were discovered by chance by state waste-management authorities whose attention was caught, while driving to an appointment at another facility, by two 55-gallon drums abandoned among weeds on GMF's property.

The owners of GMF, Joseph and Jean Sanchez, as well as Clyde Griffith, the plant manager, and Gale Dean, the production manager, were indicted for conspiracy to violate RCRA, and, individually, for violations of various sections of RCRA. At his request, Dean's trial was severed from that of the other defendants.

As production manager, Dean had day-to-day supervision of GMF's production process and employees. Among his duties was the instruction of employees on hazardous waste handling and disposal. Numerous practices at GMF violated RCRA. GMF's plating operations utilized rinse baths, contaminated with hazardous chemicals, which were drained through a pipe into an earthen lagoon outside the facility. In addition, Dean instructed employees to shovel various kinds of solid wastes from the tanks into 55-gallon drums. Dean ordered the construction of a pit, concealed behind the facility, into which 38 drums of such hazardous waste were tossed. The contents spilled onto the soil from open or corroded drums. Chemical analyses of soil and solid wastes revealed that the pit and the lagoon were contaminated with chromium. In addition, the pit was contaminated with toluene and xylene solvents. All of these substances are considered hazardous under RCRA. Drums of spent chromic acid solution were also illegally stored on the premises.

Dean was familiar with the chemicals used in each of the tanks on the production line and with the manner in which the contents of the rinse tanks were deposited in the lagoon. Material Safety Data Sheets (MSDS) provided to GMF by the chemical manufacturer clearly stated that the various chemicals in use at GMF were hazardous and were subject to federal pollution control laws. Dean was familiar with the MSDS and knowledgeable about their contents. The MSDS delivered with the chromic acid made specific reference to RCRA and to related EPA regulations. Dean told investigators that he "had read this RCRA waste code but thought it was a bunch of bull—."

Dean was convicted of conspiracy to violate RCRA as well as of (1) failure to file documentation of hazardous waste generation, storage, and disposal; (2) storage of spent chromic acid without a permit; (3) disposal of chromic acid rinse water and sludges in a lagoon without a permit; and (4) disposal of paint sludge and solvent wastes in a pit without a permit, all in violation of RCRA. Dean appealed his conviction.

Joiner, Senior District Judge

The first of the issues raised by Dean is that the trial court erred in denying his motion for acquittal on the permit-related counts because there was no evidence that Dean knew of RCRA's permit requirement. Dean's characterization of the evidence is inaccurate, but moreover, we see no basis on the face of the statute for concluding that knowledge of the permit requirement is an element of the crime. The statute penalizes:

Any person who—. . . (2) knowingly treats, stores or disposes of any hazardous waste identified or listed under this subchapter—(A) without a permit under this subchapter . . . ; or (B) in knowing violation of any material condition or requirement of such permit; or (C) in knowing violation of any applicable interim status or regulations. 42 U.S.C. section 6928(d)(2).

Dean was convicted of violating subsection 6928(d)(2)(A).

The question of interpretation presented by this provision is the familiar one of how far the initial "knowingly" travels. Other courts of appeals have divided on this question. We agree with the reasoning of the Court of Appeals for the Ninth Circuit in *United States v. Hoflin.* The "knowingly" which begins section 6928(d)(2) cannot be read as extending to the subsections without rendering nugatory the word "knowing" contained in subsections 6928(d)(2)(B) and (C). Subsection 6928(d)(2)(A) requires knowing treatment (or knowing storage, or knowing disposal) of hazardous waste. It also requires proof that the treatment, storage or disposal was done without a permit. It does not require that the person charged must have known that a permit was required, and that knowledge is not relevant.

Dean also contends that the district court should have granted his motion for acquittal because subsection 6928 (d)(2)(A) was not intended to reach employees who are not "owners" or "operators" of facilities. By its terms, the provision applies to "any person." "Person" is a defined term meaning "an individual. . . ." Dean would be hard pressed to convince the court that he is not an "individual." He argues, however, that because only owners and operators of facilities are required to obtain permits, the penalty imposed for hazardous waste handling without a permit must apply only to owners and operators.

This contention is unpersuasive for numerous reasons. Of primary importance is the fact that it is contrary to the unambiguous language of the statute.

Affirmed.

Figure 1   Sample "Uniform Hazardous Waste Manifest" Form

Please Print or type   *(Form designed for use on elite (12-pitch) typewriter)*   Form Approved OMB 2000-0404 Expires 7-31-99

UNIFORM HAZARDOUS WASTE MANIFEST	1. Generator's US EPA ID No. V A D 0 0 1 2 3 4 5 6 7 0 0 0 0 7	2. Page 1 of	Information in the shaded areas is not required by federal law

3. Generator's Name and Mailing Address
GENERAL METAL PROCESSING CO.
501 MAIN ST.
SMALLTOWN, VA 23000

A. State Manifest Document Number

4. Generator's Phone No. (804 **)** 555-0509

B. State Generator's ID

5. Transporter 1 Company Name SAFETY HAULER	6. US EPA ID Number V A D 0 0 8 9 1 2 3 4 5	C. State Transporter's ID
		D. Transporter's Phone
7. Transporter 2 Company Name	8. US EPA ID Number	E. State Transporter's ID
		F. Transporter's Phone

9. Designated Facility Name and Site Address
DISPOS-ALL, INC.
1800 NORTH AVE.
FRIENDLY TOWN, VA 2300

10. US EPA ID Number V A D 0 0 6 F 8 9 1 2 3

G. State Facility's ID

H. Facility's Phone

11. US DOT Description *(Including Proper Shipping Name, Hazard Class, and ID Number)*	12. Containers No.	Type	13. Total Quantity	13. Unit Wt/Vol	I. Waste No.
a. HAZARDOUS WASTE, LIQUID OR SOLID, NOS ORM-E NA9189	0 0 2	D M	0 0 1 1 0	GAL	
b. WASTE CYANIDE SOLUTION, NOS UN1935	0 0 1	D M	0 0 0 5 5	GAL	
c. WASTE FLAMMABLE SOLUTION, NOS UN1993	0 0 1	D M	0 0 0 5 5	GAL	
d.					

J. Additional Descriptions for Materials Listed Above

K. Handling Codes for Wastes Listed Above

15. Special Handling Instructions and Additional Information

16. Generator's Certification: I hereby declare that the contents of this consignment are fully and accurately described above by proper shipping name and classified, packed, marked, labeled, and are in all respects in proper condition for transport by highway according to applicable international and national regulations.

Unless I am a small quantity generator who has been exempted by statute or regulation from the duty to make a waste minimization certification under Section 3002(b) of RCRA, I also certify that I have a program in place to reduce the volume and toxicity of waste generated to the degree I have determined to be economically practicable and I have selected the method of treatment, storage, or disposal currently available to me which minimizes the present and future threat to human health and the environment.

Printed/ Typed Name JOSEPHINE K. DOE	Signature *Josephine K. Doe*	Month Day Year 0 8 3 0 1 0

17. Transporter 1 Acknowledgement of Receipt of Materials

Printed/Typed Name	Signature	

18. Transporter 2 Acknowledgement of Receipt of Materials

Printed/Typed Name	Signature	Month Day Year

19. Discrepancy Indication Space

20. Facility Owner or Operator: Certification of receipt of hazardous materials covered by this manifest except as noted in Item 19.

Printed/Typed Name	Signature	Month Day Year

EPA Form 8700-22 (Rev. 4-85) Previous Edition is obsolete.

Information in the shaded areas is not required by federal law, but this or other additional information may be required by your state.

The Global Business Environment

Extended Producer Responsibility

Extended producer responsibility (EPR) for consumer packaging is a part of doing business in many countries, particularly developed countries other than the United States. EPR shifts the financial burden of recycling products back to the seller or manufacturer of the products. Commonly the consumer ends up paying a fee on packaging materials that is used to support recycling programs. The concept has been adopted close to the United States as Quebec and Ontario Provinces in Canada began EPR programs in 2004. And, while there has been no broadscale adoption of such programs in the United States, in 2003, the state of California did enact EPR legislation addressing electronic products. The Electronic Waste Recycling Act of 2003 requires retailers and manufacturers to include a fee on each covered product to finance recycling and requires that manufacturers reduce the amount of toxic materials used in electronic devices.

Solid Waste

Mining, commercial, and household activities generate a large volume of waste material that can present problems if not properly disposed of. As population density has increased, causing a corresponding increase in the total volume of waste, it has become more difficult to find land or incinerators where the waste material can be disposed of properly. RCRA authorizes EPA to set minimum standards for such disposal, but states and local governments bear the primary responsibility for the siting and regulation of such activity.

As the cost and difficulty of disposing of waste increases, public attention focuses on reducing the waste to be disposed of, on looking for opportunities to recycle some of the waste material, and on changing the characteristics of the material that must ultimately be disposed of so that it poses fewer environmental problems. One of the significant challenges faced by tomorrow's businessperson will be in designing products, packaging, and production processes so as to minimize the waste products that result. A significant problem for both government and industry is the difficulty in trying to site new waste facilities. The NIMBY, or not-in-my-backyard, syndrome is pervasive as people almost universally desire to have the wastes from their everyday lives and from the economic activity in their community disposed of in someone else's neighborhood—any place but their own. As governments try to cope with the reality of finding places to dispose of wastes in an environmentally safe manner and at the same time cope with public opposition to siting new facilities, the temptation is strong to try to bar wastes from other areas from being disposed of in local facilities.

In the 1978 landmark case *City of Philadelphia v. New Jersey,* the U.S. Supreme Court struck down an attempt by the state of New Jersey to prohibit the importation of most solid waste originating outside the state. An ironic twist is that decades later, we find a number of other eastern and midwestern states trying to find ways to block the importation of wastes from New Jersey into their states. In recent years, the Supreme Court has had occasion to reiterate its holding in *City of Philadelphia v. New Jersey* in a series of new cases involving efforts by states to block or limit the flow of solid and hazardous waste from outside their state to disposal sites within the state.

Superfund

In 1980, Congress passed the Comprehensive Environmental Response, Compensation, and Liability Act (CERCLA), commonly known as Superfund, to deal with the problem of uncontrolled or abandoned hazardous waste sites. In 1986, it strengthened and expanded the law. Under the Superfund law, EPA identified and assessed the sites in the United States where hazardous wastes had been spilled, stored, or abandoned.

Eventually, EPA expects to identify 30,000 such sites. The sites are ranked on the basis of the type, quantity, and toxicity of the wastes; the number of people potentially exposed to the wastes; the different ways (e.g., in the air or drinking water) in which they might be exposed; the risks to contamination of aquifers; and other factors. The sites with the highest ranking are put on the National Priority List to receive priority federal and/or state attention for cleanup. At these sites, EPA makes careful scientific and engineering studies to determine the most appropriate cleanup plans. Once a site has been cleaned up, the state is responsible for managing it to prevent future environmental problems. EPA also has the authority to quickly initiate actions at hazardous waste sites—whether or not the site is on the priority list—to address imminent hazards such as the risk of fire, explosion, or contamination of drinking water.

The cleanup activity is financed by federal tax revenues. However, EPA is authorized to require that a site be cleaned up by those persons responsible for contaminating it, either as the **owner or operator of the site,** a **transporter of wastes to the site,** or the **owner of wastes deposited at the site.** Where EPA expends money to clean up a site, it has the legal authority to recover its costs from those who were responsible for the problem. The courts have held that such persons are "jointly and severally responsible for the cost of cleanup." Chapter 7, Negligence and Strict Liability, discusses the concept of joint liability. Of concern to many business-

people is the fact that this stringent and potentially very expensive liability can in some instances be imposed on a current owner of a site who had nothing to do with the contamination, such as a subsequent purchaser of the land.

In the case that follows, *United States v. Domenic Lombardi Realty,* a subsequent purchaser was held liable for cleaning up a property that had been contaminated, in part, by the actions of its predecessor in title.

United States v. Domenic Lombardi Realty
290 F.Supp 2d 198 (D. Rhode Island 2003)

During the early 1980s, Armand Allen acquired 31 acres of property located off of Robin Hollow Road in West Greenwich, Rhode Island. Allen began construction of a home on the property, but never completed the structure. Allen, along with his wife, lived in a 60-foot trailer on the site. Although he never obtained the licenses required to operate a junkyard, Allen stored a number of junk cars and trucks in various states of disrepair on the property. The Town of West Greenwich denied Allen's multiple applications for a junkyard license, but never ordered him to clean up his property.

In the fall of 1986 Domenic Lombardi, an employee of Lombardi Realty, approached Allen regarding a "For Sale" sign that was posted at the site. Allen indicated that his price for the property was $135,000, but that he was willing to drop the price to $85,000 in order to make a quick sale. Lombardi later testified that while he was on the property, he noticed stripped down cars and trucks as well as other solid waste. Lombardi instructed his real estate agent, Ray Walsh, to make an offer on the property of $85,000, which Allen immediately accepted on December 11, 1986.

Lombardi testified that Allen informed him that at one time he stripped electrical transformers on the site to recover copper from them. He also had a witness who claimed he had taken a load of transformers to the site sometime between 1982 and 1986; this witness was a convicted felon with a history of lying in court. Moreover, this testimony was contradicted by Allen's wife that she never saw any transformers brought on-site.

Walsh testified that in preparation for the purchase, he obtained a plat map from the city in order to estimate the future assessment of taxes that Lombardi would incur, but he did not perform any additional background investigation, such as an environmental assessment or a walk around the property, nor did he contact authorities concerning the prior use of the property.

After the purchase, Lombardi completed work on the partially constructed, single-family home. He also began renting out the trailer. The tenant testified that within a few months after she began renting the trailer, she saw transformers among the solid waste debris on the property. Other neighbors testified that they witnessed Lombardi Realty trucks dumping trash, including electrical transformers, on the site.

In November 1987, the Rhode Island Department of Environmental Management (RIDEM), believing that Lombardi Realty was permitting the property to be used for the disposal of solid waste without a permit, issued Lombardi Realty a notice of violation and ordered it to remove all solid waste that had been disposed of at the site. Subsequently, RIDEM discovered the presence of oil containing PCBs at the site. RIDEM ordered Lombardi to—among other things—submit and implement a sampling plan, to contract for the removal of all hazardous wastes from the site, and to submit and implement a cleanup plan. Lombardi Realty did not comply with any of the orders until 1989, when it arranged for the excavation of some of the PCB-contaminated soil, which it put in uncovered piles on the site.

In 1991, John Lombardi became president of Lombardi Realty when Dominic was sent to prison for the arson of the trailer on the site. John Lombardi knew little about the seriousness of the contamination on the site prior to becoming president, never having been informed about it by his father. The information withheld included the fact that children were using the piles as ramps for their dirt bikes.

In November 1994, EPA became involved at the request of RIDEM. From February though July of 1995, EPA removed the contaminated soil from the site and replaced it with clean backfill. In total, EPA excavated about 900 tons of soil. EPA then initiated an action against Lombardi Realty to recover the $481,068 "response costs" incurred in removing the hazardous substances from the site. Lombardi Realty asserted that it was an "innocent landowner" and that it should not be liable for the response costs.

Smith, Judge

The Comprehensive Environmental Response, Compensation, and Liability Act (CERCLA) provides the EPA a mechanism to compel parties associated with contaminated property to cleanup, or pay for the cleanup, of the contaminated property. In order for the EPA to successfully pursue its CERCLA claim against Lombardi Realty, it must prove (1) a release or threatened release of hazardous waste has occurred; (2) at a facility; (3) causing the EPA to incur response costs; and (4) that the defendant is a responsible party as defined by 42 U.S.C. § 9607(a). Here, it is either uncontested, or has been established at the summary judgment stage, that the EPA has met its burden with respect to these requirements. Accordingly, unless Lombardi Realty can take advantage of one of CERCLA's affirmative defenses, it will be held liable for the cleanup costs incurred by the EPA.

The affirmative defense asserted in this case is the innocent landowner defense. In 1986, Congress amended CERCLA by enacting the Superfund Amendments and Reauthorization Act ("SARA"). In these amendments, Congress provided an affirmative defense for landowners who, innocently and in good faith, purchase property without knowledge that a predecessor in the chain of title had allowed hazardous substances to be disposed on the property. The innocent landowner defense provides a statutory defense to liability where the release of hazardous substances was due to "an act or omission of a third party other than an employee or agent of the defendant, or than one whose act or omission occurs in connection with a contractual relationship, existing directly or indirectly, with the defendant. . . ."

In order to assert this defense, the statute provided that a party must demonstrate, by a preponderance of the evidence, that (1) the contamination occurred prior to the defendant's purchase of the land; (2) the defendant had "no reason to know" that the property was contaminated; (3) the defendant took "all appropriate inquiry into the previous ownership and uses of the property consistent with good commercial or customary practice" in an effort to minimize liability; and (4) once the contamination was discovered, the defendant exercised due care with respect to the hazardous substances concerned.

Subsequent to the initiation of this lawsuit, Congress enacted the Small Business Relief and Brownfields Revitalization Act ("Brownfields Amendments"), which altered elements of CERCLA's innocent landowner defense. In part, this Act was intended to encourage the purchase and development of "brownfields" by attempting to eliminate the fear of CERCLA liability often associated with the purchase of such land. The Act altered CERCLA's innocent landowner defense in three significant ways. First, the Act changed the "all appropriate inquiries" standard from one that must be "consistent with good commercial or customary practice" to one that must be "in accordance with generally accepted good commercial and customary standards and practices." Second, it established criteria for determining whether a defendant has made "all appropriate inquiries" regarding the past ownership and usage of a property. Third, a party must now demonstrate to the court that it took reasonable steps to stop any continuing release, prevent any future release, and prevent or limit exposure to any previously released hazardous substance.

In order to take advantage of the innocent landowner defense, Lombardi Realty must first meet the threshold burden of proving that the contamination at the Site was caused "*solely* by an act or omission of a third party." Accordingly, Lombardi Realty cannot avail itself of the protection of the innocent landowner defense if it contributed to the release of PCBs at the Site.

While Lombardi Realty attempted to establish that Allen had disposed of transformers on the property, that testimony was rife with credibility problems. While there is evidence to indicate that Allen operated a junk or scrap yard, there is none to establish that he contaminated the Site with PCBs. The Government, on the other hand, offered testimony from numerous credible witnesses regarding the presence of transformers on the Site during Lombardi Realty's ownership. First, Haroldean Allen testified that she never saw her husband dispose of transformers at the Robin Hollow Road property. Second, another witness testified that she witnessed Lombardi with transformers on the property on several different occasions. Third, another witness also testified that she saw broken transformers "with some kind of oil stuff" and "oil around" them. Accordingly, Lombardi Realty has not proven that the PCB contamination was caused solely by Allen or any other third party. Therefore, this Court holds that Lombardi Realty cannot avail itself of the protections of the innocent landowner defense.

Even if Lombardi Realty could establish that the release was caused solely by the act or omission of a third party, it would still be unable to prove the other elements of the innocent landowner defense. Lombardi Realty failed to offer sufficient evidence that it "had no reason to know" of the presence of PCBs on the Site. While Lombardi Realty presented no evidence as to what constituted "good commercial or customary practices" for purchasing property in Rhode Island in 1986, the Government proffered expert testimony indicating that an environmental assessment of the property would have been required. Lombardi Realty never performed an environmental assessment of the Site, nor does this Court find that Lombardi Realty made any other meaningful inquiry into the Site's environmental state. Accordingly, Lombardi Realty cannot prove that it carried out all appropriate inquiry into the prior use of the property as required.

Lombardi Realty also failed to meet its burden of establishing that it took "due care" with respect to the PCB contaminated soil. As early as 1989, RIDEM issued an NOV ordering Lombardi Realty to, *inter alia,* inform all visitors to the property of the soil contamination and its hazards. At trial, the Government submitted unrebutted testimony which established that Lombardi Realty never informed visitors or tenants living on the property of the contamination. Furthermore, the Government established that Lombardi Realty never properly stored the contaminated soil following its removal. On numerous occasions, witnesses observed the piles of soil in an uncovered state. Lombardi Realty also failed to obtain a "roll-off" container to store the contaminated soil despite the EPA's orders. Lombardi Realty is therefore unable to prove that it acted with due care in regard to the contaminated soil.

Judgment in favor of United States granting it the costs it incurred cleaning up the site.

CYBERLAW IN ACTION

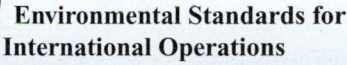

The Toxic Release Inventory Is Available Online

In 1986 the Emergency Planning and Community Right-to-Know Act (EPCRA) was enacted. A primary purpose of this legislation was to ensure that communities and citizens were aware of chemical hazards in their area. Under Section 313 of the EPCRA, the EPA and the states must annually collect data on releases and transfers of certain toxic chemicals from specific facilities. In turn, the data must be made available to the general public in a Toxics Release Inventory (TRI). Now, much of the EPCRA information and data, including data in the TRI program, is easily accessible online through the EPA Web site. In addition, many individual state environmental agency Web sites provide information on TRI for facilities within their particular state. A company's detailed toxic release data can be useful information for the company's competitors. A company could use the TRI information to determine how much of a particular chemical is being produced by their competitors, or to gain insight into what production process is being used by the competition. For more information about the TRI program, visit **www.epa.gov/tri/.**

Community Right to Know and Emergency Cleanup

As part of its 1986 amendments to Superfund, Congress enacted a series of requirements for emergency planning, notification of spills and accidents involving hazardous materials, disclosure by industry to the community of the presence of certain listed chemicals, and notification of the amounts of various chemicals being routinely released into the environment in the area of a facility. This legislation was in response to the industrial accident at Bhopal, India, in 1984 and to several similar incidents in the United States. Firms subject to the requirements have to carefully plan how they will communicate with the surrounding community what chemicals are being regularly released and what precautions the facility has taken to protect the community from regular or accidental releases. Mindful of the difficulty of explaining to a community why large emissions of hazardous substances are taking place, a significant number of companies have undertaken to reduce those emissions below levels they are currently required to meet by law.

Ethics in Action

Environmental Standards for International Operations

Suppose that a multinational chemical company with its primary manufacturing facilities in the United States plans to build a manufacturing facility in a developing country where there are few, if any, real state-imposed environmental regulations. Is it sufficient for the company to simply meet the environmental requirements of the host country? Is there any ethical obligation to do more—for example, to build the facility to meet the requirements it would have to meet in this country?

Major Environmental Laws

Act	Focus
Clean Air Act	Protects quality of ambient (outdoor) air through national ambient air quality standards, state implementation plans, control of toxic air pollutants, new source performance standards, and controls on automobiles and fuels
Clean Water Act	Protects and enhances quality of surface waters by setting water quality standards and limiting discharges by industry and municipalities to those waters through permit system; also regulates dredging and filling of wetlands
Marine Protection, Research, and Sanctuaries Act	Regulates dumping of all types of material into ocean waters
Safe Drinking Water Act	Protects and enhances quality of our drinking water. Also regulates disposal of wastes in wells
Resource Conservation and Recovery Act (RCRA)	Establishes a cradle-to-the-grave regulatory system for handling and disposal of hazardous wastes; also deals with solid waste
Comprehensive Environmental Response Compensation and Liability Act (Superfund)	Provides a program to deal with hazardous waste that was inadequately disposed of in the past

Problems and Problem Cases

1. In July 1984, Vanguard Corporation began operating a metal furniture manufacturing plant in Brooklyn, New York. The plant is located in an area that has not attained the national ambient air quality standards for ozone. The plant is a major stationary source (i.e., has the potential to emit more than 100 tons a year) of volatile organic compounds that contribute to the production of ozone in the atmosphere. The New York state implementation plan (SIP) requires that metal-coating facilities use paint that contains less than three pounds of organic solvent (minus water) per gallon at the time of coating. On August 24, 1984, EPA notified Vanguard that it was not in compliance with the SIP provision concerning coatings and issued it a notice of violation. Vanguard sought to defend against the notice of violation on the grounds that it had used its best faith efforts to comply but that full compliance was technologically and economically infeasible. It indicated that it wanted 18 more months to come into compliance. Should Vanguard be held to be in violation of the Clean Air Act?

2. In August, Tzavah Urban Renewal Corporation purchased from the city of Newark a building formerly known as the Old Military Park Hotel. While the buyer was given an opportunity to inspect the building, it was not informed by the city that the building was permeated with asbestos-containing material. At the time of the purchase, the building was in great disrepair and had been uninhabited for many years. Its proposed renovation was to be a major urban renewal project. In the following June, Tzavah contracted with Greer Industrial Corporation to "gut" the building. While the work was going on, an EPA inspector visited the site and concluded that the hotel was contaminated with asbestos. He observed Greer employees throwing asbestos-laced objects out of the windows of the building and noted an uncovered refuse pile next to the hotel that contained asbestos. The workers were not wetting the debris before heaving it out the windows and the refuse pile was also dry. As a result, asbestos dust was being released into the air. Although the hotel was located in a commercial district, there were private homes nearby. Renovation of buildings contaminated with asbestos is regulated under the Clean Air Act. The EPA regulations require building owners or operators to notify EPA before commencing renovation or demolition and prescribe various procedures for storage and removal of the

asbestos. Tzavah failed to provide the required notice or to comply with procedures required. After being notified by EPA of the violation of the law, Tzavah stopped the demolition work, left the building unsecured, and left the waste piles dry and uncovered. EPA tried informally to get Tzavah to complete the work in accordance with the asbestos regulations; when Tzavah did not take action, EPA brought a lawsuit against Tzavah to do so. Should the court issue an injunction requiring Tzavah to abate the hazard posed by the dry asbestos remaining in the hotel?

3. Mall Properties, Inc., was an organization that for many years sought to develop a shopping mall in the Town of North Haven, Connecticut, a suburb of New Haven. Because the proposed development would require the filling of some wetlands, Mall Properties was required to obtain a permit from the Corps of Engineers pursuant to section 404 of the Clean Water Act. The City of New Haven opposed development of the mall—and the granting of the permit—on the grounds it would jeopardize the fragile economy of New Haven. The Corps of Engineers found the net loss of wetlands would be substantially compensated for by a proposed on-site wetland creation. Relying primarily on the socioeconomic concerns of the City of New Haven, the district engineer rejected the proposed permit. Mall Properties then brought suit against the Corps of Engineers, claiming that the decision was arbitrary and capricious. Should the district engineer have relied on socioeconomic factors unrelated to the project's environmental impacts in making a decision on the permit?

4. Charles Hanson owned land abutting Keith Lake, a freshwater lake that was subject to some tidal flooding as a result of its connection with tidal waters. In order to minimize the detrimental effects from the tidal activities and consequent flooding, Hanson deposited a large quantity of dirt, rock, bricks, sheet metal, and other debris along the shoreline of his property. He did so without obtaining a permit from the U.S. Army Corps of Engineers under section 404 of the Clean Water Act, which controls dumping and filling activities in navigable waters of the United States. Under the law, discharges of pollutants into navigable waters without a permit are forbidden. The term *pollutant* is defined to include "dredged soil, solid waste, incinerator residue, sewage, garbage, sewage sludge, munitions, chemical wastes, biological materials, radioactive materials, heat, wrecked or

discarded equipment, rock, sand, cellar dirt, and industrial, municipal and agricultural waste discharged into water." EPA brought an enforcement action against Hanson claiming he had violated the Clean Water Act. Should the court find that Hanson violated the act?

5. Johnson & Towers, Inc., is in the business of overhauling large motor vehicles. It uses degreasers and other industrial chemicals that contain chemicals classified as "hazardous wastes" under the Resource Conservation and Recovery Act (RCRA)—for example, methylene chloride and trichloroethylene. For some period of time, waste chemicals from cleaning operations were drained into a holding tank and, when the tank was full, pumped into a trench. The trench flowed from the plant property into Parker's Creek, a tributary of the Delaware River. Under RCRA, generators of such wastes must obtain a permit for disposal from the Environmental Protection Agency (EPA). EPA had neither issued, nor received an application for, a permit for the Johnson & Towers operations. Over a three-day period, federal agents saw workers pump waste from the tank into the trench, and on the third day toxic chemicals flowed into the creek. The company and two of its employees, Jack Hopkins, a foreman, and Peter Angel, the service manager, were indicted for unlawfully disposing of hazardous wastes. The company pled guilty. The federal district court dismissed the criminal charges against the two individuals, holding that RCRA's criminal penalty provisions imposing fines and imprisonment did not apply to employees. The government appealed. Can employees of a corporation be held criminally liable if their actions on behalf of the corporation violate the federal hazardous waste law?

6. Anne Arundel County, Maryland, enacted two related ordinances. One absolutely prohibited the disposal in and the transportation through Anne Arundel County of various hazardous wastes not originating in that county. Another ordinance required a license to dispose of hazardous waste in Anne Arundel County; it also required a license to transport hazardous wastes through the county. Browning-Ferris, Inc. (BFI), is the owner and operator of a landfill located in Anne Arundel County that is licensed by the state of Maryland to receive hazardous wastes. BFI is also a hauler of hazardous wastes within the county. The county notified BFI that it expected BFI to comply with the new regulations, and BFI filed a lawsuit challenging

the ordinances and seeking to have them enjoined. How should the court rule?

7. The Royal McBee Corporation manufactured typewriters at a factory in Springfield, Missouri. As a part of the manufacturing process, Royal McBee generated cyanide-based electroplating wastes, sludge from the bottom of electroplating tanks, and spent plating bath solution. As part of their duties, Royal McBee employees dumped the wastes onto the surface of the soil on a vacant lot adjoining the factory. This took place between 1959 and 1962. Over time, the waste materials migrated outward and downward from the original dumping site, contaminating a large area. In 1970, the manufacturing facility and lot were sold to General Electric, which operated the plant but did not engage in the dumping of wastes on the vacant lot. In the mid-1980s, General Electric was required by EPA and the state of Missouri, under the authority of the federal Superfund law, to clean up the contamination at the site. General Electric then brought a lawsuit against the successor corporation of Royal McBee's typewriter business, Litton Business Systems, to recover for the costs incurred in cleaning up the site. Under the Superfund law, "any person who at the time of disposal of any hazardous substance owned or operated any facilities at which such hazardous substances were disposed of, shall be liable for any other necessary costs of response incurred by any other person" consistent with the Superfund law and regulations. Is General Electric entitled to recover its cleanup costs from Litton?

Online Research

Online Access to Toxic Release Inventory

Locate the Web site for the environmental agency in your state. Does the Web site provide Toxics Release Inventory (TRI) data for the state? What companies are the largest contributors of toxic release to the air? What companies are the largest contributors of toxic release to the water? You may look at the EPA Web site (**www.epa.gov/**) as a starting point to see if your state posts information on its TRI program. If your state does not provide such information, then use the data from a neighboring state.

Consider completing the case "ENVIRONMENTAL LAW: Digging Dogs Find Deadly Dirt" from the You Be the Judge Web site element after you have read this chapter. Visit our Web site at www.mhhe.com/mallor14e for more information and activities regarding this case segment.

THE CONSTITUTION OF THE UNITED STATES OF AMERICA

Preamble

We the People of the United States, in Order to form a more perfect Union, establish Justice, insure domestic Tranquility, provide for the common defense, promote the general Welfare, and secure the Blessings of Liberty to ourselves and our Posterity, do ordain and establish this Constitution for the United States of America.

Article I

Section 1 All legislative Powers herein granted shall be vested in a Congress of the United States, which shall consist of a Senate and House of Representatives.

Section 2 The House of Representatives shall be composed of Members chosen every second Year by the People of the several States, and the Electors in each State shall have the Qualifications requisite for Electors of the most numerous Branch of the State Legislature.

No Person shall be a Representative who shall not have attained to the age of twenty five Years, and been seven Years a Citizen of the United States, and who shall not, when elected, be an Inhabitant of that State in which he shall be chosen.

Representatives and direct Taxes shall be apportioned among the several States which may be included within this Union, according to their respective Numbers, which shall be determined by adding to the whole Number of free Persons, including those bound to Service for a Term of Years, and excluding Indians not taxed, three fifths of all other Persons.[1] The actual Enumeration shall be made within three Years after the first Meeting of the Congress of the United States, and within every subsequent Term of ten Years, in such Manner as they shall by Law direct. The Number of Representatives shall not exceed one for every thirty Thousand, but each State shall have at Least one Representative, and until such enumeration shall be made, the State of New Hampshire shall be entitled to choose three, Massachusetts eight, Rhode-Island and Providence Plantations one, Connecticut five, New York six, New Jersey four, Pennsylvania eight, Delaware one, Maryland six, Virginia ten, North Carolina five, South Carolina five, and Georgia three.

When vacancies happen in the Representation from any State, the Executive Authority thereof shall issue Writs of Election to fill such Vacancies.

The House of Representatives shall chuse their Speaker and other Officers; and shall have the sole Power of Impeachment.

Section 3 The Senate of the United States shall be composed of two Senators from each State, chosen by the Legislature thereof,[2] for six Years; and each Senator shall have one Vote.

Immediately after they shall be assembled in Consequence of the first Election, they shall be divided as equally as may be into three Classes. The Seats of the Senators of the first Class shall be vacated at the Expiration of the second Year, of the second Class at the Expiration of the fourth Year, and of the third Class at the Expiration of the sixth Year, so that one third may be chosen every second Year; and if Vacancies happen by Resignation, or otherwise, during the Recess of the Legislature of any State, the Executive thereof may make temporary Appointments until the next Meeting of the Legislature, which shall then fill such Vacancies.[3]

No Person shall be a Senator who shall not have attained to the Age of thirty Years, and been nine Years a Citizen of the United States, and who shall not, when elected, be an Inhabitant of that State for which he shall be chosen.

The Vice President of the United States shall be President of the Senate, but shall have no Vote, unless they be equally divided.

The Senate shall chuse their other Officers, and also a President pro tempore, in the Absence of the Vice President, or when he shall exercise the Office of President of the United States.

---

[1]Changed by the Fourteenth Amendment.

[2]Changed by the Seventeenth Amendment.
[3]Changed by the Seventeenth Amendment.

The Senate shall have the sole Power to try all Impeachments. When sitting for that Purpose, they shall be on Oath or Affirmation. When the President of the United States is tried, the Chief Justice shall preside: And no Person shall be convicted without the Concurrence of two thirds of the Members present.

Judgment in Cases of Impeachment shall not extend further than to removal from Office, and disqualification to hold and enjoy any Office of honor, Trust or Profit under the United States: but the Party convicted shall nevertheless be liable and subject to Indictment, Trial, Judgment and Punishment, according to Law.

Section 4 The Times, Places and Manner of holding Elections for Senators and Representatives, shall be prescribed in each State by the Legislature thereof; but the Congress may at any time by Law make or alter such Regulations, except as to the Places of chusing Senators.

The Congress shall assemble at least once in every Year, and such Meeting shall be on the first Monday in December, unless they shall by Law appoint a different Day.[4]

Section 5 Each House shall be the Judge of the Elections, Returns and Qualifications of its own Members, and a Majority of each shall constitute a Quorum to do Business; but a smaller Number may adjourn from day to day, and may be authorized to compel the Attendance of absent Members, in such Manner, and under such Penalties as each House may provide.

Each House may determine the Rules of its Proceedings, punish its Members for disorderly Behaviour, and with the Concurrence of two thirds, expel a Member.

Each House shall keep a Journal of its Proceedings, and from time to time publish the same, excepting such Parts as may in their Judgment require Secrecy; and the Yeas and Nays of the Members of either House on any question shall, at the Desire of one fifth of those Present, be entered on the Journal.

Neither House, during the Session of Congress, shall, without the Consent of the other, adjourn for more than three days, nor to any other Place than that in which the two Houses shall be sitting.

Section 6 The Senators and Representatives shall receive a Compensation for their Services, to be ascertained by Law, and paid out of the Treasury of the United States. They shall in all Cases, except Treason, Felony and Breach of the Peace, be privileged from Arrest during their Attendance at the Session of their respective Houses, and in going to and returning from the same; and for any Speech or Debate in either House, they shall not be questioned in any other Place.

No Senator or Representative shall, during the Time for which he was elected, be appointed to any civil Office under the Authority of the United States, which shall have been created, or the Emoluments whereof shall have been encreased during such time; and no Person holding any Office under the United States, shall be a Member of either House during his Continuance in Office.

Section 7 All Bills for raising Revenue shall originate in the House of Representatives; but the Senate may propose or concur with Amendments as on other Bills.

Every Bill which shall have passed the House of Representatives and the Senate, shall, before it becomes a Law, be presented to the President of the United States; If he approves he shall sign it, but if not he shall return it, with his Objections to that House in which it shall have originated, who shall enter the Objections at large on their Journal, and proceed to reconsider it. If after such Reconsideration two thirds of that House shall agree to pass the Bill, it shall be sent, together with the Objections, to the other House, by which it shall likewise be reconsidered, and if approved by two thirds of that House, it shall become a Law. But in all such Cases the Votes of both Houses shall be determined by Yeas and Nays, and the Names of the Persons voting for and against the Bill shall be entered on the Journal of each House respectively. If any Bill shall not be returned by the President within ten Days (Sundays excepted) after it shall have been presented to him, the Same shall be a Law, in like Manner as if he had signed it, unless the Congress by their Adjournment prevent its Return, in which Case it shall not be a Law.

Every Order, Resolution, or Vote to which the Concurrence of the Senate and House of Representatives may be necessary (except on a question of Adjournment) shall be presented to the President of the United States; and before the Same shall take Effect, shall be approved by him, or being disapproved by him, shall be repassed by two thirds of the Senate and House of Representatives, according to the Rules and Limitations prescribed in the Case of a Bill.

Section 8 The Congress shall have Power To lay and collect Taxes, Duties, Imposts and Excises, to pay the Debts and provide for the common Defence and general Welfare of the United States; but all Duties, Imposts and Excises shall be uniform throughout the United States.

To borrow Money on the credit of the United States;

To regulate Commerce with foreign Nations, and among the several States, and with the Indian Tribes;

To establish an uniform Rule of Naturalization, and uniform Laws on the subject of Bankruptcies throughout the United States;

---

[4]Changed by the Twentieth Amendment.

To coin Money, regulate the Value thereof, and of foreign Coin, and fix the Standard of Weights and Measures;

To provide for the Punishment of counterfeiting the Securities and current Coin of the United States;

To establish Post Offices and post Roads;

To promote the Progress of Science and useful Arts, by securing for limited Times to Authors and Inventors the exclusive Right to their respective Writings and Discoveries;

To constitute Tribunals inferior to the supreme Court;

To define and punish Piracies and Felonies committed on the high Seas, and Offences against the Law of Nations;

To declare War, grant Letters of Marque and Reprisal, and make Rules concerning Captures on Land and Water;

To raise and support Armies, but no Appropriation of Money to that Use shall be for a longer Term than two Years;

To provide and maintain a Navy;

To make Rules for the Government and Regulation of the land and naval Forces;

To provide for calling forth the Militia to execute the Laws of the Union, suppress Insurrections and repel Invasions;

To provide for organizing, arming, and disciplining, the Militia, and for governing such Part of them as may be employed in the Service of the United States, reserving to the States respectively, the Appointment of the Officers, and the Authority of training the Militia according to the discipline prescribed by Congress;

To exercise exclusive Legislation in all Cases whatsoever, over such District (not exceeding ten Miles square) as may, by Cession of particular States, and the Acceptance of Congress, become the Seat of the Government of the United States, and to exercise like Authority over all Places purchased by the Consent of the Legislature of the State in which the Same shall be, for the Erection of Forts, Magazines, Arsenals, dock-Yards, and other needful Buildings;—And

To make all Laws which shall be necessary and proper for carrying into Execution the foregoing Powers, and all other Powers vested by this Constitution in the Government of the United States, or in any Department or Officer thereof.

Section 9 The Migration or Importation of such Persons as any of the States now existing shall think proper to admit, shall not be prohibited by the Congress prior to the Year one thousand eight hundred and eight, but a Tax or duty may be imposed on such Importation, not exceeding ten dollars for each Person.

The Privilege of the Writ of Habeas Corpus shall not be suspended, unless when in Cases of Rebellion or Invasion the public Safety may require it.

No Bill of Attainder or ex post facto Law shall be passed.

No Capitation, or other direct, Tax shall be laid, unless in Proportion to the Census of Enumeration herein before directed to be taken.[5]

No Tax or Duty shall be laid on Articles exported from any State.

No Preference shall be given by any Regulation of Commerce or Revenue to the Ports of one State over those of another: nor shall Vessels bound to, or from, one State, be obliged to enter, clear, or pay Duties in another.

No Money shall be drawn from the Treasury, but in Consequence of Appropriations made by Law; and a regular Statement and Account of the Receipts and Expenditures of all public Money shall be published from time to time.

No Title of Nobility shall be granted by the United States: And no Person holding any Office of Profit or Trust under them, shall, without the Consent of the Congress, accept of any present, Emolument, Office, or Title, of any kind whatever, from any King, Prince, or foreign State.

Section 10 No State shall enter into any Treaty, Alliance, or Confederation; grant Letters of Marque and Reprisal; coin Money; emit Bills of Credit; make any Thing but gold and silver coin a Tender in Payment of Debts; pass any Bill of Attainder, ex post facto Law, or Law impairing the Obligation of Contracts, or grant any Title of Nobility.

No State shall, without the Consent of the Congress, lay any Imposts or Duties on Imports or Exports, except what may be absolutely necessary for executing its inspection Laws: and the net Produce of all Duties and Imposts, laid by any State on Imports or Exports, shall be for the Use of the Treasury of the United States; and all such Laws shall be subject to the Revision and Controul of the Congress.

No State shall, without the consent of Congress, lay any Duty of Tonnage, keep Troops, or Ships of War in time of Peace, enter into any Agreement or Compact with another State, or with a foreign Power, or engage in War, unless actually invaded, or in such imminent Danger as will not admit of delay.

Article II

Section 1 The executive Power shall be vested in a President of the United States of America. He shall hold his Office during the Term of four Years, and, together with

---

[5]Changed by the Sixteenth Amendment.

the Vice President, chosen for the same Term, be elected, as follows

Each state shall appoint, in such Manner as the Legislature thereof may direct, a Number of Electors, equal to the whole Number of Senators and Representatives to which the State may be entitled in Congress: but no Senator or Representative, or Person holding an Office of Trust or Profit under the United States, shall be appointed an Elector.

The Electors shall meet in their respective States, and vote by Ballot for two Persons, of whom one at least shall not be an inhabitant of the same State with themselves. And they shall make a List of all the Persons voted for, and of the Number of Votes for each; which List they shall sign and certify, and transmit sealed to the Seat of the Government of the United States, directed to the President of the Senate. The President of the Senate shall, in the Presence of the Senate and House of Representatives, open all the Certificates, and the Votes shall then be counted. The Person having the greatest Number of Votes shall be the President, if such Number be a Majority of the whole Number of Electors appointed; and if there be more than one who have such Majority, and have an equal Number of Votes, then the House of Representatives shall immediately chuse by Ballot one of them for President; and if no Person have a Majority, then from the five highest on the List the said House shall in like Manner chuse the President. But in chusing the President, the Votes shall be taken by States, the Representation from each State having one Vote; A quorum for this purpose shall consist of a Member or Members from two thirds of the States, and a Majority of all the States shall be necessary to a Choice. In every Case, after the Choice of the President, the Person having the greatest Number of Votes of the Electors shall be the Vice President. But if there should remain two or more who have equal Votes, the Senate shall chuse from them by Ballot the Vice President.[6]

The Congress may determine the Time of chusing the Electors, and the Day on which they shall give their Votes; which Day shall be the same throughout the United States.

No Person except a natural born Citizen, or a Citizen of the United States, at the time of the Adoption of this Constitution, shall be eligible to the Office of President; neither shall any Person be eligible to that Office who shall not have attained to the Age of thirty five Years, and been fourteen Years a Resident within the United States.

In Case of the Removal of the President from Office, or of his Death, Resignation, or Inability to discharge the Powers and Duties of the said Office, the Same shall devolve on the Vice President, and the Congress may by Law provide for the Case of Removal, Death, Resignation or Inability, both of the President and Vice President, declaring what Officer shall then act as President, and such Officer shall act accordingly, until the Disability be removed, or a President shall be elected.[7]

The President shall, at stated Times, receive for his Services, a Compensation, which shall neither be encreased nor diminished during the Period for which he shall have been elected, and he shall not receive within that Period any other Emolument from the United States, or any of them.

Before he enter on the Execution of his Office, he shall take the following Oath or Affirmation:—"I do solemnly swear (or affirm) that I will faithfully execute the Office of President of the United States, and will to the best of my Ability, preserve, protect, and defend the Constitution of the United States."

Section 2 The President shall be Commander in Chief of the Army and Navy of the United States, and of the Militia of the several States, when called into the actual Service of the United States; he may require the Opinion, in writing, of the principal Officer in each of the executive Departments, upon any Subject relating to the Duties of their respective Offices, and he shall have Power to grant Reprieves and Pardons for Offences against the United States, except in Cases of Impeachment.

He shall have Power, by and with the Advice and Consent of the Senate, to make Treaties, provided two thirds of the Senators present concur; and he shall nominate, and by and with the Advice and Consent of the Senate, shall appoint Ambassadors, other public Ministers and Consuls, Judges of the supreme Court, and all other Officers of the United States, whose Appointments are not herein otherwise provided for, and which shall be established by Law; but the Congress may by Law vest the Appointment of such inferior Officers, as they think proper, in the President alone, in the Courts of Law, or in the Heads of Departments.

The President shall have Power to fill up all Vacancies that may happen during the Recess of the Senate, by granting Commissions which shall expire at the End of their next Session.

Section 3 He shall from time to time give to the Congress Information of the State of the Union, and recommend to their Consideration such Measures as he shall judge necessary and expedient; he may, on extraordinary Occasions, convene both Houses, or either of them, and

---

[6]Changed by the Twelfth Amendment.

[7]Changed by the Twenty-fifth Amendment.

in Case of Disagreement between them, with Respect to the Time of Adjournment, he may adjourn them to such Time as he shall think proper; he shall receive Ambassadors and other public Ministers; he shall take Care that the Laws be faithfully executed, and shall Commission all the Officers of the United States.

Section 4 The President, Vice President and all civil Officers of the United States, shall be removed from Office on Impeachment for, and Conviction of, Treason, Bribery, or other high Crimes and Misdemeanors.

Article III

Section 1 The judicial Power of the United States, shall be vested in one supreme Court, and in such inferior Courts as the Congress may from time to time ordain and establish. The Judges, both of the supreme and inferior Courts, shall hold their Offices during good Behaviour, and shall, at stated Times, receive for their Services, a Compensation, which shall not be diminished during their Continuance in Office.

Section 2 The judicial Power shall extend to all Cases, in Law and Equity, arising under this Constitution, the Laws of the United States, and Treaties made, or which shall be made, under their Authority;—to all Cases affecting Ambassadors, other public Ministers and Consuls;—to all Cases of admiralty and maritime Jurisdiction;—to Controversies to which the United States shall be a party;—to Controversies between two or more States;—between a State and Citizens of another State;[8]—between Citizens of different States;—between Citizens of the same State claiming Lands under Grants of different States, and between a State, or the Citizens thereof, and foreign States, Citizens or Subjects.

In all Cases affecting Ambassadors, other public Ministers and Consuls, and those in which a State shall be Party, the supreme Court shall have original Jurisdiction. In all the other Cases before mentioned, the supreme Court shall have appellate Jurisdiction, both as to Law and Fact, with such Exceptions, and under such Regulations as the Congress shall make.

The Trial of all Crimes, except in Cases of Impeachment, shall be by Jury: and such Trial shall be held in the State where the said Crimes shall have been committed; but when not committed within any State, the Trial shall be at such Place or Places as the Congress may by Law have directed.

Section 3 Treason against the United States, shall consist only in levying War against them, or in adhering to their Enemies, giving them Aid and Comfort. No Person shall be convicted of Treason unless on the Testimony of two Witnesses to the same overt Act, or on Confession in open Court.

The Congress shall have Power to declare the Punishment of Treason, but no Attainder of Treason shall work Corruption of Blood, or Forfeiture except during the Life of the Person attainted.

Article IV

Section 1 Full Faith and Credit shall be given in each State to the public Acts, Records, and judicial Proceedings of every other State. And the Congress may by general Laws prescribe the Manner in which such Acts, Records and Proceedings shall be proved, and the Effect thereof.

Section 2 The Citizens of each State shall be entitled to all Privileges and Immunities of Citizens in the several States.

A Person charged in any State with Treason, Felony, or other Crime, who shall flee from Justice, and be found in another State, shall on Demand of the executive Authority of the State from which he fled, be delivered up, to be removed to the State having Jurisdiction of the Crime.

No Person held to Service or Labour in one State, under the Laws thereof, escaping into another, shall, in Consequence of any Law or Regulation therein, be discharged from such Service or Labour, but shall be delivered up on Claim of the Party to whom such Service or Labour may be due.[9]

Section 3 New States may be admitted by the Congress into this Union; but no new State shall be formed or erected within the Jurisdiction of any other State; nor any State be formed by the Junction of two or more States, or Parts of States, without the Consent of the Legislatures of the States concerned as well as of the Congress.

The Congress shall have Power to dispose of and make all needful Rules and Regulations respecting the Territory or other Property belonging to the United States; and nothing in this Constitution shall be so construed as to Prejudice any Claims of the United States, or of any particular State.

Section 4 The United States shall guarantee to every State in this Union a Republican Form of Government, and shall protect each of them against Invasion; and on

---

[8]Changed by the Eleventh Amendment.

[9]Changed by the Thirteenth Amendment.

Application of the Legislature, or of the Executive (when the Legislature cannot be convened) against domestic Violence.

Article V

The Congress, whenever two thirds of both Houses shall deem it necessary, shall propose Amendments to this Constitution, or, on the Application of the Legislatures of two thirds of the several States, shall call a Convention for proposing Amendments, which, in either Case, shall be valid to all Intents and Purposes, as Part of this Constitution, when ratified by the legislatures of three fourths of the several States, or by Conventions in three fourths thereof, as the one or the other Mode of Ratification may be proposed by the Congress; Provided that no Amendment which may be made prior to the Year One thousand eight hundred and eight shall in any Manner affect the first and fourth Clauses in the Ninth Section of the first Article; and that no State, without its Consent, shall be deprived of its equal Suffrage in the Senate.

Article VI

All Debts contracted and Engagements entered into, before the Adoption of this Constitution, shall be as valid against the United States under this Constitution, as under the Confederation.

The Constitution, and the Laws of the United States which shall be made in Pursuance thereof; and all Treaties made, or which shall be made, under the Authority of the United States, shall be the supreme Law of the Land; and the Judges in every State shall be bound thereby, any Thing in the Constitution or Laws of any State to the Contrary notwithstanding.

The Senators and Representatives before mentioned, and the Members of the several State Legislatures, and all executive and judicial Officers, both of the United States and of the several States, shall be bound by Oath or Affirmation, to support this Constitution; but no religious Test shall ever be required as a Qualification to any Office or public Trust under the United States.

Article VII

The Ratification of the Conventions of nine States, shall be sufficient for the Establishment of this Constitution between the States so ratifying the Same.

Done in Convention by the Unanimous Consent of the States present the Seventeenth Day of September in the Year of our Lord one thousand seven hundred and eighty

seven and of the Independance of the United States of America the Twelfth. In witness whereof We have hereunto subscribed our Names.

Amendments

[The first 10 amendments are known as the "Bill of Rights."]

Amendment I (Ratified 1791) Congress shall make no law respecting an establishment of religion, or prohibiting the free exercise thereof; or abridging the freedom of speech, or of the press; or the right of the people peaceably to assemble, and to petition the Government for a redress of grievances.

Amendment 2 (Ratified 1791) A well regulated Militia, being necessary to the security of a free State, the right of the people to keep and bear Arms, shall not be infringed.

Amendment 3 (Ratified 1791) No Soldier shall, in time of peace be quartered in any house, without the consent of the Owner, nor in time of war, but in a manner to be prescribed by law.

Amendment 4 (Ratified 1791) The right of the people to be secure in their persons, houses, papers, and effects, against unreasonable searches and seizures, shall not be violated, and no Warrants shall issue, but upon probable cause, supported by Oath or affirmation, and particularly describing the place to be searched, and the persons or things to be seized.

Amendment 5 (Ratified 1791) No person shall be held to answer for a capital, or otherwise infamous crime, unless on a presentment or indictment of a Grand Jury, except in cases arising in the land or naval forces, or in the Militia, when in actual service in time of War or public danger; nor shall any person be subject for the same offence to be twice put in jeopardy of life or limb; nor shall be compelled in any criminal case to be a witness against himself, nor be deprived of life, liberty, or property, without due process of law; nor shall private property be taken for public use, without just compensation.

Amendment 6 (Ratified 1791) In all criminal prosecutions, the accused shall enjoy the right to a speedy and public trial, by an impartial jury of the State and district wherein the crime shall have been committed, which district shall have been previously ascertained by law, and to be informed of the nature and cause of the accusation; to be confronted with the witnesses against him; to have compulsory process for obtaining Witnesses in his favor, and to have assistance of counsel for his defence.

Amendment 7 (Ratified 1791) In Suits at common law, where the value in controversy shall exceed twenty dollars, the right of trial by jury shall be preserved, and no fact tried by a jury, shall be otherwise re-examined in any Court of the United States, than according to the rules of the common law.

Amendment 8 (Ratified 1791) Excessive bail shall not be required, nor excessive fines imposed, nor cruel and unusual punishments inflicted.

Amendment 9 (Ratified 1791) The enumeration in the Constitution, of certain rights, shall not be construed to deny or disparage others retained by the people.

Amendment 10 (Ratified 1791) The powers not delegated to the United States by the Constitution, nor prohibited by it to the States, are reserved to the States respectively, or to the people.

Amendment 11 (Ratified 1795) The Judicial power of the United States shall not be construed to extend to any suit in law or equity, commenced or prosecuted against one of the United States by Citizens of another State, or by Citizens or Subjects of any Foreign State.

Amendment 12 (Ratified 1804) The Electors shall meet in their respective states, and vote by ballot for President and Vice-President, one of whom, at least, shall not be an inhabitant of the same state with themselves; they shall name in their ballots the person voted for as President, and in distinct ballots the person voted for as Vice-President, and they shall make distinct lists of all persons voted for as President, and of all persons voted for as Vice-President, and of the number of votes for each, which lists they shall sign and certify, and transmit sealed to the seat of the government of the United States, directed to the President of the Senate;—The President of the Senate shall, in the presence of the Senate and House of Representatives, open all the certificates and the votes shall then be counted;—The person having the greatest number of votes for President, shall be the President, if such number be a majority of the whole number of Electors appointed; and if no person have such majority, then from the persons having the highest numbers not exceeding three on the list of those voted for as President, the House of Representa-

tives shall choose immediately, by ballot, the President. But in choosing the President, the votes shall be taken by states, the representation from each state having one vote; a quorum for this purpose shall consist of a member or members from two-thirds of the states, and a majority of all the states shall be necessary to a choice. And if the House of Representatives shall not choose a President whenever the right of choice shall devolve upon them, before the fourth day of March next following, then the Vice-President shall act as president, as in the case of the death or other constitutional disability of the President.[10]—The person having the greatest number of votes as Vice-President, shall be the Vice-President, if such number be a majority of the whole number of Electors appointed, and if no person have a majority, then from the two highest numbers on the list, the Senate shall choose the Vice-President; a quorum for the purpose shall consist of two-thirds of the whole number of Senators, and a majority of the whole number shall be necessary to a choice. But no person constitutionally ineligible to the office of President shall be eligible to that of Vice-President of the United States.

Amendment 13 (Ratified 1865) Section 1 Neither slavery nor involuntary servitude, except as a punishment for crime whereof the party shall have been duly convicted, shall exist within the United States, or any place subject to their jurisdiction.

Section 2 Congress shall have power to enforce this article by appropriate legislation.

Amendment 14 (Ratified 1868) Section 1 All persons born or naturalized in the United States, and subject to the jurisdiction thereof, are citizens of the United States and of the State wherein they reside. No State shall make or enforce any law which shall abridge the privileges or immunities of citizens of the United States; nor shall any State deprive any person of life, liberty, or property, without due process of law; nor deny to any person within its jurisdiction the equal protection of the laws.

Section 2 Representatives shall be apportioned among the several States according to their respective numbers, counting the whole number of persons in each State, excluding Indians not taxed. But when the right to vote at any election for the choice of electors for President and Vice President of the United States, Representatives in Congress, the Executive and Judicial officers of a State, or the members of the Legislature thereof, is denied to

---

[10]Changed by the Twentieth Amendment.

any of the male inhabitants of such State, being twenty-one[11] years of age, and citizens of the United States, or in any way abridged except for participation in rebellion, or other crime, the basis of representation therein shall be reduced in the proportion which the number of such male citizens shall bear to the whole number of male citizens twenty-one years of age in such State.

Section 3 No person shall be a Senator or Representative in Congress, or elector of President and Vice President, or hold any office, civil or military, under the United States, or under any State, who, having previously taken an oath, as a member of Congress, or as an officer of the United States, or as a member of any State legislature, or as an executive or judicial officer of any State, to support the Constitution of the United States, shall have engaged in insurrection or rebellion against the same, or given aid or comfort to the enemies thereof. But Congress may by a vote of two-thirds of each House, remove such disability.

Section 4 The validity of the public debt of the United States, authorized by law, including debts incurred for payment of pensions and bounties for services in suppressing insurrection or rebellion, shall not be questioned. But neither the United States nor any State shall assume or pay any debt or obligation incurred in aid of insurrection or rebellion against the United States, or any claim for the loss or emancipation of any slave; but all such debts, obligations and claims shall be held illegal and void.

Section 5 The Congress shall have power to enforce, by appropriate legislation, the provisions of this article.

Amendment 15 (Ratified 1870)
Section 1 The right of citizens of the United States to vote shall not be denied or abridged by the United States or by any State on account of race, color, or previous condition of servitude.

Section 2 The Congress shall have power to enforce this article by appropriate legislation.

Amendment 16 (Ratified 1913)
The Congress shall have power to lay and collect taxes on incomes, from whatever source derived, without apportionment among the several States, and without regard to any census or enumeration.

Amendment 17 (Ratified 1913)
The Senate of the United States shall be composed of two Senators from each State, elected by the people thereof, for six years; and each Senator shall have one vote. The electors in each State shall have the qualifications requisite for electors of the most numerous branch of the State legislatures.

When vacancies happen in the representation of any State in the Senate, the executive authority of such State shall issue writs of election to fill such vacancies: *Provided,* That the legislature of any State may empower the executive thereof to make temporary appointments until the people fill the vacancies by election as the legislature may direct.

This amendment shall not be so construed as to affect the election or term of any Senator chosen before it becomes valid as part of the Constitution.

Amendment 18 (Ratified 1919; Repealed 1933)
Section 1 After one year from the ratification of this article the manufacture, sale, or transportation of intoxicating liquors within, the importation thereof into, or the exportation thereof from the United States and all territory subject to the jurisdiction thereof for beverage purposes is hereby prohibited.

Section 2 The Congress and the several States shall have concurrent power to enforce this article by appropriate legislation.

Section 3 This article shall be inoperative unless it shall have been ratified as an amendment to the Constitution by the legislatures of the several States, as provided in the Constitution, within seven years from the date of the submission hereof to the States by the Congress.[12]

Amendment 19 (Ratified 1920)
The right of citizens of the United States to vote shall not be denied or abridged by the United States or by any State on account of sex.

Congress shall have power to enforce this article by appropriate legislation.

Amendment 20 (Ratified 1933)
Section 1 The terms of the President and Vice President shall end at noon on the 20th day of January, and the terms of Senators and Representatives at noon on the 3d day of January, of the years in which such terms would have ended if this article had not been ratified; and the terms of their successors shall then begin.

Section 2 The Congress shall assemble at least once in every year, and such meeting shall begin at noon on the 3d day of January, unless they shall by law appoint a different day.

Section 3 If, at the time fixed for the beginning of the term of the President, the President elect shall have died, the Vice President elect shall become President. If a Pres-

---

[11]Changed by the Twenty-sixth Amendment.

[12]Repealed by the Twenty-first Amendment.

ident shall not have been chosen before the time fixed for the beginning of his term, or if the President elect shall have failed to qualify, then the Vice President elect shall act as President until a President shall have qualified; and the Congress may by law provide for the case wherein neither a President elect nor a Vice President elect shall have qualified, declaring who shall then act as President, or the manner in which one who is to act shall be selected, and such person shall act accordingly until a President or Vice President shall have qualified.

Section 4 The Congress may by law provide for the case of the death of any of the persons from whom the House of Representatives may choose a President whenever the right of choice shall have devolved upon them, and for the case of the death of any of the persons from whom the Senate may choose a Vice President whenever the right of choice shall have devolved upon them.

Section 5 Sections 1 and 2 shall take effect on the 15th day of October following the ratification of this article.

Section 6 This article shall be inoperative unless it shall have been ratified as an amendment to the Constitution by the legislatures of three-fourths of the several States within seven years from the date of its submission.

Amendment 21 (Ratified 1933)
Section 1 The eighteenth article of amendment to the Constitution of the United States is hereby repealed.

Section 2 The transportation or importation into any State, Territory, or possession of the United States for delivery or use therein of intoxicating liquors, in violation of the laws thereof, is hereby prohibited.

Section 3 This article shall be inoperative unless it shall have been ratified as an amendment to the Constitution by conventions in the several States, as provided in the Constitution, within seven years from the date of the submission hereof to the States by the Congress.

Amendment 22 (Ratified 1951)
Section 1 No person shall be elected to the office of the President more than twice, and no person who has held the office of President, or acted as President, for more than two years of a term to which some other person was elected President shall be elected to the office of the President more than once. But this Article shall not apply to any person holding the office of President when this Article was proposed by the Congress, and shall not prevent any person who may be holding the office of President, or acting as President, during the term within which this Article becomes operative from holding the office of President or acting as President during the remainder of such term.

Section 2 This Article shall be inoperative unless it shall have been ratified as an amendment to the Constitution by the legislatures of three-fourths of the several States within seven years from the date of its submission to the States by the Congress.

Amendment 23 (Ratified 1961)
Section 1 The District constituting the seat of Government of the United States shall appoint in such manner as the Congress may direct:

A number of electors of President and Vice President equal to the whole number of Senators and Representatives in Congress to which the District would be entitled if it were a State, but in no event more than the least populous State; they shall be in addition to those appointed by the States, but they shall be considered, for the purposes of the election of President and Vice President, to be electors appointed by a State; and they shall meet in the District and perform such duties as provided by the twelfth article of amendment.

Section 2 The Congress shall have power to enforce this article by appropriate legislation.

Amendment 24 (Ratified 1964)
Section 1 The right of citizens of the United States to vote in any primary or other election for President or Vice President, for electors for President or Vice President, or for Senator or Representative in Congress, shall not be denied or abridged by the United States or any State by reason of failure to pay any poll tax or other tax.

Section 2 The Congress shall have power to enforce this article by appropriate legislation.

Amendment 25 (Ratified 1967)
Section 1 In case of the removal of the President from office or of his death or resignation, the Vice President shall become President.

Section 2 Whenever there is a vacancy in the office of the Vice President, the President shall nominate a Vice President who shall take office upon confirmation by a majority vote of both Houses of Congress.

Section 3 Whenever the President transmits to the President pro tempore of the Senate and the Speaker of the House of Representatives his written declaration that he is unable to discharge the powers and duties of his office, and until he transmits to them a written declaration to the contrary, such powers and duties shall be discharged by the Vice President as Acting President.

Section 4 Whenever the Vice President and a majority of either the principal officers of the executive departments or of such other body as Congress may by law provide, transmit to the President pro tempore of the Senate and the Speaker of the House of Representatives their written declaration that the President is unable to discharge the powers and duties of his office, the Vice President shall immediately assume the powers and duties of the office as Acting President.

Thereafter, when the President transmits to the President pro tempore of the Senate and the Speaker of the House of Representatives his written declaration that no inability exists, he shall resume the powers and duties of his office unless the Vice President and a majority of either the principal officers of the executive department or of such other body as Congress may by law provide, transmit within four days to the President pro tempore of the Senate and the Speaker of the House of Representatives their written declaration that the President is unable to discharge the powers and duties of his office. Thereupon Congress shall decide the issue, assembling within forty-eight hours for that purpose if not in session. If the Congress, within twenty-one days after receipt of the latter written declaration, or, if Congress is not in session, within twenty-one days after Congress is required to assemble, determines by two-thirds vote of both Houses that the President is unable to discharge the powers and duties of his office, the Vice President shall continue to discharge the same as Acting President; otherwise, the President shall resume the powers and duties of his office.

Amendment 26 (Ratified 1971) Section 1 The right of citizens of the United States, who are eighteen years of age or older, to vote shall not be denied or abridged by the United States or by any State on account of age.

Section 2 The Congress shall have power to enforce this article by appropriate legislation.

Amendment 27 (Ratified 1992) No law, varying the compensation for the services of the Senators and Representatives, shall take effect, until an election of Representatives shall have intervened.

UNIFORM COMMERCIAL CODE

Article 2–Sales

Part 1: Short Title, General Construction and Subject Matter

§ 2–101. Short Title. This Article shall be known and may be cited as Uniform Commercial Code—Sales.

§ 2–102. Scope; Certain Security and Other Transactions Excluded from This Article. Unless the context otherwise requires, this Article applies to transactions in goods; it does not apply to any transaction which although in the form of an unconditional contract to sell or present sale is intended to operate only as a security transaction nor does this Article impair or repeal any statute regulating sales to consumers, farmers or other specified classes of buyers.

§ 2–103. Definitions and Index of Definitions.

(1) In this Article unless the context otherwise requires
  (a) "Buyer" means a person who buys or contracts to buy goods.
  (b) "Good faith" in the case of a merchant means honesty in fact and the observance of reasonable commercial standards of fair dealing in the trade.
  (c) "Receipt" of goods means taking physical possession of them.
  (d) "Seller" means a person who sells or contracts to sell goods.
(2) Other definitions applying to this Article or to specified Parts thereof, and the sections in which they appear are:

"Acceptance"	Section 2–606.
"Banker's credit"	Section 2–325.
"Between merchants"	Section 2–104.
"Cancellation"	Section 2–106(4).
"Commercial unit"	Section 2–105.
"Confirmed credit"	Section 2–325.
"Conforming to contract".	Section 2–106.
"Contract for sale"	Section 2–106.
"Cover"	Section 2–712.
"Entrusting"	Section 2–403.
"Financing agency"	Section 2–104.
"Future goods"	Section 2–105.
"Goods"	Section 2–105.
"Identification"	Section 2–501.
"Installment contract"	Section 2–612.
"Letter of Credit"	Section 2–325.
"Lot"	Section 2–105.
"Merchant"	Section 2–104.
"Overseas"	Section 2–323.
"Person in position of seller"	Section 2–707.
"Present sale"	Section 2–106.
"Sale"	Section 2–106.
"Sale on approval"	Section 2–326.
"Sale or return"	Section 2–326.
"Termination"	Section 2–106.

(3) The following definitions in other Articles apply to this Article:

"Check"	Section 3-104.
"Consignee"	Section 7-102.
"Consignor"	Section 7-102.
"Consumer goods"	Section 9-109.
"Dishonor"	Section 3-502.
"Draft"	Section 3-104.

(4) In addition Article 1 contains general definitions and principles of construction and interpretation applicable throughout this Article.

As amended in 1994.
  See Appendix XI for material relating to changes made in text in 1994.

§ 2–104. Definitions: "Merchant"; "Between Merchants"; "Financing Agency".

(1) "Merchant" means a person who deals in goods of the kind or otherwise by his occupation holds himself out as having knowledge or skill peculiar to the practices or goods involved in the transaction or to whom such knowledge or skill may be attributed by his employment of an agent or broker or other intermediary who by his occupation holds himself out as having such knowledge or skill.

(2) "Financing agency" means a bank, finance company or other person who in the ordinary course of business makes advances against goods or documents of title or who by arrangement with either the seller or the buyer intervenes in ordinary course to make or collect payment due or claimed under the contract for sale, as by purchasing or paying the seller's draft or making advances against it or by merely taking it for collection whether or not documents of title accompany the draft. "Financing agency" includes also a bank or other person who similarly intervenes between persons who are in the position of seller and buyer in respect to the goods (Section 2–707).

(3) "Between merchants" means in any transaction with respect to which both parties are chargeable with the knowledge or skill of merchants.

§ 2–105. Definitions: "Transferability"; "Goods"; "Future" Goods; "Lot"; "Commercial Unit".

(1) "Goods" means all things (including specially manufactured goods) which are movable at the time of identification to the contract for sale other than the money in which the price is to be paid, investment securities (Article 8) and things in action. "Goods" also includes the unborn young of animals and growing crops and other identified things attached to realty as described in the section on goods to be severed from realty (Section 2–107).

(2) Goods must be both existing and identified before any interest in them can pass. Goods which are not both existing and identified are "future" goods. A purported present sale of future goods or of any interest therein operates as a contract to sell.

(3) There may be a sale of a part interest in existing identified goods.

(4) An undivided share in an identified bulk of fungible goods is sufficiently identified to be sold although the quantity of the bulk is not determined. Any agreed proportion of such a bulk or any quantity thereof agreed upon by number, weight or other measure may to the extent of the seller's interest in the bulk be sold to the buyer who then becomes an owner in common.

(5) "Lot" means a parcel or a single article which is the subject matter of a separate sale or delivery, whether or not it is sufficient to perform the contract.

(6) "Commercial unit" means such a unit of goods as by commercial usage is a single whole for purposes of sale and division of which materially impairs its character or value on the market or in use. A commercial unit may be a single article (as a machine) or a set of articles (as a suite of furniture or an assortment of sizes) or a quantity (as a bale, gross, or carload) or any other unit treated in use or in the relevant market as a single whole.

§ 2–106. Definitions: "Contract"; "Agreement"; "Contract for Sales"; "Sale"; "Present Sale"; "Conforming" to Contract; "Termination"; "Cancellation".

(1) In this Article unless the context otherwise requires "contract" and "agreement" are limited to those relating to the present or future sale of goods. "Contract for sale" includes both a present sale of goods and a contract to sell goods at a future time. A "sale" consists in the passing of title from the seller to the buyer for a price (Section 2–401). A "present sale" means a sale which is accomplished by the making of the contract.

(2) Goods or conduct including any part of a performance are "conforming" or conform to the contract when they are in accordance with the obligations under the contract.

(3) "Termination" occurs when either party pursuant to a power created by agreement or law puts an end to the contract otherwise than for its breach. On "termination" all obligations which are still executory on both sides are discharged but any right based on prior breach or performance survives.

(4) "Cancellation" occurs when either party puts an end to the contract for breach by the other and its effect is the same as that of "termination" except that the cancelling party also retains any remedy for breach of the whole contract or any unperformed balance.

§ 2–107. Goods to Be Severed from Realty: Recording.

(1) A contract for the sale of minerals or the like (including oil and gas) or a structure or its materials to be removed from realty is a contract for the sale of goods within this Article if they are to be severed by the seller but until severance a purported present sale thereof which is not effective as a transfer of an interest in land is effective only as a contract to sell.

(2) A contract for the sale apart from the land of growing crops or other things attached to realty and capable of severance without material harm thereto but not described in subsection (1) or of timber to be cut is a contract for the sale of goods within this Article whether the subject matter is to be severed by the buyer or by the seller even though it forms part of the realty at the time of contracting, and the parties can by identification effect a present sale before severance.

(3) The provisions of this section are subject to any third party rights provided by the law relating to realty records, and the contract for sale may be executed and recorded as a document transferring an interest in land and shall then constitute notice to third parties of the buyer's rights under the contract for sale. As amended in 1972.

Part 2: Form, Formation and Readjustment Of Contract

§ 2–201. Formal Requirements; Statute of Frauds.

(1) Except as otherwise provided in this section a contract for the sale of goods for the price of $500 or more is not enforceable by way of action or defense unless there is some writing sufficient to indicate that a contract for sale has been made between the parties and signed by the party against whom enforcement is sought or by his authorized agent or broker. A writing is not insufficient because it omits or incorrectly states a term agreed upon but the contract is not enforceable under this paragraph beyond the quantity of goods shown in such writing.

(2) Between merchants if within a reasonable time a writing in confirmation of the contract and sufficient against the sender is received and the party receiving it has reason to know its contents, it satisfies the requirements of subsection (1) against such party unless written notice of objection to its contents is given within 10 days after it is received.

(3) A contract which does not satisfy the requirements of subsection (1) but which is valid in other respects is enforceable

   (a) if the goods are to be specially manufactured for the buyer and are not suitable for sale to others in the ordinary course of the seller's business and the seller, before notice of repudiation is received and under circumstances which reason-

ably indicate that the goods are for the buyer, has made either a substantial beginning of their manufacture or commitments for their procurement; or

   (b) if the party against whom enforcement is sought admits in his pleading, testimony or otherwise in court that a contract for sale was made, but the contract is not enforceable under this provision beyond the quantity of goods admitted; or

   (c) with respect to goods for which payment has been made and accepted or which have been received and accepted (Sec. 2–606).

§ 2–202. Final Written Expression: Parol or Extrinsic Evidence.
Terms with respect to which the confirmatory memoranda of the parties agree or which are otherwise set forth in a writing intended by the parties as a final expression of their agreement with respect to such terms as are included therein may not be contradicted by evidence of any prior agreement or of a contemporaneous oral agreement but may be explained or supplemented

   (a) by course of dealing or usage of trade (Section 1-205) or by course of performance (Section 2–208); and

   (b) by evidence of consistent additional terms unless the court finds the writing to have been intended also as a complete and exclusive statement of the terms of the agreement.

§ 2–203. Seals Inoperative.
The affixing of a seal to a writing evidencing a contract for sale or an offer to buy or sell goods does not constitute the writing a sealed instrument and the law with respect to sealed instruments does not apply to such a contract or offer.

§ 2–204. Formation in General.

(1) A contract for sale of goods may be made in any manner sufficient to show agreement, including conduct by both parties which recognizes the existence of such a contract.

(2) An agreement sufficient to constitute a contract for sale may be found even though the moment of its making is undetermined.

(3) Even though one or more terms are left open a contract for sale does not fail for indefiniteness if the parties have intended to make a contract and there is a reasonably certain basis for giving an appropriate remedy.

§ 2–205. Firm Offers.

An offer by a merchant to buy or sell goods in a signed writing which by its terms gives assurance that it will be held open is not revocable, for lack of consideration, during the time stated or if no time is stated for a reasonable time, but in no event may such period of irrevocability exceed three months; but any such term of assurance on a form supplied by the offeree must be separately signed by the offeror.

§ 2–206. Offer and Acceptance in Formation of Contract.

(1) Unless otherwise unambiguously indicated by the language or circumstances
  (a) an offer to make a contract shall be construed as inviting acceptance in any manner and by any medium reasonable in the circumstances;
  (b) an order or other offer to buy goods for prompt or current shipment shall be construed as inviting acceptance either by a prompt promise to ship or by the prompt or current shipment of conforming or non-conforming goods, but such a shipment of non-conforming goods does not constitute an acceptance if the seller seasonably notifies the buyer that the shipment is offered only as an accommodation to the buyer.
(2) Where the beginning of a requested performance is a reasonable mode of acceptance an offeror who is not notified of acceptance within a reasonable time may treat the offer as having lapsed before acceptance.

§ 2–207. Additional Terms in Acceptance or Confirmation.

(1) A definite and seasonable expression of acceptance or a written confirmation which is sent within a reasonable time operates as an acceptance even though it states terms additional to or different from those offered or agreed upon, unless acceptance is expressly made conditional on assent to the additional or different terms.
(2) The additional terms are to be construed as proposals for addition to the contract. Between merchants such terms become part of the contract unless:
  (a) the offer expressly limits acceptance to the terms of the offer;
  (b) they materially alter it; or
  (c) notification of objection to them has already been given or is given within a reasonable time after notice of them is received.
(3) Conduct by both parties which recognizes the existence of a contract is sufficient to establish a contract for sale although the writings of the parties do not otherwise establish a contract. In such case the terms of the particular contract consist of those terms on which the writings of the parties agree, together with any supplementary terms incorporated under any other provisions of this Act.

§ 2–208. Course of Performance or Practical Construction.

(1) Where the contract for sale involves repeated occasions for performance by either party with knowledge of the nature of the performance and opportunity for objection to it by the other, any course of performance accepted or acquiesced in without objection shall be relevant to determine the meaning of the agreement.
(2) The express terms of the agreement and any such course of performance, as well as any course of dealing and usage of trade, shall be construed whenever reasonable as consistent with each other; but when such construction is unreasonable, express terms shall control course of performance and course of performance shall control both course of dealing and usage of trade (Section 1-205).
(3) Subject to the provisions of the next section on modification and waiver, such course of performance shall be relevant to show a waiver or modification of any term inconsistent with such course of performance.

§ 2–209. Modification, Recission and Waiver.

(1) An agreement modifying a contract within this Article needs no consideration to be binding.
(2) A signed agreement which excludes modification or rescission except by a signed writing cannot be otherwise modified or rescinded, but except as between merchants such a requirement on a form supplied by the merchant must be separately signed by the other party.
(3) The requirements of the statute of frauds section of this Article (Section 2–201) must be satisfied if the contract as modified is within its provisions.
(4) Although an attempt at modification or rescission does not satisfy the requirements of subsection (2) or (3) it can operate as a waiver.
(5) A party who has made a waiver affecting an executory portion of the contract may retract the waiver by reasonable notification received by the other party that strict performance will be required of any term waived, unless the retraction would be unjust in view of a material change of position in reliance on the waiver.

§ 2–210. Delegation of Performance; Assignment of Rights.

(1) A party may perform his duty through a delegate unless otherwise agreed or unless the other party has a substantial interest in having his original promisor perform or control the acts required by the contract. No delegation of performance relieves the party delegating of any duty to perform or any liability for breach.

(2) Unless otherwise agreed all rights of either seller or buyer can be assigned except where the assignment would materially change the duty of the other party, or increase materially the burden or risk imposed on him by his contract, or impair materially his chance of obtaining return performance. A right to damages for breach of the whole contract or a right arising out of the assignor's due performance of his entire obligation can be assigned despite agreement otherwise.

(3) Unless the circumstances indicate the contrary a prohibition of assignment of "the contract" is to be construed as barring only the delegation to the assignee of the assignor's performance.

(4) An assignment of "the contract" or of "all my rights under the contract" or an assignment in similar general terms is an assignment of rights and unless the language or the circumstances (as in an assignment for security) indicate the contrary, it is a delegation of performance of the duties of the assignor and its acceptance by the assignee constitutes a promise by him to perform those duties. This promise is enforceable by either the assignor or the other party to the original contract.

(5) The other party may treat any assignment which delegates performance as creating reasonable grounds for insecurity and may without prejudice to his rights against the assignor demand assurances from the assignee (Section 2–609).

Part 3: General Obligation and Construction of Contract

§ 2–301. General Obligations of Parties.
The obligation of the seller is to transfer and deliver and that of the buyer is to accept and pay in accordance with the contract.

§ 2–302. Unconscionable Contract or Clause.

(1) If the court as a matter of law finds the contract or any clause of the contract to have been unconscionable at the time it was made the court may refuse to enforce the contract, or it may enforce the remainder of the contract without the unconscionable clause, or it may so limit the application of any unconscionable clause as to avoid any unconscionable result.

(2) When it is claimed or appears to the court that the contract or any clause thereof may be unconscionable the parties shall be afforded a reasonable opportunity to present evidence as to its commercial setting, purpose and effect to aid the court in making the determination.

§ 2–303. Allocation or Division of Risks.
Where this Article allocates a risk or a burden as between the parties "unless otherwise agreed", the agreement may not only shift the allocation but may also divide the risk or burden.

§ 2–304. Price Payable in Money, Goods, Realty, or Otherwise.

(1) The price can be made payable in money or otherwise. If it is payable in whole or in part in goods each party is a seller of the goods which he is to transfer.

(2) Even though all or part of the price is payable in an interest in realty the transfer of the goods and the seller's obligations with reference to them are subject to this Article, but not the transfer of the interest in realty or the transferor's obligations in connection therewith.

§ 2–305. Open Price Term.

(1) The parties if they so intend can conclude a contract for sale even though the price is not settled. In such a case the price is a reasonable price at the time for delivery if
   (a) nothing is said as to price; or
   (b) the price is left to be agreed by the parties and they fail to agree; or
   (c) the price is to be fixed in terms of some agreed market or other standard as set or recorded by a third person or agency and it is not so set or recorded.

(2) A price to be fixed by the seller or by the buyer means a price for him to fix in good faith.

(3) When a price left to be fixed otherwise than by agreement of the parties fails to be fixed through fault of one party the other may at his option treat the contract as cancelled or himself fix a reasonable price.

(4) Where, however, the parties intend not to be bound unless the price be fixed or agreed and it is not fixed or agreed there is no contract. In such a case the buyer must return any goods already received or if unable so to do must pay their reasonable value at the

time of delivery and the seller must return any portion of the price paid on account.

§ 2–306. Output, Requirements and Exclusive Dealings.

(1) A term which measures the quantity by the output of the seller or the requirements of the buyer means such actual output or requirements as may occur in good faith, except that no quantity unreasonably disproportionate to any stated estimate or in the absence of a stated estimate to any normal or otherwise comparable prior output or requirements may be tendered or demanded.

(2) A lawful agreement by either the seller or the buyer for exclusive dealing in the kind of goods concerned imposes unless otherwise agreed an obligation by the seller to use best efforts to supply the goods and by the buyer to use best efforts to promote their sale.

§ 2–307. Delivery in Single Lot or Several Lots.
Unless otherwise agreed all goods called for by a contract for sale must be tendered in a single delivery and payment is due only on such tender but where the circumstances give either party the right to make or demand delivery in lots the price if it can be apportioned may be demanded for each lot.

§ 2–308. Absence of Specified Place for Delivery.
Unless otherwise agreed

(a) the place for delivery of goods is the seller's place of business or if he has none his residence; but

(b) in a contract for sale of identified goods which to the knowledge of the parties at the time of contracting are in some other place, that place is the place for their delivery; and

(c) documents of title may be delivered through customary banking channels.

§ 2–309. Absence of Specific Time Provisions; Notice of Termination.

(1) The time for shipment or delivery or any other action under a contract if not provided in this Article or agreed upon shall be a reasonable time.

(2) Where the contract provides for successive performances but is indefinite in duration it is valid for a reasonable time but unless otherwise agreed may be terminated at any time by either party.

(3) Termination of a contract by one party except on the happening of an agreed event requires that reasonable notification be received by the other party and

an agreement dispensing with notification is invalid if its operation would be unconscionable.

§ 2–310. Open Time for Payment or Running of Credit; Authority to Ship Under Reservation.
Unless otherwise agreed

(a) payment is due at the time and place at which the buyer is to receive the goods even though the place of shipment is the place of delivery; and

(b) if the seller is authorized to send the goods he may ship them under reservation, and may tender the documents of title, but the buyer may inspect the goods after their arrival before payment is due unless such inspection is inconsistent with the terms of the contract (Section 2–513); and

(c) if delivery is authorized and made by way of documents of title otherwise than by subsection (b) then payment is due at the time and place at which the buyer is to receive the documents regardless of where the goods are to be received; and

(d) where the seller is required or authorized to ship the goods on credit the credit period runs from the time of shipment but postdating the invoice or delaying its dispatch will correspondingly delay the starting of the credit period.

§ 2–311. Options and Cooperation Respecting Performance.

(1) An agreement for sale which is otherwise sufficiently definite (subsection (3) of Section 2–204) to be a contract is not made invalid by the fact that it leaves particulars of performance to be specified by one of the parties. Any such specification must be made in good faith and within limits set by commercial reasonableness.

(2) Unless otherwise agreed specifications relating to assortment of the goods are at the buyer's option and except as otherwise provided in subsections (1)(c) and (3) of Section 2–319 specifications or arrangements relating to shipment are at the seller's option.

(3) Where such specification would materially affect the other party's performance but is not seasonably made or where one party's cooperation is necessary to the agreed performance of the other but is not seasonably forthcoming, the other party in addition to all other remedies

(a) is excused for any resulting delay in his own performance; and

(b) may also either proceed to perform in any reasonable manner or after the time for a material part of his own performance treat the failure to specify or to cooperate as a breach by failure to deliver or accept the goods.

§ 2–312. Warranty of Title and Against Infringement; Buyer's Obligation Against Infringement.

(1) Subject to subsection (2) there is in a contract for sale a warranty by the seller that
   (a) the title conveyed shall be good, and its transfer rightful; and
   (b) the goods shall be delivered free from any security interest or other lien or encumbrance of which the buyer at the time of contracting has no knowledge.

(2) A warranty under subsection (1) will be excluded or modified only by specific language or by circumstances which give the buyer reason to know that the person selling does not claim title in himself or that he is purporting to sell only such right or title as he or a third person may have.

(3) Unless otherwise agreed a seller who is a merchant regularly dealing in goods of the kind warrants that the goods shall be delivered free of the rightful claim of any third person by way of infringement or the like but a buyer who furnishes specifications to the seller must hold the seller harmless against any such claim which arises out of compliance with the specifications.

§ 2–313. Express Warranties by Affirmation, Promise, Description, Sample.

(1) Express warranties by the seller are created as follows:
   (a) Any affirmation of fact or promise made by the seller to the buyer which relates to the goods and becomes part of the basis of the bargain creates an express warranty that the goods shall conform to the affirmation or promise.
   (b) Any description of the goods which is made part of the basis of the bargain creates an express warranty that the goods shall conform to the description.
   (c) Any sample or model which is made part of the basis of the bargain creates an express warranty that the whole of the goods shall conform to the sample or model.

(2) It is not necessary to the creation of an express warranty that the seller use formal words such as "warrant" or "guarantee" or that he have a specific intention to make a warranty, but an affirmation merely of the value of the goods or a statement purporting to be merely the seller's opinion or commendation of the goods does not create a warranty.

§ 2–314. Implied Warranty: Merchantability; Usage of Trade.

(1) Unless excluded or modified (Section 2–316), a warranty that the goods shall be merchantable is implied in a contract for their sale if the seller is a merchant with respect to goods of that kind. Under this section the serving for value of food or drink to be consumed either on the premises or elsewhere is a sale.

(2) Goods to be merchantable must be at least such as
   (a) pass without objection in the trade under the contract description; and
   (b) in the case of fungible goods, are of fair average quality within the description; and
   (c) are fit for the ordinary purposes for which such goods are used; and
   (d) run, within the variations permitted by the agreement, of even kind, quality and quantity within each unit and among all units involved; and
   (e) are adequately contained, packaged, and labeled as the agreement may require; and
   (f) conform to the promise or affirmations of fact made on the container or label if any.

(3) Unless excluded or modified (Section 2–316) other implied warranties may arise from course of dealing or usage of trade.

§ 2–315. Implied Warranty: Fitness for Particular Purpose.
Where the seller at the time of contracting has reason to know any particular purpose for which the goods are required and that the buyer is relying on the seller's skill or judgment to select or furnish suitable goods, there is unless excluded or modified under the next section an implied warranty that the goods shall be fit for such purpose.

§ 2–316. Exclusion or Modification of Warranties.

(1) Words or conduct relevant to the creation of an express warranty and words or conduct tending to negate or limit warranty shall be construed wherever reasonable as consistent with each other; but subject to the provisions of this Article on parol or extrinsic evidence (Section 2–202) negation or limitation is inoperative to the extent that such construction is unreasonable.

(2) Subject to subsection (3), to exclude or modify the implied warranty of merchantability or any part of it the language must mention merchantability and in case of a writing must be conspicuous, and to exclude or modify any implied warranty of fitness the

exclusion must be by a writing and conspicuous. Language to exclude all implied warranties of fitness is sufficient if it states, for example, that "There are no warranties which extend beyond the description on the face hereof."

(3) Notwithstanding subsection (2)

    (a) unless the circumstances indicate otherwise, all implied warranties are excluded by expressions like "as is", "with all faults" or other language which in common understanding calls the buyer's attention to the exclusion of warranties and makes plain that there is no implied warranty; and

    (b) when the buyer before entering into the contract has examined the goods or the sample or model as fully as he desired or has refused to examine the goods there is no implied warranty with regard to defects which an examination ought in the circumstances to have revealed to him; and

    (c) an implied warranty can also be excluded or modified by course of dealing or course of performance or usage of trade.

(4) Remedies for breach of warranty can be limited in accordance with the provisions of this Article on liquidation or limitation of damages and on contractual modification of remedy (Sections 2–718 and 2–719).

§ 2–317. Cumulation and Conflict of Warranties Express or Implied. Warranties whether express or implied shall be construed as consistent with each other and as cumulative, but if such construction is unreasonable the intention of the parties shall determine which warranty is dominant. In ascertaining that intention the following rules apply:

    (a) Exact or technical specifications displace an inconsistent sample or model or general language of description.

    (b) A sample from an existing bulk displaces inconsistent general language of description.

    (c) Express warranties displace inconsistent implied warranties other than an implied warranty of fitness for a particular purpose.

§ 2–318. Third Party Beneficiaries of Warranties Express or Implied. Note: *If this Act is introduced in the Congress of the United States this section should be omitted. (States to select one alternative.)*

Alternative A
A seller's warranty whether express or implied extends to any natural person who is in the family or household of his buyer or who is a guest in his home if it is reasonable to expect that such person may use, consume or be affected by the goods and who is injured in person by breach of the warranty. A seller may not exclude or limit the operation of this section.

Alternative B
A seller's warranty whether express or implied extends to any natural person who may reasonably be expected to use, consume or be affected by the goods and who is injured in person by breach of the warranty. A seller may not exclude or limit the operation of this section.

Alternative C
A seller's warranty whether express or implied extends to any person who may reasonably be expected to use, consume or be affected by the goods and who is injured by breach of the warranty. A seller may not exclude or limit the operation of this section with respect to injury to the person of an individual to whom the warranty extends.

As amended in 1966.

§ 2–319. F.O.B. and F.A.S. Terms.

(1) Unless otherwise agreed the term F.O.B. (which means "free on board") at a named place, even though used only in connection with the stated price, is a delivery term under which

    (a) when the term is F.O.B. the place of shipment, the seller must at that place ship the goods in the manner provided in this Article (Section 2–504) and bear the expense and risk of putting them into the possession of the carrier; or

    (b) when the term is F.O.B. the place of destination, the seller must at his own expense and risk transport the goods to that place and there tender delivery of them in the manner provided in this Article (Section 2–503);

    (c) when under either (a) or (b) the term is also F.O.B. vessel, car or other vehicle, the seller must in addition at his own expense and risk load the goods on board. If the term is F.O.B. vessel the buyer must name the vessel and in an appropriate case the seller must comply with the provisions of this Article on the form of bill of lading (Section 2–323).

(2) Unless otherwise agreed the term F.A.S. vessel (which means "free alongside") at a named port, even though used only in connection with the stated price, is a delivery term under which the seller must

    (a) at his own expense and risk deliver the goods alongside the vessel in the manner usual in that port or on a dock designated and provided by the buyer; and

(b) obtain and tender a receipt for the goods in exchange for which the carrier is under a duty to issue a bill of lading.

(3) Unless otherwise agreed in any case falling within subsection (1)(a) or (c) or subsection (2) the buyer must seasonably give any needed instructions for making delivery, including when the term is F.A.S. or F.O.B. the loading berth of the vessel and in an appropriate case its name and sailing date. The seller may treat the failure of needed instructions as a failure of cooperation under this Article (Section 2–311). He may also at his option move the goods in any reasonable manner preparatory to delivery or shipment.

(4) Under the term F.O.B. vessel or F.A.S. unless otherwise agreed the buyer must make payment against tender of the required documents and the seller may not tender nor the buyer demand delivery of the goods in substitution for the documents.

§ 2–320. C.I.F. and C. & F. Terms.

(1) The term C.I.F. means that the price includes in a lump sum the cost of the goods and the insurance and freight to the named destination. The term C. & F. or C.F. means that the price so includes cost and freight to the named destination.

(2) Unless otherwise agreed and even though used only in connection with the stated price and destination, the term C.I.F. destination or its equivalent requires the seller at his own expense and risk to

(a) put the goods into the possession of a carrier at the port for shipment and obtain a negotiable bill or bills of lading covering the entire transportation to the named destination; and

(b) load the goods and obtain a receipt from the carrier (which may be contained in the bill of lading) showing that the freight has been paid or provided for; and

(c) obtain a policy or certificate of insurance, including any war risk insurance, of a kind and on terms then current at the port of shipment in the usual amount, in the currency of the contract, shown to cover the same goods covered by the bill of lading and providing for payment of loss to the order of the buyer or for the account of whom it may concern; but the seller may add to the price the amount of the premium for any such war risk insurance; and

(d) prepare an invoice of the goods and procure any other documents required to effect shipment or to comply with the contract; and

(e) forward and tender with commercial promptness all the documents in due form and with any indorsement necessary to perfect the buyer's rights.

(3) Unless otherwise agreed the term C. & F. or its equivalent has the same effect and imposes upon the seller the same obligations and risks as a C.I.F. term except the obligation as to insurance.

(4) Under the term C.I.F. or C. & F. unless otherwise agreed the buyer must make payment against tender of the required documents and the seller may not tender nor the buyer demand delivery of the goods in substitution for the documents.

§ 2–321. C.I.F. or C. & F.: "Net Landed Weights"; "Payment on Arrival"; Warranty of Condition on Arrival. Under a contract containing a term C.I.F. or C. & F.

(1) Where the price is based on or is to be adjusted according to "net landed weights", "delivered weights", "out turn" quantity or quality or the like, unless otherwise agreed the seller must reasonably estimate the price. The payment due on tender of the documents called for by the contract is the amount so estimated, but after final adjustment of the price a settlement must be made with commercial promptness.

(2) An agreement described in subsection (1) or any warranty of quality or condition of the goods on arrival places upon the seller the risk of ordinary deterioration, shrinkage and the like in transportation but has no effect on the place or time of identification to the contract for sale or delivery or on the passing of the risk of loss.

(3) Unless otherwise agreed where the contract provides for payment on or after arrival of the goods the seller must before payment allow such preliminary inspection as is feasible; but if the goods are lost delivery of the documents and payment are due when the goods should have arrived.

§ 2–322. Delivery "Ex-Ship".

(1) Unless otherwise agreed a term for delivery of goods "ex-ship" (which means from the carrying vessel) or in equivalent language is not restricted to a particular ship and requires delivery from a ship which has reached a place at the named port of destination where goods of the kind are usually discharged.

(2) Under such a term unless otherwise agreed

(a) the seller must discharge all liens arising out of the carriage and furnish the buyer with a direction which puts the carrier under a duty to deliver the goods; and

(b) the risk of loss does not pass to the buyer until the goods leave the ship's tackle or are otherwise properly unloaded.

§ 2–323. Form of Bill of Lading Required in Overseas Shipment; "Overseas".

(1) Where the contract contemplates overseas shipment and contains a term C.I.F. or C. & F. or F.O.B. vessel, the seller unless otherwise agreed must obtain a negotiable bill of lading stating that the goods have been loaded in board or, in the case of a term C.I.F. or C. & F., received for shipment.

(2) Where in a case within subsection (1) a bill of lading has been issued in a set of parts, unless otherwise agreed if the documents are not to be sent from abroad the buyer may demand tender of the full set; otherwise only one part of the bill of lading need be tendered. Even if the agreement expressly requires a full set

(a) due tender of a single part is acceptable within the provisions of this Article on cure of improper delivery (subsection (1) of Section 2–508); and

(b) even though the full set is demanded, if the documents are sent from abroad the person tendering an incomplete set may nevertheless require payment upon furnishing an indemnity which the buyer in good faith deems adequate.

(3) A shipment by water or by air or a contract contemplating such shipment is "overseas" insofar as by usage of trade or agreement it is subject to the commercial, financing or shipping practices characteristic of international deep water commerce.

§ 2–324. "No Arrival, No Sale" Term.
Under a term "no arrival, no sale" or terms of like meaning, unless otherwise agreed,

(a) the seller must properly ship conforming goods and if they arrive by any means he must tender them on arrival but he assumes no obligation that the goods will arrive unless he has caused the non-arrival; and

(b) where without fault of the seller the goods are in part lost or have so deteriorated as no longer to conform to the contract or arrive after the contract time, the buyer may proceed as if there had been casualty to identified goods (Section 2–613).

§ 2–325. "Letter of Credit" Term; "Confirmed Credit".

(1) Failure of the buyer seasonably to furnish an agreed letter of credit is a breach of the contract for sale.

(2) The delivery to seller of a proper letter of credit suspends the buyer's obligation to pay. If the letter of credit is dishonored, the seller may on seasonable notification to the buyer require payment directly from him.

(3) Unless otherwise agreed the term "letter of credit" or "banker's credit" in a contract for sale means an irrevocable credit issued by a financing agency of good repute and, where the shipment is overseas, of good international repute. The term "confirmed credit" means that the credit must also carry the direct obligation of such an agency which does business in the seller's financial market.

§ 2–326. Sale on Approval and Sale or Return; Consignment Sales and Rights of Creditors.

(1) Unless otherwise agreed, if delivered goods may be returned by the buyer even though they conform to the contract, the transaction is

(a) a "sale on approval" if the goods are delivered primarily for use, and

(b) a "sale or return" if the goods are delivered primarily for resale.

(2) Except as provided in subsection (3), goods held on approval are not subject to the claims of the buyer's creditors until acceptance; goods held on sale or return are subject to such claims while in the buyer's possession.

(3) Where goods are delivered to a person for sale and such person maintains a place of business at which he deals in goods of the kind involved, under a name other than the name of the person making delivery, then with respect to claims of creditors of the person conducting the business the goods are deemed to be on sale or return. The provisions of this subsection are applicable even though an agreement purports to reserve title to the person making delivery until payment or resale or uses such words as "on consignment" or "on memorandum". However, this subsection is not applicable if the person making delivery

(a) complies with an applicable law providing for a consignor's interest or the like to be evidenced by a sign, or

(b) establishes that the person conducting the business is generally known by his creditors to be substantially engaged in selling the goods of others, or

(c) complies with the filing provisions of the Article on Secured Transactions (Article 9).

(4) Any "or return" term of a contract for sale is to be treated as a separate contract for sale within the statute of frauds section of this Article (Section

2–201) and as contradicting the sale aspect of the contract within the provisions of this Article on parol or extrinsic evidence (Section 2–202).

§ 2–327. Special Incidents of Sale on Approval and Sale or Return.

(1) Under a sale on approval unless otherwise agreed
  (a) although the goods are identified to the contract the risk of loss and the title do not pass to the buyer until acceptance; and
  (b) use of the goods consistent with the purpose of trial is not acceptance but failure seasonably to notify the seller of election to return the goods is acceptance, and if the goods conform to the contract acceptance of any part is acceptance of the whole; and
  (c) after due notification of election to return, the return is at the seller's risk and expense but a merchant buyer must follow any reasonable instructions.
(2) Under a sale or return unless otherwise agreed
  (a) the option to return extends to the whole or any commercial unit of the goods while in substantially their original condition, but must be exercised seasonably; and
  (b) the return is at the buyer's risk and expense.

§ 2–328. Sale by Auction.

(1) In a sale by auction if goods are put up in lots each lot is the subject of a separate sale.
(2) A sale by auction is complete when the auctioneer so announces by the fall of the hammer or in other customary manner. Where a bid is made while the hammer is falling in acceptance of a prior bid the auctioneer may in his discretion reopen the bidding or declare the goods sold under the bid on which the hammer was falling.
(3) Such a sale is with reserve unless the goods are in explicit terms put up without reserve. In an auction with reserve the auctioneer may withdraw the goods at any time until he announces completion of the sale. In an auction without reserve, after the auctioneer calls for bids on an article or lot, that article or lot cannot be withdrawn unless no bid is made within a reasonable time. In either case a bidder may retract his bid until the auctioneer's announcement of completion of the sale, but a bidder's retraction does not revive any previous bid.
(4) If the auctioneer knowingly receives a bid on the seller's behalf or the seller makes or procures such a bid, and notice has not been given that liberty for such bidding is reserved, the buyer may at his option avoid the sale or take the goods at the price of the last good faith bid prior to the completion of the sale. This subsection shall not apply to any bid at a forced sale.

Part 4: Title, Creditors and Good Faith Purchasers

§ 2–401. Passing of Title; Reservation for Security; Limited Application of This Section.
Each provision of this Article with regard to the rights, obligations and remedies of the seller, the buyer, purchasers or other third parties applies irrespective of title to the goods except where the provision refers to such title. Insofar as situations are not covered by the other provisions of this Article and matters concerning title become material the following rules apply:

(1) Title to goods cannot pass under a contract for sale prior to their identification to the contract (Section 2–501), and unless otherwise explicitly agreed the buyer acquires by their identification a special property as limited by this Act. Any retention or reservation by the seller of the title (property) in goods shipped or delivered to the buyer is limited in effect to a reservation of a security interest. Subject to these provisions and to the provisions of the Article on Secured Transactions (Article 9), title to goods passes from the seller to the buyer in any manner and on any conditions explicitly agreed on by the parties.
(2) Unless otherwise explicitly agreed title passes to the buyer at the time and place at which the seller completes his performance with reference to the physical delivery of the goods, despite any reservation of a security interest and even though a document of title is to be delivered at a different time or place; and in particular and despite any reservation of a security interest by the bill of lading
  (a) if the contract requires or authorizes the seller to send the goods to the buyer but does not require him to deliver them at destination, title passes to the buyer at the time and place of shipment; but
  (b) if the contract requires delivery at destination, title passes on tender there.
(3) Unless otherwise explicitly agreed where delivery is to be made without moving the goods,
  (a) if the seller is to deliver a document of title, title passes at the time when and the place where he delivers such documents; or
  (b) if the goods are at the time of contracting already identified and no documents are to be delivered, title passes at the time and place of contracting.

(4) A rejection or other refusal by the buyer to receive or retain the goods, whether or not justified, or a justified revocation of acceptance revests title to the goods in the seller. Such revesting occurs by operation of law and is not a "sale".

§ 2–402. Rights of Seller's Creditors Against Sold Goods.

(1) Except as provided in subsections (2) and (3), rights of unsecured creditors of the seller with respect to goods which have been identified to a contract for sale are subject to the buyer's rights to recover the goods under this Article (Sections 2–502 and 2–716).

(2) A creditor of the seller may treat a sale or an identification of goods to a contract for sale as void if as against him a retention of possession by the seller is fraudulent under any rule of law of the state where the goods are situated, except that retention of possession in good faith and current course of trade by a merchant-seller for a commercially reasonable time after a sale or identification is not fraudulent.

(3) Nothing in this Article shall be deemed to impair the rights of creditors of the seller

   (a) under the provisions of the Article on Secured Transactions (Article 9); or

   (b) where identification to the contract or delivery is made not in current course of trade but in satisfaction of or as security for a pre-existing claim for money, security or the like and is made under circumstances which under any rule of law of the state where the goods are situated would apart from this Article constitute the transaction a fraudulent transfer or voidable preference.

§ 2–403. Power to Transfer; Good Faith Purchase of Goods; "Entrusting".

(1) A purchaser of goods acquires all title which his transferor had or had power to transfer except that a purchaser of a limited interest acquires rights only to the extent of the interest purchased. A person with voidable title has power to transfer a good title to a good faith purchaser for value. When goods have been delivered under a transaction of purchase the purchaser has such power even though

   (a) the transferor was deceived as to the identity of the purchaser, or

   (b) the delivery was in exchange for a check which is later dishonored, or

   (c) it was agreed that the transaction was to be a "cash sale", or

   (d) the delivery was procured through fraud punishable as larcenous under the criminal law.

(2) Any entrusting of possession of goods to a merchant who deals in goods of that kind gives him power to transfer all rights of the entruster to a buyer in ordinary course of business.

(3) "Entrusting" includes any delivery and any acquiescence in retention of possession regardless of any condition expressed between the parties to the delivery or acquiescence and regardless of whether the procurement of the entrusting or the possessor's disposition of the goods have been such as to be larcenous under the criminal law.

[Publisher's Editorial Note: If a state adopts the repealer of Article 6—Bulk Transfers (Alternative A), subsec. (4) should read as follows:]

(4) The rights of other purchasers of goods and of lien creditors are governed by the Articles on Secured Transactions (Article 9) and Documents of Title (Article 7).

[Publisher's Editorial Note: If a state adopts Revised Article 6—Bulk Sales (Alternative B), subsec. (4) should read as follows:]

(4) The rights of other purchasers of goods and of lien creditors are governed by the Articles on Secured Transactions (Article 9), Bulk Sales (Article 6) and Documents of Title (Article 7).

As amended in 1988.

For material relating to the changes made in text in 1988, see section 3 of Alternative A (Repealer of Article 6—Bulk Transfers) and Conforming Amendment to Section 2–403 following end of Alternative B (Revised Article 6—Bulk Sales).

Part 5: Performance

§ 2–501. Insurable Interest in Goods; Manner of Identification of Goods.

(1) The buyer obtains a special property and an insurable interest in goods by identification of existing goods as goods to which the contract refers even though the goods so identified are non-conforming and he has an option to return or reject them. Such identification can be made at any time and in any manner explicitly agreed to by the parties. In the absence of explicit agreement identification occurs

   (a) when the contract is made if it is for the sale of goods already existing and identified;

   (b) if the contract is for the sale of future goods other than those described in paragraph (c), when goods are shipped, marked or otherwise designated by the seller as goods to which the contract refers;

(c) when the crops are planted or otherwise become growing crops or the young are conceived if the contract is for the sale of unborn young to be born within twelve months after contracting or for the sale of crops to be harvested within twelve months or the next normal harvest season after contracting whichever is longer.

(2) The seller retains an insurable interest in goods so long as title to or any security interest in the goods remains in him and where the identification is by the seller alone he may until default or insolvency or notification to the buyer that the identification is final substitute other goods for those identified.

(3) Nothing in this section impairs any insurable interest recognized under any other statute or rule of law.

§ 2–502. Buyer's Right to Goods on Seller's Insolvency.

(1) Subject to subsection (2) and even though the goods have not been shipped a buyer who has paid a part or all of the price of goods in which he has a special property under the provisions of the immediately preceding section may on making and keeping good a tender of any unpaid portion of their price recover them from the seller if the seller becomes insolvent within ten days after receipt of the first installment on their price.

(2) If the identification creating his special property has been made by the buyer he acquires the right to recover the goods only if they conform to the contract for sale.

§ 2–503. Manner of Seller's Tender of Delivery.

(1) Tender of delivery requires that the seller put and hold conforming goods at the buyer's disposition and give the buyer any notification reasonably necessary to enable him to take delivery. The manner, time and place for tender are determined by the agreement and this Article, and in particular

(a) tender must be at a reasonable hour, and if it is of goods they must be kept available for the period reasonably necessary to enable the buyer to take possession; but

(b) unless otherwise agreed the buyer must furnish facilities reasonably suited to the receipt of the goods.

(2) Where the case is within the next section respecting shipment tender requires that the seller comply with its provisions.

(3) Where the seller is required to deliver at a particular destination tender requires that he comply with subsection (1) and also in any appropriate case tender documents as described in subsections (4) and (5) of this section.

(4) Where goods are in the possession of a bailee and are to be delivered without being moved

(a) tender requires that the seller either tender a negotiable document of title covering such goods or procure acknowledgment by the bailee of the buyer's right to possession of the goods; but

(b) tender to the buyer of a non-negotiable document of title or of a written direction to the bailee to deliver is sufficient tender unless the buyer seasonably objects, and receipt by the bailee of notification of the buyer's rights fixes those rights as against the bailee and all third persons; but risk of loss of the goods and of any failure by the bailee to honor the non-negotiable document of title or to obey the direction remains on the seller until the buyer has had a reasonable time to present the document or direction, and a refusal by the bailee to honor the document or to obey the direction defeats the tender.

(5) Where the contract requires the seller to deliver documents

(a) he must tender all such documents in correct form, except as provided in this Article with respect to bills of lading in a set (subsection (2) of Section 2–323); and

(b) tender through customary banking channels is sufficient and dishonor of a draft accompanying the documents constitutes non-acceptance or rejection.

§ 2–504. Shipment by Seller.
Where the seller is required or authorized to send the goods to the buyer and the contract does not require him to deliver them at a particular destination, then unless otherwise agreed he must

(a) put the goods in the possession of such a carrier and make such a contract for their transportation as may be reasonable having regard to the nature of the goods and other circumstances of the case; and

(b) obtain and promptly deliver or tender in due form any document necessary to enable the buyer to obtain possession of the goods or otherwise required by the agreement or by usage of trade; and

(c) promptly notify the buyer of the shipment.

Failure to notify the buyer under paragraph (c) or to make a proper contract under paragraph (a) is a ground for rejection only if material delay or loss ensues.

§ 2–505. Seller's Shipment Under Reservation.

(1) Where the seller has identified goods to the contract by or before shipment:
  (a) his procurement of a negotiable bill of lading to his own order or otherwise reserves in him a security interest in the goods. His procurement of the bill to the order of a financing agency or of the buyer indicates in addition only the seller's expectation of transferring that interest to the person named.
  (b) a non-negotiable bill of lading to himself or his nominee reserves possession of the goods as security but except in a case of conditional delivery (subsection (2) of Section 2–507) a non-negotiable bill of lading naming the buyer as consignee reserves no security interest even though the seller retains possession of the bill of lading.
(2) When shipment by the seller with reservation of a security interest is in violation of the contract for sale it constitutes an improper contract for transportation within the preceding section but impairs neither the rights given to the buyer by shipment and identification of the goods to the contract nor the seller's powers as a holder of a negotiable document.

§ 2–506. Rights of Financing Agency.

(1) A financing agency by paying or purchasing for value a draft which relates to a shipment of goods acquires to the extent of the payment or purchase and in addition to its own rights under the draft and any document of title securing it any rights of the shipper in the goods including the right to stop delivery and the shipper's right to have the draft honored by the buyer.
(2) The right to reimbursement of a financing agency which has in good faith honored or purchased the draft under commitment to or authority from the buyer is not impaired by subsequent discovery of defects with reference to any relevant document which was apparently regular on its face.

§ 2–507. Effect of Seller's Tender; Delivery on Condition.

(1) Tender of delivery is a condition to the buyer's duty to accept the goods and, unless otherwise agreed, to his duty to pay for them. Tender entitles the seller to acceptance of the goods and to payment according to the contract.

(2) Where payment is due and demanded on the delivery to the buyer of goods or documents of title, his right as against the seller to retain or dispose of them is conditional upon his making the payment due.

§ 2–508. Cure by Seller of Improper Tender or Delivery; Replacement.

(1) Where any tender or delivery by the seller is rejected because non-conforming and the time for performance has not yet expired, the seller may seasonably notify the buyer of his intention to cure and may then within the contract time make a conforming delivery.
(2) Where the buyer rejects a non-conforming tender which the seller had reasonable grounds to believe would be acceptable with or without money allowance the seller may if he seasonably notifies the buyer have a further reasonable time to substitute a conforming tender.

§ 2–509. Risk of Loss in the Absence of Breach.

(1) Where the contract requires or authorizes the seller to ship the goods by carrier
  (a) if it does not require him to deliver them at a particular destination, the risk of loss passes to the buyer when the goods are duly delivered to the carrier even though the shipment is under reservation (Section 2–505); but
  (b) if it does require him to deliver them at a particular destination and the goods are there duly tendered while in the possession of the carrier, the risk of loss passes to the buyer when the goods are there duly so tendered as to enable the buyer to take delivery.
(2) Where the goods are held by a bailee to be delivered without being moved, the risk of loss passes to the buyer
  (a) on his receipt of a negotiable document of title covering the goods; or
  (b) on acknowledgment by the bailee of the buyer's right to possession of the goods; or
  (c) after his receipt of a non-negotiable document of title or other written direction to deliver, as provided in subsection (4)(b) of Section 2–503.
(3) In any case not within subsection (1) or (2), the risk of loss passes to the buyer on his receipt of the goods if the seller is a merchant; otherwise the risk passes to the buyer on tender of delivery.
(4) The provisions of this section are subject to contrary agreement of the parties and to the provisions of this Article on sale on approval (Section 2–327) and on effect of breach on risk of loss (Section 2–510).

§ 2–510. Effect of Breach on Risk of Loss.

(1) Where a tender or delivery of goods so fails to conform to the contract as to give a right of rejection the risk of their loss remains on the seller until cure or acceptance.

(2) Where the buyer rightfully revokes acceptance he may to the extent of any deficiency in his effective insurance coverage treat the risk of loss as having rested on the seller from the beginning.

(3) Where the buyer as to conforming goods already identified to the contract for sale repudiates or is otherwise in breach before risk of their loss has passed to him, the seller may to the extent of any deficiency in his effective insurance coverage treat the risk of loss as resting on the buyer for a commercially reasonable time.

§ 2–511. Tender of Payment by Buyer; Payment by Check.

(1) Unless otherwise agreed tender of payment is a condition to the seller's duty to tender and complete any delivery.

(2) Tender of payment is sufficient when made by any means or in any manner current in the ordinary course of business unless the seller demands payment in legal tender and gives any extension of time reasonably necessary to procure it.

(3) Subject to the provisions of this Act on the effect of an instrument on an obligation (Section 3-310), payment by check is conditional and is defeated as between the parties by dishonor of the check on due presentment.

As amended in 1994.

See Appendix XI for material relating to changes made in text in 1994.

§ 2–512. Payment by Buyer Before Inspection. *1995 Amendments to text indicated by strikeout and underline*]

(1) Where the contract requires payment before inspection non-conformity of the goods does not excuse the buyer from so making payment unless
  (a) the non-conformity appears without inspection; or
  (b) despite tender of the required documents the circumstances would justify injunction against honor under this Act (Section 5-109(b)).

(2) Payment pursuant to subsection (1) does not constitute an acceptance of goods or impair the buyer's right to inspect or any of his remedies.

As amended in 1995.

See Appendix XIV for material relating to changes made in text in 1995.

§ 2–513. Buyer's Right to Inspection of Goods.

(1) Unless otherwise agreed and subject to subsection (3), where goods are tendered or delivered or identified to the contract for sale, the buyer has a right before payment or acceptance to inspect them at any reasonable place and time and in any reasonable manner. When the seller is required or authorized to send the goods to the buyer, the inspection may be after their arrival.

(2) Expenses of inspection must be borne by the buyer but may be recovered from the seller if the goods do not conform and are rejected.

(3) Unless otherwise agreed and subject to the provisions of this Article on C.I.F. contracts (subsection (3) of Section 2–321), the buyer is not entitled to inspect the goods before payment of the price when the contract provides
  (a) for delivery "C.O.D." or on other like terms; or
  (b) for payment against documents of title, except where such payment is due only after the goods are to become available for inspection.

(4) A place or method of inspection fixed by the parties is presumed to be exclusive but unless otherwise expressly agreed it does not postpone identification or shift the place for delivery or for passing the risk of loss. If compliance becomes impossible, inspection shall be as provided in this section unless the place or method fixed was clearly intended as an indispensable condition failure of which avoids the contract.

§ 2–514. When Documents Deliverable on Acceptance; When on Payment.
Unless otherwise agreed documents against which a draft is drawn are to be delivered to the drawee on acceptance of the draft if it is payable more than three days after presentment; otherwise, only on payment.

§ 2–515. Preserving Evidence of Goods in Dispute.
In furtherance of the adjustment of any claim or dispute

  (a) either party on reasonable notification to the other and for the purpose of ascertaining the facts and preserving evidence has the right to inspect, test and sample the goods including such of them as may be in the possession or control of the other; and

(b) the parties may agree to a third party inspection or survey to determine the conformity or condition of the goods and may agree that the findings shall be binding upon them in any subsequent litigation or adjustment.

Part 6: Breach, Repudiation and Excuse

§ 2–601. Buyer's Rights on Improper Delivery.
Subject to the provisions of this Article on breach in installment contracts (Section 2–612) and unless otherwise agreed under the sections on contractual limitations of remedy (Sections 2–718 and 2–719), if the goods or the tender of delivery fail in any respect to conform to the contract, the buyer may

(a) reject the whole; or

(b) accept the whole; or

(c) accept any commercial unit or units and reject the rest.

§ 2–602. Manner and Effect of Rightful Rejection.

(1) Rejection of goods must be within a reasonable time after their delivery or tender. It is ineffective unless the buyer seasonably notifies the seller.

(2) Subject to the provisions of the two following sections on rejected goods (Sections 2–603 and 2–604),

(a) after rejection any exercise of ownership by the buyer with respect to any commercial unit is wrongful as against the seller; and

(b) if the buyer has before rejection taken physical possession of goods in which he does not have a security interest under the provisions of this Article (subsection (3) of Section 2–711), he is under a duty after rejection to hold them with reasonable care at the seller's disposition for a time sufficient to permit the seller to remove them; but

(c) the buyer has no further obligations with regard to goods rightfully rejected.

(3) The seller's rights with respect to goods wrongfully rejected are governed by the provisions of this Article on Seller's remedies in general (Section 2–703).

§ 2–603. Merchant Buyer's Duties as to Rightfully Rejected Goods.

(1) Subject to any security interest in the buyer (subsection (3) of Section 2–711), when the seller has no agent or place of business at the market of rejection a merchant buyer is under a duty after rejection of goods in his possession or control to follow any reasonable instructions received from the seller with respect to the goods and in the absence of such instructions to make reasonable efforts to sell them for the seller's account if they are perishable or threaten to decline in value speedily. Instructions are not reasonable if on demand indemnity for expenses is not forthcoming.

(2) When the buyer sells goods under subsection (1), he is entitled to reimbursement from the seller or out of the proceeds for reasonable expenses of caring for and selling them, and if the expenses include no selling commission then to such commission as is usual in the trade or if there is none to a reasonable sum not exceeding ten per cent on the gross proceeds.

(3) In complying with this section the buyer is held only to good faith and good faith conduct hereunder is neither acceptance nor conversion nor the basis of an action for damages.

§ 2–604. Buyer's Options as to Salvage of Rightfully Rejected Goods.
Subject to the provisions of the immediately preceding section on perishables if the seller gives no instructions within a reasonable time after notification of rejection the buyer may store the rejected goods for the seller's account or reship them to him or resell them for the seller's account with reimbursement as provided in the preceding section. Such action is not acceptance or conversion.

§ 2–605. Waiver of Buyer's Objections by Failure to Particularize.

(1) The buyer's failure to state in connection with rejection a particular defect which is ascertainable by reasonable inspection precludes him from relying on the unstated defect to justify rejection or to establish breach

(a) where the seller could have cured it if stated seasonably; or

(b) between merchants when the seller has after rejection made a request in writing for a full and final written statement of all defects on which the buyer proposes to rely.

(2) Payment against documents made without reservation of rights precludes recovery of the payment for defects apparent on the face of the documents.

§ 2–606. What Constitutes Acceptance of Goods.

(1) Acceptance of goods occurs when the buyer

(a) after a reasonable opportunity to inspect the goods signifies to the seller that the goods are conforming or that he will take or retain them in spite of their non-conformity; or

(b) fails to make an effective rejection (subsection (1) of Section 2–602), but such acceptance does not occur until the buyer has had a reasonable opportunity to inspect them; or

(c) does any act inconsistent with the seller's ownership; but if such act is wrongful as against the seller it is an acceptance only if ratified by him.

(2) Acceptance of a part of any commercial unit is acceptance of that entire unit.

§ 2–607. Effect of Acceptance; Notice of Breach; Burden of Establishing Breach After Acceptance; Notice of Claim or Litigation to Person Answerable Over.

(1) The buyer must pay at the contract rate for any goods accepted.

(2) Acceptance of goods by the buyer precludes rejection of the goods accepted and if made with knowledge of a non-conformity cannot be revoked because of it unless the acceptance was on the reasonable assumption that the non-conformity would be seasonably cured but acceptance does not of itself impair any other remedy provided by this Article for non-conformity.

(3) Where a tender has been accepted

(a) the buyer must within a reasonable time after he discovers or should have discovered any breach notify the seller of breach or be barred from any remedy; and

(b) if the claim is one for infringement or the like (subsection (3) of Section 2–312) and the buyer is sued as a result of such a breach he must so notify the seller within a reasonable time after he receives notice of the litigation or be barred from any remedy over for liability established by the litigation.

(4) The burden is on the buyer to establish any breach with respect to the goods accepted.

(5) Where the buyer is sued for breach of a warranty or other obligation for which his seller is answerable over

(a) he may give his seller written notice of the litigation. If the notice states that the seller may come in and defend and that if the seller does not do so he will be bound in any action against him by his buyer by any determination of fact common to the two litigations, then unless the seller after seasonable receipt of the notice does come in and defend he is so bound.

(b) if the claim is one for infringement or the like (subsection (3) of Section 2–312) the original seller may demand in writing that his buyer turn over to him control of the litigation including settlement or else be barred from any remedy over and if he also agrees to bear all expense and to satisfy any adverse judgment, then unless the buyer after seasonable receipt of the demand does turn over control the buyer is so barred.

(6) The provisions of subsections (3), (4) and (5) apply to any obligation of a buyer to hold the seller harmless against infringement or the like (subsection (3) of Section 2–312).

§ 2–608. Revocation of Acceptance in Whole or in Part.

(1) The buyer may revoke his acceptance of a lot or commercial unit whose non-conformity substantially impairs its value to him if he has accepted it

(a) on the reasonable assumption that its non-conformity would be cured and it has not been seasonably cured; or

(b) without discovery of such non-conformity if his acceptance was reasonably induced either by the difficulty of discovery before acceptance or by the seller's assurances.

(2) Revocation of acceptance must occur within a reasonable time after the buyer discovers or should have discovered the ground for it and before any substantial change in condition of the goods which is not caused by their own defects. It is not effective until the buyer notifies the seller of it.

(3) A buyer who so revokes has the same rights and duties with regard to the goods involved as if he had rejected them.

§ 2–609. Right to Adequate Assurance of Performance.

(1) A contract for sale imposes an obligation on each party that the other's expectation of receiving due performance will not be impaired. When reasonable grounds for insecurity arise with respect to the performance of either party the other may in writing demand adequate assurance of due performance and until he receives such assurance may if commercially reasonable suspend any performance for which he has not already received the agreed return.

(2) Between merchants the reasonableness of grounds for insecurity and the adequacy of any assurance offered shall be determined according to commercial standards.

(3) Acceptance of any improper delivery or payment does not prejudice the aggrieved party's right to demand adequate assurance of future performance.

(4) After receipt of a justified demand failure to provide within a reasonable time not exceeding thirty days such assurance of due performance as is adequate under the circumstances of the particular case is a repudiation of the contract.

§ 2–610. Anticipatory Repudiation. When either party repudiates the contract with respect to a performance not yet due the loss of which will substantially impair the value of the contract to the other, the aggrieved party may

(a) for a commercially reasonable time await performance by the repudiating party; or

(b) resort to any remedy for breach (Section 2–703 or Section 2–711), even though he has notified the repudiating party that he would await the latter's performance and has urged retraction; and

(c) in either case suspend his own performance or proceed in accordance with the provisions of this Article on the seller's right to identify goods to the contract notwithstanding breach or to salvage unfinished goods (Section 2–704).

§ 2–611. Retraction of Anticipatory Repudiation.

(1) Until the repudiating party's next performance is due he can retract his repudiation unless the aggrieved party has since the repudiation cancelled or materially changed his position or otherwise indicated that he considers the repudiation final.

(2) Retraction may be by any method which clearly indicates to the aggrieved party that the repudiating party intends to perform, but must include any assurance justifiably demanded under the provisions of this Article (Section 2–609).

(3) Retraction reinstates the repudiating party's rights under the contract with due excuse and allowance to the aggrieved party for any delay occasioned by the repudiation.

§ 2–612. "Installment Contract"; Breach.

(1) An "installment contract" is one which requires or authorizes the delivery of goods in separate lots to be separately accepted, even though the contract contains a clause "each delivery is a separate contract" or its equivalent.

(2) The buyer may reject any installment which is nonconforming if the non-conformity substantially impairs the value of that installment and cannot be cured or if the non-conformity is a defect in the required documents; but if the non-conformity does not fall within subsection (3) and the seller gives adequate assurance of its cure the buyer must accept that installment.

(3) Whenever non-conformity or default with respect to one or more installments substantially impairs the value of the whole contract there is a breach of the whole. But the aggrieved party reinstates the contract if he accepts a non-conforming installment without seasonably notifying of cancellation or if he brings an action with respect only to past installments or demands performance as to future installments.

§ 2–613. Casualty to Identified Goods. Where the contract requires for its performance goods identified when the contract is made, and the goods suffer casualty without fault of either party before the risk of loss passes to the buyer, or in a proper case under a "no arrival, no sale" term (Section 2–324) then

(a) if the loss is total the contract is avoided; and

(b) if the loss is partial or the goods have so deteriorated as no longer to conform to the contract the buyer may nevertheless demand inspection and at his option either treat the contract as avoided or accept the goods with due allowance from the contract price for the deterioration or the deficiency in quantity but without further right against the seller.

§ 2–614. Substituted Performance.

(1) Where without fault of either party the agreed berthing, loading, or unloading facilities fail or an agreed type of carrier becomes unavailable or the agreed manner of delivery otherwise becomes commercially impracticable but a commercially reasonable substitute is available, such substitute performance must be tendered and accepted.

(2) If the agreed means or manner of payment fails because of domestic or foreign governmental regulation, the seller may withhold or stop delivery unless the buyer provides a means or manner of payment which is commercially a substantial equivalent. If delivery has already been taken, payment by the means or in the manner provided by the regulation discharges the buyer's obligation unless the regulation is discriminatory, oppressive or predatory.

§ 2–615. Excuse by Failure of Presupposed Conditions. Except so far as a seller may have assumed a greater obligation and subject to the preceding section on substituted performance:

(a) Delay in delivery or non-delivery in whole or in part by a seller who complies with paragraphs

(b) and (c) is not a breach of his duty under a contract for sale if performance as agreed has been made impracticable by the occurrence of a contingency the non-occurrence of which was a basic assumption on which the contract was made or by compliance in good faith with any applicable foreign or domestic governmental regulation or order whether or not it later proves to be invalid.

(b) Where the causes mentioned in paragraph (a) affect only a part of the seller's capacity to perform, he must allocate production and deliveries among his customers but may at his option include regular customers not then under contract as well as his own requirements for further manufacture. He may so allocate in any manner which is fair and reasonable.

(c) The seller must notify the buyer seasonably that there will be delay or non-delivery and, when allocation is required under paragraph (b), of the estimated quota thus made available for the buyer.

§ 2–616. Procedure on Notice Claiming Excuse.

(1) Where the buyer receives notification of a material or indefinite delay or an allocation justified under the preceding section he may by written notification to the seller as to any delivery concerned, and where the prospective deficiency substantially impairs the value of the whole contract under the provisions of this Article relating to breach of installment contracts (Section 2–612), then also as to the whole,

    (a) terminate and thereby discharge any unexecuted portion of the contract; or

    (b) modify the contract by agreeing to take his available quota in substitution.

(2) If after receipt of such notification from the seller the buyer fails so to modify the contract within a reasonable time not exceeding thirty days the contract lapses with respect to any deliveries affected.

(3) The provisions of this section may not be negated by agreement except in so far as the seller has assumed a greater obligation under the preceding section.

Part 7: Remedies

§ 2–701. Remedies for Breach of Collateral Contracts Not Impaired.
Remedies for breach of any obligation or promise collateral or ancillary to a contract for sale are not impaired by the provisions of this Article.

§ 2–702. Seller's Remedies on Discovery of Buyer's Insolvency.

(1) Where the seller discovers the buyer to be insolvent he may refuse delivery except for cash including payment for all goods theretofore delivered under the contract, and stop delivery under this Article (Section 2–705).

(2) Where the seller discovers that the buyer has received goods on credit while insolvent he may reclaim the goods upon demand made within ten days after the receipt, but if misrepresentation of solvency has been made to the particular seller in writing within three months before delivery the ten day limitation does not apply. Except as provided in this subsection the seller may not base a right to reclaim goods on the buyer's fraudulent or innocent misrepresentation of solvency or of intent to pay.

(3) The seller's right to reclaim under subsection (2) is subject to the rights of a buyer in ordinary course or other good faith purchaser under this Article (Section 2–403). Successful reclamation of goods excludes all other remedies with respect to them.

As amended in 1966.

§ 2–703. Seller's Remedies in General.
Where the buyer wrongfully rejects or revokes acceptance of goods or fails to make a payment due on or before delivery or repudiates with respect to a part or the whole, then with respect to any goods directly affected and, if the breach is of the whole contract (Section 2–612), then also with respect to the whole undelivered balance, the aggrieved seller may

    (a) withhold delivery of such goods;

    (b) stop delivery by any bailee as hereafter provided (Section 2–705);

    (c) proceed under the next section respecting goods still unidentified to the contract;

    (d) resell and recover damages as hereafter provided (Section 2–706);

    (e) recover damages for non-acceptance (Section 2–708) or in a proper case the price (Section 2–709);

    (f) cancel.

§ 2–704. Seller's Right to Identify Goods to the Contract Notwithstanding Breach or to Salvage Unfinished Goods.

(1) An aggrieved seller under the preceding section may

    (a) identify to the contract conforming goods not already identified if at the time he learned of the breach they are in his possession or control;

(b) treat as the subject of resale goods which have demonstrably been intended for the particular contract even though those goods are unfinished.

(2) Where the goods are unfinished an aggrieved seller may in the exercise of reasonable commercial judgment for the purposes of avoiding loss and of effective realization either complete the manufacture and wholly identify the goods to the contract or cease manufacture and resell for scrap or salvage value or proceed in any other reasonable manner.

§ 2–705. Seller's Stoppage of Delivery in Transit or Otherwise.

(1) The seller may stop delivery of goods in the possession of a carrier or other bailee when he discovers the buyer to be insolvent (Section 2–702) and may stop delivery of carload, truckload, planeload or larger shipments of express or freight when the buyer repudiates or fails to make a payment due before delivery or if for any other reason the seller has a right to withhold or reclaim the goods.

(2) As against such buyer the seller may stop delivery until

(a) receipt of the goods by the buyer; or

(b) acknowledgment to the buyer by any bailee of the goods except a carrier that the bailee holds the goods for the buyer; or

(c) such acknowledgment to the buyer by a carrier by reshipment or as warehouseman; or

(d) negotiation to the buyer of any negotiable document of title covering the goods.

(3) (a) To stop delivery the seller must so notify as to enable the bailee by reasonable diligence to prevent delivery of the goods.

(b) After such notification the bailee must hold and deliver the goods according to the directions of the seller but the seller is liable to the bailee for any ensuing charges or damages.

(c) If a negotiable document of title has been issued for goods the bailee is not obliged to obey a notification to stop until surrender of the document.

(d) A carrier who has issued a non-negotiable bill of lading is not obliged to obey a notification to stop received from a person other than the consignor.

§ 2–706. Seller's Resale Including Contract for Resale.

(1) Under the conditions stated in Section 2–703 on seller's remedies, the seller may resell the goods concerned or the undelivered balance thereof. Where the resale is made in good faith and in a commercially reasonable manner the seller may recover the difference between the resale price and the contract price together with any incidental damages allowed under the provisions of this Article (Section 2–710), but less expenses saved in consequence of the buyer's breach.

(2) Except as otherwise provided in subsection (3) or unless otherwise agreed resale may be at public or private sale including sale by way of one or more contracts to sell or of identification to an existing contract of the seller. Sale may be as a unit or in parcels and at any time and place and on any terms but every aspect of the sale including the method, manner, time, place and terms must be commercially reasonable. The resale must be reasonably identified as referring to the broken contract, but it is not necessary that the goods be in existence or that any or all of them have been identified to the contract before the breach.

(3) Where the resale is at private sale the seller must give the buyer reasonable notification of his intention to resell.

(4) Where the resale is at public sale

(a) only identified goods can be sold except where there is a recognized market for a public sale of futures in goods of the kind; and

(b) it must be made at a usual place or market for public sale if one is reasonably available and except in the case of goods which are perishable or threaten to decline in value speedily the seller must give the buyer reasonable notice of the time and place of the resale; and

(c) if the goods are not to be within the view of those attending the sale the notification of sale must state the place where the goods are located and provide for their reasonable inspection by prospective bidders; and

(d) the seller may buy.

(5) A purchaser who buys in good faith at a resale takes the goods free of any rights of the original buyer even though the seller fails to comply with one or more of the requirements of this section.

(6) The seller is not accountable to the buyer for any profit made on any resale. A person in the position of a seller (Section 2–707) or a buyer who has rightfully rejected or justifiably revoked acceptance must account for any excess over the amount of his security interest, as hereinafter defined (subsection (3) of Section 2–711).

§ 2–707. "Person in the Position of a Seller".

(1) A "person in the position of a seller" includes as against a principal an agent who has paid or become responsible for the price of goods on behalf of his principal or anyone who otherwise holds a security interest or other right in goods similar to that of a seller.

(2) A person in the position of a seller may as provided in this Article withhold or stop delivery (Section 2–705) and resell (Section 2–706) and recover incidental damages (Section 2–710).

§ 2–708. Seller's Damages for Non-acceptance or Repudiation.

(1) Subject to subsection (2) and to the provisions of this Article with respect to proof of market price (Section 2–723), the measure of damages for non-acceptance or repudiation by the buyer is the difference between the market price at the time and place for tender and the unpaid contract price together with any incidental damages provided in this Article (Section 2–710), but less expenses saved in consequence of the buyer's breach.

(2) If the measure of damages provided in subsection (1) is inadequate to put the seller in as good a position as performance would have done then the measure of damages is the profit (including reasonable overhead) which the seller would have made from full performance by the buyer, together with any incidental damages provided in this Article (Section 2–710), due allowance for costs reasonably incurred and due credit for payments or proceeds of resale.

§ 2–709. Action for the Price.

(1) When the buyer fails to pay the price as it becomes due the seller may recover, together with any incidental damages under the next section, the price

    (a) of goods accepted or of conforming goods lost or damaged within a commercially reasonable time after risk of their loss has passed to the buyer; and

    (b) of goods identified to the contract if the seller is unable after reasonable effort to resell them at a reasonable price or the circumstances reasonably indicate that such effort will be unavailing.

(2) Where the seller sues for the price he must hold for the buyer any goods which have been identified to the contract and are still in his control except that if resale becomes possible he may resell them at any time prior to the collection of the judgment. The net proceeds of any such resale must be credited to the buyer and payment of the judgment entitles him to any goods not resold.

(3) After the buyer has wrongfully rejected or revoked acceptance of the goods or has failed to make a payment due or has repudiated (Section 2–610), a seller who is held not entitled to the price under this section shall nevertheless be awarded damages for non-acceptance under the preceding section.

§ 2–710. Seller's Incidental Damages.

Incidental damages to an aggrieved seller include any commercially reasonable charges, expenses or commissions incurred in stopping delivery, in the transportation, care and custody of goods after the buyer's breach, in connection with return or resale of the goods or otherwise resulting from the breach.

§ 2–711. Buyer's Remedies in General; Buyer's Security Interest in Rejected Goods.

(1) Where the seller fails to make delivery or repudiates or the buyer rightfully rejects or justifiably revokes acceptance then with respect to any goods involved, and with respect to the whole if the breach goes to the whole contract (Section 2–612), the buyer may cancel and whether or not he has done so may in addition to recovering so much of the price as has been paid

    (a) "cover" and have damages under the next section as to all the goods affected whether or not they have been identified to the contract; or

    (b) recover damages for non-delivery as provided in this Article (Section 2–713).

(2) Where the seller fails to deliver or repudiates the buyer may also

    (a) if the goods have been identified recover them as provided in this Article (Section 2–502); or

    (b) in a proper case obtain specific performance or replevy the goods as provided in this Article (Section 2–716).

(3) On rightful rejection or justifiable revocation of acceptance a buyer has a security interest in goods in his possession or control for any payments made on their price and any expenses reasonably incurred in their inspection, receipt, transportation, care and custody and may hold such goods and resell them in like manner as an aggrieved seller (Section 2–706).

§ 2–712. "Cover"; Buyer's Procurement of Substitute Goods.

(1) After a breach within the preceding section the buyer may "cover" by making in good faith and without unreasonable delay any reasonable purchase of or contract to purchase goods in substitution for those due from the seller.

(2) The buyer may recover from the seller as damages the difference between the cost of cover and the contract price together with any incidental or consequential damages as hereinafter defined (Section 2–715), but less expenses saved in consequence of the seller's breach.

(3) Failure of the buyer to effect cover within this section does not bar him from any other remedy.

§ 2–713. Buyer's Damages for Non-delivery or Repudiation.

(1) Subject to the provisions of this Article with respect to proof of market price (Section 2–723), the measure of damages for non-delivery or repudiation by the seller is the difference between the market price at the time when the buyer learned of the breach and the contract price together with any incidental and consequential damages provided in this Article (Section 2–715), but less expenses saved in consequence of the seller's breach.

(2) Market price is to be determined as of the place for tender or, in cases of rejection after arrival or revocation of acceptance, as of the place of arrival.

§ 2–714. Buyer's Damages for Breach in Regard to Accepted Goods.

(1) Where the buyer has accepted goods and given notification (subsection (3) of Section 2–607) he may recover as damages for any non-conformity of tender the loss resulting in the ordinary course of events from the seller's breach as determined in any manner which is reasonable.

(2) The measure of damages for breach of warranty is the difference at the time and place of acceptance between the value of the goods accepted and the value they would have had if they had been as warranted, unless special circumstances show proximate damages of a different amount.

(3) In a proper case any incidental and consequential damages under the next section may also be recovered.

§ 2–715. Buyer's Incidental and Consequential Damages.

(1) Incidental damages resulting from the seller's breach include expenses reasonably incurred in inspection, receipt, transportation and care and custody of goods rightfully rejected, any commercially reasonable charges, expenses or commissions in connection with effecting cover and any other reasonable expense incident to the delay or other breach.

(2) Consequential damages resulting from the seller's breach include

(a) any loss resulting from general or particular requirements and needs of which the seller at the time of contracting had reason to know and which could not reasonably be prevented by cover or otherwise; and

(b) injury to person or property proximately resulting from any breach of warranty.

§ 2–716. Buyer's Right to Specific Performance or Replevin.

(1) Specific performance may be decreed where the goods are unique or in other proper circumstances.

(2) The decree for specific performance may include such terms and conditions as to payment of the price, damages, or other relief as the court may deem just.

(3) The buyer has a right of replevin for goods identified to the contract if after reasonable effort he is unable to effect cover for such goods or the circumstances reasonably indicate that such effort will be unavailing or if the goods have been shipped under reservation and satisfaction of the security interest in them has been made or tendered.

§ 2–717. Deduction of Damages from the Price. The buyer on notifying the seller of his intention to do so may deduct all or any part of the damages resulting from any breach of the contract from any part of the price still due under the same contract.

§ 2–718. Liquidation or Limitation of Damages; Deposits.

(1) Damages for breach by either party may be liquidated in the agreement but only at an amount which is reasonable in the light of the anticipated or actual harm caused by the breach, the difficulties of proof of loss, and the inconvenience or nonfeasibility of otherwise obtaining an adequate remedy. A term fixing unreasonably large liquidated damages is void as a penalty.

(2) Where the seller justifiably withholds delivery of goods because of the buyer's breach, the buyer is entitled to restitution of any amount by which the sum of his payments exceeds

(a) the amount to which the seller is entitled by virtue of terms liquidating the seller's damages in accordance with subsection (1), or

(b) in the absence of such terms, twenty per cent of the value of the total performance for which the buyer is obligated under the contract or $500, whichever is smaller.

(3) The buyer's right to restitution under subsection (2) is subject to offset to the extent that the seller establishes

    (a) a right to recover damages under the provisions of this Article other than subsection (1), and

    (b) the amount or value of any benefits received by the buyer directly or indirectly by reason of the contract.

(4) Where a seller has received payment in goods their reasonable value or the proceeds of their resale shall be treated as payments for the purposes of subsection (2); but if the seller has notice of the buyer's breach before reselling goods received in part performance, his resale is subject to the conditions laid down in this Article on resale by an aggrieved seller (Section 2–706).

§ 2–719. Contractual Modification or Limitation of Remedy.

(1) Subject to the provisions of subsections (2) and (3) of this section and of the preceding section on liquidation and limitation of damages,

    (a) the agreement may provide for remedies in addition to or in substitution for those provided in this Article and may limit or alter the measure of damages recoverable under this Article, as by limiting the buyer's remedies to return of the goods and repayment of the price or to repair and replacement of non-conforming goods or parts; and

    (b) resort to a remedy as provided is optional unless the remedy is expressly agreed to be exclusive, in which case it is the sole remedy.

(2) Where circumstances cause an exclusive or limited remedy to fail of its essential purpose, remedy may be had as provided in this Act.

(3) Consequential damages may be limited or excluded unless the limitation or exclusion is unconscionable. Limitation of consequential damages for injury to the person in the case of consumer goods is prima facie unconscionable but limitation of damages where the loss is commercial is not.

§ 2–720. Effect of "Cancellation" or "Rescission" on Claims for Antecedent Breach.

Unless the contrary intention clearly appears, expressions of "cancellation" or "rescission" of the contract or the like shall not be construed as a renunciation or discharge of any claim in damages for an antecedent breach.

§ 2–721. Remedies for Fraud.

Remedies for material misrepresentation or fraud include all remedies available under this Article for non-fraudulent breach. Neither rescission or a claim for rescission of the contract for sale nor rejection or return of the goods shall bar or be deemed inconsistent with a claim for damages or other remedy.

§ 2–722. Who Can Sue Third Parties for Injury to Goods.

Where a third party so deals with goods which have been identified to a contract for sale as to cause actionable injury to a party to that contract

    (a) a right of action against the third party is in either party to the contract for sale who has title to or a security interest or a special property or an insurable interest in the goods; and if the goods have been destroyed or converted a right of action is also in the party who either bore the risk of loss under the contract for sale or has since the injury assumed that risk as against the other;

    (b) if at the time of the injury the party plaintiff did not bear the risk of loss as against the other party to the contract for sale and there is no arrangement between them for disposition of the recovery, his suit or settlement is, subject to his own interest, as a fiduciary for the other party to the contract;

    (c) either party may with the consent of the other sue for the benefit of whom it may concern.

§ 2–723. Proof of Market Price: Time and Place.

(1) If an action based on anticipatory repudiation comes to trial before the time for performance with respect to some or all of the goods, any damages based on market price (Section 2–708 or Section 2–713) shall be determined according to the price of such goods prevailing at the time when the aggrieved party learned of the repudiation.

(2) If evidence of a price prevailing at the times or places described in this Article is not readily available the price prevailing within any reasonable time before or after the time described or at any other place which in commercial judgment or under usage of trade would serve as a reasonable substitute for the one described may be used, making any proper allowance for the cost of transporting the goods to or from such other place.

(3) Evidence of a relevant price prevailing at a time or place other than the one described in this Article offered by one party is not admissible unless and until he has given the other party such notice as the court finds sufficient to prevent unfair surprise.

§ 2–724. Admissibility of Market Quotations. Whenever the prevailing price or value of any goods regularly bought and sold in any established commodity market is in issue, reports in official publications or trade journals or in newspapers or periodicals of general circulation published as the reports of such market shall be admissible in evidence. The circumstances of the preparation of such a report may be shown to affect its weight but not its admissibility.

§ 2–725. Statute of Limitations in Contracts for Sale.

(1) An action for breach of any contract for sale must be commenced within four years after the cause of action has accrued. By the original agreement the parties may reduce the period of limitation to not less than one year but may not extend it.

(2) A cause of action accrues when the breach occurs, regardless of the aggrieved party's lack of knowledge of the breach. A breach of warranty occurs when tender of delivery is made, except that where a warranty explicitly extends to future performance of the goods and discovery of the breach must await the time of such performance the cause of action accrues when the breach is or should have been discovered.

(3) Where an action commenced within the time limited by subsection (1) is so terminated as to leave available a remedy by another action for the same breach such other action may be commenced after the expiration of the time limited and within six months after the termination of the first action unless the termination resulted from voluntary discontinuance or from dismissal for failure or neglect to prosecute.

(4) This section does not alter the law on tolling of the statute of limitations nor does it apply to causes of action which have accrued before this Act becomes effective.

Article 2A: Leases

Part 1: General Provisions

§ 2A–101. Short Title. This Article shall be known and may be cited as the Uniform Commercial Code—Leases.

See Appendix VI [following Amendment 24 therein] for material relating to changes in the Official Com-

ment to conform to the 1990 amendments to various sections of Article 2A.

§ 2A–102. Scope. This Article applies to any transaction, regardless of form, that creates a lease.

§ 2A–103. Definitions and Index of Definitions.

(1) In this Article unless the context otherwise requires:

(a) "Buyer in ordinary course of business" means a person who in good faith and without knowledge that the sale to him [or her] is in violation of the ownership rights or security interest or leasehold interest of a third party in the goods buys in ordinary course from a person in the business of selling goods of that kind but does not include a pawnbroker. "Buying" may be for cash or by exchange of other property or on secured or unsecured credit and includes receiving goods or documents of title under a preexisting contract for sale but does not include a transfer in bulk or as security for or in total or partial satisfaction of a money debt.

(b) "Cancellation" occurs when either party puts an end to the lease contract for default by the other party.

(c) "Commercial unit" means such a unit of goods as by commercial usage is a single whole for purposes of lease and division of which materially impairs its character or value on the market or in use. A commercial unit may be a single article, as a machine, or a set of articles, as a suite of furniture or a line of machinery, or a quantity, as a gross or carload, or any other unit treated in use or in the relevant market as a single whole.

(d) "Conforming" goods or performance under a lease contract means goods or performance that are in accordance with the obligations under the lease contract.

(e) "Consumer lease" means a lease that a lessor regularly engaged in the business of leasing or selling makes to a lessee who is an individual and who takes under the lease primarily for a personal, family, or household purpose[, if the total payments to be made under the lease contract, excluding payments for options to renew or buy, do not exceed $_____].

(f) "Fault" means wrongful act, omission, breach, or default.

(g) "Finance lease" means a lease with respect to which:

    (i) the lessor does not select, manufacture, or supply the goods;

(ii) the lessor acquires the goods or the right to possession and use of the goods in connection with the lease; and

(iii) one of the following occurs:

(A) the lessee receives a copy of the contract by which the lessor acquired the goods or the right to possession and use of the goods before signing the lease contract;

(B) the lessee's approval of the contract by which the lessor acquired the goods or the right to possession and use of the goods is a condition to effectiveness of the lease contract;

(C) the lessee, before signing the lease contract, receives an accurate and complete statement designating the promises and warranties, and any disclaimers of warranties, limitations or modifications of remedies, or liquidated damages, including those of a third party, such as the manufacturer of the goods, provided to the lessor by the person supplying the goods in connection with or as part of the contract by which the lessor acquired the goods or the right to possession and use of the goods; or

(D) if the lease is not a consumer lease, the lessor, before the lessee signs the lease contract, informs the lessee in writing (a) of the identity of the person supplying the goods to the lessor, unless the lessee has selected that person and directed the lessor to acquire the goods or the right to possession and use of the goods from that person, (b) that the lessee is entitled under this Article to the promises and warranties, including those of any third party, provided to the lessor by the person supplying the goods in connection with or as part of the contract by which the lessor acquired the goods or the right to possession and use of the goods, and (c) that the lessee may communicate with the person supplying the goods to the lessor and receive an accurate and complete statement of those promises and warranties, including any disclaimers and limitations of them or of remedies.

(h) "Goods" means all things that are movable at the time of identification to the lease contract, or are fixtures (Section 2A–309), but the term does not include money, documents, instruments, accounts, chattel paper, general intangibles, or minerals or the like, including oil and gas, before extraction. The term also includes the unborn young of animals.

(i) "Installment lease contract" means a lease contract that authorizes or requires the delivery of goods in separate lots to be separately accepted, even though the lease contract contains a clause "each delivery is a separate lease" or its equivalent.

(j) "Lease" means a transfer of the right to possession and use of goods for a term in return for consideration, but a sale, including a sale on approval or a sale or return, or retention or creation of a security interest is not a lease. Unless the context clearly indicates otherwise, the term includes a sublease.

(k) "Lease agreement" means the bargain, with respect to the lease, of the lessor and the lessee in fact as found in their language or by implication from other circumstances including course of dealing or usage of trade or course of performance as provided in this Article. Unless the context clearly indicates otherwise, the term includes a sublease agreement.

(l) "Lease contract" means the total legal obligation that results from the lease agreement as affected by this Article and any other applicable rules of law. Unless the context clearly indicates otherwise, the term includes a sublease contract.

(m) "Leasehold interest" means the interest of the lessor or the lessee under a lease contract.

(n) "Lessee" means a person who acquires the right to possession and use of goods under a lease. Unless the context clearly indicates otherwise, the term includes a sublessee.

(o) "Lessee in ordinary course of business" means a person who in good faith and without knowledge that the lease to him [or her] is in violation of the ownership rights or security interest or leasehold interest of a third party in the goods, leases in ordinary course from a person in the business of selling or leasing goods of that kind but does not include a pawnbroker. "Leasing" may be for cash or by exchange of other property or on secured or unsecured credit and includes receiving goods or documents of title under a preexisting lease contract but does not include a transfer in bulk or as security for or in total or partial satisfaction of a money debt.

(p) "Lessor" means a person who transfers the right to possession and use of goods under a lease. Unless the context clearly indicates otherwise, the term includes a sublessor.

(q) "Lessor's residual interest" means the lessor's interest in the goods after expiration, termination, or cancellation of the lease contract.

(r) "Lien" means a charge against or interest in goods to secure payment of a debt or performance of an obligation, but the term does not include a security interest.

(s) "Lot" means a parcel or a single article that is the subject matter of a separate lease or delivery, whether or not it is sufficient to perform the lease contract.

(t) "Merchant lessee" means a lessee that is a merchant with respect to goods of the kind subject to the lease.

(u) "Present value" means the amount as of a date certain of one or more sums payable in the future, discounted to the date certain. The discount is determined by the interest rate specified by the parties if the rate was not manifestly unreasonable at the time the transaction was entered into; otherwise, the discount is determined by a commercially reasonable rate that takes into account the facts and circumstances of each case at the time the transaction was entered into.

(v) "Purchase" includes taking by sale, lease, mortgage, security interest, pledge, gift, or any other voluntary transaction creating an interest in goods.

(w) "Sublease" means a lease of goods the right to possession and use of which was acquired by the lessor as a lessee under an existing lease.

(x) "Supplier" means a person from whom a lessor buys or leases goods to be leased under a finance lease.

(y) "Supply contract" means a contract under which a lessor buys or leases goods to be leased.

(z) "Termination" occurs when either party pursuant to a power created by agreement or law puts an end to the lease contract otherwise than for default.

(2) Other definitions applying to this Article and the sections in which they appear are:

"Accessions"	Section 2A–310(1).
"Construction mortgage"	Section 2A–309(1) (d).
"Encumbrance"	Section 2A–309(1) (e).
"Fixtures"	Section 2A–309(1) (a).
"Fixture filing"	Section 2A–309(1) (b).
"Purchase money lease"	Section 2A–309(1) (c).

(3) The following definitions in other Articles apply to this Article:

"Account"	Section 9–106.
"Between merchants"	Section 2–104(3).
"Buyer"	Section 2–103(1) (a).
"Chattel paper"	Section 9–105(1) (b).
"Consumer goods"	Section 9–109(1).
"Document"	Section 9–105(1) (f).
"Entrusting"	Section 2–403(3).
"General intangibles"	Section 9–106.
"Good faith"	Section 2–103(1) (b).
"Instrument"	Section 9–105(1) (i).
"Merchant"	Section 2–104(1).
"Mortgage"	Section 9–105(1) (j).
"Pursuant to commitment"	Section 9–105(1) (k).
"Receipt"	Section 2–103(1) (c).
"Sale"	Section 2–106(1).
"Sale on approval"	Section 2–326.
"Sale or return"	Section 2–326.
"Seller"	Section 2–103(1) (d).

(4) In addition Article 1 contains general definitions and principles of construction and interpretation applicable throughout this Article.

As amended in 1990.

§ 2A–104. Leases Subject to Other Law.

(1) A lease, although subject to this Article, is also subject to any applicable:

(a) certificate of title statute of this State: (list any certificate of title statutes covering automobiles, trailers, mobile homes, boats, farm tractors, and the like);

(b) certificate of title statute of another jurisdiction (Section 2A–105); or

(c) consumer protection statute of this State, or final consumer protection decision of a court of this State existing on the effective date of this Article.

(2) In case of conflict between this Article, other than Sections 2A–105, 2A–304(3), and 2A–305(3), and a statute or decision referred to in subsection (1), the statute or decision controls.

(3) Failure to comply with an applicable law has only the effect specified therein.

As amended in 1990.

§ 2A–105. Territorial Application of Article to Goods Covered by Certificate of Title.

Subject to the provisions of Sections 2A–304(3) and 2A–305(3), with respect to goods covered by a certificate of title issued under a statute of this State or of another jurisdiction, compliance and the effect of compliance or noncompliance with a certificate of title statute are governed by the law (including the conflict of laws rules) of the jurisdiction issuing the certificate until the earlier of (a) surrender of the certificate, or (b) four months after the goods are removed from that jurisdiction and thereafter until a new certificate of title is issued by another jurisdiction.

§ 2A–106. Limitation on Power of Parties to Consumer Lease to Choose Applicable Law and Judicial Forum.

(1) If the law chosen by the parties to a consumer lease is that of a jurisdiction other than a jurisdiction in which the lessee resides at the time the lease agreement becomes enforceable or within 30 days thereafter or in which the goods are to be used, the choice is not enforceable.

(2) If the judicial forum chosen by the parties to a consumer lease is a forum that would not otherwise have jurisdiction over the lessee, the choice is not enforceable.

§ 2A–107. Waiver or Renunciation of Claim or Right After Default.

Any claim or right arising out of an alleged default or breach of warranty may be discharged in whole or in part without consideration by a written waiver or renunciation signed and delivered by the aggrieved party.

§ 2A–108. Unconscionability.

(1) If the court as a matter of law finds a lease contract or any clause of a lease contract to have been unconscionable at the time it was made the court may refuse to enforce the lease contract, or it may enforce the remainder of the lease contract without the unconscionable clause, or it may so limit the application of any unconscionable clause as to avoid any unconscionable result.

(2) With respect to a consumer lease, if the court as a matter of law finds that a lease contract or any clause of

a lease contract has been induced by unconscionable conduct or that unconscionable conduct has occurred in the collection of a claim arising from a lease contract, the court may grant appropriate relief.

(3) Before making a finding of unconscionability under subsection (1) or (2), the court, on its own motion or that of a party, shall afford the parties a reasonable opportunity to present evidence as to the setting, purpose, and effect of the lease contract or clause thereof, or of the conduct.

(4) In an action in which the lessee claims unconscionability with respect to a consumer lease:

   (a) If the court finds unconscionability under subsection (1) or (2), the court shall award reasonable attorney's fees to the lessee.

   (b) If the court does not find unconscionability and the lessee claiming unconscionability has brought or maintained an action he [or she] knew to be groundless, the court shall award reasonable attorney's fees to the party against whom the claim is made.

   (c) In determining attorney's fees, the amount of the recovery on behalf of the claimant under subsections (1) and (2) is not controlling.

§ 2A–109. Option to Accelerate at Will.

(1) A term providing that one party or his [or her] successor in interest may accelerate payment or performance or require collateral or additional collateral "at will" or "when he [or she] deems himself [or herself] insecure" or in words of similar import must be construed to mean that he [or she] has power to do so only if he [or she] in good faith believes that the prospect of payment or performance is impaired.

(2) With respect to a consumer lease, the burden of establishing good faith under subsection (1) is on the party who exercised the power; otherwise the burden of establishing lack of good faith is on the party against whom the power has been exercised.

Part 2: Formation and Construction of Lease Contract

§ 2A–201. Statute of Frauds.

(1) A lease contract is not enforceable by way of action or defense unless:

   (a) the total payments to be made under the lease contract, excluding payments for options to renew or buy, are less than $1,000; or

   (b) there is a writing, signed by the party against whom enforcement is sought or by that party's authorized agent, sufficient to indicate that a lease contract has been made between the parties and to describe the goods leased and the lease term.

(2) Any description of leased goods or of the lease term is sufficient and satisfies subsection (1) (b), whether or not it is specific, if it reasonably identifies what is described.

(3) A writing is not insufficient because it omits or incorrectly states a term agreed upon, but the lease contract is not enforceable under subsection (1) (b) beyond the lease term and the quantity of goods shown in the writing.

(4) A lease contract that does not satisfy the requirements of subsection (1), but which is valid in other respects, is enforceable:

(a) if the goods are to be specially manufactured or obtained for the lessee and are not suitable for lease or sale to others in the ordinary course of the lessor's business, and the lessor, before notice of repudiation is received and under circumstances that reasonably indicate that the goods are for the lessee, has made either a substantial beginning of their manufacture or commitments for their procurement;

(b) if the party against whom enforcement is sought admits in that party's pleading, testimony or otherwise in court that a lease contract was made, but the lease contract is not enforceable under this provision beyond the quantity of goods admitted; or

(c) with respect to goods that have been received and accepted by the lessee.

(5) The lease term under a lease contract referred to in subsection (4) is:

(a) if there is a writing signed by the party against whom enforcement is sought or by that party's authorized agent specifying the lease term, the term so specified;

(b) if the party against whom enforcement is sought admits in that party's pleading, testimony, or otherwise in court a lease term, the term so admitted; or

(c) a reasonable lease term.

§ 2A–202. Final Written Expression: Parol or Extrinsic Evidence. Terms with respect to which the confirmatory memoranda of the parties agree or which are otherwise set forth in a writing intended by the parties as a final expression of their agreement with respect to such terms as are included therein may not be contradicted by evidence of any prior agreement or of a contemporaneous oral agreement but may be explained or supplemented:

(a) by course of dealing or usage of trade or by course of performance; and

(b) by evidence of consistent additional terms unless the court finds the writing to have been intended also as a complete and exclusive statement of the terms of the agreement.

§ 2A–203. Seals Inoperative. The affixing of a seal to a writing evidencing a lease contract or an offer to enter into a lease contract does not render the writing a sealed instrument and the law with respect to sealed instruments does not apply to the lease contract or offer.

§ 2A–204. Formation in General.

(1) A lease contract may be made in any manner sufficient to show agreement, including conduct by both parties which recognizes the existence of a lease contract.

(2) An agreement sufficient to constitute a lease contract may be found although the moment of its making is undetermined.

(3) Although one or more terms are left open, a lease contract does not fail for indefiniteness if the parties have intended to make a lease contract and there is a reasonably certain basis for giving an appropriate remedy.

§ 2A–205. Firm Offers. An offer by a merchant to lease goods to or from another person in a signed writing that by its terms gives assurance it will be held open is not revocable, for lack of consideration, during the time stated or, if no time is stated, for a reasonable time, but in no event may the period of irrevocability exceed 3 months. Any such term of assurance on a form supplied by the offeree must be separately signed by the offeror.

§ 2A–206. Offer and Acceptance in Formation of Lease Contract.

(1) Unless otherwise unambiguously indicated by the language or circumstances, an offer to make a lease contract must be construed as inviting acceptance in any manner and by any medium reasonable in the circumstances.

(2) If the beginning of a requested performance is a reasonable mode of acceptance, an offeror who is not notified of acceptance within a reasonable time may treat the offer as having lapsed before acceptance.

§ 2A–207. Course of Performance or Practical Construction.

(1) If a lease contract involves repeated occasions for performance by either party with knowledge of the nature of the performance and opportunity for objection to it by the other, any course of performance accepted or acquiesced in without objection is relevant to determine the meaning of the lease agreement.

(2) The express terms of a lease agreement and any course of performance, as well as any course of dealing and usage of trade, must be construed whenever reasonable as consistent with each other; but if that construction is unreasonable, express terms control course of performance, course of performance controls both course of dealing and usage of trade, and course of dealing controls usage of trade.

(3) Subject to the provisions of Section 2A–208 on modification and waiver, course of performance is relevant to show a waiver or modification of any term inconsistent with the course of performance.

§ 2A–208. Modification, Rescission and Waiver.

(1) An agreement modifying a lease contract needs no consideration to be binding.

(2) A signed lease agreement that excludes modification or rescission except by a signed writing may not be otherwise modified or rescinded, but, except as between merchants, such a requirement on a form supplied by a merchant must be separately signed by the other party.

(3) Although an attempt at modification or rescission does not satisfy the requirements of subsection (2), it may operate as a waiver.

(4) A party who has made a waiver affecting an executory portion of a lease contract may retract the waiver by reasonable notification received by the other party that strict performance will be required of any term waived, unless the retraction would be unjust in view of a material change of position in reliance on the waiver.

§ 2A–209. Lessee Under Finance Lease as Beneficiary of Supply Contract.

(1) The benefit of a supplier's promises to the lessor under the supply contract and of all warranties, whether express or implied, including those of any third party provided in connection with or as part of the supply contract, extends to the lessee to the extent of the lessee's leasehold interest under a finance lease related to the supply contract, but is subject to the terms of the warranty and of the supply contract and all defenses or claims arising therefrom.

(2) The extension of the benefit of a supplier's promises and of warranties to the lessee (Section 2A–209(1)) does not: (i) modify the rights and obligations of the parties to the supply contract, whether arising therefrom or otherwise, or (ii) impose any duty or liability under the supply contract on the lessee.

(3) Any modification or rescission of the supply contract by the supplier and the lessor is effective between the supplier and the lessee unless, before the modification or rescission, the supplier has received notice that the lessee has entered into a finance lease related to the supply contract. If the modification or rescission is effective between the supplier and the lessee, the lessor is deemed to have assumed, in addition to the obligations of the lessor to the lessee under the lease contract, promises of the supplier to the lessor and warranties that were so modified or rescinded as they existed and were available to the lessee before modification or rescission.

(4) In addition to the extension of the benefit of the supplier's promises and of warranties to the lessee under subsection (1), the lessee retains all rights that the lessee may have against the supplier which arise from an agreement between the lessee and the supplier or under other law.

As amended in 1990.

§ 2A–210. Express Warranties.

(1) Express warranties by the lessor are created as follows:

   (a) Any affirmation of fact or promise made by the lessor to the lessee which relates to the goods and becomes part of the basis of the bargain creates an express warranty that the goods will conform to the affirmation or promise.

   (b) Any description of the goods which is made part of the basis of the bargain creates an express warranty that the goods will conform to the description.

   (c) Any sample or model that is made part of the basis of the bargain creates an express warranty that the whole of the goods will conform to the sample or model.

(2) It is not necessary to the creation of an express warranty that the lessor use formal words, such as "warrant" or "guarantee," or that the lessor have a specific intention to make a warranty, but an affirmation merely of the value of the goods or a statement purporting to

be merely the lessor's opinion or commendation of the goods does not create a warranty.

§ 2A–211. Warranties Against Interference and Against Infringement; Lessee's Obligation Against Infringement.

(1) There is in a lease contract a warranty that for the lease term no person holds a claim to or interest in the goods that arose from an act or omission of the lessor, other than a claim by way of infringement or the like, which will interfere with the lessee's enjoyment of its leasehold interest.

(2) Except in a finance lease there is in a lease contract by a lessor who is a merchant regularly dealing in goods of the kind a warranty that the goods are delivered free of the rightful claim of any person by way of infringement or the like.

(3) A lessee who furnishes specifications to a lessor or a supplier shall hold the lessor and the supplier harmless against any claim by way of infringement or the like that arises out of compliance with the specifications.

§ 2A–212. Implied Warranty of Merchantability.

(1) Except in a finance lease, a warranty that the goods will be merchantable is implied in a lease contract if the lessor is a merchant with respect to goods of that kind.

(2) Goods to be merchantable must be at least such as

    (a) pass without objection in the trade under the description in the lease agreement;

    (b) in the case of fungible goods, are of fair average quality within the description;

    (c) are fit for the ordinary purposes for which goods of that type are used;

    (d) run, within the variation permitted by the lease agreement, of even kind, quality, and quantity within each unit and among all units involved;

    (e) are adequately contained, packaged, and labeled as the lease agreement may require; and

    (f) conform to any promises or affirmations of fact made on the container or label.

(3) Other implied warranties may arise from course of dealing or usage of trade.

§ 2A–213. Implied Warranty of Fitness for Particular Purpose.

Except in a finance lease, if the lessor at the time the lease contract is made has reason to know of any particular purpose for which the goods are required and that the lessee is relying on the lessor's skill or judgment to select or furnish suitable goods, there is in the lease contract an implied warranty that the goods will be fit for that purpose.

§ 2A–214. Exclusion or Modification of Warranties.

(1) Words or conduct relevant to the creation of an express warranty and words or conduct tending to negate or limit a warranty must be construed wherever reasonable as consistent with each other; but, subject to the provisions of Section 2A–202 on parol or extrinsic evidence, negation or limitation is inoperative to the extent that the construction is unreasonable.

(2) Subject to subsection (3), to exclude or modify the implied warranty of merchantability or any part of it the language must mention "merchantability", be by a writing, and be conspicuous. Subject to subsection (3), to exclude or modify any implied warranty of fitness the exclusion must be by a writing and be conspicuous. Language to exclude all implied warranties of fitness is sufficient if it is in writing, is conspicuous and states, for example, "There is no warranty that the goods will be fit for a particular purpose".

(3) Notwithstanding subsection (2), but subject to subsection (4),

    (a) unless the circumstances indicate otherwise, all implied warranties are excluded by expressions like "as is," or "with all faults," or by other language that in common understanding calls the lessee's attention to the exclusion of warranties and makes plain that there is no implied warranty, if in writing and conspicuous;

    (b) if the lessee before entering into the lease contract has examined the goods or the sample or model as fully as desired or has refused to examine the goods, there is no implied warranty with regard to defects that an examination ought in the circumstances to have revealed; and

    (c) an implied warranty may also be excluded or modified by course of dealing, course of performance, or usage of trade.

(4) To exclude or modify a warranty against interference or against infringement (Section 2A–211) or any part of it, the language must be specific, be by a writing, and be conspicuous, unless the circumstances, including course of performance, course of dealing, or usage of trade, give the lessee reason to know that the goods are being leased subject to a claim or interest of any person.

§ 2A–215. Cumulation and Conflict of Warranties Express or Implied.

Warranties, whether express or

implied, must be construed as consistent with each other and as cumulative, but if that construction is unreasonable, the intention of the parties determines which warranty is dominant. In ascertaining that intention the following rules apply:

(a) Exact or technical specifications displace an inconsistent sample or model or general language of description.

(b) A sample from an existing bulk displaces inconsistent general language of description.

(c) Express warranties displace inconsistent implied warranties other than an implied warranty of fitness for a particular purpose.

§ 2A–216. ThirdParty Beneficiaries of Express and Implied Warranties.

Alternative A

A warranty to or for the benefit of a lessee under this Article, whether express or implied, extends to any natural person who is in the family or household of the lessee or who is a guest in the lessee's home if it is reasonable to expect that such person may use, consume, or be affected by the goods and who is injured in person by breach of the warranty. This section does not displace principles of law and equity that extend a warranty to or for the benefit of a lessee to other persons. The operation of this section may not be excluded, modified, or limited, but an exclusion, modification, or limitation of the warranty, including any with respect to rights and remedies, effective against the lessee is also effective against any beneficiary designated under this section.

Alternative B

A warranty to or for the benefit of a lessee under this Article, whether express or implied, extends to any natural person who may reasonably be expected to use, consume, or be affected by the goods and who is injured in person by breach of the warranty. This section does not displace principles of law and equity that extend a warranty to or for the benefit of a lessee to other persons. The operation of this section may not be excluded, modified, or limited, but an exclusion, modification, or limitation of the warranty, including any with respect to rights and remedies, effective against the lessee is also effective against the beneficiary designated under this section.

Alternative C

A warranty to or for the benefit of a lessee under this Article, whether express or implied, extends to any person who may reasonably be expected to use, consume, or be affected by the goods and who is injured by breach of the warranty. The operation of this section may not be excluded, modified, or limited with respect to injury to the person of an individual to whom the warranty extends, but an exclusion, modification, or limitation of the warranty, including any with respect to rights and remedies, effective against the lessee is also effective against the beneficiary designated under this section.

§ 2A–217. Identification.
Identification of goods as goods to which a lease contract refers may be made at any time and in any manner explicitly agreed to by the parties. In the absence of explicit agreement, identification occurs:

(a) when the lease contract is made if the lease contract is for a lease of goods that are existing and identified;

(b) when the goods are shipped, marked, or otherwise designated by the lessor as goods to which the lease contract refers, if the lease contract is for a lease of goods that are not existing and identified; or

(c) when the young are conceived, if the lease contract is for a lease of unborn young of animals.

§ 2A–218. Insurance and Proceeds.

(1) A lessee obtains an insurable interest when existing goods are identified to the lease contract even though the goods identified are nonconforming and the lessee has an option to reject them.

(2) If a lessee has an insurable interest only by reason of the lessor's identification of the goods, the lessor, until default or insolvency or notification to the lessee that identification is final, may substitute other goods for those identified.

(3) Notwithstanding a lessee's insurable interest under subsections (1) and (2), the lessor retains an insurable interest until an option to buy has been exercised by the lessee and risk of loss has passed to the lessee.

(4) Nothing in this section impairs any insurable interest recognized under any other statute or rule of law.

(5) The parties by agreement may determine that one or more parties have an obligation to obtain and pay for insurance covering the goods and by agreement may determine the beneficiary of the proceeds of the insurance.

§ 2A–219. Risk of Loss.

(1) Except in the case of a finance lease, risk of loss is retained by the lessor and does not pass to the lessee. In the case of a finance lease, risk of loss passes to the lessee.

(2) Subject to the provisions of this Article on the effect of default on risk of loss (Section 2A–220), if risk of loss is to pass to the lessee and the time of passage is not stated, the following rules apply:

(a) If the lease contract requires or authorizes the goods to be shipped by carrier
  (i) and it does not require delivery at a particular destination, the risk of loss passes to the lessee when the goods are duly delivered to the carrier; but
  (ii) if it does require delivery at a particular destination and the goods are there duly tendered while in the possession of the carrier, the risk of loss passes to the lessee when the goods are there duly so tendered as to enable the lessee to take delivery.

(b) If the goods are held by a bailee to be delivered without being moved, the risk of loss passes to the lessee on acknowledgment by the bailee of the lessee's right to possession of the goods.

(c) In any case not within subsection (a) or (b), the risk of loss passes to the lessee on the lessee's receipt of the goods if the lessor, or, in the case of a finance lease, the supplier, is a merchant; otherwise the risk passes to the lessee on tender of delivery.

§ 2A–220. Effect of Default on Risk of Loss.

(1) Where risk of loss is to pass to the lessee and the time of passage is not stated:

(a) If a tender or delivery of goods so fails to conform to the lease contract as to give a right of rejection, the risk of their loss remains with the lessor, or, in the case of a finance lease, the supplier, until cure or acceptance.

(b) If the lessee rightfully revokes acceptance, he [or she], to the extent of any deficiency in his [or her] effective insurance coverage, may treat the risk of loss as having remained with the lessor from the beginning.

(2) Whether or not risk of loss is to pass to the lessee, if the lessee as to conforming goods already identified to a lease contract repudiates or is otherwise in default under the lease contract, the lessor, or, in the case of a finance lease, the supplier, to the extent of any deficiency in his [or her] effective insurance coverage may treat the risk of loss as resting on the lessee for a commercially reasonable time.

§ 2A–221. Casualty to Identified Goods. If a lease contract requires goods identified when the lease contract is made, and the goods suffer casualty without fault of the lessee, the lessor or the supplier before delivery, or the goods suffer casualty before risk of loss passes to the lessee pursuant to the lease agreement or Section 2A–219, then:

(a) if the loss is total, the lease contract is avoided; and

(b) if the loss is partial or the goods have so deteriorated as to no longer conform to the lease contract, the lessee may nevertheless demand inspection and at his [or her] option either treat the lease contract as avoided or, except in a finance lease that is not a consumer lease, accept the goods with due allowance from the rent payable for the balance of the lease term for the deterioration or the deficiency in quantity but without further right against the lessor.

Part 3: Effect of Lease Contract

§ 2A–301. Enforceability of Lease Contract. Except as otherwise provided in this Article, a lease contract is effective and enforceable according to its terms between the parties, against purchasers of the goods and against creditors of the parties.

§ 2A–302. Title to and Possession of Goods. Except as otherwise provided in this Article, each provision of this Article applies whether the lessor or a third party has title to the goods, and whether the lessor, the lessee, or a third party has possession of the goods, notwithstanding any statute or rule of law that possession or the absence of possession is fraudulent.

§ 2A–303. Alienability of Party's Interest Under Lease Contract or of Lessor's Residual Interest in Goods; Delegation of Performance; Transfer of Rights.

(1) As used in this section, "creation of a security interest" includes the sale of a lease contract that is subject to Article 9, Secured Transactions, by reason of Section 9–102(1) (b).

(2) Except as provided in subsections (3) and (4), a provision in a lease agreement which (i) prohibits the voluntary or involuntary transfer, including a transfer by sale, sublease, creation or enforcement of a security interest, or attachment, levy, or other judicial process, of an interest of a party under the lease contract or of the lessor's residual interest in the goods, or (ii) makes such a transfer an event of default, gives rise to the rights and remedies provided in subsection (5), but a transfer that is prohibited or is an event of default under the lease agreement is otherwise effective.

(3) A provision in a lease agreement which (i) prohibits the creation or enforcement of a security interest in an interest of a party under the lease contract or in the lessor's residual interest in the goods, or (ii) makes such a transfer an event of default, is not enforceable unless, and then only to the extent that, there is an actual transfer by the lessee of the lessee's right of possession or use of the goods in violation of the provision or an actual delegation of a material performance of either party to the lease contract in violation of the provision. Neither the granting nor the enforcement of a security interest in (i) the lessor's interest under the lease contract or (ii) the lessor's residual interest in the goods is a transfer that materially impairs the prospect of obtaining return performance by, materially changes the duty of, or materially increases the burden or risk imposed on, the lessee within the purview of subsection (5) unless, and then only to the extent that, there is an actual delegation of a material performance of the lessor.

(4) A provision in a lease agreement which (i) prohibits a transfer of a right to damages for default with respect to the whole lease contract or of a right to payment arising out of the transferor's due performance of the transferor's entire obligation, or (ii) makes such a transfer an event of default, is not enforceable, and such a transfer is not a transfer that materially impairs the prospect of obtaining return performance by, materially changes the duty of, or materially increases the burden or risk imposed on, the other party to the lease contract within the purview of subsection (5).

(5) Subject to subsections (3) and (4):

(a) if a transfer is made which is made an event of default under a lease agreement, the party to the lease contract not making the transfer, unless that party waives the default or otherwise agrees, has the rights and remedies described in Section 2A–501(2);

(b) if paragraph (a) is not applicable and if a transfer is made that (i) is prohibited under a lease agreement or (ii) materially impairs the prospect of obtaining return performance by, materially changes the duty of, or materially increases the burden or risk imposed on, the other party to the lease contract, unless the party not making the transfer agrees at any time to the transfer in the lease contract or otherwise, then, except

as limited by contract, (i) the transferor is liable to the party not making the transfer for damages caused by the transfer to the extent that the damages could not reasonably be prevented by the party not making the transfer and (ii) a court having jurisdiction may grant other appropriate relief, including cancellation of the lease contract or an injunction against the transfer.

(6) A transfer of "the lease" or of "all my rights under the lease", or a transfer in similar general terms, is a transfer of rights and, unless the language or the circumstances, as in a transfer for security, indicate the contrary, the transfer is a delegation of duties by the transferor to the transferee. Acceptance by the transferee constitutes a promise by the transferee to perform those duties. The promise is enforceable by either the transferor or the other party to the lease contract.

(7) Unless otherwise agreed by the lessor and the lessee, a delegation of performance does not relieve the transferor as against the other party of any duty to perform or of any liability for default.

(8) In a consumer lease, to prohibit the transfer of an interest of a party under the lease contract or to make a transfer an event of default, the language must be specific, by a writing, and conspicuous.

As amended in 1990.

§ 2A–304. Subsequent Lease of Goods by Lessor.

(1) Subject to Section 2A–303, a subsequent lessee from a lessor of goods under an existing lease contract obtains, to the extent of the leasehold interest transferred, the leasehold interest in the goods that the lessor had or had power to transfer, and except as provided in subsection (2) and Section 2A–527(4), takes subject to the existing lease contract. A lessor with voidable title has power to transfer a good leasehold interest to a good faith subsequent lessee for value, but only to the extent set forth in the preceding sentence. If goods have been delivered under a transaction of purchase, the lessor has that power even though:

(a) the lessor's transferor was deceived as to the identity of the lessor;

(b) the delivery was in exchange for a check which is later dishonored;

(c) it was agreed that the transaction was to be a "cash sale"; or

(d) the delivery was procured through fraud punishable as larcenous under the criminal law.

(2) A subsequent lessee in the ordinary course of business from a lessor who is a merchant dealing in goods of that kind to whom the goods were entrusted by the existing lessee of that lessor before the interest of the subsequent lessee became enforceable against that lessor obtains, to the extent of the leasehold interest transferred, all of that lessor's and the existing lessee's rights to the goods, and takes free of the existing lease contract.

(3) A subsequent lessee from the lessor of goods that are subject to an existing lease contract and are covered by a certificate of title issued under a statute of this State or of another jurisdiction takes no greater rights than those provided both by this section and by the certificate of title statute.

As amended in 1990.

§ 2A–305. Sale or Sublease of Goods by Lessee.

(1) Subject to the provisions of Section 2A–303, a buyer or sublessee from the lessee of goods under an existing lease contract obtains, to the extent of the interest transferred, the leasehold interest in the goods that the lessee had or had power to transfer, and except as provided in subsection (2) and Section 2A–511(4), takes subject to the existing lease contract. A lessee with a voidable leasehold interest has power to transfer a good leasehold interest to a good faith buyer for value or a good faith sublessee for value, but only to the extent set forth in the preceding sentence. When goods have been delivered under a transaction of lease the lessee has that power even though:

  (a) the lessor was deceived as to the identity of the lessee;

  (b) the delivery was in exchange for a check which is later dishonored; or

  (c) the delivery was procured through fraud punishable as larcenous under the criminal law.

(2) A buyer in the ordinary course of business or a sublessee in the ordinary course of business from a lessee who is a merchant dealing in goods of that kind to whom the goods were entrusted by the lessor obtains, to the extent of the interest transferred, all of the lessor's and lessee's rights to the goods, and takes free of the existing lease contract.

(3) A buyer or sublessee from the lessee of goods that are subject to an existing lease contract and are covered by a certificate of title issued under a statute of this State or of another jurisdiction takes no greater rights than those provided both by this section and by the certificate of title statute.

§ 2A–306. Priority of Certain Liens Arising by Operation of Law.

If a person in the ordinary course of his [or her] business furnishes services or materials with respect to goods subject to a lease contract, a lien upon those goods in the possession of that person given by statute or rule of law for those materials or services takes priority over any interest of the lessor or lessee under the lease contract or this Article unless the lien is created by statute and the statute provides otherwise or unless the lien is created by rule of law and the rule of law provides otherwise.

§ 2A–307. Priority of Liens Arising by Attachment or Levy on, Security Interests in, and Other Claims to Goods.

(1) Except as otherwise provided in Section 2A–306, a creditor of a lessee takes subject to the lease contract.

(2) Except as otherwise provided in subsections (3) and (4) and in Sections 2A–306 and 2A–308, a creditor of a lessor takes subject to the lease contract unless:

  (a) the creditor holds a lien that attached to the goods before the lease contract became enforceable;

  (b) the creditor holds a security interest in the goods and the lessee did not give value and receive delivery of the goods without knowledge of the security interest; or

  (c) the creditor holds a security interest in the goods which was perfected (Section 9–303) before the lease contract became enforceable.

(3) A lessee in the ordinary course of business takes the leasehold interest free of a security interest in the goods created by the lessor even though the security interest is perfected (Section 9–303) and the lessee knows of its existence.

(4) A lessee other than a lessee in the ordinary course of business takes the leasehold interest free of a security interest to the extent that it secures future advances made after the secured party acquires knowledge of the lease or more than 45 days after the lease contract becomes enforceable, whichever first occurs, unless the future advances are made pursuant to a commitment entered into without knowledge of the lease and before the expiration of the 45-day period.

As amended in 1990.

§ 2A–308. Special Rights of Creditors.

(1) A creditor of a lessor in possession of goods subject to a lease contract may treat the lease contract as void if as against the creditor retention of possession by the lessor is fraudulent under any statute or rule of law, but retention of possession in good faith and current course of trade by the lessor for a commercially reasonable time after the lease contract becomes enforceable is not fraudulent.

(2) Nothing in this Article impairs the rights of creditors of a lessor if the lease contract (a) becomes enforceable, not in current course of trade but in satisfaction of or as security for a preexisting claim for money, security, or the like, and (b) is made under circumstances which under any statute or rule of law apart from this Article would constitute the transaction a fraudulent transfer or voidable preference.

(3) A creditor of a seller may treat a sale or an identification of goods to a contract for sale as void if as against the creditor retention of possession by the seller is fraudulent under any statute or rule of law, but retention of possession of the goods pursuant to a lease contract entered into by the seller as lessee and the buyer as lessor in connection with the sale or identification of the goods is not fraudulent if the buyer bought for value and in good faith.

§ 2A–309. Lessor's and Lessee's Rights When Goods Become Fixtures.

(1) In this section:

(a) goods are "fixtures" when they become so related to particular real estate that an interest in them arises under real estate law;

(b) a "fixture filing" is the filing, in the office where a mortgage on the real estate would be filed or recorded, of a financing statement covering goods that are or are to become fixtures and conforming to the requirements of Section 9–402(5);

(c) a lease is a "purchase money lease" unless the lessee has possession or use of the goods or the right to possession or use of the goods before the lease agreement is enforceable;

(d) a mortgage is a "construction mortgage" to the extent it secures an obligation incurred for the construction of an improvement on land including the acquisition cost of the land, if the recorded writing so indicates; and

(e) "encumbrance" includes real estate mortgages and other liens on real estate and all other rights in real estate that are not ownership interests.

(2) Under this Article a lease may be of goods that are fixtures or may continue in goods that become fixtures, but no lease exists under this Article of ordinary building materials incorporated into an improvement on land.

(3) This Article does not prevent creation of a lease of fixtures pursuant to real estate law.

(4) The perfected interest of a lessor of fixtures has priority over a conflicting interest of an encumbrancer or owner of the real estate if:

(a) the lease is a purchase money lease, the conflicting interest of the encumbrancer or owner arises before the goods become fixtures, the interest of the lessor is perfected by a fixture filing before the goods become fixtures or within ten days thereafter, and the lessee has an interest of record in the real estate or is in possession of the real estate; or

(b) the interest of the lessor is perfected by a fixture filing before the interest of the encumbrancer or owner is of record, the lessor's interest has priority over any conflicting interest of a predecessor in title of the encumbrancer or owner, and the lessee has an interest of record in the real estate or is in possession of the real estate.

(5) The interest of a lessor of fixtures, whether or not perfected, has priority over the conflicting interest of an encumbrancer or owner of the real estate if:

(a) the fixtures are readily removable factory or office machines, readily removable equipment that is not primarily used or leased for use in the operation of the real estate, or readily removable replacements of domestic appliances that are goods subject to a consumer lease, and before the goods become fixtures the lease contract is enforceable; or

(b) the conflicting interest is a lien on the real estate obtained by legal or equitable proceedings after the lease contract is enforceable; or

(c) the encumbrancer or owner has consented in writing to the lease or has disclaimed an interest in the goods as fixtures; or

(d) the lessee has a right to remove the goods as against the encumbrancer or owner. If the lessee's right to remove terminates, the priority of the interest of the lessor continues for a reasonable time.

(6) Notwithstanding subsection (4)(a) but otherwise subject to subsections (4) and (5), the interest of a lessor of fixtures, including the lessor's residual interest, is subordinate to the conflicting interest of an encumbrancer of the real estate under a construction mortgage recorded before the goods become fixtures if the goods become fixtures before the completion of the construction. To the extent given to refinance a construction mortgage, the conflicting interest of an encumbrancer of the real estate under a mortgage has this priority to the same extent as the encumbrancer of the real estate under the construction mortgage.

(7) In cases not within the preceding subsections, priority between the interest of a lessor of fixtures, including the lessor's residual interest, and the conflicting interest of an encumbrancer or owner of the real estate who is not the lessee is determined by the priority rules governing conflicting interests in real estate.

(8) If the interest of a lessor of fixtures, including the lessor's residual interest, has priority over all conflicting interests of all owners and encumbrancers of the real estate, the lessor or the lessee may (i) on default, expiration, termination, or cancellation of the lease agreement but subject to the agreement and this Article, or (ii) if necessary to enforce other rights and remedies of the lessor or lessee under this Article, remove the goods from the real estate, free and clear of all conflicting interests of all owners and encumbrancers of the real estate, but the lessor or lessee must reimburse any encumbrancer or owner of the real estate who is not the lessee and who has not otherwise agreed for the cost of repair of any physical injury, but not for any diminution in value of the real estate caused by the absence of the goods removed or by any necessity of replacing them. A person entitled to reimbursement may refuse permission to remove until the party seeking removal gives adequate security for the performance of this obligation.

(9) Even though the lease agreement does not create a security interest, the interest of a lessor of fixtures, including the lessor's residual interest, is perfected by filing a financing statement as a fixture filing for leased goods that are or are to become fixtures in accordance with the relevant provisions of the Article on Secured Transactions (Article 9).

As amended in 1990.

§ 2A–310. Lessor's and Lessee's Rights When Goods Become Accessions.

(1) Goods are "accessions" when they are installed in or affixed to other goods.

(2) The interest of a lessor or a lessee under a lease contract entered into before the goods became accessions is superior to all interests in the whole except as stated in subsection (4).

(3) The interest of a lessor or a lessee under a lease contract entered into at the time or after the goods became accessions is superior to all subsequently

acquired interests in the whole except as stated in subsection (4) but is subordinate to interests in the whole existing at the time the lease contract was made unless the holders of such interests in the whole have in writing consented to the lease or disclaimed an interest in the goods as part of the whole.

(4) The interest of a lessor or a lessee under a lease contract described in subsection (2) or (3) is subordinate to the interest of

(a) a buyer in the ordinary course of business or a lessee in the ordinary course of business of any interest in the whole acquired after the goods became accessions; or

(b) a creditor with a security interest in the whole perfected before the lease contract was made to the extent that the creditor makes subsequent advances without knowledge of the lease contract.

(5) When under subsections (2) or (3) and (4) a lessor or a lessee of accessions holds an interest that is superior to all interests in the whole, the lessor or the lessee may (a) on default, expiration, termination, or cancellation of the lease contract by the other party but subject to the provisions of the lease contract and this Article, or (b) if necessary to enforce his [or her] other rights and remedies under this Article, remove the goods from the whole, free and clear of all interests in the whole, but he [or she] must reimburse any holder of an interest in the whole who is not the lessee and who has not otherwise agreed for the cost of repair of any physical injury but not for any diminution in value of the whole caused by the absence of the goods removed or by any necessity for replacing them. A person entitled to reimbursement may refuse permission to remove until the party seeking removal gives adequate security for the performance of this obligation.

§ 2A–311. Priority Subject to Subordination. Nothing in this Article prevents subordination by agreement by any person entitled to priority.

As added in 1990.

Part 4: Performance of Lease Contract: Repudiated, Substituted and Excused

§ 2A–401. Insecurity: Adequate Assurance of Performance.

(1) A lease contract imposes an obligation on each party that the other's expectation of receiving due performance will not be impaired.

(2) If reasonable grounds for insecurity arise with respect to the performance of either party, the insecure party may demand in writing adequate assurance of due performance. Until the insecure party receives that assurance, if commercially reasonable the insecure party may suspend any performance for which he [or she] has not already received the agreed return.

(3) A repudiation of the lease contract occurs if assurance of due performance adequate under the circumstances of the particular case is not provided to the insecure party within a reasonable time, not to exceed 30 days after receipt of a demand by the other party.

(4) Between merchants, the reasonableness of grounds for insecurity and the adequacy of any assurance offered must be determined according to commercial standards.

(5) Acceptance of any nonconforming delivery or payment does not prejudice the aggrieved party's right to demand adequate assurance of future performance.

§ 2A–402. Anticipatory Repudiation. If either party repudiates a lease contract with respect to a performance not yet due under the lease contract, the loss of which performance will substantially impair the value of the lease contract to the other, the aggrieved party may:

(a) for a commercially reasonable time, await retraction of repudiation and performance by the repudiating party;

(b) make demand pursuant to Section 2A–401 and await assurance of future performance adequate under the circumstances of the particular case; or

(c) resort to any right or remedy upon default under the lease contract or this Article, even though the aggrieved party has notified the repudiating party that the aggrieved party would await the repudiating party's performance and assurance and has urged retraction. In addition, whether or not the aggrieved party is pursuing one of the foregoing remedies, the aggrieved party may suspend performance or, if the aggrieved party is the lessor, proceed in accordance with the provisions of this Article on the lessor's right to identify goods to the lease contract notwithstanding default or to salvage unfinished goods (Section 2A–524).

§ 2A–403. Retraction of Anticipatory Repudiation.

(1) Until the repudiating party's next performance is due, the repudiating party can retract the repudiation unless, since the repudiation, the aggrieved party has cancelled the lease contract or materially changed the aggrieved party's position or otherwise indicated that the aggrieved party considers the repudiation final.

(2) Retraction may be by any method that clearly indicates to the aggrieved party that the repudiating party intends to perform under the lease contract and includes any assurance demanded under Section 2A–401.

(3) Retraction reinstates a repudiating party's rights under a lease contract with due excuse and allowance to the aggrieved party for any delay occasioned by the repudiation.

§ 2A–404. Substituted Performance.

(1) If without fault of the lessee, the lessor and the supplier, the agreed berthing, loading, or unloading facilities fail or the agreed type of carrier becomes unavailable or the agreed manner of delivery otherwise becomes commercially impracticable, but a commercially reasonable substitute is available, the substitute performance must be tendered and accepted.

(2) If the agreed means or manner of payment fails because of domestic or foreign governmental regulation:

(a) the lessor may withhold or stop delivery or cause the supplier to withhold or stop delivery unless the lessee provides a means or manner of payment that is commercially a substantial equivalent; and

(b) if delivery has already been taken, payment by the means or in the manner provided by the regulation discharges the lessee's obligation unless the regulation is discriminatory, oppressive, or predatory.

§ 2A–405. Excused Performance. Subject to Section 2A–404 on substituted performance, the following rules apply:

(a) Delay in delivery or nondelivery in whole or in part by a lessor or a supplier who complies with paragraphs (b) and (c) is not a default under the lease contract if performance as agreed has been made impracticable by the occurrence of a contingency the nonoccurrence of which was a basic assumption on which the lease contract was made or by compliance in good faith with any applicable foreign or domestic governmental regulation or order, whether or not the regulation or order later proves to be invalid.

(b) If the causes mentioned in paragraph (a) affect only part of the lessor's or the supplier's capacity to perform, he [or she] shall allocate production and deliveries among his [or her] customers but at his [or her] option may include regular customers not then under contract for sale or lease as well as his [or her] own requirements for further manufacture. He [or she] may so allocate in any manner that is fair and reasonable.

(c) The lessor seasonably shall notify the lessee and in the case of a finance lease the supplier seasonably shall notify the lessor and the lessee, if known, that there will be delay or nondelivery and, if allocation is required under paragraph (b), of the estimated quota thus made available for the lessee.

§ 2A–406. Procedure on Excused Performance.

(1) If the lessee receives notification of a material or indefinite delay or an allocation justified under Section 2A–405, the lessee may by written notification to the lessor as to any goods involved, and with respect to all of the goods if under an installment lease contract the value of the whole lease contract is substantially impaired (Section 2A–510):

(a) terminate the lease contract (Section 2A–505(2)); or

(b) except in a finance lease that is not a consumer lease, modify the lease contract by accepting the available quota in substitution, with due allowance from the rent payable for the balance of the lease term for the deficiency but without further right against the lessor.

(2) If, after receipt of a notification from the lessor under Section 2A–405, the lessee fails so to modify the lease agreement within a reasonable time not exceeding 30 days, the lease contract lapses with respect to any deliveries affected.

§ 2A–407. Irrevocable Promises: Finance Leases.

(1) In the case of a finance lease that is not a consumer lease the lessee's promises under the lease contract become irrevocable and independent upon the lessee's acceptance of the goods.

(2) A promise that has become irrevocable and independent under subsection (1):

(a) is effective and enforceable between the parties, and by or against third parties including assignees of the parties; and

(b) is not subject to cancellation, termination, modification, repudiation, excuse, or substitution without the consent of the party to whom the promise runs.

(3) This section does not affect the validity under any other law of a covenant in any lease contract making the lessee's promises irrevocable and independent upon the lessee's acceptance of the goods.

As amended in 1990.

Part 5: Default

§ 2A–501. Default: Procedure.

(1) Whether the lessor or the lessee is in default under a lease contract is determined by the lease agreement and this Article.

(2) If the lessor or the lessee is in default under the lease contract, the party seeking enforcement has rights and remedies as provided in this Article and, except as limited by this Article, as provided in the lease agreement.

(3) If the lessor or the lessee is in default under the lease contract, the party seeking enforcement may reduce the party's claim to judgment, or otherwise enforce the lease contract by self-help or any available judicial procedure or nonjudicial procedure, including administrative proceeding, arbitration, or the like, in accordance with this Article.

(4) Except as otherwise provided in Section 1–106(1) or this Article or the lease agreement, the rights and remedies referred to in subsections (2) and (3) are cumulative.

(5) If the lease agreement covers both real property and goods, the party seeking enforcement may proceed under this Part as to the goods, or under other applicable law as to both the real property and the goods in accordance with that party's rights and remedies in respect of the real property, in which case this Part does not apply.

As amended in 1990.

§ 2A–502. Notice After Default. Except as otherwise provided in this Article or the lease agreement, the lessor or lessee in default under the lease contract is not entitled to notice of default or notice of enforcement from the other party to the lease agreement.

§ 2A–503. Modification or Impairment of Rights and Remedies.

(1) Except as otherwise provided in this Article, the lease agreement may include rights and remedies for default in addition to or in substitution for those provided in this Article and may limit or alter the measure of damages recoverable under this Article.

(2) Resort to a remedy provided under this Article or in the lease agreement is optional unless the remedy is expressly agreed to be exclusive. If circumstances cause an exclusive or limited remedy to fail of its essential purpose, or provision for an exclusive remedy is unconscionable, remedy may be had as provided in this Article.

(3) Consequential damages may be liquidated under Section 2A–504, or may otherwise be limited, altered, or excluded unless the limitation, alteration, or exclusion is unconscionable. Limitation, alteration, or exclusion of consequential damages for injury to the person in the case of consumer goods is prima facie unconscionable but limitation, alteration, or exclusion of damages where the loss is commercial is not prima facie unconscionable.

(4) Rights and remedies on default by the lessor or the lessee with respect to any obligation or promise collateral or ancillary to the lease contract are not impaired by this Article.

As amended in 1990.

§ 2A–504. Liquidation of Damages.

(1) Damages payable by either party for default, or any other act or omission, including indemnity for loss or diminution of anticipated tax benefits or loss or damage to lessor's residual interest, may be liquidated in the lease agreement but only at an amount or by a formula that is reasonable in light of the then anticipated harm caused by the default or other act or omission.

(2) If the lease agreement provides for liquidation of damages, and such provision does not comply with subsection (1), or such provision is an exclusive or limited remedy that circumstances cause to fail of its essential purpose, remedy may be had as provided in this Article.

(3) If the lessor justifiably withholds or stops delivery of goods because of the lessee's default or insolvency (Section 2A–525 or 2A–526), the lessee is entitled to restitution of any amount by which the sum of his [or her] payments exceeds:

(a) the amount to which the lessor is entitled by virtue of terms liquidating the lessor's damages in accordance with subsection (1); or

(b) in the absence of those terms, 20 percent of the then present value of the total rent the lessee was obligated to pay for the balance of the lease term, or, in the case of a consumer lease, the lesser of such amount or $500.

(4) A lessee's right to restitution under subsection (3) is subject to offset to the extent the lessor establishes:

(a) a right to recover damages under the provisions of this Article other than subsection (1); and

(b) the amount or value of any benefits received by the lessee directly or indirectly by reason of the lease contract.

§ 2A–505. Cancellation and Termination and Effect of Cancellation, Termination, Rescission, or Fraud on Rights and Remedies.

(1) On cancellation of the lease contract, all obligations that are still executory on both sides are discharged, but any right based on prior default or performance survives, and the cancelling party also retains any remedy for default of the whole lease contract or any unperformed balance.

(2) On termination of the lease contract, all obligations that are still executory on both sides are discharged but any right based on prior default or performance survives.

(3) Unless the contrary intention clearly appears, expressions of "cancellation," "rescission," or the like of the lease contract may not be construed as a renunciation or discharge of any claim in damages for an antecedent default.

(4) Rights and remedies for material misrepresentation or fraud include all rights and remedies available under this Article for default.

(5) Neither rescission nor a claim for rescission of the lease contract nor rejection or return of the goods may bar or be deemed inconsistent with a claim for damages or other right or remedy.

§ 2A–506. Statute of Limitations.

(1) An action for default under a lease contract, including breach of warranty or indemnity, must be commenced within 4 years after the cause of action accrued. By the original lease contract the parties may reduce the period of limitation to not less than one year.

(2) A cause of action for default accrues when the act or omission on which the default or breach of warranty is based is or should have been discovered by the aggrieved party, or when the default occurs, whichever is later. A cause of action for indemnity accrues when the act or omission on which the claim for indemnity is based is or should have been discovered by the indemnified party, whichever is later.

(3) If an action commenced within the time limited by subsection (1) is so terminated as to leave available a remedy by another action for the same default or breach of warranty or indemnity, the other action may be commenced after the expiration of the time limited and within 6 months after the termination of the first action unless the termination resulted from voluntary discontinuance or from dismissal for failure or neglect to prosecute.

(4) This section does not alter the law on tolling of the statute of limitations nor does it apply to causes of action that have accrued before this Article becomes effective.

§ 2A–507. Proof of Market Rent: Time and Place.

(1) Damages based on market rent (Section 2A–519 or 2A–528) are determined according to the rent for the use of the goods concerned for a lease term identical to the remaining lease term of the original lease agreement and prevailing at the times specified in Sections 2A–519 and 2A–528.

(2) If evidence of rent for the use of the goods concerned for a lease term identical to the remaining lease term of the original lease agreement and prevailing at the times or places described in this Article is not readily available, the rent prevailing within any reasonable time before or after the time described or at any other place or for a different lease term which in commercial judgment or under usage of trade would serve as a reasonable substitute for the one described may be used, making any proper allowance for the difference, including the cost of transporting the goods to or from the other place.

(3) Evidence of a relevant rent prevailing at a time or place or for a lease term other than the one described in this Article offered by one party is not admissible unless and until he [or she] has given the other party notice the court finds sufficient to prevent unfair surprise.

(4) If the prevailing rent or value of any goods regularly leased in any established market is in issue, reports in official publications or trade journals or in newspapers or periodicals of general circulation published as the reports of that market are admissible in evidence. The circumstances of the preparation of the report may be shown to affect its weight but not its admissibility.

As amended in 1990.

§ 2A–508. Lessee's Remedies.

(1) If a lessor fails to deliver the goods in conformity to the lease contract (Section 2A–509) or repudiates the lease contract (Section 2A–402), or a lessee rightfully rejects the goods (Section 2A–509) or justifiably revokes acceptance of the goods (Section 2A–517), then with respect to any goods involved, and with respect to all of the goods if under an installment lease contract the value of the whole lease contract is substantially impaired (Section 2A–510), the lessor is in default under the lease contract and the lessee may:

  (a) cancel the lease contract (Section 2A–505(1));

  (b) recover so much of the rent and security as has been paid and is just under the circumstances;

  (c) cover and recover damages as to all goods affected whether or not they have been identified to the lease contract (Sections 2A–518 and 2A–520), or recover damages for nondelivery (Sections 2A–519 and 2A–520);

  (d) exercise any other rights or pursue any other remedies provided in the lease contract.

(2) If a lessor fails to deliver the goods in conformity to the lease contract or repudiates the lease contract, the lessee may also:

  (a) if the goods have been identified, recover them (Section 2A–522); or

  (b) in a proper case, obtain specific performance or replevy the goods (Section 2A–521).

(3) If a lessor is otherwise in default under a lease contract, the lessee may exercise the rights and pursue the remedies provided in the lease contract, which may include a right to cancel the lease, and in Section 2A–519(3).

(4) If a lessor has breached a warranty, whether express or implied, the lessee may recover damages (Section 2A–519(4)).

(5) On rightful rejection or justifiable revocation of acceptance, a lessee has a security interest in goods in the lessee's possession or control for any rent and security that has been paid and any expenses reasonably incurred in their inspection, receipt, transportation, and care and custody and may hold those goods and dispose of them in good faith and in a commercially reasonable manner, subject to Section 2A–527(5).

(6) Subject to the provisions of Section 2A–407, a lessee, on notifying the lessor of the lessee's intention to do so, may deduct all or any part of the damages resulting from any default under the lease contract from any part of the rent still due under the same lease contract.

As amended in 1990.

§ 2A–509. Lessee's Rights on Improper Delivery; Rightful Rejection.

(1) Subject to the provisions of Section 2A–510 on default in installment lease contracts, if the goods or the tender or delivery fail in any respect to conform to the lease contract, the lessee may reject or accept the goods or accept any commercial unit or units and reject the rest of the goods.

(2) Rejection of goods is ineffective unless it is within a reasonable time after tender or delivery of the goods and the lessee seasonably notifies the lessor.

§ 2A–510. Installment Lease Contracts: Rejection and Default.

(1) Under an installment lease contract a lessee may reject any delivery that is nonconforming if the nonconformity substantially impairs the value of that delivery and cannot be cured or the nonconformity is a defect in the required documents; but if the nonconformity does not fall within subsection (2) and the lessor or the supplier gives adequate assurance of its cure, the lessee must accept that delivery.

(2) Whenever nonconformity or default with respect to one or more deliveries substantially impairs the value of the installment lease contract as a whole there is a default with respect to the whole. But, the aggrieved party reinstates the installment lease contract as a whole if the aggrieved party accepts a nonconforming delivery without seasonably notifying of cancellation or brings an action with respect only to past deliveries or demands performance as to future deliveries.

§ 2A–511. Merchant Lessee's Duties as to Rightfully Rejected Goods.

(1) Subject to any security interest of a lessee (Section 2A–508(5)), if a lessor or a supplier has no agent or place of business at the market of rejection, a merchant lessee, after rejection of goods in his [or her] possession or control, shall follow any reasonable instructions received from the lessor or the supplier with respect to the goods. In the absence of those instructions, a merchant lessee shall make reasonable efforts to sell, lease, or otherwise dispose of the goods for the lessor's account if they threaten to decline in value speedily. Instructions are not reasonable if on demand indemnity for expenses is not forthcoming.

(2) If a merchant lessee (subsection (1)) or any other lessee (Section 2A–512) disposes of goods, he [or she]

is entitled to reimbursement either from the lessor or the supplier or out of the proceeds for reasonable expenses of caring for and disposing of the goods and, if the expenses include no disposition commission, to such commission as is usual in the trade, or if there is none, to a reasonable sum not exceeding 10 percent of the gross proceeds.

(3) In complying with this section or Section 2A–512, the lessee is held only to good faith. Good faith conduct hereunder is neither acceptance or conversion nor the basis of an action for damages.

(4) A purchaser who purchases in good faith from a lessee pursuant to this section or Section 2A–512 takes the goods free of any rights of the lessor and the supplier even though the lessee fails to comply with one or more of the requirements of this Article.

§ 2A–512. Lessee's Duties as to Rightfully Rejected Goods.

(1) Except as otherwise provided with respect to goods that threaten to decline in value speedily (Section 2A–511) and subject to any security interest of a lessee (Section 2A–508(5)):

(a) the lessee, after rejection of goods in the lessee's possession, shall hold them with reasonable care at the lessor's or the supplier's disposition for a reasonable time after the lessee's seasonable notification of rejection;

(b) if the lessor or the supplier gives no instructions within a reasonable time after notification of rejection, the lessee may store the rejected goods for the lessor's or the supplier's account or ship them to the lessor or the supplier or dispose of them for the lessor's or the supplier's account with reimbursement in the manner provided in Section 2A–511; but

(c) the lessee has no further obligations with regard to goods rightfully rejected.

(2) Action by the lessee pursuant to subsection (1) is not acceptance or conversion.

§ 2A–513. Cure by Lessor of Improper Tender or Delivery; Replacement.

(1) If any tender or delivery by the lessor or the supplier is rejected because nonconforming and the time for performance has not yet expired, the lessor or the supplier may seasonably notify the lessee of the lessor's or the supplier's intention to cure and may then make a conforming delivery within the time provided in the lease contract.

(2) If the lessee rejects a nonconforming tender that the lessor or the supplier had reasonable grounds to believe would be acceptable with or without money allowance, the lessor or the supplier may have a further reasonable time to substitute a conforming tender if he [or she] seasonably notifies the lessee.

§ 2A–514. Waiver of Lessee's Objections.

(1) In rejecting goods, a lessee's failure to state a particular defect that is ascertainable by reasonable inspection precludes the lessee from relying on the defect to justify rejection or to establish default:

   (a) if, stated seasonably, the lessor or the supplier could have cured it (Section 2A–513); or

   (b) between merchants if the lessor or the supplier after rejection has made a request in writing for a full and final written statement of all defects on which the lessee proposes to rely.

(2) A lessee's failure to reserve rights when paying rent or other consideration against documents precludes recovery of the payment for defects apparent on the face of the documents.

§ 2A–515. Acceptance of Goods.

(1) Acceptance of goods occurs after the lessee has had a reasonable opportunity to inspect the goods and

   (a) the lessee signifies or acts with respect to the goods in a manner that signifies to the lessor or the supplier that the goods are conforming or that the lessee will take or retain them in spite of their nonconformity; or

   (b) the lessee fails to make an effective rejection of the goods (Section 2A–509(2)).

(2) Acceptance of a part of any commercial unit is acceptance of that entire unit.

§ 2A–516. Effect of Acceptance of Goods; Notice of Default; Burden of Establishing Default After Acceptance; Notice of Claim or Litigation to Person Answerable Over.

(1) A lessee must pay rent for any goods accepted in accordance with the lease contract, with due allowance for goods rightfully rejected or not delivered.

(2) A lessee's acceptance of goods precludes rejection of the goods accepted. In the case of a finance lease, if made with knowledge of a nonconformity, acceptance cannot be revoked because of it. In any other case, if made with knowledge of a nonconformity, acceptance cannot be revoked because of it unless the acceptance was on the reasonable assumption that the nonconformity would be seasonably cured. Acceptance does not of itself impair any other remedy provided by this Article or the lease agreement for nonconformity.

(3) If a tender has been accepted:

   (a) within a reasonable time after the lessee discovers or should have discovered any default, the lessee shall notify the lessor and the supplier, if any, or be barred from any remedy against the party not notified;

   (b) except in the case of a consumer lease, within a reasonable time after the lessee receives notice of litigation for infringement or the like (Section 2A–211) the lessee shall notify the lessor or be barred from any remedy over for liability established by the litigation; and

   (c) the burden is on the lessee to establish any default.

(4) If a lessee is sued for breach of a warranty or other obligation for which a lessor or a supplier is answerable over the following apply:

   (a) The lessee may give the lessor or the supplier, or both, written notice of the litigation. If the notice states that the person notified may come in and defend and that if the person notified does not do so that person will be bound in any action against that person by the lessee by any determination of fact common to the two litigations, then unless the person notified after seasonable receipt of the notice does come in and defend that person is so bound.

   (b) The lessor or the supplier may demand in writing that the lessee turn over control of the litigation including settlement if the claim is one for infringement or the like (Section 2A–211) or else be barred from any remedy over. If the demand states that the lessor or the supplier agrees to bear all expense and to satisfy any adverse judgment, then unless the lessee after seasonable receipt of the demand does turn over control the lessee is so barred.

(5) Subsections (3) and (4) apply to any obligation of a lessee to hold the lessor or the supplier harmless against infringement or the like (Section 2A–211).

As amended in 1990.

§ 2A–517. Revocation of Acceptance of Goods.

(1) A lessee may revoke acceptance of a lot or commercial unit whose nonconformity substantially impairs its value to the lessee if the lessee has accepted it:

(a) except in the case of a finance lease, on the reasonable assumption that its nonconformity would be cured and it has not been seasonably cured; or

(b) without discovery of the nonconformity if the lessee's acceptance was reasonably induced either by the lessor's assurances or, except in the case of a finance lease, by the difficulty of discovery before acceptance.

(2) Except in the case of a finance lease that is not a consumer lease, a lessee may revoke acceptance of a lot or commercial unit if the lessor defaults under the lease contract and the default substantially impairs the value of that lot or commercial unit to the lessee.

(3) If the lease agreement so provides, the lessee may revoke acceptance of a lot or commercial unit because of other defaults by the lessor.

(4) Revocation of acceptance must occur within a reasonable time after the lessee discovers or should have discovered the ground for it and before any substantial change in condition of the goods which is not caused by the nonconformity. Revocation is not effective until the lessee notifies the lessor.

(5) A lessee who so revokes has the same rights and duties with regard to the goods involved as if the lessee had rejected them.

As amended in 1990.

§ 2A–518. Cover; Substitute Goods.

(1) After a default by a lessor under the lease contract of the type described in Section 2A–508(1) , or, if agreed, after other default by the lessor, the lessee may cover by making any purchase or lease of or contract to purchase or lease goods in substitution for those due from the lessor.

(2) Except as otherwise provided with respect to damages liquidated in the lease agreement (Section 2A–504) or otherwise determined pursuant to agreement of the parties (Sections 1–102(3) and 2A–503), if a lessee's cover is by a lease agreement substantially similar to the original lease agreement and the new lease agreement is made in good faith and in a commercially reasonable manner, the lessee may recover from the lessor as damages (i) the present value, as of the date of the commencement of the term of the new lease agreement, of the rent under the new lease agreement applicable to that period of the new lease term which is comparable to the then remaining term of the original lease agreement minus the present value as of the same date of the total

rent for the then remaining lease term of the original lease agreement, and (ii) any incidental or consequential damages, less expenses saved in consequence of the lessor's default.

(3) If a lessee's cover is by lease agreement that for any reason does not qualify for treatment under subsection (2), or is by purchase or otherwise, the lessee may recover from the lessor as if the lessee had elected not to cover and Section 2A–519 governs.

As amended in 1990.

§ 2A–519. Lessee's Damages for Nondelivery, Repudiation, Default, and Breach of Warranty in Regard to Accepted Goods.

(1) Except as otherwise provided with respect to damages liquidated in the lease agreement (Section 2A–504) or otherwise determined pursuant to agreement of the parties (Sections 1–102(3) and 2A–503), if a lessee elects not to cover or a lessee elects to cover and the cover is by lease agreement that for any reason does not qualify for treatment under Section 2A–518(2), or is by purchase or otherwise, the measure of damages for nondelivery or repudiation by the lessor or for rejection or revocation of acceptance by the lessee is the present value, as of the date of the default, of the then market rent minus the present value as of the same date of the original rent, computed for the remaining lease term of the original lease agreement, together with incidental and consequential damages, less expenses saved in consequence of the lessor's default.

(2) Market rent is to be determined as of the place for tender or, in cases of rejection after arrival or revocation of acceptance, as of the place of arrival.

(3) Except as otherwise agreed, if the lessee has accepted goods and given notification (Section 2A–516(3)), the measure of damages for nonconforming tender or delivery or other default by a lessor is the loss resulting in the ordinary course of events from the lessor's default as determined in any manner that is reasonable together with incidental and consequential damages, less expenses saved in consequence of the lessor's default.

(4) Except as otherwise agreed, the measure of damages for breach of warranty is the present value at the time and place of acceptance of the difference between the value of the use of the goods accepted and the value if they had been as warranted for the lease term, unless special circumstances show proximate damages of a different amount, together with

incidental and consequential damages, less expenses saved in consequence of the lessor's default or breach of warranty.

As amended in 1990.

§ 2A–520. Lessee's Incidental and Consequential Damages.

(1) Incidental damages resulting from a lessor's default include expenses reasonably incurred in inspection, receipt, transportation, and care and custody of goods rightfully rejected or goods the acceptance of which is justifiably revoked, any commercially reasonable charges, expenses or commissions in connection with effecting cover, and any other reasonable expense incident to the default.

(2) Consequential damages resulting from a lessor's default include:

(a) any loss resulting from general or particular requirements and needs of which the lessor at the time of contracting had reason to know and which could not reasonably be prevented by cover or otherwise; and

(b) injury to person or property proximately resulting from any breach of warranty.

§ 2A–521. Lessee's Right to Specific Performance or Replevin.

(1) Specific performance may be decreed if the goods are unique or in other proper circumstances.

(2) A decree for specific performance may include any terms and conditions as to payment of the rent, damages, or other relief that the court deems just.

(3) A lessee has a right of replevin, detinue, sequestration, claim and delivery, or the like for goods identified to the lease contract if after reasonable effort the lessee is unable to effect cover for those goods or the circumstances reasonably indicate that the effort will be unavailing.

§ 2A–522. Lessee's Right to Goods on Lessor's Insolvency.

(1) Subject to subsection (2) and even though the goods have not been shipped, a lessee who has paid a part or all of the rent and security for goods identified to a lease contract (Section 2A–217) on making and keeping good a tender of any unpaid portion of the rent and security due under the lease contract may recover the goods identified from the lessor if the lessor becomes insolvent within 10 days after receipt of the first installment of rent and security.

(2) A lessee acquires the right to recover goods identified to a lease contract only if they conform to the lease contract.

§ 2A–523. Lessor's Remedies.

(1) If a lessee wrongfully rejects or revokes acceptance of goods or fails to make a payment when due or repudiates with respect to a part or the whole, then, with respect to any goods involved, and with respect to all of the goods if under an installment lease contract the value of the whole lease contract is substantially impaired (Section 2A–510), the lessee is in default under the lease contract and the lessor may:

(a) cancel the lease contract (Section 2A–505(1));

(b) proceed respecting goods not identified to the lease contract (Section 2A–524);

(c) withhold delivery of the goods and take possession of goods previously delivered (Section 2A–525);

(d) stop delivery of the goods by any bailee (Section 2A–526);

(e) dispose of the goods and recover damages (Section 2A–527), or retain the goods and recover damages (Section 2A–528), or in a proper case recover rent (Section 2A–529);

(f) exercise any other rights or pursue any other remedies provided in the lease contract.

(2) If a lessor does not fully exercise a right or obtain a remedy to which the lessor is entitled under subsection (1), the lessor may recover the loss resulting in the ordinary course of events from the lessee's default as determined in any reasonable manner, together with incidental damages, less expenses saved in consequence of the lessee's default.

(3) If a lessee is otherwise in default under a lease contract, the lessor may exercise the rights and pursue the remedies provided in the lease contract, which may include a right to cancel the lease. In addition, unless otherwise provided in the lease contract:

(a) if the default substantially impairs the value of the lease contract to the lessor, the lessor may exercise the rights and pursue the remedies provided in subsections (1) or (2); or

(b) if the default does not substantially impair the value of the lease contract to the lessor, the lessor may recover as provided in subsection (2).

As amended in 1990.

§ 2A–524. Lessor's Right to Identify Goods to Lease Contract.

(1) After default by the lessee under the lease contract of the type described in Section 2A–523(1) or 2A–523(3) (a) or, if agreed, after other default by the lessee, the lessor may:

   (a) identify to the lease contract conforming goods not already identified if at the time the lessor learned of the default they were in the lessor's or the supplier's possession or control; and

   (b) dispose of goods (Section 2A–527(1)) that demonstrably have been intended for the particular lease contract even though those goods are unfinished.

(2) If the goods are unfinished, in the exercise of reasonable commercial judgment for the purposes of avoiding loss and of effective realization, an aggrieved lessor or the supplier may either complete manufacture and wholly identify the goods to the lease contract or cease manufacture and lease, sell, or otherwise dispose of the goods for scrap or salvage value or proceed in any other reasonable manner.

As amended in 1990.

§ 2A–525. Lessor's Right to Possession of Goods.

(1) If a lessor discovers the lessee to be insolvent, the lessor may refuse to deliver the goods.

(2) After a default by the lessee under the lease contract of the type described in Section 2A–523(1) or 2A–523(3) (a) or, if agreed, after other default by the lessee, the lessor has the right to take possession of the goods. If the lease contract so provides, the lessor may require the lessee to assemble the goods and make them available to the lessor at a place to be designated by the lessor which is reasonably convenient to both parties. Without removal, the lessor may render unusable any goods employed in trade or business, and may dispose of goods on the lessee's premises (Section 2A–527).

(3) The lessor may proceed under subsection (2) without judicial process if it can be done without breach of the peace or the lessor may proceed by action.

As amended in 1990.

§ 2A–526. Lessor's Stoppage of Delivery in Transit or Otherwise.

(1) A lessor may stop delivery of goods in the possession of a carrier or other bailee if the lessor discovers the lessee to be insolvent and may stop delivery of carload, truckload, planeload, or larger shipments of express or freight if the lessee repudiates or fails to make a payment due before delivery, whether for rent, security or otherwise under the lease contract, or for any other reason the lessor has a right to withhold or take possession of the goods.

(2) In pursuing its remedies under subsection (1), the lessor may stop delivery until

   (a) receipt of the goods by the lessee;

   (b) acknowledgment to the lessee by any bailee of the goods, except a carrier, that the bailee holds the goods for the lessee; or

   (c) such an acknowledgment to the lessee by a carrier via reshipment or as warehouseman.

(3) (a) To stop delivery, a lessor shall so notify as to enable the bailee by reasonable diligence to prevent delivery of the goods.

   (b) After notification, the bailee shall hold and deliver the goods according to the directions of the lessor, but the lessor is liable to the bailee for any ensuing charges or damages.

   (c) A carrier who has issued a nonnegotiable bill of lading is not obliged to obey a notification to stop received from a person other than the consignor.

§ 2A–527. Lessor's Rights to Dispose of Goods.

(1) After a default by a lessee under the lease contract of the type described in Section 2A–523(1) or 2A–523(3) (a) or after the lessor refuses to deliver or takes possession of goods (Section 2A–525 or 2A–526), or, if agreed, after other default by a lessee, the lessor may dispose of the goods concerned or the undelivered balance thereof by lease, sale, or otherwise.

(2) Except as otherwise provided with respect to damages liquidated in the lease agreement (Section 2A–504) or otherwise determined pursuant to agreement of the parties (Sections 1–102(3) and 2A–503), if the disposition is by lease agreement substantially similar to the original lease agreement and the new lease agreement is made in good faith and in a commercially reasonable manner, the lessor may recover from the lessee as damages (i) accrued and unpaid rent as of the date of the commencement of the term of the new lease agreement, (ii) the present value, as of the same date, of the total rent for the then remaining lease term of the original lease agreement minus the present value, as of the same date, of the rent under the new lease agreement applicable to that period

of the new lease term which is comparable to the then remaining term of the original lease agreement, and (iii) any incidental damages allowed under Section 2A–530, less expenses saved in consequence of the lessee's default.

(3) If the lessor's disposition is by lease agreement that for any reason does not qualify for treatment under subsection (2), or is by sale or otherwise, the lessor may recover from the lessee as if the lessor had elected not to dispose of the goods and Section 2A–528 governs.

(4) A subsequent buyer or lessee who buys or leases from the lessor in good faith for value as a result of a disposition under this section takes the goods free of the original lease contract and any rights of the original lessee even though the lessor fails to comply with one or more of the requirements of this Article.

(5) The lessor is not accountable to the lessee for any profit made on any disposition. A lessee who has rightfully rejected or justifiably revoked acceptance shall account to the lessor for any excess over the amount of the lessee's security interest (Section 2A–508(5)).

As amended in 1990.

§ 2A–528. Lessor's Damages for Nonacceptance, Failure to Pay, Repudiation, or Other Default.

(1) Except as otherwise provided with respect to damages liquidated in the lease agreement (Section 2A–504) or otherwise determined pursuant to agreement of the parties (Sections 1–102(3) and 2A–503), if a lessor elects to retain the goods or a lessor elects to dispose of the goods and the disposition is by lease agreement that for any reason does not qualify for treatment under Section 2A–527(2), or is by sale or otherwise, the lessor may recover from the lessee as damages for a default of the type described in Section 2A–523(1) or 2A–523(3) (a), or, if agreed, for other default of the lessee, (i) accrued and unpaid rent as of the date of default if the lessee has never taken possession of the goods, or, if the lessee has taken possession of the goods, as of the date the lessor repossesses the goods or an earlier date on which the lessee makes a tender of the goods to the lessor, (ii) the present value as of the date determined under clause (i) of the total rent for the then remaining lease term of the original lease agreement minus the present value as of the same date of the market rent at the place where the goods are located computed for the same lease term, and (iii) any incidental damages

allowed under Section 2A–530, less expenses saved in consequence of the lessee's default.

(2) If the measure of damages provided in subsection (1) is inadequate to put a lessor in as good a position as performance would have, the measure of damages is the present value of the profit, including reasonable overhead, the lessor would have made from full performance by the lessee, together with any incidental damages allowed under Section 2A–530, due allowance for costs reasonably incurred and due credit for payments or proceeds of disposition.

As amended in 1990.

§ 2A–529. Lessor's Action for the Rent.

(1) After default by the lessee under the lease contract of the type described in Section 2A–523(1) or 2A–523(3) (a) or, if agreed, after other default by the lessee, if the lessor complies with subsection (2), the lessor may recover from the lessee as damages:

    (a) for goods accepted by the lessee and not repossessed by or tendered to the lessor, and for conforming goods lost or damaged within a commercially reasonable time after risk of loss passes to the lessee (Section 2A–219), (i) accrued and unpaid rent as of the date of entry of judgment in favor of the lessor, (ii) the present value as of the same date of the rent for the then remaining lease term of the lease agreement, and (iii) any incidental damages allowed under Section 2A–530, less expenses saved in consequence of the lessee's default; and

    (b) for goods identified to the lease contract if the lessor is unable after reasonable effort to dispose of them at a reasonable price or the circumstances reasonably indicate that effort will be unavailing, (i) accrued and unpaid rent as of the date of entry of judgment in favor of the lessor, (ii) the present value as of the same date of the rent for the then remaining lease term of the lease agreement, and (iii) any incidental damages allowed under Section 2A–530, less expenses saved in consequence of the lessee's default.

(2) Except as provided in subsection (3), the lessor shall hold for the lessee for the remaining lease term of the lease agreement any goods that have been identified to the lease contract and are in the lessor's control.

(3) The lessor may dispose of the goods at any time before collection of the judgment for damages obtained pursuant to subsection (1). If the disposition is before the end of the remaining lease term of the lease agreement, the lessor's recovery against the lessee for damages is governed by Section 2A–527 or Section 2A–528, and the lessor will cause an appropriate credit to be provided against a judgment for damages to the extent that the amount of the judgment exceeds the recovery available pursuant to Section 2A–527 or 2A–528.

(4) Payment of the judgment for damages obtained pursuant to subsection (1) entitles the lessee to the use and possession of the goods not then disposed of for the remaining lease term of and in accordance with the lease agreement.

(5) After default by the lessee under the lease contract of the type described in Section 2A–523(1) or Section 2A–523(3) (a) or, if agreed, after other default by the lessee, a lessor who is held not entitled to rent under this section must nevertheless be awarded damages for nonacceptance under Section 2A–527 or Section 2A–528.

As amended in 1990.

§ 2A–530. Lessor's Incidental Damages. Incidental damages to an aggrieved lessor include any commercially reasonable charges, expenses, or commissions incurred in stopping delivery, in the transportation, care and custody of goods after the lessee's default, in connection with return or disposition of the goods, or otherwise resulting from the default.

§ 2A–531. Standing to Sue Third Parties for Injury to Goods.

(1) If a third party so deals with goods that have been identified to a lease contract as to cause actionable injury to a party to the lease contract (a) the lessor has a right of action against the third party, and (b) the lessee also has a right of action against the third party if the lessee:
    (i)   has a security interest in the goods;
    (ii) has an insurable interest in the goods; or
    (iii) bears the risk of loss under the lease contract or has since the injury assumed that risk as against the lessor and the goods have been converted or destroyed.

(2) If at the time of the injury the party plaintiff did not bear the risk of loss as against the other party to the lease contract and there is no arrangement between them for disposition of the recovery, his [or her] suit or settlement, subject to his [or her] own interest, is as a fiduciary for the other party to the lease contract.

(3) Either party with the consent of the other may sue for the benefit of whom it may concern.

§ 2A–532. Lessor's Rights to Residual Interest. In addition to any other recovery permitted by this Article or other law, the lessor may recover from the lessee an amount that will fully compensate the lessor for any loss of or damage to the lessor's residual interest in the goods caused by the default of the lessee.

As added in 1990.

Article 3–Negotiable Instruments

Part 1: General Provisions and Definitions

§ 3–101. Short Title. This Article may be cited as Uniform Commercial Code—Negotiable Instruments.

§ 3–102. Subject Matter.

(a) This Article applies to negotiable instruments. It does not apply to money, to payment orders governed by Article 4A, or to securities governed by Article 8.

(b) If there is conflict between this Article and Article 4 or 9, Articles 4 and 9 govern.

(c) Regulations of the Board of Governors of the Federal Reserve System and operating circulars of the Federal Reserve Banks supersede any inconsistent provision of this Article to the extent of the inconsistency.

§ 3–103. Definitions.

(a) In this Article:
    (1) "Acceptor" means a drawee who has accepted a draft.
    (2) "Consumer account" means an account established by an individual primarily for personal, family, or household purposes.
    (3) "Consumer transaction" means a transaction in which an individual incurs an obligation primarily for personal, family, or household purposes.
    (4) "Drawee" means a person ordered in a draft to make payment.
    (5) "Drawer" means a person who signs or is identified in a draft as a person ordering payment.
    (6) ["Good faith" means honesty in fact and the observance of reasonable commercial standards of fair dealing.]

(7) "Maker" means a person who signs or is identified in a note as a person undertaking to pay.

(8) "Order" means a written instruction to pay money signed by the person giving the instruction. The instruction may be addressed to any person, including the person giving the instruction, or to one or more persons jointly or in the alternative but not in succession. An authorization to pay is not an order unless the person authorized to pay is also instructed to pay.

(9) "Ordinary care" in the case of a person engaged in business means observance of reasonable commercial standards, prevailing in the area in which the person is located, with respect to the business in which the person is engaged. In the case of a bank that takes an instrument for processing for collection or payment by automated means, reasonable commercial standards do not require the bank to examine the instrument if the failure to examine does not violate the bank's prescribed procedures and the bank's procedures do not vary unreasonably from general banking usage not disapproved by this Article or Article 4.

(10) "Party" means a party to an instrument.

(11) "Principal obligor," with respect to an instrument, means the accommodated party or any other party to the instrument against whom a secondary obligor has recourse under this article.

(12) "Promise" means a written undertaking to pay money signed by the person undertaking to pay. An acknowledgment of an obligation by the obligor is not a promise unless the obligor also undertakes to pay the obligation.

(13) "Prove" with respect to a fact means to meet the burden of establishing the fact (Section 1-201(8)).

(14) ["Record" means information that is inscribed on a tangible medium or that is stored in an electroinic or other medium and is retrieveable in perceivable form.]

(15) "Remitter" means a person who purchases an instrument from its issuer if the instrument is payable to an identified person other than the purchaser.

(16) "Remotely-created consumer item" means an item drawn on a consumer account, which is not created by the payor bank and does not bear a handwritten signature purporting to be the signature of the drawer.

(17) "Secondary obligor," with respect to an instrument, means (a) an indorser or an accommodation party, (b) a drawer having the obligation described in Section 3-414(d), or (c) any other party to the instrument that has recourse against another party to the instrument pursuant to Section 3-116(b).

(b) Other definitions applying to this Article and the sections in which they appear are:

"Acceptance"	Section 3-409
"Accommodated party"	Section 3-419
"Accommodation party"	Section 3-419
"Account"	Section 4-104
"Alteration"	Section 3-407
"Anomalous indorsement"	Section 3-205
"Blank indorsement"	Section 3-205
"Cashier's check"	Section 3-104
"Certificate of deposit"	Section 3-104
"Certified check"	Section 3-409
"Check"	Section 3-104
"Consideration"	Section 3-303
"Draft"	Section 3-104
"Holder in due course"	Section 3-302
"Incomplete instrument"	Section 3-115
"Indorsement"	Section 3-204
"Indorser"	Section 3-204
"Instrument"	Section 3-104
"Issue"	Section 3-105
"Issuer"	Section 3-105
"Negotiable instrument"	Section 3-104
"Negotiation"	Section 3-201
"Note"	Section 3-104
"Payable at a definite time"	Section 3-108
"Payable on demand"	Section 3-108
"Payable to bearer"	Section 3-109
"Payable to order"	Section 3-109
"Payment"	Section 3-602
"Person entitled to enforce"	Section 3-301
"Presentment"	Section 3-501
"Reacquisition"	Section 3-207
"Special indorsement"	Section 3-205
"Teller's check"	Section 3-104

"Transfer of instrument"	Section 3-203
"Traveler's check"	Section 3-104
"Value"	Section 3-303

(c) The following definitions in other Articles apply to this Article:

"Banking day"	Section 4-104
"Clearing house"	Section 4-104
"Collecting bank"	Section 4-105
"Depositary bank"	Section 4-105
"Documentary draft"	Section 4-104
"Intermediary bank"	Section 4-105
"Item"	Section 4-104
"Payor bank"	Section 4-105
"Suspends payments"	Section 4-104

(d) In addition, Article 1 contains general definitions and principles of construction and interpretation applicable throughout this Article.

Legislative Note. A jurisdiction that enacts this statute that has not yet enacted the revised version of UCC Article 1 should add to Section 3-103 the definition of "good faith" that appears in the official version of Section 1-201(b)(20) and the definition of "record" that appears in the official version of Section 1-201(b)(31). Sections 3-103(a)(6) and (14) are reserved for that purpose. A jurisdiction that already has adopted or simultaneously adopts the revised Article 1 should not add those definitions, but should leave those numbers "reserved." If jurisdictions follow the numbering suggested here, the subsections will have the same numbering in all jurisdictions that have adopted these amendments (whether they have or have not adopted the revised version of UCC Article 1).

§ 3–104. Negotiable Instrument.

(a) Except as provided in subsections (c) and (d), "negotiable instrument" means an unconditional promise or order to pay a fixed amount of money, with or without interest or other charges described in the promise or order, if it:

(1) is payable to bearer or to order at the time it is issued or first comes into possession of a holder;

(2) is payable on demand or at a definite time; and

(3) does not state any other undertaking or instruction by the person promising or ordering payment to do any act in addition to the payment of money, but the promise or order may contain (i) an undertaking or power to give, maintain, or protect collateral to secure payment, (ii) an authorization or power to the holder to confess judgment or realize on or dispose of collateral, or (iii) a waiver of the benefit of any law intended for the advantage or protection of an obligor.

(b) "Instrument" means a negotiable instrument.

(c) An order that meets all of the requirements of subsection (a), except paragraph (1), and otherwise falls within the definition of "check" in subsection (f) is a negotiable instrument and a check.

(d) A promise or order other than a check is not an instrument if, at the time it is issued or first comes into possession of a holder, it contains a conspicuous statement, however expressed, to the effect that the promise or order is not negotiable or is not an instrument governed by this Article.

(e) An instrument is a "note" if it is a promise and is a "draft" if it is an order. If an instrument falls within the definition of both "note" and "draft," a person entitled to enforce the instrument may treat it as either.

(f) "Check" means (i) a draft, other than a documentary draft, payable on demand and drawn on a bank or (ii) a cashier's check or teller's check. An instrument may be a check even though it is described on its face by another term, such as "money order."

(g) "Cashier's check" means a draft with respect to which the drawer and drawee are the same bank or branches of the same bank.

(h) "Teller's check" means a draft drawn by a bank (i) on another bank, or (ii) payable at or through a bank.

(i) "Traveler's check" means an instrument that (i) is payable on demand, (ii) is drawn on or payable at or through a bank, (iii) is designated by the term "traveler's check" or by a substantially similar term, and (iv) requires, as a condition to payment, a countersignature by a person whose specimen signature appears on the instrument.

(j) "Certificate of deposit" means an instrument containing an acknowledgment by a bank that a sum of money has been received by the bank and a promise by the bank to repay the sum of money. A certificate of deposit is a note of the bank.

§ 3–105. Issue of Instrument.

(a) "Issue" means the first delivery of an instrument by the maker or drawer, whether to a holder or nonholder, for the purpose of giving rights on the instrument to any person.

(b) An unissued instrument, or an unissued incomplete instrument that is completed, is binding on the maker or drawer, but nonissuance is a defense. An instrument that is conditionally issued or is issued for a special purpose is binding on the maker or drawer, but failure of the condition or special purpose to be fulfilled is a defense.

(c) "Issuer" applies to issued and unissued instruments and means a maker or drawer of an instrument.

§ 3–106. Unconditional Promise or Order.

(a) Except as provided in this section, for the purposes of Section 3-104(a), a promise or order is unconditional unless it states (i) an express condition to payment, (ii) that the promise or order is subject to or governed by another record, or (iii) that rights or obligations with respect to the promise or order are stated in another record. A reference to another record does not of itself make the promise or order conditional.

(b) A promise or order is not made conditional (i) by a reference to another record for a statement of rights with respect to collateral, prepayment, or acceleration, or (ii) because payment is limited to resort to a particular fund or source.

(c) If a promise or order requires, as a condition to payment, a countersignature by a person whose specimen signature appears on the promise or order, the condition does not make the promise or order conditional for the purposes of Section 3-104(a). If the person whose specimen signature appears on an instrument fails to countersign the instrument, the failure to countersign is a defense to the obligation of the issuer, but the failure does not prevent a transferee of the instrument from becoming a holder of the instrument.

(d) If a promise or order at the time it is issued or first comes into possession of a holder contains a statement, required by applicable statutory or administrative law, to the effect that the rights of a holder or transferee are subject to claims or defenses that the issuer could assert against the original payee, the promise or order is not thereby made conditional for the purposes of Section 3-104(a); but if the promise or order is an instrument, there cannot be a holder in due course of the instrument.

§ 3–107. Instrument Payable in Foreign Money.
Unless the instrument otherwise provides, an instrument that states the amount payable in foreign money may be paid in the foreign money or in an equivalent amount in dollars calculated by using the current bank offered spot rate at the place of payment for the purchase of dollars on the day on which the instrument is paid.

§ 3–108. Payable on Demand or at Definite Time.

(a) A promise or order is "payable on demand" if it (i) states that it is payable on demand or at sight, or otherwise indicates that it is payable at the will of the holder, or (ii) does not state any time of payment.

(b) A promise or order is "payable at a definite time" if it is payable on elapse of a definite period of time after sight or acceptance or at a fixed date or dates or at a time or times readily ascertainable at the time the promise or order is issued, subject to rights of (i) prepayment, (ii) acceleration, (iii) extension at the option of the holder, or (iv) extension to a further definite time at the option of the maker or acceptor or automatically upon or after a specified act or event.

(c) If an instrument, payable at a fixed date, is also payable upon demand made before the fixed date, the instrument is payable on demand until the fixed date and, if demand for payment is not made before that date, becomes payable at a definite time on the fixed date.

§ 3–109. Payable to Bearer or to Order.

(a) A promise or order is payable to bearer if it:
  (1) states that it is payable to bearer or to the order of bearer or otherwise indicates that the person in possession of the promise or order is entitled to payment;
  (2) does not state a payee; or
  (3) states that it is payable to or to the order of cash or otherwise indicates that it is not payable to an identified person.

(b) A promise or order that is not payable to bearer is payable to order if it is payable (i) to the order of an identified person or (ii) to an identified person or order. A promise or order that is payable to order is payable to the identified person.

(c) An instrument payable to bearer may become payable to an identified person if it is specially indorsed pursuant to Section 3–205(a). An instrument payable to an identified person may become payable to bearer if it is indorsed in blank pursuant to Section 3–205(b).

§ 3–110. Identification of Person to Whom Instrument ID Payable.

(a) The person to whom an instrument is initially payable is determined by the intent of the person, whether or not authorized, signing as, or in the name or behalf of, the issuer of the instrument. The instrument is payable to the person intended by the signer even if that person is identified in the instrument by a name or other identification that is not that of the intended person. If more than one person signs in the name or behalf of the issuer of an instrument and all the signers do not intend the same person as payee, the instrument is payable to any person intended by one or more of the signers.

(b) If the signature of the issuer of an instrument is made by automated means, such as a check writing machine, the payee of the instrument is determined by the intent of the person who supplied the name or identification of the payee, whether or not authorized to do so.

(c) A person to whom an instrument is payable may be identified in any way, including by name, identifying number, office, or account number. For the purpose of determining the holder of an instrument, the following rules apply:

(1) If an instrument is payable to an account and the account is identified only by number, the instrument is payable to the person to whom the account is payable. If an instrument is payable to an account identified by number and by the name of a person, the instrument is payable to the named person, whether or not that person is the owner of the account identified by number.

(2) If an instrument is payable to:

(i) a trust, an estate, or a person described as trustee or representative of a trust or estate, the instrument is payable to the trustee, the representative, or a successor of either, whether or not the beneficiary or estate is also named;

(ii) a person described as agent or similar representative of a named or identified person, the instrument is payable to the represented person, the representative, or a successor of the representative;

(iii) a fund or organization that is not a legal entity, the instrument is payable to a representative of the members of the fund or organization; or

(iv) an office or to a person described as holding an office, the instrument is payable to the named person, the incumbent of the office, or a successor to the incumbent.

(d) If an instrument is payable to two or more persons alternatively, it is payable to any of them and may be negotiated, discharged, or enforced by any or all of them in possession of the instrument. If an instrument is payable to two or more persons not alternatively, it is payable to all of them and may be negotiated, discharged, or enforced only by all of them. If an instrument payable to two or more persons is ambiguous as to whether it is payable to the persons alternatively, the instrument is payable to the persons alternatively.

§ 3–111. Place of Payment.

Except as otherwise provided for items in Article 4, an instrument is payable at the place of payment stated in the instrument. If no place of payment is stated, an instrument is payable at the address of the drawee or maker stated in the instrument. If no address is stated, the place of payment is the place of business of the drawee or maker. If a drawee or maker has more than one place of business, the place of payment is any place of business of the drawee or maker chosen by the person entitled to enforce the instrument. If the drawee or maker has no place of business, the place of payment is the residence of the drawee or maker.

§ 3–112. Interest.

(a) Unless otherwise provided in the instrument, (i) an instrument is not payable with interest, and (ii) interest on an interest bearing instrument is payable from the date of the instrument.

(b) Interest may be stated in an instrument as a fixed or variable amount of money or it may be expressed as a fixed or variable rate or rates. The amount or rate of interest may be stated or described in the instrument in any manner and may require reference to information not contained in the instrument. If an instrument provides for interest, but the amount of interest payable cannot be ascertained from the description, interest is payable at the judgment rate in effect at the place of payment of the instrument and at the time interest first accrues.

§ 3–113. Date of Instrument.

(a) An instrument may be antedated or postdated. The date stated determines the time of payment if the instrument is payable at a fixed period after date. Except as provided in Section 4–401(c), an instrument payable on demand is not payable before the date of the instrument.

(b) If an instrument is undated, its date is the date of its issue or, in the case of an unissued instrument, the date it first comes into possession of a holder.

§ 3–114. Contradictory Terms of Instrument.

If an instrument contains contradictory terms, typewritten terms prevail over printed terms, handwritten terms prevail over both, and words prevail over numbers.

§ 3–115. Incomplete Instrument.

(a) "Incomplete instrument" means a signed writing, whether or not issued by the signer, the contents of which show at the time of signing that it is incomplete but that the signer intended it to be completed by the addition of words or numbers.

(b) Subject to subsection (c), if an incomplete instrument is an instrument under Section 3–104, it may be enforced according to its terms if it is not completed, or according to its terms as augmented by completion. If an incomplete instrument is not an instrument under Section 3–104, but, after completion, the requirements of Section 3–104 are met, the instrument may be enforced according to its terms as augmented by completion.

(c) If words or numbers are added to an incomplete instrument without authority of the signer, there is an alteration of the incomplete instrument under Section 3–407.

(d) The burden of establishing that words or numbers were added to an incomplete instrument without authority of the signer is on the person asserting the lack of authority.

§ 3–116. Joint and Several Liability; Contribution.

(a) Except as otherwise provided in the instrument, two or more persons who have the same liability on an instrument as makers, drawers, acceptors, indorsers who indorse as joint payees, or anomalous indorsers are jointly and severally liable in the capacity in which they sign.

(b) Except as provided in Section 3–419(f) or by agreement of the affected parties, a party having joint and several liability who pays the instrument is entitled to receive from any party having the same joint and several liability contribution in accordance with applicable law.

§ 3–117. Other Agreements Affecting Instrument.

Subject to applicable law regarding exclusion of proof of contemporaneous or previous agreements, the obligation of a party to an instrument to pay the instrument may be modified, supplemented, or nullified by a separate agreement of the obligor and a person entitled to enforce the instrument, if the instrument is issued or the obligation is incurred in reliance on the agreement or as part of the same transaction giving rise to the agreement. To the extent an obligation is modified, supplemented, or nullified by an agreement under this section, the agreement is a defense to the obligation.

§ 3–118. Statute of Limitations.

(a) Except as provided in subsection (e), an action to enforce the obligation of a party to pay a note payable at a definite time must be commenced within six years after the due date or dates stated in the note or, if a due date is accelerated, within six years after the accelerated due date.

(b) Except as provided in subsection (d) or (e), if demand for payment is made to the maker of a note payable on demand, an action to enforce the obligation of a party to pay the note must be commenced within six years after the demand. If no demand for payment is made to the maker, an action to enforce the note is barred if neither principal nor interest on the note has been paid for a continuous period of 10 years.

(c) Except as provided in subsection (d), an action to enforce the obligation of a party to an unaccepted draft to pay the draft must be commenced within three years after dishonor of the draft or 10 years after the date of the draft, whichever period expires first.

(d) An action to enforce the obligation of the acceptor of a certified check or the issuer of a teller's check, cashier's check, or traveler's check must be commenced within three years after demand for payment is made to the acceptor or issuer, as the case may be.

(e) An action to enforce the obligation of a party to a certificate of deposit to pay the instrument must be commenced within six years after demand for payment is made to the maker, but if the instrument states a due date and the maker is not required to pay before that date, the six-year period begins when a demand for payment is in effect and the due date has passed.

(f) An action to enforce the obligation of a party to pay an accepted draft, other than a certified check, must be commenced (i) within six years after the due date or dates stated in the draft or acceptance if the obligation of the acceptor is payable at a definite time, or

(ii) within six years after the date of the acceptance if the obligation of the acceptor is payable on demand.

(g) Unless governed by other law regarding claims for indemnity or contribution, an action (i) for conversion of an instrument, for money had and received, or like action based on conversion, (ii) for breach of warranty, or (iii) to enforce an obligation, duty, or right arising under this Article and not governed by this section must be commenced within three years after the [cause of action] accrues.

§ 3–119. Notice of Right to Defend Action. In an action for breach of an obligation for which a third person is answerable over pursuant to this Article or Article 4, the defendant may give the third person notice of the litigation in a record, and the person notified may then give similar notice to any other person who is answerable over. If the notice states (i) that the person notified may come in and defend and (ii) that failure to do so will bind the person notified in an action later brought by the person giving the notice as to any determination of fact common to the two litigations, the person notified is so bound unless after seasonable receipt of the notice the person notified does come in and defend.

Part 2: Negotiation, Transfer, and Indorsement

§ 3–201. Negotiation.

(a) "Negotiation" means a transfer of possession, whether voluntary or involuntary, of an instrument by a person other than the issuer to a person who thereby becomes its holder.

(b) Except for negotiation by a remitter, if an instrument is payable to an identified person, negotiation requires transfer of possession of the instrument and its indorsement by the holder. If an instrument is payable to bearer, it may be negotiated by transfer of possession alone.

§ 3–202. Negotiation Subject to Rescission.

(a) Negotiation is effective even if obtained (i) from an infant, a corporation exceeding its powers, or a person without capacity, (ii) by fraud, duress, or mistake, or (iii) in breach of duty or as part of an illegal transaction.

(b) To the extent permitted by other law, negotiation may be rescinded or may be subject to other remedies, but those remedies may not be asserted against a subsequent holder in due course or a person paying the

instrument in good faith and without knowledge of facts that are a basis for rescission or other remedy.

§ 3–203. Transfer of Instrument; Rights Acquired by Transfer.

(a) An instrument is transferred when it is delivered by a person other than its issuer for the purpose of giving to the person receiving delivery the right to enforce the instrument.

(b) Transfer of an instrument, whether or not the transfer is a negotiation, vests in the transferee any right of the transferor to enforce the instrument, including any right as a holder in due course, but the transferee cannot acquire rights of a holder in due course by a transfer, directly or indirectly, from a holder in due course if the transferee engaged in fraud or illegality affecting the instrument.

(c) Unless otherwise agreed, if an instrument is transferred for value and the transferee does not become a holder because of lack of indorsement by the transferor, the transferee has a specifically enforceable right to the unqualified indorsement of the transferor, but negotiation of the instrument does not occur until the indorsement is made.

(d) If a transferor purports to transfer less than the entire instrument, negotiation of the instrument does not occur. The transferee obtains no rights under this Article and has only the rights of a partial assignee.

§ 3–204. Indorsement.

(a) "Indorsement" means a signature, other than that of a signer as maker, drawer, or acceptor, that alone or accompanied by other words is made on an instrument for the purpose of (i) negotiating the instrument, (ii) restricting payment of the instrument, or (iii) incurring indorser's liability on the instrument, but regardless of the intent of the signer, a signature and its accompanying words is an indorsement unless the accompanying words, terms of the instrument, place of the signature, or other circumstances unambiguously indicate that the signature was made for a purpose other than indorsement. For the purpose of determining whether a signature is made on an instrument, a paper affixed to the instrument is a part of the instrument.

(b) "Indorser" means a person who makes an indorsement.

(c) For the purpose of determining whether the transferee of an instrument is a holder, an indorsement that transfers a security interest in the instrument is effective as an unqualified indorsement of the instrument.

(d) If an instrument is payable to a holder under a name that is not the name of the holder, indorsement may be made by the holder in the name stated in the instrument or in the holder's name or both, but signature in both names may be required by a person paying or taking the instrument for value or collection.

§ 3–205. Special Indorsement; Blank Indorsement; Anomalous Indorsement.

(a) If an indorsement is made by the holder of an instrument, whether payable to an identified person or payable to bearer, and the indorsement identifies a person to whom it makes the instrument payable, it is a "special indorsement." When specially indorsed, an instrument becomes payable to the identified person and may be negotiated only by the indorsement of that person. The principles stated in Section 3–110 apply to special indorsements.

(b) If an indorsement is made by the holder of an instrument and it is not a special indorsement, it is a "blank indorsement." When indorsed in blank, an instrument becomes payable to bearer and may be negotiated by transfer of possession alone until specially indorsed.

(c) The holder may convert a blank indorsement that consists only of a signature into a special indorsement by writing, above the signature of the indorser, words identifying the person to whom the instrument is made payable.

(d) "Anomalous indorsement" means an indorsement made by a person who is not the holder of the instrument. An anomalous indorsement does not affect the manner in which the instrument may be negotiated.

§ 3–206. Restrictive Indorsement.

(a) An indorsement limiting payment to a particular person or otherwise prohibiting further transfer or negotiation of the instrument is not effective to prevent further transfer or negotiation of the instrument.

(b) An indorsement stating a condition to the right of the indorsee to receive payment does not affect the right of the indorsee to enforce the instrument. A person paying the instrument or taking it for value or collection may disregard the condition, and the rights and liabilities of that person are not affected by whether the condition has been fulfilled.

(c) If an instrument bears an indorsement (i) described in Section 4–201(b), or (ii) in blank or to a particular bank using the words "for deposit," "for collection," or other words indicating a purpose of having the instrument collected by a bank for the indorser or for a particular account, the following rules apply:

(1) A person, other than a bank, who purchases the instrument when so indorsed converts the instrument unless the amount paid for the instrument is received by the indorser or applied consistently with the indorsement.

(2) A depositary bank that purchases the instrument or takes it for collection when so indorsed converts the instrument unless the amount paid by the bank with respect to the instrument is received by the indorser or applied consistently with the indorsement.

(3) A payor bank that is also the depositary bank or that takes the instrument for immediate payment over the counter from a person other than a collecting bank converts the instrument unless the proceeds of the instrument are received by the indorser or applied consistently with the indorsement.

(4) Except as otherwise provided in paragraph (3), a payor bank or intermediary bank may disregard the indorsement and is not liable if the proceeds of the instrument are not received by the indorser or applied consistently with the indorsement.

(d) Except for an indorsement covered by subsection (c), if an instrument bears an indorsement using words to the effect that payment is to be made to the indorsee as agent, trustee, or other fiduciary for the benefit of the indorser or another person, the following rules apply:

(1) Unless there is notice of breach of fiduciary duty as provided in Section 3–307, a person who purchases the instrument from the indorsee or takes the instrument from the indorsee for collection or payment may pay the proceeds of payment or the value given for the instrument to the indorsee without regard to whether the indorsee violates a fiduciary duty to the indorser.

(2) A subsequent transferee of the instrument or person who pays the instrument is neither given notice nor otherwise affected by the restriction in the indorsement unless the transferee or payor knows that the fiduciary dealt with the instrument or its proceeds in breach of fiduciary duty.

(e) The presence on an instrument of an indorsement to which this section applies does not prevent a purchaser of the instrument from becoming a holder in due course of the instrument unless the purchaser is a converter under subsection (c) or has notice or knowledge of breach of fiduciary duty as stated in subsection (d).

(f) In an action to enforce the obligation of a party to pay the instrument, the obligor has a defense if payment would violate an indorsement to which this section applies and the payment is not permitted by this section.

§ 3–207. Reacquisition. Reacquisition of an instrument occurs if it is transferred to a former holder, by negotiation or otherwise. A former holder who reacquires the instrument may cancel indorsements made after the reacquirer first became a holder of the instrument. If the cancellation causes the instrument to be payable to the reacquirer or to bearer, the reacquirer may negotiate the instrument. An indorser whose indorsement is canceled is discharged, and the discharge is effective against any subsequent holder.

Part 3: Enforcement of Instruments

§ 3–301. Person Entitled to Enforce Instrument. "Person entitled to enforce" an instrument means (i) the holder of the instrument, (ii) a nonholder in possession of the instrument who has the rights of a holder, or (iii) a person not in possession of the instrument who is entitled to enforce the instrument pursuant to Section 3–309 or 3–418(d). A person may be a person entitled to enforce the instrument even though the person is not the owner of the instrument or is in wrongful possession of the instrument.

§ 3–302. Holder in Due Course.

(a) Subject to subsection (c) and Section 3–106(d), "holder in due course" means the holder of an instrument if:

(1) the instrument when issued or negotiated to the holder does not bear such apparent evidence of forgery or alteration or is not otherwise so irregular or incomplete as to call into question its authenticity; and

(2) the holder took the instrument (i) for value, (ii) in good faith, (iii) without notice that the instrument is overdue or has been dishonored or that there is an uncured default with respect to payment of another instrument issued as part of the same series, (iv) without notice that the instrument contains an unauthorized signature or has

been altered, (v) without notice of any claim to the instrument described in Section 3–306, and (vi) without notice that any party has a defense or claim in recoupment described in Section 3–305(a).

(b) Notice of discharge of a party, other than discharge in an insolvency proceeding, is not notice of a defense under subsection (a), but discharge is effective against a person who became a holder in due course with notice of the discharge. Public filing or recording of a document does not of itself constitute notice of a defense, claim in recoupment, or claim to the instrument.

(c) Except to the extent a transferor or predecessor in interest has rights as a holder in due course, a person does not acquire rights of a holder in due course of an instrument taken (i) by legal process or by purchase in an execution, bankruptcy, or creditor's sale or similar proceeding, (ii) by purchase as part of a bulk transaction not in ordinary course of business of the transferor, or (iii) as the successor in interest to an estate or other organization.

(d) If, under Section 3–303(a)(1), the promise of performance that is the consideration for an instrument has been partially performed, the holder may assert rights as a holder in due course of the instrument only to the fraction of the amount payable under the instrument equal to the value of the partial performance divided by the value of the promised performance.

(e) If (i) the person entitled to enforce an instrument has only a security interest in the instrument and (ii) the person obliged to pay the instrument has a defense, claim in recoupment, or claim to the instrument that may be asserted against the person who granted the security interest, the person entitled to enforce the instrument may assert rights as a holder in due course only to an amount payable under the instrument which, at the time of enforcement of the instrument, does not exceed the amount of the unpaid obligation secured.

(f) To be effective, notice must be received at a time and in a manner that gives a reasonable opportunity to act on it.

(g) This section is subject to any law limiting status as a holder in due course in particular classes of transactions.

§ 3–303. Value and Consideration.

(a) An instrument is issued or transferred for value if:

(1) the instrument is issued or transferred for a promise of performance, to the extent the promise has been performed;

(2) the transferee acquires a security interest or other lien in the instrument other than a lien obtained by judicial proceeding;

(3) the instrument is issued or transferred as payment of, or as security for, an antecedent claim against any person, whether or not the claim is due;

(4) the instrument is issued or transferred in exchange for a negotiable instrument; or

(5) the instrument is issued or transferred in exchange for the incurring of an irrevocable obligation to a third party by the person taking the instrument.

(b) "Consideration" means any consideration sufficient to support a simple contract. The drawer or maker of an instrument has a defense if the instrument is issued without consideration. If an instrument is issued for a promise of performance, the issuer has a defense to the extent performance of the promise is due and the promise has not been performed. If an instrument is issued for value as stated in subsection (a), the instrument is also issued for consideration.

§ 3–304. Overdue Instrument.

(a) An instrument payable on demand becomes overdue at the earliest of the following times:

(1) on the day after the day demand for payment is duly made;

(2) if the instrument is a check, 90 days after its date; or

(3) if the instrument is not a check, when the instrument has been outstanding for a period of time after its date which is unreasonably long under the circumstances of the particular case in light of the nature of the instrument and usage of the trade.

(b) With respect to an instrument payable at a definite time the following rules apply:

(1) If the principal is payable in installments and a due date has not been accelerated, the instrument becomes overdue upon default under the instrument for nonpayment of an installment, and the instrument remains overdue until the default is cured.

(2) If the principal is not payable in installments and the due date has not been accelerated, the instru-

ment becomes overdue on the day after the due date.

(3) If a due date with respect to principal has been accelerated, the instrument becomes overdue on the day after the accelerated due date.

(c) Unless the due date of principal has been accelerated, an instrument does not become overdue if there is default in payment of interest but no default in payment of principal.

§ 3–305. Defenses and Claims in Recoupment; Claims in Consumer Transactions.

(a) Except as otherwise provided in this section, the right to enforce the obligation of a party to pay an instrument is subject to the following:

(1) a defense of the obligor based on (i) infancy of the obligor to the extent it is a defense to a simple contract, (ii) duress, lack of legal capacity, or illegality of the transaction which, under other law, nullifies the obligation of the obligor, (iii) fraud that induced the obligor to sign the instrument with neither knowledge nor reasonable opportunity to learn of its character or its essential terms, or (iv) discharge of the obligor in insolvency proceedings;

(2) a defense of the obligor stated in another section of this Article or a defense of the obligor that would be available if the person entitled to enforce the instrument were enforcing a right to payment under a simple contract; and

(3) a claim in recoupment of the obligor against the original payee of the instrument if the claim arose from the transaction that gave rise to the instrument; but the claim of the obligor may be asserted against a transferee of the instrument only to reduce the amount owing on the instrument at the time the action is brought.

(b) The right of a holder in due course to enforce the obligation of a party to pay the instrument is subject to defenses of the obligor stated in subsection (a)(1), but is not subject to defenses of the obligor stated in subsection (a)(2) or claims in recoupment stated in subsection (a)(3) against a person other than the holder.

(c) Except as stated in subsection (d), in an action to enforce the obligation of a party to pay the instrument, the obligor may not assert against the person entitled to enforce the instrument a defense, claim in recoupment, or claim to the instrument (Section 3-306) of another person, but the other person's claim to the instrument may be asserted by the obligor if the other person is joined in the action and personally asserts the claim against the person entitled to enforce the instrument. An obligor is not obliged to pay the instrument if the person seeking enforcement of the instrument does not have rights of a holder in due course and the obligor proves that the instrument is a lost or stolen instrument.

(d) In an action to enforce the obligation of an accommodation party to pay an instrument, the accommodation party may assert against the person entitled to enforce the instrument any defense or claim in recoupment under subsection (a) that the accommodated party could assert against the person entitled to enforce the instrument, except the defenses of discharge in insolvency proceedings, infancy, and lack of legal capacity.

(e) In a consumer transaction, if law other than this article requires that an instrument include a statement to the effect that the rights of a holder or transferee are subject to a claim or defense that the issuer could assert against the original payee, and the instrument does not include such a statement:

(1) the instrument has the same effect as if the instrument included such a statement;

(2) the issuer may assert against the holder or transferee all claims and defenses that would have been available if the instrument included such a statement; and

(3) the extent to which claims may be asserted against the holder or transferee is determined as if the instrument included such a statement.

(f) This section is subject to law other than this article that establishes a different rule for consumer transactions.

Legislative Note: If a consumer protection law in this state addresses the same issue as subsection (g), it should be examined for consistency with subsection (g) and, if inconsistent, should be amended.

§ 3–306. Claims to an Instrument. A person taking an instrument, other than a person having rights of a holder in due course, is subject to a claim of a property or possessory right in the instrument or its proceeds, including a claim to rescind a negotiation and to recover the instrument or its proceeds. A person having rights of a holder in due course takes free of the claim to the instrument.

§ 3–307. Notice of Breach of Fiduciary Duty.

(a) In this section:

(1) "Fiduciary" means an agent, trustee, partner, corporate officer or director, or other representative owing a fiduciary duty with respect to an instrument.

(2) "Represented person" means the principal, beneficiary, partnership, corporation, or other person to whom the duty stated in paragraph (1) is owed.

(b) If (i) an instrument is taken from a fiduciary for payment or collection or for value, (ii) the taker has knowledge of the fiduciary status of the fiduciary, and (iii) the represented person makes a claim to the instrument or its proceeds on the basis that the transaction of the fiduciary is a breach of fiduciary duty, the following rules apply:

(1) Notice of breach of fiduciary duty by the fiduciary is notice of the claim of the represented person.

(2) In the case of an instrument payable to the represented person or the fiduciary as such, the taker has notice of the breach of fiduciary duty if the instrument is (i) taken in payment of or as security for a debt known by the taker to be the personal debt of the fiduciary, (ii) taken in a transaction known by the taker to be for the personal benefit of the fiduciary, or (iii) deposited to an account other than an account of the fiduciary, as such, or an account of the represented person.

(3) If an instrument is issued by the represented person or the fiduciary as such, and made payable to the fiduciary personally, the taker does not have notice of the breach of fiduciary duty unless the taker knows of the breach of fiduciary duty.

(4) If an instrument is issued by the represented person or the fiduciary as such, to the taker as payee, the taker has notice of the breach of fiduciary duty if the instrument is (i) taken in payment of or as security for a debt known by the taker to be the personal debt of the fiduciary, (ii) taken in a transaction known by the taker to be for the personal benefit of the fiduciary, or (iii) deposited to an account other than an account of the fiduciary, as such, or an account of the represented person.

§ 3–308. Proof of Signatures and Status as Holder in Due Course.

(a) In an action with respect to an instrument, the authenticity of, and authority to make, each signature on the instrument is admitted unless specifically denied in the pleadings. If the validity of a signature is denied in the pleadings, the burden of establishing validity is on the person claiming validity, but the signature is presumed to be authentic and authorized unless the action is to enforce the liability of the purported signer and the signer is dead or incompetent at the time of trial of the issue of validity of the signature. If an action to enforce the instrument is brought against a person as the undisclosed principal of a person who signed the instrument as a party to the instrument, the plaintiff has the burden of establishing that the defendant is liable on the instrument as a represented person under Section 3–402(a).

(b) If the validity of signatures is admitted or proved and there is compliance with subsection (a), a plaintiff producing the instrument is entitled to payment if the plaintiff proves entitlement to enforce the instrument under Section 3–301, unless the defendant proves a defense or claim in recoupment. If a defense or claim in recoupment is proved, the right to payment of the plaintiff is subject to the defense or claim, except to the extent the plaintiff proves that the plaintiff has rights of a holder in due course which are not subject to the defense or claim.

§ 3–309. Enforcement of Lost, Destroyed, Or Stolen Instrument.

(a) A person not in possession of an instrument is entitled to enforce the instrument if:

    (1) the person seeking to enforce the instrument:

(a) was entitled to enforce the instrument when loss of possession occurred; or

(b) has directly or indirectly acquired ownership of the instrument from a person who was entitled to enforce the instrument when loss of possession occurred;

    (2) the loss of possession was not the result of a transfer by the person or a lawful seizure; and

    (3) the person cannot reasonably obtain possession of the instrument because the instrument was destroyed, its whereabouts cannot be determined, or it is in the wrongful possession of an unknown person or a person that cannot be found or is not amenable to service of process.

(b) A person seeking enforcement of an instrument under subsection (a) must prove the terms of the instrument and the person's right to enforce the instrument. If that proof is made, Section 3-308 applies to the case as if the person seeking enforcement had produced the instrument. The court may not enter judgment in favor of the person seeking enforcement unless it finds that the person required to pay the instrument is adequately protected against loss that might occur by reason of a claim by another person to enforce the instrument. Adequate protection may be provided by any reasonable means.

§ 3–310. Effect of Instrument on Obligation for Which Taken.

(a) Unless otherwise agreed, if a certified check, cashier's check, or teller's check is taken for an obligation, the obligation is discharged to the same extent discharge would result if an amount of money equal to the amount of the instrument were taken in payment of the obligation. Discharge of the obligation does not affect any liability that the obligor may have as an indorser of the instrument.

(b) Unless otherwise agreed and except as provided in subsection (a), if a note or an uncertified check is taken for an obligation, the obligation is suspended to the same extent the obligation would be discharged if an amount of money equal to the amount of the instrument were taken, and the following rules apply:

    (1) In the case of an uncertified check, suspension of the obligation continues until dishonor of the check or until it is paid or certified. Payment or certification of the check results in discharge of the obligation to the extent of the amount of the check.

    (2) In the case of a note, suspension of the obligation continues until dishonor of the note or until it is paid. Payment of the note results in discharge of the obligation to the extent of the payment.

    (3) Except as provided in paragraph (4), if the check or note is dishonored and the obligee of the obligation for which the instrument was taken is the person entitled to enforce the instrument, the obligee may enforce either the instrument or the obligation. In the case of an instrument of a third person which is negotiated to the obligee by the obligor, discharge of the obligor on the instrument also discharges the obligation.

    (4) If the person entitled to enforce the instrument taken for an obligation is a person other than the obligee, the obligee may not enforce the obligation to the extent the obligation is suspended. If the obligee is the person entitled to enforce the instrument but no longer has possession of it because it was lost, stolen, or destroyed, the obligation may not be enforced to the extent of the amount payable on the instrument, and to that extent the obligee's rights against the obligor are limited to enforcement of the instrument.

(c) If an instrument other than one described in subsection (a) or (b) is taken for an obligation, the effect is (i) that stated in subsection (a) if the instrument is one on which a bank is liable as maker or acceptor, or (ii) that stated in subsection (b) in any other case.

§ 3–311. Accord and Satisfaction by Use of Instrument.

(a) If a person against whom a claim is asserted proves that (i) that person in good faith tendered an instrument to the claimant as full satisfaction of the claim, (ii) the amount of the claim was unliquidated or subject to a bona fide dispute, and (iii) the claimant obtained payment of the instrument, the following subsections apply.

(b) Unless subsection (c) applies, the claim is discharged if the person against whom the claim is asserted proves that the instrument or an accompanying written communication contained a conspicuous statement to the effect that the instrument was tendered as full satisfaction of the claim.

(c) Subject to subsection (d), a claim is not discharged under subsection (b) if either of the following applies:

(1) The claimant, if an organization, proves that (i) within a reasonable time before the tender, the claimant sent a conspicuous statement to the person against whom the claim is asserted that communications concerning disputed debts, including an instrument tendered as full satisfaction of a debt, are to be sent to a designated person, office, or place, and (ii) the instrument or accompanying communication was not received by that designated person, office, or place.

(2) The claimant, whether or not an organization, proves that within 90 days after payment of the instrument, the claimant tendered repayment of the amount of the instrument to the person against whom the claim is asserted. This paragraph does not apply if the claimant is an organization that sent a statement complying with paragraph (1)(i).

(d) A claim is discharged if the person against whom the claim is asserted proves that within a reasonable time before collection of the instrument was initiated, the claimant, or an agent of the claimant having direct responsibility with respect to the disputed obligation, knew that the instrument was tendered in full satisfaction of the claim.

§ 3–312. Lost, Destroyed, or Stolen Cashier's Check, Teller's Check, or Certified Check.

(a) In this section:

(1) "Check" means a cashier's check, teller's check, or certified check.

(2) "Claimant" means a person who claims the right to receive the amount of a cashier's check, teller's check, or certified check that was lost, destroyed, or stolen.

(3) "Declaration of loss" means a statement, made in a record under penalty of perjury, to the effect that (i) the declarer lost possession of a check, (ii) the declarer is the drawer or payee of the check, in the case of a certified check, or the remitter or payee of the check, in the case of a cashier's check or teller's check, (iii) the loss of possession was not the result of a transfer by the declarer or a lawful seizure, and (iv) the declarer cannot reasonably obtain possession of the check because the check was destroyed, its whereabouts cannot be determined, or it is in the wrongful possession of an unknown person or a person that cannot be found or is not amenable to service of process.

(4) "Obligated bank" means the issuer of a cashier's check or teller's check or the acceptor of a certified check.

(b) A claimant may assert a claim to the amount of a check by a communication to the obligated bank describing the check with reasonable certainty and requesting payment of the amount of the check, if (i) the claimant is the drawer or payee of a certified check or the remitter or payee of a cashier's check or teller's check, (ii) the communication contains or is accompanied by a declaration of loss of the claimant with respect to the check, (iii) the communication is received at a time and in a manner affording the bank a reasonable time to act on it before the check is paid, and (iv) the claimant provides reasonable identification if requested by the obligated bank. Delivery of a declaration of loss is a warranty of the truth of the statements made in the declaration. If a claim is asserted in compliance with this subsection, the following rules apply:

(1) The claim becomes enforceable at the later of (i) the time the claim is asserted, or (ii) the 90th day following the date of the check, in the case of a cashier's check or teller's check, or the 90th day following the date of the acceptance, in the case of a certified check.

(2) Until the claim becomes enforceable, it has no legal effect and the obligated bank may pay the check or, in the case of a teller's check, may permit the drawee to pay the check. Payment to a person entitled to enforce the check discharges all liability of the obligated bank with respect to the check.

(3) If the claim becomes enforceable before the check is presented for payment, the obligated bank is not obliged to pay the check.

(4) When the claim becomes enforceable, the obligated bank becomes obliged to pay the amount of the check to the claimant if payment of the check has not been made to a person entitled to enforce the check. Subject to Section 4-302(a)(1), payment to the claimant discharges all liability of the obligated bank with respect to the check.

(c) If the obligated bank pays the amount of a check to a claimant under subsection (b)(4) and the check is presented for payment by a person having rights of a holder in due course, the claimant is obliged to (i) refund the payment to the obligated bank if the check is paid, or (ii) pay the amount of the check to the person having rights of a holder in due course if the check is dishonored.

(d) If a claimant has the right to assert a claim under subsection (b) and is also a person entitled to enforce a cashier's check, teller's check, or certified check which is lost, destroyed, or stolen, the claimant may assert rights with respect to the check either under this section or Section 3-309.

Part 4: Liability of Parties

§ 3–401. Signature.

(a) A person is not liable on an instrument unless (i) the person signed the instrument, or (ii) the person is represented by an agent or representative who signed the instrument and the signature is binding on the represented person under Section 3–402.

(b) A signature may be made (i) manually or by means of a device or machine, and (ii) by the use of any name, including a trade or assumed name, or by a word, mark, or symbol executed or adopted by a person with present intention to authenticate a writing.

§ 3–402. Signature by Representative.

(a) If a person acting, or purporting to act, as a representative signs an instrument by signing either the name of the represented person or the name of the signer, the represented person is bound by the signature to the same extent the represented person would be bound if the signature were on a simple contract. If the represented person is bound, the signature of the representative is the "authorized signature of the represented person" and the represented person is liable on the instrument, whether or not identified in the instrument.

(b) If a representative signs the name of the representative to an instrument and the signature is an authorized signature of the represented person, the following rules apply:

(1) If the form of the signature shows unambiguously that the signature is made on behalf of the represented person who is identified in the instrument, the representative is not liable on the instrument.

(2) Subject to subsection (c), if (i) the form of the signature does not show unambiguously that the signature is made in a representative capacity or (ii) the represented person is not identified in the instrument, the representative is liable on the instrument to a holder in due course that took the instrument without notice that the representative was not intended to be liable on the instrument. With respect to any other person, the representative is liable on the instrument unless the representative proves that the original parties did not intend the representative to be liable on the instrument.

(c) If a representative signs the name of the representative as drawer of a check without indication of the representative status and the check is payable from an account of the represented person who is identified on the check, the signer is not liable on the check if the signature is an authorized signature of the represented person.

§ 3–403. Unauthorized Signature.

(a) Unless otherwise provided in this Article or Article 4, an unauthorized signature is ineffective except as the signature of the unauthorized signer in favor of a person who in good faith pays the instrument or takes it for value. An unauthorized signature may be ratified for all purposes of this Article.

(b) If the signature of more than one person is required to constitute the authorized signature of an organization, the signature of the organization is unauthorized if one of the required signatures is lacking.

(c) The civil or criminal liability of a person who makes an unauthorized signature is not affected by any provision of this Article which makes the unauthorized signature effective for the purposes of this Article.

§ 3–404. Impostors; Fictitious Payees.

(a) If an impostor, by use of the mails or otherwise, induces the issuer of an instrument to issue the instrument to the impostor, or to a person acting in concert with the impostor, by impersonating the payee of the instrument or a person authorized to act for the payee, an indorsement of the instrument by any person in the name of the payee is effective as the indorsement of the payee in favor of a person who, in good faith, pays the instrument or takes it for value or for collection.

(b) If (i) a person whose intent determines to whom an instrument is payable (Section 3–110(a) or (b)) does not intend the person identified as payee to have any interest in the instrument, or (ii) the person identified as payee of an instrument is a fictitious person, the following rules apply until the instrument is negotiated by special indorsement:

   (1) Any person in possession of the instrument is its holder.

   (2) An indorsement by any person in the name of the payee stated in the instrument is effective as the indorsement of the payee in favor of a person who, in good faith, pays the instrument or takes it for value or for collection.

(c) Under subsection (a) or (b), an indorsement is made in the name of a payee if (i) it is made in a name substantially similar to that of the payee or (ii) the instrument, whether or not indorsed, is deposited in a depositary bank to an account in a name substantially similar to that of the payee.

(d) With respect to an instrument to which subsection (a) or (b) applies, if a person paying the instrument or taking it for value or for collection fails to exercise ordinary care in paying or taking the instrument and that failure substantially contributes to loss resulting from payment of the instrument, the person bearing the loss may recover from the person failing to exercise ordinary care to the extent the failure to exercise ordinary care contributed to the loss.

§ 3–405. Employer's Responsibility for Fraudulent Indorsement by Employee.

(a) In this section:

   (1) "Employee" includes an independent contractor and employee of an independent contractor retained by the employer.

   (2) "Fraudulent indorsement" means (i) in the case of an instrument payable to the employer, a forged indorsement purporting to be that of the employer, or (ii) in the case of an instrument with respect to which the employer is the issuer, a forged indorsement purporting to be that of the person identified as payee.

   (3) "Responsibility" with respect to instruments means authority (i) to sign or indorse instruments on behalf of the employer, (ii) to process instruments received by the employer for bookkeeping purposes, for deposit to an account, or for other disposition, (iii) to prepare or process instruments for issue in the name of the employer, (iv) to supply information determining the names or addresses of payees of instruments to be issued in the name of the employer, (v) to control the disposition of instruments to be issued in the name of the employer, or (vi) to act otherwise with respect to instruments in a responsible capacity.

    "Responsibility" does not include authority that merely allows an employee to have access to instruments or blank or incomplete instrument forms that are being stored or transported or are part of incoming or outgoing mail, or similar access.

(b) For the purpose of determining the rights and liabilities of a person who, in good faith, pays an instrument or takes it for value or for collection, if an employer entrusted an employee with responsibility with respect to the instrument and the employee or a person acting in concert with the employee makes a fraudulent indorsement of the instrument, the indorsement is effective as the indorsement of the person to whom the instrument is payable if it is made in the name of that person. If the person paying the instrument or taking it for value or for collection fails to exercise ordinary care in paying or taking the instrument and that failure substantially contributes to loss resulting from the fraud, the person bearing the loss may recover from the person failing to exercise ordinary care to the extent the failure to exercise ordinary care contributed to the loss.

(c) Under subsection (b), an indorsement is made in the name of the person to whom an instrument is payable if (i) it is made in a name substantially similar to the name of that person or (ii) the instrument, whether or not indorsed, is deposited in a depositary bank to an account in a name substantially similar to the name of that person.

§ 3–406. Negligence Contributing to Forged Signature or Alteration of Instrument.

(a) A person whose failure to exercise ordinary care substantially contributes to an alteration of an instrument or to the making of a forged signature on an instrument is precluded from asserting the alteration or the forgery against a person who, in good faith, pays the instrument or takes it for value or for collection.

(b) Under subsection (a), if the person asserting the preclusion fails to exercise ordinary care in paying or taking the instrument and that failure substantially contributes to loss, the loss is allocated between the person precluded and the person asserting the preclusion according to the extent to which the failure of each to exercise ordinary care contributed to the loss.

(c) Under subsection (a), the burden of proving failure to exercise ordinary care is on the person asserting the preclusion. Under subsection (b), the burden of proving failure to exercise ordinary care is on the person precluded.

§ 3–407. Alteration.

(a) "Alteration" means (i) an unauthorized change in an instrument that purports to modify in any respect the obligation of a party, or (ii) an unauthorized addition of words or numbers or other change to an incomplete instrument relating to the obligation of a party.

(b) Except as provided in subsection (c), an alteration fraudulently made discharges a party whose obligation is affected by the alteration unless that party assents or is precluded from asserting the alteration. No other alteration discharges a party, and the instrument may be enforced according to its original terms.

(c) A payor bank or drawee paying a fraudulently altered instrument or a person taking it for value, in good faith and without notice of the alteration, may enforce rights with respect to the instrument (i) according to its original terms, or (ii) in the case of an incomplete instrument altered by unauthorized completion, according to its terms as completed.

§ 3–408. Drawee Not Liable on Unaccepted Draft.
A check or other draft does not of itself operate as an assignment of funds in the hands of the drawee available for its payment, and the drawee is not liable on the instrument until the drawee accepts it.

§ 3–409. Acceptance of Draft; Certified Check.

(a) "Acceptance" means the drawee's signed agreement to pay a draft as presented. It must be written on the draft and may consist of the drawee's signature alone. Acceptance may be made at any time and becomes effective when notification pursuant to instructions is given or the accepted draft is delivered for the purpose of giving rights on the acceptance to any person.

(b) A draft may be accepted although it has not been signed by the drawer, is otherwise incomplete, is overdue, or has been dishonored.

(c) If a draft is payable at a fixed period after sight and the acceptor fails to date the acceptance, the holder may complete the acceptance by supplying a date in good faith.

(d) "Certified check" means a check accepted by the bank on which it is drawn. Acceptance may be made as stated in subsection (a) or by a writing on the check which indicates that the check is certified. The drawee of a check has no obligation to certify the check, and refusal to certify is not dishonor of the check.

§ 3–410. Acceptance Varying Draft.

(a) If the terms of a drawee's acceptance vary from the terms of the draft as presented, the holder may refuse the acceptance and treat the draft as dishonored. In that case, the drawee may cancel the acceptance.

(b) The terms of a draft are not varied by an acceptance to pay at a particular bank or place in the United States, unless the acceptance states that the draft is to be paid only at that bank or place.

(c) If the holder assents to an acceptance varying the terms of a draft, the obligation of each drawer and indorser that does not expressly assent to the acceptance is discharged.

§ 3–411. Refusal to Pay Cashier's Checks, Teller's Checks, and Certified Checks.

(a) In this section, "obligated bank" means the acceptor of a certified check or the issuer of a cashier's check or teller's check bought from the issuer.

(b) If the obligated bank wrongfully (i) refuses to pay a cashier's check or certified check, (ii) stops payment of a teller's check, or (iii) refuses to pay a dishonored teller's check, the person asserting the right to enforce the check is entitled to compensation for expenses and loss of interest resulting from the nonpayment and may recover consequential damages if the obligated bank refuses to pay after receiving notice of particular circumstances giving rise to the damages.

(c) Expenses or consequential damages under subsection (b) are not recoverable if the refusal of the obligated bank to pay occurs because (i) the bank suspends payments, (ii) the obligated bank asserts a claim or defense of the bank that it has reasonable grounds to believe is available against the person entitled to enforce the instrument, (iii) the obligated bank has a reasonable doubt whether the person demanding payment is the person entitled to enforce the instrument, or (iv) payment is prohibited by law.

§ 3–412. Obligation of Issuer of Note or Cashier's Check. The issuer of a note or cashier's check or other draft drawn on the drawer is obliged to pay the instrument (i) according to its terms at the time it was issued or, if not issued, at the time it first came into possession of a holder, or (ii) if the issuer signed an incomplete instrument, according to its terms when completed, to the extent stated in Sections 3–115 and 3–407. The obligation is owed to a person entitled to enforce the instrument or to an indorser who paid the instrument under Section 3–415.

§ 3–413. Obligation of Acceptor.

(a) The acceptor of a draft is obliged to pay the draft (i) according to its terms at the time it was accepted, even though the acceptance states that the draft is payable "as originally drawn" or equivalent terms, (ii) if the acceptance varies the terms of the draft, according to the terms of the draft as varied, or (iii) if the acceptance is of a draft that is an incomplete instrument, according to its terms when completed, to the extent stated in Sections 3–115 and 3–407. The obligation is owed to a person entitled to enforce the draft or to the drawer or an indorser who paid the draft under Section 3–414 or 3–415.

(b) If the certification of a check or other acceptance of a draft states the amount certified or accepted, the obligation of the acceptor is that amount. If (i) the certification or acceptance does not state an amount, (ii) the amount of the instrument is subsequently raised, and (iii) the instrument is then negotiated to a holder in due course, the obligation of the acceptor is the amount of the instrument at the time it was taken by the holder in due course.

§ 3–414. Obligation of Drawer.

(a) This section does not apply to cashier's checks or other drafts drawn on the drawer.

(b) If an unaccepted draft is dishonored, the drawer is obliged to pay the draft (i) according to its terms at the time it was issued or, if not issued, at the time it first came into possession of a holder, or (ii) if the

drawer signed an incomplete instrument, according to its terms when completed, to the extent stated in Sections 3–115 and 3–407. The obligation is owed to a person entitled to enforce the draft or to an indorser who paid the draft under Section 3–415.

(c) If a draft is accepted by a bank, the drawer is discharged, regardless of when or by whom acceptance was obtained.

(d) If a draft is accepted and the acceptor is not a bank, the obligation of the drawer to pay the draft if the draft is dishonored by the acceptor is the same as the obligation of an indorser under Section 3–415(a) and (c).

(e) If a draft states that it is drawn "without recourse" or otherwise disclaims liability of the drawer to pay the draft, the drawer is not liable under subsection (b) to pay the draft if the draft is not a check. A disclaimer of the liability stated in subsection (b) is not effective if the draft is a check.

(f) If (i) a check is not presented for payment or given to a depositary bank for collection within 30 days after its date, (ii) the drawee suspends payments after expiration of the 30–day period without paying the check, and (iii) because of the suspension of payments, the drawer is deprived of funds maintained with the drawee to cover payment of the check, the drawer to the extent deprived of funds may discharge its obligation to pay the check by assigning to the person entitled to enforce the check the rights of the drawer against the drawee with respect to the funds.

§ 3–415. Obligation of Indorser.

(a) Subject to subsections (b), (c), (d), (e) and to Section 3–419(d), if an instrument is dishonored, an indorser is obliged to pay the amount due on the instrument (i) according to the terms of the instrument at the time it was indorsed, or (ii) if the indorser indorsed an incomplete instrument, according to its terms when completed, to the extent stated in Sections 3–115 and 3–407. The obligation of the indorser is owed to a person entitled to enforce the instrument or to a subsequent indorser who paid the instrument under this section.

(b) If an indorsement states that it is made "without recourse" or otherwise disclaims liability of the indorser, the indorser is not liable under subsection (a) to pay the instrument.

(c) If notice of dishonor of an instrument is required by Section 3–503 and notice of dishonor complying with that section is not given to an indorser, the liability of the indorser under subsection (a) is discharged.

(d) If a draft is accepted by a bank after an indorsement is made, the liability of the indorser under subsection (a) is discharged.

(e) If an indorser of a check is liable under subsection (a) and the check is not presented for payment, or given to a depositary bank for collection, within 30 days after the day the indorsement was made, the liability of the indorser under subsection (a) is discharged.

§ 3–416. Transfer Warranties.

(a) A person who transfers an instrument for consideration warrants to the transferee and, if the transfer is by indorsement, to any subsequent transferee that:

(1) the warrantor is a person entitled to enforce the instrument;

(2) all signatures on the instrument are authentic and authorized;

(3) the instrument has not been altered;

(4) the instrument is not subject to a defense or claim in recoupment of any party which can be asserted against the warrantor;

(5) the warrantor has no knowledge of any insolvency proceeding commenced with respect to the maker or acceptor or, in the case of an unaccepted draft, the drawer; and

(6) with respect to a remotely-created consumer item, that the person on whose account the item is drawn authorized the issuance of the item in the amount for which the item is drawn.

(b) A person to whom the warranties under subsection (a) are made and who took the instrument in good faith may recover from the warrantor as damages for breach of warranty an amount equal to the loss suffered as a result of the breach, but not more than the amount of the instrument plus expenses and loss of interest incurred as a result of the breach.

(c) The warranties stated in subsection (a) cannot be disclaimed with respect to checks. Unless notice of a claim for breach of warranty is given to the warrantor within 30 days after the claimant has reason to know of the breach and the identity of the warrantor, the liability of the warrantor under subsection (b) is discharged to the extent of any loss caused by the delay in giving notice of the claim.

(d) A [cause of action] for breach of warranty under this section accrues when the claimant has reason to know of the breach.

§ 3–417. Presentment Warranties.

(a) If an unaccepted draft is presented to the drawee for payment or acceptance and the drawee pays or accepts the draft, (i) the person obtaining payment or acceptance, at the time of presentment, and (ii) a previous transferor of the draft, at the time of transfer, warrant to the drawee making payment or accepting the draft in good faith that:

(1) the warrantor is, or was, at the time the warrantor transferred the draft, a person entitled to enforce the draft or authorized to obtain payment or acceptance of the draft on behalf of a person entitled to enforce the draft;

(2) the draft has not been altered;

(3) the warrantor has no knowledge that the signature of the drawer of the draft is unauthorized; and

(4) with respect to any remotely-created consumer item, that the person on whose account the item is drawn authorized the issuance of the item in the amount for which the item is drawn.

(b) A drawee making payment may recover from any warrantor damages for breach of warranty equal to the amount paid by the drawee less the amount the drawee received or is entitled to receive from the drawer because of the payment. In addition, the drawee is entitled to compensation for expenses and loss of interest resulting from the breach. The right of the drawee to recover damages under this subsection is not affected by any failure of the drawee to exercise ordinary care in making payment. If the drawee accepts the draft, breach of warranty is a defense to the obligation of the acceptor. If the acceptor makes payment with respect to the draft, the acceptor is entitled to recover from any warrantor for breach of warranty the amounts stated in this subsection.

(c) If a drawee asserts a claim for breach of warranty under subsection (a) based on an unauthorized indorsement of the draft or an alteration of the draft, the warrantor may defend by proving that the indorsement is effective under Section 3–404 or 3–405 or the drawer is precluded under Section 3–406 or 4–406 from asserting against the drawee the unauthorized indorsement or alteration.

(d) If (i) a dishonored draft is presented for payment to the drawer or an indorser or (ii) any other instrument is presented for payment to a party obliged to pay the instrument, and (iii) payment is received, the following rules apply:

(1) The person obtaining payment and a prior transferor of the instrument warrant to the person making payment in good faith that the warrantor is, or was, at the time the warrantor transferred the instrument, a person entitled to enforce the instrument or authorized to obtain payment on behalf of a person entitled to enforce the instrument.

(2) The person making payment may recover from any warrantor for breach of warranty an amount equal to the amount paid plus expenses and loss of interest resulting from the breach.

(e) The warranties stated in subsections (a) and (d) cannot be disclaimed with respect to checks. Unless notice of a claim for breach of warranty is given to the warrantor within 30 days after the claimant has reason to know of the breach and the identity of the warrantor, the liability of the warrantor under subsection (b) or (d) is discharged to the extent of any loss caused by the delay in giving notice of the claim.

(f) A [cause of action] for breach of warranty under this section accrues when the claimant has reason to know of the breach.

§ 3–418. Payment or Acceptance by Mistake.

(a) Except as provided in subsection (c), if the drawee of a draft pays or accepts the draft and the drawee acted on the mistaken belief that (i) payment of the draft had not been stopped pursuant to Section 4–403 or (ii) the signature of the drawer of the draft was authorized, the drawee may recover the amount of the draft from the person to whom or for whose benefit payment was made or, in the case of acceptance, may revoke the acceptance. Rights of the drawee under this subsection are not affected by failure of the drawee to exercise ordinary care in paying or accepting the draft.

(b) Except as provided in subsection (c), if an instrument has been paid or accepted by mistake and the case is not covered by subsection (a), the person paying or accepting may, to the extent permitted by the law governing mistake and restitution, (i) recover the payment from the person to whom or for whose benefit payment was made or (ii) in the case of acceptance, may revoke the acceptance.

(c) The remedies provided by subsection (a) or (b) may not be asserted against a person who took the instrument in good faith and for value or who in good faith changed position in reliance on the payment or

acceptance. This subsection does not limit remedies provided by Section 3–417 or 4–407.

(d) Notwithstanding Section 4–215, if an instrument is paid or accepted by mistake and the payor or acceptor recovers payment or revokes acceptance under subsection (a) or (b), the instrument is deemed not to have been paid or accepted and is treated as dishonored, and the person from whom payment is recovered has rights as a person entitled to enforce the dishonored instrument.

§ 3–419. Instruments Signed for Accommodation.

(a) If an instrument is issued for value given for the benefit of a party to the instrument ("accommodated party") and another party to the instrument ("accommodation party") signs the instrument for the purpose of incurring liability on the instrument without being a direct beneficiary of the value given for the instrument, the instrument is signed by the accommodation party "for accommodation."

(b) An accommodation party may sign the instrument as maker, drawer, acceptor, or indorser and, subject to subsection (d), is obliged to pay the instrument in the capacity in which the accommodation party signs. The obligation of an accommodation party may be enforced notwithstanding any statute of frauds and whether or not the accommodation party receives consideration for the accommodation.

(c) A person signing an instrument is presumed to be an accommodation party and there is notice that the instrument is signed for accommodation if the signature is an anomalous indorsement or is accompanied by words indicating that the signer is acting as surety or guarantor with respect to the obligation of another party to the instrument. Except as provided in Section 3-605, the obligation of an accommodation party to pay the instrument is not affected by the fact that the person enforcing the obligation had notice when the instrument was taken by that person that the accommodation party signed the instrument for accommodation.

(d) If the signature of a party to an instrument is accompanied by words indicating unambiguously that the party is guaranteeing collection rather than payment of the obligation of another party to the instrument, the signer is obliged to pay the amount due on the instrument to a person entitled to enforce the instrument only if (i) execution of judgment against the other party has been returned unsatisfied, (ii) the other party is insolvent or in an insolvency proceeding, (iii) the other party cannot be served with process, or (iv) it is otherwise apparent that payment cannot be obtained from the other party.

(e) If the signature of a party to an instrument is accompanied by words indicating that the party guarantees payment or the signer signs the instrument as an accommodation party in some other manner that does not unambiguously indicate an intention to guarantee collection rather than payment, the signer is obliged to pay the amount due on the instrument to a person entitled to enforce the instrument in the same circumstances as the accommodated party would be obliged, without prior resort to the accommodated party by the person entitled to enforce the instrument.

(f) An accommodation party who pays the instrument is entitled to reimbursement from the accommodated party and is entitled to enforce the instrument against the accommodated party. In proper circumstances, an accommodation party may obtain relief that requires the accommodated party to perform its obligations on the instrument. An accommodated party that pays the instrument has no right of recourse against, and is not entitled to contribution from, an accommodation party.

§ 3–420. Conversion of Instrument.

(a) The law applicable to conversion of personal property applies to instruments. An instrument is also converted if it is taken by transfer, other than a negotiation, from a person not entitled to enforce the instrument or a bank makes or obtains payment with respect to the instrument for a person not entitled to enforce the instrument or receive payment. An action for conversion of an instrument may not be brought by (i) the issuer or acceptor of the instrument or (ii) a payee or indorsee who did not receive delivery of the instrument either directly or through delivery to an agent or a co-payee.

(b) In an action under subsection (a), the measure of liability is presumed to be the amount payable on the instrument, but recovery may not exceed the amount of the plaintiff's interest in the instrument.

(c) A representative, other than a depositary bank, who has in good faith dealt with an instrument or its proceeds on behalf of one who was not the person entitled to enforce the instrument is not liable in conversion to that person beyond the amount of any proceeds that it has not paid out.

Part 5: Dishonor

§ 3–501. Presentment.

(a) "Presentment" means a demand made by or on behalf of a person entitled to enforce an instrument (i) to pay the instrument made to the drawee or a party obliged to pay the instrument or, in the case of a note or accepted draft payable at a bank, to the bank, or (ii) to accept a draft made to the drawee.

(b) The following rules are subject to Article 4, agreement of the parties, and clearing-house rules and the like:

(1) Presentment may be made at the place of payment of the instrument and must be made at the place of payment if the instrument is payable at a bank in the United States; may be made by any commercially reasonable means, including an oral, written, or electronic communication; is effective when the demand for payment or acceptance is received by the person to whom presentment is made; and is effective if made to any one of two or more makers, acceptors, drawees, or other payors.

(2) Upon demand of the person to whom presentment is made, the person making presentment must (i) exhibit the instrument, (ii) give reasonable identification and, if presentment is made on behalf of another person, reasonable evidence of authority to do so, and (iii) sign a receipt on the instrument for any payment made or surrender the instrument if full payment is made.

(3) Without dishonoring the instrument, the party to whom presentment is made may (i) return the instrument for lack of a necessary indorsement, or (ii) refuse payment or acceptance for failure of the presentment to comply with the terms of the instrument, an agreement of the parties, or other applicable law or rule.

(4) The party to whom presentment is made may treat presentment as occurring on the next business day after the day of presentment if the party to whom presentment is made has established a cut-off hour not earlier than 2 p.m. for the receipt and processing of instruments presented for payment or acceptance and presentment is made after the cut-off hour.

§ 3–502. Dishonor.

(a) Dishonor of a note is governed by the following rules:

    (1) If the note is payable on demand, the note is dishonored if presentment is duly made to the maker and the note is not paid on the day of presentment.

    (2) If the note is not payable on demand and is payable at or through a bank or the terms of the note require presentment, the note is dishonored if presentment is duly made and the note is not paid on the day it becomes payable or the day of presentment, whichever is later.

    (3) If the note is not payable on demand and paragraph (2) does not apply, the note is dishonored if it is not paid on the day it becomes payable.

(b) Dishonor of an unaccepted draft other than a documentary draft is governed by the following rules:

    (1) If a check is duly presented for payment to the payor bank otherwise than for immediate payment over the counter, the check is dishonored if the payor bank makes timely return of the check or sends timely notice of dishonor or nonpayment under Section 4–301 or 4–302, or becomes accountable for the amount of the check under Section 4–302.

    (2) If a draft is payable on demand and paragraph (1) does not apply, the draft is dishonored if presentment for payment is duly made to the drawee and the draft is not paid on the day of presentment.

    (3) If a draft is payable on a date stated in the draft, the draft is dishonored if (i) presentment for payment is duly made to the drawee and payment is not made on the day the draft becomes payable or the day of presentment, whichever is later, or (ii) presentment for acceptance is duly made before the day the draft becomes payable and the draft is not accepted on the day of presentment.

    (4) If a draft is payable on elapse of a period of time after sight or acceptance, the draft is dishonored if presentment for acceptance is duly made and the draft is not accepted on the day of presentment.

(c) Dishonor of an unaccepted documentary draft occurs according to the rules stated in subsection (b)(2), (3), and (4), except that payment or acceptance may be delayed without dishonor until no later than the close of the third business day of the drawee following the day on which payment or acceptance is required by those paragraphs.

(d) Dishonor of an accepted draft is governed by the following rules:

    (1) If the draft is payable on demand, the draft is dishonored if presentment for payment is duly made to the acceptor and the draft is not paid on the day of presentment.

    (2) If the draft is not payable on demand, the draft is dishonored if presentment for payment is duly made to the acceptor and payment is not made on the day it becomes payable or the day of presentment, whichever is later.

(e) In any case in which presentment is otherwise required for dishonor under this section and presentment is excused under Section 3–504, dishonor occurs without presentment if the instrument is not duly accepted or paid.

(f) If a draft is dishonored because timely acceptance of the draft was not made and the person entitled to demand acceptance consents to a late acceptance, from the time of acceptance the draft is treated as never having been dishonored.

§ 3–503. Notice of Dishonor.

(a) The obligation of an indorser stated in Section 3–415(a) and the obligation of a drawer stated in Section 3–414(d) may not be enforced unless (i) the indorser or drawer is given notice of dishonor of the instrument complying with this section or (ii) notice of dishonor is excused under Section 3–504(b).

(b) Notice of dishonor may be given by any person; may be given by any commercially reasonable means, including an oral, written, or electronic communication; and is sufficient if it reasonably identifies the instrument and indicates that the instrument has been dishonored or has not been paid or accepted. Return of an instrument given to a bank for collection is sufficient notice of dishonor.

(c) Subject to Section 3–504(c), with respect to an instrument taken for collection by a collecting bank, notice of dishonor must be given (i) by the bank before midnight of the next banking day following the banking day on which the bank receives notice of dishonor of the instrument, or (ii) by any other person within 30 days following the day on which the person receives notice of dishonor. With respect to any other instrument, notice of dishonor must be given within 30 days following the day on which dishonor occurs.

§ 3–504. Excused Presentment and Notice of Dishonor.

(a) Presentment for payment or acceptance of an instrument is excused if (i) the person entitled to present the instrument cannot with reasonable diligence make presentment, (ii) the maker or acceptor has repudiated an obligation to pay the instrument or is dead or in insolvency proceedings, (iii) by the terms of the instrument presentment is not necessary to enforce the obligation of indorsers or the drawer, (iv) the drawer or indorser whose obligation is being enforced has waived presentment or otherwise has no reason to expect or right to require that the instrument be paid or accepted, or (v) the drawer instructed the drawee not to pay or accept the draft or the drawee was not obligated to the drawer to pay the draft.

(b) Notice of dishonor is excused if (i) by the terms of the instrument notice of dishonor is not necessary to enforce the obligation of a party to pay the instrument, or (ii) the party whose obligation is being enforced waived notice of dishonor. A waiver of presentment is also a waiver of notice of dishonor.

(c) Delay in giving notice of dishonor is excused if the delay was caused by circumstances beyond the control of the person giving the notice and the person giving the notice exercised reasonable diligence after the cause of the delay ceased to operate.

§ 3–505. Evidence of Dishonor.

(a) The following are admissible as evidence and create a presumption of dishonor and of any notice of dishonor stated:

    (1) a document regular in form as provided in subsection (b) which purports to be a protest;

    (2) a purported stamp or writing of the drawee, payor bank, or presenting bank on or accompanying the instrument stating that acceptance or payment has been refused unless reasons for the refusal are stated and the reasons are not consistent with dishonor;

    (3) a book or record of the drawee, payor bank, or collecting bank, kept in the usual course of business which shows dishonor, even if there is no evidence of who made the entry.

(b) A protest is a certificate of dishonor made by a United States consul or vice consul, or a notary public or other person authorized to administer oaths by the law of the place where dishonor occurs. It may be made upon information satisfactory to that person. The protest must identify the instrument and certify either that presentment has been made or, if not made, the reason why it was not made, and that the instrument has been dishonored by nonacceptance or nonpayment. The protest may also certify that notice of dishonor has been given to some or all parties.

Part 6: Discharge and Payment

§ 3–601. Discharge and Effect of Discharge.

(a) The obligation of a party to pay the instrument is discharged as stated in this Article or by an act or agreement with the party which would discharge an obligation to pay money under a simple contract.

(b) Discharge of the obligation of a party is not effective against a person acquiring rights of a holder in due course of the instrument without notice of the discharge.

§ 3–602. Payment.

(a) Subject to subsection (e), an instrument is paid to the extent payment is made by or on behalf of a party obliged to pay the instrument, and to a person entitled to enforce the instrument.

(b) Subject to subsection (e), a note is paid to the extent payment is made by or on behalf of a party obliged to pay the note to a person that formerly was entitled to enforce the note only if at the time of the payment the party obliged to pay has not received adequate notification that the note has been transferred and that payment is to be made to the transferee. A notification is adequate only if it is signed by the transferor or the transferee; reasonably identifies the transferred note; and provides an address at which payments subsequently are to be made. Upon request, a transferee shall seasonably furnish reasonable proof that the note has been transferred. Unless the transferee complies with the request, a payment to the person that formerly was entitled to enforce the note is effective for purposes of subsection (c) even if the party obliged to pay the note has received a notification under this paragraph.

(c) Subject to subsection (e), to the extent of a payment under subsections (a) and (b), the obligation of the party obliged to pay the instrument is discharged even though payment is made with knowledge of a claim to the instrument under Section 3-306 by another person.

(d) Subject to subsection (e), a transferee, or any party that has acquired rights in the instrument directly or indirectly from a transferee, including any such party that has rights as a holder in due course, is deemed to have notice of any payment that is made under subsection (b) after the date that the note is transferred to the transferee but before the party obliged to pay the note receives adequate notification of the transfer.

(e) The obligation of a party to pay the instrument is not discharged under subsections (a) through (d) if:

(1) a claim to the instrument under Section 3-306 is enforceable against the party receiving payment and (i) payment is made with knowledge by the payor that payment is prohibited by injunction or similar process of a court of competent jurisdiction, or (ii) in the case of an instrument other than a cashier's check, teller's check, or certified check, the party making payment accepted, from the person having a claim to the instrument, indemnity against loss resulting from refusal to pay the person entitled to enforce the instrument; or

(2) the person making payment knows that the instrument is a stolen instrument and pays a person it knows is in wrongful possession of the instrument.

(f) As used in this section, "signed," with respect to a record that is not a writing, includes the attachment to or logical association with the record of an electronic symbol, sound, or process with the present intent to adopt or accept the record.

§ 3–603. Tender of Payment.

(a) If tender of payment of an obligation to pay an instrument is made to a person entitled to enforce the instrument, the effect of tender is governed by principles of law applicable to tender of payment under a simple contract.

(b) If tender of payment of an obligation to pay an instrument is made to a person entitled to enforce the instrument and the tender is refused, there is discharge, to the extent of the amount of the tender, of the obligation of an indorser or accommodation party having a right of recourse with respect to the obligation to which the tender relates.

(c) If tender of payment of an amount due on an instrument is made to a person entitled to enforce the instrument, the obligation of the obligor to pay interest after the due date on the amount tendered is discharged. If presentment is required with respect to an instrument and the obligor is able and ready to pay on the due date at every place of payment stated in the

instrument, the obligor is deemed to have made tender of payment on the due date to the person entitled to enforce the instrument.

§ 3–604. Discharge by Cancellation or Renunciation.

(a) A person entitled to enforce an instrument, with or without consideration, may discharge the obligation of a party to pay the instrument (i) by an intentional voluntary act, such as surrender of the instrument to the party, destruction, mutilation, or cancellation of the instrument, cancellation or striking out of the party's signature, or the addition of words to the instrument indicating discharge, or (ii) by agreeing not to sue or otherwise renouncing rights against the party by a signed record.

(b) Cancellation or striking out of an indorsement pursuant to subsection (a) does not affect the status and rights of a party derived from the indorsement.

(c) In this section, "signed," with respect to a record that is not a writing, includes the attachment to or logical association with the record of an electronic symbol, sound, or process with the present intent to adopt or accept the record.

§ 3–605. Discharge of Secondary Obligors.

(a) If a person entitled to enforce an instrument releases the obligation of a principal obligor in whole or in part, and another party to the instrument is a secondary obligor with respect to the obligation of that principal obligor, the following rules apply:

(1) Any obligations of the principal obligor to the secondary obligor with respect to any previous payment by the secondary obligor are not affected. Unless the terms of the release preserve the secondary obligor's recourse, the principal obligor is discharged, to the extent of the release, from any other duties to the secondary obligor under this article.

(2) Unless the terms of the release provide that the person entitled to enforce the instrument retains the right to enforce the instrument against the secondary obligor, the secondary obligor is discharged to the same extent as the principal obligor from any unperformed portion of its obligation on the instrument. If the instrument is a check and the obligation of the secondary obligor is based on an indorsement of the check, the secondary obligor is discharged without regard to the language or circumstances of the discharge or other release.

(3) If the secondary obligor is not discharged under paragraph (2), the secondary obligor is discharged to the extent of the value of the consideration for the release, and to the extent that the release would otherwise cause the secondary obligor a loss.

(b) If a person entitled to enforce an instrument grants a principal obligor an extension of the time at which one or more payments are due on the instrument and another party to the instrument is a secondary obligor with respect to the obligation of that principal obligor, the following rules apply:

(1) Any obligations of the principal obligor to the secondary obligor with respect to any previous payment by the secondary obligor are not affected. Unless the terms of the extension preserve the secondary obligor's recourse, the extension correspondingly extends the time for performance of any other duties owed to the secondary obligor by the principal obligor under this article.

(2) The secondary obligor is discharged to the extent that the extension would otherwise cause the secondary obligor a loss.

(3) To the extent that the secondary obligor is not discharged under paragraph (2), the secondary obligor may perform its obligations to a person entitled to enforce the instrument as if the time for payment had not been extended or, unless the terms of the extension provide that the person entitled to enforce the instrument retains the right to enforce the instrument against the secondary obligor as if the time for payment had not been extended, treat the time for performance of its obligations as having been extended correspondingly.

(c) If a person entitled to enforce an instrument agrees, with or without consideration, to a modification of the obligation of a principal obligor other than a complete or partial release or an extension of the due date and another party to the instrument is a secondary obligor with respect to the obligation of that principal obligor, the following rules apply:

(1) Any obligations of the principal obligor to the secondary obligor with respect to any previous payment by the secondary obligor are not affected. The modification correspondingly modifies any other duties owed to the secondary obligor by the principal obligor under this article.

(2) The secondary obligor is discharged from any unperformed portion of its obligation to the extent that the modification would otherwise cause the secondary obligor a loss.

(3) To the extent that the secondary obligor is not discharged under paragraph (2), the secondary obligor may satisfy its obligation on the instrument as if the modification had not occurred, or treat its obligation on the instrument as having been modified correspondingly.

(d) If the obligation of a principal obligor is secured by an interest in collateral, another party to the instrument is a secondary obligor with respect to that obligation, and a person entitled to enforce the instrument impairs the value of the interest in collateral, the obligation of the secondary obligor is discharged to the extent of the impairment. The value of an interest in collateral is impaired to the extent the value of the interest is reduced to an amount less than the amount of the recourse of the secondary obligor, or the reduction in value of the interest causes an increase in the amount by which the amount of the recourse exceeds the value of the interest. For purposes of this subsection, impairing the value of an interest in collateral includes failure to obtain or maintain perfection or recordation of the interest in collateral, release of collateral without substitution of collateral of equal value or equivalent reduction of the underlying obligation, failure to perform a duty to preserve the value of collateral owed, under Article 9 or other law, to a debtor or other person secondarily liable, and failure to comply with applicable law in disposing of or otherwise enforcing the interest in collateral.

(e) A secondary obligor is not discharged under subsections (a)(3), (b), (c), or (d) unless the person entitled to enforce the instrument knows that the person is a secondary obligor or has notice under Section 3-419(c) that the instrument was signed for accommodation.

(f) A secondary obligor is not discharged under this section if the secondary obligor consents to the event or conduct that is the basis of the discharge, or the instrument or a separate agreement of the party provides for waiver of discharge under this section specifically or by general language indicating that parties waive defenses based on suretyship or impairment of collateral. Unless the circumstances indicate otherwise, consent by the principal obligor to an act that would lead to a discharge under this section constitutes consent to that act by the secondary obligor if the secondary obligor controls the principal obligor or deals with the person entitled to enforce the instrument on behalf of the principal obligor.

(g) A release or extension preserves a secondary obligor's recourse if the terms of the release or extension provide that:

(1) the person entitled to enforce the instrument retains the right to enforce the instrument against the secondary obligor; and

(2) the recourse of the secondary obligor continues as if the release or extension had not been granted.

(h) Except as otherwise provided in subsection (i), a secondary obligor asserting discharge under this section has the burden of persuasion both with respect to the occurrence of the acts alleged to harm the secondary obligor and loss or prejudice caused by those acts.

(i) If the secondary obligor demonstrates prejudice caused by an impairment of its recourse, and the circumstances of the case indicate that the amount of loss is not reasonably susceptible of calculation or requires proof of facts that are not ascertainable, it is presumed that the act impairing recourse caused a loss or impairment equal to the liability of the secondary obligor on the instrument. In that event, the burden of persuasion as to any lesser amount of the loss is on the person entitled to enforce the instrument.

Article 4–Bank Deposits and Collections

Part 1: General Provisions and Definitions

§ 4–101. Short Title. This Article may be cited as Uniform Commercial Code—Bank Deposits and Collections.

§ 4–102. Applicability.

(a) To the extent that items within this Article are also within Articles 3 and 8, they are subject to those Articles. If there is conflict, this Article governs Article 3, but Article 8 governs this Article.

(b) The liability of a bank for action or non-action with respect to an item handled by it for purposes of presentment, payment, or collection is governed by the law of the place where the bank is located. In the case of action or non-action by or at a branch or separate office of a bank, its liability is governed by the law of the place where the branch or separate office is located.

§ 4–103. Variation by Agreement; Measure of Damages; Action Constituting Ordinary Care.

(a) The effect of the provisions of this Article may be varied by agreement, but the parties to the agreement cannot disclaim a bank's responsibility for its lack of good faith or failure to exercise ordinary care or limit the measure of damages for the lack or failure. However, the parties may determine by agreement the standards by which the bank's responsibility is to be measured if those standards are not manifestly unreasonable.

(b) Federal Reserve regulations and operating circulars, clearinghouse rules, and the like have the effect of agreements under subsection (a), whether or not specifically assented to by all parties interested in items handled.

(c) Action or non-action approved by this Article or pursuant to Federal Reserve regulations or operating circulars is the exercise of ordinary care and, in the absence of special instructions, action or non-action consistent with clearinghouse rules and the like or with a general banking usage not disapproved by this Article, is prima facie the exercise of ordinary care.

(d) The specification or approval of certain procedures by this Article is not disapproval of other procedures that may be reasonable under the circumstances.

(e) The measure of damages for failure to exercise ordinary care in handling an item is the amount of the item reduced by an amount that could not have been realized by the exercise of ordinary care. If there is also bad faith it includes any other damages the party suffered as a proximate consequence.

§ 4–104. Definitions and Index of Definitions.

(a) In this Article, unless the context otherwise requires:

(1) "Account" means any deposit or credit account with a bank, including a demand, time, savings, passbook, share draft, or like account, other than an account evidenced by a certificate of deposit;

(2) "Afternoon" means the period of a day between noon and midnight;

(3) "Banking day" means the part of a day on which a bank is open to the public for carrying on substantially all of its banking functions;

(4) "Clearing house" means an association of banks or other payors regularly clearing items;

(5) "Customer" means a person having an account with a bank or for whom a bank has agreed to collect items, including a bank that maintains an account at another bank;

(6) "Documentary draft" means a draft to be presented for acceptance or payment if specified documents, certificated securities (Section 8-102) or instructions for uncertificated securities (Section 8-102), or other certificates, statements, or the like are to be received by the drawee or other payor before acceptance or payment of the draft;

(7) "Draft" means a draft as defined in Section 3-104 or an item, other than an instrument, that is an order;

(8) "Drawee" means a person ordered in a draft to make payment;

(9) "Item" means an instrument or a promise or order to pay money handled by a bank for collection or payment. The term does not include a payment order governed by Article 4A or a credit or debit card slip;

(10) "Midnight deadline" with respect to a bank is midnight on its next banking day following the banking day on which it receives the relevant item or notice or from which the time for taking action commences to run, whichever is later;

(11) "Settle" means to pay in cash, by clearing-house settlement, in a charge or credit or by remittance, or otherwise as agreed. A settlement may be either provisional or final;

(12) "Suspends payments" with respect to a bank means that it has been closed by order of the supervisory authorities, that a public officer has been appointed to take it over, or that it ceases or refuses to make payments in the ordinary course of business.

(b) Other definitions applying to this Article and the sections in which they appear are:

"Agreement for electronic presentment" Section 4-110.

"Collecting bank"	Section 4-105.
"Depositary bank"	Section 4-105.
"Intermediary bank"	Section 4-105.
"Payor bank"	Section 4-105.
"Presenting bank"	Section 4-105.
"Presentment notice"	Section 4-110.

(c) The following definitions in other Articles apply to this Article:

"Acceptance"	Section 3-409.
"Alteration"	Section 3-407.
"Cashier's check"	Section 3-104.
"Certificate of deposit"	Section 3-104.
"Certified check"	Section 3-409.
"Check"	Section 3-104.
"Good faith"	Section 3-103.
"Holder in due course"	Section 3-302.
"Instrument"	Section 3-104.
"Notice of dishonor"	Section 3-503.
"Order"	Section 3-103.
"Ordinary care"	Section 3-103.
"Person entitled to enforce"	Section 3-301.
"Presentment"	Section 3-501.
"Promise"	Section 3-103.
"Prove"	Section 3-103.
"Record"	Section 3-103.
"Remotely-Created consumer item"	Section 3-103.
"Teller's check"	Section 3-104.
"Unauthorized signature"	Section 3-403.

(d) In addition, Article 1 contains general definitions and principles of construction and interpretation applicable throughout this Article.

§ 4–105. Definitions of Types of Banks   In this Article:

(1) ["Bank" means a person engaged in the business of banking, including a savings bank, savings and loan association, credit union, or trust company;]

(2) "Depositary bank" means the first bank to take an item even though it is also the payor bank, unless the item is presented for immediate payment over the counter;

(3) "Payor bank" means a bank that is the drawee of a draft;

(4) "Intermediary bank" means a bank to which an item is transferred in course of collection except the depositary or payor bank;

(5) "Collecting bank" means a bank handling an item for collection except the payor bank;

(6) "Presenting bank" means a bank presenting an item except a payor bank.

Legislative Note: A jurisdiction that enacts this statute that has not yet enacted the revised version of UCC Article 1 should leave the definition of "Bank" in Section 4-105(1). Section 4-105(1) is reserved for that purpose. A jurisdiction that has adopted or simultaneously adopts the revised Article 1 should delete the definition of "Bank" from Section 4-105(1), but should leave those numbers "reserved." If jurisdictions follow the numbering suggested here, the subsections will have the same numbering in all jurisdictions that have adopted these amendments (whether they have or have not adopted the revised version of UCC Article 1). In either case, they should change the title of the section, as indicated in these revisions, so that all jurisdictions will have the same title for the section.

§ 4–106. Payable Through or Payable at Bank: Collecting Bank.

(a) If an item states that it is "payable through" a bank identified in the item, (i) the item designates the bank as a collecting bank and does not by itself authorize the bank to pay the item, and (ii) the item may be presented for payment only by or through the bank.

Alternative A

(b) If an item states that it is "payable at" a bank identified in the item, the item is equivalent to a draft drawn on the bank.

Alternative B

(b) If an item states that it is "payable at" a bank identified in the item, (i) the item designates the bank as a collecting bank and does not by itself authorize the bank to pay the item, and (ii) the item may be presented for payment only by or through the bank.

(c) If a draft names a nonbank drawee and it is unclear whether a bank named in the draft is a co-drawee or a collecting bank, the bank is a collecting bank.

§ 4–107. Separate Office of Bank.
A branch or separate office of a bank is a separate bank for the purpose of computing the time within which and determining the place at or to which action may be taken or notices or orders shall be given under this Article and under Article 3.

§ 4–108. Time of Receipt of Items.

(a) For the purpose of allowing time to process items, prove balances, and make the necessary entries on its books to determine its position for the day, a bank may fix an afternoon hour of 2 P.M. or later as a cutoff hour for the handling of money and items and the making of entries on its books.

(b) An item or deposit of money received on any day after a cutoff hour so fixed or after the close of the banking day may be treated as being received at the opening of the next banking day.

§ 4–109. Delays.

(a) Unless otherwise instructed, a collecting bank in a good faith effort to secure payment of a specific item drawn on a payor other than a bank, and with or without the approval of any person involved, may waive, modify, or extend time limits imposed or permitted by this [Act] for a period not exceeding two additional banking days without discharge of drawers or indorsers or liability to its transferor or a prior party.

(b) Delay by a collecting bank or payor bank beyond time limits prescribed or permitted by this [Act] or by instructions is excused if (i) the delay is caused by interruption of communication or computer facilities, suspension of payments by another bank, war, emergency conditions, failure of equipment, or other circumstances beyond the control of the bank, and (ii) the bank exercises such diligence as the circumstances require.

§ 4–110. Electronic Presentment.

(a) "Agreement for electronic presentment" means an agreement, clearing-house rule, or Federal Reserve regulation or operating circular, providing that presentment of an item may be made by transmission of an image of an item or information describing the item ("presentment notice") rather than delivery of the item itself. The agreement may provide for procedures governing retention, presentment, payment, dishonor, and other matters concerning items subject to the agreement.

(b) Presentment of an item pursuant to an agreement for presentment is made when the presentment notice is received.

(c) If presentment is made by presentment notice, a reference to "item" or "check" in this Article means the presentment notice unless the context otherwise indicates.

§ 4–111. Statute of Limitations.
An action to enforce an obligation, duty, or right arising under this Article must be commenced within three years after the [cause of action] accrues.

Part 2: Collection of Items: Depositary and Collecting Banks

§ 4–201. Status of Collecting Bank as Agent and Provisional Status of Credits; Applicability of Article; Item Indorsed "Pay Any Bank".

(a) Unless a contrary intent clearly appears and before the time that a settlement given by a collecting bank for an item is or becomes final, the bank, with respect to an item, is an agent or subagent of the owner of the item and any settlement given for the item is provisional. This provision applies regardless of the form of indorsement or lack of indorsement and even though credit given for the item is subject to immediate withdrawal as of right or is in fact withdrawn; but the continuance of ownership of an item by its owner and any rights of the owner to proceeds of the item are subject to rights of a collecting bank, such as those resulting from outstanding advances on the item and rights of recoupment or setoff. If an item is handled by banks for purposes of presentment, payment, collection, or return, the relevant provisions of this Article apply even though action of the parties clearly establishes that a particular bank has purchased the item and is the owner of it.

(b) After an item has been indorsed with the words "pay any bank" or the like, only a bank may acquire the rights of a holder until the item has been:
   (1) returned to the customer initiating collection; or
   (2) specially indorsed by a bank to a person who is not a bank.

§ 4–202. Responsibility for Collection or Return; When Action Timely.

(a) A collecting bank must exercise ordinary care in:
   (1) presenting an item or sending it for presentment;
   (2) sending notice of dishonor or nonpayment or returning an item other than a documentary draft to the bank's transferor after learning that the item has not been paid or accepted, as the case may be;
   (3) settling for an item when the bank receives final settlement; and
   (4) notifying its transferor of any loss or delay in transit within a reasonable time after discovery thereof.

(b) A collecting bank exercises ordinary care under subsection (a) by taking proper action before its midnight deadline following receipt of an item, notice, or settlement. Taking proper action within a reasonably longer time may constitute the exercise of ordinary care, but the bank has the burden of establishing timeliness.

(c) Subject to subsection (a)(1), a bank is not liable for the insolvency, neglect, misconduct, mistake, or default of another bank or person or for loss or destruction of an item in the possession of others or in transit.

§ 4–203. Effect of Instructions.
Subject to Article 3 concerning conversion of instruments (Section 3–420) and restrictive indorsements (Section 3–206), only a collecting bank's transferor can give instructions that affect the bank or constitute notice to it, and a collecting bank is not liable to prior parties for any action taken pursuant to the instructions or in accordance with any agreement with its transferor.

§ 4–204. Methods of Sending and Presenting; Sending Directly to Payor Bank.

(a) A collecting bank shall send items by a reasonably prompt method, taking into consideration relevant instructions, the nature of the item, the number of those items on hand, the cost of collection involved, and the method generally used by it or others to present those items.

(b) A collecting bank may send:
   (1) an item directly to the payor bank;
   (2) an item to a nonbank payor if authorized by its transferor; and
   (3) an item other than documentary drafts to a nonbank payor, if authorized by Federal Reserve regulation or operating circular, clearinghouse rule, or the like.

(c) Presentment may be made by a presenting bank at a place where the payor bank or other payor has requested that presentment be made.

§ 4–205. Depositary Bank Holder of Unindorsed Item.
If a customer delivers an item to a depositary bank for collection:

   (1) the depositary bank becomes a holder of the item at the time it receives the item for collection if the customer at the time of delivery was a holder of the item, whether or not the customer indorses the item, and, if the bank satisfies the other requirements of Section 3–302, it is a holder in due course; and
   (2) the depositary bank warrants to collecting banks, the payor bank or other payor, and the drawer that the amount of the item was paid to

the customer or deposited to the customer's account.

§ 4–206. Transfer Between Banks.

Any agreed method that identifies the transferor bank is sufficient for the item's further transfer to another bank.

§ 4–207. Transfer Warranties.

(a) A customer or collecting bank that transfers an item and receives a settlement or other consideration warrants to the transferee and to any subsequent collecting bank that:

   (1) the warrantor is a person entitled to enforce the item;

   (2) all signatures on the item are authentic and authorized;

   (3) the item has not been altered;

   (4) the item is not subject to a defense or claim in recoupment (Section 3–305(a)) of any party that can be asserted against the warrantor;

   (5) the warrantor has no knowledge of any insolvency proceeding commenced with respect to the maker or acceptor or, in the case of an unaccepted draft, the drawer; and

   (6) with respect to any remotely-created consumer item, that the person on whose account the item is drawn authorized the issuance of the item in the amount for which the item is drawn.

(b) If an item is dishonored, a customer or collecting bank transferring the item and receiving settlement or other consideration is obliged to pay the amount due on the item (i) according to the terms of the item at the time it was transferred, or (ii) if the transfer was of an incomplete item, according to its terms when completed as stated in Sections 3–115 and 3–407. The obligation of a transferor is owed to the transferee and to any subsequent collecting bank that takes the item in good faith. A transferor cannot disclaim its obligation under this subsection by an indorsement stating that it is made "without recourse" or otherwise disclaiming liability.

(c) A person to whom the warranties under subsection (a) are made and who took the item in good faith may recover from the warrantor as damages for breach of warranty an amount equal to the loss suffered as a result of the breach, but not more than the amount of the item plus expenses and loss of interest incurred as a result of the breach.

(d) The warranties stated in subsection (a) cannot be disclaimed with respect to checks. Unless notice of a claim for breach of warranty is given to the warran-

tor within 30 days after the claimant has reason to know of the breach and the identity of the warrantor, the warrantor is discharged to the extent of any loss caused by the delay in giving notice of the claim.

(e) A cause of action for breach of warranty under this section accrues when the claimant has reason to know of the breach.

§ 4–208. Presentment Warranties.

(a) If an unaccepted draft is presented to the drawee for payment or acceptance and the drawee pays or accepts the draft, (i) the person obtaining payment or acceptance, at the time of presentment, and (ii) a previous transferor of the draft, at the time of transfer, warrant to the drawee that pays or accepts the draft in good faith that:

   (1) the warrantor is, or was, at the time the warrantor transferred the draft, a person entitled to enforce the draft or authorized to obtain payment or acceptance of the draft on behalf of a person entitled to enforce the draft;

   (2) the draft has not been altered; and

   (3) the warrantor has no knowledge that the signature of the purported drawer of the draft is unauthorized; and

   (4) with respect to any remotely-created consumer item, that the person on whose account the item is drawn authorized the issuance of the item in the amount for which the item is drawn.

(b) A drawee making payment may recover from a warrantor damages for breach of warranty equal to the amount paid by the drawee less the amount the drawee received or is entitled to receive from the drawer because of the payment. In addition, the drawee is entitled to compensation for expenses and loss of interest resulting from the breach. The right of the drawee to recover damages under this subsection is not affected by any failure of the drawee to exercise ordinary care in making payment. If the drawee accepts the draft (i) breach of warranty is a defense to the obligation of the acceptor, and (ii) if the acceptor makes payment with respect to the draft, the acceptor is entitled to recover from a warrantor for breach of warranty the amounts stated in this subsection.

(c) If a drawee asserts a claim for breach of warranty under subsection (a) based on an unauthorized indorsement of the draft or an alteration of the draft, the warrantor may defend by proving that the indorsement is effective under Section 3–404 or 3–405 or the drawer is precluded under Section 3–406 or

4–406 from asserting against the drawee the unauthorized indorsement or alteration.

(d) If (i) a dishonored draft is presented for payment to the drawer or an indorser or (ii) any other item is presented for payment to a party obliged to pay the item, and the item is paid, the person obtaining payment and a prior transferor of the item warrant to the person making payment in good faith that the warrantor is, or was, at the time the warrantor transferred the item, a person entitled to enforce the item or authorized to obtain payment on behalf of a person entitled to enforce the item. The person making payment may recover from any warrantor for breach of warranty an amount equal to the amount paid plus expenses and loss of interest resulting from the breach.

(e) The warranties stated in subsections (a) and (d) cannot be disclaimed with respect to checks. Unless notice of a claim for breach of warranty is given to the warrantor within 30 days after the claimant has reason to know of the breach and the identity of the warrantor, the warrantor is discharged to the extent of any loss caused by the delay in giving notice of the claim.

(f) A cause of action for breach of warranty under this section accrues when the claimant has reason to know of the breach.

§ 4–209. Encoding and Retention Warranties.

(a) A person who encodes information on or with respect to an item after issue warrants to any subsequent collecting bank and to the payor bank or other payor that the information is correctly encoded. If the customer of a depositary bank encodes, that bank also makes the warranty.

(b) A person who undertakes to retain an item pursuant to an agreement for electronic presentment warrants to any subsequent collecting bank and to the payor bank or other payor that retention and presentment of the item comply with the agreement. If a customer of a depositary bank undertakes to retain an item, that bank also makes this warranty.

(c) A person to whom warranties are made under this section and who took the item in good faith may recover from the warrantor as damages for breach of warranty an amount equal to the loss suffered as a result of the breach, plus expenses and loss of interest incurred as a result of the breach.

§ 4–210. Security Interest of Collecting Bank in Items, Accompanying Documents and Proceeds.

(a) A collecting bank has a security interest in an item and any accompanying documents or the proceeds of either:

(1) in case of an item deposited in an account, to the extent to which credit given for the item has been withdrawn or applied;

(2) in case of an item for which it has given credit available for withdrawal as of right, to the extent of the credit given, whether or not the credit is drawn upon or there is a right of charge back; or

(3) if it makes an advance on or against the item.

(b) If credit given for several items received at one time or pursuant to a single agreement is withdrawn or applied in part, the security interest remains upon all the items, any accompanying documents or the proceeds of either. For the purpose of this section, credits first given are first withdrawn.

(c) Receipt by a collecting bank of a final settlement for an item is a realization on its security interest in the item, accompanying documents, and proceeds. So long as the bank does not receive final settlement for the item or give up possession of the item or accompanying documents for purposes other than collection, the security interest continues to that extent and is subject to Article 9, but:

(1) no security agreement is necessary to make the security interest enforceable (Section 9–203(1)(a));

(2) no filing is required to perfect the security interest; and

(3) **the security interest has priority over conflicting perfected security interests in the item, accompanying documents, or proceeds.**

§ 4–211. When Bank Gives Value for Purposes of Holder in Due Course.
For purposes of determining its status as a holder in due course, a bank has given value to the extent it has a security interest in an item, if the bank otherwise complies with the requirements of Section 3–302 on what constitutes a holder in due course.

§ 4-212. Presentment by Notice of Item Not Payable by, Through, or at Bank; Liability of Drawer or Indorser.

(a) Unless otherwise instructed, a collecting bank may present an item not payable by, through, or at a bank by sending to the party to accept or pay a record providing notice that the bank holds the item for acceptance or payment. The notice must be sent in time to be received on or before the day when presentment is due and the bank must meet any requirement of the party to accept or pay under Section 3-501 by the close of the bank's next banking day after it knows of the requirement.

(b) If presentment is made by notice and payment, acceptance, or request for compliance with a requirement under Section 3-501 is not received by the close of business on the day after maturity or, in the case of demand items, by the close of business on the third banking day after notice was sent, the presenting bank may treat the item as dishonored and charge any drawer or indorser by sending it notice of the facts.

§ 4–213. Medium and Time of Settlement by Bank.

(a) With respect to settlement by a bank, the medium and time of settlement may be prescribed by Federal Reserve regulations or circulars, clearinghouse rules, and the like, or agreement. In the absence of such prescription:

   (1) the medium of settlement is cash or credit to an account in a Federal Reserve bank of or specified by the person to receive settlement; and

   (2) the time of settlement, is:

      (i) with respect to tender of settlement by cash, a cashier's check, or teller's check, when the cash or check is sent or delivered;

      (ii) with respect to tender of settlement by credit in an account in a Federal Reserve Bank, when the credit is made;

      (iii) with respect to tender of settlement by a credit or debit to an account in a bank, when the credit or debit is made or, in the case of tender of settlement by authority to charge an account, when the authority is sent or delivered; or

      (iv) with respect to tender of settlement by a funds transfer, when payment is made pursuant to Section 4A–406(a) to the person receiving settlement.

(b) If the tender of settlement is not by a medium authorized by subsection (a) or the time of settlement is not fixed by subsection (a), no settlement occurs until the tender of settlement is accepted by the person receiving settlement.

(c) If settlement for an item is made by cashier's check or teller's check and the person receiving settlement, before its midnight deadline:

   (1) presents or forwards the check for collection, settlement is final when the check is finally paid; or

   (2) fails to present or forward the check for collection, settlement is final at the midnight deadline of the person receiving settlement.

(d) If settlement for an item is made by giving authority to charge the account of the bank giving settlement in the bank receiving settlement, settlement is final when the charge is made by the bank receiving settlement if there are funds available in the account for the amount of the item.

§ 4–214. Right of Charge–Back or Refund; Liability of Collecting Bank; Return of Item.

(a) If a collecting bank has made provisional settlement with its customer for an item and fails by reason of dishonor, suspension of payments by a bank, or otherwise to receive settlement for the item which is or becomes final, the bank may revoke the settlement given by it, charge back the amount of any credit given for the item to its customer's account, or obtain refund from its customer, whether or not it is able to return the item, if by its midnight deadline or within a longer reasonable time after it learns the facts it returns the item or sends notification of the facts. If the return or notice is delayed beyond the bank's midnight deadline or a longer reasonable time after it learns the facts, the bank may revoke the settlement, charge back the credit, or obtain refund from its customer, but it is liable for any loss resulting from the delay. These rights to revoke, charge back, and obtain refund terminate if and when a settlement for the item received by the bank is or becomes final.

(b) A collecting bank returns an item when it is sent or delivered to the bank's customer or transferor or pursuant to its instructions.

(c) A depository bank that is also the payor may charge back the amount of an item to its customer's account or obtain refund in accordance with the section governing return of an item received by a payor bank for credit on its books (Section 4–301).

(d) The right to charge back is not affected by:

   (1) previous use of a credit given for the item; or

   (2) failure by any bank to exercise ordinary care with respect to the item, but a bank so failing remains liable.

(e) A failure to charge back or claim refund does not affect other rights of the bank against the customer or any other party.

(f) If credit is given in dollars as the equivalent of the value of an item payable in foreign money, the dollar amount of any charge-back or refund must be calculated on the basis of the bank offered spot rate for the foreign money prevailing on the day when the person entitled to the charge-back or refund learns that it will not receive payment in ordinary course.

§ 4–215. Final Payment of Item by Payor Bank; When Provisional Debits and Credits Become Final; When Certain Credits Become Available for Withdrawal.

(a) An item is finally paid by a payor bank when the bank has first done any of the following:

(1) paid the item in cash;

(2) settled for the item without having a right to revoke the settlement under statute, clearinghouse rule, or agreement; or

(3) made a provisional settlement for the item and failed to revoke the settlement in the time and manner permitted by statute, clearinghouse rule, or agreement.

(b) If provisional settlement for an item does not become final, the item is not finally paid.

(c) If provisional settlement for an item between the presenting and payor banks is made through a clearing house or by debits or credits in an account between them, then to the extent that provisional debits or credits for the item are entered in accounts between the presenting and payor banks or between the presenting and successive prior collecting banks seriatim, they become final upon final payment of the item by the payor bank.

(d) If a collecting bank receives a settlement for an item which is or becomes final, the bank is accountable to its customer for the amount of the item and any provisional credit given for the item in an account with its customer becomes final.

(e) Subject to (i) applicable law stating a time for availability of funds and (ii) any right of the bank to apply the credit to an obligation of the customer, credit given by a bank for an item in a customer's account becomes available for withdrawal as of right:

(1) if the bank has received a provisional settlement for the item, when the settlement becomes final and the bank has had a reasonable time to receive return of the item and the item has not been received within that time;

(2) if the bank is both the depositary bank and the payor bank, and the item is finally paid, at the opening of the bank's second banking day following receipt of the item.

(f) Subject to applicable law stating a time for availability of funds and any right of a bank to apply a deposit to an obligation of the depositor, a deposit of money becomes available for withdrawal as of right at the opening of the bank's next banking day after receipt of the deposit.

§ 4–216. Insolvency and Preference.

(a) If an item is in or comes into the possession of a payor or collecting bank that suspends payment and the item has not been finally paid, the item must be returned by the receiver, trustee, or agent in charge of the closed bank to the presenting bank or the closed bank's customer.

(b) If a payor bank finally pays an item and suspends payments without making a settlement for the item with its customer or the presenting bank which settlement is or becomes final, the owner of the item has a preferred claim against the payor bank.

(c) If a payor bank gives or a collecting bank gives or receives a provisional settlement for an item and thereafter suspends payments, the suspension does not prevent or interfere with the settlement's becoming final if the finality occurs automatically upon the lapse of certain time or the happening of certain events.

(d) If a collecting bank receives from subsequent parties settlement for an item, which settlement is or becomes final and the bank suspends payments without making a settlement for the item with its customer which settlement is or becomes final, the owner of the item has a preferred claim against the collecting bank.

Part 3: Collection of Items: Payor Banks

§ 4–301. Posting; Recovery of Payment by Return of Items; Time of Dishonor; Return of Items by Payor Bank.

(a) If a payor bank settles for a demand item other than a documentary draft presented otherwise than for immediate payment over the counter before midnight of the banking day of receipt, the payor bank may revoke the settlement and recover the settlement if, before it has made final payment and before its midnight deadline, it

(1) returns the item;

(2) returns an image of the item, if the party to which the return is made has entered into an agreement to accept an image as a return of the item and the image is returned in accordance with that agreement; or

(3) sends a record providing notice of dishonor or nonpayment if the item is unavailable for return.

(b) If a demand item is received by a payor bank for credit on its books, it may return the item or send notice of dishonor and may revoke any credit given or recover the amount thereof withdrawn by its customer, if it acts within the time limit and in the manner specified in subsection (a).

(c) Unless previous notice of dishonor has been sent, an item is dishonored at the time when for purposes of dishonor it is returned or notice sent in accordance with this section.

(d) An item is returned:

(1) as to an item presented through a clearing house, when it is delivered to the presenting or last collecting bank or to the clearing house or is sent or delivered in accordance with clearing-house rules; or

(2) in all other cases, when it is sent or delivered to the bankís customer or transferor or pursuant to instructions.

§ 4–302. Payor's Bank Responsibility for Late Return of Item.

(a) If an item is presented to and received by a payor bank, the bank is accountable for the amount of:

(1) a demand item, other than a documentary draft, whether properly payable or not, if the bank, in any case in which it is not also the depositary bank, retains the item beyond midnight of the banking day of receipt without settling for it or, whether or not it is also the depositary bank, does not pay or return the item or send notice of dishonor until after its midnight deadline; or

(2) any other properly payable item unless, within the time allowed for acceptance or payment of that item, the bank either accepts or pays the item or returns it and accompanying documents.

(b) The liability of a payor bank to pay an item pursuant to subsection (a) is subject to defenses based on breach of a presentment warranty (Section 4–208) or proof that the person seeking enforcement of the liability presented or transferred the item for the purpose of defrauding the payor bank.

§ 4–303. When Items Subject to Notice, Stop-Payment Order, Legal Process, or Setoff; Order in Which Items May Be Changed or Certified.

(a) Any knowledge, notice, or stop-payment order received by, legal process served upon, or setoff exercised by a payor bank comes too late to terminate, suspend, or modify the bank's right or duty to pay an item or to charge its customer's account for the item if the knowledge, notice, stop-payment order, or

legal process is received or served and a reasonable time for the bank to act thereon expires or the setoff is exercised after the earliest of the following:

(1) the bank accepts or certifies the item;

(2) the bank pays the item in cash;

(3) the bank settles for the item without having a right to revoke the settlement under statute, clearinghouse rule, or agreement;

(4) the bank becomes accountable for the amount of the item under Section 4–302 dealing with the payor bank's responsibility for late return of items; or

(5) with respect to checks, a cutoff hour no earlier than one hour after the opening of the next banking day after the banking day on which the bank received the check and no later than the close of that next banking day or, if no cutoff hour is fixed, the close of the next banking day after the banking day on which the bank received the check.

(b) Subject to subsection (a), items may be accepted, paid, certified, or charged to the indicated account of its customer in any order.

Part 4: Relationship between Payor Bank and Its Customer

§ 4–401. When Bank May Charge Customer's Account.

(a) A bank may charge against the account of a customer an item that is properly payable from the account even though the charge creates an overdraft. An item is properly payable if it is authorized by the customer and is in accordance with any agreement between the customer and bank.

(b) A customer is not liable for the amount of an overdraft if the customer neither signed the item nor benefited from the proceeds of the item.

(c) A bank may charge against the account of a customer a check that is otherwise properly payable from the account, even though payment was made before the date of the check, unless the customer has given notice to the bank of the postdating describing the check with reasonable certainty. The notice is effective for the period stated in Section 4–403(b) for stop payment orders, and must be received at such time and in such manner as to afford the bank a reasonable opportunity to act on it before the bank takes any action with respect to the check described in Section 4–303. If a bank charges against the account of a customer a check before the date stated in the notice of postdating, the bank is liable for damages for the loss resulting from its act. The loss may include damages for dishonor of subsequent items under Section 4–402.

(d) A bank that in good faith makes payment to a holder may charge the indicated account of its customer according to:

(1) the original terms of the altered item; or

(2) the terms of the completed item, even though the bank knows the item has been completed unless the bank has notice that the completion was improper.

§ 4–402. Bankís Liability to Customer for Wrongful Dishonor, Time of Determining Insufficient of Account.

(a) Except as otherwise provided in this Article, a payor bank wrongfully dishonors an item if it dishonors an item that is properly payable, but a bank may dishonor an item that would create an overdraft unless it has agreed to pay the overdraft.

(b) A payor bank is liable to its customer for damages proximately caused by the wrongful dishonor of an item. Liability is limited to actual damages proved and may include damages for an arrest or prosecution of the customer or other consequential damages. Whether any consequential damages are proximately caused by the wrongful dishonor is a question of fact to be determined in each case.

(c) A payor bank's determination of the customer's account balance on which a decision to dishonor for insufficiency of available funds is based may be made at any time between the time the item is received by the payor bank and the time that the payor bank returns the item or gives notice in lieu of return, and no more than one determination need be made. If, at the election of the payor bank, a subsequent balance determination is made for the purpose of reevaluating the bank's decision to dishonor the item, the account balance at that time is determinative of whether a dishonor for insufficiency of available funds is wrongful.

§ 4–403. Customer's Right to Stop Payment; Burden of Proof of Loss.

(a) A customer or any person authorized to draw on the account if there is more than one person may stop payment of any item drawn on the customer's account or close the account by an order to the bank describing the item or account with reasonable certainty received at a time and in a manner that affords the bank a reasonable opportunity to act on it before any action by the bank with respect to the item described in Section 4-303. If the signature of more than one person is required to draw on an account, any of these persons may stop payment or close the account.

(b) A stop-payment order is effective for six months, but it lapses after 14 calendar days if the original order was oral and was not confirmed in a record within that period. A stop-payment order may be renewed for additional six-month periods by a record given to the bank within a period during which the stop-payment order is effective.

(c) The burden of establishing the fact and amount of loss resulting from the payment of an item contrary to a stop-payment order or order to close an account is on the customer. The loss from payment of an item contrary to a stop-payment order may include damages for dishonor of subsequent items under Section 4-402.

§ 4–404. Bank Not Obliged to Pay Check More than Six Months Old.
A bank is under no obligation to a customer having a checking account to pay a check, other than a certified check, which is presented more than six months after its date, but it may charge its customer's account for a payment made thereafter in good faith.

§ 4–405. Death or Incompetence of Customer.

(a) A payor or collecting bank's authority to accept, pay, or collect an item or to account for proceeds of its collection, if otherwise effective, is not rendered ineffective by incompetence of a customer of either bank existing at the time the item is issued or its collection is undertaken if the bank does not know of an adjudication of incompetence. Neither death nor incompetence of a customer revokes the authority to accept, pay, collect, or account until the bank knows of the fact of death or of an adjudication of incompetence and has reasonable opportunity to act on it.

(b) Even with knowledge, a bank may for 10 days after the date of death pay or certify checks drawn on or before that date unless ordered to stop payment by a person claiming an interest in the account.

§ 4–406. Customer's Duty to Discover and Report Unauthorized Signature or Alteration.

(a) A bank that sends or makes available to a customer a statement of account showing payment of items for the account shall either return or make available to the customer the items paid or provide information in the statement of account sufficient to allow the customer reasonably to identify the items paid. The statement of account provides sufficient information if the item is described by item number, amount, and date of payment.

(b) If the items are not returned to the customer, the person retaining the items shall either retain the items or, if the items are destroyed, maintain the capacity to furnish legible copies of the items until the expiration of seven years after receipt of the items. A customer may request an item from the bank that paid the item, and that bank must provide in a reasonable time either the item or, if the item has been destroyed or is not otherwise obtainable, a legible copy of the item.

(c) If a bank sends or makes available a statement of account or items pursuant to subsection (a), the customer must exercise reasonable promptness in examining the statement or the items to determine whether any payment was not authorized because of an alteration of an item or because a purported signature by or on behalf of the customer was not authorized. If, based on the statement or items provided, the customer should reasonably have discovered the unauthorized payment, the customer must promptly notify the bank of the relevant facts.

(d) If the bank proves that the customer failed, with respect to an item, to comply with the duties imposed on the customer by subsection (c), the customer is precluded from asserting against the bank:

(1) the customer's unauthorized signature or any alteration on the item, if the bank also proves that it suffered a loss by reason of the failure; and

(2) the customer's unauthorized signature or alteration by the same wrongdoer on any other item paid in good faith by the bank if the payment was made before the bank received notice from the customer of the unauthorized signature or alteration and after the customer had been afforded a reasonable period of time, not exceeding 30 days, in which to examine the item or statement of account and notify the bank.

(e) If subsection (d) applies and the customer proves that the bank failed to exercise ordinary care in paying the item and that the failure substantially contributed to loss, the loss is allocated between the customer precluded and the bank asserting the preclusion according to the extent to which the failure of the customer to comply with subsection (c) and the failure of the bank to exercise ordinary care contributed to the loss. If the customer proves that the bank did not pay the item in good faith, the preclusion under subsection (d) does not apply.

(f) Without regard to care or lack of care of either the customer or the bank, a customer who does not within one year after the statement or items are made available to the customer (subsection (a)) discover and report the customer's unauthorized signature on or any alteration on the item is precluded from asserting against the bank the unauthorized signature or alteration. If there is a preclusion under this subsection, the payor bank may not recover for breach of warranty under Section 4–208 with respect to the unauthorized signature or alteration to which the preclusion applies.

§ 4–407. Payor Bank's Right to Subrogation on Improper Payment. If a payor bank has paid an item over the order of the drawer or maker to stop payment, or after an account has been closed, or otherwise under circumstances giving a basis for objection by the drawer or maker, to prevent unjust enrichment and only to the extent necessary to prevent loss to the bank by reason of its payment of the item, the payor bank is subrogated to the rights

(1) of any holder in due course on the item against the drawer or maker;

(2) of the payee or any other holder of the item against the drawer or maker either on the item or under the transaction out of which the item arose; and

(3) of the drawer or maker against the payee or any other holder of the item with respect to the transaction out of which the item arose.

Part 5: Collection of Documentary Drafts

§ 4–501. Handling of Documentary Drafts; Duty to Send for Presentment and to Notify Customer of Dishonor. A bank that takes a documentary draft for collection shall present or send the draft and accompanying documents for presentment and, upon learning that the draft has not been paid or accepted in due course, shall seasonably notify its customer of the fact even though it may have discounted or bought the draft or extended credit available for withdrawal as of right.

§ 4–502. Presentment of "On Arrival" Drafts. If a draft or the relevant instructions require presentment "on arrival", "when goods arrive" or the like, the collecting bank need not present until in its judgment a reasonable time for arrival of the goods has expired. Refusal to pay or accept because the goods have not arrived is not dishonor; the bank must notify its transferor of the refusal but need not present the draft again until it is instructed to do so or learns of the arrival of the goods.

§ 4–503. Responsibility of Presenting Bank for Documents and Goods; Report of Reasons for Dishonor; Referee in Case of Need.
Unless otherwise instructed and except as provided in Article 5, a bank presenting a documentary draft:

(1) must deliver the documents to the drawee on acceptance of the draft if it is payable more than three days after presentment; otherwise, only on payment; and

(2) upon dishonor, either in the case of presentment for acceptance or presentment for payment, may seek and follow instructions from any referee in case of need designated in the draft or, if the presenting bank does not choose to utilize the referee's services, it must use diligence and good faith to ascertain the reason for dishonor, must notify its transferor of the dishonor and of the results of its effort to ascertain the reasons therefor, and must request instructions.

However the presenting bank is under no obligation with respect to goods represented by the documents except to follow any reasonable instructions seasonably received; it has a right to reimbursement for any expense incurred in following instructions and to prepayment of or indemnity for those expenses.

§ 4–504. Privilege of Presenting Bank to Deal with Goods; Security Interest for Expenses.

(a) A presenting bank that, following the dishonor of a documentary draft, has seasonably requested instructions but does not receive them within a reasonable time may store, sell, or otherwise deal with the goods in any reasonable manner.

(b) For its reasonable expenses incurred by action under subsection (a) the presenting bank has a lien upon the goods or their proceeds, which may be foreclosed in the same manner as an unpaid seller's lien.

Article 7–Documents of Title

Part 1: General

§ 7–101. Short Title.
This article may be cited as Uniform Commercial Code-Documents of Title.

§ 7–102. Definitions and Index of Definitions.

(a) In this article, unless the context otherwise requires:

(1) "Bailee" means a person that by a warehouse receipt, bill of lading, or other document of title acknowledges possession of goods and contracts to deliver them.

(2) "Carrier" means a person that issues a bill of lading.

(3) "Consignee" means a person named in a bill of lading to which or to whose order the bill promises delivery.

(4) "Consignor" means a person named in a bill of lading as the person from which the goods have been received for shipment.

(5) "Delivery order" means a record that contains an order to deliver goods directed to a warehouse, carrier, or other person that in the ordinary course of business issues warehouse receipts or bills of lading.

(6) "Good faith" means honesty in fact and the observance of reasonable commercial standards of fair dealing.

(7) "Goods" means all things that are treated as movable for the purposes of a contract for storage or transportation.

(8) "Issuer" means a bailee that issues a document of title or, in the case of an unaccepted delivery order, the person that orders the possessor of goods to deliver. The term includes a person for which an agent or employee purports to act in issuing a document if the agent or employee has real or apparent authority to issue documents, even if the issuer did not receive any goods, the goods were misdescribed, or in any other respect the agent or employee violated the issuer's instructions.

(9) "Person entitled under the document" means the holder, in the case of a negotiable document of title, or the person to which delivery of the goods is to be made by the terms of, or pursuant to instructions in a record under, a nonnegotiable document of title.

(10) "Record" means information that is inscribed on a tangible medium or that is stored in an electronic or other medium and is retrievable in perceivable form.

(11) "Sign" means, with present intent to authenticate or adopt a record:

(A) to execute or adopt a tangible symbol; or

(B) to attach to or logically associate with the record an electronic sound, symbol, or process.

(12) "Shipper" means a person that enters into a contract of transportation with a carrier.

(13) "Warehouse" means a person engaged in the business of storing goods for hire.

(b) Definitions in other articles applying to this article and the sections in which they appear are:

(1) "Contract for sale", Section 2–106.

(2) "Lessee in ordinary course", Section 2A-103.

(3) " 'Receipt' of goods", Section 2-103.

(c) In addition, Article 1 contains general definitions and principles of construction and interpretation applicable throughout this article.

Legislative Note: If the state has enacted Revised Article 1, the definitions of "good faith" in subsection (a)(6) and "record" in (a)(10) need not be enacted in this section as they are contained in Article 1, Section 1-201. These subsections should be marked as "reserved" in order to provide for uniform numbering of subsections.

§ 7–103. Relation of Article to Treaty or Statute.

(a) This article is subject to any treaty or statute of the United States or a regulatory statute of this State to the extent the treaty, statute, or regulatory statute is applicable.

(b) This article does not repeal or modify any law prescribing the form or contents of a document of title or the services or facilities to be afforded by a bailee, or otherwise regulating a bailee's businesses in respects not specifically treated in this article. However, violation of these laws does not affect the status of a document of title that otherwise complies with the definition of a document of title.

§ 7–104. Negotiable and Nonnegotiable Document of Title.

(a) A document of title is negotiable if by its terms the goods are to be delivered to bearer or to the order of a named person.

(b) A document of title other than one described in subsection (a) is nonnegotiable. A bill of lading that states that the goods are consigned to a named person is not made negotiable by a provision that the goods are to be delivered only against an order in a record signed by the same or another named person.

(c) A document of title is nonnegotiable if, at the time it is issued, the document has a conspicuous legend, however expressed, that it is nonnegotiable.

§ 7–105. Reissuance in Alternative Medium.

(a) Upon request of a person entitled under an electronic document of title, the issuer of the electronic document may issue a tangible document of title as a substitute for the electronic document if:

(1) the person entitled under the electronic document surrenders control of the document to the issuer; and

(2) the tangible document when issued contains a statement that it is issued in substitution for the electronic document.

(b) Upon issuance of a tangible document of title in substitution for an electronic document of title in accordance with subsection (a):

(1) the electronic document ceases to have any effect or validity; and

(2) the person that procured issuance of the tangible document warrants to all subsequent persons entitled under the tangible document that the warrantor was a person entitled under the electronic document when the warrantor surrendered control of the electronic document to the issuer.

(c) Upon request of a person entitled under a tangible document of title, the issuer of the tangible document may issue an electronic document of title as a substitute for the tangible document if:

(1) the person entitled under the tangible document surrenders possession of the document to the issuer; and

(2) the electronic document when issued contains a statement that it is issued in substitution for the tangible document.

(d) Upon issuance of the electronic document of title in substitution for a tangible document of title in accordance with subsection (c):

(1) the tangible document ceases to have any effect or validity; and

(2) the person that procured issuance of the electronic document warrants to all subsequent persons entitled under the electronic document that the warrantor was a person entitled under the tangible document when the warrantor surrendered possession of the tangible document to the issuer.

§ 7–106. Control of Electronic Document of Title.

(a) A person has control of an electronic document of title if a system employed for evidencing the transfer of interests in the electronic document reliably establishes that person as the person to which the electronic document was issued or transferred.

(b) A system satisfies subsection (a), and a person is deemed to have control of an electronic document of title, if the document is created, stored, and assigned in such a manner that:

   (1) a single authoritative copy of the document exists which is unique, identifiable, and, except as otherwise provided in paragraphs (4), (5), and (6), unalterable;

   (2) the authoritative copy identifies the person asserting control as:

     (A) the person to which the document was issued; or

     (B) if the authoritative copy indicates that the document has been transferred, the person to which the document was most recently transferred;

   (3) the authoritative copy is communicated to and maintained by the person asserting control or its designated custodian;

   (4) copies or amendments that add or change an identified assignee of the authoritative copy can be made only with the consent of the person asserting control;

   (5) each copy of the authoritative copy and any copy of a copy is readily identifiable as a copy that is not the authoritative copy; and

   (6) any amendment of the authoritative copy is readily identifiable as authorized or unauthorized.

§ 7–107. Relation to Electronic Signatures in Global and National Commerce Act. This [Act] modifies, limits, and supersedes the federal Electronic Signatures in Global and National Commerce Act (15 U.S.C. Section 7001, et. seq.) but does not modify, limit, or supersede Section 101(c) of that act (15 U.S.C. Section 7001(c)) or authorize electronic delivery of any of the notices described in Section 103(b) of that act (15 U.S.C. Section 7003(b)).

Part 2: Warehouse Receipts: Special Provisions

§ 7–201. Person That May Issue a Warehouse Receipt; Storage Under Bond.

(a) A warehouse receipt may be issued by any warehouse.

(b) If goods, including distilled spirits and agricultural commodities, are stored under a statute requiring a bond against withdrawal or a license for the issuance of receipts in the nature of warehouse receipts, a receipt issued for the goods is deemed to be a warehouse receipt even if issued by a person that is the owner of the goods and is not a warehouse.

§ 7–202. Form of Warehouse Receipt.

(a) A warehouse receipt need not be in any particular form.

(b) Unless a warehouse receipt provides for each of the following, the warehouse is liable for damages caused to a person injured by the omission:

   (1) the location of the warehouse facility where the goods are stored;

   (2) the date of issue of the receipt;

   (3) the unique identification code of the receipt;

   (4) a statement whether the goods received will be delivered to the bearer, to a named person, or to a named person or its order;

   (5) the rate of storage and handling charges, but if goods are stored under a field warehousing arrangement, a statement of that fact is sufficient on a nonnegotiable receipt;

   (6) a description of the goods or the packages containing them;

   (7) the signature of the warehouse or its agent;

   (8) if the receipt is issued for goods that the warehouse owns, either solely, jointly, or in common with others, the fact of that ownership; and

   (9) a statement of the amount of advances made and of liabilities incurred for which the warehouse claims a lien or security interest but if the precise amount of advances made or of liabilities incurred is, at the time of the issue of the receipt, unknown to the warehouse or to its agent that issued the receipt, a statement of the fact that advances have been made or liabilities incurred and the purpose of the advances or liabilities is sufficient.

(c) A warehouse may insert in its receipt any terms that are not contrary to the provisions of [the Uniform Commercial Code] and do not impair its obligation of delivery under Section 7–403 or its duty of care under Section 7–204. Any contrary provisions are ineffective.

§ 7–203. Liability for Nonreceipt or Misdescription. A party to or purchaser for value in good faith of a document of title, other than a bill of lading, that relies upon the description of the goods in the document may recover from the issuer damages caused by the nonreceipt or misdescription of the goods, except to the extent that:

(1) the document conspicuously indicates that the issuer does not know whether all or part of the goods in fact were received or conform to the description, such as a case in which the description is in terms of marks or labels or kind, quantity, or condition, or the receipt or description is qualified by "contents, condition, and quality unknown", "said to contain", or words of similar import, if the indication is true; or

(2) the party or purchaser otherwise has notice of the nonreceipt or misdescription.

§ 7–204. Duty of Care; Contractual Limitation of Warehouse's Liability.

(a) A warehouse is liable for damages for loss of or injury to the goods caused by its failure to exercise care with regard to the goods that a reasonably careful person would exercise under similar circumstances. However, unless otherwise agreed, the warehouse is not liable for damages that could not have been avoided by the exercise of that care.

(b) Damages may be limited by a term in the warehouse receipt or storage agreement limiting the amount of liability in case of loss or damage beyond which the warehouse is not liable. No such limitation is effective with respect to the warehouse's liability for conversion to its own use. The warehouse's liability, on request of the bailor in a record at the time of signing such storage agreement or within a reasonable time after receipt of the warehouse receipt, may be increased on part or all of the goods covered by the storage agreement or the warehouse receipt. In this event, increased rates may be charged based on an increased valuation of the goods.

(c) Reasonable provisions as to the time and manner of presenting claims and commencing actions based on the bailment may be included in the warehouse receipt or storage agreement.

(d) This section does not impair or repeal [Insert reference to any statute that imposes a higher responsibility upon the warehouse or invalidates contractual limitations that would be permissible under this Article.]

§ 7–205. Title Under Warehouse Receipt Defeated in Certain Cases.
A buyer in ordinary course of business of fungible goods sold and delivered by a warehouse that is also in the business of buying and selling such goods takes the goods free of any claim under a warehouse receipt even if the receipt is negotiable and has been duly negotiated.

§ 7–206. Termination of Storage at Warehouse's Option.

(a) A warehouse, by giving notice to the person on whose account the goods are held and any other person known to claim an interest in the goods, may require payment of any charges and removal of the goods from the warehouse at the termination of the period of storage fixed by the document of title or, if a period is not fixed, within a stated period not less than 30 days after the warehouse gives notice. If the goods are not removed before the date specified in the notice, the warehouse may sell them pursuant to Section 7–210.

(b) If a warehouse in good faith believes that goods are about to deteriorate or decline in value to less than the amount of its lien within the time provided in subsection (a) and Section 7–210, the warehouse may specify in the notice given under subsection (a) any reasonable shorter time for removal of the goods and, if the goods are not removed, may sell them at public sale held not less than one week after a single advertisement or posting.

(c) If, as a result of a quality or condition of the goods of which the warehouse did not have notice at the time of deposit, the goods are a hazard to other property, the warehouse facilities, or other persons, the warehouse may sell the goods at public or private sale without advertisement or posting on reasonable notification to all persons known to claim an interest in the goods. If the warehouse, after a reasonable effort, is unable to sell the goods, it may dispose of them in any lawful manner and does not incur liability by reason of that disposition.

(d) A warehouse shall deliver the goods to any person entitled to them under this article upon due demand made at any time before sale or other disposition under this section.

(e) A warehouse may satisfy its lien from the proceeds of any sale or disposition under this section but shall hold the balance for delivery on the demand of any person to which the warehouse would have been bound to deliver the goods.

§ 7–207. Goods Must Be Kept Separate; Fungible Goods.

(a) Unless the warehouse receipt provides otherwise, a warehouse shall keep separate the goods covered by each receipt so as to permit at all times identification and delivery of those goods. However, different lots of fungible goods may be commingled.

(b) If different lots of fungible goods are commingled, the good are owned in common by the persons entitled thereto and the warehouse is severally liable to each owner for that owner's share. If, because of overissue, a mass of fungible goods is insufficient to meet all the receipts the warehouse has issued against it, the persons entitled include all holders to which overissued receipts have been duly negotiated.

§ 7–208. Altered Warehouse Receipts. If a blank in a negotiable tangible warehouse receipt has been filled in without authority, a good faith purchaser for value and without notice of the lack of authority may treat the insertion as authorized. Any other unauthorized alteration leaves any tangible or electronic warehouse receipt enforceable against the issuer according to its original tenor.

§ 7–209. Lien of Warehouse.

(a) A warehouse has a lien against the bailor on the goods covered by a warehouse receipt or storage agreement or on the proceeds thereof in its possession for charges for storage or transportation, including demurrage and terminal charges, insurance, labor, or other charges, present or future, in relation to the goods, and for expenses necessary for preservation of the goods or reasonably incurred in their sale pursuant to law. If the person on whose account the goods are held is liable for similar charges or expenses in relation to other goods whenever deposited and it is stated in the warehouse receipt or storage agreement that a lien is claimed for charges and expenses in relation to other goods, the warehouse also has a lien against the goods covered by the warehouse receipt or storage agreement or on the proceeds thereof in its possession for those charges and expenses, whether or not the other goods have been delivered by the warehouse. However, as against a person to which a negotiable warehouse receipt is duly negotiated, a warehouse's lien is limited to charges in an amount or at a rate specified in the warehouse receipt or, if no charges are so specified, to a reasonable charge for storage of the specific goods covered by the receipt subsequent to the date of the receipt.

(b) The warehouse may also reserve a security interest under Article 9 against the bailor for the maximum amount specified on the receipt for charges other than those specified in subsection (a), such as for money advanced and interest. A security interest is governed by Article 9.

(c) A warehouseís lien for charges and expenses under subsection (a) or a security interest under subsection (b) is also effective against any person that so entrusted the bailor with possession of the goods that a pledge of them by the bailor to a good faith purchaser for value would have been valid. However, the lien or security interest is not effective against a person that before issuance of a document of title had a legal interest or a perfected security interest in the goods and that did not:

(1) deliver or entrust the goods or any document covering the goods to the bailor or the bailor's nominee with actual or apparent authority to ship, store, or sell; or with power to obtain delivery under Section 7–403; or with power of disposition under Sections 2-403, 2A-304(2), 2A-305(2) or 9-320 or other statute or rule of law; or

(2) acquiesce in the procurement by the bailor or its nominee of any document.

(d) A warehouse's lien on household goods for charges and expenses in relation to the goods under subsection (a) is also effective against all persons if the depositor was the legal possessor of the goods at the time of deposit. In this subsection, "household goods" means furniture, furnishings, or personal effects used by the depositor in a dwelling.

(e) A warehouse loses its lien on any goods that it voluntarily delivers or unjustifiably refuses to deliver.

§ 7–210. Enforcement of Warehouse's Lien.

(a) Except as otherwise provided in subsection (b), a warehouse's lien may be enforced by public or private sale of the goods, in bulk or in packages, at any time or place and on any terms that are commercially reasonable, after notifying all persons known to claim an interest in the goods. The notification must include a statement of the amount due, the nature of the proposed sale, and the time and place of any public sale. The fact that a better price could have been obtained by a sale at a different time or in a different method from that selected by the warehouse is not of itself sufficient to establish that the sale was not made in a commercially reasonable manner. The warehouse has sold in a commercially reasonable manner if the warehouse sells the goods in the usual manner in any recognized market therefor, sells at the price current in that market at the time of the sale, or has otherwise sold in conformity with commercially reasonable practices among dealers in the type of goods sold. A sale of more goods than apparently necessary to be offered to ensure satisfaction of the obligation is not commercially reasonable, except in cases covered by the preceding sentence.

(b) A warehouse's lien on goods, other than goods stored by a merchant in the course of its business, may be enforced only if the following requirements are satisfied:

(1) All persons known to claim an interest in the goods must be notified.

(2) The notification must include an itemized statement of the claim, a description of the goods subject to the lien, a demand for payment within a specified time not less than 10 days after receipt of the notification, and a conspicuous statement that unless the claim is paid within that time the goods will be advertised for sale and sold by auction at a specified time and place.

(3) The sale must conform to the terms of the notification.

(4) The sale must be held at the nearest suitable place to where the goods are held or stored.

(5) After the expiration of the time given in the notification, an advertisement of the sale must be published once a week for two weeks consecutively in a newspaper of general circulation where the sale is to be held. The advertisement must include a description of the goods, the name of the person on whose account the goods are being held, and the time and place of the sale. The sale must take place at least 15 days after the first publication. If there is no newspaper of general circulation where the sale is to be held, the advertisement must be posted at least 10 days before the sale in not less than six conspicuous places in the neighborhood of the proposed sale.

(c) Before any sale pursuant to this section, any person claiming a right in the goods may pay the amount necessary to satisfy the lien and the reasonable expenses incurred in complying with this section. In that event, the goods may not be sold but must be retained by the warehouse subject to the terms of the receipt and this article.

(d) A warehouse may buy at any public sale held pursuant to this section.

(e) A purchaser in good faith of goods sold to enforce a warehouse's lien takes the goods free of any rights of persons against which the lien was valid, despite the warehouse's noncompliance with this section.

(f) A warehouse may satisfy its lien from the proceeds of any sale pursuant to this section but shall hold the balance, if any, for delivery on demand to any person to which the warehouse would have been bound to deliver the goods.

(g) The rights provided by this section are in addition to all other rights allowed by law to a creditor against a debtor.

(h) If a lien is on goods stored by a merchant in the course of its business, the lien may be enforced in accordance with subsection (a) or (b).

(i) A warehouse is liable for damages caused by failure to comply with the requirements for sale under this section and, in case of willful violation, is liable for conversion.

Part 3: Bills of Lading: Special Provisions

§ 7–301. Liability for Nonreceipt or Misdescription; "Said to Contain"; "Shipper's Load and Count"; Improper Handling.

(a) A consignee of a nonnegotiable bill of lading which has given value in good faith, or a holder to which a negotiable bill has been duly negotiated, relying upon the description of the goods in the bill or upon the date shown in the bill, may recover from the issuer damages caused by the misdating of the bill or the nonreceipt or misdescription of the goods, except to the extent that the document of title indicates that the issuer does not know whether any part or all of the goods in fact were received or conform to the description, such as in a case in which the description is in terms of marks or labels or kind, quantity, or condition or the receipt or description is qualified by "contents or condition of contents of packages unknown", "said to contain", "shipper's weight, load and count" or words of similar import, if that indication is true.

(b) If goods are loaded by the issuer of the bill of lading, the issuer must count the packages of goods if shipped in packages and ascertain the kind and quantity if shipped in bulk and words such as "shipper's weight, load and count" or words of similar import indicating that the description was made by the shipper are ineffective except as to goods concealed by packages.

(c) If bulk goods are loaded by a shipper that makes available to the issuer of the bill of lading adequate facilities for weighing those goods, the issuer must ascertain the kind and quantity within a reasonable time after receiving the shipper's request in a record to do so. In that case, "shipper's weight" or words of similar import are ineffective.

(d) The issuer, by including in the bill of lading the words "shipper's weight, load and count" or words of similar import, may indicate that the goods were loaded by the shipper, and, if that statement is true, the issuer is not liable for damages caused by the improper loading. However, omission of such words does not imply liability for damages caused by improper loading.

(e) A shipper guarantees to the issuer the accuracy at the time of shipment of the description, marks, labels, number, kind, quantity, condition, and weight, as furnished by the shipper, and the shipper shall indemnify the issuer against damage caused by inaccuracies in those particulars. This right of the issuer to that indemnity does not limit its responsibility or liability under the contract of carriage to any person other than the shipper.

§ 7–302. Through Bills of Lading and Similar Documents of Title.

(a) The issuer of a through bill of lading or other document of title embodying an undertaking to be performed in part by a person acting as its agent or by a performing carrier is liable to any person entitled to recover on the document for any breach by the other person or the performing carrier of its obligation under the document. However, to the extent that the bill covers an undertaking to be performed overseas or in territory not contiguous to the continental United States or an undertaking including matters other than transportation, this liability for breach by the other person or the performing carrier may be varied by agreement of the parties.

(b) If goods covered by a through bill of lading or other document of title embodying an undertaking to be performed in part by a person other than the issuer are received by that person, the person is subject, with respect to its own performance while the goods are in its possession, to the obligation of the issuer. The person's obligation is discharged by delivery of the goods to another person pursuant to the document and does not include liability for breach by any other person or by the issuer.

(c) The issuer of a through bill of lading or other document of title described in subsection (a) is entitled to recover from the performing carrier, or other person in possession of the goods when the breach of the obligation under the document occurred:

(1) the amount it may be required to pay to any person entitled to recover on the document for the breach, as may be evidenced by any receipt, judgment, or transcript, and;

(2) the amount of any expense reasonably incurred by the issuer in defending any action commenced by any person entitled to recover on the document for the breach.

§ 7–303. Diversion; Reconsignment; Change of Instructions.

(a) Unless the bill of lading otherwise provides, a carrier may deliver the goods to a person or destination other than that stated in the bill or may otherwise dispose of the goods, without liability for misdelivery, on instructions from:

(1) the holder of a negotiable bill;

(2) the consignor on a nonnegotiable bill even if the consignee has given contrary instructions;

(3) the consignee on a nonnegotiable bill in the absence of contrary instructions from the consignor, if the goods have arrived at the billed destination or if the consignee is in possession of the tangible bill or in control of the electronic bill; or

(4) the consignee on a nonnegotiable bill, if the consignee is entitled as against the consignor to dispose of the goods.

(b) Unless instructions described in subsection (a) are included in a negotiable bill of lading, a person to which the bill is duly negotiated may hold the bailee according to the original terms.

§ 7–304. Tangible Bills of Lading in a Set.

(a) Except as customary in international transportation, a tangible bill of lading may not be issued in a set of parts. The issuer is liable for damages caused by violation of this subsection.

(b) If a tangible bill of lading is lawfully issued in a set of parts, each of which contains an identification code and is expressed to be valid only if the goods have not been delivered against any other part, the whole of the parts constitutes one bill.

(c) If a tangible negotiable bill of lading is lawfully issued in a set of parts and different parts are negotiated to different persons, the title of the holder to which the first due negotiation is made prevails as to both the document of title and the goods even if any later holder may have received the goods from the carrier in good faith and discharged the carrier's obligation by surrendering its part.

(d) A person that negotiates or transfers a single part of a tangible bill of lading issued in a set is liable to holders of that part as if it were the whole set.

(e) The bailee is obliged to deliver in accordance with Part 4 of this article against the first presented part of a tangible bill of lading lawfully issued in a set. Delivery in this manner discharges the bailee's obligation on the whole bill.

§ 7–305. Destination Bills.

(a) Instead of issuing a bill of lading to the consignor at the place of shipment, a carrier , at the request of the consignor, may procure the bill to be issued at destination or at any other place designated in the request.

(b) Upon request of any person entitled as against a carrier to control the goods while in transit and on surrender of possession or control of any outstanding bill of lading or other receipt covering the goods, the issuer, subject to Section 7–105, may procure a substitute bill to be issued at any place designated in the request.

§ 7–306. Altered Bills of Lading.
An unauthorized alteration or filling in of a blank in a bill of lading leaves the bill enforceable according to its original tenor.

§ 7–307. Lien of Carrier.

(a) A carrier has a lien on the goods covered by a bill of lading or on the proceeds thereof in its possession for charges after the date of the carrier's receipt of the goods for storage or transportation, including demurrage and terminal charges, and for expenses necessary for preservation of the goods incident to their transportation or reasonably incurred in their sale pursuant to law. However, against a purchaser for value of a negotiable bill of lading, a carrier's lien is limited to charges stated in the bill or the applicable tariffs or, if no charges are stated, a reasonable charge.

(b) A lien for charges and expenses under subsection (a) on goods that the carrier was required by law to receive for transportation is effective against the consignor or any person entitled to the goods unless the carrier had notice that the consignor lacked authority to subject the goods to those charges and expenses. Any other lien under subsection (a) is effective against the consignor and any person that permitted the bailor to have control or possession of the goods unless the carrier had notice that the bailor lacked authority.

(c) A carrier loses its lien on any goods that it voluntarily delivers or unjustifiably refuses to deliver.

§ 7–308. Enforcement of Carrier's Lien.

(a) A carrier's lien on goods may be enforced by public or private sale of the goods, in bulk or in packages, at any time or place and on any terms that are commercially reasonable, after notifying all persons known to claim an interest in the goods. The notification must include a statement of the amount due, the nature of the proposed sale, and the time and place of any public sale. The fact that a better price could have been obtained by a sale at a different time or in a different method from that selected by the carrier is not of itself sufficient to establish that the sale was not made in a commercially reasonable manner. The carrier has sold goods in a commercially reasonable manner if the carrier sells the goods in the usual manner in any recognized market therefor, sells at the price current in that market at the time of the sale, or has otherwise sold in conformity with commercially reasonable practices among dealers in the type of goods sold. A sale of more goods than apparently necessary to be offered to ensure satisfaction of the obligation is not commercially reasonable, except in cases covered by the preceding sentence.

(b) Before any sale pursuant to this section, any person claiming a right in the goods may pay the amount necessary to satisfy the lien and the reasonable expenses incurred in complying with this section. In that event, the goods may not be sold but must be retained by the carrier, subject to the terms of the bill of lading and this article.

(c) A carrier may buy at any public sale pursuant to this section.

(d) A purchaser in good faith of goods sold to enforce a carrier's lien takes the goods free of any rights of persons against which the lien was valid, despite the carrier's noncompliance with this section.

(e) A carrier may satisfy its lien from the proceeds of any sale pursuant to this section but shall hold the balance, if any, for delivery on demand to any person to which the carrier would have been bound to deliver the goods.

(f) The rights provided by this section are in addition to all other rights allowed by law to a creditor against a debtor.

(g) A carrier's lien may be enforced pursuant to either subsection (a) or the procedure set forth in subsection Section 7–210(b).

(h) A carrier is liable for damages caused by failure to comply with the requirements for sale under this section and, in case of willful violation, is liable for conversion.

§ 7–309. Duty of Care; Contractual Limitation of Carrier's Liability.

(a) A carrier that issues a bill of lading, whether negotiable or nonnegotiable, must exercise the degree of care in relation to the goods which a reasonably careful person would exercise under similar circumstances. This subsection does not affect any statute, regulation, or rule of law that imposes liability upon a common carrier for damages not caused by its negligence.

(b) Damages may be limited by a term in the bill of lading that the carrier's liability may not exceed a value stated in the bill if the carrier's rates are dependent upon value and the consignor is afforded an opportunity to declare a higher value and the consignor is advised of the opportunity. However, no such limitation is effective with respect to the carrier's liability for conversion to its own use.

(c) Reasonable provisions as to the time and manner of presenting claims and commencing actions based on the shipment may be included in a bill of lading.

Part 4: Warehouse Receipts and Bills of Lading: General Obligations

§ 7–401. Irregularities in Issue of Receipt or Bill or Conduct of Issuer.

The obligations imposed by this article on an issuer apply to a document of title even if:

(1) the document does not comply with the requirements of this article or of any other statute, rule, or regulation regarding its issue, form, or content;

(2) the issuer violated laws regulating the conduct of its business;

(3) the goods covered by the document were owned by the bailee when the document was issued; or

(4) the person issuing the document is not a warehouse but the document purports to be a warehouse receipt.

§ 7–402. Duplicate Document of Title; Overissue.

A duplicate or any other document of title purporting to cover goods already represented by an outstanding document of the same issuer does not confer any right in the goods, except as provided in the case of tangible bills of lading in a set of parts, overissue of documents for fungible goods, substitutes for lost, stolen, or destroyed documents, or substitute documents issued pursuant to Section 7–105. The issuer is liable for damages caused by its overissue or failure to identify a duplicate document by a conspicuous notation.

§ 7–403. Obligation of Warehouse or Carrier to Deliver; Excuse.

(a) A bailee shall deliver the goods to a person entitled under a document of title that complies with subsections (b) and (c), unless and to the extent that the bailee establishes any of the following:

(1) delivery of the goods to a person whose receipt was rightful as against the claimant;

(2) damage to or delay, loss, or destruction of the goods for which the bailee is not liable;

(3) previous sale or other disposition of the goods in lawful enforcement of a lien or on a warehouse's lawful termination of storage;

(4) the exercise by a seller of its right to stop delivery pursuant to Section 2–705 or by a lessor of its right to stop delivery pursuant to Section 2A-526;

(5) a diversion, reconsignment, or other disposition pursuant to Section 7–303;

(6) release, satisfaction, or any other fact affording a personal defense against the claimant; or

(7) any other lawful excuse.

(b) A person claiming goods covered by a document of title shall satisfy the bailee's lien if the bailee so requests or the bailee is prohibited by law from delivering the goods until the charges are paid.

(c) Unless a person claiming the goods is one against which the document of title does not confer a right under Section 7–503(a):

(1) the person claiming under a document shall surrender possession or control of any outstanding negotiable document covering the goods for cancellation or indication of partial deliveries; and

(2) the bailee shall cancel the document or conspicuously indicate in the document the partial delivery or be liable to any person to which the document is duly negotiated.

§ 7–404. No Liability for Good Faith Delivery Pursuant to Document of Title.

A bailee that in good faith has received goods and delivered or otherwise disposed of the goods according to the terms of a document of title or pursuant to this article is not liable for the goods even if:

(1) the person from which the bailee received the goods did not have authority to procure the document or to dispose of the goods; or

(2) the person to which the bailee delivered the goods did not have authority to receive the goods.

Part 5: Warehouse Receipts and Bills of Lading: Negotiation and Transfer

§ 7–501. Form of Negotiation and Requirements of Due Negotiation.

(a) The following rules apply to a negotiable tangible document of title:

  (1) If the document's original terms run to the order of a named person, the document is negotiated by the named person's indorsement and delivery. After the named person's indorsement in blank or to bearer, any person may negotiate the document by delivery alone.

  (2) If the document's original terms run to bearer, it is negotiated by delivery alone.

  (3) If the document's original terms run to the order of a named person and it is delivered to the named person, the effect is the same as if the document had been negotiated.

  (4) Negotiation of the document after it has been indorsed to a named person requires indorsement by the named person as well as delivery.

  (5) A document is duly negotiated if it is negotiated in the manner stated in this subsection to a holder that purchases it in good faith without notice of any defense against or claim to it on the part of any person and for value, unless it is established that the negotiation is not in the regular course of business or financing or involves receiving the document in settlement or payment of a monetary obligation.

(b) The following rules apply to a negotiable electronic document of title:

  (1) If the document's original terms run to the order of a named person or to bearer, the document is negotiated by delivery of the document to another person. Indorsement by the named person is not required to negotiate the document.

  (2) If the document's original terms run to the order of a named person and the named person has control of the document, the effect is the same as if the document had been negotiated.

  (3) A document is duly negotiated if it is negotiated in the manner stated in this subsection to a holder that purchases it in good faith without notice of any defense against or claim to it on the part of any person and for value, unless it is established that the negotiation is not in the regular course of business or financing or involves taking delivery of the document in settlement or payment of a monetary obligation.

(c) Indorsement of a nonnegotiable document of title neither makes it negotiable nor adds to the transferee's rights.

(d) The naming in a negotiable bill of lading of a person to be notified of the arrival of the goods does not limit the negotiability of the bill or constitute notice to a purchaser of the bill of any interest of that person in the goods.

§ 7–502. Rights Acquired by Due Negotiation.

(a) Subject to Sections 7–205 and 7–503, a holder to which a negotiable document of title has been duly negotiated acquires thereby:

  (1) title to the document;

  (2) title to the goods;

  (3) all rights accruing under the law of agency or estoppel, including rights to goods delivered to the bailee after the document was issued; and

  (4) the direct obligation of the issuer to hold or deliver the goods according to the terms of the document free of any defense or claim by the issuer except those arising under the terms of the document or under this article. In the case of a delivery order, the bailee's obligation accrues only upon the bailee's acceptance of the delivery order and the obligation acquired by the holder is that the issuer and any indorser will procure the acceptance of the bailee.

(b) Subject to Section 7–503, title and rights acquired by due negotiation are not defeated by any stoppage of the goods represented by the document of title or by surrender of the goods by the bailee and are not impaired even if:

  (1) the due negotiation or any prior due negotiation constituted a breach of duty;

  (2) any person has been deprived of possession of a negotiable tangible document or control of a negotiable electronic document by misrepresentation, fraud, accident, mistake, duress, loss, theft, or conversion; or

  (3) a previous sale or other transfer of the goods or document has been made to a third person.

§ 7–503. Document of Title to Goods Defeated in Certain Cases.

(a) A document of title confers no right in goods against a person that before issuance of the document had a legal interest or a perfected security interest in the goods and that did not:

  (1) deliver or entrust the goods or any document covering the goods to the bailor or the bailor's

nominee with actual or apparent authority to ship, store, or sell; with power to obtain delivery under Section 7–403; or with power of disposition under Section 2–403, 2A-304(2), 2A-305(2), or 9–320 or other statute or rule of law; or

(2) acquiesce in the procurement by the bailor or its nominee of any document.

(b) Title to goods based upon an unaccepted delivery order is subject to the rights of any person to which a negotiable warehouse receipt or bill of lading covering the goods has been duly negotiated. That title may be defeated under Section 7–504 to the same extent as the rights of the issuer or a transferee from the issuer.

(c) Title to goods based upon a bill of lading issued to a freight forwarder is subject to the rights of any person to which a bill issued by the freight forwarder is duly negotiated. However, delivery by the carrier in accordance with Part 4 pursuant to its own bill of lading discharges the carrier's obligation to deliver.

§ 7–504. Rights Acquired in Absence of Due Negotiation; Effect of Diversion; Stoppage of Delivery.

(a) A transferee of a document of title, whether negotiable or nonnegotiable, to which the document has been delivered but not duly negotiated, acquires the title and rights that its transferor had or had actual authority to convey.

(b) In the case of a nonnegotiable document of title, until but not after the bailee receives notice of the transfer, the rights of the transferee may be defeated:

(1) by those creditors of the transferor that could treat the transfer as void under Section 2–402 or 2A-308 ;

(2) by a buyer from the transferor in ordinary course of business if the bailee has delivered the goods to the buyer or received notification of the buyer's rights;

(3) by a lessee from the transferor in ordinary course of business if the bailee has delivered the goods to the lessee or received notification of the lessee's rights; or

(4) as against the bailee, by good faith dealings of the bailee with the transferor.

(c) A diversion or other change of shipping instructions by the consignor in a nonnegotiable bill of lading which causes the bailee not to deliver the goods to the consignee defeats the consignee's title to the goods if the goods have been delivered to a buyer in ordinary course of business or a lessee in ordinary course of

business and in any event defeats the consignee's rights against the bailee.

(d) Delivery of the goods pursuant to a nonnegotiable document of title may be stopped by a seller under Section 2–705 or a lessor under Section 2A-526, subject to the requirements of due notification in those sections. A bailee honoring the seller's or lessor's instructions is entitled to be indemnified by the seller or lessor against any resulting loss or expense.

§ 7–505. Indorser Not Guarantor for Other Parties.
The indorsement of a tangible document of title issued by a bailee does not make the indorser liable for any default by the bailee or previous indorsers.

§ 7–506. Delivery without Indorsement: Right to Compel Indorsement.
The transferee of a negotiable tangible document of title has a specifically enforceable right to have its transferor supply any necessary indorsement, but the transfer becomes a negotiation only as of the time the indorsement is supplied.

§ 7–507. Warranties on Negotiation or Delivery of Document of Title.
If a person negotiates or delivers a document of title for value, otherwise than as a mere intermediary under Section 7–508, unless otherwise agreed, the transferor warrants to its immediate purchaser only in addition to any warranty made in selling or leasing the goods that:

(1) the document is genuine;

(2) the transferor does not have knowledge of any fact that would impair the document's validity or worth; and

(3) the negotiation or delivery is rightful and fully effective with respect to the title to the document and the goods it represents.

§ 7–508. Warranties of Collecting Bank as to Documents of Title.
A collecting bank or other intermediary known to be entrusted with documents of title on behalf of another or with collection of a draft or other claim against delivery of documents warrants by the delivery of the documents only its own good faith and authority even if the collecting bank or other intermediary has purchased or made advances against the claim or draft to be collected.

§ 7–509. Adequate Compliance with Commercial Contract.
Whether a document of title is adequate to fulfill the obligations of a contract for sale, a contract for lease, or the conditions of a letter of credit is determined by Article 2, 2A, or 5.

Part 6: Warehouse Receipts and Bills of Lading: Miscellaneous Provisions

§ 7–601. Lost, Stolen, or Destroyed Documents of Title.

(a) If a document of title is lost, stolen, or destroyed, a court may order delivery of the goods or issuance of a substitute document and the bailee may without liability to any person comply with the order. If the document was negotiable, a court may not order delivery of the goods or issuance of a substitute document without the claimantís posting security unless it finds that any person that may suffer loss as a result of nonsurrender of possession or control of the document is adequately protected against the loss. If the document was nonnegotiable, the court may require security. The court may order payment of the bailee's reasonable costs and attorney's fees in any action under this subsection.

(b) A bailee that without court order delivers goods to a person claiming under a missing negotiable document of title is liable to any person injured thereby. If the delivery is not in good faith, the bailee is liable for conversion. Delivery in good faith is not conversion if the claimant posts security with the bailee in an amount at least double the value of the goods at the time of posting to indemnify any person injured by the delivery which files a notice of claim within one year after the delivery.

§ 7–602. Attachment of Goods Covered by Negotiable Document of Title.
Unless the document of title was originally issued upon delivery of the goods by a person that did not have power to dispose of them, a lien does not attach by virtue of any judicial process to goods in the possession of a bailee for which a negotiable document of title is outstanding unless possession or control of the document is first surrendered to the bailee or the document's negotiation is enjoined. The bailee may not be compelled to deliver the goods pursuant to process until possession or control of the document is surrendered to the bailee or to the court. A purchaser of the document for value without notice of the process or injunction takes free of the lien imposed by judicial process.

§ 7–603. Conflicting Claims; Interpleader.
If more than one person claims title to or possession of the goods, the bailee is excused from delivery until the bailee has a reasonable time to ascertain the validity of the adverse claims or to commence an action for interpleader. The bailee may assert an interpleader either in defending an action for nondelivery of the goods or by original action.

Part 7: Transition Provisions

§ 7–701. Effective Date.
This [Act] takes effect on _____, 20 ___.

§ 7–702. Repeals.
[Existing Article 7] and [Section 10-104 of the Uniform Commercial Code] are repealed.

§ 7–703. Applicability.
This [Act] applies to a document of title that is issued or a bailment that arises on or after the effective date of this [Act]. This [Act] does not apply to a document of title that is issued or a bailment that arises before the effective date of this [Act] even if the document of title or bailment would be subject to this [Act] if the document of title had been issued or bailment had arisen after the effective date of this [Act]. This [Act] does not apply to a right of action that has accrued before the effective date of this [Act].

§ 7–704. Savings Clause.
A document of title issued or a bailment that arises before the effective date of this [Act] and the rights, obligations, and interests flowing from that document or bailment are governed by any statute or other rule amended or repealed by this [Act] as if amendment or repeal had not occurred and may be terminated, completed, consummated, or enforced under that statute or other rule.

Article 9–Secured Transactions

Part 1: General Provisions

§ 9–101. Short Title.
This article may be cited as Uniform Commercial Code–Secured Transactions.

§ 9–102. Definitions and Index of Definitions.

(a) [Article 9 definitions.] In this article:
  (1) "Accession" means goods that are physically united with other goods in such a manner that the identity of the original goods is not lost.
  (2) "Account", except as used in "account for", means a right to payment of a monetary obligation, whether or not earned by performance, (i) for property that has been or is to be sold, leased,

licensed, assigned, or otherwise disposed of, (ii) for services rendered or to be rendered, (iii) for a policy of insurance issued or to be issued, (iv) for a secondary obligation incurred or to be incurred, (v) for energy provided or to be provided, (vi) for the use or hire of a vessel under a charter or other contract, (vii) arising out of the use of a credit or charge card or information contained on or for use with the card, or (viii) as winnings in a lottery or other game of chance operated or sponsored by a State, governmental unit of a State, or person licensed or authorized to operate the game by a State or governmental unit of a State. The term includes health-care-insurance receivables. The term does not include (i) rights to payment evidenced by chattel paper or an instrument, (ii) commercial tort claims, (iii) deposit accounts, (iv) investment property, (v) letter-of-credit rights or letters of credit, or (vi) rights to payment for money or funds advanced or sold, other than rights arising out of the use of a credit or charge card or information contained on or for use with the card.

(3) "Account debtor" means a person obligated on an account, chattel paper, or general intangible. The term does not include persons obligated to pay a negotiable instrument, even if the instrument constitutes part of chattel paper.

(4) "Accounting", except as used in "accounting for", means a record:
 (A) authenticated by a secured party;
 (B) indicating the aggregate unpaid secured obligations as of a date not more than 35 days earlier or 35 days later than the date of the record; and
 (C) identifying the components of the obligations in reasonable detail.

(5) "Agricultural lien" means an interest in farm products:
 (A) which secures payment or performance of an obligation for:
  (i) goods or services furnished in connection with a debtor's farming operation; or
  (ii) rent on real property leased by a debtor in connection with its farming operation;
 (B) which is created by statute in favor of a person that:
  (i) in the ordinary course of its business furnished goods or services to a debtor

in connection with a debtor's farming operation; or
  (ii) leased real property to a debtor in connection with the debtor's farming operation; and
 (C) whose effectiveness does not depend on the person's possession of the personal property.

(6) "As-extracted collateral" means:
 (A) oil, gas, or other minerals that are subject to a security interest that:
  (i) is created by a debtor having an interest in the minerals before extraction; and
  (ii) attaches to the minerals as extracted; or
 (B) accounts arising out of the sale at the wellhead or minehead of oil, gas, or other minerals in which the debtor had an interest before extraction.

(7) "Authenticate" means:
 (A) to sign; or
 (B) to execute or otherwise adopt a symbol, or encrypt or similarly process a record in whole or in part, with the present intent of the authenticating person to identify the person and adopt or accept a record.

(8) "Bank" means an organization that is engaged in the business of banking. The term includes savings banks, savings and loan associations, credit unions, and trust companies.

(9) "Cash proceeds" means proceeds that are money, checks, deposit accounts, or the like.

(10) "Certificate of title" means a certificate of title with respect to which a statute provides for the security interest in question to be indicated on the certificate as a condition or result of the security interest's obtaining priority over the rights of a lien creditor with respect to the collateral.

(11) "Chattel paper" means a record or records that evidence both a monetary obligation and a security interest in specific goods, a security interest in specific goods and software used in the goods, a security interest in specific goods and license of software used in the goods, a lease of specific goods, or a lease of specific goods and license of software used in the goods. In this paragraph, "monetary obligation" means a monetary obligation secured by the goods or owed under a lease of the goods and includes a monetary obligation with respect to software used in the goods. The term does not include (i)

charters or other contracts involving the use or hire of a vessel or (ii) records that evidence a right to payment arising out of the use of a credit or charge card or information contained on or for use with the card. If a transaction is evidenced by records that include an instrument or series of instruments, the group of records taken together constitutes chattel paper.

(12) "Collateral" means the property subject to a security interest or agricultural lien. The term includes:

   (A) proceeds to which a security interest attaches;

   (B) accounts, chattel paper, payment intangibles, and promissory notes that have been sold; and

   (C) goods that are the subject of a consignment.

(13) "Commercial tort claim" means a claim arising in tort with respect to which:

   (A) the claimant is an organization; or

   (B) the claimant is an individual and the claim:

     (i) arose in the course of the claimant's business or profession; and

     (ii) does not include damages arising out of personal injury to or the death of an individual.

(14) "Commodity account" means an account maintained by a commodity intermediary in which a commodity contract is carried for a commodity customer.

(15) "Commodity contract" means a commodity futures contract, an option on a commodity futures contract, a commodity option, or another contract if the contract or option is:

   (A) traded on or subject to the rules of a board of trade that has been designated as a contract market for such a contract pursuant to federal commodities laws; or

   (B) traded on a foreign commodity board of trade, exchange, or market, and is carried on the books of a commodity intermediary for a commodity customer.

(16) "Commodity customer" means a person for which a commodity intermediary carries a commodity contract on its books.

(17) "Commodity intermediary" means a person that:

   (A) is registered as a futures commission merchant under federal commodities law; or

   (B) in the ordinary course of its business provides clearance or settlement services for a board of trade that has been designated as a contract market pursuant to federal commodities law.

(18) "Communicate" means:

   (A) to send a written or other tangible record;

   (B) to transmit a record by any means agreed upon by the persons sending and receiving the record; or

   (C) in the case of transmission of a record to or by a filing office, to transmit a record by any means prescribed by filing-office rule.

(19) "Consignee" means a merchant to which goods are delivered in a consignment.

(20) "Consignment" means a transaction, regardless of its form, in which a person delivers goods to a merchant for the purpose of sale and:

   (A) the merchant:

     (i) deals in goods of that kind under a name other than the name of the person making delivery;

     (ii) is not an auctioneer; and

     (iii) is not generally known by its creditors to be substantially engaged in selling the goods of others;

   (B) with respect to each delivery, the aggregate value of the goods is $1,000 or more at the time of delivery;

   (C) the goods are not consumer goods immediately before delivery; and

   (D) the transaction does not create a security interest that secures an obligation.

(21) "Consignor" means a person that delivers goods to a consignee in a consignment.

(22) "Consumer debtor" means a debtor in a consumer transaction.

(23) "Consumer goods" means goods that are used or bought for use primarily for personal, family, or household purposes.

(24) "Consumer-goods transaction" means a consumer transaction in which:

   (A) an individual incurs an obligation primarily for personal, family, or household purposes; and

   (B) a security interest in consumer goods secures the obligation.

(25) "Consumer obligor" means an obligor who is an individual and who incurred the obligation as part of a transaction entered into primarily for personal, family, or household purposes.

(26) "Consumer transaction" means a transaction in which (i) an individual incurs an obligation primarily for personal, family, or household purposes, (ii) a security interest secures the obligation, and (iii) the collateral is held or acquired primarily for personal, family, or household purposes. The term includes consumer-goods transactions.

(27) "Continuation statement" means an amendment of a financing statement which:

(A) identifies, by its file number, the initial financing statement to which it relates; and

(B) indicates that it is a continuation statement for, or that it is filed to continue the effectiveness of, the identified financing statement.

(28) "Debtor" means:

(A) a person having an interest, other than a security interest or other lien, in the collateral, whether or not the person is an obligor;

(B) a seller of accounts, chattel paper, payment intangibles, or promissory notes; or

(C) a consignee.

(29) "Deposit account" means a demand, time, savings, passbook, or similar account maintained with a bank. The term does not include investment property or accounts evidenced by an instrument.

(30) "Document" means a document of title or a receipt of the type described in Section 7-201(2).

(31) "Electronic chattel paper" means chattel paper evidenced by a record or records consisting of information stored in an electronic medium.

(32) "Encumbrance" means a right, other than an ownership interest, in real property. The term includes mortgages and other liens on real property.

(33) "Equipment" means goods other than inventory, farm products, or consumer goods.

(34) "Farm products" means goods, other than standing timber, with respect to which the debtor is engaged in a farming operation and which are:

(A) crops grown, growing, or to be grown, including:

(i) crops produced on trees, vines, and bushes; and

(ii) aquatic goods produced in aquacultural operations;

(B) livestock, born or unborn, including aquatic goods produced in aquacultural operations;

(C) supplies used or produced in a farming operation; or

(D) products of crops or livestock in their unmanufactured states.

(35) "Farming operation" means raising, cultivating, propagating, fattening, grazing, or any other farming, livestock, or aquacultural operation.

(36) "File number" means the number assigned to an initial financing statement pursuant to Section 9-519(a).

(37) "Filing office" means an office designated in Section 9-501 as the place to file a financing statement.

(38) "Filing-office rule" means a rule adopted pursuant to Section 9-526.

(39) "Financing statement" means a record or records composed of an initial financing statement and any filed record relating to the initial financing statement.

(40) "Fixture filing" means the filing of a financing statement covering goods that are or are to become fixtures and satisfying Section 9-502(a) and (b). The term includes the filing of a financing statement covering goods of a transmitting utility which are or are to become fixtures.

(41) "Fixtures" means goods that have become so related to particular real property that an interest in them arises under real property law.

(42) "General intangible" means any personal property, including things in action, other than accounts, chattel paper, commercial tort claims, deposit accounts, documents, goods, instruments, investment property, letter-of-credit rights, letters of credit, money, and oil, gas, or other minerals before extraction. The term includes payment intangibles and software.

(43) "Good faith" means honesty in fact and the observance of reasonable commercial standards of fair dealing.

(44) "Goods" means all things that are movable when a security interest attaches. The term includes (i) fixtures, (ii) standing timber that is to be cut and removed under a conveyance or contract for sale, (iii) the unborn young of animals, (iv) crops grown, growing, or to be grown, even if the crops are produced on trees, vines, or bushes, and (v) manufactured homes. The term also includes a computer program embedded in goods and any supporting information provided in connection with a transaction relating to the program if (i) the program is associated with the goods in such a manner that it customarily is considered part of the goods, or (ii) by becoming the owner of the goods, a person acquires a right to use the program in connection with the goods. The term does not include a computer program embedded in goods that consist solely of the medium in which the program is embedded. The term also does not include accounts, chattel paper, commercial tort claims, deposit accounts, documents, general intangibles, instruments, investment property, letter-of-credit rights, letters of credit, money, or oil, gas, or other minerals before extraction.

(45) "Governmental unit" means a subdivision, agency, department, county, parish, municipality, or other unit of the government of the United States, a State, or a foreign country. The term includes an organization having a separate corporate existence if the organization is eligible to issue debt on which interest is exempt from income taxation under the laws of the United States.

(46) "Health-care-insurance receivable" means an interest in or claim under a policy of insurance which is a right to payment of a monetary obligation for health-care goods or services provided or to be provided.

(47) "Instrument" means a negotiable instrument or any other writing that evidences a right to the payment of a monetary obligation, is not itself a security agreement or lease, and is of a type that in ordinary course of business is transferred by delivery with any necessary indorsement or assignment. The term does not include (i) investment property, (ii) letters of credit, or (iii) writings that evidence a right to payment arising out of the use of a credit or charge card or information contained on or for use with the card.

(48) "Inventory" means goods, other than farm products, which:
  (A) are leased by a person as lessor;
  (B) are held by a person for sale or lease or to be furnished under a contract of service;
  (C) are furnished by a person under a contract of service; or
  (D) consist of raw materials, work in process, or materials used or consumed in a business.

(49) "Investment property" means a security, whether certificated or uncertificated, security entitlement, securities account, commodity contract, or commodity account.

(50) "Jurisdiction of organization", with respect to a registered organization, means the jurisdiction under whose law the organization is organized.

(51) "Letter-of-credit right" means a right to payment or performance under a letter of credit, whether or not the beneficiary has demanded or is at the time entitled to demand payment or per-

formance. The term does not include the right of a beneficiary to demand payment or performance under a letter of credit.

(52) "Lien creditor" means:
  (A) a creditor that has acquired a lien on the property involved by attachment, levy, or the like;
  (B) an assignee for benefit of creditors from the time of assignment;
  (C) a trustee in bankruptcy from the date of the filing of the petition; or
  (D) a receiver in equity from the time of appointment.

(53) "Manufactured home" means a structure, transportable in one or more sections, which, in the traveling mode, is eight body feet or more in width or 40 body feet or more in length, or, when erected on site, is 320 or more square feet, and which is built on a permanent chassis and designed to be used as a dwelling with or without a permanent foundation when connected to the required utilities, and includes the plumbing, heating, air-conditioning, and electrical systems contained therein. The term includes any structure that meets all of the requirements of this paragraph except the size requirements and with respect to which the manufacturer voluntarily files a certification required by the United States Secretary of Housing and Urban Development and complies with the standards established under Title 42 of the United States Code.

(54) "Manufactured-home transaction" means a secured transaction:
  (A) that creates a purchase-money security interest in a manufactured home, other than a manufactured home held as inventory; or
  (B) in which a manufactured home, other than a manufactured home held as inventory, is the primary collateral.

(55) "Mortgage" means a consensual interest in real property, including fixtures, which secures payment or performance of an obligation.

(56) "New debtor" means a person that becomes bound as debtor under Section 9-203(d) by a security agreement previously entered into by another person.

(57) "New value" means (i) money, (ii) money's worth in property, services, or new credit, or (iii) release by a transferee of an interest in property previously transferred to the transferee. The term does not include an obligation substituted for another obligation.

(58) "Noncash proceeds" means proceeds other than cash proceeds.

(59) "Obligor" means a person that, with respect to an obligation secured by a security interest in or an agricultural lien on the collateral, (i) owes payment or other performance of the obligation, (ii) has provided property other than the collateral to secure payment or other performance of the obligation, or (iii) is otherwise accountable in whole or in part for payment or other performance of the obligation. The term does not include issuers or nominated persons under a letter of credit.

(60) "Original debtor", except as used in Section 9-310(c), means a person that, as debtor, entered into a security agreement to which a new debtor has become bound under Section 9-203(d).

(61) "Payment intangible" means a general intangible under which the account debtor's principal obligation is a monetary obligation.

(62) "Person related to", with respect to an individual, means:

(A) the spouse of the individual;

(B) a brother, brother-in-law, sister, or sister-in-law of the individual;

(C) an ancestor or lineal descendant of the individual or the individual's spouse; or

(D) any other relative, by blood or marriage, of the individual or the individual's spouse who shares the same home with the individual.

(63) "Person related to", with respect to an organization, means:

(A) a person directly or indirectly controlling, controlled by, or under common control with the organization;

(B) an officer or director of, or a person performing similar functions with respect to, the organization;

(C) an officer or director of, or a person performing similar functions with respect to, a person described in subparagraph (A);

(D) the spouse of an individual described in subparagraph (A), (B), or (C); or

(E) an individual who is related by blood or marriage to an individual described in subparagraph (A), (B), (C), or (d) and shares the same home with the individual.

(64) "Proceeds", except as used in Section 9-609(b), means the following property:

(A) whatever is acquired upon the sale, lease, license, exchange, or other disposition of collateral;

(B) whatever is collected on, or distributed on account of, collateral;

(C) rights arising out of collateral;

(D) to the extent of the value of collateral, claims arising out of the loss, nonconformity, or interference with the use of, defects or infringement of rights in, or damage to, the collateral; or

(E) to the extent of the value of collateral and to the extent payable to the debtor or the secured party, insurance payable by reason of the loss or nonconformity of, defects or infringement of rights in, or damage to, the collateral.

(65) "Promissory note" means an instrument that evidences a promise to pay a monetary obligation, does not evidence an order to pay, and does not contain an acknowledgment by a bank that the bank has received for deposit a sum of money or funds.

(66) "Proposal" means a record authenticated by a secured party which includes the terms on which the secured party is willing to accept collateral in full or partial satisfaction of the obligation it secures pursuant to Sections 9-620, 9-621, and 9-622.

(67) "Public-finance transaction" means a secured transaction in connection with which:

(A) debt securities are issued;

(B) all or a portion of the securities issued have an initial stated maturity of at least 20 years; and

(C) the debtor, obligor, secured party, account debtor or other person obligated on collateral, assignor or assignee of a secured obligation, or assignor or assignee of a security interest is a State or a governmental unit of a State.

(68) "Pursuant to commitment", with respect to an advance made or other value given by a secured party, means pursuant to the secured party's obligation, whether or not a subsequent event of default or other event not within the secured party's control has relieved or may relieve the secured party from its obligation.

(69) "Record", except as used in "for record", "of record", "record or legal title", and "record owner", means information that is inscribed on a tangible medium or which is stored in an electronic or other medium and is retrievable in perceivable form.

(70) "Registered organization" means an organization organized solely under the law of a single State or the United States and as to which the State or the United States must maintain a public record showing the organization to have been organized.

(71) "Secondary obligor" means an obligor to the extent that:

(A) the obligor's obligation is secondary; or

(B) the obligor has a right of recourse with respect to an obligation secured by collateral against the debtor, another obligor, or property of either.

(72) "Secured party" means:

(A) a person in whose favor a security interest is created or provided for under a security agreement, whether or not any obligation to be secured is outstanding;

(B) a person that holds an agricultural lien;

(C) a consignor;

(D) a person to which accounts, chattel paper, payment intangibles, or promissory notes have been sold;

(E) a trustee, indenture trustee, agent, collateral agent, or other representative in whose favor a security interest or agricultural lien is created or provided for; or

(F) a person that holds a security interest arising under Section 2-401, 2-505, 2-711(3), 2A-508(5), 4-210, or 5-118.

(73) "Security agreement" means an agreement that creates or provides for a security interest.

(74) "Send", in connection with a record or notification, means:

(A) to deposit in the mail, deliver for transmission, or transmit by any other usual means of communication, with postage or cost of transmission provided for, addressed to any address reasonable under the circumstances; or

(B) to cause the record or notification to be received within the time that it would have been received if properly sent under subparagraph (A).

(75) "Software" means a computer program and any supporting information provided in connection with a transaction relating to the program. The term does not include a computer program that is included in the definition of goods.

(76) "State" means a State of the United States, the District of Columbia, Puerto Rico, the United States Virgin Islands, or any territory or insular possession subject to the jurisdiction of the United States.

(77) "Supporting obligation" means a letter-of-credit right or secondary obligation that supports the payment or performance of an account, chattel paper, a document, a general intangible, an instrument, or investment property.

(78) "Tangible chattel paper" means chattel paper evidenced by a record or records consisting of information that is inscribed on a tangible medium.

(79) "Termination statement" means an amendment of a financing statement which:

(A) identifies, by its file number, the initial financing statement to which it relates; and

(B) indicates either that it is a termination statement or that the identified financing statement is no longer effective.

(80) "Transmitting utility" means a person primarily engaged in the business of:

(A) operating a railroad, subway, street railway, or trolley bus;

(B) transmitting communications electrically, electromagnetically, or by light;

(C) transmitting goods by pipeline or sewer; or

(D) transmitting or producing and transmitting electricity, steam, gas, or water.

(b) **[Definitions in other articles.]** The following definitions in other articles apply to this article:

"Applicant"	Section 5-102.
"Beneficiary"	Section 5-102.
"Broker"	Section 8-102.
"Certificated security"	Section 8-102.
"Check"	Section 3-104.
"Clearing corporation"	Section 8-102.
"Contract for sale"	Section 2-106.
"Customer"	Section 4-104.
"Entitlement holder"	Section 8-102.
"Financial asset"	Section 8-102.
"Holder in due course"	Section 3-302.

"Issuer" (with respect to a
letter of credit or letter-of-credit
right)   Section 5-102.

"Issuer" (with respect to a
security)   Section 8-201.

"Lease"   Section 2A-103.

"Lease agreement"   Section 2A-103.

"Lease contract"   Section 2A-103.

"Leasehold interest"   Section 2A-103.

"Lessee"   Section 2A-103.

"Lessee in ordinary course of
business"   Section 2A-103.

"Lessor"   Section 2A-103.

"Lessorís residual interest"   Section 2A-103.

"Letter of credit"   Section 5-102.

"Merchant"   Section 2-104.

"Negotiable instrument"   Section 3-104.

"Nominated person"   Section 5-102.

"Note"   Section 3-104.

"Proceeds of a letter of credit"   Section 5-114.

"Prove"   Section 3-103.

"Sale"   Section 2-106.

"Securities account"   Section 8-501.

"Securities intermediary"   Section 8-102.

"Security"   Section 8-102.

"Security certificate"   Section 8-102.

"Security entitlement"   Section 8-102.

"Uncertificated security"   Section 8-102.

(c) **[Article 1 definitions and principles.]** Article 1 contains general definitions and principles of construction and interpretation applicable throughout this article.

§ 9–103. Purchase-Money Security Interest; Application of Payments; Burden of Establishing.

(a) **[Definitions.]** In this section:
  (1) "purchase-money collateral" means goods or software that secures a purchase-money obligation incurred with respect to that collateral; and
  (2) "purchase-money obligation" means an obligation of an obligor incurred as all or part of the price of the collateral or for value given to enable the debtor to acquire rights in or the use of the collateral if the value is in fact so used.

(b) **[Purchase-money security interest in goods.]** A security interest in goods is a purchase-money security interest:
  (1) to the extent that the goods are purchase-money collateral with respect to that security interest;
  (2) if the security interest is in inventory that is or was purchase-money collateral, also to the extent that the security interest secures a purchase-money obligation incurred with respect to other inventory in which the secured party holds or held a purchase-money security interest; and
  (3) also to the extent that the security interest secures a purchase-money obligation incurred with respect to software in which the secured party holds or held a purchase-money security interest.

(c) **[Purchase-money security interest in software.]** A security interest in software is a purchase-money security interest to the extent that the security interest also secures a purchase-money obligation incurred with respect to goods in which the secured party holds or held a purchase-money security interest if:
  (1) the debtor acquired its interest in the software in an integrated transaction in which it acquired an interest in the goods; and
  (2) the debtor acquired its interest in the software for the principal purpose of using the software in the goods.

(d) **[Consignor's inventory purchase-money security interest.]** The security interest of a consignor in goods that are the subject of a consignment is a purchase-money security interest in inventory.

(e) **[Application of payment in non-consumer-goods transaction.]** In a transaction other than a consumer-goods transaction, if the extent to which a security interest is a purchase-money security interest depends on the application of a payment to a particular obligation, the payment must be applied:
  (1) in accordance with any reasonable method of application to which the parties agree;
  (2) in the absence of the parties' agreement to a reasonable method, in accordance with any intention of the obligor manifested at or before the time of payment; or
  (3) in the absence of an agreement to a reasonable method and a timely manifestation of the obligorís intention, in the following order:
    (A) to obligations that are not secured; and
    (B) if more than one obligation is secured, to obligations secured by purchase-money

security interests in the order in which those obligations were incurred.

(f) [No loss of status of purchase-money security interest in non-consumer-goods transaction.] In a transaction other than a consumer-goods transaction, a purchase-money security interest does not lose its status as such, even if:

(1) the purchase-money collateral also secures an obligation that is not a purchase-money obligation;

(2) collateral that is not purchase-money collateral also secures the purchase-money obligation; or

(3) the purchase-money obligation has been renewed, refinanced, consolidated, or restructured.

(g) [Burden of proof in non-consumer-goods transaction.] In a transaction other than a consumer-goods transaction, a secured party claiming a purchase-money security interest has the burden of establishing the extent to which the security interest is a purchase-money security interest.

(h) [Non-consumer-goods transactions; no inference.] The limitation of the rules in subsections (e), (f), and (g) to transactions other than consumer-goods transactions is intended to leave to the court the determination of the proper rules in consumer-goods transactions. The court may not infer from that limitation the nature of the proper rule in consumer-goods transactions and may continue to apply established approaches.

§ 9–104. Control of Deposit Account.

(a) [Requirements for control.] A secured party has control of a deposit account if:

(1) the secured party is the bank with which the deposit account is maintained;

(2) the debtor, secured party, and bank have agreed in an authenticated record that the bank will comply with instructions originated by the secured party directing disposition of the funds in the deposit account without further consent by the debtor; or

(3) the secured party becomes the bank's customer with respect to the deposit account.

(b) [Debtor's right to direct disposition.] A secured party that has satisfied subsection (a) has control, even if the debtor retains the right to direct the disposition of funds from the deposit account.

§ 9–105. Control of Electronic Chattel Paper.
A secured party has control of electronic chattel paper if the record or records comprising the chattel paper are created, stored, and assigned in such a manner that:

(1) a single authoritative copy of the record or records exists which is unique, identifiable and, except as otherwise provided in paragraphs (4), (5), and (6), unalterable;

(2) the authoritative copy identifies the secured party as the assignee of the record or records;

(3) the authoritative copy is communicated to and maintained by the secured party or its designated custodian;

(4) copies or revisions that add or change an identified assignee of the authoritative copy can be made only with the participation of the secured party;

(5) each copy of the authoritative copy and any copy of a copy is readily identifiable as a copy that is not the authoritative copy; and

(6) any revision of the authoritative copy is readily identifiable as an authorized or unauthorized revision.

§ 9–106. Control of Investment Property.

(a) [Control under Section 8-106.] A person has control of a certificated security, uncertificated security, or security entitlement as provided in Section 8-106.

(b) [Control of commodity contract.] A secured party has control of a commodity contract if:

(1) the secured party is the commodity intermediary with which the commodity contract is carried; or

(2) the commodity customer, secured party, and commodity intermediary have agreed that the commodity intermediary will apply any value distributed on account of the commodity contract as directed by the secured party without further consent by the commodity customer.

(c) [Effect of control of securities account or commodity account.] A secured party having control of all security entitlements or commodity contracts carried in a securities account or commodity account has control over the securities account or commodity account.

§ 9–107. Control of Letter-of-Credit Right.
A secured party has control of a letter-of-credit right to the extent of any right to payment or performance by the issuer or any nominated person if the issuer or nominated person has consented to an assignment of proceeds of the letter of credit under Section 5-114(c) or otherwise applicable law or practice.

§ 9–108. Sufficiency of Description.

(a) [Sufficiency of description.] Except as otherwise provided in subsections (c), (d), and (e), a description of personal or real property is sufficient, whether or not it is specific, if it reasonably identifies what is described.

(b) [Examples of reasonable identification.] Except as otherwise provided in subsection (d), a description of collateral reasonably identifies the collateral if it identifies the collateral by:

(1) specific listing;

(2) category;

(3) except as otherwise provided in subsection (e), a type of collateral defined in [the Uniform Commercial Code];

(4) quantity;

(5) computational or allocational formula or procedure; or

(6) except as otherwise provided in subsection (c), any other method, if the identity of the collateral is objectively determinable.

(c) [Supergeneric description not sufficient.] A description of collateral as "all the debtorís assets" or "all the debtor's personal property" or using words of similar import does not reasonably identify the collateral.

(d) [Investment property.] Except as otherwise provided in subsection (e), a description of a security entitlement, securities account, or commodity account is sufficient if it describes:

(1) the collateral by those terms or as investment property; or

(2) the underlying financial asset or commodity contract.

(e) [When description by type insufficient.] A description only by type of collateral defined in [the Uniform Commercial Code] is an insufficient description of:

(1) a commercial tort claim; or

(2) in a consumer transaction, consumer goods, a security entitlement, a securities account, or a commodity account.

[SUBPART 2. APPLICABILITY OF ARTICLE]

§ 9–109. Scope.

(a) [General scope of article.] Except as otherwise provided in subsections (c) and (d), this article applies to:

(1) a transaction, regardless of its form, that creates a security interest in personal property or fixtures by contract;

(2) an agricultural lien;

(3) a sale of accounts, chattel paper, payment intangibles, or promissory notes;

(4) a consignment;

(5) a security interest arising under Section 2-401, 2-505, 2-711(3), or 2A-508(5), as provided in Section 9-110; and

(6) a security interest arising under Section 4-210 or 5-118.

(b) [Security interest in secured obligation.] The application of this article to a security interest in a secured obligation is not affected by the fact that the obligation is itself secured by a transaction or interest to which this article does not apply.

(c) [Extent to which article does not apply.] This article does not apply to the extent that:

(1) a statute, regulation, or treaty of the United States preempts this article;

(2) another statute of this State expressly governs the creation, perfection, priority, or enforcement of a security interest created by this State or a governmental unit of this State;

(3) a statute of another State, a foreign country, or a governmental unit of another State or a foreign country, other than a statute generally applicable to security interests, expressly governs creation, perfection, priority, or enforcement of a security interest created by the State, country, or governmental unit; or

(4) the rights of a transferee beneficiary or nominated person under a letter of credit are independent and superior under Section 5-114.

(d) [Inapplicability of article.] This article does not apply to:

(1) a landlord's lien, other than an agricultural lien;

(2) a lien, other than an agricultural lien, given by statute or other rule of law for services or materials, but Section 9-333 applies with respect to priority of the lien;

(3) an assignment of a claim for wages, salary, or other compensation of an employee;

(4) a sale of accounts, chattel paper, payment intangibles, or promissory notes as part of a sale of the business out of which they arose;

(5) an assignment of accounts, chattel paper, payment intangibles, or promissory notes which is for the purpose of collection only;

(6) an assignment of a right to payment under a contract to an assignee that is also obligated to perform under the contract;

(7) an assignment of a single account, payment intangible, or promissory note to an assignee in

full or partial satisfaction of a preexisting indebtedness;

(8) a transfer of an interest in or an assignment of a claim under a policy of insurance, other than an assignment by or to a health-care provider of a health-care-insurance receivable and any subsequent assignment of the right to payment, but Sections 9-315 and 9-322 apply with respect to proceeds and priorities in proceeds;

(9) an assignment of a right represented by a judgment, other than a judgment taken on a right to payment that was collateral;

(10) a right of recoupment or set-off, but:

(A) Section 9-340 applies with respect to the effectiveness of rights of recoupment or set-off against deposit accounts; and

(B) Section 9-404 applies with respect to defenses or claims of an account debtor;

(11) the creation or transfer of an interest in or lien on real property, including a lease or rents thereunder, except to the extent that provision is made for:

(A) liens on real property in Sections 9-203 and 9-308;

(B) fixtures in Section 9-334;

(C) fixture filings in Sections 9-501, 9-502, 9-512, 9-516, and 9-519; and

(D) security agreements covering personal and real property in Section 9-604;

(12) an assignment of a claim arising in tort, other than a commercial tort claim, but Sections 9-315 and 9-322 apply with respect to proceeds and priorities in proceeds; or

(13) an assignment of a deposit account in a consumer transaction, but Sections 9-315 and 9-322 apply with respect to proceeds and priorities in proceeds.

§ 9–110. Security Interests Arising Under Article 2 or 2A.
A security interest arising under Section 2-401, 2-505, 2-711(3), or 2A-508(5) is subject to this article. However, until the debtor obtains possession of the goods:

(1) the security interest is enforceable, even if Section 9-203(b)(3) has not been satisfied;

(2) filing is not required to perfect the security interest;

(3) the rights of the secured party after default by the debtor are governed by Article 2 or 2A; and

(4) the security interest has priority over a conflicting security interest created by the debtor.

Part 2: Effectiveness of Security Agreement; Attachment of Security Interest; Rights of Parties to Security Agreement

[SUBPART 1. EFFECTIVENESS AND ATTACHMENT]

§ 9–201. General Effectiveness of Security Agreement.

(a) [General effectiveness.] Except as otherwise provided in [the Uniform Commercial Code], a security agreement is effective according to its terms between the parties, against purchasers of the collateral, and against creditors.

(b) [Applicable consumer laws and other law.] A transaction subject to this article is subject to any applicable rule of law which establishes a different rule for consumers and [insert reference to (i) any other statute or regulation that regulates the rates, charges, agreements, and practices for loans, credit sales, or other extensions of credit and (ii) any consumer-protection statute or regulation].

(c) [Other applicable law controls.] In case of conflict between this article and a rule of law, statute, or regulation described in subsection (b), the rule of law, statute, or regulation controls. Failure to comply with a statute or regulation described in subsection (b) has only the effect the statute or regulation specifies.

(d) [Further deference to other applicable law.] This article does not:

(1) validate any rate, charge, agreement, or practice that violates a rule of law, statute, or regulation described in subsection (b); or

(2) extend the application of the rule of law, statute, or regulation to a transaction not otherwise subject to it.

§ 9–202. Title to Collateral Immaterial.
Except as otherwise provided with respect to consignments or sales of accounts, chattel paper, payment intangibles, or promissory notes, the provisions of this article with regard to rights and obligations apply whether title to collateral is in the secured party or the debtor.

§ 9–203. Attachment and Enforceability of Security Interest; Proceeds; Supporting Obligations; Formal Requisites.

(a) [Attachment.] A security interest attaches to collateral when it becomes enforceable against the debtor with respect to the collateral, unless an agreement expressly postpones the time of attachment.

(b) **[Enforceability.]** Except as otherwise provided in subsections (c) through (i), a security interest is enforceable against the debtor and third parties with respect to the collateral only if :

(1) value has been given;

(2) the debtor has rights in the collateral or the power to transfer rights in the collateral to a secured party; and

(3) one of the following conditions is met:

(A) the debtor has authenticated a security agreement that provides a description of the collateral and, if the security interest covers timber to be cut, a description of the land concerned;

(B) the collateral is not a certificated security and is in the possession of the secured party under Section 9-313 pursuant to the debtor's security agreement;

(C) the collateral is a certificated security in registered form and the security certificate has been delivered to the secured party under Section 8-301 pursuant to the debtor's security agreement; or

(D) the collateral is deposit accounts, electronic chattel paper, investment property, or letter-of-credit rights, and the secured party has control under Section 9-104, 9-105, 9-106, or 9-107 pursuant to the debtor's security agreement.

(c) **[Other UCC provisions.]** Subsection (b) is subject to Section 4-210 on the security interest of a collecting bank, Section 5-118 on the security interest of a letter-of-credit issuer or nominated person, Section 9-110 on a security interest arising under Article 2 or 2A, and Section 9-206 on security interests in investment property.

(d) **[When person becomes bound by another person's security agreement.]** A person becomes bound as debtor by a security agreement entered into by another person if, by operation of law other than this article or by contract:

(1) the security agreement becomes effective to create a security interest in the person's property; or

(2) the person becomes generally obligated for the obligations of the other person, including the obligation secured under the security agreement, and acquires or succeeds to all or substantially all of the assets of the other person.

(e) **[Effect of new debtor becoming bound.]** If a new debtor becomes bound as debtor by a security agreement entered into by another person:

(1) the agreement satisfies subsection (b)(3) with respect to existing or after-acquired property of the new debtor to the extent the property is described in the agreement; and

(2) another agreement is not necessary to make a security interest in the property enforceable.

(f) **[Proceeds and supporting obligations.]** The attachment of a security interest in collateral gives the secured party the rights to proceeds provided by Section 9-315 and is also attachment of a security interest in a supporting obligation for the collateral.

(g) **[Lien securing right to payment.]** The attachment of a security interest in a right to payment or performance secured by a security interest or other lien on personal or real property is also attachment of a security interest in the security interest, mortgage, or other lien.

(h) **[Security entitlement carried in securities account.]** The attachment of a security interest in a securities account is also attachment of a security interest in the security entitlements carried in the securities account.

(i) **[Commodity contracts carried in commodity account.]** The attachment of a security interest in a commodity account is also attachment of a security interest in the commodity contracts carried in the commodity account.

§ 9–204. After-Acquired Property; Future Advances.

(a) **[After-acquired collateral.]** Except as otherwise provided in subsection (b), a security agreement may create or provide for a security interest in after-acquired collateral.

(b) **[When after-acquired property clause not effective.]** A security interest does not attach under a term constituting an after-acquired property clause to:

(1) consumer goods, other than an accession when given as additional security, unless the debtor acquires rights in them within 10 days after the secured party gives value; or

(2) a commercial tort claim.

(c) **[Future advances and other value.]** A security agreement may provide that collateral secures, or that accounts, chattel paper, payment intangibles, or promissory notes are sold in connection with, future advances or other value, whether or not the advances or value are given pursuant to commitment.

§ 9–205. Use or Disposition of Collateral Permissible.

(a) **[When security interest not invalid or fraudulent.]** A security interest is not invalid or fraudulent against creditors solely because:

(1) the debtor has the right or ability to:

    (A) use, commingle, or dispose of all or part of the collateral, including returned or repossessed goods;

    (B) collect, compromise, enforce, or otherwise deal with collateral;

    (C) accept the return of collateral or make repossessions; or

    (D) use, commingle, or dispose of proceeds; or

(2) the secured party fails to require the debtor to account for proceeds or replace collateral.

(b) **[Requirements of possession not relaxed.]** This section does not relax the requirements of possession if attachment, perfection, or enforcement of a security interest depends upon possession of the collateral by the secured party.

§ 9–206. Security Interest Arising in Purchase or Delivery of Financial Asset.

(a) **[Security interest when person buys through securities intermediary.]** A security interest in favor of a securities intermediary attaches to a person's security entitlement if:

(1) the person buys a financial asset through the securities intermediary in a transaction in which the person is obligated to pay the purchase price to the securities intermediary at the time of the purchase; and

(2) the securities intermediary credits the financial asset to the buyer's securities account before the buyer pays the securities intermediary.

(b) **[Security interest secures obligation to pay for financial asset.]** The security interest described in subsection (a) secures the person's obligation to pay for the financial asset.

(c) **[Security interest in payment against delivery transaction.]** A security interest in favor of a person that delivers a certificated security or other financial asset represented by a writing attaches to the security or other financial asset if:

(1) the security or other financial asset:

    (A) in the ordinary course of business is transferred by delivery with any necessary indorsement or assignment; and

    (B) is delivered under an agreement between persons in the business of dealing with such securities or financial assets; and

(2) the agreement calls for delivery against payment.

(d) **[Security interest secures obligation to pay for delivery.]** The security interest described in subsection

(c) secures the obligation to make payment for the delivery.

[SUBPART 2. RIGHTS AND DUTIES]

§ 9–207. Rights and Duties of Secured Party Having Possession or Control of Collateral.

(a) **[Duty of care when secured party in possession.]** Except as otherwise provided in subsection (d), a secured party shall use reasonable care in the custody and preservation of collateral in the secured party's possession. In the case of chattel paper or an instrument, reasonable care includes taking necessary steps to preserve rights against prior parties unless otherwise agreed.

(b) **[Expenses, risks, duties, and rights when secured party in possession.]** Except as otherwise provided in subsection (d), if a secured party has possession of collateral:

(1) reasonable expenses, including the cost of insurance and payment of taxes or other charges, incurred in the custody, preservation, use, or operation of the collateral are chargeable to the debtor and are secured by the collateral;

(2) the risk of accidental loss or damage is on the debtor to the extent of a deficiency in any effective insurance coverage;

(3) the secured party shall keep the collateral identifiable, but fungible collateral may be commingled; and

(4) the secured party may use or operate the collateral:

    (A) for the purpose of preserving the collateral or its value;

    (B) as permitted by an order of a court having competent jurisdiction; or

    (C) except in the case of consumer goods, in the manner and to the extent agreed by the debtor.

(c) **[Duties and rights when secured party in possession or control.]** Except as otherwise provided in subsection (d), a secured party having possession of collateral or control of collateral under Section 9-104, 9-105, 9-106, or 9-107:

(1) may hold as additional security any proceeds, except money or funds, received from the collateral;

(2) shall apply money or funds received from the collateral to reduce the secured obligation, unless remitted to the debtor; and

(3) may create a security interest in the collateral.

(d) **[Buyer of certain rights to payment.]** If the secured party is a buyer of accounts, chattel paper, payment intangibles, or promissory notes or a consignor:

    (1) subsection (a) does not apply unless the secured party is entitled under an agreement:

        (A) to charge back uncollected collateral; or

        (B) otherwise to full or limited recourse against the debtor or a secondary obligor based on the nonpayment or other default of an account debtor or other obligor on the collateral; and

    (2) subsections (b) and (c) do not apply.

§ 9–208. Additional Duties of Secured Party Having Control of Collateral.

(a) **[Applicability of section.]** This section applies to cases in which there is no outstanding secured obligation and the secured party is not committed to make advances, incur obligations, or otherwise give value.

(b) **[Duties of secured party after receiving demand from debtor.]** Within 10 days after receiving an authenticated demand by the debtor:

    (1) a secured party having control of a deposit account under Section 9-104(a)(2) shall send to the bank with which the deposit account is maintained an authenticated statement that releases the bank from any further obligation to comply with instructions originated by the secured party;

    (2) a secured party having control of a deposit account under Section 9-104(a)(3) shall:

        (A) pay the debtor the balance on deposit in the deposit account; or

        (B) transfer the balance on deposit into a deposit account in the debtor's name;

    (3) a secured party, other than a buyer, having control of electronic chattel paper under Section 9-105 shall:

        (A) communicate the authoritative copy of the electronic chattel paper to the debtor or its designated custodian;

        (B) if the debtor designates a custodian that is the designated custodian with which the authoritative copy of the electronic chattel paper is maintained for the secured party, communicate to the custodian an authenticated record releasing the designated custodian from any further obligation to comply with instructions originated by the secured party and instructing the custodian to comply with instructions originated by the debtor; and

        (C) take appropriate action to enable the debtor or its designated custodian to make copies of or revisions to the authoritative copy which add or change an identified assignee of the authoritative copy without the consent of the secured party;

    (4) a secured party having control of investment property under Section 8-106(d)(2) or 9-106(b) shall send to the securities intermediary or commodity intermediary with which the security entitlement or commodity contract is maintained an authenticated record that releases the securities intermediary or commodity intermediary from any further obligation to comply with entitlement orders or directions originated by the secured party; and

    (5) a secured party having control of a letter-of-credit right under Section 9-107 shall send to each person having an unfulfilled obligation to pay or deliver proceeds of the letter of credit to the secured party an authenticated release from any further obligation to pay or deliver proceeds of the letter of credit to the secured party.

§ 9–209. Duties of Secured Party If Account Debtor Has Been Notified of Assignment.

(a) **[Applicability of section.]** Except as otherwise provided in subsection (c), this section applies if:

    (1) there is no outstanding secured obligation; and

    (2) the secured party is not committed to make advances, incur obligations, or otherwise give value.

(b) **[Duties of secured party after receiving demand from debtor.]** Within 10 days after receiving an authenticated demand by the debtor, a secured party shall send to an account debtor that has received notification of an assignment to the secured party as assignee under Section 9-406(a) an authenticated record that releases the account debtor from any further obligation to the secured party.

(c) **[Inapplicability to sales.]** This section does not apply to an assignment constituting the sale of an account, chattel paper, or payment intangible.

§ 9–210. Request for Accounting; Request Regarding List of Collateral or Statement of Account.

(a) **[Definitions.]** In this section:

    (1) "Request" means a record of a type described in paragraph (2), (3), or (4).

    (2) "Request for an accounting" means a record authenticated by a debtor requesting that the recipient provide an accounting of the unpaid obligations secured by collateral and reasonably

identifying the transaction or relationship that is the subject of the request.

    (3) "Request regarding a list of collateral" means a record authenticated by a debtor requesting that the recipient approve or correct a list of what the debtor believes to be the collateral securing an obligation and reasonably identifying the transaction or relationship that is the subject of the request.

    (4) "Request regarding a statement of account" means a record authenticated by a debtor requesting that the recipient approve or correct a statement indicating what the debtor believes to be the aggregate amount of unpaid obligations secured by collateral as of a specified date and reasonably identifying the transaction or relationship that is the subject of the request.

(b) **[Duty to respond to requests.]** Subject to subsections (c), (d), (e), and (f), a secured party, other than a buyer of accounts, chattel paper, payment intangibles, or promissory notes or a consignor, shall comply with a request within 14 days after receipt:

    (1) in the case of a request for an accounting, by authenticating and sending to the debtor an accounting; and

    (2) in the case of a request regarding a list of collateral or a request regarding a statement of account, by authenticating and sending to the debtor an approval or correction.

(c) **[Request regarding list of collateral; statement concerning type of collateral.]** A secured party that claims a security interest in all of a particular type of collateral owned by the debtor may comply with a request regarding a list of collateral by sending to the debtor an authenticated record including a statement to that effect within 14 days after receipt.

(d) **[Request regarding list of collateral; no interest claimed.]** A person that receives a request regarding a list of collateral, claims no interest in the collateral when it receives the request, and claimed an interest in the collateral at an earlier time shall comply with the request within 14 days after receipt by sending to the debtor an authenticated record:

    (1) disclaiming any interest in the collateral; and

    (2) if known to the recipient, providing the name and mailing address of any assignee of or successor to the recipient's interest in the collateral.

(e) **[Request for accounting or regarding statement of account; no interest in obligation claimed.]** A person that receives a request for an accounting or a request regarding a statement of account, claims no interest in the obligations when it receives the re-quest, and claimed an interest in the obligations at an earlier time shall comply with the request within 14 days after receipt by sending to the debtor an authenticated record:

    (1) disclaiming any interest in the obligations; and

    (2) if known to the recipient, providing the name and mailing address of any assignee of or successor to the recipient's interest in the obligations.

(f) **[Charges for responses.]** A debtor is entitled without charge to one response to a request under this section during any six-month period. The secured party may require payment of a charge not exceeding $25 for each additional response.

Part 3: Perfection and Priority

[SUBPART 1. LAW GOVERNING PERFECTION AND PRIORITY]

§ 9–301. Law Governing Perfection and Priority of Security Interests. Except as otherwise provided in Sections 9-303 through 9-306, the following rules determine the law governing perfection, the effect of perfection or nonperfection, and the priority of a security interest in collateral:

    (1) Except as otherwise provided in this section, while a debtor is located in a jurisdiction, the local law of that jurisdiction governs perfection, the effect of perfection or nonperfection, and the priority of a security interest in collateral.

    (2) While collateral is located in a jurisdiction, the local law of that jurisdiction governs perfection, the effect of perfection or nonperfection, and the priority of a possessory security interest in that collateral.

    (3) Except as otherwise provided in paragraph (4), while negotiable documents, goods, instruments, money, or tangible chattel paper is located in a jurisdiction, the local law of that jurisdiction governs:

        (A) perfection of a security interest in the goods by filing a fixture filing;

        (B) perfection of a security interest in timber to be cut; and

        (C) the effect of perfection or nonperfection and the priority of a nonpossessory security interest in the collateral.

    (4) The local law of the jurisdiction in which the wellhead or minehead is located governs perfection, the effect of perfection or nonperfection, and the priority of a security interest in as-extracted collateral.

§ 9–302. Law Governing Perfection and Priority of Agricultural Liens. While farm products are located in a jurisdiction, the local law of that jurisdiction governs perfection, the effect of perfection or nonperfection, and the priority of an agricultural lien on the farm products.

§ 9–303. Law Governing Perfection and Priority of Security Interests in Goods Covered by a Certificate Of Title.

(a) [Applicability of section.] This section applies to goods covered by a certificate of title, even if there is no other relationship between the jurisdiction under whose certificate of title the goods are covered and the goods or the debtor.

(b) [When goods covered by certificate of title.] Goods become covered by a certificate of title when a valid application for the certificate of title and the applicable fee are delivered to the appropriate authority. Goods cease to be covered by a certificate of title at the earlier of the time the certificate of title ceases to be effective under the law of the issuing jurisdiction or the time the goods become covered subsequently by a certificate of title issued by another jurisdiction.

(c) [Applicable law.] The local law of the jurisdiction under whose certificate of title the goods are covered governs perfection, the effect of perfection or nonperfection, and the priority of a security interest in goods covered by a certificate of title from the time the goods become covered by the certificate of title until the goods cease to be covered by the certificate of title.

§ 9–304. Law Governing Perfection and Priority of Security Interests in Deposit Accounts.

(a) [Law of bank's jurisdiction governs.] The local law of a bank's jurisdiction governs perfection, the effect of perfection or nonperfection, and the priority of a security interest in a deposit account maintained with that bank.

(b) [Bank's jurisdiction.] The following rules determine a bank's jurisdiction for purposes of this part:

(1) If an agreement between the bank and its customer governing the deposit account expressly provides that a particular jurisdiction is the bank's jurisdiction for purposes of this part, this article, or [the Uniform Commercial Code], that jurisdiction is the bankís jurisdiction.

(2) If paragraph (1) does not apply and an agreement between the bank and its customer governing the deposit account expressly provides that the agreement is governed by the law of a particular jurisdiction, that jurisdiction is the bank's jurisdiction.

(3) If neither paragraph (1) nor paragraph (2) applies and an agreement between the bank and its customer governing the deposit account expressly provides that the deposit account is maintained at an office in a particular jurisdiction, that jurisdiction is the bank's jurisdiction.

(4) If none of the preceding paragraphs applies, the bank's jurisdiction is the jurisdiction in which the office identified in an account statement as the office serving the customer's account is located.

(5) If none of the preceding paragraphs applies, the bankís jurisdiction is the jurisdiction in which the chief executive office of the bank is located.

§ 9–305. Law Governing Perfection and Priority of Security Interests in Investment Property.

(a) [Governing law: general rules.] Except as otherwise provided in subsection (c), the following rules apply:

(1) While a security certificate is located in a jurisdiction, the local law of that jurisdiction governs perfection, the effect of perfection or nonperfection, and the priority of a security interest in the certificated security represented thereby.

(2) The local law of the issuer's jurisdiction as specified in Section 8-110(d) governs perfection, the effect of perfection or nonperfection, and the priority of a security interest in an uncertificated security.

(3) The local law of the securities intermediary's jurisdiction as specified in Section 8-110(e) governs perfection, the effect of perfection or nonperfection, and the priority of a security interest in a security entitlement or securities account.

(4) The local law of the commodity intermediary's jurisdiction governs perfection, the effect of perfection or nonperfection, and the priority of a security interest in a commodity contract or commodity account.

(b) [Commodity intermediary's jurisdiction.] The following rules determine a commodity intermediary's jurisdiction for purposes of this part:

(1) If an agreement between the commodity intermediary and commodity customer governing the commodity account expressly provides that a particular jurisdiction is the commodity

intermediary's jurisdiction for purposes of this part, this article, or [the Uniform Commercial Code], that jurisdiction is the commodity intermediary's jurisdiction.

(2) If paragraph (1) does not apply and an agreement between the commodity intermediary and commodity customer governing the commodity account expressly provides that the agreement is governed by the law of a particular jurisdiction, that jurisdiction is the commodity intermediary's jurisdiction.

(3) If neither paragraph (1) nor paragraph (2) applies and an agreement between the commodity intermediary and commodity customer governing the commodity account expressly provides that the commodity account is maintained at an office in a particular jurisdiction, that jurisdiction is the commodity intermediary's jurisdiction.

(4) If none of the preceding paragraphs applies, the commodity intermediary's jurisdiction is the jurisdiction in which the office identified in an account statement as the office serving the commodity customer's account is located.

(5) If none of the preceding paragraphs applies, the commodity intermediary's jurisdiction is the jurisdiction in which the chief executive office of the commodity intermediary is located.

(c) **[When perfection governed by law of jurisdiction where debtor located.]** The local law of the jurisdiction in which the debtor is located governs:

(1) perfection of a security interest in investment property by filing;

(2) automatic perfection of a security interest in investment property created by a broker or securities intermediary; and

(3) automatic perfection of a security interest in a commodity contract or commodity account created by a commodity intermediary.

§ 9–306. Law Governing Perfection and Priority of Security Interests in Letter-of-Credit Rights.

(a) **[Governing law: issuer's or nominated person's jurisdiction.]** Subject to subsection (c), the local law of the issuer's jurisdiction or a nominated person's jurisdiction governs perfection, the effect of perfection or nonperfection, and the priority of a security interest in a letter-of-credit right if the issuer's jurisdiction or nominated person's jurisdiction is a State.

(b) **[Issuer's or nominated person's jurisdiction.]** For purposes of this part, an issuer's jurisdiction or nom-inated person's jurisdiction is the jurisdiction whose law governs the liability of the issuer or nominated person with respect to the letter-of-credit right as provided in Section 5-116.

(c) **[When section not applicable.]** This section does not apply to a security interest that is perfected only under Section 9-308(d).

§ 9–307. Location of Debtor.

(a) **["Place of business."]** In this section, "place of business" means a place where a debtor conducts its affairs.

(b) **[Debtor's location: general rules.]** Except as otherwise provided in this section, the following rules determine a debtor's location:

(1) A debtor who is an individual is located at the individual's principal residence.

(2) A debtor that is an organization and has only one place of business is located at its place of business.

(3) A debtor that is an organization and has more than one place of business is located at its chief executive office.

(c) **[Limitation of applicability of subsection (b).]** Subsection (b) applies only if a debtor's residence, place of business, or chief executive office, as applicable, is located in a jurisdiction whose law generally requires information concerning the existence of a nonpossessory security interest to be made generally available in a filing, recording, or registration system as a condition or result of the security interest's obtaining priority over the rights of a lien creditor with respect to the collateral. If subsection (b) does not apply, the debtor is located in the District of Columbia.

(d) **[Continuation of location: cessation of existence, etc.]** A person that ceases to exist, have a residence, or have a place of business continues to be located in the jurisdiction specified by subsections (b) and (c).

(e) **[Location of registered organization organized under State law.]** A registered organization that is organized under the law of a State is located in that State.

(f) **[Location of registered organization organized under federal law; bank branches and agencies.]** Except as otherwise provided in subsection (i), a registered organization that is organized under the law of the United States and a branch or agency of a bank that is not organized under the law of the United States or a State are located:

(1) in the State that the law of the United States designates, if the law designates a State of location;

(2) in the State that the registered organization, branch, or agency designates, if the law of the United States authorizes the registered organization, branch, or agency to designate its State of location; or

(3) in the District of Columbia, if neither paragraph (1) nor paragraph (2) applies.

(g) [Continuation of location: change in status of registered organization.] A registered organization continues to be located in the jurisdiction specified by subsection (e) or (f) notwithstanding:

(1) the suspension, revocation, forfeiture, or lapse of the registered organization's status as such in its jurisdiction of organization; or

(2) the dissolution, winding up, or cancellation of the existence of the registered organization.

(h) [Location of United States.] The United States is located in the District of Columbia.

(i) [Location of foreign bank branch or agency if licensed in only one state.] A branch or agency of a bank that is not organized under the law of the United States or a State is located in the State in which the branch or agency is licensed, if all branches and agencies of the bank are licensed in only one State.

(j) [Location of foreign air carrier.] A foreign air carrier under the Federal Aviation Act of 1958, as amended, is located at the designated office of the agent upon which service of process may be made on behalf of the carrier.

(k) [Section applies only to this part.] This section applies only for purposes of this part.

[SUBPART 2. PERFECTION]

§ 9–308. When Security Interest or Agricultural Lien Is Perfected; Continuity of Perfection.

(a) [Perfection of security interest.] Except as otherwise provided in this section and Section 9-309, a security interest is perfected if it has attached and all of the applicable requirements for perfection in Sections 9-310 through 9-316 have been satisfied. A security interest is perfected when it attaches if the applicable requirements are satisfied before the security interest attaches.

(b) [Perfection of agricultural lien.] An agricultural lien is perfected if it has become effective and all of the applicable requirements for perfection in Section 9-310 have been satisfied. An agricultural lien is perfected when it becomes effective if the applicable requirements are satisfied before the agricultural lien becomes effective.

(c) [Continuous perfection; perfection by different methods.] A security interest or agricultural lien is perfected continuously if it is originally perfected by one method under this article and is later perfected by another method under this article, without an intermediate period when it was unperfected.

(d) [Supporting obligation.] Perfection of a security interest in collateral also perfects a security interest in a supporting obligation for the collateral.

(e) [Lien securing right to payment.] Perfection of a security interest in a right to payment or performance also perfects a security interest in a security interest, mortgage, or other lien on personal or real property securing the right.

(f) [Security entitlement carried in securities account.] Perfection of a security interest in a securities account also perfects a security interest in the security entitlements carried in the securities account.

(g) [Commodity contract carried in commodity account.] Perfection of a security interest in a commodity account also perfects a security interest in the commodity contracts carried in the commodity account.

Legislative Note: Any statute conflicting with subsection (e) must be made expressly subject to that subsection.

§ 9–309. Security Interest Perfected upon Attachment. The following security interests are perfected when they attach:

(1) a purchase-money security interest in consumer goods, except as otherwise provided in Section 9-311(b) with respect to consumer goods that are subject to a statute or treaty described in Section 9-311(a);

(2) an assignment of accounts or payment intangibles which does not by itself or in conjunction with other assignments to the same assignee transfer a significant part of the assignor's outstanding accounts or payment intangibles;

(3) a sale of a payment intangible;

(4) a sale of a promissory note;

(5) a security interest created by the assignment of a health-care-insurance receivable to the provider of the health-care goods or services;

(6) a security interest arising under Section 2-401, 2-505, 2-711(3), or 2A-508(5), until the debtor obtains possession of the collateral;

(7) a security interest of a collecting bank arising under Section 4-210;

(8) a security interest of an issuer or nominated person arising under Section 5-118;

(9) a security interest arising in the delivery of a financial asset under Section 9-206(c);

(10) a security interest in investment property created by a broker or securities intermediary;

(11) a security interest in a commodity contract or a commodity account created by a commodity intermediary;

(12) an assignment for the benefit of all creditors of the transferor and subsequent transfers by the assignee thereunder; and

(13) a security interest created by an assignment of a beneficial interest in a decedent's estate.; and

(14) a sale by an individual of an account that is a right to payment of winnings in a lottery or other game of chance.

§ 9–310. When Filing Required to Perfect Security Interest or Agricultural Lien; Security Interests and Agricultural Liens to Which Filing Provisions Do Not Apply.

(a) [General rule: perfection by filing.] Except as otherwise provided in subsection (b) and Section 9-312(b), a financing statement must be filed to perfect all security interests and agricultural liens.

(b) [Exceptions: filing not necessary.] The filing of a financing statement is not necessary to perfect a security interest:

(1) that is perfected under Section 9-308(d), (e), (f), or (g);

(2) that is perfected under Section 9-309 when it attaches;

(3) in property subject to a statute, regulation, or treaty described in Section 9-311(a);

(4) in goods in possession of a bailee which is perfected under Section 9-312(d)(1) or (2);

(5) in certificated securities, documents, goods, or instruments which is perfected without filing or possession under Section 9-312(e), (f), or (g);

(6) in collateral in the secured party's possession under Section 9-313;

(7) in a certificated security which is perfected by delivery of the security certificate to the secured party under Section 9-313;

(8) in deposit accounts, electronic chattel paper, investment property, or letter-of-credit rights which is perfected by control under Section 9-314;

(9) in proceeds which is perfected under Section 9-315; or

(10) that is perfected under Section 9-316.

(c) [Assignment of perfected security interest.] If a secured party assigns a perfected security interest or agricultural lien, a filing under this article is not required to continue the perfected status of the security interest against creditors of and transferees from the original debtor.

§ 9–311. Perfection of Security Interests in Property Subject to Certain Statutes, Regulations, and Treaties.

(a) [Security interest subject to other law.] Except as otherwise provided in subsection (d), the filing of a financing statement is not necessary or effective to perfect a security interest in property subject to:

(1) a statute, regulation, or treaty of the United States whose requirements for a security interest's obtaining priority over the rights of a lien creditor with respect to the property preempt Section 9-310(a);

(2) [list any certificate-of-title statute covering automobiles, trailers, mobile homes, boats, farm tractors, or the like, which provides for a security interest to be indicated on the certificate as a condition or result of perfection, and any non-Uniform Commercial Code central filing statute]; or

(3) a certificate-of-title statute of another jurisdiction which provides for a security interest to be indicated on the certificate as a condition or result of the security interest's obtaining priority over the rights of a lien creditor with respect to the property.

(b) [Compliance with other law.] Compliance with the requirements of a statute, regulation, or treaty described in subsection (a) for obtaining priority over the rights of a lien creditor is equivalent to the filing of a financing statement under this article. Except as otherwise provided in subsection (d) and Sections 9-313 and 9-316(d) and (e) for goods covered by a certificate of title, a security interest in property subject to a statute, regulation, or treaty described in subsection (a) may be perfected only by compliance with those requirements, and a security interest so perfected remains perfected notwithstanding a change in the use or transfer of possession of the collateral.

(c) [Duration and renewal of perfection.] Except as otherwise provided in subsection (d) and Section 9-316(d) and (e), duration and renewal of perfection of a security interest perfected by compliance with the requirements prescribed by a statute, regulation, or treaty described in subsection (a) are governed by the statute, regulation, or treaty. In other respects, the security interest is subject to this article.

(d) **[Inapplicability to certain inventory.]** During any period in which collateral subject to a statute specified in subsection (a)(2) is inventory held for sale or lease by a person or leased by that person as lessor and that person is in the business of selling goods of that kind, this section does not apply to a security interest in that collateral created by that person.

§ 9–312. Perfection of Security Interests in Chattel Paper, Deposit Accounts, Documents, Goods Covered by Documents, Instruments, Investment Property, Letter-of-Credit Rights, and Money; Perfection by Permissive Filing; Temporary Perfection Without Filing or Transfer of Possession.

(a) **[Perfection by filing permitted.]** A security interest in chattel paper, negotiable documents, instruments, or investment property may be perfected by filing.

(b) **[Control or possession of certain collateral.]** Except as otherwise provided in Section 9-315(c) and (d) for proceeds:

   (1) a security interest in a deposit account may be perfected only by control under Section 9-314;

   (2) and except as otherwise provided in Section 9-308(d), a security interest in a letter-of-credit right may be perfected only by control under Section 9-314; and

   (3) a security interest in money may be perfected only by the secured party's taking possession under Section 9-313.

(c) **[Goods covered by negotiable document.]** While goods are in the possession of a bailee that has issued a negotiable document covering the goods:

   (1) a security interest in the goods may be perfected by perfecting a security interest in the document; and

   (2) a security interest perfected in the document has priority over any security interest that becomes perfected in the goods by another method during that time.

(d) **[Goods covered by nonnegotiable document.]** While goods are in the possession of a bailee that has issued a nonnegotiable document covering the goods, a security interest in the goods may be perfected by:

   (1) issuance of a document in the name of the secured party;

   (2) the bailee's receipt of notification of the secured party's interest; or

   (3) filing as to the goods.

(e) **[Temporary perfection: new value.]** A security interest in certificated securities, negotiable documents, or instruments is perfected without filing or the taking of possession for a period of 20 days from the time it attaches to the extent that it arises for new value given under an authenticated security agreement.

(f) **[Temporary perfection: goods or documents made available to debtor.]** A perfected security interest in a negotiable document or goods in possession of a bailee, other than one that has issued a negotiable document for the goods, remains perfected for 20 days without filing if the secured party makes available to the debtor the goods or documents representing the goods for the purpose of:

   (1) ultimate sale or exchange; or

   (2) loading, unloading, storing, shipping, transshipping, manufacturing, processing, or otherwise dealing with them in a manner preliminary to their sale or exchange.

(g) **[Temporary perfection: delivery of security certificate or instrument to debtor.]** A perfected security interest in a certificated security or instrument remains perfected for 20 days without filing if the secured party delivers the security certificate or instrument to the debtor for the purpose of:

   (1) ultimate sale or exchange; or

   (2) presentation, collection, enforcement, renewal, or registration of transfer.

(h) **[Expiration of temporary perfection.]** After the 20-day period specified in subsection (e), (f), or (g) expires, perfection depends upon compliance with this article.

§ 9–313. When Possession by or Delivery to Secured Party Perfects Security Interest Without Filing.

(a) **[Perfection by possession or delivery.]** Except as otherwise provided in subsection (b), a secured party may perfect a security interest in negotiable documents, goods, instruments, money, or tangible chattel paper by taking possession of the collateral. A secured party may perfect a security interest in certificated securities by taking delivery of the certificated securities under Section 8-301.

(b) **[Goods covered by certificate of title.]** With respect to goods covered by a certificate of title issued by this State, a secured party may perfect a security interest in the goods by taking possession of the goods only in the circumstances described in Section 9-316(d).

(c) [Collateral in possession of person other than debtor.] With respect to collateral other than certificated securities and goods covered by a document, a secured party takes possession of collateral in the possession of a person other than the debtor, the secured party, or a lessee of the collateral from the debtor in the ordinary course of the debtor's business, when:

(1) the person in possession authenticates a record acknowledging that it holds possession of the collateral for the secured party's benefit; or

(2) the person takes possession of the collateral after having authenticated a record acknowledging that it will hold possession of collateral for the secured party's benefit.

(d) [Time of perfection by possession; continuation of perfection.] If perfection of a security interest depends upon possession of the collateral by a secured party, perfection occurs no earlier than the time the secured party takes possession and continues only while the secured party retains possession.

(e) [Time of perfection by delivery; continuation of perfection.] A security interest in a certificated security in registered form is perfected by delivery when delivery of the certificated security occurs under Section 8-301 and remains perfected by delivery until the debtor obtains possession of the security certificate.

(f) [Acknowledgment not required.] A person in possession of collateral is not required to acknowledge that it holds possession for a secured party's benefit.

(g) [Effectiveness of acknowledgment; no duties or confirmation.] If a person acknowledges that it holds possession for the secured party's benefit:

(1) the acknowledgment is effective under subsection (c) or Section 8-301(a), even if the acknowledgment violates the rights of a debtor; and

(2) unless the person otherwise agrees or law other than this article otherwise provides, the person does not owe any duty to the secured party and is not required to confirm the acknowledgment to another person.

(h) [Secured party's delivery to person other than debtor.] A secured party having possession of collateral does not relinquish possession by delivering the collateral to a person other than the debtor or a lessee of the collateral from the debtor in the ordinary course of the debtor's business if the person was instructed before the delivery or is instructed contemporaneously with the delivery:

(1) to hold possession of the collateral for the secured party's benefit; or

(2) to redeliver the collateral to the secured party.

(i) [Effect of delivery under subsection (h); no duties or confirmation.] A secured party does not relinquish possession, even if a delivery under subsection (h) violates the rights of a debtor. A person to which collateral is delivered under subsection (h) does not owe any duty to the secured party and is not required to confirm the delivery to another person unless the person otherwise agrees or law other than this article otherwise provides.

§ 9–314. Perfection by Control.

(a) [Perfection by control.] A security interest in investment property, deposit accounts, letter-of-credit rights, or electronic chattel paper may be perfected by control of the collateral under Section 9-104, 9-105, 9-106, or 9-107.

(b) [Specified collateral: time of perfection by control; continuation of perfection.] A security interest in deposit accounts, electronic chattel paper, or letter-of-credit rights is perfected by control under Section 9-104, 9-105, or 9-107 when the secured party obtains control and remains perfected by control only while the secured party retains control.

(c) [Investment property: time of perfection by control; continuation of perfection.] A security interest in investment property is perfected by control under Section 9-106 from the time the secured party obtains control and remains perfected by control until:

(1) the secured party does not have control; and

(2) one of the following occurs:

(A) if the collateral is a certificated security, the debtor has or acquires possession of the security certificate;

(B) if the collateral is an uncertificated security, the issuer has registered or registers the debtor as the registered owner; or

(C) if the collateral is a security entitlement, the debtor is or becomes the entitlement holder.

§ 9–315. Secured Party's Rights on Disposition of Collateral and in Proceeds.

(a) [Disposition of collateral: continuation of security interest or agricultural lien; proceeds.] Except as otherwise provided in this article and in Section 2-403(2):

(1) a security interest or agricultural lien continues in collateral notwithstanding sale, lease, license, exchange, or other disposition thereof unless the secured party authorized the disposition free of the security interest or agricultural lien; and

(2) a security interest attaches to any identifiable proceeds of collateral.

(b) **[When commingled proceeds identifiable.]** Proceeds that are commingled with other property are identifiable proceeds:

(1) if the proceeds are goods, to the extent provided by Section 9-336; and

(2) if the proceeds are not goods, to the extent that the secured party identifies the proceeds by a method of tracing, including application of equitable principles, that is permitted under law other than this article with respect to commingled property of the type involved.

(c) **[Perfection of security interest in proceeds.]** A security interest in proceeds is a perfected security interest if the security interest in the original collateral was perfected.

(d) **[Continuation of perfection.]** A perfected security interest in proceeds becomes unperfected on the 21st day after the security interest attaches to the proceeds unless:

(1) the following conditions are satisfied:

   (A) a filed financing statement covers the original collateral;

   (B) the proceeds are collateral in which a security interest may be perfected by filing in the office in which the financing statement has been filed; and

   (C) the proceeds are not acquired with cash proceeds;

(2) the proceeds are identifiable cash proceeds; or

(3) the security interest in the proceeds is perfected other than under subsection (c) when the security interest attaches to the proceeds or within 20 days thereafter.

(e) **[When perfected security interest in proceeds becomes unperfected.]** If a filed financing statement covers the original collateral, a security interest in proceeds which remains perfected under subsection (d)(1) becomes unperfected at the later of:

(1) when the effectiveness of the filed financing statement lapses under Section 9-515 or is terminated under Section 9-513; or

(2) the 21st day after the security interest attaches to the proceeds.

§ 9–316. Continued Perfection of Security Interest Following Change in Governing Law.

(a) **[General rule: effect on perfection of change in governing law.]** A security interest perfected pursuant to the law of the jurisdiction designated in Section 9-301(1) or 9-305(c) remains perfected until the earliest of:

(1) the time perfection would have ceased under the law of that jurisdiction;

(2) the expiration of four months after a change of the debtor's location to another jurisdiction; or

(3) the expiration of one year after a transfer of collateral to a person that thereby becomes a debtor and is located in another jurisdiction.

(b) **[Security interest perfected or unperfected under law of new jurisdiction.]** If a security interest described in subsection (a) becomes perfected under the law of the other jurisdiction before the earliest time or event described in that subsection, it remains perfected thereafter. If the security interest does not become perfected under the law of the other jurisdiction before the earliest time or event, it becomes unperfected and is deemed never to have been perfected as against a purchaser of the collateral for value.

(c) **[Possessory security interest in collateral moved to new jurisdiction.]** A possessory security interest in collateral, other than goods covered by a certificate of title and as-extracted collateral consisting of goods, remains continuously perfected if:

(1) the collateral is located in one jurisdiction and subject to a security interest perfected under the law of that jurisdiction;

(2) thereafter the collateral is brought into another jurisdiction; and

(3) upon entry into the other jurisdiction, the security interest is perfected under the law of the other jurisdiction.

(d) **[Goods covered by certificate of title from this state.]** Except as otherwise provided in subsection (e), a security interest in goods covered by a certificate of title which is perfected by any method under the law of another jurisdiction when the goods become covered by a certificate of title from this State remains perfected until the security interest would have become unperfected under the law of the other jurisdiction had the goods not become so covered.

(e) **[When subsection (d) security interest becomes unperfected against purchasers.]** A security interest described in subsection (d) becomes unperfected as against a purchaser of the goods for value and is deemed never to have been perfected as against a purchaser of the goods for value if the applicable requirements for perfection under Section 9-311(b) or 9-313 are not satisfied before the earlier of:

(1) the time the security interest would have become unperfected under the law of the other jurisdiction had the goods not become covered by a certificate of title from this State; or

(2) the expiration of four months after the goods had become so covered.

(f) **[Change in jurisdiction of bank, issuer, nominated person, securities intermediary, or commodity intermediary.]** A security interest in deposit accounts, letter-of-credit rights, or investment property which is perfected under the law of the bank's jurisdiction, the issuer's jurisdiction, a nominated person's jurisdiction, the securities intermediary's jurisdiction, or the commodity intermediary's jurisdiction, as applicable, remains perfected until the earlier of:

(1) the time the security interest would have become unperfected under the law of that jurisdiction; or

(2) the expiration of four months after a change of the applicable jurisdiction to another jurisdiction.

(g) **[Subsection (f) security interest perfected or unperfected under law of new jurisdiction.]** If a security interest described in subsection (f) becomes perfected under the law of the other jurisdiction before the earlier of the time or the end of the period described in that subsection, it remains perfected thereafter. If the security interest does not become perfected under the law of the other jurisdiction before the earlier of that time or the end of that period, it becomes unperfected and is deemed never to have been perfected as against a purchaser of the collateral for value.

[SUBPART 3. PRIORITY]

§ 9–317. Interests That Take Priority Over or Take Free of Security Interest or Agricultural Lien.

(a) **[Conflicting security interests and rights of lien creditors.]** A security interest or agricultural lien is subordinate to the rights of:

(1) a person entitled to priority under Section 9-322; and

(2) except as otherwise provided in subsection (e), a person that becomes a lien creditor before the earlier of the time:

(A) the security interest or agricultural lien is perfected; or

(B) one of the conditions specified in Section 9-203(b)(3) is met and a financing statement covering the collateral is filed.

(b) **[Buyers that receive delivery.]** Except as otherwise provided in subsection (e), a buyer, other than a secured party, of tangible chattel paper, documents, goods, instruments, or a security certificate takes free of a security interest or agricultural lien if the buyer gives value and receives delivery of the collateral without knowledge of the security interest or agricultural lien and before it is perfected.

(c) **[Lessees that receive delivery.]** Except as otherwise provided in subsection (e), a lessee of goods takes free of a security interest or agricultural lien if the lessee gives value and receives delivery of the collateral without knowledge of the security interest or agricultural lien and before it is perfected.

(d) **[Licensees and buyers of certain collateral.]** A licensee of a general intangible or a buyer, other than a secured party, of accounts, electronic chattel paper, general intangibles, or investment property other than a certificated security takes free of a security interest if the licensee or buyer gives value without knowledge of the security interest and before it is perfected.

(e) **[Purchase-money security interest.]** Except as otherwise provided in Sections 9-320 and 9-321, if a person files a financing statement with respect to a purchase-money security interest before or within 20 days after the debtor receives delivery of the collateral, the security interest takes priority over the rights of a buyer, lessee, or lien creditor which arise between the time the security interest attaches and the time of filing.

§ 9–318. No Interest Retained in Right to Payment That Is Sold; Rights and Title of Seller of Account or Chattel Paper with Respect to Creditors and Purchasers.

(a) **[Seller retains no interest.]** A debtor that has sold an account, chattel paper, payment intangible, or promissory note does not retain a legal or equitable interest in the collateral sold.

(b) **[Deemed rights of debtor if buyer's security interest unperfected.]** For purposes of determining the rights of creditors of, and purchasers for value of an account or chattel paper from, a debtor that has sold an account or chattel paper, while the buyer's security interest is unperfected, the debtor is deemed to have rights and title to the account or chattel paper identical to those the debtor sold.

§ 9–319. Rights and Title of Consignee with Respect to Creditors and Purchasers.

(a) **[Consignee has consignor's rights.]** Except as otherwise provided in subsection (b), for purposes of determining the rights of creditors of, and purchasers for value of goods from, a consignee, while the goods are in the possession of the consignee, the consignee is deemed to have rights and title to the goods identical to those the consignor had or had power to transfer.

(b) **[Applicability of other law.]** For purposes of determining the rights of a creditor of a consignee, law other than this article determines the rights and title of a consignee while goods are in the consignee's possession if, under this part, a perfected security interest held by the consignor would have priority over the rights of the creditor.

§ 9–320. Buyer of Goods.

(a) **[Buyer in ordinary course of business.]** Except as otherwise provided in subsection (e), a buyer in ordinary course of business, other than a person buying farm products from a person engaged in farming operations, takes free of a security interest created by the buyer's seller, even if the security interest is perfected and the buyer knows of its existence.

(b) **[Buyer of consumer goods.]** Except as otherwise provided in subsection (e), a buyer of goods from a person who used or bought the goods for use primarily for personal, family, or household purposes takes free of a security interest, even if perfected, if the buyer buys:

(1) without knowledge of the security interest;

(2) for value;

(3) primarily for the buyer's personal, family, or household purposes; and

(4) before the filing of a financing statement covering the goods.

(c) **[Effectiveness of filing for subsection (b).]** To the extent that it affects the priority of a security interest over a buyer of goods under subsection (b), the period of effectiveness of a filing made in the jurisdiction in which the seller is located is governed by Section 9-316(a) and (b).

(d) **[Buyer in ordinary course of business at wellhead or minehead.]** A buyer in ordinary course of business buying oil, gas, or other minerals at the wellhead or minehead or after extraction takes free of an interest arising out of an encumbrance.

(e) **[Possessory security interest not affected.]** Subsections (a) and (b) do not affect a security interest in goods in the possession of the secured party under Section 9-313.

§ 9–321. Licensee of General Intangible and Lessee of Goods in Ordinary Course of Business.

(a) **["Licensee in ordinary course of business."]** In this section, "licensee in ordinary course of business" means a person that becomes a licensee of a general intangible in good faith, without knowledge that the license violates the rights of another person in the general intangible, and in the ordinary course from a person in the business of licensing general intangibles of that kind. A person becomes a licensee in the ordinary course if the license to the person comports with the usual or customary practices in the kind of business in which the licensor is engaged or with the licensor's own usual or customary practices.

(b) **[Rights of licensee in ordinary course of business.]** A licensee in ordinary course of business takes its rights under a nonexclusive license free of a security interest in the general intangible created by the licensor, even if the security interest is perfected and the licensee knows of its existence.

(c) **[Rights of lessee in ordinary course of business.]** A lessee in ordinary course of business takes its leasehold interest free of a security interest in the goods created by the lessor, even if the security interest is perfected and the lessee knows of its existence.

§ 9–322. Priorities Among Conflicting Security Interests in and Agricultural Liens on Same Collateral.

(a) **[General priority rules.]** Except as otherwise provided in this section, priority among conflicting security interests and agricultural liens in the same collateral is determined according to the following rules:

(1) Conflicting perfected security interests and agricultural liens rank according to priority in time of filing or perfection. Priority dates from the earlier of the time a filing covering the collateral is first made or the security interest or agricultural lien is first perfected, if there is no period thereafter when there is neither filing nor perfection.

(2) A perfected security interest or agricultural lien has priority over a conflicting unperfected security interest or agricultural lien.

(3) The first security interest or agricultural lien to attach or become effective has priority if conflicting security interests and agricultural liens are unperfected.

(b) **[Time of perfection: proceeds and supporting obligations.]** For the purposes of subsection (a)(1):

(1) the time of filing or perfection as to a security interest in collateral is also the time of filing or perfection as to a security interest in proceeds; and

(2) the time of filing or perfection as to a security interest in collateral supported by a supporting obligation is also the time of filing or perfection as to a security interest in the supporting obligation.

(c) **[Special priority rules: proceeds and supporting obligations.]** Except as otherwise provided in subsection (f), a security interest in collateral which qualifies for priority over a conflicting security interest under Section 9-327, 9-328, 9-329, 9-330, or 9-331 also has priority over a conflicting security interest in:

(1) any supporting obligation for the collateral; and

(2) proceeds of the collateral if:

(A) the security interest in proceeds is perfected;

(B) the proceeds are cash proceeds or of the same type as the collateral; and

(C) in the case of proceeds that are proceeds of proceeds, all intervening proceeds are cash proceeds, proceeds of the same type as the collateral, or an account relating to the collateral.

(d) **[First-to-file priority rule for certain collateral.]** Subject to subsection (e) and except as otherwise provided in subsection (f), if a security interest in chattel paper, deposit accounts, negotiable documents, instruments, investment property, or letter-of-credit rights is perfected by a method other than filing, conflicting perfected security interests in proceeds of the collateral rank according to priority in time of filing.

(e) **[Applicability of subsection (d).]** Subsection (d) applies only if the proceeds of the collateral are not cash proceeds, chattel paper, negotiable documents, instruments, investment property, or letter-of-credit rights.

(f) **[Limitations on subsections (a) through (e).]** Subsections (a) through (e) are subject to:

(1) subsection (g) and the other provisions of this part;

(2) Section 4-210 with respect to a security interest of a collecting bank;

(3) Section 5-118 with respect to a security interest of an issuer or nominated person; and

(4) Section 9-110 with respect to a security interest arising under Article 2 or 2A.

(g) **[Priority under agricultural lien statute.]** A perfected agricultural lien on collateral has priority over a conflicting security interest in or agricultural lien on the same collateral if the statute creating the agricultural lien so provides.

§ 9–323. Future Advances.

(a) **[When priority based on time of advance.]** Except as otherwise provided in subsection (c), for purposes of determining the priority of a perfected security interest under Section 9-322(a)(1), perfection of the security interest dates from the time an advance is made to the extent that the security interest secures an advance that:

(1) is made while the security interest is perfected only:

(A) under Section 9-309 when it attaches; or

(B) temporarily under Section 9-312(e), (f), or (g); and

(2) is not made pursuant to a commitment entered into before or while the security interest is perfected by a method other than under Section 9-309 or 9-312(e), (f), or (g).

(b) **[Lien creditor.]** Except as otherwise provided in subsection (c), a security interest is subordinate to the rights of a person that becomes a lien creditor to the extent that the security interest secures an advance made more than 45 days after the person becomes a lien creditor unless the advance is made:

(1) without knowledge of the lien; or

(2) pursuant to a commitment entered into without knowledge of the lien.

(c) **[Buyer of receivables.]** Subsections (a) and (b) do not apply to a security interest held by a secured party that is a buyer of accounts, chattel paper, payment intangibles, or promissory notes or a consignor.

(d) **[Buyer of goods.]** Except as otherwise provided in subsection (e), a buyer of goods other than a buyer in ordinary course of business takes free of a security interest to the extent that it secures advances made after the earlier of:

(1) the time the secured party acquires knowledge of the buyer's purchase; or

(2) 45 days after the purchase.

(e) **[Advances made pursuant to commitment: priority of buyer of goods.]** Subsection (d) does not apply if the advance is made pursuant to a commitment entered into without knowledge of the buyer's purchase and before the expiration of the 45-day period.

(f) **[Lessee of goods.]** Except as otherwise provided in subsection (g), a lessee of goods, other than a lessee in ordinary course of business, takes the leasehold interest free of a security interest to the extent that it secures advances made after the earlier of:

(1) the time the secured party acquires knowledge of the lease; or

(2) 45 days after the lease contract becomes enforceable.

(g) **[Advances made pursuant to commitment: priority of lessee of goods.]** Subsection (f) does not apply if the advance is made pursuant to a commitment entered into without knowledge of the lease and before the expiration of the 45-day period.

§ 9–324. Priority of Purchase-Money Security Interests.

(a) **[General rule: purchase-money priority.]** Except as otherwise provided in subsection (g), a perfected purchase-money security interest in goods other than inventory or livestock has priority over a conflicting security interest in the same goods, and, except as otherwise provided in Section 9-327, a perfected security interest in its identifiable proceeds also has priority, if the purchase-money security interest is perfected when the debtor receives possession of the collateral or within 20 days thereafter.

(b) **[Inventory purchase-money priority.]** Subject to subsection (c) and except as otherwise provided in subsection (g), a perfected purchase-money security interest in inventory has priority over a conflicting security interest in the same inventory, has priority over a conflicting security interest in chattel paper or an instrument constituting proceeds of the inventory and in proceeds of the chattel paper, if so provided in Section 9-330, and, except as otherwise provided in Section 9-327, also has priority in identifiable cash proceeds of the inventory to the extent the identifiable cash proceeds are received on or before the delivery of the inventory to a buyer, if:

(1) the purchase-money security interest is perfected when the debtor receives possession of the inventory;

(2) the purchase-money secured party sends an authenticated notification to the holder of the conflicting security interest;

(3) the holder of the conflicting security interest receives the notification within five years before the debtor receives possession of the inventory; and

(4) the notification states that the person sending the notification has or expects to acquire a purchase-money security interest in inventory of the debtor and describes the inventory.

(c) **[Holders of conflicting inventory security interests to be notified.]** Subsections (b)(2) through (4) apply only if the holder of the conflicting security interest had filed a financing statement covering the same types of inventory:

(1) if the purchase-money security interest is perfected by filing, before the date of the filing; or

(2) if the purchase-money security interest is temporarily perfected without filing or possession under Section 9-312(f), before the beginning of the 20-day period thereunder.

(d) **[Livestock purchase-money priority.]** Subject to subsection (e) and except as otherwise provided in subsection (g), a perfected purchase-money security interest in livestock that are farm products has priority over a conflicting security interest in the same livestock, and, except as otherwise provided in Section 9-327, a perfected security interest in their identifiable proceeds and identifiable products in their unmanufactured states also has priority, if:

(1) the purchase-money security interest is perfected when the debtor receives possession of the livestock;

(2) the purchase-money secured party sends an authenticated notification to the holder of the conflicting security interest;

(3) the holder of the conflicting security interest receives the notification within six months before the debtor receives possession of the livestock; and

(4) the notification states that the person sending the notification has or expects to acquire a purchase-money security interest in livestock of the debtor and describes the livestock.

(e) **[Holders of conflicting livestock security interests to be notified.]** Subsections (d)(2) through (4) apply only if the holder of the conflicting security interest had filed a financing statement covering the same types of livestock:

(1) if the purchase-money security interest is perfected by filing, before the date of the filing; or

(2) if the purchase-money security interest is temporarily perfected without filing or possession under Section 9-312(f), before the beginning of the 20-day period thereunder.

(f) [Software purchase-money priority.] Except as otherwise provided in subsection (g), a perfected purchase-money security interest in software has priority over a conflicting security interest in the same collateral, and, except as otherwise provided in Section 9-327, a perfected security interest in its identifiable proceeds also has priority, to the extent that the purchase-money security interest in the goods in which the software was acquired for use has priority in the goods and proceeds of the goods under this section.

(g) [Conflicting purchase-money security interests.] If more than one security interest qualifies for priority in the same collateral under subsection (a), (b), (d), or (f):

(1) a security interest securing an obligation incurred as all or part of the price of the collateral has priority over a security interest securing an obligation incurred for value given to enable the debtor to acquire rights in or the use of collateral; and

(2) in all other cases, Section 9-322(a) applies to the qualifying security interests.

§ 9–325. Priority of Security Interests in Transferred Collateral.

(a) [Subordination of security interest in transferred collateral.] Except as otherwise provided in subsection (b), a security interest created by a debtor is subordinate to a security interest in the same collateral created by another person if:

(1) the debtor acquired the collateral subject to the security interest created by the other person;

(2) the security interest created by the other person was perfected when the debtor acquired the collateral; and

(3) there is no period thereafter when the security interest is unperfected.

(b) [Limitation of subsection (a) subordination.] Subsection (a) subordinates a security interest only if the security interest:

(1) otherwise would have priority solely under Section 9-322(a) or 9-324; or

(2) arose solely under Section 2-711(3) or 2A-508(5).

§ 9–326. Priority of Security Interests Created by New Debtor.

(a) [Subordination of security interest created by new debtor.] Subject to subsection (b), a security interest created by a new debtor which is perfected by a filed financing statement that is effective solely under Section 9-508 in collateral in which a new debtor has or acquires rights is subordinate to a security interest in the same collateral which is perfected other than by a filed financing statement that is effective solely under Section 9-508.

(b) [Priority under other provisions; multiple original debtors.] The other provisions of this part determine the priority among conflicting security interests in the same collateral perfected by filed financing statements that are effective solely under Section 9-508. However, if the security agreements to which a new debtor became bound as debtor were not entered into by the same original debtor, the conflicting security interests rank according to priority in time of the new debtor's having become bound.

§ 9–327. Priority of Security Interests in Deposit Account.
The following rules govern priority among conflicting security interests in the same deposit account:

(1) A security interest held by a secured party having control of the deposit account under Section 9-104 has priority over a conflicting security interest held by a secured party that does not have control.

(2) Except as otherwise provided in paragraphs (3) and (4), security interests perfected by control under Section 9-314 rank according to priority in time of obtaining control.

(3) Except as otherwise provided in paragraph (4), a security interest held by the bank with which the deposit account is maintained has priority over a conflicting security interest held by another secured party.

(4) A security interest perfected by control under Section 9-104(a)(3) has priority over a security interest held by the bank with which the deposit account is maintained.

§ 9–328. Priority of Security Interests in Investment Property.
The following rules govern priority among conflicting security interests in the same investment property:

(1) A security interest held by a secured party having control of investment property under Section 9-106 has priority over a security interest held by a secured party that does not have control of the investment property.

(2) Except as otherwise provided in paragraphs (3) and (4), conflicting security interests held by secured parties each of which has control under Section 9-106 rank according to priority in time of:

(A) if the collateral is a security, obtaining control;

(B) if the collateral is a security entitlement carried in a securities account and:

   (i) if the secured party obtained control under Section 8-106(d)(1), the secured party's becoming the person for which the securities account is maintained;

   (ii) if the secured party obtained control under Section 8-106(d)(2), the securities intermediary's agreement to comply with the secured party's entitlement orders with respect to security entitlements carried or to be carried in the securities account; or

   (iii) if the secured party obtained control through another person under Section 8-106(d)(3), the time on which priority would be based under this paragraph if the other person were the secured party; or

(C) if the collateral is a commodity contract carried with a commodity intermediary, the satisfaction of the requirement for control specified in Section 9-106(b)(2) with respect to commodity contracts carried or to be carried with the commodity intermediary.

(3) A security interest held by a securities intermediary in a security entitlement or a securities account maintained with the securities intermediary has priority over a conflicting security interest held by another secured party.

(4) A security interest held by a commodity intermediary in a commodity contract or a commodity account maintained with the commodity intermediary has priority over a conflicting security interest held by another secured party.

(5) A security interest in a certificated security in registered form which is perfected by taking delivery under Section 9-313(a) and not by control under Section 9-314 has priority over a conflicting security interest perfected by a method other than control.

(6) Conflicting security interests created by a broker, securities intermediary, or commodity intermediary which are perfected without control under Section 9-106 rank equally.

(7) In all other cases, priority among conflicting security interests in investment property is governed by Sections 9-322 and 9-323.

§ 9–329. Priority of Security Interests in Letter-of-Credit Right. The following rules govern priority among conflicting security interests in the same letter-of-credit right:

(1) A security interest held by a secured party having control of the letter-of-credit right under Section 9-107 has priority to the extent of its control over a conflicting security interest held by a secured party that does not have control.

(2) Security interests perfected by control under Section 9-314 rank according to priority in time of obtaining control.

§ 9–330. Priority of Purchaser of Chattel Paper or Instrument.

(a) [Purchaser's priority: security interest claimed merely as proceeds.] A purchaser of chattel paper has priority over a security interest in the chattel paper which is claimed merely as proceeds of inventory subject to a security interest if:

(1) in good faith and in the ordinary course of the purchaser's business, the purchaser gives new value and takes possession of the chattel paper or obtains control of the chattel paper under Section 9-105; and

(2) the chattel paper does not indicate that it has been assigned to an identified assignee other than the purchaser.

(b) [Purchaser's priority: other security interests.] A purchaser of chattel paper has priority over a security interest in the chattel paper which is claimed other than merely as proceeds of inventory subject to a security interest if the purchaser gives new value and takes possession of the chattel paper or obtains control of the chattel paper under Section 9-105 in good faith, in the ordinary course of the purchaser's business, and without knowledge that the purchase violates the rights of the secured party.

(c) [Chattel paper purchaser's priority in proceeds.] Except as otherwise provided in Section 9-327, a purchaser having priority in chattel paper under subsection (a) or (b) also has priority in proceeds of the chattel paper to the extent that:

(1) Section 9-322 provides for priority in the proceeds; or

(2) the proceeds consist of the specific goods covered by the chattel paper or cash proceeds of the specific goods, even if the purchaser's security interest in the proceeds is unperfected.

(d) [Instrument purchaser's priority.] Except as otherwise provided in Section 9-331(a), a purchaser of an instrument has priority over a security interest in the instrument perfected by a method other than possession if the purchaser gives value and takes possession of the instrument in good faith and without knowledge that the purchase violates the rights of the secured party.

(e) **[Holder of purchase-money security interest gives new value.]** For purposes of subsections (a) and (b), the holder of a purchase-money security interest in inventory gives new value for chattel paper constituting proceeds of the inventory.

(f) **[Indication of assignment gives knowledge.]** For purposes of subsections (b) and (d), if chattel paper or an instrument indicates that it has been assigned to an identified secured party other than the purchaser, a purchaser of the chattel paper or instrument has knowledge that the purchase violates the rights of the secured party.

§ 9–331. Priority of Rights of Purchasers of Instruments, Documents, and Securities Under Other Articles; Priority of Interests in Financial Assets and Security Entitlements Under Article 8.

(a) **[Rights under Articles 3, 7, and 8 not limited.]** This article does not limit the rights of a holder in due course of a negotiable instrument, a holder to which a negotiable document of title has been duly negotiated, or a protected purchaser of a security. These holders or purchasers take priority over an earlier security interest, even if perfected, to the extent provided in Articles 3, 7, and 8.

(b) **[Protection under Article 8.]** This article does not limit the rights of or impose liability on a person to the extent that the person is protected against the assertion of a claim under Article 8.

(c) **[Filing not notice.]** Filing under this article does not constitute notice of a claim or defense to the holders, or purchasers, or persons described in subsections (a) and (b).

§ 9–332. Transfer of Money; Transfer of Funds from Deposit Account.

(a) **[Transferee of money.]** A transferee of money takes the money free of a security interest unless the transferee acts in collusion with the debtor in violating the rights of the secured party.

(b) **[Transferee of funds from deposit account.]** A transferee of funds from a deposit account takes the funds free of a security interest in the deposit account unless the transferee acts in collusion with the debtor in violating the rights of the secured party.

§ 9–333. Priority of Certain Liens Arising by Operation of Law.

(a) **["Possessory lien."]** In this section, "possessory lien" means an interest, other than a security interest or an agricultural lien:

(1) which secures payment or performance of an obligation for services or materials furnished with respect to goods by a person in the ordinary course of the person's business;

(2) which is created by statute or rule of law in favor of the person; and

(3) whose effectiveness depends on the person's possession of the goods.

(b) **[Priority of possessory lien.]** A possessory lien on goods has priority over a security interest in the goods unless the lien is created by a statute that expressly provides otherwise.

§ 9–334. Priority of Security Interests in Fixtures and Crops.

(a) **[Security interest in fixtures under this article.]** A security interest under this article may be created in goods that are fixtures or may continue in goods that become fixtures. A security interest does not exist under this article in ordinary building materials incorporated into an improvement on land.

(b) **[Security interest in fixtures under real-property law.]** This article does not prevent creation of an encumbrance upon fixtures under real property law.

(c) **[General rule: subordination of security interest in fixtures.]** In cases not governed by subsections (d) through (h), a security interest in fixtures is subordinate to a conflicting interest of an encumbrancer or owner of the related real property other than the debtor.

(d) **[Fixtures purchase-money priority.]** Except as otherwise provided in subsection (h), a perfected security interest in fixtures has priority over a conflicting interest of an encumbrancer or owner of the real property if the debtor has an interest of record in or is in possession of the real property and:

(1) the security interest is a purchase-money security interest;

(2) the interest of the encumbrancer or owner arises before the goods become fixtures; and

(3) the security interest is perfected by a fixture filing before the goods become fixtures or within 20 days thereafter.

(e) **[Priority of security interest in fixtures over interests in real property.]** A perfected security interest in fixtures has priority over a conflicting interest of an encumbrancer or owner of the real property if:

(1) the debtor has an interest of record in the real property or is in possession of the real property and the security interest:

    (A) is perfected by a fixture filing before the interest of the encumbrancer or owner is of record; and

    (B) has priority over any conflicting interest of a predecessor in title of the encumbrancer or owner;

(2) before the goods become fixtures, the security interest is perfected by any method permitted by this article and the fixtures are readily removable:

    (A) factory or office machines;

    (B) equipment that is not primarily used or leased for use in the operation of the real property; or

    (C) replacements of domestic appliances that are consumer goods;

(3) the conflicting interest is a lien on the real property obtained by legal or equitable proceedings after the security interest was perfected by any method permitted by this article; or

(4) the security interest is:

    (A) created in a manufactured home in a manufactured-home transaction; and

    (B) perfected pursuant to a statute described in Section 9-311(a)(2).

(f) [Priority based on consent, disclaimer, or right to remove.] A security interest in fixtures, whether or not perfected, has priority over a conflicting interest of an encumbrancer or owner of the real property if:

(1) the encumbrancer or owner has, in an authenticated record, consented to the security interest or disclaimed an interest in the goods as fixtures; or

(2) the debtor has a right to remove the goods as against the encumbrancer or owner.

(g) [Continuation of paragraph (f)(2) priority.] The priority of the security interest under paragraph (f)(2) continues for a reasonable time if the debtor's right to remove the goods as against the encumbrancer or owner terminates.

(h) [Priority of construction mortgage.] A mortgage is a construction mortgage to the extent that it secures an obligation incurred for the construction of an improvement on land, including the acquisition cost of the land, if a recorded record of the mortgage so indicates. Except as otherwise provided in subsections (e) and (f), a security interest in fixtures is subordinate to a construction mortgage if a record of the mortgage is recorded before the goods become fixtures and the goods become fixtures before the completion of the construction. A mortgage has this priority to the same extent as a construction mortgage to the extent that it is given to refinance a construction mortgage.

(i) [Priority of security interest in crops.] A perfected security interest in crops growing on real property has priority over a conflicting interest of an encumbrancer or owner of the real property if the debtor has an interest of record in or is in possession of the real property.

(j) [Subsection (i) prevails.] Subsection (i) prevails over any inconsistent provisions of the following statutes:

[List here any statutes containing provisions inconsistent with subsection (i).]

Legislative Note: States that amend statutes to remove provisions inconsistent with subsection (i) need not enact subsection (j).

§ 9–335. Accessions.

(a) [Creation of security interest in accession.] A security interest may be created in an accession and continues in collateral that becomes an accession.

(b) [Perfection of security interest.] If a security interest is perfected when the collateral becomes an accession, the security interest remains perfected in the collateral.

(c) [Priority of security interest.] Except as otherwise provided in subsection (d), the other provisions of this part determine the priority of a security interest in an accession.

(d) [Compliance with certificate-of-title statute.] A security interest in an accession is subordinate to a security interest in the whole which is perfected by compliance with the requirements of a certificate-of-title statute under Section 9-311(b).

(e) [Removal of accession after default.] After default, subject to Part 6, a secured party may remove an accession from other goods if the security interest in the accession has priority over the claims of every person having an interest in the whole.

(f) [Reimbursement following removal.] A secured party that removes an accession from other goods under subsection (e) shall promptly reimburse any holder of a security interest or other lien on, or owner of, the whole or of the other goods, other than the debtor, for the cost of repair of any physical injury to the whole or the other goods. The secured party need not reimburse the holder or owner for any diminution in value of the whole or the other goods caused by the absence of the accession removed or by any necessity for replacing it. A person entitled to reimbursement may refuse permission to remove until the secured party gives adequate assurance for the performance of the obligation to reimburse.

§ 9–336. Commingled Goods.

(a) **["Commingled goods."]** In this section, "commingled goods" means goods that are physically united with other goods in such a manner that their identity is lost in a product or mass.

(b) **[No security interest in commingled goods as such.]** A security interest does not exist in commingled goods as such. However, a security interest may attach to a product or mass that results when goods become commingled goods.

(c) **[Attachment of security interest to product or mass.]** If collateral becomes commingled goods, a security interest attaches to the product or mass.

(d) **[Perfection of security interest.]** If a security interest in collateral is perfected before the collateral becomes commingled goods, the security interest that attaches to the product or mass under subsection (c) is perfected.

(e) **[Priority of security interest.]** Except as otherwise provided in subsection (f), the other provisions of this part determine the priority of a security interest that attaches to the product or mass under subsection (c).

(f) **[Conflicting security interests in product or mass]** If more than one security interest attaches to the product or mass under subsection (c), the following rules determine priority:

    (1) A security interest that is perfected under subsection (d) has priority over a security interest that is unperfected at the time the collateral becomes commingled goods.

    (2) If more than one security interest is perfected under subsection (d), the security interests rank equally in proportion to the value of the collateral at the time it became commingled goods.

§ 9–337. Priority of Security Interests in Goods Covered by Certificate of Title.

If, while a security interest in goods is perfected by any method under the law of another jurisdiction, this State issues a certificate of title that does not show that the goods are subject to the security interest or contain a statement that they may be subject to security interests not shown on the certificate:

    (1) a buyer of the goods, other than a person in the business of selling goods of that kind, takes free of the security interest if the buyer gives value and receives delivery of the goods after issuance of the certificate and without knowledge of the security interest; and

    (2) the security interest is subordinate to a conflicting security interest in the goods that attaches, and is perfected under Section 9-311(b), after issuance of the certificate and without the conflicting secured party's knowledge of the security interest.

§ 9–338. Priority of Security Interest or Agricultural Lien Perfected by Filed Financing Statement Providing Certain Incorrect Information.

If a security interest or agricultural lien is perfected by a filed financing statement providing information described in Section 9-516(b)(5) which is incorrect at the time the financing statement is filed:

    (1) the security interest or agricultural lien is subordinate to a conflicting perfected security interest in the collateral to the extent that the holder of the conflicting security interest gives value in reasonable reliance upon the incorrect information; and

    (2) a purchaser, other than a secured party, of the collateral takes free of the security interest or agricultural lien to the extent that, in reasonable reliance upon the incorrect information, the purchaser gives value and, in the case of chattel paper, documents, goods, instruments, or a security certificate, receives delivery of the collateral.

§ 9–339. Priority Subject to Subordination.

This article does not preclude subordination by agreement by a person entitled to priority.

[SUBPART 4. RIGHTS OF BANK]

§ 9–340. Effectiveness of Right of Recoupment or Set-Off Against Deposit Account.

(a) **[Exercise of recoupment or set-off.]** Except as otherwise provided in subsection (c), a bank with which a deposit account is maintained may exercise any right of recoupment or set-off against a secured party that holds a security interest in the deposit account.

(b) **[Recoupment or set-off not affected by security interest.]** Except as otherwise provided in subsection (c), the application of this article to a security interest in a deposit account does not affect a right of recoupment or set-off of the secured party as to a deposit account maintained with the secured party.

(c) **[When set-off ineffective.]** The exercise by a bank of a set-off against a deposit account is ineffective against a secured party that holds a security interest in the deposit account which is perfected by control under Section 9-104(a)(3), if the set-off is based on a claim against the debtor.

§ 9–341. Bank's Rights and Duties with Respect to Deposit Account.

Except as otherwise provided in Section 9-340(c), and unless the bank otherwise agrees in an authenticated record, a bank's rights and duties with respect to a deposit account maintained with the bank are not terminated, suspended, or modified by:

(1) the creation, attachment, or perfection of a security interest in the deposit account;

(2) the bank's knowledge of the security interest; or

(3) the bank's receipt of instructions from the secured party.

§ 9–342. Bank's Right to Refuse to Enter into or Disclose Existence of Control Agreement.

This article does not require a bank to enter into an agreement of the kind described in Section 9-104(a)(2), even if its customer so requests or directs. A bank that has entered into such an agreement is not required to confirm the existence of the agreement to another person unless requested to do so by its customer.

Part 4: Rights of Third Parties

§ 9–401. Alienability of Debtor's Rights.

(a) **[Other law governs alienability; exceptions.]** Except as otherwise provided in subsection (b) and Sections 9-406, 9-407, 9-408, and 9-409, whether a debtor's rights in collateral may be voluntarily or involuntarily transferred is governed by law other than this article.

(b) **[Agreement does not prevent transfer.]** An agreement between the debtor and secured party which prohibits a transfer of the debtor's rights in collateral or makes the transfer a default does not prevent the transfer from taking effect.

§ 9–402. Secured Party Not Obligated on Contract of Debtor or in Tort.

The existence of a security interest, agricultural lien, or authority given to a debtor to dispose of or use collateral, without more, does not subject a secured party to liability in contract or tort for the debtor's acts or omissions.

§ 9–403. Agreement Not to Assert Defenses Against Assignee.

(a) **["Value."]** In this section, "value" has the meaning provided in Section 3-303(a).

(b) **[Agreement not to assert claim or defense.]** Except as otherwise provided in this section, an agreement between an account debtor and an assignor not to assert against an assignee any claim or defense that the account debtor may have against the assignor is enforceable by an assignee that takes an assignment:

(1) for value;

(2) in good faith;

(3) without notice of a claim of a property or possessory right to the property assigned; and

(4) without notice of a defense or claim in recoupment of the type that may be asserted against a person entitled to enforce a negotiable instrument under Section 3-305(a).

(c) **[When subsection (b) not applicable.]** Subsection (b) does not apply to defenses of a type that may be asserted against a holder in due course of a negotiable instrument under Section 3-305(b).

(d) **[Omission of required statement in consumer transaction.]** In a consumer transaction, if a record evidences the account debtor's obligation, law other than this article requires that the record include a statement to the effect that the rights of an assignee are subject to claims or defenses that the account debtor could assert against the original obligee, and the record does not include such a statement:

(1) the record has the same effect as if the record included such a statement; and

(2) the account debtor may assert against an assignee those claims and defenses that would have been available if the record included such a statement.

(e) **[Rule for individual under other law.]** This section is subject to law other than this article which establishes a different rule for an account debtor who is an individual and who incurred the obligation primarily for personal, family, or household purposes.

(f) **[Other law not displaced.]** Except as otherwise provided in subsection (d), this section does not displace law other than this article which gives effect to an agreement by an account debtor not to assert a claim or defense against an assignee.

§ 9–404. Rights Acquired by Assignee; Claims and Defenses Against Assignee.

(a) **[Assignee's rights subject to terms, claims, and defenses; exceptions.]** Unless an account debtor has made an enforceable agreement not to assert defenses or claims, and subject to subsections (b) through (e), the rights of an assignee are subject to:

(1) all terms of the agreement between the account debtor and assignor and any defense or claim in recoupment arising from the transaction that gave rise to the contract; and

(2) any other defense or claim of the account debtor against the assignor which accrues before the account debtor receives a notification of the assignment authenticated by the assignor or the assignee.

(b) **[Account debtor's claim reduces amount owed to assignee.]** Subject to subsection (c) and except as otherwise provided in subsection (d), the claim of an account debtor against an assignor may be asserted against an assignee under subsection (a) only to reduce the amount the account debtor owes.

(c) **[Rule for individual under other law.]** This section is subject to law other than this article which establishes a different rule for an account debtor who is an individual and who incurred the obligation primarily for personal, family, or household purposes.

(d) **[Omission of required statement in consumer transaction.]** In a consumer transaction, if a record evidences the account debtor's obligation, law other than this article requires that the record include a statement to the effect that the account debtor's recovery against an assignee with respect to claims and defenses against the assignor may not exceed amounts paid by the account debtor under the record, and the record does not include such a statement, the extent to which a claim of an account debtor against the assignor may be asserted against an assignee is determined as if the record included such a statement.

(e) **[Inapplicability to health-care-insurance receivable.]** This section does not apply to an assignment of a health-care-insurance receivable.

§ 9–405. Modification of Assigned Contract.

(a) **[Effect of modification on assignee.]** A modification of or substitution for an assigned contract is effective against an assignee if made in good faith. The assignee acquires corresponding rights under the modified or substituted contract. The assignment may provide that the modification or substitution is a breach of contract by the assignor. This subsection is subject to subsections (b) through (d).

(b) **[Applicability of subsection (a).]** Subsection (a) applies to the extent that:

(1) the right to payment or a part thereof under an assigned contract has not been fully earned by performance; or

(2) the right to payment or a part thereof has been fully earned by performance and the account debtor has not received notification of the assignment under Section 9-406(a).

(c) **[Rule for individual under other law.]** This section is subject to law other than this article which establishes a different rule for an account debtor who is an individual and who incurred the obligation primarily for personal, family, or household purposes.

(d) **[Inapplicability to health-care-insurance receivable.]** This section does not apply to an assignment of a health-care-insurance receivable.

§ 9–406. Discharge of Account Debtor; Notification of Assignment; Identification and Proof of Assignment; Restrictions on Assignment of Accounts, Chattel Paper, Payment Intangibles, and Promissory Notes Ineffective.

(a) **[Discharge of account debtor; effect of notification.]** Subject to subsections (b) through (i), an account debtor on an account, chattel paper, or a payment intangible may discharge its obligation by paying the assignor until, but not after, the account debtor receives a notification, authenticated by the assignor or the assignee, that the amount due or to become due has been assigned and that payment is to be made to the assignee. After receipt of the notification, the account debtor may discharge its obligation by paying the assignee and may not discharge the obligation by paying the assignor.

(b) **[When notification ineffective.]** Subject to subsection (h), notification is ineffective under subsection (a):

(1) if it does not reasonably identify the rights assigned;

(2) to the extent that an agreement between an account debtor and a seller of a payment intangible limits the account debtor's duty to pay a person other than the seller and the limitation is effective under law other than this article; or

(3) at the option of an account debtor, if the notification notifies the account debtor to make less than the full amount of any installment or other periodic payment to the assignee, even if:

(A) only a portion of the account, chattel paper, or payment intangible has been assigned to that assignee;

(B) a portion has been assigned to another assignee; or

(C) the account debtor knows that the assignment to that assignee is limited.

(c) [Proof of assignment.] Subject to subsection (h), if requested by the account debtor, an assignee shall seasonably furnish reasonable proof that the assignment has been made. Unless the assignee complies, the account debtor may discharge its obligation by paying the assignor, even if the account debtor has received a notification under subsection (a).

(d) [Term restricting assignment generally ineffective.] Except as otherwise provided in subsection (e) and Sections 2A-303 and 9-407, and subject to subsection (h), a term in an agreement between an account debtor and an assignor or in a promissory note is ineffective to the extent that it:

(1) prohibits, restricts, or requires the consent of the account debtor or person obligated on the promissory note to the assignment or transfer of, or the creation, attachment, perfection, or enforcement of a security interest in, the account, chattel paper, payment intangible, or promissory note; or

(2) provides that the assignment or transfer or the creation, attachment, perfection, or enforcement of the security interest may give rise to a default, breach, right of recoupment, claim, defense, termination, right of termination, or remedy under the account, chattel paper, payment intangible, or promissory note.

(e) [Inapplicability of subsection (d) to certain sales.] Subsection (d) does not apply to the sale of a payment intangible or promissory note.

(f) [Legal restrictions on assignment generally ineffective.] Except as otherwise provided in Sections 2A-303 and 9-407 and subject to subsections (h) and (i), a rule of law, statute, or regulation that prohibits, restricts, or requires the consent of a government, governmental body or official, or account debtor to the assignment or transfer of, or creation of a security interest in, an account or chattel paper is ineffective to the extent that the rule of law, statute, or regulation:

(1) prohibits, restricts, or requires the consent of the government, governmental body or official, or account debtor to the assignment or transfer of, or the creation, attachment, perfection, or enforcement of a security interest in the account or chattel paper; or

(2) provides that the assignment or transfer or the creation, attachment, perfection, or enforcement of the security interest may give rise to a default, breach, right of recoupment, claim, defense, termination, right of termination, or remedy under the account or chattel paper.

(g) [Subsection (b)(3) not waivable.] Subject to subsection (h), an account debtor may not waive or vary its option under subsection (b)(3).

(h) [Rule for individual under other law.] This section is subject to law other than this article which establishes a different rule for an account debtor who is an individual and who incurred the obligation primarily for personal, family, or household purposes.

(i) [Inapplicability to health-care-insurance receivable.] This section does not apply to an assignment of a health-care-insurance receivable.

(j) [Section prevails over specified inconsistent law.] This section prevails over any inconsistent provisions of the following statutes, rules, and regulations:[List here any statutes, rules, and regulations containing provisions inconsistent with this section.]

Legislative Note: States that amend statutes, rules, and regulations to remove provisions inconsistent with this section need not enact subsection (j).

§ 9–407. Restrictions on Creation or Enforcement of Security Interest in Leasehold Interest or in Lessor's Residual Interest.

(a) [Term restricting assignment generally ineffective.] Except as otherwise provided in subsection (b), a term in a lease agreement is ineffective to the extent that it:

(1) prohibits, restricts, or requires the consent of a party to the lease to the assignment or transfer of, or the creation, attachment, perfection, or enforcement of a security interest in, an interest of a party under the lease contract or in the lessor's residual interest in the goods; or

(2) provides that the assignment or transfer or the creation, attachment, perfection, or enforcement of the security interest may give rise to a default, breach, right of recoupment, claim, defense, termination, right of termination, or remedy under the lease.

(b) [Effectiveness of certain terms.] Except as otherwise provided in Section 2A-303(7), a term described in subsection (a)(2) is effective to the extent that there is:

(1) a transfer by the lessee of the lessee's right of possession or use of the goods in violation of the term; or

(2) a delegation of a material performance of either party to the lease contract in violation of the term.

(c) **[Security interest not material impairment.]** The creation, attachment, perfection, or enforcement of a security interest in the lessor's interest under the lease contract or the lessor's residual interest in the goods is not a transfer that materially impairs the lessee's prospect of obtaining return performance or materially changes the duty of or materially increases the burden or risk imposed on the lessee within the purview of Section 2A-303(4) unless, and then only to the extent that, enforcement actually results in a delegation of material performance of the lessor.

§ 9–408. Restrictions on Assignment of Promissory Notes, Health-Care-Insurance Receivables, and Certain General Intangibles Ineffective.

(a) **[Term restricting assignment generally ineffective.]** Except as otherwise provided in subsection (b), a term in a promissory note or in an agreement between an account debtor and a debtor which relates to a health-care-insurance receivable or a general intangible, including a contract, permit, license, or franchise, and which term prohibits, restricts, or requires the consent of the person obligated on the promissory note or the account debtor to, the assignment or transfer of, or creation, attachment, or perfection of a security interest in, the promissory note, health-care-insurance receivable, or general intangible, is ineffective to the extent that the term:

(1) would impair the creation, attachment, or perfection of a security interest; or

(2) provides that the assignment or transfer or the creation, attachment, or perfection of the security interest may give rise to a default, breach, right of recoupment, claim, defense, termination, right of termination, or remedy under the promissory note, health-care-insurance receivable, or general intangible.

(b) **[Applicability of subsection (a) to sales of certain rights to payment.]** Subsection (a) applies to a security interest in a payment intangible or promissory note only if the security interest arises out of a sale of the payment intangible or promissory note.

(c) **[Legal restrictions on assignment generally ineffective.]** A rule of law, statute, or regulation that pro-hibits, restricts, or requires the consent of a government, governmental body or official, person obligated on a promissory note, or account debtor to the assignment or transfer of, or creation of a security interest in, a promissory note, health-care-insurance receivable, or general intangible, including a contract, permit, license, or franchise between an account debtor and a debtor, is ineffective to the extent that the rule of law, statute, or regulation:

(1) would impair the creation, attachment, or perfection of a security interest; or

(2) provides that the assignment or transfer or the creation, attachment, or perfection of the security interest may give rise to a default, breach, right of recoupment, claim, defense, termination, right of termination, or remedy under the promissory note, health-care-insurance receivable, or general intangible.

(d) **[Limitation on ineffectiveness under subsections (a) and (c).]** To the extent that a term in a promissory note or in an agreement between an account debtor and a debtor which relates to a health-care-insurance receivable or general intangible or a rule of law, statute, or regulation described in subsection (c) would be effective under law other than this article but is ineffective under subsection (a) or (c), the creation, attachment, or perfection of a security interest in the promissory note, health-care-insurance receivable, or general intangible:

(1) is not enforceable against the person obligated on the promissory note or the account debtor;

(2) does not impose a duty or obligation on the person obligated on the promissory note or the account debtor;

(3) does not require the person obligated on the promissory note or the account debtor to recognize the security interest, pay or render performance to the secured party, or accept payment or performance from the secured party;

(4) does not entitle the secured party to use or assign the debtor's rights under the promissory note, health-care-insurance receivable, or general intangible, including any related information or materials furnished to the debtor in the transaction giving rise to the promissory note, health-care-insurance receivable, or general intangible;

(5) does not entitle the secured party to use, assign, possess, or have access to any trade secrets or confidential information of the person obligated

on the promissory note or the account debtor; and

(6) does not entitle the secured party to enforce the security interest in the promissory note, health-care-insurance receivable, or general intangible.

(e) **[Section prevails over specified inconsistent law.]** This section prevails over any inconsistent provisions of the following statutes, rules, and regulations:

[List here any statutes, rules, and regulations containing provisions inconsistent with this section.]

Legislative Note: States that amend statutes, rules, and regulations to remove provisions inconsistent with this section need not enact subsection (e).

§ 9–409. Restrictions on Assignment of Letter-of-Credit Rights Ineffective.

(a) **[Term or law restricting assignment generally ineffective.]** A term in a letter of credit or a rule of law, statute, regulation, custom, or practice applicable to the letter of credit which prohibits, restricts, or requires the consent of an applicant, issuer, or nominated person to a beneficiary's assignment of or creation of a security interest in a letter-of-credit right is ineffective to the extent that the term or rule of law, statute, regulation, custom, or practice:

(1) would impair the creation, attachment, or perfection of a security interest in the letter-of-credit right; or

(2) provides that the assignment or the creation, attachment, or perfection of the security interest may give rise to a default, breach, right of recoupment, claim, defense, termination, right of termination, or remedy under the letter-of-credit right.

(b) **[Limitation on ineffectiveness under subsection (a).]** To the extent that a term in a letter of credit is ineffective under subsection (a) but would be effective under law other than this article or a custom or practice applicable to the letter of credit, to the transfer of a right to draw or otherwise demand performance under the letter of credit, or to the assignment of a right to proceeds of the letter of credit, the creation, attachment, or perfection of a security interest in the letter-of-credit right:

(1) is not enforceable against the applicant, issuer, nominated person, or transferee beneficiary;

(2) imposes no duties or obligations on the applicant, issuer, nominated person, or transferee beneficiary; and

(3) does not require the applicant, issuer, nominated person, or transferee beneficiary to recognize the security interest, pay or render performance to the secured party, or accept payment or other performance from the secured party.

Part 5: Filing

[SUBPART 1. FILING OFFICE; CONTENTS AND EFFECTIVENESS OF FINANCING STATEMENT]

§ 9–501. Filing Office.

(a) **[Filing offices.]** Except as otherwise provided in subsection (b), if the local law of this State governs perfection of a security interest or agricultural lien, the office in which to file a financing statement to perfect the security interest or agricultural lien is:

(1) the office designated for the filing or recording of a record of a mortgage on the related real property, if:

(A) the collateral is as-extracted collateral or timber to be cut; or

(B) the financing statement is filed as a fixture filing and the collateral is goods that are or are to become fixtures; or

(2) the office of [ ] [or any office duly authorized by [ ]], in all other cases, including a case in which the collateral is goods that are or are to become fixtures and the financing statement is not filed as a fixture filing.

(b) **[Filing office for transmitting utilities.]** The office in which to file a financing statement to perfect a security interest in collateral, including fixtures, of a transmitting utility is the office of [ ]. The financing statement also constitutes a fixture filing as to the collateral indicated in the financing statement which is or is to become fixtures.

Legislative Note: The State should designate the filing office where the brackets appear. The filing office may be that of a governmental official (e.g., the Secretary of State) or a private party that maintains the State's filing system.

§ 9–502. Contents of Financing Statement; Record of Mortgage as Financing Statement; Time of Filing Financing Statement.

(a) **[Sufficiency of financing statement.]** Subject to subsection (b), a financing statement is sufficient only if it:

(1) provides the name of the debtor;

(2) provides the name of the secured party or a representative of the secured party; and

(3) indicates the collateral covered by the financing statement.

(b) **[Real-property-related financing statements.]** Except as otherwise provided in Section 9-501(b), to be sufficient, a financing statement that covers as-extracted collateral or timber to be cut, or which is filed as a fixture filing and covers goods that are or are to become fixtures, must satisfy subsection (a) and also:

(1) indicate that it covers this type of collateral;

(2) indicate that it is to be filed [for record] in the real property records;

(3) provide a description of the real property to which the collateral is related [sufficient to give constructive notice of a mortgage under the law of this State if the description were contained in a record of the mortgage of the real property]; and

(4) if the debtor does not have an interest of record in the real property, provide the name of a record owner.

(c) **[Record of mortgage as financing statement.]** A record of a mortgage is effective, from the date of recording, as a financing statement filed as a fixture filing or as a financing statement covering as-extracted collateral or timber to be cut only if:

(1) the record indicates the goods or accounts that it covers;

(2) the goods are or are to become fixtures related to the real property described in the record or the collateral is related to the real property described in the record and is as-extracted collateral or timber to be cut;

(3) the record satisfies the requirements for a financing statement in this section other than an indication that it is to be filed in the real property records; and

(4) the record is [duly] recorded.

(d) **[Filing before security agreement or attachment.]** A financing statement may be filed before a security agreement is made or a security interest otherwise attaches.

Legislative Note: Language in brackets is optional. Where the State has any special recording system for real property other than the usual grantor-grantee index (as, for instance, a tract system or a title registration or Torrens system) local adaptations of subsection (b) and Sec-

tion 9-519(d) and (e) may be necessary. See, e.g., Mass. Gen. Laws Chapter 106, Section 9-410.

§ 9–503. Name of Debtor and Secured Party.

(a) **[Sufficiency of debtor's name.]** A financing statement sufficiently provides the name of the debtor:

(1) if the debtor is a registered organization, only if the financing statement provides the name of the debtor indicated on the public record of the debtor's jurisdiction of organization which shows the debtor to have been organized;

(2) if the debtor is a decedent's estate, only if the financing statement provides the name of the decedent and indicates that the debtor is an estate;

(3) if the debtor is a trust or a trustee acting with respect to property held in trust, only if the financing statement:

(A) provides the name specified for the trust in its organic documents or, if no name is specified, provides the name of the settlor and additional information sufficient to distinguish the debtor from other trusts having one or more of the same settlors; and

(B) indicates, in the debtor's name or otherwise, that the debtor is a trust or is a trustee acting with respect to property held in trust; and

(4) in other cases:

(A) if the debtor has a name, only if it provides the individual or organizational name of the debtor; and

(B) if the debtor does not have a name, only if it provides the names of the partners, members, associates, or other persons comprising the debtor.

(b) **[Additional debtor-related information.]** A financing statement that provides the name of the debtor in accordance with subsection (a) is not rendered ineffective by the absence of:

(1) a trade name or other name of the debtor; or

(2) unless required under subsection (a)(4)(B), names of partners, members, associates, or other persons comprising the debtor.

(c) **[Debtor's trade name insufficient.]** A financing statement that provides only the debtor's trade name does not sufficiently provide the name of the debtor.

(d) **[Representative capacity.]** Failure to indicate the representative capacity of a secured party or representative of a secured party does not affect the sufficiency of a financing statement.

(e) [Multiple debtors and secured parties.] A financing statement may provide the name of more than one debtor and the name of more than one secured party.

§ 9–504. Indication of Collateral. A financing statement sufficiently indicates the collateral that it covers if the financing statement provides:

(1) a description of the collateral pursuant to Section 9-108; or

(2) an indication that the financing statement covers all assets or all personal property.

§ 9–505. Filing and Compliance with Other Statutes and Treaties for Consignments, Leases, Other Bailments, and Other Transactions.

(a) [Use of terms other than "debtor" and "secured party."] A consignor, lessor, or other bailor of goods, a licensor, or a buyer of a payment intangible or promissory note may file a financing statement, or may comply with a statute or treaty described in Section 9-311(a), using the terms "consignor", "consignee", "lessor", "lessee", "bailor", "bailee", "licensor", "licensee", "owner", "registered owner", "buyer", "seller", or words of similar import, instead of the terms "secured party" and "debtor".

(b) [Effect of financing statement under subsection (a).] This part applies to the filing of a financing statement under subsection (a) and, as appropriate, to compliance that is equivalent to filing a financing statement under Section 9-311(b), but the filing or compliance is not of itself a factor in determining whether the collateral secures an obligation. If it is determined for another reason that the collateral secures an obligation, a security interest held by the consignor, lessor, bailor, licensor, owner, or buyer which attaches to the collateral is perfected by the filing or compliance.

§ 9–506. Effect of Errors or Omissions.

(a) [Minor errors and omissions.] A financing statement substantially satisfying the requirements of this part is effective, even if it has minor errors or omissions, unless the errors or omissions make the financing statement seriously misleading.

(b) [Financing statement seriously misleading.] Except as otherwise provided in subsection (c), a financing statement that fails sufficiently to provide the name of the debtor in accordance with Section 9-503(a) is seriously misleading.

(c) [Financing statement not seriously misleading.] If a search of the records of the filing office under the debtor's correct name, using the filing office's standard search logic, if any, would disclose a financing statement that fails sufficiently to provide the name of the debtor in accordance with Section 9-503(a), the name provided does not make the financing statement seriously misleading.

(d) ["Debtor's correct name."] For purposes of Section 9-508(b), the "debtor's correct name" in subsection (c) means the correct name of the new debtor.

§ 9–507. Effect of Certain Events on Effectiveness of Financing Statement.

(a) [Disposition.] A filed financing statement remains effective with respect to collateral that is sold, exchanged, leased, licensed, or otherwise disposed of and in which a security interest or agricultural lien continues, even if the secured party knows of or consents to the disposition.

(b) [Information becoming seriously misleading.] Except as otherwise provided in subsection (c) and Section 9-508, a financing statement is not rendered ineffective if, after the financing statement is filed, the information provided in the financing statement becomes seriously misleading under Section 9-506.

(c) [Change in debtor's name.] If a debtor so changes its name that a filed financing statement becomes seriously misleading under Section 9-506:

(1) the financing statement is effective to perfect a security interest in collateral acquired by the debtor before, or within four months after, the change; and

(2) the financing statement is not effective to perfect a security interest in collateral acquired by the debtor more than four months after the change, unless an amendment to the financing statement which renders the financing statement not seriously misleading is filed within four months after the change.

§ 9–508. Effectiveness of Financing Statement If New Debtor Becomes Bound by Security Agreement.

(a) [Financing statement naming original debtor.] Except as otherwise provided in this section, a filed financing statement naming an original debtor is effective to perfect a security interest in collateral in which a new debtor has or acquires rights to the extent that the financing statement would have been effective had the original debtor acquired rights in the collateral.

(b) [Financing statement becoming seriously misleading.] If the difference between the name of the original debtor and that of the new debtor causes a filed financing statement that is effective under subsection (a) to be seriously misleading under Section 9-506:

(1) the financing statement is effective to perfect a security interest in collateral acquired by the new debtor before, and within four months after, the new debtor becomes bound under Section 9-203(d); and

(2) the financing statement is not effective to perfect a security interest in collateral acquired by the new debtor more than four months after the new debtor becomes bound under Section 9-203(d) unless an initial financing statement providing the name of the new debtor is filed before the expiration of that time.

(c) **[When section not applicable.]** This section does not apply to collateral as to which a filed financing statement remains effective against the new debtor under Section 9-507(a).

§ 9–509. Persons Entitled to File a Record.

(a) **[Person entitled to file record.]** A person may file an initial financing statement, amendment that adds collateral covered by a financing statement, or amendment that adds a debtor to a financing statement only if:

(1) the debtor authorizes the filing in an authenticated record or pursuant to subsection (b) or (c); or

(2) the person holds an agricultural lien that has become effective at the time of filing and the financing statement covers only collateral in which the person holds an agricultural lien.

(b) **[Security agreement as authorization.]** By authenticating or becoming bound as debtor by a security agreement, a debtor or new debtor authorizes the filing of an initial financing statement, and an amendment, covering:

(1) the collateral described in the security agreement; and

(2) property that becomes collateral under Section 9-315(a)(2), whether or not the security agreement expressly covers proceeds.

(c) **[Acquisition of collateral as authorization.]** By acquiring collateral in which a security interest or agricultural lien continues under Section 9-315(a)(1), a debtor authorizes the filing of an initial financing statement, and an amendment, covering the collateral and property that becomes collateral under Section 9-315(a)(2).

(d) **[Person entitled to file certain amendments.]** A person may file an amendment other than an amendment that adds collateral covered by a financing statement or an amendment that adds a debtor to a financing statement only if:

(1) the secured party of record authorizes the filing; or

(2) the amendment is a termination statement for a financing statement as to which the secured party of record has failed to file or send a termination statement as required by

Section 9-513(a) or (c), the debtor authorizes the filing, and the termination statement indicates that the debtor authorized it to be filed.

(e) **[Multiple secured parties of record.]** If there is more than one secured party of record for a financing statement, each secured party of record may authorize the filing of an amendment under subsection (d).

§ 9–510. Effectiveness of Filed Record.

(a) **[Filed record effective if authorized.]** A filed record is effective only to the extent that it was filed by a person that may file it under Section 9-509.

(b) **[Authorization by one secured party of record.]** A record authorized by one secured party of record does not affect the financing statement with respect to another secured party of record.

(c) **[Continuation statement not timely filed.]** A continuation statement that is not filed within the six-month period prescribed by Section 9-515(d) is ineffective.

§ 9–511. Secured Party of Record.

(a) **[Secured party of record.]** A secured party of record with respect to a financing statement is a person whose name is provided as the name of the secured party or a representative of the secured party in an initial financing statement that has been filed. If an initial financing statement is filed under Section 9-514(a), the assignee named in the initial financing statement is the secured party of record with respect to the financing statement.

(b) **[Amendment naming secured party of record.]** If an amendment of a financing statement which provides the name of a person as a secured party or a representative of a secured party is filed, the person named in the amendment is a secured party of record. If an amendment is filed under Section 9-514(b), the assignee named in the amendment is a secured party of record.

(c) **[Amendment deleting secured party of record.]** A person remains a secured party of record until the filing of an amendment of the financing statement which deletes the person.

§ 9–512. Amendment of Financing Statement.

[Alternative A]

(a) **[Amendment of information in financing statement.]** Subject to Section 9-509, a person may add or delete collateral covered by, continue or terminate the effectiveness of, or, subject to subsection (e), otherwise amend the information provided in, a financing statement by filing an amendment that:

(1) identifies, by its file number, the initial financing statement to which the amendment relates; and

(2) if the amendment relates to an initial financing statement filed [or recorded] in a filing office described in Section 9-501(a)(1), provides the information specified in Section 9-502(b).

[Alternative B]

(a) **[Amendment of information in financing statement.]** Subject to Section 9-509, a person may add or delete collateral covered by, continue or terminate the effectiveness of, or, subject to subsection (e), otherwise amend the information provided in, a financing statement by filing an amendment that:

(1) identifies, by its file number, the initial financing statement to which the amendment relates; and

(2) if the amendment relates to an initial financing statement filed [or recorded] in a filing office described in Section 9-501(a)(1), provides the date [and time] that the initial financing statement was filed [or recorded] and the information specified in Section 9-502(b).

[End of Alternatives]

(b) **[Period of effectiveness not affected.]** Except as otherwise provided in Section 9-515, the filing of an amendment does not extend the period of effectiveness of the financing statement.

(c) **[Effectiveness of amendment adding collateral.]** A financing statement that is amended by an amendment that adds collateral is effective as to the added collateral only from the date of the filing of the amendment.

(d) **[Effectiveness of amendment adding debtor.]** A financing statement that is amended by an amendment

that adds a debtor is effective as to the added debtor only from the date of the filing of the amendment.

(e) **[Certain amendments ineffective.]** An amendment is ineffective to the extent it:

(1) purports to delete all debtors and fails to provide the name of a debtor to be covered by the financing statement; or

(2) purports to delete all secured parties of record and fails to provide the name of a new secured party of record.

Legislative Note: *States whose real-estate filing offices require additional information in amendments and cannot search their records by both the name of the debtor and the file number should enact Alternative B to Sections 9-512(a), 9-518(b), 9-519(f)   and 9-522(a).*

§ 9–513. Termination Statement.

(a) **[Consumer goods.]** A secured party shall cause the secured party of record for a financing statement to file a termination statement for the financing statement if the financing statement covers consumer goods and:

(1) there is no obligation secured by the collateral covered by the financing statement and no commitment to make an advance, incur an obligation, or otherwise give value; or

(2) the debtor did not authorize the filing of the initial financing statement.

(b) **[Time for compliance with subsection (a).]** To comply with subsection (a), a secured party shall cause the secured party of record to file the termination statement:

(1) within one month after there is no obligation secured by the collateral covered by the financing statement and no commitment to make an advance, incur an obligation, or otherwise give value; or

(2) if earlier, within 20 days after the secured party receives an authenticated demand from a debtor.

(c) **[Other collateral.]** In cases not governed by subsection (a), within 20 days after a secured party receives an authenticated demand from a debtor, the secured party shall cause the secured party of record for a financing statement to send to the debtor a termination statement for the financing statement or file the termination statement in the filing office if:

(1) except in the case of a financing statement covering accounts or chattel paper that has been sold or goods that are the subject of a consignment, there is no obligation secured by the collateral covered by the financing statement and no commitment to make an advance, incur an obligation, or otherwise give value;

(2) the financing statement covers accounts or chattel paper that has been sold but as to which the account debtor or other person obligated has discharged its obligation;

(3) the financing statement covers goods that were the subject of a consignment to the debtor but are not in the debtor's possession; or

(4) the debtor did not authorize the filing of the initial financing statement.

(d) **[Effect of filing termination statement.]** Except as otherwise provided in Section 9-510, upon the filing of a termination statement with the filing office, the financing statement to which the termination statement relates ceases to be effective. Except as otherwise provided in Section 9-510, for purposes of Sections 9-519(g), 9-522(a), and 9-523(c), the filing with the filing office of a termination statement relating to a financing statement that indicates that the debtor is a transmitting utility also causes the effectiveness of the financing statement to lapse.

§ 9–514. Assignment of Powers of Secured Party of Record.

(a) **[Assignment reflected on initial financing statement.]** Except as otherwise provided in subsection (c), an initial financing statement may reflect an assignment of all of the secured party's power to authorize an amendment to the financing statement by providing the name and mailing address of the assignee as the name and address of the secured party.

(b) **[Assignment of filed financing statement.]** Except as otherwise provided in subsection (c), a secured party of record may assign of record all or part of its power to authorize an amendment to a financing statement by filing in the filing office an amendment of the financing statement which:

(1) identifies, by its file number, the initial financing statement to which it relates;

(2) provides the name of the assignor; and

(3) provides the name and mailing address of the assignee.

(c) **[Assignment of record of mortgage.]** An assignment of record of a security interest in a fixture covered by a record of a mortgage which is effective as a financing statement filed as a fixture filing under Section 9-502(c) may be made only by an assignment of record of the mortgage in the manner provided by law of this State other than [the Uniform Commercial Code].

§ 9–515. Duration and Effectiveness of Financing Statement; Effect of Lapsed Financing Statement.

(a) **[Five-year effectiveness.]** Except as otherwise provided in subsections (b), (e), (f), and (g), a filed financing statement is effective for a period of five years after the date of filing.

(b) **[Public-finance or manufactured-home transaction.]** Except as otherwise provided in subsections (e), (f), and (g), an initial financing statement filed in connection with a public-finance transaction or manufactured-home transaction is effective for a period of 30 years after the date of filing if it indicates that it is filed in connection with a public-finance transaction or manufactured-home transaction.

(c) **[Lapse and continuation of financing statement.]** The effectiveness of a filed financing statement lapses on the expiration of the period of its effectiveness unless before the lapse a continuation statement is filed pursuant to subsection (d). Upon lapse, a financing statement ceases to be effective and any security interest or agricultural lien that was perfected by the financing statement becomes unperfected, unless the security interest is perfected otherwise. If the security interest or agricultural lien becomes unperfected upon lapse, it is deemed never to have been perfected as against a purchaser of the collateral for value.

(d) **[When continuation statement may be filed.]** A continuation statement may be filed only within six months before the expiration of the five-year period specified in subsection (a) or the 30-year period specified in subsection (b), whichever is applicable.

(e) **[Effect of filing continuation statement.]** Except as otherwise provided in Section 9-510, upon timely filing of a continuation statement, the effectiveness of the initial financing statement continues for a period of five years commencing on the day on which the financing statement would have become ineffective in the absence of the filing. Upon the expiration of the five-year period, the financing statement lapses in the same manner as provided in subsection (c), unless, before the lapse, another continuation statement is filed pursuant to subsection (d). Succeeding continuation statements may be filed in the same manner to continue the effectiveness of the initial financing statement.

(f) **[Transmitting utility financing statement.]** If a debtor is a transmitting utility and a filed financing statement so indicates, the financing statement is effective until a termination statement is filed.

(g) **[Record of mortgage as financing statement.]** A record of a mortgage that is effective as a financing statement filed as a fixture filing under Section 9-502(c) remains effective as a financing statement filed as a fixture filing until the mortgage is released or satisfied of record or its effectiveness otherwise terminates as to the real property.

§ 9–516. What Constitutes Filing; Effectiveness of Filing.

(a) **[What constitutes filing.]** Except as otherwise provided in subsection (b), communication of a record to a filing office and tender of the filing fee or acceptance of the record by the filing office constitutes filing.

(b) **[Refusal to accept record; filing does not occur.]** Filing does not occur with respect to a record that a filing office refuses to accept because:

(1) the record is not communicated by a method or medium of communication authorized by the filing office;

(2) an amount equal to or greater than the applicable filing fee is not tendered;

(3) the filing office is unable to index the record because:

(A) in the case of an initial financing statement, the record does not provide a name for the debtor;

(B) in the case of an amendment or correction statement, the record:

(i) does not identify the initial financing statement as required by Section 9-512 or 9-518, as applicable; or

(ii) identifies an initial financing statement whose effectiveness has lapsed under Section 9-515;

(C) in the case of an initial financing statement that provides the name of a debtor identified as an individual or an amendment that provides a name of a debtor identified as an individual which was not previously provided in the financing statement to which the record relates, the record does not identify the debtor's last name; or

(D) in the case of a record filed [or recorded] in the filing office described in Section 9-501(a)(1), the record does not provide a sufficient description of the real property to which it relates;

(4) in the case of an initial financing statement or an amendment that adds a secured party of record, the record does not provide a name and mailing address for the secured party of record;

(5) in the case of an initial financing statement or an amendment that provides a name of a debtor which was not previously provided in the financing statement to which the amendment relates, the record does not:

(A) provide a mailing address for the debtor;

(B) indicate whether the debtor is an individual or an organization; or

(C) if the financing statement indicates that the debtor is an organization, provide:

(i) a type of organization for the debtor;

(ii) a jurisdiction of organization for the debtor; or

(iii) an organizational identification number for the debtor or indicate that the debtor has none;

(6) in the case of an assignment reflected in an initial financing statement under Section 9-514(a) or an amendment filed under Section 9-514(b), the record does not provide a name and mailing address for the assignee; or

(7) in the case of a continuation statement, the record is not filed within the six-month period prescribed by Section 9-515(d).

(c) **[Rules applicable to subsection (b).]** For purposes of subsection (b):

(1) a record does not provide information if the filing office is unable to read or decipher the information; and

(2) a record that does not indicate that it is an amendment or identify an initial financing statement to which it relates, as required by Section 9-512, 9-514, or 9-518, is an initial financing statement.

(d) **[Refusal to accept record; record effective as filed record.]** A record that is communicated to the filing office with tender of the filing fee, but which the filing office refuses to accept for a reason other than one set forth in subsection (b), is effective as a filed record except as against a purchaser of the collateral which gives value in reasonable reliance upon the absence of the record from the files.

§ 9–517. Effect of Indexing Errors.
The failure of the filing office to index a record correctly does not affect the effectiveness of the filed record.

§ 9–518. Claim Concerning Inaccurate or Wrongfully Filed Record.

(a) **[Correction statement.]** A person may file in the filing office a correction statement with respect to a record indexed there under the person's name if the person believes that the record is inaccurate or was wrongfully filed.

[Alternative A]

(b) **[Sufficiency of correction statement.]** A correction statement must:

  (1) identify the record to which it relates by the file number assigned to the initial financing statement to which the record relates;

  (2) indicate that it is a correction statement; and

  (3) provide the basis for the person's belief that the record is inaccurate and indicate the manner in which the person believes the record should be amended to cure any inaccuracy or provide the basis for the person's belief that the record was wrongfully filed.

[Alternative B]

(b) **[Sufficiency of correction statement.]** A correction statement must:

  (1) identify the record to which it relates by:

    (A) the file number assigned to the initial financing statement to which the record relates; and

    (B) if the correction statement relates to a record filed [or recorded] in a filing office described in Section 9-501(a)(1), the date [and time] that the initial financing statement was filed [or recorded] and the information specified in Section 9-502(b);

  (2) indicate that it is a correction statement; and

  (3) provide the basis for the person's belief that the record is inaccurate and indicate the manner in which the person believes the record should be amended to cure any inaccuracy or provide the basis for the person's belief that the record was wrongfully filed.

[End of Alternatives]

(c) **[Record not affected by correction statement.]** The filing of a correction statement does not affect the effectiveness of an initial financing statement or other filed record.

[SUBPART 2. DUTIES AND OPERATION OF FILING OFFICE]

§ 9–519. Numbering, Maintaining, and Indexing Records; Communicating Information Provided in Records.

(a) **[Filing office duties.]** For each record filed in a filing office, the filing office shall:

  (1) assign a unique number to the filed record;

  (2) create a record that bears the number assigned to the filed record and the date and time of filing;

  (3) maintain the filed record for public inspection; and

  (4) index the filed record in accordance with subsections (c), (d), and (e).

(b) **[File number.]** A file number [assigned after January 1, 2002,] must include a digit that:

  (1) is mathematically derived from or related to the other digits of the file number; and

  (2) aids the filing office in determining whether a number communicated as the file number includes a single-digit or transpositional error.

(c) **[Indexing: general.]** Except as otherwise provided in subsections (d) and (e), the filing office shall:

  (1) index an initial financing statement according to the name of the debtor and index all filed records relating to the initial financing statement in a manner that associates with one another an initial financing statement and all filed records relating to the initial financing statement; and

  (2) index a record that provides a name of a debtor which was not previously provided in the financing statement to which the record relates also according to the name that was not previously provided.

(d) **[Indexing: real-property-related financing statement.]** If a financing statement is filed as a fixture filing or covers as-extracted collateral or timber to be cut, [it must be filed for record and] the filing office shall index it:

  (1) under the names of the debtor and of each owner of record shown on the financing statement as if they were the mortgagors under a mortgage of the real property described; and

  (2) to the extent that the law of this State provides for indexing of records of mortgages under the name of the mortgagee, under the name of the secured party as if the secured party were the mortgagee thereunder, or, if indexing is by description, as if the financing statement were a record of a mortgage of the real property described.

(e) **[Indexing: real-property-related assignment.]** If a financing statement is filed as a fixture filing or covers as-extracted collateral or timber to be cut, the filing office shall index an assignment filed under Section 9-514(a) or an amendment filed under Section 9-514(b):

(1) under the name of the assignor as grantor; and

(2) to the extent that the law of this State provides for indexing a record of the assignment of a mortgage under the name of the assignee, under the name of the assignee.

[Alternative A]

(f) **[Retrieval and association capability.]** The filing office shall maintain a capability:

(1) to retrieve a record by the name of the debtor and by the file number assigned to the initial financing statement to which the record relates; and

(2) to associate and retrieve with one another an initial financing statement and each filed record relating to the initial financing statement.

[Alternative B]

(f) **[Retrieval and association capability.]** The filing office shall maintain a capability:

(1) to retrieve a record by the name of the debtor and:

(A) if the filing office is described in Section 9-501(a)(1), by the file number assigned to the initial financing statement to which the record relates and the date [and time] that the record was filed [or recorded]; or

(B) if the filing office is described in Section 9-501(a)(2), by the file number assigned to the initial financing statement to which the record relates; and

(2) to associate and retrieve with one another an initial financing statement and each filed record relating to the initial financing statement.

[End of Alternatives]

(g) **[Removal of debtor's name.]** The filing office may not remove a debtor's name from the index until one year after the effectiveness of a financing statement naming the debtor lapses under Section 9-515 with respect to all secured parties of record.

(h) **[Timeliness of filing office performance.]** The filing office shall perform the acts required by subsections (a) through (e) at the time and in the manner prescribed by filing-office rule, but not later than two business days after the filing office receives the record in question.

(i) **[Inapplicability to real-property-related filing office.]** Subsection[s] [(b)] [and] [(h)] do[es] not apply to a filing office described in Section 9-501(a)(1).]

§ 9–520. Acceptance and Refusal to Accept Record.

(a) **[Mandatory refusal to accept record.]** A filing office shall refuse to accept a record for filing for a reason set forth in Section 9-516(b) and may refuse to accept a record for filing only for a reason set forth in Section 9-516(b).

(b) **[Communication concerning refusal.]** If a filing office refuses to accept a record for filing, it shall communicate to the person that presented the record the fact of and reason for the refusal and the date and time the record would have been filed had the filing office accepted it. The communication must be made at the time and in the manner prescribed by filing-office rule but[, in the case of a filing office described in Section 9-501(a)(2),] in no event more than two business days after the filing office receives the record.

(c) **[When filed financing statement effective.]** A filed financing statement satisfying Section 9-502(a) and (b) is effective, even if the filing office is required to refuse to accept it for filing under subsection (a). However, Section 9-338 applies to a filed financing statement providing information described in Section 9-516(b)(5) which is incorrect at the time the financing statement is filed.

(d) **[Separate application to multiple debtors.]** If a record communicated to a filing office provides information that relates to more than one debtor, this part applies as to each debtor separately.

§ 9–522. Maintenance and Destruction of Records.

[Alternative A]

(a) **[Post-lapse maintenance and retrieval of information.]** The filing office shall maintain a record of the information provided in a filed financing statement for at least one year after the effectiveness of the financing statement has lapsed under Section 9-515 with respect to all secured parties of record. The record must be retrievable by using the name of the debtor and by using the file number assigned to the initial financing statement to which the record relates.

[Alternative B]

(a) **[Post-lapse maintenance and retrieval of information.]** The filing office shall maintain a record of the information provided in a filed financing statement for at least one year after the effectiveness of the financing statement has lapsed under Section 9-515 with respect to all secured parties of record. The record must be retrievable by using the name of the debtor and:

(1) if the record was filed [or recorded] in the filing office described in Section 9-501(a)(1), by using the file number assigned to the initial financing statement to which the record relates and the date [and time] that the record was filed [or recorded]; or

(2) if the record was filed in the filing office described in Section 9-501(a)(2), by using the file number assigned to the initial financing statement to which the record relates.

[End of Alternatives]

(b) **[Destruction of written records.]** Except to the extent that a statute governing disposition of public records provides otherwise, the filing office immediately may destroy any written record evidencing a financing statement. However, if the filing office destroys a written record, it shall maintain another record of the financing statement which complies with subsection (a).

§ 9–523. Information from Filing Office; Sale or License of Records.

(a) **[Acknowledgment of filing written record.]** If a person that files a written record requests an acknowledgment of the filing, the filing office shall send to the person an image of the record showing the number assigned to the record pursuant to Section 9-519(a)(1) and the date and time of the filing of the record. However, if the person furnishes a copy of the record to the filing office, the filing office may instead:

(1) note upon the copy the number assigned to the record pursuant to Section 9-519(a)(1) and the date and time of the filing of the record; and

(2) send the copy to the person.

(b) **[Acknowledgment of filing other record.]** If a person files a record other than a written record, the filing office shall communicate to the person an acknowledgment that provides:

(1) the information in the record;

(2) the number assigned to the record pursuant to Section 9-519(a)(1); and

(3) the date and time of the filing of the record.

(c) **[Communication of requested information.]** The filing office shall communicate or otherwise make available in a record the following information to any person that requests it:

(1) whether there is on file on a date and time specified by the filing office, but not a date earlier than three business days before the filing office receives the request, any financing statement that:

(A) designates a particular debtor [or, if the request so states, designates a particular debtor at the address specified in the request];

(B) has not lapsed under Section 9-515 with respect to all secured parties of record; and

(C) if the request so states, has lapsed under Section 9-515 and a record of which is maintained by the filing office under Section 9-522(a);

(2) the date and time of filing of each financing statement; and

(3) the information provided in each financing statement.

(d) **[Medium for communicating information.]** In complying with its duty under subsection (c), the filing office may communicate information in any medium. However, if requested, the filing office shall communicate information by issuing [its written certificate] [a record that can be admitted into evidence in the courts of this State without extrinsic evidence of its authenticity].

(e) **[Timeliness of filing office performance.]** The filing office shall perform the acts required by subsections (a) through (d) at the time and in the manner prescribed by filing-office rule, but not later than two business days after the filing office receives the request.

(f) **[Public availability of records.]** At least weekly, the [insert appropriate official or governmental agency] [filing office] shall offer to sell or license to the public on a nonexclusive basis, in bulk, copies of all records filed in it under this part, in every medium from time to time available to the filing office.

§ 9–524. Delay by Filing Office. Delay by the filing office beyond a time limit prescribed by this part is excused if:

(1) the delay is caused by interruption of communication or computer facilities, war, emergency conditions, failure of equipment, or other circumstances beyond control of the filing office; and

(2) the filing office exercises reasonable diligence under the circumstances.

§ 9–525. Fees.

(a) [Initial financing statement or other record: general rule.] Except as otherwise provided in subsection (e), the fee for filing and indexing a record under this part, other than an initial financing statement of the kind described in subsection (b), is [the amount specified in subsection (c), if applicable, plus]:

(1) $ __[X]_____ if the record is communicated in writing and consists of one or two pages;

(2) $ __[2X]_____ if the record is communicated in writing and consists of more than two pages; and

(3) $ __[1/2X]___ if the record is communicated by another medium authorized by filing-office rule.

(b) [Initial financing statement: public-finance and manufactured-housing transactions.] Except as otherwise provided in subsection (e), the fee for filing and indexing an initial financing statement of the following kind is [the amount specified in subsection (c), if applicable, plus]:

(1) $ _____ if the financing statement indicates that it is filed in connection with a public-finance transaction;

(2) $ _____ if the financing statement indicates that it is filed in connection with a manufactured-home transaction.

[Alternative A]

(c) [Number of names.] The number of names required to be indexed does not affect the amount of the fee in subsections (a) and (b).

[Alternative B]

(c) [Number of names.] Except as otherwise provided in subsection (e), if a record is communicated in writing, the fee for each name more than two required to be indexed
is $ _____.

[End of Alternatives]

(d) [Response to information request.] The fee for responding to a request for information from the filing office, including for [issuing a certificate showing] [communicating] whether there is on file any financing statement naming a particular debtor, is:

(1) $ ____ if the request is communicated in writing; and

(2) $ ____ if the request is communicated by another medium authorized by filing-office rule.

(e) [Record of mortgage.] This section does not require a fee with respect to a record of a mortgage which is effective as a financing statement filed as a fixture filing or as a financing statement covering as-extracted collateral or timber to be cut under Section 9-502(c). However, the recording and satisfaction fees that otherwise would be applicable to the record of the mortgage apply.

Legislative Notes:

1. To preserve uniformity, a State that places the provisions of this section together with statutes setting fees for other services should do so without modification.

2. A State should enact subsection (c), Alternative A, and omit the bracketed language in subsections (a) and (b) unless its indexing system entails a substantial additional cost when indexing additional names.

§ 9–526. Filing-Office Rules.

(a) [Adoption of filing-office rules.] The [insert appropriate governmental official or agency] shall adopt and publish rules to implement this article. The filing-office rules must be:

(1) consistent with this article; and

(2) adopted and published in accordance with the [insert any applicable state administrative procedure act].

(b) [Harmonization of rules.] To keep the filing-office rules and practices of the filing office in harmony with the rules and practices of filing offices in other jurisdictions that enact substantially this part, and to keep the technology used by the filing office compatible with the technology used by filing offices in other jurisdictions that enact substantially this part, the [insert appropriate governmental official or agency], so far as is consistent with the purposes, policies, and provisions of this article, in adopting, amending, and repealing filing-office rules, shall:

(1) consult with filing offices in other jurisdictions that enact substantially this part; and

(2) consult the most recent version of the Model Rules promulgated by the International Association of Corporate Administrators or any successor organization; and

(3) take into consideration the rules and practices of, and the technology used by, filing offices in other jurisdictions that enact substantially this part.

§ 9–527. Duty to Report. The [insert appropriate governmental official or agency] shall report [annually on or before _____] to the [Governor and Legislature] on the operation of the filing office. The report must contain a statement of the extent to which:

(1) the filing-office rules are not in harmony with the rules of filing offices in other jurisdictions that enact substantially this part and the reasons for these variations; and

(2) the filing-office rules are not in harmony with the most recent version of the Model Rules promulgated by the International Association of Corporate Administrators, or any successor organization, and the reasons for these variations.

Part 6: Default

[SUBPART 1. DEFAULT AND ENFORCEMENT OF SECURITY INTEREST]

§ 9–601. Rights After Default; Judicial Enforcement; Consignor or Buyer of Accounts, Chattel Paper, Payment Intangibles, or Promissory Notes.

(a) **[Rights of secured party after default.]** After default, a secured party has the rights provided in this part and, except as otherwise provided in Section 9-602, those provided by agreement of the parties. A secured party:

(1) may reduce a claim to judgment, foreclose, or otherwise enforce the claim, security interest, or agricultural lien by any available judicial procedure; and

(2) if the collateral is documents, may proceed either as to the documents or as to the goods they cover.

(b) **[Rights and duties of secured party in possession or control.]** A secured party in possession of collateral or control of collateral under Section 9-104, 9-105, 9-106, or 9-107 has the rights and duties provided in Section 9-207.

(c) **[Rights cumulative; simultaneous exercise.]** The rights under subsections (a) and (b) are cumulative and may be exercised simultaneously.

(d) **[Rights of debtor and obligor.]** Except as otherwise provided in subsection (g) and Section 9-605, after default, a debtor and an obligor have the rights provided in this part and by agreement of the parties.

(e) **[Lien of levy after judgment.]** If a secured party has reduced its claim to judgment, the lien of any levy that may be made upon the collateral by virtue of an execution based upon the judgment relates back to the earliest of:

(1) the date of perfection of the security interest or agricultural lien in the collateral;

(2) the date of filing a financing statement covering the collateral; or

(3) any date specified in a statute under which the agricultural lien was created.

(f) **[Execution sale.]** A sale pursuant to an execution is a foreclosure of the security interest or agricultural lien by judicial procedure within the meaning of this section. A secured party may purchase at the sale and thereafter hold the collateral free of any other requirements of this article.

(g) **[Consignor or buyer of certain rights to payment.]** Except as otherwise provided in Section 9-607(c), this part imposes no duties upon a secured party that is a consignor or is a buyer of accounts, chattel paper, payment intangibles, or promissory notes.

§ 9–602. Waiver and Variance of Rights and Duties.
Except as otherwise provided in Section 9-624, to the extent that they give rights to a debtor or obligor and impose duties on a secured party, the debtor or obligor may not waive or vary the rules stated in the following listed sections:

(1) Section 9-207(b)(4)(C), which deals with use and operation of the collateral by the secured party;

(2) Section 9-210, which deals with requests for an accounting and requests concerning a list of collateral and statement of account;

(3) Section 9-607(c), which deals with collection and enforcement of collateral;

(4) Sections 9-608(a) and 9-615(c) to the extent that they deal with application or payment of noncash proceeds of collection, enforcement, or disposition;

(5) Sections 9-608(a) and 9-615(d) to the extent that they require accounting for or payment of surplus proceeds of collateral;

(6) Section 9-609 to the extent that it imposes upon a secured party that takes possession of collateral without judicial process the duty to do so without breach of the peace;

(7) Sections 9-610(b), 9-611, 9-613, and 9-614, which deal with disposition of collateral;

(8) Section 9-615(f), which deals with calculation of a deficiency or surplus when a disposition is made to the secured party, a person related to the secured party, or a secondary obligor;

(9) Section 9-616, which deals with explanation of the calculation of a surplus or deficiency;

(10) Sections 9-620, 9-621, and 9-622, which deal with acceptance of collateral in satisfaction of obligation;

(11) Section 9-623, which deals with redemption of collateral;

(12) Section 9-624, which deals with permissible waivers; and

(13) Sections 9-625 and 9-626, which deal with the secured party's liability for failure to comply with this article.

§ 9–603. Agreement on Standards Concerning Rights and Duties.

(a) [**Agreed standards.**] The parties may determine by agreement the standards measuring the fulfillment of the rights of a debtor or obligor and the duties of a secured party under a rule stated in Section 9-602 if the standards are not manifestly unreasonable.

(b) [**Agreed standards inapplicable to breach of peace.**] Subsection (a) does not apply to the duty under Section 9-609 to refrain from breaching the peace.

§ 9–604. Procedure If Security Agreement Covers Real Property or Fixtures.

(a) [**Enforcement: personal and real property.**] If a security agreement covers both personal and real property, a secured party may proceed:

(1) under this part as to the personal property without prejudicing any rights with respect to the real property; or

(2) as to both the personal property and the real property in accordance with the rights with respect to the real property, in which case the other provisions of this part do not apply.

(b) [**Enforcement: fixtures.**] Subject to subsection (c), if a security agreement covers goods that are or become fixtures, a secured party may proceed:

(1) under this part; or

(2) in accordance with the rights with respect to real property, in which case the other provisions of this part do not apply.

(c) [**Removal of fixtures.**] Subject to the other provisions of this part, if a secured party holding a security interest in fixtures has priority over all owners and encumbrancers of the real property, the secured party, after default, may remove the collateral from the real property.

(d) [**Injury caused by removal.**] A secured party that removes collateral shall promptly reimburse any encumbrancer or owner of the real property, other than the debtor, for the cost of repair of any physical injury caused by the removal. The secured party need not reimburse the encumbrancer or owner for any diminution in value of the real property caused by the absence of the goods removed or by any necessity of replacing them. A person entitled to reimbursement may refuse permission to remove until the secured party gives adequate assurance for the performance of the obligation to reimburse.

§ 9–605. Unknown Debtor or Secondary Obligor.
A secured party does not owe a duty based on its status as secured party:

(1) to a person that is a debtor or obligor, unless the secured party knows:

(A) that the person is a debtor or obligor;

(B) the identity of the person; and

(C) how to communicate with the person; or

(2) to a secured party or lienholder that has filed a financing statement against a person, unless the secured party knows:

(A) that the person is a debtor; and

(B) the identity of the person.

§ 9–606. Time of Default for Agricultural Lien.
For purposes of this part, a default occurs in connection with an agricultural lien at the time the secured party becomes entitled to enforce the lien in accordance with the statute under which it was created.

§ 9–607. Collection and Enforcement by Secured Party.

(a) [**Collection and enforcement generally.**] If so agreed, and in any event after default, a secured party:

(1) may notify an account debtor or other person obligated on collateral to make payment or otherwise render performance to or for the benefit of the secured party;

(2) may take any proceeds to which the secured party is entitled under Section 9-315;

(3) may enforce the obligations of an account debtor or other person obligated on collateral and exercise the rights of the debtor with respect to the obligation of the account debtor or other person obligated on collateral to make payment or otherwise render performance to the debtor, and with respect to any property that secures the obligations of the account debtor or other person obligated on the collateral;

(4) if it holds a security interest in a deposit account perfected by control under Section 9-104(a)(1), may apply the balance of the deposit account to the obligation secured by the deposit account; and

(5) if it holds a security interest in a deposit account perfected by control under Section 9-104(a)(2) or (3), may instruct the bank to pay the balance of the deposit account to or for the benefit of the secured party.

(b) **[Nonjudicial enforcement of mortgage.]** If necessary to enable a secured party to exercise under subsection (a)(3) the right of a debtor to enforce a mortgage nonjudicially, the secured party may record in the office in which a record of the mortgage is recorded:

(1) a copy of the security agreement that creates or provides for a security interest in the obligation secured by the mortgage; and

(2) the secured party's sworn affidavit in recordable form stating that:

(A) a default has occurred; and

(B) the secured party is entitled to enforce the mortgage nonjudicially.

(C) **[Commercially reasonable collection and enforcement.]** A secured party shall proceed in a commercially reasonable manner if the secured party:

(1) undertakes to collect from or enforce an obligation of an account debtor or other person obligated on collateral; and

(2) is entitled to charge back uncollected collateral or otherwise to full or limited recourse against the debtor or a secondary obligor.

(d) **[Expenses of collection and enforcement.]** A secured party may deduct from the collections made pursuant to subsection (c) reasonable expenses of collection and enforcement, including reasonable attorney's fees and legal expenses incurred by the secured party.

(e) **[Duties to secured party not affected.]** This section does not determine whether an account debtor, bank, or other person obligated on collateral owes a duty to a secured party.

§ 9–608. Application of Proceeds of Collection or Enforcement; Liability for Deficiency and Right to Surplus.

(a) **[Application of proceeds, surplus, and deficiency if obligation secured.]** If a security interest or agricultural lien secures payment or performance of an obligation, the following rules apply:

(1) A secured party shall apply or pay over for application the cash proceeds of collection or enforcement under Section 9-607 in the following order to:

(A) the reasonable expenses of collection and enforcement and, to the extent provided for by agreement and not prohibited by law, reasonable attorney's fees and legal expenses incurred by the secured party;

(B) the satisfaction of obligations secured by the security interest or agricultural lien under which the collection or enforcement is made; and

(C) the satisfaction of obligations secured by any subordinate security interest in or other lien on the collateral subject to the security interest or agricultural lien under which the collection or enforcement is made if the secured party receives an authenticated demand for proceeds before distribution of the proceeds is completed.

(2) If requested by a secured party, a holder of a subordinate security interest or other lien shall furnish reasonable proof of the interest or lien within a reasonable time. Unless the holder complies, the secured party need not comply with the holder's demand under paragraph (1)(C).

(3) A secured party need not apply or pay over for application noncash proceeds of collection and enforcement under Section 9-607 unless the failure to do so would be commercially unreasonable. A secured party that applies or pays over for application noncash proceeds shall do so in a commercially reasonable manner.

(4) A secured party shall account to and pay a debtor for any surplus, and the obligor is liable for any deficiency.

(b) **[No surplus or deficiency in sales of certain rights to payment.]** If the underlying transaction is a sale of accounts, chattel paper, payment intangibles, or promissory notes, the debtor is not entitled to any surplus, and the obligor is not liable for any deficiency.

§ 9–609. Secured Party's Right to Take Possession After Default.

(a) **[Possession; rendering equipment unusable; disposition on debtor's premises.]** After default, a secured party:

(1) may take possession of the collateral; and

(2) without removal, may render equipment unusable and dispose of collateral on a debtor's premises under Section 9-610.

(b) **[Judicial and nonjudicial process.]** A secured party may proceed under subsection (a):

(1) pursuant to judicial process; or

(2) without judicial process, if it proceeds without breach of the peace.

(c) **[Assembly of collateral.]** If so agreed, and in any event after default, a secured party may require the debtor to assemble the collateral and make it available to the secured party at a place to be designated by the secured party which is reasonably convenient to both parties.

§ 9–610. Disposition of Collateral After Default.

(a) **[Disposition after default.]** After default, a secured party may sell, lease, license, or otherwise dispose of any or all of the collateral in its present condition or following any commercially reasonable preparation or processing.

(b) **[Commercially reasonable disposition.]** Every aspect of a disposition of collateral, including the method, manner, time, place, and other terms, must be commercially reasonable. If commercially reasonable, a secured party may dispose of collateral by public or private proceedings, by one or more contracts, as a unit or in parcels, and at any time and place and on any terms.

(c) **[Purchase by secured party.]** A secured party may purchase collateral:

(1) at a public disposition; or

(2) at a private disposition only if the collateral is of a kind that is customarily sold on a recognized market or the subject of widely distributed standard price quotations.

(d) **[Warranties on disposition.]** A contract for sale, lease, license, or other disposition includes the warranties relating to title, possession, quiet enjoyment, and the like which by operation of law accompany a voluntary disposition of property of the kind subject to the contract.

(e) **[Disclaimer of warranties.]** A secured party may disclaim or modify warranties under subsection (d):

(1) in a manner that would be effective to disclaim or modify the warranties in a voluntary disposition of property of the kind subject to the contract of disposition; or

(2) by communicating to the purchaser a record evidencing the contract for disposition and including an express disclaimer or modification of the warranties.

(f) **[Record sufficient to disclaim warranties.]** A record is sufficient to disclaim warranties under subsection (e) if it indicates "There is no warranty relating to title, possession, quiet enjoyment, or the like in this disposition" or uses words of similar import.

§ 9–611. Notification Before Disposition of Collateral.

(a) **["Notification date."]** In this section, "notification date" means the earlier of the date on which:

(1) a secured party sends to the debtor and any secondary obligor an authenticated notification of disposition; or

(2) the debtor and any secondary obligor waive the right to notification.

(b) **[Notification of disposition required.]** Except as otherwise provided in subsection (d), a secured party that disposes of collateral under Section 9-610 shall send to the persons specified in subsection (c) a reasonable authenticated notification of disposition.

(c) **[Persons to be notified.]** To comply with subsection (b), the secured party shall send an authenticated notification of disposition to:

(1) the debtor;

(2) any secondary obligor; and

(3) if the collateral is other than consumer goods:

(A) any other person from which the secured party has received, before the notification date, an authenticated notification of a claim of an interest in the collateral;

(B) any other secured party or lienholder that, 10 days before the notification date, held a security interest in or other lien on the collateral perfected by the filing of a financing statement that:

(i) identified the collateral;

(ii) was indexed under the debtor's name as of that date; and

(iii) was filed in the office in which to file a financing statement against the debtor covering the collateral as of that date; and

(C) any other secured party that, 10 days before the notification date, held a security interest in the collateral perfected by compliance with a statute, regulation, or treaty described in Section 9-311(a).

(d) **[Subsection (b) inapplicable: perishable collateral; recognized market.]** Subsection (b) does not apply if the collateral is perishable or threatens to decline speedily in value or is of a type customarily sold on a recognized market.

(e) [Compliance with subsection (c)(3)(B).] A secured party complies with the requirement for notification prescribed by subsection (c)(3)(b) if:

    (1) not later than 20 days or earlier than 30 days before the notification date, the secured party requests, in a commercially reasonable manner, information concerning financing statements indexed under the debtor's name in the office indicated in subsection (c)(3)(B); and

    (2) before the notification date, the secured party:

        (A) did not receive a response to the request for information; or

        (B) received a response to the request for information and sent an authenticated notification of disposition to each secured party or other lienholder named in that response whose financing statement covered the collateral.

§ 9–612. Timeliness of Notification Before Disposition of Collateral.

(a) [Reasonable time is question of fact.] Except as otherwise provided in subsection (b), whether a notification is sent within a reasonable time is a question of fact.

(b) [10-day period sufficient in non-consumer transaction.] In a transaction other than a consumer transaction, a notification of disposition sent after default and 10 days or more before the earliest time of disposition set forth in the notification is sent within a reasonable time before the disposition.

§ 9–613. Contents and Form of Notification Before Disposition of Collateral: General. Except in a consumer-goods transaction, the following rules apply:

    (1) The contents of a notification of disposition are sufficient if the notification:

        (A) describes the debtor and the secured party;

        (B) describes the collateral that is the subject of the intended disposition;

        (C) states the method of intended disposition;

        (D) states that the debtor is entitled to an accounting of the unpaid indebtedness and states the charge, if any, for an accounting; and

        (E) states the time and place of a public disposition or the time after which any other disposition is to be made.

    (2) Whether the contents of a notification that lacks any of the information specified in paragraph (1) are nevertheless sufficient is a question of fact.

    (3) The contents of a notification providing substantially the information specified in paragraph (1) are sufficient, even if the notification includes:

        (A) information not specified by that paragraph; or

        (B) minor errors that are not seriously misleading.

    (4) A particular phrasing of the notification is not required.

    (5) The following form of notification and the form appearing in Section 9-614(3), when completed, each provides sufficient information:

NOTIFICATION OF DISPOSITION OF COLLATERAL

To: *[Name of debtor, obligor, or other person to which the notification is sent]*

From: *[Name, address, and telephone number of secured party]*

Name of Debtor(s):   *[Include only if debtor(s) are not an addressee]*

[For a public disposition:]

We will sell [or lease or license, *as applicable*] the *[describe collateral]* [to the highest qualified bidder] in public as follows:

Day and Date:

Time:

Place:

[For a private disposition:]

We will sell [or lease or license, *as applicable*] the *[describe collateral]* privately sometime after *[day and date]* .

You are entitled to an accounting of the unpaid indebtedness secured by the property that we intend to sell [or lease or license, *as applicable*] [for a charge of $____].
You may request an accounting by calling us at *[telephone number]*

[End of Form]

§ 9–614. Contents and Form of Notification Before Disposition of Collateral: Consumer-Goods Transaction. In a consumer-goods transaction, the following rules apply:

    (1) A notification of disposition must provide the following information:

        (A) the information specified in Section 9-613(1);

        (B) a description of any liability for a deficiency of the person to which the notification is sent;

        (C) a telephone number from which the amount that must be paid to the secured party to redeem the collateral under Section 9-623 is available; and

(D) a telephone number or mailing address from which additional information concerning the disposition and the obligation secured is available.

(2) A particular phrasing of the notification is not required.

(3) The following form of notification, when completed, provides sufficient information:

[*Name and address of secured party*]

[*Date*]

NOTICE OF OUR PLAN TO SELL PROPERTY

[*Name and address of any obligor who is also a debtor*]

Subject: [*Identification of Transaction*]

We have your [*describe collateral*], because you broke promises in our agreement.

[*For a public disposition:*]

We will sell [*describe collateral*] at public sale. A sale could include a lease or license. The sale will be held as follows:

Date:

Time:

Place:

You may attend the sale and bring bidders if you want.

[*For a private disposition:*]

We will sell [*describe collateral*] at private sale sometime after [*date*] . A sale could include a lease or license.

The money that we get from the sale (after paying our costs) will reduce the amount you owe. If we get less money than you owe, you [*will or will not, as applicable*] still owe us the difference. If we get more money than you owe, you will get the extra money, unless we must pay it to someone else.

You can get the property back at any time before we sell it by paying us the full amount you owe (not just the past due payments), including our expenses. To learn the exact amount you must pay, call us at [*telephone number*] .

If you want us to explain to you in writing how we have figured the amount that you owe us, you may call us at [*telephone number*] [or write us at [*secured party's address*]] and request a written explanation. [We will charge you $_____ for the explanation if we sent you another written explanation of the amount you owe us within the last six months.]

If you need more information about the sale call us at [*telephone number*]] [or write us at [*secured party's address*]].

We are sending this notice to the following other people who have an interest in [*describe collateral*] or who owe money under your agreement: [*Names of all other debtors and obligors, if any*]

[End of Form]

(4) A notification in the form of paragraph (3) is sufficient, even if additional information appears at the end of the form.

(5) A notification in the form of paragraph (3) is sufficient, even if it includes errors in information not required by paragraph (1), unless the error is misleading with respect to rights arising under this article.

(6) If a notification under this section is not in the form of paragraph (3), law other than this article determines the effect of including information not required by paragraph (1).

§ 9–615. Application of Proceeds of Disposition; Liability for Deficiency and Right to Surplus.

(a) **[Application of proceeds.]** A secured party shall apply or pay over for application the cash proceeds of disposition under Section 9-610 in the following order to:

(1) the reasonable expenses of retaking, holding, preparing for disposition, processing, and disposing, and, to the extent provided for by agreement and not prohibited by law, reasonable attorney's fees and legal expenses incurred by the secured party;

(2) the satisfaction of obligations secured by the security interest or agricultural lien under which the disposition is made;

(3) the satisfaction of obligations secured by any subordinate security interest in or other subordinate lien on the collateral if:

(A) the secured party receives from the holder of the subordinate security interest or other lien an authenticated demand for proceeds before distribution of the proceeds is completed; and

(B) in a case in which a consignor has an interest in the collateral, the subordinate security interest or other lien is senior to the interest of the consignor; and

(4) a secured party that is a consignor of the collateral if the secured party receives from the consignor an authenticated demand for proceeds before distribution of the proceeds is completed.

(b) [Proof of subordinate interest.] If requested by a secured party, a holder of a subordinate security interest or other lien shall furnish reasonable proof of the interest or lien within a reasonable time. Unless the holder does so, the secured party need not comply with the holder's demand under subsection (a)(3).

(c) [Application of noncash proceeds.] A secured party need not apply or pay over for application noncash proceeds of disposition under Section 9-610 unless the failure to do so would be commercially unreasonable. A secured party that applies or pays over for application noncash proceeds shall do so in a commercially reasonable manner.

(d) [Surplus or deficiency if obligation secured.] If the security interest under which a disposition is made secures payment or performance of an obligation, after making the payments and applications required by subsection (a) and permitted by subsection (c):

(1) unless subsection (a)(4) requires the secured party to apply or pay over cash proceeds to a consignor, the secured party shall account to and pay a debtor for any surplus; and

(2) the obligor is liable for any deficiency.

(e) [No surplus or deficiency in sales of certain rights to payment.] If the underlying transaction is a sale of accounts, chattel paper, payment intangibles, or promissory notes:

(1) the debtor is not entitled to any surplus; and

(2) the obligor is not liable for any deficiency.

(f) [Calculation of surplus or deficiency in disposition to person related to secured party.] The surplus or deficiency following a disposition is calculated based on the amount of proceeds that would have been realized in a disposition complying with this part to a transferee other than the secured party, a person related to the secured party, or a secondary obligor if:

(1) the transferee in the disposition is the secured party, a person related to the secured party, or a secondary obligor; and

(2) the amount of proceeds of the disposition is significantly below the range of proceeds that a complying disposition to a person other than the secured party, a person related to the secured party, or a secondary obligor would have brought.

(g) [Cash proceeds received by junior secured party.] A secured party that receives cash proceeds of a dis-

position in good faith and without knowledge that the receipt violates the rights of the holder of a security interest or other lien that is not subordinate to the security interest or agricultural lien under which the disposition is made:

(1) takes the cash proceeds free of the security interest or other lien;

(2) is not obligated to apply the proceeds of the disposition to the satisfaction of obligations secured by the security interest or other lien; and

(3) is not obligated to account to or pay the holder of the security interest or other lien for any surplus.

§ 9–616. Explanation of Calculation of Surplus or Deficiency.

(a) [Definitions.] In this section:

(1) "Explanation" means a writing that:

 (A) states the amount of the surplus or deficiency;

 (B) provides an explanation in accordance with subsection (c) of how the secured party calculated the surplus or deficiency;

 (C) states, if applicable, that future debits, credits, charges, including additional credit service charges or interest, rebates, and expenses may affect the amount of the surplus or deficiency; and

 (D) provides a telephone number or mailing address from which additional information concerning the transaction is available.

(2) "Request" means a record:

 (A) authenticated by a debtor or consumer obligor;

 (B) requesting that the recipient provide an explanation; and

 (C) sent after disposition of the collateral under Section 9-610.

(b) [Explanation of calculation.] In a consumer-goods transaction in which the debtor is entitled to a surplus or a consumer obligor is liable for a deficiency under Section 9-615, the secured party shall:

(1) send an explanation to the debtor or consumer obligor, as applicable, after the disposition and:

 (A) before or when the secured party accounts to the debtor and pays any surplus or first makes written demand on the consumer obligor after the disposition for payment of the deficiency; and

 (B) within 14 days after receipt of a request; or

(2) in the case of a consumer obligor who is liable for a deficiency, within 14 days after receipt of a request, send to the consumer obligor a record waiving the secured party's right to a deficiency.

(c) [Required information.] To comply with subsection (a)(1)(B), a writing must provide the following information in the following order:

(1) the aggregate amount of obligations secured by the security interest under which the disposition was made, and, if the amount reflects a rebate of unearned interest or credit service charge, an indication of that fact, calculated as of a specified date:

(A) if the secured party takes or receives possession of the collateral after default, not more than 35 days before the secured party takes or receives possession; or

(B) if the secured party takes or receives possession of the collateral before default or does not take possession of the collateral, not more than 35 days before the disposition;

(2) the amount of proceeds of the disposition;

(3) the aggregate amount of the obligations after deducting the amount of proceeds;

(4) the amount, in the aggregate or by type, and types of expenses, including expenses of retaking, holding, preparing for disposition, processing, and disposing of the collateral, and attorney's fees secured by the collateral which are known to the secured party and relate to the current disposition;

(5) the amount, in the aggregate or by type, and types of credits, including rebates of interest or credit service charges, to which the obligor is known to be entitled and which are not reflected in the amount in paragraph (1); and

(6) the amount of the surplus or deficiency.

(d) [Substantial compliance.] A particular phrasing of the explanation is not required. An explanation complying substantially with the requirements of subsection (a) is sufficient, even if it includes minor errors that are not seriously misleading.

(e) [Charges for responses.] A debtor or consumer obligor is entitled without charge to one response to a request under this section during any six-month period in which the secured party did not send to the debtor or consumer obligor an explanation pursuant to subsection (b)(1). The secured party may require payment of a charge not exceeding $25 for each additional response.

§ 9–617. Rights of Transferee of Collateral.

(a) [Effects of disposition.] A secured party's disposition of collateral after default:

(1) transfers to a transferee for value all of the debtor's rights in the collateral;

(2) discharges the security interest under which the disposition is made; and

(3) discharges any subordinate security interest or other subordinate lien [other than liens created under [cite acts or statutes providing for liens, if any, that are not to be discharged]].

(b) [Rights of good-faith transferee.] A transferee that acts in good faith takes free of the rights and interests described in subsection (a), even if the secured party fails to comply with this article or the requirements of any judicial proceeding.

(c) [Rights of other transferee.] If a transferee does not take free of the rights and interests described in subsection (a), the transferee takes the collateral subject to:

(1) the debtor's rights in the collateral;

(2) the security interest or agricultural lien under which the disposition is made; and

(3) any other security interest or other lien.

§ 9–618. Rights and Duties of Certain Secondary Obligors.

(a) [Rights and duties of secondary obligor.] A secondary obligor acquires the rights and becomes obligated to perform the duties of the secured party after the secondary obligor:

(1) receives an assignment of a secured obligation from the secured party;

(2) receives a transfer of collateral from the secured party and agrees to accept the rights and assume the duties of the secured party; or

(3) is subrogated to the rights of a secured party with respect to collateral.

(b) [Effect of assignment, transfer, or subrogation.] An assignment, transfer, or subrogation described in subsection (a):

(1) is not a disposition of collateral under Section 9-610; and

(2) relieves the secured party of further duties under this article.

§ 9–619. Transfer of Record or Legal Title

(a) ["Transfer statement."] In this section, "transfer statement" means a record authenticated by a secured party stating:

(1) that the debtor has defaulted in connection with an obligation secured by specified collateral;

(2) that the secured party has exercised its post-default remedies with respect to the collateral;

(3) that, by reason of the exercise, a transferee has acquired the rights of the debtor in the collateral; and

(4) the name and mailing address of the secured party, debtor, and transferee.

(b) [Effect of transfer statement.] A transfer statement entitles the transferee to the transfer of record of all rights of the debtor in the collateral specified in the statement in any official filing, recording, registration, or certificate-of-title system covering the collateral. If a transfer statement is presented with the applicable fee and request form to the official or office responsible for maintaining the system, the official or office shall:

(1) accept the transfer statement;

(2) promptly amend its records to reflect the transfer; and

(3) if applicable, issue a new appropriate certificate of title in the name of the transferee.

(c) [Transfer not a disposition; no relief of secured party's duties.] A transfer of the record or legal title to collateral to a secured party under subsection (b) or otherwise is not of itself a disposition of collateral under this article and does not of itself relieve the secured party of its duties under this article.

§ 9–620. Acceptance of Collateral in Full or Partial Satisfaction of Obligation; Compulsory Disposition of Collateral.

(a) [Conditions to acceptance in satisfaction.] Except as otherwise provided in subsection (g), a secured party may accept collateral in full or partial satisfaction of the obligation it secures only if:

(1) the debtor consents to the acceptance under subsection (c);

(2) the secured party does not receive, within the time set forth in subsection (d), a notification of objection to the proposal authenticated by:

(A) a person to which the secured party was required to send a proposal under Section 9-621; or

(B) any other person, other than the debtor, holding an interest in the collateral subordinate to the security interest that is the subject of the proposal;

(3) if the collateral is consumer goods, the collateral is not in the possession of the debtor when the debtor consents to the acceptance; and

(4) subsection (e) does not require the secured party to dispose of the collateral or the debtor waives the requirement pursuant to Section 9-624.

(b) [Purported acceptance ineffective.] A purported or apparent acceptance of collateral under this section is ineffective unless:

(1) the secured party consents to the acceptance in an authenticated record or sends a proposal to the debtor; and

(2) the conditions of subsection (a) are met.

(c) [Debtor's consent.] For purposes of this section:

(1) a debtor consents to an acceptance of collateral in partial satisfaction of the obligation it secures only if the debtor agrees to the terms of the acceptance in a record authenticated after default; and

(2) a debtor consents to an acceptance of collateral in full satisfaction of the obligation it secures only if the debtor agrees to the terms of the acceptance in a record authenticated after default or the secured party:

(A) sends to the debtor after default a proposal that is unconditional or subject only to a condition that collateral not in the possession of the secured party be preserved or maintained;

(B) in the proposal, proposes to accept collateral in full satisfaction of the obligation it secures; and

(C) does not receive a notification of objection authenticated by the debtor within 20 days after the proposal is sent.

(d) [Effectiveness of notification.] To be effective under subsection (a)(2), a notification of objection must be received by the secured party:

(1) in the case of a person to which the proposal was sent pursuant to Section 9-621, within 20 days after notification was sent to that person; and

(2) in other cases:

(A) within 20 days after the last notification was sent pursuant to Section 9-621; or

(B) if a notification was not sent, before the debtor consents to the acceptance under subsection (c).

(e) [Mandatory disposition of consumer goods.] A secured party that has taken possession of collateral shall dispose of the collateral pursuant to Section 9-610 within the time specified in subsection (f) if:

(1) 60 percent of the cash price has been paid in the case of a purchase-money security interest in consumer goods; or

(2) 60 percent of the principal amount of the obligation secured has been paid in the case of a non-purchase-money security interest in consumer goods.

(f) **[Compliance with mandatory disposition requirement.]** To comply with subsection (e), the secured party shall dispose of the collateral:

(1) within 90 days after taking possession; or

(2) within any longer period to which the debtor and all secondary obligors have agreed in an agreement to that effect entered into and authenticated after default.

(g) **[No partial satisfaction in consumer transaction.]** In a consumer transaction, a secured party may not accept collateral in partial satisfaction of the obligation it secures.

§ 9–621. Notification of Proposal to Accept Collateral.

(a) **[Persons to which proposal to be sent.]** A secured party that desires to accept collateral in full or partial satisfaction of the obligation it secures shall send its proposal to:

(1) any person from which the secured party has received, before the debtor consented to the acceptance, an authenticated notification of a claim of an interest in the collateral;

(2) any other secured party or lienholder that, 10 days before the debtor consented to the acceptance, held a security interest in or other lien on the collateral perfected by the filing of a financing statement that:

(A) identified the collateral;

(B) was indexed under the debtor's name as of that date; and

(C) was filed in the office or offices in which to file a financing statement against the debtor covering the collateral as of that date; and

(3) any other secured party that, 10 days before the debtor consented to the acceptance, held a security interest in the collateral perfected by compliance with a statute, regulation, or treaty described in Section 9-311(a).

(b) **[Proposal to be sent to secondary obligor in partial satisfaction.]** A secured party that desires to accept collateral in partial satisfaction of the obligation it secures shall send its proposal to any secondary obligor in addition to the persons described in subsection (a).

§ 9–622. Effect of Acceptance of Collateral.

(a) **[Effect of acceptance.]** A secured party's acceptance of collateral in full or partial satisfaction of the obligation it secures:

(1) discharges the obligation to the extent consented to by the debtor;

(2) transfers to the secured party all of a debtor's rights in the collateral;

(3) discharges the security interest or agricultural lien that is the subject of the debtor's consent and any subordinate security interest or other subordinate lien; and

(4) terminates any other subordinate interest.

(b) **[Discharge of subordinate interest notwithstanding noncompliance.]** A subordinate interest is discharged or terminated under subsection (a), even if the secured party fails to comply with this article.

§ 9–623. Right to Redeem Collateral.

(a) **[Persons that may redeem.]** A debtor, any secondary obligor, or any other secured party or lienholder may redeem collateral.

(b) **[Requirements for redemption.]** To redeem collateral, a person shall tender:

(1) fulfillment of all obligations secured by the collateral; and

(2) the reasonable expenses and attorney's fees described in Section 9-615(a)(1).

(c) **[When redemption may occur.]** A redemption may occur at any time before a secured party:

(1) has collected collateral under Section 9-607;

(2) has disposed of collateral or entered into a contract for its disposition under Section 9-610; or

(3) has accepted collateral in full or partial satisfaction of the obligation it secures under Section 9-622.

§ 9–624. Waiver.

(a) **[Waiver of disposition notification.]** A debtor or secondary obligor may waive the right to notification of disposition of collateral under Section 9-611 only by an agreement to that effect entered into and authenticated after default.

(b) **[Waiver of mandatory disposition.]** A debtor may waive the right to require disposition of collateral under Section 9-620(e) only by an agreement to that effect entered into and authenticated after default.

(c) [Waiver of redemption right.] Except in a consumer-goods transaction, a debtor or secondary obligor may waive the right to redeem collateral under Section 9-623 only by an agreement to that effect entered into and authenticated after default.

[SUBPART 2. NONCOMPLIANCE WITH ARTICLE]

§ 9–625. Remedies for Secured Party's Failure to Comply with Article.

(a) [Judicial orders concerning noncompliance.] If it is established that a secured party is not proceeding in accordance with this article, a court may order or restrain collection, enforcement, or disposition of collateral on appropriate terms and conditions.

(b) [Damages for noncompliance.] Subject to subsections (c), (d), and (f), a person is liable for damages in the amount of any loss caused by a failure to comply with this article. Loss caused by a failure to comply may include loss resulting from the debtor's inability to obtain, or increased costs of, alternative financing.

(c) [Persons entitled to recover damages; statutory damages in consumer-goods transaction.] Except as otherwise provided in Section 9-628:

(1) a person that, at the time of the failure, was a debtor, was an obligor, or held a security interest in or other lien on the collateral may recover damages under subsection (b) for its loss; and

(2) if the collateral is consumer goods, a person that was a debtor or a secondary obligor at the time a secured party failed to comply with this part may recover for that failure in any event an amount not less than the credit service charge plus 10 percent of the principal amount of the obligation or the time-price differential plus 10 percent of the cash price.

(d) [Recovery when deficiency eliminated or reduced.] A debtor whose deficiency is eliminated under Section 9-626 may recover damages for the loss of any surplus. However, a debtor or secondary obligor whose deficiency is eliminated or reduced under Section 9-626 may not otherwise recover under subsection (b) for noncompliance with the provisions of this part relating to collection, enforcement, disposition, or acceptance.

(e) [Statutory damages: noncompliance with specified provisions.] In addition to any damages recoverable under subsection (b), the debtor, consumer obligor, or person named as a debtor in a filed record, as applicable, may recover $500 in each case from a person that:

(1) fails to comply with Section 9-208;

(2) fails to comply with Section 9-209;

(3) files a record that the person is not entitled to file under Section 9-509(a);

(4) fails to cause the secured party of record to file or send a termination statement as required by Section 9-513(a) or (c);

(5) fails to comply with Section 9-616(b)(1) and whose failure is part of a pattern, or consistent with a practice, of noncompliance; or

(6) fails to comply with Section 9-616(b)(2).

(f) [Statutory damages: noncompliance with Section 9-210.] A debtor or consumer obligor may recover damages under subsection (b) and, in addition, $500 in each case from a person that, without reasonable cause, fails to comply with a request under Section 9-210. A recipient of a request under Section 9-210 which never claimed an interest in the collateral or obligations that are the subject of a request under that section has a reasonable excuse for failure to comply with the request within the meaning of this subsection.

(g) [Limitation of security interest: noncompliance with Section 9-210.] If a secured party fails to comply with a request regarding a list of collateral or a statement of account under Section 9-210, the secured party may claim a security interest only as shown in the list or statement included in the request as against a person that is reasonably misled by the failure.

§ 9–626. Action in Which Deficiency or Surplus Is in Issue.

(a) [Applicable rules if amount of deficiency or surplus in issue.] In an action arising from a transaction, other than a consumer transaction, in which the amount of a deficiency or surplus is in issue, the following rules apply:

(1) A secured party need not prove compliance with the provisions of this part relating to collection, enforcement, disposition, or acceptance unless the debtor or a secondary obligor places the secured party's compliance in issue.

(2) If the secured party's compliance is placed in issue, the secured party has the burden of

establishing that the collection, enforcement, disposition, or acceptance was conducted in accordance with this part.

(3) Except as otherwise provided in Section 9-628, if a secured party fails to prove that the collection, enforcement, disposition, or acceptance was conducted in accordance with the provisions of this part relating to collection, enforcement, disposition, or acceptance, the liability of a debtor or a secondary obligor for a deficiency is limited to an amount by which the sum of the secured obligation, expenses, and attorney's fees exceeds the greater of:

(A) the proceeds of the collection, enforcement, disposition, or acceptance; or

(B) the amount of proceeds that would have been realized had the noncomplying secured party proceeded in accordance with the provisions of this part relating to collection, enforcement, disposition, or acceptance.

(4) For purposes of paragraph (3)(B), the amount of proceeds that would have been realized is equal to the sum of the secured obligation, expenses, and attorney's fees unless the secured party proves that the amount is less than that sum.

(5) If a deficiency or surplus is calculated under Section 9-615(f), the debtor or obligor has the burden of establishing that the amount of proceeds of the disposition is significantly below the range of prices that a complying disposition to a person other than the secured party, a person related to the secured party, or a secondary obligor would have brought.

(b) **[Non-consumer transactions; no inference.]** The limitation of the rules in subsection (a) to transactions other than consumer transactions is intended to leave to the court the determination of the proper rules in consumer transactions. The court may not infer from that limitation the nature of the proper rule in consumer transactions and may continue to apply established approaches.

§ 9–627. Determination of Whether Conduct Was Commercially Reasonable.

(a) **[Greater amount obtainable under other circumstances; no preclusion of commercial reasonableness.]** The fact that a greater amount could have been obtained by a collection, enforcement, disposition, or acceptance at a different time or in a different method from that selected by the secured party is not of itself sufficient to preclude the secured party from establishing that the collection, enforcement, disposition, or acceptance was made in a commercially reasonable manner.

(b) **[Dispositions that are commercially reasonable.]** A disposition of collateral is made in a commercially reasonable manner if the disposition is made:

(1) in the usual manner on any recognized market;

(2) at the price current in any recognized market at the time of the disposition; or

(3) otherwise in conformity with reasonable commercial practices among dealers in the type of property that was the subject of the disposition.

(c) **[Approval by court or on behalf of creditors.]** A collection, enforcement, disposition, or acceptance is commercially reasonable if it has been approved:

(1) in a judicial proceeding;

(2) by a bona fide creditorsí committee;

(3) by a representative of creditors; or

(4) by an assignee for the benefit of creditors.

(d) **[Approval under subsection (c) not necessary; absence of approval has no effect.]** Approval under subsection (c) need not be obtained, and lack of approval does not mean that the collection, enforcement, disposition, or acceptance is not commercially reasonable.

§ 9–628. Nonliability and Limitation on Liability of Secured Party; Liability of Secondary Obligor.

(a) **[Limitation of liability of secured party for noncompliance with article.]** Unless a secured party knows that a person is a debtor or obligor, knows the identity of the person, and knows how to communicate with the person:

(1) the secured party is not liable to the person, or to a secured party or lienholder that has filed a financing statement against the person, for failure to comply with this article; and

(2) the secured party's failure to comply with this article does not affect the liability of the person for a deficiency.

(b) **[Limitation of liability based on status as secured party.]** A secured party is not liable because of its status as secured party:

(1) to a person that is a debtor or obligor, unless the secured party knows:

(A) that the person is a debtor or obligor;

(B) the identity of the person; and

(C) how to communicate with the person; or

(2) to a secured party or lienholder that has filed a financing statement against a person, unless the secured party knows:

    (A) that the person is a debtor; and

    (B) the identity of the person.

(c) **[Limitation of liability if reasonable belief that transaction not a consumer-goods transaction or consumer transaction.]** A secured party is not liable to any person, and a person's liability for a deficiency is not affected, because of any act or omission arising out of the secured party's reasonable belief that a transaction is not a consumer-goods transaction or a consumer transaction or that goods are not consumer goods, if the secured party's belief is based on its reasonable reliance on:

    (1) a debtor's representation concerning the purpose for which collateral was to be used, acquired, or held; or

    (2) an obligor's representation concerning the purpose for which a secured obligation was incurred.

(d) **[Limitation of liability for statutory damages.]** A secured party is not liable to any person under Section 9-625(c)(2) for its failure to comply with Section 9-616.

(e) **[Limitation of multiple liability for statutory damages.]** A secured party is not liable under Section 9-625(c)(2) more than once with respect to any one secured obligation.

Part 7: Transition

§ 9–701. Effective Date. This [Act] takes effect on July 1, 2001.

§ 9–702. Savings Clause.

(a) **[Pre-effective-date transactions or liens.]** Except as otherwise provided in this part, this [Act] applies to a transaction or lien within its scope, even if the transaction or lien was entered into or created before this [Act] takes effect.

(b) **[Continuing validity.]** Except as otherwise provided in subsection (c) and Sections 9-703 through 9-709:

    (1) transactions and liens that were not governed by [former Article 9], were validly entered into or created before this [Act] takes effect, and would be subject to this [Act] if they had been entered into or created after this [Act] takes effect, and the rights, duties, and interests flowing from

those transactions and liens remain valid after this [Act] takes effect; and

    (2) the transactions and liens may be terminated, completed, consummated, and enforced as required or permitted by this [Act] or by the law that otherwise would apply if this [Act] had not taken effect.

(c) **[Pre-effective-date proceedings.]** This [Act] does not affect an action, case, or proceeding commenced before this [Act] takes effect.

§ 9–703. Security Interest Perfected Before Effective Date.

(a) **[Continuing priority over lien creditor: perfection requirements satisfied.]** A security interest that is enforceable immediately before this [Act] takes effect and would have priority over the rights of a person that becomes a lien creditor at that time is a perfected security interest under this [Act] if, when this [Act] takes effect, the applicable requirements for enforceability and perfection under this [Act] are satisfied without further action.

(b) **[Continuing priority over lien creditor: perfection requirements not satisfied.]** Except as otherwise provided in Section 9-705, if, immediately before this [Act] takes effect, a security interest is enforceable and would have priority over the rights of a person that becomes a lien creditor at that time, but the applicable requirements for enforceability or perfection under this [Act] are not satisfied when this [Act] takes effect, the security interest:

    (1) is a perfected security interest for one year after this [Act] takes effect;

    (2) remains enforceable thereafter only if the security interest becomes enforceable under Section 9-203 before the year expires; and

    (3) remains perfected thereafter only if the applicable requirements for perfection under this [Act] are satisfied before the year expires.

§ 9–704. Security Interest Unperfected Before Effective Date. A security interest that is enforceable immediately before this [Act] takes effect but which would be subordinate to the rights of a person that becomes a lien creditor at that time:

(1) remains an enforceable security interest for one year after this [Act] takes effect;

(2) remains enforceable thereafter if the security interest becomes enforceable under Section 9-203 when this [Act] takes effect or within one year thereafter; and

(3) becomes perfected:
  (A) without further action, when this [Act] takes effect if the applicable requirements for perfection under this [Act] are satisfied before or at that time; or
  (B) when the applicable requirements for perfection are satisfied if the requirements are satisfied after that time.

§ 9–705. Effectiveness of Action Taken Before Effective Date.

(a) **[Pre-effective-date action; one-year perfection period unless reperfected.]** If action, other than the filing of a financing statement, is taken before this [Act] takes effect and the action would have resulted in priority of a security interest over the rights of a person that becomes a lien creditor had the security interest become enforceable before this [Act] takes effect, the action is effective to perfect a security interest that attaches under this [Act] within one year after this [Act] takes effect. An attached security interest becomes unperfected one year after this [Act] takes effect unless the security interest becomes a perfected security interest under this [Act] before the expiration of that period.

(b) **[Pre-effective-date filing.]** The filing of a financing statement before this [Act] takes effect is effective to perfect a security interest to the extent the filing would satisfy the applicable requirements for perfection under this [Act].

(c) **[Pre-effective-date filing in jurisdiction formerly governing perfection.]** This [Act] does not render ineffective an effective financing statement that, before this [Act] takes effect, is filed and satisfies the applicable requirements for perfection under the law of the jurisdiction governing perfection as provided in [former Section 9-103]. However, except as otherwise provided in subsections (d) and (e) and Section 9-706, the financing statement ceases to be effective at the earlier of:
  (1) the time the financing statement would have ceased to be effective under the law of the jurisdiction in which it is filed; or
  (2) June 30, 2006.

(d) **[Continuation statement.]** The filing of a continuation statement after this [Act] takes effect does not continue the effectiveness of the financing statement filed before this [Act] takes effect. However, upon the timely filing of a continuation statement after this [Act] takes effect and in accordance with the law of the jurisdiction governing perfection as provided in Part 3, the effectiveness of a financing statement filed in the same office in that jurisdiction before this [Act] takes effect continues for the period provided by the law of that jurisdiction.

(e) **[Application of subsection (c)(2) to transmitting utility financing statement.]** Subsection (c)(2) applies to a financing statement that, before this [Act] takes effect, is filed against a transmitting utility and satisfies the applicable requirements for perfection under the law of the jurisdiction governing perfection as provided in [former Section 9-103] only to the extent that Part 3 provides that the law of a jurisdiction other than the jurisdiction in which the financing statement is filed governs perfection of a security interest in collateral covered by the financing statement.

(f) **[Application of Part 5.]** A financing statement that includes a financing statement filed before this [Act] takes effect and a continuation statement filed after this [Act] takes effect is effective only to the extent that it satisfies the requirements of Part 5 for an initial financing statement.

§ 9–706. When Initial Financing Statement Suffices to Continue Effectiveness of Financing Statement.

(a) **[Initial financing statement in lieu of continuation statement.]** The filing of an initial financing statement in the office specified in Section 9-501 continues the effectiveness of a financing statement filed before this [Act] takes effect if:
  (1) the filing of an initial financing statement in that office would be effective to perfect a security interest under this [Act];
  (2) the pre-effective-date financing statement was filed in an office in another State or another office in this State; and
  (3) the initial financing statement satisfies subsection (c).

(b) **[Period of continued effectiveness.]** The filing of an initial financing statement under subsection (a) continues the effectiveness of the pre-effective-date financing statement:
  (1) if the initial financing statement is filed before this [Act] takes effect, for the period provided in [former Section 9-403] with respect to a financing statement; and
  (2) if the initial financing statement is filed after this [Act] takes effect, for the period provided in Section 9-515 with respect to an initial financing statement.

(c) [Requirements for initial financing statement under subsection (a).] To be effective for purposes of subsection (a), an initial financing statement must:

(1) satisfy the requirements of Part 5 for an initial financing statement;

(2) identify the pre-effective-date financing statement by indicating the office in which the financing statement was filed and providing the dates of filing and file numbers, if any, of the financing statement and of the most recent continuation statement filed with respect to the financing statement; and

(3) indicate that the pre-effective-date financing statement remains effective.

§ 9–707. Amendment of Pre-Effective-Date Financing Statement.

(a) ["Pre-effective-date financing statement".] In this section, "pre-effective-date financing statement" means a financing statement filed before this [Act] takes effect.

(b) [Applicable law.] After this [Act] takes effect, a person may add or delete collateral covered by, continue or terminate the effectiveness of, or otherwise amend the information provided in, a pre-effective-date financing statement only in accordance with the law of the jurisdiction governing perfection as provided in Part 3. However, the effectiveness of a pre-effective-date financing statement also may be terminated in accordance with the law of the jurisdiction in which the financing statement is filed.

(c) [Method of amending: general rule.] Except as otherwise provided in subsection (d), if the law of this State governs perfection of a security interest, the information in a pre-effective-date financing statement may be amended after this [Act] takes effect only if:

(1) the pre-effective-date financing statement and an amendment are filed in the office specified in Section 9-501;

(2) an amendment is filed in the office specified in Section 9-501 concurrently with, or after the filing in that office of, an initial financing statement that satisfies Section 9-706(c); or

(3) an initial financing statement that provides the information as amended and satisfies Section 9-706(c) is filed in the office specified in Section 9-501.

(d) [Method of amending: continuation.] If the law of this State governs perfection of a security interest, the effectiveness of a pre-effective-date financing statement may be continued only under Section 9-705(d) and (f) or 9-706.

(e) [Method of amending: additional termination rule.] Whether or not the law of this State governs perfection of a security interest, the effectiveness of a pre-effective-date financing statement filed in this State may be terminated after this [Act] takes effect by filing a termination statement in the office in which the pre-effective-date financing statement is filed, unless an initial financing statement that satisfies Section 9-706(c) has been filed in the office specified by the law of the jurisdiction governing perfection as provided in Part 3 as the office in which to file a financing statement.

§ 9–708. Persons Entitled to File Initial Financing Statement or Continuation Statement.
A person may file an initial financing statement or a continuation statement under this part if:

(1) the secured party of record authorizes the filing; and

(2) the filing is necessary under this part:

(A) to continue the effectiveness of a financing statement filed before this [Act] takes effect; or

(B) to perfect or continue the perfection of a security interest.

§ 9–709. Priority.

(a) [Law governing priority.] This [Act] determines the priority of conflicting claims to collateral. However, if the relative priorities of the claims were established before this [Act] takes effect, [former Article 9] determines priority.

(b) [Priority if security interest becomes enforceable under Section 9-203.] For purposes of Section 9-322(a), the priority of a security interest that becomes enforceable under Section 9-203 of this [Act] dates from the time this [Act] takes effect if the security interest is perfected under this [Act] by the filing of a financing statement before this [Act] takes effect which would not have been effective to perfect the security interest under [former Article 9]. This subsection does not apply to conflicting security interests each of which is perfected by the filing of such a financing statement.

Glossary

abandonment   To intentionally give up possession or claim to property with the intent of relinquishment of any ownership or claim.

abatement   An action of stopping or removing.

ab initio   From the beginning.

abstract of title   A summary of the conveyances, transfers, and other facts relied on as evidence of title, together with all such facts appearing of record that may impair its validity.

abuse of process   An intentional tort designed to protect against the initiation of legal proceedings for a primary purpose other than the one for which such proceedings were designed.

acceleration   The shortening of the time for the performance of a contract or the payment of a note by the operation of some provision in the contract or note itself.

acceptance   The actual or implied receipt and retention of that which is tendered or offered.

accession   The acquisition of property by its incorporation or union with other property.

accommodation paper   A negotiable instrument signed without consideration by a party as acceptor, drawer, or indorser for the purpose of enabling the payee to obtain credit.

accommodation party   A person who signs a negotiable instrument for the purpose of adding his name and liability to another party to the instrument.

accord and satisfaction   A legally binding agreement to settle a disputed claim for a definite amount.

account stated   An account that has been rendered by one to another and which purports to state the true balance due and that balance is either expressly or impliedly admitted to be due by the debtor.

acquit   To set free or judicially to discharge from an accusation; to release from a debt, duty, obligation, charge, or suspicion of guilt.

actionable   Capable of being remedied by a legal action or claim.

act of God   An occurrence resulting exclusively from natural forces that could not have been prevented or whose effect could not have been avoided by care or foresight.

act of state doctrine   A doctrine of international law that no nation is permitted to judge the act of another nation committed within its own boundaries.

adjudge   To give judgment; to decide.

adjudicate   To adjudge; to settle by judicial decree.

ad litem   During the pendency of the action or proceeding.

administrator   The personal representative appointed by a probate court to settle the estate of a deceased person who died intestate (without leaving a valid will).

adoption   In corporation law, a corporation's acceptance of a preincorporation contract by action of its board of directors, by which the corporation becomes liable on the contract.

advance directive   A written document such as a living will or durable power of attorney that directs others how future health care decisions should be made in the event that the individual becomes incapacitated.

adverse possession   Open and notorious possession of real property over a given length of time that denies ownership in any other claimant.

advised letter of credit   The seller's bank acts as the seller's agent to collect against the letter of credit issued by the buyer's bank.

affidavit   A signed writing containing statements of fact to whose accuracy the signing party has sworn. Used in a variety of judicial proceedings, including the motion for summary judgment.

affirm   To confirm or uphold a former judgment or order of a court. Appellate courts, for instance, may affirm the decisions of lower courts.

after-acquired property   Property of the debtor that is obtained after a security interest in the debtor's property has been created.

agency   A legal relationship in which an agent acts under the direction of a principal for the principal's benefit. Also used to refer to government regulatory bodies of all kinds.

agent   One who acts under the direction of a principal for the principal's benefit in a legal relationship known as agency. See *principal.*

aggregate theory   In partnership law, the view that there is no distinction between a partnership and the partners who own it. See *entity theory.*

aggrieved   One whose legal rights have been invaded by the act of another. Also, one whose pecuniary interest is directly affected by a judgment, or whose right of property may be divested by an action.

alienation   The voluntary act or acts by which one person transfers his or her own property to another.

alien corporation   A corporation incorporated in one country that is doing business in another country. See *foreign corporation.*

allegation   A statement of a party to an action in a declaration or pleading of what the party intends to prove.

allege   To assert a statement of fact.

alteration   An addition or change in a document.

alter ego Other self. In corporation law, a doctrine that permits a court to pierce a corporation's veil and to hold a shareholder liable for the actions of a corporation dominated by the shareholder.

alternative dispute resolution (ADR) A general name applied to the many nonjudicial means of settling private disputes.

amortize To provide for the payment of a debt by creating a sinking fund or paying in installments.

ancillary Auxiliary to. An ancillary receiver is a receiver who has been appointed in aid of, and in subordination to, the primary receiver.

ancillary covenant not to compete A promise that is ancillary to (part of) a valid contract whereby one party to a contract agrees not to compete with the other party for a specified time and within a specified location. Also called *noncompetition clause.*

answer The pleading of a defendant in which he or she may deny any or all the facts set out in the plaintiff's declaration or complaint.

anticipatory breach A contracting party's indication before the time for performance that he cannot or will not perform the contract.

appearance The first act of the defendant in court.

appellant The party making an appeal.

appellate jurisdiction Jurisdiction to revise or correct the work of a subordinate court.

appellee A party against whom a favorable court decision is appealed. May be called the *respondent* in some jurisdictions.

applicant A petitioner; one who files a petition or application.

appurtenance An accessory; something that belongs to another thing.

arbitrate To submit some disputed matter to selected persons and to accept their decision or award as a substitute for the decision of a judicial tribunal.

argument The discussion by counsel for the respective parties of their contentions on the law and the facts of the case being tried in order to aid the jury in arriving at a correct and just conclusion.

articles of incorporation A document that must be filed with a secretary of state to create a corporation. Usually, it includes the basic rights and responsibilities of the corporation and the shareholders.

artisan's lien A common law possessory security interest arising out of the improvement of property by one skilled in some mechanical art or craft; the lien entitles the improver of the property to retain possession in order to secure the agreed-on price or the value of the work performed.

assault An intentional tort that prohibits any attempt or offer to cause harmful or offensive contact with another if it results in a well-grounded apprehension of imminent battery in the mind of the threatened person.

assent To give or express one's concurrence or approval of something done.

assignable Capable of being lawfully assigned or transferred; transferable; negotiable. Also, capable of being specified or pointed out as an assignable error.

assignee A person to whom an assignment is made.

assignment A transfer of property or some right or interest.

assignor The maker of an assignment.

assumption of risk A traditional defense to negligence liability based on the argument that the plaintiff voluntarily exposed himself to a known danger created by the defendant's negligence.

assurance To provide confidence or to inform positively.

attachment In general, the process of taking a person's property under an appropriate judicial order by an appropriate officer of the court. Used for a variety of purposes, including the acquisition of jurisdiction over the property seized and the securing of property that may be used to satisfy a debt.

attest To bear witness to; to affirm; to be true or genuine.

attorney-in-fact An agent who is given express, written authorization by his principal to do a particular act or series of acts on behalf of the principal.

at will See *employment at will* or *partnership at will.*

audit committee In corporation law, a committee of the board that recommends and supervises the public accountant who audits the corporation's financial records.

authentication Such official attestation of a written instrument as will render it legally admissible in evidence.

authority In agency law, an agent's ability to affect his principal's legal relations with third parties. Also used to refer to an actor's legal power or ability to do something. In addition, sometimes used to refer to a statute, case, or other legal source that justifies a particular result.

authorized shares Shares that a corporation is empowered to issue by its articles of incorporation.

automatic stay Under the Bankruptcy Act, the suspension of all litigation against the debtor and his property, which is triggered by the filing of a bankruptcy petition.

averment A statement of fact made in a pleading.

avoid To nullify a contractual obligation.

B

bad faith A person's actual intent to mislead or deceive another; an intent to take an unfair and unethical advantage of another.

bailee The person to whom a bailment is made.

bailment The transfer of personal property by its owner to another person with the understanding that the property will be returned to the owner in the future.

bailor The owner of bailed property; the one who delivers personal property to another to be held in bailment.

bankruptcy The state of a person who is unable to pay his or her debts without respect to time; one whose liabilities exceed his or her assets.

bar As a collective noun, those persons who are admitted to practice law, members of the bar. The court itself. A plea or defense asserted by a defendant that is sufficient to destroy a plaintiff's action.

battery An intentional tort that prohibits the harmful or offensive touching of another without his consent.

bearer A person in possession of a negotiable instrument that is payable to him, his order, or to whoever is in possession of the instrument.

bench Generally used as a synonym for the term *court* or the judges of a court.

beneficiary The person for whose benefit an insurance policy, trust, will, or contract is established. In the case of a contract, the beneficiary is called a *third-party beneficiary.*

bequest In a will, a gift of personal property or money. Also called a *legacy.*

bid To make an offer at an auction or at a judicial sale. As a noun, an offer.

bilateral contract A contract in which the promise of one of the parties forms the consideration for the promise of the other.

bill of exchange An unconditional order in writing by one person to another, signed by the person giving it, requiring the person to whom it is addressed to pay on demand or at a fixed or determinable future time a sum certain in money to order or to bearer.

bill of lading A written acknowledgment of the receipt of goods to be transported to a designated place and delivery to a named person or to his or her order.

bill of sale A written agreement by which one person assigns or transfers interests or rights in personal property to another.

binder Also called a *binding slip.* A brief memorandum or agreement issued by an insurer as a temporary policy for the convenience of all the parties, constituting a present insurance in the amount specified, to continue in force until the execution of a formal policy.

blue sky laws The popular name for state statutes that regulate securities transactions.

bona fide Made honestly and in good faith; genuine.

bona fide purchaser An innocent buyer for valuable consideration who purchases goods without notice of any defects in the title of the goods acquired.

bond A long-term debt security that is secured by collateral.

bonus shares Also called *bonus stock.* Shares issued for no lawful consideration. See *discount shares* and *watered shares.*

breaking bulk The division or separation of the contents of a package or container.

brief A statement of a party's case or legal arguments, usually prepared by an attorney. Often used to support some of the motions described in Chapter 2, and also used to make legal arguments before appellate courts. Also, an abridgement of a reported case.

broker An agent who bargains or carries on negotiations in behalf of the principal as an intermediary between the latter and third persons in transacting business relative to the acquisition of contractual rights, or to the sale or purchase of property the custody of which is not entrusted to him or her for the purpose of discharging the agency.

bulk transfer The sale or transfer of a major part of the stock of goods of a merchant at one time and not in the ordinary course of business.

burden of proof Used to refer both to the necessity or obligation of proving the facts needed to support a party's claim, and the persuasiveness of the evidence used to do so. Regarding the second sense of the term, the usual burden of proof in a civil case is a preponderance of the evidence; in a criminal case, it is proof beyond a reasonable doubt.

business judgment rule A rule protecting business managers from liability for making bad decisions when they have acted prudently and in good faith.

buy-and-sell agreement A share transfer restriction compelling a shareholder to sell his shares to the other shareholders or the corporation and obligating the other shareholders or the corporation to buy the shareholder's shares.

buyer in ordinary course of business A person who, in good faith and without knowledge that the sale to him is in violation of a third party's ownership rights or security interest in the goods, buys in ordinary course from a person who is in the business of selling goods of that kind.

bylaws In corporation law, a document that supplements the articles of incorporation and contains less important rights, powers, and responsibilities of a corporation and its shareholders, officers, and directors.

C

call See *redemption.* Also, a type of option permitting a person to buy a fixed number of securities at a fixed price at a specified time. Compare *put.*

canceled shares Previously outstanding shares repurchased by a corporation and canceled by it; such shares no longer exist.

cancellation The act of crossing out a writing. The operation of destroying a written instrument.

C&F The price of the goods includes the cost of the goods plus the freight to the named destination.

capacity The ability to incur legal obligations and acquire legal rights.

capital Contributions of money and other property to a business made by the owners of the business.

capital stock See *stated capital.*

capital surplus Also called *additional paid in capital.* A balance sheet account; the portion of shareholders' contributions exceeding the par or stated value of shares.

case law The law extracted from decided cases.

cashier's check A draft (including a check) drawn by a bank on itself and accepted by the act of issuance.

causa mortis   In contemplation of approaching death.

cause of action   A legal rule giving the plaintiff the right to obtain some legal relief once certain factual elements are proven. Often used synonymously with the terms *claim* or *theory of recovery.*

caveat emptor   "Let the buyer beware."

caveat venditor   "Let the seller beware."

certificate of deposit   An acknowledgment by a bank of the receipt of money with an engagement to pay it back.

certificate of limited partnership   A document that must be filed with a secretary of state to create a limited partnership.

certification   The return of a writ; a formal attestation of a matter of fact; the appropriate marking of a certified check.

certified check   A check that has been accepted by the drawee bank and has been so marked or certified that it indicates such acceptance.

chancellor   A judge of a court of chancery.

chancery   Equity or a court of equity.

charge   The legal instructions that a judge gives a jury before the jury begins its deliberations. In the prosecution of a crime, to formally accuse the offender or charge him with the crime.

charging order   A court's order granting rights in a partner's transferable interest to a personal creditor of the partner; a creditor with a charging order is entitled to the partner's share of partnership distributions.

charter   An instrument or authority from the sovereign power bestowing the right or power to do business under the corporate form of organization. Also, the organic law of a city or town, and representing a portion of the statute law of the state.

chattel   An article of tangible property other than land.

chattel mortgage   An instrument whereby the owner of chattels transfers the title to such property to another as security for the performance of an obligation subject to be defeated on the performance of the obligation. Under the UCC, called merely a *security interest.*

chattel paper   Written documents that evidence both an obligation to pay money and a security interest in particular goods.

check   A written order on a bank or banker payable on demand to the person named or his order or bearer and drawn by virtue of credits due the drawer from the bank created by money deposited with the bank.

chose in action   A personal right not reduced to possession but recoverable by a suit at law.

CIF   An abbreviation for cost, freight, and insurance, used in mercantile transactions, especially in import transactions.

citation of authorities   The reference to legal authorities such as reported cases or treatises to support propositions advanced.

civil action   An action brought to enforce a civil right; in contrast to a criminal action.

civil law   The body of law applicable to lawsuits involving two private parties.

class action   An action brought on behalf of the plaintiff and others similarly situated.

close corporation   A corporation with few shareholders generally having a close personal relationship to each other and participating in the management of the business.

COD   Cash on delivery. When goods are delivered to a carrier for a cash on delivery shipment, the carrier must not deliver without receiving payment of the amount due.

code   A system of law; a systematic and complete body of law.

codicil   Some addition to or qualification of one's last will and testament.

collateral   Property put up to secure the performance of a promise, so that if the promisor fails to perform as promised, the creditor may look to the property to make him whole.

collateral attack   An attempt to impeach a decree, a judgment, or other official act in a proceeding that has not been instituted for the express purpose of correcting or annulling or modifying the decree, judgment, or official act.

collateral contract   A contract in which one person agrees to pay the debt of another if the principal debtor fails to pay. See *guaranty.*

comaker   A person who with another or others signs a negotiable instrument on its face and thereby becomes primarily liable for its payment.

commercial impracticability   The standards used by the UCC, replacing the common law doctrine of impossibility, to define when a party is relieved of his or her contract obligations because of the occurrence of unforeseeable, external events beyond his or her control.

commercial law   The law that relates to the rights of property and persons engaged in trade or commerce.

commercial paper   Negotiable paper such as promissory notes, drafts, and checks that provides for the payment of money and can readily be transferred to other parties.

commercial unit   Under the UCC, any unit of goods that is treated by commercial usage as a single whole. It may, for example, be a single article or a set of articles such as a dozen, bale, gross, or carload.

common area   In landlord–tenant law, an area over which the landlord retains control but which is often used by or for the benefit of tenants. For example, hallways in an apartment building.

common carrier   One who undertakes, for hire or reward, to transport the goods of such of the public as choose to employ him.

common law   The law that is made and applied by judges.

common shareholders   Shareholders who claim the residual profits and assets of a corporation, and usually have the exclusive power and right to elect the directors of the corporation.

comparative fault   Often used synonymously with *comparative negligence.* But also sometimes used to refer to a defense that operates like comparative negligence but considers the plaintiff's and the defendant's overall fault rather than either's negligence alone.

comparative negligence The contemporary replacement for the traditional doctrine of contributory negligence. The basic idea is that damages are apportioned between the parties to a negligence action in proportion to their relative fault. The details vary from state to state.

compensatory damages Damages that will compensate a part for direct losses due to an injury suffered.

complaint The pleading in a civil case in which the plaintiff states his claim and requests relief.

composition with creditors An agreement between creditors and their common debtor and between themselves whereby the creditors agree to accept the sum or security stipulated in full payment of their claims.

concealment In contract law, taking active steps to prevent another from learning the truth.

concurrent Running with; simultaneously with.

condemn To appropriate land for public use. To adjudge a person guilty; to pass sentence on a person convicted of a crime.

condition In contract law, a future, uncertain event that creates or extinguishes a duty of performance; a provision or clause in a contract that operates to suspend or rescind a party's duty to perform.

conditional acceptance An acceptance of a bill of exchange containing some qualification limiting or altering the acceptor's liability on the bill.

conditional gift A gift that does not become absolute or complete until the occurrence of some express or implied condition.

conditional sale The term is most frequently applied to a sale in which the seller reserves the title to the goods, although the possession is delivered to the buyer, until the purchase price is paid in full.

condition precedent A condition that operates to give rise to a contracting party's duty to perform.

condition subsequent A condition that operates to relieve or discharge one from his obligation under a contract.

confession of judgment An entry of judgment on the admission or confession of the debtor without the formality, time, or expense involved in an ordinary proceeding.

confirmed letter of credit The seller's bank agrees to assume liability on the letter of credit issued by the buyer's bank.

confusion The inseparable intermixture of property belonging to different owners.

consent decree or consent order Used to refer to the order courts or administrative agencies issue when approving the settlement of a lawsuit or administrative action against some party.

consent restraint A security transfer restriction requiring a shareholder to obtain the consent of the corporation or its shareholders prior to the shareholder's sale of her shares.

consequential damages Damages that do not flow directly and immediately from an act but rather flow from the results of the act; damages that are indirect consequences of a breach of contract or certain other legal wrongs. Examples include personal injury, damage to property, and lost profits.

conservator (of an incompetent person) A person appointed by a court to take care of and oversee the person and estate of an incompetent person.

consideration In contract law, a basic requirement for an enforceable agreement under traditional contract principles, defined in this text as legal value, bargained for and given in exchange for an act or promise. In corporation law, cash or property contributed to a corporation in exchange for shares, or a promise to contribute such cash or property.

consignee A person to whom goods are consigned, shipped, or otherwise transmitted, either for sale or for safekeeping.

consignment A bailment for sale. The consignee does not undertake the absolute obligation to sell or pay for the goods.

consignor One who sends goods to another on consignment. A shipper or transmitter of goods.

conspicuous Noticeable by a reasonable person, such as a term or clause in a contract that is in bold print, in capitals, or a contrasting color or type style.

constructive eviction In landlord–tenant law, a breach of duty by the landlord that makes the premises uninhabitable or otherwise deprives the tenant of the benefit of the lease and gives rise to the tenant's right to vacate the property and terminate the lease.

construe To read a statute or document for the purpose of ascertaining its meaning and effect, but in doing so the law must be regarded.

contempt Conduct in the presence of a legislative or judicial body tending to disturb its proceedings or impair the respect due to its authority, or a disobedience to the rules or orders of such a body, which interferes with the due administration of law.

continuation statement A document, usually a multicopy form, filed in a public office to indicate the continuing viability of a financing statement. See *financing statement.*

contra Otherwise; disagreeing with; contrary to.

contract A legally enforceable promise or set of promises.

contract of adhesion A contract in which a stronger party is able to dictate terms to a weaker party, leaving the weaker party no practical choice but to adhere to the terms. If the stronger party has exploited its bargaining power to achieve unfair terms, the contract is against public policy.

contribution In business organization law, the cash or property contributed to a business by its owners.

contributory negligence A traditional defense to negligence liability based on the plaintiff's failure to exercise reasonable care for his own safety.

conversion Any distinct act of dominion wrongfully exerted over another's personal property in denial of or inconsistent with his rights therein. That tort committed by a person who deals with chattels not belonging to him in a manner that is inconsistent with the ownership of the lawful owner.

convertible securities Securities giving their holders the power to exchange those securities for other securities without paying any additional consideration.

conveyance A written instrument transferring the title to land or some interest therein from one person to another.

copartnership A partnership.

copyright A set of exclusive rights, protected by federal law, pertaining to certain creative works such as books, musical compositions, computer programs, works of art, and so forth. The rights are (1) to reproduce the work in question, (2) to prepare derivative works based on it, (3) to sell or otherwise distribute it, and (4) to perform or display it publicly.

corporation A form of business organization that is owned by owners, called shareholders, who have no inherent right to manage the business, and is managed by a board of directors that is elected by the shareholders.

corporation by estoppel A doctrine that prevents persons from denying that a corporation exists when the persons hold themselves out as representing a corporation or believe themselves to be dealing with a corporation.

corporeal Possessing physical substance; tangible; perceptible to the senses.

counterclaim A legal claim made in response to the plaintiff's initial claim in a civil suit. Unlike a defense, the counterclaim is the defendant's affirmative attempt to obtain legal relief; in effect, it states a cause of action entitling the defendant to such relief. Often, the counterclaim must arise out of the occurrence that forms the basis for the plaintiff's claim.

counteroffer A cross-offer made by the offeree to the offeror.

countertrade A buyer's purchase of the seller's goods in exchange for the seller's agreement to purchase goods of the buyer or other person; usually required as a condition to selling goods to a foreign trade corporation.

course of dealing A sequence of previous conduct between the parties to a transaction that is fairly to be regarded as establishing a common basis for interpreting their contract.

covenant A contract; a promise.

cover To obtain substitute or equivalent goods.

credible As applied to a witness, competent.

creditor A person to whom a debt or legal obligation is owed, and who has the right to enforce payment of that debt or obligation.

crime An act prohibited by the state; a public wrong.

criminal law The body of law setting out public wrongs that the government attempts to correct by prosecuting wrongdoers.

culpable Blameworthy; denotes breach of legal duty but not necessarily criminal conduct.

cumulative voting A procedure for voting for a corporation's directors that permits a shareholder to multiply the number of shares she owns by the number of directors to be elected and to cast the resulting total of votes for one or more directors. See *straight voting.*

curtesy At common law, a husband's right in property owned by his wife during her life.

custody The bare control or care of a thing as distinguished from the possession of it.

cy pres As near as possible. In the law of trusts, a doctrine applied to prevent a charitable trust from failing when the application of trust property to the charitable beneficiary designated by the settlor becomes illegal or impossible to carry out; in such a case, cy pres allows the court to redirect the distribution of trust property for some purpose that is as near as possible to the settlor's general charitable intent.

D

damages The sum of money recoverable by a plaintiff who has received a judgment in a civil case.

date of issue As applied to notes, bonds, and so on of a series, the arbitrary date fixed as the beginning of the term for which they run, without reference to the precise time when convenience or the state of the market may permit their sale or delivery.

D/B/A Doing business as; indicates the use of a trade name.

deal To engage in transactions of any kind, to do business with.

debenture A long-term, unsecured debt security.

debtor A person who is under a legal obligation to pay a sum of money to another (the creditor).

decedent A person who has died.

deceit A tort involving intentional misrepresentation or cheating by means of some device.

decision The judgment of a court; the opinion merely represents the reasons for that judgment.

declaratory judgment One that expresses the opinion of a court on a question of law without ordering anything to be done.

decree An order or sentence of a court of equity determining some right or adjudicating some matter affecting the merits of the cause.

deed A writing, sealed and delivered by the parties; an instrument conveying real property.

deed of trust A three-party instrument used to create a security interest in real property in which the legal title to the real property is placed in one or more trustees to secure the repayment of a sum of money or the performance of other conditions.

de facto In fact; actual. Often used in contrast to *de jure* to refer to a real state of affairs.

de facto corporation A corporation that has complied substantially with the mandatory conditions precedent to incorporation, taken as a whole.

defalcation The word includes both embezzlement and misappropriation and is a broader term than either.

defamation An intentional tort that prohibits the publication of false and defamatory statements concerning another.

default Fault; neglect; omission; the failure of a party to an action to appear when properly served with process; the failure to perform a duty or obligation; the failure of a person to pay money when due or when lawfully demanded.

defeasible Regarding title to property, capable of being defeated. A title to property that is open to attack or that may be defeated by the performance of some act.

defend To oppose a claim or action; to plead in defense of an action; to contest an action suit or proceeding.

defendant The party who is sued in a civil case, or the party who is prosecuted in a criminal case.

defendant in error Any of the parties in whose favor a judgment was rendered that the losing party seeks to have reversed or modified by writ of error and whom he names as adverse parties.

defense A rule of law entitling the defendant to a judgment in his favor even if the plaintiff proves all elements of his claim or cause of action.

deficiency That part of a debt that a mortgage was made to secure, not realized by the liquidation of the mortgaged property. Something that is lacking.

defraud To deprive another of a right by deception or artifice.

de jure According to the law; legitimate; by legal right.

de jure corporation A corporation that has complied substantially with each of the mandatory conditions precedent to incorporation.

delegation In constitutional law and administrative law, a process whereby a legislature effectively hands over some of its legislative power to an administrative agency that it has created, thus giving the agency power to make law within the limits set by the legislature. In contract law, a transaction whereby a person who owes a legal duty to perform under a contract appoints someone else to carry out his performance.

deliver To surrender property to another person.

demand A claim; a legal obligation; a request to perform an alleged obligation; a written statement of a claim. In corporation law, a request that the board of directors sue a person who has harmed the corporation; a prerequisite to a shareholder derivative suit.

demurrer A civil motion that attacks the plaintiff's complaint by assuming the truth of the facts stated in the complaint for purposes of the motion, and by arguing that even if these facts are true, there is no rule of law entitling the plaintiff to recovery. Roughly similar to the motion to dismiss for failure to state a claim on which relief can be granted.

de novo Anew; over again; a second time. A trial de novo, for example, is a new trial in which the entire case is retried.

deposition A form of discovery consisting of the oral examination of a party or a party's witness by the other party's attorney.

deputy A person subordinate to a public officer whose business and object is to perform the duties of the principal.

derivative suit Also called *derivative action*. A suit to enforce a corporate right of action brought on behalf of a corporation by one or more of its shareholders.

descent Hereditary succession. It is the title whereby, upon the death of an ancestor, the heir acquires the ancestor's estate under state law.

detriment Any act or forbearance by a promisee. A loss or harm suffered in person or property.

devise In a will, a gift of real property.

dictum Language in a judicial opinion that is not necessary for the decision of the case and that, while perhaps persuasive, does not bind subsequent courts. Distinguished from *holding*.

directed verdict A verdict issued by a judge who has, in effect, taken the case away from the jury by directing a verdict for one party. Usually, the motion for a directed verdict is made at trial by one party after the other party has finished presenting his evidence.

disaffirm In contract law, a party's exercise of his power to avoid a contract entered before the party reached the age of majority; a minor's cancellation of his contract.

discharge Release from liability.

discharge in bankruptcy An order or decree rendered by a court in bankruptcy proceedings, the effect of which is to satisfy all debts provable against the estate of the bankrupt as of the time when the bankruptcy proceedings were initiated.

disclaimer A term in a contract whereby a party attempts to relieve itself of some potential liability associated with the contract. The most common example is the seller's attempt to disclaim liability for defects in goods that it sells.

discount A loan on an evidence of debt, where the compensation for the use of the money until the maturity of the debt is deducted from the principal and retained by the lender at the time of making the loan.

discount shares Also called *discount stock*. Shares issued for less than their par value or stated value. See *bonus shares* and *watered shares*.

discovery A process of information gathering that takes place before a civil trial. See *deposition* and *interrogatory*.

dishonor The failure to pay or accept a negotiable instrument that has been properly presented.

dismiss To order a cause, motion, or prosecution to be discontinued or quashed.

dissenter's rights A shareholder's right to receive the fair value of her shares from her corporation when she objects to a corporate transaction that significantly alters her rights in the corporation.

dissociation In partnership law, the change in the relation of the partners caused by any partner ceasing to be associated with the carrying on of the business.

dissolution In partnership law, the commencement of the winding up process.

distribution In business organization law, a business's gratuitous transfer of its assets to the owners of the business. Includes cash and property dividends and redemptions.

divided court A court is so described when there has been a division of opinion between its members on a matter that has been submitted to it for decision.

dividends, cash or property A corporation's distribution of a portion of its assets to its shareholders, usually corresponding to current or historical corporate profits; unlike a redemption, it is not accompanied by a repurchase of shares.

dividends, share   Also called *stock dividends*. A corporation's pro rata issuance of shares to existing shareholders for no consideration.

documents of title   A classification of personal property that includes bills of lading, warehouse receipts, dock warrants, and dock receipts.

domain   The ownership of land; immediate or absolute ownership. The public lands of a state are frequently termed the *public domain*.

domicile   A place where a person lives or has his home; in a strict legal sense, the place where he has his true, fixed, permanent home and principal establishment, and to which place he has, whenever he is absent, the intention of returning.

donee   A person to whom a gift is made.

donor   A person who makes a gift.

double jeopardy clause   A constitutional provision designed to protect criminal defendants from multiple prosecutions for the same offense.

dower   The legal right or interest that a wife has in her husband's real estate by virtue of their marriage.

draft   A written order drawn on one person by another, requesting him to pay money to a designated third person.

drawee   A person on whom a draft is drawn by the drawer.

drawer   The maker of a draft.

due bill   An acknowledgment of a debt in writing, not made payable to order.

dummy   One posing or represented as acting for himself, but in reality acting for another. A tool or "straw man" for the real parties in interest.

dumping   The selling of goods by a seller in a foreign nation at unfairly low prices.

durable power of attorney   A power of attorney that is not affected by the principal's incapacity. See *power of attorney* and *attorney-in-fact*.

durable power of attorney for health care   A durable power of attorney in which the principal specifically gives the attorney-in-fact the authority to make health care decisions for her in the event that the principal should become incompetent. Also called *health care representative*.

duress   Overpowering of the will of a person by force or fear.

F

earned surplus   Also called *retained earnings*. A balance sheet account; a corporation's profits that have not been distributed to shareholders.

earnest money   Something given as part of the purchase price to bind the bargain.

easement   The right to make certain uses of another person's property or to prevent another person from making certain uses of his own property.

edict   A command or prohibition promulgated by a sovereign and having the effect of law.

e.g.   For example.

ejectment   By statute in some states, an action to recover the immediate possession of real property.

eleemosynary corporation   A corporation created for a charitable purpose or for charitable purposes.

emancipate   To release; to set free. In contract law, a parent's waiver of his rights to control and receive the services of his minor child.

embezzlement   A statutory offense consisting of the fraudulent conversion of another's personal property by one to whom it has been entrusted, with the intention of depriving the owner thereof, the gist of the offense being usually the violation of relations of a fiduciary character.

eminent domain   A governmental power whereby the government can take or condemn private property for a public purpose on the payment of just compensation.

employment at will   A rule stating that if an employment is not for a definite time period, either party may terminate the employment without liability at any time and for any reason that is not otherwise illegal.

enabling legislation   The statute by which a legislative body creates an administrative agency.

en banc (in banc)   By all the judges of a court, with all the judges of a court sitting.

encumbrance   A right in a third person that diminishes the value of the land but is consistent with the passing of ownership of the land by deed.

endorsement   See *indorsement*.

entity theory   In partnership law, the view that a partnership is a legal entity distinct from the partners who own it. See *aggregate theory*.

entry   Recordation; noting in a record; going on land; taking actual possession of land.

environmental impact statement   A document that the National Environmental Policy Act requires federal agencies to prepare in connection with any legislative proposals or proposed actions that will significantly affect the environment.

equity   A system of justice that developed in England separate from the common law courts. Few states in the United States still maintain separate equity courts, though most apply equity principles and procedures when remedies derived from the equity courts are sought. A broader meaning denotes fairness and justice. In business organization law, the capital contributions of owners plus profits that have not been distributed to the owners; stated capital plus capital surplus plus earned surplus.

equity of redemption   The right of a mortgagee to discharge the mortgage when due and to have title to the mortgaged property free and clear of the mortgage debt.

error   A mistake of law or fact; a mistake of the court in the trial of an action.

escheat   The reversion of land to the state in the event that a decedent dies leaving no heirs.

estate An interest in land. Property owned by a decedent at the time of his death.

estop To bar or stop.

estoppel That state of affairs that arises when one is forbidden by law from alleging or denying a fact because of his previous action or inaction.

et al. And another or and others. An abbreviation for the Latin *et alius,* meaning "and another"; also of *et alii,* meaning "and others."

eviction Depriving the tenant of the possession of leased premises.

evidence That which makes clear or ascertains the truth of the fact or point in issue either on the one side or the other; those rules of law whereby we determine what testimony is to be admitted and what rejected in each case and what is the weight to be given to the testimony admitted.

exception An objection; a reservation; a contradiction.

exclusionary rule The rule that bars the admissibility in criminal proceedings of evidence seized in violation of the Fourth Amendment's prohibition against unreasonable searches and seizures.

exculpatory clause A clause in a contract or trust instrument that excuses a party from some duty.

executed When applied to written instruments, synonymous with the word *signed;* more frequently, it means everything has been done to complete the transaction; that is, the instrument has been signed, sealed, and delivered. An executed contract is one in which the object of the contract is performed.

execution A process of enforcing a judgment, usually by having an appropriate officer seize property of the defendant and sell it at a judicial sale. The final consummation of a contract or other instrument, including completion of all the formalities needed to make it binding.

executive order A legal rule issued by a chief executive (e.g., the president or a state governor), usually pursuant to a delegation of power from the legislature.

executor The personal representative appointed to administer the estate of a person who died leaving a valid will.

executory Not yet executed; not yet fully performed, completed, fulfilled, or carried out; to be performed wholly or in part.

exemption A release from some burden, duty, or obligation; a grace; a favor; an immunity; taken out from under the general rule, not to be like others who are not exempt.

exhibit A copy of a written instrument on which a pleading is founded, annexed to the pleading and by reference made a part of it. Any paper or thing offered in evidence and marked for identification.

ex post facto After the fact. The U.S. Constitution prohibits ex post facto criminal laws, meaning those that criminalize behavior that was legal when committed.

express warranty A warranty made in words, either oral or written.

expropriation A government's taking of a business's assets, such as a manufacturing facility, usually without just compensation.

ex ship A shipping term that does not specify a particular ship for transportation of goods but does not place the expense and risk of transportation on the seller until the goods are unloaded from whatever ship is used.

F

face value The nominal or par value of an instrument as expressed on its face; in the case of a bond, this is the amount really due, including interest.

factor An agent who is employed to sell goods for a principal, usually in his own name, and who is given possession of the goods.

false imprisonment An intentional tort that prohibits the unlawful confinement of another for an appreciable time without his consent.

FAS An abbreviation for the expression free alongside ship.

federal supremacy The ability of federal laws to defeat inconsistent state laws in case they conflict.

fee simple absolute The highest form of land ownership, which gives the owner the right to possess and use the land for an unlimited period of time, subject only to governmental or private restrictions, and unconditional power to dispose of the property during his lifetime or upon his death.

felony As a general rule, all crimes punishable by death or by imprisonment in a state prison.

fiction An assumption made by the law that something is true that is or may be false.

fiduciary One who holds goods in trust for another or one who holds a position of trust and confidence.

field warehousing A method of protecting a security interest in the inventory of a debtor whereby the creditor or his agent retains the physical custody of the debtor's inventory, which is released to the debtor as he complies with the underlying security agreement.

financing statement A document, usually a multicopy form, filed in a public office serving as constructive notice to the world that a creditor claims a security interest in collateral that belongs to a certain named debtor.

firm offer Under the Uniform Commercial Code, a signed, written offer by a merchant containing assurances that it will be held open, and which is not revocable for the time stated in the offer, or for a reasonable time if no such time is stated.

fixture A thing that was originally personal property and that has been actually or constructively affixed to the soil itself or to some structure legally a part of the land.

FOB An abbreviation of free on board.

force majeure clause A contract provision, commonly encountered in international agreements for the sale of goods, that excuses nonperformance that results from conditions beyond the parties' control.

foreclosure   To terminate the rights of the mortgagor/owner of property.

foreign corporation   A corporation incorporated in one state doing business in another state. See *alien corporation*.

foreign trade corporation   A corporation in a NME nation that is empowered by the government to conduct the whole business of exporting or importing a particular product.

forwarder   A person who, having no interest in goods and no ownership or interest in the means of their carriage, undertakes, for hire, to forward them by a safe carrier to their destination.

franchise   A special privilege conferred by government on individuals, and which does not belong to the citizens of a country generally, of common right. Also a contractual relationship establishing a means of marketing goods or services giving certain elements of control to the supplier (franchisor) in return for the right of the franchisee to use the supplier's tradename or trademark, usually in a specific marketing area.

fraud   Misrepresentation made with knowledge of its falsity and intent to deceive. See *misrepresentation*.

freeze-out   In corporation law, a type of oppression by which only minority shareholders are forced to sell their shares.

fungible goods   Goods, any unit of which is from its nature or by mercantile custom treated as the equivalent of any other unit.

future advances   Money or other value provided to a debtor by a creditor subsequent to the time a security interest in the debtor's collateral is taken by that creditor.

futures   Contracts for the sale and future delivery of stocks or commodities, wherein either party may waive delivery, and receive or pay, as the case may be, the difference in market price at the time set for delivery.

G

garnishee   Used as a noun, the third party who is subjected to the process of garnishment. Used as a verb, to institute garnishment proceedings; to cause a garnishment to be levied on the garnishee.

garnishment   A statutory proceeding whereby money, property, wages, or credits of the defendant that are in the hands of a third party are seized to satisfy a judgment or legally valid claim that the plaintiff has against the defendant.

general partnership   See *partnership*.

gift   A voluntary transfer of property for which the donor receives no consideration in return.

good faith   Honesty in fact; an honest intention to abstain from taking an unfair advantage of another.

goodwill   The value of a business due to expected continued public patronage of the business.

grantee   A person to whom a grant is made.

grantor   A person who makes a grant.

gravamen   The gist, essence, or central point of a legal claim or argument.

gray market goods   Goods lawfully bearing trademarks or using patented or copyrighted material, but imported into a foreign market without the authorization of the owner of the trademark, patent, or copyright.

guarantor   A person who promises to perform the same obligation as another person (called the *principal*), upon the principal's default.

guaranty   An undertaking by one person to be answerable for the payment of some debt, or the due performance of some contract or duty by another person, who remains liable to pay or perform the same.

guardian   A person (in some rare cases, a corporation) to whom the law has entrusted the custody and control of the person, or estate, or both, of an incompetent person.

H

habeas corpus   Any of several common law writs having as their object to bring a party before the court or judge. The only issue it presents is whether the prisoner is restrained of his liberty by due process.

hearing   The supporting of one's contentions by argument and, if need be, by proof.

hedging   A market transaction in which a party buys a certain quantity of a given commodity at the price current on the date of the purchase and sells an equal quantity of the same commodity for future delivery for the purpose of getting protection against loss due to fluctuation in the market.

heirs   Those persons appointed by law to succeed to the estate of a decedent who has died without leaving a valid will.

holder   A person in possession of a document of title or an instrument payable or indorsed to him, his order, or to bearer.

holder in due course   A person who is a holder of a negotiable instrument who took the instrument for value, in good faith, without notice that it is overdue or has been dishonored or that there is any uncured default with respect to payment of another instrument issued as part of the same series, without notice that the instrument contains an unauthorized signature or has been altered, without notice of any claim of a property or possessory interest in it, and without notice that any party has any defense against it or claim in recoupment to it.

holding   Language in a judicial opinion that is necessary for the decision the court reached and that is said to be binding on subsequent courts. Distinguished from *dictum*.

holding company   A corporation whose purpose or function is to own or otherwise hold the shares of other corporations either for investment or control.

holographic will   A will written in the handwriting of the testator.

homestead   In a legal sense, the real estate occupied as a home and also the right to have it exempt from levy and forced sale. It is the land, not exceeding a prescribed amount, upon which the owner and his family reside, including the house in which they reside as an indispensable part.

I

i.e. That is.

illusory Deceiving or intending to deceive, as by false appearances; fallacious. An illusory promise is a promise that appears to be binding but that in fact does not bind the promisor.

immunity A personal favor granted by law, contrary to the general rule.

impanel To place the names of the jurors on a panel; to make a list of the names of those persons who have been selected for jury duty; to go through the process of selecting a jury that is to try a cause.

implied warranty A warranty created by operation of law.

implied warranty of habitability Implied warranty arising in lease or sale of residential real estate that the property will be fit for human habitation.

impossibility A doctrine under which a party to a contract is relieved of his or her duty to perform when that performance has become impossible because of the occurrence of an event unforeseen at the time of contracting.

inalienable Incapable of being alienated, transferred, or conveyed; nontransferable.

in camera In the judge's chambers; in private.

incapacity A legal disability, such as infancy or want of authority.

inception Initial stage. The word does not refer to a state of actual existence but to a condition of things or circumstances from which the thing may develop.

inchoate Imperfect; incipient; not completely formed.

incidental damages Collateral damages that result from a breach of contract, including all reasonable expenses that are incurred because of the breach; damages that compensate a person injured by a breach of contract for reasonable costs he incurs in an attempt to avoid further loss.

indenture A contract between a corporation and the holders of bonds or debentures issued by the corporation stating the rights of the holders and duties of the corporation.

independent contractor A person who contracts with a principal to perform some task according to his own methods, and who is not under the principal's control regarding the physical details of the work. Under the *Restatement (Second) of Agency,* an independent contractor may or may not be an agent.

indictment A finding by a grand jury that there is probable cause to believe an accused committed a crime.

indorsement Writing on the back of an instrument; the contract whereby the holder of an instrument (such as a draft, check, or note) or a document (such as a warehouse receipt or bill of lading) transfers to another person his right to such instrument and incurs the liabilities incident to the transfer.

infant See *minor.*

information A written accusation of crime brought by a public prosecuting officer to a court without the intervention of a grand jury.

injunction An equitable remedy whereby the defendant is ordered to perform certain acts or to desist from certain acts.

in pari delicto Equally at fault in tort or crime; in equal fault or guilt.

in personam Against a person. For example, in personam jurisdiction.

in re In the matter of.

in rem Against a thing and not against a person; concerning the condition or status of a thing; for example, in rem jurisdiction.

inside information Confidential information possessed by a person due to his relationship with a business.

insolvency In corporation law, the inability of a business to pay its currently maturing obligations.

instrument Formal or legal documents in writing, such as contracts, deeds, wills, bonds, leases, and mortgages.

insurable interest Any interest in property such that the owner would experience a benefit from the continued existence of the property or a loss from its destruction.

inter alia Among other things.

interlocutory Something not final but deciding only some subsidiary matter raised while a lawsuit is pending.

interpleader An equitable remedy applicable where one fears injury from conflicting claims. Where a person does not know which of two or more persons claiming certain property held by him has a right to it, filing a bill of interpleader forces the claimants to litigate the title between themselves.

interrogatory Written questions directed to a party, answered in writing, and signed under oath.

inter se Between or among themselves.

interstate Between or among two or more states.

intervening cause An intervening force that plays so substantial a role in causing a particular plaintiff's injury that it relieves a negligent defendant of any responsibility for that injury. Also called *superseding cause.*

intervention A proceeding by which one not originally made a party to an action or suit is permitted, on his own application, to appear therein and join one of the original parties in maintaining his cause of action or defense, or to assert some cause of action against some or all of the parties to the proceeding as originally instituted.

inter vivos A transaction between living persons.

intestate Having died without leaving a valid will.

in toto Wholly, completely.

intrastate Within a particular state.

investment contract In securities law, a type of security encompassing any contract by which an investor invests in a common enterprise with an expectation of profits solely from the efforts of persons other than the investor.

invitee A person who is on private premises for a purpose connected with the business interests of the possessor of those premises, or a member of the public who is lawfully on land open to the public.

ipso facto   By the fact itself; by the very fact.

irrevocable letter of credit   The issuing bank may not revoke the letter of credit issued by the buyer's bank.

issue   Lineal descendants such as children and grandchildren. This category of persons includes adopted children.

issued shares   A corporation's shares that a corporation has sold to its shareholders. Includes shares repurchased by the corporation and retained as treasury shares, but not shares canceled or returned to unissued status.

issuer   In securities law, a person who issues or proposes to issue a security; the person whose obligation is represented by a security.

J

joint and several liability   Liability of a group of persons in which the plaintiff may sue any member of the group individually and get a judgment against that person, or may sue all members of the group collectively.

joint bank account   A bank account of two persons so fixed that they shall be joint owners thereof during their mutual lives, and the survivor shall take the whole on the death of other.

joint liability   Liability of a group of persons in which, if one of these persons is sued, he can insist that the other liable parties be joined to the suit as codefendants, so that all must be sued collectively.

jointly   Acting together or in concert or cooperating; holding in common or interdependently, not separately. Persons are jointly bound in a bond or note when both or all must be sued in one action for its enforcement, not either one at the election of the creditor.

joint tenancy   An estate held by two or more jointly, with an equal right in all to share in the enjoyments of the land during their lives. An incident of joint tenancy is the right of survivorship.

joint venture   A form of business organization identical to a partnership, except that it is engaged in a single project, not carrying on a business.

judgment   A court's final resolution of a lawsuit or other proceeding submitted to it for decision.

judgment lien   The statutory lien on the real property of a judgment debtor that is created by the judgment itself. At common law, a judgment imposes no lien on the real property of the judgment debtor, and to subject the property of the debtor to the judgment, it was necessary to take out a writ called an *elegit*.

judgment notwithstanding the verdict   A judgment made by a judge contrary to a prior jury verdict whereby the judge effectively overrules the jury's verdict. Also called the *j.n.o.v.* or the *judgment non obstante veredicto*. Similar to the directed verdict, except that it occurs after the jury has issued its verdict.

judicial review   The courts' power to declare the actions of the other branches of government unconstitutional.

jurisdiction   The power of a court to hear and decide a case.

jurisprudence   The philosophy of law. Also sometimes used to refer to the collected positive law of some jurisdiction.

jury   A body of lay persons, selected by lot, or by some other fair and impartial means, to ascertain, under the guidance of the judge, the truth in questions of fact arising either in civil litigation or a criminal process.

K

kite   To secure the temporary use of money by issuing or negotiating worthless paper and then redeeming such paper with the proceeds of similar paper. The word is also used as a noun, meaning the worthless paper thus employed.

L

laches   The established doctrine of equity that, apart from any question of statutory limitation, its courts will discourage delay and sloth in the enforcement of rights. Equity demands conscience, good faith, and reasonable diligence.

land contract   A conditional agreement for the sale and purchase of real estate in which the legal title to the property is retained by the seller until the purchaser has fulfilled the agreement, usually by completing the payment of the agreed-on purchase price.

larceny   The unlawful taking and carrying away of personal property with the intent to deprive the owner of his property permanently.

last clear chance   Under traditional tort principles, a doctrine that allowed a contributorily negligent plaintiff to recover despite his failure to exercise reasonable care for his own safety by arguing that the defendant had the superior opportunity (last clear chance) to avoid the harm.

law merchant   The custom of merchants, or lex mercatorio, that grew out of the necessity and convenience of business, and that, although different from the general rules of the common law, was engrafted into it and became a part of it. It was founded on the custom and usage of merchants.

leading case   The most significant and authoritative case regarded as having settled and determined a point of law. Often, the first case to have done so in a definitive and complete fashion.

leading questions   Questions that suggest to the witness the answer desired or those that assume a fact to be proved that is not proved, or that, embodying a material fact, allow the witness to answer by a simple negative or affirmative.

lease   A contract for the possession and use of land or other property, including goods, on one side, and a recompense of rent or other income on the other; a conveyance to a person for life, or years, or at will in consideration of a return of rent or other recompense.

legacy   A bequest; a testamentary gift of personal property. Sometimes incorrectly applied to a testamentary gift of real property.

legal   According to the principles of law; according to the method required by statute; by means of judicial proceedings; not equitable.

letter of credit   An instrument containing a request (general or special) to pay to the bearer or person named money, or sell him or her some commodity on credit or give something of value and look to the drawer of the letter for recompense.

levy At common law, a levy on goods consisted of an officer's entering the premises where they were and either leaving an assistant in charge of them or removing them after taking an inventory. Today, courts differ as to what is a valid levy, but by the weight of authority there must be an actual or constructive seizure of the goods. In most states, a levy on land must be made by some unequivocal act of the officer indicating the intention of singling out certain real estate for the satisfaction of the debt.

libel The defamation action appropriate to printed or written defamations, or to those that have a physical form.

license A personal privilege to do some act or series of acts on the land of another, without possessing any ownership interest in the land. A permit or authorization to do something that, without a license, would be unlawful.

licensee A person lawfully on land in possession of another for purposes unconnected with the business interests of the possessor.

lien In its most extensive meaning, it is a charge on property for the payment or discharge of a debt or duty; a qualified right; a proprietary interest that, in a given case, may be exercised over the property of another.

life estate A property interest that gives a person the right to possess and use property for a time that is measured by his lifetime or that of another person.

limited liability limited partnership A limited partnership that has elected to obtain limited liability status for all of its partners, including general partners, by filing with the secretary of state. Also called *LLLP*.

limited liability partnership A partnership that has elected to obtain limited liability for its partners by filing with the secretary of state. Also called *LLP*.

limited partner An owner of a limited partnership who has no right to manage the business but who possesses liability limited to his capital contribution to the business.

limited partnership A form of business organization that has one or more general partners who manage the business and have unlimited liability for the obligations of the business and one or more limited partners who do not manage and have limited liability.

liquidated damages The stipulation by the parties to a contract of the sum of money to be recovered by the aggrieved party in the event of a breach of the contract by the other party.

liquidated debt A debt that is due and certain. That is, one that is not the subject of a bona fide dispute either as to its existence or the amount that is owed.

lis pendens A pending suit. As applied to the doctrine of lis pendens, it is the jurisdiction, power, or control that courts acquire over property involved in a suit, pending the continuance of the action, and until its final judgment.

listing contract A so-called contract whereby an owner of real property employs a broker to procure a purchaser without giving the broker an exclusive right to sell. Under such an agreement, it is generally held that the employment may be terminated by the owner at will, and that a sale of the property by the owner terminates the employment.

litigant A party to a lawsuit.

living will A document executed with specific legal formalities stating a person's preference that heroic life support measures should not be used if there is no hope of the person's recovery.

LLLP See *limited liability limited partnership*.

LLP See *limited liability partnership*.

long-arm statute A state statute that grants to a state's courts broad authority to exercise jurisdiction over out-of-state persons who have contacts with the state.

looting In corporation law, the transfer of a corporation's assets to its managers or controlling shareholders at less than fair value.

M

magistrate A word commonly applied to the lower judicial officers such as justices of the peace, police judges, town recorders, and other local judicial functionaries. In a broader sense, a magistrate is a public civil officer invested with some part of the legislative, executive, or judicial power given by the Constitution. The president of the United States is the chief magistrate of the nation.

maker A person who makes or executes an instrument. The signer of an instrument.

malfeasance The doing of an act that a person ought not to do at all. It is to be distinguished from misfeasance—the improper doing of an act that a person might lawfully do.

malicious prosecution An intentional tort designed to protect against the wrongful initiation of criminal proceedings.

mandamus We command. It is a command issuing from a competent jurisdiction, in the name of the state or sovereign, directed to some inferior court, officer, corporation, or person, requiring the performance of a particular duty therein specified, which duty results from the official station of the party to whom it is directed, or from operation of law.

margin A deposit by a buyer in stocks with a seller or a stockbroker, as security to cover fluctuations in the market in reference to stocks that the buyer has purchased but for which he has not paid. Commodities are also traded on margin.

marshals Ministerial officers belonging to the executive department of the federal government, who with their deputies have the same powers of executing the laws of the United States in each state as the sheriffs and their deputies in such state may have in executing the laws of that state.

material Important. In securities law, a fact is material if a reasonable person would consider it important in his decision to purchase shares or to vote shares.

materialman's lien A claim created by law for the purpose of securing a priority of payment of the price or value of materials furnished in erecting or repairing a building or other structure.

mechanic's lien A claim created by law for the purpose of securing a priority of payment of the price or value of work performed and materials furnished in erecting or repairing a building or other structure; as such, it attaches to the land as well as to the buildings erected therein.

memorandum A writing.

mens rea A guilty mind; criminal intent.

merchant Under the Uniform Commercial Code, one who regularly deals in goods of the kind sold in the contract at issue, or holds himself out as having special knowledge or skill relevant to such goods, or who makes the sale through an agent who regularly deals in such goods or claims such knowledge or skill.

merchantable Of good quality and salable, but not necessarily the best. As applied to articles sold, the word requires that the article shall be such as is usually sold in the market, of medium quality, and bringing the average price.

merger In corporation law, traditionally, a transaction by which one corporation acquires another corporation, with the acquiring corporation being owned by the shareholders of both corporations and the acquired corporation going out of existence. Today, loosely applied to any negotiated acquisition of one corporation by another.

merger clause A contract clause providing that the written contract is the complete expression of the parties' agreement. Also called *integration clause*.

mining partnership A form of business organization used for mining and drilling mineral resources that is identical to a partnership, except that mining partnership interests are freely transferable.

minor A person who has not reached the age at which the law recognizes a general contractual capacity (called *majority*), which is 18 in most states.

misdemeanor Any crime that is punishable neither by death nor by imprisonment in a state prison.

misrepresentation The assertion of a fact that is not in accord with the truth. A contract can be rescinded on the ground of misrepresentation when the assertion relates to a material fact or is made fraudulently and the other party actually and justifiably relies on the assertion.

mistrial An invalid trial due to lack of jurisdiction, error in selection of jurors, or some other fundamental requirement.

mitigation of damages A reduction in the amount of damages due to extenuating circumstances.

mortgage A conveyance of property to secure the performance of some obligation, the conveyance to be void on the due performance thereof.

mortgagee The creditor to whom property has been mortgaged to secure the performance of an obligation.

mortgagor The owner of the property that has been mortgaged or pledged as security for a debt.

motion to dismiss A motion made by the defendant in a civil case to defeat the plaintiff's case, usually after the complaint or all the pleadings have been completed. The most common form of motion to dismiss is the motion to dismiss for failure to state a claim on which relief can be granted, which attacks the legal sufficiency of the plaintiff's complaint. See *demurrer*.

motive The cause or reason that induced a person to commit a crime.

mutuality Reciprocal obligations of the parties required to make a contract binding on either party.

N

national ambient air quality standards Federally established air pollution standards designed to protect the public health and welfare.

natural law A body of allegedly existing ethical rules or principles that is morally superior to positive law and that prevails over positive law in case of a clash between it and the natural law. See *positive law*.

necessaries That which is reasonably necessary for a minor's proper and suitable maintenance, in view of the income level and social position of the minor's family.

negligence The omission to do something that a reasonable person, guided by those considerations that ordinarily regulate human affairs, would do, or doing something that a prudent and reasonable person would not do.

negligence per se The doctrine that provides that a conclusive presumption of breach of duty arises when a defendant has violated a statute and thereby caused a harm the statute was designed to prevent to a person the statute was designed to protect.

negotiable Capable of being transferred by indorsement or delivery so as to give the holder a right to sue in his or her own name and to avoid certain defenses against the payee.

negotiable instrument An instrument that may be transferred or negotiated, so that the holder may maintain an action thereon in his own name.

negotiation The transfer of an instrument in such form that the transferee becomes a holder.

NME A nonmarket economy; a socialist economy in which a central government owns and controls all significant means of production, thereby setting prices and the levels of production.

nolo contendere A no contest plea by the defendant in a criminal case that has much the same effect as a guilty plea but that cannot be used as an admission of guilt in other legal proceedings.

nominal damages Damages that are recoverable when a legal right is to be vindicated against an invasion that has produced no actual present loss.

non compos mentis Mentally incompetent.

nonfeasance In the law of agency, the total omission or failure of an agent to enter on the performance of some distinct duty or undertaking that he or she has agreed with the principal to do.

non obstante veredicto Notwithstanding the verdict. J.n.o.v. See *judgment notwithstanding the verdict*.

no-par value stock Stock of a corporation having no face or par value.

novation A mutual agreement, between all parties concerned, for the discharge of a valid existing obligation by the substitution of a new valid obligation on the part of the debtor or another, or a like agreement for the discharge of a debtor to his creditor by the substitution of a new creditor.

nudum pactum A naked promise, a promise for which there is no consideration.

nuisance That which endangers life or health, gives offense to the senses, violates the laws of decency, or obstructs the reasonable and comfortable use of property.

nuncupative will An oral will. Such wills are valid in some states, but only under limited circumstances and to a limited extent.

O

oath Any form of attestation by which a person signifies that he is bound in conscience to perform an act faithfully and truthfully.

obiter dictum That which is said in passing; a rule of law set forth in a court's opinion but not necessary to decide the case. See *dictum*.

objection In the trial of a case the formal remonstrance made by counsel to something that has been said or done, in order to obtain the court's ruling thereon.

obligee A person to whom another is bound by a promise or other obligation; a promisee.

obligor A person who is bound by a promise or other obligation; a promisor.

offer A proposal by one person to another that is intended to create legal relations on acceptance by the person to whom it is made.

offeree A person to whom an offer is made.

offeror A person who makes an offer.

opinion The opinion of the court represents merely the reasons for its judgment, while the decision of the court is the judgment itself.

oppression The officers, directors, or controlling shareholder's isolation of one group of shareholders for disadvantageous treatment to the benefit of another group of shareholders.

option A separate contract in which an offeror agrees not to revoke her offer for a stated period of time in exchange for some valuable consideration.

option agreement A share transfer restriction granting a corporation or its shareholders an option to buy a selling shareholder's shares at a price determined by the agreement.

ordinance A legislative enactment of a county or an incorporated city or town.

original jurisdiction The power to decide a case as a trial court.

outstanding shares A corporation's shares currently held by shareholders.

overdraft The withdrawal from a bank by a depositor of money in excess of the amount of money he or she has on deposit there.

overdue When an instrument is not paid when due or at maturity.

overplus That which remains; a balance left over.

owner's risk A term employed by common carriers in bills of lading and shipping receipts to signify that the carrier does not assume responsibility for the safety of the goods.

P

par Par means equal, and par value means a value equal to the face of a bond or a stock certificate.

parent corporation A corporation that owns a controlling interest of another corporation, called a *subsidiary corporation*.

parol Oral; verbal; by word of mouth.

parol evidence Where a written contract exists, evidence about promises or statements made prior to or during the execution of the writing that are not contained in the written contract.

parties All persons who are interested in the subject matter of an action and who have a right to make defense, control the proceedings, examine and cross-examine witnesses, and appeal from the judgment.

partition A proceeding the object of which is to enable those who own property as joint tenants or tenants in common to put an end to the tenancy so as to vest in each a sole estate in specific property or an allotment of the lands and tenements. If a division of the estate is impracticable, the estate ought to be sold and the proceeds divided.

partners The owners of a partnership.

partnership A form of business organization; specifically, an association of two or more persons to carry on a business as co-owners for profit.

partnership agreement A formal written contract between the partners of a partnership that states the rights and the responsibilities of the partners.

partnership at will A partnership whose partnership agreement does not specify any term or undertaking to be accomplished.

partnership by estoppel See *purported partnership*.

partnership interest A partner's ownership interest in a partnership which embodies the partner's transferable interest and the partner's management and other rights.

partner's transferable interest In partnership law, a partner's share of the partnership's profits and losses and right to receive partnership distributions.

party to be charged The person against whom enforcement of a contract is sought; the person who is asserting the statute of frauds as a defense.

par value An arbitrary dollar amount assigned to shares by the articles of incorporation, representing the minimum amount of consideration for which the corporation may issue the shares and the portion of consideration that must be allocated to the stated capital amount.

patent   A patent for land is a conveyance of title to government lands by the government; a patent of an invention is the right of monopoly secured by statute to those who invent or discover new and useful devices and processes.

patentee   The holder of a patent.

pawn   A pledge; a bailment of personal property as security for some debt or engagement, redeemable on certain terms, and with an implied power of sale on default.

payee   A person to whom a payment is made or is made payable.

pecuniary   Financial; pertaining or relating to money.

pendente lite   During the litigation.

per capita   A distribution of property in which each member of a group shares equally.

per curiam   By the court as a whole, without an opinion signed by a particular judge.

peremptory challenge   A challenge to a proposed juror that a defendant may make as an absolute right, and that cannot be questioned by either opposing counsel or the court.

perfection   The process or method by which a secured party obtains a priority in certain collateral belonging to a debtor against creditors or claimants of a debtor; it usually entails giving notice of the security interest, such as by taking possession or filing a financial statement.

performance   The fulfillment of a contractual duty.

periodic tenancy   The tenancy that exists when the landlord and tenant agree that rent will be paid in regular successive intervals until notice to terminate is given but do not agree on a specific duration of the lease. A typical periodic tenancy is a tenancy from month to month.

perjury   The willful and corrupt false swearing or affirming, after an oath lawfully administered, in the course of a judicial or quasi-judicial proceeding, as to some matter material to the issue or point in question.

per se   In itself or as such.

personal property   All objects and rights, other than real property, that can be owned. See *real property.*

per stirpes   A distribution in which each surviving descendant divides the share that his or her parent would have taken if the parent had survived. Also called *by right of representation.*

petition   In equity pleading, a petition is in the nature of a pleading (at least when filed by a stranger to the suit) and forms a basis for independent action.

petition (bankruptcy)   The document filed with the appropriate federal court that initiates a bankruptcy proceeding. It may be either a voluntary petition (i.e., filed by the debtor) or an involuntary petition (i.e., filed by creditors).

piercing the corporate veil   Holding a shareholder responsible for acts of a corporation due to a shareholder's domination and improper use of the corporation.

plaintiff   The party who sues in a civil case.

plaintiff in error   The unsuccessful party to the action who prosecutes a writ of error in a higher court.

plea   A plea is an answer to a declaration or complaint or any material allegation of fact therein that, if untrue, would defeat the action. In criminal procedure, a plea is the matter that the accused, on his arraignment, alleges in answer to the charge against him.

pleadings   The documents the parties file with the court when they state their claims and counterarguments early in a civil case. Examples include the complaint and the answer.

pledge   A pawn; a bailment of personal property as security for some debt or engagement, redeemable on certain terms, and with an implied power of sale on default.

pledgee   A person to whom personal property is pledged by a pledgor.

pledgor   A person who makes a pledge of personal property to a pledgee.

police power   The states' power to regulate to promote the public health, safety, morals, and welfare.

positive law   Laws actually and specifically enacted or adopted by proper authority for the government of a jural society as distinguished from principles of morality or laws of honor.

possession   Respecting real property, exclusive dominion and control such as owners of like property usually exercise over it. Manual control of personal property either as owner or as one having a qualified right in it.

postdated check   A check dated with a date later than its date of issue.

power of attorney   A written authorization by a principal to an agent to perform specified acts on behalf of the principal. See *attorney-in-fact.*

precedent   A past judicial decision relied on as authority in a present case.

preemptive right   A shareholder's option to purchase new issuances of shares in proportion to the shareholder's current ownership of the corporation.

preference   The act of a debtor in paying or securing one or more of his creditors in a manner more favorable to them than to other creditors or to the exclusion of such other creditors. In the absence of statute, a preference is perfectly good, but to be legal it must be bona fide, and not a mere subterfuge of the debtor to secure a future benefit to himself or to prevent the application of his property to his debts.

preferential   Having priority.

preferred shareholders   Shareholders who have dividend and liquidation preferences over other classes of shareholders, usually common shareholders.

prenuptial contract   A contract between prospective marriage partners respecting matters such as property ownership and division.

preponderance   Most; majority; more probable than not.

prerogative A special power, privilege, or immunity, usually used in reference to an official or his office.

presentment A demand for acceptance or payment of a negotiable instrument made on the maker, acceptor, drawee, or other payor by or on behalf of the holder.

presumption A term used to signify that which may be assumed without proof, or taken for granted. It is asserted as a self-evident result of human reason and experience.

pretermitted In the law of wills, an heir born after the execution of the testator's will.

prima facie At first sight; a fact that is presumed to be true unless disproved by contrary evidence.

prima facie case A case sufficiently strong that, unless rebutted by the defendant in some fashion, it entitles the plaintiff to recover against the defendant.

principal In agency law, one under whose direction an agent acts and for whose benefit that agent acts.

priority Having precedence or the better right.

privilege Generally, a legal right to engage in conduct that would otherwise result in legal liability. Privileges are commonly classified as absolute (unqualified) or conditional (qualified). Occasionally, privilege is also used to denote a legal right to refrain from particular behavior (e.g., the constitutional privilege against self-incrimination).

privity of contract The existence of a direct contractual relation between two parties.

probate A term used to include all matters of which probate courts have jurisdiction, which in many states are the estates of deceased persons and of persons under guardianship.

procedural law The body of law controlling public bodies such as courts, as they create and enforce rules of substantive law. See *substantive law.*

proceeds Whatever is received on the sale, exchange, collection, or other disposition of collateral.

process Generally, the summons or notice of beginning of suit.

proffer To offer for acceptance or to make a tender of.

profit An interest in land giving a person the right to enter land owned by another and remove natural resources (e.g., timber) from the land. Also called *profit à prendre.*

promisee The person to whom a promise is made.

promisor A person who makes a promise to another; a person who promises.

promissory estoppel An equitable doctrine that protects those who foreseeably and reasonably rely on the promises of others by enforcing such promises when enforcement is necessary to avoid injustice, even though one or more of the elements normally required for an enforceable agreement is absent.

promissory note Commercial paper or instrument in which the maker promises to pay a specific sum of money to another person, to his order, or to bearer.

promoter A person who incorporates a business, organizes its initial management, and raises its initial capital.

property Something that is capable of being owned. A right or interest associated with something that gives the owner the ability to exercise dominion over it.

pro rata Proportionate; in proportion.

prospectus In securities law, a document given to prospective purchasers of a security that contains information about an issuer of securities and the securities being issued.

pro tanto For so much; to such an extent.

proximate cause A legal limitation on a negligent wrongdoer's liability for the actual consequences of his actions. Such wrongdoers are said to be relieved of responsibility for consequences that are too remote or not the proximate result of their actions. Various tests for proximate cause are employed by the courts.

proxy A person who is authorized to vote the shares of another person. Also, the written authorization empowering a person to vote the shares of another person.

pseudoforeign corporation A corporation incorporated under the laws of a state but doing most of its business in one other state.

publicly held corporation A corporation owned by a large number of widely dispersed shareholders.

punitive damages Damages designed to punish flagrant wrongdoers and to deter them and others from engaging in similar conduct in the future.

purchase money security interest A security interest that is (1) taken or retained by the seller of collateral to secure all or part of its purchase price or (2) taken by a debtor to acquire rights in or the use of the collateral if the value is so used.

purported partnership The appearance of partnership when there is no partnership; it arises when a person misleads a second person into believing that the first person is a partner of a third person; a theory that allows the second person to recover from the first person all reasonable damages the second person has suffered due to his reliance on the appearance of partnership.

put A type of option permitting a person to sell a fixed number of securities at a fixed price at a specified time. Compare *call.*

Q

qualified acceptance A conditional or modified acceptance. In order to create a contract, an acceptance must accept the offer substantially as made; hence, a qualified acceptance is no acceptance at all, is treated by the courts as a rejection of the offer made, and is in effect an offer by the offeree, which the offeror may, if he chooses, accept and thus create a contract.

quantum meruit As much as is deserved. A part of a common law action in assumpsit for the value of services rendered.

quash To vacate or make void.

quasi-contract   The doctrine by which courts imply, as a matter of law, a promise to pay the reasonable value of goods or services when the party receiving such goods or services has knowingly done so under circumstances that make it unfair to retain them without paying for them.

quasi-judicial   Acts of public officers involving investigation of facts and drawing conclusions from them as a basis of official action.

quiet title, action to   An action to establish a claimant's title in land by requiring adverse claimants to come into court to prove their claim or to be barred from asserting it later.

quitclaim deed   A deed conveying only the right, title, and interest of the grantor in the property described, as distinguished from a deed conveying the property itself.

quorum   That number of persons, shares represented, or officers who may lawfully transact the business of a meeting called for that purpose.

quo warranto   By what authority. The name of a writ (and also of the whole pleading) by which the government commences an action to recover an office or franchise from the person or corporation in possession of it.

R

ratification   The adoption or affirmance by a person of a prior act that did not bind him.

real property   The earth's crust and all things firmly attached to it.

rebuttal   Testimony addressed to evidence produced by the opposite party; rebutting evidence.

receiver   One appointed by a court to take charge of a business or the property of another during litigation to preserve it and/or to dispose of it as directed by the court.

recklessness   Behavior that indicates a conscious disregard for a known high risk of probable harm to others.

recognizance   At common law, an obligation entered into before some court of record or magistrate duly authorized, with a condition to do some particular act, usually to appear and answer to a criminal accusation. Being taken in open court and entered on the order book, it was valid without the signature or seal of any of the obligors.

recorder   A public officer of a town or county charged with the duty of keeping the record books required by law to be kept in his or her office and of receiving and causing to be copied in such books such instruments as by law are entitled to be recorded.

redemption   The buying back of one's property after it has been sold. The right to redeem property sold under an order or decree of court is purely a privilege conferred by, and does not exist independently of, statute.

redemption right   Also called a call. In corporation law, the right of a corporation to repurchase shares held by existing shareholders.

redress   Remedy; indemnity; reparation.

reformation   An equitable remedy in which a court effectively rewrites the terms of a contract.

rejection   In contract law, an express or implied manifestation of an offeree's unwillingness to contract on the terms of an offer. In sales law, a buyer's refusal to accept goods because they are defective or nonconforming.

release   The giving up or abandoning of a claim or right to a person against whom the claim exists or the right is to be enforced or exercised. It is the discharge of a debt by the act of the party, in distinction from an extinguishment that is a discharge by operation of law.

remainderman   One who is entitled to the remainder of the estate after a particular estate carved out of it has expired.

remand   A process whereby an appellate court returns the case to a lower court (usually a trial court) for proceedings not inconsistent with the appellate court's decision.

remedy   The appropriate legal form of relief by which a remediable right may be enforced.

remittitur   The certificate of reversal issued by an appellate court upon reversing the order or judgment appealed from.

repatriation   An investor's removal to the investor's nation of profits from his investment in a foreign nation.

replevin   A common law action by which the owner recovers possession of his own goods.

repudiation   Indicating to another party to a contract that the party does not intend to perform his obligations.

res   The thing; the subject matter of a suit; the property involved in the litigation; a matter; property; the business; the affair; the transaction.

rescind   As the word is applied to contracts, to terminate the contract as to future transactions or to annul the contract from the beginning.

rescission   The rescinding or cancellation of a contract or transaction. In general, its effect is to restore the parties to their original precontractual position.

residue   Residuary; all that portion of the estate of a testator of which no effectual disposition has been made by his will otherwise than in the residuary clause.

res ipsa loquitur   Literally, the thing speaks for itself. A doctrine that, in some circumstances, gives rise to an inference that a defendant was negligent and that his negligence was the cause of the plaintiff's injury.

res judicata   A matter that has been adjudicated; that which is definitely settled by a judicial decision.

respondeat superior   A legal doctrine making an employer (or master) liable for the torts of an employee (servant) that are committed within the scope of the employee's employment.

respondent   A term often used to describe the party charged in an administrative proceeding. The party adverse to the appellant in a case appealed to a higher court. In this sense, often synonymous with *appellee*.

Restatement(s)   Collections of legal rules produced by the American Law Institute, covering certain subject matter areas. Although *Restatements* are often persuasive to courts, they are not legally binding unless adopted by the highest court of a particular state.

restitution   A remedy whereby one is able to obtain the return of that which he has given the other party, or an amount of money equivalent to that which he has given the other party.

restrictive covenant   An agreement restricting the use of real property.

reverse   To reject or overturn a judgment or order of a court. An appellate court, for example, may reverse the decision of a trial court. See *affirm*.

revocation   In general, the recalling or voiding of a prior action. In contract law, the withdrawal of an offer by the offeror prior to effective acceptance by the offeree.

right   An interest given and protected by law. In corporation law, an option to purchase shares given to existing shareholders, permitting them to buy quantities of newly issued securities in proportion to their current ownership.

right of appraisal   See *dissenter's rights*.

right of first refusal   In corporation law, a share transfer restriction granting a corporation or its shareholders an option to match the offer that a selling shareholder receives for her shares. See also *option agreement*.

right of survivorship   A feature of some types of co-ownership of property causing a co-owner's interest in property to be transferred on his death immediately and by operation of law to his surviving co-owner(s). See *tenancy by the entirety* and *joint tenancy*.

riparian   Pertaining to water rights or situated on the bank of a river.

S

sale of goods   The transfer of ownership to tangible personal property in exchange for money, other goods, or the performance of service.

sale on approval   A conditional sale that is to become final only in case the buyer, after a trial, approves or is satisfied with the article sold.

sale or return   A contract in which the seller delivers a quantity of goods to the buyer on the understanding that if the buyer desires to retain, use, or sell any portion of the goods, he will consider such part as having been sold to him, and that he will return the balance or hold it as bailee for the seller.

sanction   The penalty that will be incurred by a wrongdoer for the violation of a law.

satisfaction   A performance of the terms of an accord. If such terms require a payment of a sum of money, then satisfaction means that such payment has been made.

scienter   In cases of fraud and deceit, the word means knowledge on the part of the person making the representations, at the time when they are made, that they are false. In an action for deceit, scienter must be proved.

S corporation   Also called *subchapter S corporation*. A close corporation whose shareholders have elected to be taxed essentially like partners are taxed under federal income tax law.

seal   At common law, a seal is an impression on wax or some other tenacious material, but in modern practice the letters *l.s.* (locus sigilli) or the word *seal* enclosed in a scroll, either written, or printed, and acknowledged in the body of the instrument to be a seal, are often used as substitutes.

security   An instrument commonly dealt with in the securities markets or commonly recognized as a medium of investment and evidencing an obligation of an issuer or a share, participation, or other interest in an enterprise.

security agreement   An agreement that creates or provides a security interest or lien on personal property. A term used in the UCC including a wide range of transactions in the nature of chattel mortgages, conditional sales, and so on.

security interest   A lien given by a debtor to his creditor to secure payment or performance of a debt or obligation.

service   As applied to a process of courts, the word ordinarily implies something in the nature of an act or proceeding adverse to the party served, or of a notice to him.

set off   That right that exists between two parties, each of whom, under an independent contract, owes an ascertained amount to the other, to calculate their respective debts by way of mutual deduction, so that, in any action brought for the larger debt, the residue only, after such deduction, shall be recovered.

settlor   A person who creates a trust. Also called *trustor*.

severable contract   A contract that is not entire or indivisible. If the consideration is single, the contract is entire; but if it is expressly or by necessary implication apportioned, the contract is severable. The question is ordinarily determined by inquiring whether the contract embraces one or more subject matters, whether the obligation is due at the same time to the same person, and whether the consideration is entire or apportioned.

share   An equity security, representing a shareholder's ownership of a corporation.

share dividend   See *dividends, share*.

shareholder   Also called *stockholder*. An owner of a corporation, who has no inherent right to manage the corporation but has liability limited to his capital contribution.

share split   Also called *stock split*. Traditionally, a corporation's dividing existing shares into two or more shares, thereby increasing the number of authorized, issued, and outstanding shares and reducing their par value. In modern corporation law, treated like a share dividend.

sight   A term signifying the date of the acceptance or that of protest for the nonacceptance of a bill of exchange; for example, 10 days after sight.

sinking fund   A fund established by an issuer of securities to accumulate funds to repurchase the issuer's securities.

situs   Location; local position; the place where a person or thing is, is his situs. Intangible property has no actual situs, but it may have a legal situs, and for the purpose of taxation, its legal situs is at the place where it is owned and not at the place where it is owed.

slander   The defamation action appropriate to oral defamation.

sole proprietor   The owner of a sole proprietorship.

sole proprietorship   A form of business under which one person owns and controls the business.

sovereign immunity   Generally, the idea that the sovereign (or state) may not be sued unless it consents to be sued. In antitrust law, the statutory immunity from antitrust liability for governmental actions that foreign governments enjoy under the Foreign Sovereign Immunities Act of 1976.

special damages   Actual damages that would not necessarily but because of special circumstances do in fact flow from an injury.

specific performance   A contract remedy whereby the defendant is ordered to perform according to the terms of his contract.

stale check   A check more than six months past its date of issue.

standby letter of credit   The seller's bank promises to pay the buyer if the seller defaults on his contract to deliver conforming goods.

standing   The legal requirement that anyone seeking to challenge a particular action in court must demonstrate that such action substantially affects his legitimate interests before he will be entitled to bring suit.

stare decisis   A doctrine whereby a court is said to be bound to follow past cases that are like the present case on the facts and on the legal issues it presents, and that are issued by an authoritative court.

stated capital   Also called *capital stock*. A balance sheet account; shareholders' capital contributions representing the par value of par shares or stated value of no-par shares.

stated value   An arbitrary dollar amount assigned to shares by the board of directors, representing the minimum amount of consideration for which the corporation may issue the shares and the portion of consideration that must be allocated to the stated capital account.

state implementation plan   A document prepared by states in which the emissions to the air from individual sources are limited legally so that the area will meet the national ambient air quality standards.

status quo   The existing state of things. In contract law, returning a party to status quo or status quo ante means putting him in the position he was in before entering the contract.

statute of frauds   A statute that provides that no lawsuit may be brought to enforce certain classes of contracts unless there is a written note or memorandum signed by the party against whom enforcement is sought or by his agent.

statute of limitations   A statute that requires that certain classes of lawsuits must be brought within defined limits of time after the right to begin them accrued or the right to bring the lawsuit is lost.

stipulation   An agreement between opposing counsel in a pending action, usually required to be made in open court and entered on the minutes of the court, or else to be in writing and filed in the action, ordinarily entered into for the purpose of avoiding delay, trouble, or expense in the conduct of the action.

stock   A business's inventory. Also, as used in corporation and securities law, see *share*.

stock dividend   See *dividends, share*.

stockholder   See *shareholder*.

stock split   See *share split*.

stoppage in transitu   A right that the vendor of goods on credit has to recall them, or retake them, on the discovery of the insolvency of the vendee. It continues so long as the carrier remains in the possession and control of the goods or until there has been an actual or constructive delivery to the vendee, or some third person has acquired a bona fide right in them.

stop-payment order   A request made by the drawer of a check to the drawee asking that the order to pay not be followed.

straight voting   A form of voting for directors that ordinarily permits a shareholder to cast a number of votes equal to the number of shares he owns for as many nominees as there are directors to be elected. See *cumulative voting*.

strict liability   Legal responsibility placed on an individual for the results of his actions irrespective of whether he was culpable or at fault.

strike suit   In corporation law, a derivative suit motivated primarily by an intent to gain an out-of-court settlement for the suing shareholder personally or to earn large attorney's fees for lawyers, rather than to obtain a recovery for the corporation.

subchapter S corporation   See *S corporation*.

sub judice   Before a court.

sublease   A transfer of some but not all of a tenant's remaining right to possess property under a lease.

sub nom   Under the name of.

subpoena   A process for compelling a witness to appear before a court and give testimony.

subrogation   The substitution of one person in the place of another with reference to a lawful claim or right, frequently referred to as the doctrine of substitution. It is a device adopted or invented by equity to compel the ultimate discharge of a debt or obligation by the person who in good conscience ought to pay it.

subscription   In corporation law, a promise by a person to purchase from a corporation a specified number of shares at a specified price.

subsidiary corporation   A corporation owned and controlled by another corporation, called a *parent corporation*.

substantive law   The body of law setting out rights and duties that affect how people behave in organized social life. See *procedural law.*

sui generis   Of its own kind, unique, peculiar to itself.

summary judgment   A method of reaching a judgment in a civil case before trial. The standard for granting a motion for summary judgment is that there be no significant issue of material fact and that the moving party be entitled to judgment as a matter of law.

summary proceedings   Proceedings, usually statutory, in the course of which many formalities are dispensed with. But such proceedings are not concluded without proper investigation of the facts, or without notice, or an opportunity to be heard by the person alleged to have committed the act, or whose property is sought to be affected.

summons   A writ or process issued and served on a defendant in a civil action for the purpose of securing his appearance in the action.

superseding cause   See *intervening cause.*

supra   Above; above mentioned; in addition to.

surety   A person who promises to perform the same obligation as another person (the principal) and who is jointly liable along with the principal for that obligation's performance. See *guarantor.*

T

T/A   Trading as, indicating the use of a trade name.

tacking   The adding together of successive periods of adverse possession of persons in privity with each other, in order to constitute one continuous adverse possession for the time required by the statute, to establish title.

takeover   A tender offer; also applied generally to any acquisition of one business by another business.

tangible   Having a physical existence; real; substantial; evident.

tariff   A tax or duty imposed on goods by a nation when the goods are imported into that nation.

tax haven   A nation that has no or minimal taxation of personal, business, and investment income.

tenancy   General term indicating a possessory interest in property. In landlord–tenant law, a property owner's conveyance to another person of the right to possess the property exclusively for a period of time.

tenancy at sufferance   The leasehold interest that occurs when a tenant remains in possession of property after the expiration of a lease.

tenancy at will   A leasehold interest that occurs when property is leased for an indefinite period of time and is terminable at the will of either landlord or tenant.

tenancy by the entirety   A form of co-ownership of property by a married couple that gives the owners a right of survivorship and cannot be severed during life by the act of only one of the parties.

tenancy for a term   A leasehold interest that results when the landlord and tenant agree on a specific duration for a lease and fix the date on which the tenancy will terminate.

tenancy in common   A form of co-ownership of property that is freely disposable both during life and at death, and in which the co-owners have undivided interests in the property and equal rights to possess the property.

tender   An unconditional offer of payment, consisting in the actual production in money or legal tender of a sum not less than the amount due.

tender offer   A public offer by a bidder to purchase a subject company's shares directly from its shareholders at a specified price for a fixed period of time.

testament   A will; the disposition of one's property to take effect after death.

testator   A deceased person who died leaving a will.

testimony   In some contexts, the word bears the same import as the word *evidence,* but in most connections it has a much narrower meaning. Testimony is the words heard from the witness in court, and evidence is what the jury considers it worth.

thin capitalization   In corporation law, a ground for piercing the corporate veil due to the shareholders' contributing too little capital to the corporation in relation to its needs.

third-party beneficiary   A person who is not a party to a contract but who has the right to enforce it because the parties to the contract made the contract with the intent to benefit him.

title   Legal ownership; also, a document evidencing legal rights to real or personal property.

tombstone advertisement   A brief newspaper advertisement alerting prospective shareholders that an issuer is offering to sell the securities described in the advertisement.

tort   A private (civil) wrong against a person or his property.

tortfeasor   A person who commits a tort; a wrongdoer.

tortious   Partaking of the nature of a tort; wrongful; injurious.

trade fixtures   Articles of personal property that have been annexed to real property leased by a tenant during the term of the lease and that are necessary to the carrying on of a trade.

trademark   A distinctive word, name, symbol, device, or combination thereof, which enables consumers to identify favored products or services and which may find protection under state or federal law.

trade secret   A secret formula, pattern, process, program, device, method, technique, or compilation of information that is used in its owner's business and affords that owner a competitive advantage. Trade secrets are protected by state law.

transcript   A copy of a writing.

transferee   A person to whom a transfer is made.

transfer of partner's transferable interest   A partner's voluntary transfer of her transferable interest to another person, such as the partner's creditor, giving the transferee the right to receive the partner's share of distributions from the partnership.

transferor A person who makes a transfer.

treasury shares Previously outstanding shares repurchased by a corporation that are not canceled or restored to unissued status.

treble damages Three times provable damages, as may be granted to private parties bringing an action under the antitrust laws.

trespass An unauthorized entry on another's property.

trial An examination before a competent tribunal, according to the law of the land, of the facts or law put in issue in a cause, for the purpose of determining such issue. When the court hears and determines any issue of fact or law for the purpose of determining the rights of the parties, it may be considered a trial.

trust A legal relationship in which a person who has legal title to property has the duty to hold it for the use or benefit of another person. The term is also used in a general sense to mean confidence reposed in one person by another.

trustee A person in whom property is vested in trust for another.

trustee in bankruptcy The federal bankruptcy act defines the term as an officer, and he is an officer of the courts in a certain restricted sense, but not in any such sense as a receiver. He takes the legal title to the property of the bankrupt and in respect to suits stands in the same general position as a trustee of an express trust or an executor. His duties are fixed by statute. He is to collect and reduce to money the property of the estate of the bankrupt.

U

ultra vires Beyond the powers. In administrative law, it describes an act that is beyond the authority granted to an administrative agency by its enabling legislation. In corporation law, it describes a corporation's performing an act beyond the limits of its purposes as stated in its articles of incorporation.

unconscionable In contract law, a contract that is grossly unfair or one-sided; one that "shocks the conscience of the court."

undisclosed principal In agency law, a principal whom a third party lacks knowledge or the reason to know the principal's existence and identity.

unidentified principal In agency law, a principal whom a third party knows or has reason to know exists but who lacks knowledge or reason to know the principal's identity.

unilateral contract A contract formed by an offer or a promise on one side for an act to be done on the other, and a doing of the act by the other by way of acceptance of the offer or promise; that is, a contract wherein the only acceptance of the offer that is necessary is the performance of the act.

unliquidated Undetermined in amount.

usage of trade Customs and practices generally known by people in the business and usually assumed by parties to a contract for goods of that type.

usurpation In corporation law, an officer, director, or shareholder's taking to himself a business opportunity that belongs to his corporation.

usury The taking of more than the law allows on a loan or for forbearance of a debt. Illegal interest; interest in excess of the rate allowed by law.

V

valid Effective; operative; not void; subsisting; sufficient in law.

value Under the Code (except for negotiable instruments and bank collections), generally any consideration sufficient to support a simple contract.

vendee A purchaser of property. The word is more commonly applied to a purchaser of real property, the word *buyer* being more commonly applied to the purchaser of personal property.

vendor A person who sells property to a vendee. The words *vendor* and *vendee* are more commonly applied to the seller and purchaser of real estate, and the words *seller* and *buyer* are more commonly applied to the seller and purchaser of personal property.

venire The name of a writ by which a jury is summoned.

venue A requirement distinct from jurisdiction that the court be geographically situated so that it is the most appropriate and convenient court to try the case.

verdict Usually, the decision made by a jury and reported to the judge on the matters or questions submitted to it at trial. In some situations, however, the judge may be the party issuing a verdict, as, for example, in the motion for a directed verdict. See *directed verdict*.

versus Against.

vest To give an immediate fixed right of present or future enjoyment.

vicarious liability The imposition of liability on one party for the wrongs of another. Also called *imputed liability*. For example, the civil liability of a principal for the wrongs his agent commits when acting within the scope of his employment. See *respondeat superior*. Such liability is also occasionally encountered in the criminal context (e.g., the criminal liability that some regulatory statutes impose on managers for the actions of employees under their supervision).

void That which is entirely null. A void act is one that is not binding on either party and that is not susceptible of ratification.

voidable Capable of being made void; not utterly null, but annullable, and hence that may be either voided or confirmed. See *avoid*.

voidable title A title that is capable of, or subject to, being judged invalid or void.

voting trust A type of shareholder voting arrangement by which shareholders transfer their voting rights to a voting trustee.

W

waive   To throw away; to relinquish voluntarily, as a right that one may enforce, if he chooses.

waiver   The intentional relinquishment of a known right. It is a voluntary act and implies an election by the party to dispense with something of value, or to forgo some advantage that he or she might have demanded and insisted on.

warehouse receipt   A receipt issued by a person engaged in the business of storing goods for hire.

warrant   An order authorizing a payment of money by another person to a third person. Also, an option to purchase a security. As a verb, the word means to defend; to guarantee; to enter into an obligation of warranty.

warrant of arrest   A legal process issued by competent authority, usually directed to regular officers of the law, but occasionally issued to private persons named in it, directing the arrest of a person or persons on grounds stated therein.

warranty   An undertaking relating to characteristics of a thing being sold; a guaranty.

waste   The material alteration, abuse, or destructive use of property by one in rightful possession of it that results in injury to one having an underlying interest in it.

watered shares   Also called *watered stock*. Shares issued in exchange for property that has been overvalued. See *bonus shares* and *discount shares*.

will   A document executed with specific legal formalities that contains a person's instructions about the disposition of his property at his death.

winding up   In partnership and corporation law, the orderly liquidation of the business's assets.

writ   A commandment of a court given for the purpose of compelling certain action from the defendant, and usually executed by a sheriff or other judicial officer.

writ of certiorari   An order of a court to an inferior court to forward the record of a case for reexamination by the superior court.

wrongful use of civil proceedings   An intentional tort designed to protect against the wrongful initiation of civil proceedings.

Index

A

Abandoned property, 590–593
Abandonment
    lease, 660–661
    patents, 242
    trademarks, 265
ABKCO Music Inc. v. Harrisongs Music, Ltd., 902–903
Abnormally dangerous activities, 234
Abrahamson, Judge, 861
Abstract of title, 628
Abuse of process, 195
Acceptance, contracts
    goods, 553
    insurance, 688–689
    offer; *see* Contracts: acceptance
Acceptor, of drafts, 808
Accession, obtaining personal property by, 597
Accommodation party, negotiable instruments
    discharge, 866
    liability, 849–850
Accord and satisfaction, 352, 467
Acid rain controls, 1347
Acquisition
    controlling block of shares, 1151–1152
    corporations, 1151
    personal property, 597
    real property, 623–625
Action and sale, foreclosure by, 729
Act of state doctrine, 1311
Actual authority, 898, 956
Actual cash value, property insurance, 699
Actual cause, in negligence actions, 224–225
Actual reliance, in misrepresentation, 362
Act utilitarianism, 96
Adams, Judge, 279, 509
Adaptation as element of fixture classification, 614
Ademption, 668
Adhesion, contracts of, 403, 406
Adjudicative proceedings, 1226–1227
Administrative agencies
    adjudicatory powers, 1207–1208
    congressional controls on, 1208
    Constitution's applicability to, 1197–1199
    creation of, 1196–1201
    delegation of powers to, 1199–1201
    deregulation versus regulation, 1219–1220
    failure to regulate, 1206–1207
    industry influence on, 1219
    information controls, 1216–1219
    investigative powers, 1202–1203
    judicial review, 1208–1216

    legal bases for challenging actions, 1214
    nature of, 1194–1195
    organizational structure, 1202
    origins of, 1196
    powers of, 1202–1208
    presidential controls on, 1208
    regulations and standards; *see* Administrative regulations
    rulemaking powers, 1205–1207
    separation of powers principle, 1199
    types of, 1201–1202
Administrative dissolution, 1109
Administrative law judge, 1207
Administrative Procedure Act, 1202, 1205–1206, 1208
Administrative regulations
    deregulation versus regulation, 1219–1220
    historical view of changing character of, 1219
    interpretive rules, 1205
    judicial review, 1208–1216
    legal bases for challenging, 1214
    legislative rules, 1205–1206
    nature of, 5–6
    preemption of private suits, 1220–1221
    procedural rules, 1205
    rulemaking, 1205–1207
    standards of review, 1214–1216
Administrator of estate, 678
Admissions, request for, 40–41
Admission to public, duty to maintain property leased for, 653
ADR; *see* Alternative dispute resolution
Adsit Co. v. Gustin, 326–327
Adversary system, 39
Adverse opinions, 1180
Adverse possession, 623–624
Advertisements
    contract offer, 313–314
    false, 280–283
    tombstone ad, 1121, 1122
    warranties and, 507
Advised letter of credit, 551
Advisory letters, FTC, 1226
Advisory opinions, 23
Affidavit, self-proving, 678
Affirmance on appeal, 48
Affirmative defense, 39
Affirmative easements, 619
After-acquired property, 744
Age Discrimination in Employment Act, 20–22, 1330–1331
Agency decisions, 5–6
Agency law
    account, agent's duty to, 904
    act of parties, termination by, 907
    agreement, agent's liability by, 921

Agency law—*Cont.*
  authority, 898
  capacity, 897
  care and skill, agent's duty to act with, 903
  compensate agent, principal's duty to, 906–907
  confidentiality, 902
  conflicts of interest, 902
  contracts
    agent's liability, 919–923
    principal's liability, 914–919
    subagent's, 919
    suits against principal and agent, 923
  definition of agency, 896
  disclosed principal, 919
  duties
    agent to principal, 901–905
    principal to agent, 906–907
  formation of relationship, 897
  knowledge of agent imputed to principal, 917
  loyalty, duty of, 902
  nondelegable obligations, 897–898
  nonexistent principal, 920
  notification to agent binding on principal, 917
  notify principal, agent's duty to, 904
  obey instructions, agent's duty to, 903
  operation of law, termination by, 907–908
  partially disclosed principal, 920
  ratification, 917–918
  reimbursement and indemnity, principal's duty of, 907
  security, termination of agency powers given as, 908–909
  subagent, contracts by, 919
  termination of relationship, 907–910
  third parties
    notice of termination to, 910
    relations of principal and agent, 913–928
  tort liability
    agent's, 927
    independent contractor's, 926
    misrepresentation by agent, 926–927
    suits against principal and agent, 927–928
  types of agents, 899
  undisclosed principal, 920
Agent
  agency relationship; *see* Agency law
  definition of, 896
  duties to principal, 901–905
  tort liability of, 927
  types of, 899
Agricultural cooperatives and antitrust liability, 1307
Aiding and abetting, 1175
Air France v. Saks, 23
Air pollution, 1347–1352
Albin, Judge, 472
Alcohol testing of employees, 1335
Alexander, Judge, 921

Alien status, Equal Protection Clause and, 75
Alito, Justice Samuel A., 74, 75
Allstate Indemnity Co. v. Ruiz, 41–43
Alteration
  checks, 871, 877–878
  discharge of contract by, 468
Alternative dispute resolution
  arbitration, 49–50
  court-annexed arbitration, 52
  early neutral evaluation (ENE), 53
  general information, 49
  magistrates, 53
  med/arb, 53
  mediation, 52
  minitrial, 53
  private judges, 53
  private panels, 53
  settlement, 49
  summary jury trial, 52–53
Ambient air control standards, 1347
Amerada Hess Corp. v. Director of Taxation, 1014
American Federal Bank, FSB v. Parker, 865
American Insurance Association v. Garamendi, 695
American legal realism, 9–10
American Library Association v. Federal Communications Commission, 1214
Americans with Disabilities Act
  employer's responsibilities, 1331–1333
  landlord's responsibilities, 653
  modifications of property, 632
  new construction, 632
  public accommodation, applicability to places of, 631
  remedies for violations, 632
American Trucking Assns., Inc. v. Mich. Pub. Serv. Comm., 1014
American Trucking Assns., Inc. v. Scheiner, 1014
America Online, Inc. v. St. Paul Mercury Insurance Co., 707–708
Amoco Oil Co. v. Toppert, 393
Ancillary covenant not to compete, 398
Ancillary restraints, 1267
Angelini, Justice, 925
Anstead, Judge, 13
Answer, 39–40
Anticipatory repudiation/breach, 464–465, 563
Anticompetitive behavior, FTC authority over, 1226–1227
Anticybersquatting Consumer Protection Act, 273
Antidiscrimination
  credit, 1243
  employment; *see* Discrimination in employment
  housing, 626
Anti-Drug Abuse Act of 1988, 26–27
Antiterrorism legislation, 147–148
Antitrust
  Chicago School theories, 1255, 1256, 1289
  civil litigation, 1257

Clayton Act; *see* Clayton Act
concerted action to restrain trade, 1257–1273
congressional intent in legislation, 1254–1255
criminal prosecutions, 1256–1257
direct injury, importance of, 1257
exceptions and exemptions, 1306–1308
exclusive dealing agreements, 1272
group boycotts, 1268–1269
historical background, 1254–1255
horizontal division of markets, 1267
horizontal price-fixing, 1259
joint ventures by competitors, 1272–1273
mergers; *see* Mergers
monopoly power; *see* Monopolies
National Cooperative Research and Production
        Act, 1272–1273
Noerr-Pennington doctrine, 1308
per se unlawful actions, 1258, 1261
pretrial settlements, 1256
price discrimination; *see* Price discrimination
Robinson-Patman Act; *see* Robinson-Patman Act
rule of reason analysis, 1258, 1261
Sherman Act; *see* Sherman Act
traditional theories, 1255
treble damages, 1257
tying agreements, 1268–1272, 1288
vertical price-fixing, 1260–1267
vertical restraints on competition, 1267–1268
Anza v. Ideal Steel Supply Corp., 161–163
Apparent authority, 898–899, 914–915, 956–957, 973
Appeals and appellate courts
    general information, 48
    jurisdiction, 30, 36–37
Appearance in court, 39
Applications, patent, 242, 243
Approval, sale on, 496–497
Arbitrary and capricious test, 1216
Arbitration (ADR), 52
Arbitration clause, 299
Argumentum ad baculum in ethical decisions, 112
Argumentum ad hominem in ethical decisions, 112–113
Argumentum ad populum in ethical decisions, 111–112
*Armstrong Surgical Center, Inc. v. Armstrong County
        Memorial Hospital,* 1308–1310
Armstrong v. Rohm and Haas Company, Inc., 309–310
Arnhold v. Ocean Atlantic Woodland Corp., 462–464
Arnold, Circuit Judge, 193
Arraignment, in criminal law, 138
Arthur Andersen LLP v. United States, 135–137, 1186–1188
Articles of incorporation
    amendments to, 1088
    contents of, 1031
    filing of, 1031–1032
    general information, 1030–1031
    purpose clause, 1048–1049

Artisan's lien, 602, 758
Asahi Metal Industry Co. v. Superior Court, 38
Ashcroft v. American Civil Liberties Union, 132
Ashcroft v. Free Speech Coalition, 66, 132
Assault, 175–176
Asset protection trusts, Chapter 7, 779
Assignee
    definition, 435
    liability of assignor to, 441
Assignments
    contracts; *see* Contracts: assignments
    leases, 659–660
    mortgage, interest in, 729
    patents, 247
    trade secrets, 274
Assignor
    definition, 435
    liability to assignees, 441
Assumption of risk, 534
Assurance, in sales contracts, 560
Atlantic Coast Airlines v. Cook, 221–224
Attachment
    element of fixture classification, 614
    perfection of security interest by, 748–749
    security interest, 742
Attestation clause, 669
Attorney's fees as remedy, 1326
Auctions as invitation of contract offer, 314
Auditors; *see* Securities professionals
Audit requirements, 1184
Authority
    in agency law, 898
    argument from in ethical decisions, 113
Authorized shares, 1037
Automatic novation clause, 1028
Automobile liability policies, 705
Automobile pollution, 1351–1352
Auto-Owners Insurance Co. v. Harvey, 693,
        702–704
Award, in arbitration, 49

B

Back pay as remedy, 1326
Bad faith, insurance contract, 708–709
Bailments
    bailee, 598
    bailee's duties
        care of property, 599–600
        return of property, 600–601
    bailor's liability
        defects in property, 602–603
        limits on, 602
        misdelivery, 602
    common carriers, 603
    creation of, 598

Bailments—*Cont.*
  hotelkeepers, 603
  involuntary, 605
  nature and essential elements of, 598
  return of property, 600
  right to compensation, 602
  safe-deposit boxes, 605
  types of, 599
Baily-Schiffman, Judge, 837
Baker, Judge, 326
Baker v. Burlington Coat Factory Warehouse, 582–583
Baker v. International Syndicate, Inc., 569–570
Balance sheet test, dividends, 1098
Bandwagon fallacy in ethical decisions, 112
Bank One, N.A. v. Streeter, 854–856
Bankruptcy
  Chapter 7: liquidation, 771–782
  Chapter 11: reorganization, 790–794
  Chapter 12: family farms, 794–796
  Chapter 13: consumer debt adjustments, 796–800
  collective bargaining agreements, 794
  contracts discharged by, 469
  core proceeding, 770
  courts, 770–771
  debt payment as consideration barred by, 356
  discharge, 782–790, 798–800
  federal law: overview, 769–770
  reaffirmation agreements, 785–786
  repeat bankruptcies, 800
  types of proceedings, 770
Bankruptcy courts, 36
Banks
  Check 21, 886–887
  checks; *see* Checks
  death or incompetence of customer, 876
  duty to pay, 870
  electronic transfers, 887–891
  Regulation CC, 881, 886
  right to charge customer's account, 870–871, 877
  UCC provisions, 869–870, 880–881
Bargain and sale, deed of, 628
Bartle, III, Judge, 345
Basic assumptions of contract, mistakes about, 365–366
Basic Inc. v. Levinson, 1142, 1143
Basis-of-the-bargain
  damages, 526
  UCC requirement, 507
Bataillon, Chief District Judge, 511
Battery, 173–174
"Battle of the Forms," 329
Baxter v. City of Nashville, 637
Bearer paper, 823
Beatty, Judge, 402
Becknell v. Board of Education, 1324–1326
Bell, Chief Judge, 817

Belle Terre v. Boraas, 637
Beneficiary
  creditor beneficiaries, 447
  donee beneficiaries, 447
  generally, 679
  incidental beneficiaries, 446–447
  insurance, 688
  intended beneficiaries, 446–447
  third party, 446–449
  vesting of rights, 448–449
Benefit theory, 1012
Bentham, Jeremy, 96
Benton, Circuit Judge, 1174
Benton v. Cameco Corp., 38
Bequest, 668
Berdon, Associate Justice, 489
Berman v. Parker, 85, 86
Berne Convention, 268
Bersani v. U.S. Environmental Protection Agency, 1358–1359
Best efforts underwriting, 1119
Bids as invitation of contract offer, 314
Bilateral contracts
  acceptance, 334–335
  generally, 294–295
Bill of lading, negotiable, 551
Bill of Rights, 3, 57
  Eighth Amendment, 133
  Fifth Amendment, 71–80, 84–86, 148–153
  First Amendment; *see* Freedom of speech
  Fourth Amendment, 139–146
  incorporation process, 63
  Sixth Amendment, 127–128, 153–154
Bill of sale as security, 719
Bills of lading, 605, 607
Binders (insurance), 689
Black v. William Insulation Co., 225–227
Blue-sky laws, 1153
Board of directors
  advances for legal fees, 1079
  audit committee, 1050
  authority under corporation statutes, 1049
  committees, delegations to, 1049–1050
  compensation committee, 1050
  conflicts of interest, 1067–1069
  demand on directors to bring suit, 1100–1101
  dissent, right of, 1073
  duties to corporation, 1056–1073
  election of, 1050–1052, 1084–1087
  executive committee, 1049–1050
  indemnification of, 1078–1079
  meeting of, 1053–1054
  nominating committee, 1050
  oppression of minority shareholders, 1071
  proxies, 1051–1052
  removal of directors, 1053

rights and liabilities, 1050
self-dealing, 1069
shareholder litigation committee, 1050
takeovers, opposition to, 1063–1067
torts and crimes, liability for, 1074–1075
trading on inside information, 1072–1073
usurpation of company's assets, 1069
vacancies, 1053
Boehm, Justice, 529
Bohanon, Bankruptcy Judge, 742
Bombliss v. Cornelsen, 31–33
Bona fide occupational qualification (BFOQ), 1324
Bona fide purchaser, 758
Bonds, 1038
Booking, in criminal law, 137
Bowman, Presiding Justice, 507
Boyd v. United States, 152
Boyko, U.S. District Judge, 730
Braswell v. United States, 153
Breach of contract
anticipatory repudiation, 464–465
bad faith, 708–709
conditions, 453–454
divisible contracts, 465
effect on risk of loss, 496
equitable remedies for, 473–474
insurance contracts, 694
legal remedies for, 469–473
limitations on recovery for, 469–470
materiality of, 460–461
quasi-contracts, 465
recovery by person committing, 465
remedies, 468–474
timeliness of performance, 462–464
Breach of trust, 1165
Brehm v. Eisner, 1058–1063
Brendlin v. California, 140
Brentwood Academy v. Tennessee Secondary School Athletic Association, 64
Breyer, Judge, 1078
Breyer, Justice Stephen G., 72, 75, 146, 250, 1267
Bribery, 159–160
Brister, Judge, 438
Brodie v. Jordan, 1105–1107
Brooke Group Ltd. v. Brown & Williamson Tobacco Corp., 1300–1302
Brooks v. Lewin Realty III, Inc., 650–653
Brown, Vice Chancellor, 974
Browsewrap contracts, 315
Brunswick Corp. v. Pueblo Bowl-o-Mat, Inc., 1257
Bryner, Chief Justice, 387
Burke, Justice, 979
Burlington Industries, Inc. v. Ellerth, 1328
Burton v. Wilmington Parking Authority, 63
Bush v. Gore, 57

Business compulsion, in contracts, 371
Business Electronics Corp. v. Sharp Electronics Corp., 1268
Business judgment rule, 1056–1057
Business liability policies, 701, 705
Business purpose test of freeze-out, 1071
Business records, Fifth Amendment and, 152–153
Butler v. Beer Across America, 488
Buy-and-sell agreement for share sales, 1041
Buyers in ordinary course of business, 492, 758
Bylaws of corporation, 1032
Byrne, Judge, 396
Byrne v. Boadle, 231

C

Cabot Corporation v. AVX Corporation, 372–373
Cabranes, Circuit Judge, 900
Caldwell, United States District Judge, 1325
Calkins, Justice, 760
Callam, Judge, 462
Canceled shares, 1037
CAN-SPAM Act, 1232
Capacity
in agency law, 897
to contract; *see* Contracts: capacity
criminal law and, 134–135
definition, 378
testamentary, 668–669
trust creation, 680
Capital Markets Efficiency Act of 1996, 1153
Capper-Volstead Act, 1307
Cappy, Justice, 596
Care, duty of; *see* Duty of care
Care of prudent person standard, 1160
Carey Station Village Homeowners Association, Inc. v. Carey Station Village, Inc., 278–279
Cargill, Inc. & Excel Corp. v. Monfort of Colorado, Inc., 1281
Carlyle, Thomas, 96
Carriage of Goods by Sea Act (COGSA), 605
Carrow v. Arnold, 427–430
Carr v. CIGNA Securities, Inc., 1141–1142, 1175
Casebolt, Judge, 898
Case law; *see* Common law (case law)
Cashier's check, 811, 875, 876
Castillo, Judge, 347
Categorical imperative, business ethics, 93–94
Causa mortis, gift, 594
Causation in negligence actions, 221–231
Cavanaugh, U.S.D.J., 399
Caveat emptor, 505, 629
Caveat venditor, 505–506
C.B.C. Distribution & Marketing, Inc. v. Major League Baseball Advanced Media, L.P., 193–195
CBOCS West, Inc. v. Humphries, 1330
Cease and desist orders, 1116, 1226–1227

Central Bank of Denver, N.A. v. First Interstate Bank of Denver, N.A., 1172, 1175
CERCLA, 1364–1367
Certificate of authority, 1015
Certificate of limited partnership, 994
Certificate of organization (LLC), 986
Certificates of deposit, 808
Certification marks, 264
Certified check, 875, 876
Certiorari jurisdiction, 37
C & F (cost and freight), 494
Chapter 7: liquidation
    asset protection trusts (fraudulent transfer), 779
    attorney certification of petition, 771–772
    automatic stay provisions, 772
    claims, 781–782
    credit counseling requirement, 771
    debtor education requirement, 771
    duties of trustee, 773
    election of trustee, 772–773
    estate
        composition of, 773–774
        distribution of, 782
    fraudulent transfers, 778–779
    health care business, 773
    homestead exemption, 776
    interim trustee, 771
    liens, voiding of, 776–777
    means test, 786
    meeting of creditors, 772–773
    order of relief, 772
    petitions, 771
    preferential liens, 777
    preferential payment, 777
    proof of claim, 781
    relief, order of, 772
    retention bonuses (fraudulent transfer), 779
    U.S. Trustee's role, 773
Chapter 11: reorganization
    collective bargaining agreements, 794
    cram down confirmation, 791
    creditor acceptance confirmation, 790–791
    nonresidential real property, 794
    prepackaged plans, 790
    use and misuse of, 793
Chapter 12: family farms, 794–796
Charging order (partner), 947–948
Charitable subscriptions, 356
Charitable trusts, 680
Chatigny, District Judge, 303
Check Clearing for the 21st Century Act (Check 21), 886–887
Checks
    altered, 871, 877–878
    availability of funds, 885–886
    cashier's check, 811, 876

certified check, 875, 876
    collection, 880–881
    conversion of check, 8w6
    dishonored, 881
    forgeries, 877–879
    form of commercial paper, 808–811
    funds availability, 885–886
    holds, 885–886
    incomplete, 871
    indorsement; *see* Indorsement
    multiple forgeries or alterations, 877–878
    postdated, 871
    presentment of, 852–853
    stale checks, 871
    stop-payment orders, 871–873
    teller's check, 811
Checks and balances, 57
Chicago Lawyers Committee for Civil Rights Under Law, Inc. v. Craigslist, Inc., 15
Chicago School theories, 1255, 1256, 1272
Child Online Protection Act, 132
Choice of law clause, 299
Christmas Lumber Co., Inc. v. Valiga, 1034–1035
Churchich v. Duda, 27–28
Cicero, Marcus Tullius, 9
CIF (cost, insurance, and freight), 494
Circuit City Stores, Inc. v. Mantor, 404–406
Circuits
    courts of appeal; *see* Appeals and appellate courts
    federal judicial circuits, 37
Circular reasoning in ethical decisions, 111
Cisco v. King, 1340–1341
CISG; *see* Convention on Contracts for the International Sale of Goods (CISG)
City of Cleburne v. Cleburne Living Centers, 637
City of Philadelphia v. New Jersey, 1364
City of Renton v. Playtime Theaters, Inc., 637
Civil law, 8
Civil liability, torts, 170
Civil procedure, 39–49
    adversary system, 39
    affirmative defense, 39
    answer, 39–40
    class actions, 48–49
    complaint, 39
    counterclaim, 40
    demurrer, 40
    discovery, 40–45
    enforcement of judgments, 48
    interrogatories, 40–41
    judgment notwithstanding the verdict, 47
    jury trials, 47
    multiparty cases, 48–49
    new trial motion, 47
    pleadings, 39–40

preponderance of evidence standard, 39
pretrial conference, 45
reply, 40
request for admissions, 40–41
request for production of documents, 41
service, 39
summary judgment, 45
summons, 39
trials, 45–47
verdicts, 47
Civil proceedings, misuse of, 195
Civil Rights Act (1964), Title VII, 26, 1323–1334
Claims, Chapter 7, 781–782
Claims in recoupment, 833, 839
Class actions
generally, 48–49
shareholders' lawsuits, 1099–1100
Class voting, 1051
Clayton Act, 1227
congressional intent, 1287–1288
cooperatives, 1307
labor unions, 1307
Section 3, tying and exclusive dealing, 1288–1289
Section 8, interlocks, 1298–1299
Section 7 mergers, 1289–1298
Clean Air Act, 1347–1352
Clean Water Act, 1355–1358
Clickwrap contracts, 34, 294, 315
Clifford, Justice, 824
Climate change, 1352–1355
Close corporations
definition of, 1010
dissolution power of shareholder, 1110
incorporation process, 1032
management of, 1055
protection of minority shareholders, 1055
transfer of shares, 1042, 1044
Codes of ethics/conduct, 99
Codicils, 673
Coffey, Circuit Judge, 462
Coggins v. New England Patriots Football Club, Inc., 1072
Coinsurance clause, property insurance, 700
Coleman, Judge, 415
Colgate doctrine, 1261, 1268
Collateral
negotiable instruments referring to, 818
proceeds from, 744, 762–763
sale of, 761
types of, 741
Collateral contracts, 414
Collective bargaining agreements, 794
Collective marks, 264
Color discrimination, 1327
Colten v. Kentucky, 133
Coma Corporation v. Kansas Department of Labor, 393–394

Co-maker, 809
Combination to restrain trade, 1257
Commerce Clause, 59–62, 81–82
states as market participants, 82–84
Commerce power of Congress, 59–62
Commercial appropriation of name or likeness, 192–193, 280
Commercial impracticability and contract
performance, 467–468, 563
Commercial loan note, 809
Commercial paper
generally, 806–807
negotiable instruments; *see* Negotiable instruments
transfer of, 842
Commercial speech
First Amendment and, 65–70, 131
Supreme Court test for, 65–67
Commercial torts
generally, 276–279
unfair competition, 280–283
Commercial unit, 553
*Commodity Futures Trading Commission v.
Collins,* 1204–1205
Common areas, duty to maintain, 653
Common carriers, special bailments for, 603
Common law (case law)
acceptance of contract, 327
case law reasoning, 12–13
corporations, 1011
definiteness of contract terms, 310–311
exceptions to at will employment doctrine, 1338–1341
general contract requirements, 296, 298
general information, 3
modification of contract, 348–349
securities professionals' liability to third
parties, 1165–1170
Common law liens, 724
Common shares, 1036, 1085
Communications Decency Act, 15, 17–20, 132, 232
Community property, 618
Comparable worth discrimination theory, 1334
Comparative fault
generally, 233
product liability, 534–535
Comparative negligence
generally, 232–233
impostors and fictitious payees, 860
product liability, 534–535
Compassionate Use Act, 59–62
Compensation
large partnerships, 954
partner, 953–954
right to, 602
takings clause, 85
Compensatory damages
breach of contract, 470, 708–709

Compensatory damages—*Cont.*
  discrimination in employment, 1326–1327
  torts, 170
Competition, unfair business practices, 280–283
Complaint, 39
Complete Auto Transit, Inc. v. Brady, 1014
Composition agreements, 352
Comprehensive Environmental Response, Compensation, and
    Liability Act (CERCLA), 1364–1367
Comprehensive general liability policies, 701
Computer Fraud and Abuse Act, 164, 165
Computers
  code and copyrights, 252
  crimes involving, 163–165
Concealment of facts in contracts, 362
Concept reviews
  attachment (security interest), 745
  bailees and bailors, duties of, 604
  bankruptcy
    comparison of major forms, 799
    distribution of debtor's estate, 783
  consideration, 353
  contracts
    buyer's remedies, 583
    formation of contracts, 484
    misrepresentation and fraud, 366
    mistake as ground for avoidance, 370
    parol evidence rule, 427
    risk of loss, 497
    sales contracts: acceptance, revocation, rejection, 559
    seller's remedies, 575
    statute of frauds, 419
    substantial performance, 460
    termination of contract offers, 318
    time for performance, 464
    title and third parties, 493
    undue influence, 374
  corporations: roles of shareholders and board of
      directors, 1110
  distribution of debtor's estate, 783
  employment discrimination laws, 1334
  environmental laws, 1368
  equal protection and levels of scrutiny, 80
  First Amendment, 67
  indorsement, 829
  negotiability, 820
  negotiable instruments
    claims and defenses against payment, 783
    contract liability based on signature, 853
    holder in due course, 835
    multiple forgeries or alterations, 880
    presentment warranties, 858
    transfer warranties, 857
  partner's death or retirement, 982
  perfection of security interest, 752

principal's tort liability, 927
property
  fixtures, 615
  rights of finders of personal property, 595
  security interests in real property, 733
resisting requests to act unethically, 118
securities law
  due diligence defense, 1135
  exemptions from registration under 1933 Act,
      1128–1129
  information requirements for registered offerings, 1123
  liability of professional to nonclients, 1171
  liability sections of 1933 and 1934 Acts, 1176–1177
  trading on inside information, 1145
security interest
  attachment, 745
  perfection, 752
  priority rules, 762
tenancy, types of, 647
termination of contract offers, 318
Concerted action to restrain trade, 1257–1258
Concerted refusal to deal, 1268
Concurrent condition, 454–455
Concurrent jurisdiction, 36
Concurrent powers, 58
Conditional gift, 595
Condition precedent, 454
Conditions of contract, 453–459
Condition subsequent, 455
Condominium ownership, 618–619
Confidentiality
  agency law, 902
  agreements, 398
Confinement, intentional, 177–180
Confirmed letter of credit, 551, 552
Conflicts of interest
  agency law, 902
  corporate boards and officers, 1067–1069
  partnership, 952
  securities analysts, 1176–1179
Conflicts of law, 6
Confusion, obtaining personal property by, 597
Conglomerate mergers, 1297–1298
Congress, U.S.
  commerce power, 59–62
  delegation of powers, 1199–1201
  enumerated powers, 58
  regulatory powers, 58–63
  spending power, 63
  taxing power, 62–63
Consent orders, 1207–1208, 1227
Consent to contract, invalid, 360–374
Consequential damages
  breach of contract, 470
  product liability, 526

Consideration
  contracts; *see* Contracts: consideration
  insurance, 688–689
Consignment sales, 498
Consolidations, 1088
Conspiracy to restrain trade, 1257
Constitution, U.S.
  administrative agencies, applicability to, 1197–1199
  Bill of Rights, 3, 57
  checks and balances, 57
  Commerce Clause, 59–62, 81–82
  Copyright Clause, 252–253
  criminalizing behavior, limits on, 131–134
  defamation and, 186–191, 190–191
  due process; *see* Due process
  Eighth Amendment, 133
  enumerated powers, 58
  equal protection, 72–80
  executive powers, 57
  federalism, 2–3, 57
  federal supremacy, 57
  Fifth Amendment, 71–80, 84–86, 132, 148–153, 1203
  First Amendment; *see* Freedom of speech
  Fourteenth Amendment, 71–80, 84–86, 132–133
  Fourth Amendment, 139–146, 1203
  freedom of speech; *see* Freedom of speech
  government action requirement, 63–64
  independent checks, 58, 63–86
  judicial powers, 57
  legislative powers, 57
  means-end tests, 64–65, 72
  privacy right, 131, 139–142
  public function doctrine, 63–64
  safeguards, 139–154
  separation of powers, 2, 56–57, 1199
  Sixth Amendment, 127–128, 153–154
  Supreme Court's role, 57–58
  text of, Appendix A-1–A-10
  Twenty-sixth Amendment, 380
Constitutionality
  employer searches, 1335–1336
  zoning ordinances, 637
Constitutions, functions of, 2–3, 56
Constructive bailee, 605
Constructive conditions, 456
Constructive eviction, 648–649
Constructive fraud, 1170
Constructive trusts, 684
Consultants; *see* Securities professionals
Consumer debt adjustments, Chapter 13 bankruptcy, 796–800
Consumer goods, creditor's security interest in, 761
Consumer Product Safety Act, 1248
Consumer Product Safety Commission, 1248
Continuation statement, 745
Contract clause, 80–81

Contract offer
  advertisements as, 313–314
  communication to offeree, 313
  death of party terminating, 318
  definiteness of terms, 309–311
  destruction of subject matter terminating, 318
  insanity of party terminating, 318
  intent to contract, 306–307
  intervening illegality terminating, 318
  nonrevocation situations, 316–317
  objective theory of contracts, 308
  offeror as "master of the offer," 315
  option for nonrevocation, 316
  rejection, 317–318
  requirements of, 307–315
  revocation, 316–317
  specified time limitations, 315
  termination of, 315–320
  terms included in, 314
  unilateral contracts and power to revoke, 316
  unspecified time for acceptance, 315–316
Contracts
  acceptance
    of contract offer; *see* Contracts: acceptance
    of goods, 553
  adhesion, 403, 406
  assignment of contracts; *see* Contracts: assignments
  bilateral, 294–295
  breach; *see* Breach of contract
  capacity; *see* Contracts: capacity
  collateral contracts, 414
  common law application, 296, 298, 310–311
  conditions, 453–459
  consent invalidity obtained, 360–374
  consideration; *see* Contracts: consideration
  definition of, 290
  delegation of duties, 441–445
  disaffirmance; *see* Disaffirmance of contracts
  discharge, 468–469
  divisible contracts, 407–408
  elements of, 291–292
  enforcement by third-party beneficiary, 446
  evolution of law governing, 291
  exclusive dealing contracts, 487
  exculpatory clauses, 400–401
  executed, 295
  executory, 295
  express, 295
  foreseeable reliance, 302–303
  fraud, 362–365
  functions of, 290–291
  goods (UCC), 296
  governing law, 295–300
  hybrid, 296
  illegality as grounds for nonenforcement, 392–409

Contracts—*Cont.*
  implied, 295
  indemnity contracts, 699
  information contracts, 296
  insurance contracts, 688–689
  interference with, 277–278
  interpretation of contracts, 430–431
  lack of capacity, effect of, 378–379
  land contracts, 732
  listing contracts, 625–626
  merchants, standard for, 299–300
  methods of making, 291
  misrepresentation, 362–365
  mistakes, 365–369
  needs contract, 483, 485
  noncompetition clauses, 398–400
  noncontract obligations, 300–302
  nonperformance, excuses for, 465–468
  offer; *see* Contract offer
  online, 294
  oral, 412
  output contract, 483, 485
  parol evidence rule, 425–427
  performance; *see* Performance of contracts;
     Performance of sales contracts
  preincorporation contracts, 1027–1029
  promissory estoppel, 302–303, 425
  public policy, agreements violating; *see* Contracts
     violating public policy
  quasi-contract; *see* Quasi-contracts
  ratification, 360, 381
  remedies, 5
  remedy for breach of illegal agreement, 406–409
  rescission of, 360–362, 407
  Restatement (Second) of Contracts; see Restatement
     (Second) of Contracts
  restrain trade, contracts to, 1257
  revocation
     acceptance of goods, 554
     offer of contract, 316–317
  sale of real estate or intangibles, 296
  sales contracts; *see* Sales contracts
  services (common law), 296
  signature, 412
  stages of making, 292
  standard form, 291
  statutes, agreements violating, 394–397
  suits against principal and agent, 923
  surety and principal relationship, 721
  third-party rights
     assignments; *see* Contracts: assignments
     beneficiaries, 446–449
     delegation of duties, 441–445
  types of, 294–295
  unconscionable, 299, 369, 403
  undue influence, 374

  unenforceable, 295, 392–409, 412
  unfairness in, 403–406
  Uniform Commercial Code provisions, 295–296,
     298–300, 311
  unilateral, 294–295
  unjust enrichment, 301
  valid and enforceable, 295
  void, 295, 385
  voidable, 295, 360, 370, 385
  winding up of partnership, executory contracts during, 972
  writing requirement, 418
Contracts: acceptance
  ambiguous offers, 337
  "Battle of the Forms," 329
  Common law, 327
  communication of acceptance, 331–338
  defining elements, 325, 553
  implicit acceptance, 335
  intention to accept, 325–327
  mailbox rule, 332–334
  mirror image rule, 327
  persons able to accept, 338
  shipment, acceptance by, 337–338
  silence as, 335
  stipulated means of communication, 334
  Uniform Commercial Code standard, 328–330
  unilateral contracts, 334
  written agreement, 337
Contracts: assignments
  "American rule," 440
  clauses prohibiting, 439
  creation of, 437
  current law, 436–437
  defenses against assignee, 440
  "English rule," 440
  evolution of law governing, 436
  nature of, 435–436
  notification to obligor, 439–440
  requirements for, 437–439
  rights of assignee, 439–440, 811
  sales contract, 550
  subsequent assignment, 440
  successive assignments, 440–441
  terminology, 436
  warranty liability of assignor to assignee, 441
Contracts: capacity
  definition, 378
  disaffirmance; *see* Disaffirmance of contracts
  intoxicated persons, 389
  lack of capacity, effect of, 378–379
  mentally impaired persons, 369–370
  minors, 379–385
Contracts: consideration
  adequacy, 344
  bankruptcy discharge barring debt payment, 356
  "bargained-for exchange" aspect, 344–345

cancellation clause affecting, 347
charitable subscriptions as, 356
composition agreements, 352
contractual duty, performance of preexisting, 348–351
elements of, 343–345
exclusive dealing contracts affecting, 348
forbearance to sue, 352–353
illusory promises, 346
legal value, 344
marriage as consideration, 419–420
modification of contract
    under common law, 348–349
    under UCC, 351
moral obligation, promises to satisfy preexisting, 354
nominal consideration, 344
output contacts affecting, 348
past consideration, 353
performance of preexisting duties as, 348–351
preexisting duties affecting, 348–353
promissory estoppel as substitute for, 354–356
public duty, performance of preexisting, 348
requirements contracts affecting, 348
settle debts, preexisting duty to, 351–353
statutes of limitations barring debt payment, 356
termination clause affecting, 347
Contracts violating public policy
court-articulated policy, agreements violating, 397–402
criminal acts, agreements for committing, 395
family relationships, 402
general considerations, 392–393
licensing law, agreements violating, 395–396
purpose of statute, agreements violating, 395
regulatory statutes, 395–396
restraint of competition, agreements in, 398–400
statutory violations, agreements promoting, 395
Contractual liability
agency law, 914–919
negotiable instruments, 846–847
Contractual relations, interference with, 277–278
Contribution
partner's share of liability, 963
right to, 723–724
Contributory negligence, 232, 534
Contributory patent infringement, 248
Convention on Contracts for the International Sale of Goods
    (CISG), 299, 351, 498, 562
writing requirement, 413
Convention on International Bills of Exchange and
    International Promissory Notes, 828
Conversion (criminal law)
generally, 198
negotiable instruments, 863
Conversion of LPs and LLCs, 1001
Convertible debt securities, 1038
Conway, District Judge, 35
Cook, J, 312

Cooper, Justice, 219
Cooperative ownership, 619
Cooperatives and antitrust liability, 1307
Coordination, registration by, 1153
Coors v. Rubin, 67
Copperweld Corp. v. Independence Tube Corp., 1258
Copyright Act, 251–263, 266
Copyright Clause of Constitution, 252–253
Copyright Office, 252
Copyrights, 251–263
Copyright Term Extension Act (CTEA), 252–253
Cordy, Judge, 372
Core proceeding, in bankruptcy, 770
Corliss v. Wenner and Anderson, 591–593
Corporations
alien, 1012
annual report, 1032
articles of incorporation
    amendments to, 1088
    contents of, 1031
    filing of, 1031–1032
    general information, 1030–1031
    purpose clause, 1048–1049
benefits of, 1008
board of directors; *see* Board of directors
bylaws, 1032
characteristics of, 1009
circumvention of statutes, 1019
close corporations; *see* Close corporations
common law, 1011
consolidation, 1088
constituency statutes, 1048
defenses to tender offers, 1064
defrauding creditors, 1018–1019
dissolution, 1088–1089, 1109–1110
domestic, 1012
domination by shareholders for improper purpose, 1018
duties of officers to, 1056–1073
evasion of obligation, 1019
financing
    debt securities, 1038
    general considerations, 1036–1038
    shares; *see* Shares and shareholders
foreign; *see* Foreign corporations
going private, 1071
government-owned corporations, 1010
history of, 1009
incorporation
    articles of incorporation, filing of, 1031–1032
    de facto corporation, 1033
    defective attempts at, 1033–1035
    de jure corporation, 1033
    estoppel, corporation by, 1034
    liability for defective, 1034
    organization meeting, 1032
    steps in, 1030–1032

Corporations—*Cont.*
    indemnification of directors and employees, 1078–1079
    insurance, 1078, 1079
    liability
        for defective incorporation, 1034
        to promoter, 1030
        torts and crimes, 1074
    looting, 1018–1019
    mergers, 1088
    Model Business Corporation Act (MBCA), 1011
    nature of, 934–935
    nonprofit corporations; *see* Nonprofit corporations
    objectives of, 1047–1048
    officers
        conflicts of interest, 1067–1069
        duties of, 1056–1073
        indemnification of, 1078–1079
        oppression of minority shareholders, 1071
        principal positions, 1054
        torts and crimes, liability for, 1074–1075
        trading on inside information, 1072–1073
        usurpation of company's assets, 1069
    piercing the corporate veil, 1017–1023
    powers of, 1049
    preincorporation contracts, 1027–1029
    preincorporation share subscriptions, 1029
    professional corporation, 935, 1010
    promoter of, 1027–1029
    publicly held corporations, 1010
    sales of assets, 1088
    S corporations; *see* S corporations
    shares and shareholders; *see* Shares and shareholders
    social responsibility and ethical business
        practices, 91–93
    special charters, 1009
    state incorporation statutes, 1011
    takeovers, opposition to, 1063–1067
    tender offer, acquisition by, 1151
    termination, 1110
    thin capitalization, 1018
    types of, 1010
    ultra vires doctrine, 1048–1049
    Unocal test, 1067
    winding up, 1110
Corpus, in trusts, 679
Corrigan, Judge, 7
Cottle, Presiding Judge, 577
Counterclaims, 40
Counterfeit goods, 266
Course of dealing, 547
Court-annexed arbitration, 52
Court of Federal Claims, 36
Court of International Trade, 36
Courts
    appeals courts, 30

    common law, 3
    equity, 5
    federal courts, 34–37
    judicial review, 57–58
    limited jurisdiction, 29
    limits on power of, 23, 57–58
    trial courts, 29–30
Cowin, Judge, 1105
Coyle v. Schwartz, 1043–1044
Craraway, J., 293
Cratsley, Justice, 749
Crawford v. Marion County Election Board, 73
Credit
    definition, 718
    disclosure of terms, 1237–1238
    nondiscrimination in access to, 1243
    pledges, 719
    report information, 1238–1239
    secured and unsecured, 719–720
    security devices, 719–720
    surety, 720–723
Credit cards
    disclosure requirements, 1237–1238
    disputes in billing, 1243–1244
    liability for unauthorized use, 1238
Credit counseling in bankruptcy proceedings, 771
Creditor beneficiaries, 447
Creditors
    meeting of, Chapter 7, 772–773
    options on default, 761
    partnership's, 954
    potential liability of, 763–765
    proof of claim, Chapter 7, 781
Criminal law; *see also* White-collar crimes
    arraignment, 138
    booking, 137
    business records, production of, 152–153
    capacity, 134–135
    computer crime, 163–165
    Constitutional provisions, 131–134, 139–154
    corporate crimes, 1074–1075
    criminal intent, 134–135
    cruel and unusual punishment, 133
    deterrence as purpose, 126
    double jeopardy, 153
    due process restrictions, 132
    Equal Protection Clause and, 132–133
    essentials of crime, 128–137
    felonies, 126
    general information, 8
    incapacitation, 126
    incapacity, 134–135
    information, 138
    infractions, 126
    initial appearance, 138

mens rea, 134–135
misdemeanors, 126
nature of crimes, 125–126
pleas, 138
preliminary hearing, 138
premeditation, 134
prevention of crimes, 126
privacy rights and, 139–142
probable cause, 138
probation, 126
procedures, 137–154
production of records, 152–153
proof beyond a reasonable doubt, 134
public wrongs, 125
purpose of sanctions, 126–128
rehabilitation as purpose, 126
retribution as purpose, 126
self-incrimination, privilege against, 148–149
sentencing, 126–128
speedy trial, right to, 153–154
stages of prosecution, 137–138
statutory offenses, crimes as, 128
warrant requirement, 143
Crippen, Judge, 963
Critical legal studies (CLS) movement, 11
Croskey v. BMW of North America, Inc., 515–517
Crowe v. CarMax Auto Superstores, Inc., 509–510
Cruel and unusual punishment, criminal law and, 133
Cummings, Circuit Judge, 1259
Cumulative voting, 1051, 1084–1085
Cureton, Judge, 865
Currie v. Chevron U.S.A., Inc., 211–214
Curtesy, 672
Curtilage, privacy right and, 139
Cyberlaw in action
    accidental mistakes in pricing, 371
    account aggregation, 870
    bailments, online tracking of, 604
    browsewrap contracts, 315
    buyers' benefits from e-commerce, 576
    cable Internet service providers' status, 1215
    CAN-SPAM Act, 1232
    check scam, 884
    clickwrap (clickthrough) contracts, 294, 315, 534
    Communications Decency Act, 15, 232
    Computer Fraud and Abuse Act, 164
    contracts online, 294
    contracts online, modifications of, 549
    copyright infringement in Internet context, 254
    cybersquatting, 273
    defamation, 185–186
    Digital Millennium Copyright Act, 254
    e-checks, 610, 810, 890
    e-commerce's benefits for buyers, 576
    e-mails and electronic information, discoverability of, 44–45

e-payments, 814
e-signatures and the statute of frauds, 423, 485
Fair Housing Act's applicability to Web sites, 627
First Amendment issues, 66
forgery of negotiable instruments, 890
insurance coverage for defective software, 707–708
leasing of property, 646
limitation of remedy clauses, 534
negligence, 232
notification of nonacceptance of goods, 557
online permitting, 1351
passage of title, 488
real estate finance on the Internet, 728
remedy of divestiture for monopoly violation, 1281
sales transactions, modifications of, 549
secured transactions, 743
shrinkwrap contracts/licensees, 294, 315, 534
software and other information contracts, 296
toxicity data online, 1367
trespass and use of e-mail system, 199–200
Uniform Electronic Transactions Act (UETA), 549
warranty disclaimers, 534
Cybersquatting, 273
Cyr, Senior Circuit Judge, 941

D

Damages
    antitrust, 1257
    breach of contract, 470–473, 708–709
    breach of implied warranty of habitability, 649
    consequential, 578
    defamation, 190
    defective goods, damages for, 581–582
    discrimination in employment, 1327
    incidental, 578
    incidental damages, 470–471
    libel, 181
    liquidated damages, 471, 568–570, 576
    nominal damages, 471
    nondelivery, damages for, 578–579
    product liability, 526–527
    rejection or repudiation, 572–573
    slander, 181
    torts, 170–171
    treble damages, 1257
Dangerous activities, abnormally, 234
Darco Transportation v. Dulen, 1318–1319
Davenport v. Cotton Hope Plantation, 233–234
Davis v. United States, 154
*Dealer Management Systems, Inc. v. Design Automotive
        Group, Inc.,* 481–482
Death
    bank's customer, 876
    party to contract, 318
    promisor in contract, 467

Debentures, 1038
Debtor education in bankruptcy proceedings, 771
Debts
    bankruptcy; *see* Bankruptcy
    executor's payment of decedent's debt, 418–419
    garnishment of wages, 719
    judgment-proof debtor, 719
    payment as contract consideration, 351–353
Deceit, 195–196, 361
Deceptive practices, FTC regulation, 1227–1230
Declaratory judgment statutes, 24
Deductive reasoning, 12
Deed of trust
    general information, 732
    as security interest, 732
Deeds, 627–628
Defamation
    absolute privilege, 182
    conditional privilege, 182–183
    Constitution and, 186–191, 190–191
    damages, 181, 190
    defined, 181
    elements of, 181–182
    fault requirements, 190, 191
    injurious falsehood and, 277
    libel-slander distinction, 181
    malice, proof of actual, 187–188
    media-nonmedia issue, 190–191
    "of and concerning plaintiff" requirement, 181–182
    private figure plaintiff, 190
    privileges, 182–183
    publication requirement, 182
    public figure plaintiff, 187–188, 191
    public official plaintiff, 191
    truth as defense, 181, 182
Default and foreclosure, 761–765
Defects, duty to disclose hidden, 630, 653
Defenses
    affirmative defense, 39
    age discrimination, 1331
    assumption of risk, 534
    comparative fault, 534–535
    comparative negligence, 534–535
    contributory negligence, 534
    defamation actions, 181, 182
    discrimination in employment, 1324
    due diligence, 1130–1134, 1171–1172
    holder in due course, 834, 836–839
    misuse of product, 534
    negligence, 232–233
    negotiable instrument subject to, 833
    no-privity, 527–528
    patent infringement, 250–251
    preemption defense, 535
    price discrimination defenses, 1305–1306

    regulatory compliance, 535–536
    Section 11, 1130–1134
    surety's, 721
Deferred prosecution agreements, 158–159
Deficiency judgment, 762
Definiteness of contract terminology, 309–311
Delaware Block Method, 1090
Delegatee, 441
Delegation of duties
    assumption of duties by delagatee, 442–443
    contracts, 441–445
    discharge by novation, 444
    language creating a delegation, 442
    nature of, 441
    qualifying duties for delegation, 441–442
    relationship of parties (figure), 442
    terminology, 441
Delegation of power, 6, 1199–1201
Delegator, 441
Delgado v. Trax Bar & Grill, 215–218
Delivery
    basic obligation, 550
    buyer's rights on improper, 556–557
    cancellation and withholding delivery, 571–572
    place of, 550
    right to stop as remedy, 575–576
    seller's duty, 550
    terms, 487
Demurrer, 40
DeNardo v. Bax, 183–185
Denny's Marina, Inc. v. Renfro Productions, Inc., 1259–1260
De novo review, 1207, 1215
Department of Homeland Security, 1201–1202
Department of Revenue of Kentucky v. Davis, 82–84
Department of the Interior v. Klamath Water Users Protective Association, 1217–1218
Depositions, 40
Deregulation, 1219–1220
Derivative actions, shareholders', 1100–1103, 1108–1109
Design
    defective, 521
    negligent, 515–517
Destruction of subject matter and contract performance, 467
Deterrence, in criminal law, 126
Detroit Institute of Arts v. Rose and Smith, 600–601
Devise, 668
Diamond v. Diehr, 242
Dickerson, Judge, 582
Dickson, Justice, 4, 703
Difference principle, 95
Digital Millennium Copyright Act, 254
Digital signatures, 423
Dilution of trademark, 266–267
Direct economic loss, 526
Directed verdict, 47

Direct liability of principal, 924–925
Dirks v. SEC, 1144–1145
Disaffirmance of contracts
    "Benefit Rule," 382
    duties upon, 381–382
    exceptions to minor's right, 380
    general rule, 379–380
    "infancy doctrine," 382
    intoxicated persons, 389
    mentally impaired persons, 386–388
    minors, 379–385
    real estate, contracts affecting title to, 381
    restitution by disaffirming minor, 381–382
Discharge
    holder in due course, 837
    indorsers and accommodation parties, 866
    liability, 863–866
    negotiable instruments, 863–866
Discharge in bankruptcy
    acts barring, 784
    Chapter 13, 798–800
    dismissal of cases for substantial abuse, 786
    general entitlement, 782
    nondischargeable debts, 784
    objections to, 782, 784
    reaffirmation agreements, 785–786
Disclaimers
    of opinion, 1180
    in product liability, 532–533
Disclosed principal, 919
Disclose-or-refrain rule, 1143
Disclosure
    credit report information, 1239
    credit terms, 1237–1238
    hazardous chemicals, release of, 1367
    periodic disclosure under 1934 securities law, 1136
    public disclosure of private facts, 191–192
Discovery, 40–45
Discrimination in employment
    Age Discrimination in Employment Act, 20–22,
        1330–1331
    Americans with Disabilities Act, 1331–1333
    defenses to alleged, 1324
    Equal Pay Act, 1322–1323
    Executive Order 11245, 1333
    federal contractors, 1333
    proving, 1323–1324
    remedies, 1326–1327
    Section 1981, 1330
    state laws, 1333–1334
    Title VII of 1964 Civil Rights Act, 1323–1334
Discriminatory practices, FHA prohibition on, 626, 648
Dismiss, motion to, 40
Disparate impact under Title VII, 1323–1324
Disparate treatment under Title VII, 1323

Dissenters' rights, 1089–1090
Dissociation, in partnership
    continuation of business after, 975–981
    definition, 967
    effect of, 968–969
    limited liability limited partnership, 999–1001
    limited partnership, 999–1001
Dissociation, limited liability company, 990
Dissolution and winding up, 1088–1089, 1110–1111
    authority of partners, 972–973, 973–974
    borrowing money during, 972–973
    causes, 969–970
    distribution of assets, 974–975
    executory contracts during, 972
    fiduciary duties during winding up, 969
    joint ventures, 972
    limited liability company, 990–991
    mining partnerships, 972
    partnership agreement, effect on, 970
Distributional interest (LLC), 989
District court jurisdiction, 34
Diversity jurisdiction, 34
Dividend preferences, 1037
Dividends, 1096–1099
Divisible contracts, 407–408, 465
Division of markets, 1298–1299
Doctrine of employment at will, 1338–1341
Doctrine of equivalents, 248
Documents of title, 605
Dodge v. Ford Motor Co., 1097–1098
Dodson v. Shrader, 382–383
Donee, 593
Donee beneficiaries, 447
Donor, 593
Do-Not-Call Registry, 1232–1236
Donovan, U.S. Bankruptcy Judge, 787
Double jeopardy, 153
Dow Chemical Co. v. United States, 1205
Dower right, 672
Drafts, 808
Drawer and drawee, 808, 810, 847–848, 869–878
Dreher, Bankruptcy Judge, 775
Drinking water standards, 1360
Droney, District Judge, 601
Drudge Report, 28
Drug testing of employees, 1335
Due process
    Compassionate Use Act, 59–62
    criminal law and, 132
    foreign corporations, 1012
    procedural due process, 71
    substantive due process, 71–72
Dun & Bradstreet, Inc. v. Greenmoss Builders, Inc., 190
Durable power of attorney, 674–675
Duress, in contracts, 370–373

Duties
    agent to principal, 901–905
    assignment, 59
    audits, 1162
    bank's, 870, 871
    contract conditions, 453–459
    creditor's to surety, 721
    customer's duty to report forged check, 877–879
    defend insured, 705–706
    directors' to corporation, 1056–1073
    disclosure of hidden defects, 630
    fiduciary duty, 681, 833, 901–902, 951, 969, 998, 1029
    general partner's, 998
    insurer's, 705–706
    landlord's, 653–654
    limited partner's, 998
    nonprofit's directors and officers, 1073
    officers' to corporation, 1056–1073
    partner's, 951–953
    payment of sums owed by insured, 706
    principal to agent, 906–907
    promoter's to corporation, 1029
    real estate brokers, 625
    securities professionals, 1189
    tenants, 549
    trustees, 680–681, 773
Duty of care
    breach of, 206–207
    common carriers, 607
    corporate directors and officers, 1056–1058
    factors considered in evaluating, 210–211
    partner's, 952
    persons owed, 207
    reasonable care standard, 206
    reasonable foreseeability of harm standard, 210
    reasonable person test, 206, 210
Duty of confidentiality, 274, 953
Duty of good faith and fair dealing, 951–952, 998
Duty of good faith in contracts, 298–299
Duty of loyalty
    director's, 1067
    officer's, 1067
    partner's, 951
    trustee's, 681
Duty to account, partner's, 952–953
Duty to act within actual authority
    director's, 1056
    partner's, 952
Duty to defend, insurer's, 705
Duty to serve, partner's, 952
Dyson, Freeman, 92

E

Early neutral evaluation (ADR), 53
Easements
    appurtenant, 619
    creation of, 620–621
    definition of, 619
    by grant, 619
    by implication, 620
    by necessity, 620
    by prescription, 619–620
    by prior use, 620
    with a profit, 620
    by reservation, 619
    Statute of Frauds, 620
Easley, Justice, 513
East Capitol View Community Development Corporation v. Robinson, 466–467
Eastern R. R. President's Conference v. Noerr Motor Freight, Inc., 1308
eBay, Inc. v. Merc Exchange, LLC, 248, 249–250, 251
Ebel, Circuit Judge, 710, 1233
Economic duress, in contracts, 371
Edgar, Chief U.S. District Judge R. Allan, 379
Edmead, Judge, 813
Edwards v. Arizona, 153–154
Ehrlich, Eugen, 10
Eichen, Judge, 722
Eighth Amendment, criminal law and, 133
Eisenberg v. Advance Relocation & Storage, Inc., 900–901
Ejusdem generis rule, 22
Eldred v. Ashcroft, 253
Eldridge, Justice, 651, 655
Election of directors, 1050–1052, 1084–1087
Electronic banking, 887–891
Electronic Funds Transfer Act, 850, 888–890
Electronic Signature in Global and National Commerce Act (E-Sign), 423, 485
Emancipation, minors, 380–381
Embedded property, 592
Emergency Planning and Community Right-to-Know Act (EPCRA), 1367
Eminent domain, 84, 633–636
Emotional distress, intentional infliction of, 176–177
Employee Polygraph Protection Act, 1335
Employee Retirement Income Security Act of 1974 (ERISA), 1320
Employer and employee
    agent classification, 899
    collective bargaining, 1321–1322
    discrimination; *see* Discrimination in employment
    drug and alcohol tests, 1335
    ends and means employment law (chart), 1316
    equal opportunity, 1322–1334
    exceptions to at will employment doctrine, 1338–1341
    health, safety, and well being, 1316–1320
    implied covenant of good faith and fair dealing, 1340
    independent contractors, 899
    liability for employee's fraudulent indorsement, 860

liability for sexual harassment, 1328
monitoring of employees, 1336–1338
noncompetition clauses in employment contracts, 398–400
polygraph tests, 1334–1335
privacy of employees, 1334–1338
promises by employers, 1340
public policy issues, 1338–1339
records and references, 1336
searches, 1335–1336
security of employment, 1338–1341
sexual harassment, 1262–1267
union activity, 1321–1322
wages, pensions, and benefits, 1320–1321
at will employment doctrine, 1338–1341
workers' compensation, 1316–1319
Employment-at-will doctrine, 1338–1341
Enabling legislation, 1196–1197
Enforcement of judgments, 48
Enoch, Chief Judge, 569
Entrusting of goods, 492–493
Enumerated powers, 58
Environmental impact statements, 1208
Environmental Protection Agency, 1346
Environmental regulation
abandoned hazardous waste sites, 1364–1365
air pollution, 1347–1352
climate change, 1352–1355
criminal penalties, 1356
global warming, 1352–1355
greenhouse gases, 1352–1355
hazardous waste manifest, 1361, 1363
historical perspective, 1345–1346
waste disposal, 1361–1367
water pollution, 1355–1358
Equal Credit Opportunity Act, 1243
Equal Employment Opportunity Commission, 1322–1323
Equal Pay Act, 1322–1323
Equal protection
applicability, 72
"classifies or distinguishes" criterion, 72
criminal law and, 132–133
fundamental rights, stricter scrutiny for, 73–79
rational basis test, 64–65, 72
state tax rate differences, 72–73
suspect classes, stricter scrutiny for, 74–79
zoning laws and, 637
Equitable relief, 1327
Equitable remedies, 5–6
Equitable title, 679
Equity courts, 6
Equity law, 5–6
Equity of redemption, 729–730
Equity securities, 1036–1037
Erickstad, Chief Justice, 445
ERISA, 1320

Escheats, 675
Escott v. BarChris Construction Corp., 1131–1134, 1172
E-signatures and Statute of Frauds, 423, 485
Espinosa, Chief Judge, 368
Estate of McDaniel v. McDaniel, 676–677
Estate of Nelson v. Rice, 368–369
Estate of Shelly, 670–672
Estates
administrator of estate, 678
determining existence of will, 678
estate planning, 667
law of estates and trusts, 667
probate/administration process, 678–679
probate estate, 678
responsibilities of personal representative, 678–679
selecting a personal representative, 678–679
trusts; *see* Trusts
wills; *see* Wills
Estates in land, 617
Estoppel
corporation by, 1034
excuse of conditions, 457
promissory; *see* Promissory estoppel
Estray statutes, 591
Ethical business practices
alternatives in decision making, identifying, 106
appeals to pity in decision making, 111
argumentum ad hominem in decision making, 112–113
argumentum ad populum in decision making, 111–112
bandwagon fallacy in decision making, 112
bottom-line impact of decisions, 107
circular reasoning in decision making, 111
codes of ethics/conduct, 99
communicating core values, 119
complexity of issues affecting decision making, 116
corporate executives' special position, 91
corporate social responsibility, 91–93
critical thinking, 110–115
dealing with unethical situations
bosses who are unethical, 116–117
buying time, 117
intrafirm tactics, 118–119
losing job as consequence, 119
mentors, support from, 117
peer support group, 117
resisting pressure to act unethically, 116–119
strategies for, 116–119
win-win situations, 117–118
facts affecting decisions, 105–106
false analogies in decision making, 111
false cause fallacy in decision making, 113
gambler's fallacy in decision making, 113–114
goals, failure to remember, 115
good business and ethical behavior, 119
guidelines for, 105–106, 110

Ethical business practices—*Cont.*
  implementation of decisions, 109–110
  improving corporate governance/social
        responsibility, 99–105
  independence of board of directors, 101–102
  instruction for employees, 99
  internal management structure, 102
  John Rawls, 95
  judgment in decision making, 110
  justice theory, 95–96, 109
  Kantianism, 93–94
  leading ethically, 119–120
  legal compliance and ethical behavior, 98
  legal remedies, 103–105
  lure of the new in decision making, 114
  moral values underlying capitalism, 93
  non sequiturs in decision making, 110–111
  overconfidence affecting decision making, 115–116
  personal impact of decisions, 107–108
  perverse incentives, 102–103
  pity, appeals in decision making to, 111
  poor decision making characteristics, 115
  practical constraints, 109
  profit maximization, 97–99, 108
  reductio ad absurdum in decision making, 114
  reinforcement of ethical behavior, 119–120
  reverence or respect; argument to in decision
        making, 113
  rights theory, 93–95, 108–109
  Sarbanes-Oxley Act of 2002, 91
  setting an example, 119
  shareholder influence, 99, 101
  slippery slope fallacy in decision making, 114
  social impact of decisions, 106–107
  stakeholders' interests, 101, 106
  stakeholder theory of corporate responsibility, 92
  stock options, 102–103
  sunk cost fallacy in decisions, 114–115
  supervision of management, 102–103
  teleological ethical theories, 93
  theories of ethics, 93–105
  tradition; appeals to in decision making, 114
  utilitarianism, 96–97, 108
Ethics in action
  antitrust and competition, 1282
  auditor independence standards, 1165
  bankruptcy to manage liability or labor contracts, 794
  bequests in will, 672
  business form as shelter from liability, 936
  classes of shares with limited rights, 1088
  contracts
      effect of breach on payment, 465
      price fluctuation of goods subject of, 547
  corporations
      audits, 904
      constituency statutes, 1048
      indemnification of directors, 1079
      management duties and liabilities, 1073
  creditor's action on missed payments, 732
  destruction of potentially incriminating evidence, 46
  disclosures
      credit and employment history, 724
      possible hazards to tenants, 658
  discovery misconduct, 46
  dissociated partner's entitlement, 981
  donee beneficiary, in contract law, 449
  effects of white-collar crime, 155
  employee theft, 606
  entrusting goods, 494
  environmental regulation in international operations, 1367
  exemption from antitrust liability despite false
        statements, 1311
  financial statements (SOX), 1139
  finders of lost/mislaid property, 594
  foreclosure and repossession, 765
  free access to copyrighted music, 264
  gambling debt, defense of illegality against, 838
  Google's Code of Conduct, 100
  health insurance reform, 708
  hidden contract terms, 315
  homestead exemption, 778
  information disclosure under securities law, 1130
  limited liability, 1004
  limited liability partnerships, 962
  loans to corporate directors and officers, 1068
  mandatory arbitration agreements, 1334
  modification of consideration, 353
  morality and law, 12
  negligence of employer for employee's conduct, 215
  parent-subsidiary corporate structure, 1023
  parol evidence rule, 431
  pollution allowed by regulation, 1352
  principal's liability for agent's torts, 924
  Public Company Accounting Oversight Board, 1160
  purported partnership doctrine, 944
  qualifying an indorsement, 849
  quasi contract and promissory estoppel cases, 304
  "revolving door" at administrative agencies, 1220
  risk/benefit analysis, 1249
  schools of jurisprudence, 12
  securities analysts' conflicts of interest, 1179
  sexual orientation and equal protection, 74
  shareholder litigation committee recommendations, 1103
  silence as acceptance of offer, 337
  standardized form contracts, 431
  stop payment on checks, 875
  tax havens, domestic, 1031
  time scales and survival strategies, 92
  tobacco litigation, 525
  unconscionable contracts, 407

video surveillance system and privacy, 192
voluntary disclosure of material facts by sellers, 581
whistleblowing, 158
zoning ordinance and restrictive covenants, 637
European Union's Merger Regulation, 1298
Eviction
breach of lease, 660
constructive eviction, 648–649
Evidence, parol, 420–421
Evory v. RJM Acquisitions Funding, L.L.C., 1244–1248
Exclusionary rule (Fourth Amendment), 143–147
Exclusive dealing agreements, 1272, 1288–1289
Exclusive dealing contracts, 348, 487
Exculpatory clauses, 233, 400–401, 654
Excuse of conditions, 457
Excuse of performance of contract, 465–468, 563
Executed contracts, 295
Executive agencies, 1201
Executive orders
EO 11245, 1333
general information, 6
Executive powers, 57
Executor of estate, 678
Executor's payment of decedent's debt, 418–419
Executory contracts, 295
Exemptions
Chapter 7 liquidation, 774
registration under Securities Act of 1933, 1124–1129
Exhaustion of remedies, 1214
Exoneration right, 724
Expectation interest, 469
Expedited Funds Availability Act, 886
Express agreement as to fixtures, 615
Express authority, 898, 914, 956, 972
Express conditions, 456–457
Express contracts, 295
Express ratification, 917
Express trusts, 680
Express warranties, 506–508, 533
Ex-ship destination contract, 495
Exxon Corp. v. Eagerton, 81

F

Fabe, Justice, 183
FACT Act, 1242–1243
Failure to warn, negligent, 514–515
Fair Credit Billing Act, 1243–1244
Fair Credit Reporting Act, 1238–1239
Fair Debt Collection Practices Act, 1244
Fair Housing Act, 626, 648
Fair Housing Council of San Fernando Valley v. Roommate.com, LLC, 16–20
Fair Labor Standards Act, 1321
Fair trial, due process and, 71
Fair use doctrine, 258

False advertising under Lanham Act, 280–283
False analogies in ethical decisions, 111
False brokerage, 1306
False cause fallacy in ethical decisions, 113
False imprisonment, 177–180
False light publicity, 192
False representation under Lanham Act, 280
Family and Medical Leave Act, 1319–1320
Family farms, Chapter 12 bankruptcy, 794–796
Family relationships and contracts, 402
Family Video Movie Club v. Home Folks, Inc., 319–320
Faragher v. Boca Raton, 1328
Farms (family), Chapter 12 bankruptcy, 794–796
FAS (free alongside ship), 493–494
FAS (freight alongside ship), 487
Fashion Originators' Guild v. FTC, 1268
Federal Arbitration Act, 50–52
Federal Communications Commission, 1232–1236
Federal contractors, 1333
Federal courts jurisdiction, 34–38
Federal Insurance Contributions Act (FICA), 1320
Federalism, 2–3, 57
Federal judicial circuits (chart), 37
Federal question jurisdiction, 34
Federal Register, 1206
Federal regulatory powers, 58–63
Federal Reserve, 889
Federal Sentencing Guidelines, 127–128, 158
Federal supremacy, 6, 57, 84
Federal Tort Claims Act, 27
Federal Trade Commission
adjudicative proceedings, 1226–1227
consumer credit, 1237–1239
deceptive business practices, 1227–1230
enabling legislation, 1196–1197
enforcement procedures, 1226–1227
holder in due course, 839–840
identity theft protection, 1242–1243
Industry guides, 1226
powers, 1226–1227
remedies for deceptive or unfair behavior, 1231
telemarketing abuse, 1232–1236
unfair business practices, 1231
warranties, 1236
Federal Trade Commission Act
anticompetitive behavior, 1227
enactment, 1226
Section 5 deception and unfairness provisions, 1227–1231
Federal Trade Commission v. Staples, Inc., 1293–1296
Federal Trademark Dilution Act, 266–267
Federal Water Pollution Control Act, 1355
Fedwire, 889–890
Fee simple absolute, 617
Fehribach v. E&Y LLP, 1162
Feigned controversies, 23

Felley v. Singleton, 507–508
Felonies, 126
Ferris, Baker Watts, Inc. v. Ernst & Young, LLP, 1173–1175
Fictional accounts and defamation, 181
Fictitious payee rule, 859–860
Fiduciary duty, 681, 833, 901–902, 951, 969, 998, 1104–1105
Field warehousing arrangement, 748
Fifth Amendment
    business records and, 152–153
    double jeopardy, 153
    due process, 71–72, 132
    equal protection, 72–80
    Miranda warnings, 148–152
    privilege against self-incrimination, 148–149
    takings clause, 84–86
Financial firms, Chapter 7, 773
Financing statement
    form, 746–747
    general information, 744–745
Finder of lost/mislaid property, 593
Finnin v. Bob Lindsay, Inc., 327–328
Fire insurance, 696–697
First Amendment; *see* Freedom of speech
*Firstar Bank, N.A. v. First Service Title Agency,
        Inc.,* 833–834
First-to-invent rule, 242
Fischer, Judge, 179
Fisher v. United States, 153
Fitl v. Strek, 557–558
Fitness, implied warranty of, 512–514
Fitzgerald v. Racing Association of Central Iowa, 72–73
Fixed amount of money, negotiable instruments, 815
Fixtures
    definition, 589, 613
    express agreement, 615
    factors for classifying items as, 614
    priority determination, 758–759
    security interest in, 615–616, 751
Flaum, Circuit Judge, 1229
FOB (free on board), 487, 493, 495
Food and Drug Administration Modernization Act, 87
*Food and Drug Administration v. Brown & Williamson
        Tobacco Corp.,* 1214
Forbearance to sue, 352–353
Foreclosure
    default and, 761–765
    liens, 727, 734–737
    mortgages, 729, 730
Foreign commerce, 1311
Foreign corporations
    certificate of authority, 1015
    Commerce Clause requirement, 1012
    definition of, 1012
    "doing business" criterion, 1012
    due process requirements, 1012

    isolated transactions, 1015
    long-arm statutes, 1013
    pseudo-foreign corporations, 1017
    qualification requirements, 1014–1016
    regulation of, 1011–1017
    suits against, 1012–1013
    taxation of, 1014
Foreign Corrupt Practices Act, 160, 1152
Foreign Intelligence Surveillance Act, 148
Foreign Sovereign Immunities Act, 1311
Foreseeable criminal acts, 631
Foreseeable reliance, 302–303
Foreseeable users test, 1167
Foreseen users/class of users tests, 1166–1167
Forgery
    checks, 877–879
    holder in due course, 837
Formal rulemaking, 1206
Forms of businesses
    chart, general characteristics, 937
    choice of, 932
44 Liquormart v. Rhode Island, 67
Forum selection clauses, 33–34
Foti, Judge, 955
Fourteenth Amendment
    due process, 71–72, 132
    equal protection, 72–80
    takings clause, 84–86
Fourth Amendment
    exclusionary rule, 143–147
    privacy right, 139–146
    searches, 139–146
    warrant requirement, 143
Franklin v. The Monadnock Company, 1339–1340
Fraud, 195–196, 362–365
    defrauding creditors, 1018–1019
    liability for professional's fraud, 1170
    securities professionals, 1164–1165, 1170
Fraud-on-the-market theory, 1142
Frauds, Statute of; *see* Statute of Frauds
Fraudulent transfers, Chapter 7, 778–779
Freedom of Access to Clinic Entrances Act (FACE), 26–27
Freedom of contract, 291
Freedom of Information Act, 1216–1217
Freedom of speech
    commercial speech, 65–70, 131
    compelled speech decisions, 70–71
    compelled subsidy decisions, 70–71
    compelling government purpose requirement, 65
    defamation; *see* Defamation
    defamation and, 186–187
    marketplace rationale, 65
    noncommercial speech, 65, 131
    obscenity, 131–132
    political speech, 65

restrictiveness of prohibition, 65
scope, 131–132
zoning laws and, 637
Freezing out shareholders, 1071, 1104
Friedman, Bankruptcy Judge, 499
Friedman, Judge, 755
Friedman, Milton, 97
Friendly fires, 697
Full strict scrutiny (means-end test), 65
Furnished dwellings, duty to maintain, 653
Furst v. Einstein Moomjy, Inc., 471–472
Future advances, 744
FW/PBS, Inc. v. City of Dallas, 637

G

Galatia Community State Bank v. Kindy, 818–819
Gall v. United States, 128
Gambler's fallacy in ethical decisions, 113–114
Gap fillers, 483
Gardner, Judge, 455
Gardner v. Jefferys, 621–622
Garelli Wong & Associates, Inc. v. Nichols, 164
Garnishment of wages, 48, 719
Gender, Equal Protection Clause and, 75
General agent, 899
General Agreement on Tariffs and Trade (GATT), 247
General Credit Corp. v. New York Linen Co., Inc., 836–837
General Dynamics Land Systems, Inc. v. Cline, 20–22, 25, 1331
General Electric Capital Commercial Automotive Finance, Inc. v. Spartan Motors, Inc., 753–756
General public purpose in statutory interpretation, 22
General verdict, 47
Gentry v. eBay, 232
George, Chief Justice, 216
Georgia v. Randolph, 143
Gertz v. Robert Welch, Inc., 190
Gibbons, Justice, 555
Gifts
acquisition of real property by, 623
general information, 593–595
Giles v. First Virginia Credit Services, Inc., 763–765
Ginsburg, Justice Ruth Bader, 50, 75, 146, 250, 1303
Glaze, Justice, 1086
Global business environment
administrative law, 1207
antibribery statutes, 160
antitrust laws, 1274
buyer's remedies in international transactions, 581
consideration for shares, 1039
contracts
acceptance of, 338
disputes involving, 299
modification of, 351

offer to contract, 313, 318
writing or other formal requirement, 412
Convention on International Bills of Exchange and International Promissory Notes, 828
corporate directors' duties, 1074
corporations, 1011
counterfeit and gray market goods, 266
dissolution of partnership, 976
electronic agents, 915
exclusionary rule, 146–147
extended producer responsibility for consumer packaging, 1364
foreign business and U.S. laws, 104
Foreign Corrupt Practices Act, 1152
Germany
corporate governance, 1053
corporation law, 936
golden rule, 94
gray market and counterfeit goods, 266
Holocaust Victim Insurance Relief Act of 1999, 695
insecurity concerning nonperformance, 562
intellectual property, 266, 268
International Accounting Standards Board (IASB), 1161
international air problems, 1352
International Consortium of Real Estate Associations, 906
international electronic funds transfers, 891
Internet offerings, 1178
liability of carriers, 606
limited liability companies, 993
limited partnerships, 1004
long-arm statutes, 1013–1014
mergers, 1298
misleading advertising, 1228
offer to contract, 313, 318
offshore tax havens, 1015
partnership
dissolution, 976
duties of partner, 954
payment methods, 551
in personam jurisdiction, 38
piracy, 266
real estate code of ethics, 906
risk of loss, 498
securities regulation, 1136
seller's remedies in international transactions, 573
shareholder activism, 1089
shareholder power, 1109
strict liability, 518
transnational insolvency proceedings, 795
treaties, interpretation of, 23
voluntary environmental management standards, 1360
writing or other formal contract requirement, 412
Global warming, 1352–1355
Golden Years Nursing Home, Inc. v. Gabbard, 830–831
Gonzales v. Raich, 59–62

Good faith
    definition under UCC, 490
    duty of good faith and fair dealing, 951–952, 998
    holder in due course, 831–832
    in performance, 460, 547
Google's tombstone ad, 1122
Gottlieb v. Tropicana Hotel and Casino, 345–346
Government action requirement of Constitution, 63–64
Government in the Sunshine Act of 1976, 1219
Government-owned corporations, 1010
Grace Label, Inc. v. Kliff, 547–549
Grant deeds, 628
Gratuities, illegal, 159–160
Gratuitous agent, 899
Gratz v. Bollinger, 74
Gray market goods, 266
Great Atlantic and Pacific Tea Co. v. FTC, 1306
*Greater New Orleans Broadcasting Association v.
    United States,* 67
Greatest equal liberty principle, 95
Greenhouse gases, 1352–1355
Greenspan, Alan, 91, 93
*Green Wood Industrial Company v. Forceman International
    Development Group, Inc.,* 579–580
Greer, Judge, 661
Grendell, Judge, 996
Gribben v. Wal-Mart Stores, Inc., 3–5
Grimes v. Donald, 1052–1053
Griswold v. Connecticut, 131
Group boycotts, 1268
Grutter v. Bollinger, 74
Guaranty and suretyship, 720–723
Gurfein, Circuit Judge, 1182
Guth v. Loft, Inc, 1069–1070
Guy, Circuit Judge, 1329
Gyamfoah v. EG&G Dynatrend, 607–608

H

Hagan v. Coca-Cola Bottling Co., 13–14
Hague-Visby Rules, 606
Halbrooks, Judge, 919
Hall, J., 349
Hall Street Associates v. Mattel, Inc., 49
Hamer v. Sidway, 344, 353
Hammurabi's code, 938
Harbor Park Market v. Gronda, 457–459
Hargis v. Baize, 218–220
Harrington v. MacNab, 848
Hart-Scott-Rodino Antitrust Improvement Act, 1289
Hatchett, Circuit Judge, 139
Hawaii Housing Authority v. Midkiff, 85, 86
Health care
    Chapter 7 bankruptcy, 773
    durable power of attorney, 674–675
    representatives, 675

Health Insurance Portability and Accountability
    Act of 1996, 708
Hearst Corp. v. Skeen, 188–189
Heinz v. W. Kirchner, 1227
Hernandez v. Hillsides, Inc., 192
Hildreth v. Tidewater Equipment Co., 1019–1021
Hill, Justice, 226
Historical school of jurisprudence, 10
Hobbes, Thomas, 9
Hobbs, Justice, 208
Hodgson, Justice, 944
Hogan, District Judge, 1293
Holder, negotiable instruments, 811, 828–829, 833
Holder in due course
    adverse claims, notice of, 832–833
    alteration of completed instrument, 837
    altered signature, 832
    breach of fiduciary duty, notice of, 833
    changes in rule of, 839–842
    defenses and claims
        claims in recoupment, 839
        claims to the instrument, 838–839
        generally, 834, 836
        notice of, 833
        personal defenses, 837–838
        real defenses, 836–837
    disadvantages to consumers of rule of, 839
    discharge, 837
    dishonored instrument disqualifying, 832
    Federal Trade Commission regulation, 839–840
    forgery, 837
    general requirements, 829
    good faith requirement, 831–832
    irregular and incomplete instruments, 833
    rights of, 828–829, 834, 836–839
    shelter rule, 834
    state consumer protection legislation, 839
    unauthorized signature, 832
    value, 831
Holmes, Oliver Wendell, 10, 65, 138, 345
Holocaust Victim Insurance Relief Act of 1999, 695
Holographic wills, 670
Holt v. Home Depot, U.S.A., Inc., 303–304
Homeowners' policies, 702
Homestead exemption, Chapter 7, 776
Horizontal boycotts, 1268
Horizontal division of markets, 1267
Horizontal mergers
    effects of, 1292–1293
    market share of firm resulting from, 1292
Horizontal price-fixing, 1259
Horsey, Justice, 1066
Hostile environment harassment, 1328
Hostile fires, 697
Hotelkeepers, 603

Housing codes, 650
Howey test, 1116–1118
Hudson v. Michigan, 143–146
Hull, Judge, 676
Hustler Magazine, Inc. v. Falwell, 177, 186
Hybrid contracts, 296
Hybrid rulemaking, 1206
Hyundai Motor America, Inc. v. Goodin, 528–531

I

Identity theft, 1242–1243
Ikuta, Circuit Judge, 260
Illegitimate birth, Equal Protection Clause and, 75
Illinois Brick Co. v. State of Illinois, 1257
Illinois Tool Works, Inc. v. Independent Ink, Inc., 1269–1271
Illinois v. Caballes, 140
Illness of promisor in contract, 467
Impact rule, 13–14
Implied authority, 898, 914, 956, 972
Implied contracts, 295
Implied covenant of good faith and fair dealing, 460
Implied-in-fact conditions, 456
Implied ratification, 917
Implied trusts, 684
Implied warranties
    of authority, 922–923
    disclaimers, 532–533
    of fitness, 512–514
    of habitability, 629–630, 649
    of merchantability, 508–509
    of possession, 648
    of quiet enjoyment, 648
Impossibility of performance of contract, 465, 563
Impostor rule, 859–860
Improper threat, in contracts, 370–371
Incapacitation, in criminal law, 126
Incapacity, in criminal law, 134–135
Incidental beneficiaries, 446–447
Incidental damages, 470–471
Income beneficiary from trusts, 681
Incompetence, customer of bank, 876
Incorporation process of Bill of Rights provisions, 63
INCOTERMS, 498
Indemnify
    partner's duty, 953
    partner's liability to other partners, 963
Indemnity
    corporation's directors, officers, employees, 1078–1079
    principal's duty of, 907
Indemnity contracts, 699
Independent agencies, 1201
Independent checks, 58, 63–86
Independent contractors
    agent's status as, 899
    liability for torts of, 926

Indivisible contracts, 408–409
Indorsement
    altered signature, 832
    blank indorsement, 825–826
    conditional indorsement, 827
    discharge of indorsers, 866
    effects of, 825
    employee's fraudulent indorsement, liability for, 860
    mistakes in or missing, 823–824
    nature of, 823
    obligation of indorser, 849
    prohibiting further negotiation, 827
    qualified indorsement, 827–828
    rescission of, 828
    restrictive, 826–827
    special indorsement, 825
    unauthorized signature, 832
Industrial Revolution's effect on tort law, 206
Industry guides, 1226
Industrywide liability, 524–526
Infancy as incapacity; *see also* Minors
    contract law, 379–385
    criminal law, 134–135
Informal rulemaking, 1206
Information
    in criminal law, 138
    right to, 1060, 1095
Infractions, 126
Infringement
    copyright, 253–263
    patents, 248
    trade dress, 280
    trademarks, 266, 280
Inheritance
    acquisition of personal property by, 597
    acquisition of real property by, 623
Injunctions
    equitable remedy, 5
    remedy for breach of contract, 473–474
    against securities professionals, 1183
Injurious falsehood, 275–276
In personam jurisdiction, 30
In re Borden, 725–727
In re Burt, 797–798
In re Corvette Collection of Boston, Inc., 499–500
In re Foreclosure Cases, 730–731
In re Garrison-Ashburn, LC, 991–992
In re Gerhardt, 784–785
In re Hanford Nuclear Reservation Program, 235–236
In re Interbank Funding Corp. v. Chadmoore Wireless Group Inc., 922–923
In re Kyllogen, 774–775
In re Labrum & Doak, LLP, 977–978
In re Made In Detroit, Inc., 791–793
In re Manhattan Investment Fund Ltd., 779–781

In re McAllister, 756–757
In rem jurisdiction, 33
In re Shirel, 742–743
In re Siegenberg, 786–790
Insanity
    incapacity, in criminal law, 134–135
    party to contract, 318
Inside information, trading on, 1072–1073,
        1137–1138, 1143
Insiders, 1137–1138, 1143–1146
Insolvent buyer, 575
Inspection
    negligence, 514
    shareholders' right, 1108
Inspection rights
    buyers', 550–551
    shareholders', 1095
Instructions, inadequate, 521
Instrumentalist approach of courts, 11
Insurable interest, 692, 694–696
Insurance
    antitrust exemption, 1307
    benefits of, 688
    breach by insurer, 694, 708–709
    cancellation, 693
    contractual aspects, 688–689
    corporations, 1078, 1079
    form and content of contracts, 692–694
    interpretation of contracts, 693
    lapse, 693
    legality, 692
    liability insurance; *see* Liability insurance
    loss-causing event, notice and proof of, 693
    misrepresentation, 692
    nature of, 688
    nonprofit corporations, 1079
    parties, 688
    performance by insurer, 694
    product liability, 506
    property insurance; *see* Property insurance
    reformation of written policy,
        692–693
    required clauses, 693
    risk of loss, 496
    time limits, 693
    title insurance, 629
    warranties and representations distinguished, 692
    writing requirement, 692
Insured party, 688
Insurer, 688
Intangible personal property, 589
Integration clause, 426
Intel Co. v. Hamidi, 199–200
Intellectual property
    copyrights, 251–263
    patents, 242–251
    trademarks, 263–273
    trade secrets, 273–276
Intended beneficiaries, 446–447
Intent
    to accept contract, 325–327
    assault, 175
    battery, 173–174
    to contract, 307–308
    defined, 170
    element of fixture classification, 614
Inter-American Convention Against Corruption (IACAC), 160
Interbank of New York v. Fleet Bank, 813
Interest in land contracts, 415–416
Intermediate scrutiny (means-end test), 65, 75
International Consortium of Real Estate Associations, 906
International Shoe Co. v. Washington, 38, 1012, 1013
International wire transfers, 889–890
Internet
    defamation, 182
    securities fraud, 1149
    securities offerings, 1119–1120, 1127
Internet Solutions Corp. v. Marshall, 34–36
Interpretation of contracts, 430–431
Interpretive rules, 1205
Interrogatories, 40–41
Interstate commerce, power of Congress to
        regulate, 59–62, 81–82
Interstate Commerce Act, 606
Intervening cause in negligence actions, 228
Inter vivos gift, 594
Inter vivos trust, 679
Intestacy, 675, 677
In the Matter of International Harvester, 1249
Intoxication as incapacity
    contract law, 389
    criminal law, 134
Intrastate commerce, power of Congress to regulate, 59–62
Intrastate offering exemptions, 1124
Intrinsic fairness standard, 1068–1069
Invasion of privacy, torts comprising, 191–195
Inventions; *see* Patents
Inventory, perfected purchase money security interest in, 753
Inverse condemnation, 633
Investment contracts, 1116
Invitees on property, duties owed to, 214
Involuntary bailee, 605
Iredell Digestive Disease Clinic P.A. v. Petrozza, 398
Irrevocable letter of credit, 551
Irwin, Chief Judge, 197
Isolated transactions, 1015
Issue, in estates and trusts, 668
Issued shares, 1037

J

Jackson, District Judge Thomas Penfield, 1281
Jacobs, Justice, 1059, 1092

Jacobs, Vice Chancellor, 682
Jannusch v. Naffziger, 311–313
Jet Wine & Spirits, Inc. v. Bacardi & Co., Ltd., 1013–1014
Jewish Federation of Greater Des Moines v. Cedar Forrest Products Co., 574
Johanns v. Livestock Marketing Association, 70–71
Johnson, Judge, 1043
Joinder, class actions, 48
Joiner, Senior District Judge, 1362
Joint export activities, 1307
Joint tenancy, 618
Joint ventures
    authority of partners, 959
    by competitors, 1272–1273
    dissolution, winding up's effect of, 972
    fiduciary duties, 953
    partnerships distinguished, 940–941
    transfers of interests, 948
Joint wills, 670
Jones, Circuit Judge, 785
Jones v. The Baran Company, 423–425
Jordan v. Knafel, 363–365
Judge-made law; *see* Common law (case law)
Judges, private (ADR), 53
Judgment notwithstanding the verdict (judgment n.o.v.), 47
Judgment on the pleadings, motion for, 40
Judgment-proof debtor, 719
Judicial dissolution, 1109–1110
Judicial powers, 57
Judicial review, 57–58, 1205–1206, 1208–1216
Jurisdiction
    appellate courts, 30, 36–37
    concurrent jurisdiction, 36
    district courts, 34
    diversity jurisdiction, 34
    exclusive, 37
    federal courts, 34–38
    federal question jurisdiction, 34
    limited jurisdiction courts, 29
    necessity of, 30
    original, 37
    in personam, 30
    in rem, 33
    specialized federal courts, 36
    state courts, 29–34
    subject-matter, 30
    Supreme Court, U.S., 37
    trial courts, 29–30
Jurisprudence, 9–11
Jury instructions, 47
Jury trials
    general information, 47
    right to, 127–128
Just compensation in eminent domain, 633

Justice theory
    criticism of, 95–96
    decision making according to, 109
    ethical business practices, 95–96
Justifiable reliance, in misrepresentation, 362

K

Kantianism: rights theory of business ethics, 93–94
Kasky v. Nike, Inc., 68–70
Katris v. Carroll, 988–989
Kearse, Circuit Judge, 1357
Keeton v. Flying J, Inc., 1329–1330
Kelly v. Central Bank & Trust Co., 824–825
Kelo v. City of New London, 85–86, 634–636
Kenai Chrysler Center, Inc. v. Denison, 386–388
Kennard, Justice, 68
Kennedy, Justice, 146, 162, 245, 250, 1147, 1264, 1301
Kessler, J., 355
KGM Harvesting Co. v. Fresh Network, 577–578
Khan v. Parsons Global Services, Ltd., 176–177
Kilburg, Chief Judge, 757
Kimbrough v. United States, 128
Kimmelman, J.A.D., 333
Knievel v. ESPN, 185–186
Knowledge, agency law, 917
Koch Materials Co. v. Shore Slurry Seal, Inc., 560–562
Kozinski, Judge, 17
Kraft, Inc. v. Federal Trade Commission, 1228–1230
Kressel, Chief Judge, 727
Kruser v. Bank of America NT & SA, 888–889
KSR International Co. v./ Teleflex, Inc., 244–247, 251
Kulp v. Timmons, 682–683
Kyllo v. United States, 141–142

L

Labor Management Relations Act, 1322
Labor Management Reporting and Disclosure Act, 1322
Labor unions and antitrust liability, 1307
Lach v. Man O'War, LLC, 1001–1003
Laissez faire theory of capitalism, 97
Lambert v. Barron, 293–294
Land; *see* Real property
Land contracts, 732
Landlord and tenant
    condition of property, 649–650
    contractual aspects of relationship, 645
    duties of landlord, 648–649
    duties of tenant, 659
    injuries
        criminal conduct of others' causing, 658
        to third persons, 660
    leases; *see* Leases
    liabilities of landlord, 653–658
    rights of landlord, 647–648
    rights of tenant, 659

Landlord and tenant—*Cont.*
  security deposits, 647–648
  tenancies, types of, 646, 647
  tenant's liabilities, 660
  tort liability of landlord, 653–658
Landrum-Griffin Act, 1322
Land use control
  eminent domain, 633–636
  inverse condemnation, 633
  nuisance law, 632–633
  public purpose in eminent domain, 633–636
  subdivision laws, 636–637
  zoning laws, 636–637
Lanham Act, 263–273, 280–283
Law
  case law reasoning, 12–13
  classification of, 8–9
  functions of, 11
  jurisprudence, 9–11
  legal reasoning, 11–24
  mistakes of, 366–367
  types of, 2–6
Law and economics movement, 11
Law merchant, 480
Layton, Chief Justice, 1070
Leading object rule, 414–415
Leasehold estate, 646
Lease of goods, 482–483
Leases, 593
  assignment, 659–660
  constructive eviction, 648–649
  definition of, 646
  execution of, 646–647
  subleases, 659, 660
  termination
    abandonment, 660–661
    constructive eviction, 648–649
    eviction, 660–661
    landlord's breach, 649
    surrender, 660
  types of, 646, 647
Leegin Creative Leather Products v. PSKS, Inc.,
  1263–1267
Lefkowitz v. Great Minneapolis Surplus Store, 314
Legal positivism, 9
Legal proceedings, misuse of, 195
Legal realism, American, 9–10
Legal remedies; *see* Damages
Legislative history, in statutory interpretation, 16
Legislative powers, 57
Legislative purpose, in statutory interpretation, 16
Legislative rules, 1205–1206
LeHigh Presbytery v. Merchants Bancorp. Inc, 826–827
Letter of credit, 551
Leval, Circuit Judge, 494

Lewis, Justice, 42
Liability
  acceptor of draft, 847
  accommodation party, negotiable instruments, 849–850
  agent's contractual liability, 919–923
  bank's liability after stop-payment order, 872–873
  buyer inducement of discrimination, 1306
  civil liability; torts, 170
  consumer reporting agencies, 1239
  contractual liability
    agent's, 919–923
    negotiable instruments, 846–847
    securities professionals, 1160–1161
  contractual liability: negotiable instruments, 851–854
  conversions, negotiable instruments, 863
  corporate management, for torts and crimes, 1074–1075
  credit bureau officers and employees, 1239
  creditor holding security interest in collateral, 763–765
  criminal liability, securities law, 1135–1136, 1180–1183
  defective incorporation, 1034
  discharge of liability, negotiable instruments, 863–866
  disclaimers, 532–533
  drawee of check, 847–848
  drawer of check, 849
  employer for fraudulent indorsement by employee, 860
  false brokerage, 1306
  fictitious payee rule, negotiable instruments, 859–860
  fraud by professional, 1170
  fraudulent indorsement by employees, negotiable
    instruments, 860
  general information, 846
  hazardous chemicals, cleanup costs of, 1364–1365
  impostor rule, negotiable instruments, 859–860
  indorser of check, 849
  industrywide liability, 524–526
  landlord's tort liability, 653–658
  maker of promissory note, 847
  negligence, writing or signing negotiable instruments,
    858–859
  new partners, 981, 983
  "no liability outside privity of contract" principle, 505
  "no liability without fault" principle, 505
  partner's
    to creditors, 954
    dissociated partner, 976–977
    limited partnerships and LLLPs, 996–999
    successor liability, 975
    tort of other partner, 961–962
  partnership's tort liability, 961–962
  preincorporation contracts, 1027–1028
  preincorporation transactions of nonprofits, 1036
  primarily liable, 847
  principal's
    contractual liability, 914–919
    tort liability, 923–927

product liability; *see* Product liability

promoter's on preincorporation contracts, 1028

proportionate liability, 1175–1176

purported partners (LLPs), 943

secondarily liable, 847

securities law, 1122, 1129–1135, 1140–1151, 1160–1176

securities professionals
  to clients, 1160–1165
  to third persons under common law, 1165–1170
  to third persons under securities law, 1171–1176

sexual harassment, 1328

shareholders', 1103–1107

tort liability
  principal's, 923–927
  security professionals, 1161–1165

warranty liability, 854–858

Liability insurance
  covered liabilities, 702
  definition, 701
  duties of insurer, 705–706
  types of, 701
  unaffordability and "crisis" situation, 706, 708

Liacos, Justice, 1072

Libel, defined, 181

Licensee on property, duty owed to, 214

Licenses
  contracts violative of public policy, 395
  online, 294
  patent licensing, 1311
  property right accorded by, 620
  shrinkwap, 294
  trade secret, 274

Liens
  Chapter 7 bankruptcy
    exempt properties, 776
    preferential liens, 777
  common law, 724
  essential elements of, 725
  foreclosure, 727, 734–737
  materialman's, 732–737
  mechanic's, 732–737
  notice of, 734
  possessory, 724
  priorities, 734–737
  statutory, 724
  waiver of, 737

Life estate, 617

Lifland, Judge, 922

Lifland, U.S. Bankruptcy Judge, 780

Likeness, commercial appropriation of, 192–193, 280

Lillard, Judge, 297

Limitation of remedies, 533

Limitation statutes; *see* Statutes of limitations

Limited liability company (LLC)
  certificate of organization, 986

conversion to other business form, 1001

dissociation of member, 990–991

dissolution of, 980–981

distribution to creditors of dissolved LLC, 991

distribution to members, 989

duties of members, 987

formation of, 986

liability of member, 986

management rights, 986–987

manager-managed LLC, 987

member-managed LLC, 986–987

mergers, 1001

nature of, 935–936

operating agreement, effect of dissolution on, 991

ownership interest of members, 989–990

payment to dissociated member, 990

principal characteristics of, 987

tax treatment of, 986

winding up, 990–991

Limited liability limited partnership (LLLP)
  capital contributions, 996–997
  certificate of limited partnership, 994
  conversion to other business form, 1001
  creation of, 994–995
  dissociation of partner, 999–1000
  dissolution, 1000–1001
  distribution of assets, 1001
  general partners
    dissociation of, 999–1000
    fiduciary duties of, 998
    management powers and compensation, 997–998
  improper formation, 995
  liability of partners, 995, 996–999
  limited partner dissociations, 999
  limited partnership agreement, 995, 1000
  mergers, 1001
  nature of, 934, 993–994
  new partners, 997
  noncompliance with requirements, 995
  profit and loss sharing, 997
  rights of partners, 996–999
  tax treatment of, 993–994
  tort liability, general partners, 998
  transferable interest, 997
  use of, 993–994
  voting, 997
  winding up, 1000–1001
  withdrawal from, 997

Limited liability partnership (LLP)
  contractual liability, 963
  creation of, 942
  dissolution
    dissociated partner's liability, 977
    distribution of assets, 975
  lawsuits against, 962–963

Limited liability partnership (LLP)—*Cont.*
  nature of, 933–934
  new partners, 983
  partners; *see* Partners
  securities professionals, 1179–1180
  tort liability, 962
Limited partnership
  capital contributions, 996–997
  certificate of limited partnership, 994
  conversion to other business form, 1001
  creation of, 994–995
  dissociation of partner, 999–1000
  dissolution, 1000–1001
  distribution of assets, 1001
  fiduciary duties, general partners, 998
  general partners
    dissociation of, 999–1000
    functions, 993
    management powers and compensation, 997–998
    tort liability, 998
  improper formation, 995
  liability of partners, 995, 996–999
  limited partners, 993, 999
  limited partnership agreement, 995, 1000
  mergers, 1001
  nature of, 934, 993–994
  new partners, 997
  noncompliance with requirements, 995
  profit and loss sharing, 997
  rights of partners, 996–999
  tax treatment of, 993–994
  transferable interest, 997
  use of, 993–994
  voting, 997
  winding up, 1000–1001
  withdrawal from, 997
Limited partnership agreement
  dissolution's effect on, 1000
  general information, 995
Lindh v. Surman, 595–596
Lingle v. Chevron U.S.A., Inc., 639–640
Lipez, Circuit Judge, 336
Liquidated damages
  agreement for, 568–570
  breach of contract, 471, 576
Liquidated debts, 351–352
Liquidation preference, 1037
Listing contracts, 625–626
LLC; *see* Limited liability company (LLC)
LLLP; *see* Limited liability limited partnership (LLLP)
LLP; *see* Limited liability partnership (LLP)
Loans
  debt collection practices, 1244
  disclosure requirements, 1237–1238
Lochner v. New York, 71
Locke v. Ozark City Board of Education, 447–448

Long-arm statutes, 30
Looting, corporations, 1018–1019
Lorenz, Judge, 308
Lost property
  finder's responsibilities, 593
  general information, 590–593
Lotteries and money laundering, 128–131
Louis Vuitton Malletier, SA v. Haute Diggity Dog, LLC,
    269–273
Loyalty, duty of, 902, 951
Lucas v. South Carolina Coastal Council, 84–85, 638
Lure of the new in ethical decisions, 114
Lynch, District Judge, 905
Lynch, Judge, 1013

M

*M. A. Mortenson Company, Inc. v. Timberline
    Software Corp.,* 534
Magistrates (ADR), 53
Magnuson-Moss Act, 524, 533
Magnuson-Moss Warranty Act, 1236–1237
Mail fraud, 1183
Main purpose rule, 414–415
*Mainstream Marketing Services, Inc. v. Federal Trade
    Commission,* 1233–1236
Maker, promissory note, 807
Malice, defamation cases, element of, 187–188
Malicious prosecution, 195
Malpractice insurance policies, 701
Management solicitation of proxies, 1051–1052
Mandatory dividend, 1037
Manion, Circuit Judge, 917
Mann v. Abel, 181
Manufacture
  defects in, 521
  negligent, 514
Marine Protection, Research, and Sanctuaries
    Act, 1359–1360
Maritime doctrine of general average, 606
Marketable title, 628
Mark v. FSC Securities Corp., 1125–1126
Marriage as contract consideration, 419–420
Marschewski, Magistrate Judge, 491
Marsh v. Alabama, 63
Marvin v. Marvin, 402
Massachusetts v. Environmental Protection Agency, 1207,
    1209–1214, 1353–1355
Masters, special (ADR), 53
Materiality
  in misleading claims, 1228
  in misrepresentation, 362
  in mistakes, 367
  securities law, 1141
Materialmen
  liens, 732–737
  rights of, 732–733

Mathias v. Accor Economy Lodging, Inc., 171–173

Matsushita Electric Industrial Co., Ltd. v. Zenith Radio Corp., 1281

Matthews v. Amberwood Associates Limited Partnership, Inc., 654–658

Maxims, in statutory interpretation, 22

Mayer, C., 885

Mayer, Judge, 992

McAvo, Judge, 1359

McCarran-Ferguson Act, 1307

McClendon, Judge, 174

McCormack v. Brevig, 946–947

McCune v. Myrtle Beach Indoor Shooting Range, Inc., 401–402

McDade, Justice, 31

McEwen, Judge, 827

McGee, Judge, 763

McGurn v. Bell Microproducts, Inc., 335–337

McLachlan, Judge, 971

McLean, District Judge, 1132

McNeil v. Wisconsin, 154

MDM Group Associates, Inc. v. CX Reinsurance Company Ltd., 897–898

Meacham v. Knolls Atomic Power Laboratory, 1331

Means-end test, 64–65

Means test (bankruptcy), 786

Mechanic's liens, 732–737, 758

Med/arb (ADR), 53

Mediation (ADR), 52

MedImmune v. Genentech, 251

Meeting
    board of directors, 1053–1054
    Chapter 7 creditors, 772–773
    due diligence, 1134
    shareholders, 1083–1084, 1107–1108

Meinhard v. Salmon, 1067

Melvor, Bankruptcy Judge, 792

Memorandum in contracts, 420–421

Mens rea
    criminal law, 134–135
    white-collar crimes, 154

Mental examination, motion for court order requiring, 41

Mental incapacity
    effect of, 386–389
    right to disaffirm contracts, 386–389
    test for, 385–386
    void or voidable contracts, 385

Mentors; assistance from in dealing with unethical situations, 117

Meram v. MacDonald, 308–309

Merchantability, implied warranty of, 508–509

Merchants
    applicability of UCC to, 483
    contract standards for, 299–300

Merger clause, 426

Mergers, 1088
    Clayton Act provisions, 1289–1298
    competition, effect on, 1296
    conglomerate mergers, 1297–1298
    effects of, 1292–1293
    geographic market, 1292
    horizontal, 1292–1296
    limited liability companies, 1001
    limited partnerships, 1001
    line of commerce determination, 1289–1290
    market shares issues, 1292
    relevant market, 1289–1290
    relevant product market, 1289–1290
    vertical, 1296

Merit registration, 1153

Merritt, Circuit Judge, 515

Meskell v. Bertone, 749–751

Metro-Goldwyn-Mayer Studios, Inc. v. Grokster, Ltd., 255–258

Milan v. Dean Witter Reynolds, Inc., 925–926, 1161

Milkovich v. Lorain Journal Co., 186

Mill, John Stuart, 96

Miller v. California, 131, 132

Mining partnerships
    authority of partners, 959
    creation of, 942
    dissolution, winding up's effect of, 972
    fiduciary duties, 953
    transfer of interests, 948

Minitrial (ADR), 53

Minors
    capacity to contract, 379–385
    emancipation, 380–381
    "infancy doctrine," 382
    liability for necessaries, 383
    misrepresentation of age, 385
    period of minority, 380
    right to disaffirm; *see* Disaffirmance

Miranda v. Arizona, 148–149

Mirror image rule, 327

Misappropriation of trade secret, 274

Misappropriation theory, 1146

Misdemeanors, 126

Mislaid property
    finder's responsibilities, 593
    general information, 590–593

Misleading claims, FTC regulation, 1227

Misrepresentation
    general information, 362–365
    insured's, 692
    liability for agent's misrepresentation, 926–927
    minor's age, 385
    product liability recovery for, 524
    securities professionals, 1166–1170

Missouri v. Seibert, 149–152

Mistake
  in contracts, 365–369
  payment or acceptance of negotiable instrument by, 857
Misuse of legal proceedings, 195
Model Business Corporation Act (MBCA), 1011
Model Nonprofit Corporation Act (MNCA), 1011,
    1017, 1107–1108
Model statutes, 3
Modification of contracts
  performance, 549
  sales contracts, 418
  UCC provisions, 351
Money: fixed amount in negotiable instruments, 815
Money laundering and lotteries, 128–131
Monopolies
  attempted monopolization, 1280–1281
  Clayton Act, 1288–1289
  conspiracy to monopolize, 1282
  definition of "monopolization" and "monopoly power," 1273
  geographic market, 1274
  intent to monopolize, 1274–1275
  product market, 1274
  relevant market, 1274
  Sherman Act, 1273–1282
Moore v. City of East Cleveland, 637
Mootness, 23
Moraghan, Judge Trial Referee, 624
Moral values and the law, 10–11
Moren v. JAX Restaurant, 963–964
Mortgagee, 728
Mortgages
  assignment of interest, 729
  execution, 728
  foreclosure, 729, 730
  historical development of, 729
  purchase of property, 729
  recordation, 728
  redemption right, 729–730
  requirements, 728
  sale of property, 729
  security interest, 728–730
Mortgagor, 728
Moser v. Moser, 995–996
Mosk, Judge, 579, 1339
Moss v. Batesville Casket Co., 512–514
Motions
  directed verdict, 47
  dismissal, 40
  judgment on the pleadings, 40
  new trial, 47
  summary judgment, 45
Motor Carrier Act of 1980, 89
Motor vehicles, perfecting security interest, 751
Mukasey, District Judge, 553
Murdock, Judge, 384

Murray, Judge, 458
Music Acceptance Corp. v. Lofing, 841–842
Mutual agreement to discharge contract, 468
Mutual mistakes, 367
Mutual Savings Association v. Res/Com Properties, L.L.C.,
    734–737
Mutual wills, 670

N

Najam, Judge, 486
Naked restraints, 1267
Name, commercial appropriation of, 192–193
Nase Services, Inc. v. Jervis, 399–400
*National Cable and Telecommunications Association v. Brand
    X Internet Services,* 1215
National Environmental Policy Act, 1208, 1346
National Labor Relations Act, 1321–1322
National origin
  discrimination on basis of, 1327
  Equal Protection Clause and, 74–75
National Pollution Discharge Elimination System permit, 1355
Natural law, 9
*NBN Broadcasting, Inc. v. Sheridan Broadcasting Networks,
    Inc.,* 959–961
Needs contract, 483, 485
Negative easements, 619
Negligence
  actual cause, 224–225
  assumption of risk, 233
  comparative negligence, 232–233, 1162
  contributory negligence, 534, 1162
  defenses, 232–233
  defined, 170
  design, 515–517
  duty of care, 206–207
  elements of, 206
  failure to warn, 514–515
  foreseeable events after breach, 228
  injury, causation of, 221–231
  inspection, 514
  insurance applications, delay in acting on, 691–692
  intervening cause, 228
  manufacture, 514
  mistakes resulting from, 366
  origins, 206
  per se negligence, 218
  property, duties to persons on, 214–218
  proximate cause, 225
  res ipsa loquitur, 231–232, 514
  securities professionals, 1161, 1166–1170
  securities violations, 1135
  special duties, 214
  tort reform and, 236–237
Negotiable bill of lading, 551
Negotiable document of title, 608

Negotiable instruments
    acceptor, 808
    advantages of negotiability, 807, 811
    alteration, discharge by, 864–866
    ambiguous terms, 818
    assignee of a contract, rights of, 811
    authorized signature, 850–851
    basic types of, 807–811
    bearer paper, 823
    cancellation, discharge by, 864
    certificates of deposit, 808
    checks; *see* Checks
    collateral, clauses concerning, 818
    conversion, 863
    definition, 807
    discharge of, 863–866
    dishonored instruments, 832, 852
    drafts, 808, 810, 852–853
    drawer and drawee, 808, 810
    formal requirements, 811–812
    holder, 811, 822, 830
    holder in due course; *see* Holder in due course
    liability
        discharge of, 863–866
        specific obligations; *see* Liability
    maker, 807
    mistake, payment or acceptance by, 857
    note, presentment of, 852
    order paper, 823
    overdue instruments, 832
    payee, 807, 808, 810
    payment
        at definite time, 815–816
        on demand, 815
        fixed amount of money, 815
        in money, 815
        order or bearer, payable to, 816–817
    payment, discharge by, 864
    presentment of, 852–853
    promise or order, 813–815
    promissory notes, 807–811
    rights of holder, 811
    signing requirement, 812, 850–851
    time of presentment, 853–854
    transfer of order instrument, 824
    UCC provisions, 807
    unauthorized signature, 851
    undertakings or instructions disallowed, 818
    waiver of benefit of law, clauses concerning, 818
    warranty liability, 854–858
    writing requirement, 812
Negotiation
    definition under UCC, 822–823
    formal requirements, 823
    rights acquired by, 608

Newbern, Justice, 819
New Jason clauses, 606
*New Jersey Economic Development Authority v. Pavonia
    Restaurant, Inc.,* 722–723
Newkirk, Judge, 424
Newman, Justice, 596
New source controls under Clean Air Act, 1348
Newton v. Standard Candy Co., 510–511
New trial motion, 47
New York Clearinghouse Interbank Payments System
    (CHIPS), 889–890
New York Times Co. v. Sullivan, 187, 191
Niemeyer, Circuit Judge, 269
Nietzsche, Friedrich, 115
NLRB v. Bildisco and Bildisco, 794
No action letters, 1116
"No arrival, no sale" destination contract, 495
Noble, Vice Chancellor, 301
Noble Roman's, Inc. v. Pizza Boxes, Inc., 485–487
Noerr-Pennington doctrine, 1308
Nollan v. California Coastal Commissioner, 638
Nolo contendere plea, 138
Nominal damages, 471
Noncommercial speech and First Amendment, 65–67, 131
Noncompetition clauses, 398–400
Nonconforming uses in zoning, 636
Noncupative wills, 669
Nondisclosure
    agreements for, 398
    in misrepresentation, 362
Noneconomic loss, 526
Nonexistent principal, 920
Nonprofit corporations
    annual meeting, 1107–1108
    definition of, 1010
    derivative suits, 1108–1109
    dissolution, 1110–1111
    distribution of assets, 1108
    duties of directors and officers, 1073
    election of directors, 1107–1108
    expulsion of members, 1108
    financing, 1044–1045
    foreign, 1017
    incorporation, 1035–1036
    information, right to, 1108
    inspection rights, 1108
    insurance, 1079
    liability for preincorporation transaction, 1036
    management of, 1055–1056
    Model Nonprofit Corporation Act (MNCA), 1011, 1017
    piercing the corporate veil, 1017–1023
    powers of, 1049
    resignation of members, 1108
    voting rights, 1107–1108
    winding up, 1110–1111

Non sequiturs in ethical decisions, 110–111
Nonsolicitation agreements, 398–399
Nontrading partnership, 958
No-privity defense, 527–528
Norris-LaGuardia Act, 1307, 1321
North Atlantic Instruments, Inc. v. Haber, 275–276
Northwest Wholesale Stationers, Inc. v. Pacific Stationery & Printing Co., 1268
Notes, promissory
 co-maker of, 809
 general information, 807
 maker of, 807
 presentment of, 852
Notes (debt security), 1038
Not-for-profit corporations; *see* Nonprofit corporations
Notice
 adverse claims and breaches, to holder in due course, 832–833
 agency law, 917
 due process and, 71
 liens, 734
 "notice and comment" rulemaking, 1206
 to partner, 958
 shareholders meeting, 1084
 termination of agency, to third party, 910
Novation
 discharge of delagator by, 444
 general information, 976, 1028
Nozick, Roger, 95
Nuisance, private, 196
Nuisance law, 632–633
Nuss, J., 393

O

Objective theory of contracts, 308
Obligations; *see* Liability
Obligee
 definition, 435
 delegation of duties, 441
Obligor
 definition, 435
 delegation of duties, 441
 notification to, 439–440
O'Brien, Justice, 382
Obscenity and freedom of speech, 131–132
Occupational Safety and Health Act, 1319
Occupational Safety and Health Administration, 1319
Ocean dumping, 1359–1360
O'Connor, Justice, 74, 639, 1118, 1261
Offer
 contract; *see* Contract offer
 insurance, 688–689
Offeree, 307
Offeror, 307
Office of Management and Budget (OMB), 1208

Okosa v. Hall, 332–333
Olbekson v. Huber, 614–615
Olin Corporation v. Federal Trade Commission, 1290–1291
Olympic Airways v. Husain, 23
Oncale v. Sundowner Offshore Services, Inc, 1328
O'Neil, Jr., Judge, 607
Opala, Judge, 1318
Open policies, property insurance, 699–700
Opinion letter, 1180
Opp v. Wheaton Van Lines, Inc., 916–917
Option agreement for share sales, 1041
Oral contracts
 legality, 412
 sale of land, 415–416
Order of relief, Chapter 7, 772
Order paper, 823
Ordinances, 6
Original jurisdiction, 37
Orlovsky, District Judge, 561
Ostrander, Chief Justice, 1097
Output contracts, 348, 483, 485
Outrageousness, 176, 177
Outstanding shares, 1037
Owner and ownership
 copyrights, 253–254
 in insurance, 688
 patents, 247–248
 personal property, 589–598
 trademarks, 265
 trade secrets, 274

P

Paciaroni v. Crane, 973–974
Pack v. Damon Corp., 533
Palese v. Delaware State Lottery Office, 301–302
Palmer, Judge, 1016
Palmer v. Claydon, 944
"Palming off" tort claims, 280
Paramount Communications, Inc. v. Time, Inc., 1065–1067
Parents Involved in Community Schools v. Seattle School District No. 1, 75–79
Parent-subsidiary transactions, 1069
Paris Convention for the Protection of Industrial Property, 268
Parker v. Brown, 1307–1308
Parol evidence rule, 425–427
Parsons, Vice Chancellor, 428
Partially disclosed principal, 920
Participating preferred shares, 1037
Partners
 admissions by, 958
 authority of, 956–957, 972–973
 borrowing money
  from partnership, 957–958
  during winding up, 972–973
 buyout of dissociated partners, 978

charging order, 947–948
compensation of, 953–954
competing against partnership, 952
conflict of interest, 952
consequences of being, 940
conveyance of partnership real property, 957
definition, 933
disagreements among, 958
disputes during winding up, 973
dissolution, 969–975
duties of, 951–953
executory contracts during winding up, 972
handling negotiable instruments, 958
interest adverse to partnership, 952
issuing negotiable instruments, 958
lawsuits by and against, 962–963
liability
    dissociated partner's, 976–977
    joint and several liability, 963
    new partner's, 981, 983
    to partnership creditors, 954
    for partner's torts and crimes, 961–962
    remaining partners' after dissociation, 975
liability of, 933
management powers of, 956–961
new partners, 981, 983
notice to, 958
ordinary course of business decisions, 958
ownership interest, 947–948
partnership agreement and management powers, 959
partnership interest, 947–948
purported partners, 942–943
ratification of unauthorized acts of, 957
transferable interest, 947–948
unanimity requirement, 958–959
winding up, authority during, 972–973
Partnerships
    agreement to restrict transfers, 948
    capital, 945
    "carrying on a business" requirement, 939
    continuation after dissociation, 975–981
    co-ownership requirement, 939–940
    creation of, 938–939
    crime, liability for partner's, 962
    dissociation
        continuation after, 975–981
        effect of, 968–969
        right of partner, 967–968
    dissolution, 969–975
    distribution of assets at dissolution, 974–975
    "intention to create relationship" requirement, 940
    joint ventures; see Joint ventures
    lawsuits by and against, 962–963
    limited liability limited partnership (LLLP), 934
    limited liability partnerships (LLPs); see Limited liability partnership (LLP)
    limited partnership, 934
    mining partnerships; see Mining partnerships
    nature of, 933, 938
    negligence, liability for partner's intentional, 962
    nontrading partnership, 958
    nonwrongful dissociation, 968
    partners; see Partners
    partnership agreement
        dissociation's effect on, 969
        dissolution/winding up's effect on, 970
    principal characteristics of, 938
    profit-sharing requirement, 939–940, 953–954
    property, 945
    purported partners, 942–943
    termination, 975
    tort, liability for partner's intentional, 962
    trading partnership, 957–958
    transferable interest, 947–948
    voluntary and consensual association requirement, 939
    winding up, 969–975
    wrongful dissociation, 968–969
Partnerships, tenancy in, 618
"Passing off" tort claims, 280
Pass v. Shelby Aviation, 297–298
Past consideration, 353
Patent and Trademark Office, 243, 250–251, 265
Patents
    abandonment, 242
    application, 242, 243
    criteria for patentability, 242
    current issues, 251
    defenses to infringement, 250–251
    infringement, 248
    inventions, 242–251
    licensing, 1311
    misuse of patent by patentee, 251
    ownership, 247–248
    specification, 243
    transfer of rights, 247–248
Patient Self-Determination Act, 675
Payee
    checks, 810
    drafts, 808
    promissory note, 807, 809
Payment
    negotiable instruments, 815–817
    in sales contracts, 552
Pearson v. Shalala, 1197–1199
Pelican National Bank v. Provident Bank of Maryland, 817–818
Per capita, in estates and trusts, 668
Peremptory challenges, 45
Perfect 10, Inc. v. Amazon.com, Inc., 259–263
Perfection of security interest
    by attachment, 748–749
    automatic, 748–749

Perfection of security interest—*Cont.*
   by control by secured party, 748
   financing statement, 744–747
   fixtures, 751
   motor vehicles, 751
   by possession by secured party, 745, 748
   by public filing, 744–745
Performance of contracts
   anticipatory repudiation, 464–465
   discharge of promisor's duties, 459–460
   excuses for nonperformance, 465–468
   good faith performance, 460
   insurance contracts, 694
   late performance, 461
   oral contracts for sale of land, 415–416
   sales contracts; *see* Performance of sales contracts
   specific performance as remedy, 473
   strict performance standard, 459
   substantial performance standard, 459–460
   time for, 461, 487
Performance of sales contracts
   acceptance of goods, 553
   anticipatory repudiation, 563
   assignment, 550
   assurance, 560
   commercial impracticability, 563
   course of dealing, 547
   delivery, 487, 550
   duties of buyer
      after acceptance, 554
      after rejection, 559–560
   excuses for nonperformance, 563
   failure to object constituting waiver, 549–550
   general rules, 546–550
   good faith, 547
   impossibility of, 563
   improper delivery, rights of buyer on, 556–557
   inspection right of buyer, 550–551
   payment, 552
   rejection of goods, 553, 557
   seller's right to cure nonconformance, 559
   usage of trade, 547
   waiver, 549–550
Periodic tenancy, 646
Perlman v. Feldman, 1104
Permits
   Clean Air Act, 1350–1351
   hazardous wastes, 1361
   industrial discharges, 1355
Per se negligence, 218
Per se unlawful antitrust actions, 1258, 1261
Personal injuries
   damages, product liability, 526
   negligence actions, 221
Personal liability policies, 701

Personal property
   acquiring ownership of, 589–598
   bailments; *see* Bailments
   classifications of, 589
   leasing, 593
   redemption of, Chapter 7, 773
   title documents, 605
Personal property insurance, 697
Personal rights, interference with, 173–196
Per stirpes, in estates and trusts, 668
Petitions, Chapter 7, 771
Pfaff v. Wells Electronics, Inc., 242, 243–244
Phillips v. E.I. DuPont de Nemours & Co., 235–236
Physical examination, motion for court order requiring, 41
Pierce, Circuit Judge, 903
Piercing the corporate veil, 1017–1023
Piracy, 266
Pity, appeals in ethical decisions to, 111
Plain meaning, in statutory interpretation, 16
Pleadings, 39–40
Pleas, in criminal law, 138
Pledges as security, 719
Police power, 58, 589
Policy limits, property insurance, 699
Political speech and First Amendment, 65
Pollack, Judge, 961
Pollution control, 1347–1352
Polygraph tests of employees, 1334–1335
Pope v. Rostraver Shop and Save, 178–180
Popovich, Judge, 670
Pornography and freedom of speech, 131–132
Posner, Chief Judge, 1142
Posner, Circuit Judge, 171, 1163, 1245
Posner, Judge, 1204
Possessory liens, 724
Potential reciprocity in conglomerate mergers, 1297
Pound, Roscoe, 10
Powell, Justice, 1144
Power of sale, foreclosure under, 729
PPG Industries, Inc. v. JMB/Houston Center, 437–438
Precedents, 3, 12–13
Preemption, federal, 57, 84
   defense of, 534
   regulations that preempt private suits, 1220–1221
Preferential liens, Chapter 7, 777
Preferential payments, Chapter 7, 777
Preferred shares, 1036–1037, 1085
Pregerson, Circuit Judge, 404
Preliminary hearing, in criminal law, 138
Premeditation, in criminal law, 134
Premium, in insurance, 688
Preponderance of evidence standards, 39, 170, 1207
Presentment warranties, 856–858
President of corporation, 1054
Preston v. Ferrer, 50–52

Presumed damages in slander and libel, 181
Presumption of reviewability, 1209
Pretermitted children, 673
Pretrial conference, 45
Prevention, in criminal law, 126
Prezeau, District Judge, 615
Price discrimination
    anticompetitive effect, 1300
    applicability to like grade and quality, 1300
    buyer inducement of discrimination, 1306
    changing conditions defense, 1305
    cost justification defense, 1305
    false brokerage, 1306
    functional discounts, 1299–1300
    indirect, 1306
    meeting competition in good faith defense, 1305–1306
    payments and services, discriminatory, 1306
    violative acts, 1299–1300
Price-fixing, 1259–1267, 1298–1299
Price terms, sales contracts, 483
Primary benefit test, 1166
Principal
    agency relationship; *see* Agency law
    definition, 896
Principe v. McDonald's Corp., 1271
Prior decisions, in statutory interpretation, 22
Priority claims, Chapter 7, 781–782
Priority rules for law conflicts, 6
Priority rules for security interest
    artisan's liens, 758
    bona fide purchaser, 758
    buyers in ordinary course of business, 758
    consumer goods, liens on, 758
    fixtures, 758–759
    general rules, 753
    inventory, perfected purchase money security
        interest in, 753–756
    mechanic's liens, 758
    need for, 752–753
    noninventory collateral, purchase money security interests
        in, 756–757
    rationale for protecting, 757–758
Priority systems for recording deeds, 629
Privacy Act of 1974, 1219
Privacy right
    antiterrorism legislation and, 147–148
    criminal law and, 139–146
    curtilage, 139
    employees, 1334–1338
    limit on criminalizing behavior, 131
    torts comprising invasion of, 191–195
Private judging (ADR), 53
Private law, 9
Private nuisance, 196, 633
Private offering exemptions, 1124–1126

Private panels (ADR), 53
Private property, 589
Private Securities Litigation Reform Act of 1995,
    1175–1176, 1194
Privileges
    defamation actions, 182–183
    professional-client, 1185
    against self-incrimination, 148–149
Privity
    of contract, 1166
    no-privity defense, 527–528
    UCC provisions, 528–531
Probable cause, in criminal law, 138
Probate estate, 678
Probation, in criminal law, 126
Procedural law, 8–9
Procedural rules, 1205
Procedural unconscionability, 403–404
Proceeds from collateral, 744, 762–763
Production, acquiring personal property by, 589
Production of documents, request for, 41
Product liability
    assumption of risk defense, 534
    contributory negligence, 534
    damages, 526–527
    defenses, 527–528, 533–539
    disclaimers, 532–533
    express warranties, 506–508
    historical development of law, 505–506
    industrywide liability, 524–526
    insurance costs affecting, 506
    Magnuson-Moss Act, 524, 533
    misrepresentation, recovery for, 524
    misuse of product defense, 534
    negligence suits, 515–517
    no-privity defense, 527–528
    recovery theories, 506–526
    remedy limitations, 532, 533
    Restatement (Second) of Torts, Section 402A,
        517–518
    Restatement (Third) of Torts: Product
        Liability, 520–521
    statutes of limitations, 526
    strict liability, 517–518
Product safety regulation, 1249
Professional-client privilege, 1185
Professional corporation, 935
Professional duties, negligence and, 214
Professional liability policies, 701, 705
Profit maximization
    ethical business practices, 108
    generally, 97–99
Profits, easement with, 620
Profit sharing, partnerships, 939–940, 953–954, 997
Prohibition, 88–89

Promise or order, negotiable instruments, 813–815
Promissory estoppel
    generally, 302–303
    power to revoke contract offer, 316–317
    Statute of Frauds and, 425
    substitute for consideration, 354–356
Promissory notes
    co-maker of, 809
    generally, 807
    maker of, 807
    presentment of, 852
Promoter of corporation, 1027–1029
Proof
    age discrimination, 1331
    beyond a reasonable doubt, 134
    malice, 187–188
    preponderance of evidence, 39
    Rule 10b-5 actions, 1141
    tort law, 170
Proof of claim, Chapter 7, 781
Property
    classifications of, 589
    Constitutional protection of ownership, 589
    definition of, 588
    duties owed to persons on, 214–218
    personal property; *see* Personal property
    procedural due process and, 71
    real property; *see* Real property
Property damage
    negligence actions, 221
    product liability, 526
Property insurance
    additional coverages, 697
    cancellation, 701
    coinsurance clause, 699–700
    covered perils, 696–697
    duration, 701
    excluded perils, 696–697
    fire insurance, 696–697
    insurable interest requirement, 694–696
    insurer's payment obligation, 699–701
    open policies, 699–700
    personal property, 697
    policy limits, 699
    pro rata clause, 700–701
    subrogation right, 701
    valued policies, 699–700
Property rights, interference with, 196–198
Pro rata clause, property insurance, 700–701
Prospective advantage, interference with, 278
Prospectus, securities, 1120, 1122
Protect Act (child pornography), 66
Proxies
    appointment by shareholder, 1086
    proxy contests, 1138
    proxy statement, 1138
        shareholder proposals, 1140
        solicitation, 1051–1052, 1138, 1140
Proximate cause in negligence actions, 225, 231
Prudent person standard, 1159–1160
Pseudo-foreign corporations, 1017
Public Company Accounting Oversight Board, 1160
Public disclosure of private facts, 191–192
Public figure plaintiff in defamation case, 187–188
Public function doctrine, 63–64
Publicity, false light, 192
Public law, 9
Public nuisance, 633
Public official plaintiff in defamation case, 187–188
Public property, 589
Public purpose
    in statutory interpretation, 22
    takings clause and, 85–86
Public purpose in eminent domain, 634–636
Public use, takings clause and, 85
Public wrongs, 125
Punitive damage
    breach of contract, 473, 708–709
    discrimination in employment, 1327
    product liability, 526–527
    torts, 170–171
Purchase money security interest
    after-acquired property, 744
    consumer goods, 748
    inventory, 753
    noninventory collateral, 756–757
    rationale for protection of, 757–758
Purchases
    acquiring personal property by, 589
    of real property, 623

Q

Qualified opinions, 1180
Quality terms, sales contracts, 483
Quanta Computer v. LG Electronics, 247, 251
Quasi-contracts
    breach of contract, 465
    minor's liability for necessaries, 383
    purpose, 300–3–1
    recovery of value from unenforceable contract, 413
Questions of fact or policy, 1214–1215
Questions of law, 1214
Quid pro quo sexual harassment, 1328
Quiet period, securities offerings, 1120
Quill Corp. v. North Dakota, 1014
Quillen, Justice, 1102
Quitclaim deeds, 627
Quorum, shareholders meetings, 1084

R

Race and Equal Protection Clause, 74–79
Racial discrimination, 1327

Racketeer Influenced and Corrupt Organizations Act (RICO), 160–163, 1183
Railway Labor Act, 1321
Raker, Judge, 651
Raleigh v. Performance Plumbing and Heating, Inc., 207–210
Ratification
    agency law, 917–918
    unauthorized acts of partners, 957
Rational basis test (means-end test), 64–65, 72
Rawls, John, 95
Reaffirmation agreements, 785–786
Real defenses of holder in due course, 836–837
Real estate brokers, 625
Real property
    acquisition of, 623–625
    Americans with Disabilities Act, 631–632
    deeds, 627–628
    definition, 613
    definition of, 589
    fixtures; *see* Fixtures
    governing law, 296
    land use control, 632–640
    oral contracts for sale, 415–416
    partner's power to convey, 957
    personal property distinguished, 589
    premises liability, 630–631
    regulation denying economic benefit, 638
    residential property, seller's responsibilities for, 629–630
    rights and interests in
        co-ownership, 617–619
        others, property owned by, 619–623
        possessory interests, 617
        security interest, 616–617
    sale of, 625–629
    security precautions, 631
    takings, 638–640
    title, 628–629
    trade fixtures, 615
    transfer by sale, 625–629
Reasonable alternatives, in duress, 371
Reasonable care in premises liability, 630–631
Reasonable care standard, 206
Reasonable consumer test, 1227–1228
Reasonable expectation of privacy, 139–142
Reasonable foreseeability of harm standard, 210
Reasonableness standard (UCC), 298
Reasonable person test, 206, 210
Reciprocal dealing agreements, 1272
Recklessness, defined, 170
Recording deeds, 628
Recording statutes, 628
Recoupment, negotiable instruments subject to claims in, 833, 839
Recovery of purchase price as remedy, 572

Redemption
    Chapter 7 bankruptcy: personal property redemption, 773
    right of, 729–730
Reductio ad absurdum arguments in ethical decisions, 114
Reformation, 5
Refusal to deal, 1268
Registration of securities
    coordination, registration by, 1153
    merit registration, 1153
    Securities Act of 1933, 1119–1123
    Securities Act of 1934, 1136–1137
    state statutes, 1153
Registration statement
    1933 law, 1120, 1171–1172
    1934 law, 1136
Regulation CC (dishonored checks), 881
Regulation FD (Fair Disclosure), 1149–1150
Regulatory compliance defense, 535–536
Regulatory Flexibility Act, 1208
Regulatory offenses by corporations, 159
Regulatory powers of government
    federal, 58–63
    state, 58
Regulatory statutes, 395–396
Rehabilitation, in criminal law, 126
Rehnquist, Chief Justice, 74, 136, 1187
Reimbursement
    principal's duty of, 907
    right to, 723
Rejection
    contract offer, 317–318
    damages for, 572–573
    goods, 553, 557
Reliance interest, 469
Religious discrimination, 1327
Remaindermen, 681
Remand on appeal, 48
Remedies
    age discrimination, 1331
    Americans with Disabilities Act, 632
    Consumer Product Safety Act, 1249
    credit reporting violations, 1239
    deceptive or unfair business practices, 1231
    discrimination in employment, 1326–1327
    fraud, 361
    implied warranty of habitability, breach of, 649–650
    limitations in product liability, 533
    reformation as remedy for contract mistake, 366–367
    specific performance as remedy, 416
    trade secret misappropriation, 274
    unjust dismissal, 1338
    wrongful discharge, 1338
Remedies for breach of contract
    equitable remedies, 473–474
    legal remedies, 469–473

Remedies for breach of contract—*Cont.*
  sales contracts; *see* Remedies for breach of sales contract
  types of, 468
Remedies for breach of sales contract
  agreements between parties, 568–570, 582–583
  buyer's remedies, 576–583
  cancellation and withholding of delivery, 571–572
  damages
    buyer's remedies, 578–582
    rejection or repudiation, 572–573
    seller's remedies, 576
  insolvent buyer, 575
  liquidated damages, 576
  recovery of purchase price, 572
  resale of goods, 572
  right to cover, 577
  seller's remedies, 571–576
  specific performance, 582
  statute of limitations, 571
  stop delivery, 575–576
Removal of case, 36
Rendell-Baker v. Cohn, 64
Reno v. American Civil Liberties Union, 132
Rent
  abatement, 649–650
  tenant's duty to pay, 659
Repairs
  cost of, property insurance, 699
  duty of reasonable care in making, 653
  repair-and-deduct, 650
Replacement cost, property insurance, 699
Reply, 40
Reporting requirements, securities law, 1137
Repudiation
  anticipatory repudiation, 464–465, 563
  damages for, 572–573
Requests for admissions, 40–41
Requests for documents and things, 41
Requirements contracts, 348, 463, 465
Res, in trusts, 679
Resale of goods as remedy, 572
Rescission
  contracts, 360–362
  indorsement, 828
  prior to performance of illegal act, 407
  as remedy, 5
Residential property; *see also* Landlord and tenant
  Fair Housing Act, 626
  seller's responsibilities for, 629–630
Residuary, 668
Res ipsa loquitur, 231–232, 514
Resisting pressure to act unethically, 116–119
Resource Conservation and Recovery Act, 1361
Respondeat superior doctrine
  business liability policies, 705
  corporate torts, 1074

partnerships and partners, 961–962
principal's tort liability, 923–924
scope-of-employment requirement, 924
white-collar crimes, 154
Restatement of Security: Suretyship, 723
Restatements, generally, 3
Restatement (Second) of Agency, 914, 915
Restatement (Second) of Contracts, 300
  acceptance, 336
  assignments, 440–441
  damages for breach, 472
  delegation of duties, 442
  improper threat, 370
  interest in land contracts, 416
  justifiable reliance, 362
  mailbox rule, 332
  mentally impaired persons capacity to contract, 386
  mistakes, 366, 368–369
  negligence in making mistakes, 366
  promissory estoppel, 425
  risk from mistakes, 367–369
  unconscionability, 403
Restatement (Second) of Property: landlord's duty to keep
    premises in repair, 651
Restatement (Second) of Torts
  abnormally dangerous activities, 235–236
  accountant liability, 1167
  injurious falsehood, 276
  intentional infliction of emotional distress, 176
  nuisance, 197
  product liability, 517–518
  professional negligence, 1166–1167
Restatement (Third) of Agency, 914, 915, 923
Restatement (Third) of Property: restrictive covenants, 622
Restatement (Third) of Torts: product liability,
    520–521, 527
Restitution
  disaffirmance of contract by minor, 381–382
  interest protected by contract remedies, 469
  remedy for breach of contract, 474
Restraints of trade (Sherman Act), 1257–1273
Restricted securities, 1127
Restrictive covenants, 620–621
Restrictive indorsement, 826–827
Resulting trusts, 684
Retention bonuses, Chapter 7, 779
Retribution, in criminal law, 126
Return, sale or, 497–498
Revenue-raising statutes, 395–396
Reverence or respect; argument to in ethical decisions, 113
Reversal on appeal, 48
Reverse splitting of shares, 1099
Reves v. Ernst & Young, 1117
Revised Uniform Limited Liability Company Act of 1996
    (RULLCA), 985–986
Revised Uniform Partnership Act (RUPA), 938

Revocation
offer of contracts, 316–317
sale of goods, 317
wills, 673
Reward, as contract offer, 314
Reynolds Health Care Services, Inc. v. HMNM, Inc., 1086–1087
Rice, Justice, 883, 946
Ricketts v. Scothorn, 302
RICO (Racketeer Influenced and Corrupt Organizations Act), 160–163
Riegel v. Medtronic, 536–539
Riggs v. Woman to Woman, P.C., 396–397
Right, preemptive, 1095–1096
Right of appraisal, 1071
Right of exoneration, 724
Right of first refusal, 1041
Right of inspection, shareholders', 1095, 1108
Right of privacy, 131
antiterrorism legislation and, 147–148
criminal law and, 139–142
torts comprising invasion of, 191–195
Right of redemption, 729–730, 1099
Right of subrogation, 723
Right of survivorship, 618
Rights, dissenters', 1089–1090
Rights, securities option, 1038
Rights acquired by negotiation, 608
Rights of assignee, 811
Rights of holder of a negotiable instrument, 811
Rights of partners, 996–999
Rights theory of business ethics
criticism of, 95
decision making according to, 108–109
Kantianism, 93–94
modern rights theory, 94–95
Right to compensation, 602
Right to cover, 577
Right to disaffirm; *see* Disaffirmance
Right to information, 1060, 1095
Right to possession, 761
Right to privacy; *see* Privacy right
Right to reimbursement, 723
Right to speedy trial, 153–154
Right to stop delivery as remedy, 575–576
Riley, Circuit Judge, 698
Ripeness, 23, 1214
Ripple, Circuit Judge, 1168
Risk
assumption of risk defense, 534
of loss, 493–496
from mistake in contract, 367–369
socialization-of-risk rationale, 506
Rita v. United States, 128
River and Harbor Act of 1866, 1355
Roberts, Chief Justice John G., 74, 75, 76, 250

Robinson-Patman Act, 1227
jurisdiction, 1299
relation to Clayton Act, 1299–1300
Section 2(a)
defenses to, 1305–1306
price discrimination, 1299–1305
Section 2(c), false brokerage, 1306
Section 2(d), discriminatory payments, 1306
Section 2(f), buyer inducement, 1306
Rodowsky, Judge, 657
Rodriquez, Judge, 1029
Roe v. Wade, 131
Rogers, Circuit Judge, 177
Rosenberg v. Son, Inc., 444–445
Ross v. May Company, 349–351
Rucker, Justice, 222
Rulemaking, administrative agency, 1205–1207
Rule of reason analysis, 1258–1259, 1261
Rule utilitarianism, 96
Rulon, Chief Justice, 735
Ryan v. Cerullo, 1016–1017

S

Safeco Insurance Co. of America v. Burr, 1239–1242
Safe-deposit boxes, 605
Safe Drinking Water Act, 1360
Sale of goods; *see* Sales contracts
Sale of real estate or intangibles, 280; *see also* Real property
Sale on approval, 496–497
Sale on consignment, 498
Sale or return, 497–498
Sales contracts
applicability of UCC, 296, 480–481
approval, sale on, 496–497
breach; *see* Breach of contract; Remedies for breach of sales contract
commercial unit, 553
consignment sales, 498
destination contracts, 495–496
exclusive dealing contracts, 348, 487
$500-plus contracts, 418, 421–425
gap fillers, 483
general contract provisions applicable to, 483
modification of, 418, 549
needs contract, 463, 465
output contract, 463, 465
performance; *see* Performance of contracts
price terms, 483
quality terms, 483
real property, 626
remedies for breach; *see* Remedies for breach of sales contract
return, sale or, 497–498
revocation of acceptance of goods, 554
risk of loss, 493–496

Sales contracts—*Cont.*
   shipment contracts, 493–495
   third parties; *see* Third parties
   title, 487–489
   trial sales, 496–500
   Uniform Commercial Code, 421–425
   writing requirement, 418
Sales talk and warranties, 506–507
Sanders v. Madison Square Garden L.P., 905–906
Sarbanes-Oxley Act of 2002, 91, 98, 103, 104–105, 159,
      1068, 1073, 1115, 1139, 1160, 1165, 1178–1179, 1184
Sargus, Judge, 1349
Satirical accounts and defamation, 181
Satisfaction
   personal, 456–457
   third parties, 456
Savigny, Friedrich Karl von, 10
Saylor, District Judge, 310
Scalia, Justice, 75, 129, 141, 144, 250, 537, 1200
Schaadt v. St. Jude Medical S.C., Inc., 417–418
Schermer, Bankruptcy Judge, 725
Schlichting v. Cotter, 624–625
Schlitz, U.S. District Judge, 417
Scholl, Justice, 977
Schroeder, Circuit Judge, 235
Schwartzman, Chief Judge, 591
Schwartz v. Family Dental Group, P.C., 970–972
Scienter, 361, 1135, 1141, 1164
Scirica, Chief Judge, 330
S corporations, 1010
Scott, Justice, 1002
Search and seizure
   administrative agency, 1205
   Fourth Amendment, 139–146
SEC. v. Edwards, 1117–1119
SEC. v. W. J. Howey Co., 1116
Seclusion, intrusion on, 191
Secretary of corporation, 1054
Secured claims, Chapter 7, 781
Secured credit, 719–720
Securities Act of 1933
   applicability, 1119
   consequences of transaction exemption, 1128–1129
   content of offers, 1120–1122
   criminal liability, 1180–1181
   defenses to Section 11 liability, 1130–1134,
         1171–1172
   exemption from registration, 1124–1129
   final prospectus, 1122
   free-writing prospectus, 1120
   "free writings," 1120, 1122
   Internet offerings, 1119–1120, 1127
   liability provisions
      misstatements or omissions, 1129–1135
      Section 5, offerings, 1122
      Section 11, false or misleading statements, 1171–1172

Section 11, misstatements or omissions, 1129–1135
Section 24, criminal liability, 1135–1136
Section 12(a)(2), misstatements or omissions, 1135, 1172
Section 17(a)(2), negligence and scienter, 1135,
      1172–1173
   methods of making offers, 1120–1122
   nonissuers, exemption for, 1127
   post-effective period, 1122
   pre-filing period, 1120, 1122
   preliminary prospectus, 1122
   private offering exemptions, 1124–1126
   prospectus, 1120, 1122
   purpose, 1115
   quiet period, 1120
   registration of securities, 1119–1123
   registration statement
      defective, 1129–1135, 1171–1172
      requirements, 1120
   Regulation A offerings, 1126–1127
   restricted securities, 1127
   Rule 504 offerings, 1126
   Rule 505 offerings, 1126
   Rule 506 offerings, 1124–1126, 1127
   Section 5 regulation of offerings, 1120–1122
   small offering exemptions, 1126–1127
   timing of offers, 1120–1122
   transaction exemptions, 1124–1129
   underwriting arrangements, 1119–1120
   waiting period, 1122
Securities Act of 1934
   continuous disclosure obligation, 1143
   criminal liability, 1180–1182
   false or misleading statements, 1140
   insider trading, 1137–1138, 1143–1146
   liability provisions
      aiding and abetting, 1146
      criminal liability, 1151
      insider trading, 1143–1146
      Section 18, false or misleading statements, 1140, 1173
      Section 10(b)/Rule 10b-5, deceptive or manipulative
            devices, 1140–1149, 1173–1175
   misstatements or omissions, 1140
   periodic reports, 1137
   proof in Rule 10b-5 actions, 1141
   proxy solicitation, 1138, 1140
   purpose, 1115, 1136, 1143
   registration of securities, 1136–1137
   registration statement, 1136
   Regulation FD (Fair Disclosure), 1149–1150
   termination of registration, 1136–1137
   Williams Act amendments, 1151
Securities and Exchange Commission (SEC)
   administrative proceedings, 1183–1184
   authority of, 1115–1116
Securities professionals
   administrative proceedings, 1183–1184

audit engagements, 1162
audit requirements, 1184
breach of trust, 1165
conflicts of interest, 1176–1179
fraud, 1164–1165, 1170
general performance standard, 1159–1160
injunctions against, 1183
internal control report, 1184
liability
    to clients, 1160–1165
    criminal, 1180–1183
    limiting by incorporation and LLPs, 1179–1180
    to third persons, 1165–1176
misrepresentation, negligent, 1166–1170
negligence, 1166–1170
opinion letter, 1180
professional-client privilege, 1185
unaudited statements, 1180
working papers, 1185
Securities regulation
    definition of "security," 1116–1117
    disclosure scheme, 1115
    federal regulation; *see* Securities Act of 1933; Securities
        Act of 1934
    historical background, 1115
    purpose, 1115
    rights of action, 1165
    state regulation, 1152–1153
Security agreement
    future advances, 744
    nature of, 742
Security deposits, 647–648
Security devices, 719–720
Security interest
    after-acquired property, 744
    agency powers given as, termination of, 908–909
    artisan's and mechanic's liens, priority rule for, 758
    attachment of, 742
    buyer in ordinary course of business, priority rule for, 758
    deed of trust, 732
    definition, 741
    financing statement, 744–747
    fixtures, 616–617, 751
    inventory, priority rule for interest in, 753–756
    land contracts, 732
    mortgage, 728–730
    noninventory collateral, priority rule for interest in,
        756–757
    perfection of, 744–752
    personal property, 720
    priority rules, 752–761
    proceeds from collateral, 744
    purchase money security interest; *see* Purchase money
        security interest
    real property, 616–617, 720, 727–732
    types of collateral, 741

SEC v. Texas Gulf Sulphur Co., 1141
Sedima, S.P.R.L. v. Imrex Co., 161
See, Justice, 447
Seigel v. Merrill Lynch, Pierce, Fenner & Smith, Inc.,
    873–875
Self-incrimination, privilege against, 148–149
Self-proving affidavit, 678
Selya, Circuit Judge, 336
Sentencing
    federal guidelines, 127–128, 158
    state approaches, 126
Sentencing Reform Act of 1984, 127–128
Separation of powers, 2, 56–57
Service marks, 264
Service of summons, 39
Settlement (ADR), 49
Settlor, 679
Sex (gender)
    discrimination based on, 1327–1328
    Equal Protection Clause and, 75
Shannon v. The State, 593
Shares and shareholders
    action without meeting, 1084
    annual meeting, 1083
    bona fide purchaser of shares, 1041
    buy-and-sell agreement for share sales, 1041
    capital surplus, 1039
    class actions suits, 1099–1100
    close corporation transfers of shares, 1042, 1044
    control block of shares, sale of, 1103–1104
    corporate debts, liability for, 1103
    defense of corporation by, 1103
    demand on directors, 1100–1101
    derivative actions, 1100–1103
    directors of corporation; *see* Board of directors
    discount shares, 1039
    disqualified purchasers of shares, 1042
    dissenters' rights, 1089–1090
    distributions to, 1096–1099
    dividends, 1096–1099
    double derivative suit, 1100
    election of directors, 1050–1052, 1084–1087
    exchanges of shares, compulsory, 1088
    expenses of litigation, 1102–1103
    fair value, 1039
    fiduciaries, shareholders as, 1104–1105
    freezing out minority shareholders, 1071, 1104
    illegal distributions, liability for, 1103
    individual lawsuits, 1099
    information, right to, 1095
    inspection right, 1095
    issuance of shares, 1040
    lawsuits, 1099–1100
    liability of shareholders, 1103–1107
    litigation committee, 1101
    meetings, 1083–1084

Shares and shareholders—*Cont.*
    nonprofit corporations, rights and duties, 1107–1108
    oppression of minority shareholders, 1071, 1104
    option agreements, 1041
    par value, 1039
    postincorporation subscription, 1040
    preemptive right, 1095–1096
    preincorporation subscription, 1029, 1040
    private acquisition of controlling block of shares, 1151–1152
    procedural requirements, 1089
    proposals in proxy statement, 1140
    quality of consideration, 1038
    quantity of consideration, 1038–1040
    real value, 1038
    repurchase of shares, 1099
    resales, 1039–1040
    restrictions on transfers of shares, 1041–1042
    return on investment, 1099
    reverse splitting of shares, 1098–1099
    right of first refusal, 1041
    rights, 1038
    share dividend, 1098
    share subscription, 1040
    splitting of shares, 1098–1099
    tender offer, 1151–1153
    transfer of shares, 1040–1042
    types of shares, 1036–1037, 1085
    voting agreements, 1085
    warrants, 1038
    watered shares, 1039
Shelley v. Kraemer, 63
Shelter Mutual Insurance Co. v. Maples, 698–699
Shelter rule, 834
Sherman Act
    FTC authority, 1227
    jurisdiction, 1256
    Noerr-Pennington doctrine, 1308
    Section 1, restraints of trade, 1257–1273
    Section 2, monopolization, 1273–1282
    standing, 1257
    types of cases, 1256
Shlensky v. Wrigley, 1057
Shop right doctrine, 248
Short-form merger, 1089
Shrinkwrap contracts or licensees, 294, 315
Sigler v. Patrick, 27–28
Signature requirement, 412
    e-signatures, 423
    negotiable instruments, 812, 850–851
    Statute of Frauds, 420
Silberman, Circuit Judge, 1197
Simo v. Mitsubishi Motors North America, Inc., 518–520
Simultaneous death, 677–678

Sixth Amendment, 127–128
    general information, 153–154
    jury trial, right to, 127–128
Skebba v. Kasch, 354–356
Skill-of-prudent-person standard, 1159
Slander defined, 181
Slippery slope fallacy in ethical decisions, 114
Smalkin, District Judge, 848
Small offering exemptions, 1126–1127
Smith, Adam, 97, 1257
Smith, Judge, 1366
SmithStearn Yachts, Inc. v. Gyrographic Communications, inc., 1028–1029
Smith v. Carter & Burgess, Inc., 455–456
Smith v. City of Jackson, 1331
Smith v. Van Gorkom, 1057
Social Security, 1320
Sociological jurisprudence, 10–11
Sole proprietor defined, 932
Sole proprietorship, nature of, 932–933
Solid waste disposal, 1364
Solitude, intrusion on, 191
Solvency test, dividends, 1098
Souter, Justice David, 21, 75, 82, 146, 150, 250, 256, 1217, 1240
Southex Exhibitions, Inc. v. Rhode Island Builders Association, Inc., 941–942
Sovereign compulsion doctrine, 1311
Sovereign immunity, 1311
Sowell, Thomas, 97
Sparks, Associate Justice, 841
Special agent, 899
Special charters, 1009
Special damages
    breach of contract, 470
    slander and libel, 181
Specialized federal courts, 36
Special masters (ADR), 53
Special verdict, 47
Specific performance as remedy, 5, 416, 473, 582
Specific restitution as remedy, 474
Spector v. Konover, 955–956
Spending power of Congress, 63
Spendthrift trust, 681–683
Splitting of shares, 1098–1099
Spoliation of evidence, 3–5
Stahlecker v. Ford Motor Co., 228–231
Stakeholder theory of corporate responsibility, 92
Stale checks, 871
Standard Bent Glass Corporation v. Glassrobots Oy, 330–331
Standard Oil Co. v. United States, 1288
Standards, environmental
    ambient air control, 1347
    automobile pollution, 1351–1352
    water quality, 1356

Standby underwriting, 1119
Standing to sue, 23, 1209
Stapleton, Circuit Judge, 1309
Stare decisis, 3, 12, 58
Star-Shadow Productions, Inc. v. Super 8 Sync Sound System, 570–571
State courts
    jurisdiction, 29–34
Stated capital account, 1039
Statement of Denial, 956
Statement of Partnership Authority, 956
State of Connecticut v. Cardwell, 488–489
State of New York v. Burger, 1205
State Oil Co. v. Khan, 1261–1263
States
    ambient air quality standards, 1347
    antitrust exemption for state action, 1307–1308
    employment discrimination laws, 1333–1334
    enforcement of air quality standards, 1351
    independent checks applicable only to, 81–82
    regulatory powers, 58
    securities laws, 1152–1153, 1176
    tender offers, regulation of, 1152–1153
    waste disposal, 1361
    water pollution control, 1355–1356
Statue of Liberty–Ellis Island Commemorative Coin Act, 323
Statute of Frauds
    applicability, 413–420
    easements and, 620
    e-signatures and, 423, 485
    history of, 413
    insurance contracts, 692
    marriage as consideration, 419–420
    memorandum requirements, 420–421
    one-year rule, 416–418
    payment of decedent's debt, 418–419
    promissory estoppel and, 425
    purposes of, 413
    requirements, 420–425
    sale of goods for $500 or more, 418
    signature requirement, 420
Statutes, generally, 3
    constitutional restrictions, 58–59
    federal regulatory power, 58–59
    state regulatory power, 58
Statutes of limitations
    debt payment as contracts consideration, 356
    discharge of contracts by, 468
    product liability, 526
    remedies for breach of sales contract, 571
    Rule 10b-5 liability, 1149
    Section 11 liability, 1134–1135
Statutory interpretation, 15–24
Statutory liens, 724
Statutory strict liability, 236

Staub, Circuit Judge, 275
Steadman, Associate Judge, 874
Stephens v. Pillen, 196–198
Stevens, Justice John Paul, 60, 75, 85, 86, 146, 243, 250, 634, 1210, 1353
Stock options, 102–103
Stone, Associate Justice, 889
Stone, Christopher, 102
Stoneridge Investment Partners, LLC v. Scientific-Atlanta, Inc., 1146–1149, 1175
Stoshak v. East Baton Rouge Parish School Board, 174–175
Straight voting, 1050, 1084
Strict foreclosure, 729
Strict liability
    defined, 170
    generally, 234
    Section 402A, *Restatement (Second) of Torts,* 517–518
Strict performance standard, 459
Stroupes v. The Finish Line, Inc., 379–380
Subagent, 899
Subassignee, 440
Subcontractors, rights of, 732–733
Subdivision laws, 636–637
Subject matter jurisdiction, 30
Subleases, 659, 660
Subpoenas, administrative agency, 1203
Subrogation right
    nature of, 723
    property insurance, 701
Substantial evidence test, 1215–1216
Substantial performance standard, 459–460
Substantive law, 8
Substantive unconscionability, 404
Substitutionary restitution as remedy for breach of contract, 474
Summary judgment, 45
Summary jury trial (ADR), 52–53
Summons, 39
Sunk cost fallacy in ethical decisions, 114–115
Superfund, 1364–1367
Supervening illegality and contract performance, 467
Supremacy, federal, 6
Supreme Court
    commercial speech, test for, 65–67
    Constitution, role with respect to, 57–58
    jurisdiction, 37
    means-end test, 64–65
Surety, 720–723
Suretyship and guaranty, 720–723
Surrender of lease, 660
Survivorship, right of, 618
Suspect classes, 74–79
Sutton v. United Airlines, 1333
Swiney, Judge, 1035
Syllogistic reasoning, 12
Sylva Shops Limited Partnership v. Hibbard, 661–663

T

Taft-Hartley Act, 1322
Takings Clause
    eminent domain, 84, 633
    just compensation, 85
    land use regulation, 638–640
    public purpose, 85–86
    public use, 85
    rent cap provision, 639–640
    scope, 84–86
Tampa Electric Co. v. Nashville Coal Co., 1289
Tang, Circuit Judge, 1290
Tangible personal property, 589
Tariff Act of 1930, 266
Taxes
    Congress, taxing power of, 62–63
    foreign corporations, 1014
    limited liability company, 986
    limited partnership, 993–994
Tax sale, acquisition of real property by, 623
*TBG Insurance Services Corp. v. Superior
        Court,* 1336–1338
Telecommunications Act of 1996, 1215
Telemarketing
    Do-Not-Call Registry, 1232–1236
    Telemarketing and Consumer Fraud and Abuse Prevention
        Act, 1231–1232
    Telemarketing Sales Rule, 1231–1232
Teleological ethical theories, 93
Teller's check, 811
*Tempur-Pedic International, Inc. v. Waste to Charity,
        Inc.,* 490–492
Tenancies
    in common, 617–618
    by the entirety, 618
    at sufferance, 646
    for a term, 646
    types of, 646, 647
    at will, 646
    for years, 646
Tenancy in partnership, 618
Tender offer regulation, 1151–1153
Termination
    agency relationship, 907–910
    agent's authority, effect on, 909–910
    contract offer, 315–320
    corporations, winding up and termination, 1110–1111
    employment, 1338–1341
    leases; *see* Leases
    partnerships, 975
    registration of securities, 1136–1137
    restrictive covenant, 623
    trusts, 684
Termination statement, 745

Ternus, Justice, 521
Testamentary capacity, 668–669
Testamentary trust, 679
Theis, J., 363
A Theory of Justice (John Rawls), 95
The Wealth of Nations, 1257
*The Work Connection, Inc. v. Universal Forest Products
        Co.,* 918–919
Thin capitalization, corporations, 1018
Third parties
    assignment of contracts, 435–441
    beneficiaries, 446–449
    contract beneficiaries, 446–449
    delegation of contract duties, 441–445
    express condition of contracts, 456
    goods in possession of, 496
    securities professionals' liability to
        common law, 1165–1171
            securities law, 1171–1176
    termination of agency relationship, notice to, 910
    title to goods, 490–492
Thomas, Justice Clarence, 75, 249
Thompson, Judge, 443
Thorne v. Deas, 343
Thurman, U.S. Bankruptcy Judge, 797
Time for performance of contracts, 487
Times-Picayune Co. v. United States, 1255
Time Warner Cable, Inc. v. DIRECTV, Inc., 280–283
Tippees, 1143–1146
Title documents, 605, 608
Title to goods
    buyers in ordinary course of business, 492
    entrusting of goods, 492–493
    identity of holder, 487–488
    passage of, 487–488
    third parties, 490–492
    voidable, 490
Title to real property, 628–629
Title VII, 1964 Civil Rights Act, 1323–1334
Toal, Judge, 233
Tombstone ad, securities offering
    general information, 1121
    sample ad, 1122
Torrens system of title assurance, 629
Tort immunity of landlords, 653
Tort law
    agent's liability, 927
    bad faith breach of contract, 708–709
    civil liability, 170
    commercial torts, 276–279
    damages, 170–171
    deceit, 361
    definitions, 170
    disclaimers of liability, 533
    independent contractor's liability, 926

Industrial Revolution's effect on, 206
intent, 170
interference with personal rights, 173–196
interference with property rights, 196–198
joint and several liability, 927–928
landlord's tort liability, 653–658
misrepresentation by agent, 926–927
negligence; *see* Negligence
principal's liability, 923–927
privity determinations, 527
recklessness, 170
reform of tort law
    liability insurance and, 706, 708
    negligence and, 236–237
securities law rights of action, 1165
securities professionals' tort liability, 1161–1165
standard of proof, 170
strict liability, 170
suits against principal and agent, 927–928
Total fairness test of freeze-out, 1071
Totten trusts, 680
Toxic substances: air pollutants, 1347–1348
Toyota Manufacturing Co. v. Williams, 1333
Trade fixtures, 615
Trademark Counterfeiting Act of 1984, 266
Trademarks, 263–273
    definition, 263
    dilution, 266–267
    distinctiveness, 264–265
    infringement, 266
    licensing use of, 265
    registration, 265
    term of protection, 265
    transfer of rights, 265
Trade regulation rules, FTC, 1226
Trade secrets, 273–276
Trading on inside information, 1072–1073
Trading partnership, 957–958
Tradition, appeals in ethical decisions to, 114
Transaction exemptions, 1124–1129
Transactions in ordinary course of business:
    Chapter 7, 777–778
Transfer of interests, partnerships, 947–948, 997
Transferred intent: battery, 173–174
Transfer warranties, 854, 857–858
Traxler, Circuit Judge, 519
Treadwell v. J.D. Construction Co.,
    920–921
Treasurer of corporation, 1054
Treasure trove, 591–593
Treasury shares, 1037
Treaties, 6
Treble damages, 1257
Trentadue v. Gorton, 6–8
Trepanier v. Bankers Life & Casualty Co., 909

Trespass to land
    duty owed to trespasser, 214–215
    generally, 196
Trial courts, 29–30
Trials
    generally, 45–47
    jury trials, 47
    speedy trial, right to, 153–154
Tricontinental Industries, Ltd. v. PricewaterhouseCoopers,
    LLP, 1167–1170
Trustees
    allocating principal and income, 681
    Chapter 7 bankruptcy, 772–773
    definition of, 679
    liabilities of, 681
    powers and duties, 680–681
    U.S. Trustee, 773
Trusts
    asset protection trusts, 779
    charitable trusts, 680
    constructive trusts, 684
    creation, requirements for, 680
    cy pres doctrine, 680
    definition of, 679
    express trusts, creation of, 680
    implied trusts, 684
    income beneficiary, 681
    inter vivos trust, 679
    modification, 684
    purpose of, 679–680
    remaindermen, 681
    resulting trusts, 684
    spendthrift trust, 681–683
    termination, 684
    testamentary trust, 679
    Totten trusts, 680
Truth in Lending Act, 1237–1239
Twenty-first Amendment, 88–89
Twenty-sixth Amendment, 380
Tying agreements, 1268–1272, 1288

U

Ultramares Corp. v. Touche, 1166, 1170
Ultra vires doctrine, 1048–1049
Unaudited statements, 1180
Unconscionable contracts, 299, 369, 403
Unconscionable disclaimers, 533
Underground storage tanks, regulation of, 1361
Underwriting, securities, 1119–1120
Undisclosed principal, 920
Undue influence, in contracts, 374
Unemployment compensation, 1320
Unenforceable contracts, 295, 392–409
Unfair competition (Lanham Act), 280–283
Unfair persuasion, in contracts, 374

Uniform acts, 3
Uniform Commercial Code
    acceptance of contract, 328–330
    Article 9, 740–765
    assignment, 436–437, 439
    commercial impracticability and contract performance, 467
    definiteness of contract terms, 311
    delegation of duties, 442
    discharge of liability, negotiable instruments, 863–864
    disclaimers of implied warranty, 532–533
    drawee's liability, 847–848
    drawer-drawee relationship, 869–878
    express warranties, 506–508
    fitness, implied warranty of, 512–514
    fund transfers, 890
    general contract requirements, 295–296, 298–300
    holder in due course personal defenses, 837–838
    leases, 483, 593
    limitation of remedies, 533
    mailbox rule, 333–334
    memorandum in contracts, 420
    merchantability, implied warranty of, 508–509
    merchants, 483
    modification of contract, 351
    negotiable instruments, 807, 831–832
    negotiation, 822–823
    no-privity defense, 527–528
    origin and purpose, 295–296
    parol evidence rule, 426
    privity, 528–531
    risk of loss, 493–496
    sale of goods; see Sales contracts
    sales contracts, 421–425
    security interest, 740–765
    shares, issuance of, 1040
    shelter rule, 834
    software and other information contracts, 296
    stop payment orders, 874
    text of, Appendix B-1–B-154
    unauthorized signatures, 877–878
    unconscionability of contract, 403
Uniform Computer Information Transactions
        Act (UCITA), 296
Uniform Electronic Transactions Act (UETA), 423, 549
Uniform Limited Liability Company Act of 1996, Revised
        (RULLCA), 985–986
Uniform Limited Partnership Acts (ULPA), 993
Uniform Probate Code (UPC), 667
Uniform Simultaneous Death Act, 677–678
Uniform Transfers to Minors Act, 597
Unilateral contracts
    acceptance, 334
    general information, 294–295
    power to revoke contract offer, 316
Unilateral mistakes, 369

Unilateral refusals to deal, 1260–1261
Union Labor Life Insurance Co. v. Pireno, 1307
Union Planters Bank, N.A. v. Rogers, 878–879
Unions, 1321–1322
Unissued status of shares, 1037
United Housing Foundation Inc. v. Forman, 1116–1117
United Mine Workers v. Pennington, 1308
U.S. Trustee, 773
United States v. Aluminum Co. of America,
        Inc., 1255, 1275
United States v. Booker, 127–128, 158
United States v. Chiarella, 1143
United States v. Dean, 1361–1362
United States v. Doe, 153
United States v. Domenic Lombardi Realty, 1365–1367
United States v. E. I. du Pont de Nemours and Co., 1274
United States v. General Electric Company, 1311
United States v. Grinnell Corp., 1273
United States v. Hall, 139–140
United States v. Hopkins, 1356–1358
United States v. Jensen, 1075–1078
United States v. Microsoft Corp., 1275–1280, 1281
United States v. Morton Salt, 1203
United States v. Natelli, 1181–1182
United States v. Ohio Edison Company, 1348–1350
United States v. Park, 156, 157
United States v. Philadelphia National Bank, 1292
United States v. Place, 140
United States v. Santos, 128–131
United States v. Socony-Vacuum Oil, 1259
United States v. Topco Associates, Inc., 1267
United States v. Twombly, 133
United States v. U.S. Gypsum Co., 1256
United States v. Williams, 66, 132
Universal City Studios, Inc. v. Corley, 254
Unjust dismissal, 1338
Unjust enrichment, 301
Unliquidated debts, 352
Unocal Corp. v. Mesa Petroleum Co., 1063
Unowned property, 590
Unsecured credit, 719
Untrue assertion of fact, 361–362
Usage of trade, 547
USA PATRIOT Act, 147–148
Utilitarianism
    ethical business practices, 108
    generally, 96–97

V

Vaidik, Judge, 319
Valley Bank of Ronan v. Hughes, 882–885
Valued policies, property insurance, 699–700
Variances from zoning rules, 636
Vaught, Judge, 1341
Veasey, Chief Justice, 1052

Venue
   general information, 33
   requirements, 30
Verdicts, 47
Vertical boycotts, 1268
Vertical mergers, 1296
Vertical price-fixing, 1260–1267
Vertical restraints on distribution, 1267–1268
Vice president of corporation, 1054
Victory Clothing Co., Inc. v. Wachovia Bank,
       N.A., 860–863
Vining v. Enterprise Financial Group, Inc., 709–712
Violence Against Women Act, 88
Virginia v. Moore, 143
Vogel, Justice, 1337
Vogel, Presiding Judge, 574
Voidable contracts, 295
Void contracts, 295
Voir dire, 45
Voluntary dissolution, 1109
Volvo Trucks North America, Inc. v. Reeder-Simco GMC, Inc.,
       1302–1305
Voting for board of directors, 1050–1052, 1107–1108
Voting rights, preferred shares, 1037
Voting trusts, 1085

W

Waddell v. L.V.R.V. Inc., 554–555
Wagering contracts, 692
Wagner Act, 1321–1322
Waiver
   benefit of law, negotiable instruments, 818
   discharge of contract by, 468
   excuse of conditions, 457
   failure to object creating, 549–550
   liens, 737
   restrictive covenants, 623
Walker, Chief Judge, 690
Waller, Presiding Justice, 878
Wall Street rule, 1051
Walters, Chief United States Magistrate Judge, 548
Warehouse receipts, 605
Warner-Jenkinson Co. v. Hilton Davis Chemical Co., 248
Warnick v. Warnick, 979–981
Warnings
   inadequate, 521
   negligent failure to provide, 514–515
Warranties
   advertisements, 507
   assignor's liability in contracts, 441
   authority, implied warranty of, 922–923
   basis-of-the-bargain requirement, 507
   disclaimers, 532–533
   document of title, 609
   express warranties, 506–508

fitness, implied warranty of, 512–514
FTC authority, 1236–1237
habitability, implied warranty of, 629–630
information requirements, 1236–1237
insurance policies, 692
merchantability, implied warranty of, 508–509
multiple express warranties, 507
negotiable instruments, 854–858
no-privity defense, 527–528
possession, implied warranty of, 648
quiet enjoyment, implied warranty of, 648
sales talk, 506–507
statements of value or opinion, 506–507
Warrant requirement (Fourth Amendment), 143
Warrants (securities), 1038
Warranty deeds, 627–628
Warsaw Convention, 606
Washington, Chief Judge, 466
Waste, tenant's duty not to commit, 659
Watered shares, 1039
Water pollution, 1355–1358
Watts v. Simpson, 443–444
Webb-Pomerene Act, 1307
Weil v. Murray, 553–554
Weinberger v. UOP, 1090
Wetlands, protection of, 1358
Whistleblowing, 158, 1338
White-collar crimes
   bribery, 159–160
   corporate criminal liability, 155–156
   deferred prosecution agreements, 158–159
   early approaches, 154–155
   fraudulent acts, 159
   future directions, 157–159
   gratuities, illegal, 159–160
   liability of individuals, 156–157
   mail fraud, 1183
   mens rea, 154
   nature of, 154
   problems with individual liability, 156–157
   problems with punishing corporations, 155–156
   regulatory offenses, 159
   respondeat superior doctrine, 154
   RICO, 160–163, 1183
   securities law, 1180–1183
   tax law violations, 1182
Whitman v. American Trucking Associations, 1199–1201
Williams Act, 1151
Wills
   acquisition of personal property by, 597
   acquisition of real property by, 623
   advance directives, 673–675
   codicils, 673
   construction of, 670
   durable form of attorney for health care, 675

Wills—*Cont.*
  durable power of attorney, 674–675
  execution of, 669
  extrinsic documents, 669
  form of living will declaration, 674
  holographic wills, 670
  incorporation by reference, 669
  joint wills, 670
  limitation on disposition by, 672–673
  living wills, 673–674
  mutual wills, 670
  noncupative wills, 669
  pretermitted children, 673
  revocation, 673
  right of disposition by, 667–668
  simultaneous death, 677–678
  surviving spouse, 673
  terminology, 668
  testamentary capacity, 668–669
Wilner, Judge, 1020
Winding up; *see* Dissolution and winding up
Windows, Inc. v. Jordan Panel Systems Corp.,
    494–495
Wineries, out-of-state shipment by, 88–89
Wintersport Ltd. v. Millionaire.com, Inc., 414–415
Wire transfers, 889–890

Workers' compensation, 701, 705, 1316–1319
Working papers, ownership of, 1185
Work product material, 41–43
Works for hire, 253
World Trade Center Properties, LLC v. Hartford Fire
    Insurance Co., 689–691
World Trade Organization, 268
Wright, Justice, 558
Wright v. Brooke Group Limited, 521–524
Writing requirement
  insurance contracts, 692
  negotiable instruments, 812
  sales contracts, 418
  Statute of Frauds; *see* Statute of Frauds
Writ of execution, 48
Wrongful discharge, 1338

Y

Yeadon Fabric Domes, Inc. v. Maine Sports Complex,
    LLC, 759–761
Young v. Weaver, 384–385

Z

Zapata Corp. v. Maldonado, 1101–1102
Zoning laws, 636–637